GERMANS ★TO AMERICA

Volume 56
May 1888—November 1888

Other *Germans to America* Publications available from Scholarly Resources (Series ISBN 0-8420-2279-1)

Vol. No.	Dates	ISBN (0-8420-)	Vol. No.	Dates	ISBN (0-8420-)
1	1/2/1850–5/24/1851	2315-1	29	1/2/1873–5/31/1873	2406-9
2	5/24/1851–6/5/1852	2316-X	30	6/2/1873–11/28/1873	2407-7
3	6/5/1852–9/21/1852	2317-8	31	12/1/1873–12/29/1874	2408-5
4	9/22/1852–5/28/1853	2318-6	32	1/4/1875–9/30/1876	2409-3
5	5/28/1853–10/24/1853	2319-4	33	10/2/1876–9/30/1878	2410-7
6	10/24/1853–5/4/1854	2320-8	34	10/1/1878–12/31/1879	2411-5
7	5/5/1854–8/4/1854	2321-6	35	1/2/1880–6/30/1880	2412-3
8	8/4/1854–12/11/1854	2322-4	36	7/1/1880–11/29/1880	2501-4
9	12/12/1854–12/31/1855	2323-2	37	12/1/1880–4/14/1881	2502-2
10	1/3/1856–4/27/1857	2355-0	38	4/16/1881–5/31/1881	2503-0
11	4/27/1857–11/30/1857	2356-9	39	6/1/1881–8/6/1881	2504-9
12	11/2/1857–7/29/1859	2357-7	40	8/8/1881–10/31/1881	2505-7
13	8/1/1859–12/31/1860	2358-5	41	11/1/1881–3/27/1882	2506-5
14	1/2/1861–5/29/1863	2359-3	42	3/28/1882–5/18/1882	2507-3
15	6/1/1863–10/31/1864	2360-7	43	5/19/1882–8/9/1882	2508-1
16	11/1/1864–11/2/1865	2361-5	44	8/10/1882–11/15/1882	2509-X
17	11/4/1865–6/12/1866	2384-4	45	11/16/1882–4/19/1883	2510-3
18	6/13/1866–12/27/1866	2385-2	46	4/20/1883–6/30/1883	2565-0
19	1/2/1867–8/15/1867	2386-0	47	7/2/1883–10/31/1883	2566-9
20	8/19/1867–5/14/1868	2387-9	48	11/1/1883–4/14/1884	2567-7
21	5/15/1868–9/29/1868	2388-7	49	4/15/1884–6/30/1884	2568-5
22	10/2/1868–5/31/1869	2389-5	50	7/2/1884–11/29/1884	2569-3
23	6/1/1869–12/31/1869	2390-9	51	12/1/1884–6/30/1885	2614-2
24	1/3/1870–12/31/1870	2401-8	52	7/1/1885–4/29/1886	2615-0
25	1/2/1871–9/30/1871	2402-6	53	5/1/1886–1/3/1887	2616-9
26	10/2/1871–4/30/1872	2403-4	54	1/3/1887–6/30/1887	2617-7
27	5/2/1872–7/31/1872	2404-2	55	7/1/1887–4/30/1888	2618-5
28	8/1/1872–12/31/1872	2405-0	56	5/1/1888–11/30/1888	2619-3

GERMANS ★TO AMERICA

Lists of Passengers Arriving
at U.S. Ports

Volume 56
May 1888—November 1888

Edited by
Ira A. Glazier
and
P. William Filby

SR Scholarly Resources Inc.
Wilmington, Delaware

The paper used in this publication meets the minimum requirements of the American National Standard for permanence of paper for printed library materials, Z39.48, 1984.

©1997 by Scholarly Resources Inc.
All rights reserved
First printed 1997
Printed and bound in the United States of America

Scholarly Resources Inc.
104 Greenhill Avenue
Wilmington, Delaware 19805-1897

Series ISBN 0-8420-2279-1

Library of Congress Cataloging-in-Publication Data

Germans to America: lists of passengers arriving at U.S.
        ports / edited by Ira A. Glazier, P. William Filby
        p.   cm.
        Includes indexes.
        ISBN 0-8420-2315-1 (v. 1)
        1. German Americans—Genealogy. 2. Ships—
United States—Passenger lists. 3. United States—
Emigration and immigration. 4. Immigrants—United
States—Registers. 5. Germany—Emigration and
immigration. I. Glazier, Ira A. II. Filby, P. William, 1911-
E184.G3G38 1988
929'.3'08931–dc19   87-35442
                                                          CIP

CONTENTS

FOREWORD

As a speaker at many major genealogical conferences, I am aware of the enormous interest in German immigration, particularly after 1840. Most of the questions at these conferences and in my correspondence concern the search for German immigrants. About four million Germans came to the United States between 1850 and 1893. Although they are recorded in the National Archives, their names remain unindexed and therefore unfindable unless the researcher knows the ship on which the person arrived and the exact date of arrival. What has been needed is a list of immigrants, arranged first by ship at the port of debarkation and then indexed by family name.

The original passenger lists for 1850 through 1893, prepared by shipping agents and ships' officers, are now deposited at the Temple-Balch Institute's Center for Immigration Research in Philadelphia and are reproduced chronologically in these volumes by date of each ship's arrival. This arrangement will greatly aid genealogical researchers as will the volume-by-volume index of passenger surnames.

Why was there such a great mass of people wishing to quit their homeland for the unknown United States? Emigration from Germany was spurred by a variety of factors, including crop failures, a lack of industrial employment, overpopulation, social discontent and political repression and upheaval, as well as the lure of cheap land and the chance to make a fresh start in a new country. The lists, starting from 1850, were chosen for publication because that year begins a period when immigration to the United States was swelling, touched off by the departure of political refugees, liberals, and intellectuals and by stories about a better life sent back by those who had emigrated previously. Most of the immigrants found the trip worthwhile, and few returned to Germany.

The two main German ports of embarkation were Bremen and Hamburg, where German officials prepared lists of emigrants. For various reasons the Bremen lists have been destroyed or otherwise made unavailable, but, since the lists reproduced here record arrivals in all U.S. ports, the loss of the Bremen lists does not present as serious a problem as it might be otherwise. The great majority of immigrants came to New York, but many went to New Orleans and Baltimore, with fewer going to Boston and Philadelphia.

P. William Filby
Former director, Maryland Historical Society
Fellow of the Society of Genealogists, London
Fellow of the National Genealogical Society

INTRODUCTION

Germans to America provides both the historian and the genealogist with an extensive data base of German immigrants who came to the United States from 1850 through 1893. This data base derives from the original ship manifest schedules, currently housed at the Temple-Balch Institute's Center for Immigration Research. These schedules were filed by all vessels entering U.S. ports in accordance with the act of Congress of 1819.

The passenger lists reproduced in these volumes are arranged in chronological order by date of arrival. In the 1850-1855 volumes, these lists contain a minimum of 80 percent German surnames and are published in their entirety. Starting in 1856 the selection criterion changes to include all ships with German passengers, regardless of the percentage. Unlike the previous volumes, only those calling themselves Germans are now listed; all other passenger names are deleted. It should be noted that after 1856 these German immigrants include those coming not only from German states or territories but also from countries such as France, Switzerland, or Luxemburg.

According to the act of 1819, lists of all passengers were to be delivered upon arrival to the local collector of customs, who made copies that were then transmitted to the secretary of state and subsequently reported to Congress.[1] The secretary of state also published quarterly and annual summaries under the title of **Statement of the Number and Description of Passengers Arriving in the United States** between 1820 and 1870. These reports were later published by the Bureau of Statistics of the Treasury Department from 1867 to 1895 and by the Office of Immigration, now the Immigration and Naturalization Service, after 1895.

The passenger lists make possible a detailed reconstruction of the movement of population from the major sender countries, in the present case the German states, by including information on the age, sex, occupation, and nationality of each passenger and residence and putative destination. Analysis of this information enables the researcher to identify U.S. citizens returning to their country of origin, persons transitting the United States, and immigrants. The manifests record deaths during the voyage, although information on mortality is not reproduced in these volumes. The lists herein also indicate the name of the ship, the port of embarkation, and the date of arrival in the U.S. port.

Although the manifests provide significant information about nineteenth-century immigration, we know little about the compilation of these lists; we do not know who made the lists originally, or if there was any uniform standard applied in collecting the data at the various ports. Some evidence suggests that the lists were compiled first by shipping agents at the port of embarkation and initially contained the names of all prepaid passengers; the names of additional passengers were added on board, after which clerks copied the lists before depositing them with U.S. authorities at the port of debarkation.

Historical Background of German Migration in the Nineteenth Century

Population increased rapidly in Germany during the period of relative stability that followed the conclusion of the Napoleonic Wars. Although German-speaking immigrants had been coming to the United States since the middle of the eighteenth century, the number of German arrivals in a single year did not exceed 10,000 until 1832. The numbers increased rapidly thereafter, reaching 60,000 in 1846, 150,000 in 1852, and 196,000 in 1854.[2] Immigration declined during the period of the Civil War but revived between 1866 and 1873, decreased slightly during the depression of the later 1870s, and rose to its high point between 1880 and 1885.

Table 1
German Immigration to the U.S. and Total German Emigration, 1820–1914

Years	German Immigration to U.S. (000)	Germans as % of Immigration to U.S.	Total Emigration (000)	Percent to U.S.
1820–24	1.9	4.9	9.8	19.4
1825–29	3.8	4.3	12.7	29.9
1830–34	39.3	17.0	51.1	76.9
1835–39	85.5	27.8	94.0	91.0
1840–44	100.5	25.1	110.6	90.9
1845–49	284.9	27.7	308.2	92.4
1850–54	654.3	34.1	728.3	89.8
1855–59	321.8	35.9	372.0	86.5
1860–64	204.1	28.9	225.9	90.3
1865–69	519.6	37.8	542.7	95.2
1870–74	450.5	23.9	484.6	93.0
1875–79	120.0	14.0	143.3	83.7
1880–84	797.9	26.3	864.3	92.3
1885–89	452.6	20.5	498.2	90.8
1890–94	428.8	18.5	462.2	92.8
1895–99	120.2	8.8	142.4	84.4
1900–04	128.6	3.9	140.8	91.3
1905–09	123.5	2.5	135.7	91.0
1910-14	84.1	1.6	104.3	80.6

Source: P. Marschalk, *Deutsche Uberseewanderung im 19 Jahrhundert*, p. 48.

German emigration to the United States, prior to the 1830s, had come almost exclusively from southwest Germany, Wurtemberg, Baden, Bavaria, and the Rhineland-Palatinate, which were the areas of greatest demographic increase. This was a region predominantly of small farms, in which inheritance laws resulted in the equal division of family property among the surviving children. This, combined with the effects of peasant emancipation, resulted in a steadily declining economic base for much of the increasing population. German industry had not developed sufficiently to enable urban areas to absorb the surplus population, thereby providing a stimulus to overseas migration.

In the 1840s emigration spread to northwest Germany. Although this was an area characterized by more sizable landholdings, the local textile industry was unable to compete with English imports, and industrial and agricultural depression forced unemployed artisans, tenant farmers, and agricultural laborers to emigrate. By the 1850s peasant emancipation in the eastern and northeastern parts of Germany, Schleswig Holstein, Mecklenburg, and East Prussia led to the dispossession of former serfs from the great estates,[3] and to large-scale emigration of peasants and artisans after 1865.[4] Although the population of the German states doubled between 1840 and 1910, from 32.8 million to 64.9 million, emigration carried off approximately one third of this increase.[5] The great exodus between 1847 and 1855 was the result of a combination of crop failures, the increase in the price of food, famine, political instability; and the general decline in the standard of living of a predominantly rural population.

Table 2
Geographic Origins of German Emigration, 1871–1910

Years	North-east	North-west	South-west	Center	South-east	West	Hanseatic States
1871–75	39.6	15.4	25.6	3.8	5.2	8.3	2.1
1876–80	35.4	15.2	25.3	4.2	7.2	9.8	3.1
1881–85	38.2	14.4	24.1	3.8	6.3	10.6	2.6
1886–90	37.7	12.0	28.9	3.2	5.1	10.1	3.0
1891–95	34.8	13.3	25.3	4.4	7.1	10.7	4.4
1896–1900	28.6	14.8	26.1	4.8	6.9	10.8	8.0
1901–05	30.7	13.8	23.6	5.0	7.8	14.1	5.0
1906–10	27.5	13.3	23.4	5.2	8.7	15.7	6.2

Source: W. Mönckmeier, *Die deutsche überseeische Auswanderung* (Jena, 1912), pp. 128–29, 133.

German overseas emigration falls into two phases in the nineteenth century. Between 1815 and 1865 families of small farmers, artisans, and tradesmen from the southwest and agricultural laborers from the northwest left Germany in search of cheap land, which was abundant in the United States. Preliminary analysis of data for the period 1850–51 indicates that two thirds of the departures were male and that over 80 percent were either farmers or laborers. Between 1865 and 1895 peasants and unemployed industrial workers, largely from eastern Germany, left the country looking for employment, attracted by the demand for cheap labor during a period of rapid U.S. industrialization that followed the Civil War. The era of massive overseas migration came to an end in the mid-1890s as German industry matured and absorbed surplus agricultural and industrial population.

Bremen and Hamburg served as the primary German ports of embarkation throughout the nineteenth century, but French ports, such as Le Havre, and Antwerp and Rotterdam, in the Low Countries, were also major points of departure.

Table 3
German Arrivals at U.S. Ports, 1850–90
(000)

	1850	1860	1870	1880	1890
New York	49.90	38.96	75.66	67.98	70.38
Boston	0.07	0.127	2.99	0.91	0.30
Philadelphia	0.23	0.372	0.69	3.69	3.61
Baltimore	3.30	3.47	9.18	9.08	17.98
New Orleans	5.70	5.35	1.54	1.16	0.13
Other	–	6.22	–	1.81	0.02
Total	59.20	54.49	89.45	84.67	92.42

Source: House Executive Documents, 1850–90.

The most important ports of arrival in the United States were New York, from which the immigrants dispersed via Albany and Troy throughout the western part of the country, and Baltimore and New Orleans, from which they reached the Mississippi. However, the Civil War abruptly ended New Orleans's position as a leading port of entry and its predominance as a commercial center. New railroad routes from the East now ran to St. Louis and the Mississippi River, and therefore many immigrants landing in New York after the war could find direct railroad passage to the Midwest. Philadelphia and Boston, though, remained secondary ports throughout the latter half of the nineteenth century.

Conclusion

Genealogists and historians in the field of immigration have relied on aggregate-level data to examine the development, extent, and characteristics of population movements. With the information available in this volume, researchers will be able to go beyond gross statistical profiles to study these movements at the level of microhistory—to follow individuals and families from their place of origin to their destination and to focus on their personal circumstances.[6] This, in turn, will enable scholars to assess the push-and-pull factors that contributed to the migration phenomenon and to give a more human dimension to this mass movement.

The editor would like to express his appreciation to the students and staff at the Temple-Balch Institute's Center for Immigration Research who have worked so diligently and conscientiously on this project. A special debt is owed to the systems manager, Nancy Smart.

Ira A. Glazier
Director, Temple-Balch Institute's Center
for Immigration Research

NOTES

1. For material dealing with the Passenger Acts see Edith Abbot, *Immigration: Select Documents and Case Records*, Part 1 (Chicago, 1924).
2. F. Burgdorfer, "Migration across the Frontiers of Germany," p. 333, in W. W. Wilcox, ed., *International Migrations*, vol. 2, *Interpretations* (New York, 1931); P. Marschalk, *Deutsche Uberseewanderung im 19 Jahrhundert* (Stuttgart, 1973), p. 10.
3. Marschalk, *Deutsche Uberseewanderung*, pp. 41-44.

4. W. Kollman and P. Marschalk, "German Emigration to the United States," in *Perspectives in American History* 7 (1973): 524–41.

5. Burgdorfer, "Migration," pp. 315-16.

6. W. Kamphoefner, *Westfalen in der Neuen Welt, Eine Sozialgeschichte der Auswanderung im 19 Jahrhundert* (Munster, 1982). Also papers of Robert Swierenga, Deirdre Mageean, and Julianna Puskas, in I. A. Glazier and L. De Rosa, *Migration across Time and Nations* (New York, 1986).

ABSR	AMBASSADOR	BRG	BURGESS
ACCT	ACCOUNTANT	BRK	BARKEEPER
ACHTT	ARCHITECT	BRKR	BROKER
ACROBAT	ACROBAT	BRKSTR	BRICK SETTER
ADJ	ADJUSTER	BRM	BRUSH MAKER
ADLR	ANTIQUE DEALER	BRN	BARON
ADV	ADVOCATE	BRR	BREWER
AGNT	AGENT	BRRGM	BARGEMAN
AGNTTH	THEATRICAL AGENT	BRSMKR	BRUSH MAKER
AGRC	AGRICULTURIST	BRWKR	BRASS WORKER
AGRT	AGRICULTURALIST	BRZ	BRAZIER
AGT	RETIRED	BSCKMR	BISCUIT MAKER
AHR	AUTHOR	BSKM	BASKETMAKER
AMR	ARMOURER	BSP	BISHOP
ANT	AERONAUT	BST	BLASTER
APDST	APPRENTICE	BTBLK	BOOTBLACK
APTC	APOTHECARY	BTC	BOOT CLOSER
AR	ACTOR	BTDR	BARTENDER
ART	ARTIST	BTH	BATHER
ASST	ASSISTANT	BTL	BUTLER
ASTR	ASTRONOMER	BTLMKR	BOTTLE MAKER
ATH	ATHLETE	BTM	BIT MAKER
ATR	ACTUARY	BTMK	BOATMAKER
ATSN	ARTISAN	BTMKR	BOOTMAKER
ATTEND	ATTENDANT	BTNM	BUTTON MAKER
ATTNY	ATTORNEY	BXMR	BOX MAKER
AUC	AUCTIONEER	BY	BOY
AXMKR	AX MAKER	BYR	BUYER
AY	ARMY	C	COUSIN
AY-LT	ARMY OFFICER	CABL	CABLER
B	BROTHER	CADR	CARDER
BALR	BAILER	CAGT	COMMERCIAL AGENT
BAR	BARRISTER	CAND	CANDIDATE
BARRELMKR	BARRELMAKER	CAR	CARRIER
BAT	BATTER	CASEMAKER	CASE MAKER
BBR	BARBER	CBDR	CABDRIVER
BCHR	BUTCHER	CBLDR	CARRIAGE BUILDER/MAKER
BCK	BACKER	CBLR	COBBLER
BCKM	BRICK MAKER	CBMKR	CLOG AND BUTTON MAKER
BCKMKR	BUCKLE MAKER	CBTMKR	CABINET MAKER
BDM	BIRD MAN	CCHBLDR	COACH BUILDER
BDMKR	BEAD MAKER	CCHMKR	COACH MAKER
BDS	BIRD SELLER	CCHMN	COACHMAN
BGR	BAGGER	CCHPNTR	COACHPAINTER
BILLPOSTER	BILL POSTER	CCMCHT	COMMERCIAL MERCHANT
BKBNDR	BOOKBINDER	CDN	COMEDIAN
BKLYR	BRICKLAYER	CDR	CAR DRIVER
BKMKR	BRICK MAKER	CDTR	CORD CUTTER
BKMN	BOOK DEALER	CDW	CORD WINDER
BKMR	BOOKMAKER	CDWN	CORDWAINER
BKPR	BOOKKEEPER	CFEKPP	COFFEEHOUSE KEEPER
BKR	BAKER	CFNMK	COFFIN MAKER
BKRB	BREAD BAKER	CGR	CHARGER
BKRC	CAKE BAKER	CGRMKR	CIGAR MAKER
BKSL	BOOKSELLER	CGRTW	CIGAR TWISTER
BL	BLEACHER	CH	CHILD
BLDMKR	BLADE MAKER	CHAIR	CHAIR MAKER
BLDR	BUILDER	CHAR	CHARWOMAN
BLKGMKR	BLACKING MAKER	CHASE	CHAISE MAKER
BLKMKR	BLOCK MAKER	CHBRMD	CHAMBER MAID
BLKSMH	BLACKSMITH	CHD	CHEESE DEALER
BLMKR	BOWL MAKER	CHFRMN	CHIEF FOREMAN
BLMN	BELLMAN	CHIMKR	CHINAMAKER
BLR	BOILER MAKER	CHMAK	CHEESE MAKER
BMKR	BROOM MAKER	CHMGR	CHEESE MANAGER
BND	BINDER	CHMKR	CLOTH MAKER
BNKR	BANKER	CHMKRR	CHEST MAKER
BOAT	BOATMAN	CHMMTR	CHEMICAL MANUFACTURER
BOMKR	BONNET MAKER	CHND	CHANDLER
BOO	BOOKER	CHND	CHILD MAID
BOTT	BOTANIST	CHR	CHASER
BR	BARKER	CHRMKR	CHAIRMAKER
BRCMKR	BRACE MAKER	CHSWP	CHIMNEY SWEEPER
BRDE	BRIDE	CHTMR	COACH TRIMMER
BRDKP	BOARDINGHOUSE KEEPER	CHWKR	CLOTH WORKER
BRF	BRASS FOUNDER	CK	COOK
BRFHR	BRASS FINISHER	CKCTR	CORK CUTTER

CKM	COOK MAID	CVR-GLDR	CARVER AND GILDER
CKR	CHECKER	D	DAUGHTER
CL	CLERK	DARY	DAIRYMAN
CLCMKR	COUCH LACE MAKER	DCT	DECORATOR
CLDRS	CLOTH DRESSER	DETECTIVE	DETECTIVE
CLGMKR	CLOGMAKER	DFTMN	DRAFTSMAN
CLGYMN	CLERGYMAN	DGR	DIGGER
CLK	CLICKER	DIACTR	DIAMOND SETTER
CLKMKR	CLOCK MAKER	DIP	DIPLOMAT
CLLMN	CELLAR MAN	DIR	DIVER
CLLR	COLLECTOR	DISP	DISPATCHER
CLMKR	COLOR MAKER	DLR	DEALER
CLMNFTR	CLOTH MANUFACTURER	DMS	DOMESTIC
CLNT	COLONISATOR	DNC	DANCING MASTER/TEACHER
CLR	COLLIER	DPR	DRAPER
CLRMKR	COLLAR MAKER	DPRASST	DRAPER ASSISTANT
CLSH	CLOTH SHEARER	DR	DOCTOR
CLWN	CLOWN	DRG	DRUGGIST
CMAGT	COMMISSION AGENT	DRKP	DOORKEEPER
CMDR	COMMODORE	DRMR	DRUMMER
CMMR	COMMERCE MAN	DRS	DRESSER
CMMSR	COMMISSIONER	DRSMKR	DRESSMAKER
CMN	COALMAN	DRV	DROVER
CMP	COMPOSER	DRVR	DRIVER
CMPR	COMPOSITOR	DSGR	DESIGNER
CMST	CHEMIST	DSTLR	LIQUOR MAKER
CNDL	CANDLE MAKER	DT	DENTIST
CNF	CONFECTIONER	DTR	DIRECTOR
COL	COLONEL	DYR	DYER
COMP	COMPANION	ECON	ECONOMIST
CON	CONDUCTOR	ED	EDITOR
COUM	COUCHMAN	EGR	ENGRAVER
COUMKR	COUCH MAKER	ELN	ELECTRICIAN
CPMKR	CAP MAKER	EMBD	EMBROIDERER
CPR	COOPER	EMBL	EMBELLISHER
CPRMNR	COPPER MINER	EMBS	EMBOSSER
CPRSMH	COPPERSMITH	EMPL	EMPLOYEE
CPSPNGMKR	CAPSPRING MAKER	ENGD	ENGINE DRIVER
CPT	CAPTAIN	ENGMN	ENGINEMAN
CPTLT	CAPITALIST	ENGR	ENGINEER
CPTR	CARPENTER	ENMKR	ENGINE MAKER
CPYR	COPIER	ENMLR	ENAMELLER
CRBLDR	CAR BUILDER	EQ	EQUESTRIAN
CRDMKR	CARD MAKER	EXCV	EXCAVATOR
CRMN	CAR MAN	F	STEPDAUGHTER
CRNDLR	CORN DEALER	FA	FATHER
CRPM	CARPET MAKER	FAB	FABRICANT
CRR	COURIER	FCTR	FILE CUTTER
CRT	CARTER	FDR	FOUNDER
CRTMK	CART MAKER	FDRS	FUR DRESSER
CRTMN	CARTMAN	FEFNDR	IRON FOUNDER
CRTR	CROFTER	FELMO	FELLMONGER
CSHR	CASHIER	FFMR	FRUIT GROWER
CSL	CONSUL	FGR	FIGURIST
CSLR	COUNSELOR	FHAD	FARM HAND
CSTR	CASTER	FID	FIDDLER
CTHR	CLOTHIER	FIL	FILER
CTL	CUTLER	FINA	FINANCE AGENT
CTLDLR	CATTLE DEALER	FLABR	FARM LABORER
CTLDR	CATTLE DRIVER	FLC	FLOCK MAKER
CTLMN	CATTLE ATTENDANT	FLINTMAKER	FLINT MAKER
CTM	CATTLE MAN	FLMLR	FLOUR MILLER
CTMKR	CRATE MAKER	FLSH	FLESHER
CTNPTR	COTTON PRINTER	FLSMH	FILE SMITH
CTNSP	COTTON SPINNER	FLST	FLORIST
CTR	CUTTER	FLUMR	FLUTE MAKER
CTRMN	MOUNTAIN CUTTER	FLWMKR	FLOWER MAKER
CTRV	COMMERCIAL TRAVELLER	FLWSLR	FLOWER SELLER
CTTR	CONTRACTOR	FLXNR	FLAXENER
CTW	CARTWRIGHT	FMGR	FISH MERCHANT
CTYM	COUNTRY MAN	FMR	FARMER
CULT	CULTIVATOR	FMR-MECH	FARMER AND MECHANIC
CUR	CURRIER	FMSTWD	FARM STEWARD
CURE	CURER	FNR	FANNER
CVER	CIVIL ENGINEER	FORMN	FOREMAN
CVMKR	COVER MAKER	FRD	FRUIT DEALER, SELLER
CVR	CARVER	FRDYR	FUR DYER

FRG	FORGEMAN		HP	HELPER
FRMKR	FRAME MAKER		HPNTR	HOUSE PAINTER
FRMN	FIREMAN		HRCTR	HAIRCUTTER
FRNGMR	FRINGE MAKER		HRDRS	HAIRDRESSER
FRR	FARRIER		HRHRCR	HORSE-HAIR CURLER
FRWKR	FRAME WORKER		HRNSNR	HORN SHINER
FSHMN	FISHERMAN		HRPR	HARPER
FSR	FORESTER		HRSB	HARNESS MAKER
FSVNT	FARM SERVANT		HRSDLR	HORSE DEALER
FT	FACTOR		HRSKPR	HORSE KEEPER
FTMN	FOOTMAN		HRSM	HARNESS MAKER
FTR	FITTER		HRSMN	HORSEMAN
FUL	FULLER		HS	HOSIER
FUNSHR	FURNISHER		HSKPR	HOUSEKEEPER
FUR	FURRIER		HSMD	HOUSE MAID
FURNM	FURNITURE MAKER		HSPTR	HOUSE CARPENTER
FWKR	FACTORY WORKER		HSTLR	HOSTLER
FY	FOYER		HSW	HOUSE WORKER
FYMN	FOUNDRYMAN		HSWF	HOUSEWIFE
G	STEPSON		HSWR	HOUSEWRIGHT
GALVANIZER	GALVANIZER		HTDRS	HATDRESSER
GAMB	GAMBLER		HTL	HOSTLER
GCR	GROCER		HTLKPR	HOTEL KEEPER
GCRCL	GROCERY CLERK		HTLMGR	HOTEL MANAGER
GDBT	GOLDBEATER		HTR	HATTER
GDMRMK	GAS METER MAKER		HTTR	HAT TRIMMER
GDNR	GARDENER,GROWER		HUSB	HUSBAND
GDR	GRINDER		HWK	HAWKER
GDSM	GOLDSMITH		IMKR	INSTRUMENT MAKER
GDWK	GOLDWORKER		IMPLIT	IMPRINTER, LITHOGRAPHER
GEN	GENERAL		IND	INDEPENDENT
GENT	GENTLEMAN		INDT	INDUSTRIALIST
GEOL	GEOLOGIST		INF	INFANT
GEOM	GEOMETER		INKP	INNKEEPER
GKPR	GAMESKEEPER		INMKR	IRON MAKER
GL	GIRL		INMNGR	IRON MONGER
GLABR	GOLD LABORER		INS	INSURANCE BROKER
GLDR	GILDER		INSTR	INSTITUTOR
GLMK	GLOVE MAKER		INSTRU	INSTRUCTOR
GLSBR	GLASS BLOWER		INT-B	FAMILY-GOING TO BROTHER
GLSCTR	GLASS CUTTER		INT-FA	INTENDING TO GO TO FAMILY
GLSGDR	GLASS GRINDER		INT-H	FAMILY-GOING TO HUSBAND
GLSL	GLASS SELLER		INT-S	FAMILY-GOING TO SON
GLSMKR	GLASS MAKER		INTP	INTERPRETER
GLSR	GLASSER		INWKR	IRON WORKER
GLSSTR	GLASS STAINER		IPTR	IMPORTER
GLVR	GLOVER		IRDR	IRON DRESSER
GM	GROOM		IRGR	IRON GROVER
GNGMKR	GINGER MAKER		IRN	IRONER
GNMKR	GUN MAKER		IRNMLDR	IRON MOULDER
GNR	GRAINER		IRNT	IRON TURNER
GRL	GIRDLER		IRSMH	IRON SMITH
GRN-GCR	GREEN GROCER		ISP	INSPECTOR
GRVMKR	GROVE MAKER		JAP	JAPANNER
GSF	GASFITTER		JCK	JOCKEY
GSMH	GUNSMITH		JDG	JUDGE
GSMN	GAS MAN		JLR	JAILER
GSW	GAS WORKER		JNLST	JOURNALIST
GTFTR	GRATE FITTER		JNR	JOINER
GUL	GUILDER		JNTR	JANITOR
GUNNR	US NAVY GUNNER		JRNM	JOURNEYMAN
GVNS	GOVERNESS		JRNW	JOURNEYWOMAN
GVR	GRAVER		JRT	JURIST
GVTS	GOVERNMENT SERVICES		JUG	JUGGLER
GYMN	GYMNAST		JUR	JURIST
GYP	GYPSER		JWLR	JEWELLER
GZR	GLAZIER		KEMK	KEY MAKER
H	HUSBAND		KMNFTR	KNIFE MANUFACTURER
HAMF	HAT MANUFACTURER		KNGR	KNIFE GRINDER
HARB	HARBOR MASTER		KNR	KEENER
HBRDSR	HABERDASHER		KNSMH	KNIFESMITH
HD	HERD		KNTR	KNITTER
HDWMR	HARDWARE MERCHANT		KPR	KEEPER
HJNR	HOUSE JOINER		KTM	KETTLE MAKER
HKR	HACKER		L	IN LAW
HMRMN	HAMMER MAN		LABR	LABORER
HNTR	HUNTER		LAD	LAUNDRY WORKER

LANDMAN	LANDMAN	MNTL	MANTLE MAKER
LCMKR	LACE MAKER	MNTR	MOUNTER
LCT	LECTOR	MOD	MODELER
LDGHKPR	LODGINGHOUSE KEEPER	MODIST	MODIST
LDMA	LADY'S MAID	MODMKR	MODEL MAKER
LDOWR	LAND OWNER	MON	MONK
LDPR	LINEN DRAPER	MPOL	MARBLE POLISHER
LDY	LADY	MRCR	MERCER
LEDLR	LEATHER DEALER	MRMKR	MIRROR MAKER
LFNDR	LETTER FOUNDER	MRNR	MARINER
LITGR	LITHOGRAPHER	MSMK	MASON MAKER
LKMKR	LOCKMAKER	MSN	MASON
LKSH	LOCKSMITH	MSNY	MISSIONARY
LLD	LANDLORD	MSR	MEASURER
LMBRM	LUMBERMAN	MST	MASTER
LMKR	LOOM MAKER	MSTMKR	MILLSTONE MAKER
LMNFTR	LEATHER MANUFACTURER	MSVNT	MANSERVANT
LMP	LUMPER	MTE	MATE
LNG	LINGUIST	MTH	MATCHMAKER
LNM	LINEN WORKER	MTLDLR	METAL DEALER
LNWVR	LINEN WEAVER	MTMKR	MANTEAU MAKER
LPLTR	LAMP LIGHTER	MTMLDR	METAL MOLDER
LPMKR	LAMP MAKER	MTWKR	METAL WORKER
LPR	LAPPER	MUSDIR	MUSICAL DIRECTOR
LQT	LIQUORIST	MUSMR	MASTER OF MUSIC
LRCTR	LEATHER CUTTER	MUSN	MUSICIAN
LRDR	LARD RENDERER	MUSTCHR	MUSIC TEACHER
LRDRS	LEATHER DRESSER	MYR	MAYOR
LSORT	LETTER SORTER	N	NIECE/NEPHEW
LSPNR	LACE SPINNER	NDM	NEEDLE MANUFACTURER
LSTDNT	LAW STUDENT	NDMKR	NEEDLEMAKER
LT	LIEUTENANT	NLR	NAILER
LTRCRR	LETTER CARRIER	NLRM	NAIL MAKER
LTRMN	LITERARY MAN	NLSMH	NAILSMITH
LWYR	LAWYER	NN	NONE
M	MOTHER	NOTPUB	NOTARY PUBLIC
MA	MATRON	NRS	NURSE
MACH	MACHINIST	NRSN	NIGHT NURSE
MACHMKR	MACHINE MAKER	NRSYMN	NURSERYMAN
MAGISTRAT	MAGISTRATE	NTRL	NATURALIST
MAR	MARRIER	NVGT	NAVIGATOR
MARMSN	MARBLE MASON	NVOF	NAVAL OFFICER
MARN	MARINE	NVYLT	NAVY LIEUTENANT
MARWKR	MARBLE WORKER	NWP	NEWSPAPER
MAT	MATTRESS MAKER	OFF	OFFICER
MCHR	MARBLE CUTTER	OGNBDR	ORGAN BUILDER
MCHT	MERCHANT	OGNMK	ORGAN MAKER
MCHT-CL	MERCHANT AND CLERK	OGNST	ORGANIST
MCTR	MARBLE CUTTER	OLM	OILMAN
MD	PHYSICIAN	OLMKR	OIL MAKER
MDW	MIDWIFE	OLREF	OIL REFINER
ME	MEALER	OP	OPERATIVE
MECH	MECHANIC	OPSGR	OPERA SINGER
MED	MEDICAL WORKER	OPTC	OPTICIAN
METLGT	METALLURGIST	OST	OSTLER
MGR	MANAGER	OVRSR	OVERSEER
MILT	MILITARY	PASM	PASTRY MAKER
MKDLR	MILK DEALER	PAST	POST ASSISTANT
MKMD	MILKMAID	PBL	PUBLICAN
MKMN	MILKMAN	PCR	PIECER
MKR	MAKER	PDLR	PEDDLER
MLBLDR	MILL BUILDER	PEN	PENSIONER
MLCCHR	MOLE CATCHER	PFNL	PROFESSIONAL
MLDR	MOLDER	PH	PHOTOGRAPHER
MLHND	MILL HAND	PHD	DOCTOR OF PHILOSOPHY
MLKPR	MULE KEEPER	PHLG	PHILOLOGIST
MLNR	MILLINER	PHRS	PHARMACIST
MLR	MILLER BAKER	PHS	PHILOSOPHER
MLSTR	MALTSTER	PIMK	PIPE MAKER
MLW	MILL WORKER	PINST	PIANIST
MLWR	MILLWRIGHT	PK	PACKER
MMRNR	MASTER MARINER	PKBCHR	PORK CUTTER
MNFTR	MANUFACTURER	PLGM	PLOUGHMAN
MNLG	MINERALOGIST	PLH	PLOW HOLDER
MNR	MINER	PLMN	POLICEMAN
MNRES	MINING ENGINEER	PLN	PLANER
MNSTR	MINISTER	PLNTR	PLANTER

PLR	PLAITER	RPTR	REPORTER
PLSTR	PLASTERER	RR	RENTER
PLT	POLITICIAN	RRCL	RAILWAY CLERK
PLTR	POULTERER	RROFF	RAILWAY OFFICER
PLTWKR	PLATE WORKER	RRWKR	RAILWAY WORKER
PLTYR	PLATE LAYER	RST	RESTORER
PMBR	PLUMBER	RTR	RENTIER
PMKR	PIANO MAKER	RVR	RIVETER
PMM	PORTMANTEAU MAKER	RZMKR	RAZOR MAKER
PMNFTR	PIANO MANUFACTURER	S	SON
PNM	PIN MAKER	S-FRM	SON OF FARMER
PNR	POINTER	SALT	SALTER
PNTR	PAINTER	SCH	SCHOLAR
PORKMAN	PORK MAN	SCHM	SCHOOL MASTER
POST	POST OFFICER	SCHMS	SCHOOL MISTRESS
POT	PILOT	SCM	SCALE MAKER
POUT	UNKNOWN	SCMKR	SCREW MAKER
PPHGR	PAPER HANGER	SCP	SCULPTOR
PPMFR	PAPER MANUFACTURER	SCR	SCOURER
PPMKR	PAPER MAKER	SCRBLR	SCRIBBLER
PPNTMKR	PRINT MAKER	SCRV	SCRIVENER
PPNTR	PORTRAIT PAINTER	SDLMKR	SADDLE MAKER
PPR	PIPER	SDLR	SADDLER
PPTR	PROPRIETOR	SDM	SEEDMAN
PRCH	PREACHER	SDWM	SODA WATER MAKER
PREST	PRIEST	SDYR	SILK DYER
PRF	PERFUMER	SEALMAKER	SEAL MAKER
PRNTR	PRINTER	SEC	SECRETARY
PROF	PROFESSOR	SEMN	SEAMAN
PROF-MUS	PROFESSOR OF MUSIC	SGL	SINGLE
PRS	PRESSMAN	SGN	SURGEON
PRSR	PRESSER	SGNMKR	SIGN MAKER
PRTR	PORTER	SHAGNT	SHIP AGENT
PRWKR	PRINT WORKER	SHCHND	SHIP CHANDLER
PSMK	PASTE MAKER	SHDL	SHEEP JOBBER
PSN	PARSON	SHFM	SHEPHERD
PSNT	PEASANT	SHGLR	SHINGLER
PSP	LAPIDARY	SHIBRO	SHIP BROKER
PSR	PURSER	SHMK	SHOEMAKER
PSSR	PROPRIETOR	SHMST	SHIP MASTER
PST	PASTER	SHNR	SHINER
PSTR	PASTOR	SHPAST	SHOP ASSISTANT
PT	POTTER	SHPC	SHIP'S CARPENTER
PTLON	POSTILION	SHPKR	SHOPKEEPER
PTMKR	PATTERN MAKER	SHPMKR	SHIP MAKER
PTNR	PIANO TUNER	SHPMN	SHOPMAN
PTR	PUTTER	SHPNTR	SHIP PAINTER
PTYM	POTTERY MAKER	SHPO	SHIP OWNER
PUB	PUBLISHER	SHPR	SHIPPER
PUD	PUDDLER	SHPWRT	SHIPWRIGHT
PUMK	PUMP MAKER	SHR	SHEARER
PURMKR	PURSE MAKER	SHSM	SHIPSMITH
PVMT	PROVISION MERCHANT	SHUMK	SHUTTLE MAKER
PVR	PAVER	SHV	SHAVER
PVTM	PRIVATE MAN	SHW	SHOWMAN
PVTR	PRIVATIER	SI	SISTER
PVTW	PRIVATE WOMAN	SING	SINGER
PWT	PEWTERER	SJNR	SHIP JOINER
QA	QUAY WORKER	SKDR	SKIN DRESSER
QRYMN	QUARRYMAN	SKR	SKINNER
R	RELATIVE	SLD	SOLDIER
RAB	RABBI	SLKDRS	SILK DRESSER
RBM	RIBBON MAKER	SLKP	SALOON KEEPER
RCR	RANCHER	SLL	SELLER
RDMKR	ROAD MAKER	SLMK	SALESPERSON
RE	RELIGIOUS	SLMKR	SAIL MAKER
RE-MERCY	SISTER OF MERCY	SLPL	SILVER PLATER
REAGT	REAL ESTATE AGENT	SLPMK	SLIPPER MAKER
REF	REFINER	SLR	SAILOR
REST	RESTAURANT	SLSMH	SILVERSMITH
RFMK	ROOF MAKER	SLSMN	SALESMAN
RGM	RAGMAN	SLT	SLATER
RKCTR	ROCK CUTTER	SMH	SMITH
RKMKR	RAKE MAKER	SML	SMELTER
RMKR	RULE MAKER	SMNFTR	SILK MANUFACTURER
RNGR	RANGER	SMSTS	SEAMSTRESS
RPR	ROPE MAKER	SP	SPINSTER

SPB	SOAP BOILER	TIREMN	TIRE DEALER
SPDLR	SOAP DEALER	TKMKR	TRUNK MAKER
SPM	SOAP MAKER	TKR	TINKER
SPMKR	SPADE MAKER	TLKPR	TOLL KEEPER
SPMNFTR	SOAP MANUFACTURER	TLR	TAILOR
SPNMK	SPOON MAKER	TLRW	WAISTCOAT MAKER
SPNMSTR	SPINNING MASTER	TMKR	THREAD MAKER
SPNR	SPINNER	TNG	TECHNOLOGIST
SPNTR	SIGN PAINTER	TNM	TINMAN
SPRTMN	SPORTSMAN	TNMICH	TIN MAN,IRON WORKER,COPPER SMITH
SRTMKR	SHIRT MAKER	TNMK	TIN MAKER
SSPNR	SILK SPINNER	TNR	TANNER
STAMKR	STAMP MAKER	TNSTH	TINSMITH
STB	STONE BREAKER	TPCTR	TYPE CUTTER
STBLR	STABLER	TPGPH	TYPOGRAPHER
STCL	STORE CLERK	TPMK	TAPE MAKER
STCLR	STREET CLEANER	TPS	TYPESETTER
STCTR	STONE CUTTER	TR	TILER
STDNT	STUDENT	TRANSLATOR	TRANSLATOR
STDR	STAGE DRIVER	TRDM	MAN OF TRADE
STGKPR	STAGE KEEPER	TRDSMN	TRADESMAN
STK	STOKER	TRMM	TRIMMING MAKER
STKB	STOCK BROKER	TRMR	TRIMMER
STKPR	STOREKEEPER	TRNR	TRAINER
STKR	STOCK RAISER	TRSR	TREASURER
STKW	STOCKING WEAVER	TRVLR	TRAVELLER
STLMN	STABLEMAN	TSLMK	TASSEL MAKER
STLR	STONE LAYER	TT	TOURIST
STMAKR	STICK MAKER	TU	TURNER
STMKR	STEEL MAKER	TUT	TUTOR
STMN	STATESMAN	TVN	TAVERNER
STMSN	STONE MASON	TYMN	TOYMAN
STNER	STATIONER	U	UNCLE
STNG	STENOGRAPHER	UMKR	UMBRELLA MAKER
STNR	STONER	UNDTKR	UNDERTAKER
STPLH	STONE POLISHER	UPHST	UPHOLSTERER
STRK	STRIKER	VAL	VALET
STRW	SILK THROWSTER	VAR	VARNISHER
STRY	STATUARY	VET	VETERINARIAN
STVMKR	STOVE MANUFACTURER	VINM	VINEGAR MAKER
STW	SILK TWISTER	VIOL	VIOLINIST
STWD	STEWARD	VLNTR	VOLUNTEER
STWPR	STRAW PRESSER	VLT	VELVET WORKER
STWS	STEWARDESS	VND	VENDER
STWVR	STEAM WEAVER	VNDRS	VINE-DRESSER
SUGB	SUGAR BAKER	VNT	VINTNER
SUGBBLR	SUGAR BOILER	VSGN	VETERINARIAN SURGEON
SUGF	SUGAR REFINER	W	WIFE
SUGM	SUGAR MAKER	W-FMR	WIFE OF FARMER
SVNT	SERVANT	W-SHMK	WIFE OF SHOEMAKER
SVYR	SURVEYOR	WCHMKR	WATCHMAKER
SWMKR	SAW MAKER	WDCDR	WOOD CORDER
SWP	SWEEPER	WDCTR	WOOD CUTTER
SWR	SAWYER	WDCV	WOOD CARVER
SWVR	SILK WEAVER	WDMCHT	WOOD MERCHANT
SXT	SEXTON	WDMN	WOOD MAN
TAPMKR	TAPESTRY MAKER	WDRNGR	WOOD RANGER
TBCL	TOBACCO LABORER	WDTU	WOOD TURNER
TBCMNFTR	TOBACCO MANUFACTURER	WET	WATERMAN
TBCNST	TOBACCONIST	WGGM	WAGON MAKER
TBKR	TABLE MAKER	WGHR	WEIGHER
TBMR	TUBE MAKER	WGNR	WAGONER
TCH	TECHNICIAN	WGR	WINE GROWER
TCHR	TEACHER	WGT	WRIGHT
TCHRL	TEACHER OF LANGUAGES	WHLR	WHEELER
TDR	TRADER	WHR	WHEELWRIGHT
TECH	TECHNICIAN	WI	WIDOW/WIDOWER
TELG	TELEGRAPHER	WI-FMR	WIDOW/WIDOWER-FARMER
TER	TEAMSTER	WIDLR	WIRE DEALER
TERM	TERRACE MAKER	WIDR	WIRE DRAWER
TGC	TELEGRAPH CLERK	WIWKR	WIRE WORKER
THEO	THEOLOGIAN	WIWVR	WIRE WEAVER
THPROF	THEOLOGY PROFESSOR	WLCR	WALL CLEANER
THR	THATCHER	WLD	WELDER
TIL	TILLER	WLDPR	WOOL DRAPER
TILM	TILE MAKER	WLS	WOOL SPINNER
TIR	TINNER	WLSR	WOOL SORTER

xxii

LIST OF OCCUPATIONS WITH CODES

WLST	WOOL STAPLER	WSHR	WASHER
WLWRK	WOOL WORKER	WSMH	WHITESMITH
WMCHT	WINE MERCHANT	WTR	WAITER
WMN	WATCHMAN	WTRPR	WATERPROOF MAKER
WO	WOMAN	WTRS	WAITRESS
WPMKR	WHIP MAKER	WVR	WEAVER
WPRTR	WINE PORTER	WWSH	WHITE WASHER
WRHSMN	WAREHOUSE MAN	WXM	WAX MAKER
WRMKR	WIRE MAKER	Y	GRANDPARENT
WRT	WRITER	ZWKR	ZINC WORKER

AB	ANHALT BERNBURG		MK	MECKLENBURG
AC	ALSACE		MW	MECKLENBURG SCHWERIN
AD	ANHALT DESSAU		MZ	MECKLENBURG STRELITZ
AL	ALSACE LORRAINE		OB	UPPER FRANCONIA
AN	ANHALT		OL	OLDENBURG
BD	BADEN		PM	POMERANIA
BP	UPPER BAVARIA		PR	PRUSSIA
BR	BREMEN		RE	REUSS
BU	BRANDENBURG		SA	SILESIA
BV	BAVARIA		SB	SCHWARZBURG RUDOLSTADT
BW	BRUNSWICK		SC	SAXONY COBURG GOTHA
FF	FRANKFURT		SD	SCHWARZBURG SONDERSHAUSEN
FR	FRANCE		SG	SAXONY MEININGEN
GR	GERMANY		SH	SCHLESWIG HOLSTEIN
HB	HAMBURG		SL	LIPPE SCHAUMBURG
HC	HESSE CASSEL		SR	SWITZERLAND
HD	HESSE DARMSTADT		SS	SWABIA
HH	HESSE HOMBURG		SW	SAXONY WEIMAR EISENACH
HN	WALDECK HESSE NASSAU		SX	SAXONY ALTENBURG
HO	HANOVER		SY	SAXONY
HS	HESSE		SZ	SCHWARZBURG
HZ	HOHENZOLLERN		TG	THURINGIA
LG	LAUENBURG		UN	UNKNOWN
LP	LIPPE DETMOLD		UP	PALATINATE
LU	LUEBECK		WM	WURTEMBERG
LX	LUXEMBURG		WP	WESTPHALIA

**The alphabetical codes listed above for provinces
and countries apply to this volume only.**

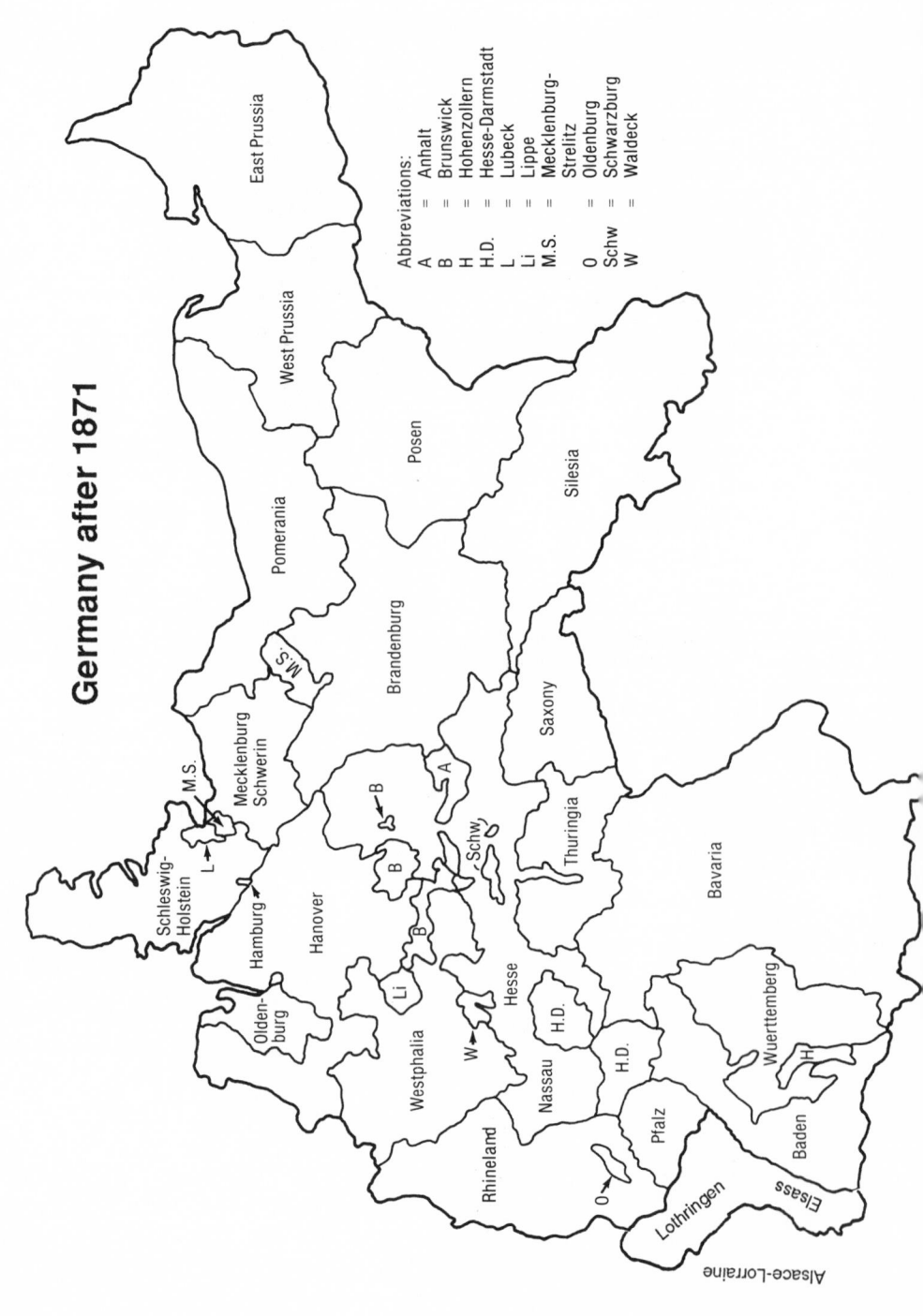

Germany after 1871

Abbreviations:

A = Anhalt
B = Brunswick
H = Hohenzollern
H.D. = Hesse-Darmstadt
L = Lubeck
Li = Lippe
M.S. = Mecklenburg-Strelitz
O = Oldenburg
Schw = Schwarzburg
W = Waldeck

East Prussia

West Prussia

Posen

Silesia

Pomerania

Brandenburg

Saxony

Schleswig-Holstein

M.S.

Mecklenburg Schwerin

M.S.

L

Hamburg

Hanover

B

B

A

Schw,

Thuringia

Bavaria

Oldenburg

Li

W

Hesse

H.D.

Westphalia

Nassau

H.D.

Pfalz

Wuerttemberg

H

Rhineland

O

Baden

Lothringen

Elsass

Alsace-Lorraine

AAAA	AACH	AADA	ALTERSHAUSEN	AAGA	AUMA
AAAB	AACHEN	AADB	ALTHAUSEN	AAGB	AURA
AAAC	AALEN	AADC	ALTHEIM	AAGC	AURICH
AAAD	ABBENSEN	AADD	ALTIGEN	AAGD	AUSTIN
AAAE	ABENHEIM	AADE	ALTONA	AAGE	BABENHAUSEN
AAAF	ABTERODE	AADF	ALTRIP	AAGF	BACH
AAAG	ACHERN	AADG	ALTSTADT	AAGG	BACHARACH
AAAH	ACHIM	AADH	ALTWASSER	AAGH	BACHHAUSEN
AAAI	ACHTRUP	AADI	ALZENAU	AAGI	BACHLINGEN
AAAJ	ACKENHAUSEN	AADJ	ALZEY	AAGJ	BACKNANG
AAAK	ADELEBSEN	AADK	AMBRAND	AAGK	BADBERGEN
AAAL	ADELMANNSFELDEN	AADL	AMELITH	AAGL	BADEN
AAAM	ADELSDORF	AADM	AMELUNXEN	AAGM	BADEN BADEN
AAAN	ADELSHEIM	AADN	AMOENEBURG	AAGN	BADINGEN
AAAO	ADENDORF	AADO	AMORBACH	AAGO	BAECHLINGEN
AAAP	ADENSTEDT	AADP	AMSHAUSER	AAGP	BAGBAND
AAAQ	AERZEN	AADQ	AMSTERDAM	AAGQ	BAIENFURT
AAAR	AFFINGHAUSEN	AADR	ANDELFINGEN	AAGR	BAIERSBRONN
AAAS	AGLASTERHAUSEN	AADS	ANDORF	AAGS	BAIERSDORF
AAAT	AHAUS	AADT	ANDRAZ	AAGT	BAITZ
AAAU	AHE	AADU	ANDREASBERG	AAGU	BALDENBURG
AAAV	AHLDEN	AADV	ANGENROD	AAGV	BALEN
AAAW	AHLE	AADW	ANGERSBACH	AAGW	BALINGEN
AAAX	AHLEN	AADY	ANHAUSEN	AAGX	BALKHAUSEN
AAAY	AHLUM	AADZ	ANKUM	AAGY	BALLHAUSEN
AAAZ	AHORN	AAEA	ANNABERG	AAGZ	BALLRECHTEN
AABA	AHORNBERG	AAEB	ANSBACH	AAHA	BALTIMORE
AABB	AICH	AAEC	ANTWERP	AAHB	BAMBERG
AABC	ALBACHTEN	AAED	APEN	AAHC	BANKWITZ
AABD	ALBANY	AAEE	APENSEN	AAHD	BANN
AABE	ALBERSHAUSEN	AAEF	APOLDA	AAHE	BARBECKE
AABF	ALBERSLOH	AAEG	ARENDSEE	AAHF	BARCHEL
AABG	ALBIG	AAEH	ARENSBERG	AAHG	BARCHFELD
AABH	ALBIS	AAEI	ARHEILGEN	AAHH	BARGEN
AABI	ALBISHEIM	AAEJ	ARHOLZEN	AAHI	BARGSTEDT
AABJ	ALBSHAUSEN	AAEK	ARLESHEIM	AAHJ	BARKENHOLM
AABK	ALDINGEN	AAEL	ARMSEN	AAHK	BARKHAUSEN
AABL	ALFELD	AAEM	ARMSHEIM	AAHL	BARMEN
AABM	ALFHAUSEN	AAEN	ARNEGG	AAHM	BARNHAUSEN
AABN	ALFSTEDT	AAEO	ARNHEIM	AAHN	BARNSTORF
AABO	ALLEGHENY	AAEP	ARNSBERG	AAHO	BARSKAMP
AABP	ALLENBACH	AAEQ	ARNSTADT	AAHP	BARTENSTEIN
AABQ	ALLENBURG	AAER	ARNSTEIN	AAHQ	BARTH
AABR	ALLENDORF	AAES	ARNSWALDE	AAHR	BARTOW
AABS	ALLERSHAUSEN	AAET	AROLSEN	AAHS	BARUM
AABT	ALLSTEDT	AAEU	ARRACH	AAHU	BASEL
AABU	ALMSTEDT	AAEV	ARSTEN	AAHV	BASSUM
AABV	ALPERSBACH	AAEW	ARTERN	AAHW	BATTENBERG
AABW	ALSDORF	AAEX	ARZBERG	AAHX	BAUDENBACH
AABX	ALSENZ	AAEY	ARZHEIM	AAHY	BAUERBACH
AABY	ALSFELD	AAEZ	ASBACH	AAHZ	BAUMBACH
AABZ	ALSLEBEN	AAFA	ASBERG	AAIA	BAUMGARTEN
AACA	ALTBACH	AAFB	ASCH	AAIB	BAUMHOLDER
AACB	ALTDORF	AAFC	ASCHAFFENBURG	AAIC	BAUSENDORF
AACD	ALTENA	AAFD	ASCHEBERG	AAID	BAUTZEN
AACE	ALTENBACH	AAFE	ASCHENDORF	AAIE	BAVARIA
AACF	ALTENBAMBERG	AAFF	ASCHWARDEN	AAIF	BAYREUTH
AACG	ALTENBEKEN	AAFG	ASEL	AAIG	BEBELSHEIM
AACH	ALTENBERG	AAFH	ASLAU	AAIH	BEBRA
AACI	ALTENBERGE	AAFI	ASMUSHAUSEN	AAII	BECHLINGEN
AACJ	ALTENBREITUNGEN	AAFJ	ASSELN	AAIJ	BECHTHEIM
AACK	ALTENBRUCH	AAFK	ASSEN	AAIK	BECHTOLSHEIM
AACL	ALTENBRUCK	AAFL	ASSENHEIM	AAIL	BECK
AACM	ALTENBUCH	AAFM	ASSLAR	AAIM	BECKSTEIN
AACN	ALTENBUEREN	AAFN	ATENS	AAIN	BECKUM
AACO	ALTENBURG	AAFO	ATTENDORF	AAIO	BEDERKESA
AACP	ALTENDORF	AAFP	AU	AAIP	BEDESBACH
AACQ	ALTENGESEKE	AAFQ	AUE	AAIQ	BEEK
AACR	ALTENGRONAU	AAFR	AUENHEIM	AAIR	BEELEN
AACS	ALTENHAGEN	AAFS	AUENSTEIN	AAIS	BEERFELDEN
AACT	ALTENHEIM	AAFT	AUERBACH	AAIT	BEESKOW
AACU	ALTENHOF	AAFU	AUFENAU	AAIU	BEESTEN
AACV	ALTENHUNTORF	AAFV	AUFHAUSEN	AAIV	BEILSTEIN
AACW	ALTENKIRCHEN	AAFW	AUFSESS	AAIW	BEISEFOERTH
AACX	ALTENKUNSTADT	AAFX	AUGSBURG	AAIX	BELGARD
AACY	ALTENSTADT	AAFY	AUGUSTA	AAIY	BELGRAD
AACZ	ALTENSTEIG	AAFZ	AUHAGEN	AAIZ	BELKE

Code	Village	Code	Village	Code	Village
AAJA	BELLINGEN	AAMB	BIERBACH	AAPD	BOENNINGHAUSEN
AAJB	BELM	AAMC	BIERDE	AAPE	BOFFZEN
AAJC	BELTHEIM	AAMD	BIERDEN	AAPF	BOHLEN
AAJD	BELUM	AAME	BIEREN	AAPG	BOHLINGEN
AAJE	BENDELEBEN	AAMF	BIERINGEN	AAPH	BOHMTE
AAJF	BENDORF	AAMG	BIESENDORF	AAPI	BOITZEN
AAJG	BENHORN	AAMH	BIETIGHEIM	AAPJ	BOITZENBURG
AAJH	BENKEN	AAMI	BILLERBECK	AAPK	BOKE
AAJI	BENNIN	AAMJ	BILLIGHEIM	AAPL	BOKEL
AAJJ	BENNINGEN	AAMK	BILLINGHAUSEN	AAPM	BOLLINGEN
AAJK	BENRATH	AAML	BILSHAUSEN	AAPN	BOLLINGHAUSEN
AAJL	BENSEN	AAMM	BINDE	AAPO	BOLLMANN
AAJM	BENSHAUSEN	AAMN	BINGEN	AAPP	BONAMES
AAJN	BENSHEIM	AAMO	BINNEN	AAPQ	BONFELD
AAJO	BENTHEIM	AAMP	BINSWANGEN	AAPR	BONLANDEN
AAJP	BENZ	AAMQ	BIPPEN	AAPS	BONN
AAJQ	BENZEN	AAMR	BIRK	AAPT	BOOKHOFF
AAJR	BEREL	AAMS	BIRKACH	AAPU	BOOS
AAJS	BERENBOSTEL	AAMT	BIRKENAU	AAPV	BOPFINGEN
AAJT	BERENT	AAMU	BIRKENFELD	AAPW	BORAU
AAJU	BERG	AAMV	BIRNBAUM	AAPX	BORGENTREICH
AAJV	BERGA	AAMW	BIRNFELD	AAPY	BORGFELD
AAJW	BERGE	AAMX	BISCHBERG	AAPZ	BORGHOLZHAUSEN
AAJX	BERGEN	AAMY	BISCHHAUSEN	AAQA	BORGHORST
AAJY	BERGHAUSEN	AAMZ	BISCHLEBEN	AAQB	BORGLOH
AAJZ	BERGHEIM	AANA	BISCHOFFERODE	AAQC	BORKEN
AAKA	BERGKIRCHEN	AANB	BISCHOFSBURG	AAQD	BORNHEIM
AAKB	BERGWITZ	AANC	BISCHOFSDHRON	AAQE	BORRINGHAUSEN
AAKC	BERINGHAUSEN	AAND	BISCHOFSGRUEN	AAQF	BORSTEL
AAKD	BERK	AANE	BISCHOFSHEIM	AAQG	BOSSEL
AAKE	BERKA	AANF	BISCHOFSWERDER	AAQH	BOSTON
AAKF	BERKAU	AANG	BISCHWEIER	AAQI	BOTHEL
AAKG	BERLEBURG	AANH	BISENZ	AAQJ	BOVENDEN
AAKH	BERLIN	AANI	BISMARCK	AAQK	BRAACH
AAKI	BERLINCHEN	AANK	BISSENDORF	AAQM	BRACKEL
AAKJ	BERN	AANL	BITBURG	AAQN	BRACKENHEIM
AAKK	BERNBACH	AANM	BITTERFELD	AAQO	BRAEUNSDORF
AAKL	BERNBURG	AANN	BLANKENAU	AAQP	BRAKE
AAKM	BERNCASTEL	AANO	BLANKENBACH	AAQQ	BRAKEL
AAKN	BERNDORF	AANP	BLANKENBURG	AAQR	BRAMBERG
AAKO	BERNE	AANQ	BLANKENHAGEN	AAQS	BRAMSCHE
AAKP	BERNHOF	AANR	BLANKENHAIN	AAQT	BRAMSTADT
AAKQ	BERNSEE	AANS	BLASHEIM	AAQU	BRAMSTEDT
AAKR	BERNSTEIN	AANT	BLAUBEUREN	AAQV	BRAND
AAKS	BERNTERODE	AANU	BLECKEDE	AAQW	BRANDAU
AAKT	BERSENBRUECK	AANV	BLEICHENBACH	AAQX	BRANDEISL
AAKU	BERUM	AANW	BLEICHERODE	AAQY	BRANDENBURG
AAKV	BESENFELD	AANX	BLEIDENROD	AAQZ	BRANDOBERNDORF
AAKW	BESENKAMP	AANY	BLEISTADT	AARA	BRANDT
AAKX	BESIGHEIM	AANZ	BLENDER	AARB	BRANOWITZ
AAKY	BESSE	AAOA	BLERSUM	AARC	BRAUNFELS
AAKZ	BESSINGEN	AAOB	BLEXEN	AARD	BRAUNHAUSEN
AALA	BETHEN	AAOC	BLOMBERG	AARE	BRAUNLAGE
AALB	BETHLEHEM	AAOD	BLOWITZ	AARF	BRAUNLINGEN
AALC	BETTENHAUSEN	AAOE	BLUMBERG	AARG	BRAUNWEILER
AALD	BETTINGEN	AAOF	BLUMENTHAL	AARH	BREDBECK
AALE	BETZIESDORF	AAOG	BOBENHAUSEN	AARI	BREDDORF
AALF	BEUERN	AAOH	BOBERG	AARJ	BREDENBORN
AALG	BEUTELSBACH	AAOI	BOBSTADT	AARK	BREGENZ
AALH	BEVERGERN	AAOJ	BOCHINGEN	AARL	BREISACH
AALI	BEVERSTEDT	AAOK	BOCHOLT	AARM	BREITENBACH
AALJ	BEVERUNGEN	AAOL	BOCHUM	AARN	BREITENBRUNN
AALK	BEYERSDORF	AAOM	BOCKEL	AARO	BREITENHOLZ
AALL	BIBERACH	AAON	BOCKELAU	AARP	BREITENSTEIN
AALN	BIBERSFELD	AAOO	BOCKENHEIM	AARQ	BREITSCHEID
AALO	BIBLIS	AAOQ	BOCKHOP	AARR	BREMEN
AALP	BIBRA	AAOR	BOCKHORST	AARS	BREMERHAVEN
AALQ	BICKENBACH	AAOS	BOCKWA	AART	BREMERVOERDE
AALR	BICKENRIEDE	AAOT	BODELSHAUSEN	AARU	BREMGARTEN
AALS	BIEBELNHEIM	AAOU	BODENBURG	AARV	BREMKA
AALT	BIEBER	AAOV	BODENDORF	AARW	BREMKE
AALU	BIEBRICH	AAOW	BODENFELDE	AARX	BRENKEN
AALV	BIEDENKOPF	AAOX	BODENROD	AARY	BRESIN
AALW	BIEDESHEIM	AAOY	BODENWERDER	AARZ	BRESLAU
AALX	BIEL	AAOZ	BODES	AASA	BRETTEN
AALY	BIELEFELD	AAPA	BOEDIGHEIM	AASB	BRETTHAUSEN
AALZ	BIELEN	AAPC	BOEHMENKIRCH	AASC	BRETZENHEIM
AAMA					

Code	Name	Code	Name	Code	Name
AASD	BRETZINGEN	AAVE	BUNDORF	AAYF	COLMAR
AASE	BRICKWEDE	AAVF	BUOCHS	AAYG	COLOGNE
AASF	BRIDGEPORT	AAVG	BURG	AAYH	COLORADO
AASG	BRIEG	AAVH	BURGDORF	AAYI	COLUMBUS
AASH	BRILL	AAVI	BURGEL	AAYJ	CONNECTICUT
AASI	BRINGHAUSEN	AAVJ	BURGFELDEN	AAYK	COPENHAGEN
AASJ	BRINKUM	AAVK	BURGHAUSEN	AAYL	COPPENBRUEGGE
AASK	BRNO	AAVL	BURGHEIM	AAYM	CORBACH
AASL	BROCHTERBECK	AAVM	BURGHOLZHAUSEN	AAYN	CORSICA
AASM	BROCK	AAVN	BURGLENGENFELD	AAYO	COSWIG
AASN	BROCKEL	AAVO	BURGWEDEL	AAYP	COTTBUS
AASO	BROCKHAGEN	AAVP	BURGWEILER	AAYQ	COUVET
AASP	BROCKHAUSEN	AAVQ	BURHAVE	AAYR	CRAILSHEIM
AASQ	BROCKSTREK	AAVR	BURKHEIM	AAYS	CRIMMITSCHAU
AASR	BROKHAUSEN	AAVS	BUSCHKAU	AAYT	CRIVITZ
AASS	BROMBERG	AAVT	BUSENBERG	AAYU	CRONE
AAST	BROME	AAVU	BUSENDORF	AAYV	CRONENBERG
AASV	BROMSKIRCHEN	AAVV	BUTTELSTEDT	AAYW	CRONHEIM
AASW	BRONN	AAVW	BUTTENHAUSEN	AAYX	CROSSEN
AASX	BRONNEN	AAVX	BUTTENHEIM	AAYY	CRUMBACH
AASY	BROOKLYN	AAVY	BUTTENWIESEN	AAYZ	CULM
AASZ	BROSEWITZ	AAVZ	BUTTERFELDE	AAZA	CULMBACH
AATA	BROSTAU	AAWA	BUTTLAR	AAZB	CULMIKAU
AATB	BRUCH	AAWB	BUTZBACH	AAZC	CUXHAVEN
AATC	BRUCHHAGEN	AAWC	CADENBERGE	AAZD	CZARNIKAU
AATD	BRUCHHAUSEN	AAWD	CALBE	AAZE	DAADEN
AATF	BRUCHSAL	AAWG	CALCAR	AAZF	DAHLEN
AATG	BRUCHSTEDT	AAWH	CALIFORNIA	AAZG	DAHLHEIM
AATH	BRUCK	AAWI	CALLE	AAZH	DAHLINGHAUSEN
AATI	BRUECK	AAWJ	CALLNBERG	AAZI	DAISBERG
AATJ	BRUECKEN	AAWK	CALMBACH	AAZJ	DALHAUSEN
AATK	BRUECKENAU	AAWL	CALVESLAGE	AAZK	DALHEIM
AATL	BRUEGGEN	AAWM	CALVOERDE	AAZL	DAMBACH
AATM	BRUEMSEL	AAWN	CALW	AAZM	DAMM
AATN	BRUENN	AAWO	CAMBERG	AAZN	DAMME
AATO	BRUMATH	AAWP	CAMBURG	AAZO	DANKERSEN
AATP	BRUNN	AAWQ	CAMIN	AAZP	DANNENBERG
AATQ	BRUNSBROCK	AAWR	CAMPE	AAZQ	DANZIG
AATR	BRUNSHAUSEN	AAWS	CANNEWITZ	AAZR	DARDESHEIM
AATS	BRUNSWICK	AAWT	CANNSTATT	AAZS	DARMSTADT
AATT	BRUSSELS	AAWU	CANUM	AAZT	DASCHITZ
AATU	BUBENHEIM	AAWV	CAPPEL	AAZU	DASEBURG
AATV	BUCH	AAWW	CAPPELN	AAZV	DASSEL
AATW	BUCHAU	AAWX	CARDEN	AAZW	DEBSTEDT
AATX	BUCHBACH	AAWY	CARLOWITZ	AAZX	DECKBERGEN
AATY	BUCHEN	AAWZ	CARLSBAD	AAZY	DECKENBACH
AATZ	BUCHENAU	AAXA	CARLSHAFEN	AAZZ	DEDESDORF
AAUA	BUCHENBACH	AAXB	CARLSRUHE	ABAA	DEGGINGEN
AAUB	BUCHENBERG	AAXC	CARZIG	ABAB	DEIDERODE
AAUC	BUCHHEIM	AAXD	CASEL	ABAC	DEINSTE
AAUD	BUCHHOF	AAXE	CASLAU	ABAD	DELBRUECK
AAUE	BUCHHOLZ	AAXF	CASSEL	ABAG	DELMENHORST
AAUF	BUCKAU	AAXG	CASTEL	ABAH	DEMMIN
AAUG	BUCKOW	AAXH	CELLE	ABAI	DENKENDORF
AAUH	BUECHES	AAXI	CHALON	ABAJ	DENSBERG
AAUI	BUECKENBERG	AAXJ	CHARLESTON	ABAK	DENZLINGEN
AAUJ	BUECKEN	AAXK	CHEMNITZ	ABAL	DERMBACH
AAUK	BUEDEN	AAXL	CHICAGO	ABAM	DERNE
AAUL	BUEDINGEN	AAXM	CHINOW	ABAN	ANHALT-DESSAU
AAUM	BUEHL	AAXN	CHUR	ABAO	DETERN
AAUN	BUEHLER	AAXO	CINCINNATI	ABAP	DETMOLD
AAUO	BUEHNE	AAXP	CISTA	ABAQ	DETROIT
AAUP	BUEHREN	AAXQ	CLADOW	ABAR	DETTINGEN
AAUQ	BUELKAU	AAXR	CLAUEN	ABAS	DEUTZ
AAUR	BUENDE	AAXS	CLAUSEN	ABAT	DEVENTER
AAUS	BUER	AAXT	CLAUSTHAL	ABAU	DEXBACH
AAUT	BUEREN	AAXU	CLEVE	ABAV	DIEBURG
AAUU	BUERGEL	AAXV	CLEVELAND	ABAW	DIEDELSHEIM
AAUV	BUESUM	AAXW	CLOPPENBURG	ABAX	DIEDORF
AAUW	BUETTELBORN	AAXX	COBLENZ	ABAY	DIELHEIM
AAUX	BUETTSTEDT	AAXY	COBURG	ABAZ	DIELINGEN
AAUY	BUFFALO	AAXZ	COELBE	ABBA	DIEMARDEN
AAUZ	BUG	AAYA	COELLN	ABBB	DIEPENAU
AAVA	BUIR	AAYB	COESFELD	ABBC	DIEPHOLZ
AAVB	BUKE	AAYC	COETHEN	ABBD	DIERHAGEN
AAVC	BUNDE	AAYD	COLBITZ	ABBE	DIESBACH
AAVD	BUNDENTHAL	AAYE	COLLIN	ABBF	DIESSEN

ABBG	DIETERSDORF	ABEH	DUESSELDORF	ABHH	EISENACH
ABBH	DIETZ	ABEI	DUETZEN	ABHI	EISENBERG
ABBI	DIJON	ABEJ	DUISBERG	ABHJ	EISLEBEN
ABBJ	DILLBRECHT	ABEK	DUISENBURG	ABHK	EISLINGEN
ABBK	DILLENBURG	ABEM	DURLACH	ABHL	EISSELN
ABBL	DILLICH	ABEN	DUSSLINGEN	ABHM	EITERFELD
ABBM	DILLINGEN	ABEO	DUTTWEILER	ABHN	EITZE
ABBN	DINGEN	ABEP	EAST FRIESLAND	ABHO	EITZENDORF
ABBO	DINKELSBUEHL	ABEQ	EBELEBEN	ABHP	EITZUM
ABBP	DINKLAGE	ABER	EBENSFELD	ABHQ	ELB
ABBQ	DIRMSTEIN	ABES	EBERN	ABHS	ELBEBERG
ABBR	DISSEN	ABET	EBERSBACH	ABHT	ELBERFELD
ABBS	DITTELSHEIM	ABEU	EBERSTADT	ABHU	ELBING
ABBT	DITTERSBACH	ABEV	EBHAUSEN	ABHV	ELDAGSEN
ABBV	DITTERSDORF	ABEW	EBINGEN	ABHW	ELDERN
ABBW	DITZUM	ABEX	EBNAT	ABHX	ELEND
ABBX	DOBRA	ABEY	ECHTE	ABHY	ELFERSHAUSEN
ABBY	DOEHLAU	ABEZ	ECHZELL	ABHZ	ELGERSHAUSEN
ABBZ	DOEHLEN	ABFA	ECKARTHAUSEN	ABIA	ELLA
ABCA	DOEHREN	ABFB	ECKEL	ABIB	ELLENBERG
ABCB	DOERBACH	ABFC	ECKERDE	ABIC	ELLENSTEDT
ABCC	DOERNBERG	ABFD	ECKERSDORF	ABID	ELLINGHAUSEN
ABCD	DOERZBACH	ABFE	ECKWEISBACH	ABIE	ELLERSHAUSEN
ABCE	DOESBURG	ABFF	ED	ABIF	ELM
ABCF	DOGERN	ABFG	EDENKOBEN	ABIG	ELMSHORN
ABCG	DOHM	ABFH	EDESHEIM	ABIH	ELMSTEIN
ABCH	DOHNSEN	ABFI	EDEWECHT	ABII	ELPERSHEIM
ABCI	DOHR	ABFJ	EFFELDER	ABIJ	ALSACE
ABCJ	DOMNITZ	ABFK	EFFINGEN	ABIK	ELSENBERG
ABCK	DONAUWOERTH	ABFL	EGELN	ABIL	ELSENDORF
ABCL	DONNERSTEDT	ABFM	EGEN	ABIM	ELSENFELD
ABCM	DORF	ABFN	EGENHAUSEN	ABIN	ELSENZ
ABCN	DORFBAUERSCHAFT	ABFO	EGER	ABIO	ELSFLETH
ABCO	DORFMARK	ABFP	EGGENRIED	ABIP	ELSHEIM
ABCP	DORHEIM	ABFQ	EGLOFFSTEIN	ABIQ	ELSOFF
ABCQ	DORLAR	ABFR	EHEIM	ABIR	ELSTEN
ABCR	DORMETTINGEN	ABFS	EHINGEN	ABIS	ELSTERBERG
ABCS	DORNBERG	ABFT	EHLEN	ABIT	ELSTRA
ABCT	DORNBIRN	ABFU	EHMEN	ABIU	ELTERN
ABCU	DORNDORF	ABFV	EHNINGEN	ABIV	ELTMANN
ABCV	DORNHEIM	ABFW	EHRDISSEN	ABIW	ELZE
ABCW	DORNUM	ABFX	EHRENBREITSTEIN	ABIX	EMBSEN
ABCX	DORTMUND	ABFY	EHRENBURG	ABIY	EMDEN
ABCY	DORUM	ABFZ	EHRINGEN	ABJA	EMMENDINGEN
ABCZ	DOSSENHEIM	ABGA	EIB	ABJB	EMMINGEN
ABDA	DOTTERNHAUSEN	ABGB	EIBELSTADT	ABJC	EMPEDE
ABDB	DOTTINGEN	ABGC	EIBENSTOCK	ABJD	EMPFINGEN
ABDC	DRACHHAUSEN	ABGD	EICHA	ABJE	EMS
ABDD	DRAMBURG	ABGE	EICHBERG	ABJF	EMSDETTEN
ABDE	DRANSFELD	ABGF	EICHELHAIN	ABJG	EMSEN
ABDF	DREETZ	ABGG	EICHELSACHSEN	ABJH	EMSKIRCHEN
ABDG	DREIDORF	ABGH	EICHELSDORF	ABJI	EMTINGHAUSEN
ABDH	DREIS	ABGI	EICHENBERG	ABJJ	EN
ABDI	DREISBACH	ABGJ	EICHENHEIM	ABJK	ENDINGEN
ABDK	DRENSTEINFURT	ABGK	EICHENHOF	ABJL	ENDORF
ABDL	DRENTWEDE	ABGL	EICHENHOFEN	ABJM	ENGE
ABDM	DRESDEN	ABGM	EICHENREID	ABJN	ENGEL
ABDN	DRESEL	ABGN	EICHHOLZ	ABJO	ENGELN
ABDO	DREYEN	ABGO	EICHLING	ABJP	ENGELREICHING
ABDP	DRIESEN	ABGP	EICHSTADT	ABJQ	ENGELSDORF
ABDQ	DROSEDOW	ABGQ	EICHSTETTEN	ABJR	ENGELSTADT
ABDR	DROSENDORF	ABGR	EICKEDORF	ABJS	ENGEN
ABDS	DROSSEN	ABGS	EICKENDORF	ABJT	ENGER
ABDT	DRUEBER	ABGT	EICKHORST	ABJU	ENGERS
ABDU	DUBEN	ABGU	EIENBACH	ABJV	ENGSTLATT
ABDV	DUDENHOFEN	ABGV	EIERSHAUSEN	ABJW	ENGTER
ABDW	DUDENSEN	ABGW	EIFA	ABJX	ENNIGERLOH
ABDX	DUDERSTADT	ABGX	EILSEN	ABJY	ENSINGEN
ABDY	DUDWEILER	ABGY	EILSHAUSEN	ABJZ	ENTRINGEN
ABDZ	DUEHREN	ABGZ	EILSUM	ABKA	EPE
ABEA	DUELMEN	ABHA	EIMBECK	ABKB	EPFENBACH
ABEB	DUENSBACH	ABHB	EIME	ABKC	EPPE
ABEC	DUEREN	ABHC	EINBECK	ABKD	EPPELSHEIM
ABED	DUERKHEIM	ABHD	EININGEN	ABKE	EPPENDORF
ABEE	DUERRENWAID	ABHE	EININGHAUSEN	ABKF	EPPERTSHAUSEN
ABEF	DUERRWANGEN	ABHF	EINOED	ABKG	EPPINGEN
ABEG	DUESHORN	ABHG	EISBERGEN	ABKH	ERBACH

XXX

ABKI	ERBBACH	ABNI	FILZEN	ABQH	FRILE
ABKJ	ERDA	ABNJ	FIRREL	ABQI	FRILLE
ABKK	ERDBACH	ABNK	FISCHBACH	ABQJ	FRISCHBORN
ABKL	ERDEN	ABNL	FISCHERDORF	ABQK	FRITZLAR
ABKM	ERDER	ABNM	FISCHERHUDE	ABQL	FROEMERN
ABKN	ERDMANNRODE	ABNN	FLACHT	ABQM	FROHNBACH
ABKO	ERDMANNSDORF	ABNO	FLATOW	ABQN	FROHNBERG
ABKP	ERFURT	ABNP	FLECHTORF	ABQO	FROHNHAUSEN
ABKQ	ERICHSHAGEN	ABNQ	FLECHUM	ABQP	FROHNSDORF
ABKR	ERLANGEN	ABNR	FLEIN	ABQQ	FUCHSBERG
ABKS	ERLAU	ABNS	FLENSBURG	ABQR	FUCHSSTADT
ABKT	ERLBACH	ABNT	FLERZHEIM	ABQS	FUECHTORF
ABKU	ERLEN	ABNU	FLIEDEN	ABQT	FUENFHAUSEN
ABKV	ERLENBACH	ABNV	FLOH	ABQU	FUENFSTETTEN
ABKW	ERNDTEBRUECK	ABNW	FLORENCE	ABQV	FUERSTENAU
ABKX	ERNSTHAUSEN	ABNX	FLORIDA	ABQW	FUERSTENBERG
ABKY	ERNSTMUEHL	ABNY	FLOSS	ABQX	FUERSTENWALD
ABKZ	ERPOLZHEIM	ABNZ	FOEHR	ABQY	FUERSTENWALDE
ABLA	ERSHAUS	ABOA	FOELSEN	ABQZ	FUERTH
ABLB	ERSINGEN	ABOB	FOERDEN	ABRA	FULDA
ABLC	ERTE	ABOC	FOERSTE	ABRB	FURT
ABLD	ERZINGEN	ABOD	FORCHHEIM	ABRC	FURTH
ABLE	ESBECK	ABOE	FORST	ABRD	GABEL
ABLF	ESBERG	ABOF	FORT WAYNE	ABRE	GABLONZ
ABLG	ESCHAU	ABOG	FRANCE	ABRF	GAGGENAU
ABLH	ESCHBACH	ABOH	FRANK	ABRG	GAILHOF
ABLI	ESCHE	ABOI	FRANKEN	ABRH	GAILINGEN
ABLJ	ESCHELBACH	ABOJ	FRANKENAU	ABRI	GAIS
ABLK	ESCHENAU	ABOK	FRANKENBERG	ABRJ	GALLINGEN
ABLL	ESCHER	ABOL	FRANKENBRUNN	ABRK	GALVESTON
ABLM	ESCHWEGE	ABOM	FRANKENHAUSEN	ABRL	GANDERKESEE
ABLN	ESEBECK	ABON	FRANKENHEIM	ABRM	GANDERSHEIM
ABLP	ESENS	ABOO	FRANKENSTEIN	ABRO	GARDELEGEN
ABLQ	ESLOHE	ABOP	FRANKENTHAL	ABRP	GARTOW
ABLR	ESPASINGEN	ABOQ	FRANKFURT	ABRQ	GARTZ
ABLS	ESPELKAMP	ABOR	FRANKFURT AM MAIN	ABRR	GASSELDORF
ABLT	ESSEN	ABOS	FRANZBURG	ABRS	GAUPEL
ABLU	ESSINGEN	ABOT	FRAUENBORN	ABRT	GAUSELFINGEN
ABLV	ESSLINGEN	ABOU	FRAUENSEE	ABRU	GEBERSDORF
ABLW	ESTORF	ABOV	FRAUENSTEIN	ABRV	GEBROTH
ABLX	ETELSEN	ABOW	FRAUSTADT	ABRW	GEDERN
ABLY	ETTENHEIM	ABOX	FRECHEN	ABRX	GEESDORF
ABLZ	ETZ	ABOY	FRECKENHORST	ABRY	GEESTDORF
ABMA	ETZEN GESAESS	ABOZ	FREDELSLOH	ABRZ	GEESTEMUENDE
ABMB	EUBIGHEIM	ABPA	FREDEN	ABSA	GEHAU
ABMC	EUDORF	ABPB	FREEST	ABSB	GEHAUS
ABMD	EUTIN	ABPC	FREIBURG	ABSC	GEHOFEN
ABME	EVANSVILLE	ABPD	FREIENHAGEN	ABSD	GEHRDE
ABMF	EVERSBERG	ABPE	FREIENOHL	ABSE	GEHRDEN
ABMG	EVERSWINKEL	ABPF	FREIENSTEINAU	ABSF	GEHREN
ABMH	EWATTINGEN	ABPG	FREIENWALDE	ABSG	GEISA
ABMI	EXING	ABPH	FREISBACH	ABSH	GEISFELD
ABMJ	EXTER	ABPI	FREISTETT	ABSI	GEISINGEN
ABMK	EYSTRUP	ABPJ	FRENSDORF	ABSJ	GEISLINGEN
ABML	FACHINGEN	ABPK	FRENZ	ABSK	GEISMAR
ABMM	FAHR	ABPL	FREREN	ABSL	GELDERN
ABMN	FAHRENHOLZ	ABPM	FREUDENSTADT	ABSM	GELLERSHAUSEN
ABMO	FALKENAU	ABPN	FREUDENTHAL	ABSN	GELM
ABMP	FALKENBERG	ABPO	FREYBURG	ABSO	GELNHAUSEN
ABMQ	FALKENBURG	ABPP	FRIEDBERG	ABSP	GEMBITZ
ABMR	FALKENSTEIN	ABPQ	FRIEDEBURG	ABSQ	GEMMRIGHEIM
ABMS	FALLINGBOSTEL	ABPR	FRIEDELSHEIM	ABSR	GEMUEND
ABMT	FALLS	ABPS	FRIEDENSDORF	ABSS	GEMUENDEN
ABMU	FAMBACH	ABPT	FRIEDEWALD	ABSU	GENEVA
ABMV	FASSOLDSHOF	ABPU	FRIEDEWALDE	ABSW	GENTHIN
ABMW	FAURNDAU	ABPV	FRIEDLAND	ABSX	GEPPERSDORF
ABMX	FAUTENBACH	ABPW	FRIEDLOS	ABSY	GERA
ABMY	FECHENBACH	ABPX	FRIEDRICHORST	ABSZ	GERBERSDORF
ABMZ	FEHRENBACH	ABPY	FRIEDRICHRODE	ABTA	GERDEN
ABNA	FEIL	ABPZ	FRIEDRICHSDORF	ABTB	GERHAUSEN
ABNB	FELDE	ABQA	FRIEDRICHSHAUSEN	ABTC	GERHELM
ABNC	FELDKIRCHEN	ABQB	FRIEDRICHSTADT	ABTD	GERMANNSBERG
ABND	FELL	ABQC	FRIEDRICHSTHAL	ABTE	GERMERSHEIM
ABNE	FELSBERG	ABQD	FRIEDRICHSWALDE	ABTF	GERNSHEIM
ABNF	FENNE	ABQE	FRIELINGEN	ABTG	GERODE
ABNG	FERNSDORF	ABQF	FRIEMEN	ABTH	GEROLDSGRUEN
ABNH	FEUCHTWANGEN	ABQG	FRIESLAND	ABTI	GERRA

ABTJ	GERSFELD	ABWJ	GRAISCH	ABZK	CUXHAGEN
ABTK	GERSHEIM	ABWK	GRAMBKE	ABZL	HAAG
ABTL	GERSTETTEN	ABWL	GRAMZOW	ABZM	HAAGEN
ABTM	GERSTUNGEN	ABWM	GRANDORF	ABZN	HABELSCHWERDT
ABTN	GERSWALDE	ABWN	GRASTE	ABZO	HACHENBURG
ABTO	GESCHWEND	ABWO	GRAUDENZ	ABZP	HADAMAR
ABTP	GESENBERG	ABWP	GREBENAU	ABZQ	HADDENHAUSEN
ABTQ	GESMOLD	ABWQ	GREFEL	ABZR	HADEMARSCHEN
ABTR	GIEBELSTADT	ABWR	GREIFENDORF	ABZS	HADERSLEBEN
ABTS	GIESEBITZ	ABWS	GREIFENHAGEN	ABZT	HAETZINGEN
ABTT	GIESEN	ABWT	GREIFFENBERG	ABZU	HAFENPREPPACH
ABTU	GIESSEN	ABWU	GREIZ	ABZV	HAGEN
ABTV	GILDEHAUS	ABWV	GRENDEL	ABZW	HAGENAU
ABTW	GILSERBERG	ABWW	GRETTSTADT	ABZX	HAGENBACH
ABTX	GILTEN	ABWX	GREUSSEN	ABZY	HAGENBURG
ABTY	GIMBSHEIM	ABWY	GREVEN	ABZZ	HAGENOW
ABTZ	GINGEN	ABWZ	GRIESBACH	ACAA	HAHAUSEN
ABUA	GINSHEIM	ABXA	GRIESHEIM	ACAB	HAHLEN
ABUB	GIRKHAUSEN	ABXB	GRIMMEN	ACAC	HAHN
ABUC	GITTELDE	ABXD	GROEBZIG	ACAD	HAHNBACH
ABUD	GLADBACH	ABXE	GROEMBACH	ACAE	HAHNHEIM
ABUE	GLADENBACH	ABXF	GROHN	ACAF	HAIBACH
ABUF	GLANDORF	ABXG	GROMADEN	ACAG	HAID
ABUG	GLARUS	ABXH	GRONAU	ACAH	HAILER
ABUH	GLATT	ABXI	GROSS ASCHEN	ACAI	HAINA
ABUI	GLATTEN	ABXJ	GROSS BERKEL	ACAJ	HAINBACH
ABUJ	GLATZ	ABXK	GROSS BERSEN	ACAK	HAINCHEN
ABUK	GLAUCHAU	ABXL	GROSS GERAU	ACAL	HAINEBACH
ABUL	GLEICHEN	ABXM	GROSS RECHTENBACH	ACAM	HAINSBACH
ABUM	GLEICHENBERG	ABXN	GROSS SOTTRUM	ACAO	HAINSFARTH
ABUN	GLEIDINGEN	ABXO	GROSS STEINHEIM	ACAP	HAINSPITZ
ABUO	GLEWITZ	ABXP	GROSSALMERODE	ACAQ	HAINSTADT
ABUP	GLISSSEN	ABXQ	GROSSALTORF	ACAR	HALBERSTADT
ABUQ	GLOEVZIN	ABXR	GROSSASPACH	ACAS	HALDEN
ABUR	GMAIN	ABXS	GROSSBOCKENHEIM	ACAU	HALDORF
ABUS	GMUEND	ABXT	GROSSBREITENBACH	ACAV	HALL
ABUT	GNESEN	ABXU	GROSSEICHOLZHEIM	ACAW	HALLE
ABUU	GNEWIKOW	ABXV	GROSSENDORF	ACAX	HALLSTADT
ABUV	GNEWIN	ABXW	GROSSENHAIN	ACAY	HALSDORF
ABUW	GODRAMSTEIN	ABXX	GROSSENLUEDER	ACAZ	HALSTEIN
ABUX	GOEDENROTH	ABXY	GROSSENSTEIN	ACBA	HALTERN
ABUY	GOEGGINGEN	ABXZ	GROSSFELD	ACBB	HALVERDE
ABUZ	GOEHREN	ABYA	GROSSGARNSTADT	ACBC	HAMBACH
ABVA	GOELLHEIM	ABYB	GROSSGARTACH	ACBD	HAMBERG
ABVB	GOENNERN	ABYC	GROSSHEPPACH	ACBE	HAMBERGEN
ABVC	GOENNHEIM	ABYD	GROSSKARBEN	ACBF	HAMBURG
ABVD	GOEPPINGEN	ABYE	GROSSROSEN	ACBG	HAMELN
ABVE	GOERLITZ	ABYF	GROTTKAU	ACBH	HAMILTON
ABVF	GOES	ABYG	GRUEN	ACBI	HAMM
ABVG	GOESSWEINSTEIN	ABYH	GRUENBERG	ACBJ	HAMMELBACH
ABVH	GOETTINGEN	ABYI	GRUENEBERG	ACBK	HAMMELBURG
ABVI	GOETZINGEN	ABYJ	GRUENENPLAN	ACBL	HAMMER
ABVJ	GOHLIS	ABYK	GRUENHOF	ACBM	HAMMERSTEIN
ABVK	GOLDBACH	ABYL	GRUENOW	ACBO	HANAU
ABVL	GOLDBERG	ABYN	GRUENSTADT	ACBP	HANDORF
ABVM	GOLDENSTEDT	ABYO	GRUENWALD	ACBQ	HANKENSBUETTEL
ABVN	GOLDKRONACH	ABYP	GRUEPPENBUEHREN	ACBR	HANNOVER
ABVO	GOLDLAUTER	ABYQ	GRUMBACH	ACBT	HANWEILER
ABVP	GOLDMUEHL	ABYR	GRUNAU	ACBU	HARBACH
ABVQ	GOLLANCZ	ABYS	GUBEN	ACBV	HARBKE
ABVR	GONDELSHEIM	ABYT	GUDENSBERG	ACBW	HARBURG
ABVS	GORSLEBEN	ABYU	GUENTERSLEBEN	ACBX	HARDEGSEN
ABVT	GOSBERG	ABYV	GUENTHERS	ACBY	HARDT
ABVU	GOSLAR	ABYW	GUESTROW	ACBZ	HAREN
ABVV	GOSSNITZ	ABYX	GUETERSDORF	ACCA	HARGESHEIM
ABVW	GOTHA	ABYY	GUETERSLOH	ACCB	HARPENFELD
ABVX	GOTTENHEIM	ABYZ	GUHRAU	ACCC	HARPSTEDT
ABVY	GRABAU	ABZA	GUMBINNEN	ACCD	HARSEWINKEL
ABVZ	GRABEN	ABZB	GUNDERSHEIM	ACCE	HARTA
ABWA	GRABOW	ABZC	GUNTERSBLUM	ACCF	HARTENROD
ABWB	GRABOWEN	ABZD	GUNZENHAUSEN	ACCG	HARTERSHAUSEN
ABWC	GRAEFENBERG	ABZE	GUSOW	ACCH	HARTFORD
ABWD	GRAETZ	ABZF	GUTENBERG	ACCI	HARTHAUSEN
ABWE	GRAFE	ABZG	GUTENBURG	ACCJ	HARTHEIM
ABWF	GRAFENBERG	ABZH	GUTENSTEIN	ACCK	HARTMANNSDORF
ABWG	GRAFENDORF	ABZI	GUTMANNSHAUSEN	ACCL	HARTUM
ABWH	GRAFENHAUSEN	ABZJ	GUTTENBERG	ACCM	HARZ

ACCN	HASBERGEN	ACFN	HEMELINGEN	ACIN	HOFSTAEDTEN
ACCO	HASELBACK	ACFO	HEMER	ACIO	HOHENBERG
ACCP	HASELUENNE	ACFP	HEMHOFFEN	ACIP	HOHENEBRA
ACCQ	HASENBERG	ACFQ	HEMMELTE	ACIQ	HOHENEGGELSEN
ACCR	HASLACH	ACFR	HEMMENDORF	ACIR	HOHENFELS
ACCS	HASLAU	ACFS	HENGSTFELD	ACIS	HOHENHAMELN
ACCT	HASLOCH	ACFT	HENKENHAGEN	ACIT	HOHENHAUSEN
ACCU	HASPERDE	ACFU	HENNEBERG	ACIU	HOHENKIRCHEN
ACCV	HASSEL	ACFV	HENNERSDORF	ACIV	HOHENSTADT
ACCW	HASSELBACH	ACFW	HEPPENHEIM	ACIW	HOHENSTEIN
ACCX	HASSENDORF	ACFX	HEPSTEDT	ACIX	HOHENWEILER
ACCY	HASSLOCH	ACFY	HERBELHAUSEN	ACIY	HOLLEN
ACCZ	HASTE	ACFZ	HERBOLZHEIM	ACIZ	HOLLENSTEDT
ACDA	HASTEN	ACGA	HERBORN	ACJA	HOLLSTADT
ACDB	HATTEN	ACGB	HERBSTEIN	ACJB	HOLSEN
ACDC	HATTENDORFF	ACGC	HERDECKE	ACJC	HOLSTEN
ACDD	HATTENHEIM	ACGD	HERFORD	ACJD	HOLTDORF
ACDE	HATTENHOFEN	ACGF	HERFORST	ACJE	HOLTE
ACDF	HATTERODE	ACGG	HERINGEN	ACJF	HOLTENSEN
ACDG	HATTINGEN	ACGH	HERMANNSTADT	ACJG	HOLTGAST
ACDH	HATTORF	ACGI	HERMANNSTEIN	ACJH	HOLTROP
ACDI	HATTSTEDT	ACGJ	HERMSDORF	ACJI	HOLZHAUSEN
ACDJ	HATZBACH	ACGK	HERRENBERG	ACJJ	HOLZHEIM
ACDK	HAUBERSBRONN	ACGL	HERSCHWEILER	ACJK	HOLZINGEN
ACDL	HAUSACH	ACGM	HERSFELD	ACJL	HOLZMADEN
ACDM	HAUSDORF	ACGN	HERSTE	ACJM	HOLZMINDEN
ACDN	HAUSEN	ACGO	HERSTELLE	ACJO	HOMBERG
ACDP	HAUSTENBECK	ACGP	HERZBERG	ACJP	HOMBURG
ACDQ	HAVANA	ACGQ	HESEPE	ACJQ	HONOLULU
ACDR	HAVIXBECK	ACGR	HESSEN	ACJR	HOPFGARTEN
ACDS	HAVRE	ACGS	HESSLOCH	ACJS	HORB
ACDT	HEBEL	ACGT	HETTINGEN	ACJT	HORK
ACDU	HECHINGEN	ACGU	HEUBACH	ACJU	HORN
ACDV	HECHTHAUSEN	ACGV	HEUSENSTAMM	ACJV	HORNBACH
ACDW	HECKLINGEN	ACGW	HEUTHEN	ACJW	HORNBERG
ACDX	HEDDESHEIM	ACGX	HILBERSDORF	ACJX	HORNBURG
ACDY	HEGENDORF	ACGY	HILCHENBACH	ACJZ	HORNHAUSEN
ACDZ	HEGENHEIM	ACGZ	HILDBURGHAUSEN	ACKA	HORSTEIN
ACEA	HEGENSDORF	ACHA	HILDESHEIM	ACKB	HORSTEN
ACEB	HEIDEBERG	ACHB	HILLE	ACKC	HOSTAU
ACEC	HEIDELBACH	ACHC	HILTER	ACKD	HOSTENBACH
ACED	HEIDELBERG	ACHD	HIMMELKRON	ACKE	HOTTENBACH
ACEE	HEIDENHEIM	ACHE	HIMMELPFORTEN	ACKF	HOU
ACEF	HEIDMUEHLEN	ACHF	HIMMELREICH	ACKG	HOVEN
ACEG	HEILBRONN	ACHG	HINSBECK	ACKH	HOYA
ACEH	HEILIGENBERG	ACHH	HINTERNAH	ACKI	HUCHEM
ACEI	HEILIGENSTADT	ACHI	HINTERPOMMERN	ACKJ	HUDE
ACEJ	HEIMARSHAUSEN	ACHJ	HINTSCHINGEN	ACKK	HUECKESWAGEN
ACEK	HEIMBACH	ACHK	HIRRLINGEN	ACKL	HUEFINGEN
ACEL	HEIMSEN	ACHL	HIRSCHAID	ACKM	HUEMME
ACEM	HEINA	ACHM	HIRSCHAU	ACKN	HUESEDE
ACEN	HEINERSBERG	ACHN	HIRSCHBACH	ACKP	HUETTEN
ACEO	HEINERSDORF	ACHO	HIRSCHBERG	ACKQ	HUETTENBACH
ACEP	HEININGEN	ACHP	HIRSCHFELD	ACKR	HUETTENBUSCH
ACEQ	HEINRICHAU	ACHQ	HITZKIRCH	ACKS	HUETTENHEIM
ACER	HEINRICHS	ACHR	HOBOKEN	ACKT	HUNDHEIM
ACES	HEINSDORF	ACHS	HOCHBERG	ACKU	HUNDSBACH
ACET	HEINSEN	ACHT	HOCHDORF	ACKV	HUNDSFELD
ACEU	HEINSHEIM	ACHU	HOCHELHEIM	ACKW	HUNDSHAUSEN
ACEV	HEISE	ACHV	HOCHFELDEN	ACKX	HUNGEN
ACEW	HEISEBECK	ACHW	HOCHHAUSEN	ACKY	HUSUM
ACEX	HEITLAND	ACHX	HOCHHEIM	ACKZ	HUTZDORF
ACEY	HELDBURG	ACHY	HOCHSTADT	ACLA	IBA
ACEZ	HELLENDORF	ACHZ	HOCHSTETTEN	ACLB	IBER
ACFA	HELLINGEN	ACIA	HOCKENHEIM	ACLC	IBURG
ACFB	HELLSTEIN	ACIB	HOECHST	ACLD	ICKERN
ACFC	HELMARSHAUSEN	ACIC	HOEFLES	ACLE	IDAR
ACFD	HELMBRECHTS	ACID	HOEG	ACLF	IDEN
ACFE	HELMERN	ACIE	HOERINGEN	ACLH	IFFENS
ACFF	HELMERSHAUSEN	ACIF	HOERINGHAUSEN	ACLJ	IHN
ACFG	HELMINGHAUSEN	ACIG	HOERSTE	ACLK	ILBESHAUSEN
ACFH	HELMSHAUSEN	ACIH	HOERSTEL	ACLL	ILBESHEIM
ACFI	HELMSHEIM	ACII	HOEXTER	ACLM	ILERG
ACFJ	HELMSTADT	ACIJ	HOF	ACLN	ILFELD
ACFK	HELMSTEDT	ACIK	HOFEN	ACLO	ILLINGEN
ACFL	HELSEN	ACIL	HOFGEISMAR	ACLQ	ILSEN BERG
ACFM	HELVETIA	ACIM	HOFHEIM	ACLR	IMBSEN

ACLS	IMHAUSEN	ACPB	KAPPELRODECK	ACSE	KOENIGSBURG
ACLT	IMMENDINGEN	ACPC	KAPPELWINDECK	ACSF	KOENIGSDORF
ACLU	IMMENHAUSEN	ACPD	KARBOW	ACSG	KOENIGSHAIN
ACLV	IMMENRODE	ACPE	KARLSRUHE	ACSH	KOENIGSHOFEN
ACLW	IMMERSIEBEN	ACPF	KARSEE	ACSI	KOENIGSHUETTE
ACLX	IMSHAUSEN	ACPG	KASCHAU	ACSJ	KOENIGSLUTTER
ACMC	INGELHEIM	ACPH	KASTORF	ACSK	KOENIGSWALD
ACMD	INGENHEIM	ACPI	KATOWITZ	ACSL	KOENIGSWALDE
ACME	INGOLSTADT	ACPJ	KATZENELNBOGEN	ACSM	KOENIGSWART
ACMF	INGWEILER	ACPK	KATZENFURTH	ACSO	KOERNER
ACMG	INNSBRUCK	ACPL	KAULBACH	ACSP	KOESEN
ACMH	INOWRACLAW	ACPM	KELLBERG	ACSQ	KOETHEN
ACMI	INS	ACPO	KELLINGHUSEN	ACSR	KOETZSCHENBRODA
ACMK	IPHOFEN	ACPP	KEMBERG	ACSS	KOHDEN
ACML	IRCHWITZ	ACPQ	KEMNADE	ACST	KOHLBERG
ACMM	IRMELSHAUSEN	ACPR	KEMNATH	ACSU	KOHLENBACH
ACMN	IRRENDORF	ACPS	KEMPEN	ACSV	KOLENFELD
ACMO	IRSLINGEN	ACPT	KEMPENICH	ACSW	KOLZIG
ACMP	ISE	ACPU	KEMPTEN	ACSX	KONITZ
ACMQ	ISENBUETTEL	ACPV	KENN	ACSY	KONSTANZ
ACMR	ISENSTEDT	ACPW	KENTUCKY	ACSZ	KORB
ACMS	ISERLOHN	ACPX	KESTEN	ACTA	KORK
ACMT	ISERNHAGEN	ACPY	KETSCH	ACTB	KOTHEN
ACMU	ISERT	ACPZ	KEULA	ACTC	KRAKAU
ACMV	ISMANING	ACQA	KIEL	ACTD	KRATZEBURG
ACMW	ISNY	ACQB	KINDENHEIM	ACTE	KRAUSNICK
ACMX	ISTHA	ACQC	KIRBEG	ACTF	KRAUTHEIM
ACMY	ISTRUP	ACQD	KIRCHARDT	ACTG	KREIMBACH
ACMZ	ITTEL	ACQE	KIRCHBERG	ACTH	KREMPE
ACNA	ITTLINGEN	ACQF	KIRCHDORF	ACTI	KREUTZ
ACNB	ITZ	ACQG	KIRCHEN	ACTJ	KREUZ
ACNC	ITZUM	ACQH	KIRCHENBERG	ACTK	KREUZBERG
ACND	IWITZ	ACQI	KIRCHENKIRNBERG	ACTL	KREUZNACH
ACNE	IXHEIM	ACQJ	KIRCHGELLERSEN	ACTM	KRIEGSFELD
ACNF	JACOBS	ACQK	KIRCHHAIN	ACTN	KROESBACH
ACNG	JAGSTBERG	ACQL	KIRCHHAM	ACTO	KROJANKE
ACNH	JAGSTHAUSEN	ACQM	KIRCHHATTEN	ACTP	KRONACH
ACNI	JANKENDORF	ACQN	KIRCHHAUSEN	ACTQ	KROTOSCHIN
ACNJ	JANOWITZ	ACQO	KIRCHHEIM	ACTR	KRUMBACH
ACNK	JAROSZEWO	ACQP	KIRCHHEIMBOLANDEN	ACTS	KRUMBECK
ACNL	JAUER	ACQQ	KIRCHHOFEN	ACTT	KRUMMENDIECH
ACNM	JEBSHEIM	ACQR	KIRCHRODE	ACTU	KUCHEN
ACNN	JECHNITZ	ACQS	KIRCHWEYHE	ACTV	KUEHRSTEDT
ACNO	JEDDELOH	ACQT	KIRCHZELL	ACTW	KUELLSTEDT
ACNP	JEDDINGEN	ACQU	KIRDORF	ACTX	KUEPS
ACNR	JEHSEN	ACQV	KIRN	ACTY	KUHSTEDT
ACNS	JEINSEN	ACQW	KIRRWEILER	ACUA	KULM
ACNT	JENA	ACQX	KIRTORF	ACUB	KUMMERFELD
ACNV	JERSEY CITY	ACQY	KISSINGEN	ACUC	KUNITZ
ACNW	JEVER	ACQZ	KITZBEN	ACUD	KUPPENHEIM
ACNX	JOCKGRIM	ACRA	KITZINGEN	ACUE	KUSEL
ACNY	JOELLENBECK	ACRB	KLATTAU	ACUF	KUTTENBERG
ACNZ	JOHANNISTHAL	ACRC	KLEEFELD	ACUG	LAAR
ACOA	JOLLENBECK	ACRD	KLEEKAMP	ACUH	LABUHN
ACOB	JONAS	ACRF	KLEINBERG	ACUI	LACHE
ACOC	JUELICH	ACRG	KLEINBOTTWAR	ACUJ	LADBERGEN
ACOD	JUNGHOLZ	ACRH	KLEINEN	ACUK	LADENBURG
ACOE	JUNGHOLZHAUSEN	ACRI	KLEINGARTACH	ACUL	LAER
ACOF	JUNGNAU	ACRJ	KLEINHAUSEN	ACUM	LAGE
ACOG	JUNKERSDORF	ACRK	KLEINHENBACH	ACUN	LAHN
ACOH	KAICHEN	ACRL	KLEINOSTHEIM	ACUO	LAHR
ACOI	KAIERDE	ACRM	KLEINWALLSTADT	ACUP	LAHRBACH
ACOJ	KAISERSBACH	ACRN	KLEINWENKHEIM	ACUQ	LAIBACH
ACOL	KALADEY	ACRO	KLENGEN	ACUR	LAMBACH
ACOM	KALDORF	ACRP	KLEPTOW	ACUS	LAMERDEN
ACON	KALISCH	ACRQ	KLINGEN	ACUT	LAMMERSHAGEN
ACOO	KALKHORST	ACRR	KLITZSCHEN	ACUU	LAMPERTHEIM
ACOP	KALTENBORN	ACRT	KLOSTER OESEDE	ACUV	LAMSPRINGE
ACOQ	KALTENSUNDHEIM	ACRU	KLOSTERHOLTE	ACUW	LAMSTEDT
ACOR	KALWARYA	ACRV	KNETZGAU	ACUX	LANDAU
ACOS	KAMMER	ACRW	KNIELINGEN	ACUY	LANDECK
ACOT	KAMNITZ	ACRX	KOBYLIN	ACUZ	LANDEN
ACOU	KAMPEN	ACRY	KOEDDINGEN	ACVA	LANDESHUT
ACOV	KANDEL	ACSA	KOENIG	ACVB	LANDORF
ACOW	KANSAS	ACSB	KOENIGINHOF	ACVC	LANDSBERG
ACOZ	KAPPEL	ACSC	KOENIGSBACH	ACVE	LANDSTUHL
ACPA	KAPPELN	ACSD	KOENIGSBERG	ACVF	LANGDORF

ACVG	LANGEN	ACYI	LENNEP	ADBI	LOEWENSTEIN
ACVH	LANGENAU	ACYJ	LENZEN	ADBJ	LOH
ACVI	LANGENBERG	ACYK	LENZKIRCH	ADBK	LOHE
ACVJ	LANGENBERNSDORF	ACYL	LEOBSCHUETZ	ADBL	LOHMA
ACVK	LANGENBRUCK	ACYM	LEONBERG	ADBM	LOHN
ACVL	LANGENBRUECK	ACYN	LESCHEDE	ADBN	LOHNE
ACVM	LANGENELZ	ACYO	LESSEN	ADBO	LOHR
ACVN	LANGENHAGEN	ACYP	LESUM	ADBP	LOHRE
ACVO	LANGENHAUSEN	ACYQ	LETTEN	ADBQ	LONDON
ACVP	LANGENHEIM	ACYR	LEUCHTENBERG	ADBR	LONDORF
ACVQ	LANGENHOLZ	ACYS	LEUN	ADBS	LONG ISLAND
ACVR	LANGENHOLZHAUSEN	ACYT	LEUSEL	ADBT	LORCH
ACVS	LANGENSALZA	ACYU	LEUSTETTEN	ADBU	LORSCH
ACVT	LANGENSCHWARZ	ACYV	LEUTMANNSDORF	ADBV	LOSSBURG
ACVU	LANGENSTEIN	ACYW	LEVERN	ADBW	LOTHRINGEN
ACVV	LANGENTHAL	ACYX	LHOTKA	ADBX	LOTTE
ACVW	LANGFOERDEN	ACYY	LICH	ADBY	LOTZEN
ACVX	LANGHEIM	ACYZ	LICHTEN	ADBZ	LOUISENDORF
ACVY	LANGNAU	ACZA	LICHTENAU	ADCC	LOWIN
ACVZ	LANGSDORF	ACZB	LICHTENBERG	ADCD	LOXSTEDT
ACWA	LANGWEDEL	ACZC	LICHTENBORN	ADCF	LOXTEN
ACWB	LANZ	ACZD	LICHTENFELD	ADCH	LUCHSINGEN
ACWC	LARET	ACZE	LICHTENFELS	ADCI	LUCKA
ACWD	LASEL	ACZF	LICHTENSTEIN	ADCJ	LUDWIGSBURG
ACWE	LASTRUP	ACZG	LICHTENTHAL	ADCK	LUDWIGSDORF
ACWF	LAUBACH	ACZH	LIEBAU	ADCL	LUDWIGSHAFEN
ACWG	LAUDA	ACZI	LIEBENAU	ADCM	LUDWIGSHOF
ACWH	LAUENBERG	ACZJ	LIEBENBURG	ADCN	LUDWIGSLUST
ACWI	LAUENBURG	ACZK	LIEBENSTEIN	ADCO	LUDWIGSTADT
ACWJ	LAUENFOERDE	ACZL	LIEBENZELL	ADCP	LUDWIGSTHAL
ACWK	LAUENHAGEN	ACZM	LIEBESCHITZ	ADCQ	LUEBARS
ACWL	LAUENSTEIN	ACZN	LIEBLOS	ADCR	LUEBBECKE
ACWM	LAUF	ACZO	LIEGNITZ	ADCU	LUEBLOW
ACWN	LAUFACH	ACZP	LIEME	ADCV	LUEBOW
ACWO	LAUFENBURG	ACZQ	LIENEN	ADCW	LUEBZ
ACWP	LAUFFEN	ACZR	LIENHEIM	ADCX	LUEDENSCHLID
ACWQ	LAUN	ACZS	LIESBORN	ADCY	LUEDERSFELD
ACWR	LAUPHEIM	ACZT	LIESKAU	ADCZ	LUEDINGHAUSEN
ACWS	LAUTENBACH	ACZU	LILIENFELD	ADDB	LUEDINGWORTH
ACWT	LAUTENBERG	ACZV	LILIENTHAL	ADDC	LUEGDE
ACWU	LAUTENTHAL	ACZW	LIMBACH	ADDD	LUENEBURG
ACWW	LAUTERBACH	ACZX	LIMBERGEN	ADDE	LUENINGHAUSEN
ACWX	LAUTERSHEIM	ACZY	LIMBURG	ADDF	LUESSEM
ACWY	LAVELSLOH	ACZZ	LINDAU	ADDG	LUETHORST
ACWZ	LAVIN	ADAA	LINDEN	ADDH	LUETZEL
ACXA	LECK	ADAB	LINDENAU	ADDI	LUETZEN
ACXC	LEEDEN	ADAC	LINDHEIM	ADDJ	LUSTENAU
ACXD	LEER	ADAD	LINDHORST	ADDK	LUZERN
ACXE	LEESE	ADAE	LINGELBACH	ADDL	LYCK
ACXF	LEESTE	ADAF	LINGEN	ADDM	MAAR
ACXG	LEGDEN	ADAG	LINGENFELD	ADDN	MADEN
ACXH	LEHE	ADAH	LINNE	ADDP	MAEHREN
ACXI	LEHESTEN	ADAI	LINSBURG	ADDQ	MAGDEBURG
ACXJ	LEHMEN	ADAJ	LINSEN	ADDR	MAGSTADT
ACXK	LEHRE	ADAK	LINTEL	ADDS	MAHLBERG
ACXL	LEHRTE	ADAL	LINTORF	ADDT	MAHNDORF
ACXM	LEIBERTINGEN	ADAM	LINUM	ADDU	MAINROTH
ACXN	LEICHLINGEN	ADAN	LINZ	ADDV	MAINSTOCKHEIM
ACXO	LEIDERSBACH	ADAO	LIPPOLDSWEILER	ADDW	MAINZ
ACXP	LEIDHECKEN	ADAP	LIPPRAMSDORF	ADDX	MAINZLAR
ACXQ	LEIFERDE	ADAQ	LIPPSTADT	ADDY	MALBERGEN
ACXR	LEIHGESTERN	ADAR	LISDORF	ADDZ	MALCHIN
ACXS	LEIMBACH	ADAS	LISPENHAUSEN	ADEA	MALCHOW
ACXT	LEIMERSHEIM	ADAT	LISSA	ADEB	MALIX
ACXV	LEIPZIG	ADAU	LISSBERG	ADEC	MALSCH
ACXW	LEITMAR	ADAV	LITTAU	ADED	MANCHESTER
ACXX	LEMBACH	ADAW	LITTLE ROCK	ADEE	MANDELSLOH
ACXY	LEMBECK	ADAX	LIVERPOOL	ADEF	MANHEIM
ACXZ	LEMBERG	ADAY	LOBENSTEIN	ADEH	MANNENBACH
ACYA	LEMFOERDE	ADAZ	LOBSENS	ADEI	MANNHEIM
ACYB	LEMGO	ADBA	LOCCUM	ADEK	MANSLAGT
ACYC	LEMKE	ADBB	LOCKHAUSEN	ADEL	MARBACH
ACYD	LEMMIE	ADBC	LOCKSTEDT	ADEM	MARBURG
ACYE	LEMSTEDT	ADBD	LOEBAU	ADEN	MARGONIN
ACYF	LENGAU	ADBE	LOEHNE	ADEO	MARIAZELL
ACYG	LENGERICH	ADBF	LOENINGEN	ADEP	MARIENBURG
ACYH	LENGNAU	ADBG	LOEWEN	ADEQ	MARIENFELD

Code	Village	Code	Village	Code	Village
ADER	MARIENSEE	ADHW	MICHELBACH	ADLD	MUNICH
ADES	MARIENTHAL	ADHX	MICHELSDORF	ADLE	MUNSTER
ADET	MARIENWERDER	ADHY	MICHELSROMBACH	ADLF	MUNSTER AN DER NAHE
ADEU	MARKDORF	ADHZ	MICHELSTADT	ADLG	MUNZINGEN
ADEV	MARKE	ADIB	MIDLUM	ADLH	MURAU
ADEW	MARKENDORF	ADIC	MIEL	ADLI	MUSKAU
ADEX	MARKGROENINGEN	ADID	MIES	ADLJ	MUTTERSTADT
ADEZ	MARKOLDENDORF	ADIE	MIESTERHORST	ADLK	NACKENHEIM
ADFA	MARKT BIBART	ADIF	MILITSCH	ADLL	NAENSEN
ADFB	MARKTBREIT	ADIH	MIMMENHAUSEN	ADLM	NAGOLD
ADFC	MARTFELD	ADII	MINDELHEIM	ADLN	NAILA
ADFD	MARTHIL	ADIJ	MINDEN	ADLO	NAKEL
ADFE	MARTINFELD	ADIK	MINKEN	ADLP	NANNDORF
ADFF	MARTINHAGEN	ADIM	MIROSLAW	ADLR	NASSAU
ADFH	MARZ	ADIN	MIROWITZ	ADLS	NAUGARD
ADFI	MASAN	ADIP	MISTELBACH	ADLU	NAUMBURG
ADFJ	MASCHEN	ADIQ	MISTELGAU	ADLV	NAUSIS
ADFL	MASSENBACHHAUSEN	ADIR	MITTELBACH	ADLX	NECKARHAUSEN
ADFM	MASSENHAUSEN	ADIS	MITTELDORF	ADLY	NECKARSTEINACH
ADFN	MASSENHEIM	ADIT	MITTELFRANKEN	ADLZ	NEDLITZ
ADFO	MASSOW	ADIU	MITTELHAUSEN	ADMA	NEERLAGE
ADFQ	MAUER	ADIV	MITTELSDORF	ADMB	NEERMOOR
ADFR	MECKLENBURG	ADIW	MITTELSEEMEN	ADMC	NEFTENBACH
ADFS	MEERANE	ADIX	MITTWEIDA	ADMD	NEIDERWEISEL
ADFT	MEERHOLZ	ADIY	MITWITZ	ADME	NEIDLINGEN
ADFU	MEHLINGEN	ADIZ	MIXDORF	ADMF	NEISSE
ADFV	MEHNA	ADJB	MOEHRINGEN	ADMG	NEMDEN
ADFW	MEHRHOLZ	ADJC	MOELLN	ADMH	NEMMERSDORF
ADFX	MEHRINGEN	ADJD	MOELSHEIM	ADMI	NENDINGEN
ADFY	MEICHES	ADJE	MOEMLINGEN	ADMK	NENNDORF
ADFZ	MEILEN	ADJF	MOENCHSROTH	ADML	NENTERSHAUSEN
ADGA	MEINERSHAGEN	ADJG	MOERLENBACH	ADMM	NESSE
ADGC	MEININGEN	ADJH	MOESE	ADMN	NESSELBACH
ADGD	MEISENHEIM	ADJI	MOIDE	ADMO	NESSELROEDEN
ADGE	MEISSEN	ADJJ	MOLLEN	ADMP	NESSMERSIEL
ADGF	MEISSENHEIM	ADJK	MOLSDORF	ADMQ	NETRA
ADGG	MELBACH	ADJL	MOLZEN	ADMS	NETTELSTEDT
ADGH	MELDORF	ADJN	MONZINGEN	ADMT	NETZE
ADGI	MELKENDORF	ADJO	MOOR	ADMU	NEUARENBERG
ADGJ	MELLE	ADJP	MOORBURG	ADMV	NEUBRANDENBURG
ADGK	MELLRICHSTADT	ADJQ	MOORDORF	ADMW	NEUBRUCHHAUSEN
ADGL	MELS	ADJR	MOOS	ADMX	NEUBRUECK
ADGM	MELSDORF	ADJS	MOOSBACH	ADMY	NEUBULACH
ADGN	MELSUNGEN	ADJT	MOOSBURG	ADMZ	NEUBURG
ADGO	MEMEL	ADJU	MORBACH	ADNA	NEUDINGEN
ADGQ	MENDEN	ADJV	MORINGEN	ADNB	NEUDORF
ADGR	MENGERSKIRCHEN	ADJW	MORSBACH	ADNC	NEUENBRUNSLAR
ADGS	MENGSHAUSEN	ADJX	MOSBACH	ADND	NEUENBURG
ADGT	MENSFELDEN	ADJY	MOSCHENDORF	ADNE	NEUENDORF
ADGU	MENSLAGE	ADJZ	MOSELLE	ADNF	NEUENHAUS
ADGV	MENZINGEN	ADKA	MOSHEIM	ADNG	NEUENHEERSE
ADGW	MEPPEN	ADKB	MOTZLAR	ADNH	NEUENHEIM
ADGX	MERCHINGEN	ADKC	MUCKENSCHOPF	ADNI	NEUENKIRCHEN
ADGY	MERGENTHEIM	ADKD	MUEDEN	ADNJ	NEUENLANDE
ADGZ	MERKEN	ADKE	MUEHLBACH	ADNK	NEUENWALDE
ADHA	MERKENFRITZ	ADKF	MUEHLBERG	ADNL	NEUFFEN
ADHB	MERKLIN	ADKG	MUEHLBURG	ADNM	NEUFRA
ADHC	MERKLINGEN	ADKH	MUEHLEN	ADNN	NEUHAMMER
ADHD	MERLAU	ADKI	MUEHLFELD	ADNO	NEUHAUS
ADHE	MERSEBURG	ADKJ	MUEHLHAUSEN	ADNP	NEUHAUSEN
ADHF	MERZALBEN	ADKK	MUEHLHEIM	ADNQ	NEUHEIM
ADHG	MERZEN	ADKL	MUEHRINGEN	ADNR	NEUHOF
ADHH	MERZHAUSEN	ADKM	MUELHEIM	ADNS	NEUHUETTEN
ADHI	MESCHEDE	ADKN	MUENCHAURACH	ADNT	NEUKIRCH
ADHJ	MESERITZ	ADKO	MUENCHBERG	ADNU	NEUKIRCHEN
ADHK	MESSELHAUSEN	ADKP	MUENCHEHOF	ADNV	NEULAND
ADHL	MESSENKAMP	ADKR	MUENCHHAUSEN	ADNW	NEULUSSHEIM
ADHM	MESSINGHAUSEN	ADKS	MUENCHINGEN	ADNX	NEUMARK
ADHN	MESSKIRCH	ADKT	MUENCHWEILER	ADNY	NEUMARKT
ADHO	MESSLINGEN	ADKU	MUENDEN	ADNZ	NEUMORSCHEN
ADHP	MESSSTETTEN	ADKV	MUENNERSTADT	ADOA	NEUMUENSTER
ADHQ	METTINGEN	ADKW	MUENSTER	ADOB	NEUNDORF
ADHR	METZINGEN	ADKX	MUENSTERBERG	ADOC	NEUNKIRCH
ADHS	METZLOS	ADKZ	MUENZENBERG	ADOD	NEUNKIRCHEN
ADHT	MEYENBURG	ADLA	MUESCHEN	ADOE	NEURODE
ADHU	MIASTECZKO	ADLB	MUETTERSHOLZ	ADOG	NEUSES
ADHV	MICHELAU	ADLC	MULSUM	ADOH	NEUSS

Code	Village	Code	Village	Code	Village
ADOI	NEUSTADT	ADRU	OBERBACH	ADUT	OETINGHAUSEN
ADOJ	NEUSTETTIN	ADRV	OBERBERGEN	ADUU	OETISHEIM
ADOK	NEUSTRELITZ	ADRW	OBERBIEBER	ADUV	OETTINGEN
ADOL	NEUWEILER	ADRX	OBERBOIHINGEN	ADUW	OEVELGOENNE
ADOM	NEUWIED	ADRY	OBERBRECHEN	ADUX	OFFENBACH
ADON	NEUZELLE	ADRZ	OBERBRUCK	ADUY	OFFENWARDEN
ADOX	NICKERN	ADSA	OBERDORF	ADUZ	OFFSTEIN
ADOY	NIDDA	ADSB	OBERDORLA	ADVB	OHLAU
ADOZ	NIED	ADSC	OBEREHRENBACH	ADVC	OHLSPACH
ADPA	NIEDENSTEIN	ADSD	OBERELSBACH	ADVD	OHRDRUFF
ADPB	NIEDER SAULHEIM	ADSE	OBERFINKENBACH	ADVE	OKEL
ADPC	NIEDERAUERBACH	ADSF	OBERFLOERSHEIM	ADVF	OLBERSLEBEN
ADPD	NIEDERAULA	ADSG	OBERFRANKEN	ADVH	OLDENBURG
ADPE	NIEDERBACH	ADSH	OBERG	ADVI	OLDENDORF
ADPF	NIEDERESCHBACH	ADSI	OBERGEBRA	ADVJ	OLDENSTADT
ADPG	NIEDERGRUENDAU	ADSJ	OBERGRAEFENHAIN	ADVK	OLDESLOE
ADPH	NIEDERHAUSEN	ADSK	OBERHARMERSBACH	ADVL	OLDHAM
ADPI	NIEDERHOCHSTADT	ADSL	OBERHAUSEN	ADVM	OLDISLEBEN
ADPJ	NIEDERHOF	ADSM	OBERHILBERSHEIM	ADVN	OLDSUM
ADPK	NIEDERHOFEN	ADSN	OBERHOFEN	ADVO	OLFEN
ADPL	NIEDERHOLSTEN	ADSO	OBERJOSSA	ADVP	OLPE
ADPM	NIEDERKAUFUNGEN	ADSP	OBERKALBACH	ADVQ	OLTEN
ADPN	NIEDERKLEEN	ADSQ	OBERKIRCHEN	ADVS	OOS
ADPO	NIEDERKLEIN	ADSR	OBERKORN	ADVT	OPFENBACH
ADPP	NIEDERLINDACH	ADSS	OBERLAND	ADVU	OPPAU
ADPQ	NIEDERMOSCHEL	ADST	OBERLANGENSTADT	ADVV	OPPELN
ADPR	NIEDERNDORF	ADSU	OBERLAUCHRINGEN	ADVW	OPPENAU
ADPS	NIEDERNEUNKIRCHEN	ADSV	OBERLENNINGEN	ADVX	OPPERSDORF
ADPT	NIEDERNHALL	ADSW	OBERLIND	ADVY	OPPURG
ADPU	NIEDERNTUDORF	ADSX	OBERLINDELBACH	ADWA	ORSOY
ADPV	NIEDERORSCHEL	ADSY	OBERLISTINGEN	ADWB	ORTSHAUSEN
ADPW	NIEDERRAD	ADSZ	OBERLUNGWITZ	ADWC	OSCHERSLEBEN
ADPX	NIEDERRODENBACH	ADTA	OBERMAESSING	ADWD	OSCHITZ
ADPY	NIEDERSCHLEMA	ADTB	OBERMEHNEN	ADWE	OSIEK
ADPZ	NIEDERSTEIN	ADTC	OBERMENDIG	ADWF	OSNABRUECK
ADQA	NIEDERSTETTEN	ADTD	OBERMERZBACH	ADWG	OSSWEIL
ADQB	NIEDERWEGSCHEID	ADTE	OBERNAU	ADWH	OSTELSHEIM
ADQC	NIEDERWEILER	ADTF	OBERNBERG	ADWI	OSTEN
ADQD	NIEDERWEIMAR	ADTG	OBERNBREIT	ADWJ	OSTENDE
ADQE	NIEDERWETTER	ADTH	OBERNBURG	ADWK	OSTENLAND
ADQF	NIEDERWOELLSTADT	ADTI	OBERNDORF	ADWL	OSTERAU
ADQG	NIEDERZWEHREN	ADTJ	OBERNKIRCHEN	ADWM	OSTERCAPPELN
ADQH	NIEFERN	ADTK	OBERODERWITZ	ADWN	OSTEREISTEDT
ADQI	NIEHEIM	ADTL	OBERPFALZ	ADWO	OSTERHOLZ
ADQJ	NIEMASCHKLEBA	ADTM	OBERRAD	ADWP	OSTERLINDE
ADQK	NIENBERGE	ADTN	OBERRAMSTADT	ADWQ	OSTERNBURG
ADQL	NIENBURG	ADTO	OBERREICHENBACH	ADWR	OSTERODE
ADQM	NIENHAGEN	ADTP	OBERSASBACH	ADWS	OSTERWICK
ADQN	NIERSTEIN	ADTQ	OBERSCHEFFLENZ	ADWT	OSTHEIM
ADQO	NIESTEDT	ADTR	OBERSCHLESIEN	ADWU	OSTHOFEN
ADQP	NITTENAU	ADTS	OBERSCHWARZACH	ADWV	OTTENBERG
ADQQ	NOERDLINGEN	ADTT	OBERSTEIN	ADWW	OTTENDORF
ADQR	NOERTEN	ADTU	OBERSTREU	ADWX	OTTENHAUSEN
ADQS	NORDECK	ADTV	OBERTUERKHEIM	ADWY	OTTENHEIM
ADQT	NORDEICH	ADTW	OBERWEILER	ADWZ	OTTENSEN
ADQU	NORDEL	ADTX	OBERWESEL	ADXA	OTTENSTEIN
ADQV	NORDEN	ADTY	OBERWEYER	ADXB	OTTERBACH
ADQW	NORDENBERG	ADTZ	OBERZELL	ADXC	OTTERNDORF
ADQX	NORDHALBEN	ADUA	OBING	ADXE	OTTERSBERG
ADQY	NORDHAMMERN	ADUB	OBRIGHEIM	ADXF	OTTERSHAUSEN
ADQZ	NORDHAUSEN	ADUC	OCHSENFURT	ADXG	OTTERSHEIM
ADRA	NORDHEIM	ADUD	OCHTRUP	ADXH	OTTERSWEIER
ADRB	NORDHOLZ	ADUE	ODENHEIM	ADXI	OTTING
ADRC	NORDHORN	ADUF	OEDING	ADXJ	OTTMARSHEIM
ADRD	NORDLEDA	ADUG	OEFLINGEN	ADXK	OTTRAU
ADRE	NORDSTETTEN	ADUH	OELDE	ADXL	OTZING
ADRF	NORDWALDE	ADUI	OELSHAUSEN	ADXM	OVELGOENNE
ADRG	NORF	ADUJ	OELZE	ADXN	OY
ADRJ	NORTHEIM	ADUK	OENSBACH	ADXO	OYLE
ADRK	NORTRUP	ADUL	OEPFERSHAUSEN	ADXP	PADERBORN
ADRM	NOVA SCOTIA	ADUM	OERDINGHAUSEN	ADXQ	PANTAU
ADRO	NUERNBERG	ADUN	OESDORF	ADXR	PAPENBURG
ADRP	OBBACH	ADUO	OESE	ADXS	PAPPENDORF
ADRQ	OBENHEIM	ADUP	OESEDE	ADXT	PAPPENHEIM
ADRR	OBENKIRCHEN	ADUQ	OESFELD	ADXU	PARADIES
ADRS	OBER RAMSTADT	ADUR	OESTERWEG	ADXV	PARCHIM
ADRT	OBERAULA	ADUS	OESTHEIM	ADXW	PARIS

ADXX	PARKSTEIN	AEBI	RACZKI	AEEL	RHENA
ADXY	PAS DE CALAIS	AEBJ	RADE	AEEM	RHEYDT
ADXZ	PASEWALK	AEBK	RADEBURG	AEEN	RHINA
ADYA	PASSAU	AEBL	RADLIN	AEEP	RHODEN
ADYC	PATTENSEN	AEBM	RADMUEHL	AEEQ	RICHELSDORF
ADYD	PATZIG	AEBN	RADUHN	AEES	RICKERT
ADYE	PECKELSHEIM	AEBO	RAHDEN	AEET	RIEDE
ADYF	PEGNITZ	AEBP	RAHMEL	AEEU	RIEDEN
ADYG	PEINE	AEBQ	RAIN	AEEV	RIEDENBURG
ADYH	PEITZ	AEBR	RAINROD	AEEW	RIEGEL
ADYI	PENKUN	AEBS	RAMBERG	AEEX	RIEHE
ADYL	PERLACH	AEBT	RAMSTEIN	AEEY	RIELASINGEN
ADYM	PERLEBERG	AEBU	RANIS	AEEZ	RIELINGSHAUSEN
ADYN	PETERSBERG	AEBV	RANSTADT	AEFA	RIEMSLOH
ADYP	PETERSDORF	AEBW	RAPPENAU	AEFB	RIEPHOLM
ADYQ	PETERSHAGEN	AEBX	RASCHA	AEFC	RIEPING
ADYR	PETERZELL	AEBY	RASTATT	AEFD	RIESA
ADYS	PETZEWO	AEBZ	RATZENBURG	AEFE	RIESBACH
ADYT	PFAFFENWEILER	AECA	RAUBACH	AEFF	RIESENBECK
ADYU	PFALZ	AECB	RAUDNITZ	AEFG	RIESENBURG
ADYW	PFALZDORF	AECC	RAUSCHENBERG	AEFH	RIESTE
ADYX	PFEDDERSHEIM	AECD	RAVENSBURG	AEFI	RIETBERG
ADYY	PFORZHEIM	AECE	RECHENBERG	AEFJ	RIETHEIM
ADZA	PHILIPPSBURG	AECF	RECHTENFLETH	AEFK	RIETSCHEN
ADZB	PIDING	AECG	RECKE	AEFL	RIGA
ADZC	PILSEN	AECH	RECKENDORF	AEFM	RIMBACH
ADZD	PILSUM	AECI	RECKINGEN	AEFN	RIMBECK
ADZE	PINNOW	AECJ	RECKLINGHAUSEN	AEFO	RINGELHEIM
ADZF	PIRACH	AECK	REDWITZ	AEFP	RINGEN
ADZG	PIRK	AECL	REGEN	AEFQ	RINGSHEIM
ADZH	PIRMASENS	AECM	REGENSBURG	AEFR	RINGSTEDT
ADZI	PIRNA	AECN	REGENWALDE	AEFS	RINTELN
ADZJ	PIRNITZ	AECO	REHBURG	AEFT	RITTERHUDE
ADZK	PISTIN	AECP	REHDEN	AEFU	RITTERSBACH
ADZM	PLANIG	AECQ	REHE	AEFV	RITZE
ADZN	PLATHE	AECR	REHER	AEFW	RIXFELD
ADZO	PLAUEN	AECS	REHME	AEFX	ROCHAU
ADZP	PLESCHE	AECT	REHNA	AEFZ	ROCHLITZ
ADZQ	PLOCHINGEN	AECU	REHREN	AEGA	RODA
ADZR	POEHLDE	AECV	REHWEILER	AEGB	RODACH
ADZS	POESSNECK	AECW	REICH	AEGC	RODEN
ADZT	POLLE	AECX	REICHELSHEIM	AEGD	RODENBACH
ADZU	POLZIN	AECY	REICHENAU	AEGE	RODENBERG
ADZV	POMERANIA	AECZ	REICHENBACH	AEGF	RODENKIRCHEN
ADZW	POMMERSFELDEN	AEDA	REICHENBERG	AEGG	RODEWALD
ADZX	POPPENBUETTEL	AEDB	REICHENSACHSEN	AEGH	RODHEIM
ADZY	POPPENHAUSEN	AEDD	REICHSHOFEN	AEGI	ROEBEL
ADZZ	POPPENLAUER	AEDE	REICHSTADT	AEGJ	ROEDDENAU
AEAB	POSEN	AEDF	REICHTHAL	AEGK	ROEDINGHAUSEN
AEAC	POTSDAM	AEDG	REILINGEN	AEGL	ROEHRENFUERTH
AEAE	POTTSVILLE	AEDH	REINBACH	AEGM	ROEHRSDORF
AEAF	PRAGUE	AEDI	REINBERG	AEGN	ROEMERSHAUSEN
AEAG	PRATAU	AEDJ	REINHEIM	AEGO	ROENNEBECK
AEAH	PRELLWITZ	AEDK	REINSHAGEN	AEGP	ROETTINGEN
AEAI	PREMSLAFF	AEDL	REISBACH	AEGQ	ROETZ
AEAJ	PRENZLAU	AEDM	REISELFINGEN	AEGR	ROGAESEN
AEAK	PRESSBURG	AEDN	REMELS	AEGS	ROHR
AEAL	PRETZFELD	AEDO	REMPTENDORF	AEGT	ROHRBACH
AEAM	PRICHSENSTADT	AEDP	REMSCHEID	AEGU	ROLLSHAUSEN
AEAN	PROELSDORF	AEDQ	RENCHEN	AEGV	ROMANSHOF
AEAP	PRUSSIA	AEDR	RENDEL	AEGW	ROMROD
AEAQ	PUDEWITZ	AEDS	RENDSBURG	AEGX	ROMSTHAL
AEAR	PUSCHENDORF	AEDT	RENNINGEN	AEGY	RONNEBURG
AEAS	PUTZIG	AEDU	REPELEN	AEGZ	RONSDORFF
AEAT	PYRMONT	AEDV	REPPNER	AEHA	RONSHAUSEN
AEAU	QUACKENBURG	AEDW	RETHEM	AEHB	RONSPERG
AEAV	QUAKENBRUECK	AEDX	REUSSEN	AEHC	ROPPERHAUSEN
AEAX	QUECKBORN	AEDY	REUTH	AEHD	ROSBACH
AEAY	QUEDLINBURG	AEDZ	REUTHEN	AEHE	ROSDORF
AEAZ	QUERFURT	AEEA	REUTLINGEN	AEHF	ROSENBERG
AEBA	QUETZEN	AEEB	RHADE	AEHG	ROSENFELD
AEBC	QUITZOW	AEEC	RHEDA	AEHH	ROSENFELDE
AEBD	RAASDORF	AEED	RHEDEN	AEHI	ROSENHAGEN
AEBE	RABBER	AEEE	RHEIN	AEHJ	ROSENTHAL
AEBF	RABENAU	AEEF	RHEINBISCHOFSHEIM	AEHK	ROSSBERG
AEBG	RABENSTEIN	AEEG	RHEINE	AEHL	ROSSDORF
AEBH	RABI	AEEH	RHEINPFALZ	AEHM	ROSSLAU

AEHN	ROSSLEBEN	AEKW	SAYN	AENV	SCHOENLIND
AEHO	ROSSOW	AEKX	SCHAAR	AENW	SCHOENOW
AEHP	ROSSWEIN	AEKY	SCHAFFHAUSEN	AENX	SCHOENSTADT
AEHQ	ROSTOCK	AEKZ	SCHAFHAUS	AENY	SCHOENTHAL
AEHR	ROTENBACH	AELA	SCHAIDT	AENZ	SCHOENWALD
AEHS	ROTENBURG	AELB	SCHALE	AEOA	SCHOENWALDE
AEHT	ROTH	AELC	SCHANDAU	AEOB	SCHOEPPINGEN
AEHU	ROTHENBACH	AELD	SCHARFENBERG	AEOC	SCHOMBERG
AEHV	ROTHENBERG	AELE	SCHARMBECK	AEOD	SCHONINGEN
AEHW	ROTHENBERGA	AELF	SCHARMEDE	AEOE	SCHOPFLOCH
AEHX	ROTHENBURG	AELG	SCHEESSEL	AEOF	SCHORNDORF
AEHY	ROTHENFELDE	AELH	SCHEIDT	AEOH	SCHOTTEN
AEHZ	ROTHENFELS	AELI	SCHELLENBERG	AEOI	SCHRAMBERG
AEIA	ROTHENKIRCHEN	AELJ	SCHEMMERN	AEOJ	SCHRECKSBACH
AEIC	ROTHHAUSEN	AELK	SCHERFEDER	AEOK	SCHREIBENDORF
AEID	ROTHSELBERG	AELL	SCHESSLITZ	AEOL	SCHRIMM
AEIE	ROTTENBACH	AELM	SCHIFFDORF	AEOM	SCHROZBERG
AEIF	ROTTENBURG	AELN	SCHIFFERSTADT	AEON	SCHUBIN
AEIG	ROTTERDAM	AELO	SCHIFFWEILER	AEOO	SCHUBY
AEIH	ROTTWEIL	AELP	SCHILDESCHE	AEOP	SCHUEREN
AEII	RUDELSDORF	AELQ	SCHILLINGEN	AEOQ	SCHUETTORF
AEIJ	RUDEN	AELR	SCHILLINGSTADT	AEOR	SCHURGAST
AEIK	RUDOLFSTADT	AELS	SCHIRGISWALDE	AEOS	SCHUTTERN
AEIL	RUDOLSTADT	AELT	SCHIRUM	AEOT	SCHWAAN
AEIM	RUECKERS	AELU	SCHLADEN	AEOU	SCHWABACH
AEIO	RUEGENWALDE	AELV	SCHLAGENTHIN	AEOV	SCHWABEN
AEIP	RUESSEN	AELW	SCHLAN	AEOW	SCHWALBACH
AEIQ	RUHLA	AELX	SCHLANGEN	AEOY	SCHWANDORF
AEIR	RUHLKIRCHEN	AELY	SCHLATT	AEOZ	SCHWANFELD
AEIS	RUHRORT	AELZ	SCHLAUPITZ	AEPA	SCHWANGAU
AEIT	RULLE	AEMA	SCHLAWE	AEPB	SCHWANHEIM
AEIU	RUPPERSDORF	AEMB	SCHLEDEHAUSEN	AEPC	SCHWANN
AEIV	RUPPERTENROD	AEMC	SCHLEID	AEPD	SCHWARZA
AEIW	RUPPERTSBURG	AEMD	SCHLEISSHEIM	AEPE	SCHWARZBURG
AEIX	RUSS	AEME	SCHLEITHEIM	AEPF	SCHWARZENBERG
AEIY	RUSSDORF	AEMF	SCHLEMMIN	AEPG	SCHWARZENBORN
AEIZ	RUST	AEMG	SCHLETTAU	AEPH	SCHWARZENFELD
AEJA	SAALDORF	AEMH	SCHLEUSINGEN	AEPI	SCHWARZENFELS
AEJB	SAALFELD	AEMI	SCHLEWECKE	AEPJ	SCHWASTORF
AEJC	SAARBRUECKEN	AEMJ	SCHLICHTEN	AEPK	SCHWEBHEIM
AEJD	SAARBURG	AEMK	SCHLIEBEN	AEPL	SCHWEDT
AEJF	SAARLOUIS	AEML	SCHLIERBACH	AEPN	SCHWEI
AEJG	SABBENHAUSEN	AEMM	SCHLINGEN	AEPO	SCHWEIDNITZ
AEJH	SABOW	AEMN	SCHLITZ	AEPP	SCHWEIGHAUSEN
AEJJ	SACHSENBURG	AEMO	SCHLOPPE	AEPQ	SCHWEINA
AEJK	SACHSENDORF	AEMP	SCHLOTHEIM	AEPR	SCHWEINAU
AEJL	SACHSENHAGEN	AEMQ	SCHLUCHTERN	AEPS	SCHWEINBERG
AEJM	SACHSENHAUSEN	AEMR	SCHLUECHTERN	AEPT	SCHWEINFURT
AEJO	SALINGEN	AEMS	SCHLUESSELBURG	AEPU	SCHWEINHEIM
AEJP	SALMUENSTER	AEMT	SCHMALKALDEN	AEPV	SCHWEINSDORF
AEJQ	SALZ	AEMU	SCHMALWASSER	AEPW	SCHWELM
AEJR	SALZBACH	AEMV	SCHMERIKON	AEPX	SCHWENNINGEN
AEJS	SALZBRUNN	AEMW	SCHMOELLN	AEPY	SCHWENTE
AEJT	SALZBURG	AEMX	SCHNATOW	AEPZ	SCHWERIN
AEJU	SALZDETFURTH	AEMY	SCHNEEBERG	AEQA	SCHWERINGEN
AEJW	SALZGITTER	AEMZ	SCHNEEREN	AEQB	SCHWETZINGEN
AEJX	SALZKOTTEN	AENA	SCHNEIDEMUEHL	AEQC	SCHWIEGERSHAUSEN
AEJY	SALZUNGEN	AENB	SCHNEIDERHOF	AEQD	SCRANTON
AEJZ	SALZWEDEL	AENC	SCHNELLDORF	AEQE	SECKENHAUSEN
AEKB	SANDAU	AEND	SCHNEY	AEQG	SEDELSBERG
AEKC	SANDBERG	AENE	SCHODEN	AEQH	SEDLETZ
AEKD	SANDE	AENF	SCHOENAU	AEQI	SEDLEC
AEKE	SANDERSHAUSEN	AENG	SCHOENBACH	AEQJ	SEEDORF
AEKF	SANDHAUSEN	AENH	SCHOENBECK	AEQK	SEEFELD
AEKG	SANDHEIM	AENI	SCHOENBERG	AEQL	SEEGREHNA
AEKH	SANDHOFEN	AENJ	SCHOENBRUNN	AEQM	SEELBACH
AEKI	SANDSTEDT	AENK	SCHOENBUSCH	AEQN	SEESEN
AEKJ	SANGERHAUSEN	AENL	SCHOENEBERG	AEQO	SEEWIS
AEKM	SARSTEDT	AENM	SCHOENECKEN	AEQP	SEHLDE
AEKN	SARTOWITZ	AENN	SCHOENEFELD	AEQQ	SEIDEL
AEKO	SASBACH	AENO	SCHOENEGRUEND	AEQR	SEIDORF
AEKP	SASBACHWALDEN	AENP	SCHOENERMARK	AEQS	SEIFERTS
AEKQ	SAULGAU	AENQ	SCHOENFELD	AEQT	SEITINGEN
AEKR	SAUSENHEIM	AENR	SCHOENFLIESS	AEQU	SELCHOW
AEKT	SAVERNE	AENS	SCHOENHAGEN	AEQV	SELIGENTHAL
AEKU	SAVOY	AENT	SCHOENINGEN	AEQW	SELLNOW
AEKV	SAXONY	AENU	SCHOENLANKE	AEQX	SELLSTEDT

Code	Village	Code	Village	Code	Village
AEQY	SELSINGEN	AETZ	SPRINGFELD	AEXJ	STRALSUND
AEQZ	SELTERS	AEUB	SPROTTAU	AEXK	STRASSBURG
AERA	SENDEN	AEUD	ST.LOUIS	AEXL	STRAUBING
AERB	SENNFELD	AEUE	ST.ETIENNE	AEXM	STRECK
AERC	SENSBURG	AEUG	ST.GEORGES	AEXN	STREITAU
AERD	SENTHEIM	AEUH	ST.GOAR	AEXO	STRELITZ
AERE	SEULINGEN	AEUI	ST.JOHANN	AEXP	STRESSENHAUSEN
AERF	SEVERY	AEUL	ST.MAGNUS	AEXQ	STRIEGAU
AERG	SICHENHAUSEN	AEUM	ST.MARTIN	AEXR	STROEHEN
AERH	SIEBENEICHEN	AEUN	ST.MAURITZ	AEXS	STROMBERG
AERI	SIEBER	AEUP	ST.PETER	AEXT	STRUTH
AERJ	SIEBLEBEN	AEUR	ST.THOMAS	AEXU	STUBBEN
AERK	SIECKE	AEUS	ST.VITH	AEXV	STUHM
AERL	SIEDENBURG	AEUT	ST.WENDEL	AEXW	STUTTGART
AERM	SIEGELSBACH	AEUU	STAAB	AEXX	SUDHEIM
AERN	SIEGELSDORF	AEUV	STADE	AEXY	SUEDHEMMERN
AERO	SIEGEN	AEUW	STADELHOFEN	AEXZ	SUEDLOHN
AERP	SIEKER	AEUX	STADEN	AEYA	SUELZ
AERQ	SIEVERN	AEUY	STADTHAGEN	AEYB	SUELZBACH
AERR	SIEVERSHAUSEN	AEUZ	STADTILM	AEYC	SUESTEDT
AERS	SILESIA	AEVA	STADTLOHN	AEYD	SUHL
AERT	SIMMERN	AEVB	STADTOLDENDORF	AEYE	SULINGEN
AERU	SINDELFINGEN	AEVC	STAFFELBACH	AEYF	SULSDORF
AERV	SINDLINGEN	AEVD	STAFFELDE	AEYG	SULZBACH
AERW	SINDRINGEN	AEVE	STAHL	AEYH	SULZDORF
AERX	SINGEN	AEVF	STAHLE	AEYI	SULZFELD
AERY	SINSHEIM	AEVH	STAMMBACH	AEYJ	SWITZERLAND
AERZ	SINZHEIM	AEVI	STAMMHEIM	AEYK	SYKE
AESA	SIPPERSFELD	AEVK	STANGENROD	AEYM	TABOR
AESB	SITTEN	AEVM	STARGARD	AEYN	TACHAU
AESC	SLATE	AEVN	STASSFURT	AEYO	TAMMHAUSEN
AESD	SCHLESWIG	AEVO	STEDESDORF	AEYP	TANN
AESE	SMASIN	AEVP	STEIERMARK	AEYQ	TANNENBERG
AESF	SMOLENSK	AEVQ	STEIN	AEYR	TARMSTEDT
AESG	SODEN	AEVR	STEINACH	AEYS	TATING
AESH	SOEMMERDA	AEVS	STEINAU	AEYT	TAUBENBACH
AESI	SOEST	AEVT	STEINBACH	AEYU	TAUBERRETTERSHEIM
AESJ	SOETERN	AEVU	STEINBECK	AEYV	TAURA
AESK	SOHREN	AEVV	STEINBERG	AEYW	TAUTENHAIN
AESL	SOLDIN	AEVW	STEINDORF	AEYX	TECKLENBURG
AESM	SOLINGEN	AEVX	STEINENBRONN	AEYY	TEGERNAU
AESN	SOLMS	AEVY	STEINFELD	AEYZ	TEGERNBACH
AESO	SOLOTHURN	AEVZ	STEINFURTH	AEZA	TELGTE
AESP	SOLPKE	AEWA	STEINHAUSEN	AEZB	TENNSTEDT
AESQ	SOLTAU	AEWB	STEINHEIM	AEZD	TEPLITZ
AESR	SOLZ	AEWC	STEINHOFEN	AEZE	TESCHENDORF
AESS	SOMMERACH	AEWD	STEINSDORF	AEZF	TESSIN
AEST	SOMMERAU	AEWE	STEINWEILER	AEZG	TETTENS
AESU	SOMMERFELD	AEWF	STEINWIESEN	AEZH	TEUCHERN
AESV	SOMMERHAUSEN	AEWG	STEMMEN	AEZI	TEUFELSMOOR
AESW	SOMMERSDORF	AEWH	STEMMENREUTH	AEZJ	TEUFENTHAL
AESX	SONDERSHAUSEN	AEWI	STEPPACH	AEZK	TEUNZ
AESY	SONDHEIM	AEWJ	STERNENFELS	AEZL	TEVEREN
AESZ	SONNEBERG	AEWK	STERZHAUSEN	AEZN	THAL
AETA	SONNEBORN	AEWL	STETTEN	AEZO	THALHEIM
AETC	SONNEFELD	AEWM	STETTIN	AEZP	THALMAESSING
AETD	SONNENBORN	AEWN	STIEG	AEZQ	THAMSBRUECK
AETE	SONTRA	AEWO	STIEGLITZ	AEZR	THEDINGHAUSEN
AETF	SOODEN	AEWP	STOCKELSDORF	AEZS	THEILHEIM
AETG	SOPHIENTHAL	AEWQ	STOCKHAUSEN	AEZT	THEMAR
AETH	SORAU	AEWR	STOCKHEIM	AEZU	THIERGARTEN
AETI	SORGE	AEWS	STOCKHOLM	AEZV	THORN
AETK	SOUTHAMPTON	AEWT	STOCKSTADT	AEZX	THULBA
AETL	SPADEN	AEWU	STOCKUM	AEZY	THUN
AETM	SPAICHINGEN	AEWV	STOEVEN	AEZZ	THURNAU
AETN	SPANDAU	AEWW	STOEWEN	AFAA	TIEFENORT
AETO	SPANGENBEG	AEWX	STOLBERG	AFAB	TILSIT
AETP	SPELDORF	AEWY	STOLLHAMM	AFAC	TIRSCHENREUTH
AETQ	SPELLE	AEWZ	STOLP	AFAD	TITTING
AETR	SPENGE	AEXA	STOLPE	AFAE	TITTLING
AETS	SPEYER	AEXB	STOLZ	AFAF	TODENMANN
AETT	SPICH	AEXC	STOLZENAU	AFAG	TODTENHAUSEN
AETU	SPIEGELBERG	AEXE	STORNDORF	AFAH	TOLEDO
AETV	SPIEKA	AEXF	STOTEL	AFAI	TOLLHAUSEN
AETW	SPREMBERG	AEXG	STOTTERNHEIM	AFAJ	TORGAU
AETX	SPRENDLINGEN	AEXH	STRACKHOLT	AFAK	TORONTO
AETY	SPRINGE	AEXI	STRAHLENFELS	AFAL	TRABELSDORF

AFAM	TREBBIN	AFDS	VENNEBECK	AFGU	WALLENHAUSEN
AFAN	TREFFURT	AFDT	VENNIGEN	AFGV	WALLENSTEDT
AFAO	TREIS	AFDU	VERA CRUZ	AFGW	WALLERFANGEN
AFAP	TRENDELBURG	AFDW	VERDEN	AFGX	WALLERSDORF
AFAQ	TREPTOW	AFDX	VERLIEHAUSEN	AFGY	WALLERSTEIN
AFAR	TREUEN	AFDZ	VERNA	AFGZ	WALLHAUSEN
AFAS	TRIER	AFEA	VERONA	AFHA	WALSDORF
AFAU	TRINS	AFEB	VERSBACH	AFHB	WALSLEBEN
AFAV	TROCKENERFURTH	AFEC	VERSMOLD	AFHC	WALSRODE
AFAW	TROGEN	AFED	VESTRUP	AFHD	WALTERSDORF
AFAX	TROPPAU	AFEE	VIENNA	AFHE	WALTERSHOF
AFAY	TROSSINGEN	AFEF	VIENNE	AFHF	WAMBEL
AFBA	TRUNSTADT	AFEG	VILBEL	AFHG	WANGEN
AFBB	TUCHEL	AFEH	VILLARS	AFHH	WANHEIM
AFBC	TUCHLA	AFEI	VILLINGEN	AFHI	WANNA
AFBD	TUEBINGEN	AFEJ	VILLMAR	AFHJ	WANNE
AFBE	TURKAH	AFEK	VILSEN	AFHK	WANNENBERG
AFBF	TUTTLINGEN	AFEL	VINSEBECK	AFHL	WANSLEBEN
AFBG	TYROL	AFEN	VISBECK	AFHM	WANZLEBEN
AFBH	UCHTDORF	AFEO	VLOTHO	AFHN	WARBURG
AFBI	UCHTE	AFEP	VLUYN	AFHO	WARDENBURG
AFBJ	UDENHAUSEN	AFEQ	VOERSTETTEN	AFHP	WARENDORF
AFBK	UEBERLINGEN	AFER	VOGELSANG	AFHQ	WARIN
AFBM	UEDINGEN	AFES	VOGT	AFHR	WARNSDORF
AFBN	UEFFELN	AFET	VOIGTSTEDT	AFHS	WARSINGSFEHN
AFBO	UELDE	AFEU	VOLKERSHAUSEN	AFHT	WARSTEIN
AFBP	UELSEN	AFEV	VOLKMARSEN	AFHU	WARTENBERG
AFBR	UENZEN	AFEW	VOLLMER	AFHV	WARTENFELS
AFBS	UFFELN	AFEX	VOLLMERZ	AFHW	WARZENBACH
AFBT	UFFHOFEN	AFEY	VOLMERDINGSEN	AFHX	WASCH
AFBU	UHLINGEN	AFEZ	VORDERWEIDENTHAL	AFHZ	WASSEN
AFBV	ULM	AFFA	VORRA	AFIA	WASUNGEN
AFBW	ULMBACH	AFFB	VORSTADT	AFIB	WATTENBACH
AFBX	ULMEN	AFFC	VORWERK	AFIC	WATTENHEIM
AFBY	UNADINGEN	AFFD	WABERN	AFID	WATTENS
AFBZ	UNGEDANKEN	AFFE	WACHAU	AFIE	WATZUM
AFCA	UNLINGEN	AFFF	WACHBACH	AFIF	WECHOLD
AFCB	UNTERBALZHEIM	AFFG	WACHENBUCHEN	AFIG	WEDEL
AFCD	UNTEREBERSBACH	AFFH	WACHENHEIM	AFIH	WEENER
AFCE	UNTEREICHEN	AFFI	WACHENROTH	AFII	WEFERLINGEN
AFCF	UNTERFRANKEN	AFFJ	WACKHOFEN	AFIJ	WEHDEL
AFCG	UNTERKESSACH	AFFK	WADENDORF	AFIK	WEHDEM
AFCH	UNTERLEINACH	AFFL	WADERSLOH	AFIL	WEHRENDORF
AFCI	UNTERLENNINGEN	AFFM	WADGASSEN	AFIM	WEHRSDORF
AFCJ	UNTERLUEBBE	AFFN	WAGENFELD	AFIN	WEICHERSBACH
AFCK	UNTERMUENKHEIM	AFFO	WAGENSCHWEND	AFIO	WEID MOOS
AFCL	UNTERSCHEFFLENZ	AFFP	WAGENSTADT	AFIP	WEIDA
AFCM	UNTERSCHLEICHACH	AFFQ	WAHLEN	AFIQ	WEIDENAU
AFCN	UNTERSCHWANINGEN	AFFR	WAHLERT	AFIR	WEIDENBACH
AFCO	UNTERSTKOPPEL	AFFS	WAHNBEK	AFIS	WEIDENHAUSEN
AFCP	UNTERWEISSENBACH	AFFT	WAIBLINGEN	AFIT	WEIDENTHAL
AFCQ	UNTERWELLENBORN	AFFU	WAIBSTADT	AFIU	WEIER
AFCR	UNTERZAUNSBACH	AFFV	WAIN	AFIV	WEIERBACH
AFCS	UPHUSUM	AFFW	WALD	AFIW	WEIKERSHEIM
AFCT	URACH	AFFX	WALDANGELLOCH	AFIX	WEIL
AFCU	URBACH	AFFY	WALDAU	AFIY	WEILAR
AFCV	URBERACH	AFFZ	WALDBURG	AFIZ	WEILBURG
AFCW	URLAU	AFGA	WALDECK	AFJA	WEILER
AFCX	URSPRUNG	AFGB	WALDENBUCH	AFJB	WEILERSTEUSSLINGEN
AFCY	USINGEN	AFGC	WALDENBURG	AFJC	WEILHEIM
AFCZ	USLAR	AFGD	WALDHAUSEN	AFJD	WEIMAR
AFDB	VACHA	AFGE	WALDHEIM	AFJE	WEIMERSHEIM
AFDC	VALLENDAR	AFGF	WALDKIRCH	AFJF	WEINBERG
AFDD	VAREL	AFGG	WALDLAUBERSHEIM	AFJG	WEINGARTEN
AFDE	VARENHOLZ	AFGH	WALDMICHELBACH	AFJH	WEINHEIM
AFDF	VECHTA	AFGI	WALDMUENCHEN	AFJI	WEINSDORF
AFDG	VECHTEL	AFGJ	WALDORF	AFJJ	WEINSFELD
AFDH	VECKENSTEDT	AFGK	WALDSEE	AFJK	WEISBACH
AFDI	VECKERHAGEN	AFGL	WALDSHUT	AFJL	WEISENDORF
AFDJ	VEERSE	AFGM	WALHAUSEN	AFJM	WEISENHEIM
AFDK	VEGESACK	AFGN	WALLAU	AFJN	WEISSDORF
AFDM	VEHLAGE	AFGO	WALLDORF	AFJO	WEISSENBACH
AFDN	VEHRTE	AFGP	WALLE	AFJP	WEISSENBERG
AFDO	VELEN	AFGQ	WALLENBRUECK	AFJQ	WEISSENBORN
AFDP	VELMEDE	AFGR	WALLENBRUNN	AFJR	WEISSENDORF
AFDQ	VELPKE	AFGS	WALLENDORF	AFJS	WEISSENFELD
AFDR	VENNE	AFGT	WALLENFELS	AFJT	WEISSENFELS

AFJU	WEISSENHASEL	AFMW	WIBLINGEN	AFPY	WOLF
AFJV	WEISSENHAUS	AFMX	WICHTE	AFPZ	WOLFAHRTSWEILER
AFJW	WEISSENSEE	AFMY	WIDDERN	AFQA	WOLFEN
AFJX	WEISSENSTADT	AFMZ	WIEBLINGEN	AFQB	WOLFENBUETTEL
AFJY	WEISSENSTEIN	AFNA	WIEDENBRUECK	AFQC	WOLFERSDORF
AFJZ	WEISSENTHURM	AFNB	WIEDENSAHL	AFQD	WOLFERSGRUEN
AFKA	WEISWEIL	AFNC	WIEHE	AFQE	WOLFERSTADT
AFKB	WELKENDORF	AFNE	WIERBORN	AFQF	WOLFHAGEN
AFKC	WELLEN	AFNF	WIERSCHUTZIN	AFQG	WOLFSEGG
AFKD	WELLENDINGEN	AFNG	WIERSEN	AFQH	WOLFSHAGEN
AFKE	WELLHEIM	AFNH	WIERSHAUSEN	AFQI	WOLFSKEHLEN
AFKF	WELLINGEN	AFNI	WIERUP	AFQJ	WOLKENDORF
AFKG	WELLINGHOLZHAUSEN	AFNJ	WIESACH	AFQK	WOLLGAST
AFKH	WELSEDE	AFNK	WIESBADEN	AFQL	WOLLIN
AFKJ	WELZHEIM	AFNL	WIESECK	AFQM	WOLLMATINGEN
AFKK	WENDEBURG	AFNM	WIESEDE	AFQN	WOLLSTEIN
AFKL	WENDELSHEIM	AFNN	WIESEDERMEER	AFQO	WOLTERSDORF
AFKM	WENDELSTEIN	AFNO	WIESENBACH	AFQP	WOLTERSHAUSEN
AFKN	WENDEN	AFNP	WIESENFELD	AFQQ	WOLTRINGHAUSEN
AFKO	WENDENBORSTEL	AFNQ	WIESENTHAL	AFQR	WON
AFKP	WENDISCH BUCHHOLZ	AFNR	WIESENTHAU	AFQS	WONSOWO
AFKQ	WENDTHAGEN	AFNS	WIESENTHEIT	AFQT	WOQUARD
AFKR	WENGENHAUSEN	AFNT	WIESETH	AFQU	WORMDITT
AFKS	WENINGS	AFNU	WIESLOCH	AFQV	WORMS
AFKT	WENNEBOSTEL	AFNV	WIESWEILER	AFQW	WORPSWEDE
AFKU	WENNIGSTEDT	AFNW	WIETZEN	AFQX	WORRINGEN
AFKV	WENSE	AFNX	WILDBERG	AFQY	WORTH
AFKW	WERBIG	AFNY	WILDEMANN	AFQZ	WOTERSEN
AFKX	WERDAU	AFNZ	WILDENAU	AFRA	WREMEN
AFKY	WERDEN	AFOA	WILDESHAUSEN	AFRB	WRESCHEN
AFKZ	WERDER	AFOB	WILDUNGEN	AFRC	WRESCHERODE
AFLA	WERDORF	AFOC	WILHELMSDORF	AFRD	WRISSE
AFLB	WERDUM	AFOD	WILHELMSFELD	AFRE	WUELLEN
AFLC	WERL	AFOE	WILHELMSHAUSEN	AFRF	WUERGES
AFLD	WERNAU	AFOF	WILHELMSHAVEN	AFRG	WUERZBURG
AFLE	WERNE	AFOG	WILLERSDORF	AFRH	WUESTEN
AFLF	WERNIGERODE	AFOH	WILLIAMSBURG	AFRI	WUESTENSACHSEN
AFLG	WERNSBACH	AFOI	WILLINGEN	AFRJ	WULFSTAHL
AFLH	WERNSDORF	AFOK	WILSDRUFF	AFRK	WULFTEN
AFLI	WERSABE	AFOL	WILSTEDT	AFRL	WULMSTORF
AFLJ	WERSCHE	AFOM	WILSTEDTER MOOR	AFRM	WULSDORF
AFLK	WERSCHETZ	AFON	WIMMER	AFRN	WUNSIEDEL
AFLL	WERSEN	AFOO	WIMPFEN	AFRO	WUNSTORF
AFLM	WERTHEIM	AFOP	WINCHESTER	AFRP	WURMLINGEN
AFLN	WERTHER	AFOQ	WINDECKEN	AFRQ	WURMSDORF
AFLO	WESEL	AFOR	WINDHEIM	AFRR	WURTHFLETH
AFLP	WESERITZ	AFOS	WINDORF	AFRS	WYK
AFLQ	WESSUM	AFOT	WINDSBACH	AFRT	YORK
AFLR	WESTBARTHAUSEN	AFOU	WINKEL	AFRU	ZAINHAMMER
AFLS	WESTBEVERN	AFOV	WINKELDORF	AFRV	ZATTEN
AFLT	WESTE	AFOW	WINKELSHUETTEN	AFRW	ZEBHAUSEN
AFLU	WESTEN	AFOX	WINNENDEN	AFRX	ZEIL
AFLV	WESTENDORF	AFOY	WINNINGEN	AFRY	ZEILHARD
AFLW	WESTENHOLZ	AFOZ	WINSEN	AFRZ	ZEILITZHEIM
AFLX	WESTERCAPPELN	AFPA	WINTERBACH	AFSA	ZEITZ
AFLY	WESTEREIDEN	AFPB	WINTERHAGEN	AFSB	ZELL
AFLZ	WESTERHAUSEN	AFPC	WINTERLINGEN	AFSC	ZELLA
AFMA	WESTERHEIM	AFPD	WINTERSCHEID	AFSD	ZELLERFELD
AFMB	WESTERHOLTE	AFPE	WINZLAR	AFSE	ZELLINGEN
AFMC	WESTERHOLZ	AFPF	WIPPENBACH	AFSF	ZEMPELBURG
AFMD	WESTERLOH	AFPG	WIRSITZ	AFSG	ZENTBECHHOFEN
AFME	WESTERMARSCH	AFPH	WISCHIN	AFSH	ZEPFENHAN
AFMF	WESTERSTEDE	AFPJ	WISSEK	AFSI	ZERBST
AFMG	WESTERWANNA	AFPK	WISSEL	AFSJ	ZERNIKOW
AFMH	WESTERWIEHE	AFPL	WITTELSBERG	AFSK	ZERNIN
AFMI	WESTHEIM	AFPM	WITTENBERG	AFSL	ZETEL
AFMJ	WESTHOFEN	AFPN	WITTERSHAUSEN	AFSM	ZEULENRODA
AFMK	WESTPHALIA	AFPO	WITTGENSTEIN	AFSN	ZEVEN
AFMM	WESTRUM	AFPP	WITTLAGE	AFSO	ZIEGELBRONN
AFMN	WESTRUP	AFPQ	WITTMUND	AFSP	ZIEGENHAGEN
AFMO	WETTEN	AFPR	WITTORF	AFSQ	ZIEGENHAIN
AFMP	WETTER	AFPS	WITTSTEDT	AFSR	ZIERIKZEE
AFMQ	WETTERFELD	AFPT	WITZENHAUSEN	AFSS	ZILSHAUSEN
AFMR	WETTMAR	AFPU	WITZIN	AFST	ZIMMERN
AFMS	WETTRINGEN	AFPV	WOELMEN	AFSU	ZIMMERSRODE
AFMT	WETZLAR	AFPW	WOERPEDORF	AFSV	ZIMMET
AFMU	WEYER	AFPX	WOHRA	AFSW	ZINKEN

Code	Name	Code	Name	Code	Name
AFSX	ZIRKWITZ	AFWF	UECKERMUENDE	AFZK	SCHILDE
AFSY	ZITTAU	AFWG	UNGARN	AFZL	SCHLOCHAU
AFSZ	ZOTZENBACH	AFWI	WANGERIN	AFZM	SCHOENSEE
AFTA	ZUEHLSDORF	AFWJ	WARSAW	AFZN	SCHORIN
AFTB	ZUELZ	AFWK	WIELLE	AFZO	SCHWEBEN
AFTC	ZULTENBERG	AFWL	ALM	AFZQ	SEMEROW
AFTD	ZURICH	AFWM	ALTHAMMER	AFZS	SOPHIENBERG
AFTE	ZUZENHAUSEN	AFWN	AMBERG	AFZT	ST.GALLEN
AFTF	ZWEIBRUECKEN	AFWO	ANDERNACH	AFZU	STAFFELHAGEN
AFTG	ZWESTEN	AFWP	APPELWERDER	AFZV	STEINFURT
AFTI	ZWICKAU	AFWQ	ARNOLDSDORF	AFZW	TADDEN
AFTJ	ALEXANDRIA	AFWR	BARGFELD	AFZX	TANGEN
AFTK	ALLENSTEIN	AFWS	BEIERN	AFZY	TEKLENBURG
AFTL	AURORA	AFWT	BENTSCHEN	AGAA	TOULOUSE
AFTM	AUSTRIA	AFWU	BITOV	AGAB	ULRICHSTEIN
AFTN	BARVER	AFWV	BOLL	AGAC	UTTRICHSHAUSEN
AFTO	BATH	AFWW	BORDEAUX	AGAD	VALPARAISO
AFTP	BELFAST	AFWX	BOSEN	AGAE	WACHSMUTH
AFTQ	BELLEVILLE	AFWY	BRATTWIN	AGAF	WADERN
AFTR	BOGENSE	AFWZ	BRAUNSCHWEIG	AGAG	WATERLOO
AFTS	BOHEMIA	AFXB	BUGEWITZ	AGAH	WEISSENBURG
AFTT	BONNE	AFXC	BURGSINN	AGAI	WIEGENDORF
AFTU	BRIESEN	AFXD	CZARNOWO	AGAL	WUERTEMBERG
AFTV	BURLINGTON	AFXE	DARGEBANZ	AGAM	ZACHAN
AFTW	CAMMIN	AFXF	DEICHSENDE	AGAN	ZEMLIN
AFTX	CARLSKRONA	AFXG	DENZIN	AGAO	ZNIN
AFTY	CARLSTHAL	AFXH	EISENBACH	AGAP	ZUCHAU
AFTZ	COLUMBIA	AFXI	ELTVILLE	AGAQ	ZUCKEN
AFUA	DENVER	AFXJ	ESSEL	AGAR	POLAJEWO
AFUB	DEUTSCH-KRONE	AFXK	FEGERSHEIM	AGAS	BUETOW
AFUC	DRAWEHN	AFXL	FRIEDENDORF	AGAT	DAMERFITZ
AFUD	EBENDORF	AFXM	GENSUNGEN	AGAU	DEUTSCHEYLAU
AFUE	ESCHERSHAUSSEN	AFXN	GERHARDSHOFEN	AGAW	DIRSCHAU
AFUF	GEORGIA	AFXO	GEROLZHOFEN	AGAX	DRESCHWITZ
AFUG	GREEN BAY	AFXP	GESORKE	AGAY	FRANKENFELDE
AFUH	GREIFENBERG	AFXQ	GIFHORN	AGBA	GESTIEN
AFUI	GREIFSWALD	AFXR	GLEIWITZ	AGBB	GLASHUETTE
AFUJ	HARPERS FERRY	AFXS	GRODITZ	AGBC	GUETZKOW
AFUK	HARRISBURG	AFXT	GRONE	AGBE	HABORN
AFUL	HELGOLAND	AFXU	GUETZ	AGBF	HEINRICHSHAGEN
AFUM	HELSINGOER	AFXV	GUSTEN	AGBG	HOLBECK
AFUN	HINDENBURG	AFXW	HARMELSDORF	AGBH	HOLDORF
AFUO	HOHENWALDE	AFXX	HARRE	AGBI	IBBENBUEREN
AFUP	JELTSCH	AFXY	HASELBACH	AGBK	KALLIES
AFUR	LABENZ	AFXZ	HILGERSHAUSEN	AGBL	KLEIN NAKEL
AFUS	LAMBSBORN	AFYA	HOLLSTEIN	AGBM	KNAPENDORF
AFUT	LANCASTER	AFYB	JASTROW	AGBN	KORNA
AFUU	LIPPE	AFYC	KARBACH	AGBO	KRATZWIECK
AFUV	LIPPE-DETMOLD	AFYD	KARLSDORF	AGBP	KREFELD
AFUW	LOMNITZ	AFYE	KITZEROW	AGBQ	LEBUSA
AFUX	MARIENAU	AFYF	KOERLIN	AGBR	LUEBBEN
AFUY	NAURU	AFYH	KRAMPE	AGBS	LUEKEN
AFUZ	NEBRA	AFYI	LANGEBOESE	AGBU	MARSEILLE
AFVA	NEMITZ	AFYJ	LANGENBRUCH	AGBV	MOHROW
AFVF	ODENSE	AFYK	LANGENDORF	AGBW	MOLLENSTORF
AFVG	ODESSA	AFYL	LAUTERECKEN	AGBX	NORDHEMMERN
AFVH	OXFORD	AFYM	LETSCHIN	AGBY	NORGAU
AFVI	PAPENHAGEN	AFYN	LICHTENHAGEN	AGCA	PEGAU
AFVL	RAPPIN	AFYO	LINDENBERG	AGCB	PFERDSDORF
AFVM	RECKOW	AFYP	LONZIG	AGCC	PREUSSISCH FRIEDLAND
AFVN	REDEN	AFYQ	LORRAINE	AGCD	PYRITZ
AFVO	REETZ	AFYR	LUGGEWIESE	AGCE	RADOM
AFVP	REHBERG	AFYS	MAHREN	AGCG	RUEDERSHAUSEN
AFVQ	RIESENKIRCH	AFYU	MILDENITZ	AGCH	SCHIVELBEIN
AFVR	ROTTENDORF	AFYV	MONTREAL	AGCI	SCHOENWERDER
AFVS	SAAL	AFYW	MOSEL	AGCJ	SCHOKKEN
AFVT	SACHSEN-COBURG	AFYX	NAUGART	AGCK	SCHROTTHAUS
AFVU	SACHSEN-MEININGEN	AFYY	NEUENSUND	AGCL	SCHURBACH
AFVV	SEIBELSDORF	AFYZ	OBERLAUTERBACH	AGCN	SILLIGSDORF
AFVW	SELLISTRAU	AFZB	ORB	AGCO	SPIESEN
AFVX	SLAGELSE	AFZC	ORNSHAGEN	AGCQ	STOVE
AFVY	SPECK	AFZD	POLAND	AGCR	STRZELEWO
AFVZ	SANTO DOMINGO	AFZF	ROEDEN	AGCS	THIEMENDORF
AFWA	STAVEN	AFZG	ROGASEN	AGCT	THIENDORF
AFWB	STEGLIN	AFZH	RUEBER	AGCU	TRIEBUSCH
AFWC	STEINORT	AFZI	RUMMELSBURG	AGCV	TRZEMESZNO
AFWD	TANGER	AFZJ	SCHADEWINKEL	AGCX	UHLKAU

AGCY	UJAST	AGGA	PROVENCE	AGJH	MUEHLAU
AGCZ	URWEILER	AGGB	SACHSENBERG	AGJI	NACHTSHEIM
AGDA	VARGOW	AGGC	WARSIN	AGJJ	OBERSUHL
AGDB	VORSFELDE	AGGD	SCHWETZIN	AGJK	OTTERSWEILER
AGDC	WERRICH	AGGE	WERLAU	AGJL	PUENDERICH
AGDD	WIELITZ	AGGF	WIECK	AGJM	RICKLING
AGDE	WINDORP	AGGG	WASHINGTON	AGJN	RIPPBERG
AGDF	ZUELLCHOW	AGGH	ZEMPELKOWO	AGJO	RIVE-DE-GIER
AGDG	BELKOW	AGGI	ZERRIN	AGJP	ROANNE
AGDH	KOESLIN	AGGJ	WISCONSIN	AGJQ	RUPPERTSHUETTEN
AGDI	WOLFISHEIM	AGGK	ZOLL	AGJR	RUPPERTSWEILER
AGDJ	ABLACH	AGGL	ZUG	AGJS	SCHECHINGEN
AGDK	ALBERSWEILER	AGGM	ZETHLINGEN	AGJT	SCHEIBERHARDT
AGDM	ANGERMUENDE	AGGN	BAIERSBRUNN	AGJU	SISSACH
AGDO	BARTENHEIM	AGGO	BECHEN	AGJV	ST.SEBASTIAN
AGDP	BAUMGARTH	AGGP	BERNSDORF	AGJW	UNERBRUCH
AGDQ	BERGWALDE	AGGQ	BEWERSDORF	AGJX	UNTERGROENINGEN
AGDR	BORNTUCHEN	AGGR	EHRENBERG	AGJY	UNTERWAIZ
AGDS	BREDOW	AGGU	ETTELBRUECK	AGJZ	WALDASCHAFF
AGDT	BUESCHDORF	AGGV	FRIEDERIKA	AGKA	WANDSBEK
AGDU	CZERSK	AGGX	GERNEWITZ	AGKB	WELSCHBILLIG
AGDW	DAMEROW	AGGY	GOLLANTSCH	AGKC	WIEHL
AGDX	DARGISLAFF	AGHA	GOSTITZ	AGKD	ASCHBACH
AGDY	DETZEM	AGHB	GROSS-LATZKOW	AGKE	ASPACH
AGDZ	DRENOW	AGHC	GRUENWALDE	AGKF	AUCH
AGEA	ESCHDORF	AGHD	GUENTHERSDORF	AGKG	BALLWEILER
AGEB	ESCHENFELDEN	AGHE	HARDEBEK	AGKH	BELFORT
AGEC	ETTISWEILER	AGHF	HAUSBERGE	AGKI	BERLICHINGEN
AGED	FINKENSTEIN	AGHG	KOMMERAU	AGKJ	BIRNDORF
AGEE	GERSDORF	AGHH	KRAUCHENWIES	AGKK	BLEICKHEIM
AGEF	GOEFFINGEN	AGHJ	MEHLEN	AGKL	BONDORF
AGEG	GORGAST	AGHK	NUSSDORF	AGKM	BREST
AGEH	GRAVENHORST	AGHL	OBERKOTZAU	AGKN	BURGSTEINFURT
AGEI	GRIES	AGHM	REICHENBUCH	AGKO	CAROW
AGEJ	BERGEN-OP-ZOOM	AGHN	ROHRBECK	AGKP	CETTE
AGEK	HEINRICHSWALDE	AGHO	SAARGEMUEND	AGKQ	CHRISTIANSTADT
AGEL	HOHENFELDE	AGHP	SCHWARZENBACH	AGKR	DELEMONT
AGEM	BISSINGEN	AGHR	SEITENBERG	AGKS	DIETERHAUSEN
AGEN	KLEINWALDE	AGHS	SINGWITZ	AGKT	DONAUESCHINGEN
AGEO	KLINGBECK	AGHT	STRAUSBERG	AGKU	DURMERSCHEIM
AGEP	KRAIN	AGHU	WASCHOW	AGKV	ECHTERNACH
AGEQ	DAMEN	AGHV	WELSCHINGEN	AGKW	EHRENFELD
AGER	LEBBIN	AGHW	WILLMERSBACH	AGKX	ERSTEIN
AGES	DURHAM	AGHY	ZIEGENDORF	AGKY	FREDERICIA
AGET	EICHELSBACH	AGHZ	ZUELLICHAU	AGKZ	FRIESEN
AGEU	LISTRUP	AGIA	ALTDAMM	AGLA	GREIN
AGEV	FRIEDRICHSHAFEN	AGIB	ALTSTAETTEN	AGLB	GRENOBLE
AGEW	LOUISENHOF	AGIC	ATTENHOFEN	AGLC	GROEDE
AGEX	GENOA	AGID	BECKEDORF	AGLD	HARGARTEN
AGEY	HAMMERSBACH	AGIE	BERSCHWEILER	AGLE	HASPE
AGEZ	MARIENBERG	AGIF	BESANCON	AGLF	HEITERSHEIM
AGFA	HERZFELD	AGIG	BRUESSOW	AGLG	HILSBACH
AGFB	HOHENLANDIN	AGIH	BUEDESHEIM	AGLH	HOLSTEIN
AGFC	MERSIN	AGII	BURGSPONHEIM	AGLI	IRRHAUSEN
AGFD	METZ	AGIJ	CHALONS-SUR-MARNE	AGLJ	KADELBURG
AGFE	IOWA	AGIK	DAHLENBERG	AGLK	KALTHAUSEN
AGFF	KASSEL	AGIM	GERMAU	AGLL	KLEINBUNDENBACH
AGFG	KLEIN-BENZ	AGIN	GERTSCHEN	AGLM	LEUTKIRCH
AGFH	NEUWEDEL	AGIO	GRANDVILLARD	AGLN	LINDACH
AGFI	LIBAU	AGIP	GROSSNEUHAUSEN	AGLO	LORIENT
AGFJ	OTTERBERG	AGIQ	GUDOW	AGLP	LOTTSTETTEN
AGFK	PARLIN	AGIR	HANDSCHUHSHEIM	AGLQ	LUCERNE
AGFL	MENGEN	AGIS	HARTEFELD	AGLR	LUNGERN
AGFM	MICHIGAN	AGIT	HILFARTH	AGLS	LUXEMBURG
AGFN	MIESENBACH	AGIU	HUNTENBERG	AGLT	LYON
AGFO	MILWAUKEE	AGIV	KALTENWESTHEIM	AGLU	MECHENRIED
AGFP	MISSOURI	AGIW	KAUDER	AGLV	MEIENDORF
AGFQ	MONTKEN	AGIX	KLINGENMUENSTER	AGLW	MILDENBERG
AGFR	NEBRASKA	AGIY	KOENIGSBRONN	AGLX	MONTAUBAN
AGFS	SEELEN	AGIZ	KRIENS	AGLY	NANCY
AGFT	SENNHEIM	AGJA	KUENZELSAU	AGLZ	NEIDENBURG
AGFU	NEW YORK	AGJB	LANGENPROZELTEN	AGMA	NIEDERURNEN
AGFV	OHIO	AGJC	LOERRACH	AGMB	NIMES
AGFW	PENNSYLVANIA	AGJD	LOTZWIL	AGMC	NITTEL
AGFX	PHILADELPHIA	AGJE	LUECHINGEN	AGMD	OBERFLACHT
AGFY	PITTSBURGH	AGJF	MAULBURG	AGME	OBERRIED
AGFZ	PRIEMEN	AGJG	MONTBELIARD	AGMF	OBERSCHLETTENBACH

AGMG	ORLEANS	AGPG	KROKAU	AGSF	ERMSTADT
AGMH	ORSIERES	AGPH	KURTATSCH	AGSG	ERNSTRODE
AGMI	OTTOBERG	AGPI	LANDWEHR	AGSH	GRESSEN
AGMJ	RANDOW	AGPJ	LEKNO	AGSI	GR.SOLT
AGMK	RANNENBERG	AGPK	LERBACH	AGSJ	HITTESAU
AGML	REINSFELD	AGPL	LILLE	AGSK	KOMOSOWO
AGMM	RIED	AGPM	LOCHUM	AGSL	LANDSES
AGMN	ROBE	AGPN	LOEWENBERG	AGSM	LANSES
AGMO	RODT	AGPO	LOHRBACH	AGSN	LEIDRINGER
AGMP	SAATZIG	AGPP	LYONS	AGSO	LEPIN
AGMQ	SCHLIERSTADT	AGPQ	MEDERNACH	AGSP	BOURBON-LES-BAINS
AGMR	SCHWAIGEN	AGPR	MENTON	AGSQ	MEGGE
AGMS	SIGMARINGEN	AGPS	MEUSELBACH	AGSR	MUNKPRARUP
AGMT	ST.FIDEN	AGPT	MIROW	AGSS	OSTRA
AGMU	ST.MAURICE	AGPU	MOMBACH	AGST	RETTERBACH
AGMV	STEDUM	AGPV	MORAVIA	AGSU	RIEBE
AGMW	STEINEN	AGPW	MUELLHEIM	AGSV	RISANA
AGMX	SULZ	AGPX	MUELSEN	AGSW	ROSTADT
AGMY	SUMISWALD	AGPY	NIDA	AGSX	SCHWANDI
AGMZ	TRARBACH	AGPZ	NIEBLUM	AGSY	SIMONSWALD
AGNA	TROIS-VIERGES	AGQA	NIEDERROSSBACH	AGSZ	TWISTE
AGNB	UDERN	AGQB	NIEDERZIER	AGTA	WARGOLDHAUSEN
AGNC	UHM	AGQC	OBERLAURINGEN	AGTB	WELDAU
AGND	VINCENNES	AGQD	OSTERBURG	AGTC	WIRSCHEIDT
AGNE	WEINSBERG	AGQE	OSTERMOOR	AGTD	WOERSTADT
AGNF	WERSCHEN	AGQF	OSTERWOHLE	AGTE	ALLING
AGNH	AARAU	AGQG	PENZBERG	AGTF	ANNECY
AGNI	AESCH	AGQH	PERL	AGTG	ANTIBES
AGNJ	AIXHEIM	AGQI	PFAFFENHOFEN	AGTH	ARCH
AGNK	ALBERSDORF	AGQJ	PILGRAMSDORF	AGTI	ARDECHE
AGNL	ALKERSUM	AGQK	POPOWO	AGTJ	ARRAS
AGNM	ALSENBORN	AGQL	PREETZ	AGTK	AUSBACH
AGNN	ALTENLINGEN	AGQM	QUENDORF	AGTL	AUVERNIER
AGNO	AURACH	AGQN	RANSDORF	AGTM	AVRANCHES
AGNP	BACKUM	AGQO	RAUTENBERG	AGTO	BASSES-PYRENEES
AGNQ	BAHLINGEN	AGQP	REINACH	AGTP	BEARN
AGNR	BARKEN	AGQQ	REISSDORF	AGTQ	BEAUFORT
AGNS	BERINGEN	AGQR	RETZBACH	AGTR	BELMONT
AGNT	BESSEN	AGQS	RINGLEBEN	AGTS	BISSEN
AGNU	BIERSTADT	AGQT	ROMANSHORN	AGTT	BLEDESBACH
AGNV	BIESHEIM	AGQU	ROTENBERG	AGTU	BLOIS
AGNW	BLANKENMOOR	AGQV	ROTHENBUCH	AGTV	BOLLENDORF
AGNX	BLOEDESHEIM	AGQW	ROUBAIX	AGTW	BREDA
AGNY	BREDSTEDT	AGQX	RUNOWO	AGTX	CALVI
AGNZ	BRODERSDORF	AGQY	SADKE	AGTY	CANTAL
AGOA	BROKDORF	AGQZ	SAMOTSCHIN	AGTZ	CHAMPAGNE
AGOB	BRUGES	AGRA	SCHADOW	AGUA	CHATILLON
AGOC	BRUNSBUETTEL	AGRB	SCHLAGETEN	AGUB	CHAUNY
AGOD	BUENOS AIRES	AGRC	SCHWABSTEDT	AGUC	CHER
AGOE	CLAUSDORF	AGRD	SCHWENTEN	AGUD	CHERBOURG
AGOF	DAVENPORT	AGRE	SCHWIEBUS	AGUE	CLERMONT-FERRAND
AGOG	DIEDERSDORF	AGRF	SILENEN	AGUF	CREUSE
AGOH	DIENHEIM	AGRG	SIMMENAU	AGUG	DAGERSHEIM
AGOI	ECKERNFOERDE	AGRH	SITTARD	AGUH	DALLAU
AGOJ	EISCHEID	AGRI	SOEGEL	AGUI	DIPPACH
AGOK	ESCHWEILER	AGRJ	STANS	AGUJ	DOMBASH
AGOL	ESSMANSDORF	AGRK	STENDENBACH	AGUK	DOUBS
AGOM	FAHREN	AGRL	TASCHENBERG	AGUL	DUNKERQUE
AGON	FELDBERG	AGRM	TECHRITZ	AGUM	DYON
AGOO	FESSENHEIM	AGRN	VAALE	AGUN	ECK
AGOP	FLUMS	AGRO	VEHLEN	AGUO	EIKEN
AGOQ	FRAUENBERG	AGRP	WECHSELBURG	AGUP	EINSIEDELN
AGOR	GABER	AGRQ	WEHINGEN	AGUQ	ELBINGEN
AGOS	GAILDORF	AGRR	WEISSENHOEHE	AGUR	EMBRACH
AGOT	GARZ	AGRS	WETTSTETTEN	AGUS	ENGI
AGOU	GOHRA	AGRT	WILNA	AGUT	ESCHOLZMATT
AGOV	HANDRUP	AGRU	WILSTER	AGUU	FELLBACH
AGOW	HARD	AGRV	WITTINGEN	AGUV	FRAUENFELD
AGOX	HELMSDORF	AGRW	WOLFTERODE	AGUW	FRIBOURG
AGOY	HERBITZHEIM	AGRX	ZEHDEN	AGUX	GARD
AGOZ	HOLLENBACH	AGRY	ASPERG-WURTEMBERG	AGUY	GEISENHEIM
AGPA	HOLTHAUSEN	AGRZ	BARMSTED	AGUZ	GOTHENBURG
AGPB	HUSSEN	AGSA	BOEGEL	AGVA	GROSS-UMSTADT
AGPC	IDESHEIM	AGSB	BOETRINGEN	AGVB	HEINSBERG
AGPD	KALTENHAUSEN	AGSC	CAROLINIENSIEL	AGVC	HERDERN
AGPE	KOLPIN	AGSD	CATHARINA	AGVD	HILBRINGEN
AGPF	KREMPENDORF	AGSE	DAMMIN	AGVE	HOERDT

Code	Village	Code	Village	Code	Village
AGVF	HOETTINGEN	AGYF	NEUBREISACH	AHBH	MORLESAU
AGVG	HOHENSEE	AGYG	WINTERSCHEIM	AHBI	FINISTERE
AGVH	INDRE	AGYH	OBEREGG	AHBJ	FORBACH
AGVI	ISERE	AGYI	RUPERTSHAIN	AHBL	DINTIKON
AGVJ	IVRY	AGYJ	RUFACH	AHBM	DINSHEIM
AGVK	JURA	AGYK	ROTHENFLIESS	AHBN	BETSCHWANDEN
AGVL	KAHL	AGYL	WIESENHOFFEN	AHBO	BAISINGEN
AGVM	KEHL	AGYM	WIESENSTETTEN	AHBP	BITSCH
AGVN	KLOSTERS	AGYN	ROYN	AHBQ	BREMBERG
AGVO	LACHEN	AGYO	WILSTEN	AHBR	BRENNSBACH
AGVP	LANDER	AGYP	NEDDENSTEIN	AHBS	AYER
AGVQ	LAUSANNE	AGYQ	RUBENHEIM	AHBT	ATTING
AGVR	LEINBACH	AGYR	SEUZACH	AHBU	ABELLIENEN
AGVS	LISIEUX	AGYS	SPIES	AHBV	ALPES MARITIMES
AGVT	LODER	AGYT	MUEHLWAND	AHBW	ARGEN
AGVU	LORSCHEID	AGYU	YONNE	AHBX	ARPSDORF
AGVV	LOSHEIM	AGYV	ZILLIS	AHBY	BRIENNE
AGVW	LUDWIGSWINKEL	AGYW	ZUROW	AHBZ	BRITTNAU
AGVX	LUGANO	AGYX	STE.MARIE AUX MINES	AHCA	DECHENGRUEN
AGVY	MACON	AGYY	ZWOLLE	AHCB	CHAMBERY
AGVZ	MILTENBERG	AGYZ	WUNSCHWITZ	AHCC	DETTENHOFEN
AGWA	MITLODI	AGZA	SANGEBACH	AHCD	DIETFURT
AGWB	MUEHLENBACH	AGZB	OBERHALLAU	AHCE	DEFFINGEN
AGWC	MUTTENZ	AGZC	SPREICHER	AHCF	BUTZEN
AGWD	NANTES	AGZD	MUNDINGEN	AHCG	BROICH
AGWE	NECKAR	AGZE	RUTTERSHAUSEN	AHCH	BUDENINGKEN
AGWF	NECKARTENZLINGEN	AGZF	VAUX	AHCI	BULSTEN
AGWG	NEHREN	AGZG	SCHRIESHEIM	AHCJ	BURGEN
AGWH	NIDEGGEN	AGZH	WEILKIRCHEN	AHCK	GROENINGEN
AGWI	OBERSCHEFFACH	AGZI	PORT SUR SAONE	AHCL	FARGE
AGWJ	ODENBACH	AGZJ	WECKHOVEN	AHCM	KALTENTAL
AGWK	OISE	AGZK	ULZBURG	AHCN	KENZINGEN
AGWL	OLM	AGZL	PLATTEN	AHCO	KIRCHENTELLINSFURT
AGWM	OPFINGEN	AGZM	WEINFELDEN	AHCP	KREUZBACH
AGWN	OPPENHEIM	AGZN	WAHREN	AHCQ	JESSEN
AGWO	ORENHOFEN	AGZO	WATTENWIL	AHCR	IRLENBORN
AGWP	RAMBOW	AGZP	PYRENEES	AHCS	HUELSCHEID
AGWQ	RAUNVITER	AGZQ	PYRENEES ORIENTALES	AHCT	HUESTAN
AGWR	REIDEN	AGZR	RELLINGEN	AHCU	HUTTENHEIM
AGWS	REIN	AGZS	VALZEINA	AHCV	KREUZPULLACH
AGWT	RHEIMS	AGZT	SARREGUEMINES	AHCW	GUEGLINGEN
AGWU	RHEINFELD	AGZU	UNTERBOIHINGEN	AHCX	LEISELHEIM
AGWW	RODENTHAL	AGZV	UZWIL	AHCY	LENTERSHAGEN
AGWX	ROSHEIM	AGZW	TROYES	AHCZ	LULEC
AGWY	ROSIAN	AGZX	TRIBERG	AHDA	LORSBACH
AGWZ	ROUEN	AGZY	SCHMARFENDORF	AHDB	LEBUS
AGXA	RUTESHEIM	AGZZ	OTTENHOEFFEN	AHDC	MARIENHEIDE
AGXB	SARNEN	AHAA	OERATH	AHDD	KUEBELBERG
AGXC	SARTHE	AHAB	TAULEN	AHDE	LANDSWEILER
AGXD	SCHLETTSTADT	AHAC	TARBECK	AHDF	HIDDENHAUSEN
AGXE	SCHWANDEN	AHAD	PAINDORF	AHDG	KISSEL BERG
AGXF	SCHWARZBACH	AHAE	PARSOW	AHDH	HAUTE MARNE
AGXG	SEINE	AHAF	RHEINSHAGEN	AHDI	HARSKIRCHEN
AGXH	SPIELBERG	AHAG	VOSGES	AHDJ	HARTING
AGXI	ST.CROIX	AHAH	SARREBURG	AHDK	GUNNINGEN
AGXJ	ST.DENIS	AHAI	RIESELFINGEN	AHDL	HAUTVILLE
AGXK	ST.GERMAIN	AHAJ	VANGERIN	AHDM	HERISAU
AGXL	ST.QUENTIN	AHAL	REUDCHEN	AHDN	HAUPTSTUHL
AGXM	STADEKEN	AHAM	LEINZELL	AHDO	MOMMENHEIM
AGXN	THURINGIA	AHAN	EMMISHOFFEN	AHDP	HAUTE GARONNE
AGXO	TOULON	AHAO	ELBEN	AHDQ	GUTACH
AGXP	TRIESTE	AHAQ	EPPENHAIN	AHDR	ALPE
AGXQ	TWISTRINGEN	AHAR	ESCHENBACH	AHDS	NEUCHATEL
AGXR	URLOFFEN	AHAS	EISENTAL	AHDT	PUY DE DOME
AGXS	VALENCE	AHAT	EINSIEDEL	AHDU	ST.BRIEUC
AGXT	VAR	AHAU	DORFPROZELTE	AHDV	TICINO
AGXU	VERTH	AHAV	DOMATSCHINE	AHDW	WALDBREITBACH
AGXV	VIVIERS	AHAW	DURNHAN	AHDX	BAS RHIN
AGXW	WASSERALFINGEN	AHAX	ECKHAUSEN	AHDY	BITSCHWEILLER
AGXX	WASSERBILLIG	AHAY	EICHENTHAL	AHEA	CHAUX DE FONDS
AGXY	WAXWEILER	AHAZ	EURE	AHEB	HAUT RHIN
AGXZ	WEIBE	AHBA	EUTZEN	AHEC	HAUTE SAONE
AGYA	WEIHER	AHBB	GEBWEILER	AHED	LENKERSHEIM
AGYB	WEST PRUSSIA	AHBD	GORLEN	AHEE	LIEDOLSHEIM
AGYC	WIELBERG	AHBE	GANTHEN	AHEF	ALTENSHEIM
AGYD	WOLFGANZ	AHBF	FRIXHEIM	AHEG	ALTERSBACH
AGYE	OBERDIELFEN	AHBG	FRETT	AHEH	ALTMARK

AHEI	ANGERS	AHII	HARSCHEID	AHLJ	PRUESSBERG
AHEJ	BLUE ISLAND	AHIK	HEBELERMEER	AHLK	RAMMELBURG
AHEL	DUSSELDORF	AHIL	HEIDE	AHLL	RHEINBACK
AHEM	HESSE	AHIM	HEIDEN	AHLM	RIESWEILER
AHEN	INDIANAPOLIS	AHIN	HEILIGENHAFEN	AHLN	RIXDORF
AHEO	LOUISVILLE	AHIO	HENSTEDT	AHLO	ROGALLEN
AHEP	MARYLAND	AHIP	HERICOURT	AHLP	ROGGOW
AHEQ	NAPERVILLE	AHIQ	HESELWANGEN	AHLQ	RONCHAMPS
AHER	NEW ORLEANS	AHIR	HIRSCHLANDEN	AHLR	ROSCHBERG
AHES	OMAHA	AHIS	HOCHFELDE	AHLS	ROXEL
AHET	PHOENIXVILLE	AHIT	HOFFENHEIM	AHLT	RUEHEN
AHEU	REIMS	AHIU	HOLSTENNIENDORF	AHLU	SAGAN
AHEV	RICHMOND	AHIV	HOYERN	AHLV	SAGERITZ
AHEW	SAN SALVADOR	AHIW	HUEBLINGEN	AHLW	SALESKE
AHEX	SPRINGFIELD	AHIX	HUEGELHEIM	AHLX	SANDWEIER
AHEY	ST.PAUL	AHIY	HUTTENGUM	AHLY	SCHAFSTAEDT
AHEZ	TEXAS	AHIZ	JESINGEN	AHLZ	SCHINKENBERG
AHFA	TRINIDAD	AHJA	KAFFERTAL	AHMA	SCHOLASTIKOWO
AHFB	SAVANNAH	AHJB	KAETERHAGEN	AHMB	SEDAN
AHFC	MOBILE	AHJC	KANDERN	AHMC	SEESTERMUEHL
AHFD	VERSAILLES	AHJD	KAESEMARK	AHMD	SEVRES
AHFE	YOKOHAMA	AHJE	KLEIN GLUCHEY	AHME	SOCHOW
AHFF	AGENBACH	AHJF	KLEIN NENNDORF	AHMF	SONDERBACH
AHFG	ALTHOF	AHJG	KLEIN STEIN	AHMG	SOSSENHEIM
AHFH	ALTENWERDER	AHJH	KLEIN UMSTADT	AHMH	SPEICHER
AHFI	APPENZELL	AHJI	KLEIN ZABRZE	AHMI	SPRINGBERG
AHFJ	AVRICOURT	AHJJ	KLETZKE	AHMJ	ST.PIERRE-DE-ALBIGNY
AHFK	BABBIN	AHJK	KOENIGSHEIM	AHMK	ST.PIERRE-MIQUELON
AHFL	BALLENSTEDT	AHJL	KOENIGSTEIN	AHML	STAHLBERG
AHFM	BAMMEMTHAL	AHJM	KREUZKRUG	AHMM	STOLPEN
AHFN	BEBER	AHJN	KRUCKENBECK	AHMN	STORKOW
AHFO	BECKINGEN	AHJO	KRUSEMARK	AHMO	SUEDERAU
AHFP	BENAN	AHJP	KUPFERBERG	AHMP	TEETZ
AHFQ	BERTHELSDORF	AHJQ	LA-ROCHELLE	AHMQ	THUROW
AHFR	BICHL	AHJR	LABEHN	AHMR	TIEGE
AHFS	BIRKENDORF	AHJS	LANGENBIELAU	AHMS	TIEGENHAGEN
AHFT	BOEBLINGEN	AHJT	LETZKAU	AHMT	TOENNING
AHFU	BOEHLENDORF	AHJU	LIEGE	AHMU	TUERKHEIM
AHFV	BOSSOW	AHJV	LINDERODE	AHMV	TUERMITZ
AHFW	BUDZIN	AHJW	LINDEWERRA	AHMW	UNTERBERG
AHFX	BUELOW	AHJX	LINDENWALD	AHMX	UNTERHOHENRIED
AHFY	BUERRIG	AHJY	LOEWITZ	AHMY	URI
AHFZ	BUESSOW	AHJZ	LOIT	AHMZ	VALAIS
AHGA	BUROW	AHKA	BASSES ALPES	AHNA	VELTEN
AHGB	CHARLEVILLE	AHKB	LUDENBERG	AHNB	VIARTLUM
AHGC	CHRISTBURG	AHKC	MALSCHENBERG	AHNC	VIRGINIA
AHGD	DEININGEN	AHKD	MARIENHOF	AHND	VORDORF
AHGE	DOEBERN	AHKE	MARKERSBACH	AHNE	WALLMOW
AHGF	EBSTORF	AHKF	MAYEN	AHNF	WANGERITZ
AHGG	EISENBRUECK	AHKG	MELZOW	AHNG	WARNOW
AHGH	ELLERBECK	AHKH	MENNINGEN	AHNH	WATTENSCHEID
AHGI	ELLERSHAGEN	AHKJ	MICHELFELD	AHNI	WEIDEN
AHGJ	EHREN	AHKK	MINDERSBACH	AHNJ	WERTHAUSEN
AHGK	ESCHENROD	AHKL	MORATZ	AHNK	WESTERLAND
AHGL	ETTERWINDEN	AHKM	MOESCHEN	AHNL	WESTERWEYHE
AHGM	FINKEL	AHKN	MUECKENBERG	AHNM	WINTERSDORF
AHGN	FRIEDELHAUSEN	AHKO	NEBRINGEN	AHNN	WINZELN
AHGO	FRIEDRICHSFELD	AHKP	NECKARAU	AHNO	WISMAR
AHGP	FRIESENHEIM	AHKQ	NEDDEMIN	AHNP	WITTENBURG
AHGQ	GAP	AHKR	NEUFERISACH	AHNQ	WOLLENBERG
AHGR	GELSENKIRCHEN	AHKS	NEUFREISTETT	AHNR	WULKSFELDE
AHGS	GLOTTAU	AHKT	NEUKAHLEN	AHNS	WUTZKOW
AHGT	GROSS DALLENTHIN	AHKU	NICE	AHNT	ZIEGELHAUSEN
AHGU	GROSS DAMMER	AHKV	NIENDORF	AHNU	ADELSHOFEN
AHGV	GROSS DOBERN	AHKW	NIEWEDDE	AHNV	ALF
AHGW	GROSS DRENSEN	AHKX	NIEMIETZKE	AHNW	BUEHLERTAL
AHGX	GROSS STREHLITZ	AHKY	NITTINGEN	AHNX	JAMAICA
AHGY	GRAFENAU	AHKZ	NITZE	AHNY	KAISERSTUHL
AHGZ	GRAND FORKS	AHLA	NONNENWEIER	AHNZ	LACHERSHOF
AHIA	GRANOW	AHLB	OBER WALDENBURG	AHOA	MAINE
AHIB	GREVESMUEHLEN	AHLC	OBERWALDE	AHOB	MOGHILEV
AHIC	GRIBBOHM	AHLD	ODERBERG	AHOC	TRONDHEIM
AHID	GRICHEM	AHLE	OEDINGEN	AHOD	CANADA
AHIE	GRUBEN	AHLF	OGGERSHEIN	AHOE	MASSACHUSETTS
AHIF	HAUTES ALPES	AHLG	OMMERSHEIM	AHOF	OREGON
AHIG	HALLENBERG	AHLH	ORTENBERG	AHOG	TOURS
AHIH	HAMMELWARDEN	AHLI	PETERSWALDE	AHOH	USA

xlvii

AHOI	ABBENDORF	AHRI	FREDERSDORF	AHUH	LUBOW
AHOK	ABENBERG	AHRJ	FREUDENBERG	AHUI	LUDERSHEIM
AHOL	AHRENSBURG	AHRK	FRICKHOFEN	AHUJ	LUEBTHEEN
AHOM	ALT-GRAPE	AHRL	FRIEDENTHAL	AHUK	MACHERN
AHON	ALT-KARIN	AHRM	FRIESENHAUSEN	AHUL	MALENTE
AHOO	ALTENHAUSEN	AHRN	FUCHSMUEHL	AHUM	MALKEN
AHOP	ALTENSTEIN	AHRO	GAARDEN	AHUN	MARZAHN
AHOQ	AMEL	AHRP	GAMBACH	AHUO	MASTRUP
AHOR	ANGERBURG	AHRQ	GEISLING	AHUP	MATZWITZ
AHOS	ARFELD	AHRR	GELLIN	AHUQ	MAULBACH
AHOT	ASCHEFFEL	AHRS	GEMLITZ	AHUR	MECHTERSHEIM
AHOU	BACHENHEIM	AHRT	GIERSDORF	AHUS	MELNO
AHOV	BARNTRUP	AHRU	GILSA	AHUT	MERGELSTETTEN
AHOW	BARSKEWITZ	AHRV	GIMBESHEIM	AHUU	METTEN
AHOX	BARTELSDORF	AHRW	GINGST	AHUV	METTERNICH
AHOY	BATENHORST	AHRX	GLADAU	AHUW	MIESTE
AHOZ	BAUM	AHRY	GLASEWITZ	AHUX	MILDSTEDT
AHPA	BELLHEIM	AHRZ	GLASGOW	AHUY	MOERSEN
AHPB	BERGEDORF	AHSA	GLUECKSTADT	AHUZ	MOGILNO
AHPC	BERKHOLZ	AHSB	GNODSTAD	AHVA	MONTOWO
AHPD	BERSTADT	AHSC	GOLUB	AHVB	MOTZEN
AHPE	BERWANGEN	AHSD	GORITZ	AHVC	MULDA
AHPF	BEUTHEN	AHSE	GRANZIN	AHVD	MUTTERHAUSEN
AHPG	BEVERINGEN	AHSF	GRONENBERG	AHVE	NAGEL
AHPH	BIALKEN	AHSG	HEDELFINGEN	AHVF	NETZTHAL
AHPI	BIESENBROW	AHSH	HEDERSLEBEN	AHVG	NEUMUEHL
AHPJ	BIRKWEILER	AHSI	HEIDERSDORF	AHVH	NEUSATZ
AHPK	BIRNBACH	AHSJ	HEIDINGSFELD	AHVI	NOTTINGHAM
AHPL	BISSEL	AHSK	HEIMBERG	AHVJ	NYBORG
AHPM	BITTBURG	AHSL	HEISINGEN	AHVK	OBERKOCHEN
AHPN	BLANKENHOF	AHSM	HEMME	AHVL	OBERSTAUFEN
AHPO	BLASCHEWITZ	AHSN	HERBSLEBEN	AHVM	OBERSTETTEN
AHPP	BLESKODE	AHSO	HERDORF	AHVN	OBORNIK
AHPQ	BLUMENHAGEN	AHSP	HERMANNSBURG	AHVO	ODENDORF
AHPR	BORECK	AHSQ	HEUBERG	AHVP	ODERNHEIM
AHPS	BRAUNSWALDE	AHSR	HINTERSTEINAU	AHVQ	ODISHEIM
AHPT	BRETTACH	AHSS	HIRZENHAIN	AHVR	PALZIG
AHPU	BRILON	AHST	HOEFINGEN	AHVS	PASING
AHPV	BRITZ	AHSU	HOHENDORF	AHVT	PAULSDORF
AHPW	BUCHAREST	AHSV	HOLLE	AHVU	PERSANZIG
AHPX	BUDAPEST	AHSW	HOLLFELD	AHVV	PETERWITZ
AHPY	BUTOW	AHSX	HOLZ	AHVW	PEWSUM
AHPZ	CALAIS	AHSY	HOLZKIRCHEN	AHVX	PFULLINGEN
AHQA	CHARLOTTENBURG	AHSZ	HORNEBURG	AHVY	PICHER
AHQB	DAHME	AHTA	HOYM	AHVZ	PLATTLING
AHQC	DAMGARTEN	AHTB	JABLONOWO	AHWA	PLEINTING
AHQD	DARGUN	AHTC	KARBY	AHWB	POLLITZ
AHQE	DARUP	AHTD	KARLSTADT	AHWC	RABENKIRCHEN
AHQF	DATTELN	AHTE	KAROW	AHWD	RADDACH
AHQG	DEGGENDORF	AHTF	KARSCHAU	AHWE	RADEGAST
AHQH	DEIDESHEIM	AHTG	KELTSCH	AHWF	RAKOW
AHQI	DEILLINGEN	AHTH	KETZIN	AHWG	RASDORF
AHQJ	DETTWEILER	AHTI	KIETZ	AHWH	RASSELWITZ
AHQK	DEUBEN	AHTJ	KOEHLEN	AHWI	RATZEBUHR
AHQL	DIERSBURG	AHTK	KOENIGSMUEHL	AHWJ	REPENOW
AHQM	DIXMUDE	AHTL	KOTZENAU	AHWK	RITTERSHAUSEN
AHQN	DOBRZYCA	AHTM	KOWNO	AHWL	RODALBEN
AHQO	DORFBACH	AHTN	KUNZENDORF	AHWM	ROSA
AHQP	DORNITZ	AHTO	LABISCHIN	AHWN	SACHSENHEIM
AHQQ	DORZBACH	AHTP	LABOE	AHWO	SAMTENS
AHQR	DRATZIG	AHTQ	LAM	AHWP	SANDHAGEN
AHQS	EDDERSHEIM	AHTR	LANGMEIL	AHWQ	SCHARNHORST
AHQT	EIDINGHAUSEN	AHTS	LAUBAN	AHWR	SCHEYERN
AHQU	ELBERGEN	AHTT	LEBA	AHWS	SCHMIEGEL
AHQV	ELBERSROTH	AHTU	LEHNIN	AHWT	SCHNEIDLINGEN
AHQW	ELDENA	AHTV	LEIDERSDORF	AHWU	SCHORSTEDT
AHQX	ELLERWALD	AHTW	LEMWERDER	AHWV	SCHRODA
AHQY	ENGELSBERG	AHTX	LENDERSDORF	AHWW	SCHROTZ
AHQZ	ERDORF	AHTY	LENGEFELD	AHWX	SEGEBERG
AHRA	ERNSBACH	AHTZ	LIEBEMUEHL	AHWY	SELIGENSTADT
AHRB	EULAU	AHUA	LIPPERSDORF	AHWZ	SINZLOW
AHRC	FILEHNE	AHUB	LOCHAU	AHXA	SOMMERSTEDT
AHRD	FLUORN	AHUC	LOITZ	AHXB	ST.PETERSBURG
AHRE	FRANKENBACH	AHUD	LOTTIN	AHXC	ST.PETERSBURGH
AHRF	FRANKENDORF	AHUE	LOUISENTHAL	AHXD	STAVENHAGEN
AHRG	FRAUENTHAL	AHUF	LUBBEN	AHXE	STEGLITZ
AHRH	FREDENBECK	AHUG	LUBEN	AHXF	STEINBRUECKEN

xlviii

Code	Village	Code	Village	Code	Village
AHXG	STEINHAGEN	AIAG	BURLAFINGEN	AIDI	LOBSTAEDT
AHXH	STELLE	AIAH	CRANZ	AIDJ	LOUVAIN
AHXI	STENDAL	AIAI	DAMBECK	AIDK	LUBASCHAU
AHXJ	STETTFELD	AIAJ	DAMNITZ	AIDL	LUBOTIN
AHXK	STOLZENHAGEN	AIAK	DEISSLINGEN	AIDM	LUETZELHAUSEN
AHXL	STREHLEN	AIAL	DESSAU	AIDN	MALLERSDORF
AHXM	STREUDORF	AIAM	DOLINIK	AIDO	MARNE
AHXN	STROHKIRCHEN	AIAN	DUBRAU	AIDP	MEINBREXEN
AHXO	SYDOW	AIAO	DUEDELSHEIM	AIDQ	MEINE
AHXP	TANKOW	AIAP	ECHTERNACHERBRUECK	AIDR	MENIN
AHXQ	TEMPLIN	AIAQ	ECKWEILER	AIDT	MIETESHEIM
AHXR	TETEROW	AIAR	EILENBURG	AIDU	MIL
AHXS	THARDEN	AIAS	EISCHEN	AIDV	MISKOWITZ
AHXT	THIERSTEIN	AIAT	EPERNAY	AIDW	MOHRKIRCH OSTERHOLZ
AHXU	TINGLEFF	AIAU	EPPSTEIN	AIDX	NAUNHEIM
AHXV	TORNOW	AIAV	ERBESBUEDESHEIM	AIDY	NIEBUEL
AHXW	TREBRA	AIAW	ERNSDORF	AIDZ	NIEDERKIRCHEN
AHXX	TREYSA	AIAX	FINSTERWALDE	AIEA	NIEDERSTEINBACH
AHXY	UETERSEN	AIAY	FLUELEN	AIEB	NIEDERWERDEN
AHXZ	UETZHAUSEN	AIAZ	FOCKBEK	AIEC	NIEDERWIES
AHYA	UNTER-HARMERSBACH	AIBA	GALLIN	AIED	NOELL
AHYB	UNTERSTEINACH	AIBB	GAMBURG	AIEE	NOSSEN
AHYC	UNTERSTEINBACH	AIBC	GANSINGEN	AIEF	NUSSBACH
AHYD	URSPRINGEN	AIBD	GASTEIN	AIEG	OBERDACHSTETTEN
AHYE	VAIHINGEN	AIBE	GEINSHEIM	AIEH	OBERKAUFUNGEN
AHYF	VIERNHEIM	AIBF	GEROLDSTEIN	AIEI	OBERRUETI
AHYG	VIETNITZ	AIBG	GESEKE	AIEJ	OBERZWEHREN
AHYH	WAHN	AIBJ	GOTSCHDORF	AIEK	OLSCHOEWKEN
AHYI	WALLISFURTH	AIBK	GRANITZ	AIEL	OPPENWEHE
AHYJ	WARBENDE	AIBL	GRASSAU	AIEM	OPPENWEILER
AHYK	WAREN	AIBM	GROSS KNOPKEN	AIEN	OSTERBRUCH
AHYL	WATTWEILER	AIBN	GROSS NEUDORF	AIEO	OSTROW
AHYM	WEDDINGSTEDT	AIBO	GROSS PANKOW	AIEP	PANKLAU
AHYN	WEGELEBEN	AIBP	GROSS PLAUTH	AIEQ	PARCHAU
AHYO	WEGGUN	AIBQ	GROSSPETERWITZ	AIER	PETERSBACH
AHYP	WEISKIRCHEN	AIBR	GRUNEWALD	AIES	PFULLENDORF
AHYQ	WEISSKIRCHEN	AIBS	GUMBIN	AIET	PINNEBERG
AHYR	WERBACH	AIBT	GUSTORF	AIEU	PLANAN
AHYS	WERBEN	AIBU	HADMERSLEBEN	AIEV	PLUSKAU
AHYT	WERNSTEIN	AIBV	HARTAU	AIEW	PROSNITZ
AHYU	WERSAU	AIBW	HASSENBERG	AIEX	RADEWITSCH
AHYV	WETTSCHEWELL	AIBX	HECHTSHEIM	AIEY	RANKAU
AHYW	WIESENBERG	AIBY	HEINRICHSRUH	AIEZ	REICHACH
AHYX	WIESTHAL	AIBZ	HERMANNSRUHE	AIFA	REISTINGEN
AHYY	WILDEGG	AICA	HETTSTADT	AIFB	REMICH
AHYZ	WILDENSTEIN	AICB	HETZBACH	AIFC	REMLINGEN
AHZB	WILSNACK	AICC	HOHENFRIEDEBERG	AIFD	REPTICH
AHZC	WINDESHEIM	AICD	HOHENKAMMER	AIFE	REWAHL
AHZD	WINGEN	AICE	HOHENWARTE	AIFF	ROENSAHL
AHZE	WINZIG	AICF	HOHNE	AIFG	RUSSHEIM
AHZF	WITTKOW	AICG	HOLLENBECK	AIFH	SANITZ
AHZG	WITTSTOCK	AICH	HORSTE	AIFI	SARNOW
AHZH	WOLFACH	AICI	HOTHEN	AIFJ	SCHAALBY
AHZI	WOLFSTEIN	AICJ	HUTTE	AIFK	SCHEIPNITZ
AHZJ	WOLKENSTEIN	AICK	JACOBSDORF	AIFL	SCHOENBORN
AHZK	WOLMESHEIM	AICL	JAGERSDORF	AIFM	SCHOLLBRONN
AHZL	ABSTATT	AICM	JUEGESHEIM	AIFN	SCHONSTETT
AHZM	ALTGANDERSHEIM	AICN	KAISERSFELDE	AIFO	SCHROEDERSHOF
AHZN	AMERIKA	AICO	KAMEN	AIFP	SCHULAU
AHZO	ANTONINHOF	AICP	KARLBURG	AIFQ	SCHUTTERWALD
AHZP	APPENRODE	AICQ	KELLENHUSEN	AIFR	SCHUTTSCHENOFEN
AHZQ	ARGOS	AICR	KINZENBACH	AIFS	SCHWABHAUSEN
AHZR	ARNBACH	AICS	KNITTLINGEN	AIFT	SCHWADORF
AHZS	ASCHERSLEBEN	AICT	KOBELAU	AIFU	SCHWARTOW
AHZT	AUGUSTENBURG	AICU	KOENIGGRAETZ	AIFV	SCHWERZEN
AHZU	BARGTEHEIDE	AICV	KOEPPLIN	AIFW	SEIFEN
AHZV	BARKELSBY	AICW	KOHLHAUSEN	AIFX	SELBACH
AHZW	BERGERHAUSEN	AICX	KOSSEBADE	AIFY	SELLIN
AHZX	BIALYSTOK	AICY	KOSSOWO	AIFZ	SILKERODE
AHZY	BIBERIST	AICZ	KRONBURG	AIGA	SINDELSDORF
AHZZ	BITZ	AIDA	KURZIG	AIGB	SIPIORY
AIAA	BLANKENSEE	AIDB	LANGENFELDE	AIGC	SMOLNITZ
AIAB	BLASWEILER	AIDC	LANGENSTEINBACH	AIGD	SOBERNHEIM
AIAC	BLAUFELDEN	AIDD	LANGFELD	AIGE	SOELLMNITZ
AIAD	BRESTAU	AIDE	LANKEN	AIGF	STEUDEN
AIAE	BROMBACH	AIDG	LAURENBERG	AIGG	STOECKELSBERG
AIAF	BURGHOLZ	AIDH	LIEBSTADT	AIGH	STOLLHOFEN

Code	Name	Code	Name	Code	Name
AIGI	STOLPMUENDE	AIJH	NACKEL	AIMI	ARNSTORF
AIGJ	STRADEM	AIJI	LANGENSEE	AIMJ	ARZFELD
AIGK	SUELBECK	AIJJ	OFFENBURG	AIMK	ASHEIM
AIGL	SZARADOWO-ZALESIE	AIJK	LIGGERSDORF	AIML	ASTEDE
AIGM	TEMPELHOF	AIJL	LOUISIANA	AIMM	ASTHEIM
AIGN	TETTAU	AIJM	POLSCHEN	AIMN	ATZELRODE
AIGO	THALDORF	AIJN	PRILLWITZ	AIMO	AUENWALDE
AIGP	THOMASDORF	AIJO	PRINOWEN	AIMP	AUGGEN
AIGQ	THOMASWALDAU	AIJP	RELZOW	AIMQ	AUGUSTENHOF
AIGR	TIEDMANNSDORF	AIJQ	RETZIN	AIMR	AUGUSTENTHAL
AIGS	TOELL	AIJR	RIETH	AIMS	AUGUSTFEHN
AIGT	TREBOW	AIJS	SCHIPPENBEIL	AIMT	AUGUSTFELDE
AIGU	TREMPEN	AIJT	NEUHOFF	AIMU	AUSSEN
AIGV	TROSSENFURT	AIJU	NEW JERSEY	AIMV	AUSTERLITZ
AIGW	TZEMIETOWO	AIJV	SONNENBERG	AIMW	BABITZ
AIGX	UCHTENHAGEN	AIJW	SWINEMUENDE	AIMX	BACKENBERG
AIGY	UMMERSTADT	AIJX	TIEFENTHAL	AIMZ	BAERWEILER
AIGZ	UNTERDORF	AIJY	TRIBSOW	AINA	BAGDAD
AIHA	UNTERLEITERBACH	AIJZ	UFHOVEN	AINB	BAGNOWEN
AIHB	UNTERZELL	AIKA	VENHAUS	AINC	BALDENBERG
AIHC	VASILE LUPU	AIKB	VILSINGEN	AIND	BALKUM
AIHD	VEHLINGEN	AIKC	VOERDEN	AINE	BALOW
AIHE	VIELAU	AIKD	SAN FRANCISCO	AINF	BALSTER
AIHF	WACHENDORF	AIKE	WELLERODE	AING	BANGSCHIN
AIHG	WACKERN	AIKF	TENNESSEE	AINH	BARBELROTH
AIHH	WAFFENSEN	AIKG	THIONVILLE	AINI	BARKENFELDE
AIHI	WALDOWO	AIKH	WINNWEILER	AINJ	BARKOW
AIHJ	WARNIN	AIKI	WIESBACH	AINK	BARMBECK
AIHK	WEITENHAGEN	AIKJ	WITTEN	AINL	BARMES
AIHL	WENGERZ	AIKK	WOHLEN	AINM	BARMSTEDT
AIHM	WESSENDORF	AIKL	ADELWITZ	AINN	BARTMANNSHAGEN
AIHN	WESTERBURG	AIKM	ZURZACH	AINO	BARUTH
AIHO	WESTHALTEN	AIKN	ST.MENEHOULD	AINP	BASBECK
AIHP	WICKERSHAIN	AIKO	SYRAU	AINQ	BATTWEILER
AIHQ	WIDDERSHAUSEN	AIKP	GREIZ DOELAU	AINR	BAUHOF
AIHR	WIEROW	AIKQ	CAEN	AINS	BAUMGARTNER
AIHS	WILDENFELS	AIKR	LE MANS	AINT	BECHERBACH
AIHT	WILLEN	AIKS	KAISERLAUTERN	AINU	BEDSTEDT
AIHU	WILLENBERG	AIKT	ABBENHAUSEN	AINV	BEGGENDOF
AIHV	WITTENBERGEN	AIKU	AARANS	AINW	BEKUM
AIHW	WOLKERSDORF	AIKV	ABBACH	AINX	BELKAU
AIHX	WOMMELSHAUSEN	AIKW	ACHEN	AINY	BELLEN
AIHY	WONGROWITZ	AIKX	ACHENDORF	AINZ	BELLIN
AIHZ	ZIRKEL	AIKY	ADAMSDORF	AIOA	BELOW
AIIA	ZORNHEIM	AIKZ	ADAMSHOF	AIOB	BENDFELD
AIIB	LUNDEBORG	AILA	ADAMSTHAL	AIOC	BENTIN
AIIC	OBERGRIES	AILB	ADELNAU	AIOD	BENTRUP
AIID	RHEIDT	AILC	ADELSHEIN	AIOE	BEREND
AIIE	ROELLINGSEN	AILD	ADENAU	AIOF	BERGDORF
AIIF	STRZALKOWO	AILE	ADLERSHORST	AIOG	BERGENHUSEN
AIIG	STUEBENDORF	AILF	ADORF	AIOH	BERGFELD
AIIH	TEMPELBURG	AILG	AFFOLTERN	AIOI	BERGHOFEN
AIII	TUREK	AILH	AHAUSEN	AIOJ	BERGSDORF
AIIJ	SCHEINFELD	AILI	AICHHALDEN	AIOK	BERGSTEDT
AIIK	ARKANSAS	AILJ	AISTAIG	AIOL	BERLINGEN
AIIL	GROSSBURG	AILK	ALBACH	AIOM	BERNA
AIIM	BERGZABERN	AILL	ALBENDORF	AION	BERNAU
AIIN	BISMARCKSFELD	AILM	ALEXANDERHOF	AIOO	BERNSTADT
AIIO	KEMPFENBRUNN	AILN	ALEXEN	AIOP	BEROD
AIIP	BRUCHEN	AILO	ALSBACH	AIOQ	BERTINGEN
AIIQ	CARNAP	AILP	ALSHEIM	AIOR	BESANDTEN
AIIR	CHUDOW	AILQ	ALSMANNSDORF	AIOS	BETZDORF
AIIS	LABES	AILR	ALT-STETTIN	AIOT	BEVENSEN
AIIT	DENMARK	AILS	ALTEN-BUSECK	AIOU	BIADKI
AIIU	LEINE	AILT	ALTEN-EBSTORF	AIOV	BIEBERACH
AIIV	LESSE	AILU	ALTENHOFEN	AIOW	BIENAU
AIIW	FRANKENHAIN	AILV	ALTENSITTENBACH	AIOX	BIENDORF
AIIX	LITTFELD	AILW	ALTHUETTE	AIOY	BIERFELD
AIIY	FRIEDRICHSHOF	AILX	AMALIENHOF	AIOZ	BIESELSBERG
AIIZ	LUESSEN	AILY	AMALIENRUH	AIPA	BIESENTHAL
AIJA	MANOW	AILZ	AMPFERBACH	AIPB	BIRGEN
AIJB	HELBSHEIM	AIMA	ANNABURG	AIPC	BIRKEN
AIJC	MECHOW	AIMB	ANTEN	AIPD	BISCHDORF
AIJD	MERSCH	AIME	ARBACH	AIPE	BISCHOFFEN
AIJE	ILLINOIS	AIMF	ARGENAU	AIPF	BISCHOFFSTEIN
AIJF	INDIANA	AIMG	ARNSBACH	AIPG	BISCHOFSWALDE
AIJG	MITTELBERG	AIMH	ARNSTEDT	AIPH	BITSCHIN

1

AIPI	BLADEN	AISH	DEHLENTRUP	AIVG	ESSERHAUSEN
AIPJ	BLASEWITZ	AISI	DEICHSHAUSEN	AIVH	ESTERWEGEN
AIPK	BLIESEN	AISJ	DELLINGEN	AIVI	ETTLINGEN
AIPL	BOBENTHAL	AISK	DELLSTEDT	AIVJ	EUSKIRCHEN
AIPM	BOCKHORN	AISL	DELLWIG	AIVK	EUTINGEN
AIPN	BODEN	AISM	DENOW	AIVL	EYBACH
AIPO	BOEHLEN	AISN	DERENDINGEN	AIVM	EYDTKUHNEN
AIPP	BOENITZ	AISO	DESTEL	AIVN	FAEHR
AIPQ	BOERGER	AISP	DETERSHAGEN	AIVO	FELBACH
AIPR	BOETTINGEN	AISQ	DETTELBACH	AIVP	FELDHAUSEN
AIPS	BOLDEKOW	AISR	DETTENHAUSEN	AIVQ	FERDINANDSHOF
AIPT	BOLLEN	AISS	DIEDESHEIM	AIVR	FEUERBACH
AIPU	BOLLSTADT	AIST	DIEDRICHSDORF	AIVS	FINKEN
AIPV	BOLZ	AISU	DIERSHEIM	AIVT	FINKENBACH
AIPW	BONNEWEG	AISV	DILL	AIVU	FINTEL
AIPX	BORDESHOLM	AISW	DINGOLFING	AIVV	FLONHEIM
AIPY	BORGSUM	AISX	DINSLAKEN	AIVW	FORCHTENBERG
AIPZ	BORK	AISY	DISCHINGEN	AIVX	FRANKWEILER
AIQA	BORKOW	AISZ	DOBERAN	AIVY	FREISING
AIQB	BORUSCHIN	AITA	DOBRILUGK	AIVZ	FREIST
AIQC	BRAAK	AITB	DOELITZ	AIWA	FRESDORF
AIQD	BRAAKE	AITC	DOERPEN	AIWB	FREYHAN
AIQE	BREITENBURG	AITD	DOERVERDEN	AIWC	FRICHTWANGER
AIQF	BREITENFELDE	AITE	DOLGESHEIM	AIWD	FRIEBERG
AIQG	BRESEGARD	AITF	DONAUSTAUF	AIWE	FRIEBURG
AIQH	BRIEDEN	AITG	DORDRECHT	AIWF	FRIEDENFELS
AIQI	BRIENZ	AITH	DORGENDORF	AIWG	FRIEDFELD
AIQJ	BRINNITZ	AITI	DORMITZ	AIWH	FRIEDINGEN
AIQK	BRODY	AITJ	DORNDIEL	AIWI	FRIEDRICHBERG
AIQL	BROOK	AITK	DORNHOLZHAUSEN	AIWJ	FRIEDRICHSBERG
AIQM	BRUCHWEILER	AITL	DORPHAGEN	AIWK	FRIEDRICHSBURG
AIQN	BRUEGGE	AITM	DORSTEN	AIWL	FRIEDRICHSKOOG
AIQO	BRUEHL	AITN	DOVER	AIWM	FUNKENHAGEN
AIQP	BRUN	AITO	DRAGE	AIWN	GABLENBERG
AIQQ	BRUNNEN	AITP	DRANGSTEDT	AIWO	GABOW
AIQR	BUBLITZ	AITQ	DREISEN	AIWP	GALEN
AIQS	BUCHDORF	AITR	DUERRENBUECHIG	AIWQ	GALIZIEN
AIQT	BUCHENDORF	AITS	DUERRMENZ	AIWR	GALLEN
AIQU	BUCHENTHAL	AITT	DURANT-IOWA	AIWS	GALLENSOW
AIQV	BUCHFELDE	AITU	DUVENSTEDT	AIWT	GALLNAU
AIQW	BUCHHORST	AITV	EBERNBURG	AIWU	GALWAY
AIQX	BUCHWALD	AITW	EBERSDORF	AIWV	GAMERSHEIM
AIQY	BUDDENDORF	AITX	EBERSHAUSEN	AIWW	GAMMENDORF
AIQZ	BUDENHEIM	AITY	EBERSTEIN	AIWX	GAND
AIRA	BUDWEISS	AITZ	EBERTSHEIM	AIWY	GANSE
AIRB	BUECHENBACH	AIUA	EDELBACH	AIWZ	GANZER
AIRC	BUEDERICH	AIUB	EDIGER	AIXA	GOLLNOW
AIRD	BUEHLERZELL	AIUC	EDINGHAUSEN	AIXA	GARCHING
AIRE	BUELTE	AIUD	EGENDORF	AIXB	GARDEN
AIRF	BUKOWINE	AIUE	EICH	AIXC	GARDING
AIRG	BULACH	AIUF	EICHLOCH	AIXD	GARTENDORF
AIRH	BULLENDORF	AIUG	EIGELTINGEN	AIXE	GEIST
AIRI	BUNZLAU	AIUH	EINLAGE	AIXF	GEISTENDORF
AIRJ	BURGSCHWALBACH	AIUI	EISENTEIN	AIXG	GERBACH
AIRK	CAASCHWITZ	AIUJ	EISFELD	AIXH	GERDSHAGEN
AIRL	CARLSHOF	AIUK	EISTEN	AIXI	GERNACH
AIRM	CAROLINENHOF	AIUL	ELCHESHEIM	AIXJ	GEYER
AIRN	CARTAGENA	AIUM	ELISENHOF	AIXK	GIEHLERMOOR
AIRO	CARUM	AIUN	ELLINGEN	AIXL	GIESENTHAL
AIRP	CASHAGEN	AIUO	ELLMENDINGEN	AIXM	GILGENBURG
AIRQ	CHARLOTTENHOF	AIUP	ELLWANGEN	AIXN	GILSDORF
AIRR	CISMAR	AIUQ	ELSTORF	AIXO	GILSENBERG
AIRS	COLBERG	AIUR	ELTINGEN	AIXP	GLASER
AIRT	CONCORDIA-MO	AIUS	EMMERICH	AIXQ	GLEISZELLEN
AIRU	CONNEWITZ	AIUT	EMSLOH	AIXR	GLUMEN
AIRV	COSEL	AIUU	ENDERSBACH	AIXS	GOCH
AIRW	CRIEWEN	AIUV	ENSEN	AIXT	GOERKE
AIRX	CRIMEA	AIUW	ERBENHAUSEN	AIXU	GOERKEN
AIRY	DACHOW	AIUX	ERFDE	AIXV	GOESDORF
AIRZ	DAHLWITZHOF	AIUY	ERLABRUNN	AIXW	GOLDBECK
AISA	DALOW	AIUZ	ERLACH	AIXX	GOLLENBURG
AISB	DANNSTADT	AIVA	ERLE	AIXY	GOLLIN
AISC	DARGELIN	AIVB	ERLINGEN	AIYA	GOLLNOWSHAGEN
AISD	DARGEZIN	AIVC	ERLINGHAUSEN	AIYB	GOLTOFT
AISE	DARSIN	AIVD	ERSTFELD	AIYC	GORAY
AISF	DASOW	AIVE	ESCHEDE	AIYD	GORMA
AISG	DEERSHEIM	AIVF	ESSENBERG	AIYE	GORROW

Code	Name	Code	Name	Code	Name
AIYF	GR.BLANKENBACH	AJBE	HEINRICHSDORF	AJED	KEMPENDORF
AIYG	GR.DUBBEROW	AJBF	HEINRICHSFELDE	AJEE	KESSELBACH
AIYH	GR.GARDE	AJBG	HEITMANSHAUSEN	AJEF	KETSCHENDORF
AIYI	GR.GOHLAU	AJBH	HELDRUNGEN	AJEG	KETTENHEIM
AIYJ	GR.HEIDE	AJBI	HELLER	AJEH	KIEDRICH
AIYK	GR.JESTIN	AJBJ	HELZENDORF	AJEI	KIENITZ
AIYL	GR.KARBEN	AJBK	HEMSDORF	AJEJ	KILBURG
AIYM	GR.KREBS	AJBL	HEMSEN	AJEK	KIPPENHEIM
AIYN	GR.KRIEN	AJBM	HENGERSBERG	AJEL	KIRCHHEILIGEN
AIYO	GR.NIENHAGEN	AJBN	HENNINGSDORF	AJEM	KIST
AIYP	GR.RUNOR	AJBO	HERBEDE	AJEN	KISZKOWO
AIYQ	GR.SABOW	AJBP	HERBERTINGEN	AJEO	KLEIST
AIYR	GR.SILKOW	AJBQ	HERMANNSHAGEN	AJEP	KLEMPIN
AIYS	GR.SPIEGELBERG	AJBR	HERNE	AJEQ	KLEVE
AIYT	GR.STAERKENAU	AJBS	HERRLINGEN	AJER	KLINGENBERG
AIYU	GR.TUCHEN	AJBT	HERSCHBACH	AJES	KLINGENTHAL
AIYV	GR.WECKOW	AJBU	HESEDORF	AJET	KLINKEN
AIYW	GR.ZUENDER	AJBV	HESELBACH	AJEU	KLINT
AIYX	GRAEFENBUCH	AJBW	HESLACH	AJEV	KLOETZEN
AIYY	GRAMKOW	AJBX	HESSELBACH	AJEW	KLOSTERSEE
AIYZ	GRAMMEN	AJBY	HESSHEIM	AJEX	KLOSTERWALD
AIZA	GRAMMERLIN	AJBZ	HESSLAR	AJEY	KLOTZEN
AIZB	GRAMSDORF	AJCA	HESSLINGEN	AJEZ	KLUKOWO
AIZC	GRANSTEDT	AJCB	HEUCHLINGEN	AJFA	KLUS
AIZD	GRANZOW	AJCC	HEUDORF	AJFB	KLUSS
AIZE	GRAPPERSHOFEN	AJCD	HINSDORF	AJFC	KNAPP
AIZF	GRASSDORF	AJCE	HITZDORF	AJFD	KNIEBIS
AIZG	GRAUDENHEIM	AJCF	HOBBACH	AJFE	KNOWAXLAW
AIZH	GRAULINGEN	AJCG	HOCHHEIDE	AJFF	KOEHN
AIZI	GREBENHAIN	AJCH	HOCHTZEIT	AJFG	KOENDRINGEN
AIZJ	GREBIN	AJCI	HOEFEN	AJFH	KOHLENDORF
AIZK	GREENE	AJCJ	HOERNE	AJFI	KOHLKRIESSE
AIZL	GREMERSDORF	AJCK	HOFWEIER	AJFJ	KOKEMEHL
AIZM	GRIFTE	AJCL	HOHENSELCHOW	AJFK	KOLBERMOOR
AIZN	GRIMMA	AJCM	HOHENWESTEDT	AJFL	KOLBNITZ
AIZO	GROEPELINGEN	AJCN	HOLBACH	AJFM	KOSCHMIN
AIZP	GROOTHUSEN	AJCO	HOLLERN	AJFN	KOSLOW
AIZQ	GROSS-GRABEN	AJCP	HOLM	AJFO	KOSSDORF
AIZR	GROSS-PODEL	AJCQ	HOLT	AJFP	KOSSOW
AIZS	GROSSBETTLINGEN	AJCR	HOLZFELD	AJFQ	KOSTENTHAL
AIZT	GROSSENBACH	AJCS	HONAU	AJFR	KOTTOW
AIZU	GROSSILBER	AJCT	HOPTRUP	AJFS	KRAMSK
AIZV	GRUB	AJCU	HOSENFELD	AJFT	KRATZIG
AIZW	GRUENFELD	AJCV	HRAIENBURG	AJFU	KRAY
AIZX	GRUENHAGEN	AJCW	HUDDESTORF	AJFV	KRESSIN
AIZY	GRUENSTEIN	AJCX	HUETTENRODE	AJFW	KREUZEBER
AIZZ	GRUNDOLDENDORF	AJCY	HUMPTRUP	AJFX	KROEFFELBACH
AJAA	GUENTERSHAGEN	AJCZ	HYGENDORF	AJFY	KRONENBERG
AJAB	GUILDORF	AJDA	HYMENDORF	AJFZ	KRONSBERG
AJAC	GUNDELFINGEN	AJDB	IBIND	AJGA	KROPP
AJAD	GUNZENDORF	AJDC	ICHENCHEIM	AJGB	KROSSNOW
AJAE	GUTENDORF	AJDD	IDUNG	AJGC	KUECHEN
AJAF	HAALE	AJDE	IGGELHEIM	AJGD	KUELSHEIM
AJAG	HAAN	AJDF	IGGENBACH	AJGE	KUERN
AJAH	HAAREN	AJDG	IGLAU	AJGF	KURSDORF
AJAI	HAASSEL	AJDH	IMMENTHAL	AJGG	KUSSEN
AJAJ	HABKIRCHEN	AJDI	INSTERBERG	AJGH	KUTENHOLZ
AJAK	HAGENDORF	AJDJ	INZLINGEN	AJGI	KYRITZ
AJAL	HAIG	AJDK	JAMBER	AJGJ	LAAGE
AJAM	HAIGER	AJDL	JANIKOW	AJGK	LAATZIG
AJAN	HAITERBACH	AJDM	JETTENBACH	AJGL	LACHENDORF
AJAO	HAMBRUECHEN	AJDN	JEZEWO	AJGM	LADENTHIN
AJAP	HANSEN	AJDO	JUNGFERNDORF	AJGN	LAHM
AJAQ	HARMSDORF	AJDP	KAHLAU	AJGO	LANDENHAUSEN
AJAR	HARTENHEIM	AJDQ	KAILBACH	AJGP	LANDKERN
AJAS	HARTHA	AJDR	KAILEN	AJGQ	LANDKIRCHEN
AJAT	HARZGERODE	AJDS	KAISERSWALDE	AJGR	LANDSHEID
AJAU	HASEN	AJDT	KALLSTADT	AJGS	LANGENHORN
AJAV	HASENBURG	AJDU	KALTWASSER	AJGT	LANGENLOHE
AJAW	HASTEDT	AJDV	KARL	AJGU	LANGENWEDDIGEN
AJAX	HAVELBERG	AJDW	KARTHAUS	AJGV	LANGERHORN
AJAY	HAYINGEN	AJDX	KARWITZ	AJGW	LAUCHHEIM
AJAZ	HAYNO	AJDY	KARZIN	AJGX	LAUTERBERG
AJBA	HEDDERSDORF	AJDZ	KAUFBACH	AJGY	LAUTERN
AJBB	HEDDINGHAUSEN	AJEA	KAULSDORF	AJGZ	LEEHEIM
AJBC	HEEDE	AJEB	KEHLEN	AJHA	LEHNSTEDT
AJBD	HEINEBACH	AJEC	KELBRA	AJHB	LEHRBACH

AJHC	LEHSEN	AJKB	NEGAST	AJNA	PALSCHAU
AJHD	LEIMEN	AJKC	NEIDENFELS	AJNB	PAMPOW
AJHE	LEINEFELDE	AJKD	NELLINGEN	AJNC	PANZIN
AJHF	LEINSWEILER	AJKE	NEN.PANZIN	AJND	PAREY
AJHG	LEISNIG	AJKF	NEU DAMM	AJNE	PARNOW
AJHH	LEMNITZ	AJKG	NEU WIEDENTHAL	AJNF	PEESELIN
AJHI	LENSIN	AJKH	NEU-ULM	AJNG	PENIG
AJHJ	LENZ	AJKI	NEUBRONN	AJNH	PETERHOF
AJHK	LESUMSTOTEL	AJKJ	NEUBRUNN	AJNI	PETKUM
AJHL	LETZIN	AJKK	NEUDERSUM	AJNJ	PFORTZ
AJHM	LEUTENDORF	AJKL	NEUEMUENSTER	AJNK	PFUHL
AJHN	LEVIN	AJKM	NEUENHOF	AJNL	PFUNGSTADT
AJHO	LIEBSTHAL	AJKN	NEUENKRUG	AJNM	PILLIG
AJHP	LINDENTHAL	AJKO	NEUHAEUSEL	AJNN	PLATZIG
AJHQ	LISCHNITZ	AJKP	NEUHAUSER	AJNO	PLEIDELSHEIM
AJHR	LITZENDORF	AJKQ	NEUKALEN	AJNP	PLETTENBURG
AJHS	LOBBERICH	AJKR	NEUKLENZ	AJNQ	PLOCK
AJHT	LOBKOWITZ	AJKS	NEUKOPPE	AJNR	POBLOTZ
AJHU	LODZ	AJKT	NEUMUEHLEN	AJNS	PODEWILS
AJHV	LOEFFINGEN	AJKU	NEUSALZ	AJNT	POGUM
AJHW	LOUISENBERG	AJKV	NEUSTETTEN	AJNU	POHL
AJHX	LUCKENWALDE	AJKW	NEVIGES	AJNV	POLCH
AJHY	LUCKOW	AJKX	NEWCASTLE	AJNW	POLKA
AJHZ	LUDORF	AJKY	NIECHOWO	AJNX	POLSNITZ
AJIA	LUECHOW	AJKZ	NIEDERBROMBACH	AJNY	POMBSEN
AJIB	LUELLEMIN	AJLA	NIEDERHORBACH	AJNZ	PORST
AJIC	LUETGENDORF	AJLB	NIEDERLAHNSTEIN	AJOA	POSSENDORF
AJID	LUETTE	AJLC	NIEDERWALD	AJOB	PRAUST
AJIE	MAASHOHN	AJLD	NIEDERWEISS	AJOC	PRESSATH
AJIF	MAHNWITZ	AJLE	NIEDERWINDEN	AJOD	PRESSECK
AJIG	MAIBACH	AJLF	NIEVERN	AJOE	PRESSEN
AJIH	MAINBERG	AJLG	NIMPTSCH	AJOF	PRESSSTIN
AJII	MAISBORSTEL	AJLH	NIPPERWIESE	AJOG	PRITZWALK
AJIJ	MALCHEN	AJLI	NIPPES	AJOH	PROCKENDORF
AJIK	MARL	AJLJ	NORDENHAMMER	AJOI	PROKELWITZ
AJIL	MARNHEIM	AJLK	NORDSTRAND	AJOJ	PRUST
AJIM	MAROLDSWEISACH	AJLL	NORTORF	AJOK	PUSTAMIN
AJIN	MASSBACK	AJLM	NUSSLOCH	AJOL	PUTLITZ
AJIO	MAUENFELDE	AJLN	NUTTELN	AJOM	PYRBAUM
AJIP	MAULBRONN	AJLO	OBEHLISCHKEN	AJON	QUATZOW
AJIQ	MAUSDORF	AJLP	OBER-SCHMITTEN	AJOO	QUERNHEIM
AJIR	MECKLAR	AJLQ	OBERENSE	AJOP	RACKWITZ
AJIS	MEGGERKOOG	AJLR	OBERFROHNA	AJOQ	RADEWITZ
AJIT	MEHLBACH	AJLS	OBERKIRCH	AJOR	RADHEIM
AJIU	MEICHOW	AJLT	OBERNEULAND	AJOS	RADISLEBEN
AJIV	MEIERHOF	AJLU	OBERNHOF	AJOT	RAEDNITZ
AJIW	MEINSEN	AJLV	OBERSGEGEN	AJOU	RAIBACH
AJIX	MERNES	AJLW	OBERSITZKO	AJOV	RAMIN
AJIY	MESSBACH	AJLX	OBERTHAL	AJOW	RAMMINGEN
AJIZ	METTENDORF	AJLY	OBERURSEL	AJOX	RATH
AJJA	MEUSEN	AJLZ	OBERWANGEN	AJOY	RATIBOR
AJJB	MEYERHOF	AJMA	OBERWEISSENBRUNN	AJOZ	RATTELSDORF
AJJC	MIDDELS	AJMB	OBERWIDDERSHEIM	AJPA	RAUDEN
AJJD	MIEHLEN	AJMC	OBERWINDEN	AJPB	RAUENBERG
AJJE	MILMERSDORF	AJMD	OCHSHAUSEN	AJPC	RAUENSTEIN
AJJF	MISSEN	AJME	OELS	AJPD	RAWITSCH
AJJG	MITTELFELD	AJMF	OETZE	AJPE	REDEL
AJJH	MOCKER	AJMG	OEYNHAUSEN	AJPF	REGNITZ
AJJI	MOECKMUEHL	AJMH	OFAFFENDORF	AJPG	REHBORN
AJJJ	MOEGELTONDERN	AJMI	OFTRINGEN	AJPH	REHLINGEN
AJJK	MOESSINGEN	AJMJ	OKARBEN	AJPI	REICHENWALD
AJJL	MOHREN	AJMK	OLCHING	AJPJ	REIFFENHAUSEN
AJJM	MORITZFELDE	AJML	OLDHAUS	AJPK	REIL
AJJN	MORSUM	AJMM	OLIVA	AJPL	REIMERSWALDE
AJJO	MOSEBECK	AJMN	ORSCHWEIER	AJPM	REINBEK
AJJP	MROTSCHEN	AJMO	ORZECHOWKO	AJPN	REINHARDSHAUSEN
AJJQ	MUEHLENDORF	AJMP	OSDORF	AJPO	REKUM
AJJR	MUENZESHEIM	AJMQ	OSLEBSHAUSEN	AJPP	REMPEN
AJJS	MUGGENSTRUM	AJMR	OSTENDORF	AJPQ	REMSE
AJJT	MURR	AJMS	OSTERBERG	AJPR	RENSDORF
AJJU	MUSDORF	AJMT	OSTERFELD	AJPS	REPPEN
AJJV	MYSLOWITZ	AJMU	OSTERHORN	AJPT	REUDNITZ
AJJW	NAEHERSTILLE	AJMV	OSTWALD	AJPU	REULBACH
AJJX	NAPLES	AJMW	OTTERSTADT	AJPV	REUSS
AJJY	NARZYM	AJMX	OTTERWITSCH	AJPW	REXIN
AJJZ	NARZYN	AJMY	OWEN	AJPX	RHEINHEIM
AJKA	NATTHEIM	AJMZ	OYTEN	AJPY	RHEINSHEIM

AJPZ	RHEINWEILER	AJSY	SECKLENDORF	AJVX	TOTTLEBEN
AJQA	RIBNITZ	AJSZ	SEEBA	AJVY	TRAUSTADT
AJQB	RICHENWALDE	AJTA	SEEBURG	AJVZ	TREBLIN
AJQC	RICHTENBERG	AJTB	SEEHAUSEN	AJWA	TREBNITZ
AJQD	RITTERSDORF	AJTC	SEHL	AJWB	TRENNFELD
AJQE	RITTERSHOFEN	AJTD	SELB	AJWC	TRENT
AJQF	RITZOW	AJTE	SELBITZ	AJWD	TRETTSTADT
AJQG	ROCKENHAUSEN	AJTF	SIEDEN	AJWE	TRIEBENSRUTH
AJQH	ROCKSTEDT	AJTG	SIEGBURG	AJWF	TRIPPSTADT
AJQI	ROCKWINKEL	AJTH	SIELHORST	AJWG	TRIPTIS
AJQJ	ROEHL	AJTI	SILBER	AJWH	TROCKENHUETTE
AJQK	ROGZOW	AJTJ	SILBERBERG	AJWI	TROLLENHAGEN
AJQL	ROLLWITZ	AJTK	SILBERG	AJWJ	TROPHAGEN
AJQM	ROMAN	AJTL	SILBERSTEDT	AJWK	TRUPE
AJQN	ROMBERG	AJTM	SOBBOWITZ	AJWL	TUSCHENDORF
AJQO	ROSEN	AJTN	SOELLINGEN	AJWM	UBSTADT
AJQP	ROSENBACH	AJTO	SONDERNAU	AJWN	UDENHEIM
AJQQ	ROSENOW	AJTP	SPALT	AJWO	UELZEN
AJQR	ROTHA	AJTQ	SPANDAN	AJWP	UESCHERSDORF
AJQS	ROTTWERNDORF	AJTR	SPANTEKOW	AJWQ	UFFENHEIM
AJQT	RUEBGARTEN	AJTS	SPARNECK	AJWR	UNBESANDTEN
AJQU	RUETZENHAGEN	AJTT	SPECHTSBRUNN	AJWS	UNNA
AJQV	RUFEN	AJTU	SPIESHEIM	AJWT	UNSEBURG
AJQW	RUHSTORF	AJTV	ST.-INGBERT	AJWU	UNTERBRUEDEN
AJQX	RUSCHENDORF	AJTW	ST.INGBERT	AJWV	UNTERDERTINGEN
AJQY	RUSTOW	AJTX	ST.JUERGEN	AJWW	UNTERMASSFELD
AJQZ	SACHSA	AJTY	ST.MARGARETHEN	AJWX	UNTERMICHELBACH
AJRA	SAGEMUEHL	AJTZ	STABITZ	AJWY	UNTERRODAEN
AJRB	SAINT-INGBERT	AJUA	STAHRINGEN	AJWZ	UNTERROHN
AJRC	SAINT-JOSEPH	AJUB	STANGENDORF	AJXA	UNTERTUERKHEIM
AJRD	SALENBURG	AJUC	STAPEL	AJXB	USCH
AJRE	SALZHAUSEN	AJUD	STAUDHEIM	AJXC	VADERSDORF
AJRF	SALZWEG	AJUE	STAUFEN	AJXD	VEITSBERG
AJRG	SASEL	AJUF	STEINMAUERN	AJXE	VELSOW
AJRH	SASSENBURG	AJUG	STERNBERG	AJXF	VENUSBERG
AJRI	SATTELBOGEN	AJUH	STINSTEDT	AJXG	VIETZ
AJRJ	SCHALKE	AJUI	STOLTENBERG	AJXH	VIETZIG
AJRK	SCHALLODENBACH	AJUJ	STOLZENBERG	AJXI	VIRCHOW
AJRL	SCHAMBECK	AJUK	STOLZENBURG	AJXJ	VOGELHEIM
AJRM	SCHANGAM	AJUL	STOLZENFELDE	AJXK	VOLKMARSHAUSEN
AJRN	SCHAUDORF	AJUM	STRASSFORTH	AJXL	VOLKSTEDT
AJRO	SCHAUEN	AJUN	STRIEGUN	AJXM	VOLTLAGE
AJRP	SCHEIBE	AJUO	STRUECKEN	AJXN	VORBURG
AJRQ	SCHELINGEN	AJUP	STRUPPEN	AJXO	VORHEIDE
AJRR	SCHELLENBURG	AJUQ	STRZELNO	AJXP	VRESS
AJRS	SCHERNECK	AJUR	STUBA	AJXQ	WAHRENHOLZ
AJRT	SCHIFFELBACH	AJUS	STUHR	AJXR	WAHRHAUSEN
AJRU	SCHIPPACH	AJUT	SUDERSTAPEL	AJXS	WALDBACH
AJRV	SCHIRNDING	AJUU	SUDURGEN	AJXT	WALDFISCHBACH
AJRW	SCHLAGTOW	AJUV	SUEDERBRARUP	AJXU	WALDSTETTEN
AJRX	SCHLEBUSCH	AJUW	SUEDERSTAPEL	AJXV	WALHEIM
AJRY	SCHLEITHAL	AJUX	SUELLDORF	AJXW	WALLEN
AJRZ	SCHLEIZ	AJUY	SULZHEIM	AJXX	WALLSTADT
AJSA	SCHLESEN	AJUZ	SULZTHAL	AJXY	WALSHAUSEN
AJSB	SCHLOSS	AJVA	SUNDSTEDT	AJXZ	WALTERSHAUSEN
AJSC	SCHLOTTAU	AJVB	SUWALKEN	AJYA	WARMSEN
AJSD	SCHLUESSELFELD	AJVC	SZELDKEHMEN	AJYB	WARNITZ
AJSE	SCHMIDTHEIM	AJVD	TAAKEN	AJYC	WARZELN
AJSF	SCHMIE	AJVE	TABEN	AJYD	WARZENRIED
AJSG	SCHMITTEN	AJVF	TARNAU	AJYE	WASENBURG
AJSH	SCHNAITTACH	AJVG	TARP	AJYF	WASSMUTHAUSEN
AJSI	SCHOENHAIDE	AJVH	TAUBENHEIM	AJYG	WEBENHEIM
AJSJ	SCHOENLAGE	AJVI	TAUBERBISCHOFSHEIM	AJYH	WEDENDORF
AJSK	SCHOENRADE	AJVJ	TECHNOW	AJYI	WEENERMOOR
AJSL	SCHOETZOW	AJVK	TELLINGSTEDT	AJYJ	WEETZEN
AJSM	SCHOPP	AJVL	TESCHENHAGEN	AJYK	WEGEZIN
AJSN	SCHROECK	AJVM	TETENHUSEN	AJYL	WEHLDORF
AJSO	SCHUELP	AJVN	TEUPITZ	AJYM	WEISENBACH
AJSP	SCHURA	AJVO	THALBERG	AJYN	WEISENBERG
AJSQ	SCHUROW	AJVP	THANNHAUSEN	AJYO	WEISS
AJSR	SCHWABSBURG	AJVQ	THONBERG	AJYP	WEISSACH
AJSS	SCHWACHENWALDE	AJVR	THOREN	AJYQ	WEISSBACH
AJST	SCHWACHHAUSEN	AJVS	THURN	AJYR	WEISSINSTEIN
AJSU	SCHWARME	AJVT	TIEFENBACH	AJYS	WELLMERSDORF
AJSV	SCHWARZENAU	AJVU	TIEFENSTEIN	AJYT	WENGELN
AJSW	SCHWARZHOLZ	AJVV	TIEGENHOF	AJYU	WENTORF
AJSX	SCHWETZ	AJVW	TODENDORF	AJYV	WERNSHAUSEN

AJYW	WESSIN	AKQV	AMALIENTHAL	AKTV	BRANNENBURG
AJYX	WESSINGEN	AKQW	AMERDINGEN	AKTW	BRARUPHOLZ
AJYY	WESTER	AKQX	ANHOLT	AKTX	BREBACH
AJYZ	WESTERBECK	AKQY	APLERBECK	AKTY	BREITENTHAL
AJZA	WESTERMOOR	AKQZ	ARBERG	AKTZ	BRESLAWITZ
AJZB	WESTERODE	AKRA	ARKONA VITTE	AKUA	BRILLIT
AJZC	WICKENDORF	AKRB	ARLEN	AKUB	BUCHET
AJZD	WIEMERSDORF	AKRC	ARRESTING	AKUC	BUCHHAGAEN
AJZE	WIENAU	AKRD	ASPISHEIM	AKUD	BUCHHAGEN
AJZF	WIENHAUSEN	AKRE	AUGUSTWALDE	AKUE	BUECHENBRONN
AJZG	WIENSDORF	AKRF	AXELHOF	AKUF	BUELLINGHAUSEN
AJZH	WIESENHEIM	AKRG	BACHEM	AKUG	BUENKENBERG
AJZI	WIESENSTEIG	AKRH	BACHHEIM	AKUH	BUESCHEID
AJZJ	WILDBAD	AKRI	BADEKOW	AKUI	BUNDEN
AJZK	WILDENBERG	AKRJ	BALERSBRONN	AKUJ	BUNDERHAMMRICH
AJZL	WILDENHAGEN	AKRK	BALTRUM	AKUK	BURGAU
AJZM	WILDSTEIN	AKRL	BANDAU	AKUM	BURGSTAEDT
AJZN	WILHELMSHOEHE	AKRM	BANDERSOW	AKUN	BURGTONNA
AJZO	WILHELMSTHAL	AKRN	BANSIN	AKUO	BURKERSDORF
AJZP	WILHEMSBURG	AKRO	BARENBRUCH	AKUP	BUSDORF
AJZQ	WILKERSDORF	AKRP	BASTHEIM	AKUQ	CHERSON
AJZR	WINTERBERG	AKRQ	BEBRICH	AKUR	CHOJNO
AJZS	WINTERHAUSEN	AKRR	BECHTOLDSWEILLER	AKUS	CHORANGER
AJZT	WIPPINGEN	AKRS	BEDNARKEN	AKUT	CHRISTIANENHOF
AJZU	WIRBALLEN	AKRT	BEDRA	AKUU	CLENNEN
AJZV	WISSEN	AKRU	BEGGENDORF	AKUV	CLENZE
AJZW	WISSINGEN	AKRV	BEIDL	AKUW	CLINGEN
AJZX	WITTENHOF	AKRW	BEITSCH	AKUX	COCHEN
AJZY	WITTKIEL	AKRX	BELG	AKUY	DALLWITZ
AJZZ	WITZLEBEN	AKRY	BENHAUSEN	AKUZ	DAMENDORF
AKPA	WITZWORT	AKRZ	BENKHEIM	AKVA	DAMERAU
AKPB	WOELCHINGEN	AKSA	BENZIN	AKVB	DAMMRATSCHHAMMER
AKPC	WOERLITZ	AKSB	BERCHTESGADEN	AKVC	DAMSDORF
AKPD	WOESSINGEN	AKSC	BERGESHOEVDE	AKVD	DAMSUM
AKPE	WOHLENHAUSEN	AKSD	BERSCHEID	AKVE	DARNEBECK
AKPF	WOLDISCH	AKSE	BERTLINGEN	AKVF	DAUBHAUSEN
AKPG	WOLFENHAUSEN	AKSF	BESSENICH	AKVG	DAZENDORF
AKPH	WOLFERSHAUSEN	AKSG	BICKEN	AKVH	DEBRONG
AKPI	WOLLERSDORF	AKSH	BICKENDORF	AKVI	DECHSEL
AKPJ	WRIEDEL	AKSI	BIESELBERG	AKVJ	DEGTOW
AKPK	WUELFLINGEN	AKSJ	BILLBERGE	AKVK	DEHRENTRUP
AKPL	WURCHOW	AKSK	BISCHOFFINGEN	AKVL	DELSTEDT
AKPM	WUROW	AKSL	BISCHOFFSWERDER	AKVM	DEMMINGEN
AKPN	WURZEN	AKSM	BISCHWIND	AKVN	DEPPEN
AKPO	ZAHLBACH	AKSN	BISSENBERG	AKVO	DETTENDORF
AKPP	ZECHIN	AKSO	BLANKWITT	AKVP	DETTMANSDORF
AKPQ	ZESELBERG	AKSP	BOBAU	AKVQ	DEUTSCHKAMITZ
AKPR	ZEYER	AKSQ	BOCKENBACH	AKVR	DEUTSCHWETTE
AKPS	ZIEGENHALS	AKSR	BOEBBELIN	AKVS	DEVIN
AKPT	ZOPPOT	AKSS	BOECKELT	AKVT	DIELE
AKPU	ZUELZEFITZ	AKST	BOEHMERWALD	AKVU	DIENSDORF
AKPV	ZUESCHEN	AKSU	BOINGHAUSEN	AKVV	DIESBURG
AKPW	ZWINGENBERG	AKSV	BOJANOW	AKVW	DIETKIRCHEN
AKPX	ABTSGEMUEND	AKSW	BOLLENSEN	AKVX	DINGELSTEDT
AKPY	ADELSBERG	AKSX	BOLTHAUS	AKVY	DITTINGEN
AKPZ	AFFALTRACH	AKSY	BOMBACH	AKVZ	DOBBRIKOW
AKQA	AHLDORF	AKSZ	BOMMERN	AKWB	DOBRYZIN
AKQB	AILINGEN	AKTA	BONIN	AKWC	DOEHLE
AKQC	ALLMANSDORF	AKTB	BONNEBERG	AKWD	DOMBROWSKEN
AKQD	ALSERWURP	AKTC	BONSWEIHER	AKWE	DORNSTETTEN
AKQE	ALSTAETTE	AKTD	BORBECK	AKWF	DORSHEIM
AKQF	ALSTERDORF	AKTE	BOREK	AKWG	DRAHANY
AKQG	ALT BESTENDORF	AKTF	BORG	AKWH	DREBKAU
AKQH	ALT GLIETZEN	AKTG	BORGEFELD	AKWI	DREWITZ
AKQI	ALT GUHRAU	AKTH	BORNRETHE	AKWJ	DUBENSKO
AKQJ	ALT HELDENSDORF	AKTI	BOROWEN	AKWK	DUDENROTH
AKQK	ALT LAUSKE	AKTJ	BOROWIAN	AKWL	DUEPOW
AKQL	ALT PLESTLIN	AKTK	BORSUM	AKWM	EBELSBACH
AKQM	ALT SCHLAGE	AKTL	BOSGENTHIN	AKWN	EBERGOENS
AKQN	ALT SCHLAWIN	AKTM	BOSSBORN	AKWO	ECHALLENS
AKQO	ALT TESCHEN	AKTN	BOSSIN	AKWP	ECKDORF
AKQP	ALTENESSEN	AKTO	BOTHAU	AKWQ	ECKERSBACH
AKQQ	ALTENFLIESS	AKTP	BOTTMINGEN	AKWR	ECKERSMUEHLEN
AKQR	ALTLEINGEN	AKTQ	BOXBERG	AKWS	EDELSBERG
AKQS	ALTMANNSHOFEN	AKTS	BRACHTENBECK	AKWT	EFFELN
AKQT	ALTSANSKOW	AKTT	BRANDENBERG	AKWU	EGERKINGEN
AKQU	ALTVERDISSEN	AKTU	BRANDERODE	AKWV	EIBAU

Code	Village	Code	Village	Code	Village
AKWW	EINSELTHUM	AKZV	GROSSOLDENDORF	ALCV	KELZ
AKWX	ELGEN	AKZW	GROSZSCHWARZENLOHE	ALCW	KINDELBRUCK
AKWY	EMMERSHAUSEN	AKZX	GRUEMPEN	ALCX	KIRCHLEIN
AKWZ	ENERICH	AKZY	GRUENFOH	ALCY	KRONPRINZENKOOG
AKXA	ERKRATH	AKZZ	GRUNDAU	ALCZ	KUESTRIN
AKXB	ESCHENBERGEN	ALAA	GRUSEN	ALDA	KLADRUM
AKXC	ESCHLEKAM	ALAB	GRYBOWEN	ALDB	KLATTERSDORF
AKXD	ETTELN	ALAC	GUSTAEDT	ALDC	KLEIN BOELKAU
AKXE	EVERSDORF	ALAD	GUSTAEVEL	ALDD	KLEIN BUTZING
AKXF	EXTEN	ALAE	GUSTOW	ALDE	KLEIN GARDE
AKXG	FALDO	ALAF	HAARDENSETTEN	ALDF	KLEIN KLESCHKAU
AKXH	FALLERSLEBEN	ALAG	HABSCHIED	ALDG	KLEIN KOENIGSFOERDE
AKXI	FELSENHAGEN	ALAH	HAEDER	ALDH	KLEIN NEUDORF
AKXJ	FIER	ALAI	HAHENFELD	ALDI	KLEIN POBLOTH
AKXK	FLUSSBACH	ALAJ	HAHNENBERG	ALDJ	KLEIN SILBER
AKXL	FOHRE	ALAK	HALBEMOND	ALDK	KLEIN VIELEN
AKXM	FORNBACH	ALAL	HALLWANGEN	ALDL	KLEINEISLINGEN
AKXN	FRAUENDORF	ALAM	HAMELSPRINCE	ALDM	KLEINWOKERN
AKXO	FREIES	ALAN	HAMFELDE	ALDN	KLOCKOW
AKXP	FREIHUNG	ALAO	HAMMELSHAN	ALDO	KLOSTERHAUSER
AKXQ	FREISHEIM	ALAP	HAMMERMUEHLE	ALDP	KNURRBUSCH
AKXR	FRIEDRICKSHAVEN	ALAQ	HARDINGEN	ALDQ	KOENIGSHAUS
AKXS	FUSSINGEN	ALAR	HARLINGERODE	ALDR	KOEPERNITZ
AKXT	GAARDE	ALAS	HARTMUTHSACKSEN	ALDS	KOLBA
AKXU	GABERSDORF	ALAT	HAUSBACH	ALDT	KOLLSFREE
AKXV	GAMMELIN	ALAU	HAUSTADT	ALDU	KOMPITTEN
AKXW	GANSCHOW	ALAV	HEINRICHSHAUS	ALDV	KOWALEWSKEN
AKXX	GANZKOW	ALAW	HEINRICHSHOEFEN	ALDW	KRAAK
AKXY	GARNSEE	ALAX	HEINRICHSKIRCHEN	ALDX	KRAILBURG
AKXZ	GAUERNITZ	ALAZ	HELBA	ALDY	KRAMES
AKYA	GEDDELSBACK	ALBA	HELLENBERG	ALDZ	KREBES
AKYB	GEHRENRODE	ALBB	HELPENSTEIN	ALEA	KRKUMMWISCH
AKYC	GEILSDORF	ALBC	HELSUNGEN	ALEB	KRUSCHINNEN
AKYD	GENNERBRECK	ALBD	HEMBERGEN	ALEC	KUEMKEN
AKYE	GERBSTEDT	ALBE	HERCHENHAIN	ALED	KUETZIN
AKYF	GERNSBACK	ALBF	HERGERSHAUSEN	ALEE	KULMAIN
AKYG	GERSHASEN	ALBG	HERKHEIM	ALEF	KUTZDORF
AKYH	GHENT	ALBH	HERMANNSKIRCHEN	ALEG	LACKENHAUSER
AKYI	GIEBICHENSTEIN	ALBI	HERRENZIMERN	ALEH	LADEKOPP
AKYJ	GIELAU	ALBJ	HERRN-ALPE	ALEI	LAEHDEN
AKYK	GIESENHORST	ALBK	HERSBRUCK	ALEJ	LAMBSCHEIM
AKYL	GINSBERG	ALBL	HERSCHEID	ALEK	LANDSCHAFTESPOLDER
AKYM	GITTERSEE	ALBM	HERSSUM	ALEL	LANG NEUNDORF
AKYN	GLADEBECK	ALBN	HERZOGENREUTH	ALEM	LANGEN BROMBACH
AKYO	GLASEHAGEN	ALBO	HILPERTSAU	ALEN	LANGENSTEINACH
AKYP	GLUTZOW	ALBP	HINTERBRUCH	ALEO	LANGWEILER
AKYQ	GNARRENBURG	ALBQ	HOCHA	ALEP	LAPPACH
AKYR	GNOTTAU	ALBR	HOCHSPEYER	ALEQ	LASSERG
AKYS	GOEL	ALBS	HOCHSTEDT	ALER	LATDORF
AKYT	GOLLAU	ALBT	HOECKER	ALES	LAUCHDORF
AKYU	GORNSDORF	ALBU	HOEGERING	ALET	LEBRADE
AKYV	GOSCHUETZ	ALBV	HOHENMIN	ALEU	LECKOW
AKYW	GOSTEWITZ	ALBW	HOLPERDORF	ALEV	LEIPNIG
AKYX	GOTZING	ALBX	HOLZGERLINGEN	ALEW	LEIZEN
AKYY	GR.BODEN	ALBY	HOOGSTEDE	ALEX	LESSNICK
AKYZ	GR.GIESEN	ALBZ	HORATH	ALEY	LINDENHARDT
AKZA	GR.GLADEBRUEGGE	ALCA	HORLITZ	ALEZ	LINDENSCHIED
AKZB	GR.GRESSINGEN	ALCB	HOLZAPPEL	ALFA	LINDERWIESE
AKZC	GR.HEHLEN	ALCC	HUCKINGEN	ALFB	LOBAS
AKZD	GR.LINICHEN	ALCD	HUISBERDEN	ALFC	LOBITZSCH
AKZE	GR.MARKOW	ALCE	IBERSHEIM	ALFD	LOEFFELSTELZEN
AKZF	GR.OSTHEIM	ALCF	IHRHOVE	ALFE	LOESCHWITZ
AKZG	GR.OTTLAU	ALCG	IMMENSTADT	ALFF	LOFLING
AKZH	GR.SALZE	ALCH	JACOBSEND	ALFG	LOSSOW
AKZI	GR.SCHOENEBECK	ALCI	JAWOR	ALFH	LOTHE
AKZJ	GR.SONNENBURG	ALCJ	JAWOROW	ALFI	LOVERICH
AKZK	GR.TREBBOW	ALCK	JESAU	ALFJ	LUBEK
AKZL	GRAMMENTIN	ALCL	JOACHIMSTHAL	ALFK	LUBIATH
AKZM	GRASBERG	ALCM	JOHANNESDORF	ALFL	LUCHAU
AKZN	GRAUDSZEN	ALCN	JUSTINGEN	ALFM	LUDWIGSHORST
AKZO	GREBELWITZ	ALCO	KAISING	ALFN	LUEDERSHAGEN
AKZP	GRENDERICH	ALCP	KAMBERG	ALFO	LUETZELINDEN
AKZQ	GROENENBACH	ALCQ	KANNEWORT	ALFP	LULZHAUSEN
AKZR	GROSSBOTHEN	ALCR	KARDORF	ALFQ	LUNKE
AKZS	GROSSE MOOR	ALCS	KARSAU	ALFR	LUPITZ
AKZT	GROSSMOELSEN	ALCT	KATHARINENBERG	ALFS	LUSAN
AKZU	GROSSMOENSDORF	ALCU	KEHNERT	ALFT	LUSCHEN

ALFU	LUTTENWANG	ALIU	NEUWELT	ALLT	RATHSDAMNITZ
ALFV	MAASTRICHT	ALIV	NIEDERBRUNN	ALLU	REHFELD
ALFW	MACHTOLSHEIM	ALIW	NIEDERFLOERSHEIM	ALLV	REITZENHAIN
ALFX	MAHLOW	ALIX	NIEDERHONE	ALLW	RENNERTEHAUSEN
ALFY	MAHLSTETTEN	ALIY	NIEDERMUEHLSEN	ALLX	REPKE
ALFZ	MAINABULLAU	ALIZ	NIEDERVORSCHUETZ	ALLY	RETTKAU
ALGA	MALSTEDT	ALJA	NIEDR LIPKA	ALLZ	REUDEN
ALGB	MANGOLDSALL	ALJB	NIEMEGK	ALMA	REUDERN
ALGC	MANNEBACH	ALJC	NOHEN	ALMB	REUTERN
ALGD	MANZE	ALJD	NORDBURG	ALMC	REVENOW
ALGE	MARCZYNOWEN	ALJE	NORDENSTADT	ALMD	RHPR
ALGF	MARKKOEBEL	ALJF	NOSKOVICI	ALME	RICHELBACH
ALGG	MARLOW	ALJG	NOWAWES	ALMF	RICKLINGEN
ALGH	MARSOW	ALJH	OBER SCHMITTEN	ALMG	RIMPAR
ALGI	MARTENSDORF	ALJI	OBERACHERN	ALMH	ROEDDELN
ALGJ	MASSLOW	ALJJ	OBERDING	ALMI	ROEDEL BACH
ALGK	MASSTRICHT	ALJK	OBERELSUNGEN	ALMJ	ROGAU
ALGL	MEBRITZ	ALJL	OBEREMMEL	ALMK	ROHDEN
ALGM	MECHAU	ALJM	OBERENZEN	ALML	ROHNDORF
ALGN	MECHELSDORF	ALJN	OBERESSFELD	ALMM	ROLTZHEIM
ALGO	MEIDERICH	ALJO	OBERGRUNA	ALMN	ROSCHWITZWALD
ALGP	MEIERBERG	ALJP	OBERNHAGEN	ALMO	ROSENWEIDE
ALGQ	MENGERS	ALJQ	OBERREISSEN	ALMP	RUBITZ
ALGR	MENKIN	ALJR	OBERRONING	ALMQ	RUCKEN
ALGS	MENZ	ALJS	OBERWEISSBACH	ALMR	RUESCHELD
ALGT	MERGELHEIDE	ALJT	OBERWIESEN	ALMS	RUHLEBEN
ALGU	MERING	ALJU	OCKSTADT	ALMT	RUMBECK
ALGV	MESEBERG	ALJV	OEDERAN	ALMU	RUMBESKE
ALGW	MIECHOWEN	ALJW	OESCHL	ALMV	RUNDEWIESE
ALGX	MIESCHKOW	ALJX	OFFERDINGEN	ALMW	RUNZEN
ALGY	MIETINGEN	ALJY	OFFINGEN	ALMX	RUPPERTSECKEN
ALGZ	MIETZELFELDE	ALJZ	OHL	ALMY	RUSCHBERG
ALHA	MIGEHNEN	ALKA	OHLIGS	ALMZ	RUSCHKOWITZ
ALHB	MILANO	ALKB	OHR	ALNA	RUSSOW
ALHC	MILDENAU	ALKC	OHRENBERG	ALNB	RUTHENBECK
ALHD	MILKENDORF	ALKD	OLDENBUETTEL	ALNC	RUTZKAU
ALHE	MILOSTIN	ALKE	OLSCHEWEN	ALND	RYMKEN
ALHF	MITTELSTEINE	ALKF	ORMESHEIM	ALNE	SAABEN
ALHG	MITTENFELDE	ALKG	ORTELSBERG	ALNF	SAARBECK
ALHH	MOKRZ	ALKH	ORTMANNSDORF	ALNG	SACHEN
ALHI	MONSCHAU	ALKI	PALESCHKEN	ALNH	SADDEK
ALHJ	MOORBRUECKE	ALKJ	PARUSCHKE	ALNI	SADEWITZ
ALHK	MOOSHAM	ALKK	PAULIENEN	ALNJ	SAINT JULIAN
ALHL	MORDAU	ALKL	PENTING	ALNK	SALINE
ALHM	MORGENROTH	ALKM	PERMAUERN	ALNL	SALLMANNSHAUSEN
ALHN	MORRN	ALKN	PERUSCHEN	ALNM	SALM
ALHO	MROZY	ALKO	PETTING	ALNN	SALZAU
ALHP	MUELHOF	ALKP	PEUCKER	ALNO	SALZBERGEN
ALHQ	MUENCHENSBERNSDORF	ALKQ	PFAFFENHAUSEN	ALNP	SALZDERHEIDEN
ALHR	MUESLERINGEN	ALKR	PFARRWEISACH	ALNQ	SALZMUENDE
ALHS	MUESSOW	ALKS	PHILLIPSTHAL	ALNR	SANDOW
ALHT	MUNDELFINGEN	ALKT	PIASKEN	ALNS	SANNE
ALHU	MUNDOLSHEIM	ALKU	PIERHEIM	ALNT	SARBSKE
ALHW	NAUENDORF	ALKV	PITTERSDORF	ALNU	SARNEKOW
ALHX	NAUNDORF	ALKW	PLESCHEN	ALNV	SATTLERN
ALHY	NECKARRENS	ALKX	PLETNITZ	ALNW	SAUDEN
ALHZ	NECKARTAILFINGEN	ALKY	PLUTOWO	ALNX	SAUERHOF
ALIA	NECKARZIMMERN	ALKZ	POGOSCH	ALNY	SCHAAKEN
ALIB	NEIRSTEDT	ALLA	POLAK	ALNZ	SCHAEFEREI
ALIC	NELLINGHOF	ALLB	POLKOWITZ	ALOA	SCHAFSBERG
ALID	NENSA	ALLC	POPELAU	ALOB	SCHALINGEN
ALIE	NETTE	ALLD	POPPENBACH	ALOC	SCHALKAU
ALIF	NEU BUCKOW	ALLE	POTZEHN	ALOD	SCHALKEN
ALIG	NEU BUDKOWITZ	ALLF	PRAGSDORF	ALOE	SCHAMMELSDORF
ALIH	NEU DIEDERSDORF	ALLG	PRAMSDORF	ALOF	SCHAUREN
ALII	NEU DOLLSTAEDT	ALLH	PREDEL	ALOG	SCHEDDERNDORF
ALIJ	NEU GLIENICKE	ALLI	PRETSCHEN	ALOH	SCHEER
ALIK	NEU GRUEN	ALLJ	PREUSSISCH HOLLAND	ALOI	SCHEUERN
ALIL	NEU MARKT	ALLK	PULLITZ	ALOJ	SCHIEGAU
ALIM	NEU PLACHT	ALLL	QUEICHHAMBACH	ALOK	SCHILKOWITZ
ALIN	NEU PROCHNOW	ALLM	RACHLAU	ALOL	SCHILLINGSFUERST
ALIO	NEU REICHENAU	ALLN	RACKAU	ALOM	SCHINCHOW
ALIP	NEU VORWERK	ALLO	RADAWNITZ	ALON	SCHIWINNEN
ALIQ	NEU WILMSDORF	ALLP	RADWANITZ	ALOO	SCHKEUDITZ
ALIR	NEUBORNA	ALLQ	RAGOW	ALOP	SCHLESWITZ
ALIS	NEUNLANDE	ALLR	RALOW	ALOQ	SCHLOSSIG
ALIT	NEUSTADTGOEDENS	ALLS	RAMTEN	ALOR	SCHMACHTENBERG

ALOS	SCHMALBACH	ALRR	STOEDTLEN	ALUQ	UNTERTHALLEN
ALOT	SCHMARSAU	ALRS	STOLHOFEN	ALUR	UPHOEFEN
ALOU	SCHMECKTEN	ALRT	STOLZENBACH	ALUS	URNSHAUSEN
ALOV	SCHMELLENTHIN	ALRU	STOLZENFELD	ALUT	UTAH
ALOW	SCHMIEDEBACH	ALRV	STOMMELN	ALUU	VARREL
ALOX	SCHMIEDEFELD	ALRW	STOPPENBERG	ALUV	VASBUEHL
ALOY	SCHMOELZ	ALRX	STRENZ	ALUW	VELBERT
ALOZ	SCHNEIDHAIN	ALRY	STRETENSEE	ALUX	VENEDIEN
ALPA	SCHNITTEN	ALRZ	STRICHE	ALUY	VETSCHAU
ALPB	SCHOENDORF	ALSA	STUEDNITZ	ALUZ	VIENAU
ALPC	SCHOENENKAMP	ALSB	SUBZOW	ALVA	VIERECK
ALPD	SCHOENHEIDE	ALSC	SUCHAU	ALVB	VILICH
ALPE	SCHOENMOHR	ALSD	SUDWALDE	ALVC	VILLKOW
ALPF	SCHOENSTEIN	ALSE	SUNDERN	ALVD	VILSHOFEN
ALPG	SCHOEPS	ALSF	SUNGER	ALVE	VINZLER
ALPH	SCHOLWIN	ALSG	SUSSNICK	ALVF	VISSELHOEVDE
ALPI	SCHORKENDORF	ALSH	SWAINEN	ALVG	VISSUM
ALPJ	SCHRSCHOW	ALSI	TAETENDORF	ALVH	VOLKBACH
ALPK	SCHULLWITZ	ALSJ	TANNAU	ALVI	VOLKENSHAGEN
ALPL	SCHUTTERZELL	ALSK	TAPLAU	ALVJ	VOLKERS
ALPM	SCHUZBACH	ALSL	TEGLINGEN	ALVK	VOLKERZEN
ALPN	SCHWABTHAL	ALSM	TEISTUNGEN	ALVL	VOLLERSRODA
ALPO	SCHWACHENSALDE	ALSN	TELLIG	ALVM	VORDAMM
ALPP	SCHWALINGEN	ALSO	TEMMEN	ALVN	WACHENHAUSEN
ALPQ	SCHWANEWEDE	ALSP	TEMNICK	ALVO	WACKENHAUSEN
ALPR	SCHWARZ	ALSQ	TESCHENAU	ALVP	WACKERSDORF
ALPS	SCHWARZHOFEN	ALSR	THALBACH	ALVQ	WADRILL
ALPT	SCHWARZMUEHLE	ALSS	THALE	ALVR	WAGNERN
ALPU	SCHWARZSEE	ALST	THALFINGEN	ALVS	WAHRLANG
ALPV	SCHWARZWALDAU	ALSU	THANN	ALVT	WALDHOF
ALPW	SCHWECKEN	ALSV	THEININGSEN	ALVU	WALDKATHEN
ALPX	SCHWEIGHOF	ALSW	THERESIA	ALVV	WALDULM
ALPY	SCHWEIZERTHAL	ALSX	THIELAU	ALVW	WALGENBACH
ALPZ	SCHWELLE	ALSY	THOMA	ALVX	WALLBACH
ALQA	SCHWERINSBURG	ALSZ	THUENGEN	ALVY	WALSHEIM
ALQB	SCHWESKAU	ALTA	THUERUNGEN	ALVZ	WALTRINGEN
ALQC	SCHWIENE	ALTB	THUMBY	ALWA	WANFRIED
ALQD	SEELIG	ALTC	TILLWAIDE	ALWB	WANGERSHAUSEN
ALQE	SELIGGEN	ALTD	TIMMENHAGEN	ALWC	WANSDORF
ALQF	SELKENTROP	ALTE	TINGE	ALWD	WANSEN
ALQG	SENDELBACH	ALTF	TODENBUETTEL	ALWE	WASCHENBACK
ALQH	SESSENBACH	ALTG	TONDORF	ALWF	WASSERBURG
ALQI	SEVERIN	ALTH	TRANATENBURG	ALWG	WASSERHAUSEN
ALQJ	SHALKOWITZ	ALTI	TRAVEMUENDE	ALWH	WASSERSUPPE
ALQK	SHORBACH	ALTJ	TREMMEN	ALWI	WATKENDORF
ALQL	SHORTEWITZ	ALTK	TREPPENDORF	ALWJ	WATTERDINGEN
ALQM	SHOSSOW	ALTL	TRIBBEVITZ	ALWK	WEBAU
ALQN	SHROECK	ALTM	TRIEBS	ALWL	WEBERN
ALQO	SIBLIN	ALTN	TRIMMAU	ALWM	WECHINGEN
ALQP	SICKELS	ALTO	TRIPS	ALWN	WECKESHEIM
ALQQ	SICKENHOF	ALTP	TROEBES	ALWO	WEHLEN
ALQR	SILBERKOPF	ALTQ	TROPPLOWITZ	ALWP	WEHRBLECK
ALQS	SITTENBACH	ALTR	TRUCHSEN	ALWQ	WEIBERG
ALQT	SITZERATH	ALTS	TRUEB	ALWR	WEIDELBACH
ALQU	SKARSINE	ALTT	TRUSEN	ALWS	WEIGENHOFEN
ALQV	SOEDER	ALTU	TUERRENFELD	ALWT	WEIHERSBERG
ALQW	SPITZE	ALTV	TUETINGEN	ALWU	WEILACK
ALQX	ST. BARBARA	ALTW	TUNINGEN	ALWV	WEINHAUSEN
ALQY	ST. MARGARETHEN	ALTX	TURNOW	ALWW	WEIPERZ
ALQZ	STADEL	ALTY	TURZIG	ALWX	WELGESHEIM
ALRA	STAMMELN	ALTZ	TUTSCHEN	ALWY	WELKENBACH
ALRB	STANGENBERG	ALUA	UDENHAIN	ALWZ	WELLBERGEN
ALRC	STARKOW	ALUB	UEBERRAU	ALXA	WENDORF
ALRD	STASCHWITZ	ALUC	ULLERSDORF	ALXB	WERLESHAUSEN
ALRE	STATZEN	ALUD	ULRICHSBERG	ALXC	WERMELSKIRCHEN
ALRF	STECHAU	ALUE	UNTERBREIZBACH	ALXD	WESELBURG
ALRG	STEGELITZ	ALUF	UNTERDETTINGEN	ALXE	WESSELSHOEFEN
ALRH	STEINBUECHEL	ALUG	UNTERDORNBACH	ALXF	WESTERSCHEPS
ALRI	STEINWARD	ALUH	UNTERHARMERSBACH	ALXG	WESTRHAUDERFEHN
ALRJ	STEMMERMUEHLEN	ALUI	UNTERIGLING	ALXH	WETZE
ALRK	STERBENIN	ALUJ	UNTERKIRNACH	ALXI	WICKEN
ALRL	STERNIN	ALUK	UNTERLIND	ALXJ	WIENBERGEN
ALRM	STIBBE	ALUL	UNTERMUSBACH	ALXK	WILHELMSAUE
ALRN	STIERBERG	ALUM	UNTERRUHLDINGEN	ALXL	WILHELMSHORST
ALRO	STIMBERN	ALUN	UNTERSCHLECHTBACH	ALXM	WILKAU
ALRP	STIMPFACH	ALUO	UNTERSCHNEIDHEIM	ALXN	WILKOWEN
ALRQ	STIRPE	ALUP	UNTERSENNE	ALXO	WILME

ALXP	WINDERATT	ALZB	ZUENDORF	AMAL	NEUDOERFCHEN
ALXQ	WINDSCHEIM	ALZC	AHRENSBACH	AMAM	NEUNBURG
ALXR	WINDSCHLAEG	ALZD	ALLRODE	AMAN	NEUWERK
ALXS	WIRTENBACH	ALZE	ANTWEILER	AMAO	NIEDERMOOS
ALXT	WISCHENHOFEN	ALZF	AUGUSTENDORF	AMAP	OBERBAUERSCHAFT
ALXU	WISCHKE	ALZG	BADEM	AMAQ	OBERWARTH
ALXV	WISSERHEIM	ALZH	BARANOWEN	AMAR	OSTERENDE
ALXW	WITTKEN	ALZI	BARNIN	AMAS	PELPIN
ALXX	WLOSTEN	ALZJ	BASSELSCHELDE	AMAT	PRIBBERNOW
ALXY	WOBENSIN	ALZK	BASSOW	AMAU	QUEICHHEIM
ALXZ	WOBESER	ALZL	BOLLSCHWEIL	AMAV	RADOSCHAU
ALYA	WOEBBERMIN	ALZM	BROCKHOEFE	AMAW	RENTSCHEN
ALYB	WOLDENBURG	ALZN	BUXTEHUDE	AMAX	ROBEN
ALYC	WOLTHUSEN	ALZO	DABER	AMAY	ROEDELHEIM
ALYD	WOPERSNOW	ALZP	DOMBROWA	AMAZ	RYDZEWEN
ALYE	WRIEZEN	ALZQ	ECKARTSWEILLER	AMBA	SAALBURG
ALYF	WRIXUM	ALZR	EIDELSTEDT	AMBB	SCHERNBERG
ALYG	WRONKEN	ALZS	ELLEFELD	AMBC	SCHWIENKUHLEN
ALYJ	WUESATERGIERSDORF	ALZT	FLEDERBORN	AMBD	SEELIGSTADT
ALYK	WURZBACH	ALZU	GARZIGER	AMBE	SEGELHORST
ALYL	WYLER	ALZV	GERADSTETTEN	AMBF	STALLUPONEN
ALYM	ZACHOW	ALZW	GERSROD	AMBG	STERNHOF
ALYN	ZAHMEN	ALZX	GERSTEN	AMBH	STRELOW
ALYO	ZAMBORST	ALZY	GR. BREMBACH	AMBI	TONNDORF
ALYP	ZANDERSDORF	ALZZ	GRIEFSWALD	AMBJ	TUELLINGEN
ALYQ	ZEHNHAUSEN	AMAA	GRINDERWALD	AMBK	WALLACHSEE
ALYR	ZELLENDORF	AMAB	HEDWIGSHOF	AMBL	WASCHKULKEN
ALYS	ZETTWEIL	AMAC	HENNINGEN	AMBM	WIESSEE
ALYT	ZIEGENBACH	AMAD	KAMIONKA	AMBN	WITTLOHE
ALYU	ZIEGENBERG	AMAE	KLEINEBERSDORF	AMBO	WOLLMAR
ALYV	ZIETLOW	AMAF	KOHLAU	AMBP	ZACHENBERG
ALYW	ZINNA	AMAG	KORNITZ	AMBQ	ZELLHAUSEN
ALYX	ZINTZEN	AMAH	MALTERDINGEN	AMBR	ZIPPLAU
ALYY	ZOEBINGEN	AMAI	MINSK	ZZZZ	UNKNOWN
ALYZ	ZOLLEN	AMAJ	MITTELGRUENDEN	****	BORN AT SEA
ALZA	ZSCALTEN	AMAK	MUELLENDORF		

[Ed. Note: The village codes include some apparent anomalies. The inclusion of cities or states, such as Albany or California, indicates that passengers calling themselves German nationals previously had emigrated from their homeland; settled in either Albany or California, for instance; returned to Germany; and then once more voyaged to the United States. Therefore, when asked their nationality they responded "German," but when asked to list their village the answer was "Albany."]

ABG	ALTENBURG		BUE	BUENOS AYRES		DES	DESPLAINES
ACC	APPLE CREEK		BUF	BUFFALO		DET	DETROIT
ADA	ADAMS		BUR	BURTON		DIX	DIXON
ADD	ADDISON		CA	CENTRAL AMERICA		DKK	DUNKIRK
ADR	ADRIAN		CAA	CANAAN		DMK	DENMARK
AGT	ARGENTINA		CAB	CANBY		DOR	DORCHESTER
AIO	ALBION		CAC	CANON CITY		DRE	DRESDEN
AKR	AKRON		CAE	CALEDONIA		DUB	DUBLIN
AL	ALABAMA		CAI	CAIRO		DYE	DYERSVILLE
ALB	ALBANY		CAL	CALIFORNIA		DYT	DAYTON
ALE	ALLEGHENY		CAM	CAMBRIDGE		EAU	EAU CLAIRE
ALI	ALLIANCE		CAN	CANADA		EB	ELIZABETH
ALL	ALLENTOWN		CAO	CAROLINA		EBT	ELIZABETHTOWN
ALP	ALPENA		CAR	CAMERON		EDG	EDGARTOWN
ALT	ALTOONA		CAS	CASSELTON		EDI	EDINA
ALX	ALEXANDRIA		CAT	CANTON		EI	EAST INDIES
AMS	AMSTERDAM		CBA	CUBA		ELD	ELDORADO
ANN	ANN ARBOR		CDE	CAMDEN		ELG	ELGIN
ANT	ATLANTIC		CEA	CEDAR FALLS		ELK	ELK RIVER
AOA	AURORA		CEB	CEDARBURG		ELL	ELLWOOD
APP	APPLETON		CED	CEDAR RAPIDS		ELP	EL PASO
AR	ARKANSAS		CEG	CEDAR GROVE		ELY	ELYRIA
ARM	ARMSTRONG		CEN	CENTRALIA		EMA	ELMIRA
ASH	ASHLAND		CER	CANTERBURY		EME	EMERSON
AST	ASTORIA		CGD	CAPE GIRARDEAU		EMP	EMPORIA
ATC	ATCHISON		CH	CHICAGO		EN	ENGLAND
ATK	ATKINSON		CHA	CHARLES CITY		ERE	ERIE
ATL	ATLANTA		CHE	CHESTER		ESC	ESCANABA
ATO	ALTON		CHI	CHILTON		EVA	EVANSVILLE
ATR	AUSTRALIA		CHL	CHILE		EXC	EXCELSIOR
ATT	ATTICA		CHN	CHINA		FAI	FAIRFIELD
AUB	AUBURN		CHO	CHEROKEE TOWN		FAL	FALMOUTH
AUG	AUGUSTA		CHR	CHARLESTON		FAS	FALLS CITY
AUS	AUSTRIA		CIA	CHRISTIAN		FDE	FREDONIA
AZ	ARIZONA		CIN	CINCINNATI		FDG	FORT DODGE
BAA	BATAVIA		CLA	CLARENDON		FKL	FRANKLIN GROVE
BAD	BADEN		CLE	CLEVELAND		FL	FLORIDA
BAL	BALTIMORE		CLF	CLEARFIELD		FOE	FOREST
BAR	BARCELONA		CLI	CLINTON		FOR	FORDHAM
BAT	BATTLE CREEK		CLN	CLINTONVILLE		FOT	FORT ATKINSON
BAV	BAVARIA		CLR	CLARKSVILLE		FR	FRANCE
BAW	BALDWIN		CME	CAMETA		FRA	FRANKFORT
BCK	BECKUM		CNN	CANNON		FRE	FREMONT
BEA	BEACONSFIELD		CO	COLORADO		FRK	FRANKLIN
BED	BEDFORD		COA	CORONA		FRO	FERNANDO
BEE	BELLE PLAINE		COC	COLCHESTER		FRP	FREEPORT
BEL	BELLEVILLE		COD	COLD WATER		FRS	FRESNO
BEM	BERMUDA		COE	CONNELLSVILLE		FRY	FRYEBURG
BEN	BENSENVILLE		COI	CORNING		FTL	FORT LANDING
BER	BEREA		COL	COLUMBIA		FTM	FORT MADISON
BET	BETHLEHEM		CON	CONCORD		FTP	FORT PLAIN
BEV	BELLEVUE		COO	COLON		FUL	FULTON
BGL	BURLINGTON		COR	CONCORDIA		FWY	FORT WAYNE
BGM	BELGIUM		COS	COSTA RICA		GA	GEORGIA
BIL	BILBAO		COT	CORINTH		GAI	GALICIA
BIS	BLUE ISLAND		COU	COLUMBUS		GAL	GALVESTON
BKL	BUNKER HILL		COV	COVINGTON		GAP	GALLIPOLIS
BLO	BLOOMINGTON		CPO	CITYPOINT		GBY	GREEN BAY
BLV	BELLVILLE		CRC	COSTA RICA		GEN	GENOA
BMG	BIRMINGHAM		CRE	CIRCLEVILLE		GES	GREEN ISLAND
BNG	BRANDENBURG		CRK	CROOKSTON		GFD	GREENFIELD
BO	BOSTON		CRM	CARMEL		GHV	GRAND HAVEN
BOI	BOLIVIA		CRO	CROWN POINT		GIR	GIRARD
BOL	BOLLINGTON		CRS	CHARLESTOWN		GLA	GALENA
BON	BOONEVILLE		CT	CONNECTICUT		GLO	GLOUCESTER
BOO	BLOOMFIELD		CUM	CUMBERLAND		GR	GERMANY
BRA	BRAZIL		CUR	CURACAO		GRA	GRAFTON
BRC	BRANCH		CVL	CHARLESVILLE		GRE	GREENWICH
BRD	BRIDGEPORT		DAD	DAVID CITY		GRL	GREEN LEE
BRE	BREMEN		DAK	DAKOTA		GRN	GRAND RAPIDS
BRH	BRENHAM		DAN	DANVILLE		GRS	GREENSBURG
BRI	BRISTOL		DAV	DAVENPORT		GRT	GREAT BRITAIN
BRL	BERLIN		DBQ	DUBUQUE		GTR	GERMANTOWN
BRN	BRANDON		DE	DELAWARE		GUA	GUAYAQUIL
BRO	BROOKLYN		DEE	DUNDEE		GUD	GUADELOUPE
BRT	BRITISH COLUMBIA		DEL	DELANO		GUE	GUATEMALA
BTL	BUTLER		DER	DERBY		GUT	GUTTENBERG

GVE	GREENVILLE	KNX	KNOXVILLE	MPS	MEMPHIS
HAA	HARLAN	KS	KANSAS	MRE	MONROE
HAI	HARRISON	KY	KENTUCKY	MRL	MONTREAL
HAK	HACKENSACK	LA	LOUISIANA	MRQ	MARQUETTE
HAL	HALIFAX	LAA	LACKAWANNA	MRR	MORRIS
HAM	HAMBURG	LAB	LABRADOR	MS	MISSISSIPPI
HAN	HENDERSON	LAC	LA CROSSE	MSN	MADISON
HAR	HARRISBURG	LAI	LANSING	MT	MONTANA
HAS	HASTINGS	LAM	LA MARZE	MTA	MANITOBA
HAT	HAMILTON	LAN	LANCASTER	MTC	MT. CARROLL
HAV	HAVRE	LAS	LA SALLE	MTO	MILTON
HAZ	HAZELTON	LAW	LAWRENCE	MTR	MONTROSE
HBI	HANNIBAL	LEA	LEAVENWORTH	MTS	MARTINSBURG
HBK	HOBOKEN	LEB	LEBANON	MTV	MT. VERNON
HDT	HERMANNSTADT	LEM	LEMONT	MUC	MUSCATINE
HEL	HELENA	LER	LE MARS	MUS	MUSKEGON
HES	HESSE	LEX	LEXINGTON	MVL	MELVILLE
HFT	HATFIELD	LGH	LONGHILL	MX	MEXICO
HIG	HIGHLAND	LIB	LIBERTY	NAN	NANCY
HII	HIGGINSVILLE	LIM	LIMA	NAS	NASHVILLE
HIN	HINSDALE	LIP	LIVERPOOL	NAT	NANTICOKE
HLU	HONOLULU	LIS	LONG ISLAND	NAU	NAUVOO
HMN	HARMON	LIT	LITTLE FALLS	NBG	NEWBURG
HMR	HOMER	LIV	LIVINGSTON	NBH	NEWBURGH
HMY	HARMONY	LOB	LOUISBURG	NBR	NEW BERLIN
HOA	HOWARD CITY	LOG	LOGANSPORT	NC	NORTH CAROLINA
HOD	HONDURAS	LON	LONDON	NCY	NEW CITY
HOG	HONG KONG	LOR	LORRAINE	ND	NORTH DAKOTA
HOL	HOLLAND	LOS	LOS ANGELES	NDF	NEW BEDFORD
HOM	HOMESTEAD	LOU	LOUISVILLE	NE	NEBRASKA
HON	HUNGARY	LOW	LOWELL	NEB	NEBRASKA CITY
HOU	HOUSTON	LPE	LA PORTE	NEF	NEWFOUNDLAND
HOW	HOWARD	LPR	LA PRAIRIE	NEH	NEW HAMPTON
HRL	HARLEM	LRT	LITTLE ROCK	NEL	NELSONVILLE
HRW	HAVERSTRAW	LUX	LUXEMBURG	NEW	NEW LEXINGTON
HTD	HARTFORD	LWG	LAWRENCEBURG	NEZ	NATCHEZ
HTI	HAITI	LYE	LAFAYETTE	NFA	NIAGARA FALLS
HTO	HAMPTON	LYO	LYON	NFF	NEW BUFFALO
HTT	HUNTINGTON	MA	MASSACHUSETTS	NFK	NORFOLK
HUD	HUDSON	MAA	MAYAGUEZ	NFL	NEW BRAUNFELS
HUM	HUMBOLDT	MAD	MADELIA	NGD	NEW GRANADA
HUR	HURON	MAE	MANISTEE	NH	NEW HAMPSHIRE
HVA	HAVANA	MAG	MARENGO	NHB	NEW HAMBURG
HVR	HANNOVER	MAH	MARSHFIELD	NJ	NEW JERSEY
IA	IOWA	MAI	MASSILLON	NLB	NEW ALBANY
ICE	ICELAND	MAN	MANCHESTER	NLO	NEW LONDON
ID	IDAHO	MAR	MARION	NM	NEW MEXICO
IL	ILLINOIS	MAS	MANSFIELD	NME	NEW BREMEN
IN	INDIANA	MAT	MATAMOROS	NO	NEW ORLEANS
INA	INDIA	MAY	MARYSVILLE	NOL	NEW HOLSTEIN
IND	INDIANAPOLIS	MCK	MC KEESPORT	NOO	NORWOOD
INE	INDEPENDENCE	MCL	MT. CARMEL	NOR	NORTHWOOD
IRE	IRELAND	MD	MARYLAND	NOT	NOTRE DAME
IVH	IVANHOE	ME	MAINE	NOV	NOVA SCOTIA
JAE	JASPER	MEA	MEADVILLE	NOW	NORWALK
JAI	JAMAICA	MEC	MECKLENBURG	NPO	NAPOLEON
JAK	JACKSONVILLE	MEL	MELLEN	NPT	NEWPORT
JAM	JAMESTOWN	MEN	MENDOTA	NRD	NEW MADRID
JAP	JAPAN	MEO	MENOMINEE	NRW	NORWICH
JAS	JASONVILLE	MER	MERIDIAN	NSS	NASSAU
JDA	JORDAN	MET	METROPOLIS	NST	NEW AMSTERDAM
JEF	JEFFERSON	MI	MICHIGAN	NUE	NEUSTADT
JER	JERSEY	MID	MIDDLETOWN	NUL	NEW ULM
JKS	JACKSON	MIL	MILWAUKEE	NUV	NEUVILLE
JOH	JOHNSTON	MIN	MINNEAPOLIS	NV	NEVADA
JON	JOHNSTOWN	MIQ	MIQUELON	NVE	NEW HAVEN
JRV	JERSEYVILLE	MIT	MITCHELL	NW	NEWARK
JSB	JAMESBURG	MLL	MARSCHALLTOWN	NWK	NEW BRUNSWICK
JUN	JUNCTION CITY	MN	MINNESOTA	NWY	NORWAY
KAL	KALAMAZOO	MO	MISSOURI	NY	NEW YORK
KAN	KANKAKEE	MOB	MOBILE	NZL	NEW ZEALAND
KAS	KANSAS CITY	MOI	MONTICELLO	OAK	OAK HARBOR
KEL	KELLOGG	MOL	MOLINE	ODE	ODESSA
KEN	KENSINGTON	MON	MONTCLAIR	OH	OHIO
KEO	KENOSHA	MOO	MONROEVILLE	OIL	OIL CITY
KEW	KEWANEE	MOR	MORRILTON	OLD	OLDENBURG
KIN	KINGSTON	MOT	MONTGOMERY	OLY	OLNY

Code	Destination	Code	Destination	Code	Destination
OMA	OMAHA	SAJ	SAN JOSE	TRE	TRENTON
ONE	ONEIDA	SAL	SALISBURY	TRI	TRINIDAD
OR	OREGON	SAM	SALAMANCA	TRN	TURNER
ORA	ORANGE CITY	SAN	SANDUSKY	TRY	TROY
ORG	ORANGE	SAO	SANTO DOMINGO	TWD	TONAWANDA
ORO	OROVILLE	SAR	SARATOGA	TX	TEXAS
OSC	OSCEOLA	SAS	SAN SALVADOR	UNK	UNKNOWN
OSH	OSHKOSH	SAT	SAN ANTONIO	UON	UNION
OSS	OSSINING	SAU	SAUK RAPIDS	UPC	UPPER CANADA
OSW	OSWEGO	SAV	SAVANNAH	URB	URBANA
OTT	OTTAWA	SAX	SAXONY	USA	UNITED STATES
OWS	OWENS	SBG	SHEBOYGAN	USY	UPPER SANDUSKY
OXF	OXFORD	SC	SOUTH CAROLINA	UT	UTICA
PA	PENNSYLVANIA	SCH	SCHENECTADY	VA	VIRGINIA
PAL	PALMYRA	SCR	SCRANTON	VAC	VERACRUZ
PAN	PANAMA	SCT	SCOTLAND	VAN	VAN WERT
PAR	PARIS	SCU	SCHULENBURG	VCK	VICKSBURG
PAT	PATERSON	SDH	SANDWICH ISLAND	VLP	VALPARAISO
PE	PERU	SED	SEDGWICK	VMT	VERMONT
PEE	PETERBOROUGH	SEG	SEGUIN	VUL	VULCAN
PEM	PEMBROKE	SFC	SAN FRANCISCO	VZU	VENEZUELA
PEO	PEORIA	SFE	SANTA FE	WAB	WABASH
PER	PERTH AMBOY	SGN	SOUTHINGTON	WAC	WASECA
PET	PETERSBURG	SHA	SHANGHAI	WAE	WATERTOWN
PHI	PHILADELPHIA	SHE	SHEBOYGAN FALLS	WAL	WALNUT
PIT	PITTSBURGH	SHH	SOUTHAMPTON	WAR	WARSAW
PJV	PORT JERVIS	SHL	SHELDON	WAS	WASHINGTON
PKE	POUGHKEEPSIE	SHM	SHAMOKIN	WAT	WATERLOO
PLA	PLATTSMOUTH	SHN	SHENANDOAH	WBK	WESTBROOK
PLR	PALMER	SHR	SHERBORNE	WDC	WASHINGTON D.C.
PLT	PLATTEVILLE	SID	SIDNEY	WDV	WOODVILLE
PLY	PLYMOUTH	SIO	SIOUX CITY	WEB	WEBSTER
PMT	PYRMONT	SIS	STATEN ISLAND	WEF	WESTFIELD
POE	POTTER	SLG	STERLING	WEI	WELLINGTON
POM	POMERANIA	SOT	SOUTH AMERICA	WES	WESTERLY
POR	PORTUGAL	SOU	SOUTH BEND	WET	WEST NEWTON
POS	POTTSTOWN	SP	ST. PAUL	WFD	WATERFORD
POT	POTTSVILLE	SPA	SPARTA	WGT	WILLINGTON
PRI	PRINCETON	SPI	SPAIN	WHE	WHEELING
PRU	PRUSSIA	SPP	ST. PIERRE	WI	WISCONSIN
PSN	PATTERSON	SPR	SPRINGFIELD	WIK	WILKES BARRE
PTL	PORTLAND	SRB	SHARPSBURG	WIL	WILLIAMSBURG
PTS	PORTSMOUTH	SRE	SACRAMENTO	WIM	WILMINGTON
PTT	PITTSFIELD	SRY	ST. MARY	WIN	WINDSOR
PTW	PORT WASHINGTON	SSB	STRASBOURG	WIO	WINONA
PUE	PUERTO RICO	STA	ST. LAURENT	WIT	WILMINGTON
PUR	PORT HURON	STC	ST. CHARLES	WOD	WOODLAND
PVD	PROVIDENCE	STE	STERLING	WOH	WOODHAVEN
PVX	PHOENIXVILLE	STF	STRATFORD	WOO	WOODSTOCK
QBC	QUEBEC	STG	ST. PIERRE MIQUELON	WOS	WOOSTER
QUI	QUINCY	STI	STILLWATER	WPA	WESTPHALIA
RAC	RACINE	STJ	ST. JOSEPH	WPT	WEST POINT
RAD	RADOM	STL	ST. LOUIS	WRR	WATERBURY
RAY	RAYMOND	STO	ST. CLOUD	WRT	WUERTEMBERG
RBI	RUBICON	STP	ST. PETER	WTM	WESTMINSTER
RCI	ROCK ISLAND	STR	STREATOR	WTP	WESTPORT
RDE	RIO DE JANEIRO	STU	STURGIS	WV	WEST VIRGINIA
RDG	READING	STV	STEVENS POINT	WY	WYOMING
RDT	RONDOUT	STW	STONEWALL	WYA	WYANDOTTE
REP	REPUBLIC	STZ	SCHWEIDNITZ	WYC	WYCKOFF
REY	REYNOLDSVILLE	SVT	ST. VINCENT	YAN	YANKTON
RI	RHODE ISLAND	SW	SWITZERLAND	YOK	YOKOHAMA
RIC	RICHMOND	SWD	SWEDEN	YOR	YORKVILLE
RIP	RIPON	SY	SYRACUSE	YOU	YOUNGSTOWN
RKV	ROCKVILLE	SYL	SCHUYLER	ZAN	ZANESVILLE
RME	ROME	TAH	TAHITI	***	DIED ON BOARD
ROC	ROCHESTER	TAY	TARRYTOWN		
ROK	ROCKAWAY	TFF	TIFFIN		
ROS	ROSEVILLE	THO	THOMASTON		
RSS	RUSSIA	THT	TERRE HAUTE		
RUS	RUSH	THU	THURINGIA		
SAA	SAARLOUIS	TKY	TURKEY		
SAC	ST. CLAIR	TN	TENNESSEE		
SAD	SANDWICH	TOL	TOLEDO		
SAE	SALEM	TOP	TOPEKA		
SAG	SAGINAW	TOR	TORONTO		
SAI	SALINAS	TRA	TRAVERSE CITY		

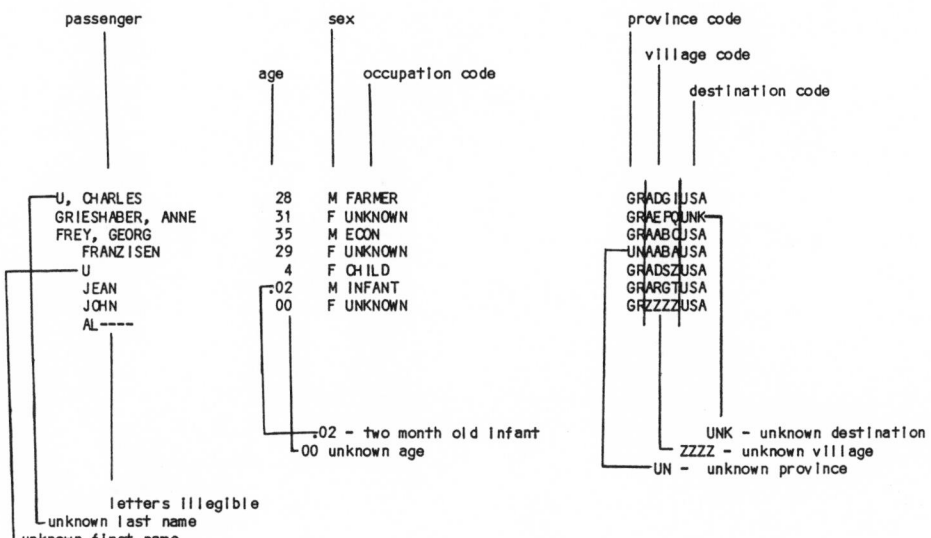

* Information in the above fields is as it appears in the document. For this reason, information on the provinces and villages can often be the same. Information on occupation may also include data on personal status.

PASSENGER	AGE	SEX	OCCUPATION	PRVVL	DES
SHIP: BRAUNSCHWEIG					
FROM: BREMEN					
TO: BALTIMORE					
ARRIVED: 01 MAY 1888					
CZARNEKI, WOJCIECH	49	M	LABR		GRZZZZBAL
MARIANNA	47	F	W		GRZZZZBAL
U	15	M	S		GRZZZZBAL
WOJCIECH	00	M	CH		GRZZZZBAL
JOSEF	6	M	CHILD		GRZZZZBAL
KUEGER, JOHANN	28	M	LABR		GRZZZZMD
JOHANNA	29	F	W		GRZZZZMD
BUMASZEK, JACOB	22	M	LABR		GRZZZZMD
LEMAN, JOSEF	54	M	LABR		GRZZZZMD
ANNA	54	F	W		GRZZZZMD
BARBARA	22	F	D		GRZZZZMD
AUGUST	18	M	S		GRZZZZMD
BERUHEND	11	M	S		GRZZZZMD
TUCHOWSKA, ANTONIA	33	F	UNKNOWN		GRZZZZMD
PELAGINA	5	F	CHILD		GRZZZZMD
JOKAKIUS	3	M	CHILD		GRZZZZMD
SOPHIE	.11	F	INFANT		GRZZZZMD
SCHULTZ, EMIL	16	M	LABR		GRZZZZMD
HENRY	14	M	LABR		GRZZZZMD
WESTPHAL, LUDOWIKA	19	F	UNKNOWN		GRZZZZMD
FAUST, AUGUST	33	M	LABR		GRZZZZMD
CHARLOTTE	30	F	W		GRZZZZMD
BERTHA	19	F	D		GRZZZZMD
RAUPECKE, AUGUSTE	14	F	UNKNOWN		GRZZZZMD
JAUSH, CARL	9	M	CHILD		GRZZZZMD
AUGUSTE	7	F	CHILD		GRZZZZMD
GUSTAV	4	M	CHILD		GRZZZZMD
AUGUST	.03	M	INFANT		GRZZZZMD
MISZKOWSKA, JULIANA	25	F	SVNT		GRZZZZMD
BLASZACK, WOIJCIEH	24	M	LABR		GRZZZZMD
RYBUCKA, MICHAELINA	17	F	SVNT		GRZZZZMD
WICZKI, THEKLA	50	F	UNKNOWN		GRZZZZMD
STACHOWIAK, FRANZ	24	M	LABR		GRZZZZMD
HELLWIG	21	F	SVNT		GRZZZZMD
LADZICK, PAULINE	20	F	SVNT		GRZZZZMD
KRAUSE, MARIANNA	25	F	UNKNOWN		GRZZZZMD
JOS.	3	F	CHILD		GRZZZZMD
FRANZ	.03	M	INFANT		GRZZZZMD
WASILEWSKI, ADAM	29	M	LABR		GRZZZZMD
LEPKOWSKI, WOIJCE-	24	M	LABR		GRZZZZMD
WUTSHIK, JOSEF	28	M	LABR		GRZZZZMD
TAFELSKI, JOHANN	29	M	LABR		GRZZZZMD
FEDERAN, FRANZ	31	M	LABR		GRZZZZMD
AUGUSTE	31	F	W		GRZZZZMD
BERTHA	4	F	CHILD		GRZZZZMD
OTTO	.11	M	INFANT		GRZZZZMD
ZILINSKI, ANDRZY	62	M	LABR		GRZZZZMD
ANTONIA	60	F	W		GRZZZZMD
FRANZISKA	20	F	D		GRZZZZMD
GRABOWSKI, ANTON	25	M	LABR		GRZZZZMD
ANGELIKA	18	F	SVNT		GRZZZZMD
SYKUCZYNSKI, ADAM	42	M	LABR		GRZZZZMD
WENDT, JACOB	33	M	LABR		GRZZZZMD
ANNA	37	F	W		GRZZZZMD
MARIA	4	F	CHILD		GRZZZZMD
PAUL	2	M	CHILD		GRZZZZMD
FRANZ	.08	M	INFANT		GRZZZZMD
CIMANOWSKI, MARIA	76	F	Y		GRZZZZMD
JENDRYEWSKI, VALENTIN	50	M	LABR		GRZZZZMD
ROSALIE	50	F	W		GRZZZZMD
MARIANNE	22	F	D		GRZZZZMD
JOSEFA	2	F	CHILD		GRZZZZMD
STANISLAW	.06	M	INFANT		GRZZZZMD
JOSEF	4	M	CHILD		GRZZZZMD
MULLER, JULIUS	40	M	LABR		GRZZZZMD
ROSALIE	40	F	W		GRZZZZMD
ANTONIE	6	F	CHILD		GRZZZZMD
SCHELTMANN, MARYANNA	66	F	UNKNOWN		GRZZZZMD
AMRIA	18	F	D		GRZZZZMD
NEUMANN, MARIA	18	F	SVNT		GRZZZZMD
ROSALIE	17	F	SVNT		GRZZZZMD
NAEFE, FRIEDRICH	18	M	LABR		GRZZZZMD
AUGUSTE	16	F	SVNT		GRZZZZMD
JULIUS	17	M	LABR		GRZZZZMD
ALBERTZKI, FERDINAND	24	M	LABR		GRZZZZMD
ZITTE, HENRICH	16	M	LABR		GRZZZZMD
GEHLE, ERST.	17	M	LABR		GRZZZZMD
ZADANOWSKI, ANDREAS	22	M	LABR		GRZZZZMD
QUNSNEY, ALEXANDER	37	M	LABR		GRZZZZMD
PAULINE	33	F	W		GRZZZZMD
EMMA	11	F	CH		GRZZZZMD
HERMANN	9	M	CHILD		GRZZZZMD
EMIL	8	M	CHILD		GRZZZZMD
MAX	4	M	CHILD		GRZZZZMD
ROBERT	2	M	CHILD		GRZZZZMD
AUGUST	.11	M	INFANT		GRZZZZMD
SAHNKE, GOTTLIEBE	57	F	UNKNOWN		GRZZZZMD
ELISE	21	F	D		GRZZZZMD
AUGUST	.09	M	INFANT		GRZZZZMD
BROOGE, AUGUST	32	M	LABR		GRZZZZMD
JOHANNA	23	F	W		GRZZZZMD
HERMANN	.11	M	INFANT		GRZZZZMD
FISCHER, JULIUS	45	M	LABR		GRZZZZMD
EMILIE	30	F	W		GRZZZZMD
BERTHA	11	F	CH		GRZZZZMD
PAUL	9	M	CHILD		GRZZZZMD
WILHELM	3	M	CHILD		GRZZZZMD
ANNA	1	F	CHILD		GRZZZZMD
ZESCHKE, U	18	F	SVNT		GRZZZZMD
ZKAJADA, U	65	M	LABR		GRZZZZMD
U	60	F	W		GRZZZZMD
FRANZ	17	M	S		GRZZZZMD
KLIMPERT, JOHANNA	20	F	UNKNOWN		GRZZZZMD
JOSEF	1	M	CHILD		GRZZZZMD
ROGANSKI, JACOB	45	M	LABR		GRZZZZMD
MARIA	44	F	W		GRZZZZMD
ROSA	20	F	D		GRZZZZMD
MARIA	12	F	CH		GRZZZZMD
CECIL	9	M	CHILD		GRZZZZMD
JULIANNA	7	F	CHILD		GRZZZZMD
FRANZ	8	M	CHILD		GRZZZZMD
HELENE	.04	F	INFANT		GRZZZZMD
GORDON, APOLLONIA	27	F	SVNT		GRZZZZMD
MICHAELINA	18	F	SVNT		GRZZZZMD
CEZAP, LEON	30	M	LABR		GRZZZZMD
MARIANNA	30	F	W		GRZZZZMD
JACOB	4	M	CHILD		GRZZZZMD
THOMAS	3	M	CHILD		GRZZZZMD
ANTONIA	.09	F	INFANT		GRZZZZMD
GENDICHAN, HENRIETTE	17	F	SVNT		GRZZZZMD
ROESKE, CAROLINE	53	F	UNKNOWN		GRZZZZMD
MATHILDE	10	F	CH		GRZZZZMD
HEIDKE, BERTHA	27	F	UNKNOWN		GRZZZZMD
U	2	F	CHILD		GRZZZZMD
POGES, U	43	F	UNKNOWN		GRZZZZMD
U	00	F	D		GRZZZZMD
U	10	M	S		GRZZZZMD
ANASY, U	32	M	LABR		GRZZZZMD
LIZENSKI, JOHANN	30	M	LABR		GRZZZZMD
JOHANN	27	M	LABR		GRZZZZMD
DREWS, WILHELM	21	M	LABR		GRZZZZMD
URLANB, JOHANA	24	F	SVNT		GRZZZZMD
AUGUST	32	M	LABR		GRZZZZMD
RICHARD	15	M	LABR		GRZZZZMD
JOHANNA	61	F	M		GRZZZZMD
LUCK, BERTHA	17	F	SVNT		GRZZZZMD
VANDERSEE, CARL	28	M	LABR		GRZZZZMD
REIMER, CHRISTIAN	29	M	LABR		GRZZZZMD
CAROLINE	27	F	W		GRZZZZMD
ELSA	3	F	CHILD		GRZZZZMD
LOUISE	1	F	CHILD		GRZZZZMD
RATAEZAK, FRANZICECK	22	M	LABR		GRZZZZMD
KEESKI, MICHAEL	28	M	LABR		GRZZZZMD

PASSENGER	AGE	SEX	OCCUPATION	PRVL	DES
MARIANNA	20	F	W		GRZZZZMD
LEWANDOWSKA, ANNA	29	F	SVNT		GRZZZZMD
GRZELAK, MARIANNA	24	F	W		GRZZZZMD
JOSEF	28	M	LABR		GRZZZZMD
FRANCISCA	50	F	M		GRZZZZMD
VICTORIA	4	F	CHILD		GRZZZZMD
FRANCISCA	2	F	CHILD		GRZZZZMD
STANISLAWA	.08	F	INFANT		GRZZZZMD
JAMUZECKI, KATARZYNA	19	F	SVNT		GRZZZZMD
KOLINSKI, BERNARD	24	M	LABR		GRZZZZMD
BLUME, ANNA	14	F	SVNT		GRZZZZMD
SCHMIDT, ANTON	28	M	LABR		GRZZZZMD
AUGUSTE	23	F	W		GRZZZZMD
PAUL	.11	M	INFANT		GRZZZZMD
PIASKOWSKI, VICTOR	27	M	LABR		GRZZZZMD
BERTHA	22	F	W		GRZZZZMD
U, U	00	M	LABR		GRZZZZMD
--LSCHEWITZ, U	00	F	SVNT		GRZZZZMD
STANGE, FRANZ	50	M	LABR		GRZZZZMD
BULCHEWITZ, LEOCADIA	4	F	CHILD		GRZZZZMD
ANTONIA	3	F	CHILD		GRZZZZMD
FRANCISCA	2	F	CHILD		GRZZZZMD
MARIA	.10	F	INFANT		GRZZZZMD
BAROWIAK, JACOB	37	M	LABR		GRZZZZMD
MARIANNA	33	F	W		GRZZZZMD
JOSEF	9	M	CHILD		GRZZZZMD
STANILSAUS	7	M	CHILD		GRZZZZMD
GEORG	3	M	CHILD		GRZZZZMD
AGNES	.11	F	INFANT		GRZZZZMD
KUPTZ, JOSEF	25	M	LABR		GRZZZZMD
WOLFF, IGNAZ	36	M	LABR		GRZZZZMD
BARBARA	35	F	W		GRZZZZMD
STASEK, AUGUSTA	17	F	SVNT		GRZZZZBAL
CZEMSKI, FRANZISKA	60	F	M		GRZZZZBAL
BARBARA	35	F	D		GRZZZZBAL
STERN, CARL	23	M	LABR		GRZZZZBAL
SCHUMACHER, IDA	16	F	SVNT		GRZZZZBAL
LINMANN, HEINRICH	25	M	LABR		GRZZZZBAL
ZIPPEL, WILHELM	26	M	LABR		GRZZZZBAL
WIEMUND, SIMON	26	M	LABR		GRZZZZBAL
CZOLBE, MICHAIL	39	M	LABR		GRZZZZBAL
LAURA	21	F	W		GRZZZZBAL
EMMA	.06	F	INFANT		GRZZZZBAL
SCHMIDT, U	60	F	UNKNOWN		GRZZZZBAL
U	00	F	UNKNOWN		GRZZZZBAL
AN.	25	F	UNKNOWN		GRZZZZBAL
HEDWIG	10	F	CH		GRZZZZBAL
ANNA	8	F	CHILD		GRZZZZBAL
WALCZEK, MARTIN	34	M	LABR		GRZZZZBAL
PIVEH, FERDINAND	25	M	LABR		GRZZZZBAL
JOHANNE	29	F	W		GRZZZZBAL
SELMA	.03	F	INFANT		GRZZZZBAL
REICH, ANNA	35	F	SVNT		GRZZZZBAL
KUBIAK, ANDREUS	21	M	LABR		GRZZZZBAL
TRAPP, EMIL	17	M	LABR		GRZZZZBAL
GIRONDY, HENRICH	42	M	LABR		GRZZZZMD
PAULINE	39	F	W		GRZZZZMD
HELENE	19	F	D		GRZZZZMD
ANTOINE	10	F	CH		GRZZZZMD
EMMA	7	F	CHILD		GRZZZZMD
FRITZ	4	M	CHILD		GRZZZZMD
EILHELM	.04	M	INFANT		GRZZZZMD
FALEK, AUGUST	38	M	LABR		GRZZZZMD
BERTHA	38	F	W		GRZZZZMD
WILHELM	11	M	CH		GRZZZZMD
MARTHA	5	F	CHILD		GRZZZZMD
MARIA	.09	F	INFANT		GRZZZZMD
STAMEMANN, MINNA	61	F	M		GRZZZZMD
SZCZESNY, BARTHOLOMEN	47	M	LABR		GRZZZZMD
HEDWIG	48	F	W		GRZZZZMD
THOMAS	11	M	CH		GRZZZZMD
CATHARINA	7	F	CHILD		GRZZZZMD
MICHAEL	4	M	CHILD		GRZZZZMD
PALENTIA	4	F	CHILD		GRZZZZMD
BOENKE, CARL	51	M	LABR		GRZZZZMD
WILHELM	22	M	LABR		GRZZZZMD
SEMANUKOSKA, ANASTASIA	20	F	SVNT		GRZZZZMD
SOWA, JOHANN	32	M	LABR		GRZZZZMD
CZIZEWSKI, U	17	M	LABR		GRZZZZMD
MOSCHEK, U	24	M	LABR		GRZZZZMD
MODOZENSKI, FRANZISKA	20	F	SVNT		GRZZZZMD
JULIANNA	17	F	SVNT		GRZZZZMD
KORNOWSKI, JOSEF	25	M	LABR		GRZZZZMD
KATHARINE	30	F	W		GRZZZZMD
JACHEWSKI, ANTON	33	M	LABR		GRZZZZMD
HERZOG, AUGUSTE	18	F	SVNT		GRZZZZMD
LOWA, FRIEDERIKE	23	F	UNKNOWN		GRZZZZMD
FREDERICH	3	M	CHILD		GRZZZZMD
AUGUST	.06	M	INFANT		GRZZZZMD
GRAEZIK, JOHANN	33	M	LABR		GRZZZZMD
GOTTLIEBE	26	F	W		GRZZZZMD
FRIEDRICH	2	M	CHILD		GRZZZZMD
ANNA	.09	F	INFANT		GRZZZZMD
OMNITZ, CARL	16	M	LABR		GRZZZZMD
KUKOWSKY, GUSTAV	35	M	LABR		GRZZZZOH
SCHWEDA, MARTIN	25	M	LABR		GRZZZZOH
JOSEF	33	M	LABR		GRZZZZOH
KUNME, AUGUST	45	M	LABR		GRZZZZOH
AUGUSTA	36	F	W		GRZZZZOH
BERTHA	13	F	CH		GRZZZZOH
WILHELM	10	M	CH		GRZZZZOH
CARL	8	M	CHILD		GRZZZZOH
MINNA	3	F	CHILD		GRZZZZOH
RUTZEN, EMILIE	25	F	SVNT		GRZZZZOH
UNTERBERGER, DAVID	37	M	LABR		GRZZZZOH
WANZEWIEZ, ALEXANA	24	F	SVNT		GRZZZZOH
STRZYZESKI, U	16	F	SVNT		GRZZZZOH
DERNIG, FRANZ	51	M	LABR		GRZZZZOH
FRANZISKA	51	F	W		GRZZZZOH
FRANZ	27	M	S		GRZZZZOH
RUDOLF	8	M	CHILD		GRZZZZOH
BERNHARD	6	M	CHILD		GRZZZZOH
BUSSE, MATHILDE	17	F	SVNT		GRZZZZOH
CZAMOWSKY, HERMINE	22	F	SVNT		GRZZZZOH
GRUHN, ADOLF	62	M	LABR		GRZZZZOH
LOUISE	57	F	W		GRZZZZOH
BRATKOWSKY, JOSEF	44	M	LABR		GRZZZZOH
MARIE	41	F	W		GRZZZZOH
JULIANNE	16	F	D		GRZZZZOH
PAULINE	4	F	CHILD		GRZZZZOH
AGNES	3	F	CHILD		GRZZZZOH
LEO	.09	M	INFANT		GRZZZZOH
VOSS, BERNHARD	31	M	LABR		GRZZZZOH
U	29	F	W		GRZZZZOH
U	6	M	CHILD		GRZZZZOH
MARTHA	.04	F	INFANT		GRZZZZOH
PODGURSKA, EMMA	22	F	SVNT		GRZZZZOH
JUGANG, MAX	30	M	LABR		GRZZZZOH
HALMANN, AUGUST	24	M	LABR		GRZZZZOH
ZINKEL, JOHANN	26	M	LABR		GRZZZZOH
FRANZISKA	23	F	W		GRZZZZOH
AUGUSTE	4	F	CHILD		GRZZZZOH
JULIUS	3	M	CHILD		GRZZZZOH
MARIE	1	F	CHILD		GRZZZZOH
BARUCKI, JOSEF	23	M	LABR		GRZZZZOH
LONNENBERG, AUGST	30	M	LABR		GRZZZZOH
BRACKREMIE	26	F	W		GRZZZZOH
MARIANNA	.03	F	INFANT		GRZZZZOH
WEGENER, EDUARD	23	M	LABR		GRZZZZOH
EMIL	16	M	LABR		GRZZZZOH
JOHAM.	33	M	LABR		GRZZZZOH
ROSINE	39	F	W		GRZZZZOH
BLADZIK, MARTIN	56	M	LABR		GRZZZZOH
MARIANNA	51	F	W		GRZZZZOH
MARIANNA	17	F	D		GRZZZZOH
JOSEF	14	M	S		GRZZZZOH
MARTIN	10	M	CH		GRZZZZOH
JOSEFA	8	F	CHILD		GRZZZZOH
SCHULZ, FLORA	31	F	UNKNOWN		GRZZZZOH
MARIE	6	F	CHILD		GRZZZZOH

PASSENGER	AGE	SEX	OCCUPATION	PRVL	DES
HELENE	4	F	CHILD		GRZZZZOH
REINHARD	2	M	CHILD		GRZZZZOH
CZARNEZKA, MAIRA	21	F	SVNT		GRZZZZOH
SOLORZGINSKI, MARIANNA	50	F	UNKNOWN		GRZZZZOH
MICHALINA	17	F	D		GRZZZZOH
KODAYSKI, VICENT	77	M	UNKNOWN		GRZZZZOH
KATHARINA	67	F	W		GRZZZZOH
DOOR, FRNZISKA	46	F	D		GRZZZZOH
ELISABETH	39	F	D		GRZZZZOH
JZAEPSKI, JOHANN	32	M	LABR		GRZZZZOH
MICHELINA	22	F	W		GRZZZZOH
STANISLAUS	.11	M	INFANT		GRZZZZOH
CZENNEKA, VALENTINE	21	F	SVNT		GRZZZZOH
WITUCKI, WOJCIECH	36	M	LABR		GRZZZZOH
CATHARINA	29	F	W		GRZZZZOH
VICENTINE	.03	F	INFANT		GRZZZZOH
DACLUNZ, HENRIETTE	53	F	UNKNOWN		GRZZZZBAL
U	26	F	D		GRZZZZBAL
SELLIN, AUGUST	55	M	LABR		GRZZZZBAL
AUGUSTE	56	F	W		GRZZZZBAL
HERMANN	20	M	S		GRZZZZBAL
CARL	18	M	S		GRZZZZBAL
BERTHA	16	F	D		GRZZZZBAL
RADLOFF, GUSTAV	34	M	LABR		GRZZZZBAL
MARIA	28	F	W		GRZZZZBAL
ANNA	6	F	CHILD		GRZZZZBAL
MARTHA	4	F	CHILD		GRZZZZBAL
MARIA	3	F	CHILD		GRZZZZBAL
CARL	.11	M	INFANT		GRZZZZBAL
BISCHOFF, WILHELM	69	M	FARMER		GRZZZZMD
FREDRICKE	59	F	W		GRZZZZMD
AUGUSTE	24	F	D		GRZZZZMD
LANGE, HERMANN	20	M	LABR		GRZZZZMD
HOLPPNER, JOHANN	49	M	FARMER		GRZZZZMD
U	47	F	W		GRZZZZMD
U	17	M	S		GRZZZZMD
BERTHA	15	F	D		GRZZZZMD
THEODOR	11	M	CH		GRZZZZMD
ALBERT	8	M	CHILD		GRZZZZMD
MARIE	5	F	CHILD		GRZZZZMD
WILHELM	3	M	CHILD		GRZZZZMD
ROBERT	.11	M	INFANT		GRZZZZMD
SCHLEGER, WILHELM	42	M	LABR		GRZZZZOH
FRANZISKA	37	F	W		GRZZZZOH
HENRICH	11	M	CH		GRZZZZOH
FREDERICH	10	M	CH		GRZZZZOH
MARIE	9	F	CHILD		GRZZZZOH
LOUISE	4	F	CHILD		GRZZZZOH
MELCHERT, BERTHA	38	F	UNKNOWN		GRZZZZOH
ANNA	15	F	D		GRZZZZOH
BERTHA	8	F	CHILD		GRZZZZOH
U	6	M	CHILD		GRZZZZOH
MARIE	3	F	CHILD		GRZZZZOH
PIVEH, HULDA	26	F	UNKNOWN		GRZZZZOH
BERTHA	9	F	CHILD		GRZZZZOH
SIWERT, MINNA	21	F	SVNT		GRZZZZBAL
DRZESDOW, FRANZISKA	16	F	SVNT		GRZZZZBAL
ANARYWSKI, IGNAZ	27	M	LABR		GRZZZZBAL
ROHRSDORFF, FRITZ	14	M	LABR		GRZZZZBAL
ANDREE, ALBERT	15	M	LABR		GRZZZZBAL
ATUFF, MANE	20	F	SVNT		GRZZZZBAL
KOCH, JULIA	25	F	SVNT		GRZZZZBAL
MASCHKE, WILHELM	48	M	LABR		GRZZZZOH
CAROLINE	49	F	W		GRZZZZOH
BERTHA	23	F	D		GRZZZZOH
MINNA	15	F	D		GRZZZZOH
GRABUREK, ANTON	32	M	LABR		GRZZZZOH
KAMINSKA, ANNA	63	F	UNKNOWN		GRZZZZOH
NYBACH, JOSEF	17	M	BKR		GRZZZZOH
HOPPE, AUGUST	28	M	LABR		GRZZZZOH
MATHILDE	24	F	W		GRZZZZOH
ANNA	6	F	CHILD		GRZZZZOH
MARTHA	5	F	CHILD		GRZZZZOH
MARHARETHA	3	F	CHILD		GRZZZZOH
PAUL	.10	M	INFANT		GRZZZZOH
HAPKE, GOTTLIEB	50	M	LABR		GRZZZZOH
TESSMANN, IDA	23	F	SVNT		GRZZZZOH
NEMITZ, REINHARD	16	M	BCHR		GRZZZZOH
MARG, FREDERICH	54	M	LABR		GRZZZZOH
HENRIETTE	57	F	W		GRZZZZOH
U	25	F	D		GRZZZZOH
HULDA	2	F	CHILD		GRZZZZOH
ELSKE, CARL	30	M	LABR		GRZZZZOH
BRUNKE, ERNESTINE	19	F	SVNT		GRZZZZOH
RINGER, ANTON	29	M	LABR		GRZZZZOH
AMALIE	27	F	W		GRZZZZOH
ANNA	5	F	CHILD		GRZZZZOH
OTTO	5	M	CHILD		GRZZZZOH
MINNA	3	F	CHILD		GRZZZZOH
AUGUSTE	.07	F	INFANT		GRZZZZOH
KARKOWSKI, AUGUST	23	M	LABR		GRZZZZOH
KOLASINSKI, JOHANN	52	M	LABR		GRZZZZOH
MARYANNA	40	F	W		GRZZZZOH
MICHAEL	15	M	S		GRZZZZOH
JOSEF	8	M	CHILD		GRZZZZOH
U	75	F	Y		GRZZZZOH
CZAPSKA, U	50	F	UNKNOWN		GRZZZZOH
BONEZKOWSKI, JOSEF	38	M	LABR		GRZZZZOH
JOSEFA	36	F	W		GRZZZZOH
ANDREUS	11	M	CH		GRZZZZOH
STANISLAWA	5	F	CHILD		GRZZZZOH
FRANZ	4	M	CHILD		GRZZZZOH
REDEMANN, GUSTAV	31	M	LABR		GRZZZZOH
BERTHA	30	F	W		GRZZZZOH
ZBYTOSKI, MICHAEL	47	M	LABR		GRZZZZOH
FRANZISKA	44	F	W		GRZZZZOH
WENDORF, AUGUST	23	M	TLR		GRZZZZBAL
ERNESTINE	22	F	W		GRZZZZBAL
MARTHA	3	F	CHILD		GRZZZZBAL
LUDSKE, JOHANN	39	M	FARMER		GRZZZZBAL
WILHELMINA	40	F	W		GRZZZZBAL
HERMANN	11	M	CH		GRZZZZBAL
OTTO	8	M	CHILD		GRZZZZBAL
BERTHA	6	F	CHILD		GRZZZZBAL
AUGUST	14	M	S		GRZZZZBAL
ZIRBEL, JOHANN	17	M	LABR		GRZZZZBAL
BERGMANN, EMILIE	22	F	SVNT		GRZZZZBAL
MELHNKE, JOHANN	40	M	LABR		GRZZZZOH
DIRDA, MICHAEL	35	M	LABR		GRZZZZOH
HILDELRANDT, WILHELM	30	M	LABR		GRZZZZOH
WILHELMINE	26	F	W		GRZZZZOH
ANNA	6	F	CHILD		GRZZZZOH
AUGUST	4	M	CHILD		GRZZZZOH
WILHELM	2	M	CHILD		GRZZZZOH
KRAUSE, AUGUST	28	M	BKR		GRZZZZOH
ANNA	25	F	BKR		GRZZZZOH
GUSTAV	2	M	CHILD		GRZZZZOH
HERMANN	1	M	CHILD		GRZZZZOH
RUDE, JULIUS	25	M	CL		GRZZZZOH
THAR, CARL	56	M	LABR		GRZZZZOH
AUGUSTE	50	F	W		GRZZZZOH
FRIEDRICH	16	M	CH		GRZZZZOH
LUDWIG	9	M	CHILD		GRZZZZOH
ERNST	7	M	CHILD		GRZZZZOH
ALWINE	5	F	CHILD		GRZZZZOH
HOPP, CARL	66	M	LABR		GRZZZZOH
CHARLOTTE	46	F	W		GRZZZZOH
ALWINE	23	F	D		GRZZZZOH
WILHELM	11	M	CH		GRZZZZOH
OTTO	9	M	CHILD		GRZZZZOH
CARL	.06	M	INFANT		GRZZZZOH
LIEBERT, HENRIETTE	36	F	UNKNOWN		GRZZZZOH
OTTILIE	11	F	CH		GRZZZZOH
EMILIE	10	F	CH		GRZZZZOH
ANNA	5	F	CHILD		GRZZZZOH
HENRIETTE	3	F	CHILD		GRZZZZOH
JENNY	.11	F	INFANT		GRZZZZOH
HINZ, FRIEDERICH	55	M	LABR		GRZZZZOH
WILHELMINE	44	F	W		GRZZZZOH
ALBERTINE	19	F	D		GRZZZZOH

PASSENGER	AGE	SEX	OCCUPATION	PRVL	DES
EMILIE	16	F	D		GRZZZZOH
HERMANN	14	M	S		GRZZZZOH
WILHELM	12	M	CH		GRZZZZOH
AUGUST	8	M	CHILD		GRZZZZOH
MARIE	4	F	CHILD		GRZZZZOH
ALBERT	.08	M	INFANT		GRZZZZOH
MUNSKY, OTTO	25	M	LABR		GRZZZZOH
SAMARAZNOSKA, MARIANNA	70	F	UNKNOWN		GRZZZZOH
KATHARINA	38	F	UNKNOWN		GRZZZZOH
STANISLAW	6	M	CHILD		GRZZZZOH
MARIANNA	4	F	CHILD		GRZZZZOH
STANISLAWA	3	F	CHILD		GRZZZZOH
VICTORIA	1	F	CHILD		GRZZZZOH
WILKE, JOSEF	26	M	BKR		GRZZZZOH
POLANGE, CARL	27	M	BLKSMH		GRZZZZOH
AUGUSTE	23	F	W		GRZZZZOH
FRIEDERIKE	63	F	Y		GRZZZZOH
ANNA	4	F	CHILD		GRZZZZOH
CARL	1	M	CHILD		GRZZZZOH
THOMAS, FERDINAND	54	M	LABR		GRZZZZOH
FRIEDERIKE	53	F	W		GRZZZZOH
WILHELMINE	28	F	D		GRZZZZOH
ERNESTINE	23	F	D		GRZZZZOH
HERMANN	16	M	S		GRZZZZOH
U	11	F	CH		GRZZZZOH
MIELKE, JOHANN	46	M	LABR		GRZZZZOH
CAROLINE	44	F	W		GRZZZZOH
BERTHA	20	F	D		GRZZZZOH
FRITZ	11	M	CH		GRZZZZOH
HERMANN	9	M	CHILD		GRZZZZOH
WILHELM	7	M	CHILD		GRZZZZOH
REINHOLD	5	M	CHILD		GRZZZZOH
GERSH, FRIEDERIKE	58	F	UNKNOWN		GRZZZZOH
AUGUST	16	M	S		GRZZZZOH
JOHANN	12	M	CH		GRZZZZOH
JEWORSKA, ANNA	57	F	UNKNOWN		GRZZZZOH
WYSOCKI, JOHN	16	M	LABR		GRZZZZOH
PARUSKWIECZ, STANISLAUS	33	M	LABR		GRZZZZOH
JOSEFA	26	F	W		GRZZZZOH
WILHELMINE	9	F	CHILD		GRZZZZOH
JOSEF	1	M	CHILD		GRZZZZOH
MODUSKI, ANTON	50	M	LABR		GRZZZZMN
WANDA	10	F	CH		GRZZZZMN
WITZKE, JOHANN	29	M	LABR		GRZZZZMN
EMILIE	31	F	W		GRZZZZMN
WALTER	3	M	CHILD		GRZZZZMN
PUNITZKIE, VALENTINE	26	F	UNKNOWN		GRZZZZMN
THEODOR	4	M	CHILD		GRZZZZMN
KELABUNDA, HENRICH	33	M	LABR		GRZZZZMN
ELISABETH	32	F	W		GRZZZZMN
AUGUST	9	M	CHILD		GRZZZZMN
JOHANN	6	M	CHILD		GRZZZZMN
HENRICH	4	M	CHILD		GRZZZZMN
LEMANIZUCK, PAUL	26	M	LABR		GRZZZZBAL
STIWE, GUTTEW	28	M	LABR		GRZZZZBAL
PAULINE	28	F	W		GRZZZZBAL
MARIA	3	F	CHILD		GRZZZZBAL
HERMANN	2	M	CHILD		GRZZZZBAL
AUGUSTE	.03	F	INFANT		GRZZZZBAL
GUTZMER, HERMANN	24	M	LABR		GRZZZZBAL
BERTHA	23	F	W		GRZZZZBAL
MINNA	1	F	CHILD		GRZZZZBAL
ROSENERUNZ, THEOPHIL	24	M	LABR		GRZZZZBAL
STRECH, ALBERT	27	M	BBR		GRZZZZBAL
CHARLOTTE	25	F	W		GRZZZZBAL
KONIG, MARIA	26	F	UNKNOWN		GRZZZZBAL
PAUL	4	M	CHILD		GRZZZZBAL
FRITZ	1	M	CHILD		GRZZZZBAL
UECKERT, ELISE	32	F	UNKNOWN		GRZZZZBAL
PAUL	12	M	CH		GRZZZZBAL
ANNA	8	F	CHILD		GRZZZZBAL
MENZEL, PAULINE	39	F	SVNT		GRZZZZBAL
HORN, AMALIE	33	F	UNKNOWN		GRZZZZBAL
BERTHA	8	F	CHILD		GRZZZZBAL
GUSTAC	7	M	CHILD		GRZZZZBAL
SAHNKE, CARL	30	M	LABR		GRZZZZMN
ANNA	26	F	W		GRZZZZMN
KUPSCH, FRANZ	39	M	LABR		GRZZZZMN
FRIEDERIKE	37	F	W		GRZZZZMN
ANNA	15	F	D		GRZZZZMN
WILHLEMINE	13	F	D		GRZZZZMN
BERTHA	10	F	CH		GRZZZZMN
WILHELM	6	M	CHILD		GRZZZZMN
MINNA	3	F	CHILD		GRZZZZMN
CLARA	1	F	CHILD		GRZZZZMN
ZENIDER, WILHWLM	41	M	LABR		GRZZZZOH
ANNA	34	F	W		GRZZZZOH
U	10	F	CH		GRZZZZOH
U	8	M	CHILD		GRZZZZOH
CLARA	5	F	CHILD		GRZZZZOH
MARIA	4	F	CHILD		GRZZZZOH
ALFRED	3	M	CHILD		GRZZZZOH
LOUISE	2	F	CHILD		GRZZZZOH
HAFNER, FRIDOLIN	16	M	LABR		GRZZZZOH
HOMBERGER, GEORG	25	M	TLR		GRZZZZOH
RICK, JOHANN	24	M	BKR		GRZZZZIN
CAROLINE	22	F	W		GRZZZZIN
ROWA, MARIE	19	F	SVNT		GRZZZZIN
BERGER, JOHANN	27	M	FARMER		GRZZZZBAL
SCHATKE, ANNA	25	F	SVNT		GRZZZZBAL
HINDORF, HERMANN	32	M	SHFM		GRZZZZBAL
MARIE	39	F	W		GRZZZZBAL
SCHLIEBS, AUGUST	32	M	LABR		GRZZZZBAL
PRANGA, AUGUST	22	M	LABR		GRZZZZIL
NERGER, AUGUST	53	M	FARMER		GRZZZZTX
PAULINE	54	F	W		GRZZZZTX
PAUL	16	M	S		GRZZZZTX
PSZYBELSKI, THOMAS	30	M	LABR		GRZZZZMI
BARANIEK, ANTON	37	M	LABR		GRZZZZIL
KATARINA	25	F	W		GRZZZZIL
ANAREUS	3	M	CHILD		GRZZZZIL
UKLYN, FRANZ	31	M	LABR		GRZZZZIL
BRIGITTE	25	F	W		GRZZZZIL
THOMAS	4	M	CHILD		GRZZZZIL
BOROWSKI, FRANZ	27	M	LABR		GRZZZZIL
U, U	31	F	SVNT		GRZZZZWI
ZIPPEL, MARIE	26	F	UNKNOWN		GRZZZZMN
CARL	3	M	CHILD		GRZZZZMN
LOUISE	1	F	CHILD		GRZZZZMN
NIMEMUNN, CARL	27	M	LABR		GRZZZZIL
HERMANN	25	M	BCHR		GRZZZZIL
LEISSING, FRIEDERICH	25	M	LABR		GRZZZZDAK
MARIE	28	F	W		GRZZZZDAK
FRIEDERICH	1	M	CHILD		GRZZZZDAK
HOPPE, ROBERT	16	M	LABR		GRZZZZWI
SCHMIDT, JOHANN	42	M	LABR		GRZZZZWI
JOHANNA	36	F	W		GRZZZZWI
CARL	11	M	CH		GRZZZZWI
JOHAMUUS	7	M	CHILD		GRZZZZWI
KNOP, CARL	22	M	LABR		GRZZZZWI
HAPKE, JOHANNE	45	F	UNKNOWN		GRZZZZWI
EMILIE	23	F	SVNT		GRZZZZWI
ERNESTINE	21	F	SVNT		GRZZZZWI
BERTHA	18	F	SVNT		GRZZZZWI
BRUNO	10	M	CH		GRZZZZWI
WILM, LENA	18	F	SVNT		GRZZZZWI
ZEILSDORF, HERMANN	25	M	LABR		GRZZZZDAK
AUGUSTE	25	F	W		GRZZZZDAK
BRENSKE, IGNAZ	58	M	LABR		GRZZZZIL
ANNA	56	F	W		GRZZZZIL
JULIA	8	F	CHILD		GRZZZZIL
ANNA	3	F	CHILD		GRZZZZIL
BORUFLETH, HERMANN	28	M	LABR		GRZZZZWI
GENDRICHAN, JOHANNE	45	F	LABR		GRZZZZMI
BERTHA	15	F	D		GRZZZZMI
RETZLAFF, FERDINAND	32	M	LABR		GRZZZZWI
TOINNES, WILLY	25	M	BKR		GRZZZZIL
BERCK, MICHAEL	23	M	BLKSMH		GRZZZZOH
GURSKI, PILAGNA	19	M	LABR		GRZZZZOH
U, U	00	F	SVNT		GRZZZZMI

4

PASSENGER	AGE	SEX	OCCUPATION	PRVL	DES
WEGENER, JOSEF	30	M	LABR	GRZZZZNE	
MASCHE, GUSTAV	25	M	LABR	GRZZZZWI	
HARMS, HEMRICH	28	M	LABR	GRZZZZWI	
DOROTHEA	32	F	W	GRZZZZWI	
MASCHALKOWSKA, FRANZKE.	25	F	SVNT	GRZZZZWI	
LENZ, JOHANN	32	M	LABR	GRZZZZWI	
FELICIA	25	F	W	GRZZZZWI	
STEPHANIE	4	F	CHILD	GRZZZZWI	
THEODOR	2	M	CHILD	GRZZZZWI	
MAXIMILIAN	.03	M	INFANT	GRZZZZWI	
BLOCK, CARL	26	M	LABR	GRZZZZIL	
TRETTIN, RUDORF	30	M	LABR	GRZZZZIL	
HENRIETTE	32	F	W	GRZZZZIL	
BERTHA	8	F	CHILD	GRZZZZIL	
EMILIE	6	F	CHILD	GRZZZZIL	
ANNA	2	F	CHILD	GRZZZZIL	
IDA	.03	F	INFANT	GRZZZZIL	
POATH, JOACHIM	70	M	Y	GRZZZZWI	
BLOCK, WILHELM	36	M	LABR	GRZZZZWI	
HENRIETTE	36	F	W	GRZZZZWI	
LOUISE	12	F	CH	GRZZZZWI	
OTTO	10	M	CH	GRZZZZWI	
KARL	8	M	CHILD	GRZZZZWI	
GUSTAV	3	M	CHILD	GRZZZZWI	
WILHELM	.06	M	INFANT	GRZZZZWI	
HINZ, FRIEDERICH	70	M	Y	GRZZZZWI	
STEFFEN, REINHARD	16	M	LABR	GRZZZZWI	
VALCK, U	22	M	LABR	GRZZZZWI	
BAUSKE, BERTHA	18	F	LABR	GRZZZZDAK	
VETT, AUGUST	39	M	LABR	GRZZZZIL	
BERTHA	37	F	W	GRZZZZIL	
HAMRICH	70	M	Y	GRZZZZIL	
MEISSNER, HERMANN	35	M	CL	GRZZZZIL	
WARCEWSKI, WLADISLAW	25	M	LABR	GRZZZZMI	
FRANZISKA	20	F	W	GRZZZZMI	
SCHUMAN, AUGUST	55	M	FARMER	GRZZZZDAK	
MARIE	54	F	W	GRZZZZDAK	
EMIL	9	M	CHILD	GRZZZZDAK	
KUNDE, IDA	24	F	SVNT	GRZZZZIA	
GAST, BERTHA	17	F	SVNT	GRZZZZOH	
BERNHARDT, FREIDERICH	19	M	LABR	GRZZZZMI	
KESSLER, JOHANN	23	M	LABR	GRZZZZMI	
RAUF, AUGUST	17	M	LABR	GRZZZZOH	
KLEIVER, JAN	59	M	LABR	GRZZZZIL	
EVERDINA	55	F	W	GRZZZZIL	
BRANDES, BERTHA	25	F	UNKNOWN	GRZZZZIL	
EMIL	3	M	CHILD	GRZZZZIL	
FRANZ	.09	M	INFANT	GRZZZZIL	
PRIETT, DORA	20	F	SVNT	GRZZZZUNK	
SCHULZ, HERMANN	26	M	LABR	GRZZZZMD	
AUGUSTA	21	F	W	GRZZZZMD	
ALBERT	.05	M	INFANT	GRZZZZMD	
NERTZEL, LOUISE	21	F	UNKNOWN	GRZZZZMD	
ANNA	.11	F	INFANT	GRZZZZMD	
REICHEL, FERDINAND	55	M	LABR	GRZZZZMD	
EMILIE	55	F	W	GRZZZZMD	
OTTO	15	M	S	GRZZZZMD	
ANNA	18	F	D	GRZZZZMD	
JAN	12	M	CH	GRZZZZMD	
JULIUS	12	M	CH	GRZZZZMD	
ALBERT	9	M	CHILD	GRZZZZMD	
LUCHT, U	54	M	FARMER	GRZZZZMD	
AUGUSTE	42	F	W	GRZZZZMD	
FRANZ	14	M	CH	GRZZZZMD	
ALBERT	12	M	CH	GRZZZZMD	
LOUISE	9	F	CHILD	GRZZZZMD	
WENKE, CARL	45	M	FARMER	GRZZZZMD	
WILHELME.	39	F	W	GRZZZZMD	
JOHANN	72	M	Y	GRZZZZMD	
HERMANN	14	M	S	GRZZZZMD	
GUSTAV	11	M	CH	GRZZZZMD	
WILHELM	7	M	CHILD	GRZZZZMD	
EMIL	4	M	CHILD	GRZZZZMD	
ANNA	2	F	CHILD	GRZZZZMD	
MINNA	.09	F	INFANT	GRZZZZMD	
BENTZ, HERMANN	26	M	LABR	GRZZZZMD	
RUPP, GEORG	17	M	LABR	GRZZZZMD	
HARRER, LOUISE	22	F	SVNT	GRZZZZMD	
FREDERIKE	22	F	SVNT	GRZZZZMD	
BUCH, CAROLINE	18	F	SVNT	GRZZZZMD	
KLIWER, JOHANN	16	M	LABR	GRZZZZMD	
NIKUM, JACOB	68	M	LABR	GRZZZZMD	
CATHARINA	60	F	W	GRZZZZMD	
NICOLAUS	23	M	S	GRZZZZMD	
VONNIEDA, JOCOB	24	M	LABR	GRZZZZMD	
HASKIN, WILHELM	21	M	LABR	GRZZZZMD	
WESSELMANN, CAROLINE	17	F	SVNT	GRZZZZMD	
PFEIFFER, PAULINE	16	F	SVNT	GRZZZZMD	
WILKEUS, BERNHARD	28	M	LABR	GRZZZZMD	
ALMUS, U	26	M	LABR	GRZZZZMD	
SCHMIDT, U	35	F	UNKNOWN	GRZZZZMD	
JOHANN	5	M	CHILD	GRZZZZMD	
DIEDERICH	.11	M	INFANT	GRZZZZMD	
FUCHS, SOPHIA	21	F	SVNT	GRZZZZMD	
HAMER, ERNESTINE	17	F	SVNT	GRZZZZMD	
ZAISER, ROBERT	21	M	LABR	GRZZZZMD	
HARTMANN, GERTUDE	20	F	SVNT	GRZZZZMD	
HAMEL, ANNA	16	F	SVNT	GRZZZZMD	
SCHNEIDER, HEMRICH	24	M	LABR	GRZZZZMD	
ROSENER, HEINRICH	23	M	TLR	GRZZZZMD	
GERAES, HEINRICH	30	M	FARMER	GRZZZZMD	
NIESKE	35	F	W	GRZZZZMD	
GRESJEDINA	6	F	CHILD	GRZZZZMD	
FRANKE	4	M	CHILD	GRZZZZMD	
HENCURIKE	2	F	CHILD	GRZZZZMD	
FICK, MARGARETHA	21	F	SVNT	GRZZZZMD	
LANG, CATHARINA	25	F	SVNT	GRZZZZMD	
WACHENDORF, HEMRICH	45	M	LABR	GRZZZZIL	
AMALIE	48	F	W	GRZZZZIL	
JOHN, INNA	24	F	SVNT	GRZZZZIL	
WACHENDORF, HEMRICH	17	M	LABR	GRZZZZPA	
NOWICKI, JAN	65	M	LABR	GRZZZZPA	
JOSEFA	62	F	W	GRZZZZPA	
MICHAELINA	21	F	D	GRZZZZPA	
FRANZISKA	.09	F	INFANT	GRZZZZPA	
STEPHAN	28	M	LABR	GRZZZZPA	
JOSEFA	24	F	W	GRZZZZPA	
MARIANNA	.09	F	INFANT	GRZZZZPA	
SHEZELICKI, JOSEF	28	M	LABR	GRZZZZPA	
FUNG, AUGUST	30	M	LABR	GRZZZZPA	
KUPFERMALLER, ANDREUS	53	M	FARMER	GRZZZZPA	
FANNY	48	F	W	GRZZZZPA	
ANDREUS	15	M	S	GRZZZZPA	
EUGEN	12	M	S	GRZZZZPA	
MARIE	10	F	CH	GRZZZZPA	
JOHANN	4	M	CHILD	GRZZZZPA	
ANNA	2	F	CHILD	GRZZZZPA	
BACHMEIER, JOSEF	22	M	LABR	GRZZZZOH	
RUNDT, JOHANN	43	M	LABR	GRZZZZWI	
ANNA	43	F	W	GRZZZZWI	
HEMRICH	15	M	S	GRZZZZWI	
AUGUSTE	11	F	CH	GRZZZZWI	
JOHANN	6	M	CHILD	GRZZZZWI	
JUSTINE	4	F	CHILD	GRZZZZWI	
LOUISE	1	F	CHILD	GRZZZZWI	
MONDL, FERDINAND	24	M	LABR	GRZZZZWI	
KUHLMANN, JULIUS	35	M	LABR	GRZZZZIL	
OTTILIE	24	F	W	GRZZZZIL	
WALTER	.06	M	INFANT	GRZZZZIL	
LUHN, AUGUST	32	M	LABR	GRZZZZIL	
MARIE	32	F	W	GRZZZZIL	
AUGUST	2	M	CHILD	GRZZZZIL	
CLARA	.06	F	INFANT	GRZZZZIL	
BROHS, ROSALIA	20	F	SVNT	GRZZZZIL	
KRUGER, AGUSTE	21	F	SVNT	GRZZZZIL	
ROLLER, ANNA	19	F	SVNT	GRZZZZIL	
KEMPER, JOSEF	46	M	LABR	GRZZZZPA	
KREIDELER, BERNARD	43	M	LABR	GRZZZZOH	
ANNA	38	F	W	GRZZZZOH	
LESETTE	4	F	CHILD	GRZZZZOH	

5

PASSENGER	AGE	SEX	OCCUPATION	PRVVL DES
CATHARINA	60	F	Y	GRZZZZOH
REHKAMP, HEMRICH	51	M	LABR	GRZZZZMN
GERTRUD	50	F	W	GRZZZZMN
MINNA	13	F	CH	GRZZZZMN
HEMRICH	10	M	CH	GRZZZZMN
KORTEKAMP, LISETTE	24	F	SVNT	GRZZZZOH
WILKENS, ANNA	22	F	SVNT	GRZZZZMN
SCHWER, GERHARD	28	M	LABR	GRZZZZIL
ROSENWINCKIL, DIETRICH	19	M	LABR	GRZZZZIL
MEINKING, DIETRICH	18	M	LABR	GRZZZZIL
WILHELM	16	M	LABR	GRZZZZOH
HOFMANN, CHRISTIAN	15	M	LABR	GRZZZZOH
GEYER, MARGARETHA	23	F	SVNT	GRZZZZOH
HRIERGARTNER, FRIEDERIC	22	M	BCHR	GRZZZZOH
BREHM, JOHANN	25	M	LABR	GRZZZZBAL
HEIJE	38	F	UNKNOWN	GRZZZZBAL
JURGEN	14	M	S	GRZZZZBAL
MARTIN	11	M	CH	GRZZZZBAL
WEHR, SUSANNA	19	F	SVNT	GRZZZZOH
GOOS, JOHANN	15	M	LABR	GRZZZZOH
REICHEL, HEINRICH	25	M	LABR	GRZZZZOH
VESHOTT, WILHELM	31	M	LABR	GRZZZZBAL
RABE, ALBERT	35	M	LABR	GRZZZZBAL
PATZNIK, WILHELM	26	M	LABR	GRZZZZMN
AUGUSTE	26	F	W	GRZZZZMN
WRITJES, HENDERKUS	52	M	FARMER	GRZZZZMN
STECHTJE	42	F	W	GRZZZZMN
JOOHANN	20	M	S	GRZZZZMN
ALVYANIA	18	F	D	GRZZZZMN
JOHANNA	16	F	D	GRZZZZMN
HEMRICH	10	M	CH	GRZZZZMN
AISSO	3	M	CHILD	GRZZZZMN
VOLCK, ADALBUS	30	M	PNTR	GRZZZZMN
MARIE	28	F	W	GRZZZZMN
WITTE, HEINRICH	34	M	LABR	GRZZZZMN
U, U	00	F	UNKNOWN	GRZZZZMN
U	8	M	CHILD	GRZZZZMN
ANNA	6	F	CHILD	GRZZZZMN
HEINRICH	.10	M	INFANT	GRZZZZBAL
BURZIK, JACOB	38	M	LABR	GRZZZZBAL
JULIE	30	F	W	GRZZZZBAL
MARIANNA	10	F	CH	GRZZZZBAL
MARTHA	8	F	CHILD	GRZZZZBAL
JOHANN	3	M	CHILD	GRZZZZBAL
VERONIKA	.06	F	INFANT	GRZZZZBAL
ECKDEIN, KARL	80	M	Y	GRZZZZBAL
MITZNER, KARL	21	M	LABR	GRZZZZOH
SZEZERNEY, ELIZABETH	30	F	SVNT	GRZZZZOH
SZYPIRSKI, FRANZ	28	M	LABR	GRZZZZOH
ANDREAS	24	M	LABR	GRZZZZOH
KUNKEL, FRANZ	46	M	LABR	GRZZZZIL
SCHMIDT, JOHANN	37	M	LABR	GRZZZZPA
MARIA	14	F	D	GRZZZZPA
IGNATZ	10	M	CH	GRZZZZPA
STEWTLANAN, KARL	48	M	LABR	GRZZZZBAL
JOHANNE	48	F	W	GRZZZZBAL
CHRISTIAN	17	M	S	GRZZZZBAL
JOHANN	11	M	CH	GRZZZZBAL
CARL	9	M	CHILD	GRZZZZBAL
JOHANNA	7	F	CHILD	GRZZZZBAL
JAN	4	M	CHILD	GRZZZZBAL
BERTUS	2	M	CHILD	GRZZZZBAL
NISSEN, AUG.	25	M	FARMER	GRZZZZBAL
U, U	37	F	UNKNOWN	GRZZZZBAL
U	00	F	CH	GRZZZZBAL
THIERGEIRTNER, CHRUSTIA	55	M	LABR	GRZZZZBAL
THIERGEIRTNER, ANNA	56	F	W	GRZZZZBAL
DETZEL, ELISABETH	29	F	UNKNOWN	GRZZZZBAL
MARGARETTE	7	F	CHILD	GRZZZZBAL
LEONHARD	3	M	CHILD	GRZZZZBAL
WIECHERT, HEINRIETTE	32	F	UNKNOWN	GRZZZZBAL
ALMA	11	F	CH	GRZZZZBAL
NOWICKI, STANISLAWA	19	M	LABR	GRZZZZBAL
BEIR, CONRAD	74	M	LABR	GRZZZZBAL
HENRIETTE	31	F	W	GRZZZZBAL
BLASS, KATHARINA	55	F	UNKNOWN	GRZZZZIL
MARIE	27	F	D	GRZZZZIL
KATHARINA	21	F	D	GRZZZZIL
HOFMANN, MARIE	18	F	SVNT	GRZZZZIL
KOHLER, MARIE	24	F	SVNT	GRZZZZIL
STOLPKE, CARL	26	M	LABR	GRZZZZWI
BUDEICHERA, DINA	55	F	UNKNOWN	GRZZZZWI
JOSEF	14	M	LABR	GRZZZZWI
MEISTER, CARL	24	M	LABR	GRZZZZWI
WELAGE, FRANZ	15	M	LABR	GRZZZZWI
SCHWIDERING, BERNHEND	20	M	LABR	GRZZZZWI
BIEDENTORN, JOHANN	20	M	LABR	GRZZZZWI
STEINER, AUGUST	46	M	LABR	GRZZZZMN
PAULINE	46	F	W	GRZZZZMN
ANNA	20	F	D	GRZZZZMN
BERTHA	20	F	D	GRZZZZMN
ALBERT	13	M	S	GRZZZZMN
LOUISE	8	F	CHILD	GRZZZZMN
SCHMIDT, GEORG	39	M	FARMER	GRZZZZOH
MOLLER, HEINRICH	45	M	FARMER	GRZZZZIL
MARIE	43	F	W	GRZZZZIL
ELISABETH	13	F	D	GRZZZZIL
U	00	M	S	GRZZZZIL
BERNARD	4	M	CHILD	GRZZZZIL
KAROLINE	2	F	CHILD	GRZZZZIL
MICHAELOWISCH, MICHAEL	29	M	LABR	GRZZZZOH
GRUB, FERDINAND	17	M	LABR	GRZZZZBAL
POCHENKA, MARIE	58	F	UNKNOWN	GRZZZZIL
CATHARINA	22	F	D	GRZZZZIL
AGNES	17	F	D	GRZZZZIL
STRECH, MARIE	31	F	W	GRZZZZIL
GEORG	31	M	LABR	GRZZZZIL
GEORG	3	M	CHILD	GRZZZZIL
MARTHA	2	F	CHILD	GRZZZZIL
MARIA	68	F	Y	GRZZZZIL
SCHMIDT, FRANZ	23	M	LABR	GRZZZZIL
SCHON, BARBARA	16	F	SVNT	GRZZZZBAL
MARGARETHE	48	F	UNKNOWN	GRZZZZBAL
ERNSHOFF, CHRISTIAN	17	M	LABR	GRZZZZBAL
SPIRA, FRANTE	27	M	LABR	GRZZZZBAL
MARIANNA	28	F	W	GRZZZZBAL
JOSEF	7	M	CHILD	GRZZZZBAL
META	2	F	CHILD	GRZZZZBAL
THERESE	.03	F	INFANT	GRZZZZBAL
NAPMALSKI, MICHAIL	60	M	LABR	GRZZZZOH
LUCEE	50	F	W	GRZZZZOH
JADWIGA	14	F	D	GRZZZZOH
KATHARINA	10	F	CH	GRZZZZOH
PETER	18	M	S	GRZZZZOH
TAKOWIACK, ANASTASIA	39	F	UNKNOWN	GRZZZZOH
U	9	M	CHILD	GRZZZZOH
GRZEZINSKI, NEPOMUCH	39	M	FARMER	GRZZZZOH
HELENE	39	F	W	GRZZZZOH
MAISLAW	9	M	CHILD	GRZZZZOH
JOSEPHA	7	F	CHILD	GRZZZZOH
EDUARD	5	M	CHILD	GRZZZZOH
STANISLAWA	3	F	CHILD	GRZZZZOH
CASLAW	.11	M	INFANT	GRZZZZOH
STOLARSKI, JOHANN	56	M	LABR	GRZZZZOH
MARIANNA	55	F	W	GRZZZZOH
LEHECHT	24	M	S	GRZZZZOH
JOHANN	21	M	S	GRZZZZOH
CATHARINA	20	F	D	GRZZZZOH
MARYANN	18	F	D	GRZZZZOH
BEHNKE, JULIUS	32	M	LABR	GRZZZZOH
ANNA	30	F	W	GRZZZZOH
ANNA	60	F	Y	GRZZZZOH
CHRISTIAN	3	M	CHILD	GRZZZZOH
JULIUS	.06	M	INFANT	GRZZZZOH
KRON, CHRISIAN	23	M	BCHR	GRZZZZBAL
KULASENSKI, JAN	19	M	LABR	GRZZZZOH
ROSELWECK, HERMANN	20	M	LABR	GRZZZZOH
KOHLES, AUGUST	17	M	LABR	GRZZZZOH
SAWITZKI, PAUL	18	M	LABR	GRAGFVBAL
PATZNIK, GUSTAV	00	M	INF	GR****BAL

PASSENGER	AGE	SEX	OCCUPATION	PRVL DES
BATKOWSKY, CATHARINA	00	F	INF	GR****BAL

SHIP: ELBE

FROM: BREMEN AND SOUTHAMPTON
TO: NEW YORK
ARRIVED: 02 MAY 1888

PASSENGER	AGE	SEX	OCCUPATION	PRVL DES
KUEPER, FRITZ	32	M	TT	GRZZZZUSA
GUMBACHEN, FRITZ	36	M	TT	GRZZZZUSA
ALEXANDER, LOUIS	50	M	TT	GRZZZZUSA
JUST, L.	19	F	TT	GRZZZZUSA
SCHWEPPE, GEORG	36	M	TT	GRZZZZUSA
V. S.	28	M	TT	GRZZZZUSA
BUECHNER, FRIEDKE.	35	F	TT	GRZZZZUSA
NONEWMACHER, SOPHIE	28	F	TT	GRZZZZUSA
ERNST	7	M	CHILD	GRZZZZUSA
OSTEN--, FERD.	51	M	CH	GRADLDUSA
BRANDES, EMMA	20	F	CH	GRZZZZUSA
BOTHNER, H.MAX	36	M	CH	GRAEILUSA
R---MAN, LINDA	21	F	CH	GRZZZZUSA
LA---, JOHN.	23	M	CH	GRADLDUSA
ALB.	21	M	CH	GRADLDUSA
ASMUS, GUST.	26	M	CH	GRZZZZUSA
--LING, U	55	F	CH	GRZZZZUSA
SCHAP--, ERNSTE.	28	F	W	GRAHCKNY
LOUISE	60	F	W	GRAHCKNY
PETER	28	M	BBR	GRAHCKNY
BALSER, CARL	26	M	LABR	GRZZZZNY
HELLER, GEORG	42	M	LABR	GRZZZZNY
LEIDICH, HEINR.	10	M	CH	GRZZZZNY
MARIE	34	F	W	GRZZZZNY
LORENZ	30	M	FARMER	GRZZZZNY
HENRIETTE	11	F	CH	GRZZZZNY
CARL	7	M	CHILD	GRZZZZNY
WILH.	6	M	CHILD	GRZZZZNY
BOSCHEN, META	14	F	SVNT	GRZZZZNY
WANCKE, ANNE	21	F	SVNT	GRZZZZNY
SCHOMAKER, HERM.	14	M	LABR	GRACFXNY
MATZLEWSICZ, MICHE.	40	M	LABR	GRZZZZNY
MALKOWSKY, LUKAS	28	M	LABR	GRZZZZNY
ANNA	30	F	W	GRZZZZNY
JULIE	.09	F	INFANT	GRZZZZNY
BOROWSKI, STEFAN	28	M	LABR	GRZZZZNY
MALANOWSKI, IWRENZ	27	M	LABR	GRZZZZNY
JOSEFA	28	F	W	GRZZZZNY
EVA	.08	F	INFANT	GRZZZZNY
RORDALSKI, ADAM	27	M	LABR	GRZZZZNY
PETRIKOWSKI, JOH.	28	M	LABR	GRZZZZNY
PADGORSKI, MAX	16	M	LABR	GRZZZZNY
SWOLLINSKI, GGN.	34	M	LABR	GRAARRNY
BOROWSKI, GOTTF.	57	M	LABR	GRZZZZNY
MINNA	56	F	W	GRZZZZNY
BEISKE, PAUL	24	M	LABR	GRZZZZNY
SAMMEK, WILHNE.	25	F	W	GRZZZZNY
ROSA	19	F	SVNT	GRZZZZNY
KOWNATZKI, KONST.	25	M	LABR	GRAHSCNY
TODDE, AUGTE.	18	F	SVNT	GRAICONY
SCHWARZ, GOTTL.	26	M	BBR	GRZZZZNY
--MMER, CHRIST	25	M	FARMER	GRZZZZNY
HORTNER, ANNA	25	F	UNKNOWN	GRZZZZNY
EHRENTREICH, CARL	24	M	TCHR	GRZZZZNY
ERDTEN, OTTO	16	M	LABR	GRZZZZNY
APEL, EGIDUS	23	M	LABR	GRZZZZNY
ANNA	34	F	W	GRZZZZNY
ROHN, JOHN	48	M	FARMER	GRZZZZNY
KUNIG.	45	F	W	GRZZZZNY
PHILIPP	15	M	LABR	GRZZZZNY
CATH.	11	F	CH	GRZZZZNY
MARIE	11	F	CH	GRZZZZNY
JOH.	10	M	CH	GRZZZZNY
FRIEDR.	7	M	CHILD	GRZZZZNY
GEORG	6	M	CHILD	GRZZZZNY
PETER	.06	M	INFANT	GRZZZZNY
BERGERSDOERFER, FRITZ	19	M	BCHR	GRZZZZNY
BOSCH, CONRAD	18	M	FARMER	GRZZZZNY
ELENBERGER, BARBARA	20	F	SVNT	GRZZZZNY
BECKER, HEINR.	19	M	LABR	GRZZZZNY
METZGER, JOS.	19	M	LABR	GRZZZZNY
DUDLIK, MARA	25	F	SVNT	GRAARZNY
HOFFMANN, CARL	19	M	UNKNOWN	GRAARZNY
NEUMANN, GUST.	35	M	UNKNOWN	GRZZZZNY
MARIE	12	F	CH	GRZZZZNY
FRIED.	10	F	CH	GRZZZZNY
HELENE	7	F	CHILD	GRZZZZNY
CARL	5	M	CHILD	GRZZZZNY
BENCH.	.01	M	INFANT	GRZZZZNY
RATLUK, AND.	25	M	LABR	GRZZZZNY
MUELLER, ELNA	50	F	W	GRAAXKNY
ELNA	13	F	CH	GRAAXKNY
GUST.	7	M	CHILD	GRAAXKNY
KLEIN, FRITZ	5	M	CHILD	GRAARRNY
LEMKE, AUG.	24	M	FARMER	GRZZZZNY
MATHDE.	25	F	W	GRZZZZNY
FRANZ	2	M	CHILD	GRZZZZNY
ALB.	.03	M	INFANT	GRZZZZNY
AUGTE.	16	F	SVNT	GRZZZZNY
KONIGER, FRANZ	18	M	LABR	GRADVHNY
EMERICH, EILHM.	83	M	FARMER	GRZZZZNY
MARGA.	75	F	W	GRZZZZNY
RASPERKA, JOSEFA	21	F	SVNT	GRZZZZNY
EBERHARDT, FRIED.	18	M	BCHR	GRZZZZNY
SCHIRMACHER, JOH.	24	M	FARMER	GRZZZZNY
DORBALSKI, JOS.	23	M	LABR	GRZZZZNY
LORGER, GUST.	35	M	LABR	GRZZZZNY
CAROLE.	42	F	W	GRAGLZNY
RUKOWSKI, JOH.	29	M	LABR	GRZZZZNY
KOEMER, SEBAST.	28	M	FARMER	GRZZZZNY
NORVICKI, ANNA	30	F	W	GRZZZZNY
ANTON	5	M	CHILD	GRZZZZNY
ANNA	3	F	CHILD	GRZZZZNY
MARIE	.06	F	INFANT	GRZZZZNY
GEVER, GUSTAV	44	M	FARMER	GRABOQNY
ALEX	11	M	CH	GRABOQNY
WILLY	6	M	CHILD	GRABOQNY
ADOLPH	.11	M	INFANT	GRABOQNY
HEROLD, KUNIGDE.	21	F	SVNT	GRABOQNY
CHRIST, MARGA.	18	F	SVNT	GRABLTNY
MINNA	16	F	SVNT	GRABLTNY
RUEBE, ALBERT	26	M	LABR	GRABLTNY
SCHLOETTER, MICHAEL	22	M	FARMER	GRAFRGNY
MARIE	22	F	W	GRAFRGNY
SCHOEDEL, ANDRAS	39	M	BKR	GRAHYDNY
HEIN, MATHILDE	14	F	SVNT	GRZZZZNY
MAIER, MARIE	15	F	SVNT	GRAFRGNY
WAGNER, FRIEDR.	25	M	CPTR	GRABKVNY
KAHN, LEOPOLD	39	M	FARMER	GRAEHUNY
BRAUN, WILHELM.	30	F	SVNT	GRAFQYNY
SCHMIDT, ANNA	16	F	SVNT	GRAFQYNY
HELD, FRIED.	66	M	FARMER	GRAHGANY
HAPP, WILHELMINE	13	M	FARMER	GRAHGANY
AC-LIN, KARL	24	M	LABR	GRABSYNY
MARYKIEWIECZ, STAN	28	M	LABR	GRZZZZNY
DEJA, ANDRAS	23	M	UNKNOWN	GRAICOIL
RUMMINSKY, EVA	33	F	W	GRAICOIL
FREITAG, GOTTFRIED	22	M	FARMER	GRZZZZIL
AUGUSTE	22	F	W	GRZZZZIL
GRABSKI, ANTON	25	M	LABR	GRZZZZIL
MIEDLICKE, JOSEF	44	M	FARMER	GRZZZZBUF
GEIBEL, ELISE	48	F	W	GRZZZZIL
ELISE	7	F	CHILD	GRZZZZIL
WEGNER, JOH.	28	M	SHMK	GRZZZZIL
FUHRMANN, HEINR.	39	M	DRVR	GRAEMAIL
MIECK, GOTTL.	52	M	LABR	GRAEMAIL
PAUKIL, AUGUST	30	M	LABR	GRZZZZIL

PASSENGER	AGE	SEX	OCCUPATION	PRVL	DES
GRETZMANN, ALEX	30	M	LABR	GRZZZZUSA	
ROGOZINSKI, THOM.	29	M	LABR	GRAEABBUF	
PFAFF, FRIEDR.	34	F	W	GRZZZZPA	
DULAR, ANNA	14	F	SVNT	GRZZZZPA	
MORGENSTERN, PH.	12	F	CH	GRZZZZPA	
PFAFF, ERNST	4	M	CHILD	GRZZZZPA	
OTTO	.11	M	INFANT	GRZZZZPA	
WIEGMANN, HEIN	23	M	CPTR	GRAAXWOH	
HEMPEL, EMILIE	19	F	SVNT	GRABSOPA	
SCHOURING, HEINRICH	57	M	FARMER	GRZZZZOH	
SCHAUER, GOTTL.	57	M	FARMER	GRZZZZNE	
EILHELME.	50	F	W	GRZZZZNE	
WILHELM	14	M	CH	GRZZZZNE	
MARTHA	5	F	CHILD	GRZZZZNE	
TUSCHLING, HENRIETTE	50	F	W	GRZZZZNE	
PENNSYLVANIA, HENRIETTE	50	F	W	GRZZZZNE	
BERTHA	28	F	W	GRZZZZNE	
HERMANN	00	M	SVNT	GRZZZZNE	
CARL	11	M	CH	GRZZZZNE	
GUSTAV	7	M	CHILD	GRZZZZNE	
ALWINE	37	F	W	GRZZZZNE	
MASCH, EMILIE	22	F	SVNT	GRZZZZMI	
WYROZUNIALSKA, JOHANN	46	M	FARMER	GRZZZZUNK	
MARTINA	22	F	W	GRZZZZUNK	
ANTON	16	M	LABR	GRZZZZUNK	
AGNES	11	F	CH	GRZZZZUNK	
MART.	7	M	CHILD	GRZZZZUNK	
JOSEF	3	M	CHILD	GRZZZZUNK	
MARIE	.10	F	INFANT	GRZZZZUNK	
ZIOLKOWSKY, ADALB.	28	M	FARMER	GRZZZZUNK	
MARIANNE	21	F	W	GRZZZZUNK	
MARIANNE	.10	F	INFANT	GRZZZZUNK	
BUTMANN, MARIE	23	F	SVNT	GRZZZZROC	
BOGASCH, BERNH.	27	M	TLR	GRZZZZROC	
DAUER, KUNIGUNDE	27	F	SVNT	GRZZZZUSA	
WOLF, MARIE	27	F	W	GRZZZZPA	
JOSEF	.09	M	INFANT	GRZZZZPA	
VOJER, LEONHARD	22	M	LABR	GRZZZZMN	
SCHNEIDER, BARBARA	20	F	SVNT	GRZZZZOH	
MEYER, WILHM.	31	M	FARMER	GRACBRWI	
JETTE	35	F	W	GRACBRWI	
FRITZ	10	M	CH	GRACBRWI	
LUESCHEN, JOH.	22	M	FARMER	GRZZZZIL	
MUELLER, MAX	16	M	FARMER	GRADLDPA	
HELD, HEINRICH	23	M	FARMER	GRZZZZOH	
VI-GT, OTTO	21	M	SHMK	GRZZZZMI	
SEIFFERLEIN, BARBARA	55	F	W	GRAEPKOH	
O-RTEL, RICHD.	20	M	TCHR	GRAAXKNY	
AGAHD, ROSA	15	F	CH	GRZZZZNY	
GERGD.	7	F	CHILD	GRZZZZNY	
RUEGGE, CARL	18	M	GDNR	GRAARRNY	
BAIER, JOHN	42	M	PH	GRAAKHNY	
MUELLER, MAGDALENE	23	F	SVNT	GRZZZZNY	
BOZER, MARGA.	20	F	SVNT	GRACZZNY	
PRUBE, AUGUSTE	14	F	SVNT	GRABVHNY	
C--DES, DIEDR.	26	M	LABR	GRACKRNY	
STENECK, CONRAD	16	M	LABR	GRZZZZNY	
-HRENS, ERNST	27	M	LABR	GRAARTNY	
D-RKING, G.H.	45	M	BCHR	GRAARTNY	
---EMANN, HEINR.	15	M	FARMER	GRAARTNY	
FINK, WILHELM	19	M	FARMER	GRADRDNY	
WENDELKEN, DIEDRICH	20	M	LABR	GRADRDNY	
ROEMER, HERMANN	21	M	LABR	GRZZZZNY	
WOIGH, JOH.	14	M	LABR	GRACNWNY	
JOOSTEN, FRIEDR.	23	M	FARMER	GRACNWNY	
KRAKE, ERNST	24	M	BKR	GRACNWNY	
WENBOLDT, CAROLINE	22	F	SVNT	GRACXHNY	
REHM, MAX	26	M	JNR	GRAARSNY	
BEHRENS, DIEDRICH	20	M	LABR	GRAAIONY	
ALDAG, KATHARINE	20	F	SVNT	GRAARSNY	
CLAASEN, MUNDA	23	F	SVNT	GRZZZZNY	
SOHL, PETER	36	M	LABR	GRZZZZNY	
KIRCHHEIMER, NICOL	24	M	LABR	GRZZZZNY	
VOIGT, CAROLINE	33	F	W	GRABLVNY	
ROSSELL, SOPHIE	18	F	SVNT	GRABOQNY	
BRAUN, ANDRAS	29	M	GDNR	GRZZZZNY	
KUEFNER, JOH.	28	M	FARMER	GRZZZZUNK	
MARGARETHE	24	F	W	GRZZZZUNK	
KATHARINE	.06	F	INFANT	GRZZZZUNK	
MARGA.	20	F	W	GRZZZZUNK	
KONRAD	.06	M	INFANT	GRZZZZUNK	
FUCHS, KATHA.	22	F	SVNT	GRZZZZUNK	
MOHRAT, KUNIGUNDE	17	F	SVNT	GRZZZZUNK	
KURTZ, JOH.	50	M	LABR	GRZZZZWI	
LEINBERGER, MAX	17	M	LABR	GRZZZZPA	
BAUER, BARBARA	51	F	W	GRZZZZNY	
ANNA	10	F	CH	GRZZZZNY	
KUEHRER, LISETTE	18	F	SVNT	GRAAANNY	
STEINBACH, CAROLIN.	16	F	SVNT	GRAAANNY	
SCHMIDT, JOHANN	69	M	FARMER	GRACWFNY	
--AF, ROSINE	17	F	SVNT	GRZZZZNY	
GUMPLE, JOS.	19	M	SMH	GRZZZZNY	
MUELLER, ROSINE	23	F	W	GRZZZZNY	
PAUL	6	M	CHILD	GRZZZZNY	
FRIEDR.	.11	M	INFANT	GRZZZZNY	
WEBER, SEB.	16	M	LABR	GRZZZZNY	
WEIDNER, BABETTE	18	F	SVNT	GRABOQNY	
KOESTER, JOH.	14	M	LABR	GRAEZGNY	
PETER	16	M	LABR	GRAEZGNY	
FRENZ, HEINR.	15	M	LABR	GRZZZZNY	
SCHAEF, ERNST	40	M	DLR	GRZZZZNY	
MINNA	17	F	SVNT	GRZZZZNY	
FRIEDA	11	F	CH	GRZZZZNY	
KAHL, EMIEL	21	M	MNR	GRZZZZNY	
BAUER, MARTIN	40	M	FARMER	GRZZZZNY	
FRANZKA.	31	F	W	GRZZZZNY	
BARBARA	7	F	CHILD	GRZZZZNY	
MARGARETHA	4	F	CHILD	GRZZZZNY	
VE--HLER, ALBT.	12	M	CH	GRACAVNY	
--LAND, LOUISE	23	F	SVNT	GRZZZZNY	
--IEN, ERNST	30	M	WTR	GRAAWTNY	
CATHAR.	29	F	W	GRAAWTNY	
ANNA	4	F	CHILD	GRAAWTNY	
BERTHA	.11	F	INFANT	GRAAWTNY	
BAUER, WALBURGA	.09	F	INFANT	GRZZZZNY	
HACKEL, ANDRAS	61	M	FARMER	GRAEYGNY	
GLOECKLER, CARL	13	M	LABR	GRAEYGNY	
GOLDNER, CARL	22	M	LABR	GRZZZZNY	
IETTINGER, WILHELM	16	M	LABR	GRAEYGNY	
KAUFMANN, GOTTB.	16	M	LABR	GRZZZZNY	
LAIDIG, FRIEDR.	18	M	LABR	GRZZZZNY	
CHRISTINE	16	F	SVNT	GRACQONY	
BINDER, GOTTF.	26	M	CPTR	GRACQONY	
LAIDIG, FRIEDERIDE	7	F	CHILD	GRACQONY	
LASKOWSKY, STANISL.	27	M	LABR	GRAEABNY	
KNEISSLER, CHARLOTTE	24	F	W	GRAEABNY	
LISA	4	F	CHILD	GRAEABNY	
LEPINSKY, IGNATZ	26	M	LABR	GRZZZZNY	
MARIANNE	24	F	W	GRZZZZNY	
ANNISCHKA	56	F	W	GRZZZZNY	
MARIANNE	2	F	CHILD	GRZZZZNY	
ANNISCHKA	.11	F	INFANT	GRZZZZNY	
JOSEF	.01	M	INFANT	GRZZZZNY	
KAIDAS, ANDRA.	36	M	LABR	GRAHWVBUF	
HEDW.	30	F	W	GRAHWVBUF	
MARTIN	7	M	CHILD	GRAHWVBUF	
LUDWIG	3	M	CHILD	GRAHWVBUF	
MARIE	.01	F	INFANT	GRAHWVBUF	
RUMMEL, JOSEF	29	M	FARMER	GRZZZZNY	
LEWANDOWSKY, JOH.	26	M	LABR	GRZZZZNY	
MARIANNE	22	F	W	GRZZZZNY	
LORENZ	2	M	CHILD	GRZZZZNY	
STANISL.	.06	M	INFANT	GRZZZZNY	
WILHELMSEN, HERM.	22	M	LABR	GRZZZZIA	
SAUERWEIN, JAC.	52	M	JNR	GRABLTNE	
ANNA	52	F	W	GRABLTNE	
JACOB	19	M	JNR	GRABLTNE	
ANNA	17	F	SVNT	GRABLTNE	
JOSEPHA	15	F	SVNT	GRABLTNE	
AUGUST	7	M	CHILD	GRABLTNE	

PASSENGER	AGE	SEX	OCCUPATION	PRVVL	DES	PASSENGER	AGE	SEX	OCCUPATION	PRVVL	DES
REINHARDT, LOUIS	28	M	LABR	GRZZZZNY		VINCENT	26	M	UNKNOWN	GRZZZZMN	
FRIEDR.	24	M	LABR	GRZZZZNY		KOSIEDOWSKY, AUGUST	26	M	UNKNOWN	GRZZZZMN	
HUBER, SEBASTIAN	24	M	CPTR	GRAARRPA		ZEIG, WILHELM	28	M	UNKNOWN	GRZZZZMN	
CATHARINE	23	F	W	GRAARRPA		KNOLL, EMIEL	25	M	UNKNOWN	GRZZZZMN	
POMOLKI, JOS.	40	M	LABR	GRAARRNY		MAISSEL, CARL	32	M	UNKNOWN	GRZZZZMN	
BLUCUSKY, FRANZ	37	M	LABR	GRZZZZIL		FALKENSTEIN, FRIEDRKE.	25	F	SVNT	GRAAKHPA	
JUST, VELANTI	31	M	LABR	GRZZZZIL		LEH, JACOB	36	M	FARMER	GRACEDNY	
BERAITER, LORENZ	42	M	LABR	GRZZZZPA		STOPSCHINSKY, JOS.	24	M	FARMER	GRACEDPA	
BL-SZYK, ANDRAS	30	M	LABR	GRZZZZUNK		BOLSELER, JULIUS	30	M	FARMER	GRZZZZOH	
MALOBESCHKE, ANDRAS	50	M	LABR	GRAARRIL		CHRISTINE	23	F	W	GRZZZZOH	
MICHALINE	22	F	W	GRAARRIL		KREMER, JOHN	60	M	FARMER	GRAFHVNY	
KATH, CLAUS	27	M	BCHR	GRAARRUSA		MARGURETHA	54	F	UNKNOWN	GRAFHVNY	
SCHLAMEYER, JOH.	17	M	FARMER	GRAEABUSA		U	14	M	UNKNOWN	GRAFHVNY	
CYGAUCK, MICHAEL	25	M	LABR	GRAEABBUF		JOHANNE	5	F	CHILD	GRAFHVNY	
ARMASINSKI, JOSEFA	28	F	SVNT	GRAEABBUF		PAULUS	30	M	FARMER	GRAFHVNY	
MAINDAL, CARL	26	M	DLR	GRADLDNY		LEEGE, ROBERT	29	M	GDNR	GRZZZZWI	
MARIE	23	F	W	GRADLDNY		LUEVING, LUDWIG	29	M	UNKNOWN	GRZZZZOH	
CZECGUNSKY, JAN	26	M	LABR	GRADLDNY		GUST.	14	M	LABR	GRZZZZOH	
SCHLICHTEMAYER, ROSA	44	F	W	GRADLDKS		FUERSTENAU, EMMA	17	F	SVNT	GRZZZZWI	
JACOB	16	M	LABR	GRADLDKS		BRINDZA, MATZAR	38	M	LABR	GRZZZZNY	
WILHELM	5	M	CHILD	GRADLDKS		GAMISCHEFSKY, PAVEL	50	M	LABR	GRZZZZNY	
JESCHER, CHARLOTTE	26	F	W	GRAARRNY		FRANZISKA	17	F	SVNT	GRZZZZNY	
LINA	5	F	CHILD	GRAARRNY		SKITSCH, FRANZ	25	M	LABR	GRZZZZNY	
TOLLE, FRIEDR.	23	F	SVNT	GRAARRNY		HOFFMANN, MARGARETHA	25	F	W	GRAAQDNY	
MORGEBERGER, CHRIST	26	M	FARMER	GRZZZZNY		KOCH, WILHELM	34	M	BCHR	GRZZZZNY	
WINARSKI, PETER	23	M	UNKNOWN	GRAASSNY		ZITTLOSEN, META	20	F	SVNT	GRAHTWNY	
HOFFMANN, ANNA	29	F	UNKNOWN	GRAASSNY		SEGBYORUSEN, OLGA	28	F	SVNT	GRAHTWNY	
B---, MARIE	21	F	UNKNOWN	GRAASSNY		BLOHM, HEINRICH	11	M	CH	GRAHTWNY	
--HARFER, MALWINE	30	F	UNKNOWN	GRAASSNY		RUMPNER, GERHARD	29	M	LABR	GRZZZZNY	
SPRADA, FRANZ	30	M	UNKNOWN	GRZZZZBUF		HERM.	25	M	LABR	GRZZZZNY	
AUGUSTE	30	F	UNKNOWN	GRZZZZBUF		GASSNER, JOHANN	20	M	SLR	GRADOINY	
FRANZ	3	M	CHILD	GRZZZZBUF		HEINDLE, GEORG	17	M	ATR	GRADOINY	
THONIE	1	F	CHILD	GRAECZBUF		ZITZER, LOUIS	22	M	LABR	GRABKHNY	
AMALIE	.05	F	INFANT	GRAARRBUF		HUPP, FRIEDR.	15	M	LABR	GRABKHNY	
KAUL, MARIE	22	F	SVNT	GRAFTSBUF		KNOPP, CATHARINE	19	F	SVNT	GRABKHNY	
REICHE, HERMANN	27	M	UNKNOWN	GRAFTSBUF		BAR, ELIAS	26	M	BKR	GRACIJNY	
HULDA	19	F	W	GRAFTSBUF		SIMON, GEORG	44	M	SEMN	GRACIJUNK	
HULDA	.11	F	INFANT	GRAFTSBUF		MATTHIAS	46	M	SEMN	GRACIJUNK	
BUNGE, JOHANN	58	M	FARMER	GRAFTSOH		LOUISE	17	F	SVNT	GRACIJUNK	
AUGUSTE	42	F	UNKNOWN	GRAFTSIL		SIEVERS, CLAUS	22	M	FSHMN	GRZZZZUNK	
ERNESTINE	20	F	UNKNOWN	GRAFTSNY		ALTMANN, HUGO	28	M	UNKNOWN	GRABDMNY	
ADOLF	7	M	CHILD	GRAFTSNY		---MUELLER, B---	40	M	UNKNOWN	GRABDMNY	
WANDA	4	F	CHILD	GRAFTSNY		U. HEINR.	25	M	UNKNOWN	GRACBRNV	
RUDOLF	24	M	UNKNOWN	GRAFTSNY		GRONALA, CASPAR	56	M	FARMER	GRAKTENY	
AREND, JOSEF	30	M	UNKNOWN	GRABVWNY		CONSTANTINE	44	F	W	GRAKTENY	
ERNST, KARL	17	M	UNKNOWN	GRZZZZPA		VERONICA	17	F	SVNT	GRAKTENY	
KIESLING, MICHAL	34	M	UNKNOWN	GRZZZZNY		ANTON	13	M	CH	GRAKTENY	
VOIGT, FRIDA	20	F	SVNT	GRAARRNY		STANISLE	10	M	CH	GRAKTENY	
KIMMERER, FRIEDR.	30	M	CPR	GRZZZZIL		ANASTASIA	7	F	CHILD	GRAKTENY	
STEMMER, GOTTFRIED	26	M	CPTR	GRZZZZOH		WANTIKE, HERM.	28	M	LABR	GRZZZZNY	
KELM, GOTTF.	28	M	MCHT	GRACBFWI		HAEFNER, CAROLINE	23	F	SVNT	GRZZZZNY	
THEIS, ELISAB.	22	F	SVNT	GRZZZZMI		ENGELHARDT, FRIEDR.	19	M	JNR	GRZZZZNY	
BARDY, CHRIST.	19	M	LABR	GRADVVIL		U, FRI--	17	M	UNKNOWN	GRZZZZOH	
KUPTZ, FRANZ	23	M	LABR	GRZZZZIL		U	13	F	UNKNOWN	GRAEGBOH	
PIKRON, JOHANN	26	M	SMH	GRZZZZIL		KAISER, MARGARETHE	13	F	UNKNOWN	GRAEGBNY	
POIL, JACOB	15	M	LABR	GRZZZZIL		SCHMIDT, ALBERT	13	M	LABR	GRAEGBNY	
LIEB, JACOB	24	M	TCHR	GRZZZZBUF		BEHN, JOHANN	16	M	LABR	GRAEETNY	
SCHAFER, HEINR.	38	M	FARMER	GRADKAIA		KROPF, JANNY	23	M	LABR	GRZZZZNY	
CATHARINE	36	F	W	GRADKAIA		GROSS, H.F.	16	M	LABR	GRACBRNY	
WILHELMINE	64	M	W	GRADKAIA		DROGE, BETA	14	F	SVNT	GRACBRNY	
LUDW.	11	M	CH	GRADKAIA		BURMEISTER, JOHANN	15	M	SVNT	GRAAZWNY	
MARTHA	7	F	CHILD	GRADKAIA		OSTERNDORF, JOHANNE	17	F	SVNT	GRACXHNY	
CONRAD	6	M	CHILD	GRADKAIA		SCHROEDER, META	17	F	SVNT	GRZZZZNY	
ELIDABETH	4	F	CHILD	GRADKAIA		HERMANN	20	M	SMH	GRZZZZNY	
ANNA	3	F	CHILD	GRADKAIA		RJOEVER, DIEDRICH	17	M	LABR	GRACTYNY	
WILHELM	.11	M	INFANT	GRADKAIA		GRIEN, NATALIE	31	F	W	GRAEXWNY	
STAEDLER, AUGUST	25	M	MCHT	GRZZZZNY		ALFONS	4	M	CHILD	GRAEXWNY	
KOSIEDOWSKY, JOSEF	25	M	LABR	GRZZZZMN		VOCK, PAULA.	60	F	W	GRAEXWNY	
JOSEFINE	20	F	W	GRZZZZMN		SCHMIDT, ELISABETH	55	F	W	GRACURNY	
IGNATZ	.10	M	INFANT	GRZZZZMN		PHILIPP	23	M	BCHR	GRACURNY	
WERA, THERESIA	53	F	W	GRZZZZMN		BOCKHAUS, PETER	20	M	TCHR	GRACURNY	
CACILIE	17	F	UNKNOWN	GRZZZZMN		SENGER, PAUL	24	M	JNR	GRAHSINY	
PIPLINSKY, FRANZ	27	M	UNKNOWN	GRZZZZMN		JOST, OTTO	26	M	TNR	GRZZZZNY	
FRANZISKA	21	F	UNKNOWN	GRZZZZMN		ROTHENBURG, HERM.	28	M	MCHT	GRAARZNY	
JOHANN	.10	M	INFANT	GRZZZZMN		SCHULZ, MATHILDE	24	F	SVNT	GRAEABNY	

PASSENGER	AGE	SEX	OCCUPATION	PRVL	DES
ALBACH, WILHELM	26	M	LABR	GRAARRNY	
HARTUNG, FRIEDR.	38	M	FARMER	GRZZZZNY	
ANNA	39	F	W	GRZZZZNY	
ROSILIE	11	F	CH	GRZZZZNY	
ALBERT	9	M	CHILD	GRZZZZNY	
MATHILDE	7	F	CHILD	GRZZZZNY	
ALINE	5	F	CHILD	GRZZZZNY	
HELMUTH	3	M	CHILD	GRZZZZNY	
OLGA	.11	F	INFANT	GRZZZZNY	
RIELZ, JOH.	78	M	FARMER	GRABRANY	
BINDER, WILHELM	28	M	FARMER	GRZZZZOH	
MOSBACHER, BARBARA	28	F	W	GRZZZZOH	
GROPPBOCKER, HEINR.	18	M	LABR	GRAHQHNY	
ESCHMANN, ADAM	18	M	LABR	GRAHQHNY	
BARBARA	21	F	SVNT	GRAHQHNY	
WEISSENBERGER, JOH.	34	M	FARMER	GRZZZZNY	
AUG.	16	M	FARMER	GRZZZZMI	
EBERLE, CATHARINE	40	F	W	GRACGKMI	
GOTTLOB	14	M	CH	GRACGKNY	
MARIA	7	F	CHILD	GRACGKNY	
KIENTSCH, DAVIED	28	M	BCHR	GRZZZZNY	
MEYER, JACOB	45	M	MLR	GRACBRNY	
GRETJE	7	F	CHILD	GRACBRNY	
BOHLIN, THEODOR	15	M	LABR	GRAFTSNY	
MASSER, JACOB	46	M	UNKNOWN	GRAARRNY	
BAROLINE	10	F	CH	GRAARRNY	
ELIDABETH	7	F	CHILD	GRAARRNY	
HERZLINGER, KAROL.	48	F	W	GRAARRNY	
MATHES, MAGDALENE	34	F	W	GRAARRNY	
NEES, JOH.	41	M	LABR	GRAARRNY	
RUST, JAC.	24	M	DLR	GRZZZZNY	
U, AUGUST	26	M	UNKNOWN	GRADNDPA	
EN---, KARL	18	M	UNKNOWN	GRAIUNNY	
STRECKER, LUDW.	17	M	CH	GRZZZZNY	
HOEFLER, JOH.	15	M	CH	GRZZZZNY	
KRAEMER, FRANZISKA	20	F	SVNT	GRACFWNY	
WERNEBERG, ELSE	16	F	SVNT	GRAEMTNY	
ERNST	14	M	LABR	GRAEMTNY	
KUENDSEN, JORG.	61	M	FARMER	GRZZZZMT	
ANE	59	F	W	GRZZZZMT	
CICILIE	25	F	SVNT	GRZZZZMT	
PAWLOWSKY, HERM.	28	M	LABR	GRZZZZOH	
BAUER, HANS	27	M	LABR	GRZZZZWI	
BOEHM, MARGARETHE	36	F	W	GRACIJNY	
ELISE	7	F	CHILD	GRACIJNY	
LORENZ	4	M	CHILD	GRACIJNY	
ZEINMER, FRIEDA	17	F	SVNT	GRZZZZNY	
HEMPEL, ALWIN	17	M	LABR	GRZZZZNY	
GROIS, HALENE	21	F	W	GRZZZZNY	
MARTIN	.08	M	INFANT	GRZZZZNY	
WINNER, MICHAEL	30	M	LABR	GRZZZZNY	
HERWIG, ALBERT	20	F	SVNT	GRABVHNY	
PECHLER, LEONHARD	44	M	LABR	GRZZZZWI	
JOHANNE	31	F	W	GRZZZZWI	
FRANZ	10	M	CH	GRZZZZWI	
WOLFGANG	7	M	CHILD	GRZZZZWI	
GEORG	3	M	CHILD	GRZZZZWI	
CATHARINE	.09	F	INFANT	GRZZZZWI	
CHRASTIL, MARIE	31	F	UNKNOWN	GRAARRNY	
THOMA, HENRIETTE	30	F	W	GRZZZZNY	
REINHARD	.11	M	INFANT	GRZZZZNY	
MAJDEREK, STANISL	37	M	LABR	GRZZZZNY	
ANTONIO	33	F	W	GRZZZZNY	
KATHARINE	7	F	CHILD	GRZZZZNY	
ANTONIO	6	F	CHILD	GRZZZZNY	
FRANZ	4	M	CHILD	GRZZZZNY	
JOHANN	.10	M	INFANT	GRZZZZNY	
MARK, ELISABETH	20	F	SVNT	GRAADJNY	
DRUHM, FRANZ	23	M	LABR	GRZZZZNY	
ROCKHOFF, MARIE	16	F	SVNT	GRZZZZNY	
MICKEL, PAUL	17	M	FARMER	GRABDMNY	
WLECLINCKI, WLAD.	24	M	FARMER	GRZZZZNY	
REINEKE, LORENZ	24	M	FARMER	GRZZZZNY	
MAHLER, HERMANN	16	M	LABR	GRACBRNY	
GANDER, AUGUST	26	M	LABR	GRZZZZNY	
HULDA	26	F	W	GRZZZZNY	
PAUL	2	M	CHILD	GRZZZZNY	
MARTHA	.06	F	INFANT	GRZZZZNY	
DEN---, SOPHIA	14	F	UNKNOWN	GRACBRNY	
EVE----, HEINR.	18	M	DLR	GRACBRNY	
MUELLER, LINA	16	F	SVNT	GRAEWMNY	
WANSELOW, JRANZ	27	M	LABR	GRAEWMNY	
SUNKEL, META	16	F	SVNT	GRABIYNY	
CAMULSKA, MAGDALENE	34	F	W	GRADOINY	
STANISLE	7	M	CHILD	GRADOINY	
WUTKE, MARIE	23	F	SVNT	GRZZZZNY	
BURK, ANNA	17	F	SVNT	GRZZZZNY	
STREICHERT, CAROLINE	33	F	W	GRACYVNY	
EMMA	7	F	CHILD	GRACYVNY	
SELMA	5	F	CHILD	GRACYVNY	
ARTHUR	.10	M	INFANT	GRACYVNY	
HOHMANN, MARTHA	18	F	UNKNOWN	GRZZZZNY	
WE---, PHILIPP	24	M	UNKNOWN	GRACSDNY	
U, VALESKA	27	F	UNKNOWN	GRACSDNY	
ZEOLKIW--, MICH.	46	F	UNKNOWN	GRZZZZNY	
ELISABETH	7	F	CHILD	GRAEABNY	
WLADISLA	6	F	CHILD	GRABUTNY	
JOHANN	4	M	CHILD	GRABUTNY	
MARIANNE	14	F	CH	GRABUTNY	
UHLMANN, ADOLF	29	M	UNKNOWN	GRABUTNY	
GROSSMANN, LOUISE	32	F	W	GRZZZZTX	
DAHNENHAUER, JOHANN	30	M	LABR	GRZZZZNY	
AUSTEDT, FRANZ	33	M	LABR	GRZZZZNY	
LINK, GOTTL.	17	M	LABR	GRZZZZNY	
WILHELMINE	16	F	SVNT	GRZZZZNY	
GOLY, MARIE	36	F	W	GRZZZZNY	
EMIL	7	M	CHILD	GRZZZZNY	
JULIE	.02	F	INFANT	GRZZZZNY	
WEIGEL, DANIEL	18	M	SHMK	GRZZZZNY	
BAER, PAUL	15	F	SVNT	GRABDVNY	
HOOCK, ADOLF	26	M	LABR	GRABDVNY	
MOENIG, CONRAD	21	M	LABR	GRABDVNY	
DRANGENSTEIN, JOS.	18	M	LABR	GRABHJNY	
SAUMER, CHRICT	28	M	LABR	GRABHJNY	
DZIK, PETER	23	M	LABR	GRABHJWI	
DOTJAUER, K.	22	M	LABR	GRAFEENY	
ARENDT, JOSEF	36	M	LABR	GRAAKHNY	
BINDER, GOTTFRIED	40	M	LABR	GRAAKHNY	
MEYER, ANTON	50	M	UNKNOWN	GRABDMNY	
BENDER, PETER	24	M	UNKNOWN	GRACXVNY	
BRUNING, AUGUST	52	M	UNKNOWN	GRAAXKNY	
EBEL, WM.	26	M	UNKNOWN	GRAARRNY	
SKOMROC, MARHTA	18	M	UNKNOWN	GRZZZZNY	
A-HENK, H.B.	36	M	TT	GRADBQNY	

SHIP: IOWA

FROM: LIVERPOOL
TO: BOSTON
ARRIVED: 03 MAY 1888

PASSENGER	AGE	SEX	OCCUPATION	PRVL	DES
KLEIN, ABRAM	55	M	SHMK	GRZZZZUSA	
FANNIE	50	F	W	GRZZZZUSA	
WOHLGEMUTH, JACOB	39	M	LABR	GRZZZZUSA	
JULIANNE	48	F	W	GRZZZZUSA	
BERGEN, LOUIS	79	M	TLR	GRZZZZUSA	
WHILIMENE	39	F	W	GRZZZZUSA	
GORABOWYKI, WOYSICK	30	M	LABR	GRZZZZUSA	
MAGDALINE	32	F	W	GRZZZZUSA	
LAMBRECHT, FRED.	32	M	MACH	GRZZZZUSA	
CAROLINE	33	F	W	GRZZZZUSA	
RODANSKI, AUG.	55	M	LABR	GRZZZZUSA	
JOHANNA	54	F	W	GRZZZZUSA	
GIELS, AUG.	24	M	LABR	GRZZZZUSA	
AMALIE	24	F	W	GRZZZZUSA	

PASSENGER	AGE	SEX	OCCUPATION	PRVL DES
MARTEN, EDWARD	36	M	LABR	GRZZZZUSA
AUGUSTE	28	F	W	GRZZZZUSA
JACOBSEN, JANS	42	M	LABR	GRZZZZUSA
HEDWIG	41	F	W	GRZZZZUSA
RUDAILIE, JOHN	26	M	UNKNOWN	GRZZZZUSA
OIRSULE	25	F	W	GRZZZZUSA
ARROWS, ISAAC	24	M	JNR	GRZZZZUSA
RACHEL	24	F	W	GRZZZZUSA
GOLDFINGER, RIFKE	23	F	W	GRZZZZUSA
HOCKHAUSEN, SUSA	11	F	SCH	GRZZZZUSA
STANKA, SCHASKA	19	F	SP	GRZZZZUSA
WARSHOLSK, DOMANTA	20	F	SP	GRZZZZUSA
RIBNER, FEIGE	15	F	SP	GRZZZZUSA
GOHN, CHRISTINE	25	F	SP	GRZZZZUSA
HOPPE, MARIA	18	F	SP	GRZZZZUSA
RODANKI, BERTHA	15	F	SP	GRZZZZUSA
JOHANNA	16	F	SP	GRZZZZUSA
SCHIERALLINE, MARTHA	59	F	W	GRZZZZUSA
JACOBSEN, LOUISE	15	F	SP	GRZZZZUSA
WALESK, HIGWIGA	22	F	W	GRZZZZUSA
TOPNICK, MARCILA	23	F	SP	GRZZZZUSA
KLEIN, THOMAS	8	M	CHILD	GRZZZZUSA
TOSKO	11	M	CH	GRZZZZUSA
GOLDFINGER, FEIGE	5	F	CHILD	GRZZZZUSA
SARI	3	F	CHILD	GRZZZZUSA
LEIBSCH	.11	F	INFANT	GRZZZZUSA
WOHLGEMUTH, EMIL	8	M	CHILD	GRZZZZUSA
MAN	4	M	CHILD	GRZZZZUSA
WEINSTEIN, CHAIN	8	M	CHILD	GRZZZZUSA
BERGEN, HEDWIG	11	M	SCH	GRZZZZUSA
EMIL	16	M	TLR	GRZZZZUSA
GORABOWYK, MARY-A.	3	F	CHILD	GRZZZZUSA
JADWIGA	2	F	CHILD	GRZZZZUSA
LAMBRECHT, MARIA	5	F	CHILD	GRZZZZUSA
RICKARD	.05	M	INFANT	GRZZZZUSA
GIELS, JOHN	9	M	CHILD	GRZZZZUSA
AUG.	7	M	CHILD	GRZZZZUSA
BERTHA	5	F	CHILD	GRZZZZUSA
GUSTAV	.04	M	INFANT	GRZZZZUSA
MARTIN, HADA	4	F	CHILD	GRZZZZUSA
GUSTAV	3	M	CHILD	GRZZZZUSA
MARTHA	1	F	CHILD	GRZZZZUSA
JANE	.02	F	INFANT	GRZZZZUSA
JACOBSEN, CARL	11	M	SCH	GRZZZZUSA
HANS	9	M	CHILD	GRZZZZUSA
SELINA	4	F	CHILD	GRZZZZUSA
ANNA	3	F	CHILD	GRZZZZUSA
DORA	1	F	CHILD	GRZZZZUSA
FERZNGER, HERSCH	11	M	SCH	GRZZZZUSA
RUDAIHE, JOSEPH	.06	M	INFANT	GRZZZZUSA
ARROWS, ELPHA	.11	F	INFANT	GRZZZZUSA
GORABOWONYK, SNEFAN	1	M	CHILD	GRZZZZUSA
HOCHSTER, WILHELM	45	M	LABR	GRZZZZUSA
MIERS, MAX	18	M	LABR	GRZZZZUSA
POZEGO, JANKO	25	M	BKLYR	GRZZZZUSA
ADDLER, FRANK	24	M	LABR	GRZZZZUSA
NEILSON, MARIANES	23	M	JNR	GRZZZZUSA
LUMBRECHT, WILHELM	27	M	MACH	GRZZZZUSA
LANGE, RIKE	30	M	LABR	GRZZZZUSA
HOPPE, WILHELM	16	M	LABR	GRZZZZUSA
RODANKI, CARL	23	M	LABR	GRZZZZUSA
FREDK.	21	M	LABR	GRZZZZUSA
AUG.	17	M	LABR	GRZZZZUSA
PUSETT, ALWIN	21	M	LABR	GRZZZZUSA
KERSTNEY, FREDK.	23	M	LABR	GRZZZZUSA
GICKLER, ALB.	50	M	MACH	GRZZZZUSA
REITZ, CHRISTIAN	40	M	LKSH	GRZZZZUSA
FIRZINGER, GALMAN	27	M	LABR	GRZZZZUSA
BLUM, JOSEF	19	M	TLR	GRZZZZUSA
KEMNISKY, ISAAC	19	M	TLR	GRZZZZUSA
FREEDMAN, LOUIS	30	M	PNTR	FRZZZZUSA

SHIP: BRITANNIC

FROM: LIVERPOOL AND QUEENSTOWN
TO: NEW YORK
ARRIVED: 04 MAY 1888

PASSENGER	AGE	SEX	OCCUPATION	PRVL DES
RICHTEL, HERSCH	27	M	LABR	FRADAXUSA
WISHAUSKEY, SCHERIE	26	M	LABR	FRADAXUSA
ABRAHAM, ESTER	33	F	W	FRADAXUSA
KOLINON	00	M	INF	FRADAXUSA
RODA, JOSEPH	33	M	LABR	FRADAXUSA
SALZ, PESSEL	11	M	CH	FRADAXUSA
LYFENFERD, PERSEL	16	F	SP	FRADAXUSA
EVILNER, EISIG	22	M	FARMER	FRADAXUSA
KRASKER, LEBAE	16	M	LABR	FRADAXUSA
HERSCH	10	M	CH	FRADAXUSA
DICK, BIMISCH	1	M	CHILD	FRADAXUSA
SCHSBEL, LEA	32	F	W	FRADAXUSA
DWORE	10	F	CH	FRADAXUSA
GITTE	7	F	CHILD	FRADAXUSA
MOSES	5	M	CHILD	FRADAXUSA
CHRIST	3	M	CHILD	FRADAXUSA
LINE	1	F	CHILD	FRADAXUSA
LANGER, SALI	24	F	SVNT	FRADAXUSA
RIJKE	1	F	CHILD	FRADAXUSA
CRESKOWNER, MARIA	20	F	SVNT	FRADAXUSA
ROSENBAUM, LEIH	11	F	CH	FRADAXUSA
MERCHWEWITZ, JOSEPHA	35	M	STNR	FRADAXUSA
SILBERSTEIN, REGINA	18	F	SP	FRADAXUSA
RAPPEL, SAINVALET	41	M	LABR	FRADAXUSA
RACSKOUSKI, JUDSE	33	F	W	FRADAXUSA
CHA--	10	M	CH	FRADAXUSA
FREID, EDHER	18	F	SP	FRADAXUSA
LE, FRANZ	24	M	LABR	FRADAXUSA
GERTZEN, S	21	M	LABR	FRADAXUSA
GAROWSKI, U	1	M	CHILD	FRADAXUSA
MAGNUS, A	47	M	MCHT	FRADAXUSA

SHIP: GALLIA

FROM: LIVERPOOL AND QUEENSTOWN
TO: NEW YORK
ARRIVED: 04 MAY 1888

PASSENGER	AGE	SEX	OCCUPATION	PRVL DES
VIEBRANG, ALFRED	24	M	HRDRS	FRACBFUSA
SAUER, EMIL	23	M	HRDRS	FRACBFUSA
MATERN, HAMANN	24	M	LABR	FRACBFUSA
U, U	00	U	MA	FRACBFUSA
U	00	U	INF	FRACBFUSA
KONBAN, U	65	M	LABR	FRACBFUSA
DORA	54	F	W	FRACBFUSA
AUG	21	M	LABR	FRACBFUSA
CHRIS	18	M	LABR	FRACBFUSA
HARMANN	13	M	CH	FRACBFUSA
FREDEREICK	11	M	CH	FRACBFUSA
STAHK, AUG	37	M	CPTR	FRACBFUSA
DOROTHEA	36	F	W	FRACBFUSA
MINA	17	F	SP	FRACBFUSA
HERMANNIE	11	M	CH	FRACBFUSA
BERTHA	10	F	CH	FRACBFUSA
EVALD	9	F	CHILD	FRACBFUSA
FRED	5	M	CHILD	FRACBFUSA
LANGE, ALBERTINA	36	F	MA	FRACBFUSA
REINHOLD	11	M	CH	FRACBFUSA
ALLAIN	9	M	CHILD	FRACBFUSA
LEIDE	3	F	CHILD	FRACBFUSA
SCHINDLER, HADES	17	M	SVNT	FRACBFUSA

SHIP: LAHN

FROM: BREMEN AND SOUTHAMPTON
TO: NEW YORK
ARRIVED: 04 MAY 1888

PASSENGER	AGE	SEX	OCCUPATION	PRVL	DES
---MANN, M	20	F	UNKNOWN	FRADLDGR	
MECKE, ANT	57	F	W	FRAARRGR	
VANROSENBERG, ROB	61	M	TT	FRAARRGR	
----ING, ALFRED	31	M	TT	FRAARRGR	
LOENING, A	25	F	W	FRAARRGR	
RUDOLPH	4	M	CHILD	FRAARRGR	
ABB	2	M	CHILD	FRAARRGR	
GOWOERNEUR, IRMA	28	F	GVNS	FRAARRGR	
ILGENER, EDW	47	M	TT	FRAAKHGR	
---RK, JOS	37	M	TT	GRZZZZGR	
FREUDENBERG, FRIEDR	60	M	TT	GRZZZZGR	
BACHENHEIM, HUGO	15	M	TT	GRZZZZGR	
-AARDT, OTTO	24	M	TT	GRAAPSGR	
---AEGER, HEDW	25	F	UNKNOWN	GRZZZZGR	
CUMME, WALTER	17	M	TT	GRAARRGR	
POSSELT, FRIEDR	40	M	TT	GRADOIGR	
GOETTSCH, GEORG	30	M	TT	GRAGOIGR	
MARTHA	24	F	W	GRAGOIGR	
SAFT, HENRIETTE	30	F	W	GRAAKHGR	
MAXIMILIAN	5	M	CHILD	GRAAKHGR	
SIEGMAR	4	M	CHILD	GRAAKHGR	
BIANKA	.08	F	INFANT	GRAAKHGR	
HORN, BERNHARD	17	M	TT	GRACKSGR	
SAM	19	M	TT	GRACKSGR	
---ESEL, MAX	32	M	TT	GRAARRGR	
--LARDI, CARL	30	M	TT	GRAAXKGR	
PFALZER, FLORUS	17	M	TT	GRAFHPGR	
URY, MATHILDE	36	F	W	GRAAWTGR	
FELIX	10	M	CH	GRAAWTGR	
JULIAN	7	M	CHILD	GRAAWTGR	
GEORGE, FRIEDA	27	F	UNKNOWN	GRAAWTGR	
--UNTNER, ALBERT	16	M	TT	GRAEXWGR	
---HULTE, ANTON	30	M	TT	GRZZZZGR	
KOR--ES, H	32	M	TT	GRAGNNGR	
FRITZ, CARL	24	M	TT	GRZZZZGR	
SIEBER, CHRISTOPH	34	M	TT	GRAARRGR	
VANGAYERN, OLOF	27	M	TT	GRAFEESW	
HASHAGEN, ERICH	30	M	SEMN	GRAAOFGR	
META	28	F	W	GRAAOFGR	
KROESING, GUSTAV	32	M	LABR	GRAEWMUSA	
JANKOWSKI, WLADISLAW	15	M	UNKNOWN	GRAEABUSA	
ZUBA, ANTONIA	43	F	W	GRZZZZUSA	
MICHAELA	7	F	CHILD	GRZZZZUSA	
MARIANNA	6	F	CHILD	GRZZZZUSA	
STANISLAV	5	M	CHILD	GRZZZZUSA	
PITRENELLA	3	F	CHILD	GRZZZZUSA	
MARTIN	.11	M	INFANT	GRZZZZUSA	
--MANSKA, CATH	45	F	W	GRAECPUSA	
THEOPHILA	7	F	CHILD	GRAECPUSA	
ANNA	6	F	CHILD	GRAECPUSA	
LANGOWSKA, JULIANA	18	F	UNKNOWN	GRAECPUSA	
SZYMANSKI, JOHANN	17	M	LABR	GRAECPUSA	
STROZYNSKI, ANTON	28	M	LABR	GRZZZZUSA	
PASTVA, IGNATZ	60	M	LABR	GRZZZZUSA	
JOSEFA	70	F	W	GRZZZZUSA	
JULIA	30	F	W	GRZZZZUSA	
FRANZ	7	M	CHILD	GRZZZZUSA	
JULIA	2	F	CHILD	GRZZZZUSA	
JOHANN	.09	M	INFANT	GRZZZZUSA	
KRUEGER, BALTHASAR	60	M	LABR	GRZZZZUSA	
ANNA	66	F	W	GRZZZZUSA	
KONICZKA, JOSEF	60	M	LABR	GRZZZZUSA	
ANTONIA	30	F	W	GRZZZZUSA	
STOSCHINSKI, ANTONIA	21	F	W	GRZZZZUSA	
STANISLAWA	.10	F	INFANT	GRZZZZUSA	
KONIECZKA, JOSEPHA	20	F	W	GRZZZZUSA	
SZCEPAN	7	M	CHILD	GRZZZZUSA	
BRANDTA, JOSEF	23	M	LABR	GRZZZZUSA	
STARCZEWSKI, FRANZ	22	M	LABR	GRZZZZUSA	
GUFKA, JAN	24	M	LABR	GRAFRBUSA	
PIETROWSKA, STANISL	7	M	CHILD	GRAFRBUSA	
MARIANNE	5	F	CHILD	GRAFRBUSA	
APOLONIA	.09	F	INFANT	GRAFRBUSA	
SCHNEIDER, JENDRZY	52	M	LABR	GRZZZZUSA	
MICHAL	26	F	W	GRZZZZUSA	
---TOWSKI, HERM	22	M	LABR	GRZZZZUSA	
JANOWIAK, WOJCIECH	22	M	LABR	GRZZZZUSA	
ROMANN, FRANZ	33	M	LABR	GRADENUSA	
ANNA	29	F	W	GRADENUSA	
SOBECKI, VALENTY	28	M	LABR	GRZZZZUSA	
NOWAK, FRANZ	35	M	LABR	GRZZZZUSA	
KLEWIN, PAULINE	25	F	W	GRZZZZUSA	
AUGUST	3	M	CHILD	GRZZZZUSA	
OTTILIE	.10	F	INFANT	GRZZZZUSA	
KUSTAN, ANTONIE	7	F	CHILD	GRZZZZUSA	
MANTHIER, HERM	13	M	UNKNOWN	GRZZZZUSA	
BUKOWSKI, ANDR	68	M	LABR	GRZZZZUSA	
JUST	57	F	W	GRZZZZUSA	
FRANZ	6	M	CHILD	GRZZZZUSA	
LABIENSKI, WILH	24	M	LABR	GRZZZZUSA	
MEYER, CHRIST	15	M	UNKNOWN	GRAEBOUSA	
--MOHS, ANNA	31	F	W	GRZZZZUSA	
MARTHA	7	F	CHILD	GRZZZZUSA	
MALISCHEWSKA, ERNEST	42	F	W	GRZZZZUSA	
VALERIA	5	F	CHILD	GRZZZZUSA	
DONATA	.08	F	INFANT	GRZZZZUSA	
KARSKI, JOHANN	32	M	LABR	GRZZZZUSA	
ROSINSKI, ANNA	23	F	UNKNOWN	GRZZZZUSA	
SULEY, WOJCIECH	37	M	LABR	GRZZZZUSA	
SZYBATH, JAKOB	84	M	PVTR	GRZZZZUSA	
SULEY, CATH	30	F	W	GRZZZZUSA	
STANISL	7	M	CHILD	GRZZZZUSA	
FRANZ	6	F	CHILD	GRZZZZUSA	
ANDR	4	M	CHILD	GRZZZZUSA	
ANNA	.10	F	INFANT	GRZZZZUSA	
PADZINSKA, ELISAB	18	F	UNKNOWN	GRZZZZUSA	
MAGD	54	F	W	GRZZZZUSA	
WISNIESKA, JOSEF	40	M	LABR	GRZZZZUSA	
VICTORIA	26	F	W	GRZZZZUSA	
STEFAN	6	M	CHILD	GRZZZZUSA	
FRANZ	4	M	CHILD	GRZZZZUSA	
VALENTIN	2	M	CHILD	GRZZZZUSA	
FRANZ	.09	F	INFANT	GRZZZZUSA	
PADZINSKA, MARIANNA	21	F	UNKNOWN	GRZZZZUSA	
JENDRZEJEWSKI, JACOB	28	M	LABR	GRZZZZUSA	
MARIANNA	30	F	W	GRZZZZUSA	
KASKA, MARIANNA	30	F	W	GRZZZZUSA	
FRANZ	7	F	CHILD	GRZZZZUSA	
MARIANNA	6	F	CHILD	GRZZZZUSA	
ROSALIE	.11	F	INFANT	GRZZZZUSA	
WLADISLAW	1	M	CHILD	GRZZZZUSA	
---OLINSKI, IGNATZ	36	M	LABR	GRZZZZUSA	
BORANSKI, IGNATZ	26	M	LABR	GRZZZZUSA	
DOBROWSKI, STEFAN	25	M	LABR	GRZZZZUSA	
LLUKACZEWICZ, KAT	49	F	UNKNOWN	GRZZZZUSA	
YARZEBOWSKI, MICH	42	M	LABR	GRZZZZUSA	
JOSEFA	38	F	W	GRZZZZUSA	
ANTON	7	M	CHILD	GRZZZZUSA	
JAPKOWSKI, MARIANNA	22	F	W	GRZZZZUSA	
YARZEBOWSKI, ANTONIA	6	F	CHILD	GRZZZZUSA	
MARTIN	5	M	CHILD	GRZZZZUSA	
BRONISLAW	.09	M	INFANT	GRZZZZUSA	
JAPKOWSKI, PETER	.09	M	INFANT	GRZZZZUSA	
KOTOWSKI, FRANZ	30	M	LABR	GRZZZZUSA	
KWIATKOWSKA, JOSEFA	23	M	LABR	GRZZZZUSA	
SENKEL, KARL	30	M	LABR	GRZZZZUSA	
KLATZKO, JORE	23	F	W	GRAGRTUSA	
CHAWE	.04	F	INFANT	GRAGRTUSA	
GUDERIAN, FRIEDR	42	M	LABR	GRZZZZUSA	
HERM	7	M	CHILD	GRZZZZUSA	
GUNEMANN, META	24	F	UNKNOWN	GRAJAWUSA	
JANKOWSKA, STANISL	38	F	W	GRZZZZUSA	
FELICIA	7	F	CHILD	GRZZZZUSA	

PASSENGER	AGE	SEX	OCCUPATION	PRVL DES
CZESLAWA	5	F	CHILD	GRZZZZUSA
HELENA	.11	F	INFANT	GRZZZZUSA
SKRZYPCZAK, FRANZ	29	M	UNKNOWN	GRZZZZUSA
PAWLAK, ROSALIE	19	F	UNKNOWN	GRZZZZUSA
BROCKMANN, SOPHIE	24	F	UNKNOWN	GRAARRUSA
SCHROEDER, ANNA	15	F	UNKNOWN	GRAACKUSA
MILES, ADOLF	15	M	UNKNOWN	GRABCYUSA
MEYER, MINNIE	23	F	UNKNOWN	GRZZZZUSA
DOESCHER, LISETTE	53	F	UNKNOWN	GRZZZZUSA
BUERGER, HEIINR	30	M	LABR	GRZZZZUSA
LOEWEKAMP, CARL	19	M	LABR	GRZZZZUSA
LOEWER, JOH	25	M	LABR	GRZZZZUSA
RATHJEN, OTTO	17	M	BKR	GRABRYUSA
FRIEDR	14	M	UNKNOWN	GRABRYUSA
KNOCHE, HEINR	16	M	UNKNOWN	GRABRYUSA
SCHRIEVER, FRIEDR	31	M	LABR	GRAEFSUSA
MARIE	21	F	W	GRAEFSUSA
KOPPMANN, HEINR	25	M	LABR	GRAEFSUSA
EMMA	27	F	W	GRAEFSUSA
HUESKER, LUDWIG	30	M	LABR	GRAEFSUSA
KOENEMANN, CARL	24	M	LABR	GRAEFSUSA
MICHEL, CRESCENZ	24	M	LABR	GRZZZZUSA
RAAB, JOSEF	8	M	CHILD	GRZZZZUSA
CORDES, REBECKA	18	F	UNKNOWN	GRAFWZUSA
MEYERHOLZ, JOH	60	M	LABR	GRAFWZUSA
SOPHIE	60	F	W	GRAFWZUSA
THOELE, ANNA	20	F	UNKNOWN	GRAFWZUSA
BECK, WILH	34	M	LABR	GRADYYUSA
CAROL	34	M	LABR	GRADYYUSA
WILH	7	M	CHILD	GRADYYUSA
CARL	5	M	CHILD	GRADYYUSA
JOHANN	2	M	CHILD	GRADYYUSA
ETZLER, JOH	33	M	LABR	GRADYYUSA
SUSANNE	31	F	W	GRADYYUSA
ADOLF	4	M	CHILD	GRADYYUSA
BERTHA	.06	F	INFANT	GRADYYUSA
FLATHMANN, CARL	14	M	UNKNOWN	GRAELEUSA
GROSSMEYER, MATH	26	F	W	GRAJTDUSA
LUDWIG	2	M	CHILD	GRAJTDUSA
CARL	.04	M	INFANT	GRAJTDUSA
GIEBLER, OTTO	38	M	JNR	GRAESQUSA
HARTL, HEINR	24	M	LABR	GRZZZZUSA
MATH	25	F	W	GRZZZZUSA
THERESE	3	F	CHILD	GRZZZZUSA
SKONICKA, IGNACZ	30	M	LABR	GRAEABUSA
ANTONIE	26	F	W	GRAEABUSA
JOHANN	2	M	CHILD	GRAEABUSA
WANDA	.10	F	INFANT	GRAEABUSA
SULETZKY, JOSEF	33	M	LABR	GRZZZZUSA
FRANZ	27	F	W	GRZZZZUSA
HELENA	2	F	CHILD	GRZZZZUSA
ELISAB	.06	F	INFANT	GRZZZZUSA
WOLANDT, MARIA	25	F	UNKNOWN	GRZZZZUSA
ZALEZ, PETER	24	M	LABR	GRZZZZUSA
KOTKE, GUSTAV	39	M	LABR	GRADNPUSA
WELLBROCK, HEINR	13	M	UNKNOWN	GRACBGUSA
JUEDEL, JULIUS	44	M	LABR	GRZZZZUSA
GEILER, CARL	30	M	BCHR	GRABYQUSA
HOPPMANN, SOPHIE	15	F	UNKNOWN	GRZZZZUSA
BARG, WILH	16	F	UNKNOWN	GRZZZZUSA
COLLMANN, RUPRECHT	25	M	LABR	GRACBRUSA
KUHLMANN, HEINR	25	M	LABR	GRAALZUSA
GRABERMANN, WILH	24	F	UNKNOWN	GRAALZUSA
EHRLICH, FRIEDR	55	M	LABR	GRZZZZUSA
CHRIST	50	F	W	GRZZZZUSA
GEORGE	27	M	LABR	GRZZZZUSA
GREWE, CATH	22	F	UNKNOWN	GRZZZZUSA
HARKE, JOHANN	27	M	LABR	GRZZZZUSA
KLOPPENBURG, JOH	24	M	LABR	GRZZZZUSA
MUELLER, WILHELM	26	M	LABR	GRABCYUSA
HAAKE, GUSTAV	16	M	LABR	GRABCYUSA
ANNA	20	F	UNKNOWN	GRZZZZUSA
SEIDEL, ALFRED	17	M	LABR	GRZZZZUSA
EVERS, HEINR	15	M	UNKNOWN	GRZZZZUSA
HASPER, HEINR	50	M	LABR	GRZZZZUSA
WUNDERLICH, MARIEE	19	F	UNKNOWN	GRAFSBUSA
GREIM, ELISAB	16	F	UNKNOWN	GRZZZZUSA
SCHNEIDER, KAT	18	F	UNKNOWN	GRZZZZUSA
SCHOERNER, MARIE	16	F	UNKNOWN	GRZZZZUSA
WERMUTH, MARIE	26	F	UNKNOWN	GRZZZZUSA
WATTES, CHRIST	23	F	UNKNOWN	GRZZZZUSA
MILES, GEORG	14	M	UNKNOWN	GRACBFUSA
RINGE, GEORG	14	M	UNKNOWN	GRACBFUSA
HENCK, ALMA	18	F	UNKNOWN	GRACBFUSA
JENTZ, OTTO	14	M	UNKNOWN	GRACBFUSA
ROGGE, AUGUSTE	20	F	UNKNOWN	GRZZZZUSA
DRUEKSTEIN, DORA	19	F	UNKNOWN	GRZZZZUSA
WISCHHUSEN, GEORG	21	M	FARMER	GRABWKUSA
HOFMANN, CARL	30	M	LKSH	GRACZWUSA
JUNGWALTER, THERESE	37	F	UNKNOWN	GRZZZZUSA
POSLER, PETER	40	M	SMH	GRZZZZUSA
ERTEL, JOHANN	27	M	LABR	GRZZZZUSA
KOLP, GEORGE	25	M	LABR	GRZZZZUSA
GROESER, THEVES	27	M	LABR	GRZZZZUSA
LEVI, TAUBE	50	F	W	GRAFZGUSA
SILBERBERG, JACOB	17	M	LABR	GRAFZGUSA
KACZMAREK, EGIDIUS	28	M	LABR	GRZZZZUSA
PLAHASCH, JOSEF	23	M	LABR	GRZZZZUSA
MISCHEK, VALENT	24	M	LABR	GRZZZZUSA
JASCH, JACOB	24	M	LABR	GRZZZZUSA
PASCHIKOWSKY, WLADISL	25	M	LABR	GRZZZZUSA
SZENDA, NICL	24	M	LABR	GRZZZZUSA
KESSLER, BERTHA	24	F	UNKNOWN	GRZZZZUSA
HEITMANN, MARIE	23	F	UNKNOWN	GRZZZZUSA
KRDEMER, LOUIS	23	M	LABR	GRAAKGUSA
MUELLER, MARRIE	23	F	UNKNOWN	GRZZZZUSA
STEFFE, MINNA	20	F	UNKNOWN	GRAEROUSA
ROSENTHAL, AUG	20	F	UNKNOWN	GRAEROUSA
BEHNKEN, FRIEDR	10	M	CH	GRAARRUSA
DENEKE, WILH	26	M	TLR	GRADVHUSA
TEPPENJOHANNES, FRIEDR	26	M	MCHT	GRADVHUSA
BARTELS, HERM	16	M	UNKNOWN	GRZZZZUSA
KREBS, JOHANN	15	M	UNKNOWN	GRABRYUSA
SEEKAMP, ADELH	65	F	W	GRAIBTUSA
FEDERWITZ, ANNA	20	F	UNKNOWN	GRAELEUSA
BLENDERMANN, HERM	14	M	UNKNOWN	GRAELEUSA
MARTHA	14	F	UNKNOWN	GRAELEUSA
WENDELKEN, ADELHEID	14	F	UNKNOWN	GRAELEUSA
BORWEGEN, EMMA	16	F	UNKNOWN	GRAELEUSA
LEHR, WILH	26	F	UNKNOWN	GRZZZZUSA
BLOECHL, PETER	25	M	LABR	GRZZZZUSA
SCHMITKUNZ, MARIE	20	F	UNKNOWN	GRACBRUSA
KIZON, MARIE	20	F	UNKNOWN	GRACBRUSA
KLEIN, MARIE	18	M	LABR	GRZZZZUSA
STEINBACH, JOHANN	54	M	LABR	GRABOQUSA
MARG	53	F	W	GRABOQUSA
BUDE, LOUISE	16	F	UNKNOWN	GRZZZZUSA
NAU, CATH	19	F	UNKNOWN	GRZZZZUSA
KRALL, CATH	20	F	UNKNOWN	GRZZZZUSA
JAEGER, CATH	21	F	W	GRZZZZUSA
WILH	24	M	LABR	GRZZZZUSA
DOELL, OTTO	21	F	FARMER	GRZZZZUSA
EHRMANN, MARG	18	F	UNKNOWN	GRZZZZUSA
BRAUN, JOHANN	17	M	LKSH	GRZZZZUSA
MAERZ, JOHANN	32	M	LKSH	GRZZZZUSA
MARIE	32	F	W	GRZZZZUSA
MARIE	7	F	CHILD	GRZZZZUSA
KATH	.08	F	INFANT	GRZZZZUSA
MARIE	36	F	UNKNOWN	GRZZZZUSA
SCHUETZ, ELISAB	25	F	UNKNOWN	GRZZZZUSA
RIEDMUELLER, JACOB	23	M	LABR	GRZZZZUSA
SCHMITT, HERM	20	M	LABR	GRZZZZUSA
SIEDENTOPF, WILH	35	M	LABR	GRZZZZUSA
HEDERICH, PHILIPP	13	M	LABR	GRZZZZUSA
SCHEU, WILLIAM	15	M	LABR	GRZZZZUSA
SCHNEIDER, HEIN	25	M	LABR	GRZZZZUSA
HAUENSTEIN, LUD	17	M	LABR	GRZZZZUSA
LUNDRUG, MARIE	24	F	UNKNOWN	GRZZZZUSA
BRICK, ANNE	20	F	UNKNOWN	GRZZZZUSA
THOMSEN, CARL	24	M	LABR	GRZZZZUSA

PASSENGER	AGE	SEX	OCCUPATION	PVL	DES
BECKER, CATH	15	F	UNKNOWN		GRZZZZUSA
GOERLACH, ELISAB	16	F	UNKNOWN		GRZZZZUSA
BOERNER, OSWALD	30	M	LABR		GRZZZZUSA
BERTHA	28	F	W		GRZZZZUSA
RAAB, MARIA	28	F	UNKNOWN		GRZZZZUSA
SCHAIBLEIN, EGENIE	21	F	UNKNOWN		GRZZZZUSA
ROSSMANN, ANDREAS	51	M	LABR		GRZZZZUSA
ANNA	53	F	W		GRZZZZUSA
LORENZ	6	M	CHILD		GRZZZZUSA
SCHMIDT, JOHANN	18	M	LABR		GRZZZZUSA
WINDOLPH, FRANZ	25	M	LABR		GRABODUSA
RAMMGER, ED	17	M	LABR		GRZZZZUSA
MARTIN, AUGUSTIN	16	M	LABR		GRZZZZUSA
PANKRATZ, RIPPEL	16	M	LABR		GRZZZZUSA
SCHREINER, PHILIPP	39	M	LABR		GRZZZZUSA
HOLZER, BARB	21	F	UNKNOWN		GRAKPIUSA
SCHNEIDER, CARL	17	M	LABR		GRAFWNUSA
STRAUSS, MORITZ	25	M	MCHT		GRACZYUSA
STEIGERWALD, LORENZ	50	M	LABR		GRZZZZUSA
ROSINE	40	F	W		GRZZZZUSA
BERTHA	9	F	CHILD		GRZZZZUSA
EDUARD	7	M	CHILD		GRZZZZUSA
CARL	6	M	CHILD		GRZZZZUSA
APOLONIA	5	F	CHILD		GRZZZZUSA
AMANDA	4	F	CHILD		GRZZZZUSA
ANTON	2	M	CHILD		GRZZZZUSA
EICHINE	.09	F	INFANT		GRZZZZUSA
SEIGERTH, GEORG	16	M	UNKNOWN		GRADNOUSA
WITTMANN, EMILIE	14	F	UNKNOWN		GRAHGPUSA
MUELLER, MARG	59	F	UNKNOWN		GRAKPEUSA
SCHWARZ, MARG	21	F	UNKNOWN		GRZZZZUSA
GEIS, KAETCHEN	24	F	UNKNOWN		GRABLGUSA
GROSS, GEORG	16	M	UNKNOWN		GRADLDUSA
KOPP, ALOIS	53	M	LABR		GRADLDUSA
MARIA	21	F	UNKNOWN		GRADLDUSA
HELLA, GUSTAV	10	M	CH		GRZZZZUSA
FRANZEN, MARIE	19	F	UNKNOWN		GRACBRUSA
WALLENSTEIN, SOPHIE	52	F	UNKNOWN		GRACBRUSA
MAEGERLEIN, TOBIAS	25	M	LABR		GRAJWQUSA
HERTZLER, SIEGFR	21	M	LABR		GRABUTUSA
FRENZ, FRIEDR	23	M	LABR		GRZZZZUSA
LAY, JOHANN	17	M	LABR		GRZZZZUSA
LEIPPOLD, HERM	23	M	LABR		GRZZZZUSA
WURST, JOHANN	25	M	LABR		GRZZZZUSA
KUEBLER, HEINR	24	M	LABR		GRZZZZUSA
FAHRION, LOUISE	22	F	UNKNOWN		GRZZZZUSA
KAUFMANN, KATIE	20	F	UNKNOWN		GRZZZZUSA
KIEFER, WILH	40	M	SMH		GRAEXWUSA
BARB	42	F	W		GRAEXWUSA
WILH	6	M	CHILD		GRAEXWUSA
BERTHA	5	F	CHILD		GRAEXWUSA
CARL	4	M	CHILD		GRAEXWUSA
PAUL	3	M	CHILD		GRAEXWUSA
STUHBACH, JOSEF	38	M	WCHMKR		GRAEXWUSA
KLEIN, HEINR	30	M	MCHT		GRAEXWUSA
KNOLL, MAX	16	M	UNKNOWN		GRZZZZUSA
ALBERT, ANNA	21	F	UNKNOWN		GRZZZZUSA
KRALL, KATH	21	F	UNKNOWN		GRZZZZUSA
WEISS, ELISABETH	22	F	UNKNOWN		GRAFQVUSA
WIND, BURGHARDT	14	M	UNKNOWN		GRADXKUSA
PFAFF, ANNA	24	F	UNKNOWN		GRAGEEUSA
REIKER, ANNE	22	F	UNKNOWN		GRAGEEUSA
BAHNTGE, CHRIST	22	M	BKR		GRAHNOUSA
LENZ, GEORG	49	M	LABR		GRZZZZUSA
REGINA	22	F	UNKNOWN		GRZZZZUSA
HACKER, KUNIG	20	F	UNKNOWN		GRAGBBUSA
HAGEN, JOHANN	34	M	LABR		GRAGBBUSA
RICHTER, JACOB	19	M	LABR		GRZZZZUSA
HAUB, CONRAD	17	M	LABR		GRZZZZUSA
HILDEBRANDT, ELISE	15	F	UNKNOWN		GRZZZZUSA
REUTER, KATH	18	F	UNKNOWN		GRZZZZUSA
MOHR, WILH	11	M	CH		GRZZZZUSA
HAGEMANN, FERD	15	M	UNKNOWN		GRZZZZUSA
HAUSMANN, ELISAB	13	F	UNKNOWN		GRAIEFUSA
FRANKE, GUST	27	M	LABR		GRAHZFUSA
POPP, NIKOL	56	M	LABR		GRABYGUSA
EVA	56	F	W		GRABYGUSA
GEORG	7	M	CHILD		GRABYGUSA
JOHANN	5	M	CHILD		GRABYGUSA
KWEIZER, ANDR	24	M	LABR		GRZZZZUSA
CACILIE	22	F	W		GRZZZZUSA
BRONISLAWA	.06	F	INFANT		GRZZZZUSA
DEUTSCH, CLARA	27	F	UNKNOWN		GRAAKHUSA
JOCHNER, BLASIUS	28	M	LABR		GRADLDUSA
GRIMM, LUDWIG	24	M	LABR		GRADLDUSA
KAROL	26	F	W		GRADLDUSA
WILH	.06	F	INFANT		GRADLDUSA
TREU, WILH	24	F	UNKNOWN		GRADLDUSA
ZIMMERMANN, ADAM	42	M	LABR		GRZZZZUSA
BERGER, ANTON	23	M	LABR		GRZZZZUSA
LEONHARDT, ADOLF	15	M	LABR		GRABVHUSA
LEITNER, MATH	37	M	LABR		GRZZZZUSA
SCHUSTER, FILOMINA	39	F	W		GRZZZZUSA
PETER	7	M	CHILD		GRZZZZUSA
ZILLENBILLED, ANNA	26	F	UNKNOWN		GRZZZZUSA
MOELTER, SUSANNA	31	F	W		GRZZZZUSA
MATH	.09	F	INFANT		GRZZZZUSA
ALBIN	24	M	CPTR		GRZZZZUSA
DUENISCH, ADOLPH	17	M	CPTR		GRZZZZUSA
GESSNER, ADAM	50	M	LABR		GRZZZZUSA
ANTONIA	21	F	UNKNOWN		GRZZZZUSA
HOCHGERANG, KATH	44	F	UNKNOWN		GRZZZZUSA
LEMKE, ERNST	27	M	FARMER		GRZZZZUSA
HACH, RUFINE	21	F	UNKNOWN		GRZZZZUSA
ZWIRLEIN, SUSANNA	19	F	UNKNOWN		GRZZZZUSA
LINK, REG	19	F	UNKNOWN		GRADKIUSA
HELMERICH, SABINA	13	F	UNKNOWN		GRADKIUSA
KRESS, CLARA	19	F	UNKNOWN		GRADKIUSA
HARTING, MARIA	58	F	W		GRADKIUSA
KATH	7	F	CHILD		GRADKIUS.\
EUGEN	6	M	CHILD		GRADKIUSA
PFANNER, BARBARA	16	F	UNKNOWN		GRADKIUSA
LUDWIG, WILH	38	M	BKR		GRACZYUSA
HENRIETTE	35	F	W		GRACZYUSA
ANNA	9	F	CHILD		GRACZYUSA
HEINR	7	M	CHILD		GRACZYUSA
WILLY	6	M	CHILD		GRACZYUSA
MARIE	5	F	CHILD		GRACZYUSA
HILDA	4	F	CHILD		GRACZYUSA
MATH	3	F	CHILD		GRACZYUSA
JOHANN	2	M	CHILD		GRACZYUSA
JOSEF	11	M	INF		GRACZYUSA
KAETCHEN	.01	F	INFANT		GRACZYUSA
STIEHL, MARG	19	F	UNKNOWN		GRZZZZUSA
APPEL, JOHANN	28	M	BKLYR		GRAAJZUSA
EIGENBROD, WILH	32	M	CPTR		GRAAJZUSA
SYRING, LOUISE	19	F	UNKNOWN		GRAAJZUSA
BETZ, SOPHIE	14	F	UNKNOWN		GRAARSUSA
ARDAG, HANS	25	M	LABR		GRAFZLUSA
BOEHMKE, CARL	62	M	LABR		GRAFZLUSA
WILH	58	F	W		GRAFZLUSA
THEODOR	26	M	LABR		GRAFZLUSA
SCHULZ, HEINR	27	M	BKR		GRZZZZUSA

SHIP: LESSING

FROM: HAMBURG
TO: NEW YORK
ARRIVED: 04 MAY 1888

PASSENGER	AGE	SEX	OCCUPATION	PVL	DES
SWART, HERM.	16	M	UNKNOWN		GRACBFUSA
WEINSCHENK, WILH.	26	M	LABR		MKZZZZUSA
ALBRAHT, CARL	26	M	TLR		MKZZZZUSA
POSTEL, AMANDUS	23	M	LABR		MKACBRUSA
MEYER, EMMA	32	F	WO		MKACBFUSA

PASSENGER	AGE	SEX	OCCUPATION	PRIVL	DES
TYGARSKA, VICTOEIA	23	F	WO		PRZZZZUSA
CHRISTENSEN, LORENZ	62	M	TLR		PRABNSUSA
CHRISTINE	60	F	W		PRABNSUSA
MARIE	30	F	D		PRABNSUSA
REDLIN, MAX	24	M	UNKNOWN		PRACGZUSA
DAHM, CACSAR	20	M	UNKNOWN		PRACBFUSA
CZITUCH, STNISLAUS	28	M	LABR		PRAJFMUSA
GOLA, AUGUST	44	M	LABR		PRAJFMUSA
JOSEF	19	M	LABR		PRAJFMUSA
ANISKA	20	F	SGL		PRAJFMUSA
ANNA	18	F	SGL		PRAJFMUSA
KOSMALSKI, VALENTIN	24	M	LABR		PRAJFMUSA
MARIANNA	23	F	W		PRAJFMUSA
STANISLAWA	00	F	INF		PRAJFMUSA
AUGUSTYNIAK, JOH.	24	M	LABR		PRAJFMUSA
MARIANNA	19	F	W		PRAJFMUSA
NOVAK, STEFAN	28	M	LABR		PRZZZZUSA
BEHRENS, WILH.	35	M	LABR		PRZZZZUSA
JFACUBONSKY, MARIE	51	F	WO		PRAEONUSA
JULS.	16	M	BBR		PRAEONUSA
KATSCHMAREK, PETER	30	M	LABR		PRZZZZUSA
FRANKE, PAUL	28	M	WCHMKR		PRABPCUSA
DAHNKE, CARL	52	M	LABR		PRAEDIUSA
MARIE	64	F	W		PRAEDIUSA
HILMER, JOHANN	26	M	FARMER		PRZZZZUSA
KLOSE, JOSEF	18	M	JNR		PRACGJUSA
V, PETER	32	M	FARMER		PRADNIUSA
META	26	F	SGL		PRADNIUSA
PEHLKE, WILH.	18	M	UNKNOWN		PRZZZZUSA
NISSEN, FEDDER	16	M	UNKNOWN		PRZZZZUSA
PINJER, BABETTE	28	F	SGL		PRZZZZUSA
CHRISTENSEN, LAURITZ	17	M	FARMER		PRZZZZUSA
FLUEGGE, PAULE.	20	F	SGL		PRAADEUSA
MEYER, RICHARD	17	M	LABR		PRAADEUSA
BUCZYNSKI, STANISLAUS	36	M	LABR		PRZZZZUSA
BARTEL, MARIE	38	F	WO		PRZZZZUSA
WESOLOWSKY, MICHAL	35	M	LABR		PRZZZZUSA
BUDSKOWSKY, ANTONIE	22	F	SGL		PRZZZZUSA
FRANZISKA	9	F	CHILD		PRZZZZUSA
GRZYB, GRETCHEN	42	F	WO		PRACBFUSA
ALBERT	14	M	S		PRACBFUSA
GUZYB, ANNA	7	F	CHILD		PRACBFUSA
TEMCZAK, SOFIA	21	F	SGL		PRZZZZUSA
MAKOZAK, MARIANNE	21	F	SGL		PRZZZZUSA
LASECKA, JOSEFA	22	F	SGL		PRZZZZUSA
KOZAK, JADWIGA	21	F	SGL		PRZZZZUSA
SANER, HEINR.	34	M	FARMER		PRAEUBUSA
EMMA	34	F	W		PRAEUBUSA
EMIL	00	M	INF		PRAEUBUSA
MARIE	.01	F	INFANT		PRAEUBUSA
HILMERS, AUGUST	24	M	CPR		PRABDMUSA
RICHTER, OTTO	39	M	WCHMKR		PRABPCUSA
HARDLER, HEINR.	39	M	WCHMKR		PRAJNXUSA
STECHMANN, HEINR.	30	M	FARMER		PRZZZZUSA
WELDECKER, LOUISE	19	F	SGL		PRZZZZUSA
DE, DOROTHEA	62	F	WO		PRACBFUSA
MOSES, CHARLOTTE	18	F	SGL		PRAASSUSA
SAGAEZ, EMILIE	54	F	WO		PRAAKHUSA
BYLEDBAL, JOS.	28	M	LABR		PRZZZZUSA
MICOLAICZAK, JOSEF	27	M	LABR		PRZZZZUSA
PONSCHITZKY, STANISL.	31	M	LABR		PRZZZZUSA
VERONICA	32	F	W		PRZZZZUSA
MICHALINE	3	F	CHILD		PRZZZZUSA
MARIANNE	00	F	INF		PRZZZZUSA
WESOLOWSKI, CATHA.	18	F	SGL		PRZZZZUSA
SCHNEIDER, BERNHD.	43	M	FARMER		PRZZZZUSA
LEGNER, ERNST	57	M	FARMER		PRZZZZUSA
ANTONIA	53	F	W		PRZZZZUSA
OTTO	9	M	CHILD		PRZZZZUSA
STENISCHEWSKY, FRANZ	34	M	FARMER		PRAHLPUSA
ANNA	28	F	W		PRAHLPUSA
KASIMIR	9	M	CHILD		PRAHLPUSA
JOSEF	6	M	CHILD		PRAHLPUSA
FRANZISKA	4	F	CHILD		PRAHLPUSA
MICHAL	00	M	INF		PRAHLPUSA
HELENE	.01	F	INFANT		PRAHLPUSA
JASICKA, PELATIA	17	F	SGL		PRAHLPUSA
KULISCH, BRUNO	26	M	SHMK		PRZZZZUSA
HERING, GEORG	24	M	LABR		PRAEPZUSA
THIELVOLDT, CATHA.	17	F	SGL		PRZZZZUSA
TIMM, CAROLINE	61	F	WO		PRADZOUSA
NIELSEN, MARIE	60	F	WO		PRAHZPUSA
SCHRAPP, FRANZ	17	M	MSN		BDZZZZUSA
HIRSCH, CARL	29	M	LABR		BDAGLSUSA
JOSEPHE.	32	F	W		BDAGLSUSA
GUSTAV	4	M	CHILD		BDAGLSUSA
KORA	3	F	CHILD		BDAGLSUSA
HEINR.	00	M	INF		BDAGLSUSA
KURZ, WILHE.	16	F	SGL		MKZZZZUSA
DIBBERT, CHRIST	15	M	LABR		MKAIFYUSA
NORDBLUM, DOROTHEA	31	F	WO		PRZZZZUSA
EMIL	9	M	CHILD		PRZZZZUSA
AMANDA	8	F	CHILD		PRZZZZUSA
BEATE	7	F	CHILD		PRZZZZUSA
BERNHD.	6	M	CHILD		PRZZZZUSA
FRIEDRIKE	4	F	CHILD		PRZZZZUSA
KARL	00	M	INF		PRZZZZUSA
MAIER, JOHN	43	M	HTR		PRZZZZUSA
SOERENSEN, PETER	33	M	SLR		MKACBFUSA
FRIEDA	28	F	W		MKACBFUSA
MARIE	4	F	CHILD		MKACBFUSA
ADOLF	00	M	INF		MKACBFUSA
REPENNING, ELISE	19	F	SGL		PRZZZZUSA
TIMM, CARL	24	M	LABR		PRADZOUSA
DORIS	28	F	W		PRADZOUSA
GUSTAV	00	M	INF		PRADZOUSA
BECK, WILH.	7	M	CHILD		PRADZOUSA
KRAUSE, WALDEMAR	16	M	BCHR		PRZZZZUSA
LORENZEN, JENS	52	M	FARMER		PRZZZZUSA
MARIE	42	F	W		PRZZZZUSA
JOHE.	19	F	CH		PRZZZZUSA
CARL	17	M	CH		PRZZZZUSA
EMMA	14	F	CH		PRZZZZUSA
JACOB	9	M	CHILD		PRZZZZUSA
ANNIE	8	F	CHILD		PRZZZZUSA
JULS.	2	M	CHILD		PRZZZZUSA
ANNA	80	F	M		PRZZZZUSA
KAHL, WILH.	15	M	LABR		PRAIFYUSA
ANDRESEN, JENS	30	M	LABR		PRZZZZUSA
ANDRA	29	F	W		PRZZZZUSA
FRIEDERIE	3	F	CHILD		PRZZZZUSA
HERLICH	00	M	INF		PRZZZZUSA
CHRISTENSEN, PAUL	9	M	CHILD		PRZZZZUSA
RICHERT, ADAM	25	M	FARMER		HSZZZZUSA
SCHAEFER, JOHS.	26	M	FARMER		HSZZZZUSA
WUNDER, ANTON	16	M	TLR		BVZZZZUSA
HAILBRONNER, LUDWIG	27	M	MCHT		BVACWRUSA
SCHENK, CARL	17	M	BCHR		BVADTIUSA
BREIDING, GUSTAV	25	M	FARMER		WMZZZZUSA
MATTES, LIBOR	34	M	FARMER		WMZZZZUSA
FRANZISKA	26	F	SGL		WMZZZZUSA
JURDAN, LUDWIG	26	M	CPTR		WMZZZZUSA
SCHLECHT, JOH.	25	M	FARMER		WMACIWUSA
STROH, HERMANN	28	M	UNKNOWN		WMACQAUSA
MAGNER, ERNESTINE	50	F	WO		WMACBFUSA
MARTENS, C.J.	56	M	FARMER		PRZZZZUSA
EDELSTEIN, CHANE	44	F	WO		PRAMAIUSA
GEDALJE	2	F	CHILD		PRAMAIUSA
ROSA	9	F	CHILD		PRAMAIUSA
SIMON	8	M	CHILD		PRAMAIUSA
LENA	5	F	CHILD		PRAMAIUSA
BUSSILO, ANDREY	33	M	MCHT		PRZZZZUSA
SAMILSKA, SCHAJE	30	M	MCHT		PRZZZZUSA
KISISCHA, JORAS	24	M	MCHT		PRZZZZUSA
LEIKUS, MATH.	18	M	MCHT		PRZZZZUSA
ROSENBLUTH, ADOLF	23	M	TLR		PRZZZZUSA
ANDERSON, ANNA	28	F	WO		PRACBFUSA
MERZ, EMMA	22	F	WO		PRAIKSUSA
BERGECST, JOH.	34	M	MCHT		PRACBRUSA
EBELT, WILH.	23	M	MCHT		SYZZZZUSA

PASSENGER	AGE	SEX	OCCUPATION	PRVL / DES
LEUSCHEL, RICHARD	22	M	MCHT	SYAFIPUSA
WOLF, JOACHIM	24	M	MSN	SYALGGUSA
FRDK.	19	F	W	SYALGGUSA
ANNA	00	F	INF	SYALGGUSA
SCHNEIDER, DORA	19	F	SGL	SYAAVGUSA
GRETL, HEINR.	16	M	FARMER	SYAAVGUSA
ASSMANN, BERTHA	26	F	SGL	PRZZZZUSA
RICHERT, JOHS.	15	M	FARMER	PRZZZZUSA
KOCH, OTTILIE	37	F	WO	PRAAKHUSA
AMALIE	9	F	CHILD	PRAAKHUSA
KRAEMER, MARIA	22	F	SGL	BVZZZZUSA
GESSNER, EVA	25	F	SGL	BVZZZZUSA
RIEDEL, HERM.	35	M	MCHT	PRZZZZUSA
DOROTHEA	22	F	W	PRZZZZUSA
PETRY, ELISABETH	58	F	WO	PRZZZZUSA
HELLER, CATHA.	16	F	SGL	PRZZZZUSA
WITTENBERG, LUSWIG	18	M	LABR	PRADYGUSA
RIEMENSCHNEIDER, WILH.	18	M	LABR	PRADYGUSA
SCHOEN, MARIANNE	20	F	WO	PRAAZQUSA
VOLLACZINSKOVO, CATH.	20	F	SGL	PRZZZZUSA
DENERLING, WILHE.	17	F	SGL	BVZZZZUSA
HAHN, MARGARETHA	24	F	SGL	BVZZZZUSA
KROENER, GEORG	15	M	MSN	BVZZZZUSA
ALSDORF, WULH.	27	M	LKSH	BVAAXFUSA
MUELLER, AUGUSTE	54	F	WO	BVAAKHUSA
WOHLERS, HEINR.	50	M	FARMER	PRZZZZUSA
MARGR.	57	F	W	PRZZZZUSA
WIRTH, DORA	9	F	CHILD	PRZZZZUSA
SPORK, REBECCA	18	F	SGL	PRZZZZUSA
HEDWIG, HEINR.	32	M	FARMER	PRZZZZUSA
BRATAK, JACOB	24	M	LABR	PRZZZZUSA
THIELE, CLARA	17	F	SGL	PRAAKHUSA
BAVEL, CHRISTE	30	F	WO	PRAIYMUSA
IDA	4	F	CHILD	PRAIYMUSA
OTTO	00	M	INF	PRAIYMUSA
KARLA, MARTHA	32	F	WO	PRAEWZUSA
ANNA	7	F	CHILD	PRAEWZUSA
ARTHUR	3	M	CHILD	PRAEWZUSA
MAX	2	M	CHILD	PRAEWZUSA
ELISE	00	F	INF	PRAEWZUSA
STRAUS, JOSEF	15	M	TLR	PRAEXKUSA
LIEBONSKY, WILHE.	66	F	WO	PRZZZZUSA
GIESE, HERM.	32	M	LABR	PRZZZZUSA
WILHE.	30	F	W	PRZZZZUSA
EMILIE	5	F	CHILD	PRZZZZUSA
FRIEDR.	00	M	INF	PRZZZZUSA
KRYSSAK, MICHAEL	24	M	LABR	PRZZZZUSA
MOELLER, CONRAD	46	M	LABR	PRABPTUSA
CATHA.	40	F	W	PRABPTUSA
FRIEDR.	15	M	CH	PRABPTUSA
CONRAD	13	M	CH	PRABPTUSA
MARIE	9	F	CHILD	PRABPTUSA
WILH.	5	M	CHILD	PRABPTUSA
PETER	00	M	INF	PRABPTUSA
ANDRESEN, JOH.CHR.	16	M	LABR	PRACKYUSA
BACK, CARSEN	15	M	LABR	PRAIXCUSA
WALCZAK, ANTONIA	25	F	WO	PRZZZZUSA
ANTONI	6	M	CHILD	PRZZZZUSA
STANISLAWA	3	F	CHILD	PRZZZZUSA
JAN	.11	M	INFANT	PRZZZZUSA
BRAKS, JOH.	23	M	LABR	PRZZZZUSA
PRYBYT, AGNISKA	36	F	WO	PRZZZZUSA
MARIANNA	13	F	CH	PRZZZZUSA
ROSALIE	9	F	CHILD	PRZZZZUSA
LEOKADIA	7	F	CHILD	PRZZZZUSA
FRANZISKA	4	F	CHILD	PRZZZZUSA
STANISLAUS	00	M	INF	PRZZZZUSA
KIESOW, JULUS	34	M	LABR	PRZZZZUSA
ANNA	34	F	W	PRZZZZUSA
ERNST	4	M	CHILD	PRZZZZUSA
HERM.	2	M	CHILD	PRZZZZUSA
DALLMANN, PAUL	29	M	LABR	PRZZZZUSA
EWER, FRIEDR.	24	M	LABR	PRZZZZUSA
KUHR, EMIL	28	M	BKR	PRAAKHUSA
PETZNIK, AUGUSTE	54	F	WO	PRZZZZUSA

PASSENGER	AGE	SEX	OCCUPATION	PRVL / DES
SZWENGA, JAN	57	M	LABR	PRZZZZUSA
MARIANNA	45	F	W	PRZZZZUSA
JOSEF	20	M	CH	PRZZZZUSA
ROSALIE	9	F	CHILD	PRZZZZUSA
ANTONIE	8	F	CHILD	PRZZZZUSA
FRANZISKA	6	F	CHILD	PRZZZZUSA
VINCENT	4	M	CHILD	PRZZZZUSA
PODLEWSKI, JOSEPH	27	M	LABR	PRZZZZUSA
LARKOWSKY, FRANZ	27	M	LABR	PRZZZZUSA
V, ELISE	44	F	SGL	PRABOQUSA
KOPF, SIEGFRIEDE	26	F	SGL	PRZZZZUSA
BERUDT, JULS.	36	M	MCHT	PRZZZZUSA
DOMERASKI, JOH.	31	M	BCHR	PRZZZZUSA
FEIGE, HEINR.	22	M	LABR	PRZZZZUSA
SIEVERS, GESCHE	27	F	FARMER	PRZZZZUSA
ZWEIGBAUM, ABR.	33	F	SGL	PRZZZZUSA
PJESKE, WILH.	24	M	LABR	PRZZZZUSA
WARMINSKI, ANTON	25	M	LABR	PRZZZZUSA
HARS, HEINR.	34	M	CPTR	PRAHPBUSA
BRUKUS, FERDA.	36	M	MCHT	PRAHPBUSA
ZWINGENBERG, GUSTAV	26	M	LABR	PRAAKLUSA
MUELLER, IDA	23	F	SGL	PRZZZZUSA
BUDESHEIM, JOH.	36	M	FARMER	PRZZZZUSA
CIESLIEWITZ, JAN	40	M	LABR	PRZZZZUSA
FRANZISKA	33	F	W	PRZZZZUSA
JOSEF	9	M	CHILD	PRZZZZUSA
WALENZY	8	M	CHILD	PRZZZZUSA
AGNES	6	F	CHILD	PRZZZZUSA
FRANZ	.11	M	INFANT	PRZZZZUSA
DZIADASZEK, CATHA.	9	F	CHILD	PRZZZZUSA
HEDRICH, PAULINE	33	F	WO	PRZZZZUSA
FRANZ	4	M	CHILD	PRZZZZUSA
PAUL	.11	M	INFANT	PRZZZZUSA
BERTELSMANN, KONRAD	22	M	MCHT	PRZZZZUSA
HENGOLD, OTTILIE	37	F	W	PRAASSUSA
KURT	.11	M	INFANT	PRAASSUSA
WEUSTHOFF, HUGO	31	M	MD	PRAAFTUSA
ELISABETH	28	F	W	PRAAFTUSA
ANNA	4	F	CHILD	PRAAFTUSA
RIEMANN, HERM.	31	M	PVTM	HBZZZZUSA
HENKELMANN, EMMA	24	F	SGL	HBAEUXUSA
WITEPSKI, HELENE	24	F	SGL	HBAAKHUSA
SCHNEIDER, OTTO	46	M	MCHT	HBABOQUSA
MARIE	16	F	D	HBABOQUSA
PAUL	9	M	CHILD	HBABOQUSA
SCHAPER, MAX	25	M	MCHT	HBACBFUSA
LIENAU, FRITZ	16	M	SCH	HBACBFUSA
CASPARY, CAECILIE	17	F	SGL	HBAEWMUSA
HAMPEL, WILH.	31	M	MCHT	HBABHTUSA
SCHULTZ, AUGUST	24	M	MCHT	HBAAKHUSA
MICHELSEN, OTTO	33	M	FARMER	HBACBFUSA
LUCIE	29	F	W	HBACBFUSA
HEIN, RUDOLF	14	M	SCH	HBACBFUSA
SCHAETZELL, PAUL	33	M	MCHT	HBAAKHUSA
ANNA	30	F	W	HBAAKHUSA
MARGR.	5	F	CHILD	HBAAKHUSA
CHARLOTTE	4	F	CHILD	HBAAKHUSA
PAUL	.11	M	INFANT	HBAAKHUSA
ANGER, EMMA	22	F	SGL	HBACBFUSA
KOFSE, HENRIETTE	54	F	W	HBAAKHUSA
SCHWADERER, CARL	34	M	FARMER	HBADLDUSA

SHIP: POLARIA

FROM: HAMBURG
TO: NEW YORK
ARRIVED: 04 MAY 1888

PASSENGER	AGE	SEX	OCCUPATION	PRVL / DES
JABLONSKY, JULIANA	46	F	WO	PRZZZZUSA
JOH	23	M	CH	PRZZZZUSA

PASSENGER	AGE	SEX	OCCUPATION	PRVL	DES
JULIANE	20	F	CH		PRZZZZUSA
ANNA	9	F	CHILD		PRZZZZUSA
VINCENT	8	M	CHILD		PRZZZZUSA
ANTON	5	M	CHILD		PRZZZZUSA
GAPENOSKY, JOHANN	23	M	LABR		PRZZZZUSA
LITZAN, CARL	32	M	MLR		PRZZZZUNK
CATH	29	F	W		PRZZZZUNK
ARNTUR	6	M	CHILD		PRZZZZUNK
REINHOLD	4	M	CHILD		PRZZZZUNK
EDW	35	M	LABR		PRZZZZUNK
ALBERT	36	M	UNKNOWN		PRZZZZUNK
PAUL	8	M	CHILD		PRZZZZUNK
ANNA	4	F	CHILD		PRZZZZUNK
MARG	.07	F	INFANT		PRZZZZUNK
SELL, WILH	30	M	SGL		PRZZZZUNK
ENGLER, BERTHA	30	F	WO		PRZZZZNY
MARTHA	11	F	CH		PRZZZZNY
OTTO	1	M	CHILD		PRZZZZNY
WOLFSKY, ANTON	44	M	LABR		PRZZZZUNK
PROESE, HENRIETTE	20	F	SGL		PRZZZZUNK
SUTTKONSKY, FRANZ	30	M	LABR		PRZZZZNY
JULIANNE	25	F	W		PRZZZZNY
MARIANNE	.03	F	INFANT		PRZZZZNY
MUCHHALLER, LEONHARD	26	M	FARMER		PRZZZZUNK
WENGLIKOWSKY, ANTONIA	22	F	W		PRZZZZNY
STANISLAUS	.03	M	INFANT		PRZZZZNY
LUETHANOSKY, BARTHOLOMA	56	M	LABR		PRZZZZNY
LUETHANOSKY, ELISABETH	50	F	W		PRZZZZNY
SOPHIE	3	F	CHILD		PRZZZZNY
LEO	6	M	CHILD		PRZZZZNY
NAMROW, ALEXANDER	29	M	LABR		PRZZZZNY
WENOWITZ, FRANC	43	M	LABR		PRZZZZNY
SITCK, LORENTZ	28	M	LABR		PRZZZZUSA
HABIENSKY, MICHAEL	14	M	LABR		PRZZZZUSA
KLUMP, HENRIETTE	24	F	SGL		PRZZZZNY
AMALIA	9	F	CHILD		PRZZZZNY
GIETZ, REINHARD	27	M	LABR		PRZZZZNY
JOH	28	F	W		PRZZZZNY
ANNA	5	M	CHILD		PRZZZZNY
BERTHOLD	.10	M	INFANT		PRZZZZNY
ENGELLAND, WILH	14	M	SGL		PRZZZZNY
GIERZ, AUGUST	28	M	LABR		PRZZZZNY
ERNST	4	M	CHILD		PRZZZZNY
AUGUST	2	M	CHILD		PRZZZZNY
DRESSING, FRANZ	27	M	LABR		PRZZZZNY
MARIE	26	F	W		PRZZZZNY
FRANZ	5	M	CHILD		PRZZZZNY
JOSEF	2	M	CHILD		PRZZZZNY
FRANZ	.06	M	INFANT		PRZZZZNY
NERRET, GUSTAV	32	M	SHMK		PRZZZZNY
BALZENAK, HYRONIMUS	23	M	LABR		PRZZZZNY
MOELLER, ELISABETH	54	F	WO		PRZZZZNY
ELISE	15	F	D		PRZZZZNY
WALTER, CARL	17	M	FARMER		PRZZZZNY
SCHOENNING, HEINRICH	14	M	LABR		PRZZZZNY
LARSEN, CARL	32	M	PNTR		PRZZZZMIL
FRENDENBERG, PETER	27	M	FARMER		PRZZZZNY
FINKLER, JOHN	16	M	STDNT		PRZZZZNY
CLAUSEN, HERM	27	M	SCP		PRZZZZNY
TAMMS, HEINRICH	9	M	CHILD		PRZZZZMIL
IDA	8	F	CHILD		PRZZZZMIL
EMMA	8	F	CHILD		PRZZZZMIL
OTTO	4	F	CHILD		PRZZZZMIL
JOERGENSEN, JUERGEN	24	M	CH		PRZZZZMIL
HARDER, MINNA	24	F	FARMER		PRZZZZCH
GIETZ, AUGUSTE	30	F	WO		PRZZZZNY
MARTHA	.06	F	INFANT		PRZZZZNY
VOIGT, WILH	38	M	SHMK		PRZZZZNY
HENRIETTE	38	F	W		PRZZZZNY
PAUL	9	M	CHILD		PRZZZZNY
GUSTAV	6	M	CHILD		PRZZZZNY
ANNA	4	F	CHILD		PRZZZZNY
RICHARD	.11	M	INFANT		PRZZZZNY
STARKER, JOH	16	M	BCHR		WMZZZZNY
MUELLER, FRIEDR	70	M	LABR		PRZZZZNY

PASSENGER	AGE	SEX	OCCUPATION	PRVL	DES
ERNESTINE	68	F	W		PRZZZZNY
HAMANN, HEINRICH	22	M	LABR		PRZZZZNY
CAROL	64	F	W		PRZZZZNY
CARL	35	M	LABR		PRZZZZNY
MARIE	24	F	W		PRZZZZNY
RICHARD	.01	M	INFANT		PRZZZZNY
SCHUETT, GRDKE	36	F	WO		PRZZZZNY
FRIEDA	8	F	CHILD		PRZZZZNY
WILH	1	M	CHILD		PRZZZZNY
MARTHA	5	F	CHILD		PRZZZZNY
HERMANN	3	M	CHILD		PRZZZZNY
OTTO	.11	M	INFANT		PRZZZZNY
LENWARENZ, HERM	24	M	LABR		PRZZZZNY
KARPINSKY, MARIAN	24	M	WHR		PRZZZZNY
GOLUMBINOSKY, FRANZ	40	M	LABR		PRZZZZNY
BENDER, PAUL	20	M	LABR		PRZZZZPHI
FISCHER, FRANZ	22	M	BCHR		PRZZZZNY
BAY, FRIEDR	21	M	MCHT		WMZZZZNY
LEMBERT, DACAR	16	M	JNR		SYZZZZNY
LUETH, WILH	42	M	LABR		PRZZZZNY
LENA	39	F	W		PRZZZZNY
GUSTAV	9	M	CHILD		PRZZZZNY
ANNIE	8	F	CHILD		PRZZZZNY
DORA	5	F	CHILD		PRZZZZNY
KOLOER, DINA	19	F	WO		PRZZZZNY
KREPSTEIN, LUDWIG	36	M	FARMER		MKZZZZNY
SOFIE	29	F	W		MKZZZZNY
PAUL	00	M	INF		MKZZZZNY
MOELLER, CAROLINE	57	F	W		MKZZZZNY
OFFENHAGEN, AUGUSTE	23	F	W		MKZZZZNY
AUG	00	M	INF		MKZZZZNY
LUDWIG	19	M	LABR		MKZZZZNY
WERNER, LOUISE	26	F	W		HBZZZZNY
MARIE	00	F	INF		HBZZZZNY
PRUEGER, HEINR	23	M	TLR		MKZZZZNY
HARM, HEINRICH	28	M	LABR		MKZZZZTOL
WICHMANN, JAKOB	54	M	LABR		PRZZZZNY
HARRY	15	M	LABR		PRZZZZNY
NITECHT, GUSTAV	22	M	TLR		PRZZZZNY
WARCINKOWSKY, LORENZ	24	M	LABR		PRZZZZNY
JUSCHKOWIAK, MARIANNE	38	F	LABR		PRZZZZNY
KAJDOSCH, FRANZ	28	M	LABR		PRZZZZNY
AGNES	24	F	W		PRZZZZNY
ROSALIA	4	F	CHILD		PRZZZZNY
PIOTR	2	M	CHILD		PRZZZZNY
ANTON	00	M	INF		PRZZZZNY
MOCH, EMILIE	26	F	WO		PRZZZZNY
FRITZ	7	M	CHILD		PRZZZZNY
HERMAN	3	M	CHILD		PRZZZZNY
MARTHA	.11	F	INFANT		PRZZZZNY
KARDSCH, MICHAEL	36	M	LABR		PRZZZZWI
AUGUSTE	40	F	W		PRZZZZWI
JOH	6	M	CHILD		PRZZZZWI
MARIE	4	F	CHILD		PRZZZZWI
JOSEF	.09	M	INFANT		PRZZZZWI
GAARDE, JORGEN	24	M	SMH		PRZZZZNY
SZORA, SIMON	24	M	LABR		PRZZZZNY
PICHULA, FELIX	36	M	LABR		PRZZZZWI
ELISABETH	36	F	W		PRZZZZWI
JOH	9	M	CHILD		PRZZZZWI
PETER	8	M	CHILD		PRZZZZWI
FRANZ	6	M	CHILD		PRZZZZWI
ALBERT	4	M	CHILD		PRZZZZWI
MARIE	2	F	CHILD		PRZZZZWI
DAWID, SOPHIE	9	F	CHILD		PRZZZZWI
FISCHER, AUGUSTE	22	F	SGL		PRZZZZWI
SPRINGER, STANISL	24	M	LABR		PRZZZZNY
MARIANNE	29	F	W		PRZZZZNY
NOWIKI, FRANZ	28	M	LABR		PRZZZZNY
STANISL	25	F	W		PRZZZZNY
JOH	.10	M	INFANT		PRZZZZNY
NIKOLAI, JOH	15	M	LABR		PRZZZZNY
FRANZ	15	M	B		PRZZZZNY
KARL	4	M	CHILD		PRZZZZNY
PIELSKI, JOSEF	34	M	LABR		PRZZZZNY

PASSENGER	AGE	SEX	OCCUPATION	PRVL	DES
JESSEN, PETER	16	M	LABR	PRZZZZNY	
KRAMER, MARIE	22	F	JNR	PRZZZZNY	
WISMINSKI, FRANZ	60	M	LABR	PRZZZZNY	
CATH	50	M	LABR	PRZZZZNY	
ANNA	17	M	LABR	PRZZZZNY	
JAN	9	M	CHILD	PRZZZZNY	
ANTON	5	M	CHILD	PRZZZZNY	
ABRAMCZEK, FRAN	22	M	LABR	PRZZZZNY	
ELISABETH	22	F	W	PRZZZZNY	
NAUENNEKI, MARTIN	25	M	LABR	PRZZZZNY	
FRANZISKA	31	M	LABR	PRZZZZNY	
MARYANNA	9	F	CHILD	PRZZZZNY	
ANTON	4	M	CHILD	PRZZZZNY	
NAWREK, JOHN	.11	M	INFANT	PRZZZZNY	
MODRYKA, JOSEFA	24	F	SGL	PRZZZZNY	
ADANZYK, VALENTIN	25	M	LABR	PRZZZZNY	
FILAR, JACOB	31	M	LABR	PRZZZZNY	
MARIE	31	F	W	PRZZZZNY	
JAN	4	M	CHILD	PRZZZZNY	
MURJEWSKI, ANTON	36	M	LABR	PRZZZZNY	
JIKAWSKI, FRANZ	27	M	LABR	PRZZZZNY	
WEINSDORF, MAX	21	M	MCHT	PRZZZZCH	
NITZSCHHE, PAUL	23	M	LABR	SYZZZZNY	
EIKEL, BERTHA	29	F	WO	PRZZZZNY	
OLGA	9	F	CHILD	PRZZZZNY	
GRETE	9	F	CHILD	PRZZZZNY	
ELSE	3	F	CHILD	PRZZZZNY	
EMOND	.09	M	INFANT	PRZZZZNY	
CZARETZKY, JOS	25	M	LABR	PRZZZZNY	
PAWLAK, LUDW	18	M	LABR	PRZZZZNY	
GROTMANN, GUST	25	M	LABR	PRZZZZNY	
LUEHRS, CATH	17	F	SGL	PRZZZZNY	
STEFFENS, CLAUS	29	M	SHMK	PRZZZZNY	
ANNA	25	F	W	PRZZZZNY	
ZIMMERMANN, HEINRICH	16	M	FARMER	PRZZZZUSA	
LUTTICH, JOACHIM	38	M	LABR	PRZZZZUNK	
LISETTE	29	F	W	PRZZZZUNK	
GERNER, EMIL	29	M	FARMER	PRZZZZNY	
LIEBARDT, HERM	23	M	LABR	PRZZZZNY	
WIEDERMANN, GUSTAV	27	M	UNKNOWN	PRZZZZBUF	
WINTER, ADAM	30	M	CGRMKR	BDZZZZNY	
KAZMIRZAK, WIEZEND	24	M	LABR	PRZZZZNY	
MAZUREK, WOJEICK	47	M	LABR	PRZZZZCH	
CATH	34	F	W	PRZZZZCH	
ANTONIA	9	F	CHILD	PRZZZZCH	
JOSEFA	9	F	CHILD	PRZZZZCH	
MARIANNE	8	F	CHILD	PRZZZZCH	
FRANZ	5	M	CHILD	PRZZZZCH	
STANISLAUS	.11	M	INFANT	PRZZZZCH	
PASLEV, ERNST	26	M	LABR	PRZZZZCH	
HOLST, ELFRIDE	15	M	SGL	PRZZZZCH	
SCHUEFFER, GEORG	20	M	LABR	WMZZZZNY	
GEHRIKE, AUGUST	15	M	LABR	PRZZZZNY	
BYLEBGT, WOYTECH	46	M	LABR	PRZZZZNY	
DARNACH, JOHANN	32	M	LABR	PRZZZZNY	
DRZEWETZKI, FRANZ	28	M	LABR	PRZZZZBUF	
MARTHA	9	F	CHILD	PRZZZZUSA	
DAVID	.06	M	INFANT	PRZZZZUSA	
SCHEMIENSKA, ANTONIA	40	F	W	HBZZZZUSA	
WOJCICH	8	M	CHILD	HBZZZZUSA	
VASIL	7	M	CHILD	HBZZZZUSA	
JENDRZY	4	M	CHILD	HBZZZZUSA	
ROSALIE	.11	F	INFANT	HBZZZZUSA	
JINTECK, ANASTASIA	42	F	W	PRZZZZUSA	
TEKLA	18	F	CH	PRZZZZUSA	
ROSALIA	15	F	CH	PRZZZZUSA	
FRANZ	9	M	CHILD	PRZZZZUSA	
CAECILIE	8	F	CHILD	PRZZZZUSA	
VALENTIN	6	M	CHILD	PRZZZZUSA	
ROHLF, WILH.	15	M	FARMER	PRZZZZUSA	
BROCHINSKY, NIPOMUCENA	48	F	W	PRZZZZUSA	
BRUNISLAWA	22	F	CH	PRZZZZUSA	
SIEGMUEND	24	M	CH	PRZZZZUSA	
CLEMENTINE	18	F	CH	PRZZZZUSA	
KUELPER, JULIUS	22	M	FARMER	HBZZZZUSA	
MEYER, FERD.	52	M	LABR	PRZZZZUSA	
EGGERS, WILHE.	20	F	WO	PRZZZZUSA	
BOHNSACK, CHR.	53	M	LABR	PRZZZZUSA	
ERNESTINE	53	F	W	PRZZZZUSA	
CAROLINE	20	F	CH	PRZZZZUSA	
HEINR.	16	M	CH	PRZZZZUSA	
CARL	9	M	CHILD	PRZZZZUSA	
JORASZEWSKY, MICHAL	29	M	LABR	PRZZZZUSA	
WINKLER, ALBERT	28	M	MCHT	PRZZZZUSA	
BUCHELT, HEINR.	45	M	MSN	PRZZZZUSA	
PAULINE	44	F	W	PRZZZZUSA	
PAUL	16	M	CH	PRZZZZUSA	
BERTHA	9	F	CHILD	PRZZZZUSA	
U	8	M	CHILD	PRZZZZUSA	
MAECHTER, HEINR.	31	M	FARMER	PRZZZZUSA	
ANNA	29	F	W	PRZZZZUSA	
OSCAR	4	M	CHILD	PRZZZZUSA	
ROBERT	3	M	CHILD	PRZZZZUSA	
EMMA	2	F	CHILD	PRZZZZUSA	
HAUS	.11	M	INFANT	PRZZZZUSA	
SAMUEL, THEODOR	39	M	CPTR	PRZZZZUSA	
KOEZELSKI, MICHAEL	36	M	LABR	PRZZZZUSA	
BOCHART, JOSEF	60	M	LABR	PRZZZZUSA	
FRANZISKA	60	F	W	PRZZZZUSA	
ANDRAS	26	M	UNKNOWN	PRZZZZUSA	
JOSEFA	23	F	W	PRZZZZUSA	
FRANZISKA	.11	F	INFANT	PRZZZZUSA	
BADE, WILH.	30	M	FARMER	PRZZZZUSA	
EMMA	20	F	W	PRZZZZUSA	
CATHA.	.09	F	INFANT	PRZZZZUSA	
JOHS.	1	M	CHILD	PRZZZZUSA	
CATHA.	63	F	M	PRZZZZUSA	
ROHDE, MADGALA.	24	F	WO	PRZZZZUSA	
HAUSEN, FRIEDR.	45	M	FARMER	PRZZZZUSA	
DOROTHEA	49	F	W	PRZZZZUSA	
THOMS, MARTIN	00	F	UNKNOWN	PRZZZZUSA	
SCHLUETER, PETER	25	M	FARMER	PRZZZZUSA	
BLOCK, HEINR.	25	M	LABR	PRZZZZUSA	
FALKNER, CHRIST.	18	M	TNM	BVZZZZUSA	
RICHTER, JUL.	32	M	LABR	SYZZZZUSA	
EMILIE	30	F	W	SYZZZZUSA	
HOLSTEIN, CLARA	33	F	W	SYZZZZUSA	
PAUL	9	M	CHILD	SYZZZZUSA	
KIHN, JOHANN	30	M	MLR	GRZZZZUSA	
DANZIGER, HERRM.	25	M	MLR	GRZZZZUSA	
FINE	26	F	W	GRZZZZUSA	
KLAWIKOWSKI, FRANZ	27	M	LABR	GRZZZZUSA	
BARANSKI, ALBRECHT	57	M	LABR	GRZZZZUSA	
REUSS, EDUARD	35	M	FARMER	GRZZZZUSA	
MAGDALENA	40	F	W	GRZZZZUSA	
JULIANE	9	F	CHILD	GRZZZZUSA	
LUDWIG	8	M	CHILD	GRZZZZUSA	
ELISABETH	4	M	CHILD	GRZZZZUSA	
FRANZISKA	.09	F	INFANT	GRZZZZUSA	
MOELLER, HEINR.	29	M	CPTR	GRZZZZUSA	
AUGUSTE	27	F	W	GRZZZZUSA	

SHIP: RHAETIA

FROM: HAMBURG AND HAVRE
TO: NEW YORK
ARRIVED: 04 MAY 1888

PASSENGER	AGE	SEX	OCCUPATION	PRVL	DES
CHRISTENSEN, CARL	20	M	FARMER	PRZZZZUSA	
PODLECH, FRANZ	21	M	LABR	PRZZZZUSA	
SCHWARTZ, FRIEDR.	55	M	LABR	PRZZZZUSA	
WILHNE.	54	F	W	PRZZZZUSA	
ANNA	22	F	CH	PRZZZZUSA	
LEOPOLD	16	M	CH	PRZZZZUSA	
FRIEDRA.	9	F	CHILD	PRZZZZUSA	

PASSENGER	AGE	SEX	OCCUPATION	PRVL	DES
ARTHUR	.06	M	INFANT	GRZ	ZZZUSA
BREITFELD, CARL	30	M	FARMER	GRZ	ZZZUSA
STAISCHAK, MATHILDE	22	F	WO	GRZ	ZZZUSA
MESCHKE, LORENZ	24	M	LABR	GRZ	ZZZUSA
MIELOSCH, JACOB	27	M	LABR	GRZ	ZZZUSA
MICHALSKI, NICOLAUS	29	M	LABR	GRZ	ZZZUSA
MARIANNE	24	F	UNKNOWN	GRZ	ZZZUSA
SMIGAJ, FRANZ	25	M	LABR	GRZ	ZZZUSA
MARIANNE	21	F	W	GRZ	ZZZUSA
MANEWSKA, AGNES	18	F	WO	GRZ	ZZZUSA
ZASCHKE, PAULINE	32	F	WO	GRZ	ZZZUSA
MIELKE, BERTHA	24	F	WO	GRZ	ZZZUSA
WANELISKA, WOJCECH	60	M	LABR	GRZ	ZZZUSA
WIECZAREK, VALENTI	28	M	LABR	GRZ	ZZZUSA
MARIE	28	F	W	GRZ	ZZZUSA
FRANZISKA	2	F	CHILD	GRZ	ZZZUSA
VONROBERT, WLADISLAW	30	M	LABR	GRZ	ZZZUSA
CLEMENTINE	25	F	W	GRZ	ZZZUSA
WLADISLAW	.06	M	INFANT	GRZ	ZZZUSA
GOLATA, JOHANN	27	M	LABR	GRZ	ZZZUSA
APOLONIA	22	F	W	GRZ	ZZZUSA
WAWRZYN	.09	M	INFANT	GRZ	ZZZUSA
PERECZAK, MICHAEL	30	M	LABR	GRZ	ZZZUSA
WESLOWSKY, ANDRAS	35	M	LABR	GRZ	ZZZUSA
ANELIA	24	F	W	GRZ	ZZZUSA
FRANS	9	M	CHILD	GRZ	ZZZUSA
JENISKA	6	F	CHILD	GRZ	ZZZUSA
VERENKA	3	F	CHILD	GRZ	ZZZUSA
CLEMENTINE	.11	F	INFANT	GRZ	ZZZUSA
WIESE, JOSEF	33	M	SMH	GRZ	ZZZUSA
MARIANNE	23	F	W	GRZ	ZZZUSA
CASIMIR	.10	M	INFANT	GRZ	ZZZUSA
KROPACZINSKI, JOH.	59	M	LABR	GRZ	ZZZUSA
GARZTZEWSKI, THOMAS	28	M	LABR	GRZ	ZZZUSA
WISNEWSKY, ADAM	42	M	LABR	GRZ	ZZZUSA
SMUDZINSKI, IGNATZ	30	M	LABR	GRZ	ZZZUSA
VICTORIA	28	F	UNKNOWN	GRZ	ZZZUSA
KOBITZKI, PETER	28	M	LABR	GRZ	ZZZUSA
RUSZKIEWITZ, STANISL.	34	M	CPR	GRZ	ZZZUSA
LORENZ	30	M	CPR	GRZ	ZZZUSA
BOBECK, THOMAS	40	M	LABR	GRZ	ZZZUSA
ZIELINSKI, JOS.	36	M	UNKNOWN	GRZ	ZZZUSA
KUBIAK, VALENTIN	24	M	UNKNOWN	GRZ	ZZZUSA
KREFFT, PETER	35	M	UNKNOWN	GRZ	ZZZUSA
HAGARSKI, JOH.	35	M	UNKNOWN	GRZ	ZZZUSA
WIECZNIEWSKI, ANTON	32	M	UNKNOWN	GRZ	ZZZUSA
WIENIEWSKI, FRANZISKA	33	F	UNKNOWN	GRZ	ZZZUSA
FRANZ	5	M	CHILD	GRZ	ZZZUSA
WIECZNIEWSKI, JOH.	3	M	CHILD	GRZ	ZZZUSA
MARIE	1	F	CHILD	GRZ	ZZZUSA
NAGARSKI, JOH.	35	M	UNKNOWN	GRZ	ZZZUSA
FRANZISKA	27	F	UNKNOWN	GRZ	ZZZUSA
FRANZ	8	M	CHILD	GRZ	ZZZUSA
JOHANN	5	M	CHILD	GRZ	ZZZUSA
ALOIS	3	M	CHILD	GRZ	ZZZUSA
JOSEFA	.08	F	INFANT	GRZ	ZZZUSA
RASZINSKI, MICHAL	48	M	LABR	GRZ	ZZZUSA
KUEHLBARS, EMIL	39	M	MCHT	GRZ	ZZZUSA
EMILIE	32	F	W	GRZ	ZZZUSA
PAUL	19	M	CH	GRZ	ZZZUSA
IDA	13	F	CH	GRZ	ZZZUSA
MARIE	9	F	CHILD	GRZ	ZZZUSA
EMIL	8	M	CHILD	GRZ	ZZZUSA
CLARA	7	F	CHILD	GRZ	ZZZUSA
ANNA	5	F	CHILD	GRZ	ZZZUSA
FRIEDA	4	F	CHILD	GRZ	ZZZUSA
EMMA	2	F	CHILD	GRZ	ZZZUSA
HEDWIG	1	F	CHILD	GRZ	ZZZUSA
JOHANNA	.03	F	INFANT	GRZ	ZZZUSA
HINDERSEN, ANNA	28	F	W	GRZ	ZZZUSA
ELLA	3	F	CHILD	GRZ	ZZZUSA
GERTRUDE	.10	F	INFANT	GRZ	ZZZUSA
HAUSCHE, LOUISE	34	F	W	GRZ	ZZZUSA
ELISE	15	F	CH	GRZ	ZZZUSA
HEDWIG	6	F	CHILD	GRZ	ZZZUSA
HESSE, AUGUSTE	38	F	W	GRZ	ZZZUSA
PAUL	9	M	CHILD	GRZ	ZZZUSA
RICHARD	5	M	CHILD	GRZ	ZZZUSA
AGNES	2	F	CHILD	GRZ	ZZZUSA
MAGDEFRAU, CLARA	16	F	WO	GRZ	ZZZUSA
KRAWCZEK, VALENTIN	36	M	LABR	GRZ	ZZZUSA
STACHOWIAZ, STANISL.	44	M	LABR	GRZ	ZZZUSA
SKLEJSIK, VALENTIN	24	M	LABR	GRZ	ZZZUSA
SZUMINSKY, MIHAL	24	M	UNKNOWN	GRZ	ZZZUSA
STRASZAK, MIHAL	35	M	UNKNOWN	GRZ	ZZZUSA
CHAJNICKI, JOHANN	36	F	UNKNOWN	GRZ	ZZZUSA
ANNA	26	F	W	GRZ	ZZZUSA
STANISL.	5	M	CHILD	GRZ	ZZZUSA
JOSEF	3	M	CHILD	GRZ	ZZZUSA
MARIA	.11	F	INFANT	GRZ	ZZZUSA
SCHEFFLER, CARL	31	M	LABR	GRZ	ZZZUSA
MATHILDE	28	F	LABR	GRZ	ZZZUSA
BERTHA	4	F	CHILD	GRZ	ZZZUSA
OTTO	3	M	CHILD	GRZ	ZZZUSA
WILHE.	.10	F	INFANT	GRZ	ZZZUSA
JANUSZIAK, VALENTIN	34	M	LABR	GRZ	ZZZUSA
JOSEFA	28	F	W	GRZ	ZZZUSA
MICHALINE	9	F	CHILD	GRZ	ZZZUSA
MARCIN	8	M	CHILD	GRZ	ZZZUSA
FRANZISKA	7	F	CHILD	GRZ	ZZZUSA
FRANZ	4	F	CHILD	GRZ	ZZZUSA
MICHAEL	.08	M	INFANT	GRZ	ZZZUSA
JOSEFA	.08	M	INFANT	GRZ	ZZZUSA
WIECZIKOWSKI, MICHAEL	32	M	LABR	GRZ	ZZZUSA
LEOVADIA	24	F	W	GRZ	ZZZUSA
JOSEF	5	M	CHILD	GRZ	ZZZUSA
STANISL.	4	M	CHILD	GRZ	ZZZUSA
VICTORIA	.11	F	INFANT	GRZ	ZZZUSA
KUNIGUNDA	73	F	WO	GRZ	ZZZUSA
BLOEDAU, FRIEDRICH	38	M	LABR	GRZ	ZZZUSA
EMILIE	34	F	W	GRZ	ZZZUSA
OTTILIE	10	F	CH	GRZ	ZZZUSA
IDA	8	F	CHILD	GRZ	ZZZUSA
EMMA	6	F	CHILD	GRZ	ZZZUSA
MARTHA	4	F	CHILD	GRZ	ZZZUSA
WANDA	.09	F	INFANT	GRZ	ZZZUSA
DIETRICH, JOHANN	29	M	LABR	GRZ	ZZZUSA
SCHOLTZ, CARL	22	M	SHMK	GRZ	ZZZUSA
BARGMANN, ANNA	23	F	SGL	GRZ	ZZZUSA
WICZIOLEK, MARTIN	30	M	LABR	GRZ	ZZZUSA
MARKITOW, FRANZ	30	M	LABR	GRZ	ZZZUSA
FRANZISKA	30	F	W	GRZ	ZZZUSA
MARIE	4	F	CHILD	GRZ	ZZZUSA
CAECILIE	.09	F	INFANT	GRZ	ZZZUSA
KACZNUREK, FRANZ	23	M	LABR	GRZ	ZZZUSA
KURLINSKI, STANISL.	24	M	LABR	GRZ	ZZZUSA
GAROZYNSKA, CONSTANZIA	23	F	SGL	GRZ	ZZZUSA
CISZENSKI, THOMAS	27	M	LABR	GRZ	ZZZUSA
ELISABETH	26	F	W	GRZ	ZZZUSA
STANISLAWA	.11	F	INFANT	GRZ	ZZZUSA
RADEMACHER, SOPHIE	15	F	SGL	GRZ	ZZZUSA
OWERZET, ADAM	45	M	LABR	GRZ	ZZZUSA
MARIANNE	36	F	W	GRZ	ZZZUSA
EVA	15	F	CH	GRZ	ZZZUSA
KOCHANSKI, JAN	30	M	LABR	GRZ	ZZZUSA
PECKA, IGNATZ	30	M	LABR	GRZ	ZZZUSA
BOGASINSKI, MAXIMILIAN	33	M	SMH	GRZ	ZZZUSA
VERONICA	26	F	W	GRZ	ZZZUSA
FRANZISCA	4	F	CHILD	GRZ	ZZZUSA
MARIANNE	3	F	CHILD	GRZ	ZZZUSA
JOH.	.11	M	INFANT	GRZ	ZZZUSA
KOSMALSKI, JOSEF	30	M	LABR	GRZ	ZZZUSA
FRANZISKA	26	F	W	GRZ	ZZZUSA
JOH.	4	M	CHILD	GRZ	ZZZUSA
STANISLAWA	2	F	CHILD	GRZ	ZZZUSA
STANISLAUS	1	M	CHILD	GRZ	ZZZUSA
KAZIMIR	.01	M	INFANT	GRZ	ZZZUSA
CREZYKOWSKY, FRANZ	34	M	LABR	GRZ	ZZZUSA
SCHMARTZ, IGNATZ	32	M	LABR	GRZ	ZZZUSA
ROHS, HEINR.	26	F	SHMK	GRZ	ZZZUSA

PASSENGER	AGE	SEX	OCCUPATION	PRVL	DES
ANNA	22	F	W	GRZZZZUSA	
RADMACHER, CATHA.	51	F	WO	GRZZZZUSA	
ADELHEID	14	F	CH	GRZZZZUSA	
FIGLER, JOSEF	24	M	LABR	GRZZZZUSA	
PINARSKI, ROCH	37	M	LABR	GRZZZZUSA	
PAWLACZAK, MACIEJ	35	M	LABR	GRZZZZUSA	
MAGDALE.	38	F	W	GRZZZZUSA	
MICH.	4	M	CHILD	GRZZZZUSA	
FRANZISZEK	.06	M	INFANT	GRZZZZUSA	
WINTER, FRITZ	28	M	UNKNOWN	GRZZZZUSA	
ZILINSKI, KASIMIR	26	M	LABR	GRZZZZUSA	
BRAUN, MARGA.	27	F	SGL	GRZZZZUSA	
SZYMCZAK, KASIMIR	22	M	LABR	GRZZZZUSA	
KULA, ANTON	24	M	LABR	GRZZZZUSA	
CIEZLISKA, MARIANNE	24	F	SGL	GRZZZZUSA	
BIBLEWSKY, FRANZ	38	M	LABR	GRZZZZUSA	
CATHA.	28	F	W	GRZZZZUSA	
SALKOWSKY, JOSEF	35	M	LABR	GRZZZZUSA	
ANNA	35	F	W	GRZZZZUSA	
ALBERT	4	M	CHILD	GRZZZZUSA	
MARIE	2	F	CHILD	GRZZZZUSA	
JOSEF	1	M	CHILD	GRZZZZUSA	
MARTHA	.06	F	INFANT	GRZZZZUSA	
SOEZYNSKY, JAN	27	M	FARMER	GRZZZZUSA	
OCHAZRINSKI, MARTIN	27	M	TLR	GRZZZZUSA	
DEALICK, JAN	24	M	FARMER	GRZZZZUSA	
WARZIKOWSKI, JOH.	28	M	LABR	GRZZZZUSA	
FOTH, AUG.	26	M	MCHT	GRZZZZUSA	
KOZLECKI, BRONISLAW	28	M	LABR	GRZZZZUSA	
OLSEWSKI, MICHEL	26	M	LABR	GRZZZZUSA	
MICHALINE	19	F	W	GRZZZZUSA	
DARRIS, SIMON	32	M	FARMER	GRZZZZUSA	
THULKE, LOUIS	17	M	LABR	GRZZZZUSA	
GRANZ, RUDOLF	32	M	LABR	GRZZZZUSA	
AMALIE	32	F	W	GRZZZZUSA	
HILDEGARD	.06	F	INFANT	GRZZZZUSA	
HENRIETTE	26	F	W	GRZZZZUSA	
ERICH	.08	M	INFANT	GRZZZZUSA	
HOROWITZ, SIEGFRIED	45	M	MCHT	GRZZZZUSA	
JULIE	28	F	W	GRZZZZUSA	
GERTRUD	8	F	CHILD	GRZZZZUSA	
KACZMIRACZAK, STANISL.	30	M	LABR	GRZZZZUSA	
ANTONIA	24	F	W	GRZZZZUSA	
ANDRZY	3	M	CHILD	GRZZZZUSA	
PIETR.	.09	M	INFANT	GRZZZZUSA	
KRANTE, JOHANN	21	M	LABR	GRZZZZUSA	
KOWALEWSKY, JOSEF	24	M	LABR	GRZZZZUSA	
KOPERSKI, ANTON	28	M	LABR	GRZZZZUSA	
MARIANNE	21	F	W	GRZZZZUSA	
MARIANNA	.03	F	INFANT	GRZZZZUSA	
JUDWASCHEK, MICHEL	25	M	LABR	GRZZZZUSA	
MATUSZAK, THOMAS	25	M	LABR	GRZZZZUSA	
MARIANNA	19	F	W	GRZZZZUSA	
BERGNER, KONSTANTYN	9	M	CHILD	GRZZZZUSA	
PATZOLDT, WILHE.	62	F	WO	GRZZZZUSA	
HAHN, ISIDOR	44	M	MCHT	GRZZZZUSA	
GOLDE	43	F	W	GRZZZZUSA	
PAULE.	16	F	CH	GRZZZZUSA	
SOPHIE	13	F	CH	GRZZZZUSA	
WIENA	9	F	CHILD	GRZZZZUSA	
FANNY	8	F	CHILD	GRZZZZUSA	
GERTRUD	4	F	CHILD	GRZZZZUSA	
MICHEL, ANNA	18	F	SGL	SRZZZZUSA	
THORMANN, JUSTINA	20	F	SGL	GRZZZZUSA	
MUCKENSTURM, MARIA	22	F	SGL	GRZZZZUSA	
ZELTNER, ARNOLD	28	M	LABR	SRZZZZUSA	
ROSINE	39	F	W	SRZZZZUSA	
JACOB	17	M	CH	SRZZZZUSA	
ADIELA	12	M	CH	SRZZZZUSA	
WANNENMOCHER, CARL	39	M	FARMER	GRZZZZUSA	
CHRISTINE	30	F	W	GRZZZZUSA	
GOTTLIEB	10	M	CH	GRZZZZUSA	
JACOB	6	M	CHILD	GRZZZZUSA	
CAROLE.	4	F	CHILD	GRZZZZUSA	
MARIE	3	F	CHILD	GRZZZZUSA	

PASSENGER	AGE	SEX	OCCUPATION	PRVL	DES
ROSINE	.09	F	INFANT	GRZZZZUSA	
ZEIGER, LOUISE	9	F	CHILD	GRZZZZUSA	
GAERTNER, MARTIN	25	M	GZR	GRZZZZUSA	
BAUMGARTEN, LORENZ	28	M	GZR	GRZZZZUSA	
ECKER, CLEMENTINE	26	F	SGL	GRZZZZUSA	
BURGERT, CONSTANTIN	22	M	BRR	GRZZZZUSA	
KERN, M.THERESE	18	F	SGL	GRZZZZUSA	
GUTMANN, JOHANN	25	M	FARMER	GRZZZZUSA	
SPEICH, MATHILDE	18	F	SGL	GRZZZZUSA	
VAUBAN, CATHARINE	40	F	SGL	GRZZZZUSA	
HUGO, GOTTFRIED	22	M	LABR	SRZZZZUSA	
HEINIS, EUGENE	23	M	TLR	GRZZZZUSA	
GRAF, ANDREAS	65	M	FARMER	SRZZZZUSA	
HAENGI, MARIE	24	F	SGL	SRZZZZUSA	
HAENER, JACOB	32	M	LABR	SRZZZZUSA	
ROSALIE	32	F	W	SRZZZZUSA	
EMMA	10	F	CH	SRZZZZUSA	
HAEFTLI, ANTON	26	M	FARMER	SRZZZZUSA	
HERRMANN, ANTON	17	M	FARMER	SRZZZZUSA	
CASANOVA, ANTON	18	M	FARMER	SRZZZZUSA	
ELSENBERG, JOSEF	19	M	LABR	SRZZZZUSA	
PHILIPP, IVAN	29	M	FARMER	GRZZZZUSA	
BLIND, JOSEF	19	M	FARMER	GRZZZZUSA	
SCHENKEL, HERRM.	22	M	BCHR	SRZZZZUSA	
BOHNER, ANTON	27	M	BBR	SRZZZZUSA	
GREGORI, HANS	38	M	MCHT	SRZZZZUSA	
MARTINET, ANTOINE	42	M	FARMER	GRZZZZUSA	
SEUFTEN, MARIE	32	F	W	GRZZZZUSA	
ARNOLD	.09	M	INFANT	GRZZZZUSA	
HUEGLI, ARNOLD	31	M	LABR	SRZZZZUSA	
ARFORT, FERDINAND	21	M	MSN	FRZZZZUSA	
LALLEMAND, JULES	22	M	FARMER	FRZZZZUSA	
BRANDT, HUGO	19	M	WCHMKR	GRZZZZUSA	
WIEZAREK, VALENTI	.06	M	INFANT	GRZZZZUSA	
MOWSCHTER, BRUNO-R.	00	M	INF	GR****USA	
WESSOTOWSKI, MARIANE	00	F	INF	GR****USA	
U, U	00	F	UNKNOWN	SRZZZZUSA	
SCHNEIDER, AMALIA	28	F	WO	SRZZZZUSA	

SHIP: NOVA SCOTIAN

FROM: LIVERPOOL
TO: BALTIMORE
ARRIVED: 05 MAY 1888

PASSENGER	AGE	SEX	OCCUPATION	PRVL	DES
SETURER, ISYDOR	43	M	SHMK	GRZZZZBAL	
KORN, FER	43	M	TRVLR	GRZZZZBAL	
WINTZET, ERNEST	28	M	LABR	GRZZZZBAL	
KNITTEL, HEINRICH	29	M	SMH	GRZZZZNY	
AKSELAWIZ, HELENE	19	F	DRSMKR	GRZZZZPIT	
GARFUNKEL, JOSKEEL	31	M	FARMER	GRZZZZPHI	
SAPPEITEWIS, SCHUNI	18	F	DRSMKR	GRZZZZBAL	
GARFUNKEL, MOSES	38	F	FARMER	GRZZZZNY	
ISAAK	17	M	FARMER	GRZZZZNY	
MALKE	24	F	UNKNOWN	GRZZZZNY	
TYNN, ERNEST	30	M	LABR	GRZZZZBAL	
AUG	27	M	LABR	GRZZZZBAL	
FRIEDRICK	36	M	LABR	GRZZZZBAL	
HESS, PAUL	22	M	UMKR	GRZZZZBAL	
SCHWARZ, JOHN	39	M	MSN	GRZZZZPA	
LOUISE	28	F	W	GRZZZZPA	
LOUISE	2	F	CHILD	GRZZZZPA	

PASSENGER	AGE	SEX	OCCUPATION	PRVL	DES
SHIP: STATE OF NEVADA					
FROM: GLASGOW AND LARNE					
TO: NEW YORK					
ARRIVED: 05 MAY 1888					
FALKENBERG, MINNA	24	F	SVNT	GRZZZZUSA	
MASLUKOWSK, FRANZISKA	19	F	SVNT	GRZZZZUSA	
NALIDZINSKY, ANDRAS	63	M	LABR	GRZZZZUSA	
MARIA	59	F	W	GRZZZZUSA	
FRANZ	29	M	LABR	GRZZZZUSA	
STANISLAUS	28	M	LABR	GRZZZZUSA	
MARIA	.09	F	INFANT	GRZZZZUSA	
ROSENMAN, MINNA	26	F	MRNR	GRZZZZUSA	
FEIGE	10	F	CH	GRZZZZUSA	
MENDEL	1	M	CHILD	GRZZZZUSA	
STRUCK, DETLEF	21	M	FARMER	GRZZZZUSA	
STONIWITZKI, ANTON	25	M	LABR	GRZZZZUSA	
JOHANNA	24	F	W	GRZZZZUSA	
JOHAN	.06	M	INFANT	GRZZZZUSA	
MICHEL	36	M	LABR	GRZZZZUSA	
ANTONIE	24	F	W	GRZZZZUSA	
ANTONIE	7	F	CHILD	GRZZZZUSA	
MARIE	3	F	CHILD	GRZZZZUSA	
WESPHALEN, GERH.	19	M	CL	GRZZZZUSA	
WEISS, FANNY	23	M	UNKNOWN	GRZZZZUSA	
GUSTA	10	F	CH	GRZZZZUSA	
DAVID	3	M	CHILD	GRZZZZUSA	
FRIEDR.	1	F	CHILD	GRZZZZUSA	
KAUFMAN, HEINR.	22	M	MCHT	GRZZZZUSA	
SHIP: EMS					
FROM: BREMEN					
TO: NEW YORK					
ARRIVED: 07 MAY 1888					
RACHEWSKY, AUGUSTE	49	F	W	GRZZZZUNK	
AUGUSTE	9	F	CHILD	GRZZZZUNK	
W--ZEL, RUDOLF	22	M	LABR	GRZZZZUNK	
--NSKA, MARSKA	14	F	UNKNOWN	GRADEICLE	
WIZICKI, FRANZISKA	30	F	UNKNOWN	GRADEICH	
TYROWSKI, FRIEDRICH	17	M	FARMER	GRADEIUNK	
POKROJEKI, ANTON	45	M	FARMER	GRZZZZSTL	
JOSEFINA	43	F	W	GRZZZZSTL	
FRANZ	15	M	FARMER	GRZZZZSTL	
ANNA	9	F	CHILD	GRZZZZSTL	
JOHANN	7	M	CHILD	GRZZZZSTL	
JOSEFINA	.01	F	INFANT	GRZZZZSTL	
NABAKOWSKI, GOTTLIEB	40	M	LABR	GRZZZZMIL	
MAICHUZAK, MICHAEL	43	M	LABR	GRZZZZUNK	
EHRLICH, GUSTAV	30	M	LABR	GRZZZZUNK	
---ROEDER, MICHAEL	40	M	FARMER	GRZZZZBAL	
AUG--	40	F	W	GRZZZZBAL	
KARTIN	9	M	CHILD	GRZZZZBAL	
MANE	8	F	CHILD	GRZZZZBAL	
LIVANCE, ANNA	17	F	UNKNOWN	GRAAEABAL	
IGLINSKI, JOSEF	26	M	LABR	GRZZZZCH	
QUASTASIA	24	F	W	GRZZZZCH	
MARIA	.01	F	INFANT	GRZZZZCH	
SZEINA, CARL	28	M	PNTR	GRAAKHUNK	
MARIA	23	F	UNKNOWN	GRAAKHUNK	
KUCZBORSKI, JOHANN	37	M	FARMER	GRAEAFCH	
AGNES	20	F	UNKNOWN	GRAEAFCH	
WICENTY	8	M	CHILD	GRAEAFCH	
ANTONI	2	M	CHILD	GRAEAFCH	
KOWATZKI, ANTON	24	M	JNR	GRAEAFPHI	
HOFFMANN, MARIE	10	F	CH	GRAAKHCH	
CHUDZICHI, JOHANN	25	M	UNKNOWN	GRAAKHBAL	
CHUDZICKI, MARIE	37	F	W	GRAAKHBAL	
CEGILSKA, JOSEPH	10	F	CH	GRAAKHBAL	
ANTON	8	M	CHILD	GRAAKHBAL	
CHUDZICKI, STANISLAUS	.03	M	INFANT	GRAAKHBAL	
JORDAN, HERM.	30	M	JNR	GRAAKHBAL	
BONSCHKIEWICZ, FRANZ	31	M	TLR	GRAAKHBAL	
HERTEL, AUGUSTE	47	F	UNKNOWN	GRAAEAUNK	
LAURA	17	F	UNKNOWN	GRAAEAUNK	
STIBINSKI, KATHARINA	30	F	UNKNOWN	GRAEABUNK	
MARIA	8	F	CHILD	GRAEABUNK	
WEGE, KATCHEN	24	F	UNKNOWN	GRZZZZUNK	
GERBER, WILHELMINA	21	F	UNKNOWN	GRZZZZWAS	
DO--BECK, CATHARINA	32	F	UNKNOWN	GRZZZZBAL	
STANISL.	.11	F	INFANT	GRZZZZBAL	
WITUZKY, MICHAL	20	M	LABR	GRADYMUNK	
MARGARETHA	17	F	UNKNOWN	GRADYMUNK	
JARMUSCH, FRIEDRICH	47	M	LABR	GRZZZZUNK	
AUGUSTE	16	F	UNKNOWN	GRZZZZUNK	
WOZNIAK, ANDREAS	23	M	LABR	GRAFDDCH	
STEPHAN--	25	M	W	GRAFDDCH	
--ZULAK, MARIANNE	47	F	UNKNOWN	GRZZZZPIT	
KYDZYNSKI, AGNES	27	F	W	GRZZZZBUF	
JOHANN	5	M	CHILD	GRZZZZBUF	
THOMAS	4	M	CHILD	GRZZZZBUF	
ANTON	35	M	FARMER	GRZZZZBUF	
ROSALIA	.11	F	INFANT	GRZZZZBUF	
-ICHALECK, ANDRYG	25	M	LABR	GRZZZZCH	
LE--NDOWSKA, MARIA	20	F	UNKNOWN	GRAAKHUNK	
W--BLESKA, SIMON	33	M	FARMER	GRAAKHUSA	
WOLINSKA, MARIANNE	19	F	UNKNOWN	GRAARZOH	
FAGIELSKA, ASBIETA	19	F	UNKNOWN	GRAARZCH	
SCHWARZ, EMILIE	20	F	UNKNOWN	GRAARZDET	
GOLIBIESKA, JAGNIESCA	42	F	UNKNOWN	GRAARZDET	
FRANZ	9	M	CHILD	GRAARZDET	
MICHAL	7	M	CHILD	GRAARZDET	
ROSALIE	5	F	CHILD	GRAARZDET	
VICTORIA	3	F	CHILD	GRAARZDET	
JOSEPHA	.11	F	INFANT	GRAARZDET	
WISNOEWSKA, CONSTANCIA	36	F	W	GRADYMPIT	
BOGANICA	11	F	UNKNOWN	GRADYMPIT	
WAZLAW	3	M	CHILD	GRADYMPIT	
ORESLAW	2	M	CHILD	GRADYMPIT	
MARIA	.11	F	INFANT	GRADYMPIT	
WOJNOWSKI, PETER	23	M	FARMER	GRAARZMIL	
SZESCYCKI, MARIA	28	F	UNKNOWN	GRAARZCH	
PIMION, WAWRZYN	28	M	FARMER	GRAARZMN	
WALCZAK, KATHIAS	35	M	FARMER	GRAARZCH	
RUZULAK, MARTIN	47	M	FARMER	GRAARZPIT	
BALM, CONR.	20	M	LABR	GRAARRBAL	
GRESKOWIAK, IGNATZ	45	M	LABR	GRAARRBAL	
CATHARINA	27	F	UNKNOWN	GRAARRBAL	
MICHAEL	16	M	LABR	GRAARRBAL	
STANISLAWA	8	F	CHILD	GRAARRBAL	
FRANZ	4	M	CHILD	GRAARRBAL	
JOSEPH	2	M	CHILD	GRAARRBAL	
ZIPLINSKY, JACOB	25	M	SHMK	GRAARRBAL	
KYSZYKOWSKI, JACOB	30	M	LABR	GRAARRBAL	
ANTONIE	28	F	W	GRAARRBAL	
FRANZ	24	M	LABR	GRAARRBAL	
PRIEBE, ERNST	61	M	BOO	GRAARRBAL	
LOUISE	58	F	W	GRAARRBAL	
OTTO	3	M	CHILD	GRAARRBAL	
WORMS, CARL	25	M	LABR	GRAARRBAL	
GUZENSKI, ANDRO	31	M	LABR	GRAIVMCH	
ANNA	28	F	W	GRAIVMCH	
LEOCADIA	5	F	CHILD	GRAIVMCH	
FRANZISCA	3	F	CHILD	GRAIVMCH	
FOIGHT	.11	M	INFANT	GRAIVMCH	
KATZ, MINNA	20	F	UNKNOWN	GRAIVMBAL	
DOLKA, FRANZ	24	M	LABR	GRAIVMBAL	
JENDRUSHAK, VALENTINE	.10	F	INFANT	GRAIVMBAL	
BUCKOWICKI, FRANZ	26	M	LABR	GRAIVMSOU	
MAGDALENE	30	F	W	GRAIVMSOU	
ANNA	9	F	CHILD	GRAIVMSOU	
KATHARINA	6	F	CHILD	GRAIVMSOU	

PASSENGER	AGE	SEX	OCCUPATION	PRVL	DES
DOLKA, FRANZISKA	25	F	W		GRAIVMSOU
BUDKOWICKI, WOJECH	5	M	CHILD		GRAIVMSOU
ROMAN	3	M	CHILD		GRAIVMSOU
JON	.11	M	INFANT		GRAIVMSOU
PETEZINSKA, MARIANNE	22	F	UNKNOWN		GRADGOSOU
ROESSLER, EVA	50	F	W		GRACNTBAL
AUGUSTA	11	F	CH		GRACNTBAL
AUSTRIA	9	F	CHILD		GRACNTBAL
FRANZISKA	5	F	CHILD		GRACNTBAL
FRANZ	2	M	CHILD		GRACNTBAL
WILHELM	50	M	FARMER		GRACNTBAL
NEUBAUER, KARL	29	M	BKPR		GRACNTPIT
AUGUSTE	22	F	W		GRACNTPIT
SCHWIEJA, FRISCH	26	M	LABR		GRZZZZBAL
TOKARSKY, JOSEPH	36	M	LABR		GRZZZZBAL
JENDRUSHAK, VINCENSKY	34	M	LABR		GRADVBBAL
MICHALAK, MICHAL	29	M	LABR		GRAAYGBAL
EDENHARTEN, ANNA	17	F	UNKNOWN		GRAAYGBAL
SCHULZ, JOHANN	49	M	FARMER		GRAAYGBAL
WALOZEK, ANTOAN	25	M	DRVR		GRZZZZBAL
SOKOTA, JOHANN	39	M	PNTR		GRZZZZBAL
CILLIAN, LUCAS	27	M	MNR		GRAARRUNK
MARIA	30	F	W		GRAEZVUNK
VICTORIA	4	F	CHILD		GRAEZVUNK
JOSEFA	3	M	CHILD		GRAEZVUNK
FISCHER, THEODOR	14	M	UNKNOWN		GRACBFBAL
MATUCHEWSKA, VICTORIA	56	F	W		GRAESFTOL
LORENZ	54	M	LABR		GRAESFTOL
OLENYIK, MARIANNE	53	F	W		GRZZZZCOE
FRISKE, JADWIGA	52	F	W		GRAEAFUNK
KOZAL, MARIE	27	F	W		GRZZZZUNK
NOWAK, JOSEFA	57	F	W		GRZZZZUNK
FILIPSKI, JAN	43	M	LABR		GRZZZZUNK
FELIXIA	37	F	W		GRZZZZUNK
ANTON	7	M	CHILD		GRZZZZUNK
FRANZ	5	M	CHILD		GRZZZZUNK
NOVICKI, FRANZ	28	M	PDLR		GRZZZZUSA
ECKE, LEONHARDT	18	M	SDLR		GRZZZZCH
RING, CARL	27	M	TLR		GRAAKHUNK
NEUBAUER, GUSTAV	3	M	CHILD		GRADVBPIT
EMILIE	2	F	CHILD		GRADVBPIT
CAROLINE	.11	F	INFANT		GRADVBPIT
BJOENING, GUSTAV	16	M	STWD		GRZZZZUNK
DRECKMAYER, JOAHNNE	25	F	UNKNOWN		GRZZZZMIL
WISCHMEYER, CL.	18	M	TIR		GRAARZCLE
WILH.	17	M	SMH		GRAARZCLE
FORTSCH, JOSEF	14	M	UNKNOWN		GRZZZZCH
WERNER, LOUISE	49	F	W		GRAAKHUNK
CLARA	17	F	UNKNOWN		GRACBRUNK
GOLLIWAS, FRANZISKA	25	F	W		GRADYGUNK
PETER	.11	M	INFANT		GRADYGUNK
GREGER, DOROTHEA	18	F	UNKNOWN		GRZZZZSP
ERNESTINE	20	F	UNKNOWN		GRZZZZSP
RUTHKOWSKY, MARG.	17	F	UNKNOWN		GRADYMUNK
HABERMANN, HERM.	23	M	SDLR		GRADYMSP
LECIEJEWSKY, JOHANN	28	M	SHMK		GRABRCBAL
BEITRAG, ROSIN	44	F	W		GRAEXKSOU
MEYER, CHRISTIAN	19	M	UNKNOWN		GRAEXKUNK
KLOSOWSKA, FRANZISKA	24	F	UNKNOWN		GRACQAHEL
MAGNOSKA, HEINRICH	43	M	PNTR		GRACQADET
BORKOWICKZ, JOHANN	24	M	FARMER		GRACQADET
BORKOWICZ, PELEGIA	21	F	W		GRACQADET
BAGROWSKA, MARIANNE	33	F	UNKNOWN		GRZZZZBAL
SOPHIA	5	F	CHILD		GRZZZZBAL
MALINOWSKI, STANISLAUS	25	M	LABR		GRZZZZBAL
JOSEFA	20	F	W		GRZZZZBAL
BIKOWICS, MICHAEL	25	M	LABR		GRABHUBAL
PROUDZINSKI, PAUL	35	M	LABR		GRABHUBAL
STREZELEWITZ, AGNATZ	70	M	LABR		GRAAXLBAL
CHMILEWSKA, CONSTANCYA	17	F	UNKNOWN		GRADGOPIT
SCHULZ, FERD.	26	M	CMST		GRAEXLCH
GRABARKIEWICZ, JOSEF	19	M	MNR		GRZZZZCH
TUSHOLSKI, JOHN	22	M	MNR		GRZZZZDET
VERONIKA	18	F	W		GRZZZZDET
HABERMANN, AUGUST	29	M	MNR		GRZZZZWAE
KATHILDE	24	F	W		GRZZZZWAE
EMILIE	2	F	CHILD		GRZZZZWAE
KARL	.10	M	INFANT		GRZZZZWAE
MUCKOWIAK, KASPAR	6	M	CHILD		GRZZZZTOL
KATHARINA	69	F	W		GRZZZZTOL
WILKOWSKA, JULIANA	75	F	PVTR		GRAEXLUNK
JOSEFA	24	F	W		GRAEXLUNK
JADJEJEWSKI, PETER	38	M	LABR		GRAEXLLIT
JOSEFINE	26	F	W		GRAEXLLIT
GOLINSKI, JOHANN	36	M	LABR		GRADYMCH
ANNA	30	F	W		GRADYMCH
FRANZ	9	M	CHILD		GRADYMCH
MARIANNA	7	F	CHILD		GRADYMCH
ROSALIE	5	F	CHILD		GRADYMCH
REGINA	.02	F	INFANT		GRADYMCH
PLATH, EMMA	18	F	UNKNOWN		GRACBRTRN
WILHELM	53	M	FARMER		GRACBRTRN
JUSTINE	53	F	W		GRACBRTRN
EDUARD	17	M	LABR		GRACBRTRN
ADA	13	F	UNKNOWN		GRACBRTRN
HOEFT, EMMA	40	F	UNKNOWN		GRZZZZUNK
HENRIETTE	39	F	UNKNOWN		GRZZZZUNK
HUEBNER, AUGUSTE	18	F	UNKNOWN		GRADZOUNK
WILHELMINE	16	F	UNKNOWN		GRADZOUNK
JULIUS	22	M	LABR		GRADZOUNK
HANRIETTE	11	F	UNKNOWN		GRZZZZUNK
MATHILDE	10	F	CH		GRZZZZUNK
OTTILIE	7	F	CHILD		GRZZZZUNK
EMMA	.11	F	INFANT		GRZZZZUNK
FADJEJEWSKA, MAIRANNE	5	F	CHILD		GRAEXLLIT
AUGUST	3	M	CHILD		GRAEXLLIT
ANNA	.11	F	INFANT		GRAEXLLIT
KOERING, MARTIN	32	M	CPTR		GRADDWLIT
SPICZAK, MARTIN	42	M	CPTR		GRADDWLIT
LOSIK, CASIMIR	24	M	FARMER		GRADDWTOL
SZTUREMBIKI, JOHANN	30	M	FARMER		GRADDWCH
AGNES	26	F	W		GRADDWCH
LEON	.11	M	INFANT		GRADDWCH
ROZEWICZ, KORDULA	24	F	UNKNOWN		GRZZZZCH
MALECKI, THOMAS	39	M	CPR		GRZZZZDET
BUKOWSKY, JAN	27	M	SMH		GRADVHPIT
JAWORSKA, ROSALIE	60	F	W		GRAAQPCH
MASCHOKA, ALBERT	23	M	TIR		GRZZZZBAL
PLOKA, ANTON	25	M	BCHR		GRZZZZBAL
KOTTE, ANNA	17	F	UNKNOWN		GRZZZZBAL
FAHNZA, JOSEF	23	M	CPTR		GRABVUBAL
TAMMER, GERHARD	24	M	CPTR		GRAEXWBAL
MERGLER, CLARA	23	F	UNKNOWN		GRAEXWBAL
SCHMIDT, WILHELM	14	M	UNKNOWN		GRADLDUNK
MARIE	20	F	UNKNOWN		GRABDMUNK
WEISWEBER, SOPHIE	22	F	UNKNOWN		GRACXVTOL
RISCHMUXLLER, KAROLIN	18	F	UNKNOWN		GRACXVBAL
KRUMDICK, DOROTHEA	16	F	UNKNOWN		GRAEAPBAL
SUCHTING, DORALINE	17	F	UNKNOWN		GRZZZZBAL
THEINER, ALMUTH	17	M	LABR		GRAEXWSTE
BENS, MIINKE	24	M	LABR		GRAEXWUNK
OLTMANUS, GEESKE	18	M	LABR		GRAEXWBAT
FRAHMANN, HELENE	22	F	UNKNOWN		GRADDWUNK
HEINR.	.11	M	INFANT		GRADDWUNK
HARMS, META	23	F	UNKNOWN		GRAAYGUNK
NOWAK, JOHANN	22	M	LABR		GRZZZZUNK
ZIELINSKI, WOJCSICH	27	M	LABR		GRAAZCUNK
CATHARINA	26	F	W		GRAAZCUNK
JOSEPH	.11	M	INFANT		GRAAZCUNK
STANISLAWA	3	M	CHILD		GRAAZCUNK
WOJESICH	.11	M	INFANT		GRAAZCUNK
FANKOWSKY, JOHANN	29	M	LABR		GRACBFTOL
IGNAZ	26	M	LABR		GRACBFTOL
BOCHANSKI, ADALBERT	36	M	LABR		GRAAZQUNK
KOCH, KATHARINA	26	F	UNKNOWN		GRAAZQCH
STEIGENBERGER, JOHANN	25	M	LABR		GRAAZQUNK
ULFERS, JOHANN	16	M	LABR		GRAAZQUNK
KRUMDIECK, ERNST	15	M	LABR		GRAAXLUNK
STIEGLITZ, HEINRICH	17	M	MCHT		GRZZZZUNK
LAUM, ANNA	24	F	UNKNOWN		GRZZZZUNK

PASSENGER	AGE	SEX	OCCUPATION	PRVL	DES
REICHERT, THERESE	22	F	UNKNOWN		GRZZZZBAL
HORACEK, JOAEF	30	M	CPR		GRZZZZCH
MARIE	28	F	UNKNOWN		GRZZZZCH
PAUL	8	M	CHILD		GRZZZZCH
EMMA	7	F	CHILD		GRZZZZCH
MAX	5	M	CHILD		GRZZZZCH
FRIEDA	3	F	CHILD		GRZZZZCH
CLARA	2	F	CHILD		GRZZZZCH
HUGO	.11	M	INFANT		GRZZZZCH
GIENSBERG, PETER	24	M	CPR		GRABDMUNK
NAAB, GEORG	16	M	SMH		GRACXVEVA
GRUSZENSKI, THOMAS	25	M	FARMER		GRZZZZTOL
MALVINE	20	F	W		GRZZZZTOL
JOSEFINE	.11	F	INFANT		GRZZZZTOL
OSOWSKA, AGNISKA	60	F	UNKNOWN		GRAFSITOL
KAWINSKA, JULIA	63	F	UNKNOWN		GRAIRIDET
MARTIN	10	M	CH		GRAIRIDET
WALKOWIAK, IGNATZ	26	M	FARMER		GRAIEUBAL
GERTZEN, FRIEDRIKE	26	F	W		GRZZZZCLI
PAULINE	.11	F	INFANT		GRZZZZCLI
CHRISTINE	2	F	CHILD		GRZZZZCLI
MODENBACH, MINNA	22	F	UNKNOWN		GRZZZZCLE
PLAPHAL, HERMANN	25	M	SMH		GRAAZSBAL
SCHMIDTKAMER, BARB.	23	F	UNKNOWN		GRAAZSBAL
MUSAWSKI, JOSEF	26	M	TIR		GRAAZSBAL
KAEMPER, KATHARINE	16	F	UNKNOWN		GRAAGLBAL
KATHARINE	75	F	UNKNOWN		GRAAGLBAL
MINNA	38	F	UNKNOWN		GRAAGLBAL
SCHOETTLER, REGINA	43	F	W		GRZZZZBAL
LOUIS	17	M	LABR		GRZZZZBAL
LINA	13	F	CH		GRZZZZBAL
GEORG	11	M	CH		GRZZZZBAL
KUWALKE, JOHANNES	37	M	LABR		GRZZZZBAL
HENRIETTE	39	F	W		GRZZZZBAL
GUISAR	11	M	CH		GRZZZZBAL
AUGUSTE	9	F	CHILD		GRZZZZBAL
FRIEDRICH	5	M	CHILD		GRZZZZBAL
EMILIE	3	F	CHILD		GRZZZZBAL
PAULINE	.09	F	INFANT		GRZZZZBAL
WOZESCINSKI, MARTIN	28	M	FARMER		GRAEABBAL
MARRIE	25	F	W		GRAEABBAL
ANNA	4	F	CHILD		GRAEABBAL
JOSEF	2	M	CHILD		GRAEABBAL
ANASTASIA	.11	F	INFANT		GRAEABBAL
WUJAK, THOMAS	30	M	LABR		GRAEABBAL
AGNITZKA	27	F	W		GRAEABBAL
ANTONIA	4	F	CHILD		GRAEABBAL
WASORGIN	3	M	CHILD		GRAEABBAL
MANONIN	2	F	CHILD		GRAEABBAL
MARTIN	.06	M	INFANT		GRAEABBAL
MATUSZAK, ANTON	16	M	LABR		GRZZZZBAL
MATUZAK, BARTOLOM.	23	M	LABR		GRZZZZBAL
KLOSS, AUGUST	26	M	GDNR		GRAHNOUNK
BORN, FRANZ	26	M	CPTR		GRADCRUNK
BIRR, BERTHA	15	F	UNKNOWN		GRAEPTUNK
SCHWANKE, JOHANN	28	M	SMH		GRZZZZUNK
CAROLINE	20	F	UNKNOWN		GRZZZZUNK
BRUAN, WILHELMINE	23	F	UNKNOWN		GRAAZQUNK
SCHWANKE, EHMK	.10	M	INFANT		GRACSDUNK
BARZ, AUGUST	31	M	GDNR		GRZZZZCH
HEYER, FERD.	29	M	GDNR		GRADVBUNK
THERESE	29	F	W		GRADVBUNK
JULIE	5	F	CHILD		GRADVBUNK
PAUL	3	M	CHILD		GRADVBUNK
LIBKE, PAUL	65	M	PVTM		GRADVBUNK
HENRIETTE	44	F	W		GRADVBUNK
WILHEMINE	35	F	UNKNOWN		GRADVBUNK
LINA	22	F	UNKNOWN		GRADVBUNK
MARIE	11	F	CH		GRADVBUNK
MARIANNE	3	F	CHILD		GRADVBUNK
NADOLNY, JOHN	58	M	PNTR		GRACSDDET
ROSALIA	50	F	W		GRACSDDET
THEOPHILA	21	F	UNKNOWN		GRACSDDET
FRANZISKA	17	F	UNKNOWN		GRACSDDET
JOSIEFA	15	F	UNKNOWN		GRACSDDET
CASEMIR	8	M	CHILD		GRACSDDET
SCHOLZ, ADOLPH	35	M	BTMKR		GRZZZZCH
LUTOMSKA, KATARZYNA	16	F	UNKNOWN		GRZZZZPIT
DOBBECK, ANDREAS	23	M	LABR		GRZZZZCH
SWIDERSKA, KATARZYNA	21	F	LABR		GRADEPUNK
GRZEYOZEWICZ, WALENTY	57	M	LABR		GRZZZZUNK
SPEK, PAUL	30	M	LABR		GRZZZZCH
MARIANNE	20	F	W		GRZZZZCH
LOUISE	60	F	UNKNOWN		GRZZZZCH
MARIA	.11	F	INFANT		GRZZZZCH
STAWICKI, ANTON	26	M	DPR		GRAEABUNK
LONGOWSKI, JACOB	33	M	STDNT		GRZZZZCH
UFERMANN, HEINR.	30	M	LABR		GRZZZZUNK
JOSEFINE	24	F	W		GRZZZZUNK
KATHARINE	2	F	CHILD		GRZZZZUNK
GESINE	.11	F	INFANT		GRZZZZUNK
ROSZAK, JOSEF	29	M	FARMER		GRAHLDCH
AGNES	22	F	W		GRAHLDCH
FRANZISKA	2	F	CHILD		GRAHLDCH
VICTORIA	.11	F	INFANT		GRAHLDCH
WALKOWIAK, MICHAEL	46	M	LABR		GRAHLDCH
FRANZISKA	41	F	W		GRAHLDCH
CONSTANTIA	19	F	UNKNOWN		GRAHLDCH
JOSEF	11	M	UNKNOWN		GRAHLDCH
MARIA	9	F	CHILD		GRAHLDCH
ANNA	6	F	CHILD		GRAHLDCH
SALOMONA	4	F	CHILD		GRAHLDCH
ROSZAK, AGNISKA	22	F	UNKNOWN		GRAHLDCH
RIERK, HERMANN	22	M	MNR		GRAHLDAUG
KSIAZKIEWICS, MICHAEL	32	M	MNR		GRADLDUNK
JOSEFA	23	F	W		GRADLDUNK
VALENTIN	6	M	CHILD		GRADLDUNK
STANISLAWA	4	F	CHILD		GRADLDUNK
MARIANNE	2	F	CHILD		GRADLDUNK
ROSALIE	.11	F	INFANT		GRADLDUNK
SOCZEPANIAK, MARIA	32	F	UNKNOWN		GRAEXWUNK
SOLAREYK, TONASZ	57	M	PDLR		GRAAIFTOL
ANTONIA	55	F	W		GRAAIFTOL
KLEIN, JULIA	52	F	W		GRZZZZCH
ALBERTINA	16	F	UNKNOWN		GRZZZZCH
JOHANNE	55	F	W		GRZZZZCH
JOHANN	9	M	CHILD		GRZZZZCH
AUGUST	7	M	CHILD		GRZZZZCH
WESTERMANN, MARIE	13	F	UNKNOWN		GRAEVVELG
UPHOFF, HERMANN	52	M	MNR		GRZZZZSP
MOELLER, MAGDALENE	22	F	UNKNOWN		GRZZZZPIT
ZOECKLEIN, JOHANN	17	M	PNTR		GRZZZZPIT
MARGA	15	F	UNKNOWN		GRZZZZPIT
ALBERT, MARIA	14	F	UNKNOWN		GRZZZZBAL
WESTERMANN, CONRAD	16	M	CPTR		GRAAEQELG
KOSFELD, HEINRICH	25	M	CPTR		GRZZZZELG
SCHWERMANN, KATHAR.	65	F	UNKNOWN		GRZZZZBAL
BEILMANN, LINA	22	F	UNKNOWN		GRZZZZCIN
BOCKOCKI, PETER	33	M	MNR		GRADVBCH
JOHANNA	27	F	W		GRADVBCH
FRANZISKA	.11	F	INFANT		GRADVBCH
DANK, WILHELM	29	M	TLR		GRADYACH
BENKERT, GEORG	43	M	BTDR		GRADYAUNK
DANKHAENDER, JOSEF	21	M	BTDR		GRADYASPR
MARIA	15	M	UNKNOWN		GRADYASPR
ZIEGLER, MARIA	17	F	UNKNOWN		GRADYABAL
KOENZPEICHLER, FRANZ	25	M	FARMER		GRZZZZTFF
MARIA	24	F	W		GRZZZZTFF
ORLOWICZ	.09	M	INFANT		GRZZZZTFF
TESSNER, GUSTAV	27	M	LABR		GRADYAUNK
SCHMIDT, AUGUST	37	M	LABR		GRADYACH
HEIDELMANN, CARL	45	M	LABR		GRADYACH
KORNMUETTER, BERNH.	24	M	LABR		GRADYAPIT
THERESE	19	F	UNKNOWN		GRADYAPIT
GEORG, SEIFRIED	17	M	LABR		GRAEZVPIT
DENZLER, JOSEF	24	M	LABR		GRAEZVPIT
ROTH, MARGAR.	22	F	UNKNOWN		GRAEZVPIT
WEBER, MICHAEL	27	M	LABR		GRZZZZBAL
FRANK, HEINRICH	22	M	LABR		GRAARZCLE
ANNA	20	F	UNKNOWN		GRAARZCLE

PASSENGER	AGE	SEX	OCCUPATION	PRVVL	DES
AICHNER, JOSEF	36	M	LABR		GRAARRBAL
PIRCYNSKI, IGNAZ	36	M	LABR		GRAARRCH
ENAZI	30	M	W		GRAARRCH
MARIA	4	F	CHILD		GRAARRCH
CATHARINA	2	F	CHILD		GRAARRCH
VICTORIA	.06	F	INFANT		GRAARRCH
MAHLKE, FRIEDRICH	51	M	LABR		GRAARRMIL
WILHEMINE	44	F	W		GRAARRMIL
EMILIE	18	F	UNKNOWN		GRAARRMIL
IDA	15	F	UNKNOWN		GRAARRMIL
MATHILDE	.11	F	INFANT		GRAARRMIL
KNORR, WILHELM	35	M	LABR		GRAHLDUNK
AUGUSTE	19	F	W		GRAHLDUNK
OTTILIE	.11	F	INFANT		GRAHLDUNK
ALBRECHT, AUGUST	26	M	LABR		GRADYGUNK
LOUISE	24	F	W		GRADYGUNK
SASS, KARL	29	M	UNKNOWN		GRACHAUNK
POPP, WILHELM	55	M	FARMER		GRADVBMIL
ALBERT	30	M	FARMER		GRADVBMIL
EMILIE	27	F	W		GRADVBMIL
BERTHA	21	F	UNKNOWN		GRADVBMIL
RICHARD	9	M	CHILD		GRADVBMIL
SCHMIDT, WILHELM	16	M	CPR		GRZZZZUNK
SUEDTZKE, ERNST	63	M	FARMER		GRABCYMIL
DOROTHEA	57	F	W		GRABCYMIL
ICILIE	18	F	UNKNOWN		GRABCYMIL
FRANZ	15	M	UNKNOWN		GRABCYMIL
HILGENDORFF, HERM.	32	M	CPTR		GRADYAUNK
EMILIE	32	F	W		GRADYAUNK
BERTHA	4	F	CHILD		GRADYAUNK
ANNA	.11	F	INFANT		GRADYAUNK
HUBRICH, FRANZ	27	M	LABR		GRADHEUNK
WILHELMINE	24	F	W		GRAAZSUNK
WENDT, CARL	71	M	PVTM		GRAAZSUNK
LOUISE	51	F	W		GRAAZSUNK
WEGNER, IDA	23	F	UNKNOWN		GRAAZSUNK
WENDT, WILHELMINE	17	F	UNKNOWN		GRAAZSUNK
ALBERTINE	16	F	UNKNOWN		GRAAZSUNK
OTTO	11	M	UNKNOWN		GRAAZSUNK
ALWIN	4	M	CHILD		GRAAZSUNK
MAX	4	M	CHILD		GRAAZSUNK
LAURA	3	F	CHILD		GRAAZSUNK
WEGNER, FRANZ	.11	M	INFANT		GRAAZSUNK
ROSANKA, WILHELM	31	M	LABR		GRAAZSUNK
MOELLERKE, CARL	27	M	DRVR		GRAAZSUNK
MATHILDE	24	F	W		GRAAZSUNK
HEINRICH	13	M	CH		GRAAZSUNK
GEHRHOLZ, FRIEDRICH	24	M	LABR		GRADYAUNK
EMMA	21	F	W		GRADYAUNK
OTTO	.11	M	INFANT		GRADYAUNK
FREITAG, JULIUS	26	M	LABR		GRADYAUNK
EMILIE	28	F	W		GRADYAUNK
ANNA	8	F	CHILD		GRADYAUNK
FRANZ	6	M	CHILD		GRADYAUNK
BERTHA	.09	F	INFANT		GRADYAUNK
BARG, FRIEDRICH	61	M	FARMER		GRAETHUNK
HENRIETTE	62	F	W		GRAETHUNK
WINKELMANN, CARL	68	M	FARMER		GRAETHMIL
RUEGE, FRANZ	21	M	LABR		GRAETHMIL
BERNDT, AUGUSTE	30	F	UNKNOWN		GRAAYGCH
HILDEBRANDT, CARL	28	M	BKR		GRAAYGCH
TRAPP, AUGUSTE	29	F	UNKNOWN		GRAAYGLOS
MUELLWER, GUSTAV	27	M	JNR		GRZZZZBAL
BERTHA	27	F	W		GRZZZZBAL
ALBERECHT	2	M	CHILD		GRZZZZBAL
EMMA	.11	F	INFANT		GRZZZZBAL
SCHULZ, ALBERTINE	7	F	CHILD		GRADUXBAL
BUCK, CARL	60	M	FARMER		GRZZZZBAL
CAROLINE	60	F	W		GRZZZZBAL
FRIEDRIKE	20	F	UNKNOWN		GRZZZZBAL
APPELT, ERNESTINE	29	F	UNKNOWN		GRADGOBAL
VENTZKI, GUSTAV	25	M	MUSN		GRZZZZBAL
WETTER, JOHANN	27	M	MUSN		GRZZZZBAL
VENTZKI, MARTHA	22	F	UNKNOWN		GRZZZZBAL
BERTHA	11	F	UNKNOWN		GRZZZZBAL
KLOPFER, JOH.GOTTL.	17	M	TLR		GRZZZZBAL
REDEMSKI, ALBERT	32	M	BKLYR		GRZZZZBAL
WERNER, FRITZ	14	M	LABR		GRAARRBAL
KIPPER, WILHELM	30	M	LABR		GRADLDBAL
GRUBER, ANNA	32	F	UNKNOWN		GRADLDBAL
LUKOWSKI, JOSEF	30	M	LABR		GRADLDBAL
JULIANE	29	F	W		GRADLDBAL
ANDREAS	4	M	CHILD		GRADLDBAL
MARTIN	4	M	CHILD		GRADLDBAL
VALENTIN	.11	M	INFANT		GRADLDBAL
WALKOWIAK, JOSEF	30	M	LABR		GRAETNBAL
STODOLNA, ROSALIA	25	F	UNKNOWN		GRAETNBAL
CATHARINA	.11	F	INFANT		GRAETNBAL
KRACZKOWSKI, JACOB	24	M	LABR		GRZZZZBAL
DIMMIENSKI, JOHANN	33	M	LABR		GRZZZZBAL
BAHR, CHARLOTTE	63	F	W		GRADDQBAL
MIELLERKE, ALBERT	36	M	TIR		GRACBRBAL
STENZEL, EMIL	29	M	SMH		GRAEXWBAL
SCHENDEL, GUSTAV	39	M	SMH		GRAHXIBAL
WILHELM	34	M	SMH		GRAJWOBAL
EMMA	11	F	UNKNOWN		GRAAKHBAL
MARIE	5	F	CHILD		GRAAKHBAL
WILHELM	4	M	CHILD		GRAAKHBAL
CARL	3	M	CHILD		GRAAKHBAL
MARTHA	.11	F	INFANT		GRAAKHBAL
BRAUN, EDUARD	22	M	LABR		GRADLDBAL
KRANIG, CARL	28	M	SMH		GRADLDBAL
EVA	3	F	CHILD		GRADLDBAL
FEHRMANN, CONRAD	19	M	BBR		GRAEXWBAL
HOFFMANN, JOHANN	15	M	BBR		GRZZZZBAL
BABETTE	19	F	NRS		GRZZZZBAL
KUANIG, LOUIS	29	M	TIR		GRADLDBAL
MASEK, MICHAEL	40	M	MNR		GRAEWMBAL
MICHEL	10	M	CH		GRAEWMBAL
SOKOLOWSKY, WALENTY	28	M	MNR		GRAEABCH
LUBECKI, JOHANN	22	M	MNR		GRAEABCH
FEZAK, WALENTY	53	M	MNR		GRAEABCH
AUGUST	18	M	MNR		GRAEABCH
ANNIKA	20	F	UNKNOWN		GRAEABCH
MAGALIN	11	M	CH		GRAEABCH
FARZYNSKI, ANDR.	37	M	MNR		GRZZZZBAL
MARIE	30	F	W		GRZZZZBAL
JOHANN	6	M	CHILD		GRZZZZBAL
JOSEF	3	M	CHILD		GRZZZZBAL
JOHANN	2	M	CHILD		GRZZZZBAL
FRANZISKA	.11	F	INFANT		GRZZZZBAL
KOWALSKA, JULIANE	23	F	UNKNOWN		GRZZZZUNK
---ACWOSKA, MATHIAS	32	M	MNR		GRZZZZMIL
STODOLNY, STANISL.	25	M	MNR		GRZZZZBAL
KACZMAREK, JOSEF	23	M	LABR		GRZZZZCH
FRANZISKA	23	F	W		GRZZZZCH
JOSEF	.11	F	INFANT		GRZZZZCH
MICHAEL	26	M	LABR		GRZZZZCH
WOZESINSKI, JOSEF	32	M	LABR		GRZZZZTOL
JULIANE	21	F	W		GRZZZZTOL
FRANZ	.11	M	INFANT		GRZZZZTOL
FASKULSKI, JACOB	24	M	LABR		GRZZZZMIL
LEWANDOWSKI, JOSEF	25	M	LABR		GRZZZZUNK
JOSEFA	20	F	W		GRZZZZUNK
LISS, FRANZ	67	M	FARMER		GRZZZZUNK
CATHARINA	60	F	W		GRZZZZUNK
STRAUSHIN, FRANZ	25	M	FARMER		GRZZZZUNK
MILOSZYK, MATHIAS	28	M	FARMER		GRZZZZUNK
ROSENBAUM, FRANZISKA	17	F	UNKNOWN		GRZZZZUNK
POHL, JULIANE	20	F	UNKNOWN		GRZZZZUNK
HENRIETTE	17	F	UNKNOWN		GRZZZZUNK
GUENTHER, ANNA	25	F	UNKNOWN		GRZZZZUNK
SARNOWSKY, JOHANN	28	M	LABR		GRZZZZUNK
ADRIENNE	38	F	W		GRZZZZUNK
CARL	8	M	CHILD		GRZZZZUNK
FRANZ	6	M	CHILD		GRZZZZUNK
KARTHA	3	F	CHILD		GRZZZZUNK
ANGELA	3	F	CHILD		GRZZZZUNK
ANNA	5	F	CHILD		GRZZZZUNK
PAULINE	.11	F	INFANT		GRZZZZUNK

PASSENGER	AGE	SEX	OCCUPATION	PRVL	DES
WITKOWSKI, MICHAEL	25	M	SMH		GRZZZZALP
LEWANDOWSKI, MARIANNE	26	F	UNKNOWN		GRZZZZPHI
ANNA	2	F	CHILD		GRZZZZPHI
ADAM	.11	M	INFANT		GRZZZZPHI
KACZNAREK, WALENTY	26	M	MNR		GRADYACH
MARIANNE	25	F	W		GRADYACH
ANNA	.10	F	INFANT		GRADYACH
OBERKIRSCH, WILHELM	31	M	BTMKR		GRADYACH
AUGUSTE	38	F	W		GRADYACH
EMMA	8	F	CHILD		GRADYACH
LUCKER, ANNA	57	F	W		GRACUXCH
WENSMANN, BERNHARD	17	M	STWD		GRZZZZCH
ETZEL, KARL	26	M	STWD		GRACBRCLE
STEPHANIK, JOSEF	26	M	LABR		GRZZZZPHI
BUDDE, FRITZ	26	M	LABR		GRZZZZCH
CHRISTIANE	26	F	W		GRZZZZCH
BARHORST, JOHANNA	20	F	UNKNOWN		GRZZZZUNK
BERNHARD	16	M	LABR		GRZZZZUNK
MAZUREK, WOJCECH	58	M	LABR		GRZZZZCH
PAULINE	40	F	W		GRZZZZCH
LADISLAUS	8	M	CHILD		GRZZZZCH
MARIE	5	F	CHILD		GRZZZZCH
KIERCZENSKA, STANISLAW	33	M	LABR		GRACUXUNK
ANNA	60	F	W		GRACUXUNK
HENKENBERNS, BERNHARD	67	M	FARMER		GRAEXUCIN
ELISABETH	17	F	UNKNOWN		GRAEXUCIN
CZUPINSKI, JOSEF	38	M	LABR		GRAHLDCH
KATH.	31	F	W		GRAHLDCH
STANISLAUS	6	M	CHILD		GRAHLDCH
JOHANN	3	M	CHILD		GRAHLDCH
FRANZ	.11	M	INFANT		GRAHLDCH
LALUTERBACH, MARIE	56	F	LABR		GRADVBTOP
MARIE	21	F	W		GRADVBTOP
KURATKOWSKI, ANTON	25	M	LABR		GRAAXLTOP
HEDWIG	21	F	W		GRAAXLTOP
WANDA	.03	F	INFANT		GRAAXLTOP
BALHORN, CARL	20	M	TLR		GRAAXLBAL
FOK, THOMAS	18	M	TLR		GRAAXLCH
SIEVERT, CARL	44	M	FARMER		GRAAXLCH
WILHELMINE	45	F	W		GRAAXLCH
BARTHA	19	F	UNKNOWN		GRAAXLCH
WILHELM	11	M	CH		GRAAXLCH
GUSTAV	10	M	CH		GRAAXLCH
WILHELMINE	8	F	CHILD		GRAAXLCH
ALWINE	9	F	CHILD		GRAAXLCH
CARL	4	M	CHILD		GRAAXLCH
NEUMANN, MARIE	19	F	UNKNOWN		GRZZZZCLE
PAUL	.11	M	INFANT		GRZZZZCLE
ARNDT, AUGUST	33	M	LABR		GRZZZZBAL
AUGUSTE	24	F	W		GRZZZZBAL
FRIEDA	4	F	CHILD		GRZZZZBAL
LISBETH	2	F	CHILD		GRZZZZBAL
IDA	.10	F	INFANT		GRZZZZBAL
MOCHR, JOHANNE	26	F	W		GRAAWZBAL
LISBETH	.11	F	INFANT		GRAAWZBAL
HOLMANN, GESINA	54	F	W		GRAHJKUNK
JOHANN	20	M	LABR		GRAHJKUNK
PACEK, LUKAR	45	M	PNTR		GRZZZZCLE
MIKODEON, MICHAEL	27	M	PNTR		GRZZZZUNK
JOHANNE	25	F	W		GRZZZZUNK
JOHANN	.10	M	INFANT		GRZZZZUNK
FLEISCHER, ANNA	19	F	UNKNOWN		GRAFDWUNK
FESCHKE, JOHANN	17	M	PNTR		GRAFDWUNK
STUEWER, KAROLINE	19	F	UNKNOWN		GRAFDWUNK
WENDA, JOSEFINE	16	F	UNKNOWN		GRAFDWCLE
GEDANITZ, KATHARINE	23	F	UNKNOWN		GRAEABDET
JOSEF	21	M	BCHR		GRAEABDET
MARTHA	16	F	UNKNOWN		GRAEABDET
PLUZINSKY, ANDREAS	43	M	LABR		GRAHLDCH
ANNA	42	F	W		GRAHLDCH
FRANZ	17	M	LABR		GRAHLDCH
PROSZEWICH, AUGUST	30	M	LABR		GRADXZPIT
KASPZAK, JOSEF	25	M	LABR		GRADXZMN
SACHOWICZ, WLADISLAW	25	M	LABR		GRADXZDET
ANNA	24	F	W		GRADXZDET

PASSENGER	AGE	SEX	OCCUPATION	PRVL	DES
LEONORE	.10	F	INFANT		GRADXZDET
PACHOLSKI, JOSEF	32	M	FARMER		GRACBRCH
FRANZ	7	M	CHILD		GRACBRCH
JOSEF	3	M	CHILD		GRACBRCH
WOICECH	2	M	CHILD		GRACBRCH
STANISLAUS	.09	M	INFANT		GRACBRCH
ANTONIE	32	F	W		GRACBRCH
PLACINSKA, PELAZIA	9	F	CHILD		GRAAXXCH
JOSEFA	6	F	CHILD		GRAAXXCH
STANISLAWA	.08	F	INFANT		GRAAXXCH
ROZANSKA, MICHALINA	35	F	UNKNOWN		GRZZZZCH
EDWIN	11	M	UNKNOWN		GRZZZZCH
FRANZ	6	M	CHILD		GRZZZZCH
LUDWIG	9	M	CHILD		GRZZZZCH
STANISLAUS	3	M	CHILD		GRZZZZCH
WITALKA, CONSTANCIE	19	F	UNKNOWN		GRZZZZLAS
FRANZISKA	27	F	UNKNOWN		GRZZZZLAS
VALENTINA	.09	F	INFANT		GRZZZZLAS
SCHIMPF, JOHANN	29	M	BKR		GRZZZZALX
GROSSMAN, JOHANNA	57	M	LABR		GRAAKHIN
WILHELM	26	M	LABR		GRAAKHIN
WILHELMINE	24	F	W		GRAAKHIN
AUGUST	18	M	LABR		GRAAKHIN
BUENGER, HELENE	52	F	UNKNOWN		GRZZZZMIL
HELENA	16	M	LABR		GRZZZZMIL
HERMANN	15	M	LABR		GRZZZZMIL
OTTO	10	M	CH		GRZZZZMIL
ANNA	5	F	CHILD		GRZZZZMIL
AUGUSTA	29	F	UNKNOWN		GRZZZZMIL
WILHELM	28	M	LABR		GRZZZZMIL
FRANZ	3	M	CHILD		GRZZZZMIL
WANORZYNSKI, EMIL	23	M	LABR		GRAARZMIL
CIBULZKA, FRANZISKA	22	F	UNKNOWN		GRAARZCH
GARDT, WILHELM	27	M	LABR		GRADCRWAE
CAROLINE	29	F	W		GRADCRWAE
ELISABETH	3	F	CHILD		GRADCRWAE
FRANZ	.11	M	INFANT		GRADCRWAE
PISKE, AUGUST	39	M	FARMER		GRACQAUNK
CAROLINE	37	F	W		GRACQAUNK
WILHELM	60	M	FARMER		GRACQAUNK
FRANZ	11	M	CH		GRACQAUNK
ELBERT	5	M	CHILD		GRACQAUNK
HERMANN	4	M	CHILD		GRACQAUNK
EMIL	3	M	CHILD		GRACQAUNK
PAUL	.10	M	INFANT		GRACQAUNK
SCHULTZ, WILH.FERD.	27	M	LABR		GRACQAUNK
FANIZEWSKA, MINNA	34	F	W		GRACQABAL
HELENE	9	F	CHILD		GRACQABAL
FRANZ	6	M	CHILD		GRACQABAL
ROSENTRETER, JOHANN	66	M	FARMER		GRACQAUNK
WILHELMINE	60	F	W		GRACQAUNK
ALWINE	24	F	UNKNOWN		GRACQAUNK
PELKOWSKI, JOSEF	23	M	LABR		GRACQAUNK
PALZER, LOUISE	18	F	UNKNOWN		GRACQACH
WEBER, WOLFGANG	20	M	BRZ		GRZZZZOXF
GROSS, CARL	16	M	SMH		GRZZZZKAS
DANER, PETER	24	M	PNTR		GRZZZZUNK
JACEK, SYMEN	14	M	PDLR		GRAEXWBAL
SKRYPINSKI, JOHANN	58	M	MCHT		GRZZZZUNK
FLORENTINA	45	F	W		GRZZZZUNK
CASPAR	23	M	LABR		GRZZZZUNK
CATHARINA	20	F	UNKNOWN		GRZZZZUNK
MOWEK, GOTTGRIED	26	M	LABR		GRAEZVBAL
WURPINSKI, ANNA	28	F	UNKNOWN		GRAEZVDET
KLEMENT, MARIE	28	F	W		GRZZZZPIT
CARLOS	2	M	CHILD		GRZZZZPIT
DEKLOFF, FRIEDRICH	23	M	FARMER		GRABOQBAL
ANNA	22	F	W		GRABOQBAL
GUSTAV	.11	M	INFANT		GRABOQBAL
FRIEDRICH	.11	M	INFANT		GRABOQBAL
OTTRUMBACHER, GOTTLIEB	60	M	PVTR		GRADZCBAL
STEENHARDT, KLAAS	51	M	FARMER		GRADIJIA
OLTY	55	M	FARMER		GRADIJIA
KLAAS	15	M	UNKNOWN		GRADIJIA
ZIEGERT, WILHELM	30	M	LABR		GRAEABSTJ

PASSENGER	AGE	SEX	OCCUPATION	PRVL	DES
HENRIETTE	28	F	UNKNOWN		GRAEABSTJ
KAMENTZKI, ADELINE	11	F	CH		GRAEABSTJ
JANICKE, CARL	17	M	STDNT		GRAEABUNK
BERGMANN, WILHELM	48	M	LABR		GRZZZZUNK
SOPHIE	55	F	W		GRZZZZUNK
ANNA	16	F	UNKNOWN		GRZZZZUNK
KLENKERT, ANNE	19	F	UNKNOWN		GRZZZZUNK
PASNER, MARIA	35	F	UNKNOWN		GRZZZZUNK
GIESEKING, AUG.	41	M	MNR		GRADHEUNK
SOPHIE	41	F	W		GRADHEUNK
HEINRICH	15	M	CH		GRADHEUNK
GEORG	13	M	CH		GRADHEUNK
AUGUST	11	M	CH		GRADHEUNK
CHARLOTTE	10	F	CH		GRADHEUNK
ANEDA	8	F	CHILD		GRADHEUNK
WILHELM	7	M	CHILD		GRADHEUNK
HENRIETTE	.09	F	INFANT		GRADHEUNK
MARIE	.09	F	INFANT		GRADHEUNK
DZINK, LEOCADIA	22	F	UNKNOWN		GRADXZBAL
VIGANZKY, GOTTLIEB	55	M	FARMER		GRZZZZSTJ
CAROLINE	52	F	W		GRZZZZSTJ
ALWINE	21	F	UNKNOWN		GRZZZZSTJ
AUGUSTE	15	F	UNKNOWN		GRZZZZSTJ
WATHNER, JOHANNA	22	F	NRS		GRADYMUNK
HERBSLEW, ANNA	29	M	LABR		GRZZZZPHI
ERNSTINE	28	F	W		GRZZZZPHI
JOHANNA	.09	F	INFANT		GRZZZZPHI
RAABE, ALBERT	49	M	TIR		GRZZZZUNK
MARIA	48	F	W		GRZZZZUNK
CARL	11	M	CH		GRZZZZUNK
HEDWIG	8	F	CHILD		GRZZZZUNK
BACK, FRANZ	26	M	JNR		GRZZZZMIL
FRIEDRICH	18	M	BKR		GRZZZZMIL
EMMA	22	F	UNKNOWN		GRZZZZMIL
BUCHOLSKY, ANNA	23	F	UNKNOWN		GRAAGLCIN
CZESCHELSKA, AUGUSTA	20	F	UNKNOWN		GRZZZZCLE
MAX	3	M	CHILD		GRZZZZCLE
SCHATZSCHNEIDER, GOTTLI	30	M	DPR		GRZZZZUNK
SCHATZSCHNEIDER, THERES	32	F	W		GRZZZZUNK
SCHATZSCHNEIDER, ALBERT	.10	M	INFANT		GRZZZZUNK
GREEN, CARL	52	M	LABR		GRZZZZUNK
HENRIETTE	46	F	W		GRZZZZUNK
ALBERT	23	M	LABR		GRZZZZUNK
HERMANN	18	M	TLR		GRZZZZUNK
ANNA	13	F	NRS		GRZZZZUNK
BERTHA	8	F	CHILD		GRZZZZUNK
FRIEDERIKE	56	F	W		GRZZZZUNK
JOOS, CAROLINA	19	F	UNKNOWN		GRACBRAOA
EFFEC, JACOB	16	M	PNTR		GRAAKHZAN
HEBELE, MARCIO	11	M	CH		GRZZZZZAN
EPPLE, TEROWE	18	M	UNKNOWN		GRZZZZWAT
GREINER, PAULINE	18	F	NRS		GRZZZZUNK
SCHAEFER, MARIA	18	F	NRS		GRAEACUNK
SCHOCH, GOTTFRIED	15	M	BBR		GRAEZVUNK
DIEHLE, MARIE	18	F	UNKNOWN		GRZZZZSTL
NICKELSKIE, JOSEF	37	M	LABR		GRADZCCH
JULIANE	58	F	W		GRADZCCH
LOUISE	4	F	CHILD		GRADZCCH
AUGUST	.10	M	INFANT		GRADZCCH
PUTTKAMER, ROSALIE	25	F	UNKNOWN		GRAAGLCH
VERONICA	24	F	W		GRAAGLCH
ANNA	2	F	CHILD		GRAAGLCH
ANTON	.09	M	INFANT		GRAAGLCH
LESCHINSKI, ANDREAS	47	M	FARMER		GRACHXSP
WILHELMINE	42	F	W		GRACHXSP
ANNA	20	F	UNKNOWN		GRACHXSP
MARIE	18	F	UNKNOWN		GRACHXSP
MATHILDE	16	F	UNKNOWN		GRACHXSP
JULIUS	12	M	UNKNOWN		GRACHXSP
BERNHARD	9	M	CHILD		GRACHXSP
PAULINE	.11	F	INFANT		GRACHXSP
BENKIE, ANNA	18	F	UNKNOWN		GRZZZZCH
NACZKIE, JULIUS	23	M	PNTR		GRZZZZCH
DENZ, PAWELL	32	M	LABR		GRZZZZCH
BANDERSEN, AUGUSTE	22	F	UNKNOWN		GRZZZZCH
BORSCHKIE, JOSEF	42	M	LABR		GRZZZZCH
GRUBBA, MARTIN	50	M	LABR		GRZZZZCH
TRAVINSKI, ANTONIE	34	F	UNKNOWN		GRZZZZCH
KLUTZ, STANISLAUS	25	M	FARMER		GRAEABSOU
CATHARINA	19	F	W		GRAEABSOU
PELAGIA	.11	F	INFANT		GRAEABSOU
MUSHINSKI, ADONIS	25	M	CPTR		GRZZZZDET
KIEHLE, HEINRICH	17	M	BBR		GRZZZZSTL
FRIEDRICH, AMALIA	11	F	CH		GRZZZZBAL
TRZESIELSKI, JOSEFA	11	F	UNKNOWN		GRAAKOUNK
TESKA, AGNES	79	F	W		GRAHLDUNK
POPPELBAUM, THOMAS	38	M	MNR		GRADVHBAL
BOEKENS, GEORG	16	M	BTDR		GRABIONY
FEHRMANN, CONRAD	17	M	BTDR		GRZZZZBAL
WILKE, AUGUST	37	M	LABR		GRAEABBAL
JOSEFINE	32	F	W		GRAEABBAL
MARTHA	7	F	CHILD		GRAEABBAL
FRANCISKA	.10	F	INFANT		GRAEABBAL
KOZAL, ANDREAS	25	M	LABR		GRZZZZNY
FRISKE, FRANZISKA	11	F	CH		GRADUXNY
ALBERS, ANNA	19	F	UNKNOWN		GRZZZZUNK
STRUNK, EMMA	21	F	UNKNOWN		GRADDWUNK
FISCHER, ELISE	21	F	UNKNOWN		GRAAGLCH
PESKA, JOSEF	13	M	CH		GRZZZZLAS
MALA	7	F	CHILD		GRZZZZLAS
AGNES	.09	M	INFANT		GRZZZZLAS
NOLK, GUSTAV	33	M	SMH		GRZZZZUNK
LOUISE	26	F	W		GRZZZZUNK
EMMA	7	F	CHILD		GRZZZZUNK
EMILIE	3	F	CHILD		GRZZZZUNK
AUGUST	.09	M	INFANT		GRZZZZUNK
URBANSKI, MICHAEL	33	M	LABR		GRZZZZUNK
BARBARA	23	F	W		GRZZZZUNK
STANISLAW	11	M	CH		GRZZZZUNK
PELAGIA	.11	F	INFANT		GRZZZZUNK
GONDSCHAAL, ANTJE	20	M	TIR		GRZZZZUNK
PIOTROASKI, ADAM	22	M	LABR		GRAHLDBAL
ARANOWSKI, ANTON	27	M	LABR		GRAHLDBAL
KEMPER, BERNARD	10	M	CH		GRZZZZBAL
AGNES	6	F	CHILD		GRZZZZBAL
HINRICH	4	M	CHILD		GRZZZZBAL
KOSLOWSKI, JOHANNES	45	M	PNTR		GRADYAUNK
ANASTASIA	34	F	W		GRADYAUNK
PELAGIA	8	F	CHILD		GRADYAUNK
FRANZ	6	M	CHILD		GRADYAUNK
NOWAKOWSKI, CARL	39	M	FARMER		GRAEAFUNK
KLINDEWITSCH, MARTHA	18	F	UNKNOWN		GRAEAFCIN
HUMMEL, MARGARETHA	18	F	UNKNOWN		GRAEAFIN
PLOTZ, JOHANN	18	M	LABR		GRADXZBAL
ZAGECK, JOSEPH	18	M	BBR		GRZZZZMIN
RENECKER, HEINRICH	72	M	FARMER		GRAARZUNK
GEORG	29	M	FARMER		GRAARZUNK
JOHANN	27	M	FARMER		GRAARZUNK
CATH.	30	F	W		GRAARZUNK
HINRICH	9	M	CHILD		GRAARZUNK
META	5	F	CHILD		GRAARZUNK
JOHANN	3	M	CHILD		GRAARZUNK
MARTIN	2	M	CHILD		GRAARZUNK
CATHARINA	.06	F	INFANT		GRAARZUNK
ROESTER, JOHANN	15	M	CPTR		GRZZZZUSA
WAETJEN, JOHANN	16	M	TLR		GRZZZZUSA
RATHENAU, JOSEPH	17	M	BBR		GRAFDWBUF
KLEIN, AUG.	24	M	CPR		GRAAAHBUF
CAROLINE	28	F	UNKNOWN		GRAAAHBUF
WESSELLOWSKY, FRANZ	24	M	TLR		GRAAAHBAL
BELMER, META	22	F	UNKNOWN		GRAFTSHOM
EHLERT, FRIEDRICH	28	M	LABR		GRZZZZCLE
HIRSCH, HERM.	13	M	LABR		GRABCYCH
IMHOFF, SOPHIE	19	F	UNKNOWN		GRZZZZCH
WILCOSCH, VALENTIN	28	M	LABR		GRABDMNY
STANISLAUS	2	M	CHILD		GRABDMNY
STENZEL, RIENHARD	18	M	LABR		GRZZZZCLE
STORNKOWSKI, MICHAEL	23	M	LABR		GRACXVBAL
JULIANE	26	F	W		GRACXVBAL
MARIANNE	.11	F	INFANT		GRACXVBAL

PASSENGER	AGE	SEX	OCCUPATION	PRVL	DES
REIMANN, FRANZ	23	M	LABR		GRZZZZUNK
FIETZKE, MARIE	45	F	W		GRAFWZBAL
LOUIS	20	M	BKR		GRAFWZBAL
DAMMS, IGNATZ	55	M	LABR		GRAFQBUNK
ANNA	52	F	W		GRAFQBUNK
JULUIS	16	M	LABR		GRAFQBUNK
THEODORE	10	F	CH		GRAFQBUNK
GRAEPER, CARL	62	M	FARMER		GRZZZZPRI
SCHUETTE, WILH.	17	M	LABR		GRADYMPRI
KOENEMANN, SOPHIE	19	F	NRS		GRAETNUNK
CAROLINE	13	F	UNKNOWN		GRAETNUNK
KRUEGER, WILHELM	57	M	FARMER		GRAEACUNK
CATHARINA	30	F	W		GRAEACUNK
LINA	10	F	CH		GRAEACUNK
RECKWEG, AUGUST	25	M	BKR		GRADDQUSA
HAESEMEIER, ERNST	17	M	BBR		GRAJAXSTL
GLAESER, ALBERT	10	M	CH		GRAEZVDET
ANNA	11	F	CH		GRAEZVDET
WROBLEWITZ, JOSEF	28	M	PNTR		GRADDWDET
BANNASCH, WILHELM	26	M	PRNTR		GRADUXDET
SIKORSKI, ROBERT	31	M	LABR		GRAEXWPLA
PINT, JOHANN	66	M	FARMER		GRZZZZUNK
MARIE	54	F	W		GRZZZZUNK
SEETZEN, MARIE	17	F	UNKNOWN		GRZZZZCH
SCHUH, JOHANN	26	M	BTMK		GRZZZZBAL
BLECK, CARL	32	M	SDLR		GRADDQCH
JOHANN	28	M	TLR		GRADDQCH
AGNES	4	F	CHILD		GRADDQCH
WILLY	2	M	CHILD		GRADDQCH
CIESBOIZA, JOHANN	27	M	MNR		GRZZZZBAL
HEDWIGH	22	F	UNKNOWN		GRZZZZBAL
DOBERKOSZKI, JOSEF	23	M	MNR		GRAETHBAL
SCHLEIMER, FREDRIKE	17	F	NRS		GRAJWOUNK
WIENER, MARIA	11	F	UNKNOWN		GRZZZZUNK
HUGO	4	M	CHILD		GRZZZZUNK
BARKOWSKI, MICHAEL	27	M	LABR		GRZZZZBAL
MARIANNE	27	F	W		GRZZZZBAL
FRANZ	2	M	CHILD		GRZZZZBAL
CARL	.10	M	INFANT		GRZZZZBAL
MICIAK, KASIMIR	18	M	MNR		GRZZZZCH
STANISLAWA	17	F	UNKNOWN		GRZZZZCH
WURSCHINSKI, JOSEF	56	M	LABR		GRZZZZDET
CHRISTINE	52	F	W		GRZZZZDET
AUGUSTE	17	F	UNKNOWN		GRZZZZDET
FRIEDRICH	11	M	CH		GRZZZZDET
DANKMEYER, JOHANN	18	M	MCHT		GRZZZZCLE
BEHRENS, HEINR.	16	M	LABR		GRADWQMIL
HOECKER, HEINR.	17	M	JNR		GRZZZZCLE
VIENTKER, ERNST	19	M	LABR		GRAAKHCLE
SCHMIDT, HEINRICH	26	M	LABR		GRAETNCH
MINA	26	F	W		GRAETNCH
CASPAR	.09	M	INFANT		GRAETNCH
BROKMEYER, HEINR.	29	M	LABR		GRAAIFCH
SOPHIE	23	F	W		GRAAIFCH
HEINRICH	2	M	CHILD		GRAAIFCH
WILHELM	.10	M	INFANT		GRAAIFCH
GRUEBMEYER, CONRAD	31	M	LABR		GRADROCH
SOPHIE	32	F	W		GRADROCH
WILHELM	7	M	CHILD		GRADROCH
FRITZ	2	M	CHILD		GRADROCH
KOHLSTADT, FRITZ	30	M	DLR		GRZZZZUNK
KORTEMEYER, AUGUST	27	M	MCHT		GRZZZZMIL
WINZER, FRIEDRICH	34	M	PPTR		GRZZZZCH
RUNDA, JOHANN	26	M	LABR		GRZZZZCH
RAMMER, HEINRICH	16	M	JNR		GRZZZZBAL
MIX, ELONORE	54	F	W		GRZZZZCH
EMILIE	19	F	UNKNOWN		GRZZZZCH
JOHANNE	11	F	CH		GRZZZZCH
ROLZIN, JOHANNE	16	F	UNKNOWN		GRZZZZCH
PONTOW, LUDWIG	37	M	LABR		GRZZZZCH
PUSCH, CARL	32	M	MNR		GRAAZSUNK
THERESE	31	F	W		GRAAZSUNK
ALOISIA	6	F	CHILD		GRAAZSUNK
IGNATZ	4	M	CHILD		GRAAZSUNK
KARL	.10	M	INFANT		GRAAZSUNK

PASSENGER	AGE	SEX	OCCUPATION	PRVL	DES
FERMER, AMALIE	21	F	UNKNOWN		GRZZZZUNK
KNAUER, GEORG	28	M	LABR		GRAETHUNK
FRANZMANN, JACOB	18	M	LABR		GRAEROSP
HECK, MINNA	15	F	UNKNOWN		GRAAZSBAL
KLEINHENN, OTTO	16	M	UNKNOWN		GRAAZSBAL
CHRISTIANSEN, DOROTHE	29	F	UNKNOWN		GRAAZSCIN
CARL	.10	M	INFANT		GRAAZSCIN
DESICKIE, IGNATZ	25	M	CPR		GRAAZSUNK
ECKERT, PAULINE	23	F	UNKNOWN		GRZZZZBUF
BOETTGER, WOLBERT	30	M	CPTR		GRAEZVMIL
SCHROEDER, MICHAEL	40	M	CPR		GRAAEABAL
JASNICA	40	F	W		GRAAEABAL
STUEMKE, AUGUSTE	23	F	UNKNOWN		GRZZZZNY
WILHELM	16	M	UNKNOWN		GRZZZZNY
SCHRAND, GERHARD	23	M	LABR		GRADIJNY
GERDES, HEINRICH	60	M	FARMER		GRADWFSTL
GESINA	50	F	W		GRADWFSTL
HEINRICH	20	M	UNKNOWN		GRADWFSTL
BEHNER, GERHARD	40	M	FARMER		GRZZZZSTL
THEKLA	40	F	W		GRZZZZSTL
BERNHARD	10	M	CH		GRZZZZSTL
EILISABETH	6	F	CHILD		GRZZZZSTL
HEINRICH	4	M	CHILD		GRZZZZSTL
JULIUS	.11	M	INFANT		GRZZZZSTL
HOLTHAUS, EILISABETH	66	F	W		GRADROSTL
PREISS, MARGARETHE	17	F	UNKNOWN		GRADEIPHI
GOESSLING, AUGUST	21	M	LABR		GRAERONY
MOENK, JOHANN	16	M	LABR		GRAAJXCIN
DRUEHE, BERNHD.	24	M	MCHT		GRZZZZCIN
VOLKERDINY, JAS.	24	M	LABR		GRABDMCIN
BREMER, FRIEDR.	36	M	LABR		GRAFBVNY
WITZKI, REINHARD	24	M	BRR		GRAFBVCH
WITTE, DOROTHEA	17	F	UNKNOWN		GRZZZZNPO
ROEHRS, MARIE	17	F	UNKNOWN		GRZZZZNPO
DAEHNERT, FRIEDRICH	27	M	BRR		GRAEZVUNK
MARIA	26	F	W		GRAEZVUNK
CARL	3	M	CHILD		GRAEZVUNK
OTTO	2	M	CHILD		GRAEZVUNK
AUERNHEIMER, CARL	29	M	DRVR		GRAFWZCIN
VALENTA, VOJT	38	M	LABR		GRAAWZBAL
FILIP, JOSEF	25	M	LABR		GRAAWZBAL
DOBIHAL, ANTON	30	M	LABR		GRAAWZBAL
MIKUTA, THOMAS	33	M	LABR		GRAAWZBAL
KORASEK, BARBARA	26	F	UNKNOWN		GRACBRSAG
DUFEK, KAROLINA	16	F	UNKNOWN		GRACBRBAL
MAULE, MATHIAS	28	M	LABR		GRACBRBAL
GORIUK, MARTZIN	29	M	LABR		GRAARZBAL
STANISKO	6	M	CHILD		GRAARZBAL
JAJKO, MARIA	20	F	NRS		GRAEPZBAL
FAWORSKI, WASLAW	16	M	LABR		GRAARRNY
BODENSTEIN, LOUIS	32	M	BDM		GRAARSNY

SHIP: WERRA

FROM: BREMEN AND SOUTHAMPTON
TO: NEW YORK
ARRIVED: 09 MAY 1888

PASSENGER	AGE	SEX	OCCUPATION	PRVL	DES
U, CARL	19	M	MCHT		GRABOQGR
ELISE	53	F	W		GRAEVMGR
SOPHIE	23	F	NN		GRAEVMGR
--LTER, AMALIE	44	F	NN		GRAEVMGR
SCHNEE, PAUL	11	M	CH		GRAEVMGR
ED.	9	M	CHILD		GRAEVMGR
GEBHARDI, LAURA	29	F	W		GRAEBUGR
ELSE	7	F	CHILD		GRAEBUGR
EMMA	5	F	CHILD		GRAEBUGR
CARL	3	M	CHILD		GRAEBUGR
FRIEDA	.10	F	INFANT		GRAEBUGR
KNELLER, LAURA	23	F	W		GRACEDGR

PASSENGER	AGE	SEX	OCCUPATION	PRVL DES
JULIA	.09	F	INFANT	GRACEDGR
LOBENSTEIN, AD.	17	M	TT	BDZZZZGR
WEHSE, CARL	27	M	TT	BDZZZZGR
EMILIE	28	F	W	BDZZZZGR
DORA	3	F	CHILD	BDZZZZGR
KERN, CAROLE.	20	F	NN	BDABOQGR
FAZLER, JOH.	40	M	TT	BDACPEGR
LICHTENFELS, J.	55	M	MCHT	BDABVHGR
HENRIETTE	12	F	CH	BDABVHGR
HOFELER, EMMA	39	F	W	BDZZZZGR
DAVID	11	M	CH	BDZZZZGR
AMOS, FRIEDKE.	19	F	NN	BDAAXYGR
LANGBEIN, MORITZ	42	M	TT	BDAFTFGR
FRANK, LUDW.	60	M	TT	BDAFTFGR
BUCHER, ADOLF	24	M	TT	BDAFTFGR
MILLER, EMIL	26	M	TT	BDAEXWGR
NIEDERGESAESS, ROBERT	42	M	TT	BDAEXWGR
REGENHARDT, F.	35	M	TT	BDAAKHGR
MARIE	31	F	W	BDAAKHGR
FRITZ	9	M	CHILD	BDAAKHGR
ALBERT	5	M	CHILD	BDAAKHGR
FRANZ	3	M	CHILD	BDAAKHGR
FRANK, WILH.	18	M	TT	BDAAKHGR
BAHRS, ANNA	18	F	NN	BDAAHVUSA
SCHNABEL, KARL	17	M	LABR	GRZZZZUSA
CZAIKOWSKI, OTTILIE	23	F	W	GRADNRUSA
MAX	.03	M	INFANT	GRADNRUSA
U, ANTON	25	M	LABR	GRADNRUSA
M---NSKA, MART.	19	M	LABR	GRZZZZUSA
--LLER, MINNA	23	F	NN	GRADYYUSA
U, ELISAB.	34	F	W	GRAAZPUSA
LAN, HEINR.	4	M	CHILD	GRAAZPUSA
STROMER, CARL	61	M	LABR	GRAAGCUSA
MARIE	59	F	W	GRAAGCUSA
WILH.	18	M	FARMER	GRAAGCUSA
REUSS, ANNA	41	F	NN	GRZZZZUSA
STEPPKE, AUG.	27	M	LABR	GRABHUUSA
ELISAB.	29	F	W	GRABHUUSA
ANNA	2	F	CHILD	GRABHUUSA
ROSA	.08	F	INFANT	GRABHUUSA
REIMANN, REGA.	61	F	W	GRABHUUSA
GESSNER, FRIEDR.	49	M	LABR	GRABHUUSA
MARIA	47	F	W	GRABHUUSA
ELISAB.	16	F	NN	GRABHUUSA
EMMA	14	F	NN	GRABHUUSA
ADELT, AUG.	24	M	LABR	GRZZZZUSA
SUSSBACH, ANNA	27	F	NN	GRZZZZUSA
WENZEL, REINHOLD	15	M	NN	GRZZZZUSA
FELLBAUM, EMILIE	16	F	NN	GRZZZZUSA
STEPHAN, WILH.	27	M	LABR	GRAHJSUSA
SKUSU, ED.	46	M	LABR	GRZZZZUSA
WILHE.	37	F	W	GRZZZZUSA
HOFFMANN, IDA	20	F	NN	GRZZZZUSA
KNOPP, WILHE.	14	F	NN	GRZZZZUSA
SCHAEFFER, KILL.	62	M	LABR	BVZZZZUSA
MARGUARDT, HEINR.	26	M	LABR	GRZZZZUSA
MENIKEN, HERM.	13	M	NN	GRAAAHUSA
GRABOWSKI, HENRIETTE	27	F	NN	GRZZZZUSA
TROENDLER, LOUISE	23	F	NN	BDZZZZUSA
CZYZ, ANTONIA	25	F	W	GRZZZZUSA
VICTORIA	2	F	CHILD	GRZZZZUSA
FRANZISKA	.09	F	INFANT	GRZZZZUSA
THIEBE, MICH.	58	M	LABR	GRZZZZUSA
CAROLE.	58	F	W	GRZZZZUSA
THIEBLE, CAROLE.	16	F	NN	BDZZZZUSA
LEMKE, EMIL	22	M	LABR	GRZZZZUSA
OTTILIE	21	F	W	GRZZZZUSA
ROSENTRETTER, EMMA	7	F	CHILD	GRZZZZUSA
WILL, ALOIS	24	M	FARMER	BVZZZZUSA
BOSCH, JOH.	14	M	NN	BVAARRUSA
BAETJER, FRIEDR.	14	M	NN	BVAARRUSA
SCHILDER, ANNASTASIA	11	F	CH	BVAFTUUSA
BUEHLER, ERNST	23	M	LABR	BVABVDUSA
BREUSCH, GUST.	23	M	BRR	BVABVDUSA
WOTTKE, CLARA	25	F	NN	GRZZZZUSA
KOWALSKI, JACOB	18	M	LABR	GRZZZZUSA
MUND, MALWE.	24	F	W	GRAHNMUSA
ALBTE.	2	F	CHILD	GRAHNMUSA
KREBER, BARBA.	6	F	CHILD	GRAHNMUSA
FISCHER, ROBERT	16	M	NN	GRAEGTUSA
KAUTZMANN, ANTON	13	M	NN	GRAEGTUSA
EISENHUTH, JOS.	25	M	LABR	GRAEGTUSA
VOGES, MINNA	21	F	NN	GRZZZZUSA
VONTOENNERMANN, ALFONS	23	M	FARMER	GRAFHPUSA
PAPPERT, AUGE.	22	F	NN	GRZZZZUSA
BAUMANN, OTTILIE	23	F	NN	GRZZZZUSA
THAN, ANTON	28	M	LABR	GRABHUUSA
BARBA.	24	F	W	GRABHUUSA
THAM, MARTHA	2	F	CHILD	GRABHUUSA
OTTO	.02	M	INFANT	GRABHUUSA
VORSTEIN, HEINR.	17	M	LABR	GRAAKHUSA
PERLING, CARL	30	M	LABR	GRAKPTUSA
HEENRIETTE	39	F	W	GRAKPTUSA
GROSSMANN, J.H.	31	M	FARMER	BVZZZZUSA
HANBAUER, ROSA.	23	F	W	BVZZZZUSA
JOH.	.09	M	INFANT	BVZZZZUSA
REIFENBERGER, GEORG	18	M	BRR	BVZZZZUSA
MALZER, ANNA	17	F	NN	BVZZZZUSA
ZERNER, GUST.	25	M	FARMER	BVAFOFUSA
MEYER, JOH.	18	M	FARMER	BVAFDDUSA
LANG, HERM.	35	M	FARMER	GRZZZZUSA
BREIDENBACH, MICH.	40	M	FARMER	BVZZZZUSA
ELISAB.	12	F	CH	BVZZZZUSA
CARL	5	M	CHILD	BVZZZZUSA
JOH.	5	M	CHILD	BVZZZZUSA
FECHER, ANNA	28	F	NN	BVADTEUSA
BORN, PAULUS	21	M	FARMER	BVZZZZUSA
ZELLER, MARIA	47	F	NN	BVAAFCUSA
KWAPISCH, ANTON	36	M	LABR	GRZZZZUSA
CATHA.	30	F	W	GRZZZZUSA
FRANZKA.	5	F	CHILD	GRZZZZUSA
JOH.	.09	M	INFANT	GRZZZZUSA
KUBIAK, ANTONIE	19	F	NN	GRZZZZUSA
RICHTER, ARDI-	17	F	NN	GRZZZZUSA
LEWIN, F.	25	M	LABR	GRZZZZUSA
MALKE	.11	F	INFANT	GRZZZZUSA
IGYNAL, JAN	16	M	NN	GRAJSVUSA
RADLOFF, CHRIST.	32	M	LABR	GRAAUDUSA
GRONNER, ALOIS	26	M	LABR	BVZZZZUSA
BABETTE	24	F	W	BVZZZZUSA
GEBHARD, FRITZ	15	M	NN	BVZZZZUSA
INDISCH, WILHE.	48	F	W	BVAETWUSA
ANNA	5	F	CHILD	BVAETWUSA
GUST.	3	M	CHILD	BVAETWUSA
ARTHUR	2	M	CHILD	BVAETWUSA
ELISE	.11	F	INFANT	BVAETWUSA
ZAGATA, ANNA	17	F	NN	BVAARRUSA
STANISLAUS	13	M	NN	BVAARRUSA
KOMROWSKI, ANT.	33	M	LABR	GRZZZZUSA
TILLMANN, FRIEDR.	39	M	LABR	GRAFVVUSA
HERIETTE	39	F	W	GRAFVVUSA
MARIE	7	F	CHILD	GRAFVVUSA
OTTILIE	6	F	CHILD	GRAFVVUSA
BERTHA	4	F	CHILD	GRAFVVUSA
ELISE	3	F	CHILD	GRAFVVUSA
IDA	2	F	CHILD	GRAFVVUSA
EMILIE	.09	F	INFANT	GRAFVVUSA
ANDRZEJEWSKA, WLAWIA	22	F	W	GRAEONUSA
JOHA.	3	F	CHILD	GRAEONUSA
STANISLAWA	.11	F	INFANT	GRAEONUSA
GRZECHULSKA, MAGDE.	28	F	W	GRZZZZUSA
MARIANNA	.09	F	INFANT	GRZZZZUSA
KOSMACZEWSKI, JOS.	26	M	LABR	GRZZZZUSA
BRZYKYY, JACOB	25	M	LABR	GRZZZZUSA
MARIANNE	25	F	W	GRZZZZUSA
WOJCIECH	.03	M	INFANT	GRZZZZUSA
PYRCZYNSKI, FRANZ	27	M	LABR	GRZZZZUSA
GRGESCHOLSKI, FRANZIS	28	M	LABR	GRZZZZUSA
KARCZEWSKA, ANTONIA	24	F	W	GRZZZZUSA
JOH.	2	M	CHILD	GRZZZZUSA

PASSENGER	AGE	SEX	OCCUPATION	PRVL	DES	PASSENGER	AGE	SEX	OCCUPATION	PRVL	DES
ALINA	.09	F	INFANT	GRZZZZUSA		JULIE	30	F	W	GRAIHYUSA	
MUSIELAK, WAWRZIN	27	M	LABR	GRZZZZUSA		POESL, XAVER	38	M	LABR	BVZZZZUSA	
WALISCHEWSKA, FRIEDR.	27	M	LABR	GRZZZZUSA		KATHA.	38	F	W	BVZZZZUSA	
MARIE	29	F	W	GRZZZZUSA		ALOIS	7	M	CHILD	BVZZZZUSA	
MIENE	3	F	CHILD	GRZZZZUSA		BARBA.	4	F	CHILD	BVZZZZUSA	
OTTO	.11	M	INFANT	GRZZZZUSA		CATHA.	.11	F	INFANT	BVZZZZUSA	
PIOTRAWSKI, STEFAN	28	M	LABR	GRZZZZUSA		BRONOLD, MICH.	16	M	LABR	BVZZZZUSA	
KATHA.	26	F	W	GRZZZZUSA		ALT, JOH.	40	M	LABR	BVZZZZUSA	
MICHALA.	6	F	CHILD	GRZZZZUSA		FINSTER, MICH.	15	M	LABR	BVAEWLUSA	
MARIANNE	.09	F	INFANT	GRZZZZUSA		BAHRS, FDRIEDR.	26	M	LABR	BVACBRUSA	
DOLOTA, KATHA.	24	F	NN	GRZZZZUSA		ORTH, ANTON	18	M	BCHR	BVZZZZUSA	
DRZEWIECKI, KAZMIEZ	37	M	FARMER	GRABUTUSA		HELLER, THEODOR	36	M	LABR	BVAEWMUSA	
RAJTAJCZAK, ANDRO	40	M	FARMER	GRZZZZUSA		BUCK, HEINR.	19	M	LABR	BVAIELUSA	
ANDRZYEWSKI, STANISLAW	30	M	FARMER	GRZZZZUSA		HASELOFF, EMILIE	27	F	NN	BVAAKHUSA	
MEHRING, BERTHA	21	F	NN	GRAIWJUSA		DINSEN, JOSIAS-SILBERG	42	F	NN	GRZZZZUSA	
GENKE, JULIUS	16	M	NN	GRAGIAUSA		SANDER, CHRISTOPH	35	F	NN	GRZZZZUSA	
JUL.	39	M	FARMER	GRAGIAUSA		WIEDEMANN, WM.	24	F	NN	GRAGXWUSA	
GIESE, CHR.	44	M	FARMER	GRZZZZUSA		KLOPFER, JOSEF	26	F	NN	GRAGXWUSA	
LOUISE	34	F	W	GRZZZZUSA		HENKEL, LOUIS	20	F	NN	GRADOIUSA	
BERTHA	4	F	CHILD	GRZZZZUSA		GAYER, CARL	15	M	NN	WMZZZZUSA	
EMMA	2	F	CHILD	GRZZZZUSA		STEIFF, MARIE	28	F	NN	WMABSJUSA	
GIEBEL, FERD.	34	M	LABR	GRAEWMUSA		ZIMMERMANNN, HERM.	24	M	LABR	GRZZZZUSA	
FRIEDKE.	29	F	W	GRAEWMUSA		ANTONIE	12	F	CH	GRZZZZUSA	
EMIL	4	M	CHILD	GRAEWMUSA		OTTO	6	M	CHILD	GRZZZZUSA	
ELLA	.11	F	INFANT	GRAEWMUSA		WILH.	4	M	CHILD	GRZZZZUSA	
ALMA	6	F	CHILD	GRAEWMUSA		MARTHA	2	F	CHILD	GRZZZZUSA	
TOM	3	M	CHILD	GRAEWMUSA		BERTHA	21	F	W	GRZZZZUSA	
KETTEL, REINHOLD	29	M	LABR	GRAEWMUSA		SCHRODER, CARL	29	M	LABR	GRZZZZUSA	
AUGUSTE	29	F	W	GRAEWMUSA		MARIE	28	F	W	GRZZZZUSA	
BERTHA	.11	F	INFANT	GRAEWMUSA		ADELHEID	4	F	CHILD	GRZZZZUSA	
ANNA	.03	F	INFANT	GRAEWMUSA		JOSEF	2	M	CHILD	GRZZZZUSA	
STEFFAN, EMILIA	36	F	W	GRZZZZUSA		MARIE	.09	F	INFANT	GRZZZZUSA	
OTTO	6	M	CHILD	GRZZZZUSA		WIRTH, JOSEF	56	M	LABR	GRADJXUSA	
CARL	4	M	CHILD	GRZZZZUSA		RIPPEL, JOH.	26	M	LABR	BVZZZZUSA	
MARIA	.11	F	INFANT	GRZZZZUSA		GABRIEL, CARL	44	M	LABR	GRZZZZUSA	
BULOW, AUG.	29	M	FARMER	GRAEWMUSA		ERNST	4	M	CHILD	GRZZZZUSA	
ANDRE, WILH.	24	M	FARMER	GRAEWMUSA		HARTUNG, GEORG	30	M	FARMER	BVZZZZUSA	
AUGUSTE	29	F	W	GRAEWMUSA		MARGA.	25	F	W	BVZZZZUSA	
AUGUSTE	5	F	CHILD	GRAEWMUSA		GEORG	.06	M	INFANT	BVZZZZUSA	
ELISE	.11	F	INFANT	GRAEWMUSA		GRIESSMANN, BARBA.	35	F	NN	BVACYRUSA	
SCHULZ, FRIEDR.	27	M	FARMER	GRAKQMUSA		MARX, WALBURGA	22	F	NN	BVACYRUSA	
ANNA	24	F	W	GRAKQMUSA		RAM, MARIA	25	F	NN	BVACYRUSA	
HELENE	.11	F	INFANT	GRAKQMUSA		BAIER, MARIA	17	F	NN	BVAFFYUSA	
GUSTAV	3	M	CHILD	GRAKQMUSA		REGER, JOH.	26	M	LABR	BVADSWUSA	
WILH.	30	M	FARMER	GRZZZZUSA		VOELKL, WOLFGANG	23	M	LABR	BVADSWUSA	
JOHA.	30	F	W	GRZZZZUSA		MARX, JOHANN	24	M	LABR	BVADSWUSA	
BERTHA	7	F	CHILD	GRZZZZUSA		GROESS, JACOB	26	M	LABR	BVZZZZUSA	
ANNA	4	F	CHILD	GRZZZZUSA		MASCHEK, REGA.	34	F	W	BVACYRUSA	
EMILIE	2	F	CHILD	GRZZZZUSA		CLEMENT	7	M	CHILD	BVACYRUSA	
WILH.	.09	M	INFANT	GRZZZZUSA		REGA.	.02	F	INFANT	BVACYRUSA	
SCHMIDT, WILH.	29	M	LABR	GRZZZZUSA		KIECK, FRANZ	47	M	LABR	BVACYRUSA	
GEHRKE, CARL	24	M	LABR	GRAJKVUSA		MARGA.	50	F	W	BVACYRUSA	
WOLFGRAM, WILHE.	63	F	W	GRAJKVUSA		FRANZ	6	M	CHILD	BVACYRUSA	
GOBOWSKI, MICHAL	27	M	LABR	GRZZZZUSA		ROSINE	4	F	CHILD	BVACYRUSA	
FESCHKE, HERM.	17	M	LABR	GRACVHUSA		WARNKE, HINRICH	17	M	BKR	BVADRDUSA	
FORSTER, ROSA	35	F	W	GRACYRUSA		HARMS, JOHA.	20	F	NN	GRZZZZUSA	
BARBA.	7	F	CHILD	GRACYRUSA		HELMKE, HINR.	17	M	PNTR	GRAFHIUSA	
MICH.	5	M	CHILD	GRACYRUSA		SUDEN, HINR.	17	M	FARMER	GRAFHIUSA	
BAUER, ANNA	24	F	NN	GRACYRUSA		MOELLER, AUGUSTE	16	F	NN	GRAACKUSA	
WAGNER, THERESIA	16	F	NN	GRACYRUSA		RUESCH, BERTHA	19	F	NN	GRAACKUSA	
MEYER, ANNA	17	F	NN	GRADHXUSA		SEHLMEIER, JOH.	14	M	NN	GRAACKUSA	
BARBA.	7	F	CHILD	GRADHXUSA		WILHE.	16	F	NN	GRAACKUSA	
KOLASSIN, FRANZISZEK	30	M	LABR	BVZZZZUSA		SCHULTZ, ANNA	40	F	W	GRADNJUSA	
SKWERES, TOMACZ	26	M	LABR	BVZZZZUSA		HERM.	12	M	NN	GRADNJUSA	
MALGORZATA	24	F	W	BVZZZZUSA		HEINR.	7	M	CHILD	GRADNJUSA	
NORCHOWIAK, ANTON	45	M	LABR	BVABUTUSA		JOHE.	4	F	CHILD	GRADNJUSA	
GUCIAK, JOSEFA	58	F	NN	BVABUTUSA		JOHANN	3	M	CHILD	GRADNJUSA	
SCHULZ, JOSEF	23	M	LABR	BVABUTUSA		FRIEDR.	2	M	CHILD	GRADNJUSA	
EMIL	14	M	NN	BVABUTUSA		FERDINAND	.03	M	INFANT	GRADNJUSA	
THIEL, FRANZ	22	M	LABR	BVAEZFUSA		SCHROEDER, JOHE.	15	F	NN	GRAACKUSA	
KWIATKOWSKI, VALENTIN	39	M	LABR	BVZZZZUSA		BARTH, CARL	24	M	LABR	GRAFNKUSA	
STRUSS, HEINR.W.	16	M	FARMER	GRZZZZUSA		JOHE.	24	F	W	GRAFNKUSA	
RUSS, ERNST	16	M	FARMER	GRZZZZUSA		WARCHOWSKI, SCHNA.	18	F	NN	BDZZZZUSA	
MEINKEN, HEINR.	15	M	FARMER	GRZZZZUSA		KANT, ANDR.	30	M	LABR	BDACIJUSA	
SZCZSZYNSKI, JOSEF	31	M	FARMER	GRAIHYUSA		HANENSTEIN, HEINR.	26	M	LABR	BDACIJUSA	

29

PASSENGER	AGE	SEX	OCCUPATION	PRVL	DES
FUEHRBASS, LEOP.	33	M	LABR		BVZZZZUSA
DEURING, CAROLE.	28	F	W		WMZZZZUSA
CAROLE.	.11	F	INFANT		WMZZZZUSA
PESOLLO, PAUL	33	M	FARMER		WMABNOUSA
BAUER, PUINO	25	M	FARMER		WMAGQIUSA
TITEL, MARGA.	20	F	NN		WMAGQIUSA
ROEHRS, JOH.	26	M	FARMER		BVZZZZUSA
SCHMIDT, JACOB	18	M	FARMER		BVZZZZUSA
LASCHINGER, ALOIS	24	M	FARMER		BVZZZZUSA
LIMBRUNER, KATHA.	23	F	NN		BVZZZZUSA
RAMSAUER, JOS.	26	M	LABR		BVZZZZUSA
THERESIA	7	F	CHILD		BVZZZZUSA
GEBHARDT, JOH.	30	M	FARMER		BVAJADUSA
BECK, JOH.	16	M	FARMER		BVZZZZUSA
BORCH, JUL.	32	M	FARMER		BVABYHUSA
BLOCK, DORIS	28	M	FARMER		BVAAAHUSA
HERM.	14	M	NN		BVAAAHUSA
SCHUETT, ANNA	16	F	NN		BVABPZUSA
VONBOHR, PHA.	21	F	NN		BVAAPUUSA
HOEHN, MARIA	16	F	NN		BVAAPUUSA
SCHLECHTWEG, ROSALIA	18	F	NN		GRZZZZUSA
LINA	15	F	NN		GRZZZZUSA
JUNGE, GERTR.	23	F	NN		GRADWOUSA
FINK, CATHE.	20	F	NN		BVZZZZUSA
LAPP, CARL	34	M	LABR		BVAFIAUSA
MARIE	14	F	NN		BVAFIAUSA
KRENZ, WILH.	14	M	NN		BVAEHSUSA
BLASCHKE, ANTON	65	M	LABR		BVZZZZUSA
JUENGER, ROSINE	57	F	W		BVZZZZUSA
THERESE	27	F	NN		BVZZZZUSA
EDUARD	7	M	CHILD		BVZZZZUSA
SKVOBANEK, JOHANN	37	M	LABR		BVZZZZUSA
ANNA	37	F	W		BVZZZZUSA
ANNA	11	F	CH		BVZZZZUSA
FRIEDKE.	7	F	CHILD		BVZZZZUSA
JULIE	6	F	CHILD		BVZZZZUSA
OTTILIE	4	F	CHILD		BVZZZZUSA
ADOLF	2	M	CHILD		BVZZZZUSA
IDA	.11	F	INFANT		BVZZZZUSA
MUEHR, FRANZ	19	M	BKR		BVAHTNUSA
MENDL, EDWARD	7	M	CHILD		BVAHTNUSA
MALCHER, FRANZ	64	M	FARMER		BVZZZZUSA
THERESE	50	F	W		BVZZZZUSA
BLASCHKA, JOHANN	34	M	FARMER		BVZZZZUSA
ANNA	30	F	W		BVZZZZUSA
JOHANN	7	M	CHILD		BVZZZZUSA
ANNA	4	F	CHILD		BVZZZZUSA
FERDINAND	.07	M	INFANT		BVZZZZUSA
DAVID, MARIA	26	F	NN		BVZZZZUSA
FROER, MARGA.	24	F	W		BVAIKSUSA
CARL	.10	M	INFANT		BVAIKSUSA
BOTSCHGANG, GRETCHEN	20	F	NN		BVAIKSUSA
SCHARF, KATHA.	21	F	NN		BVZZZZUSA
SCHNEIDER, MARIA	23	F	NN		BVZZZZUSA
GLASS, JACOB	16	M	LABR		GRZZZZUSA
STRECK, JOHANN	22	M	LABR		GRAGAPUSA
PAPROKI, ZALENTY	39	M	LABR		GRZZZZUSA
GRALLA, FRANZ	16	M	LABR		GRZZZZUSA
LITKA, JOSEPH	33	M	LABR		GRZZZZUSA
JERZEWSKA, FRANZISKA	21	F	NN		GRAEXKUSA
CILHOCKA, ANNA	31	F	W		GRZZZZUSA
JOSEPH	7	M	CHILD		GRZZZZUSA
STANISLAUS	3	M	CHILD		GRZZZZUSA
KOWALEWSKY, VALENTIN	24	M	LABR		GRAFZGUSA
GRABAFSKI, EMILIE	19	F	NN		GRADHVUSA
SLACHCIAK, JOSEF	26	M	LABR		GRZZZZUSA
MARIA	21	F	W		GRZZZZUSA
APOLINIA	.11	F	INFANT		GRZZZZUSA
NIEBEL, EMMA	21	F	NN		GRAFZGUSA
KIRSCH, OSCAR	25	M	FARMER		GRAEHJUSA
MANTHEI, FRIEDR.	42	M	FARMER		GRALZTUSA
HENRIETTE	39	F	W		GRALZTUSA
CARL	9	M	CHILD		GRALZTUSA
WILHELMINE	6	F	CHILD		GRALZTUSA
KOSINSKI, JUSTIN	24	M	LABR		GRZZZZUSA
KASPROWICZ, ANTON	23	M	LABR		GRZZZZUSA
GRZESZKOWIAK, MART.	26	M	LABR		GRZZZZUSA
BASCHADRACK, FRANZISA.	20	F	NN		GRZZZZUSA
SCHROEDER, CHRISTOPH	27	M	FARMER		GRZZZZUSA
MEYER, HENRY	15	M	NN		GRZZZZUSA
KAMPS, HELENE	19	F	NN		GRAARRUSA
NAGTS, HEINR.	23	M	FARMER		GRZZZZUSA
MONSEES, JOH.	16	M	FARMER		GRZZZZUSA
KIRSTEIN, DORIS	20	M	FARMER		GRAARRUSA
FINK, WILHELM	16	M	FARMER		GRZZZZUSA
WERNER, AUGUST	24	M	FARMER		GRAACKUSA
IND, GUSTAV	14	M	NN		GRAACKUSA
FICK, AUGUST	19	M	FARMER		GRAACKUSA
TIMMERMANN, MARIA	21	F	NN		GRAACKUSA
WORIESCHEK, JOSEPH	24	M	LABR		GRAFRMUSA
MONSEES, PETER	16	M	LABR		GRAAIOUSA
HERR, G.	26	M	LABR		GRABRZUSA
MOSER, JACOB	22	M	LABR		GRZZZZUSA
BRANDENBERGER, JULE.	15	F	NN		WMZZZZUSA
BOSE, LUDOLF	20	M	LABR		GRZZZZUSA
BICKEL, ELISAB.	17	F	NN		BDZZZZUSA
WOLPERT, RICH.	14	M	NN		BDZZZZUSA
KUEHN, THEKLA	15	F	NN		BDZZZZUSA
GROTE, GABRIEL	15	M	NN		BDZZZZUSA
ERTER, JOHANN	34	M	FARMER		BDABLDUSA
KERN, PHILIPP	23	M	FARMER		BDZZZZUSA
WIEDEMANN, EMIL	17	M	FARMER		GRZZZZUSA
WISSICH, GEORG	23	M	FARMER		GRZZZZUSA
STAHL, LUDWIG	27	M	FARMER		GRZZZZUSA
KATHA.	27	F	W		GRZZZZUSA
PHILIPPINE	5	F	CHILD		GRZZZZUSA
SCHUCHEN, WILH.	23	M	LABR		GRZZZZUSA
STAHL, CONRAD	26	M	FARMER		GRZZZZUSA
SUELZ, GEORGE	16	M	FARMER		GRAJJKUSA
BAUER, FRIEDR.	17	M	FARMER		WMZZZZUSA
CATHA.	18	F	NN		WMZZZZUSA
PFAU, FRIEDKA.	20	F	NN		WMAEHVUSA
BLUST, JOHN	16	M	NN		WMAIAKUSA
SOURWINE, MARY	21	M	NN		WMAIAKUSA
PAULINE	18	M	NN		WMAIAKUSA
STIEGEL, LOUISE	20	M	NN		WMZZZZUSA
SIEGEL, MARIE	31	M	NN		WMZZZZUSA
MUELLER, JOSEPH	53	M	LABR		WMZZZZUSA
CRESCENZ	46	M	W		WMZZZZUSA
LOUISE	7	F	CHILD		WMZZZZUSA
MATHILDE	6	F	CHILD		WMZZZZUSA
PAULINE	4	F	CHILD		WMZZZZUSA
GISTERN, CAROLINE	19	F	NN		WMZZZZUSA
RUDOLF, FRIEDKE.	26	F	NN		WMZZZZUSA
MATHILDE	18	F	NN		WMZZZZUSA
ZAVODNY, MART.	27	M	LABR		GRZZZZUSA
UTHNEMER, JOH.	25	M	LABR		GRAARRUSA
GANZENMUELLER, MARGA.	35	F	NN		GRAHGDUSA
JANIKULA, ED.	26	M	LABR		GRADVVUSA
VONHALTEN, OTTO	16	M	LABR		GRAAZCUSA
FRELS, MATHILDE	19	F	NN		GRZZZZUSA
WALZ, PAULINE	21	F	NN		WMZZZZUSA
DIENER, FRIEDR.	17	M	FARMER		WMAAMFUSA
SCHWAB, WILH.	23	M	FARMER		WMAAMFUSA
HELD, JOHANNES	27	M	FARMER		WMZZZZUSA
MARIA	23	F	W		WMZZZZUSA
CATHA.	.06	F	INFANT		WMZZZZUSA
CATHA.	.06	F	INFANT		WMZZZZUSA
HANNINGS, MARIE	29	F	W		WMAEJWUSA
WILLI	6	M	CHILD		WMAEJWUSA
ELISE	4	F	CHILD		WMAEJWUSA
MARIE	.04	F	INFANT		WMAEJWUSA
WOLTERS, CARL	36	M	FARMER		WMAEJWUSA
MARIE	34	F	W		WMAEJWUSA
MAGDA.	6	F	CHILD		WMAEJWUSA
CARL	4	F	CHILD		WMAEJWUSA
HEINR.	2	F	CHILD		WMAEJWUSA
WILH.	.10	M	INFANT		WMAEJWUSA
STEFANSKI, ANTONIE	44	F	W		GRZZZZUSA
IGNATZ	3	M	CHILD		GRZZZZUSA

PASSENGER	AGE	SEX	OCCUPATION	PRVVL	DES
EICHHORN, ROCHUS	27	M	LABR	GRAIENUSA	
MARIA	27	F	W	GRAIENUSA	
DINA	3	F	CHILD	GRAIENUSA	
OTTILIA	2	F	CHILD	GRAIENUSA	
CARL	.03	M	INFANT	GRAIENUSA	
ECKERT, IGNAZ	18	M	MCHT	GRAIENUSA	
CARL	17	M	FARMER	GRAEHVUSA	
KLAUSMANN, WEND	19	M	FARMER	WMZZZZUSA	
HESS, ANDR.	16	M	FARMER	WMZZZZUSA	
HAENSSLER, GEORG	36	M	FARMER	WMAIAKUSA	
KAUTH, CATHA.	17	F	NN	WMAILIUSA	
KLAUSMANN, ELISE	16	F	NN	WMZZZZUSA	
GEISS, JACOB	13	M	UNKNOWN	WMZZZZUSA	
MOHR, CONR.	14	M	NN	WMAIALUSA	
ROSSE, ANNA	26	F	W	WMAIALUSA	
ALFRED	3	M	CHILD	WMAIALUSA	
OTTO	.11	M	INFANT	WMAIALUSA	
ROESKE, BERTHA	33	F	NN	GRZZZZUSA	
DOEPP, ELISE	39	F	W	GRAAHWUSA	
KARL	6	M	CHILD	GRAAHWUSA	
CONRAD	4	M	CHILD	GRAAHWUSA	
KINKEL, ELISE	16	F	NN	GRAAHWUSA	
JAHN, FRIEDKE.	30	F	NN	GRABLVUSA	
HELD, CARL	36	M	LABR	WMZZZZUSA	
RASS, FRIEDR.	17	M	LABR	BVZZZZUSA	
DEUBEL, GEORG	16	M	LABR	BVZZZZUSA	
MENKENS, JOHANN	62	M	LABR	GRZZZZUSA	
ANNA	65	F	W	GRZZZZUSA	
KUENNEMANN, HEINR.	17	M	FARMER	GRZZZZUSA	
BEHNKE, ERNESTNE.	23	F	NN	GRAHFWUSA	
HELMERS, HENRY	15	M	NN	GRZZZZUSA	
WISSEL, CHRISTE.	24	F	W	GRAHRJUSA	
BERTHA	2	F	CHILD	GRAHRJUSA	
LINA	.11	F	INFANT	GRAHRJUSA	
HUMMER, NICOLAUS	18	M	FARMER	BVZZZZUSA	
HEBRANT, HEINR.	24	M	LABR	BVZZZZUSA	
FELDMAIER, WILH.	29	M	LABR	BVZZZZUSA	
HERTER, CHRISTOF	16	M	LABR	BVAJJKUSA	
EBERLE, JACOB	31	M	LABR	BVZZZZUSA	
BREITENSTEIN, MARIE	21	F	NN	BVADYXUSA	
KOCH, ANNA	22	F	NN	BVADYUUSA	
WEIGELT, MAX	14	M	NN	GRZZZZUSA	
WEIGAND, MARIA	21	F	NN	GRADBOUSA	
FESER, MICH.	28	M	FARMER	BVZZZZUSA	
WOLF, OTTO	23	M	FARMER	BVALQGUSA	
DEGENHARDT, LIBORIUS	22	M	FARMER	BVAFANUSA	
ZINSEL, CONRAD	28	M	FARMER	BVAEYGUSA	
FISCHER, HEINR.	40	M	FARMER	BVADOIUSA	
BARBA.	40	F	W	BVADOIUSA	
HEINR.	5	M	CHILD	BVADOIUSA	
LUDWIG	3	M	CHILD	BVADOIUSA	
WIENEKE, PETER	27	M	FARMER	GRZZZZUSA	
FISCHER, MARY	7	F	CHILD	GRADOIUSA	
GILBERT, JOSEF	37	M	LABR	GRZZZZUSA	
LEUSMANN, CARL	46	M	LABR	GRZZZZUSA	
KLIPPEL, FERD.	34	M	LABR	GRABEDUSA	
WILKENS, GESINE	19	M	LABR	GRAARRUSA	
LACHENAUER, MINNA	18	M	LABR	BDZZZZUSA	
ARNOLD, JOHANN	28	M	FARMER	BDZZZZUSA	
TIETJE, HERM.	43	M	FARMER	BDAAAHUSA	
MINNA	44	F	W	BDAAAHUSA	
AUGUSTE	9	F	CHILD	BDAAAHUSA	
MINNA	6	F	CHILD	BDAAAHUSA	
BERTHA	4	F	CHILD	BDAAAHUSA	
JOHANNE	2	F	CHILD	BDAAAHUSA	
STERNHAGEN, ANNA	38	F	W	BDAARRUSA	
ADOLF	11	M	CH	BDAARRUSA	
HESS, LAURA	20	F	NN	BDACZAUSA	
PAWLAK, MARIA	22	F	NN	BDABUTUSA	
KOROWSKA, ANNA	19	F	NN	GRZZZZUSA	
JUERGENSEN, ELIZABETH	23	F	NN	GRAENQUSA	
BEYE, MARIE	28	F	NN	GRABPVUSA	
APELT, FRIEDR.	53	M	LABR	GRACXVUSA	
GEMPEL, CHRIST.	26	M	LABR	GRAGAHUSA	
SCHNEIDER, JACOB	23	M	LABR	GRAAIKUSA	
BUEHLER, JACOB	24	M	LABR	WMZZZZUSA	
SCHLICHENMAIER, FRIEDE.	19	F	NN	WMZZZZUSA	
SANDHERR, CARL	16	F	NN	WMZZZZUSA	
KUGLER, GOTTLIEB	27	M	FARMER	WMZZZZUSA	
ROSENBERGER, MICH.	51	M	FARMER	BVZZZZUSA	
MARIE	48	F	W	BVZZZZUSA	
PAULINE	11	F	CH	BVZZZZUSA	
DOROTHEA	9	F	CHILD	BVZZZZUSA	
AUGUSTE	7	F	CHILD	BVZZZZUSA	
ANDREAS	4	M	CHILD	BVZZZZUSA	
VALENTIN	2	M	CHILD	BVZZZZUSA	
MARIE	.11	F	INFANT	BVZZZZUSA	
HOFMANN, FRANZ	32	M	LABR	BVZZZZUSA	
KATHA.	30	F	W	BVZZZZUSA	
ANTON	7	M	CHILD	BVZZZZUSA	
NEES, EVA	20	F	NN	BVZZZZUSA	
GANS, FRANZCA.	15	M	NN	GRZZZZUSA	
WEILAND, MATHIAS	34	M	LABR	GRALXNUSA	
KULCZAK, KATHA.	25	F	W	GRZZZZUSA	
STANISLAUS	4	M	CHILD	GRZZZZUSA	
STRANZ, MARTHA	24	F	W	GRZZZZUSA	
ALFRED	3	M	CHILD	GRACMHUSA	
WUEDTKE, SELMA	21	F	NN	GRZZZZUSA	
PIMPLER, PAULINE	39	F	W	GRZZZZUSA	
WILH.	7	M	CHILD	GRZZZZUSA	
BERTHA	5	F	CHILD	GRZZZZUSA	
GUSTAV	3	M	CHILD	GRZZZZUSA	
LIS, PAULINE	19	F	NN	GRZZZZUSA	
SCHMELTER, ALBERT	45	M	LABR	GRZZZZUSA	
WEILAND, THERESIA	34	F	W	GRZZZZUSA	
IGNATZ	5	M	CHILD	GRZZZZUSA	
JOSEF	3	M	CHILD	GRZZZZUSA	
THEOPHIL	.09	M	INFANT	GRZZZZUSA	
WIRTH, ALBERT	19	M	FARMER	GRADJXUSA	
LOSKOWFSKI, FRIEDR.	27	M	FARMER	GRZZZZUSA	
FLORENTINE	24	F	W	GRZZZZUSA	
JOHANN	3	M	CHILD	GRZZZZUSA	
FRIEDRICH	.11	M	INFANT	GRZZZZUSA	
SCHULZ, LOUISE	16	F	NN	GRZZZZUSA	
HEINKE, AUGUST	35	M	LABR	GRAARZUSA	
OLGA	28	F	W	GRAARZUSA	
OSKAR	6	M	CHILD	GRAARZUSA	
HENDRICK, BETTY	11	F	CH	BDZZZZUSA	
HILLER, JUSTINA	24	F	W	BDZZZZUSA	
RICHARD	2	M	CHILD	BDZZZZUSA	
MAX	.09	M	INFANT	BDZZZZUSA	
WISNIEWSKA, CONST.	19	M	LABR	BDZZZZUSA	
FISCHER, CRESZENT	18	M	LABR	BVZZZZUSA	
RAPP, MARIA	18	F	NN	BVZZZZUSA	
SCHERGER, AGNES	16	F	NN	BVZZZZUSA	
RATER, EDMUND	16	F	NN	BVZZZZUSA	
FREUTHEIM, OTTILIE	15	F	NN	BVZZZZUSA	
SCHMIDT, FRANZA.	20	F	NN	BVZZZZUSA	
FLOHR, MICHAEL	2	M	CHILD	BVADTEUSA	
MUELLER, KARL	16	M	NN	BVAJCFUSA	
WETZEL, JOSEF	16	M	NN	BVACRMUSA	
HELM, MICHAEL	50	M	FARMER	BVACRMUSA	
JULIANA	45	F	W	BVACRMUSA	
SCHARF, MARGA.	19	F	NN	BVACRMUSA	
REICHARDS, MARGA.	52	F	W	BVZZZZUSA	
FRIEDR.	7	M	CHILD	BVZZZZUSA	
KATHE.	7	F	CHILD	BVZZZZUSA	
MARIE	5	F	CHILD	BVZZZZUSA	
LEHR, MARIE	16	F	NN	BVZZZZUSA	
MARIE	19	F	NN	BVZZZZUSA	
FICHTNER, ANNA	26	F	W	BVACFDUSA	
ANNA	.05	F	INFANT	BVACFDUSA	
NEUBAUER, CHRIST.	23	M	LABR	BVAAHBUSA	
FLESS--, LOUISE	18	F	NN	BVACFDUSA	
NEUBAUER, KATHA.	40	F	W	BVAAHBUSA	
ADAM	7	M	CHILD	BVAAHBUSA	
JOHANN	5	M	CHILD	BVAAHBUSA	
HEINR.	3	M	CHILD	BVAAHBUSA	
RUETH, ENGELBERTH	17	M	CH	BVACRMUSA	
HUBER, ALOIS	28	M	CH	BVAHQGUSA	

PASSENGER	AGE	SEX	OCCUPATION	PRIVL/DES
MARIA	25	F	W	BVAHQGUSA
FRANZISCA	.10	F	INFANT	BVAHQGUSA
JOHAN	21	M	FARMER	BVZZZZUSA
SCHERER, JOHANN	39	M	FARMER	BVZZZZUSA
THERESE	41	F	W	BVZZZZUSA
ELISABETH	65	F	W	BVZZZZUSA
JOHANN	6	M	CHILD	BVZZZZUSA
LUTZ, ANTON	17	M	FARMER	BDZZZZUSA
ROPP, HEINR.	48	M	FARMER	BDAEOHUSA
LETOILE, HERM.	30	M	FARMER	BDADEIUSA
LIZZIE	30	F	W	BDADEIUSA
BARTMANN, ANNA	27	F	NN	BDAMAMUSA
MEHLTRETTER, KARL	14	M	NN	BDAMAMUSA
BERGER, ALOISA	24	F	W	GRZZZZUSA
JOSEF	.10	M	INFANT	GRZZZZUSA
PAULER, ROSA	23	F	NN	GRZZZZUSA
FUCHS, ERNESTE.	29	F	NN	GRZZZZUSA
HENRIETTE	19	F	NN	GRZZZZUSA
SCHERER, MICHAEL	7	M	CHILD	GRAACPUSA
SCHECKENER, HEINR.	42	M	FARMER	GRAARRUSA
HEINTZ, LUDW.	27	M	FARMER	GRZZZZUSA
BODE, AUG.	24	M	FARMER	GRADAAUSA
BOROWSKY, ANNA	24	F	NN	GRAGDHUSA
SABATOWSKI, WENZEL	24	M	FARMER	GRZZZZUSA
HELLWIG, PETER	32	M	FARMER	GRZZZZUSA
BERR, CARL	17	M	LABR	GRAAPSUSA
MOELLER, CARL	29	M	LABR	GRZZZZUSA
SEIDEL, KAROLE.	30	F	W	GRAHRTUSA
WILH.	3	M	CHILD	GRAHRTUSA
MARY	.11	F	INFANT	GRAHRTUSA
KRUEGER, MARIE	24	F	NN	GRAHUCUSA
GRAMERS, ANNA	45	F	NN	GRAHUCUSA
LEGGUS, BERTHA	18	F	NN	GRAEXWUSA
STRZELECKA, MARIA	22	F	W	GRZZZZUSA
STANISL.	.06	M	INFANT	GRZZZZUSA
PEILTE, JACOB	23	M	LABR	GRZZZZUSA
BOEHMISCH, W.	27	M	LABR	GRZZZZUSA
RADTKA, WLADISLAW	7	M	CHILD	GRZZZZUSA
STANISLAUS	5	M	CHILD	GRZZZZUSA
ANNA	3	F	CHILD	GRZZZZUSA
DOBLER, JACOBINE	28	F	W	GRZZZZUSA
SUSANNE	7	F	CHILD	GRZZZZUSA
MATHIAS	5	M	CHILD	GRZZZZUSA
JOHANN	3	M	CHILD	GRZZZZUSA
REINHOLD	.09	M	INFANT	GRZZZZUSA
JANTA, FRANZ	37	M	FARMER	GRZZZZUSA
FRANZCA.	30	F	W	GRZZZZUSA
EVA	4	F	CHILD	GRZZZZUSA
MARIANNE	.11	F	INFANT	GRZZZZUSA
JOHANN	.02	M	INFANT	GRZZZZUSA
DEUTSCHLE, HEINR.	22	M	FARMER	BVZZZZUSA
RADTKE, DAVID	32	M	LABR	GRZZZZUSA
MARIE	36	F	W	GRZZZZUSA
STANISLAUS	6	M	CHILD	GRZZZZUSA
IDA	.09	F	INFANT	GRZZZZUSA
KUEHNLE, ERNST	15	M	NN	WMZZZZUSA
KITZ, FRANZ	37	M	MCHT	WMACXVUSA
JACOB	35	M	MCHT	WMACXVUSA

SHIP: DEVONIA

FROM: GLASGOW
TO: NEW YORK
ARRIVED: 09 MAY 1888

PASSENGER	AGE	SEX	OCCUPATION	PRIVL/DES
FINK, CHRISTIAN	60	M	LABR	WMADZVUSA
AUGUSTE	40	M	NN	WMADZVUSA
AUGT.	17	M	LABR	WMADZVUSA
KAROLINE	9	F	CHILD	WMADZVUSA
ALBERT	7	M	CHILD	WMADZVUSA

PASSENGER	AGE	SEX	OCCUPATION	PRIVL/DES
KUTOFSKI, AUST.	46	M	LABR	WMADZVUSA
JOHANNA	38	F	NN	WMADZVUSA
ANISLA	17	F	NN	WMADZVUSA
AUGT.	15	M	NN	WMADZVUSA
GEO	.11	M	INFANT	WMADZVUSA
SORZEWIAK, VALENTIN	28	M	CCHMN	GRZZZZUSA
ANTONIE	23	F	NN	GRZZZZUSA
MARIE-ANN	1	F	CHILD	GRZZZZUSA
MAREAN	.03	F	INFANT	GRZZZZUSA
STREUBING, WILHME.	29	F	INF	GRADZVUSA
IDA	1	F	CHILD	GRADZVUSA
KARL	.02	M	INFANT	GRADZVUSA
HOLKIN, RACHEL	20	F	NN	GRACBFUSA
EGGERT, ANNA	14	F	SVNT	GRADZVUSA
FINK, CARL	19	M	LABR	GRADZVUSA
GORMY, MARTIN	40	M	LABR	GRADZVUSA
GISDE, FERD.	20	M	MECH	GRZZZZUSA
HAUSEN, PETER	49	M	SEMN	GRACBFUSA
HEIMBUCHER, JOHAN	24	M	BBR	GRACBFUSA
JOHAN, CARL	38	M	WVR	BVZZZZUSA
KAELICKI, JACENTY	29	M	BKR	BVAEABUSA
KRIPCZAK, JAKOB	41	M	LABR	BVZZZZUSA
MAZEK, HUGO	17	M	MNR	BVZZZZUSA
PRECHOCKI, WADISLAW	20	M	FSHMN	BVAEABUSA
SCHLAPKO, FRANZ	30	M	SHMK	BVAEABUSA
SOLL, WM.	27	M	JNR	BVAEABUSA
STORZ, WM.	27	M	BCHR	BVAEABUSA

SHIP: MICHIGAN

FROM: LIVERPOOL
TO: BOSTON
ARRIVED: 09 MAY 1888

PASSENGER	AGE	SEX	OCCUPATION	PRIVL/DES
SARITZKY, MICHEAL	24	M	CPTR	GRZZZZUSA
FOGEL, ISAAC	40	M	TLR	GRZZZZUSA
KAHAN, RUBEN	27	M	BTMKR	GRZZZZUSA
ZUCHONITZKY, ISRAEL	20	M	BTMKR	GRZZZZUSA
ISAAC	11	M	SCH	GRZZZZUSA
ROEJEUTES, MOSES	27	M	BTMKR	GRZZZZUSA
STAROZINSKY, LEIB	28	M	CPTR	GRZZZZUSA
NEUMAN, ADERIK	38	M	WCHMKR	GRZZZZUSA
REYNIK, BERIL	41	M	CPTR	GRZZZZUSA
POZAH, VINCENTY	31	M	TLR	GRZZZZUSA
LUPROUSKI, CHAMI	21	M	BTMKR	GRZZZZUSA
HIFFMAN, EYGENE	23	M	TLR	GRZZZZUSA
MARGULUS, SHOLOME	35	M	CPTR	GRZZZZUSA
URDANSKI, MOSKA	35	M	TLR	GRZZZZUSA
NISTRICK, LEON	28	M	SP	GRZZZZUSA
SEGERL, HERTZKE	44	M	TLR	GRZZZZUSA
SHAWLAWSKY, SALUM	25	M	BTMKR	GRZZZZUSA
DAWALKA, JOSEPH	23	M	TLR	GRZZZZUSA
WAGMAI, CHAIM	33	M	CRBLDR	GRZZZZUSA
BERSAU, ISAAC	22	M	UNKNOWN	GRZZZZUSA
NAMOSVITZ, SIOTE	33	M	TLR	GRZZZZUSA
CHARVATAK, JOEL	35	M	BTMKR	GRZZZZUSA
SAPOLWITZ, AB.	27	M	BTMKR	GRZZZZUSA
LINTON, KASIMIR	25	M	BTMKR	GRZZZZUSA
JANKOWSKI, JOSEPH	29	M	LABR	GRZZZZUSA
MARCUS, CHEJER	37	M	TLR	GRZZZZUSA
GINSBERG, BENJ	17	M	CL	GRZZZZUSA
LOWENORTH, ESK	14	F	SCH	GRZZZZUSA
DOCHROWITZ, MOSES	45	M	CPTR	GRZZZZUSA
CLARA	18	F	W	GRZZZZUSA
GRUNEVAER, ANNA	25	F	W	GRZZZZUSA
NEMROWSKI, MOSES	26	M	TLR	GRZZZZUSA
MACHLE	20	F	W	GRZZZZUSA
NUIDORFF, SLZLOMA	30	M	TLR	GRZZZZUSA
LIBE	28	F	W	GRZZZZUSA
RACHINAUZIK, RIFKE	26	F	W	GRZZZZUSA

PASSENGER	AGE	SEX	OCCUPATION	PRVL	DES
BARCHE	17	F	W	GRZZZZUSA	
LOWENORTH, PITEL	38	F	W	GRZZZZUSA	
RACHOWINZIK, HIBEL	.09	F	INFANT	GRZZZZUSA	
HINCKEL	.09	F	INFANT	GRZZZZUSA	
LOWENORTH, ANN	7	F	CHILD	GRZZZZUSA	
GRUNAEVAER, JOSEF	4	M	CHILD	GRZZZZUSA	
LOWENORTH, MANI	10	M	CH	GRZZZZUSA	
SAMIE	8	M	CHILD	GRZZZZUSA	
ABRAHAM	7	M	CHILD	GRZZZZUSA	
DAVID	.08	M	INFANT	GRZZZZUSA	

SHIP: PENNSYLVANIA

FROM: ANTWERP
TO: NEW YORK
ARRIVED: 09 MAY 1888

PASSENGER	AGE	SEX	OCCUPATION	PRVL	DES
BUBEL, MARIE	7	F	CHILD	GRZZZZUNK	
JOSEF	5	M	CHILD	GRZZZZUNK	
BABULJA, ROSA	39	M	LABR	BVZZZZNY	
BAUNMANN, D	26	M	LABR	BVZZZZNY	
BOCHEBER, H	29	M	LABR	PRZZZZNY	
BEUKER, J	40	M	LABR	BVZZZZNY	
BOERSCH, J	45	M	LABR	BVZZZZNY	
MARG	40	F	W	BVZZZZNY	
JOH	11	M	CH	BVZZZZNY	
MICH	.06	M	INFANT	BVZZZZNY	
BOKROVSKI, EVA	15	F	SP	PRZZZZNY	
BABEL, F	24	M	LABR	BVZZZZNY	
BAER, HEIN	24	M	LABR	BVZZZZNY	
CALLUGARI, G	27	M	JNLST	GRZZZZNY	
M	20	M	CL	GRZZZZNY	
DEUGEL, H	29	M	LABR	PRZZZZNY	
CAROLINE	32	F	W	PRZZZZNY	
H	9	M	CHILD	PRZZZZNY	
J	6	M	CHILD	PRZZZZNY	
O	3	M	CHILD	PRZZZZNY	
CARL	.06	F	INFANT	PRZZZZNY	
DEUTSCHMANN, A	25	M	LABR	PRZZZZNY	
DOMINOWSKY, J	17	M	LABR	PRZZZZCH	
EHRENSAAL, J	17	M	LABR	GRZZZZNY	
ENGLER, M	25	M	LABR	GRZZZZNY	
JUHR, H	24	M	LABR	GRZZZZNY	
D	28	M	LABR	GRZZZZNY	
J	33	M	LABR	GRZZZZNY	
FIRLIT, J	40	M	LABR	GRZZZZNY	
FEG, E	36	M	LABR	BVZZZZNY	
FARSLER, C	24	M	LABR	PRZZZZNY	
MARIA	22	F	W	PRZZZZNY	
GOLLEZ, M	28	M	LABR	GRZZZZNY	
GUMOKS, P	18	M	LABR	GRZZZZNY	
GOJLUMIS, A	27	M	LABR	GRZZZZNY	
GUENTER, F	46	M	LABR	BVZZZZNY	
GOCHREI, J	57	M	LABR	GRZZZZNY	
HEIDENREICH, K	36	M	LABR	GRZZZZNY	
K	15	M	LABR	GRZZZZNY	
A	11	M	CH	GRZZZZNY	
F	9	M	CHILD	GRZZZZNY	
C	4	M	CHILD	GRZZZZNY	
M	.09	M	INFANT	GRZZZZNY	
HEIVER, W	24	M	LABR	PRZZZZNY	
HAACK, H	27	M	LABR	SYZZZZCH	
JACOBOWSKI, D	18	M	LABR	GRZZZZCH	
JABLONSKI, A	43	M	LABR	PRZZZZCH	
JASYKOWAK, M	50	F	WI	PRZZZZCH	
KLEIN, MARG	36	F	WI	ACZZZZIN	
M	8	F	CHILD	ACZZZZIN	
J	7	M	CHILD	ACZZZZIN	
M	4	F	CHILD	ACZZZZIN	
KANDEL, G	38	M	LABR	GRZZZZNY	
J	11	M	CH	GRZZZZNY	
KOPUCZMSKI, MAR	20	F	SVNT	GRZZZZNY	
KARYEN, A	26	M	LABR	GRZZZZNY	
KWIATKOWSKY, M	38	M	LABR	GRZZZZNY	
KOTZ, J	25	M	LABR	GRZZZZNY	
KOENIG, A	23	M	LABR	GRZZZZNY	
KOLL, CATH	22	F	SP	PRZZZZNY	
KOBLER, PETER	18	M	LABR	HSZZZZNY	
KAISERSBERGER, M	48	M	LABR	HSZZZZNY	
LEID, F	30	M	LABR	GRZZZZNY	
JOHN	29	F	W	GRZZZZNY	
JANOS	5	M	CHILD	GRZZZZNY	
LINSLER, BARB	46	F	WI	BVZZZZNY	
FR	20	M	LABR	BVZZZZNY	
MARIE	18	F	SP	BVZZZZNY	
LINA, F	57	M	LABR	PRZZZZNY	
ANNA	60	F	W	PRZZZZNY	
F	26	M	LABR	PRZZZZNY	
MARIE	26	F	W	PRZZZZNY	
FELIX	3	M	CHILD	PRZZZZNY	
M	1	F	CHILD	PRZZZZNY	
LANGE, O	28	M	LABR	SYZZZZUSA	
R	28	F	W	SYZZZZUSA	
P	2	F	CHILD	SYZZZZUSA	
MJOTTKE, JOH	26	M	LABR	PRZZZZNY	
M	24	F	W	PRZZZZNY	
J	3	M	CHILD	PRZZZZNY	
R	5	M	CHILD	PRZZZZNY	
MARTIN, H	34	M	LABR	GRZZZZNY	
MEYER, R	17	M	LABR	GRZZZZROC	
MOREZELLA, L	26	M	LABR	PRZZZZNY	
J	20	F	W	PRZZZZNY	
E	9	F	CHILD	PRZZZZNY	
M	6	M	CHILD	PRZZZZNY	
F	1	M	CHILD	PRZZZZNY	
MALT, A	26	M	LABR	GRZZZZNY	
MOSER, C	36	M	LABR	GRZZZZNY	
RUNCHOW, A	33	M	FARMER	GRZZZZCH	
OCHAUSEN, J	24	M	LABR	BVZZZZCH	
B	17	F	SP	BVZZZZCH	
J	16	M	LABR	BVZZZZCH	
CATH	18	F	SP	BVZZZZCH	
PRABUSKA, F	56	F	WI	PRZZZZNY	
ANA	19	F	SP	PRZZZZNY	
H	16	M	LABR	PRZZZZNY	
F	11	M	CH	PRZZZZNY	
PALUS, F	22	M	LABR	GRZZZZNY	
PASQUALL, A	26	M	LABR	FRZZZZNY	
PAVO, G	24	M	LABR	FRZZZZNY	
PRZJBYLINSKA, W	26	M	LABR	PRZZZZCH	
POTZLITNER, J	28	M	LABR	PRZZZZNY	
ROTH, G	18	M	LABR	GRZZZZNY	
RUDER, F	27	M	LABR	GRZZZZUNK	
RICHTER, S	37	M	LABR	PRZZZZNY	
REECK, W	24	M	LABR	PRZZZZNY	
SREC, F	36	M	LABR	GRZZZZNY	
STANEK, J	43	M	LABR	GRZZZZNY	
AGNES	34	F	W	GRZZZZNY	
JOSEFA	10	F	CH	GRZZZZNY	
J	4	M	CHILD	GRZZZZNY	
M	3	M	CHILD	GRZZZZNY	
MARIE	2	F	CHILD	GRZZZZNY	
SVEHLA, F	26	M	LABR	GRZZZZNY	
STEFAN, K	17	M	LABR	BVZZZZNY	
STEFFEN, CATH	39	F	W	LXZZZZNY	
A	18	M	LABR	LXZZZZNY	
CATH	10	F	CH	LXZZZZNY	
JAN	7	M	CHILD	LXZZZZNY	
SCIPIAROWSKI, L	17	M	LABR	GRZZZZNY	
SCHMIDT, J	34	M	LABR	BVZZZZNY	
SBCOEDE, A	28	M	LABR	PRZZZZCH	
J	19	F	W	PRZZZZCH	
URBAN, JOS	35	M	LABR	BVZZZZNY	
WOSFIEL, G	29	M	LABR	PRZZZZNY	
WOHLFART, J	26	M	LABR	HSZZZZNY	

PASSENGER	AGE	SEX	OCCUPATION	PRVL	DES
WAGNER, G	26	M	LABR	HSZZZZWI	
MARIE	20	F	W	HSZZZZWI	
WOLF, B	55	M	LABR	BVZZZZUNK	
WAYLER, E	39	M	LABR	BVZZZZNY	
RICHTER, L	29	M	LABR	PRZZZZNY	
A	26	F	W	PRZZZZNY	
L	3	F	CHILD	PRZZZZNY	
J	.08	M	INFANT	PRZZZZNY	

SHIP: RHEIN

FROM: BREMEN
TO: BALTIMORE
ARRIVED: 09 MAY 1888

PASSENGER	AGE	SEX	OCCUPATION	PRVL	DES
MACHOWAK, WALENTY	27	M	LABR	GRZZZZUSA	
MACKOWIAK, AGNES	24	F	W	GRZZZZUSA	
MARIANNA	.09	F	INFANT	GRZZZZUSA	
DWORESACK, BARB	20	F	UNKNOWN	GRZZZZUSA	
KAMIENSKI, MARIE	20	F	UNKNOWN	GRZZZZUSA	
PAWLOWSKI, JAN	21	M	LABR	GRZZZZUSA	
ANNA	22	F	UNKNOWN	GRZZZZUSA	
SCHWERKOWSKI, JOSEF	48	M	LABR	GRZZZZUSA	
GEORGE, JOSEPH	32	M	LABR	GRZZZZUSA	
BERENT, ANDRE	50	M	LABR	GRZZZZUSA	
ANNA	40	F	W	GRZZZZUSA	
ANTON	7	M	CHILD	GRZZZZUSA	
MARIE	7	F	CHILD	GRZZZZUSA	
KATH	5	F	CHILD	GRZZZZUSA	
IGNATZ	4	M	CHILD	GRZZZZUSA	
FRANZ	2	M	CHILD	GRZZZZUSA	
MARTIN	1	M	CHILD	GRZZZZUSA	
STANISLAUS	.04	M	INFANT	GRZZZZUSA	
BEHRENDT, MARTIN	50	M	LABR	GRZZZZUSA	
MARIE	50	F	W	GRZZZZUSA	
ELSBIEDA	7	F	CHILD	GRZZZZUSA	
STANISLAWA	6	F	CHILD	GRZZZZUSA	
ANDRYCZAKA, JOHANN	22	M	LABR	GRZZZZUSA	
MACZESEWSKA, IGNATZ	23	M	LABR	GRZZZZUSA	
NOWAKOWSKI, THEOPHIL	24	M	LABR	GRZZZZUSA	
MAGD	24	F	W	GRZZZZUSA	
WLADISLAW	.11	M	INFANT	GRZZZZUSA	
LANGE, ANTON	23	M	PNTR	GRZZZZUSA	
HABIECHT, RUDOLF	27	M	GDNR	GRZZZZUSA	
GARTNER, AUGUST	5	M	CHILD	GRZZZZUSA	
WILH	.05	M	INFANT	GRZZZZUSA	
MIHALY, KREHELY	35	M	LABR	GRZZZZBAL	
DERY, BALTOMIEJ	20	M	LABR	GRZZZZBAL	
MELCHERT, JOHANN	45	M	JNR	GRZZZZBAL	
HENRIETTE	42	F	W	GRZZZZBAL	
JOHANNE	10	F	CH	GRZZZZBAL	
HANS	7	M	CHILD	GRZZZZBAL	
ROBERT	5	M	CHILD	GRZZZZBAL	
WILH	2	F	CHILD	GRZZZZBAL	
LUECHEN	.07	F	INFANT	GRZZZZBAL	
KOZERSKI, PIOTR	32	M	LABR	GRZZZZBAL	
STANISLAWA	24	F	W	GRZZZZBAL	
JOHANN	.11	M	INFANT	GRZZZZBAL	
MICHAEL	.01	M	INFANT	GRZZZZBAL	
GINDERA, WALENTY	42	M	LABR	GRZZZZBAL	
HARMES, B	20	M	LABR	GRZZZZBAL	
LIUSS, ANNA	24	F	UNKNOWN	GRZZZZBAL	
FREESE, JOHN	28	M	TLR	GRZZZZBAL	
GROSEZEKOREK, MARIANNA	60	F	UNKNOWN	GRZZZZBAL	
STOCHOWIAK, RICH	26	M	LABR	GRZZZZBAL	
BOETCHER, ADAM	58	M	LABR	GRZZZZBAL	
MINNA	30	F	W	GRZZZZBAL	
WILH	.09	F	INFANT	GRZZZZBAL	
GRUSZEZENSKI, JAKOB	35	M	LABR	GRZZZZBAL	
ROSALIA	27	F	W	GRZZZZBAL	
MARIANNE	7	F	CHILD	GRZZZZBAL	
JACOB	5	M	CHILD	GRZZZZBAL	
MICHAEL	3	M	CHILD	GRZZZZBAL	
VICTORIA	.09	F	INFANT	GRZZZZBAL	
GRZEGOREK, GERTRUD	19	F	UNKNOWN	GRZZZZBAL	
WOJWOTZKI, JOHANN	30	M	LABR	GRZZZZBAL	
BTRIGITTA	27	F	W	GRZZZZBAL	
JOSEF	3	M	CHILD	GRZZZZBAL	
JOHANN	.09	M	INFANT	GRZZZZBAL	
ADAMKEWITSCH, MICH	26	M	LABR	GRZZZZBAL	
ZIELINSKI, PETER	45	M	LABR	GRZZZZBAL	
SKARNPIENSKI, JOSEFA	23	F	UNKNOWN	GRZZZZBAL	
PACER, JACOB	29	M	LABR	GRZZZZBAL	
URSULA	18	F	UNKNOWN	GRZZZZBAL	
TYLLMANN, ANDR	18	M	LABR	GRZZZZBAL	
OLSEWSKA, FRANZ	50	F	UNKNOWN	GRZZZZBAL	
KRIKANT, JOHANN	29	M	LABR	GRZZZZBAL	
JOSEFINE	30	F	W	GRZZZZBAL	
MARIANNE	3	F	CHILD	GRZZZZBAL	
FRANZ	.04	M	INFANT	GRZZZZBAL	
JOSEFINE	.04	F	INFANT	GRZZZZBAL	
MUSZANOWSKI, JAN	34	M	FARMER	GRZZZZBAL	
ANASTASIA	27	F	W	GRZZZZBAL	
FRANZ	4	M	CHILD	GRZZZZBAL	
MARTHA	.02	F	INFANT	GRZZZZBAL	
MARIANNA	1	F	CHILD	GRZZZZBAL	
BANDURSKI, MARTIN	28	M	LABR	GRZZZZBAL	
VICTORIA	19	F	W	GRZZZZBAL	
BARKOWICZ, JAN	11	M	CH	GRZZZZBAL	
SCHWENSCHIKOWSKA, MARIA	22	F	UNKNOWN	GRZZZZBAL	
BOLTER, WILH	27	M	HTR	GRZZZZBAL	
AMALIE	23	F	W	GRZZZZBAL	
FLISOWSKI, ROSALIA	19	F	SVNT	GRZZZZBAL	
KUEHN, AUGUSTE	22	F	SVNT	GRZZZZBAL	
WICHERT, ANNA	33	F	UNKNOWN	GRZZZZBAL	
FRANZ	7	M	CHILD	GRZZZZBAL	
STANISLAWA	7	F	CHILD	GRZZZZBAL	
HEDWIG	5	F	CHILD	GRZZZZBAL	
ANTONIE	4	F	CHILD	GRZZZZBAL	
LEO	.10	M	INFANT	GRZZZZBAL	
GALL, CAROLINRE	47	F	UNKNOWN	GRZZZZBAL	
AMALIE	14	F	CH	GRZZZZBAL	
DRECKA, APOLONIA	16	F	UNKNOWN	GRZZZZBAL	
JESEWSKA, FRANCISCA	28	M	LABR	GRZZZZBAL	
FRANZ	28	F	W	GRZZZZBAL	
JOSEPH	.11	M	INFANT	GRZZZZBAL	
KARPUS, FRANZ	32	F	UNKNOWN	GRZZZZBAL	
ROSALIA	60	F	UNKNOWN	GRZZZZBAL	
JOHANN	5	M	CHILD	GRZZZZBAL	
MARIA	.08	F	INFANT	GRZZZZBAL	
SROCKI, JOSEPH	32	M	LABR	GRZZZZBAL	
FENSKI, WILH	19	F	UNKNOWN	GRZZZZBAL	
SCHMETKE, WALENTY	40	M	LABR	GRZZZZBAL	
KOY, ANDREAS	31	M	LABR	GRZZZZBAL	
FRANZ	25	F	W	GRZZZZBAL	
JOHANN	3	M	CHILD	GRZZZZBAL	
FRANZ	.08	M	INFANT	GRZZZZBAL	
PILANSKI, IGNATZ	29	M	LABR	GRZZZZBAL	
ABRAHAM, VERONIKA	45	F	UNKNOWN	GRZZZZBAL	
ANNA	19	F	UNKNOWN	GRZZZZBAL	
ANTON	17	M	UNKNOWN	GRZZZZBAL	
ELISABETH	10	F	CH	GRZZZZBAL	
GORTATEWSKI, FRANK	33	M	LABR	GRZZZZBAL	
ANNA	28	F	W	GRZZZZBAL	
FRANZ	6	M	CHILD	GRZZZZBAL	
ANTON	4	M	CHILD	GRZZZZBAL	
BERNHARD	.11	M	INFANT	GRZZZZBAL	
OGRODOWSKI, JOHN	28	M	LABR	GRZZZZBAL	
MARIANNA	28	F	W	GRZZZZBAL	
LEO	3	M	CHILD	GRZZZZBAL	
STANISLAWA	.02	F	INFANT	GRZZZZBAL	
LUCZAK, SZYMON	29	M	LABR	GRZZZZBAL	
GRZESIAK, MARYANNA	18	F	UNKNOWN	GRZZZZBAL	
MICHAEL	30	M	LABR	GRZZZZBAL	
STEFANSKI, THOMAS	44	M	SMH	GRZZZZBAL	

PASSENGER	AGE	SEX	OCCUPATION	PRVL	DES
ANTONIE	44	F	W		GRZZZZBAL
JOHANN	7	M	CHILD		GRZZZZBAL
STANISL	5	M	CHILD		GRZZZZBAL
IGNATZ	3	M	CHILD		GRZZZZBAL
KACZMIRCZAK, FRANZ	24	M	LABR		GRZZZZBAL
PIEGAN, HULDA	43	F	UNKNOWN		GRZZZZBAL
AGNIS	10	F	CH		GRZZZZBAL
RICHARD	7	M	CHILD		GRZZZZBAL
LEOPOLD	6	M	CHILD		GRZZZZBAL
WILHELM	4	M	CHILD		GRZZZZBAL
RZEPEZENSKI, FRANZISZEK	28	M	LABR		GRZZZZBAL
OLSIESKI, JOHANN	27	M	LABR		GRZZZZBAL
AGNES	23	F	W		GRZZZZBAL
MICHEL	.11	M	INFANT		GRZZZZBAL
GEZERNI, MICH	25	M	LABR		GRZZZZBAL
FRANZ	.04	F	INFANT		GRZZZZBAL
WISNESKI, FRANZISZ	24	M	LABR		GRZZZZBAL
FRANZ	22	F	W		GRZZZZBAL
JAN	.01	M	INFANT		GRZZZZBAL
LASZKIEWICZ, MARIANNA	23	F	UNKNOWN		GRZZZZBAL
GROCKE, FRANZ	28	F	UNKNOWN		GRZZZZBAL
MARIANNA	53	F	UNKNOWN		GRZZZZBAL
ISIDOR	.09	M	INFANT		GRZZZZBAL
JOHANN	.09	M	INFANT		GRZZZZUNK
SANTOWSKI, JULIUS	38	M	CPTR		GRZZZZUSA
AUGUSTE	33	F	W		GRZZZZUSA
MINE	6	F	CHILD		GRZZZZUSA
HERMANN	5	M	CHILD		GRZZZZUSA
BERTHA	.10	F	INFANT		GRZZZZUSA
G---SKI, IGNACZ	26	M	LABR		GRZZZZUSA
JOSEFA	18	F	UNKNOWN		GRZZZZUSA
KENDZIORA, FRANMCZIZEK	28	M	LABR		GRZZZZUSA
JULIANNA	29	F	W		GRZZZZUSA
FRANCZIZEK	.11	M	INFANT		GRZZZZUSA
TIM, IGNATZ	30	M	LABR		GRZZZZUSA
JOSEFA	27	F	W		GRZZZZUSA
JAN	3	M	CHILD		GRZZZZUSA
AGATHE	.11	F	INFANT		GRZZZZUSA
RIPICKI, PIOTR	29	M	LABR		GRZZZZUSA
JEZIERNA, MARIE	23	F	UNKNOWN		GRZZZZUSA
SCHUMARSKI, MIKOLAY	22	M	LABR		GRZZZZUSA
FACH, PAULINA	18	F	UNKNOWN		GRZZZZUSA
GABRIEL, MICHAEL	25	M	LABR		GRZZZZUSA
RATAJEZAK, LUDWIG	18	M	LABR		GRZZZZUSA
PIELARSKI, ANTON	35	M	LABR		GRZZZZUSA
ROSALIA	24	F	W		GRZZZZUSA
MARIA	.09	F	INFANT		GRZZZZUSA
GRUCZA, BERNARD	34	M	BKR		GRZZZZUSA
JOHANNE	29	F	W		GRZZZZUSA
JOHANN	4	M	CHILD		GRZZZZUSA
JOHANNE	2	F	CHILD		GRZZZZUSA
JOSEPH	.06	M	INFANT		GRZZZZUSA
SULINSKY, ANDRZY	23	M	LABR		GRZZZZUSA
KRUCZEWSKI, FRANZ	29	M	BCHR		GRZZZZUSA
JULIANNA	23	F	W		GRZZZZUSA
MARIANNA	60	F	UNKNOWN		GRZZZZUSA
DREWS, CARL	31	M	LABR		GRZZZZUSA
JOHANNA	31	F	W		GRZZZZUSA
ALBERT	.11	M	INFANT		GRZZZZUSA
KROGULSKA, FRANZ	31	F	UNKNOWN		GRZZZZUSA
ANNA	7	F	CHILD		GRZZZZUSA
FRANZ	5	M	CHILD		GRZZZZUSA
JULA	3	F	CHILD		GRZZZZUSA
PAULINE	1	F	CHILD		GRZZZZUSA
ANNASTASIA	.03	F	INFANT		GRZZZZUSA
KROLSKI, MARTIN	26	M	LABR		GRZZZZUSA
CONSTANZIA	27	F	W		GRZZZZUSA
WOITSCHEK	.04	M	INFANT		GRZZZZUSA
BLINKOWICZ, JOSEPHA	24	F	UNKNOWN		GRZZZZUSA
VALENTIN	.11	M	INFANT		GRZZZZUSA
JENDRASZKIEWICZ, ANNA	53	F	UNKNOWN		GRZZZZUSA
MARIANNA	16	F	UNKNOWN		GRZZZZUSA
ROCHNOWSKI, MARIANNA	50	F	UNKNOWN		GRZZZZUSA
SOHPIA	7	F	CHILD		GRZZZZUSA
WLADISLAUS	7	M	CHILD		GRZZZZUSA
STRZELEZKA, MAGD	45	F	UNKNOWN		GRZZZZUSA
ANTON	6	M	CHILD		GRZZZZUSA
ANDREAS	38	M	SHMK		GRZZZZUSA
LASSIN, ALBERT	38	M	SHMK		GRZZZZUSA
ELISAB	33	F	W		GRZZZZUSA
MARIA	7	F	CHILD		GRZZZZUSA
PAUL	7	M	CHILD		GRZZZZUSA
JOSEF	3	M	CHILD		GRZZZZUSA
AGNES	.09	F	INFANT		GRZZZZUSA
NAWROSKI, WICENTY	27	M	LABR		GRZZZZUSA
LEOKADIA	22	F	W		GRZZZZUSA
VALENTINA	4	F	CHILD		GRZZZZUSA
ROSALIA	.06	F	INFANT		GRZZZZUSA
LIERCK, KATARZYNA	30	F	UNKNOWN		GRZZZZUSA
GREITSCHEK, ANDREAS	25	M	LABR		GRZZZZUSA
LASSIN, JOHANN	72	M	LABR		GRZZZZUSA
BOROWSKI, MACZY	42	M	LABR		GRZZZZUSA
MARIANNA	43	F	W		GRZZZZUSA
JOHANN	6	M	CHILD		GRZZZZUSA
PETER	4	M	CHILD		GRZZZZUSA
STANISLAW	2	M	CHILD		GRZZZZUSA
AGNES	.09	F	INFANT		GRZZZZUSA
STRZELSKI, JACOB	56	M	CPTR		GRZZZZUSA
JAEGER, JOHANN	28	M	LABR		GRZZZZUSA
AUGUST	.09	M	INFANT		GRZZZZUSA
JOHANNE	.09	F	INFANT		GRZZZZUSA
SPITZKOPF, JACOB	32	M	LABR		GRZZZZUSA
CIACINEK, ANDRZY	29	M	LABR		GRZZZZUSA
CZAPALSKI, MICHAEL	25	M	LABR		GRZZZZUSA
OPIELINSKI, FRANS	46	M	LABR		GRZZZZUSA
MORITZ	6	M	CHILD		GRZZZZUSA
CZAPALSKI, ANNA	26	F	UNKNOWN		GRZZZZUSA
LEISNER, MARIANNA	62	F	UNKNOWN		GRZZZZUSA
CZAPALSKI, STANISL	5	M	CHILD		GRZZZZUSA
VINZENS	.04	M	INFANT		GRZZZZUSA
OIELINSKA, MARG	7	F	CHILD		GRZZZZUSA
SPORNY, FRANZ	16	M	PNTR		GRZZZZUSA
SZKUDLAREK, ROSALIA	25	F	UNKNOWN		GRZZZZUSA
MAZURKISWIZC, STANISLAW	17	M	LABR		GRZZZZUSA
TALARCZYK, MAX	30	M	LABR		GRZZZZUSA
LUKASIEWICZ, JOSEFA	20	F	UNKNOWN		GRZZZZUSA
WISNIEFSKI, MARG	38	F	UNKNOWN		GRZZZZUSA
PELAGIA	6	F	CHILD		GRZZZZUSA
CATHARINA	4	F	CHILD		GRZZZZUSA
FRANZ	2	F	CHILD		GRZZZZUSA
STANISLAUS	.05	M	INFANT		GRZZZZUSA
JANOWICZ, FRANZ	26	F	UNKNOWN		GRZZZZUSA
JOHANN	4	M	CHILD		GRZZZZUSA
ANTON	.01	M	INFANT		GRZZZZUSA
KOLACZKOWSKI, JOSEPH	23	M	LABR		GRZZZZUSA
ZAGAJESKI, KONR	23	M	LABR		GRZZZZUSA
WALCZAK, WOJCIECH	48	M	LABR		GRZZZZUSA
WIEAZCHOLSKI, JACOB	22	M	LABR		GRZZZZUSA
STACHOWIAK, ANDR	13	M	LABR		GRZZZZUSA
NAWAKOWSKI, KASRER	36	M	LABR		GRZZZZUSA
JOSEPHA	26	F	W		GRZZZZUSA
KASPAR	.11	M	INFANT		GRZZZZUSA
PINARKIEWICZ, JOSEPH	25	M	LABR		GRZZZZUSA
MACZKOWIAK, LORENZ	37	M	LABR		GRZZZZUSA
HOYNACKI, STANISL	36	M	LABR		GRZZZZUSA
GORNY, FRANZ	23	M	LABR		GRZZZZUSA
NOWICKI, FRANZ	25	M	LABR		GRZZZZUSA
VICTORIA	21	F	W		GRZZZZUSA
MIKOLAJCZAK, FRANZ	26	M	LABR		GRZZZZUSA
CZARNECKI, LIO	36	M	LABR		GRZZZZUSA
GORNIK, ANTONIE	33	F	UNKNOWN		GRZZZZUSA
STANISL	2	M	CHILD		GRZZZZUSA
ANNA	.04	F	INFANT		GRZZZZUSA
WOZNIAK, APOLONIA	30	F	UNKNOWN		GRZZZZUSA
WERNER, HERM	25	M	BKBNDR		GRZZZZWI
CZIJEWSKI, FRANZ	32	M	LABR		GRZZZZIL
MARIE	28	F	W		GRZZZZIL
HELENE	5	F	CHILD		GRZZZZIL
MARTHA	3	F	CHILD		GRZZZZIL
FRANZ	.09	M	INFANT		GRZZZZIL

PASSENGER	AGE	SEX	OCCUPATION	PRVVL	DES
LOUTKOWSKI, MARTHA	18	F	UNKNOWN	GRZZZZIL	
KOWALSKI, ANDRZEJ	24	M	FARMER	GRZZZZMN	
SPERRA, JOHANN	24	M	LABR	GRZZZZMN	
LIPINSKI, VINCENT	16	M	LABR	GRZZZZLIT	
OSTROWSKI, MARTIN	36	M	LABR	GRZZZZLIT	
VERONICA	30	F	W	GRZZZZLIT	
VERONICA	4	F	CHILD	GRZZZZLIT	
ALBERT	.11	M	INFANT	GRZZZZLIT	
EVA	.01	F	INFANT	GRZZZZLIT	
MRUCH, WAWRZIN	58	M	FARMER	GRZZZZMI	
CATHARINA	51	F	W	GRZZZZMI	
MAGD	16	F	UNKNOWN	GRZZZZMI	
MICHALINA	20	F	UNKNOWN	GRZZZZMI	
LERCZAK, MARIE	22	F	UNKNOWN	GRZZZZMN	
BONIK, JOHANN	24	M	LABR	GRZZZZIL	
ROSALIA	29	F	W	GRZZZZIL	
SULNISKA, MARIANNA	23	F	UNKNOWN	GRZZZZOH	
LUDWIG	3	M	CHILD	GRZZZZOH	
MICHAEL	.06	M	INFANT	GRZZZZOH	
MANTHEI, BERTHA	46	F	UNKNOWN	GRZZZZMN	
ZIELSKI, AUGUST	44	M	JNR	GRZZZZOH	
ROSALIE	37	F	W	GRZZZZOH	
ADELINA	10	F	CH	GRZZZZOH	
MINNA	7	F	CHILD	GRZZZZOH	
BERTHA	4	F	CHILD	GRZZZZOH	
SIEFERT, FRIEDR	38	M	TLR	GRZZZZMI	
WILH	39	F	W	GRZZZZMI	
ERNSTINE	6	F	CHILD	GRZZZZMI	
WILHELM	4	M	CHILD	GRZZZZMI	
FRITZ	2	M	CHILD	GRZZZZMI	
TOMAS, JOSEF	28	M	LABR	GRZZZZIL	
STAGERT, FERDIN	44	M	BKR	GRZZZZOH	
WOLOWSKI, JOHANN	16	M	LABR	GRZZZZMI	
GREITSCHEK, MARTIN	60	M	LABR	GRZZZZOH	
VICTORIA	60	F	W	GRZZZZOH	
LEWANDOWSKI, JOSEF	41	M	LABR	GRZZZZMO	
ROSALIE	26	F	W	GRZZZZMO	
EVA	.11	F	INFANT	GRZZZZMO	
BRONISLAW	.11	M	INFANT	GRZZZZMO	
JANOWICZ, JACOB	33	M	LABR	GRZZZZMO	
LADEWSKI, WLADISL	27	M	LABR	GRZZZZPA	
KWIATKOWSKI, JOHANN	27	M	LABR	GRZZZZIL	
KLUSMANN, CARL	15	M	FARMER	GRZZZZIL	
RICH	17	M	FARMER	GRZZZZIL	
KUNSEN, WILH	19	F	UNKNOWN	GRZZZZIL	
PETROLAT, MINNA	20	F	UNKNOWN	GRZZZZIL	
GWILINSKI, PETER	33	M	LABR	GRZZZZIL	
BARANOWSKA, ANT	28	F	UNKNOWN	GRZZZZIL	
WOLSKI, ANTON	40	M	LABR	GRZZZZIL	
HERZ, WILH	40	M	FARMER	GRZZZZIL	
AUGUSTE	35	F	W	GRZZZZIL	
JOHANNE	7	F	CHILD	GRZZZZIL	
LAURA	5	F	CHILD	GRZZZZIL	
KOPITOWSKI, ANASTASIA	24	F	UNKNOWN	GRZZZZIL	
HANSEN, JULIUS	50	M	SMH	GRZZZZIL	
INGEBORG	55	M	LABR	GRZZZZIL	
SLUPKA, MARYANNA	54	F	UNKNOWN	GRZZZZIL	
STAWSKA, JULIA	28	F	UNKNOWN	GRZZZZIL	
SEMRAN, JAC	65	M	LABR	GRZZZZIL	
KATH	58	F	W	GRZZZZIL	
ANASTASIA	22	F	UNKNOWN	GRZZZZIL	
JOSEPHA	20	F	UNKNOWN	GRZZZZIL	
BRONISLAWA	15	F	UNKNOWN	GRZZZZIL	
WOJTECKI, MICHAEL	25	M	LABR	GRZZZZIL	
RICHLITZKA, MARG	64	F	UNKNOWN	GRZZZZIL	
JOHANN	48	M	LABR	GRZZZZIL	
ROSPLOCH, VERONIKA	21	F	UNKNOWN	GRZZZZIL	
MENZEL, PAULINE	35	F	UNKNOWN	GRZZZZIL	
ANNA	7	F	CHILD	GRZZZZIL	
JULIUS	5	M	CHILD	GRZZZZIL	
MARTHA	2	F	CHILD	GRZZZZIL	
EMMA	.10	F	INFANT	GRZZZZIL	
SCHILINSKA, THOMAS	33	M	CPTR	GRZZZZIL	
MARIANNA	26	F	W	GRZZZZIL	
KAZIMIR	4	M	CHILD	GRZZZZIL	
WACLAW	2	M	CHILD	GRZZZZIL	
HELENA	.11	F	INFANT	GRZZZZIL	
SYPNIESKA, ANTONIA	30	F	UNKNOWN	GRZZZZIL	
JOSEFA	5	F	CHILD	GRZZZZIL	
FRASZESKY, MICH	25	M	LABR	GRZZZZIL	
MARIANNA	21	F	W	GRZZZZIL	
STANISLAWA	5	F	CHILD	GRZZZZIL	
CHROSNIAK, BARTH	25	M	LABR	GRZZZZIL	
JENDRZCJEWSKI, CONST	29	M	LABR	GRZZZZIL	
CATH	25	F	W	GRZZZZIL	
MARIANNA	.09	F	INFANT	GRZZZZIL	
FUCHS, CAROLINE	19	F	UNKNOWN	GRZZZZIL	
DUSCHEL, CATH	7	F	CHILD	GRZZZZIL	
JOSEF	5	M	CHILD	GRZZZZIL	
KASMTSCHKE, MARIA	26	F	UNKNOWN	GRZZZZIL	
SCHLOETZER, KATHA	26	F	UNKNOWN	GRZZZZIL	
HABEGGER, JACOB	21	M	LABR	SRZZZZIL	
SCHMIDT, ANNA	18	F	CK	GRZZZZIL	
ROSINA	28	F	CK	GRZZZZIL	
RAMMEL, MARIA	26	F	SVNT	GRZZZZIL	
MOEHRING, OTTO	21	M	LABR	GRZZZZIL	
FISCHER, CARL	16	M	CL	GRZZZZIL	
KRANC, IGNATZ	46	M	LABR	GRZZZZIL	
URSULLA	36	F	W	GRZZZZIL	
MARIANNA	9	F	CHILD	GRZZZZIL	
SIBILLA	7	F	CHILD	GRZZZZIL	
APOLONIA	7	F	CHILD	GRZZZZIL	
VERONIKA	5	F	CHILD	GRZZZZIL	
JOSEFA	.10	F	INFANT	GRZZZZIL	
LIEBRENZ, FERD	16	M	FARMER	GRZZZZBAL	
FRIEDR	15	M	FARMER	GRZZZZBAL	
KITTL, MARIE	30	F	UNKNOWN	GRZZZZPA	
MARIE	.07	F	INFANT	GRZZZZPA	
KERSCHBAUM, MARIE	50	F	UNKNOWN	GRZZZZPA	
BRAUNS, AUG	30	M	LABR	GRZZZZIL	
ANNA	28	F	W	GRZZZZIL	
DAHL, ELISAB	55	F	UNKNOWN	GRZZZZIL	
RISCH, HERM	23	M	LABR	GRZZZZOH	
SCHWENNSEN, HEINR	18	M	MLR	GRZZZZIA	
FLUIZ, FERD	25	M	BCHR	GRZZZZOH	
MARTIN	.10	M	INFANT	GRZZZZOH	
OLTMANN, MAGD	31	F	UNKNOWN	GRZZZZBAL	
ANDREAS	5	M	CHILD	GRZZZZBAL	
FRANZ	2	M	CHILD	GRZZZZBAL	
SZILLAT, MARTIN	62	M	LABR	GRZZZZBAL	
ELISE	65	F	W	GRZZZZBAL	
EDUARD	7	M	CHILD	GRZZZZBAL	
ZELLMANN, ANNA	19	F	UNKNOWN	GRZZZZBAL	
MAREWSKI, TOMAS	39	M	LABR	GRZZZZBAL	
FRANCISCA	34	F	W	GRZZZZBAL	
VALENTIN	6	M	CHILD	GRZZZZBAL	
ALOISSINS	.06	M	INFANT	GRZZZZBAL	
FILIPSKA, ROSALIE	19	F	UNKNOWN	GRZZZZBAL	
HASKE, FRIEDR	15	M	CL	GRZZZZBAL	
SOBWERCKA, VALERIA	26	F	UNKNOWN	GRZZZZBAL	
FELCKA, ANNA	32	F	UNKNOWN	GRZZZZBAL	
DEMSKA, MARIANNA	26	F	UNKNOWN	GRZZZZBAL	
BREZICKI, FRANZ	23	M	LABR	GRZZZZBAL	
JANISCHEWSKI, FRANZ	36	M	LABR	GRZZZZBAL	
GALL, FRANZISZAK	39	M	LABR	GRZZZZBAL	
MARIANNA	38	F	W	GRZZZZBAL	
ANNA	6	F	CHILD	GRZZZZBAL	
JAKOB	4	M	CHILD	GRZZZZBAL	
MARTIN	2	M	CHILD	GRZZZZBAL	
FRANZ	.09	M	INFANT	GRZZZZBAL	
JANISCHEWSKA, MARIE	27	F	UNKNOWN	GRZZZZBAL	
BECKER, EMIL	25	M	MLR	GRZZZZBAL	
PUKOWSKI, JACOB	46	M	BRR	GRZZZZBAL	
LAMPARSKI, JOH	27	M	LABR	GRZZZZBAL	
VICTORIA	20	F	W	GRZZZZBAL	
BRANISLAWA	.05	F	INFANT	GRZZZZBAL	
THOMAS	31	M	PRNTR	GRZZZZBAL	
KATHARINA	40	F	W	GRZZZZBAL	
VALERIA	.10	F	INFANT	GRZZZZBAL	
JOHANN	.10	M	INFANT	GRZZZZBAL	

PASSENGER	AGE	SEX	OCCUPATION	PRVL	DES
PREIS, JOSEF	48	M	CPR		GRZZZZBAL
KATHARINA	30	F	W		GRZZZZBAL
VERONIKA	.05	F	INFANT		GRZZZZBAL
CZEPANSKI, ANTON	33	M	LABR		GRZZZZBAL
SUSANNA	20	F	W		GRZZZZBAL
LEONI	.11	F	INFANT		GRZZZZBAL
GOLDENSTEIN, ANTONI	28	M	DYR		GRZZZZIL
GAJEWSKY, SIMON	38	M	LABR		GRZZZZBAL
PAROLOWSKY, ADAM	26	M	LABR		GRZZZZBAL
FILITZKY, MARCIN	58	M	LABR		GRZZZZBAL
TWAROZOWSKY, THEODOR	24	M	LABR		GRZZZZBAL
KALINOWSKY, ANDRZI	26	M	LABR		GRZZZZBAL
TWARGOWSKY, STANISLAW	36	M	LABR		GRZZZZBAL
JANKI, CARL	26	M	LABR		GRZZZZBAL
OSELMEIER, AUGUSTE	16	F	UNKNOWN		GRZZZZBAL
MUELLER, ANTON	16	M	HTR		GRZZZZBAL
ASELMEIER, HELENE	19	F	UNKNOWN		GRZZZZBAL
FISCHER, CHRISTINE	40	F	UNKNOWN		GRZZZZBAL
FRANZ	10	M	CH		GRZZZZBAL
HERMANN	7	M	CHILD		GRZZZZBAL
WILH	5	F	CHILD		GRZZZZBAL
EMMA	2	F	CHILD		GRZZZZBAL
CARL	.07	F	INFANT		GRZZZZBAL
ANNA	.07	F	INFANT		GRZZZZBAL
WOLF, PAULINA	36	F	UNKNOWN		GRZZZZBAL
MAX	6	M	CHILD		GRZZZZBAL
MARIE	3	F	CHILD		GRZZZZBAL
ELISE	1	F	CHILD		GRZZZZUNK
ALBERT	.03	M	INFANT		GRZZZZUNK
SELLING, FANNY	16	F	CK		GRZZZZUSA
FLEISCHAUER, CARL	16	M	SLR		GRZZZZUSA
MELZIAN, ERNST	15	M	CL		GRZZZZUSA
SAUER, GRETCHEN	21	F	CK		GRZZZZUSA
KLICSCHIES, MARTIN	34	M	LABR		GRZZZZUSA
ANNA	37	F	W		GRZZZZUSA
MARTHA	6	F	CHILD		GRZZZZUSA
ZIELINSKI, ADAM	20	M	GDR		GRZZZZUSA
CZELWSIK, WOJCICEK	42	M	LABR		GRZZZZUSA
MARIANNA	40	F	W		GRZZZZUSA
WASCHIM	9	M	CHILD		GRZZZZUSA
MARIANNA	7	F	CHILD		GRZZZZUSA
CASPER	6	M	CHILD		GRZZZZUSA
SOPHIE	6	F	CHILD		GRZZZZUSA
CATH	3	F	CHILD		GRZZZZUSA
FRANZ	.03	M	INFANT		GRZZZZUSA
SOSNOSKI, MICHAEL	28	M	LABR		GRZZZZUSA
PLATZ, ANNA	17	F	UNKNOWN		GRZZZZUSA
JABLONSKI, CAROLINA	55	F	UNKNOWN		GRZZZZUSA
AUGUST	29	M	LABR		GRZZZZUSA
GUSTAV	4	M	CHILD		GRZZZZUSA
JOHANNE	.03	F	INFANT		GRZZZZUSA
FETTING, FRANZ	33	M	MSN		GRZZZZUSA
WILHELMINE	42	F	W		GRZZZZUSA
LOUISE	77	F	UNKNOWN		GRZZZZUSA
AUGUST	7	M	CHILD		GRZZZZUSA
WILHELM	5	M	CHILD		GRZZZZUSA
HERMANN	3	M	CHILD		GRZZZZUSA
CARL	1	M	CHILD		GRZZZZUSA
BINASZESKA, JOSEPHA	24	F	UNKNOWN		GRZZZZUSA
JOSEPH	5	M	CHILD		GRZZZZUSA
JOHANN	2	M	CHILD		GRZZZZUSA
LEYK, KAROLINE	33	F	UNKNOWN		GRZZZZUSA
ADAM	6	M	CHILD		GRZZZZUSA
MINNA	4	F	CHILD		GRZZZZUSA
FRIEDR	2	M	CHILD		GRZZZZUSA
GOTTLIEB	.04	M	INFANT		GRZZZZUSA
BECKER, FRIEDR	53	M	FARMER		GRZZZZBAL
CAROLINE	53	F	W		GRZZZZBAL
JULIUS	7	M	CHILD		GRZZZZBAL
HULDA	5	F	CHILD		GRZZZZBAL
EDUARD	3	M	CHILD		GRZZZZBAL
REINHOLD	2	M	CHILD		GRZZZZBAL
FRIEDR	25	M	FARMER		GRZZZZBAL
WILH	27	F	W		GRZZZZBAL
FRIEDR	6	M	CHILD		GRZZZZBAL
AUGUST	2	M	CHILD		GRZZZZBAL
CARL	.06	M	INFANT		GRZZZZBAL
RODA, FRANZ	6	M	CHILD		GRZZZZBAL
CZENSTOCHOSKI, FELIX	36	M	LABR		GRZZZZBAL
MARIE	26	F	W		GRZZZZBAL
JOSEF	3	M	CHILD		GRZZZZBAL
JOHANN	.11	M	INFANT		GRZZZZBAL
WARNHOLZ, AUGUST	33	M	DYR		GRZZZZBAL
AMMENDA, JOHN	39	M	JNR		GRZZZZBAL
MALINOWSKY, FRANZ	35	M	LABR		GRZZZZBAL
MARIE	32	F	W		GRZZZZBAL
MARIE	7	F	CHILD		GRZZZZBAL
ANASTASIA	5	F	CHILD		GRZZZZBAL
ANNA	3	F	CHILD		GRZZZZBAL
STEFAN	1	M	CHILD		GRZZZZBAL
ROSALIE	.02	F	INFANT		GRZZZZBAL
BANK, FRIEDR	42	M	FARMER		GRZZZZBAL
LINA	39	F	W		GRZZZZBAL
RUDOLF	6	M	CHILD		GRZZZZBAL
LINA	5	F	CHILD		GRZZZZBAL
KAROLINE	3	F	CHILD		GRZZZZBAL
MARTHA	2	F	CHILD		GRZZZZBAL
ALBERT	.09	M	INFANT		GRZZZZBAL
CHARLOTTE	.09	F	INFANT		GRZZZZBAL
HARING, MARIE	22	F	CK		GRZZZZBAL
PALUCZAK, MICHALINA	38	F	UNKNOWN		GRZZZZBAL
ADAM	.05	M	INFANT		GRZZZZBAL
BARTODZIG, HELENE	22	F	UNKNOWN		GRZZZZBAL
KUCHORCZYK, STEPHAN	27	M	LABR		GRZZZZBAL
STEPHAN	.09	M	INFANT		GRZZZZBAL
BARTTODZIE, THOMAS	29	M	LABR		GRZZZZBAL
MARIA	27	F	W		GRZZZZBAL
JOSEF	.07	F	INFANT		GRZZZZBAL
RADKE, JACOB	56	M	FARMER		GRZZZZBAL
HERM	16	M	FARMER		GRZZZZBAL
FRANZ	7	M	CHILD		GRZZZZBAL
HULDA	5	F	CHILD		GRZZZZBAL
AUGUSTE	37	F	W		GRZZZZBAL
ERDMANN, GUST	23	M	SMH		GRZZZZBAL
KOHL, GOTTL	23	M	SDLR		GRZZZZBAL
MEIER, MARG	30	F	UNKNOWN		GRZZZZBAL
JOHANN	30	M	LABR		GRZZZZBAL
SCHRAML, MARIA	41	F	UNKNOWN		GRZZZZBAL
JOSEF	6	M	CHILD		GRZZZZBAL
CAMILA	4	F	CHILD		GRZZZZBAL
MARIA	4	F	CHILD		GRZZZZBAL
FRANZ	2	M	CHILD		GRZZZZBAL
CARL	1	M	CHILD		GRZZZZBAL
MICHEL	.01	M	INFANT		GRZZZZBAL
SMANDZIK, FRANZ	24	M	PRNTR		GRZZZZIL
SGRAI, CHRISTIAN	26	M	LABR		GRZZZZIL
MANJURKA, FRANZ	21	F	UNKNOWN		GRZZZZIL
APELT, LOUISE	45	F	UNKNOWN		GRZZZZIL
PAURUCKER, FRANZ	48	M	LABR		GRZZZZWI
KANLEN, FERDIN	34	M	LABR		GRZZZZIA
PRZIREMBL, ROZALIE	33	F	UNKNOWN		GRZZZZIL
CARL	5	M	CHILD		GRZZZZIL
MARIE	2	F	CHILD		GRZZZZIL
LUDWIG	.09	M	INFANT		GRZZZZIL
BARTODZIG, JOSEF	44	M	LABR		GRZZZZIL
MARIA	38	F	W		GRZZZZIL
JOSEF	6	M	CHILD		GRZZZZIL
MARIA	4	F	CHILD		GRZZZZIL
DIECKS, CARL	30	M	LABR		GRZZZZBAL
LOUISE	30	F	W		GRZZZZBAL
HAUBOLD, ERNST	33	M	JNR		GRZZZZBAL
DOROTHEA	32	F	W		GRZZZZBAL
MARIA	4	F	CHILD		GRZZZZBAL
IDA	2	F	CHILD		GRZZZZBAL
WILH	.01	M	INFANT		GRZZZZBAL
LIHS, ANATASIA	22	F	UNKNOWN		GRZZZZBAL
DEMLER, MARTHA	24	F	UNKNOWN		GRZZZZBAL
PRANGA, FRANZ	29	F	UNKNOWN		GRZZZZBAL
JOHANN	6	M	CHILD		GRZZZZBAL
MARIE	3	F	CHILD		GRZZZZBAL

PASSENGER	AGE	SEX	OCCUPATION	PVL	DES
JULIUS	1	M	CHILD		GRZZZZBAL
JULIANE	.11	F	INFANT		GRZZZZBAL
DYBOWSKI, JOH	38	M	LABR		GRZZZZBAL
JULIANE	30	F	W		GRZZZZBAL
MARIE	6	F	CHILD		GRZZZZBAL
FRANZ	4	M	CHILD		GRZZZZBAL
LINDEMANN, FRANZ	16	M	FARMER		GRZZZZBAL
OTTILIE	15	F	FARMER		GRZZZZBAL
JOHN	51	M	FARMER		GRZZZZBAL
HANNE	49	F	W		GRZZZZBAL
WILH	5	F	CHILD		GRZZZZBAL
BERTHA	4	F	CHILD		GRZZZZBAL
LIESKE, LUKUCZYA	17	F	UNKNOWN		GRZZZZBAL
PIONKE, AUG	28	M	LABR		GRZZZZBAL
SUCHOWSKI, JOH	39	M	LABR		GRZZZZBAL
AUG	30	F	W		GRZZZZBAL
FREDERICH, CATH	24	F	UNKNOWN		GRZZZZBAL
FRIEDR	.01	M	INFANT		GRZZZZBAL
RUPNOW, FRIEDR	26	M	CPR		GRZZZZBAL
EMILIE	23	F	W		GRZZZZBAL
HERMANN	.04	M	INFANT		GRZZZZBAL
FRIEDR	64	M	LABR		GRZZZZBAL
CAROLINA	61	F	W		GRZZZZBAL
SCHMIDT, ALB	22	M	LABR		GRZZZZBAL
LORENZ, AUGUST	29	M	LABR		GRZZZZBAL
MARIA	27	F	W		GRZZZZBAL
ANNA	2	F	CHILD		GRZZZZBAL
HERM	.09	M	INFANT		GRZZZZBAL
FIERFOS, MARYANNA	20	F	UNKNOWN		GRZZZZBAL
PASZKIEWICZ, STANISLAUS	28	M	LABR		GRZZZZBAL
KUKLA, MICHAEL	70	M	LABR		GRZZZZBAL
GROSEINIAK, MARCIN	49	M	LABR		GRZZZZBAL
SATRUSZINKI, CARL	47	M	LABR		GRZZZZBAL
ANNA	47	F	W		GRZZZZBAL
ANNA	5	F	CHILD		GRZZZZBAL
AUGUSTE	3	F	CHILD		GRZZZZBAL
ERNST	.01	M	INFANT		GRZZZZBAL
LIMAN, MARIA	7	F	CHILD		GRZZZZBAL
BOETCHER, CARL	37	M	PNTR		GRZZZZBAL
AUGUSTE	37	F	W		GRZZZZBAL
LOUISE	50	F	UNKNOWN		GRZZZZBAL
AUGUST	7	M	CHILD		GRZZZZBAL
AUGUSTE	4	F	CHILD		GRZZZZBAL
ROBATZEK, EMILIE	25	F	UNKNOWN		GRZZZZBAL
WROBLEWSKI, JOH	40	M	FARMER		GRZZZZBAL
JOHANNA	34	F	W		GRZZZZBAL
FRANZ	6	F	CHILD		GRZZZZBAL
STANISLAUS	4	M	CHILD		GRZZZZBAL
JULIANE	.10	F	INFANT		GRZZZZBAL
FLORIAK, FRANSKA	20	M	CCHMN		GRZZZZBAL
URBAN, STANISLAUS	28	M	LABR		GRZZZZBAL
SIWAJEK, MICH	35	M	LABR		GRZZZZBAL
MARIANNE	26	F	W		GRZZZZBAL
FRANZ	7	F	CHILD		GRZZZZBAL
JOSEPHA	2	F	CHILD		GRZZZZBAL
JAN	.09	M	INFANT		GRZZZZBAL
URBAN, STANISL	6	M	CHILD		GRZZZZBAL
MILLBRODT, MARIA	18	F	UNKNOWN		GRZZZZBAL
HELENA	20	F	UNKNOWN		GRZZZZBAL
KACZMAREK, BOLESLAW	21	M	LABR		GRZZZZBAL
JEKEL, MARIE	28	F	W		GRZZZZBAL
HERMANN	.02	M	INFANT		GRZZZZBAL
KARKAN, WILH	38	F	UNKNOWN		GRZZZZBAL
PAULINE	3	F	CHILD		GRZZZZBAL
GUSTAV	.11	M	INFANT		GRZZZZUNK
KAPRINSKA, AGNISZKA	31	F	UNKNOWN		GRZZZZUSA
JOHANN	4	M	CHILD		GRZZZZUSA
MARQUARDT, CARL	45	M	FARMER		GRZZZZUSA
WILH	35	F	W		GRZZZZUSA
FRIEDR	7	M	CHILD		GRZZZZUSA
ADOLF	6	M	CHILD		GRZZZZUSA
EWALD	3	M	CHILD		GRZZZZUSA
OTTILIE	3	F	CHILD		GRZZZZUSA
EMILIE	2	F	CHILD		GRZZZZUSA
EMMA	.06	F	INFANT		GRZZZZUSA
SOBOLEWSKA, WILH	65	M	LABR		GRZZZZBAL
MARIA	35	F	UNKNOWN		GRZZZZBAL
FRANZ	.09	M	INFANT		GRZZZZBAL
MARQURDT, EDUARD	46	M	PNTR		GRZZZZBAL
ANNA	45	F	W		GRZZZZBAL
EDUARD	11	M	CH		GRZZZZBAL
ANNA	7	F	CHILD		GRZZZZBAL
POTTANG, CARL	42	M	FARMER		GRZZZZBAL
ANNA	41	F	W		GRZZZZBAL
ERNSTINE	7	F	CHILD		GRZZZZBAL
CAROLINE	5	F	CHILD		GRZZZZBAL
ANNA	2	F	CHILD		GRZZZZBAL
CARL	.10	M	INFANT		GRZZZZBAL
BERTHA	.10	F	INFANT		GRZZZZBAL
KUROWSKI, TOMASZ	38	M	LABR		GRZZZZBAL
GURSCHULA	28	F	W		GRZZZZBAL
GARTWIGA	5	F	CHILD		GRZZZZBAL
LUDWIKA	3	F	CHILD		GRZZZZBAL
MARIA	.01	F	INFANT		GRZZZZBAL
ORTMANN, JOH	17	M	CL		GRZZZZBAL
TSARMOK, THOMAS	28	M	LABR		GRZZZZBAL
MARIE	28	F	W		GRZZZZBAL
JOHANN	.11	M	INFANT		GRZZZZBAL
HAHN, WILH	29	M	LABR		GRZZZZBAL
EMIL	5	M	CHILD		GRZZZZBAL
SZEPANAK, JACOB	27	M	LABR		GRZZZZBAL
CATH	27	F	W		GRZZZZBAL
MARG	60	F	UNKNOWN		GRZZZZBAL
ANTONIA	30	F	UNKNOWN		GRZZZZBAL
JAN	.09	M	INFANT		GRZZZZBAL
JOSEPHA	.06	F	INFANT		GRZZZZBAL
NAPIERALSKI, JOSEF	23	M	LABR		GRZZZZBAL
NOWAK, WOJCIECH	30	M	LABR		GRZZZZBAL
VICTORIA	25	F	W		GRZZZZBAL
CATH	.06	F	INFANT		GRZZZZBAL
MIELKE, AUG	30	M	LABR		GRZZZZBAL
HTE	26	F	W		GRZZZZBAL
MARG	4	F	CHILD		GRZZZZBAL
WILH	.01	F	INFANT		GRZZZZBAL
WITKOPF, JOHANN	15	M	HTR		GRZZZZBAL
BEHNKE, JOHANNE	22	F	UNKNOWN		GRZZZZBAL
EICHMANN, FERD	23	M	JNR		GRZZZZBAL
CHUDOBBA, MICH	60	M	LABR		GRZZZZBAL
MATHILDE	29	F	UNKNOWN		GRZZZZBAL
BRZENINSKY, WALENTY	20	M	LABR		GRZZZZBAL
STRALL, GOTTLIEB	35	M	FARMER		GRZZZZBAL
LOUISE	28	F	W		GRZZZZBAL
EMILIE	7	F	CHILD		GRZZZZBAL
EMIL	4	M	CHILD		GRZZZZBAL
FRIEDR	.06	M	INFANT		GRZZZZBAL
ZUBE, AUGUSTE	25	F	CK		GRZZZZBAL
PIETROWSKI, CARL	28	M	LABR		GRZZZZBAL
WACHS, PAULINE	16	F	UNKNOWN		GRZZZZBAL
BETHKE, FRIEDR	20	M	PNTR		GRZZZZBAL
LEBNISKI, WILH	26	M	MLR		GRZZZZBAL
LANGNER, JOH	26	M	BBR		GRZZZZBAL
AUGUSTE	29	F	W		GRZZZZBAL
FRANZ	2	M	CHILD		GRZZZZBAL
RUDOLF	.03	M	INFANT		GRZZZZUNK
RHODE, WILH	36	M	FRR		GRZZZZUSA
THERESE	34	F	W		GRZZZZUSA
FRANZ	.04	M	INFANT		GRZZZZUSA
ZYGOWSKA, JOH	23	M	LABR		GRZZZZUSA
BUCHHOLZ, WILH	32	M	LABR		GRZZZZUSA
BARKA, CLEMENTINE	18	F	UNKNOWN		GRZZZZUSA
DAHLKE, AGNES	21	F	UNKNOWN		GRZZZZUSA
VALESKI, JULIUS	25	M	LABR		GRZZZZUSA
MANING, ALBERT	38	M	LABR		GRZZZZUSA
NOREK, JOH	24	M	LABR		GRZZZZUSA
JULIANE	22	F	W		GRZZZZUSA
PRZYBYS, ANTON	30	M	LABR		GRZZZZUSA
MARIANNA	24	F	W		GRZZZZUSA
STANISLAW	.06	M	INFANT		GRZZZZUSA
WISNIEWSKI, JOSEF	45	M	LABR		GRZZZZUSA
LUKOWSKI, ADAM	27	M	LABR		GRZZZZUSA

PASSENGER	AGE	SEX	OCCUPATION	PRVL	DES
PRONDZINSKI, THOMAS	27	M	LABR	GRZZZZ	USA
VERONICA	21	F	W	GRZZZZ	USA
JOHANN	.06	M	INFANT	GRZZZZ	USA
ZABOROWSKI, JOSEPH	22	M	LABR	GRZZZZ	USA
MASGAJ, MICHAEL	27	M	LABR	GRZZZZ	USA
MASKOWSKA, MARYANNA	33	F	UNKNOWN	GRZZZZ	USA
V, WILH	28	M	LABR	GRZZZZ	USA
MIELKE, GOTTL	58	M	LABR	GRZZZZ	WI
WANGERIN, WILH	24	M	LABR	GRZZZZ	WI
WILH	22	F	W	GRZZZZ	WI
EBENDT, AUG	16	M	CVR	GRZZZZ	IL
SCHENNEMANN, JOHANNA	23	F	CK	GRZZZZ	MI
MINNA	54	F	UNKNOWN	GRZZZZ	MI
MARZKE, ALBERT	30	M	PMBR	GRZZZZ	OH
ZALINSKI, ANTON	25	M	LABR	GRZZZZ	IL
CZARNOWSKI, MARTIN	25	M	LABR	GRZZZZ	IL
RYNGWELSKY, ANDTZY	29	M	LABR	GRZZZZ	IL
RYBOCZENSKI, MARTIN	28	M	LABR	GRZZZZ	NY
JULE	27	F	W	GRZZZZ	NY
LEWANDOWSKI, LORENZ	23	M	LABR	GRZZZZ	NY
TANDETZKI, IGNATZ	32	M	LABR	GRZZZZ	IL
MROSZIK, ANDRZY	29	M	LABR	GRZZZZ	IL
RATAJCZAK, JOH	27	M	LABR	GRZZZZ	IL
MUSIALOWSKI, JAN	30	M	LABR	GRZZZZ	IL
NOWAK, ANTONI	30	M	LABR	GRZZZZ	IL
ZAGIELSKA, STANISLAWA	23	F	UNKNOWN	GRZZZZ	IL
NEMITZ, MINNA	5	F	CHILD	GRZZZZ	WI
RUTZ, EMIL	15	M	CH	GRZZZZ	IL
PAWLAK, CARL	38	M	LABR	GRZZZZ	WI
HEBEL, FRANZ	60	M	LABR	GRZZZZ	IL
SCHMIDT, WILH	26	M	LABR	GRZZZZ	WI
SCHIMPF, CARL	21	M	LABR	GRZZZZ	WI
STANGE, MONIKA	24	F	UNKNOWN	GRZZZZ	WI
EBEL, ADOLF	26	M	LABR	GRZZZZ	IA
BAIER, MICH	16	M	LABR	GRZZZZ	IL
EICHHORN, JOH	27	M	LABR	GRZZZZ	IL
EGERER, JOH	28	M	LABR	GRZZZZ	IL
FISCHER, WOLFGANG	69	M	LABR	GRZZZZ	MN
MARG	68	F	W	GRZZZZ	MN
HOCHWART, SABINE	21	F	UNKNOWN	GRZZZZ	PA
BUTTGER, ESKE	46	M	UNKNOWN	GRZZZZ	BAL
LINA	5	F	CHILD	GRZZZZ	BAL
JOHANN	3	M	CHILD	GRZZZZ	BAL
CATH	1	F	CHILD	GRZZZZ	BAL
HERM	.02	M	INFANT	GRZZZZ	BAL
TOETGER, MAGD	20	F	UNKNOWN	GRZZZZ	BAL
HEIN	.11	M	INFANT	GRZZZZ	BAL
VEDDER, EMMA	25	F	UNKNOWN	GRZZZZ	BAL
BARCZYNSKI, JOHANN	25	M	LABR	GRZZZZ	BAL
MEYER, HEINR	35	M	LABR	GRZZZZ	BAL
KANNE, HEINR	47	M	LABR	GRZZZZ	BAL
HERMINE	4	F	CHILD	GRZZZZ	BAL
KUEHN, RICH	6	M	CHILD	GRZZZZ	BAL
WARNKE, WILH	62	F	UNKNOWN	GRZZZZ	BAL
NEUMANN, AUG	28	M	JNR	GRZZZZ	WI
EMILIE	21	F	W	GRZZZZ	WI
GUSTAV	.03	M	INFANT	GRZZZZ	WI
HARTMANN, CARL	63	M	FARMER	GRZZZZ	MN
HERMINE	26	F	UNKNOWN	GRZZZZ	MN
BASKE, JOSEF	29	M	LABR	GRZZZZ	MI
PAULINA	25	F	W	GRZZZZ	MI
EVA	.01	F	INFANT	GRZZZZ	MI
GORCZISZA, FRIEDR	57	M	LABR	GRZZZZ	MI
BERTHA	3	F	CHILD	GRZZZZ	MI
YARKE, WILH	41	F	UNKNOWN	GRZZZZ	BAL
HELENE	7	F	CHILD	GRZZZZ	BAL
FRANZ	5	M	CHILD	GRZZZZ	BAL
WILH	4	F	CHILD	GRZZZZ	BAL
OTTO	2	M	CHILD	GRZZZZ	BAL
GOTTLIEB	.01	M	INFANT	GRZZZZ	BAL
EILRICH, HERM	22	M	HTR	GRZZZZ	BAL
ZADY, EVA	36	F	UNKNOWN	GRZZZZ	BAL
JOHANN	9	M	CHILD	GRZZZZ	BAL
FRANZ	7	F	CHILD	GRZZZZ	BAL
ANTONIE	4	F	CHILD	GRZZZZ	BAL
JOHANN	2	M	CHILD	GRZZZZ	BAL
ANNA	1	F	CHILD	GRZZZZ	BAL
MICHEL	.04	M	INFANT	GRZZZZ	BAL
KOWALSKI, JAN	56	M	LABR	GRZZZZ	BAL
KATH	51	F	W	GRZZZZ	BAL
KOWALSKY, FRANZ	24	M	LABR	GRZZZZ	BAL
ANTON	19	M	LABR	GRZZZZ	BAL
WARDETZKA, JUSTINE	44	F	UNKNOWN	GRZZZZ	BAL
MEYER, GEORG	15	M	TU	GRZZZZ	BAL
SOYKE, MARIE	23	F	UNKNOWN	GRZZZZ	BAL
FETZLAFF, ALEX	22	M	LABR	GRZZZZ	BAL
EGGER, LOUISE	18	F	UNKNOWN	GRZZZZ	BAL
KOENIG, JOHANNE	16	F	UNKNOWN	GRZZZZ	BAL
KITTNER, THERESE	20	F	UNKNOWN	GRZZZZ	BAL
LIETZ, FERD	50	M	MLR	GRZZZZ	BAL
LOUISE	35	F	W	GRZZZZ	BAL
AUGUSTE	9	F	CHILD	GRZZZZ	BAL
AUGUST	7	M	CHILD	GRZZZZ	BAL
MATHILDE	6	F	CHILD	GRZZZZ	BAL
JULIUS	4	M	CHILD	GRZZZZ	BAL
GUSTAV	2	M	CHILD	GRZZZZ	BAL
IDA	.06	F	INFANT	GRZZZZ	BAL
BERTHA	20	F	UNKNOWN	GRZZZZ	BAL
TUCHOLKA, JOSEFA	28	F	UNKNOWN	GRZZZZ	BAL
LUECK, AUGUSTE	37	F	UNKNOWN	GRZZZZ	BAL
GENRICH, BERTHA	10	F	CH	GRZZZZ	BAL
LUECK, MARIE	6	F	CHILD	GRZZZZ	BAL
GRIMM, CHRIST	19	M	LABR	GRZZZZ	BAL
RAEHN, PETER	18	M	LABR	GRZZZZ	BAL
VOIGT, CARL	40	M	LABR	GRZZZZ	BAL
LOUISE	32	F	W	GRZZZZ	BAL
HERM	4	M	CHILD	GRZZZZ	BAL
MINNA	.01	F	INFANT	GRZZZZ	BAL
STUCKY, CATH	20	F	UNKNOWN	GRZZZZ	BAL
KLONICH, ANNA	15	F	UNKNOWN	GRZZZZ	BAL
BOUQUET, FRIEDR	18	M	LABR	GRZZZZ	BAL
NILHAS, CHRISTINA	18	F	UNKNOWN	GRZZZZ	BAL
ANKENER, CATH	50	F	UNKNOWN	GRZZZZ	BAL
CATH	7	F	CHILD	GRZZZZ	BAL
UDEN, WILH	43	M	FARMER	GRZZZZ	BAL
MINNA	46	F	W	GRZZZZ	BAL
ENGELINA	10	F	CH	GRZZZZ	BAL
WILHELM	6	M	CHILD	GRZZZZ	BAL
HILKE	4	F	CHILD	GRZZZZ	BAL
JACOB	1	M	CHILD	GRZZZZ	BAL
GRETHE	.02	F	INFANT	GRZZZZ	BAL
KUEHLER, HILKE	24	F	UNKNOWN	GRZZZZ	NE
LUETKE, ANNA	62	F	UNKNOWN	GRZZZZ	NE
WILLY	6	M	CHILD	GRZZZZ	NE
MUELLER, CARL	37	M	SDLR	GRZZZZ	IL
KRUSE, WILH	24	M	JNR	GRZZZZ	KS
DUERE, JOH	28	M	LABR	GRZZZZ	KS
OTTILIE	21	F	W	GRZZZZ	KS
BOSCH, JACOB	32	M	GDNR	GRZZZZ	KS
CAROLINE	30	F	W	GRZZZZ	KS
JACOB	4	M	CHILD	GRZZZZ	KS
EMILIE	2	F	CHILD	GRZZZZ	KS
EDUARD	1	M	CHILD	GRZZZZ	KS
ADINA	.02	F	INFANT	GRZZZZ	KS
WEIDNER, TH	24	M	HTR	GRZZZZ	MN
BEYER, JOH	54	M	SMH	GRZZZZ	MN
SCHAPER, HEINR	32	M	FARMER	GRZZZZ	BAL
CARL	27	M	FARMER	GRZZZZ	BAL
WILH	20	F	W	GRZZZZ	BAL
FRIEDR	.11	M	INFANT	GRZZZZ	BAL
LANGHALS, FRANZ	22	M	DYR	GRZZZZ	BAL
KOSUTTIS, MICH	33	M	LABR	GRZZZZ	MO
KOEHLER, MARIA	24	F	UNKNOWN	GRZZZZ	BAL
LOUISE	.06	F	INFANT	GRZZZZ	BAL
WOLFF, JOH	63	M	LABR	GRZZZZ	BAL
LANGHALS, JOH	24	M	JNR	GRZZZZ	BAL
KRANZ, SOPHIE	27	F	UNKNOWN	GRZZZZ	BAL
ERNET, WILH	31	M	FARMER	GRZZZZ	IN
WILH	29	F	W	GRZZZZ	IN
WILH	6	F	CHILD	GRZZZZ	IN

PASSENGER	AGE	SEX	OCCUPATION	PRVL	DES
EMMA	3	F	CHILD	GRZZZZIN	
CAROL	3	F	CHILD	GRZZZZIN	
EDUARD	2	M	CHILD	GRZZZZIN	
AUGUSTE	.11	F	INFANT	GRZZZZIN	
SCHAEFER, NICOLAUS	24	M	CPR	GRZZZZIL	
DORNERT, MARIA	32	F	UNKNOWN	GRZZZZBAL	
KOEHLER, ANNA	19	F	CK	GRZZZZKS	

SHIP: WISCONSIN

FROM: LIVERPOOL AND QUEENSTOWN
TO: NEW YORK
ARRIVED: 10 MAY 1888

PASSENGER	AGE	SEX	OCCUPATION	PRVL	DES
HENMANN, HEINRICH	31	M	FARMER	GRZZZZUSA	
FRANZISCA	28	F	W	GRZZZZUSA	
WINKLA, ROBITI	25	F	SP	GRZZZZUSA	
MIKELSOHN, CHAIE	24	F	W	GRZZZZUSA	
MASCHE	3	F	CHILD	GRZZZZUSA	
GOLDE	.10	F	INFANT	GRZZZZUSA	
KRINZKAS, JOS	36	M	LABR	GRZZZZUSA	
BAUER, JOHANN	16	M	PMBR	GRZZZZUSA	
CASSELBERG, AUG	28	M	FARMER	GRZZZZUSA	
ROSALIE	.08	F	INFANT	GRZZZZUSA	

SHIP: ITALY

FROM: LIVERPOOL AND QUEENSTOWN
TO: NEW YORK
ARRIVED: 11 MAY 1888

PASSENGER	AGE	SEX	OCCUPATION	PRVL	DES
BUCHE, J	44	M	LABR	GRACBFNY	
HERMAR, MARY	30	F	CNF	GRZZZZNY	

SHIP: ALLER

FROM: BREMEN AND SOUTHAMPTON
TO: NEW YORK
ARRIVED: 12 MAY 1888

PASSENGER	AGE	SEX	OCCUPATION	PRVL	DES
RIES--AT, A	40	M	RTR	GRZZZZUSA	
LOUISE	38	F	W	GRZZZZUSA	
-AHN, CLAUSSEN	45	M	OFF	GRZZZZUSA	
U, H	31	M	MCHT	GRZZZZUSA	
SCHRADER, V	18	M	MCHT	GRZZZZUSA	
BORNEMANN, MINNI	22	F	NN	GRZZZZUSA	
-----MACHER, U	24	F	NN	GRZZZZUSA	
----MUELLER, ------NT	23	M	MCHT	GRZZZZUSA	
V, FRITZ	23	M	MCHT	GRZZZZUSA	
LOEVENTHAL, MAX	20	M	MCHT	GRZZZZUSA	
STUCKE, OTTO	20	M	MCHT	GRZZZZUSA	
LIMKOS, ANDREAS	28	M	MCHT	GRZZZZUSA	
-HONAMUS, MARIE	60	F	NN	GRZZZZUSA	
MARIE	34	F	NN	GRZZZZUSA	
LUDWIG	32	M	NN	GRZZZZUSA	
-LIGER, CHRISTOF	70	M	MCHT	GRZZZZUSA	
----LOH, ELISABETH	20	F	NN	GRZZZZUSA	
---MING, GESINE	26	F	NN	GRZZZZUSA	
WEIL, LUDWIG	16	M	BRR	GRZZZZUSA	
MICHEL, LEONHARD	20	M	MCHT	GRZZZZUSA	

PASSENGER	AGE	SEX	OCCUPATION	PRVL	DES
HIRSCHFELD, ISIDOR	31	M	MCHT	GRZZZZUSA	
BORK, MAX	22	M	MCHT	GRZZZZUSA	
SAMMELS, MAGNUS	57	M	MCHT	GRZZZZUSA	
SCHNID--, HENRY	40	M	MCHT	GRZZZZUSA	
WI--Y, JOHN	20	M	MCHT	GRZZZZUSA	
B---N-M, GUSTAV	17	M	MCHT	GRZZZZUSA	
----BURG, HERMAN	50	M	MCHT	GRZZZZUSA	
CONCORDIA	50	F	W	GRZZZZUSA	
---MA	4	F	CHILD	GRZZZZUSA	
KIESSLING, ERNST	45	M	BRR	GRZZZZUSA	
SONDHIEM, -OEL	26	M	MCHT	GRZZZZUSA	
BENDKA	66	F	NN	GRZZZZUSA	
HAMBURGER, BABETTE	22	F	NN	GRZZZZUSA	
KUNTMANN, WILHELM	22	M	BCHR	GRZZZZUSA	
HUSCH, SIMON	15	M	MCHT	GRZZZZUSA	
KLEIN, JOSEF	22	M	MCHT	GRZZZZUSA	
GIESECKE, AGNES	20	F	NN	GRZZZZUSA	
HIRSCH, JULIE	20	F	NN	GRZZZZUSA	
-O--T-, WILHELM	24	M	MCHT	GRZZZZUSA	
BAER, MINNA	33	F	NN	GRZZZZUSA	
VICTOR	3	M	CHILD	GRZZZZUSA	
GERSTLE, RATZ-K	35	M	MCHT	GRZZZZUSA	
GRUBE, AUGUSTE	20	F	NN	GRZZZZUSA	
WEINSTEIN, MORRIS	25	M	BCHR	GRZZZZUSA	
MEYER, TILLY	17	F	NN	GRZZZZUSA	
--NEMANN, HEINRICH	16	M	FARMER	GRZZZZUSA	
CIEPINSKY, ANTON	19	M	FARMER	GRZZZZUSA	
RUSKE, GERHARD	38	M	FARMER	GRZZZZUSA	
-IENER, CARL	15	M	FARMER	GRZZZZUSA	
LANG, ANDREAS	20	M	BRR	GRZZZZUSA	
BERNHARE, JOSEF	26	M	BRR	GRZZZZUSA	
BAUER, EUGEN	32	M	BRR	GRZZZZUSA	
-EITER, GEORG	23	M	BCHR	GRZZZZUSA	
K-RBER, FRIDRICH	24	M	BCHR	GRZZZZUSA	
ZEI-EN-ASSER, WILHELM	25	M	FARMER	GRZZZZUSA	
-RIEG, CARL	20	M	FARMER	GRZZZZUSA	
BAN--, ANSELM	25	M	MCHT	GRZZZZUSA	
DECK, HEINR	18	M	FARMER	GRZZZZUSA	
KOERNER, FRANZ	16	M	FARMER	GRZZZZUSA	
STRANDBERG, HUGO	19	M	FARMER	GRZZZZUSA	
NELSON, CARL	32	M	FARMER	GRZZZZUSA	
SEEGERS, CHRISTIAN	15	M	BRR	GRZZZZUSA	
BISCHOFF, EMIL	68	M	BRR	GRZZZZUSA	
NIEMANN, FRITZ	16	M	BRR	GRZZZZUSA	
H--, JOSEF	40	M	BRR	GRZZZZUSA	
SCH----, SAHAN	33	M	FARMER	GRZZZZUSA	
NIEBANK, LUEDER	20	M	FARMER	GRZZZZUSA	
K-CKMANN, NICOLAUS	14	M	FARMER	GRZZZZUSA	
HO--IS, NICOLAUS	26	M	FARMER	GRZZZZUSA	
WE---ER, JOHAN	16	M	MCHT	GRZZZZUSA	
ERNST	14	M	MCHT	GRZZZZUSA	
BUECKER, JOHAN	23	M	MCHT	GRZZZZUSA	
VOGT, HEINRICH	25	M	MCHT	GRZZZZUSA	
SPECKER, HEINRICH	22	M	MCHT	GRZZZZUSA	
OBENDORF, HEINRICH	19	M	FARMER	GRZZZZUSA	
DANKENBRUEK, HEINRICH	50	M	FARMER	GRZZZZUSA	
WIND-ORST, WILHELM	16	M	FARMER	GRZZZZUSA	
MESSNER, CHRISTIAN	20	M	FARMER	GRZZZZUSA	
GREBE, GUSTAV	22	M	BCHR	GRZZZZUSA	
F-A--NG, JOHAN	16	M	BCHR	GRZZZZUSA	
BO--, PHILIPP	41	M	BCK	GRZZZZUSA	
-----ER, CARL	43	M	FARMER	GRZZZZUSA	
STEINHAGE, JOSEF	14	M	FARMER	GRZZZZUSA	
-AINA-T, HEINRICK	23	M	TLR	GRZZZZUSA	
SUSEBR-NK, FRIDRICH	27	M	TLR	GRZZZZUSA	
A-BACHER, JOHAN	61	M	TLR	GRZZZZUSA	
KURZ, JOHAN	16	M	TLR	GRZZZZUSA	
BAEHRINGER, FRIDRICH	14	M	FARMER	GRZZZZUSA	
HUEGEL, OSCAR	20	M	FARMER	GRZZZZUSA	
SCHLEGER, JACOB	24	M	FARMER	GRZZZZUSA	
STAHL, CONRAD	15	M	FARMER	GRZZZZUSA	
STEINKILBER, ABRAHAM	15	M	FARMER	GRZZZZUSA	
SAUER, MICHAEL	16	M	FARMER	GRZZZZUSA	
ZIEGLER, ERNST	17	M	FARMER	GRZZZZUSA	
KNAMER, FRIDRICH	15	M	FARMER	GRZZZZUSA	

PASSENGER	AGE	SEX	OCCUPATION	PRVL	DES
WEBER, AUGUST	16	M	BBR	GRZZZZUSA	
U, HEINRICH	16	M	BCHR	GRZZZZUSA	
WEBER, MICHAEL	31	M	FARMER	GRZZZZUSA	
FOR-TER, ANDREAS	18	M	FARMER	GRZZZZUSA	
DIEDRICH, ADOLPH	52	M	FARMER	GRZZZZUSA	
BINDER, HEINRICH	23	M	FARMER	GRZZZZUSA	
VALK, ARMIN	22	M	FARMER	GRZZZZUSA	
LOCHNER, FRIDRICH	4	M	CHILD	GRZZZZUSA	
ROTH, HEINRICH	39	M	BRR	GRZZZZUSA	
KOUSE, HERMAN	16	M	FARMER	GRZZZZUSA	
FRENNENT, CARL	18	M	FARMER	GRZZZZUSA	
SCHUECKER, HEINRICH	30	M	FARMER	GRZZZZUSA	
BAEHLER, JOSEF	36	M	FARMER	GRZZZZUSA	
WENDT, STENBEND	23	M	FARMER	GRZZZZUSA	
VOIGT, ADAM	22	M	FARMER	GRZZZZUSA	
GARLISCH, FRIDRICH	16	M	MCHT	GRZZZZUSA	
SIEMENACHT, DANIEL	25	M	MCHT	GRZZZZUSA	
STRAUSS, CARL	17	M	BRR	GRZZZZUSA	
THIEMIG, HERMAN	22	M	FARMER	GRZZZZUSA	
WILKEN, HEINRICH	28	M	FARMER	GRZZZZUSA	
BEHRMANN, FERDINAND	26	M	FARMER	GRZZZZUSA	
SCHEN--ER, EDUARD	24	M	FARMER	GRZZZZUSA	
SCHILD-TSKY, THEODOR	34	M	MCHT	GRZZZZUSA	
WENDERLICH, WILHELM	18	M	FARMER	GRZZZZUSA	
FEDER, JOSEF	7	M	CHILD	GRZZZZUSA	
HILL, JACOB	36	M	FARMER	GRZZZZUSA	
STUESSER, HEINRICH	6	M	CHILD	GRZZZZUSA	
BAH-MANN, FELIX	18	M	FARMER	GRZZZZUSA	
HERMANN, EUGEN	26	M	FARMER	GRZZZZUSA	
GIEBEL, FIUS	28	M	FARMER	GRZZZZUSA	
HUBER, CARL	25	M	BRR	GRZZZZUSA	
ST--ACH, FRANZ	16	M	FARMER	GRZZZZUSA	
SACK, GUSTAV	55	M	FARMER	GRZZZZUSA	
NIEDLING, JOHAN	30	M	FARMER	GRZZZZUSA	
STIERHAF, GEORG	32	M	BCK	GRZZZZUSA	
SCH-OER, HEINRICH	25	M	BCK	GRZZZZUSA	
MORNASCH, PETER	27	M	BCHR	GRZZZZUSA	
EUTER, HEINRICH	22	M	BCHR	GRZZZZUSA	
PETER	19	M	FARMER	GRZZZZUSA	
BEHRENS, HEINRICH	14	M	FARMER	GRZZZZUSA	
MEIER, HEINRICH	32	M	FARMER	GRZZZZUSA	
COSANKE, FRANZ	16	M	MCHT	GRZZZZUSA	
WIND-OR-E, FERDINAND	14	M	MCHT	GRZZZZUSA	
KNA--, ADOLF	18	M	MCHT	GRZZZZUSA	
KUEHNEL, JOSEF	23	M	MCHT	GRZZZZUSA	
ZEI----, PAUL	28	M	MCHT	GRZZZZUSA	
-ISSER, RUDOLPH	24	M	MCHT	GRZZZZUSA	
HARMS, HERMAN	20	M	MCHT	GRZZZZUSA	
T-PE, HEINRICH	26	M	MCHT	GRZZZZUSA	
STEFFENS, AUGUST	22	M	MCHT	GRZZZZUSA	
GREFE, HERMAN	18	M	BCHR	GRZZZZUSA	
S-INDLER, CARL	14	M	BCHR	GRZZZZUSA	
DIR-AM, PETER	19	M	TLR	GRZZZZUSA	
STETTER, GEORG	16	M	TLR	GRZZZZUSA	
SIEMERS, FRIDRICH	27	M	BRR	GRZZZZUSA	
BACHMEIER, JOSEF	17	M	BRR	GRZZZZUSA	
MUELLER, BERNHARD	28	M	FARMER	GRZZZZUSA	
SCHAEFER, JOHAN	32	M	FARMER	GRZZZZUSA	
DURNER, U	16	M	FARMER	GRZZZZUSA	
SCHMIDT, CARL	27	M	FARMER	GRZZZZUSA	
MEYER, DIEDRICH	16	M	FARMER	GRZZZZUSA	
WILD, ALOIS	27	M	FARMER	GRZZZZUSA	
SCHUSTER, PETER	24	M	FARMER	GRZZZZUSA	
SOMMER, FRANZ	46	M	FARMER	GRZZZZUSA	
DREIMANN, RUDOLPH	23	M	MCHT	GRZZZZUSA	
MUELLER, HERMAN	25	M	MCHT	GRZZZZUSA	
FLEU--, CARL	26	M	MCHT	GRZZZZUSA	
KERWIN, CARL	35	M	MCHT	GRZZZZUSA	
BRENNE, AUGUST	50	M	MCHT	GRZZZZUSA	
CARL	15	M	FARMER	GRZZZZUSA	
SALINGER, DAVID	30	M	FARMER	GRZZZZUSA	
STARK, AUGUST	18	M	FARMER	GRZZZZUSA	
HILDEBRAND, NICOLAUS	23	M	FARMER	GRZZZZUSA	
-ARKE, HEINRICH	23	M	FARMER	GRZZZZUSA	
HEINBERCKEL, JOHAN	16	M	FARMER	GRZZZZUSA	
LANDERS, FRITZ	21	M	BCK	GRZZZZUSA	
KNEWZWIES, MICHAEL	24	M	BCHR	GRZZZZUSA	
DEILE, JACOB	17	M	BCHR	GRZZZZUSA	
KNOCKER, FRANZ	45	M	TLR	GRZZZZUSA	
BACH, AUGUST	25	M	FARMER	GRZZZZUSA	
KLEMMER, JULIUS	53	M	FARMER	GRZZZZUSA	
KLOSE, WILHELM	42	M	FARMER	GRZZZZUSA	
LESHZINGER, -ONIS	27	M	FARMER	GRZZZZUSA	
WESTPHAL, BERNHARD	16	M	FARMER	GRZZZZUSA	
UHLERS, JOHAN	16	M	FARMER	GRZZZZUSA	
WINTER, WILHELM	14	M	FARMER	GRZZZZUSA	
MUELLER, HEINRICH	16	M	FARMER	GRZZZZUSA	
CONRAD	17	M	FARMER	GRZZZZUSA	
GUSTAV	19	M	MCHT	GRZZZZUSA	
B--R, GEORG	28	M	UNKNOWN	GRZZZZUSA	
--THAAL, WILHELM	29	M	TLR	GRZZZZUSA	
EINHAUS, WILHELM	27	M	TLR	GRZZZZUSA	
--KE, JOHAN	17	M	BCHR	GRZZZZUSA	
-SE, JOHAN	18	M	BRR	GRZZZZUSA	
---CKELMANN, GEORG	14	M	BRR	GRZZZZUSA	
--TJEN, FIDEL	32	M	BCK	GRZZZZUSA	
JOHAN	36	M	BCK	GRZZZZUSA	
NEO--A, ANDRES	32	M	FARMER	GRZZZZUSA	
SU-ANIK, JOHAN	39	M	FARMER	GRZZZZUSA	
RUDAN, JOHAN	23	M	FARMER	GRZZZZUSA	
TATONIK, JOHAN	26	M	FARMER	GRZZZZUSA	
WANGER, GIORGI	42	M	FARMER	GRZZZZUSA	
WASKO, ANDREAS	18	M	FARMER	GRZZZZUSA	
RAEHLING, HEINRICH	36	M	GDNR	GRZZZZUSA	
ABETS, EDUARD	22	M	GDNR	GRZZZZUSA	
KAMMEYER, JOHAN	38	M	MCHT	GRZZZZUSA	
KI----E, JOHAN	23	M	MCHT	GRZZZZUSA	
-ESER, ERNST	14	M	FARMER	GRZZZZUSA	
-TEIN, WILHELM	18	M	FARMER	GRZZZZUSA	
TENFEL, HERMAN	30	M	FARMER	GRZZZZUSA	
--RENS, ADOLF	18	M	BCHR	GRZZZZUSA	
--NOSBAUER, CARL	25	M	BRR	GRZZZZUSA	
--OEDTEL, WILHELM	16	M	BCK	GRZZZZUSA	
GETKEN, HERMAN	15	M	SLR	GRZZZZUSA	
--TENSSEN, HEINRICH	26	M	FARMER	GRZZZZUSA	
BICH-ER, MARY	22	F	NN	GRZZZZUSA	
-IRCH, ANNA	25	F	NN	GRZZZZUSA	
-ETJEN, ANNA	19	F	NN	GRZZZZUSA	
EDEL, THERESE	30	F	NN	GRZZZZUSA	
GLESSMANN, WEHE	22	F	NN	GRZZZZUSA	
ENGELHARDT, MARIE	31	F	NN	GRZZZZUSA	
ME--NER, GIORGINE	18	F	NN	GRZZZZUSA	
-EUER, RUTH	15	F	NN	GRZZZZUSA	
KLENK, META	17	F	NN	GRZZZZUSA	
-I-EBRANER, CATHRINE	15	F	NN	GRZZZZUSA	
GRAVENSTETTER, LOUISE	23	F	NN	GRZZZZUSA	
--TTEND, AUGUSTE	19	F	NN	GRZZZZUSA	
SCHMIDTMANN, CAROLINE	20	F	NN	GRZZZZUSA	
BAUER, LOUISE	25	F	NN	GRZZZZUSA	
LA---, ELISE	22	F	NN	GRZZZZUSA	
--LAM, APPOLONIA	23	F	NN	GRZZZZUSA	
STEIN---ILBER, MARIE	21	F	NN	GRZZZZUSA	
S--CHER, CHRISTINE	21	F	NN	GRZZZZUSA	
LIN---ANN, ANNA	17	F	NN	GRZZZZUSA	
U--R, WILHELMINE	18	F	NN	GRZZZZUSA	
KU---, MARIE	18	F	NN	GRZZZZUSA	
ROEH---GER, CATI	15	F	NN	GRZZZZUSA	
STE---, EVA	22	F	NN	GRZZZZUSA	
GREM--STMEYER, MINNA	27	F	NN	GRZZZZUSA	
SCH--GER, CATHI	65	F	NN	GRZZZZUSA	
HU--ER, EVA	20	F	NN	GRZZZZUSA	
--MIDA, BARBARA	25	F	NN	GRZZZZUSA	
-UTZ, EMMA	22	F	NN	GRZZZZUSA	
HOEHM, ROSINE	20	F	NN	GRZZZZUSA	
ZIEGLER, LOUISE	17	F	NN	GRZZZZUSA	
MAIER, FRIDRIKE	25	F	NN	GRZZZZUSA	
OCKERMANN, CAROLINE	18	F	NN	GRZZZZUSA	
--AMME, PAULINE	19	F	NN	GRZZZZUSA	
BUEHM, MARIE	17	F	NN	GRZZZZUSA	
SCHAEFER, MARIE	24	F	NN	GRZZZZUSA	

PASSENGER	AGE	SEX	OCCUPATION	PRVL	DES
BEYER, CAROLINE	24	F	NN	GRZZZZ	USA
BLUMENSTEIN, EVA	18	F	NN	GRZZZZ	USA
HUEBLER, BERTHA	21	F	NN	GRZZZZ	USA
ULLRICH, THEODORE	24	F	NN	GRZZZZ	USA
FAUST, MARIE	7	F	CHILD	GRZZZZ	USA
SCHOCH, LOUISE	25	F	CH	GRZZZZ	USA
KNAPP, CHRISTINE	25	F	CH	GRZZZZ	USA
ARBELE, THERESE	27	F	CH	GRZZZZ	USA
ROTH, ANNA	47	F	CH	GRZZZZ	USA
FRIDRICH, MARIE	14	F	CH	GRZZZZ	USA
MUELLER, AUGUSTE	20	F	CH	GRZZZZ	USA
--AFF, BARBARA	42	F	CH	GRZZZZ	USA
SAN---, MARIE	23	F	CH	GRZZZZ	USA
HA--EIS, JENNY	15	F	CH	GRZZZZ	USA
-----NNDS, JOSEPHA	20	F	CH	GRZZZZ	USA
G-----MANN, CATHI	21	F	CH	GRZZZZ	USA
NE---S, ANNA	54	F	CH	GRZZZZ	USA
HENMUELLER, ANNA	20	F	CH	GRZZZZ	USA
MAEBUS, CATHI	18	F	CH	GRZZZZ	USA
MUTH, ELISE	26	F	CH	GRZZZZ	USA
NEUSCHAEFER, MARIE	30	F	CH	GRZZZZ	USA
EGGERT, MARIE	20	F	CH	GRZZZZ	USA
KESSLER, ANNETTE	26	F	CH	GRZZZZ	USA
SCHWAB, ELISE	24	F	CH	GRZZZZ	USA
PETERSEN, ELISE	23	F	CH	GRZZZZ	USA
M--, PHILIPPA	22	F	CH	GRZZZZ	USA
BENTRAM, JOHANNE	30	F	CH	GRZZZZ	USA
ROTHSCHILD, SINA	15	F	CH	GRZZZZ	USA
BISCHER, ANNA	16	F	CH	GRZZZZ	USA
CO--ES, MARIE	16	F	CH	GRZZZZ	USA
U--TI, BERTHA	21	F	CH	GRZZZZ	USA
--NG, FRANCISCA	19	F	CH	GRZZZZ	USA
BOCK, MARIE	7	F	CHILD	GRZZZZ	USA
NEV, ANNA	55	F	NN	GRZZZZ	USA
HO--, AMALIE	23	F	NN	GRZZZZ	USA
CATHI	26	F	NN	GRZZZZ	USA
-ERBST, PHILOMETA	32	F	NN	GRZZZZ	USA
----TE, JOHANNE	27	F	NN	GRZZZZ	USA
--GE, HEDWIG	19	F	NN	GRZZZZ	USA
D-HME, META	7	F	CHILD	GRZZZZ	USA
BRAUN, MARIE	20	F	NN	GRZZZZ	USA
LUEBECK, BERTHA	18	F	NN	GRZZZZ	USA
FRENN-, MAGDA	21	F	NN	GRZZZZ	USA
KATHEL, MARIE	27	F	NN	GRZZZZ	USA
HOFFMANN, CATHI	20	F	NN	GRZZZZ	USA
KINZENBERG, JOHANNE	58	F	NN	GRZZZZ	USA
NEUBERGER, EMMA	23	F	NN	GRZZZZ	USA
ITZEL, CLAUDIEN	7	F	CHILD	GRZZZZ	USA
EL---, ANNA	15	F	CH	GRZZZZ	USA
---EL, CHRISTINE	15	F	CH	GRZZZZ	USA
AU---KA, MARIA	22	F	CH	GRZZZZ	USA
WEN--, LUCIE	37	F	CH	GRZZZZ	USA
WEISSB-NDT, --ONA	20	F	CH	GRZZZZ	USA
HAMMER, HELENE	22	F	CH	GRZZZZ	USA
HANSEN, MARIE	22	F	CH	GRZZZZ	USA
SIGMONDE, ANTONIE	50	F	CH	GRZZZZ	USA
KRAETE, ELISE	19	F	CH	GRZZZZ	USA
HEISE, WILHELME	6	F	CHILD	GRZZZZ	USA
SUNDMACHER, ELISE	19	F	NN	GRZZZZ	USA
SA-E, -ETCHEN	24	F	NN	GRZZZZ	USA
FICK, ANNA	20	F	NN	GRZZZZ	USA
WA-NCKE, AMALIE	21	F	NN	GRZZZZ	USA
KUECKEN, MARIE	15	F	NN	GRZZZZ	USA
-ECKER, WILHELME	21	F	NN	GRZZZZ	USA
----SEN, GESINE	21	F	NN	GRZZZZ	USA
M----ELS, EMMA	17	F	NN	GRZZZZ	USA
BEIMBRUECK, ANNA	58	F	NN	GRZZZZ	USA
BROCKMANN, ANNA	21	F	NN	GRZZZZ	USA
BLENDERMANN, META	28	F	NN	GRZZZZ	USA
BEN-ER, MAGDA	24	F	NN	GRZZZZ	USA
CATHI	22	F	NN	GRZZZZ	USA
BERBI--E, SOPHIE	20	F	NN	GRZZZZ	USA
-ESCHMACHER, GESINE	14	F	NN	GRZZZZ	USA
WEI--AUCH, AMALIE	23	F	NN	GRZZZZ	USA
PAULINE	20	F	NN	GRZZZZ	USA
KE--S, MARIE	6	F	CHILD	GRZZZZ	USA
-----ER, PELAGIA	17	F	NN	GRZZZZ	USA
LEOCADIA	15	F	NN	GRZZZZ	USA
----SS, HELENE	28	F	NN	GRZZZZ	USA
G----ERE, CAROLA	22	F	NN	GRZZZZ	USA
W-----S, HELENE	24	F	NN	GRZZZZ	USA
U, VICTORIA	39	F	NN	GRZZZZ	USA
H-----KENBACH, JOHANNE	17	F	NN	GRZZZZ	USA
THERESE	20	F	NN	GRZZZZ	USA
ROSE, MARIE	7	F	CHILD	GRZZZZ	USA
BONE, BERTHA	14	F	NN	GRZZZZ	USA
HORMANN, LOUISE	12	F	CH	GRZZZZ	USA
KUEMMER, MARIE	22	F	NN	GRZZZZ	USA
STRUSS, ANNA	23	F	NN	GRZZZZ	USA
MAIC--NA, MARIE	24	F	NN	GRZZZZ	USA
JAN	.11	M	INFANT	GRZZZZ	USA
GRASS, HEINRICH	27	M	FARMER	GRZZZZ	USA
FRANCISCA	23	F	W	GRZZZZ	USA
FRIDA	.09	F	INFANT	GRZZZZ	USA
WEIMAR, THEODOR	41	M	FARMER	GRZZZZ	USA
PHILIPPA	38	F	W	GRZZZZ	USA
FRIDA	7	F	CHILD	GRZZZZ	USA
LORENZ	6	M	CHILD	GRZZZZ	USA
MARIE	5	F	CHILD	GRZZZZ	USA
D---ARELT, JOHAN	31	M	FARMER	GRZZZZ	USA
MARIE	27	F	W	GRZZZZ	USA
ANNA	5	F	CHILD	GRZZZZ	USA
MARIE	3	F	CHILD	GRZZZZ	USA
WOLFGANG	.10	M	INFANT	GRZZZZ	USA
--IG, PHILIPP	26	M	MCHT	GRZZZZ	USA
CAROLINE	27	F	W	GRZZZZ	USA
OSTER--AN-, CLAUS	44	M	FARMER	GRZZZZ	USA
ANNA	46	F	W	GRZZZZ	USA
CORNELIUS	10	M	CH	GRZZZZ	USA
PAULINE	7	F	CHILD	GRZZZZ	USA
ANDREAS	6	M	CHILD	GRZZZZ	USA
WILHELM	.06	M	INFANT	GRZZZZ	USA
-----TEL, MAX	37	M	MCHT	GRZZZZ	USA
JENNY	32	F	W	GRZZZZ	USA
OTTO	5	M	CHILD	GRZZZZ	USA
RICHARD	.06	M	INFANT	GRZZZZ	USA
HELKER, HEINRICH	23	M	FARMER	GRZZZZ	USA
CATHI	22	F	W	GRZZZZ	USA
KRONCKE, MALVINE	38	F	NN	GRZZZZ	USA
DORA	7	F	CHILD	GRZZZZ	USA
NEURICH, JACOB	26	M	GDNR	GRZZZZ	USA
CHRISTINE	25	F	W	GRZZZZ	USA
CARL	.05	M	INFANT	GRZZZZ	USA
FEIS, PHILIPINE	47	F	NN	GRZZZZ	USA
HEINRICH	21	M	NN	GRZZZZ	USA
PHILIPP	18	M	NN	GRZZZZ	USA
ELISABETH	7	F	CHILD	GRZZZZ	USA
BARBARA	6	F	CHILD	GRZZZZ	USA
APOLONIA	4	F	CHILD	GRZZZZ	USA
WALTHER	.04	M	INFANT	GRZZZZ	USA
TRAUB, CHRISTOPH	28	M	FARMER	GRZZZZ	USA
CAROLINE	28	F	W	GRZZZZ	USA
FRIDRIKE	3	F	CHILD	GRZZZZ	USA
WILHELME	.11	F	INFANT	GRZZZZ	USA
CAROLINE	.11	F	INFANT	GRZZZZ	USA
SABKE, HERMAN	35	M	FARMER	GRZZZZ	USA
AUGUSTE	32	F	W	GRZZZZ	USA
BERTHA	5	F	CHILD	GRZZZZ	USA
ERNESTINE	3	F	CHILD	GRZZZZ	USA
GUSTAV	25	M	NN	GRZZZZ	USA
CAROLINE	69	F	NN	GRZZZZ	USA
MON--EN, WILHELM	50	M	GDNR	GRZZZZ	USA
MARIE	44	F	W	GRZZZZ	USA
BERTHA	7	F	CHILD	GRZZZZ	USA
ANNA	6	F	CHILD	GRZZZZ	USA
PAUL	5	M	CHILD	GRZZZZ	USA
HERMAN	.09	M	INFANT	GRZZZZ	USA
H-----, ERNST	00	M	FARMER	GRZZZZ	USA
WILHELME	24	F	W	GRZZZZ	USA
BERNHARD	.06	M	INFANT	GRZZZZ	USA

PASSENGER	AGE	SEX	OCCUPATION	PRVL	DES
LEEMANN, CHRISTIAN	64	M	MCHT	GRZZZZ	USA
DOROTHEA	53	F	W	GRZZZZ	USA
HADEM--, CHRISTIANE	58	F	NN	GRZZZZ	USA
CATHI	16	F	NN	GRZZZZ	USA
HOOPS, HINRICH	56	M	FARMER	GRZZZZ	USA
EMMA	7	F	CHILD	GRZZZZ	USA
MINNA	.06	F	INFANT	GRZZZZ	USA
SZ---EWSKY, PAULINE	23	F	NN	GRZZZZ	USA
LOUISE	.06	F	INFANT	GRZZZZ	USA
FU----, MARIE	43	F	NN	GRZZZZ	USA
THERESE	20	F	NN	GRZZZZ	USA
MINNA	16	F	NN	GRZZZZ	USA
FERDINAND	7	M	CHILD	GRZZZZ	USA
FRIDRICH	6	M	CHILD	GRZZZZ	USA
FRANZ	5	M	CHILD	GRZZZZ	USA
EMMA	2	F	CHILD	GRZZZZ	USA
IDA	.10	F	INFANT	GRZZZZ	USA
-AUCH, EMIL	34	M	FARMER	GRZZZZ	USA
EMILIE	30	F	W	GRZZZZ	USA
JOSEF	7	M	CHILD	GRZZZZ	USA
WILD, FERDINAND	36	M	FARMER	GRZZZZ	USA
MARIE	30	F	W	GRZZZZ	USA
EMIL	7	M	CHILD	GRZZZZ	USA
MARTHA	6	F	CHILD	GRZZZZ	USA
ALBERT	4	M	CHILD	GRZZZZ	USA
ELISABETH	.09	F	INFANT	GRZZZZ	USA
RAL--, SOPHIE	39	F	NN	GRZZZZ	USA
LUDWIG	16	M	NN	GRZZZZ	USA
BERTHA	14	F	NN	GRZZZZ	USA
L------, ALFRED	31	M	FARMER	GRZZZZ	USA
CATHRINE	26	F	W	GRZZZZ	USA
M---ZAHR, ADOLPH	40	M	BRR	GRZZZZ	USA
ROSA	34	F	W	GRZZZZ	USA
CATHRINE	7	F	CHILD	GRZZZZ	USA
U	.06	F	INFANT	GRZZZZ	USA
HEI---CHNER, ALBAN	31	M	FARMER	GRZZZZ	USA
SOPHIE	33	F	W	GRZZZZ	USA
MARIE	3	F	CHILD	GRZZZZ	USA
EMMA	.09	F	INFANT	GRZZZZ	USA
SCHMIDT, CATHRINE	22	F	NN	GRZZZZ	USA
MARIE	16	F	NN	GRZZZZ	USA
CAROLINE	6	F	CHILD	GRZZZZ	USA
ZWEINER, IDA	34	F	NN	GRZZZZ	USA
ELFRIDE	.02	F	INFANT	GRZZZZ	USA
BERKOWITZ, -AUBE	22	F	NN	GRZZZZ	USA
MOESCHE	7	F	CHILD	GRZZZZ	USA
LEIB	3	M	CHILD	GRZZZZ	USA
SALLY	.09	F	INFANT	GRZZZZ	USA
WEISSKAMPF, HULDA	27	F	NN	GRZZZZ	USA
HERMAN	.11	M	INFANT	GRZZZZ	USA
BAUMENT, CARL	28	M	FARMER	GRZZZZ	USA
ANNA	23	F	W	GRZZZZ	USA
-LMA	2	F	CHILD	GRZZZZ	USA
KLARA	.06	F	INFANT	GRZZZZ	USA
HEDWIG	.06	F	INFANT	GRZZZZ	USA
MEIER, SOPHIE	25	F	NN	GRZZZZ	USA
HEINRICH	.11	M	INFANT	GRZZZZ	USA
-LATHMANN, JOHAN	63	M	FARMER	GRZZZZ	USA
GESCHE	63	F	W	GRZZZZ	USA
HARMS, CLAUS	38	M	FARMER	GRZZZZ	USA
CATHI	35	F	W	GRZZZZ	USA
JOHAN	7	M	CHILD	GRZZZZ	USA
CLAUS	.10	M	INFANT	GRZZZZ	USA
ROEHRS, WILHELM	46	M	GDNR	GRZZZZ	USA
CHRISTINE	41	F	W	GRZZZZ	USA
MARIE	7	F	CHILD	GRZZZZ	USA
MINNA	.06	F	INFANT	GRZZZZ	USA
EMMA	.06	F	INFANT	GRZZZZ	USA
GIETZEN, CATHI	44	F	NN	GRZZZZ	USA
CATHI	18	F	NN	GRZZZZ	USA
MARIE	7	F	CHILD	GRZZZZ	USA
JOSEF	.06	M	INFANT	GRZZZZ	USA
BERNHARDT, ROSA	48	F	NN	GRZZZZ	USA
MARIE	22	F	NN	GRZZZZ	USA
MINNA	20	F	NN	GRZZZZ	USA

PASSENGER	AGE	SEX	OCCUPATION	PRVL	DES
-----WSKY, ROBERT	35	M	FARMER	GRZZZZ	USA
LOUISE	30	F	W	GRZZZZ	USA
LOUISE	7	F	CHILD	GRZZZZ	USA
EMILIE	5	F	CHILD	GRZZZZ	USA
FRIDA	.04	F	INFANT	GRZZZZ	USA
TREUSS, WILHELME	38	F	NN	GRZZZZ	USA
LOUISE	7	F	CHILD	GRZZZZ	USA
OTTO	6	M	CHILD	GRZZZZ	USA
HERMINE	3	F	CHILD	GRZZZZ	USA
CARL	2	M	CHILD	GRZZZZ	USA
EMILIE	.09	F	INFANT	GRZZZZ	USA
BECKER, CONRAD	50	M	MCHT	GRZZZZ	USA
ANNA	18	F	CH	GRZZZZ	USA
HERMAN	6	M	CHILD	GRZZZZ	USA
BAUER, CATHRINE	41	F	NN	GRZZZZ	USA
ROSINE	15	F	NN	GRZZZZ	USA
CATHI	7	F	CHILD	GRZZZZ	USA
CAROLINE	7	F	CHILD	GRZZZZ	USA
JACOB	6	M	CHILD	GRZZZZ	USA
WILHELMINE	.11	F	INFANT	GRZZZZ	USA
OBERMEYER, CHARLES	27	M	MCHT	GRZZZZ	USA

SHIP: BOHEMIA

FROM: HAMBURG AND HAVRE
TO: NEW YORK
ARRIVED: 12 MAY 1888

PASSENGER	AGE	SEX	OCCUPATION	PRVL	DES
OTT, FRIEDRICH	25	M	FARMER	PRZZZZ	NY
KRUEGER, AUGUSTE	24	F	SGL	PRZZZZ	NY
MOHRMANN, AUGUST	37	M	LKSH	MKZZZZ	NY
JONAS, JOH	17	M	BKR	MKAIAH	NY
MRACH, WILHELMINE	50	F	WO	MKAHAE	NY
JOLKMANN, AUGUSTE	23	F	SGL	MKAHAE	NY
BERTHA	17	F	SGL	MKAHAE	NY
SUPLE, FERD	42	M	UNKNOWN	MKAAKH	NY
THUMA, AMALIA	28	F	UNKNOWN	PRZZZZ	NY
RUBIEN, EMILIE	9	F	CHILD	HBZZZZ	NY
PLOTZKI, EMIL	24	M	FARMER	HBAICN	IL
VOLLMAR, EMIL	28	M	BRR	HBAIES	OH
DYSCHINSKY, THOMAS	22	M	TLR	PRZZZZ	OH
KOPERA, JAN	22	M	UNKNOWN	PRZZZZ	OH
KONZAL, VALENTIN	31	M	UNKNOWN	PRZZZZ	OH
SPRAWA, IGNATZ	22	M	UNKNOWN	PRZZZZ	OH
OTTO, ANT	30	M	UNKNOWN	PRACWL	BUF
CZARNETZKI, DOMINIK	34	M	UNKNOWN	PRZZZZ	BUF
SCHIRNDING, ADALBERT	24	M	MCHT	PRADRO	BUF
JAN	65	M	LABR	PRADRO	BUF
WACISZAK, KATH	21	F	SGL	PRADRO	BUF
GABRIEL, EUGENE	17	M	WCHMKR	PRAGCH	BUF
LEO	15	M	UNKNOWN	PRAGCH	BUF
HOCHMANN, MICHAEL	36	M	UNKNOWN	BVZZZZ	BUF
KATH	34	F	W	BVZZZZ	BUF
MARIANNE	9	F	CHILD	BVZZZZ	BUF
VERONIKA	8	F	CHILD	BVZZZZ	BUF
CONSTANTIN	7	M	CHILD	BVZZZZ	BUF
NOVICKI, IGNATZ	22	M	LABR	BVZZZZ	BUF
KATH	24	F	W	BVZZZZ	BUF
RESSEL, MATHILDE	23	F	SGL	BVAAKH	BUF
HOFFMANN, EVA	21	F	SGL	BVACED	NY
KRAMPFORT, ELISE	18	F	SGL	BVACED	NY
AMM, CHRISTIAN	56	M	HTR	SYZZZZ	PA
FRDKE	50	F	W	SYZZZZ	PA
SOPHIE	16	F	W	SYZZZZ	PA
MANKOWSKI, MICHAEL	65	M	LABR	PRZZZZ	IL
MARIANNE	77	F	W	PRZZZZ	IL
KACZMIERCZAK, FRANZ	35	M	LABR	PRZZZZ	IL
FRANZISKA	39	F	W	PRZZZZ	IL
ANDR	12	M	S	PRZZZZ	IL
FEUERSTEIN, BERNH	27	M	MCHT	PRAAKH	IL

PASSENGER	AGE	SEX	OCCUPATION	PRIVL	DES
WENTZEL, JOH	34	M	UNKNOWN	PRZZZZIL	
SPRINGER, MARIANNE	24	F	UNKNOWN	PRZZZZIL	
BIERNACKI, VINCENTY	35	M	LABR	PRZZZZIL	
MICHALINE	26	F	W	PRZZZZIL	
ANTONIA	9	F	CHILD	PRZZZZIL	
STEFAN	7	M	CHILD	PRZZZZIL	
CONSTANTIN	2	M	CHILD	PRZZZZIL	
SEVERIN	.03	M	INFANT	PRZZZZIL	
KOROLEWSKI, PETER	27	M	LABR	PRZZZZNY	
POBLOEKI, IGNATZ	28	M	LABR	PRZZZZNY	
ANNA	24	F	W	PRZZZZNY	
ANNA	.09	F	INFANT	PRZZZZNY	
SCHWIEGERLING, WALTER	49	M	LABR	PRAJTBOH	
HENRIETTE	44	F	W	PRAJTBOH	
FRDKE	21	F	CH	PRAJTBOH	
LOUISE	19	F	CH	PRAJTBOH	
AUGUSTE	8	F	CHILD	PRAJTBOH	
ERNST	.11	M	INFANT	PRAJTBOH	
MINNA	.01	F	INFANT	PRAJTBOH	
NOLTE, CARL	17	M	FARMER	PRZZZZNY	
JAROVINSKA, FRANZISKA	24	F	WO	PRZZZZNY	
JADWIGA	.11	F	INFANT	PRZZZZNY	
VIETZEN, CARL	27	M	FARMER	PRZZZZNY	
LANGE, ROSALIE	17	F	SGL	PRZZZZNY	
JOERGENSEN, ANNA	20	F	UNKNOWN	PRZZZZNY	
KRUSE, JOHANN	15	M	UNKNOWN	PRZZZZNY	
KOHLENMEYER, BERTHA	22	F	SGL	PRZZZZNY	
HOFFMANN, JOH	45	M	LABR	BVZZZZNY	
KUMMROW, GUSTAV	31	M	FARMER	BVAFUHWI	
ARP, HEINR	25	M	LABR	HBZZZZIL	
SCHLICKER, CAECILIE	21	F	SGL	HBZZZZIL	
WYSOCKY, LUCIAN	27	M	LABR	PRZZZZNY	
ANNA	28	F	W	PRZZZZNY	
VICTOR	2	M	CHILD	PRZZZZNY	
UEBERLE, FRIEDR	27	M	GDNR	PRZZZZNY	
KNUDSEN, HANS	14	M	UNKNOWN	PRZZZZNY	
ERICHSON, BERTHOLD	14	M	UNKNOWN	PRZZZZNY	
KIENE, HERM	23	M	LABR	HBZZZZNY	
KUFAHL, MINNA	20	F	SGL	HBAADENY	
BIRKNER, ERNST	23	M	SMH	SYZZZZCH	
WAETJE, HERMANN	28	M	MLR	SYADTIMN	
FRDKE	21	F	W	SYADTIMN	
EBSEN, CHR	16	M	FARMER	SYADTIIL	
MARKWALDT, AUG	15	M	FARMER	SYAAUQMN	
WOZNIAK, MARIANNA	26	F	W	PRZZZZBUF	
JOSEF	4	M	CHILD	PRZZZZBUF	
VALENTIN	2	M	CHILD	PRZZZZBUF	
JAN	.11	M	INFANT	PRZZZZBUF	
CLUNIEL, FRANZISKA	27	F	SGL	PRZZZZBUF	
WESTPHAL, HUGO	32	M	SLR	PRACHOIL	
GAURAN, VINCENT	24	M	LABR	PRZZZZIL	
PELEGIA	21	F	W	PRZZZZIL	
MERCINEK, TOMS	40	M	LABR	PRZZZZBUF	
MAJEWSKY, STANSL	61	M	LABR	PRAHWVBUF	
MARGA	58	F	W	PRAHWVBUF	
ALBERT	8	M	CHILD	PRAHWVBUF	
PAYSEN, SCHWENN	16	M	FARMER	PRZZZZUNK	
JESSEN, PETER	15	M	FARMER	PRZZZZUNK	
CLEMENZ, ERICH	21	M	SLR	PRZZZZUNK	
JOHANNSEN, B	16	M	FARMER	PRAHNKUNK	
WEPPLER, PETER	16	M	FARMER	PRZZZZUNK	
MURAWSKY, STEFAN	24	M	LABR	PRZZZZUNK	
MARIANNA	22	F	W	PRZZZZUNK	
VICTORIA	.11	F	INFANT	PRZZZZUNK	
ANNA	.01	F	INFANT	PRZZZZUNK	
BRAUN, ANNA	17	F	SGL	PRZZZZUNK	
LEWIN, NATALIE	17	F	LABR	PRZZZZIL	
LANDSVERGER, HERM	24	M	BKR	PRAGHAIL	
MEYER, FRIEDR	28	M	FARMER	PRAJSVIL	
EMMA	25	F	W	PRAJSVIL	
MUELLER, HERM	37	M	FARMER	PRZZZZIL	
IWERSEN, HANS	34	M	LABR	PRZZZZIL	
HELENE	28	F	W	PRZZZZIL	
SOFIE	5	F	CHILD	PRZZZZIL	
U	3	F	CHILD	PRZZZZIL	
JENS	.11	M	INFANT	PRZZZZIL	
CHRISTENSEN, IWER	15	M	FARMER	PRZZZZNY	
ANDERS, CARL	62	M	FARMER	PRZZZZNY	
CAROLINE	32	F	SGL	PRZZZZNY	
MARKS, MARIE	58	F	W	SYZZZZNY	
DORATHEA	18	F	CH	SYZZZZNY	
CARL	16	F	CH	SYZZZZNY	
LOUIS	14	F	CH	SYZZZZNY	
RAU, ROESLE	17	F	SGL	PRZZZZNY	
OTTERBACH, BABETTE	22	F	SGL	PRZZZZNY	
WIELAND, KATH	16	F	SGL	PRZZZZNY	
HONERT, HERM	32	F	FARMER	PRZZZZPA	
BERTHA	30	F	W	PRZZZZPA	
MARTHA	7	F	CHILD	PRZZZZPA	
EMIL	6	M	CHILD	PRZZZZPA	
BERTHA	2	F	CHILD	PRZZZZPA	
HERM	.11	M	INFANT	PRZZZZPA	
JOHNSEN, HANS	41	M	FARMER	PRZZZZPA	
STUEWE, ROBERT	23	M	FARMER	PRZZZZPA	
WERNER, ERNST	33	M	FARMER	PRAAKHPA	
ANNA	31	F	W	PRAGIAPA	
NISSEN, MARIE	21	F	SGL	PRZZZZIL	
PIEPER, HANS	23	M	MCHT	HBZZZZIL	
BEHRENBRUCH, ALBERT	39	M	FARMER	PRZZZZPA	
JENNY	34	F	W	PRZZZZPA	
META	9	F	CHILD	PRZZZZPA	
ELSE	7	F	CHILD	PRZZZZPA	
GELMUTH	6	F	CHILD	PRZZZZPA	
GUSTAV	5	M	CHILD	PRZZZZPA	
BRUNO	.11	M	INFANT	PRZZZZPA	
SCHWING, HEINRICH	24	M	FARMER	PRZZZZPA	
MARTENS, GERH	33	M	SLR	PRZZZZIL	
PETERSEN, AUG	46	M	FARMER	PRZZZZIL	
CATH	28	F	W	PRZZZZIL	
JUSTIN	3	M	CHILD	PRZZZZIL	
HELENE	2	F	CHILD	PRZZZZIL	
LORENZ	.09	M	INFANT	PRZZZZIL	
GRUENTHAL, WILH	35	M	LABR	PRABMQMI	
ANNA	25	F	W	PRABMQMI	
WILH	4	M	CHILD	PRABMQMI	
FRITZ	2	M	CHILD	PRABMQMI	
OTTO	8	M	CHILD	PRABMQMI	
ANDERSEN, ANDRAS	45	M	FARMER	PRZZZZIL	
ANNA	51	F	W	PRZZZZIL	
JENS	14	M	CH	PRZZZZIL	
ERICH	9	M	CHILD	PRZZZZIL	
CHRISTINE	8	F	CHILD	PRZZZZIL	
LUDWIGSEN, HANS	48	M	FARMER	PRZZZZIL	
CHR	14	M	S	PRZZZZIL	
THOMSEN, MARTIN	31	M	FARMER	PRZZZZIL	
ANNA	22	F	W	PRZZZZIL	
JOHNSEN, HANSINE	19	F	SGL	PRZZZZIL	
LAGONS, PAULINE	23	F	SGL	PRZZZZIL	
HOLST, GEORG	21	M	FARMER	PRZZZZIL	
ANDERSEN, HANS	27	M	FARMER	PRZZZZIL	
THOMSEN, TOMAS	24	M	SLR	PRZZZZIA	
MIKKELSEN, MAGD	22	F	SGL	PRZZZZIA	
MAD	21	M	FARMER	PRZZZZIA	
LUDWIGSEN, JENS	17	M	FARMER	PRZZZZIA	
NISSEN, HANS	16	M	FARMER	PRZZZZIA	
HOLST, GEORG	20	M	FARMER	PRZZZZMI	
EBBESEN, LAURITZ	36	M	FARMER	PRZZZZIL	
CHRISTINE	32	F	W	PRZZZZIL	
HANNE	9	F	CHILD	PRZZZZIL	
HOLGEN	7	F	CHILD	PRZZZZIL	
HANS	6	M	CHILD	PRZZZZIL	
HELENE	.09	F	INFANT	PRZZZZIL	
HOLM, CARL	35	M	FARMER	PRZZZZIA	
JOHNSEN, REGINE	36	F	W	PRZZZZIA	
HANS	8	M	CHILD	PRZZZZIA	
REINH	6	M	CHILD	PRZZZZIA	
ANTON	7	M	CHILD	PRZZZZIA	
HANSEN, HANS	26	M	FARMER	PRZZZZIL	
HANSINE	26	F	W	PRZZZZIL	
MARIE	.03	F	INFANT	PRZZZZIL	

PASSENGER	AGE	SEX	OCCUPATION	PRVVL	DES
SOERENSEN, HEINRICH	26	M	FARMER		PRZZZZIL
ANDERSEN, ANNA	30	F	SGL		PRZZZZIA
SCHMIDT, JEP	25	M	FARMER		PRZZZZIA
FERMANSSEN, ANNA	27	F	SGL		PRAHZPIA
NIELSEN, JEGGE	16	M	FARMER		PRZZZZIA
DOSE, EMIL	15	M	FARMER		PRZZZZIL
GUSTAV	16	M	FARMER		PRZZZZIL
LOUISE	18	F	SGL		PRZZZZIL
SCHMIDT, FERD	16	M	FARMER		PRZZZZIL
TUECKIS, GERROT	48	M	FARMER		PRAHXYIA
CLARA	15	F	CH		PRAHXYIA
MARIE	14	F	CH		PRAHXYIA
CHARLES	8	M	CHILD		PRAHXYIA
SIBBERT, JOH	15	M	FARMER		PRZZZZIA
SOUKSEN, PETER	16	M	FARMER		PRZZZZIA
MOLZEN, JOHANN	23	M	FARMER		PRZZZZIA
MARG	20	F	W		PRZZZZIA
MIKKELSEN, NIELS	24	M	FARMER		PRABRDIA
SELBRECHT, ALBERT	24	M	LABR		PRZZZZIL
MIELCZOZEK, PETER	29	M	LABR		PRZZZZMN
JENSEN, JENS	43	M	LABR		PRAJJNOR
KUBIAK, KASPAR	35	M	LABR		PRZZZZOR
DERINDA, FRANZ	26	M	LABR		PRZZZZOR
CATH	20	F	W		PRZZZZOR
MICHAEL	.06	M	INFANT		PRZZZZOR
HESELOW, FRIEDR	37	M	LABR		PRZZZZIL
FRIEDRE	33	F	W		PRZZZZIL
WILH	8	M	CHILD		PRZZZZIL
FRIEDR	6	M	CHILD		PRZZZZIL
ANNA	2	F	CHILD		PRZZZZIL
GUSTAV	8	M	CHILD		PRZZZZIL
SEPKE, HERM	28	M	LABR		PRZZZZIL
WILH	29	F	W		PRZZZZIL
MARTHA	4	F	CHILD		PRZZZZIL
HERM	2	M	CHILD		PRZZZZIL
IDA	.06	F	INFANT		PRZZZZIL
HIRSCH, GWORG	30	M	SHMK		WMZZZZNY
KOOH, MARTIN	23	M	FARMER		WMAIVBNY
RADETZKI, JOSEF	45	M	LABR		PRZZZZNY
CASEMIR	16	M	LABR		PRZZZZNY
JOSEF	8	M	CHILD		PRZZZZNY
SCHWING, CATH	46	F	WO		PRAEVIIL
MARIE	18	F	CH		PRAEVIIL
CARL	8	M	CHILD		PRAEVIIL
CATH	4	F	CHILD		PRAEVIIL
KOERNER, MARIE	22	F	SGL		WMZZZZIL
WIELAND, GEORG	24	M	FARMER		WMZZZZIL
RASSLER, MARIE	19	F	SGL		WMZZZZIL
SCHMIDT, WILH	22	M	FARMER		WMAHIRIL
RAU, WILH	28	M	BOAT		WMAEVIIL
MARG	29	F	W		WMAEVIIL
SCHINSK, JONS	19	M	LABR		WMAEVIIL
WYPI, VICTOR	31	M	LABR		PRZZZZIL
VICTORINE	31	F	W		PRZZZZIL
MARIANNE	3	F	CHILD		PRZZZZIL
ANTONIE	2	F	CHILD		PRZZZZIL
CATH	60	F	WO		PRZZZZIL
MUELLER, GUSTAV	24	M	BCHR		PRABOVIL
FOLKMAR, ILADE	37	M	LABR		PRABDMIL
BAROWSKY, EMIL	23	M	CL		PRZZZZIL
MEINZEL, ERNESTINE	48	F	WO		PRACHOIL
TOPOELL, HEINRICH	25	M	BKR		PRAAHQNY
STACHOWSKI, FRANZ	24	M	LABR		PRZZZZNY
STORJOHANN, HERM	15	M	LABR		PRADOANY
KNOZYNSKI, JACOB	36	M	LABR		PRZZZZNY
MARIANNE	30	F	W		PRZZZZNY
VALERIA	5	F	CHILD		PRZZZZNY
ANTON	3	M	CHILD		PRZZZZNY
JOH	11	M	INF		PRZZZZNY
BLOHM, HEINR	15	M	LABR		HBZZZZNY
MEYER, ERNST	27	M	FARMER		MKZZZZWI
BERNSDORFF, MARTHA	16	F	SGL		MKABDMWI
RICHARD	9	M	CHILD		MKABDMWI
BINDING, WILH	30	M	CGRMKR		MKACHOWI
CLEMENTINE	28	F	W		MKACHOWI
GRAEDEL, JOH	16	M	FARMER		BVZZZZWI
SKOTARCHZAK, JOH	38	M	LABR		PRZZZZNY
MARIANNE	23	F	W		PRZZZZNY
JOSEF	16	M	LABR		PRZZZZNY
FISCH, STEFAN	35	M	LABR		PRZZZZNY
VALENTINA	25	F	W		PRZZZZNY
ANNA	11	F	INF		PRZZZZNY
GALL, CARL	29	M	FARMER		PRZZZZNY
JOHANN	28	F	W		PRZZZZNY
DALLMANN, WILH	65	M	FARMER		PRZZZZNY
KONICZKA, ANDREAS	28	M	LABR		PRZZZZNY
MICHALINE	50	F	WO		PRZZZZNY
BARZENSKI, FRANZ	32	M	LABR		PRZZZZNY
JOSEPHA	38	F	W		PRZZZZNY
STANISLAUS	11	M	INF		PRZZZZNY
KLABON, ANTONIA	25	F	SGL		PRAFTUNY
SCHARMER, LEOPOLD	38	M	LABR		PRZZZZNY
WILH	26	F	W		PRZZZZNY
RICHARD	3	M	CHILD		PRZZZZNY
SCHECKER, WM	16	M	LABR		PRADNONY
SLOMA, MICHAEL	24	M	LABR		PRZZZZNY
AUERBACH, MORITZ	32	M	ENGR		PRABDMNY
SIETAS, ERNST	14	M	FARMER		PRZZZZIL
SCHAARS, JOH	14	M	FARMER		PRZZZZIL
STACKOWSKI, MARIANNA	26	F	WO		PRZZZZIL
ANDR	.11	M	INFANT		PRZZZZIL
EINFELDT, CHRISTIAN	16	M	WVR		PRZZZZIL
HINST, ANNA	18	F	SGL		PRZZZZIL
CATH	14	F	SGL		PRZZZZIL
RASZAREK, LUDWIG	28	M	LABR		PRZZZZWI
JULIANE	21	F	W		PRZZZZWI
MARIANNE	2	F	CHILD		PRZZZZWI
FRANZISKA	.03	F	INFANT		PRZZZZWI
BERNDT, WILH	39	M	LABR		PRZZZZWI
MARIE	41	F	W		PRZZZZWI
BESTMANN, MARIE	21	F	SGL		PRZZZZWI
PAHL, HEINR	16	M	FARMER		PRZZZZWI
ROCZACK, JACOB	33	M	LABR		PRZZZZPA
SCHECKER, AUGUST	15	M	FARMER		PRADNOPA
ROSINSKI, PAUL	41	M	LABR		PRZZZZOH
VICTORIA	32	F	W		PRZZZZOH
MARTHA	9	F	CHILD		PRZZZZOH
JOH	9	M	CHILD		PRZZZZOH
FUHRMANN, CARL	28	M	LABR		PRZZZZIL
BARTECKI, THOMAS	29	M	LABR		PRZZZZPA
CATH	26	F	W		PRZZZZPA
MICH	6	M	CHILD		PRZZZZPA
FRANZISKA	4	F	CHILD		PRZZZZPA
LORENZ	3	M	CHILD		PRZZZZPA
CONSTANTIN	.11	M	INFANT		PRZZZZPA
DRZIWETZKI, JADWIGA	21	F	SGL		PRZZZZPA
ADAMOWICZ, MICHAEL	26	M	LABR		PRACTQPA
MARCHALLKIEWICH, MICH	38	M	LABR		PRACTQPA
MAGDALENE	26	F	W		PRACTQPA
STEFAN	9	M	CHILD		PRACTQPA
VALENTIN	2	M	CHILD		PRACTQPA
SCHOBER, ANDREAS	42	M	LABR		PRZZZZPA
TRZECKI, FRANZ	34	M	LABR		PRZZZZBUF
MARIANNE	22	F	W		PRZZZZBUF
NAROZNY, MIHAL	25	M	LABR		PRZZZZOH
LEPPEN, HERMANN	24	M	SVNT		PRAAKHOH
RADZIMANOWSKI, IDA	24	F	SGL		PRABTNOH
LITTMANN, GEORG	23	M	MCHT		HBZZZZOH
KUJAWA, MICHAEL	47	M	LABR		PRZZZZOH
VERONIKA	30	F	W		PRZZZZOH
JOSEFA	9	F	CHILD		PRZZZZOH
MARIANNE	3	F	CHILD		PRZZZZOH
KONTECK, PETER	34	M	LABR		PRZZZZMI
ANNA	38	F	W		PRZZZZMI
MAGD	9	F	CHILD		PRZZZZMI
PAUL	8	F	CHILD		PRZZZZMI
JOH	4	M	CHILD		PRZZZZMI
FRANZ	3	M	CHILD		PRZZZZMI
STEPHAN	1	M	CHILD		PRZZZZMI
KAUTHACK, FRANZ	24	M	LABR		PRZZZZMI

PASSENGER	AGE	SEX	OCCUPATION	PRVL	DES
SCHULZ, ANTON	28	M	LABR	PRZZZZNY	
ROSALIE	28	F	W	PRZZZZNY	
JOHANN	4	M	CHILD	PRZZZZNY	
FRANZ	.01	M	INFANT	PRZZZZNY	
MATHIAS	52	M	LABR	PRZZZZNY	
SUSANNA	52	F	W	PRZZZZNY	
WOLLENBERG, GOTTLIEB	34	M	LABR	PRZZZZNY	
AUGUSTE	44	F	W	PRZZZZNY	
BERHA	9	F	CHILD	PRZZZZNY	
KAUTHACK, JOSEPH	28	M	LABR	PRZZZZMI	
HULDA	26	F	W	PRZZZZMI	
BERN	2	M	CHILD	PRZZZZMI	
FRANZ	.11	M	INFANT	PRZZZZMI	
OSTBERG, AUGUST	26	M	CL	PRAAKHNY	
HANISCH, JOHANNA	23	F	SGL	PRAAKHOH	
ALBRECHT, ANNA	22	F	SGL	PRABWAOH	
STOLP, AUGUST	24	M	WHLR	PRACTOOH	
LUEDTKE, WILH	40	M	LABR	PRZZZZMI	
AMALIE	37	F	W	PRZZZZMI	
PAUL	9	M	CHILD	PRZZZZMI	
WILH	8	M	CHILD	PRZZZZMI	
OLGA	7	F	CHILD	PRZZZZMI	
HEDWIG	4	F	CHILD	PRZZZZMI	
MARTHA	4	F	CHILD	PRZZZZMI	
MAX	3	M	CHILD	PRZZZZMI	
IDA	.11	M	INFANT	PRZZZZMI	
FRITZ, RICHARD	15	M	LABR	PRZZZZMI	
LIEBERS, PAUL	27	M	BKR	PRAEZONE	
FRIEDA	9	F	CHILD	PRAEZONE	
LOAKE, HERM	22	M	SLR	PRZZZZIA	
JENSEN, ANNA	53	F	WO	PRZZZZIA	
NIELSINE	18	F	SGL	PRZZZZIA	
KINSK, CAROLINE	22	F	SGL	PRZZZZNE	
CHRISTENSEN, BADIL	16	F	SGL	PRZZZZIL	
WALEZAK, LUDWIG	30	M	LABR	PRZZZZPA	
HAMMER, ALBERT	33	M	CMPR	PRAEXWBUF	
STOHLK, THEODOR	22	M	FARMER	PRADNUIL	
MARIE	22	F	W	PRADNUIL	
WEGNER, HEINR	24	M	FARMER	PRZZZZIL	
PULLS, JOHANN	30	M	FARMER	PRZZZZIL	
MARIE	28	F	W	PRZZZZIL	
EMMA	4	F	CHILD	PRZZZZIL	
CARL	3	M	CHILD	PRZZZZIL	
HEINR	.09	M	INFANT	PRZZZZIL	
MUELLER, KARL	14	M	FARMER	PRZZZZIL	
BRANDT, KARL	33	M	FARMER	BWZZZZWI	
SCHUBERT, GOTTFRIED	24	M	FARMER	PRZZZZIA	
BOETHERS, AUGUST	29	M	BRR	PRADYMIA	
MIELKE, CARL	24	M	LABR	PRZZZZMO	
WILH	26	F	W	PRZZZZMO	
HULDA	2	F	CHILD	PRZZZZMO	
EMMA	.04	F	INFANT	PRZZZZMO	
MUELLER, FRIEDR	17	M	FARMER	PRZZZZIL	
SOEKEN, CATH	71	F	WO	PRACXDMO	
MARIE	36	F	SGL	PRACXDMO	
HERCHO, TELKE	35	F	SGL	PRACXDMO	
SCHMUND, FERDINAND	30	M	LABR	PRAELVNY	
CAROLINE	30	F	W	PRAELVNY	
EMILIE	8	F	CHILD	PRAELVNY	
DONNER, WILHELM	40	M	LABR	PRZZZZUNK	
JOHANNE	45	F	W	PRZZZZUNK	
FRANZ	16	M	CH	PRZZZZUNK	
WILH	9	M	CHILD	PRZZZZUNK	
HERM	8	M	CHILD	PRZZZZUNK	
MARTHA	7	F	CHILD	PRZZZZUNK	
EMILIE	5	F	CHILD	PRZZZZUNK	
OTTO, HERMANN	40	M	LABR	PRZZZZMI	
WILH	38	F	W	PRZZZZMI	
CARL	17	M	CH	PRZZZZMI	
WILH	9	M	CHILD	PRZZZZMI	
BERTHA	8	F	CHILD	PRZZZZMI	
DONNER, JOHANNA	64	F	WO	PRZZZZMI	
ZIMMERMANN, AUGUST	62	M	LABR	PRAGCIMI	
MARIE	61	F	W	PRAGCIMI	
EMILIE	24	F	CH	PRAGCIMI	
HERM	21	M	CH	PRAGCIMI	
EMILIE	21	F	CH	PRAGCIMI	
BUTENHOF, HERM	26	M	BLKSMH	PRZZZZMI	
PEETZ, CARL	28	M	LABR	PRZZZZMI	
HENRIETTE	31	F	W	PRZZZZMI	
WILH	4	M	CHILD	PRZZZZMI	
OTTILIE	2	F	CHILD	PRZZZZMI	
EMMA	66	F	WO	PRZZZZMI	
EMIL	66	M	LABR	PRZZZZMI	
FRITZ, LOUISE	28	F	WO	PRZZZZMI	
SCHAHMANN, CARL	56	M	LABR	PRABUZMI	
HENRIETTE	54	F	W	PRABUZMI	
FRIEDR	19	M	CH	PRABUZMI	
AUGUSTE	16	F	CH	PRABUZMI	
LOUISE	14	F	CH	PRABUZMI	
KLINGBEIL, JULIUS	26	M	LABR	PRABUZMI	
AUGUSTE	22	F	W	PRABUZMI	
EMMA	2	F	CHILD	PRABUZMI	
EMIL	.06	M	INFANT	PRABUZMI	
BLANK, FRIEDR	29	M	LABR	PRZZZZMI	
WILH	22	F	W	PRZZZZMI	
ERNST	4	M	CHILD	PRZZZZMI	
MINNA	3	F	CHILD	PRZZZZMI	
SCHNEIDER, ANNA	24	F	WO	PRZZZZNY	
AUGUSTE	2	F	CHILD	PRZZZZNY	
FISCHER, WILH	26	M	LABR	PRAECZNY	
EMILIE	24	F	W	PRAECZNY	
AUGUSTE	1	F	CHILD	PRAECZNY	
ANNA	.03	F	INFANT	PRAECZNY	
RIES, MARIANNE	36	F	SGL	PRZZZZWI	
WEINKE, JULIUS	32	M	LABR	PRAAZQWI	
NIEMZICK, JOHANN	36	M	LABR	PRZZZZWI	
ROSALIE	24	F	W	PRZZZZWI	
VICTOR	15	M	LABR	PRZZZZWI	
ANNA	2	F	CHILD	PRZZZZWI	
JOSEF	1	M	CHILD	PRZZZZWI	
ANNA	.06	F	INFANT	PRZZZZWI	
KROPTOWSKA, ANTONIA	68	F	WO	PRZZZZIL	
TESSMANN, AUGUST	56	M	LABR	PRAICKIL	
THERESE	58	F	W	PRAICKIL	
GUSTAV	18	M	CH	PRAICKIL	
BERTHA	9	F	CHILD	PRAICKIL	
MARTHA	.09	F	INFANT	PRAICKIL	
JANESCHEFSKI, ANTON	34	M	LABR	PRZZZZBUF	
PASCH, CAROLINE	21	F	SGL	PRZZZZBUF	
BUSSE, MARIE	20	F	SGL	PRZZZZBUF	
DAMASKE, EVALINE	23	F	SGL	PRZZZZNY	
NEUBIESER, WILH	35	M	FARMER	PRAGASNY	
JOHANNA	50	F	W	PRAGASNY	
PAULINE	9	F	CHILD	PRAGASNY	
GUSTAV	8	M	CHILD	PRAGASNY	
HERM	5	M	CHILD	PRAGASNY	
WILH	4	M	CHILD	PRAGASNY	
ROBERT	.08	M	INFANT	PRAGASNY	
WETTA, JOHANN	52	M	LABR	PRZZZZMI	
VERONIKA	48	F	W	PRZZZZMI	
MARIE	16	F	CH	PRZZZZMI	
FRANZISKA	12	F	CH	PRZZZZMI	
FRANZ	8	M	CHILD	PRZZZZMI	
ANTON	4	M	CHILD	PRZZZZMI	
SCHNEIDER, MARIE	19	F	SGL	PRZZZZMI	
KACZMARECK, JACOB	45	M	LABR	PRZZZZIL	
ROSALIE	40	F	W	PRZZZZIL	
NEPOMIKA	20	F	SGL	PRZZZZIL	
MICKO	9	M	CHILD	PRZZZZIL	
CASIMIR	8	M	CHILD	PRZZZZIL	
PLAHM, WILH	45	M	LABR	PRZZZZOH	
WILH	40	F	W	PRZZZZOH	
AUGUSTE	19	F	CH	PRZZZZOH	
JOHANNA	17	F	CH	PRZZZZOH	
FRITZ	14	M	CH	PRZZZZOH	
CARL	9	M	CHILD	PRZZZZOH	
MATHILDE	7	F	CHILD	PRZZZZOH	
BERTHA	5	F	CHILD	PRZZZZOH	
OTTO	2	F	CHILD	PRZZZZOH	

PASSENGER	AGE	SEX	OCCUPATION	PRV VIL DES
MOLDENHAUER, EMILIE	19	F	SGL	PRZZZZNY
LUEDER, FERD	25	M	LABR	PRZZZZMI
EMILIE	23	F	W	PRZZZZMI
AUGUST	1	M	CHILD	PRZZZZMI
HERMANN	.03	M	INFANT	PRZZZZMI
BLOEDOM, WILH	61	M	LABR	PRZZZZMI
BOHM, JOH	38	M	LABR	PRZZZZIL
EMILIE	38	F	W	PRZZZZIL
HERM	8	M	CHILD	PRZZZZIL
EMILIE	7	F	CHILD	PRZZZZIL
ALBERT	4	F	CHILD	PRZZZZIL
ERNESTINE	2	F	CHILD	PRZZZZIL
AUGUSTE	.06	F	INFANT	PRZZZZIL
BOORTZ, WILH	68	M	LABR	PRZZZZIL
WILH	18	F	SGL	PRZZZZIL
KRUMREY, HERMANN	29	M	LABR	PRZZZZWI
WILHELMINE	26	F	W	PRZZZZWI
JOHANN	26	M	LABR	PRZZZZWI
BERTHA	4	F	CHILD	PRZZZZWI
MINNA	3	F	CHILD	PRZZZZWI
FRANZ	.10	M	INFANT	PRZZZZWI
BETHKE, WILH	26	M	FARMER	PRAINJNY
FRDKE	33	F	W	PRAINJNY
RICHARD	.11	M	INFANT	PRAINJNY
KRUEGER, FRIED	68	M	LABR	PRAINJNY
MIELOSTON, JOSEPH	24	M	LABR	PRZZZZNY
MARIANNA	24	F	W	PRZZZZNY
MARIANNE	.06	F	INFANT	PRZZZZNY
BARTKOWSIAK, VERONIKA	17	F	SGL	PRZZZZPA
WERNER, MICHAEL	48	M	LABR	PRZZZZPA
ANNA	58	F	W	PRZZZZPA
ROSALIE	9	F	CHILD	PRZZZZPA
KUSCH, JOSEPH	27	M	LABR	PRZZZZNY
AUGUSTE	26	F	W	PRZZZZNY
ALBERT	3	M	CHILD	PRZZZZNY
FRANZ	.11	M	INFANT	PRZZZZNY
HENKE, FRIEDR	46	M	SVNT	PRZZZZWI
MARIE	46	F	W	PRZZZZWI
FRANZ	19	M	CH	PRZZZZWI
OTTO	12	M	CH	PRZZZZWI
PAUL	9	M	CHILD	PRZZZZWI
ELSKE, JOHANN	48	M	FARMER	PRALNRWI
JOHANNE	48	F	W	PRALNRWI
FRANZ	19	M	CH	PRALNRWI
ROBERT	16	M	CH	PRALNRWI
OTTO	9	M	CHILD	PRALNRWI
WILHELM	8	M	CHILD	PRALNRWI
HERMANN	7	M	CHILD	PRALNRWI
STACHEL, AUGUST	35	M	LABR	PRZZZZWI
SOPHIE	33	F	W	PRZZZZWI
MARIE	9	F	CHILD	PRZZZZWI
CHARLOTTE	8	F	CHILD	PRZZZZWI
WILH	4	M	CHILD	PRZZZZWI
EMILIE	3	F	CHILD	PRZZZZWI
FERDINAND	2	M	CHILD	PRZZZZWI
HERMANN	.11	M	INFANT	PRZZZZWI
SZELINSKY, JOSEPH	29	M	LABR	PRZZZZWI
EVA	27	F	W	PRZZZZWI
ANNA	3	F	CHILD	PRZZZZWI
GERTRUDE	.09	F	INFANT	PRZZZZWI
KOEHLER, AUGUST	55	M	LABR	PRZZZZWI
BERTHA	37	F	W	PRZZZZWI
CARL	9	M	CHILD	PRZZZZWI
OTTO	8	M	CHILD	PRZZZZWI
WIENKE, BERTHA	22	F	SGL	PRZZZZWI
KUBIAK, JACOB	16	M	LABR	PRZZZZWI
DITTMER, FRIEDRICH	42	M	LABR	PRZZZZWI
HENRIETTE	45	F	W	PRZZZZWI
AUGUSTE	32	F	SGL	PRZZZZWI
WILH	18	F	CH	PRZZZZWI
AUGUSTE	17	F	CH	PRZZZZWI
CARL	14	F	CH	PRZZZZWI
AUGUSTE	13	F	CH	PRZZZZWI
ROBERT	9	M	CHILD	PRZZZZWI
CARL	7	M	CHILD	PRZZZZWI
FRANZ	6	M	CHILD	PRZZZZWI
GENSKE, WILHELM	44	M	WHLR	PRAHKDMI
WILH	43	F	W	PRAHKDMI
WILH	16	F	W	PRAHKDMI
OTTO	14	M	CH	PRAHKDMI
EMIL	9	M	CHILD	PRAHKDMI
BERTHA	8	F	CHILD	PRAHKDMI
LISBETH	7	F	CHILD	PRAHKDMI
RUDOLPH	4	M	CHILD	PRAHKDMI
EMMA	3	F	CHILD	PRAHKDMI
GAWRONSKY, MAURZYN	34	M	LABR	PRAEABNY
MARIANNE	24	F	W	PRAEABNY
MARTIN	9	M	CHILD	PRAEABNY
FRANZISKA	7	M	CHILD	PRAEABNY
TELLEA	3	F	CHILD	PRAEABNY
STANISLAWA	.06	F	INFANT	PRAEABNY
EITNER, PAUB	24	M	LKSH	PRAAKHIL
EMMA	27	F	W	PRAAKHIL
HEDWIG	.11	F	INFANT	PRAAKHIL
PANKOW, GUSTAV	34	M	LABR	PRZZZZWI
ALWINE	32	F	W	PRZZZZWI
ANNA	7	F	CHILD	PRZZZZWI
GEORG	2	M	CHILD	PRZZZZWI
RUETTING, FERD	50	M	LABR	PRZZZZWI
ALWINE	19	F	W	PRZZZZWI
KUCHTA, MARIANNE	34	F	WO	PRZZZZWI
ROSALIE	17	F	SGL	PRZZZZWI
NESS, CHRISTINE	39	F	WO	PRZZZZWI
CARL	9	M	CHILD	PRZZZZWI
HERMANN	8	M	CHILD	PRZZZZWI
RAGCINSKA, AGNIKA	40	F	WO	PRADENIL
MARIANNE	14	F	CH	PRADENIL
ANNA	9	F	CHILD	PRADENIL
ROSALIE	8	F	CHILD	PRADENIL
MICHAEL	7	M	CHILD	PRADENIL
CATH	.02	F	INFANT	PRADENIL
ZORNOW, JOHANNA	38	F	W	PRZZZZWI
EMMA	8	F	CHILD	PRZZZZWI
HEINRICH	16	M	LABR	PRZZZZWI
THRUN, HERMANN	40	M	LABR	PRZZZZWI
BERTHA	30	F	W	PRZZZZWI
CARL	15	M	CH	PRZZZZWI
HERMANN	9	M	CHILD	PRZZZZWI
GUSTAV	8	M	CHILD	PRZZZZWI
MATHILDE	6	F	CHILD	PRZZZZWI
OTTO	3	M	CHILD	PRZZZZWI
ARNDT, CARL	35	M	CCHMN	PRZZZZMI
FRDKE	30	F	W	PRZZZZMI
CARL	4	M	CHILD	PRZZZZMI
MARTHA	2	F	CHILD	PRZZZZMI
JOCHEN, JOHANN	23	M	LABR	PRAKPRMI
JAUSCH, JOSEF	30	M	LABR	PRZZZZBUF
JOSEFA	24	F	W	PRZZZZBUF
MICHAEL	.06	M	INFANT	PRZZZZBUF
ADAMSKY, JOSEF	30	M	LABR	PRZZZZBUF
MUECH, NICALOUS	29	M	LABR	PRZZZZBUF
UFNOWSKI, MARTIN	25	M	LABR	PRZZZZIL
JULIANNE	28	F	W	PRZZZZIL
MACHUSKI, ANDREAS	27	M	LABR	PRZZZZBUF
KOSTRCZKI, JOSEPH	28	M	LABR	PRZZZZNY
GRZENIA, IGNATZ	25	M	LABR	PRZZZZNY
SCHLINK, ANTONIA	21	F	SGL	PRZZZZNY
LEU, JOHANN	47	M	LABR	PRAFUXIL
WILH	49	F	W	PRAFUXIL
BERTHA	19	F	CH	PRAFUXIL
HERMANN	17	M	CH	PRAFUXIL
ALBERT	9	M	CHILD	PRAFUXIL
ZACHOW, WILHELM	22	M	FARMER	PRAFUXWI
KOSTERZEWSKI, ANNA	20	F	WO	PRZZZZWI
PELAGIA	.09	F	INFANT	PRZZZZWI
JOSEPHA	9	F	CHILD	PRZZZZWI
PIWINSKY, JOHANN	50	M	LABR	PRZZZZWI
MARIANNE	49	F	W	PRZZZZWI
THERESIA	9	F	CHILD	PRZZZZWI
JOHANN	.11	M	INFANT	PRZZZZWI

PASSENGER	AGE	SEX	OCCUPATION	PRIVL	DES
NEUMANN, PAULINE	16	F	SGL		PRZZZZOH
KINOWSKA, KATH	68	F	WO		PRZZZZOH
ZAIS, ROSALIE	28	F	SGL		PRAFHUOH
BARTEL, EDUARD	28	M	LABR		PRZZZZOH
WESTPHAL, MATHDE	58	F	WO		PRZZZZOH
ADELINE	16	F	D		PRZZZZOH
HEBEL, HENRIETTE	25	F	SGL		PRZZZZOH
NEUMANN, EMIL	42	M	LABR		PRZZZZWI
AUGUSTE	43	F	W		PRZZZZWI
HERMANN	16	M	CH		PRZZZZWI
OTTILIE	14	F	CH		PRZZZZWI
AUGUSTE	8	F	CHILD		PRZZZZWI
ARNOLD	4	M	CHILD		PRZZZZWI
ALEXANDER	.11	M	INFANT		PRZZZZUNK
SCHWARZ, ROBERT	32	M	LABR		PRACNIMD
OTTILIE	26	F	W		PRACNIMD
ANNA	2	F	CHILD		PRACNIMD
PAUL	.06	M	INFANT		PRACNIMD
JACUBOWSKI, JUSTINE	40	F	WO		PRACNINY
POETZKE, CARL	43	M	BKLYR		PRAAKHNY
CAROLINE	42	F	W		PRAAKHNY
BERTHA	19	F	CH		PRAAKHNY
ANNA	15	F	CH		PRAAKHNY
EMIL	9	M	CHILD		PRAAKHNY
BZISKI, FRANZ	27	M	LABR		PRZZZZPA
MARIANNA	24	F	W		PRZZZZPA
STANISLAUS	3	M	CHILD		PRZZZZPA
JASZM	.11	M	INFANT		PRZZZZPA
GOHR, LEBRECHT	30	M	LLD		PRABWAROC
MINNA	28	F	W		PRABWAROC
GERDA	2	F	CHILD		PRABWAROC
ERNA	.09	F	INFANT		PRABWAROC
BORCHARDT, AUGUST	29	M	LABR		PRZZZZWI
SOHPIE	32	F	W		PRZZZZWI
HERMANN	9	M	CHILD		PRZZZZWI
ANNA	4	F	CHILD		PRZZZZWI
OTTO	2	M	CHILD		PRZZZZWI
AMANDA	.11	F	INFANT		PRZZZZWI
WIRKUS, WILHELM	30	M	LABR		PRZZZZNY
ZABBAK, FRANZ	16	M	LABR		PRZZZZNY
SKIBA, JOHANN	27	M	LABR		PRZZZZNY
MARTSCHINSKI, CARL	48	M	LABR		PRZZZZMI
FLORENTINE	48	F	W		PRZZZZMI
LUDWIG	19	M	CH		PRZZZZMI
JUL	16	M	CH		PRZZZZMI
CARL	9	M	CHILD		PRZZZZMI
EMILIE	8	F	CHILD		PRZZZZMI
MATHILDE	6	F	CHILD		PRZZZZMI
GUSTAV	3	M	CHILD		PRZZZZMI
SCHARMER, CARL	35	M	LABR		PRZZZZUNK
OTTILIE	32	F	W		PRZZZZUNK
CARL	60	M	LABR		PRZZZZUNK
HENRIETTE	55	F	W		PRZZZZUNK
BERTHA	4	F	CHILD		PRZZZZUNK
RICHARD	3	M	CHILD		PRZZZZUNK
ALWINE	2	F	CHILD		PRZZZZUNK
HEDWIG	.11	F	INFANT		PRZZZZUNK
THIEDE, JOHANN	30	M	LABR		PRZZZZNY
PAULINE	25	F	W		PRZZZZNY
BERTHA	.11	F	INFANT		PRZZZZNY
SENGER, ANNA	50	F	WO		PRZZZZNY
BOTH, GUSTAV	24	M	LABR		PRZZZZNY
AFFELDT, MARIE	20	F	LABR		PRAJNNNY
SCHULTZ, JOH	16	M	LABR		PRAJNNNY
MATEJEWSKY, ANDRZY	29	M	LABR		PRZZZZNY
MARIE	26	F	W		PRZZZZNY
PELAGIA	2	F	CHILD		PRZZZZNY
VERONIKA	.06	F	INFANT		PRZZZZNY
JANKOWSKI, WILH	60	M	LABR		PRZZZZIL
JUSTINE	50	F	W		PRZZZZIL
JULIUS	16	M	CH		PRZZZZIL
FRIEDR	14	M	CH		PRZZZZIL
CARL	19	M	CH		PRZZZZIL
BERTHA	9	F	CHILD		PRZZZZIL
AUGUSTE	7	F	CHILD		PRZZZZIL

PASSENGER	AGE	SEX	OCCUPATION	PRIVL	DES
ANDRYSIAK, MARIE	21	F	SGL		PRZZZZNY
NAGEL, HENRIETTE	50	F	WO		PRAAGUNY
BRAUN, JOHANNE	25	F	SGL		PRAAGUNY
HOFFMANN, ALBERT	25	M	LABR		PRAAKHCH
PAULINE	22	F	W		PRAAKHCH
MARG	.11	F	INFANT		PRAAKHCH
PAUL	.01	M	INFANT		PRAAKHUNK
NIERWINK, JACOB	35	M	LABR		PRZZZZNE
MARIANNE	36	F	W		PRZZZZNE
JOH	7	M	CHILD		PRZZZZNE
JOSEF	3	M	CHILD		PRZZZZNE
ROSALIE	.06	F	INFANT		PRZZZZNE
VOIGT, AUGUST	16	M	LABR		PRZZZZNE
PRZYBILEK, ANDREAS	24	M	LABR		PRZZZZPIT
ANTONIA	24	F	W		PRZZZZPIT
AGNES	6	F	CHILD		PRZZZZPIT
ZIEROTZKI, JOSEF	30	M	LABR		PRABSYNY
OTTILIE	28	F	W		PRABSYNY
ANNA	3	F	CHILD		PRABSYNY
JOH	.09	M	INFANT		PRABSYNY
GESCHKE, BENATTE	73	F	WO		PRADOINY
FRIEDR	25	M	LABR		PRADOINY
AUGUSTE	19	F	SGL		PRADOINY
TEWS, FRANZ	29	M	LABR		PRZZZZIN
AUGUSTE	26	F	W		PRZZZZIN
MARIE	3	F	CHILD		PRZZZZIN
IDA	.06	F	INFANT		PRZZZZUNK
NIESWIADONY, FRANZ	16	M	LABR		PRZZZZBUF
SCHLOWA, AUGUST	28	M	LABR		PRZZZZBUF
AUGUSTE	39	F	W		PRZZZZBUF
OTTO	9	M	CHILD		PRZZZZBUF
CARL	6	M	CHILD		PRZZZZBUF
AUGUST	4	M	CHILD		PRZZZZBUF
FRITZ	2	M	CHILD		PRZZZZBUF
WOJTOSCH, AUGUST	34	M	LABR		PRZZZZIL
JULIANNE	28	F	W		PRZZZZIL
BARBARA	2	F	CHILD		PRZZZZIL
CATH	.09	F	INFANT		PRZZZZIL
SCHULZ, HERMANN	32	M	LABR		PRABMQIL
EMILIE	33	F	W		PRABMQIL
BERTHA	8	F	CHILD		PRABMQIL
ALBERT	6	M	CHILD		PRABMQIL
AUGUSTE	4	F	CHILD		PRABMQIL
ANNA	.08	F	INFANT		PRABMQIL
BYTHIN, AUGUST	34	M	LABR		PRZZZZNY
ROSALIE	36	F	W		PRZZZZNY
HEREDWIG	.05	F	INFANT		PRZZZZNY
LADEWIG, GUSTAV	45	M	LABR		PRAHMNCH
WILH	35	F	W		PRAHMNCH
AUGUST	9	M	CHILD		PRAHMNCH
EMILIE	8	F	CHILD		PRAHMNCH
ANNA	.11	F	INFANT		PRAHMNCH
LASS, AUGUST	34	M	LABR		PRZZZZUNK
MUELLER, CARL	26	M	LABR		PRAJIAUNK
STRASSMANN, CARL	46	M	LABR		PRZZZZMIL
AUGUSTE	43	F	W		PRZZZZMIL
MARTHA	9	F	CHILD		PRZZZZMIL
WILH	68	F	WO		PRZZZZMIL
EMILIE	25	F	SGL		PRZZZZMIL
TESCH, FRANZ	35	M	LABR		PRAFTWMI
ALWINE	35	F	W		PRAFTWMI
OTTO	7	M	CHILD		PRAFTWMI
MARTHA	6	F	CHILD		PRAFTWMI
GRETHE	.06	F	INFANT		PRAFTWMI
KUHN, FRIEDR	36	M	LABR		PRABZWWI
PAULINE	30	F	W		PRABZWWI
FRIEDR	5	M	CHILD		PRABZWWI
PAULINE	3	F	CHILD		PRABZWWI
MARIE	3	F	CHILD		PRABZWWI
ADOLF	.03	M	INFANT		PRABZWWI
WOCKENFUSS, ERNST	39	M	LABR		PRZZZZIL
EMILIE	36	F	W		PRZZZZIL
PAULINE	9	F	CHILD		PRZZZZIL
FRANZ	8	M	CHILD		PRZZZZIL
EMIL	4	M	CHILD		PRZZZZIL

PASSENGER	AGE	SEX	OCCUPATION	PRVL	DES
FRIEDR	2	M	CHILD		PRZZZZIL
ROMER, AUGUST	26	M	LABR		PRZZZZIL
MOWS, JOHANNA	24	F	SGL		PRZZZZIL
FICK, FRIEDR	47	M	LABR		PRZZZZIL
WILH	46	F	W		PRZZZZIL
JOH	18	F	CH		PRZZZZIL
MARIE	5	F	CHILD		PRZZZZIL
NEUKNFELDT, FRIEDR	63	M	LABR		PRZZZZIL
CARLOTTE	69	F	W		PRZZZZIL
BOELTER, FRIEDR	32	M	FARMER		PRAAMIWI
PAULINE	30	F	W		PRAAMIWI
EMMA	5	F	CHILD		PRAAMIWI
HELENE	4	F	CHILD		PRAAMIWI
HELLMUTH	2	M	CHILD		PRAAMIWI
IDA	.06	F	INFANT		PRAAMIWI
LUEBKE, FRIEDR	27	M	LABR		PRAAMIWI
BERTHA	34	F	W		PRAAMIWI
BRZCZINSKY, MARIANNE	22	F	LABR		PRADLOWI
LEWIN, LUDWIG	50	M	LABR		PRAEIOWI
SAWATZKI, PAULINE	18	F	SGL		PRZZZZWI
KRUMREI, CARL	36	M	FARMER		PRALSCWI
AUGUSTE	35	F	W		PRALSCWI
ERNESTINE	5	F	CHILD		PRALSCWI
FRIEDR	3	M	CHILD		PRALSCWI
SCHWAHN, MARIE	16	F	SGL		PRAEWMNY
GOLKE, HERM	24	M	JNR		PRAAKHCH
JEDEMOWSKI, JACOB	26	M	DLR		PRAFZMCH
SMENTEK, JOSEFA	15	F	SGL		PRZZZZCH
REICH, ERNST	46	M	LABR		PRZZZZCH
LOUISE	45	F	W		PRZZZZCH
ANNA	17	F	CH		PRZZZZCH
ROSALIE	9	F	CHILD		PRZZZZCH
JOSEPHA	8	F	CHILD		PRZZZZCH
STANISLAWA	7	F	CHILD		PRZZZZCH
CONSTANTIN	4	M	CHILD		PRZZZZCH
BELKE, HENRIETTE	48	F	WO		PRZZZZWI
HERM	16	M	CH		PRZZZZWI
JOH	14	M	CH		PRZZZZWI
AUGUSTE	9	F	CHILD		PRZZZZWI
EMILIE	8	F	CHILD		PRZZZZWI
SZCZEPANSKA, ANTONIA	36	F	WO		PRZZZZNE
IGNATZ	12	M	CH		PRZZZZNE
PELKA	9	M	CHILD		PRZZZZNE
JAGUSCA	8	F	CHILD		PRZZZZNE
WLADISLAWA	6	F	CHILD		PRZZZZNE
JAN	4	M	CHILD		PRZZZZNE
BROECKER, ERNST	39	M	LABR		PRZZZZNE
LUBINSKY, MICHAEL	34	M	LABR		PRACMHNE
BRANDT, FRIEDR	56	M	FARMER		PRAJJQMI
HENRIETTE	52	F	W		PRAJJQMI
OTTO	15	M	CH		PRAJJQMI
JULS	13	M	CH		PRAJJQMI
ALBERT	9	M	CHILD		PRAJJQMI
AUGUST	7	M	CHILD		PRAJJQMI
ANNA	19	F	CH		PRAJJQMI
GURICH, FRIEDR	24	M	FARMER		PRZZZZIL
JOHANNA	29	F	W		PRZZZZIL
AUGUSTE	.11	F	INFANT		PRZZZZIL
KOHN, FRANZ	24	M	LABR		PRAEVMOH
AUGUSTE	22	F	W		PRAEVMOH
ALBERT	3	M	CHILD		PRAEVMOH
IDA	.09	F	INFANT		PRAEVMOH
BELL, FRIEDR	45	M	FARMER		PRZZZZWI
ALBERTINE	42	F	W		PRZZZZWI
MARIE	18	F	CH		PRZZZZWI
EMILIE	17	F	CH		PRZZZZWI
OTTO	14	F	CH		PRZZZZWI
ANNA	13	F	CH		PRZZZZWI
HERMANN	9	M	CHILD		PRZZZZWI
MULSAT, FRANZ	22	M	LABR		PRZZZZWI
PRZYBILEK, SIMON	32	M	LABR		PRZZZZBUF
RADTKE, AUGUSTE	32	F	LABR		PRAELVWI
FRDKE	31	F	W		PRAELVWI
FRIEDR	5	M	CHILD		PRAELVWI
CARL	3	M	CHILD		PRAELVWI
KOCASINSKI, JOH	26	M	LABR		PRZZZZNE
KOWALSKI, JOH	28	M	LABR		PRZZZZBUF
MARIANNE	25	F	W		PRZZZZBUF
STANISLAWA	.09	F	INFANT		PRZZZZBUF
FALENCZIK, VICTORIA	27	F	SGL		PRZZZZMI
FRANZ	32	M	LABR		PRZZZZMI
ANASTASIA	25	F	W		PRZZZZMI
JOHANN	5	M	CHILD		PRZZZZMI
FRANZISKA	4	F	CHILD		PRZZZZMI
WLADISLAW	.11	M	INFANT		PRZZZZMI
VERONIKA	59	F	WO		PRZZZZMI
ABRAHAM, AUGUST	44	M	LABR		PRADIMOH
HEDWIG	38	F	W		PRADIMOH
ANDREAS	16	M	CH		PRADIMOH
HEDWIG	9	F	CHILD		PRADIMOH
SAMUEL	8	M	CHILD		PRADIMOH
AUGUSTE	6	F	CHILD		PRADIMOH
MATHILDE	1	F	CHILD		PRADIMOH
KRAUSE, JULIUS	32	M	FSHMN		PRAFTWMIL
BERTHA	30	F	W		PRAFTWMIL
JULS	9	M	CHILD		PRAFTWMIL
ROBERT	5	M	CHILD		PRAFTWMIL
MAX	3	M	CHILD		PRAFTWMIL
KARRL, HUGO	23	M	WCHMKR		PRAEWMOH
BARTHEL, PULINE	38	F	WO		PRZZZZWI
KATKE, BERTHA	4	F	CHILD		PRZZZZUNK
LUECK, AUGUSTE	18	F	WO		PRZZZZWI
KLINGBEIL, FERD	50	M	LABR		PRZZZZNY
EMILIE	47	F	W		PRZZZZNY
FRITZ	9	M	CHILD		PRZZZZNY
EMILIE	8	F	CHILD		PRZZZZNY
ANNA	5	F	CHILD		PRZZZZNY
EMMA	3	F	CHILD		PRZZZZNY
FARCHMIN, FRIEDR	25	M	LABR		PRAEWMNY
CLARA	23	F	W		PRAEWMNY
KARCHIS, LEMJON	27	M	LABR		PRZZZZPA
EMILIE	25	F	W		PRZZZZPA
EMIL	2	F	CHILD		PRZZZZPA
SCHMALZ, ADELINE	24	F	SGL		PRZZZZNY
PADOLSKI, VINCENT	28	M	LABR		PRZZZZNY
AUGUSTE	30	F	W		PRZZZZNY
GOLIAT, HEINRICH	63	M	FARMER		PRZZZZNY
SUSANNE	56	F	W		PRZZZZNY
FRIEDR	26	M	CH		PRZZZZNY
JULIANNE	20	F	CH		PRZZZZNY
ZASTROW, EMIL	20	M	FARMER		PRZZZZNY
KALES, JOSEF	37	M	LABR		PRZZZZPA
AUGUSTE	35	F	W		PRZZZZPA
IDA	8	F	CHILD		PRZZZZPA
KRYSCHEWSKI, JOHANN	27	M	LABR		PRZZZZNY
KUEHN, AUGUST	31	M	BLKSMH		PRAAESNY
PETERS, FERD	57	M	LABR		PRAAZQCO
THERESE	18	F	D		PRAAZQCO
PEC, MARIE	28	F	SGL		PRAAZQCO
BOTHKE, JOHANN	24	M	LABR		PRZZZZMO
MARIE	14	F	SGL		PRZZZZMO
ENGLER, ROBERT	34	M	LABR		PRZZZZWI
BERTHA	29	F	W		PRZZZZWI
CARL	8	M	CHILD		PRZZZZWI
ROBERT	4	M	CHILD		PRZZZZWI
PINKE, ALWINE	18	F	SGL		PRZZZZWI
KLABUNDE, ALBERT	29	M	LABR		PRZZZZMN
AUGUSTE	24	F	W		PRZZZZMN
WALZER, FRANZ	32	M	LABR		PRZZZZMN
CAROLINE	30	F	W		PRZZZZMN
IDA	4	F	CHILD		PRZZZZMN
OTTO	.09	M	INFANT		PRZZZZMN
WASIAK, RUDOLPH	30	M	BRR		PRAEWMIL
LOUISE	28	F	W		PRAEWMIL
ROBERT	3	M	CHILD		PRAEWMIL
BRUNO	2	M	CHILD		PRAEWMIL
RINDFLEISCH, AUGUSTE	43	F	WO		PRAEWMNY
ELSE	5	F	CHILD		PRAEWMNY
SCHELESDAN, MINNA	23	F	WO		PRAASSNY
ANNA	16	F	SGL		PRAASSNY

PASSENGER	AGE	SEX	OCCUPATION	PRVVL	DES
LISCHNEWSKI, MICHAEL	53	M	LABR		PRZZZZDET
BOBRUCKI, JOSEPH	25	M	LABR		PRZZZZDET
NAPIENTEK, LEO	29	M	BKLYR		PRZZZZCH
ANGLIKA	20	F	W		PRZZZZCH
ZALADECK, FRANZ	24	M	LABR		PRACSFWI
SCHAULAND, AUGUSTE	24	F	SGL		PRZZZZWI
FERD	60	M	LABR		PRZZZZWI
DORATH	59	F	W		PRZZZZWI
JOH	26	M	S		PRZZZZWI
KUCHENBECKER, ELISABETH	20	F	SGL		PRZZZZEMA
SELKE, FERD	41	M	LABR		PRZZZZEMA
NAFFKE, WILH	24	M	SMH		PRAJNRROC
ORLOWSKY, JOSEPH	41	M	LABR		PRZZZZPA
MIHAL	16	M	LABR		PRZZZZPA
OPALINSKY, VALENTIN	48	M	LABR		PRZZZZPA
BRAUN, HERM	43	M	LABR		PRAEABPA
FRASE, WILH	27	M	LABR		PRZZZZPA
MARUNGE, ALBERT	16	M	LABR		PRZZZZOH
SOMMER, PAUL	30	M	LABR		PRAEWMWI
SZAFRANSKI, MICHAEL	29	M	CCHMN		PRZZZZWI
JOSEFA	24	F	W		PRZZZZWI
JOSEPH	2	M	CHILD		PRZZZZWI
FRANZ	.11	M	INFANT		PRZZZZWI
THIEDE, PAULINE	9	F	CHILD		PRAJNNWI
SKIBA, EMILIE	27	F	WO		PRAJNNWI
JOHANN	8	M	CHILD		PRAJNNWI
AUGUSTE	3	F	CHILD		PRAJNNWI
MARTHA	.09	F	INFANT		PRAJNNWI
PAKULU, CATHARINA	50	F	WO		PRZZZZWI
GRIESCHKE, CARL	27	M	LABR		PRZZZZIN
JENSEN, CHRISTINE	16	F	SGL		PRAJJNIN
WIES, FRANZ	22	M	LABR		PRZZZZIA
MEYER, LOUIS	25	M	LABR		PRZZZZIA
WINKLER, SAMUEL	24	M	LABR		PRZZZZIA
WERNER, HERM	21	M	LABR		PRZZZZIA
REBER, PETER	31	M	LABR		SRZZZZOH
ANNA	28	F	W		SRZZZZOH
ROSA	4	F	CHILD		SRZZZZOH
CHRISTIAN	3	M	CHILD		SRZZZZOH
LINA	2	F	CHILD		SRZZZZOH
ANNA	.08	F	INFANT		SRZZZZOH
BITTON, GEORGES	30	M	DLR		SRAAHUOH
MARIE	20	F	W		SRAAHUOH
UHLAND, CHRISTIANA	40	M	LABR		SRZZZZOH
MINNA	30	F	W		SRZZZZOH
FRIEDR	10	M	CH		SRZZZZOH
RIKA	9	F	CHILD		SRZZZZOH
LOUIS	7	M	CHILD		SRZZZZOH
CARL	4	M	CHILD		SRZZZZOH
CHRISTIAN	.07	M	INFANT		SRZZZZOH
SCHERESCHEWSKY, MAX	44	M	LABR		SRAAHUOH
CLIMENT, SIMON	28	M	LABR		SRAAHUOH
STEEN, NICOLAUS	62	M	LABR		SRAAHUOH
VUGET, JOSEPH	26	M	LABR		SRZZZZOH
TURNIER, GERMAIN	23	M	LABR		SRZZZZOH
ELVINA	39	F	WO		SRZZZZOH
KLEIN, EUGEMIE	19	F	SGL		SRZZZZIL
MOCHETTAN, PASIFIQUE	22	M	LABR		SRZZZZIL
REAL, BARTH	32	M	LABR		SRZZZZIL
STALDER, PHILIP	36	M	LABR		SRZZZZIL
PANZERI, EUGENIA	39	F	WO		SRZZZZIL
TANNER, CONRAD	24	M	LABR		SRAAKJIL
GREUB, JOHANN	21	M	LABR		SRAAHUIL
HANETER, JACK	23	M	LABR		SRACVYIL
BELLI, HEINR	20	M	LABR		SRZZZZIL
VOGTLI, URSULA	20	F	SGL		SRZZZZIL
ZEGGIO, PIETRO	52	M	LABR		SRZZZZCAL
CAMASTRAL, JACOB	32	M	LABR		SRZZZZCAL
BELLINGER, LISETTE	24	F	SGL		SRAGNSCAL
BELLI, ALEX	42	M	LABR		SRZZZZCAL
URSULA	39	F	W		SRAGNSCAL
BARBARA	17	F	CH		SRAGNSOH
ANNA	16	F	CH		SRAGNSOH
LAURA	14	F	CH		SRAGNSOH
ALBERT	11	F	CH		SRAGNSOH
JOHANN	9	M	CHILD		SRAGNSOH
HEINRICH	6	M	CHILD		SRAGNSOH
JACOB	4	M	CHILD		SRAGNSOH
MARIE	.11	F	INFANT		SRAGNSOH
IBALI, IGNATZ	29	M	LABR		SRAGNSOH
BELLINGER, URSULA	67	F	WO		SRAGNSOH
LANG, EMILIE	26	F	SGL		SRZZZZOH
LOHRMANN, RICHARD	29	M	STDNT		SRAEXWPHI
GASSER, WILHELM	20	M	LABR		SRAAHUPA
HERMANN, ANDREAS	31	M	LABR		SRAAHUPA
HAFNER, RUDOLF	26	M	LABR		SRAAHUPA
MISERREZ, MARIE	23	F	SGL		SRAAHUNY
JOSEPH	18	M	LABR		SRAAHUNY
PAUL	15	M	LABR		SRAAHUNY
LEON	13	M	LABR		SRAAHUNY
MAURER, FRITZ	26	M	LABR		SRAAHUNY
MATTI, EMANUEL	26	M	LABR		SRZZZZUNK
EGGER, JOHANN	25	M	LABR		SRZZZZPA
STEINER, HUGO	28	M	LABR		SRZZZZPA
PLATTTEN, EMIL	26	M	CL		SRZZZZPA
ZUEGER, BENEDICT	30	M	LABR		SRZZZZPA
GENOFEVA	27	F	W		SRZZZZPA
ALBERT	2	M	CHILD		SRZZZZPA
GENOFEVA	.07	F	INFANT		SRZZZZPA
MARGUERETTI, FERD	29	M	LABR		SRZZZZNY
FIGEORD, SERAPHINE	26	F	UNKNOWN		SRZZZZNY
CONRAD, JUL	31	M	LABR		SRAAHUNY
REAL, FERDINAND	35	M	LABR		SRAAHUNY
HOOHMANN, MICHAEL	.03	M	INFANT		PRZZZZNY
WYSOKY, LUCIAN	.03	M	INFANT		PRZZZZNY
MEIER, OLGA	.07	F	INFANT		PRZZZZNY
MAROHALLKIEWICZ, MICHAE	.02	F	INFANT		PRZZZZNY
DITTMAR, HANRY	64	M	CNF		PRAARZNY
ANNA	55	F	W		PRAARZNY
MITTELSTADT, ELLA	48	F	UNKNOWN		PRAAKHCH
DAEBELER, ERNST	25	M	UNKNOWN		MKZZZZCH
SCHLUNK, BERN	29	M	STDNT		PRZZZZNY
OSWALD, ROBERT	17	M	MCHT		PRAAZSMO
WEISS, MARTHA	15	F	SGL		PRAEWMCH
TRZECKI, FRANZ	2	M	CHILD		PRZZZZNY
KUSCH, JOSEF	.01	M	INFANT		PRZZZZNY
GRUENEBAUM, JETTOHEN	27	F	SGL		PRZZZZCH
PRZYBYTEK, STANISLAW	00	M	INF		PR****CH
KOWALSKI, JOHANN	.02	M	INFANT		PR****CH
KUCZINSKI, THOMAS	.03	M	INFANT		PR****CH
ARNDT, ANNA	.04	F	INFANT		PR****CH

SHIP: SERVIA

FROM: LIVERPOOL AND QUEENSTOWN
TO: NEW YORK
ARRIVED: 14 MAY 1888

PASSENGER	AGE	SEX	OCCUPATION	PRVVL	DES
KASSEN, GEORGE	29	M	MCHT		PRADAXCIN

SHIP: SORRENTO

FROM: HAMBURG
TO: NEW YORK
ARRIVED: 14 MAY 1888

PASSENGER	AGE	SEX	OCCUPATION	PRVVL	DES
SCHLICKE, CARL	37	M	LABR		PRZZZZUSA
BARTKOWIAK, CASIMIR	29	M	LABR		PRZZZZCH
MAGDAL.	27	F	W		PRZZZZCH
FRANZ	3	M	CHILD		PRZZZZCH

PASSENGER	AGE	SEX	OCCUPATION	PRVL	DES
JOSEF	.11	M	INFANT		PRZZZZCH
BUBISICK, IGNATZ	28	M	LABR		PRZZZZCH
JOSEFA	25	F	W		PRZZZZNY
MARIANNA	3	F	CHILD		PRZZZZNY
ZAWERSKY, JOH.	30	M	LABR		PRZZZZNY
STRYZEWSKI, MICHAEL	32	M	LABR		PRZZZZNY
AGNISKA	23	F	W		PRZZZZNY
ANTONI	.11	M	INFANT		PRZZZZNY
FRANZ	.11	M	INFANT		PRZZZZNY
ABRAMSOHN, HERRMAN	26	M	TLR		PRZZZZNY
NOVAK, VINCENTY	32	M	LABR		PRZZZZNY
MARIANNA	27	F	W		PRZZZZNY
JOSEFA	4	F	CHILD		PRZZZZNY
BOCHLKE, EMIL	9	M	CHILD		SYZZZZNY
FRIEDRICH	6	M	CHILD		SYZZZZNY
ADOLPH	4	M	CHILD		SYZZZZNY
FRIEDMANN, TOBIAS	31	M	DLR		PRZZZZNY
DZEWKA, PEISSACH	20	M	TLR		PRZZZZNY
BARSIK, FRANZ	20	M	JNR		PRZZZZNY
DRANCEWICZ, JOH.	25	M	LABR		PRZZZZNY
LISCHNEVSKY, ANTON	24	M	LABR		PRZZZZNY
NAWICZKI, WIN.	27	M	LABR		WMZZZZNY
CATHA.	28	F	W		WMZZZZNY
HEDWIG	2	M	CHILD		WMZZZZNY
JOHANN	.11	M	INFANT		WMZZZZNY
FRANZ	.11	M	INFANT		PRZZZZNY
KOWALSKI, JOSEFA	40	F	W		PRZZZZIL
ANDRAS	15	M	CH		PRZZZZIL
STANISLAUS	9	M	CHILD		PRZZZZIL
JOSEFA	5	F	CHILD		PRZZZZBUF
STANISLAUS	2	M	CHILD		PRZZZZBUF
IGNATZ	.03	M	INFANT		PRZZZZBUF
NAPIROLSKI, MARIANNA	42	F	WO		WMZZZZNY
JOSEFA	8	F	CHILD		WMZZZZNY
GABILOWITZ, SCHUL	30	M	DLR		WMZZZZNY
GILSPERN, BEREL	36	M	DLR		PRZZZZNY
MEYER, ABR.	30	M	GLSR		PRZZZZNY
VALENTOKANECZ, H.	22	M	LABR		PRZZZZNY
SLODZINSKY, ST.	45	M	LABR		PRZZZZNY
STERMFNITZ, V.	27	M	LABR		PRZZZZNY
SVIRTSEK, JENDRI	26	M	LABR		PRZZZZNY
HODAU, JOHANN	30	M	LABR		PRZZZZNY
SKODAU, MICHAEL	34	M	LABR		PRZZZZNY
REHAK, JAN	28	M	FARMER		PRZZZZNY
STRACHER, JENTE	22	F	WO		PRZZZZNY
RACHEL	.06	F	INFANT		PRZZZZNY
MALECKY, WLADISLAW	26	M	LABR		PRZZZZBUF
WILMINSKY, V.	29	M	LABR		PRAGFUBUF
PETERSEN, ANNA	28	F	WO		PRAGFUBUF
WILLI	5	M	CHILD		PRAGFUBUF
TONI	.11	M	INFANT		PRAGFUBUF
SILBERMANN, ANNA	33	F	WO		PRAGFUBUF
SARA	9	F	CHILD		PRAGFUBUF
FRAHSE, AUGUST	7	M	CHILD		PRAGFUBUF
PASIMENSKI, LEISER	19	M	TNR		PRAGFUBUF
SCHABER, GOTTL.	35	F	WO		PRAGFUBUF
ANNA	9	F	CHILD		PRAGFUBUF
MINNA	8	F	CHILD		PRAGFUBUF
HERMANN	7	M	CHILD		PRAGFUBUF
PIONTCK, JULA	60	F	WO		PRAGFUBUF
JORBLUM, MOSES	31	M	LABR		PRAGFUBUF
HAMMAN, WILH.	28	M	GDNR		PRAGFUBUF
EMMA	23	F	W		PRAGFUBUF
MARGAR.	.11	F	INFANT		PRAGFUBUF
MUELLER, WILH.	62	M	FARMER		PRAGFUBUF
BERTHA	54	F	W		PRAGFUBUF
IDA	24	F	CH		PRAGFUBUF
BOFINGER, CATHA.	29	F	WO		PRAGFUBUF
ANNA	9	F	CHILD		PRAGFUBUF
BARTSCH, AUGUSTA	21	F	SGL		PRAGFUBUF
KOWALSKI, JOSEF	18	M	LABR		PRAGFUBUF
BARTKOWIAK, F.	35	M	LABR		PRAGFUBUF
PETZOLD, J.	29	M	CGRMKR		PRAGFUBUF
DOROTHEA	27	F	W		PRAGFUBUF
ELFRIEDE	5	F	CHILD		PRAGFUBUF
ELSA	2	F	CHILD		PRAGFUBUF
DODENHOF, AUGUST	15	M	FARMER		PRAGFUBUF
KLIE, GEORG	46	M	LABR		PRAGFUIA
CATHA.	51	F	W		PRAGFUIA
MARIE	15	F	CH		PRAGFUIA
ELLERBROCH, GUSTAV	30	M	MCHT		PRAGFUNY
PRESTIEN, MARIE	48	F	WO		PRAGFUNY
MARTHA	16	F	CH		PRAGFUNY
ALPHONS	14	M	CH		PRAGFUNY
OTTO	9	M	CHILD		PRAGFUNY
JULIUS	8	M	CHILD		PRAGFUNY
NEUMANN, MAX	21	M	MCHT		PRAGFUNY
GLASSHOF, HENRY	26	M	MSN		PRAGFUNY
WILHE.	29	F	W		PRAGFUNY
EMMA	8	F	CHILD		PRAGFUNY
MINNA	.11	F	INFANT		PRAGFUNY
NEUNZIG, JOH.	28	M	BKR		PRAGFUNY
ELISE	23	F	W		PRAGFUNY
HANS	.03	M	INFANT		PRAGFUNY
ORTE, PETER	44	M	LABR		PRAGFUCH
CATHA.	48	F	W		PRAGFUCH
ANNA	14	F	CH		PRAGFUCH
CHR.	8	M	CHILD		PRAGFUCH
CHR.H.	8	M	CHILD		PRAGFUCH
HELENE	4	F	CHILD		PRAGFUCH
JESSEN, CHR.H.	26	M	FARMER		PRAGFUNY
JENSEN, ELLEN	27	M	FARMER		PRAGFUNY
MOELLER, J.H.	15	M	FARMER		PRAGFUPHI
WILLESIN, ANNA	25	F	SGL		PRAGFUPHI
JENSEN, NISS	27	M	FARMER		PRAGFUNY
DEERTZ, ANNA	21	F	SGL		PRAGFUNY
BETTI	15	F	SGL		PRAGFUCH
NORDSTROEM, PETER	22	M	SHMK		PRAGFUCH
STROSMEYER, HEINRICH	35	M	TNR		PRAGFUPHI
MEYER, CARL	73	M	FARMER		PRAGFUIA
EMILY	19	F	SGL		PRAGFUPHI
KRAUSE, OTTO	16	M	FARMER		PRAGFUPHI
DEWALD, CLARA	21	F	SGL		PRAGFUNY
HEIDER, PAULINE	21	F	SGL		PRAGFUNY
FASSNACHT, BERTHA	26	F	SGL		PRAGFUNY
FINNC, WILH.	38	M	CTHR		PRAGFUNY
ANNA	37	F	W		PRAGFUNY
RICHARD	9	M	CHILD		PRAGFUNY
HELENE	8	F	CHILD		PRAGFUNY
ANNA	.09	F	INFANT		PRAGFUNY
OTTO, CARL	63	M	LABR		PRAGFUTX
HENRIETTE	58	F	W		PRAGFUTX
AUGUSTE	21	M	CH		PRAGFUTX
ANNA	19	F	CH		PRAGFUTX
KOLBE, AUGUST	35	M	LABR		PRAGFUBUF
ELISABETH	25	F	W		PRAGFUBUF
PAULINE	5	F	CHILD		PRAGFUBUF
ANNA	3	F	CHILD		PRAGFUBUF
FRIEDRICH	.03	M	INFANT		PRAGFUBUF
SZYMANCK, MARTIN	30	M	FARMER		PRAGFUNY
CONSTANTIA	30	F	W		PRAGFUNY
MARIANNA	.09	F	INFANT		PRAGFUNY
LITSCHKE, PAULINE	22	F	SGL		PRAGFUNY
CHMIELARZ, FRANZISKA	29	F	SGL		PRAGFUNY
ROCHE	17	F	SGL		PRAGFUNY
ELISABETH	6	F	CHILD		PRAGFUNY
CATHARINA	15	F	SGL		PRAGFUNY
JAFFKE, JOHANN	48	M	LABR		PRAGFUMI
CAROLINE	44	F	W		PRAGFUMI
BERTHOLD	9	M	CHILD		PRAGFUMI
OTTO	8	M	CHILD		PRAGFUMI
HUGO	4	M	CHILD		PRAGFUMI
ADOLF	2	M	CHILD		PRAGFUMI
SELKE, FRANZ	15	M	LABR		PRAGFUMI
RUNG, HIMRICH	50	M	LABR		PRAGFUNY
KAPITKE, RUDOLPH	23	M	LABR		PRAGFUNY
JACOBSOHN, CHRIST.	28	M	FARMER		PRAGFUNY
SIEVERS, WILH.	32	M	FARMER		PRAGFUNY
SCHMIGLINSKY, MARTIN	57	M	FARMER		PRAGFUNY
ANTONIA	43	F	W		PRAGFUNY

PASSENGER	AGE	SEX	OCCUPATION	PRIVL	DES
AGNISKA	20	F	CH		PRAGFUNY
JACOB	18	M	CH		PRAGFUNY
PRAXIDA	16	F	CH		PRAGFUNY
STANISLAWA	14	F	CH		PRAGFUNY
CATHA.	9	F	CHILD		PRAGFUNY
ANTON	8	M	CHILD		PRAGFUNY
FRANZ	6	M	CHILD		PRAGFUNY
FRANZ	4	M	CHILD		PRAGFUNY
FRANZISKA	.11	F	INFANT		PRAGFUNY
ROHS, HEINRICH	26	M	SHMK		PRAGFUBUF
ANNA	22	F	W		PRAGFUBUF
DAWIDOWICZ, MOSES	21	M	JNR		PRAGFUNY
GOVINSKY, MARIANNA	18	F	SGL		PRAGFUNY
JOHLE, PAULINE	29	F	WO		PRAGFUNY
OTTO	4	F	CHILD		PRAGFUNY
WERTH, JACOB	28	M	SMH		PRAGFUNY
HUMBURG, WILH.	29	M	JNR		PRAGFUDAK
ELISABETH	30	F	W		PRAGFUDAK
ANNA	4	F	CHILD		PRAGFUDAK
HEINRICH	2	M	CHILD		PRAGFUDAK
JOHANN	37	M	FARMER		PRAGFUDAK
HELLWIG, HEINRICH	34	M	LKSH		PRAGFUNY
CATHA.	42	F	W		PRAGFUNY
ELISABETH	9	F	CHILD		PRAGFUNY
HEINRICH	7	M	CHILD		PRAGFUNY
MATHILDE	.06	F	INFANT		PRAGFUNY
DAMM, CAROLINE	9	F	CHILD		PRAGFUNY
MUELLER, MARGR.	35	F	WO		PRAGFYNY
HEINRICH	9	M	CHILD		PRAGFYNY
FRIEDR.	8	M	CHILD		PRAGFYNY
CHRISTE.	5	M	CHILD		PRAGFYNY
WILHE.	.11	F	INFANT		PRAGFYNY
SCHMIDT, GUSTAV	18	M	BKR		PRAGFYCH
SCHROEDER, FRANZ	27	M	LABR		PRAGFYNY
BIERWISCH, WILH.	35	M	SMH		PRAGFYNY
BYCKOWSKI, ADOLF	20	M	BCHR		PRAGFYPHI
MOESER, AUGUST	26	M	SMH		PRAGFYBUF
MATHILDE	22	F	W		PRAGFYBUF
KRANEPFUL, WILH.	30	M	SLR		PRAGFYNY
HENRIETTE	29	F	W		PRAGFYNY
ELISE	.11	F	INFANT		PRAGFYNY
KETELSEN, CATHA.	17	F	SGL		PRAGFY***
WOLLMERS, ANNA	52	F	WO		PRAGFYNY
MARIE	17	F	CH		PRAGFYNY
FRITZ	15	M	CH		PRAGFYNY
WITTKOWSKY, JOSEF	36	M	LABR		PRAGFYNY
ANTONIA	31	F	W		PRAGFYNY
JOHANN	9	M	CHILD		PRAGFYNY
STANISLAUS	7	M	CHILD		PRAGFYNY
PELAGIA	.02	F	INFANT		PRAGFYNY
RATAPSAK, STANISLAW	26	M	LABR		PRAGFYNY
MARCZINSKI, JAN	56	M	LABR		PRAGFYNY
ANASTASIA	40	F	W		PRAGFYNY
MARIE	14	F	CH		PRAGFYNY
ANNA	9	F	CHILD		PRAGFYNY
GORRA, ANNA	26	F	SGL		PRAGFYNY
LEHNARDT, CARL	28	M	LABR		PRAGFYNY
ELEONORE	30	F	W		PRAGFYNY
OTTO	6	M	CHILD		PRAGFYNY
EMMA	4	F	CHILD		PRAGFYNY
LAURA	3	F	CHILD		PRAGFYNY
EMMA	2	F	CHILD		PRAGFYNY
STANISLAW	.04	M	INFANT		PRAGFYNY
HARENZA, MICHALINE	40	F	WO		PRAGFYNY
MICHAEL	9	M	CHILD		PRAGFYNY
CATHA.	7	F	CHILD		PRAGFYNY
RYCHLEWICZ, W.	40	M	LABR		PRAGFYNY
ANTONI	9	M	CHILD		PRAGFYNY
FRANKFURT, WALD.	24	M	PNTR		PRAGFYNY
ARNDT, AUGUSTE	22	F	SGL		PRAGFYNY
NOWAKI, MIKOLAY	58	M	LABR		PRAGFYNY
MARY	50	F	W		PRAGFYNY
JOHA.	16	M	CH		PRAGFYNY
LEON	.11	M	INFANT		PRAGFYNY
IRBANSKI, WLADISL.	33	M	LABR		PRAGFYNY
APOLLONIA	28	F	W		PRAGFYNY
STEFANIE	7	F	CHILD		PRAGFYNY
VICENTI	4	F	CHILD		PRAGFYNY
JULE.	3	F	CHILD		PRAGFYNY
JOHN	.11	M	INFANT		PRAGFYNY
WISNIEWSKY, ANNA	25	F	WO		PRAGFYNY
BRONISLAWA	.11	F	INFANT		PRAGFYNY
DIERKER, ADOLF	15	M	FARMER		PRAGFYNY
WOLTER, VALENTIN	23	M	LABR		PRAGFYNY
GUSE, HERMAN	16	M	LABR		PRAGFYNY
KROPSKY, CATHA.	28	F	SGL		PRAGFYNY
CATHA.	54	F	WO		PRAGFYNY
STRYSZAK, ROBERT	16	M	LABR		PRAGFYNY
TOMASZAK, ANTON	27	M	LABR		PRAGFYNY
MICHALINE	27	F	W		PRAGFYNY
ROGANOWSKI, JOS.	35	M	TLR		PRAGFYNY
STEINKE, ERNST	27	M	LABR		PRAGFYNY
MARCHLANSKA, ANNA	25	F	WO		PRAGFYNY
PETER	.11	M	INFANT		PRAGFYNY
MATTHE	.11	M	INFANT		PRAGFYNY
SCHULZ, MARIANNA	23	F	WO		PRAGFYNY
MARIE	.09	F	INFANT		PRAGFYNY
GOHINOSKA, MARY	28	F	WO		PRAGFYNY
MICHAEL	5	M	CHILD		PRAGFYNY
MARY	3	F	CHILD		PRAGFYNY
KOEPP, MARTHA	9	F	CHILD		PRAGFYNY
PANTOWSKA, PAULE.	25	F	SGL		PRAGFYNY
SCHILLER, JULIUS	19	M	MCHT		PRAGFYDAK
NAWROTZKI, ANTON	30	M	LABR		PRAGFYNY
STEKAWSKI, JOHAN	28	M	LABR		PRAGFYNY
WENKE, DOROTHEA	22	F	SGL		PRAGFYNY
HASSLAU, JOHANN	26	M	LABR		PRAGFYSFC
CATHA.	23	F	W		PRAGFYSFC
HEINRICH	2	M	CHILD		PRAGFYSFC
CATHA.	23	F	SI		PRAGFYSFC
LOUISE	.11	F	INFANT		PRAGFYSFC
NICOLAUS	.11	M	INFANT		PRAGFYSFC
PETERSEN, THOMAS	28	M	LABR		PRAGFYNY
JOHE.	19	F	SGL		PRAGFYNY
PETER	25	M	LABR		PRAGFYNY
FUGE, ANNA	22	F	SGL		PRAGFYNY
GUENTHER, JOH.F.	58	M	LABR		PRAGFYNY
MAZAWE, LOUISE	24	F	SGL		PRAGFYNY
HELBIOF, IDA	22	F	SGL		PRAGFYNY
HEMPE, MARTHA	20	F	SGL		PRAGFYNY
PILAKOWSKI, ANDRAS	39	M	LABR		PRAGFYCH
SZYPERSKI, TEOFIL	28	M	LABR		PRAGFYNY
VALERIA	31	F	W		PRAGFYNY
NOWECKA, ELSBETHA	61	F	WO		PRAGFYNY
KROLIK, PETER	37	M	LABR		PRAGFYNY
SPROTZ, WILH.	42	M	LABR		PRAGFYWI
DOROTHEA	40	F	W		PRAGFYWI
TRINA	15	F	CH		PRAGFYWI
ANNA	9	F	CHILD		PRAGFYWI
WILHELM	7	M	CHILD		PRAGFYWI
ELISE	4	F	CHILD		PRAGFYWI
EMMA	2	F	CHILD		PRAGFYWI
KIMME, JOSEF	51	M	WVR		PRAGFYNY
MARIE	48	F	W		PRAGFYNY
WOLTER, JOSEFA	23	F	WO		PRAGFYUNK
MARIANNA	.11	F	INFANT		PRAGFYUNK
KACZMARCH, MICHAEL	29	M	LABR		PRAGFYSRE
ANTONIA	23	F	W		PRAGFYSRE
SCHMIDT, AUGUSTE	36	F	WO		PRAGFYNY
HANS	3	M	CHILD		PRAGFYNY
GRETCHEN	.11	F	INFANT		PRAGFYNY
GOLDMANN, ARTHUR	18	M	MCHT		PRAGFYNY
SWIETLICK, AGNES	17	F	SGL		PRAGFYCH
FRANZISKA	23	F	SGL		PRAGFYCH
MENDELSOHN, MARIE	29	F	WO		PRAGFYNY
DORIS	4	F	CHILD		PRAGFYNY
BIALK, LEO	23	M	LABR		PRAGFYCH
FUERSTENAU, CARL	27	M	LABR		PRAGFYNY
SCHUNKE, GUSTAV	42	M	LABR		PRAGFYNY
FLORENTINE	41	F	W		PRAGFYNY

PASSENGER	AGE	SEX	OCCUPATION	PRVL	DES
EMMA	18	F	CH		PRAGFYNY
BERTHA	9	F	CHILD		PRAGFYNY
HULDA	8	F	CHILD		PRAGFYNY
OLGA	3	F	CHILD		PRAGFYNY
ADOLF	.09	M	INFANT		PRAGFYNY
SEMRAU, DOROTHEA	21	F	SGL		PRAGFYNY
VOPELIUS, CARL	40	M	DYR		PRAGFYNY
THERESE	32	F	W		PRAGFYNY
AGNES	9	F	CHILD		PRAGFYNY
ANNA	8	F	CHILD		PRAGFYNY
OTTO	7	M	CHILD		PRAGFYNY
LOUISE	4	F	CHILD		PRAGFYNY
STEPHAN, FRIEDR.	49	M	LABR		PRAGFYCH
ROSA	52	F	W		PRAGFYCH
FRIEDR.	16	M	CH		PRAGFYCH
MERKEL, EMILIE	21	F	SGL		PRAGFYCH
MINNA	14	F	SGL		PRAGFYCH
KUNZ, OTTO	23	M	LABR		PRAGFYNY
MAIWALD, JOSEF	25	M	LABR		PRAGFYNY
SURANSKY, JACOB	38	M	LABR		PRAGFYNY
BUCHHOLZ, CHRISTE.	53	F	WO		PRAGFYBUF
CHRISTE.	26	F	SGL		PRAGFYBUF
CIESLEWITZ, FELIX	56	M	LABR		PRAGFYNY
FRANZISKA	54	F	W		PRAGFYNY
CIESLEWICZ, STEFAN	15	M	CH		PRAGFYNY
THEODORA	14	F	CH		PRAGFYNY
KOEHLER, DORIS	21	F	WO		PRZZZZUSA
HEROLD, AUGUST	14	M	LABR		PRACBFUSA
SCHNOOR, CLAUS	42	M	LABR		PRACBFUSA
REGINA	40	F	W		PRACBFUSA
WINZEN, JOHANN	26	M	BKR		PRACBWUSA
FINSTERWALDER, RICH	26	M	CL		SYZZZZUSA
RUDOLF, OTTO	16	M	LABR		PRZZZZUSA
ZAPT, PHILIPP	16	M	BKR		BDZZZZUSA
WALFF, MINNA	22	F	SGL		WMZZZZUSA
PAULINE	17	F	SGL		WMZZZZUSA
DOTTILIJE, ROSA	29	F	SGL		WMACBFUSA
RICHERER, CAROLE	30	F	WO		WMACQOUSA
CARL	9	M	CHILD		WMACQOUSA
PAUL	7	M	CHILD		WMACQOUSA
EUGEN	4	M	CHILD		WMACQOUSA
FELDMAIER, GOTTLIEB	58	M	BKR		WMZZZZUSA
LOUISE	45	F	W		WMZZZZUSA
ADOLF	7	M	CHILD		WMZZZZUSA
RAUSCHER, CATH	15	F	SGL		WMAAVWUSA
MUELLER, WM	59	M	LABR		PRZZZZUSA
EMILIE	51	F	UNKNOWN		PRZZZZUSA
AUGUST	19	M	CH		PRZZZZUSA
AUGUSTE	13	F	CH		PRZZZZUSA
WILH	9	M	CHILD		PRZZZZUSA
BUTTER, CARL	37	M	SHMK		PRAAKHUSA
BAER, JOHANN	35	M	LABR		BVZZZZUSA
BARBA	39	F	W		BVZZZZUSA
MARG	9	F	CHILD		BVZZZZUSA
JOH	8	F	CHILD		BVZZZZUSA
J	7	F	CHILD		BVZZZZUSA
MARGR	.11	F	INFANT		BVZZZZUSA
HACKBARTH, BERTHA	16	F	SGL		PRZZZZUSA
SPANDE, ANNA	18	F	SGL		PRAIQXUSA
SCHOBERTH, BARBA	34	F	WO		PRAIQXUSA
MARGR	9	F	CHILD		PRAIQXUSA
JOH	4	M	CHILD		PRAIQXUSA
MENZEL, ALBERT	15	M	FARMER		PRZZZZUSA
STEENHUSEN, CATHA	21	F	SGL		PRACKYUSA

SHIP: SUEVIA

FROM: HAMBURG AND HAVRE
TO: NEW YORK
ARRIVED: 14 MAY 1888

PASSENGER	AGE	SEX	OCCUPATION	PRVL	DES
CREUTZMANN, WILH	33	M	TLR		PRACBFUSA
WOZNIAK, MARTIN	30	M	TLR		PRZZZZUSA
PRIGGE, HEINR	24	M	TLR		PRZZZZUSA
RUNGE, EMMA	24	F	WO		PRAEXJUSA
KNOCHE, AUG	26	M	BCHR		PRADVMUSA
SCHEEL, MARIE	38	F	WO		PRAINKUSA
SOMMER, CARL	38	M	LABR		PRAINKUSA
JANOWIAK, LUKAS	26	M	LABR		PRAEONUSA
BRZYCHY, JACOB	40	M	LABR		PRZZZZUSA
BLOHM, CHRISTIAN	31	M	LABR		PRACBFUSA
HELENA	24	F	W		PRACBFUSA
BECK, ERNST	46	M	LABR		PRAADEUSA
ANDREA	36	F	W		PRAADEUSA
GROESE, CLARA	32	F	W		PRACBFUSA
WILH	8	M	CHILD		PRACBFUSA
ROBERT	4	M	CHILD		PRACBFUSA
SOFIE	3	F	CHILD		PRACBFUSA
OSCAR	00	M	INF		PRACBFUSA
BRUNNERHOFF, FRIEDR	23	M	MSN		PRACBRUSA
PORNHAGEN, SOFIE	49	F	W		PRAINKUSA
WEDE, AUGUSTE	14	F	CH		PRAINKUSA
NAEFTKE, AMANDA	2	F	CHILD		PRAINKUSA
POMMERANCE, JUL	38	M	CPT		PRAASSUSA
BREUER, CLAUS	16	M	LABR		PRACBRUSA
SCHMIDT, GERHARD	24	M	PNTR		PRACBFUSA
BAYER, HERM	35	M	MCHT		PRABPPUSA
ITALIENER, NATHAN	48	M	MCHT		PRACBFUSA
TAMMY	38	F	W		PRACBFUSA
ARNOLD	23	M	CH		PRACBFUSA
ALEXE	15	M	CH		PRACBFUSA
JETTCHEN	8	F	CHILD		PRACBFUSA
JOS	7	M	CHILD		PRACBFUSA
MARIE	6	F	CHILD		PRACBFUSA
BELLA	5	F	CHILD		PRACBFUSA
SENNY	3	F	CHILD		PRACBFUSA
SOFIE	2	F	CHILD		PRACBFUSA
MARE	00	M	INF		PRACBFUSA
ZABOROWSKY, MAGDALENA	60	F	WO		PRABDMUSA
ANTON	18	M	S		PRABDMUSA
STREMPEL, GOTTFRIED	24	M	LABR		PRZZZZUSA
LUDWIG	3	M	CHILD		PRZZZZUSA
SIECHTLING, MARIANNA	22	F	WO		PRZZZZUSA
PETER	.08	M	INFANT		PRZZZZUSA
DRECKHAHN, FRIEDA	8	F	CHILD		PRZZZZUSA
KAUTZEN, BLANKEN	15	F	SGL		PRABMPUSA
JAEGER, HERM	16	M	LABR		PRAAMVUSA
-URTH, KATI	28	F	WO		PRZZZZUSA
ELZA	4	F	CHILD		PRZZZZUSA
META	3	F	CHILD		PRZZZZUSA
MATUELLE, ALWINE	16	F	SGL		PRZZZZUSA
PSZCZOTH, IGNATZ	19	M	LABR		PRZZZZUSA
MUELLER, JACOB	16	M	LABR		PRZZZZUSA
SCHULZ, SOPHIE	35	F	SGL		PRAEHQUSA
GAILUS, ELSE	25	F	SGL		PRZZZZUSA
WALTER, BENJAMIN	16	M	LABR		PRZZZZUSA
BROCKMOELLER, ANTON	27	M	MCHT		PRACBFUSA
LOUISE	22	F	W		PRACBFUSA
HERM	.11	M	INFANT		PRACBFUSA
VICTOR	.01	M	INFANT		PRACBFUSA
MUELLER, OTTO	27	M	SMH		PRZZZZUSA
WILKEN, HANS	53	M	MUSN		PRADYPUSA
CATHA	53	F	W		PRADYPUSA
ROEPKE, CARL	9	M	CHILD		PRADYPUSA
MAASS, HEINR	23	M	MUSN		PRADYPUSA
METSCHER, ANNA	67	F	WO		PRZZZZUSA
KERSTEN, CARL	22	M	LABR		PRADYQUSA
KAPPLER, FRANZ	28	M	BCHR		SYZZZZUSA
HIRSCH, JOHN	27	M	MCHT		SYAAFCUSA
SCHUCH, MICHAEL	52	M	SHMK		BVZZZZUSA
BABETTE	40	F	W		BVZZZZUSA
LORENZ	9	M	CHILD		BVZZZZUSA
KALINKA	7	F	CHILD		BVZZZZUSA
KAUPP, CATHA	19	F	SGL		BVZZZZUSA
LEMBACH, MAGDALENA	31	F	WO		BVZZZZUSA

PASSENGER	AGE	SEX	OCCUPATION	PRV VIL DES
MARGAR	9	F	CHILD	BVZZZZUSA
JORGENSEN, RASMUS	23	M	LABR	BVZZZZUSA
MARKSHAUSEN, HEINR	25	M	PNTR	BVADWZUSA
MARIE	23	F	W	BVADWZUSA
KASCHEFSKI, BERNHD	37	M	MCHT	PRZZZZUSA
MIK-APZAK, ANTON	24	M	LABR	PRZZZZUSA
PIECKEL, JOHANN	28	M	LABR	PRZZZZUSA
PELARK, FRANZ	27	M	LABR	PRZZZZUSA
ANNA	27	F	W	PRZZZZUSA
SPLITT, PETER	32	M	LABR	PRZZZZUSA
DUDSZUS, AMALIE	25	F	WO	PRZZZZUSA
BERTJE-OCKEN, SIEBERTS	21	F	SGL	PRABBZUSA
-NSORGE, FRIEDERIKE	26	F	WO	PRZZZZUSA
HAINKE, HERM	27	M	LABR	PRZZZZUSA
FAUST, EMMA	33	F	WO	PRADGXUSA
ADOLF	5	M	CHILD	PRADGXUSA
----STE	3	F	CHILD	PRADGXUSA
EUGEN	.09	M	INFANT	PRADGXUSA
SCHMIDT, EMMA	20	F	SGL	PRZZZZUSA
BLANKENBURG, FRIEDR	32	M	MUSN	PRZZZZUSA
LASZ, JOH	22	M	LABR	PRZZZZUSA
MUENCH, ADOLF	43	M	LABR	PRZZZZUSA
ANNA	26	F	W	PRZZZZUSA
JOHS	9	M	CHILD	PRZZZZUSA
GUSTAV	5	M	CHILD	PRZZZZUSA
ERNST	.11	M	INFANT	PRZZZZUSA
KROEGER, ALWINE	22	F	SGL	PRAHPYUSA
WINKELMANN, MARGR	42	F	WO	PRZZZZUSA
MARG	9	F	CHILD	PRZZZZUSA
BERTHA	8	F	CHILD	PRZZZZUSA
MINNA	5	F	CHILD	PRZZZZUSA
GUSTAV	3	M	CHILD	PRZZZZUSA
SCHAEFER, ALFRED	16	M	MCHT	PRZZZZUSA
DELFS, JUERGEN	15	M	FARMER	PRZZZZUSA
WILENS, ANNA	18	F	WO	PRZZZZUSA
WILTING, HEINR	16	M	LABR	PRZZZZUSA
DIEDR	14	M	LABR	PRZZZZUSA
GLAWE, HEINR	47	M	FARMER	PRZZZZUSA
WILH	29	F	W	PRZZZZUSA
WILHE	8	F	CHILD	PRZZZZUSA
HERMAN	7	M	CHILD	PRZZZZUSA
FRIEDR	6	M	CHILD	PRZZZZUSA
HEINRICH	5	F	CHILD	PRZZZZUSA
CARL	3	M	CHILD	PRZZZZUSA
JOH	00	M	INF	PRZZZZUSA
HOFFMANN, AMALIE	23	F	WO	PRZZZZUSA
JORDAN, HERM	15	M	FARMER	PRZZZZUSA
THOEM, CLAUS	15	M	FARMER	PRZZZZUSA
UMLAND, AUG	16	M	LABR	PRAACPUSA
ADOLF	17	F	WO	PRZZZZUSA
WEDEMEYER, CATHA	20	F	WO	PRZZZZUSA
PE-K, LUDW	54	M	FARMER	PRADEQUSA
MUNN, WILH	56	M	FARMER	PRZZZZUSA
ANTJE	53	F	W	PRZZZZUSA
MAGDALENA	21	F	CH	PRZZZZUSA
JACOB	19	M	CH	PRZZZZUSA
HERM	13	M	CH	PRZZZZUSA
FRITZ	8	M	CHILD	PRZZZZUSA
MARIE	4	F	CHILD	PRZZZZUSA
GROTH, ANNA	19	F	WO	PRZZZZUSA
INGWERSEN, JOHA	26	F	W	PRZZZZUSA
JOHANN	4	M	CHILD	PRZZZZUSA
INGEBORG	00	M	INF	PRZZZZUSA
LORENZEN, JACOB	28	M	FARMER	PRZZZZUSA
HARDER, HEINRICH	25	M	LABR	PRZZZZUSA
ANNA	20	F	W	PRZZZZUSA
STUETZA, FELIX	29	M	LABR	PRZZZZUSA
SEEBAS, ALEX	25	M	MCHT	SYZZZZUSA
MALSKEIT, AUG	15	M	LABR	PRZZZZUSA
-UDSZUS, AUG	1	M	CHILD	PRZZZZUSA
LOUIS	00	M	INF	PRZZZZUSA
SCHROEDER, JOHANN	23	M	LABR	PRZZZZUSA
WIDEMANN, JOSEFINE	22	F	WO	PRZZZZUSA
EDELMANN, ALFONS	16	M	LABR	PRZZZZUSA
WALKERREIT, CARL	18	M	LKSH	PRAFNKUSA
STAUDENMEIER, CARL	23	M	MCHT	WMZZZZUSA
FLECKENSTEIN, CATHA	21	F	WO	BVZZZZUSA
MATTELER, MARIE	21	F	WO	WMZZZZUSA
ZOERNER, CHRISTIAN	54	M	FARMER	WMZZZZUSA
CHRISTINE	48	F	W	WMZZZZUSA
CARL	19	M	S	WMZZZZUSA
JOH	20	M	S	WMZZZZUSA
EMMA	00	F	INF	WMZZZZUSA
BOTTCHER, IDA	14	M	UNKNOWN	PRZZZZUSA
ERNST, ALBERT	43	M	LABR	PRAAIXUSA
BOESEL, HERM	34	M	LABR	PRZZZZUSA
MEYER, AUGUST	25	M	LABR	PRZZZZUSA
NITSCHKE, ADOLF	47	M	JNR	PRAARZUSA
LABINSKA, WENDEL	35	M	LABR	PRAFRBUSA
MEYER, FRIEDR	15	M	FARMER	PRZZZZUSA
STOECKENBERGER, JOH	17	M	FARMER	PRAFBVUSA
KUEHN, FRIEDR	17	M	FARMER	BVZZZZUSA
JACOBSEN, MARGR	19	F	SGL	PRZZZZUSA
HENGST, IDA	21	F	SGL	PRAAXKUSA
FEDDERSEN, MARGR	15	F	SGL	PRZZZZUSA
MADOLIN, ELISABETH	48	F	WO	PRZZZZUSA
GLADCZAK, VALENTY	34	M	LABR	PRZZZZUSA
MUENSTER, ANNA	18	F	SGL	PRZZZZUSA
SCHROEDER, WILH	27	M	LABR	PRZZZZUSA
JOZWIAK, CATHA	32	F	WO	PRZZZZUSA
JOSEF	7	M	CHILD	PRZZZZUSA
IGNATZ	4	M	CHILD	PRZZZZUSA
STANISLAWA	.09	F	INFANT	PRZZZZUSA
CLEMENS, OSWALD	18	M	UNKNOWN	SYZZZZUSA
TIPKE, JOHANN	29	M	UNKNOWN	PRZZZZUSA
MAASS, ERNST	15	M	UNKNOWN	PRZZZZUSA
TRAEGER, AGNES	25	F	SGL	PRACBRUSA
LENZ, ALBERT	19	M	LABR	PRZZZZUSA
DRUCKER, FANNY	22	F	SGL	PRABNOUSA
LABUISKA, DORA	34	F	WO	PRAFRBUSA
ROSA	7	F	CHILD	PRAFRBUSA
SALI	5	M	CHILD	PRAFRBUSA
HEINR	2	M	CHILD	PRAFRBUSA
NATHALIE	.10	F	INFANT	PRAFRBUSA
WOYIESCZAK, JACOB	23	M	LABR	PRZZZZUSA
ABRAHAM, EMILIE	26	F	WO	PRAEABUSA
MARIE	18	F	SGL	PRAEABUSA
SALI	.03	M	INFANT	PRAEABUSA
KALUPA, ANTON	30	M	SMH	PRZZZZUSA
COHN, LIEBCHEN	55	F	WO	PRAIFVUSA
PERETZ, OTTILIE	22	F	SGL	PRAFRBUSA
BERTHA	20	F	SGL	PRAFRBUSA
SEELIG, BRUNO	17	M	MCHT	PRAARZUSA
MEYER, ROSA	28	F	WO	PRAAKHUSA
ANNA	4	F	CHILD	PRAAKHUSA
SOFIE	.11	F	INFANT	PRAAKHUSA
ELLA	.01	F	INFANT	PRAAKHUSA
HUEBNER, GEORG	18	M	GDNR	PRAAKHUSA
BRENK, MICHAEL	26	M	LABR	PRZZZZUSA
ROST, HEINR	55	M	MNFTR	PRAAKHUSA
MARIE	42	F	W	PRAAKHUSA
FRIEDE	9	F	CHILD	PRAAKHUSA
SCHUMANN, CARL	28	M	TLR	PRAAKHUSA
GREVE, FRANZ	25	M	LABR	PRZZZZUSA
HENPEL, FRIEDR	54	M	WVR	PRAAXKUSA
ZIMMERLING, CARL	57	M	FARMER	PRZZZZUSA
HARTKOPT, AUGUST	27	M	MCHT	PRZZZZUSA
WENDT, MAX	38	M	MCHT	PRACBFUSA
MUELLER, ROSALIA	57	M	WO	PRADHXUSA
HILDENBRAND, CARL	19	M	BKBNDR	PRACPEUSA
SCHOCKEL, HEINR	32	M	BKR	PRZZZZUSA
MAUMANN, PAUL	17	M	FARMER	PRABOKUSA
LEONHARDT, AUGUST	51	M	LABR	SYZZZZUSA
SCHOLL, CAROLE	25	F	SGL	SYAFCTUSA
KLEIN, CATHA	20	F	SGL	SYAFCTUSA
KULL, AUGUST	16	M	BKR	SYAFCTUSA
HAAS, NANE	21	F	SGL	WMZZZZUSA
KLUEGEL, GUSTAV	17	M	LABR	WMABDMUSA
STENDA, SOPHIE	20	F	SGL	WMZZZZUSA
FRIEDECK, CARL	45	M	LABR	WMAARZUSA

PASSENGER	AGE	SEX	OCCUPATION	PRVL	DES
IDA	36	F	W	WMAARZUSA
CARL	6	M	CHILD	WMAARZUSA
IDA	2	F	CHILD	WMAARZUSA
HUAS	.09	M	INFANT	WMAARZUSA
CHRISTIANSEN, JENS	26	M	LABR	PRZZZZUSA
CAROLE	26	F	W	PRZZZZUSA
KRISTE	.11	F	INFANT	PRZZZZUSA
WACHOWIAK, PETER	23	M	LABR	PRZZZZUSA
MARIANNA	22	F	W	PRZZZZUSA
ANTON	.03	M	INFANT	PRZZZZUSA
POCHERDIN, HEINR	23	M	WVR	SRZZZZUSA
KRAUS, JACOB	31	M	WVR	SRZZZZUSA
ANNA	29	F	W	SRZZZZUSA
FRIDA	4	F	CHILD	SRZZZZUSA
ROSA	.04	F	INFANT	SRZZZZUSA
JINHOF, EMIL	24	M	LABR	SRAAKJUSA
KRAUS, MARIE	.01	F	INFANT	SRAAKJUSA
S--HOF, MELANIE	22	F	W	SRAAKJUSA
GERUM, JAN	33	M	CPTR	SRZZZZUSA
HOTZ, JOSEF	24	M	CPTR	SRZZZZUSA
LUDWIG, CONRAD	20	M	LKSH	SRAAHUUSA
PERIER, L--DES	24	F	LABR	SRAAHUUSA
MATHILDE	23	F	UNKNOWN	SRAESOUSA
MUECK, JOHANN	26	M	LKSH	SRAAHUUSA
BROT, ROBERT	26	M	LABR	SRAAHUUSA
HENRY, LUDWIG	17	M	LABR	SRAAHUUSA
JARIE, ANNA	36	F	WO	SRAAHUUSA
ROSA	11	F	CH	SRAAHUUSA
CHRISTIAN	10	F	CH	SRAAHUUSA
MELCHIOR	9	M	CHILD	SRAAHUUSA
MARGARITHE	7	F	CHILD	SRAAHUUSA
ANTON	4	M	CHILD	SRAAHUUSA
CHRISTOFFERT, GEORGE	21	M	LABR	SRAAHUUSA
RUEDI, HEINRICH	27	M	FARMER	SRZZZZUSA
HILDBOLD, ADOLF	27	M	FARMER	SRZZZZUSA
EMMA	21	F	W	SRZZZZUSA
FRIDA	.09	F	INFANT	SRZZZZUSA
----STEN, ELISA	25	F	UNKNOWN	SRAAKJUSA
CANIMADA, LUIGI	43	M	LABR	SRAAKJUSA
HIRT, JACOB	26	M	LABR	SRZZZZUSA
STIEFENHOFER, VALENINE	32	M	FARMER	SRZZZZUSA
ALOISE	29	M	FARMER	SRZZZZUSA
GOSSER, ALBERT	21	M	UNKNOWN	SRZZZZUSA
SACHER, ANTONI	39	M	LABR	SRZZZZUSA
FRIDOLENE	44	M	LABR	SRZZZZUSA
HERZOG, LINA	37	F	WO	SRZZZZUSA
REICHLE, ADOLF	28	M	LABR	SRZZZZUSA
VETSCH, CARL	18	M	FARMER	SRZZZZUSA
MOSER, ANNA	20	F	SGL	SRAAKJUSA
AMBORDT, PETER	42	M	FARMER	SRZZZZUSA
LOUISE	42	F	W	SRZZZZUSA
BIDERBROT, ANTON	21	M	FARMER	SRZZZZUSA
FRANZ	26	M	FARMER	SRZZZZUSA
ZANG, CHARLES	18	M	FARMER	SRZZZZUSA
JARDIN, JULIA	44	F	WO	SRAAHUUSA
MA--GOLD, THEOPHIL	18	M	LABR	SRAAHUUSA
HA-FLEIN, CARL	48	M	LABR	SRAAKJUSA
MARSINI, BATTISTA	30	F	W	SRAAKJUSA
CORLAZ, LOUIS	28	M	LABR	PRZZZZUSA
CHRISTO, FRANZOIS	23	M	LABR	PRZZZZUSA
ORICZ, LOUIS	20	M	LABR	PRZZZZUSA
FROSSARD, JOSEF	18	M	LABR	PRAAHUUSA
SCHA-NLLE, HERM	26	M	LABR	PRAAHUUSA
BRUNNER, CATHERINE	25	F	W	PRAAHUUSA
AMAN-, CRISTOMUS	22	M	LABR	PRAAHUUSA
KOHLER, ELISE	21	F	W	PRAAHUUSA
SPOHN, JACQUES	21	M	LABR	PRAAHUUSA
H--M-KER, HERM	23	M	LABR	PRAAHUUSA
R-THISBERGER, GOTTLIEB	41	M	LABR	PRAAHUUSA
ROSETTE	43	F	WO	PRAAHUUSA
ALBERT	11	M	CH	PRAAHUUSA
MARIE	10	F	CH	PRAAHUUSA
EMILIE	7	F	CHILD	PRAAHUUSA
MARTH	6	M	CHILD	PRAAHUUSA
MARTHA	4	F	CHILD	PRAAHUUSA
ERNEST	2	M	CHILD	PRAAHUUSA
ARNOLD	1	M	CHILD	PRAAHUUSA
SCHAAD, SAMUEL	21	M	LABR	PRAAKJUSA
JOHANN	20	F	W	PRAAKJUSA
WELTER, JOH	44	M	LABR	PRAGFDUSA
STEINBRENNER, LEO	17	M	LABR	PRAGFDUSA
KLENK, MARIE	20	F	SGL	PRAGFDUSA
PAULINE	15	F	SGL	PRAGFDUSA
GR--NN, ADAM	22	M	LABR	PRAGFDUSA
ZELTMANN, JOH	46	M	LABR	PRAGFDUSA
CATH	33	F	W	PRAGFDUSA
CATH	19	F	CH	PRAGFDUSA
LOUISE	15	F	CH	PRAGFDUSA
FRED	12	M	CH	PRAGFDUSA
SCHWEICKHAIDT, GOTTLIEB	17	M	LABR	PRAGFDUSA
DIETZ, LOUISE	36	F	WO	PRAGFDUSA
CHRIST	9	M	CHILD	PRAGFDUSA
HENRI	7	M	CHILD	PRAGFDUSA
FRED	5	F	CHILD	PRAGFDUSA
JAC	4	M	CHILD	PRAGFDUSA
LOUISE	1	F	CHILD	PRAGFDUSA
LEHMANN, MARIE	12	F	CH	PRAGFDUSA
ZELTMANN, PAULINE	8	F	CHILD	PRAGFDUSA
FRED	4	M	CHILD	PRAGFDUSA
CHARLES	2	M	CHILD	PRAGFDUSA
EMILIE	2	F	CHILD	PRAGFDUSA
AUGUSTE	.06	F	INFANT	PRAGFDUSA
BERTHA	.06	F	INFANT	PRAGFDUSA
SCHWEICKHAEDT, LUDV	26	M	LABR	PRAGFDUSA
RONNI	22	F	W	PRAGFDUSA
MARI	2	F	CHILD	PRAGFDUSA
CHARLES	.06	M	INFANT	PRAGFDUSA
LUDW	60	M	LABR	PRAGFDUSA
CATH	56	F	W	PRAGFDUSA
ELIS	16	F	D	PRAGFDUSA
H-CHULE, WILLY	16	M	LABR	PRAGFDUSA
GOLL, CRET	18	M	LABR	PRAGFDUSA
JUELLE, CAROLINE	16	F	SGL	PRAGFDUSA
KELLER, GOTTLOB	16	M	LABR	PRAGFDUSA
MOUNENNAEBER, CRET	24	M	LABR	PRAGFDUSA
HOHENLOSER, LOUISE	25	F	SGL	PRAGFDUSA
SCHWARZ, WEDELIN	33	F	SGL	PRAGFDUSA
SOULOUSSI, SUKELARIOS	25	F	SGL	PRAGFDUSA
SIEFART, PAULINE	52	F	WO	PRAAFCUSA
NACHTER, CLARA	36	F	WO	PRACVAUSA
HEULS, HEDWIG	17	F	SGL	PRAAVWUSA
PIEDGE, MARIE	28	M	LABR	PRAALZUSA
V., GUSTAV	31	M	PVTM	SYZZZZUSA
SAULIAN, GEORG	9	M	CHILD	PRZZZZUSA
ANDERSSON, ERNST	23	M	MCHT	PRAARZUSA
HMMER, ANNA	36	F	SGL	SRZZZZUSA
GARTNER, J	46	M	MCHT	SRAARZUSA

SHIP: CIRCASSIA

FROM: GLASGOW AND MOVILLE
TO: NEW YORK
ARRIVED: 15 MAY 1888

PASSENGER	AGE	SEX	OCCUPATION	PRVL	DES
DOCH, FRANZ	26	M	LABR	GRZZZZUSA
GRABORS-YZK, MARCUS	35	M	LABR	GRZZZZUSA
SKONROSKI, MICH	23	M	LABR	GRZZZZUSA
BAUMAN, EVALD	17	M	LABR	GRZZZZUSA
HENSCHKE, AUG	32	M	LABR	GRZZZZUSA
PAULAK, PIETRO	31	M	LABR	GRZZZZUSA
WIESNIESKY, WALENTZ	28	M	LABR	GRZZZZUSA
-DKOWSKI, ANT	26	M	LABR	GRZZZZUSA
GRAKOWSKI, JAN	32	M	LABR	GRZZZZUSA
FRANZ	35	M	LABR	GRZZZZUSA
ZIMMERMANN, NIKOLAS	14	M	CL	GRZZZZUSA

PASSENGER	AGE	SEX	OCCUPATION	PRVL	DES	PASSENGER	AGE	SEX	OCCUPATION	PRVL	DES
KOULASKI, JAN	39	M	LABR	GRZZZZ	USA	SHIP: HUNGARIA					
KARLINSKI, JOSEF	30	M	LABR	GRZZZZ	USA						
SILINKI, IGNATZ	26	M	LABR	GRZZZZ	USA	FROM: HAMBURG					
CIENCZYK, JAN	27	M	LABR	GRZZZZ	USA	TO: NEW YORK					
JORGENS, PETER	49	M	LABR	GRZZZZ	USA	ARRIVED: 15 MAY 1888					
RAK, PAUL	28	M	LABR	GRZZZZ	USA						
WEEKE, EMIL	22	M	DLR	GRZZZZ	USA						
MILKE, CARL	28	M	LABR	GRZZZZ	USA	SCHLECHT, WILHELM	30	M	CPTR	PRZZZZ	USA
BARIENSZKI, JOSEF	24	M	LABR	GRZZZZ	USA	AUGUSTE	40	F	W	PRZZZZ	USA
SZEDLIKOWSKI, JOSEF	24	M	LABR	GRZZZZ	USA	MINNIE	16	F	CH	PRZZZZ	USA
JOHAN	49	M	LABR	GRZZZZ	USA	AMANDA	14	F	CH	PRZZZZ	USA
STAZKOWI-CZ, MAX	28	M	LABR	GRZZZZ	USA	JOHANN	9	M	CHILD	PRZZZZ	USA
HELLSTERN, EUGENE	14	M	LABR	GRZZZZ	USA	EMMA	4	F	CHILD	PRZZZZ	USA
-WEATKOWSKY, WALENTZ	35	M	LABR	GRZZZZ	USA	GUSTAV	.06	M	INFANT	PRZZZZ	USA
BEDNARIK, WOCECH	32	M	LABR	GRZZZZ	USA	WILHELM	.06	M	INFANT	PRZZZZ	USA
MEYEROWITZ, MAX	28	M	BLKSMH	GRZZZZ	USA	WALCZAK, STANISLAUS	55	M	LABR	PRZZZZ	USA
BRANTZEN, SIMON	60	M	LABR	GRZZZZ	USA	TRIEBEK, ANTON	43	M	LABR	PRZZZZ	USA
BENTHER, TIMOTHENS	14	M	CL	GRZZZZ	USA	MARY	43	F	W	PRZZZZ	USA
ZIMMERMANN, GREGOR	13	M	LABR	GRZZZZ	USA	FRANZISKA	16	F	CH	PRZZZZ	USA
HAMMER, R	24	M	LKSH	GRZZZZ	USA	CATHA	7	F	CHILD	PRZZZZ	USA
KLEIN, BERNHARD	26	M	LABR	GRZZZZ	USA	JOSEF	7	M	CHILD	PRZZZZ	USA
BRUSSEN, WALLENTIN	25	M	LABR	GRZZZZ	USA	VICTORIA	2	F	CHILD	PRZZZZ	USA
ROSING, AMANDE	17	F	HP	GRZZZZ	USA	S-KOLOWSKY, FRANZ	19	M	LABR	PRZZZZ	USA
ANSBERG, MENICKE	58	F	W	GRZZZZ	USA	BLUEMEL, HERMANN	42	M	LABR	PRZZZZ	USA
PAULIKE	8	F	CHILD	GRZZZZ	USA	ERNESTINE	42	F	W	PRZZZZ	USA
HEINE-, JULIANNA	52	F	HP	GRZZZZ	USA	MARTHA	8	F	CHILD	PRZZZZ	USA
GRAPE, MINA	22	F	HP	GRZZZZ	USA	KENGELSKA, MARIE	22	F	SGL	PRZZZZ	USA
GOEZ, FRANSESCA	30	F	HP	GRZZZZ	USA	BELLER, MICHAEL	20	M	LABR	SYZZZZ	USA
JAREK, MARIA	30	F	CK	GRZZZZ	USA	FREY, MINNA	37	F	WO	SYZZZZ	USA
HELLSTERN, JAK-MEDA	20	F	HP	GRZZZZ	USA	FRANZISKA	7	F	CHILD	SYZZZZ	USA
SYZMONIAK, AND	26	M	LABR	GRZZZZ	USA	GRAULICH, WILHELM	17	M	SGL	PRZZZZ	USA
ANASTA	22	F	W	GRZZZZ	USA	BERHAUPT, JOHS	22	M	FARMER	WMZZZZ	USA
BO----	.11	F	INFANT	GRZZZZ	USA	MAYN, JOHANNES	37	M	UNKNOWN	PRZZZZ	USA
GAWRICH, ANT	27	M	JNR	GRZZZZ	USA	JESSEN, LUDWIG	46	M	FARMER	PRZZZZ	USA
ANASTAS	24	F	W	GRZZZZ	USA	CAECILIA	16	F	D	PRZZZZ	USA
B-GES	4	M	CHILD	GRZZZZ	USA	WIENOLD, ERNESTINE	51	F	W	SYZZZZ	USA
ANT	4	M	CHILD	GRZZZZ	USA	PAUL	9	M	CHILD	SYZZZZ	USA
ANGLECIA	1	F	CHILD	GRZZZZ	USA	GRAUPNER, MAX	24	M	LABR	SYZZZZ	USA
SZE-OMOWSKA, EVA	22	F	HP	GRZZZZ	USA	ROZA, -EDOR	31	F	WO	PRZZZZ	USA
HELLSTERN, BARTH	60	M	LABR	GRZZZZ	USA	HEISER, ERNST	28	M	SHMK	SYZZZZ	USA
SARA	54	F	W	GRZZZZ	USA	REIMANN, FRIEDR	30	M	UNKNOWN	SYZZZZ	USA
MATHILDA	11	F	CH	GRZZZZ	USA	MILKOWSKY, THEODOR	23	M	BCHR	PRZZZZ	USA
MELKE, MICH	38	M	LABR	GRZZZZ	USA	JULIANE	25	F	W	PRZZZZ	USA
JOSEFA	27	F	W	GRZZZZ	USA	KOSCHINSKY, FRANZ	24	M	LABR	PRZZZZ	USA
ANT	.08	M	INFANT	GRZZZZ	USA	JAKES, CASIMIR	22	M	LABR	PRZZZZ	USA
GRETCH, A	51	M	GDNR	GRZZZZ	USA	MUSI-LOWSKY, JOH	36	M	LABR	PRZZZZ	USA
ELIZ	42	F	W	GRZZZZ	USA	NONA, WOJECH	31	M	LABR	PRZZZZ	USA
CARL	3	M	CHILD	GRZZZZ	USA	HANNEMANN, LOUIS	34	M	FARMER	PRZZZZ	USA
KISPERT, JOHAN	44	M	LABR	GRZZZZ	USA	JANSKI, ALBERTINE	23	F	WO	PRZZZZ	USA
ANNA	25	F	W	GRZZZZ	USA	LISNECKI, LUCIAN	26	M	LABR	PRZZZZ	USA
GRABOWSKI, IGNATZ	43	M	LABR	GRZZZZ	USA	JAWBROCK, JACOB	30	M	LABR	PRZZZZ	USA
APOLLINA	34	F	W	GRZZZZ	USA	AGNES	26	F	W	PRZZZZ	USA
ZUCHLINSKI, MICH	28	M	BRR	GRZZZZ	USA	FRANZ	4	M	CHILD	PRZZZZ	USA
MARIANNE	25	F	W	GRZZZZ	USA	WAWRZYN	3	M	CHILD	PRZZZZ	USA
ROSALIE	.03	F	INFANT	GRZZZZ	USA	JOSEFA	.11	F	INFANT	PRZZZZ	USA
TUREK, WO-CECH	24	M	TLR	GRZZZZ	USA	SIMANA, VALENTY	25	M	LABR	PRZZZZ	USA
MARGT	24	F	W	GRZZZZ	USA	PACHE, HEINR	17	M	LABR	PRZZZZ	USA
STEPHAN	.06	M	INFANT	GRZZZZ	USA	HENTSCHEL, OTTO	32	M	WHR	PRZZZZ	USA
HERBORM, HERMAN	28	M	LABR	GRAHRZ	USA	MUELLER, RUDOLF	33	M	SHMK	PRZZZZ	USA
JOHANNA	24	F	W	GRAHRZ	USA	DOSCH, MICHAL	24	M	BCHR	BVZZZZ	USA
U	00	M	INF	GR****U	USA	FREUNTLEIN, BARBARA	24	F	WO	BVZZZZ	USA
MICH	3	M	CHILD	GRAHRZ	USA	ULRICH, BABETTE	23	F	SGL	BVZZZZ	USA
JULIUS	2	M	CHILD	GRAHRZ	USA	DEMUTH, WILHELMINE	17	F	SGL	PRZZZZ	USA
BOGDA, FERD	58	M	LABR	GRAHRZ	USA	FRIEDRICH	15	M	MSN	PRZZZZ	USA
WILHA	56	F	W	GRAHRZ	USA	OLZEWSKY, JOSEF	26	M	LABR	PRZZZZ	USA
JOHANN	28	M	LABR	GRAHRZ	USA	MITTELHAEUSER, RUDOLF	30	M	LABR	PRZZZZ	USA
AUGUSTA	26	F	W	GRAHRZ	USA	SUESSMILCH, HEINRICH	35	M	TLR	PRZZZZ	USA
ALVINE	6	F	CHILD	GRAHRZ	USA	KUTZNER, WILHELMINE	50	F	W	PRZZZZ	USA
ANNA	1	F	CHILD	GRAHRZ	USA						

```
                        A  S          P V  D                               A  S          P V  D
                        G  E OCCUPATION R I  E                              G  E OCCUPATION R I  E
PASSENGER               E  X          V L  S     PASSENGER                  E  X          V L  S
--------------------------------------------     --------------------------------------------
SHIP:   EIDER                                    LENZ, WILLIAM             16 M GCR        GRZZZZUSA
                                                 BJUCKOWSKI, JOSEF         24 M LABR       GRZZZZUSA
FROM:   BREMEN AND SOUTHAMPTON                   LEWANDOWSKA, AGNZISZKA    34 F W          GRZZZZUSA
TO:     NEW YORK                                   JULIA                    7 F CHILD      GRZZZZUSA
ARRIVED: 16 MAY 1888                              JOHANN                   6 M CHILD       GRZZZZUSA
                                                  FRANZ                    4 M CHILD       GRZZZZUSA
                                                  MARIANNA                .09 F INFANT     GRZZZZUSA
RUSS, F.                41 F UNKNOWN  UNZZZZUSA ROTH, MARIA               49 F NN         GRZZZZUSA
FREI, LINA              16 F NN       GRZZZZGR  MAIER, AUG.               15 M NN         GRZZZZUSA
WEHN, TONI              22 F NN       GRZZZZGR  NEUNER, MARIE             23 F SVNT       GRZZZZUSA
KOSNAPFE, HELENE        25 F NN       GRZZZZGR  WOLF, WALDEMAR            17 M LABR       GRZZZZUSA
MARKWALD, ERNST         29 M UNKNOWN  GRZZZZGR  SCHUMANN, THERESIA        19 F SVNT       GRZZZZUSA
MEINHARDT, MARIE        53 F NN       GRZZZZGR  STERBENZ, JOSEPH          38 M LABR       GRZZZZUSA
ADLER, CAROLINE         23 F NN       GRZZZZGR  KOCH, MARIE               21 F SVNT       GRZZZZUSA
WAHLE, FRIEDERKE.       19 F NN       GRZZZZGR  GUETTLER, SIMON           34 M MCHT       GRZZZZUSA
BOETTCHER, MARG.        49 F NN       GRZZZZGR  SPRANGER, HAVER           29 M MCHT       GRZZZZUSA
BYER, L.                23 M UNKNOWN  GRZZZZGR  RAUCH, KARL               31 M CNF        GRZZZZUSA
WISSEL, CONRAD          62 M UNKNOWN  GRZZZZGR  GRUNDLE, WOLFG.            6 M CHILD       GRZZZZUSA
   CAECILIE             54 F NN       GRZZZZGR  BUERNER, KUNIGUNDE        23 F NN         GRZZZZUSA
GRUENWALD, MATHILDE     28 F NN       GRZZZZGR  STREHLE, MARIA            18 F SVNT       GRZZZZUSA
SPALDING, CARL          64 M NN       GRZZZZGR  SOMMERFELD, HERM.         17 M FARMER     GRZZZZUSA
   MARIE                17 F NN       GRZZZZGR  SCHROEDER, HEINR.         16 M FARMER     GRZZZZUSA
SCHOENFELD, MINNA       20 F NN       GRZZZZGR  KUEHLB---, CHR.           14 M FARMER     GRZZZZUSA
HALLE, ALBERT           17 M NN       GRZZZZGR  LAMPRECHT, LOUISE         23 F NN         GRZZZZUSA
LUEHRSEN, MARIE         66 F NN       GRZZZZGR     GRETCHEN              .11 F INFANT     GRZZZZUSA
KRUETZFELDT, AUGUSTE    29 F NN       GRZZZZGR  SCHWEDLOWSKI, MICH.       28 M LABR       GRZZZZUSA
LIND, PH.               44 M NN       GRZZZZGR  BUCHERT, PAUL             19 M LABR       GRZZZZUSA
   LOUISE               44 F W        GRZZZZGR  SCHREINER, JOHANN         19 M LABR       GRZZZZUSA
LUHTMANN, CHARL.        31 F UNKNOWN  GRZZZZGR  MUELLER, META             16 F NN         GRZZZZUSA
HINSCH, HEINR.          28 M UNKNOWN  GRZZZZGR  JAEGER, ANNA              16 F NN         GRZZZZUSA
AUERBACH, SELMA         23 F UNKNOWN  GRZZZZGR  HEINRICHS, CONRAD         26 M FARMER     GRZZZZUSA
BUETHEFISCH, ANNA       17 F UNKNOWN  GRZZZZGR  STAWETZKI, ANDRAS         68 M FARMER     GRZZZZUSA
ULASZEWSKI, WALENTY     15 M LABR     GRZZZZUSA TRE----, HEINR.           26 M FARMER     GRZZZZUSA
KUSINSKY, FRANZ         25 M LABR     GRZZZZUSA SCHEUNEMANN, ALB.         30 M UNKNOWN    GRZZZZUSA
LAKOMECKI, VALENTZ      17 M LABR     GRZZZZUSA OTTO, FRIEDR.             26 M UNKNOWN    GRZZZZUSA
GAZYBOSKI, MICHALL      27 M LABR     GRZZZZUSA GROEPLER, MART.           22 M UNKNOWN    GRZZZZUSA
SKOZVANSKI, FRANZ       20 M LABR     GRZZZZUSA STEINDEL, AUGUSTE         18 F SVNT       GRZZZZUSA
ERHARDT, KUNIGUNDE      28 F NN       GRZZZZUSA BRUER, HEINR.             15 M FARMER     GRZZZZUSA
   JOHANN              .11 M INFANT   GRZZZZUSA KREUZ, ADAM               43 M FARMER     GRZZZZUSA
SCOZRANSKI, ANTONI      20 M LABR     GRZZZZUSA WOLF, ALEX                30 M FARMER     GRZZZZUSA
DEHLER, WILHELMINE      18 F SVNT     GRZZZZUSA JOOSTEN, REMMER           48 M FARMER     GRZZZZUSA
GOETZ, EVA              16 F SVNT     GRZZZZUSA    SOPHIE                 46 F W          GRZZZZUSA
OFFENBACHER, ELISAB.    68 F NN       GRZZZZUSA    JOHANN                 14 M NN         GRZZZZUSA
TRAEGER, ANNA           30 F NN       GRZZZZUSA    HEINRICH                8 M CHILD      GRZZZZUSA
KLEIN, ANNA             27 F NN       GRZZZZUSA    WILHELM                 6 M CHILD      GRZZZZUSA
KEMPA, FRANZ            35 M LABR     GRZZZZUSA    MARTHA                  5 F CHILD      GRZZZZUSA
LUNANDOWSKI, FRANZ      33 M LABR     GRZZZZUSA D-AKER, ADELHEID          25 F SVNT       GRZZZZUSA
TIEBELKORN, MICHEL      31 M LABR     GRZZZZUSA LUNDI, MARTIN             75 M FARMER     GRZZZZUSA
   PAULINE              31 F W        GRZZZZUSA VONHASSELN, HERM.         14 M FARMER     GRZZZZUSA
   AGNES                 4 F CHILD    GRZZZZUSA HOOPS, ANNA               18 F SVNT       GRZZZZUSA
   CLARA                 3 F CHILD    GRZZZZUSA SCHULDT, FRIEDERIKE       19 F SVNT       GRZZZZUSA
   ELISABETH           .11 F INFANT   GRZZZZUSA VONGLAHN, SOPHIE          19 F SVNT       GRZZZZUSA
   MARGARETHE          .06 F INFANT   GRZZZZUSA VONHOLLEN, IDA            18 F SVNT       GRZZZZUSA
BIERWALT, AUGUST        28 M FARMER   GRZZZZUSA BEHRENS, HEINR.           24 M LABR       GRZZZZUSA
   MARIA                29 F NN       GRZZZZUSA HORMANN, LUDW.            23 M LABR       GRZZZZUSA
   MARIA               .09 F INFANT   GRZZZZUSA WIEBLEN, MARIE            49 F NN         GRZZZZUSA
LIEMPKIC, ROZALIE       22 F NN       GRZZZZUSA    ERNST                   8 M CHILD      GRZZZZUSA
ESCHENBACH, FRANZ       28 M PNTR     GRZZZZUSA HOFFMANN, CATHAR.         21 F SVNT       GRZZZZUSA
SCHMIDT, CATHAR.        20 F SVNT     GRZZZZUSA GRUENE, ANNA              23 F SVNT       GRZZZZUSA
GOERKE, HERM.           25 M FARMER   GRZZZZUSA BRUNKHORST, MARIA         15 F SVNT       GRZZZZUSA
   HENRIETTE            23 F W        GRZZZZUSA SEEHASE, AUGUST           18 F SVNT       GRZZZZUSA
VIEREGGE, FRIEDRICH     28 F NN       GRZZZZUSA MEIS---, WILH.            14 M SVNT       GRZZZZUSA
   SIMON                31 M FARMER   GRZZZZUSA SIEN----, ANNA            44 F NN         GRZZZZUSA
   FRIEDERIKE           48 F NN       GRZZZZUSA    SOPHIE                  7 F CHILD      GRZZZZUSA
   WILHELM               5 M CHILD    GRZZZZUSA OLTMANN, GERHD.           30 M SMH        GRZZZZUSA
   HEINRICH              3 M CHILD    GRZZZZUSA KUHLMANN, JOHANNE         14 F CNF        GRZZZZUSA
   SIMON               .09 M INFANT   GRZZZZUSA SCHOMAKER, MARGAR.        18 F SVNT       GRZZZZUSA
GROSS, WILH.            31 M HTR      GRZZZZUSA QUELLEN, JOHANN           23 M LABR       GRZZZZUSA
LEWANDOWSKA, ROSALIE    26 F NN       GRZZZZUSA    MARGAR.                18 F W          GRZZZZUSA
   ANNA                  7 F CHILD    GRZZZZUSA SCHUMAYER, CARL           14 M NN         GRZZZZUSA
   VERONICA              5 F CHILD    GRZZZZUSA FRIKEN, META               8 F CHILD      GRZZZZUSA
   MARIANNA              3 F CHILD    GRZZZZUSA KRITTLER, ANNA            33 F NN         GRZZZZUSA
   ANASTASIA           .11 F INFANT   GRZZZZUSA HEUSSLER, ROSE            21 F SVNT       GRZZZZUSA
   CATHARINA            63 F NN       GRZZZZUSA BAUER, CHRISTINE          21 F SVNT       GRZZZZUSA
PAULI, FRANZ            29 M FARMER   GRZZZZUSA MAYER, WILH.              25 M CPTR       GRZZZZUSA

                                         57
```

PASSENGER	AGE	SEX	OCCUPATION	PRVL	DES
DIEHL, GEORG	29	M	CPTR	GRZZZZUSA
JOHANNES	27	M	CPTR	GRZZZZUSA
WITTICH, CLARA	19	F	SVNT	GRZZZZUSA
WABNER, MARIE	38	F	SVNT	GRZZZZUSA
JAGEL, IDA	30	F	SVNT	GRZZZZUSA
PEPER, KAROLINE	15	F	SVNT	GRZZZZUSA
SCHAMPER, PHILIPP	16	M	FARMER	GRZZZZUSA
SOMMER, ANTONIE	46	F	NN	GRZZZZUSA
STAAKE, CARL	18	M	FARMER	GRZZZZUSA
EHLERS, CARL	8	M	CHILD	GRZZZZUSA
SCHRANDT, ANNA	24	F	SVNT	GRZZZZUSA
MEIER, MARIE	14	F	SVNT	GRZZZZUSA
FLATH, FRIEDR.	22	M	BKLYR	GRZZZZUSA
GRAZEWSKI, JOSEF	26	M	BKLYR	GRZZZZUSA
GRIMM, JULIUS	17	M	BKLYR	GRZZZZUSA
FEINER, JULIANNE	19	F	SVNT	GRZZZZUSA
U, A.MARIA	7	F	CHILD	GRZZZZUSA
LAMB---, JULIUS	17	M	MCHT	GRZZZZUSA
DA-----, MARIE	23	F	NN	GRZZZZUSA
SCHAEFER, REGINA	18	F	NN	GRZZZZUSA
GRAU, ROSE	30	F	NN	GRZZZZUSA
THIERAOLF, MARG.	20	F	NN	GRZZZZUSA
KATHAR.	17	F	NN	GRZZZZUSA
SOMMER, MARIE	18	F	SVNT	GRZZZZUSA
WOERNER, JACOB	16	M	LABR	GRZZZZUSA
SCHOENLEBER, GOTTLIEBEN	20	F	SVNT	GRZZZZUSA
MOLLENBERG, JOH.	25	F	SVNT	GRZZZZUSA
MAST, AGATHE	50	F	NN	GRZZZZUSA
MARIE	18	F	NN	GRZZZZUSA
GEORG	5	F	CHILD	GRZZZZUSA
ANDREAS	7	F	CHILD	GRZZZZUSA
HEUSSLER, FRIEDERIKE	26	F	NN	GRZZZZUSA
KONZELMANN, PAULINE	16	F	LABR	GRZZZZUSA
HOCH, ANNA	18	F	NN	GRZZZZUSA
LAUTER, ROSE	21	F	SVNT	GRZZZZUSA
KRIMEL, ANNA	57	F	SVNT	GRZZZZUSA
MERZ, MARIA	26	F	NN	GRZZZZUSA
MARIE	5	F	CHILD	GRZZZZUSA
BOHN, GEORG	24	M	CPTR	GRZZZZUSA
WALTER, JOHANNE	23	F	SVNT	GRZZZZUSA
BARTH, ANNA	57	F	NN	GRZZZZUSA
NEHER, GOTTLIEB	15	M	NN	GRZZZZUSA
ROSENER, JACOB	19	M	WCHMKR	GRZZZZUSA
SCHOBER, ROSINE	21	F	UNKNOWN	GRZZZZUSA
HOELLE, JOSEF	16	M	UNKNOWN	GRZZZZUSA
EHRLE, JOHANN	16	M	UNKNOWN	GRZZZZUSA
SCHWEIZ, MARIE	25	F	SVNT	GRZZZZUSA
LOTTERER, ERWIN	6	M	CHILD	GRZZZZUSA
RAU, JACOB	16	M	CNF	GRZZZZUSA
SPOHN, CATHAR.	16	F	SVNT	GRZZZZUSA
JETTER, AUG.	16	M	WTR	GRZZZZUSA
WOLFF, BABETTE	18	F	SVNT	GRZZZZUSA
VESER, CATHAR.	16	F	SVNT	GRZZZZUSA
ALLMENDINGER, JOH.	14	M	NN	GRZZZZUSA
BUESHELER, ELISE	20	F	SVNT	GRZZZZUSA
HAUSCH, MARIA	8	F	CHILD	GRZZZZUSA
JETTER, CATHAR.	23	F	SVNT	GRZZZZUSA
EPPLER, BARBARA	22	F	SVNT	GRZZZZUSA
MUENCHINGEN, EUGEN	14	M	NN	GRZZZZUSA
VONDERHEIDE, CLEMENS	24	M	FARMER	GRZZZZUSA
TRAUTH, CONRAD	53	M	FARMER	GRZZZZUSA
DANNEMANN, ROSE	23	F	NN	GRZZZZUSA
GAUSS, ANNA	41	F	NN	GRZZZZUSA
BIEDLINGMAIER, J.G.	36	M	BRR	GRZZZZUSA
STICHELE, MATHILDE	47	F	NN	GRZZZZUSA
CHRISTINE	7	F	CHILD	GRZZZZUSA
LUTZ, JOHANN	15	M	NN	GRZZZZUSA
UTTROEDT, MARIA	67	F	NN	GRZZZZUSA
STERZ, MARIA	41	F	NN	GRZZZZUSA
FAUST, JACOB	14	M	NN	GRZZZZUSA
URBAN, THEKLA	24	F	NN	GRZZZZUSA
OTTO	2	F	CHILD	GRZZZZUSA
THEKLA	.09	F	INFANT	GRZZZZUSA
MAURER, JOHS.	16	M	NN	GRZZZZUSA
CWETKO, FRANZ	33	M	CGRMKR	GRZZZZUSA
KRAMMENDOHE, CHRISTINE	17	F	SVNT	GRZZZZUSA
EVA	5	F	CHILD	GRZZZZUSA
HEES, JACOB	48	M	FARMER	GRZZZZUSA
RIES, PHILIPPINE	26	F	SVNT	GRZZZZUSA
MAJER, IGNATZ	19	M	MCHT	GRZZZZUSA
BOCKRATH, GEORG	31	M	FARMER	GRZZZZUSA
ROTHE, CARL	65	M	FARMER	GRZZZZUSA
HOECH, HEINR.	25	M	FARMER	GRZZZZUSA
RUFA, FRANZISKA	19	F	SVNT	GRZZZZUSA
HORST, RICH.	13	M	NN	GRZZZZUSA
ZIMMERMANN, JOH.	56	M	FARMER	GRZZZZUSA
ELISABETH	57	F	W	GRZZZZUSA
HELENE	19	F	NN	GRZZZZUSA
KAISER, EMILIE	22	F	SMSTS	GRZZZZUSA
WILH.	7	M	CHILD	GRZZZZUSA
MARIE	8	F	CHILD	GRZZZZUSA
SCHUELE, WILH.	16	M	NN	GRZZZZUSA
UEBELE, CHRIST.	16	M	NN	GRZZZZUSA
BLESSING, AUGUST	14	M	NN	GRZZZZUSA
HOEGER, MARIE	20	F	SMSTS	GRZZZZUSA
NESTMANN, ED.	48	M	MCHT	GRZZZZUSA
OSWALD	7	M	CHILD	GRZZZZUSA
WENDT, ELISE	42	F	NN	GRZZZZUSA
ELISE	11	F	CH	GRZZZZUSA
EUST	7	M	CHILD	GRZZZZUSA
MOELLER, CHRIST.	16	M	NN	GRZZZZUSA
ILLIG, BERNHD.	29	M	TLR	GRZZZZUSA
SCHAEFER, HEINR.	27	M	HTR	GRZZZZUSA
STEINHAEUSER, K.	24	M	PNTR	GRZZZZUSA
RATHER, ELISAB.	20	F	SVNT	GRZZZZUSA
GERNLEIN, MARTHA	17	F	SVNT	GRZZZZUSA
NAEGELE, JOH.	21	M	BRR	GRZZZZUSA
STROBEL, FERDD.	17	M	FARMER	GRZZZZUSA
GIEGERICH, CARL	24	M	FARMER	GRZZZZUSA
MUEHLER, MAGDAL.	30	F	SVNT	GRZZZZUSA
HUGENROTH, JOS.	27	M	FARMER	GRZZZZUSA
KUHN, GUST.	20	M	FARMER	GRZZZZUSA
OSTHOFF, BERNARD	24	M	FARMER	GRZZZZUSA
SUHLING, ALOIS	23	M	FARMER	GRZZZZUSA
SCHAEFER, ANNA	18	F	SVNT	GRZZZZUSA
WITTEKIND, REGINE	28	F	NN	GRZZZZUSA
AUGUSTE	4	F	CHILD	GRZZZZUSA
EBERHARDT, JUSTUS	31	M	FARMER	GRZZZZUSA
MARTHA	24	F	W	GRZZZZUSA
FRITZ	4	M	CHILD	GRZZZZUSA
EMMA	3	F	CHILD	GRZZZZUSA
AUGUSTE	.11	F	INFANT	GRZZZZUSA
ELISE	20	F	SVNT	GRZZZZUSA
KRAFT, JULIUS	16	M	MCHT	GRZZZZUSA
AUGUSTE	17	F	NN	GRZZZZUSA
STEINHAUER, H.	16	M	WTR	GRZZZZUSA
FEROIN, GAOIN	37	M	SHMK	GRZZZZUSA
EMILIE	31	F	W	GRZZZZUSA
PIEPER, HENRIETTE	28	F	NN	GRZZZZUSA
GOERNER, AUG.	51	M	FARMER	GRZZZZUSA
THERESE	49	F	W	GRZZZZUSA
REICHELT, LENA	14	F	SVNT	GRZZZZUSA
LAERZER, MINNA	23	F	SVNT	GRZZZZUSA
KARMANN, WALBURGA	21	F	SVNT	GRZZZZUSA
ZIMANSKI, PETRONELLA	20	F	SVNT	GRZZZZUSA
KUHN, DOROTHEA	18	F	SVNT	GRZZZZUSA
BENKER, RICHARD	7	M	CHILD	GRZZZZUSA
HIPPLER, JOHANN	50	M	FARMER	GRZZZZUSA
ANNA	50	F	W	GRZZZZUSA
MARGAR.	20	F	NN	GRZZZZUSA
STOCKMANN, CASPAR	25	M	BRR	GRZZZZUSA
WAHLER, JOHANN	26	M	CK	GRZZZZUSA
WEHRMANN, MICH.	18	M	TLR	GRZZZZUSA
VIEREILIG, KUNIGUNDE	18	F	SVNT	GRZZZZUSA
ZWIEFEL, BARBARA	18	F	SVNT	GRZZZZUSA
KROEKEL, JOHANN	50	M	FARMER	GRZZZZUSA
THERESE	42	F	W	GRZZZZUSA
DOROTHEA	53	F	NN	GRZZZZUSA
JOHANN	15	M	NN	GRZZZZUSA
PHILOMENA	10	F	NN	GRZZZZUSA

PASSENGER	AGE	SEX	OCCUPATION	PRVL	DES	PASSENGER	AGE	SEX	OCCUPATION	PRVL	DES
MARIA	8	F	CHILD	GRZZZZUSA		VINCENTZ	.03	M	INFANT	GRZZZZUSA	
MARGARETHE	7	F	CHILD	GRZZZZUSA		GAJEWSKI, FRANZ	38	M	FARMER	GRZZZZUSA	
LUDWIG	3	M	CHILD	GRZZZZUSA		ROSA	37	F	W	GRZZZZUSA	
ENGLERT, KATHARINE	56	F	NN	GRZZZZUSA		FRIEDR.	10	M	CH	GRZZZZUSA	
BECKER, KUNIGUNDE	18	F	SVNT	GRZZZZUSA		ROSALIA	8	F	CHILD	GRZZZZUSA	
SCHALLER, LEONHARD	27	M	MCHT	GRZZZZUSA		ELISABETH	7	F	CHILD	GRZZZZUSA	
TEIGL, THERESE	19	F	SVNT	GRZZZZUSA		PAUL	.09	M	INFANT	GRZZZZUSA	
GRUBER, MARGAR.	22	F	SVNT	GRZZZZUSA		FIGANITT, VALENTY	36	M	LABR	GRZZZZUSA	
BODER, MARGAR.	18	F	SVNT	GRZZZZUSA		SCHRAMME, JUSTINE	68	F	NN	GRZZZZUSA	
KEES, KAROLINE	20	F	SVNT	GRZZZZUSA		VELKE, AUGUSTE	12	F	CH	GRZZZZUSA	
VONMALOTKE, ALB.	38	M	CK	PRZZZZUSA		MISTKOWSKA, HELENE	26	F	NN	GRZZZZUSA	
KOHLENBERG, AUG.	73	M	NN	PRZZZZUSA		KEISTER, JACOB	55	M	LABR	GRZZZZUSA	
VETTER, MARIE	20	F	SVNT	PRZZZZUSA		MICHNA, FRANZ	39	M	LABR	GRZZZZUSA	
NIKLAS, ANTONIA	15	F	SVNT	PRZZZZUSA		GRZYWACZ, ROSALIE	48	F	NN	GRZZZZUSA	
JESSEN, EDWALD	23	M	PNTR	PRZZZZUSA		JACUBOWSKI, JOH.	25	M	FARMER	GRZZZZUSA	
RIEBE, HERM.	17	M	PNTR	PRZZZZUSA		U, DOROTHEA	43	F	NN	GRZZZZUSA	
ERNESTINE	49	F	NN	PRZZZZUSA		PALZIN, BERNHARD	25	M	PNTR	GRZZZZUSA	
AUGUST	51	M	FARMER	PRZZZZUSA		CAECILIA	8	F	CHILD	GRZZZZUSA	
MASIJEWSKI, GUSTAV	24	M	FARMER	PRZZZZUSA		HENNIG, MICHEL	44	M	LABR	GRZZZZUSA	
DIETRICH, HERM.	32	M	FARMER	PRZZZZUSA		JOSEFA	45	F	W	GRZZZZUSA	
HENRIETTE	34	F	W	PRZZZZUSA		OTTO	18	M	LABR	GRZZZZUSA	
HERM.	7	M	CHILD	PRZZZZUSA		JOSEFA	9	F	CHILD	GRZZZZUSA	
OTTO	3	M	CHILD	PRZZZZUSA		VALESKA	8	F	CHILD	GRZZZZUSA	
KA---HKE, AUGUST	44	M	FARMER	PRZZZZUSA		FIGANIAK, FRANZISKA	35	F	NN	GRZZZZUSA	
BERTHA	31	F	W	PRZZZZUSA		MARTIN	6	M	CHILD	GRZZZZUSA	
CARL	10	M	CH	PRZZZZUSA		VALENTINE	3	F	CHILD	GRZZZZUSA	
OTTO	8	M	CHILD	PRZZZZUSA		IGNATZ	.10	M	INFANT	GRZZZZUSA	
EMIL	7	M	CHILD	PRZZZZUSA		VOIGT, JOHANN	25	M	SHMK	GRZZZZUSA	
EMMA	6	F	CHILD	PRZZZZUSA		ANNA	26	F	UNKNOWN	GRZZZZUSA	
ERNST	.11	M	INFANT	PRZZZZUSA		MARIE	.09	F	INFANT	GRZZZZUSA	
HIEBER, MARIE	38	F	NN	PRZZZZUSA		LEIBSEN, U	14	M	NN	GRZZZZUSA	
BOCHARDT, MARIE	24	F	NN	PRZZZZUSA		HECKMANN, FERDD.	14	M	NN	GRZZZZUSA	
-ESTLER, ANDREAS	27	M	ENGR	GRZZZZUSA		THADEN, HUGO	29	M	PNTR	GRZZZZUSA	
U, WILH.	26	M	ENGR	GRZZZZUSA		HUNDINGER, FRANZ	16	M	PNTR	GRZZZZUSA	
MOESSEN, JOH.	27	M	FARMER	GRZZZZUSA		TASTO, CARL	25	M	TUT	GRZZZZUSA	
JOHANNA	20	F	W	GRZZZZUSA		LUEBKEMANN, FRIEDR.	5	M	CHILD	GRZZZZUSA	
RODEWALD, BERTHA	32	F	NN	GRZZZZUSA		WOLTEMEIER, WILH.	27	M	MCHT	GRZZZZUSA	
JOHANNE	7	F	CHILD	GRZZZZUSA		MUELLER, JOH.	15	M	BBR	GRZZZZUSA	
EMMA	3	F	CHILD	GRZZZZUSA		HEUMANN, BERNHD.	28	M	SHMK	GRZZZZUSA	
MAX	1	M	CHILD	GRZZZZUSA		FRIED, JOH.	31	M	SHMK	GRZZZZUSA	
MARIA	.03	F	INFANT	GRZZZZUSA		CAROLINE	31	F	W	GRZZZZUSA	
DAUS, WALDEMAR	25	M	PNTR	GRZZZZUSA		GOTTLIEB	3	M	CHILD	GRZZZZUSA	
SCHROER, WILHELM	37	M	LABR	GRZZZZUSA		WILHELMINE	4	F	CHILD	GRZZZZUSA	
MARIE	29	F	W	GRZZZZUSA		JACOB	.09	M	INFANT	GRZZZZUSA	
LOUISE	7	F	CHILD	GRZZZZUSA		ZIRK, SEB.	24	M	LABR	GRZZZZUSA	
EMMA	6	F	CHILD	GRZZZZUSA		BERTHA	21	F	W	GRZZZZUSA	
WILHELM	2	M	CHILD	GRZZZZUSA		HENER, HEINR.	7	M	CHILD	GRZZZZUSA	
MARIE	.09	F	INFANT	GRZZZZUSA		LOESCH, HEINR.	35	M	BRR	GRZZZZUSA	
MUSWEILER, FRANZ	29	M	BLKSMH	GRZZZZUSA		THOMANN, LOUISE	24	F	SMSTS	GRZZZZUSA	
KATTHE, JACUB	69	M	FARMER	GRZZZZUSA		COHN, SALOMON	37	M	LABR	GRZZZZUSA	
BERTHA	61	F	W	GRZZZZUSA		HERFORTH, HERM.	25	M	LABR	GRZZZZUSA	
KATHARINA	33	F	NN	GRZZZZUSA		KLINGELHOEFER, LOUIS	17	M	FSR	GRZZZZUSA	
BERTHA	8	F	CHILD	GRZZZZUSA		LOCHMANN, ANNA	20	F	SVNT	GRZZZZUSA	
MARTHA	7	F	CHILD	GRZZZZUSA		BACKHAUS, HERMINE	30	F	NN	GRZZZZUSA	
FRANZ	2	M	CHILD	GRZZZZUSA		HERMANN	2	M	CHILD	GRZZZZUSA	
MARIE	.02	F	INFANT	GRZZZZUSA		MARIE	.06	F	INFANT	GRZZZZUSA	
REINHARD, ROSA	14	M	SVNT	GRZZZZUSA		SINGLE, CATHAR.	21	F	SVNT	GRZZZZUSA	
ROGENGREIF, VALENTIN	35	M	PNTR	GRZZZZUSA		WIDMANN, ANNA	30	F	NN	GRZZZZUSA	
CAROLINE	48	F	W	GRZZZZUSA		FRIDA	4	F	CHILD	GRZZZZUSA	
WILL, FRIEDR.	38	M	PNTR	GRZZZZUSA		GUSTAV	2	M	CHILD	GRZZZZUSA	
U, JOHANNE	42	F	SVNT	GRZZZZUSA		BENDER, CARL	17	M	CH	GRZZZZUSA	
KIRSCH, ANNA	23	F	SVNT	GRZZZZUSA		EPPLER, KATHAR.	30	F	NN	GRZZZZUSA	
KOWALEWSKA, VICTORIA	20	F	SVNT	GRZZZZUSA		KATHAR.	7	F	CHILD	GRZZZZUSA	
RENK, ANDREAS	34	M	FARMER	GRZZZZUSA		BINDER, JOHS.	25	M	BRR	GRZZZZUSA	
PAULINE	33	F	W	GRZZZZUSA		TIMMERMANNN, ANNA	56	F	NN	GRZZZZUSA	
JOHANN	8	F	CHILD	GRZZZZUSA		GOEHNER, GOTTL.	14	M	NN	GRZZZZUSA	
CARL	5	M	CHILD	GRZZZZUSA		LINPPOLD, LOUISE	15	F	NN	GRZZZZUSA	
FRANZ	.10	M	INFANT	GRZZZZUSA		REIFFEL, VALENTIN	19	M	PNTR	GRZZZZUSA	
BOS, MARGAR.	23	F	SVNT	GRZZZZUSA		MICHEL, JACOB	32	M	BCHR	GRZZZZUSA	
KOLLMER, ANTON	22	M	TLR	GRZZZZUSA		DEUBLER, LOUISE	22	F	SVNT	GRZZZZUSA	
ZIEMKIWICZ, MARYANNA	32	F	SMSTS	GRZZZZUSA		SCHMIDT, WILHE.	27	F	SVNT	GRZZZZUSA	
KAMINSKA, MARYANNA	19	F	SMSTS	GRZZZZUSA		CHRISTIAN	.03	M	INFANT	GRZZZZUSA	
KUJAWA, WOJCIECH	38	M	LABR	GRZZZZUSA		WIEDMAYER, WILHELMINE	20	F	NN	GRZZZZUSA	
KRA---, EDUARD	26	M	LABR	GRZZZZUSA		CAROLINE	19	F	NN	GRZZZZUSA	
KRAUSE, VACLAVA	25	F	NN	GRZZZZUSA		MUELLER, ROSINE	22	F	SVNT	GRZZZZUSA	

PASSENGER	AGE	SEX	OCCUPATION	PRVVL	DES
RAPP, LOUISE	27	F	SVNT	GRZZZZ	USA
ORTH, GOTTL.	31	M	SHMK	GRZZZZ	USA
MICHAELIS, ADAM	18	M	SHMK	GRZZZZ	USA
KNIERIM, MARG.	22	F	SVNT	GRZZZZ	USA
ZIEN, MARTHA	20	F	SVNT	GRZZZZ	USA
HAHN, ELISE	20	F	SVNT	GRZZZZ	USA
CATHARINE	15	F	SVNT	GRZZZZ	USA
KATTENBORN, HEINR.	60	M	FARMER	GRZZZZ	USA
PFLETSCHINGER, ANNA	26	F	SVNT	GRZZZZ	USA
ROSINE	17	F	SVNT	GRZZZZ	USA
VOGEL, MARIA	25	F	SVNT	GRZZZZ	USA
WEBER, CHRIST.	46	M	LABR	GRZZZZ	USA
CATHARINE	49	F	W	GRZZZZ	USA
MARIA	20	F	SVNT	GRZZZZ	USA
CATHARINE	18	F	UNKNOWN	GRZZZZ	USA
ANNA	3	F	CHILD	GRZZZZ	USA
MARTHA	6	F	CHILD	GRZZZZ	USA
CONRAD	2	M	CHILD	GRZZZZ	USA
EIPELE, ANNA	19	F	SMSTS	GRZZZZ	USA
GRUBER, ALOIS	17	M	BCHR	GRZZZZ	USA
HOLSBERG, HERM.	17	M	BCHR	GRZZZZ	USA
GISCH, JACOB	29	M	LABR	GRZZZZ	USA
MEIER, JOHANN	60	M	BCHR	GRZZZZ	USA
WALBURGA	53	F	W	GRZZZZ	USA
PETER	7	M	CHILD	GRZZZZ	USA
AUKENBRAND, BARBARA	37	F	NN	GRZZZZ	USA
JOHANN	8	M	CHILD	GRZZZZ	USA
ARMENDINGER, MICH.	32	M	SHMK	GRZZZZ	USA
MARTHA	18	F	W	GRZZZZ	USA
MASCHMEIER, FRIEDR.	17	M	LABR	GRZZZZ	USA
SOPHIE	23	F	NN	GRZZZZ	USA
GUETHE, JOHANNA	24	F	SVNT	GRZZZZ	USA
SEEMANN, SOPHIE	25	F	SVNT	GRZZZZ	USA
DANZ, HEINR.	31	M	BKLYR	GRZZZZ	USA
ANNA	29	F	W	GRZZZZ	USA
LOUISE	4	F	CHILD	GRZZZZ	USA
AUGUST	.06	M	INFANT	GRZZZZ	USA
ALBERT	17	M	CPTR	GRZZZZ	USA
ULRICH, ERNST	21	M	CPTR	GRZZZZ	USA
VALENTIN, JOHANN	31	M	FARMER	GRZZZZ	USA
MARIE	33	F	W	GRZZZZ	USA
LYPECKI, ANESTASY	31	M	MNR	GRZZZZ	USA
THEKLA	21	F	W	GRZZZZ	USA
LEONA	2	F	CHILD	GRZZZZ	USA
ARMANSKI, JOSE	26	M	MNR	GRZZZZ	USA
MARIANNE	26	F	W	GRZZZZ	USA
HEDWIG	.06	F	INFANT	GRZZZZ	USA
SLUPSKI, FRANZ	23	M	MNR	GRZZZZ	USA
FEURDT, JOH.	26	M	BCHR	GRZZZZ	USA
HAUSCHILD, GEORG	15	M	PNTR	GRZZZZ	USA
HEINEMEIER, LOUIS	16	M	PNTR	GRZZZZ	USA
LINA	22	F	W	GRZZZZ	USA
MUELLER, PETER	6	M	CHILD	GRZZZZ	USA
TIETJEN, HINR.	19	M	LABR	GRZZZZ	USA
KUEBELER, ALB.	14	M	NN	GRZZZZ	USA
HILLEBRANDT, HEINR.	17	M	WTR	GRZZZZ	USA
VOGES, WILH.	17	M	TLR	GRZZZZ	USA
BARSCHE, JAN	28	M	LABR	GRZZZZ	USA
WENDT, OTTO	17	M	SHMK	GRZZZZ	USA
WEYHAUSEN, HEINR.	30	M	SHMK	GRZZZZ	USA
MARIE	29	F	W	GRZZZZ	USA
ELISE	.07	F	INFANT	GRZZZZ	USA
GERDES, ANNA	16	F	SMSTS	GRZZZZ	USA
HINCK, WILH.	3	M	CHILD	GRZZZZ	USA
DOESCHER, CHRIST.	60	M	FARMER	GRZZZZ	USA
DOMFORDE, LUDW.	50	M	FARMER	GRZZZZ	USA
FAUERT, HEINR.	27	M	FARMER	GRZZZZ	USA
PUTZ, THILLMANN	31	M	FARMER	GRZZZZ	USA
KUPPFEL, HERMINE	60	F	NN	GRZZZZ	USA
HEINRICH	24	M	LABR	GRZZZZ	USA
LUEBBERT, JULIANE	21	F	SVNT	GRZZZZ	USA
MERTSCHING, CAROLINE	35	F	NN	GRZZZZ	USA
REINHARD	8	M	CHILD	GRZZZZ	USA
THEODOR	7	M	CHILD	GRZZZZ	USA
MARIE	6	F	CHILD	GRZZZZ	USA
CLARA	5	F	CHILD	GRZZZZ	USA
VAHL, AUGUST	19	M	LABR	GRZZZZ	USA
HENK, WILH.	35	M	LABR	GRZZZZ	USA
TOELLE, FRITZ	30	M	LABR	GRZZZZ	USA
HACHLER, FR.W.	28	M	LABR	GRZZZZ	USA
LEHMANN, SAMUEL	7	M	CHILD	GRZZZZ	USA
DAY, WILH.	22	M	LABR	GRZZZZ	USA
SCHONDLOWSKI, JOH.	33	M	LABR	GRZZZZ	USA
ANNA	34	F	W	GRZZZZ	USA
ANNA	7	F	CHILD	GRZZZZ	USA
MARIE	5	F	CHILD	GRZZZZ	USA
ROSALIE	2	F	CHILD	GRZZZZ	USA
JUSTINE	.03	F	INFANT	GRZZZZ	USA
DETTMER, MARIE	29	F	NN	GRZZZZ	USA
ROSAMUENDE	2	F	CHILD	GRZZZZ	USA
HERBIG, MARIE	30	F	NN	GRZZZZ	USA
AUGUST	8	M	CHILD	GRZZZZ	USA
CARL	7	M	CHILD	GRZZZZ	USA
GERTRUD	6	F	CHILD	GRZZZZ	USA
WILHELM	.09	M	INFANT	GRZZZZ	USA
DEPPE, HERM.	32	M	LABR	GRZZZZ	USA
SCHUELER, ADOLF	25	M	LABR	GRZZZZ	USA
KONIMATH, PAUL	28	M	LABR	GRZZZZ	USA
TARNECHLADER, ALBERT	32	M	BCHR	GRZZZZ	USA
SOLBACH, JOHANNES	29	M	PNTR	GRZZZZ	USA
DORMANN, EBERHARD	24	M	SHMK	GRZZZZ	USA
BEHRMANN, WILH.	23	M	FARMER	GRZZZZ	USA
BEHRENS, HINRICH	15	M	NN	GRZZZZ	USA
WOHLERS, JOHANN	24	M	BKLYR	GRZZZZ	USA
ALTENSTEIN, ANNA	20	F	SMSTS	GRZZZZ	USA
GREITKE, WILH.	29	M	CK	GRZZZZ	USA
FRITZSCH, JOSEF	18	M	BCHR	GRZZZZ	USA
JOSEFA	58	F	W	GRZZZZ	USA
MAX	8	M	CHILD	GRZZZZ	USA
PROEZCHEN, JOHS.	69	M	FARMER	GRZZZZ	USA
CHRISTINE	23	F	NN	GRZZZZ	USA
HELLER, ANNA	29	F	NN	SRZZZZ	USA
HEITMANN, JOHANN	17	M	LABR	GRZZZZ	USA
HUEBENTHAL, HEINR.	13	M	LABR	GRZZZZ	USA
BLANKE, LOUIS	18	M	BBR	GRZZZZ	USA
RODIEK, HEINR.	18	M	WTR	GRZZZZ	USA
PFRITZ, LISETTE	19	F	SVNT	GRZZZZ	USA
BAUMANN, JOHANN	46	M	FARMER	GRZZZZ	USA
GOTTLIEBE	50	F	NN	GRZZZZ	USA
KATHARINE	18	F	NN	GRZZZZ	USA
MARGARETHA	2	F	CHILD	GRZZZZ	USA
LONA	7	F	CHILD	GRZZZZ	USA
SCHUMACHER, DREWES	45	M	FARMER	GRZZZZ	USA
SCHLECHE, FRIEDR.	32	M	FARMER	GRZZZZ	USA
GAETZE, GOERGE	28	M	FARMER	GRZZZZ	USA
BARDENHAGEN, WILLY	33	M	FARMER	GRZZZZ	USA
BAUMANN, HEINR.	43	M	GDNR	GRZZZZ	USA
WULFF, HEINR.	27	M	BCHR	GRZZZZ	USA
TAMKE, LUETJE	35	M	FARMER	GRZZZZ	USA
MARGARETHE	30	F	W	GRZZZZ	USA
ANNA	8	F	CHILD	GRZZZZ	USA
META	7	F	CHILD	GRZZZZ	USA
FRIEDRICH	5	M	CHILD	GRZZZZ	USA
VONDERLIETH, CAROLINE	23	F	SVNT	GRZZZZ	USA
HOLST, CATHARINE	24	F	SVNT	GRZZZZ	USA
WULFF, FRIEDRICH	35	M	LABR	GRZZZZ	USA
GLUECKMANN, B.	25	F	SVNT	GRZZZZ	USA

PASSENGER	AGE	SEX	OCCUPATION	PRVL	DES

SHIP: STATE OF NEVADA

FROM: LIVERPOOL AND QUEENSTOWN
TO: NEW YORK
ARRIVED: 16 MAY 1888

PASSENGER	AGE	SEX	OCCUPATION	PRVL	DES
BOTWINICH, BONICH	26	M	LABR	GRZZZZ	USA
GAWLIK, GREGORY	30	M	FARMER	GRZZZZ	USA
KASDIN, BENJ	24	M	LABR	GRZZZZ	USA
KOKOSET, IOSSEL	50	M	FARMER	GRZZZZ	USA
ETKIN, WOLF	25	M	TLR	GRZZZZ	USA
HERZBERG, WOLEK	25	M	TLR	GRZZZZ	USA
BECH, FERDINNAD	27	M	FARMER	GRZZZZ	USA
JENTLER, CHAIM	31	M	BKR	GRZZZZ	USA
KLEINBERG, MICH	27	M	LABR	GRZZZZ	USA
GUMBERG, BERMAN	18	M	LABR	GRZZZZ	USA
PERLMANN, MORDCHE	45	M	TLR	GRZZZZ	USA
BIRMANN, SCHAIE	25	M	TLR	GRZZZZ	USA
PETERSBERG, SAM	35	M	FARMER	GRZZZZ	USA
WEMBERG, HIZIG	27	M	FARMER	GRZZZZ	USA
HILMARD, CHIAM	17	M	LABR	GRZZZZ	USA
INDIKT, SCHAI	26	M	LABR	GRZZZZ	USA
BRAUMSTEIN, BERL	23	M	LABR	GRZZZZ	USA
HIRSCH, ISAAC	27	M	PNTR	GRZZZZ	USA
WEISSBERG, MICHAEL	26	M	PNTR	GRZZZZ	USA
RENA, ISAAC	26	M	BKR	GRZZZZ	USA
DOW, MOUR	46	M	BKR	GRZZZZ	USA
KAPLAN, MEIER	36	M	GZR	GRZZZZ	USA
SCHLESINGER, SAM	36	M	LABR	GRZZZZ	USA
KLUFFS, DISRAEL	33	M	LABR	GRZZZZ	USA
SCHIFFER, CHAIM	24	M	LABR	GRZZZZ	USA
TEPER, ABRAM	22	M	PNTR	GRZZZZ	USA
HIRSCH	7	M	CHILD	GRZZZZ	USA
FUELDER, SAM	21	M	LABR	GRZZZZ	USA
REMR, CARL	18	M	LABR	GRZZZZ	USA
BLUMENSTEIN, CHAIN	22	M	TLR	GRZZZZ	USA
MIELKE, ALBERT	23	M	TLR	GRZZZZ	USA
ILDTKE, JANKEL	28	M	LABR	GRZZZZ	USA
LEWMANN, DANIEL	22	M	LABR	GRZZZZ	USA
MALSMED, KOPEK	22	M	LABR	GRZZZZ	USA
HEDBERG, CA	26	M	FARMER	GRZZZZ	USA
MARTINSEN, JULIUS	21	M	LABR	GRZZZZ	USA
DUHE, ALEX	22	M	LABR	GRZZZZ	USA
STRAND, KUN	20	M	LABR	GRZZZZ	USA
NOSHEIM, AMIND	18	M	LABR	GRZZZZ	USA
KLEIN, PEPI	18	F	SP	GRZZZZ	USA
WEINCHHOLN, SELMA	21	F	SP	GRZZZZ	USA
GERDA	17	F	SP	GRZZZZ	USA
LEWIN, KATI	14	F	SP	GRZZZZ	USA
DEUTSEK, EILE	16	F	SP	GRZZZZ	USA
PERLEUNTLER, REIZEL	17	F	SP	GRZZZZ	USA
FEIGE	7	F	CHILD	GRZZZZ	USA
BERBERG, CHANI	21	F	W	GRZZZZ	USA
ITE	.06	F	INFANT	GRZZZZ	USA
PER, SCHEINE	30	F	W	GRZZZZ	USA
ROCHEL	7	F	CHILD	GRZZZZ	USA
WOLF	.06	M	INFANT	GRZZZZ	USA
LINA	.06	F	INFANT	GRZZZZ	USA
GERBER, SORE	38	F	W	GRZZZZ	USA
HIRSCH	7	M	CHILD	GRZZZZ	USA
CHAINE	6	F	CHILD	GRZZZZ	USA
MOSES	3	M	CHILD	GRZZZZ	USA
SUMKE	.06	F	INFANT	GRZZZZ	USA
NEWMANN, ETRENNE	43	F	W	GRZZZZ	USA
VILEIN, GALIE	40	F	UNKNOWN	GRZZZZ	USA
PEPPI	16	F	SP	GRZZZZ	USA
GULAISKA, ALEXANDER	31	F	W	GRZZZZ	USA
STANISLAUS	3	F	CHILD	GRZZZZ	USA
SEIGMUND	.06	F	INFANT	GRZZZZ	USA
AMBURTER, ESTER	19	F	SP	GRZZZZ	USA
MARK, CHIVIE	18	F	SP	GRZZZZ	USA
BERG, MARTIN	37	M	FARMER	GRZZZZ	USA
LISA	43	F	W	GRZZZZ	USA
LYDER	4	F	CHILD	GRZZZZ	USA
WIMBERG, PER	21	M	LABR	GRZZZZ	USA
BOAS, CAROLINE	28	F	SP	GRZZZZ	USA
JANDEA, EUGENIA	18	F	SP	GRZZZZ	USA
SELMA	22	F	SP	GRZZZZ	USA
THORTEJONIESEN, GRO	22	F	SP	GRZZZZ	USA
DELHI, LAURA	21	F	SP	GRZZZZ	USA
JOHANSON, B	23	F	SP	GRZZZZ	USA
HAGEN, BERGIT	25	F	SP	GRZZZZ	USA
VAR, GEO	22	F	SP	GRZZZZ	USA
RADBERG, JENUINE	21	F	SP	GRZZZZ	USA
KARISON, BLANDA	22	F	SP	GRZZZZ	USA
RADBERG, AMANDA	20	F	SP	GRZZZZ	USA
AVENDT, MARIE	38	F	W	GRZZZZ	USA
EDUARD	18	F	SP	GRZZZZ	USA
PAUL	7	M	CHILD	GRZZZZ	USA
OTTO	5	F	CHILD	GRZZZZ	USA
KLUGER, ABRAM	30	M	FARMER	GRZZZZ	USA
LEA	30	F	W	GRZZZZ	USA
DEBRA	7	F	CHILD	GRZZZZ	USA
DAVID	5	M	CHILD	GRZZZZ	USA
EMGER, ISRAEL	55	M	FARMER	GRZZZZ	USA
MIETTA	53	F	W	GRZZZZ	USA
REGOSIA	18	F	SP	GRZZZZ	USA
CHAINE	7	F	CHILD	GRZZZZ	USA
BAUMANN, PINCAS	59	M	FARMER	GRZZZZ	USA
KRENIE	7	F	CHILD	GRZZZZ	USA
SIMCHE	6	F	CHILD	GRZZZZ	USA
SACHMARD, ISAAC	19	M	LABR	GRZZZZ	USA
MORE	20	F	SP	GRZZZZ	USA
NEWMAN, BEILE	18	F	SP	GRZZZZ	USA
RUDD, MARG	20	F	SP	GRZZZZ	USA
REGNALUDA	17	M	LABR	GRZZZZ	USA

SHIP: ENGLAND

FROM: LIVERPOOL AND QUEENSTOWN
TO: NEW YORK
ARRIVED: 17 MAY 1888

PASSENGER	AGE	SEX	OCCUPATION	PRVL	DES
OFFMAN, HAMMOND	20	M	LABR	GRZZZZ	NY
REILLY, PATRICK	30	M	LABR	GRZZZZ	UNK
STOKES, ALFRED	41	M	LABR	GRZZZZ	UNK
HESSMANN, BERL	18	M	LABR	GRAGFU	NY
KORNREICH, MOSES	25	M	LABR	GRAGFU	NY
MARGUELIS, MEYER	18	M	LABR	GRAGFU	PHI
SCHARTZ, WOLFF	11	M	CH	GRAGFU	NY
SPRINGER, LEIB	38	M	LABR	GRAGFU	NY
GERCHON	36	M	LABR	GRAGFU	NY
SCHMIDT, S	41	M	LABR	GRAGFU	NY
PHILLIPS, GEORGE	30	M	LABR	GRAGFU	NY
EISEN, LEIB	17	M	LABR	GRAGFU	NY
-INHARD, JOHAN	29	M	LABR	GRAGFU	NY
BYRAN, CARL	20	M	LABR	GRAGFU	BO
LEMBECH, LEIB	23	M	LABR	GRAGFU	BO
-IEBER, BER	11	M	CH	GRAGFU	BO
DAMMERT, WILHELM	46	M	LABR	GRAGFU	OH
HALLER, HENRICH	26	M	LABR	GRAGFU	OH
HOLE, PETER	20	M	LABR	GRAGFU	MN
SCHAFER, LESSER	17	M	LABR	GRAGFU	PHI
SAUERBIER, HANS	30	M	LABR	GRAGFU	WI
-L-DAL, SEVER--	20	M	LABR	GRAGFU	NY
KRONSENBERG, MORRIS	36	M	LABR	GRAGFU	NY
FUCHS, ABAH	31	M	LABR	GRAGFU	NY
BRENDAR, BERL	36	M	LABR	GRAGFU	NY
MARTINSSON, MARL	31	M	LABR	GRAGFU	NY
MISS	26	F	SP	GRAGFU	NY
SCHON, MR	36	M	LABR	GRAGFU	NY
PITZALE, CHIEL	25	M	LABR	GRAGFU	NY
AXELRAEL, BERNT	36	M	LABR	GRAGFU	NY
PICIUS, BENJ	17	M	LABR	GRAGFU	NY

PASSENGER	AGE	SEX	OCCUPATION	PRVL	DES
GALEF, JACOB	26	M	LABR		GRAGFUNY
FINKIN, MOSES	11	M	CH		GRAGFUNY
BRANKSTEIN, RICHD	27	M	LABR		GRAGFUNY
RICHD	6	M	CHILD		GRAGFUNY
FUERMANN, AB	23	M	LABR		GRAGFUNY
STEINBERG, JACOB	30	M	LABR		GRAGFUNY
CHA-KE	8	M	CHILD		GRAGFUNY
GOLDSTEIN, MARK	30	M	LABR		GRAGFUBO
BAER, GEZA	17	M	LABR		GRAGFUNY
BO-STEIN, LEIB	35	M	LABR		GRAGFUNY
ABRAH	8	M	CHILD		GRAGFUNY
RECHT, JACOB	51	M	LABR		GRAGFUNY
ISRAEL	16	M	LABR		GRAGFUNY
BEILE	9	M	CHILD		GRAGFUNY
ENGVIG, KNUD	25	M	LABR		GRAGFUWI
PERLITZ, EISIG	22	M	LABR		GRAGFUNY
DICKSKIN, LEIB	30	M	LABR		GRAGFUNY
MINKSOFSKY, JACOB	17	M	LABR		GRAGFUNY
H--LSON, LOUIS	25	M	LABR		GRAGFUCRS
AXELROD, BERNT	35	M	LABR		GRAGFUNY
KORNBLEIT, BERIL	25	M	LABR		GRAGFUNY
GRERN, JACOB	48	M	LABR		GRAGFUNY
GLASSMAN, SOHRE	11	M	CH		GRAGFUNY
BOBINSKY, JACOB	18	M	LABR		GRAGFUNY
PIERRE, -USEL	24	M	LABR		GRAGFUNY
DE---ICO, MICHEL	30	M	LABR		GRAGFUNY
ALEXR	23	F	SVNT		GRAGFUNY
MARIE	20	F	SVNT		GRAGFUNY
RAPHEL	25	M	LABR		GRAGFUNY
LABO-IE, MICHEL	22	M	LABR		GRAGFUNY
KVACAIKES, ANTON	23	M	LABR		GRAGFUNY
ELLIS, J	23	M	LABR		GRAGFUNY
MINGAR, SCHIEL	25	M	LABR		GRAGFUNY
ADULTY, JACOB	38	M	LABR		GRAGFUBAL
VANDEM, JOSEPH	47	M	LABR		GRAGFUNY
TODE, CHRISTIAN	39	M	LABR		GRAGFUNY
DAHN, JOHANNES	57	M	LABR		GRAGFUOR
MAGDALEN	44	F	W		GRAGFUOR
DALLE-	16	F	SP		GRAGFUOR
SOFIA	15	F	SP		GRAGFUOR
ANNA	11	F	CH		GRAGFUOR
TUNNERMANN, MARIE	59	F	MA		GRAGFUNY
FELDMAN, EPHRAIM	37	M	LABR		GRAGFUNY
JEANNETTE	17	F	SP		GRAGFUNY
REBECCA	15	F	SP		GRAGFUNY
F-ORNAN, HENRY	26	M	LABR		GRAGFUNY
ADELAIDE	23	F	W		GRAGFUNY
THEODORE	.07	F	INFANT		GRAGFUNY
PHILLIPS, ABRAHAM	35	M	PNTR		GRAGFUNY
MIRIAM	35	F	W		GRAGFUNY
BETSY	16	F	SP		GRAGFUNY
SAMUEL	11	M	CH		GRAGFUNY
ESTER	7	F	CHILD		GRAGFUNY
JACOB	4	M	CHILD		GRAGFUNY
BERTHA	1	F	CHILD		GRAGFUNY

SHIP: PERUVIAN

FROM: LIVERPOOL AND QUEENSTOWN
TO: BALTIMORE
ARRIVED: 17 MAY 1888

PASSENGER	AGE	SEX	OCCUPATION	PRVL	DES
FREY, BERNT	52	M	LABR		GRZZZZIL
HRABAK, ALB.	19	M	LABR		GRZZZZCLE
FISER, KAROL	43	M	LABR		GRZZZZOH
JACOB, AUGUSTE	36	M	LABR		GRZZZZBAL
FREY, JULIUS	52	M	LABR		GRZZZZBAL
JOHANN	24	F	W		GRZZZZBAL
JOSEFINE	56	F	HSWF		GRZZZZIL
U, JOSEFA	27	F	HSWF		GRZZZZIL

PASSENGER	AGE	SEX	OCCUPATION	PRVL	DES
ANTON	3	M	CHILD		GRZZZZIL
EMIL	3	M	CHILD		GRZZZZIL
ALOIS	.04	M	INFANT		GRZZZZIL
KARLSTEN, KARL	43	M	LABR		GRZZZZNY
KEMER, FREDRICK	40	M	LABR		GRZZZZSTL
METZGER, CARL	28	M	LABR		GRZZZZBAL
KNOP, KARL	25	M	LABR		GRZZZZBAL
GALL, HEINRICH	42	M	LABR		GRZZZZBAL
MARIA	40	F	W		GRZZZZBAL
ANNA	17	F	CH		GRZZZZBAL
FRITZ	11	M	CH		GRZZZZBAL
MARIA	9	F	CHILD		GRZZZZBAL
BERTHA	3	F	CHILD		GRZZZZBAL
KROWRATZ, J.	21	F	DMS		GRZZZZBAL
RAZIPKI, F.	20	F	DMS		GRZZZZBAL

SHIP: ROMAN

FROM: LIVERPOOL
TO: BOSTON
ARRIVED: 17 MAY 1888

PASSENGER	AGE	SEX	OCCUPATION	PRVL	DES
NEDERSON, JOHN	22	M	MCHT		GRZZZZBO
LISTONIZ, A.	22	M	LABR		GRZZZZNY
IVEL, CHR.	22	M	LABR		GRZZZZNY

SHIP: STATE OF INDIANA

FROM: GLASGOW AND LARNE
TO: NEW YORK
ARRIVED: 17 MAY 1888

PASSENGER	AGE	SEX	OCCUPATION	PRVL	DES
PILS, FRANZ	34	M	LABR		GRZZZZUSA
GLUOK, MOSES	16	M	LABR		GRZZZZUSA
KOWALZESKI, ISAAC	30	M	LABR		GRZZZZUSA
GREEN, HARRIS	24	M	CL		GRZZZZUSA
ROGALSKI, ANNA	17	F	DMS		GRZZZZUSA
GRASSBERG, CLARA	26	F	DMS		GRZZZZUSA
JINFER, ESTER	15	F	DMS		GRZZZZUSA
GRUNBERGER, JOHANNA	19	F	DMS		GRZZZZUSA
MILLINGER, RESI	16	F	DMS		GRZZZZUSA
ROSENBERG, ESSI	11	F	UNKNOWN		GRZZZZUSA
SCHLESINGER, ESSI	16	F	DMS		GRZZZZUSA
GOEDE, ERNST	51	M	MLR		GRZZZZUSA
LOUISE	45	F	W		GRZZZZUSA
MINNA	11	F	CH		GRZZZZUSA
EMMA	9	F	CHILD		GRZZZZUSA
ROBERT	3	M	CHILD		GRZZZZUSA

SHIP: GOTHIA

FROM: STETTIN
TO: NEW YORK
ARRIVED: 18 MAY 1888

PASSENGER	AGE	SEX	OCCUPATION	PRVL	DES
KLEMPKE, ALBERTINE	21	F	SGL		PRZZZZUSA
ZELBE, ERNST	30	M	LABR		PRZZZZUSA
NADOLSKI, JOHANN	14	M	BY		PRZZZZUSA
ZUHL, WILHELM	62	M	FARMER		PRZZZZUSA
CAROLINE	62	F	W		PRZZZZUSA

PASSENGER	AGE	SEX	OCCUPATION	PRVL	DES
AUGUST	24	M	CH		PRZZZZUSA
MARIE	16	F	CH		PRZZZZUSA
MAX	1	M	CHILD		PRZZZZUSA
TOPEL, LOUISE	15	F	SGL		PRZZZZUSA
TREPTOW, LOUISE	15	F	SGL		PRZZZZUSA
KILINSKI, ROCHUS	36	M	LABR		PRZZZZUSA
CARL	80	M	UNKNOWN		PRZZZZUSA
JOSEFA	30	F	W		PRZZZZUSA
JOHANN	9	M	CHILD		PRZZZZUSA
ANDREAS	6	M	CHILD		PRZZZZUSA
FRANZ	4	M	CHILD		PRZZZZUSA
VALENTIN	2	M	CHILD		PRZZZZUSA
MARIANA	24	F	SI		PRZZZZUSA
DAU, MATHILDE	24	F	SGL		PRZZZZUSA
KOWALSKI, JOSEPHA	24	F	W		PRZZZZUSA
STANISLAUS	3	M	CHILD		PRZZZZUSA
MARIANNA	1	F	CHILD		PRZZZZUSA
SCHOLZ, HERMANN	29	M	PNTR		PRZZZZUSA
JOHANNA	33	F	W		PRZZZZUSA
ANNA	10	F	CH		PRZZZZUSA
REICHOW, AUGUSTE	18	F	SGL		PRZZZZUSA
JANKOWSKI, JOHANN	55	M	LABR		PRZZZZUSA
SCHNABEL, EDUARD	31	M	LABR		PRZZZZUSA
MAGDALENA	29	F	W		PRZZZZUSA
ANNA	2	F	CHILD		PRZZZZUSA
PAULINE	.03	F	INFANT		PRZZZZUSA
WINKLER, CARL	15	M	BY		PRZZZZUSA
STANKIEWICEZ, VALENTINE	24	F	SGL		PRZZZZUSA
PAPENFUSS, CARL	51	M	FARMER		PRZZZZUSA
MARIE	56	F	W		PRZZZZUSA
AUGUSTE	24	F	D		PRZZZZUSA
BERTHA	21	F	D		PRZZZZUSA
KALINOWSKI, JOSEPH	27	M	LABR		PRZZZZUSA
MARIANNA	25	F	W		PRZZZZUSA
KATHARINA	39	F	W		PRZZZZUSA
ANTON	.03	M	INFANT		PRZZZZUSA
LUBAWSKI, SIOFIL	42	M	UNKNOWN		PRZZZZUSA
SCHROCK, JOHANNA	18	F	SGL		PRZZZZUSA
LEWISKI, ALBIN	32	M	SHMK		PRZZZZUSA
KWIZAWSKI, THECLA	26	F	SGL		PRZZZZUSA
DOMRESS, JOHANN	25	M	LABR		PRZZZZUSA
EVA	25	F	W		PRZZZZUSA
MARIE	.06	F	INFANT		PRZZZZUSA
PRUSTROWSKA, EVA	41	F	W		PRZZZZUSA
JOSEF	.03	M	INFANT		PRZZZZUSA
CENRONKE, ALBERT	32	M	LABR		PRZZZZUSA
ALBERTINE	37	F	W		PRZZZZUSA
MARTHA	20	F	CH		PRZZZZUSA
JOHANN	5	M	CHILD		PRZZZZUSA
MATHILDE	3	F	CHILD		PRZZZZUSA
LEO	1	M	CHILD		PRZZZZUSA
MICHALSKI, PETER	33	M	LABR		PRZZZZUSA
VERONIKA	28	F	W		PRZZZZUSA
MARYANNA	4	F	CHILD		PRZZZZUSA
VERONIKA	2	F	CHILD		PRZZZZUSA
JOHANN	.06	M	INFANT		PRZZZZUSA
CZECHOWSKA, PAULINE	22	F	SGL		PRZZZZUSA
KAPHEIM, WILHELMINE	44	F	W		PRZZZZUSA
WILHELMINE	15	F	CH		PRZZZZUSA
FRIEDRICH	11	M	CH		PRZZZZUSA
MARTHA	.10	F	INFANT		PRZZZZUSA
NIEMANN, AUGUST	36	M	LABR		PRZZZZUSA
BERTHA	32	F	W		PRZZZZUSA
OTTO	10	M	CH		PRZZZZUSA
ANNA	8	F	CHILD		PRZZZZUSA
HERMANN	5	M	CHILD		PRZZZZUSA
GRONKE, CHARLOTTE	59	F	W		PRZZZZUSA
ALBERTINE	25	F	CH		PRZZZZUSA
AUGUSTE	4	F	CHILD		PRZZZZUSA
FEDKE, CARL	25	M	FARMER		PRZZZZUSA
MWZYNKI, AUGUST	28	M	LABR		PRZZZZUSA
MICHALINE	27	F	W		PRZZZZUSA
SCHULL, CARL	17	M	LABR		PRZZZZUSA
DREYER, BERTHA	29	F	W		PRZZZZUSA
PAWLAK, JOSEPH	45	M	LABR		PRZZZZUSA
JOSEPHA	47	F	W		PRZZZZUSA
JACOB	16	M	CH		PRZZZZUSA
MARIANNA	10	F	CH		PRZZZZUSA
IGNATZ	7	M	CHILD		PRZZZZUSA
KOWALSKI, FRANZ	16	M	LABR		PRZZZZUSA
DETTOFF, WILHELM	47	M	FARMER		PRZZZZUSA
CAROLINE	47	F	W		PRZZZZUSA
HENRIETTE	16	F	CH		PRZZZZUSA
FRIEDRICH	11	M	CH		PRZZZZUSA
CARL	9	M	CHILD		PRZZZZUSA
AUGUSTE	7	F	CHILD		PRZZZZUSA
PAULINE	5	F	CHILD		PRZZZZUSA
NOWATZKI, MARIANNA	30	F	W		PRZZZZUSA
STANISLAUS	4	M	CHILD		PRZZZZUSA
JOSEF	1	M	CHILD		PRZZZZUSA
MUENN, FRIEDRIKE	40	F	W		PRZZZZUSA
WILHELM	17	M	CH		PRZZZZUSA
EMILIE	15	F	CH		PRZZZZUSA
PAUL	9	M	CHILD		PRZZZZUSA
BERTHA	5	F	CHILD		PRZZZZUSA
FRITZ	2	M	CHILD		PRZZZZUSA
MILKA, MARTIN	25	M	FARMER		PRZZZZUSA
ANASTASIA	30	F	W		PRZZZZUSA
KRUTZ, ANNA	45	F	W		PRZZZZUSA
JOHANN	16	M	CH		PRZZZZUSA
AUGUSTINA	10	M	CH		PRZZZZUSA
SCHOFFELKE, BERTHA	18	F	SGL		PRZZZZUSA
STEINKE, MARIA	60	F	W		PRZZZZUSA
NITUHMANN, HERRMANN	30	M	LABR		PRZZZZUSA
WILHELMINE	27	F	W		PRZZZZUSA
MARGARETHE	4	F	CHILD		PRZZZZUSA
HERMANN	3	M	CHILD		PRZZZZUSA
FRITZ	1	M	CHILD		PRZZZZUSA
EDUARD	.03	M	INFANT		PRZZZZUSA
ZIELKE, NATHALIE	18	F	SGL		PRZZZZUSA
SASS, JULIANNA	54	F	W		PRZZZZUSA
AUGUST	18	M	CH		PRZZZZUSA
ANNA	14	F	CH		PRZZZZUSA
BUCHOLZ, FRIEDERIKE	55	F	W		PRZZZZUSA
FRIEDRICH	23	M	CH		PRZZZZUSA
AUGUSTE	16	M	CH		PRZZZZUSA
MAZURI, JOHANN	34	M	SMH		PRZZZZUSA
FRANZISKA	23	F	W		PRZZZZUSA
JAN	4	M	CHILD		PRZZZZUSA
WEIDNER, JOHANN	34	M	LABR		PRZZZZUSA
HENRIETTE	31	F	W		PRZZZZUSA
AUGUSTE	7	F	CHILD		PRZZZZUSA
GUSTAV	4	M	CHILD		PRZZZZUSA
ERNST	2	M	CHILD		PRZZZZUSA
ANNA	4	F	CHILD		PRZZZZUSA
AUGUSTE	25	F	SI		PRZZZZUSA
VOSS, AMALIE	39	F	W		PRZZZZUSA
GUSTAV	15	M	CH		PRZZZZUSA
IDA	11	F	CH		PRZZZZUSA
LOUISE	10	F	CH		PRZZZZUSA
EMIL	7	M	CHILD		PRZZZZUSA
KAZMICZAK, WOICIECK	28	M	LABR		PRZZZZUSA
MICHALINE	23	F	W		PRZZZZUSA
ROSALIE	2	F	CHILD		PRZZZZUSA
MAX	.03	M	INFANT		PRZZZZUSA
LIPINSKA, KATHARINA	40	F	W		PRZZZZUSA
GRUNA, AGNES	19	F	SGL		PRZZZZUSA
KIEWERT, WILHELM	17	M	LABR		PRZZZZUSA
MAUSKA, PAUL	15	M	LABR		PRZZZZUSA
FALK, EMMA	17	F	SGL		PRZZZZUSA
KEMP, WILHELM	41	M	MSN		PRZZZZUSA
WILHELMINE	41	F	W		PRZZZZUSA
BERTHA	10	F	CH		PRZZZZUSA
ALMA	9	F	CHILD		PRZZZZUSA
THEODOR	6	M	CHILD		PRZZZZUSA
OTTO	4	M	CHILD		PRZZZZUSA
MARTHA	3	F	CHILD		PRZZZZUSA
PAUL	1	M	CHILD		PRZZZZUSA
HUEBNER, GUSTAV	33	M	LABR		PRZZZZUSA
ADELINE	29	F	W		PRZZZZUSA

PASSENGER	AGE	SEX	OCCUPATION	PRVL	DES	PASSENGER	AGE	SEX	OCCUPATION	PRVL	DES
ERNST	5	M	CHILD	PRZZZZUSA		MECLEWSKA, PELAGIA	21	F	SGL	PRZZZZUSA	
BERNHARDT	.03	M	INFANT	PRZZZZUSA		WEINER, MARIANNA	21	F	SGL	PRZZZZUSA	
POEPPEL, FRANZ	29	M	LABR	PRZZZZUSA		RUDZINSKI, JOHANN	40	M	LABR	PRZZZZUSA	
WILHELMINE	27	F	W	PRZZZZUSA		ANTONIA	40	F	W	PRZZZZUSA	
GEORG	3	M	CHILD	PRZZZZUSA		MARIANNA	5	F	CHILD	PRZZZZUSA	
RICHARD	3	M	CHILD	PRZZZZUSA		HEDWIG	3	F	CHILD	PRZZZZUSA	
GOETZE, ADOLF	15	M	LABR	PRZZZZUSA		KLOSIN, THOMAS	30	M	LABR	PRZZZZUSA	
SACKSCHEWSKY, ANTON	44	M	LABR	PRZZZZUSA		DUSCHINSKY, ANNA	20	F	SGL	PRZZZZUSA	
MARIE	41	F	W	PRZZZZUSA		PATEWALSKI, IGNATZ	46	M	LABR	PRZZZZUSA	
MARIE	12	F	UNKNOWN	PRZZZZUSA		UNMACH, WILHELMINE	24	F	SGL	PRZZZZUSA	
FRANZISKA	8	F	CHILD	PRZZZZUSA		WILL, AUGUSTE	20	F	SGL	PRZZZZUSA	
JACOB	5	M	CHILD	PRZZZZUSA		DORSZ, SIMON	68	M	LABR	PRZZZZUSA	
JOSEF	3	M	CHILD	PRZZZZUSA		STANISLAUS	12	M	CH	PRZZZZUSA	
ELISABETH	.03	F	INFANT	PRZZZZUSA		ROLKE, ADOLF	30	M	LABR	PRZZZZUSA	
MAUTZKE, JOHANNA	39	F	W	PRZZZZUSA		PIEGUSCH, GUSTAV	43	M	LABR	PRZZZZUSA	
FRANZ	17	M	CH	PRZZZZUSA		HENRIETTE	46	F	W	PRZZZZUSA	
ANNA	14	F	CH	PRZZZZUSA		BERTHA	8	F	CHILD	PRZZZZUSA	
OTTO	12	F	CH	PRZZZZUSA		KOLSCHOWSKY, ANNA	26	F	SGL	PRZZZZUSA	
AUGUST	6	M	CHILD	PRZZZZUSA		CAROLINE	22	F	SGL	PRZZZZUSA	
ALBERT	3	M	CHILD	PRZZZZUSA		POLZIN, WILHELM	42	M	CPTR	PRZZZZUSA	
BINHOFF, JOHANNA	20	F	SGL	PRZZZZUSA		EMILIE	41	F	W	PRZZZZUSA	
ZYLKA, VERONIKA	22	F	SGL	PRZZZZUSA		EMIL	15	M	CH	PRZZZZUSA	
JAHNKE, FERDINAND	16	M	LABR	PRZZZZUSA		BERTHA	14	F	CH	PRZZZZUSA	
REHBEIN, CARL	51	M	LABR	PRZZZZUSA		WEGNER, AUGUST	36	M	DLR	PRZZZZUSA	
PELOWSKY, LORENZ	34	M	FARMER	PRZZZZUSA		BERTHA	37	F	W	PRZZZZUSA	
LISS, VALENTIN	23	M	LABR	PRZZZZUSA		WILHELM	11	M	CH	PRZZZZUSA	
ZILLMER, MARTHA	14	F	SGL	PRZZZZUSA		IDA	10	F	CH	PRZZZZUSA	
CZOSKE, FRANZ	26	M	LABR	PRZZZZUSA		EMIL	9	M	CHILD	PRZZZZUSA	
ANNA	27	F	W	PRZZZZUSA		OTTO	6	M	CHILD	PRZZZZUSA	
AUGUST	.01	M	INFANT	PRZZZZUSA		KLOEHN, LUDWIG	34	M	LABR	PRZZZZUSA	
LEBAU, AUGUST	38	M	LABR	PRZZZZUSA		SCHULZ, WILHELM	24	M	FARMER	PRZZZZUSA	
AUGUSTE	27	F	W	PRZZZZUSA		FERDINAND	28	M	FARMER	PRZZZZUSA	
ANNA	4	F	CHILD	PRZZZZUSA		ZIESEMANN, ALBERT	34	M	JNR	PRZZZZUSA	
WILHELM	3	M	CHILD	PRZZZZUSA		ALBERTINE	34	F	W	PRZZZZUSA	
AUGUST	1	M	CHILD	PRZZZZUSA		EMIL	6	M	CHILD	PRZZZZUSA	
WITTHAUS, PAUL	19	M	LABR	PRZZZZUSA		LUTZKE, EMILIE	23	F	SGL	PRZZZZUSA	
SCHOCK, JOSEF	24	M	LABR	PRZZZZUSA		RASCH, FRIEDRICH	30	M	LABR	PRZZZZUSA	
DORA	25	F	SGL	PRZZZZUSA		EMILIE	18	F	W	PRZZZZUSA	
TROSCHINSKE, MICHAEL	47	M	LABR	PRZZZZUSA		EMILIE	.01	F	INFANT	PRZZZZUSA	
GROSS, EMILIE	25	F	SGL	PRZZZZUSA		PAETZ, ROBERT	16	M	LABR	SYZZZZUSA	
KLENOWSKI, VERONIKA	15	F	SGL	PRZZZZUSA		WATZDORF, CARL	17	M	LABR	SYZZZZUSA	
RURIE, ANTONIE	43	F	W	PRZZZZUSA		WEBER, OTTO	14	M	LABR	SYZZZZUSA	
EMMA	18	F	CH	PRZZZZUSA		BAUMGERTEL, BERNHARD	16	M	LABR	SYZZZZUSA	
JULIUS	16	M	CH	PRZZZZUSA		ROTHBART, ADOLF	49	M	LABR	PRZZZZUSA	
JOHANN	14	M	CH	PRZZZZUSA		FRIEDERIKE	47	F	W	PRZZZZUSA	
RASIMIR	8	M	CHILD	PRZZZZUSA		CAROLINE	18	F	CH	PRZZZZUSA	
MARTHA	6	F	CHILD	PRZZZZUSA		ANNA	4	F	CHILD	PRZZZZUSA	
BLOCK, JOHANN	24	M	LABR	PRZZZZUSA		JANSEN, RUDOLF	17	M	MSN	PRZZZZUSA	
WISEZOREK, WILHELMINE	17	F	SGL	PRZZZZUSA		KOSCHNIK, EMIL	22	M	PNTR	PRZZZZUSA	
JOHANN	14	M	LABR	PRZZZZUSA		MERZENGER, JOHANN	47	M	SHMK	PRZZZZUSA	
LANGFIEL, LOUISE	23	F	SGL	PRZZZZUSA		VERONIKA	47	F	W	PRZZZZUSA	
HOFFMANN, KATHARINA	16	F	SGL	PRZZZZUSA		IDA	17	F	CH	PRZZZZUSA	
PRODOEHL, FRANZ	22	M	LABR	PRZZZZUSA		BERNHARD	8	M	CHILD	PRZZZZUSA	
KIEP, JOHANN	45	M	LABR	PRZZZZUSA		KADDATZ, EMIL	26	M	LABR	PRZZZZUSA	
JOHANNA	49	F	W	PRZZZZUSA		GRIWATZ, FRIEDRICH	56	M	LABR	PRZZZZUSA	
KRASKA, ALBERT	32	M	LABR	PRZZZZUSA		MARIA	54	F	W	PRZZZZUSA	
MARIE	30	F	W	PRZZZZUSA		FERDINAND	25	M	S	PRZZZZUSA	
VICTORIA	14	F	CH	PRZZZZUSA		TIEDEMANN, CARL	28	M	LABR	PRZZZZUSA	
ROCH	7	M	CHILD	PRZZZZUSA		AUGUSTE	29	F	W	PRZZZZUSA	
JOSEF	4	M	CHILD	PRZZZZUSA		OTTILIE	.11	F	INFANT	PRZZZZUSA	
REUTER, GUSTAV	22	M	BKR	PRZZZZUSA		JESIKEWICZ, ALEXANDER	27	M	LABR	PRZZZZUSA	
KUSCHINSKY, JOHANN	58	M	LABR	PRZZZZUSA		AUGUSTE	25	F	W	PRZZZZUSA	
EVA	41	F	W	PRZZZZUSA		LEOKADIA	2	F	CHILD	PRZZZZUSA	
ANNA	16	F	D	PRZZZZUSA		JOHANN	.06	M	INFANT	PRZZZZUSA	
BERTHA	11	F	CH	PRZZZZUSA		HAKMANN, WILHELM	26	M	FARMER	PRZZZZUSA	
JOHANN	7	M	CHILD	PRZZZZUSA		SCHUETZ, AUGUST	24	M	UNKNOWN	PRZZZZUSA	
GRUNST, HEINRICH	67	M	SMH	PRZZZZUSA		HINZ, WILHELM	17	M	LABR	PRZZZZUSA	
CAROLINE	53	F	W	PRZZZZUSA		KEMPFERT, AMALIE	38	F	W	PRZZZZUSA	
WINKLER, AUGUST	22	M	LABR	PRZZZZUSA		HERMANN	.05	M	INFANT	PRZZZZUSA	
LAURA	22	F	W	PRZZZZUSA		KNAAK, AUGUST	56	M	JNR	PRZZZZUSA	
GRUNST, HERRMANN	17	M	CH	PRZZZZUSA		LAURETTE	49	F	W	PRZZZZUSA	
MARIA	11	F	CH	PRZZZZUSA		AUGUSTE	17	F	CH	PRZZZZUSA	
MINNA	10	F	CH	PRZZZZUSA		LOUISE	14	F	CH	PRZZZZUSA	
KNABE, AUGUSTE	22	F	W	PRZZZZUSA		MINNA	9	F	CHILD	PRZZZZUSA	
OSCAR	1	M	CHILD	PRZZZZUSA		FRAEDRICH, AUGUSTE	23	F	W	PRZZZZUSA	

PASSENGER	AGE	SEX	OCCUPATION	PRVL	DES
RUDOLF	.03	M	INFANT	PRZZZZUSA
TREDUP, JOHANN	35	M	LABR	PRZZZZUSA
MARIE	34	F	W	PRZZZZUSA
ELISE	8	F	CHILD	PRZZZZUSA
JOHANNES	6	M	CHILD	PRZZZZUSA
HELENE	2	F	CHILD	PRZZZZUSA
WEGNER, ALBERT	47	M	MCHT	PRZZZZUSA
FELLMANN, CARL	16	M	LABR	SYZZZZUSA
KLUETZ, PAUL	26	M	SLR	PRZZZZUSA
HINZ, BERTHA	16	F	SGL	PRZZZZUSA
ZICK, AUGUST	30	M	LABR	PRZZZZUSA
RIPS, FRANZ	30	M	MCHT	PRZZZZUSA
RIEBE, HERRMANN	30	M	SHMK	PRZZZZUSA
GERIMMSCH, CAROLINE	26	F	W	PRZZZZUSA
FRIEDRICH	.11	M	INFANT	PRZZZZUSA
ROHLOFF, FRIEDRICH	27	M	INF	PRZZZZUSA
MALIK, JOHANN	56	M	SDLR	PRZZZZUSA
JOHANNA	48	F	W	PRZZZZUSA
FRANZ	14	M	CH	PRZZZZUSA
ALBERT	11	M	CH	PRZZZZUSA
HEDWIG	9	F	CHILD	PRZZZZUSA
EMMA	7	F	CHILD	PRZZZZUSA
ARTHUR	5	M	CHILD	PRZZZZUSA
REIFSCHLAEGER, CARL	30	M	LABR	PRZZZZUNK
DOUNER, FRANZ	24	M	FARMER	PRZZZZUNK
LOUISE	23	F	W	PRZZZZUNK
KRUEGER, FRANZ	40	M	FARMER	PRZZZZUNK
EMILIE	38	F	W	PRZZZZUNK
EMMA	15	F	CH	PRZZZZUNK
ANNA	13	F	CH	PRZZZZUNK
MARIE	12	F	CH	PRZZZZUNK
MARTHA	10	F	CH	PRZZZZUNK
ERNST	9	M	CHILD	PRZZZZUNK
FRANZ	7	M	CHILD	PRZZZZUNK
FRITZ	2	M	CHILD	PRZZZZUNK
WILHELM	.06	M	INFANT	PRZZZZUNK
ANDERS, EMILIE	30	F	W	PRZZZZUNK
HULDA	10	F	CH	PRZZZZUNK
SELMA	7	F	CHILD	PRZZZZUNK
HUGO	4	M	CHILD	PRZZZZUNK
OTTILIE	.03	F	INFANT	PRZZZZUNK
ROSE, WILHELM	17	M	LABR	PRZZZZUNK
BERG, FERDINNAD	24	M	FARMER	PRZZZZUNK
THEEL, AUGUST	26	M	LABR	PRZZZZUNK
JOHANNA	30	F	W	PRZZZZUNK
BERTHA	7	F	CHILD	PRZZZZUNK
ALBERT	3	M	CHILD	PRZZZZUNK
FRIEDERIKE	25	F	SI	PRZZZZUNK
WILHELM	.06	M	INFANT	PRZZZZUNK
BARFKNECHT, LOUISE	18	F	SGL	PRZZZZUNK
LAUGNEFF, FRANZ	35	M	LABR	PRZZZZUNK
DZIEATKIEWICZ, ALBERT	29	M	LABR	PRZZZZUNK
WOTTRICH, BIANCA	28	F	SGL	PRZZZZUNK
GRIGUSCHAT, THERESE	23	F	SGL	PRZZZZUNK
BOENISCH, OTTILIE	25	F	SGL	PRZZZZUNK
SCHMIDT, FRANZ	23	M	LABR	PRZZZZUNK
ANNA	27	F	W	PRZZZZUNK
KINKOR, ANNA	19	F	W	PRZZZZUNK
MARIE	8	F	CHILD	PRZZZZUNK
ROSALIE	5	F	CHILD	PRZZZZUNK
LUZINSKA, ALEXANDRINE	20	F	SGL	PRZZZZUNK
LATZKE, CARL	36	M	LABR	PRZZZZUNK
WILHELMINE	38	F	W	PRZZZZUNK
HERMANN	10	M	CH	PRZZZZUNK
CARL	8	M	CHILD	PRZZZZUNK
ALWINE	6	F	CHILD	PRZZZZUNK
EMIL	.03	F	INFANT	PRZZZZUNK
SCHRAMKE, JOSEF	28	M	LABR	PRZZZZUNK
ROSALIE	26	F	W	PRZZZZUNK
MARIE	.03	F	INFANT	PRZZZZUNK
ANNA	3	F	CHILD	PRZZZZUNK
BISCHOFF, JOHANNA	29	F	W	PRZZZZUNK
ADOLF	1	M	CHILD	PRZZZZUNK
VERCH, JOHANNA	57	F	W	PRZZZZUNK
WILHELM	16	M	S	PRZZZZUNK
SESMANSKI, PAULINE	40	F	W	PRZZZZUNK
AMALIE	14	F	D	PRZZZZUNK
OTTO, RICHARD	23	M	LABR	PRZZZZUNK
BENTIN, WILHELM	25	M	FARMER	PRZZZZUNK
DOBRUNZ, WILHELMINE	19	F	SGL	PRZZZZUNK
FUHRMANN, LOUISE	22	F	SGL	PRZZZZUNK
SALZWEDEL, CARL	24	M	CTW	PRZZZZUNK
KLEMKE, DOROTHEA	65	F	W	PRZZZZUNK
HERMINE	18	F	D	PRZZZZUNK
RAHN, BERTHA	18	F	SGL	PRZZZZUNK
KRUCK, WILHELM	25	M	LABR	PRZZZZUNK
FOLKSDORF, LOISE	21	F	SGL	PRZZZZUNK
AGNES	19	F	SGL	PRZZZZUNK
MUTZ, ANNA	46	F	W	PRZZZZUNK
SUSANNE	11	F	D	PRZZZZUNK
MARIE	4	F	CHILD	PRZZZZUNK
PASCHOLKE, FRIEDRICH	29	M	LABR	PRZZZZUNK
NEUITZ, JOHANN	29	M	LABR	PRZZZZUNK
BARTSCH, BERTHA	21	F	SGL	PRZZZZUNK
NEUBAUER, ALEX	30	M	BKPR	PRZZZZUNK
HORUK, WILHELMINE	27	F	SGL	PRZZZZUNK
GEHRKE, EMILIE	21	F	SGL	PRZZZZUNK
KAATZ, CARL	18	M	UNKNOWN	PRZZZZUNK
NOWAK, FRANZ	29	M	UNKNOWN	PRZZZZUNK
ANNA	29	F	W	PRZZZZUNK
JAN	2	M	CHILD	PRZZZZUNK
WLADISLAW	.06	M	INFANT	PRZZZZUNK
ZAHN, FRANZ	26	M	FARMER	PRZZZZUNK
ENGLER, OTTO	29	M	LABR	PRZZZZUNK
MATHILDE	28	F	W	PRZZZZUNK
MAX	3	M	CHILD	PRZZZZUNK
MINNA	1	F	CHILD	PRZZZZUNK
BARTELS, JOHANN	32	M	LABR	PRZZZZUNK
EMILIE	30	F	W	PRZZZZUNK
PAUL	4	M	CHILD	PRZZZZUNK
ELISABETH	2	F	CHILD	PRZZZZUNK
JOHANNES	.03	M	INFANT	PRZZZZUNK
BORCHARDT, ANNA	13	F	L	PRZZZZUNK
PIOCK, BERTHA	21	F	SGL	PRZZZZUNK
SCHULZ, ARTHUR	25	M	FARMER	PRZZZZUNK
BRAUN, BERTHA	21	F	SGL	PRZZZZUNK
NEHRING, FRIEDERIKE	49	F	W	PRZZZZUNK
ANNA	18	F	CH	PRZZZZUNK
ALBERT	15	M	CH	PRZZZZUNK
HELENE	11	F	CH	PRZZZZUNK
MACHNOWSKI, JOSEF	48	M	LABR	PRZZZZUNK
WIRTALLA, AUGUST	30	M	TLR	PRZZZZUNK
WILHELMINE	29	F	W	PRZZZZUNK
AUGUST	7	M	CHILD	PRZZZZUNK
RUDOLF	5	M	CHILD	PRZZZZUNK
JOHANN	.03	M	INFANT	PRZZZZUNK
GOSTOMSKI, FRANZ	28	M	FARMER	PRZZZZUNK
WARDINSKI, AUGUST	22	M	LABR	PRZZZZUNK
KIEHN, JOHANN	23	M	LABR	PRZZZZUNK
MIKOLEIT, ANNA	17	F	SGL	PRZZZZUNK
KOSLOWSKI, AUGUST	30	M	BKPR	PRZZZZUNK
MUELLER, CARL	16	M	BY	PRZZZZUNK
ERDMANN, U	29	M	LABR	PRZZZZUNK
PZSCHEBESCHEWSKI, STANI	40	M	LABR	PRZZZZUNK
CERWJONKE, JOSEF	27	M	LABR	PRZZZZUNK
GERTRUDE	1	F	CHILD	PRZZZZUNK
ANASTASIA	1	F	CHILD	PRZZZZUNK
MURZYNSKI, LUDWIG	.03	M	INFANT	PRZZZZUNK
BAUER, MARIA	41	F	SGL	HSZZZZUSA
LOEWENHEIM, OLGA	18	F	SGL	PRZZZZUSA
ROSE, EDUARD	22	M	MCHT	PRZZZZUSA
VOLKMANN, JULIUS	13	M	MCHT	PRZZZZUSA
WILLY	10	M	CH	PRZZZZUSA
HEIDTMANN, MARIE	47	F	W	PRZZZZUSA
MAX	16	M	S	PRZZZZUSA

SHIP: RHYNLAND

FROM: ANTWERP
TO: NEW YORK
ARRIVED: 18 MAY 1888

PASSENGER	AGE	SEX	OCCUPATION	CODE
D------, SEVERIN	24	M	SLR	GRZZZZNY
MARGOT, MR	42	M	UNKNOWN	FRZZZZNY
AB	10	M	CH	FRZZZZNY
M	8	F	CHILD	FRZZZZNY
SINGER, C	20	F	SVNT	GRZZZZNY
STOLZKE, M	40	M	LABR	GRZZZZNY
COHN, C	17	M	TLR	GRZZZZNY
SJCOKIN, M	17	M	TLR	GRZZZZNY
MULINSKY, B	17	M	TLR	GRZZZZNY
STEPHALATIS, P	23	M	LABR	GRZZZZNY
RABINOWITZ, J	38	M	TLR	GRZZZZNY
E	9	M	CHILD	GRZZZZNY
L-OSCHERZ, M	18	M	TLR	GRZZZZNY
BALLIN, S	16	M	LABR	GRZZZZNY
SOMMERFELD, U	20	M	BCHR	GRZZZZNY
HENKEL, C	22	M	CGRMKR	GRZZZZNY
STEINER, W	22	M	CGRMKR	GRZZZZNY
SCHMIEL, G	23	M	LABR	GRZZZZNY
BRIESEMEISTER, W	24	M	LABR	GRZZZZNY
E	23	F	W	GRZZZZNY
F	00	M	INF	GRZZZZNY
REISER, W	22	M	BCHR	GRZZZZMIL
KEROPIDLOWSKI, J	38	M	LABR	GRZZZZMIL
C	27	F	W	GRZZZZMIL
F	00	M	INF	GRZZZZMIL
RYSCHK, A	26	M	SHMK	GRZZZZUNK
HEROLD, C	25	F	SVNT	GRZZZZALT
KRAUTE, J	23	M	LABR	GRZZZZBUF
TAUBER, G	19	M	LABR	GRZZZZUNK
BAUMGARTNER, A	27	F	SVNT	GRZZZZCH
ME-IOL, M	43	F	W	GRZZZZNY
M	9	F	CHILD	GRZZZZNY
FRANK	5	M	CHILD	GRZZZZNY
AUGUST	00	M	INF	GRZZZZNY
SILVERKAMP, W	22	M	LABR	GRZZZZPIT
SACOSECK, M	36	M	LABR	GRZZZZPIT
PERSCHUERON, T	60	F	SVNT	GRZZZZUNK
EMMERICH, B	16	M	NN	GRZZZZNY
BAILY, M	23	M	MCHT	GRZZZZNY
RUDHOFF, M	19	F	SVNT	GRZZZZNY
DIEHL, A	26	M	LABR	GRZZZZNY
M	28	F	W	GRZZZZNY
HEPFINGER, S	18	M	MLR	GRZZZZMIL
RUMPF, F	35	M	SMH	GRZZZZUNK
PRADLE, F	23	M	LABR	GRZZZZCH
WEITZ, F	56	M	LABR	GRZZZZUNK
WEBER, J	33	M	LABR	GRZZZZNY
M	8	F	CHILD	GRZZZZNY
J	7	F	CHILD	GRZZZZNY
J	5	M	CHILD	GRZZZZNY
F	3	M	CHILD	GRZZZZNY
L	2	F	CHILD	GRZZZZNY
HANSEL, S	21	F	SVNT	GRZZZZNY
WALTER, J	17	M	LABR	GRZZZZNY
PRAUM, G	21	M	LABR	GRZZZZNY
PFEIFFER, J	46	M	TRVLR	GRZZZZNY
C	40	F	W	GRZZZZNY
J	16	M	CH	GRZZZZNY
F	14	M	CH	GRZZZZNY
A	4	F	CHILD	GRZZZZNY
SCHNEIDER, E	20	F	SVNT	GRZZZZUNK
SCHULEIN, J	18	M	LABR	GRZZZZBUF
GESTNER, J	18	M	BKR	GRZZZZBAL
MULLER, A	32	M	LABR	GRZZZZDBQ
A	28	F	W	GRZZZZDBQ
A	00	F	INF	GRZZZZDBQ
EISENHAUER, V	26	M	LABR	SRZZZZSAN
ALBERGINI, G	46	M	LABR	SRZZZZBO
L	37	F	W	SRZZZZBO
V	10	M	CH	SRZZZZBO
-ENFINAS, F	40	M	MSN	GRZZZZNY
H	16	M	MSN	GRZZZZNY
E	11	M	CH	GRZZZZNY
E	9	M	CHILD	GRZZZZNY
A	4	F	CHILD	GRZZZZNY
SCHMIDT, J	30	M	MSN	GRZZZZNY
SCHOLL, C	22	F	SVNT	GRZZZZNY
FORST, H	24	F	SVNT	GRZZZZCH
C	18	F	SVNT	GRZZZZCH
BADENDISTEL, M	34	M	LABR	GRZZZZNY
-OLASCHINSKI, M	52	M	LABR	GRZZZZNY
ROWICH, FRANZ	24	M	LABR	GRZZZZNY
SCHEIKER, TH	42	M	LABR	GRZZZZNY
SLACKOWITZ, J	28	M	LABR	GRZZZZNY
DOMAK, L	47	M	LABR	GRZZZZNY
RING, J	38	M	LABR	GRZZZZNY
DOMAK, L	11	M	LABR	GRZZZZNY
RING, MAGD	34	F	W	GRZZZZNY
HRISE	6	M	CHILD	GRZZZZNY
HAMMOWSKI, J	23	M	LABR	GRZZZZNY
BILANSKI, TH	48	M	LABR	GRZZZZCH
MARTIN, H	19	F	W	GRZZZZPIT
LINA	15	F	SVNT	GRZZZZPIT
LOUISE	48	F	SVNT	GRZZZZPIT
HUNTINGEN, F	27	M	BCHR	GRZZZZNY
PINGLER, W	28	M	LABR	GRZZZZNY
E	27	F	W	GRZZZZNY
C	00	M	INF	GRZZZZNY
A	60	F	M	GRZZZZNY
OCHEKI, JEAN	30	M	TRVLR	FRZZZZNY
MARIE	26	F	W	FRZZZZNY
RHEIN, ED	21	M	JNR	GRZZZZNY
HERMAN, J	17	M	BCHR	GRZZZZCH
FISCHER, H	21	F	SVNT	GRZZZZUSA
STISS, J	25	M	FARMER	GRZZZZUSA
EMMLICH, F	29	M	CPTR	GRZZZZNY
TRACHE, E	21	F	SVNT	GRZZZZNY
HERMES, J	32	M	TRVLR	GRZZZZSP
M	37	F	W	GRZZZZSP
P	2	M	CHILD	GRZZZZSP
M	00	F	INF	GRZZZZSP
VERTEGGEN, C	30	F	W	FRZZZZNY
J	00	F	INF	FRZZZZNY
SCHLOCH, J	22	M	LABR	SRZZZZNY
STRASSER, J	45	M	LABR	SRZZZZNY
ESCHMICKEL, A	15	F	SVNT	SRZZZZNY
DESILVESTER, C	40	M	LABR	SRZZZZNY
ORELLO, G	38	M	LABR	SRZZZZNY
H-RZE, J	46	M	LABR	SRZZZZNY
WIDEMANN, M	28	M	CPRSMH	GRZZZZWIK
DIEFENBACH, C	29	M	BCHR	GRZZZZNY
LAUBER, C	25	F	SVNT	GRZZZZNY
WIRTH, C	25	F	SVNT	GRZZZZNY
KAPPOLD, O	15	F	SVNT	GRZZZZNY
KAGMAIER, J	23	M	LABR	GRZZZZNY
SEBANTIO, C	15	F	SVNT	GRZZZZNY
BAUER, H	25	F	SVNT	GRZZZZNY
DITWER, V	23	M	LABR	GRZZZZNY
HELLMANN, E	35	M	LABR	GRZZZZNY
FELIX	19	M	LABR	GRZZZZNY
ARONSON, H	40	M	TLR	GRZZZZNY
OLISCHKEWITZ, D	43	M	TLR	GRZZZZNY
BLITZ, H	38	M	CGRMKR	GRZZZZNY
LEMPORT, B	32	M	TLR	GRZZZZNY
E	30	F	W	GRZZZZNY
TISCHLER, M	28	M	TRVLR	GRZZZZNY
J	28	F	W	GRZZZZNY
POVE--SIL, F	24	M	NN	GRZZZZNY
H-LIC--, J	27	M	MCHT	GRZZZZNY
HUCERA, J	18	M	LABR	GRZZZZNY
RYTINA, M	18	M	LABR	GRZZZZNY
BRAFER, J	21	M	LABR	GRZZZZNY
HOSEK, J	23	F	SVNT	GRZZZZNY

PASSENGER	AGE	SEX	OCCUPATION	PRVL	DES
-ILKA, J	23	M	LABR	GRZZZZNY	
F	26	F	W	GRZZZZNY	
J	5	M	CHILD	GRZZZZNY	
M	3	F	CHILD	GRZZZZNY	
B	00	F	INF	GRZZZZNY	
HE-NIK, M	17	F	SVNT	GRZZZZNY	
SINDELAR, A	19	M	LABR	GRZZZZNY	
HERZA, W	25	M	LABR	GRZZZZNY	
CERVENSKY, F	38	M	LABR	GRZZZZNY	
MED-EA, A	26	M	LABR	GRZZZZNY	
K	28	F	W	GRZZZZNY	
J	5	M	CHILD	GRZZZZNY	
M	2	F	CHILD	GRZZZZNY	
DAMMET, J	29	M	BKR	GRZZZZNY	
LYROVA, M	21	F	SVNT	GRZZZZNY	
CEREMY, W	26	M	TLR	GRZZZZNY	
M	29	F	W	GRZZZZNY	
CAPEK, F	21	M	LABR	GRZZZZNY	
HARMIK, A	16	F	SVNT	GRZZZZNY	
HUBERT, J	39	M	LABR	GRZZZZNY	
CORK, J	30	M	NN	GRZZZZNY	
HABADA, F	21	F	SVNT	GRZZZZNY	
PATEK, M	22	F	SVNT	GRZZZZNY	
SEIFELDER, C	23	M	LABR	GRZZZZNY	
CROCUES, E	21	F	SVNT	GRZZZZNY	
SERVAIS, M	73	F	SVNT	GRZZZZNY	
BRANDENBERGER, A	34	M	LABR	GRZZZZNY	
SEIFERMANN, B	21	M	FARMER	GRZZZZNY	
P	20	M	FARMER	GRZZZZNY	
KICHNER, W	25	M	NN	GRZZZZNY	
GUISEPPE, S	45	M	LABR	SRZZZZNY	
SARAVITO, G	45	F	LABR	SRZZZZNY	
GIOVINO, MARINE	32	F	SVNT	SRZZZZNY	
DEPORA, GIACOMO	26	M	LABR	SRZZZZNY	
CANUSSI, AMEDEO	33	M	LABR	SRZZZZNY	
RINADOSSI, FAUSTINO	25	M	LABR	SRZZZZNY	
BAISIMIO, GIOR	33	M	LABR	SRZZZZNY	
CESCUTTI, GIOV	40	M	LABR	SRZZZZPIT	
MACHINI, LORENZ	33	M	LABR	SRZZZZPIT	
CLEVA, GIOB	34	F	SVNT	SRZZZZPIT	
SCHARF, M	20	F	SVNT	GRZZZZPIT	
STOCKMEYER, G	16	F	SVNT	GRZZZZPIT	
DOERFLER, R	23	F	SVNT	GRZZZZUNK	
BUHR, P	30	M	LABR	GRZZZZUT	
LANG, J	17	M	LABR	GRZZZZUT	
GRIMMER, J	15	F	SVNT	GRZZZZNY	
GRIMET, B	20	F	SVNT	GRZZZZNY	
HEMPLING, J	15	F	SVNT	GRZZZZNY	
WEBER, J	34	M	FARMER	GRZZZZNY	
KOSSAS, C	38	F	SVNT	GRZZZZNY	
PETER, G	30	M	LABR	GRZZZZNY	
-ANDERICK, E	36	M	JNR	GRZZZZNY	
WILH	19	F	SVNT	GRZZZZNY	
STILLER, J	43	M	BBR	GRZZZZNY	
OELSEN, J	21	M	LABR	GRZZZZNY	
TERRASSON, P	41	M	LABR	FRZZZZNY	
SPENCK, H	27	M	SMH	GRZZZZNY	
MEYER, A	23	F	SVNT	GRZZZZNY	
BRITZ, M	22	M	LABR	FRZZZZNY	
M	21	F	W	FRZZZZNY	
GUILPAIN, L	44	M	UNKNOWN	FRZZZZCH	
PFLEGER, POTTCHEN	14	F	SVNT	GRZZZZNY	
HESS, M	15	F	SVNT	GRZZZZNY	
DONGES, E	29	F	W	GRZZZZNY	
J	6	F	CHILD	GRZZZZNY	
W	4	F	CHILD	GRZZZZNY	
PFARRINS, H	16	M	MCHT	GRZZZZNY	
MAES, J	21	M	BKBNDR	GRZZZZNY	
MULLER, C	25	M	BKR	GRZZZZNY	
RUSSIE, E	22	F	SVNT	GRZZZZNY	
KEIL, L	15	M	MECH	GRZZZZNY	
FELLEISEN, A	29	M	LABR	GRZZZZNY	
SCHAFER, T	25	F	SVNT	GRZZZZNY	
REICHERT, L	21	F	SVNT	GRZZZZNY	
HERTLEIN, R	19	F	SVNT	GRZZZZNY	

PASSENGER	AGE	SEX	OCCUPATION	PRVL	DES
J	16	M	LABR	GRZZZZNY	
SCHILLS, M	31	M	LABR	GRZZZZNY	
PFEIFFER, M	30	M	LABR	GRZZZZNY	
SCHLEIMER, G	24	M	LABR	GRZZZZNY	
J	7	M	CHILD	GRZZZZNY	
EPPICH, F	24	M	LABR	GRZZZZNY	
RIES, C	23	F	SVNT	GRZZZZNY	
HERM, J	18	M	LABR	GRZZZZNY	
LOHMAN, M	43	F	SVNT	GRZZZZSTL	
C	19	M	TRVLR	GRZZZZSTL	
J	17	M	TRVLR	GRZZZZSTL	
RUEHLER, G	17	M	LABR	GRZZZZSTL	
----TEL, U	52	M	LABR	GRZZZZUNK	
ELIZA	40	F	W	GRZZZZUNK	
BRUMMELN, CATH	24	M	LABR	GRZZZZUNK	
SCHULLHORN, AD	32	M	LABR	GRZZZZUNK	
KUHN, H	16	M	BCHR	GRZZZZCOU	
JASSINS, C	27	M	LABR	GRZZZZNY	
REICHER, J	25	M	LABR	GRZZZZPIT	
G	24	F	W	GRZZZZPIT	
J	00	F	INF	GRZZZZPIT	
HA-ER, J	30	M	LABR	GRZZZZUNK	
BUCHE, TH	25	F	UNKNOWN	GRZZZZSTL	
HUMING, C	36	F	SVNT	GRZZZZNY	
E	22	F	SVNT	GRZZZZNY	
BROST, G	39	M	LABR	GRZZZZNY	
ZICO-HAGEN, A	23	M	APTC	GRZZZZNY	
STOCK, C	27	M	LABR	GRZZZZNY	
HOBLER, G	21	M	NN	GRZZZZNY	
KELLER, A	29	F	SVNT	GRZZZZNY	
BESCHMANN, H	19	F	SVNT	GRZZZZKAS	
SUGG, M	22	F	SVNT	GRZZZZLOU	
SOMMERBERG, A	43	M	LABR	GRZZZZNY	
GRETENMEYER, C	24	M	TLR	GRZZZZNY	
MOHLEMERAFT, J	27	M	LABR	GRZZZZNY	
BRUCKER, M	28	F	SVNT	GRZZZZNY	
SCOMODAN, H	32	M	SHMK	GRZZZZNY	
VOLKER, H	32	M	SHMK	GRZZZZPAT	
MUELLER, C	31	M	LABR	GRZZZZNY	
SCHADEN, J	38	M	LABR	GRZZZZCLE	
MAYER, M	23	F	SVNT	GRZZZZNY	
MAUF, C	19	F	UNKNOWN	GRZZZZNY	
ROLL, G	25	M	BCHR	GRZZZZPEO	
LINGENMAYER, G	36	M	TRVLR	GRZZZZNY	
C	26	F	W	GRZZZZNY	
C	11	M	BY	GRZZZZNY	
PFENGER, G	22	M	LABR	GRZZZZNY	
ECKERT, A	16	M	LABR	GRZZZZNY	
-URDTER, MARG	28	F	SVNT	GRZZZZNY	
BRENNER, M	16	F	SVNT	GRZZZZNY	
STREBEL, J	48	M	LABR	GRZZZZNY	
LENK, J	32	M	LABR	GRZZZZUNK	
KRAUTLEIN, J	28	M	FARMER	GRZZZZNY	
WISCHMULLER, J	17	M	LABR	GRZZZZNY	
BAUER, J	19	M	BCHR	GRZZZZNY	
KRELZ, W	24	F	SVNT	GRZZZZNY	
STE--GLEIN, J	16	M	BKR	GRZZZZNY	
STENGEL, F	26	F	M	GRZZZZNY	
H	00	F	INF	GRZZZZNY	
KRUMM--IECK, P	26	F	FARMER	GRZZZZNY	
KRUPP, B	26	F	SVNT	GRZZZZNY	
DOER, G	16	M	BCHR	GRZZZZNY	
LIEBEN, G	28	M	GZR	GRZZZZNY	
BIRCHEN, LUTZEN	36	M	LABR	GRAFWJNY	
WIRGES, J	34	M	LABR	GRAFWJNY	
HEIMANN, C	21	F	W	GRAFWJCH	
E	20	F	BCHR	GRAFWJCH	
KE--ST, A	45	F	SVNT	GRAFWJNY	
OTTO	22	M	LABR	GRAFWJNY	
E	8	M	CHILD	GRAFWJNY	
RENNY, J	27	M	FARMER	GRAFWJUSA	
LA-IO, H	17	M	BKBNDR	GRAFWJKAS	
CARLIER, A	27	F	M	GRAFWJUNK	
A	5	F	CHILD	GRAFWJUNK	
M	00	F	INF	GRAFWJUNK	

PASSENGER	AGE	SEX	OCCUPATION	PRVVL	DES
MASSMER, J	25	M	LABR		GRAFWJNY
OTTERBACH, F	53	M	LABR		GRAFWJNY
G	47	F	W		GRAFWJNY
G	24	M	LABR		GRAFWJNY
M	15	F	SVNT		GRAFWJNY
H	13	M	LABR		GRAFWJNY
F	8	M	CHILD		GRAFWJNY
M	5	F	CHILD		GRAFWJNY
GRAF, U	27	F	M		GRAFWJNY
D	50	M	LABR		GRAFWJNY
C	5	M	CHILD		GRAFWJNY
O	3	M	CHILD		GRAFWJNY
J	00	F	INF		GRAFWJNY
PREVVT, B	64	M	TRVLR		GRAFWJUNK
A	60	F	W		GRAFWJUNK
ZUBRA, LEPREUN	11	F	SVNT		GRAFWJUNK
CHRZ, J	17	F	SVNT		GRAFWJNY
LORNZ, A	22	F	SVNT		GRAFWJNY
SVEJKOWSKY, J	19	F	SVNT		GRAFWJNY
-IEDRIGEER, F	27	M	LABR		GRAFWJNY
SK-AS, B	38	M	LABR		GRAFWJNY
GRODZINSKI, F	20	M	LABR		GRAFWJBUF
KRUSZYSNKI, F	21	M	LABR		GRAFWJCH
A	16	M	TRVLR		GRAFWJCH
KRUSIEWSKI, J	37	M	LABR		GRAFWJUNK
HERMANN, J	21	M	LABR		GRAFWJNY
STINE, JOS	25	M	LABR		GRAFWJNY
KOLM--, A	27	M	LABR		GRAFWJNY
WITTIG, J	22	M	LABR		GRAFWJNY
DRANGOSCH, L	17	F	SVNT		GRAFWJNY
KISCHLE, M	50	F	SVNT		GRAFWJNY
J	14	F	SVNT		GRAFWJNY
M	18	F	SVNT		GRAFWJNY
BRA-----, F	27	M	BKR		GRAFWJNY
SIEBERT, F	19	M	BCHR		GRAFWJNY
PUSCH, H	18	M	MLR		GRAFWJUNK
HOELZENS, M	27	M	MCHT		GRAFWJNY
HERTZ, MAX	27	M	GCR		GRAFWJNY
KLEIN, PAUL	21	F	NN		GRAFWJHBK
GLUECK, MARY	24	F	NN		GRAFWJBRO
VERLAGE, VALENTIN	38	M	GCR		GRAFWJTOR
LANG, OTTO	21	M	FARMER		GRAFWJUNK
KORDES, ANNA	23	F	LDY		GRAFWJNY
KROC---, JULIUS	24	M	GCR		GRAFWJNY
W------, EMILIE	00	F	NN		GRAFWJNY
JOSEPHINE	3	F	CHILD		GRAFWJNY
U	.08	F	INFANT		GRAFWJNY
KOERNER, MISS	22	F	LDY		GRAFWJDET

SHIP: SAALE

FROM: BREMEN AND SOUTHAMPTON
TO: NEW YORK
ARRIVED: 18 MAY 1888

PASSENGER	AGE	SEX	OCCUPATION	PRVVL	DES
VONSCHUCKMANN, BRUNO	30	M	OFF		GRZZZZGR
RU----, EDW.	45	M	MCHT		GRZZZZGR
LOUIS	24	M	MCHT		GRZZZZGR
ROSENTHAL, LOUIS	38	M	MCHT		GRZZZZGR
ZIEGELE, ALB.	55	M	TT		GRZZZZGR
DERNBERG, FRIEDR.	42	M	TT		GRZZZZGR
CLASON, HANS	20	M	CL		GRZZZZGR
COX, GEORG	20	M	MCHT		GRZZZZGR
MINNA	40	F	W		GRZZZZGR
ANNIE	6	F	CHILD		GRZZZZGR
DOROTI	5	F	CHILD		GRZZZZGR
RUEPF, ANNA	45	F	NN		GRZZZZGR
HOLDE-, ANNA	24	F	NN		GRZZZZGR
KAMPMANN, THEOD.	30	M	FARMER		GRZZZZGR
SIEGLER, ANNA	21	F	NN		GRZZZZGR

PASSENGER	AGE	SEX	OCCUPATION	PRVVL	DES
KROEN-IN, AUGUSTE	28	F	NN		GRZZZZGR
NOLTE, ELISE	58	F	NN		GRZZZZGR
WIEBE, PETER	00	M	GCR		GRZZZZGR
BUDKE, MARIE	50	F	NN		GRZZZZGR
FRIEDLAENDER, CLARA	30	F	NN		GRZZZZGR
PAUL	6	M	CHILD		GRZZZZGR
RUCKWEID, CHRISTE.	26	F	NN		GRZZZZGR
LANDECKER, SIMON	16	M	CL		GRZZZZGR
MOHRMANN, CARL	32	M	CLGYMN		GRZZZZGR
RIPPE, HERM.	21	M	MSNY		GRZZZZGR
RIBOTE, FRITZ	35	M	MCHT		GRZZZZGR
SOPHIE	00	F	W		GRZZZZGR
KAETCHEN	00	F	CH		GRZZZZGR
OTTILIE	00	F	CH		GRZZZZGR
STOLL, GUST	15	M	CL		GRZZZZGR
BAETJER, GERD.	16	M	CL		GRZZZZGR
EUCHLER, WILH.	24	M	GZR		GRZZZZGR
HOLM, EBERHARD	28	M	PNTR		GRZZZZGR
HAENISCH, MINNA	21	F	NN		GRZZZZGR
FROEHLICH, FANNY	14	F	NN		GRZZZZGR
ADLER, MINNA	19	F	NN		GRZZZZGR
KOHN, JEANETTE	48	F	NN		GRZZZZGR
KUPFER, BERNHD.	24	M	MCHT		GRZZZZGR
WEISTKOPF, BERNHD.	24	M	MCHT		GRZZZZGR
FLORENA	22	F	W		GRZZZZGR
LOUIS	.06	M	INFANT		GRZZZZGR
DOSE, GUSTAV	28	M	GCR		GRZZZZGR
SALOMON, JULIE	23	F	NN		GRZZZZGR
LYKKE, MAGDA.	30	F	W		GRZZZZGR
EMIL	6	M	CHILD		GRZZZZGR
ELLA	3	F	CHILD		GRZZZZGR
JOAC----, ANNA	16	F	NN		GRZZZZGR
JARETZ----, WILH.	24	M	BKBNDR		GRZZZZGR
BLEY, LEOPOLD	18	M	BKBNDR		GRZZZZGR
HELDMAIER, FRIEDKE.	68	F	NN		GRZZZZGR
REITZENSTEIN, PAUL	41	M	CPT		GRZZZZGR
STERKE, RUD.	27	M	WRT		GRZZZZGR
KLEIN, JULIUS	27	M	WRT		GRZZZZGR
THELE--, LUDW.	36	M	TRVLR		GRZZZZGR
ALGE, ROBERT	18	M	CL		GRZZZZGR
HENLE, ALB.	16	M	BKR		GRZZZZGR
ROOS, ADOLF	31	M	MD		GRZZZZGR
BARTENSTEIN, CARL	12	M	NN		GRZZZZGR
DIPPEL, CHRIST.	24	M	DPR		GRZZZZGR
PETERSEN, ANNA	25	F	NN		GRZZZZGR
CATRINE	20	F	NN		GRZZZZGR
SCHMIDT, IVER	27	M	MCHT		GRZZZZGR
KOHN, JOSEF	25	M	MCHT		GRZZZZGR
PIESEN, ALFRED	27	M	MCHT		GRZZZZGR
CERMAK, JAN	29	M	BCHR		GRZZZZGR
ULLMANN, GUST.	19	M	SMH		GRZZZZGR
DOERFLER, CATHE.	31	F	NN		GRZZZZGR
CZAPS--, BENO	20	M	MSNY		GRZZZZGR
CASTENDY-K, RICH.	29	M	POST		GRZZZZGR
MILLER, SOPHIE	20	F	NN		GRZZZZGR
KRONCKE, ANNA	20	F	NN		GRZZZZUSA
SCH---DT, HEINR.	15	M	NN		GRZZZZUSA
STUEHRMANN, MART.	16	M	NN		GRZZZZUSA
CHUDPICKI, MIKOLAJ	28	M	LABR		GRZZZZUSA
FINKE, DEDERICH	20	M	BCHR		GRZZZZUSA
STIERING, AUG.	14	M	NN		GRZZZZUSA
GOETZ, MARGA.	37	F	NN		GRZZZZUSA
JUNGE, MARIE	54	F	NN		GRZZZZUSA
MEYER, FRIEDR.	67	M	FARMER		GRZZZZUSA
REINERT, ANNA	16	F	NN		GRZZZZUSA
FORM--, FRANZ	36	M	JNR		GRZZZZUSA
MARKS, JOH.	35	M	TLR		GRZZZZUSA
SOKOLOWSKI, ANTON	30	M	TLR		GRZZZZUSA
SANGMEISTER, HERM.	28	M	SMH		GRZZZZUSA
DE-BOER, FOLKERT	40	M	SHMK		GRZZZZUSA
BRUECKMEIER, XAVER	33	M	LABR		GRZZZZUSA
KARL	12	M	CH		GRZZZZUSA
KOEFERL, MARGA.	20	F	NN		GRZZZZUSA
DIETRICH, GOTTL.	34	M	BBR		GRZZZZUSA
RAUSCH, RICH.	15	M	JNR		GRZZZZUSA

PASSENGER	AGE	SEX	OCCUPATION	PRVL	DES
HENKEL, OTTO	29	M	BKR	GRZZZZ	USA
KEIL, JOH.	25	M	TLR	GRZZZZ	USA
SCHMIDT, MARGA.	18	F	NN	GRZZZZ	USA
KOECHER, CATHA.	17	F	NN	GRZZZZ	USA
WOEBBECKE, KARL	24	M	JNR	GRZZZZ	USA
WEIDEMAN, HERM.	49	M	FARMER	GRZZZZ	USA
FLORENA	47	F	W	GRZZZZ	USA
FRIEDR.	6	M	CHILD	GRZZZZ	USA
WAWRZYNIAK, ANNA	22	F	NN	GRZZZZ	USA
THOMAS	50	M	FARMER	GRZZZZ	USA
AGNES	3	F	CHILD	GRZZZZ	USA
WAWRZYNIAK, JOSEF	.01	M	INFANT	GRZZZZ	USA
PAWLACK, JAKOB	55	M	LABR	GRZZZZ	USA
ANTA	50	F	W	GRZZZZ	USA
KATARINA	21	F	NN	GRZZZZ	USA
WOIZECH	15	M	NN	GRZZZZ	USA
LUDWIG	7	M	CHILD	GRZZZZ	USA
GLUCKMANN, MORITZ	18	M	PNTR	GRZZZZ	USA
REI--NN, SALOMON	45	M	FARMER	GRZZZZ	USA
WILHE.	44	F	W	GRZZZZ	USA
REINOLD	12	M	CH	GRZZZZ	USA
ANNA	7	F	CHILD	GRZZZZ	USA
FRIEDR.	5	M	CHILD	GRZZZZ	USA
SCHOENFELDT, FRIEDR.	24	M	GZR	GRZZZZ	USA
LABINSKI, VALENTIN	46	M	TCHR	GRZZZZ	USA
JACOBS, EMMA	34	F	NN	GRZZZZ	USA
ZEP--R, GUSTAV	25	M	JNR	GRZZZZ	USA
CZIRSKEFSKA, MARGA.	21	F	NN	GRZZZZ	USA
STERN, MATHE.	17	F	NN	GRZZZZ	USA
ZIENTECH, ROSALIE	20	F	NN	GRZZZZ	USA
ELISAB.	18	F	NN	GRZZZZ	USA
MEIER, PAUL	14	M	SMH	GRZZZZ	USA
ANTKOWIAK, VALENTY	28	M	CPTR	GRZZZZ	USA
MGDA.	20	F	NN	GRZZZZ	USA
SKRZEPOZAK, FRANZ	40	M	BCHR	GRZZZZ	USA
SCHIMANOWSKI, ANDR.	29	M	BCHR	GRZZZZ	USA
WITTKOWSKI, MATHE.	22	F	NN	GRZZZZ	USA
SAGERT, MICH.	71	M	SMH	GRZZZZ	USA
SCHABER, JUL.	22	M	TLR	GRZZZZ	USA
LACKOWSKI, ANT.	34	M	JNR	GRZZZZ	USA
SCHUNITZLER, CHRIST.	15	M	BKR	GRZZZZ	USA
BAUMGAERTNER, JOH.	15	M	BKR	GRZZZZ	USA
DIETEL, KATHA.	26	F	NN	GRZZZZ	USA
WEBER, MARIA	25	F	W	GRZZZZ	USA
MART.	.11	M	INFANT	GRZZZZ	USA
SATZ, CHRIST.	25	M	SHMK	GRZZZZ	USA
SOBEZAK, ANDRYZ	60	M	FARMER	GRZZZZ	USA
MARIANNE	64	F	W	GRZZZZ	USA
FRANZISKA	21	F	NN	GRZZZZ	USA
BARWIKOWSKI, BARTHOL.	46	M	JNR	GRZZZZ	USA
KRAUSE, JOHA.	24	F	NN	GRZZZZ	USA
WITOMSKI, MART.	28	M	MLR	GRZZZZ	USA
EBERS, WILH.	38	M	BCHR	GRZZZZ	USA
GLEIZMANN, HEINR.	15	M	BCHR	GRZZZZ	USA
SCHMIDT, CHRIST.	26	M	SMH	GRZZZZ	USA
TUMMER, JOH.	67	M	FARMER	GRZZZZ	USA
ANNA	56	F	W	GRZZZZ	USA
ADELHEIDE	24	F	NN	GRZZZZ	USA
JOHA.	19	F	NN	GRZZZZ	USA
JOHS.	7	M	CHILD	GRZZZZ	USA
HOLTJES, DORIS	15	F	NN	GRZZZZ	USA
KRONSHAGE, HENRY	15	M	TLR	GRZZZZ	USA
GEISELER, U	14	M	NN	GRZZZZ	USA
HAASE, HEINR.	16	M	TLR	GRZZZZ	USA
NUEBEL, HEINR.	17	M	BKR	GRZZZZ	USA
SCHROEDER, HEINR.	14	M	NN	GRZZZZ	USA
HEISSENBUETTEL, BETTY	18	F	NN	GRZZZZ	USA
PRIGGE, JOH.	16	M	BKR	GRZZZZ	USA
RUNNE, DIEDR.	14	M	BKR	GRZZZZ	USA
FEIL, ANNA	28	F	BKR	GRZZZZ	USA
SIEM, RICH.	27	M	JNR	GRZZZZ	USA
FINKE, CATHA.	20	F	NN	GRZZZZ	USA
CORDES, HEINR.	16	M	JNR	GRZZZZ	USA
SCHOENEBAUM, CHRIST.	14	M	NN	GRZZZZ	USA
FENNSING, JOH.	18	M	JNR	GRZZZZ	USA
BOENING, HERM.	24	M	TLR	GRZZZZ	USA
BEHRMANN, MARIE	17	F	NN	GRZZZZ	USA
BUETTELMANN, JOH.	17	M	TLR	GRZZZZ	USA
EHLER, MINNA	16	F	NN	GRZZZZ	USA
WITTEN, HERM.	20	M	SMH	GRZZZZ	USA
SEEBECK, DIEDR.	25	M	SMH	GRZZZZ	USA
HUELSBACH, FRIEDR.	23	M	SMH	GRZZZZ	USA
HINCK, DIEDR.	21	M	CPTR	GRZZZZ	USA
STUEWEN, ANNA	21	F	NN	GRZZZZ	USA
KRIETE, FRIEDR.	26	M	BKLYR	GRZZZZ	USA
KRACKE, THEOB.	24	M	BKLYR	GRZZZZ	USA
REISERT, DOROTHEA	24	F	NN	GRZZZZ	USA
GRIEBEN, GUST.	24	M	MLR	GRZZZZ	USA
SCHROEDER, MARIE	14	F	NN	GRZZZZ	USA
BUSCHMANN, HINR.	16	M	PNTR	GRZZZZ	USA
SCHMIDT, SUSANNA	16	F	NN	GRZZZZ	USA
KNOPF, RICH.	38	M	FARMER	GRZZZZ	USA
CARL	16	M	FARMER	GRZZZZ	USA
FRIEDA	15	F	NN	GRZZZZ	USA
SEIDEL, MINNA	16	F	NN	GRZZZZ	USA
SCHULZE, MINNA	28	F	W	GRZZZZ	USA
MARIA	10	F	CH	GRZZZZ	USA
MINNA	7	F	CHILD	GRZZZZ	USA
FRIEDR.	4	M	CHILD	GRZZZZ	USA
SOPHIE	2	F	CHILD	GRZZZZ	USA
CZYKOWSKI, IGNATZ	30	M	TCHR	GRZZZZ	USA
KRZYWODZINSKI, JOS.	26	M	CK	GRZZZZ	USA
SEMMLER, IDA	19	F	NN	GRZZZZ	USA
ZEMPEL, HEINR.	21	M	BCHR	GRZZZZ	USA
BECKMANN, HEINR.	26	M	BCHR	GRZZZZ	USA
NOWAKOWSKI, PETER	26	M	CPTR	GRZZZZ	USA
VICTORIA	27	F	W	GRZZZZ	USA
FRANZ	.07	M	INFANT	GRZZZZ	USA
WOESTE, JOS.	28	M	BKR	GRZZZZ	USA
BISCHOFF, ROSA	21	F	NN	GRZZZZ	USA
MEYER, ANNA	15	F	NN	GRZZZZ	USA
ROEMKE, LINA	32	F	W	GRZZZZ	USA
ADOLF	.10	M	INFANT	GRZZZZ	USA
BAUMANN, FRIEDR.	27	M	SMH	GRZZZZ	USA
BECKER, ADAM	33	M	FARMER	GRZZZZ	USA
EVA	41	F	W	GRZZZZ	USA
JACOB	14	M	NN	GRZZZZ	USA
U	7	M	CHILD	GRZZZZ	USA
ELISE	6	F	CHILD	GRZZZZ	USA
ADAM	4	M	CHILD	GRZZZZ	USA
ANNA	.11	F	INFANT	GRZZZZ	USA
REUSCH, ANT.	31	M	GZR	GRZZZZ	USA
PFEIFFER, HEINR.	31	M	BKLYR	GRZZZZ	USA
ELISAB.	32	F	W	GRZZZZ	USA
MARIA	4	F	CHILD	GRZZZZ	USA
ADAM	.09	M	INFANT	GRZZZZ	USA
LAGERIN, JUL.	46	M	JNR	GRZZZZ	USA
EVA	46	F	W	GRZZZZ	USA
CATHA.	6	F	CHILD	GRZZZZ	USA
OLT, LEONHARD	18	M	LABR	GRZZZZ	USA
GAUL, JACOB	19	M	WRT	GRZZZZ	USA
SCHAEFER, JACOB	19	M	WRT	GRZZZZ	USA
FINKE, HEINR.	14	M	NN	GRZZZZ	USA
MEYER, ANT.	23	M	FARMER	GRZZZZ	USA
HILLMANN, JOH.	31	M	GCR	GRZZZZ	USA
PLUMP, BEHREND	16	M	GZR	GRZZZZ	USA
PRUEFERT, AUGSTE.	57	F	NN	GRZZZZ	USA
JULIA	30	F	NN	GRZZZZ	USA
MARIE	24	F	NN	GRZZZZ	USA
LUCIE	18	F	NN	GRZZZZ	USA
WEDEMEYER, RICH.	23	M	MSNY	GRZZZZ	USA
WEBER, HERM.	16	M	TLR	GRZZZZ	USA
SUNDERMANN, ERNST	17	M	TLR	GRZZZZ	USA
MAHLER, CARL	14	M	NN	GRZZZZ	USA
STRUNCK, MARIE	15	F	NN	GRZZZZ	USA
ROESCH, HINR.	22	M	JNR	GRZZZZ	USA
JOH.	20	M	SMH	GRZZZZ	USA
MEYER, ANNA	24	F	NN	GRZZZZ	USA
BRINKMANN, CORD.	23	M	MLR	GRZZZZ	USA
PAULSEN, MATHS.	44	M	MLR	GRZZZZ	USA

PASSENGER	AGE	SEX	OCCUPATION	PRVL	DES
CHRISTIANSEN, NIC.	28	M	BCHR	GRZZZZ	USA
ANT.	26	M	PNTR	GRZZZZ	USA
NIELSEN, NIELS	45	M	SHMK	GRZZZZ	USA
CLEMENS	7	M	CHILD	GRZZZZ	USA
BLOCK, JACOB	18	M	SHMK	GRZZZZ	USA
HARTWIGSEN, HANS	32	M	SHMK	GRZZZZ	USA
CHRISTE.	41	F	W	GRZZZZ	USA
HEINSEN, PETER	19	M	SLR	GRZZZZ	USA
HARTWIGSEN, CHRISTE.	6	F	CHILD	GRZZZZ	USA
DIEDR.	2	M	CHILD	GRZZZZ	USA
ANDR.	.03	M	INFANT	GRZZZZ	USA
CHRISTENSEN, CATHA.	27	F	NN	GRZZZZ	USA
JACOBSEN, JACOBE.	18	F	NN	GRZZZZ	USA
DIERKS, CHRIST.	25	M	BKR	GRZZZZ	USA
HANSEN, HANS-OLSEN	16	M	BKR	GRZZZZ	USA
HANS-OLSEN	24	F	NN	GRZZZZ	USA
NIELSEN, ANNA	22	F	NN	GRZZZZ	USA
NISSEN, ANNA	51	F	NN	GRZZZZ	USA
CHRISTENSEN, JUERGEN	18	M	LABR	GRZZZZ	USA
CARL, JOERG	15	M	LABR	GRZZZZ	USA
JENSEN, MART.	16	M	LABR	GRZZZZ	USA
NISSEN, META	27	F	W	GRZZZZ	USA
ANNA	4	F	CHILD	GRZZZZ	USA
ELISE	.08	F	INFANT	GRZZZZ	USA
NIELSEN, MATH.	33	M	LABR	GRZZZZ	USA
ANNA	40	F	W	GRZZZZ	USA
U	.11	M	INFANT	GRZZZZ	USA
KLEE, ELISE	19	F	NN	GRZZZZ	USA
HAEUSER, SOPHIE	23	F	NN	GRZZZZ	USA
JENSEN, SOPHIE	20	F	NN	GRZZZZ	USA
PETERSEN, ESTER	17	M	JNR	GRZZZZ	USA
JENSEN, JOH.	16	M	NN	GRZZZZ	USA
NISSEN, CHRIST.	49	M	FARMER	GRZZZZ	USA
WOLLESEN, JOHA.	34	F	NN	GRZZZZ	USA
CHRISTENSEN, ANNA	17	F	NN	GRZZZZ	USA
MEYER, GEO	14	M	NN	GRZZZZ	USA
BUDELMANN, DIRK.	16	M	NN	GRZZZZ	USA
MAHKUEN, GEORG	16	M	NN	GRZZZZ	USA
STROBEL, MAGDA	24	M	NN	GRZZZZ	USA
HEEREN, JOACHIM	54	M	FARMER	GRZZZZ	USA
MARIE	27	F	NN	GRZZZZ	USA
JOHE.	23	F	NN	GRZZZZ	USA
GESINE	18	F	NN	GRZZZZ	USA
HUGO	5	M	CHILD	GRZZZZ	USA
TASCHLEIN, FRIEDR.	17	M	LABR	GRZZZZ	USA
FEURER, MARIE	24	F	NN	GRZZZZ	USA
SCHMIDT, ALB.	29	M	CPTR	GRZZZZ	USA
FRIEDRICH, GUST.	25	M	SMH	GRZZZZ	USA
WEBER, PHIL.	33	M	FARMER	GRZZZZ	USA
HEYNEMANN, ANNA	21	F	NN	GRZZZZ	USA
PANTEL, ANNA	25	F	NN	GRZZZZ	USA
THIELBAHR, REBECKA	17	F	NN	GRZZZZ	USA
MURTEN, ANNA	17	F	NN	GRZZZZ	USA
WESSEL, ANNA	17	F	NN	GRZZZZ	USA
BROHAMMER, NATH.	54	M	BKR	GRZZZZ	USA
LEMKE, ADOLF	25	M	JNR	GRZZZZ	USA
WILH.	18	M	JNR	GRZZZZ	USA
BOECK, GOTTLOB	24	M	BKLYR	GRZZZZ	USA
CARL	26	M	BCHR	GRZZZZ	USA
WILBE, ARTHUR	15	M	NN	GRZZZZ	USA
ESAR, JOH.	28	M	PNTR	GRZZZZ	USA
HEINR.	20	M	PNTR	GRZZZZ	USA
GEIB, JOHS.	45	M	FARMER	GRZZZZ	USA
ELISAB.	42	F	W	GRZZZZ	USA
CATHA.	16	F	NN	GRZZZZ	USA
CATHA.	7	M	CHILD	GRZZZZ	USA
ELISAB.	6	F	CHILD	GRZZZZ	USA
MUELLER, MAGDA	18	F	NN	GRZZZZ	USA
GERLACH, AUG.	40	M	FARMER	GRZZZZ	USA
LINA	15	F	NN	GRZZZZ	USA
SCHWEIKERT, WILH.	27	M	CK	GRZZZZ	USA
HAAS, BERNH.	16	M	NN	GRZZZZ	USA
SCHMIDT, CHRIST.	30	M	BCHR	GRZZZZ	USA
HUBER, KAROLE.	23	F	NN	GRZZZZ	USA
ARNOLD, LINA	20	F	NN	GRZZZZ	USA
HAUG, U	17	F	NN	GRZZZZ	USA
SIMMEL, FRIEDR.	23	M	SMH	GRZZZZ	USA
KAROLA.	21	F	NN	GRZZZZ	USA
KRAUSS, KARL	36	M	FARMER	GRZZZZ	USA
MARIE	37	F	W	GRZZZZ	USA
KARL	7	M	CHILD	GRZZZZ	USA
BORN, KAROLE.	19	F	NN	GRZZZZ	USA
LEBER, LOUISE	21	F	NN	GRZZZZ	USA
DUNG, LOUISE	38	F	W	GRZZZZ	USA
WILH.	7	M	CHILD	GRZZZZ	USA
FICK, WILH.	16	M	BKR	GRZZZZ	USA
NUERNBERG, HEINR.	16	M	BKR	GRZZZZ	USA
WERNER, HERM.	16	M	BKR	GRZZZZ	USA
STRUCZ, MATHDE.	19	F	NN	GRZZZZ	USA
WALTER, FRIEDR.	14	M	NN	GRZZZZ	USA
MUCKLENBERG, CARL	14	M	NN	GRZZZZ	USA
BLOCK, JOH.	16	M	NN	GRZZZZ	USA
HAAG, CONRAD	22	M	FARMER	GRZZZZ	USA
GEORG	25	M	FARMER	GRZZZZ	USA
MARIE	20	F	NN	GRZZZZ	USA
NAEDELE, URSULA	50	F	NN	GRZZZZ	USA
SCHMIDT, URSULA	19	F	NN	GRZZZZ	USA
REHMS, CATHA.	22	F	NN	GRZZZZ	USA
CLAUS, WILH.	60	M	LABR	GRZZZZ	USA
KUECKS, JOH.	26	M	PNTR	GRZZZZ	USA
BOESCHE, OTTO	23	M	SMH	GRZZZZ	USA
DANZBERG, HEINR.	10	M	CH	GRZZZZ	USA
GOPPELT, JOH.	48	M	FARMER	GRZZZZ	USA
MARGA.	44	F	W	GRZZZZ	USA
CARL	7	M	CHILD	GRZZZZ	USA
PAULE.	6	F	CHILD	GRZZZZ	USA
WILH.	4	M	CHILD	GRZZZZ	USA
EMILIE	3	F	CHILD	GRZZZZ	USA
PUETTERICH, JOH.	57	M	FARMER	GRZZZZ	USA
BARBA.	53	F	W	GRZZZZ	USA
BURKHARDT, MARIE	43	F	NN	GRZZZZ	USA
BUEHLER, JACOB	32	M	FARMER	GRZZZZ	USA
BARBA.	32	F	W	GRZZZZ	USA
KONRAD	7	M	CHILD	GRZZZZ	USA
WEISS, ANDR.	24	M	JNR	GRZZZZ	USA
SCHUMACHER, MARGA.	15	F	NN	GRZZZZ	USA
DANKERMANN, CATHA.	16	F	NN	GRZZZZ	USA
SCHUMACHER, JACOB	68	M	BCHR	GRZZZZ	USA
CATHA.	70	F	W	GRZZZZ	USA
WOLFF, HEINR.	17	M	BCHR	GRZZZZ	USA
HIPPELIN, CATHE.	28	F	NN	GRZZZZ	USA
SCHANKENBERG, CHARLTE.	17	F	NN	GRZZZZ	USA
TIEDEMANN, CATHA.	44	F	NN	GRZZZZ	USA
CATHA.	14	F	NN	GRZZZZ	USA
HEIMBOVKEL, JOH.	21	M	JNR	GRZZZZ	USA
FICK, WILH.	39	M	BCHR	GRZZZZ	USA
WILHE.	29	F	W	GRZZZZ	USA
WILH.	.01	M	INFANT	GRZZZZ	USA
HINSCH, WILH.	60	M	FARMER	GRZZZZ	USA
FROEHLING, PETER	23	M	CPTR	GRZZZZ	USA
HILD, JOSEPHA	21	F	NN	GRZZZZ	USA
BRAUN, FRANZ	46	M	FARMER	GRZZZZ	USA
DOROTHEA	40	F	W	GRZZZZ	USA
CASPER	15	M	NN	GRZZZZ	USA
FRIEDR.	6	M	CHILD	GRZZZZ	USA
JOSEPH	4	M	CHILD	GRZZZZ	USA
HAMMEL, JOHS.	50	M	FARMER	GRZZZZ	USA
ANNA	48	F	W	GRZZZZ	USA
JOHS.	19	M	FARMER	GRZZZZ	USA
CATHA.	16	F	NN	GRZZZZ	USA
MARGA.	14	F	NN	GRZZZZ	USA
HELENE	6	F	CHILD	GRZZZZ	USA
JOH.	.09	M	INFANT	GRZZZZ	USA
HEYMANN, PETER	29	M	PNTR	GRZZZZ	USA
CATHA.	27	F	W	GRZZZZ	USA
WILH.	4	M	CHILD	GRZZZZ	USA
KIND, CATHA.	18	F	NN	GRZZZZ	USA
STRUP, ANNA	18	F	NN	GRZZZZ	USA
DROEGE, CLAUS	15	M	JNR	GRZZZZ	USA
SCHRIEFER, ADELHE.	15	F	NN	GRZZZZ	USA

PASSENGER	AGE	SEX	OCCUPATION	PRVL	DES
WILKENS, PETER	16	M	JNR		GRZZZZUSA
DOESCHER, HEINR.	16	M	JNR		GRZZZZUSA
JOH.	16	M	JNR		GRZZZZUSA
DETJEN, JOH.	16	M	JNR		GRZZZZUSA
ROSITZKI, HERM.	15	M	JNR		GRZZZZUSA
SCHMIDT, HEINR.	17	M	TLR		GRZZZZUSA
BETHY	19	F	NN		GRZZZZUSA
LUNCHEN, ANNA	23	F	NN		GRZZZZUSA
SCHAEFER, CHRISTE.	22	F	NN		GRZZZZUSA
TIENKEN, HEINR.	16	M	TLR		GRZZZZUSA
GRIESE, HEINR.	24	M	SMH		GRZZZZUSA
DANNENBOOM, LOUISE	24	F	NN		GRZZZZUSA
WANDT, HEINR.	27	M	JNR		GRZZZZUSA
REIDEL, CARL	32	M	BKR		GRZZZZUSA
FRIEDE.	27	F	W		GRZZZZUSA
FRIEDR.	5	M	CHILD		GRZZZZUSA
KOCH, WILH.	15	M	NN		GRZZZZUSA
ENGELKING, DIEDR.	15	M	NN		GRZZZZUSA
SCHEFFEL, EMILIE	26	F	NN		GRZZZZUSA
BROSZIO, FRIEDR.	28	M	TCHR		GRZZZZUSA
KNAPP, EMILIE	29	F	W		GRZZZZUSA
ALMA	3	F	CHILD		GRZZZZUSA
WILLI	.11	M	INFANT		GRZZZZUSA
WAEGELEIN, LOUIS	17	M	LABR		GRZZZZUSA
DAUG, CATHA.	46	F	W		GRZZZZUSA
JOH.	17	M	LABR		GRZZZZUSA
--ST.	11	M	CH		GRZZZZUSA
WAGNER, CHRISTE.	14	F	NN		GRZZZZUSA
REX, FRANZ	38	M	PNTR		GRZZZZUSA
EBERHARDT, EHRICH	40	M	PNTR		GRZZZZUSA
FRIEDE.	41	F	W		GRZZZZUSA
ROB.	16	M	TLR		GRZZZZUSA
ALB.	13	M	NN		GRZZZZUSA
EMILIE	6	F	CHILD		GRZZZZUSA
GUIRE, EMILIE	19	F	NN		GRZZZZUSA
TRAUTMANN, HEINR.	38	M	FARMER		GRZZZZUSA
LOUISE	33	F	W		GRZZZZUSA
GUST.	25	M	FARMER		GRZZZZUSA
IDA	11	F	CH		GRZZZZUSA
BERTHA	6	F	CHILD		GRZZZZUSA
MINNA	2	F	CHILD		GRZZZZUSA
MEYER, HEINR.	63	M	FARMER		GRZZZZUSA
LUCIE	63	F	W		GRZZZZUSA
KORNHAUSER, HEINR.	33	M	SMH		GRZZZZUSA
DORIS	28	F	W		GRZZZZUSA
GEORG	.03	M	INFANT		GRZZZZUSA
SIEMER, HEINR.	54	M	FARMER		GRZZZZUSA
HEINR.	14	M	NN		GRZZZZUSA
WUEHLMANN, ALB.	16	M	LABR		GRZZZZUSA
SCHMIDT, HEINR.	16	M	LABR		GRZZZZUSA
LUEDEKE, HEINR.	15	M	LABR		GRZZZZUSA
BLOCK, GEORG	15	M	LABR		GRZZZZUSA
WINDELS, META	25	F	NN		GRZZZZUSA
MEYER, META	16	F	NN		GRZZZZUSA
HILDEBRANDT, META	20	F	NN		GRZZZZUSA
KOHL, BETA	26	F	NN		GRZZZZUSA
PETSCHOW, ALFRED	21	M	BCHR		GRZZZZUSA
LINDERKAMP, SOPHIE	25	F	NN		GRZZZZUSA
RESSENNA, MATH.	20	M	JNR		GRZZZZUSA
JESPERSEN, JENS	33	M	JNR		GRZZZZUSA
KLEMM, HERM.	39	M	CPTR		GRZZZZUSA
PETRAA	47	F	W		GRZZZZUSA
DAVIDSEN, MARIA	14	F	NN		GRZZZZUSA
OTTO	9	M	CHILD		GRZZZZUSA
HANS	7	M	CHILD		GRZZZZUSA
HAEMMERLE, ANTON	23	M	BCHR		GRZZZZUSA
ALGE, RUD.	45	M	SMH		GRZZZZUSA
FIEDERLEIN, FILOMENE	16	F	NN		GRZZZZUSA
WETZEL, IDA	30	F	W		GRZZZZUSA
LOUISE	10	F	CH		GRZZZZUSA
HENKER, MARIE	18	F	NN		GRZZZZUSA
MUELLER, KATH.	16	F	NN		GRZZZZUSA
STEINHOELBER, --ST	16	M	LABR		GRZZZZUSA
GILLMANN, JOHS.	55	M	LABR		GRZZZZUSA
THEOD.	7	M	CHILD		GRZZZZUSA

PASSENGER	AGE	SEX	OCCUPATION	PRVL	DES
VAIHINGER, LOUISE	23	F	NN		GRZZZZUSA
HAEGELE, ALB.	15	M	LABR		GRZZZZUSA
KOENIG, RICH.	27	M	TLR		GRZZZZUSA
MARIE	24	F	W		GRZZZZUSA
EUGEN	2	M	CHILD		GRZZZZUSA
HUESING, HEINR.	26	M	TLR		GRZZZZUSA
KUKUK, U	23	M	SMH		GRZZZZUSA
FLEISCHMANN, HEINR.	25	M	BKR		GRZZZZUSA
JOH.	14	M	NN		GRZZZZUSA
KERSCH, PAULE.	16	F	NN		GRZZZZUSA
EULER, ANNA	24	F	NN		GRZZZZUSA
BERG, LOUISE	36	F	NN		GRZZZZUSA
KNIE, MARIE	16	F	NN		GRZZZZUSA
NILL, ANNA	17	F	NN		GRZZZZUSA
FREUND, ADOLF	28	M	BCHR		GRZZZZUSA
SEHER, SUSANNE	58	F	W		GRZZZZUSA
CHRIST.	14	M	NN		GRZZZZUSA
ELSAESSER, MARIE	58	F	W		GRZZZZUSA
CAROLE.	21	F	NN		GRZZZZUSA
TAUSEL, BARBA.	22	F	NN		GRZZZZUSA
GUTBROD, ANNA	7	F	CHILD		GRZZZZUSA
SCHMIDT, BARBA.	17	F	NN		GRZZZZUSA
HERBST, JOHA.	16	F	NN		GRZZZZUSA
LUENEBRUECK, GERH.	16	M	LABR		GRZZZZUSA
MIDDING, HERM.	28	M	LABR		GRZZZZUSA
SATTLER, LUDWIG	22	M	SDLR		GRZZZZUSA
ELISE	24	F	NN		GRZZZZUSA
BREUNINGER, WILH.	53	M	FARMER		GRZZZZUSA
SOPHIE	16	F	NN		GRZZZZUSA
HUSS, CATHA.	18	F	NN		GRZZZZUSA
MUELLER, CHRIST.	21	M	SHMK		GRZZZZUSA
BARBA.	17	F	NN		GRZZZZUSA
STEINERT, LOUISE	17	F	NN		GRZZZZUSA
LILLER, ELISAB.	25	F	NN		GRZZZZUSA
FESER, MICH.	19	M	BKR		GRZZZZUSA
WISCH, CHRISTE.	15	F	NN		GRZZZZUSA
CHOISSAN, KATHA.	22	F	NN		GRZZZZUSA
VOGEL, JOH.	19	M	TLR		GRZZZZUSA
ZWIRLEIN, CAECILIE	19	F	NN		GRZZZZUSA
FUCKERER, EVA	22	F	NN		GRZZZZUSA
GLUECKER, MARIA	23	F	NN		GRZZZZUSA
SCHMIDT, CHRIST.	15	M	NN		GRZZZZUSA
WALZ, U	14	M	NN		GRZZZZUSA
HERBERTH, AMALIE	24	F	W		GRZZZZUSA
GLOGER, HEDWIG	25	F	W		GRZZZZUSA
THEISING, JOH.	13	M	W		GRZZZZUSA
MESTER, JOH.	40	M	FARMER		GRZZZZUSA
MARIA	37	F	W		GRZZZZUSA
LINA	6	F	CHILD		GRZZZZUSA
HENRTE.	3	F	CHILD		GRZZZZUSA
PAUL	.11	M	INFANT		GRZZZZUSA
HEROLD, ED.	16	M	JNR		GRZZZZUSA
HARTUNG, EDW.	17	M	TLR		GRZZZZUSA
BUDENZ, JOSEF	15	M	NN		GRZZZZUSA
MUNDEL, CAROLE.	26	F	NN		GRZZZZUSA
U	22	F	NN		GRZZZZUSA
BOEHME, ---NZ	52	F	CPTR		GRZZZZUSA
NORDMANN, MARIA	25	F	W		GRZZZZUSA
FRANZ	.04	M	INFANT		GRZZZZUSA
BECKER, MARIA	22	F	W		GRZZZZUSA
ANNA	20	F	W		GRZZZZUSA
EMMA	15	F	W		GRZZZZUSA
MEISTER, CATHA.	16	F	NN		GRZZZZUSA
KRONE, ELISAB.	16	F	NN		GRZZZZUSA
KASTENS, AUG.	18	M	JNR		GRZZZZUSA
SCHWEDHELM, U	16	M	PNTR		GRZZZZUSA
WIEDERMANN, U	50	F	W		GRZZZZUSA
MARGA.	19	F	NN		GRZZZZUSA
ANGELA	15	F	NN		GRZZZZUSA
CATHA.	7	F	CHILD		GRZZZZUSA
HERMINE	5	F	CHILD		GRZZZZUSA
ANNA	4	F	CHILD		GRZZZZUSA
RIEGER, AUGSTE.	28	F	NN		GRZZZZUSA
DAYEN, MARGA.	28	F	NN		GRZZZZUSA
VOGES, ELISABETH	14	F	NN		GRZZZZUSA

PASSENGER	AGE	SEX	OCCUPATION	PRVL	DES
WOLMERSHAUSEN, MARIA	18	F	NN		GRZZZZUSA
GERLAND, HERM.	17	M	SDLR		GRZZZZUSA
MEINDERS, BERD.	17	M	SDLR		GRZZZZUSA
SCHWELM, JOH.	27	M	SDLR		GRZZZZUSA
BALTZ, ---ES	44	F	W		GRZZZZUSA
LINA	20	F	NN		GRZZZZUSA
AUGSTE.	18	F	NN		GRZZZZUSA
RUDOLPH	16	M	NN		GRZZZZUSA
ARMANT, MARIA	20	F	NN		GRZZZZUSA
BUTTLER, JEAN	20	M	GZR		GRZZZZUSA
BUESSLER, CARL	20	M	BKR		GRZZZZUSA
WESTERWICK, JOHS.	24	M	SMH		GRZZZZUSA
KETZER, MATH.	36	M	TLR		GRZZZZUSA
FEHR, GEORG	24	M	JNR		GRZZZZUSA
FASSOLD, MARGA.	17	F	NN		GRZZZZUSA
LEIDECKER, PETER	30	M	BCHR		GRZZZZUSA
PAULINE	30	F	W		GRZZZZUSA
KADEN, HERM.	23	M	PNTR		GRZZZZUSA
GRAU, ALEX	29	M	SDLR		GRZZZZUSA
JULIUS	23	M	MLR		GRZZZZUSA
MAYFORTH, ADAM	15	M	LABR		GRZZZZUSA
LUEPKE, ULRICH	27	M	CPTR		GRZZZZUSA
KOCH, JOHANN	26	M	SHMK		GRZZZZUSA
FRIEDLAENDER, JETTE	17	F	NN		GRZZZZUSA
SCHOLZ, AUGSTE.	21	F	NN		GRZZZZUSA
REIMANN, WILH.	44	M	FARMER		GRZZZZUSA
CATHA.	43	F	W		GRZZZZUSA
MARGA.	6	F	CHILD		GRZZZZUSA
FICK, MICHAEL	46	M	FARMER		GRZZZZUSA
OTTO	15	M	NN		GRZZZZUSA
REMLER, FRANZ	14	M	NN		GRZZZZUSA
STRECKER, IDA	19	F	NN		GRZZZZUSA
WUSTRACK, WILH.	24	M	PNTR		GRZZZZUSA
MARIE	23	F	W		GRZZZZUSA
KARL	.10	M	INFANT		GRZZZZUSA
FRIEDR.	61	M	FARMER		GRZZZZUSA
MARTHA	19	F	NN		GRZZZZUSA
FLEISCHMANN, BARBA.	21	F	NN		GRZZZZUSA
BOEHLER, JEAN	26	M	CPTR		GRZZZZUSA
LONDON, ELLEN	22	F	NN		GRZZZZGR
HAMBURGER, MORITZ	18	M	MCHT		GRZZZZGR

SHIP: CITY OF CHICAGO

FROM: LIVERPOOL AND QUEENSTOWN
TO: NEW YORK
ARRIVED: 19 MAY 1888

PASSENGER	AGE	SEX	OCCUPATION	PRVL	DES
ALLERSCHT, PETER	27	M	CPTR		GRACBFNY
HOLERATH, W	38	M	LABR		GRACBFNY
SCHUMELDIFFEL, MARTIN	21	M	LABR		GRACBFIL
PETERSEN, ANDERS	18	M	LABR		GRACBFOH
GOTTHARDT, MATH	34	F	W		GRAAECIL
CATH	10	F	CH		GRAAECIL
JACOB	8	M	CHILD		GRAAECIL
GEO	6	M	CHILD		GRAAECIL
MAT	00	F	INF		GRAAECIL
THOMAS, ALBERT	28	M	FARMER		GRZZZZIA
PAULINE	25	F	W		GRZZZZIA
LENA	3	F	CHILD		GRZZZZIA
BER	00	M	INF		GRZZZZIA
IDA	00	F	INF		GRZZZZIA
STYNALD, VICTOR	30	F	W		GRZZZZNY
VALENTY	11	M	CH		GRZZZZNY
MICHAEL	9	M	CHILD		GRZZZZNY
MADELINE	6	F	CHILD		GRZZZZNY
MOSES	00	F	INF		GRZZZZNY
MIKLOEZ, JACOB	26	M	LABR		GRZZZZPA
JULIANA	25	F	W		GRZZZZPA
FRANZ	5	M	CHILD		GRZZZZPA

PASSENGER	AGE	SEX	OCCUPATION	PRVL	DES
ANTON	4	M	CHILD		GRZZZZPA
JAHNSEN, INGBERG	37	F	W		GRACBFNY
AUG	33	M	LABR		GRACBFNY
HOEFER, NATTAN	35	M	LABR		GRACBFNY
BETH	28	F	W		GRACBFNY
WINGENBACH, ELISE	23	F	W		GRACBFNY
ARTUR	27	M	LABR		GRACBFNY
KAUF, L	21	F	LDY		GRACBFNY
SCHULTH, J	25	F	LDY		GRACBFNY

SHIP: MARSALA

FROM: HAMBURG
TO: NEW YORK
ARRIVED: 19 MAY 1888

PASSENGER	AGE	SEX	OCCUPATION	PRVL	DES
FLIEGE, CARL	26	M	LABR		PRZZZZNY
WILHELMINE	30	F	W		PRZZZZNY
HELENE	22	F	SGL		PRZZZZNY
FRANZ	.11	M	INFANT		PRZZZZNY
CLAUSEN, PETER	23	M	SMH		PRZZZZNY
KLAR, SOPHIE	23	F	SGL		SYZZZZNY
JENSEN, MARGARETHE	18	F	SGL		PRZZZZNY
HO---CK, U	19	F	SGL		PRZZZZCH
SCHROEDER, WILH	16	M	LABR		PRZZZZNY
PAULSEN, JOH	24	M	SMH		PRZZZZDAV
RUMBAUER, ERNST	23	M	MCHT		PRZZZZNY
PHILIPP, AMALIA	50	F	WO		PRZZZZNY
EMMY	9	F	CHILD		PRZZZZNY
CARL	8	M	CHILD		PRZZZZNY
TROECK, DORA	26	F	WO		PRZZZZNY
MARTHA	26	F	WO		PRZZZZNY
COHN, ITZIG	26	M	DLR		PRZZZZNY
WIESENER, ENGEL	39	F	WO		PRZZZZNY
DIERCKS, AUGUST	17	M	LABR		PRZZZZNY
SCHROEDE, HERMANN	31	M	LABR		PRZZZZWI
LUISE	23	F	W		PRZZZZWI
PAUL	.06	M	INFANT		PRZZZZWI
WILHELM	76	M	LABR		PRZZZZWI
BETTSCHLEG, WILHELM	41	M	LABR		PRZZZZWI
WILHELMINE	52	F	W		PRZZZZWI
GUSTAV	9	M	CHILD		PRZZZZWI
BRUENNSTEIN, HANS	28	M	FARMER		PRZZZZUSA
SOMMER, ALBERT	27	M	MLR		PRZZZZUNK
KAEMMER, AUGUST	22	M	MSN		PRZZZZOMA
MALWITZ, LUDIKA	49	F	WO		PRZZZZNY
IDA	21	F	CH		PRZZZZNY
EDUARD	23	M	S		PRZZZZNY
HERM	9	M	CHILD		PRZZZZNY
OTTO	8	M	CHILD		PRZZZZNY
FRANZ	7	M	CHILD		PRZZZZNY
MERTINS, AUGUST	43	M	LABR		PRZZZZNY
RICHARD	15	M	LABR		PRZZZZNY
LANCUKI, VALENTIN	46	M	BCHR		PRZZZZNY
JAN	19	M	S		PRZZZZNY
LOEBER, THEKLA	25	F	SGL		BVZZZZNY
U, FRITZ	48	M	SHMK		PRZZZZNY
MARIA	44	F	W		PRZZZZNY
MARTHA	9	F	CHILD		PRZZZZNY
EMIL	.11	M	INFANT		PRZZZZNY
BRIX, GUSTAV	16	M	LABR		PRZZZZNY
EISERMANN, CATHAR	18	F	SGL		WMZZZZNY
BIRGL, JOCHANN	14	M	LABR		BVZZZZNY
CORDSEN, JOHS	32	M	FARMER		PRZZZZMIL
CARLE, MAGDAL	19	F	SGL		WMZZZZROC
OCHMER, FRIEDR	25	M	LABR		BDZZZZNY
JACOBSEN, LAURITZ	28	M	FARMER		PRZZZZMIL
HENRIETTE	28	F	W		PRZZZZMIL
CARL	6	M	CHILD		PRZZZZMIL
JOACHIM	4	M	CHILD		PRZZZZMIL

PASSENGER	AGE	SEX	OCCUPATION	PRVL	DES
HENRIETTE	.03	F	INFANT		PRZZZZMIL
KATZ, JACOB	16	M	BCHR		PRZZZZNY
PANOWSKI, STANISL	26	M	LABR		PRZZZZNY
HELENE	22	F	W		PRZZZZNY
NONNEMNACHER, GUSTAV	32	M	LABR		PRZZZZNY
WILH	28	F	W		PRZZZZNY
HERM	5	M	CHILD		PRZZZZNY
EMMA	2	F	CHILD		PRZZZZNY
ERICH	.11	M	INFANT		PRZZZZNY
DRAWAL, MARIALA	58	F	SGL		PRZZZZNY
JOERSTNER, HERMANN	32	M	SHMK		PRZZZZNY
HEIDENREICH, ANNA	17	F	SGL		PRZZZZNY
HOECK, GUSTAV	50	M	LABR		PRZZZZNY
AUGUSTE	50	F	W		PRZZZZNY
GUSTAV	20	F	CH		PRZZZZNY
WILHELM	14	M	CH		PRZZZZNY
JOHN	9	M	CHILD		PRZZZZNY
HERMANN	8	M	CHILD		PRZZZZNY
TISCHBEIN, JOH	45	M	LABR		PRZZZZNY
CATHAR	46	F	W		PRZZZZNY
RUDOLPH	9	M	CHILD		PRZZZZNY
JULA	8	F	CHILD		PRZZZZNY
ALEXANDER	7	F	CHILD		PRZZZZNY
THEOPHIL	2	M	CHILD		PRZZZZNY
ANNA	2	F	CHILD		PRZZZZNY
KERSTEN, WILHELMINE	50	F	WO		PRZZZZNY
GUSTAV	23	M	LABR		PRZZZZNY
AUGUST	17	M	LABR		PRZZZZNY
ANNA	9	F	CHILD		PRZZZZNY
SCHULZ, FRITZ	40	M	LABR		PRZZZZNY
MARIA	39	F	W		PRZZZZNY
BRUNO	10	M	CH		PRZZZZNY
GERTRUD	4	F	CHILD		PRZZZZNY
BAECKERMANN, ZIWA	27	F	WO		PRZZZZNY
FEIGE	6	F	CHILD		PRZZZZNY
BENJAMIN	5	M	CHILD		PRZZZZNY
LEIBUSCH	.10	M	INFANT		PRZZZZNY
BORCHMANN, JOH	57	M	SLR		PRZZZZNY
JOHANSEN, MAGNUS	39	M	LABR		PRZZZZNY
KIEHNSOP, JOH	25	M	LABR		PRZZZZNY
AUGUSTE	.09	F	INFANT		PRZZZZNY
MARTHA	.09	F	INFANT		PRZZZZNY
MATZENSKA, ANNA	19	F	SGL		PRZZZZNY
WASALSKA, MARIANNA	30	F	WO		PRZZZZNY
MARIANNA	6	F	CHILD		PRZZZZNY
STANISLAWA	4	F	CHILD		PRZZZZNY
FRANZ	2	M	CHILD		PRZZZZNY
JOSEPH	.06	M	INFANT		PRZZZZNY
DRAWS, GUSTAV	37	M	LABR		PRZZZZNY
READER, GUSTAV	16	M	LABR		PRZZZZNY
BOLCHOW, LUISE	50	F	WO		PRZZZZNY
WITT, JACOB	17	M	FARMER		PRZZZZNY
HANSEN, JOHANN	18	M	FARMER		PRZZZZOMA
CHRIST	18	M	FARMER		PRZZZZOMA
WAGENER, HENRIETTE	56	F	WO		PRZZZZNY
PAULINE	21	F	D		PRZZZZNY
KOELLN, MICHAEL	16	M	LABR		PRZZZZNY
THIESEN, CLAUS	28	M	LABR		PRZZZZNY
GIESE, MARIA	15	F	SGL		PRZZZZDAV
WINKELMANN, WILHELMINE	19	F	SGL		PRZZZZIA
ANNA	17	F	SGL		PRZZZZIA
BOCHMKE, NICOLAUS	44	M	FARMER		PRZZZZIA
JOHANNA	38	F	W		PRZZZZIA
WILH	9	M	CHILD		PRZZZZIA
MARIA	8	F	CHILD		PRZZZZIA
HERM	7	M	CHILD		PRZZZZIA
EMMA	4	F	CHILD		PRZZZZIA
LUISE	3	F	CHILD		PRZZZZIA
ALWINA	.11	F	INFANT		PRZZZZIA
PAEPER, DETLAF	48	M	FARMER		PRZZZZNY
HENRIETTE	46	F	W		PRZZZZNY
ANNA	9	F	CHILD		PRZZZZNY
AUGUST	7	M	CHILD		PRZZZZNY
WINKELMANN, WIEBKE	44	F	WO		PRZZZZUNK
HERM	15	M	CH		PRZZZZUNK
BERTHA	13	F	CH		PRZZZZUNK
WILHELMINE	9	F	CHILD		PRZZZZUNK
SIERK, MATHILDE	17	F	SGL		PRZZZZUNK
KOCK, AGNES	17	F	SGL		PRZZZZNY
KRUSE, MARIE	17	F	SGL		PRZZZZOAK
KOCH, JOHANN	22	M	LABR		PRZZZZNY
SIMENSKI, JOSEF	23	M	LABR		PRZZZZUNK
CATHA	20	F	W		PRZZZZUNK
FRANZISKA	.11	F	INFANT		PRZZZZUNK
MARIE	1	F	CHILD		PRZZZZUNK
QUANDT, WILH	26	M	LABR		PRZZZZSPR
SCHMIDT, LUISE	31	F	SGL		PRZZZZNY
MEYER, EMMA	24	F	SGL		PRZZZZNY
SIMKOVIAK, THERESE	23	F	W		PRZZZZPHI
MARTHENS	29	M	LABR		PRZZZZPHI
PLATZ, JOSEPHINA	17	F	SGL		BVZZZZNY
SCHMEHLING, HERMANN	36	M	TLR		PRZZZZNY
PROKOPP, JOHANN	25	M	LABR		PRZZZZDET
WILDE, ROBERT	25	M	BCHR		PRZZZZCH
HUEBNER, EMMA	24	F	SGL		PRZZZZCH
CONRAD, BRUNO	8	M	CHILD		PRZZZZNY
JANNSCHOWSKI, JOH	31	M	LABR		PRZZZZUNK
JOSEFA	27	F	W		PRZZZZUNK
SOBECKI, VALENTIN	58	M	LABR		PRZZZZUNK
MARIANNE	27	F	W		PRZZZZUNK
THEKLA	4	F	CHILD		PRZZZZUNK
FRANZ	3	M	CHILD		PRZZZZUNK
JULIANE	.11	F	INFANT		PRZZZZUNK
BRONIKOWSKI, MARGARETHE	15	F	SGL		PRZZZZNY
MICHAL	46	M	LABR		PRZZZZNY
NEUMANN, CARL	50	M	CTHR		PRZZZZNY
CARL	18	M	CTHR		PRZZZZNY
KRUEGER, ALBERT	40	M	WVR		PRZZZZNY
MUELLER, CLARA	31	F	WO		PRZZZZNY
ARTHUR	5	M	CHILD		PRZZZZNY
MITTMANN, AUGUSTE	53	F	WO		PRZZZZNY
DANIELEWICZ, JACOB	40	M	LABR		PRZZZZPHI
VERONIKA	34	F	W		PRZZZZPHI
LUDWIG	16	M	CH		PRZZZZPHI
FRANZISKA	14	F	CH		PRZZZZPHI
STANISLAWA	9	F	CHILD		PRZZZZPHI
JOSEF	8	M	CHILD		PRZZZZPHI
ANTONIA	6	M	CHILD		PRZZZZPHI
SONNENBERGER, EWALD	36	M	LABR		PRZZZZCIN
CHRISTINE	34	F	W		PRZZZZCIN
CLARA	9	F	CHILD		PRZZZZCIN
SCHEEL, CAROLINE	22	F	JNR		PRZZZZCIN
PETROLL, WILHELM	48	M	MSN		PRZZZZCIN
WILHELMINE	42	F	W		PRZZZZCIN
WILHELM	14	M	CH		PRZZZZCIN
ROBERT	9	M	CHILD		PRZZZZCIN
AUGUST	8	M	CHILD		PRZZZZCIN
MAX	7	M	CHILD		PRZZZZCIN
EUGEN	.11	F	INFANT		PRZZZZCIN
PAUL	.11	M	INFANT		PRZZZZCIN
PAWLOWSKI, LUCAS	31	M	LABR		PRZZZZCIN
MARIANNE	23	F	W		PRZZZZCIN
JOSEF	.03	M	INFANT		PRZZZZCIN
NOWAK, MICHALINE	9	F	CHILD		PRZZZZCIN
MOMBERGER, HEINR	23	M	MCHT		PRZZZZCIN
HERMANN, ANNA	19	F	SGL		BVZZZZCIN
SENF, PETER	17	M	TLR		BVZZZZCIN
SCHREINER, GEORG	30	M	BCHR		BVZZZZCIN
THIEME, ERNST	23	M	UNKNOWN		PRZZZZCIN
DAEHNE, HEDWIG	30	F	WO		PRZZZZCIN
CURT	4	M	CHILD		PRZZZZCIN
MARTHA	3	F	CHILD		PRZZZZCIN
BERGMANN, CARL	42	M	LABR		PRZZZZNY
MINNA	49	F	W		PRZZZZNY
HERMANN	16	M	S		PRZZZZNY
SCHLOTTMANN, JOHANNA	24	F	WO		PRZZZZNY
DOROTHEA	.09	F	INFANT		PRZZZZNY
BARDENHAGEN, JOHANN	16	M	LABR		PRZZZZNY
MARGUARDT, NICOLAUS	68	M	LABR		PRZZZZNY
DOROTHEA	67	F	W		PRZZZZNY

PASSENGER	AGE	SEX	OCCUPATION	PRVVL	DES
BERTHA	28	F	W		PRZZZZNY
MARTHA	6	F	CHILD		PRZZZZNY
EMIL	27	M	LABR		PRZZZZNY
HANS	.11	M	INFANT		PRZZZZNY
PIONTEK, OTTILIE	15	F	SGL		PRZZZZNY
OTTO	6	M	CHILD		PRZZZZNY
WETZEL, AMALIE	29	F	SGL		PRZZZZCH
VARSCHINSKI, EMILIE	25	F	SGL		PRZZZZNY
SPLETZER, AUGUST	15	M	LABR		PRZZZZNY
NOWICKI, JUS	23	M	LABR		PRZZZZNY
SWIATKOWSKA, JOHANNE	60	F	WO		PRZZZZNY
FISCHEL, SENDER	14	M	DLR		PRZZZZNY
SCHERKOWSKI, SCHIEL	23	M	TLR		PRZZZZNY
SUSZKE, FRANZ	28	M	SHMK		PRZZZZBUF
HELL, LIZZIE	17	F	W		PRZZZZNY
DRESSLER, FRANZ	34	M	LABR		PRZZZZNY
MINNA	27	F	WO		PRZZZZNY
CARL	5	M	CHILD		PRZZZZNY
CARL	.09	M	INFANT		PRZZZZNY
ANNA	3	F	CHILD		PRZZZZNY

SHIP: RUGIA

FROM: HAMBURG
TO: NEW YORK
ARRIVED: 19 MAY 1888

PASSENGER	AGE	SEX	OCCUPATION	PRVVL	DES
GEIST, PAULINE	28	F	WO	WMZZZZUSA
BENDEK, ARON	26	M	MCHT	PRZZZZUSA
DAZGELOH, EMIL	26	M	UNKNOWN	GRZZZZUSA
PAAP, EDUARD	18	M	LABR	PRZZZZUSA
CLEMENT, MARIE	23	F	SGL	FRZZZZUSA
GLEICHPINE, VICTOR	20	M	LABR	WMZZZZUSA
RASE, MARIE	18	F	SGL	WMZZZZUSA
LERITZ, JOS	19	M	LABR	WMZZZZUSA
MERRI, FELIX	24	M	LABR	SRZZZZUSA
LERDA, LUIGI	32	M	LABR	SRZZZZUSA
MARIA	20	F	LABR	SRZZZZUSA
MEYER, ALBERT	19	M	UNKNOWN	SRZZZZUSA
STEISS, JOHANNA	18	F	SGL	SRZZZZUSA
ZELLER, CRETIEN	24	M	LABR	WMZZZZUSA
DIETZ, CRETIEN	18	M	LABR	WMZZZZUSA
STURM, EVA	27	F	SGL	WMZZZZUSA
BURKER, GEORG	16	M	LABR	WMZZZZUSA
WAYDER, MAGD	20	F	SGL	WMZZZZUSA
EISELE, A	18	M	LABR	WMZZZZUSA
KUKUCK, FRIED	37	M	LABR	PRZZZZUSA
PAUL	26	F	W	PRZZZZUSA
GUSTAV	7	M	CHILD	PRZZZZUSA
EDUARD	2	M	CHILD	PRZZZZUSA
MARTHA	4	F	CHILD	PRZZZZUSA
ADELE	00	F	INF	PRZZZZUSA
HERZAG, ANE	29	F	W	BVZZZZUSA
THERESE	2	F	CHILD	BVZZZZUSA
HEINRICH	00	M	INF	BVZZZZUSA
LORENZ, MAGNUS	25	M	TCHR	SYZZZZUSA
MOECKEL, CLEMENS	19	M	LKSH	SYZZZZUSA
MUELLER, EMANUEL	37	M	LABR	SYZZZZUSA
LOUISE	40	F	W	SYZZZZUSA
EMMA	8	F	CHILD	SYZZZZUSA
GRAF, THERESE	21	F	WO	BVZZZZUSA
WINTER, FRIEDR	29	M	MSN	SYZZZZUSA
HENRIETTE	30	F	W	SYZZZZUSA
PAUL	5	M	CHILD	SYZZZZUSA
ANDERSEN, THERESE	19	F	SGL	PRZZZZUSA
FRICKE, ERNST	58	M	CPTR	PRZZZZUSA
ARP, CLAUS	21	M	FARMER	PRZZZZUSA
AGNES	22	F	W	PRZZZZUSA
META	3	F	CHILD	PRZZZZUSA
HERM	2	M	CHILD	PRZZZZUSA

PASSENGER	AGE	SEX	OCCUPATION	PRVVL	DES
JUL	.06	M	INFANT	PRZZZZUSA
PERKSEN, CHRIST	18	F	FARMER	PRZZZZUSA
GAENSLE, CARL	18	M	TLR	WMZZZZUSA
SCHNEIDER, MARIE	18	F	SGL	WMZZZZUSA
GERTRUDE	15	F	SGL	PRZZZZUSA
ULLRICHSEN, HELGA	22	F	SGL	PRZZZZUSA
QUELL, AUGUSTE	26	F	SGL	PRZZZZUSA
HUEBNER, HEINR	16	M	LABR	PRZZZZUSA
WIESE, PETER	59	M	FARMER	PRZZZZUSA
LENE	54	F	W	PRZZZZUSA
BERTHA	19	F	D	PRZZZZUSA
KOESTER, EMIL	20	M	UNKNOWN	PRZZZZUSA
NOATBAR, PAUL	47	M	DLR	PRZZZZUSA
MARG	21	F	D	PRZZZZUSA
RABSCH, WILH	24	F	SGL	PRZZZZUSA
SANDERGARD, INGE	17	F	SGL	PRZZZZUSA
HAGEDORN, JOH	14	F	SGL	PRZZZZUSA
JANSEN, ADOLF	18	M	FARMER	PRZZZZUSA
JENNING, THEODOR	23	M	LABR	PRZZZZUSA
HEINBOCKEL, CLAUS	27	M	LABR	PRZZZZUSA
HENNINGSEN, CHRIST	16	M	FARMER	PRZZZZUSA
PETERSEN, ANNA	25	F	SGL	PRZZZZUSA
MADSEN, OLENE	22	F	SGL	PRZZZZUSA
CHRISTIANSEN, THEODOR	19	M	FARMER	PRZZZZUSA
BRENCK, ELISE	39	F	WO	PRZZZZUSA
JEPSEN, JEP	40	M	LABR	PRZZZZUSA
JOAST, WILH	29	M	FARMER	PRZZZZUSA
ANNE	25	F	W	PRZZZZUSA
GUSTAV	2	M	CHILD	PRZZZZUSA
SIEMSEN, HANS	25	M	FARMER	PRZZZZUSA
ANNA	23	F	W	PRZZZZUSA
THOMSEN, JOH	16	M	FARMER	PRZZZZUSA
KOCH, CHRISTIAN	32	M	FARMER	PRZZZZUSA
REDLE, GEORG	30	M	FARMER	PRZZZZUSA
SAHM, JOH	39	M	TLR	PRZZZZUSA
MARGR	39	F	W	PRZZZZUSA
MICH	9	M	CHILD	PRZZZZUSA
ADAM	8	M	CHILD	PRZZZZUSA
ELISAB	7	F	CHILD	PRZZZZUSA
BARB	3	F	CHILD	PRZZZZUSA
PETERSEN, AUGUSTE	53	F	W	PRZZZZUSA
DETLER	16	M	FARMER	PRZZZZUSA
GOEHRING, JOH	35	M	FARMER	WMZZZZUSA
EHMAN, WILH	20	F	SGL	WMZZZZUSA
GUSTAV	14	M	FARMER	WMZZZZUSA
KOCH, MARIE	23	F	SGL	WMZZZZUSA
SCHMIDT, ADAM	49	M	LABR	WMZZZZUSA
PAUL	56	F	W	WMZZZZUSA
STECHER, GOTTLIEB	15	M	UNKNOWN	WMZZZZUSA
ROSE	19	F	UNKNOWN	WMZZZZUSA
KRAUSS, MATTHIAS	25	M	UNKNOWN	WMZZZZUSA
HOMMEL, MARIE	20	F	UNKNOWN	WMZZZZUSA
SCHICK, JOH	21	M	UNKNOWN	WMZZZZUSA
KESSLER, JACOB	17	M	BKR	BVZZZZUSA
BEYERSDOERFER, MAGD	25	F	SGL	BVZZZZUSA
JOPP, JOH	16	M	BBR	BVZZZZUSA
HEINSHANDT, MARIE	16	F	SGL	BVZZZZUSA
HAUSSMANN, CARL	28	M	JNR	WMZZZZUSA
CLAUSNITZER, WILH	52	F	W	SYZZZZUSA
LAASE, ZILLA	25	F	SGL	SYZZZZUSA
HEDSTROM, PETER	50	M	LABR	PRZZZZUSA
EUG	48	F	W	PRZZZZUSA
CARL	9	M	CHILD	PRZZZZUSA
SCHULTZ, CARL	32	M	LABR	PRZZZZUSA
LAURA	25	F	W	PRZZZZUSA
ALBERT	2	M	CHILD	PRZZZZUSA
FRITZ	.03	M	INFANT	PRZZZZUSA
BRUENERT, MARTIN	58	M	LABR	PRZZZZUSA
LOUISE	59	F	W	PRZZZZUSA
PAUL	20	F	D	PRZZZZUSA
WIETZYKOSKA, JADWIGA	45	F	WO	PRZZZZUSA
FRANZ	9	M	CHILD	PRZZZZUSA
CATH	5	F	CHILD	PRZZZZUSA
GRIMMER, JOH	14	M	LABR	BDZZZZUSA
STOCKMANN, CARL	32	M	LABR	PRZZZZUSA

PASSENGER	AGE	SEX	OCCUPATION	PV RIVL	DES
HERMINE	34	F	W		PRZZZZUSA
ROB	.11	M	INFANT		PRZZZZUSA
WILKOOWSKY, WLADISLAW	15	M	LABR		PRZZZZUSA
PREUSS, AUGUST	24	M	UNKNOWN		PRZZZZUSA
WILH	22	M	UNKNOWN		PRZZZZUSA
MARIE	.06	F	INFANT		PRZZZZUSA
CZEPANSKI, LOUISE	62	F	WO		PRZZZZUSA
BARTHAUSKI, ANASTASIA	17	F	SGL		PRZZZZUSA
REGULSKA, FRANZ	28	F	WO		PRZZZZUSA
PELAGIA	8	F	CHILD		PRZZZZUSA
FRANZ	6	M	CHILD		PRZZZZUSA
THEODOR	4	M	CHILD		PRZZZZUSA
STEPHAN	.08	M	INFANT		PRZZZZUSA
KAUL, ANNA	19	F	SGL		PRZZZZUSA
SCHMITZ, HUGO	36	M	MCHT		PRZZZZUSA
JACOBS, HERM	16	F	UNKNOWN		PRZZZZUSA
LEWKOWITZ, BERH	25	M	BCHR		PRZZZZUSA
HENRIETTE	22	F	W		PRZZZZUSA
BORMAN, ARTHUR	24	M	UNKNOWN		PRZZZZUSA
PARADIES, ADOLF	32	M	MCHT		PRZZZZUSA
JEZWRSKY, CSEPANI	28	M	LABR		PRZZZZUSA
LACHS, FRIED	52	F	LABR		PRZZZZUSA
MANKE, ALBERT	23	M	LABR		PRZZZZUSA
SCHWANDT, GOTTFRIED	46	M	LABR		PRZZZZUSA
WIEBEN, CATH	23	F	SGL		HBZZZZUSA
STOEPEL, JOHANN	41	M	MLR		PRZZZZUSA
CAROL	41	F	W		PRZZZZUSA
MARIE	16	F	W		PRZZZZUSA
LANGHOF, FRITZ	24	M	LABR		PRZZZZUSA
HAXOL, FRITZ	49	M	LABR		PRZZZZUSA
ANNA	47	F	W		PRZZZZUSA
REICHELT, FRIEDR	31	M	LKSH		PRZZZZUSA
ROTH, CLAUS	41	M	LABR		HBZZZZUSA
HACKRODT, CARL	25	M	CL		HBZZZZUSA
LAMPE, JOHN	25	M	CL		HBZZZZUSA
KORNEFFEL, FRIEDRICH	27	M	TNM		HBZZZZUSA
MEHLHOSE, MARIE	31	F	WO		HBZZZZUSA
PAUL	5	M	CHILD		HBZZZZUSA
FISCHER, WILH	51	M	MCHT		HBZZZZUSA
MUCS, HERM	28	M	MCHT		PRZZZZUSA
MIKULSKY, MALCAN	29	M	LABR		PRZZZZUSA
ANTONIA	21	F	W		PRZZZZUSA
MIHAL	.11	M	INFANT		PRZZZZUSA
LILIENTHAL, SAM	31	M	LABR		PRZZZZUSA
SEBOLD, HEINRICH	30	M	MCHT		PRZZZZUSA
HELEN	19	F	W		PRZZZZUSA
KRIPPNER, GEORG	17	M	SMH		BVZZZZUSA
SCHAPIRO, ROCHE	.11	F	INFANT		BVZZZZUSA
PLUEDDEMANN, HERM	22	M	MCHT		PRZZZZUSA
GAERSDORF, EMIL	25	M	LABR		PRZZZZUSA
BELASZ, MIHALY	51	M	LABR		PRZZZZUSA
IHLE, GUSTAV	36	M	FARMER		PRZZZZUSA
MARIE	45	F	W		PRZZZZUSA
CARL	8	M	CHILD		PRZZZZUSA
JOH	6	F	CHILD		PRZZZZUSA
LIBERA, AUG	24	F	W		PRZZZZUSA
ALFRED	3	M	CHILD		PRZZZZUSA
FRITZ	2	M	CHILD		PRZZZZUSA
LANG, ANNA	33	F	W		BVZZZZUSA
ANNA	8	F	CHILD		BVZZZZUSA
ELISABETH	5	F	CHILD		BVZZZZUSA
BADEN, ANNA	16	F	SGL		PRZZZZUSA
SCHLINGEN, JUL	23	M	LABR		PRZZZZUSA
MICHELSEN, MARG	25	F	SGL		PRZZZZUSA
LANG, EMMA	3	F	CHILD		BVZZZZUSA
CATH	00	F	INF		BVZZZZUSA
LIETZ, FRANZ	18	F	WO		PRZZZZUSA
HOOPS, SOFIA	17	F	WO		PRZZZZUSA
HERTZ, EMIL	26	M	MCHT		PRZZZZUSA
MIKOLSKA, MARIA	22	F	WO		PRZZZZUSA
WENZEL, MAX	24	M	BKR		SYZZZZUSA
WIERSBITZKI, ED	40	M	LABR		PRZZZZUSA
MARIA	35	F	W		PRZZZZUSA
ZIEBARTH, PAULINE	22	F	WO		PRZZZZUSA
LORZ, RICHARD	30	M	FARMER		SYZZZZUSA
IDA	26	F	W		SYZZZZUSA
ZBORAWSKI, LORENZ	52	M	FARMER		PRZZZZUSA
MAAG, ANDREAS	37	M	SHMK		WMZZZZUSA
ALBERT	5	M	CHILD		WMZZZZUSA
GONCHOWSKA, JOSEPHINE	56	F	W		PRZZZZUSA
FRANZ	23	M	S		PRZZZZUSA
SAULSON, CASPER	24	M	SHMK		PRZZZZUSA
HENKE, GUSTAV	16	M	LABR		PRZZZZUSA
BUDEZINSKA, GENOFEVA	24	F	WO		PRZZZZUSA
PICCHOWSKA, ANNA	23	F	WO		PRZZZZUSA
KLINGER, ANNA	24	F	WO		PRZZZZUSA
KRAUSE, EMILIE	53	F	WO		PRZZZZUSA
AUGUSTE	24	F	WO		PRZZZZUSA
HENSCHKE, CAROLINE	60	F	WO		SYZZZZUSA
BOCK, ERNST	29	M	TCHR		SYZZZZUSA
AUGUSTE	27	F	W		SYZZZZUSA
MADAUS, PAULINE	30	F	W		HBZZZZUSA
HEINR	00	M	INF		HBZZZZUSA
BARLAW, BARBARA	36	F	WO		WMZZZZUSA
HABENICHT, MARTHA	31	F	W		PRZZZZUSA
ALBERT	8	M	CHILD		PRZZZZUSA
FRIED	3	F	CHILD		PRZZZZUSA
FRANKOWSAK, JOS	27	M	LABR		PRZZZZUSA
WERNER, GUSTAV	23	M	BCHR		PRZZZZUSA
AGNES	20	F	W		PRZZZZUSA
LENKERSDORFER, HEINR	40	M	WVR		SYZZZZUSA
SIDONA	30	F	W		SYZZZZUSA
MINNI	00	F	INF		SYZZZZUSA
EILSNER, JOH	60	F	W		SYZZZZUSA
KORN, EMMA	21	F	WO		SYZZZZUSA
LOUISE	18	F	WO		SYZZZZUSA
HEILEMAN, MAX	26	M	LKSH		SYZZZZUSA
HELDT, PETER	20	M	LABR		PRZZZZUSA
THIEBE, MICHAEL	30	M	LABR		PRZZZZUSA
WOLF, CARL	33	M	LABR		PRZZZZUSA
MARCHAND, LOUISE	18	F	SGL		WMZZZZUSA
BICKEL, HENRY	50	M	LABR		SRZZZZUSA
CATH	48	F	W		SRZZZZUSA
AUG	19	M	S		SRZZZZUSA
CATH	17	F	D		SRZZZZUSA
HENRY	14	M	S		SRZZZZUSA
JOH	9	M	CHILD		SRZZZZUSA
LOUISE	7	F	CHILD		SRZZZZUSA
PERSEM, CHRIST	51	M	LABR		WMZZZZUSA
CHRIST	43	F	W		WMZZZZUSA
JEAN	18	M	S		WMZZZZUSA
BARBE	17	F	D		WMZZZZUSA
CHRISTINE	15	F	D		WMZZZZUSA
GUSTAVE	6	M	CHILD		WMZZZZUSA
MARLOT, FRIEDR	32	M	LABR		SRZZZZUSA
ANNA	33	F	W		SRZZZZUSA
FRIEDR	7	M	CHILD		SRZZZZUSA
EDUARD	.09	M	INFANT		SRZZZZUSA
SCHWARZ, MATHILDE	19	F	SGL		SRZZZZUSA
STEHLI, KARL	24	M	LABR		SRZZZZUSA
WIDMER, REINLY	26	M	LABR		SRZZZZUSA
ADRESSA, U	19	M	LABR		SRZZZZUSA
FEDEL, PASQUNIO	27	M	LABR		SRZZZZUSA
WALLHARDT, ARNOLD	25	M	LABR		SRZZZZUSA
HARTMAN, FRIEDR	26	M	LABR		SRZZZZUSA
KALTENBACH, LOUIS	26	M	LABR		SRZZZZUSA
SEIBEL, JEAN	33	M	LABR		SRZZZZUSA
MAYER, ELISAB	38	F	W		SRZZZZUNK
BRIGG, ULRICH	21	M	LABR		SRZZZZUSA
WALTNER, U	18	F	SGL		HNZZZZUSA
MASEL, EMILIE	63	F	WO		PRZZZZUSA
ALICE	23	F	D		PRZZZZUSA
HAGERFELD, RUDOLF	16	M	STDNT		LUZZZZUSA
SCHOLL, MARTHA	24	F	SGL		BVZZZZUSA
SILBERNAGEL, MAGDALENA	30	F	SGL		BVZZZZUSA
WOLTMANN, JOH	61	M	CPT		HBZZZZUSA
ANNA	64	F	W		HBZZZZUSA
SELLSCHOPP, W	27	M	MCHT		PRZZZZUSA
EBERLEIN, IDA	24	F	WO		PRZZZZUSA
SATTLER, EMMA	23	F	SGL		PRZZZZUSA

PASSENGER	AGE	SEX	OCCUPATION	PRVVL	DES
KOESTER, MARIE	19	F	SGL		PRZZZZUSA
MEISSNER, ANNA	27	F	SGL		PRZZZZUSA
BURMESTER, WILH	26	M	MCHT		PRZZZZUSA
KIES, WILH	48	M	MCHT		WMZZZZUSA
DENNER, CARL	24	M	PVTR		PRZZZZUSA
ROHLOFF, EMILIE	28	F	SGL		PRZZZZUSA
LEMKE, THEODOR	29	M	UNKNOWN		PRZZZZUSA
MARIE	31	F	W		PRZZZZUSA
ELSE	6	F	CHILD		PRZZZZUSA
ERWIN	5	M	CHILD		PRZZZZUSA
LIEMAN, MARTIN	27	M	MLR		PRZZZZUSA
FISCHER, JOHANN	31	M	UNKNOWN		PRZZZZUSA
HEYER, FRANZ	6	M	CHILD		PRZZZZUSA
ALFRED	4	M	CHILD		PRZZZZUSA
CLAUSNITZER, AUG	62	M	LABR		SYZZZZUSA
KRABBENHOFF, ELISABETH	18	F	SGL		PRZZZZUSA
REESE, HEINR	17	M	LABR		HBZZZZUSA
PICKER, HARALD	22	M	FARMER		PRZZZZUSA
POGRZEBA, JOSEF	33	M	FARMER		PRZZZZUSA
JOSEFA	30	F	W		PRZZZZUSA
CATH	8	F	CHILD		PRZZZZUSA
JUL	4	F	CHILD		PRZZZZUSA
STANISLAUS	3	M	CHILD		PRZZZZUSA
GLATKI, VALENTIN	29	M	FARMER		PRZZZZUSA
BERTHA	26	F	W		PRZZZZUSA
THEODOR	.04	M	INFANT		PRZZZZUSA
KOMOR, SIMON	34	M	FARMER		PRZZZZUSA
MARIE	45	F	W		PRZZZZUSA
FRANZISKA	23	F	UNKNOWN		PRZZZZUSA
FRUEHMARK, FRANZISKA	15	F	UNKNOWN		PRZZZZUSA
HOFFMANN, ERNESTE	40	F	WO		SYZZZZUSA
LEVERENZ, LINE	23	F	SGL		PRZZZZUSA
ELISE	19	F	SGL		PRZZZZUSA
JUNGE, GEORG	18	M	MLR		PRZZZZUSA
BRUST, WLADISLAUS	25	M	BRR		PRZZZZUSA
POHRKE, ERNEST	18	F	SGL		PRZZZZUSA
KOPINKE, ALWINE	20	F	SGL		PRZZZZUSA
REISS, ADOLF	18	M	MCHT		PRZZZZUSA
GALOW, AUGUST	37	M	LABR		PRZZZZUSA
CAROL	28	F	W		PRZZZZUSA
WILH	3	F	CHILD		PRZZZZUSA
BERTHA	.11	F	INFANT		PRZZZZUSA
MIKLAY, MARIE	38	F	UNKNOWN		PRZZZZUSA
SEIDLER, AUGUSTE	52	F	WO		PRZZZZUSA
ELISE	21	F	SGL		PRZZZZUSA
CURTIAS, FRIEDR	19	M	BKBNDR		PRZZZZUSA
JOAP, JULS	33	M	LABR		PRZZZZUSA
ANNA	32	F	W		PRZZZZUSA
OTTILIE	4	F	CHILD		PRZZZZUSA
EMMA	2	F	CHILD		PRZZZZUSA
WILHELM	.11	M	INFANT		PRZZZZUSA
KRISMALSKI, PETER	38	M	LABR		PRZZZZUSA
BUDJEWSKI, CASIMIR	33	M	LABR		PRZZZZUSA
WENDLAND, JULIE	21	F	SGL		PRZZZZUSA
RADOWSKY, JOHANN	30	M	LABR		PRZZZZUSA
POHL, FLORENTE	17	F	SGL		PRZZZZUSA
LOPATKA, MATHEUS	28	M	LABR		PRZZZZUSA
MARIANNA	25	F	W		PRZZZZUSA
JAN	25	M	LABR		PRZZZZUSA
NIEDRICH, JACOB	46	M	LABR		PRZZZZUSA
KRAMPITZ, RUDOLF	24	M	MCHT		PRZZZZUSA
OTTA	30	M	MLR		PRZZZZUSA
KARBAWSKI, MICHAEL	34	M	LABR		PRZZZZUSA
FISCHER, CAROL	37	F	WO		PRZZZZUSA
ANNA	9	F	CHILD		PRZZZZUSA
THOMAS, HEINRICH	17	M	LABR		PRZZZZUSA
RMGELS, OSCAR	25	M	LABR		HBZZZZUSA
PATZ, EMMA	18	F	SGL		PRZZZZUSA
TENSCH, EMMA	14	F	SGL		PRZZZZUSA
SCHREMMER, FRANZ	35	M	WVR		PRZZZZUSA
ANDERS, AUGUST	31	M	LABR		PRZZZZUSA
JENDROW, MATHEUS	45	M	FARMER		PRZZZZUSA
CATH	40	F	W		PRZZZZUSA
JOH	18	F	CH		PRZZZZUSA
FRANZISKA	16	F	CH		PRZZZZUSA
WILH	13	M	CH		PRZZZZUSA
VALENTIN	9	M	CHILD		PRZZZZUSA
AGNES	4	M	CHILD		PRZZZZUSA
PAUL	3	M	CHILD		PRZZZZUSA
WELTNA, JOHANN	23	M	LABR		PRZZZZUSA
SOLLARZ, FRANZ	44	M	FARMER		PRZZZZUSA
ELISABETH	38	F	W		PRZZZZUSA
ROSALIE	18	F	UNKNOWN		PRZZZZUSA
STNISLAUS	14	M	UNKNOWN		PRZZZZUSA
PETER	9	M	CHILD		PRZZZZUSA
JOSEPHE	8	F	CHILD		PRZZZZUSA
MARIANNE	4	F	CHILD		PRZZZZUSA
FRANZISKA	3	F	CHILD		PRZZZZUSA
JOH	.03	M	INFANT		PRZZZZUSA
PIONTEK, SIMON	30	M	FARMER		PRZZZZUSA
FRANCISKA	28	F	W		PRZZZZUSA
JACOB	4	M	CHILD		PRZZZZUSA
FRANZ	3	M	CHILD		PRZZZZUSA
MARIE	.06	F	INFANT		PRZZZZUSA
AHRENKEIL, HANSINE	18	F	SGL		PRZZZZUSA
MOELLER, HERM	15	M	FARMER		PRZZZZUSA
TENNER, THEA	18	F	SGL		PRZZZZUSA
ZBORALSKY, SOFIE	18	F	SGL		PRZZZZUSA
KOERNER, EMMA	23	F	SGL		PRZZZZUSA
MEYER, WILH	39	F	WO		PRZZZZUSA
EMILIE	18	F	CH		PRZZZZUSA
OTTO	14	M	CH		PRZZZZUSA
MINNA	13	F	CH		PRZZZZUSA
PAUL	9	M	CHILD		PRZZZZUSA
AMANDA	4	F	CHILD		PRZZZZUSA
BERTHA	.09	F	INFANT		PRZZZZUSA
SCHIPPER, MARIE	18	F	SGL		PRZZZZUSA
EGGERS, MARG	19	F	SGL		PRZZZZUSA
KORAS, HYPALIT	25	M	LABR		PRZZZZUSA
WATTENBERG, JOH	22	F	SGL		PRZZZZUSA
SCHUR, CARL	18	M	WTR		PRZZZZUSA
HUEHNE, CARL	14	M	LABR		PRZZZZUSA
SCHEER, GOTLIEB	50	M	BCHR		PRZZZZUSA
AUGUSTE	35	F	W		PRZZZZUSA
BERTHA	9	F	CHILD		PRZZZZUSA
OTTO	7	M	CHILD		PRZZZZUSA
HELENE	4	F	CHILD		PRZZZZUSA
ANNA	2	F	CHILD		PRZZZZUSA
WEGNER, OTTO	16	M	FARMER		PRZZZZUSA
JEDAMSKI, GOTT	33	M	LABR		PRZZZZUSA
CHARLOTTE	30	F	W		PRZZZZUSA
EMIL	4	M	CHILD		PRZZZZUSA
GUSTAV	.11	M	INFANT		PRZZZZUSA
KNIFKA, CHRISTOF	37	M	LABR		PRZZZZUSA
MARIE	36	F	W		PRZZZZUSA
EMILIE	7	F	CHILD		PRZZZZUSA
MAR--	3	F	CHILD		PRZZZZUSA
WILH	.09	F	INFANT		PRZZZZUSA
BIELSKI, KATH	22	F	SGL		PRZZZZUSA
SCHOENKNECHT, CARL	65	M	UNKNOWN		PRZZZZUSA
AHLERS, CARL	34	M	FARMER		OLZZZZUSA
ELISE	21	F	W		OLZZZZUSA
HUSFELD, ARTHUR	24	M	MCHT		PRZZZZUSA
FRENCHHOFF, WILH	36	M	LABR		SYZZZZUSA
STERNBERG, ERNESTINE	22	F	SGL		PRZZZZUSA
HARTS, HELENE	17	F	SGL		PRZZZZUSA
U, U	27	U	UNKNOWN		PRZZZZUSA
U	23	U	UNKNOWN		PRZZZZUSA
BERENNISKA, ---NI	24	U	UNKNOWN		PRZZZZUSA
POMASZEWISH, ---RA	27	U	UNKNOWN		PRZZZZUSA
FRANICH, GIOVANI	25	U	UNKNOWN		PRZZZZUSA
CATTICH, NICCOLAO	36	U	UNKNOWN		PRZZZZUSA
GUSEPPE, MATTEO	34	U	UNKNOWN		PRZZZZUSA
LUSICH, ANTONIO	36	U	UNKNOWN		PRZZZZUSA
ZITOWICH, BALDOSSAVE	50	U	UNKNOWN		PRZZZZUSA
SKORTUSA, GIOVANNI	25	U	UNKNOWN		PRZZZZUSA
NAVOCOWICH, RISTANO	32	U	UNKNOWN		PRZZZZUSA
LEJAK, ANTONIO	24	U	UNKNOWN		PRZZZZUSA
LALICH, INO	30	U	UNKNOWN		PRZZZZUSA
STANICH, ABRAM	34	U	UNKNOWN		PRZZZZUSA

PASSENGER	AGE	SEX	OCCUPATION	PRVL	DES
ELLECOVICH, GIOVANNI	20	U	UNKNOWN	PRZZZZ	USA
LUSICH, NICOLA	18	U	UNKNOWN	PRZZZZ	USA
STANCOWICH, PIETRO	18	U	UNKNOWN	PRZZZZ	USA
NIDUCH, GIOVANNI	38	U	UNKNOWN	PRZZZZ	USA
PETRIS, LUCCA	23	U	UNKNOWN	PRZZZZ	USA
MITROWIC, GIOV	17	U	UNKNOWN	PRZZZZ	USA
MATIGA, MATTEO	17	U	UNKNOWN	PRZZZZ	USA
MOTACHINIC, GIOGIO	17	U	UNKNOWN	PRZZZZ	USA
OPOSITCH, INO	18	U	UNKNOWN	PRZZZZ	USA
KINKEL, INO	9	U	CHILD	PRZZZZ	USA
WIDOCK, PAWLO	9	U	CHILD	PRZZZZ	USA
NAIVODA, LOZIA	23	F	WO	PRZZZZ	USA
LIPINA, STEFANO	25	M	SLR	PRZZZZ	USA
MARIENCOWITSCH, NICOLA	51	M	SLR	PRZZZZ	USA
FELIE	47	M	SLR	PRZZZZ	USA

SHIP: AMERICA

FROM: BREMEN
TO: BALTIMORE
ARRIVED: 20 MAY 1888

PASSENGER	AGE	SEX	OCCUPATION	PRVL	DES
OSTROWSKI, IGNATZ	26	M	LABR	GRZZZZ	NE
CATHARINE	24	F	UNKNOWN	GRZZZZ	NE
STEFAN	.03	M	INFANT	GRZZZZ	NE
DOBRIKOWSKI, ADELINE	33	F	UNKNOWN	GRZZZZ	NE
ABRAHAM, WILHELMINE	68	F	UNKNOWN	GRZZZZ	NE
DOBRIKOWSKI, MARIA	8	F	CHILD	GRZZZZ	NE
FRANZ	7	M	CHILD	GRZZZZ	NE
PAUL	5	M	CHILD	GRZZZZ	NE
BERTHA	3	F	CHILD	GRZZZZ	NE
KREUTZBERGER, CAROLINE	66	F	UNKNOWN	GRZZZZ	WI
CIESIELSKI, JAN	24	M	GZR	GRZZZZ	WI
VICTORIA	25	F	UNKNOWN	GRZZZZ	WI
HEDWIG	.11	F	INFANT	GRZZZZ	WI
JOSEPHA	.01	F	INFANT	GRZZZZ	WI
SIEWERT, CARL	65	M	UNKNOWN	GRZZZZ	WI
NOEVICKI, ANTON	24	M	PNTR	GRZZZZ	WI
KLONOWSKI, MARIANNA	37	F	UNKNOWN	GRZZZZ	WI
MARIAN	4	M	CHILD	GRZZZZ	WI
ADAM	39	M	LABR	GRZZZZ	WI
ANTON	.06	M	INFANT	GRZZZZ	WI
THECKLA	.06	F	INFANT	GRZZZZ	WI
WITZINSKA, CATHARINA	23	F	UNKNOWN	GRZZZZ	MI
FRANZ	.11	M	INFANT	GRZZZZ	MI
KRUSZKOWSKI, MARTIN	11	M	CH	GRZZZZ	MI
KARP, ALBERT	22	M	FARMER	GRZZZZ	MI
NEUMANN, CLARA	16	F	SVNT	GRZZZZ	MI
DAMKE, EMILIE	17	F	SVNT	GRZZZZ	MI
MALACHOWIECZ, ALBERT	32	M	MSN	GRZZZZ	OH
JOHANNE	35	F	UNKNOWN	GRZZZZ	OH
FRANZ	7	M	CHILD	GRZZZZ	OH
HELENE	4	M	CHILD	GRZZZZ	OH
ALBERT	.07	M	INFANT	GRZZZZ	OH
FESNER, EMMA	16	F	SVNT	GRZZZZ	MD
ROEHR, ANTON	23	M	MCHT	GRZZZZ	MD
MINNA	18	F	UNKNOWN	GRZZZZ	MD
PI----SKI, MARY	16	F	UNKNOWN	GRZZZZ	MD
KITOFSKI, JACOB	60	M	FARMER	GRZZZZ	DAK
MARIE	54	F	UNKNOWN	GRZZZZ	DAK
LISZEZYNSKI, LUDWIG	20	M	LABR	GRZZZZ	DAK
KACHELSKY, MARTIN	49	M	LABR	GRZZZZ	MI
ANNA	45	F	UNKNOWN	GRZZZZ	MI
WOJCEICK	14	M	UNKNOWN	GRZZZZ	MI
MARIANNA	9	F	CHILD	GRZZZZ	MI
JOSEPHA	5	F	CHILD	GRZZZZ	MI
ANNA	4	F	CHILD	GRZZZZ	MI
FABIARINSKA, MARY	19	F	SVNT	GRZZZZ	KS
PANLOWSKA, CONSTANTIA	24	F	LABR	GRZZZZ	KS
MATIK, AUGUST	26	M	UNKNOWN	GRZZZZ	KS
SCHWARZ, ADAM	36	M	UNKNOWN	GRZZZZ	KS
MARIE	34	F	UNKNOWN	GRZZZZ	KS
BERTHA	.09	F	INFANT	GRZZZZ	KS
GRABOWSKY, PETER	31	M	TLR	GRZZZZ	OH
MARIE	22	F	UNKNOWN	GRZZZZ	OH
MARIE	5	F	CHILD	GRZZZZ	OH
PETER	4	M	CHILD	GRZZZZ	OH
KOSLOWSKI, ELISABETH	50	F	UNKNOWN	GRZZZZ	OH
SEITZ, HENRIETTE	59	F	UNKNOWN	GRZZZZ	OH
GOREELITZ, CARL	22	M	LABR	GRZZZZ	IA
LOUISE	25	F	SVNT	GRZZZZ	IA
REICHERT, ALBERT	21	M	MCHT	GRZZZZ	MN
KOWALSKI, WLADEK	22	M	LABR	GRZZZZ	MN
KORNATH, AUGUST	39	M	LABR	GRZZZZ	MN
EMILIE	00	F	UNKNOWN	GRZZZZ	MN
AUGUSTE	11	F	CH	GRZZZZ	MN
MINNA	7	F	CHILD	GRZZZZ	MN
BERTHA	4	F	CHILD	GRZZZZ	MN
ALBERT	2	M	CHILD	GRZZZZ	MN
IDA	.06	F	INFANT	GRZZZZ	MN
LENE	.06	F	INFANT	GRZZZZ	MN
MUELLER, HERMANN	30	M	FARMER	GRZZZZ	IL
BEIFUSS, JOHANN	29	M	FARMER	GRZZZZ	IL
KURZHALS, ROMAN	27	M	FARMER	GRZZZZ	IL
HOFFMANN, FRIEDRICH	61	M	FARMER	GRZZZZ	MI
PAULINE	51	F	UNKNOWN	GRZZZZ	MI
ANNA	18	F	UNKNOWN	GRZZZZ	MI
ALBERT	15	M	UNKNOWN	GRZZZZ	MI
EMIL	7	M	CHILD	GRZZZZ	MI
THEODOR	5	M	CHILD	GRZZZZ	MI
WILHELM	3	M	CHILD	GRZZZZ	MI
KLAWIKOWSKA, U	34	F	UNKNOWN	GRZZZZ	MI
DEMSKY, AUGUST	29	M	LABR	GRZZZZ	MI
WILHELMINE	26	F	UNKNOWN	GRZZZZ	MI
JOHANN	4	M	CHILD	GRZZZZ	MI
AUGUST	.07	M	INFANT	GRZZZZ	MI
OSTROFSKI, FLORENTINA	62	F	UNKNOWN	GRZZZZ	MI
HUCK, OTTO	18	M	UNKNOWN	GRZZZZ	MD
KNUEPPEL, WILHELM	27	M	UNKNOWN	GRZZZZ	MD
HAIN, CAROLINE	27	F	UNKNOWN	GRZZZZ	KY
FRANZ	4	M	CHILD	GRZZZZ	KY
BEILKE, ALBERT	25	M	LABR	GRZZZZ	NE
BORCHARDT, BERTHA	23	F	SVNT	GRZZZZ	NE
RECK, PAUL	28	M	GDNR	GRZZZZ	NE
HARTWIG, ANNA	25	F	SVNT	GRZZZZ	NE
LANGERMANN, ALBERT	16	M	UNKNOWN	GRZZZZ	NE
U, U	26	F	MLNR	GRZZZZ	NE
HALNBFUSS, U	16	F	MLNR	GRZZZZ	NE
PIPKORN, AUGUST	28	M	SHMK	GRZZZZ	IN
WILHELMINE	24	F	UNKNOWN	GRZZZZ	IN
JULIUS	3	M	CHILD	GRZZZZ	IN
BERTHA	2	F	CHILD	GRZZZZ	IN
MARTHA	.01	F	INFANT	GRZZZZ	IN
RUEFFER, CAROLINE	68	F	UNKNOWN	GRZZZZ	IN
ROCHOW, FRANZ	32	M	STCTR	GRZZZZ	SC
WANDA	7	F	CHILD	GRZZZZ	SC
OTTO	6	M	CHILD	GRZZZZ	SC
ANNA	4	F	CHILD	GRZZZZ	SC
MARIA	2	F	CHILD	GRZZZZ	SC
STALLAN, ALBERTINE	22	F	SVNT	GRZZZZ	KS
FUNK, MARIA	31	F	SVNT	GRZZZZ	KS
FICK, MARIE	17	F	SVNT	GRZZZZ	MD
HARKE, EMILIE	21	F	SVNT	GRZZZZ	MD
SKULSKI, JULIE	23	F	SVNT	GRZZZZ	MD
BENZ, ANNA	22	F	SVNT	GRZZZZ	MD
ANNA	.11	F	INFANT	GRZZZZ	MD
BACH, FRIEDERIKE	24	F	UNKNOWN	GRZZZZ	IL
MARTHA	.06	F	INFANT	GRZZZZ	IL
PETRY, BERTHA	22	F	UNKNOWN	GRZZZZ	WI
ELSBETH	3	F	CHILD	GRZZZZ	WI
HEHE, JULIE	24	F	UNKNOWN	GRZZZZ	NE
EMILIE	5	F	CHILD	GRZZZZ	NE
JANOS, MATHILDE	27	F	SVNT	GRZZZZ	NE
U, U	28	M	MCHT	GRZZZZ	OH
SEKORSKY, FRANZ	32	M	LABR	GRZZZZ	OH

PASSENGER	AGE	SEX	OCCUPATION	PRIVL	DES
FAUBNER, AUGUST	60	M	FARMER	GRZZZZ	OH
WILZINOZKOWSKI, ANTON	48	M	SHMK	GRZZZZ	KS
MARIANNA	43	F	UNKNOWN	GRZZZZ	KS
WLADISLAUS	18	M	UNKNOWN	GRZZZZ	KS
CONSTANTIN	15	M	CH	GRZZZZ	KS
MARINANNA	6	F	CHILD	GRZZZZ	KS
FRANZ	4	M	CHILD	GRZZZZ	KS
JOHANNE	.11	F	INFANT	GRZZZZ	KS
MODZEWSKY, CATHERINE	63	F	UNKNOWN	GRZZZZ	MD
GOLKOWSKI, THOMAS	36	M	UNKNOWN	GRZZZZ	MO
JOHANNE	34	F	UNKNOWN	GRZZZZ	MO
FRANZISKA	6	F	CHILD	GRZZZZ	MO
GELEMBROWSKI, JOHANNE	35	F	UNKNOWN	GRZZZZ	PA
PAULINE	24	F	UNKNOWN	GRZZZZ	PA
CAROLINE	.10	F	INFANT	GRZZZZ	PA
U, U	21	F	UNKNOWN	GRZZZZ	PA
WILZIEWZKOWSKI, ANTONIE	.11	F	INFANT	GRZZZZ	KS
SCHNELL, AGATHA	21	F	SVNT	GRZZZZ	MD
BIEGAISKI, JOHANN	32	M	SDLR	GRZZZZ	OH
VICTORIA	35	F	UNKNOWN	GRZZZZ	OH
ANASTASIA	11	F	CH	GRZZZZ	OH
JOHANN	7	M	CHILD	GRZZZZ	OH
WILHELM	4	M	CHILD	GRZZZZ	OH
WLADISLAW	.10	M	INFANT	GRZZZZ	OH
KALNZUG, ALBERT	34	M	FARMER	GRZZZZ	AZ
MELINA	27	F	UNKNOWN	GRZZZZ	AZ
ALBERT	6	M	CHILD	GRZZZZ	AZ
IGNATZ	4	M	CHILD	GRZZZZ	AZ
STANISLAWA	2	F	CHILD	GRZZZZ	AZ
MARTIN	.04	M	INFANT	GRZZZZ	AZ
STACHINSKI, JOHANN	50	M	BBR	GRZZZZ	DAK
EICHSTEDT, ANIELA	18	F	UNKNOWN	GRZZZZ	MD
U, U	54	F	UNKNOWN	GRZZZZ	MD
ANNA	20	F	UNKNOWN	GRZZZZ	MD
TEOFIL	15	M	UNKNOWN	GRZZZZ	MD
BALBINA	.05	F	INFANT	GRZZZZ	MD
MARCKOWSKY, MARYANNA	19	F	UNKNOWN	GRZZZZ	OH
HUDZINSKA, AGNISKA	21	F	SVNT	GRZZZZ	OH
SZIDLOWSKA, HEDWIG	7	F	CHILD	GRZZZZ	OH
LEIMBRUNNER, JOSEF	31	M	BRR	GRZZZZ	OH
BIRNER, EVA	23	F	UNKNOWN	GRZZZZ	OH
JOHANNA	.11	F	INFANT	GRZZZZ	OH
OETTMEIER, JETTA	15	F	UNKNOWN	GRZZZZ	OH
GREB, JOSEFA	20	F	SVNT	GRZZZZ	KY
NEPPINGER, JOHANN	47	M	TLR	GRZZZZ	MI
CATHARINE	37	F	UNKNOWN	GRZZZZ	MI
MICHAEL	11	M	CH	GRZZZZ	MI
CATHARINA	10	F	CH	GRZZZZ	MI
NICOLAUS	6	M	CHILD	GRZZZZ	MI
FIEDEL, U	37	M	UNKNOWN	GRZZZZ	MI
CHRISTIAN, DANIEL	55	M	LABR	GRZZZZ	OR
EVA	17	F	UNKNOWN	GRZZZZ	OR
MARGARETHE	15	F	UNKNOWN	GRZZZZ	OR
ANNA	13	F	UNKNOWN	GRZZZZ	OR
JOHANN	9	M	CHILD	GRZZZZ	OR
JANSSEN, UNKA	16	F	UNKNOWN	GRZZZZ	MD
KURAK, JULIUS	25	M	TLR	GRZZZZ	IL
ANNA	13	F	UNKNOWN	GRZZZZ	IL
EMMA	.06	F	INFANT	GRZZZZ	IL
CHEMINSKA, JOSEFINA	15	F	UNKNOWN	GRZZZZ	IL
CICIELAK, ANTONIA	20	F	SVNT	GRZZZZ	IL
RUKONSKA, ROSALIA	50	F	UNKNOWN	GRZZZZ	IL
MARIANNA	5	F	CHILD	GRZZZZ	IL
DOROTHEA	3	F	CHILD	GRZZZZ	IL
BECKS, ANDREAS	.09	M	INFANT	GRZZZZ	IL
NASTALIE, FRANZ	24	M	MCHT	GRZZZZ	MN
ROSALIE	18	F	SVNT	GRZZZZ	MN
GALITZKI, LOUISE	40	F	UNKNOWN	GRZZZZ	IA
CLARA	7	F	CHILD	GRZZZZ	IA
FRITZ	5	M	CHILD	GRZZZZ	IA
HARZINAK, MICHAEL	36	M	SHFM	GRZZZZ	TX
ANNA	37	F	UNKNOWN	GRZZZZ	TX
WOJEICK	7	M	CHILD	GRZZZZ	TX
JOSEF	6	M	CHILD	GRZZZZ	TX
CASIMIR	6	M	CHILD	GRZZZZ	TX
AGENCA	3	F	CHILD	GRZZZZ	TX
JAN	.11	M	INFANT	GRZZZZ	TX
MICHAEL	.11	M	INFANT	GRZZZZ	TX
LAMPARSKI, LEO	33	M	MCHT	GRZZZZ	MD
EISENMANN, BABETTE	19	F	SVNT	GRZZZZ	OH
HAHN, JOHANN	21	M	MCHT	GRZZZZ	LA
KAHNLE, AUGUST	14	M	UNKNOWN	GRZZZZ	OR
SOMMER, MARTHA	18	F	SVNT	GRZZZZ	OR
SOSHKA, ADELINE	25	F	UNKNOWN	GRZZZZ	IL
WILHELM	3	M	CHILD	GRZZZZ	IL
PALLAS, BERTHA	19	F	MLNR	GRZZZZ	IL
GWADE, WILHELMINE	25	F	UNKNOWN	GRZZZZ	IL
ERNSTINE	25	F	UNKNOWN	GRZZZZ	IL
AUGUST	.02	M	INFANT	GRZZZZ	IL
HOFT, JULIUS	18	M	LABR	GRZZZZ	CIN
FISCHER, AUGUST	33	M	LABR	GRZZZZ	CIN
TOPPE, LUDWIG	28	M	FARMER	GRZZZZ	NE
BERTHA	28	F	UNKNOWN	GRZZZZ	NE
HERMANN	5	M	CHILD	GRZZZZ	NE
BERTHA	4	F	CHILD	GRZZZZ	NE
HARTMANN, JOHANNA	27	F	UNKNOWN	GRZZZZ	IN
FRANZ	.10	M	INFANT	GRZZZZ	IN
MISKLE, FERDINAND	24	M	LABR	GRZZZZ	MO
HABERMANN, ALBERTINE	22	F	UNKNOWN	GRZZZZ	KS
AUGUST	35	M	CPTR	GRZZZZ	KS
CHRISTIAN	.11	M	INFANT	GRZZZZ	KS
ENZNER, MARY	17	F	SVNT	GRZZZZ	MD
EVA	5	F	CHILD	GRZZZZ	MD
KUNIGUNDE	19	F	MLNR	GRZZZZ	MD
GASSENHUBER, XAVER	54	M	LABR	GRZZZZ	VA
ANNA	45	F	UNKNOWN	GRZZZZ	VA
DONHARL, ALOIS	16	M	LABR	GRZZZZ	VA
REIF, CONRAD	15	M	LABR	GRZZZZ	VA
LEIBINGER, ERHARDT	26	M	LABR	GRZZZZ	VA
SCHORR, JOSEFA	20	F	DRSMKR	GRZZZZ	AR
LEINBRUNNER, JOSEF	32	M	SDLR	GRZZZZ	IL
HANNWAKER, MARGARETHE	22	F	SVNT	GRZZZZ	IL
KERN, KONRAD	18	M	LABR	GRZZZZ	IL
GEHRKE, MARIE	30	F	DRSMKR	GRZZZZ	IL
KRAMER, HERMANN	27	M	MCHT	GRZZZZ	IL
KUEHNS, ELISABETH	32	F	UNKNOWN	GRZZZZ	NE
ANNA	7	F	CHILD	GRZZZZ	NE
MAX	5	M	CHILD	GRZZZZ	NE
BABETTA	.10	F	INFANT	GRZZZZ	NE
HALLDOERFER, KUNIGUNDE	55	F	UNKNOWN	GRZZZZ	SC
KUNIGUNDE	17	F	UNKNOWN	GRZZZZ	SC
FRANZEN, JACOB	42	M	JNR	GRZZZZ	MD
MARGARETHE	40	F	UNKNOWN	GRZZZZ	MD
BARBARA	18	F	UNKNOWN	GRZZZZ	MD
MARIA	6	F	CHILD	GRZZZZ	MD
MARTHA	.04	F	INFANT	GRZZZZ	MD
HASBERGF, WILHELM	23	M	TLR	GRZZZZ	MO
IHDE, WILHELM	25	M	TLR	GRZZZZ	MO
GIEGLER, JOHANN	22	M	TLR	GRZZZZ	MO
TREPTE, MAX	36	M	TLR	GRZZZZ	MO
HEUDLER, EDUARD	22	M	TLR	GRZZZZ	MO
KEMPEL, GNIDE	23	M	TLR	GRZZZZ	MO
PRAEGER, CARL	26	M	TLR	GRZZZZ	MO
CZAKOWSKI, RUDOLPH	35	M	TLR	GRZZZZ	MO
DEIZACH, FRANZ	29	M	TLR	GRZZZZ	MO
GUENTHER, CARL	29	M	TLR	GRZZZZ	MO
RICK, CHRISTIAN	29	M	TLR	GRZZZZ	MO
ZIETZ, FRITZ	26	M	TLR	GRZZZZ	MO
PFAEFLE, GOTTLOB	40	M	LABR	GRZZZZ	WI
FRANZISKA	39	F	UNKNOWN	GRZZZZ	WI
GOTTLOB	16	M	LABR	GRZZZZ	WI
CAROLINE	13	F	CH	GRZZZZ	WI
CHRISTIAN	9	M	CHILD	GRZZZZ	WI
JOHANNE	7	F	CHILD	GRZZZZ	WI
FRIEDERICKE	5	F	CHILD	GRZZZZ	WI
CHRISTOPH	3	M	CHILD	GRZZZZ	WI
GUSTAV	2	M	CHILD	GRZZZZ	WI
HAFNER, ANNA	18	F	SVNT	GRZZZZ	OH
ZIEFLE, MARIE	.09	F	INFANT	GRZZZZ	OH
MUELLER, ANNA	32	F	DRSMKR	GRZZZZ	OH

PASSENGER	AGE	SEX	OCCUPATION	PRVVL DES
KLEUK, MARIA	21	F	DRSMKR	GRZZZZOH
BAESSLER, SOPHIE	17	F	SVNT	GRZZZZOH
HABEL, LEONHARD	27	M	UNKNOWN	GRZZZZDAK
KLEIBER, URSULA	17	F	SVNT	GRZZZZCIN
SEEGER, MARIE	15	F	SVNT	GRZZZZCIN
REMMEL, CONRAD	18	M	MCHT	GRZZZZCIN
PALSTER, JOHANN	24	M	MCHT	GRZZZZCIN
ARZBARGER, MARY	33	F	MLNR	GRZZZZCIN
DAUM, JOHANN	23	M	MSN	GRZZZZIL
HELLDOERFER, JOHANN	28	M	MSN	GRZZZZIL
PROBST, CAROLINE	21	F	SVNT	GRZZZZIL
KNAUER, AUGUST	24	M	JNR	GRZZZZIL
MERZ, FRIEDRICH	21	M	CL	GRZZZZIL
ROSINE	14	F	UNKNOWN	GRZZZZIL
DOPHIE	50	F	UNKNOWN	GRZZZZIL
SCHMIDT, JACOB	16	M	UNKNOWN	GRZZZZIL
BURGDORFF, CARL	18	M	LABR	GRZZZZMI
GEDALIUS, JEANETTE	25	F	DRSMKR	GRZZZZMD
KASZANK, JOSEFA	18	F	SVNT	GRZZZZMD
GERAWSKI, MARTIN	21	M	LABR	GRZZZZWV
MARIANNA	26	F	SVNT	GRZZZZWV
LICHTEC, CARL	52	M	FARMER	GRZZZZWV
NOWAKOWSKI, JOSEF	33	M	FARMER	GRZZZZWV
PAYZYNSKA, FRANZISKA	48	F	UNKNOWN	GRZZZZIN
CATHARINE	11	F	CH	GRZZZZIN
STANISLAWA	7	F	CHILD	GRZZZZIN
STANISLAW	4	M	CHILD	GRZZZZIN
MARTIN	2	M	CHILD	GRZZZZIN
HELENA	.11	F	INFANT	GRZZZZIN
RATZKOWSKI, JOSEPH	45	M	LABR	GRZZZZMN
ORLOWSKI, FELIX	16	M	LABR	GRZZZZMN
WALTER, FRANZ	28	M	LABR	GRZZZZMN
FRANZ	5	M	CHILD	GRZZZZMN
GUDERBY, ELISABETH	28	F	SVNT	GRZZZZMN
SZUMSKY, JOHN	16	M	UNKNOWN	GRZZZZIA
ANNA	21	F	SVNT	GRZZZZIA
REELMER, JOHANNA	24	F	SVNT	GRZZZZIA
MACOISZEK, PIETER	48	M	FARMER	GRZZZZIA
GRASILIENZKA, JOSEF	19	M	LABR	GRZZZZIA
LASCH, ANNA	16	F	UNKNOWN	GRZZZZIA
BORCHERT, AUGUST	56	M	FARMER	GRZZZZIA
JULIUS	26	M	UNKNOWN	GRZZZZIA
AUGUSTA	6	F	CHILD	GRZZZZIA
GOLTZ, HERMANN	25	M	SHMK	GRZZZZIA
KOTLOWSKA, ANNA	23	F	SVNT	GRZZZZIA
WURZER, ANDREA	36	F	SMSTS	SRZZZZCH
MARKESCHOFSKI, AUGUST	32	M	JNR	GRZZZZNE
ANNA	32	F	UNKNOWN	GRZZZZNE
AUGUSTE	3	F	CHILD	GRZZZZNE
LINA	.06	F	INFANT	GRZZZZNE
WEBER, BARBARA	18	F	SVNT	GRZZZZMD
LEWINSKY, NATHAN	26	M	SVNT	GRZZZZMD
KABACINSKA, STANISLAWA	20	F	UNKNOWN	GRZZZZIL
MUSZENSKY, ANTON	27	M	LABR	GRZZZZIL
LYDUCH, ANDREAS	18	M	TLR	GRZZZZIL
SZABLEWSKI, MICHAEL	60	M	JNR	GRZZZZIL
DOROTHEA	59	F	UNKNOWN	GRZZZZIL
MARIA	20	F	UNKNOWN	GRZZZZIL
ANTONIA	3	F	CHILD	GRZZZZIL
JOHANN	.11	M	INFANT	GRZZZZIL
ZAWORKA, JOSEFA	24	F	UNKNOWN	GRZZZZIL
STANISLAUS	.09	M	INFANT	GRZZZZIL
LEWANDOWSKI, BABESLAW	24	M	SHMK	GRZZZZIL
SCHUETZ, JOHANNE	60	F	UNKNOWN	GRZZZZIL
BARTHOL, IGNATZ	26	M	LABR	GRZZZZIL
KNOELLER, JULIUS	37	M	LABR	GRZZZZIL
CHARLOTTE	30	F	UNKNOWN	GRZZZZIL
AUGUST	16	M	UNKNOWN	GRZZZZIL
PLOCICH, CONSTANCIA	16	F	UNKNOWN	GRZZZZIL
STRAUSS, JOHANN	27	M	PNTR	GRZZZZIL
HELENA	26	F	UNKNOWN	GRZZZZIL
HELENA	.09	F	INFANT	GRZZZZIL
DEMSKY, MINNA	24	F	SVNT	GRZZZZDAK
MALKECWICZ, ADALIA	22	F	SVNT	GRZZZZDAK
BENDOWSKI, AUGUST	26	M	LABR	GRZZZZOH
JOSEFA	27	F	UNKNOWN	GRZZZZOH
AUGUST	.09	M	INFANT	GRZZZZOH
LESESKI, MARIANNA	23	F	UNKNOWN	GRZZZZOH
ANTON	.09	M	INFANT	GRZZZZOH
SOTREMBERG, WILHELMINE	39	F	UNKNOWN	GRZZZZOH
OTTILIE	36	F	UNKNOWN	GRZZZZOH
EMILIE	7	F	CHILD	GRZZZZOH
EMIL	5	M	CHILD	GRZZZZOH
ESCHEL, WILHELMINE	28	F	UNKNOWN	GRZZZZPA
ANNA	6	F	CHILD	GRZZZZPA
MARIA	.09	F	INFANT	GRZZZZPA
JAROSCHINSKI, VALENTIN	30	M	MSN	GRZZZZPA
JAROCZEWSKA, MICHALINA	31	F	UNKNOWN	GRZZZZPA
JOSEF	3	M	CHILD	GRZZZZPA
JOHANN	2	M	CHILD	GRZZZZPA
CATHARINE	.09	F	INFANT	GRZZZZPA
PAWLOWKA, JOSEFA	30	F	CK	GRZZZZIN
KATZLAH, ANDREZEI	28	M	LABR	GRZZZZIN
WISNIEWSKI, STANISLAUS	24	M	LABR	GRZZZZIN
NOWAK, FRANZISKA	21	F	SVNT	GRZZZZIN
STEINCKE, PAULINE	41	F	UNKNOWN	GRZZZZIN
HULDA	12	F	CH	GRZZZZIN
AMANDE	7	F	CHILD	GRZZZZIN
PAUL	6	M	CHILD	GRZZZZIN
BERTHA	.11	F	INFANT	GRZZZZIN
SEMRAM, WILHELM	29	M	LABR	GRZZZZPA
WEHMANN, SOPHIE	4	F	CHILD	GRZZZZOH
SIEBE, AUGUST	21	M	MSN	GRZZZZOH
THIE, HEINRICH	17	M	LABR	GRZZZZOH
RIETH, VALENTIN	32	M	LABR	GRZZZZOH
KAFATH, ALBERT	27	M	LABR	GRZZZZOH
WILHELMINE	19	F	UNKNOWN	GRZZZZOH
WIEZNCEWSKA, VERONIKA	22	F	SVNT	GRZZZZOH
WESTERHAMP, CHRISTIAN	32	M	LABR	GRZZZZOH
CATHRINE	31	F	UNKNOWN	GRZZZZOH
ELISE	7	F	CHILD	GRZZZZOH
DOROTHEA	6	F	CHILD	GRZZZZOH
LOUISE	4	F	CHILD	GRZZZZOH
U	2	F	CHILD	GRZZZZOH
HEINRICH	.10	M	INFANT	GRZZZZOH
HEHMANN, MARIA	16	F	UNKNOWN	GRZZZZOH
FISCHER, HEINRICH	25	M	MSN	GRZZZZMD
KOHN, ESTER	34	F	UNKNOWN	GRZZZZMD
HAEUSLE	7	F	CHILD	GRZZZZMD
GERSCHEN	4	F	CHILD	GRZZZZMD
SCHEULICK	.11	M	INFANT	GRZZZZMD
GOLKOWSKY, LUCIA	7	F	CHILD	GRZZZZMD
ANASTASIA	6	F	CHILD	GRZZZZMD
JOHANNA	4	F	CHILD	GRZZZZMD
PAULINE	.11	F	INFANT	GRZZZZMD
MUELLER, AUGUST	22	M	PNTR	GRZZZZMD
MARIA	19	M	PNTR	GRZZZZMD
MARTHA	.03	F	INFANT	GRZZZZMD
WALKOWSKY, FRANK	26	M	LABR	GRZZZZOH
SUSANNA	26	F	UNKNOWN	GRZZZZOH
STANISLAW	.01	M	INFANT	GRZZZZOH
JAN	.11	M	INFANT	GRZZZZOH
WENDZEWSKI, JAN	27	M	TLR	GRZZZZMD
BLASZIZAK, JOSEFA	26	F	UNKNOWN	GRZZZZIL
MAUSCHEFSKY, ALBERTINE	6	F	CHILD	GRZZZZIL
WISSEL, LINA	40	F	UNKNOWN	GRZZZZIN
LINA	6	F	CHILD	GRZZZZIN
BUDE, FRITZ	26	M	LABR	GRZZZZIN
GRUENWALD, AUGUST	60	M	PVTM	GRZZZZOH
LEINWANDT, ANDREAS	37	M	MCHT	GRZZZZOH
RENATE	27	F	UNKNOWN	GRZZZZOH
MARTHA	6	F	CHILD	GRZZZZOH
MATHILDE	3	F	CHILD	GRZZZZOH
GUSTAV	.11	M	INFANT	GRZZZZOH
BAUER, ANNA	44	F	UNKNOWN	GRZZZZPA
AUGUST	18	M	MSN	GRZZZZPA
MARTHA	16	F	MSN	GRZZZZPA
JOHANN	14	M	MSN	GRZZZZPA
CARL	11	M	CH	GRZZZZPA
MARIE	7	F	CHILD	GRZZZZPA

PASSENGER	AGE	SEX	OCCUPATION	PRVL DES
GUSTAV	3	M	CHILD	GRZZZZPA
WEISS, XAVER	29	M	LABR	GRZZZZWI
MARGARETHE	62	F	UNKNOWN	GRZZZZWI
ANNA	30	F	UNKNOWN	GRZZZZWI
KUNIGUNDE	.03	F	INFANT	GRZZZZWI
STRAHBERGER, MATTHIAS	61	M	FARMER	GRZZZZWI
ELISABETH	57	F	UNKNOWN	GRZZZZWI
MARIA	26	F	UNKNOWN	GRZZZZWI
ANTONIA	18	F	UNKNOWN	GRZZZZWI
MARIA	7	F	CHILD	GRZZZZWI
FETSCH, CRESCENZ	20	M	JNR	GRZZZZWI
HOECH, JOHANN	23	M	JNR	GRZZZZKY
KLEIN, AUGUST	25	M	MCHT	GRZZZZOH
GLAHN, HEINRICH	28	M	MCHT	GRZZZZWI
SIEBERT, ANNA	27	F	UNKNOWN	GRZZZZWI
U	3	F	CHILD	GRZZZZWI
JOSEF	.11	M	INFANT	GRZZZZWI
KUHLMANN, WILHELMINE	39	F	UNKNOWN	GRZZZZMN
THERESE	7	F	CHILD	GRZZZZMN
DOROTHEA	6	F	CHILD	GRZZZZMN
CARL	4	M	CHILD	GRZZZZMN
AUGUST	3	M	CHILD	GRZZZZMN
WILHELMINE	.11	F	INFANT	GRZZZZMN
HEINKEL, CATHRINE	25	F	UNKNOWN	GRZZZZKS
DORMANN, WILHELM	6	M	CHILD	GRZZZZKS
HELWIG, ERNSTINE	30	F	UNKNOWN	GRZZZZIL
KOCH, MARTIN	21	M	LABR	GRZZZZIL
MATUSCHECK, JOHANN	30	M	LABR	GRZZZZPA
KRABLEWSKY, FRANZ	50	M	LABR	GRZZZZIN
MARIANNA	50	F	UNKNOWN	GRZZZZIN
KROBLEWSKI, WLADISLAUS	7	M	CHILD	GRZZZZIN
KLEINSCHMIDT, JOSEFA	50	F	UNKNOWN	GRZZZZWI
MARTHA	4	F	CHILD	GRZZZZWI
STUPSKI, LEON	34	M	FARMER	GRZZZZKS
PIETCHOWSKI, CONSTANTIN	28	M	LABR	GRZZZZIL
PIETROWSKI, STANISLAW	28	M	FARMER	GRZZZZIL
TUCHLER, FRIEDRICH	41	M	JNR	GRZZZZIL
JULIE	38	F	UNKNOWN	GRZZZZIL
SIKORSKI, FRANZ	31	M	CHMAK	GRZZZZIL
FRANCISCA	31	F	UNKNOWN	GRZZZZIL
LEOCADIA	2	F	CHILD	GRZZZZIL
MERNIKA	.06	F	INFANT	GRZZZZIL
KNILLER, U	14	F	UNKNOWN	GRZZZZPA
FRIEDRICH	2	M	CHILD	GRZZZZPA
WICHLACZ, NICOLAUS	40	M	LABR	GRZZZZOH
FABIANKE, FRANZ	7	M	CHILD	GRZZZZIL
TOTSCHECK, MARKUS	21	M	TLR	GRZZZZWI
WAESEMANN, ELISE	15	F	UNKNOWN	GRZZZZMN
DREBER, JOHANN	49	M	JNR	GRZZZZMN
WILHELMINE	45	F	UNKNOWN	GRZZZZMN
CARL	6	M	CHILD	GRZZZZMN
FRIEDRICH	7	M	CHILD	GRZZZZMN
KRAUSE, ERNESTINE	18	F	SVNT	GRZZZZIL
STINSKY, HERMANN	38	M	GDNR	GRZZZZMN
ROSA	35	F	UNKNOWN	GRZZZZMN
FRIEDA	4	F	CHILD	GRZZZZMN
HEDWIG	.10	F	INFANT	GRZZZZMN
DREBE, WILHELMINE	6	F	CHILD	GRZZZZMN
KATZEL, HEINRICH	54	M	LABR	GRZZZZMN
HENRIETTE	58	F	UNKNOWN	GRZZZZMN
FRANZ	24	M	UNKNOWN	GRZZZZMN
PAUL	4	M	CHILD	GRZZZZMN
WENDT, BERTHA	24	F	SVNT	GRZZZZMN
PIESKE, OTTILIE	27	F	CK	GRZZZZMN
DREDER, CARL	25	M	SHMK	GRZZZZPA
EMMA	5	F	CHILD	GRZZZZPA
NEUBAUER, FRIEDRICH	36	M	FARMER	GRZZZZPA
AUGUSTE	33	F	UNKNOWN	GRZZZZPA
FRANZ	2	M	CHILD	GRZZZZPA
HELENE	.09	F	INFANT	GRZZZZPA
BAROWIAK, FRANZ	40	M	FARMER	GRZZZZIL
CATHARINE	33	F	UNKNOWN	GRZZZZIL
STANISLAUS	6	M	CHILD	GRZZZZIL
MARIE	3	F	CHILD	GRZZZZIL
WLADISLAUS	.06	M	INFANT	GRZZZZIL
IWANDOWSKI, JACOB	26	M	LABR	GRZZZZMI
SCHIDLOWSKI, VALENTIN	25	M	LABR	GRZZZZIL
SEIDEL, ENDLICH	34	M	LABR	GRZZZZIL
GOLDSTEIN, CURT	11	M	CH	GRZZZZIL
PFLUG, JOHANNE	43	F	UNKNOWN	GRZZZZIL
HERMANN	6	M	CHILD	GRZZZZIL
THOMAS, JOSEF	25	M	LABR	GRZZZZMD
BALBINA	69	F	UNKNOWN	GRZZZZMD
KUSCHMILOH, AUGUST	25	M	LABR	GRZZZZMD
AUGUSTE	29	F	UNKNOWN	GRZZZZMD
KUSCHMILEK, ANNA	.07	F	INFANT	GRZZZZMD
JANKOWSKI, AGNES	46	F	UNKNOWN	GRZZZZOH
KOENIG, JOSEF	36	M	LABR	GRZZZZOH
KLEINSCHMITH, JACOB	42	M	LABR	GRZZZZIL
FRANZ	7	M	CHILD	GRZZZZIL
LOUISE	6	F	CHILD	GRZZZZIL
KOENIG, MARDE	28	F	UNKNOWN	GRZZZZOH
FRANZ	.11	M	INFANT	GRZZZZOH
ANTON	3	M	CHILD	GRZZZZOH
SCHMIDT, WILHELM	32	M	JNR	GRZZZZKS
LINA	28	F	UNKNOWN	GRZZZZKS
BERTHA	2	F	CHILD	GRZZZZKS
U	.09	F	INFANT	GRZZZZKS
HARTMANN, GEORG	16	M	UNKNOWN	GRZZZZMO
STOERMER, RONDOLF	21	M	LABR	GRZZZZMD
FLOEHR, OSCAR	28	M	LABR	GRZZZZMD
CLARA	30	F	UNKNOWN	GRZZZZMD
MARGARETHE	.10	F	INFANT	GRZZZZMD
GROENERT, OTTILIE	29	F	UNKNOWN	GRZZZZMD
MARTHA	7	F	CHILD	GRZZZZMD
GEORG	3	M	CHILD	GRZZZZMD
GERKEN, CATHARINE	19	F	SVNT	GRZZZZPA
SCHWICH, FRITZ	28	M	TLR	GRZZZZPA
BUSCH, JOHANN	6	M	CHILD	GRZZZZPA
AROLD, FRIEDRICH	24	M	SHMK	GRZZZZPA
HUVELT, ANDRES	38	M	MSN	GRZZZZIL
FRANCISCA	38	F	UNKNOWN	GRZZZZIL
ANDREAS	60	M	UNKNOWN	GRZZZZIL
JOSEFA	7	F	CHILD	GRZZZZIL
ELISE	6	F	CHILD	GRZZZZIL
JOSEF	5	M	CHILD	GRZZZZIL
MARIA	3	F	CHILD	GRZZZZIL
ANDREAS	.07	M	INFANT	GRZZZZIL
STADLE, ALOIS	15	M	UNKNOWN	GRZZZZMI
BAUER, CONRAD	57	M	FARMER	GRZZZZMN
PAULINE	21	F	UNKNOWN	GRZZZZMN
ANNA	17	F	UNKNOWN	GRZZZZMN
JOSEF	15	M	UNKNOWN	GRZZZZMN
MARIE	11	F	CH	GRZZZZMN
CHRISTOPF	10	M	CH	GRZZZZMN
BAISCH, WILHELMINE	24	F	SVNT	GRZZZZMD
FLEMMING, HEINRICH	43	M	LABR	GRZZZZIN
CATHARINE	43	F	UNKNOWN	GRZZZZIN
CARL	14	M	UNKNOWN	GRZZZZIN
ELISE	10	F	CH	GRZZZZIN
GERHARDT	6	M	CHILD	GRZZZZIN
HELMICH, MARIA	22	F	UNKNOWN	GRZZZZIN
ELISE	6	F	CHILD	GRZZZZIN
SEEMANN, JOHANN	27	M	SLR	GRZZZZMD
MARIA	20	F	UNKNOWN	GRZZZZMD
MANSOLF, IDA	20	F	SVNT	GRZZZZMD
MUELLER, CONRAD	14	M	UNKNOWN	GRZZZZMD
LORENZ, JOSEF	16	M	UNKNOWN	GRZZZZMD
POPENFUSS, AUGUST	29	M	LABR	GRZZZZMD
AUGUSTE	31	F	UNKNOWN	GRZZZZMD
WILHELMINE	.11	F	INFANT	GRZZZZMD
BUCHHOLZ, JOSEFA	26	F	UNKNOWN	GRZZZZMD
STANISLAUS	5	M	CHILD	GRZZZZMD
MAKOURKA, STANISLAWA	54	F	UNKNOWN	GRZZZZMD
KASZAK, MARIANNA	33	F	UNKNOWN	GRZZZZPA
HEDWIG	6	F	CHILD	GRZZZZPA
ROSALIE	.11	F	INFANT	GRZZZZPA
PLICHTA, U	27	M	MCHT	GRZZZZMI
MALBURG, EUGEN	18	M	MCHT	GRZZZZMI
DROSZONOWSKI, STEFAN	25	M	LABR	GRZZZZMI

PASSENGER	AGE	SEX	OCCUPATION	PRVVL	DES
ANNA	23	F	UNKNOWN	GRZZZZ	MI
ZANIK, JOSEF	36	M	LABR	GRZZZZ	IL
FRANZISKA	28	F	UNKNOWN	GRZZZZ	IL
MARIANNA	7	F	CHILD	GRZZZZ	IL
WLADISLAUS	6	M	CHILD	GRZZZZ	IL
LUDWIG	.06	M	INFANT	GRZZZZ	IL
BRZEZINSKI, FRANZ	23	M	LABR	GRZZZZC	IN
SCHNEIDER, ERNESTINE	23	F	UNKNOWN	GRZZZZC	IN
WILHELMINE	5	F	CHILD	GRZZZZC	IN
PROCHMIEWSKI, ANTON	36	M	JNR	GRZZZZ	OH
MARGARETHE	28	F	UNKNOWN	GRZZZZ	OH
MICHALENKO	2	M	CHILD	GRZZZZ	OH
STEFAN	.04	M	INFANT	GRZZZZ	OH
GOERKE, WILHELMINE	50	F	UNKNOWN	GRZZZZ	IN
ASCHBREUNER, PAULINA	20	F	UNKNOWN	GRZZZZ	IN
FRITZ	18	M	UNKNOWN	GRZZZZ	IN
KONKOLEWSKA, ANNA	27	F	UNKNOWN	GRZZZZ	OH
CHOJUSKI, BERNARD	23	M	LABR	GRZZZZ	OH
ROTHKEGEL, ALOIS	35	M	LABR	GRZZZZ	WI
CONSTANTINE	35	F	UNKNOWN	GRZZZZ	WI
AGNES	7	F	CHILD	GRZZZZ	WI
PAUL	4	M	CHILD	GRZZZZ	WI
ALOIS	.11	M	INFANT	GRZZZZ	WI
PATSCHKOWSKI, CARL	16	M	UNKNOWN	GRZZZZD	AK
STRAUSS, JOHANN	36	M	FARMER	GRZZZZ	OH
CONCORDIA	33	F	UNKNOWN	GRZZZZ	OH
JOHANN	7	M	CHILD	GRZZZZ	OH
MARIA	6	F	CHILD	GRZZZZ	OH
ANNA	5	F	CHILD	GRZZZZ	OH
CARL	4	M	CHILD	GRZZZZ	OH
LOUISE	.11	F	INFANT	GRZZZZ	OH
WIEMER, PAUL	16	M	INF	GRZZZZ	OH
FEBBEN, CAROLINE	24	F	SVNT	GRZZZZ	OH
STOKELMANN, BERNHARD	44	M	FARMER	GRZZZZ	OH
ELISABETH	42	F	UNKNOWN	GRZZZZ	OH
HEINRICH	7	M	CHILD	GRZZZZ	OH
FRANZ	5	M	CHILD	GRZZZZ	OH
LOEWNER, JOHANN	58	M	JNR	GRZZZZ	IA
ZIESMER, AUGUSTE	20	F	SVNT	GRZZZZ	IA
KOSLOWSKI, GOTTFRIED	37	M	LABR	GRZZZZ	IA
MARIE	40	F	UNKNOWN	GRZZZZ	IA
BERTHA	2	F	CHILD	GRZZZZ	IA
ALBERT	.06	M	INFANT	GRZZZZ	IA
STRAUSS, CARL	33	M	FARMER	GRZZZZ	OH
ANNA	26	F	UNKNOWN	GRZZZZ	OH
MARIA	6	F	CHILD	GRZZZZ	OH
FRANZ	5	M	CHILD	GRZZZZ	OH
ELISABETH	2	F	CHILD	GRZZZZ	OH
ANNA	.09	F	INFANT	GRZZZZ	OH
HARZEMBECK, JOHANN	26	M	MSN	GRZZZZ	IL
POSTRACH, JOSEF	38	M	STCTR	GRZZZZ	IL
JOHANNA	18	F	UNKNOWN	GRZZZZ	IL
FELIX	6	M	CHILD	GRZZZZ	IL
MARIE	4	F	CHILD	GRZZZZ	IL
JOSEF	.11	M	INFANT	GRZZZZ	IL
ANNA	.11	F	INFANT	GRZZZZ	IL
THIE--, JOHANN	25	M	WTR	GRZZZZ	USA
KLEINOWSKY, ANTON	27	M	GZR	GRZZZZ	IL
MANCKE, ALBRECHT	40	M	LABR	GRZZZZ	IL
TOMANOWSKA, EMMA	28	F	CK	GRZZZZ	IL
LACZKOWSKI, JOHANN	20	M	LABR	GRZZZZ	IL
MATHEWS, GEORG	52	M	LABR	GRZZZZ	MD
MARGARETHE	45	F	UNKNOWN	GRZZZZ	MD
ELISABETH	15	F	UNKNOWN	GRZZZZ	MD
JOHANN	7	M	CHILD	GRZZZZ	MD
DERGANZ, MARTHA	30	F	UNKNOWN	GRZZZZ	MD
AUGUSTE	5	F	CHILD	GRZZZZ	MD
LANGE, REINHARD	4	M	CHILD	GRZZZZ	MD
FROEGER, ERNST	14	M	UNKNOWN	GRZZZZ	MD
PETZ, OTTO	14	M	UNKNOWN	GRZZZZ	MD
BERGMANN, LINA	22	F	MLNR	GRZZZZ	MD
HUETTL, MICHAEL	59	M	LABR	GRZZZZ	MD
BLECHSCHMIDT, ANTONIE	38	F	UNKNOWN	GRZZZZ	MD
MARIANNA	6	F	CHILD	GRZZZZ	MD
EBERHARD, FRIEDRIKE	28	F	CH	GRZZZZ	MD

PASSENGER	AGE	SEX	OCCUPATION	PRVVL	DES
EHLERS, REBEKA	25	F	UNKNOWN	GRZZZZ	MN
LANG, MARGARETE	57	F	UNKNOWN	GRZZZZ	OH
SCHLEE, JOHANN	7	M	CHILD	GRZZZZ	MD
SCHELL, AUGUST	48	M	JNR	GRZZZZ	MD
GRAF, OSWALD	48	M	FARMER	GRZZZZ	MN
JOSEF	24	M	FARMER	GRZZZZ	MN
NASER, JACOB	48	M	FARMER	GRZZZZ	OH
STROSSE, MARIE	20	F	SVNT	GRZZZZ	IN
KRAZSINIAK, MARTIN	46	M	LABR	GRZZZZ	IN
G-OLLONIA	64	F	UNKNOWN	GRZZZZ	IN
GRUNDBERG, OTTO	32	M	LABR	GRZZZZ	WI
ROGASE, ELISABETH	7	F	CHILD	GRZZZZ	IL
PLEGE, ROBERT	32	M	LABR	GRZZZZ	MD
BRAST, WILHELM	59	M	FARMER	GRZZZZ	WI
CAROLINE	47	F	UNKNOWN	GRZZZZ	WI
MARTHA	17	F	UNKNOWN	GRZZZZ	WI
RAKOWSKI, GUSTAV	24	M	JNR	GRZZZZ	WI
HAKER, MARIE	31	F	UNKNOWN	GRZZZZ	MD
BERTHA	5	F	CHILD	GRZZZZ	MD
WILHELM	3	F	CHILD	GRZZZZ	MD
KREUTZER, JOHANN	32	M	MCHT	GRZZZZ	WI
ZISCHALTZ, ALBERT	56	M	LABR	GRZZZZ	WI
ANTONIA	56	F	UNKNOWN	GRZZZZ	WI
PAULINA	19	F	UNKNOWN	GRZZZZ	WI
AUGUST	.05	M	INFANT	GRZZZZ	WI
WURSTER, MARIA	18	F	SVNT	GRZZZZ	MI
SCHILLING, WILHELM	22	M	SMH	GRZZZZ	MN
MENKE, JOHANN	24	M	FARMER	GRZZZZ	IL
HEDT, EDUARD	5	M	CHILD	GRZZZZ	MN
STUERMER, JOHANN	57	M	FARMER	GRZZZZ	IL
ANNA	53	F	UNKNOWN	GRZZZZ	IL
GEORG	20	M	FARMER	GRZZZZ	IL
HEINRICH	16	M	FARMER	GRZZZZ	IL
KLEINFELD, EDUARD	25	M	SHMK	GRZZZZ	WI
OTTO	30	M	SHMK	GRZZZZ	WI
AUGUSTE	25	F	UNKNOWN	GRZZZZ	WI
OTTO	3	M	CHILD	GRZZZZ	WI
ANNA	.06	F	INFANT	GRZZZZ	WI
RAKOFSKY, MATTHIAS	26	M	LABR	GRZZZZ	IL
MARGARETHE	24	F	UNKNOWN	GRZZZZ	IL
KALK, FRIEDRICH	47	M	MSN	GRZZZZ	KY
BRANDT, HERMAN	6	M	CHILD	GRZZZZ	KY
LUEBBERS, CAROLINE	37	F	UNKNOWN	GRZZZZ	IL
ADOLF	5	M	CHILD	GRZZZZ	IL
MEIERSOHN, EMMA	23	F	SVNT	GRZZZZ	BAL
WALTER, MINNA	25	F	UNKNOWN	GRZZZZ	IL
EMIL	6	M	CHILD	GRZZZZ	IL
STIELAW, CARL	61	M	FARMER	GRZZZZ	PA
FRIEDA	54	F	UNKNOWN	GRZZZZ	PA
HULDA	26	F	SVNT	GRZZZZ	PA
OTTO	5	M	CHILD	GRZZZZ	PA
HERMANN	26	M	FARMER	GRZZZZ	PA
WIETZKE, HEINRICH	33	M	SHMK	GRZZZZ	PA
JOHANNA	32	F	UNKNOWN	GRZZZZ	PA
PAUL	6	M	CHILD	GRZZZZ	PA
ANNA	5	F	CHILD	GRZZZZ	PA
MINNA	2	F	CHILD	GRZZZZ	PA
ELSA	.02	F	INFANT	GRZZZZ	PA
ZIEGLER, GERTRUD	22	F	UNKNOWN	GRZZZZ	IA
CATHARINA	2	F	CHILD	GRZZZZ	IA
VOGEL, FRANCISCA	28	F	UNKNOWN	GRZZZZ	OH
PAUL	6	M	CHILD	GRZZZZ	OH
MUELLER, WILHELM	60	M	FARMER	GRZZZZ	KY
HEINRICH	27	M	FARMER	GRZZZZ	KY
WILHELM	33	M	FARMER	GRZZZZ	KY
FRIEDRICH	20	M	FARMER	GRZZZZ	KY
ELISABETH	15	F	FARMER	GRZZZZ	KY
CATHARINA	7	F	CHILD	GRZZZZ	KY
DERGANZ, AUGUSTE	2	F	CHILD	GRZZZZ	MD
MARINE	.07	F	INFANT	GRZZZZ	MD
ALMS, WILHELM	28	M	MCHT	GRZZZZ	MD
WEHLING, HERMANN	32	M	MLR	GRZZZZ	MD
KNACH, AUGUST	35	M	UNKNOWN	GRZZZZ	NE
HERMINE	37	F	UNKNOWN	GRZZZZ	NE
MARIE	6	F	CHILD	GRZZZZ	NE

PASSENGER	AGE	SEX	OCCUPATION	PRVL	DES
FERDINAND	4	M	CHILD	GRZZZZNE	
ROBERT	00	M	UNKNOWN	GRZZZZNE	
BERTHA	.09	F	INFANT	GRZZZZNE	
LAWRENZ, JULIUS	24	M	MSN	GRZZZZOH	
OTTO	22	M	MSN	GRZZZZOH	
POLOWSKI, ANNA	00	F	CH	GRZZZZOH	
GUSTAV	5	M	CHILD	GRZZZZOH	
GELHAUS, FRIEDRICH	34	M	CPTR	GRZZZZIL	
LANG, MARGARETHE	6	F	CHILD	GRZZZZIL	
FIBKE, CLAUS	54	M	FARMER	GRZZZZIA	
META	29	F	UNKNOWN	GRZZZZIA	
ENGEL	4	F	CHILD	GRZZZZIA	

SHIP: ALASKA

FROM: LIVERPOOL AND QUEENSTOWN
TO: NEW YORK
ARRIVED: 21 MAY 1888

PASSENGER	AGE	SEX	OCCUPATION	PRVL	DES
PURSCHIS, MARCUS	42	M	LABR	GRZZZZUSA	
SZIGALS, CHENE	43	F	MA	GRZZZZUSA	
BASCHE	10	M	CH	GRZZZZUSA	
SCHEPSEL	9	M	CHILD	GRZZZZUSA	
RIWKE	7	M	CHILD	GRZZZZUSA	
SALOMON	4	M	CHILD	GRZZZZUSA	
KATZ, ROSCHE	19	F	SP	GRZZZZUSA	
FRIEDMAN, CHAIE	40	F	MA	GRZZZZUSA	
LEIB	7	M	CHILD	GRZZZZUSA	
JACOB	4	M	CHILD	GRZZZZUSA	
LEBERFARB, JOSEF	30	M	LABR	GRZZZZUSA	
LEWIS, LIMCHE	50	M	LABR	GRZZZZUSA	
ISAAC	17	M	LABR	GRZZZZUSA	
KANTON, SCHEME	21	F	SP	GRZZZZUSA	
ROPIEN, SCHEINE	30	F	SP	GRZZZZUSA	
STURMAN, CHAIE	23	F	MA	GRZZZZUSA	
JOCHEN	6	M	CHILD	GRZZZZUSA	
CHAIM	3	M	CHILD	GRZZZZUSA	
MIFFAIL, JOSEPH	38	M	LABR	GRZZZZUSA	
WEISZ, CHAIE	18	F	SP	GRZZZZUSA	
GREENWALD, CHAI	50	F	SP	GRZZZZUSA	
HARRILYOK, ANNA	20	F	SP	GRZZZZUSA	
LORENIG, THERESIA	50	F	MA	GRZZZZUSA	
ANNA	15	F	SP	GRZZZZUSA	
KATHARINA	11	F	CH	GRZZZZUSA	
WEISSBERG, CHAIE	11	F	CH	GRZZZZUSA	
STURMAN, BROCHE	.10	F	INFANT	GRZZZZUSA	
FREDMAN, RACHEL	.08	F	INFANT	GRZZZZUSA	
ROSENTHAL, CARL	51	M	GENT	GRZZZZUSA	
BERTHA	40	F	W	GRZZZZUSA	
SPREGEL, REBECCA	21	F	SP	GRZZZZUSA	
WEISS, NATHAN	27	M	TLR	GRZZZZUSA	
CHAIMOWICZ, MENDEL	48	M	GENT	GRZZZZUSA	
RADSICK, ABRAHAM	11	M	CH	GRZZZZUSA	
CHAIMOWICZ, MANASSEL	25	M	FARMER	GRZZZZUSA	
GITTEL	20	F	W	GRZZZZUSA	
LIMENJEW, MOSES	30	M	FARMER	GRZZZZUSA	
ROSA	25	F	W	GRZZZZUSA	
GARG, SOLOMON	19	M	LABR	GRZZZZUSA	
SCHEINE	18	F	W	GRZZZZUSA	
FRIEDLAND, W.	30	M	FARMER	PRZZZZUSA	

SHIP: EGYPT

FROM: LIVERPOOL
TO: NEW YORK
ARRIVED: 21 MAY 1888

PASSENGER	AGE	SEX	OCCUPATION	PRVL	DES
SMITHSON, JOSEF	25	M	LABR	PRAARRUSA	
NELSON, JONS	21	M	LABR	PRAARRUSA	
BENGT	24	M	LABR	PRAARRUSA	
KRUKMANS, L.	45	M	LABR	PRAARRUSA	
PEHL, MARTEN	19	M	LABR	PRAARRUSA	
HWILIS, MIKAS	27	M	LABR	PRAARRUSA	
FERTILSCEON, SAML.	45	M	LABR	PRAARRUSA	
VAL, OLAF	19	M	LABR	PRAARRUSA	
MARTENSEN, KE--T	19	M	LABR	PRAARRUSA	
MACHE, SCHLOME	31	M	LABR	PRAARRUSA	
MANSON, MAES	36	M	LABR	PRAARRUSA	
JONSON, A.	30	M	LABR	PRAARRUSA	
JOHANSON, HOF	27	M	LABR	PRAARRUSA	
ROGNAN, ALE-L.	19	M	LABR	PRAARRUSA	
AUTERHOLM, N.	22	M	LABR	PRAARRUSA	
LARSON, A.	20	M	LABR	PRAARRUSA	
ROSENGREA, U	35	M	LABR	PRAARRUSA	
ANDERSON, ALDREW	25	M	LABR	PRAARRUSA	
NILSSON, PEHR.	25	M	LABR	PRAARRUSA	
OLSON, PEHR.	18	M	LABR	PRAARRUSA	
FARLESTEIN, JOSEPH	25	M	LABR	PRAARRUSA	
KOLESCHI, ELEWISTIAN	20	M	LABR	PRAARRUSA	
GRANDE, BRODER	35	M	LABR	PRAARRUSA	
JOHANSON, J.A.	21	M	LABR	PRAARRUSA	
EKSTADO, J.A.	19	M	LABR	PRAARRUSA	
LARSSON, PETER	22	M	LABR	PRAARRUSA	
CHERCHUSIN, ISAAC	37	M	LABR	PRAARRUSA	
BULITER, ADONIS	30	M	LABR	PRAARRUSA	
CHATSON	25	M	LABR	PRAARRUSA	
HASSELGVEST, K.A.	25	M	LABR	PRAARRUSA	
OLSSON, AUG.	21	M	LABR	PRAARRUSA	
JOHANNAN, J.A.	31	M	LABR	PRAARRUSA	
ROSESGREEN, OLA	17	M	LABR	PRAARRUSA	
LONBRONITZ, MALES	22	M	LABR	PRAARRUSA	
MENDEL	21	M	LABR	PRAARRUSA	
NILSON, ANDREW	25	M	LABR	PRAARRUSA	
PAULSSEN, JOHANNES	28	M	LABR	PRAARRUSA	
VALSTED, O.	21	M	LABR	PRAARRUSA	
ROBBE, J.	22	M	LABR	PRAARRUSA	
GAZENKA, ENDRIS	30	M	LABR	PRAARRUSA	
NAKNELAS, ANTONAS	25	M	LABR	PRAARRUSA	
BAKLAM, F.O.	26	M	LABR	PRAARRUSA	
LARSON, A.G.	28	M	LABR	PRAARRUSA	
JOHNSON, DANIEL	25	M	LABR	PRAARRUSA	
SOLOMONSON, JOHN	30	M	LABR	PRAARRUSA	
GOLDBERG, MEIER	38	M	LABR	PRAARRUSA	
ERIKSEN, ROB.	26	M	LABR	PRAARRUSA	
GROSSEMETE, MOSES	21	M	LABR	PRAARRUSA	
HOPFENBACH, JOSEPH	23	M	LABR	PRAARRUSA	
SMITH, MICHAEL	27	M	LABR	PRAARRUSA	
MERLIS, SAML.	18	M	LABR	PRAARRUSA	
SKROBONS, JOSEF	29	M	LABR	PRAARRUSA	
ZELNOST, JACOB	32	M	LABR	PRAARRUSA	
PETROSSON, JOHN	32	M	LABR	PRAARRUSA	
BENGSTON, SVERE	20	M	LABR	PRAARRUSA	
SCHUMSKA, JONAS	24	M	LABR	PRAARRUSA	
LARSON, NELS	29	M	LABR	PRAARRUSA	
PEARSON, A.	38	M	LABR	PRAARRUSA	
A.	17	M	LABR	PRAARRUSA	
HANSEN, PETER	37	M	LABR	PRAARRUSA	
AMUNDSEN, JULIUS	28	M	LABR	PRAARRUSA	
PETERSON, OLAF	18	M	LABR	PRAARRUSA	
HANDLAND, MICHAEL	20	M	LABR	PRAARRUSA	
WANDE, O--IG	20	M	LABR	PRAARRUSA	
ANAREWKENITZ, F.	28	M	LABR	PRAARRUSA	
AMUNDSON, A.	33	M	LABR	PRAARRUSA	
SCHILSKONSKY, ABR.	26	M	LABR	PRAARRUSA	
RUCKS, FRED.	23	M	LABR	PRAARRUSA	

PASSENGER	AGE	SEX	OCCUPATION	PRVL	DES
NAMRRO, PAULUS	25	M	LABR		PRAARRUSA
FHEORD, JOHAN	35	M	LABR		PRAARRUSA
FLYNN, THOS.	20	M	LABR		PRAARRUSA
JOHNSON, JOHAN	26	M	LABR		PRAARRUSA
KELSSON, HANS	19	M	LABR		PRAARRUSA
BUZINSKA, ADOMS	25	M	LABR		PRAARRUSA
GOLDKOOS, CH.	20	M	LABR		PRAARRUSA
FREDFIELD, MOSES	40	M	LABR		PRAARRUSA
FRUEL, ITZEK	18	M	LABR		PRAARRUSA
RUSSFIELD, LEIB	25	M	LABR		PRAARRUSA
SCHWARTZ, W.	24	M	LABR		PRAARRUSA
REIST, HERMAN	32	M	LABR		PRAARRUSA
WILSKY, JACOB	17	M	LABR		PRAARRUSA
SEGAL, CHONA	24	M	LABR		PRAARRUSA
STRANBERGER, MORDCHEL	42	M	LABR		PRAARRUSA
VOIT, CHAS.	18	M	LABR		PRAARRUSA
MATUSEWITZ, STAN.	23	M	LABR		PRAARRUSA
BRESTOW, SCHLOME	25	M	LABR		PRAARRUSA
MALONEY, JOHN	16	M	LABR		PRAARRUSA
HOLING-EN, CARL-N.	20	M	LABR		PRAARRUSA
FRIBERG, CARL-A.	19	M	LABR		PRAARRUSA
BALSCHAR, JOSEF	23	M	LABR		PRAARRUSA
WALWALIS, MICHAEL	30	M	LABR		PRAARRUSA
DARCHOWSKY, MENDEL	14	M	LABR		PRAARRUSA
GR-P-KES, O.P.	28	M	LABR		PRAARRUSA
JURI	28	M	LABR		PRAARRUSA
OZERNE-, PETER	38	M	LABR		PRAARRUSA
BUTREMONWITZ, J.	30	M	LABR		PRAARRUSA
JOHNSON, ANDREW	17	M	LABR		PRAARRUSA
KELSSEN, JONS	19	M	LABR		PRAARRUSA
MORDIKAN, M.	20	M	LABR		PRAARRUSA
JAMES, RICHARD	24	M	LABR		PRAARRUSA
CARLSON, ADOLF	22	M	LABR		PRAARRUSA
MALSTROM, JOHAN	27	M	LABR		PRAARRUSA
ANDERSON, C.P.	16	M	LABR		PRAARRUSA
WETTELAND, THORWALD	17	M	LABR		PRAARRUSA
BROOMSHABERS, THORWALD	20	M	LABR		PRAARRUSA
FRANK, S.	22	M	LABR		PRAARRUSA
JOHNSSON, GUSLOF	21	M	LABR		PRAARRUSA
ARENWAILER, MARCUS	20	M	LABR		PRAARRUSA
JONSON, P.A.	45	M	LABR		PRAARRUSA
JOHNSON, F.	35	M	LABR		PRAARRUSA
WERONOWITZ, PETER	21	M	LABR		PRAARRUSA
POSTOWSKY, MARKUS	17	M	LABR		PRAARRUSA
SUCCUSSON, J.E.	24	M	LABR		PRAARRUSA
BENGSON, B.K.	24	M	LABR		PRAARRUSA
SVENSSON, A.	21	M	LABR		PRAARRUSA
ANDLERCON, E.	24	M	LABR		PRAARRUSA
MYNDAS, PARK	43	M	LABR		PRAARRUSA
FACHNER, JOSEF	30	M	LABR		PRAARRUSA
JOHANSON, JULY	26	M	LABR		PRAARRUSA
SNELLSON, PETER	32	M	LABR		PRAARRUSA
LUCASSON, SVEN	41	M	LABR		PRAARRUSA
MATHEASSON, W.	25	M	LABR		PRAARRUSA
WAHLGOUST, AUG.	22	M	LABR		PRAARRUSA
ANDERSON, J.A.	25	M	LABR		PRAARRUSA
PETERSON, CARL	26	M	LABR		PRAARRUSA
JOHNSON, J.E.	23	M	LABR		PRAARRUSA
LARSON, J.W.	20	M	LABR		PRAARRUSA
EMANUELSON, J.	19	M	LABR		PRAARRUSA
HALBERG, J.B.	33	M	LABR		PRAARRUSA
STEVENSON, DAN	21	M	LABR		PRAARRUSA
ALMAN, CARL	20	M	LABR		PRAARRUSA
SMUALA, J.	24	M	LABR		PRAARRUSA
GISTOPSON, C.A.	17	M	LABR		PRAARRUSA
OLSSEN, EMIL	20	M	LABR		PRAARRUSA
GRANTON, FOM	24	M	LABR		PRAARRUSA
HAUSSEN, HACKEN	32	M	LABR		PRAARRUSA
OLSEN, NILS	20	M	LABR		PRAARRUSA
PENSON, HAZBARTH	19	M	LABR		PRAARRUSA
BROWN, JOSEF	27	M	LABR		PRAARRUSA
NILSON, CARL	27	M	LABR		PRAARRUSA
WITTKORFF, KARIL	18	M	LABR		PRAARRUSA
RYCHWORT, C.	66	M	LABR		PRAARRUSA
SCHNELBERG, SCHOEL	27	M	LABR		PRAARRUSA

PASSENGER	AGE	SEX	OCCUPATION	PRVL	DES
HARWITZ, MICHL.	23	M	LABR		PRAARRUSA
EDINA, ESSI	25	M	LABR		PRAARRUSA
KYPLAN, ABRAH.	22	M	LABR		PRAARRUSA
DOBRUSCHI	10	M	CH		PRAARRUSA
LASSON, ERIN	20	M	LABR		PRAARRUSA
SOLOMON, JACOB	28	M	LABR		PRAARRUSA
MARTENSEN, GUSTAF-ELOF	19	M	LABR		PRAARRUSA
PRUSKI, ABRAH.	36	M	LABR		PRAARRUSA
ANDERSON, JONS	27	M	LABR		PRAARRUSA
OLOSSE, NILS	22	M	LABR		PRAARRUSA
JORKEWITZ, MARTIN	22	M	LABR		PRAARRUSA
LANE, ADOLF	19	M	LABR		PRAARRUSA
WINKAR, KASPAR	45	M	LABR		PRAARRUSA
KENNEDY, JAMES	18	M	LABR		PRAARRUSA
SEPPA, AUH.	39	M	LABR		PRAARRUSA
OKEGNAN, ANDERS	24	M	LABR		PRAARRUSA
PERSSON, P.	22	M	LABR		PRAARRUSA
RASCHKOWSKY, C.	26	M	LABR		PRAARRUSA
HOLM, MIKOLM	20	M	LABR		PRAARRUSA
BERNSKER, C.A.	19	M	LABR		PRAARRUSA
JOHNSSON, HERMANN	22	M	LABR		PRAARRUSA
WATLGROIST, G.A.	22	M	LABR		PRAARRUSA
LARSON, A.	49	M	LABR		PRAARRUSA
BENSTON, A.	18	M	LABR		PRAARRUSA
MIKULSKY, KAROL.	23	M	LABR		PRAARRUSA
BRONISY, CH.	30	M	LABR		PRAARRUSA
C.	20	M	LABR		PRAARRUSA
ANDERSON, S.J.	22	M	LABR		PRAARRUSA
AUSTRIA, STANISH	23	M	LABR		PRAARRUSA
GRODZANSKY, J.	29	M	LABR		PRAARRUSA
FECHORCHOW, ABR.	28	M	LABR		PRAARRUSA
ISCHERCHOW, ZEZOK	14	M	LABR		PRAARRUSA
WEIWETZKI, A.	29	M	LABR		PRAARRUSA
BIGOMSON, CHRISTIAN	30	M	LABR		PRAARRUSA
M.M.	17	M	LABR		PRAARRUSA
JAMS, JAS.A.	11	M	LABR		PRAARRUSA
SAM.	10	M	LABR		PRAARRUSA
ANDERSEN, CARL	26	M	LABR		PRAARRUSA
BERG, J.A.	22	M	LABR		PRAARRUSA
CARL	18	M	LABR		PRAARRUSA
JEKLAM	16	M	LABR		PRAARRUSA

SHIP: FURNESSIA

FROM: GLASGOW AND MOVILLE
TO: NEW YORK
ARRIVED: 21 MAY 1888

PASSENGER	AGE	SEX	OCCUPATION	PRVL	DES
BRUNN, MAX	25	M	MUSN		GRZZZZUSA
ROSHMAN, R	45	F	DMS		GRZZZZUSA
ROSE	19	F	DMS		GRZZZZUSA
SANDLER, N	33	F	DMS		GRZZZZUSA
WALTER, WILHELMINE	30	F	UNKNOWN		GRZZZZUSA
U	00	F	INF		GRZZZZUSA
WEINSTEIN, SIMA	19	F	DMS		GRZZZZUSA
KROF, JOSEPHINE	25	F	NRS		GRZZZZUSA
GREGORRANSKI, W	28	M	FRMN		GRZZZZUSA
HELLVIG, GEO	19	M	JNR		GRZZZZUSA
KALLER, JOSEF	26	M	TLR		GRZZZZUSA
KAMMINSKI, U	30	M	LABR		GRZZZZUSA
KAHAN, MENDEL	30	M	LABR		GRZZZZUSA
KUMMER, G	20	M	LABR		GRZZZZUSA
LEIBLI, CARL	21	M	TLR		GRZZZZUSA
MAIER, JOSEF	26	M	LABR		GRZZZZUSA
NOLITSERAK, FRANZ	21	M	LABR		GRZZZZUSA
SERTGAUGER, HEINRICH	26	M	LABR		GRZZZZUSA
SILBERMAN, SOLOMON	33	M	TLR		GRZZZZUSA
SAUDER, EDUARD	36	M	SCHM		GRZZZZUSA
JEHNEL, HERMEN	25	M	LABR		GRZZZZUSA
WOLF, JACOB	26	M	LABR		GRZZZZUSA

SHIP: UMBRIA

FROM: LIVERPOOL AND QUEENSTOWN
TO: NEW YORK
ARRIVED: 21 MAY 1888

PASSENGER	AGE	SEX	OCCUPATION	PRVL/DES
KLEUTHWOUTH, JOHN	24	M	LABR	GRAAKHUSA
SALTZWEDEL, WILHELM	25	M	FARMER	GRAAKHUSA
HERRMAN, WILLIAM	22	M	CL	GRADLDUSA
SELS, DETER	18	M	LABR	GRACBFUSA
WESTPHAL, CARL	19	M	LABR	GRACBFUSA
KUNSE, CATHERINE	24	F	SVNT	GRACBFUSA
LOKKEN, BOUNKE	50	M	FARMER	GRAAKHUSA
RENNE	40	F	W	GRAAKHUSA
RENNE	11	F	CH	GRAAKHUSA
GESCHE	9	F	CHILD	GRAAKHUSA
ANTGA	5	F	CHILD	GRAAKHUSA
JURREN	3	M	CHILD	GRAAKHUSA
HENRY	.11	M	INFANT	GRAAKHUSA
GUSHECK, JOSIAH	18	M	LABR	GRAAKHUSA
RICHTER, RACHEL	50	F	MA	GRAAKHUSA
KARAFRNY, KATHERINA	25	F	SVNT	GRACBFUSA
BUNDLIN, FRANK	55	M	MECH	GRZZZZUSA
LOKKEN, TALLKE	7	F	CHILD	GRAAKHUSA
L---OLFER, CAROLINE	40	F	SVNT	GRAAKHUSA
RICHTER	7	M	CHILD	GRAAKHUSA
MERMOOD, AUGUST-S.	62	M	UNKNOWN	SRZZZZSW
BOOS, GEORGE	29	M	TRVLR	SRADLDGR
ALEXANDER, EDMUND	26	M	ACCT	SRADBQFR
U, RENE	46	F	UNKNOWN	SRADBQFR
MABELOTRE, LONIE	30	F	SVNT	SRADBQFR

SHIP: AUSTRALIA

FROM: HAMBURG
TO: NEW YORK
ARRIVED: 22 MAY 1888

PASSENGER	AGE	SEX	OCCUPATION	PRVL/DES
HEIDORN, FRIEDR.	16	M	LABR	PRZZZZNY
MUSALL, MARTIN	60	M	LABR	PRZZZZNY
WILHE.	26	F	CH	PRZZZZNY
AMELIE	22	F	CH	PRZZZZNY
BRAESEN, WILH.	19	M	LABR	HBZZZZNY
ECKE, WILH.	28	M	SHMK	PRZZZZNY
LUETT, CARL	24	M	FARMER	PRZZZZNY
LECKSCHEID, CARL	25	M	FARMER	PRZZZZNY
HEIDORN, HEINR.	19	M	GDNR	PRZZZZNY
POKARSKY, ANDREAS	42	M	LABR	PRZZZZNY
MARIANNE	32	F	W	PRZZZZNY
MACIEJEWSKY, WOYCICH	24	M	LABR	PRZZZZNY
NOWICKY, FRANZ	16	M	LABR	PRZZZZNY
BLANCK, HEINR.	57	M	CPT	HBZZZZPIT
HOPPE, ALBERT	23	M	FARMER	PRZZZZNY
HINZ, AUGUST	34	M	LABR	PRZZZZNY
ELIS.	30	F	W	PRZZZZUNK
MARIE	6	F	CHILD	PRZZZZUNK
JOH.	3	M	CHILD	PRZZZZUNK
PAUL	.11	M	INFANT	PRZZZZUNK
SANDT, CARL	40	M	LABR	PRZZZZUNK
PAULE.	38	F	W	PRZZZZUNK
MARTHE.	16	F	CH	PRZZZZUNK
ALBERT	9	M	CHILD	PRZZZZUNK
IDA	8	F	CHILD	PRZZZZUNK
FRIEDRICH	7	M	CHILD	PRZZZZUNK
BOEHMKE, WILH.	14	M	LABR	PRZZZZMSN
STEINBECK, FRIED.	53	M	SHMK	HBZZZZNY
BECKMANN, WILH.	33	M	BKBNDR	PRZZZZNY
DIETRICHSON, EDUARD	24	M	LABR	PRZZZZNY
CARSTENSON, ANDREAS	22	M	SMH	PRZZZZNY
JOHANNESON, AUGUST	30	M	FARMER	PRZZZZNY
GUSTAVSON, FRANZ	25	M	FARMER	PRZZZZUNK
JAHNKE, AUGUST	34	M	FARMER	PRZZZZNY
WENSKO, AUGUSTE	24	F	SVNT	PRZZZZNY
GROMKOWSKA, JULIANE	28	F	WO	PRZZZZNY
JAN	8	M	CHILD	PRZZZZNY
FALKOWSKY, PETER	20	M	FARMER	PRZZZZNY
TRUPPECK, EUGEN	17	M	LABR	PRZZZZNY
HENTZE, FELIX	21	M	MCHT	PRZZZZNY
LOESER, CARL-FR.	38	M	CPTR	PRZZZZNY
MARG.	35	F	W	PRZZZZNY
CARL	9	M	CHILD	PRZZZZNY
WILHE.	8	F	CHILD	PRZZZZNY
FRIEDA	7	F	CHILD	PRZZZZNY
CATH.	5	F	CHILD	PRZZZZNY
AUG.	2	M	CHILD	PRZZZZNY
JOH.	.09	M	INFANT	PRZZZZNY
KUNASZKIEWICZ, WYCIK	32	M	LABR	PRZZZZNY
POKARSKY, STANISLAUS	23	M	LABR	PRZZZZNY
JOHE.	8	F	CHILD	PRZZZZNY
LORENZ	5	M	CHILD	PRZZZZNY
WLADISLAWA	.09	F	INFANT	PRZZZZNY
FREITAG, KATH.	28	F	WO	BVZZZZNY
OELSCHLAEGEL, GEORG	16	M	SMH	BVZZZZNY
LEMBERG, HERM.	16	M	LABR	PRZZZZNY
KORNELIUS, ELIS.	25	F	SVNT	BVZZZZNY
MELSEN, JUERGEN	27	M	LABR	PRZZZZNY
JOENS, CATHR.	57	F	WO	PRZZZZNY
HERM.	18	F	CH	PRZZZZNY
DANKER, GUSTAV	16	M	LABR	PRZZZZNY
LORENZEN, PETER	56	M	PNTR	PRZZZZNY
SOPHIE	52	F	W	PRZZZZNY
PETER	16	M	CH	PRZZZZNY
GRIMME, DANIEL	41	M	SHMK	PRZZZZNY
DUYSEN, GRIMME-DUYE	32	M	LABR	PRZZZZNY
SCHMIDT, FERDIN.	29	M	LABR	PRZZZZNY
MARIE	30	F	W	PRZZZZNY
ANNA	6	F	CHILD	PRZZZZNY
FRIEDR.	4	M	CHILD	PRZZZZNY
QUANTE, WILH.	28	M	FARMER	PRZZZZNY
HOELZER, JOH.	21	M	MCHT	PRZZZZNY
JADAMOWSKY, ANTON	48	M	CPTR	PRZZZZNY
KLEVER, MARIE	57	F	WO	PRZZZZPLY
JOH.	20	M	CH	PRZZZZPLY
WILH.	15	M	CH	PRZZZZPLY
FRIEDRKE.	22	F	CH	PRZZZZPLY
BAECKER, LOUISE	28	F	CH	PRZZZZMIL
STOLP, ALMA	20	F	SVNT	PRZZZZNY
ANTONIE	16	F	SVNT	PRZZZZNY
MAYER, EUGEN	16	M	MCHT	WMZZZZNY
LAUR, MARIE	35	F	SVNT	WMZZZZNY
WERNER, CHARLOTTE	22	F	SVNT	PRZZZZNY
DOELL, BERTHA	21	F	SVNT	PRZZZZNY
PFEIFFER, CONRAD	55	M	FARMER	PRZZZZNY
CHRISTE.	53	F	W	PRZZZZNY
PETER	9	F	CHILD	PRZZZZNY
HENRIETTE	6	F	CHILD	PRZZZZNY
NISKILOWSKA, MARIE	24	F	SVNT	PRZZZZNY
CASRIEL, BERNH.	16	M	LABR	PRZZZZNY
KALKA, FRANZ	17	M	TLR	PRZZZZNY
RASPEDA, CONST.	20	M	LABR	PRZZZZNY
THIEL, JOHE.	14	M	SVNT	PRZZZZUNK
FRIED.	9	M	CHILD	PRZZZZNY
NOR, PETER	47	M	LABR	PRZZZZNY
BOHNHAUSEN, FRIEDR.	35	M	LABR	PRZZZZNY
BERTHA	34	F	W	PRZZZZNY
FRANZ	9	M	CHILD	PRZZZZNY
WEICHERT, GEORG	22	M	SMH	SYZZZZNY
FRITZ, ALBERT	28	M	MSN	PRZZZZNY
IDA	23	F	W	PRZZZZNY
FRIDA	.01	F	INFANT	PRZZZZNY
HUNKE, ANNA	50	F	WO	PRZZZZNY
NATHAN, SALLY	22	F	LABR	PRZZZZNY
CZAJKA, CATHRINE	40	F	WO	PRZZZZNY
FRANZ	9	M	CHILD	PRZZZZNY

PASSENGER	AGE	SEX	OCCUPATION	PRVL	DES
MARIANE	6	F	CHILD		PRZZZZNY
STANISLAV	.11	M	INFANT		PRZZZZNY
SCHMIDT, ALBERT	18	M	LABR		PRZZZZNY
KUECHEL, BERTHA	30	F	WO		PRZZZZNY
GERT.	3	F	CHILD		PRZZZZNY
DEJA, STANISLAUS	16	M	LABR		PRZZZZNY
ANNE	19	F	SVNT		PRZZZZNY
HARTMANN, JOHANN	35	M	LABR		PRZZZZNY
ANNA	32	F	W		PRZZZZNY
FRITZ	9	M	CHILD		PRZZZZNY
HUGO	8	M	CHILD		PRZZZZNY
ANNA	7	F	CHILD		PRZZZZNY
ERNST	5	M	CHILD		PRZZZZNY
ADOLF	.10	M	INFANT		PRZZZZNY
SCHWALBE, OTTILIE	22	F	SVNT		PRZZZZNY
MOTZKE, ANDRAS	28	M	LABR		PRZZZZNY
HEDWIG	25	F	W		PRZZZZNY
ANTON	.11	M	INFANT		PRZZZZNY
ADAMCZYK, JOH.	48	M	TLR		PRZZZZNY
SCHROEDER, HEINRICH	47	M	FARMER		PRZZZZCH
MARGARETHE	47	F	W		PRZZZZCH
WILHELM	18	M	CH		PRZZZZCH
THIEL, HANS	26	M	FARMER		PRZZZZUNK
MAGD.	22	F	W		PRZZZZUNK
WILLERS, FRIED.	31	M	LABR		PRZZZZUNK
WITTROCK, HEINRICH	16	M	LABR		PRZZZZUNK
WILLMAN, FNRANZ	26	M	FARMER		PRZZZZNY
DIESTERHOFF, ALBERTINE	35	F	SVNT		PRZZZZNY
BOEGE, WILHELM	46	M	SVNT		PRZZZZNY
DZIEMBOWSKY, ROMAN	49	M	LABR		PRZZZZNY
OTTILIE	49	F	W		PRZZZZNY
KNAAK, HERMANN	21	M	FARMER		PRZZZZNY
LONG-PRAIRIEPELOWSKYARR	44	M	FARMER		PRZZZZCAT
JAEGER, FRANZ	23	M	BKR		ACZZZZNY
APELT, LOUISE	56	F	WO		ACZZZZDYT
BERTH	16	F	CH		ACZZZZDYT
KAPELKE, HUGO	23	M	WCHMKR		ACZZZZNY
LEHMAN, OSKAR	30	M	FARMER		ACZZZZUNK
GASIOR, ANDRAS	33	M	LABR		ACZZZZUNK
NIKOLAJEZYZ, MATHEUS	24	M	LABR		ACZZZZUNK
BRUNN, MAX	27	M	CPTR		ACZZZZCH
ANNA	28	F	W		ACZZZZCH
BUCHHOLZ, VICTOR	23	M	MCHT		ACZZZZNY
LERCH, OTTO	32	M	FARMER		ACZZZZNY
HERBST, AUGUST	30	M	FARMER		ACZZZZNY
WEIDNER, GUSTAV	26	M	SMH		ACZZZZCH
LANGNER, WILHELM	33	M	LABR		ACZZZZUNK
AUGUSTE	31	F	W		ACZZZZUNK
OLGA	5	F	CHILD		ACZZZZUNK
FRIEDR.	3	M	CHILD		ACZZZZUNK
SENKOWICZ, EISIG	50	M	LABR		ACZZZZUNK
GROSS, GUSTAV	18	M	LABR		ACZZZZNY
PUDLEWSKY, MICHAL	32	M	LABR		ACZZZZNY
MARIANNE	33	F	W		ACZZZZNY
JAN	8	M	CHILD		ACZZZZNY
ANTON	4	M	CHILD		ACZZZZNY
JULIANE	.11	F	INFANT		ACZZZZNY
DRZDZYNSKY, LORENZ	26	M	FARMER		ACZZZZNY
CONSTANTIA	23	F	SVNT		ACZZZZNY
REXIN, JULIUS	39	M	JNR		ACZZZZNY
JULIA	31	F	W		ACZZZZNY
LUDWIG	9	M	CHILD		ACZZZZNY
RUDOLF	8	M	CHILD		ACZZZZNY
FRIED.	6	M	CHILD		ACZZZZNY
IDA	.11	F	INFANT		ACZZZZNY
GAECKLE, EMIL	16	M	SMH		BDZZZZNY
BASKE, GUSTAV	24	M	LABR		PRZZZZNY
JOHANN	23	F	W		PRZZZZNY
ELLA	.06	F	INFANT		PRZZZZNY
ERBER, ANTON	20	M	LABR		BVZZZZNY
HOFFMANN, CARL	23	M	BBR		PRZZZZNY
AUGUSTE	29	F	W		PRZZZZNY
FRITSCHE, FRIED.	50	M	DLR		SYZZZZNY
FIEHN, WILHELM	29	M	LABR		LUZZZZNY
DUEKER, JOHANNE	16	F	SVNT		PRZZZZNY
VALENTIN, ED.	20	M	FARMER		PRZZZZNY
HANSEN, JOHE.	18	F	SVNT		PRZZZZNY
SCHWARZ, HERM.	57	M	TIR		PRZZZZNY
VINTER, PETER-N.	23	M	TIR		PRZZZZNY
RAMM, JOHE.	28	F	WO		PRZZZZNY
WILHELM	.09	M	INFANT		PRZZZZNY
GIERZ, CHRISTIAN	33	M	LABR		PRZZZZNY
MARIE	29	F	W		PRZZZZNY
JAKOB	5	F	CHILD		PRZZZZNY
EMMA	3	F	CHILD		PRZZZZNY
WILHELME.	.09	F	INFANT		PRZZZZNY
PUPPA--, SOPHIE	00	M	UNKNOWN		WMZZZZNY
HINRICH, JOH.	20	M	LABR		PRZZZZNY
BRAEUNING, CARL	39	M	FARMER		PRZZZZNY
U	35	F	W		PRZZZZNY
AUGUST	17	M	CH		PRZZZZNY
EMILIE	9	F	CHILD		PRZZZZNY
MINNA	8	F	CHILD		PRZZZZNY
CARL	7	M	CHILD		PRZZZZNY
MAX	6	M	CHILD		PRZZZZNY
ELISE	3	F	CHILD		PRZZZZNY
HEDWIG	.11	F	INFANT		PRZZZZNY
FISCHER, ROBERT	29	M	LABR		SYZZZZNY
KURZ, GOTTFRIED	31	M	BCHR		WMZZZZNY
BRUEGGERT, MARIE	63	F	WO		PRZZZZCH
GROSSMANN, WILH.	24	F	WO		PRZZZZCH
WILHE.	21	F	W		PRZZZZCH
REINHARDT	.09	M	INFANT		PRZZZZCH
CYBART, JOSEF	47	M	LABR		PRZZZZNY
SWICEZYNSKA, STANISLAWA	19	F	SVNT		PRZZZZNY
RIETH, FRANZ	26	M	CPR		PRZZZZNY

SHIP: FULDA

FROM: BREMEN AND SOUTHAMPTON
TO: NEW YORK
ARRIVED: 22 MAY 1888

PASSENGER	AGE	SEX	OCCUPATION	PRVL	DES
WHITELHEAD, RICHARD	16	M	UNKNOWN		GRZZZZGR
MEYER, ROBERT	48	F	UNKNOWN		GRZZZZGR
MORTIZ	17	M	TT		GRZZZZGR
KLINGENBERG, U-MR	19	M	ACHTT		GRZZZZGR
FRIEDENTHA, BERTHA	18	F	UNKNOWN		GRZZZZGR
ESLAESSER, MARIA	19	F	UNKNOWN		GRZZZZGR
GUHRAUER, HERMANN	40	M	MCHT		GRZZZZGR
LOEB, MOSES	8	M	CHILD		GRZZZZGR
SIEBERG, LENA	36	F	UNKNOWN		GRZZZZGR
DODY	7	F	CHILD		GRZZZZGR
MENSER, THERESE	18	F	UNKNOWN		GRZZZZGR
SCHLICHMEIER, THERESE	64	F	UNKNOWN		GRZZZZGR
MARTHA	.09	F	INFANT		GRZZZZGR
NIEMEYER, CARL	19	M	FARMER		GRZZZZUSA
KARAN, JUL.	25	M	FARMER		GRZZZZUSA
CZEKLISKI, THEOPHIL	24	M	FARMER		GRZZZZUSA
CZEPETZ, MARTIN	25	M	FARMER		GRZZZZUSA
ARNDT, ADOLF	25	M	LABR		GRZZZZUSA
NOVAK, STANISLAUS	32	M	LABR		GRZZZZUSA
SAREMBACH, JOSEF	25	M	LABR		GRZZZZUSA
WALTER, AUGUST	50	M	LABR		GRZZZZUSA
LOUISE	28	F	UNKNOWN		GRZZZZUSA
AUGUST	6	M	CHILD		GRZZZZUSA
ARTHUR	3	M	CHILD		GRZZZZUSA
ERNA	.01	F	INFANT		GRZZZZUSA
KASCHKE, AUGUST	30	M	MSN		GRZZZZUSA
KRUEGER, LOUISE	36	F	UNKNOWN		GRZZZZUSA
WANDA	13	F	CH		GRZZZZUSA
MINNA	8	F	CHILD		GRZZZZUSA
CLARA	7	F	CHILD		GRZZZZUSA
JOHANNE	7	F	CHILD		GRZZZZUSA
FRITZ	4	M	CHILD		GRZZZZUSA

PASSENGER	AGE	SEX	OCCUPATION	PRVL	DES
KRIEGER, BERTHA	2	F	CHILD	GRZZZZ	USA
HULDA	.06	F	INFANT	GRZZZZ	USA
GONSERKOWSKI, AUGUST	27	M	PNTR	GRZZZZ	USA
NIEMANN, HANNY	24	F	UNKNOWN	GRZZZZ	USA
OTTO	.11	M	INFANT	GRZZZZ	USA
PUTZKE, ANNA	30	F	UNKNOWN	GRZZZZ	USA
ZIEGLER, MARTIN	15	F	UNKNOWN	GRZZZZ	USA
LOUISE	13	F	UNKNOWN	GRZZZZ	USA
BLERSCH, CARL	14	M	LABR	GRZZZZ	USA
HAEFNER, GOTTLIEB	42	M	LABR	GRZZZZ	USA
ROSINE	35	F	UNKNOWN	GRZZZZ	USA
GOTTFRIED	15	M	PNTR	GRZZZZ	USA
CATHARINA	7	F	CHILD	GRZZZZ	USA
FRIEDRICH	00	M	UNKNOWN	GRZZZZ	USA
CAROLINE	5	F	CHILD	GRZZZZ	USA
WILHELM	2	M	CHILD	GRZZZZ	USA
ELISE	.03	F	INFANT	GRZZZZ	USA
PFITZER, JACOB	41	M	PNTR	GRZZZZ	USA
JANSS, LOUISE	25	F	UNKNOWN	GRZZZZ	USA
REUTER, JOHANN	16	M	MSN	GRZZZZ	USA
DAUTEL, ALBERT	16	M	MSN	GRZZZZ	USA
SCHMID, GOTTFIED	15	M	FARMER	GRZZZZ	USA
RECK, GEORG	25	M	UNKNOWN	GRZZZZ	USA
HAUFMANN, PAULINE	31	F	UNKNOWN	GRZZZZ	USA
STECK, PAULINE	17	F	UNKNOWN	GRZZZZ	USA
NASS, PAULINE	20	F	UNKNOWN	GRZZZZ	USA
BENZEL, CHRISTINE	16	F	UNKNOWN	GRZZZZ	USA
HAEUSSLER, BARBARA	20	F	UNKNOWN	GRZZZZ	USA
AUER, CATHARINA	60	F	UNKNOWN	GRZZZZ	USA
MARIE	17	F	UNKNOWN	GRZZZZ	USA
SCHMIDT, WILHELMINE	19	F	UNKNOWN	GRZZZZ	USA
BINDER, LOUIS	17	M	BCHR	GRZZZZ	USA
ANNA	7	F	CHILD	GRZZZZ	USA
LOEFFLER, MARTIN	17	M	FARMER	GRZZZZ	USA
SCHOEPF, JOHANNES	14	M	FARMER	GRZZZZ	USA
DIETZ, DAVID	16	M	FARMER	GRZZZZ	USA
VEIT, GOTTFRIED	17	M	FARMER	GRZZZZ	USA
FRANK, LENE	23	F	UNKNOWN	GRZZZZ	USA
DAEUBLE, CATHARINE	30	F	UNKNOWN	GRZZZZ	USA
LINK, ANNA	15	F	UNKNOWN	GRZZZZ	USA
BARTHOLOMAE, WILHELM	17	M	FARMER	GRZZZZ	USA
BORT, CHRISTINE	21	F	UNKNOWN	GRZZZZ	USA
MARIE	16	F	UNKNOWN	GRZZZZ	USA
MUELLER, MICHAEL	25	M	BCHR	GRZZZZ	USA
CHRISTINE	26	F	UNKNOWN	GRZZZZ	USA
CHRISTINE	.07	F	INFANT	GRZZZZ	USA
KLEIN, WILHELM	14	M	FARMER	GRZZZZ	USA
FRECH, JACOB	16	M	FARMER	GRZZZZ	USA
KURZ, ADOLF	16	M	FARMER	GRZZZZ	USA
STERN, MARIA	15	F	UNKNOWN	GRZZZZ	USA
MYLLERSCHOEN, LOUISE	18	F	UNKNOWN	GRZZZZ	USA
MUELLER, SOREN	22	M	PNTR	GRZZZZ	USA
ANDERSEN, THEODOR	17	F	FARMER	GRZZZZ	USA
NIELSEN, HELENE	21	F	UNKNOWN	GRZZZZ	USA
CLAUSSEN, CARL	27	M	MSN	GRZZZZ	USA
ANNE	22	F	UNKNOWN	GRZZZZ	USA
HELENE	.09	F	INFANT	GRZZZZ	USA
MORTENSEN, SOPHIE	22	M	PDLR	GRZZZZ	USA
LUND, PETER	63	M	FARMER	GRZZZZ	USA
PETERSEN, MAREN	22	M	FARMER	GRZZZZ	USA
NICOLAISEN, HELENE	54	F	UNKNOWN	GRZZZZ	USA
DUHOHN, JURE	16	M	FARMER	GRZZZZ	USA
META	23	F	UNKNOWN	GRZZZZ	USA
MAAS, JENS	40	M	CPTR	GRZZZZ	USA
ANDERSEN, CARL	37	M	CPTR	GRZZZZ	USA
MOLLER, CATHARINA	19	F	UNKNOWN	GRZZZZ	USA
MAAS, MARIE	28	F	UNKNOWN	GRZZZZ	USA
SCHREIBER, PETER	16	M	LABR	GRZZZZ	USA
THEWS, ANDREAS	28	M	LABR	GRZZZZ	USA
ANNA	27	F	UNKNOWN	GRZZZZ	USA
JOSEF	2	M	CHILD	GRZZZZ	USA
JOHANN	.06	M	INFANT	GRZZZZ	USA
MAROTZ, CARL	24	M	SMH	GRZZZZ	USA
ANDERSEN, CARL	21	M	SMH	GRZZZZ	USA
HOLM, SINE	16	F	UNKNOWN	GRZZZZ	USA
LUEHMANN, MARIE	15	F	UNKNOWN	GRZZZZ	USA
HEINZ, MARIE	26	F	UNKNOWN	GRZZZZ	USA
DOTJEN, CATHARINE	19	F	UNKNOWN	GRZZZZ	USA
DITTMER, HERMANN	60	M	FARMER	GRZZZZ	USA
MARIE	49	F	UNKNOWN	GRZZZZ	USA
FRIEDRICH	17	M	LABR	GRZZZZ	USA
MARIE	20	F	UNKNOWN	GRZZZZ	USA
RADTKE, MARIANNA	23	F	UNKNOWN	GRZZZZ	USA
BOYSON, ANDREAS	58	M	LABR	GRZZZZ	USA
MINNE	60	F	UNKNOWN	GRZZZZ	USA
KASSHUBE, FRIEDRICH	25	M	PNTR	GRZZZZ	USA
LIGARZEWSKA, KONSTANCIE	22	F	UNKNOWN	GRZZZZ	USA
JULIUS	7	M	CHILD	GRZZZZ	USA
ZBORALSKA, MARIE	23	F	UNKNOWN	GRZZZZ	USA
KUESEL, ANNA	16	F	UNKNOWN	GRZZZZ	USA
-AGORSKY, IGNATZ	35	M	FARMER	GRZZZZ	USA
WEGENER, CARL	24	M	FARMER	GRZZZZ	USA
KAHRS, HEINRICH	28	M	MSN	GRZZZZ	USA
HOFMANN, ERYST	19	M	FARMER	GRZZZZ	USA
WEITZ, HEINRICH	16	M	FARMER	GRZZZZ	USA
SCHREIBER, GUSTAV	26	M	FARMER	GRZZZZ	USA
SOERENSSEN, SOEREN	29	M	FARMER	GRZZZZ	USA
RUDEBEK, THOMAS	66	M	LABR	GRZZZZ	USA
NIELSEN, ANE	24	F	UNKNOWN	GRZZZZ	USA
JOERGENSEN, CHR.	16	M	PNTR	GRZZZZ	USA
METZ, KASPER	30	M	FARMER	GRZZZZ	USA
BRUECKNER, ERNST	14	M	UNKNOWN	GRZZZZ	USA
SCHMIDT, SCHMIDT	14	M	CPTR	GRZZZZ	USA
PIONKE, EMMA	23	F	UNKNOWN	GRZZZZ	USA
AMANDA	20	F	UNKNOWN	GRZZZZ	USA
PIOCH, ALBERT	22	M	FARMER	GRZZZZ	USA
HULDA	20	F	UNKNOWN	GRZZZZ	USA
KOSNICKI, STANISLAUS	50	M	BRR	GRZZZZ	USA
ROSALIE	48	F	UNKNOWN	GRZZZZ	USA
FRANZISCA	23	F	UNKNOWN	GRZZZZ	USA
JOSEFA	20	F	UNKNOWN	GRZZZZ	USA
BERNARD	15	M	LABR	GRZZZZ	USA
AUGUSTE	8	F	CHILD	GRZZZZ	USA
LANG, JOHANNA	44	F	UNKNOWN	GRZZZZ	USA
AUGUSTE	18	F	CH	GRZZZZ	USA
ALWINE	8	F	CHILD	GRZZZZ	USA
WILHELMINE	7	F	CHILD	GRZZZZ	USA
FRIEDRICH	.11	M	INFANT	GRZZZZ	USA
JOHANNA	33	F	UNKNOWN	GRZZZZ	USA
MAKONSKI, JULIUS	16	M	JNR	GRZZZZ	USA
MANKE, HERMANN	26	M	MCHT	GRZZZZ	USA
AUGUSTE	25	F	UNKNOWN	GRZZZZ	USA
HELENE	8	F	CHILD	GRZZZZ	USA
ERICH	7	M	CHILD	GRZZZZ	USA
MARIE	4	F	CHILD	GRZZZZ	USA
PAUL	.09	M	INFANT	GRZZZZ	USA
WILHELMINE	36	F	UNKNOWN	GRZZZZ	USA
WEIHING, FRIEDRICH	16	M	MSN	GRZZZZ	USA
ZAWIELAK, JOSEF	26	M	FARMER	GRZZZZ	USA
MANIAK, JACOB	42	M	FARMER	GRZZZZ	USA
HANSEN, HANS	17	M	FARMER	GRZZZZ	USA
SCHMIDT, PETER	23	M	FARMER	GRZZZZ	USA
ILESEN, OLE-PETER	17	M	FARMER	GRZZZZ	USA
JEPSEN, JAKOBINE	16	F	UNKNOWN	GRZZZZ	USA
RIES, JAKOBINE	20	F	UNKNOWN	GRZZZZ	USA
ANNE	27	F	UNKNOWN	GRZZZZ	USA
FLUEGSANG, SIMON	19	M	LABR	GRZZZZ	USA
SOMMERER, CHR.	17	M	LABR	GRZZZZ	USA
ROHR, JOSEF	50	M	LABR	GRZZZZ	USA
KATARZYNA	43	F	UNKNOWN	GRZZZZ	USA
ANNA	2	F	CHILD	GRZZZZ	USA
ROCKSTROH, FR.	60	M	FARMER	GRZZZZ	USA
DOROTHEA	60	F	UNKNOWN	GRZZZZ	USA
WEGEL, LOUIS	47	M	PNTR	GRZZZZ	USA
BODINUS, ANNA	15	F	UNKNOWN	GRZZZZ	USA
WEGEL, ALBERT	5	M	CHILD	GRZZZZ	USA
GERLAD, AUGUST	22	M	FARMER	GRZZZZ	USA
PAUL, FRIEDRICH	24	M	FARMER	GRZZZZ	USA
GYDESEN, LENE	22	F	UNKNOWN	GRZZZZ	USA
HAAS, JACOB	38	M	PNTR	GRZZZZ	USA

PASSENGER	AGE	SEX	OCCUPATION	PRVL	DES
ROSINE	37	F	UNKNOWN	GRZZZZUSA	
FRIEDRICH	8	M	CHILD	GRZZZZUSA	
EMIL	7	M	CHILD	GRZZZZUSA	
LINA	5	F	CHILD	GRZZZZUSA	
ROSA	.10	F	INFANT	GRZZZZUSA	
GULDE, ALOANSA	30	F	UNKNOWN	GRZZZZUSA	
BARTH, LOUISE	19	F	UNKNOWN	GRZZZZUSA	
REUZ, MARTIN	14	M	LABR	GRZZZZUSA	
FISCHER, CATHARINA	17	F	UNKNOWN	GRZZZZUSA	
REUCHLE, BARBARA	16	F	UNKNOWN	GRZZZZUSA	
KOEHLER, ADAM	13	M	PNTR	GRZZZZUSA	
TEUFEL, GOTTLIEB	24	M	LABR	GRZZZZUSA	
REBER, JOHANN	29	M	LABR	GRZZZZUSA	
LEIPERSPERGEN, CAROLINE	21	F	UNKNOWN	GRZZZZUSA	
SCHLENKE, EMILIE	29	F	UNKNOWN	GRZZZZUSA	
SCHAEFFLER, EUGEN	17	M	MSN	GRZZZZUSA	
RAPP, GEORG	23	M	FARMER	GRZZZZUSA	
SCHNEIDER, CAROLINE	16	F	UNKNOWN	GRZZZZUSA	
KOTTMANN, FRANZISCA	19	F	UNKNOWN	GRZZZZUSA	
BREINER, CHR.	57	M	SMH	GRZZZZUSA	
MARIE	19	F	UNKNOWN	GRZZZZUSA	
IMHOFF, THERESE	18	F	UNKNOWN	GRZZZZUSA	
RUF, AGATHE	22	F	UNKNOWN	GRZZZZUSA	
HAMM, FR.	27	M	BCHR	GRZZZZUSA	
HELLER, WILHELMINE	22	F	UNKNOWN	GRZZZZUSA	
EMINGER, MARIE	7	F	CHILD	GRZZZZUSA	
RENZ, GOTTLOB	17	M	FARMER	GRZZZZUSA	
HANZ, PAULINE	20	F	UNKNOWN	GRZZZZUSA	
MANELL, MARIE	16	F	UNKNOWN	GRZZZZUSA	
HUBER, SARAH	24	F	UNKNOWN	GRZZZZUSA	
CAROLINA	21	F	UNKNOWN	GRZZZZUSA	
HOFMANN, ELISABETH	19	F	UNKNOWN	GRZZZZUSA	
MOHR, KATHARINA	17	F	UNKNOWN	GRZZZZUSA	
NOETH, MAGDALENE	17	F	UNKNOWN	GRZZZZUSA	
NEIDERT, CATHARINA	48	F	UNKNOWN	GRZZZZUSA	
JOSEF	17	M	LABR	GRZZZZUSA	
ANNA	15	F	UNKNOWN	GRZZZZUSA	
REGINA	3	F	CHILD	GRZZZZUSA	
JOSEPHINE	6	F	CHILD	GRZZZZUSA	
SCHWARZ, GEORG	18	M	CPTR	GRZZZZUSA	
WOLSIFFER, JOHANN	20	M	JNR	GRZZZZUSA	
BEXROTH, JACOB	28	M	BRR	GRZZZZUSA	
ROTHENBACH, WILHELM	40	M	FARMER	GRZZZZUSA	
PEORSINGER, MARGARETHA	16	F	UNKNOWN	GRZZZZUSA	
AUMANN, GEORG	61	M	PNTR	GRZZZZUSA	
MARGARETRHA	56	F	UNKNOWN	GRZZZZUSA	
HEINRICH	8	M	CHILD	GRZZZZUSA	
JOHANES	6	M	CHILD	GRZZZZUSA	
MOHR, CATHARINA	20	F	UNKNOWN	GRZZZZUSA	
HOCHBRUECKNER, THERESIA	25	F	UNKNOWN	GRZZZZUSA	
EHRHARDT, BABETTA	28	F	UNKNOWN	GRZZZZUSA	
GEORG	26	M	FARMER	GRZZZZUSA	
BACH, KATHARINA	19	F	UNKNOWN	GRZZZZUSA	
MARKO, LUDWIG	18	M	LABR	GRZZZZUSA	
MUENZINGER, WILHELM	27	M	LABR	GRZZZZUSA	
GUETLING, MARIANNA	20	F	UNKNOWN	GRZZZZUSA	
KIRELMER, MARIE	19	F	UNKNOWN	GRZZZZUSA	
GRUEN, ANNA	50	F	UNKNOWN	GRZZZZUSA	
MARIE	23	F	UNKNOWN	GRZZZZUSA	
CHRISTINE	19	F	UNKNOWN	GRZZZZUSA	
PETER	14	M	FARMER	GRZZZZUSA	
SEUBERT, ANTON	29	M	FARMER	GRZZZZUSA	
HEIMMANN, MARGARETHE	31	F	UNKNOWN	GRZZZZUSA	
NOLL, JOHANN	40	M	BCHR	GRZZZZUSA	
MARIE	39	F	UNKNOWN	GRZZZZUSA	
EVA	7	F	CHILD	GRZZZZUSA	
PETER	6	M	CHILD	GRZZZZUSA	
SCHUER, HINRICH	51	M	GDNR	GRZZZZUSA	
MARGARETHA	49	F	UNKNOWN	GRZZZZUSA	
JEPSEN, ANNA	19	F	UNKNOWN	GRZZZZUSA	
MARGARETHA	18	F	UNKNOWN	GRZZZZUSA	
ANDREAS	6	M	CHILD	GRZZZZUSA	
HERSKIND, CHRISTIAN	43	M	LABR	GRZZZZUSA	
RAON, NIELS	46	M	LABR	GRZZZZUSA	
KIESTE.	42	F	UNKNOWN	GRZZZZUSA	
ANNE	19	F	UNKNOWN	GRZZZZUSA	
LUND, ANDERS	7	M	CHILD	GRZZZZUSA	
RAON, JOERGLINE	2	F	CHILD	GRZZZZUSA	
BERGSTEDT, HANS	34	M	FARMER	GRZZZZUSA	
THIES, HEINRICH	30	M	FARMER	GRZZZZUSA	
MATHI	19	F	UNKNOWN	GRZZZZUSA	
BONDE, LAURITZ	18	M	FARMER	GRZZZZUSA	
HANSEN, CHR.	18	M	FARMER	GRZZZZUSA	
DOLL, WILHELMINE	18	F	UNKNOWN	GRZZZZUSA	
CHRISTENSEN, CHRISTEN	27	M	PNTR	GRZZZZUSA	
BYERNIN, ANNE	19	F	UNKNOWN	GRZZZZUSA	
BOLMAN, ANNA	18	F	UNKNOWN	GRZZZZUSA	
THORNSEN, MATHIAS	58	M	LABR	GRZZZZUSA	
HELENE	59	F	UNKNOWN	GRZZZZUSA	
MATHILDE	5	F	CHILD	GRZZZZUSA	
LEINER, LOUIS	56	M	BRR	GRZZZZUSA	
FALLER, LUDWIG	32	M	CPTR	GRZZZZUSA	
FRIEDERIKE	41	F	UNKNOWN	GRZZZZUSA	
AUGUST	4	M	CHILD	GRZZZZUSA	
MARIE	3	F	CHILD	GRZZZZUSA	
MAYER, KATIE	22	F	UNKNOWN	GRZZZZUSA	
W--NER, HENRIETTE	19	F	UNKNOWN	GRZZZZUSA	
RUEGE, WILHELMINE	18	F	UNKNOWN	GRZZZZUSA	
MEJKA, ANNA	24	F	UNKNOWN	GRZZZZUSA	
SCHLUMANN, CARL	28	M	LABR	GRZZZZUSA	
POHDE, MARIE	23	F	UNKNOWN	GRZZZZUSA	
EDUARD	3	M	CHILD	GRZZZZUSA	
NIEMEYER, ELISE	22	F	UNKNOWN	GRZZZZUSA	
WOLSEEFER, CHRISTIAN	25	M	FARMER	GRZZZZUSA	
THERESE	25	F	UNKNOWN	GRZZZZUSA	
RAUTH, MARIA	23	F	UNKNOWN	GRZZZZUSA	
ENGELHARDT, MARGARETHA	20	F	UNKNOWN	GRZZZZUSA	
AROLIE, KATHARINA	25	F	UNKNOWN	GRZZZZUSA	
FRIEDERIKE	20	F	UNKNOWN	GRZZZZUSA	
JESPERSEN, JENS	22	M	FARMER	GRZZZZUSA	
MATHIESEN, METTE	22	M	FARMER	GRZZZZUSA	
THOMSEN, HANS	53	M	GDNR	GRZZZZUSA	
DOROTHEA	57	F	UNKNOWN	GRZZZZUSA	
MARIE	24	F	UNKNOWN	GRZZZZUSA	
ANNA	20	F	UNKNOWN	GRZZZZUSA	
WERNER, CHRISTIAN	18	M	UNKNOWN	GRZZZZUSA	
SKOTT, PAUL	16	M	UNKNOWN	GRZZZZUSA	
SPITZ, CATH.	13	F	CH	GRZZZZUSA	
ALBER, JOHANNES	17	M	SMH	GRZZZZUSA	
SCHMIDT, CARL	17	M	FARMER	GRZZZZUSA	
MUELLER, FRIEDERIKE	19	F	UNKNOWN	GRZZZZUSA	
GLUNZ, MARIE	47	F	UNKNOWN	GRZZZZUSA	
WOLZ, GOTTLIEBIN	17	M	FARMER	GRZZZZUSA	
MASS, CATHARINA	16	F	UNKNOWN	GRZZZZUSA	
GANSS, CHRISTINE	17	F	UNKNOWN	GRZZZZUSA	
MARTIN, FRIEDERIKE	17	F	UNKNOWN	GRZZZZUSA	
SCHMID, JACOB	28	M	FARMER	GRZZZZUSA	
HITZINGER, JACOB	18	M	FARMER	GRZZZZUSA	
HEINZIG, FR.	23	M	FARMER	GRZZZZUSA	
LOWENSTERN, MAX	17	M	MCHT	GRZZZZUSA	
MEINICKE, NETTCHEN	45	F	UNKNOWN	GRZZZZUSA	
MUELLER, CHR.	33	M	TLR	GRZZZZUSA	
BERTHA	18	F	UNKNOWN	GRZZZZUSA	
MEYER, HEINRICH	52	M	BCHR	GRZZZZUSA	
MARIA	45	F	UNKNOWN	GRZZZZUSA	
MARGARETHA	18	F	UNKNOWN	GRZZZZUSA	
HEINRICH	15	M	PNTR	GRZZZZUSA	
GESINE	6	F	CHILD	GRZZZZUSA	
FEILER, GEORG	23	M	LABR	GRZZZZUSA	
KUNIGUNDE	22	F	UNKNOWN	GRZZZZUSA	
BECKER, EDUARD	28	M	PNTR	GRZZZZUSA	
LUEDDECKE, FRITZ	28	M	JNR	GRZZZZUSA	
FROEHLICH, JOHANNES	28	M	JNR	GRZZZZUSA	
SOPHIE	22	F	UNKNOWN	GRZZZZUSA	
MARIE	.08	F	INFANT	GRZZZZUSA	
BUEHLER, JOHANN	42	M	FARMER	GRZZZZUSA	
AGATHE	46	F	UNKNOWN	GRZZZZUSA	
JOHANN	14	M	FARMER	GRZZZZUSA	
MUSCHERT, FRITZ	17	M	PNTR	GRZZZZUSA	
WALZ, CATHARINA	24	F	UNKNOWN	GRZZZZUSA	

PASSENGER	AGE	SEX	OCCUPATION	PRV/IVL/DES
WIEDEMANN, BRIGITTA	19	F	UNKNOWN	GRZZZZUSA
DEISCHE, JOSEPH	40	M	FARMER	GRZZZZUSA
JACOBIEN, MARIE	33	F	UNKNOWN	GRZZZZUSA
ANNA	8	F	CHILD	GRZZZZUSA
CLAUSSEN, ELISABETH	7	F	CHILD	GRZZZZUSA
JESPERSEN, CHRISTINE	30	F	UNKNOWN	GRZZZZUSA
KIEFER, CHRISTINE	4	F	CHILD	GRZZZZUSA
WILHELM	3	M	CHILD	GRZZZZUSA
KARL	.10	M	INFANT	GRZZZZUSA
LINA	18	F	UNKNOWN	GRZZZZUSA
HALB, AMANDA	30	F	UNKNOWN	GRZZZZUSA
PITTERICH, WERNER	30	M	FARMER	GRZZZZUSA
MARIE	7	F	CHILD	GRZZZZUSA
ELISABETH	.03	F	INFANT	GRZZZZUSA
JOHANNE	54	M	FARMER	GRZZZZUSA
PROTSCH, KUNIGIUNDE	29	F	UNKNOWN	GRZZZZUSA
SCHRENKER, JOHANN	61	M	LABR	GRZZZZUSA
GOEHL, PHILIPPINA	19	F	UNKNOWN	GRZZZZUSA
KLAAS, MINNA	20	F	UNKNOWN	GRZZZZUSA
VONKROEMER, MARIE	19	F	UNKNOWN	GRZZZZUSA
KLUGE, GERTRUD	26	F	UNKNOWN	GRZZZZUSA
BLAKEMEYER, CHRIST.	15	M	MSN	GRZZZZUSA
ELISE	17	F	UNKNOWN	GRZZZZUSA
ANDREWSKA, JULIANNA	25	F	UNKNOWN	GRZZZZUSA
CATHARINA	22	F	UNKNOWN	GRZZZZUSA
HAHN, KAROLINE	59	F	UNKNOWN	GRZZZZUSA
LENDER, JUSTINE	16	F	UNKNOWN	GRZZZZUSA
KLAGE, OTTO	26	M	FARMER	GRZZZZUSA
FROEHLICH, EMMA	18	F	UNKNOWN	GRZZZZUSA
NEUBERT, EMILIE	34	F	UNKNOWN	GRZZZZUSA
ALEX	7	M	CHILD	GRZZZZUSA
ELMIRA	5	F	CHILD	GRZZZZUSA
GERTTMANN, FRANZ	18	M	FARMER	GRZZZZUSA
FLORIN, MAX	15	M	FARMER	GRZZZZUSA
PFRIELITZ, JOHANN	25	M	FARMER	GRZZZZUSA
IRZIBOWSKI, WOJCIECH	31	M	FARMER	GRZZZZUSA
KLUGE, OLGA	16	F	UNKNOWN	GRZZZZUSA
ANNA	24	F	UNKNOWN	GRZZZZUSA
SCHIMANSKI, JOHANN	41	M	SMH	GRZZZZUSA
KLAAS, HEINRICH	40	M	SMH	GRZZZZUSA
DREIER, JOHANN	23	M	MCHT	GRZZZZUSA
SCHLOH, HERMANN	55	M	CPTR	GRZZZZUSA
MARIE	48	F	UNKNOWN	GRZZZZUSA
HERMANN	17	M	JNR	GRZZZZUSA
HEINRICH	16	M	GDNR	GRZZZZUSA
JOHANN	6	M	CHILD	GRZZZZUSA
LEMBACH, GUSTAV	22	M	BRR	GRZZZZUSA
ELLMANCH, MARIA	16	F	UNKNOWN	GRZZZZUSA
LEMBACH, JULIAN	48	M	BCHR	GRZZZZUSA
ADELHEID	41	F	UNKNOWN	GRZZZZUSA
FRANZ	16	M	FARMER	GRZZZZUSA
WILLKOMEN, PETER	53	M	FARMER	GRZZZZUSA
KATHARINA	59	F	UNKNOWN	GRZZZZUSA
MARTINA	7	F	CHILD	GRZZZZUSA
GIGL, ANNA	25	F	UNKNOWN	GRZZZZUSA
MAX	6	M	CHILD	GRZZZZUSA
FRANZ	4	M	CHILD	GRZZZZUSA
WANINGER, WILHELM	17	M	PNTR	GRZZZZUSA
KLEINHARZ, JOHANN	25	M	FARMER	GRZZZZUSA
POESCHL, BENEDIKT	29	M	FARMER	GRZZZZUSA
GEHRES, DANIEL	30	M	FARMER	GRZZZZUSA
FADEL, CATHARINA	26	F	UNKNOWN	GRZZZZUSA
GEHRES, EDUARD	5	M	CHILD	GRZZZZUSA
CARL	3	M	CHILD	GRZZZZUSA
ALBERT	.11	M	INFANT	GRZZZZUSA
KUNZ, LUDWIG	8	M	CHILD	GRZZZZUSA
SOEDER, GEORG	24	M	FSHMN	GRZZZZUSA
LORENZ	27	M	FSHMN	GRZZZZUSA
RUMPF, AUGUST	24	M	MSN	GRZZZZUSA
STEFFENS, JACOB	23	M	MCHT	GRZZZZUSA
HINK, HERMANN	25	M	MCHT	GRZZZZUSA
BORCHER, HEINRICH	23	M	FARMER	GRZZZZUSA
POPPE, ANNA	14	F	UNKNOWN	GRZZZZUSA
MARGARETHA	16	F	UNKNOWN	GRZZZZUSA
PLATH, MAX	30	M	BCHR	GRZZZZUSA
KOFFMANN, MARTHA	00	F	UNKNOWN	GRZZZZUSA
BENEDIX, IDA	19	F	UNKNOWN	GRZZZZUSA
SCHEDA, THOMAS	29	M	FARMER	GRZZZZUSA
KUEHFUSS, JOH.GOTTL.	30	M	FARMER	GRZZZZUSA
WAGNER, MARIE	27	F	UNKNOWN	GRZZZZUSA
JEHRLE, FRIEDR.	29	M	LABR	GRZZZZUSA
CATHARINA	25	F	UNKNOWN	GRZZZZUSA
MARGARETHA	.09	F	INFANT	GRZZZZUSA
BECK, JOHANNES	28	M	PNTR	GRZZZZUSA
CATHARINA	26	F	UNKNOWN	GRZZZZUSA
MARGARETHA	2	F	CHILD	GRZZZZUSA
GUSTAV	.03	M	INFANT	GRZZZZUSA
CHRISTIAN	33	M	CPTR	GRZZZZUSA
KLEICH, JOHS.	21	M	CPTR	GRZZZZUSA
HOLZ, JOHANNES	26	M	JNR	GRZZZZUSA
VATER, THERESE	35	F	UNKNOWN	GRZZZZUSA
MOGGE, LINA	32	F	UNKNOWN	GRZZZZUSA
MARIA	50	F	UNKNOWN	GRZZZZUSA
BECK, JACOB	17	M	FARMER	GRZZZZUSA
KRUEGENER, WILHELMINE	30	F	UNKNOWN	GRZZZZUSA
RIESE, ALFRED	18	M	FARMER	GRZZZZUSA
KLUTHE, WILHELMINE	18	F	UNKNOWN	GRZZZZUSA
WITTE, ELISABETH	18	F	UNKNOWN	GRZZZZUSA
WEDEMEYER, GEORG-LAFREN	14	M	FARMER	GRZZZZUSA
ROHDE, HEINRICH	24	M	SMH	GRZZZZUSA
BUCHHOLZ, LOUISE	19	F	UNKNOWN	GRZZZZUSA
STAHLER, CHRISTOPH	34	M	LABR	GRZZZZUSA
MOLL, CHRISTIAN	29	M	WTR	GRZZZZUSA
BABETTE	18	F	UNKNOWN	GRZZZZUSA
KUHFUSS, PHILIP-JACOB	47	M	FARMER	GRZZZZUSA
SEIDEL, CHRISTOPH	28	M	FARMER	GRZZZZUSA
ABRAHAM, HENRIETTE	59	F	UNKNOWN	GRZZZZUSA
ERNESTINE	21	F	UNKNOWN	GRZZZZUSA
ALBERT	16	M	MCHT	GRZZZZUSA
FRIEDRICH	14	M	MCHT	GRZZZZUSA
CARL	7	M	CHILD	GRZZZZUSA
WIESE, HULDA	17	F	UNKNOWN	GRZZZZUSA
ALBERS, BERNHARD	47	M	LABR	GRZZZZUSA
FRIEDERIKE	17	F	UNKNOWN	GRZZZZUSA
ALWINE	15	F	UNKNOWN	GRZZZZUSA
BEHNER, ANNA	59	F	UNKNOWN	GRZZZZUSA
JOHANNES	28	M	PNTR	GRZZZZUSA
HESSER, MARIA	23	F	UNKNOWN	GRZZZZUSA
HAUSER, MARTIN	25	M	LABR	GRZZZZUSA
KUTZKI, BARBAR.	20	F	UNKNOWN	GRZZZZUSA
WOHLLEBER, MARIA	14	F	UNKNOWN	GRZZZZUSA
HAUSER, ROSINE	20	F	UNKNOWN	GRZZZZUSA
BILFINGER, BERTHA	21	F	UNKNOWN	GRZZZZUSA
KILGUS, ANNA	24	F	UNKNOWN	GRZZZZUSA
BERTHA	18	F	UNKNOWN	GRZZZZUSA
SCHWARZ, LOUISE	20	F	UNKNOWN	GRZZZZUSA
HOEHL, LUISE	19	F	UNKNOWN	GRZZZZUSA
MOHRBACHER, HENRIETTE	17	F	UNKNOWN	GRZZZZUSA
SPIESS, KATHARINA	18	F	UNKNOWN	GRZZZZUSA
MEYER, HEINRICH	27	M	FSHMN	GRZZZZUSA
SOMMERHALTER, MARIE	21	F	UNKNOWN	GRZZZZUSA
PFAFF, FRIEDERIKE	17	F	UNKNOWN	GRZZZZUSA
ROHR, LUDWIG	18	M	FARMER	GRZZZZUSA
CHRISTMANN, BARBARA	34	F	UNKNOWN	GRZZZZUSA
MARGARETHE	8	F	CHILD	GRZZZZUSA
HEINRICH	6	M	CHILD	GRZZZZUSA
GEORG	5	M	CHILD	GRZZZZUSA
MOHRMANN, HEINR.	15	M	MSN	GRZZZZUSA
FELLER, CARL	38	M	MSN	GRZZZZUSA
HUETTGER, AUGUST	25	M	MCHT	GRZZZZUSA
REIF, ROSA	27	F	UNKNOWN	GRZZZZUSA
EMIG, ANNA	26	F	UNKNOWN	GRZZZZUSA
LESCH, MARGARETHA	19	F	UNKNOWN	GRZZZZUSA
MATTHARI, HEINRICH	29	M	JNR	GRZZZZUSA
ANNA	45	F	UNKNOWN	GRZZZZUSA
ELISE	15	F	UNKNOWN	GRZZZZUSA
CONRAD	13	M	LABR	GRZZZZUSA
KLUTHE, THERSE	21	F	UNKNOWN	GRZZZZUSA
DIETRICH, PHILIPP	40	M	FARMER	GRZZZZUSA
FISCHER, ELISE	20	F	UNKNOWN	GRZZZZUSA

PASSENGER	AGE	SEX	OCCUPATION	PRVL	DES
REINSCHUESSEL, MARIA	51	F	UNKNOWN	GRZZZZ	USA
FRIDOLIN	6	M	CHILD	GRZZZZ	USA
CAROLINE	4	F	CHILD	GRZZZZ	USA
FRAUCK, CAROLINE	17	F	UNKNOWN	GRZZZZ	USA
CLEMEN, FRIEDRICH	24	M	PNTR	GRZZZZ	USA
BAUMANN, KARL	41	M	GDNR	GRZZZZ	USA
FRIEDRICH	38	M	FARMER	GRZZZZ	USA
MARIE	18	F	UNKNOWN	GRZZZZ	USA
CAROLINE	16	F	UNKNOWN	GRZZZZ	USA
REGINE	14	F	UNKNOWN	GRZZZZ	USA
WILHELM	7	M	CHILD	GRZZZZ	USA
CARL	3	M	CHILD	GRZZZZ	USA
PAULINE	.01	F	INFANT	GRZZZZ	USA
RATHJE, BERTHA	16	F	UNKNOWN	GRZZZZ	USA
BROCKELMANN, META	27	F	UNKNOWN	GRZZZZ	USA
WREDE, AUGUST	15	M	PNTR	GRZZZZ	USA
BAHR, SOPHIE	14	F	UNKNOWN	GRZZZZ	USA
VAGT, BERTHA	37	F	UNKNOWN	GRZZZZ	USA
TIMME, BERTHA	18	F	UNKNOWN	GRZZZZ	USA
POPPE, ALBERT	24	M	LABR	GRZZZZ	USA
VIGOLD, FRIEDERIKE	15	F	UNKNOWN	GRZZZZ	USA
HELENE	7	F	CHILD	GRZZZZ	USA
AGNES	5	F	CHILD	GRZZZZ	USA
HOLTMANN, AUGUSTE	24	F	UNKNOWN	GRZZZZ	USA
EHLERS, ADELINE	26	F	UNKNOWN	GRZZZZ	USA
NIELSEN, JOHANN	26	M	FARMER	GRZZZZ	USA
ANNE	22	F	UNKNOWN	GRZZZZ	USA
LEISER, EDUARD	22	M	LABR	GRZZZZ	USA
STEINHAGEN, V.	23	M	LABR	GRZZZZ	USA
LANG, KARL	23	M	LABR	GRZZZZ	USA
HECKWOLF, KATHARINA	22	F	UNKNOWN	GRZZZZ	USA
GRIMM, FRITZ	16	M	WTR	GRZZZZ	USA
WOLHDORF, JETCHEN	16	F	UNKNOWN	GRZZZZ	USA
SALOMON	14	M	LABR	GRZZZZ	USA
ADRIAN, KATHRINA	19	F	UNKNOWN	GRZZZZ	USA
RICHTER, DOROTHEA	21	F	UNKNOWN	GRZZZZ	USA
HIMMLER, SOPHIE	18	F	UNKNOWN	GRZZZZ	USA
OTT, MARGARETHA	23	F	UNKNOWN	GRZZZZ	USA
NIEDERSCHMIDT, MINNA	17	F	UNKNOWN	GRZZZZ	USA
LECHER, MAGDALENA	18	F	UNKNOWN	GRZZZZ	USA
HAASE, MINNA	29	F	UNKNOWN	GRZZZZ	USA
FRIEDA	4	F	CHILD	GRZZZZ	USA
SOPHIE	.10	F	INFANT	GRZZZZ	USA
ZIMMERMANN, MARGARETHE	21	F	UNKNOWN	GRZZZZ	USA
VAETTER, KAETCHEN	24	F	UNKNOWN	GRZZZZ	USA
RICHTER, ANNA	18	F	UNKNOWN	GRZZZZ	USA
LAMBRECHT, AUGUST	22	M	MCHT	GRZZZZ	USA
CZAPLENSKA, MARIA	20	F	UNKNOWN	GRZZZZ	USA
OFITZER, ANTON	21	M	PNTR	GRZZZZ	USA
VOGT, FRIEDRICH	22	M	FARMER	GRZZZZ	USA
DENZ, PETER	27	M	FARMER	GRZZZZ	USA
TRAUTWEIN, KAROLINE	18	F	UNKNOWN	GRZZZZ	USA
GROTE, AUGUST	15	M	LABR	GRZZZZ	USA
HASSELHORN, ADOLF	24	M	LABR	GRZZZZ	USA
HILMERS, GERD.	20	M	LABR	GRZZZZ	USA
MICHAEL, D.	22	M	LABR	GRZZZZ	USA
WIECKER, FRIEDRICH	00	M	LABR	GRZZZZ	USA
NAGLER, ROBERT	31	M	LABR	GRZZZZ	USA
HOFFMANN, MARIE	21	F	UNKNOWN	GRZZZZ	USA
ISTERTAG, THERESE	59	F	UNKNOWN	GRZZZZ	USA
SCHMIDT, ROSINE	29	F	UNKNOWN	GRZZZZ	USA
NETZEL, MARIE	17	F	UNKNOWN	GRZZZZ	USA
DOEHLE, C.	27	F	UNKNOWN	GRZZZZ	USA
ENGELBERT	7	M	CHILD	GRZZZZ	USA
KATHI	2	F	CHILD	GRZZZZ	USA
HENRIETTE	.09	F	INFANT	GRZZZZ	USA
FISCHER, ELIS.	14	F	UNKNOWN	GRZZZZ	USA
ZWINK, DIEDRICH	30	M	AGT	GRZZZZ	USA
ALIDIA	4	F	CHILD	GRZZZZ	USA
KONIG, IDA	17	F	UNKNOWN	GRZZZZ	USA
KUHNLE, MARIE	17	F	UNKNOWN	GRZZZZ	USA
SCHWEIERLE, LOUISE-DEUT	19	F	UNKNOWN	GRZZZZ	USA
DETTINGER, PAULINE	20	F	UNKNOWN	GRZZZZ	USA
HEINRICH, MARIE	27	F	UNKNOWN	GRZZZZ	USA
LAUER, JOHANN	32	M	UNKNOWN	GRZZZZ	USA
EVA	28	F	UNKNOWN	GRZZZZ	USA
ERNST	2	M	CHILD	GRZZZZ	USA
GAUS, TONI	30	F	UNKNOWN	GRZZZZ	USA
WILHELMINE	7	F	CHILD	GRZZZZ	USA
TONI	5	F	CHILD	GRZZZZ	USA
BAMBERG, BERTHA	24	F	UNKNOWN	GRZZZZ	USA
OTTILIE	24	F	UNKNOWN	GRZZZZ	USA
EDMUND	3	M	CHILD	GRZZZZ	USA
WILHELM	.06	M	INFANT	GRZZZZ	USA
ALBERS, JOSEF	27	M	FARMER	GRZZZZ	USA
BR---EL, RICHARD	28	M	FARMER	GRZZZZ	USA
PLATE, SEGELKE	54	M	FARMER	GRZZZZ	USA
HERTZL, FRITZ	40	M	FARMER	GRZZZZ	USA
HEINRICH, F.E.	51	M	FARMER	GRZZZZ	USA
HELD, LOUISE	27	F	UNKNOWN	GRZZZZ	USA
BRAEUNLINGER, SATWIN	26	M	LABR	GRZZZZ	USA
SCHROEDER, CORD	15	M	LABR	GRZZZZ	USA
VIEBROCK, JACOB	16	M	LABR	GRZZZZ	USA
BERTRAM, CLAUS	22	M	LABR	GRZZZZ	USA
SECKE, JOHANNES	14	M	LABR	GRZZZZ	USA
SELKE, ADOLF	15	M	LABR	GRZZZZ	USA
SCHMANER, FRIEDRICH	14	M	LABR	GRZZZZ	USA
BUCK, CATHARINA	18	F	UNKNOWN	GRZZZZ	USA
STEIN, LAURA	24	F	UNKNOWN	GRZZZZ	USA
GOHL, MARIANNA	56	F	UNKNOWN	GRZZZZ	USA
STOECKER, FRANZ	35	M	SMH	GRZZZZ	USA
MARGARETHE	32	F	UNKNOWN	GRZZZZ	USA
KATHARINA	7	F	CHILD	GRZZZZ	USA
JOSEPH	5	M	CHILD	GRZZZZ	USA
MARGARETHA	3	F	CHILD	GRZZZZ	USA
ELISE	.09	F	INFANT	GRZZZZ	USA
GROSS, LISETTE	16	F	UNKNOWN	GRZZZZ	USA
EHMANN, CATHARINA	63	F	UNKNOWN	GRZZZZ	USA
FUHRLAND, FRIEDRICH	21	M	FARMER	GRZZZZ	USA
BAHLMANN, HEINRICH	31	M	FARMER	GRZZZZ	USA
HERMANN	34	M	FARMER	GRZZZZ	USA
TALLEN, REGINA	33	F	UNKNOWN	GRZZZZ	USA
KOCK, GESINE	26	F	UNKNOWN	GRZZZZ	USA
HAASKEN, JOHN-B.	70	M	LABR	GRZZZZ	***
BOEHM, CONRAD	23	M	UNKNOWN	GRZZZZ	USA
RAN, AUGUST	20	M	UNKNOWN	GRZZZZ	USA
WAGNER, MARTIN	28	M	PNTR	GRZZZZ	USA
RACK, CHRISTIAN	16	M	LABR	GRZZZZ	USA
REBER, FRANZ	16	M	LABR	GRZZZZ	USA
GRISTEDE, CARL	17	M	SMH	GRZZZZ	USA
DIEDRICH	15	M	LABR	GRZZZZ	USA
FEDDEN, NICOLAUS	17	M	FARMER	GRZZZZ	USA
FUCHTER, NICOLAUS	16	M	FARMER	GRZZZZ	USA
RAMM, O.H.	24	M	FARMER	GRZZZZ	USA
GULDEN, HERMANN	26	M	FARMER	GRZZZZ	USA
VOGTS, DOROTHEA	17	F	UNKNOWN	GRZZZZ	USA
STEIN, AMANDUS	16	M	PNTR	GRZZZZ	USA
JACOBI, E.	23	M	MCHT	GRZZZZ	USA
AMANS, ANNA	20	F	UNKNOWN	GRZZZZ	USA
ROLAND, WILHELM	16	M	FARMER	GRZZZZ	USA
WIRTH, ROSALIE	18	F	UNKNOWN	GRZZZZ	USA
WESSEL, ELISE	64	F	UNKNOWN	GRZZZZ	USA
REEG, U-MRS	42	F	UNKNOWN	GRZZZZ	USA
GERHARD	7	M	CHILD	GRZZZZ	USA
LEONHARD	5	M	CHILD	GRZZZZ	USA
HERMANN, KARL	26	M	JNR	GRZZZZ	USA
KAROLINE	25	F	JNR	GRZZZZ	USA
KATHARINA	2	F	CHILD	GRZZZZ	USA
KARL	.03	M	INFANT	GRZZZZ	USA
MEHL, HANS	40	M	GDNR	GRZZZZ	USA
MUELLER, KATHA.	24	F	UNKNOWN	GRZZZZ	USA
U	22	U	UNKNOWN	GRZZZZ	USA
GEISS, FELIX	29	M	LABR	GRZZZZ	USA
SOMMER, LOUISE	24	F	UNKNOWN	GRZZZZ	USA
MEHLHORN, GUSTAV	17	M	CPTR	GRZZZZ	USA
SCHAU, ADOLF	49	M	TLR	GRZZZZ	USA
PHILIPPINE	51	F	UNKNOWN	GRZZZZ	USA
ADOLF	21	M	BCHR	GRZZZZ	USA
MARGARETHE	16	F	UNKNOWN	GRZZZZ	USA
CHARLES	17	M	LABR	GRZZZZ	USA

PASSENGER	AGE	SEX	OCCUPATION	PRVL	DES
PETER	7	M	CHILD	GRZZZZ	USA
HEINRICH	6	M	CHILD	GRZZZZ	USA
EMILIE	29	F	UNKNOWN	GRZZZZ	USA
SIEBER, CATHARINE	17	F	UNKNOWN	GRZZZZ	USA
HEINRICH, E.	24	M	PNTR	GRZZZZ	USA
MOELLER, SOEREN	27	M	LABR	GRZZZZ	USA
MEYER, ERNST	13	M	MCHT	GRZZZZ	USA

SHIP: WESTERNLAND

FROM: ANTWERP
TO: NEW YORK
ARRIVED: 23 MAY 1888

PASSENGER	AGE	SEX	OCCUPATION	PRVL	DES
THEIS, JACQUES	40	M	BRR	LXZZZZ	NY
KLEINODI, JOSEF	38	M	FARMER	GRZZZZ	NY
BRAKMANN, WM	34	M	BCHR	GRZZZZ	CLE
HEINRICH	26	M	BRR	GRZZZZ	CLE
SCHULER, JOHAN	37	M	FARMER	GRZZZZ	CLE
HERMANN, JOH	25	M	FARMER	GRZZZZ	UNK
ANASTASIA	25	F	UNKNOWN	GRZZZZ	UNK
HARTMANN, JOS	25	M	FARMER	GRZZZZ	UNK
WEICHSELBERGER, WENZEL	25	M	FARMER	GRZZZZ	UNK
SCHULZ, HERMAN	32	M	CL	GRZZZZ	UNK
FASEON, FIED	36	M	BRR	GRZZZZ	NY
OPITZ, ALBERT	33	M	BRR	GRZZZZ	NY
MIDEAK, CARL	29	M	FARMER	GRZZZZ	NY
THALHOFF, MATHILDE	49	F	UNKNOWN	GRZZZZ	NY
BAUMANN, CATHA	58	F	UNKNOWN	GRZZZZ	NY
MARIE	15	F	UNKNOWN	GRZZZZ	NY
STARK, EVA	21	F	UNKNOWN	GRZZZZ	NY
HERBER, MARK	17	M	LABR	GRZZZZ	NY
KUTSCHOLL, OTTO	28	M	LABR	GRZZZZ	UNK
IDA	20	F	UNKNOWN	GRZZZZ	UNK
HEDWIG	1	M	CHILD	GRZZZZ	UNK
BUSCHKE, ANNA	19	F	UNKNOWN	GRZZZZ	CH
FEPPER, STANISL	29	M	FARMER	GRZZZZ	UNK
THOMAS	22	M	FARMER	GRZZZZ	UNK
SOEBRICH, WM	16	M	LABR	GRZZZZ	UNK
PERCY, CATH	34	F	UNKNOWN	GRZZZZ	CH
LINA	9	F	CHILD	GRZZZZ	CH
JOHANN	4	M	CHILD	GRZZZZ	CH
LEOPOLD	1	M	CHILD	GRZZZZ	CH
ZIRNDER, NATCH	29	F	UNKNOWN	GRZZZZ	NY
ALEX	1	M	CHILD	GRZZZZ	NY
KAUFMANN, MAX	36	M	CL	GRZZZZ	NY
APPEL, RICHARD	18	M	FARMER	GRZZZZ	NY
KLEIN, WILHELM	20	M	MSN	GRZZZZ	NY
SCHEURING, GG	26	M	FARMER	GRZZZZ	NY
CATHA	28	F	UNKNOWN	GRZZZZ	NY
GEORG	1	M	CHILD	GRZZZZ	NY
COIN, THOMAS	42	M	LABR	GRZZZZ	NY
THIELENHAUS, RUDOLF	18	M	CL	GRZZZZ	NY
HANBERWEISER, ADOLPHE	22	F	UNKNOWN	GRZZZZ	NY
HEINES, ANGELA	19	F	UNKNOWN	GRZZZZ	USA
SCHMIDT, NICOL	43	M	LABR	GRZZZZ	UNK
BRUNSFELD, JOHN	30	M	FARMER	GRZZZZ	CH
HAUSER, WM	24	M	FARMER	GRZZZZ	BUF
LEMDECKER, ANNA	17	F	UNKNOWN	GRZZZZ	UNK
CATHA	15	F	UNKNOWN	GRZZZZ	UNK
MICHEL	11	M	UNKNOWN	GRZZZZ	UNK
THIELMANN, JOH	21	M	FARMER	GRZZZZ	BUF
WELZMER, NIC	19	M	LABR	GRZZZZ	UNK
HOFFMANN, PET	23	M	FARMER	GRZZZZ	CH
BURG, PAUL	25	M	FARMER	GRZZZZ	CH
LINS, NIC	30	M	FARMER	GRZZZZ	UNK
SCHANY, MARG	22	F	UNKNOWN	GRZZZZ	UNK
GILBERT, CLEMENS	27	M	LABR	GRZZZZ	PHI
CARL	24	M	LABR	GRZZZZ	PHI
LEWY, CAROLINE	18	F	UNKNOWN	GRZZZZ	NY
STAICH, JOHN	20	M	CL	GRZZZZ	NY
EMMA	30	F	UNKNOWN	GRZZZZ	NY
HAUTH, HEINRICH	25	M	FARMER	GRZZZZ	NY
GERHARD, HEINRICH	20	M	FARMER	GRZZZZ	NY
KINS, DOMINIKO	21	M	FARMER	GRZZZZ	UNK
SEUBERT, ANTON	24	M	LABR	GRZZZZ	NY
STEUP, OTTOLIE	43	F	UNKNOWN	GRZZZZ	NY
EUGENIE	21	F	UNKNOWN	GRZZZZ	NY
EUGEN	6	M	CHILD	GRZZZZ	NY
LINE	8	F	CHILD	GRZZZZ	NY
ELFRIDE	2	F	CHILD	GRZZZZ	NY
HELFENSTEIN, JACOB	18	M	FARMER	GRZZZZ	NY
VANTHENEN, HUBERT	54	M	FARMER	GRZZZZ	NY
WOLOHY	17	M	FARMER	GRZZZZ	NY
WOLPERT, MARIA	19	F	UNKNOWN	GRZZZZ	NY
HODECKER, FRIDA	15	F	UNKNOWN	GRZZZZ	NY
SCHMIDE, CAROLINE	21	F	UNKNOWN	GRZZZZ	NY
WEISS, HUGO	6	M	CHILD	GRZZZZ	NY
WAMBACH, CATHE	28	F	UNKNOWN	GRZZZZ	NY
SCHERER, JACOB	27	M	LABR	GRZZZZ	NY
SCHMIDT, PAUL	24	M	FARMER	GRZZZZ	NY
FAUER, CATHA	20	F	UNKNOWN	GRZZZZ	NY
WIESNER, ANNA	46	F	UNKNOWN	GRZZZZ	UNK
THEISS, JOSEF	14	M	UNKNOWN	GRZZZZ	UNK
BECHLER, JULEANA	17	F	UNKNOWN	GRZZZZ	UNK
WOLFSJAGER, FRZ	27	M	SMH	GRZZZZ	NY
KLESER, PETER	43	M	LABR	GRZZZZ	NY
MITTERMEYER, JOSEF	43	M	LABR	GRZZZZ	NY
PARE, JOH	58	M	LABR	GRZZZZ	UNK
REBULL, AUGUST	23	M	FARMER	GRZZZZ	UNK
KINNE, MICHAEL	43	M	FARMER	GRZZZZ	CLE
HUTS, PETER	22	M	LABR	GRZZZZ	NY
PFRUDEL, BENJ	19	M	FARMER	GRZZZZ	NY
NOWACK, OTTO	15	M	UNKNOWN	GRZZZZ	NY
GRZENKOWITZ, JOH	26	M	LABR	GRZZZZ	NY
WEIDINGER, ROBERT	43	M	MSN	GRZZZZ	NY
SCHWERGER, HELENE	50	F	UNKNOWN	GRZZZZ	UNK
FRANZ	13	M	UNKNOWN	GRZZZZ	UNK
HOGLMANN, GG	34	M	FARMER	GRZZZZ	PHI
CLARA	21	F	UNKNOWN	GRZZZZ	PHI
BRUGEL, JOSEF	33	M	FARMER	GRZZZZ	PHI
HELENE	33	F	UNKNOWN	GRZZZZ	PHI
JOSEF	4	M	CHILD	GRZZZZ	PHI
HELENE	1	F	CHILD	GRZZZZ	PHI
MERTEN, AUGUSTIN	27	M	CL	GRZZZZ	PHI
KLEIMER, HERMANN	36	M	BRR	GRZZZZ	UNK
SPRUNK, HELENA	24	F	UNKNOWN	GRZZZZ	NY
GOLDINI, MEDR	71	M	UNKNOWN	GRZZZZ	DET
VANMAELE, SOPHIE	73	M	UNKNOWN	GRZZZZ	DET
SAP, AMANDE	33	F	UNKNOWN	GRZZZZ	DET
KLEMSTAUBER, ANNA	25	F	UNKNOWN	GRZZZZ	DET
STRAUSS, FRANZ	29	M	LABR	GRZZZZ	NY
BURKHAR, JULIUS	28	M	CBTMKR	GRZZZZ	NY
ALMA	25	F	UNKNOWN	GRZZZZ	NY
MARIE	6	F	CHILD	GRZZZZ	NY
BURKHARDT, DOROTHEA	4	F	CHILD	GRZZZZ	NY
ETTY	3	F	CHILD	GRZZZZ	NY
SIEBLER, JOSEF	17	M	LABR	GRZZZZ	NY
HENMANN, MAX	26	M	MACH	GRZZZZ	NY
SATTLER, CHR	19	M	CL	GRZZZZ	NY
RIANKEWITZ, ANNA	19	F	UNKNOWN	GRZZZZ	NY
WIRTZ, THEOD	32	M	BKR	GRZZZZ	NY
KOHLER, JOH	17	M	BKR	GRZZZZ	NY
MULLER, STOFFEL	51	M	LABR	GRZZZZ	NY
KOPPELLE, J	26	M	LABR	GRZZZZ	BUF
FEITINK, JOH	26	M	FARMER	GRZZZZ	BUF
WIESKAMP, WM	28	M	FARMER	GRZZZZ	BUF
FEITINK, BERN	24	M	FARMER	GRZZZZ	BUF
SCHARZ, GOTH	55	M	MCHT	GRZZZZ	NY
M	56	F	UNKNOWN	GRZZZZ	NY
LAMBERT	20	F	UNKNOWN	GRZZZZ	NY
GUST	16	M	UNKNOWN	GRZZZZ	NY
N	14	F	UNKNOWN	GRZZZZ	NY
BOHN, GUILLE	43	M	MSN	FRZZZZ	IA
ZELEGMANN, G	22	M	LABR	GRZZZZ	NY

90

PASSENGER	AGE	SEX	OCCUPATION	PRVL	DES	PASSENGER	AGE	SEX	OCCUPATION	PRVL	DES
HELLMANN, DAVID	24	M	LABR	GRZZZZNY		HAAP, PETER	20	M	FARMER	SRZZZZNY	
ROTMANN, KELMEN	20	M	LABR	GRZZZZNY		RENNER, HERM	17	M	FARMER	SRZZZZNY	
SENIE	20	F	UNKNOWN	GRZZZZNY		OSMAS, PETER	30	M	LABR	SRZZZZNY	
WEISS, MARTIN	21	M	FARMER	GRZZZZNY		GEIGIS, ANTON	28	M	LABR	SRZZZZNY	
LAUGWEIL, MICHEL	22	M	FARMER	GRZZZZNY		HINDEN, WERENA	20	F	UNKNOWN	SRZZZZNY	
BIERBAUM, KELMAN	23	M	FARMER	GRZZZZNY		GEISBEIGER, JEAN	56	M	STKPR	SRZZZZNY	
BERGER, PAUL	26	M	LABR	GRZZZZNY		HUGGLER, ANDREAS	69	M	FARMER	SRZZZZNY	
SUSSMANN, ABRAH	28	M	LABR	GRZZZZNY		ANNA	40	F	UNKNOWN	SRZZZZNY	
SCHWARTZ, HERMAN	20	M	UNKNOWN	GRZZZZNY		SAUER, JOSEF	23	M	FARMER	SRZZZZNY	
LAHN, N	29	M	LABR	GRZZZZNY		ZEHLE, MARIA	23	F	UNKNOWN	SRZZZZNY	
HAUSEN, AND	33	M	FARMER	GRZZZZCH		BAILE, EMIL	25	M	LABR	SRZZZZNY	
THE---, JOSEF	18	M	LABR	GRZZZZNY		DENOTH, WALENTI	33	M	FARMER	SRZZZZNY	
SKALA, FRANZ	20	M	FARMER	GRZZZZNY		KALIN, EMMA	22	F	UNKNOWN	SRZZZZNY	
CERMOHOWSKI, ANTON	34	M	MSN	GRZZZZNY		HENTSCHEL, HUGO	30	M	CPR	SRZZZZNY	
GOEBEL, FRIED	43	M	FARMER	GRZZZZNY		KELLER, TH	41	M	FARMER	SRZZZZNY	
ELSA	28	F	UNKNOWN	GRZZZZNY		POER, ADEL	31	F	UNKNOWN	SRZZZZNY	
JACOB	14	M	CH	GRZZZZNY		RUCH, HANS	16	M	LABR	SRZZZZNY	
CATH	11	F	UNKNOWN	GRZZZZNY		BRITSCHGI, WERNER	49	M	FARMER	SRZZZZNY	
ELISA	9	F	CHILD	GRZZZZNY		FURRER, JOSEF	22	M	FARMER	SRZZZZNY	
FRIED	4	M	CHILD	GRZZZZNY		FANETT, BARBA	42	F	UNKNOWN	SRZZZZNY	
LUDW	3	M	CHILD	GRZZZZNY		JOHANN	11	M	UNKNOWN	SRZZZZNY	
MATHIAS	1	M	CHILD	GRZZZZNY		AGATHE	8	F	CHILD	SRZZZZNY	
FRIED	24	M	FARMER	GRZZZZNY		BLUMER, MARIE	63	F	UNKNOWN	SRZZZZNY	
PHILPE	18	F	UNKNOWN	GRZZZZNY		RHINER, H	48	M	FARMER	SRZZZZNY	
ELLNER, MARTIN	23	M	FARMER	GRZZZZNY		KRUSI, JAC	20	M	FARMER	SRZZZZNY	
ARMBRUSTER, PHILIP	23	M	FARMER	GRZZZZNY		ZCHUDER, HAAS	26	M	FARMER	SRZZZZNY	
FATER, JOSEF	22	M	LABR	GRZZZZNY		ROSINA	24	F	UNKNOWN	SRZZZZNY	
CORK, JOHANN	23	M	SMH	GRZZZZNY		RUDOLF	22	M	FARMER	SRZZZZNY	
PESID--, JOHANN	26	M	MSN	GRZZZZNY		CARL	17	M	CH	SRZZZZNY	
KARL, ANTON	25	M	LABR	GRZZZZNY		BUSTEN, AND	61	M	FARMER	SRZZZZNY	
RABIN, JOH	25	M	LABR	GRZZZZNY		LINA	37	F	UNKNOWN	SRZZZZNY	
VAUCK, MARIA	24	F	UNKNOWN	GRZZZZNY		FLUER, RUD	00	M	FARMER	SRZZZZNY	
JOHANNS, GOTTL	32	M	FARMER	GRZZZZNY		MEUK, LINDER	21	M	FARMER	SRZZZZNY	
DUIGELS, LEONHARD	22	M	MLR	GRZZZZNY		THONI, JOHANN	22	M	FARMER	SRZZZZNY	
RAUSCH, MATH	20	M	LABR	GRZZZZNY		BOHLMANN, FRITZ	19	M	FARMER	SRZZZZNY	
MULLER, PHILIPP	29	M	SMH	GRZZZZNY		ABEGGLEN, FRITZ	20	M	FARMER	SRZZZZNY	
LUIDEN, MATH	22	M	CBTMKR	GRZZZZNY		AMACHER, FRITZ	19	M	FARMER	SRZZZZNY	
BOEKER, AUGUST	20	M	FARMER	GRZZZZNY		IRBOF, CATHA	46	F	UNKNOWN	SRZZZZNY	
SCH---, PHILIPP	00	M	LABR	GRZZZZNY		CHRIST	23	F	UNKNOWN	SRZZZZNY	
RATTONY, ADELINE	28	F	UNKNOWN	GRZZZZNY		ANNA	21	F	UNKNOWN	SRZZZZNY	
WALDBILLIG, ANNA	24	M	LABR	GRZZZZNY		FRITZ	19	M	FARMER	SRZZZZNY	
HAUSEN, JEAN	25	M	FARMER	GRZZZZNY		ALBERT	18	M	FARMER	SRZZZZNY	
ARENDT, PAUL	27	M	FARMER	GRZZZZNY		ADOLF	11	M	FARMER	SRZZZZNY	
MARIE	27	F	UNKNOWN	GRZZZZNY		ELISA	9	F	CHILD	SRZZZZNY	
NICOLAS	3	M	CHILD	GRZZZZNY		CARL	1	M	CHILD	SRZZZZNY	
CATHERINE	1	F	CHILD	GRZZZZNY		KNABINT, FRANZ	18	M	LABR	SRZZZZNY	
BRAUN, HENRI	38	M	LABR	GRZZZZNY		NAGEL, ROSINA	24	F	UNKNOWN	SRZZZZNY	
ARENDT, FRANCISCE	34	F	UNKNOWN	GRZZZZNY		SCHNEIDER, HAVER	32	M	LABR	SRZZZZNY	
BRAUN, ELISA	9	F	CHILD	GRZZZZNY		WINKLER, HERM	23	M	LABR	SRZZZZNY	
MARIA	8	F	CHILD	GRZZZZNY		HECHLER, JOH	19	M	LABR	SRZZZZNY	
CATHERINE	5	F	CHILD	GRZZZZNY		NAGELE, ERNST	21	M	LABR	SRZZZZNY	
HENRI	3	M	CHILD	GRZZZZNY		MULLER, JACOB	25	M	LABR	SRZZZZNY	
SCHWARZ, MATHIAS	40	M	MSN	GRZZZZNY		REMHART, F	35	M	LABR	SRZZZZNY	
KAITZ, MICHAEL	28	M	LABR	GRZZZZNY		FRITZ, WILH	21	M	LABR	SRZZZZNY	
SCHMIDE, ALBERT	22	M	CL	GRZZZZNY		BATLER, JACOB	21	M	LABR	SRZZZZNY	
DREDUCH, ADOLF	20	M	MSN	GRZZZZNY		SCHAFER, MARIA	39	F	UNKNOWN	SRZZZZNY	
REUTZ, JEAN	19	M	LABR	GRZZZZNY		KECHELE, LINA	19	F	UNKNOWN	SRZZZZNY	
LAUX, JOHANN	18	M	LABR	GRZZZZNY		WESCHENMOSER, G	65	M	UNKNOWN	SRZZZZNY	
ROTTENBACH, PHILIPP	20	M	LABR	GRZZZZNY		BISCHOF, LINA	21	F	UNKNOWN	SRZZZZNY	
HENCITZ, NICOL	45	M	LABR	GRZZZZNY		SCHIOFF, MATHILDE	22	F	UNKNOWN	SRZZZZNY	
WETTER, JOSEPH	39	M	LABR	GRZZZZNY		MULLER, MARIA	23	F	UNKNOWN	SRZZZZNY	
GLAESENER, ANNA	28	F	UNKNOWN	GRZZZZNY		JOSEPHINE	14	F	UNKNOWN	SRZZZZNY	
WETTER, ELISA	8	F	CHILD	GRZZZZNY		MAUCHLI, MARIE	49	F	UNKNOWN	SRZZZZNY	
ANGELA	7	F	CHILD	GRZZZZNY		REBER, JOSEF	29	M	FARMER	SRZZZZNY	
KOH--, JOHN	21	F	UNKNOWN	GRZZZZNY		MAUCHLI, ALFRED	24	M	FARMER	SRZZZZNY	
GLAESNER, MARIA	19	F	UNKNOWN	GRZZZZNY		MARIA	27	M	FARMER	SRZZZZNY	
SUSANNA	15	F	UNKNOWN	GRZZZZNY		JOHANN	23	M	FARMER	SRZZZZNY	
WELTER, ANNA	3	F	CHILD	GRZZZZNY		MOCK, ALB	21	M	FARMER	SRZZZZNY	
BECK, FRED	27	M	LABR	GRZZZZNY		WOGET, GG	48	M	FARMER	SRZZZZNY	
GEORG	26	M	LABR	GRZZZZNY		PAUL	17	M	FARMER	SRZZZZNY	
WASSMUS, WILH	25	M	FARMER	GRZZZZNY		MAUGLE, JOS	23	M	FARMER	SRZZZZNY	
DAUB, NICOLAS	28	M	LABR	GRZZZZNY		HEMMETER, GOTTL	25	M	LABR	SRZZZZNY	
MARAYNKOWSKI, JOH	24	M	FARMER	GRZZZZNY		HUZEL, JOHAN	24	M	LABR	SRZZZZNY	
MOMEL, JOH	23	M	FARMER	GRZZZZNY		GUBLER, EDUARD	20	M	SMH	SRZZZZNY	
MORBACH, GEORG	19	M	MLR	GRZZZZNY		PFLEGHART, ALOIS	28	M	FARMER	SRZZZZNY	

PASSENGER	AGE	SEX	OCCUPATION	PRVL	DES
KISSLER, ANNA	28	F	UNKNOWN		SRZZZZNY
ALBERT	10	M	CH		SRZZZZNY
LEIBINGER, LOUISE	20	F	UNKNOWN		SRZZZZNY
SCHMID, JOH	23	M	FARMER		SRZZZZNY
HARTEGGER, BEN	33	M	FARMER		SRZZZZNY
SCHUTERER, JOH	22	M	FARMER		SRZZZZNY
LEUCHS, EDUARD	33	M	FARMER		SRZZZZNY
LAUTENBACH, JOH	42	M	FARMER		SRZZZZNY
WM	16	M	FARMER		SRZZZZNY
ROGG, MARIE	23	F	UNKNOWN		SRZZZZNY
BEER, LOUIS	28	M	FARMER		SRZZZZNY
ROGG, ANNA	19	F	UNKNOWN		SRZZZZNY
WINZENRICH, DAVID	54	M	FARMER		SRZZZZNY
CHRISTINE	57	F	UNKNOWN		SRZZZZNY
ANNA	30	F	UNKNOWN		SRZZZZNY
ALPLANDORF, ANDR	24	M	FARMER		SRZZZZNY
FLOHMANN, JAC	20	M	FARMER		SRZZZZNY
THONI, MELCHIOR	45	M	FARMER		SRZZZZNY
ALPLANOLZ, M	30	M	FARMER		SRZZZZNY
WEHRLI, CASPAR	20	M	FARMER		SRZZZZNY
AGI, SUSANNA	70	F	UNKNOWN		SRZZZZNY
DAVID	42	M	FARMER		SRZZZZNY
CARL	15	M	FARMER		SRZZZZNY
ELISE	13	F	UNKNOWN		SRZZZZNY
AARBURGER, MARIE	25	F	UNKNOWN		SRZZZZNY
MADER, SAMUEL	30	M	LABR		SRZZZZNY
CAROLINE	30	F	UNKNOWN		SRZZZZNY
ZUCHER, LINA	20	F	UNKNOWN		SRZZZZNY
ELISE	19	F	UNKNOWN		SRZZZZNY
MOSER, JOHANN	38	M	LABR		SRZZZZNY
DEOZ, EMILIE	32	F	UNKNOWN		SRZZZZNY
PAULINE	28	F	UNKNOWN		SRZZZZNY
DINA	15	F	UNKNOWN		SRZZZZNY
ERNST	4	M	CHILD		SRZZZZNY
SAMUEL	2	M	CHILD		SRZZZZNY
LINA	.06	F	INFANT		SRZZZZNY
SCHUMACHER, EVA	34	F	UNKNOWN		GRZZZZCH
FRIED	11	M	UNKNOWN		GRZZZZCH
HERMAN	9	M	CHILD		GRZZZZCH
CARL	6	M	CHILD		GRZZZZCH
PETER	2	M	CHILD		GRZZZZCH
BERGEL, CATH	19	F	UNKNOWN		GRZZZZPIT
STUPP, CATH	65	F	UNKNOWN		GRZZZZPIT
KRAMER, GERT	22	F	UNKNOWN		GRZZZZPIT
HEMERLI, ANNA	19	F	UNKNOWN		GRZZZZPAT
BRIEG, SUSANNA	21	F	UNKNOWN		GRZZZZPAT
GACHOT, MARGA	15	F	UNKNOWN		GRZZZZASH
DEHER, JOHANN	28	M	FARMER		GRZZZZASH
SCHWEIZER, ELISA	39	F	UNKNOWN		GRZZZZUNK
ELISA	9	F	CHILD		GRZZZZUNK
BARBA	6	F	CHILD		GRZZZZUNK
ELISA	3	F	CHILD		GRZZZZUNK
JOSEF	2	M	CHILD		GRZZZZUNK
KAISER, JOHANN	27	M	MSN		GRZZZZUNK
WEILICHER, CAROLA	22	F	UNKNOWN		GRZZZZUNK
LEVY, OSWALD	18	M	LABR		GRZZZZUNK
MARTIN, PETER	48	M	FARMER		GRZZZZUNK
MARGA	43	F	UNKNOWN		GRZZZZUNK
ANNA	20	F	UNKNOWN		GRZZZZUNK
GEORG	11	M	UNKNOWN		GRZZZZUNK
BERTHA	4	F	CHILD		GRZZZZUNK
WALK, MARIA	19	F	UNKNOWN		GRZZZZUNK
ZIEGLMEIER, MICHAEL	53	M	FARMER		GRZZZZPEO
MARIA	39	F	UNKNOWN		GRZZZZPEO
JOHANN	13	M	UNKNOWN		GRZZZZPEO
ANDREAS	11	M	UNKNOWN		GRZZZZPEO
ANNA	7	F	CHILD		GRZZZZPEO
MICHEL	6	M	CHILD		GRZZZZPEO
LUDWIG	3	M	CHILD		GRZZZZPEO
KRONINGER, MICHAEL	43	M	LABR		GRZZZZPEO
ABERGFELL, JOH	24	M	FARMER		GRZZZZPEO
WOLPERT, CARL	16	M	FARMER		GRZZZZPEO
HELFRICH, CATHA	69	F	UNKNOWN		GRZZZZPEO
WAHL, BARBA	13	F	UNKNOWN		GRZZZZPEO
ERHARD, APOLLA	20	F	UNKNOWN		GRZZZZPEO
ROTHSCHMIDE, CHRISTE	19	F	UNKNOWN		GRZZZZPEO
AMNINT, JOHANN	24	M	LABR		GRZZZZPEO
HENNERT, CASPAR	17	M	LABR		GRZZZZPEO
LERNER, JACOB	17	M	LABR		GRZZZZPEO
STOCKLE, MED	25	M	CPTR		GRZZZZPEO
SUSANNA	23	F	UNKNOWN		GRZZZZPEO
SCHUNK, GEORG	37	M	FARMER		GRZZZZPEO
CATHA	35	F	UNKNOWN		GRZZZZPEO
PHILIPP	8	M	CHILD		GRZZZZPEO
FRED	4	M	CHILD		GRZZZZPEO
THEOD	2	M	CHILD		GRZZZZPEO
ACKER, MARTIN	17	M	FARMER		GRZZZZUNK
BOCKER, CARL	25	M	LABR		GRZZZZSRE
JOH	17	M	LABR		GRZZZZSRE
SILL, JOHANN	25	M	FARMER		GRZZZZNY
RESLING, AMALIE	22	F	UNKNOWN		GRZZZZNY
LESCH, ADAM	17	M	LABR		GRZZZZNY
SCHIMPF, MARG	46	F	UNKNOWN		GRZZZZNY
BERTHA	17	F	UNKNOWN		GRZZZZNY
LEONORA	6	F	CHILD		GRZZZZNY
CARL	3	M	CHILD		GRZZZZNY
FRUND, JOHANNA	17	M	FARMER		GRZZZZNY
EMERT, NATALIE	39	F	UNKNOWN		GRZZZZNY
LORENZ, WILHELM	22	M	LABR		GRZZZZBAL
FRIEDA	19	F	UNKNOWN		GRZZZZBAL
LEHMANN, CHRIST	19	M	FARMER		GRZZZZBAL
WEBER, CARL	15	M	FARMER		GRZZZZCIN
CATH	13	F	UNKNOWN		GRZZZZCIN
BEISEL, MINA	22	F	UNKNOWN		GRZZZZUNK
JACOB	18	M	LABR		GRZZZZUNK
SCHUMPF, SIMON	13	M	UNKNOWN		GRZZZZUNK
HELFRICH, ELISA	20	F	UNKNOWN		GRZZZZNY
DORNER, MARTIN	27	M	LABR		GRZZZZNY
BECKER, ELISA	20	F	UNKNOWN		GRZZZZNY
ANNA	2	F	CHILD		GRZZZZNY
KREILMEIER, LISETTE	25	F	UNKNOWN		GRZZZZNY
WINTER, MAGD	19	F	UNKNOWN		GRZZZZNY
MULLER, ELISAB	24	F	UNKNOWN		GRZZZZNY
BRANDT, CATHA	28	F	UNKNOWN		GRZZZZNY
ELSA	26	F	UNKNOWN		GRZZZZNY
BERTHA	11	F	UNKNOWN		GRZZZZNY
DIHL, PAULINE	15	F	UNKNOWN		GRZZZZNY
WIEBELT, HEINRICH	17	M	LABR		GRZZZZCLE
SCHOF, EMIL	17	M	LABR		GRZZZZUNK
MULLNER, LUDW	33	M	FARMER		GRZZZZNY
STENAD, ADELBERT	27	M	FARMER		GRZZZZNY
POMMERSENNIG, CARL	21	M	FARMER		GRZZZZNY
WILHELM	26	M	FARMER		GRZZZZNY
KAPLAN, CHS	55	M	LABR		GRZZZZNY
GOTTSCHAL, HENRY	21	M	SDLR		GRZZZZNY
VOLLMANN, JACOB	44	M	LABR		GRZZZZNY
ESTHER	47	F	UNKNOWN		GRZZZZNY
FISCHER, JULIENNE	17	F	UNKNOWN		GRZZZZNY
SCHILD, PETER	15	M	FARMER		GRZZZZNY
GRUNWALD, VALT	47	M	FARMER		GRZZZZNY
FREUS, MICHAEL	60	M	FARMER		GRZZZZNY
KIRTZ, JEAN	25	M	FARMER		GRZZZZNY
KERTZER, PETER	21	M	FARMER		GRZZZZNY
MICHELS, PIERRE	28	M	FARMER		GRZZZZNY
PAUL, MICHEL	30	M	FARMER		GRZZZZNY
ANNA	22	F	UNKNOWN		GRZZZZNY
KREMER, PETER	25	M	FARMER		GRZZZZNY
BARTHEL, SUSAN	16	F	UNKNOWN		GRZZZZNY
SEFFEN, CHRIST	25	M	FARMER		GRZZZZNY
SCHMAL, EVA	18	F	UNKNOWN		GRZZZZNY
PETERS, MARIE	26	F	UNKNOWN		GRZZZZNY
HAAS, DOM	18	M	LABR		GRZZZZNY
MARGA	20	F	UNKNOWN		GRZZZZNY
CORNELIN, JACOB	21	M	LABR		GRZZZZNY
HIRSCH, NICOL	20	M	WTR		GRZZZZNY
KOPPES, NIC	30	M	LABR		GRZZZZNY
HORD, MARG	24	F	UNKNOWN		GRZZZZNY
BRETZ, BERNARD	16	M	LABR		GRZZZZNY
NINERBURG, BERNARD	48	M	LABR		GRZZZZNY
MARIE	44	F	UNKNOWN		GRZZZZNY

PASSENGER	AGE	SEX	OCCUPATION	PRVVL DES
NICOLAS	11	M	UNKNOWN	GRZZZZNY
CATH	8	F	CHILD	GRZZZZNY
JOHANN	4	M	CHILD	GRZZZZNY
BARTHOLOME, ANDRE	22	M	LABR	GRZZZZNY
GRISENAUER, JOSEF	24	M	LABR	GRZZZZNY
WENZL, JOH	38	M	FARMER	GRZZZZNY
CATH	34	F	UNKNOWN	GRZZZZNY
MICH	16	M	UNKNOWN	GRZZZZNY
NIC	13	M	UNKNOWN	GRZZZZNY
JOH	11	M	UNKNOWN	GRZZZZNY
MARIE	9	F	CHILD	GRZZZZNY
AND	7	M	CHILD	GRZZZZNY
MARG	4	F	CHILD	GRZZZZNY
COMOK, NIC	25	M	LABR	GRZZZZNY
DOLEIDEN, K	21	F	UNKNOWN	GRZZZZNY
QUARZ, FRANZ	16	M	UNKNOWN	GRZZZZNY
ANNA	17	F	UNKNOWN	GRZZZZNY
HESEINALD, MAX	26	M	LABR	GRZZZZNY
REMHAIDT, HCH	19	M	LABR	GRZZZZNY
RIES, J	39	M	LABR	GRZZZZNY
KEISCH, MAGD	38	F	UNKNOWN	GRZZZZNY
RIES, DOMINIQUE	10	M	CH	GRZZZZNY
JOSEPHINE	5	M	CHILD	GRZZZZNY
JACOB	4	M	CHILD	GRZZZZNY
RAULES, LEONARD	58	M	FARMER	FRZZZZNY
M	47	F	UNKNOWN	FRZZZZNY
J	19	M	LABR	FRZZZZNY
MARIE	16	F	UNKNOWN	FRZZZZNY
JOSEF	11	M	UNKNOWN	FRZZZZNY
EMILIE	7	F	CHILD	FRZZZZNY
DUBOIS, LOUIS	26	M	LABR	FRZZZZNY
NAU, PIERRE	45	M	LABR	GRZZZZNY
FELTGEN, ANNA	50	F	UNKNOWN	GRZZZZNY
NAU, EMIL	17	M	LABR	GRZZZZNY
MARIE	14	F	UNKNOWN	GRZZZZNY
JOH	11	M	UNKNOWN	GRZZZZNY
MARIE	7	F	CHILD	GRZZZZNY
BRUCK, NIC	21	M	LABR	GRZZZZNY
TUTSANN, AND	23	M	FARMER	GRZZZZNY
CATHA	24	F	UNKNOWN	GRZZZZNY
MULLER, MICH	23	M	FARMER	GRZZZZNY
EBERLE, CARL	14	M	UNKNOWN	GRZZZZNY
HENRI	11	M	UNKNOWN	GRZZZZNY
BERTEN, PETER	16	M	LABR	GRZZZZCH
REUTEN, PH	22	M	LABR	GRZZZZCH
BREIDECKER, HCH	26	M	CL	GRZZZZCH
DIEHL, OTTO	19	M	FARMER	GRZZZZCH
ABEL, CARL	15	M	FARMER	GRZZZZCH
MAUER, AUGUST	15	M	FARMER	GRZZZZCH
KUPFERER, MARIA	30	F	UNKNOWN	GRZZZZNY
CARL	6	M	CHILD	GRZZZZNY
MARIA	4	F	CHILD	GRZZZZNY
EUGEN	3	M	CHILD	GRZZZZNY
ELISAB	1	F	CHILD	GRZZZZNY
TRAUER, E	15	M	FARMER	GRZZZZNY
GROSS, LOUISA	16	F	UNKNOWN	GRZZZZNY
MOHR, GEO	15	M	FARMER	GRZZZZNY
KRULE, CAROLINE	22	F	UNKNOWN	GRZZZZNY
LOUISE	19	F	UNKNOWN	GRZZZZNY
KETZCHER, AMALIA	20	F	UNKNOWN	GRZZZZNY
GREENER, PAULINE	21	F	UNKNOWN	GRZZZZNY
ROSA	19	F	UNKNOWN	GRZZZZNY
URSEL, ERNST	21	M	LABR	GRZZZZNY
ROSENBERGER, ADOLF	19	M	LABR	GRZZZZSY
NIKUTTA, ADAM	28	M	LABR	GRZZZZUNK
BERTHA	24	F	UNKNOWN	GRZZZZUNK
FRANZ	1	M	CHILD	GRZZZZUNK
JOSS, IDA	25	M	UNKNOWN	SRZZZZUNK
IDA	3	F	CHILD	SRZZZZUNK
ANATOLE	1	F	CHILD	SRZZZZUNK
CHATELLEIN, EMIL	26	M	FARMER	SRZZZZUNK
RIES, MARG	20	F	UNKNOWN	SRZZZZCIN
SCHELLDORFER, BARB	00	F	UNKNOWN	SRZZZZPHI
SCHUG, ANNA	15	F	UNKNOWN	GRZZZZNY
MULLER, JOSEPHINE	20	F	UNKNOWN	GRZZZZNY
ORF, CATHA	33	F	UNKNOWN	GRZZZZNY
MARC	7	M	CHILD	GRZZZZNY
JOHANN	5	M	CHILD	GRZZZZNY
CAROLA	3	F	CHILD	GRZZZZNY
SIMON	2	M	CHILD	GRZZZZNY
HELENE	.09	F	INFANT	GRZZZZNY
HOFFARTH, LOUISA	20	F	UNKNOWN	GRZZZZPIT
STASHELINE, FR	25	F	UNKNOWN	GRZZZZPIT
DIESE, ERNST	21	M	FARMER	GRZZZZUNK
OSTER, FRANZ	23	M	MSN	GRZZZZBUF
BACH, JACOB	19	M	SMH	GRZZZZCRM
THOMAS, JOSEF	19	M	LABR	GRZZZZPIT
HEYMANN, M	19	M	LABR	GRZZZZNY
SCHMIDT, ANNA	19	F	UNKNOWN	GRZZZZNY
FLEISCHER, ELISA	19	F	UNKNOWN	GRZZZZNY
RIEGER, FRANZ	24	M	LABR	GRZZZZUNK
SCHREIBER, MICHEL	32	M	FARMER	GRZZZZUNK
MARIE	37	F	UNKNOWN	GRZZZZUNK
THERESE	9	F	CHILD	GRZZZZUNK
JOSEF	7	M	CHILD	GRZZZZUNK
LUDWIG	4	M	CHILD	GRZZZZUNK
ANNA	2	F	CHILD	GRZZZZUNK
CATH	.09	F	INFANT	GRZZZZUNK
LEMGUNG, AND	19	M	LABR	GRZZZZNY
ADAM	18	M	LABR	GRZZZZNY
SCHNEIDER, PH	25	M	FARMER	GRZZZZNY
LINZ, THEOD	16	M	FARMER	GRZZZZNY
MARIA	15	F	UNKNOWN	GRZZZZNY
KOERPER, ANNA	21	F	UNKNOWN	GRZZZZNY
HIEBUR, AUGUST	25	M	FARMER	GRZZZZNY
GUBENER, JOS	25	M	FARMER	GRZZZZNY
WOLFER, SEB	24	M	FARMER	GRZZZZNY
BERNIUS, JACOB	16	M	FARMER	GRZZZZNY
EHRHARDT, JOH	8	M	CHILD	GRZZZZNY
SCHAFFT, CAROL	16	F	UNKNOWN	GRZZZZNY
DAUER, BARBA	21	F	UNKNOWN	GRZZZZNY
KRUMERNACKER, MAGD	19	F	UNKNOWN	GRZZZZNY
SUSS, ANA	20	F	UNKNOWN	GRZZZZNY
WITTE, EMILIE	19	F	UNKNOWN	GRZZZZNY
MESSMER, MARIA	25	F	UNKNOWN	GRZZZZNY
SCHAFER, HEINR	58	M	FARMER	GRZZZZNY
ANNA	55	F	UNKNOWN	GRZZZZNY
JOHANNE	15	F	UNKNOWN	GRZZZZNY
SCHWEBER, JOHANN	43	M	FARMER	GRZZZZWHE
MAGDA	37	F	UNKNOWN	GRZZZZWHE
AUGUST	7	M	CHILD	GRZZZZWHE
MAGDA	5	F	CHILD	GRZZZZWHE
SCHELL, EVA	22	F	UNKNOWN	GRZZZZNY
SCHLICK, BERNH	24	M	LABR	GRZZZZNY
LAUTH, CATHA	20	F	UNKNOWN	GRZZZZNY
BECKER, JACOB	21	M	MSN	GRZZZZNY
BRIZINS, NICOL	32	M	CL	GRZZZZNY
MERGES, MATH	17	M	LABR	GRZZZZNY
GIBBERS, JOH	16	M	LABR	GRZZZZNY
HERES, CATH	49	F	UNKNOWN	GRZZZZNY
ROSA	22	F	UNKNOWN	GRZZZZNY
JOH	14	M	UNKNOWN	GRZZZZNY
ANGELA	11	F	UNKNOWN	GRZZZZNY
SCHNEIDER, CATH	51	F	UNKNOWN	GRZZZZNY
BACH, A	26	F	UNKNOWN	GRZZZZNY
THOMMEL, MATH	25	M	FARMER	GRZZZZNY
HAUDT, BRIZIUS	44	M	FARMER	GRZZZZNY
HELENE	38	F	UNKNOWN	GRZZZZNY
JACOB	16	M	UNKNOWN	GRZZZZNY
HELENE	11	F	UNKNOWN	GRZZZZNY
AU	9	M	CHILD	GRZZZZNY
PETER	3	F	CHILD	GRZZZZNY
MARG	.10	F	INFANT	GRZZZZNY
LIESER, ANDR	39	M	FARMER	GRZZZZNY
BERMANN, M	22	F	UNKNOWN	GRZZZZNY
JOSEPHER, MARIANNA	17	F	UNKNOWN	GRZZZZNY
NUSBAUM, ADELE	20	F	UNKNOWN	GRZZZZNY
KAUFMANN, BRUNETTE	23	F	UNKNOWN	GRZZZZNY
HENGELSBERG, PET	31	M	FARMER	GRZZZZNY
HOFMAN, FRZ	20	M	ENGR	GRZZZZNY

PASSENGER	AGE	SEX	OCCUPATION	PRIVL	DES
ZENGERL, OTTO	17	M	FARMER	GRZZZZPHI	
MULSER, HEINR	34	M	FARMER	GRZZZZNY	
BRECHTEFELD, W	44	F	UNKNOWN	GRZZZZNY	
LUT, LUDW	25	M	LABR	GRZZZZNY	
STEGLER, LEONARD	32	M	FARMER	GRZZZZUNK	
GIERDEN, JOSEF	24	M	FARMER	GRZZZZUNK	
RETTER, CARL	16	M	LABR	GRZZZZUSA	
MULLER, JOH	17	M	LABR	GRZZZZNY	
MYRTER, LOUISE	15	F	UNKNOWN	GRZZZZNY	
RUPP, FRIEDR	11	M	UNKNOWN	GRZZZZUNK	
JACOB	10	M	CH	GRZZZZUNK	
HCH	9	M	CHILD	GRZZZZUNK	
RUSS, CHRISSTOF	61	M	FARMER	GRZZZZUSA	
DOROTHEA	57	F	UNKNOWN	GRZZZZUSA	
JOHANN	20	M	FARMER	GRZZZZUSA	
CATH	18	M	FARMER	GRZZZZUSA	
JOHANNE	14	F	FARMER	GRZZZZUSA	
REICHERL, JACOB	67	M	FARMER	GRZZZZERE	
FRED	44	F	UNKNOWN	GRZZZZERE	
CAROLINE	21	F	UNKNOWN	GRZZZZERE	
JACOB	19	M	FARMER	GRZZZZERE	
WILHELMINE	14	F	UNKNOWN	GRZZZZERE	
SOPHIE	11	F	UNKNOWN	GRZZZZERE	
HETTENBACH, CHRISTIAN	26	M	CL	GRZZZZLAN	
HOERGER, CHRIST	18	F	UNKNOWN	GRZZZZLAN	
SCHUSTER, JOH	15	M	UNKNOWN	GRZZZZLAN	
JOERNSTED, ROSINE	19	F	UNKNOWN	GRZZZZLAN	
SCHILLER, SOPHIE	16	F	UNKNOWN	GRZZZZLAN	
GRAUER, GG	18	M	LABR	GRZZZZNY	
HOFMANN, JOH	16	M	LABR	GRZZZZNY	
POPP, ELISAB	24	F	UNKNOWN	GRZZZZNY	
SCHOELLBORN, HELENE	23	F	UNKNOWN	GRZZZZNY	
WM	8	F	CHILD	GRZZZZNY	
JOOS, ROSINE	17	F	UNKNOWN	GRZZZZNY	
MULLERSCHON, CARL	15	M	LABR	GRZZZZPIT	
BARTH, DAVID	14	M	UNKNOWN	GRZZZZPHI	
LINDAUER, CATHA	22	F	UNKNOWN	GRZZZZPHI	
WIESE, ADAM	30	M	FARMER	GRZZZZPHI	
MULLERSCHON, CATH	25	F	UNKNOWN	GRZZZZNY	
HENZLER, ELISA	18	F	UNKNOWN	GRZZZZNY	
LEPUND, SOPHIE	18	F	UNKNOWN	GRZZZZNY	
BAER, BARBA	60	F	UNKNOWN	GRZZZZNY	
WIBEL, LOUISE	46	F	UNKNOWN	GRZZZZNY	
CARL	24	M	FARMER	GRZZZZNY	
THEOD	15	M	FARMER	GRZZZZNY	
ERNST	3	M	CHILD	GRZZZZNY	
CHRISTINE	66	F	UNKNOWN	GRZZZZNY	
HERZOG, ANNA	19	F	UNKNOWN	GRZZZZNY	
PENOPP, JOH	17	M	LABR	GRZZZZNY	
GOYPERT, CATHA	16	F	UNKNOWN	GRZZZZNY	
BECK, VALENT	72	M	LABR	GRZZZZNY	
JOSEPHINE	66	F	UNKNOWN	GRZZZZNY	
MATHILDE	39	F	UNKNOWN	GRZZZZNY	
ZITHA	11	F	UNKNOWN	GRZZZZNY	
ZIEGELMANN, WM	25	M	CPTR	GRZZZZNY	
KAUM, CARL	25	M	LABR	GRZZZZNY	
HELLER, GOTTL	26	M	FARMER	GRZZZZNY	
CATHA	23	F	UNKNOWN	GRZZZZNY	
CARL	1	M	CHILD	GRZZZZNY	
DEER, JOS	22	M	MSN	GRZZZZBUF	
REISHERT, MARTIN	55	M	FARMER	GRZZZZDYT	
MAGDALENE	41	F	UNKNOWN	GRZZZZDYT	
ANAN	18	F	UNKNOWN	GRZZZZDYT	
FRANZ	15	M	UNKNOWN	GRZZZZDYT	
AUGUST	11	M	UNKNOWN	GRZZZZDYT	
JOSEF	7	M	CHILD	GRZZZZDYT	
BARBARA	4	F	CHILD	GRZZZZDYT	
HUMER, REGE	20	F	UNKNOWN	GRZZZZNY	
GRASSER, GEORGE	17	M	FARMER	GRZZZZNY	
BUCHLER, NIC	25	M	FARMER	GRZZZZNY	
STRASSER, HCH	32	M	FARMER	GRZZZZNY	
ERCHER, HAVER	22	M	FARMER	GRZZZZNY	
GOLSDUKA, MICH	26	M	FARMER	GRZZZZNY	
JUNG, FRED	16	M	FARMER	GRZZZZPHI	
ZONER, CAROLINE	17	F	UNKNOWN	GRZZZZPHI	
SIEGLE, GG	22	M	MSN	GRZZZZCOU	
BETZ, CARL	15	M	CL	GRZZZZCOU	
KACHEL, SOPHIE	16	F	UNKNOWN	GRZZZZCOU	
FUCHS, GOTTLIEB	15	M	LABR	GRZZZZNY	
RUCK, JULIUS	19	M	BRR	GRZZZZNY	
KOLB, WM	25	M	BRR	GRZZZZNY	
KIELMAIER, CAROLINA	16	F	UNKNOWN	GRZZZZNY	
AUCH, CATHA	19	F	UNKNOWN	GRZZZZNY	
NECKER, CATHA	18	F	UNKNOWN	GRZZZZNY	
CATH	20	F	UNKNOWN	GRZZZZNY	
RUCH, CARL	18	M	LABR	GRZZZZNY	
GOTH	18	M	LABR	GRZZZZNY	
JOHANNE	15	F	UNKNOWN	GRZZZZNY	
FISCHER, ROSA	13	F	UNKNOWN	GRZZZZNY	
KOLKUS, FRIDA	16	F	UNKNOWN	GRZZZZNY	
FRITZ, MARIE	16	F	UNKNOWN	GRZZZZNY	
BETZ, HER	18	M	LABR	GRZZZZNY	
SUMMENDINGER, M	24	F	UNKNOWN	GRZZZZNY	
MARTIN, ANTON	30	M	FARMER	GRZZZZNY	
ANNA	21	F	UNKNOWN	GRZZZZNY	
BITZEL, HCH	22	M	FARMER	GRZZZZNY	
STOCKLE, JOSEF	38	M	BRR	GRZZZZNY	
MAURER, JOH	28	M	CL	GRZZZZNY	
KESSLENBERG, EWALD	35	M	FARMER	GRZZZZNY	
SCHOFF, JOSEF	16	M	FARMER	GRZZZZNY	
BETSAMER, ANT	17	M	FARMER	GRZZZZNY	
HIRSCH, ROSA	19	F	UNKNOWN	GRZZZZNY	
ANMULLER, LORENZ	20	M	FARMER	GRZZZZNY	
LAUCH, CATH	20	M	UNKNOWN	GRZZZZNY	
ENDRES, MARIA	18	F	UNKNOWN	GRZZZZNY	
ANMUELLER, VAL	25	M	FARMER	GRZZZZNY	
BAB	25	F	UNKNOWN	GRZZZZNY	
GAERTNER, JOH	16	M	LABR	GRZZZZPIT	
BREHM, JOH	22	M	CBTMKR	GRZZZZSP	
ENGELHARDT, FRED	28	M	LABR	GRZZZZSP	
LOUISE	27	F	UNKNOWN	GRZZZZSP	
WRUZIG, CONRAD	30	M	FARMER	GRZZZZCIN	
KARGES, MARIA	21	F	UNKNOWN	GRZZZZCIN	
WEBER, JOSEF	32	M	FARMER	GRZZZZBUF	
CATH	26	F	UNKNOWN	GRZZZZBUF	
LIMEL, HER	23	M	LABR	GRZZZZBUF	
VEITH, DAN	38	M	FARMER	GRZZZZNY	
ANNA	37	F	UNKNOWN	GRZZZZNY	
LINA	14	F	UNKNOWN	GRZZZZNY	
CARL	8	M	CHILD	GRZZZZNY	
ADOLF	5	M	CHILD	GRZZZZNY	
RAUCH, CAROLINE	27	F	UNKNOWN	GRZZZZNY	
MARIA	5	F	CHILD	GRZZZZNY	
LUDWIG	3	M	CHILD	GRZZZZNY	
MARG	.09	F	INFANT	GRZZZZNY	
NORKE, MARTHE	23	F	UNKNOWN	GRZZZZNY	
MARTENS, ERNST	29	M	CPTR	GRZZZZNY	
SCHWARZ, E	25	F	UNKNOWN	GRZZZZNY	
FRESE, HECH	26	M	CPTR	GRZZZZNY	
FELDTUSCH, CASPAR	26	M	FARMER	GRZZZZNY	
RICKE, JOSEF	22	M	MSN	GRZZZZNY	
VANTHERN, F	15	M	UNKNOWN	GRZZZZNY	
RAST, HCH	21	M	BRR	GRZZZZNY	
BRENNIG, HER	19	M	FARMER	GRZZZZNY	
RAU, MAGD	19	M	FARMER	GRZZZZNY	
DAMM, BARBA	18	F	UNKNOWN	GRZZZZNY	
HUNGEMRINKER, PH	19	M	LABR	GRZZZZNY	
APPEL, EVA	13	F	UNKNOWN	GRZZZZNY	
HELFIECH, ANNA	18	F	UNKNOWN	GRZZZZNY	
HERTZIG, MARTIN	53	M	BKR	GRZZZZNY	
ANNA	49	F	UNKNOWN	GRZZZZNY	
EVA	20	F	UNKNOWN	GRZZZZNY	
JULIUS	13	M	UNKNOWN	GRZZZZNY	
JOSEF	11	M	UNKNOWN	GRZZZZNY	
EDEL, BERTHA	21	F	UNKNOWN	GRZZZZNY	
DIETZ, GEORG	48	M	FARMER	GRZZZZNY	
ANASTASIA	40	F	UNKNOWN	GRZZZZNY	
ELISA	19	F	UNKNOWN	GRZZZZNY	
MARIA	16	F	UNKNOWN	GRZZZZNY	
ENGELBERT	12	M	UNKNOWN	GRZZZZNY	

PASSENGER	AGE	SEX	OCCUPATION	PRVL	DES
EMIL	16	M	UNKNOWN		GRZZZZNY
EMMA	4	F	CHILD		GRZZZZNY
ANTONIA	7	F	CHILD		GRZZZZNY
BUSTNER, CATHA	00	F	UNKNOWN		GRZZZZNY
BERTHA	15	F	UNKNOWN		GRZZZZNY
HOID, RUD	15	M	CL		GRZZZZNY
HUBER, JOSEF	16	M	LABR		GRZZZZNY
KLOPF, ALWIN	16	M	LABR		GRZZZZLOU
FREY, GEORG	48	M	FARMER		GRZZZZSP
MARGA	45	F	UNKNOWN		GRZZZZSP
THERESE	13	F	UNKNOWN		GRZZZZSP
MARG	11	F	UNKNOWN		GRZZZZSP
FRANCISCA	6	F	CHILD		GRZZZZSP
ANNA	3	F	CHILD		GRZZZZSP
MOHL, EVA	27	F	UNKNOWN		GRZZZZUNK
LINA	6	F	CHILD		GRZZZZUNK
MARG	4	F	CHILD		GRZZZZUNK
GEORG	.09	M	INFANT		GRZZZZUNK
ZAUGL, MICH	54	M	FARMER		GRZZZZBUF
MARGA	47	F	UNKNOWN		GRZZZZBUF
FRANCISCA	17	F	UNKNOWN		GRZZZZBUF
ANTON	7	M	CHILD		GRZZZZBUF
FRANZ	3	M	CHILD		GRZZZZBUF
BAUER, CARL	25	M	LABR		GRZZZZNY
GOTTL	26	M	LABR		GRZZZZNY
OBOCHT, ANNA	17	F	UNKNOWN		GRZZZZLOU
HOLDENBACH, HER	25	M	LABR		GRZZZZNY
SCHOLL, CATHA	17	M	UNKNOWN		GRZZZZNY
BAUER, CATHA	16	F	UNKNOWN		GRZZZZNY
FRANCISCA	27	F	UNKNOWN		GRZZZZNY
WOLTERMANN, LUDWIG	17	M	FARMER		GRZZZZNY
KUCH, HERM	17	M	FARMER		GRZZZZNY
FETTER, CHRIST	14	M	FARMER		GRZZZZNY
WURZ, RUFRIA	46	F	UNKNOWN		GRZZZZUNK
LUTZ, MAGDA	24	F	UNKNOWN		GRZZZZUNK
HATTIG, OTTO	26	M	LABR		GRZZZZCLE
BECK, JOSEF	18	M	LABR		GRZZZZROC
MUKER, ANNA	14	F	UNKNOWN		GRZZZZROC
SCHULZ, JOH	28	M	FARMER		GRZZZZROC
MARGA	23	F	UNKNOWN		GRZZZZROC
CHRISTMAN, JOH	52	M	FARMER		GRZZZZROC
BARBA	49	F	UNKNOWN		GRZZZZROC
CARL	13	M	UNKNOWN		GRZZZZROC
WALTER, JOSEF	15	M	LABR		GRZZZZROC
HELFER, JACOB	51	M	FARMER		GRZZZZROC
WETER, MARIE	20	F	UNKNOWN		GRZZZZROC
HEISS, GEORG	18	M	FARMER		GRZZZZROC
VESPER, FRANZ	26	M	FARMER		GRZZZZROC
BRECHALTER, CATHA	21	F	UNKNOWN		GRZZZZROC
LERTEL, PHIL	24	M	LABR		GRZZZZROC
MOGG, MARIE	23	F	UNKNOWN		GRZZZZROC
JAUER, JOSEPHINE	25	F	UNKNOWN		GRZZZZROC
HAUSEN, NICOL	62	M	FARMER		GRZZZZUNK
PETER	45	M	FARMER		GRZZZZUNK
ANNA	37	F	UNKNOWN		GRZZZZUNK
THOMAS	7	M	CHILD		GRZZZZUNK
JOHANN	4	M	CHILD		GRZZZZUNK
MARGA	1	F	CHILD		GRZZZZUNK
ANNA	16	F	UNKNOWN		GRZZZZUNK
ROENMAIER, CHRIST	24	M	LABR		GRZZZZSTL
ABEL, BARTHA	18	F	UNKNOWN		GRZZZZNY
ZIMERER, HCH	26	M	CPTR		GRZZZZNY
LEOPOLDINE	32	F	UNKNOWN		GRZZZZNY
ADOLF	5	M	CHILD		GRZZZZNY
EMMA	1	F	CHILD		GRZZZZNY
GRUSEK, LORENZ	17	M	MSN		GRZZZZNY
WINKLER, THERESE	35	F	UNKNOWN		GRZZZZNY
LEHRER, CAROLINE	55	F	UNKNOWN		GRZZZZNY
CAROLINE	25	F	UNKNOWN		GRZZZZNY
LOUISE	18	F	UNKNOWN		GRZZZZNY
WILHELM	20	M	FARMER		GRZZZZNY
AUGUST	12	M	UNKNOWN		GRZZZZNY
HOEBELE, SALOM	36	M	LABR		GRZZZZNY
PFLEIG, URSULA	26	F	UNKNOWN		GRZZZZNY
MULLER, CATHA	58	F	UNKNOWN		GRZZZZNY
KLISE, UMAND	25	M	FARMER		GRZZZZNY
MULLER, HER	29	M	FARMER		GRZZZZNY
HEGEMANN, HCH	26	M	FARMER		GRZZZZNY
FLICKE, AND	38	M	FARMER		GRZZZZNY
HAM, ELISE	18	F	UNKNOWN		GRZZZZNY
WALSCH, NIC	36	M	LABR		GRZZZZNY
REITZ, JOS	26	M	FARMER		GRZZZZNY
DERCKA, KJOH	26	M	FARMER		GRZZZZNY
NAGEL, NIC	32	M	FARMER		GRZZZZNY
GAST, JOSEPH	24	M	MSN		GRZZZZNY
BABET, EMILIE	19	F	UNKNOWN		GRZZZZPHI
KNECHT, MICH	43	M	CPTR		GRZZZZBUF
MICH	10	M	CH		GRZZZZBUF
STRECHLER, JOSEL	21	M	UNKNOWN		GRZZZZBUF
REUDLER, PETER	17	M	LABR		GRZZZZNY
MERKEL, ROSA	20	F	UNKNOWN		GRZZZZNY
GERTH, FRIED	44	M	CBTMKR		GRZZZZNY
WINNER, BERNHARD	15	M	FARMER		GRZZZZNY
THERESA	22	F	UNKNOWN		GRZZZZNY
STEPHAN, REGINE	28	F	UNKNOWN		GRZZZZNY
CAROLINE	5	F	CHILD		GRZZZZNY
WM	3	M	CHILD		GRZZZZNY
THERESE	1	F	CHILD		GRZZZZNY
LIETTLER, AGNES	52	F	UNKNOWN		GRZZZZNY
NIEMANN, CARL	15	M	UNKNOWN		GRZZZZNY
ARBOGAST, SALOME	18	F	UNKNOWN		GRZZZZNY
MECHELER, EVA	22	F	UNKNOWN		GRZZZZNY
JUND, ANDREAS	27	M	FARMER		GRZZZZNY
CAROLINE	24	F	UNKNOWN		GRZZZZNY
MICHAEL	4	M	CHILD		GRZZZZNY
CAROLINE	3	F	CHILD		GRZZZZNY
ANDREAS	1	M	CHILD		GRZZZZNY
LOBSTEIN, PHIL	26	M	CPTR		GRZZZZNY
HOFFARTH, JOH	18	M	LABR		GRZZZZNY
SCHILLINGER, CAROLE	17	F	UNKNOWN		GRZZZZNY
MEIER, MARIE	40	F	UNKNOWN		GRZZZZNY
RUDOLF, HELENE	18	F	UNKNOWN		GRZZZZNY
REUSCHER, CATHA	21	F	UNKNOWN		GRZZZZNY
KUSIAN, JOH	27	M	LABR		GRZZZZNY
NECHER, CARL	35	M	UNKNOWN		GRZZZZNY
VECK, ERNST	13	M	UNKNOWN		GRZZZZNY
LAMBRECHT, JOH	43	M	FARMER		GRZZZZNY
RENNIG, LUDW	25	M	FARMER		GRZZZZNY
ROMMEL, NIC	28	M	FARMER		GRZZZZNY
ANNA	28	F	UNKNOWN		GRZZZZNY
ELISA	7	F	CHILD		GRZZZZNY
EMMA	2	F	CHILD		GRZZZZNY
MAGD	.09	F	INFANT		GRZZZZNY
REIM, SERAPHIM	34	M	FARMER		GRZZZZNY
PAULINE	32	F	UNKNOWN		GRZZZZNY
MARIA	11	F	UNKNOWN		GRZZZZNY
SERAPHIN	9	M	CHILD		GRZZZZNY
JOSEF	7	M	CHILD		GRZZZZNY
NIC	4	M	CHILD		GRZZZZNY
PAULINE	2	F	CHILD		GRZZZZNY
KLEIN, JOH	21	F	UNKNOWN		GRZZZZNY
BAUER, MINA	20	F	UNKNOWN		GRZZZZPHI
KLEIN, JOHAN	44	M	BCHR		GRZZZZMIL
CATH	36	F	UNKNOWN		GRZZZZMIL
JOH	15	M	UNKNOWN		GRZZZZMIL
OTTO	6	M	CHILD		GRZZZZMIL
ELISE	4	F	CHILD		GRZZZZMIL
FRANZ	3	M	CHILD		GRZZZZMIL
JOSEFINE	1	F	CHILD		GRZZZZMIL
U, ELISE	36	F	UNKNOWN		GRZZZZMIL
FRIEDGEN, MATH	22	M	LABR		GRZZZZMIL
DIDION, MAGD	36	F	UNKNOWN		GRZZZZNY
ROSA	11	F	UNKNOWN		GRZZZZNY
CARL	3	M	CHILD		GRZZZZNY
WEISS, W	25	M	FARMER		GRZZZZNY
KOWELOSKI, CHARLOTTE	25	F	UNKNOWN		GRZZZZUSA
AUGUST	2	M	CHILD		GRZZZZUSA
CARL	1	M	CHILD		GRZZZZUSA
HOFFMANN, CHARLOTTE	26	F	UNKNOWN		GRZZZZUSA
BRODA, EMILIE	10	F	CH		GRZZZZUSA

PASSENGER	AGE	SEX	OCCUPATION	PRVL	DES
HOFFMANN, BERTHA	5	F	CHILD	GRZZZZ	USA
WM	2	M	CHILD	GRZZZZ	USA
MARGARETEN, HUBERT	54	M	FARMER	GRZZZZ	UNK
LAMBERT	15	M	UNKNOWN	GRZZZZ	UNK
FRIED	10	M	CH	GRZZZZ	UNK
MARIA	6	F	CHILD	GRZZZZ	UNK
FUSEINICH, SIBILLA	28	F	UNKNOWN	GRZZZZ	UNK
ESCH, JOSEFE	30	F	UNKNOWN	GRZZZZ	UNK
WERKARDT, LINA	14	F	UNKNOWN	GRZZZZ	UNK
DOMER, KASP	14	M	UNKNOWN	GRZZZZ	UNK
SCHLAUG, ANN	17	M	LABR	GRZZZZ	UNK
PFEIL, LUDW	60	M	FARMER	GRZZZZ	UNK
ELISA	60	F	UNKNOWN	GRZZZZ	UNK
ROSINE	17	F	UNKNOWN	GRZZZZ	UNK
ANTON	29	M	FARMER	GRZZZZ	UNK
SUSE	26	F	UNKNOWN	GRZZZZ	UNK
HCH	3	M	CHILD	GRZZZZ	UNK
ELISE	1	F	CHILD	GRZZZZ	UNK
EMMA	.09	F	INFANT	GRZZZZ	UNK
DOMER, LOUISE	53	F	UNKNOWN	GRZZZZ	CLE
KARL	11	M	UNKNOWN	GRZZZZ	CLE
KONRAD, HERM	20	M	MSN	GRZZZZ	CLE
BOTH, BAB	19	F	UNKNOWN	GRZZZZ	CLE
SCHOTH, EVA	15	F	UNKNOWN	GRZZZZ	CLE
KADWEISS, JAC	17	M	LABR	GRZZZZ	ROC
SCHNEIDER, MAX	28	M	CPTR	GRZZZZ	NY
FRIEDGEN, JOSEPH	26	M	LABR	GRZZZZ	NY
SEVENIST, MAG	26	F	UNKNOWN	GRZZZZ	UNK
GERT	5	F	CHILD	GRZZZZ	UNK
ELISAB	3	F	CHILD	GRZZZZ	UNK
LENA	.11	F	INFANT	GRZZZZ	UNK
CORON, LOUISE	35	F	UNKNOWN	GRZZZZ	UNK
LEON	10	M	CH	GRZZZZ	UNK
VEDAL	7	M	CHILD	GRZZZZ	UNK
LOUISE	4	F	CHILD	GRZZZZ	UNK
JOSEPH	.11	F	INFANT	GRZZZZ	UNK
GUGGSBERG, MAR	22	F	UNKNOWN	GRZZZZ	UNK
PANKOKE, CARL	17	M	LABR	GRZZZZ	PIT
CUERM, JOSEPHINA	20	M	UNKNOWN	SRZZZZ	CLE
FAULEY, A	38	M	ART	GRZZZZ	NY
HAUF, J	45	M	MCHT	GRZZZZ	NY
NEUMANN, U	25	F	SVNT	GRZZZZ	NY
C	35	M	MCHT	GRZZZZ	NY
U	31	F	UNKNOWN	GRZZZZ	NY
MULLER, E	35	F	UNKNOWN	GRZZZZ	NY
OTTO	1	M	CHILD	GRZZZZ	NY
ERNST, A	40	F	UNKNOWN	GRZZZZ	NY
OTTO	10	M	CH	GRZZZZ	NY
BEIL, JOH	29	M	ART	GRZZZZ	NY
HEYMANN, JOH	36	M	MCHT	GRZZZZ	NY
WOBKE, H	26	F	UNKNOWN	GRZZZZ	NY
WIEDEMANN, L	28	F	UNKNOWN	GRZZZZ	NY
MULLER, M	26	F	UNKNOWN	GRZZZZ	NY
HUBER, E	30	F	UNKNOWN	GRZZZZ	NY
SIDLER, J	25	F	UNKNOWN	GRZZZZ	NY
GUBELMANN, S	27	F	UNKNOWN	GRZZZZ	NY
ARNET, M	25	F	SI	GRZZZZ	NY
SIDDLER, M	28	F	UNKNOWN	GRZZZZ	NY
REINER, M	23	F	UNKNOWN	GRZZZZ	NY
SIMER, M	24	F	UNKNOWN	GRZZZZ	NY
VANEY, M	15	M	UNKNOWN	GRZZZZ	NY
BECK, A	29	F	UNKNOWN	GRZZZZ	NY
KAUFMANN, J	24	F	UNKNOWN	GRZZZZ	NY
MATLER, M	23	F	UNKNOWN	GRZZZZ	NY
WYMINGER, E	22	F	UNKNOWN	GRZZZZ	NY
AMBUL, C	27	F	UNKNOWN	GRZZZZ	NY
HOLLINGER, U	25	F	UNKNOWN	GRZZZZ	NY
SCHO---, CARL	30	M	UNKNOWN	GRZZZZ	NY
BRAUN, C	25	F	UNKNOWN	GRZZZZ	NY
BAUER, ANNA	23	F	UNKNOWN	GRZZZZ	NY
HEISS, H	27	F	UNKNOWN	GRZZZZ	NY
HOFFMANN, F	25	F	UNKNOWN	GRZZZZ	NY
MEIER, E	21	F	UNKNOWN	GRZZZZ	NY
MEINDL, B	26	F	UNKNOWN	GRZZZZ	NY
MESSNE, F	24	F	UNKNOWN	GRZZZZ	NY
STUBER, M	28	F	UNKNOWN	GRZZZZ	NY
MEIERER, T	21	F	UNKNOWN	GRZZZZ	NY
MARCHUER, A	25	F	SI	GRZZZZ	NY
BINDER, A	23	F	UNKNOWN	GRZZZZ	NY
GOLLER, B	26	F	UNKNOWN	GRZZZZ	NY
BAUER, J	27	F	UNKNOWN	GRZZZZ	NY
SIMON, W	20	M	BBR	GRZZZZ	NY
GAERTNER, A	38	M	TLR	GRZZZZ	NY
E	37	F	UNKNOWN	GRZZZZ	NY
E	12	F	UNKNOWN	GRZZZZ	NY
STIEFEL, E	45	F	UNKNOWN	GRZZZZ	NY
WAGNER, A	32	M	ENGR	GRZZZZ	NY
HENMANN, C	26	F	UNKNOWN	GRZZZZ	NY
WERTZ, M	27	F	UNKNOWN	GRZZZZ	NY
BLESSING, A	25	F	UNKNOWN	GRZZZZ	NY
SIMNETT, A	40	F	UNKNOWN	GRZZZZ	NY
BLANETT, J	55	F	UNKNOWN	GRZZZZ	NY
K	26	F	UNKNOWN	GRZZZZ	NY
H	22	F	UNKNOWN	GRZZZZ	NY
F	17	F	UNKNOWN	GRZZZZ	NY
L	15	M	UNKNOWN	GRZZZZ	NY
P	13	M	UNKNOWN	GRZZZZ	NY
JEAN	1	M	CHILD	GRZZZZ	NY
KIMEN, M	25	F	UNKNOWN	GRZZZZ	NY
BRANDT, S	26	F	UNKNOWN	GRZZZZ	NY
KING, A	21	F	UNKNOWN	GRZZZZ	NY
HINMUGER, J	28	M	MCHT	GRZZZZ	NY
LORETA, J	26	F	UNKNOWN	GRZZZZ	NY
KRAUS, G	35	M	PREST	GRZZZZ	NY
THIESE, D	29	M	PREST	GRZZZZ	NY
BART, M	21	F	UNKNOWN	GRZZZZ	NY
SCHOSER, C	25	F	SI	GRZZZZ	NY
OPITZ, A	30	M	FARMER	GRZZZZ	NY
SCHMELJLE, M	29	F	UNKNOWN	GRZZZZ	NY
U	00	F	INF	GRZZZZ	NY

```
SHIP:     MORAVIA

FROM:     HAMBURG
TO:       NEW YORK
ARRIVED:  24 MAY 1888
```

PASSENGER	AGE	SEX	OCCUPATION	PRVL	DES
KULINSKI, STANISLAUS	17	M	PTR	GRAJVY	USA
NEUMANN, --EIDE	22	F	SGL	GRACSE	USA
DOBBRODT, CAROLE	50	F	WO	GRAIOE	USA
PITZNAS, HEINR	4	M	CHILD	PRZZZZ	USA
OSTROWSKY, FRANZ	24	M	LABR	PRACWT	USA
STACHOWSKY, ANTON	34	M	LABR	PRZZZZ	USA
CONSTANTINE	32	F	W	PRZZZZ	USA
GEORG	7	M	CHILD	PRZZZZ	USA
STANISLAV	00	M	CH	PRZZZZ	USA
U	.06	M	INFANT	PRZZZZ	USA
SAWIEKI, WAW-ZIN	25	M	LABR	PRZZZZ	USA
-ANOS, PETER	57	M	MCHT	PRZZZZ	USA
NOWDTZKI, ALEXANDER	34	M	LABR	PRZZZZ	USA
HACHE, CARL	21	M	LABR	PRAAKH	USA
LEISER, ARTHUR	00	M	UNKNOWN	PRACXV	USA
BRAND, CARL	19	M	MCHT	PRAAXK	USA
SOHNEIDER, CARL	17	M	LABR	PRAAXK	UNK
LEVY, CAMILLA	18	F	SGL	PRAAXK	UNK
AHLFELD, JOH	35	M	FARMER	PRZZZZ	UNK
ELISE	25	F	W	PRZZZZ	UNK
JOH	3	M	CHILD	PRZZZZ	UNK
RESCHENBERG, THEODOR	30	M	SMH	PRZZZZ	UNK
SALEWSKA, CARL	36	M	LABR	PRACJU	UNK
CHRISTE	33	F	W	PRACJU	UNK
LEOPOLD	9	M	CHILD	PRACJU	UNK
OTTO	8	M	CHILD	PRACJU	UNK
AUGUSTE	4	F	CHILD	PRACJU	UNK
OTTILIE	3	F	CHILD	PRACJU	UNK

PASSENGER	AGE	SEX	OCCUPATION	PRVVL	DES	PASSENGER	AGE	SEX	OCCUPATION	PRVVL	DES
ALBERT	2	M	CHILD	PRACJUUNK		ONALISCH, STANISLAUS	30	M	LABR	GRZZZZWI
KAUSTKA, EDUARD	23	M	FARMER	PRZZZZUNK		LIEBNER, ANTON	25	M	LABR	GRZZZZPA
PITZN-R, GUSTAV	44	M	LABR	PRZZZZUNK		TETZLAFF, JOHANN	28	M	FARMER	GRZZZZPA
REGINE	53	F	W	PRZZZZUNK		MARIA	26	F	UNKNOWN	GRZZZZPA
LOUISE	8	F	CHILD	PRZZZZUNK		ANNA	5	F	CHILD	GRZZZZPA
WOLFF, LOUIS	19	M	CL	PRAEABUNK		THERESE	3	F	CHILD	GRZZZZPA
BEVELSKY, THEODOR	50	M	SHMK	PRAENAUNK		MARIA	.02	F	INFANT	GRZZZZPA
VIELHAUER, JOH	17	M	TNM	PRAENAUNK		TOPEL, JOHN	28	M	JNR	GRZZZZMI
LEVY, HEINRICH	16	M	MCHT	BVZZZZUNK		ALBERTINA	24	F	UNKNOWN	GRZZZZMI
SCHMIDT, FERD	43	M	CPTR	BVAAKHUNK		OTTO	4	M	CHILD	GRZZZZMI
OCHOCKI, MICHAEL	58	M	LABR	PRZZZZUNK		ALBRECHT	.09	M	INFANT	GRZZZZMI
PETER	18	M	S	PRZZZZUNK		MATHILDE	.09	F	INFANT	GRZZZZMI
ROMAN	9	M	CHILD	PRZZZZUNK		KRAMP, HEINR	16	M	WTR	GRZZZZMD
KEMPT, LUDWIG	24	M	SHMK	PRACHSUNK		GILECKI, MICHAEL	32	M	LABR	GRZZZZOH
RIPPE, HEINR	17	M	MCHT	PRAARRUNK		MARIANNA	25	F	UNKNOWN	GRZZZZOH
PERSCHMANN, ALBERT	33	M	LABR	PRAAKHUNK		MARIA	6	F	CHILD	GRZZZZOH
PAULE	40	F	W	PRAAKHUNK		FRANZ	4	M	CHILD	GRZZZZOH
RA-ERJEZAK, LORENZ	25	M	LABR	PRZZZZUNK		FRANZ	5	M	CHILD	GRZZZZOH
LASKOWSKI, JOH	25	M	LABR	PRAEZVUNK		REMUS, HENRIETTE	42	F	UNKNOWN	GRZZZZIL
PLASZUKOWSKI, ANDR	29	M	LABR	PRZZZZUNK		SOLTA, THOMAS	25	M	LABR	GRZZZZIL
MARTIENSSEN, MARTIN	36	M	LABR	PRZZZZUNK		HIRSCH, FRIEDR	23	M	LABR	GRZZZZIL
ANDERS, CHRIST	34	M	LABR	PRZZZZUNK		NIELSEN, CHRISTIAN	20	M	LABR	GRZZZZCAL
BISANG, DANIEL	35	M	JNR	PRZZZZUNK		LITERSKY, ANTON	42	M	LABR	GRZZZZCAL
MARIE	28	F	W	PRZZZZUNK		GROMZEWSKY, MICHAEL	35	M	LABR	GRZZZZNE
ERNESTE	4	F	CHILD	PRZZZZUNK		ROSALIE	28	F	UNKNOWN	GRZZZZNE
CAROLE	3	F	CHILD	PRZZZZUNK		FRANZ	8	M	CHILD	GRZZZZNE
HEINRICH	.09	M	INFANT	PRZZZZUNK		ANDREAS	4	M	CHILD	GRZZZZNE
WITTKOWSKY, FRANZ	38	M	LABR	PRZZZZUNK		ANNA	2	F	CHILD	GRZZZZNE
NIEZGORSKY, -----AL	40	M	LABR	PRZZZZUNK		PEPLINSKY, MATHIAS	28	M	LABR	GRZZZZNE
-ICKEN, FRIEDR	42	M	FARMER	PRAJYLUNK		MARIANNA	28	F	UNKNOWN	GRZZZZNE
ZIMMERMANN, CATHA	26	F	SGL	WMZZZZUNK		FRANZ	3	M	CHILD	GRZZZZNE
MENDLER, MARIA	18	F	SGL	WMAGLMUNK		JOHANN	.11	M	INFANT	GRZZZZNE
KOPT, FRANZ	29	M	LABR	BVZZZZUNK		JOSEPH	.01	M	INFANT	GRZZZZNE
KICKMANN, RICHARD	22	M	TLR	BVABDMUNK		ZIGELSKY, JOHANN	34	M	LABR	GRZZZZOH
EUGENIE	15	F	WO	BVABDMUNK		STANISLAUS	20	M	LABR	GRZZZZOH
WENDEL, ERNST	42	M	PRNTR	BVAAKHUNK		BARKOWSKY, ALBERT	40	M	LABR	GRZZZZOH
JEHRENBACH, GEORG	18	M	MCHT	BVAELSUNK		ANNA	38	F	UNKNOWN	GRZZZZOH
SCHULZ, JOHANN	25	F	SGL	PRZZZZUNK		SAWELSKA, PAULINA	19	F	UNKNOWN	GRZZZZOH
S-OEBE, HERM	26	M	BBR	PRADZIUNK		STOBBE, JUSTIN	30	F	UNKNOWN	GRZZZZWI
G--OSDZ, FRANZ	23	M	UNKNOWN	PRZZZZUNK		MARTHA	5	F	CHILD	GRZZZZWI
BITTNEV, GERTRUD	17	F	SGL	PRZZZZUNK		HANS	3	M	CHILD	GRZZZZWI
JASKULSKA, VICTORIA	18	F	SGL	PRZZZZUNK		PAUL	.03	M	INFANT	GRZZZZWI
WOSZIZINSKI, KITAU	42	M	FARMER	PRZZZZUNK		PUSCH, EMIL	20	M	BBR	GRZZZZMO
ZAMMISKI, FRAN	26	M	LABR	PRZZZZUNK		ZAKZEWSKY, PETER	44	M	LABR	GRZZZZPA
ANNA	20	F	W	PRZZZZUNK		HEYN, AUGUST	23	F	UNKNOWN	GRZZZZMD
ALTER, LEISER	30	M	LABR	PRZZZZUNK		ANNA	15	F	UNKNOWN	GRZZZZMD
WYESINSKI, ANTON	17	M	LABR	PRZZZZUNK		BOLDA, JOSEPH	23	M	LABR	GRZZZZMD
						JOHANN	8	M	CHILD	GRZZZZMD
						WINKLER, FRANZ	15	M	MCHT	GRZZZZMN
						MARIA	13	F	UNKNOWN	GRZZZZMN
						LEHMANN, CARL	30	M	MCHT	GRZZZZMN
SHIP: WESER						WILH	31	F	UNKNOWN	GRZZZZMN
						HERMANN	7	M	CHILD	GRZZZZMN
FROM: BREMEN						EMIL	5	M	CHILD	GRZZZZMN
TO: BALTIMORE						ANNA	2	F	CHILD	GRZZZZMN
ARRIVED: 24 MAY 1888						MUELLER, CHRISTINE	75	F	UNKNOWN	GRZZZZIL
						ZYWITZKA, ANNA	30	F	UNKNOWN	GRZZZZOH
						MUELLER, ADOLF	25	M	PNTR	GRZZZZOH
						IWANSKY, VALENTIN	24	M	LABR	GRZZZZPA
SEVERS, DIEDR	31	M	TNR	GRZZZZMD		NAPARSTEN, JAN	45	M	LABR	GRZZZZPA
SCHULZ, SOPHIA	30	F	UNKNOWN	GRZZZZMD		MISKO, CATHARINA	19	F	UNKNOWN	GRZZZZPA
U. MARG	34	F	UNKNOWN	GRZZZZMD		CEIOSKY, AUGUST	15	M	LABR	GRZZZZPA
ROSA	8	F	CHILD	GRZZZZMD		DURALSKA, JULIANA	26	F	UNKNOWN	GRZZZZMT
ELISABETH	7	F	CHILD	GRZZZZMD		STANISLAUS	6	M	CHILD	GRZZZZMT
WALTER	5	M	CHILD	GRZZZZMD		MARIANNA	5	F	CHILD	GRZZZZMT
OSCAR	3	M	CHILD	GRZZZZMD		PEIKA, VICTORIA	20	F	UNKNOWN	GRZZZZOH
WILHELM	2	M	CHILD	GRZZZZMD		LEWANDOWSKY, ANDREAS	33	M	LABR	GRZZZZOH
RICHARD	.02	M	INFANT	GRZZZZMD		JANKOWSKI, JOHANN	30	M	LABR	GRZZZZPA
GUENTHER, THERESE	52	F	UNKNOWN	GRZZZZMD		ANNA	28	F	UNKNOWN	GRZZZZPA
LENZ, JOHANN	31	M	BKR	GRZZZZIL		MAYKOWSKY, ROSALIE	11	F	UNKNOWN	GRZZZZPA
HOTTENBACHER, ERNST	57	M	LABR	GRZZZZIL		APOLLNIA	6	F	CHILD	GRZZZZPA
CATH	54	F	UNKNOWN	GRZZZZIL		MUSIELACK, CATH	24	F	UNKNOWN	GRZZZZPA
ELISE	17	F	UNKNOWN	GRZZZZIL		ANTONIA	25	F	UNKNOWN	GRZZZZPA
ZARADKA, JOSEPH	23	M	LABR	GRZZZZWI		KONKOWSKA, FRIEDR	17	M	FARMER	GRZZZZIL
LIEBNER, JOSEPH	30	M	LABR	GRZZZZWI		MASCHKE, CAROLINA	55	F	UNKNOWN	GRZZZZIL

PASSENGER	AGE	SEX	OCCUPATION	PRVL	DES	PASSENGER	AGE	SEX	OCCUPATION	PRVL	DES
HERMANN	14	M	UNKNOWN	GRZZZZIL		KURZOWSKA, ANNA	26	F	UNKNOWN	GRZZZZPA	
LANGE, JOSEPH	30	M	CPTR	GRZZZZKY		LETTMANN, SOPHIE	15	F	UNKNOWN	GRZZZZMA	
PAUKONEN, AUGUSTE	19	F	UNKNOWN	GRZZZZKY		LENZ, EMIL	25	M	FARMER	GRZZZZPA	
SCHNEILING, CARL	25	M	LABR	GRZZZZKY		MARIA	26	F	UNKNOWN	GRZZZZPA	
CHRIST, PAULINA	25	F	UNKNOWN	GRZZZZIA		FRANZ	3	M	CHILD	GRZZZZPA	
JUERKEWIECZ, JOSEPHINE	18	F	UNKNOWN	GRZZZZIA		RICHARD	2	M	CHILD	GRZZZZPA	
KOCH, FERDINAND	39	M	BCHR	GRZZZZMA		KALIS, FRIEDR	39	M	FARMER	GRZZZZMI	
HOLZMANN, CAROLINA	30	F	UNKNOWN	GRZZZZMA		EVA	37	F	UNKNOWN	GRZZZZMI	
GRUNKE, ALBERT	26	M	FARMER	GRZZZZKY		AUGUST	9	M	CHILD	GRZZZZMI	
AMMANDA, WILHELMINA	22	F	UNKNOWN	GRZZZZKS		ERNESTINA	8	F	CHILD	GRZZZZMI	
PAWLAWSKI, FRANZ	35	M	FARMER	GRZZZZMN		FRIEDR	6	M	CHILD	GRZZZZMI	
ANNA	30	F	UNKNOWN	GRZZZZMN		KOEHLER, ALBERTINA	37	F	UNKNOWN	GRZZZZIL	
THOMAS	8	M	CHILD	GRZZZZMN		MARQUARDT, MARGARETA	49	F	UNKNOWN	GRZZZZIL	
JOHANN	7	M	CHILD	GRZZZZMN		SOPHIA	16	F	UNKNOWN	GRZZZZIL	
CONSTANTIN	2	M	CHILD	GRZZZZMN		ANNA	9	F	CHILD	GRZZZZIL	
JOSEPH	.03	M	INFANT	GRZZZZMN		MAWARD, WILHELM	60	M	LABR	GRZZZZNE	
KOCH, MARIANNA	38	F	UNKNOWN	GRZZZZIL		HOFFMANN, PAULINA	33	F	UNKNOWN	GRZZZZMO	
ANNA	5	F	CHILD	GRZZZZIL		ANNA	6	F	CHILD	GRZZZZMO	
VALERIA	3	F	CHILD	GRZZZZIL		PAUL	4	M	CHILD	GRZZZZMO	
POTRATZ, WILHELM	26	M	LABR	GRZZZZIL		CATHARINA	.02	F	INFANT	GRZZZZMO	
MARIA	21	F	UNKNOWN	GRZZZZIL		KUBIAK, JULIANE	60	F	UNKNOWN	GRZZZZPA	
MARIA	.03	F	INFANT	GRZZZZIL		GUNDZINSKY, JOSEPH	39	M	LABR	GRZZZZPA	
PLECKE, FRANZ	39	M	LABR	GRZZZZOH		STANISLAUS	8	M	CHILD	GRZZZZPA	
KUSCHMANN, HIRSCH	17	M	DLR	GRZZZZOH		JONITZ, BRIGITTE	36	F	UNKNOWN	GRZZZZIL	
SCHLUETER, MARIA	26	F	UNKNOWN	GRZZZZKY		AUGUSTE	28	F	UNKNOWN	GRZZZZIL	
MARG	6	F	CHILD	GRZZZZKY		JUSTIN	6	F	CHILD	GRZZZZIL	
BERG, HERMANN	24	M	SHMK	GRZZZZPA		ALBERT	3	M	CHILD	GRZZZZIL	
MUELLER, WILH	17	M	LABR	GRZZZZCAL		WENDT, JOHANN	46	M	FARMER	GRZZZZIL	
KOENECKE, HEINR	64	M	LABR	GRZZZZMO		EMILIA	36	F	UNKNOWN	GRZZZZIL	
WILHELMINE	57	F	UNKNOWN	GRZZZZMO		ALBERTINE	12	F	UNKNOWN	GRZZZZIL	
MOELLER, JOOSEPH	27	M	FARMER	GRZZZZIA		MATHILDE	7	F	CHILD	GRZZZZIL	
CATHARINA	26	F	UNKNOWN	GRZZZZIA		AUGUSTE	5	F	CHILD	GRZZZZIL	
JOSEPH	4	M	CHILD	GRZZZZIA		CARL	3	M	CHILD	GRZZZZIL	
MALWINA	2	F	CHILD	GRZZZZIA		SCHORMACK, FRANZISCA	26	F	UNKNOWN	GRZZZZIL	
SOPHIA	.03	F	INFANT	GRZZZZIA		ROSALIA	3	F	CHILD	GRZZZZIL	
LANGE, MARIA	68	F	UNKNOWN	GRZZZZIA		HAASE, MARTHA	20	F	UNKNOWN	GRZZZZMA	
WALINSKI, JAN	31	M	LABR	SRZZZZIA		SCHWANZ, ANNA	41	F	UNKNOWN	GRZZZZMA	
PATZKE, OTTO	26	M	LABR	GRZZZZMI		AUGUST	36	M	PNTR	GRZZZZMA	
CAROLINE	30	F	UNKNOWN	GRZZZZMI		GUSTAV	7	M	CHILD	GRZZZZMA	
CARL	2	M	CHILD	GRZZZZMI		OTTO	5	M	CHILD	GRZZZZMA	
EMMA	.05	F	INFANT	GRZZZZMI		BERTHA	3	F	CHILD	GRZZZZMA	
LOOS, LOUISE	60	F	UNKNOWN	GRZZZZMD		EMILIA	.09	F	INFANT	GRZZZZMA	
HOSSLI, JOHANN	20	M	LABR	SRZZZZMI		SCHARLINSKY, HERNMANN	21	M	LABR	GRZZZZOH	
MARTIN	23	M	LABR	SRZZZZMI		KLINECK, FRANZISCA	37	F	UNKNOWN	GRZZZZIL	
BAERLA, PHILIPP	23	M	LABR	SRZZZZMI		STANISLAUS	33	M	LABR	GRZZZZIL	
POLAKOWSKI, JOHANN	38	M	LABR	GRZZZZNE		FRANZISCA	8	F	CHILD	GRZZZZIL	
FLORENTINE	32	F	UNKNOWN	GRZZZZNE		MARIANNA	6	F	CHILD	GRZZZZIL	
JOHANN	8	M	CHILD	GRZZZZNE		CATHARINA	3	F	CHILD	GRZZZZIL	
MARTIN	5	M	CHILD	GRZZZZNE		EVA	.04	F	INFANT	GRZZZZIL	
MARIA	2	F	CHILD	GRZZZZNE		KLUMP, EMIL	23	M	BCHR	GRZZZZVA	
ANNA	3	F	CHILD	GRZZZZNE		KAZULSKI, CASPAR	50	M	LABR	GRZZZZPA	
PAUL	.10	M	INFANT	GRZZZZNE		GRAZYCK, MARTIN	29	M	LABR	GRZZZZPA	
KRATZKE, AUGUSTE	32	F	UNKNOWN	GRZZZZNE		CACILIA	27	F	UNKNOWN	GRZZZZPA	
DEMBECK, JOHANN	58	M	SMH	GRZZZZKY		MARIANNA	4	F	CHILD	GRZZZZPA	
CATH	54	F	UNKNOWN	GRZZZZKY		FRANZ	2	M	CHILD	GRZZZZPA	
POPLANSKY, FRANZISCA	54	F	UNKNOWN	GRZZZZOH		JOSEPH	.03	M	INFANT	GRZZZZPA	
MARIANNA	10	F	CH	GRZZZZOH		NEMITZ, AUGUTE	20	F	UNKNOWN	GRZZZZMO	
VALENTIN	5	M	CHILD	GRZZZZOH		STEIN, HEINR	30	M	LABR	GRZZZZMO	
GRAMS, WALENTIN	16	M	PNTR	GRZZZZPA		WILHELMINE	19	F	UNKNOWN	GRZZZZMO	
FISCHER, ALBERT	23	M	PNTR	GRZZZZMO		JOSEPH	16	M	FARMER	GRZZZZMO	
MACIZEWSKY, MICHALINA	53	F	UNKNOWN	GRZZZZMO		RIOE, EMILIA	41	F	UNKNOWN	GRZZZZWI	
ARNDT, EMMA	19	F	UNKNOWN	GRZZZZIA		OTTILIA	9	F	CHILD	GRZZZZWI	
DEMBROWSKI, JOSEPHA	20	F	UNKNOWN	GRZZZZMI		OTTO	7	M	CHILD	GRZZZZWI	
SOBIESKY, MRIANNA	17	F	UNKNOWN	GRZZZZMI		MINNA	6	F	CHILD	GRZZZZWI	
MARIANA	25	F	UNKNOWN	GRZZZZMI		EMIL	4	M	CHILD	GRZZZZWI	
WALZEWSKA, CATH	80	F	UNKNOWN	GRZZZZMO		EDUARD	.09	M	INFANT	GRZZZZWI	
LASS, JACOB	37	M	FARMER	GRZZZZKY		GLANE, ANTONIA	17	F	UNKNOWN	GRZZZZKY	
MARIANNA	30	F	UNKNOWN	GRZZZZKY		KEDZIERSKY, MICHAEL	34	M	SMH	GRZZZZPA	
JOSEPH	7	M	CHILD	GRZZZZKY		STANGENBERG, CATHARINA	48	F	UNKNOWN	GRZZZZMA	
ROSALIA	3	F	CHILD	GRZZZZKY		AUGUSTE	14	F	UNKNOWN	GRZZZZMA	
ISIDOR	6	M	CHILD	GRZZZZKY		SCHUMANN, EMIL	29	M	FARMER	GRZZZZIA	
GUETLEIN, GEORG	65	M	LABR	GRZZZZOH		AUGUSTE	26	F	UNKNOWN	GRZZZZIA	
ROPP, ALOISIA	16	F	UNKNOWN	GRZZZZOH		OSCAR	6	M	CHILD	GRZZZZIA	
ANNA	8	F	CHILD	GRZZZZOH		MARG	4	F	CHILD	GRZZZZIA	
ORTH, KUNIGUNDE	23	F	UNKNOWN	GRZZZZPA		JOHANN	3	M	CHILD	GRZZZZIA	

PASSENGER	AGE	SEX	OCCUPATION	PVRVL DES
ERNST	.09	M	INFANT	GRZZZZIA
STASZAK, THOMAS	39	M	LABR	GRZZZZPA
CATH	24	F	UNKNOWN	GRZZZZPA
JOHANN	5	M	CHILD	GRZZZZPA
CATH	.05	F	INFANT	GRZZZZPA
HOLODZIAK, IGNATZ	53	M	LABR	GRZZZZOH
TRANYZACK, MATHIAS	37	M	LABR	GRZZZZOH
CATHARINA	31	F	UNKNOWN	GRZZZZOH
CATHARINA	.09	F	INFANT	GRZZZZOH
KEMSKI, WLADISLAUS	26	M	LABR	GRZZZZTN
EMILIA	23	F	UNKNOWN	GRZZZZTN
CLARA	.09	F	INFANT	GRZZZZTN
WASIK, MARIA	22	F	UNKNOWN	GRZZZZCO
KONIEMRA, MARIA	38	F	UNKNOWN	GRZZZZCO
VERONICA	17	F	UNKNOWN	GRZZZZCO
WALZACK, FRANZ	17	M	LABR	GRZZZZPA
DERKOWSKY, JOHN	60	M	LABR	GRZZZZPA
MOTTKE, JOSEPH	68	M	LABR	GRZZZZPA
SCHADE, HEIN	25	M	JNR	GRZZZZUNK
WASCH, WOYCIECH	26	M	LABR	GRZZZZIA
LABUDA, JOHN	26	M	LABR	GRZZZZKY
PREDKOWSKY, JOHANN	30	M	GDNR	GRZZZZKY
JOHANNA	25	F	UNKNOWN	GRZZZZKY
VALENTIN	5	M	CHILD	GRZZZZKY
LEWANDOWSKA, MARIANNA	33	F	UNKNOWN	GRZZZZOH
JAN	8	M	CHILD	GRZZZZOH
DEMBECK, MARIE	19	F	UNKNOWN	GRZZZZOH
MELSCHEWSKY, FRANZISCA	65	F	UNKNOWN	GRZZZZOH
THEODOR	18	M	PNTR	GRZZZZOH
VOGT, MARIA	40	F	UNKNOWN	GRZZZZOH
SCHAUPETER, WILHELMINA	36	F	UNKNOWN	GRZZZZOH
LIESE	8	F	CHILD	GRZZZZOH
GRETHA	6	F	CHILD	GRZZZZOH
MARIA	3	F	CHILD	GRZZZZOH
NARMFELD, CARL	19	M	FARMER	GRZZZZWI
JAZUMBECK, ANTON	25	M	LABR	GRZZZZIL
ZIENKORZ, MASE	23	M	LABR	GRZZZZMI
LASKOWSKY, ANTON	30	M	LABR	GRZZZZMI
ZAZEWSKI, THEOPHIL	32	M	LABR	GRZZZZMI
WUTSCHKE, AUGUST	33	M	BKLYR	GRZZZZMN
AUGUSTE	32	F	UNKNOWN	GRZZZZMN
BERTHA	8	F	CHILD	GRZZZZMN
AUGUSTE	6	F	CHILD	GRZZZZMN
ALBERT	4	M	CHILD	GRZZZZMN
MAX	.02	M	INFANT	GRZZZZMN
TESKE, FRIEDERIKE	66	F	UNKNOWN	GRZZZZMN
HABERSATH, AUGUST	24	M	LABR	GRZZZZWI
BERNDT, ALBERTINA	40	F	UNKNOWN	GRZZZZCO
MARTHA	7	F	CHILD	GRZZZZCO
CLARA	6	F	CHILD	GRZZZZCO
FRANZ	3	M	CHILD	GRZZZZCO
PRENZYCA, VALENTIN	36	M	LABR	GRZZZZIL
ANNA	27	F	UNKNOWN	GRZZZZIL
JOSEPHINA	2	F	CHILD	GRZZZZIL
SELMA	.01	F	INFANT	GRZZZZIL
KRAUS, CARL	29	M	FARMER	GRZZZZIL
JOHANNA	27	F	UNKNOWN	GRZZZZIL
EMILIA	4	F	CHILD	GRZZZZIL
RICHARD	2	M	CHILD	GRZZZZIL
HELENE	.02	F	INFANT	GRZZZZIL
KETTERER, ELISABETH	70	F	UNKNOWN	GRZZZZWI
WALTER, MAGARETHA	18	F	UNKNOWN	GRZZZZIL
SCHUNK, JOHANN	23	M	SHMK	GRZZZZWI
ZIMMERMANN, DORIS	18	F	UNKNOWN	GRZZZZWI
JOHANN	.01	M	INFANT	GRZZZZWI
LEONHARD	17	M	LABR	GRZZZZWI
HOFFMANN, CAROLLINE	24	F	UNKNOWN	GRZZZZIL
FUNKE, AUGUSTE	43	F	UNKNOWN	GRZZZZIL
GLASER, AUGUST	35	M	JNR	GRZZZZIL
RESCH, HEINR	32	M	WCHMKR	GRZZZZMN
WOLLMER, JOHANN	43	M	WCHMKR	GRZZZZMN
PITTORF, BERNHARD	18	M	LABR	GRZZZZMN
MANE, ANNA	20	F	UNKNOWN	GRZZZZIL
HOPPE, HERMANN	34	M	MCHT	GRZZZZMO
MEIKOWSKA, FRANZISCA	18	F	UNKNOWN	GRZZZZKS
KARPOWSKY, CARL	47	M	FARMER	GRZZZZCAL
KUESTER, FANNY	21	F	UNKNOWN	GRZZZZOH
HUSMANN, LOUISE	29	F	UNKNOWN	GRZZZZOH
SOPHIA	7	F	CHILD	GRZZZZOH
ERNST	.03	M	INFANT	GRZZZZOH
BOCK, LINA	19	F	UNKNOWN	GRZZZZMD
KOWALSKY, LUDWIG	53	M	LABR	GRZZZZMD
ERDMANN, ERNST	18	M	MUSN	GRZZZZPA
KNUEPPEL, ERNST	18	M	MUSN	GRZZZZPA
HEIDSIECK, ELISE	20	F	UNKNOWN	GRZZZZOH
KOLNICK, JOHANNA	22	F	UNKNOWN	GRZZZZIL
SCHWOMACK, AUGUST	25	M	LABR	GRZZZZMI
SPLINTER, CARL	36	M	LABR	GRZZZZIL
PAUL	8	M	CHILD	GRZZZZIL
BARANOWSKA, MARG	23	F	UNKNOWN	GRZZZZNY
STANISLAWA	.03	F	INFANT	GRZZZZNY
ZAHL, AGATHE	44	F	UNKNOWN	GRZZZZWI
ANNA	8	F	CHILD	GRZZZZWI
MARTHA	15	F	UNKNOWN	GRZZZZWI
HEDWIG	6	F	CHILD	GRZZZZWI
ENNER, GEORG	43	M	FARMER	GRZZZZOH
THERESE	39	F	UNKNOWN	GRZZZZOH
WEINBERGER, MARIA	18	F	UNKNOWN	GRZZZZOH
EBNER, ALZEY	10	F	CH	GRZZZZOH
LENI	8	F	CHILD	GRZZZZOH
FRANZ	7	F	CHILD	GRZZZZOH
THERESE	5	F	CHILD	GRZZZZOH
ANNA	3	F	CHILD	GRZZZZOH
MARIA	.09	F	INFANT	GRZZZZOH
GIX, JOSEPH	38	M	BKR	GRZZZZOH
THERESIA	34	F	UNKNOWN	GRZZZZOH
HEDWIG	9	F	CHILD	GRZZZZOH
ELISABETH	6	F	CHILD	GRZZZZUNK
CAECILIA	4	F	CHILD	GRZZZZUNK
JOSEPH	.01	M	INFANT	GRZZZZUNK
GOLKA, ADAM	37	M	LABR	GRZZZZPA
GERZENKOWITZ, ANDREAS	63	M	LABR	GRZZZZMD
WILHELMINE	61	F	UNKNOWN	GRZZZZMD
PAUL	16	M	LABR	GRZZZZMD
RENCH	7	M	CHILD	GRZZZZMD
MILKA, JOSEPH	52	M	LABR	GRZZZZMD
MARIANNA	40	F	UNKNOWN	GRZZZZMD
JOSEPH	12	M	UNKNOWN	GRZZZZMD
LEON	8	M	CHILD	GRZZZZMD
FRANZ	5	F	CHILD	GRZZZZMD
JOSEFINA	.05	F	INFANT	GRZZZZMD
SCHULZ, RUDOLF	29	M	CPTR	GRZZZZMI
EMILIA	32	F	UNKNOWN	GRZZZZMI
ANNA	3	F	CHILD	GRZZZZMI
OTTO	.04	M	INFANT	GRZZZZMI
BOROVSKI, WILHELMINE	23	F	UNKNOWN	GRZZZZMI
POTRATZ, AUGUST	28	M	LABR	GRZZZZMI
KLUSCHINSKY, FRANZ	18	M	LABR	GRZZZZOH
KRUEGER, AUGUST	20	F	UNKNOWN	GRZZZZMI
SCHMIDT, ANNA	24	F	UNKNOWN	GRZZZZIL
REMUS, B	38	M	MCHT	GRZZZZIL
DANNENBERG, EMMA	62	F	UNKNOWN	GRZZZZMD
ADOLF	42	M	FARMER	GRZZZZMD
GUTH, WILHELMINA	68	F	UNKNOWN	GRZZZZMD
HERWAGEN, CARL	43	M	BCHR	GRZZZZIL
OTTO	8	M	CHILD	GRZZZZIL
GRIMM, AUGUSTE	23	F	UNKNOWN	GRZZZZMD
STOEVER, FERD	39	M	SLR	GRZZZZMI
WEISE, WENZEL	27	M	TLR	GRZZZZPA
WOLFF, BERTHA	21	F	UNKNOWN	GRZZZZPA
BROVER, OTTO	16	M	TLR	GRZZZZDAK
BOCHNKE, WM	27	M	LABR	GRZZZZDAK
ZIBULSKI, VICTOR	28	M	LABR	GRZZZZMD
WAREZINSKI, VALENTIN	28	M	LABR	GRZZZZMD
HEDWIG	49	F	UNKNOWN	GRZZZZMD
STANISLAWA	14	F	UNKNOWN	GRZZZZMD
MARIANNA	8	F	CHILD	GRZZZZMD
KREMPEL, ANNA	20	F	CH	GRZZZZMD
POSTNELKA, FRANZ	20	M	LABR	GRZZZZIL
EUCHNER, DOROTHEA	19	F	UNKNOWN	GRZZZZUNK

PASSENGER	AGE	SEX	OCCUPATION	PRV VL	DES
BAUSCH, FRIEDRICH	20	F	UNKNOWN		GRZZZZUNK
HUEBNER, PAUL	4	M	CHILD		GRZZZZUNK
RENNER, PHILIPP	24	M	PNTR		GRZZZZOH
WINKLER, GUSTAV	28	M	FARMER		GRZZZZOR
ANNA	22	F	UNKNOWN		GRZZZZOR
MAX	6	M	CHILD		GRZZZZOR
CLARA	4	F	CHILD		GRZZZZOR
CARL	.03	M	INFANT		GRZZZZOR
LEBHARDT, FRANZ	25	M	FARMER		GRZZZZWI
LENZ, MARTIN	44	M	FARMER		GRZZZZMI
CAROLINA	40	F	UNKNOWN		GRZZZZMI
BERTHA	8	F	CHILD		GRZZZZMI
ANNA	7	F	CHILD		GRZZZZMI
GUSTAV	5	M	CHILD		GRZZZZMI
ALMA	3	F	CHILD		GRZZZZMI
EMIL	.04	M	INFANT		GRZZZZMI
WUSTKE, CARL	46	M	FARMER		GRZZZZWI
WILHELMINE	40	F	UNKNOWN		GRZZZZWI
FRITZ	10	M	CH		GRZZZZWI
MARTHA	8	F	CHILD		GRZZZZWI
THEODOR	6	M	CHILD		GRZZZZWI
MINNA	5	F	CHILD		GRZZZZWI
ELISABETH	3	F	CHILD		GRZZZZWI
CARL	.02	M	INFANT		GRZZZZWI
MARIA	15	F	UNKNOWN		GRZZZZWI
HUNTEBRINGER, JOHANN	74	M	FARMER		GRZZZZMO
CATH	40	F	UNKNOWN		GRZZZZMO
MARIA	18	F	UNKNOWN		GRZZZZMO
LOUISE	8	F	CHILD		GRZZZZMO
FRANZ	6	M	CHILD		GRZZZZMO
CATH	4	F	CHILD		GRZZZZMO
BOENK, JOHANN	32	M	SMH		GRZZZZPA
HINRICH, MICHAEL	30	M	LABR		GRZZZZNE
LUECK, EMILIE	24	F	UNKNOWN		GRZZZZMN
MATHIAS	20	M	BBR		GRZZZZMN
KUJAROWSKY, FRANZ	38	M	LABR		GRZZZZOH
MARIA	37	F	UNKNOWN		GRZZZZOH
MARIE	8	F	CHILD		GRZZZZOH
PERSCHAN, CATH	68	F	UNKNOWN		GRZZZZOH
REIMANN, AUG	29	M	TLR		GRZZZZOH
LOUISE	38	F	UNKNOWN		GRZZZZOH
LANGE, MATHILDE	23	F	UNKNOWN		GRZZZZMD
ELSA	.03	F	INFANT		GRZZZZMD
GRIMM, JOHANNA	20	F	UNKNOWN		GRZZZZMD
WEBER, CRESENZ	20	M	MCHT		GRZZZZMI
HOEB, CHRISTIAN	32	M	PNTR		GRZZZZIN
BUECHMANN, ANTON	40	M	SMH		GRZZZZOH
MARG	40	F	UNKNOWN		GRZZZZOH
MARIANNA	7	F	CHILD		GRZZZZOH
MARG	3	F	CHILD		GRZZZZOH
BOCKHOP, SOPHIE	16	F	UNKNOWN		GRZZZZNE
HUSMANN, SOPHIE	6	F	CHILD		GRZZZZNE
LENZ, JACOB	19	M	MCHT		GRZZZZMD
THUROWSKY, ADAM	29	M	LABR		GRZZZZMD
LORENZ, EMMA	41	F	UNKNOWN		GRZZZZMD
LINDEBOOM, JOHANN	43	M	MCHT		GRZZZZCAL
NIEMEYER, BERNH	30	M	LABR		GRZZZZCAL
BOLWIN, EBERHARD	43	M	JNR		GRZZZZCAL
SCHNIEDERS, DANIEL	14	M	UNKNOWN		GRZZZZCAL
DOBBER, JOHANN	50	M	LABR		GRZZZZMD
MUELLER, HEINR	33	M	LABR		GRZZZZOH
MARIA	34	F	UNKNOWN		GRZZZZOH
HEINRICH	4	M	CHILD		GRZZZZOH
BERNI	.11	M	INFANT		GRZZZZOH
MEESE, BERNHARD	25	M	TLR		GRZZZZOH
ELISABETH	26	F	UNKNOWN		GRZZZZOH
ANNA	27	F	UNKNOWN		GRZZZZOH
ROBJON, AUGUST	55	M	LABR		GRZZZZMD
WEBER, BERTHA	24	F	UNKNOWN		GRZZZZMD
MEESE, HERMANN	75	M	UNKNOWN		GRZZZZOH
KLATTE, LINA	20	F	UNKNOWN		GRZZZZOH
RUETHER, ELISABETH	23	F	UNKNOWN		GRZZZZOH
NEUSCHWANGER, JOHANN	54	M	FARMER		GRZZZZOH
BARBARA	54	F	UNKNOWN		GRZZZZOH
GUSTAV	19	M	FARMER		GRZZZZOH
CLARA	20	F	UNKNOWN		GRZZZZOH
KLAUS, REINHARD	14	M	UNKNOWN		GRZZZZOH
STEIL, CHARLOTTE	22	F	UNKNOWN		GRZZZZMD
KLOSS, PETER	20	M	LABR		GRZZZZMD
BECKER, CARL	15	M	WTR		GRZZZZIL
SOEDERN, GOTTFR	23	M	BKLYR		GRZZZZIL
SAMMET, WILH	24	M	MCHT		GRZZZZOH
ECKERT, CARL	24	M	MCHT		GRZZZZOH
ZIEGLER, JOHANN	23	M	MCHT		GRZZZZOH
DOEDERER, CARL	25	M	LABR		GRZZZZOH
SCHADER, FRANZ	48	F	UNKNOWN		GRZZZZMD
LINA	18	F	UNKNOWN		GRZZZZMD
MARIA	7	F	CHILD		GRZZZZMD
SAMMET, ALBERT	23	M	MCHT		GRZZZZOH
BENDER, ALBERTINA	31	F	UNKNOWN		GRZZZZWI
CARL	.08	M	INFANT		GRZZZZWI
GERTRUDE	3	F	CHILD		GRZZZZWI
WERMELSKIRCHEN, JOHANN	17	M	PNTR		GRZZZZKY
WERTZ, JEAN	35	M	MCHT		GRZZZZKY
GEZENSKI, JOHANN	36	M	LABR		GRZZZZMD
JULIANA	31	F	UNKNOWN		GRZZZZMD
MARIANNA	8	F	CHILD		GRZZZZMD
JOHANN	6	M	CHILD		GRZZZZMD
WALADIA	4	F	CHILD		GRZZZZMD
ANTON	3	M	CHILD		GRZZZZMD
LOUIS	.01	M	INFANT		GRZZZZMD
ZIEGENHAGEN, JOHANN	60	M	JNR		GRZZZZMD
HENRIETTE	50	F	UNKNOWN		GRZZZZMD
SALLER, HERMANN	28	M	DLR		GRZZZZMD
SCHODMIACK, JOSEPH	31	M	LABR		GRZZZZMD
BISCHOFF, BABETTE	17	F	UNKNOWN		GRZZZZMD
LOERNZEN, ANNA	25	F	UNKNOWN		GRZZZZMI
WILHE	.06	F	INFANT		GRZZZZMI
GROTSCHLITZKY, WILH	64	M	LABR		GRZZZZMI
LOUISE	66	F	UNKNOWN		GRZZZZMI
BERTHA	7	F	CHILD		GRZZZZMI
C---	31	M	LABR		GRZZZZMI
U	.01	M	INFANT		GRZZZZMI
U	20	F	UNKNOWN		GRZZZZMI
U, U	00	F	UNKNOWN		GRZZZZIL
CZARNECKI, U	26	M	LABR		GRZZZZPA
JANSEN, U	14	M	LABR		GRZZZZNE
GADE, ---LH	18	M	BCHR		GRZZZZMD
LANGKARD, THADAEUS	48	M	FARMER		GRZZZZWI
CATH	47	F	UNKNOWN		GRZZZZWI
MATHILDE	20	F	UNKNOWN		GRZZZZWI
AUGUSTE	12	F	UNKNOWN		GRZZZZWI
ROBERT	8	M	CHILD		GRZZZZWI
HEDWIG	6	F	CHILD		GRZZZZWI
OTTO	2	M	CHILD		GRZZZZWI
BRANDT, HEINRICH	28	M	FARMER		GRZZZZNE
JUSTINE	22	F	UNKNOWN		GRZZZZNE
HEINR	5	M	CHILD		GRZZZZNE
JUSTIN	3	F	CHILD		GRZZZZNE
ANDREAS	.06	M	INFANT		GRZZZZNE
DIERKS, SIEBELT	58	M	FARMER		GRZZZZNE
SIERCKS, MARGARETHA	48	F	UNKNOWN		GRZZZZNE
HEINRICH	19	M	FARMER		GRZZZZNE
EDUARD	13	M	UNKNOWN		GRZZZZNE
SIEBELT	8	M	CHILD		GRZZZZNE
WILHELM	6	M	CHILD		GRZZZZNE
AUKEA	5	F	CHILD		GRZZZZNE
DOLOTA, THEOPHILA	31	F	UNKNOWN		GRZZZZKY
STANISLAUS	7	M	CHILD		GRZZZZKY
PETER	2	M	CHILD		GRZZZZKY
MICHAEL	.06	M	INFANT		GRZZZZKY
PIONTEK, ANNA	38	F	UNKNOWN		GRZZZZMO
ANNA	17	F	UNKNOWN		GRZZZZMO
MARIA	9	F	CHILD		GRZZZZMO
WLADISLAUS	7	M	CHILD		GRZZZZMO
ALEXANDER	5	M	CHILD		GRZZZZMO
STANISLAUS	3	M	CHILD		GRZZZZMO
PELAGIA	.06	F	INFANT		GRZZZZMO
NOWACK, MICHAEL	14	M	UNKNOWN		GRZZZZPA
SMAZINSKY, FRANZ	43	M	LABR		GRZZZZPA

PASSENGER	AGE	SEX	OCCUPATION	PRVL	DES
GULZINSKY, CASPAR	24	M	LABR		GRZZZZPA
COMET, JOHANN	28	M	LABR		GRZZZZPA
BRSCHILISKA, CATH	32	F	UNKNOWN		GRZZZZIL
HARMS, THEODOR	16	M	BKR		GRZZZZCAL
STRUSS, JOHAN	17	M	BKR		GRZZZZCAL
SCHOEFF, WILH	15	M	MCHT		GRZZZZIA
SCHWANZ, HERMANN	19	M	BKPR		GRZZZZKS
ALBERT	16	M	BKPR		GRZZZZKS
ZIRKELLACH, ELISE	19	F	UNKNOWN		GRZZZZMO
MARIA	7	F	CHILD		GRZZZZMO
KRAUSS, EVA	26	F	UNKNOWN		GRZZZZMO
THIEL, ROBERT	35	M	FARMER		GRZZZZIA
AUGUSTE	24	F	UNKNOWN		GRZZZZIA
BERTHA	5	F	CHILD		GRZZZZIA
EMMA	3	F	CHILD		GRZZZZIA
BISCHOFF, FRIEDR	40	M	FARMER		GRZZZZIL
BERTHA	39	F	UNKNOWN		GRZZZZIL
HELENE	10	F	CH		GRZZZZIL
RICHARD	8	M	CHILD		GRZZZZIL
ANNA	2	F	CHILD		GRZZZZIL
SCHEEL, WILH	27	M	FARMER		GRZZZZIA
NERTHA	22	F	UNKNOWN		GRZZZZIA
MEISCH, ERNST	25	M	FARMER		GRZZZZWI
ALBERTINE	25	F	UNKNOWN		GRZZZZWI
ERNST	6	M	CHILD		GRZZZZWI
FRIEDR	77	M	UNKNOWN		GRZZZZWI
CHRISTINA	69	F	UNKNOWN		GRZZZZWI
ACHTERBERG, CARL	40	M	FARMER		GRZZZZWI
WILHELMINA	38	F	UNKNOWN		GRZZZZWI
ERNST	8	M	CHILD		GRZZZZWI
ALWINE	5	F	CHILD		GRZZZZWI
LOUISE	3	F	CHILD		GRZZZZWI
BARTELD, ANNA	27	F	UNKNOWN		GRZZZZWI
JOHANNE	6	F	CHILD		GRZZZZWI
AGATHE	5	F	CHILD		GRZZZZWI
MINNA	3	F	CHILD		GRZZZZWI
LOUISE	.06	F	INFANT		GRZZZZWI
KAMPFMEIER, FRANZ	16	M	BBR		GRZZZZIL
SCHULZ, AUGUST	29	M	CPTR		GRZZZZWI
MOEHRKE, FERDINAND	30	M	CPTR		GRZZZZWI
KRUEGER, WILHELM	27	M	LABR		GRZZZZWI
KAISER, OTTO	17	M	LABR		GRZZZZOH
MAROCHA, MARIE	20	F	UNKNOWN		GRZZZZOH
WERNER, ANNA	22	F	UNKNOWN		GRZZZZOH
POWAS, CARL	36	M	FARMER		GRZZZZNE
U, LOUISE	26	F	UNKNOWN		GRZZZZNE
BERTHA	8	F	CHILD		GRZZZZNE
CARL	7	M	CHILD		GRZZZZNE
ERNST	5	M	CHILD		GRZZZZNE
ALBERT	4	M	CHILD		GRZZZZNE
OTTO	2	M	CHILD		GRZZZZNE
HUGO	.03	M	INFANT		GRZZZZNE
TERTACHA, GOTTLIEB	33	M	LABR		GRZZZZOH
ANNA	31	F	UNKNOWN		GRZZZZOH
BERTHA	8	F	CHILD		GRZZZZOH
GOTTFRIED	4	M	CHILD		GRZZZZOH
EDUARD	2	M	CHILD		GRZZZZOH
MINNA	.06	F	INFANT		GRZZZZOH
NAGEL, AUGUSTE	39	F	UNKNOWN		GRZZZZVA
FRITZ	6	M	CHILD		GRZZZZVA
OTT, ANNA	16	F	UNKNOWN		GRZZZZVA
BUCKMACKOWSKI, AUG	18	M	MUSN		GRZZZZKY
HEINRICH, ANNA	16	F	UNKNOWN		GRZZZZKY
BUCHHOLZ, AMALIA	25	F	UNKNOWN		GRZZZZKY
BRUEDER, LUDWIG	17	M	PH		GRZZZZKY
KIDROWSKY, ANNA	24	F	UNKNOWN		GRZZZZOH
FRANZISCA	.01	F	INFANT		GRZZZZOH
GIESE, IDA	21	F	UNKNOWN		GRZZZZOH
DIABERT, EMILIE	20	F	UNKNOWN		GRZZZZOH
GOLZ, ADELINA	18	F	UNKNOWN		GRZZZZOH
KRUESEL, HULDA	18	F	UNKNOWN		GRZZZZIL
BERTHA	9	F	CHILD		GRZZZZIL
SYZECK, VINCENTY	25	M	LABR		GRZZZZPA
RETZLAFF, ELISE	16	F	UNKNOWN		GRZZZZPA
BRODKE, WILH	67	M	LABR		GRZZZZMD
BLOCH, BERTHA	20	F	UNKNOWN		GRZZZZMD
WORDELMANN, HENRIETTE	86	F	UNKNOWN		GRZZZZVA
SASS, ALBERTINE	39	F	UNKNOWN		GRZZZZIA
AUGUSTE	13	F	UNKNOWN		GRZZZZIA
IDA	7	F	CHILD		GRZZZZIA
SEEFELD, ALBERTINE	28	F	UNKNOWN		GRZZZZIA
MARTHA	.02	F	INFANT		GRZZZZIA
HERMANN	2	M	CHILD		GRZZZZIA
ELLFELD, WILHELM	17	M	SHMK		GRZZZZKS
REDMANN, WILHELM	35	M	SMH		GRZZZZMO
CAROLINE	50	F	UNKNOWN		GRZZZZMO
BUENGERMEISTER, PAULINE	18	F	UNKNOWN		GRZZZZMO
JUNG, CAROLINE	26	F	UNKNOWN		GRZZZZMO
STERN, HERMANN	19	M	MCHT		GRZZZZMI
SAATMANN, JOHANNA	31	F	UNKNOWN		GRZZZZLA
OTTO	6	M	CHILD		GRZZZZLA
HELMUTH	3	F	CHILD		GRZZZZLA
ERNST	.11	M	INFANT		GRZZZZLA
KUHREICH, WILH	46	M	FARMER		GRZZZZTX
MARIA	34	F	UNKNOWN		GRZZZZTX
AUGUST	12	F	UNKNOWN		GRZZZZTX
ANNA	8	F	CHILD		GRZZZZTX
AUGUSTE	6	F	CHILD		GRZZZZTX
MARIA	4	F	CHILD		GRZZZZTX
WILHELM	.01	M	INFANT		GRZZZZTX
TONN, MICHAEL	64	M	LABR		GRZZZZMD
NOWACK, JOSEPH	28	M	LABR		GRZZZZMN
JULIANA	25	F	UNKNOWN		GRZZZZMN
JOHAN	2	M	CHILD		GRZZZZMN
U	.03	F	INFANT		GRZZZZMN
KLUNDER, ROSALIE	30	F	UNKNOWN		GRZZZZMN
FRANZ	3	M	CHILD		GRZZZZMN
NASTASIA	.01	F	INFANT		GRZZZZMN
SCHAWITZ, ELSA	32	F	UNKNOWN		GRZZZZMN
KNITTER, ROMAN	31	M	FARMER		GRZZZZNE
MARIANNA	33	F	UNKNOWN		GRZZZZNE
JOSEPH	6	M	CHILD		GRZZZZNE
FRANZISCA	5	F	CHILD		GRZZZZNE
ANGELICA	3	F	CHILD		GRZZZZNE
MARIANNA	1	F	CHILD		GRZZZZNE
MEYER, MARIE	32	F	UNKNOWN		GRZZZZPA
MARIE	3	F	CHILD		GRZZZZPA
CATH	.03	F	INFANT		GRZZZZPA
ENGELMANN, ELISE	30	F	UNKNOWN		GRZZZZPA
HERMANN	4	M	CHILD		GRZZZZPA
JOHANN	3	M	CHILD		GRZZZZPA
ANDREAS	.01	M	INFANT		GRZZZZPA
META	.01	F	INFANT		GRZZZZPA
STRAHTMANN, FRITZ	26	M	BCHR		GRZZZZMO
STRYZEWSKY, RUTHA	25	F	UNKNOWN		GRZZZZMO
SPRADO, ENGELINE	16	F	UNKNOWN		GRZZZZMO
HAUSES, HEINR	25	M	CPTR		GRZZZZOH
RADEMACHER, EZARDINE	18	F	UNKNOWN		GRZZZZKY
SCHMID, HELENE	21	F	UNKNOWN		GRZZZZKY
KETTLER, LOUISE	21	F	UNKNOWN		GRZZZZMD
SPOONE, JOHANN	16	M	MCHT		GRZZZZKS
WUESTENFELD, CARL	14	M	UNKNOWN		GRZZZZKS
HENKESIEFKEN, FRIEDR	18	M	FARMER		GRZZZZKS
GEORG	16	M	FARMER		GRZZZZKS
KAEMPF, OTTO	14	M	FARMER		GRZZZZKS
SCHMIDT, WILH	34	M	GDNR		GRZZZZMD
HAUPT, CONRAD	24	M	BCHR		GRZZZZMD
KOERBER, ELISABETH	24	F	UNKNOWN		GRZZZZMN
WILHELM	3	M	CHILD		GRZZZZMN
ELISE	.11	F	INFANT		GRZZZZMN
ELISE	15	F	UNKNOWN		GRZZZZMO
HAIGES, JOSEPH	25	M	LABR		GRZZZZMO
KROTHBIEREN, MARTIN	21	M	LABR		GRZZZZMO
RITTER, HAVER	16	M	LABR		GRZZZZMO
UBRICH, JACOB	16	M	WCHMKR		GRZZZZKY
SPRINGMANN, CAROLINE	16	F	UNKNOWN		GRZZZZKY
REIZ, FRIEDERIKE	45	F	UNKNOWN		GRZZZZOH
BANER, WLHELMINE	17	F	UNKNOWN		GRZZZZOH
SCHNABEL, JULIUS	17	M	PNTR		GRZZZZOH
KOH, CARL	18	F	UNKNOWN		GRZZZZVA

PASSENGER	AGE	SEX	OCCUPATION	PRVL	DES
MARIE	18	F	UNKNOWN		GRZZZZVA
BERG, THERESIA	26	F	UNKNOWN		GRZZZZVA
RUDOLF	3	M	CHILD		GRZZZZKS
SCHERER, PAUL	30	M	DLR		GRZZZZKS
ADELHEID	28	F	UNKNOWN		GRZZZZKS
ROSA	.09	F	INFANT		GRZZZZKS
KESSLER, ROSA	21	F	UNKNOWN		GRZZZZKS
STEINHILBER, JACOB	17	M	LABR		GRZZZZIL
EBERHARDT, ANNA	49	F	UNKNOWN		GRZZZZIL
GEORG	19	M	BRR		GRZZZZIL
BARB	7	F	CHILD		GRZZZZIL
BERNHARD	6	M	CHILD		GRZZZZIL
DINSE, FRIEDERICK	34	F	UNKNOWN		GRZZZZIL
ALFRED	3	M	CHILD		GRZZZZIL
MARIE	.09	F	INFANT		GRZZZZIL
GLATZ, ROMAN	36	M	JNR		GRZZZZIL
LINN, MINNA	14	F	UNKNOWN		GRZZZZMI
PELOI, CATH	28	F	UNKNOWN		GRZZZZMI
CHRIST	3	M	CHILD		GRZZZZMI
FRIEDR	.09	M	INFANT		GRZZZZMI
KOCH, MATHIAS	44	M	BKLYR		GRZZZZNY
MUELLER, ANDREAS	51	M	LABR		GRZZZZMD
ELLERAN, HEINR	15	M	LABR		GRZZZZFL
CULLMANN, LISETTE	17	F	UNKNOWN		GRZZZZKY
PHILIPP	15	M	MCHT		GRZZZZKY
PIPPLE, MARIA	35	F	UNKNOWN		GRZZZZOH
VETTER, LEOPOLD	16	M	PH		GRZZZZOH
LEWANDOWSKY, ANDREAS	30	M	LABR		GRZZZZOH
URBANOWITZ, JOSEPH	29	M	LABR		GRZZZZOH
JULIANA	28	F	UNKNOWN		GRZZZZOH
BIALKE, MARIA	65	F	UNKNOWN		GRZZZZPA
JOHANNA	24	F	UNKNOWN		GRZZZZPA
MALPERT, HERMANN	37	M	FARMER		GRZZZZNE
GEELKE	35	F	UNKNOWN		GRZZZZNE
LISCHEN	8	F	CHILD		GRZZZZNE
GERD	6	M	CHILD		GRZZZZNE
ALKE	4	M	CHILD		GRZZZZNE
JOHANNA	2	F	CHILD		GRZZZZNE
TALKE	.09	F	INFANT		GRZZZZNE
LUGENBIEL, CAROLINE	17	F	UNKNOWN		GRZZZZOH
HERMANITZ, BERNH	29	M	FARMER		GRZZZZMO
SPECHER, GERRUDE	21	F	UNKNOWN		GRZZZZMO
WALTER, MARIE	19	F	UNKNOWN		GRZZZZOH
SCHAFFERT, CONRAD	17	M	TLR		GRZZZZOH
SHOENLEBER, CHRISTIAN	24	M	LABR		GRZZZZMN
FUGMANN, ANNA	25	F	UNKNOWN		GRZZZZMO
MOESSER, HEINR	40	M	FARMER		GRZZZZPA
MARG	36	F	UNKNOWN		GRZZZZPA
HEINR	11	M	UNKNOWN		GRZZZZPA
FRIEDR	8	M	CHILD		GRZZZZPA
OTTO	6	M	CHILD		GRZZZZPA
MARGA	5	F	CHILD		GRZZZZPA
WILHELM	3	M	CHILD		GRZZZZPA
HERMANN	2	M	CHILD		GRZZZZPA
ADOLF	2	M	CHILD		GRZZZZPA
PICKEL, ERNST	53	M	CPTR		GRZZZZPA
LOHMUELLER, GEORG	53	M	CPTR		GRZZZZPA
KITZINGER, ANTON	71	M	LABR		GRZZZZKY
VICHTERMANN, FRITZ	22	M	LABR		GRZZZZIL
SCHAENBLEIN, JOSEFA	21	F	UNKNOWN		GRZZZZIL
SCHWAB, MARIA	55	F	UNKNOWN		GRZZZZIL
RUEDIGER, CARL	36	M	CGRMKR		GRZZZZIL
BERTHA	32	F	UNKNOWN		GRZZZZIL
GUSTAV	7	M	CHILD		GRZZZZIL
CARL	5	M	CHILD		GRZZZZIL
FISCHER, THERESIA	58	F	UNKNOWN		GRZZZZIL
KOWALKOWSKY, JOSEPH	29	M	LABR		GRZZZZIA
EVA	27	F	UNKNOWN		GRZZZZIA
JOHN	.10	M	INFANT		GRZZZZIA
NEUBOWSKI, FRANZISCA	28	F	UNKNOWN		GRZZZZIA
EVA	23	F	UNKNOWN		GRZZZZIA
JOHN	.03	M	INFANT		GRZZZZIA
RIEDEL, RICHARD	34	M	FARMER		GRZZZZNE
JOHANE	29	F	UNKNOWN		GRZZZZNE
MAX	4	M	CHILD		GRZZZZNE
ELISABETH	.09	F	INFANT		GRZZZZNE
KLAER, CARL	26	M	LABR		GRZZZZNE
ANNA	24	F	UNKNOWN		GRZZZZNE
EMMA	2	F	CHILD		GRZZZZNE
WENGLEWSKY, JOHANN	29	M	LABR		GRZZZZMI
VERONICA	28	F	UNKNOWN		GRZZZZMI
JOHANN	.11	M	INFANT		GRZZZZMI
ZALETZKY, ANTON	33	M	LABR		GRZZZZMI
ANNA	30	F	UNKNOWN		GRZZZZMI
MARIANNA	3	F	CHILD		GRZZZZMI
VALERIA	.03	F	INFANT		GRZZZZMI
VALTER, BENJAMIN	33	M	FARMER		GRZZZZKS
MARIA	30	F	UNKNOWN		GRZZZZKS
BABETTA	7	F	CHILD		GRZZZZKS
JOHANN	3	M	CHILD		GRZZZZKS
CHRISTIANA	2	F	CHILD		GRZZZZKS
KOSSWAR, CARL	24	M	LABR		GRZZZZMI
CLUCY, FRANK	43	M	FARMER		GRZZZZMI
CATHA	31	F	UNKNOWN		GRZZZZMI
MARIANNA	11	F	UNKNOWN		GRZZZZMI
LADISLAW	8	M	CHILD		GRZZZZMI
MARTHA	6	F	CHILD		GRZZZZMI
JOSEPH	4	M	CHILD		GRZZZZMI
FRANZ	.03	M	INFANT		GRZZZZMI
OPPERMANN, OTTILIE	30	F	UNKNOWN		GRZZZZMI
OSCAR	4	M	CHILD		GRZZZZMI
MARIA	3	F	CHILD		GRZZZZMI
SCHENKEL, CHRISTINA	22	F	UNKNOWN		GRZZZZMI
KUNKE, JACOB	51	M	LABR		GRZZZZMD
SOBOTA, WOYCIECH	53	M	LABR		GRZZZZIL
VICTORIA	53	F	UNKNOWN		GRZZZZIL
IGNATZ	22	M	LABR		GRZZZZIL
STANISLAWA	3	F	CHILD		GRZZZZIL
MAZANY, FRANZISCA	24	F	UNKNOWN		GRZZZZIL
KREISE, CARL	14	M	UNKNOWN		GRZZZZMO
GEIKE, CARL	14	M	UNKNOWN		GRZZZZMO
GRIESER, SOPHIE	16	F	UNKNOWN		GRZZZZPA
DIETZE, EUGENIE	20	F	UNKNOWN		GRZZZZPA
HOFFMANN, BERTHA	42	F	UNKNOWN		GRZZZZOH
ADOLF	8	M	CHILD		GRZZZZOH
BRANDENBURG, AUGUST	31	M	MCHT		GRZZZZCAL
SCHAUKIN, VICTOR	26	M	LABR		GRZZZZCAL
MOSINSKI, JOHANN	24	M	LABR		GRZZZZIN
TONSKA, ANZIELA	25	F	UNKNOWN		GRZZZZMD
KWOSECK, MICHALINE	36	F	UNKNOWN		GRZZZZMD
MARIANNA	6	F	CHILD		GRZZZZMD
VICTORIA	.06	F	INFANT		GRZZZZMD
GASCHINSKY, ANDREAS	53	M	LABR		GRZZZZMD
WENZLEWSKY, STANISLAUS	29	M	LABR		GRZZZZMD
RESCHKE, GOTTFRIED	24	M	LABR		GRZZZZMD
WASCHOWIAK, JOSEPH	32	M	LABR		GRZZZZMD
ZUMENDSA, WAWSZIN	22	M	LABR		GRZZZZOH
PIPER, ANNA	26	F	UNKNOWN		GRZZZZOH
EVA	56	F	UNKNOWN		GRZZZZOH
ANTON	17	M	LABR		GRZZZZOH
TILIKI, JAN	28	M	LABR		GRZZZZPA
BRZINSKA, JOSEFA	19	F	UNKNOWN		GRZZZZPA
ZELUBSKI, JACOB	34	M	LABR		GRZZZZPA
LANGANKE, CARL	17	M	SHMK		GRZZZZIN
JANOWSKI, FANNY	53	F	UNKNOWN		GRZZZZPA
STANISLAUS	27	M	LABR		GRZZZZPA
LACHAIZAK, VALENTY	23	M	LABR		GRZZZZMI
MIELKA, AUGUST	50	M	LABR		GRZZZZMI
JULIUS	16	M	LABR		GRZZZZMI
TEPPER, LUDWIG	36	M	LABR		GRZZZZMN
ANASTASIA	25	F	UNKNOWN		GRZZZZMN
MARIANNA	3	F	CHILD		GRZZZZMN
FRANZ	.11	M	INFANT		GRZZZZMN
STANISLAUS	.11	M	INFANT		GRZZZZMN
WALZ, AUGUST	36	M	FARMER		GRZZZZMN
LOUISE	32	F	UNKNOWN		GRZZZZMN
EMMA	6	F	CHILD		GRZZZZMN
AUGUSTE	4	F	CHILD		GRZZZZMN
BERTHA	2	F	CHILD		GRZZZZMN
STOLOWSKI, MICHAEL	26	M	LABR		GRZZZZPA

PASSENGER	AGE	SEX	OCCUPATION	PVL DES
PRONKOWSKI, JOSEPH	26	M	LABR	GRZZZZPA
BADASCHEWSKI, AND	24	M	LABR	GRZZZZPA
WOLNICK, THOMAS	42	M	LABR	GRZZZZPA
KWIATKOWSKA, ANTONIA	24	F	UNKNOWN	GRZZZZPA
KLOS, JOHANN	45	M	FARMER	GRZZZZMI
WILH	38	F	UNKNOWN	GRZZZZMI
WILHELMINE	10	F	CH	GRZZZZMI
FRANZ	8	M	CHILD	GRZZZZMI
STANISLAUS	5	M	CHILD	GRZZZZMI
JOSEPH	2	M	CHILD	GRZZZZMI
ANTON	.03	M	INFANT	GRZZZZMI
LEWINSKA, CATH	35	F	UNKNOWN	GRZZZZIA
LUDWIG	34	M	FARMER	GRZZZZIA
JOSEPHINA	8	F	CHILD	GRZZZZIA
APOLLONIA	7	F	CHILD	GRZZZZIA
MARIANNA	5	F	CHILD	GRZZZZIA
STANISLAUS	3	M	CHILD	GRZZZZIA
FRANZISCA	2	F	CHILD	GRZZZZIA
BINGEL, JACOB	17	M	SHMK	GRZZZZMO
GOHWEIS, ANTONIA	14	F	UNKNOWN	GRZZZZMO
SALLER, MATHIAS	15	M	WTR	GRZZZZOH
MALINOWSKY, JACOB	28	M	LABR	GRZZZZKY
CATH	22	F	UNKNOWN	GRZZZZKY
FRANZ	2	M	CHILD	GRZZZZKY
JOHANNA	.03	F	INFANT	GRZZZZKY
SARNOWSKA, FRANZ	26	M	LABR	GRZZZZPA
GRAH, MARIA	17	F	UNKNOWN	GRZZZZMD
WILKA, MINNA	45	F	UNKNOWN	GRZZZZTX
FRIEDR	17	M	JNR	GRZZZZTX
ANNA	14	F	UNKNOWN	GRZZZZTX
MRUZOWSKA, MARIANNA	23	F	UNKNOWN	GRZZZZOH
JANOS, STANISLAVA	15	F	UNKNOWN	GRZZZZOH
CIESNICK, MARTHA	23	F	UNKNOWN	GRZZZZPA
KWOSEK, MICHAEL	45	M	LABR	GRZZZZOH
WOLNICK, CATH	39	F	UNKNOWN	GRZZZZPA
ADAM	10	M	CH	GRZZZZPA
EVA	8	F	CHILD	GRZZZZPA
VALERIA	2	F	CHILD	GRZZZZPA
GRAH, JOSEPH	15	M	LABR	GRZZZZPA
LENGEN, JOHANN	30	M	LABR	GRZZZZIL
SALOWSKI, CARL	41	M	FARMER	GRZZZZIL
FLORENTINA	31	F	UNKNOWN	GRZZZZIL
CARL	7	M	CHILD	GRZZZZIL
FRANZ	3	M	CHILD	GRZZZZIL
EDUARD	.05	M	INFANT	GRZZZZIL
ZINDORSCH, JOSEPH	30	M	LABR	GRZZZZMI
TANNHOLD, PETER	29	M	LABR	GRZZZZIL
FRANKE	27	F	UNKNOWN	GRZZZZIL
FRIEDA	2	F	CHILD	GRZZZZIL
PETER	.03	M	INFANT	GRZZZZIL
HINRICHSEN, HENN	22	M	BKR	GRZZZZIL
JULIA	22	F	UNKNOWN	GRZZZZIL
HENN	.02	M	INFANT	GRZZZZIL
BLUMHOFER, GEORG	18	M	BKLYR	GRZZZZDAK
KARLOWSKY, WILH	36	M	LABR	GRZZZZDE
ZAKZEWSKY, FRANZ	44	M	LABR	GRZZZZDE
KUBE, AUGUST	29	M	LABR	GRZZZZMN
BROCKMEYER, HERM	72	M	LABR	GRZZZZIL
ANNA	68	F	UNKNOWN	GRZZZZIL
BIEL, CARL	24	M	MCHT	GRZZZZWI
EISEMANN, BABETTE	24	F	UNKNOWN	GRZZZZDE
BRAUN, ELISE	23	F	UNKNOWN	GRZZZZOH
VELTEN, JOSEPH	28	M	LABR	GRZZZZOH
JURKIEWICZ, PAULINE	21	F	UNKNOWN	GRZZZZIL
WILKE, THEOD	30	M	LABR	GRZZZZIL
KUPFER, HERMANN	53	M	FARMER	GRZZZZIL
GESINA	45	F	UNKNOWN	GRZZZZIL
BERNHARD	12	M	UNKNOWN	GRZZZZIL
WILHELM	8	M	CHILD	GRZZZZIL
MARIA	6	F	CHILD	GRZZZZIL
ELISE	5	F	CHILD	GRZZZZIL
BURGHARDT, BERNARDINA	60	F	UNKNOWN	GRZZZZWI
PROHOFSKY, JOSEPH	70	M	LABR	GRZZZZMN
DARSOW, FRIEDR	50	M	LABR	GRZZZZMN
EDUARD	.09	M	INFANT	GRZZZZMN
LUTZE, FRIEDR	26	M	BCHR	GRZZZZMD
BEZEK, STEFAN	18	M	LABR	GRZZZZIL
VIKAMP, HERM	24	M	CPTR	GRZZZZMO
MANTEY, FRANZ	41	M	SHMK	GRZZZZMI
CATH	40	F	UNKNOWN	GRZZZZMI
FRANZ	4	M	CHILD	GRZZZZMI
FRANZISCA	.01	F	INFANT	GRZZZZMI
OLIANNE	2	F	CHILD	GRZZZZMI
SHUEDT, GESINE	42	F	UNKNOWN	GRZZZZOH
ANNA	11	F	UNKNOWN	GRZZZZOH
HEINRICH	8	M	CHILD	GRZZZZOH
GESINE	6	F	CHILD	GRZZZZOH
MEINHARDT	3	M	CHILD	GRZZZZOH
ANGELICA	2	F	CHILD	GRZZZZOH
WEISS, ROSALIA	30	F	UNKNOWN	GRZZZZKS
MARTHA	7	F	CHILD	GRZZZZKS
JOSEPH	.02	M	INFANT	GRZZZZKS
PONDRO, ROSALIA	70	F	UNKNOWN	GRZZZZPA
WAGENKNECHT, MORITZ	62	M	LABR	GRZZZZMD
MORITZ	16	M	LABR	GRZZZZMD
JULIUS	10	M	CH	GRZZZZMD
HEIN, MARG	30	F	UNKNOWN	GRZZZZKY
---L	2	M	CHILD	GRZZZZKY
DAROW, WILHELMINA	27	F	UNKNOWN	GRZZZZMI
EMIL	6	M	CHILD	GRZZZZMI
BERTHA	3	F	CHILD	GRZZZZMI
LOUISE	2	F	CHILD	GRZZZZMI
TOLODZIECKI, JOHANN	25	M	LABR	GRZZZZIA
ADLESIC, JOHANN	25	M	LABR	GRZZZZIL
ZECH, FRANK	18	M	LABR	GRZZZZIL
KADAN, BARBARA	14	F	UNKNOWN	GRZZZZIL
ZOSKE, RUDOLF	40	M	LABR	GRZZZZIL
PUDKOWSKY, STANISLAUS	.06	M	INFANT	GRZZZZPA

SHIP: ADRIATIC

FROM: LIVERPOOL AND QUEENSTOWN
TO: NEW YORK
ARRIVED: 25 MAY 1888

PASSENGER	AGE	SEX	OCCUPATION	PVL DES
SABATZKY, EMIL	25	M	MCHT	GRADAXUSA

SHIP: HAMMONIA

FROM: HAMBURG AND HAVRE
TO: NEW YORK
ARRIVED: 25 MAY 1888

PASSENGER	AGE	SEX	OCCUPATION	PVL DES
PASCH, DORA	16	F	UNKNOWN	PRZZZZUSA
ALBRAND, LUDW	16	M	BCHR	PRZZZZUSA
BOESER, MARIA	18	F	SGL	HBZZZZUSA
WULF, THOMAS	16	M	FARMER	PRZZZZUSA
ST-SZ, LOUIS	16	M	FARMER	PRZZZZUSA
BARTOLOMAUS, JOHS	16	M	FARMER	PRZZZZUSA
RANCHE, JOH	36	M	FARMER	PRZZZZUSA
LORENZ, CATH	29	F	SGL	PRZZZZUSA
HAGEDORN, DORIS	23	F	SGL	PRZZZZUSA
JOHANNSEN, CHR	46	M	FARMER	PRZZZZUSA
AGNES	43	F	W	PRZZZZUSA
LUDWIG	14	M	S	PRZZZZUSA
CLAUSEN, HEINR	15	M	FARMER	PRZZZZUSA
KOEHLER, HEINR	62	M	LABR	PRZZZZUSA
CATHR	50	F	W	PRZZZZUSA
DOROTHEA	15	F	D	PRZZZZUSA
HAHN, AUG	24	M	FARMER	PRZZZZUSA

PASSENGER	AGE	SEX	OCCUPATION	PRVL DES
MOELLER, CARH	57	F	W	PRZZZZUSA
GU--CHE, BERNHARD	29	M	IMKR	SYZZZZUSA
SPIEGELBERG, OTTO	27	M	FARMER	PRZZZZUSA
MI-, JOHANN	42	M	LABR	PRZZZZUSA
JUSTINE	48	F	W	PRZZZZUSA
MARIE	15	F	D	PRZZZZUSA
-EPP, GEORG	17	M	LABR	BVZZZZUSA

SHIP: TRAVE

FROM: BREMEN AND SOUTHAMPTON
TO: NEW YORK
ARRIVED: 26 MAY 1888

PASSENGER	AGE	SEX	OCCUPATION	PRVL DES
BALKAR, HENRY	40	M	MCHT	GRZZZZUSA
ADOLF	29	M	MCHT	GRZZZZUSA
MEYER, ERNST	26	M	MCHT	GRZZZZUSA
NIEHAUS, H.W.	75	M	MCHT	GRZZZZUSA
LARSEN, F.W.	49	M	MCHT	GRZZZZUSA
ANSCHUETZ, JOH.	22	M	MCHT	GRZZZZUSA
TILLER, MAX	18	M	MCHT	GRZZZZUSA
MORAW, RUD.	36	M	MCHT	GRZZZZUSA
BENDEL, FABIAN	25	M	MCHT	GRZZZZUSA
MARX, LINA	20	F	UNKNOWN	GRZZZZUSA
GRONBACH, MARIA	52	F	UNKNOWN	GRZZZZUSA
TEUTSCH, LOUISE	18	F	UNKNOWN	GRZZZZUSA
BERBICH, REGINA	21	F	UNKNOWN	GRZZZZUSA
JAEGER, MAGA.	45	F	UNKNOWN	GRZZZZUSA
HAEGER, ANNA	16	F	UNKNOWN	GRZZZZUSA
HELDMANN, ERNST	22	M	FARMER	GRZZZZUSA
HOECH, CHRISTINE	39	M	FARMER	GRZZZZUSA
ZIRONEITH, GUSTAV	19	M	FARMER	GRZZZZUSA
BECK, DORA	22	F	UNKNOWN	GRZZZZUSA
HELMBACHER, CARL	17	M	FARMER	GRZZZZUSA
MARIE	16	F	UNKNOWN	GRZZZZUSA
FEHRENBACH, WILH.	22	M	MCHT	GRZZZZUSA
SCHMITZ, ANNA	16	F	UNKNOWN	GRZZZZUSA
WEICHSEL, MOSES	16	M	MCHT	GRZZZZUSA
SCHMIDT, MAGDA.	22	F	UNKNOWN	GRZZZZUSA
LEMINGER, MARGA.	22	F	UNKNOWN	GRZZZZUSA
LIESCHEN	24	F	UNKNOWN	GRZZZZUSA
WOLD, SARDA.	36	F	UNKNOWN	GRZZZZUSA
TENGMANN, CAROL.	20	F	UNKNOWN	GRZZZZUSA
KRONGR-ST, MAGDA.	20	F	UNKNOWN	GRZZZZUSA
WOLD, ERNEST	4	M	CHILD	GRZZZZUSA
FISCHER, MARIE	16	F	UNKNOWN	GRZZZZUSA
RITTER, LYDIA	30	F	UNKNOWN	GRZZZZUSA
GROSS, B.	20	M	FARMER	GRZZZZUSA
ZINDORF, MELANIE	30	F	UNKNOWN	GRZZZZUSA
JOHANN	24	M	FARMER	GRZZZZUSA
FLEISCHER, SIGMUND	25	M	MCHT	GRZZZZUSA
REINBOLD, RUD.	19	M	MCHT	GRZZZZUSA
BALBIAN, FR.	24	M	MCHT	GRZZZZUSA
KUHLMANN, FR.	36	M	FARMER	GRZZZZUSA
WELLE, FRD.	19	M	FARMER	GRZZZZUSA
WILLIE	16	M	FARMER	GRZZZZUSA
EDDIE	14	F	UNKNOWN	GRZZZZUSA
FRANKENFELD, GEORG	6	M	CHILD	GRZZZZUSA
KRIEGL, ANNA	17	F	UNKNOWN	GRZZZZUSA
SCHREIB, ANNA	20	F	UNKNOWN	GRZZZZUSA
FRIES, ELISE	26	F	UNKNOWN	GRZZZZUSA
ARMBRUST, SOPHIE	18	F	UNKNOWN	GRZZZZUSA
AUERBACH, U-MRS	40	F	UNKNOWN	GRZZZZUSA
SCHULZE, ANNA	18	F	UNKNOWN	GRZZZZUSA
WEISS, ANNA	20	F	UNKNOWN	GRZZZZUSA
HOPPE, HENRI	18	F	UNKNOWN	GRZZZZUSA
BISNECK, EMMA	17	F	UNKNOWN	GRZZZZUSA
BRACKENBUCH, GUENTHER	32	M	MCHT	GRZZZZUSA
WEDELL, F.	30	M	FARMER	GRZZZZUSA
ANDRAC, G.	41	M	FARMER	GRZZZZUSA
FRANKENBERG, THEOD.	22	M	FARMER	GRZZZZUSA
SCHRADER, G.A.	22	M	MCHT	GRZZZZUSA
CRONER, WOLF	40	M	MCHT	GRZZZZUSA
LINDBERG, C.W.	31	M	MCHT	GRZZZZUSA
GOETTSCHE, ELISE	20	F	UNKNOWN	GRZZZZUSA
WURZINIAK, F.	44	M	LABR	GRZZZZUSA
MYTKO, WOWRZYN	16	M	LABR	GRZZZZUSA
ROFMOSKY, JOSEF	23	M	LABR	GRZZZZUSA
WERKOWSKI, THOMAS	32	M	LABR	GRZZZZUSA
HOZNOTSKI, MIHAL	16	M	LABR	GRZZZZUSA
MARIANNA	13	F	UNKNOWN	GRZZZZUSA
STANISLAUS	6	M	CHILD	GRZZZZUSA
SEMERAN, PETRONELLA	25	F	UNKNOWN	GRZZZZUSA
CORNELIA	3	F	CHILD	GRZZZZUSA
LUDWIG	2	M	CHILD	GRZZZZUSA
WADISLAW	.06	M	INFANT	GRZZZZUSA
SCHREIBER, ALEX	23	M	CPTR	GRZZZZUSA
PAWLACZYK, THOMAS	38	M	LABR	GRZZZZUSA
KEIMANN, LOUISE	20	F	UNKNOWN	GRZZZZUSA
WAREMBIER, GOTTL.	15	M	CL	GRZZZZUSA
ADOLF	5	M	CHILD	GRZZZZUSA
ECK, CHRISTOF	24	M	LABR	GRZZZZUSA
ELIZABETH	16	F	UNKNOWN	GRZZZZUSA
FISCHMANN, GIDEL	35	F	UNKNOWN	GRZZZZUSA
MICZKOWSKA, FRANZA.	35	F	UNKNOWN	GRZZZZUSA
KRAPJILOWSKI, AUG.	25	M	LABR	GRZZZZUSA
KOLTEN, RASKA	18	F	UNKNOWN	GRZZZZUSA
WOYCIECHOSKI, JAN	44	M	TIR	GRZZZZUSA
THOMAS	15	M	TIR	GRZZZZUSA
KNOPFSKI, JAN	27	M	LABR	GRZZZZUSA
MARIANNE	24	F	UNKNOWN	GRZZZZUSA
WLADISLAUS	.10	M	INFANT	GRZZZZUSA
KRUEGER, GUST.	36	M	CPTR	GRZZZZUSA
MAJCHRZAK, VALENTIN	58	M	LABR	GRZZZZUSA
AGNES	53	F	UNKNOWN	GRZZZZUSA
DREWS, GOTTLIEB	55	M	LABR	GRZZZZUSA
PAKULSKA, MARGE.	40	F	UNKNOWN	GRZZZZUSA
SANTHEIM, ANNA	21	F	UNKNOWN	GRZZZZUSA
DAUNER, ELISA	20	F	UNKNOWN	GRZZZZUSA
BIERNACKI, STANISL.	22	M	LABR	GRZZZZUSA
SOFKE, VICTORIA	21	F	UNKNOWN	GRZZZZUSA
BONIKENSKI, MARTIN	55	M	UNKNOWN	GRZZZZUSA
ANNA	50	F	UNKNOWN	GRZZZZUSA
JOHANN	.02	M	INFANT	GRZZZZUSA
BORNCKA, MARGANNA	20	F	UNKNOWN	GRZZZZUSA
LEICHNITZ, MINNA	19	F	UNKNOWN	GRZZZZUSA
KOBIAK, JOSEF	24	M	LABR	GRZZZZUSA
KLEIN, JOHN	30	M	LABR	GRZZZZUSA
ROSALIE	27	F	UNKNOWN	GRZZZZUSA
JOHANN	.05	M	INFANT	GRZZZZUSA
ROSALIE	4	F	CHILD	GRZZZZUSA
JANKOWIAK, JOHAN	27	M	LABR	GRZZZZUSA
MARIE	26	F	UNKNOWN	GRZZZZUSA
ZUCKERMANN, BETSY	25	F	UNKNOWN	GRZZZZUSA
HERMINE	.05	F	INFANT	GRZZZZUSA
KOHLMANN, CATHA.	26	F	UNKNOWN	GRZZZZUSA
TENKE, PETER	48	M	FARMER	GRZZZZUSA
ELISABETH	38	F	UNKNOWN	GRZZZZUSA
ANNA	13	F	UNKNOWN	GRZZZZUSA
ANNA	6	F	CHILD	GRZZZZUSA
GERTRUDE	.06	F	INFANT	GRZZZZUSA
PREUSS, J.	23	M	FARMER	GRZZZZUSA
KOCH, BARBARA	18	F	UNKNOWN	GRZZZZUSA
SCHUCK, MARIE	21	F	UNKNOWN	GRZZZZUSA
HAVERSTRUMPF, MARGARETH	17	F	UNKNOWN	GRZZZZUSA
HOFFMANN, MARGA.	21	F	UNKNOWN	GRZZZZUSA
GEBELSEN, SOPHIE	17	F	UNKNOWN	GRZZZZUSA
JAHN, JOHANN	25	M	FARMER	GRZZZZUSA
CHRISTINE	25	F	UNKNOWN	GRZZZZUSA
CHRISTIAN	5	M	CHILD	GRZZZZUSA
FLECKENSTEIN, GEORG	30	M	FARMER	GRZZZZUSA
HASENSTAB, THEODOR	6	M	CHILD	GRZZZZUSA
HAUN, MARGA.	20	F	UNKNOWN	GRZZZZUSA
SCHMITTNER, MARGA.	17	F	UNKNOWN	GRZZZZUSA
SCHNEPF, BABETTA	29	F	UNKNOWN	GRZZZZUSA

PASSENGER	AGE	SEX	OCCUPATION	PRVL	DES
ENGEL, BABETTE	13	F	UNKNOWN	GRZZZZUSA	
WEIMER, HEINRICH	64	M	FARMER	GRZZZZUSA	
FRIEDKE	57	F	UNKNOWN	GRZZZZUSA	
EMILIE.	19	F	UNKNOWN	GRZZZZUSA	
MATHE.	18	F	UNKNOWN	GRZZZZUSA	
JAISER, ELISE	23	F	UNKNOWN	GRZZZZUSA	
KOST, AUG.	7	M	CHILD	GRZZZZUSA	
LORCH, MARGA.	30	F	UNKNOWN	GRZZZZUSA	
DUPHSIN, MARIE	55	F	UNKNOWN	GRZZZZUSA	
WOLLENS, AD.	21	M	FARMER	GRZZZZUSA	
SIEMER, ALEX	7	M	CHILD	GRZZZZUSA	
DAEBELE, MATHE.	16	F	UNKNOWN	GRZZZZUSA	
AHNES, MARIE	17	F	UNKNOWN	GRZZZZUSA	
BRAUTIGAM, ELISE	23	F	UNKNOWN	GRZZZZUSA	
KRITZMOELLER, LOUIS	30	M	FARMER	GRZZZZUSA	
NATALIE	26	F	UNKNOWN	GRZZZZUSA	
CLARA	2	F	CHILD	GRZZZZUSA	
FANNY	.01	F	INFANT	GRZZZZUSA	
SWIERCZINSKA, THEOPHILA	27	F	INF	GRZZZZUSA	
HOLLEIN, MARIA	20	F	INF	GRZZZZUSA	
ROCK, EMMA	18	F	INF	GRZZZZUSA	
MOELLER, BABETTE	20	F	UNKNOWN	GRZZZZUSA	
OECKER, JOH.	14	M	LABR	GRZZZZUSA	
FRANK, JACOB	70	M	LABR	GRZZZZUSA	
CATHA.	60	F	UNKNOWN	GRZZZZUSA	
SCHREIBER, ANNA	21	F	UNKNOWN	GRZZZZUSA	
DAMROW, CHRIST.	67	M	FARMER	GRZZZZUSA	
WILHNE.	64	F	UNKNOWN	GRZZZZUSA	
WEBER, HERMANN	24	M	FARMER	GRZZZZUSA	
WILHE.	27	F	UNKNOWN	GRZZZZUSA	
MARIE	2	F	CHILD	GRZZZZUSA	
LOUISE	.11	F	INFANT	GRZZZZUSA	
SCHULZ, ERNST	27	M	FARMER	GRZZZZUSA	
MARIE	23	F	UNKNOWN	GRZZZZUSA	
LOUISE	2	F	CHILD	GRZZZZUSA	
WILHELM	.01	M	INFANT	GRZZZZUSA	
DACHAUER, GG.	24	M	LABR	GRZZZZUSA	
GMEINWIESER, XAV.	29	M	LABR	GRZZZZUSA	
RAFFER, JOSEF	25	M	LABR	GRZZZZUSA	
FROHLICH, ERNST	19	M	LABR	GRZZZZUSA	
HUMMER, MARIA	50	F	UNKNOWN	GRZZZZUSA	
REITMEIER, MARIE	27	F	LABR	GRZZZZUSA	
LISIAK, FRANCISKA	22	F	LABR	GRZZZZUSA	
RASZMARK, VALENZ	60	M	LABR	GRZZZZUSA	
WAWRZYNIAK, FRANZ	27	M	LABR	GRZZZZUSA	
KIKEWICZ, THOMAS	26	M	LABR	GRZZZZUSA	
STESNIAK, JOSEFA	31	F	UNKNOWN	GRZZZZUSA	
JADWIGA	7	F	CHILD	GRZZZZUSA	
SCHIMMEL, JOHAN	43	M	LABR	GRZZZZUSA	
STEINHAGEN, JULIANE	47	F	UNKNOWN	GRZZZZUSA	
FLORENTINE	20	F	UNKNOWN	GRZZZZUSA	
GRUPE, JOHA.	20	F	UNKNOWN	GRZZZZUSA	
MEYER, FRIEDR.	16	M	FARMER	GRZZZZUSA	
KREYE, ADOLF	15	M	FARMER	GRZZZZUSA	
MORITZ	23	M	FARMER	GRZZZZUSA	
ALTHOFF, RUD.	16	M	FARMER	GRZZZZUSA	
HEINR.	6	M	CHILD	GRZZZZUSA	
FERD.	4	M	CHILD	GRZZZZUSA	
TWELMEIER, ANNA	33	F	UNKNOWN	GRZZZZUSA	
FRITZ	7	M	CHILD	GRZZZZUSA	
HERMANN	5	M	CHILD	GRZZZZUSA	
AUGUSTE	4	F	CHILD	GRZZZZUSA	
JOHANNE	2	F	CHILD	GRZZZZUSA	
JOHA.	25	F	UNKNOWN	GRZZZZUSA	
BOESCHLEIN, MARIE	18	F	UNKNOWN	GRZZZZUSA	
JAEGER, CARL	20	M	LABR	GRZZZZUSA	
BOEMANN, CHRIST.	25	M	LABR	GRZZZZUSA	
HASSELBACH, HEINR.	25	M	LABR	GRZZZZUSA	
WEISS, MAGDA.	60	F	UNKNOWN	GRZZZZUSA	
JOHANNE	22	F	UNKNOWN	GRZZZZUSA	
PETERS, HENRY	14	M	LABR	GRZZZZUSA	
TIETSCHEN, HEINRICH	18	M	LABR	GRZZZZUSA	
BREDE, WILHELM	20	M	LABR	GRZZZZUSA	
GEISSWETTER, JOHANN	17	M	LABR	GRZZZZUSA	
HOLTERMANN, DIEDR.	45	M	LABR	GRZZZZUSA	

PASSENGER	AGE	SEX	OCCUPATION	PRVL	DES
TRAPHOEFFER, JOH.	30	M	LABR	GRZZZZUSA	
BLINDERMANN, JACOB	14	M	LABR	GRZZZZUSA	
JAEGER, DIEDR.	24	M	LABR	GRZZZZUSA	
ANNA	21	F	UNKNOWN	GRZZZZUSA	
MARIE	.06	F	INFANT	GRZZZZUSA	
VONBARGEN, CHRIST.	21	M	FARMER	GRZZZZUSA	
SCHUERMANN, B.	18	M	FARMER	GRZZZZUSA	
SCHILLING, REBECCA	17	F	UNKNOWN	GRZZZZUSA	
BREMER, HERMANN	25	M	FARMER	GRZZZZUSA	
MUELLER, ERNST	20	M	FARMER	GRZZZZUSA	
LUERSSEN, ANNA	6	F	CHILD	GRZZZZUSA	
EMMA	00	F	CH	GRZZZZUSA	
KREUZ, HEINR.	24	M	BKLYR	GRZZZZUSA	
MANN, HERMINE	21	F	UNKNOWN	GRZZZZUSA	
STULGITAS, FRANK	20	M	LABR	GRZZZZUSA	
THOMAS, HERMANN	28	M	LABR	GRZZZZUSA	
RATHGEBER, JULIE	23	F	UNKNOWN	GRZZZZUSA	
FRIEDR.	3	M	CHILD	GRZZZZUSA	
AUGUSTE	.01	F	INFANT	GRZZZZUSA	
ZAPF, EMMA	47	F	UNKNOWN	GRZZZZUSA	
ALBERT	48	M	FARMER	GRZZZZUSA	
HEDWIG	.05	F	INFANT	GRZZZZUSA	
WEILER, FRIEDRICH	24	M	LABR	GRZZZZUSA	
WILHELM, CONRAD	30	M	LABR	GRZZZZUSA	
BERG, LINA	18	F	UNKNOWN	GRZZZZUSA	
KUELTHAN, FRIEDKE.	18	F	UNKNOWN	GRZZZZUSA	
FRITZ, EMMA	24	F	UNKNOWN	GRZZZZUSA	
GRADL, WILHELM	25	M	LABR	GRZZZZUSA	
DEKOTZ, KRESENZ	22	M	LABR	GRZZZZUSA	
GUTEKUNST, JACOB	26	M	LABR	GRZZZZUSA	
FISCHTER, CHRIST.	31	M	LABR	GRZZZZUSA	
KARLSON, EMILIA	22	F	UNKNOWN	GRZZZZUSA	
JOHANSSON, KARL-J.	22	M	LABR	GRZZZZUSA	
ELFVING, ERIK	19	M	LABR	GRZZZZUSA	
OLOF-G.	6	M	CHILD	GRZZZZUSA	
BATINGER, SOPHIE	18	F	UNKNOWN	GRZZZZUSA	
MUENZENMEYER, CAROLINE	14	F	UNKNOWN	GRZZZZUSA	
MANGLER, MARIA	19	F	UNKNOWN	GRZZZZUSA	
STENDINGER, PHILIPPE.	19	F	UNKNOWN	GRZZZZUSA	
DOLLFINGER, FR.	15	M	BCHR	GRZZZZUSA	
SCHANZ, CARL	16	M	LABR	GRZZZZUSA	
WILTZ, JOS.	16	M	LABR	GRZZZZUSA	
THERESE	22	F	UNKNOWN	GRZZZZUSA	
LIPP, ALBERT	16	M	CPTR	GRZZZZUSA	
DITERLE, PAULINE	27	F	UNKNOWN	GRZZZZUSA	
IDA	6	F	CHILD	GRZZZZUSA	
WEINEMANN, CHRIST.	18	M	BKR	GRZZZZUSA	
FLAD, JOH.	61	M	FARMER	GRZZZZUSA	
ZIMMERER, CATHA.	18	F	UNKNOWN	GRZZZZUSA	
HERT, LINUS	26	M	BBR	GRZZZZ***	
MUENZENMAIER, CATHA.	17	F	UNKNOWN	GRZZZZUSA	
GUENTHER, CAROLINE	52	F	UNKNOWN	GRZZZZUSA	
-ERST, ELISE	41	F	UNKNOWN	GRZZZZUSA	
MINK, PAUL	22	M	FARMER	GRZZZZUSA	
EMIL	24	M	FARMER	GRZZZZUSA	
ICKERMANN, SOPHIE	20	F	UNKNOWN	GRZZZZUSA	
BILL, CATHA.	26	F	UNKNOWN	GRZZZZUSA	
ROLLER, FRIEDR.	16	M	BCHR	GRZZZZUSA	
LOUISE	20	F	UNKNOWN	GRZZZZUSA	
LEONHARDT, WILHELM	40	M	LABR	GRZZZZUSA	
SCHUHMANN, ELISABETH	20	F	UNKNOWN	GRZZZZUSA	
JENDE, FRIEDRICH	20	M	FARMER	GRZZZZUSA	
JULIANE	23	F	UNKNOWN	GRZZZZUSA	
LOUISE	4	F	CHILD	GRZZZZUSA	
FRIEDRICH	2	M	CHILD	GRZZZZUSA	
ROEMER, JOHS.	24	M	LABR	GRZZZZUSA	
NICOLAUS	18	M	LABR	GRZZZZUSA	
KAUFMANN, BERTHA	21	F	UNKNOWN	GRZZZZUSA	
CHRISTIAN	16	M	BKR	GRZZZZUSA	
PURK, JOH.	30	M	FARMER	GRZZZZUSA	
RUPPERT, MARTHA	24	F	UNKNOWN	GRZZZZUSA	
ELISABETH	.06	F	INFANT	GRZZZZUSA	
HEIDECKE, IDA	15	F	UNKNOWN	GRZZZZUSA	
MAYER, EUGEN	32	M	BCHR	GRZZZZUSA	
THUM, THEOD.	32	M	FARMER	GRZZZZUSA	

PASSENGER	AGE	SEX	OCCUPATION	PRVL	DES
KOEBERLE, FRANZ	32	M	FARMER	GRZZZZ	USA
MANUEL, FRIEDKE.	48	F	UNKNOWN	GRZZZZ	USA
ULLRICH, ELISE	19	F	UNKNOWN	GRZZZZ	USA
LEUCHTENBERG, ELISE	17	F	UNKNOWN	GRZZZZ	USA
SCHNEIDER, JOACHIM	16	M	LABR	GRZZZZ	USA
MEHLER, CAROLA.	15	F	UNKNOWN	GRZZZZ	USA
NEICHEL, CHRISTE.	30	F	UNKNOWN	GRZZZZ	USA
THIERGAERTNER, FRIEDA.	17	F	UNKNOWN	GRZZZZ	USA
LOHMUELLER, CAROLA.	29	F	UNKNOWN	GRZZZZ	USA
HAAS, BARBARA	73	F	UNKNOWN	GRZZZZ	USA
SCHINDWOLF, FERD.	17	M	FARMER	GRZZZZ	USA
GRASBERGER, MARIE	45	F	UNKNOWN	GRZZZZ	USA
JOHANN	46	M	FARMER	GRZZZZ	USA
JOSEPHINE	.03	F	INFANT	GRZZZZ	USA
FRANZISCA	6	F	CHILD	GRZZZZ	USA
HERTH, HEDWIG	16	F	UNKNOWN	GRZZZZ	USA
SCHUSTER, MARIANNE	30	F	UNKNOWN	GRZZZZ	USA
HANKE, EMILIE	20	F	UNKNOWN	GRZZZZ	USA
RUPPERT, ELISABETH	19	F	UNKNOWN	GRZZZZ	USA
PFEIFFER, MARIA	19	F	UNKNOWN	GRZZZZ	USA
WIRTH, CARL	17	M	BKR	GRZZZZ	USA
SCHWEGLER, PAULE	20	F	UNKNOWN	GRZZZZ	USA
SCHWENGER, CAROLE.	29	F	UNKNOWN	GRZZZZ	USA
HUBER, EUGEN	29	M	BCHR	GRZZZZ	USA
DEISENROTH, DOROTHEA	50	F	UNKNOWN	GRZZZZ	USA
BECKER, ANNA	36	F	UNKNOWN	GRZZZZ	USA
SOPHIE	13	F	CH	GRZZZZ	USA
ROBERT	6	M	CHILD	GRZZZZ	USA
BRUNO	7	M	CHILD	GRZZZZ	USA
AUGUSTE	4	F	CHILD	GRZZZZ	USA
HUGO	2	M	CHILD	GRZZZZ	USA
ETZHORN, RUD.	44	M	FARMER	GRZZZZ	USA
CHRISTE.	43	F	UNKNOWN	GRZZZZ	USA
RUD.	.02	M	INFANT	GRZZZZ	USA
MARIE	15	F	UNKNOWN	GRZZZZ	USA
OSCAR	6	M	CHILD	GRZZZZ	USA
ETHZHORN, DINA	5	F	CHILD	GRZZZZ	USA
CAMILLA	4	F	CHILD	GRZZZZ	USA
SCHRET, ANNA	16	F	UNKNOWN	GRZZZZ	USA
LEIMBACH, ANNA	21	F	UNKNOWN	GRZZZZ	USA
RUPPE, CATHA.	23	F	UNKNOWN	GRZZZZ	USA
SONTHEIMER, MARIE	19	F	UNKNOWN	GRZZZZ	USA
SCHUELTHEIS, GUST.	16	F	UNKNOWN	GRZZZZ	USA
REITHEL, CHRIST.	17	F	UNKNOWN	GRZZZZ	USA
HIRSCHMANN, FR.	16	F	UNKNOWN	GRZZZZ	USA
BRAUN, WILH.	17	F	UNKNOWN	GRZZZZ	USA
BRUSCHARD, JACOB	21	F	UNKNOWN	GRZZZZ	USA
FRITZ, MAGDA	20	F	UNKNOWN	GRZZZZ	USA
GEBHARDT, ROBT.	16	M	LABR	GRZZZZ	USA
BRASCHMANN, RUD.	16	M	LABR	GRZZZZ	USA
PONGRATZ, GEORG	46	M	LABR	GRZZZZ	USA
MARIE	30	F	UNKNOWN	GRZZZZ	USA
HEINRICH	5	M	CHILD	GRZZZZ	USA
WEISSHAUPL, JACOB	62	M	FARMER	GRZZZZ	USA
MARIE	18	F	UNKNOWN	GRZZZZ	USA
EISENREICH, MARGA.	56	F	UNKNOWN	GRZZZZ	USA
HEINRICH	18	M	LABR	GRZZZZ	USA
SCHREINER, FRANZISCA	21	F	UNKNOWN	GRZZZZ	USA
HIRTREITTER, MAGDA.	18	F	UNKNOWN	GRZZZZ	USA
CORDES, AUG.	17	M	FARMER	GRZZZZ	USA
SCHMIDT, HEINRICH	34	M	FARMER	GRZZZZ	USA
HEINE, FRITZ	46	M	FARMER	GRZZZZ	USA
HIENRICH	17	M	FARMER	GRZZZZ	USA
FRIEDRICH	15	M	FARMER	GRZZZZ	USA
CULLMANN, CARL	13	M	UNKNOWN	GRZZZZ	USA
DAVIDOVITZ, H.	26	M	LABR	GRZZZZ	USA
LEESER, IDA	22	F	UNKNOWN	GRZZZZ	USA
MINNA	21	F	UNKNOWN	GRZZZZ	USA
PEUZEL, BERTHA	17	F	UNKNOWN	GRZZZZ	USA
PINKER, MARGA.	24	F	UNKNOWN	GRZZZZ	USA
MUDERER, JOHANN	25	M	LABR	GRZZZZ	USA
MAILINDER, DANIEL	30	M	LABR	GRZZZZ	USA
REIF, PETER	46	M	LABR	GRZZZZ	USA
ELISABETH	46	F	UNKNOWN	GRZZZZ	USA
PETER	.02	M	INFANT	GRZZZZ	USA
JOHANN	6	M	CHILD	GRZZZZ	USA
SEIFERT, WILHE.	22	F	UNKNOWN	GRZZZZ	USA
SCHUNER, LINA	20	F	UNKNOWN	GRZZZZ	USA
KRAUSS, TERESIA	16	F	UNKNOWN	GRZZZZ	USA
SZEZYNSKI, CLAUDIUS	32	M	TIR	GRZZZZ	USA
GALBELEIN, MARIE	25	F	UNKNOWN	GRZZZZ	USA
FEISE, CARL	18	M	FARMER	GRZZZZ	USA
KLIER, ANDR.	17	M	FARMER	GRZZZZ	USA
PIONTEK, KATHA.	23	F	UNKNOWN	GRZZZZ	USA
MARIANNE	20	F	UNKNOWN	GRZZZZ	USA
DZIERZINSKI, ZYPRIAN	40	M	LABR	GRZZZZ	USA
MICHALINA	30	F	UNKNOWN	GRZZZZ	USA
HACKEMEYER, PAUL	25	M	LABR	GRZZZZ	USA
JOEST, LISETTE	18	F	UNKNOWN	GRZZZZ	USA
BOSZ, JOSEFA	19	F	UNKNOWN	GRZZZZ	USA
SPIEGEL, MARIE	18	F	UNKNOWN	GRZZZZ	USA
KUEPER, PETER	23	M	BKR	GRZZZZ	USA
UHDE, AUGUST	24	M	BBR	GRZZZZ	USA
WEILER, BARBARA	17	F	UNKNOWN	GRZZZZ	USA
MENKEN, CLAUS	16	M	FARMER	GRZZZZ	USA
GRAEFELD, ELISE	20	F	UNKNOWN	GRZZZZ	USA
WEISENS, ANNA	22	F	UNKNOWN	GRZZZZ	USA
REINHARD, PETER	25	M	LABR	GRZZZZ	USA
GRIESBACH, HEINR.	27	M	LABR	GRZZZZ	USA
HAENEL, SIDONIE	18	F	UNKNOWN	GRZZZZ	USA
TIEKOTTER, HEINR.	17	M	SMH	GRZZZZ	USA
DITTMER, JOACH.	41	M	FARMER	GRZZZZ	USA
MARIE	32	F	UNKNOWN	GRZZZZ	USA
HEINR.	7	M	CHILD	GRZZZZ	USA
JOH.	6	M	CHILD	GRZZZZ	USA
ANNA	4	F	CHILD	GRZZZZ	USA
HABERMANN, LINA	22	F	UNKNOWN	GRZZZZ	USA
FREYN, JUL.	38	M	LABR	GRZZZZ	USA
GRANER, ALB.	16	M	LABR	GRZZZZ	USA
EILERS, SOFIE	18	F	UNKNOWN	GRZZZZ	USA
BERNER, BIENCHE	24	M	LABR	GRZZZZ	USA
HEMERICH, ELISE	35	F	UNKNOWN	GRZZZZ	USA
HOFMANN, MATHE.	25	M	UNKNOWN	GRZZZZ	USA
LUBER, PAULUS	26	M	LABR	GRZZZZ	USA
SCHENKEL, THEKLA	20	F	UNKNOWN	GRZZZZ	USA
FREIN, PHILIPPINE	42	F	UNKNOWN	GRZZZZ	USA
LOUIS	44	M	FARMER	GRZZZZ	USA
ANNA	.05	F	INFANT	GRZZZZ	USA
CARL	9	M	CHILD	GRZZZZ	USA
KULLMANN, EMMA	24	F	UNKNOWN	GRZZZZ	USA
REINECKE, LUDWIG	31	M	FARMER	GRZZZZ	USA
NEBEL, MINNA	20	F	UNKNOWN	GRZZZZ	USA
BRENNER, B.	35	M	FARMER	GRZZZZ	USA
CARL	6	M	CHILD	GRZZZZ	USA
CAUDE, PETER	21	M	BCHR	GRZZZZ	USA
ELISABETH	24	F	UNKNOWN	GRZZZZ	USA
ELISABETH	50	F	UNKNOWN	GRZZZZ	USA
ZOBEL, CARL	19	M	LABR	GRZZZZ	USA
HOERNER, MARIE	18	F	UNKNOWN	GRZZZZ	USA
STEIN, FRIEDR.	16	M	FARMER	GRZZZZ	USA
WILH.	15	M	FARMER	GRZZZZ	USA
USANSKY, MORITZ	16	M	FARMER	GRZZZZ	USA
RIESE, JOH.	19	M	FARMER	GRZZZZ	USA
BENDEL, JOH.	17	M	FARMER	GRZZZZ	USA
HOLSING, LINA	24	F	UNKNOWN	GRZZZZ	USA
CHARLOTTE	20	F	UNKNOWN	GRZZZZ	USA
REINHARDT, PH.	42	M	FARMER	GRZZZZ	USA
ELISAB.	44	F	UNKNOWN	GRZZZZ	USA
PHILIPP	6	M	CHILD	GRZZZZ	USA
BARBARA	7	F	CHILD	GRZZZZ	USA
HERMANN	4	M	CHILD	GRZZZZ	USA
BARBARA	.03	F	INFANT	GRZZZZ	USA
SEMLER, ELISE	19	F	UNKNOWN	GRZZZZ	USA
DIERS, HEINR.	35	M	LABR	GRZZZZ	USA
BADKUHLE, HEINRICH	42	M	LABR	GRZZZZ	USA
PFAFF, JACOB	43	M	LABR	GRZZZZ	USA
ELISABETH	42	F	UNKNOWN	GRZZZZ	USA
OTTO	6	M	CHILD	GRZZZZ	USA
ANNA	3	F	CHILD	GRZZZZ	USA
AUGUST	7	M	CHILD	GRZZZZ	USA

PASSENGER	AGE	SEX	OCCUPATION	PRVL DES	PASSENGER	AGE	SEX	OCCUPATION	PRVL DES
LINA	5	F	CHILD	GRZZZZUSA	LORENZ	27	M	LABR	GRZZZZUSA
KRUSE, PAULINE	19	F	UNKNOWN	GRZZZZUSA	FRITZ	14	M	LABR	GRZZZZUSA
GUNZELMANN, GRETCHEN	19	F	UNKNOWN	GRZZZZUSA	STUBENRAUCH, WILHELM	16	M	LABR	GRZZZZUSA
SCHMITT, JOHANN	16	M	LABR	GRZZZZUSA	JANKOWSKY, JOSEF	19	M	LABR	GRZZZZUSA
PETERSEN, MINNA	20	F	UNKNOWN	GRZZZZUSA	RUBIAK, JAN	27	M	LABR	GRZZZZUSA
WEBER, FRIEDRICH	23	M	LABR	GRZZZZUSA	FIGANEK, LORENZ	39	M	LABR	GRZZZZUSA
WERNER, MATH.	32	M	LABR	GRZZZZUSA	RUBIAK, STANISLAW	31	M	LABR	GRZZZZUSA
HERMANN, GEORG	26	M	LABR	GRZZZZUSA	ZEIDERBAUM, OSIP	20	M	LABR	GRZZZZUSA
SAUER, JOHANN	26	M	LABR	GRZZZZUSA	ENKE, ED.	38	M	LABR	GRZZZZUSA
ANNA	20	F	UNKNOWN	GRZZZZUSA	JOHANN	7	M	CHILD	GRZZZZUSA
HERMANN, ANNA	32	F	UNKNOWN	GRZZZZUSA	RONDEL, CAROLINE	21	F	UNKNOWN	GRZZZZUSA
MARIE	5	F	CHILD	GRZZZZUSA	WEBER, WILH.	17	M	FARMER	GRZZZZUSA
MARTIN	3	M	CHILD	GRZZZZUSA	LINK, ROBERT	15	M	FARMER	GRZZZZUSA
JOHANN	2	M	CHILD	GRZZZZUSA	MANN, ROBERT	16	M	FARMER	GRZZZZUSA
WILHELM	1	M	CHILD	GRZZZZUSA	LINK, LUDW.	15	M	FARMER	GRZZZZUSA
GEORG	6	M	CHILD	GRZZZZUSA	SCHMIDT, FRIEDRICH	24	M	FARMER	GRZZZZUSA
CARL	4	M	CHILD	GRZZZZUSA	SCHLOEMER, LOUIS	29	M	FARMER	GRZZZZUSA
ENGELHARDT, META	25	F	UNKNOWN	GRZZZZUSA	TAPPER, WILHELM	28	M	FARMER	GRZZZZUSA
WERNER, AUGUSTE	26	F	UNKNOWN	GRZZZZUSA	SCHLAB, ELISABETH	36	F	UNKNOWN	GRZZZZUSA
HEINRICH	2	M	CHILD	GRZZZZUSA	OSOTKA, JOH.	29	M	LABR	GRZZZZUSA
OTTO	.06	M	INFANT	GRZZZZUSA	BRESKA, CONST.	26	M	LABR	GRZZZZUSA
SCHULZ, HEINRICH	25	M	LABR	GRZZZZUSA	ROES, JOHANN	17	M	LABR	GRZZZZUSA
MAUREN, GITEL	40	M	LABR	GRZZZZUSA	GARTELMANN, DIEDRICH	15	M	LABR	GRZZZZUSA
PINTUS	15	M	LABR	GRZZZZUSA	JAEGER, JOHANN	24	M	LABR	GRZZZZUSA
HERBSMANN, HERSCH	20	M	LABR	GRZZZZUSA	MATHIAS	14	M	LABR	GRZZZZUSA
FALLBACH, WILLIAM	25	M	LABR	GRZZZZUSA	WILHELM	6	M	CHILD	GRZZZZUSA
MARIA	24	F	UNKNOWN	GRZZZZUSA	STUERMANN, GEORG	15	M	CH	GRZZZZUSA
LUCIE	.08	F	INFANT	GRZZZZUSA	KREISSIG, BERNHD.	40	M	CH	GRZZZZUSA
LEVANSKY, HERMANN	33	M	LABR	GRZZZZUSA	ANNA	30	F	UNKNOWN	GRZZZZUSA
PAUL	.09	M	INFANT	GRZZZZUSA	E.	7	F	CHILD	GRZZZZUSA
REISS, JOSEF	18	M	LABR	GRZZZZUSA	REUTER, OSWALD	29	M	FARMER	GRZZZZUSA
KAUFMANN, LOUIS	20	M	LABR	GRZZZZUSA	KUNZE, ANNA	21	F	UNKNOWN	GRZZZZUSA
EHLEN, CLAUS	33	M	LABR	GRZZZZUSA	GOSSLER, CARL	14	M	LABR	GRZZZZUSA
TOKARSKI, FRANZ	31	M	LABR	GRZZZZUSA	TETZNER, HERM.	44	M	CPTR	GRZZZZUSA
EVA	29	F	UNKNOWN	GRZZZZUSA	TIMMANN, REINHD.	16	M	BKR	GRZZZZUSA
CLARA	.04	F	INFANT	GRZZZZUSA	BACH, CONRAD	34	M	FARMER	GRZZZZUSA
FRANZISKA	18	F	UNKNOWN	GRZZZZUSA	SCHUETER, HEINRICH	18	M	FARMER	GRZZZZUSA
MATHE.	15	F	UNKNOWN	GRZZZZUSA	HEILIGENBERG, FR.	14	M	LABR	GRZZZZUSA
AUG.	5	M	CHILD	GRZZZZUSA	WALLMANN, ANNA	22	F	UNKNOWN	GRZZZZUSA
ROSALIE	6	F	CHILD	GRZZZZUSA	WIEDEMEYER, PHILIP	20	M	LABR	GRZZZZUSA
MUHL, MAX	6	M	CHILD	GRZZZZUSA	KRATOCHSIL, FRANTISEK	26	M	LABR	GRZZZZUSA
LEVANSKY, ANASTASIA	29	F	UNKNOWN	GRZZZZUSA	DETTMER, MARIE	18	F	UNKNOWN	GRZZZZUSA
ANNA	42	F	UNKNOWN	GRZZZZUSA	GEISLINGER, LEOP.	26	M	LABR	GRZZZZUSA
MARGA	4	F	CHILD	GRZZZZUSA	PAA, FRANZ	28	M	LABR	GRZZZZUSA
SOFZ, CAROLINE	63	F	CH	GRZZZZUSA	NEUMANN, HEINRICH	44	M	LABR	GRZZZZUSA
MUELLER, MARGA.	14	F	CH	GRZZZZUSA	BRY, JUL.	20	M	LABR	GRZZZZUSA
ACKERMANN, GEORG	3	M	CHILD	GRZZZZUSA	SEYERLEM, FRANZISKA	22	F	UNKNOWN	GRZZZZUSA
WEBER, CARL	14	M	LABR	GRZZZZUSA	SUENKENBERG, AUG.	30	M	LABR	GRZZZZUSA
MUELLER, JOHANN	17	M	LABR	GRZZZZUSA	BODE, WM.	14	M	LABR	GRZZZZUSA
ORTMANN, ALFRED	37	M	LABR	GRZZZZUSA	HUEBNER, ED.	24	M	LABR	GRZZZZUSA
SCHNEIDER, BERTHA	21	F	UNKNOWN	GRZZZZUSA	RISCH, CARL	22	M	LABR	GRZZZZUSA
WESEMANN, MARIE	14	F	UNKNOWN	GRZZZZUSA	EIBER, ANNA	22	F	UNKNOWN	GRZZZZUSA
SIEVERS, WILH.	29	M	LABR	GRZZZZUSA	WOLF, THERESE	18	F	UNKNOWN	GRZZZZUSA
HEINR.	31	M	LABR	GRZZZZUSA	KORNER, MICHAEL	48	M	LABR	GRZZZZUSA
SCHIERENBECK, HEINR.	36	M	LABR	GRZZZZUSA	GAREIS, ELISABETH	16	F	UNKNOWN	GRZZZZUSA
KAMMANN, LINA	18	F	UNKNOWN	GRZZZZUSA	KOERNER, JOHANN	00	M	LABR	GRZZZZUSA
WESEMANN, DORETTE	18	F	UNKNOWN	GRZZZZUSA	HAUERSTEIN, BABETTE	15	F	UNKNOWN	GRZZZZUSA
BEHE, MATH.	56	M	LABR	GRZZZZUSA	SCHMID, JOH.	30	M	FARMER	GRZZZZUSA
VETTER, FRANZ	16	M	LABR	GRZZZZUSA	GROETTSCH, MICH.	37	M	FARMER	GRZZZZUSA
ZAEHRINGER, ROSALIE	22	F	UNKNOWN	GRZZZZUSA	SCHLEGEL, KUNIGDE.	23	F	UNKNOWN	GRZZZZUSA
FETTIG, JOSEFA	16	F	UNKNOWN	GRZZZZUSA	SCHRAMM, MAGA.	21	F	UNKNOWN	GRZZZZUSA
HOFMANN, BARBARA	17	F	UNKNOWN	GRZZZZUSA	RUSSNER, MARGA.	19	F	UNKNOWN	GRZZZZUSA
ADAM	6	M	CHILD	GRZZZZUSA	WAILER, KUNIGDE.	18	F	UNKNOWN	GRZZZZUSA
RITZER, FR.	22	M	FARMER	GRZZZZUSA	HARRER, KONRAD	25	M	TIR	GRZZZZUSA
CHRISTINE	22	F	UNKNOWN	GRZZZZUSA	RAUER, KUNIGDE.	20	F	UNKNOWN	GRZZZZUSA
EMILIE	.08	F	INFANT	GRZZZZUSA	STEGMANN, BABETTE	20	F	UNKNOWN	GRZZZZUSA
STAPP, SUSANNA	42	F	UNKNOWN	GRZZZZUSA	TRUMPF, MICH.	34	M	SMH	GRZZZZUSA
U	4	M	CHILD	GRZZZZUSA	BABETTE	32	F	UNKNOWN	GRZZZZUSA
SCHOLZ, EMMA	15	M	UNKNOWN	GRZZZZUSA	WILHELM	5	M	CHILD	GRZZZZUSA
NENNINGER, LISETTE	17	M	UNKNOWN	GRZZZZUSA	FRIEDRICH	2	M	CHILD	GRZZZZUSA
GERIETS, CARL	25	M	UNKNOWN	GRZZZZUSA	LAMM, FRIEDRICH	72	M	FARMER	GRZZZZUSA
ALBERT	14	M	UNKNOWN	GRZZZZUSA	ANNA	17	F	UNKNOWN	GRZZZZUSA
BECKER, JOH.	33	M	UNKNOWN	GRZZZZUSA	STAND, ELISABETH	22	F	UNKNOWN	GRZZZZUSA
SCHAUMLOEFFEL, CONR.	75	M	UNKNOWN	GRZZZZUSA	WAIGAND, CASPAR	25	M	LABR	GRZZZZUSA
HEINRICH, BARBA.	54	F	UNKNOWN	GRZZZZUSA	KNORR, FRIEDRICH	29	M	CPTR	GRZZZZUSA

PASSENGER	AGE	SEX	OCCUPATION	PRVL	DES
MARIANNE	23	F	UNKNOWN	GRZZZZ	USA
U	.10	F	INFANT	GRZZZZ	USA
WEILER, MARGA.	21	F	UNKNOWN	GRZZZZ	USA
SCHULZ, CHRISTINE	35	F	UNKNOWN	GRZZZZ	USA
PAUL	5	M	CHILD	GRZZZZ	USA
ELISE	4	F	CHILD	GRZZZZ	USA
EMILIE	2	F	CHILD	GRZZZZ	USA
LUDWIG	.09	M	INFANT	GRZZZZ	USA
BAUER, JOS.	29	M	LABR	GRZZZZ	USA
MESSNER, MARIE	32	F	UNKNOWN	GRZZZZ	USA
JOSEF	7	M	CHILD	GRZZZZ	USA
PLAEGER, LORENZ	39	M	FARMER	GRZZZZ	USA
BECKER, SUSANNA	19	F	UNKNOWN	GRZZZZ	USA
KIRCHNER, ROMAN	35	M	FARMER	GRZZZZ	USA
RONE-, ELENO-R.	19	M	BKR	GRZZZZ	USA
CHRISTIANSEN, OLE	31	M	FARMER	GRZZZZ	USA
THUNSEN, HEINR.	14	M	FARMER	GRZZZZ	USA
HANSEN, CLAUS	52	M	FARMER	GRZZZZ	USA
ROTHE	46	F	UNKNOWN	GRZZZZ	USA
CARL	.03	M	INFANT	GRZZZZ	USA
FRIEDRICH	6	M	CHILD	GRZZZZ	USA
HANS	4	M	CHILD	GRZZZZ	USA
WEIMER, BERTHA	30	F	UNKNOWN	GRZZZZ	USA
CLAUSS, OTTO	31	M	CPTR	GRZZZZ	USA
HULDA	31	F	UNKNOWN	GRZZZZ	USA
MAX	3	M	CHILD	GRZZZZ	USA
HELENE	.06	F	INFANT	GRZZZZ	USA
TURPE, EMIL	20	M	LABR	GRZZZZ	USA
CLAUSS, ANTON	16	M	LABR	GRZZZZ	USA
RICHARD	25	M	LABR	GRZZZZ	USA
BEHLAU, EMILIE	20	F	UNKNOWN	GRZZZZ	USA
KIRCHNER, FRITZ	29	M	BCHR	GRZZZZ	USA
SEIDLER, EMILIE	27	F	UNKNOWN	GRZZZZ	USA
FLISSOWSKA, MARIE	36	F	UNKNOWN	GRZZZZ	USA
MICHAELA	72	F	UNKNOWN	GRZZZZ	USA
BROMMUNDT, GUSTAV	32	M	LABR	GRZZZZ	USA
GATTER, FRIEDRICH	42	M	LABR	GRZZZZ	USA
DOEPNER, JULIUS	22	M	LABR	GRZZZZ	USA
HESSE, ANNA	28	F	UNKNOWN	GRZZZZ	USA
HERMANN	26	M	LABR	GRZZZZ	USA
RUSS, PAULINE	18	F	UNKNOWN	GRZZZZ	USA
ULZHOEPFER, LOUISE	17	F	UNKNOWN	GRZZZZ	USA
KUCKER, JOSEF	18	M	LABR	GRZZZZ	USA
U, U	16	U	UNKNOWN	GRZZZZ	USA
HEUSSINGER, BERNARDA	25	F	UNKNOWN	GRZZZZ	USA
STUMPF, GRESSENZIA	25	F	UNKNOWN	GRZZZZ	USA
KRAUSS, ANNA	19	F	UNKNOWN	GRZZZZ	USA
KARSCH, MARIA	19	F	UNKNOWN	GRZZZZ	USA
SCHNEIDER, FANNY	21	F	UNKNOWN	GRZZZZ	USA
SEEDORF, FRITZ	21	M	FARMER	GRZZZZ	USA
REINHARDT, EVA	6	F	CHILD	GRZZZZ	USA

SHIP: AURANIA

FROM: LIVERPOOL AND QUEENSTOWN
TO: NEW YORK
ARRIVED: 28 MAY 1888

PASSENGER	AGE	SEX	OCCUPATION	PRVL	DES
LELENTHAL, CARL	19	M	LABR	GRZZZZ	CAL
ZELLERBERG, MAURITZ	19	M	LABR	GRZZZZ	NY
MARTENSEN, MADS.	21	M	LABR	GRZZZZ	NY
SHULTZ, CARL	23	M	LABR	GRZZZZ	NY
BALDWIN, WILLIAM	38	M	JNR	GRZZZZ	NY
ISLAUB, ADOLPH	25	M	CK	GRZZZZ	NY
MARSH, ALLEN-B.	36	M	MCHT	FRZZZZ	NY
HESS, LOUIS	30	M	MCHT	FRZZZZ	NY
GUITER, MENE	23	F	SVNT	GRZZZZ	NY
HERZ, M.	35	M	MCHT	GRZZZZ	NY
U-MRS	25	F	W	GRZZZZ	NY
BERTHOLD	3	M	CHILD	GRZZZZ	NY

SHIP: LEERDAM

FROM: ROTTERDAM
TO: NEW YORK
ARRIVED: 28 MAY 1888

PASSENGER	AGE	SEX	OCCUPATION	PRVL	DES
RUPRECHT, J.	48	M	MCHT	GRZZZZ	USA
WELZ, A.	28	M	MCHT	GRZZZZ	USA
A.	22	F	MCHT	GRZZZZ	USA
KOHL, H.	25	F	MCHT	GRZZZZ	USA
SCHLUFALER, E.	28	M	MCHT	GRZZZZ	USA
SERGOTZ, M.	30	M	MCHT	GRZZZZ	USA
STRACHLE, E.	22	F	UNKNOWN	GRZZZZ	USA
ZORN, M.	22	M	MCHT	GRZZZZ	USA
BUCHERT, L.	21	M	MCHT	GRZZZZ	USA
L.	19	F	UNKNOWN	GRZZZZ	USA
GIESEN, U-MR	20	M	MCHT	GRZZZZ	USA
PACHGUSER, U-MR	49	M	MCHT	GRZZZZ	USA
U-MR	00	M	MCHT	GRZZZZ	USA
SCHOCK, C.	18	M	LABR	GRZZZZ	USA
BICHLE, J.	18	M	LABR	GRZZZZ	USA
KLEINHAINZ, A.	30	M	MCHT	GRZZZZ	USA
SCHULE, J.	19	M	MCHT	GRZZZZ	USA
BOELUM, F.	48	M	MCHT	GRZZZZ	USA
REISS, J.	36	M	MCHT	GRZZZZ	USA
GRUNER, C.	34	M	MCHT	GRZZZZ	USA
VONMANK, L.	18	M	MCHT	GRZZZZ	USA
EGGERT, M.L.	50	F	UNKNOWN	GRZZZZ	USA
H.	20	F	UNKNOWN	GRZZZZ	USA
M.	18	F	CH	GRZZZZ	USA
F.	11	M	CH	GRZZZZ	USA
E.	10	M	CH	GRZZZZ	USA
A.	4	F	CHILD	GRZZZZ	USA
HOLTGREIFE, F.	20	M	MCHT	GRZZZZ	USA
EBERHARDT, O.	23	M	MCHT	GRZZZZ	USA
F.	22	M	MCHT	GRZZZZ	USA
HAINZ	19	M	MCHT	GRZZZZ	USA
L.	18	F	MCHT	GRZZZZ	USA
REY, U-MRS	58	F	MCHT	GRZZZZ	USA
KLEINVELER, B.	20	F	LABR	GRZZZZ	USA
KNAUSS, C.	20	F	LABR	GRZZZZ	USA
SCHENIE, H.	29	F	LABR	GRZZZZ	USA
KENKER, K.F.	22	M	FARMER	GRZZZZ	USA
SOKOLOWSKI, F.	45	M	LABR	GRZZZZ	USA
K.	45	F	LABR	GRZZZZ	USA
M.	16	F	LABR	GRZZZZ	USA
LEUZYET, J.	15	M	LABR	GRZZZZ	USA
K.	14	M	LABR	GRZZZZ	USA
J.	11	F	LABR	GRZZZZ	USA
SMYRNAK, A.	26	M	LABR	GRZZZZ	USA
MIEZKEWITZ, L.	40	M	LABR	GRZZZZ	USA
DUNDASZ, M.	36	M	LABR	GRZZZZ	USA
KAPLER, A.	40	M	LABR	GRZZZZ	USA
GRAWINESKI, J.	30	M	LABR	GRZZZZ	USA
ZAGOROSHI, A.	25	M	LABR	GRZZZZ	USA
PELERUES, L.	26	M	LABR	GRZZZZ	USA
JACUBOINET, E.	19	M	LABR	GRZZZZ	USA
GARKANZ, S.	18	M	LABR	GRZZZZ	USA
JEGUNSKI, A.	30	M	LABR	GRZZZZ	USA
MEUER, N.	24	M	LABR	GRZZZZ	USA
SZIGEL, H.	24	F	LABR	GRZZZZ	USA
BLASES, J.	30	F	LABR	GRZZZZ	USA
TWORDOWSKY, F.	30	M	LABR	GRZZZZ	USA
NA-DER, M.	40	M	LABR	GRZZZZ	USA
BAGDANOWITZ, U	26	M	LABR	GRZZZZ	USA
TCHES, F.	23	M	LABR	GRZZZZ	USA
GAJECHI, J.	29	M	LABR	GRZZZZ	USA
ROZAWSKI, M.	20	M	LABR	GRZZZZ	USA
DUBOWSKI, C.	26	M	LABR	GRZZZZ	USA
GOLDFARB, S.	21	M	LABR	GRZZZZ	USA
KRIKSTEIN, M.	20	M	LABR	GRZZZZ	USA
SITNICHI, S.	20	M	LABR	GRZZZZ	USA
PERIZAN, J.	18	M	LABR	GRZZZZ	USA
PLETHIN, M.	20	M	LABR	GRZZZZ	USA

PASSENGER	AGE	SEX	OCCUPATION	PROV	DES
FRIEDMAN, J.	26	M	LABR	GRZZZZUSA	
KANTER, A.	22	M	LABR	GRZZZZUSA	
KIRMAN, B.	32	M	LABR	GRZZZZUSA	
SCHUKALI, P.	24	M	LABR	GRZZZZUSA	
KARSADOWSKI, A.	19	M	LABR	GRZZZZUSA	
KOLBUSCH, M.	29	M	LABR	GRZZZZUSA	
JANKELOWITZ, N.	25	M	LABR	GRZZZZUSA	
BARDAMOWITZ, J.	24	M	LABR	GRZZZZUSA	
BERMAN, J.	33	M	LABR	GRZZZZUSA	
S.	26	M	LABR	GRZZZZUSA	
KIRMANN, C.	40	F	LABR	GRZZZZUSA	
H.	9	F	CHILD	GRZZZZUSA	
D.	7	F	CHILD	GRZZZZUSA	
SCHOENFELD, L.	26	F	LABR	GRZZZZUSA	
KASLA, J.	23	M	LABR	GRZZZZUSA	
SCHILNETZKI, S.	38	M	LABR	GRZZZZUSA	
SCHUMACHER, L.	23	M	LABR	GRZZZZUSA	
LEITZMICK, A.	18	M	LABR	GRZZZZUSA	
BRONGAL, S.	23	M	LABR	GRZZZZUSA	
GIERUT, W.	25	M	LABR	GRZZZZUSA	
SALICHLIN, A.	25	M	LABR	GRZZZZUSA	
JAWEISIS, J.	28	M	LABR	GRZZZZUSA	
TOMASK, W.	20	M	LABR	GRZZZZUSA	
REUTER, S.	33	M	LABR	GRZZZZUSA	
PIETERUCHE, V.	21	M	LABR	GRZZZZUSA	
SKENDAL, D.	26	M	LABR	GRZZZZUSA	
DOBROWSKY, S.	30	M	LABR	GRZZZZUSA	
S.	26	F	LABR	GRZZZZUSA	
A.	00	M	INF	GRZZZZUSA	
TULITZKI, P.	19	M	INF	GRZZZZUSA	
KOWALSKI, FR.	36	M	INF	GRZZZZUSA	
AMBROSCHE, V.	18	M	INF	GRZZZZUSA	
ENVARSCHEN, J.	24	M	INF	GRZZZZUSA	
WOLZYNSKI, J.	26	M	INF	GRZZZZUSA	
LUBOWITZ, A.	21	M	INF	GRZZZZUSA	
LINK, J.	28	M	INF	GRZZZZUSA	
DOBROWOLSKI, A.	00	M	INF	GRZZZZUSA	
U, U	00	M	INF	GRZZZZUSA	
U	00	M	INF	GRZZZZUSA	
SHA-IEZK, M.	22	M	INF	GRZZZZUSA	
JAGORSKI, S.	24	M	INF	GRZZZZUSA	
RABA, J.	32	M	INF	GRZZZZUSA	
NIEBICKI, J.	28	M	INF	GRZZZZUSA	
KOWALSKI, V.	26	F	INF	GRZZZZUSA	
LAUTER, J.	23	M	INF	GRZZZZUSA	
PASCHULSKI, S.	25	M	INF	GRZZZZUSA	

SHIP: CITY OF RICHMOND

FROM: LIVERPOOL AND QUEENSTOWN
TO: NEW YORK
ARRIVED: 28 MAY 1888

PASSENGER	AGE	SEX	OCCUPATION	PROV	DES
TOMEWITZ, JOHN	22	M	LABR	GRACBFNY	
WIESEN, SABINA	20	F	SVNT	GRACBFNY	
BLECHNER, FANNY	19	F	W	GRACBFNY	
HEINNICK	35	M	LABR	GRACBFNY	
LUGWER, SALOMON	32	M	LABR	GRACBFNY	
GITEL	26	M	TLR	GRACBFNY	
FROST, JUDA	24	F	W	GRACBFNY	
WEISS, REICHEL	19	F	W	GRACBFNY	
ALTER, FANNI	18	F	UNKNOWN	GRACBFNY	
SZIMELES, BARUCH	21	M	JNR	GRACBFCH	
SUSSMAN, FANNY	24	F	LABR	GRACBFNY	
SMILEWITZ, ISAAC	32	M	SHMK	GRACBFNY	
HERSCHKOWITZ, MOSES	20	M	LABR	GRACBFNY	
GROSSMANN, BETTY	18	F	DRSMKR	GRACBFNY	
OSNOWITZ, BREINDEL	26	F	W	GRACBFNY	
ROTH, ROSA	28	F	W	GRACBFNY	
SANDOR	.11	F	INFANT	GRACBFNY	

PASSENGER	AGE	SEX	OCCUPATION	PROV	DES
BOUME, MAREO	18	M	LABR	GRADXWNY	
STRASSMANN, JULES	37	M	MCHT	GRZZZZNY	
DREYER, ANNIE	20	F	UNKNOWN	GRADAXNY	
HEUSER, LENA	23	F	SP	GRZZZZUNK	
PERNAUX, MARIE	25	F	SP	SRZZZZNY	

SHIP: ELBE

FROM: BREMEN AND SOUTHAMPTON
TO: NEW YORK
ARRIVED: 29 MAY 1888

PASSENGER	AGE	SEX	OCCUPATION	PROV	DES
COTTRINGER, MARG.	42	F	UNKNOWN	SRAFWZUSA	
CAROLNE.	20	F	UNKNOWN	SRAFWZUSA	
MARDA	17	F	UNKNOWN	SRAFWZUSA	
GOODMANN, A.	32	M	UNKNOWN	SRAFWZUSA	
SUTOR, EMMA	22	F	UNKNOWN	SRACUOUSA	
LAMMERS, GUST.	18	M	UNKNOWN	SRAAEBUSA	
REISS, BARBA.	29	F	UNKNOWN	SRAIKSUSA	
LENCHEN	7	F	CHILD	SRAIKSUSA	
CARL	5	M	CHILD	SRAIKSUSA	
BRENDEL, MARIE	28	F	TT	GRZZZZUSA	
SCHMIDT, EVA	32	F	TT	GRAFKJUSA	
MURRY, C.A.	31	M	TT	GRACNTUSA	
SCHUBERT, FELIX	32	M	TT	GRZZZZUSA	
SAMUEL, CAESAR	31	M	TT	GRAAKHUSA	
HEISS, ERNST	18	M	TT	GRAEXLUSA	
KUBIAK, JOSEF	30	M	FARMER	PRZZZZUSA	
ANTONIA	23	F	W	PRZZZZUSA	
XAVERIANNA	.11	F	INFANT	PRZZZZUSA	
STANISLAW	.11	M	INFANT	PRZZZZUSA	
SCHUDY, ANDRZY	58	M	LABR	PRZZZZUSA	
MARIANNE	46	F	W	PRZZZZUSA	
JOSEFA	20	F	CH	PRZZZZUSA	
FRANZISKA	16	F	CH	PRZZZZUSA	
STANISLAW	7	M	CHILD	PRZZZZUSA	
SONOWSKI, KAROLINE	46	F	W	GRZZZZUSA	
OTTO	14	M	CH	GRZZZZUSA	
KOWALSKI, JOSEF	16	M	LABR	GRZZZZUSA	
BENZIN, ALWINE	40	F	W	GRAAHQUSA	
ALBERT	14	F	W	GRAAHQUSA	
AUGUST	7	F	CHILD	GRAAHQUSA	
EMMA	6	F	CHILD	GRAAHQUSA	
MIEDTBRODT, SOPHIE	35	F	W	GRAAHQUSA	
ERNST	14	M	CH	GRAAHQUSA	
HEDWIG	7	F	CHILD	GRAAHQUSA	
DREWES, LOUISE	30	F	W	GRAAHQUSA	
CARL	3	M	CHILD	GRAAHQUSA	
OTTO	2	M	CHILD	GRAAHQUSA	
HERMANN	.11	M	INFANT	GRAAHQUSA	
GRUSINSKI, JAN	16	M	FARMER	GRZZZZUSA	
MICHALSKA, KATARYNA	21	F	FARMER	GRZZZZUSA	
RYCICKA, CATHARZINA	23	F	W	GRZZZZUSA	
JOSEPH	.01	M	INFANT	GRZZZZUSA	
FREUZLER, WILH.	32	M	LABR	PRZZZZMN	
LEMKE, CARL	35	M	LABR	PRZZZZOH	
EMILIE	26	F	W	PRZZZZOH	
EMIL	4	M	CHILD	PRZZZZOH	
ADOLF	.10	M	INFANT	PRZZZZOH	
JULIUS	36	M	BLKSMH	PRZZZZOH	
MACHOLL, ALEX	26	M	LABR	PRZZZZIL	
BIESCHKE, ANTONIO	60	F	W	PRZZZZIL	
ANTON	26	M	LABR	PRZZZZIL	
COSKE, ANTON	30	M	PNTR	PRZZZZIL	
ALBERNINE	32	F	W	PRZZZZIL	
FRANZ	4	M	CHILD	PRZZZZIL	
AUGUST	.11	M	INFANT	PRZZZZIL	
PATELRUK, FRANZ	33	M	BKR	PRZZZZIL	
MATHILDE	26	F	W	PRZZZZIL	
MARTHA	.11	F	INFANT	PRZZZZIL	

PASSENGER	AGE	SEX	OCCUPATION	PRVL	DES
SCHNEIDER, AUGUSTIN	28	M	LABR		BVZZZZMT
ANGEMSSEN, BRIGITTA	22	F	SVNT		BVZZZZUNK
WEGGEL, KONRAS	28	M	LABR		BVZZZZUNK
VORDEMEYER, VALENTIN	26	M	BKLYR		BVADLDMT
ZECHELMAIER, KATHA.	56	F	W		SYZZZZMT
THERESE	20	F	W		SYZZZZMT
RICHTER, CARL	59	M	SHMK		SYZZZZMT
FRIEDERIKE	67	F	W		SYZZZZMT
SPERL, HEINRICH	16	M	LABR		BVZZZZWI
SCHLESEL, MICHAEL	28	M	LABR		BVZZZZIA
CATHARINE	20	F	W		BVZZZZIA
ACHATZ, ANTON	25	M	CPR		BVZZZZMN
RIED, MATHIAS	51	M	CPR		BVALSUIA
KATHARINE	41	F	W		BVALSUIA
NITZHEIM, KATHARINE	19	F	SVNT		BVALSUIA
BARBA.	17	F	SVNT		BVALSUIA
ADAM	15	M	FARMER		BVALSUIA
JOSEF	7	M	CHILD		BVALSUIA
ANDRAS	6	M	CHILD		BVALSUIA
KATHA.	27	F	W		BVALSUIA
ACHATZ, FRANZKA.	27	F	FARMER		BVZZZZMN
BRANDEL, JOSEF	27	M	LABR		BVZZZZWI
ELLIGEROTH, ELISABETH	65	F	W		PRZZZZNY
JANSEN, ANNA	18	F	SVNT		PRZZZZNY
KRANZ, ANNA	19	F	SVNT		SYZZZZNY
HEIM, ANNA	40	F	W		SYADZONY
HELENE	17	F	SVNT		SYADZONY
ANNA	15	F	SVNT		SYADZONY
ALBERT	11	M	CH		SYADZONY
CLEMENS	7	M	CHILD		SYADZONY
ELISE	6	F	CHILD		SYADZONY
WAGNER, SCHOLESTIKA	52	F	W		SYAARMNY
BACHUS, CHRIST.	23	M	BRR		SYAARMNY
PFEIFFER, ALFRED	16	M	LABR		SGZZZZNY
POHL, JAN	21	M	SHMK		PRZZZZNY
MRUSKA, JOH.	23	M	LABR		PRZZZZNY
OSTROWSKA, ANTONIO	39	F	W		PRALTJNY
HELENE	.10	F	INFANT		PRZZZZNY
LATOUSINSKA, CATHA.	19	F	SVNT		PRZZZZNY
PAWLOWSKI, JACOB	34	M	FARMER		PRZZZZNY
LASKOWSKA, BERTHA	23	F	SVNT		PRAAKHNY
KUSSMANN, JUSTINA	59	F	W		PRZZZZNY
JULIANE	30	F	W		PRZZZZNY
ROSTOCK, AUGUST	50	M	FARMER		PRZZZZNY
OTTO	16	M	CH		PRZZZZNY
JETTE	14	F	CH		PRZZZZNY
CARL	.11	M	INFANT		PRZZZZNY
SYDEL, MARTHA	19	F	SVNT		PRZZZZPA
REHM, WILHELM	14	M	DRVR		PRZZZZNY
FICKE, MARTIN	14	M	LABR		PRAARSNY
CARL	14	M	LABR		PRAARSNY
HARENBERG, ELISE	16	F	SVNT		PRZZZZNY
TIEDEMANN, MARTIN	15	M	LABR		PRAJGHNY
EICKHOFF, JOH.	20	M	MCHT		PRAARTNY
BAUER, JEAN	23	M	CL		PRZZZZNY
JACOB	17	M	LABR		HSZZZZNY
ZUERN, KATHARINA	17	F	SVNT		HSABENNY
HILLER, WILHELM	23	M	MUSN		WMZZZZNY
UNKAUF, MARIA	22	F	SVNT		WMAEXWNY
HESSERMAUER, KATHA.	16	F	SVNT		WMACFSNY
FAUL, EMILIE	21	F	SVNT		WMAEEANY
GOLDERER, WILHNE.	16	F	SVNT		WMZZZZNY
SCHILLING, MARIE	19	F	SVNT		WMZZZZNY
EHMANN, KATHA.	22	F	SVNT		WMZZZZNY
KRAUTER, GOTTHILF	14	M	LABR		GRZZZZNY
MUELLER, JOHS.	16	M	LABR		GRZZZZNY
NETH, CONRAD	16	M	LABR		GRZZZZNY
HAPP, FRIEDRICH	14	M	LABR		GRZZZZNY
HORNUNG, JOHA.	47	M	LABR		GRZZZZNY
CHRISTINE	43	F	W		GRZZZZNY
SOPHIE	12	F	CH		GRZZZZNY
MARIE	5	F	CHILD		GRZZZZNY
WM.	6	M	CHILD		GRZZZZNY
CAROLINE	3	F	CHILD		GRZZZZNY
SCHAEFER, LOUISE	23	F	CH		GRAEEANY
SCHWOERER, CHRISTIAN	18	M	BKLYR		GRZZZZNY
HARTENSTEIN, JOHANN	25	M	BKR		GRZZZZNY
SCHNITZER, ALBERT	24	M	LABR		GRZZZZNY
SAUER, MARIA	17	F	SVNT		GRZZZZNY
WINTER, MATHIAS	67	M	FARMER		GRZZZZNY
SCHNEIDER, BERNHARD	16	M	FARMER		GRZZZZNY
MAIER, GEORG	14	M	FARMER		GRZZZZNY
ALBERT-MERK	15	M	FARMER		GRZZZZNY
MOEUSSNERT, FRIEDERICKE	50	F	W		GRZZZZNY
SOPHIE	11	F	CH		GRZZZZNY
ANNA	4	F	CHILD		GRZZZZNY
JOHE.	6	M	CHILD		GRZZZZNY
RUNGER, ELISE	25	F	SVNT		GRAEXWNY
BERNER, CHRISTIAN	23	M	GLSR		GRAEXWNY
GRAU, GEORG	23	M	PNTR		GRABLHNY
SCHUHMANN, MARIE	29	F	SVNT		GRZZZZNY
MUELLER, EMMA	36	F	SVNT		GRABJKNY
GAYKE, OTTO	35	M	TLR		GRZZZZNY
EMILIE	27	F	W		GRZZZZNY
ELSE	6	F	CHILD		GRZZZZNY
GRETE	5	F	CHILD		GRZZZZNY
EHRICH	4	M	CHILD		GRZZZZNY
FRIEDRICH	.03	M	INFANT		GRZZZZNY
MIETSCH, LINA	17	F	SVNT		GRABLVNY
HEIDROTH, HEINR.	17	M	CPR		GRAHRUNY
SEPP, MARGA.	42	F	W		GRADNHNY
HEINR.	11	M	CH		GRADNHNY
MARTHA	6	F	CHILD		GRADNHNY
ELISE	4	F	CHILD		GRADNHNY
ULBRICH, ELISE	22	F	SVNT		GRABOQNY
HAMPF, GEORG	40	M	BCHR		GRAARRNY
SCHMIDT, BARBARA	29	F	W		BVZZZZNY
MARGARETHA	26	F	SVNT		BVZZZZNY
JOH.	6	M	CHILD		BVZZZZNY
PEISKER, IDA	29	F	W		SYZZZZNY
HERMANN	4	M	CHILD		SYZZZZNY
MARTHA	.11	F	INFANT		SYZZZZNY
DIETZMANN, ROSALIE	28	F	W		SYZZZZNY
ANNA	6	F	CHILD		SYZZZZNY
HULDA	4	F	CHILD		SYZZZZNY
SELMA	3	F	CHILD		SYZZZZNY
LINA	2	F	CHILD		SYZZZZNY
OTTO	.09	M	INFANT		SYZZZZNY
KUBIS, MARTIN	23	M	LABR		PRZZZZNY
KARCZ, MICHALINE	29	F	W		PRZZZZNY
MARIANNA	3	F	CHILD		PRZZZZNY
STANISLAW	.09	M	INFANT		PRZZZZNY
URBANSKI, MARIANNE	26	F	W		PRZZZZNY
STANISLAW	.08	M	INFANT		PRZZZZNY
HEILMANN, MARTHA	18	F	SVNT		PRAEABNY
OPPELT, MARGA.	32	F	W		PRABOKNY
FELLER, THERESE	18	F	SVNT		PRABOKNY
ZIRKELBACH, LOUISE	18	F	SVNT		BVZZZZNY
SCHAUDER, AGNES	19	F	SVNT		BVZZZZNY
EEDER, EDW.	26	M	CGRMKR		BVZZZZNY
THERESE	19	F	W		BVZZZZNY
AUGUST	.09	M	INFANT		BVZZZZNY
KUHNLEIN, PAUK	21	M	LABR		BVZZZZNY
SCHMIDT, ANDREAS	30	M	LABR		BVZZZZNY
HARTMANN, ANNA	19	F	SVNT		BVZZZZNY
HOCH, DOROTHEA	15	F	SVNT		BVZZZZNY
MUELLER, MARIE	25	F	SVNT		BVZZZZNY
KARRMANN, NAM.	45	F	W		BVABSHNY
EVA	20	F	CH		BVABSHNY
BABET	17	F	CH		BVABSHNY
ANNA	16	F	CH		BVABSHNY
BARBARA	10	F	CH		BVABSHNY
ANDREAS	6	M	CHILD		BVABSHNY
JOHANN	4	M	CHILD		BVABSHNY
KUNIGUNDE	2	F	CHILD		BVABSHNY
DOBMAIER, ANNA	14	F	SVNT		BVABOENY
WEISS, BARBARA	14	F	SVNT		BVACSTNY
KAUPL, BARBARA	24	F	SVNT		BVABDMNY
KUPFER, ANNA	23	F	SVNT		BVABDMNY
NESTMANN, OTTO	23	M	PNTR		BVABDMNY

PASSENGER	AGE	SEX	OCCUPATION	PRVL	DES
KLEFELD, BERTHA	45	F	W		BVAAKHNY
ALFRED	7	M	CHILD		BVAAKHNY
WALTER	5	M	CHILD		BVAAKHNY
WOJEWODKA, ELISABETH	35	F	W		BVAEONNY
STANISLAW	4	M	CHILD		BVAEONNY
ZIELINSKI, MARGANNE	32	F	W		BVAIHINY
BEJA, ANTONIO	26	F	W		BVAEONNY
PAZKET, NAPOMAZINA	50	F	W		BVAEONNY
BELJA, BALAZI	.11	F	INFANT		BVAEONNY
PAZKET, MARIA	.10	F	INFANT		BVAEONNY
EGGERS, JOH.	54	M	FARMER		SYZZZZNY
HEFFNER, BABETTA	29	F	SVNT		SYZZZZNY
LEHR, LUDW.	15	M	LABR		SYABTUNY
BAUER, KATHA.	46	F	W		HSZZZZNY
TREN, GUST.	20	M	CPR		HSABLHNY
POPHAGEN, AUGUSTE	26	F	W		HSADVHNY
MARIE	6	F	CHILD		HSADVHNY
RAAB, BARBA.	21	F	SVNT		BVZZZZNY
LUENBACH, GEORG	14	M	LABR		BVZZZZNY
RAUCH, GEORG	30	M	SMH		BVZZZZNY
BARBARA	40	F	W		BVZZZZNY
JOSEF	7	M	CHILD		BVZZZZNY
STENGLEIN, GEORG	50	M	BKR		BVZZZZNY
ROTHLAUF, JOHANN	18	M	JNR		BVZZZZNY
EINWICH, MARIANNE	25	F	SVNT		BVZZZZNY
KOSANKE, THERESE	21	F	SVNT		PRZZZZNY
HUEBSCHMANN, MARIANNE	25	F	SVNT		BVZZZZNY
DUERR, EVA	25	F	SVNT		BVZZZZNY
NAGENGARD, MARIE	16	F	SVNT		BVZZZZNY
KUNIGUNDE	18	F	SVNT		BVZZZZNY
FORST, GEORG	16	M	LABR		BVZZZZNY
GUNDLOCH, MARIANNE	56	F	W		GRZZZZNY
MARGA.	7	F	CHILD		GRZZZZNY
GOCKSTATTER, MICH.	30	M	FARMER		GRZZZZWI
FRANCISCA	41	F	W		GRZZZZWI
MARIA	17	F	SVNT		GRZZZZWI
FRANCISKA	7	F	CHILD		GRZZZZWI
FRANZ	6	M	CHILD		GRZZZZWI
JOHANN	5	M	CHILD		GRZZZZWI
KRISTINA	.11	F	INFANT		GRZZZZWI
KABELE, JOSEF	32	M	FARMER		GRZZZZWI
ANNA	32	F	W		GRZZZZWI
WENZEL	7	M	CHILD		GRZZZZWI
JOSEF	4	M	CHILD		GRZZZZWI
VINCENC	3	M	CHILD		GRZZZZWI
ANTON	.09	M	INFANT		GRZZZZWI
LANGER, EMILE	26	F	SVNT		GRZZZZNY
TRICUCEL, IDA	20	F	SVNT		GRZZZZNY
FEY, ADAM	20	M	MCHT		GRZZZZNY
BOLFEN, BERLIN	26	M	SVNT		GRACBRNY
AHNERT, AUGUSTE	36	F	W		GRZZZZWI
MARTHA	17	F	CH		GRZZZZWI
PAUL	14	M	CH		GRZZZZWI
OTTO	7	M	CHILD		GRZZZZWI
LUDWIG	5	M	CHILD		GRZZZZWI
HELENE	3	F	CHILD		GRZZZZWI
WILHELM	.11	M	INFANT		GRZZZZWI
HILCAREK, JACOB	30	M	LABR		GRAEABNY
LAUER, JOHN.NIC	23	M	DLR		GRAAMKNY
SANDAK, PHILIPP	46	M	LABR		GRAAMKNY
LOCKEMAISER, MARGA.	22	F	SVNT		GRAAMKNY
PROSCH, ANNA	21	F	SVNT		GRAAMKNY
IGNATZ	14	M	LABR		GRAAMKNY
KUEHRT, EMMA	20	F	SVNT		GRZZZZNY
EISENSCHINK, KATHARINE	20	F	W		GRZZZZNY
DORN, ANDRAS	18	M	LABR		GRADKWIN
GREUBEL, BARBA.	15	F	SVNT		GRADKWPA
ZIEGLER, FRANZISKA	15	F	SVNT		GRADKWPA
KARL	11	M	CH		GRADKWPA
TOBEN, LARS	30	M	SEMN		GRZZZZNY
WISSMANN, GOTTLOB	22	M	BKR		GRZZZZNY
UTZMANN, BERTHA	19	F	SVNT		GRZZZZNY
GIESSEL, THERESIA	25	F	W		GRZZZZNY
GREIS, PAULE.	7	F	CHILD		GRZZZZNY
KUCHOOST, JULIANE	36	F	W		GRZZZZNY
REINHOLD	4	M	CHILD		GRZZZZNY
SEMNAU, MARIA	18	F	SVNT		GRZZZZMI
ROISA	17	F	SVNT		GRZZZZMI
CLARA	15	F	SVNT		GRZZZZMI
KLETT, MARGA.	35	F	W		GRABENNY
MARIE	7	F	CHILD		GRABENNY
MORALLER, LUDWIG	40	M	FARMER		GRADKGNY
ANNA	46	F	W		GRADKGNY
EDUARD	15	M	W		GRADKGNY
MAX	7	M	CHILD		GRADKGNY
ELMICH	6	M	CHILD		GRADKGNY
LAMPRECHT, BERTHA	28	F	SVNT		GRADKGOH
HAUSMANN, A.F.	38	M	LABR		GRAARRPA
BOHNEN, GOTTL.	21	M	LABR		GRAABKMO
MERKT, CHRIST.	26	M	LABR		GRAETMNY
TIESING, ADOLF	16	M	LABR		GRAARRROC
ERTEL, JOSEF	15	M	LABR		GRZZZZMI
MESSERSCHMIDT, ABRAHAM	51	M	LABR		GRZZZZMI
DIENER, JOH.	17	M	LABR		GRZZZZMI
BOETCHER, SALOMEA	50	F	W		GRAICOMI
ANNA	22	F	CH		GRAICOMI
MARIE	20	F	CH		GRAICOMI
FRANCISCA	18	F	CH		GRAICOMI
PAULINA	15	F	CH		GRAICOMI
ROSA	7	F	CHILD		GRAICOMI
PAUL	6	M	CHILD		GRAICOMI
ANTON	.02	M	INFANT		GRAICOMI
HOERNER, PETER	29	M	LABR		GRZZZZNY
POOCH, WILH.	34	M	DRVR		GRZZZZNY
AUGUSTE	31	F	W		GRZZZZNY
FRIEDR.	7	M	CHILD		GRZZZZNY
SCHAEFER, MARTIN	45	M	JNR		GRZZZZNY
JOHANNE	52	F	W		GRZZZZNY
MARIE	18	F	CH		GRZZZZNY
FRIEDERIKE	16	F	CH		GRZZZZNY
HIPPILI, AUGUST	24	M	SHMK		GRZZZZNY
GUMPRECHT, CHRISTIANE	25	F	SVNT		GRZZZZNY
BARTH, AUGUST	31	M	LKSH		GRAADGNY
BRODY, JACOB	28	M	LKSH		GRZZZZNY
SCHNEIDER, AUGUST	52	M	TLR		GRAEIJWI
AUGUSTE	27	F	W		GRAEIJWI
FRITZ	2	F	CHILD		GRAEIJWI
IDA	.06	F	INFANT		GRAEIJWI
GUSTAV	20	M	TLR		GRAEIJWI
DOERNER, KATHA.	18	F	SVNT		GRZZZZWI
HOFFMANN, THERESIA	17	F	SVNT		GRADNIWI
DUERR, FRIEDR.	41	M	CPR		GRADNIWI
KAROLNE	15	F	SVNT		GRADNIWI
SOPHIE	14	F	SVNT		GRADNIWI
WILHELM	7	M	CHILD		GRADNIWI
STREITBERGER, JACOB	16	M	LABR		GRADNIWI
ULBRICH, EMMA	21	F	SVNT		GRZZZZWI
KRAUSE, ANNA	23	F	SVNT		GRZZZZWI
KEIM, JOS.	39	M	LABR		GRADOIWI
SEILER, AUGUST	27	M	BKR		GRZZZZNY
DICK, PAULUS	25	M	WCHMKR		GRZZZZNY
BAUER, FRANZ-F	42	M	JNR		GRZZZZAR
ANNA	40	F	W		GRZZZZAR
MAX	65	M	JNR		GRZZZZAR
MATHIAS	7	M	CHILD		GRZZZZAR
JOSEF	7	M	CHILD		GRZZZZAR
MARKUS	6	M	CHILD		GRZZZZAR
JOHANN	5	M	CHILD		GRZZZZAR
ANNA	4	F	CHILD		GRZZZZAR
MARIE	4	F	CHILD		GRZZZZAR
THERESE	2	F	CHILD		GRZZZZAR
KATHARINE	.09	F	INFANT		GRZZZZAR
FULL, KATHARINE	20	F	W		GRZZZZAR
CACILIE	7	F	CHILD		GRZZZZAR
DANIEL	6	M	CHILD		GRZZZZAR
BAUER, JOHANN	24	M	FARMER		GRZZZZAR
SCHELL, CLARA	32	F	W		GRADLDPA
MICHAEL	7	M	CHILD		GRADLDPA
BOCHME, JOH.	14	M	NN		GRAEETOH
ADAMZEWSKY, STANISL.	40	M	LABR		GRZZZZMN

111

PASSENGER	AGE	SEX	OCCUPATION	PRVL	DES
JUNKER, MARIA	7	F	CHILD	GRZZZZNY	
EICKMEYER, HEINR.	47	M	MCHT	GRZZZZNY	
CAROLINE	38	F	W	GRZZZZNY	
CHARLOTTE	7	F	CHILD	GRZZZZNY	
CARL	.09	M	INFANT	GRZZZZNY	
NOLLAC, GOTTFRIED	57	M	LABR	GRZZZZNY	
JOHANN	36	M	W	GRZZZZNY	
LUDW.	16	M	CH	GRZZZZNY	
MARIE	10	M	CH	GRZZZZNY	
KARL	7	M	CHILD	GRZZZZNY	
JACOB	5	M	CHILD	GRZZZZNY	
BEYER, GOTTFRIED	36	M	CPTR	GRZZZZNY	
MARGA.	28	F	W	GRZZZZNY	
JACOB	7	M	CHILD	GRZZZZNY	
CHRISTIAN	.09	M	INFANT	GRZZZZNY	
BELSCHNER, CATHA.	20	F	SVNT	GRZZZZIN	
RICKENS, FRIEDR.	16	M	LABR	GRAEETNY	
TRINA	14	F	SVNT	GRAEETNY	
ROEBL, CHRISTOPH	22	M	CL	GRZZZZNY	
BAUERNFEIND, FRANZISKA	28	F	W	GRZZZZNY	
MEIER, JOSEF	56	M	FARMER	GRZZZZNY	
FRANZISKA	50	F	W	GRZZZZNY	
MAX	16	M	CH	GRZZZZNY	
ARTHUR	15	M	CH	GRZZZZNY	
JOHANN	13	M	CH	GRZZZZNY	
GRINNINGER, ALOIS	7	M	CHILD	GRZZZZNY	
ZIPS, ENGEL	23	M	LABR	GRZZZZNY	
SCHRAMM, ALOIS	45	M	LABR	GRZZZZNY	
GUENTHER, AUGUST	52	M	LABR	GRAAXENY	
MARIE	16	F	SVNT	GRAAXENY	
CHRIST, CAROLINE	40	M	LABR	GRZZZZNY	
GEIPEL, ROBERT	28	M	TLR	GRAILFPA	
JAGUSCH, MATHIAS	45	M	BKLYR	GRZZZZMN	
FRZKA.	43	F	W	GRZZZZMN	
MARIE	19	F	CH	GRZZZZMN	
ANNA	17	F	CH	GRZZZZMN	
JACOB	15	M	CH	GRZZZZMN	
JULIE	7	F	CHILD	GRZZZZMN	
FRZKA.	6	F	CHILD	GRZZZZMN	
SIEB, HERM.	17	M	LABR	SYZZZZNY	
HAESLOB, BETTY	18	F	SVNT	SYAARRNY	
HOFFMANN, ROBERT	18	M	CL	SYADLUNY	
GAWRUNSKI, ALBERT	25	M	PNTR	GRZZZZNY	
CATHA.	21	F	W	GRZZZZNY	
NARUSEWICZ, STANISL.	35	M	LABR	GRZZZZNY	
OGRINTZ, JOSEPH	26	M	LABR	GRZZZZNY	
KOPSCHE, MARTIN	29	M	LABR	GRZZZZNY	
STAHIRA, JOSEF	25	M	LABR	GRZZZZNY	
WEBELHORST, HEINRICH	26	M	FARMER	GRAARTNY	
SCHOENBERGER, JOHANN	29	M	BKR	GRAARRNY	
ALTHOFF, ANTON	28	M	FARMER	GRAARRNY	
MARIA	25	F	W	GRAARRNY	
JOSEF, MORTIZ	29	M	LABR	GRAARRNY	
MEYER, JULIE	30	F	SVNT	GRAARRNY	

SHIP: ETHIOPIA

FROM: GLASGOW
TO: NEW YORK
ARRIVED: 29 MAY 1888

PASSENGER	AGE	SEX	OCCUPATION	PRVL	DES
HOPPNER, TH.	22	M	CGRMKR	GRZZZZUSA	
ZISCHOWSKY, JULIUS	33	M	SDLR	GRZZZZUSA	
MARIANNE	32	F	UNKNOWN	GRZZZZUSA	
FRANCISKA	8	F	CHILD	GRZZZZUSA	
JOSEF	6	M	CHILD	GRZZZZUSA	
MAX	1	M	CHILD	GRZZZZUSA	
LEZADIA	.02	F	INFANT	GRZZZZUSA	
WISKOFSKY, STANISLAW	22	M	LABR	GRZZZZUSA	
BRANDNER, CARL	17	M	JNR	GRZZZZUSA	

PASSENGER	AGE	SEX	OCCUPATION	PRVL	DES
KALERPSER, ULEJANA	22	F	UNKNOWN	GRZZZZUSA	
JOHAN	.08	M	INFANT	GRZZZZUSA	
KALJASMEK, MARIANA	24	F	UNKNOWN	GRZZZZUSA	
A---, MAGDAKENA	28	F	UNKNOWN	GRZZZZUSA	
ADAM	.06	M	INFANT	GRZZZZUSA	
BRUCKNER, SOFE	44	F	HP	GRZZZZUSA	
GRIM, JACOB	32	M	BCHR	GRZZZZUSA	
TERTEN, FRANZ	48	M	LABR	GRZZZZUSA	
SALZER, CHRISTIAN	20	M	MLR	GRZZZZUSA	
NAERTEMEG, JOSEF	40	M	LABR	GRZZZZUSA	
HERKEGER, PAUL	22	M	LABR	GRZZZZUSA	
PACHER, PAUL	27	M	LABR	GRZZZZUSA	
IDZWICH, JOSEPH	42	M	LABR	GRZZZZUSA	
HEDWIGA	32	F	UNKNOWN	GRZZZZUSA	
JAN	11	M	UNKNOWN	GRZZZZUSA	
THEODOR	10	M	CH	GRZZZZUSA	
MARIANNA	7	F	CHILD	GRZZZZUSA	
STEPHAN	.09	M	INFANT	GRZZZZUSA	
PETER	4	M	CHILD	GRZZZZUSA	
SOFIA	3	F	CHILD	GRZZZZUSA	
STEPHAN	.09	M	INFANT	GRZZZZUSA	
JOSEPHA	.09	F	INFANT	GRZZZZUSA	
TUREK, ADALBERT	47	M	LABR	GRZZZZUSA	
JOSEPH	10	M	CH	GRZZZZUSA	
MASZWSEK, ANDREUS	32	M	LABR	GRZZZZUSA	
LEBUKOWSKY, IGNAZ	29	M	LABR	GRZZZZUSA	
SCHANDOSKE, ANTON	35	M	LABR	GRZZZZUSA	
ZELAZKO, ANTON	36	M	LABR	GRZZZZUSA	
PREMUS, FRIEDRICH	31	M	LABR	GRZZZZUSA	
JETTE	31	F	UNKNOWN	GRZZZZUSA	
AUGUST	10	M	CH	GRZZZZUSA	
FRIEDRICH	2	M	CHILD	GRZZZZUSA	
EMMA	.03	F	INFANT	GRZZZZUSA	
TUREK, THEOPILA	28	F	UNKNOWN	GRZZZZUSA	
WLADESLAWA	3	F	CHILD	GRZZZZUSA	
RUSE, ANNA	55	F	UNKNOWN	GRZZZZUSA	
MARYANNE	.11	F	INFANT	GRZZZZUSA	
SZAKOWSKI, IGNATZ	18	M	LABR	GRZZZZUSA	
JUNKOWSKI, LEOPOLD	27	M	LABR	GRZZZZUSA	
LESHOKI, PAULINE	37	F	UNKNOWN	GRZZZZUSA	
BRONISLAW	.09	M	INFANT	GRZZZZUSA	
JOSEF	15	M	UNKNOWN	GRZZZZUSA	
JOSEFA	20	F	UNKNOWN	GRZZZZUSA	
ANNA	.03	F	INFANT	GRZZZZUSA	
WLADISLAW	18	M	UNKNOWN	GRZZZZUSA	
SENKO, LEON	25	M	LABR	GRZZZZUSA	
CHADY, JOHN	19	M	LABR	GRZZZZUSA	
SZAJORESK, ANDERS	45	M	LABR	GRZZZZUSA	
LABERT, JEAN	52	M	WTR	FRZZZZUSA	

SHIP: MAIN

FROM: BREMEN
TO: BALTIMORE
ARRIVED: 30 MAY 1888

PASSENGER	AGE	SEX	OCCUPATION	PRVL	DES
WALZLEIN, JOH.	26	M	MCHT	BVZZZZBAL	
MUFFINGER, JOHANNES	15	M	FARMER	GRZZZZMD	
WYCIECHOWSKI, JOSEF	25	M	FARMER	GRZZZZMD	
KACZMIERCZAK, JOHANN	22	M	FARMER	GRZZZZMD	
WOJTECKA, MICHAEL	26	M	FARMER	GRZZZZMD	
FENTSAHM, HEINR.	29	M	FARMER	GRZZZZMD	
RYBICKI, JAN	17	M	FARMER	GRZZZZMD	
SCHISCHETSCKY, JOSEF	24	M	FARMER	GRZZZZMD	
KLEINSCHMIDT, CARL	24	M	FARMER	GRZZZZMD	
BLODORN, HEINR.	25	M	FARMER	GRZZZZMD	
BROUMOND, HERM.	24	M	FARMER	GRZZZZMD	
KNUTH, ERNST	21	M	FARMER	GRZZZZMD	
HERMANN, FRIEDR.	26	M	FARMER	GRZZZZMD	
KRUEGER, ALBERT	23	M	STWD	GRZZZZMD	

PASSENGER	AGE	SEX	OCCUPATION	PRVVL	DES
KRZIWDZINSKI, ANTON	24	M	STWD	GRZZZZ	MD
ANDRUKEWICZ, FELIX	41	M	FARMER	GRZZZZ	MD
GOTSCHI, FRANZ	17	M	FARMER	GRZZZZ	MD
KOTHERA, WENZL	40	M	FARMER	GRZZZZ	PA
HEINERL, JOSEF	44	M	FARMER	GRZZZZ	PA
KRIEGEL, MICHAEL	27	M	FARMER	GRZZZZ	PA
FREITAG, DANIEL	30	M	FARMER	GRZZZZ	WI
POST, ERNST	24	M	FARMER	GRZZZZ	WI
HASSE, HERM.	28	M	FARMER	GRZZZZ	WI
HIRSCH, SIEGFR.	18	M	FARMER	GRZZZZ	WI
THOMAS, GOTTFR.	26	M	FARMER	GRZZZZ	TX
WENDLER, MAX	23	M	FARMER	GRZZZZ	VA
SARA, JOHANN	25	M	FARMER	GRZZZZ	WI
HENKE, FRANZ	23	M	FARMER	GRZZZZ	MD
VONNAHME, JOSEF	19	M	FARMER	GRZZZZ	MD
HESSE, WILH.	18	M	FARMER	GRZZZZ	MD
WUESTERFELD, HEINR.	18	M	FARMER	GRZZZZ	IN
TRIMPER, HEINR.	35	M	FARMER	GRZZZZ	MO
CIZEK, VACLAV	17	M	FARMER	GRZZZZ	MO
TAENGER, AUGUST	27	M	FARMER	GRZZZZ	IL
BADEN, JOH.	26	M	FARMER	GRZZZZ	MD
STRAIN, JOSEF	25	M	FARMER	GRZZZZ	MD
ZINNTL, JOHANN	24	M	FARMER	GRZZZZ	MD
KOCH, MICHAEL	25	M	FARMER	GRZZZZ	MD
LEMBERG, DIEDR.	15	M	FARMER	GRZZZZ	MD
SIMON, CHRISTIAN	14	M	FARMER	GRZZZZ	MD
REIL, FRIEDR.	17	M	FARMER	GRZZZZ	MD
ERB, HERM.	20	M	FARMER	GRZZZZ	MD
WILHELM	18	M	FARMER	GRZZZZ	MD
CHRISTIAN	16	M	FARMER	GRZZZZ	MD
KRUEGER, WM.	28	M	FARMER	GRZZZZ	MD
SAWIESTROWSKI, JOSEF	31	M	FARMER	GRZZZZ	MD
UTECHT, FRITZ	20	M	FARMER	GRZZZZ	MD
LUEPKE, WILH.	9	M	CHILD	GRZZZZ	MD
BARTKOWICZ, WOJCEK	24	M	FARMER	GRZZZZ	MD
WINTER, RUDOLF	17	M	FARMER	GRZZZZ	MD
RUEHMSTEDT, LOUIS	52	M	FARMER	GRZZZZ	MD
BOSIKOWSKI, IGNATZ	26	M	MCHT	GRZZZZ	MD
WOJACYK, JAN	44	M	FARMER	GRZZZZ	MD
ORZEWSKI, JOSEF	37	M	FARMER	GRZZZZ	MD
URBANSKI, WADJRATAYCZAK	18	M	FARMER	GRZZZZ	MD
KATAYCZAK, JOHANN	16	M	FARMER	GRZZZZ	MD
PROTZ, CHRISTOPH	35	M	FARMER	GRZZZZ	MD
KOSKOWSKI, STANISLAW	22	M	FARMER	GRZZZZ	MD
KLATT, GUSTAV	30	M	FARMER	GRZZZZ	MD
NEITZEL, OTTO	24	M	FARMER	GRZZZZ	MD
BROND, IGNATZ	18	M	FARMER	GRZZZZ	MD
RANTZ, AUGUST	37	M	FARMER	GRZZZZ	MD
KLEMP, EMIL	16	M	FARMER	GRZZZZ	MD
NICOLAI, LUDWIG	24	M	FARMER	GRZZZZ	MD
FLIGELMANN, SIMON	9	M	CHILD	GRZZZZ	MD
PINCOWITZ, WILLY	13	M	FARMER	GRZZZZ	MD
ISIDOR	14	M	FARMER	GRZZZZ	MD
FATELBAUM, ARON	17	M	FARMER	GRZZZZ	MD
MOSES	15	M	FARMER	GRZZZZ	MD
HENNEKENS, CORT	66	M	FARMER	GRZZZZ	MD
RIEDEL, WILH.	60	M	FARMER	GRZZZZ	MD
KLEIN, JACOB	59	M	FARMER	GRZZZZ	MD
BECKER, HE-E	13	M	NN	GRZZZZ	MD
SMID, GERHARDUS	70	M	NN	GRZZZZ	MD
PALM, HEINR.	30	M	NN	GRZZZZ	MD
MACIJEWSKI, STANISL.	24	M	NN	GRZZZZ	MD
RUDOWSKI, ADAM	29	M	NN	GRZZZZ	PA
ZABLOCKI, WALENTY	24	M	NN	GRZZZZ	IL
JOCKEL, STANISL.	27	M	NN	GRZZZZ	OH
WODTKE, ERHARD	27	M	NN	GRZZZZ	NE
PUSCHERT, ALBERT	27	M	NN	GRZZZZ	NE
FRIEDRICH	38	M	NN	GRZZZZ	NE
DOMMACH, JOSEF	22	M	NN	GRZZZZ	IL
SCHWANETT, WILH.	52	M	NN	GRZZZZ	MI
SCHIESSEL, JOH.	22	M	NN	GRZZZZ	IA
HORSTMANN, EMIL	21	M	NN	GRZZZZ	PA
WEBER, MICHEL	43	M	NN	GRZZZZ	MI
REINHARD, JOHANN	29	M	NN	GRZZZZ	MI
NIKLAS, SAMUEL	19	M	NN	GRZZZZ	OH
SCHMITZIK, JOHANN	37	M	NN	GRZZZZ	OH
SCHWIATKOWSKI, STANISLA	27	M	NN	GRZZZZ	MI
RUTSCHINSKY, ALBERT	27	M	NN	GRZZZZ	MI
KOSLOWSKY, JAN	28	M	NN	GRZZZZ	IL
WITTHUHN, CARL	33	M	NN	GRZZZZ	WI
BUSE, WILH.	18	M	NN	GRZZZZ	IL
KREUTZER, CARL	26	M	NN	GRZZZZ	MD
REINHARD, JOHN	38	M	NN	GRZZZZ	MD
KUNGEL, FRANZ	19	M	NN	GRZZZZ	MD
MACIPAN, JAN	16	M	NN	GRZZZZ	MD
BRANDT, JEAN	16	M	NN	GRZZZZ	MD
MUENDER, HERMANN	16	M	NN	GRZZZZ	MD
UHRIG, LEO	15	M	NN	GRZZZZ	MD
EHRHARD, BERNARD	15	M	NN	GRZZZZ	MD
KIND, THEODOR	26	M	NN	GRZZZZ	MD
BOETTCHER, FRIEDR.	25	M	NN	GRZZZZ	MD
GRUENING, HERMANN	25	M	NN	GRZZZZ	MD
SEBASTIAN, HERMANN	39	M	NN	GRZZZZ	MD
GERLING, OTTO	26	M	NN	GRZZZZ	MD
KALWA, ANTON	33	M	NN	GRZZZZ	MD
KITEWICZ, JOSEF	29	M	NN	GRZZZZ	MD
SCHEMM, GEORG	50	M	NN	GRZZZZ	MD
JOHANN	29	M	NN	GRZZZZ	MD
HELLER, AUGUST	20	M	NN	GRZZZZ	MD
CHACHAROWSKA, ANTON	32	M	NN	GRZZZZ	MD
MUELICH, CARL	27	M	NN	GRZZZZ	MD
BRILL, HEINR.	17	M	NN	GRZZZZ	MD
RONSCHEIN, JECHESKEL	18	M	NN	GRZZZZ	MD
SCHLUETER, WILH.	17	M	NN	GRZZZZ	MD
HEER, HERMANN	50	M	NN	GRZZZZ	MD
SCHOTT, MARTIN	28	M	NN	GRZZZZ	MI
ROMANNOWSKI, FRANZ	22	M	NN	GRZZZZ	MI
BENZNIK, GERHARD	21	M	NN	GRZZZZ	MI
PILLE, JOHANN	35	M	NN	GRZZZZ	OH
BLUST, CARL	30	M	NN	GRZZZZ	MO
VOELLM, GUSTAV	14	M	NN	GRZZZZ	KS
RANGE, JOHS.	25	M	NN	GRZZZZ	KS
HENNING, FRIEDR.	25	M	NN	GRZZZZ	WI
KOWALEWSKI, JOHANN	29	M	NN	GRZZZZ	BAL
WIESMANN, JOSEF	27	M	NN	GRZZZZ	BAL
HOCHSTRAUER, ANDREAS	14	M	NN	GRZZZZ	BAL
FRANK, JOSEF	18	M	NN	GRZZZZ	BAL
HELLER, JACOB	22	M	NN	GRZZZZ	BAL
CUTTNER, JOHS.	38	M	NN	GRZZZZ	BAL
RATKA, LUDWIG	30	M	NN	GRZZZZ	BAL
ROCHOWIAK, MARTIN	30	M	NN	GRZZZZ	BAL
RUCHAY, MICHAL	29	M	NN	GRZZZZ	BAL
REINKE, ROBERT	15	M	NN	GRZZZZ	BAL
KLATT, AUGUST	22	M	NN	GRZZZZ	BAL
MUCHE, GUSTAV	11	M	CH	GRZZZZ	BAL
WEISSMUELLER, VALENTIN	21	M	FARMER	GRZZZZ	BAL
JAGER, JOHN	18	M	FARMER	GRZZZZ	BAL
CHEHMINSKI, LUDWIG	26	M	FARMER	GRZZZZ	BAL
BRASMEN, CHRISTIAN	27	M	FARMER	GRZZZZ	BAL
ELMINOWSKI, STEPHAN	30	M	FARMER	GRZZZZ	BAL
POKOZENSKI, VALENTIN	24	M	FARMER	GRZZZZ	IL
GYZENSKI, IGNATZ	41	M	FARMER	GRZZZZ	MI
GROSSMANN, MICHEL	23	M	FARMER	GRZZZZ	IL
SOMETH, MICOL.	30	M	FARMER	GRZZZZ	BAL
STRICHER, WILLIAM	30	M	FARMER	GRZZZZ	BAL
JABLONSKI, VALENTIN	44	M	FARMER	GRZZZZ	BAL
SCHMIDT, ANDREAS	34	M	FARMER	GRZZZZ	BAL
HELFERICH, JOH.G.	42	M	FARMER	GRZZZZ	BAL
WOLFF, AUG.	17	M	FARMER	GRZZZZ	BAL
WALTER, GOTTLIEB	22	M	FARMER	GRZZZZ	BAL
SCHNEIDER, JOSEPH	25	M	FARMER	GRZZZZ	BAL
SCHMEISER, HINRICH	24	M	FARMER	GRZZZZ	BAL
NACHENGAST, HEINR.	24	M	FARMER	GRZZZZ	BAL
BORK, JULIE	18	F	SVNT	GRZZZZ	IL
BONSACK, ANNA	12	F	CH	GRZZZZ	BAL
MARIA	15	F	SVNT	GRZZZZ	BAL
NEUBERGER, BABETTE	26	F	SVNT	GRZZZZ	BAL
OFF, LEDWINA	16	F	SVNT	GRZZZZ	BAL
RUCK, BABETTE	17	F	SVNT	GRZZZZ	BAL
SUPPAU, SOPHIA	24	F	W	GRZZZZ	BAL

PASSENGER	AGE	SEX	OCCUPATION	PRVL	DES
ANNA	.03	F	INFANT	GRZZZZBAL	
STAAB, BARBARA	63	F	W	GRZZZZBAL	
LANKES, JOSEPHINE	25	F	W	GRZZZZBAL	
SABORASCH, WILHNE.	17	F	SVNT	GRZZZZBAL	
STICKEL, PAULINE	40	F	W	GRZZZZBAL	
ALBERTINE	16	F	CH	GRZZZZBAL	
LEOPOLD	2	M	CHILD	GRZZZZBAL	
ANNA	.11	F	INFANT	GRZZZZBAL	
WOJTECKA, AGNES	21	F	SVNT	GRZZZZBAL	
STRAUSS, GRETCHEN	16	F	SVNT	GRZZZZBAL	
BALACHOWSKY, MARIA	18	F	SVNT	GRZZZZBAL	
KLOTZ, HULDA	17	F	SVNT	GRZZZZBAL	
RAKUSEN, SARAH	19	F	SVNT	GRZZZZBAL	
STRAHL, FRANZKA.	15	F	SVNT	GRZZZZBAL	
PAGEL, JULIE	23	F	W	GRZZZZBAL	
WILHELM	.01	M	INFANT	GRZZZZBAL	
SACK, ANNA	23	F	SVNT	GRZZZZBAL	
MUELLER, MATHILDE	22	F	SVNT	GRZZZZBAL	
MINNA	27	F	SVNT	GRZZZZBAL	
HAAK, MATHILDE	21	F	SVNT	GRZZZZBAL	
HERBST, ELISAB.	21	F	SVNT	GRZZZZBAL	
LEWANDOWSKA, MARIANNA	30	F	W	GRZZZZBAL	
JOSEF	3	M	CHILD	GRZZZZBAL	
WLADISLAWA	.01	F	INFANT	GRZZZZBAL	
HELMKE, CATHA.	54	F	W	GRZZZZBAL	
RADEMACHER, HENRIETTE	29	F	W	GRZZZZBAL	
BURKARD, CATHR.	40	F	W	GRZZZZBAL	
WILH.	9	M	CHILD	GRZZZZBAL	
BAUMGART, DOROTHEA	20	F	SVNT	GRZZZZBAL	
HOLLANDER, EVA	28	F	W	GRZZZZBAL	
FUCHS, CATHR.	20	F	SVNT	GRZZZZBAL	
PROSCHINSKY, OTTILIE	24	F	SVNT	GRZZZZBAL	
WOLFF, AGNES	16	F	SVNT	GRZZZZBAL	
PLEHN, EHRICH	10	M	CH	GRZZZZBAL	
RUETER, ELISE	22	F	SVNT	GRZZZZBAL	
MEZERA, MARIA	3	F	CHILD	GRZZZZBAL	
BLANZ, BALTRA	23	F	SVNT	GRZZZZBAL	
STEIN, ANNA	24	F	W	GRZZZZBAL	
GLATZEL, THERESE	60	F	W	GRZZZZBAL	
KLIER, FRANCISCA	20	F	SVNT	GRZZZZBAL	
KLOCKGETER, HELENE	40	F	W	GRZZZZBAL	
MARTIN, MINNA	20	F	SVNT	GRZZZZBAL	
BARTSCH, TEOPHILE	25	F	SVNT	GRZZZZBAL	
BODE, MARIA	49	F	W	GRZZZZMO	
SCHLEGEL, JOHANNE	72	F	W	GRZZZZBAL	
GOERTZ, CAECILIA	26	F	W	GRZZZZBAL	
EBERHARD, FRANZKA.	20	F	SVNT	GRZZZZIL	
ROSENTRETER, SOPHIE	19	F	SVNT	GRZZZZIL	
KLEHN, MATHILDA	25	F	SVNT	GRZZZZIL	
FRIESKE, MARIA	17	F	SVNT	GRZZZZMI	
FISCHER, EMILIE	30	F	W	GRZZZZBAL	
ANNA	.01	F	INFANT	GRZZZZBAL	
ZDROZEWKSA, AGNES	21	F	SVNT	GRZZZZBAL	
MENDYROSKA, MARIANNA	54	F	W	GRZZZZBAL	
IFFLAND, ELISAB.	34	F	W	GRZZZZBAL	
HEINZE, IDA	20	F	SVNT	GRZZZZBAL	
HUBENTHAL, ELISE	23	F	SVNT	GRZZZZBAL	
KOEHLER, IDA	17	F	SVNT	GRZZZZBAL	
SIKORA, THEOPHILE	27	F	W	GRZZZZBAL	
GRACZYK, ANNA	27	F	W	GRZZZZBAL	
JACZYNSKA, FRANZKA.	21	F	W	GRZZZZBAL	
JOHANN	.06	M	INFANT	GRZZZZBAL	
MAAJS, AUGUSTE	46	F	W	GRZZZZBAL	
LUDE	17	F	CH	GRZZZZBAL	
LEHMANN, MARIA	42	F	W	GRZZZZBAL	
MARTHA	12	F	CH	GRZZZZBAL	
GUSTAV	10	M	CH	GRZZZZBAL	
OTTO	8	M	CHILD	GRZZZZBAL	
BREMER, AUGUSTE	19	F	SVNT	GRZZZZBAL	
LIPPKE, AMELIA	20	F	SVNT	GRZZZZBAL	
BOTTKE, MATHILDE	18	F	SVNT	GRZZZZBAL	
SCHAEFER, MARTHA	28	F	SVNT	GRZZZZBAL	
HORKENBACH, MINNA	22	F	W	GRZZZZBAL	
WALTER	.10	F	INFANT	GRZZZZBAL	
SMUTNY, SOPHIE	23	F	W	GRZZZZBAL	
MARIA	13	F	CH	GRZZZZBAL	
BIANKA	5	F	CHILD	GRZZZZBAL	
EMILIE	2	F	CHILD	GRZZZZBAL	
RUDOLF	.11	M	INFANT	GRZZZZBAL	
SOPHIE	23	F	W	GRZZZZBAL	
JAROSLAW	.11	M	INFANT	GRZZZZBAL	
KAUTZ, WILHNE.	33	F	W	GRZZZZBAL	
SCHALLENBERG, ELISE	20	F	SVNT	GRZZZZBAL	
GIESE, HERMINE	25	F	W	GRZZZZBAL	
CIESIELSKA, JOSEFA	26	F	W	GRZZZZBAL	
SCHERNEIT, AUGUSTE	21	F	SVNT	GRZZZZBAL	
KEMKER, THERESE	19	F	SVNT	GRZZZZBAL	
MATTIL, MARGR.	60	F	W	GRZZZZBAL	
SCHULENBERG, ELISE	18	F	SVNT	GRZZZZBAL	
NICLON, MARGR.	21	F	SVNT	GRZZZZBAL	
MICHAEL	12	M	CH	GRZZZZBAL	
BONECZKA, MARGA.	30	F	W	GRZZZZOH	
ROGALIN, CAROLINA	29	F	W	GRZZZZOH	
KAUTZ, ALBERTINE	60	F	W	GRZZZZOH	
MARTHA	4	F	CHILD	GRZZZZOH	
FRITZ	2	M	CHILD	GRZZZZOH	
ANNA	.03	F	INFANT	GRZZZZOH	
BOHRER, MARTHA	21	F	SVNT	GRZZZZOH	
KIEFER, ELISAB.	65	F	W	GRZZZZOH	
OTTILIE	21	F	CH	GRZZZZOH	
HERMANN, CATHA.	26	F	W	GRZZZZMI	
KOSLOWSKA, BRONISLAWA	19	F	SVNT	GRZZZZWI	
MARIANNA	17	F	SVNT	GRZZZZWI	
BOEHMER, MAGDLE.	26	F	SVNT	GRZZZZPA	
HERMANNSDOTTER, BARBA.	23	F	SVNT	GRZZZZPA	
KAMRADT, JOHANNE	26	F	SVNT	GRZZZZMI	
VONSTEMPEL, MARIA	17	F	SVNT	GRZZZZMI	
SYKYRA, MARIA	15	F	SVNT	GRZZZZBAL	
SEITEK, ANTONIE	34	F	W	GRZZZZBAL	
CAROLINE	11	F	CH	GRZZZZBAL	
JOSEFINE	9	F	CHILD	GRZZZZBAL	
ANTONIE	8	F	CHILD	GRZZZZBAL	
MARIA	3	F	CHILD	GRZZZZBAL	
MUNST, ANNA	16	F	SVNT	GRZZZZBAL	
ROSENZWEIG, BARBA.	39	F	W	GRZZZZBAL	
SCHWOBIG, MARG.	18	F	SVNT	GRZZZZBAL	
BARBA.	15	F	SVNT	GRZZZZBAL	
FRITZ, ANTONIA	27	F	SVNT	GRZZZZBAL	
ZIELKOSKA, NATALIA	19	F	SVNT	GRZZZZBAL	
MACFALDA, ANTONIA	30	F	W	GRZZZZBAL	
MARIA	5	F	CHILD	GRZZZZBAL	
ANASTASIA	.11	F	INFANT	GRZZZZBAL	
ANTON	26	M	FARMER	GRZZZZBAL	
OESTERLE, PAULINE	22	F	SVNT	GRZZZZBAL	
SCHULTHEISS, CATHR.	15	F	SVNT	GRZZZZBAL	
STEINER, MARGR.	43	F	W	GRZZZZBAL	
MARGR.	14	F	CH	GRZZZZBAL	
FRIEDRKE.	10	F	CH	GRZZZZBAL	
FRIEDR.	5	M	CHILD	GRZZZZBAL	
LEIB, ANNA	20	F	SVNT	GRZZZZBAL	
SCHAD, BARBARA	25	F	SVNT	GRZZZZBAL	
DENZLEIN, MARGA.	23	F	SVNT	GRZZZZBAL	
SAFFERT, ANNA	21	F	SVNT	GRZZZZMN	
SANDER, MARIA	27	F	W	GRZZZZBAL	
LIESCHEN	3	F	CHILD	GRZZZZBAL	
FRIEDR.	.01	M	INFANT	GRZZZZBAL	
ZIENSBIONKA, ANNA	16	F	SVNT	GRZZZZBAL	
EULER, ELISE	16	F	SVNT	GRZZZZBAL	
ELISE	18	F	SVNT	GRZZZZBAL	
ELSNER, ANNA	22	F	SVNT	GRZZZZMI	
GOFFERT, HENRIETTE	11	F	CH	GRZZZZMN	
GOSTOWSKA, SUSANNA	23	F	SVNT	GRZZZZIL	
APPEL, MARGR.	15	F	SVNT	GRZZZZOH	
SCHULTHEISS, URSULA	15	F	SVNT	GRZZZZOH	
SOPHIA	12	F	CH	GRZZZZOH	
FABELING, LINA	22	F	SVNT	GRZZZZIA	
HEIDEMANN, DINA	29	F	W	GRZZZZOH	
ANKER, BERTHA	23	F	SVNT	GRZZZZPA	
LINK, MARIE	24	F	SVNT	GRZZZZPA	
BONNIKSEN, CAROLINE	25	F	SVNT	GRZZZZNE	

PASSENGER	AGE	SEX	OCCUPATION	PRV VLS DES
KOENIG, ROSINE	33	F	W	GRZZZZWI
EICKHOFF, HENRIETTE	19	F	SVNT	GRZZZZBAL
TOSZEWSKA, KONSTANZE	23	F	SVNT	GRZZZZBAL
BALBINE	21	F	SVNT	GRZZZZBAL
GRZYWA, CHARLOTTE	18	F	SVNT	GRZZZZBAL
NEIMANN, KATHR.	36	F	W	GRZZZZBAL
WLADISLAW	7	M	CHILD	GRZZZZBAL
LEONHARD	5	M	CHILD	GRZZZZBAL
SIGMUND	.10	M	INFANT	GRZZZZBAL
GRUETZEN, BERTHA	35	F	W	GRZZZZBAL
OTTO	11	M	CH	GRZZZZBAL
KNOTT, KUNIGUNDE	22	F	SVNT	GRZZZZBAL
ZIMMERLIN, LOUISE	20	F	SVNT	GRZZZZBAL
HELL, MARIA	18	F	SVNT	GRZZZZBAL
APRILL, MARGA.	23	F	SVNT	GRZZZZBAL
BECKERT, LOUISE	22	F	SVNT	GRZZZZBAL
CONSTANCIA	18	F	SVNT	GRZZZZBAL
GANS, WILHNE.	61	F	W	GRZZZZBAL
GERDES, MARGR.	26	F	W	GRZZZZBAL
MAURER, HEDWIG	23	F	SVNT	GRZZZZBAL
MONTKOSKA, TROFILA	21	F	SVNT	GRZZZZBAL
LUTZENRATH, LOUISE	50	F	W	GRZZZZBAL
BERTHA	11	F	CH	GRZZZZBAL
MINNA	8	F	CHILD	GRZZZZBAL
NOWACKA, FRASNZISCA	18	F	SVNT	GRZZZZBAL
OSOWICZKA, FRANZISKA	18	F	SVNT	GRZZZZBAL
BUSE, BERTHA	26	F	W	GRZZZZIL
CICHOWITZ, MARGR.	50	F	W	GRZZZZBAL
ERB, FRIEDERIKE	42	F	W	GRZZZZBAL
CHRISTINE	14	F	CH	GRZZZZBAL
GAZKIL, MARGR.	20	F	SVNT	GRZZZZBAL
KWIATKOWSKI, MARIE	24	F	W	GRZZZZBAL
AUGUST	3	M	CHILD	GRZZZZBAL
DOMOGALSKA, JULIANA	56	F	W	GRZZZZBAL
CATHR.	16	F	CH	GRZZZZBAL
POKOZENSKY, MARIANNA	26	F	W	GRZZZZBAL
BOLESLAW	3	M	CHILD	GRZZZZBAL
LEO	.05	M	INFANT	GRZZZZBAL
KADASKA, KAROLINA	22	F	SVNT	GRZZZZBAL
BOGUNS, META	41	F	W	GRZZZZBAL
TEMKE	11	F	CH	GRZZZZBAL
EDO	10	M	CH	GRZZZZBAL
MENNO	9	M	CHILD	GRZZZZBAL
GESCHE	7	F	CHILD	GRZZZZBAL
JOHANNE	4	F	CHILD	GRZZZZBAL
EMIL	1	M	CHILD	GRZZZZBAL
DELING, JOHANNE	24	F	W	GRZZZZBAL
CHRISTIAN	6	M	CHILD	GRZZZZBAL
ENGELMANN, JOHANNA	17	F	SVNT	GRZZZZBAL
TREBING, LOUISE	21	F	W	GRZZZZBAL
FRITZ	2	M	CHILD	GRZZZZBAL
GISSING, LOUISE	19	F	SVNT	GRZZZZBAL
HARTMANN, ANNA	17	F	SVNT	GRZZZZBAL
PICKEL, ELISE	29	F	SVNT	GRZZZZBAL
MARGA.	15	F	SVNT	GRZZZZBAL
BACHTOLD, MARGA.	18	F	SVNT	GRZZZZBAL
KOPP, ELISABETH	53	F	W	GRZZZZBAL
KREMS, SERZE	16	F	W	GRZZZZBAL
GEBHARDT, KATHR.	21	F	W	GRZZZZOH
BOEHMER, MARGA.	24	F	W	GRZZZZOH
UKARCHEFSKY, MARTIN	21	M	FARMER	GRZZZZBAL
MARIANNE	19	F	W	GRZZZZBAL
ROHDE, FRANZ	30	M	FARMER	GRZZZZBAL
MARIANNE	5	F	CHILD	GRZZZZBAL
VERONICA	3	F	CHILD	GRZZZZBAL
FRANZKA.	25	F	W	GRZZZZBAL
JOHANN	.11	M	INFANT	GRZZZZBAL
LEWAKOSKI, MACIEJ	24	M	FARMER	GRZZZZBAL
MARIANNE	25	F	W	GRZZZZBAL
JOHANN	.06	M	INFANT	GRZZZZBAL
SAMMANN, JOH.	46	M	FARMER	GRZZZZBAL
SOPHIA	42	F	W	GRZZZZBAL
OLIKOWSKI, MICHAEL	44	M	FARMER	GRZZZZBAL
JULIE	40	F	W	GRZZZZBAL
CARL	11	M	CH	GRZZZZBAL
BERNHARD	10	M	CH	GRZZZZBAL
FOERSTER, JOSEF	28	M	FARMER	GRZZZZBAL
ANNA	23	F	W	GRZZZZBAL
JOHANN	.04	M	INFANT	GRZZZZBAL
HUJARA, KASPAR	44	M	FARMER	GRZZZZBAL
ANTONIA	35	F	W	GRZZZZBAL
MARIANNA	16	F	CH	GRZZZZBAL
JOSEPH	12	M	CH	GRZZZZBAL
STANISLAW	11	M	CH	GRZZZZBAL
MICHEL	9	M	CHILD	GRZZZZBAL
FRANZISCA	5	F	CHILD	GRZZZZBAL
FRANZ	.01	M	INFANT	GRZZZZBAL
BEHLING, AUGUST	45	M	FARMER	GRZZZZBAL
EMILIE	34	F	W	GRZZZZBAL
EMILIE	12	F	CH	GRZZZZBAL
PAUL	11	M	CH	GRZZZZBAL
AUGUST	8	M	CHILD	GRZZZZBAL
ANNA	9	F	CHILD	GRZZZZBAL
AGUNDE	3	F	CHILD	GRZZZZBAL
OTTO	.03	M	INFANT	GRZZZZBAL
BORKOWSKI, ANTON	30	M	FARMER	GRZZZZBAL
JOSEFA	27	F	W	GRZZZZBAL
MARIANNE	.01	F	INFANT	GRZZZZBAL
LANKES, JOSEFINE	25	F	SVNT	GRZZZZBAL
MUELLER, RUBERTUS	25	M	FARMER	GRZZZZBAL
TIEDEMANN, AUGUST	40	M	FARMER	GRZZZZBAL
WILHNE.	44	F	W	GRZZZZBAL
AUGUST	18	M	FARMER	GRZZZZBAL
BERTHA	13	F	CH	GRZZZZBAL
ANNA	5	F	CHILD	GRZZZZBAL
KLEIST, AUGUST	36	M	FARMER	GRZZZZBAL
JOHANNE	36	F	W	GRZZZZBAL
CARL	5	M	CHILD	GRZZZZBAL
MARIA	.10	F	INFANT	GRZZZZBAL
BRANDT, CHRISTIAN	61	M	FARMER	GRZZZZBAL
ELISE	56	F	W	GRZZZZBAL
AUGUST	16	M	FARMER	GRZZZZBAL
FOLCHER, CARL	13	M	CH	GRZZZZBAL
HENRIETTE	9	F	CHILD	GRZZZZBAL
EPP, CARL	40	M	FARMER	GRZZZZBAL
ERNESTINE	40	F	W	GRZZZZBAL
ELISE	8	F	CHILD	GRZZZZBAL
HEINR.	4	M	CHILD	GRZZZZBAL
MARGR.	3	F	CHILD	GRZZZZBAL
MARIA	.09	F	INFANT	GRZZZZBAL
GUSTAV	.03	M	INFANT	GRZZZZBAL
KALAMARSKY, JOHN	27	M	FARMER	GRZZZZBAL
SOPHIE	26	F	W	GRZZZZBAL
FRANZ	2	M	CHILD	GRZZZZBAL
MARIA	.01	F	INFANT	GRZZZZBAL
WIELEWIDZKI, STANISL.	69	M	FARMER	GRZZZZBAL
ANNA	67	F	W	GRZZZZBAL
CATHRINE	24	F	CH	GRZZZZBAL
LEWANDOWSKA, MARIANNE	30	F	W	GRZZZZBAL
JOSEF	3	M	CHILD	GRZZZZBAL
WLADISLAW	.01	M	INFANT	GRZZZZBAL
ZASTUDIL, JOHANN	43	M	FARMER	GRZZZZPA
MARIA	38	F	W	GRZZZZPA
WENZL	15	M	FARMER	GRZZZZPA
FRANZ	10	M	CH	GRZZZZPA
JOHANN	6	M	CHILD	GRZZZZPA
MARIA	3	F	CHILD	GRZZZZPA
STRUSKA, MATHIAS	32	M	FARMER	GRZZZZPA
KATHARINE	27	F	W	GRZZZZPA
EMILIE	4	F	CHILD	GRZZZZPA
MARIA	2	F	CHILD	GRZZZZPA
ANTON	.06	M	INFANT	GRZZZZPA
SKLENARCH, WENZL	64	M	FARMER	GRZZZZPA
JOSEFA	62	F	W	GRZZZZPA
PERTL, JOHANN	25	M	FARMER	GRZZZZPA
EDUARD	17	M	FARMER	GRZZZZPA
WENZL	24	M	FARMER	GRZZZZPA
VANI	19	F	SVNT	GRZZZZPA
HOLLANDER, JOH.	63	M	FARMER	GRZZZZIL
JUSTINE	60	F	W	GRZZZZIL

PASSENGER	AGE	SEX	OCCUPATION	PRVL	DES	PASSENGER	AGE	SEX	OCCUPATION	PRVL	DES
PISCHNER, CARL	40	M	FARMER		GRZZZZMN	BERNHARD	15	M	FARMER		GRZZZZBAL
JOHANNA	38	F	W		GRZZZZMN	BRUNO	14	M	NN		GRZZZZBAL
PAULINE	9	F	CHILD		GRZZZZMN	OLK, JACOB	27	M	NN		GRZZZZBAL
HERMANN	6	M	CHILD		GRZZZZMN	MARIA	29	F	W		GRZZZZBAL
MARIA	4	F	CHILD		GRZZZZMN	GUSTAV	5	M	CHILD		GRZZZZBAL
WILHELM	.09	M	INFANT		GRZZZZMN	ELISABETH	70	F	W		GRZZZZBAL
SCHUETZ, CARL	66	M	FARMER		GRZZZZWI	YTATTERNY, GOTTLIEB	26	M	FARMER		GRZZZZBAL
DOROTHEA	65	F	W		GRZZZZWI	GOTTLIEBE	28	M	W		GRZZZZBAL
DIPPMANN, AUGUST	54	M	FARMER		GRZZZZWI	WILHNE.	.01	F	INFANT		GRZZZZBAL
CHRISTINE	44	F	W		GRZZZZWI	PETER, WILHELM	50	M	FARMER		GRZZZZBAL
BRUNO	11	M	CH		GRZZZZWI	AUGUSTE	45	F	W		GRZZZZBAL
JOHANNE	56	F	W		GRZZZZWI	EMMA	19	F	CH		GRZZZZBAL
BERGER, EMIL	27	M	FARMER		GRZZZZWI	WILHELM	17	M	FARMER		GRZZZZBAL
ANNA	28	F	W		GRZZZZWI	AUGUSTE	5	F	CHILD		GRZZZZBAL
MITSCHERLING, HERM.	46	M	FARMER		GRZZZZMD	DOMINIK, FRITZ	30	M	FARMER		GRZZZZBAL
PAULINE	46	F	W		GRZZZZMD	WILHELMINE	29	F	W		GRZZZZBAL
GUSTAV	12	M	CH		GRZZZZMD	WILDE, FRANZ	27	M	FARMER		GRZZZZBAL
HEDWIG	10	F	CH		GRZZZZMD	BERTHA	24	F	W		GRZZZZBAL
MAX	11	M	CH		GRZZZZMD	DIEKMANN, JOHANNE	22	F	CH		GRZZZZBAL
ELISABETH	9	F	CHILD		GRZZZZMD	WOLF, WILLIAM	14	M	CL		GRZZZZBAL
EHLING, GOTTL.F.	23	M	FARMER		GRZZZZOH	SOCZINSKA, JOHN	15	M	CL		GRZZZZBAL
CHRISTINE	20	F	W		GRZZZZOH	KATERZINA	12	F	CH		GRZZZZBAL
BORCHEWSKY, CARL	28	M	FARMER		GRZZZZIL	LESNIWSKI, FRANZ	31	M	FARMER		GRZZZZBAL
ANNA	24	F	W		GRZZZZIL	LOUISE	31	F	W		GRZZZZBAL
ROBERT	1	M	CHILD		GRZZZZIL	SCHRAMM, JULIUS	36	M	FARMER		GRZZZZBAL
JOHANNE	.06	F	INFANT		GRZZZZIL	BERTHA	32	F	W		GRZZZZBAL
FUNKE, ANNA	39	F	W		GRZZZZIL	IDA	7	F	CHILD		GRZZZZBAL
ANCHEN	11	F	CH		GRZZZZIL	RICHARD	5	M	CHILD		GRZZZZBAL
ANNA	5	F	CHILD		GRZZZZIL	MARIA	16	F	CH		GRZZZZBAL
GERHARDINE	3	F	CHILD		GRZZZZIL	LENZ, JULIUS	30	M	FARMER		GRZZZZBAL
JOHANN	1	M	CHILD		GRZZZZIL	BERTHA	32	F	W		GRZZZZBAL
MENKE, HEINR.	54	M	FARMER		GRZZZZBAL	OLGA	2	F	CHILD		GRZZZZBAL
CATHR.	52	F	W		GRZZZZBAL	MARGR.	.01	F	INFANT		GRZZZZBAL
HUHN, PAUL	30	M	FARMER		GRZZZZBAL	KABAZINSKI, FRANZ	25	M	FARMER		GRZZZZBAL
MARIA	25	F	W		GRZZZZBAL	RECKNAGEL, EDWARD	29	M	FARMER		GRZZZZBAL
JANSSEN, HEINR.	36	M	FARMER		GRZZZZNE	BERTHA	28	F	W		GRZZZZBAL
META	38	F	W		GRZZZZNE	KULLING, JOH.	61	M	FARMER		GRZZZZBAL
HELENE	9	F	CHILD		GRZZZZNE	STARK, ANNA	38	F	W		GRZZZZBAL
ANNA	7	F	CHILD		GRZZZZNE	JOHANN	18	M	FARMER		GRZZZZBAL
META	.06	F	INFANT		GRZZZZNE	DE-VRIES, JACOB	74	M	FARMER		GRZZZZBAL
EILERS, EILERT	66	M	FARMER		GRZZZZIN	GERD	43	M	FARMER		GRZZZZBAL
MARIA	51	F	W		GRZZZZIN	ELISABETH	45	F	W		GRZZZZBAL
KRAEMER, CEDERIA	11	F	CH		GRZZZZIN	TRINTJE	11	F	CH		GRZZZZBAL
SCHAEFER, WILHELM	26	M	FARMER		GRZZZZBAL	AREND	9	M	CHILD		GRZZZZBAL
HELENE	29	F	W		GRZZZZBAL	JAN	7	M	CHILD		GRZZZZBAL
DANIEL	11	M	CH		GRZZZZBAL	GERD	3	M	CHILD		GRZZZZBAL
ROSALIE	00	F	CH		GRZZZZBAL	HEGI, PHILIPP	56	M	FARMER		GRZZZZBAL
SCHMUGGE, MATHIAS	41	M	FARMER		GRZZZZBAL	LOUISE	54	F	W		GRZZZZBAL
CATHR.	25	F	W		GRZZZZBAL	HINR.	20	M	FARMER		GRZZZZBAL
JAGUSCH, MATHIAS	45	M	FARMER		GRZZZZMN	NEMITZ, FRIEDR.	30	M	FARMER		GRZZZZIL
FRANZKE.	43	F	W		GRZZZZMN	AUGUSTE	29	F	W		GRZZZZIL
MARIA	19	F	CH		GRZZZZMN	OTTO	4	M	CHILD		GRZZZZIL
ANNA	17	F	CH		GRZZZZMN	MARIA	.09	F	INFANT		GRZZZZIL
JACOB	15	M	FARMER		GRZZZZMN	MUSIELAK, JOHANN	35	M	FARMER		GRZZZZOH
JULIE	11	F	CH		GRZZZZMN	JOSEFA	38	F	W		GRZZZZOH
FRANZISKA	6	F	CHILD		GRZZZZMN	MARIANNA	14	F	CH		GRZZZZOH
BEYER, WILHELM	30	M	FARMER		GRZZZZBAL	FRANCISKA	10	F	CH		GRZZZZOH
MATHILDE	.28	F	W		GRZZZZBAL	PELAGIA	8	F	CHILD		GRZZZZOH
EMILIE	.11	F	INFANT		GRZZZZBAL	BOLESKAW	.01	F	INFANT		GRZZZZOH
ZIEMANN, CARL	17	M	FARMER		GRZZZZBAL	BIBAK, PETER	39	M	FARMER		GRZZZZMN
ALBERTINE	53	F	W		GRZZZZBAL	JUSTINE	34	F	W		GRZZZZMN
GUSTAV	10	M	CH		GRZZZZBAL	HELENE	9	F	CHILD		GRZZZZMN
HAUFT, MAX	27	M	FARMER		GRZZZZBAL	ALOISE	4	F	CHILD		GRZZZZMN
LINA	22	F	W		GRZZZZBAL	LESKADIA	.11	F	INFANT		GRZZZZMN
GEORG	3	M	CHILD		GRZZZZBAL	SCHAF, CONRAD	27	M	FARMER		GRZZZZOH
ELSE	.11	F	INFANT		GRZZZZBAL	ANNA	21	F	W		GRZZZZOH
KLOTZ, WILHELM	34	M	FARMER		GRZZZZBAL	EHEMANN, JOH.	49	M	BBR		GRZZZZCO
LOUISE	34	F	W		GRZZZZBAL	ANNA	49	F	W		GRZZZZCO
OTTO	13	M	CH		GRZZZZBAL	SIMON	20	M	BBR		GRZZZZCO
LEO	8	M	CHILD		GRZZZZBAL	MARGR.	14	F	CH		GRZZZZCO
REINHOLD	5	M	CHILD		GRZZZZBAL	ANNA	11	F	CH		GRZZZZCO
DUDEI, JOHANN	26	M	FARMER		GRZZZZBAL	PAHL, FRIEDR.	60	M	CPTR		GRZZZZIL
CAROLINE	27	F	W		GRZZZZBAL	FRIEDERIKE	40	F	W		GRZZZZIL
AUGUSTE	2	F	CHILD		GRZZZZBAL	HERMANN	18	M	CPTR		GRZZZZIL
ANNA	17	F	CH		GRZZZZBAL	AMANDA	16	F	CH		GRZZZZIL

PASSENGER	AGE	SEX	OCCUPATION	PRVVL	DES
REINHOLD	14	M	CPTR	GRZZZZIL	
THERESE	9	F	CHILD	GRZZZZIL	
EMMA	5	F	CHILD	GRZZZZIL	
FRANZ	3	M	CHILD	GRZZZZIL	
HEROLD, MICHAEL	55	M	SMH	GRZZZZPA	
LISABETHA	46	F	W	GRZZZZPA	
EVA	16	F	CH	GRZZZZPA	
MARGR.	11	F	CH	GRZZZZPA	
URSULA	9	F	CHILD	GRZZZZPA	
STAMBORSKI, TOMAS	24	M	FARMER	GRZZZZOH	
MARIANNE	22	F	W	GRZZZZOH	
FRANZ	2	M	CHILD	GRZZZZOH	
KREUTZEL, KARL	26	M	TLR	GRZZZZBAL	
REINHARD, JOHN	38	M	SHMK	GRZZZZBAL	
KUNIGUNDE	34	F	W	GRZZZZBAL	
HEINRICH	6	M	CHILD	GRZZZZBAL	
ELSEN, THEODOR	22	M	FARMER	GRZZZZBAL	
MARY	22	F	W	GRZZZZBAL	
MENKE, WILH.	26	M	FARMER	GRZZZZBAL	
ELISE	18	F	W	GRZZZZBAL	
VOSS, MICHAEL	54	M	FARMER	GRZZZZBAL	
MARGR.	47	F	W	GRZZZZBAL	
CAROLINE	16	F	CH	GRZZZZBAL	
JOHANNE	11	F	CH	GRZZZZBAL	
WILHELM	9	M	CHILD	GRZZZZBAL	
MARTHA	7	F	CHILD	GRZZZZBAL	
FABIJANS, FRANZ	29	M	MSN	GRZZZZBAL	
MARIE	27	F	W	GRZZZZBAL	
SENKBEIL, GEORG	47	M	MSN	GRZZZZBAL	
CAROLINE	32	F	W	GRZZZZBAL	
THOMA, CHRISTIAN	65	M	FARMER	GRZZZZBAL	
MARIA	8	F	CHILD	GRZZZZBAL	
ALBRECHT, FRIEDR.	35	M	TLR	GRZZZZBAL	
MARIA	18	F	W	GRZZZZBAL	
SENKBEIL, AUGUST	15	M	MSN	GRZZZZBAL	
BERTHA	10	F	CH	GRZZZZBAL	
SYNK, JOHANN	59	M	SMH	GRZZZZBAL	
JOHANNE	56	F	W	GRZZZZBAL	
BERNARD	26	M	SMH	GRZZZZBAL	
BERNHARD, JOSEF	25	M	LKSH	GRZZZZMN	
SOPHIE	21	F	W	GRZZZZMN	
KLINGBEIL, FRIEDR.	28	M	MSN	GRZZZZBAL	
CAROLINE	29	F	W	GRZZZZBAL	
PAUL	3	M	CHILD	GRZZZZBAL	
ANNA	.01	F	INFANT	GRZZZZBAL	
PAWLOWSKI, JULIUS	36	M	BCHR	GRZZZZBAL	
WILHNE.	36	F	W	GRZZZZBAL	
ADOLF	10	M	CH	GRZZZZBAL	
MARIA	5	F	CHILD	GRZZZZBAL	
WILHELM	2	M	CHILD	GRZZZZBAL	
SCHLAGE, FRANZ	29	M	BCHR	GRZZZZBAL	
LUCIE	29	F	W	GRZZZZBAL	
AUGUST	4	M	CHILD	GRZZZZBAL	
FRANZ	.01	M	INFANT	GRZZZZBAL	
KOCH, JOHANN	55	M	SHMK	GRZZZZBAL	
ROSINA	51	F	W	GRZZZZBAL	
CAROLINA	22	F	CH	GRZZZZBAL	
KLEIN, ERNST	44	M	BBR	GRZZZZBAL	
LOUISE	44	F	W	GRZZZZBAL	
AUGUSTE	7	F	CHILD	GRZZZZBAL	
PENSKI, AUGUST	57	M	UPHST	GRZZZZBAL	
PAULINE	47	F	W	GRZZZZBAL	
OTTO	11	M	CH	GRZZZZBAL	
GERTRUD	10	F	CH	GRZZZZBAL	
HEINRICH	7	M	CHILD	GRZZZZBAL	
FRIEDA	4	F	CHILD	GRZZZZBAL	
WULFF, REINHARD	48	M	WCHMKR	GRZZZZBAL	
WILHELMINE	48	F	W	GRZZZZBAL	
CHEMINSKI, LUDWIG	26	M	WCHMKR	GRZZZZBAL	
SOBIECK, WILHELM	57	M	BCHR	GRZZZZBAL	
CAROLINE	53	F	W	GRZZZZBAL	
JOHNE.	16	F	CH	GRZZZZBAL	
MATHILDE	18	F	CH	GRZZZZBAL	
HERMANN	11	M	CH	GRZZZZBAL	
ADELHEID	9	F	CHILD	GRZZZZBAL	
ZAMZOW, WILHELM	28	M	MSN	GRZZZZNE	
JOHANNE	28	F	W	GRZZZZNE	
MARGE.	4	F	CHILD	GRZZZZNE	
AMANDA	.11	F	INFANT	GRZZZZNE	
RUDOLPHI, GUSTAV	47	M	FARMER	GRZZZZNE	
MINNA	40	F	W	GRZZZZNE	
GUSTAV	11	M	CH	GRZZZZNE	
WILHELM	9	M	CHILD	GRZZZZNE	
ANNA	8	F	CHILD	GRZZZZNE	
ELISE	.09	F	INFANT	GRZZZZNE	
TAFELSKI, JAN	29	M	FARMER	GRZZZZNE	
MARIANNA	27	F	W	GRZZZZNE	
ANNA	5	F	CHILD	GRZZZZNE	
JOSEFA	3	F	CHILD	GRZZZZNE	
AGNES	.09	F	INFANT	GRZZZZNE	
MARGUARDT, EDUARD	21	M	FARMER	GRZZZZIL	
AUGUSTE	20	F	W	GRZZZZIL	
KRUEGER, HENRY	39	M	FARMER	GRZZZZBAL	
WILHELMINE	38	F	W	GRZZZZBAL	
AUGUSTE	14	F	CH	GRZZZZBAL	
EDUARD	7	M	CHILD	GRZZZZBAL	
BERTHA	5	F	CHILD	GRZZZZBAL	
OLGA	.11	F	INFANT	GRZZZZBAL	
MATYSIK, FRANK	34	M	LABR	GRZZZZBAL	
HELENE	25	F	W	GRZZZZBAL	
ANNA	2	F	CHILD	GRZZZZBAL	
KURZ, HEINR.	57	M	FARMER	GRZZZZBAL	
KATHR.	57	F	W	GRZZZZBAL	
ELISABETH	15	F	CH	GRZZZZBAL	
BROETZMANN, HEINR.	57	M	FARMER	GRZZZZBAL	
ALBERTINE	26	F	W	GRZZZZBAL	
HEDWIG	15	F	CH	GRZZZZBAL	
EMILIE	14	F	CH	GRZZZZBAL	
REINHARD	11	M	CH	GRZZZZBAL	
HEINR.	8	M	CHILD	GRZZZZBAL	
MARIA	3	F	CHILD	GRZZZZBAL	
ROBERT	.06	M	INFANT	GRZZZZBAL	
SCHMEISER, HEINR.	24	M	FARMER	GRZZZZBAL	
SCHNEIDER, JOSEPH	25	M	FARMER	GRZZZZBAL	
KOPP, MARGARETHE	40	F	W	GRZZZZBAL	
MARIA	17	F	CH	GRZZZZBAL	
MINNA	15	F	CH	GRZZZZBAL	
CARL	13	M	CH	GRZZZZBAL	
DOROTHEA	10	F	CH	GRZZZZBAL	
ELSABETH	9	F	CHILD	GRZZZZBAL	
LOUISE	7	F	CHILD	GRZZZZBAL	
MARGARETHE	4	F	CHILD	GRZZZZBAL	
WILHELM	2	M	CHILD	GRZZZZBAL	

SHIP: NOORDLAND

FROM: ANTWERP
TO: NEW YORK
ARRIVED: 31 MAY 1888

PASSENGER	AGE	SEX	OCCUPATION	PRVVL	DES
SEIDENSTICKER, B.	39	F	PVTW	GRADLDNY	
F.	17	F	PVTW	GRADLDNY	
A.	10	M	CH	GRADLDNY	
WAGNER, E.	35	M	DR	GRAFTDNY	
U	32	F	PVTW	GRAFTDNY	
O.	6	M	CHILD	GRAFTDNY	
KITZINGER, R.	23	F	CH	GRADLDNY	
SCHVONHART, F.	21	F	CH	GRADLDNY	
HUELLSTRUNG, J.	37	M	BRR	GRAHELNY	
A.	33	F	W	GRAHELNY	
J.	11	M	UNKNOWN	GRAHELNY	
W.	8	M	CHILD	GRAHELNY	
J.	36	M	BRR	GRAHELNY	
V.	32	F	W	GRAHELNY	
STOCK, TH.	33	M	PVTM	GRACBRNY	

PASSENGER	AGE	SEX	OCCUPATION	PRVL	DES
NICKEL, E.	60	F	PVTW	GRZZZZNY	
BRAND, J.	58	M	UNKNOWN	GRZZZZNY	
KUEILE, S.	17	F	PVTW	GRZZZZNY	
HEBELER, P.	30	M	ENGR	GRAAXXNY	
REICHERT, M.	68	F	PVTW	GRACXVNY	
TIEDEMANN, A.	37	F	PVTW	GRACPSNY	
HERRENBRUCK, C.W.	55	F	PVTW	GRACVFNY	
STUEHLEN, A.	11	F	PVTW	GRAAECNY	
JANSSENS, THEO.	18	M	MCHT	GRADBQNY	
SEWCZYK, M.	23	F	SVNT	GRAFZDBUF	
WOSZKISKYS, J.	25	M	LABR	GRZZZZBUF	
SCHULZ, C.	21	M	LABR	GRZZZZNY	
WEIL, E.	24	M	LABR	GRZZZZNY	
KLEIN, H.	33	M	LABR	GRADDWNY	
BENDER, A.	30	M	LABR	GRZZZZNY	
SAREM, C.F.	19	M	LABR	GRZZZZNY	
PFEIFFER, C.T.	28	M	LABR	GRZZZZNY	
FILLENZ, M.	33	M	LABR	GRZZZZNY	
E.	26	F	W	GRZZZZNY	
KORNWOLFF, EL.	69	F	W	GRZZZZUSA	
B.	40	F	W	GRZZZZUSA	
F.	38	M	LABR	GRZZZZUSA	
F.	34	F	W	GRZZZZUSA	
M.	21	M	LABR	GRZZZZUSA	
CH.	29	M	LABR	GRZZZZUSA	
BUCHLER, CH.	25	M	LABR	GRZZZZNY	
MAGEN, B.	15	M	LABR	GRZZZZUSA	
GUXLEWSKA, V.	19	M	LABR	GRZZZZUSA	
MICSCYZEWRORSKI, J.	22	M	LABR	GRZZZZUSA	
HURTZ, J.	31	M	LABR	GRZZZZTRE	
BAK, P.	19	M	LABR	GRZZZZBUF	
DISHLER, E.	30	M	LABR	GRZZZZNY	
A.	24	F	W	GRZZZZNY	
K.	3	F	CHILD	GRZZZZNY	
SPILLMANN, H.	24	M	LABR	GRAGMOUNK	
CH.	24	F	W	GRAGMOUNK	
E.	00	F	INF	GRAGMOUNK	
HENNRICH, J.	24	M	LABR	GRZZZZUSA	
CASPARY, J.	19	M	LABR	GRADDWCH	
TOLSS, A.	25	M	LABR	GRADDWCH	
SENKBEIL, A.	16	M	LABR	GRACGJUSA	
GIESE, H.	19	F	SVNT	GRACGJUSA	
H.	8	F	CHILD	GRACGJUSA	
ASSMUSS, A.	24	M	LABR	GRACGJUSA	
SUSEN, A.	24	M	LABR	GRAGBPNY	
HAINERMANN, J.	22	M	LABR	GRAGBPNY	
FISCHER, M.	55	F	W	GRAGBPSP	
MULLER, N.	50	M	LABR	GRABLTPIT	
SCHENDLER, A.	25	M	LABR	GRZZZZPHI	
KOHLMANN, C.	26	F	SVNT	GRZZZZNY	
GRABOWSKY, F.	29	M	LABR	GRZZZZCH	
LUNN, N.	25	M	LABR	GRZZZZCH	
HAFFNER, M.	22	F	SVNT	GRZZZZNY	
PAULIN	29	F	SVNT	GRZZZZNY	
GERNER, M.	19	F	SVNT	GRZZZZNY	
OHLBACH, L.	21	F	SVNT	GRZZZZNY	
LETZGUS, M.	20	F	SVNT	GRZZZZPHI	
BRAITSCH, S.	30	M	LABR	GRADDWBO	
BAITNEGER, G.	17	M	LABR	GRADDWSTL	
C.	24	M	LABR	GRADDWSTL	
WEBER, CH.	55	F	W	GRAAOLUSA	
BOHN, H.	26	M	LABR	GRZZZZNY	
MOHR, G.	25	M	LABR	GRZZZZNY	
HOFFMANN, L.	14	F	SVNT	GRZZZZNY	
BLASER, R.	20	M	LABR	GRZZZZUNK	
U	8	F	CHILD	GRZZZZUNK	
U	6	M	CHILD	GRZZZZUNK	
U	4	M	CHILD	GRZZZZUNK	
BACH, C.	47	M	LABR	GRZZZZDET	
KNOBEL, M.	42	F	W	GRZZZZPIT	
M.	10	F	CH	GRZZZZPIT	
HELDE, M.	26	M	LABR	GRZZZZUSA	
ROY, L.	54	F	W	GRZZZZUNK	
FR.	17	M	LABR	GRZZZZUNK	
MULLER, J.	00	M	LABR	GRABDMCH	
LANGE, P.	26	M	LABR	GRABDMCH	
M.	26	F	W	GRABDMCH	
GEROLD, FR.	58	M	LABR	GRZZZZNY	
FR.	17	M	LABR	GRZZZZNY	
C.	20	F	UNKNOWN	GRZZZZNY	
L.	13	F	UNKNOWN	GRZZZZNY	
KNOBEL, H.	24	M	LABR	GRZZZZNY	
HITZINGER, E.	20	F	SVNT	GRAFOLPIT	
FITZ, A.	29	F	SVNT	GRAGFDPIT	
BEKER, S.	33	M	LABR	GRAGFDUSA	
BEST, E.	15	F	SVNT	GRACDLUNK	
BAER, FR.	16	M	LABR	GRACDLNY	
GERMANN, P.	48	M	LABR	GRZZZZAKR	
W.	46	F	W	GRZZZZAKR	
M.	15	M	UNKNOWN	GRZZZZAKR	
M.	17	F	UNKNOWN	GRZZZZAKR	
A.	11	F	UNKNOWN	GRZZZZAKR	
J.	10	M	CH	GRZZZZAKR	
FRANZ, FR.	31	M	LABR	GRZZZZBEL	
E.	27	F	W	GRZZZZBEL	
A.	5	M	CHILD	GRZZZZBEL	
F.	3	M	CHILD	GRZZZZBEL	
G.	00	M	INF	GRZZZZBEL	
PERLOWSKI, C.	24	M	LABR	GRZZZZUSA	
J.	21	M	LABR	GRZZZZUSA	
E.	21	F	SVNT	GRZZZZUSA	
STULLICH, C.	18	M	LABR	GRZZZZUSA	
C.	54	M	LABR	GRZZZZUSA	
J.	46	F	W	GRZZZZUSA	
J.	14	F	SVNT	GRZZZZUSA	
C.	8	F	CHILD	GRZZZZUSA	
MAIDEWETZKI, L.	24	M	LABR	GRZZZZNY	
FURST, A.	20	M	BKR	GRZZZZNY	
GRUNEWALD, C.	24	M	SMH	GRZZZZNY	
DE, P.	20	M	SEMN	GRZZZZNY	
GRUNBERGER, A.	30	F	W	GRADLDNY	
A.	8	F	CHILD	GRADLDNY	
S.	1	M	CHILD	GRADLDNY	
KASPRZAK, A.	22	F	W	GRADLDCH	
PREDZYAK, N.	22	M	LABR	GRADLDCH	
REIBEL, J.	00	M	LABR	GRAHELNY	
YOON, I.	28	F	W	FRZZZZNY	
BUSIERE, H.	4	M	CHILD	FRZZZZNY	
S.	2	F	CHILD	FRZZZZNY	
KASTNER, J.	26	M	LABR	GRZZZZUNK	
V.	35	M	LABR	GRZZZZUNK	
WEIGE, M.	11	F	UNKNOWN	GRZZZZUNK	
SIGRIN, M.	41	M	LABR	GRZZZZUNK	
MELZER, H.	25	M	LABR	GRZZZZUNK	
KITZ, J.	21	M	LABR	GRAAOOBAA	
M.	28	F	SVNT	GRAAOOBAA	
RINKLER, L.	34	F	SVNT	GRAAOOCH	
E.	11	F	SVNT	GRAAOOCH	
URBAUX, FR.	36	M	LABR	GRZZZZNY	
LEGNER, C.	23	M	LABR	GRZZZZUNK	
BECK, M.	00	M	LABR	GRZZZZNY	
WOLFF, M.	33	M	LABR	GRZZZZPHI	
GROSS, W.	29	M	LABR	GRZZZZNW	
ROTSCHAWSKY, H.	19	F	SVNT	GRZZZZNY	
V.	18	F	SVNT	GRZZZZNY	
BRENER, J.	31	M	LABR	GRACXVNY	
M.	20	F	W	GRACXVNY	
SERBUS, A.	46	F	W	GRACXVNY	
M.	11	F	UNKNOWN	GRACXVNY	
A.	9	F	CHILD	GRACXVNY	
A.	3	F	CHILD	GRACXVNY	
SLAVICEK, J.	37	M	LABR	GRACXVNY	
BASAUT, S.	40	M	LABR	GRACXVNY	
SOWICK, M.	23	F	SVNT	GRACXVNY	
WAJRITH, J.	30	M	LABR	GRACXVNY	
KRIDLA, F.	35	M	LABR	GRACXVNY	
TUREK, J.	33	M	LABR	GRACXVNY	
GREGER, J.	34	M	LABR	GRACXVNY	
VOWIDEK, J.	25	M	LABR	GRACXVNY	
WINTER, C.	28	M	LABR	GRZZZZNY	

PASSENGER	AGE	SEX	OCCUPATION	PRVL	DES
M.	31	F	W		GRZZZZNY
M.	9	F	CHILD		GRZZZZNY
H.	7	F	CHILD		GRZZZZNY
V.	2	F	CHILD		GRZZZZNY
E.	00	F	INF		GRZZZZNY
BEROTH, M.	20	F	SVNT		GRAFLMNY
R.	17	F	SVNT		GRAFLMNY
KRESS, K.	18	F	SVNT		GRAFLMPHI
SWAUTSCHITSCH, M.	41	M	LABR		GRAFLMNY
STAKER, J.	14	M	LABR		GRAAHUNY
KRAKER, G.	31	M	LABR		GRAAHUNY
SCHAKEL, M.	24	M	LABR		GRAAHUNY
JOHANN, G.	26	M	LABR		GRAAHUNY
FERDRBER, J.	30	M	LABR		GRAAHUNY
STEGER, G.	52	M	LABR		GRZZZZNY
MICHEL, M.	35	F	SVNT		GRZZZZNY
STORCK, C.	27	M	MCHT		GRAAHUNY
MAURER, J.	48	M	MCHT		GRZZZZNY
J.	43	F	W		GRZZZZNY
M.	22	F	UNKNOWN		GRZZZZNY
A.	5	M	CHILD		GRZZZZNY
SHAUEBLIN, M.	24	F	SVNT		GRZZZZNY
FREI, J.	22	M	LABR		GRZZZZNY
SCHAERER, R.	22	M	LABR		GRZZZZNY
ZIERCHER, J.	55	M	LABR		GRZZZZNY
L.	25	F	W		GRZZZZNY
AMBROSIUS, C.	37	M	UNKNOWN		GRAAHUNY
JUNAGLIA, R.	34	M	UNKNOWN		GRAAHUNY
KAPPELER, M.	38	F	SVNT		GRAAHUNY
SCHOBINGER, H.	34	M	SMH		GRAAHUNY
GROB, J.	47	M	SMH		GRAAHUNY
STOCKLIN, L.	26	M	LABR		GRAAHUNY
CUENY, F.	51	M	LABR		GRAAHUNY
E.	10	M	CH		GRAAHUNY
ESSIG, G.	17	M	CH		GRAAHUUSA
EGLI, M.	29	F	SVNT		GRAAHUCLE
U	00	M	INF		GRAAHUCLE
JUNCK, H.	21	M	LABR		GRZZZZNY
VALENTIN, E.	19	F	W		GRAAHUNY
J.	00	M	INF		GRAAHUNY
KRUER, M.	38	F	W		GRAAHUNY
A.	10	M	CH		GRAAHUNY
J.	7	M	CHILD		GRAAHUNY
N.	5	M	CHILD		GRAAHUNY
M.	3	M	CHILD		GRAAHUNY
M.	00	F	INF		GRAAHUNY
FRANKHEUSEN, F.	58	M	LABR		GRAAHUNY
E.	57	F	W		GRAAHUNY
S.	19	F	UNKNOWN		GRAAHUNY
S.	17	M	UNKNOWN		GRAAHUNY
J.	11	M	UNKNOWN		GRAAHUNY
F.	5	M	CHILD		GRAAHUNY
GIER, J.	21	M	LABR		GRAAHUNY
ALMEYER, N.	25	M	LABR		GRAAHUNY
BATTINY, N.	41	M	FARMER		GRAAHUNY
APILLER, J.	29	M	FARMER		GRAAHUNY
HUG, C.	59	F	W		GRZZZZNY
M.	27	F	W		GRZZZZNY
TH.	24	F	W		GRZZZZNY
HERRESTAL, A.	30	F	SVNT		GRZZZZNY
ZIEGELR, K.	19	M	LABR		GRZZZZNY
ERHOLD, G.	19	M	LABR		GRZZZZNY
CHRISTMANN, E.	14	F	SVNT		GRZZZZNY
ARUBUST, C.	16	F	SVNT		GRZZZZNY
CROM, C.	34	M	FARMER		GRADOINY
ARMBRUSH, E.	58	F	W		GRZZZZUSA
C.	16	M	LABR		GRZZZZUSA
E.	9	F	CHILD		GRZZZZUSA
KOSH, J.	33	M	LABR		GRZZZZUSA
J.	20	F	SVNT		GRZZZZUSA
REIF, J.	26	M	TLR		GRZZZZNY
SCHRECK, M.W.	24	F	SVNT		GRZZZZNY
HENNINGS, G.	23	M	LABR		GRZZZZNY
GILLIG, J.	39	M	CMST		GRZZZZNY
OHNANUS, R.	25	M	LABR		GRZZZZNY
REIS, J.	25	M	LABR		GRZZZZTOL
SCHLEGER, TH.	24	M	LABR		GRZZZZCH
L.	27	F	W		GRZZZZCH
BISCHOFF, J.	27	F	W		GRZZZZCH
G.	8	M	CHILD		GRZZZZCH
A.	6	F	CHILD		GRZZZZCH
G.	00	M	INF		GRZZZZCH
TH.ARNOLD	25	M	LABR		GRZZZZPHI
JAEGER, K.	21	F	SVNT		GRZZZZSFC
FRANZ, C.	46	F	W		GRADEFNY
C.	16	M	LABR		GRADEFNY
RAPP, K.H.	22	M	LABR		GRAIVKNY
FISCHER, J.	36	M	LABR		GRAIVKNY
CHRISTMANN, M.	30	F	W		GRAIVKSAN
J.	00	M	INF		GRAIVKSAN
KROEDER, H.	17	M	LABR		GRZZZZNY
SIESKE, F.	28	F	W		GRZZZZNY
A.	2	F	CHILD		GRZZZZNY
F.	3	M	CHILD		GRZZZZNY
A.	00	M	INF		GRZZZZNY
BAKKER, M.	24	M	CPTR		GRZZZZUSA
SCHULBUS, N.	45	M	LABR		GRZZZZNY
M.	43	F	W		GRZZZZNY
M.	18	F	SVNT		GRZZZZNY
J.	13	M	UNKNOWN		GRZZZZNY
E.	11	F	UNKNOWN		GRZZZZNY
J.	9	M	CHILD		GRZZZZNY
E.	7	M	CHILD		GRZZZZNY
PETRY, S.	21	F	SVNT		GRZZZZNY
SAUX, A.	22	F	SVNT		GRAFGSNY
MARES, J.	27	M	LABR		GRAFGSNY
M.	21	F	W		GRAFGSNY
VLACH, J.	38	M	LABR		GRAFGSNY
ROHAECK, FR.	37	M	LABR		GRAFGSNY
VOSTA, J.	30	M	LABR		GRAFGSNY
B.	26	F	W		GRAFGSNY
M.	3	F	CHILD		GRAFGSNY
BRUZEK, J.	19	M	LABR		GRAFGSNY
LEONHARD, FR.	29	M	LABR		GRZZZZNY
GUTHIES, P.J.	25	M	LABR		GRZZZZNY
KOOB, M.	30	M	LABR		GRZZZZNY
DUNDTAEDTER, M.	16	M	LABR		GRZZZZNY
MEHL, C.	21	F	SVNT		GRZZZZNY
U	00	F	INF		GRZZZZNY
KRENTZER, J.	15	M	LABR		GRZZZZSTL
DENUERLEIN, J.	34	M	LABR		GRZZZZSTL
FISCHER, M.	26	F	SVNT		GRZZZZSTL
DUNERLEIN, J.	26	M	SVNT		GRZZZZSTL
HORETH, J.	20	F	SVNT		GRZZZZSTL
ZAPF, A.	22	M	LABR		GRZZZZSTL
KIEDEL, C.	20	F	W		GRZZZZSTL
HAASE, C.	21	M	LABR		GRZZZZUNK
PIEDER, M.	27	F	W		GRZZZZNY
M.	2	F	CHILD		GRZZZZNY
MAIER, J.	27	M	LABR		GRZZZZNY
ROESCH, A.	56	M	LABR		GRZZZZNY
U	00	F	W		GRZZZZNY
C.	25	F	UNKNOWN		GRZZZZNY
YANTZ, W.	23	F	SVNT		GRZZZZCIN
V.	21	F	SVNT		GRZZZZCIN
ERSING, B.	21	M	LABR		GRAALNMIL
WEINSCHEIT, E.	23	M	LABR		GRAALNCH
KECKEISEN, M.	15	M	LABR		GRAALNPHI
J.	13	F	SVNT		GRAALNPHI
VOLK, C.	25	M	LABR		GRAALNNY
BOUETINGER, C.	55	F	W		GRZZZZSTL
G.	25	M	LABR		GRZZZZSTL
M.	27	F	W		GRZZZZSTL
C.	1	M	CHILD		GRZZZZSTL
SCHMERBER, G.	34	M	LABR		GRZZZZNY
VOGT, L.	42	M	LABR		GRZZZZNY
KURTEN, W.	28	M	LABR		GRZZZZUNK
NEISER, J.	32	M	LABR		GRAEYGPIT
M.	30	F	W		GRAEYGPIT
R.	4	M	CHILD		GRAEYGPIT

119

PASSENGER	AGE	SEX	OCCUPATION	PRVL	DES	PASSENGER	AGE	SEX	OCCUPATION	PRVL	DES
J.	2	M	CHILD	GRAEYGPIT		GAIER, C.	21	F	SVNT	FRAEVRAKR	
A.	00	F	INF	GRAEYGPIT		BEIRKHARDT, P.	34	M	LABR	FRAEVRNY	
SCHMIDT, C.	24	F	W	GRAEYGPIT		SCHULZ, A.	27	M	LABR	GRZZZZUSA	
L.	4	F	CHILD	GRAEYGPIT		M.	21	F	W	GRZZZZUSA	
M.	2	F	CHILD	GRAEYGPIT		J.	00	F	INF	GRZZZZUSA	
L.	00	M	INF	GRAEYGPIT		SCHMITH, S.	24	M	BKR	GRACWFNY	
BEUDER, G.	57	M	LABR	GRZZZZNY		HARTER, C.	58	M	BKR	GRZZZZUSA	
R.	57	M	W	GRZZZZNY		M.	54	F	W	GRZZZZUSA	
R.	14	F	UNKNOWN	GRZZZZNY		C.	40	M	LABR	GRZZZZUSA	
F.	7	F	CHILD	GRZZZZNY		G.	26	M	LABR	GRZZZZUSA	
WAGNER, C.	26	M	LABR	GRZZZZNY		S.	18	M	LABR	GRZZZZUSA	
RIMELE, C.	46	M	LABR	GRZZZZNY		STEIGE, E.	21	M	LABR	GRAFEENY	
MULLER, J.	15	M	LABR	GRAFASUSA		HUBER, J.	32	M	LABR	GRZZZZNY	
WORTMANN, A.	18	M	LABR	GRAFASNY		ULMER, L.	25	M	LABR	GRZZZZNY	
STEIGER, J.	28	M	LABR	GRAFASNY		GYSEN, J.	00	M	LABR	GRZZZZCH	
BRAING, S.	48	M	LABR	GRAFASNY		DRIXTER, CH.	37	M	LABR	GRZZZZPHI	
A.	45	F	W	GRAFASNY							
A.	19	M	LABR	GRAFASNY							
N.	18	M	LABR	GRAFASNY							
J.	5	M	CHILD	GRAFASNY							
COESFELD, W.	64	M	LABR	GRAFASNY							
H.	29	M	LABR	GRAFASNY		SHIP: STATE OF GEORGIA					
A.	28	F	W	GRAFASNY							
W.	19	M	LABR	GRAFASNY		FROM: GLASGOW AND LARNE					
HAUM, W.	21	M	LABR	GRAFASNY		TO: NEW YORK					
H.	4	M	CHILD	GRAFASNY		ARRIVED: 31 MAY 1888					
W.	3	M	CHILD	GRAFASNY							
COESFELD, H.	00	M	INF	GRAFASNY							
ROSSBACH, P.	26	M	LABR	GRZZZZUNK		BRODERSEN, PETER	22	M	LABR	GRZZZZUSA	
VIEBRAUS, D.	21	M	LABR	GRZZZZUNK		DAHLMANN, ROBT.	32	M	MCHT	GRZZZZUSA	
EGLE, E.	28	F	SVNT	GRADECCH		DOMRAETIS, ERNST	28	M	LABR	GRZZZZUSA	
SKECHTER, A.	18	M	LABR	GRZZZZNY		EITENEN, HERMAN	36	M	LABR	GRZZZZUSA	
KELLER, FR.	18	M	LABR	GRZZZZNY		FASMER, FR.WILH.	20	M	LABR	GRZZZZUSA	
HANG, J.	49	M	LABR	GRZZZZNY		HADINOVA, ANNA	19	F	SVNT	GRZZZZUSA	
HEEG, V.	25	M	LABR	GRZZZZNY		HARZ, BERNH.	20	M	MCHT	GRZZZZUSA	
BREMER, A.	23	M	LABR	GRZZZZNY		HELLER, LOUISE	22	F	TLR	GRZZZZUSA	
SOBAN, H.	28	M	LABR	GRZZZZNY		THERESE	20	F	TLR	GRZZZZUSA	
STRASSER, R.	17	F	SVNT	GRZZZZPIT		KRAUS, ALFRED	10	M	CH	GRZZZZUSA	
G.	17	M	LABR	GRZZZZPIT		KOHN, BERTHA	22	F	SVNT	GRZZZZUSA	
HOF, G.	39	M	LABR	GRZZZZNY		LORENTZEN, HENRIK	20	F	FARMER	GRZZZZUSA	
C.	25	F	W	GRZZZZNY		MAHLETEIN, MENDEL	40	M	TLR	GRZZZZUSA	
M.	10	F	CH	GRZZZZNY		MARTENSEN, CHRISTEN	21	M	FARMER	GRZZZZUSA	
F.	8	M	CHILD	GRZZZZNY		PETERSEN, PETER	23	M	MSN	GRZZZZUSA	
F.	3	M	CHILD	GRZZZZNY		SOHEFFKIN, JOEL	17	M	LABR	GRZZZZUSA	
J.	00	F	INF	GRZZZZNY		VOGELSANG, MARIE	22	F	SVNT	GRZZZZUSA	
CLAUS, F.	46	M	LABR	GRZZZZNY							
L.	48	F	W	GRZZZZNY							
L.	21	F	SVNT	GRZZZZNY							
C.	19	M	UNKNOWN	GRZZZZNY							
F.	15	F	UNKNOWN	GRZZZZNY		SHIP: WIELAND					
C.	14	F	UNKNOWN	GRZZZZNY							
C.	21	F	UNKNOWN	GRZZZZNY		FROM: HAMBURG					
BEYER, A.	19	M	LABR	GRAHLXNY		TO: NEW YORK					
FISCHHAUSER, A.	24	M	LABR	GRAHLXNY		ARRIVED: 31 MAY 1888					
ROSENBERGER, M.	22	F	SVNT	GRADXWNY							
WEBER, A.	28	M	LABR	FRZZZZNY							
H.	22	F	W	FRZZZZNY							
SCHOUFOEFER, C.	30	F	W	FRZZZZUSA		FORBED, MARIUS	25	M	PNTR	PRZZZZUSA	
L.	6	M	CHILD	FRZZZZUSA		ELISE	30	F	SGL	PRZZZZUSA	
M.	4	M	CHILD	FRZZZZUSA		OHRMANN, CARL	27	M	PVTR	PRZZZZUSA	
NICODEMUS, J.	20	M	LABR	FRZZZZNY		MATHILDE	26	F	W	PRZZZZUSA	
WEICHEL, H.	21	F	SVNT	FRZZZZNY		KLEINER, CARL	48	M	UNKNOWN	HBZZZZUSA	
FORSTER, A.	19	M	LABR	FRZZZZNY		SCHMIDT, LOUISE	21	F	SGL	PRZZZZUSA	
BRUSNMER, U	19	M	LABR	FRZZZZNY		JERKE, FERDINAND	19	M	FARMER	PRZZZZUSA	
RICHTER, A.	30	F	W	FRZZZZNY		MAREK, FRANZ	16	M	LABR	PRZZZZUSA	
METZLER, C.	49	F	W	FRADDWNY		MARTENS, CATH	26	F	SGL	PRZZZZUSA	
KARST, A.	23	F	PVTW	FRADDWNY		DRAEGER, CAROLINE	62	F	WO	PRZZZZUSA	
HANEMGROSS, M.	32	M	LABR	FRADKKCIN		HULDA	24	F	WO	PRZZZZUSA	
R.	24	M	LABR	FRADKKCIN		KORSNIKOWSKY, OTTO	33	M	LABR	PRZZZZUSA	
BREMER, M.	26	M	LABR	FRADKKUSA		BOROWANSKY, ANTONIN	17	M	LABR	PRZZZZUSA	
PFISTER, M.	19	F	SVNT	FRADOINY		KRUKOW, FERD	33	M	LABR	PRZZZZUSA	
SEWUR, J.	18	M	LABR	FRADOINY		EMILIE	28	F	LABR	PRZZZZUSA	
MINDER, G.	23	M	LABR	FRADOINY		GIZIEWSKI, MICHAEL	36	M	LABR	PRZZZZUSA	
KIENZLE, L.	21	F	SVNT	FRAEVRNY		ANNA	34	F	W	PRZZZZUSA	
KOHMANN, E.	16	F	SVNT	FRAEVRNY		FRIEDR	7	M	CHILD	PRZZZZUSA	

120

PASSENGER	AGE	SEX	OCCUPATION	PRVL	DES
GOERLITZ, THERESE	25	F	SGL		PRZZZZUSA
RIEP, AUGUSTE	34	F	WO		PRZZZZUSA
ERNST	9	M	CHILD		PRZZZZUSA
VANDAMROESE, HELMUTH	16	M	LABR		PRZZZZUSA
BRAUN, ANNA	33	F	SGL		PRZZZZUSA
MUELLER, EMILIE	23	F	SGL		PRZZZZUSA
WENDT, FRDK	32	F	WO		PRZZZZUSA
ALBRECHT, U	24	F	UNKNOWN		PRZZZZUSA
MAX	4	M	CHILD		PRZZZZUSA
GERTRUD	2	F	CHILD		PRZZZZUSA
BEITSCH, MAX	23	M	SMH		PRZZZZUSA
SCHNAEKER, PAULINE	28	F	WO		PRZZZZUSA
HAUDE, OTTO	17	M	MCHT		PRZZZZUSA
KONOPATZKI, ERNST	25	M	MCHT		PRZZZZUSA
SPIESS, FRANZ	27	M	LABR		PRZZZZUSA
FRUID, ANTON	33	M	JNR		SYZZZZUSA
JOH	16	M	JNR		SYZZZZUSA
MARTENBAUM, BAER	26	M	MCHT		PRZZZZUSA
MALWINE	30	F	W		PRZZZZUSA
ENGEL, GUSTAV	25	M	SLR		PRZZZZUSA
SCHUMANN, OTTO	26	M	UNKNOWN		SYZZZZUSA
FEDDERSON, HANS	21	M	LABR		PRZZZZUSA
OTTO, LOUISE	29	F	SGL		PRZZZZUSA
MOSES, JOSEF	59	M	TCHR		PRZZZZUSA
HENRIETTE	55	F	W		PRZZZZUSA
SARA	21	F	D		PRZZZZUSA
KURLAENDER, DEBORA	15	F	SGL		PRZZZZUSA
RAHN, HELENE	18	F	WO		PRZZZZUSA
HANNEMANN, CARL	24	M	FARMER		PRZZZZUSA
WILH	22	F	SGL		PRZZZZUSA
WARACZEWSKI, PETER	16	M	LABR		PRZZZZUSA
MISCH, HEINR	15	M	FARMER		PRZZZZUSA
FISCHER, WILH	38	M	JNR		PRZZZZUSA
WIESER, LUDWIG	39	M	LABR		PRZZZZUSA
OTTILIE	40	F	W		PRZZZZUSA
ROBERT	7	M	CHILD		PRZZZZUSA
PAUL	5	M	CHILD		PRZZZZUSA
ALMA	3	F	CHILD		PRZZZZUSA
FLORA	.11	F	INFANT		PRZZZZUSA
PETRASCHEWSKY, MICHAEL	50	M	LABR		PRZZZZUSA
FRANZISZEK	14	M	S		PRZZZZUSA
KETELSEN, DORIS	28	F	SGL		PRZZZZUSA
RAHN, OTTO	27	M	MLR		PRZZZZUSA
BRAUN, CAROLINE	17	F	SGL		BDZZZZUSA
KLEMPS, NANE	17	F	SGL		BDZZZZUSA
HERMLE, JULIE	12	F	SGL		BDZZZZUSA
SCHMIDT, PETER	23	M	FARMER		BDZZZZUSA
STOCK, WILH	26	M	SCP		BVZZZZUSA
BISCHOFF, ANNA	17	F	SGL		PRZZZZUSA
LANGERICKEL, AUGUST	24	M	PNTR		PRZZZZUSA
SIEMERS, JOHS	45	M	FARMER		PRZZZZUSA
KRUEGER, JOH	29	M	AGNT		PRZZZZUSA
MAASS, CLAUS	15	M	FARMER		PRZZZZUSA
HEDRICH, ALOIS	36	M	FARMER		PRZZZZUSA
HEICK, EMMA	24	F	SGL		HBZZZZUSA
RING, MARG	21	F	SGL		BVZZZZUSA
STEINHAUFF, ANNA	24	F	SGL		PRZZZZUSA
ROTHER, JOSEFA	15	F	UNKNOWN		PRZZZZUSA
FROMMEL, ROSA	19	F	SGL		PRZZZZUSA
ZAWODSKY, KATH	37	F	WO		PRZZZZUSA
JOSEF	14	M	CH		PRZZZZUSA
MARIE	7	F	CHILD		PRZZZZUSA
FRANZ	6	M	CHILD		PRZZZZUSA
CARL	5	M	CHILD		PRZZZZUSA
JAROSLAV	.06	M	INFANT		PRZZZZUSA
STTRATZUSKA, MARIANNA	24	F	SGL		PRZZZZUSA
THIMM, LOUISE	47	F	WO		PRZZZZUSA
FRANZ	7	M	CHILD		PRZZZZUSA
MARIE	6	F	CHILD		PRZZZZUSA
FRIEDR	3	M	CHILD		PRZZZZUSA
GRAJEWSKY, ALOLY	26	F	SGL		PRZZZZUSA
TAMM, DOROTHEA	26	F	SGL		PRZZZZUSA
MARIE	16	F	SGL		PRZZZZUSA
SCHNORR, ELISE	55	F	WO		HBZZZZUSA
BERTHA	19	F	D		HBZZZZUSA
POEHL, THERESE	23	F	WO		BVZZZZUSA
CATH	.03	F	INFANT		BVZZZZUSA
MADEST, CATH	56	F	WO		PRZZZZUSA
CZERGUT, HELENE	25	F	SGL		PRZZZZUSA
SCHIFKA, ANTONIE	19	F	SGL		PRZZZZUSA
MARIE	13	F	SGL		PRZZZZUSA
GERLACH, ELISABETH	64	F	WO		PRZZZZUSA
LAMMER, AMALIE	19	F	SGL		BVZZZZUSA
WELZENBACH, MARG	19	F	SGL		BVZZZZUSA
RUETZEL, ROSALIE	15	F	SGL		BVZZZZUSA
LINDSCHAU, PETER	15	M	FARMER		PRZZZZUSA
KRAUSE, FRIEDR	18	M	LABR		PRZZZZUSA
WILLBROTH, HEINR	16	M	FARMER		PRZZZZUSA
KESSLER, REGINE	20	F	SGL		PRZZZZUSA
WYZLITZ, HELENE	21	F	SGL		PRZZZZUSA
NIESKE, FRANZISKA	21	F	SGL		PRZZZZUSA
WILK, WALTHER	27	M	CPTR		SRZZZZUSA
HEIDMANN, ALPHONS	29	M	MCHT		HBZZZZUSA
BEITHNER, ERNST	17	F	SGL		PRZZZZUSA
WAIDMANN, AUGUST	28	M	TU		HBZZZZUSA
PAULSEN, CHRIST	27	M	TU		HBZZZZUSA
BOEGE, PHILIPP	24	M	FARMER		PRZZZZUSA
MEWIS, CHRIST	25	F	SGL		PRZZZZUSA
HONBORG, JOERGEN	21	M	FARMER		PRZZZZUSA
SCHAFER, LOUISE	45	M	TNM		PRZZZZUSA
BOMBIN, HANS	30	M	ADV		PRZZZZUSA
HOFFMANN, JOH	26	M	JNR		PRZZZZUSA
HUSARSKI, VICTOR	24	M	LABR		PRZZZZUSA
LANDAU, HENRIETTE	24	F	SGL		PRZZZZUSA
HORRMANN, CHRISTIAN	67	M	LABR		PRZZZZUSA
JULIE	61	F	W		PRZZZZUSA
LOUISE	33	F	SGL		PRZZZZUSA
WILH	31	M	LABR		PRZZZZUSA
PAUL	28	M	SGL		PRZZZZUSA
HERMANN, JOSEF	27	M	UNKNOWN		PRZZZZUSA
RITTER, MARIE	43	F	W		PRZZZZUSA
WEPOLEK, EDUARD	30	M	LABR		PRZZZZUSA
MARTHA	24	F	W		PRZZZZUSA
WANDA	.09	F	INFANT		PRZZZZUSA
BERTHA	24	F	WO		PRZZZZUSA
JAEGER, CARL	9	M	CHILD		PRZZZZUSA
KNANS, FRANZ	43	M	FARMER		BVZZZZUSA
WILL, MARIE	17	F	WO		BVZZZZUSA
STEINER, JOSEF	31	M	UNKNOWN		PRZZZZUSA
SCHACHTSCHNEIDER, BERTH	22	F	SGL		PRZZZZUSA
GRAUMANN, WILH	47	M	LABR		PRZZZZUSA
MARIE	50	F	W		PRZZZZUSA
BENGMER, JACOB	34	M	MSN		PRZZZZUSA
RATHJE, INGA	16	F	SGL		PRZZZZUSA
WEIDERMANN, EMIL	30	M	ENGR		PRZZZZUSA
BERTHA	31	F	W		PRZZZZUSA
PAUL	5	M	CHILD		PRZZZZUSA
ANNA	3	F	CHILD		PRZZZZUSA
HEDWIG	.07	F	INFANT		PRZZZZUSA
FRAULSEN, ERNESTE	19	F	SGL		PRZZZZUSA
WIELAND, JOH	24	M	FARMER		WMZZZZUSA
JESS, ELISE	22	F	SGL		PRZZZZUSA
JUNGE, AUGUST	23	M	FARMER		PRZZZZUSA
TIMMERMANN, MARIE	16	F	SGL		PRZZZZUSA
DUNKER, CHRIST	17	M	FARMER		PRZZZZUSA
MOENG, FRANZ	29	M	LABR		PRZZZZUSA
MARIE	28	F	W		PRZZZZUSA
JOSEPH	2	M	CHILD		PRZZZZUSA
VALERIA	.06	F	INFANT		PRZZZZUSA
ARRIENS, MARG	20	F	SGL		PRZZZZUSA
HOLM, GUSTAW	35	M	LABR		PRZZZZUSA
ANNA	20	F	UNKNOWN		PRZZZZUSA
HAMLOT, JOHN	25	M	FARMER		PRZZZZUSA
HOLLESEN, BAYE	65	M	FARMER		PRZZZZUSA
DOROTHEA	57	F	W		PRZZZZUSA
BOTHILDE	16	F	D		PRZZZZUSA
BUSCHOW, HELENE	23	F	SGL		PRZZZZUSA
BRUHN, H	50	M	FARMER		PRZZZZUSA
ANNA	26	F	W		PRZZZZUSA
CARL	.07	M	INFANT		PRZZZZUSA

PASSENGER	AGE	SEX	OCCUPATION	PRVL	DES
THOMSEN, JENS	32	M	FARMER	PRZZZZUSA	
MARIE	27	F	W	PRZZZZUSA	
HANSINE	3	F	CHILD	PRZZZZUSA	
CHRISTINE	.11	F	INFANT	PRZZZZUSA	
WINTERMANTEL, LORENZ	23	M	SHMK	WMZZZZUSA	
KAN, ANNA	41	F	W	PRZZZZUSA	
NISS	8	M	CHILD	PRZZZZUSA	
MAREN	7	F	CHILD	PRZZZZUSA	
ENGELLAND, JUERGEN	16	M	FARMER	PRZZZZUSA	
BAHNSEN, ANNA	50	F	WO	PRZZZZUSA	
BERTHA	19	F	CH	PRZZZZUSA	
LUDWIG	8	M	CHILD	PRZZZZUSA	
CHRISTIANSEN, JOH	70	M	LABR	PRZZZZUSA	
SORENSEN, ANNA	35	F	W	PRZZZZUSA	
HERM	4	M	CHILD	PRZZZZUSA	
PAULSEN, HANS	17	M	FARMER	PRZZZZUSA	
KOLM, ANNA	17	F	WO	PRZZZZUSA	
MOELLER, ANDRAS	16	M	FARMER	PRZZZZUSA	
KRUEGER, MARIE	17	F	WO	PRZZZZUSA	
JENSEN, JENS	18	M	LABR	PRZZZZUSA	
PETERSEN, ANNA	20	F	WO	PRZZZZUSA	
BRODERSEN, BODNIG	64	M	LABR	PRZZZZUSA	
LOUISE	17	F	D	PRZZZZUSA	
SCHELLING, CHRIST	18	M	SMH	WMZZZZUSA	
JAC	16	M	LABR	WMZZZZUSA	
FUCHS, MARIE	30	F	WO	WMZZZZUSA	
FRANZ	7	M	CHILD	WMZZZZUSA	
MARTIN	5	M	CHILD	WMZZZZUSA	
WENGLER, SIBART	32	M	FARMER	WMZZZZUSA	
JUNG, JOH	33	M	FARMER	WMZZZZUSA	
MARIE	31	F	W	WMZZZZUSA	
BRAUN, ADAM	22	M	FARMER	WMZZZZUSA	
BLANK, CARL	34	M	MSN	WMZZZZUSA	
KLEIN, CAROLINE	44	F	W	WMZZZZUSA	
ANNA	19	F	D	WMZZZZUSA	
HELD, FR	27	M	LABR	WMZZZZUSA	
STELZER, CAECILIE	27	F	WO	WMZZZZUSA	
SCHMIDT, CARL	32	M	UNKNOWN	PRZZZZUSA	
NITZ, ALBERT	28	M	FARMER	PRZZZZUSA	
SOBIERY, BARTHOLOMANY	33	M	LABR	PRZZZZUSA	
BAUER, HEINR	33	M	LABR	PRZZZZUSA	
LINNECKE, CATH	58	F	UNKNOWN	PRZZZZUSA	
DORIS	19	F	UNKNOWN	PRZZZZUSA	
GELLENER, WILH	51	F	WO	SYZZZZUSA	
ROBERT	16	M	CH	SYZZZZUSA	
MARTHA	9	F	CHILD	SYZZZZUSA	
REISS, HEINR	16	M	LABR	BVZZZZUSA	
KRETZER, ANNA	15	F	SGL	PRZZZZUSA	
SCHUBERT, WILH	32	M	FARMER	PRZZZZUSA	
MAGDALENA	23	F	W	PRZZZZUSA	
RUD	2	M	CHILD	PRZZZZUSA	
STURK, ANNA	22	F	SGL	PRZZZZUSA	
PIONTKIEWIZ, MARTIN	23	M	FARMER	PRZZZZUSA	
SEIPERT, JOH	32	F	SGL	PRZZZZUSA	
GAUL, KARL	29	M	SHMK	PRZZZZUSA	
NOVAK, VALENTY	45	M	LABR	PRZZZZUSA	
BABER, HERRM	33	M	CPTR	PRZZZZUSA	
SKIBINSKI, LUZIE	20	F	SGL	PRZZZZUSA	
STUMPF, CLEMENS	23	M	FARMER	PRZZZZUSA	
LEMKE, JOH	22	M	LABR	PRZZZZUSA	
SCHMIDT, MARIE	28	F	WO	PRZZZZUSA	
ANNA	6	F	CHILD	PRZZZZUSA	
PAULINE	4	F	CHILD	PRZZZZUSA	
PABST, HERRM	24	M	SMH	PRZZZZUSA	
BURLAGE, JOSEF	23	M	LABR	PRZZZZUSA	
HERZBERG, LOUISE	31	F	LABR	PRZZZZUSA	
GERTRUD	5	F	CHILD	PRZZZZUSA	
ZELLMER, FRIEDR	55	M	FARMER	PRZZZZUSA	
ANDRESEN, INGELBORG	40	F	WO	PRZZZZUSA	
ANDRAS	8	M	CHILD	PRZZZZUSA	
SELMA	4	F	CHILD	PRZZZZUSA	
BERTHA	2	F	CHILD	PRZZZZUSA	
INGWER	.11	M	INFANT	PRZZZZUSA	
JOH	24	F	W	PRZZZZUSA	
LIEDKE, HERRM	20	M	LABR	PRZZZZUSA	
MICHLOWITZ, MARTHA	19	F	SGL	PRZZZZUSA	
KUKELE, SUSANNE	39	F	WO	BDZZZZUSA	
LOUIS	8	M	CHILD	BDZZZZUSA	
JACOB	7	M	CHILD	BDZZZZUSA	
ANNA	6	F	CHILD	BDZZZZUSA	
ALOYS	3	M	CHILD	BDZZZZUSA	
SCHAEFER, MARIE	24	F	SGL	BDZZZZUSA	
KUTTNER, JULS	28	M	MCHT	PRZZZZUSA	
RUECKERT, GUSTAV	24	M	LABR	PRZZZZUSA	
HELENE	29	F	W	PRZZZZUSA	
CURT	.11	M	INFANT	PRZZZZUSA	
SHMIDT, FRANZ	23	M	MCHT	PRZZZZUSA	
DOERFER, MARIE	18	F	SGL	BVZZZZUSA	
WOLFERT, THEOD	42	M	UNKNOWN	BVZZZZUSA	
KRUG, ADELHEID	20	F	UNKNOWN	BVZZZZUSA	
CASPAR, ANNA	18	F	SGL	PRZZZZUSA	
ZIMMERMANN, CARL	25	M	GDNR	WMZZZZUSA	
BLASS, PETER	36	M	LKSH	PRZZZZUSA	
EVA	36	F	WO	PRZZZZUSA	
THEODOR	7	M	CHILD	PRZZZZUSA	
JACOB	6	M	CHILD	PRZZZZUSA	
PHILIPP	2	M	CHILD	PRZZZZUSA	
GEORG	.06	M	INFANT	PRZZZZUSA	
ANDRZYEWSKI, FRANZ	34	M	LABR	PRZZZZUSA	
VOLMER, GEORG	31	M	BCKM	ACZZZZUSA	
SCHOEN, JACOB	23	M	LABR	ACZZZZUSA	
JOS	30	M	LABR	ACZZZZUSA	
RUTZ, ANNA	00	F	UNKNOWN	ACZZZZUSA	
LANGER, ANNA	00	F	UNKNOWN	ACZZZZUSA	
BIANOHI, ARTHUR	00	M	UNKNOWN	ACZZZZUSA	
CAROLINE	00	F	UNKNOWN	ACZZZZUSA	
LOUISE	00	F	UNKNOWN	ACZZZZUSA	
BOLLER, GOTTL	33	M	BKR	SRZZZZUSA	
LINA	33	F	W	SRZZZZUSA	
OSCAR	6	M	CHILD	SRZZZZUSA	
LINA	1	F	CHILD	SRZZZZUSA	
EBERLE, JOSEPH	21	M	FARMER	SRZZZZUSA	
HAAS, MARIA	29	F	SGL	ACZZZZUSA	
SCHACHER, EMIL	23	M	LKSH	SRZZZZUSA	
BECHTHOLD, HAVER	24	M	BRR	BDZZZZUSA	
RITZENHOFER, MARIE	26	F	W	BDZZZZUSA	
BECHTHOLD, JOSEPHINE	.02	F	INFANT	BDZZZZUSA	
SCHWARZ, EMIL	22	M	LABR	ACZZZZUSA	
ROLL, MODEST	18	M	FARMER	ACZZZZUSA	
BUELLMANN, LUDWIG	29	M	MLR	BDZZZZUSA	
LAASLI, DANIEL	41	M	LABR	SRZZZZUSA	
ELAUER, KARL	34	M	FARMER	BDZZZZUSA	
HAAS, JOSEPH	33	M	FARMER	ACZZZZUSA	
FISCHER, JOHANN	65	M	LABR	SRZZZZUSA	
FELLER, GOTTLIEB	23	M	FARMER	SRZZZZUSA	
STALDER, ROSA	19	F	SGL	SRZZZZUSA	
FREMAGET, FRANCOIS	28	M	UNKNOWN	FRZZZZUSA	
LUTZ, GOTTL	37	M	GDNR	WMZZZZUSA	
GEIGER, AUGUST	22	M	MLR	WMZZZZUSA	
WEISSLER, VALENTIN	38	M	CPR	BDZZZZUSA	
HIRT, ENGELBERT	32	M	FARMER	BDZZZZUSA	
DINGINGER, JACOB	26	M	FARMER	ACZZZZUSA	
HUG, JOHANN	74	M	FARMER	BDZZZZUSA	
CHINA, PIERRA	41	M	MSN	FRZZZZUSA	
FANGIN, PIERRE	36	M	UNKNOWN	FRZZZZUSA	
KLOSE, GUSTAV	39	M	JNR	SRZZZZUSA	
LINA	11	F	D	SRZZZZUSA	
MAAG, ANNA	24	F	W	SRZZZZUSA	
SCHNEIDER, ROSALIE	21	F	SGL	SRZZZZUSA	
LUEPOLD, ALBERT	17	M	GDNR	BDZZZZUSA	
HIRSCHZ, FRITZ	55	M	FARMER	SRZZZZUSA	
WIENER, SAM	21	M	MCHT	HBZZZZUSA	
SEIDT, GEORGES	37	M	BRR	FRZZZZUSA	
LINA	30	F	W	FRZZZZUSA	
LUICIAN	4	M	CHILD	FRZZZZUSA	
GEORGE	2	M	CHILD	FRZZZZUSA	
KOHRS, ANNA	25	F	SGL	HBZZZZUSA	
MATTERN, EMMA	33	F	WO	HBZZZZUSA	
ANNA	3	F	CHILD	HBZZZZUSA	
SCHMIDT, ANNA	15	F	UNKNOWN	PRZZZZUSA	

PASSENGER	AGE	SEX	OCCUPATION	PROV/VIL/DES
FRESE, ELISE	24	F	SGL	PRZZZZUSA
BUSCH, ANNA	50	F	WO	HBZZZZUSA
IPLAND, M	36	M	SLR	PRZZZZUSA
LESSER, HELENE	28	F	SGL	PRZZZZUSA
PENNECKE, C	29	M	PNTR	PRZZZZUSA
MINNA	39	F	WO	PRZZZZUSA
CARL	16	M	CH	PRZZZZUSA
WILH	9	M	CHILD	PRZZZZUSA
EMIL	8	M	CHILD	PRZZZZUSA
RENNER, J	35	M	BKR	PRZZZZUSA
EMMA	23	F	W	PRZZZZUSA
ELSA	9	F	CHILD	PRZZZZUSA
RICHARD	.09	M	INFANT	PRZZZZUSA
KUEHL, CLARA	21	F	SGL	PRZZZZUSA
DOSE, ANNA	20	F	SGL	PRZZZZUSA
SEEMANN, CARL	45	M	CPT	HBZZZZUSA
RABEN, AGNES	25	F	SGL	PRZZZZUSA
DIAMANT, MAX	18	M	WCHMKR	PRZZZZUSA
GROTH, ALBRECHT	21	M	GDNR	HBZZZZUSA
VANTHUN, FRANZ	23	M	MCHT	PRZZZZUSA
AMBLING, ANNA	24	F	SGL	PRZZZZUSA
LEHMANN, JOH	28	M	MCHT	HBZZZZUSA
NEUMANN, CARL	35	M	MACH	HBZZZZUSA
LOESSER, OLGA	21	F	SGL	PRZZZZUSA
WAITZ, CAROLINE	25	F	SGL	SRZZZZUSA

SHIP: AMALFI

FROM: HAMBURG
TO: NEW YORK
ARRIVED: 01 JUNE 1888

PASSENGER	AGE	SEX	OCCUPATION	PROV/VIL/DES
DETLESSEN, MAGDALENE	35	F	WO	PRZZZZUSA
EMMA	4	F	CHILD	PRZZZZUSA
MARKUS	2	M	CHILD	PRZZZZUSA
STRAUB, MATHILDE	20	F	SGL	BVZZZZUSA
EBBERT, MAGDALENE	19	F	SGL	BVZZZZUSA
JACOBI, RUDOLPH	33	M	FARMER	PRZZZZUSA
ANNA	35	F	W	PRZZZZUSA
ALBERT	8	M	CHILD	PRZZZZUSA
JULIUS	5	M	CHILD	PRZZZZUSA
FRANZISKA	.03	F	INFANT	PRZZZZUSA
PETERSEN, MARIE	19	F	SGL	PRZZZZUSA
ARP, ANNA	20	F	SGL	PRAHTPUSA
ALVINE	15	F	SGL	PRAHTPUSA
HARMS, CATHA.	22	F	SGL	PRAAHIUSA
KLOETZER, FLORENTINE	39	F	WO	PRAKWQUSA
GERTRUD	5	F	CHILD	PRAKWQUSA
EMMA	3	F	CHILD	PRAKWQUSA
MEINEL, THERESE	18	F	SGL	PRAKWQUSA
HUGO	13	M	B	PRAKWQUSA
MEGGER, LORENZ	52	M	LABR	PRZZZZUSA
ALBERTINA	35	F	W	PRZZZZUSA
ROZALIE	14	F	CH	PRZZZZUSA
LEON	9	M	CHILD	PRZZZZUSA
JOH.	7	M	CHILD	PRZZZZUSA
MARIANNA	4	F	CHILD	PRZZZZUSA
ANASTASIA	3	F	CHILD	PRZZZZUSA
PICTO	1	M	CHILD	PRZZZZUSA
SCHMIDT, METTE	18	F	SGL	PRZZZZUSA
ABELO, MARIE	20	F	SGL	PRZZZZUSA
SORGE, FRIEDRICH	28	M	FARMER	PRZZZZUSA
BERTHA	26	F	W	PRZZZZUSA
GUSTAV	.06	M	INFANT	PRZZZZUSA
WENDLAND, CAROLINE	43	F	WO	PRAAIXUSA
ADE	11	F	CH	PRAAIXUSA
LISBET	10	F	CH	PRAAIXUSA
PAUL	9	M	CHILD	PRAAIXUSA
ANNA	7	F	CHILD	PRAAIXUSA
GUSTAV	4	M	CHILD	PRAAIXUSA

PASSENGER	AGE	SEX	OCCUPATION	PROV/VIL/DES
KAHN, WILLI	18	M	LABR	PRADNXUSA
BEHRENS, HELENE	19	F	SGL	PRAJCMUSA
STAWICKA, AGNISKA	36	F	WO	PRAEIOUSA
FRANZISKA	9	F	CHILD	PRAEIOUSA
JOSEF	7	M	CHILD	PRAEIOUSA
MONIKA	5	F	CHILD	PRAEIOUSA
SIERSZYNSKI, MICHAEL	30	M	LABR	PRAEIOUSA
JUHL, MARIE	18	F	SGL	PRZZZZUSA
JOHANNSEN, HEINRICH	24	M	LABR	PRZZZZUSA
LASSA, STANISLAW	30	M	LABR	PRZZZZUSA
JOHANNA	29	F	W	PRZZZZUSA
JOSEF	5	M	CHILD	PRZZZZUSA
LUDWIG	3	M	CHILD	PRZZZZUSA
STACHNIK, MAXIMILIAN	5	M	CHILD	PRZZZZUSA
SCHULZ, FRIEDERIKE	49	F	WO	PRAEWMUSA
ANNA	4	F	CHILD	PRAEWMUSA
FELTZKOWSKI, IGNATZ	42	M	LABR	PRZZZZUSA
JENSEN, CHRISTIAN	28	M	SMH	PRZZZZUSA
NOTZKE, AUGUSTE	38	F	WO	PRAGFKUSA
FRIEDRICH	4	M	CHILD	PRAGFKUSA
EMIL	.11	M	INFANT	PRAGFKUSA
HANSEN, MARIE	19	F	SGL	PRZZZZUSA
SOERENSEN, HANS	25	M	LABR	PRAEFRUSA
SCHMIDT, JOHANN	38	M	LABR	PRZZZZUSA
MARTHA	44	F	W	PRZZZZUSA
BERTHA	6	F	CHILD	PRZZZZUSA
EMMA	2	F	CHILD	PRZZZZUSA
CYEGLER, AGNISKA	40	F	WO	PRAGAOUSA
STANISLAW	14	M	CH	PRAGAOUSA
MARIANNA	9	F	CHILD	PRAGAOUSA
JADWIGA	7	F	CHILD	PRAGAOUSA
THEODOR	4	M	CHILD	PRAGAOUSA
SCHULZ, CARL	25	M	JNR	PRACWIUSA
GUVTZ, PAULA	20	F	SGL	PRACWIUSA
ERNST, AUGUSTE	51	F	WO	PRADNOUSA
COHRS, JOH.	34	M	SLR	PRZZZZUSA
HEINS, MARG.	37	F	WO	PRAEAPUSA
STOPPERAN, WILHELM	30	M	CGRMKR	PRACYJUSA
HEINRICHT, JOHANN	25	M	FARMER	PRZZZZUSA
SEIBEL, CARL	64	M	SHMK	PRZZZZUSA
BERTHA	67	F	W	PRZZZZUSA
LANGHOLZ, WILHELM	23	M	UNKNOWN	PRAJGAUSA
TAUBERT, CARL	26	M	LABR	PRZZZZIL
JACOBSEN, JULIUS	19	M	MCHT	PRALJDPA
RHOSE, HANS	62	M	FARMER	PRZZZZPA
JERTRUM, PETER	46	M	CPTR	PRZZZZPA
CATHA.	34	F	WO	PRZZZZPA
PETER	9	M	CHILD	PRZZZZPA
BERTHA	3	F	CHILD	PRZZZZPA
JACOBSEN, JOHS.	56	M	LABR	PRZZZZPA
CARL	12	M	CH	PRZZZZPA
BENEDIC	10	M	CH	PRZZZZPA
CORNELIUS	7	M	CHILD	PRZZZZPA
JULIANNE	3	F	CHILD	PRZZZZPA
LILIENTHAL, JOHANN	30	M	LABR	PRZZZZIL
ELISE	22	F	W	PRZZZZIL
MARGAR.	72	F	WO	PRZZZZIL
HEINRICH	3	M	CHILD	PRZZZZIL
WEIGERT, EMMA	15	F	SGL	PRADCRIL
MEYER, JOHANN	46	M	FARMER	PRZZZZIA
JOHA.	45	F	W	PRZZZZIA
MARIANNA	16	F	CH	PRZZZZIA
DANIEL	11	M	CH	PRZZZZIA
FRIEDRICH	5	M	CHILD	PRZZZZIA
PETERSEN, MARIA	16	F	SGL	PRZZZZIA
RUHSERT, ELISE	20	F	SGL	PRZZZZNE
SUDEN, GEORG	14	M	LABR	PRZZZZNE
PAULSEN, FRIEDRICH	24	M	LABR	PRZZZZIA
PAGERSEN, MARIE	47	F	WO	PRZZZZMI
JOHA.	17	M	CH	PRZZZZMI
MAGD.	11	F	CH	PRZZZZMI
JETTE	7	F	CHILD	PRZZZZMI
JENS	4	M	CHILD	PRZZZZMI
CHRIST.	3	M	CHILD	PRZZZZMI
CHRISTENSEN, DOROTHEA	18	F	SGL	PRAGNYIL

PASSENGER	AGE	SEX	OCCUPATION	PRVVL DES
EHLERS, HEINRICH	16	M	LABR	PRZZZZNE
HANSEN, HANS	30	M	LABR	PRZZZZNE
SCHURGER, ANNA	27	F	WO	PRAINKPA
ANNA	6	F	CHILD	PRAINKPA
MARIA	4	F	CHILD	PRAINKPA
HICHULSKA, ANNA	52	F	SGL	PRAINKPA
WASLER, ANNA	17	F	SGL	PRAINKPA
BRIZ, CATHA.	26	F	SGL	PRZZZZNE
WALTTER, ERNESTINE	57	F	WO	PRZZZZNE
THOMSEN, GORGEN	21	M	FARMER	PRZZZZNE
JUNKER, ANTON	19	M	LABR	PRZZZZIA
PERP, MARIA	64	F	WO	PRZZZZDAK
BOETCHER, METTE	66	F	WO	PRZZZZNY
HANSEN, ASMUR	43	M	LABR	PRZZZZNY
FERDINAD	11	M	S	PRZZZZNY
BORCHARDT, JOHANN	43	M	LABR	PRAAZQPA
ELISABETH	47	F	W	PRAAZQPA
REDMANN, JOH.	23	M	LABR	PRALKBPA
WESELOWSKI, WILHELMINE	46	F	WO	PRAAZQPA
JOH.	18	M	CH	PRAAZQPA
AMANDE	11	F	CH	PRAAZQPA
GRUNWALD, IDA	26	F	SGL	PRAAZQIL
EBERHARDT, ERNST	42	M	LABR	PRAAZQMD
WIESE, OTTO	32	M	LABR	PRADYMMD
KLAUS, FRIEDRICH	44	M	LABR	PRADEPIL
ALBERT	15	M	S	PRADEPIL
KUEHNAPFEL, GUSTAV	33	M	LABR	PRZZZZIL
HAPRICH, JOSEF	64	M	LABR	PRAARZKS
WANDTKE, RICHARD	16	M	TLR	PRZZZZKS
HEINNOLD, RUDOLJER	38	M	LABR	PRACMHIL
STEPPKE, DOROTHEA	28	F	WO	PRZZZZMN
AUGUSTE	2	F	CHILD	PRZZZZMN
MARIE	.03	F	INFANT	PRZZZZMN
GEBHARDT, GOTTFRIED	35	M	LABR	PRZZZZMN
CHARLOTTE	31	F	W	PRZZZZMN
OTTO	5	M	CHILD	PRZZZZMN
GUSTAV	4	M	CHILD	PRZZZZMN
MINNA	2	F	CHILD	PRZZZZMN
HUGO	1	M	CHILD	PRZZZZMN
JOHANNA	67	M	SGL	PRZZZZMN
GUETNER, AUGUST	50	M	LABR	PRZZZZMN
LIPPKE, AUGUSTE	18	F	SGL	PRZZZZNY
HAYN, ELISABETH	23	F	SGL	PRAAKHNY
KERSTEN, ALBERT	35	M	UNKNOWN	PRAAKHNY
KNABE, ERNST	35	M	LABR	PRZZZZNY
SEWADE, HERMANN	36	M	LABR	PRZZZZNY
SELIGER, BRUNO	20	M	LABR	PRAAKHNY
FRIEDLAUDER, VICTOR	31	M	LABR	PRAAKHNY
SCHEEL, HERMANN	26	M	JNR	PRAAKHDAK
ZANDER, AUGUST	28	M	LABR	PRZZZZDAK
AUGUSTE	29	F	W	PRZZZZDAK
HERMANN	8	M	CHILD	PRZZZZDAK
EMILIE	6	F	CHILD	PRZZZZDAK
BERTHA	4	F	CHILD	PRZZZZDAK
GUSTAV	3	M	CHILD	PRZZZZDAK
IDA	.09	F	INFANT	PRZZZZDAK
SCHROEDER, MATHILDE	19	M	SGL	PRZZZZDAK
GEINKE, ALBIN	18	M	SGL	PRZZZZDAK
MROZ, VALENTIN	25	M	LABR	PRZZZZDAK
GUROLEK, THOMAS	26	M	LABR	PRZZZZDAK
GROKE, HEINRICH	24	M	LABR	PRZZZZWI
CLARA	21	F	W	PRZZZZWI
HUEBNER, CATHA.	57	F	SGL	PRZZZZWI
SCHLIEPER, ERNST	26	M	LABR	PRACXVWI
KUPTSCHINAS, ANTON	20	M	LABR	PRZZZZWI
KEWELIZKY, ISAAK	20	M	LABR	PRZZZZWI
FISCHER, CATHE.	56	F	WO	PRZZZZWI
WALBURGA	22	M	CH	PRZZZZWI
MARIE	14	F	CH	PRZZZZWI
WALBURGA	1	M	CHILD	PRZZZZWI
VETTER, FRANZ	34	M	LABR	PRACBKWI
SCHELLER, MAGRAL.	17	F	SGL	PRACBKWI
KUSSINS, ANNE	17	F	SGL	PRZZZZWI
BAUMANN, ANNA	23	F	SGL	BVZZZZWI
HOCK, JOHANN	31	M	FARMER	PRZZZZPA
PROHL, HEINRIETTA	18	F	SGL	PRZZZZPA
GEHENMANN, PAUL.	21	F	SGL	PRZZZZPA
KKLOTZ, FRIEDRICH	44	M	FARMER	WMZZZZTX
SCHAD, FRIEDRICH	24	M	LABR	WMZZZZTX
MUELLER, GEORG	76	M	FARMER	WMAFFTTX
BAUMANN, WILHELM	27	M	WVR	WMAFPCTX
ANDERSEN, PETER	26	M	LABR	PRZZZZTX
SCHAAL, FRIEDRICH	50	M	LABR	PRZZZZTX
LOUISE	43	F	W	PRZZZZTX
MOHR, EDMUND	15	M	LABR	PRAAEFPA
RICHARD	12	M	B	PRAAEFPA
SCHULER, SIMON	37	M	WCHMKR	WMZZZZPA
SCHNEIDER, MARIE	31	F	SGL	WMZZZZPA
OSDOBER, JACOB	28	M	LABR	PRZZZZNY
LUCIA	25	F	W	PRZZZZNY
STEFAN	2	M	CHILD	PRZZZZNY
GREGOR	.09	M	INFANT	PRZZZZNY
PRIGGE, MARIA	22	F	SGL	PRZZZZNY
SCHANER, FRANZ	28	M	LABR	PRZZZZWI
ANNA	30	F	W	PRZZZZWI
ANNA	7	F	CHILD	PRZZZZWI
MARIE	.09	F	INFANT	PRZZZZWI
VOSS, GETHARD	46	M	LABR	PRZZZZIN
LIPPKE, HELENE	20	F	WO	PRZZZZIN
FRIEDRITH	.09	M	INFANT	PRZZZZIN

SHIP: GALLIA

FROM: LIVERPOOL AND QUEENSTOWN
TO: NEW YORK
ARRIVED: 01 JUNE 1888

PASSENGER	AGE	SEX	OCCUPATION	PRVVL DES
HOLZ, AUGUST	31	M	CPTR	PRAEIGUSA
GERSCH, WOLF	14	M	TLR	PRACBFUSA
KRIEGER, SALOMON	33	M	UNKNOWN	PRACBFUSA
SCHMEIDER, CARL	23	M	LABR	PRACBFUSA
KRWAZI, JAN	50	M	SHMK	PRACBFUSA
TER.	11	M	CH	PRACBFUSA
SIMAN, ABRAM	34	M	TLR	PRACBFUSA
LICHTENSTEN, JULIUS	24	M	PNTR	PRAAKHUSA
MATERSYEWSKI, JAN	24	M	LABR	PRACBFUSA
MAGALSKY, FRANS	22	M	LABR	PRAEXKUSA
BLIER, RUDORF	27	M	LABR	PRAEXKUSA
MULLER, EUSTACE	25	M	GLDR	PRACBFUSA
WILHA	32	M	GLDR	PRACBFUSA
WEBER, GUSTAV	21	M	LABR	PRACBFUSA
CARL	24	M	LABR	PRACBFUSA
MULLER, FRANZ	29	M	LABR	PRACBFUSA
STARM, EUSTACE	17	M	FARMER	GRZZZZUSA
SCHULST, OTTO	16	M	LABR	GRACBFUSA
GOENING, JOSEF	42	M	LABR	GRZZZZUSA
ELFENBEIN, SILIG	31	M	LABR	GRACBFUSA
LOBERSGSKI, FRANZ	24	M	LABR	GRACBFUSA
LANIN, MARNIE	19	F	SVNT	GRACBFUSA
GIRSCH, RACHEL	15	F	SVNT	GRACBFUSA
PAPSBERG, MARI	17	F	SVNT	GRACBFUSA
CHAGT, SISYEL	20	F	SVNT	GRACBFUSA
SIMAN, LEHA	14	F	SVNT	GRACBFUSA
CARL	11	M	CH	GRACBFUSA
PINKUS, P.	18	F	SVNT	GRACBFUSA
RACHEL	14	F	SVNT	GRACBFUSA
JOSEF	10	M	CH	GRACBFUSA
RUSSEL, SARAH	15	F	SVNT	GRACBFUSA
BERKOWITZ, FANNY	17	F	SVNT	GRACBFUSA
SEYANKI, AGNISKA	17	F	SVNT	GRACBFUSA
SCHWARYMAN, BEILE	19	F	SVNT	GRACBFUSA
TIGE, JOS.	22	M	SHMK	GRACBFUSA
WILMA	20	F	SVNT	GRACBFUSA
DORFMANN, HILLEL	33	M	TCHR	GRACBFUSA
SCHABREL	17	M	FARMER	GRACBFUSA

PASSENGER	AGE	SEX	OCCUPATION	PRVL DES
SCHWELL, PERL	22	F	W	GRACBFUSA
ESHER	.11	F	INFANT	GRACBFUSA
MEIXLER, MOOR	48	M	SHMK	GRACBFUSA
SALI	45	F	W	GRACBFUSA
RABINOWITZ, LEB	11	M	CH	GRACBFUSA
ROTH, SALY	40	F	MA	GRACBFUSA
ESTER	18	F	SP	GRACBFUSA
ALBERT	9	M	CHILD	GRACBFUSA
WILMUSCH	9	M	CHILD	GRACBFUSA
TONI	6	F	CHILD	GRACBFUSA
NATHAN	2	M	CHILD	GRACBFUSA
SALI	2	F	CHILD	GRACBFUSA
ROTTI, MARTON	.08	M	INFANT	GRACBFUSA
KAPUSTA, DAVID	7	M	CHILD	GRACBFUSA
SCHMANN, CARL	43	M	CPTR	GRAAKHUSA
MARIE	43	F	W	GRAAKHUSA
CARL	20	M	LABR	GRAAKHUSA
CARL	20	M	LABR	GRAAKHUSA
THERESIA	20	F	SP	GRAAKHUSA
MARTHA	16	F	SP	GRAAKHUSA
ALBERT	14	M	SP	GRAAKHUSA
BERTHA	11	F	CH	GRAAKHUSA
PAUL	10	M	CH	GRAAKHUSA
CARL	7	M	CHILD	GRAAKHUSA
COLOMBOWITCH, BALSUS	36	M	FARMER	GRACBFUSA
ELISA	26	F	W	GRACBFUSA
DANIELA	3	F	CHILD	GRACBFUSA
MAGDALENA	2	F	CHILD	GRACBFUSA
WEISELBERG, SIMON	45	M	TLR	GRACBFUSA
AMALIE	19	F	SVNT	GRACBFUSA
ELISA	15	F	SVNT	GRACBFUSA
PAULINE	11	F	CH	GRACBFUSA
JULIUS	9	M	CHILD	GRACBFUSA
PAVHJKA, VALENTZ	50	M	LABR	GRACBFUSA
BRONUSLAW	14	M	LABR	GRACBFUSA
MARTHA	.11	F	INFANT	GRACBFUSA
SCHULZ, JOHAN	35	M	LABR	GRACBFUSA
CATH.	27	F	W	GRACBFUSA
ANASTASIA	3	F	CHILD	GRACBFUSA
FRANZISKA	2	F	CHILD	GRACBFUSA
CONRAD	.11	M	INFANT	GRACBFUSA
KOROLAUKS, LEVIC	33	M	MA	GRACBFUSA
CHANI	.11	M	INFANT	GRACBFUSA
DORFINAN, LERA	30	F	MA	GRACBFUSA
GOTE	9	F	CHILD	GRACBFUSA
ISAAC	7	M	CHILD	GRACBFUSA
SAM	5	M	CHILD	GRACBFUSA
CLARA	.10	F	INFANT	GRACBFUSA
GOLDFAUB, MARC	55	M	GDSM	GRACBFUSA
IADEL	40	F	W	GRACBFUSA
ETLER	45	F	SVNT	GRACBFUSA
ETLER	20	F	SP	GRACBFUSA
ANNA	12	F	CH	GRACBFUSA
CHALOCK, SCHAGE	43	M	UNKNOWN	GRACBFUSA
MARIA	43	F	W	GRACBFUSA
MENNEHL	14	F	SVNT	GRACBFUSA
MOSES	8	M	CHILD	GRACBFUSA
FRIEDLANN, EMMA	37	F	W	GRZZZUSA
LOUIS	17	M	NN	GRAARRGR
ALTSCHUELER, M.	19	F	NN	GRAARRGR
WITTE, OTTO-W.	16	M	NN	GRADVHGR
FABER, CARL	25	M	TT	GRADROGR
HOFFMEISTER, CARL	22	M	TT	GRAGFUGR
FROEHLICH, SARA	19	F	NN	GRZZZZGR
ROSENSTOCK, BERTHA	24	F	NN	GRACHWGR
SPEYER, A.	52	F	W	GRZZZZGR
JENNY	20	F	NN	GRZZZZGR
SCHILDMANN, GEORG	21	M	TT	GRAALZGR
KEENER, HERM.	20	M	TT	GRAARRGR
MAEHLER, FRIEDA	18	F	NN	GRACHAGR
STELLJES, A.	22	F	NN	GRAARRGR
NETTEKOVEN, CARL	28	M	TT	GRAAYGGR
BENEDIKT, LUDWIG	13	M	TT	GRAAFVGR
RODILK, FRIEDR.	20	M	TT	GRAARRGR
LEONHARDT, HEINR.	21	M	TT	GRADUXGR
HEINE, CHRIST.	32	M	TT	GRACXVGR
HEUMANN, ALEXANDER	19	M	TT	GRZZZZGR
NEUBERGER, MOSES	17	M	TT	GRADGKGR
CAROLE.	27	F	NN	GRADGKGR
ELISE	16	F	NN	GRADGKGR
MAYER, PAUL	18	M	TT	GRADGKGR
KAUFMANN, ADOLF	15	M	TT	GRACAQGR
KOLLINER, ROBERT	22	M	TT	GRACAQGR
BERTHA	51	F	W	GRACAQGR
RUCKERT, FRIEDR.	40	F	W	GRAAXYGR
MEYER, MARIE	22	F	NN	GRABDMGR
HAHN, HANNCHEN	19	F	NN	GRAJGDGR
SCHIFF, SARA	16	F	NN	GRZZZZGR
METZGER, ZIPORA	23	F	NN	GRACHXGR
ROSER, HERMANN	29	M	TT	GRAEXWGR
MARIA	23	F	W	GRAEXWGR
SCHRADER, ANNA	19	F	NN	GRAARRGR
STEIN, JEANETTE	19	F	NN	GRALSZGR
METZGER, CLARA	62	F	W	GRZZZZGR
ZIPORA	21	F	NN	GRZZZZGR
HUMANN, IDA-WALLY	15	F	NN	GRZZZZGR
MEYER, JOH.F.C.	53	M	TT	GRADWOGR
GRAAF, PETER-M.	75	M	TT	GRZZZZGR
SCHOLL, ELISE	30	F	NN	GRAAXXGR
JOBST, PAULINE	17	F	NN	GRZZZZGR
MUESER, BERTHA	17	F	NN	GRABCXGR
MERGENTHAU, SIMON	27	M	TT	GRADDWGR
COHN, EMANUEL	45	M	TT	GRAARRGR
STEINMANN, EMILIE	23	F	NN	GRACAVGR
HESSE, MARIE	51	F	W	GRAARTGR
NEEF, FRANKIE	11	M	CH	GRACXDGR
PETERS, ANNA	22	F	NN	GRAAKHGR
OLDENBURG, CARL	28	M	TT	GRADCRGR
FISCH, IDA	19	F	NN	GRADGXGR
MICHALSKY, ANTON	50	M	TT	GRZZZZGR
CHRISTINE	58	F	W	GRZZZZGR
LANGE, HEINR.R.	45	M	TT	GRADYQGR
WORSCHEIN, SOPHIE	54	F	W	GRZZZZGR
CLARA	14	F	NN	GRZZZZGR
KAETHE	18	F	NN	GRZZZZGR
RIEKER, MAX	63	M	TT	GRAFWVGR
MESSERICH, PHILIPP	20	M	TT	GRAAABGR
RIEKER, BARBARA	24	F	NN	GRAFWVGR
HEINE, MATHE.	29	F	W	GRACXVGR
KAUFMANN, JOSEF	68	M	LABR	GRAEGXUSA
REGINE	50	F	W	GRAEGXUSA
ROSA	15	F	NN	GRAEGXUSA
JULIUS	11	M	CH	GRAEGXUSA
MINNA	9	F	CHILD	GRAEGXUSA
KUEHNEMANN, ERNST	14	M	NN	GRZZZZUSA
RUEFFEL, CATHA.	28	F	W	GRABOQUSA
JOHA.	8	F	CHILD	GRABOQUSA
SAUTHER, THEODOR	18	M	LABR	GRABOQUSA
WINKELSTEIN, BERTHA	21	F	NN	GRABZPUSA
HOFMANN, SABINA	16	F	NN	GRAHRKUSA
AMALIE	21	F	NN	GRAHRKUSA
POLAWCZYNSKA, ROSALIE	21	F	NN	GRAHRKUSA
SCHMIDT, SOEREN	28	M	LABR	GRAFPGUSA

SHIP: LAHN

FROM: BREMEN AND SOUTHAMPTON
TO: NEW YORK
ARRIVED: 01 JUNE 1888

PASSENGER	AGE	SEX	OCCUPATION	PRVL DES
SCHWENKE, HELENE	23	F	NN	GRALSZGR
ASSMANN, J.AD.	30	M	TT	GRACBFGR
HEILBRONN, MARIANNA	20	F	NN	GRAARRGR
GRAU, LOUISE	20	F	NN	GRAARRGR
MOHR, IDA	19	F	NN	GRAARRGR

PASSENGER	AGE	SEX	OCCUPATION	PRVVL/DES
SCHERER, ELSE	31	F	NN	GRABZSUSA
SCHARPF, CARL	21	M	JNR	GRZZZZUSA
GERSTUNG, GEORG	17	M	LABR	GRAAXFUSA
RAUSCH, FERDINAND	34	M	LABR	GRACEDUSA
CAROLINA	30	F	W	GRACEDUSA
ANNA	8	F	CHILD	GRACEDUSA
BREISCH, PETER	60	M	LABR	GRZZZZUSA
KAETHE	57	F	W	GRZZZZUSA
GERHARD	3	M	CHILD	GRZZZZUSA
KAETHE	2	F	CHILD	GRZZZZUSA
JUNG, WILHELM	16	M	MCHT	GRAAWBUSA
KELGUS, LOUISE	24	F	NN	GRACQOUSA
MAIER, PAULINE	23	F	NN	GRACQOUSA
BAUER, MARIE	32	F	W	GRAFJCUSA
FRIEDRICH	10	M	CH	GRAFJCUSA
ALBERT	9	M	CHILD	GRAFJCUSA
LOUISE	6	F	CHILD	GRAFJCUSA
MARIE	8	F	CHILD	GRAFJCUSA
ANNA	3	F	CHILD	GRAFJCUSA
SIEGLE, FANNY	18	F	NN	GRAFWVUSA
HOFMANN, ANNA	19	F	NN	GRZZZZUSA
HERMANN	14	M	NN	GRZZZZUSA
HOEFLINGER, CARL	16	M	JNR	GRACQOUSA
BRAUN, CONRAD	17	M	JNR	GRAGEMUSA
EKERT, JOHANN	14	M	NN	GRZZZZUSA
JAKOB	16	M	SHMK	GRZZZZUSA
HUBER, ROSA	49	F	NN	GRAFRG***
WERNER, JUSTIN	22	M	JNR	GRZZZZUSA
HOLSCHER, BERNHD.	26	M	LABR	GRADDEUSA
FENZL, JOHANN	32	M	BKR	GRADNDUSA
RUGEN, HARM	14	M	BKR	GRZZZZUSA
DIERS, GEORG	16	M	BKR	GRAEVSUSA
ERNST	14	M	BKR	GRAEVSUSA
CALMAN, FERDINAND	24	M	LABR	GRACBRUSA
MEIER, FRITZ	20	M	LABR	GRACBRUSA
FRIEDKE.	15	F	NN	GRACBRUSA
LANGNER, CONRAD	22	M	LABR	GRABPCUSA
GOETZ, FRANZ	36	M	LABR	GRADGYUSA
FRIEDA	28	F	W	GRADGYUSA
ALPHONS	11	M	W	GRADGYUSA
OSCAR	.11	M	INFANT	GRADGYUSA
EMIL	2	M	CHILD	GRADGYUSA
KOPPE, CARL	28	M	LABR	GRAAKHUSA
TAU, PHILIPP	30	M	MCHT	GRACTOUSA
DOROTHEA	56	F	W	GRAEYKUSA
SCHAEFER, LOUIS	22	M	LABR	GRAIVCUSA
WERNING, FRIEDKE.	26	F	NN	GRZZZZUSA
THIELKER, LINA	14	F	NN	GRZZZZUSA
ULMER, CATHA.	18	F	NN	GRADGYUSA
PFUND, FRIEDR.	27	M	LABR	GRADGYUSA
SOPHIE	27	F	W	GRADGYUSA
WILHM.	.11	M	INFANT	GRADGYUSA
EUGEN	.05	M	INFANT	GRADGY***
GOLDSCHMIDT, ISIDOR	18	M	MCHT	GRZZZZUSA
MAAS, JOHANN	23	M	LABR	GRAFJCUSA
MARIE	20	F	W	GRAFJCUSA
BAREIS, GOTTFRIED	26	M	LABR	GRZZZZUSA
RUFF, KATHA.	19	F	NN	GRZZZZUSA
GETZ, MAGDA.	17	F	NN	GRACQOUSA
FRIEDRICH, ROSA	20	F	NN	GRADLDUSA
SCHMIDT, THERESE	28	F	W	GRAEWSUSA
JOSEFINE	2	F	CHILD	GRAEWSUSA
WILHELMINE	.06	F	INFANT	GRAEWSUSA
HOH, GEORG	27	M	BRR	GRAEWSUSA
GAD, MANE	25	F	NN	GRAEWSUSA
NENNER, GEORG	21	M	LABR	GRAEWSUSA
SCHUER, ELEONORA	30	F	NN	GRABKRUSA
MARIA	27	F	NN	GRABKRUSA
EPPERS, LUDOLPH	14	M	NN	GRADWFUSA
STOCK, LOUIS	19	M	WTR	GRAARRUSA
KEMPES, JOHANN	19	M	LABR	GRAARRUSA
WIELERS, BERNHD.	23	M	LABR	GRAARRUSA
FELDMANN, ANT.	15	M	NN	GRAARRUSA
BECKMANN, CARL	14	M	NN	GRADQLUSA
MUELLER, ALEXANDRE.	30	F	W	GRAARRUSA
FRIEDA	9	F	CHILD	GRAARRUSA
KOHL, CHRISTOPH	14	M	NN	GRABKRUSA
FRAUENSCHLAEGER, FRIEDR	19	M	NN	GRABKRUSA
BENKERT, MARIA	21	F	NN	GRADYAUSA
LANG, KATHERINA	21	F	NN	GRADYAUSA
HAGEN, HELENE	45	F	W	GRAAYGUSA
PAUL	11	M	CH	GRAAYGUSA
JOHANN	9	M	CHILD	GRAAYGUSA
HELENE	8	F	CHILD	GRAAYGUSA
LEUSMANN, MARIA	24	F	NN	GRAEATUSA
SCHMIDT, KILIAN	15	M	TLR	GRZZZZUSA
BAUM, MARCUS	43	M	LABR	GRZZZZUSA
KOEHLER, CARL	15	M	NN	GRACEDUSA
SILBERMANN, IDA	21	M	NN	GRZZZZUSA
AMBRUNN, ROSA	17	M	NN	GRZZZZUSA
HAHN, LEOPOLD	15	M	NN	GRZZZZUSA
SCHEUER, HIRSCH	16	M	NN	GRZZZZUSA
ISAK	15	M	NN	GRZZZZUSA
HORN, EUGEN	15	M	NN	GRZZZZUSA
INNIG, ANNA	55	F	W	GRAAYGUSA
ELISE	20	F	NN	GRAAYGUSA
FLORA	18	F	NN	GRAAYGUSA
HENRY	14	M	NN	GRAAYGUSA
KUELLNER, DAVID	46	M	BCHR	GRABLMUSA
ELISE	48	F	W	GRABLMUSA
CHRISTOPH	15	M	NN	GRABLMUSA
MARIE	11	F	CH	GRABLMUSA
CARL	8	M	CHILD	GRABLMUSA
UTHE, SABINE	17	F	NN	GRABSYUSA
SCHUBACH, RICHARD	37	M	LABR	GRABSYUSA
ELISE	33	F	W	GRABSYUSA
CLARA	11	F	CH	GRABSYUSA
RYBACZYK, JOH.	31	M	LABR	GRACSDUSA
SALOMON	30	M	W	GRACSDUSA
HELENE	6	F	CHILD	GRACSDUSA
FELIX	3	M	CHILD	GRACSDUSA
AGATHE	.02	F	INFANT	GRACSDUSA
SCHMITH, LORENZ	34	M	LABR	GRAEKCUSA
MENZEL, ELISE	12	F	CH	GRAAXFUSA
BLOCH, HERMANN	26	M	LABR	GRACSDUSA
BREISCH, CATHA.	29	F	W	GRZZZZUSA
JOHANN	11	M	CH	GRZZZZUSA
NAAS, BABETTE	18	F	NN	GRACIBUSA
ISAAC, SALOMON	18	M	LABR	GRZZZZUSA
HAFNER, MARGE.	27	F	NN	GRADDWUSA
GERSTENHAUER, CARL	18	M	LABR	GRZZZZUSA
HAHN, FRIEDR.	14	M	NN	GRADHWUSA
WEGER, CATHA.	20	F	NN	GRZZZZUSA
STAMMER, CARL	16	M	NN	GRAJJIUSA
DATZ, CARL	16	M	NN	GRAJJIUSA
WITTMANN, MARGE.	20	F	NN	GRZZZZUSA
LEONHD.	16	M	NN	GRZZZZUSA
MANZ, JOHANNA	32	F	W	GRAFJCUSA
ANNA	5	F	CHILD	GRAFJCUSA
FRIEDRICH	4	M	CHILD	GRAFJCUSA
GEORG	2	M	CHILD	GRAFJCUSA
ELISE	.03	F	INFANT	GRAFJCUSA
MUELLER, GESCHE	14	F	NN	GRACNWUSA
WEHMEYER, JOH.	18	M	LABR	GRAARRUSA
ONASCH, CARL	15	M	NN	GRAARRUSA
NEUBIG, PAUL	12	M	CH	GRZZZZUSA
WITTE, MATHILDE	22	F	NN	GRAGSQUSA
SCHANERTE, MINNA	20	F	NN	GRAGSQUSA
FLOEPER, THERESIA	23	F	NN	GRAGSQUSA
MEYER, WILH.	23	M	PTR	GRZZZZUSA
SEMRAU, MINNA	21	F	NN	GRZZZZUSA
FUNKE, BARBARA	47	F	W	GRAFIPUSA
ANNA	44	F	W	GRAFIPUSA
CARL	15	M	NN	GRAFIPUSA
JENSON, HUGO	65	M	LABR	GRZZZZUSA
LOUISE	53	F	W	GRZZZZUSA
CATHA.	16	F	NN	GRZZZZUSA
LAMBERT	11	M	CH	GRZZZZUSA
ANNA	11	F	CH	GRZZZZUSA
PETERS, JOH.G.	16	M	LABR	GRZZZZUSA

PASSENGER	AGE	SEX	OCCUPATION	PRVVL	DES		PASSENGER	AGE	SEX	OCCUPATION	PRVVL	DES
HINRICH	15	M	NN	GRZZZZUSA			STAUSBIER, CHRISTA.	18	F	NN	GRZZZZUSA	
BARTELS, ERNST	17	M	LABR	GRZZZZUSA			ABERLE, MATH.	18	M	LABR	GRZZZZUSA	
FREESE, WILHELM	30	M	FARMER	GRAAPLUSA			REITH, GREGOR	25	M	SMH	GRZZZZUSA	
BAUER, ANNA	31	F	NN	GRZZZZUSA			SCHWOLOW, BERTHA	22	F	NN	GRAEIOUSA	
BINDER, NOTHBURGA	30	F	NN	GRZZZZUSA			KATZ, DAVID	15	M	NN	GRZZZZUSA	
BODE, AUGUST	30	M	SEMN	GRACFJUSA			ROTHSCHILD, MATHILDE	16	F	NN	GRZZZZUSA	
MAYER, GRETCHEN	26	F	W	GRADHCUSA			SCHULZE, AEXIS	18	M	MCHT	GRAAKHUSA	
ELISE	9	F	CHILD	GRADHCUSA			ERBER, REGINA	17	F	NN	GRZZZZUSA	
DEMMER, HERM.D.	27	M	LABR	GRAAYGUSA			GEISEL, CHRISTIAN	16	M	LABR	GRZZZZUSA	
TIMKE, CATHA.	18	F	NN	GRAAPSUSA			BINGOLD, JOH.	24	M	FARMER	GRABQZUSA	
GOETZ, SABINE	17	F	NN	GRACQOUSA			WEINSTOCK, JOSNA	16	M	NN	GRACHWUSA	
MAU, FRITZ	15	M	NN	GRAARRUSA			BURGHARDT, MARIE	27	F	W	GRACBRUSA	
GRODIS, MATRUCH	46	M	LABR	GRADIMUSA			FRITZ	4	M	CHILD	GRACBRUSA	
ADAM	23	M	LABR	GRADIMUSA			CLAUS, CONRAD	22	M	LABR	GRZZZZUSA	
ENDRE, NAZY	24	M	LABR	GRZZZZUSA			NOLL, WILHELM	18	M	LABR	GRZZZZUSA	
KORBELY, JOSEF	25	M	LABR	GRZZZZUSA			WEBER, PHILIPP	18	M	LABR	GRZZZZUSA	
MEISTER, KATHARINA	19	F	NN	GRADLDUSA			BIEBER, MARIE	40	F	W	GRACSHUSA	
ANNA	15	F	NN	GRADLDUSA			JOHANN	9	M	CHILD	GRACSHUSA	
BAUER, MARTIN	16	F	NN	GRADLDUSA			LUDWIG	7	M	CHILD	GRACSHUSA	
SOEHNLEIN, ANNA	20	F	NN	GRADLDUSA			MARIE	4	F	CHILD	GRACSHUSA	
RUHKOPF, HERM.	50	M	FARMER	GRACBRUSA			BAWEDA	3	F	CHILD	GRACSHUSA	
DOBEREINEN, MICHAEL	15	M	NN	GRZZZZUSA			MARG.	1	F	CHILD	GRACSHUSA	
HEIM, LOUISE	17	F	NN	GRAAXFUSA			WINKELMANN, CONRAD	27	M	LABR	GRADBLUSA	
FRICKE, EMMA	35	F	W	GRAARRUSA			ELISE	18	F	W	GRADBLUSA	
HEDWIG	11	F	CH	GRAARRUSA			BARBARA	.10	F	INFANT	GRADBLUSA	
ROBERT	9	M	CHILD	GRAARRUSA			MEYER, CARL	25	M	STCTR	GRAAXKUSA	
ZEPP, WILHELM	30	M	LABR	GRZZZZUSA			KRAFT, HEINR.	23	M	BCHR	GRZZZZUSA	
ELISABETH	29	F	W	GRZZZZUSA			SCHOENHERR, SELMA	24	F	NN	GRACZEUSA	
KATHARINA	4	F	CHILD	GRZZZZUSA			HARDEN, MARGE.	30	F	NN	GRACBFUSA	
STAEBNER, ELISAB.	21	F	NN	GRZZZZUSA			SCHWOLOW, CARL	17	M	LABR	GRAEIOUSA	
EHRLINGER, JOH.	26	M	CPTR	GRACZYUSA			VALLEY, GRAF	47	M	UNKNOWN	GRADBQGR	
SCHWERDFEGER, MALCHE	15	F	NN	GRACZYUSA			KURT, HEINR.	33	M	VAL	GRADBQGR	
CHRISTMANN, KATHA.	48	F	W	GRACZYUSA			HENRICH, O.	24	M	TT	GRADBQGR	
ANNA	14	F	NN	GRACZYUSA								
MAGDA.	12	F	CH	GRACZYUSA								
KATHA.	10	F	CH	GRACZYUSA								
SCHWARZ, KATHA.	40	F	NN	GRACZYUSA								
GUENTHER, CARL	21	M	LABR	GRZZZZUSA			SHIP: NORSEMAN					
KRAEUZLEIN, JOHANN	29	M	BKR	GRZZZZUSA								
SPRINGER, MICHAEL	38	M	CPTR	GRZZZZUSA			FROM: LIVERPOOL AND LONDON					
LINDHAUER, MARIE	19	F	NN	GRZZZZUSA			TO: BOSTON					
KAUPER, MARIE	44	F	NN	GRZZZZUSA			ARRIVED: 02 JUNE 1888					
SCHWABELMEIER, MATHIAS	10	M	CH	GRZZZZUSA								
TAXES, GUSTAV	22	M	BKR	GRZZZZUSA								
GLUF, CARL	17	M	LABR	GRZZZZUSA			LIEBAUL, CHLS.	24	M	LABR	GRZZZZUSA	
STROBEL, BARBARA	19	F	NN	GRZZZZUSA			ANNIE	19	F	W	GRZZZZUSA	
KALTENBACH, ROSINE	20	F	NN	GRZZZZUSA			BOROWAN, JOHN	30	M	LABR	GRZZZZNY	
HEINS, JOHANN	15	M	NN	GRZZZZUSA			KRAM, HENRY	44	M	LABR	GRZZZZNY	
SAUTER, MARIE	19	F	NN	GRZZZZUSA			B-ARD, A.	44	M	LABR	GRZZZZNY	
SCHROEDER, EDMUND	27	M	ENGR	GRZZZZUSA			ME-ELSTINE, H.	24	M	LABR	GRZZZZNY	
HERZOG, BERTHA	32	F	W	GRAAXYUSA			SCHRUCK, MARUF	19	F	SVNT	GRZZZZUSA	
DORA	7	F	CHILD	GRAAXYUSA			DUFOS, MARIA	30	F	W	GRZZZZNY	
GABEL, HEINR.	26	M	FARMER	GRZZZZUSA			IFNOTSDIAK, MARTIN	30	M	LABR	GRZZZZNY	
MEYERHOLZ, HERM.	16	M	NN	GRZZZZUSA			HIAN	19	F	W	GRZZZZNY	
WILPERN, ANNA	28	F	NN	GRAARTUSA			IWATRY	00	M	INF	GRZZZZNY	
RUDOLPHI, HERM.	14	M	NN	GRAARTUSA			DORIBRONE, BERTHOLD	23	M	LABR	GRZZZZNY	
BRANTJEN, GEORGE	16	M	NN	GRAALJUSA								
ROES, JOHN	16	M	NN	GRAALJUSA								
SULEWSKI, JOSEFE.	46	F	W	GRABRYUSA								
MARTHA	6	F	CHILD	GRABRYUSA								
JACHENS, LOUISE	15	F	NN	GRACXHUSA			SHIP: ANCHORIA					
WILKENS, JOHANNE	20	F	NN	GRACXHUSA								
GABEL, MARIANNA	20	F	NN	GRACSZUSA			FROM: GLASGOW					
FLADT, AUGUST	16	M	NN	GRZZZZUSA			TO: NEW YORK					
BLATZ, FRANZ	63	M	LABR	GRAJGDUSA			ARRIVED: 04 JUNE 1888					
CAROLINE	48	F	W	GRAJGDUSA								
JACOBINE	28	F	NN	GRAJGDUSA								
CARL	10	M	CH	GRAJGDUSA			RAIT, IGNATZ	50	M	JNR	GRZZZZUSA	
WOLPERT, FRANZ	16	M	SHMK	GRAJGDUSA			IGNATZ	15	M	JNR	GRAEABUSA	
WUERZBERGER, GEORGE	32	M	TLR	GRAJGDUSA			SOMERFELD, OTTO	25	M	LABR	GRAEABUSA	
WILD, LOUISE	16	F	NN	GRADGXUSA			GUSTAV	26	M	LABR	GRZZZZUSA	
SCHUELER, WILH.	15	M	NN	GRADGXUSA			GUGEHOV, PAUL	18	M	GLSBR	GRZZZZUSA	
TILLY, JOHANN	14	M	NN	GRAAZSUSA			FELLNER, PSIAS	24	M	LABR	GRZZZZUSA	
FAHRBACH, LOUISE	18	M	NN	GRZZZZUSA								
ZWEIG, LOUISE	20	F	NN	GRZZZZUSA								

PASSENGER	AGE	SEX	OCCUPATION	PRVL	DES
PRIESS, WILH	23	M	SHMK	GRADCRUSA
BRAND, GEORG	20	M	UNKNOWN	GRAAIEUSA
DRAHEIM, MATHILDE	17	F	HP	GRAAIEUSA
SCHLEZEL, CARL	29	M	UNKNOWN	GRZZZZUSA
KRUPP, CARL	36	M	UNKNOWN	GRZZZZUSA
U	24	F	UNKNOWN	GRZZZZUSA

SHIP: ARIZONA

FROM: LIVERPOOL AND QUEENSTOWN
TO: NEW YORK
ARRIVED: 04 JUNE 1888

PASSENGER	AGE	SEX	OCCUPATION	PRVL	DES
ROGGENDORF, ADILE	19	F	SP	GRACBFUSA
RIX, LAURA	15	F	SP	GRACBFUSA
GUNTHER, HERMAN	30	M	ATSN	GRACBFUSA
ENFERTIG, MORITZ	20	M	PNTR	GRACBFUSA
KNUTKL, OTTO	27	M	FARMER	GRACBFUSA
REHDER, WILHELM	17	M	LABR	GRACBFUSA
FISCHER, SALOMON	20	M	LABR	GRACBFUSA
RUCZ, THEODOR	28	M	MSN	GRACBFUSA
SCHMIDT, SOPHIE	17	F	SP	GRACBFUSA
LAMBRECHLER, MATHIAS	35	M	FARMER	GRACBFUSA
MILLNER, HIRCH	19	M	FARMER	GRACBFUSA
DAVID	11	M	CH	GRACBFUSA
WAICULIS, MARCUS	36	M	FARMER	GRACBFUSA
GERNHARDT, KORA	32	F	W	GRACBFUSA
SOPHIE	14	F	SP	GRACBFUSA
FREDERIKE	10	F	CH	GRACBFUSA
PAULINA	7	F	CHILD	GRACBFUSA
CHRISTIAN	6	M	CHILD	GRACBFUSA
FREDERICK	4	M	CHILD	GRACBFUSA
MARTHA	.10	F	INFANT	GRACBFUSA
MAKIKMIS, SACABAS	20	M	SHPMN	GRACBFUSA
STAUFFER, JOHN	52	M	ATSN	GRAAECUSA
SUSANNA	53	F	W	GRAAECUSA
ALBERT	15	M	LABR	GRAAECUSA
MOLLER, H.	40	F	LDY	GRACBFUSA
SPORI, M.	37	F	LDY	SRZZZZUSA
ANNA	29	F	LDY	SRZZZZUSA
J.	11	M	CH	SRZZZZUSA
M.	10	F	CH	SRZZZZUSA
L.	9	F	CHILD	SRZZZZUSA
DE, S.A.	45	M	GENT	SRADBQFR
BLONDIN, CHEOL.J.F.	60	M	GENT	SRADBQFR
HENRI	32	M	GENT	SRADBQFR

SHIP: DUPUY DE LOME

FROM: ANTWERP
TO: NEW ORLEANS
ARRIVED: 04 JUNE 1888

PASSENGER	AGE	SEX	OCCUPATION	PRVL	DES
WIELAND, NICOLAS	40	M	FARMER	GRZZZZUSA
ELISE	40	F	NN	GRZZZZUSA
KLE---DT, FRANZ	43	M	CPTR	GRZZZZUSA
WERNLI, GOTTLIEB	24	M	CPTR	GRZZZZUSA
KORMAYER, CARL	19	M	MCHT	GRZZZZUSA
HEARTNER, JOHANNA	30	F	NN	GRZZZZUSA
-ILL, AUGUST	17	M	PH	GRZZZZUSA
ELKAS, ADOLPH	34	M	FARMER	GRZZZZUSA
-OSEVER, LEOPOLD	29	M	FARMER	GRZZZZUSA
DANSK, BONIFACIOUS	34	M	FARMER	GRZZZZUSA
NUERNBERG, RUDOLF	16	M	NN	GRZZZZUSA
EDWARD	9	M	CHILD	GRZZZZUSA

PASSENGER	AGE	SEX	OCCUPATION	PRVL	DES
GRIMM, HERMAN	43	M	MCHT	GRZZZZUSA
LEPLAT, JULES	40	M	PH	FRZZZZUSA
VILOE, JULE	24	M	APTC	FRZZZZUSA
PARAGNET, MARIA	18	F	NN	FRZZZZUSA
COM-ALINE, LOUISE	18	F	NN	FRZZZZUSA
AR-OIZ, CADE-	19	M	CL	FRZZZZUSA
CO-CART, ANTOINE	24	M	CPR	FRZZZZUSA
--CANA, PIERRE	26	M	BLKSMH	FRZZZZUSA
ITOURBOURON, JEAN	20	M	BKR	FRZZZZUSA
DELAGNES, PIERRE	42	M	MNR	FRZZZZUSA
JOSEPH	19	M	CL	FRZZZZUSA
LAURENT, JOACHIM	28	M	CCHMN	FRZZZZUSA
FA--, LOUIS	29	M	CCHMN	FRZZZZUSA
DUG--S, EMILE	29	M	CBTMKR	FRZZZZUSA
REGNIER, MARIE	40	F	NRS	FRZZZZUSA
LE-CURE, AUGETE	23	F	SMSTS	FRZZZZUSA
DU-O-OMB, CHIRITE	27	F	NRS	FRZZZZUSA
GUILLEBASTRE, BAPTISTE	28	M	JNR	FRZZZZUSA
PRADAL, GERMAN	23	M	CPTR	FRZZZZUSA
LAMON, JEAN	42	M	MSN	FRZZZZUSA
PIERRE	16	M	CL	FRZZZZUSA
DUMERTRE, FELICIE	18	F	SMSTS	FRZZZZUSA
MEDUS, FRANCOIS	42	M	FARMER	FRZZZZUSA
DELPHINE	42	F	HSKPR	FRZZZZUSA
POLYMMIE	7	F	CHILD	FRZZZZUSA
EDUARD	9	M	CHILD	FRZZZZUSA
DAURIGNAE, ROSE	24	F	NN	FRZZZZUSA
MARIE	22	F	NN	FRZZZZUSA
AVERED, EUPHRA---	27	F	NN	FRZZZZUSA
ROUTTE, -ABIER	19	M	CL	FRZZZZUSA
GERE, BAPTISTE	21	M	CCHMN	FRZZZZUSA
GA-DE, JOSEPH	31	M	FARMER	FRZZZZUSA
BARRET, GUSTAVE	32	M	FARMER	FRZZZZUSA
BOUI, JACQUES	27	M	FARMER	FRZZZZUSA
BERGEROT, JEAN	20	M	CL	FRZZZZUSA
DUBOIS, JEAN	28	M	CBTMKR	FRZZZZUSA
PACCIONETTI, FILIPPO	29	M	CBTMKR	FRZZZZUSA
CAZENEUBE, AMIELE	22	F	NN	FRZZZZUSA
ST, JN	28	M	WHR	FRZZZZUSA
LOUERRY, LARRAJEDIEU-AE	28	M	WHR	FRZZZZUSA
MON-AT, FRANCOIS	18	M	CL	FRZZZZUSA
SALLENAVE, JEAN	32	M	MSN	FRZZZZUSA
LAMANET, JEAN	19	M	CL	FRZZZZUSA
ABAROUETTE, JEAN	18	M	CL	FRZZZZUSA
PARGADE, MARCEL	26	M	STMSN	FRZZZZUSA
LOUBERT, JEAN	29	M	CCHMN	FRZZZZUSA
BARBE, JACQUES	21	M	CCHMN	FRZZZZUSA
LAMARAT, MARIE	19	F	NRS	FRZZZZUSA
BIRO--, JEAN	18	M	TLR	FRZZZZUSA
BRO-UA, AUGUSTE	29	M	UNKNOWN	FRZZZZUSA
-ELLET, JEAN	26	M	PNTR	FRZZZZUSA
CARE-AVE, LOLINE	20	M	CPTR	FRZZZZUSA
-O-EMME, MELINA	20	F	SMSTS	FRZZZZUSA
CAZA-D-ME---, JEAN	19	M	CL	FRZZZZUSA
-AITHUR, LOUIS	18	M	CL	FRZZZZUSA
DAVANCERS, HENRI	18	M	CL	FRZZZZUSA
CASTAGNIE, MARIE	24	F	SMSTS	FRZZZZUSA
E--UERRE, GR-T	29	M	CPR	FRZZZZUSA
PAYONAPE, JEAN	18	M	BKR	FRZZZZUSA
LATAPIE, PAUL	44	M	SHMK	FRZZZZUSA
CRAVERO, PIERRE	40	M	FARMER	FRZZZZUSA
BOLDATTINI, ANGELO	50	M	FARMER	FRZZZZUSA
MAGNANINI, ANGELO	50	M	FARMER	FRZZZZUSA
ROSA, GIOVANNI	50	M	FARMER	FRZZZZUSA
PAOLO	11	M	NN	FRZZZZUSA
ANTONIO, VINCENZO	30	M	SHPC	FRZZZZUSA
BURRIANO, JOSEPH	35	M	SHPC	FRZZZZUSA
MARCELLI, RAFAELE	36	M	BCHR	FRZZZZUSA

PASSENGER	AGE	SEX	OCCUPATION	PRVL	DES
SHIP: WERRA					
FROM: BREMEN AND SOUTHAMPTON					
TO: NEW YORK					
ARRIVED: 05 JUNE 1888					
BENNDT, --RY	54	M	TT	FRABDMUSA	
SCHLEISER, ---D	38	M	TT	FRADUXUSA	
BERGERCHEN, ROBERT	22	M	TT	FRACXVUSA	
BONDY, S	42	M	TT	FRAARRUSA	
ZAHN, JOHN	22	M	TT	FRAFBTUSA	
ZIEGLER, LAMBERT	24	M	TT	WMZZZZUSA	
HAUSSLEIN, BERTHA	21	F	UNKNOWN	WMACEHUSA	
HEIDE, HEINR	25	M	TT	GRZZZZUSA	
BUETTNER, ERNST	22	M	TT	GRZZZZUSA	
FRANK, LEO	15	M	TT	GRACRAUSA	
FLEISCHMANN, SIM	16	M	TT	BVZZZZUSA	
SCHWALD, SIM	16	M	TT	BVZZZZUSA	
VANTUMETI, HANS	21	M	TT	BVADIJUSA	
OTTO, ANTONIETTE	20	F	UNKNOWN	BVAAQPUSA	
HENKEL, PAULINE	47	F	UNKNOWN	BVAGLGUSA	
KORTA, JOSEPH	25	F	UNKNOWN	BVACOZUSA	
NIEDERMAIER, HERM	34	M	TT	BVADLDUSA	
ROESSGEN, BERTHA	34	F	W	BVAEACUSA	
OTTO	11	M	CH	BVAEACUSA	
LOUIS	9	M	CHILD	BVAEACUSA	
GEIPEL, GERTRUD	20	F	UNKNOWN	BVAEACUSA	
HANER, ANNA	23	F	UNKNOWN	BVAEACUSA	
ARNDT, MARG	23	F	UNKNOWN	BVAEACUSA	
NIESING, HERM	15	M	UNKNOWN	BVACNWUSA	
OBERGFELL, ANTON	28	M	TT	BDZZZZUSA	
JOSEFA	25	F	W	BDZZZZUSA	
MEYER, IDA	17	F	UNKNOWN	BDZZZZUSA	
HIRSCH, BARUCH	17	M	TT	BDZZZZUSA	
SCHMIDT, P	27	M	TT	BDZZZZUSA	
HENNIG, MARY	30	F	UNKNOWN	BDAARRUSA	
TIEDT, ANNA	13	F	UNKNOWN	BDAARRUSA	
OETJEN, HEIN	15	M	UNKNOWN	GRZZZZUSA	
HEINR	15	M	UNKNOWN	GRZZZZUSA	
REINHEIMER, ROSA	18	F	UNKNOWN	GRACVEUSA	
MENKEL, BERTHA	33	F	W	GRZZZZUSA	
BENNNY	10	F	CH	GRZZZZUSA	
OTTO	8	M	CHILD	GRZZZZUSA	
EMIL	6	M	CHILD	GRZZZZUSA	
HENRIETTE	4	F	CHILD	GRZZZZUSA	
FISCHER, HEINR	27	M	LABR	GRAAGLUSA	
NEDOR, MARIE	28	F	W	GRABPSUSA	
BARB	3	F	CHILD	GRABPSUSA	
ELNMER, JOH	27	M	LABR	GRAEVTUSA	
BARB	12	F	UNKNOWN	GRAEVTUSA	
HEINLEIN, AGNES	19	M	LABR	BVZZZZUSA	
HOLZMANN, MARG	18	F	UNKNOWN	BVABPSUSA	
LARSEN, JOH	28	M	UNKNOWN	BVAAKHUSA	
WESER, ERNST	60	M	LABR	GRZZZZUSA	
HENRIETTE	58	F	W	GRZZZZUSA	
SELMA	27	F	UNKNOWN	GRZZZZUSA	
CLARA	25	F	UNKNOWN	GRZZZZUSA	
RICHARD	15	M	UNKNOWN	GRZZZZUSA	
FRIEDR	7	F	CHILD	GRZZZZUSA	
ALMA	3	F	CHILD	GRZZZZUSA	
HEDWIG	.10	F	INFANT	GRZZZZUSA	
ERLER, NANI	40	F	W	GRADFSUSA	
CARL	14	M	CH	GRADFSUSA	
SCHAEFFLER, ERNST	13	M	CH	GRZZZZUSA	
HULDA	21	F	UNKNOWN	GRZZZZUSA	
GLATZKE, AUGUSTE	22	F	UNKNOWN	GRZZZZUSA	
KUFFERT, WILH	70	F	W	GRZZZZUSA	
BOETTCHER, JOH	30	M	FARMER	GRZZZZUSA	
MAX	5	M	CHILD	GRZZZZUSA	
LIEWANDOWSKY, WALERYA	19	F	UNKNOWN	GRZZZZUSA	
KAMIEWSKI, WACLAW	25	M	LABR	GRZZZZUSA	
SEGELKEN, GESCHE	50	F	W	GRZZZZUSA	
GRIM, ANNA	19	F	UNKNOWN	WRZZZZUSA	
DRYNER, HEIM	29	M	LABR	GRZZZZUSA	
NEUMANN, HENRIETTE	41	F	W	GRZZZZUSA	
EMILIE	18	F	UNKNOWN	GRZZZZUSA	
JULIUS	16	M	UNKNOWN	GRZZZZUSA	
JOHN, GERMANN	16	M	UNKNOWN	GRZZZZUSA	
KRAEFT, BERTHA	24	F	W	GRZZZZUSA	
ANNA	2	F	CHILD	GRZZZZUSA	
LOUISE	.09	F	INFANT	GRZZZZUSA	
PAUTZ, HERM	23	M	LABR	GRZZZZUSA	
ROEHDER, CAROL.	17	F	UNKNOWN	GRAARRUSA	
SONNEMANN, LNDA	19	F	UNKNOWN	GRAFQBUSA	
GLASER, WILH	22	M	LABR	GRADWYUSA	
ZWICKIRSCH, EMIL	24	M	UNKNOWN	GRAFGCUSA	
-ATHA	25	F	W	GRAFGCUSA	
WRYCZA, STANISLAUS	22	M	LABR	GRZZZZUSA	
BOROWSKI, ALEXANDER	39	M	LABR	GRABMIUSA	
WIRTH, AUGUSTE	20	F	UNKNOWN	GRABMIUSA	
GARDELLI, AUG	35	M	LABR	GRZZZZUSA	
SCHUBERT, AUGUSTE	22	F	UNKNOWN	GRZZZZUSA	
ALEXANDER, JOH	21	M	LABR	GRZZZZUSA	
CIEMIENSKA, FRANZISKA	21	F	W	GRZZZZUSA	
WANDA	2	F	CHILD	GRZZZZUSA	
ANTON	.01	M	INFANT	GRZZZZUSA	
ZIEHM, AUGUST	38	M	FARMER	GRAEFGUSA	
CAROLE	36	F	W	GRAEFGUSA	
FRITZ	8	M	CHILD	GRAEFGUSA	
AUGUSTE	6	F	CHILD	GRAEFGUSA	
GRETHE	.11	F	INFANT	GRAEFGUSA	
SALIN, ANNA	55	F	W	GRZZZZUSA	
ANNA	16	F	UNKNOWN	GRZZZZUSA	
FRANZ	7	M	CHILD	GRZZZZUSA	
LENTZ, PAULINE	20	F	UNKNOWN	GRZZZZUSA	
FIEDLER, AUGUSTE	26	F	UNKNOWN	GRZZZZUSA	
GEYER, MGRT	16	M	FARMER	GRZZZZUSA	
LANGE, HEINR	16	M	FARMER	GRZZZZUSA	
BRUECKNER, HEINR	21	M	FARMER	GRZZZZUSA	
MARIE	36	F	W	GRZZZZUSA	
ANDR	10	M	CH	GRZZZZUSA	
OSCAR	.09	M	INFANT	GRZZZZUSA	
BAUER, JACOB	30	M	LABR	GRADROUSA	
MARIA	25	F	W	GRADROUSA	
EBER, MARTHA	25	F	UNKNOWN	GRADROUSA	
ZENSCHEL, KUNIG	34	F	UNKNOWN	BVZZZZUSA	
GOLDFUSS, MARG	15	F	UNKNOWN	BVAGBBUSA	
HOFFMANN, KONRAD	26	M	BRR	BVZZZZUSA	
BOETTCHER, EMILE	27	F	W	GRZZZZUSA	
OTTO	.09	M	INFANT	GRZZZZUSA	
WALTER, CARL	17	M	LABR	GRADWYUSA	
STARK, HERM	28	M	LABR	GRABOQUSA	
HEIN	37	M	LABR	GRABOQUSA	
HEINRICH, JUL	21	M	LABR	GRZZZZUSA	
MAN, HERM	24	M	LABR	GRZZZZUSA	
LECK, HELENE	17	F	UNKNOWN	GRZZZZUSA	
GROTSCHANN, GEORG	26	M	FARMER	GRZZZZUSA	
WOLTMANN, BERNH	27	M	FARMER	GRACBEUSA	
ADICKS, ED	32	M	FARMER	GRZZZZUSA	
LEPPIN, MARTIN	24	M	FARMER	GRZZZZUSA	
AHRENS, GEO	34	M	FARMER	GRAARRUSA	
FANTZEN, GEO	14	M	UNKNOWN	GRABRYUSA	
STEINEMANN, TRINA	22	F	UNKNOWN	GRACBRUSA	
KOOPMANN, SOPHIE	18	F	UNKNOWN	GRZZZZUSA	
NOWISCKA, JULIA	26	F	W	GRZZZZUSA	
THEOPHILA	5	F	CHILD	GRZZZZUSA	
ANTON	2	M	CHILD	GRZZZZUSA	
KOLDENBURG, MART	36	M	FARMER	GRZZZZUSA	
ELFERS, GESCHE	16	F	UNKNOWN	GRZZZZUSA	
RAPP, SOPHIE	14	F	UNKNOWN	WMZZZZUSA	
MOTZER, GOTTLIEB	15	M	UNKNOWN	WMZZZZUSA	
KURZ, CATH	15	F	UNKNOWN	WMZZZZUSA	
FINK, GEORG	16	F	UNKNOWN	WMZZZZUSA	
DAMKEN, ANNA	21	F	UNKNOWN	GRZZZZUSA	
ETTA	18	F	UNKNOWN	GRACXHUSA	
ILG, EMMA	22	F	UNKNOWN	GRAEQTUSA	
SCHARLE, SOPHIE	15	F	UNKNOWN	WMZZZZUSA	
MAIER, THEODOR	36	M	LABR	WMADKJUSA	
PFERSCH, MARIA	60	F	W	WMAAXFUSA	

129

PASSENGER	AGE	SEX	OCCUPATION	PRVL DES
RINGEISEN, JOSEPH	16	M	UNKNOWN	BDZZZZUSA
HERMANN, MATHILDE	18	M	UNKNOWN	BDZZZZUSA
BARTH, GEORG	25	M	LABR	BVZZZZUSA
LIND, MICH	26	M	LABR	BVZZZZUSA
STRAUSS, LUDW	29	M	LABR	BVABOQUSA
HOEFNER, ANNA	15	F	UNKNOWN	GRZZZZUSA
WITTE, FRIEDR	14	M	UNKNOWN	GRABLTUSA
FUELLING, HENRIETE	45	F	UNKNOWN	GRAFILUSA
HINRICHS, FRIEDR	39	M	FARMER	GRAFILUSA
ANNA	49	F	W	GRAFILUSA
HEINRICH	11	M	CH	GRAFILUSA
ANNA	10	F	CH	GRAFILUSA
SCHALLHANER, MARIA	34	F	UNKNOWN	WMZZZZUSA
STOEPPELMANN, LOUISE	18	F	UNKNOWN	GRZZZZUSA
MARIA	16	F	UNKNOWN	GRZZZZUSA
AUGUSTE	9	F	CHILD	GRZZZZUSA
STRAKELJAHR, LOUISE	15	M	UNKNOWN	GRABCAUSA
KARL	16	M	UNKNOWN	GRABCAUSA
ALBZEGER, PHILIPP	24	F	UNKNOWN	BVZZZZUSA
FEDERKEIL, BARB	60	F	W	BVZZZZUSA
FELLER, MARIE	18	F	UNKNOWN	BDZZZZUSA
HETTINGER, CATH	19	F	UNKNOWN	BDZZZZUSA
WOLFER, BARB	25	F	UNKNOWN	BDZZZZUSA
DIEFENBACK, HERM	24	M	LABR	BDADDWUSA
KAISER, FREDERICH	17	M	LABR	BDADDWUSA
SCHENERMANN, JOH	19	M	LABR	BDADDWUSA
KOBER, HEIN	16	M	LABR	BDAABYUSA
BAUER, FRIEDR	14	M	UNKNOWN	BDAABYUSA
RUPP, CARL	16	M	UNKNOWN	GRZZZZUSA
LANBENGAIER, LOUISE	40	F	UNKNOWN	GRAHFTUSA
EGELER, JUSTINE	25	F	UNKNOWN	WMZZZZUSA
FRICK, MARIE	18	F	UNKNOWN	WMZZZZUSA
RUOFF, CATH	30	F	UNKNOWN	WMAAGWUSA
M---, CATH	17	F	UNKNOWN	WMZZZZUSA
BAUER, WOLFHANG	18	M	LABR	BVZZZZUSA
LIEBIG, ROB	33	M	LABR	BVAEGYUSA
FROST, ANDR	28	M	LABR	BVACBRUSA
FORTUNA, STEFAN	26	M	LABR	BVZZZZUSA
MARIA	16	F	UNKNOWN	BVZZZZUSA
KINDLE, PAUL.	17	F	UNKNOWN	WMZZZZUSA
GOMPPER, GOTTLOB	24	M	LABR	WMACWPUSA
KOENIG, FERD	22	M	LABR	WMACWPUSA
RAPP, CHR	18	M	LABR	WMACWPUSA
WINST, CARL	17	M	LABR	WMACBFUSA
SCHAIBLE, SABINE	60	F	W	WMACBFUSA
MARIA	3	F	CHILD	WMACBFUSA
EGEN, MARIA	22	F	UNKNOWN	WMACBFUSA
SCHOETTLE, JACOB	66	M	LABR	WMACBFUSA
HAIN, JOH	26	M	LABR	WMACBFUSA
STOEKEL, KUNIG	15	F	UNKNOWN	WMACBFUSA
MARG	4	F	CHILD	WMACBFUSA
BAUM, KATH	19	F	UNKNOWN	WMACBFUSA
STOECK, ELISAB	16	F	UNKNOWN	WMACBFUSA
HABIG, SUSANNA	9	F	CHILD	WMACBFUSA
PASTETENBEDEN, ELISAB	20	F	UNKNOWN	WMACBFUSA
SCHWARZ, FRIED.	15	F	UNKNOWN	WMZZZZUSA
MUELLER, MARIE	16	F	UNKNOWN	WMZZZZUSA
GEBELE, CAROL	20	F	UNKNOWN	WMZZZZUSA
RUF, MARIE	15	F	UNKNOWN	WMZZZZUSA
KOPP, CHR	26	M	LABR	WMZZZZUSA
GRAF, CARL	30	M	LABR	WMZZZZUSA
FRIEDEL, GUST	15	M	LABR	WMZZZZUSA
KLENK, FRIED	18	F	UNKNOWN	WMZZZZUSA
SCHUSTER, JACOB	39	M	LABR	WMZZZZUSA
KOCH, BARB	44	F	W	WMACWPUSA
WILH	14	M	UNKNOWN	WMACWPUSA
MARIE	11	F	CH	WMACWPUSA
AMALIE	10	F	CH	WMACWPUSA
LOUISE	9	F	CHILD	WMACWPUSA
BARB	8	F	CHILD	WMACWPUSA
CHRIST	7	M	CHILD	WMACWPUSA
HUBER, ANNA	17	F	UNKNOWN	WMZZZZUSA
FRANTWEIN, LOUISE	20	F	UNKNOWN	WMZZZZUSA
SCHWAB, CATH	20	F	UNKNOWN	WMZZZZUSA
OBT, LOUISE	17	F	UNKNOWN	WMZZZZUSA
BILGER, MARIA	18	F	UNKNOWN	WMAFAYUSA
MESSNER, MICH	18	M	LABR	WMAFAYUSA
MUELLER, DAMIAN	9	M	CHILD	GRZZZZUSA
MAYSER, OTTO	21	M	LABR	WMZZZZUSA
SEYFRIED, ADOLF	26	M	LABR	WMAEXWUSA
WAIDELICH, CATH	21	F	UNKNOWN	WMAEXWUSA
SCHURR, GUST	14	M	UNKNOWN	WMAEXWUSA
SCHAAL, PAUL.	18	F	UNKNOWN	WMAEXWUSA
IRMLEY, LINA	20	F	UNKNOWN	WMABRHUSA
REIS, ALVIT	26	M	LABR	BVZZZZUSA
MARIE	11	F	UNKNOWN	BVZZZZUSA
VANINI, CAROL	33	F	UNKNOWN	BVAEDSUSA
KAULBACH, JACOB	19	M	LABR	BVAESGUSA
SCHWABE, KILIAN	22	M	LABR	BVZZZZUSA
KOEGEL, JOHN	28	M	LABR	BVZZZZUSA
WOLTERS, FRIEDR	16	M	LABR	BVABHOUSA
BRUNS, AUGUST	16	M	LABR	BVABHOUSA
STASSER, KUNIG	24	F	W	BVZZZZUSA
JOH	2	M	CHILD	BVZZZZUSA
GREGOR, BARTHOLD	28	M	FARMER	BVADABUSA
WIRTH, EVA	38	F	W	BVZZZZUSA
MARG	19	F	UNKNOWN	BVZZZZUSA
CHRIST	11	F	CH	BVZZZZUSA
BABETTA	8	F	CHILD	BVZZZZUSA
HERM	5	M	CHILD	BVZZZZUSA
JOH	.09	M	INFANT	BVZZZZUSA
FASCHLOTTER, WILH	23	F	UNKNOWN	GRZZZZUSA
KRAUSE, FRANZ	45	M	LABR	GRZZZZUSA
KITZER, FRITZ	30	M	LABR	GRZZZZUSA
MOELLER, BARB	18	F	UNKNOWN	GRZZZZUSA
KALCHTHALER, FRIEDA	18	F	UNKNOWN	BDZZZZUSA
STROEHLER, JOH	26	F	UNKNOWN	GRZZZZUSA
BOELTER, HEINR	29	M	FARMER	GRZZZZUSA
JULIANE	18	F	UNKNOWN	GRZZZZUSA
ADOLF	3	M	CHILD	GRZZZZUSA
HERM	.06	M	INFANT	GRZZZZUSA
ZEUCH, CARL	23	M	FARMER	GRZZZZUSA
LINDGRIBE, JOH	16	M	FARMER	GRADOIUSA
SPIELER, MARG	24	F	UNKNOWN	GRADLDUSA
KAPPELMAIER, WALBURGA	31	F	UNKNOWN	GRADLDUSA
LORENZ	29	M	LABR	GRADLDUSA
WEINSTEIGER, JOHN	34	M	LABR	GRADOIUSA
EICHHORN, JOH	11	M	CH	GRADOIUSA
HOFFMANN, KATH	43	F	UNKNOWN	BVZZZZUSA
EISENREICH, JOS	18	M	BCHR	BVZZZZUSA
MART	16	M	LABR	BVZZZZUSA
HUENERT, ELEONORE	20	F	UNKNOWN	GRZZZZUSA
SCHNEIDER, APOLLONIA	29	F	UNKNOWN	GRADLDUSA
REICH, MARIE	18	F	UNKNOWN	BVZZZZUSA
JANISCHOWSKI, IGNATZ	37	M	LABR	GRZZZZUSA
SCHMIEL, ANDR	24	M	LABR	GRZZZZUSA
VIERLICK, VALENTY	43	M	LABR	GRZZZZUSA
GRABOWSKI, ANDR	29	M	LABR	GRZZZZUSA
METZGER, BABETTE	22	F	UNKNOWN	GRAAWTUSA
WALKER, DAVID	24	M	LABR	GRAAWTUSA
BANN, JOHS	27	M	LABR	WMZZZZUSA
HEIL, HEIN	25	M	LABR	WMAEMNUSA
GERBIG, GEORG	27	M	LABR	WMAEMNUSA
HOEPAS, JOH	35	M	LABR	WMALBSUSA
MAG	30	F	W	WMALBSUSA
MARIA	10	F	CH	WMALBSUSA
JOH	9	M	CHILD	WMALBSUSA
BABETTE	7	F	CHILD	WMALBSUSA
MARG	.11	F	INFANT	WMALBSUSA
STRAKA, ALBINE	28	F	UNKNOWN	GRZZZZUSA
OTTEN, HISKA	24	F	UNKNOWN	GRZZZZUSA
ENGELKE, HEINR	14	M	UNKNOWN	GRZZZZUSA
MARIE	14	F	UNKNOWN	GRZZZZUSA
KULERSER, MARYANNA	35	F	W	GRZZZZUSA
MARG	6	F	CHILD	GRZZZZUSA
JOH	4	M	CHILD	GRZZZZUSA
JOSEF	2	M	CHILD	GRZZZZUSA
MAUSER, GOTTLIEBIN	18	F	UNKNOWN	WMZZZZUSA
FRAENKE, JOH	16	M	PNTR	WMZZZZUSA
SCHNEIDER, ERNST	31	M	LABR	WMADNMUSA

PASSENGER	AGE	SEX	OCCUPATION	PRVL	DES
FRANZ	31	F	W		WMADNMUSA
CATH	3	F	CHILD		WMADNMUSA
WILH	2	M	CHILD		WMADNMUSA
ANTON	.06	M	INFANT		WMADNMUSA
KOEHLER, MOSULA	28	F	UNKNOWN		WMZZZZUSA
WEBER, WILH	35	M	LABR		GRZZZZUSA
MARG	30	F	W		GRZZZZUSA
MARIA	4	F	CHILD		GRZZZZUSA
MARG	3	F	CHILD		GRZZZZUSA
FRITZ, EMMA	17	F	UNKNOWN		GRAEDAUSA
BRUGGER, ULRICH	10	M	CH		GRAEDAUSA
WINKLER, CHRIST	35	M	W		WMZZZZUSA
FRIEDR	8	M	CHILD		WMZZZZUSA
JAKOB	5	M	CHILD		WMZZZZUSA
CARL	3	M	CHILD		WMZZZZUSA
FRIED	2	F	CHILD		WMZZZZUSA
SCHULZE, BERN	16	M	BCHR		WMACXVUSA
MICHL, MARIE	29	F	UNKNOWN		BVZZZZUSA
PFEFFER, GEORG	28	M	LABR		BVZZZZUSA
KNABENBAUM, THERESIA	36	F	W		BVADLDUSA
THERESIA	11	F	CH		BVADLDUSA
JOH	1	M	CHILD		BVADLDUSA
FAHDE, THERESE	17	F	UNKNOWN		BVADLDUSA
DETERDING, HEINR	64	M	LABR		GRZZZZUSA
GERDES, JOH	19	M	LABR		GRZZZZUSA
VOELKE, LUDW	15	M	UNKNOWN		GRAJZMUSA
WILDERMUTH, FRIEDR	48	M	FARMER		WMZZZZUSA
REGINA	45	F	W		WMZZZZUSA
WILHELM	11	M	CH		WMZZZZUSA
GOTTLIEB	7	M	CHILD		WMZZZZUSA
CAROL.	.06	F	INFANT		WMZZZZUSA
HERTKORN, RUDOLF	19	M	LABR		GRZZZZUSA
GOETTLER, CARL	26	M	LABR		WMZZZZUSA
MAUSER, CAROL	20	F	UNKNOWN		WMZZZZUSA
ROMMEL, ERNST	17	M	LABR		WMZZZZUSA
SEPLER, SOFIE	26	F	UNKNOWN		WMZZZZUSA
MAIER, PAUL	19	F	UNKNOWN		WMZZZZUSA
MUELLER, URSULA	21	F	UNKNOWN		BVZZZZUSA
EICHMANN, JOH	16	M	FARMER		BVZZZZUSA
ANGERSEN, GEORG	23	M	FARMER		BVZZZZUSA
MUENCH, JOH	34	M	FARMER		BVZZZZUSA
MARTHA	32	F	W		BVZZZZUSA
ELISAB	11	F	CH		BVZZZZUSA
DOROTHEA	9	F	CHILD		BVZZZZUSA
MARG	8	F	CHILD		BVZZZZUSA
THOMAS	5	M	CHILD		BVZZZZUSA
BARB	4	F	CHILD		BVZZZZUSA
GRUBER, WILH	17	M	LABR		GRZZZZUSA
KNIPPENBERG, HEINR	20	M	LABR		GRZZZZUSA
FRIEDR	19	M	LABR		GRZZZZUSA
SPECHT, HEINR	22	M	LABR		GRAITQUSA
UTTER, FR	24	M	LABR		BVZZZZUSA
JANNOCH, OTTO	34	M	LABR		BVAAKHUSA
AHRENS, CLEMENT	18	F	UNKNOWN		BVACBRUSA
NEDDERMEYER, STEPH	23	M	FARMER		BVACBRUSA
KARL, PETER	25	M	FARMER		BVACBRUSA
ADAM	20	M	FARMER		BVACBRUSA
MARG	37	F	UNKNOWN		BVACBRUSA
HUTWOLT, JUL	37	M	FARMER		BVZZZZUSA
PAUL, ADAM	27	M	FARMER		BVZZZZUSA
NAUERT, STEPHAN	21	M	FARMER		BVZZZZUSA
CZWELLING, JOH	45	M	LABR		GRZZZZUSA
THERESIA	32	F	W		GRZZZZUSA
MARIE	6	F	CHILD		GRZZZZUSA
ANNA	3	F	CHILD		GRZZZZUSA
STADLER, KATH	20	M	UNKNOWN		GRAFWNUSA
MARG	18	M	UNKNOWN		GRAFWNUSA
LIND, SOPHIE	18	F	UNKNOWN		GRAAJNUSA
FAHLE, MARIA	21	F	UNKNOWN		GRZZZZUSA
STECHMANN, MARIE	21	F	UNKNOWN		GRZZZZUSA
KURZ, DAVID	14	M	UNKNOWN		WMZZZZUSA
APP, WALBURGA	16	F	UNKNOWN		GRZZZZUSA
BEITTER, CATH	15	F	UNKNOWN		WMZZZZUSA
GEIER, GEORG	16	M	FARMER		WMAAAMUSA
HAASE, HEINR	16	M	FARMER		WMZZZZUSA
MEYER, CATH	21	F	UNKNOWN		BVZZZZUSA
RUSCHMEYER, CATH	20	F	UNKNOWN		GRZZZZUSA
DREYER, HINR	15	M	UNKNOWN		GRZZZZUSA
LAUTENBACH, ELISE	30	F	UNKNOWN		GRZZZZUSA
NIERMANN, AUG	28	M	LABR		GRZZZZUSA
BREDENFOERDER, HEINR	27	M	LABR		GRZZZZUSA
CRAMER, WILH	14	M	UNKNOWN		GRZZZZUSA
RANH, ELISAB	21	F	UNKNOWN		BVZZZZUSA
REINERT, AUGUST	21	F	UNKNOWN		GRZZZZUSA
HUBER, LOUISE	17	F	UNKNOWN		BDZZZZUSA
SPINKE, BARB	18	F	UNKNOWN		BDZZZZUSA
BASSLER, CATH	20	F	UNKNOWN		WMZZZZUSA
HERZOG, MART	14	M	UNKNOWN		WMZZZZUSA
HERMANN, HEINR	18	M	LABR		GRZZZZUSA
MEYER, JOHANN	24	M	LABR		GRZZZZUSA
HEINR	17	M	LABR		GRACBRUSA
BOCKELMANN, CATH	22	F	UNKNOWN		GRADLNUSA
REICHERT, SABINE	25	F	UNKNOWN		GRAKSMUSA
BINDER, BARB	28	F	UNKNOWN		GRAKSMUSA
KRATZER, ANDR	25	M	LABR		GRALBKUSA
ZIMMER, FRIDOLIN	38	M	LABR		GRABVWUSA
DOROTHEA	38	F	W		GRABVWUSA
MICHL	65	M	LABR		GRABVWUSA
HUGO	16	M	LABR		GRABVWUSA
MINNA	14	F	UNKNOWN		GRABVWUSA
PAUL	9	M	CHILD		GRABVWUSA
RICHARD	2	M	CHILD		GRABVWUSA
SCHULER, ROSA	25	F	UNKNOWN		GRACEGUSA
ANFRECHT, JOH	24	F	UNKNOWN		GRACEGUSA
WITTMANN, MARG	29	F	W		GRACEGUSA
LUDW	.11	M	INFANT		GRACEGUSA
GRETCHEN	.05	F	INFANT		GRACEGUSA
BECK, MATHIAS	17	M	FARMER		GRACEGUSA
POSER, HERM	50	M	FARMER		GRACVSUSA
SCHMIDT, JOH	16	M	FARMER		GRABYNUSA
KAMPF, ALWIN	25	M	FARMER		GRACBRUSA
BAUER, ANNA	26	F	UNKNOWN		BVZZZZUSA
GITTL, ANNA	25	F	UNKNOWN		BVZZZZUSA
STROBL, GEORGE	30	M	FARMER		BVZZZZUSA
MARG	26	F	W		BVZZZZUSA
ADAM	6	M	CHILD		BVZZZZUSA
ELISAB	.11	F	INFANT		BVZZZZUSA
VOELKL, JOH	26	M	FARMER		BVZZZZUSA
NOBEL, ELISE	22	F	UNKNOWN		BVAARRUSA
ELZENBEIK, GORG	25	M	LABR		BVZZZZUSA
MAESCHER, AUG	32	M	LABR		GRZZZZUSA
HENNIGHAUS, HEIN	35	M	LABR		GRZZZZUSA
MECKERT, ANNA	24	F	UNKNOWN		GRZZZZUSA
MARTHA	20	F	UNKNOWN		GRZZZZUSA
FRERS, HEINR	16	M	FARMER		GRADIBUSA
LUEHMANN, DIEDR	16	M	FARMER		GRALUUUSA
FISCHER, JOSEF	30	M	FARMER		GRAAHUUSA
GRETL, HEINR	29	M	FARMER		GRAAHUUSA
STUMM, FRAN	64	F	W		GRACLEUSA
KIENTSCH, ROB	17	M	LABR		WMZZZZUSA
SCHNEIDER, CHARLOTTE	20	F	UNKNOWN		GRZZZZUSA
HENSEL, H	17	M	FARMER		GRZZZZUSA
WEBER, FRANZ	23	M	FARMER		BDZZZZUSA
BRANDT, CLEMENS	26	M	FARMER		BDZZZZUSA
STANKEWITZ, ANDR	45	M	FARMER		BDAASSUSA
PAUL	9	M	CHILD		BDAASSUSA
WENDT, JOHN	31	M	LABR		BDAASSUSA
HONN, KARL	41	M	LABR		BDAASSUSA
THEKLA	34	M	W		BDAASSUSA
HUGO	14	M	UNKNOWN		BDAASSUSA
ADOLF	11	M	UNKNOWN		BDAASSUSA
ANNA	8	F	CHILD		BDAASSUSA
EMMA	.06	F	INFANT		BDAASSUSA
KOLLBARZ, CARL	51	M	LABR		GRZZZZUSA
U, CARL	48	M	LABR		GRABPCUSA
SCHULZ, EMILIE	22	F	UNKNOWN		GRZZZZUSA
HAUSCH, EMILIE	17	F	UNKNOWN		WMZZZZUSA
ZDZEBKOWSKI, WLADISLAW	16	M	LABR		GRZZZZUSA
GRAEGE, FRANZ	38	M	LABR		GRZZZZUSA
MARIE	20	F	UNKNOWN		GRZZZZUSA

PASSENGER	AGE	SEX	OCCUPATION	PRVLDES
MANKOWSKI, BOGUSLAW	36	M	LABR	GRZZZZUSA
REJMONIAK, WORZYN	36	M	LABR	GRZZZZUSA
DUCK, PAUL	32	M	LABR	GRZZZZUSA
CHAMPIOMONT, HEINR	14	M	FARMER	GRAARRUSA
HAAKE, ELISE	24	F	UNKNOWN	GRAARRUSA
HEMPEN, META	22	F	UNKNOWN	GRAARRUSA
REHTERT, FRIEDR	29	M	FARMER	GRAARRUSA
URBANSKI, JOS	31	M	LABR	GRZZZZUSA
AGNES	37	F	W	GRZZZZUSA
WLADISLAUS	7	M	CHILD	GRZZZZUSA
STANISLAUS	3	M	CHILD	GRZZZZUSA
MARIANNA	.06	F	INFANT	GRZZZZUSA
DIEMER, MARIA	56	F	UNKNOWN	GRAGNMUSA
WILH	16	F	UNKNOWN	GRAGNMUSA
GRETCHEN	15	F	UNKNOWN	GRAGNMUSA
HOFSTADT, JOH	16	M	UNKNOWN	GRAGNMUSA
STEIN, CATH	17	F	UNKNOWN	BVZZZZUSA
PRUETER, GEORG	26	M	LABR	BVACBRUSA
BERGLER, ANDR	16	M	LABR	BVZZZZUSA
GERDES, AUG	21	M	LABR	GRZZZZUSA
SIEVERS, ALBERT	31	M	LABR	GRACBRUSA
WETT, JOH	26	M	LABR	WMZZZZUSA
WUNSCH, EMIL	24	M	LABR	WMAMBHUSA
STOCKLEIN, LEONARD	40	M	LABR	WMAMBHUSA
WEBER, BERH	18	M	MCHT	GRZZZZUSA
DIENSTMAIER, MATHILDE	27	F	UNKNOWN	GRABOQUSA
BECKER, ALBERT	18	M	MCHT	GRADVHUSA
MEYER, WILH	15	M	MCHT	GRAARRUSA
BUDZYNSKI, FRANZ	39	M	LABR	GRAARRUSA
ROSALIE	33	F	W	GRAARRUSA
MARIE	2	F	CHILD	GRAARRUSA
ROSALIE	.05	F	INFANT	GRAARRUSA
DOLNA, FRANZISKA	20	F	UNKNOWN	GRAARRUSA
KOTETZKI, ANTON	53	M	LABR	GRZZZZUSA
THOMAS	35	M	LABR	GRZZZZUSA
VOSS, ALFRED	20	M	TT	GRACBWUSA

SHIP: BRAUNSCHWEIG

FROM: BREMEN
TO: BALTIMORE
ARRIVED: 06 JUNE 1888

PASSENGER	AGE	SEX	OCCUPATION	PRVLDES
BUCHOLLY, LUCY	11	F	UNKNOWN	GRZZZZBAL
LEICK, JOACHIM	32	M	FARMER	GRZZZZBAL
KULF, U	00	U	UNKNOWN	GRZZZZBAL
FUNGE, FRIEDRIKE	17	F	SVNT	GRZZZZBAL
GUR, ARON	34	M	MCHT	GRZZZZBAL
NACKENHORST, CARL	17	M	LABR	GRZZZZBAL
BUCHOLTZ, FRIEDERICH	21	M	FARMER	GRZZZZBAL
KNOBEL, CARL	19	M	FARMER	GRZZZZBAL
SOBINASCH, MICHEILINA	63	F	UNKNOWN	GRZZZZBAL
JOHANNES	27	M	FARMER	GRZZZZBAL
ANTONIA	23	F	W	GRZZZZBAL
PAKULA, VALENTIN	28	M	SVNT	GRZZZZBAL
WOSOLOWSKI, STANISLAUS	38	M	FARMER	GRZZZZBAL
HEUNSCH, BERNHARD	44	M	FARMER	GRZZZZBAL
MARTHA	32	F	W	GRZZZZBAL
PAULA	.09	F	INFANT	GRZZZZBAL
WALINSKI, JACOB	38	M	FARMER	GRZZZZBAL
SEFERINA	26	F	W	GRZZZZBAL
STANILAWA	5	F	CHILD	GRZZZZBAL
MARYANNA	.11	F	INFANT	GRZZZZBAL
STANISCH, LAURA	32	F	UNKNOWN	GRZZZZBAL
JOHANN	3	M	CHILD	GRZZZZBAL
LAURA	.01	F	INFANT	GRZZZZBAL
GRANITZKI, FRIEDERICH	35	M	FARMER	GRZZZZBAL
CAROLINE	35	F	W	GRZZZZBAL
JOHANNE	11	F	CH	GRZZZZBAL
HERMANN	9	M	CHILD	GRZZZZBAL

PASSENGER	AGE	SEX	OCCUPATION	PRVLDES
MARYANNA	7	F	CHILD	GRZZZZBAL
FRITZ	3	M	CHILD	GRZZZZBAL
AUGUST	.10	M	INFANT	GRZZZZBAL
BESLER, LUDWIG	38	M	FARMER	GRZZZZBAL
CAROLINE	35	F	W	GRZZZZBAL
ROCKEL, BERTHA	20	F	SVNT	GRZZZZBAL
SOPKOWIAK, ANASTASIA	18	F	SVNT	GRZZZZBAL
VICTORIA	10	F	S	GRZZZZBAL
B--USZICK, FRANZISKA	29	F	UNKNOWN	GRZZZZBAL
--CENZ	8	M	CHILD	GRZZZZBAL
BASZYNSKI, MARYANNA	24	F	SVNT	GRZZZZBAL
SCHMITKE, JULIUS	32	M	FARMER	GRZZZZBAL
CAROLINE	30	F	W	GRZZZZBAL
HELENE	6	F	CHILD	GRZZZZBAL
OTTO	4	M	CHILD	GRZZZZBAL
EMMA	2	F	CHILD	GRZZZZBAL
EMIL	.11	M	INFANT	GRZZZZBAL
HOFFMANN, FRANZ	30	M	BKBNDR	GRZZZZBAL
NOGAZEWSKI, LUDWIG	40	M	FARMER	GRZZZZBAL
PIESKICZ, BALBINA	23	F	SVNT	GRZZZZBAL
KATHARINA	20	F	SVNT	GRZZZZBAL
BEYER, CARL	25	M	WCHMKR	GRZZZZBAL
BORUTZKA, PETRONELIA	36	F	UNKNOWN	GRZZZZBAL
MARIANNA	7	F	CHILD	GRZZZZBAL
JOSEF	4	M	CHILD	GRZZZZBAL
JOHANN	2	M	CHILD	GRZZZZBAL
STANISAWA	.09	F	INFANT	GRZZZZBAL
DETLOFF, CARL	54	M	FARMER	GRZZZZOH
EMMA	43	F	W	GRZZZZOH
PAULA	8	F	CHILD	GRZZZZOH
FREIDA	6	F	CHILD	GRZZZZOH
GEORG	5	M	CHILD	GRZZZZOH
IDA	.09	F	INFANT	GRZZZZOH
BRECKI, LOUISA	49	F	UNKNOWN	GRZZZZMI
AUGUSTE	22	F	SVNT	GRZZZZMI
AUGUST	15	M	SVNT	GRZZZZMI
U	11	F	CH	GRZZZZMI
IDA	10	F	CH	GRZZZZMI
REKITZKI, FRIEDERICH	35	M	FARMER	GRZZZZOH
WILHELMINE	38	F	W	GRZZZZOH
OTTO	9	M	CHILD	GRZZZZOH
RUDOLPH	1	M	CHILD	GRZZZZOH
HERMINE	.02	F	INFANT	GRZZZZOH
LISCHOFSKI, MARIE	18	F	SVNT	GRZZZZBAL
BYLINSKI, WOIJCIECH	27	M	FARMER	GRZZZZOH
THEODORE	20	F	W	GRZZZZOH
WICHOWSKA, ANTOINE	11	F	UNKNOWN	GRZZZZOH
USLAR, AGNES	50	F	UNKNOWN	GRZZZZOH
JOHANNE	23	F	SVNT	GRZZZZOH
ANNA	17	F	SVNT	GRZZZZOH
VERONICA	15	F	SVNT	GRZZZZOH
IGNAZ	10	M	CH	GRZZZZOH
FRANZ, AUGUST	66	M	FARMER	GRZZZZOH
WILHEMINE	55	F	W	GRZZZZOH
EMIL	15	M	S	GRZZZZOH
FABLOWSKI, ALEXANDER	32	M	FARMER	GRZZZZWI
FRANZISKA	28	F	W	GRZZZZWI
ANNA	9	F	CHILD	GRZZZZWI
MARIE	5	F	CHILD	GRZZZZWI
BERNHARD	1	M	CHILD	GRZZZZWI
KIPP, JACOB	42	M	TLR	GRZZZZWI
PETZKE, MARTIN	51	M	FARMER	GRZZZZWI
CHRISTINE	53	F	W	GRZZZZWI
BALZER, MARIE	22	F	UNKNOWN	GRZZZZWI
PAULINE	.09	F	INFANT	GRZZZZWI
LEIMHAS, WILHELM	16	M	BCHR	GRZZZZMI
STEMI---, ADAM	32	M	CL	GRZZZZMI
KRAFT, JOHANN	17	M	FARMER	GRZZZZMI
HACHSCHILD, CARL	39	M	FARMER	GRZZZZMI
ZICK, FERDINAND	59	M	FARMER	GRZZZZWI
CAROLINE	51	F	W	GRZZZZWI
AMALIE	23	F	D	GRZZZZWI
FRIEDERICH	16	M	S	GRZZZZWI
HEINRICH	14	M	S	GRZZZZWI
MARIE	11	F	CH	GRZZZZWI

PASSENGER	AGE	SEX	OCCUPATION	PRVVL	DES
AHUTHOLTZ, DIETRICH	15	M	FARMER	GRZZZZWI	
HOEFT, HENRIETTE	52	F	UNKNOWN	GRZZZZWI	
ALWINA	21	F	SVNT	GRZZZZWI	
BERTHA	17	F	SVNT	GRZZZZWI	
SCHULZ, MARIA	20	F	SVNT	GRZZZZWI	
NORLLHOFF, MINNE	22	F	SVNT	GRZZZZBAL	
EICKEMEYER, CARL	15	M	PNTR	GRZZZZBAL	
MEYER, EILERT	64	M	FARMER	GRZZZZNE	
JOHANN	24	F	D	GRZZZZNE	
JACOB, FRIEDERIKE	40	F	UNKNOWN	GRZZZZNE	
ELISE	17	F	D	GRZZZZNE	
FRIOBEL, WILHELMINE	45	F	UNKNOWN	GRZZZZBAL	
WILHELM	11	M	S	GRZZZZBAL	
HEINE, HEINRICH	17	M	FARMER	GRZZZZBAL	
SCHLEICHER, JOHANN	38	M	FARMER	GRZZZZMD	
CAROLINE	42	F	W	GRZZZZMD	
IDA	3	F	CHILD	GRZZZZMD	
SUNDERMANN, MINNA	24	F	SVNT	GRZZZZIN	
BURDORF, WILHELM	27	M	PNTR	GRZZZZIN	
SCHLIEMANN, HEINRICH	36	M	BRR	GRZZZZBAL	
GUTZKE, JOHANN	28	M	FARMER	GRZZZZBAL	
WALBEL, AUGUST	36	M	FARMER	GRZZZZBAL	
WILHELMINE	23	F	W	GRZZZZBAL	
U	.01	F	INFANT	GRZZZZBAL	
SCHLEIMANN, FRIEDRICH	23	M	FARMER	GRZZZZBAL	
UTECHT, AUGUST	32	M	FARMER	GRZZZZBAL	
JOHANNE	36	F	W	GRZZZZBAL	
LOUISE	.09	F	INFANT	GRZZZZBAL	
GEORG	.09	M	INFANT	GRZZZZBAL	
BERNDT, IDA	19	F	SVNT	GRZZZZUNK	
TIETZ, HULDA	20	F	SVNT	GRZZZZUNK	
SCHERBARTH, WILHELM	58	M	FARMER	GRZZZZUSA	
HENRIETTE	56	F	W	GRZZZZUSA	
ZOBEL, MINNA	21	F	SVNT	GRZZZZOH	
EMIL	17	M	BCHR	GRZZZZOH	
GUSTAV	12	M	BCHR	GRZZZZOH	
SCHUFBERGER, THERESE	33	F	UNKNOWN	GRZZZZOH	
JOSEF	5	M	CHILD	GRZZZZOH	
JOHANNE	3	F	CHILD	GRZZZZOH	
HAVER	1	M	CHILD	GRZZZZOH	
HEINDL, RASMUS	26	M	BCHR	GRZZZZOH	
EYGEL, MARIA	28	F	UNKNOWN	GRZZZZWI	
THERESIA	3	F	CHILD	GRZZZZWI	
KUSLER, GEORG	14	M	UNKNOWN	GRZZZZWI	
SCHLUFLEIN, BENEDICT	22	M	FARMER	GRZZZZWI	
BARBARA	24	F	W	GRZZZZWI	
SUSANNA	.09	F	INFANT	GRZZZZWI	
ZENK, JOHANN	28	M	FARMER	GRZZZZWI	
HERTLEIN, MARGARETHE	25	F	SVNT	GRZZZZWI	
SCHNICK, FRIEDRICH	45	M	FARMER	GRZZZZIN	
SIEBOLD, ADOLF	16	M	FARMER	GRZZZZIN	
GUNTHER, NICOLAUS	40	M	FARMER	GRZZZZIN	
JOHANNE	43	F	W	GRZZZZIN	
GEORG	12	M	CH	GRZZZZIN	
MATHILDE	2	F	CHILD	GRZZZZIN	
ZIEGLER, MARIE	18	F	SVNT	GRZZZZBAL	
VERGANER, GEORG	24	M	FARMER	GRZZZZBAL	
SCHMITTELOSCH, FRIEDRIC	24	M	FARMER	GRZZZZBAL	
SCHWAMMER, ANDREUS	15	M	FARMER	GRZZZZBAL	
RAUSCHENBUGER, ANNA	17	F	SVNT	GRZZZZBAL	
KRENTZER, GEORG	25	M	TLR	GRZZZZIA	
LEIN, JOHANN	30	M	BRR	GRZZZZIA	
JAST, MARIA	26	F	SVNT	GRZZZZIA	
KORDING, JUSTINE	16	F	SVNT	GRZZZZIA	
KNOST, ELISE	25	F	SVNT	GRZZZZBAL	
STRACIL-, JOSEF	24	M	FARMER	GRZZZZBAL	
TANACH, JULIUS	23	M	FARMER	GRZZZZBAL	
WENGELEIT, MARYANNA	33	F	UNKNOWN	GRZZZZWI	
LUDWIG	9	M	CHILD	GRZZZZWI	
ANNA	3	F	CHILD	GRZZZZWI	
MIKIS, ELISABETH	25	F	UNKNOWN	GRZZZZOH	
ELISABETH	.11	F	INFANT	GRZZZZOH	
FLAX, MARGARITHE	19	F	SVNT	GRZZZZOH	
RUASHINSKI, JAN	18	M	FARMER	GRZZZZTX	
OZNISKI, WOIZECH	32	M	FARMER	GRZZZZTX	
NAETEYEWSKI, AUGUSTE	32	F	UNKNOWN	GRZZZZTX	
STEFAN	.06	M	INFANT	GRZZZZTX	
PILTZ, VICTORIA	34	F	UNKNOWN	GRZZZZWI	
ANNA	5	F	CHILD	GRZZZZWI	
MARYANNA	2	F	CHILD	GRZZZZWI	
FISKUS, ELISE	23	F	SVNT	GRZZZZWI	
SULER, FRIEDRICH	50	M	FARMER	GRZZZZMD	
SIEHLER, MARIE	15	F	SVNT	GRZZZZMD	
MULLER, OTTO	43	M	FARMER	GRZZZZPA	
WILHELMINE	42	F	W	GRZZZZPA	
ADOLF	11	M	CH	GRZZZZPA	
LINCHEN	8	F	CHILD	GRZZZZPA	
MARIE	4	F	CHILD	GRZZZZPA	
OTTO	3	M	CHILD	GRZZZZPA	
ANNA	2	F	CHILD	GRZZZZPA	
ERNST	1	M	CHILD	GRZZZZPA	
JABLOUSKI, STANISLAUS	24	M	FARMER	GRZZZZUSA	
REZENT, PAUL	43	M	BRR	GRZZZZPA	
KETZ, GORRFRIED	38	M	FARMER	GRZZZZPA	
HENRIETTE	40	F	W	GRZZZZPA	
BERTHA	12	F	CH	GRZZZZPA	
EMMA	3	F	CHILD	GRZZZZPA	
LUTZKI, THOMAS	26	M	FARMER	GRZZZZPA	
AGNES	25	F	W	GRZZZZPA	
MARIE	.07	F	INFANT	GRZZZZPA	
HUNGERBICHL, FRIEDERICH	19	M	TLR	GRZZZZOH	
BERTSCH, EMILIE	20	F	SVNT	GRZZZZIA	
SCHAFER, MARIA	17	F	SVNT	GRZZZZIA	
SEILER, CATHARINA	24	F	SVNT	GRZZZZIA	
OTZEN, AGNES	23	F	SVNT	GRZZZZBAL	
FRASIK, CECILIA	28	F	SVNT	GRZZZZMN	
MULLER, BERTHA	17	F	SVNT	GRZZZZMN	
FEUCHLER, CAROLINE	22	F	SVNT	GRZZZZMN	
GRIEPENSHOH, CHRISTIAN	16	M	FARMER	GRZZZZMI	
DOEHLER, TRANGOTT	56	M	FARMER	GRZZZZMI	
FREESE, HEINRICH	16	M	FARMER	GRZZZZOH	
LEISER, ALOIS	22	M	TLR	GRZZZZOH	
DIEHL, FRANZ	13	M	UNKNOWN	GRZZZZOH	
SCHMUCK, LOUISE	43	F	UNKNOWN	GRZZZZNE	
BORCK, JOHANNES	13	M	UNKNOWN	GRZZZZNE	
BERGNER, GEORG	17	M	FARMER	GRZZZZNE	
KENDRUP, CHRISTIAN	30	M	FARMER	GRZZZZNE	
ANNA	39	F	W	GRZZZZNE	
HEINRICH	8	M	CHILD	GRZZZZNE	
FUENG, VINCENZ	27	M	BCHR	GRZZZZPA	
SCHAFER, WILHELM	24	M	FARMER	GRZZZZPA	
WEDEMANN, FERDINAND	20	M	FARMER	GRZZZZIL	
FEFSE, FIEDERICH	43	M	FARMER	GRZZZZIL	
EMILIE	42	F	W	GRZZZZIL	
THEODOR	18	M	S	GRZZZZIL	
EDUARD	11	M	CH	GRZZZZIL	
OLGA	8	F	CHILD	GRZZZZIL	
BERTHA	7	F	CHILD	GRZZZZIL	
JULIUS	4	M	CHILD	GRZZZZIL	
ADOLF	3	M	CHILD	GRZZZZIL	
GUSTAV	.11	M	INFANT	GRZZZZIL	
FEIGER, EMILIE	28	F	UNKNOWN	GRZZZZIL	
KARL	4	M	CHILD	GRZZZZIL	
PAUL	2	M	CHILD	GRZZZZIL	
OTTO	.09	M	INFANT	GRZZZZIL	
STRAUP, OSCAR	27	M	CL	GRZZZZBAL	
KELLNER, ALBERT	22	M	BCHR	GRZZZZPA	
LIEBHARDT, LOUIS	27	M	BKLYR	GRZZZZPA	
HELGENS, JOHANN	18	M	SHMK	GRZZZZPA	
EICHHORER, OTTO	38	M	FARMER	GRZZZZIA	
LUDWIG, KONRAD	17	M	BRR	GRZZZZUSA	
HAFKE, JRANZ	38	M	FARMER	GRZZZZIA	
MARGARETHE	43	F	W	GRZZZZIA	
WILKE, FERDINAND	22	M	SHMK	GRZZZZIA	
BAROSINSKI, MATTHEUS	36	M	FARMER	GRZZZZMD	
MARYANNA	40	F	W	GRZZZZMD	
MARYANNA	11	F	CH	GRZZZZMD	
VERONICA	1	F	CHILD	GRZZZZMD	
LEOCADIA	.02	F	INFANT	GRZZZZMD	
SCHEIN, ELISABETH	43	F	UNKNOWN	GRZZZZMD	

PASSENGER	AGE	SEX	OCCUPATION	PVL	DES
ELISABETH	16	F	D		GRZZZZMD
BARBARA	9	F	CHILD		GRZZZZMD
MARIE	4	F	CHILD		GRZZZZMD
BOTTCHER, WILHELM	23	M	FARMER		GRZZZZMD
MICHULKE, FRANZ	34	M	FARMER		GRZZZZIL
HULDA	28	F	W		GRZZZZIL
CECILIA	4	F	CHILD		GRZZZZIL
ALBERT	3	M	CHILD		GRZZZZIL
MARIA	.11	F	INFANT		GRZZZZIL
SCHALK, JOHANN	28	M	BKR		GRZZZZIL
ANGERMEIER, JOSEF	26	M	FARMER		GRZZZZIL
FRANZISKA	24	F	W		GRZZZZIL
DEPANER, CARL	42	M	SMH		GRZZZZPA
CARL	16	M	S		GRZZZZPA
FRIEDERICH	9	M	CHILD		GRZZZZPA
THEIP, DANIEL	21	M	CL		GRZZZZPA
ELISABETH	15	F	S		GRZZZZPA
KRAUTH, ELISABETH	22	F	SVNT		GRZZZZPA
BEILTHUS, BEREND	28	M	FARMER		GRZZZZNE
ROTHER, ANNA	21	F	SVNT		GRZZZZAL
RIEGER, CARL	18	M	FARMER		GRZZZZPA
PACHEL, AUGUST	24	M	PNTR		GRZZZZPA
FUCHS, GOTTFRIED	55	M	FARMER		GRZZZZWI
JUSTINE	50	F	W		GRZZZZWI
BEIMLER, THOMAS	30	M	BKR		GRZZZZMN
REGER, MARIA	30	F	UNKNOWN		GRZZZZMN
ANNA	2	F	CHILD		GRZZZZMN
ZIMMERMANN, THERESE	27	F	SVNT		GRZZZZMN
BAUSER, CATHARINA	58	F	SVNT		GRZZZZMN
WEGIEL, FRANZISKA	23	F	SVNT		GRZZZZBAL
WULF, ELISE	18	F	SVNT		GRZZZZBAL
KUPTY, JOHANN	19	M	FARMER		GRZZZZBAL
WALDOW, EMIL	16	M	CL		GRZZZZBAL
ULRIKE	14	F	S		GRZZZZBAL
WOLF, HERMANN	39	M	FARMER		GRZZZZWI
LOUISE	35	F	W		GRZZZZWI
ALWINE	16	F	D		GRZZZZWI
HEDWIG	9	F	CHILD		GRZZZZWI
ARNDE.	7	M	CHILD		GRZZZZWI
CHRISTIAN	4	M	CHILD		GRZZZZWI
AUGUSTE	.11	F	INFANT		GRZZZZWI
DOPKIN, ANNA	24	F	SVNT		GRZZZZIL
SULLER, JOHANN	16	M	FARMER		GRZZZZMI
LAMPERT, WILHELM	21	M	FARMER		GRZZZZMI
VOIGL, JOSEF	22	M	FARMER		GRZZZZMI
BRUCKMEYER, FRIEDERICH	18	M	SHMK		GRZZZZNE
GOTHALLMANN, SOPHIE	20	F	SVNT		GRZZZZNE
BARTEL, GUSTAV	25	M	FARMER		GRZZZZTX
ADELINE	26	F	W		GRZZZZTX
PICHL, EMILIE	18	F	SVNT		GRZZZZBAL
METZKER, FRIEDERICH	48	M	FARMER		GRZZZZWI
MARIANNA	48	F	W		GRZZZZWI
CHRISTIAN	18	M	S		GRZZZZWI
JENNNETTE	14	F	D		GRZZZZWI
EDUARD	9	M	CHILD		GRZZZZWI
EVA	4	F	CHILD		GRZZZZWI
PINNER, PETER	29	M	FARMER		GRZZZZWI
WILHELMINE	25	F	W		GRZZZZWI
SCHMIDT, PHILIPINE	22	F	UNKNOWN		GRZZZZWI
CHARLOTTE	.03	F	INFANT		GRZZZZWI
REGENSBURGER, ALOIS	28	M	TLR		GRZZZZBAL
UTECHT, CARL	63	M	FARMER		GRZZZZNE
HEINRIETTE	59	F	W		GRZZZZNE
AUGUSTE	17	F	D		GRZZZZNE
FERDINAND	25	M	FARMER		GRZZZZNE
BERTHA	27	F	W		GRZZZZNE
FERDINAND	6	M	CHILD		GRZZZZNE
TIFILSKI, THECKLA	27	F	UNKNOWN		GRZZZZIL
JOHANN	6	M	CHILD		GRZZZZIL
MARIE	4	F	CHILD		GRZZZZIL
MAX	3	M	CHILD		GRZZZZIL
MARTHA	.11	F	INFANT		GRZZZZIL
KESSEL, PHILOPP	15	M	UNKNOWN		GRZZZZIL
HAUBACH, AUGUST	25	M	BKR		GRZZZZMI
HEIN, LEONHARD	21	M	SMH		GRZZZZMI
HARTUNG, ELISE	55	F	UNKNOWN		GRZZZZMI
HOCHSCHILD, JOHANN	35	M	FARMER		GRZZZZMI
EMILIE	25	F	W		GRZZZZMI
HERMANN	8	M	CHILD		GRZZZZMI
ROBERT	4	M	CHILD		GRZZZZMI
MATHILDE	2	F	CHILD		GRZZZZIA
MEITZEL, AUGUST	24	M	FARMER		GRZZZZIA
HERMANN, FRANZ	25	M	FARMER		GRZZZZIA
SLOTTAG, HERMANN	16	M	FARMER		GRZZZZMI
PAJEKOWSKI, ANTON	40	M	FARMER		GRZZZZMI
MARYANNA	37	F	W		GRZZZZMI
JULIANNA	11	F	CH		GRZZZZMI
SALOMEN	9	F	CHILD		GRZZZZMI
WLADISLAW	3	M	CHILD		GRZZZZMI
PAUL	.03	M	INFANT		GRZZZZMI
KUTTER, PAULINE	23	F	SVNT		GRZZZZMI
SCHUPRITT, MARIE	23	F	SVNT		GRZZZZMI
SCHMOTZER, JOHANN	25	M	PNTR		GRZZZZWI
FESCHER, CARL	58	M	FARMER		GRZZZZKS
CAROLINE	57	F	W		GRZZZZKS
JENRIETTE	32	F	L		GRZZZZKS
CARL	10	M	CH		GRZZZZKS
WALLMULLER, FRIEDRICH	28	M	BRR		GRZZZZIL
REGENSBURGER, CARL	26	M	BCHR		GRZZZZIL
SCHILLING, JACOB	23	M	FARMER		GRZZZZIL
FRIEDMANN, BARBARA	24	F	SVNT		GRZZZZMI
MARCK, MARGARETHA	27	F	UNKNOWN		GRZZZZMI
ANNA	2	F	CHILD		GRZZZZMI
FRISHOLZ, CATHARINA	15	F	SVNT		GRZZZZIN
SILKER, ANNA	28	F	UNKNOWN		GRZZZZIN
JOHANN	3	M	CHILD		GRZZZZIN
WILHELM	.09	M	INFANT		GRZZZZIN
DIETZ, JOHANN	56	M	FARMER		GRZZZZWI
MULLER, ADAM	38	M	FARMER		GRZZZZPA
ANNA	31	F	W		GRZZZZPA
ELISABETH	9	F	CHILD		GRZZZZPA
CLARA	7	F	CHILD		GRZZZZPA
MARIA	5	F	CHILD		GRZZZZPA
APOLLONIA	2	F	CHILD		GRZZZZPA
WICKENHOFER, MARIA	25	F	UNKNOWN		GRZZZZIA
EMIL	8	M	CHILD		GRZZZZIA
WEMPE, FRITZ	33	M	FARMER		GRZZZZMD
MARIA	31	F	W		GRZZZZMD
HEINRICH	7	M	CHILD		GRZZZZMD
MARIA	5	F	CHILD		GRZZZZMD
ANNA	4	F	CHILD		GRZZZZMD
FRIEDRICH	2	M	CHILD		GRZZZZMD
THEODOR	6	M	CHILD		GRZZZZMD
WOLTER, CARL	40	M	BKLYR		GRZZZZBAL
SCHEMANSKI, JOHANN	17	M	TLR		GRZZZZBAL
MANKOFSKI, FRANZ	17	M	FARMER		GRZZZZIA
STRUBE, HENRIETTE	21	F	SVNT		GRZZZZBAL
PAWLOWSKA, JOSEFA	22	F	UNKNOWN		GRZZZZIA
MARTIN	.09	M	INFANT		GRZZZZIA
POWIERSKA, JULIANA	28	F	UNKNOWN		GRZZZZIA
FRANZ	9	M	CHILD		GRZZZZIA
ROSALIE	7	F	CHILD		GRZZZZIA
SZYEWSKA, MARUANNA	30	F	UNKNOWN		GRZZZZOH
JOSEF	8	M	CHILD		GRZZZZOH
PREUSS, MICHAEL	44	M	FARMER		GRZZZZOH
DICK, HERMANN	60	M	FARMER		GRZZZZWI
FRANZISKA	57	F	W		GRZZZZWI
SIMON, JOHANNA	28	F	UNKNOWN		GRZZZZBAL
HERMANN	7	M	CHILD		GRZZZZBAL
EMMA	4	F	CHILD		GRZZZZBAL
MATHILDE	.01	F	INFANT		GRZZZZBAL
JALEK, JOHANN	61	M	FARMER		GRZZZZBAL
CARL	28	M	FARMER		GRZZZZBAL
MATHILDE	20	F	W		GRZZZZBAL
ALBRECHT, RICHARD	32	M	FARMER		GRZZZZBAL
MARTHA	20	F	W		GRZZZZBAL
RICHARD	.02	M	INFANT		GRZZZZBAL
MICHAELSKI, ANTON	25	M	SHMK		GRZZZZBAL
BOHNEUSTECK, MARGARETHA	18	F	SVNT		GRZZZZBAL
LENZ, WILHELM	34	M	FARMER		GRZZZZIA

PASSENGER	AGE	SEX	OCCUPATION	PRVL	DES
AUGUSTE	30	F	W		GRZZZZIA
GUSTAV	5	M	CHILD		GRZZZZIA
BERTHA	.10	F	INFANT		GRZZZZIA
TRAHN, GUSTAV	17	M	FARMER		GRZZZZIA
SPIHRER, JOHANN	38	M	FARMER		GRZZZZWI
SEIFERT, BARBARA	23	F	SVNT		GRZZZZOH
LIPPOLD, MARGARETHE	24	F	SVNT		GRZZZZOH
LUHER, ELISABETH	28	F	SVNT		GRZZZZOH
SIESS, SIMON	22	M	CL		GRZZZZCH
SCHWEIGER, JOHANN	19	M	BKR		GRZZZZCH
WLETSCHALK, MICHAEL	27	M	FARMER		GRZZZZOH
HENRIETTE	27	F	W		GRZZZZOH
ANNA	4	F	CHILD		GRZZZZOH
PAULINE	.11	F	INFANT		GRZZZZOH
REUZELSKI, MICHAEL	28	M	FARMER		GRZZZZWI
FRANZISKA	27	F	W		GRZZZZWI
ANTON	2	M	CHILD		GRZZZZWI
JOSEF	.09	M	INFANT		GRZZZZWI
VOSS, FRANZISKA	26	F	UNKNOWN		GRZZZZBAL
PAULINE	3	F	CHILD		GRZZZZBAL
KOHLER, MATTHEAS	26	M	FARMER		GRZZZZMD
BERCKUNER, DIETRICH	29	M	FARMER		GRZZZZMD
SCHULTZ, CHRISIAN	26	M	FARMER		GRZZZZMD
ADOLF	22	M	MUSN		GRZZZZMD
BLASSE, EMILIE	40	F	UNKNOWN		GRZZZZMD
AMALIE	18	F	D		GRZZZZMD
ROSALIE	10	F	CH		GRZZZZMD
FRANZ	7	M	CHILD		GRZZZZMD
JOSEF	4	M	CHILD		GRZZZZMD
GUSTAV	1	M	CHILD		GRZZZZMD
ZEMKE, CARL	33	M	FARMER		GRZZZZWI
AUGUSTE	27	F	W		GRZZZZWI
MATHILDE	7	F	CHILD		GRZZZZWI
ELISE	4	F	CHILD		GRZZZZWI
ANNA	2	F	CHILD		GRZZZZWI
GERTRUD	.06	F	INFANT		GRZZZZWI
MEINHARDT, KARL	27	M	FARMER		GRZZZZOH
AUGUSTE	22	F	W		GRZZZZOH
KARL	4	M	CHILD		GRZZZZOH
MARIE	.10	F	INFANT		GRZZZZOH
STEMBAUER, LEONHARD	50	M	FARMER		GRZZZZOH
MARGARETHE	48	F	W		GRZZZZOH
KUNIGUNDE	22	F	D		GRZZZZOH
JOHANN	19	M	S		GRZZZZOH
MARIA	16	F	D		GRZZZZOH
MARGARETHA	15	F	D		GRZZZZOH
BABETTE	14	F	D		GRZZZZOH
BAUM, CARLINE	84	F	UNKNOWN		GRZZZZBAL
RENATA	23	F	D		GRZZZZBAL
BEHLKE, HERMANN	15	M	PNTR		GRZZZZBAL
EMILIE	20	F	SVNT		GRZZZZBAL
HILLMANN, CARL	60	M	FARMER		GRZZZZBAL
RIEGER, VERONIKA	21	F	SVNT		GRZZZZMD
HILSE, GOTTFRIED	60	M	FARMER		GRZZZZMD
ANNA	55	F	W		GRZZZZMD
WENZEL, IDA	18	F	SVNT		GRZZZZMD
MOST, EMIL	18	M	BKR		GRZZZZMD
LEUCHTMANN, EDUARD	33	M	SHMK		GRZZZZWI
GATH, ERNESTINE	23	F	SVNT		GRZZZZIA
FLEISCHER, BERTHA	23	F	SVNT		GRZZZZIA
BUSCH, MARGARETHA	20	F	SVNT		GRZZZZIA
DOETTERMANN, CARL	30	M	FARMER		GRZZZZMI
BUCHNER, FIEDA	36	F	SVNT		GRZZZZMI
GRAF, ELISABETH	14	F	SVNT		GRZZZZMN
PILENZ, OTTO	28	M	FARMER		GRZZZZMN
MICHAELSKI, STEFAN	26	M	FARMER		GRZZZZMN
JOSEFA	21	F	W		GRZZZZMN
VICTORIA	.06	F	INFANT		GRZZZZMN
KUZKOWSKA, JULIAN	25	M	BKLYR		GRZZZZOH
DEYN, MARIE	20	F	SVNT		GRZZZZOH
MATHILDE	18	F	SVNT		GRZZZZOH
PUFHL, HENRIETTE	26	F	SVNT		GRZZZZMN
KUMPTZ, AUGUST	23	M	CK		GRZZZZIA
MAKOSKI, JOHANES	14	M	SHMK		GRZZZZIA
MARGARETHA	10	F	S		GRZZZZIA

PASSENGER	AGE	SEX	OCCUPATION	PRVL	DES
LEIMEN, HEINRICH	15	M	FARMER		GRZZZZTX
BOLUCZUTE, ANNA	22	F	SVNT		GRZZZZNE
BARANOWSKA, FRANZISKA	38	F	UNKNOWN		GRZZZZBAL
ANNA	.11	F	INFANT		GRZZZZBAL
SABLAWSKA, MARIE	19	F	SVNT		GRZZZZMD
SCHWANTKOWSKA, ANNA	51	F	UNKNOWN		GRZZZZIN
DORA	14	F	CH		GRZZZZIN
ROSALIE	6	F	CHILD		GRZZZZIN
RINGEL, ANNA	18	F	SVNT		GRZZZZWI
LOMKER, FRITZ	36	M	FARMER		GRZZZZNE
MARIE	34	F	W		GRZZZZNE
FRITZ	15	M	S		GRZZZZNE
MARIE	11	F	CH		GRZZZZNE
JOHANN	4	M	CHILD		GRZZZZNE
HELENE	2	F	CHILD		GRZZZZNE
GEISENBERGER, JOHANN	17	M	BCHR		GRZZZZBAL
TEWS, FRIEDERIKE	63	F	UNKNOWN		GRZZZZOH
DANIEL	24	M	FARMER		GRZZZZOH
GALL, JOHANN	40	M	PNTR		GRZZZZOH
IDA	36	F	W		GRZZZZOH
ANNA	10	F	CH		GRZZZZOH
EPPICH, M.	23	M	UNKNOWN		GRZZZZIA
HOGE, ANTON	25	M	BKR		GRZZZZIA
GLASER, JOHANN	27	M	FARMER		GRZZZZIA
STANICHEWSKI, JOHANN	19	M	FARMER		GRZZZZIA
VETTER, JOHANNE	35	F	UNKNOWN		GRZZZZBAL
SCHWEINNER, GEORG	17	M	FARMER		GRZZZZMN
HUNOWIE, JOHANN	18	M	LABR		GRZZZZKS

SHIP: STATE OF NEVADA

FROM: GLASGOW AND LARNE
TO: NEW YORK
ARRIVED: 06 JUNE 1888

PASSENGER	AGE	SEX	OCCUPATION	PRVL	DES
DORER, WM.	37	M	WCHMKR		GRAHRZUSA
DORA	20	F	UNKNOWN		GRAHRZUSA
CARL	6	M	CHILD		GRAHRZUSA
WILHELM	4	M	CHILD		GRAHRZUSA
LOUISE	.08	F	INFANT		GRAHRZUSA
SELBIGER, JOSEF	22	M	MCHT		GRAHRZUSA

SHIP: THE QUEEN

FROM: LIVERPOOL AND QUEENSTOWN
TO: NEW YORK
ARRIVED: 06 JUNE 1888

PASSENGER	AGE	SEX	OCCUPATION	PRVL	DES
ALEXANDER, MORVAN	18	M	LABR		FRZZZZBO
SMIDT, HERMAN	28	M	LABR		GRZZZZBO
HEINER, JAMES	31	M	LABR		GRACBFNY
MARTENS, FRED	36	M	LABR		GRACBFNY
SCHMIDT, PAULINE	48	F	SP		GRZZZZNY
WEISS, JOSEPH	24	M	LABR		GRZZZZPHI
NOWICKI, AGNES	16	F	SP		GRZZZZNY
STEIN	14	F	SP		GRZZZZNY
MENDELSOHN, JACOB	17	M	LABR		GRZZZZNY
JERWASCOMA, S.	17	M	LABR		GRZZZZNY

135

PASSENGER	AGE	SEX	OCCUPATION	PRVL	DES

SHIP: CITY OF ROME

FROM: LIVERPOOL AND QUEENSTOWN
TO: NEW YORK
ARRIVED: 07 JUNE 1888

PASSENGER	AGE	SEX	OCCUPATION	PRVL	DES
MENGES, A.	37	M	GENT		GRADAXUSA
SPIELER, FAVONI	35	F	SVNT		GRADAXUSA
MUSAS, ILZIG	30	M	PNTR		GRADAXUSA
VIETORSDHER, ISRAEL	52	M	FARMER		GRADAXUSA
CHAIE	52	F	W		GRADAXUSA
FRIEDE	10	M	CH		GRADAXUSA
DAVID	9	M	CHILD		GRADAXUSA
LANSDMAN, ADOLF	30	M	CL		GRADAXUSA
LINDBERG, PETER	19	M	LABR		GRADAXUSA
BORNIK, MICHLINE	50	F	W		GRADAXUSA
TAYBE	11	F	CH		GRADAXUSA
KOHN, ISAK	20	M	LABR		GRADAXUSA
SILLERMAN, CLARA	23	F	SVNT		GRADAXUSA
ZARASKI, ALEX	24	M	LABR		GRADAXUSA
TELS, JOHN	20	M	LABR		GRADAXUSA
COCK, EVANGELINE	27	M	FARMER		GRADAXUSA
ALLEN, W.	31	M	LABR		GRADAXUSA

SHIP: AMSTERDAM

FROM: ROTTERDAM
TO: NEW YORK
ARRIVED: 08 JUNE 1888

PASSENGER	AGE	SEX	OCCUPATION	PRVL	DES
ELSEN, BERTHA	32	F	NN		GRZZZZUSA
KLINGHORST, WILLEM	17	M	MCHT		GRZZZZUSA
HAGEN, JOHAN	60	M	SHMK		GRZZZZUSA
CATHA	58	F	NN		GRZZZZUSA
HOFFMAN, JOSEF	36	M	CLLR		GRZZZZUSA
KLENK, JOHAN	22	M	AHR		GRZZZZUSA
KARG, U	24	M	MCHT		GRZZZZUSA
HOLL, U	16	M	MCHT		GRZZZZUSA
SCHERR, GERARD	30	M	AHR		GRZZZZUSA
ARMANN, ANNA	14	F	NN		GRZZZZUSA
THEO	17	F	NN		GRZZZZUSA
BRIUNEY, CATH	24	F	NN		GRZZZZUSA
WERTZ, MARTHA	21	F	NN		GRZZZZUSA
STEIN, AUGUST	22	M	MCHT		GRZZZZUSA
SCHLANDEROCH, ALFRED	23	M	MCHT		GRZZZZUSA
STEINHARDT, JOHANNA	39	F	NN		GRZZZZUSA
OLGA	19	M	NN		GRZZZZUSA
ELISE	8	M	CHILD		GRZZZZUSA
KRAFT, ABRAM	31	M	MCHT		GRZZZZUSA
KILGUS, CAT-	26	F	NN		GRZZZZUSA
SIEGLER, ABRAM	17	M	NN		GRZZZZUSA
METZ, JOHAN	23	M	LABR		GRZZZZUSA
VETTER, JOSEF	27	M	LABR		GRZZZZUSA
-AFER, CAREL	65	M	CPTR		GRZZZZUSA
BRUESSEL, LOUISE	23	F	NN		GRZZZZUSA
--ALLONE, SALVATORE	32	M	LABR		FRZZZZUSA
RINALDI, ANTONIO	30	M	LABR		FRZZZZUSA
RITACCA, LUIGI	30	M	LABR		FRZZZZUSA
CUR--O, SABINO	27	M	LABR		FRZZZZUSA
CARAMICO, JACINTO	27	M	LABR		FRZZZZUSA
GENIGONE, GERARDO	25	M	LABR		FRZZZZUSA
MARZUCO, ROSIANCO	22	M	LABR		FRZZZZUSA
TAMBORINO, GUISEPPI	23	M	LABR		FRZZZZUSA
P-PPI, ALDERICO	30	M	LABR		FRZZZZUSA
LENGOTTI, LUIGI	34	M	LABR		FRZZZZUSA
CARLO	23	M	LABR		FRZZZZUSA
BERTOGLEO, FRANCESCO	28	M	LABR		FRZZZZUSA
JANBLANC, ARSENE	35	M	LABR		FRZZZZUSA
GARTE, CHARLES	54	M	LABR		FRZZZZUSA

PASSENGER	AGE	SEX	OCCUPATION	PRVL	DES
PUTART, PETRURS	55	M	LABR		FRZZZZUSA
MACHESIELLE, GIULIANO	25	M	LABR		FRZZZZUSA
ROCCO	8	M	CHILD		FRZZZZUSA
VES-AVO, GUI-ES	28	M	LABR		FRZZZZUSA
-ERASSO, FRANCESCO	19	M	LABR		FRZZZZUSA
ORECCHIO, ANTONIO	23	M	LABR		FRZZZZUSA
PIEDRADO--O, TOR-ASO	20	M	LABR		FRZZZZUSA
GENANO, PERILLO	30	M	LABR		FRZZZZUSA
-ETTOLO, GIOVANNI	23	M	LABR		FRZZZZUSA
SCHUER, OTTO	18	M	LABR		FRZZZZUSA
COSTANTINE, GIUSEPPE	30	M	LABR		FRZZZZUSA
FRESI, PIETRO	36	M	LABR		FRZZZZUSA
FERRARI, ANTONIO	40	M	LABR		FRZZZZUSA
MIUNCK, CHARLES	25	M	LABR		FRZZZZUSA
COUTI, PAOLO	32	M	LABR		FRZZZZUSA
CELLA, LUIGI	40	M	LABR		FRZZZZUSA
-ACOMAUNA, PASQUALI	29	M	LABR		FRZZZZUSA
FRANCESCO	24	M	LABR		FRZZZZUSA
ZANELLI, GIUSEPPE	40	M	LABR		FRZZZZUSA
TORELLI, GIUSEPPE	25	M	LABR		FRZZZZUSA
CORBELLINI, DOMINICO	25	M	LABR		FRZZZZUSA
MARCELLINA	17	F	NN		FRZZZZUSA
TERESA	13	F	NN		FRZZZZUSA
ARMADINI, PIETRO	30	M	LABR		FRZZZZUSA
PALMINA	23	F	NN		FRZZZZUSA
MORELLI, GIUSEPPE	26	M	LABR		FRZZZZUSA
MARIANI, GENOVEVA	51	F	SVNT		FRZZZZUSA
CATHERINA	48	F	SVNT		FRZZZZUSA
ARMALINGER, JOSEPH	18	M	LABR		GRZZZZUSA
GROSZ, JOSEPH	20	M	LABR		GRZZZZUSA
FRIEMANN, JULIE	36	F	SVNT		GRZZZZUSA
ES-I	18	F	SVNT		GRZZZZUSA
ESHE--A	15	F	SVNT		GRZZZZUSA
SAMUEL	11	M	CH		GRZZZZUSA
ISIDOR	7	M	CHILD		GRZZZZUSA
DAVID	5	M	CHILD		GRZZZZUSA
VERONIKA	4	F	CHILD		GRZZZZUSA
ANNA	2	F	CHILD		GRZZZZUSA
ESTER	.06	F	INFANT		GRZZZZUSA
ZUCKER, FANNY	20	F	SVNT		GRZZZZUSA
HOLZMANN, HERMINA	22	F	SVNT		GRZZZZUSA
ECKHARDT, LOUIS	17	M	LABR		GRZZZZUSA
LECHOWITZ, LEON	35	M	LABR		GRZZZZUSA
CORDES, HERWANA	22	M	LABR		GRZZZZUSA
AR-DY--IS, PAULES	40	M	LABR		GRZZZZUSA
OL-, GEORGE	32	M	LABR		GRZZZZUSA
PALINSKY, ANDREAS	32	M	LABR		GRZZZZUSA
JANOWSKI, ERNST	26	M	LABR		GRZZZZUSA
-IGLE-IS, IGNACE	34	M	LABR		GRZZZZUSA
KULOWITZ, FLORIAN	30	M	LABR		GRZZZZUSA
ZA-IDSKI, ISRAEL	44	M	LABR		GRZZZZUSA
RUDKOWSKY, SAMUEL	35	M	LABR		GRZZZZUSA
KOWALSKI, KASIMIR	37	M	LABR		GRZZZZUSA
SZOLODSKI, KASIMIR	38	M	LABR		GRZZZZUSA
CHONOWSKI, VINCENT	18	M	LABR		GRZZZZUSA
RUETZKIN, FRITZ	25	M	LABR		GRZZZZUSA
F--ND, BER-E	20	M	LABR		GRZZZZUSA
SENTHEIL, CARL	25	M	LABR		GRZZZZUSA
-UKAK, CONSTANTIN	24	M	LABR		GRZZZZUSA
SWITZ, ISAAC	26	M	LABR		GRZZZZUSA
SANDMANN, GUSTAV	17	M	LABR		GRZZZZUSA
LUDWIG	17	M	LABR		GRZZZZUSA
W---ROWSKY, JAN	40	M	LABR		GRZZZZUSA
PETER	40	M	LABR		GRZZZZUSA
JANOWITZ, JOHAN	28	M	LABR		GRZZZZUSA
KLOPPENBURG, EILERT	22	M	LABR		GRZZZZUSA
BERENDS, BERNARD	22	M	LABR		GRZZZZUSA
WOLFF, JULIUS	24	M	LABR		GRZZZZUSA
VOLZ, JAN	29	M	LABR		GRZZZZUSA
NEULAND, FRITZ	22	M	LABR		GRZZZZUSA
MORDEKI, WYAT	30	M	LABR		GRZZZZUSA
GZYWALOSKI, ANTON	36	M	LABR		GRZZZZUSA
WENGERT, JOHANN	25	M	LABR		GRZZZZUSA
LAMB, CARL	27	M	LABR		GRZZZZUSA
BARUICH, JOSEF	23	M	LABR		GRZZZZUSA

PASSENGER	AGE	SEX	OCCUPATION	PRVL	DES
UMAND, JULIUS	23	M	LABR		GRZZZZUSA
BLA-ANES, MARTIN	43	M	LABR		GRZZZZUSA
SAMUELSOHN, ABRAM	35	M	LABR		GRZZZZUSA
RAPPORT, HIRSCH	39	M	LABR		GRZZZZUSA
JOSEF	10	M	LABR		GRZZZZUSA
HOLUWGRISZ, KARL	20	M	LABR		GRZZZZUSA
CHAULZKI, JOSEPH	29	M	LABR		GRZZZZUSA
JANCKEL, J--SEN	32	M	LABR		GRZZZZUSA
THEURSER, FRIEDRICH	27	M	LABR		GRZZZZUSA
SCHWEITZEN, JACOB	30	M	LABR		GRZZZZUSA
GOLDEN, LAIS--	30	M	LABR		GRZZZZUSA
-ASTROU, TONI	20	M	LABR		GRZZZZUSA
JANCKEL, MARK	40	M	LABR		GRZZZZUSA
WEIER, BUR	35	M	LABR		GRZZZZUSA
KURY, JOSEF	28	M	LABR		GRZZZZUSA
INDELMANN, ERIK	38	M	LABR		GRZZZZUSA
SKUDRING, JOHAN	24	M	LABR		GRZZZZUSA
RU--IMON, MARCUS	25	M	LABR		GRZZZZUSA
SHENOWSKI, MA----	23	M	LABR		GRZZZZUSA
RUSLAND, JOSEF	26	M	LABR		GRZZZZUSA
ROTH, SAMUEL	21	M	LABR		GRZZZZUSA
GLOSUIS, SIMON	47	M	LABR		GRZZZZUSA
BERNAS, ---KAS	25	M	LABR		GRZZZZUSA
VOGEL, HEINRICH	18	M	LABR		GRZZZZUSA
REICH, JOHANN	28	M	LABR		GRZZZZUSA
DUPLESSI, FRANCESCO	48	M	LABR		GRZZZZUSA
LEWIKAN, HENACH	30	M	LABR		GRZZZZUSA
KOLNRED, SIMON	30	M	LABR		GRZZZZUSA
MUELLER, OTTO	29	M	LABR		GRZZZZUSA
WEISS, MARTIN	58	M	LABR		GRZZZZUSA
SCHWEITZER, FREDERIKE	26	F	SVNT		GRZZZZUSA
GERUSCH, WLADISLAV	25	M	LABR		GRZZZZUSA
CAROLINE	25	F	NN		GRZZZZUSA
BOE---, SUSANNA	30	F	NN		GRZZZZUSA
BRAUNN, CATHARINE	25	F	SVNT		GRZZZZUSA
SCHLAK, JOHAN	44	M	LABR		GRZZZZUSA
ROSINE	40	F	NN		GRZZZZUSA
JOHAN	5	M	CHILD		GRZZZZUSA
ROSINE	3	F	CHILD		GRZZZZUSA
KUG, FREDERIKE	30	F	SVNT		GRZZZZUSA
SCHACTER, JOSEPHINE	20	F	SVNT		GRZZZZUSA
WURTZ, KATHARINE	17	F	SVNT		GRZZZZUSA
TRIPOLSKI, HIRSCH	40	M	LABR		GRZZZZUSA
CHAIE	35	F	NN		GRZZZZUSA
ZALE	16	F	NN		GRZZZZUSA
ELKE	13	F	NN		GRZZZZUSA
MOSES	9	M	CHILD		GRZZZZUSA
JOSEF	7	M	CHILD		GRZZZZUSA
ARON	3	M	CHILD		GRZZZZUSA
BUEZE	1	M	CHILD		GRZZZZUSA
JAN-EL	.01	M	INFANT		GRZZZZUSA
FREUDENACHER, PETER	29	M	LABR		GRZZZZUSA
HERENI	27	F	NN		GRZZZZUSA
HERENI	1	F	CHILD		GRZZZZUSA
CHEIMOWITZ, PRE	23	M	LABR		GRZZZZUSA
KOENIG, ANNA	13	F	SVNT		GRZZZZUSA
ZIMMERMANN, LUCIA	22	F	SVNT		GRZZZZUSA
PFAENDER, MARGARETHE	38	F	SVNT		GRZZZZUSA
MART-	3	M	CHILD		GRZZZZUSA
PRISCH---A, ISAAK	28	M	LABR		GRZZZZUSA
SARAH	26	F	SVNT		GRZZZZUSA
MARIA	.06	F	INFANT		GRZZZZUSA
---IESRATH, JOHAN	50	M	FARMER		GRZZZZUSA
WILHELM	20	F	NN		GRZZZZUSA
PELIZENKO, LEIB	48	M	LABR		GRZZZZUSA
SCHIFFRE	28	F	NN		GRZZZZUSA
HENOCH	18	M	LABR		GRZZZZUSA
JESCHIE	16	M	LABR		GRZZZZUSA
ABRAM	9	M	CHILD		GRZZZZUSA
SCHIFRE	6	M	CHILD		GRZZZZUSA
TRUME	4	M	CHILD		GRZZZZUSA
REISEL	16	M	LABR		GRZZZZUSA
SARAH	3	F	CHILD		GRZZZZUSA
MOSES	1	M	CHILD		GRZZZZUSA
MENDEL	22	M	LABR		GRZZZZUSA

PASSENGER	AGE	SEX	OCCUPATION	PRVL	DES
-ONE	21	M	LABR		GRZZZZUSA
TEN-ULA, JAN	23	M	LABR		GRZZZZUSA
-AST, ELISA	20	F	NN		GRZZZZUSA
SCHMOLZES, CHARLES	44	F	TCHR		GRZZZZUSA
A-UB-S, FRIEDRICH	12	M	LABR		GRZZZZUSA
HUMMEL, FREDERIKA	59	F	NN		GRZZZZUSA
JOHAN	25	M	FARMER		GRZZZZUSA
KUEPNER, CHARLOTTE	23	F	NN		GRZZZZUSA
EDUARD	3	M	CHILD		GRZZZZUSA
ANNA	.06	F	INFANT		GRZZZZUSA
GAENSHE, CATHARINA	47	F	NN		GRZZZZUSA
JOHAN	21	M	NN		GRZZZZUSA
B--DRUM, JOHANN	40	M	LABR		GRZZZZUSA
CATHARINE	40	F	NN		GRZZZZUSA
MARY	15	F	NN		GRZZZZUSA
ANNA	10	F	NN		GRZZZZUSA
LUDWIG	8	M	CHILD		GRZZZZUSA
ANTONIE	7	F	CHILD		GRZZZZUSA
JOHANN	5	M	CHILD		GRZZZZUSA
FANNY	3	F	CHILD		GRZZZZUSA
CATHARINE	.06	F	INFANT		GRZZZZUSA
KARNOWSKY, NOCHEIM	40	M	LABR		GRZZZZUSA
GITTEL	32	F	NN		GRZZZZUSA
GOVE	55	F	NN		GRZZZZUSA
RIKE	46	F	NN		GRZZZZUSA
ARIEL	19	F	NN		GRZZZZUSA
SCHEIM	9	F	CHILD		GRZZZZUSA
SCHIFRA	5	F	CHILD		GRZZZZUSA
CHAIE	2	F	CHILD		GRZZZZUSA
CHAIE	9	F	CHILD		GRZZZZUSA

SHIP: CALIFORNIA

FROM: HAMBURG
TO: NEW YORK
ARRIVED: 08 JUNE 1888

PASSENGER	AGE	SEX	OCCUPATION	PRVL	DES
FISCHER, MATHAUS	25	M	LABR		BVZZZZNY
MAGDALENA	23	F	UNKNOWN		BVZZZZNY
VOIGTMANN, PAUL	22	M	CGRMKR		PRZZZZNY
FUNK, ANNA	20	F	UNKNOWN		PRZZZZNY
VALERIA	9	F	CHILD		PRZZZZNY
CATHARINA	5	F	CHILD		PRZZZZNY
TYZENSKI, AUGUSTE	18	F	DRSMKR		PRZZZZNY
RENNEISEN, FRANZISKA	55	F	CK		HBZZZZNY
KAISER, ANDREAS	46	M	CGRMKR		SRZZZZNY
HAISCH, GOTTLIEB	42	M	JNR		HBZZZZUNK
HOEPFNER, THEODOR	29	M	LABR		PRZZZZNY
POHL, CARL	19	M	UNKNOWN		PRZZZZNY
LOOCK, RICHARD	27	M	MCHT		PRZZZZNY
JEHNISCH, EMIL	22	M	LABR		PRZZZZNY
KRAUS, MARTIN	17	M	LABR		PRZZZZNY
STRAUCH, FRANZ	42	M	LABR		PRZZZZSP
KUMINSKY, JULIUS	35	M	LABR		PRZZZZCH
ANNA	22	F	W		PRZZZZCH
THEODOR	2	M	CHILD		PRZZZZCH
PINNER, GUSTAV	24	M	UNKNOWN		PRZZZZDET
HUBLER, CATHARINA	27	F	UNKNOWN		PRZZZZDET
JEKANIN, JOSEF	24	M	LABR		PRZZZZDET
KRUEDENER, AUG.	14	M	LABR		PRZZZZDET
GABER, MELON	26	M	LABR		PRZZZZDET
LAEGE, ANNA	26	F	UNKNOWN		PRZZZZDET
ANDERSCHEFSKI, LEONORE	44	F	UNKNOWN		PRZZZZNY
-BARIA	16	F	UNKNOWN		PRZZZZNY
CATHARINA	9	F	CHILD		PRZZZZNY
U	8	M	CHILD		PRZZZZNY
FRANZISKA	5	F	CHILD		PRZZZZNY
FRANZ	3	M	CHILD		PRZZZZNY
JOSEFA	.06	F	INFANT		PRZZZZNY
JANISCHOWSKY, KASIMIR	44	M	LABR		PRZZZZNY

PASSENGER	AGE	SEX	OCCUPATION	PRVL	DES
STANISL.	16	M	UNKNOWN		PRZZZZNY
ZWIENER, AGNES	62	F	UNKNOWN		PRZZZZUSA
PAULINE	23	F	D		PRAGFUUSA
ALBERT	15	M	S		PRAGFUUSA
KRENS, FRIEDRICH	24	M	LABR		PRAGFUUSA
GOLDSTEIN, OISER	23	M	LKSH		PRAGFUUSA
KOGELMANN, OTTO	17	M	MCHT		PRAGFUUSA
KUNDSEN, CATHAR.	21	F	SVNT		PRAGFUUSA
BYLLING, AUGUSTE	33	F	SVNT		PRAGFUUSA
BEYERSDORF, LOUISE	24	F	UNKNOWN		PRAGFUNY
EGGERT, GOTFRIED	30	M	LABR		PRAGFUNY
IDA	27	F	W		PRAGFUNY
BERTHA	6	F	CHILD		PRAGFUNY
HERMANN	2	M	CHILD		PRAGFUNY
JALINGER, U	15	F	SGL		PRAGFUNY
KRUEGER, HERMANN	18	M	UNKNOWN		PRAGFUNY
MOLLER, CARL	25	M	LABR		PRAGFUNY
META	23	F	W		PRAGFUNY
DORA	3	F	CHILD		PRAGFUNY
ANNA	1	F	CHILD		PRAGFUNY
HEINRICH	.06	M	INFANT		PRAGFUNY
JANTZEN, ANTONIE	21	F	SGL		PRAGFUNY
NOSIEKA, MARIANNE	24	F	WO		PRAGFUNY
STANISLAV	3	M	CHILD		PRAGFUNY
JOSEFA	.11	F	INFANT		PRAGFUNY
FREHSE, FRIEDA	25	F	SVNT		PRAGFUNY
KRUEGER, ERICH	14	M	LABR		PRAGFUNY
SCHLUETER, HEINRICH	16	M	FARMER		PRAGFUNY
SCHULZ, HERMANN	36	M	LABR		PRAGFUNY
BUHMANN, HASCHE	24	M	LABR		PRAGFUNY
WIERSGALLE, BARBARA	40	F	WO		PRAGFUNY
GOLINSZI, ROSINA	37	F	SVNT		PRAGFUNY
PAULINE	7	F	CHILD		PRAGFUNY
CAROLINE	2	F	CHILD		PRAGFUNY
SUDA, MARIANNA	27	F	SVNT		PRAGFUNY
JOH.	2	M	CHILD		PRAGFUNY
ANNA	.11	F	INFANT		PRAGFUNY
STIEWE, AGNES	20	F	SGL		PRAGFUNY
SZEGEPANSKY, WOJCECH	24	M	UNKNOWN		PRAGFUNY
KUESS, CAROL.	60	F	WO		PRAGFUNY
BECK, GUSTAV	38	M	UNKNOWN		PRAGFUNY
LEDZINSKY, JOSEF	46	M	LABR		PRAGFUNY
BLUTHMANN, OTTO	20	M	LABR		PRAGFUNY
SETHMANN, MARTHA	50	F	UNKNOWN		PRAGFUNY
MARIE	14	F	UNKNOWN		PRAGFUNY
DIEDRICH	9	M	CHILD		PRAGFUNY
BLASZAK, MICHALIZA	40	F	WO		PRAGFUNY
WOJCICH	9	M	CHILD		PRAGFUNY
FELDMANN, HENRIETTE	16	F	SVNT		PRAGFUNY
HAMANNSEN, NICOLINE	16	F	SVNT		PRAGFUNY
SCHMIDT, AUGUST	24	M	BCHR		PRAGFUNY
MEIER, ANTON	24	M	LABR		PRAGFUNY
SCHULTZE, AUGUST	45	M	SMH		PRAGFUNY
SCHMIDT, PAULINE	33	F	WO		PRAGFUNY
ANNA	9	F	CHILD		PRAGFUNY
KWIATKOWSKI, MARIAN	35	M	LABR		PRAGFUNY
MALIZEWSKI, PAULINE	34	F	WO		PRAGFUNY
JULIA	9	F	CHILD		PRAGFUNY
MARIANNA	7	F	CHILD		PRAGFUNY
SCHWALONIS, GEORG	32	M	LABR		PRAGFUNY
BERTHA	27	F	W		PRAGFUNY
MERTENS, CHRISIAN	59	M	LABR		PRAGFUNY
FRIEDERIKE	59	F	W		PRZZFUNY
CAROLINA	39	F	UNKNOWN		PRAGFUNY
EMMA	15	F	SGL		PRAGFUNY
MARIE	6	F	CHILD		PRAGFUNY
ADOLF	4	M	CHILD		PRAGFUNY
EMIL	.11	M	INFANT		PRAGFUNY
TOMSEN, AUGUST	46	M	FARMER		PRAGFUNY
HANSEN, MARTHA	19	F	SVNT		PRAGFUNY
JOEHNK, RUDOLF	22	M	FARMER		PRAGFUNY
CAROLINA	20	F	W		PRAGFUNY
BOERCHARDT, ANDREUS	26	M	LABR		PRAGFUNY
EMILIE	26	F	W		PRAGFUNY
JOERGENSEN, ASMUS	24	M	FARMER		PRAGFUNY
ANNE	23	F	SVNT		PRAGFUNY
SCHUETH, CLAUS	14	M	LABR		PRAGFUNY
QUAST, WILHELM	25	M	FARMER		PRAGFUSTL
TIETJE, JOHANN	64	M	FARMER		PRAGFUSTL
ANNA	60	F	W		PRAGFUSTL
STROEH, FRIEDRICH	48	M	FARMER		PRAGFUUSA
LOUISE	40	F	W		PRAGFUUSA
LOUISE	17	F	CH		PRAGFUUSA
LUDWIG	15	M	CH		PRAGFUUSA
ERNST	9	M	CHILD		PRAGFUUSA
ELLA	8	F	CHILD		PRAGFUUSA
FRIEDRICH	7	M	CHILD		PRAGFUUSA
EMIL	6	M	CHILD		PRAGFUUSA
CARL	4	M	CHILD		PRAGFUUSA
META	3	F	CHILD		PRAGFUUSA
OTTMANN, CARL	31	M	UNKNOWN		PRAGFUUSA
AMALIA	31	F	W		PRAGFUUSA
ARTHUR	7	M	CHILD		PRAGFUUSA
RICHARD	4	M	CHILD		PRAGFUUSA
PAUL	2	M	CHILD		PRAGFUUSA
SCHOENJAHN, CARL	64	M	MSN		PRAGFUNY
CATHARINA	62	F	W		PRAGFUNY
CARL	23	M	CH		PRAGFUNY
FRIEDERIKE	17	F	CH		PRAGFUNY
AUGUST	9	M	CHILD		PRAGFUNY
WENZLAN, OTTO	26	M	BCHR		PRAGFUNY
VOLKMANN, FRANZ	33	M	FARMER		PRAGFUCH
HULDA	28	F	W		PRAGFUCH
MINNA	8	F	CHILD		PRAGFUCH
WILLIBALD	2	M	CHILD		PRAGFUCH
EMIL	.11	M	INFANT		PRAGFUCH
REINFELD, HANNA	60	F	WO		PRAGFUNY
BUALKE, FRIEDRICH	36	M	FARMER		PRAGFUNY
LOUISE	38	F	W		PRAGFUNY
EMMA	9	F	CHILD		PRAGFUNY
OTTO	8	M	CHILD		PRAGFUNY
HULDA	5	F	CHILD		PRAGFUNY
BERTHA	4	F	CHILD		PRAGFUNY
FRIEDRICH	2	M	CHILD		PRAGFUNY
BIKARSKI, CONSTANTIN	24	M	SMH		PRAGFUNY
HELA, GUSTAV	42	M	MLR		PRAGFUNY
GRYCZAK, ANTON	38	M	LABR		PRAGFUNY
CATHAR.	28	F	W		PRAGFUNY
GEORG	9	M	CHILD		PRAGFUNY
APOLLONIA	7	F	CHILD		PRAGFUNY
MARIANNA	5	F	CHILD		PRAGFUNY
FRANZ	3	M	CHILD		PRAGFUNY
ANTON	.11	M	INFANT		PRAGFUNY
MARTHA	.01	F	INFANT		PRAGFUNY
PAWLAK, JOSEF	60	M	LKSH		PRAGFUNY
MARIANNA	67	F	UNKNOWN		PRAGFUNY
PIETREZYNSKA, EMILIE	54	F	WO		PRAGFUNY
PETER	18	M	S		PRAGFUNY
KASIMIR	16	M	S		PRAGFUNY
SHULZ, VINCENT	32	M	TNM		PRAGFUNY
DOBLER, AUGUSTE	30	F	SVNT		PRAGFUNY
BITTERICH, CARL	54	M	WVR		PRAGFUNY
WILHELMINE	54	F	W		PRAGFUNY
ECKSTEIN, JULIUS	32	M	FARMER		PRAGFUNY
BUHL, PAUL	31	M	WVR		PRAGFUNY
MARIANNE	27	F	W		PRAGFUNY
JOSEF	5	M	CHILD		PRAGFUNY
JOHANNA	2	F	CHILD		PRAGFUNY
MARIE	.06	F	INFANT		PRAGFUNY
KANDUH, NICOLAUS	26	M	FARMER		PRAGFUSP
HEIK, ADOLF	29	M	BKR		PRAGFUSP
BUKOWSKI, PAUL	17	M	LABR		PRAGFUSP
BUERGEL, GOTTLIEB	28	M	JNR		PRAGFUSP
SCHOTT, JULIANE	46	F	UNKNOWN		PRAGFUPHI
WLADISLAV	9	M	CHILD		PRAGFUPHI
JOSEF	8	M	CHILD		PRAGFUPHI
MARIA	7	F	CHILD		PRAGFUPHI
ROMAN	6	M	CHILD		PRAGFUPHI
AUGUST	4	M	CHILD		PRAGFUPHI
BLUMENTHAL, PAULINE	24	F	SGL		PRAGFUPHI

PASSENGER	AGE	SEX	OCCUPATION	PRVL	DES
NEUMANN, JULIA	40	F	WO		PRAGFUPHI
ERNST	9	M	CHILD		PRAGFUPHI
FRIEDRICH	7	M	CHILD		PRAGFUPHI
AUGUSTE	3	M	CHILD		PRAGFUPHI
ELMER, FRIEDRICH	27	M	FARMER		PRAGFUUSA
SOBALOWSKY, JOSEF	21	M	LABR		PRAGFUUSA
SCHWENKBECK, JOHANNES	15	M	SHMK		PRAGFUUSA
GERNE, MARIE	20	F	UNKNOWN		PRAGFUUSA
ZOELLER, PETER	28	M	LABR		PRAGFUUSA
WENDLER, ANNA	30	F	SVNT		PRAGFUSTL
RINNER, GEORG	34	M	JNR		PRAGFUNY
JLANGENFELDER, CONRAD	16	M	LABR		PRAGFUNY
SAWINA	19	F	SVNT		PRAGFUNY
HARTMANN, HUGO	17	M	BCHR		PRAGFUNY
MARKERT, FRANZ	24	M	TCHR		PRAGFUNY
FISCHER, WILHELM	27	M	TLR		PRAGFUNY
MARY	31	F	W		PRAGFUNY
RIESCH, BABETTE	21	F	UNKNOWN		PRAGFUNY
ERDMANN, GUSTAW	9	M	CHILD		PRAGFUNY
BOYE, AMALIE	46	F	WO		PRAGFUCLE
MINNA	9	F	CHILD		PRAGFUCLE
JOHANN	7	M	CHILD		PRAGFUCLE
EMMA	5	F	CHILD		PRAGFUCLE
BERNHARD	.09	M	INFANT		PRAGFUCLE
REINKE, ROBERT	29	M	LABR		PRAGFUCH
MARIE	23	F	W		PRAGFUCH
MARTHA	3	F	CHILD		PRAGFUCH
REINHOLD	.11	M	INFANT		PRAGFUCH
JOHANN	.01	M	INFANT		PRAGFUCH
HUELSBERG, CARL	24	M	LABR		PRAGFUCH
BERTHA	17	F	W		PRAGFUCH
GLOYE, CLAUS	30	M	JNR		PRAGFUUSA
ANNA	28	F	W		PRAGFUUSA
MAX	3	M	CHILD		PRAGFUUSA
DREYER, HANS	27	M	LABR		PRAGFUCH
MARIA	24	F	W		PRAGFUCH
CHRISTINE	.09	F	INFANT		PRAGFUCH
HAFFMANN, CATHARINA	24	F	SGL		PRAGFUCH
GORDON, ELLE	41	M	DLR		PRAGFUCH
BEILE	27	F	SVNT		PRAGFUCH
JUERGENFSEN, ANNA	47	F	WO		PRAGFUUSA
CLAUSEN, ANDERS	30	M	LABR		PRAGFUCH
ANTONETTE	36	F	W		PRAGFUCH
PETER	5	M	CHILD		PRAGFUCH
HANS	3	M	CHILD		PRAGFUCH
CHRISTINE	.06	F	INFANT		PRAGFUCH
LARSEN, KAREN	19	F	SVNT		PRAGFUCH
GATZA, JEANNETTE	28	F	WO		PRAGFUCH
MARIA	.09	F	INFANT		PRAGFUCH

SHIP: GEISER

FROM: COPENHAGEN
TO: NEW YORK
ARRIVED: 08 JUNE 1888

PASSENGER	AGE	SEX	OCCUPATION	PRVL	DES
ANDERSEN, HANS	11	M	CH		GRZZZZUSA
MAGM---	10	M	CH		GRZZZZUSA
MARIE	9	F	CHILD		GRZZZZUSA
ANNA	2	F	CHILD		GRZZZZUSA
MARIE	.06	F	INFANT		GRZZZZUSA
RUENDAHL, NILS	20	M	LABR		GRZZZZUSA
ANDERSEN, ANNA	26	F	W		GRZZZZUSA
RASMUSSEN, MARIE	76	F	WI		GRZZZZUSA
HANNE	36	F	UNKNOWN		GRZZZZUSA
BONDE, HANS	21	M	FARMER		GRZZZZUSA

SHIP: WAESLAND

FROM: ANTWERP
TO: NEW YORK
ARRIVED: 08 JUNE 1888

PASSENGER	AGE	SEX	OCCUPATION	PRVL	DES
STRASS, F.	50	M	MCHT		GRZZZZHAL
GROTTA, G.	41	M	MCHT		GRZZZZNY
HOCHSTRATE, U-MISS	22	F	UNKNOWN		GRZZZZNY
HENSCHEL, MAX	32	M	DCT		GRZZZZNY
U-MRS	31	F	DCT		GRZZZZNY
F.	5	M	CHILD		GRZZZZNY
HELENE	22	F	DCT		GRZZZZNY
VOGEL, JOHN	28	M	SLSMN		GRZZZZPHI
VANDENDRIECH, U-MISS	21	F	UNKNOWN		GRZZZZNY
GENKINGER, W.	28	M	MCHT		GRZZZZCLE
LENZ, L.	21	M	UNKNOWN		GRZZZZCLE
M.	23	F	UNKNOWN		GRZZZZCLE
OSBORN, U-MR	26	M	TRVLR		FRZZZZPHI
LUTZBACH, L.	26	F	UNKNOWN		GRZZZZNY
LOUISE	24	F	UNKNOWN		GRZZZZNY
E.	22	F	UNKNOWN		GRZZZZNY
MULLER, A.	28	M	SMH		GRZZZZUNK
EVERTZ, R.	31	F	UNKNOWN		GRZZZZNY
U	1	F	CHILD		GRZZZZNY
WINDROTH, C.	30	M	MCHT		GRZZZZNY
RUSSE, H.	30	M	LITGR		GRZZZZNY
KUCHLER, C.	21	F	LITGR		GRZZZZNY
BLUM, M.	44	F	GLSBR		GRZZZZPIT
L.	13	M	GLSBR		GRZZZZPIT
BECKEL, PETER	18	M	MECH		GRZZZZNY
HAENDLER, MICH.	19	M	MECH		GRZZZZNY
BEUTZ, NIC.	18	M	MECH		GRZZZZNY
WIELAND, GOTTL.	27	M	MECH		GRZZZZNY
DEWALD, HER.	19	M	SMH		GRZZZZNY
HELWIG, M.	22	M	CBTMKR		GRZZZZNY
ANNA	24	F	CBTMKR		GRZZZZNY
WILH.	00	M	INF		GRZZZZNY
KIELPIKOWSKI, WLAD.	21	M	FARMER		GRZZZZNY
GOLLNAST, HERM.	24	M	LABR		GRZZZZMIL
MASUS, MARIA	35	F	W		GRZZZZHAZ
JOHN	13	F	CH		GRZZZZHAZ
ANDRI	11	M	CH		GRZZZZHAZ
MARIA	2	F	CHILD		GRZZZZHAZ
BURCHARD, HERRM.	20	M	CPTR		GRZZZZTRY
HATZFELD, DANIEL	17	M	BTMKR		GRZZZZPIT
LINA	18	F	BTMKR		GRZZZZPIT
MULLER, FRIED.	16	M	BBR		GRZZZZPHI
BEYER, MAGDE.	19	M	BBR		GRZZZZPHI
SIMOWSKI, MICH.	19	M	LABR		GRZZZZMI
KRIRILLA, JOH.	33	M	LABR		GRZZZZCH
HERZINGER, JOHN	24	M	BCHR		GRZZZZCH
LINA	26	F	BCHR		GRZZZZCH
KLEIN, JOHN	27	M	LABR		GRZZZZCH
KRATZ, CAROLINE	16	F	UNKNOWN		GRZZZZCIN
KRUMRIG, HELENA	16	F	UNKNOWN		GRZZZZNY
WILH.	11	M	CH		GRZZZZNY
LANGENBACHER, MARIE	17	F	UNKNOWN		GRZZZZNY
SCHWARTZTRAUER, P.	17	M	BTMKR		GRZZZZNY
WEIMER, JOSEPH	16	M	FARMER		GRZZZZUNK
CATHA.	20	F	FARMER		GRZZZZUNK
MAI, JOHANN	36	M	MACH		GRZZZZUT
SPETZ, LUDWIG	17	M	CBTMKR		GRZZZZNY
SCHUELLER, WME.	19	F	UNKNOWN		GRZZZZNY
MOHR, AND.	24	M	BBR		GRZZZZNY
GROBHOLZ, PETER	22	M	BL		GRZZZZNY
STROHMAYER, LEON.	17	M	GLSMKR		GRZZZZUNK
PIERRE, JEAN	22	M	TLR		GRZZZZAOA
SNYDER, JOSEF	20	M	PNTR		GRZZZZTRE
HOFFMANN, CAROLINE	20	F	SVNT		GRZZZZBUF
ADAM, LUDWIG	18	M	CGRMKR		GRZZZZPIT
RAILLAND, ELISE	20	F	UNKNOWN		GRZZZZUSA
HUNGERHOEFER, MARIE	20	F	UNKNOWN		GRZZZZUNK
EHMANN, FRKE.	20	F	UNKNOWN		GRZZZZNY

PASSENGER	AGE	SEX	OCCUPATION	PRVL	DES
BECK, CARL	16	M	BTMKR	GRZZZZNY	
BOCHARD, JOHN	43	M	SMH	SRZZZZNY	
STEINTHAL, ISAAC	16	M	BCHR	GRZZZZNY	
TEUFEL, JOSEF	00	M	MLR	SRZZZZNY	
DECK, ELISAB.	19	F	UNKNOWN	GRZZZZAKR	
ANNA	16	F	UNKNOWN	GRZZZZAKR	
PETER	9	M	CHILD	GRZZZZAKR	
CAMMISCH, CHRIST.	16	M	LABR	SRZZZZCH	
HANSEN, J.P.	20	M	LABR	GRZZZZCH	
ASSEL, JOH.	19	M	CBTMKR	GRZZZZNY	
BRANDT, WILH.	27	M	CBTMKR	GRZZZZNY	
REIS, FERD.	21	M	FARMER	GRZZZZSTL	
BRANDT, IGNATZ	00	M	BTMKR	GRZZZZNY	
ROCKINGER, PETER	41	M	BTMKR	GRZZZZPIT	
FRANKOSKI, ANTON	17	M	SLMKR	GRZZZZCH	
KLINCK, JACOB	25	M	WTR	GRZZZZMIL	
WIEZIELESZEK, WOJ.	27	M	LABR	GRZZZZNY	
MICH.	22	F	LABR	GRZZZZNY	
FRANZ	00	M	INF	GRZZZZNY	
LENHARD, JACOB	24	M	CBTMKR	GRZZZZROC	
WACHTER, CATHA.	16	F	UNKNOWN	GRZZZZNY	
BOHRER, HENRIETTE	21	F	UNKNOWN	GRZZZZNY	
LICK, MARIA	23	F	UNKNOWN	GRZZZZNY	
BOUBEL, PHILIPE.	30	F	UNKNOWN	GRZZZZNY	
ERLENBACH, STEFAN	22	M	MCHT	GRZZZZNY	
SCHLALTER, MATH.	27	M	LABR	GRZZZZNY	
STADLER, ULRICH	25	M	MCHT	SRZZZZNY	
WUCHER, JOSEF	27	M	AGT	GRZZZZNY	
KLINGER, MAGD.	21	F	UNKNOWN	GRZZZZNY	
HOFFER, JOSEF	26	M	BTMKR	GRZZZZNY	
FRIES, CARL	31	M	PLH	GRZZZZNY	
U., FRANZK.	16	M	PLH	GRZZZZASH	
REINARTZ, HUB.	37	M	MLR	GRZZZZNY	
HARTMANN, B.	19	M	MCHT	GRZZZZNY	
GERHARD, HCH.	26	M	LABR	GRZZZZCIN	
WEISEL, PET.	26	M	LABR	GRZZZZCIN	
WODATSCHAK, VAL.	36	M	LABR	GRZZZZNY	
KEUZIN, MICH.	27	M	LABR	GRZZZZNY	
GOTKE, CARL	21	M	CPTR	GRZZZZTRY	
HELMUTH, FRANZ	52	M	WVR	GRZZZZNY	
BOLINGER, CARL	22	M	WVR	GRZZZZNY	
BAIER, MICH.	31	M	FARMER	GRZZZZNY	
EICHELMANN, CHRIST.	54	M	BCHR	GRZZZZNY	
HOREN, VICTOR	45	M	CGRMKR	GRZZZZNY	
MANGES, LOUIS	25	M	BCHR	GRZZZZNY	
MASELL, WILL.	24	M	BCHR	GRZZZZNY	
WOOLF, EMIL	27	M	HRDRS	GRZZZZNY	
GOODMANN, MARIA	27	F	W	GRZZZZNY	
THEOBALD, FRANZ	28	M	MSN	GRZZZZUNK	
BAZIK, JOSEF	37	M	LABR	GRZZZZNY	
RAUFEN-OLL, PETER	45	M	LABR	SRZZZZNY	
SOPHIE	40	F	LABR	SRZZZZNY	
RUDOLPH	14	M	LABR	SRZZZZNY	
MARIE	9	F	CHILD	SRZZZZNY	
ELISA	5	F	CHILD	SRZZZZNY	
ROSA	3	F	CHILD	SRZZZZNY	
ALFRED	00	M	INF	SRZZZZNY	
BARTH, JOHANN	28	M	MLR	SRZZZZNY	
HINTERMANN, REG.	25	F	SVNT	SRZZZZNY	
EISENRING, ADOLF	23	M	MLR	SRZZZZNY	
SPOERRI, HCH.	38	M	BRR	SRZZZZNY	
EBERHARD, VAL.	40	M	LABR	SRZZZZNY	
WARP.	10	F	CH	SRZZZZNY	
GRIMM, GEO	27	M	BTMKR	SRZZZZNY	
WEBER, CASPAR	48	M	WCHMKR	SRZZZZNY	
BUTMANN, PH.	21	M	FARMER	GRZZZZNY	
WEIHRICH, PET.	30	M	FARMER	GRZZZZNY	
TEUMA, CARL	18	M	BKR	GRZZZZNY	
SPANFELDER, ED.	31	M	BTMKR	GRZZZZNY	
RUPP, ANTON	26	M	BKR	GRZZZZNY	
HILDEBRAND, CARL	48	M	MCHT	GRZZZZNY	
HOELZER, MARTIN	31	M	SMH	GRZZZZPIT	
SOHN, HCH.	18	M	SMH	GRZZZZNY	
FRANK, CATHA.	42	F	W	GRZZZZNY	
REGA.	5	F	CHILD	GRZZZZNY	
CULLMANN, JACOB	13	M	UNKNOWN	GRZZZZNY	
MEIGEL, ROSA	15	F	FAB	GRZZZZNY	
SCHOEN, CARL	63	M	SMH	GRZZZZNY	
JULIANNE	65	F	SMH	GRZZZZNY	
SCHMIDT, WILH.	28	F	SMH	GRZZZZNY	
JULIUS	2	M	CHILD	GRZZZZNY	
MATHILDE	00	F	INF	GRZZZZNY	
CAROLINE	16	F	SMSTS	GRZZZZNY	
HELLVOGEL, PHILE.	25	F	SVNT	GRZZZZNY	
KAUFMANN, FERD.	21	M	LABR	GRZZZZNY	
HOFMANN, SEBAST.	30	M	BCHR	GRZZZZNY	
FOHRINGER, JOH.	30	M	CGRMKR	GRZZZZNY	
KATHA.	31	F	CGRMKR	GRZZZZNY	
LINK, CHRISTINE	12	F	CH	GRZZZZNY	
CARL	24	M	CGRMKR	GRZZZZNY	
FREUDENBERGER, HCH.	28	M	LABR	GRZZZZNY	
WALTHER, PHILIPP	17	M	BCHR	GRZZZZNY	
ADELMANN, APOLLONIA	69	F	W	GRZZZZNY	
WOLF, JOSEFINE	4	F	CHILD	GRZZZZNY	
WINKLER, ADAM	43	M	CPTR	GRZZZZNY	
KATHA.	23	F	CPTR	GRZZZZNY	
ELISAB.	15	F	CPTR	GRZZZZNY	
FRIDA	10	F	CH	GRZZZZNY	
ANNA	2	F	CHILD	GRZZZZNY	
JACOB	4	M	CHILD	GRZZZZNY	
LINA	2	F	CHILD	GRZZZZNY	
BABETTE	00	F	INF	GRZZZZNY	
VOLLMAR, LUDWIG	26	M	BTMKR	GRZZZZCH	
KOHRBACHER, HCH.	33	M	LABR	GRZZZZCH	
KLEIN, CATHA.	53	F	W	GRZZZZBUF	
VOLLMAR, PETER	35	M	LABR	GRZZZZNY	
MULLER, MARIE	29	F	W	GRZZZZNY	
ERPELDING, CATHA.	55	F	W	GRZZZZNY	
FUNCH, JEAN	15	M	W	GRZZZZNY	
ANNA	11	F	CH	GRZZZZNY	
MARIE	10	F	CH	GRZZZZNY	
DEEANTECHER, GG.	23	M	LABR	GRZZZZNY	
DUCKAERT, MA.	31	F	W	GRZZZZNY	
MAAS, A.	31	M	BKR	GRZZZZNY	
BARTHEL, J.P.	20	M	FARMER	GRZZZZNY	
BISCHOF, CHRIST.	51	M	FARMER	GRZZZZNY	
ELISAB.	15	F	FARMER	GRZZZZNY	
ATTMEYER, JUL.	19	M	CPR	GRZZZZNY	
ELISA	17	F	CPR	GRZZZZNY	
HOLLINGER, PH.	18	F	SVNT	GRZZZZNY	
WEBER, CATH.	18	F	SVNT	GRZZZZBLO	
MEYER, W.	14	M	LABR	GRZZZZCLE	
WERNER, PET.	51	M	LABR	GRZZZZSY	
MARIE	51	F	LABR	GRZZZZSY	
SOPHIE	17	F	LABR	GRZZZZSY	
AMWOERTER, ELISAB.	15	F	W	GRZZZZPHI	
KLEINKNECHT, ELISAB.	15	F	CH	GRZZZZPHI	
MASSA, CONS.	39	M	GZR	GRZZZZPHI	
MARIA	14	F	GZR	GRZZZZPHI	
SCHOEBER, AUG.	15	M	SHMK	GRZZZZPHI	
GOTZ, ANDREAS	36	M	CBTMKR	GRZZZZPHI	
MARIE	32	F	CBTMKR	GRZZZZPHI	
MARIE	3	F	CHILD	GRZZZZPHI	
CARL	2	M	CHILD	GRZZZZPHI	
VOSSELER, JACOB	38	M	CH	GRZZZZPHI	
JACOB	15	M	CH	GRZZZZPHI	
GOLL, ANTON	27	M	CH	GRZZZZPHI	
ROSCH, GEO	26	M	CPR	GRZZZZPHI	
MARIE	26	F	CPR	GRZZZZPHI	
GUSTAV	3	M	CHILD	GRZZZZPHI	
WEBER, GEO	34	M	DLR	GRZZZZPHI	
MOZER, FREDKE.	26	F	DLR	GRZZZZPHI	
WALTER, MARIA	62	F	DLR	GRZZZZPHI	
MEYER, ALBT.	4	M	CHILD	GRZZZZLOS	
KLESER, CATHA.	18	F	UNKNOWN	GRZZZZLOS	
KRON, JACOB	24	M	PNTR	GRZZZZUNK	
CATHA.	26	F	PNTR	GRZZZZUNK	
ANNA	3	F	CHILD	GRZZZZUNK	
SIEBER, ANNA	21	F	CH	GRZZZZUNK	
DARMSTAEDT, CHRISTIEN	18	M	UNKNOWN	GRZZZZNY	

PASSENGER	AGE	SEX	OCCUPATION	PRVL	DES
KNUSSMANN, CLARA	26	F	UNKNOWN	GRZZZZUSA	
ROESCH, PH.	15	M	FAB	GRZZZZUNK	
SPANFELDER, SUSD.	37	F	UNKNOWN	GRZZZZNY	
SUSD.	00	F	INF	GRZZZZNY	
GRASER, OTTO	35	M	FARMER	GRZZZZNY	
BODEN, ANNA	18	F	SVNT	GRZZZZNY	
SABEIL, ERNST	20	M	CRPM	GRZZZZNY	
MAUER, CARL	33	M	LABR	GRZZZZNY	
VONHAGEN, MARTHA	18	F	SVNT	GRZZZZNY	
KLEMENCZ, JOHA.	22	F	W	GRZZZZNY	
BERTHA	2	F	CHILD	GRZZZZNY	
GAUTER, SABINE	21	F	UNKNOWN	GRZZZZNY	
SCHMIDT, HUBERT	52	F	W	GRZZZZNY	
LANGLE, RICH.	14	M	UNKNOWN	GRZZZZNY	
NEU, ANNA	18	F	SVNT	GRZZZZNY	
LANGELE, CRECZENZ	00	F	SVNT	GRZZZZNY	
BEUSINGER, G.A.	16	M	LABR	GRZZZZNY	
ENRESS, CAROLINE	26	F	SVNT	GRZZZZNY	
LEVIGARD, MARTIN	16	M	WVR	GRZZZZNY	
CHRISTNACHT, HCH.	49	M	BCHR	GRZZZZNY	
SEYFFERLE, F.	23	F	UNKNOWN	GRZZZZNY	
MARIE	14	F	UNKNOWN	GRZZZZNY	
KLEIN, OTTO	17	M	SHMK	GRZZZZNY	
MOSBACH, ANNA	16	F	CH	GRZZZZNY	
WENZ, ANNA	17	F	SVNT	GRZZZZNY	
ELISE	19	F	SVNT	GRZZZZNY	
STEITZ, VAL.	17	M	CH	GRZZZZNY	
MARKL, JACOB	26	M	WGNR	GRZZZZNY	
MEIER, MICH.	19	M	WGNR	GRZZZZNY	
RANTENBERG, ROB.	31	M	SCP	GRZZZZNY	
DOROTHEA	24	F	SCP	GRZZZZNY	
WEISS, HCH.	16	M	CH	GRZZZZNY	
REICHERT, CHRIST.	14	M	CH	GRZZZZNY	
KLOTZ, EMIL	15	M	CH	GRZZZZNY	
EBERLE, GUSTAV	16	M	CH	GRZZZZNY	
BECHTOLD, MARGA.	25	F	SVNT	GRZZZZNY	
LA-, FRANZ	31	M	BRR	GRZZZZNY	
ELISAB.	35	F	BRR	GRZZZZNY	
LICHTENBERGER, ANTON	27	M	SHMK	GRZZZZNY	
GESELWAUTMER, GUS.	17	M	CPR	GRZZZZNY	
LEGE, HCH.	34	M	PLH	GRZZZZNY	
SIEMES, WM.	31	M	PLH	GRZZZZNY	
HANTISEL, FREIDK.	31	F	W	GRZZZZNY	
HAUTISCH, FREIDK.	31	F	W	GRZZZZNY	
MENTGES, JOH.	8	M	CHILD	GRZZZZNY	
HAUTISCH, ERI-ST	00	M	INF	GRZZZZNY	
BRUCKMANN, CHRIST.	32	M	INF	GRZZZZNY	
DOROTHEA	36	F	INF	GRZZZZNY	
JOHANN	10	M	CH	GRZZZZNY	
JACOB	8	M	CHILD	GRZZZZNY	
ADAM	5	M	CHILD	GRZZZZNY	
RITTENAUER, KILIAN	26	M	FARMER	GRZZZZNY	
ZIMMER, HCH.	45	M	FARMER	GRZZZZNY	
MARTIN, ELISE	21	F	SVNT	GRZZZZNY	
KRIEGER, ELISE	23	F	SVNT	GRZZZZNY	
JENKEN, PFILIPP	17	M	WCHMKR	GRZZZZUSA	
MENDEL, MARTIN	32	F	W	GRZZZZUSA	
SLOIBER, CATHA.	23	F	W	GRZZZZUSA	
MAX	00	F	INF	GRZZZZUSA	
VOGEL, CATHA.	28	F	W	GRZZZZUSA	
STOIBER, JOSEF	17	M	LABR	GRZZZZSP	
EBAUER, CRESCENZ	00	F	SVNT	GRZZZZUSA	
HIRSCH, DOMINICK	36	M	TLR	GRZZZZBUF	
JOSEFINA	29	F	TLR	GRZZZZBUF	
CONRAD	8	M	CHILD	GRZZZZBUF	
ELISE	6	F	CHILD	GRZZZZBUF	
WEBER, MARIE	21	F	CH	GRZZZZBUF	
ZAUGL, G.	52	M	CPTR	GRZZZZBUF	
THERES.	21	F	CPTR	GRZZZZBUF	
ANTON	19	M	CPTR	GRZZZZUNK	
BARTOLOMEW	14	M	CPTR	GRZZZZUNK	
ROSINA	11	F	CH	GRZZZZUNK	
DREXLER, BONASENTURA	18	M	FARMER	GRZZZZNY	
ZOLLNER, XAVER	23	M	MSN	GRZZZZNY	
MITTERREITTER, JOSEF	31	M	FARMER	GRZZZZNY	
MARIA	28	F	FARMER	GRZZZZNY	
JOSEF	4	M	CHILD	GRZZZZNY	
PFRANK, IGNATZ	17	M	LABR	GRZZZZNY	
BENZINGER, LEOP.	22	M	LABR	GRZZZZNY	
ZELENKA, JOSEF	27	M	LABR	GRZZZZNY	
SIMON, PHIL.	23	M	BBR	GRZZZZNY	
GEISS, JOS.	26	M	CL	GRZZZZNY	
RUEDEL, ANNA	23	F	SVNT	GRZZZZNY	
FAHRBACH, MARIA	21	F	SVNT	GRZZZZPHI	
WELLER, EVA	52	F	W	GRZZZZPHI	
MARIE	16	F	CH	GRZZZZPHI	
GOTTLOB	12	M	CH	GRZZZZPHI	
HOLZWARTH, GOTT.	24	M	BTMKR	GRZZZZPHI	
FRIZ, CHRISTINE	66	F	UNKNOWN	GRZZZZCH	
FRIED.	38	M	CH	GRZZZZCH	
MUHLBERGER, CATHA.	17	F	SVNT	GRZZZZNY	
REBENECK, GEO	17	M	GZR	GRZZZZIN	
MARG.	19	F	GZR	GRZZZZIN	
GIEGER, BARB.	19	F	GZR	GRZZZZIN	
JUNG, JAC.	17	M	PDLR	GRZZZZCH	
EICHBAKER, ERNST	18	M	CK	GRZZZZNY	
LANGERER, WM.	61	M	TLR	GRZZZZNY	
WME.	53	F	TLR	GRZZZZNY	
ROSINE	16	F	TLR	GRZZZZNY	
MAGD.	11	F	TLR	GRZZZZNY	
RUDOLF	10	M	TLR	GRZZZZNY	
LINA	8	F	CHILD	GRZZZZNY	
ERNST	7	M	CHILD	GRZZZZNY	
SCHWEGER, MAG.	21	F	SVNT	GRZZZZPHI	
SOHN, BARB.	16	F	UNKNOWN	GRZZZZPIT	
LANG, MARG.	31	F	UNKNOWN	GRZZZZWIT	
FRIED.	7	M	CHILD	GRZZZZWIT	
CAMILLE	6	M	CHILD	GRZZZZWIT	
SOLOMON	3	M	CHILD	GRZZZZWIT	
HCH.	00	M	INF	GRZZZZWIT	
WEIDENIER, MICH.	26	M	FARMER	GRZZZZPHI	
TEIPEL, NIC.	40	M	CGR	GRZZZZNY	
KERFEL, CARL	28	M	MCHT	GRZZZZNY	
JAKUTZEIT, JURGEN	27	M	MCHT	GRZZZZNY	
MOLDANER, ARON	27	M	MCHT	GRZZZZNY	
WIPPE, Z.	21	M	CL	GRZZZZNY	
ROTH, ROCHEL	27	F	SVNT	GRZZZZNY	
MONTAG, ABERHAM	21	M	CL	GRZZZZNY	
CHRAB, ISAC	38	M	MCHT	GRZZZZNY	
KALB, ABRAHAM	24	M	LABR	GRZZZZNY	
RIROEKA	22	M	LABR	GRZZZZNY	
ROSENBLATT, MENDEL	21	M	LABR	GRZZZZNY	
LUPIN	19	M	LABR	GRZZZZNY	
WOLF, MOSES	31	M	LABR	GRZZZZNY	
SCHUSSELFEL-, NATHAN	22	M	LABR	GRZZZZNY	
COHN, LINA	18	F	HSKPR	GRZZZZNY	
GRIES, PESEL	22	F	FHAD	GRZZZZNY	
GRUNFELDT, J.M.	18	M	LABR	GRZZZZNY	
NEUMANN, ERNST	34	M	LABR	GRZZZZNY	
AURSCHOVITZ, SARA	24	F	W	GRZZZZNY	
ARON	00	M	INF	GRZZZZNY	
SALOMON	00	M	INF	GRZZZZNY	
BALL---T, BEILE	19	F	CH	GRZZZZNY	
WUTZER, KREINTZA	25	F	UNKNOWN	GRZZZZNY	
CH.	35	F	UNKNOWN	GRZZZZNY	
BEILE	30	F	FARMER	GRZZZZNY	
GITSCHA	5	F	CHILD	GRZZZZNY	
TWOYNE	3	F	CHILD	GRZZZZNY	
DALKO	9	F	CHILD	GRZZZZNY	
HORSCH	00	M	INF	GRZZZZNY	
MAUSS, SIEGRIIED	18	M	BTMKR	GRZZZZNY	
HERSCHKOWITZ, JULI	18	M	LABR	GRZZZZNY	
BENMI	21	M	LABR	GRZZZZNY	
ELFANDOWITZ, MOSES	49	M	LABR	GRZZZZNY	
NEUG-T, PINOIS	26	M	TCHR	GRZZZZNY	
LICHTENSTEIN, RIFKE	15	F	SVNT	GRZZZZNY	
ZELDHEIM, LEIB	47	M	LABR	GRZZZZNY	
JANKEL	19	M	LABR	GRZZZZNY	
GLODFKI, NECHER	34	M	LABR	GRZZZZNY	
BRUSTEL, JOHANN	24	M	SMH	GRZZZZCLE	

PASSENGER	AGE	SEX	OCCUPATION	PRVL	DES
JOHANN	24	M	SMH	GRZZZZCLE	
MOCK, JOHANN	16	M	BCHR	GRZZZZCH	
IMROTH, ALB.	31	M	CGRMKR	GRZZZZCH	
KUCHENBECKER, AUG.	25	M	CGRMKR	GRZZZZMIL	
KROLI, JOSEF	20	M	CGRMKR	GRZZZZNY	
WEIS, WILH.	19	M	STCTR	GRZZZZUSA	
LINDER, SOFIA	22	F	UNKNOWN	GRZZZZTRE	
ALLARD, JEAN	43	M	FARMER	FRZZZZPIT	
MARIE	43	F	FARMER	FRZZZZPIT	
ISIDORE	16	F	FARMER	FRZZZZPIT	
ELEONORE	16	F	FARMER	FRZZZZPIT	
VICTOR	10	M	CH	FRZZZZPIT	
ZELIE	8	F	CHILD	FRZZZZPIT	
JEAN	5	M	CHILD	FRZZZZPIT	
LOUIS	4	M	CHILD	FRZZZZPIT	
HAT---, BERNARD	00	M	BCHR	FRZZZZUSA	
U, U	00	U	UNKNOWN	GRZZZZUSA	
HUBER, AUG.	47	M	MSN	GRZZZZUNK	
CATH.	46	F	MSN	GRZZZZUNK	
FRITZ	17	M	MSN	GRZZZZUNK	
ELISAB.	15	F	MSN	GRZZZZUNK	
TH.	12	M	MSN	GRZZZZUNK	
JACOB	11	M	MSN	GRZZZZUNK	

SHIP: ALLER

FROM: BREMEN
TO: NEW YORK
ARRIVED: 09 JUNE 1888

PASSENGER	AGE	SEX	OCCUPATION	PRVL	DES
GAERTLER, ANNA	25	F	UNKNOWN	GRZZZZUSA	
KEMPNER, ANDREAS	35	M	MCHT	GRZZZZUSA	
ANNI	29	F	UNKNOWN	GRZZZZUSA	
WALF, SAMUEL	40	M	MCHT	GRZZZZUSA	
ROSA	36	F	W	GRZZZZUSA	
SIMON, ESAAK	68	M	MCHT	GRZZZZUSA	
CAROLINE	62	F	W	GRZZZZUSA	
EMANUEL	25	M	CH	GRZZZZUSA	
MULLER, EMMA	25	F	UNKNOWN	GRZZZZUSA	
ROSENBERG, JACOB	23	M	MCHT	GRZZZZUSA	
ENGLAENDER, ROSA	36	F	UNKNOWN	GRZZZZUSA	
HATZHANER, ABRAHAM	64	M	MCHT	GRZZZZUSA	
CAROLINE	65	F	W	GRZZZZUSA	
KORB, CARL	37	M	MCHT	GRZZZZUSA	
ROSS, JONATHAN	29	M	MCHT	GRZZZZUSA	
STOCOKER, VICTOR	59	M	MCHT	GRZZZZUSA	
BALWERKE, THEOD.	48	M	MCHT	GRZZZZUSA	
JACOBSOHN, ROSA	24	F	UNKNOWN	GRZZZZUSA	
BAUM, EMILIE	36	F	UNKNOWN	GRZZZZUSA	
SCHORS, MARCUS	34	M	MCHT	GRZZZZUSA	
RICHARDSEN, CHRISTIAN	26	M	MCHT	GRZZZZUSA	
MEINECKE, WILHELM	30	M	MCHT	GRZZZZUSA	
EILENBERG, BENTHOLD	44	M	MCHT	GRZZZZUSA	
BORK, ANDREAS	15	M	FARMER	GRZZZZUSA	
BENDIG, FRANCISCA	70	F	UNKNOWN	GRZZZZUSA	
BRAMM, CARL	17	M	FARMER	GRZZZZUSA	
WILHELM	17	M	FARMER	GRZZZZUSA	
SUEGSENGEL, EMMA	14	F	UNKNOWN	GRZZZZUSA	
ADLER, GAETH	15	M	MCHT	GRZZZZUSA	
HANSEN, CHRISTIAN	36	M	MCHT	GRZZZZUSA	
FLANT, EMMA	23	F	UNKNOWN	GRZZZZUSA	
MUTSCHLER, AMMA	29	F	UNKNOWN	GRZZZZUSA	
FURWIN, JOHANNE	35	F	UNKNOWN	GRZZZZUSA	
EMMA	5	F	CHILD	GRZZZZUSA	
FANNY	4	F	CHILD	GRZZZZUSA	
JULIE	.11	F	INFANT	GRZZZZUSA	
SLOWICKA, HELENE	21	F	UNKNOWN	GRZZZZUSA	
HELENE	2	F	CHILD	GRZZZZUSA	
CATHI	19	F	UNKNOWN	GRZZZZUSA	
BLUMER, WILHELM	28	M	MCHT	GRZZZZUSA	

PASSENGER	AGE	SEX	OCCUPATION	PRVL	DES
BEINHOLD, ELISE	11	F	UNKNOWN	GRZZZZUSA	
HANSEN, MARIAN	32	M	MCHT	GRZZZZUSA	
SIEGEL, SIGMUND	40	M	MCHT	GRZZZZUSA	
DANN--, HEINR.	00	M	MCHT	GRZZZZUSA	
CONDINER, HEINR.	00	M	MCHT	GRZZZZUSA	
BERSEBACH, JOHANN	17	M	FARMER	GRZZZZUSA	
KRETE, HEINR.	17	M	FARMER	GRZZZZUSA	
GUENDEL, FRIED	25	M	FARMER	GRZZZZUSA	
KUHLMANN, CONRAD	16	M	FARMER	GRZZZZUSA	
BENSE, LUDWIG	18	M	FARMER	GRZZZZUSA	
LOUIS	43	M	FARMER	GRZZZZUSA	
BENCHENT, OTTO	23	M	FARMER	GRZZZZUSA	
SZOZEPANSKY, ANTON	62	M	BCHR	GRZZZZUSA	
FRITSCH, FRANZ	27	M	MCHT	GRZZZZUSA	
HIRSCHMANN, JOHAN	23	M	MCHT	GRZZZZUSA	
STEINER, MAX	24	M	MCHT	GRZZZZUSA	
FAUTHNER, ANDR.	41	M	FARMER	GRZZZZUSA	
FEITROWSKY, VLADISLAV	7	M	CHILD	GRZZZZUSA	
STRASSER, FRIEDR.	24	M	FARMER	GRZZZZUSA	
ELSNER, CONRAD	7	M	CHILD	GRZZZZUSA	
VALKMANN, PAUL	16	M	FARMER	GRZZZZUSA	
WICHMANN, AUG.	27	M	FARMER	GRZZZZUSA	
TOEBELMANN, WILLI	17	M	FARMER	GRZZZZUSA	
MAKORDES, GEORG	15	M	FARMER	GRZZZZUSA	
KUTTING, FRANZ	25	M	FARMER	GRZZZZUSA	
GENT, ROBERT	42	M	FARMER	GRZZZZUSA	
KOZIMRITSKY, RUD.	25	M	FARMER	GRZZZZUSA	
HAVERMANN, RUD.	27	M	FARMER	GRZZZZUSA	
RADBERG, JAH.	30	M	FARMER	GRZZZZUSA	
HAMJE, HEINR.	18	M	FARMER	GRZZZZUSA	
SEHMKUHL, WILH.	16	M	FARMER	GRZZZZUSA	
MICHALLIS, JOHN	7	M	CHILD	GRZZZZUSA	
BORNUK, JOHN	25	M	FARMER	GRZZZZUSA	
LOWINGER, JAN.	35	M	MCHT	GRZZZZUSA	
MATTHEY, JAN.	7	M	CHILD	GRZZZZUSA	
MORIUS, JAN.	31	M	FARMER	GRZZZZUSA	
PFEIFFER, AUG.	00	M	FARMER	GRZZZZUSA	
HERRMANN, FRIEDR.	19	M	SHMK	GRZZZZUSA	
GRASS, HEINR.	18	M	SHMK	GRZZZZUSA	
WIETRSJICHOWSKY, CHRIST	17	M	BCHR	GRZZZZUSA	
KRANS, WILHELM	5	M	CHILD	GRZZZZUSA	
SCHENINGER, FRIEDR.	16	M	FARMER	GRZZZZUSA	
BISCHOFF, HEINR.	31	M	FARMER	GRZZZZUSA	
BAUGERT, LUDW.	35	M	FARMER	GRZZZZUSA	
HEINR.	25	M	LABR	GRZZZZUSA	
ISRAEL, ADOLF	17	M	LABR	GRZZZZUSA	
KRAIMER, WILHELM	17	M	LABR	GRZZZZUSA	
LAHSE, GERHARD	19	M	LABR	GRZZZZUSA	
MEYER, CHRISTIAN	20	M	LABR	GRZZZZUSA	
LESSEAN, AUGUST	14	M	GDNR	GRZZZZUSA	
DULLE, HEINR.	14	M	GDNR	GRZZZZUSA	
NAETH, GEORG	14	M	GDNR	GRZZZZUSA	
SCHMIDT, FRIEDR.	17	M	GDNR	GRZZZZUSA	
HOLLENBACH, ADOLPH	24	M	UNKNOWN	GRZZZZUSA	
EISKANS, JOSEF	21	M	UNKNOWN	GRZZZZUSA	
MANGALD, BERNHD.	29	M	UNKNOWN	GRZZZZUSA	
RENZ, LUDWIG	28	M	UNKNOWN	GRZZZZUSA	
BECK, FRIEDR.	30	M	FARMER	GRZZZZUSA	
RUDOLPH, CARL	14	M	FARMER	GRZZZZUSA	
HAFMANN, JOHN	17	M	FARMER	GRZZZZUSA	
METZ, HEINR.	26	M	GDNR	GRZZZZUSA	
SENSLEIN, FRIEDR.	25	M	GDNR	GRZZZZUSA	
HAHNER, GEORG	27	M	GDNR	GRZZZZUSA	
OSMANN, JAHANN	23	M	GDNR	GRZZZZUSA	
NOWUSCH, CARL	23	M	MCHT	GRZZZZUSA	
STANG, ADOLPH	17	M	MCHT	GRZZZZUSA	
KATZMUELLER, JAS	18	M	FARMER	GRZZZZUSA	
SCHLEICH, PETER	20	M	FARMER	GRZZZZUSA	
RUDOLPH, JENS	17	M	FARMER	GRZZZZUSA	
SIMON, JAHANN	14	M	LABR	GRZZZZUSA	
ALEXANDER, DAVID	18	M	LABR	GRZZZZUSA	
NICKSCH, AUG.	21	M	LABR	GRZZZZUSA	
BARTHEL, GEORG	52	M	GDNR	GRZZZZUSA	
CARL	23	M	GDNR	GRZZZZUSA	
SCHALLMEYER, IGNATZ	29	M	GDNR	GRZZZZUSA	

PASSENGER	AGE	SEX	OCCUPATION	PRVVLS	DES	PASSENGER	AGE	SEX	OCCUPATION	PRVVLS	DES
ZEITLER, JOHANN	27	M	GDNR	GRZZZZ	USA	CORDES, FRIEDRIKE	17	F	UNKNOWN	GRZZZZ	USA
SUHL, CLAUS	17	M	GDNR	GRZZZZ	USA	JMMER, LOUISE	22	F	UNKNOWN	GRZZZZ	USA
BUNDE, JAS	18	M	GDNR	GRZZZZ	USA	SCHONFELD, MINNA	7	F	CHILD	GRZZZZ	USA
JAGUET, FRANZ	11	M	UNKNOWN	GRZZZZ	USA	CORDES, THEODORE	15	F	UNKNOWN	GRZZZZ	USA
LENZ, JOHANN	24	M	FARMER	GRZZZZ	USA	DOERFLER, MARG.	20	F	UNKNOWN	GRZZZZ	USA
LUEHN, AUGUST	25	M	FARMER	GRZZZZ	USA	FROESCHHOLZ, URSULA	26	F	UNKNOWN	GRZZZZ	USA
BIRCKNSTOCK, HEINR.	18	M	FARMER	GRZZZZ	USA	JAEGER, ALBERTE	18	F	UNKNOWN	GRZZZZ	USA
PETERSEN, HANS	17	M	FARMER	GRZZZZ	USA	VALK, ANNA	18	F	UNKNOWN	GRZZZZ	USA
SKARPL--, THEOPHIL	15	M	MCHT	GRZZZZ	USA	KRAUS, BARBARA	56	F	UNKNOWN	GRZZZZ	USA
DRAHEIM, GALLIEL	68	M	MCHT	GRZZZZ	USA	FITELINS, FRIEDRKE.	16	F	UNKNOWN	GRZZZZ	USA
HAUSSMANN, FRIEDR.	42	M	MCHT	GRZZZZ	USA	ECKER, LINA	17	F	UNKNOWN	GRZZZZ	USA
BOCKERS, EDUARD	25	M	GDNR	GRZZZZ	USA	BAETZNER, CAROLA	19	F	UNKNOWN	GRZZZZ	USA
BROWN, CONRAD	15	M	GDNR	GRZZZZ	USA	DERCKER, ANNA	19	F	UNKNOWN	GRZZZZ	USA
BINISZKIWICZ, JOH.	00	M	GDNR	GRZZZZ	USA	KALBE, THEKLA	18	F	UNKNOWN	GRZZZZ	USA
BAHR, WILH.	24	M	FARMER	GRZZZZ	USA	ZACHMANN, PAULINE	18	F	UNKNOWN	GRZZZZ	USA
DOERSAM, JOH.	21	M	FARMER	GRZZZZ	USA	SICHTENBERGER, FRANK.	23	F	UNKNOWN	GRZZZZ	USA
PASCHKE, HEINR.	37	M	FARMER	GRZZZZ	USA	BRODBECK, NANA	17	F	UNKNOWN	GRZZZZ	USA
LANGE, CHRIST	18	M	FARMER	GRZZZZ	USA	NIES, ANNA	17	F	UNKNOWN	GRZZZZ	USA
ELLRODT, LEONH.	21	M	FARMER	GRZZZZ	USA	SEIDEL, MARIE	20	F	UNKNOWN	GRZZZZ	USA
REICHENBACH, JOH.	16	M	FARMER	GRZZZZ	USA	BRENNER, BABETE	27	F	UNKNOWN	GRZZZZ	USA
MUEHLHAFER, FRITZ	35	M	FARMER	GRZZZZ	USA	RATH, CATHI	26	F	UNKNOWN	GRZZZZ	USA
DORMANN, MICHAEL	27	M	FARMER	GRZZZZ	USA	VIERHELLER, CATHI	19	F	UNKNOWN	GRZZZZ	USA
HEINLEIN, LEO	23	M	FARMER	GRZZZZ	USA	KRAEMER, CATHI	28	F	UNKNOWN	GRZZZZ	USA
RUETER, HERM.	16	M	FARMER	GRZZZZ	USA	BRODBECK, ROSINE	14	F	UNKNOWN	GRZZZZ	USA
NIEMEYER, WILH.	15	M	FARMER	GRZZZZ	USA	HANANER, CLARA	26	F	UNKNOWN	GRZZZZ	USA
BARTHALOMAC, GUST.	29	M	FARMER	GRZZZZ	USA	FOERSTER, ANNA	23	F	UNKNOWN	GRZZZZ	USA
REITZ, ERNST	30	M	FARMER	GRZZZZ	USA	EXMEIER, DORATHE	18	F	UNKNOWN	GRZZZZ	USA
WENZ, RUDOLPH	36	M	FARMER	GRZZZZ	USA	PFOENTSCH, KUNIGE.	20	F	UNKNOWN	GRZZZZ	USA
LANER, HEINR.	37	M	FARMER	GRZZZZ	USA	SCHMIDT, HENRIETTE	21	F	UNKNOWN	GRZZZZ	USA
REIDERS, BERNH.	27	M	FARMER	GRZZZZ	USA	KUERR, MARIE	25	F	UNKNOWN	GRZZZZ	USA
STEINBACH, JOH.	27	M	FARMER	GRZZZZ	USA	SCHLETTE, SOPHIE	25	F	UNKNOWN	GRZZZZ	USA
FRANER, JACOB	16	M	FARMER	GRZZZZ	USA	GONG, KATHI	16	F	UNKNOWN	GRZZZZ	USA
STEINMEYER, WILH.	51	M	FARMER	GRZZZZ	USA	BECKER, LISETTE	16	F	UNKNOWN	GRZZZZ	USA
SCHATTENSPIEL, W.	68	M	MCHT	GRZZZZ	USA	HAHLWEG, MAGDA	19	F	UNKNOWN	GRZZZZ	USA
FRITZ, ENGELB	24	M	MCHT	GRZZZZ	USA	STUBLING, EMILIE	21	F	UNKNOWN	GRZZZZ	USA
BROOKS, HEINR.	32	M	BCHR	GRZZZZ	USA	GRUENHAGEN, EMMA	15	F	UNKNOWN	GRZZZZ	USA
DEIERL, JOSEF	16	M	GDNR	GRZZZZ	USA	SCHAETT, ANNA	22	F	UNKNOWN	GRZZZZ	USA
LANG, HEINR.	23	M	GDNR	GRZZZZ	USA	FERSCH, THERESE	29	F	UNKNOWN	GRZZZZ	USA
BARZKOWSKY, M-RT	00	M	GDNR	GRZZZZ	USA	SANTRUP, LAURA	28	F	UNKNOWN	GRZZZZ	USA
LUCZAK, BO-ESL	23	M	GDNR	GRZZZZ	USA	KAY, ANNA	25	F	UNKNOWN	GRZZZZ	USA
DABROWSLU, FRANZ	27	M	GDNR	GRZZZZ	USA	STOCK, ESTHER	23	F	UNKNOWN	GRZZZZ	USA
SCHACKENMEIER, HEINR.	25	M	GDNR	GRZZZZ	USA	JOCHENSEN, CATHI	19	F	UNKNOWN	GRZZZZ	USA
CHRIST, FRIEDR.	28	M	GDNR	GRZZZZ	USA	SCHIESSE, MARIE	23	F	UNKNOWN	GRZZZZ	USA
FEDDEN, CARL	15	M	FARMER	GRZZZZ	USA	RUNGE, MARIE	21	F	UNKNOWN	GRZZZZ	USA
HEFERS, FRITZ	16	M	FARMER	GRZZZZ	USA	ASMUSSEN, HELENE	24	F	UNKNOWN	GRZZZZ	USA
NORPEL, JOHANN	28	M	FARMER	GRZZZZ	USA	WETZEL, WILHEL.	19	F	UNKNOWN	GRZZZZ	USA
ALDACH--, J.H.	00	M	GDNR	GRZZZZ	USA	GAEHR, CATHI	23	F	UNKNOWN	GRZZZZ	USA
GRAHN, WILH.	14	M	GDNR	GRZZZZ	USA	SEIPEL, SIBILLA	22	F	UNKNOWN	GRZZZZ	USA
SCHEMANN, MAX	14	M	GDNR	GRZZZZ	USA	KRANE, ANNASTASCE	18	F	UNKNOWN	GRZZZZ	USA
BORZ, MAX	16	M	GDNR	GRZZZZ	USA	RAEHRS, MARIE	19	F	UNKNOWN	GRZZZZ	USA
MATULIATIS, JONAS	31	M	GDNR	GRZZZZ	USA	MAJA, EMMA	32	F	UNKNOWN	GRZZZZ	USA
OSMANS, HINR.	15	M	GDNR	GRZZZZ	USA	RATHAUS, AUGUSTE	21	F	UNKNOWN	GRZZZZ	USA
KACHADT, ALBERT	16	M	GDNR	GRZZZZ	USA	DROSTE, FRIEDRK.	17	F	UNKNOWN	GRZZZZ	USA
JUNIG, GEORG	30	M	GDNR	GRZZZZ	USA	HELFRICH, DORATH.	14	F	UNKNOWN	GRZZZZ	USA
BISCHOFF, HEINR.	16	M	GDNR	GRZZZZ	USA	GROSCH, ANNA	25	F	UNKNOWN	GRZZZZ	USA
HERMEYER, AUGUST	24	M	FARMER	GRZZZZ	USA	ASCHMANN, MARIE	23	F	UNKNOWN	GRZZZZ	USA
ROSENBAUM, GUST.	14	M	FARMER	GRZZZZ	USA	LUETZ, MAGDA	23	F	UNKNOWN	GRZZZZ	USA
V. HERM.	27	M	FARMER	GRZZZZ	USA	BRAUN, HELENE	20	F	UNKNOWN	GRZZZZ	USA
BANERLEIN, JOSEF	25	M	GDNR	GRZZZZ	USA	SCHRAGENHEIM, IDA	22	F	UNKNOWN	GRZZZZ	USA
STANDINGER, ROBERT	32	M	GDNR	GRZZZZ	USA	GRUNWALD, LIESCHEN	7	F	CHILD	GRZZZZ	USA
VENNUS, JOSEF	28	M	GDNR	GRZZZZ	USA	RODICK, HELENE	21	F	UNKNOWN	GRZZZZ	USA
FENKER, CARL	22	M	GDNR	GRZZZZ	USA	RADKE, MAGDA	17	F	UNKNOWN	GRZZZZ	USA
LANGE, META	17	F	UNKNOWN	GRZZZZ	USA	KABE, KATE	18	F	UNKNOWN	GRZZZZ	USA
WEHLING, AUGUSTE	18	F	UNKNOWN	GRZZZZ	USA	WALTERS, KATE	28	F	UNKNOWN	GRZZZZ	USA
WOSCSAK, AGNES	17	F	UNKNOWN	GRZZZZ	USA	BURCK, ELISE	17	F	UNKNOWN	GRZZZZ	USA
SAMMET, MARIE	25	F	UNKNOWN	GRZZZZ	USA	RATH, MARIE	20	F	UNKNOWN	GRZZZZ	USA
BAELL, MARIE	18	F	UNKNOWN	GRZZZZ	USA	VAGEL, MARIE	16	F	UNKNOWN	GRZZZZ	USA
BERNER, CATHI	14	F	UNKNOWN	GRZZZZ	USA	FADEL, PAULA	25	F	UNKNOWN	GRZZZZ	USA
BAUMEISTER, LENA	29	F	UNKNOWN	GRZZZZ	USA	ALWEN, RACHEL	48	F	UNKNOWN	GRZZZZ	USA
BERBERICH, CAROLA	19	F	UNKNOWN	GRZZZZ	USA	RUCK, WILHE.	19	F	UNKNOWN	GRZZZZ	USA
FRIES, ANNA	6	F	CHILD	GRZZZZ	USA	SCHMIDT, WILHE.	20	F	UNKNOWN	GRZZZZ	USA
BORNZKA, LWONORE	22	F	UNKNOWN	GRZZZZ	USA	HAPOLD, WILHELE.	26	F	UNKNOWN	GRZZZZ	USA
KRAUS, AUGUSTE	26	F	UNKNOWN	GRZZZZ	USA	GURHANER, MARIE	46	F	UNKNOWN	GRZZZZ	USA
FENNER, CATHI	8	F	CHILD	GRZZZZ	USA	EDER, LABINE	14	F	UNKNOWN	GRZZZZ	USA
KORDKAMP, KORIS	14	F	UNKNOWN	GRZZZZ	USA	BUHLMEIER, MARIE	24	F	UNKNOWN	GRZZZZ	USA

PASSENGER	AGE	SEX	OCCUPATION	PVRIVL	DES
MAIER, MARIE	25	F	UNKNOWN	GRZZZZUSA	
STALH, META	18	F	UNKNOWN	GRZZZZUSA	
RALFS, SOPHIE	18	F	UNKNOWN	GRZZZZUSA	
KLUG, REGINE	18	F	UNKNOWN	GRZZZZUSA	
LIEBERMANN, BERTHA	16	F	UNKNOWN	GRZZZZUSA	
FLUNCHER, CHRIST	24	F	UNKNOWN	GRZZZZUSA	
DASCKING, WILHE.	17	F	UNKNOWN	GRZZZZUSA	
NADL, KATHI	24	F	UNKNOWN	GRZZZZUSA	
DORNREISER, MARIE	16	F	UNKNOWN	GRZZZZUSA	
KAUFMANN, SARA	19	F	UNKNOWN	GRZZZZUSA	
JUELLER, MARIE	21	F	UNKNOWN	GRZZZZUSA	
RAN, MARTHA	14	F	UNKNOWN	GRZZZZUSA	
FEIPEL, ANNA	24	F	UNKNOWN	GRZZZZUSA	
STRUCK, ELLY	14	F	UNKNOWN	GRZZZZUSA	
SOHAUSEN, ELFRIEDE	17	F	UNKNOWN	GRZZZZUSA	
SEGEL, MORDCKE	30	F	UNKNOWN	GRZZZZUSA	
BORNEMANN, CAROLA	14	F	UNKNOWN	GRZZZZUSA	
A-RACHEN, CAROLA	41	F	UNKNOWN	GRZZZZUSA	
SEIDEL, MARIE	24	F	UNKNOWN	GRZZZZUSA	
FREY, ELISE	27	F	UNKNOWN	GRZZZZUSA	
WORMSEK, FERD.	26	M	FARMER	GRZZZZUSA	
WILHE.	23	F	W	GRZZZZUSA	
SCHLAARD, HERMINE	24	F	UNKNOWN	GRZZZZUSA	
HESCHEN	.10	F	INFANT	GRZZZZUSA	
RATHBUCHNER, ANNA	22	F	UNKNOWN	GRZZZZUSA	
ELISE	13	F	UNKNOWN	GRZZZZUSA	
AUGUST	.06	M	INFANT	GRZZZZUSA	
BECKER, ELISE	21	F	UNKNOWN	GRZZZZUSA	
MAGDA	.06	F	INFANT	GRZZZZUSA	
RUDEL, ANNA	28	F	UNKNOWN	GRZZZZUSA	
GEORG	6	M	CHILD	GRZZZZUSA	
SENF, CHARLOTTE	30	F	UNKNOWN	GRZZZZUSA	
HEINR.	7	M	CHILD	GRZZZZUSA	
FRIEDR.	3	M	CHILD	GRZZZZUSA	
MINNA	1	F	CHILD	GRZZZZUSA	
WAGNER, BARBARA	62	F	UNKNOWN	GRZZZZUSA	
CHRISTE.	22	F	UNKNOWN	GRZZZZUSA	
BANTEL, MARIA	52	F	UNKNOWN	GRZZZZUSA	
CHARLOTTE	22	F	UNKNOWN	GRZZZZUSA	
ELISE	7	F	CHILD	GRZZZZUSA	
CONRAD	40	M	FARMER	GRZZZZUSA	
CARL	4	M	CHILD	GRZZZZUSA	
STENERNAGEL, PETER	48	M	MCHT	GRZZZZUSA	
CHRISTIAN	16	M	CH	GRZZZZUSA	
MARIA	7	F	CHILD	GRZZZZUSA	
SCHLAFFEL, ELISE	52	F	UNKNOWN	GRZZZZUSA	
ANNA	11	F	UNKNOWN	GRZZZZUSA	
MARY	7	F	CHILD	GRZZZZUSA	
SCHLANFUS, MORITZ	43	M	FARMER	GRZZZZUSA	
CAROLA	37	F	W	GRZZZZUSA	
ELISE	7	F	CHILD	GRZZZZUSA	
FRIEDRK.	4	F	CHILD	GRZZZZUSA	
EMIL	.10	M	INFANT	GRZZZZUSA	
ASCHMANN, MARY	25	F	UNKNOWN	GRZZZZUSA	
GUSTAV	.11	M	INFANT	GRZZZZUSA	
PFAFF, CARL	28	M	FARMER	GRZZZZUSA	
CATHI	4	F	CHILD	GRZZZZUSA	
FUERST, JAN	27	M	GDNR	GRZZZZUSA	
CUNIGUNDE	30	F	W	GRZZZZUSA	
BARBARA	49	F	UNKNOWN	GRZZZZUSA	
ANDRES	6	M	CHILD	GRZZZZUSA	
STANISLAWA	.04	F	INFANT	GRZZZZUSA	
WISHNIEWSKY, MARTIN	42	M	FARMER	GRZZZZUSA	
CLARA	35	F	W	GRZZZZUSA	
OTTMEYER, JOH.	37	M	FARMER	GRZZZZUSA	
JACOB	6	F	CHILD	GRZZZZUSA	
TOZYBILATZ, STANISL.	24	M	GDNR	GRZZZZUSA	
JADWIGA	21	F	W	GRZZZZUSA	
FASSHAUER, ELIAS	52	M	FARMER	GRZZZZUSA	
ANNA	41	F	W	GRZZZZUSA	
MARY	7	F	CHILD	GRZZZZUSA	
KAELBERER, GEORG	36	M	FARMER	GRZZZZUSA	
CATHI	32	F	W	GRZZZZUSA	
CAROLA	10	F	CH	GRZZZZUSA	
HEINR.	7	M	CHILD	GRZZZZUSA	
ADOLF	4	M	CHILD	GRZZZZUSA	
GUSTAV	.06	M	INFANT	GRZZZZUSA	
UTZ, SCHOLASTICA	60	F	UNKNOWN	GRZZZZUSA	
ANNA	22	F	UNKNOWN	GRZZZZUSA	
THERESE	7	F	CHILD	GRZZZZUSA	
RUNGE, JOHANNE	48	F	UNKNOWN	GRZZZZUSA	
ROBERT	16	M	UNKNOWN	GRZZZZUSA	
LOUISE	7	F	CHILD	GRZZZZUSA	
MEYER, CARL	47	M	FARMER	GRZZZZUSA	
LOUISE	46	F	W	GRZZZZUSA	
FRIEDRIKE	24	F	CH	GRZZZZUSA	
ELISE	7	F	CHILD	GRZZZZUSA	
HANS	4	M	CHILD	GRZZZZUSA	
KATHE	.10	F	INFANT	GRZZZZUSA	
KOCHERER, BARBARA	38	F	UNKNOWN	GRZZZZUSA	
BARBARA	7	F	CHILD	GRZZZZUSA	
GEORG	5	M	CHILD	GRZZZZUSA	
THERESE	3	F	CHILD	GRZZZZUSA	
ADAM	.09	M	INFANT	GRZZZZUSA	
PERITZ, ZARDIK	50	M	FARMER	GRZZZZUSA	
LEO	11	M	CH	GRZZZZUSA	
NATHAN	7	M	CHILD	GRZZZZUSA	
HASELMANN, SOPHIE	20	F	UNKNOWN	GRZZZZUSA	
ERHARD	14	M	UNKNOWN	GRZZZZUSA	
TODLICH, WILHELM	40	M	FARMER	GRZZZZUSA	
AUGUSTE	4	F	CHILD	GRZZZZUSA	
HOLZERLAND, CHR.	45	M	GDNR	GRZZZZUSA	
JOHANNE	58	F	W	GRZZZZUSA	
EMIL	15	M	CH	GRZZZZUSA	
RUDOLPH	7	M	CHILD	GRZZZZUSA	
HEDWIG	4	F	CHILD	GRZZZZUSA	
FRIDA	.11	F	INFANT	GRZZZZUSA	
DEGENER, ALBERT	32	M	FARMER	GRZZZZUSA	
CLEMENTE.	25	F	W	GRZZZZUSA	
MARIE	3	F	CHILD	GRZZZZUSA	
ROSENBLUM, MORITZ	17	M	MCHT	GRZZZZUSA	
WOLF	16	M	MCHT	GRZZZZUSA	
EHMANN, GOTTFRIED	38	M	GDNR	GRZZZZUSA	
BERTA	35	F	W	GRZZZZUSA	
CARL	10	M	CH	GRZZZZUSA	
GOTTLIEB	7	M	CHILD	GRZZZZUSA	
GOTTHILF	4	M	CHILD	GRZZZZUSA	
EMILIE	2	F	CHILD	GRZZZZUSA	
KIERZKOWSKY, JOH.	22	M	FARMER	GRZZZZUSA	
ANTONIE	38	F	UNKNOWN	GRZZZZUSA	
JEPSEN, SEH.	33	M	FARMER	GRZZZZUSA	
CHRISTE.	29	F	W	GRZZZZUSA	
CATHI	3	F	CHILD	GRZZZZUSA	
NICOLAUS	.10	M	INFANT	GRZZZZUSA	
MEYER, HEINR.	31	M	FARMER	GRZZZZUSA	
CAROLA	21	F	W	GRZZZZUSA	
CHRIST	.09	M	INFANT	GRZZZZUSA	
ULLRICH, CARL	26	M	GDNR	GRZZZZUSA	
MARIA	20	F	W	GRZZZZUSA	
NIGRIN, EILH.	24	M	FARMER	GRZZZZUSA	
ANNA	22	F	W	GRZZZZUSA	
WILHELM	4	M	CHILD	GRZZZZUSA	
BERG, CARL	29	M	FARMER	GRZZZZUSA	
WILHE.	32	F	W	GRZZZZUSA	
WILH.	3	M	CHILD	GRZZZZUSA	
GRETHE	2	F	CHILD	GRZZZZUSA	
ERNA	.03	F	INFANT	GRZZZZUSA	
DETERLING, MARIA	27	F	UNKNOWN	GRZZZZUSA	
SOPHIE	23	F	UNKNOWN	GRZZZZUSA	
RUCK, WILHE.	39	F	UNKNOWN	GRZZZZUSA	
CHARLOTTE	7	F	CHILD	GRZZZZUSA	
SCHLAGINTWEIT, FANNY	32	F	UNKNOWN	GRZZZZUSA	
FERRI	9	U	CHILD	GRZZZZUSA	
ALBERTE	5	F	CHILD	GRZZZZUSA	
FANNY	7	F	CHILD	GRZZZZUSA	
BERTHA	.11	F	INFANT	GRZZZZUSA	
BECKER, ANNA	25	F	UNKNOWN	GRZZZZUSA	
CAROLA	4	F	CHILD	GRZZZZUSA	
SCHMIDT, JOSEF	41	M	FARMER	GRZZZZUSA	
ANNA	41	F	W	GRZZZZUSA	

PASSENGER	AGE	SEX	OCCUPATION	PRVVL	DES
BARBARA	10	F	CH	GRZZZZUSA	
MELCHIOR	7	M	CHILD	GRZZZZUSA	
MARGARE.	3	F	CHILD	GRZZZZUSA	
JOSEF	2	M	CHILD	GRZZZZUSA	
MARIA	.08	F	INFANT	GRZZZZUSA	
MOOSBACH, WILH.	25	M	GDNR	GRZZZZUSA	
LISETTE	18	F	W	GRZZZZUSA	
JULIE	.11	F	INFANT	GRZZZZUSA	
FRAD, JOHANNE	29	F	UNKNOWN	GRZZZZUSA	
JOH.	5	M	CHILD	GRZZZZUSA	
SAGERER, SANNY	24	F	UNKNOWN	GRZZZZUSA	
MAX	.06	M	INFANT	GRZZZZUSA	
SCHUERMANN, GUSTAV	24	M	FARMER	GRZZZZUSA	
AUGUSTE	20	F	W	GRZZZZUSA	
WOLF, FRANZ	45	M	FARMER	GRZZZZUSA	
ELISE	43	F	W	GRZZZZUSA	
GERTRUD	7	F	CHILD	GRZZZZUSA	
HELENE	3	F	CHILD	GRZZZZUSA	
FRANZ	.11	M	INFANT	GRZZZZUSA	
LACKMANN, HENR.	62	M	GDNR	GRZZZZUSA	
HINR.	15	M	CH	GRZZZZUSA	
FULD, SIEGFRIED	19	M	FARMER	GRZZZZUSA	
SABINE	16	F	W	GRZZZZUSA	
WOLFF, HERMANN	33	M	FARMER	GRZZZZUSA	
U	34	F	W	GRZZZZUSA	
RICHARD	7	M	CHILD	GRZZZZUSA	
MARTHA	6	F	CHILD	GRZZZZUSA	
MAX	.11	M	INFANT	GRZZZZUSA	
WISNIEWSKA, ANTONIE	27	F	UNKNOWN	GRZZZZUSA	
JAN	.11	M	INFANT	GRZZZZUSA	
MUELLER, LENA	32	F	UNKNOWN	GRZZZZUSA	
ESTHER	7	F	CHILD	GRZZZZUSA	
LEONHARD	6	M	CHILD	GRZZZZUSA	
EMIL	4	M	CHILD	GRZZZZUSA	
LEA	3	F	CHILD	GRZZZZUSA	

SHIP: CITY OF BERLIN

FROM: LIVERPOOL AND QUEENSTOWN
TO: NEW YORK
ARRIVED: 09 JUNE 1888

PASSENGER	AGE	SEX	OCCUPATION	PRVVL	DES
FARZKEWITZ, JERINARD	29	M	LABR	GRACBFNY	
PRUSCHWOFSKY, NUSEN	28	M	LABR	GRACBFNY	
WEISS, HERMAN	18	M	LABR	GRACBFNY	
ITCIKOWITZ, SAUL	24	M	TLR	GRACBFNY	
ZULLINGER, ALEX	30	M	LABR	GRACBFNY	
SCHWARZ, HERMAN	40	M	LABR	GRACBFNY	
NEIDERMAN, MALI	20	F	SVNT	GRACBFNY	
DAVIS, HERMAN	24	M	LABR	GRACBFNY	
GOLDBERG, B	26	M	LABR	GRACBFNY	
GREENWALD, MARI	16	F	LABR	GRACBFNY	
ZIGATHA, ANNA	17	F	LABR	GRACBFNY	
SALTKIN, CHAIE	25	F	W	GRACBFNY	
GISCHE	00	F	INF	GRACBFNY	
PULSIGWER, ABT.	46	M	GENT	GRACBFNY	
BERUST--ON, LEOPLD	35	M	GENT	GRZZZZNY	

SHIP: GELLERT

FROM: HAMBURG AND HAVRE
TO: NEW YORK
ARRIVED: 09 JUNE 1888

PASSENGER	AGE	SEX	OCCUPATION	PRVVL	DES
LEWIN, ELCAS	52	M	CGRMKR	HBZZZZUSA	
ROETHHOLZ, BERTHA	19	F	SGL	PRZZZZUSA	
PETER, HERMANN	17	M	JNR	PRZZZZUSA	
ZIMS, PAUL	14	M	FARMER	PRZZZZUSA	
HABIOR, FRANZ	42	M	LABR	PRZZZZUSA	
SCHAUB, JOHANNAS	19	M	LABR	PRZZZZUSA	
BETFREUND, GERHARD	64	M	SMH	PRZZZZUSA	
HEDWIG	54	F	W	PRZZZZUSA	
BOUGORT, ADOLPH	22	M	BKR	PRZZZZUSA	
BERUTH, FREDERIKE	31	F	WO	HBZZZZUSA	
UFFEN, HEINRICH	28	M	MCHT	PRZZZZUSA	
HERMANN	32	M	LABR	PRZZZZUSA	
HOFMANN, HEINRICH	51	M	LABR	HBZZZZUSA	
GITTMER, ADOLPHINE	19	F	SGL	PRZZZZUSA	
BUTTNER, LEONARD	21	M	BKR	BVZZZZUSA	
FIGINSCHE, KATHARINA	22	F	SGL	BVZZZZUSA	
NISSEN, ANNA	28	F	WO	PRZZZZUSA	
CACECILIE	5	F	CHILD	PRZZZZUSA	
ANDREAS	3	M	CHILD	PRZZZZUSA	
PETER	.11	M	INFANT	PRZZZZUSA	
HEIKMANN, WILHELM	33	M	LABR	HBZZZZUSA	
HASSE, MATHILDE	16	F	SGL	PRZZZZUSA	
LAU, DOROTHEA	54	F	WO	PRZZZZUSA	
AMALIA	20	F	D	PRZZZZUSA	
WEHRENT, ANNA	5	F	CHILD	PRZZZZUSA	
FINKELSTEIN, CHAIE	40	F	WO	PRZZZZUSA	
JUTE	15	F	WO	PRZZZZUSA	
SIMON	7	M	CHILD	PRZZZZUSA	
MARCUS	5	M	CHILD	PRZZZZUSA	
STAHLBOHM, JOHANNA	23	F	SGL	PRZZZZUSA	
FIEDLER, THEODORIA	33	F	WO	PRZZZZUSA	
TASCHENBERGER, CARL	33	M	UPHST	HBZZZZUSA	
GUNDLACH, AUGUST	61	M	LABR	PRZZZZUSA	
FRANCISCA	61	F	W	PRZZZZUSA	
MARIE	17	F	D	PRZZZZUSA	
NICKE, LOUIS	23	M	LABR	PRZZZZUSA	
SCHUB, AUGUST	22	M	LABR	PRZZZZUSA	
EHLERT, CARL	22	M	LABR	PRZZZZUSA	
LINDFNER, CARL	38	M	LABR	PRZZZZUSA	
HINTZ, AUGUSTE	35	F	WO	PRZZZZUSA	
ADOLF	36	M	LABR	PRZZZZUSA	
BAATS, JOHANN	34	M	JNR	PRZZZZUSA	
BAAK, MARIE	30	F	W	PRZZZZUSA	
EMMA	8	F	CHILD	PRZZZZUSA	
ROSA	4	F	CHILD	PRZZZZUSA	
WILHELM	.03	M	INFANT	PRZZZZUSA	
CATHARINA	65	F	WO	PRZZZZUSA	
HANSEN, CHRISTINE	20	F	SGL	PRZZZZUSA	
SCHUERDER, JULIUS	23	M	CPTR	PRZZZZUSA	
ELISABETH	22	F	W	PRZZZZUSA	
MARTHA	2	F	CHILD	PRZZZZUSA	
ZEIDLER, JUSTINE	27	F	SGL	BVZZZZUSA	
HILDENBRANDT, MARIE	18	F	SGL	BDZZZZUSA	
WISNIEWSKA, FRANZISKA	40	F	WO	PRZZZZUSA	
KERSTING, EMILIE	53	F	WO	SYZZZZUSA	
FRIEDRICH	15	M	S	SYZZZZUSA	
WOLFF, MICHEL	24	M	LABR	PRZZZZUSA	
BISCHOFF, MARGARETHE	20	F	SGL	PRZZZZUSA	
JACOB, ROBERT	14	M	LABR	PRZZZZUSA	
GITL, JOSEPH	33	M	SHMK	BVZZZZUSA	
OFF, GOFFL	27	M	LABR	WMZZZZUSA	
NIKEL, MARIE	36	F	SGL	PRZZZZUSA	
ROTHER, AMALIE	15	F	SGL	PRZZZZUSA	
BRONISLAW	18	M	LABR	PRZZZZUSA	
PLIEFKE, CAROLINE	54	F	WO	PRZZZZUSA	
PAUL	18	M	S	PRZZZZUSA	
HERMANN	15	M	S	PRZZZZUSA	
HEIDORN, WILHELM	23	M	TLR	PRZZZZUSA	

PASSENGER	AGE	SEX	OCCUPATION	PRVL	DES
KRUEGER, ADAM	25	M	LABR	PRZZZZUSA	
AURICH, BERTHA	27	F	WO	PRZZZZUSA	
ANNA	7	F	CHILD	PRZZZZUSA	
PAUL	4	M	CHILD	PRZZZZUSA	
AUGUSTE	.11	F	INFANT	PRZZZZUSA	
BETTI	.01	F	INFANT	PRZZZZUSA	
CORECK, RUDOLPH	25	M	MCHT	PRZZZZUSA	
HEINKE, AUGUSTE	24	F	SGL	PRZZZZUSA	
ERP, JOHANN	27	M	SMH	PRZZZZUSA	
SCHROEDER, GOTTHARD	23	M	MCHT	PRZZZZUSA	
HOLTINGER, JOHANN	24	M	LABR	BVZZZZUSA	
SCHRAMM, LINA	22	F	SGL	PRZZZZUSA	
BLANK, WILHELM	28	M	LABR	HBZZZZUSA	
MARGARETHE	28	F	W	HBZZZZUSA	
MARTHA	.11	F	INFANT	HBZZZZUSA	
HOLTZ, DORA	22	F	SGL	HBZZZZUSA	
WAHLEN, PETER	43	M	FARMER	PRZZZZUSA	
CHRISTINE	36	F	W	PRZZZZUSA	
OTTO	9	M	CHILD	PRZZZZUSA	
MARTHA	8	F	CHILD	PRZZZZUSA	
PETER	4	M	CHILD	PRZZZZUSA	
ARNOLD	3	M	CHILD	PRZZZZUSA	
ERNST	.11	M	INFANT	PRZZZZUSA	
KAHRS, GUSTAV	16	M	FARMER	PRZZZZUSA	
FINKELSTEIN, MORITZ	9	M	CHILD	PRZZZZUSA	
PAULSEN, NIELS	19	M	FARMER	PRZZZZUSA	
STUHR, WILHELM	23	M	WTR	PRZZZZUSA	
EPSTEIN, ERNESTINE	20	F	SGL	PRZZZZUSA	
MUELLER, FRIEDRICH	27	M	SMH	PRZZZZUSA	
SISZCZYNSKA, DOROTHEA	30	F	SGL	PRZZZZUSA	
ELSNER, HELENE	27	F	SGL	PRZZZZUSA	
KRAJEWSKA, APOLONIA	22	F	SGL	PRZZZZUSA	
LEYDEL, CARL	40	M	LABR	PRZZZZUSA	
EMILIE	33	F	W	PRZZZZUSA	
RICHARD	18	M	CH	PRZZZZUSA	
AUGUSTE	4	M	CHILD	PRZZZZUSA	
HULDA	2	F	CHILD	PRZZZZUSA	
CARL	.08	M	INFANT	PRZZZZUSA	
ETELSOHN, CHAIE	9	F	CHILD	PRZZZZUSA	
KLOAK, GEORG	29	M	JNR	PRZZZZUSA	
ANNA	25	F	W	PRZZZZUSA	
HERMANN	2	M	CHILD	PRZZZZUSA	
FRITZ	.06	M	INFANT	PRZZZZUSA	
MEINS, HEINRICH	58	M	LLD	PRZZZZUSA	
WILMOWICZ, ANNA	20	F	SGL	PRZZZZUSA	
KAISER, JOHANN	23	M	JNR	PRZZZZUSA	
SZYMANSKI, TOMAS	24	M	LABR	PRZZZZUSA	
BOETEL, THEODOR	34	M	FARMER	PRZZZZUSA	
FREDERIKE	9	F	CHILD	PRZZZZUSA	
ELISE	7	F	CHILD	PRZZZZUSA	
ANNA	4	F	CHILD	PRZZZZUSA	
BECKER, CATHARINA	19	F	SGL	WMZZZZUSA	
DETHLEFSEN, JOHANNE	22	F	SGL	PRZZZZUSA	
KRAEMER, CARL	14	M	FARMER	PRZZZZUSA	
ERDMANN, MAGNUS	16	M	PH	PRZZZZUSA	
KUEHL, FRITZ	22	M	FARMER	PRZZZZUSA	
ZELLER, FREDRICH	9	M	CHILD	PRZZZZUSA	
RAHN, ADOLF	30	M	SHMK	PRZZZZUSA	
AMTER, ANNA	21	F	SGL	PRZZZZUSA	
STEINBRENNER, AUGUST	9	M	CHILD	WMZZZZUSA	
HAERLE, FRIEDRICH	16	M	GDNR	WMZZZZUSA	
WEISS, MARIE	21	F	SGL	PRZZZZUSA	
BOCK, CHRISTINE	15	F	SGL	PRZZZZUSA	
JESSEN, JOERGEN	24	M	LABR	PRZZZZUSA	
CLAUSSEN, ASMUSS	37	M	FARMER	PRZZZZUSA	
VELTE, KARL	13	M	LABR	PRZZZZUSA	
DUL, MARTIN	36	M	SLR	PRZZZZUSA	
ROERDEN, ARENDT	16	M	FARMER	PRZZZZUSA	
PAULSEN, META	16	F	SGL	PRZZZZUSA	
KRAEMER, WILHELMINE	18	F	SGL	PRZZZZUSA	
WILLERT, ANNA	32	F	SGL	PRZZZZUSA	
ARFSTEN, KECKI	24	F	SGL	PRZZZZUSA	
HAUSEN, HANS	17	M	FARMER	PRZZZZUSA	
HINRICHSEN, MARGARETHE	18	F	SGL	PRZZZZUSA	
HAUSEN, HEINRICH	25	M	LABR	PRZZZZUSA	
INGWER	15	M	LABR	PRZZZZUSA	
DOROTHEA	17	F	SGL	PRZZZZUSA	
HOHN, MORITZ	15	M	FARMER	PRZZZZUSA	
RIEWERTS, ROSCHE	27	F	WO	PRZZZZUSA	
ROSINE	6	F	CHILD	PRZZZZUSA	
BLEEY, CHRISTIAN	15	M	FARMER	PRZZZZUSA	
CHRISTIANSEN, ANTONIE	17	F	SGL	PRZZZZUSA	
HAUSEN, MARIE	22	M	SGL	PRZZZZUSA	
HOLNIERS, JESS	16	M	FARMER	PRZZZZUSA	
FULLESEN, HANNE	16	F	SGL	PRZZZZUSA	
NIELSEN, ROSINE	22	F	SGL	PRZZZZUSA	
JESSEN, PETER	49	M	FARMER	PRZZZZUSA	
PAULINE	40	F	W	PRZZZZUSA	
CATHARINA	20	F	CH	PRZZZZUSA	
ANDREAS	18	M	CH	PRZZZZUSA	
CHRISTIAN	16	M	CH	PRZZZZUSA	
PAUL	9	M	CHILD	PRZZZZUSA	
CARL	4	M	CHILD	PRZZZZUSA	
MARTIN	3	M	CHILD	PRZZZZUSA	
HAUSEN, LORENZ	36	M	FARMER	PRZZZZUSA	
CLAUSEN, PETER	9	M	CHILD	PRZZZZUSA	
BRANDT, WILHELM	45	M	FARMER	PRZZZZUSA	
CLAUSEN, RESMUS	46	M	FARMER	PRZZZZUSA	
JACOB	8	M	CHILD	PRZZZZUSA	
CHRISTINE	5	M	CHILD	PRZZZZUSA	
JENS	4	M	CHILD	PRZZZZUSA	
RASMUS	.11	M	INFANT	PRZZZZUSA	
LUETKE, HERMANN	28	M	MLR	SYZZZZUSA	
LOEW, GEORG	54	M	WVR	WMZZZZUSA	
ELISABETH	39	F	W	WMZZZZUSA	
VOELK, CARL	21	M	MSN	WMZZZZUSA	
GASSNER, JANATZ	28	M	LABR	WMZZZZUSA	
VOLLMAR, PAULINE	17	F	SGL	WMZZZZUSA	
ELISABETH	27	F	SGL	WMZZZZUSA	
KAHL, ROSA	26	F	SGL	BDZZZZUSA	
FABRI, HELENE	21	F	SGL	BDZZZZUSA	
AMTHER, MARIE	20	F	SGL	BVZZZZUSA	
KLEIN, LUDWIG	24	M	FARMER	WMZZZZUSA	
GOEHNER, ANNA	29	F	SGL	WMZZZZUSA	
MUNSINGER, JACOB	29	M	SMH	WMZZZZUSA	
MARIE	28	F	W	WMZZZZUSA	
CARL	.03	M	INFANT	WMZZZZUSA	
HAUSCH, PAULINE	20	F	SGL	WMZZZZUSA	
WEIDLE, MARTIN	9	M	CHILD	WMZZZZUSA	
SACHS, MAGDALENA	17	F	SGL	WMZZZZUSA	
FRIEDRICH, CARL	25	M	BCHR	WMZZZZUSA	
OTTENBACHER, CHRISTINE	51	F	WO	WMZZZZUSA	
SAUER, FRIEDERIKE	23	F	SGL	WMZZZZUSA	
CAROLINE	21	F	SGL	WMZZZZUSA	
SCHAEFER, ELISE	17	F	SGL	WMZZZZUSA	
NILL, JULIE	40	F	WO	WMZZZZUSA	
HERMANN	9	M	CHILD	WMZZZZUSA	
MUELLER, MARIE	21	F	SGL	WMZZZZUSA	
HOELLE, CONRAD	41	M	FARMER	WMZZZZUSA	
METZNER, OTTO	18	M	MCHT	SYZZZZUSA	
NILL, ROSINE	17	F	SGL	WMZZZZUSA	
GAEHM, GEORG	47	M	FARMER	WMZZZZUSA	
CATHARINA	44	F	W	WMZZZZUSA	
FRIEDRICH	19	M	CH	WMZZZZUSA	
LEONHARD	17	M	CH	WMZZZZUSA	
ROSINE	14	F	CH	WMZZZZUSA	
CATHARINA	9	F	CHILD	WMZZZZUSA	
REGINE	8	F	CHILD	WMZZZZUSA	
GAEHN, GEORG	7	M	CHILD	WMZZZZUSA	
JOHN	6	M	CHILD	WMZZZZUSA	
CAROLINE	4	F	CHILD	WMZZZZUSA	
WARM, JOHANN	24	M	GDSM	PRZZZZUSA	
EMMA	30	F	W	PRZZZZUSA	
SOLEWSKY, JACOB	18	M	LABR	PRZZZZUSA	
KAESTNER, FRIEDERIKE	17	F	WO	PRZZZZUSA	
RICHTER, MARTHA	19	F	SGL	PRZZZZUSA	
WITTE, CLARA	18	F	WO	PRZZZZUSA	
PAUL	14	M	LABR	PRZZZZUSA	
PETERS, RIEWERT	45	M	LABR	PRZZZZUSA	
RICKMERS, RIEWERT	15	M	LABR	PRZZZZUSA	

PASSENGER	AGE	SEX	OCCUPATION	PRVL	DES
PETERSEN, CATHARINA	30	F	WO		PRZZZZUSA
NIELSEN, CHRIATIAN	25	M	FARMER		PRZZZZUSA
LIERANKA, MARIANNA	18	F	WO		PRZZZZUSA
CICZPIK, HIPPOLIT	17	M	LABR		PRZZZZUSA
STRUCK, JOHANN	21	M	LABR		PRZZZZUSA
RICHAN, MINNA	22	F	WO		PRZZZZUSA
ZICHINSKI, MATHILDE	21	F	SGL		PRZZZZUSA
JOSEPHA	18	F	SGL		PRZZZZUSA
LAWRCUZ, ALBERT	25	M	LABR		PRZZZZUSA
MEYER, OTTILIE	18	F	SGL		PRZZZZUSA
PHILIPSKI, RUDOLF	36	M	LABR		PRZZZZUSA
STIEWE, CARL	31	M	LABR		PRZZZZUSA
MAKOWSKY, JACOB	26	M	LABR		PRZZZZUSA
GORSKA, MARIANNA	71	F	WO		PRZZZZUSA
HOPPE, HEINRICH	26	M	LABR		PRZZZZUSA
EILER, CARL	26	M	FARMER		PRZZZZUSA
ANDERSEN, ERICH	45	M	FARMER		PRZZZZUSA
TASCHITKY, SOPHIE	57	F	WO		PRZZZZUSA
BOHN, CORNELIUS	16	M	FARMER		PRZZZZUSA
HAUSEN, CHRISTIANE	23	F	SGL		PRZZZZUSA
MATHIEEN, INGEBORG	22	F	SGL		PRZZZZUSA
FRIEDERIKE	15	F	SGL		PRZZZZUSA
HARTZ, CARL	24	M	MCHT		PRZZZZUSA
DEIKOV, OTTO	32	M	FARMER		PRZZZZUSA
BOEGE, SOPHIE	27	F	SGL		PRZZZZUSA
JAURTZKA, STANISLAVA	19	F	SGL		PRZZZZUSA
JANKOWSKA, MARIE	20	F	SGL		PRZZZZUSA
BERNSTEIN, ERNESTINE	19	F	SGL		PRZZZZUSA
SCHAUM, WILHELMINE	31	F	WO		PRZZZZUSA
MAX	9	M	CHILD		PRZZZZUSA
MARTHA	8	F	CHILD		PRZZZZUSA
KCYHA, HELENE	20	F	SGL		PRZZZZUSA
TONN, FRIEDRICH	30	M	LABR		PRZZZZUSA
SCHLESINGER, MAX	22	M	MCHT		PRZZZZUSA
JAEHN, HERMANN	25	M	LKSH		HBZZZZUSA
KEPPISCH, FRANZ	31	M	LABR		PRZZZZUSA
ALWINE	32	F	W		PRZZZZUSA
EMMA	9	F	CHILD		PRZZZZUSA
KLUGE, KARL	23	M	WVR		SYZZZZUSA
ZSCHACHE, LOUISE	31	F	SGL		SYZZZZUSA
GOD, WILHELM	29	M	SHMK		BDZZZZUSA
ENGLER, ARTHUR	20	M	BRR		PRZZZZUSA
UEBNER, AUGUSTE	36	F	SGL		PRZZZZUSA
PUNKE, AUGUSTE	15	F	SGL		PRZZZZUSA
WESTERSEN, PETER	30	M	LABR		PRZZZZUSA
ZINSER, JOHANN	27	M	WCHMKR		WMZZZZUSA
NAGELDINGER, JACOB	16	M	LABR		BVZZZZUSA
ZIER, HCH.	26	M	BRR		BDZZZZUSA
ANZIGO, J	38	M	WTR		FRZZZZUSA
VETTER, LORENZ	55	M	FARMER		PRZZZZUSA
HELENE	23	F	W		PRZZZZUSA
SEBASTIAN	18	M	FARMER		PRZZZZUSA
WALD, GAMIL	28	M	SHMK		PRZZZZUSA
EMILIE	.08	F	INFANT		PRZZZZUSA
MEYER, ALBERTINE	21	F	SGL		SRZZZZUSA
ZEPF, EDUARD	21	M	SHMK		WMZZZZUSA
ERLACHER, GERDAS	24	M	LABR		BDZZZZUSA
EHERENZ, GERHARD	24	M	LKSH		BDZZZZUSA
SCHIEBER, OSWALD	25	M	FARMER		BDZZZZUSA
BOHN, ANNA	24	F	SGL		BDZZZZUSA
SCHISESS, AMALIE	25	F	SGL		BDZZZZUSA
STICHLER, THEODOR	26	M	LABR		BDZZZZUSA
SCHMIDT, FRIEDRICH	22	M	BKR		BDZZZZUSA
HAUANER, MARTIN	24	M	TLR		BDZZZZUSA
KROMER, FLORENTINE	21	F	SGL		BDZZZZUSA
U, U	26	M	BCHR		BDZZZZUSA
U	00	M	BKR		BDZZZZUSA
JETZER, AUGUSTE	24	F	SGL		BDZZZZUSA
MUELLER, CARL	24	M	JNR		BDZZZZUSA
KRETS, BERTHA	21	F	SGL		BDZZZZUSA
LEHMANN, JAKEL	33	M	BCHR		SRZZZZUSA
KELLER, ALBERT	18	M	BKR		BDZZZZUSA
GESSLER, JACOB	22	M	FARMER		BDZZZZUSA
MEYER, JEAN	34	M	BRR		BDZZZZUSA
ERDMANN, CLARLES	48	M	LABR		FRZZZZUSA

PASSENGER	AGE	SEX	OCCUPATION	PRVL	DES
GEIGER, AMALIE	21	F	SGL		WMZZZZUSA
MEZGER, HENDRIK	22	F	SGL		WMZZZZUSA
FAULHABER, CATHARINE	19	F	SGL		WMZZZZUSA
GEIGER, JOHANNS	44	M	JNR		WMZZZZUSA
BUERKEL, CARL	17	M	TLR		BDZZZZUSA
TEUFEL, JAC	17	M	TLR		BDZZZZUSA
BAAS, MICHAEL	17	M	BKR		PRZZZZUSA
LALLEMEUT, AUGUST	29	M	FARMER		PRZZZZUSA
EBER, MARIE	48	F	WO		FRZZZZUSA
SELIGMANN, LINA	24	F	SGL		HBZZZZUSA
HAMMEL, BERNHARD	60	M	MCHT		PRZZZZUSA
DOROTHEA	60	F	W		PRZZZZUSA
HOLTZ, SOPHIE	19	F	WO		PRZZZZUSA
DOURTZ, HERMANN	34	M	ACHTT		HBZZZZUSA
MARIE	34	F	W		HBZZZZUSA
HEEG, PETRONELLA	18	F	SGL		BVZZZZUSA
SOMMER, FRIEDA	18	F	SGL		BVZZZZUSA
HEINEN, JOHANNA	54	F	WO		PRZZZZUSA
SIEVERS, MARGARETHE	29	F	SGL		HBZZZZUSA
MOELLER, IDA	22	F	SGL		PRZZZZUSA
KREUTER, CHRISTINE	9	F	CHILD		PRZZZZUSA
HERMINE	8	F	CHILD		PRZZZZUSA
U	8	F	CHILD		PRZZZZUSA
U, U	27	F	SGL		PRZZZZUSA
MEEL, LISETTE	22	F	SGL		BDZZZZUSA
V, FRIEDRICH	27	M	FARMER		SYZZZZUSA
SCHILLING, OTTO	16	M	STDNT		PRZZZZUSA
HERMS, PAUL	30	M	CNF		PRZZZZUSA
AHRENT, MATHILDE	25	F	WO		PRZZZZUSA
SCHRAMM, ROBERT	32	M	UNKNOWN		PRZZZZUSA

SHIP: DEVONIA

FROM: GLASGOW AND MOVILLE
TO: NEW YORK
ARRIVED: 11 JUNE 1888

PASSENGER	AGE	SEX	OCCUPATION	PRVL	DES
THOMAS, ERNST	43	M	MLR		PRAHRZUSA
CAROLINE	38	F	UNKNOWN		PRAHRZUSA
LUDVIG	15	M	UNKNOWN		PRAHRZUSA
CARL	10	M	CH		PRAHRZUSA
MINNIE	9	F	CHILD		PRAHRZUSA
ALMA	3	F	CHILD		PRAHRZUSA
ANNA	.11	F	INFANT		PRAHRZUSA
JANKOWIAK, FRANCISCHEK	48	M	UNKNOWN		PRAHRZUSA
MARIANNE	10	F	CH		PRAHRZUSA
STANISLAW	2	M	CHILD		PRAHRZUSA
KAUPTMANN, ANNA	24	F	SVNT		PRAHRZUSA
KOCH, AUGUSTA	44	F	SVNT		PRAHRZUSA
KAMINSKY, MARIE	19	F	SVNT		PRAHRZUSA
OLFSCHEFSKA, MARIE	9	F	CHILD		PRAHRZUSA
SPERBER, BREINDEL	19	F	SVNT		PRAHRZUSA
LIPSCHE	17	F	SVNT		PRAHRZUSA
AMON, JOHAN	41	M	STCTR		PRAHRZUSA
BULLERT, AB.	31	M	LABR		PRAHRZUSA
KWIDA, ANTON	17	M	BKR		PRAHRZUSA
LESINTZKI, PETER	27	M	MNR		PRAHRZUSA
MALKOWSKI, FRANZ	15	M	UNKNOWN		PRAHRZUSA
NAGEL, HERMAN	24	M	LABR		PRAHRZUSA
STAPEL, LABRECH	21	M	LABR		PRAHRZUSA
SALOMOWITZ, JAN	16	M	LABR		PRAHRZUSA
JANSOVIAK, MARCIN	45	M	LABR		PRAHRZUSA

147

PASSENGER	AGE	SEX	OCCUPATION	PRVL	DES

SHIP: SERVIA

FROM: LIVERPOOL AND QUEENSTOWN
TO: NEW YORK
ARRIVED: 11 JUNE 1888

PASSENGER	AGE	SEX	OCCUPATION	PRVL DES
DABERGOTZ, RENBOLD	28	M	LABR	SRZZZZNY
ALESAAT, GUSTAV	32	M	MACH	GRZZZZNY
KIEHN, JOHAN	41	M	LABR	GRZZZZNY
KOHFUHL, HEINRICH	56	M	LABR	GRZZZZNY
SUCLES, CARL	21	M	LABR	GRZZZZNY
MAY, FRIEDRICH	30	M	LABR	GRZZZZNY
LEWANDOWSKY, FRANZ	38	M	LABR	GRZZZZNY
CHLEBOWITZ, JULIAN	24	M	TLR	GRZZZZNY
NEUMANN, EMIL	19	M	CL	GRZZZZNY
SAUTER, JACOB	28	M	BKR	GRZZZZNY
BELLMAN, LOTTIE	22	F	SP	GRZZZZNY
DETOURBE, MAURICE	27	M	MCHT	FRZZZZNY

SHIP: EIDER

FROM: BREMEN AND SOUTHAMPTON
TO: NEW YORK
ARRIVED: 12 JUNE 1888

PASSENGER	AGE	SEX	OCCUPATION	PRVL DES
GRAETZEL, CR	29	M	TT	GRZZZZUSA
GROSS, JULIUS	28	M	TT	GRZZZZUSA
WIEGNER, ALWIN	28	M	TT	GRZZZZUSA
EGBERDING, FRANZ	26	M	TT	GRZZZZUSA
SCHMIE--, BERNH	13	M	TT	GRZZZZUSA
SEIFERT, ADAM	40	M	UNKNOWN	GRZZZZUSA
EIM, KAETCHEN	24	F	UNKNOWN	GRZZZZUSA
LIEDTKE, MARIE	53	F	UNKNOWN	GRZZZZUSA
LIND, KATHARINE	52	F	UNKNOWN	GRZZZZUSA
MARIE	22	F	UNKNOWN	GRZZZZUSA
PHILIPP	19	M	TT	GRZZZZUSA
KATHARINE	10	F	CH	GRZZZZUSA
PFEIL, IDA	19	F	UNKNOWN	GRZZZZUSA
KRAUSS, EMIL	32	M	TT	GRZZZZUSA
KIMBLE, G	56	M	TT	GRZZZZUSA
K	29	M	TT	GRZZZZUSA
ECKER, LINA	25	F	UNKNOWN	GRZZZZUSA
SCHROEDER, LOUISE	20	F	UNKNOWN	GRZZZZUSA
RATHIEN, EMMA	11	F	UNKNOWN	GRZZZZUSA
HOLLER, JOSEF	19	M	TT	GRZZZZUSA
ROES, CHALLI	30	M	TT	GRZZZZUSA
DEICHMANN, EMILIE	30	F	UNKNOWN	GRZZZZUSA
HAENPTNER, OSCAR	35	M	TT	GRZZZZUSA
FISCHEL, ELISABETH	50	F	UNKNOWN	GRZZZZUSA
THOMAS, FRANZ	23	M	TT	GRZZZZUSA
BURGHARDT, G	45	M	TT	GRZZZZUSA
VOGEL, META	18	F	UNKNOWN	GRZZZZUSA
GEHL, EREMREICH	28	M	TT	GRZZZZUSA
WEISE, MINNA	18	F	SVNT	GRZZZZUSA
FR	40	M	DLR	GRZZZZUSA
BENKER, JOH	21	M	LABR	GRZZZZUSA
WALFISCH, MALI	25	F	UNKNOWN	GRZZZZUSA
LOTTIE	18	F	UNKNOWN	GRZZZZUSA
ADOLF	5	M	CHILD	GRZZZZUSA
ISIDOR	3	M	CHILD	GRZZZZUSA
TONI	.08	F	INFANT	GRZZZZUSA
LOEHN, FERDINAND	36	M	LABR	GRZZZZUSA
AMANDA	33	F	W	GRZZZZUSA
AUGUSTE	10	F	CH	GRZZZZUSA
GUESTAV	00	M	UNKNOWN	GRZZZZUSA
RICHARD	6	M	CHILD	GRZZZZUSA
KLEIMEL, WILH	16	M	LABR	GRZZZZUSA
ARTMANN, RICHARD	24	M	PNTR	GRZZZZUSA
KOTENBENTEL, AUGUSTE	25	F	SVNT	GRZZZZUSA
MOSINSKY, ANDR	41	M	MLR	GRZZZZUSA
SCHNELL, HERM	19	M	MLR	GRZZZZUSA
BRATZ, MICH	44	M	FARMER	GRZZZZUSA
FABER, JULIUS	15	M	FARMER	GRZZZZUSA
MARKO, OTTO	12	M	UNKNOWN	GRZZZZUSA
GAWRONSKI, ANTON	28	M	LABR	GRZZZZUSA
NENENFELDT, CARL	36	M	JNR	GRZZZZUSA
EMMA	33	F	W	GRZZZZUSA
ANNA	9	F	CHILD	GRZZZZUSA
ALBERT	4	M	CHILD	GRZZZZUSA
JAHN, WILH	24	M	LKSH	GRZZZZUSA
HAGER, GEORG	18	M	MCHT	GRZZZZUSA
LORENZ, BERTHA	18	F	SVNT	GRZZZZUSA
KALWER, JOHANNA	48	F	LABR	GRZZZZUSA
CAROLINE	46	F	W	GRZZZZUSA
MARIE	20	F	UNKNOWN	GRZZZZUSA
GALEWSKA, ELEONORE	23	F	UNKNOWN	GRZZZZUSA
STANISLAUS	.02	M	INFANT	GRZZZZUSA
BUCHHOLZ, LOUISE	18	F	SVNT	GRZZZZUSA
RIESENBURG, ERNSTINE	34	F	UNKNOWN	GRZZZZUSA
FELIX	4	M	CHILD	GRZZZZUSA
ISIDOR	2	M	CHILD	GRZZZZUSA
GERTRUD	.04	F	INFANT	GRZZZZUSA
KRZYZANOWSKY, IGNATZ	32	M	LABR	GRZZZZUSA
GLISCZYNSKA, ANNA	25	F	UNKNOWN	GRZZZZUSA
MARYANNA	.10	F	INFANT	GRZZZZUSA
DREWS, FRIEDR	35	M	LABR	GRZZZZUSA
LUCHTER, AUG	16	M	LABR	GRZZZZUSA
KALWA, FRIEDR	11	M	UNKNOWN	GRZZZZUSA
AUGUSTE	8	F	CHILD	GRZZZZUSA
LOUISE	4	F	CHILD	GRZZZZUSA
DOBERSTEIN, APOLLONIA	17	F	UNKNOWN	GRZZZZUSA
BANICK, OTTILIE	16	F	UNKNOWN	GRZZZZUSA
WEBER, HEINR	25	M	LABR	GRZZZZUSA
MARIA	18	F	W	GRZZZZUSA
BROTHAG, HUGO	34	M	PNTR	GRZZZZUSA
ANDERS, JOH	36	M	CPTR	GRZZZZUSA
AUGUSTE	25	F	W	GRZZZZUSA
KARL	.10	M	INFANT	GRZZZZUSA
PAWLOWSKY, IGNATZ	32	M	LABR	GRZZZZUSA
MATHILDE	36	F	W	GRZZZZUSA
PAULINE	.06	F	INFANT	GRZZZZUSA
TARCZEWSKI, JULIANNE	74	F	UNKNOWN	GRZZZZUSA
FOERSTER, WILH	13	M	UNKNOWN	GRZZZZUSA
STRANG, ANDR	41	M	LKSH	GRZZZZUSA
JOSEFA	36	F	W	GRZZZZUSA
JOSEF	10	M	CH	GRZZZZUSA
CARL	11	M	CH	GRZZZZUSA
SCHAEFER, WALLY	25	F	SVNT	GRZZZZUSA
BAUCK, CAROLINE	58	F	SVNT	GRZZZZUSA
HAMHORDT, DORIS	20	F	UNKNOWN	GRZZZZUSA
PETRI, ANNA	24	F	UNKNOWN	GRZZZZUSA
HERMINE	5	F	CHILD	GRZZZZUSA
CAROLINE	1	F	CHILD	GRZZZZUSA
HOREIS, MINNA	18	F	SVNT	GRZZZZUSA
ERCK, CHRIST	29	M	FARMER	GRZZZZUSA
ERK, JOH	5	F	CHILD	GRZZZZUSA
WILH	.09	M	INFANT	GRZZZZUSA
GERKEN, GARADINE	23	F	SMSTS	GRZZZZUSA
GUETHNER, LEONH	16	M	FARMER	GRZZZZUSA
LUITHLE, CARL	16	M	FARMER	GRZZZZUSA
OTTWEIN, OTTILIE	25	F	SVNT	GRZZZZUSA
BUHLMAIER, CATH	20	F	SVNT	GRZZZZUSA
SCHOEHEN, LOUISE	29	F	UNKNOWN	GRZZZZUSA
LOUISE	5	F	CHILD	GRZZZZUSA
ROTH, KATH	20	F	SWR	GRZZZZUSA
ZIPF, FRIED	20	F	SWR	GRZZZZUSA
KERN, JOH	17	M	FARMER	GRZZZZUSA
BAREIFT, GOTTFRIED	23	M	FARMER	GRZZZZUSA
OCKEN, CAROLINE	19	F	SMSTS	GRZZZZUSA
UNANGOT, MARIE	17	F	UNKNOWN	GRZZZZUSA
LINK, WILH	16	M	FARMER	GRZZZZUSA
SCHULZ, WILH	15	M	FARMER	GRZZZZUSA
BECKER, ANNA	40	F	W	GRZZZZUSA
M	30	M	MLR	GRZZZZUSA

PASSENGER	AGE	SEX	OCCUPATION	PRVL	DES
A	7	M	CHILD		GRZZZZUSA
DEMSKI, CASPAR	34	M	BCHR		GRZZZZUSA
KRAMER, WILHELM	18	F	SMSTS		GRZZZZUSA
BEHR, HINR	15	M	LABR		GRZZZZUSA
HOLSING, FRIEDR	77	M	LABR		GRZZZZUSA
RICHTER, MAGDALINE	10	F	CH		GRZZZZUSA
WUENSCHE, ANNA	22	F	SMSTS		GRZZZZUSA
HULDA	17	F	SMSTS		GRZZZZUSA
SCHAEFER, ADAM	29	F	BKR		GRZZZZUSA
HEIN, SOPHIE	33	F	UNKNOWN		GRZZZZUSA
HERMINE	7	F	CHILD		GRZZZZUSA
JOHANNE	1	F	CHILD		GRZZZZUSA
BOEHRLE, SOPHIE	17	F	UNKNOWN		GRZZZZUSA
VELZ, EVA	18	F	UNKNOWN		GRZZZZUSA
GILDNER, ANDREAS	27	M	LABR		GRZZZZUSA
WILKER, ELISAB	18	F	SMSTS		GRZZZZUSA
SCHWING, JOST	17	M	FARMER		GRZZZZUSA
SCHOTT, ANDREAS	16	M	FARMER		GRZZZZUSA
PENS, JOH	29	F	UNKNOWN		GRZZZZUSA
MARIE	.03	F	INFANT		GRZZZZUSA
POHL, ELISE	16	F	SMSTS		GRZZZZUSA
SAUM, KATH	25	F	SMSTS		GRZZZZUSA
NORDMANN, ANKE	57	F	SMSTS		GRZZZZUSA
FRIEDERIKE	14	F	SMSTS		GRZZZZUSA
SAAL, JOH	38	M	FARMER		GRZZZZUSA
ELISE	27	F	W		GRZZZZUSA
JOHAN	.01	M	INFANT		GRZZZZUSA
MEYER, HEINR	17	M	LABR		GRZZZZUSA
KRAMER, CHRIST	26	M	LABR		GRZZZZUSA
WEIDT, SOFIA	34	F	UNKNOWN		GRZZZZUSA
ALBERT	5	M	CHILD		GRZZZZUSA
EMIL	3	M	CHILD		GRZZZZUSA
MAZA, JAN	26	M	LABR		GRZZZZUSA
PAULINE	21	F	W		GRZZZZUSA
FRANZ	.06	M	INFANT		GRZZZZUSA
WARCECKA, LEON	27	M	DLR		GRZZZZUSA
FELDMANN, ADELE	19	F	SMSTS		GRZZZZUSA
SWIECICHOSKE, ANTOINE	36	F	UNKNOWN		GRZZZZUSA
GROTH, HERM	16	M	TNM		GRZZZZUSA
NOVICKI, ANTOINIE	25	F	UNKNOWN		GRZZZZUSA
BADERSBACH, MICHAEL	23	M	FARMER		GRZZZZUSA
KRAATZ, JONES	30	M	LABR		GRZZZZUSA
ZAGELOW, PAUL	17	M	LABR		GRZZZZUSA
BANNE, GEORG	52	M	LABR		GRZZZZUSA
REGEL, HERM	34	M	LABR		GRZZZZUSA
IDA	44	F	W		GRZZZZUSA
HELENE	14	F	UNKNOWN		GRZZZZUSA
GERTRUD	11	F	CH		GRZZZZUSA
BLIEFENICHT, FRIEDERIKE	28	F	UNKNOWN		GRZZZZUSA
HERMANN, ERNST	19	M	WTR		GRZZZZUSA
WALDHEHN, GEORG	61	M	FARMER		GRZZZZUSA
MARIA	60	F	W		GRZZZZUSA
JOST, PH	76	M	FARMER		GRZZZZUSA
LAUNG, JOH	25	M	FARMER		GRZZZZUSA
MATISKIEWICZ, ANDR	37	M	FARMER		GRZZZZUSA
BRZELT, JEANETTE	20	F	UNKNOWN		GRZZZZUSA
FREUND, EVA	16	F	UNKNOWN		GRZZZZUSA
HOFFMANN, U	17	M	BKR		GRZZZZUSA
U, U	28	M	LABR		GRZZZZUSA
KERN, EMIL	16	M	LABR		GRZZZZUSA
FISCHER, CARL	14	M	LABR		GRZZZZUSA
NENTZE, ANNA	19	F	UNKNOWN		GRZZZZUSA
GELLERT, MARIE	18	F	UNKNOWN		GRZZZZUSA
STANBER, GEORG	23	M	FARMER		GRZZZZUSA
BEYER, CAROLINE	21	F	UNKNOWN		GRZZZZUSA
BULLEIER, PHIL	44	M	FSHMN		GRZZZZUSA
WOLPERT, ROSINE	30	F	UNKNOWN		GRZZZZUSA
MICHAEL	9	M	CHILD		GRZZZZUSA
CHRISTINE	4	F	CHILD		GRZZZZUSA
JOHANN	.06	M	INFANT		GRZZZZUSA
HEFKE, JOH	28	M	MCHT		GRZZZZUSA
HERDEGER, ARNOLD	50	M	MCHT		GRZZZZUSA
MARIE	48	F	W		GRZZZZUSA
CATHARINE	80	F	UNKNOWN		GRZZZZUSA
SCHMIDT, KATHARINA	28	F	UNKNOWN		GRZZZZUSA
LISA	6	F	CHILD		GRZZZZUSA
FISCHEL, BERTHA	16	F	UNKNOWN		GRZZZZUSA
LEDERER, SIMON	35	M	FARMER		GRZZZZUSA
THERESIA	33	F	W		GRZZZZUSA
CAMILLA	7	F	CHILD		GRZZZZUSA
CLARA	6	F	CHILD		GRZZZZUSA
ERNST	5	M	CHILD		GRZZZZUSA
SCHWARZ, SOPHIE	30	F	UNKNOWN		GRZZZZUSA
ZANNE, FRIEDR	17	M	LABR		GRZZZZUSA
PICK, GUSTAV	13	M	UNKNOWN		GRZZZZUSA
EPSTEIN, FANNI	26	M	UNKNOWN		GRZZZZUSA
KRABAK, ALOIS	28	M	BRR		GRZZZZUSA
KRIL, WENZEL	27	M	ENGR		GRZZZZUSA
PRASCZKY, WENZEL	17	M	LABR		GRZZZZUSA
HERMANN, FRANZISCA	27	F	SMSTS		GRZZZZUSA
VEITH, JOH	18	M	LABR		GRZZZZUSA
NOWAK, JOSEF	27	M	LABR		GRZZZZUSA
BEHONNEK, KATH	70	F	UNKNOWN		GRZZZZUSA
KAUFMANN, DAVID	24	M	MCHT		GRZZZZUSA
JEDLICKA, WENZEL	20	M	LABR		GRZZZZUSA
HAAS, JOSEF	26	M	CPTR		GRZZZZUSA
CAROLINE	18	F	W		GRZZZZUSA
VOHANCK, ARNOSTA	24	F	W		GRZZZZUSA
CECKA, JOHANNE	27	F	UNKNOWN		GRZZZZUSA
SCHWABE, LEONH	36	M	LABR		GRZZZZUSA
MARIE	36	F	W		GRZZZZUSA
ANDR	9	F	CHILD		GRZZZZUSA
FRANZ	4	M	CHILD		GRZZZZUSA
KATHAR	2	F	CHILD		GRZZZZUSA
MARIE	.02	F	INFANT		GRZZZZUSA
ABEL, HEINR	32	M	LABR		GRZZZZUSA
VICTORIA	25	F	W		GRZZZZUSA
FELIX	4	M	CHILD		GRZZZZUSA
LEOCARDIA	3	F	CHILD		GRZZZZUSA
ELISAB	1	F	CHILD		GRZZZZUSA
MARTHA	.06	F	INFANT		GRZZZZUSA
DUDAR, MICHAEL	60	M	LABR		GRZZZZUSA
ELISAB	47	F	W		GRZZZZUSA
MARIANNE	30	F	UNKNOWN		GRZZZZUSA
STANISL	16	M	UNKNOWN		GRZZZZUSA
ROSALIE	11	F	UNKNOWN		GRZZZZUSA
FRANZ	9	M	CHILD		GRZZZZUSA
ADALBERT	7	M	CHILD		GRZZZZUSA
BERGEMANN, JUL	32	M	LABR		GRZZZZUSA
MEYER, LOUISE	16	F	UNKNOWN		GRZZZZUSA
STUEBS, FERD	52	M	FARMER		GRZZZZUSA
MATH	45	F	UNKNOWN		GRZZZZUSA
HULDA	13	F	UNKNOWN		GRZZZZUSA
MARTHA	9	F	CHILD		GRZZZZUSA
CAROLINE	4	F	CHILD		GRZZZZUSA
SCHMIDT, AUG	43	M	FARMER		GRZZZZUSA
JULIANE	43	F	W		GRZZZZUSA
WILHELM	14	M	UNKNOWN		GRZZZZUSA
MARIE	11	F	UNKNOWN		GRZZZZUSA
AMANDA	7	F	CHILD		GRZZZZUSA
OTTO	7	M	CHILD		GRZZZZUSA
REINHARDT, AUGUST	66	M	FARMER		GRZZZZUSA
THERESE	66	F	W		GRZZZZUSA
KOCH, CARL	43	M	FARMER		GRZZZZUSA
EMILIE	43	F	W		GRZZZZUSA
ALBERT	11	M	UNKNOWN		GRZZZZUSA
AUGUST	10	M	CH		GRZZZZUSA
ANNA	8	F	CHILD		GRZZZZUSA
ROCH, HUGO	4	M	CHILD		GRZZZZUSA
GAIL, KATHAR	17	F	UNKNOWN		GRZZZZUSA
DANER, JOSEF	29	M	CPTR		GRZZZZUSA
NIEMEYER, AUG	43	M	LABR		GRZZZZUSA
FELDMANN, DORA	26	F	UNKNOWN		GRZZZZUSA
LOUISE	4	F	CHILD		GRZZZZUSA
MINNA	2	F	CHILD		GRZZZZUSA
ETZMUSS, AUG	24	M	LABR		GRZZZZUSA
GRIESSHEIMER, FRIEDR	26	M	LABR		GRZZZZUSA
MAAS, MARIE	21	F	UNKNOWN		GRZZZZUSA
MEHRENS, CLAUS	57	M	FARMER		GRZZZZUSA
ANNA	42	F	W		GRZZZZUSA

PASSENGER	AGE	SEX	OCCUPATION	PRVL	DES
CHRISTIAN	21	M	FARMER		GRZZZZUSA
ERNSTINE	11	F	UNKNOWN		GRZZZZUSA
WENDEL, JOHANN	17	M	BKR		GRZZZZUSA
SPAETH, JOSEF	33	M	FARMER		GRZZZZUSA
THERESE	35	F	W		GRZZZZUSA
SCHENBECK, LIZZIE	19	F	UNKNOWN		GRZZZZUSA
ANNA	11	F	UNKNOWN		GRZZZZUSA
KOENIG, JOSEPH	14	M	UNKNOWN		GRZZZZUSA
ROEHNBERG, EMILIE	17	F	UNKNOWN		GRZZZZUSA
WAHLERS, HINR	15	M	BKLYR		GRZZZZUSA
SCHWABE, THERESIA	27	F	UNKNOWN		GRZZZZUSA
JOHANN	8	M	CHILD		GRZZZZUSA
JOHANN	4	M	CHILD		GRZZZZUSA
JOSEF	3	M	CHILD		GRZZZZUSA
PIELER, MARGAR	54	F	UNKNOWN		GRZZZZUSA
JOSITZKA, FRANCISCA	22	F	UNKNOWN		GRZZZZUSA
JAN	.11	M	INFANT		GRZZZZUSA
MAJEWSKI, JOSEF	30	M	FARMER		GRZZZZUSA
MARIANNE	22	F	W		GRZZZZUSA
STANISLAUS	.11	M	INFANT		GRZZZZUSA
VARSEL, ADAM	29	M	LABR		GRZZZZUSA
GIRA, STEFAN	30	M	LABR		GRZZZZUSA
TINNO, JANOS	36	M	LABR		GRZZZZUSA
ROLKMANN, HELENE	22	F	UNKNOWN		GRZZZZUSA
APEL, AUG	16	M	CNF		GRZZZZUSA
HEMM, CARL	50	M	LABR		GRZZZZUSA
FRIEDERIKE	46	F	W		GRZZZZUSA
MARIE	18	F	UNKNOWN		GRZZZZUSA
OSCAR	8	M	CHILD		GRZZZZUSA
CLARA	6	F	CHILD		GRZZZZUSA
HARTJE, DIEDR	16	M	LABR		GRZZZZUSA
DOHNEKE, META	16	F	UNKNOWN		GRZZZZUSA
BERCHERS, LINA	16	F	UNKNOWN		GRZZZZUSA
SCHWALBACH, JOH	60	M	LABR		GRZZZZUSA
NORDMANN, ALB	18	M	LABR		GRZZZZUSA
FELDMANN, FRIEDR	46	M	FARMER		GRZZZZUSA
EMMA	47	F	UNKNOWN		GRZZZZUSA
FRIEDR	11	M	UNKNOWN		GRZZZZUSA
PAUL	8	M	CHILD		GRZZZZUSA
PAULA	8	F	CHILD		GRZZZZUSA
SELMA	17	F	UNKNOWN		GRZZZZUSA
IDA	14	F	UNKNOWN		GRZZZZUSA
MIRWALD, FRANZ	34	M	FARMER		GRZZZZUSA
JOHANNA	38	F	W		GRZZZZUSA
KATHAR	18	F	UNKNOWN		GRZZZZUSA
THERESE	26	F	UNKNOWN		GRZZZZUSA
FRANZ	2	M	CHILD		GRZZZZUSA
MARIE	.02	F	INFANT		GRZZZZUSA
ONINTING, AUG	25	M	FARMER		GRZZZZUSA
EICHENGRUEN, DINA	23	F	UNKNOWN		GRZZZZUSA
HERZOG, ANNA	23	F	UNKNOWN		GRZZZZUSA
MEYER, CARL	14	M	LABR		GRZZZZUSA
KAPPLER, FRANZ	26	M	LABR		GRZZZZUSA
BAUMANN, U	21	M	LABR		GRZZZZUSA
RISSMEYER, AMALIE	25	F	SMSTS		GRZZZZUSA
AUGUST	23	M	LABR		GRZZZZUSA
WESTERMANN, ELISE	21	F	UNKNOWN		GRZZZZUSA
HIWRE, FRIEDR	25	M	LABR		GRZZZZUSA
LETKOWSKY, JAN	28	M	LABR		GRZZZZUSA
JOHANNE	26	F	W		GRZZZZUSA
FRANCISCA	3	F	CHILD		GRZZZZUSA
PIPFERWEIN, WILHELM	31	F	SMSTS		GRZZZZUSA
ROEHRIG, CATH	16	F	UNKNOWN		GRZZZZUSA
VOLZ, JACOB	30	M	LABR		GRZZZZUSA
ZEH, HEINR	29	M	JNR		GRZZZZUSA
BAILHARZ, CHRIST	35	M	UNKNOWN		GRZZZZUSA
ANAN	7	F	CHILD		GRZZZZUSA
ROM---ER, GEORG	28	M	LABR		GRZZZZUSA
ELIASCHOWICZ, SISLE	16	F	UNKNOWN		GRZZZZUSA
GITEL	14	F	UNKNOWN		GRZZZZUSA
LENA	18	F	UNKNOWN		GRZZZZUSA
HURWITZ, BERTHA	17	F	UNKNOWN		GRZZZZUSA
DUESTERDIECK, DIEDR	27	M	JNR		GRZZZZUSA
ROTTWACHS, JUDA	20	F	UNKNOWN		GRZZZZUSA
OTTEN, JOH	8	M	CHILD		GRZZZZUSA

PASSENGER	AGE	SEX	OCCUPATION	PRVL	DES
PREUSS, JOH	33	M	FARMER		GRZZZZUSA
ANDERS, HANS	.01	M	INFANT		GR****USA

SHIP: NEWPORT

FROM: ASPINWALL
TO: NEW YORK
ARRIVED: 12 JUNE 1888

PASSENGER	AGE	SEX	OCCUPATION	PRVL	DES
RIEHNOLD, F	38	M	JWLR		GRZZZZUSA
ELLIS, B	50	M	MCHT		GRZZZZUSA
GEHSE, F	21	F	NN		GRZZZZUSA
MULLER, F	28	M	MCHT		GRZZZZUSA
F	23	F	NN		GRZZZZUSA
ECHADI, M	34	M	UNKNOWN		FRZZZZUSA
VALLARINO, B	45	M	MD		FRZZZZUSA
VARILLA, B	29	M	UNKNOWN		FRZZZZUSA
ROUSE, V	30	M	UNKNOWN		FRZZZZUSA
GOETSCHEL, S	42	M	MCHT		FRZZZZUSA
GRONING, P	35	M	PINST		GRZZZZUSA
NEEBE, E	31	M	UNKNOWN		GRZZZZUSA
LOWEY, E	38	F	NN		GRZZZZUSA
E	15	F	NN		GRZZZZUSA
G	12	M	NN		GRZZZZUSA
L	10	F	CH		GRZZZZUSA
THEO	5	M	CHILD		GRZZZZUSA
B	1	M	CHILD		GRZZZZUSA
DORFLER, H	31	M	BCHR		GRZZZZUSA
HAIDER, A	19	M	WLWRK		FRZZZZUSA
BOWDIN, E	40	M	CK		FRZZZZUSA
FISHER, W	20	M	NN		GRZZZZUSA
KAUFMAN, C	42	M	ENGR		GRZZZZUSA

SHIP: SPAIN

FROM: LIVERPOOL AND QUEENSTOWN
TO: NEW YORK
ARRIVED: 12 JUNE 1888

PASSENGER	AGE	SEX	OCCUPATION	PRVL	DES
REPALIAN, SAUMAN	27	M	LABR		GRAAECUSA
CARABIDIAN, AUSTIN	26	M	LABR		GRAAECUSA
BENGACIEN, STEPPHAM	25	M	LABR		GRAAECUSA
REDMONIAN, OEVANES	30	M	LABR		GRAAECUSA
ARCESSEM, MOSSES	19	M	LABR		GRAAECUSA
KUKMANE, ARM.	26	M	LABR		GRAAECUSA
U, U	29	M	LABR		FRZZZZUSA
LAINE, A.	19	F	LDY		FRZZZZPAR

SHIP: DONAU

FROM: BREMEN
TO: BALTIMORE
ARRIVED: 13 JUNE 1888

PASSENGER	AGE	SEX	OCCUPATION	PRVL	DES
FRIEDRICH, GOTTLIEF	26	M	FARMER		GRZZZZMO
JUERGENS, HEINR	38	M	TLR		GRZZZZIA
AGNES	28	F	UNKNOWN		GRZZZZIA
OLGA	10	F	CH		GRZZZZIA
FURCH, OTTILIE	15	F	UNKNOWN		GRZZZZMD
BRANDAN, BARBARA	17	F	UNKNOWN		GRZZZZWAS

PASSENGER	AGE	SEX	OCCUPATION	PRVL DES
HOFFMANN, MARY	25	F	UNKNOWN	GRZZZZMD
BOETTINGER, KATH	68	F	UNKNOWN	GRZZZZMD
WERNER, FRIEDR	60	M	LABR	GRZZZZMD
ENKE, HERMAN	25	M	DYR	GRZZZZWAS
DEUSCHER, KATH	18	F	UNKNOWN	GRZZZZWI
KOSNICK, MARIA	50	F	UNKNOWN	GRZZZZMI
RICHUT, PAULINE	21	F	UNKNOWN	GRZZZZMI
SLUZEWSKA, MARTHA	56	F	UNKNOWN	GRZZZZIL
FIEBRONZ, HEINR	52	M	FARMER	GRZZZZMN
AUGUSTE	49	F	UNKNOWN	GRZZZZMN
MARIA	3	F	CHILD	GRZZZZMN
WEIDNER, GOTTFRIED	26	M	LABR	GRZZZZMI
STADLER, BABETTA	13	F	UNKNOWN	GRZZZKS
GALL, AUGUST	25	M	LABR	GRZZZZMD
OTT, MARIA	15	F	UNKNOWN	GRZZZZMD
JOHAN	11	M	CH	GRZZZZMD
BAEIRLE, JACOB	17	M	LABR	GRZZZZMI
HALTERMANN, DANIEL	16	M	FARMER	GRZZZZIL
GESINE	18	F	UNKNOWN	GRZZZZIL
SAGITZKI, RUD	22	M	CPTR	GRZZZZMI
NIEHAUS, AUGUSTA	18	F	UNKNOWN	GRZZZZMI
GROTE, WILH.	18	F	UNKNOWN	GRZZZZMI
GUCHS, CONRAD	24	M	LABR	GRZZZZNE
HINZ, MINNA	49	F	UNKNOWN	GRZZZZMD
HEFDWIG	10	M	CH	GRZZZZMD
GOLINSKI, JOSEF	33	M	LABR	GRZZZZIL
BLECK, WILH	22	M	LABR	GRZZZZIL
MUELLER, EMILIE	18	F	UNKNOWN	GRZZZZUNK
JULIN	16	M	UNKNOWN	GRZZZZUNK
LANGHEINRICH, ROB.	15	M	UNKNOWN	GRZZZZOH
LAWRENH, LINA	18	F	UNKNOWN	GRZZZZMD
JOPP, EDUARD	37	M	ART	GRZZZZMD
HEDWIG	30	F	UNKNOWN	GRZZZZMD
MAX	7	M	CHILD	GRZZZZMD
WERNER, THERESE	51	F	UNKNOWN	GRZZZZDAK
RODOLF	11	M	UNKNOWN	GRZZZZDAK
MARTHA	9	F	CHILD	GRZZZZDAK
ROBERT	27	M	GDNR	GRZZZZDAK
MARIE	22	F	UNKNOWN	GRZZZZDAK
HAASE, BERNH.	23	M	WVR	GRZZZZWI
HOFFMANN, GEORG	57	M	WVR	GRZZZZIL
HENRIETTE	63	F	UNKNOWN	GRZZZZIL
HACKBERTH, ALWINE	21	F	UNKNOWN	GRZZZZDAK
TAGEITZ, DOROTHEA	67	F	UNKNOWN	GRZZZZDAK
STIENKE, OTTO	27	M	FARMER	GRZZZZDAK
BERTHA	28	F	UNKNOWN	GRZZZZDAK
ANNA	4	F	CHILD	GRZZZZDAK
GUSTAV	1	M	CHILD	GRZZZZDAK
MIELKE, JOHAN	65	M	FARMER	GRZZZZDAK
WILH	56	F	UNKNOWN	GRZZZZDAK
KARNIEWSKA, ANIELA	20	F	UNKNOWN	GRZZZZIL
FRANZ	1	M	CHILD	GRZZZZIL
WLADISLAUS	.03	M	INFANT	GRZZZZIL
GROSS, FRIEDR	26	M	BCHR	GRZZZZMI
SEEMANN, ERNST	31	M	BCHR	GRZZZZMI
BERTHA	21	F	UNKNOWN	GRZZZZMI
KOECHER, HEINRICH	37	M	CK	GRZZZZMI
HENRIETTE	28	F	UNKNOWN	GRZZZZMI
OTTO, CHRISTIAN	63	M	LABR	GRZZZZMI
STOECKER, ANTON	17	M	LABR	GRZZZZMI
KOECHER, ALWIN	9	M	CHILD	GRZZZZMI
ANNA	.06	F	INFANT	GRZZZZMI
HOERNKE, AUGUST	53	M	LABR	GRZZZZIL
ROEDER, CAROLINE	50	F	UNKNOWN	GRZZZZIL
HOERNKE, BERTHA	23	F	UNKNOWN	GRZZZZIL
WILH	18	F	UNKNOWN	GRZZZZIL
EMILIE	11	F	UNKNOWN	GRZZZZIL
FRANZ	20	M	LABR	GRZZZZIL
BUSCH, EMIL	48	M	CGRMKR	GRZZZZMD
EBERHARDT	16	M	CGRMKR	GRZZZZMD
PETERSEN, CLAUS	18	M	CPTR	GRZZZZNE
HARGES, SOPHIE	18	M	CCHMN	GRZZZZWI
GANSKE, CARL	18	M	CCHMN	GRZZZZWI
SMYDZINSLKI, PAWL	32	M	BKR	GRZZZZIL
MARQUARDT, EMILIE	31	F	UNKNOWN	GRZZZZIL
PAUL	4	M	CHILD	GRZZZZIL
SEEFELD, LOUISE	25	F	UNKNOWN	GRZZZZPA
EGGELBRECHT, KAROLINE	36	F	UNKNOWN	GRZZZZIN
JOHANN	4	M	CHILD	GRZZZZIN
WOIWOD, ROSA	24	F	UNKNOWN	GRZZZZPA
ENDERMANN, FRANZ	17	F	UNKNOWN	GRZZZZOH
BELZ, HERMAN	30	M	WVR	GRZZZZOH
CHRISTINA	29	F	UNKNOWN	GRZZZZOH
MARIE	4	F	CHILD	GRZZZZOH
PAUL	3	M	CHILD	GRZZZZOH
PREUSSS, THERESE	20	F	UNKNOWN	GRZZZZMI
RAHN, AUGUSTA	19	F	UNKNOWN	GRZZZZWI
CONRAD, AGNES	19	F	UNKNOWN	GRZZZZIL
ADLOFF, MARIA	19	F	UNKNOWN	GRZZZZMI
TOTZKE, HERMAN	30	M	BCHR	GRZZZZMA
RUBITZKI, EMILIE	22	F	UNKNOWN	GRZZZZMD
REICH, EDUARD	24	M	BKR	GRZZZZIL
WEELEWSKI, K.	24	M	MCHT	GRZZZZIL
THIELE, CARL	41	M	SHFM	GRZZZZIL
AUGUSTE	36	F	UNKNOWN	GRZZZZIL
GUSTAV	14	M	UNKNOWN	GRZZZZIL
WILHELM	11	M	UNKNOWN	GRZZZZIL
BERTHA	10	F	CH	GRZZZZIL
HERMAN	8	M	CHILD	GRZZZZIL
ANNA	4	F	CHILD	GRZZZZIL
OTTO	.11	M	INFANT	GRZZZZIL
BOCKE, WILHELM	15	M	FARMER	GRZZZZIA
BROEKERS, ADELHEID	68	F	UNKNOWN	GRZZZZKY
BARTSCH, AUGUSTE	20	F	UNKNOWN	GRZZZZOH
SCHWANKE, WILH.	25	F	UNKNOWN	GRZZZZMN
FRIEDRICH	16	M	UNKNOWN	GRZZZZMN
HULDA	10	F	CH	GRZZZZMN
KRAJETZKI, JOHAN	38	M	LABR	GRZZZZIL
HOPPE, ANNA	23	F	UNKNOWN	GRZZZZIL
PUS, JUSTINA	41	F	UNKNOWN	GRZZZZIL
ANNA	6	F	CHILD	GRZZZZIL
EMILIE	3	F	CHILD	GRZZZZIL
JAWOROWSKA, JUSTINE	25	F	UNKNOWN	GRZZZZIL
PAUL	.09	M	INFANT	GRZZZZIL
KRUEGER, CARL	60	M	SHFM	GRZZZZMN
DOROTHEA	63	F	UNKNOWN	GRZZZZMN
KOHN, BERTHA	17	F	UNKNOWN	GRZZZZMN
WILKENING, DORA	14	F	UNKNOWN	GRZZZZMD
BRUELLE, FRITZ	17	M	LABR	GRZZZZMD
ROESSL, WOLFGANG	45	M	CPR	GRZZZZMN
SCHINLATZ, GEORG	33	M	LABR	GRZZZZMN
AELLER, WILHELM	17	M	MCHT	GRZZZZOH
LICHTENBERG, JULIUS	58	M	LABR	GRZZZZMN
JETTE	59	F	UNKNOWN	GRZZZZMN
MARTHA	17	F	UNKNOWN	GRZZZZMN
GEHRKE, EMIL	26	M	MLR	GRZZZZWI
WITAKOWSKA, MARIANNA	26	F	UNKNOWN	GRZZZZMN
VOEGEL, HENRY	17	M	LABR	GRZZZZMN
SCHLAGOWSKI, JOHAN	56	M	BKLYR	GRZZZZMD
AUGUSTE	40	F	UNKNOWN	GRZZZZMD
GENRICH, FERDINAND	36	M	LABR	GRZZZZKS
WILH	35	F	UNKNOWN	GRZZZZKS
HENRIETTE	15	F	UNKNOWN	GRZZZZKS
AUGUST	14	M	UNKNOWN	GRZZZZKS
BERTHA	9	F	CHILD	GRZZZZKS
HERMAN	7	M	CHILD	GRZZZZKS
ANNA	5	F	CHILD	GRZZZZKS
MARIA	4	F	CHILD	GRZZZZKS
JULIUS	.06	M	INFANT	GRZZZZKS
WILHELM	.06	M	INFANT	GRZZZZKS
BORCHARDT, MARIE	37	F	UNKNOWN	GRZZZZIL
HEFLER, ALWINE	17	F	UNKNOWN	GRZZZZIL
MUELLER, MARIA	18	F	UNKNOWN	GRZZZZMI
SEGMANN, HERMAN	24	M	FARMER	GRZZZZMN
LOUISE	22	F	UNKNOWN	GRZZZZMN
MAGEDANZ, HERMAN	29	M	LABR	GRZZZZMD
AUGUSTE	28	F	UNKNOWN	GRZZZZMD
WILH	61	M	UNKNOWN	GRZZZZMD
MARIA	5	F	CHILD	GRZZZZMD
MARTHA	3	F	CHILD	GRZZZZMD

PASSENGER	AGE	SEX	OCCUPATION	PRVL	DES
GUSTAV	.06	M	INFANT	GRZZZZ	MD
GUMM, FRITZ	17	M	UNKNOWN	GRZZZZ	MD
LESCHMANN, CARL	26	M	LABR	GRZZZZ	IL
MARTHA	00	U	UNKNOWN	GRZZZZ	IL
MARTHA	00	U	UNKNOWN	GRZZZZ	IL
STUEWE, MARIA	24	F	UNKNOWN	GRZZZZ	MN
BERNHARDT	.09	M	INFANT	GRZZZZ	MN
BARTSCH, GOTTLIEB	33	M	MLR	GRZZZZ	MN
CAROLINE	32	F	UNKNOWN	GRZZZZ	MN
OSCAR	5	M	CHILD	GRZZZZ	MN
REINHOLD	4	M	CHILD	GRZZZZ	MN
BERTHA	2	F	CHILD	GRZZZZ	MN
KOUPP, GUTAV	25	M	LABR	GRZZZZ	WI
BERTHA	23	F	UNKNOWN	GRZZZZ	WI
PAULINE	6	F	CHILD	GRZZZZ	WI
MARTHA	.06	F	INFANT	GRZZZZ	WI
WEIHER, AUGUST	17	M	LABR	GRZZZZ	OH
CIBELLA, CONSTANTIA	20	F	UNKNOWN	GRZZZZ	WI
AUGUSTE	18	F	UNKNOWN	GRZZZZ	WI
ALBERT	16	M	UNKNOWN	GRZZZZ	WI
HOPPA, ANTONIE	49	F	UNKNOWN	GRZZZZ	IL
SORENTINE	10	F	CH	GRZZZZ	IL
MARIANNA	5	F	CHILD	GRZZZZ	IL
JOSEPH	4	M	CHILD	GRZZZZ	IL
KAREZYNSKI, JAN	24	M	LABR	GRZZZZ	PA
BELAN, GUSTAF	22	M	LABR	GRZZZZ	OH
BENBANSKI, LEON	48	M	CPTR	GRZZZZ	IL
WICENTY	16	M	CPTR	GRZZZZ	MI
HOLASZINSKI, ANTON	28	M	LABR	GRZZZZ	MI
MILLER, ADAM	67	M	FARMER	GRZZZZ	MI
ANNA	56	F	UNKNOWN	GRZZZZ	MI
NE---, ROSALIE	00	U	UNKNOWN	GRZZZZ	IL
MATERNOWSKI, ANDREAS	29	M	LABR	GRZZZZ	IL
ANTONIA	28	F	UNKNOWN	GRZZZZ	IL
JOSEPHA	4	F	CHILD	GRZZZZ	IL
ANASTASIA	2	F	CHILD	GRZZZZ	IL
MARYANA	.03	F	INFANT	GRZZZZ	IL
JOHAN	21	M	UNKNOWN	GRZZZZ	IL
WOJCIECH	.02	M	INFANT	GRZZZZ	IL
FROEMING, FRIEDRICH	25	M	BLKSMH	GRZZZZ	MA
BLANK, ERNST	21	M	TLR	GRZZZZ	WI
ANNA	29	F	UNKNOWN	GRZZZZ	WI
HUGO	5	M	CHILD	GRZZZZ	WI
MAX	4	M	CHILD	GRZZZZ	WI
LISBETH	.03	F	INFANT	GRZZZZ	WI
SCHMITTKE, HERMAN	42	M	FARMER	GRZZZZ	IA
CAROLINE	52	F	UNKNOWN	GRZZZZ	IA
BERTHA	15	F	UNKNOWN	GRZZZZ	IA
MINNA	13	F	UNKNOWN	GRZZZZ	IA
LUTHER, LEONH	20	M	LABR	GRZZZZ	MD
SCHALK, OTTILIE	20	F	UNKNOWN	GRZZZZ	MD
SCHUELZ, ANNA	24	F	UNKNOWN	GRZZZZ	PA
BAUER, ALOS	15	M	UNKNOWN	GRZZZZ	MD
JOHANNES, LIENE	18	F	UNKNOWN	GRZZZZ	IL
DORIS	11	F	UNKNOWN	GRZZZZ	IL
BORCHARDT, ERNST	16	M	LABR	GRZZZZ	IL
CARL	10	M	CH	GRZZZZ	IL
ANNA	9	F	CHILD	GRZZZZ	IL
OTTO	.03	M	INFANT	GRZZZZ	IL
HEILMAN, U	40	M	BKLYR	GRZZZZ	KY
KLAWON, FRANZ	32	M	BLKSMH	GRZZZZ	PA
LATEWSKI, JOSEPH	25	M	MCHT	GRZZZZ	IL
KRAJECKA, FRANZ	17	M	MCHT	GRZZZZ	IL
KALIMOWSKI, JACOB	24	M	GDNR	GRZZZZ	PA
SODERGREN, EMIL	21	M	TLR	GRZZZZ	MD
JOHNSON, EMMA	27	F	UNKNOWN	GRZZZZ	IL
CARLSON, JOHAN	39	M	FARMER	GRZZZZ	MO
TELLANDER, JOHAN	59	M	FARMER	GRZZZZ	IL
OETERS, HELENE	36	F	UNKNOWN	GRZZZZ	IL
WILHEL	6	F	CHILD	GRZZZZ	IL
ANNA	3	F	CHILD	GRZZZZ	IL
WAGNER, LEONHARDT	30	M	LABR	GRZZZZ	MD
HOCHDUECHTER, CONRAD	24	M	SHMK	GRZZZZ	MO
SCHAEFER, ANTON	24	M	PNTR	GRZZZZ	MO
BAUMANN, BARBARA	22	F	UNKNOWN	GRZZZZ	IL
ENGELBERT	15	M	UNKNOWN	GRZZZZ	IL
HEUSEL, CASPAR	38	M	LABR	GRZZZZ	IN
KAMINSKI, AUGUST	30	M	LABR	GRZZZZ	IN
BLENKNER, ANNA	60	F	UNKNOWN	GRZZZZ	IN
SCHMIDT, LISETTE	26	F	UNKNOWN	GRZZZZ	IN
WAGNER, ELISABETH	25	F	UNKNOWN	GRZZZZ	IN
SCHLAEFFER, MICHAEL	23	M	LABR	GRZZZZ	IN
KOLLER, ANNA	49	F	UNKNOWN	GRZZZZ	IN
GUTZMUEHL, LUDWIG	48	M	LABR	GRZZZZ	MD
PUSELEITNER, LUDWIG	47	U	UNKNOWN	GRZZZZ	MD
RIECHERS, FRITZ	29	U	UNKNOWN	GRZZZZ	IL
SCHREINER, LUDWIG	16	M	JNR	GRZZZZ	PA
KAINL, MARIE	19	F	UNKNOWN	GRZZZZ	PA
SCHAEFER, ANNA	19	F	UNKNOWN	GRZZZZ	KY
MUELLER, DANIEL	25	M	LABR	GRZZZZ	KY
NEUMEYER, FRIEDRICH	27	M	BLKSMH	GRZZZZ	MD
HELENE	25	F	UNKNOWN	GRZZZZ	MD
KAHLE, WILHELM	26	M	SHMK	GRZZZZ	OH
STEFFEN, META	20	F	UNKNOWN	GRZZZZ	MI
HENZE, FRITZ	17	M	LABR	GRZZZZ	KY
POLENTZ, GUSTAV	38	M	LABR	GRZZZZ	OH
MALWINE	40	F	UNKNOWN	GRZZZZ	OH
ELISABETH	9	F	CHILD	GRZZZZ	OH
JOHANNE	7	F	CHILD	GRZZZZ	OH
AUGUSTE	.11	F	INFANT	GRZZZZ	OH
BRUNO	.02	M	INFANT	GRZZZZ	OH
RAUTER, AUGUST	38	M	LABR	GRZZZZ	OH
ROSALIA	38	F	UNKNOWN	GRZZZZ	OH
PIRSCH, DOROTHEA	30	F	UNKNOWN	GRZZZZ	OH
SCHWOEDER, ADOLF	28	M	LABR	GRZZZZ	OH
MARIE	24	F	UNKNOWN	GRZZZZ	OH
STEINKRAUSS, H.	34	M	JNR	GRZZZZ	MD
BRAUER, CARL	23	M	SHMK	GRZZZZ	MO
REBMANN, JEREMIAS	21	M	MLR	GRZZZZ	WI
FULLE, AUGUST	17	M	LABR	GRZZZZ	NE
EIFERT, MARG	25	F	UNKNOWN	GRZZZZ	WI
ANTES, KATH	25	F	UNKNOWN	GRZZZZ	WI
WINTER, ESTER	20	F	UNKNOWN	GRZZZZ	MD
HOMILINS, OSWALD	17	M	BKR	GRZZZZ	OH
DURBECK, KATH	19	F	UNKNOWN	GRZZZZ	MD
MARG	16	F	UNKNOWN	GRZZZZ	MD
HANKEN, ELISE	19	F	UNKNOWN	GRZZZZ	NE
WIRSPECKER, MARIE	16	F	UNKNOWN	GRZZZZ	OH
LEMMERTZ, ELISABETH	17	F	UNKNOWN	GRZZZZ	WI
KAUSTEDT, GOTTHOLD	42	M	SHMK	GRZZZZ	MN
JOHANNE	39	F	UNKNOWN	GRZZZZ	MN
FRANZISKA	14	F	UNKNOWN	GRZZZZ	MN
GOTTHOLD	12	M	UNKNOWN	GRZZZZ	MN
SOPHIE	8	F	CHILD	GRZZZZ	MN
ROBERT	5	M	CHILD	GRZZZZ	MN
MINNA	4	F	CHILD	GRZZZZ	MN
CAROLINE	2	F	CHILD	GRZZZZ	MN
AUGUST	.06	M	INFANT	GRZZZZ	MN
FISCHER, JACOB	21	M	TLR	GRZZZZ	MN
METZ, MARTIN	24	M	CCHMN	GRZZZZ	IA
KRAFT, LINA	16	F	UNKNOWN	GRZZZZ	MA
ZINK, CHRISTINA	17	F	UNKNOWN	GRZZZZ	IL
GMAEHLE, CAROLINA	19	F	UNKNOWN	GRZZZZ	PA
KIMMERLING, FRANZ	17	M	SHMK	GRZZZZ	PA
KRIEGER, EMILIE	19	F	UNKNOWN	GRZZZZ	MD
KENNER, ANNA	34	F	UNKNOWN	GRZZZZ	OH
BOPP, MARIE	19	F	UNKNOWN	GRZZZZ	MD
NIKSWEG, JOHAN	27	M	TLR	GRZZZZ	PA
RUMANN, W.	50	F	UNKNOWN	GRZZZZ	IL
AUGUST	20	M	FARMER	GRZZZZ	IL
LOUISE	18	F	UNKNOWN	GRZZZZ	IL
ANNA	13	F	UNKNOWN	GRZZZZ	IL
AIBE, HERMAN	16	M	LABR	GRZZZZ	IA
BLEICHER, ROSA	41	F	UNKNOWN	GRZZZZ	MO
MAX	9	M	CHILD	GRZZZZ	MO
OSWALD	3	M	CHILD	GRZZZZ	MO
ELISE	1	F	CHILD	GRZZZZ	MO
LAURITZEN, JOHANNES	17	M	LABR	GRZZZZ	IN
JAEHNKE, BERTHA	33	F	UNKNOWN	GRZZZZ	WI
MARTHA	9	F	CHILD	GRZZZZ	WI

PASSENGER	AGE	SEX	OCCUPATION	PRVVL	DES
EMIL	7	M	CHILD	GRZZZZWI	
HULDA	5	F	CHILD	GRZZZZWI	
AMANDA	3	F	CHILD	GRZZZZWI	
OSTERBUS, HELENE	17	F	UNKNOWN	GRZZZZIL	
SCHMIDT, AUGUST	17	M	LABR	GRZZZZMI	
HEINRICH	15	M	UNKNOWN	GRZZZZMI	
MUTSCHLER, MARIE	18	F	UNKNOWN	GRZZZZPA	
ERNST	13	M	UNKNOWN	GRZZZZPA	
RUEBMANN, ANNA	60	F	UNKNOWN	GRZZZZVA	
PIETZSCH, ALBIN	20	M	FARMER	GRZZZZVA	
HEITMANN, JOHAN	32	M	LABR	GRZZZZWI	
WILH	31	F	UNKNOWN	GRZZZZWI	
FRIEDA	6	F	CHILD	GRZZZZWI	
CARL	2	M	CHILD	GRZZZZWI	
ADLER, CARL	25	M	MCHT	GRZZZZWI	
JUCH, CARL	24	M	SHMK	GRZZZZOH	
CHARLOTTA	25	F	UNKNOWN	GRZZZZOH	
HOLZMANN, MARIA	30	F	UNKNOWN	GRZZZZMD	
KRUG, DOROTHEA	3	F	CHILD	GRZZZZMD	
ZIEGLER, ANNA	28	F	UNKNOWN	GRZZZZOH	
GEORG	6	M	CHILD	GRZZZZOH	
ALTMANN, MICHAEL	45	M	BKLYR	GRZZZZKY	
ROSINA	43	F	UNKNOWN	GRZZZZKY	
FRANZISKA	13	F	UNKNOWN	GRZZZZKY	
THEUERL, THERESIA	55	F	UNKNOWN	GRZZZZMD	
FRIEDRICH	24	M	FARMER	GRZZZZMD	
GEORG	10	M	CH	GRZZZZMD	
FRANZ	6	M	CHILD	GRZZZZMD	
THERESIA	4	F	CHILD	GRZZZZMD	
FRANZISKA	8	F	CHILD	GRZZZZMD	
MERTEL, MARIA	11	F	CH	GRZZZZMD	
FEULNER, BARBARA	16	F	UNKNOWN	GRZZZZMD	
KAUFMANN, CATH	18	F	UNKNOWN	GRZZZZMD	
KOLPZTZKI, FRANZ	37	M	CPTR	GRZZZZMI	
VICTORIA	29	F	UNKNOWN	GRZZZZMI	
CATH	5	F	CHILD	GRZZZZMI	
JOHANNA	4	F	CHILD	GRZZZZMI	
LADISLAUS	3	M	CHILD	GRZZZZMI	
ANNA	.03	F	INFANT	GRZZZZMI	
VARWIG, JOHANNA	18	F	UNKNOWN	GRZZZZMO	
ADOLF	14	M	UNKNOWN	GRZZZZMO	
JASIENSKY, JAN	40	M	LABR	GRZZZZOH	
MARCEL	17	M	LABR	GRZZZZWI	
CLARA	12	F	UNKNOWN	GRZZZZWI	
WOJIECH	9	M	CHILD	GRZZZZWI	
KOSOBATZKI, FRANZISZEK	57	M	SDLR	GRZZZZIL	
EVA	56	F	UNKNOWN	GRZZZZIL	
ANTON	22	M	LABR	GRZZZZIL	
LEOKADIA	20	F	UNKNOWN	GRZZZZIL	
WINKLER, KARL	30	M	LABR	GRZZZZMI	
WILH	35	F	UNKNOWN	GRZZZZMI	
ALBERT	6	M	CHILD	GRZZZZMI	
HERMANN	2	M	CHILD	GRZZZZMI	
KRAUSE, AUGUSTE	23	F	UNKNOWN	GRZZZZMI	
ALWINE	.03	F	INFANT	GRZZZZMI	
WURTMANN, BERNH	11	M	UNKNOWN	GRZZZZIL	
UHL, KAROLINE	26	F	UNKNOWN	GRZZZZOH	
KOLLS, HEINR	22	M	LABR	GRZZZZIL	
MATHEUS, FRANZ	27	M	BLKSMH	GRZZZZPA	
STEENKEN, ADELINE	20	F	UNKNOWN	GRZZZZOH	
LUEHRS, HEINRICH	48	M	FARMER	GRZZZZIL	
PAULY, MARIA	24	F	UNKNOWN	GRZZZZIL	
RUNKEL, JOHAN	34	M	LABR	GRZZZZIL	
KRAFT, MARIA	14	F	UNKNOWN	GRZZZZMA	
UERKWITZ, ANNA	24	F	UNKNOWN	GRZZZZNY	
OETERS, HEINR	36	M	ENGR	GRZZZZMD	
OSMERS, U	19	F	UNKNOWN	GRZZZZMD	
BEFERS, ANNA	24	F	UNKNOWN	GRZZZZMI	
BRUCKMANN, MATHIAS	34	M	BKLYR	GRZZZZMI	
CATH	31	F	UNKNOWN	GRZZZZMI	
WILHELM	10	M	CH	GRZZZZMI	
CATHARINA	8	F	CHILD	GRZZZZMI	
JOHAN	6	M	CHILD	GRZZZZMI	
ELISABETH	2	F	CHILD	GRZZZZMI	
MATHIAS	.03	M	INFANT	GRZZZZMI	
VOSS, JOHANN	55	M	LABR	GRZZZZMI	
CAROLINE	54	F	UNKNOWN	GRZZZZMI	
MINNA	11	F	UNKNOWN	GRZZZZMI	
DOESS, GEORG	18	M	LABR	GRZZZZOH	
ULRICH, HENRY	17	M	LABR	GRZZZZMI	
STEINKRAUS, WILH	35	M	LABR	GRZZZZMD	
ELISABETH	5	F	CHILD	GRZZZZMD	
JOHANNES	2	M	CHILD	GRZZZZMD	
ERNST	.07	M	INFANT	GRZZZZMD	
KRUEGER, JOSEPH	28	M	LABR	GRZZZZUNK	
HOEFNER, FRIEDERIKE	15	F	UNKNOWN	GRZZZZMD	
METZGER, MARG.	16	F	UNKNOWN	GRZZZZIL	
BLEICHER, WILH	18	F	UNKNOWN	GRZZZZMD	
AUGUSTE	17	F	UNKNOWN	GRZZZZMD	
KRUEGER, MARY	33	F	UNKNOWN	GRZZZZMI	
KATHARINA	23	F	UNKNOWN	GRZZZZMI	
WALPURGA	14	F	UNKNOWN	GRZZZZMI	
ROSA	8	F	CHILD	GRZZZZMI	
ANNA	3	F	CHILD	GRZZZZMI	
RAHN, KATH	25	F	UNKNOWN	GRZZZZMD	
JOH	3	M	CHILD	GRZZZZMD	
WILHELM	1	M	CHILD	GRZZZZMD	
CATH	.04	F	INFANT	GRZZZZMD	
KNOCHE, WILHELM	41	M	CGRMKR	GRZZZZIL	
LINA	63	F	UNKNOWN	GRZZZZIL	
SEIER, H--	20	M	LABR	GRZZZZIN	
SETZLER, CATH	20	F	UNKNOWN	GRZZZZOH	
OTTO, EDUARD	46	M	WVR	GRZZZZWI	
AUGUSTE	42	F	UNKNOWN	GRZZZZWI	
SELMA	16	F	UNKNOWN	GRZZZZWI	
MINNA	12	F	UNKNOWN	GRZZZZWI	
ALFRED	6	M	CHILD	GRZZZZWI	
EMIL	.03	M	INFANT	GRZZZZWI	
HENRIETTE	38	F	UNKNOWN	GRZZZZMD	
HENRIETTE	8	F	CHILD	GRZZZZMD	
PAUL	6	M	CHILD	GRZZZZMD	
BEHAUSER, JACOB	11	M	UNKNOWN	GRZZZZOH	
MUELLER, JOHAN	17	M	FARMER	GRZZZZOH	
SCHORSCH, MARIA	15	F	UNKNOWN	GRZZZZIL	
RICHTER, IDA	33	F	UNKNOWN	GRZZZZPA	
URBANSKI, MICH	23	M	WTR	GRZZZZIL	
RICHTER, CLARA	22	F	UNKNOWN	GRZZZZDAK	
MITTELSTADT, CARL	29	M	LABR	GRZZZZMN	
MARIE	21	F	UNKNOWN	GRZZZZMN	
HERMAN	2	M	CHILD	GRZZZZMN	
MARIE	1	F	CHILD	GRZZZZMN	
ANNA	.03	F	INFANT	GRZZZZMN	
CAROLINE	60	F	UNKNOWN	GRZZZZMN	
SELONEK, DANIEL	24	M	FARMER	GRZZZZIL	
BEHNE, WM.	65	F	UNKNOWN	GRZZZZIL	
RAUSCH, EMMA	20	F	UNKNOWN	GRZZZZMN	
EMILIE	18	F	UNKNOWN	GRZZZZMN	
KRUEGER, AUGUSTA	42	F	UNKNOWN	GRZZZZMD	
MARTHA	15	F	UNKNOWN	GRZZZZMD	
GUSTAV	8	M	CHILD	GRZZZZMD	
EMILIE	5	F	CHILD	GRZZZZMD	
LISTMANN, HEINRICH	17	M	MCHT	GRZZZZMD	
BASS, SUSMANN	22	M	TLR	GRZZZZMD	
ROSE, BERNARD	25	M	FARMER	GRZZZZOH	
KUERENS, ANNA	28	F	UNKNOWN	GRZZZZIL	
JANICZEWSKI, VICTOR	32	M	JNR	GRZZZZIL	
JOSEPHA	26	F	UNKNOWN	GRZZZZIL	
ROMAN	5	M	CHILD	GRZZZZIL	
WLADILAUS	3	M	CHILD	GRZZZZIL	
HEINRICH	.11	M	INFANT	GRZZZZIL	
HELENA	.11	F	INFANT	GRZZZZIL	
JABLOWICZ, JAN	25	M	LABR	GRZZZZIL	
MUELLER, MARG	17	F	UNKNOWN	GRZZZZVA	
LANGHEIM, JULIA	34	F	UNKNOWN	GRZZZZPA	
U	7	M	CHILD	GRZZZZPA	
WILHELM.	7	F	CHILD	GRZZZZPA	
AUGUSTE	5	F	CHILD	GRZZZZPA	
ALBERT	.10	M	INFANT	GRZZZZPA	
POHLMEIER, KAROLINE	19	F	UNKNOWN	GRZZZZMD	
MOLSKI, ANDREAS	51	M	LABR	GRZZZZMD	

PASSENGER	AGE	SEX	OCCUPATION	PRVL	DES
DRATCHKEWIE, HEDWIG	10	F	CH		GRZZZZMD
JAHNKE, FRIEDRICH	43	M	LABR		GRZZZZMD
ROZMAITY, SIMON	28	M	LABR		GRZZZZWI
MATHILDE	28	F	UNKNOWN		GRZZZZWI
ZOGELOW, JOHAN	67	M	GDNR		GRZZZZWI
EDUARD	25	M	GDNR		GRZZZZWI
ANNA	27	F	UNKNOWN		GRZZZZWI
AMANDA	30	F	UNKNOWN		GRZZZZWI
MAJEWSKI, JAN	23	M	LABR		GRZZZZPA
MARIANNA	64	F	UNKNOWN		GRZZZZPA
SUCHY, THOMAS	40	M	LABR		GRZZZZPA
ANASTASIA	41	F	UNKNOWN		GRZZZZDAK
ANTONIA	12	F	UNKNOWN		GRZZZZDAK
SOPHIE	10	F	CH		GRZZZZDAK
MARIA	8	F	CHILD		GRZZZZDAK
MARIANA	4	F	CHILD		GRZZZZDAK
JULIE	.10	F	INFANT		GRZZZZDAK
KONICZZUY, JOSEF	30	M	LABR		GRZZZZDAK
MARIANNA	30	F	UNKNOWN		GRZZZZDAK
FRANZ	11	M	UNKNOWN		GRZZZZDAK
JACOB	8	M	CHILD		GRZZZZDAK
AURELA	2	F	CHILD		GRZZZZDAK
HELENE	.06	F	INFANT		GRZZZZDAK
ZIEHR, GEORG	24	M	TLR		GRZZZZMD
SOEHNLEIN, JOHAN	18	M	FARMER		GRZZZZKY
KAISER, ERNST	32	M	BKLYR		GRZZZZMD
BECKER, AUGUST	35	M	LABR		GRZZZZMD
PAULINE	30	F	UNKNOWN		GRZZZZMD
PAUL	4	M	CHILD		GRZZZZMD
MAX	.11	M	INFANT		GRZZZZMD
ROWALSKY, EDUARD	45	M	LABR		GRZZZZMD
MARIANNA	40	F	UNKNOWN		GRZZZZMD
SEVERIN	15	M	UNKNOWN		GRZZZZMD
LADISLAUS	10	M	CH		GRZZZZMD
WLADISLAUS	4	M	CHILD		GRZZZZMD
WLADISLAWA	3	F	CHILD		GRZZZZMD
PELAGIA	.09	F	INFANT		GRZZZZMD
ENGELER, ALBERT	29	M	HTR		GRZZZZMD
STOELTZING, MARTIN	16	M	UNKNOWN		GRZZZZIA
STARCK, CARL	10	M	CH		GRZZZZIA
BREDER, CARL	15	M	UNKNOWN		GRZZZZIA
KOLLISCHEWSKY, LOUISE	27	F	UNKNOWN		GRZZZZKS
HENRIETTE	3	F	CHILD		GRZZZZKS
HEIL, KATHARINA	18	F	UNKNOWN		GRZZZZMD
ZINN, MARG	19	F	UNKNOWN		GRZZZZMD
HASSE, AUGUSTE	31	F	UNKNOWN		GRZZZZIL
EMMA	7	F	CHILD		GRZZZZIL
FRITZ	4	M	CHILD		GRZZZZIL
CARL	.09	M	INFANT		GRZZZZIL
SWIEDERSKI, JAN	16	M	UNKNOWN		GRZZZZMD
GUTZKI, AUGUSTA	50	F	UNKNOWN		GRZZZZMD
HERMAN	11	M	UNKNOWN		GRZZZZMD
WISCHEWSKY, KATH	42	F	UNKNOWN		GRZZZZPA
FRANZ	15	M	UNKNOWN		GRZZZZPA
ROSALIE	11	F	UNKNOWN		GRZZZZPA
HELENE	9	F	CHILD		GRZZZZPA
HERONIN	8	M	CHILD		GRZZZZPA
KAMINSKI, JOHAN	32	M	LABR		GRZZZZMI
SCHALLER, ANNA	27	F	LABR		GRZZZZMD
KOCHLER, PAUL	25	M	BKLYR		GRZZZZPA
WITTWER, EMIL	27	M	TLR		GRZZZZMI
MARQUARDT, CAROLINE	65	F	UNKNOWN		GRZZZZMI
HABERLAND, DOROTHEA	38	F	UNKNOWN		GRZZZZPA
LOUISA	12	F	UNKNOWN		GRZZZZPA
GUSTAV	10	M	CH		GRZZZZPA
ANNA	6	F	CHILD		GRZZZZPA
RASZUBKIEWITZ, KONSTANZ	18	F	UNKNOWN		GRZZZZMD
NEYMARK, SARAH	35	F	UNKNOWN		GRZZZZIA
ANNA	10	F	CH		GRZZZZIA
JACOB	8	M	CHILD		GRZZZZIA
SAMUEL	6	M	CHILD		GRZZZZIA
DAVID	4	M	CHILD		GRZZZZIA
GERMA, LINA	19	F	UNKNOWN		GRZZZZMD
REICELT, BERTHA	16	F	UNKNOWN		GRZZZZDAK
GASS, JUSTINE	20	F	UNKNOWN		GRZZZZWAS
DIETRICH, KAROLINE	51	F	UNKNOWN		GRZZZZMD
EGERSKI, FRANZ	74	M	BLKSMH		GRZZZZMD
BOROWZAK, CASIMIR	53	M	LABR		GRZZZZWI
ROSALIE	7	F	CHILD		GRZZZZWI
JARMUSCH, KAROLINE	57	F	UNKNOWN		GRZZZZOH
WILH.	26	F	UNKNOWN		GRZZZZOH
GOERKE, EMMA	18	F	UNKNOWN		GRZZZZMD
NELKOWSKI, JOHAS	51	M	LABR		GRZZZZMD
OWILKEN, CARL	30	M	LABR		GRZZZZOH
BERTHA	32	F	UNKNOWN		GRZZZZOH
HELMUTH	1	M	CHILD		GRZZZZOH
BRAND, CAROLINE	16	F	UNKNOWN		GRZZZZOH
PATZKE, GOTTLIEB	36	M	CCHMN		GRZZZZWI
HUFNAGEL, EMIL	17	M	CCHMN		GRZZZZWI
KAMP, WILH	54	F	UNKNOWN		GRZZZZWI
EMILIE	14	F	UNKNOWN		GRZZZZWI
BAUER, FRANZISKA	23	F	UNKNOWN		GRZZZZWI
WAGNER, ANNA	29	F	UNKNOWN		GRZZZZWI
HOLZMANN, KILIAN	20	M	LABR		GRZZZZWI
MERK, GEORG	29	M	JNR		GRZZZZWI
DIEDRICH, OTTO	11	M	UNKNOWN		GRZZZZWI
LUBS, JOHANNA	18	F	UNKNOWN		GRZZZZWI
FRIEDERIKE	13	F	UNKNOWN		GRZZZZMI
HADER, HERMAN	9	M	CHILD		GRZZZZMI
OSSNSCHMAN, U	27	F	UNKNOWN		GRZZZZIA
ANNA	10	F	CH		GRZZZZIA
KALINOWSKI, STANISLAUS	30	M	LABR		GRZZZZIA
NEDER, FRANZISKA	58	F	UNKNOWN		GRZZZZIL
HIMMER, MARG	54	F	UNKNOWN		GRZZZZMD
GEISSLER, HENRIETTE	38	F	UNKNOWN		GRZZZZMD
FANNY	4	F	CHILD		GRZZZZMD
PAUL	3	M	CHILD		GRZZZZMD
ADAMZEK, TMAS	33	M	JNR		GRZZZZMD
TOMCZAK, LUDWIG	32	M	JNR		GRZZZZMD
HEUSEL, CASPAR	38	M	FARMER		GRZZZZIN

SHIP: STATE OF NEBRASKA

FROM: GLASGOW AND LARNE
TO: NEW YORK
ARRIVED: 13 JUNE 1888

PASSENGER	AGE	SEX	OCCUPATION	PRVL	DES
COPPERSMITH, SEBASTIAN	19	M	LABR		GRZZZZUSA
KREISS, JOHANN	19	M	CL		GRZZZZUSA
BUCHNOWITZ, HERMANN	40	M	PDLR		GRZZZZUSA
BEER, JOHAN	22	M	LABR		GRZZZZUSA
BUGLER, MAGDALENE	20	F	SP		GRZZZZUSA
VERONIKA	19	F	SP		GRZZZZUSA
PECHL, ROSA	17	F	SP		GRZZZZUSA
THOMPSON, MARTHA	26	F	SP		GRZZZZUSA
MUELLER, SAHAN	24	F	SP		GRZZZZUSA
KELLERMANN, JOHANN	66	M	LABR		GRZZZZUSA
WILHELMINE	65	F	W		GRZZZZUSA
MARIE	11	F	CH		GRZZZZUSA
EMIL	7	M	CHILD		GRZZZZUSA
VALENTIN	3	M	CHILD		GRZZZZUSA
WILHELMINE	2	F	CHILD		GRZZZZUSA
GRANDAME, LOUIS	54	M	LABR		FRZZZZUSA
PREWOST, ZEPHER	26	M	LABR		FRZZZZUSA
IRMA	22	F	W		FRZZZZUSA
ZENOLE	2	M	CHILD		FRZZZZUSA
ZENOLA	4	F	CHILD		FRZZZZUSA
GRANDEME, MARIE	11	F	CH		FRZZZZUSA
LACOMTE, LOUISE	27	F	W		FRZZZZUSA
STEPHANIE	9	F	CHILD		FRZZZZUSA
LOUISE	4	F	CHILD		FRZZZZUSA
AUGUSTIN	.06	M	INFANT		FRZZZZUSA
PREWOST, OLMA	.02	F	INFANT		FRZZZZUSA

154

PASSENGER	AGE	SEX	OCCUPATION	PRVVL	DES

SHIP: WISCONSIN

FROM: LIVERPOOL AND QUEENSTOWN
TO: NEW YORK
ARRIVED: 13 JUNE 1888

PASSENGER	AGE	SEX	OCCUPATION	PRVVL	DES
SEIDT, FILIP	31	M	TLR		GRZZZZUSA
BOS, DERK	22	M	LABR		GRZZZZUSA
HERZ, F.	34	M	GENT		GRZZZZGR
HEINERTH, J.	25	F	LDY		GRZZZZGR
BOGER, R.	30	M	GENT		GRZZZZGR

SHIP: BELGENLAND

FROM: ANTWERP
TO: NEW YORK
ARRIVED: 14 JUNE 1888

PASSENGER	AGE	SEX	OCCUPATION	PRVVL	DES
SCHIER, F.	44	M	MCHT		GRAAECNY
KRAUSEN, FRITZ	25	M	MCHT		GRABEHNY
HOFFSUEMMER, J.	37	M	UNKNOWN		GRZZZZNY
HANEBURGER, ADOLF	52	M	MCHT		GRABOQNY
U-MRS	40	F	UNKNOWN		GRABOQNY
ZERLINE	12	F	CH		GRABOQNY
RICH.	8	M	CHILD		GRABOQNY
ALF	5	M	CHILD		GRABOQNY
MAX	16	M	CH		GRABOQNY
EMIL	15	M	CH		GRABOQNY
BRAND, GUSTE	20	M	PRNTR		GRAAYGNY
HAEBERLE, JACOB	19	M	BKR		GRAAYGNY
KESSELRING, CATHA.	27	M	LABR		GRAAECNY
JAEGER, CARL	27	M	BKR		GRZZZZNY
KOCH, ANNA	21	F	UNKNOWN		GRAAFXNY
ALBERT	4	M	CHILD		GRAAFXNY
ANNA	00	F	INF		GRAAFXNY
SCHALTHUN, FRIED.	23	M	BKBNDR		GRZZZZNY
GUSTAV	21	M	BKBNDR		GRZZZZNY
SCHWEIZER, GEO	42	M	PUB		GRZZZZNY
BRENICKER, HEINR.	20	M	SMH		GRZZZZNY
JURK, ADOLF	19	M	CGRMKR		GRZZZZNY
STREITBERGER, JOSEF	27	M	TNSTH		GRADLDUNK
SPECKMANN, FRIED.	34	M	GDNR		GRZZZZNY
KNOBB, CATH.	19	F	SVNT		GRZZZZLEB
KUPKOSKI, PAUL	25	M	LABR		GRZZZZMIL
ANNA	23	F	UNKNOWN		GRZZZZMIL
VALERIA	3	F	CHILD		GRZZZZMIL
FRANCESCA	.01	F	INFANT		GRZZZZMIL
SPEISER, EVA	20	F	SVNT		GRZZZZCH
MEYER, MARIE	14	F	UNKNOWN		GRADKJNY
RUSSA, JACOB	16	M	LABR		GRZZZZBUF
MARTENS, HEINR.	21	M	WVR		GRZZZZNY
CZECH, JOH.	28	M	LABR		GRZZZZWEB
ANTONIE	22	F	UNKNOWN		GRZZZZWEB
IGNATZ	2	M	CHILD		GRZZZZWEB
MARTHA	00	F	INF		GRZZZZWEB
WEINBRECKT, BERTHA	19	F	SVNT		GRZZZZTRE
SUSEMICHEL, ANDREAS	17	M	LABR		GRZZZZLOU
KOSMOROSKI, JOHN	23	M	LABR		GRZZZZUSA
BRUTONT, MATHILDE	22	F	UNKNOWN		FRZZZZUNK
OSCAR	00	M	INF		FRZZZZUNK
BETZ, ANNA	20	F	SVNT		FRAGKDNY
HECHTENBERG, WILH.	20	M	CPTR		GRZZZZNY
SCHEIDT, PETER	18	M	LABR		GRAEWXUSA
PETERS, U	18	M	LABR		GRAEWXUSA
MACHLER, MARIA	27	F	UNKNOWN		GRZZZZAKR
NICOLAS	7	M	CHILD		GRZZZZAKR
GRAF, ANNA	30	F	CK		GRAAHABAL
HUMMEL, FRIED.	16	M	LABR		GRADUCBUF
SCHWARZMUELLER, MAGD.	62	F	UNKNOWN		GRZZZZPIT
HOFFMANN, HEINR.	31	M	UNKNOWN		GRZZZZNY
NEUHOFF, HEINR.	24	M	BCHR		GRZZZZNY
STRASSER, CATH.	33	F	UNKNOWN		GRZZZZBO
WILH.	10	M	CH		GRZZZZBO
EMIL	8	M	CHILD		GRZZZZBO
AUG.	6	M	CHILD		GRZZZZBO
CARL	3	M	CHILD		GRZZZZBO
KEUL, JOHAN	22	M	LABR		GRZZZZCH
HINZINGER, PETER	20	M	LABR		GRZZZZCH
PHILIPPI, LUDW.	51	M	LABR		GRAGPDCH
MGDA.	50	F	UNKNOWN		GRAGPDCH
ANNA	11	F	CH		GRAGPDCH
CHAS.	9	M	CHILD		GRAGPDCH
JOSEPH	8	M	CHILD		GRAGPDCH
MATHES, CHRISTINE	19	F	SVNT		GRACTLCH
BUHL, CATH.	16	F	SVNT		GRACTLCH
HAMOT, NORBERT	45	M	MLDR		FRZZZZUNK
AUIGUST	17	M	MLDR		FRZZZZUNK
WAHL, MARIE-C.	26	F	CK		GRZZZZSTR
SILBEREISER, MARTHA-S.	16	F	SVNT		GRADYYNY
KNOERZER, GOTTF.	27	M	LABR		GRZZZZPIT
VOGEL, FR.	40	M	LABR		GRAGVWUSA
GEISSEL, HCH.	18	M	CGRMKR		GRAGVWNY
PETER, EMIL-G.	17	M	STMSN		GRAEXKNY
BUSCH, FRZ.	24	M	BKR		GRZZZZNY
DUDEL, GEO	18	M	BKR		GRZZZZNY
LINSMEIER, GEORGE	19	M	LABR		GRACYRBUF
GORISCH, CASIMIR	22	F	SVNT		GRACJUMIL
KALTHOF, THERESE	27	F	CK		GRACJUMIL
THIELE, FRIEDR.	43	M	LABR		GRZZZZNY
JOSEPHINE	41	F	UNKNOWN		GRZZZZNY
FRIEDR.	11	M	CH		GRZZZZNY
JOHAN	5	M	CHILD		GRZZZZNY
CLARA	2	F	CHILD		GRZZZZNY
HACHMEIER, HEINR.	42	M	LABR		GRZZZZNY
MARIA	42	F	UNKNOWN		GRZZZZNY
HUGO	11	M	CH		GRZZZZNY
OTTO	11	M	CH		GRZZZZNY
FRANZ	9	M	CHILD		GRZZZZNY
MARIA	6	F	CHILD		GRZZZZNY
HEINR.	4	M	CHILD		GRZZZZNY
ANNA	10	F	CH		GRZZZZNY
TRATZ, ANDREAS	23	M	CH		GRAAFCNY
KRUEGER, GEORGE	39	M	CH		GRZZZZNY
BLUM, WILH.	28	M	GLSMKR		GRZZZZNY
U. K.	29	M	MNR		GRAJBRSAU
KUMAROWSKI, EDW.	26	M	MNR		GRAJBRSAU
LANGE, JACOB	45	M	BBR		GRZZZZNY
BAUMGARTEN, RUD.	27	M	CNF		GRZZZZNY
EFFENBURGER, KARL	18	M	CNF		GRZZZZNY
KREIS, GEO	27	M	ENGR		GRZZZZNY
GAUSEN, H.	47	M	CL		GRZZZZNY
FITZER, AUGUST	23	M	HRDRS		GRZZZZNY
EINSBERG, SOLOMON	22	M	GZR		GRADBQNY
RAYNER	23	M	GZR		GRADBQNY
KLEIN, HEINR.	26	M	BKR		GRADBQNY
HELEN	27	F	UNKNOWN		GRADBQNY
HENRY	4	M	CHILD		GRADBQNY
HELEN	2	F	CHILD		GRADBQNY
GERT	00	F	INF		GRADBQNY
BERTZAM, JOHN	42	M	BKR		GRADBQNY
PENDERWASSER, AARON	29	M	LABR		GRADBQPHI
HINDE	25	F	UNKNOWN		GRADBQPHI
WETZNER, JOHAN	25	M	CL		GRADBQPIT
FISCH, JOSH.	30	M	SHMK		GRADBQCLE
REBECCA	26	F	UNKNOWN		GRADBQCLE
ELLIS	4	M	CHILD		GRADBQCLE
SARAH	3	F	CHILD		GRADBQCLE
ABRA	2	M	CHILD		GRADBQCLE
WOOLF	00	M	INF		GRADBQCLE
KALTENMEIER, CAROL.	19	F	SVNT		GRAEVZNY
GEIB, PHIL.	24	M	SMH		GRZZZZPHI
MARIA	21	F	UNKNOWN		GRZZZZPHI
PHIL.	1	M	CHILD		GRZZZZPHI
GOGOL, EUG.	35	F	CK		GRAJBRSAU

PASSENGER	AGE	SEX	OCCUPATION	PRVVL	DES
WOLF, MICH.	34	M	HRDRS	GRZZZZNY	
SCHLENGER, CONRAD	28	M	LABR	GRZZZZNY	
ZIPPENFELD, SOPHIOE	20	F	SVNT	GRAEWXNY	
SPO-, HUBERT	28	M	LABR	GRAEWXNY	
GITZEN, JACOB	25	M	LABR	GRACHACH	
SCHLOESSER, JOSEF	38	M	LABR	GRACHACH	
NAPIONTEK, NOCHEM	43	M	SHMK	GRZZZZUNK	
CARL	16	M	SHMK	GRZZZZUNK	
TAUBENSER, EDW.	26	M	UNKNOWN	GRABHUCH	
TURTLETAUB, ELIAS	55	M	CL	GRZZZZNY	
ABRAH	9	M	CHILD	GRZZZZNY	
ZURAWJICKY, JOSEPH	30	M	SMH	GRZZZZNY	
SIROKA, THEODOR	36	M	LKSH	GRZZZZNY	
HAUBENREISER, CARL-O.	26	M	BKR	GRACXVNY	
TELLER, CAROL.	17	F	UNKNOWN	GRACXVNY	
SCHROBBACK, AUGUST	30	M	TLR	GRABOQNY	
LUCIA	7	F	CHILD	GRABOQNY	
KNIES, MARG.	24	F	SVNT	GRAFXONY	
EVA	21	F	SVNT	GRAFXONY	
HERMAN, CRESZA.	21	F	CK	GRZZZZNY	
FAHRSDORFER, JOHAN	37	M	BCHR	GRAECMBUF	
BENDER, FRIED.	00	M	BKR	GRZZZZMIL	
SCHLACHTER, CHRIST.	23	M	BKR	GRZZZZNY	
MICH, MARIE	68	F	UNKNOWN	GRZZZZNY	
MINERI, XAVER	29	M	UNKNOWN	GRAAHUNY	
MOEHRLE, U	27	M	CPTR	GRAAHUNY	
U, U	24	F	SVNT	GRAAHUNY	
PECCHAMANI, GIOV.	34	M	HTLKPR	GRAAHUNY	
GAUSS, CATH.	31	M	LABR	GRAFTDNY	
HERTENSTEIN, CASPAR	41	M	LABR	SRZZZZNY	
SUSANNA	40	F	UNKNOWN	SRZZZZNY	
EMMA	16	F	UNKNOWN	SRZZZZNY	
ANNA	14	F	UNKNOWN	SRZZZZNY	
EMIL	9	M	CHILD	SRZZZZNY	
HERM.	7	M	CHILD	SRZZZZNY	
GRUNTZ, ALPH.	29	M	UNKNOWN	SRAAHUNY	
GERBER, GOTTL.	33	M	STMSN	SRAAHUSAN	
WAHL, NIC.	00	M	FARMER	LXZZZZNY	
KIND	7	M	CHILD	LXZZZZNY	
HOLBACH, CHAS.	25	M	MSN	GRZZZZNY	
MARG.	24	F	UNKNOWN	GRZZZZNY	
MARG.	.02	F	INFANT	GRZZZZNY	
WAGNER, WILH.	19	M	CL	GRACVENY	
BOM, PETER	32	M	BKR	GRZZZZNY	
HECHEL, NICOLAS	23	M	LABR	GRZZZZNY	
BUDERER, CHRIST.	28	M	BRR	GRAECZNY	
KIEFFER, NIC.	27	M	FARMER	LXZZZZNY	
HENTGES, WILHELM	27	M	LABR	LXZZZZNY	
GRAF, CARL	10	M	CH	LXZZZZNY	
GEIGER, DOROTH.	54	F	UNKNOWN	LXZZZZNY	
MARGA.	10	F	CH	LXZZZZNY	
PFEIFER, CARL	27	M	LABR	LXZZZZPIT	
MARG.	26	F	UNKNOWN	LXZZZZPIT	
ANNA	3	F	CHILD	LXZZZZPIT	
CATH.	.11	F	INFANT	LXZZZZPIT	
LIEBLER, THERESE	17	F	UNKNOWN	LXAIBBNY	
BAUER, MARIE	23	F	UNKNOWN	LXADZAHEL	
JULIUS	5	M	CHILD	LXADZAHEL	
LOUISE	2	F	CHILD	LXADZAHEL	
SCHIMSING, PAULINE	27	F	UNKNOWN	LXADZAHEL	
STEIMER, FRZ.	33	M	BKBNDR	LXADZACH	
ELISE	30	F	UNKNOWN	LXADZACH	
EUGA.	7	F	CHILD	LXADZACH	
FRIEDR.	5	M	CHILD	LXADZACH	
GUSTAV	3	M	CHILD	LXADZACH	
GOTTE, BERNARD	28	M	CPTR	GRZZZZUNK	
BECKSTEIN, HCH.	31	M	CL	GRADLNNY	
JUNG, A.	29	M	CPTR	GRZZZZNY	
PHIL.	25	F	UNKNOWN	GRZZZZNY	
BUERGENHEIMER, PETER	31	M	GDNR	GRAGWNNY	
GERON, JACOB	26	M	LABR	GRZZZZNY	
CATH.	26	F	UNKNOWN	GRZZZZNY	
ELISAB.	4	F	CHILD	GRZZZZNY	
EVA	00	F	INF	GRZZZZNY	
GIEHL, JOHANN	27	M	CPTR	GRZZZZNY	
WEISS, JOH.	30	M	WHLR	GRZZZZNY	
LAUTH, IRZGOS	24	M	FARMER	GRZZZZUSA	
MEIER, FRZ.	24	M	LABR	GRALGASP	
LOUISE	28	F	UNKNOWN	GRALGASP	
GOERGEN	11	F	CH	GRALGASP	
MARIE	9	F	CHILD	GRALGASP	
FRZ.	00	M	INF	GRALGASP	
SCHMIDT, JOSEF	23	M	BCHR	GRZZZZSP	
STORK, LOUIS	26	M	CPTR	GRADOISP	
HELENE	21	F	UNKNOWN	GRADOISP	
HEREM, CONRAD	25	M	LABR	GRACPYSP	
RIEHM, CHRISTO	39	M	CPTR	GRADOISP	
MARIA	39	F	UNKNOWN	GRADOISP	
ADAM	17	M	UNKNOWN	GRADOISP	
RUDOLF	11	M	CH	GRADOISP	
CARL	9	M	CHILD	GRADOISP	
LUDW.	5	M	CHILD	GRADOISP	
U, U	4	M	CHILD	GRADOISP	
BAUER, U	31	M	CH	GRZZZZSP	
THERESE	10	F	CH	GRZZZZSP	
JOHAN	2	M	CHILD	GRZZZZSP	
GEORGE	1	M	CHILD	GRZZZZSP	
FRITZ, ANDREAS	27	M	MSN	GRALIASP	
KREBS, SAM.	31	M	CPTR	GRZZZZDET	
MARIA	32	F	UNKNOWN	GRZZZZDET	
ANNA	8	F	CHILD	GRZZZZDET	
JULIUS	6	M	CHILD	GRZZZZDET	
RUDOLF	4	M	CHILD	GRZZZZDET	
HCH.	3	M	CHILD	GRZZZZDET	
MINA	1	F	CHILD	GRZZZZDET	
SCHWALL, JUSTINE	27	M	CPTR	GRZZZZDET	
THERESIA	24	F	UNKNOWN	GRZZZZDET	
LOUISE	3	F	CHILD	GRZZZZDET	
PROBST, MATH.	24	M	LABR	GRZZZZCH	
VATTER, JOH.G.	39	M	LABR	GRZZZZNY	
WONN, LOUISE	18	F	LABR	GRZZZZNY	
FELD	9	F	CHILD	GRZZZZNY	
IDA	7	F	CHILD	GRZZZZNY	
KLEIN, DOROTHEA	29	F	CK	GRAAKHUNK	
NEHR, FRZ.	28	M	LABR	GRZZZZNY	
ELISAB.	20	F	UNKNOWN	GRZZZZNY	
ANNA	00	F	INF	GRZZZZNY	
KRAMER, LORENZ	24	M	BCHR	GRZZZZNY	
LORENZ	24	M	BCHR	GRZZZZNY	
HOPFENMULLER, LORENZ	21	M	TLR	GRACAXNY	
BAUER, MARG.	19	F	SVNT	GRZZZZNY	
BOCHIN, MICH.	24	M	BBR	GRAGKDNY	
WERNER, ELISA	19	F	SVNT	GRADUXNY	
ORTH, LEONHARD	21	M	LABR	GRZZZZNY	
WOLFSCHNEIDER, BALTH.	27	M	BKR	GRZZZZCH	
ELISAB.	23	F	UNKNOWN	GRZZZZCH	
KIND	.04	F	INFANT	GRZZZZCH	
MARG, MARIE	55	F	UNKNOWN	GRZZZZCH	
MOG, HCH.	21	M	LABR	GRALBRCH	
HABERLE, ROBERT	00	M	UNKNOWN	GRZZZZNY	
VOGTMANN, PETER	47	M	LABR	GRZZZZCH	
KIMES, NIC.	33	M	LABR	LXZZZZNY	
BARBA.	26	F	UNKNOWN	LXZZZZNY	
BARBA.	.10	F	INFANT	LXZZZZNY	
KAPP, PETER	27	M	MNR	LXZZZZPIT	
MENKE, THEODORE	30	M	LKSH	LXZZZZPIT	
KAFFENBERGER, JOH.	25	M	BKR	LXAEVTNY	
HAUN, STEFAN	23	M	BKR	LXAHYRNY	
KOBE, CARL	31	M	BKR	GRZZZZNY	
KUEHNER, MARIE	40	F	UNKNOWN	GRACUONY	
EMILIE	14	F	UNKNOWN	GRACUONY	
KARL	11	M	CH	GRACUONY	
LUDW.	8	M	CHILD	GRACUONY	
HERM.	6	M	CHILD	GRACUONY	
LEONE	2	M	CHILD	GRACUONY	
GRUNDNER, PHIL.	35	M	LABR	GRZZZZNY	
CHARLTE.	31	F	UNKNOWN	GRZZZZNY	
RICH.	7	M	CHILD	GRZZZZNY	
RAIMOND	3	M	CHILD	GRZZZZNY	
MATHILDE	.02	F	INFANT	GRZZZZNY	

PASSENGER	AGE	SEX	OCCUPATION	PRIVVL	DES	PASSENGER	AGE	SEX	OCCUPATION	PRIVVL	DES
SCHERER, WM.	30	M	GDSM	GRAMAMNY		FRIEGLER, HULDA	22	F	W	GRZZZZNY	
MECH, KARL	23	M	GDSM	GRAMAMNY		EMMA	3	F	CHILD	GRZZZZNY	
ZWICK, JACOB	50	M	LABR	GRABALNY		IDA	19	F	UNKNOWN	GRZZZZNY	
JOH.	17	M	LABR	GRABALNY		SCHILBINGER, LINA	24	F	UNKNOWN	GRAEXWNY	
ASEL, JOHAN	24	M	MUSN	GRAJSMNY		HELD, GEORG	28	M	BKLYR	GRZZZZNY	
WAGNER, MARIANNE	16	F	UNKNOWN	GRAGFBNY		LINA	19	F	W	GRZZZZNY	
LEICK, JEAN	26	M	MLR	LXZZZZNY		MINNA	.01	F	INFANT	GRZZZZNY	
KRAUSS, WILHM.	27	M	PNTR	GRZZZZNY		MUELLER, OTTO	35	M	TNM	GRZZZZNY	
KUEBGEN, B.	26	M	PDLR	GRAGLSNY		SCHMEIDER, FRANZ	17	M	TNM	GRACXVNY	
MANIET, LOUIS	25	M	LKSH	GRADXWNY		FUCHS, EMILIE	36	F	W	GRZZZZNY	
APPEZ, SCHEZ	43	M	LABR	GRADXWCH		ALBIN	11	M	UNKNOWN	GRZZZZNY	
MUND, HEIN	46	M	TU	GRACBRNY		ALBERT	6	M	CHILD	GRZZZZNY	
GRUSAT, CHRISTOF	40	M	LABR	GRZZZZNY		OTTO	3	M	CHILD	GRZZZZNY	
GIESE, FRIED.	32	M	BKR	GRZZZZNY		WEBER, CARL	19	M	CL	GRZZZZNY	
ABERLE, ADELE	27	F	UNKNOWN	FRZZZZNY		SCHILLER, JULIANNA	50	F	W	GRADBDNY	
WELER, CATH.	20	F	UNKNOWN	FRZZZZNY		IDA	17	F	UNKNOWN	GRADBDNY	
BRANDMEYER, LOUISE	20	F	UNKNOWN	FRZZZZNY		MEYER, GEORG	24	M	CL	GRZZZZNY	
ABERLE, CHAS.	4	M	CHILD	FRZZZZNY		LUEC, LOUISE	66	F	W	GRZZZZNY	
EUG.	.11	M	INFANT	FRZZZZNY		MAYFARTH, HEINR.	16	M	LABR	GRZZZZNY	
MEYER, JACOB	45	M	MLDR	FRAAECNY		KRYWICKA, DOMINSK	30	M	LABR	GRZZZZNY	
PETTIG, AUG.	23	M	LABR	GRZZZZNY		SCHOBERT, ALBRECHT	33	M	LABR	GRZZZZNY	
KOLBENSCHLAG, JOSEPH	30	M	LABR	GRZZZZNY		ALWA	33	F	W	GRZZZZNY	
ENGEL, JAC.	22	M	BCHR	SRZZZZNY		LINA	11	F	UNKNOWN	GRZZZZNY	
						MAX	7	M	CHILD	GRZZZZNY	
						REINHARDT, JOHANNA	45	F	W	GRZZZZNY	
						THEODOR	21	M	CPTR	GRZZZZNY	
SHIP: EMS						ALMA	18	F	UNKNOWN	GRZZZZNY	
						OTTO	8	M	CHILD	GRZZZZNY	
FROM: BREMEN AND SOUTHAMPTON						GNASS, KATHARINA	24	F	UNKNOWN	GRAFNKNY	
TO: NEW YORK						GEHDE, RUDOLF	36	M	JNR	GRZZZZUNK	
ARRIVED: 14 JUNE 1888						FRIEDERIKE	30	F	W	GRZZZZUNK	
						HERSCHER, EMMA	17	F	UNKNOWN	GRZZZZUNK	
						AMALIA	32	F	UNKNOWN	GRZZZZUNK	
HOFFMANN, HEUPTMANN	50	M	CPTR	SRAARRNY		CLOVS, CATHARINA	24	F	UNKNOWN	GRZZZZUSA	
GASCH, EMIL	28	M	MCHT	GRZZZZNY		SOLLEDER, JOSEF	37	M	BRZ	GRZZZZWI	
MARIE	23	F	W	GRZZZZNY		SEDLMEIER, JACOB	34	M	BRZ	GRZZZZWI	
JAGER, WALBURGA	26	F	UNKNOWN	GRACUXNY		MICHLICH, THERESE	22	F	UNKNOWN	GRAAHBCH	
DIETRICH, ALBIN	37	M	MCHT	GRZZZZNY		SCHILD, JOSEFA	34	F	UNKNOWN	GRAAHBCH	
SCHNNITZ, PAUL	19	M	MCHT	GRAAHLNY		SEMPFHNBER, JOSEF	18	M	CL	GRZZZZMN	
STROETER, ADOLF	20	M	MCHT	GRAAHLNY		FIDLER, JULIANNA	17	F	UNKNOWN	GRAARRNY	
HAHN, ANNA	28	F	UNKNOWN	GRAJKDNY		GRUENWALD, EMMA	18	F	UNKNOWN	GRAARRNY	
WILLENBROCKEL, MARIE	24	F	UNKNOWN	GRZZZZNY		SCHUELZ, HELENA	19	F	UNKNOWN	GRAARRNY	
MOSSNER, ALFRED	29	M	MCHT	GRAARRNY		SCHADE, MATHAUS	29	M	LABR	GRZZZZNY	
STEFFEN, MARIEJ	20	F	UNKNOWN	GRAARRNY		BISCHOFF, CARL	55	M	FARMER	GRZZZZOH	
ELISABETH	19	F	UNKNOWN	GRAARRNY		ROSINA	54	F	W	GRZZZZOH	
GEISER, JOHANN	30	M	SVNT	GRAARRNY		LENA	11	F	UNKNOWN	GRZZZZOH	
RUPP, JACOB	30	M	GZR	GRZZZZUNK		KETTMANN, KATHARINA	20	F	UNKNOWN	GRZZZZOH	
KNOBLANCH, JOHANN	10	M	MCHT	GRZZZZUNK		GUTMANN, KATHARINA	32	F	W	GRZZZZIL	
PORH, CATHARINE	30	F	W	GRZZZZNY		CARL	4	M	CHILD	GRZZZZIL	
STELJES, ADELHEID	19	F	UNKNOWN	GRZZZZNY		KONRAD	2	M	CHILD	GRZZZZIL	
BESKMANN, ALINE	32	F	W	GRZZZZNY		FRIEDR.	.03	M	INFANT	GRZZZZIL	
BERTHOELD	11	M	UNKNOWN	GRZZZZNY		SCHMIDT, JACOB	16	M	BKR	GRZZZZIL	
LOUISE	10	F	CH	GRZZZZNY		BISCHOFF, FRIEDRICH	27	M	FARMER	GRZZZZOH	
EMILIE	7	F	CHILD	GRZZZZNY		LECHMER, MARGARETHA	28	F	W	GRZZZZOH	
HEDWIG	5	F	CHILD	GRZZZZNY		KARL	27	M	BLKSMH	GRZZZZOH	
KRENZBERGER, FRANZ	27	M	TNM	GRAAKHNY		HANSSLER, DOROTHEA	26	F	UNKNOWN	GRZZZZPA	
KOEHNKEN, META	22	F	UNKNOWN	GRAARRNY		PFENHEISSER, GEORG	22	M	CPTR	GRZZZZNY	
GERINO, CATHARINA	17	F	UNKNOWN	GRZZZZNY		GERMAN, ELISABETH	28	F	UNKNOWN	GRAEAFIL	
MERKEL, GEORG	23	M	FARMER	GRADLNNY		FLATHMANN, HEINR.	26	M	LABR	GRZZZZNY	
FIEDLER, HEINRICH	21	M	LABR	GRADLNNY		GRINDELMANN, FRITZ	30	M	FARMER	GRACXHNY	
FISCHER, NICLS	22	M	LABR	GRADLNNY		DAMHORSH, MARIA	20	F	UNKNOWN	GRADAQMN	
WILFERT, HEINRICH	25	M	LABR	GRADLNNY		WOERDEMANN, BERNHD.	18	M	FARMER	GRZZZZNE	
LAKNER, PETER	27	M	LABR	GRAFBVMT		WENSING, GERTRUDE	26	F	UNKNOWN	GRAFMKWI	
ROSENBOHM, ANNA	18	F	UNKNOWN	GRACBRNY		GROSSASCHOFF, ERNST	36	M	FARMER	GRACBRNE	
WEIBEZAHL, AMALIE	51	F	W	GRZZZZNY		KLEINHAKENKAMP, KASPER	25	M	FARMER	GRAFMKNE	
HELENE	21	F	UNKNOWN	GRZZZZNY		ORTMANN, HEIRN.	29	M	TNM	GRAFMKNE	
LYDIA	18	F	UNKNOWN	GRZZZZNY		ACKFELD, JOSEF	16	M	LABR	GRAFMKMN	
REHOR, ERNST	16	M	LABR	GRZZZZNY		HECKS, ALFRED	38	M	LABR	GRAFMKNY	
GEICR, GEORG	26	M	SHMK	GRADRONY		JULIE	30	F	W	GRAFMKNY	
MUELLER, ELISABETH	22	F	UNKNOWN	GRZZZZNY		TROTTINA, DAVID	28	M	CL	GRAFMKNY	
TRENHEIT, CONRAD	29	M	CPR	GRADRONY		KALLMANN, CATHARINA	40	F	W	GRAFMKNY	
SCHRECK, ANNA	22	F	UNKNOWN	GRADRONY		MORITZ	10	M	CH	GRAFMKNY	
ALTMANN, JOHANN	64	M	LABR	GRADRONY		SCHANFLER, NANE	18	F	UNKNOWN	GRZZZZOH	
						WURZ, MINE	20	F	UNKNOWN	GRZZZZNY	
						EISEMEYER, ROSLE	21	F	UNKNOWN	GRZZZZNY	

PASSENGER	AGE	SEX	OCCUPATION	PRIVL	DES
HERB, FRANZ	19	M	BBR	GRZZZZNY	
SCHWANK, MARGARETHA	29	F	UNKNOWN	GRACPUNY	
WERNINGER, MARTHA	20	F	UNKNOWN	GRAEYGNY	
CATHARINA	18	F	UNKNOWN	GRAEYGNY	
SCHMID, CRESCENZIA	64	F	W	GRZZZZNY	
MESSERLE, OTTO	20	M	CL	GRAEYGNY	
FREY, FRIEDRICH	18	M	JNR	GRAEYGNY	
KUNZ, WILHWLMINE	24	F	UNKNOWN	GRAEYGNY	
STRAUSS, CHRISTIAN	16	M	CPTR	GRAEYGNY	
AUCH, MARIA	23	F	UNKNOWN	GRAEYGNY	
ANNAOERTER, MARIE	31	F	UNKNOWN	GRZZZZNY	
OFNER, JEANNETTE	18	F	UNKNOWN	GRAEXWNY	
DREYFUFS, BERTHA	18	F	UNKNOWN	GRZZZZNY	
NEUWELT, ISIDOR	24	M	SHMK	GRZZZZNY	
SCHMIDT, CATHARINA	22	F	UNKNOWN	GRZZZZNY	
GOTTFARDT, JOHANN	28	M	FARMER	GRAIACNY	
RIPPS, HEINRICH	29	M	FARMER	GRABOQNY	
SCHUELER, ADAM	17	M	TLR	GRAAZSNY	
ACKER, JACOB	18	M	LABR	GRAFZVNY	
WEBER, JACOB	26	M	LABR	GRAEOHNY	
STENBERGER, FRIEDR.	16	M	LABR	GRAEOHNY	
WEBER, GEORG	50	M	FARMER	GRAEOHNY	
LANER, ANTON	18	M	CL	GRAFZVNY	
KAMMERSCHMIDT, FERD.	17	M	LABR	GRABEDNY	
THOENGES, PHILLIP	26	M	JNR	GRAFZVNY	
JOCKEL, CHRISIAN	17	M	BBR	GRAFZVNY	
VILLHARD, MARIA	24	F	UNKNOWN	GRZZZZPA	
STUDT, JOHANN	27	M	BKLYR	GRZZZZMN	
CERANEWSKA, MARYANNA	20	F	UNKNOWN	GRZZZZNY	
KUCHLER, LUDWIG	21	M	LABR	GRZZZZNY	
SCHMIDT, WILHELM	26	M	JNR	GRAARRNY	
MARTENS, ROBERT	16	M	FARMER	GRZZZZNY	
RIKE, META	18	F	UNKNOWN	GRZZZZNY	
DIERKING, HEINR.	18	M	FARMER	GRZZZZNY	

SHIP: NOVA SCOTIAN

FROM: LIVERPOOL
TO: BALTIMORE
ARRIVED: 14 JUNE 1888

PASSENGER	AGE	SEX	OCCUPATION	PRIVL	DES
RANDAL, ERNST	23	M	NN	GRZZZZNY	
BERGE, KLARA	22	F	NN	GRZZZZNY	
SERDING, JAS.	22	M	PNTR	GRZZZZNY	
DOEHLER, ELIAS	23	F	W	GRZZZZBAL	
WALTER	1	M	CHILD	GRZZZZBAL	
BIRKET, MAGGIE	18	F	SVNT	GRZZZZPIT	
SCHMIDT, E.	22	F	SVNT	GRZZZZBAL	
LEIBEL, ISRAEL	28	M	LABR	GRZZZZBAL	
KRUMZBERGER, LOUISE	20	F	SVNT	GRZZZZPIT	
VOLLMAN, JOH.	17	M	LABR	GRZZZZNY	
LEWRITTEN, EISIK	43	M	CH	GRZZZZBAL	
DISEFELD, HENRICH	22	M	BLKSMH	GRZZZZNY	

SHIP: POLYNESIA

FROM: HAMBURG
TO: NEW YORK
ARRIVED: 15 JUNE 1888

PASSENGER	AGE	SEX	OCCUPATION	PRIVL	DES
ASMUS, CAESAR	18	M	CL	HBZZZZNY	
MUELLER, WILH	18	M	LABR	PRZZZZNY	
ALBERTINE	19	F	W	PRZZZZNY	
SASS, CLAUS	27	M	CGRMKR	PRZZZZNY	
GRABOWSKA, AGNISKA	24	F	WO	PRZZZZNY	

PASSENGER	AGE	SEX	OCCUPATION	PRIVL	DES
KOCH, MARIE	50	F	W	PRZZZZNY	
BERTHA	26	F	D	PRZZZZNY	
MARTIN	8	M	CHILD	PRZZZZNY	
PETRAT, AUGUST	33	M	LABR	PRZZZZNY	
REINDL, JOSEF	24	M	FARMER	BVZZZZNY	
FRANZISKA	55	F	W	BVZZZZNY	
HAVENUS	15	M	S	BVZZZZNY	
WILLKENS, HEINRICH	30	M	MLR	PRZZZZNY	
MARIE	29	F	W	PRZZZZNY	
GAEBEL, ANNA	19	F	WO	MKZZZZNY	
TIMM, ANNA	20	F	WO	MKZZZZNY	
SIVEITS, FRIEDR	20	M	CL	PRZZZZNY	
TIMM, MARIE	20	F	WO	MKZZZZNY	
HESSE, ELISABETH	18	F	SGL	PRZZZZNY	
CATHARINA	15	F	SGL	PRZZZZNY	
UHRIG, KARL	27	M	SDLR	BVZZZZNY	
MUELLER, LUISE	65	F	WO	WMZZZZNY	
SCHLUETER, MATHILDE	24	F	SGL	PRZZZZNY	
KINTKEL, MARIE	51	F	UNKNOWN	HBZZZZNY	
NOLLE, BERNH	30	M	JNR	HBZZZZNY	
DRGAK, WILH	61	M	LABR	PRZZZZNY	
JOH.	60	F	W	PRZZZZNY	
EMMA	9	F	CHILD	PRZZZZNY	
SACHTMANN, JACOB	48	M	TLR	PRZZZZNY	
EGGERS, ROBERT	42	M	TLR	PRZZZZNY	
LORENZ, CARL	31	M	TLR	PRZZZZNY	
SPITZKEIT, HERMANN	30	M	ENGR	PRZZZZNY	
HENNIG, ALBERT	27	M	BCHR	PRZZZZNY	
BADE, WILH	42	F	WO	HBZZZZNY	
FRIEDR	8	M	CHILD	HBZZZZNY	
HERMAN	7	M	CHILD	HBZZZZNY	
JOHANNES	6	M	CHILD	HBZZZZNY	
AMANDA	4	F	CHILD	HBZZZZNY	
PALAZINSKI, SOPHIE	23	F	WO	PRZZZZNY	
JOSEFA	.11	F	INFANT	PRZZZZNY	
BADE, WILH	9	F	CHILD	PRZZZZNY	
KOCH, PETER	36	M	LABR	PRZZZZNY	
ANNA	33	F	W	PRZZZZNY	
BRUNZEL, WALTER	28	M	TCHR	HBZZZZNY	
CLAUSSEN, WILH	23	M	LABR	PRZZZZNY	
BETTY	22	F	W	PRZZZZNY	
BABBE, MARG	64	F	WO	PRZZZZNY	
WENZKE, REINHOLD	37	M	BCHR	PRZZZZNY	
PAUL	38	F	W	PRZZZZNY	
ARTHUR	8	M	CHILD	PRZZZZNY	
WILLY	6	M	CHILD	PRZZZZNY	
ARTHUR	.09	M	INFANT	PRZZZZNY	
SANDBERG, OTTO	36	M	LKSH	PRZZZZNY	
SIEGEL, FRANZ	28	M	WVR	SYZZZZNY	
MARIE	24	F	W	SYZZZZNY	
ANNA	.03	F	INFANT	SYZZZZUNK	
BUSCHNER, CHR	43	M	DLR	SYZZZZUSA	
EMILIE	35	F	W	SYZZZZUSA	
HERMES, CAROL	56	F	UNKNOWN	PRZZZZUSA	
CARL	33	M	UNKNOWN	PRZZZZUSA	
JOSEPH	9	M	CHILD	PRZZZZUSA	
GIPPERT, BERNH	16	M	LABR	PRZZZZUSA	
SCHORNER, BRUNO	37	M	SDLR	SYZZZZUSA	
BRAUN, JACOB	17	M	MECH	WMZZZZUSA	
NILL, CHRISTIAN	17	M	BKR	WMZZZZUSA	
MARIE	19	F	SGL	WMZZZZUSA	
DOECHSLWER, GEORG	58	M	FARMER	WMZZZZUSA	
KLEINDIENST, MARG	28	F	SGL	BVZZZZUSA	
ARPS, HELENE	17	F	SGL	SYZZZZUSA	
VEITH, MARTHA	43	F	WO	WMZZZZUSA	
JOH	4	M	CHILD	WMZZZZUSA	
KUENKE, ALBRECHT	16	M	LABR	PRZZZZUSA	
EHLERT, CARL	49	M	FARMER	PRZZZZUSA	
CAROLINE	36	F	W	PRZZZZUSA	
GUSTAV	9	M	CHILD	PRZZZZUSA	
FRITZ	7	M	CHILD	PRZZZZUSA	
MARIE	4	F	CHILD	PRZZZZUSA	
PAUL	3	M	CHILD	PRZZZZUSA	
HEDWIG	.08	F	INFANT	PRZZZZUSA	
HAGE, HERMAN	14	M	LABR	PRZZZZUSA	

PASSENGER	AGE	SEX	OCCUPATION	PRIVL	DES
FRIDA	9	F	CHILD	PRZZZZ	USA
DREWS, AXEL	20	M	SCP	PRZZZZ	USA
LIEBELT, CARL	23	M	LABR	PRZZZZ	USA
SCHULZ, JOHANN	36	M	LABR	PRZZZZ	USA
LUISA	32	F	W	PRZZZZ	USA
EMIL	9	M	CHILD	PRZZZZ	USA
JOHANN	8	M	CHILD	PRZZZZ	USA
FRIEDRICH	3	M	CHILD	PRZZZZ	USA
AUGUSTE	.11	F	INFANT	PRZZZZ	USA
MIERZYKOWSKI, MARIANNE	30	F	SGL	PRZZZZ	USA
WENTZEL, FRITZ	24	M	PNTR	PRZZZZ	USA
MUNK, BERTHA	22	F	WO	PRZZZZ	USA
ALFRED	.11	M	INFANT	PRZZZZ	USA
ELSA	.01	F	INFANT	PRZZZZ	USA
PRECKEL, WILH	68	F	WO	PRZZZZ	USA
WROBLENSKI, APOLLINARI	26	M	BCHR	PRZZZZ	USA
PACKOWA, JOSEF	35	M	LABR	PRZZZZ	USA
BURKHARDT, EMIL	27	M	BKR	PRZZZZ	USA
SIMBOLD, IDA	65	F	WO	PRZZZZ	USA
MOLZEN, CHRIST	21	F	SGL	PRZZZZ	USA
KOWALCZYK, THOMAS	32	M	LABR	PRZZZZ	USA
CATH.	34	F	W	PRZZZZ	USA
MYRECKI, FRANZ	9	M	CHILD	PRZZZZ	USA
JAN	5	M	CHILD	PRZZZZ	USA
NEIERWSKY, KASIMIR	24	M	LABR	PRZZZZ	USA
KILL, THOMAS	28	M	LABR	PRZZZZ	USA
MICHALINE	24	F	W	PRZZZZ	USA
RADKE, MARIE	22	F	SGL	PRZZZZ	USA
WILCZEK, JOHANN	28	M	LKSH	PRZZZZ	USA
MAAS, AUGUST	29	M	LABR	PRZZZZ	USA
MARIE	26	F	W	PRZZZZ	USA
HERMANSOHN, ADOLF	18	M	MCHT	PRZZZZ	USA
ZUERSCHEN, ANNA	44	F	WO	PRZZZZ	USA
ZABICKI, CASIMIR	31	M	MCHT	PRZZZZ	USA
SUCHARZEWSKI, JOHANN	25	M	LABR	PRZZZZ	USA
GRAHL, MAX	17	M	LABR	PRZZZZ	USA
BINECK, VALENTIN	38	M	FARMER	PRZZZZ	USA
MARIE	38	F	W	PRZZZZ	USA
JOSEF	12	M	CH	PRZZZZ	USA
JULIE	9	F	CHILD	PRZZZZ	USA
MARIE	8	F	CHILD	PRZZZZ	USA
AGNES	6	F	CHILD	PRZZZZ	USA
JOH	4	M	CHILD	PRZZZZ	USA
PETER	2	M	CHILD	PRZZZZ	USA
MARTIN	.03	M	INFANT	PRZZZZ	USA
CHASKEL, SALLY	18	M	UNKNOWN	PRZZZZ	USA
NICKEL, AUGUST	32	M	LABR	PRZZZZ	USA
MATTEY, ADOLF	25	M	LABR	PRZZZZ	USA
WALTER, AUGUST	30	M	CPTR	PRZZZZ	USA
LUISE	27	F	W	PRZZZZ	USA
AUGUST	4	M	CHILD	PRZZZZ	USA
APPEL, CARL	30	M	FARMER	PRZZZZ	USA
ANNA	27	F	W	PRZZZZ	USA
GUSTAV	3	M	CHILD	PRZZZZ	USA
LUISE	2	F	CHILD	PRZZZZ	USA
ERNST	.11	M	INFANT	PRZZZZ	USA
ERNST	70	M	WO	PRZZZZ	USA
BEIN, WILLY	33	M	LABR	PRZZZZ	USA
BEIL, ARTHUR	25	M	LKSH	SYZZZZ	USA
THEKLA	20	F	W	SYZZZZ	USA
PITTER, OSCAR	35	M	MCHT	SYZZZZ	USA
EMILIE	32	F	W	SYZZZZ	USA
CURT	8	M	CHILD	SYZZZZ	USA
GERTRUD	4	F	CHILD	SYZZZZ	USA
FRIDA	2	F	CHILD	SYZZZZ	USA
HOFFMANN, ERNST	24	M	LABR	SYZZZZ	USA
FRANKE, EMIL	31	M	LABR	SYZZZZ	USA
SCHAARSCHMIDT, HERMAN	53	M	LABR	SYZZZZ	USA
ZIEGLER, BARB	55	F	WO	BVZZZZ	USA
MARIE	14	F	CH	BVZZZZ	USA
MICHAEL	6	F	CHILD	BVZZZZ	USA
WOLF, AUGISTE	49	F	WO	BVZZZZ	USA
ANNA	26	F	UNKNOWN	BVZZZZ	USA
PAUL	22	F	D	BVZZZZ	USA
MARTHA	3	F	CHILD	BVZZZZ	USA
OSCAR	9	M	CHILD	BVZZZZ	USA
GLEICHSNER, JOSEF	46	M	MSN	BVZZZZ	USA
CATH	33	F	W	BVZZZZ	USA
JOSEF	9	M	CHILD	BVZZZZ	USA
BARBARA	8	F	CHILD	BVZZZZ	USA
FRANZ	2	M	CHILD	BVZZZZ	USA
MARIE	.11	F	INFANT	BVZZZZ	USA
ANDRAS	5	M	CHILD	BVZZZZ	USA
BAUER, JOSEF	16	M	BKR	BVZZZZ	USA
GOLA, CARL	17	M	LABR	PRZZZZ	USA
EHLERT, CARL	20	M	LABR	PRZZZZ	USA
DIEDDRICH, JOH.	39	M	LABR	PRZZZZ	USA
JOH	45	F	W	PRZZZZ	USA
WILH	16	F	UNKNOWN	PRZZZZ	USA
ANNA	4	F	CHILD	PRZZZZ	USA
ELISE	3	F	CHILD	PRZZZZ	USA
CAROL	.06	F	INFANT	PRZZZZ	USA
BARK, HEINRICH	30	M	TNM	PRZZZZ	USA
EMILIE	30	F	W	PRZZZZ	USA
FRITZ	3	M	CHILD	PRZZZZ	USA
MARG	.09	F	INFANT	PRZZZZ	USA
SCHULZ, HERMANN	28	M	JNR	PRZZZZ	USA
AUGUSTE	32	F	W	PRZZZZ	USA
FRANZ	.04	M	INFANT	PRZZZZ	USA
HOFFMANN, MARIE	56	F	WO	PRZZZZ	USA
SCHNEIDER, MARIE	26	F	SGL	PRZZZZ	USA
SCHLAACK, WILHELM	26	M	JNR	PRZZZZ	USA
SCHWIERTZ, FRANZ	29	M	LABR	PRZZZZ	USA
MITTE, HERMANN	33	M	LABR	PRZZZZ	USA
FURMANN, JOSEF	41	M	LKSH	PRZZZZ	USA
WEINERT, ELISABETH	6	F	CHILD	SYZZZZ	USA
KENSA, VALENTY	35	M	LABR	PRZZZZ	USA
SMENCZAK, FRAN	35	M	LABR	PRZZZZ	USA
BOZMAREK, MICHAEL	30	M	LABR	PRZZZZ	USA
TOMS, AUGUSTE	17	F	UNKNOWN	PRZZZZ	USA
BLUM, AUGUST	49	M	MLR	PRZZZZ	USA
MARIE	45	F	W	PRZZZZ	USA
EMILIE	25	F	D	PRZZZZ	USA
HERMANN	9	M	CHILD	PRZZZZ	USA
EMIL	8	M	CHILD	PRZZZZ	USA
AUGUSTE	.08	F	INFANT	PRZZZZ	USA
MENGER, AQUILIN	34	M	SHMK	BVZZZZ	USA
STOECKEL, AUGUSTE	57	F	W	PRZZZZ	USA

SHIP: CITY OF CHESTER

FROM: LIVERPOOL AND QUEENSTOWN
TO: NEW YORK
ARRIVED: 16 JUNE 1888

PASSENGER	AGE	SEX	OCCUPATION	PRIVL	DES
REITH, LORENZ	28	M	BRR	GRZZZZ	NY
TACKLE, WILHELM	27	M	WCHMKR	GRZZZZ	OH
WEINSTEIN, MELECH	19	M	TLR	GRACBF	NY
WOLLMANN, ZINNIE	22	F	W	GRACBF	OH
LENK, KATH	58	F	W	GRAARR	OH
JURKA, EVA	25	F	W	GRAARR	OH
JURA, JANOS	11	M	CH	GRAARR	OH
MARIA	2	F	CHILD	GRAARR	OH
MISKO	.09	M	INFANT	GRAARR	OH
EINHORN, CHANE	18	F	W	GRAARR	OH
BELA	.06	F	INFANT	GRAARR	OH

159

PASSENGER	AGE	SEX	OCCUPATION	PVL	DES
SHIP: SAALE					
FROM: BREMEN AND SOUTHAMPTON					
TO: NEW YORK					
ARRIVED: 16 JUNE 1888					
LEHMANN, LEOP	40	M	LABR		GRABOQUSA
WIERICHS, BERTHA	40	F	UNKNOWN		GRABOQUSA
HOEDER, OTTO	54	M	MCHT		GRABOQUSA
KUEHL, ELISAB	39	F	UNKNOWN		GRABOQUSA
HORN, LEONARDO	20	M	MCHT		GRAGFUUSA
FREUND, JOH	17	M	MCHT		GRZZZZUSA
HORN, ANNA	21	F	UNKNOWN		GRAGFUUSA
STEINRUCK, LOUISE	40	F	UNKNOWN		GRAAXYUSA
ROSA	27	F	UNKNOWN		GRAAXYUSA
OSTLOFF, FRIEDA	20	F	UNKNOWN		GRAAXYUSA
WALLMANN, ELIS	27	F	UNKNOWN		GRZZZZUSA
LEVY, MAX	32	M	MCHT		GRAAKHUSA
GAILE, CHRIST	38	F	UNKNOWN		GRAEXWUSA
ANNA	23	F	UNKNOWN		GRAEXWUSA
MARIE	22	F	UNKNOWN		GRAEXWUSA
MARTHA	10	F	CH		GRAEXWUSA
COHN, ISIDOR	16	M	MCHT		GRAAKHUSA
LADANUI, AUGUSTE	26	F	UNKNOWN		GRAAKHUSA
KOHNSTAMM, JAKOB	16	M	JNR		GRABQZUSA
KRAUSE, MARG	21	F	UNKNOWN		GRABDMUSA
LIPPSCHUETZ, ALB	14	M	MCHT		GRAAFCUSA
SELMA	11	F	UNKNOWN		GRAAFCUSA
KEHR, MINNA	36	F	UNKNOWN		GRAIKSUSA
AMANDA	11	F	UNKNOWN		GRAIKSUSA
RUDOLF	11	M	UNKNOWN		GRAIKSUSA
ERNST	9	M	CHILD		GRAIKSUSA
HAGEN, MINNA	27	F	UNKNOWN		GRZZZZUSA
MARTIN	14	M	MCHT		GRZZZZUSA
DAEHM, HUGO	15	M	MCHT		GRZZZZUSA
HELLINGER, HERM	15	M	TLR		GRABLVUSA
RETZLAFF, CHRIST	23	F	UNKNOWN		GRABLVUSA
MEINSEN, WILH	51	M	FARMER		GRADIJUSA
WURTMANN, HEINR	40	M	MCHT		GRZZZZUSA
ADELH	20	F	W		GRZZZZUSA
ANNA	.06	F	INFANT		GRZZZZUSA
COMONA, ADOLF	28	M	JNR		GRZZZZUSA
HERM	20	F	UNKNOWN		GRZZZZUSA
STOCKMEYER, HEINR	28	M	BCHR		GRACEGUSA
VOIGT, JEANETTE	30	F	UNKNOWN		GRAARRUSA
GEORG	4	M	CHILD		GRAARRUSA
EMIL	2	M	CHILD		GRAARRUSA
AGNES	.06	F	INFANT		GRAARRUSA
DOLINCK, EUGEN	23	M	MCHT		GRACEGUSA
SCHRAMM, HERM	20	M	MCHT		GRACEGUSA
GEPP, WALDEMAR	35	M	SMH		GRAAZQUSA
BECKER, FRANZ	28	M	SMH		GRZZZZUSA
CONRAD, SOPHIE	20	F	UNKNOWN		GRZZZZUSA
POCK, CARL	30	M	MCHT		GRACTHUSA
BECKER, HENRIETE	13	F	UNKNOWN		GRZZZZUSA
WULLE, JACOB	51	M	FARMER		GRZZZZUSA
LEXOW, OSCAR	23	M	BKR		GRACBFUSA
WOLFF, HUGO	27	M	MCHT		GRADTTUSA
SEYDEL, ADOLPH	13	M	UNKNOWN		GRAARRUSA
JOHANNA	50	F	UNKNOWN		GRAARRUSA
ANCHEN	6	F	CHILD		GRAARRUSA
GOTTLIEB	4	M	CHILD		GRAARRUSA
SCHARNAGEL, EMILIE	28	F	UNKNOWN		GRAARRUSA
STEGE, WILH	15	M	FARMER		GRAEFTUSA
NOESER, CARL	15	M	FARMER		GRAEFTUSA
KATTENHORN, ERNST	16	M	FARMER		GRACYPUSA
BOEFF, PETER	61	M	GDNR		GRABOQUSA
DETERING, HEINR	17	M	FARMER		GRADIJUSA
AUGUSTE	15	F	UNKNOWN		GRADIJUSA
STADTLANDER, GEORG	18	M	JNR		GRAEFTUSA
GROSS, HEINR	23	M	JNR		GRZZZZUSA
LENZ, MARIE	53	F	UNKNOWN		GRAFGDUSA
KAMM, EVA	18	F	UNKNOWN		GRAADFUSA
KOEHLER, MAG	13	F	UNKNOWN		GRAADFUSA
SIMON, ALFRED	26	M	TLR		GRZZZZUSA
SCHOEFFER, SOPHIE	18	F	UNKNOWN		GRZZZZUSA
RUEGER, FRIEDR	37	M	BRR		GRAARRUSA
KEHRER, WILH	23	M	BRR		GRAFBDUSA
KALTEISEN, WILH	22	M	SHMK		GRAFBDUSA
HOFFMANN, DOROTHEA	25	F	UNKNOWN		GRZZZZUSA
MAUG, FERD	23	M	GZR		GRZZZZUSA
CAROL	28	F	UNKNOWN		GRZZZZUSA
REBMANN, LUDW	30	M	MCHT		GRABYCUSA
HERRMANN, BABETTE	21	F	UNKNOWN		GRZZZZUSA
HOLL, LOUISE	19	F	UNKNOWN		GRZZZZUSA
MARIA	1	F	CHILD		GRZZZZUSA
NIETFELDT, ORNOLD	47	M	FARMER		GRABBPUSA
DIEKMANN, WILH	19	F	UNKNOWN		GRABBPUSA
KULBE, AUGUSTE	24	F	UNKNOWN		GRZZZZUSA
LULZMANN, GERTRUDE	27	F	UNKNOWN		GRACVGUSA
JOH	7	F	CHILD		GRACVGUSA
JACOB	4	M	CHILD		GRACVGUSA
CHRISTOPH	3	M	CHILD		GRACVGUSA
MARIE	1	F	CHILD		GRACVGUSA
KAETCHEN	.10	F	INFANT		GRACVGUSA
GREUDEL, JOH	15	M	CL		GRAHTWUSA
CWIKLINSKI, ANTON	39	M	PNTR		GRZZZZUSA
BROMMER, JOS	29	M	CPTR		GRZZZZUSA
BUERKHARDTSMAIER, GUST	28	M	CPTR		GRZZZZUSA
SCHMIDT, CATH	24	F	UNKNOWN		GRAEVYUSA
BOEHNER, ANNA	45	F	UNKNOWN		GRAEVYUSA
MARIE	6	F	CHILD		GRAEVYUSA
KILIAN	5	M	CHILD		GRAEVYUSA
DEIFEL, ELISAB	24	F	UNKNOWN		GRZZZZUSA
BUERGI, ALB	21	M	MLR		SRZZZZUSA
STERN, BERNH	16	M	CL		SRABTRUSA
SCHMID, EMMA	18	F	UNKNOWN		SRAEXWUSA
GEISSER, CHRIST	23	M	WTR		SRABETUSA
KRAPPEMANN, AUG	16	M	WTR		SRAAHBUSA
HOEPPEL, GEORG	16	M	WTR		GRZZZZUSA
BOETSCH, JOH	16	M	WTR		GRACOGUSA
SOEBERG, METTE	47	F	UNKNOWN		GRABZSUSA
RETZLAFF, JOH	24	M	FARMER		GRZZZZUSA
VOELKER, GEORG	22	M	FARMER		GRZZZZUSA
MAIER, ANNA	32	F	UNKNOWN		GRZZZZUSA
BALTHASAR	8	M	CHILD		GRZZZZUSA
LORENZ	5	M	CHILD		GRZZZZUSA
HOEFLER, MARIA	20	F	UNKNOWN		GRZZZZUSA
KILIAN	16	M	TLR		GRZZZZUSA
SCHWARTZ, KATHI	25	F	UNKNOWN		GRAEGQUSA
SELIG, U	53	M	FARMER		GRZZZZUSA
SOPHIA	49	F	W		GRZZZZUSA
MAYER	15	M	UNKNOWN		GRZZZZUSA
ISIDOR	10	M	CH		GRZZZZUSA
BAER, JETTCHEN	19	F	UNKNOWN		GRZZZZUSA
BAEER, LINA	17	F	UNKNOWN		GRZZZZUSA
VOIGTR, EDUARD	48	M	FARMER		GRZZZZUSA
PAUL	16	M	FARMER		GRZZZZUSA
SCHOELLHAMER, GUST	16	M	TLR		GRZZZZUSA
WAGNER, CARL	40	M	TLR		GRZZZZUSA
ENGELFRIED, CARL	23	M	MCHT		GRAAPMUSA
FALLER, BRIGITA	20	F	UNKNOWN		GRZZZZUSA
BRIEM, MAX	29	M	FARMER		GRZZZZUSA
KOSWELNY, PETER	24	M	FARMER		GRZZZZUSA
KRAUSMANN, WILH	23	M	FARMER		GRZZZZUSA
TINSCHERT, MARIA	17	F	UNKNOWN		GRAADGUSA
KLAIBER, JOH	23	M	FARMER		GRAJAPUSA
BIEGER, ELISAB	73	F	UNKNOWN		GRADCLUSA
GLASER, CARL	16	M	PNTR		GRZZZZUSA
REICHERT, JOH	52	M	PNTR		GRAEXWUSA
JOH	50	F	W		GRAEXWUSA
PETERSEN, CATH	28	F	UNKNOWN		GRZZZZUSA
PETER	1	M	CHILD		GRZZZZUSA
PETER	75	M	FARMER		GRZZZZUSA
DORA	67	F	W		GRZZZZUSA
MIERSCH, ERNST	30	M	FARMER		GRZZZZUSA
BROEDBECK, WILH	21	F	UNKNOWN		GRZZZZUSA
PETERSEN, BATH	21	F	UNKNOWN		GRZZZZUSA
JAKOBKE, ED	27	M	FARMER		GRZZZZUSA

PASSENGER	AGE	SEX	OCCUPATION	PRVL DES
NEBUS, BARB	30	F	UNKNOWN	GRZZZZUSA
LUDWIG	7	M	CHILD	GRZZZZUSA
ANTONIE	3	F	CHILD	GRZZZZUSA
HARMS, HINRICH	14	M	FARMER	GRACBRUSA
MEYER, FRIEDR	17	M	CL	GRAARRUSA
FUNK, ANNA	54	F	UNKNOWN	GRZZZZUSA
ELGA	16	F	UNKNOWN	GRZZZZUSA
PETER	10	M	CH	GRZZZZUSA
GAST, BERNH	33	M	JNR	GRADIUUSA
WIEGAND, FRITZ	15	M	JNR	GRACEGUSA
BUEHRMANN, DIEDR	16	M	CL	GRAARRUSA
HORN, RICH	32	M	FARMER	GRZZZZUSA
POLLAK, ANT	28	M	FARMER	GRZZZZUSA
IDA	28	F	W	GRZZZZUSA
ALB	5	M	CHILD	GRZZZZUSA
FRIEDA	.03	F	INFANT	GRZZZZUSA
JAEKLE, CATH	19	F	UNKNOWN	GRZZZZUSA
JACOB	16	M	FARMER	GRZZZZUSA
BAUM, HEINR	11	M	UNKNOWN	GRZZZZUSA
HOFMANN, MAX	29	M	FARMER	GRZZZZUSA
ANNA	28	F	W	GRZZZZUSA
FRIEDA	3	F	CHILD	GRZZZZUSA
HILDEGARD	.09	F	INFANT	GRZZZZUSA
MAX	.09	M	INFANT	GRZZZZUSA
LEIPSERING, LINA	22	F	UNKNOWN	GRZZZZUSA
BEHRENS, DIEDR	16	M	FARMER	GRAARRUSA
WOLLBRECHT, GEORG	17	M	FARMER	GRZZZZUSA
KLEIN, JOH	37	M	FARMER	GRZZZZUSA
AMALIA	29	F	W	GRZZZZUSA
MAG	2	F	CHILD	GRZZZZUSA
MUELLER, MARIA	22	F	UNKNOWN	GRABDMUSA
OSTROWITZKY, MARIANNA	26	F	UNKNOWN	GRZZZZUSA
PEKOWSKY, JOH	25	M	FARMER	GRZZZZUSA
HAAS, BERNH	28	M	FARMER	GRADGXUSA
STAADECKER, SAM	16	M	FARMER	GRADGXUSA
OSTHEIMER, JUL	16	M	SMH	GRADGXUSA
THALHEIMER, ZACHARAS	15	M	SMH	GRADGXUSA
MAI, ADOLPH	15	M	SMH	GRADGXUSA
RIECHTER, AGNES	21	F	UNKNOWN	GRAHLNUSA
STROBEL, WILH	30	F	UNKNOWN	GRADLNUSA
KREISS, FRIEDR	27	M	FARMER	GRADGKUSA
HENRIETTE	27	F	W	GRADGKUSA
SUSANNE	64	F	UNKNOWN	GRADGKUSA
LOUISE	.09	F	INFANT	GRADGKUSA
TEUBERG, GERH	34	M	FARMER	GRADHQUSA
BERNH	32	F	W	GRADHQUSA
POETTER, JOSEPHA	19	F	UNKNOWN	GRADHQUSA
MEYER, CHRIST	16	M	FARMER	GRAAHNUSA
RIEDMANN, DORIS	21	F	UNKNOWN	GRAAHNUSA
HAGEN, GEORG	24	M	BRR	GRADQXUSA
ZACHOW, FRIEDR	50	M	SMH	GRZZZZUSA
MARIE	40	F	W	GRZZZZUSA
MINNA	17	F	UNKNOWN	GRZZZZUSA
GEYER, BERNH	33	M	MCHT	GRABDMUSA
WEBER, BARB	38	F	UNKNOWN	GRZZZZUSA
HELENE	15	F	UNKNOWN	GRZZZZUSA
NICOLAUS	11	M	UNKNOWN	GRZZZZUSA
BARB	10	F	CH	GRZZZZUSA
MARG	9	F	CHILD	GRZZZZUSA
EMILIE	6	F	CHILD	GRZZZZUSA
CHRISTINE	4	F	CHILD	GRZZZZUSA
OTTO	2	M	CHILD	GRZZZZUSA
FUCHS, HERM	34	M	FARMER	GRAFRGUSA
ELISE	23	F	W	GRAFRGUSA
MARIE	.11	F	INFANT	GRAFRGUSA
LEHMANN, FRITZ	33	M	BCHR	GRZZZZUSA
IDA	28	F	W	GRZZZZUSA
CARL	11	M	UNKNOWN	GRZZZZUSA
CURT	9	M	CHILD	GRZZZZUSA
MAX	5	M	CHILD	GRZZZZUSA
MARIE	3	F	CHILD	GRZZZZUSA
ELLA	.09	F	INFANT	GRZZZZUSA
GOTTSMANN, JOH	23	M	FARMER	GRZZZZUSA
KILIAN, GEORG	11	M	UNKNOWN	GRZZZZUSA
SCHNEIDER, ALOIS	16	M	FARMER	GRZZZZUSA

PASSENGER	AGE	SEX	OCCUPATION	PRVL DES
OMELKE, REMUND	34	M	FARMER	GRZZZZUSA
JOSEPH	8	M	CHILD	GRZZZZUSA
WISSMANN, CARL	25	M	LABR	GRAEFSUSA
NIEMANN, GOTTL	30	M	LABR	GRAEFSUSA
STEINBAUER, JAC	25	M	LABR	GRZZZZUSA
RIEDL, BARB	17	F	UNKNOWN	GRZZZZUSA
JOSEPH	24	M	SMH	GRZZZZUSA
BRUMMER, GEORG	27	M	BKLYR	GRZZZZUSA
PREIS, BARB	18	F	UNKNOWN	GRZZZZUSA
NOE, CATH	16	F	UNKNOWN	GRZZZZUSA
MARIE	14	F	UNKNOWN	GRZZZZUSA
WALBURGA	45	F	UNKNOWN	GRZZZZUSA
ANGELIN	10	M	CH	GRZZZZUSA
GEORG	9	M	CHILD	GRZZZZUSA
WAGNER, MICHEL	16	M	SHMK	GRZZZZUSA
DUECHTING, CHARLOTTE	51	F	UNKNOWN	GRACJMUSA
GLINSKA, MARIANNA	19	F	UNKNOWN	GRZZZZUSA
FREDERICH, MARTHA	15	F	UNKNOWN	GRAHVFUSA
GRAF, WILH	19	F	UNKNOWN	GRZZZZUSA
MARIE	15	F	UNKNOWN	GRZZZZUSA
REINKE, EMIL	33	M	FARMER	GRZZZZUSA
MARIE	19	F	UNKNOWN	GRZZZZUSA
ROESSKE, IDA	22	F	UNKNOWN	GRZZZZUSA
REINKE, CHRIST	73	F	UNKNOWN	GRZZZZUSA
KOCH, JOH	46	M	LABR	GRAEXWUSA
CATH	47	F	W	GRAEXWUSA
ALB	11	M	UNKNOWN	GRAEXWUSA
EMILIE	9	F	CHILD	GRAEXWUSA
WULFF, ANTON	29	M	LABR	GRABBPUSA
JUNGBAUER, MARIA	40	F	UNKNOWN	GRADLDUSA
EUFROSINE	5	F	CHILD	GRADLDUSA
JOH	7	M	CHILD	GRADLDUSA
MAX	8	M	CHILD	GRADLDUSA
MARIE	9	F	CHILD	GRADLDUSA
THERESE	10	F	CH	GRADLDUSA
JANKOWSKI, THOMAS	30	M	FARMER	GRZZZZUSA
KUHLMANN, CARL	18	M	CL	GRAAURUSA
DROSTE, ERNST	17	M	CL	GRZZZZUSA
ERNST	17	M	CL	GRACBRUSA
KARCH, ANNA	18	F	UNKNOWN	GRZZZZUSA
GOEHRING, JACOB	31	M	FARMER	GRZZZZUSA
SCHEITLER, CARL	32	M	FARMER	GRZZZZUSA
BEDEKER, AUG	55	M	FARMER	GRZZZZUSA
HELFFENSTEIN, JOH	29	M	FARMER	GRAEJCUSA
MIARA, MICH	31	M	LKSH	GRZZZZUSA
HERRMANN, LOUISE	30	F	UNKNOWN	GRADZHUSA
KAZMIEZCZAK, FRANZ	23	M	BCHR	GRZZZZUSA
BOEHM, ANDR	22	M	FARMER	GRADROUSA
KOEHLER, BERNH	29	M	FARMER	GRAFMDUSA
WILLNER, STEPHAN	18	M	FARMER	GRAFMDUSA
HEYMANN, WILH	60	M	FARMER	GRAFMDUSA
PAULSEN, LORENZ	29	M	FARMER	GRZZZZUSA
KUHN, GOTTLIEB	25	M	PNTR	GRAARRUSA
SCHEITHE, PHILIPP	16	M	FARMER	GRABKRUSA
LOEHMANN, CARL	25	M	BKLYR	GRABTTUSA
UHLMANN, FRIEDR	30	M	MCHT	GRABQZUSA
ALIZ, GEO	38	M	MCHT	GRAAKJUSA
FRANZ	9	M	CHILD	GRAAKJUSA
SCHNOERR, GUST	28	M	LKSH	GRZZZZUSA

SHIP: SCYTHIA

FROM: LIVERPOOL AND QUEENSTOWN
TO: NEW YORK
ARRIVED: 16 JUNE 1888

PASSENGER	AGE	SEX	OCCUPATION	PRVL DES
HURVITCH, MARY	25	F	UNKNOWN	GRZZZZUSA
KLRIN, SNNS	16	F	SP	GRZZZZUSA
ARNOLD, MICHEAL	45	M	UNKNOWN	GRZZZZUSA
JOHANNA	42	F	W	GRZZZZUSA

PASSENGER	AGE	SEX	OCCUPATION	PRVL	DES
EIFERT, JOHAN	47	M	CK		GRZZZZUSA
CATRINA	46	F	W		GRZZZZUSA
EMMA	17	F	SP		GRZZZZUSA
MARIA	11	F	CH		GRZZZZUSA
KRIZ, MARY	32	F	SVNT		GRZZZZUSA
FRANZ	9	M	CHILD		GRZZZZUSA
JOSEPH	4	M	CHILD		GRZZZZUSA
U	.07	F	INFANT		GRZZZZUSA
MINTZ, U	40	F	SVNT		GRZZZZUSA
GUSTAF	11	M	CH		GRZZZZUSA
ALBERT	9	M	CHILD		GRZZZZUSA
LISA	1	F	CHILD		GRZZZZUSA
HAMMERMAN, JOSEPH	28	M	LABR		GRZZZZUSA
SLEITER, ADAM	48	M	FARMER		GRZZZZUSA
DIETZE	48	F	FARMER		GRZZZZUSA
SWOLINSKY, JOSEF	39	M	TLR		GRZZZZUSA
GOLD, HIRSCH	20	M	LABR		GRZZZZUSA

SHIP: RHAETIA

FROM: HAMBURG AND HAVRE
TO: NEW YORK
ARRIVED: 18 JUNE 1888

PASSENGER	AGE	SEX	OCCUPATION	PRVL	DES
MEYER, FRIDA	15	F	SGL		GRZZZZUSA
PREUSS, AUGUSTE	23	F	UNKNOWN		GRZZZZUSA
VECKLER, RICHARD	24	M	UNKNOWN		GRZZZZUSA
DNESEL, OTTO	16	M	UNKNOWN		GRZZZZUSA
SCHUBERT, PAUL	26	M	JNR		GRZZZZUSA
JUENG, BENJAMIN	62	M	BCHR		GRZZZZUSA
GENTZSCH, HENRIETTE	40	F	WO		GRZZZZUSA
ELISABETH	7	F	CHILD		GRZZZZUSA
EMMA	7	F	CHILD		GRZZZZUSA
ANNA	.11	F	INFANT		GRZZZZUSA
PEEMOELLER, COMORDIA	43	F	UNKNOWN		GRZZZZUSA
CHRISTOPH	15	M	CH		GRZZZZUSA
LOMPARSKA, KATHA.	19	F	SGL		GRZZZZUSA
GUENTHER, ALBIN	16	M	LABR		GRZZZZUSA
WENZEL, CARL	38	M	LABR		GRZZZZUSA
ELISABETH	29	F	W		GRZZZZUSA
CAROLE.	5	F	CHILD		GRZZZZUSA
FRITZ	.11	M	INFANT		GRZZZZUSA
SIMONSKA, FRANZISKA	19	F	LABR		GRZZZZUSA
WITT, CATHA.	54	F	WO		GRZZZZUSA
AURICH, ADOLF	30	M	GLSR		GRZZZZUSA
MUELLER, JOHN	24	M	SLR		GRZZZZUSA
BUENGER, BERNHD.	24	M	ACHTT		GRZZZZUSA
DELFS, ALBERT	15	M	FARMER		GRZZZZUSA
SIEBERT, CARL	26	M	LABR		GRZZZZUSA
MEYER, ROSA	60	F	WO		GRZZZZUSA
HOLST, BERTHA	34	F	SGL		GRZZZZUSA
JUENG, CAROLE.	39	F	WO		GRZZZZUSA
ANNA	9	F	CHILD		GRZZZZUSA
KOENTOPP, FRANZ	34	M	LABR		GRZZZZUSA
BEROLZHEIMER, JOHANNE	35	F	WO		GRZZZZUSA
GERTRUDE	5	F	CHILD		GRZZZZUSA
DAVID	4	M	CHILD		GRZZZZUSA
GUSTAV	2	M	CHILD		GRZZZZUSA
JULS.	.06	M	INFANT		GRZZZZUSA
ROETHER, HERM.	27	M	MCHT		GRZZZZUSA
BALLMANN, CARL	18	M	PNTR		GRZZZZUSA
TIEDEMANN, HIRSCH	18	M	SHMK		GRZZZZUSA
VOSS, CARL	23	M	JNR		GRZZZZUSA
SCHMIDT, HEINR.	30	M	FARMER		GRZZZZUSA
BABETTE	33	F	W		GRZZZZUSA
GEUTZSCH, ANNA	15	F	SGL		GRZZZZUSA
FALK, FRDKE.	31	F	WO		GRZZZZUSA
OLGA	6	F	CHILD		GRZZZZUSA
BORSCHE, AUGUST	24	M	CPTR		GRZZZZUSA
KAEMMERER, PAUL	25	M	CPTR		GRZZZZUSA

PASSENGER	AGE	SEX	OCCUPATION	PRVL	DES
GOLD, JACOB	17	M	LABR		GRZZZZUSA
SCHUMANN, THEODOR	16	M	LABR		PRZZZZUSA
WEBER, GERTRUD	65	F	W		GRZZZZUSA
ANNA	7	F	CHILD		GRZZZZUSA
ROTH, JOS.	16	M	LABR		GRZZZZUSA
BEYER, CAROLE.	34	F	W		GRZZZZUSA
CAROLE.	.11	F	INFANT		GRZZZZUSA
GRIMSMUNEN, JOHANNA	25	F	WO		GRZZZZUSA
SCHARFF, ELISAB.	30	F	WO		GRZZZZUSA
GLUESING, ANTONIE	22	F	WO		GRZZZZUSA
BUEHRIG, AUG.	21	M	MCHT		GRZZZZUSA
LIBUDZIEWSKY, ANTON	48	M	LABR		GRZZZZUSA
ROSALIE	47	F	W		GRZZZZUSA
BERTHA	22	F	CH		GRZZZZUSA
EVA	19	F	CH		GRZZZZUSA
WLADISL.	8	M	CHILD		GRZZZZUSA
FRANZ	7	M	CHILD		GRZZZZUSA
ANNA	6	F	CHILD		GRZZZZUSA
VALENTY	2	M	CHILD		GRZZZZUSA
ANTON	.08	M	INFANT		GRZZZZUSA
TEMPLIN, MARIE	44	F	W		GRZZZZUSA
EMILIE	8	F	CHILD		GRZZZZUSA
FRITZ	6	M	CHILD		GRZZZZUSA
ERNST	.10	M	INFANT		GRZZZZUSA
HELENIAK, JACOB	26	M	LABR		GRZZZZUSA
EMILIE	23	F	W		GRZZZZUSA
BERTHA	3	F	CHILD		GRZZZZUSA
THERESE	.11	F	INFANT		GRZZZZUSA
NAKOLNY, JAN	30	M	LABR		GRZZZZUSA
IGNACZAK, JOSEFA	39	F	W		GRZZZZUSA
ROSALIE	15	F	CH		GRZZZZUSA
THOMAS	8	M	CHILD		GRZZZZUSA
THERESE	7	F	CHILD		GRZZZZUSA
LEONORA	5	F	CHILD		GRZZZZUSA
LANGFELD, DORA	16	F	SGL		HBZZZZUSA
GREUDE, WILHE.	26	F	WO		GRZZZZUSA
SOMPOLINSKI, WILHE.	20	F	WO		GRZZZZUSA
BLASIUS, MARIE	45	F	W		GRZZZZUSA
MARIE	19	F	CH		GRZZZZUSA
NICOLAUS	17	M	CH		GRZZZZUSA
ANNA	13	F	CH		GRZZZZUSA
MARGA.	8	F	CHILD		GRZZZZUSA
WITTFOTH, SOPHIE	21	F	SGL		GRZZZZUSA
SCHUESSLER, HERRM.	16	M	LABR		GRZZZZUSA
HOEFTMANN, KARL	33	M	LABR		GRZZZZUSA
MATUSZAK, MARTIN	26	M	LABR		GRZZZZUSA
EVA	20	F	W		GRZZZZUSA
BAGOSINSKA, GOLDE	15	F	SGL		GRZZZZUSA
VOLLMANN, AMALIE	20	F	SGL		GRZZZZUSA
SCHULZ, WILH.	18	M	TNM		GRZZZZUSA
REIFF, JOHANN	26	M	SMH		GRZZZZUSA
KRUSE, JOHS.	21	M	SDLR		GRZZZZUSA
PAEPER, JOHANN	25	M	TLR		GRZZZZUSA
GERTTENBERGER, ROBERT	15	M	LABR		GRZZZZUSA
KOCH, WILH.	19	M	FARMER		GRZZZZUSA
LORENZEN, JACOB	27	M	FARMER		GRZZZZUSA
DIERCKE, HANS	64	M	TLR		GRZZZZUSA
SITTIG, OTTO	28	M	FARMER		GRZZZZUSA
HEUZLER, JOSEF	40	M	FARMER		GRZZZZUSA
THERESE	28	F	W		GRZZZZUSA
ANNA	.03	F	INFANT		GRZZZZUSA
HALBERG, FRITZ	21	M	UNKNOWN		GRZZZZUSA
RICHTER, JOHANN	47	M	BCHR		GRZZZZUSA
KOLLMEYER, FRANZ	18	M	DLR		GRZZZZUSA
KAISER, GUSTAV	40	M	TNM		GRZZZZUSA
BLASEWICZ, ALPHONS	14	M	LABR		GRZZZZUSA
PFEFFER, BERNHD.	17	M	LABR		GRZZZZUSA
BOROWSKY, VALENTI	9	M	CHILD		GRZZZZUSA
MICHAEL	8	M	CHILD		GRZZZZUSA
SACHS, CHRIST	37	M	LABR		GRZZZZUSA
LANG, GEORG	33	M	FARMER		GRZZZZUSA
MAGDALENA	32	F	W		GRZZZZUSA
KSCHILA, JOH.	43	M	TLR		GRZZZZUSA
MUNTOWSKI, VERONA	28	F	SGL		GRZZZZUSA
THOMSEN, LOUISE	18	F	SGL		GRZZZZUSA

PASSENGER	AGE	SEX	OCCUPATION	PRVL DES
HAJ, CHRISTE.	16	F	SGL	GRZZZZUSA
KOPP, JONATHAN	28	M	FARMER	GRZZZZUSA
DENSO, FRANZ	28	M	LABR	GRZZZZUSA
BERG, LORENZ	23	M	FARMER	GRZZZZUSA
CAROLE.	23	F	W	GRZZZZUSA
HANS	2	M	CHILD	GRZZZZUSA
SCHELLACK, HEINR.	28	M	BCHR	GRZZZZUSA
WESTRICH, ELISABETH	68	F	WO	GRZZZZUSA
KRAATZ, HELLMUTH	27	M	TLR	GRZZZZUSA
HERM.	9	M	CHILD	GRZZZZUSA
WILHE.	65	F	WO	GRZZZZUSA
ROEDIGER, CARL	15	M	LABR	GRZZZZUSA
STAHL, HULDA	21	F	SGL	GRZZZZUSA
KOEPP, WILH.	22	M	FARMER	GRZZZZUSA
STAHL, CHR.	36	M	FARMER	GRZZZZUSA
MATHE.	42	F	W	GRZZZZUSA
MATHE.	9	F	CHILD	GRZZZZUSA
ANNA	3	F	CHILD	GRZZZZUSA
FRANZ	1	M	CHILD	GRZZZZUSA
HERRMAN	16	M	CH	GRZZZZUSA
MARTHA	7	F	CHILD	GRZZZZUSA
GIESE, ROBERT	24	M	FARMER	GRZZZZUSA
GOOS, FRIEDR.	15	M	FARMER	GRZZZZUSA
SCHEIDE, CARL	25	M	BKR	GRZZZZUSA
BESKE, FRIEDRICH	42	M	FARMER	GRZZZZUSA
FRDKE.	45	F	W	GRZZZZUSA
ALBERT	14	M	CH	GRZZZZUSA
ANNA	9	F	CHILD	GRZZZZUSA
MARTHA	8	F	CHILD	GRZZZZUSA
IDA	7	F	CHILD	GRZZZZUSA
AMANDA	2	F	CHILD	GRZZZZUSA
KRONEMANN, ERNESTE.	34	F	WO	GRZZZZUSA
MAX	13	M	CH	GRZZZZUSA
EDMUEND	9	M	CHILD	GRZZZZUSA
ISDA	8	F	CHILD	GRZZZZUSA
GROZINGER, JOHANN	51	M	FARMER	GRZZZZUSA
CHRISTE.	48	F	W	GRZZZZUSA
LOUISE	15	F	CH	GRZZZZUSA
CARL	13	M	CH	GRZZZZUSA
CAROLE.	9	F	CHILD	GRZZZZUSA
PAULE.	7	F	CHILD	GRZZZZUSA
MARIE	3	F	CHILD	GRZZZZUSA
WIEDEMANN, FRANZ	44	M	CPTR	GRZZZZUSA
LUND, FRIEDR.	17	M	FARMER	GRZZZZUSA
ERICHKORN, HEINR.	18	M	CGRTW	GRZZZZUSA
DITTMAR, ELISABETH	64	F	WO	GRZZZZUSA
KOOPMANN, AUGUSTE	14	F	SGL	GRZZZZUSA
NOSSEK, BERTHA	16	F	SGL	GRZZZZUSA
SCHULZ, MATHA	21	F	SGL	GRZZZZUSA
GOETZ, EMILIE	17	F	SGL	GRZZZZUSA
RUDING, IDA	16	F	SGL	GRZZZZUSA
THOMSEN, JOCHUN	32	M	FARMER	GRZZZZUSA
NOLTING, DOROTHEA	64	F	WO	GRZZZZUSA
NOWAK, FRITZ	29	M	FARMER	GRZZZZUSA
EMILIE	27	F	W	GRZZZZUSA
MARTHA	2	F	CHILD	GRZZZZUSA
ARTHUR	.06	M	INFANT	GRZZZZUSA
MURAWSKY, CATHA.	55	F	WO	GRZZZZUSA
BUROW, FRITZ	41	M	SHMK	GRZZZZUSA
PTACHECKI, WLADISLAW	33	M	LABR	GRZZZZUSA
SORGENFREI, HEINR.	28	M	LABR	GRZZZZUSA
MARIE	25	F	W	GRZZZZUSA
CHRIST.	2	M	CHILD	GRZZZZUSA
MARGA.	.09	F	INFANT	GRZZZZUSA
STIBBE, FERD.	15	M	LABR	GRZZZZUSA
ANNA	50	F	WO	GRZZZZUSA
EMMA	13	F	CH	GRZZZZUSA
KSIARKEWICZ, PETRONELLA	28	F	WO	GRZZZZUSA
STEFAN	4	M	CHILD	GRZZZZUSA
MARIANNE	2	F	CHILD	GRZZZZUSA
STANISLAWA	.06	F	INFANT	GRZZZZUSA
HEOPP, LOUIS	15	M	LABR	GRZZZZUSA
NAWARTAT, AUGUST	36	M	LABR	GRZZZZUSA
RABOLD, AUGUSTE	31	F	WO	GRZZZZUSA
ROSA	.11	F	INFANT	GRZZZZUSA
SIEWERT, MARIE	60	F	WO	GRZZZZUSA
SMOLINSKI, HERRM.	16	M	BBR	GRZZZZUSA
BRODERSEN, CLAUS	74	M	FARMER	GRZZZZUSA
LOUISE	33	F	W	GRZZZZUSA
RINSCHER, MAX	26	M	FARMER	GRZZZZUSA
LANGE, MARIE	19	F	SGL	GRZZZZUSA
ZANDER, GEORG	38	M	WTR	GRZZZZUSA
HENNIG, FRIEDRICH	48	M	UNKNOWN	GRZZZZUSA
FRIEDA	43	F	UNKNOWN	GRZZZZUSA
WILHE.	9	F	CHILD	GRZZZZUSA
VONRHADE, IDA	27	F	WO	GRZZZZUSA
ROSENGART, FRIEDR.	34	M	LABR	GRZZZZUSA
GOERCKI, GUSTAV	30	M	LLD	GRZZZZUSA
BUSSE, EMILIE	26	F	WO	GRZZZZUSA
ELSA	.09	F	INFANT	GRZZZZUSA
HARTMANN, JOS.	33	M	LABR	GRZZZZUSA
LOCKER, BENEDICT	22	M	MLR	GRZZZZUSA
SERAFIN	26	M	JNR	GRZZZZUSA
LARIN, SIMON	26	M	LABR	GRZZZZUSA
SKRZENSKIEWIZ, MIHAL	34	M	LABR	GRZZZZUSA
LIEBENOW, JULIUS	68	M	FARMER	GRZZZZUSA
MATAUSCH, JOSEF	26	M	SLR	GRZZZZUSA
SIEVERT, LIESCHEN	19	F	SGL	GRZZZZUSA
WOLTER, JOSEF	48	M	FARMER	GRZZZZUSA
BERNHD.	15	M	CH	GRZZZZUSA
ANNA	9	F	CHILD	GRZZZZUSA
MARIA	8	F	CHILD	GRZZZZUSA
DIETRICH, GEORG	30	M	WTR	GRZZZZUSA
ELISABETH	4	F	CHILD	GRZZZZUSA
FREYMANN, ISIDOR	28	M	LABR	GRZZZZUSA
HENRIETTE	5	F	CHILD	GRZZZZUSA
DIETERICH, OSCAR	28	M	UPHST	GRZZZZUSA
BECK, PETER	68	M	FARMER	GRZZZZUSA
HERRMANN, ALWIN	17	M	FARMER	GRZZZZUSA
MARINKEWITZ, MARIANE	23	F	SGL	GRZZZZUSA
SEEGER, RICHARD	29	M	BRR	GRZZZZUSA
HOLM, ANNA	20	F	SGL	GRZZZZUSA
HARTMANN, JOH.	26	M	FARMER	GRZZZZUSA
KALTENBACH, PIUS	24	M	BKR	GRZZZZUSA
BEHRICH, CARL	61	M	LABR	GRZZZZUSA
OPITZ, JOHE.	27	F	WO	GRZZZZUSA
MAX	9	M	CHILD	GRZZZZUSA
LIDDY	5	F	CHILD	GRZZZZUSA
MARGA.	3	F	CHILD	GRZZZZUSA
SCHWABEROW, WILH.	40	M	FARMER	GRZZZZUSA
ANNA	36	F	W	GRZZZZUSA
HEINR.	14	M	CH	GRZZZZUSA
CHWABEROW, WM.	9	M	CHILD	GRZZZZUSA
HERMAN	2	M	CHILD	GRZZZZUSA
CHRISTIANSEN, CHR.	24	M	FARMER	GRZZZZUSA
JACOBSEN, ANNA	25	F	SGL	GRZZZZUSA
SCHLEGEL, GUSTAV	30	M	BKBNDR	GRZZZZUSA
BARTSCH, JOH.FR.	51	M	MCHT	GRZZZZUSA
HEDWIG	46	F	W	GRZZZZUSA
ALFRED	9	M	CHILD	GRZZZZUSA
TONI	8	M	CHILD	GRZZZZUSA
FRIEDR.	7	M	CHILD	GRZZZZUSA
BETTI	4	F	CHILD	GRZZZZUSA
CIEZEMKA, AMELIA	20	F	SGL	GRZZZZUSA
BRILL, LOUISE	18	F	SGL	GRZZZZUSA
KELLER, KATHA.	17	F	SGL	GRZZZZUSA
TRUMM, ADOLF	24	M	BKR	GRZZZZUSA
ORKEPP, ARTHUR	18	M	INF	GRZZZZUSA
SCHMUETZ, GOTTFRIED	25	M	FARMER	SRZZZZUSA
ELISABETH	28	F	W	SRZZZZUSA
GOTTFRIED	2	M	CHILD	SRZZZZUSA
BURKHALTER, JOHANN	23	M	MECH	SRZZZZUSA
CAVIEZEL, JOH.BALZER	32	M	LABR	SRZZZZUSA
LACHER, ANTON	19	M	LABR	SRZZZZUSA
WOERTZ, CARL-AUGST.	19	M	LABR	GRZZZZUSA
BACH, GEORG	34	M	DYR	GRZZZZUSA
WALTER, HUBERT	46	M	DYR	GRZZZZUSA
ANDREOLI, JOSEF	22	M	SMH	SRZZZZUSA
DOHLER, FRIDOLIN	28	M	SMH	SRZZZZUSA
HENBERGER, ELISE	19	F	SGL	SRZZZZUSA

PASSENGER	AGE	SEX	OCCUPATION	PRIVL	DES
MARX, JOSEF	22	M	SMH		GRZZZZUSA
BRIELMAYER, AD.	50	M	FARMER		GRZZZZUSA
FR.	50	F	W		GRZZZZUSA
MEYER, MEINRAD	41	M	FARMER		GRZZZZUSA
BERTHA	43	F	W		GRZZZZUSA
BERTHA	6	F	CHILD		GRZZZZUSA
LANG, JOSEF	21	M	BKR		GRZZZZUSA
WERNER, GUSTAV	21	M	SHMK		GRZZZZUSA
DORING, JULIUS	21	M	MECH		GRZZZZUSA
LE-CANTELLA, GILLES	24	M	MSN		FRZZZZUSA
KOCH, JOSEF	24	M	FARMER		GRZZZZUSA
SCHUERCH, ERNST	23	M	RPR		SRZZZZUSA
BERTSCHI, ALBERT	26	M	SMH		SRZZZZUSA
LUETHI, ALFRED	30	M	HTR		SRZZZZUSA
MEUDER, FREDRIC	30	M	LABR		SRZZZZUSA
KELLER, NICOLAUS	27	M	LABR		GRZZZZUSA
WULF, CATHA.	32	F	UNKNOWN		GRZZZZUSA
BRINKFELD, WILHE.	32	F	WO		GRZZZZUSA
WILLI	.11	M	INFANT		GRZZZZUSA
HASENBAL-, CARL	93	M	MCHT		GRZZZZUSA
SENGER, MAX	22	M	MCHT		GRZZZZUSA
KISTEL, ALBERT	29	M	MCHT		GRZZZZUSA
BURGER, XAVER	25	M	MCHT		GRZZZZUSA
SCHLUMPERT, BERTHA	54	F	WO		GRZZZZUSA
MUEHLHAU, SOFIE	59	F	WO		GRZZZZUSA
KOEHLER, ANNA	27	F	SGL		GRZZZZUSA
RUDIGER, ADOLPHINE	56	F	WO		GRZZZZUSA
MATHILDE	25	F	SGL		GRZZZZUSA
JORDAN, E.R.	32	M	MCHT		GRZZZZUSA
EBBETS, LINE	29	F	WO		GRZZZZUSA
GRACE	8	F	CHILD		GRZZZZUSA
BESSIE	6	F	CHILD		GRZZZZUSA
EDUARD	.11	M	INFANT		GRZZZZUSA
SCHMELTZER, U	37	M	MD		GRZZZZUSA
MARGA.	27	F	W		GRZZZZUSA
TILLY	7	M	CHILD		GRZZZZUSA
JULIUS	.02	M	INFANT		GRZZZZUSA
LINCAS, MARGE.	18	F	SVNT		GRZZZZUSA

SHIP: CIRCASSIA

FROM: GLASGOW AND MOVILLE
TO: NEW YORK
ARRIVED: 19 JUNE 1888

PASSENGER	AGE	SEX	OCCUPATION	PRIVL	DES
GOHLKE, ALBERT	21	M	MCHT		GRZZZZUSA
MICHALOWSKY, ADAM	46	M	FARMER		GRZZZZUSA
WASILERS, WINCENT	20	M	LABR		GRZZZZUSA
DRUGALIS, AND.	22	M	LABR		GRZZZZUSA
BENDECK, PETER	35	M	LABR		GRZZZZUSA
BELZKI, IWAN	45	M	LABR		GRZZZZUSA
KROBB, JACOB	23	M	LKSH		GRZZZZUSA
BRILO, KASIMIR	27	M	LABR		GRZZZZUSA
KETRY, ANDRUSH	26	M	LABR		GRZZZZUSA
DESTEPHANS, GUISEPE	21	M	LABR		GRZZZZUSA
HARWITZ, CHAJE	11	M	LABR		GRZZZZUSA
MICHALSKI, ANT.	23	M	JNR		GRZZZZUSA
BES, MARCUS	16	M	DLR		GRZZZZUSA
FRANICK, JOSEF	49	M	DLR		GRZZZZUSA
JOHAN	14	M	DLR		GRZZZZUSA
BAUMANN, FRANZ	18	M	DLR		GRZZZZUSA
SCHONE, FERDINAND	29	M	TLR		GRZZZZUSA
KILINSKI, ADAM	29	M	LABR		GRZZZZUSA
MANSOR, JOS	22	M	LABR		GRZZZZUSA
BOTTCHE, JOHN	20	M	LABR		GRZZZZUSA
FORMANCH, ANDREAS	37	M	JNR		GRZZZZUSA
MAUSER, FRANZ	24	M	LABR		GRZZZZUSA
KINHOPF, JOSEF	20	M	LABR		GRZZZZUSA
JACOBSON, ISRAEL	27	M	DLR		GRZZZZUSA
ZUMAKER, AUG	36	M	DLR		GRZZZZUSA

PASSENGER	AGE	SEX	OCCUPATION	PRIVL	DES
TANNENBAUM, G	24	M	DLR		GRZZZZUSA
SWARZ, JAN	31	M	DLR		GRZZZZUSA
DORANDOWKY, FRANZ	25	M	DLR		GRZZZZUSA
SACKS, MICH	25	M	DLR		GRZZZZUSA
GIHY, HEIN.	11	M	DLR		GRZZZZUSA
RUKMANN, TOBIAS	28	M	DLR		GRZZZZUSA
LESSMANN, C	26	M	DLR		GRZZZZUSA
PRUSACH, FRANZ	33	M	DLR		GRZZZZUSA
NEGMURA, WID.	30	M	DLR		GRZZZZUSA
WOMRATH, WOJ.	23	M	LABR		GRZZZZUSA
SAM, BEER	38	M	LABR		GRZZZZUSA
MUSCHA, FRANZ	24	M	LABR		GRZZZZUSA
WEBAMAK, TH.	28	M	LABR		GRZZZZUSA
MARIA	18	F	HP		GRZZZZUSA
MICHAEL, SCHOR	23	M	LABR		GRZZZZUSA
MOSCHKOWITZ, ROSA	21	M	W		GRZZZZUSA
GERLACK, FRANZ	33	M	MCHT		GRZZZZUSA
CATHE	26	M	W		GRZZZZUSA
WILH	7	M	CHILD		GRZZZZUSA
AUG	2	M	CHILD		GRZZZZUSA
FRANTMANN, FERD	37	M	FARMER		GRZZZZUSA
GERTRUDE	38	F	W		GRZZZZUSA
BERNHARD	11	M	UNKNOWN		GRZZZZUSA
MAX	10	M	CH		GRZZZZUSA
GERTRUD	9	M	CHILD		GRZZZZUSA
BELACKOWITZ, VICTOR	27	M	LABR		GRZZZZUSA
AMALIE	25	F	W		GRZZZZUSA
FRANZISKA	2	M	CHILD		GRZZZZUSA
PAULINA	.06	F	INFANT		GRZZZZUSA
SLOWINSKA, SOFIA	22	F	HP		GRZZZZUSA
DEKOSZ, AGNISKA	18	F	HP		GRZZZZUSA
GOSEMBSINSKY, OTTO	27	M	FARMER		GRZZZZUSA
MARIA	27	F	W		GRZZZZUSA
SILOKA, MARIA	17	F	HP		GRZZZZUSA
HOCHMANN, JETTE	50	F	W		GRZZZZUSA
JERSE	9	M	CHILD		GRZZZZUSA
SARAH	7	F	CHILD		GRZZZZUSA
DAVID	11	M	CH		GRZZZZUSA
GOLDSTEIN, FEIGE	18	F	HP		GRZZZZUSA
TAUBE	6	M	CHILD		GRZZZZUSA
DESTAFAND, ELISABETTE	41	F	HP		GRZZZZUSA
REISMAN, FANNY	11	F	HP		GRZZZZUSA
MICHELSOHN, DORA	20	F	HP		GRZZZZUSA
LINA	20	F	HP		GRZZZZUSA
GRANLISK, MARTHA	18	F	HP		GRZZZZUSA
WOLPCEATR, CATH	17	F	HP		GRZZZZUSA
ISAK, PESCHE	16	F	HP		GRZZZZUSA

SHIP: FULDA

FROM: BREMEN AND SOUTHAMPTON
TO: NEW YORK
ARRIVED: 19 JUNE 1888

PASSENGER	AGE	SEX	OCCUPATION	PRIVL	DES
BUETEL, FRITZ	31	M	OFF		GRZZZZUSA
FLOHR, AUGUST	30	M	MCHT		GRZZZZUSA
JANSEN, FANNY	24	F	UNKNOWN		GRZZZZUSA
GUSDORF, FELLI	17	M	MCHT		GRZZZZUSA
MAYER, ADOLF	17	M	MCHT		GRZZZZUSA
KERER, MARIE	17	F	UNKNOWN		SRZZZZUSA
HEPPBERGER, ALEX	22	M	ART		SRZZZZUSA
REINAUER, BERNHARD	16	M	CL		GRZZZZUSA
PAWEL, ROESCHEN	33	F	UNKNOWN		GRZZZZUSA
GEORG	3	M	CHILD		GRZZZZUSA
BERTHA	.11	F	INFANT		GRZZZZUSA
IMRODE, WILHELM	7	M	CHILD		GRZZZZUSA
MUENCH, AUGUST	60	M	FARMER		GRZZZZUSA
CONCORDIA	50	F	UNKNOWN		GRZZZZUSA
HERMAN	23	M	FARMER		GRZZZZUSA
ROSA	14	F	UNKNOWN		GRZZZZUSA

PASSENGER	AGE	SEX	OCCUPATION	PRVL	DES	PASSENGER	AGE	SEX	OCCUPATION	PRVL	DES
GOEPEL, HEDWIG	19	F	UNKNOWN		GRZZZZUSA	FRIEDRICH	7	M	CHILD		GRZZZZUSA
HERMANN, ABRAHAM	17	M	LABR		GRZZZZUSA	SCHOEPPEL, CATHARINA	23	F	UNKNOWN		GRZZZZUSA
LETSCH, JOHANN	18	M	LABR		GRZZZZUSA	REINHARDT, BARBA.	18	F	UNKNOWN		GRZZZZUSA
SCHWEDLER, MAX	19	M	JNR		GRZZZZUSA	LINKS, RAHEL	23	M	PNTR		GRZZZZUSA
GUSTAV	18	M	LKSH		GRZZZZUSA	SCHEVER, LOUISE	16	F	UNKNOWN		GRZZZZUSA
ZILINSKI, ANTON	24	M	LKSH		GRZZZZUSA	BECK, CLARA	17	F	UNKNOWN		GRZZZZUSA
HERBERT, AGNES	20	F	UNKNOWN		GRZZZZUSA	PRENZ, MATHILDE	19	F	UNKNOWN		GRZZZZUSA
ITTLINGER, JOSEPH	19	M	LABR		GRZZZZUSA	BEYER, LEOPOLD	16	M	BKLYR		GRZZZZUSA
STICH, ANDREAS	26	M	BCHR		GRZZZZUSA	SCHNEIDER, HEINRICH-HAR	17	M	FARMER		GRZZZZUSA
ZICK, JOH.	64	M	SMH		GRZZZZUSA	SCHNEIDER, THOMAS	16	M	FARMER		GRZZZZUSA
POTZANY, ALOIS	25	M	FARMER		GRZZZZUSA	GILBERT, JACOB	14	M	FARMER		GRZZZZUSA
KRAFT, LOUISA	46	F	UNKNOWN		GRZZZZUSA	SCHWANER, FRIEDRICH	15	M	LABR		GRZZZZUSA
BRUNO	15	M	FARMER		GRZZZZUSA	BALZ, LOUIS	16	M	CPTR		GRZZZZUSA
AQUGUSTE	6	F	CHILD		GRZZZZUSA	KITZ, JOHANN	47	M	LABR		GRZZZZUSA
JOHE.	7	F	CHILD		GRZZZZUSA	KATHARINA	41	F	UNKNOWN		GRZZZZUSA
NIEDERLENDEN, KARL	48	M	MLR		GRZZZZUSA	MARGARETHA	17	F	UNKNOWN		GRZZZZUSA
AUGUSTE	48	F	UNKNOWN		GRZZZZUSA	KATHARINA	14	F	UNKNOWN		GRZZZZUSA
EMMA	16	F	UNKNOWN		GRZZZZUSA	LEOPOLD	5	M	CHILD		GRZZZZUSA
IDA	14	F	UNKNOWN		GRZZZZUSA	RUEHL, JOHANNETTE	20	F	UNKNOWN		GRZZZZUSA
GRETHE	7	F	CHILD		GRZZZZUSA	BOEHNISCH, FRANZ	33	M	MUSN		GRZZZZUSA
PAUL	4	M	CHILD		GRZZZZUSA	MEYER, THOMAS	31	M	MUSN		GRZZZZUSA
NITZKA, ALWINA	20	F	UNKNOWN		GRZZZZUSA	LESZINSKY, JOSEF	45	M	SHMK		GRZZZZUSA
BOJANOWSKA, PAULE	23	F	UNKNOWN		GRZZZZUSA	MARTHA	35	F	UNKNOWN		GRZZZZUSA
BRAUER, FRIEDRICH	37	M	PNTR		GRZZZZUSA	KEUSWY, BARTHOLOMEY	56	M	LABR		GRZZZZUSA
BERTHA	30	F	UNKNOWN		GRZZZZUSA	MARIANNA	54	F	UNKNOWN		GRZZZZUSA
SELMA	6	F	CHILD		GRZZZZUSA	MICHAEL	27	M	LABR		GRZZZZUSA
MARTHA	3	F	CHILD		GRZZZZUSA	ANNA	18	F	UNKNOWN		GRZZZZUSA
HANNA	.04	F	INFANT		GRZZZZUSA	FRANZISKA	6	F	CHILD		GRZZZZUSA
GELLERT, ISAAC	30	M	LABR		GRZZZZUSA	MOLINOWSKA, JOSEFA	30	F	UNKNOWN		GRZZZZUSA
SCHNEIDER, PAULINE	28	F	UNKNOWN		GRZZZZUSA	ANTONIE	6	F	CHILD		GRZZZZUSA
HAMER, FRANZISKA	23	F	UNKNOWN		GRZZZZUSA	ANTON	4	M	CHILD		GRZZZZUSA
RUEHLE, FERDIN	41	M	MLR		GRZZZZUSA	JOSEPHA	3	F	CHILD		GRZZZZUSA
WILHELMINE	41	F	UNKNOWN		GRZZZZUSA	PELAGIA	.01	F	INFANT		GRZZZZUSA
MARTHA	13	F	UNKNOWN		GRZZZZUSA	MICHAEL, SOPHIA	64	F	UNKNOWN		GRZZZZUSA
LISBETH	7	F	CHILD		GRZZZZUSA	PALITZKA, MARIANE	26	F	UNKNOWN		GRZZZZUSA
CARL	6	M	CHILD		GRZZZZUSA	DIETZ, ANNA	21	F	UNKNOWN		GRZZZZUSA
MOELLER, MARGA.	7	F	CHILD		GRZZZZUSA	HELGERT, ANNA	19	F	UNKNOWN		GRZZZZUSA
BRODER, MORITZ	16	M	FARMER		GRZZZZUSA	WENNINGER, MAGDALENA	52	F	UNKNOWN		GRZZZZUSA
BAUM, SALOMON	20	M	FARMER		GRZZZZUSA	JOSEPH	18	M	FARMER		GRZZZZUSA
ESCH, JOSEPH	25	M	FARMER		GRZZZZUSA	ANNA	6	F	CHILD		GRZZZZUSA
HOFFMANN, ANDREAS	32	M	LABR		GRZZZZUSA	RELHAN, BARBA.	24	F	UNKNOWN		GRZZZZUSA
THERESE	20	F	UNKNOWN		GRZZZZUSA	BABETTE	19	F	UNKNOWN		GRZZZZUSA
SCHULZ, FRIEDKE.	68	F	UNKNOWN		GRZZZZUSA	BARBA	58	F	UNKNOWN		GRZZZZUSA
LETHUSEN, CATHERINA	16	F	UNKNOWN		GRZZZZUSA	STANDECHER, BARBA	22	F	UNKNOWN		GRZZZZUSA
TIEDEMANN, DOROTHEA	30	F	UNKNOWN		GRZZZZUSA	HELGET, ROSINA	60	F	UNKNOWN		GRZZZZUSA
BOHMKE, H.	28	M	TLR		GRZZZZUSA	HASENSTAL, MONIKA	19	F	UNKNOWN		GRZZZZUSA
KEUNE, LINA	20	F	UNKNOWN		GRZZZZUSA	STEGMANN, JACOB	28	M	BCHR		GRZZZZUSA
RUNNER, REBECCA	18	F	UNKNOWN		GRZZZZUSA	HASENSTAL, JOHANN	48	M	LABR		GRZZZZUSA
REESE, HENRY	36	M	DLR		GRZZZZUSA	PHILIPP	50	M	SHMK		GRZZZZUSA
MAGDALENE	28	F	UNKNOWN		GRZZZZUSA	EVA	46	F	UNKNOWN		GRZZZZUSA
CATHARINA	2	F	CHILD		GRZZZZUSA	DIENER, AUGUSTE	7	F	CHILD		GRZZZZUSA
OELLRICH, JUERGEN	18	M	BCHR		GRZZZZUSA	HASENSTAL, VALBURGA	6	F	CHILD		GRZZZZUSA
KATZ, JOHANNA	24	F	UNKNOWN		GRZZZZUSA	NICOLAUS	5	M	CHILD		GRZZZZUSA
LECKE, HEINRICH	25	M	FARMER		GRZZZZUSA	CHRISTOPH	4	M	CHILD		GRZZZZUSA
VORHAUER, JOHANNES	26	M	FARMER		GRZZZZUSA	OLMANN, MARGARETHE	24	F	UNKNOWN		GRZZZZUSA
KOSZELNIK, JOSEF	23	M	FARMER		GRZZZZUSA	THEIMER, CAROLINE	19	F	UNKNOWN		GRZZZZUSA
TOLLKAMP, FRIEDRICH	31	M	DLR		GRZZZZUSA	SPAETH, JOACHIM	28	M	BCHR		GRZZZZUSA
FAUST, KONRAD	32	M	LABR		GRZZZZUSA	LERNER, JOHANN	23	M	LABR		GRZZZZUSA
KATHARINA	7	F	CHILD		GRZZZZUSA	FRIEDRICH, KATHARINA	20	F	UNKNOWN		GRZZZZUSA
JANICKE, JOSEPH	37	M	PNTR		GRZZZZUSA	WIRSING, JOSEFA	25	F	UNKNOWN		GRZZZZUSA
GRAFFIN, HERMANN	23	M	FARMER		GRZZZZUSA	SEEL, MARIE	18	F	UNKNOWN		GRZZZZUSA
EBERLE, MATHILDE	19	F	UNKNOWN		GRZZZZUSA	RIESS, MARGARETHE	19	F	UNKNOWN		GRZZZZUSA
SCHWEGLER, GOTTLIEB	16	M	GDNR		GRZZZZUSA	KRAPP, JOHANN	48	M	LABR		GRZZZZUSA
GOETZ, GUSTAV	18	M	PNTR		GRZZZZUSA	ELISABETH	46	F	UNKNOWN		GRZZZZUSA
STADMANN, WILHELM	17	M	BKR		GRZZZZUSA	MICHAEL	7	M	CHILD		GRZZZZUSA
KLENK, JACOB	24	M	BKR		GRZZZZUSA	VALENTIN	6	M	CHILD		GRZZZZUSA
HELLER, WILHELM	18	M	LKSH		GRZZZZUSA	ELEONORA	5	F	CHILD		GRZZZZUSA
FESSMANN, FRIEDR.	16	M	FARMER		GRZZZZUSA	ELISABETH	4	F	CHILD		GRZZZZUSA
MUELLER, GUSTAV	5	M	CHILD		GRZZZZUSA	NOWAK, ANDRZY	23	M	DLR		GRZZZZUSA
OELLRICH, LENA	20	F	UNKNOWN		GRZZZZUSA	GLERK, JOHANNE	14	F	UNKNOWN		GRZZZZUSA
DORA	7	F	CHILD		GRZZZZUSA	SCHENKEL, CAROLE.	58	F	UNKNOWN		GRZZZZUSA
MANDEL, HENRIETTE	14	F	UNKNOWN		GRZZZZUSA	LANGE, AUGUSTE	27	F	UNKNOWN		GRZZZZUSA
FRENTEL, CARL	68	M	LABR		GRZZZZUSA	BERTHA	.11	F	INFANT		GRZZZZUSA
HENSINGER, EMIL	15	M	LABR		GRZZZZUSA	PIKURITZ, PAUL	28	M	FARMER		GRZZZZUSA
MUELLER, EMIL	14	M	LABR		GRZZZZUSA	FICK, CONRAD	26	M	FARMER		GRZZZZUSA

PASSENGER	AGE	SEX	OCCUPATION	PRVVL	DES
WETTHAUFER, KATHA.	21	F	UNKNOWN	GRZZZZ	USA
PROBST, WILHELM	25	M	LABR	GRZZZZ	USA
HOEHL, PETER	65	M	LABR	GRZZZZ	USA
BERNHARDT, JACOB	28	M	LABR	GRZZZZ	USA
ANNA	21	F	UNKNOWN	GRZZZZ	USA
WOLFF, ALMA	26	F	UNKNOWN	GRZZZZ	USA
RUDERICH, MARIANE	24	F	UNKNOWN	GRZZZZ	USA
MUELLER, WILHELM	16	M	FARMER	GRZZZZ	USA
SCHENKEL, AUG.	17	M	UNKNOWN	GRZZZZ	USA
BIEBER, HULDA	38	F	UNKNOWN	GRZZZZ	USA
ADELE	7	F	CHILD	GRZZZZ	USA
WALTER	6	M	CHILD	GRZZZZ	USA
EMANA	5	F	CHILD	GRZZZZ	USA
MICE	4	F	CHILD	GRZZZZ	USA
EUGEN	.11	M	INFANT	GRZZZZ	USA
LOESSL, JOH.	25	M	LABR	GRZZZZ	USA
ENGERT, MARTIN	31	M	MCHT	GRZZZZ	USA
MALA, JOSEFE.	15	F	UNKNOWN	GRZZZZ	USA
DUEMMLER, MICH.	16	M	LABR	GRZZZZ	USA
NUNKE, ALWINE	17	F	UNKNOWN	GRZZZZ	USA
FUELSKE, EMILIE	18	F	UNKNOWN	GRZZZZ	USA
BLUM, MATHILDE	24	F	UNKNOWN	GRZZZZ	USA
HRANAS, EMMA	27	F	UNKNOWN	GRZZZZ	USA
RICHARD	3	M	CHILD	GRZZZZ	USA
FRIEDA	2	F	CHILD	GRZZZZ	USA
EMILIE	.01	F	INFANT	GRZZZZ	USA
EMILIE	67	F	UNKNOWN	GRZZZZ	USA
GAFFKE, ALBRECHT	25	M	LABR	GRZZZZ	USA
FUHRMANN, EMMA	18	F	UNKNOWN	GRZZZZ	USA
FLEISCHMANN, ANNA	18	F	UNKNOWN	GRZZZZ	USA
WILHELM, CAROLINE	30	F	UNKNOWN	GRZZZZ	USA
MINNA	6	F	CHILD	GRZZZZ	USA
MATHILDE	2	F	CHILD	GRZZZZ	USA
SCHAEFER, KATE	18	F	UNKNOWN	GRZZZZ	USA
NORYSKIEWITZ, JOSEPH	35	M	LABR	GRZZZZ	USA
MILLER, LAURA	18	F	UNKNOWN	GRZZZZ	USA
PAPKE, AUGUST	57	M	FARMER	GRZZZZ	USA
MARIN	56	F	UNKNOWN	GRZZZZ	USA
EMILIE	7	F	CHILD	GRZZZZ	USA
GEMBITZKY, SAL.	18	M	FARMER	GRZZZZ	USA
HEINSIUS, ISIDOR	25	M	BCHR	GRZZZZ	USA
DAHLE, LINA	32	F	UNKNOWN	GRZZZZ	USA
OTT, JOHANNES	26	M	LABR	GRZZZZ	USA
ISRAEL, PHILIPP	26	M	LABR	GRZZZZ	USA
GROTELUSCHEN, JOHANN	28	M	FARMER	GRZZZZ	USA
BLIESE, JOS.	44	M	LABR	GRZZZZ	USA
ROMINGER, REINHOLD	25	M	LABR	GRZZZZ	USA
HARTWEG, SOPHIA	20	F	FARMER	GRZZZZ	USA
DORSCH, LORENZ	35	M	LABR	GRZZZZ	USA
ANNA	60	F	UNKNOWN	GRZZZZ	USA
SCHMINCKE, LOUISE	26	F	UNKNOWN	GRZZZZ	USA
E-CO	4	F	CHILD	GRZZZZ	USA
WILHELM	.01	M	INFANT	GRZZZZ	USA
CHARLOTTE	2	F	CHILD	GRZZZZ	USA
FRECH, ELISABETH	17	F	UNKNOWN	GRZZZZ	USA
BILLENWILMS, WILHELM	25	M	FARMER	GRZZZZ	USA
HOFFMANN, WILHELM	27	M	FARMER	GRZZZZ	USA
RIXE, HEINRICH	22	M	LABR	GRZZZZ	USA
BAEHR, MOSES	17	M	LABR	GRZZZZ	USA
GRUNDMANN, CHRISTOPH	64	M	FARMER	GRZZZZ	USA
FISCHER, CARL	26	M	SMH	GRZZZZ	USA
STEINBOECK, HEINRICH	17	M	BKR	GRZZZZ	USA
SCHEPPER, MICHAEL	30	M	BKR	GRZZZZ	USA
HEINRICH, HERMANN	61	M	BBR	GRZZZZ	USA
THERESE	67	F	UNKNOWN	GRZZZZ	USA
RAUSCH, RUDOLF	7	M	CHILD	GRZZZZ	USA
GUENTHER, MICHAEL	38	M	FARMER	GRZZZZ	USA
MARIANNE	33	F	UNKNOWN	GRZZZZ	USA
MARTHA	7	F	CHILD	GRZZZZ	USA
IGNATZ	5	M	CHILD	GRZZZZ	USA
JOSEF	4	M	CHILD	GRZZZZ	USA
JOHANN	2	M	CHILD	GRZZZZ	USA
WALERA	.02	F	INFANT	GRZZZZ	USA
RUNKOWSKY, FRANZ	17	M	LABR	GRZZZZ	USA
BLUME, ADOLF	48	M	TLR	GRZZZZ	USA
SCHRADER, WILHELM	41	M	MLR	GRZZZZ	USA
HOLTHAUSEN, CLAUS	15	M	LABR	GRZZZZ	USA
SCHONTAG, PHILIPP	24	M	LABR	GRZZZZ	USA
MOLLENTOPF, HEINRICH	25	M	FARMER	GRZZZZ	USA
SCHLOPP, FRIEDRICH	25	M	FARMER	GRZZZZ	USA
CAROLINE	25	F	UNKNOWN	GRZZZZ	USA
MUEHLEISEN, MARIE	21	F	UNKNOWN	GRZZZZ	USA
RIESS, KORDULA	19	F	UNKNOWN	GRZZZZ	USA
MAUSER, FRTIZ	17	M	FARMER	GRZZZZ	USA
KAROLINE	22	F	UNKNOWN	GRZZZZ	USA
LEUTBECHER, MARIE	25	F	UNKNOWN	GRZZZZ	USA
BACH, THEKLA	22	F	UNKNOWN	GRZZZZ	USA
KEUSS, MATHILDE	21	F	UNKNOWN	GRZZZZ	USA
SATOR, ANNA	38	F	UNKNOWN	GRZZZZ	USA
THEKLA	6	F	CHILD	GRZZZZ	USA
FREDI	5	F	CHILD	GRZZZZ	USA
ROELBE, FRANZ	21	M	LABR	GRZZZZ	USA
GRUBER, PAULINE	21	F	UNKNOWN	GRZZZZ	USA
FRITZ, PAULINE	21	F	UNKNOWN	GRZZZZ	USA
LAIER, GOTTLIEB	30	M	LABR	GRZZZZ	USA
SCHERER, JACOB	29	M	LABR	GRZZZZ	USA
HAASSEL, FRIEDRICH	26	M	LABR	GRZZZZ	USA
HARTWIG, LINA	26	F	UNKNOWN	GRZZZZ	USA
LINA	2	F	CHILD	GRZZZZ	USA
HIEINRICH	.01	M	INFANT	GRZZZZ	USA
DILLER, LOUISE	22	F	UNKNOWN	GRZZZZ	USA
STEINHAGEN, CARL	24	M	LABR	GRZZZZ	USA
STOLL, MATHAEUS	23	M	LABR	GRZZZZ	USA
LANGHAUS, CARL	22	M	LABR	GRZZZZ	USA
ANNA	21	F	UNKNOWN	GRZZZZ	USA
GRAF, JOSEF	31	M	FARMER	GRZZZZ	USA
SCHREITLER, CARL	19	M	DLR	GRZZZZ	USA
LEIER, JOHN	28	M	FARMER	GRZZZZ	USA
SAATHOFF, U	30	F	W	GRZZZZ	USA
LOUISE	7	F	CHILD	GRZZZZ	USA
LUDWIG	.10	M	INFANT	GRZZZZ	USA
GOLLERT, LEONHARD	15	M	FARMER	GRZZZZ	USA
KUHL, MARIA	29	F	UNKNOWN	GRZZZZ	USA
GEYER, GUSTAV	25	M	LABR	GRZZZZ	USA
SCHUERMANN, HERMANN	24	M	LABR	GRZZZZ	USA
ANNA	20	F	UNKNOWN	GRZZZZ	USA
JUST, JOHANN	64	M	LABR	GRZZZZ	USA
AUGUST	17	M	LABR	GRZZZZ	USA
BREITHAUPT, JOHANNES	41	M	FARMER	GRZZZZ	USA
ANNA	25	F	UNKNOWN	GRZZZZ	USA
WELDE, CHRISTOFFER	16	M	FARMER	GRZZZZ	USA
DITZ, FRIEDRICH	17	M	BKR	GRZZZZ	USA
MAUL, GEORG	44	M	LABR	GRZZZZ	USA
SCHNEIDER, HEINRICH	24	M	LABR	GRZZZZ	USA
KLATT, BERTHA	22	F	UNKNOWN	GRZZZZ	USA
BIRK, JOHANN	40	M	LABR	GRZZZZ	USA
KRAEMER, ROBERT	16	M	LABR	GRZZZZ	USA
MAISKEN, GEORG	25	M	LABR	GRZZZZ	USA
TENK, MARIE	24	F	UNKNOWN	GRZZZZ	USA
OPFERMANN, HULDA	18	F	UNKNOWN	GRZZZZ	USA
HECKENDORF, EMILIE	26	F	UNKNOWN	GRZZZZ	USA
KAPTUR, JOHANN	23	M	LABR	GRZZZZ	USA
BONCZAK, WALENTY	40	M	LABR	GRZZZZ	USA
GEISLER, MAX	24	M	TIR	GRZZZZ	USA
MARTIN, CARL	44	M	BKR	GRZZZZ	USA
WISNIEWSKI, JOHANN	31	M	BKR	GRZZZZ	USA
MICHAEL	65	M	BKR	GRZZZZ	USA
MARIANNA	24	F	UNKNOWN	GRZZZZ	USA
MICHAEL	3	M	CHILD	GRZZZZ	USA
ROSALIE	.08	F	INFANT	GRZZZZ	USA
JOACHIM, FERDINAND	16	M	BKR	GRZZZZ	USA
LALASIEWICZ, AGNESZKA	69	F	UNKNOWN	GRZZZZ	USA
SCHILLER, GERHARD	17	M	PRNTR	GRZZZZ	USA
OTTO	16	M	PRNTR	GRZZZZ	USA
ELISE	7	F	CHILD	GRZZZZ	USA
WEGESCY, WINCENTZ	24	M	BRR	GRZZZZ	USA
SACHER, M.	32	M	BRR	GRZZZZ	USA
SUSANNA	4	F	CHILD	GRZZZZ	USA
WUCHTER, JOHANN	16	M	LABR	GRZZZZ	USA
DORNBUSCH, JOHANNA	24	F	FARMER	GRZZZZ	USA

PASSENGER	AGE	SEX	OCCUPATION	PRVL	DES
KALB, JOHANN	25	M	TLR	GRZZZZ	USA
DZIENKOPOT, MARIA	20	F	UNKNOWN	GRZZZZ	USA
MARIA	.11	F	INFANT	GRZZZZ	USA
SCHUESSLER, JOHANN	59	F	LABR	GRZZZZ	USA
PLATT, DOROTHEA	20	F	UNKNOWN	GRZZZZ	USA
SEIDE, ARTHUR	16	M	LABR	GRZZZZ	USA
SUESSMANN, GUSTAV	24	M	LABR	GRZZZZ	USA
KRONKE, DIEDRICH	36	M	LABR	GRZZZZ	USA
STUBER, MANE	22	F	UNKNOWN	GRZZZZ	USA
EMIL	.10	M	INFANT	GRZZZZ	USA
SALZBERGER, JOSEF	39	M	FARMER	GRZZZZ	USA
MARIA	39	F	UNKNOWN	GRZZZZ	USA
ELISABETH	7	F	CHILD	GRZZZZ	USA
JOSEF	4	M	CHILD	GRZZZZ	USA
SCHALBACH, KATHARINA	23	F	UNKNOWN	GRZZZZ	USA
KIKULSKY, STEPHAN	25	M	LABR	GRZZZZ	USA
MESSER, EMIL	46	M	LABR	GRZZZZ	USA
SCHWALLBACH, HEINRICH	43	M	LABR	GRZZZZ	USA
DANGIERD, FRANZ	25	M	LABR	GRZZZZ	USA
LUDWIG, NATHAN	59	M	FARMER	GRZZZZ	USA
NEUBER, MAX	6	M	CHILD	GRZZZZ	USA
JESSNER, DAVID	30	M	FARMER	GRZZZZ	USA
GRZEBETA, ROSALIA	22	F	UNKNOWN	GRZZZZ	USA
JULIA	16	F	UNKNOWN	GRZZZZ	USA
SCHWEITZER, JOHANN	43	M	BCHR	GRZZZZ	USA
HELENIUS, M.C.	24	M	BKR	GRZZZZ	USA
TALPIN, M.F.	28	M	LABR	GRZZZZ	USA
KUEHRT, REINHOLD	36	M	LABR	GRZZZZ	USA
BEUEFELD, CHRIST.	48	M	BCHR	GRZZZZ	USA
MINNA	46	F	UNKNOWN	GRZZZZ	USA
AUGUSTE	6	F	CHILD	GRZZZZ	USA
EMMA	7	F	CHILD	GRZZZZ	USA
QUASTDORF, ADOLF	16	M	LABR	GRZZZZ	USA
SCHMIEDICHER, JOHANN-FR	29	M	LABR	GRZZZZ	USA
MAUSER, FRIEDRICH	50	M	LABR	GRZZZZ	USA
SCHUBECK, U-MR	47	M	LABR	GRZZZZ	USA
SCHOLTE, THEODOR	34	M	LABR	GRZZZZ	USA
WULFSTEIN, ADOLF	29	M	MCHT	GRZZZZ	USA
DOMBROWSKY, HERMAN	27	M	LABR	GRZZZZ	USA
WELCKER, JOHANN	30	M	LABR	GRZZZZ	USA
OELLRICHS, MARTIN	29	M	FARMER	GRZZZZ	USA
GRETCHEN	22	F	UNKNOWN	GRZZZZ	USA

PASSENGER	AGE	SEX	OCCUPATION	PRVL	DES
ROBERT	5	M	CHILD	SRZZZZ	USA
IDA	4	F	CHILD	SRZZZZ	USA
WALTER	2	M	CHILD	SRZZZZ	USA
IRWIN	.06	M	INFANT	SRZZZZ	USA
BARTHLOME, JOHANN	27	M	FARMER	SRZZZZ	USA
ELIZA	29	F	W	SRZZZZ	USA
JOHANN	4	M	CHILD	SRZZZZ	USA
RONNA	2	F	CHILD	SRZZZZ	USA
JOHN	.06	M	INFANT	SRZZZZ	USA
HUNZIKER, VERENA	31	F	W	SRZZZZ	USA
JULIA	5	F	CHILD	SRZZZZ	USA
BEUTLER, LOUISE	26	F	SP	SRZZZZ	USA
MICHEL, MARIA	21	F	SP	SRZZZZ	USA
MURI, MARIA	22	F	SP	SRZZZZ	USA
ZEENDER, ANNA-M.	43	F	SP	SRZZZZ	USA
WYLER, BERTHA	18	F	SP	SRZZZZ	USA
BEUTLER, MARIA	18	F	SP	SRZZZZ	USA
KANER, JOHANN	42	F	W	SRZZZZ	USA
EMIL	5	M	CHILD	SRZZZZ	USA
MOSER, HANS	6	M	CHILD	SRZZZZ	USA
BARFUSS, ANDRAS	7	M	CHILD	SRZZZZ	USA
MOSER, ULRICH	30	M	FARMER	SRZZZZ	USA
ELISA	30	F	W	SRZZZZ	USA
ANNA	7	F	CHILD	SRZZZZ	USA
FRANZ	7	F	CHILD	SRZZZZ	USA
ELISA	5	F	CHILD	SRZZZZ	USA
OTTO	5	M	CHILD	SRZZZZ	USA
ROSA	3	F	CHILD	SRZZZZ	USA
AUGUST	2	M	CHILD	SRZZZZ	USA
MARTHA	.06	M	INFANT	SRZZZZ	USA
WAGI, LOUSE	25	F	SP	SRZZZZ	USA
SCHWAB, PAULINE-W.	37	F	W	SRZZZZ	USA
PAULINE-K.	17	F	SP	SRZZZZ	USA
ANNA-M.	3	F	CHILD	SRZZZZ	USA
KAROLINE	.06	F	INFANT	SRZZZZ	USA
KUTTERER, CONRAD	48	M	FARMER	SRZZZZ	USA
BRAND, ELIZA	60	F	MA	SRZZZZ	USA
RIPPLINGER, JEAN	27	M	FARMER	SRZZZZ	USA
EYGI, RUDOLF	21	M	FARMER	SRZZZZ	USA
MICHEL, ALBERT	24	M	FARMER	SRZZZZ	USA

SHIP: NEVADA

FROM: LIVERPOOL AND QUEENSTOWN
TO: NEW YORK
ARRIVED: 20 JUNE 1888

PASSENGER	AGE	SEX	OCCUPATION	PRVL	DES
THESEGOR, ABRAHAM	24	M	FARMER	GRACBF	USA
EMILY	22	F	W	GRACBF	USA
HOLLIGER, FREDERICH	35	M	FARMER	SRZZZZ	USA
EMMA	33	F	W	SRZZZZ	USA
ADOLF	7	M	CHILD	SRZZZZ	USA
MARIE	6	F	CHILD	SRZZZZ	USA
GUSTAF-A.	5	M	CHILD	SRZZZZ	USA
ROSA	3	F	CHILD	SRZZZZ	USA
EMMA	2	F	CHILD	SRZZZZ	USA
FREDRICK	.06	M	INFANT	SRZZZZ	USA
RIEDELBAUCH, MARGARET	36	F	W	SRACBF	USA
JOHN-K.	7	M	CHILD	SRACBF	USA
ANDREAS	5	M	CHILD	SRACBF	USA
ELIZABETH	3	F	CHILD	SRACBF	USA
JOHANN-G.	2	M	CHILD	SRACBF	USA
JOHANNE-B.	.09	F	INFANT	SRACBF	USA
WEBER, SAMUEL	37	M	FARMER	SRZZZZ	USA
VERINA	33	F	W	SRZZZZ	USA
MARY	68	F	MA	SRZZZZ	USA
EUGENE	7	F	CHILD	SRZZZZ	USA
LINA	5	F	CHILD	SRZZZZ	USA

SHIP: SAMARIA

FROM: LIVERPOOL AND QUEENSTOWN
TO: BOSTON
ARRIVED: 20 JUNE 1888

PASSENGER	AGE	SEX	OCCUPATION	PRVL	DES
LESNAN, LEVI	19	M	TLR	GRZZZZ	CT
GELEWITSCH, ROHIL	19	M	LABR	GRZZZZ	CT
KOTILA, JOH	19	M	LABR	GRZZZZ	CT
KOPSOLA, JOH	28	M	LABR	GRZZZZ	CT
GROF, ADRIAN	26	M	MSN	GRZZZZ	CT
ENST, JOSEF	18	M	MSN	GRZZZZ	CT
KEMASSER, GAB.	23	M	LABR	GRZZZZ	CT
HANNUS, CARL	31	M	LABR	GRZZZZ	CT
NISULA, JOH	18	M	LABR	GRZZZZ	CT
MAKI, JOHAN	27	M	FARMER	GRZZZZ	CT
ROTTER, THOMAS	28	M	LABR	GRZZZZ	CT
KOPSALA, WM.	19	M	LABR	GRZZZZ	CT
HUKARI, MATTS	17	M	LABR	GRZZZZ	CT
TEIR, MARIA	27	F	SP	GRZZZZ	CT
KOPSALA, MARIAN	23	F	SP	GRZZZZ	CT
KOTILA, CAJSA	24	F	SP	GRZZZZ	CT
OFREMAIER, JOHANNA	19	F	SP	GRZZZZ	CT
KERTOLA, MAJA	22	F	SP	GRZZZZ	CT
TRASKAHE, ANNA	25	F	SP	GRZZZZ	CT
OVAVER, MUESE	21	F	SP	GRZZZZ	CT
KONIS, MACHLE	22	F	W	GRZZZZ	MA
ABEL	.10	M	INFANT	GRZZZZ	MA
LJUNGGRIST, AXEL	22	M	MSN	GRZZZZ	MA

167

PASSENGER	AGE	SEX	OCCUPATION	PRVL	DES
MARIA	20	F	W	GRZZZZMA	
MATTILA, ERIK	38	M	MSN	GRZZZZMA	
MARIA	22	F	SP	GRZZZZMA	
MARIA	16	F	SP	GRZZZZMA	
HENRI	6	M	CHILD	GRZZZZMA	
STROM, LENA	23	F	W	GRZZZZMA	
PETER	7	M	CHILD	GRZZZZMA	
BERENSTEIN, MOLKE	36	F	W	GRZZZZMA	
MAX	14	M	LABR	GRZZZZMA	
RACHAEL	11	F	CH	GRZZZZMA	
JACOB	9	M	CHILD	GRZZZZMA	
CHRIS.	7	M	CHILD	GRZZZZMA	
SCHOLEM	2	M	CHILD	GRZZZZMA	
BESCHE	.11	F	INFANT	GRZZZZMA	
LEVI, SAM.	17	M	TLR	GRZZZZMA	
EHLERS, LOUISA	60	F	MA	GRZZZZMA	
MARY	20	F	SP	GRZZZZMA	
CHRISTINE	22	F	W	GRZZZZMA	
HENRICH	.11	M	INFANT	GRZZZZMA	

SHIP: ITALY

FROM: LIVERPOOL AND QUEENSTOWN
TO: NEW YORK
ARRIVED: 21 JUNE 1888

PASSENGER	AGE	SEX	OCCUPATION	PRVL	DES
CHAPLEWSKY, W.	53	M	FARMER	GRAARZNY	
POCKOLA, MARIA	23	F	SP	GRACBFNY	
SOFIA	19	F	SP	GRACBFNY	
LADKKONEN, MARIA	20	F	SP	GRACBFNY	
SCHUBETOWSKI, JOS.	25	M	LABR	GRACBFNY	
COLVIZ, FRIEDRICH	38	M	FARMER	GRACBFNY	
SEPTENOLA, KAISER	26	M	LABR	GRACBFNY	
FLUCK, MARIE	26	F	SP	GRAAKHNY	
WINCK, JOS.	27	M	BRR	GRAAKHNY	
EFFRET, ISAAK	21	M	LABR	GRACBFPHI	

SHIP: RHEIN

FROM: BREMEN
TO: BALTIMORE
ARRIVED: 21 JUNE 1888

PASSENGER	AGE	SEX	OCCUPATION	PRVL	DES
KOCH, JOHANN	25	M	HTR	GRZZZZBAL	
PETZLAFF, MARTIN	45	M	FARMER	GRZZZZBAL	
ABLONIA	45	F	W	GRZZZZBAL	
AUGUST	18	M	FARMER	GRZZZZBAL	
MARTIN	15	M	FARMER	GRZZZZBAL	
MARIA	14	F	CH	GRZZZZBAL	
PAUL	9	M	CHILD	GRZZZZBAL	
JOSEPH	4	M	CHILD	GRZZZZBAL	
GEHRMANN, LOUISE	43	F	NN	GRZZZZBAL	
JOHANN	11	M	CH	GRZZZZBAL	
BRIESCH, JOHANN	66	M	LABR	GRZZZZBAL	
AUGUST	24	M	LABR	GRZZZZBAL	
JESCHKE, ANNA	35	F	NN	GRZZZZBAL	
LUDOWIKA	33	F	NN	GRZZZZBAL	
ODATSCHAK, MARIANNA	28	F	NN	GRZZZZBAL	
JOSEPH	7	M	CHILD	GRZZZZBAL	
ANTONIA	4	F	CHILD	GRZZZZBAL	
HEIMANN, EVA	40	F	NN	GRZZZZBAL	
MINNA	9	F	CHILD	GRZZZZBAL	
KORDITZ, CHARLOTTE	21	F	NN	GRZZZZBAL	
RACZKOSKA, PETRONELA	28	F	NN	GRZZZZBAL	
WACHNOWSKI, AMALIE	19	F	SVNT	GRZZZZBAL	
PAPKE, LOUISA	57	F	NN	GRZZZZBAL	
ERNSTINE	18	F	SVNT	GRZZZZBAL	
GAWROWSKY, JACOB	44	M	FARMER	GRZZZZBAL	
ERNSTINE	42	F	W	GRZZZZBAL	
GABROWSKY, AUGUST	18	M	PRNTR	GRZZZZBAL	
MINNA	16	F	CK	GRZZZZBAL	
FRANZ	13	M	CH	GRZZZZBAL	
BERTHA	7	F	CHILD	GRZZZZBAL	
JOSEPHINE	4	F	CHILD	GRZZZZBAL	
ANNA	2	F	CHILD	GRZZZZBAL	
FIRST, JOHN	37	M	FARMER	GRZZZZBAL	
WILHE.	33	F	W	GRZZZZBAL	
MARIE	10	F	CH	GRZZZZBAL	
FRANZ	7	M	CHILD	GRZZZZBAL	
JOHANN	.01	M	INFANT	GRZZZZBAL	
FREYER, CARL	45	M	CPTR	GRZZZZBAL	
JOHANN	75	M	NN	GRZZZZBAL	
NOWAK, MAGDALENA	20	F	NN	GRZZZZBAL	
MARYANNA	17	F	NN	GRZZZZBAL	
MACHALINSKA, BARBA.	25	F	CK	GRZZZZBAL	
BERN.	10	M	CH	GRZZZZBAL	
SALEKA, CICILIA	25	F	NN	GRZZZZBAL	
RAMISCHERZKA, PAULINE	14	F	NN	GRZZZZBAL	
LITKA, JOHANN	24	M	PNTR	GRZZZZBAL	
SEILER, AUGUST	32	M	GDNR	GRZZZZBAL	
HERZBERG, KATH.	40	M	BRR	GRZZZZBAL	
STEIN, FRIEDR.	24	M	BKR	GRZZZZBAL	
BECKER, WILHE.	29	F	NN	GRZZZZBAL	
ANNA	5	F	CHILD	GRZZZZBAL	
OTTO	4	M	CHILD	GRZZZZBAL	
MARTHA	.03	F	INFANT	GRZZZZBAL	
TREJWALD, HERM.	36	M	MLR	GRZZZZBAL	
WILHE.	35	F	W	GRZZZZBAL	
JOHANNES	3	M	CHILD	GRZZZZBAL	
LOUISE	2	F	CHILD	GRZZZZBAL	
EMIL	.04	M	INFANT	GRZZZZBAL	
KRUEGER, ANNA	18	F	NN	GRZZZZBAL	
WACHTMEISTER, FRANZ	45	M	WVR	GRZZZZBAL	
NEIMANN, RICHARD	43	M	FARMER	GRZZZZBAL	
ALBERTINE	33	F	W	GRZZZZBAL	
EMMA	4	F	CHILD	GRZZZZBAL	
MARTHA	.07	F	INFANT	GRZZZZBAL	
WUSSOW, ALBERT	29	M	JNR	GRZZZZBAL	
WILHE.	29	F	W	GRZZZZBAL	
WEIGEL, ALBIN	27	M	DYR	GRZZZZBAL	
MINNA	28	F	W	GRZZZZBAL	
MEIER, CARL	40	M	SDLR	GRZZZZBAL	
MARIE	31	F	W	GRZZZZBAL	
WILH.	9	M	CHILD	GRZZZZBAL	
SOGORSKI, FRIEDR.	73	M	LABR	GRZZZZBAL	
TOPEL, JOHANNA	19	F	NN	GRZZZZBAL	
HOHN, ANTONIE	30	F	NN	GRZZZZBAL	
DOMINSKA, ANTON	56	M	CPR	GRZZZZBAL	
JOSEPHA	50	F	W	GRZZZZBAL	
JOSEPH	60	M	LABR	GRZZZZBAL	
MARY	30	F	NN	GRZZZZBAL	
KULNISKI, VACLAV	16	M	JNR	GRZZZZBAL	
GROSJEAN, WILHM.	21	M	PNTR	GRZZZZBAL	
NEUMANN, MARTHA	23	F	CK	GRZZZZBAL	
BORKOWSKI, JOHN	56	M	FARMER	GRZZZZBAL	
WILHE.	51	F	W	GRZZZZBAL	
ANNA	15	F	CH	GRZZZZBAL	
MARGA.	7	F	CHILD	GRZZZZBAL	
WEISE, ADOLF	28	M	BCHR	GRZZZZBAL	
SCHWARZKE, AUGUSTE	17	F	NN	GRZZZZBAL	
ZACKRZEWSKI, JOSEF	26	M	CPR	GRZZZZBAL	
ANNA	19	F	W	GRZZZZBAL	
MAKOWSKI, BERKA	40	F	NN	GRZZZZBAL	
MARGA.	10	F	CH	GRZZZZBAL	
BALDWIN	5	M	CHILD	GRZZZZBAL	
KOWALIK, JOSEFA	26	F	NN	GRZZZZBAL	
MICHAEL	11	M	CH	GRZZZZBAL	
CATHA.	6	F	CHILD	GRZZZZBAL	
JOHANN	3	M	CHILD	GRZZZZBAL	
STEFAN	.11	M	INFANT	GRZZZZBAL	

PASSENGER	AGE	SEX	OCCUPATION	PRVL	DES
CZERNIAK, ANNA	19	F	NN	GRZZZZBAL	
OTT, BENJAMIN	26	M	TLR	GRZZZZBAL	
ROSALIE	25	F	W	GRZZZZBAL	
ZIEMANN, CARL	38	M	FARMER	GRZZZZBAL	
FLORENTINE	30	F	W	GRZZZZBAL	
GUSTAV	13	M	CH	GRZZZZBAL	
FRIEDRICH	9	M	CHILD	GRZZZZBAL	
RICHARD	7	M	CHILD	GRZZZZBAL	
JULIUS	5	M	CHILD	GRZZZZBAL	
HULDA	2	F	CHILD	GRZZZZBAL	
CARL	.02	M	INFANT	GRZZZZBAL	
MANSKE, GUSTAV	28	M	TCHR	GRZZZZBAL	
HELLWIG, MARIE	63	F	NN	GRZZZZBAL	
ANNA	19	F	SVNT	GRZZZZBAL	
HAAS, FRANZ	35	M	SDLR	GRZZZZBAL	
ZICENOFSKY, MARIA	17	F	NN	GRZZZZBAL	
BAUMGART, PAULINA	45	F	NN	GRZZZZBAL	
AUGUSTE	19	F	NN	GRZZZZBAL	
CARL	15	M	NN	GRZZZZBAL	
BERTHA	11	F	CH	GRZZZZBAL	
HULDA	9	F	CHILD	GRZZZZBAL	
LEHRKE, AUGUSTE	19	F	NN	GRZZZZBAL	
MAHRKOWSKI, WOJCIECH	70	M	LABR	GRZZZZBAL	
JOSEFA	21	F	NN	GRZZZZBAL	
GUTTKE, WILH.	15	M	HTR	GRZZZZBAL	
KLOHN, EMILIE	19	F	NN	GRZZZZBAL	
KUGOTH, ELEONORE	23	F	NN	GRZZZZBAL	
STAPEL, ROBERT	27	M	BKR	GRZZZZBAL	
GEHRKE, ERNST	21	M	SHMK	GRZZZZBAL	
FRIEDRICE, AUGUSTE	18	F	NN	GRZZZZBAL	
WESTPHAL, MARIA	21	F	NN	GRZZZZBAL	
GLUBA, VICTORIA	40	F	NN	GRZZZZBAL	
THERSA	11	F	CH	GRZZZZBAL	
ANNA	9	F	CHILD	GRZZZZBAL	
SEDEA	4	F	CHILD	GRZZZZBAL	
MICHAEL	3	M	CHILD	GRZZZZBAL	
PRIEBE, LUDW.	39	M	FARMER	GRZZZZBAL	
ERNSTINE	40	F	W	GRZZZZBAL	
AUGUSTE	11	F	CH	GRZZZZBAL	
EMIL	9	M	CHILD	GRZZZZBAL	
BERTHA	6	F	CHILD	GRZZZZBAL	
MARTHA	.01	F	INFANT	GRZZZZBAL	
HINZ, HULDA	19	F	CK	GRZZZZBAL	
SCHIRK, WILHE.	45	F	NN	GRZZZZBAL	
FRANZ, ANNA	21	F	NN	GRZZZZBAL	
STRIESE, ANNA	19	F	NN	GRZZZZBAL	
KOPPMEIER, KONR.	32	M	BBR	GRZZZZOH	
HOEHN, ANNA	20	F	NN	GRZZZZOH	
WALTHER, ANNA	19	F	NN	GRZZZZOH	
SEIFERT, HERM.	26	M	TLR	GRZZZZIL	
WILHE.	28	F	W	GRZZZZIL	
PAUL	.11	M	INFANT	GRZZZZIL	
SPRENGER, ANNA	58	F	NN	GRZZZZIL	
DREIFKE, HERMINE	22	F	NN	GRZZZZWI	
OTTO, AUGUST	32	M	CVR	GRZZZZNE	
OTTILIA	25	F	W	GRZZZZNE	
LANGE, ADOLF	26	M	GLSR	GRZZZZWI	
GAERTNER, ROBERT	64	M	FARMER	GRZZZZWI	
CAROLINE	66	F	W	GRZZZZWI	
AGNES	28	F	NN	GRZZZZWI	
MARIE	32	F	NN	GRZZZZWI	
OSCAR	7	M	CHILD	GRZZZZWI	
JOHANN	4	M	CHILD	GRZZZZWI	
FANNY	2	F	CHILD	GRZZZZWI	
MALLON, PAULINE	21	F	NN	GRZZZZIL	
SCHULZ, MARTINE	21	F	NN	GRZZZZPA	
WESTPHAL, AUG.	50	M	GDNR	GRZZZZMN	
JULIANA	50	F	W	GRZZZZMN	
AUGUSTE	17	F	NN	GRZZZZMN	
JOHANNE	14	F	CH	GRZZZZMN	
EMMA	4	F	CHILD	GRZZZZMN	
WALDT, CATH.M.	19	F	NN	GRZZZZWI	
DEHLING, JOH.	27	M	CPR	GRZZZZWI	
ANNA	25	F	W	GRZZZZWI	
CATHA.	.06	F	INFANT	GRZZZZWI	
MARGA.	.06	F	INFANT	GRZZZZWI	
PIRNER, JOHANN	15	M	FARMER	GRZZZZWI	
WEDEL, ANDREAS	32	M	FARMER	GRZZZZWI	
MARGA.	31	F	W	GRZZZZWI	
KRAUSS, MARGA.	8	F	CHILD	GRZZZZWI	
POHL, CARL	30	M	FARMER	GRZZZZOH	
WILHE.	27	F	W	GRZZZZOH	
AUGUST	4	M	CHILD	GRZZZZOH	
CARL	2	M	CHILD	GRZZZZOH	
MATZMOHR, ANNA	18	F	CK	GRZZZZOH	
BERBOLZ, CARL	61	M	FARMER	GRZZZZWI	
THERESE	47	F	W	GRZZZZWI	
BERTHA	19	F	NN	GRZZZZWI	
MARTHA	16	F	NN	GRZZZZWI	
MARIE	9	F	CHILD	GRZZZZWI	
PAUL	4	M	CHILD	GRZZZZWI	
REINHARDT, ERNST	26	M	CPR	GRZZZZIL	
BOEDER, ANNA	19	F	NN	GRZZZZWI	
RATKE, EVA	23	F	NN	GRZZZZMO	
SERSENEWSKI, IGNATZ	41	M	LABR	GRZZZZWI	
PAULINA	31	F	W	GRZZZZWI	
JACOB	47	M	LABR	GRZZZZWI	
JULIAN	4	M	CHILD	GRZZZZWI	
SOPHIA	2	F	CHILD	GRZZZZWI	
STRAHL, FRANZ	36	M	GDNR	GRZZZZROC	
CATHARINA	23	F	W	GRZZZZROC	
JOHANN	7	M	CHILD	GRZZZZROC	
LEOKADIA	.09	F	INFANT	GRZZZZROC	
BUSCHE, ERNST	15	M	TU	GRZZZZIN	
RIPKEN, HEINR.	16	M	PNTR	GRZZZZBAL	
JORDAN, HERM.	25	M	FARMER	GRZZZZBAL	
LOUISA	26	F	W	GRZZZZBAL	
FERDINAND	21	M	FARMER	GRZZZZBAL	
FOLPP, BARBARA	53	F	NN	WMZZZZBAL	
POLL---, SUSANNA	20	F	NN	GRZZZZBAL	
MUELLER, FERD.	66	M	LABR	GRZZZZBAL	
LINCK, HEINR.	14	M	CH	GRZZZZBAL	
MARIA	11	F	CH	GRZZZZBAL	
SCHMIDT, KASPAR	21	M	CPR	GRZZZZBAL	
ROEDIGER, PHILIPPINE	19	F	NN	GRZZZZBAL	
LICHTFELD, AUG.	25	M	MNR	GRZZZZBAL	
BOTTMANN, LOUISE	17	F	CK	GRZZZZBAL	
WILK, JACOB	28	M	FARMER	GRZZZZBAL	
VORDEMANN, HERM.	24	M	FARMER	GRZZZZBAL	
BUETTNER, JOH.	24	M	FARMER	GRZZZZBAL	
BARTZSCH, SOFIA	46	F	NN	GRZZZZBAL	
RASCHKA, MINNA	28	F	NN	GRZZZZBAL	
BOLLMANN, SOPHIA	18	F	NN	GRZZZZBAL	
EDLER, HEINR.	29	M	FARMER	GRZZZZBAL	
MINNA	32	F	W	GRZZZZBAL	
MINNA	10	F	CH	GRZZZZBAL	
FRIEDR.	8	M	CHILD	GRZZZZBAL	
LINA	5	F	CHILD	GRZZZZBAL	
JOHANN	4	M	CHILD	GRZZZZBAL	
HEINR.	3	M	CHILD	GRZZZZBAL	
VONLUND, KATH.	19	F	NN	GRZZZZBAL	
BERCH, GEORG	22	M	JNR	GRZZZZBAL	
DEYE, MARIA	55	F	UNKNOWN	GRZZZZBAL	
JULIE	16	F	NN	GRZZZZBAL	
FRANZ	14	M	CH	GRZZZZBAL	
ELSA	7	F	CHILD	GRZZZZBAL	
MIARA, MICHANT	30	M	FARMER	GRZZZZBAL	
MUELLER, AUGUSTE	26	F	NN	GRZZZZBAL	
CHOJNACKI, FRANTISZEK	23	M	FARMER	GRZZZZBAL	
LASCHINSKI, FERD.	58	M	FARMER	GRZZZZBAL	
ANNA	60	F	W	GRZZZZBAL	
AUGUST	.11	M	INFANT	GRZZZZBAL	
MURENZ, ADAM	39	M	CPTR	GRZZZZBAL	
ANNA	36	F	W	GRZZZZBAL	
ANNA	.03	F	INFANT	GRZZZZBAL	
BRZEZINSKA, FRANZA.	27	F	NN	GRZZZZBAL	
JAN	.11	M	INFANT	GRZZZZBAL	
JAKOWSKI, GOTTFRIED	28	M	FARMER	GRZZZZBAL	
MINNA	30	F	W	GRZZZZBAL	
EMMA	5	F	CHILD	GRZZZZBAL	

PASSENGER	AGE	SEX	OCCUPATION	PRVL	DES
OTTO	3	M	CHILD		GRZZZZBAL
BERTHA	.02	F	INFANT		GRZZZZBAL
LEHR, MARG.	23	M	SVNT		GRZZZZBAL
KORMANSEK, FRANZ	32	M	FARMER		GRZZZZBAL
GERTRUDE	30	F	W		GRZZZZBAL
MARIE	3	F	CHILD		GRZZZZBAL
FORENSKY, IGNATZ	30	M	LABR		GRZZZZBAL
POKORA, MASC.	38	M	FARMER		GRZZZZBAL
VERONICA	33	F	W		GRZZZZBAL
ZOLKOWSKI, LEON	23	M	FARMER		GRZZZZBAL
MARON, EMILIE	20	F	NN		GRZZZZBAL
NEUMANN, LOUISE	66	F	NN		GRZZZZBAL
ANNA	23	F	NN		GRZZZZBAL
PODLEWSKI, MATHIAS	34	M	PRNTR		GRZZZZBAL
MICHALINA	26	F	W		GRZZZZBAL
HELENA	3	F	CHILD		GRZZZZBAL
FRANZ	2	M	CHILD		GRZZZZBAL
LUDWIG	1	M	CHILD		GRZZZZBAL
ROUSCH, THOMAS	24	M	JNR		GRZZZZBAL
KELLER, FRITZ	16	M	HTR		GRZZZZBAL
METZGER, ANNA	41	F	NN		GRZZZZBAL
CHRISTINE	18	F	NN		GRZZZZBAL
CAROLINE	7	F	CHILD		GRZZZZBAL
EMMA	5	F	CHILD		GRZZZZBAL
SKOWRONEK, EMANUEL	25	M	FARMER		GRZZZZBAL
PAULINE	28	F	W		GRZZZZBAL
MOHR, CARL	16	M	HTR		GRZZZZBAL
MARIE	18	F	NN		GRZZZZBAL
WEISE, HELENE	22	F	NN		GRZZZZBAL
KOMBER, JOHANN	17	M	CPR		GRZZZZBAL
BAER, MINNA	19	F	NN		GRZZZZBAL
LULF, HEINR.	17	M	BKBNDR		GRZZZZBAL
MUELLER, HELENE	22	F	NN		GRZZZZBAL
PRANSCHKI, FRANZ	45	M	FARMER		GRZZZZBAL
RUDOLF	17	M	FARMER		GRZZZZBAL
ROGOMANN, FRIEDA	20	F	NN		GRZZZZBAL
LIEBCHEN, AUGUST	24	M	FARMER		GRZZZZOH
STROMOSSKY, JOHANN	23	M	FARMER		GRZZZZDAK
KLIPTOFSKY, MARIANNA	18	F	NN		GRZZZZDAK
AREN, CATHA.	25	F	NN		GRZZZZIA
KLODT, HERM.	30	M	FARMER		GRZZZZIL
KRONE, CARL	39	M	FARMER		GRZZZZBAL
REICHENBERGER, KATCHEN	19	F	NN		GRZZZZIL
HENNINGER, MAT.	16	M	FUR		GRZZZZIL
HUEBNER, THERESE	20	F	NN		GRZZZZIL
KRATZ, EMMA	22	F	NN		GRZZZZIL
PRIEN, EMMA	21	F	NN		GRZZZZMI
VENGASS, MAX	25	M	GLSR		GRZZZZBAL
GROSCH, BALTHASAR	46	M	TNR		GRZZZZOH
MARTHA	22	F	NN		GRZZZZOH
KREUTZER, GEORG	46	M	STCTR		GRZZZZPA
BARBARA	40	F	W		GRZZZZPA
GEORG	.11	M	INFANT		GRZZZZPA
PETER	71	M	LABR		GRZZZZPA
DETSCH, KATHARINA	17	F	NN		GRZZZZPA
REISS, BARBARA	52	F	NN		GRZZZZPA
JOH.	18	M	CMST		GRZZZZPA
PORSCH, GEORG	21	M	CLLR		GRZZZZPA
PUTZ, MARGA.	18	F	NN		GRZZZZMI
SCHROEDEL, JOHANNES	27	M	BCHR		GRZZZZPA
MARGA.	26	F	W		GRZZZZPA
ADAM	4	M	CHILD		GRZZZZPA
NELSON, EUGEN	34	M	MCHT		GRZZZZWI
HUGE, ANNA	21	F	NN		GRZZZZOH
RUMMEL, BERTHA	29	F	NN		GRZZZZIL
SCHWEER, HEINR.	24	M	PNTR		GRZZZZWV
BARTELS, FRIEDR.	16	M	PRNTR		GRZZZZIL
FRANKE, HEINR.	17	M	LABR		GRZZZZIL
ROHRKOLX, SOPHIE	44	F	NN		GRZZZZIL
DEMINGER, JOH.	26	M	CPR		GRZZZZMI
BERG, MARG.	26	F	NN		GRZZZZMI
BARBA.	.11	F	INFANT		GRZZZZMI
WALBURGA	.11	F	INFANT		GRZZZZMI
HECHT, KATHA.	20	F	NN		GRZZZZMI
BRAFMANN, MOSES	25	M	JNR		GRZZZZBAL
WEISSENFELD, ADOLF	26	M	FARMER		GRZZZZMO
ZANDER, ERNST	21	M	HTR		GRZZZZOH
BRELICH, ANTON	26	M	PNTR		GRZZZZCAL
HARTMANN, ANT.	25	M	CL		GRZZZZCAL
HEINZ, JOSEF	31	M	TLR		GRZZZZIL
MATHILDE	25	F	NN		GRZZZZIL
LAREM, CONRAD	30	M	FARMER		GRZZZZIL
REUS, GEORG	14	M	CH		GRZZZZIL
ROIS, JULIANE	34	F	NN		GRZZZZBAL
MARIE	14	F	CH		GRZZZZBAL
JOHANN	11	M	CH		GRZZZZBAL
JOSEPH	9	M	CHILD		GRZZZZBAL
ENGELBERT	8	M	CHILD		GRZZZZBAL
LUDWIG	6	M	CHILD		GRZZZZBAL
MAX	2	M	CHILD		GRZZZZBAL
FRANZ	.09	M	INFANT		GRZZZZBAL
DEMBINSKI, MARYA	18	F	NN		GRZZZZBAL
SADOWSKI, AUG.	39	M	FARMER		GRZZZZBAL
MARIANNA	34	F	W		GRZZZZBAL
SUSANNA	4	F	CHILD		GRZZZZBAL
ANNA	2	F	CHILD		GRZZZZBAL
ALWINA	.02	F	INFANT		GRZZZZBAL
TOMKOWIAT, FRANCISCA	19	F	NN		GRZZZZBAL
GARZYNSKA, FRANCISKA	60	F	NN		GRZZZZBAL
FRANCISCA	17	F	NN		GRZZZZBAL
STASIAK, SZEZEPAN	47	M	FARMER		GRZZZZBAL
KATHARINA	37	F	W		GRZZZZBAL
FRANZ	15	M	CH		GRZZZZBAL
STANISLAV	13	M	CH		GRZZZZBAL
ROSALIA	11	F	CH		GRZZZZBAL
MARIANNA	9	F	CHILD		GRZZZZBAL
KALINA	6	F	CHILD		GRZZZZBAL
ANTON	2	M	CHILD		GRZZZZBAL
IGNATZ	.11	M	INFANT		GRZZZZBAL
ZISKOWSKI, NIKODEM	28	M	FARMER		GRZZZZBAL
KLONOWSKY, ANTON	26	M	FARMER		GRZZZZBAL
MARIA	19	F	W		GRZZZZBAL
FLORKOWSKI, FRANZ	28	M	FARMER		GRZZZZBAL
JULIANE	26	F	W		GRZZZZBAL
WLADISLAW	.01	M	INFANT		GRZZZZBAL
GRAEVENITZ, FELIX	17	M	HTR		GRZZZZBAL
DUTKIEWICZ, MARIANNA	20	F	NN		GRZZZZBAL
WITT, THERESE	19	F	NN		GRZZZZBAL
KRUEGER, HERM.	36	M	MLR		GRZZZZBAL
SCHWERT, BERTE	14	F	NN		GRZZZZBAL
LIGOWSKI, HERM.	39	M	FARMER		GRZZZZBAL
NATHALIA	34	F	W		GRZZZZBAL
HEDWIG	11	F	CH		GRZZZZBAL
FRANZ	10	M	CH		GRZZZZBAL
ROSINSKI, WOJCISCH	46	M	BKR		GRZZZZBAL
KREMARIK, JOH.	17	M	CPR		GRZZZZBAL
KARLOWA, JOSEFA	22	F	NN		GRZZZZBAL
ANTON	.08	M	INFANT		GRZZZZBAL
RAUTENBERG, JOHANNA	35	F	NN		GRZZZZBAL
LUDW.	16	M	CH		GRZZZZBAL
WILH.	10	M	CH		GRZZZZBAL
MARTHA	7	F	CHILD		GRZZZZBAL
BARBA.	4	F	CHILD		GRZZZZBAL
MARIA	3	F	CHILD		GRZZZZBAL
EMMA	.06	F	INFANT		GRZZZZBAL
ZENKIEWICZ, JOSEFA	20	F	NN		GRZZZZBAL
LINDE, MINNA	23	F	NN		GRZZZZBAL
GEYER, HERM.	18	M	DYR		GRZZZZWI
GEISEL, HEINR.	14	M	PRNTR		GRZZZZWV
KRAMER, CARL	28	M	JNR		GRZZZZIL
PAPROWSKA, AGNES	34	F	NN		GRZZZZOH
IGNATZ	9	M	CHILD		GRZZZZOH
JULIAN	7	M	CHILD		GRZZZZOH
LEON	3	M	CHILD		GRZZZZOH
JOHANNA	.09	F	INFANT		GRZZZZOH
KWIATKOWSKI, STANISL.	30	M	BRR		GRZZZZOH
KARPUS, ANDREAS	52	M	BRR		GRZZZZMI
SUSANNA	45	F	W		GRZZZZMI
WILH.	20	M	CPTR		GRZZZZMI
JOSEF	17	M	CPTR		GRZZZZMI

170

PASSENGER	AGE	SEX	OCCUPATION	PRVVLS	DES
STEFAN	11	M	CH		GRZZZZMI
FRANZ	10	M	CH		GRZZZZMI
JOHANN	7	M	CHILD		GRZZZZMI
PETER	6	M	CHILD		GRZZZZMI
MARIANNA	4	F	CHILD		GRZZZZMI
MARTHA	2	F	CHILD		GRZZZZMI
SOMMER, DAVID	15	M	FARMER		GRZZZZIL
STOCK, ESDERDINA	28	F	NN		GRZZZZIL
SCHROEDER, JOHANN	25	M	GDNR		GRZZZZKS
RAUSCH, MARGA.	24	F	NN		GRZZZZOH
KAMM, AUGUSTE	25	F	NN		GRZZZZWI
GORSKI, JOSEF	53	M	FARMER		GRZZZZKS
MARIE	39	F	W		GRZZZZKS
MARIE	15	F	CH		GRZZZZKS
FRANZ	11	M	CH		GRZZZZKS
JOSEF	10	M	CH		GRZZZZKS
VERONICA	7	F	CHILD		GRZZZZKS
JOHANN	4	M	CHILD		GRZZZZKS
ANTON	.11	M	INFANT		GRZZZZKS
SCHWERT, SOPHIE	25	F	NN		GRZZZZOH
CHUELEWSKI, JACOB	50	M	FARMER		GRZZZZIL
BERTHA	20	F	CK		GRZZZZIL
ELISE	58	F	W		GRZZZZIL
NITSCH, FRANZ	30	M	BKR		GRZZZZTX
GURSKI, JOSEPH	34	M	JNR		GRZZZZTX
KOLBE, CARL	15	M	FARMER		GRZZZZBAL
MARIA	17	F	NN		GRZZZZBAL
MEYER, OTTILIE	16	F	NN		GRZZZZBAL
ROSEBROCK, SHTR.	16	M	WVR		GRZZZZBAL
BULLER, FELIX	24	M	SMH		GRZZZZMO
BORKOWSKY, MARIE	24	F	CK		GRZZZZIL
GNENETZKY, JOHANN	34	M	FARMER		GRZZZZBAL
OLGANOWITZ, ANDREAS	27	M	CPR		GRZZZZBAL
RASCHKE, THEOVILL	28	M	BKR		GRZZZZBAL
LIPSCHITZ, ISRAEL	55	M	FARMER		GRZZZZBAL
WEFELMEYER, LOUISE	26	F	NN		GRZZZZBAL
LOSLEIN, GERH.	24	M	PNTR		GRZZZZIL
BABETTE	20	F	NN		GRZZZZIL
PIECHOKA, MARTHA	17	F	NN		GRZZZZKS
GRUENDINGER, ALOIS	16	M	FARMER		GRZZZZOH
ROSENBERGER, FRANZ	18	M	FARMER		GRZZZZKS
BLATZLE, OTTO	34	M	ENGR		GRZZZZBAL

SHIP: RHYNLAND

FROM: ANTWERP
TO: NEW YORK
ARRIVED: 21 JUNE 1888

PASSENGER	AGE	SEX	OCCUPATION	PRVVLS	DES
JANSEN, WILLY-G.	22	M	UNKNOWN		GRZZZZNY
STEFFENS, L.	39	F	PVTR		GRZZZZPHI
MERKELBACH, A.	36	F	PVTR		GRZZZZMIL
MOASSOW, R.	26	M	GCR		GRZZZZNY
GOETZ, HEINR.	17	M	UNKNOWN		GRZZZZNY
ENGERS, JOHANN	31	M	LKSH		GRZZZZNY
HABER, PAUL	36	M	UNKNOWN		GRZZZZNY
EMMA	21	F	UNKNOWN		GRZZZZNY
MANDELIUS, E.	45	F	UNKNOWN		GRAAQHNY
SCHOENHARDT, GOTTLOB	19	M	UNKNOWN		GRAAQHPVD
BUENCK, PH.	18	M	GCR		GRAAQHBET
KLEIBER, ARSEN	20	M	CMST		GRAAQHNY
STROFRONCK, EMANUEL	25	M	BCHR		GRAAQHNY
ANNA	23	F	W		GRAAQHNY
SCHUPP, ADAM	19	M	LABR		GRAAQHNY
KRAUERTZ, PETER	38	M	MACH		GRAAQHNY
HESS, CARL	19	M	TLR		GRAAQHNY
VANHULLE, JULIE	43	F	LDY		GRAAQHNY
MAIER, EVA	36	F	W		GRAHEONY
JOSEF	12	M	CH		GRAHEONY
ANNA	11	F	CH		GRAHEONY
ROMAN	10	M	CH		GRAHEONY
MARIA	7	F	CHILD		GRAHEONY
REINHARD	4	M	CHILD		GRAHEONY
SIMON	1	M	CHILD		GRAHEONY
WESS, WILH.	25	M	LABR		GRAHEOUSA
LEIPSKI, GUSTAV	26	M	LABR		GRAHEOUNK
EMILIE	20	F	W		GRAHEOUNK
MARIE	00	F	INF		GRAHEOUNK
ORGASA, HENRIETTE	13	F	CH		GRAHEOUNK
DEUZ, JOHANN	41	M	LABR		GRAHEOCH
THLEIN, JOHANN	32	M	LABR		GRAHEOCH
SECHNER, CECILIA	15	F	SVNT		GRAHEODBQ
TRAUTMAN, CHRISTIANA	22	F	SVNT		GRAHEOUNK
BABETTA	00	F	CH		GRAHEOUNK
PROSSI, VIRGINIA	30	F	SVNT		GRAHEOUNK
BOBECK, MICHAEL	23	M	LABR		GRAHEOBUF
MIMMERT, JULIUS	18	M	LABR		GRAHEOPHI
HAAS, WALPURGA	28	F	SVNT		GRAHEOIL
SCHNEIDER, WILH.	29	M	MNR		GRAHEOSCR
DROS, BABETTA	25	F	W		GRAHEONY
ELISE	2	F	CHILD		GRAHEONY
BARTHELEMY, PIERRE	28	M	LABR		GRAHEOPIT
CATH.	26	F	W		GRAHEOPIT
GERTRUDE	3	F	CHILD		GRAHEOPIT
PIERRE	2	M	CHILD		GRAHEOPIT
MICHWEL	00	M	INF		GRAHEOPIT
TISCHBACH, JOHANN	24	M	LABR		GRAHEOUNK
MUELLER, LOUIS	31	M	LABR		GRAHEOPHI
BECKER, JOHANNA	22	F	SVNT		GRAHEOCH
SCHABER, FRIED.	16	M	LABR		GRAHEOCH
BAUSCHLEICHER, CHRIST.	19	M	LABR		GRAHEOCH
SIGRIST, MEINARD	23	M	LABR		GRAHEOALT
GROSMICKLAUS, MARIA	20	F	LABR		GRAHEOPIT
MOERCH, TRAUGOTT	00	M	CL		GRAHEONY
VOEGELI, JACOB	21	M	LABR		GRAHEONY
HOERFER, SERAPHINE	44	F	W		GRAHEONY
HUBERT	16	M	CH		GRAHEONY
PAUL	10	M	CH		GRAHEONY
WERRA, ALEONIE	50	F	SVNT		GRAHEOUNK
WIELAND, GOTTL.	18	M	PNTR		GRAHEOBO
RUEDER, AUG.	23	F	SP		GRAHEOUSA
MONSHEIM, WILH.	19	M	LABR		GRAHEOUSA
NIED, MAED.	76	F	SVNT		GRAHEONY
GEIGER, RICHARD	32	M	LABR		GRAHEOCH
SZARLOTA, AND.	34	M	LABR		GRAHEOBUF
MAR.	28	F	W		GRAHEOBUF
HOSSOUN, JOH.	40	M	BKLYR		GRAHEONY
OHLIGER, AUG.	26	M	CPTR		GRAHEONY
CATH.	59	F	SVNT		GRAHEONY
EMMA	16	F	SVNT		GRAHEONY
MUELLER, LINA	16	F	SVNT		GRAHEONY
STELLWAGEN, EVA	11	F	CH		GRAHEONY
WEIDENBACH, HCH.	22	M	LABR		GRAHEOCIN
PERSON, IGNATZ	24	M	PSNT		GRAHEONY
FISCHER, REINHOLD	37	M	BTMKR		GRAHEONY
HENE, JOH.	22	M	LABR		GRAHEONY
PAUL	18	M	LABR		GRAHEONY
SCHMIDT, WM.	37	M	BKR		GRAHEONY
WERA, MINA	20	F	SVNT		GRAHEONY
FRITZ, MAGD.	38	F	W		GRAHEOBUF
VICTOR	14	M	CH		GRAHEOBUF
LAURENT	12	M	CH		GRAHEOBUF
ALPHONSE	9	M	CHILD		GRAHEOBUF
JOSEFINE	7	F	CHILD		GRAHEOBUF
VIRGINIA	5	F	CHILD		GRAHEOBUF
LEON	3	M	CHILD		GRAHEOBUF
AMBROSINE	1	F	CHILD		GRAHEOBUF
METZ, BRUNO	25	M	LABR		GRAHEONY
JOSEFA	23	F	W		GRAHEONY
GIESEN, WILH.	28	M	LABR		GRAHEOSCR
GRUBAU, JOH.	26	M	LABR		GRAHEOCH
BICKMANN, HCH.	19	M	LABR		GRAHEONY
BAUDING, AUG.	35	M	LABR		GRAHEONY
SCHERZ, LOUISE	25	F	SVNT		GRAHEONY
ULLMANN, MAX	32	M	MCHT		GRAHEONY

171

PASSENGER	AGE	SEX	OCCUPATION	PRVL	DES
TRAUT, PETER	49	M	LABR		GRAHEOCH
CHRISTINE	44	F	W		GRAHEOCH
JUL.	17	M	CH		GRAHEOCH
ELISA	13	F	CH		GRAHEOCH
OTILIA	10	F	CH		GRAHEOCH
CLEMENS	8	F	CHILD		GRAHEOCH
WAGNER, BARBA.	46	F	WI		GRAHEOCH
MATHIAS	18	M	LABR		GRAHEOCH
HCH.	10	M	CH		GRAHEOCH
JOHANN	4	M	CHILD		GRAHEOCH
PORTEN, BARBA.	25	F	SVNT		GRAHEOCH
GEISEN, ELIZABETH	19	F	SVNT		GRAHEOCH
HECK, MARIA	28	F	W		GRAHEOUSA
MARIA	4	F	CHILD		GRAHEOUSA
GERTRUD	3	F	CHILD		GRAHEOUSA
FRANZ	2	M	CHILD		GRAHEOUSA
CATHA.	00	F	INF		GRAHEOUSA
BAYER, MIC.	20	M	LABR		GRAHEOUSA
CATHA.	14	F	SVNT		GRAHEOUSA
HIRSCH, LEA	13	F	CH		GRAHEONY
LIPPKE	9	M	CHILD		GRAHEONY
BLINE	8	F	CHILD		GRAHEONY
KROMER, MARCUS	26	M	TLR		GRAHEONY
TEICHERT, FRIED.	42	M	FARMER		GRAHEOCH
PAUL	10	M	CH		GRAHEOCH
RUETER, HERM.	26	M	GLSR		GRZZZZCH
FEDERSPIEL, JEAN	42	M	FARMER		GRZZZZNLB
MARIE	32	F	W		GRZZZZNLB
MARG.	00	F	INF		GRZZZZNLB
WATGEN, PIERRE	24	M	LABR		GRZZZZUNK
MARGA.	25	F	W		GRZZZZUNK
MUELLER, JACOB	29	M	MCHT		GRZZZZNY
DORAN, WILL.	31	M	BKR		GRZZZZNY
KLEIN, JOHN	30	M	BKR		GRZZZZNY
GEORGE	27	M	BKR		GRZZZZNY
PLUM, MARTIN	27	M	BKR		GRZZZZNY
KRAUTZ, FRITZ	26	M	BKR		GRZZZZNY
STROMBACH, JUL.	30	M	LABR		GRZZZZNY
EMILIO, ANTONELLI	29	M	LABR		SRZZZZNY
PFISTER, ANNA	20	F	W		SRZZZZNY
STRESS, EUGEN	18	M	LABR		SRZZZZNY
STEECHER, BAEBETTE	19	M	LABR		SRZZZZNY
NEUBRAND, JOS.	24	M	LABR		SRZZZZNY
ROSETTE, CHRISTEN	23	M	LABR		SRZZZZNY
HILLER, JOH.	40	M	BCHR		SRZZZZNY
DAVATZ, JACOB	36	M	FARMER		SRZZZZNY
CATHE.	67	F	M		SRZZZZNY
ELSB.	37	F	W		SRZZZZNY
URSULA	29	F	SVNT		SRZZZZNY
STAUFFER, ALB.	19	M	WCHMKR		SRZZZZPIT
TOSNE, SIBOLD	22	M	LABR		SRZZZZCIN
SUETOLF, JOSEF	20	M	STWD		SRZZZZSTL
WETZEL, JACOB	27	M	CPTR		SRZZZZCOL
PELAN, FRANZ	19	M	TLR		GRZZZZNY
ZIB, ANTON	37	M	TLR		GRZZZZNY
CHALONPKA, FRZ.	27	M	LABR		GRZZZZNY
MEDLINGER, JOHANN	39	M	LABR		GRZZZZNY
CATHARINE	39	F	W		GRZZZZNY
GEORGE	11	M	CH		GRZZZZNY
MARGA.	9	F	CHILD		GRZZZZNY
JOHANNA	6	F	CHILD		GRZZZZNY
VOTRUBA, ANDR.	17	M	LABR		GRZZZZNY
PLACHY, ANNA	26	F	SVNT		GRZZZZNY
KUZERA, WENZL	34	M	MUSN		GRZZZZNY
BAUER, FRANZ	29	M	BKR		GRZZZZNY
FRANZA	28	F	W		GRZZZZNY
FRANZ	3	M	CHILD		GRZZZZNY
JOSEF	2	M	CHILD		GRZZZZNY
CATHA.	00	F	INF		GRZZZZNY
SCHUMANN, FRANZ	29	M	SHMK		GRZZZZNY
HIRSCHNER, ANTON	38	M	BKR		GRZZZZNY
WENZARA, JOSEF	30	M	HTR		GRZZZZNY
DUERR, ANNA	33	F	SVNT		GRZZZZNY
KAETCHEN	6	F	CHILD		GRZZZZNY
ZIEGLER, ELISE	25	F	SMSTS		GRZZZZNY
HELLER, THOMAS	18	M	FARMER		GRZZZZCH
LOEMPEL, DOROTHEA	24	F	SVNT		GRZZZZCH
ELIZA	18	F	SVNT		GRZZZZCH
NAUERT, PETER	27	M	LABR		GRZZZZCH
KAETH.	20	F	SVNT		GRZZZZCH
MARTIN, JOH.	37	M	LABR		GRZZZZCH
HOFER, KAETH.	21	F	SVNT		GRZZZZNY
KOEBEL, CATHE.	50	F	M		GRZZZZCIN
LUDWIG	20	M	LABR		GRZZZZCIN
RAIMOND	18	M	LABR		GRZZZZCIN
JOSEFINE	21	F	SVNT		GRZZZZCIN
ROSA	16	F	SVNT		GRZZZZCIN
MAGDALENA	13	F	SVNT		GRZZZZCIN
SZAROLOTTA, FRANZISCA	10	F	CH		GRZZZZNY
VALENTIN	8	M	CHILD		GRZZZZNY
FRANZ	3	M	CHILD		GRZZZZNY
KRAUS, ADOLF	23	M	CL		GRZZZZNY
HASOK, JOSEF	22	M	LABR		GRZZZZNY
ROTAS, CARL	18	M	CBTMKR		GRZZZZNY
KAVRIK, JOSEF	36	M	LABR		GRZZZZNY
BARBARA	36	F	W		GRZZZZNY
JOSEF	11	F	CH		GRZZZZNY
JOHANN	9	F	CHILD		GRZZZZNY
VINZENT	17	F	SVNT		GRZZZZNY
HUSTER, AUG.	35	M	SMH		GRZZZZNY
JANCOCK, JOS.	38	M	LABR		GRZZZZNY
ANNA	35	F	W		GRZZZZNY
JOSEF	15	M	CH		GRZZZZNY
MARIA	14	F	CH		GRZZZZNY
KATHA.	11	F	CH		GRZZZZNY
FRANZ	7	M	CHILD		GRZZZZNY
JOHAN	5	M	CHILD		GRZZZZNY
WENZL	6	M	CHILD		GRZZZZNY
STASTNY, MATHIAS	56	M	LABR		GRZZZZNY
ANNA	49	F	W		GRZZZZNY
MARIA	24	F	SVNT		GRZZZZNY
JOHANN	14	M	LABR		GRZZZZNY
ANTON	7	M	CHILD		GRZZZZNY
HACKMAIER, WME.	53	F	WI		GRZZZZNY
WM.	11	M	CH		GRZZZZNY
ISENSCHMIDT, IDA	14	F	CH		GRZZZZNY
GUENTHER, ADOLF	21	M	MCHT		GRZZZZNY
HENE, KAROLIC	18	F	SVNT		GRZZZZNY
ANNA	18	F	SVNT		GRZZZZNY
SCHMIDT, LUDWIG	18	M	FARMER		GRZZZZNY
GABERT, JOSEF	26	M	SHMK		GRZZZZSRB
KLEIN, PIERRE	22	M	LABR		FRZZZZNY
ETIENNE, P.	24	M	LABR		FRZZZZNY
KRAUTH, HCH.	21	M	SMH		GRZZZZNY
KNEIP, FRANZ	24	M	ENGR		GRZZZZPIT
WIDMANN, J.CH.	24	M	BCHR		GRZZZZNY
ALDINGER, GOTTL.	24	M	BKR		GRZZZZNY
LICHTENBERGER, FRIED	17	M	LABR		GRZZZZCH
EIFLER, SOPHIE	23	F	SVNT		GRZZZZNY
FEUCHT, JACOB	26	M	SMH		GRZZZZNY
KERN, JOH.	25	M	LABR		GRZZZZNY
SCHMIDT, EMMA	19	F	SVNT		GRZZZZNY
FAHNER, CHRISTINE	16	F	SVNT		GRZZZZNY
LEHN, CARL	31	M	LABR		GRZZZZNY
ANNA	28	F	W		GRZZZZNY
SUSANNA	8	F	CHILD		GRZZZZNY
GRAFFNER, MAX	29	M	FARMER		GRZZZZNY
MINE	29	F	W		GRZZZZNY
ALOIS	2	M	CHILD		GRZZZZNY
EUGHAUSEN, BARBA.	16	F	SVNT		GRZZZZNY
MUELLER, CAROLINE	20	F	SVNT		GRZZZZNY
DE-K, MARDA.	21	F	SVNT		GRZZZZNY
XAVER	17	M	TLR		GRZZZZNY
JOHAMANN, PETER	22	M	FWKR		GRZZZZNY
LENZ, JOHANNA	13	F	CH		GRZZZZNY
JOHANN	10	M	CH		GRZZZZNY
ROSA	6	F	CHILD		GRZZZZNY
TRAUETHEIM, AUG.TH.	48	M	LITGR		GRZZZZCH
SCHMIDGALL, G.	40	M	LABR		GRZZZZPEO
DRABKIN, LEWER	30	M	BKLYR		GRZZZZNY

PASSENGER	AGE	SEX	OCCUPATION	PRVL	DES
SIMON, JACOB	19	M	MCHT	GRZZZZ	STJ
SCHONBERGER, VALENTIN	34	M	LABR	GRZZZZ	NY
JENDRICK, JOH.	16	M	SHMK	GRZZZZ	NY
HACH, TH.W.	17	M	BKR	GRZZZZ	NY
BUCHBERGER, JOSEF	16	M	CL	GRZZZZ	NY
WEBER, ALOIS	28	M	LABR	GRZZZZ	NY
KIRSCHENBAUER, JOSEF	29	M	LABR	GRZZZZ	CH
JOSEF	18	M	LABR	GRZZZZ	CH
JACOB, LEONHARD	30	M	LABR	GRZZZZ	NY
LAUTENBACHER, AND.	24	M	LABR	GRZZZZ	NY
VATH, VATTINE	27	M	LABR	GRZZZZ	NY
SCHMIT, VALENTIN	26	M	BTL	GRZZZZ	OH
STELLA, CARL-PH.	19	M	MCHT	GRZZZZ	NY
WEISS, G.AD.	22	M	TRVLR	GRZZZZ	NY
VOLK, JOSEF	18	M	LABR	GRZZZZ	PHI
SCHULER, ANDR.	40	M	LABR	GRZZZZ	NY
MARGA.	41	F	W	GRZZZZ	NY
WAGNER, RICH.	3	M	CHILD	GRZZZZ	NY
HERKERT, LUCAS	16	M	CL	GRZZZZ	NY
HESSENMAUER, JACOB	18	M	BCHR	GRZZZZ	NY
RUNZ, JULIUS	18	M	NN	GRZZZZ	NY
SIEGEL, G.	22	M	NN	GRZZZZ	NY
WAGNER, JACOB	25	M	LABR	GRZZZZ	NY
GIGL, ANDREAS	24	M	LABR	GRZZZZ	NY
BACHMANN, FANNY	18	F	SVNT	GRZZZZ	NY
WASS, CAROLIE	47	F	SVNT	GRZZZZ	NY
OECHSTE, GOSWIN	19	M	STLR	GRZZZZ	NY
HAEGELE, FR.CARL	18	M	LABR	GRZZZZ	NY
HASSLER, JOHANN	51	M	LABR	GRZZZZ	NY
ANNA	51	F	W	GRZZZZ	NY
MARIA	9	F	CHILD	GRZZZZ	NY
HANG, CHRISTINE	19	F	SVNT	GRZZZZ	NY
SONSDORF, PETER	60	M	LABR	FRZZZZ	UNK
BRODMEYER, RUD.	29	M	TLR	GRZZZZ	PHI
TRATOR, CHR.	40	M	BBR	GRZZZZ	NY
ALFF, FRANZ	27	M	LABR	GRZZZZ	NY
LEIDWANGER, AUG.	60	M	LABR	GRZZZZ	NY
WELSCH, ANDR.	19	M	LABR	GRZZZZ	NY
FICHTER, IGNAZ	34	M	LABR	GRZZZZ	NY
WEISSENBACH, MIC.	45	M	PUB	GRZZZZ	NY
WILHELM, EMIL	7	M	CHILD	GRZZZZ	NY
MEIER, MAGD.	38	F	SVNT	GRZZZZ	NY
SCHAEFER, JOH.	00	M	SMH	GRZZZZ	NY
ELIENNE, ARL.	28	M	LABR	GRZZZZ	NY
FLAIN, PIETRO	30	M	LABR	GRZZZZ	UNK
TERRARI, GIORGIO	18	M	LABR	GRZZZZ	UNK
CLAUSER, DAVIDE	21	M	LABR	GRZZZZ	UNK
DELMONEGO, FELICE	36	M	NN	GRZZZZ	UNK
WELTERS, ANSON	30	M	LABR	GRZZZZ	UNK
ERPELDING, JEAN	27	M	LABR	FRZZZZ	UNK
GUTZ, MICH.	37	M	SHMK	GRZZZZ	UNK
WESSEL, LOUISE	48	F	SVNT	GRZZZZ	UNK
KARULEWSKY, SUS.	29	F	SVNT	GRZZZZ	CH
ANNA	19	F	UNKNOWN	GRZZZZ	CH
BUKOWSKA, MARIANNA	22	F	SVNT	GRZZZZ	CH
TIERRE, HCH.	19	M	LABR	GRZZZZ	CH
BURCKEL, NICOL	28	M	MCHT	GRZZZZ	NY
MARTIN, HERM.	50	M	LABR	GRZZZZ	NY
STRENZKI, L.	25	M	LABR	GRZZZZ	CH
WALTER, JACOB	00	M	FARMER	GRZZZZ	SY
ALDMAN, JOSEPH	32	M	FARMER	GRZZZZ	NY

SHIP: ROMAN

FROM: LIVERPOOL AND LONDON
TO: BOSTON
ARRIVED: 21 JUNE 1888

PASSENGER	AGE	SEX	OCCUPATION	PRVL	DES
KENGIES, ANDRES	23	M	LABR	GRZZZZ	NY

PASSENGER	AGE	SEX	OCCUPATION	PRVL	DES

SHIP: STATE OF INDIANA

FROM: GLASGOW AND LARNE
TO: NEW YORK
ARRIVED: 22 JUNE 1888

PASSENGER	AGE	SEX	OCCUPATION	PRVL	DES
WILDERMANN, ISAAC	22	M	PDLR	GRZZZZ	USA
ROHRLOK, MOSES	19	M	PDLR	GRZZZZ	USA
GOLDSTEIN, -OSCKE	28	M	LABR	GRZZZZ	USA
LAPSODES, ZABEL	15	M	LABR	GRZZZZ	USA
WENZSKOWSKY, ALBERT	20	M	LABR	GRZZZZ	USA
RESS, HIRSCH	17	M	LABR	GRZZZZ	USA
JEZOWITZ, NIPOCHUTZ	30	M	LABR	GRZZZZ	USA
CHOROWITSCH, PIOK	30	M	LABR	GRZZZZ	USA
SCHARFS, MEYER	24	M	LABR	GRZZZZ	USA
WEINGART, SUFFE	24	M	LABR	GRZZZZ	USA
HERMANN, MARDUCH	28	M	PDLR	GRZZZZ	USA
LEMUSCH, SCHEIE	30	M	LABR	GRZZZZ	USA
HATNICK, ITSCHAK	23	M	PDLR	GRZZZZ	USA
JISKONE, DAVID	23	M	LABR	GRZZZZ	USA
SALTZMANN, LIPPE	44	M	PDLR	GRZZZZ	USA
LURSKY, ABRAHAM	20	M	PDLR	GRZZZZ	USA
NASCHATTER, MOSES	25	M	PDLR	GRZZZZ	USA
GOTTFRIED, LEIB	23	M	PDLR	GRZZZZ	USA
BULKEVICH, ALX.	23	M	PDLR	GRZZZZ	USA
STEINLAUF, PIMUS	16	M	LABR	GRZZZZ	USA
WINCKWE, MEIER	43	M	PDLR	GRZZZZ	USA
UDES, JECHIEL	23	M	LABR	GRZZZZ	USA
LIPSCHKY, SALOMON	33	M	LABR	GRZZZZ	USA
SACHS, ISIDOR	22	M	PDLR	GRZZZZ	USA
DOBBER, GERHARD	27	M	PDLR	GRZZZZ	USA
KERIL, MOSES	36	M	LABR	GRZZZZ	USA
SARAH	34	F	W	GRZZZZ	USA
TIEBE	18	F	DMS	GRZZZZ	USA
SAMUEL	11	M	CH	GRZZZZ	USA
BLUME	8	M	CHILD	GRZZZZ	USA
MALE	6	F	CHILD	GRZZZZ	USA
SCHEINE	1	M	CHILD	GRZZZZ	USA
GOLDBERG, MENUSKE	35	F	W	GRZZZZ	USA
SARAH	9	F	CHILD	GRZZZZ	USA
HINDE	8	F	CHILD	GRZZZZ	USA
SLATE	1	F	CHILD	GRZZZZ	USA
AUERBACH, RIWCKE	36	F	W	GRZZZZ	USA
MARENS	11	F	CH	GRZZZZ	USA
JACOB	8	M	CHILD	GRZZZZ	USA
APPELBAUM, JOSEPH	24	M	LABR	GRZZZZ	USA
LEAH	21	F	W	GRZZZZ	USA
SCHONBERG, RIWKE	60	F	DMS	GRZZZZ	USA
RAPPEPORT, SALMEN	30	M	CPTR	GRZZZZ	USA
ESTHER	30	F	W	GRZZZZ	USA
PERCEL	5	M	CHILD	GRZZZZ	USA
POTE	1	F	CHILD	GRZZZZ	USA
RESVIK, KNOSIEL	20	F	DMS	GRZZZZ	USA
LEIBE	19	F	DMS	GRZZZZ	USA
WILKE, HEIGE	19	F	DMS	GRZZZZ	USA
ADLER, CHAIE	16	F	DMS	GRZZZZ	USA
CONRS, HANNE	22	F	DMS	GRZZZZ	USA
MEISEL, SARAH	20	F	DMS	GRZZZZ	USA
CANTOR, ROSALIE	20	F	DMS	GRZZZZ	USA
PASNER, ANNA	20	F	DMS	GRZZZZ	USA
SARAH	22	F	DMS	GRZZZZ	USA
ROBIN, ROCHE-C.	44	M	DMS	GRZZZZ	USA
PEREL	17	M	DMS	GRZZZZ	USA
LURIN, LEID	19	M	DMS	GRZZZZ	USA
FRIEDMANN, REGI	18	F	DMS	GRZZZZ	USA

PASSENGER	AGE	SEX	OCCUPATION	PRVL	DES

SHIP: TRAVE

FROM: BREMEN AND SOUTHAMPTON
TO: NEW YORK
ARRIVED: 22 JUNE 1888

PASSENGER	AGE	SEX	OCCUPATION	PRVL	DES
MENSING, CPT.	41	F	MCHT	GRZZZZ	USA
U	15	F	UNKNOWN	GRZZZZ	USA
ELFRIEDE	4	F	CHILD	GRZZZZ	USA
ALICE	2	F	CHILD	GRZZZZ	USA
KRUEGER, MINNA	25	F	MCHT	GRZZZZ	USA
V. BLOCH	38	M	MCHT	GRZZZZ	USA
KAISER, HELENE	36	F	MCHT	GRZZZZ	USA
EMIL	4	M	CHILD	GRZZZZ	USA
KEMMLER, NANETTE	23	F	MCHT	GRZZZZ	USA
FRUEDLAENDER, ROSA	25	F	MCHT	GRZZZZ	USA
SCHAECHOW, OSER	68	M	MCHT	GRZZZZ	USA
BRANDT, MATH	22	F	MCHT	GRZZZZ	USA
RANK, HERM	30	M	BCHR	GRZZZZ	USA
AUST, PETER	78	M	MCHT	GRZZZZ	USA
STERNBAUER, THERESE	28	F	MCHT	GRZZZZ	USA
KRAMER, LUDWIG	16	M	FARMER	GRZZZZ	USA
MUNTER, CLARA	22	F	FARMER	GRZZZZ	USA
RIECKE, HEINRICH	31	M	MCHT	GRZZZZ	USA
WENZEL, PAUL	40	M	MCHT	GRZZZZ	USA
IDA	30	F	UNKNOWN	GRZZZZ	USA
KOCK, CHR	24	M	MCHT	GRZZZZ	USA
ECKSTEIN, NATHAN	15	M	MCHT	GRZZZZ	USA
OESTREICHER, BERTHA	20	F	MCHT	GRZZZZ	USA
HAENIGHAUSEN, ANNA	18	F	UNKNOWN	GRZZZZ	USA
HAASE, LIPKE	65	M	UNKNOWN	GRZZZZ	USA
WIENS, ERNST	25	M	FARMER	GRZZZZ	USA
TRAUER, GEORG	23	M	MCHT	GRZZZZ	USA
THIEME, CARL	27	M	MCHT	GRZZZZ	USA
HEINZE, HEINRICH	30	M	MCHT	GRZZZZ	USA
ALINE	25	F	UNKNOWN	GRZZZZ	USA
RETTBERG, LOUISE	30	F	UNKNOWN	GRZZZZ	USA
SIMONN, MART	15	M	LABR	GRZZZZ	USA
GUTMANN, NICOL	16	M	LABR	GRZZZZ	USA
VORNDRAN, ADELE	27	M	LABR	GRZZZZ	USA
SEUZLEIN, CARL	17	M	LABR	GRZZZZ	USA
MIETSCHIN, SCHAUN	35	M	LABR	GRZZZZ	USA
BAUSEWEIN, JOHANN	15	M	LABR	GRZZZZ	USA
SAUBER, LISETTE	16	F	UNKNOWN	GRZZZZ	USA
KOPP, HANS	15	M	FARMER	GRZZZZ	USA
SVOBODA, MATEJ	23	M	TNM	GRZZZZ	USA
ARENSTEIN, JUL	19	M	FARMER	GRZZZZ	USA
MUELLER, JELLY	19	F	UNKNOWN	GRZZZZ	USA
PETRORIUS, GEO	15	M	LABR	GRZZZZ	USA
EGGERS, JOHANN	45	M	FARMER	GRZZZZ	USA
SAWATZKI, FRANZISCA	22	F	UNKNOWN	GRZZZZ	USA
ROST, MARIE	17	F	UNKNOWN	GRZZZZ	USA
WIRSTEK, ANNA	29	F	UNKNOWN	GRZZZZ	USA
DAERFLER, AD	75	M	FARMER	GRZZZZ	USA
FRIEDR	46	M	FARMER	GRZZZZ	USA
JAESERICH, CLARA	20	F	UNKNOWN	GRZZZZ	USA
SCHMIDT, HEINRICH	14	M	UNKNOWN	GRZZZZ	USA
WIESER, JOSEF	20	M	LABR	GRZZZZ	USA
MAYER, LORENZ	18	M	LABR	GRZZZZ	USA
FELLER, CARL	24	M	LABR	GRZZZZ	USA
WEBER, CHARLOTTE	24	F	UNKNOWN	GRZZZZ	USA
DAPPE, U	45	F	UNKNOWN	GRZZZZ	USA
DOPPE, JOHANN	17	M	FARMER	GRZZZZ	USA
KLINGENBIEL, EDUARD	31	M	FARMER	GRZZZZ	USA
WEYHAUSEN, DIEDRICH	14	M	FARMER	GRZZZZ	USA
THOMSEN, JOERGEN	22	M	FARMER	GRZZZZ	USA
PULS, CATHRIN	21	F	FARMER	GRZZZZ	USA
BOEGE, CLAUS	23	M	LABR	GRZZZZ	USA
KUEHL, CATHARINA	17	F	UNKNOWN	GRZZZZ	USA
SALAMON, MARIA	24	F	UNKNOWN	GRZZZZ	USA
BREMER, MARIA	20	F	UNKNOWN	GRZZZZ	USA
BETZ, CATH	18	F	UNKNOWN	GRZZZZ	USA
NEUMEISTER, JACOB	16	M	LABR	GRZZZZ	USA
MUELLER, REINH	18	M	LABR	GRZZZZ	USA
HERMANN, GOTTLIEB	23	M	LABR	GRZZZZ	USA
SCHUELER, WILHELM	20	M	LABR	GRZZZZ	USA
ALBERT	16	M	LABR	GRZZZZ	USA
FISCHER, JACOB	30	M	LABR	GRZZZZ	USA
HERNIG, WILHELM	28	M	LABR	GRZZZZ	USA
CHARLOTTE	25	F	UNKNOWN	GRZZZZ	USA
ERNST	.04	M	INFANT	GRZZZZ	USA
RAICHEN, LENCHEN	43	F	UNKNOWN	GRZZZZ	USA
HOFFMANN, CHRIST	15	F	UNKNOWN	GRZZZZ	USA
LOUISE	6	F	CHILD	GRZZZZ	USA
ROESSEL, CASPAR	18	M	LABR	GRZZZZ	USA
SCHAEFER, JOH	25	M	LABR	GRZZZZ	USA
BAMBERGER, ADOLF	16	M	LABR	GRZZZZ	USA
JUBELT, MAX	20	M	LABR	GRZZZZ	USA
AIBLE, BLASIUS	56	M	LABR	GRZZZZ	USA
SCHAEFER, JOH	42	M	LABR	GRZZZZ	USA
CHRISTINA	53	M	LABR	GRZZZZ	USA
UEBELE, SOH	16	M	LABR	GRZZZZ	USA
SCHAEFER, HERMANN	7	M	CHILD	GRZZZZ	USA
BARZ, CLARA	21	F	UNKNOWN	GRZZZZ	USA
SCHREIBER, WILH	25	M	FARMER	GRZZZZ	USA
GOTTLIEB	23	M	MLR	GRZZZZ	USA
HIRSCH, ADOLF	16	M	BCHR	GRZZZZ	USA
TRAUTWEIN, JOH	26	M	BCHR	GRZZZZ	USA
KAMP, WILH	71	F	UNKNOWN	GRZZZZ	USA
CLARA	.11	F	INFANT	GRZZZZ	USA
CERNOWSKI, PAULINE	42	F	UNKNOWN	GRZZZZ	USA
RICHARD	7	M	CHILD	GRZZZZ	USA
MARGARETHE	6	F	CHILD	GRZZZZ	USA
PAUL	5	M	CHILD	GRZZZZ	USA
WILLY	4	M	CHILD	GRZZZZ	USA
HERZING, FRIEDRICH	40	M	FARMER	GRZZZZ	USA
WAGNER, MINNA	19	F	UNKNOWN	GRZZZZ	USA
SCHWORM, ELISE	23	F	UNKNOWN	GRZZZZ	USA
MUEHLEISEN, CASPAR	27	M	LABR	GRZZZZ	USA
DANGLMAYER, JOS	18	M	LABR	GRZZZZ	USA
LUECKE, MARIA	6	F	CHILD	GRZZZZ	USA
BENDER, LENE	17	M	LABR	GRZZZZ	USA
WACHTER, LINA	17	F	UNKNOWN	GRZZZZ	USA
SCHULER, CATH	15	F	UNKNOWN	GRZZZZ	USA
BECKENBACH, ELISA	18	F	UNKNOWN	GRZZZZ	USA
STADELMANN, EMMA	20	F	UNKNOWN	GRZZZZ	USA
OBERBERGFELL, ROBERT	37	M	FARMER	GRZZZZ	USA
MARTHA	37	F	FARMER	GRZZZZ	USA
RICHARD	7	M	CHILD	GRZZZZ	USA
JOSEF	6	M	CHILD	GRZZZZ	USA
REGINA	5	F	CHILD	GRZZZZ	USA
ALFRED	3	M	CHILD	GRZZZZ	USA
BALDAUF, WILH	45	M	FARMER	GRZZZZ	USA
GERHARD	14	M	FARMER	GRZZZZ	USA
SEIFERT, OSCAR	22	M	LABR	GRZZZZ	USA
MOENCH, M	56	F	UNKNOWN	GRZZZZ	USA
MOWWE, GEORG	15	M	UNKNOWN	GRZZZZ	USA
SCHULZ, FRIEDR	20	M	LABR	GRZZZZ	USA
PIERNER, WILHELM	26	M	LABR	GRZZZZ	USA
BERTHA	17	F	UNKNOWN	GRZZZZ	USA
KNAPP, MARIE	22	F	UNKNOWN	GRZZZZ	USA
HOLZINGER, ANNA	16	F	UNKNOWN	GRZZZZ	USA
VOGLER, OTTILIE	45	F	UNKNOWN	GRZZZZ	USA
ADAM	16	M	LABR	GRZZZZ	USA
ANTON	23	M	LABR	GRZZZZ	USA
WOLFERMANN, ROSA	25	F	UNKNOWN	GRZZZZ	USA
SPITZNAGEL, JOSEPH	20	M	FARMER	GRZZZZ	USA
BARB	19	F	UNKNOWN	GRZZZZ	USA
SCHMIDT, GEORG	18	M	SMH	GRZZZZ	USA
KNAPP, PHILIPP	66	M	TLR	GRZZZZ	USA
OPEL, JOHN	31	M	LABR	GRZZZZ	USA
LUDOLPH, GESINE	19	F	UNKNOWN	GRZZZZ	USA
HAEBER, WILHELM	41	M	LABR	GRZZZZ	USA
MAX	7	M	CHILD	GRZZZZ	USA
SCHEFER, HEINRICH	27	M	FARMER	GRZZZZ	USA
ELISE	3	F	CHILD	GRZZZZ	USA
SCHULZ, BERTHA	25	F	FARMER	GRZZZZ	USA
HANDSCHUHMACHER, EMMA	18	F	UNKNOWN	GRZZZZ	USA
SCHUMACHER, CONRAD	23	M	LABR	GRZZZZ	USA

PASSENGER	AGE	SEX	OCCUPATION	PRVL	DES	PASSENGER	AGE	SEX	OCCUPATION	PRVL	DES
OBERMEYER, U	26	F	UNKNOWN	GRZZZZ	USA	CAROLINE	16	F	UNKNOWN	GRZZZZ	USA
WEINDEL, CATH	20	F	UNKNOWN	GRZZZZ	USA	CONRAD	7	M	CHILD	GRZZZZ	USA
OTT, CATH	29	F	UNKNOWN	GRZZZZ	USA	CATH	4	F	CHILD	GRZZZZ	USA
HEIDIG, MARTIN	16	M	TNM	GRZZZZ	USA	MARIE	6	F	CHILD	GRZZZZ	USA
SEEFELD, ANNA	29	F	UNKNOWN	GRZZZZ	USA	JOSEPH	5	M	CHILD	GRZZZZ	USA
SCHOMACKER, DREWES	33	M	CPTR	GRZZZZ	USA	MATHAEUS	4	M	CHILD	GRZZZZ	USA
ARING, ANNA	16	F	UNKNOWN	GRZZZZ	USA	CARL	3	M	CHILD	GRZZZZ	USA
JAEGER, JOSEF	17	M	FARMER	GRZZZZ	USA	HERMANN, MATHAŁUS	14	F	UNKNOWN	GRZZZZ	USA
DRUCER, BERTHA	17	F	UNKNOWN	GRZZZZ	USA	THOMAS, MICH	42	F	FARMER	GRZZZZ	USA
BERRETH, GEORG	49	M	LABR	GRZZZZ	USA	LORENZ	50	M	FARMER	GRZZZZ	USA
FREYBLER, SOPHIE	19	F	UNKNOWN	GRZZZZ	USA	RETTENMAIER, ALOIS	16	M	FARMER	GRZZZZ	USA
GROSSKURTH, REINH	16	M	LABR	GRZZZZ	USA	SCHNEIDER, WILH	17	M	FARMER	GRZZZZ	USA
FROEGER, ADAM	25	M	LABR	GRZZZZ	USA	F	17	M	FARMER	GRZZZZ	USA
SCHMIDT, HEINRICH	26	M	LABR	GRZZZZ	USA	MEIER, HEINR	19	M	FARMER	GRZZZZ	USA
FLESSA, HEINRICH	37	M	LABR	GRZZZZ	USA	HESS, ROBERT	19	M	FARMER	GRZZZZ	USA
GROWITZKI, MICHAEL	34	M	LABR	GRZZZZ	USA	NAUMDOUF, AD	27	M	FARMER	GRZZZZ	USA
SCHMIDT, MARTHA	26	F	UNKNOWN	GRZZZZ	USA	LINA	27	F	UNKNOWN	GRZZZZ	USA
STRITT, MARTHA	16	F	UNKNOWN	GRZZZZ	USA	WETTENGEL, CLARA	32	F	UNKNOWN	GRZZZZ	USA
HULLER, JOSEF	17	M	LABR	GRZZZZ	USA	RUSS, ALFRED	17	M	LABR	GRZZZZ	USA
SCHNEEWEIS, JUSTIN	18	M	LABR	GRZZZZ	USA	FRICKIN, JOH	19	F	UNKNOWN	GRZZZZ	USA
ROSER, ANTON	56	M	FARMER	GRZZZZ	USA	MUEHLENBRUCH, J	17	M	LABR	GRZZZZ	USA
BRANDT, ELSE	22	F	UNKNOWN	GRZZZZ	USA	BRANEL, AUG	27	M	LABR	GRZZZZ	USA
COORESEN, AD	22	F	UNKNOWN	GRZZZZ	USA	WERSEBE, ANTON	29	M	LABR	GRZZZZ	USA
GUTSLAR, LAURA	30	F	UNKNOWN	GRZZZZ	USA	WINTERS, MARTIN	15	M	LABR	GRZZZZ	USA
LENE	7	F	CHILD	GRZZZZ	USA	WILHELM	15	M	LABR	GRZZZZ	USA
MARIE	4	F	CHILD	GRZZZZ	USA	TISCHLER, MARG	30	F	UNKNOWN	GRZZZZ	USA
FORSTENBACH, PHILIPP	39	M	FARMER	GRZZZZ	USA	ALFRED	4	M	CHILD	GRZZZZ	USA
EMMA	37	F	UNKNOWN	GRZZZZ	USA	MOTHA	.11	F	INFANT	GRZZZZ	USA
IDA	15	F	UNKNOWN	GRZZZZ	USA	RADULSKY, DAVID	49	M	FARMER	GRZZZZ	USA
CARL	6	M	CHILD	GRZZZZ	USA	VEITH, CARL	38	M	FARMER	GRZZZZ	USA
HERMANN	5	M	CHILD	GRZZZZ	USA	LINA	28	F	UNKNOWN	GRZZZZ	USA
EMMA	7	F	CHILD	GRZZZZ	USA	CARL	7	M	CHILD	GRZZZZ	USA
LENZ, H	16	M	CL	GRZZZZ	USA	LINA	6	F	CHILD	GRZZZZ	USA
BRAUN, CARL	37	M	LABR	GRZZZZ	USA	AMALIE	4	F	CHILD	GRZZZZ	USA
KAESTNER, WILH	23	M	LABR	GRZZZZ	USA	REINHOLD	3	M	CHILD	GRZZZZ	USA
BAETZ, FRIEDR	16	M	LABR	GRZZZZ	USA	RUDOLF	.05	M	INFANT	GRZZZZ	USA
MAYR, PAUL	36	M	LABR	GRZZZZ	USA	BRAUN, EMILIE	62	F	UNKNOWN	GRZZZZ	USA
THERESE	38	F	UNKNOWN	GRZZZZ	USA	HUEG, F	15	M	UNKNOWN	GRZZZZ	USA
STORCH, CARL	52	M	FARMER	GRZZZZ	USA	BECKER, AUGUST	31	M	FARMER	GRZZZZ	USA
RICH	26	M	FARMER	GRZZZZ	USA	MECKER, ELISE	22	F	UNKNOWN	GRZZZZ	USA
MATH	14	F	UNKNOWN	GRZZZZ	USA	ELISE	16	F	UNKNOWN	GRZZZZ	USA
MINNA	7	F	CHILD	GRZZZZ	USA	WALDECK, SIEGFRIED	16	M	BKR	GRZZZZ	USA
KLEPPE, HEINRICH	41	M	FARMER	GRZZZZ	USA	JUNKER, FRIEDRICH	14	M	BKR	GRZZZZ	USA
ANNA	33	F	UNKNOWN	GRZZZZ	USA	THEISEN, CATH	20	F	UNKNOWN	GRZZZZ	USA
WILHELM	6	M	CHILD	GRZZZZ	USA	JUNKER, ELISABETH	16	F	UNKNOWN	GRZZZZ	USA
CARL	5	M	CHILD	GRZZZZ	USA	RIEGEL, MARG	45	F	UNKNOWN	GRZZZZ	USA
ELISE	7	F	CHILD	GRZZZZ	USA	HERDER, EMMA	18	F	UNKNOWN	GRZZZZ	USA
CHRIST	4	M	CHILD	GRZZZZ	USA	HARTH, AUG	16	M	BBR	GRZZZZ	USA
CATH	3	F	CHILD	GRZZZZ	USA	HAUBERT, PETER	15	M	FARMER	GRZZZZ	USA
MINNA	.06	F	INFANT	GRZZZZ	USA	VOELLINGER, JOS	25	M	FARMER	GRZZZZ	USA
ROSENBROCK, WILH	26	M	LABR	GRZZZZ	USA	ROTHSCHILD, LEOPOLD	22	M	FARMER	GRZZZZ	USA
PUTENJAK, LANZEM	27	M	LABR	GRZZZZ	USA	MORITZ, JOHANNA	18	F	UNKNOWN	GRZZZZ	USA
AGNES	24	F	UNKNOWN	GRZZZZ	USA	MEERING, JOHANN	31	M	FARMER	GRZZZZ	USA
GEORG	4	M	CHILD	GRZZZZ	USA	MARIA	28	F	UNKNOWN	GRZZZZ	USA
CATH	2	F	CHILD	GRZZZZ	USA	ELVIRA	4	F	CHILD	GRZZZZ	USA
APOLONIA	.06	F	INFANT	GRZZZZ	USA	MARTHA	.03	F	INFANT	GRZZZZ	USA
DOHRA, CHRIST	33	M	LABR	GRZZZZ	USA	BAUER, FR	23	M	FARMER	GRZZZZ	USA
SZWAK, FRANZ	48	M	LABR	GRZZZZ	USA	CAROL	21	F	UNKNOWN	GRZZZZ	USA
CATH	42	F	UNKNOWN	GRZZZZ	USA	SIEGERT, JUL	44	M	LABR	GRZZZZ	USA
MARIA	17	F	UNKNOWN	GRZZZZ	USA	FRIEDKE	38	F	UNKNOWN	GRZZZZ	USA
ANTON	13	M	UNKNOWN	GRZZZZ	USA	MATH	.10	F	INFANT	GRZZZZ	USA
MARTHA	6	F	CHILD	GRZZZZ	USA	BUETTNER, JOH	27	M	LABR	GRZZZZ	USA
PETER	4	M	CHILD	GRZZZZ	USA	TROEBS, JOH	22	M	LABR	GRZZZZ	USA
SCHOELZEL, PAUL	15	M	CL	GRZZZZ	USA	DIECKMANN, HERM	16	M	LABR	GRZZZZ	USA
LANG, LINA	49	F	UNKNOWN	GRZZZZ	USA	WOHLERS, AUG	25	M	LABR	GRZZZZ	USA
HEINZ, FRIEDKE	16	M	UNKNOWN	GRZZZZ	USA	WILHELM	16	M	LABR	GRZZZZ	USA
SCHAEFER, FR	47	M	FARMER	GRZZZZ	USA	KERSCHINSKY, HENRIETTE	24	F	UNKNOWN	GRZZZZ	USA
ELISAB	37	F	UNKNOWN	GRZZZZ	USA	MATHA	3	F	CHILD	GRZZZZ	USA
FRIEDRICH	7	M	CHILD	GRZZZZ	USA	BRUNO	.10	M	INFANT	GRZZZZ	USA
MARGARETH	4	F	CHILD	GRZZZZ	USA	MORITZ, H	17	M	BKR	GRZZZZ	USA
MARIA	3	F	CHILD	GRZZZZ	USA	MOHR, ANNA	3	F	CHILD	GRZZZZ	USA
BARZWEDA	2	F	CHILD	GRZZZZ	USA	IDA	.10	F	INFANT	GRZZZZ	USA
LIDIA	.03	F	INFANT	GRZZZZ	USA	WAFFERT, CARL	6	M	CHILD	GRZZZZ	USA
SEIBOLD, JOH	30	M	CPTR	GRZZZZ	USA	CONRAD, PH	23	M	FARMER	GRZZZZ	USA
BAUER, ROSINE	46	F	UNKNOWN	GRZZZZ	USA	ILLUWITZ, ISER	19	M	FARMER	GRZZZZ	USA

PASSENGER	AGE	SEX	OCCUPATION	PRVL	DES
PESE	19	M	FARMER	GRZZZZ	USA
ZEYELNITZKI, ISRAEL	18	M	LABR	GRZZZZ	USA
WOLACH, ABRAHAM	30	M	LABR	GRZZZZ	USA
SMARKOWITZ, DWORA	18	M	LABR	GRZZZZ	USA
UFTRING, ANDRAS	29	M	LABR	GRZZZZ	USA
ZARN, MARGARETHE	25	F	UNKNOWN	GRZZZZ	USA
KESSLER, GERTRUD	70	F	UNKNOWN	GRZZZZ	USA
SCHAEFER, GEORG	41	M	FARMER	GRZZZZ	USA
KOCH, LOUISE	21	F	UNKNOWN	GRZZZZ	USA
CHRONEGK, HUFRATH	45	M	MCHT	GRZZZZ	USA
FITZGERALD, JAS	26	M	LABR	GRZZZZ	USA
MAYER, CHRIST	31	M	LABR	GRZZZZ	USA
MARIE	27	F	UNKNOWN	GRZZZZ	USA
ERNST	6	M	CHILD	GRZZZZ	USA
SCHMUETTER, THEOPH	30	M	LABR	GRZZZZ	USA
RANK, MARIE	26	F	UNKNOWN	GRZZZZ	USA
FEIL, GUSTAV	35	M	LABR	GRZZZZ	USA
NICOLAS, PERE	48	M	LABR	GRZZZZ	USA

SHIP: CITY OF CHICAGO

FROM: LIVERPOOL AND QUEENSTOWN
TO: NEW YORK
ARRIVED: 23 JUNE 1888

PASSENGER	AGE	SEX	OCCUPATION	PRVL	DES
BLANK, GOLDE	20	F	SP	GRACBF	NY
RUBENSTEIN, ANNILH	19	F	SP	GRACBF	NY
EPSTEIN, SCHASSE	28	F	SP	GRACBF	NY
BEILE	26	F	W	GRACBF	NY
CHAIE	6	F	CHILD	GRACBF	NY
SCHER	00	M	INF	GRACBF	NY
LUKENTHAL, ZILINE	39	F	W	GRACBF	NY
THEKLA	11	F	CH	GRACBF	NY
LIDE	9	F	CHILD	GRACBF	NY
ANA	7	M	CHILD	GRACBF	NY
HANNA	3	F	CHILD	GRACBF	NY
ZUTTEN, MARIANA	45	F	W	GRACBF	NY
CHESSKE	6	F	CHILD	GRACBF	NY
PESCHE	3	F	CHILD	GRACBF	NY
LANGS, HANS	30	M	PDLR	GRACBF	NY
ANNA	22	F	W	GRACBF	NY
DORA	00	F	INF	GRACBF	NY
KNUSS, U	34	F	W	GRADBQ	NY
ADELA	3	F	CHILD	GRADBQ	NY

SHIP: ALASKA

FROM: LIVERPOOL AND QUEENSTOWN
TO: NEW YORK
ARRIVED: 25 JUNE 1888

PASSENGER	AGE	SEX	OCCUPATION	PRVL	DES
ROSENWIEG, GEORGE	25	M	LABR	GRZZZZ	USA
BERTHA	22	F	SP	GRZZZZ	USA
IRODTZOCH, ALB.	30	M	BKPR	GRZZZZ	USA
JANVISKY, JAN	37	M	LABR	PRZZZZ	USA
PAULINA	23	F	W	PRZZZZ	USA
FRANZ	.10	M	INFANT	PRZZZZ	USA
SAPKOWSKY, JAN	28	M	LABR	PRZZZZ	USA
OHVEZARZIEK, SZEPON	23	M	LABR	GRZZZZ	USA
STYPEREK, WOJSEEK	30	M	LABR	PRZZZZ	USA
BLUMBERG, JANKEL	18	M	GZR	GRZZZZ	USA
JACOBS, HENRY	50	M	MRNR	GRZZZZ	USA

SHIP: AURANIA

FROM: LIVERPOOL AND QUEENSTOWN
TO: NEW YORK
ARRIVED: 25 JUNE 1888

PASSENGER	AGE	SEX	OCCUPATION	PRVL	DES
LANKUITIS, TERZY	27	M	LABR	GRZZZZ	NY
ALEX-D.	19	M	LABR	GRZZZZ	NY
PAMAELS, PAUL	18	M	LABR	GRZZZZ	NY
KANTFELH, HENRY	28	M	LABR	GRZZZZ	NY
BEYER, ADOLF	26	M	LABR	GRZZZZ	NY
SCHLOLUT, ALBERT	35	M	LABR	GRZZZZ	NY
RUBINOWESKY, MEIR	30	M	LABR	GRZZZZ	NY
SUHOLIS, STANISLAW	22	M	LABR	GRZZZZ	NY
JASDOWSKY, BRONISLAW	28	M	LABR	GRZZZZ	NY
JENSEN, CHRISTIAN	23	M	LABR	GRZZZZ	NY
WEGENER, AUGUST	44	M	LABR	GRZZZZ	NY
U-MRS	39	F	W	GRZZZZ	NY
THERESA	12	F	CH	GRZZZZ	NY
AUGUST	11	M	CH	GRZZZZ	NY
WILHELM	9	M	CHILD	GRZZZZ	NY
MARIE	5	F	CHILD	GRZZZZ	NY
CARL	3	M	CHILD	GRZZZZ	NY
GARGUN, M.	47	M	MKR	SRZZZZ	ATR
EBUSCHMEILER, CHAS.	46	M	CLGYMN	GRZZZZ	ATR
GRENDT, CHAS.	40	M	GENT	FRZZZZ	ATR

SHIP: BOHEMIA

FROM: HAMBURG AND HAVRE
TO: NEW YORK
ARRIVED: 25 JUNE 1888

PASSENGER	AGE	SEX	OCCUPATION	PRVL	DES
KUNTZE, MAX	21	M	LABR	FRAAKH	IL
KIELMA, ANDRZY	63	M	LABR	PRZZZZ	IL
MATGURZATA	55	F	LABR	PRZZZZ	IL
KLEIN, MARIE	32	F	WO	PRZZZZ	IL
FRANZISKA	9	F	CHILD	PRZZZZ	IL
SOFIE	8	F	CHILD	PRZZZZ	IL
BERTHA	7	F	CHILD	PRZZZZ	IL
VONNORDHEIM, EMILIE	17	F	UNKNOWN	PRZZZZ	IL
GROBIEN, CATHA.	40	F	WO	PRABMD	IL
MARTHA	21	F	SGL	PRABMD	IL
BANDER, LINE	20	F	SGL	PRZZZZ	IL
KATZ, TAUBE	20	F	SGL	PRZZZZ	IL
WINGBERG, HELENE	18	F	UNKNOWN	PRAAVGUN	K
GELLERT, HENRIETTE	64	F	WO	PRACTQ	IL
GROTH, SOPHIE	43	F	WO	PRACON	IL
WILLY	13	M	CH	PRACON	IL
ANNA	9	F	CHILD	PRACON	IL
FRIEDR.	8	M	CHILD	PRACON	IL
WELLER, ADAM	33	M	PNTR	PRACBK	IL
KUNIGUNDE	34	F	W	PRACBK	IL
MARGULINER, MORITZ	18	M	LABR	PRAEAB	NY
MUELLER, LUDWIG	63	M	LABR	PRZZZZ	NY
ELISABETH	29	F	W	PRZZZZ	NY
MARIE	15	F	CH	PRZZZZ	NY
POBURSKI, ANTONIE	20	M	TLR	PRACWT	NY
MARTEN, AUGUST	39	M	LABR	PRZZZZ	NY
HENRIETTE	38	F	W	PRZZZZ	NY
ALBERT	9	M	CHILD	PRZZZZ	NY
LINE	8	F	CHILD	PRZZZZ	NY
FRITZ	7	M	CHILD	PRZZZZ	NY
OTTO	3	M	CHILD	PRZZZZ	NY
MINNA	.06	F	INFANT	PRZZZZ	NY
WEBER, GEORG	16	M	SHMK	PRAAYY	NY
MEYER, CHR.	39	M	SLR	PRZZZZ	NY
HAUTH, AUG.	14	M	MCHT	PRAGGF	NY
WAHLERS, HEINR.	44	M	LABR	PRZZZZ	NY

PASSENGER	AGE	SEX	OCCUPATION	PRIVL	DES
VALENTIN, JOH.	28	M	FARMER		PRZZZZIL
ANNA	27	F	W		PRZZZZIL
MARIE	4	F	CHILD		PRZZZZIL
FRIEDR.	2	M	CHILD		PRZZZZIL
ERNST	.11	M	INFANT		PRZZZZIL
GRANDT, ANNA	63	F	WO		PRZZZZIL
BUNKHOLZ, ANTON	39	M	ACHTT		PRAARRNY
ELLI	28	F	W		PRAARRNY
ELIMAR	.10	M	INFANT		PRAARRNY
JACOBS, DIRK	16	M	FARMER		PRAITOUNK
LEMPERTZ, ALBERT	17	M	MCHT		PRAIDOUNK
GREGERSEN, HEINR.	22	M	CL		PRACPANE
LUDA, AUG.	38	M	SDLR		PRZZZZNE
CAROLE.	18	F	W		PRZZZZNE
GEMBITZKA, MARIE	26	F	WO		PRAEABNE
HERM.	3	M	CHILD		PRAEABNE
SELMA	2	F	CHILD		PRAEABNE
BIANKA	.11	F	INFANT		PRAEABNE
JARAISEWER, HEDWIG	18	F	SGL		PRACTQUNK
TRAUSCHKE, CARL	68	M	LABR		PRABVEUNK
ALTMANN	49	F	W		PRABVEUNK
ALFRED	19	M	CH		PRABVEUNK
EMMA	18	F	CH		PRABVEUNK
PAASCH, OTTO	28	M	JNR		PRAAQYUNK
FEDRAHN, MARIE	66	F	WO		PRAADEUNK
TROBS, ALBERT	26	M	WHR		PRZZZZNY
DINA	22	F	W		PRZZZZNY
STEFFEN, ANNA	21	F	SGL		PRZZZZIL
SIMONSEN, CHRISTE.	59	M	FARMER		PRZZZZIL
CLAUSEN, KATHA.	15	F	SGL		PRAGSRIL
HANSEN, ANNA	46	F	WO		PRAGSRIL
MARGR.	.07	F	INFANT		PRAGSRIL
GIERLOFF, WILH.	42	M	FARMER		PRADDZIL
LINE	39	F	W		PRADDZIL
EMMA	18	F	CH		PRADDZIL
WILHE.	16	F	CH		PRADDZIL
LOUISE	9	F	CHILD		PRADDZIL
MINE	8	F	CHILD		PRADDZIL
DORIS	6	F	CHILD		PRADDZIL
FUHRMEISTER, HERM.	31	M	LLD		WMZZZZOH
JENSEN, JACOB	47	M	LABR		WMABNSOH
LENE	47	F	W		WMABNSOH
CAROLE.	13	F	CH		WMABNSOH
FROST, RUD.	50	M	ACHTT		WMACSDOH
RUDOLF, MAX	17	M	ENGR		WMAAFTNY
GOMMEL, AUGUST	27	M	FARMER		WMZZZZNE
HAMMERSCHMIDT, SUSANNA	23	F	SGL		PRZZZZPA
BETZ, JOH.	17	M	FARMER		BVZZZZNN
SOHNMACHER, CATHA.	48	F	WO		BVACQOMN
CATHA.	7	F	CHILD		BVACQOMN
PFUNDHELLER, OTTO	29	M	MLR		BVAFAQMN
DRAWS, HELENE	25	F	SGL		BVADYDMI
NEUMANN, NATHAN	16	M	LABR		BVACPSNY
FRIESE, LOUIS	16	F	WO		BVABDMNY
WAETJE, CARSTEN	36	M	FARMER		BVADGHNY
ANNA	37	F	W		BVADGHNY
MARGA.	8	F	CHILD		BVADGHNY
JOH.	7	M	CHILD		BVADGHNY
ELISE	5	F	CHILD		BVADGHNY
HEINRICH	3	M	CHILD		BVADGHNY
MARTHA	.11	F	INFANT		BVADGHNY
CARL	.01	M	INFANT		BVADGHNY
HAASE, M.	60	M	TDR		BVALZNPA
GRIEBE, WIEBLE	21	F	SGL		BVAHIOPA
BRANDT, MARGA.	8	F	CHILD		BVAHIOPA
PIOTROFSKI, JOS.	40	M	LABR		PRZZZZUNK
DOROTHEA	41	F	W		PRZZZZUNK
FRANCISKA	5	F	CHILD		PRZZZZUNK
DUMIN, CATHA.	22	F	WO		PRZZZZUNK
JOH.	7	M	CHILD		PRZZZZUNK
WOLFGANG	69	M	LABR		PRZZZZUNK
SCHLEYMER, MINNA	18	F	WO		PRZZZZUNK
MEGGERS, CHRISTINE	22	F	WO		PRZZZZIA
MACHOT, HENRIETTE	19	F	WO		PRAJJPIA
MARIE	22	F	WO		PRAJJPIA
RANK, JOH.	15	M	LABR		BVZZZZIA
CHROPLEWSKI, ERNESTINE	30	M	LABR		BVAIHYNE
SCHERNER, VILENE	27	F	W		PRZZZZIL
PETER	7	M	CHILD		PRZZZZIL
ELFRIEDE	2	F	CHILD		PRZZZZIL
WILHE.	16	F	SGL		PRZZZZIL
DRIESEN, MARTHA	13	F	SGL		PRZZZZNY
KOELN, BERTHA	18	F	SGL		PRZZZZNY
THOMSON, PETER	28	M	SHMK		PRZZZZNE
CATHA.	22	F	W		PRZZZZNE
THOMAS	.11	M	INFANT		PRZZZZNE
BRAACK, JOH.	23	M	FARMER		PRZZZZIA
MAGNUSSEN, HANS	27	M	BKR		PRZZZZIA
CHRISTENSEN, CHR.	26	M	FARMER		PRZZZZIA
HICK, WILH.	22	M	MCHT		PRAGTSNE
SELIG, ERNESTINE	21	F	SGL		PRZZZZCAL
LEEFT, KIWE	69	F	WO		PRABNOGA
DYCK, RUDOLF	22	M	BKR		PRAAKHNY
BOETTCHER, CARL	46	M	CPTR		PRAAKHNY
BLUMBERG, HERM.	26	M	LABR		PRZZZZIL
ENGEL, CARL	33	M	LABR		PRACEOWI
MATHILDE	23	F	W		PRACEOWI
KRAJEWSKI, MARTIN	45	M	FARMER		PRZZZZPA
BUDZIN, IGNATZ	33	M	LABR		PRZZZZPA
MATYSIAK, LUDWIG	22	M	LABR		PRZZZZPA
WEIDNER, ANNA	28	F	W		PRZZZZNY
GERTRUD	3	F	CHILD		PRZZZZNY
PINKUS, DORA	20	F	SGL		PRAFRBIL
LEHMANN, BERTHA	22	F	SGL		PRAFRBIL
SCHAUB, FRED.	48	M	LABR		BDZZZZOH
SUSA.	47	F	W		BDZZZZOH
DAWETZ, ANNA	27	F	SGL		BDAAYSNY
FRANZENBURG, GEORG	14	M	STDNT		BDAESDNY
OHLSEN, MATTS	35	M	SLR		PRZZZZUNK
ECKERT, PAULINE	20	F	SGL		WMZZZZIL
PAULE.	42	F	SGL		WMAGPOIL
UMNUS, FRIDR.	29	M	FARMER		WMALYMIA
MARIE	21	F	W		WMALYMIA
PAUL	.07	M	INFANT		WMALYMIA
TESCH, WILH.	24	M	FARMER		WMALYMWI
MACHOL, JENNY	24	F	SGL		WMACXVNY
GOTTLIEB, SAMUEL	15	M	MCHT		WMAAKHNY
ZEGELNITZKY, ISAAC	33	M	LABR		WMAKUQIA
RIVKE	20	F	W		WMAKUQIA
SARAH	.07	F	INFANT		WMAKUQIA
BOLARAJE, JOHN	28	M	LABR		PRZZZZIA
MAZULSKI, VINCENTY	33	M	LABR		PRZZZZPA
DOMBROSKI, ADOLF	21	M	LABR		PRZZZZPA
IWANOFF, SARNELLI	19	M	LABR		PRZZZZPA
NOVIKOFF, AMEFIEL	23	M	LABR		PRZZZZPA
MISUKEWITZ, BERNAT	27	M	LABR		PRZZZZPA
MARIANNE	20	F	W		PRZZZZPA
JEANOVITS, BOLESLAW	22	M	LABR		PRZZZZPA
IGNATOVITS, JOS.	31	M	LABR		PRZZZZPA
OWARDYCKI, BARTOLOMAUS	22	M	LABR		PRZZZZPA
KATZ, MARCUS	36	M	BCHR		PRAGRTPA
LIPPE	9	M	CHILD		PRAGRTPA
SWENDIMANN, ROSINE	22	F	SGL		PRAAKJPA
STIEGLER, FRANZ	32	M	SGL		PRAAGLNY
FRANZ	4	M	CHILD		PRAAGLNY
SCHELL, CARL	27	M	CH		PRAAGLNY
EMIL	25	M	CH		PRAAGLNY
OBERT, ANNA	21	F	SGL		PRAAGLNY
OBERGFOELL, LINA	20	F	SGL		PRAAGLNY
SCHLEGEL, JOH.	29	M	LABR		PRAAGLNY
RUHE, LOUISE	24	F	SGL		PRAAGLOH
ZIEGEBOT, JOHANN	24	M	LABR		GRZZZZOH
WOLF, EMIL	30	M	LABR		GRAANGOH
HUGENEL, WILHELM	40	M	LABR		GRAANGOH
MORITZ, FREUND	36	M	LABR		GRADLDOH
FREUND, MINNA	26	F	SGL		GRADLDOH
SCHOELLER, LORENZ	32	M	LABR		GRZZZZIL
WEISS, THERESE	20	F	SGL		GRZZZZIL
SCHMEIKENBERGER, L.	27	M	LABR		GRZZZZIL
VOLZ, MARIA	27	F	WO		GRZZZZIL

PASSENGER	AGE	SEX	OCCUPATION	PRVL	DES
GENOVEVA	17	F	SGL	GRZZZZIL	
FUCHS, JEAN	33	M	LABR	GRAAHUIA	
GROSSENBACHER, ERNST	20	M	LABR	GRAAKJIA	
HAUS	20	M	LABR	GRAAKJIA	
BORELLI, PIETRO	35	M	LABR	SRZZZZIA	
WIPF, HERMANN	39	M	LABR	SRAAHUIA	
JOSEPH, MARTE	24	M	LABR	SRZZZZIA	
AMMAN, IDA	21	F	SGL	SRZZZZIA	
RENOGLI, LOUISE	22	F	SGL	SRZZZZIA	
GEISSER, JOHANN	40	M	LABR	SRAAKJIA	
ELISABETH	38	F	W	SRAAKJIA	
EUSEBERON	16	M	CH	SRAAKJIA	
MARIA	9	F	CHILD	SRAAKJIA	
LINA	7	F	CHILD	SRAAKJIA	
HERMINE	4	F	CHILD	SRAAKJIA	
RUDOLPH	.06	M	INFANT	SRAAKJIA	
BECKERMANN, FRANZ	19	M	LABR	SRAAGLIA	
STUDI, AUGUSTE	20	M	LABR	SRZZZZIA	
WAGNER, LOUIS	30	M	LABR	SRADQLIA	
BERTOSI, JOSEPH	42	M	LABR	SRZZZZIA	
DOGE, SAMUEL	34	M	LABR	SRZZZZIA	
BONA, RINSINI	36	M	LABR	SRZZZZIA	
HOFNER, LOUISE	24	F	SGL	SRZZZZIA	
BACHOFNER, MARIE	27	F	SGL	SRAAHUOH	
MARIE	5	F	CHILD	SRAAHUOH	
ELMILIE	3	F	CHILD	SRAAHUOH	
MONTUBE, LOUIS	30	M	LABR	FRZZZZMI	
SALADIN, ALOIS	22	M	FARMER	SRZZZZIL	

SHIP: SLAVONIA

FROM: SWINEMUNDE
TO: NEW YORK
ARRIVED: 25 JUNE 1888

PASSENGER	AGE	SEX	OCCUPATION	PRVL	DES
NEUMANN, BERTHA	18	F	UNKNOWN	PRZZZZUSA	
ANNA	17	F	UNKNOWN	PRZZZZUSA	
GEHRICKE, AUGUSTE	72	F	WO	PRZZZZUSA	
KOEJYRE, MARIE	40	F	WO	PRZZZZUSA	
BRAUN, AUGST	40	M	LABR	PRABWAUSA	
ANNA	25	F	W	PRABWAUSA	
MARIE	8	F	CHILD	PRABWAUSA	
RICHARD	.03	M	INFANT	PRABWAUSA	
GEHRICKE, PAULINE	36	F	D	PRAEWMUSA	
KEIDKE, JOHANN	36	M	LABR	PRZZZZUSA	
URSULA	28	F	W	PRZZZZUSA	
STANISLAUS	4	M	CHILD	PRZZZZUSA	
JOSEPH	3	M	CHILD	PRZZZZUSA	
CAECILIE	1	F	CHILD	PRZZZZUSA	
BREWKA, MICHAEL	25	M	LABR	PRAHUZUSA	
GALSTER, AUGUSTE	26	F	SVNT	PRAHUZUSA	
WILDE, ERNST	31	M	MSN	PRADESUSA	
EILHELMINE	31	F	W	PRADESUSA	
HEINRICH	2	M	CHILD	PRADESUSA	
BLIESATH, JOHANN	30	M	LABR	PRAHUCUSA	
MARIE	29	F	W	PRAHUCUSA	
TESCH, MATHILDE	23	F	SVNT	PRZZZZUSA	
IGNASIAK, LUSAS	25	M	LABR	PRZZZZUSA	
NEUMANN, JULIUS	33	M	MSN	PRADESUSA	
LOUISE	33	F	W	PRADESUSA	
NOHRING, FRIEDERIKE	68	F	WI	PRADESUSA	
NEUMANN, EMILIE	11	F	CH	PRADESUSA	
WILHELMINE	8	F	CHILD	PRADESUSA	
ANNA	6	F	CHILD	PRADESUSA	
FRANZ	4	M	CHILD	PRADESUSA	
MATHILDE	2	F	CHILD	PRADESUSA	
SADOWSKY, AUGUSTE	43	F	WO	PRZZZZUSA	
OTTO	12	M	CH	PRZZZZUSA	
ADOLPH	9	M	CHILD	PRZZZZUSA	
GUSTAV	6	M	CHILD	PRZZZZUSA	
EMMA	4	F	CHILD	PRZZZZUSA	
GYDERIAN, EMILIE	18	F	UNKNOWN	PRZZZZUSA	
THIESS, ANNA	17	F	UNKNOWN	PRZZZZUSA	
MOUDRA, MARTIN	40	M	LABR	PRZZZZUSA	
CATHARINA	27	F	W	PRZZZZUSA	
HAUSCH, JOHANN	38	M	LABR	PRZZZZUSA	
MOUDRA, MARYANNA	6	F	CHILD	PRZZZZUSA	
THOMAS	4	M	CHILD	PRZZZZUSA	
STASIA	.03	F	INFANT	PRZZZZUSA	
CARMESIN, WILHELM	38	M	SLR	PRZZZZUSA	
WILHELMINE	29	F	W	PRZZZZUSA	
EMMA	6	F	CHILD	PRZZZZUSA	
EUGEN	2	M	CHILD	PRZZZZUSA	
WILLY	1	M	CHILD	PRZZZZUSA	
MARTHA	.01	F	INFANT	PRZZZZUSA	
GOETZ, WILHELMINE	32	F	WO	PRZZZZUSA	
PAUL	8	M	CHILD	PRZZZZUSA	
ROBERT	3	M	CHILD	PRZZZZUSA	
PUTZER, OTTILIE	22	F	UNKNOWN	PRZZZZUSA	
KAZIK, WILHELM	36	M	BLKSMH	PRZZZZUSA	
AUGUSTE	35	F	W	PRZZZZUSA	
EMIL	9	M	CHILD	PRZZZZUSA	
FRIEDRICH	5	M	CHILD	PRZZZZUSA	
ALFRED	2	M	CHILD	PRZZZZUSA	
BUKOFYNSKI, LUISA	17	F	SVNT	PRZZZZUSA	
PETER	16	M	B	PRZZZZUSA	
WESCHKE, ANNA	18	F	UNKNOWN	PRZZZZUSA	
SIMON, EVA	20	F	UNKNOWN	PRZZZZUSA	
TANDT, WILHELMINE	19	F	UNKNOWN	PRZZZZUSA	
KLATTE, PAUL	26	M	UNKNOWN	PRAAKHUSA	
MARIE	31	F	W	PRAAKHUSA	
EMMA	10	F	CH	PRAAKHUSA	
ALBERT	7	M	CHILD	PRAAKHUSA	
KROHN, JOHANN	62	M	LABR	PRAFVMUSA	
CHRISTINE	60	F	W	PRAFVMUSA	
CARL	24	M	LABR	PRAFVMUSA	
FRIEDRICH	22	M	CH	PRAFVMUSA	
BERTHA	19	F	CH	PRAFVMUSA	
SPYCHALSKY, FRANZISOCK	33	M	LABR	PRZZZZUSA	
SUSANNE	30	F	W	PRZZZZUSA	
IGNATZ	6	M	CHILD	PRZZZZUSA	
VICTORIA	4	F	CHILD	PRZZZZUSA	
FRANCZISCECK	2	M	CHILD	PRZZZZUSA	
WEDLOWSKY, JOHANN	24	M	BKR	PRZZZZUSA	
KALFF, MARIA	25	F	SVNT	PRZZZZUSA	
BRYLLA, PAUL	32	M	LABR	PRZZZZUSA	
MARIA	29	F	W	PRZZZZUSA	
MARIA	27	F	S	PRZZZZUSA	
SCHULZ, AUGUSTE	16	F	SVNT	PRZZZZUSA	
HULDA	9	F	CHILD	PRZZZZUSA	
RHODE, JOSEPH	27	M	LABR	PRADEQUSA	
AUGUSTE	24	F	W	PRADEQUSA	
WILHELM	3	M	CHILD	PRADEQUSA	
GUSTAV	.11	M	INFANT	PRADEQUSA	
CHRISTIAN	63	M	LABR	PRADEQUSA	
THERESE	57	F	W	PRADEQUSA	
MARIA	11	F	CH	PRADEQUSA	
BICKHOLZ, ALBERTINE	37	F	WO	PRZZZZUSA	
MATHILDE	14	F	CH	PRZZZZUSA	
AUGUST	10	M	CH	PRZZZZUSA	
ANNA	4	F	CHILD	PRZZZZUSA	
LEHMANN, LOUISE	18	F	UNKNOWN	PRZZZZUSA	
TYBARCYK, MICHAEL	39	M	LABR	PRZZZZUSA	
VALERIA	36	F	W	PRZZZZUSA	
JADWIGE	18	F	CH	PRZZZZUSA	
MAROINA	11	F	CH	PRZZZZUSA	
ADAM	9	M	CHILD	PRZZZZUSA	
JULIE	7	F	CHILD	PRZZZZUSA	
ANNA	5	F	CHILD	PRZZZZUSA	
VICTORIA	4	F	CHILD	PRZZZZUSA	
ANGELIA	2	F	CHILD	PRZZZZUSA	
MARIANNA	.10	F	INFANT	PRZZZZUSA	
BURO, GUSTAV	16	M	LABR	PRZZZZUSA	
CZAJKA, MICHELINE	24	F	SVNT	PRZZZZUSA	
SISICKI, JACOB	30	M	CPTR	PRZZZZUSA	

PASSENGER	AGE	SEX	OCCUPATION	PRVVL DES
EBERT, FRIEDRICH	53	M	LABR	PRZZZZUSA
BEISTER, OTTILIE	24	F	D	PRZZZZUSA
ALBERT	1	M	CHILD	PRZZZZUSA
WUESKE, CAROLINE	63	F	WI	PRZZZZUSA
BERTHA	30	F	D	PRZZZZUSA
WILLKOMM, FRIEDRICH	28	M	MSN	PRAIGJUSA
MARIA	24	F	W	PRAIGJUSA
MARIA	.07	F	INFANT	PRAIGJUNK
KANFINS, FLORENTINE	39	F	WO	PRAAKHUNK
HERMANN	19	M	CH	PRAAKHUNK
ANNA	18	F	CH	PRAAKHUNK
ARNOLD	17	M	CH	PRAAKHUNK
KAMRETH, AUGUST	24	M	LABR	PRZZZZUNK
ZOCH, JOHANNA	22	F	SVNT	PRABGIUNK
KRUGER, CARL	25	M	FARMER	PRAECNUNK
RUDUSCHEWSKY, EDUARD	38	M	CPTR	PRAEZVUNK
KOSCHSCHMIEDER, HEINRIC	51	M	LABR	PRZZZZUNK
KOSCHSCHMIEDER, CHRISTI	42	F	W	PRZZZZUNK
KOSCHSCHMIEDER, NERMANN	18	M	CH	PRZZZZUNK
ANNA	18	F	CH	PRZZZZUNK
HEINRICH	16	M	CH	PRZZZZUNK
ANNA	5	F	CHILD	PRZZZZUNK
WILHELM	3	M	CHILD	PRZZZZUNK
EMMA	1	F	CHILD	PRZZZZUNK
TOBST, ANTON	33	M	DSTLR	BVZZZZUNK
JESCHKE, JOHANN	58	M	SHFM	BVAGMLUNK
KUEHL, EMIL	27	M	LABR	BVAGDRUNK
JOHANNA	30	F	W	BVAGDRUNK
BERTHA	4	F	CHILD	BVAGDRUNK
HULDA	1	F	CHILD	BVAGDRUNK
STEINACKER, PAULINE	44	F	WO	PRZZZZUNK
AMANDA	12	F	CH	PRZZZZUNK
FRITZ	10	M	CH	PRZZZZUNK
CHILMANSKA, MARIANNA	43	F	WO	PRACYOUNK
ANASTASIA	11	F	CH	PRACYOUNK
ROSALIE	9	F	CHILD	PRACYOUNK
WINDZINSKY, MAROIN	41	M	LABR	PRZZZZUNK
CATHARINE	32	F	W	PRZZZZUNK
JOSEPH	12	M	CH	PRZZZZUNK
STANISLAUS	3	M	CHILD	PRZZZZUNK
WILHELM	.03	M	INFANT	PRZZZZUNK
SCHOELLNER, AGNES	15	F	UNKNOWN	PRAGDHUNK
WINDZINSKY, ANTONIA	6	F	CHILD	PRZZZZUNK
SCHOELLNER, U	15	F	CH	PRZZZZUNK
HANS	12	M	CH	PRZZZZUNK
JULIUS	9	M	CHILD	PRZZZZUNK
PAUL	6	M	CHILD	PRZZZZUNK
FISCHER, ALBERTINE	28	F	UNKNOWN	PRZZZZUNK
HELENE	2	F	CHILD	PRZZZZUNK
ZANOW, WILHELMINE	20	F	SVNT	PRAIXTUNK
CARL	2	M	CHILD	PRAIXTUNK
KINDT, ELWINE	49	F	LDY	PRZZZZUNK
ELSE	14	F	CH	PRZZZZUNK
GEORG	9	M	CHILD	PRZZZZUNK
KROLL, MARIA	38	F	WO	PRAEQUUNK
LORENZ	12	M	CH	PRAEQUUNK
ROBERT	9	M	CHILD	PRAEQUUNK
DIX, ALBERT	30	M	LABR	PRZZZZUNK
ANTONIE	28	F	W	PRZZZZUNK
JOHANN	5	M	CHILD	PRZZZZUNK
EVA	3	F	CHILD	PRZZZZUNK
JOSEPH	2	M	CHILD	PRZZZZUNK
DALLI, HULDA	21	F	UNKNOWN	PRZZZZUNK
MARTHA	17	F	UNKNOWN	PRZZZZUNK
HANS, BERTHA	25	F	W	PRAECNUNK
WALTHER	4	M	CHILD	PRAECNUNK
HEINRICH	32	M	MUSN	PRAECNUNK
OTTO	3	M	CHILD	PRAECNUNK
PAUL	.09	M	INFANT	PRAECNUNK
JESCHKE, WILHELMINE	53	F	WO	PRAGMLUNK
AUGUST	16	M	CH	PRAGMLUNK
ERNESTINE	13	F	CH	PRAGMLUNK
JAEDICKE, MARIE	25	F	UNKNOWN	PRAAKHUNK
RUDIES, MINNA	50	F	UNKNOWN	PRZZZZUNK
MARQUARDT, FRIEDERIKE	32	F	WO	PRZZZZUNK
JOHANNES	10	M	CH	PRZZZZUNK
FRIEDRICH	8	M	CHILD	PRZZZZUNK
ALBERTINE	1	F	CHILD	PRZZZZUNK
BAHR, EILISABETH	64	F	WO	PRAEWZUNK
BOHNENSTENGEL, MARIE	22	F	UNKNOWN	PRAEWZUNK
JANZ, CAROLINE	37	F	WO	PRAKSAUNK
FRANZ	10	M	CH	PRAKSAUNK
BERTHA	8	F	CHILD	PRAKSAUNK
STEFFENHAGEN, FRANZ	39	M	LABR	PRADLSUNK
EMILIE	39	F	W	PRADLSUNK
HEDWIG	9	F	CHILD	PRADLSUNK
GEORG	7	M	CHILD	PRADLSUNK
FRANZ	4	M	CHILD	PRADLSUNK
MARTHA	.01	F	INFANT	PRADLSUNK
SCHMIDT, CARL	31	M	LABR	PRZZZZUNK
EMILIE	27	F	W	PRZZZZUNK
ANNA	3	F	CHILD	PRZZZZUNK
OTTO	.06	M	INFANT	PRZZZZUNK
BINDEMANN, ERNESTINE	65	F	WO	PRAEWZUNK
DALL, MARTHA	16	F	UNKNOWN	PRAEWZUNK
SUMOSKY, JOHANN	49	M	CPTR	PRAAZQUNK
CAROLINE	40	F	W	PRAAZQUNK
PAUL	2	M	CHILD	PRAAZQUNK
SPINANSKY, JOHANN	17	M	LABR	PRZZZZUNK
RUTKOWSKA, MICHELINA	38	F	WO	PRAEZVUNK
EDUARD	7	M	CHILD	PRAEZVUNK
BOLESLAW	7	M	CHILD	PRAEZVUNK
RADEMACHER, ANNA	18	F	UNKNOWN	PRZZZZUNK
MARIE	16	F	UNKNOWN	PRZZZZUNK
KERMANSKY, JOSEPHA	38	F	WO	PRZZZZUNK
MARYANNA	10	F	CH	PRZZZZUNK
VERONICA	9	F	CHILD	PRZZZZUNK
WLADISLAW	9	M	CHILD	PRZZZZUNK
FELIX	5	M	CHILD	PRZZZZUNK
KAROWSKY, PAUL	19	M	LABR	PRAFFYUNK
TITZE, ADOLPH	18	M	BLKSMH	PRZZZZUNK
JPIESCHKE, JOHANNA	20	F	UNKNOWN	PRAAKHUNK
EMMA	.06	F	INFANT	PRAAKHUNK
KUBALL, CARL	39	M	LABR	PRAIWJUNK
AUGUSTE	31	F	W	PRAIWJUNK
GUSTAV	8	M	CHILD	PRAIWJUNK
FRANZ	7	M	CHILD	PRAIWJUNK
WILHELM	3	M	CHILD	PRAIWJUNK
MARTHA	.09	F	INFANT	PRAIWJUNK
MAVIJEWSKY, FRANC	26	M	LABR	PRZZZZUNK
GRZYBOWSKY, MAROIN	28	M	LABR	PRZZZZUNK
SPITULSKY, VALENTIN	45	M	SHFM	PRZZZZUNK
REGINA	42	F	W	PRZZZZUNK
MARIANNE	11	F	CH	PRZZZZUNK
KRUMREY, HERMANN	57	M	LABR	PRZZZZUNK
HENRIETTE	53	F	W	PRZZZZUNK
IDA	20	F	CH	PRZZZZUNK
GUSTAV	17	M	CH	PRZZZZUNK
FRANZ	17	M	CH	PRZZZZUNK
HERMINE	10	F	CH	PRZZZZUNK
RINKE, HEINRICH	21	M	JNR	PRAAKHUNK
BEIER, AUGUST	17	M	LABR	PRZZZZUNK
GLOWACKY, ANTON	43	M	LABR	PRZZZZUNK
MARIANNA	33	F	W	PRZZZZUNK
MICHAEL	12	M	CH	PRZZZZUNK
STANISLAUS	9	M	CHILD	PRZZZZUNK
VICTORIA	4	F	CHILD	PRZZZZUNK
MARIANNA	66	F	M	PRZZZZUNK
NICKEL, AUGUST	29	M	MSN	PRZZZZUNK
ANNA	29	F	W	PRZZZZUNK
OTTO	.07	M	INFANT	PRZZZZUNK
LUCK, WILHELM	16	M	LABR	PRZZZZUNK
HENRIETTE	76	F	WI	PRZZZZUNK
LEWANDOWSKA, CATHARINA	30	F	WO	PRZZZZUNK
WANDA	10	F	CH	PRZZZZUNK
SCHULZ, LUDWIG	57	M	SHFM	PRZZZZUNK
CHRISTINE	54	F	W	PRZZZZUNK
AUGUSTE	18	F	CH	PRZZZZUNK
FERDINAND	16	M	CH	PRZZZZUNK
WILHELMINE	13	F	CH	PRZZZZUNK

PASSENGER	AGE	SEX	OCCUPATION	PRVL	DES
EBELT, CARL	28	M	LABR	PRAIAJUNK	
MARIA	24	F	W	PRAIAJUNK	
MARIA	.06	F	INFANT	PRAIAJUNK	
FLORIAN, PAUL	23	M	MCHT	PRACSDUNK	
GOSTKOWSKY, MICHAEL	31	M	BCHR	PRZZZZUNK	
PAULINE	29	F	W	PRZZZZUNK	
FRANZ	4	M	CHILD	PRZZZZUNK	
HELENE	2	F	CHILD	PRZZZZUNK	
AL-CHONS	1	M	CHILD	PRZZZZUNK	
BRIGILSKY, ANNA	54	F	WO	PRZZZZUNK	
JULIE	10	F	CH	PRZZZZUNK	
LADRACH, EDUARD	44	M	LABR	PRZZZZUNK	
FRIEDERIKE	37	F	W	PRZZZZUNK	
ANNA	16	F	CH	PRZZZZUNK	
ELISABETH	6	F	CHILD	PRZZZZUNK	
MARIA	1	F	CHILD	PRZZZZUNK	
HINZ, JOHANN	22	M	LABR	PRZZZZUNK	
FRANZISKA	18	F	W	PRZZZZUNK	
HUBNER, CARL	46	M	FARMER	PRAAZQUNK	
MARTHA	14	F	CH	PRAAZQUNK	
JANKOWSKA, MARIANNA	50	F	WO	PRZZZZUNK	
ZAHLMANN, LUDWIG	24	M	LABR	PRZZZZUNK	
BERTHA	30	F	W	PRZZZZUNK	
RUDOLPH	4	M	CHILD	PRZZZZUNK	
GUSTAV	2	M	CHILD	PRZZZZUNK	
GUDAT, ERDMUTE	38	F	WO	PRZZZZUNK	
ANNA	7	F	CHILD	PRZZZZUNK	
GONDRAS, JOHANN	23	M	LABR	PRZZZZUNK	
SCHLEITER, META	19	F	UNKNOWN	PRZZZZUNK	
RUCKERT, ALBERT	23	M	LABR	PRZZZZUNK	
TOEFFLINGER, OSWALD	24	M	LABR	PRZZZZUNK	
MARIE	34	F	W	PRZZZZUNK	
KLAUS, ANNA	36	F	WO	PRZZZZUNK	
ADAM, AUGUSTE	20	F	UNKNOWN	PRAGDSUNK	
ANNA	10	F	S	PRAGDSUNK	
BAESTE, THEODOR	40	M	LKSH	PRAFWIUNK	
KAZUBOWSKY, MATHIAS	28	M	LABR	PRZZZZUNK	
TAUBE, WILHELM	48	M	FARMER	PRAAKHUNK	
MARIE	49	F	W	PRAAKHUNK	
BERTHA	20	F	CH	PRAAKHUNK	
GUSTAV	18	M	CH	PRAAKHUNK	
KUHLMANN, CARL	25	M	JNR	PRAAKHUNK	
WILLY	9	M	CHILD	PRAAKHUNK	
HINRICHSEN, ANNA	37	F	SVNT	PRAAKHUNK	
GOHLKE, IDA	21	F	SVNT	PRAAKHUNK	
MARCUS, MARTIN	20	M	GDSM	PRAAKHUNK	
KAISER, JOSEPHINE	57	F	WO	PRABWOUNK	
THEODOR	23	M	THR	PRABWOUNK	
DREWCK, IGNATZ	16	M	LABR	PRZZZZUNK	
REIMER, DANIEL	53	M	LKSH	PRZZZZUNK	
HETZ, ROBERT	24	M	SHFM	PRZZZZUNK	
BORCHARDT, FRANZ	16	M	LABR	PRAEMAUNK	
BOTTIN, ALBERTINE	27	F	UNKNOWN	PRZZZZUNK	
PUFAHL, AUGUSTE	23	F	UNKNOWN	PRZZZZUNK	
SCHNEIDER, HUGO	14	M	BY	PRZZZZUNK	
KLEIN, F.G.	24	M	BLKSMH	PRZZZZUNK	
RUTZ, CARL	30	M	CL	PRALMPUNK	
THERESE	26	F	W	PRALMPUNK	
SZAIKA, ANDREI	33	M	LABR	PRZZZZUNK	
MARTIN, OTTO	40	M	FARMER	PRAAKHUNK	
BERNEKER, FERDINAND	36	M	TU	PRAIIYUNK	
MORGENSTERN, BENNO	12	M	BY	PRZZZZUNK	
RESKE, AMALIE	23	F	SVNT	PRZZZZUNK	
SCHWEICHERT, WALDEMAR	28	M	CL	PRAAKHUNK	
GRABOWSKY, MARIE	28	F	WO	PRZZZZUNK	
IDA	4	F	CHILD	PRZZZZUNK	
MARTHA	2	F	CHILD	PRZZZZUNK	
ZUHL, ALBERT	23	M	LABR	PRZZZZUNK	
WILL, BERTHA	35	F	WO	PRZZZZUNK	
GOTTFRIED	10	M	CH	PRZZZZUNK	
MARGARETHE	9	F	CHILD	PRZZZZUNK	
WILHELM	7	M	CHILD	PRZZZZUNK	
CARL	.06	M	INFANT	PRZZZZUNK	

SHIP: TAORMINA

FROM: HAMBURG
TO: NEW YORK
ARRIVED: 25 JUNE 1888

PASSENGER	AGE	SEX	OCCUPATION	PRVL	DES
ALBRECHT, WILH.	34	M	UNKNOWN	PRZZZZNY	
WILHELMINE	37	F	UNKNOWN	PRZZZZNY	
FRANZ	15	M	CH	PRZZZZNY	
EMILIE	13	F	CH	PRZZZZNY	
AUGUSTE	7	F	CHILD	PRZZZZNY	
BERTHA	5	F	CHILD	PRZZZZNY	
GERTH, MARIANNA	28	F	W	PRZZZZNY	
MATHILDE	5	F	CHILD	PRZZZZNY	
MARTHA	3	F	CHILD	PRZZZZNY	
ALOIS	00	M	INF	PRZZZZNY	
M-REIT, ALBERT	48	M	BKR	PRZZZZNY	
ALTMEYER, JOHANNE	27	F	W	PRZZZZNY	
KORTETZI, GUSTAV	31	M	JNR	PRZZZZNY	
KIRSCHSTEIN, ALBERT	22	M	CL	PRZZZZNY	
SEEMANN, PETER	27	M	LABR	PRZZZZNY	
FRANZ	25	M	LABR	PRZZZZNY	
FRIEDRICH, WENZEL	29	M	LABR	PRZZZZNY	
PROSTOWSKY, AGNES	21	F	WO	PRZZZZNY	
NURERK, MARIA	45	F	W	PRZZZZNY	
FRANCISKA	21	F	CH	PRZZZZNY	
BRUNO	16	M	CH	PRZZZZNY	
JOSEPH	4	M	CHILD	PRZZZZNY	
FRANK	3	M	CHILD	PRZZZZNY	
WENZKE, JOH.	38	M	LABR	PRZZZZNY	
ELISABETH	42	F	W	PRZZZZNY	
ROSA	9	F	CHILD	PRZZZZNY	
MARSCHAUG, LINA	28	F	SGL	PRZZZZNY	
BOELSTROW, JUL.	40	M	LABR	PRZZZZNY	
MAX	5	M	CHILD	PRZZZZNY	
BORK, DORA	18	F	SGL	PRZZZZNY	
ROSENBERG, MENDEL	27	M	LABR	PRZZZZNY	
RAUTENHAUS, SOPHIE	54	F	WO	PRZZZZNY	
SCHULTES, MICHAEL	17	M	PNTR	BVZZZZROC	
STARK, GEORG	23	M	FARMER	BVZZZZROC	
BENDER, EDUARD	38	M	SHMK	PRZZZZROC	
GUSTAV	32	M	BKR	PRZZZZROC	
GELLSAU, CAROLE.	28	F	WO	PRZZZZROC	
EMMA	8	F	CHILD	PRZZZZROC	
ROBERT	6	M	CHILD	PRZZZZROC	
ANNA	3	F	CHILD	PRZZZZROC	
BETTI	.11	F	INFANT	PRZZZZROC	
VALLSTEDT, MAGDAL.	40	F	SGL	PRZZZZROC	
MORTENSEN, JENS	24	M	LABR	PRZZZZROC	
THYGESEN, CHRISTE.	21	F	SGL	PRZZZZROC	
MEINCKE, FRIEDRICH	69	M	FARMER	PRZZZZROC	
LACHMANN, NATHAN	29	M	MCHT	PRZZZZROC	
STEFFEN, HERM.	38	M	UNKNOWN	PRZZZZROC	
TALAGA, LUDWIG	45	M	LABR	PRZZZZROC	
SKARUPSKI, VINCENT	38	M	LABR	PRZZZZROC	
FLEISCHMANN, JENNY	20	F	SGL	PRZZZZROC	
EMIL	9	M	CHILD	PRZZZZROC	
MEYER, SOPHIE	16	F	SGL	WMZZZZROC	
GOETTLING, PAULINE	20	F	UNKNOWN	WMZZZZROC	
BERNHARDT, JOSEFA	56	F	WO	WMZZZZROC	
THERESE	22	F	CH	WMZZZZROC	
JACOB	16	M	CH	WMZZZZROC	
JOSEF	9	M	CHILD	WMZZZZROC	
SCHMIDT, ANTON	27	M	LABR	WMZZZZROC	
LINE	23	F	W	WMZZZZROC	
EUGEN	2	M	CHILD	WMZZZZROC	
GUSTAV	.09	M	INFANT	WMZZZZROC	
KOPF, ANNA	22	F	SGL	WMZZZZROC	
GEIGER, BRIGITTE	23	F	SGL	WMZZZZROC	
LOHR, CATHA.	41	F	WO	WMZZZZROC	
JOH.	16	M	CH	WMZZZZROC	
FRANZISKA	14	F	CH	WMZZZZROC	
CHRISTE.	13	F	CH	WMZZZZROC	
DANIEL	9	M	CHILD	WMZZZZROC	

PASSENGER	AGE	SEX	OCCUPATION	PRVL DES
ROESSLER, ERNST	25	M	UNKNOWN	WMZZZZROC
MATHES, ANDR.	24	M	UNKNOWN	WMZZZZROC
STANBESAND, JOH.	24	M	SDLR	PRZZZZROC
KUANER, EDUARD	17	M	TU	SYZZZZROC
SANDER, LAURA	36	F	WO	SYZZZZROC
ARNO	9	M	CHILD	SYZZZZROC
ERNO	8	M	CHILD	SYZZZZROC
LAURA	8	F	CHILD	SYZZZZROC
CURT	6	M	CHILD	SYZZZZROC
WALLI	3	F	CHILD	SYZZZZROC
RICHD.	.11	M	INFANT	SYZZZZROC
FLEGENHEIMER, SIMON	16	M	BCHR	BDZZZZROC
HAERING, HEINRICH	48	M	FARMER	WMZZZZROC
BEZNER, CAROLE.	18	F	SGL	WMZZZZROC
PATSCH, JOSEF	30	M	LABR	PRZZZZROC
KLUSE, WILH.	34	M	LABR	PRZZZZROC
KERS, ANTON	23	M	LABR	PRZZZZROC
WEIRNERT, ANNA	19	F	SGL	PRZZZZROC
DEPPE, OTTO	23	M	LABR	PRZZZZROC
PLAKTIES, DOROTHEA	59	F	WO	PRZZZZROC
STEINGRAEBER, CARL	43	M	LABR	PRZZZZROC
LOUISE	44	F	W	PRZZZZROC
FRANZ	16	M	CH	PRZZZZROC
GUSTAV	9	M	CHILD	PRZZZZROC
MARIE	8	F	CHILD	PRZZZZROC
KARASCH, ALWINE	32	F	WO	PRZZZZROC
LAURA	6	F	CHILD	PRZZZZROC
WM.	4	M	CHILD	PRZZZZROC
KARL	2	M	CHILD	PRZZZZROC
BERTHA	.08	F	INFANT	PRZZZZROC
KUNKEL, FRANZ	16	M	LABR	PRZZZZROC
FLUEGGE, AUGUST	16	M	LABR	PRZZZZROC
ADAMZIK, ANTON	38	M	LABR	PRZZZZROC
PADOLSKI, RUDOLF	34	M	LABR	PRZZZZROC
KARTSEN, LUDWIKA	18	F	SGL	PRZZZZROC
WENDEBORN, ALINE	43	F	WO	SYZZZZROC
OTTO	2	M	CHILD	SYZZZZROC
PINKUS, AUGUSTE	24	F	SGL	PRZZZZROC
MOSES, FANNY	19	M	LKSH	PRZZZZROC
LANG, AUG.	27	M	LABR	PRZZZZROC
PLUSKAT, JOH.	22	M	LABR	PRZZZZROC
PICKARSKI, FRANZ	46	M	BKR	PRZZZZROC
TEOPHILA	38	F	W	PRZZZZROC
VICTORIA	9	F	CHILD	PRZZZZROC
ADAM	8	M	CHILD	PRZZZZROC
JOSEF	7	M	CHILD	PRZZZZROC
ROMAN	6	M	CHILD	PRZZZZROC
BOLESLAUS	3	M	CHILD	PRZZZZROC
LEWIN, PESSE	26	M	SGL	PRZZZZROC
BEURMANN, FRIEDR.	41	M	SCP	PRZZZZROC
HANSEN, AUG.	25	M	BCHR	PRZZZZROC
ROSS, JOH.	15	M	FARMER	PRZZZZROC
GG.	18	M	MCHT	PRZZZZROC
HARDER, HANS	24	M	SMH	PRZZZZROC
PETERSEN, PETER	31	M	UNKNOWN	PRZZZZROC
ROEGUER, RICHARD	16	M	SCP	SYZZZZROC
SCHUMACHER, IDA	30	F	SGL	PRZZZZCH
KADISCH, BERHARDT	15	M	CL	PRZZZZNY
HEIGENBARTH, STEFAN	36	M	LABR	PRZZZZNY
JOSEFA	34	F	W	PRZZZZNY
KAZ.	9	M	CHILD	PRZZZZNY
JOH.	6	M	CHILD	PRZZZZNY
MARIANNA	.11	F	INFANT	PRZZZZNY
STANISLAWA	.01	F	INFANT	PRZZZZNY
EICHSTADT, WILH.	57	M	SLR	PRZZZZNY
MURCHE, FRANZ	27	M	BRR	PRZZZZNY
DROZDOWSKA, KATHA.	57	F	WO	PRZZZZNY
MARIANNA	27	F	D	PRZZZZNY
GNOSSA, CARL	27	M	BCHR	PRZZZZNY
LOEHRCKE, CHARLOTTE	28	F	WO	PRZZZZNY
GERTRUD	2	F	CHILD	PRZZZZNY
HENNIG, ROBERT	17	M	MCHT	PRZZZZNY
LOWINNECK, MORITZ	23	M	MCHT	PRZZZZNY
WENDEBAUM, PAUL	28	F	MCHT	PRZZZZNY
BERG, JOH.	25	M	MSN	PRZZZZNY
CICHOCKI, MATH.	58	F	LABR	PRZZZZNY
DOMBROWSKA, BALBINE	27	F	WO	PRZZZZNY
WLADISLAV	7	M	CHILD	PRZZZZNY
BARTEKOWSKI, MOTEL	19	M	LABR	PRZZZZNY
DLOINAK, FRANZ	54	M	LABR	PRZZZZNY
LEIEWSKA, JADWIGA	30	F	LABR	PRZZZZBUF
STEFAN	9	M	CHILD	PRZZZZBUF
FRANZISKA	.09	F	INFANT	PRZZZZBUF
SWORECK, MARIANNA	55	F	WO	PRZZZZBUF
ROLL, MARIE	21	F	SGL	WMZZZZNY
DREHER, CAROLE.	15	F	SGL	WMZZZZNY
BERGNER, BRUNO	27	M	LABR	BVZZZZNY
GERTRUD	23	F	W	BVZZZZNY
BRUNO	.06	M	INFANT	BVZZZZNY
BRAUN, CHRISTIAN	29	M	LABR	WMZZZZNY
MARIE	28	F	W	WMZZZZNY
WILH.	12	M	S	WMZZZZNY
DEININGER, MICH.	14	M	CH	WMZZZZNY
LINA	9	F	CHILD	WMZZZZNY
FRIEDRICH, VERONIKA	42	F	WO	WMZZZZNY
SCHUELE, BARBA.	19	F	SGL	WMZZZZNY
DEIRINGER, GEORG	46	M	LABR	WMZZZZNY
MAGDALENA	35	F	W	WMZZZZNY
RUDOLF	16	M	CH	WMZZZZNY
MARIE	9	F	CHILD	WMZZZZNY
GEORG	6	M	CHILD	WMZZZZNY
CARL	.09	M	INFANT	WMZZZZNY
SCHILLING, ALB.	34	M	LABR	SYZZZZPHI
ROSSIGER, ERNST	21	M	LABR	SYZZZZNY
FONTANA, FAUSTINO	40	M	LABR	SYZZZZNY
SAUSONI, LACCARIA	30	M	LABR	SYZZZZNY
SHWEINGRUBER, RUDOLF	29	M	FARMER	SYZZZZNY
ALBERTINE	26	F	W	SYZZZZNY
OTTILIE	2	F	CHILD	SYZZZZNY
OTTO	.01	M	INFANT	SYZZZZNY
KUEHN, KUNIGUNDE	28	F	W	BVZZZZNY
HERM.	7	F	CHILD	BVZZZZNY
DOROTHEA	6	F	CHILD	BVZZZZNY
FRIEDA	2	F	CHILD	BVZZZZNY
CAROLE.	.11	F	INFANT	BVZZZZNY
SCHULTZ, ERNSTE.	19	F	SGL	PRZZZZCH
EICHJOFF, JOACHIM	23	M	FARMER	PRZZZZNY
BALITZKA, MARIANNA	30	F	WO	PRZZZZCLE
JOHANN	3	M	CHILD	PRZZZZCLE
MARIANNA	.06	F	INFANT	PRZZZZCLE
KUJAWSKI, JOSEF	48	M	LABR	PRZZZZCLE
MARIANNA	46	F	W	PRZZZZCLE
ANNA	18	F	CH	PRZZZZCLE
MARIANNA	9	F	CHILD	PRZZZZCLE
STANISL.	4	M	CHILD	PRZZZZCLE
ANTONIETE	3	F	CHILD	PRZZZZCLE
MAIER, FERDINAND	50	M	LABR	PRZZZZDET
CHARLOTTE	49	F	W	PRZZZZDET
MARIE	18	F	CH	PRZZZZDET
JONATHAN	8	M	CHILD	PRZZZZDET
FRANK, KARL	24	M	LABR	WMZZZZNY
JAEHRLING, KATHA.	32	F	WO	PRZZZZNY
JACOB	8	M	CHILD	PRZZZZNY
JOHE.	6	F	CHILD	PRZZZZUNK
GEORG	4	M	CHILD	PRZZZZNY
CHRIST.	2	M	CHILD	PRZZZZNY
VALENTIN	.03	M	INFANT	PRZZZZNY
SENDLINGER, MARIE	15	F	SGL	WMZZZZNY
KUNOW, ULRICH	21	M	CL	PRZZZZNY
MOUSCHL, JOH.	30	M	LABR	PRZZZZNY
BAKASKI, WAWRZYN	39	M	LABR	PRZZZZNY
JOSEFA	32	F	W	PRZZZZNY
JOSEF	7	M	CHILD	PRZZZZNY
U	3	F	CHILD	PRZZZZNY
STANISL.	.09	M	INFANT	PRZZZZNY

SHIP: ZAANDAM

FROM: AMSTERDAM
TO: NEW YORK
ARRIVED: 25 JUNE 1888

PASSENGER	AGE	SEX	OCCUPATION	PRIVL	DES
STONE, MAD.	29	F	NN		FRZZZZUSA
MUR, H.	30	M	ENGR		FRZZZZUSA
KOHL, PH.	67	F	NN		GRZZZZUSA
WAGNER, H.	60	M	MCHT		GRZZZZUSA
T.	57	F	NN		GRZZZZUSA
TRAPOLD, IGN.	25	M	MCHT		GRZZZZUSA
EH.	21	F	NN		GRZZZZUSA
GRIMM, M.	47	M	BLKSMH		GRZZZZUSA
RUHMS, JULIUS	24	M	MCHT		GRZZZZUSA
GOLL, A.	23	M	MCHT		GRZZZZUSA
KUCHLER, MARGARETHE	15	F	SVNT		GRZZZZUSA
KORNMAYER, FRITZ	18	M	LABR		GRZZZZUSA
EHEMANN, GEORGE	17	M	LABR		GRZZZZUSA
KUEHL, FRIEDR.	18	M	LABR		GRZZZZUSA
HAEUSTMANN, VICTOR-FRIE	47	M	LABR		GRZZZZUSA
ABRAHMSON, MAYER-MAX	42	M	LABR		GRZZZZUSA
SCHAEFER, LUDWIG	34	M	LABR		GRZZZZUSA
SCHAFER, KAETCHEN	31	F	SVNT		GRZZZZUSA
MARGARETHE	20	F	SVNT		GRZZZZUSA
AUGUST	3	M	CHILD		GRZZZZUSA
HEINRICH	.04	M	INFANT		GRZZZZUSA
LAMB, FRITZ	13	M	LABR		GRZZZZUSA
SCHAEFER, THEODOR	38	M	LABR		GRZZZZUSA
HUEBER, JACOB	24	M	LABR		GRZZZZUSA
PETRI, HEINRICH	19	M	LABR		GRZZZZUSA
ELISABETH	20	F	SVNT		GRZZZZUSA
FUECHS, ANNA	27	F	SVNT		GRZZZZUSA
STROEHE, JOHS.	27	M	LABR		GRZZZZUSA
GREINER, WILH.FRIEDR.	47	M	LABR		GRZZZZUSA
SAUTTER, CARL	15	M	LABR		GRZZZZUSA
WINKLER, ADOLF	39	M	FARMER		GRZZZZUSA
PAULINE	32	F	SVNT		GRZZZZUSA
BERTHA	.06	F	INFANT		GRZZZZUSA
UMMER, ELISABETH	00	F	SVNT		GRZZZZUSA
MATHILDE	8	F	CHILD		GRZZZZUSA
KARL	4	M	CHILD		GRZZZZUSA
MARTIN	2	M	CHILD		GRZZZZUSA
BETEN, AUGUST	26	M	FARMER		GRZZZZUSA
ANNA	20	F	SVNT		GRZZZZUSA
ANASTJA	00	F	NN		GRZZZZUSA
RAAB, J.	44	M	LABR		GRZZZZUSA
ESSER, ERNST	00	M	LABR		GRZZZZUSA
LIPPS, FERDINAND	21	M	LABR		GRZZZZUSA
ROSER, LUDWIG	28	M	LABR		GRZZZZUSA
U, U	00	F	SVNT		GRZZZZUSA
U	00	M	LABR		GRZZZZUSA
U	00	F	SVNT		GRZZZZUSA
U	00	M	MCHT		GRZZZZUSA
U	00	M	LABR		GRZZZZUSA
U	00	M	MUSN		GRZZZZUSA
HIRSCHNER, ELISE	00	F	SVNT		GRZZZZUSA
JACHNITZ, PAUL	00	M	LABR		GRZZZZUSA
AMALIA	45	F	SVNT		GRZZZZUSA
DORFLEIN, HEINRICH	26	M	LABR		GRZZZZUSA
SCHLEICHER, AUG.	16	M	LABR		GRZZZZUSA
DORFLEIN, LEOPOLD	17	M	LABR		GRZZZZUSA
SCHULTE, GUSTAV	18	M	BTMKR		GRZZZZUSA
SCHNETER, BENNO	20	M	MCHT		GRZZZZUSA
MUERZWIEK, JOSEF	18	M	LABR		GRZZZZUSA
BOGUSESKA, BRONISLAWA	17	F	SVNT		GRZZZZUSA
HELFERT, KATHI	22	F	SVNT		GRZZZZUSA
JOHANN	14	M	LABR		GRZZZZUSA
LEZZIE	10	F	CH		GRZZZZUSA
WRUECK, MAX	19	M	LABR		GRZZZZUSA
KOENEN, PETER	36	M	LABR		GRZZZZUSA
MARGA.	00	F	SVNT		GRZZZZUSA
HEINRICH	4	M	CHILD		GRZZZZUSA
WILHELM	00	M	CH		GRZZZZUSA
SCHREPFE, CASPAR	42	M	LABR		GRZZZZUSA
MULLER, HCH.SR.	48	M	FARMER		GRZZZZUSA
HCH.JR	24	M	FARMER		GRZZZZUSA
SPOHRER, M.B.	19	M	LABR		GRZZZZUSA
REIF, J.	18	M	LABR		GRZZZZUSA
BETZ, DRINA	17	F	SVNT		GRZZZZUSA
BURKHARDT, OTTILIE	16	F	SVNT		GRZZZZUSA
GILLES, PETER	35	M	FARMER		GRZZZZUSA
CATHARINA	34	F	SVNT		GRZZZZUSA
JOSEPH	14	M	LABR		GRZZZZUSA
SEBASTIAN	11	M	CH		GRZZZZUSA
PETER	10	M	CH		GRZZZZUSA
DOROTHEA	5	F	CHILD		GRZZZZUSA
CATHARINA	4	F	CHILD		GRZZZZUSA
MARIE	17	F	NN		GRZZZZUSA
KLAUS, JACOB	00	M	LABR		GRZZZZUSA
GERTRUDE	00	F	SVNT		GRZZZZUSA
MATTHIAS	00	M	NN		GRZZZZUSA
CATHRINE	00	F	NN		GRZZZZUSA
MARGARETHE	7	F	CHILD		GRZZZZUSA
ANNA	4	F	CHILD		GRZZZZUSA
JACOB	3	M	CHILD		GRZZZZUSA
HOOK, ANNA-MARIA	56	F	SVNT		GRZZZZUSA
PH.	19	M	LABR		GRZZZZUSA
SCHILI, FRANCISCA	18	F	SVNT		GRZZZZUSA
WALDVOGEL, ADAM	22	M	LABR		GRZZZZUSA
DRINHAUS, CHRIST.	28	M	LABR		GRZZZZUSA
MARG.	37	F	SVNT		GRZZZZUSA
SCHAUB, FRANZ	28	M	LABR		GRZZZZUSA
MEBUS, CHRISTINA	7	F	CHILD		GRZZZZUSA
STEINEKE, CARL	11	M	CH		GRZZZZUSA
SCHOTTEN, HINRICH	59	M	LABR		GRZZZZUSA
RIEHM, CHRISTOPH	33	M	LABR		GRZZZZUSA
CHRISTOPH	8	M	CHILD		GRZZZZUSA
KUCHLER, ROSINA	63	F	SVNT		GRZZZZUSA
PAULINE	18	F	SVNT		GRZZZZUSA
KOHL, JOSEPH	19	M	LABR		GRZZZZUSA
BARBARA	38	F	SVNT		GRZZZZUSA
HEIL, THERESIA	00	F	SVNT		GRZZZZUSA
HEESER, JOHANN	28	M	LABR		GRZZZZUSA
BABETT	34	F	SVNT		GRZZZZUSA
JOHANN	4	M	CHILD		GRZZZZUSA
PHILIPINE	1	F	CHILD		GRZZZZUSA
LUDWIG	23	M	LABR		GRZZZZUSA
HOFRATH, HEINRICH	21	M	LABR		GRZZZZUSA
HOECKER, CHRIST.	34	M	LABR		GRZZZZUSA
ANNA	27	F	SVNT		GRZZZZUSA
EGGER, CRIST.	18	M	LABR		GRZZZZUSA
BRAUN, CATHARINA	20	F	SVNT		GRZZZZUSA
SCHMUDLING, JOHANN	30	M	LABR		GRZZZZUSA
BRAUN, ELISABETH	64	F	SVNT		GRZZZZUSA
SCHILLING, GOTTLIEB	23	M	LABR		GRZZZZUSA
MARGHARDT, BERTHA	16	F	SVNT		GRZZZZUSA
GOETZ, WILH.	28	M	LABR		GRZZZZUSA
SCHWARZ, EMMA	16	F	SVNT		GRZZZZUSA
HELENA	19	F	SVNT		GRZZZZUSA
MULLER, MARIE	15	F	SVNT		GRZZZZUSA
SANDTEN, WILHELM	32	M	LABR		GRZZZZUSA
EISINGER, GUSTAV	24	M	LABR		GRZZZZUSA
HENZLER, MARIE	15	F	SVNT		GRZZZZUSA
MAYER, GOTTLIEB	17	M	LABR		GRZZZZUSA
CATHRINE	15	F	SVNT		GRZZZZUSA
FRIEDRIKA	13	F	SVNT		GRZZZZUSA
FISCHER, FRANCISCA	25	F	SVNT		GRZZZZUSA
JOSEPH	6	M	CHILD		GRZZZZUSA
JOSEPHINA	4	F	CHILD		GRZZZZUSA
JOHANN	1	M	CHILD		GRZZZZUSA
ARAKAU, JOSEPH	00	M	LABR		FRZZZZUSA
CHARBONNIER, AUGUST	00	M	LABR		FRZZZZUSA
CABIAS, HENRY	00	M	LABR		FRZZZZUSA
MARIE	22	F	SVNT		FRZZZZUSA
FRANK, KAETCHEN	15	F	SVNT		GRZZZZUSA
DANER, GEORGE	18	M	LABR		GRZZZZUSA
WALZER, ODILIE	26	F	SVNT		GRZZZZUSA
SCHUTT, BERN.	26	M	BCHR		GRZZZZUSA

PASSENGER	AGE	SEX	OCCUPATION	PRVVL	DES
ROSACJACH, MARIANNE	29	F	SVNT		GRZZZZUSA
VALENTY	.10	M	INFANT		GRZZZZUSA
VONSCHEVEN, PETER	00	M	LABR		GRZZZZUSA
CAECIEL	60	F	SVNT		GRZZZZUSA
JOSEPHINE	24	F	SVNT		GRZZZZUSA
UNTENER, JOSEPH	30	M	LABR		GRZZZZUSA
PREMER, BALTHASAR	42	M	LABR		GRZZZZUSA
SCHREINER, FRZ.	36	M	LABR		GRZZZZUSA
MALECKER, JOHANN	32	M	LABR		GRZZZZUSA
ZIMMERMANN, FRANCISCA	18	F	SVNT		GRZZZZUSA
PATAC, MARIA	19	F	SVNT		GRZZZZUSA
SILLIES, J.	29	M	LABR		GRZZZZUSA
SEMRAM, OTTO	39	M	LABR		GRZZZZUSA
HOPPE, FRANZ-AND.	21	F	SVNT		GRZZZZUSA
SCHMIDT, WILH.	20	M	LABR		GRZZZZUSA
ROCK, HENRY	33	M	LABR		GRZZZZUSA
NEUBERT, GEORGE	26	M	LABR		GRZZZZUSA
SCHUEHMACHER, MICHEL	20	M	LABR		GRZZZZUSA

SHIP: PERUVIAN

FROM: LIVERPOOL
TO: BALTIMORE
ARRIVED: 26 JUNE 1888

PASSENGER	AGE	SEX	OCCUPATION	PRVVL	DES
EDELSTEIN, JEMME	25	F	DRSMKR		GRZZZZUNK
ZABLOHNY, JOSEF	22	M	LABR		GRZZZZUNK
LORENZ, FRNCISEK	23	M	LABR		GRZZZZUNK
MARIAB	22	M	LABR		GRZZZZUNK
NEWLAND, THODORE	38	M	FARMER		GRZZZZBAL
ROSENSBOCK, FEIGE	23	F	W		GRZZZZBAL
DIVORI	3	M	CHILD		GRZZZZBAL
FREDA	00	F	INF		GRZZZZBAL
PFISTER, CHRISTIAN	24	M	JNR		GRZZZZBAL
GOLDBERGER, WOLF	48	M	BTMKR		GRZZZZNY

SHIP: RUGIA

FROM: HAMBURG
TO: NEW YORK
ARRIVED: 26 JUNE 1888

PASSENGER	AGE	SEX	OCCUPATION	PRVVL	DES
PETERSEN, ERNST	24	M	SHMK		HBZZZZUSA
FLEISCHER, ELISABETH	19	F	LABR		PRZZZZUSA
BULL, HINR.	34	M	UNKNOWN		PRZZZZUSA
ANNA	36	F	W		PRZZZZUSA
FRIDA	9	F	CHILD		PRZZZZUSA
HEINR	8	M	CHILD		PRZZZZUSA
DORA	6	F	CHILD		PRZZZZUSA
WILLI	.11	M	INFANT		PRZZZZUSA
JABLOUSKI, WOIZECH	16	M	LABR		PRAMBHUSA
BEULHARZ, NANE	18	F	SGL		WMZZZZUSA
PETERS, ERNST	47	M	GDNR		HBZZZZUSA
CAROLINE	46	F	W		HBZZZZUSA
WILH	19	M	CH		HBZZZZUSA
CARL	9	M	CHILD		HBZZZZUSA
EMILIE	8	F	CHILD		HBZZZZUSA
ELISABETH	7	F	CHILD		HBZZZZUSA
ANNA	5	F	CHILD		HBZZZZUSA
POEHL, WILH	27	M	CNF		HBACBFUSA
DAUCKERT, HANS	45	M	WHR		HBAHNPUSA
WILHELMINE	35	F	W		HBAHNPUSA
HEINR	14	M	CH		HBAHNPUSA
BERTHA	9	F	CHILD		HBAHNPUSA
ADAMHEIT, CHRISTOPH	47	M	TNM		HBAAKHUSA

PASSENGER	AGE	SEX	OCCUPATION	PRVVL	DES
KIESEBYL, HENRIETTE	22	F	SGL		PRZZZZUSA
BUGHHOLZ, HANS	16	M	FARMER		PRZZZZUSA
NIELSEN, CHRIST	16	M	FARMER		PRZZZZUSA
THODE, WILH	15	M	FARMER		PRZZZZUSA
BORNHOLDT, CLAUS	50	M	MLR		HBZZZZUSA
JABLONSKI, FRANZ	40	M	UNKNOWN		HBAEABUSA
MARIE	37	F	W		HBAEABUSA
FRANZISKA	16	F	UNKNOWN		HBAEABUSA
KASIMIR	9	M	CHILD		HBAEABUSA
STANISLAW	8	M	CHILD		HBAEABUSA
HELENE	.11	F	INFANT		HBAEABUSA
BRANK, LUDWIG	34	M	PNTR		PRZZZZUSA
GERKE, HELENE	24	F	SGL		PRZZZZUSA
SCHEBEROWSKI, WILH	24	F	SGL		PRZZZZUSA
WOLF, MAX	23	M	BKR		PRADFSUSA
GOLDSCHMIDT, ISRAEL	16	M	LABR		PRACDNUSA
BARKHOLZ, FRITZ	30	M	FARMER		PRZZZZUSA
JOH	23	F	W		PRZZZZUSA
WILH	3	M	CHILD		PRZZZZUSA
FRIDA	.11	F	INFANT		PRZZZZUSA
AHRENDT, CHR	60	M	FARMER		PRZZZZUSA
JOH	59	F	W		PRZZZZUSA
FRAUENBERGER, EMIL	23	M	BKR		HBZZZZUSA
BROECKER, AUGUSTE	29	F	SGL		PRZZZZUSA
JOENSON, BENGT.	36	M	LABR		PRAHROUSA
IDA	27	F	W		PRAHROUSA
HILDA	8	F	CHILD		PRAHROUSA
BLUMENTHAL, ALFRED	17	M	FARMER		PRZZZZUSA
MAUTE, LOUISE	20	F	SGL		WMZZZZUSA
KNOBEL, ELISE	30	F	SGL		WMZZZZUSA
SCHUESSLER, GUSTAV	35	M	SHMK		PRZZZZUSA
FRD.	50	F	W		PRZZZZUSA
ANNA	17	F	CH		PRZZZZUSA
MAREN	9	F	CHILD		PRZZZZUSA
HERM	8	M	CHILD		PRZZZZUSA
KOTZKE, FRIEDR	59	M	LABR		PRAIIHUSA
ROHLOFF, ALBERT	16	M	UNKNOWN		PRZZZZUSA
SELLMANN, MARIA	28	F	SGL		HBZZZZUSA
MARTHA	22	F	SGL		HBZZZZUSA
SKORZENSKI, LUDWIG	30	M	TLR		PRZZZZUSA
MARIE	27	F	W		PRZZZZUSA
SKORZEWSKI, WILH	2	F	CHILD		PRZZZZUSA
AUGUSTE	.09	F	INFANT		PRZZZZUSA
STANK, WILH	26	M	FARMER		PRZZZZUSA
FLEISCHMANN, AUGUST	39	M	SHMK		PRZZZZUSA
AUGUSTE	35	F	W		PRZZZZUSA
LOUISE	9	F	CHILD		PRZZZZUSA
OTTO	8	M	CHILD		PRZZZZUSA
AUGUST	7	M	CHILD		PRZZZZUSA
FRANZ	6	M	CHILD		PRZZZZUSA
HELENE	5	F	CHILD		PRZZZZUSA
AUGUST	3	M	CHILD		PRZZZZUSA
GUSTAV	.09	M	INFANT		PRZZZZUSA
RICKE, WILH	60	M	FARMER		PRZZZZUSA
BREDIES, MARIE	19	F	SGL		PRZZZZUSA
LETMONIK, STANISLAW	35	M	LABR		PRZZZZUSA
WANDEL, CONRAD	22	M	MCHT		PRAARZUSA
HOCK, JENATZ	31	M	SMH		PRAGJZUSA
HELMKE, JOH	21	M	LABR		PRADCNUSA
CAMMELY, MARY	22	F	SGL		PRAIALUSA
SCHUBERT, HERM	22	M	MLR		PRZZZZUSA
BEHRMANN, JOH	14	M	LABR		PRAACKUSA
JAAKEL, JOHANNA	47	F	WO		PRAACKUSA
ADLER, MARIE	18	F	SGL		PRZZZZUSA
IDA	9	F	CHILD		PRZZZZUSA
MUELLER, CARL	22	M	LABR		PRAEXKUSA
ARLT, JOSEF	27	M	MCHT		PRZZZZUSA
SALENSKI, PAUL	26	M	CPTR		PRALKBUSA
KNITTER, FRIEDR	28	M	MSN		PRALKBUSA
BASTIAN, EMMA	27	F	SGL		PRZZZZUSA
LANGE, EMIL	24	M	CTW		PRZZZZUSA
SCHLESER, FABIAN	21	M	TLR		PRAAKHUSA
SCHMIDT, RICHARD	25	M	LABR		PRZZZZUSA
GRZENZIEKA, VERONIKA	18	F	WO		PRZZZZUSA
BRONISLAW	.11	M	INFANT		PRZZZZUSA

PASSENGER	AGE	SEX	OCCUPATION	PRVL	DES
ULRICH, WALT	67	M	FARMER	PRAGZGUSA	
CATH	67	F	W	PRAGZGUSA	
KAMINSKA, BARBARA	40	F	WO	PRZZZZUSA	
ERNESTINE	16	F	WO	PRZZZZUSA	
ALEXANDER	15	M	CH	PRZZZZUSA	
THEOPHIL	9	M	CHILD	PRZZZZUSA	
EMILIE	8	F	CHILD	PRZZZZUSA	
JOSEFA	5	F	CHILD	PRZZZZUSA	
IGNATZ	2	M	CHILD	PRZZZZUSA	
MARIANNE	.11	F	INFANT	PRZZZZUSA	
GROSCHOPFF, CONRAD	31	M	LABR	PRAGKZUSA	
KLING, ANNA	15	F	SGL	PRAGZGUSA	
BRECHT, CATH	22	F	SGL	BDZZZZUSA	
DAVID, FRITZ	25	M	LABR	PRZZZZUSA	
FRDKE	27	F	W	PRZZZZUSA	
LANGER, BERTHA	27	F	WO	PRAFUHUSA	
ERICH	.09	M	INFANT	PRAFUHUSA	
SCHALTZ, HERM	22	M	LABR	PRABHUUSA	
BERR, HEINR	64	M	LABR	PRAFUHUSA	
BIALLAS, JOSEF	27	M	FARMER	PRZZZZUSA	
NOVA, JOHANN	29	M	LABR	PRZZZZUSA	
JANOSKI, THOMAS	23	M	LABR	PRZZZZUSA	
SAVADNIK, JACOB	42	M	LABR	PRZZZZUSA	
RESI	6	F	CHILD	PRZZZZUSA	
DOSTATNY, ANTON	26	M	LABR	PRZZZZUSA	
KAUFMANN, CARL	23	M	BCHR	PRZZZZUSA	
SEETON, OTTO	58	M	FARMER	PRAAKHUSA	
OTTO	28	M	FARMER	PRAAKHUSA	
BAUMANN, FRANZ	32	M	TLR	PRAAFXUSA	
LASKOWSKA, BRONISLAWA	21	F	WO	PRZZZZUSA	
FRANZISKA	2	F	CHILD	PRZZZZUSA	
NASTASIA	.06	F	INFANT	PRZZZZUSA	
SLOMKE, EDUARD	15	M	LABR	PRAESTUSA	
RUDOLF, WM	56	M	DLR	PRAEWZUSA	
JOHANNE	60	F	W	PRAEWZUSA	
ELISABETH	26	F	D	PRAEWZUSA	
ZAEZABONSKA, MARY	25	F	SGL	PRACUAUSA	
KRAKONSKI, FRANZISKA	32	F	WO	PRZZZZUSA	
WLADISLAW	4	M	CHILD	PRZZZZUSA	
LOTTE	2	F	CHILD	PRZZZZUSA	
JAN	.06	M	INFANT	PRZZZZUSA	
HELBING, MARIE	21	F	SGL	PRZZZZUSA	
BODEWIG, C	45	M	DR	PRZZZZUSA	
LORENZ, OSCAR	48	M	PVTR	PRAARZUSA	
FRIEDA	33	F	W	PRAARZUSA	
FRITZ	9	M	CHILD	PRAARZUSA	
OSCAR	7	M	CHILD	PRAARZUSA	
JOH	6	M	CHILD	PRAARZUSA	
ELFRIEDE	4	F	CHILD	PRAARZUSA	
THEODOR	2	M	CHILD	PRAARZUSA	
GOLDBERG, LIPMANN	62	M	MCHT	PRAGQZUSA	
REBECCA	50	F	W	PRAGQZUSA	
DAVID	13	M	CH	PRAGQZUSA	
LOUIS	9	M	CHILD	PRAGQZUSA	
LUSKEY, MARY	40	F	SGL	PRACBRUSA	

SHIP: AMERICA

FROM: BREMEN
TO: BALTIMORE
ARRIVED: 27 JUNE 1888

PASSENGER	AGE	SEX	OCCUPATION	PRVL	DES
SCHLENNES, U	21	F	UNKNOWN	GRZZZZUNK	
ENGEL, CATHARINA	55	F	UNKNOWN	GRZZZZUNK	
EMO, MARIA	20	F	SVNT	GRZZZZUNK	
NEUMANN, FREDRICK	26	M	MLR	GRZZZZIA	
WIRLITZKI, EMMA	56	F	UNKNOWN	GRZZZZMD	
ANNA	17	F	UNKNOWN	GRZZZZMD	
WELLMANN, AUGUST	61	M	FARMER	GRZZZZMI	
SCHMIDT, CATHRINA	20	F	SVNT	GRZZZZMD	

PASSENGER	AGE	SEX	OCCUPATION	PRVL	DES
KRYEGER, EMMA	28	F	UNKNOWN	GRZZZZNE	
ELSA	1	F	CHILD	GRZZZZNE	
WEHEL, MARTHA	18	F	SVNT	GRZZZZNE	
SCHMID, MINNA	20	F	UNKNOWN	GRZZZZNE	
ANNA	6	F	CHILD	GRZZZZNE	
BERNDT, MARIA	25	F	UNKNOWN	GRZZZZNE	
PAUL	2	M	CHILD	GRZZZZNE	
KOECK, CRESCENTZ	37	F	UNKNOWN	GRZZZZOH	
MARIA	11	F	UNKNOWN	GRZZZZOH	
FRIEDRICH	8	M	CHILD	GRZZZZOH	
ANNA	4	F	CHILD	GRZZZZOH	
JOSEF	2	M	CHILD	GRZZZZOH	
CATHARINA	.11	F	INFANT	GRZZZZOH	
BAROWSKI, JOSEF	35	M	FARMER	GRZZZZIL	
PETER	11	M	UNKNOWN	GRZZZZIL	
SCHROEDER, JOHANN	14	M	UNKNOWN	GRZZZZPA	
ANNA	16	F	UNKNOWN	GRZZZZPA	
MEINERS, JOHANNA	46	F	UNKNOWN	GRZZZZPA	
WILHELM	11	M	UNKNOWN	GRZZZZPA	
AUGUST	10	M	CH	GRZZZZPA	
ERNST	8	M	CHILD	GRZZZZPA	
BATZKE, CHARLOTTE	65	F	UNKNOWN	GRZZZZOH	
WRUBLEWICZ, HEROMIN	15	F	UNKNOWN	GRZZZZOH	
KLINEK, VICTORIA	20	F	SVNT	GRZZZZOH	
NA----, ROSALIA	00	F	UNKNOWN	GRZZZZOH	
FRANCISCA	17	F	UNKNOWN	GRZZZZOH	
BARAWSKI, JOHN	29	M	FARMER	GRZZZZIN	
ANNA	24	F	UNKNOWN	GRZZZZIN	
GLAESER, ALFRED	5	M	CHILD	GRZZZZIN	
ONANDT, ALBERT	43	M	LABR	GRZZZZIN	
MATHILDE	42	F	UNKNOWN	GRZZZZIN	
THIELE, LEBRECHT	27	M	TLR	GRZZZZIN	
AUGUSTE	24	F	UNKNOWN	GRZZZZIN	
MARIA	2	F	CHILD	GRZZZZIN	
FRIEDA	.11	F	INFANT	GRZZZZIN	
BENDER, ROBERT	18	M	TLR	GRZZZZIN	
BATHKE, ANTONIE	37	F	UNKNOWN	GRZZZZMN	
LUCIA	47	F	UNKNOWN	GRZZZZMN	
MARIA	19	F	UNKNOWN	GRZZZZMN	
EVA	17	F	UNKNOWN	GRZZZZMN	
LORENZ	11	M	UNKNOWN	GRZZZZMN	
ZURCHER, ELISA	25	F	SVNT	SRZZZZMD	
ZEEGE, OTTO	23	M	BKLYR	GRZZZZMD	
QUANDT, MASE	14	M	UNKNOWN	GRZZZZIN	
ALBRECHT	9	M	CHILD	GRZZZZIN	
SCHWARZ, MARIA	19	F	SVNT	GRZZZZMD	
LEITNER, JOHANN	53	M	FARMER	GRZZZZIN	
MARGARETHE	39	F	UNKNOWN	GRZZZZIN	
LABINA	18	F	UNKNOWN	GRZZZZIN	
BARBARA	14	F	UNKNOWN	GRZZZZIN	
ANNA	8	F	CHILD	GRZZZZIN	
GEORG	6	M	CHILD	GRZZZZIN	
KORBER, LEONHARD	15	M	FARMER	GRZZZZOH	
HE---, ULRIKA	00	F	SVNT	GRZZZZPA	
ENGEL, THOMAS	28	M	MSN	GRZZZZMN	
BATZKE, HERMANN	43	M	UNKNOWN	GRZZZZMD	
DOERR, RICHARD	29	M	LABR	GRZZZZMI	
SCHRADER, FRIEDRIKE	43	F	UNKNOWN	GRZZZZMI	
CONRAD, ANNA	17	F	UNKNOWN	GRZZZZMI	
IDA	15	F	UNKNOWN	GRZZZZMI	
EMMA	11	F	UNKNOWN	GRZZZZMI	
AUGUSTE	8	F	CHILD	GRZZZZMI	
SCHRADER, CARL	4	M	CHILD	GRZZZZMI	
LINNA	3	F	CHILD	GRZZZZMI	
WILLY	.11	M	INFANT	GRZZZZMI	
WETTIG, ANNA	30	F	UNKNOWN	GRZZZZUNK	
ARTHUR	.11	M	INFANT	GRZZZZUNK	
DENDERLE, JOSEPH	27	M	LABR	GRZZZZOH	
SIEBER, JACOB	43	M	FARMER	GRZZZZAL	
EVA	36	F	UNKNOWN	GRZZZZAL	
BABETTA	11	F	UNKNOWN	GRZZZZAL	
ANNA	5	F	CHILD	GRZZZZAL	
MUELLER, CARL	29	M	LABR	GRZZZZWI	
JOHANNE	27	F	UNKNOWN	GRZZZZWI	
MINNA	3	F	CHILD	GRZZZZWI	

PASSENGER	AGE	SEX	OCCUPATION	PRVL	DES	PASSENGER	AGE	SEX	OCCUPATION	PRVL	DES
FRITZ	.03	M	INFANT	GRZZZZWI		ZIMMER, EMILIE	29	F	UNKNOWN	GRZZZZKS	
BUETAW, JULIUS	28	M	LABR	GRZZZZIN		HAEFNER, BABETTE	24	F	SVNT	GRZZZZMI	
BEILKE, FRIEDRICH	25	M	LABR	GRZZZZIN		DENKER, CATHARINA	20	F	SVNT	GRZZZZMD	
KRUPPI, WILHELM	40	M	MLR	GRZZZZMI		WALZ, FRIEDRIKE	18	F	SVNT	GRZZZZMD	
AUGUSTE	35	F	UNKNOWN	GRZZZZMI		CZARNEKA, BALWINA	40	F	SVNT	GRZZZZMD	
WILLY	9	M	CHILD	GRZZZZMI		MARIANNA	8	F	CHILD	GRZZZZMD	
CATHARINA	7	F	CHILD	GRZZZZMI		PLETA, MARIA	21	F	SVNT	GRZZZZMD	
KORN, DOROTHEA	68	F	UNKNOWN	GRZZZZIL		SAINZMEWSKA, JOHANN	56	M	LABR	GRZZZZOH	
BUTZIN, EMILIE	56	F	UNKNOWN	GRZZZZWI		MAGDALENE	51	F	UNKNOWN	GRZZZZOH	
MINNA	31	F	UNKNOWN	GRZZZZWI		VAGT, WILHELM	60	M	UNKNOWN	GRZZZZOH	
NEUMANN, RUDOLF	55	F	FARMER	GRZZZZMI		MICHALSKI, JACOB	33	M	MLR	GRZZZZPA	
ERNSTINE	41	F	UNKNOWN	GRZZZZMI		ANTONIE	28	F	UNKNOWN	GRZZZZPA	
PAULINE	17	F	UNKNOWN	GRZZZZMI		ADALBERT	6	M	CHILD	GRZZZZPA	
HERMANN	15	M	UNKNOWN	GRZZZZMI		ANTON	3	M	CHILD	GRZZZZPA	
ERNST	11	M	CH	GRZZZZMI		STANISLAUS	.09	M	INFANT	GRZZZZPA	
JOHANN	9	M	CHILD	GRZZZZMI		GERHARD, CATHARINA	51	F	UNKNOWN	GRZZZZKY	
RUDOLPH	7	M	CHILD	GRZZZZMI		JOHANN	16	F	UNKNOWN	GRZZZZKY	
THEODOR	4	M	CHILD	GRZZZZMI		BERTHA	15	F	UNKNOWN	GRZZZZKY	
OTTO	2	M	CHILD	GRZZZZMI		JULIANNA	13	F	UNKNOWN	GRZZZZKY	
ALBERT	.06	M	INFANT	GRZZZZMI		FRIEDRICH	8	M	CHILD	GRZZZZKY	
JAKOB, ALBERT	38	M	MCHT	GRZZZZIL		MARTIN	7	M	CHILD	GRZZZZKY	
DOROCH, EMMA	22	F	SVNT	GRZZZZMI		PAULUS, JOHANN	18	M	MCHT	GRZZZZOH	
MUELLER, WILHELM	43	M	LABR	GRZZZZWI		ZERDLER, ANTON	20	M	MCHT	GRZZZZOH	
WILHELMINE	45	F	UNKNOWN	GRZZZZWI		DOERING, CHRISTIAN	37	M	FARMER	GRZZZZNE	
BERTHA	21	F	UNKNOWN	GRZZZZWI		JUSTINA	37	F	UNKNOWN	GRZZZZNE	
ROBERT	11	M	CH	GRZZZZWI		ERNSTINA	10	F	CH	GRZZZZNE	
GERTRUD	7	F	CHILD	GRZZZZWI		EMMA	8	F	CHILD	GRZZZZNE	
WILHELM	3	M	CHILD	GRZZZZWI		ELISE	6	F	CHILD	GRZZZZNE	
REICHHARDT, OTTO	15	M	FARMER	GRZZZZCAL		PAULINE	4	F	CHILD	GRZZZZNE	
OSTREGA, STANISLAW	27	M	FARMER	GRZZZZMD		ADOLF	.11	M	INFANT	GRZZZZNE	
BRUHN, JOHANN	16	M	FARMER	GRZZZZMD		MALLE, ERNST	24	M	FARMER	GRZZZZNE	
JACOB	15	M	FARMER	GRZZZZMD		ANNA	22	F	UNKNOWN	GRZZZZNE	
ODEFEY, FRIEDRICH	16	M	FARMER	GRZZZZMD		ANNA	2	F	CHILD	GRZZZZNE	
BETE, HEINRICH	26	M	FARMER	GRZZZZMD		GUSTAV	.03	M	INFANT	GRZZZZUNK	
SOPHIE	23	F	UNKNOWN	GRZZZZMD		UNOEELAK, JOSEFA	21	F	UNKNOWN	GRZZZZIL	
LUDWIG	.06	M	INFANT	GRZZZZMD		MICHALINA	.03	F	INFANT	GRZZZZIL	
MUELLER, AUGUST	21	M	LABR	GRZZZZOH		KLANKOWSKI, ALBERT	23	M	SMH	GRZZZZOH	
CAROLINE	21	F	SVNT	GRZZZZOH		KLAUSCH, JOSEPH	58	M	SMH	GRZZZZIN	
MATT, CAROLINE	62	F	UNKNOWN	GRZZZZOH		FELIX	24	M	SMH	GRZZZZIN	
JAUCH, CHRISTIAN	52	M	SHMK	GRZZZZIL		ROSALIE	28	F	UNKNOWN	GRZZZZIN	
MARIA	55	F	UNKNOWN	GRZZZZIL		SOFIA	2	F	CHILD	GRZZZZIN	
AUGUST	5	M	CHILD	GRZZZZIL		JOSEPH	.03	M	INFANT	GRZZZZIN	
KANDERER, KATHARINA	28	F	UNKNOWN	GRZZZZIL		HELLERMANN, AUGUST	42	M	TLR	GRZZZZMN	
MARIA	4	F	CHILD	GRZZZZIL		BERTHA	30	F	UNKNOWN	GRZZZZMN	
LENA	3	F	CHILD	GRZZZZIL		OTTO	11	M	CH	GRZZZZMN	
LUDWIG	.01	M	INFANT	GRZZZZIL		FRIEDRICH	9	M	CHILD	GRZZZZMN	
KABEL, MARGARETHE	19	F	SVNT	GRZZZZMD		MARTHA	8	F	CHILD	GRZZZZMN	
KELLER, CATHARINA	26	F	UNKNOWN	GRZZZZMD		WILHELM	4	M	CHILD	GRZZZZMN	
KOENIG, PHILIPP	23	M	FARMER	GRZZZZMD		NETZ, GUSTAV	24	M	MSN	GRZZZZMI	
KNAUTZ, JULIUS	24	M	FARMER	GRZZZZMD		BALLER, ERNST	32	M	MSN	GRZZZZNE	
KABEL, MAIRA	17	F	SVNT	GRZZZZMD		EMILIE	30	F	UNKNOWN	GRZZZZNE	
HALLMANN, LAURA	45	F	UNKNOWN	GRZZZZIL		ANNA	7	F	CHILD	GRZZZZNE	
BERTHA	11	F	UNKNOWN	GRZZZZIL		ERNST	4	M	CHILD	GRZZZZNE	
LEICHTENMACHER, JOHANN	24	M	LABR	GRZZZZAL		HEDWIG	.09	F	INFANT	GRZZZZNE	
POTORATZKY, MARIA	24	F	SVNT	GRZZZZKY		EMILIE	24	F	SVNT	GRZZZZNE	
FILEWSKA, JOSEPHINA	35	F	SVNT	GRZZZZKY		BORDIK, WILHELM	16	M	UNKNOWN	GRZZZZIL	
FREUBLE, FRANZISCA	24	F	UNKNOWN	GRZZZZKY		PHMOTEDE, AUGUST	32	M	FARMER	GRZZZZNE	
FRANZISCA	.03	F	INFANT	GRZZZZKY		META	33	F	UNKNOWN	GRZZZZNE	
COMOPAGNA, FRANZ	17	M	LABR	GRZZZZVA		MARIA	6	F	CHILD	GRZZZZNE	
LIPINSKI, MAREINA	21	F	SVNT	GRZZZZMD		EMMA	4	F	CHILD	GRZZZZNE	
OSTROWSKA, MARTHA	23	F	SVNT	GRZZZZMD		AUGUST	3	M	CHILD	GRZZZZNE	
SEIDEL, WILHELM	38	M	FARMER	GRZZZZIL		LANISE	.03	F	INFANT	GRZZZZNE	
FRANZISCA	34	F	UNKNOWN	GRZZZZIL		SCHORNAK, AUGUST	32	M	FARMER	GRZZZZMI	
LOHMANN, JOHANN	33	M	FARMER	GRZZZZMI		FRANKE, ADOLF	44	M	FARMER	GRZZZZIL	
FLORENTINE	32	F	UNKNOWN	GRZZZZMI		ZITZELSBERGER, MARIE	35	F	UNKNOWN	GRZZZZWI	
FRANZ	5	M	CHILD	GRZZZZMI		HASER	11	M	CH	GRZZZZWI	
MARIE	.09	F	INFANT	GRZZZZMI		ALOIS	8	M	CHILD	GRZZZZWI	
WANOFSKI, ANNA	66	F	UNKNOWN	GRZZZZMI		THERESE	6	F	CHILD	GRZZZZWI	
CZERWINKA, JOHANNA	18	F	SVNT	GRZZZZMI		MARIA	4	F	CHILD	GRZZZZWI	
HELWIG, AUGUSTE	20	F	SVNT	GRZZZZMI		BENNO	3	M	CHILD	GRZZZZWI	
ORZECHOWSKI, ANNA	29	F	UNKNOWN	GRZZZZKS		ANNA	.11	F	INFANT	GRZZZZUNK	
PETER	6	M	CHILD	GRZZZZKS		KRAUSS, ROSA	.07	F	INFANT	GRZZZZWI	
FRANZ	4	M	CHILD	GRZZZZKS		LIEB, MARIA	19	F	SVNT	GRZZZZMD	
MARTIN	2	M	CHILD	GRZZZZKS		HERZOG, JOHANN	32	M	BRR	GRZZZZMD	
MARTHA	.07	F	INFANT	GRZZZZKS		MUELLER, FRANZ	20	M	FARMER	GRZZZZIL	

PASSENGER	AGE	SEX	OCCUPATION	PRVVL	DES
ADAMSKY, AUGUST	31	M	FARMER	GRZZZZIL	
HENSER, PETER	36	M	FARMER	GRZZZZPA	
MARIA	31	F	UNKNOWN	GRZZZZPA	
SEVERIN	2	M	CHILD	GRZZZZPA	
ANNA	.07	F	INFANT	GRZZZZPA	
MILDNER, FRANZ	22	M	LABR	GRZZZZPA	
JARECKI, JOHANN	59	M	LABR	GRZZZZMI	
CATHARINE	60	F	UNKNOWN	GRZZZZMI	
JAN	35	M	LABR	GRZZZZMI	
JOSEFA	30	F	UNKNOWN	GRZZZZMI	
STANISLAUS	9	M	CHILD	GRZZZZMI	
JOSEFA	4	F	CHILD	GRZZZZMI	
AMENDT, JOSEPH	36	M	FARMER	GRZZZZPA	
MATHILDE	32	F	UNKNOWN	GRZZZZPA	
CHRISTIAN	10	M	CH	GRZZZZPA	
CATHARINE	6	F	CHILD	GRZZZZPA	
HUBERT	4	M	CHILD	GRZZZZPA	
ELISABETH	2	F	CHILD	GRZZZZPA	
ANNA	.11	F	INFANT	GRZZZZPA	
WAHLRAB, OTTO	25	M	TLR	GRZZZZKS	
BRUN, WENZEL	26	M	TLR	GRZZZZKS	
GUTZEIT, LESETTE	48	F	UNKNOWN	GRZZZZKS	
RAJAHN, ANNA	18	F	UNKNOWN	GRZZZZKS	
VOLKMANN, ROBERT	34	M	FARMER	GRZZZZIL	
JOHANNA	37	F	UNKNOWN	GRZZZZIL	
FRANCISCA	14	F	UNKNOWN	GRZZZZIL	
BENNO	16	M	UNKNOWN	GRZZZZIL	
ROBERT	11	M	CH	GRZZZZIL	
EMIL	9	M	CHILD	GRZZZZIL	
LEA	7	M	CHILD	GRZZZZIL	
PAUL	4	M	CHILD	GRZZZZIL	
WANDA	3	F	CHILD	GRZZZZIL	
EILHELM	.11	M	INFANT	GRZZZZIL	
KRAUSE, IDA	19	F	UNKNOWN	GRZZZZIL	
HILLE, OTTO	15	M	UNKNOWN	GRZZZZIL	
FELSKE, ELISE	17	F	UNKNOWN	GRZZZZIL	
HEDWIG	16	F	UNKNOWN	GRZZZZIL	
HAAS, ANDREAS	29	M	FARMER	GRZZZZMD	
SCHLEGEL, ANNA	25	F	SVNT	GRZZZZMD	
LETZNER, GUSTAV	24	M	FARMER	GRZZZZMD	
AUGUSTE	23	F	UNKNOWN	GRZZZZMD	
EMMA	1	F	CHILD	GRZZZZMD	
LAURA	3	F	CHILD	GRZZZZMD	
RADKE, CARL	16	M	UNKNOWN	GRZZZZWAS	
GRZECHOWIAK, FRANCIS	29	M	LABR	GRZZZZIL	
BLAZEJEWSKI, MARIANNA	32	F	UNKNOWN	GRZZZZOH	
VINCENZ	10	M	CH	GRZZZZOH	
MARTHA	8	F	CHILD	GRZZZZOH	
ANTON	5	M	CHILD	GRZZZZOH	
BERNHARD	3	M	CHILD	GRZZZZOH	
WELHELM, ROBERT	26	M	LABR	GRZZZZPA	
PUHLE, OTTO	23	M	LABR	GRZZZZPA	
MOOTLER, MARTIN	23	M	LABR	GRZZZZWI	
KOPP, HULDA	18	F	UNKNOWN	GRZZZZWI	
PAST, BERTHA	35	F	UNKNOWN	GRZZZZMI	
ERNST	8	M	CHILD	GRZZZZMI	
MARTHA	6	F	CHILD	GRZZZZMI	
FRANCISCA	3	F	CHILD	GRZZZZMI	
JOHANNES	.11	M	INFANT	GRZZZZMI	
WARNKE, FRANZ	23	M	BKR	GRZZZZUNK	
SCHEFLER, HULDA	35	F	UNKNOWN	GRZZZZUNK	
WENTA, MARIANNA	27	F	UNKNOWN	GRZZZZOH	
BATTIN, HERMANN	29	M	LABR	GRZZZZOH	
FALKODORF, ANDREAS	23	M	LABR	GRZZZZMD	
WEOTPHAL, FRIEDRICH	27	M	TU	GRZZZZMD	
FAGENS, MARIANNA	36	F	UNKNOWN	GRZZZZMD	
CATHARINA	8	F	CHILD	GRZZZZMD	
HEIN, BERNHARD	24	M	FARMER	GRZZZZMD	
KRAUS, ELISABETH	47	F	UNKNOWN	GRZZZZMD	
ELISABETH	9	F	CHILD	GRZZZZMD	
WILHELMINE	5	F	CHILD	GRZZZZMD	
DCHMIDT, AUGUSTE	51	F	UNKNOWN	GRZZZZMD	
MATTAUSD, LINA	26	F	UNKNOWN	GRZZZZMD	
GERTRUD	.11	F	INFANT	GRZZZZMD	
HAIDEMANN, WILHELM	36	M	HTR	GRZZZZCAL	
MIETH, HEENRIETTE	55	F	UNKNOWN	GRZZZZOH	
PAUL	15	F	UNKNOWN	GRZZZZOH	
OTTO	13	F	UNKNOWN	GRZZZZOH	
PETERS, AUGUST	16	F	UNKNOWN	GRZZZZPA	
STAMERCILERS, JOHN	18	M	CPR	GRZZZZPA	
STREKER, THERESE	55	F	UNKNOWN	GRZZZZPA	
MARTHA	17	F	UNKNOWN	GRZZZZPA	
ROSALIA	15	F	UNKNOWN	GRZZZZPA	
KILLA, ANTON	52	M	FARMER	GRZZZZIL	
JOSEPHINE	50	F	UNKNOWN	GRZZZZIL	
ALBERT	14	M	UNKNOWN	GRZZZZIL	
HUETTER, ANTON	26	M	UNKNOWN	GRZZZZIL	
MARIA	44	F	UNKNOWN	GRZZZZIL	
MEYER, WILHELM	23	M	MCHT	GRZZZZAL	
GOTTSCHINSKA, ANGELIKA	16	F	UNKNOWN	GRZZZZKS	
GRZYWACZ, BARBARA	15	F	UNKNOWN	GRZZZZOH	
UEKER, GOTTLIEB	57	M	FARMER	GRZZZZOH	
CAROLINE	57	F	UNKNOWN	GRZZZZOH	
RUDOLPH	17	M	FARMER	GRZZZZOH	
DAHRMANN, HERMANN	39	M	LABR	GRZZZZMD	
SZWIDT, STANISLAUS	24	M	LABR	GRZZZZUNK	
MARGARETHE	19	F	UNKNOWN	GRZZZZUNK	
MICHAEL	16	M	UNKNOWN	GRZZZZUNK	
SCHWEDT, ANDRZEI	50	M	LABR	GRZZZZMD	
BALLING, AUGUST	16	M	UNKNOWN	GRZZZZOH	
HAPP, ENGELBART	17	M	MCHT	GRZZZZOH	

SHIP: ELBE

FROM: BREMEN AND SOUTHAMPTON
TO: NEW YORK
ARRIVED: 27 JUNE 1888

PASSENGER	AGE	SEX	OCCUPATION	PRVVL	DES
VONRESTORFF, COL.MRS	36	F	UNKNOWN	GRAAKHNY	
TUHY, FANY	39	F	UNKNOWN	GRACBRNY	
SCHWARZ, PAULINE	16	F	UNKNOWN	GRACBRNY	
EPPENSTEIN, CHRIST.	70	M	UNKNOWN	GRZZZZNY	
CAROLINE	40	F	UNKNOWN	GRZZZZNY	
WILHELM	9	M	CHILD	GRZZZZNY	
GUENTHER, TIEDEL	58	M	UNKNOWN	GRAGALNY	
CLAUSING, MARIE	34	F	UNKNOWN	GRACBRNY	
URBAN, HEINR.	53	M	UNKNOWN	GRACBRNY	
MERGER, MARIE	30	F	UNKNOWN	GRACBRNY	
LEO	10	M	CH	GRACBRNY	
ARTHUR	8	M	CHILD	GRACBRNY	
GRETCHEN	4	F	CHILD	GRACBRNY	
ELSCHEN	.10	F	INFANT	GRACBRNY	
BERNHEIM, SIEGFRIED	34	F	INF	GRACBRNY	
KERSCHER, PETER	38	M	INF	GRZZZZNY	
AMALIE	23	F	INF	GRZZZZNY	
MURKEN, META	47	F	UNKNOWN	GRACZVNY	
TIETJEN, KAETHIE	20	F	UNKNOWN	GRACZVNY	
MURKEN, MARTIN	53	M	UNKNOWN	GRACZVNY	
TIETJEN, GEORG	14	M	UNKNOWN	GRACZVNY	
MUELLER, LUEDER	17	M	UNKNOWN	GRACZVNY	
WINTER, UDO	19	M	UNKNOWN	GRACBRNY	
AHLERS, HERM.	40	M	UNKNOWN	GRAFOANY	
DORIS	35	F	UNKNOWN	GRAFOANY	
ADELE	4	F	CHILD	GRAFOANY	
CLARA	2	F	CHILD	GRAFOANY	
LOHMAYER, HELENE	17	F	CH	GRAFOANY	
HIRSCHBERG, HEINR.	40	M	UNKNOWN	GRAAKHNY	
CACILIE	30	F	UNKNOWN	GRAAKHNY	
FANNY	16	F	UNKNOWN	GRAAKHNY	
WAGNER, MINNA	19	F	SVNT	GRAENFNY	
WENZEL, MINNA	21	F	SVNT	GRAENFNY	
HOERING, PH.	27	M	TLR	GRADRONY	
WILKLER, FRIEDR.	29	M	LABR	GRADBBNY	
KACZMARK, MARIANNE	29	F	LABR	GRADIMNY	
JOH.	.09	M	INFANT	GRADIMNY	

PASSENGER	AGE	SEX	OCCUPATION	PRVL	DES
SZEFFNER, SALAMEA	18	F	LABR	GRADIMNY	
ENGEL, ANNA	18	F	SVNT	GRAJHPNY	
RENTZLEV, FRANZ	27	M	LABR	GRZZZZNY	
ZOLL, EMILIE	21	F	SVNT	GRAAZQNY	
KOLACKI, MICH.	25	M	LABR	GRZZZZNY	
KIENZLE, ERNESTINE	19	F	FARMER	GRZZZZNY	
SPIER, FANNY	24	F	UNKNOWN	GRZZZZNY	
RIEKCHEN	19	F	UNKNOWN	GRZZZZNY	
JAHNKE, LUDWIG	56	M	LABR	GRZZZZMN	
HENRIETTE	56	F	UNKNOWN	GRZZZZMN	
ANNA	26	F	UNKNOWN	GRZZZZMN	
STIEF, JOSEF	28	M	LABR	GRZZZZMO	
MENTZ, RICH.	19	M	CPTR	GRZZZZMO	
KLING, SOPHIE	22	F	UNKNOWN	GRADCJMO	
HAMER, WILHELM	13	M	LABR	GRADCJNY	
KOELLE, RICHARD	14	M	LABR	GRADCJNY	
BAUMGAERTNER, BERTHA	22	F	UNKNOWN	GRADCJNY	
BOTHEL, ELEONORE	16	F	UNKNOWN	GRADCJNY	
HERMANN, MATHILDE	18	F	UNKNOWN	GRAEYGNY	
LEUTSCH, ANNA	16	F	UNKNOWN	GRAEYGNY	
BAUER, MAGDALENE	26	F	UNKNOWN	GRZZZZNY	
DUERR, ANNA	19	F	UNKNOWN	GRZZZZNY	
DUESS, GOTTL.	14	M	LABR	GRZZZZNY	
UMNACHT, JACOB	14	M	LABR	GRZZZZNY	
SCHICHT, JOH.	24	M	LABR	GRZZZZNY	
FINZ, THERESE	43	F	UNKNOWN	GRZZZZNY	
SOMMER, CAROLINE	16	F	UNKNOWN	GRZZZZNY	
WAGNER, ROSE	18	F	UNKNOWN	GRABLVNY	
DENZLER, ROSE	18	F	UNKNOWN	GRABLVNY	
KROMER, BERTHA	15	F	UNKNOWN	GRABLVNY	
WEISS, CHRISTIANE	15	F	UNKNOWN	GRABENNY	
HESS, MARIE	15	F	UNKNOWN	GRABENNY	
MEZGER, JULIUS	24	M	MECH	GRAGMDNY	
JACOB, MARIE	18	F	UNKNOWN	GRAGMDNY	
WENDEL, KATHARINE	23	F	UNKNOWN	GRZZZZNY	
SCHAEFER, JULIA	17	F	UNKNOWN	GRZZZZNY	
MAIER, ROSINE	45	F	W	GRZZZZNY	
CHRIST.	13	M	CH	GRZZZZNY	
MARIE	10	F	CH	GRZZZZNY	
SOPHIE	8	F	CHILD	GRZZZZNY	
CARL	.04	M	INFANT	GRZZZZNY	
RUNDSCHUH, WILHELMINE	24	F	UNKNOWN	GRZZZZNY	
GIES, GUST.	18	M	LABR	GRZZZZNY	
WALTER, GEORG	16	M	LABR	GRZZZZWI	
LOHRMANN, JACOB	18	M	LABR	GRZZZZMO	
ZIEGLER, MINA	21	F	UNKNOWN	GRZZZZMO	
LEHR, ROSINE	20	F	UNKNOWN	GRZZZZMO	
BUSCH, REGINE	15	F	UNKNOWN	GRZZZZMO	
STOCKER, JACOB	14	M	CPR	GRZZZZPA	
STOLL, CARL	11	M	CH	GRZZZZIL	
STAEHLE, JOH.	57	M	LABR	GRZZZZWI	
JULIE	59	F	W	GRZZZZWI	
JULIE	19	F	CH	GRZZZZWI	
MARIE	7	F	CHILD	GRZZZZWI	
RENTZEL, WILHELM	46	M	SMH	GRADHZOH	
FRIEDA	38	F	W	GRADHZOH	
MARIE	14	F	CH	GRADHZOH	
FRIEDR.	11	M	CH	GRADHZOH	
FERDINAND	10	M	CH	GRADHZOH	
ANNA	8	F	CHILD	GRADHZOH	
KARL	2	M	CHILD	GRADHZOH	
FRITZ, ROSINE	25	F	UNKNOWN	GRZZZZOH	
HEILMANN, MARIE	52	F	W	GRABKVNY	
MARIE	16	F	CH	GRABKVNY	
MARGARETHA	15	F	CH	GRABKVNY	
LEONHARDT	10	F	CH	GRABKVNY	
MIDTER, ELISA	20	F	UNKNOWN	GRZZZZNY	
GRIMM, ELISABETH	47	F	W	GRZZZZNY	
WILHELM	15	M	CH	GRZZZZNY	
ALBERT	13	M	CH	GRZZZZNY	
ELISABETH	9	F	CHILD	GRZZZZNY	
KOZUBSKA, MARIANNE	20	F	UNKNOWN	GRAILBNY	
MUELLER, WILHELM	30	M	LABR	GRAILBNY	
ADLER, AUGUSTE	18	F	UNKNOWN	GRAARRNY	
MAGERSDORFER, SEBAST.	16	M	LABR	GRZZZZNY	
GENZLER, EUGEN	27	M	LABR	GRADYANY	
STOLL, MARIA	23	F	UNKNOWN	GRADYANY	
MARGA.	56	F	UNKNOWN	GRADYANY	
BRASCH, JOSEF	15	M	UNKNOWN	GRZZZZNY	
MIESBACH, ALOIS	24	M	UNKNOWN	GRZZZZNY	
STREBER, LORENZ	20	M	UNKNOWN	GRZZZZNY	
MOHR, BAPTIST	16	M	UNKNOWN	GRZZZZNY	
ULMKE, CARL	25	M	FARMER	GRZZZZNY	
WINKLER, ANNA	17	F	UNKNOWN	GRACPUNY	
ROTT, ANNA	36	F	UNKNOWN	GRACXVNY	
NOWRASKO, ANTONIO	24	F	UNKNOWN	GRAEABNY	
LORCH, BERTHA	19	F	UNKNOWN	GRABMBNY	
BELL, ANNA	22	F	UNKNOWN	GRABMBNY	
HERHAMMER, FRIEDR.	13	M	CH	GRABMBNY	
CATHARINE	14	F	UNKNOWN	GRABMBNY	
FREUDENBERGER, MINA	20	F	UNKNOWN	GRZZZZNY	
SCHLEGEL, LUDWIG	27	M	UNKNOWN	GRADUXNY	
ANNA	24	F	UNKNOWN	GRADUXNY	
OTT, HELENE	18	F	UNKNOWN	GRAARRNY	
WEINMANN, AUGUST	16	M	UNKNOWN	GRZZZZNY	
GEORG	26	M	UNKNOWN	GRZZZZNY	
BRUNNER, CONRAD	18	M	LABR	GRALBKCH	
SCHOTT, GEORG	18	M	BKR	GRALBKCAN	
KULOW, HERM.	48	M	BKR	GRZZZZNY	
CAROLINE	36	F	W	GRZZZZNY	
ANNIE	9	F	CHILD	GRZZZZNY	
MARIE	7	F	CHILD	GRZZZZNY	
OTTO	3	M	CHILD	GRZZZZNY	
MINNIE	.09	F	INFANT	GRZZZZNY	
DUECK, JOH.	28	M	BRR	GRZZZZNY	
KOERTH, WILH.	32	M	FARMER	GRZZZZNY	
DRA-----A, SALOMEA	22	F	MUSN	GRZZZZNY	
BUTZ, FLORENTINE	49	F	W	GRZZZZNY	
JOS.	15	M	CH	GRZZZZNY	
AUGUST	5	M	CHILD	GRZZZZNY	
GLAESS, CARL	57	M	BCHR	GRZZZZNY	
AUGUSTE	50	F	UNKNOWN	GRZZZZNY	
KAISER, NANA	63	F	UNKNOWN	GRZZZZNY	
GUMMINGER, PAUL	50	M	TLR	GRZZZZNY	
ALOIS	19	M	UNKNOWN	GRZZZZNY	
FRANZ	18	M	UNKNOWN	GRZZZZNY	
SCHNEIDER, THERESIA	62	F	UNKNOWN	GRACUYNY	
AUGUSTE	25	F	UNKNOWN	GRACUYNY	
LINDENTHAL, ANNA	20	F	UNKNOWN	GRACUYNY	
KUSEL, WILHELMINE	20	F	UNKNOWN	GRACUYNY	
GREHL, JOS.	39	M	LABR	GRACUYNY	
MAGD.	33	F	UNKNOWN	GRACUYNY	
PAUL	10	M	CH	GRACUYNY	
MARIA	7	F	CHILD	GRACUYNY	
HERM.	4	M	CHILD	GRACUYNY	
WILH.	2	M	CHILD	GRACUYNY	
SCHAAD, HERM.	16	M	LABR	GRACUYNY	
ZIMMERMANN, JULIUS	29	M	FSHMN	GRZZZZNE	
PAULINE	22	F	UNKNOWN	GRZZZZNE	
ALBERT	3	M	CHILD	GRZZZZNE	
JULIUS	2	M	CHILD	GRZZZZNE	
BERTHA	.05	F	INFANT	GRZZZZNE	
RIESENWEBER, HERMINE	21	F	UNKNOWN	GRAJCLIL	
KLEMKE, WILHELMINE	27	F	UNKNOWN	GRAJCLIL	
ELISE	3	F	CHILD	GRAJCLIL	
KOERTH, ADOLPHINE	27	F	UNKNOWN	GRZZZZPA	
HELENA	4	F	CHILD	GRZZZZPA	
EMILIE	3	F	CHILD	GRZZZZPA	
HERM.	2	M	CHILD	GRZZZZPA	
SCHEDLER, HERM.	51	M	BSKM	GRZZZZPA	
ANNA	44	F	UNKNOWN	GRZZZZPA	
PAUL	18	M	FARMER	GRZZZZPA	
PETERSEN, MARIE	50	F	UNKNOWN	GRZZZZWI	
POPKOWITZ, IDA	19	F	UNKNOWN	GRZZZZNY	
HOFFMANN, MAX	23	M	BBR	GRZZZZNY	
ROHDE, ANDR.	25	M	FARMER	GRZZZZNY	
HAHN, EMMA	23	F	UNKNOWN	GRADCJMA	
BAUMEISTER, AUGUST	24	M	MCHT	GRAHGRPA	
HELMSTAEDTER, GUST.	22	M	CPTR	GRAKUMPA	
HINRICHS, HELENE	25	F	UNKNOWN	GRZZZZNY	

PASSENGER	AGE	SEX	OCCUPATION	PRIVL	DES
FROMANN, HUGO	39	M	BRR	GRAAXYNY	
ROEDER, BONIFACIUS	30	M	FARMER	GRZZZZNY	
HOMEYER, WILHELM	17	M	MCHT	GRAARRNY	
STUEVER, HERM.	17	M	UNKNOWN	GRAARRNY	
MEYER, HERM.	16	M	UNKNOWN	GRAARRNY	
PREISEL, JOSEF	21	M	LKSH	GRAFWNNY	
EGERER, JOSEFA	24	F	UNKNOWN	GRAFWNNY	
ZUNNER, BERNH.	12	M	FARMER	GRAFWNNY	
BRENNECKE, CATHARINE	55	F	UNKNOWN	GRAFWNCAO	
BIERMANN, FRIEDR.	17	M	UNKNOWN	GRAFWNCAO	
SILBER, MAX	16	M	MCHT	GRAFRGNY	
MARTIN, MARIA	20	F	UNKNOWN	GRZZZZNY	
HEIMANN, FRIEDR.	16	F	UNKNOWN	GRABESNY	
KATHARINE	11	F	CH	GRABESNY	
PREUSS, MARTHA	23	F	UNKNOWN	GRAAKHNY	
MUELLER, ELISE	8	F	CHILD	GRAAKHNY	
MAREK, TEOFIL	37	M	LABR	GRAEABNY	
ZYDORZIK, ANDRAS	18	M	LABR	GRAEABNY	
GOTOWIC, LORENZ	24	M	LABR	GRZZZZNY	
HESSELBARTH, FRANZ	36	M	LABR	GRZZZZMO	
LOUISE	36	F	UNKNOWN	GRZZZZMO	
DOMIKI, SIMON	22	M	UNKNOWN	GRZZZZPA	
JACOB, MORITZ	22	M	UNKNOWN	GRZZZZPA	
GABLIC, MARK	35	M	UNKNOWN	GRAAQAPA	
ARMBROESTER, J.H.	24	M	UNKNOWN	GRAAQAPA	
NIEMANN, AUGUST	24	M	UNKNOWN	GRAAQAPA	
LINDHAUS, JOH.	25	M	UNKNOWN	GRZZZZIL	
LILIENBECKER, BERNH.	32	M	UNKNOWN	GRZZZZOH	
LEIDIG, JOH.	14	M	UNKNOWN	GRZZZZIL	
SECKEL, SOPHIE	22	F	UNKNOWN	GRZZZZOH	
EHRMANN, GOTTLIEB	28	M	UNKNOWN	GRZZZZNY	
KOCHENDOERFER, LENE	19	F	UNKNOWN	GRZZZZNY	
GEFKEN, DIERK	16	M	FARMER	GRZZZZNY	
FIECHTL, OTTO	27	M	SGL	GRAEXKNY	
ELSA	19	F	UNKNOWN	GRAEXKNY	
THERESE	18	F	UNKNOWN	GRAEXKNY	
ROSKE, ED.	37	M	PNTR	GRAAKHNY	
ADELE	33	F	UNKNOWN	GRAAKHNY	
HAASEMANN, LOUIS	34	M	SHMK	GRAAKHNY	
LAURA	34	F	UNKNOWN	GRAAKHNY	
OTTO	8	M	CHILD	GRAAKHNY	
PLATH, PAUL	20	M	TLR	GRAAKHNY	
KELLER, MAX	31	M	FARMER	GRALBSNY	
BOEHMFALK, FRIEDR.	26	M	FARMER	GRAFOANY	
SETZEPANDT, GUST.	26	M	FARMER	GRAFOANY	
GRELLA, KUNIGIUNDE	22	F	UNKNOWN	GRZZZZPA	
GRIEMA, ADOLF	13	M	LABR	GRABAGNY	
GESINE	11	F	CH	GRABAGNY	
NAUER, ANNA	27	F	UNKNOWN	GRACEENY	
ALBERT	3	M	CHILD	GRAHPUNY	
RAMROTH, MAGNUS	48	M	LABR	GRAHPUOH	
ELISABETH	18	F	UNKNOWN	GRAHPUOH	
FRITZ	11	M	CH	GRAHPUOH	
MAGNUS	28	M	LABR	GRAHPUOH	
SCHULTE, THERESIA	28	F	UNKNOWN	GRAHPUOH	
HELLFRITZSCH, JOH.	16	M	FARMER	GRZZZZPA	
DIEDRICH, MAX	26	M	FARMER	GRZZZZIL	
BENTZEN, S.	30	M	BRR	GRACTLOH	
LEVY, LEOPOLD	17	M	MCHT	GRAARROR	
EHMANN, JOH.	33	M	SHMK	GRACHTOR	
RAUSER, ANNA	21	F	UNKNOWN	GRACHTOR	
ROTTENBERGER, KATHARINE	45	F	UNKNOWN	GRZZZZOR	
MARIE	11	F	CH	GRZZZZOR	
KATHARINE	9	F	CHILD	GRZZZZOR	
THERESIA	7	F	CHILD	GRZZZZOR	
OTTO	.11	M	INFANT	GRZZZZOR	
WIEDERING, HANES	19	M	SEMN	GRZZZZNY	
BOEHLER, JACOB	38	M	MCHT	GRADLMNY	
JACOB	14	M	MCHT	GRADLMNY	
GRABHORN, WILHELM	24	M	FARMER	GRZZZZCAL	
SCHULZ, ALBERT	26	M	FARMER	GRZZZZIL	
AUGUSTE	25	F	UNKNOWN	GRZZZZIA	
FRANK, JACOB	15	M	SDLR	GRZZZZWI	
MARX, ALEX	24	M	LABR	GRZZZZWI	
WAECKER, XAVER	42	M	FARMER	GRZZZZPA	
ANNA	41	F	UNKNOWN	GRZZZZPA	
MICHE.	11	M	CH	GRZZZZPA	
XAVER	10	M	CH	GRZZZZPA	
KRESZENZ	5	M	CHILD	GRZZZZPA	
JOSEF	5	M	CHILD	GRZZZZPA	
ANNA	3	F	CHILD	GRZZZZPA	
KATHARINE	.11	F	INFANT	GRZZZZPA	
SCHNEIDER, ROSA	35	F	UNKNOWN	GRZZZZPA	
ROSA	35	F	UNKNOWN	GRZZZZPA	
HEINR.	10	M	CH	GRZZZZPA	
ROSA	9	F	CHILD	GRZZZZPA	
FRANZISKA	7	F	CHILD	GRZZZZPA	
ANNA	4	F	CHILD	GRZZZZPA	
JOSEF	2	M	CHILD	GRZZZZPA	
KRAEMER, GEORG	49	M	FARMER	GRZZZZNY	
EVA, MARGARETHA	41	F	UNKNOWN	GRZZZZNY	
BABETTE	11	F	CH	GRZZZZNY	
GEORG	9	M	CHILD	GRZZZZNY	
ADAM	6	M	CHILD	GRZZZZNY	
FRIEDR.	.11	M	INFANT	GRZZZZNY	
KISTER, BARBARA	67	F	UNKNOWN	GRZZZZNY	
ACHTERNKAMP, BERNH.	29	M	FARMER	GRZZZZNY	
AGNES	26	F	UNKNOWN	GRZZZZNY	
FREDERKING, HEINR.	23	M	CPR	GRACBRNY	
PICKEL, ROSA	27	F	UNKNOWN	GRZZZZNY	
HOLM, MARIE	18	F	UNKNOWN	GRZZZZCH	
LYBECK, LARS	36	M	LABR	GRZZZZCH	
LENE	30	F	UNKNOWN	GRZZZZCH	
NILS	10	M	CH	GRZZZZCH	
DAMM, HANS	17	M	BKR	GRZZZZCH	
FUERSTE, GERHD.	15	M	LABR	GRABSDCH	
BUECHLER, GEORG	17	M	LABR	GRAAMTNY	
MAY, ADAM	34	M	LABR	GRZZZZNY	
EBERHARDT, FRANZISKA	11	F	CH	GRZZZZPA	
HULL, JOS.	11	M	CH	GRZZZZPA	
HARICH, OTTO	16	M	LABR	GRZZZZPA	
NIGGEL, THERESIA	18	F	UNKNOWN	GRZZZZCAL	
THERESIA	20	F	UNKNOWN	GRZZZZNY	
STAEHLI, WILHELMINE	26	F	UNKNOWN	GRZZZZNY	
NIGGEL, HEDWIG	18	F	UNKNOWN	GRZZZZNY	
SCHLOTTERBECK, HEINR.	24	M	LABR	GRAFOANY	
BIETZ, KAETCHEN	18	F	UNKNOWN	GRAAMTNY	
SCHUETZ, ADAM	20	M	LABR	GRAAMTNY	
KESSLING, EDUARD	18	M	LABR	GRAAMTNY	
STANTOWIAK, THOMAS	68	M	LABR	GRZZZZNY	
PITRONELLA	73	F	UNKNOWN	GRZZZZNY	
SINGER, FRANZ	24	M	BKR	GRACBRNY	
SCHRISTOF, CARL	26	M	FARMER	GRACBRNY	
HOFMANN, JOSEF	25	M	FARMER	GRZZZZNY	
OVENBECK, FERD.	25	M	LABR	GRZZZZNY	
ZAREMBA, FRANZ	30	M	LABR	GRZZZZNY	
SCHIBROWSKY, HERM.	46	M	LABR	GRZZZZNY	
KOSZUTOSKA, PELAGIA	18	F	UNKNOWN	GRAHJJNY	
GRABIAK, MARIANNE	22	F	UNKNOWN	GRAHJJNY	
CATHARINE	10	F	CH	GRAHJJNY	
ALLINGER, HEINR.	35	M	PNTR	GRZZZZNY	
FRIEDRE.	10	F	CH	GRZZZZNY	
BRINGS, LUDW.	18	M	LABR	GRZZZZNY	
SUFFA, LISETTA	20	F	UNKNOWN	GRZZZZNY	
BAUER, MARIA	36	F	UNKNOWN	GRZZZZNY	
MARIE	6	F	CHILD	GRZZZZNY	
JOHANNE	5	F	CHILD	GRZZZZNY	
AUGUST	.06	M	INFANT	GRZZZZNY	

```
                    A S          P V  D                            A S          P V  D
                    G E OCCUPATION R I  E                          G E OCCUPATION R I  E
PASSENGER           E X          V L  S        PASSENGER           E X          V L  S
```

SHIP: ENGLAND

FROM: LIVERPOOL AND QUEENSTOWN
TO: NEW YORK
ARRIVED: 27 JUNE 1888

PASSENGER	AGE	SEX	OCCUPATION	PRVL DES
HERMAN, REICHT	37	M	LABR	GRZZZZPHI
SCHROCK, ERNEST	17	M	LABR	GRZZZZNY
KOLTINSKY, MAX	17	M	LABR	GRZZZZNY
SIEBER, BERTHA	19	F	SVNT	GRZZZZNY
LUDWIG, OTILIGE	18	F	SVNT	GRZZZZWI
ROSENBAUM, NOCHEM	24	F	W	GRZZZZNY
SEAH	.06	F	INFANT	GRZZZZNY
GOLDBERG, MARTHA	26	F	SVNT	GRZZZZNY
KLEMG, BERTHA	18	F	SVNT	GRZZZZEMA
GOLDBERGER, CHANE	25	F	SVNT	GRZZZZNY
SYLVESTER, THOMAS	34	M	LABR	FRZZZZUSA
ROSA	30	F	W	FRZZZZUSA
MARIE	2	F	CHILD	FRZZZZUSA
ALBERT	1	M	CHILD	FRZZZZUSA
POKORSKA, SCHEINDEL	.11	F	INFANT	FRZZZZUSA

SHIP: ST. OF PENNSYLVANIA

FROM: GLASGOW AND LARNE
TO: NEW YORK
ARRIVED: 27 JUNE 1888

PASSENGER	AGE	SEX	OCCUPATION	PRVL DES
KIRCHER, BENJAMIN	32	M	SHMK	GRZZZZUSA
KOANIG, ALBERT	36	M	TLR	GRZZZZUSA
BLAMIS, MICHEL	22	M	SMH	GRZZZZUSA
LAGERMANN, BERNARD	31	M	MNR	GRZZZZUSA
BLUM, LAMECH	15	M	PDLR	GRZZZZUSA
LEGALL, MINNA	10	F	SP	GRZZZZUSA
HEDONG, ETTE	22	F	SP	GRZZZZUSA
HAAS, LINA	20	F	SP	GRZZZZUSA
KRAWITZ, IDA	20	F	SP	GRZZZZUSA
FANNY	22	F	SP	GRZZZZUSA
ROSA	22	F	SP	GRZZZZUSA

SHIP: KANSAS

FROM: LIVERPOOL AND LONDON
TO: BOSTON
ARRIVED: 28 JUNE 1888

PASSENGER	AGE	SEX	OCCUPATION	PRVL DES
JOSEPH, J	26	M	LABR	FRZZZZBO
STEAD, C	27	M	LABR	FRZZZZBO
ISAACS, L	32	M	LABR	GRZZZZNY
ARMINS, ANM.	19	M	LABR	HBZZZZBO
MENDEL	9	M	CHILD	HBZZZZBO
PERNKI, JOSEPH	40	M	MSN	SRZZZZNY

SHIP: GALLIA

FROM: LIVERPOOL AND QUEENSTOWN
TO: NEW YORK
ARRIVED: 29 JUNE 1888

PASSENGER	AGE	SEX	OCCUPATION	PRVL DES
FALERIKAUS, BERL	28	M	PDLR	SRACBFUSA
KOSMAN, JACOB	18	M	MLR	SRACBFUSA
BERTSCHER, BER.	19	M	LABR	SRACBFUSA
DEALADE, ABRAHAM	47	M	BBR	SRACBFUSA
GOOTTLIEBE, HY.	30	M	TLR	SRACBFUSA
LANGER, JULIUS	23	M	LABR	SRACBFUSA
MARKUS	30	M	LABR	SRACBFUSA
BULNER, ALOIS	30	M	TLR	SRACBFUSA
STREICHER, ARON	28	M	TLR	SRACBFUSA
PAPPER, ADOLF	19	M	LABR	SRACBFUSA
FROST, LEIE	15	F	SP	SRACBFUSA
KERSCHEABAUN, LEIE	21	F	SP	SRACBFUSA
LINK, AUGUSTA	38	F	MA	SRACBFUSA
AIGISTA	8	F	CHILD	SRACBFUSA
MONICA	6	F	CHILD	SRACBFUSA
MILLER, TIKE	30	F	MA	SRACBFUSA
ABRAM	8	M	CHILD	SRACBFUSA
CHANIE	3	M	CHILD	SRACBFUSA
MALUC	.10	M	INFANT	SRACBFUSA
HENOF, W.	35	M	STMSN	SRACBFUSA
BERTHE	33	F	W	SRACBFUSA
ELIZABETH	9	F	CHILD	SRACBFUSA
MARTHA	3	F	CHILD	SRACBFUSA
MARIE	2	F	CHILD	SRACBFUSA
CHRISTO, FLORES	40	M	HTLKPR	FRZZZZUSA
MARIE	30	F	W	FRZZZZUSA
GOEDICKE, WM.	34	M	FARMER	FRABOQUSA
FOKMOOCK, MARTHA	28	F	SVNT	FRABOQUSA

SHIP: HAMMONIA

FROM: HAMBURG AND HAVRE
TO: NEW YORK
ARRIVED: 29 JUNE 1888

PASSENGER	AGE	SEX	OCCUPATION	PRVL DES
MOHR, HERMANN	46	M	UNKNOWN	PRZZZZUSA
REBEKKA	50	F	UNKNOWN	PRZZZZUSA
JOH.	8	M	CHILD	PRZZZZUSA
MULLER, LYDIA	38	F	UNKNOWN	PRACBFUSA
MOHR, MATH.	16	F	UNKNOWN	PRACBFUSA
FREDLER, MARIE	64	F	UNKNOWN	PRACBFUSA
HARDER, JOH.	17	M	LABR	PRZZZZUSA
BONINGER, FRIEDKE.	30	F	W	PRZZZZUSA
JULNE.	.11	F	INFANT	PRZZZZUSA
GELLERMANN, BENJIN	38	M	TLR	PRZZZZUSA
CHAJE	20	F	W	PRZZZZUSA
LASZINER, SELIG.	24	M	UNKNOWN	PRZZZZUSA
KLEINMANN, TAUBE	20	F	SGL	PRZZZZUSA
HINSZE, ARTHUR	25	M	UNKNOWN	PRZZZZUSA
STOLTENBERG, PETER	35	M	LABR	PRZZZZUSA
JOHNA.	31	F	W	PRZZZZUSA
AGNES	4	F	CHILD	PRZZZZUSA
PETERSEN, CATH.	63	F	W	PRZZZZUSA
CALLESEN, MARTIN	19	M	UNKNOWN	PRZZZZUSA
CHRISTIAN	17	M	LABR	PRZZZZUSA
JUERGENSEN, HELENE	33	F	W	PRAAKHUSA
EMMA	6	F	CHILD	PRAAKHUSA
ELTA	3	F	CHILD	PRAAKHUSA
HANS	.11	M	INFANT	PRAAKHUSA
RAMM, EDUARD	20	M	UNKNOWN	PRAAKHUSA
MATTHRESSEN, PETER	16	M	UNKNOWN	PRAAKHUSA
MULLER, MARGARETHA	24	F	SGL	PRAAKHUSA
YSCHINSKI, STEFAN	14	M	SHMK	PRZZZZUSA

PASSENGER	AGE	SEX	OCCUPATION	PRV VLS DES
SCHEWRINER, ISIDOR	15	M	UNKNOWN	PRZZZZUSA
SCHULZ, CARL	23	M	SHMK	PRACBFUSA
STURRE, AUG.	25	M	UNKNOWN	WMZZZZUSA
SOPHIE	21	F	W	WMZZZZUSA
BERTHA	1	F	CHILD	WMZZZZUSA
PETT, JOACHIM	34	M	FARMER	PRZZZZUSA
LOUISE	26	F	W	PRZZZZUSA
AUGUST	.06	M	INFANT	PRZZZZUSA
FRANZ	2	M	CHILD	PRZZZZUSA
BLOHM, ANNA	65	F	SGL	PRZZZZUSA
BRUNS, JOHS.	15	M	FARMER	PRZZZZUSA
HAKE, JOH.	24	M	BKR	PRZZZZUSA
FINDEISEN, EDUARD	55	M	UNKNOWN	SYZZZZUSA
SCHAEDEL, JOH.	17	M	UNKNOWN	BVZZZZUSA
KOBF, GEORG	28	M	SMH	SYZZZZUSA
NEUMANN, ROSALIE	18	F	W	SYZZZZUSA
CURT	.11	M	INFANT	SYZZZZUSA
JACOBSOHN, ERNESTINE	28	F	SGL	PRZZZZUSA
HANSEL, NICOL	18	M	TLR	BVZZZZUSA
KLEIN, JOHA.	18	F	SGL	BVZZZZUSA
GRIEPHAHN, CARL	15	M	LABR	HBZZZZUSA
SPOV, H.	28	M	LABR	PRZZZZUSA
DILGAARD, ELISABETH	29	F	SGL	BVZZZZUSA
ERICHSEN, AUGUSTE	20	F	SGL	PRZZZZUSA
BADZOM, ROBT.S.	31	M	TLR	PRZZZZUSA
MINE	22	F	W	PRZZZZUSA
HARDTHE, CAROLINE	25	F	SGL	PRZZZZUSA
JOHA.	15	F	SGL	PRZZZZUSA
SOIFER, BACHEL	23	F	SGL	PRZZZZUSA
SPLITTE, RICHARD	23	M	MCHT	SYZZZZUSA
WESSPHAL, WILH.	28	M	UNKNOWN	HBZZZZUSA
CLAUSEN, CHR.	23	M	MCHT	PRZZZZUSA
SCHROEDER, HENRIETTE	38	F	W	MKZZZZUSA
OTTO	8	M	CHILD	MKZZZZUSA
HUGO	6	M	CHILD	MKZZZZUSA
TUCHSEN, WILHME.	24	F	SGL	PRZZZZUSA
FUCHSLOCKER, ROSINE	14	F	SGL	WMZZZZUSA
MAISCH, ROSA	29	F	W	WMZZZZUSA
CATHERINE	21	F	SGL	WMZZZZUSA
RUFF, BERNH.	30	M	LABR	WMZZZZUSA
KIPPS, ANNA	17	F	SGL	WMZZZZUSA
JOHS.	16	M	LABR	WMZZZZUSA
MUELLER, ANNA	19	F	SGL	WMZZZZUSA
LWILLING, HERM.	23	M	MCHT	PRZZZZUSA
ZWERMAN, SHCODOR	31	M	UNKNOWN	PRZZZZUSA
EVA	26	F	W	PRZZZZUSA
KUENSTLER, ANNA	72	F	W	WMZZZZUSA
KLEIN, CHRISTINE	16	F	SGL	BVZZZZUSA
HOFFELDER, CAROLINE	23	F	SGL	BVZZZZUSA
LANGE, WILH.	18	M	SMH	PRZZZZUSA
FAESZOLD, ERNST	23	M	MCHT	PRZZZZUSA
BLUMENTAL, NATAN	17	M	MCHT	PRZZZZUSA
LORENZ, ELISABETH	22	F	SGL	BVZZZZUSA
CARSTENS, JOHA.	22	F	SGL	PRZZZZUSA
HEINRICH, BARBARA	24	F	SGL	BVZZZZUSA
NELL, ADELE	15	F	SGL	PRZZZZUSA
LUNSTRETT, HENRIKE	27	F	SGL	BDZZZZUSA
ANSER, HELENE	25	F	W	BDZZZZUSA
CAROLINE	16	F	SGL	BDZZZZUSA
NOLD, CAHTRA.	22	F	SGL	BDZZZZUSA
PETTIG, LUDWIG	21	M	FARMER	BDZZZZUSA
GROH, JOHN	17	M	TLR	BVZZZZUSA
GRIES, BAPTIST	21	M	LABR	BVZZZZUSA
BOLTER, ELISE	22	F	SGL	WMZZZZUSA
ROSS, MAX	21	M	UNKNOWN	PRZZZZUSA
KUHNLEIN, ADAM	43	M	UNKNOWN	BVZZZZUSA
KELZ, HERM.	36	M	UNKNOWN	PRZZZZUSA
HANSEN, ELISABETH	18	F	SGL	PRZZZZUSA
RUSCH, CHRISTINE	21	F	SGL	HBZZZZUSA
WILDERFELDER, FRANZ	20	M	SMH	HBZZZZUSA
KRAFFCZYLE, PHILIPP	55	M	LABR	PRZZZZUSA
MARIE	55	F	W	PRZZZZUSA
CAROLINA	20	F	SGL	PRZZZZUSA
JOSEFA	16	F	SGL	PRZZZZUSA
JONITT, JOH.	18	M	FARMER	PRZZZZUSA
BECKLMANN, MINNIE	17	F	UNKNOWN	PRADNVUSA
MEYER, BERTHA	29	F	UNKNOWN	PRADNVUSA
GOTTLER, HILLER	28	M	UNKNOWN	PRADNVUSA
ROTH, SAMUEL	26	M	UNKNOWN	PRADNVUSA
HOYER, JOHANNA	20	F	UNKNOWN	PRADNVUSA
BUCHSPAN, SALOMON	8	M	CHILD	PRADNVUSA
BLOCH, CHAZKEL	8	M	CHILD	PRADNVUSA
GRINBLATT, CATH.	16	F	UNKNOWN	PRADNVUSA
CLASSEN, JOACHIM	47	M	UNKNOWN	SYZZZZUSA
LOUISE	41	F	UNKNOWN	SYZZZZUSA
HEINR.	8	M	CHILD	SYZZZZUSA
CAROLINE	7	F	CHILD	SYZZZZUSA
MARIE	6	F	CHILD	SYZZZZUSA
AUGUST	5	M	CHILD	SYZZZZUSA
DWORSKY, BASCHE	45	F	UNKNOWN	BWZZZZUSA
SONE	15	F	UNKNOWN	BWZZZZUSA
SALOMON	8	M	CHILD	BWZZZZUSA
ARON	7	M	CHILD	BWZZZZUSA
DAVID	3	M	CHILD	BWZZZZUSA
LOTTE	5	F	CHILD	BWZZZZUSA
ARONSOHN, SAMUEL	23	M	UNKNOWN	BWZZZZUSA
SCHPSEL	19	M	UNKNOWN	BWZZZZUSA
GUSMANN, SCHOEL	16	M	UNKNOWN	HBZZZZUSA
PETERSEN, PETER	49	M	UNKNOWN	PRZZZZUSA
HINSCH, MARGARETHE	19	F	SGL	HBZZZZUSA
FREUDENBERG, JOH.	15	M	UNKNOWN	HBZZZZUSA
ERICHSEN, JES	59	M	UNKNOWN	HBADWZUSA
SCHLESINGER, EMMA	29	F	UNKNOWN	HBZZZZUSA
HURLEBUSCH, MARIA	8	F	CHILD	HBZZZZUSA
FRENKELBACH, MARIE	36	F	UNKNOWN	HBZZZZUSA
AUG.	16	M	UNKNOWN	HBZZZZUSA
LOUIS	14	M	UNKNOWN	HBZZZZUSA
WILLI	8	M	CHILD	HBZZZZUSA
ROSA	.06	F	INFANT	HBZZZZUSA
ULSEN, MARIE	30	F	SGL	PRZZZZUSA
LORENZ, ELISABETH	22	F	SGL	BVZZZZUSA
HAMMER, CATHR.	75	F	W	PRZZZZUSA
WICH, AUGUSTE	22	F	SGL	PRZZZZUSA
TUROWSKI, ADALBERS.	66	M	LABR	PRZZZZUSA
PTISK, DORA	52	F	W	PRZZZZUSA
SCHLUCK, ROBERT	24	M	LABR	PRZZZZUSA
NADOLSKA, JULIANE	20	F	W	PRZZZZUSA
MAXIMILIAN	.05	M	INFANT	PRZZZZUSA
WIMPFHEIMER, FRIEDR.	24	M	LABR	WMZZZZUSA
REINHE, MAX	16	M	LABR	PRZZZZUSA
WECHTRYCHOWITZ, MINE	25	F	SGL	PRZZZZUSA
SZEMANSKA, CONSTANCIA	53	F	W	PRZZZZUSA
LETSCHE, WILHELM	14	M	LABR	WMZZZZUSA
CARL	15	M	LABR	WMZZZZUSA
DITTMAR, CATH.	23	F	W	PRZZZZUSA
CHR.	.06	F	INFANT	PRZZZZUSA
FRANZEN, MARG.	23	F	W	PRZZZZUSA
ASMUS	.06	M	INFANT	PRZZZZUSA
JACOBSON, DORA	7	F	CHILD	PRZZZZUSA
WASAK, FRANZISKA	23	F	SGL	PRZZZZUSA
BERTHMANE, CHARLOTTE	20	F	SGL	PRZZZZUSA
MOSES, MINNA	28	F	SGL	PRZZZZUSA
KNIGER, JOHANNA	25	F	SGL	PRAAKHUSA
PIONTEK, ELISABETH	63	F	W	PRAAKHUSA
BASLER, AUGUSTE	50	F	W	PRZZZZUSA
PAULE.	17	F	SGL	PRZZZZUSA
BADEWEIN, HERMANN	15	M	LABR	PRZZZZUSA
GUSE, ALBERT	31	M	FARMER	PRZZZZUSA
FISCHER, CARL	45	M	FARMER	PRZZZZUSA
LOUISE	38	F	W	PRZZZZUSA
LOUISE	14	F	CH	PRZZZZUSA
CHRIST.	9	F	CHILD	PRZZZZUSA
CARL	8	M	CHILD	PRZZZZUSA
BERTHA	.11	F	INFANT	PRZZZZUSA
SETTER, JOHS.	14	M	LABR	WMZZZZUSA
STROJWASIEWICZ, AGNES	28	F	W	WMZZZZUSA
FRANZ	4	M	CHILD	WMZZZZUSA
ALEXANDER	3	M	CHILD	WMZZZZUSA
CASIMIR	.11	M	INFANT	WMZZZZUSA
SAARI, METTI	17	M	FARMER	PRZZZZUSA

PASSENGER	AGE	SEX	OCCUPATION	PRVL	DES
WIMRTHEIMER, CHRISTIANE	22	F	SGL	WMZZZZ	USA
MOEFSMER, ANNA	19	F	SGL	WMZZZZ	USA
HELFFERICH, JACOB	21	M	UNKNOWN	WMZZZZ	USA
STEINER, MARIE	20	F	SGL	WMZZZZ	USA
GRUENINGER, PAUL	17	M	BKR	WMZZZZ	USA
BUCH, HEINRICH	26	M	BCHR	WMZZZZ	USA
MAIER, CATH.	24	F	SGL	WMZZZZ	USA
MAIBIER, EMILIE	26	M	SGL	SYZZZZ	USA
SEITZ, CAROLINE	32	F	W	WMZZZZ	USA
GUSTAV	7	M	CHILD	WMZZZZ	USA
ADOLF	5	M	CHILD	WMZZZZ	USA
LINE	3	F	CHILD	WMZZZZ	USA
IDA	.11	F	INFANT	WMZZZZ	USA
VOLZ, CATH.	18	F	SGL	WMZZZZ	USA
ROCHOWSKI, PETER	17	M	UNKNOWN	PRZZZZ	USA
WOLFF, LOUISE	22	F	SGL	PRZZZZ	USA
CLZEWSKI, ANTONIE	20	F	SGL	PRAGKM	USA
DULNISKI, IGNATZ	21	M	LABR	PRAGKM	USA
MUELHAUSEN, AUG.	22	M	UNKNOWN	PRAGKM	USA
HISSEN, ANNA	16	F	SGL	PRAGKM	USA
BUETTNER, ANNA	34	F	W	PRAGKM	USA
MARTA	15	F	CH	PRAGKM	USA
CLARA	9	F	CHILD	PRAGKM	USA
HEDWIG	8	F	CHILD	PRAGKM	USA
PAUL	7	M	CHILD	PRAGKM	USA
IDA	3	F	CHILD	PRAGKM	USA
HENNE, BERTA	22	F	SGL	PRAGKM	USA
MUELLER, WILH.	19	M	UNKNOWN	PRAGKM	USA
JAWORSKI, ANNA	22	F	SGL	PRAGKM	USA
SANCA, VACLAV	20	M	SGL	PRAGKM	USA
GEBELIN, THERESE	21	F	SGL	PRAGKM	USA
MUNZERT, WILHME.	18	F	SGL	PRAGKM	USA
TKACYK, CLARA	21	F	SGL	PRAGKM	USA
GELZINNIS, WILHME.	34	F	W	PRAGKM	USA
BERTA	4	F	CHILD	PRAGKM	USA
ANNA	.04	F	INFANT	PRAGKM	USA
BLUM, EMIL	16	M	UNKNOWN	PRAGKM	USA
USCHOLD, CATH.	23	F	UNKNOWN	PRAGKM	USA
FIEDLER, EMIL	14	M	UNKNOWN	PRAGKM	USA
EISNER, SUSANNE	49	F	UNKNOWN	PRAGKM	USA
IDA	15	F	UNKNOWN	PRAGKM	USA
PAUL	9	M	CHILD	PRAGKM	USA
RUSS, FLORA	29	F	SGL	PRAGKM	USA
WOGT, CAROLINE	26	F	UNKNOWN	PRAGKM	USA
RUPPRECHT, FRIEDA	23	F	UNKNOWN	PRAGKM	USA
PUFAHL, ADOLF	28	M	LABR	PRAGKM	USA
ROSS, EMIL	26	M	LABR	PRZZZZ	USA
SCHMIDT, HULDA	17	F	SGL	PRZZZZ	USA
RAETTKE, GUSTAV	16	M	UNKNOWN	PRZZZZ	USA
JACOB	24	M	UNKNOWN	PRZZZZ	USA
ARRISON, GOTTE	17	M	UNKNOWN	PRZZZZ	USA
HANNIG, FRANZISKA	27	F	SGL	PRZZZZ	USA
CAMILITIN, HIPPOLITE	31	M	LABR	PRADDK	USA
CIAN, JEAN	32	M	LABR	PRADDK	USA
CATHIRINE	22	F	WO	PRADDK	USA
RUPPAUER, ANNA	31	F	WO	PRADDK	USA
GOTTLIEB	7	M	CHILD	PRADDK	USA
ANNA	6	F	CHILD	PRADDK	USA
CATARINA	5	F	CHILD	PRADDK	USA
KUNIGUNDE	.02	F	INFANT	PRADDK	USA
HASLER, LISETTE	25	F	SGL	PRADDK	USA
KESSELE, JOSEF	19	M	LABR	PRADDK	USA
WEGGING, JOSEF	37	M	LABR	PRADDK	USA
AMALIE	9	F	CHILD	PRADDK	USA
SCHLEGEL, J.GEORGE	29	M	LABR	PRADDK	USA
-AUSEL, LOUISE	32	F	W	SRZZZZ	USA
FRANZ	25	M	LABR	SRZZZZ	USA
BADER, JACOB	31	M	LABR	SRZZZZ	USA
ENDRES, JOSEF	26	M	BRR	SRAAHU	USA
SALZMANN, ELISE	29	F	W	SRAAHU	USA
MARTHA	5	F	CHILD	SRAAHU	USA
EMMA	4	F	CHILD	SRAAHU	USA
IDA	.06	F	INFANT	SRAAHU	USA
BLEISS, CARL	23	M	LABR	SRAAHU	USA
LAYER, CAROLINE	20	F	SGL	SRAAHU	USA
DUSS, MARIE	23	F	SGL	SRAAHU	USA
HOFFARTH, THERESE	29	F	SGL	SRAAHU	USA
MUELLER, JOHANNES	31	M	LABR	SRAAHU	USA
SCHMIDT, ROSALIE	16	F	SGL	SRAAHU	USA
BECHTEL, ERNST	16	M	LABR	SRAAHU	USA
SCHOBERT, FLORENTINE	23	F	SGL	SRAAHU	USA
CALLE, JACQUES	19	M	LABR	SRAAHU	USA
GILLIES, CELESTINE	31	F	SGL	SRAAHU	USA
CHRISTOF, AUGUST	23	M	LABR	SRAAHU	USA
KNUT, CHRISTF	52	M	MCHT	SRAAHU	USA
CATERINE	62	F	W	SRAAHU	USA
VOGE, EMMA	31	F	SGL	SRAAHU	USA
DE, BELLY	20	F	SGL	SRAAHU	USA
SANDERS, SOFIE	19	F	SGL	SRAAHU	USA
LEHMKUHL, THEODOR	35	M	MCHT	SRAAHU	USA
MINNA	32	F	W	SRAAHU	USA
FRINA	3	F	CHILD	SRAAHU	USA
RIWALSKY, LINA	60	F	W	SRAAKH	USA
WEBER, AUG.	52	F	W	HBZZZZ	USA
GOETISCH, HERMINE	18	F	SGL	HBZZZZ	USA
PETERS, CHRISTINE	21	F	SGL	HBAIDO	USA
WAJRATLIER, U	36	F	SGL	HBZZZZ	USA
SCHICHLER, HERM.	16	M	STDNT	HBZZZZ	USA
HOFFMEISLER, ANNA	25	F	SGL	HBAAKH	USA
HEYL, CARL	40	M	DR	HBAAKH	USA
HILMERS, OTTILIE	29	F	SGL	HBAEDS	USA
DETLEFS, WILH.	32	F	SGL	OLZZZZ	USA
PREISER, LOIUSE	41	F	W	OLACBR	USA
JACOBSOHN, EMILIE	63	F	W	OLAEAB	USA
RANUBACHER, BABETTE	49	F	W	BVZZZZ	USA
DORA	17	F	SGL	BVZZZZ	USA
HOID, CELINA	39	F	SGL	PRZZZZ	USA
LUDWIG, ELISABETH	29	F	WO	PRAAKH	USA
HEYN, ROBERT	33	M	MCHT	HBZZZZ	USA
SOBELMANN, HERM.	9	M	CHILD	HBACQA	USA
WINDER, LOUIS	30	M	UNKNOWN	HBADXW	USA

SHIP: LAHN

FROM: BREMEN AND SOUTHAMPTON
TO: NEW YORK
ARRIVED: 29 JUNE 1888

PASSENGER	AGE	SEX	OCCUPATION	PRVL	DES
HOPF, HERMANN	34	M	TT	HBAARR	GR
KIRCHNER, C	35	M	TT	HBAARR	GR
DOMMERICH, FRIEDKE	45	F	NN	HBAAXF	GR
NIEWALDT, FRIEDR	42	M	TT	HBACAW	GR
MOLEMAAR, GUST	31	M	TT	HBAGBP	GR
NUNGESSER, HENRY	39	M	TT	HBABXA	GR
KAHN, EMMA	27	F	NN	HBACPE	GR
LEFERS, T	39	M	TT	HBACPE	GR
ZOCHOCH, MARGE	45	F	W	HBABDM	GR
BLICKE, OSCAR	32	M	TT	HBAIVV	GR
MARGA	26	F	W	HBAIVV	GR
ABRAHAM, JULIUS	40	M	TT	HBAIMF	GR
MINNA	52	F	W	HBAIMF	GR
JENNY	15	F	NN	HBAIMF	GR
ROSA	13	F	NN	HBAIMF	GR
SANDER, EMMA	31	F	W	HBAIPJ	GR
ROBERT	10	M	CH	HBAIPJ	GR
MARTHA	9	F	CHILD	HBAIPJ	GR
GEORG	8	M	CHILD	HBAIPJ	GR
GERTRUD	4	F	CHILD	HBAIPJ	GR
PABST, WM	29	M	TT	GRZZZZ	GR
DRESSEL, C	31	M	TT	GRAGFU	GR
KAUN, MARIANNA	47	F	W	GRAATK	GR
VON, META	20	F	NN	GRAARR	GR
DE, GRETIE	70	F	W	GRABCY	GR
WEBERS, PAUL	27	M	TT	GRACBR	GR
GELDERSCHEIMER, BERTHA	17	F	NN	GRAATF	GR

PASSENGER	AGE	SEX	OCCUPATION	PRVL	DES
FANNY	56	F	W	GRAATFGR	
ROOS, THEKLA	20	F	NN	GRACBRGR	
FELGENTREFF, MAX	26	M	TT	GRAEVMGR	
SCHEIDL, CHAS	27	M	TT	GRADEMGR	
BUERGER, WM	19	M	TT	GRADLDGR	
SCHRAYER, C	35	M	TT	GRAAKHGR	
WEINSCHENK, JOSEPHE	16	F	NN	GRAATFGR	
NIEPER, AUGE	22	F	W	GRZZZZGR	
MARIA	1	F	CHILD	GRZZZZGR	
WEIL, CAROLA	19	F	NN	GRACNAGR	
BONNHEIM, BERTHOLD	8	M	CHILD	GRACNAGR	
CARRY, CARL	36	M	TT	GRZZZZGR	
KERWIN, M	30	M	TT	GRAAKHGR	
GROSSMANN, SAML	68	M	TT	GRAAKHGR	
SCHLICK, AUGA	19	F	NN	GRABWXGR	
HELENA	17	F	NN	GRABWXGR	
LIEBES, CARL	19	M	TT	GRACPSGR	
LOEWENFELS, AMALIE	20	F	NN	GRZZZZGR	
SCHWARZ, CLARA	21	F	NN	GRABDMGR	
DUNKEKAK, MARGA	61	F	W	GRACKHGR	
GRUEB, BABETTE	22	F	NN	GRAFRGGR	
SCHOTT, LUDWIG	14	M	NN	GRABOQGR	
FANNY	16	F	NN	GRABOQGR	
MARCUS, BERTHA	18	F	NN	GRABOQGR	
SCHEUER, ISIDOR	15	M	NN	GRABOQGR	
LE----, CARL	17	M	NN	GRADWFGR	
LOESCHER, OSWALD	18	M	TT	GRZZZZGR	
DRESCHER, MARIE	30	F	W	GRAARRGR	
SCHMILLING, CARL	28	M	TT	GRAAKHSWD	
TRAUTH, KATHIE	20	F	SVNT	GRABOQSWD	
SCHUNK, JOHANN	26	M	FARMER	GRABBGUSA	
ANDR	10	M	CH	GRABBGUSA	
MOSBACHER, BENNO	17	M	LABR	GRAGVZUSA	
WAGNER, JOHANN	19	M	SMH	GRAEHXUSA	
WILD, ADOLF	22	M	LABR	GRABZDUSA	
SCHUBERT, JOHANN	38	M	LABR	GRABFQUSA	
LUCZAK, MICH	24	M	FARMER	GRAGCJUSA	
CASIMIRA	20	F	W	GRAGCJUSA	
CASIMIR	2	M	CHILD	GRAGCJUSA	
BEHNKE, WILH	29	M	LKSH	GRZZZZUSA	
THERESE	26	F	W	GRZZZZUSA	
ALFRED	5	M	CHILD	GRZZZZUSA	
ALMA	3	F	CHILD	GRZZZZUSA	
HEDWIG	.01	F	INFANT	GRZZZZUSA	
WEISSBRODT, BERHD	24	M	LABR	GRZZZZUSA	
GUELKER, HEINR	20	M	LABR	GRZZZZUSA	
KLAUSNER, OTTO	40	M	FARMER	GRAFSBUSA	
KELLER, HERM	22	M	MCHT	GRAAWNUSA	
ROCKSTROH, PAULUS	53	M	PVTM	GRZZZZUSA	
KUGL, GEORG	29	M	FARMER	GRADBLUSA	
GRUBER, EVA	23	F	W	GRADBLUSA	
OTTO	3	M	CHILD	GRADBLUSA	
WITT, AUGUST	23	M	LABR	GRZZZZUSA	
EMILIE	27	F	W	GRZZZZUSA	
WILHELM	3	M	CHILD	GRZZZZUSA	
HERMANN	.11	M	INFANT	GRZZZZUSA	
RUTZ, IDA	25	F	W	GRAFWCUSA	
HORNBERGER, JOHANN	25	M	FARMER	GRZZZZUSA	
BRUECKER, SOFIE	15	F	NN	GRZZZZUSA	
HOECKER, MARGA	16	F	NN	GRZZZZUSA	
BOCHINSKA, ROSALIA	25	F	NN	GRAFWCUSA	
ZASTROW, FRANZ	35	M	LABR	GRAFWCUSA	
HERME	30	F	W	GRAFWCUSA	
OTTO	7	M	CHILD	GRAFWCUSA	
EMIL	6	M	CHILD	GRAFWCUSA	
RICHARD	4	M	CHILD	GRAFWCUSA	
EMMA	3	F	CHILD	GRAFWCUSA	
FORSTER, JOHANN	39	M	MCHT	GRAEYGUSA	
MARIA	30	F	W	GRAEYGUSA	
FRITZ	9	M	CHILD	GRAEYGUSA	
MARGA	7	F	CHILD	GRAEYGUSA	
BABETTA	4	F	CHILD	GRAEYGUSA	
HEINRICH	2	M	CHILD	GRAEYGUSA	
KOESTER, CONRAD	24	M	LABR	GRZZZZUSA	
BAUHOLZER, ANTON	16	M	NN	GRZZZZUSA	
ZERWECK, FRIEDR	17	M	LABR	GRACQOUSA	
SCHMIDT, JOHANN	25	M	FARMER	GRZZZZUSA	
HOFACKER, LUDWIG	29	M	FARMER	GRZZZZUSA	
GRIESHABER, JOSEPH	17	M	LABR	GRZZZZUSA	
RUPP, LOUIS	15	M	NN	GRAAGJUSA	
WIRTH, PHILIPPINE	31	F	W	GRACEDUSA	
KARL	.09	M	INFANT	GRACEDUSA	
PRZITOWSKI, CAROLE	23	F	NN	GRZZZZUSA	
SONDERGELS, HEINR	14	M	NN	GRAFDKUSA	
SCHAEFER, JOSEPH	24	M	FARMER	GRZZZZUSA	
KLEINDIENST, BERTHA	25	F	NN	GRABJDUSA	
KLEIN, CATHA	24	F	NN	GRZZZZUSA	
MESSNER, MICHAEL	15	M	NN	GRZZZZUSA	
KOGLER, FRIEDR	15	M	NN	GRZZZZUSA	
SCHWARZ, FRIEDR.	47	M	LABR	GRZZZZUSA	
EDEL, CONSTANTIN	47	M	FARMER	GRZZZZUSA	
MINK, PAULINE	23	F	NN	GRZZZZUSA	
ROSA	22	F	NN	GRZZZZUSA	
ELISABETH	20	F	NN	GRZZZZUSA	
PAUL	15	M	NN	GRZZZZUSA	
ANNA	11	F	CH	GRZZZZUSA	
EDEL, THOMAS	8	M	CHILD	GRZZZZUSA	
MINK, MARIA	.11	F	INFANT	GRZZZZUSA	
BRECHT, HELENE	18	F	NN	GRAATFUSA	
CONSTANTIN, FRIEDKE	16	F	NN	GRACGMUSA	
CARL	14	M	NN	GRACGMUSA	
DRESSEL, AUG	24	M	BBR	GRADDWUSA	
RUEBS-MEN, KATHA	40	F	W	GRAAWBUSA	
GEORG	10	M	CH	GRAAWBUSA	
MARIE	9	F	CHILD	GRAAWBUSA	
SCHMIDT, ANNA	20	F	NN	GRAKPWUSA	
DECKER, ANNA	30	F	W	GRACWMUSA	
FRIEDR	3	M	CHILD	GRACWMUSA	
THOMAS, ERNST	21	M	LABR	GRAEMTUSA	
EISENACHER, ERNESTE	20	F	NN	GRAEMTUSA	
TOMESCHAT, WILH	29	M	LABR	GRAIVMUSA	
WAGNER, THEOD	29	M	GDNR	GRZZZZUSA	
ALMA	22	F	W	GRZZZZUSA	
EMSKAMP, FRITZ	19	M	LABR	GRABQVUSA	
KOSLOWSKI, AUGE	36	F	NN	GRAIVMUSA	
EMILIE	25	F	W	GRAIVMUSA	
OTTO	5	M	CHILD	GRAIVMUSA	
WALDEMAR	3	M	CHILD	GRAIVMUSA	
MAX	.11	M	INFANT	GRAIVMUSA	
KOBE, FRANZ	41	M	FARMER	GRZZZZUSA	
SEMIZA, ANTON	32	M	FARMER	GRZZZZUSA	
SIGELER, JOSEFINE	36	F	W	GRAEXWUSA	
WILHELM	3	M	CHILD	GRAEXWUSA	
BOERNER, FRIEDR	42	M	LABR	GRACBFUSA	
BAUMANN, JOSEF	39	M	BKR	GRZZZZUSA	
CAROLE	36	F	W	GRZZZZUSA	
AGATHE	.11	F	INFANT	GRZZZZUSA	
KUHFUSS, GOTTLIEB	14	M	FARMER	GRALHZUSA	
DUERR, LOUISE	22	F	NN	GRALHZUSA	
BEUTLER, FRIEDKE	18	F	NN	GRALHZUSA	
FALTER, WILHELM	16	M	NN	GRALHZUSA	
BAUER, MARIA	15	F	NN	GRALHZUSA	
THIELE, LOUIS	14	M	NN	GRAAAHUSA	
KRAFT, ELIZA	11	F	CH	GRABQZUSA	
SCHOENECKER, CHRISTOPH	16	M	BCHR	GRABQZUSA	
KLEEMEYER, GESINE	17	F	NN	GRAFDWUSA	
HASE, MARGE	21	F	NN	GRAARZUSA	
MOSSNER, FRANZKA	23	F	NN	GRZZZZUSA	
CONRAEDNER, HEINR	26	M	FARMER	GRAAAHUSA	
RECKOSIAK, MARIE	24	F	NN	GRAAKHUSA	
MAY, CARL	25	M	BCHR	GRAAKHUSA	
KOENIG, VERONICA	23	F	W	GRZZZZUSA	
ROSA	.05	F	INFANT	GRZZZZUSA	
MIHM, CLOTILDE	22	F	NN	GRAHSNUSA	
EHRLICH, CARL	31	M	BKLYR	GRAAKHUSA	
BILINSKY, JOHANN	65	M	LABR	GRAAKHUSA	
ANNA	61	F	W	GRAAKHUSA	
LEVY, EMILIE	21	F	NN	GRADZEUSA	
WEBER, MARIE	21	F	NN	GRAAOOUSA	
KOSCIOLEK, ANTONINA	20	F	W	GRACWTUSA	

PASSENGER	AGE	SEX	OCCUPATION	PRVL DES
JOHANN	.02	M	INFANT	GRACWTUSA
DOHLE, CARL	25	M	BCHR	GRABLMUSA
WEBER, EMILIE	19	F	NN	GRABLMUSA
RUCKHARDT, LOUISE	22	F	NN	GRABLMUSA
HEINEMANN, LINA	17	F	NN	GRABLMUSA
ANNA	15	F	NN	GRABLMUSA
BALLING, CHRIST	17	M	SHMK	GRACJAUSA
ECKERT, ANDR	15	M	NN	GRADTUUSA
MOCK, CLARA	18	F	NN	GRADTUUSA
GOTTWALD, KARLA	48	F	W	GRADTUUSA
SCHUBERT, DOROTHEA	11	F	CH	GRZZZZUSA
KUEN, CARL	15	M	NN	GRACMGUSA
ANTONIA	11	F	CH	GRACMGUSA
ZERKOWSKA, MARYANNA	56	F	W	GRZZZZUSA
HEYMACH, CATHA	40	F	W	GRABOQUSA
PICKARECK, JULIANNA	31	F	W	GRZZZZUSA
JOHANNA	3	F	CHILD	GRZZZZUSA
LEONHARD	.09	M	INFANT	GRZZZZUSA
REINSCH, JOSEPH	25	F	NN	GRZZZZUSA
FLEISCHHAUER, ANNA	25	F	NN	GRZZZZUSA
BEHNKEN, JOHN	15	M	NN	GRAAGLUSA
FRANK, CLARA	22	F	NN	GRZZZZUSA
ARNOLD, LUDWIG	24	M	PNTR	GRAEVTUSA
WEISS, CATHA	49	F	W	GRZZZZUSA
CARL	11	M	CH	GRZZZZUSA
KUHFUSS, CATHA	56	F	W	GRALHZUSA
JOHA	29	F	NN	GRALHZUSA
MARIA	17	F	NN	GRALHZUSA
LEISSA, JULIANNA	25	F	NN	GRZZZZUSA
HERMANN, MARIA	30	F	NN	GRAAWBUSA
MUEHLBAUER, ALOIS	29	M	FARMER	GRZZZZUSA
LICHTENAUER, ROSINE	15	F	NN	GRZZZZUSA
GEISLER, GUSTAV	20	M	LABR	GRADNOUSA
FREY, CARL	18	M	LABR	GRACPEUSA
BECK, ANTOINETTE	20	F	NN	GRACPEUSA
DIETER, ANNA	14	F	NN	GRACPEUSA
BREITBARTH, KATHINKA	50	F	W	GRAAXFUSA
MARIA	25	F	NN	GRAAXFUSA
GOTTFRIED	24	M	FARMER	GRAAXFUSA
MARTHA	21	F	NN	GRAAXFUSA
HELENE	21	F	NN	GRAAXFUSA
SCHANDER, WOLFGANG	23	M	MCHT	GRAAXFUSA
STIPPING, AUGUSTE	30	F	NN	GRAFPTUSA
HOFFMANN, MARIE	22	F	W	GRABEDUSA
EMILIE	.06	F	INFANT	GRABEDUSA
EBEL, FRIEDR	31	F	STCTR	GRABEDUSA
EHRLICH, DOROTHEA	30	F	W	GRZZZZUSA
AUGUSTE	6	F	CHILD	GRZZZZUSA
OTTO	4	M	CHILD	GRZZZZUSA
LINA	2	F	CHILD	GRZZZZUSA
ALBERT	.06	M	INFANT	GRZZZZUSA
LUECKE, HERMANN	64	M	MCHT	GRAARRUSA
HAASE, JUERGEN	28	M	FARMER	GRZZZZUSA
ALBERS, MARGA	21	F	NN	GRALITUSA
CATHA	19	F	NN	GRALITUSA
HEINEMANN, HEINR	53	M	LABR	GRAARRUSA
VOGLER, GEORG	14	M	NN	GRABLMUSA
HOFMANN, HANS	14	M	NN	GRZZZZUSA
OHLMEYER, ANNA	16	F	NN	GRZZZZUSA
FOLDA, HERM	15	M	NN	GRZZZZUSA
FISCHER, THERESIA	30	F	W	GRZZZZUSA
THERESIA	4	F	CHILD	GRZZZZUSA
JOSEF	.09	M	INFANT	GRZZZZUSA
FUNDERS, ANNA	19	F	W	GRZZZZUSA
ZECHMANN, LUDWIG	26	M	BKR	GRZZZZUSA
GOLDENSTEIN, HARM	16	M	NN	GRZZZZUSA
GREIF, ANNA	24	F	NN	GRZZZZUSA
BRIECHLE, AFRA	25	F	NN	GRZZZZUSA
SCHMIDT, WILHELM	24	M	MCHT	GRZZZZUSA
BUENNING, HEINR	15	M	NN	GRAAAHUSA
SUHREN, FRITZ	16	M	NN	GRAAAHUSA
BLOCK, CORD	15	M	NN	GRAAAHUSA
BARTELS, HEINR	24	M	LABR	GRAARRUSA
MEYER, JOHANN	34	M	LABR	GRAARRUSA
KOPF, ERNST	15	M	NN	GRAEFRUSA
FUETTERER, VALENT	20	M	MCHT	GRACLOUSA
HECK, FRANZKA	19	F	NN	GRACLOUSA
JOSEF	19	M	LABR	GRACLOUSA
NIKLAUS, MARZELL	26	M	LABR	GRACLOUSA
LAPPERT, CHRIST	23	M	BKR	GRABLTUSA
WERNER, AGNES	20	F	NN	GRABDMUSA
BURZELE, JOSEF	14	M	NN	GRABCKUSA
ACKERMANN, CAROLE	21	F	NN	GRAFASUSA
BERTHA	21	F	NN	GRAFASUSA
HOLZWARTH, CLEMENTE	17	F	NN	GRAGVZUSA
WELISCH, PAUL	15	M	FARMER	GRACEGUSA
WITTMER, ISIDOR	17	M	FARMER	GRZZZZUSA
WALDHEIM, MARIA	62	F	W	GRZZZZUSA
JETTE	24	F	NN	GRZZZZUSA
CARL	10	M	CH	GRZZZZUSA
GES-LEIN, DOROTHEA	53	F	NN	GRZZZZUSA
HAHN, JOH	38	M	FARMER	GRZZZZUSA
MUELLER, LUDWIG	25	M	FARMER	GRZZZZUSA
WIEDMANN, JOH	29	M	BCHR	GRZZZZUSA
KURTZ, CATHA	29	F	NN	GRZZZZUSA
SIEH, HANS	40	M	FARMER	GRZZZZUSA
KUMMERFELD, WILH	22	M	FARMER	GRZZZZUSA
MARKET, JOHANN	14	M	NN	GRZZZZUSA
WEISENSELL, JOH	26	M	LABR	GRZZZZUSA
REGA	27	F	W	GRZZZZUSA
STEINERT, ADALBERT	34	M	FARMER	GRZZZZUSA
DOROTHEA	23	F	W	GRZZZZUSA
DOROTHEA	8	F	CHILD	GRZZZZUSA
MARGA	6	F	CHILD	GRZZZZUSA
ADALB	4	M	CHILD	GRZZZZUSA
LOUISA	2	F	CHILD	GRZZZZUSA
GEORG	.09	M	INFANT	GRZZZZUSA
LIEB, MARIE	22	F	NN	GRZZZZUSA
STOECKER, VALENTIN	25	M	BCHR	GRZZZZUSA
CHOLEWA, CONSTANT	25	M	CPTR	GRZZZZUSA
SCHWEDA, JOHANN	27	M	CPTR	GRZZZZUSA
MAAS, DIEDRICH	15	M	NN	GRZZZZUSA
FRANZE, MARIE	17	F	NN	GRZZZZUSA
KUENZEL, PAULINE	17	F	NN	GRZZZZUSA
PIRCUS, JACOB	19	M	LABR	GRACPSUSA
HECKLAU, REINHOLD	9	M	CHILD	GRZZZZUSA
LOUISE	4	F	CHILD	GRZZZZUSA
OTTO, MAX	27	M	LABR	GRAAXKUSA
FINSTER, KUNIGDE	28	F	NN	GRABOQUSA
RAUL, KATHA	22	F	NN	GRABOQUSA
FINSTER, HEDWIG	24	F	NN	GRABOQUSA
KIEWE, CHARLOTTE	21	F	NN	GRACPSUSA
URBANSKI, FRANZISEK	24	F	NN	GRAARZUSA
ROSENFELD, THERESE	17	F	NN	GRZZZZUSA
KATHE	15	F	NN	GRZZZZUSA
HUCK, CARL	26	M	MCHT	GRAFWZUSA
REICHEL, JOHANN	39	M	FARMER	GRZZZZUSA
ELISABETH	32	F	W	GRZZZZUSA
KARL	10	M	CH	GRZZZZUSA
GOTTLIEB	6	M	CHILD	GRZZZZUSA
ANNA	3	F	CHILD	GRZZZZUSA
EMMA	1	F	CHILD	GRZZZZUSA
GEGENFURTNER, JOSEPH	30	M	FARMER	GRAEXLUSA
ZITMANN, FRANZ	30	M	LABR	GRACAZUSA
EISMANN, PAUL	18	M	MCHT	GRABSYUSA
SCHIRMER, CARL	17	M	FARMER	GRAAXYUSA
ZOELLER, MARIA	50	F	W	GRZZZZUSA
ALOIS	16	M	NN	GRZZZZUSA
AUGUST	13	M	NN	GRZZZZUSA
FRANZ	11	M	CH	GRZZZZUSA
FRANZ	11	M	CH	GRZZZZUSA
LEUCHS, MARTIN	25	M	LABR	GRZZZZUSA
SCHOENBERGER, ANNA	23	F	W	GRACQEUSA
ROSA	2	F	CHILD	GRACQEUSA
LANGNER, REINHOLD	22	M	FARMER	GRADOIUSA
ANNA	24	F	W	GRADOIUSA
PAUL	1	M	CHILD	GRADOIUSA
FLEIM, JOHANN	18	M	LABR	GRACMGUSA
JOHANN	17	M	LABR	GRACMGUSA
FERLIN, FERDINAND	28	M	LABR	GRACMGUSA

PASSENGER	AGE	SEX	OCCUPATION	PRVVL	DES
FLEIN, THOMAS	18	M	LABR	GRACMGUSA
FLEIMANN, JOHANN	26	M	LABR	GRACMGUSA
DUJINI, AUGUST	24	M	LABR	GRACMGUSA
MARTINI, JOHANN	36	M	LABR	GRACMGUSA
MAX	33	M	LABR	GRACMGUSA
WACKER, MARIA	20	F	NN	GRACMGUSA
KLINGE, PAUL	15	M	LABR	GRAARRUSA
KRAPOTH, MATHIAS	21	M	LABR	GRAEABUSA
KLIANOWSKY, ANTON	25	M	LABR	GRZZZZUSA
MEYER, MINNA	18	F	NN	GRAEPXUSA
SIMMER, J	40	M	MACH	GRABRAUSA
LORTZING, RICHARD	24	M	FARMER	GRAAXFUSA
HEINEMANN, GERHARD	17	M	WTR	GRADVHUSA
SEYDEWITZ, EMMA	20	F	NN	GRACSPUSA
LOESCHINGK, WM	29	M	TT	GRADBQGR
SCHOELLER, EWALD	29	M	TT	GRADBQGR
ELSAESSER, THEODOR	27	M	TT	GRADBQGR
PRAETORIUS, CARL	28	M	TT	GRAAXUGR

SHIP: CITY OF RICHMOND

FROM: LIVERPOOL AND QUEENSTOWN
TO: NEW YORK
ARRIVED: 02 JULY 1888

PASSENGER	AGE	SEX	OCCUPATION	PRVVL	DES
MESINKIEMIER, U	26	F	W	GRACBFPA
MAGDALINE	4	F	CHILD	GRACBFPA
PENRIG, SCHAJE	19	M	LABR	GRACBFNY
VAUKOWSKI, STEFAN	27	M	LABR	GRACBFNY
SCHILLING, FRANZ	25	M	LABR	GRACBFCH
FERNBERG, MINA	22	F	LABR	GRACBFMN
TOMSAMAN, MARIE	23	F	W	GRACBFMI
IDA	2	F	CHILD	GRACBFMI
ANNA	.11	F	INFANT	GRACBFMI
RABOWSKI, MARTIN	32	M	LABR	GRACBFALB
BOEIAN, MYARE	19	F	SVNT	GRACBFNY
ROSAK, JOSE	30	F	W	GRACBFNY
MICHAEL	8	M	CHILD	GRACBFNY
WILME	3	M	CHILD	GRACBFNY
ANTON	.11	M	INFANT	GRACBFNY
POLTERMANN, NACHMEN	22	M	LABR	GRACBFPHI
GRUSINSKI, F	24	M	LABR	GRACBFBAL
MASCHE	24	F	W	GRACBFBAL
JOSEF	.11	M	INFANT	GRACBFBAL
GACKOWSKI, MATEUS	35	M	LABR	GRAAKHBAL
BEIBER, JOHANNA	28	F	W	GRACBFBAL
HERMANN	8	M	CHILD	GRACBFBAL
ALBERT, ISAAC	40	M	TLR	GRAAKHNY
SCHOLZ, CARL	50	M	JNR	GRAAKHPHI
TUROWSKA, ANGELA	19	F	LABR	GRACBFNY
GOLDFINGER, HEIME	18	F	LABR	GRACBFNY
MIRWITZ, MARIANN	35	F	W	GRACBFNY
SARA	14	F	LABR	GRACBFNY
BERTHA	10	F	CH	GRACBFNY
BENJAMIN	6	M	CHILD	GRACBFNY
HERSCH	4	M	CHILD	GRACBFNY
GERSON	2	M	CHILD	GRACBFNY
ROBERT	8	M	CHILD	GRACBFNY
LOEWENSTEIN, BEILE	20	F	W	GRACBFNY
DAVID	.11	M	INFANT	GRACBFNY
MISINKIWIER, MARY	.11	F	INFANT	GRACBFPA
KOHAN, GERSON	29	M	SHMK	GRACBFPA
CHASCHE	24	F	W	GRACBFPA
ELKE	3	F	CHILD	GRACBFPA
JANKEL	.11	F	INFANT	GRACBFPA
LARWINTZKY, LEIB	33	M	SHMK	GRACBFNY
DWURE	20	F	W	GRACBFNY
HERSCH	.11	F	INFANT	GRACBFNY
GARNITZ, HINDE	19	F	LABR	GRACBFNY
TRANOJTIS, MARCY	27	F	LABR	GRACBFNY

PASSENGER	AGE	SEX	OCCUPATION	PRVVL	DES
JURGENSOHN, JOHANNES	25	M	FARMER	GRACBFCH
LONDON, ABRAHAM	56	M	JNR	GRACBFNY
VOGT, U	30	F	TCHR	GRADBQNY
COLINS, RICHARD	18	M	WTR	GRAAKHNY
RYDER, WILLIAM	47	M	MCHT	GRAAYKNY

SHIP: ETRURIA

FROM: LIVERPOOL AND QUEENSTOWN
TO: NEW YORK
ARRIVED: 02 JULY 1888

PASSENGER	AGE	SEX	OCCUPATION	PRVVL	DES
AWNER, DAVID	31	M	LABR	GRACBFNY
LOMAN, BERNARD	29	M	LABR	GRACBFPHI
POSIS, ISRAEL	44	M	LABR	GRACBFPHI
HUSCHNISKY, MEYER	19	M	LABR	GRACBFMN
BRILI	20	M	LABR	GRACBFMN
LEWIN, JETTI	20	M	SP	GRACBFMN
RUOLIN, CHAIM	18	M	SP	GRACBFNY
TRUMAN, WOLF	11	M	CH	GRACBFPA
SARA	20	F	SP	GRACBFPA
BAHRENBURG, MARIE	34	F	SP	GRADAXPA
FONTAINE, ROSE	8	F	CHILD	FRZZZZCT
REITER, CARL	30	M	LABR	FRACBFCT
LOUISE	24	F	W	FRACBFCT
LAFFARQUE, GEORGE	29	M	LABR	FRZZZZCT
CELINA	24	F	HP	FRACBFNY
GERRARD	2	M	CHILD	FRACBFNY
CRUSE, HENRI	26	M	MCHT	FRADXWUSA
HEILL, MORRIS	52	M	MCHT	BVZZZZNY
NYSSEN, MORRIS	39	M	MCHT	BVADBQNY
KOENIG, ADOLPH	30	M	MCHT	BVADBQNY
BACHUR, BROWHEAD	39	M	MCHT	BVACBFNY
KIRCHBRAUER, ABRAHM	57	M	MCHT	BVADBQNY
SIMON	27	M	MCHT	BVADBQNY
FISCHER, LUIS	25	F	SVNT	GRZZZZNY
FALCK, HERMAN	68	M	MCHT	GRADAXNY
BAURWILL, MOIS	18	M	VAL	GRZZZZNY
WALTER, FREDERICKA	32	M	MSNY	GRZZZZNY
SCHAER, ELIAS	55	M	MCHT	GRZZZZBAL
WAYRECK, WILLIAM	54	M	MCHT	GRZZZZNY
KAMP, WILLIAM	50	M	CL	PRZZZZNY

SHIP: POLARIA

FROM: HAMBURG
TO: NEW YORK
ARRIVED: 02 JULY 1888

PASSENGER	AGE	SEX	OCCUPATION	PRVVL	DES
CHRISTIANSEN, HEINR.	56	M	UNKNOWN	HBZZZZUSA
THEODA.	50	F	W	HBZZZZUSA
SCHEUBECK, JOSEF	31	M	BRR	BVZZZZUSA
KITZINGER, ERNST	24	M	GDNR	BVACBFUSA
HAHN, JOH.M.	27	M	FARMER	BVACBFUNK
HEIMBEIN, KATH.	26	F	W	BVAEHXUNK
BAIER, WILHE.	19	F	UNKNOWN	BVZZZZUNK
BANK, JOH.	28	M	FARMER	BVZZZZUNK
SCHMELZ, JOSEFA	25	F	SGL	BVZZZZUNK
STIEPER, HANNA	33	F	SGL	BVACBFUNK
MARG.	3	F	CHILD	BVACBFUNK
DAMMER, JOSEPHA	20	F	W	BVZZZZUNK
HAGEN, PAULA	32	F	SGL	PRZZZZUNK
EMIG, BARBA.	17	F	SGL	PRZZZZUNK
KERBEIN, PAULINE	19	F	UNKNOWN	PRZZZZUNK
KLEMM, VICTORIA	22	F	UNKNOWN	PRZZZZUNK

```
                     A S        P V  D                                  A S        P V  D
                     G E OCCUPATION R I E           PASSENGER           G E OCCUPATION R I E
PASSENGER            E X        V L  S                                  E X        V L  S
----------------------------------------------      ----------------------------------------------
WRABLAESKY, KASTUSLE  21 F UNKNOWN    PRZZZZUNK        LEO               6 M CHILD     PRAAKHOH
   PALASA              9 M CHILD      PRZZZZUNK        HERM.             5 M CHILD     PRAAKHOH
FESCHKE, BERTHA       44 F WO         PRZZZZUNK        NATHALIE         .11 F INFANT   PRAAKHOH
   META               9 F CHILD       PRZZZZUNK      SPRUETTEA, GEORG   25 M LABR     LPZZZZOH
   HUGO               8 M CHILD       PRZZZZUNK      NOVAK, ANTON       28 M LABR     PRZZZZOH
GRAU, JOHANN          34 M LABR       PRACWTUNK      DUSCHUNSKY, JOSEF  25 M LABR     PRZZZZOH
HINZE, LOUISE         27 M LABR       PRAAKHUNK      BAUMGARTEN, AUGUST 29 M BCHR     PRZZZZOH
   LUCCIE             4 F CHILD       PRAAKHUNK
   HUNY               3 F CHILD       PRAAKHUNK
   WALLY             .10 M INFANT     PRAAKHUNK
SMOROWSKY, STANISLAUS 14 M LABR       PRAMBHUNK
SENFT, WALTER        18 M MUSN        PRAEWZUNK
DIDZIN, AUGUST       25 M LABR        PRAAKHUNK      SHIP:    SCHIEDAM
VICTOR, MARIE        20 F SGL         PRAAZDUNK
KAMM, HERM.          27 M FARMER      PRZZZZUNK      FROM:    AMSTERDAM
REIMUTH, KARL        19 M WTR         PRACBWUNK      TO:      NEW YORK
FOESTER, FRANZ       36 M TLR         PRAFTUUNK      ARRIVED: 02 JULY 1888
   IDA               29 F W           PRAFTUUNK
   HERM.             6 M CHILD        PRAFTUUNK
   JOHE.             4 F CHILD        PRAFTUUNK      GEMBITZ, FLORA     17 F PVTW     GRZZZZUSA
STORK, HERM.         14 M FARMER      PRAACEUNK      BERG, A.M.         30 F PVTW     GRZZZZUSA
VOELKER, EMIL        29 M UNKNOWN     PRAAKHUNK      LINDER, K.         25 F PVTW     GRZZZZUSA
KOWANDY, BARTHOL.    25 M WHR         PRZZZZUNK      BETZMAN, K.        24 F PVTW     GRZZZZUSA
HAASCH, FERD.        59 F WHR         PRZZZZUNK      KERCHEN, M.        20 F PVTW     GRZZZZUSA
   AUGUSTE           48 F W           PRZZZZUNK      SCHEFER, EMMA      35 F PVTW     GRZZZZUSA
   OLGA              25 F CH          PRZZZZUNK         EMMA            10 F CH       GRZZZZUSA
   MARIE             17 F CH          PRZZZZUNK      ZREGLER, ROBERT    22 M UNKNOWN  GRZZZZUSA
   GEORG             9 M CHILD        PRZZZZUNK      WENFENBOHLER, AUG. 26 M DCT      GRZZZZUSA
WITTE, R.            25 M BCHR        PRAHRIUNK      MEYER, MARIA       20 F PVTW     GRZZZZUSA
KUBIAK, JOS.         40 M LABR        PRZZZZUNK      MARS, AGNES        42 F PVTW     GRZZZZUSA
HINTZ, CARL          31 M LABR        PRZZZZUNK         ANTOINE         19 F PVTW     GRZZZZUSA
FREUND, ALFRED       46 M LABR        PRAARZUNK      LEINERT, BERNHARDT 29 M LABR     GRZZZZUSA
BARCZAK, CONSTANTIN  47 M LABR        PRZZZZUNK      HOLTJE, MARIA      18 F SVNT     GRZZZZUSA
JANUSZIAK, FRANZ     59 M LABR        PRAJNQUNK      SIPPEL, CORN.      21 M LABR     GRZZZZUSA
   ROSALIE           58 F W           PRAJNQUNK      FULHOWSKI, FRANZ   27 M LABR     GRZZZZUSA
LEMKE, WILHELMINE    61 F WO          PRAJHLUNK      ROZINSKY, MAVIZEN  38 M LABR     GRZZZZUSA
GRUETZMACHER, AUGUSTE 22 F WO         PRAKPPUNK      DREWERS, MARIE     16 F SVNT     GRZZZZUSA
   HEDWIG           .11 F INFANT      PRAKPPUNK         BELLIE          14 F SVNT     GRZZZZUSA
   CLARA             9 F CHILD        PRAKPPUNK      THEIL, CAROLINE    24 F SVNT     GRZZZZUSA
METTKE, HERM.        27 M LABR        PRAAKHUNK      ACHS, GREGOR       30 M LABR     GRZZZZUSA
SCHUELKE, FRIEDR.    45 F WO          PRAECNUNK         ROSINE          30 F UNKNOWN  GRZZZZUSA
   BERTHA            49 F W           PRAECNUNK         ELISABETH       4 F CHILD     GRZZZZUSA
   ANNA              15 M CH          PRAECNUNK         GREGOR          1 M CHILD     GRZZZZUSA
   THEODOR           8 M CHILD        PRAECNUNK      JERABEK, ELISABETH 56 F UNKNOWN  GRZZZZUSA
   ARTHUR            3 M CHILD        PRAECNUNK         ELISABETH       17 F SVNT     GRZZZZUSA
SCHWANZ, FERD.       35 M LABR        PRZZZZUNK      KAPSA, STEFAN      23 M LABR     GRZZZZUSA
FRANZ, AUGUST        29 M LABR        PRZZZZUNK      KLEIN, ROBERT      20 M BKR      GRZZZZUSA
DAMBOROG, IGNATZ     45 M SMH         PRZZZZUNK      ALTENDORF, FRANZ   27 M LABR     GRZZZZUSA
   JOHE.             40 F W           PRZZZZUNK         FRANZ           35 M LABR     GRZZZZUSA
   JOH.              19 M CH          PRZZZZUNK         FRAN            33 F UNKNOWN  GRZZZZUSA
   AGNES             16 F CH          PRZZZZUNK         AMALIA          9 F CHILD     GRZZZZUSA
   VINCENT           9 M CHILD        PRZZZZUNK         HENRICH         4 M CHILD     GRZZZZUSA
   AGATHE            8 F CHILD        PRZZZZUNK         LOUISE          4 F CHILD     GRZZZZUSA
   LORENZ            7 M CHILD        PRZZZZUNK         GUSTAV          2 M CHILD     GRZZZZUSA
   ANTON             3 M CHILD        PRZZZZUNK         CARL            1 M CHILD     GRZZZZUSA
KOLANOWSKI, AGNES    30 F WO          PRZZZZUNK         WIELAND        .02 M INFANT   GRZZZZUSA
   ANDR.             8 M CHILD        PRZZZZUNK      WERNER, MARIE      18 F SVNT     GRZZZZUSA
   JOSEF             6 M CHILD        PRZZZZUNK      MACK, BERTHA       19 F SVNT     GRZZZZUSA
BUDNIK, MARCIN       50 M LABR        PRZZZZUNK      VOTTINER, FREDERICKE 28 F SVNT   GRZZZZUSA
JAZWIAK, MIHALINE    30 F WO          PRZZZZUNK      HILDENBRAND, ANNA  18 F SVNT     GRZZZZUSA
   ANTON             9 M CHILD        PRZZZZUNK      ZELLER, GUSTAV     19 M LABR     GRZZZZUSA
   STANISLAWA        8 F CHILD        PRZZZZUNK      CLANT, CATHARINA   53 F UNKNOWN  GRZZZZUSA
   JOH.              3 M CHILD        PRZZZZUNK         WALPINGA        19 F SVNT     GRZZZZUSA
   VERONIKA         .11 F INFANT      PRZZZZUNK      HANSELMAN, JACOB   21 M FARMER   GRZZZZUSA
SCHUMINSKA, JULIE    36 F WO          PRAASSOH       EISELE, PAULINE    21 F SVNT     GRZZZZUSA
   CLARA             9 F CHILD        PRAASSOH       SCHOBEL, SIGMUND   34 M JNR      GRZZZZUSA
   FRANZ             8 M CHILD        PRAASSOH          MARIE           33 F UNKNOWN  GRZZZZUSA
   MARIE             5 F CHILD        PRAASSOH          ELISE           11 F UNKNOWN  GRZZZZUSA
   MARTHA            4 F CHILD        PRAASSOH       ACHEMANN, ELISE    9 F CHILD     GRZZZZUSA
RICHTER, OSCAR       31 M LKSH        PRAASSOH          JOHANNA        .05 M INFANT   GRZZZZUSA
   CATHA.            25 F W           PRAASSOH       HA--, CARL         20 M UNKNOWN  GRZZZZUSA
   CLARA             4 F CHILD        PRAASSOH       SCHWARZ, GUSTAV    17 M BLKSMH   GRZZZZUSA
   RICHARD          .08 M INFANT      PRAASSOH          PAUL            11 M UNKNOWN  GRZZZZUSA
KEDZIVEK, LIPPMANN   34 M LABR        PRAAKHOH       SCHWARTZ, DAVID    46 M LABR     GRZZZZUSA
   MINNA             32 F W           PRAAKHOH          FREDERIKE       48 F UNKNOWN  GRZZZZUSA
```

PASSENGER	AGE	SEX	OCCUPATION	PRIVL	DES
BLOCHER, PAULINE	16	F	SVNT	GRZZZZ	USA
HOPF, IDA	17	F	SVNT	GRZZZZ	USA
HORN, JACOB	17	M	LABR	GRZZZZ	USA
LEH, GUSTAV	25	M	LABR	GRZZZZ	USA
KERCHER, HEINRICH	24	M	LABR	GRZZZZ	USA
ECK, ROSA	20	F	UNKNOWN	GRZZZZ	USA
ICLOCHLAEGER, ANNA	19	F	UNKNOWN	GRZZZZ	USA
BAUHOLZER, MELCHIOR	30	M	LABR	GRZZZZ	USA
SENFERT, ANDREAS	59	M	FARMER	GRZZZZ	USA
HAAARTER, WILHELMINA	18	F	SVNT	GRZZZZ	USA
GEHRLACH, GONJT	14	M	LABR	GRZZZZ	USA
ECK, ANNA	24	F	UNKNOWN	GRZZZZ	USA
ECHL, FRANZ	.04	M	INFANT	GRZZZZ	USA
SIEHENIUS, LUDWIG	32	M	LABR	GRZZZZ	USA
ANNA	31	F	UNKNOWN	GRZZZZ	USA
SCHMIDT, PHILOPS	16	M	UNKNOWN	GRZZZZ	USA
LECHENIUS, MICHAEL	8	M	CHILD	GRZZZZ	USA
MARGARETHE	6	F	CHILD	GRZZZZ	USA
WEID, MARIE	21	F	SVNT	GRZZZZ	USA
GINSBERG, EDUARD	28	M	LABR	GRZZZZ	USA
WEID, ROSINI	18	F	SVNT	GRZZZZ	USA
BARBARA	11	F	UNKNOWN	GRZZZZ	USA
WILHELM	6	M	CHILD	GRZZZZ	USA
CONSTATIN, WOLFRALH	39	M	LABR	GRZZZZ	USA
MODLE, JOSEPHINE	22	F	UNKNOWN	GRZZZZ	USA
GEIFLER, ELISAD	17	F	SVNT	GRZZZZ	USA
MULLER, ANNA	26	F	SVNT	GRZZZZ	USA
SMIDT, KARL	26	M	LABR	GRZZZZ	USA
WILHELM	10	M	CH	GRZZZZ	USA
LANG, KATHARINA	23	F	SVNT	GRZZZZ	USA
MURLOWSKY, VALANT	23	M	LABR	GRZZZZ	USA
KLEINMANN, JOSES	25	M	LABR	GRZZZZ	USA
KAURDOWICZ, PINCHAS	55	M	LABR	GRZZZZ	USA
BLASCHAIK, KAZUMER	40	M	LABR	GRZZZZ	USA
WICKERMANN, F.	22	M	LABR	GRZZZZ	USA
PFAFF, LEOP.	22	M	LABR	GRZZZZ	USA
WEILER, JOSEPHINE	16	F	SVNT	GRZZZZ	USA
JESINHE, HENDEL	23	M	LABR	GRZZZZ	USA
BIEBELHORN, WENDELIN	21	M	LABR	GRZZZZ	USA
SCHINMEK, A.	28	M	LABR	GRZZZZ	USA
ADOLF	26	M	LABR	GRZZZZ	USA
SCHLUPPERT, HERMAN	26	M	MCHT	GRZZZZ	USA
PRAN	25	F	UNKNOWN	GRZZZZ	USA
ALFRED	.05	M	INFANT	GRZZZZ	USA
KUMPF, ERNESTINE	21	F	SVNT	GRZZZZ	USA
ERNST, SALOME	33	F	UNKNOWN	GRZZZZ	USA
JACOB	8	M	CHILD	GRZZZZ	USA
HEINRICH	4	M	CHILD	GRZZZZ	USA
HERMANN	2	M	CHILD	GRZZZZ	USA
SELMA	1	M	CHILD	GRZZZZ	USA
TROMMER, MARTIN	21	M	LABR	GRZZZZ	USA
KRAUSER, JOSEF	18	M	LABR	GRZZZZ	USA
KIEHECHOF, ANDREAS	29	M	LABR	GRZZZZ	USA
GEBAUER, OTTO	21	M	LABR	GRZZZZ	USA
SCHNEIDER, CARL	45	M	LABR	GRZZZZ	USA
WENDEL, MAGTT.	26	F	SVNT	GRZZZZ	USA
MENDELSOHN, LENA	19	F	SVNT	GRZZZZ	USA
ROSSI, ANDREA	49	M	LABR	FRZZZZ	USA
GUAMERI, OTTILIO	21	M	LABR	FRZZZZ	USA
SCHROLL, JOHN	28	M	JNR	GRZZZZ	USA
SHROLL, LOUISE	27	F	UNKNOWN	GRZZZZ	USA
JOHN	10	M	CH	GRZZZZ	USA
RUTCHEN	2	F	CHILD	GRZZZZ	USA
KOSS, ELISABETH	24	F	SVNT	GRZZZZ	USA
LUBENAU, CONRAD	21	M	LABR	GRZZZZ	USA
FIEGLER, LUDWIG	25	M	LABR	GRZZZZ	USA
MILLA, ELISABETH	22	F	UNKNOWN	GRZZZZ	USA
SCHMIDT, MAYER	18	M	LABR	GRZZZZ	USA
KLEMPHE, KARL	26	M	LABR	GRZZZZ	USA
HAHL, JACOB	21	M	LABR	GRZZZZ	USA
JOLS, U	00	U	UNKNOWN	GRZZZZ	USA
GRUMM, ANT.	26	M	LABR	GRZZZZ	USA
BARNSCHLEGEL, EVA	19	F	SVNT	GRZZZZ	USA
KNORR, ANNA	66	F	UNKNOWN	GRZZZZ	USA
KRASSWEIS, ANNA	57	F	UNKNOWN	GRZZZZ	USA

PASSENGER	AGE	SEX	OCCUPATION	PRIVL	DES
STEFANS, CONTI	27	M	LABR	FRZZZZ	USA
PASQUALE, CARANO	27	M	FARMER	FRZZZZ	USA
MARIANTANIO, PUSPERIO	24	M	FARMER	FRZZZZ	USA
GIEVANNI, MOW	30	M	FARMER	FRZZZZ	USA
MUNZIO, GRASSI	17	M	FARMER	FRZZZZ	USA
GIOVANI, JAMBANO	41	M	FARMER	FRZZZZ	USA
ANGELS	35	M	FARMER	FRZZZZ	USA
DOMENICO	37	M	FARMER	FRZZZZ	USA
MICHELO	11	M	UNKNOWN	FRZZZZ	USA
SICILI, ANGLO	21	M	FARMER	FRZZZZ	USA
ALTIMARE, ANGLO	38	M	FARMER	FRZZZZ	USA
GABRIELLE, GUISEPPE	28	M	FARMER	FRZZZZ	USA
GIAWBBE, BERROTTINI	40	M	FARMER	FRZZZZ	USA
GUISEPPE, ROMOLFI	24	M	FARMER	FRZZZZ	USA
HONOREN, ANGELE	16	F	SVNT	FRZZZZ	USA
LOUS	46	M	FARMER	FRZZZZ	USA
SEMAND	10	M	CH	FRZZZZ	USA
PATECHORTEN, SEROFINE	19	M	LABR	GRZZZZ	USA
KUFOUR, FELIX	22	M	LABR	GRZZZZ	USA

SHIP: WYOMING

FROM: LIVERPOOL AND QUEENSTOWN
TO: NEW YORK
ARRIVED: 02 JULY 1888

PASSENGER	AGE	SEX	OCCUPATION	PRIVL	DES
PETKO--, JOHAN	52	M	LABR	GRZZZZ	USA
OLSEN, JOH	22	F	W	GRZZZZ	USA
AMUNDSEN, H	25	F	SP	GRZZZZ	USA
HUKANSON, J	20	M	LABR	GRZZZZ	USA
PERSDOTTER, BERTHA	7	F	CHILD	GRZZZZ	USA
ANDERSON, KAPA	40	F	SP	GRZZZZ	USA
DANIELSON, ANNA	7	F	CHILD	GRZZZZ	USA
PERS, HANNAH	30	U	UNKNOWN	GRZZZZ	USA
CEABSTIER, B	51	M	FARMER	GRZZZZ	USA
GROSSMAN, SALLY	18	F	SP	GRZZZZ	USA
JOS	16	M	LABR	GRZZZZ	USA
KHEN, ESTI.	16	F	SP	GRZZZZ	USA
PENZIG, MORDCKE	47	F	W	GRZZZZ	USA
JOSEPH	5	M	CHILD	GRZZZZ	USA
ROWN, ISAK	34	M	LABR	GRZZZZ	USA
JORGEMAN, JOS.	00	M	INF	GRZZZZ	USA
EITS, ROH.	28	M	FARMER	GRZZZZ	USA

SHIP: EGYPT

FROM: LIVERPOOL AND QUEENSTOWN
TO: NEW YORK
ARRIVED: 03 JULY 1888

PASSENGER	AGE	SEX	OCCUPATION	PRIVL	DES
KINE, S	50	F	W	GRZZZZ	USA
S	9	F	CHILD	GRZZZZ	USA
JOSEF	8	M	CHILD	GRZZZZ	USA
S	6	M	CHILD	GRZZZZ	USA
ROLU-, HERMAN	24	M	LABR	GRACBF	USA
HELENE	28	F	W	GRACBF	USA
M	2	F	CHILD	GRACBF	USA
H	00	F	INF	GRACBF	USA
WOLF, R	36	M	LABR	GRACBF	USA
O	23	F	W	GRACBF	USA
WANDA	00	F	INF	GRACBF	USA
RAMBACH, A	26	M	LABR	GRACBF	USA
MARGR	21	F	W	GRACBF	USA
JOSEPH	46	M	LABR	GRACBF	USA
CHRIS	45	F	W	GRACBF	USA

PASSENGER	AGE	SEX	OCCUPATION	PRVL	DES
PAULINE	10	F	CH		GRACBFUSA
KROTHI, S	31	M	LABR		GRACBFUSA
ROSA	25	F	W		GRACBFUSA
W	4	F	CHILD		GRACBFUSA
B	3	F	CHILD		GRACBFUSA
CASA-	00	F	INF		GRACBFUSA
BINSK, B	20	F	SP		GRACBFUSA
MI-ETT, KATI	26	F	SP		GRACBFUSA
WEISS, FANNY	19	F	SP		GRACBFUSA
BJORKBAKKA, MARIA	21	F	SP		GRACBFUSA
KAVISTA, ANNA	26	F	SP		GRACBFUSA
---NSON, HANNAH	31	F	SP		GRACBFUSA
SCHLESIKOUSKA, SOFIA	23	F	SP		GRACBFUSA
GREICHLEN, ALBERT	42	M	LABR		GRACBFUSA
BECKOUTSECH, MOSES	44	M	LABR		GRACBFUSA
WA--LKOUSKI, C	29	M	LABR		GRACBFUSA
SCHWARTZ, A	21	M	LABR		GRACBFUSA
SELIKOW, SOL	33	M	LABR		GRACBFUSA
LEBOWITZ, SAM	34	M	LABR		GRACBFUSA
-----SON, ANDERS	25	M	LABR		GRACBFUSA
ROM, HERMAN	11	M	CH		GRACBFUSA
FICHMANN, ABRAM	16	M	LABR		GRACBFUSA
SCHELEITER, H	26	M	LABR		GRACBFUSA
NEUDELOUSKY, ELIAS	27	M	LABR		GRACBFUSA
BRA-FORD, ED	21	M	LABR		GRACBFUSA
WALTER, U	20	M	LABR		GRACBFUSA
LEONIN, C	24	M	LABR		GRACBFUSA
J	2	M	CHILD		GRACBFUSA
GUNDERON, G	16	M	LABR		GRACBFUSA
GRAYE-OK, C	16	M	LABR		GRACBFUSA
GARABETH, E	18	M	LABR		GRACBFUSA
-UNKFELD, A	16	M	LABR		GRACBFUSA
WACHS, ABRAM	30	M	LABR		GRACBFUSA
GRIMFELD, CH	32	M	LABR		GRACBFUSA
MULLNER, MEYER	41	M	LABR		GRACBFUSA
ABRAMS, ABRAM	30	M	LABR		GRACBFUSA
WANDT, JACOB	48	M	LABR		GRACBFUSA
NOURIN, MENDEL	20	M	LABR		GRACBFUSA
NOLNIK, JOSEF	40	M	LABR		GRACBFUSA
DAHL, J	39	M	LABR		GRACBFUSA
HELENA, S	18	M	LABR		GRACBFUSA
MICHELSON, RALE	16	M	LABR		GRACBFUSA
REOURKOW, LEIB	18	M	LABR		GRACBFUSA
NUATIMAKI, U	27	M	LABR		GRACBFUSA
KAJET, H	27	M	LABR		GRACBFUSA
R	18	M	LABR		GRACBFUSA
SCHMERKOWI-, BALE	21	M	LABR		GRACBFUSA
--HTA, M	37	M	LABR		GRACBFUSA
RISKI, M	37	M	LABR		GRACBFUSA
S	9	M	CHILD		GRACBFUSA
LENG, JACOB	16	M	LABR		GRACBFUSA
ROSENTHA-, HERMAN	19	M	LABR		GRACBFUSA
J	7	M	CHILD		GRACBFUSA
SALKIN, J	20	M	LABR		GRACBFUSA
GROSSMAN, ELIAS	15	M	LABR		GRACBFUSA
KARR, M	32	M	LABR		GRACBFUSA
KOSLYENSKY, V	36	M	LABR		GRACBFUSA
-OKENNITZ, A	23	M	LABR		GRACBFUSA
BERTHI-, G	25	M	LABR		GRACBFUSA
SCHULTZ, FAN---	24	M	LABR		GRACBFUSA
LUKKA, URIGAN	32	M	LABR		GRACBFUSA
ROSENBARR, J	22	M	LABR		GRACBFUSA
KRINK, H	18	M	LABR		GRACBFUSA
FUCHS, ALEX	17	M	LABR		GRACBFUSA
AVERBUCH, ABRAM	27	M	LABR		GRACBFUSA
GEORG, GALA	33	M	LABR		GRACBFUSA
JANOS, J	36	M	LABR		GRACBFUSA
WE-IES, M	17	M	LABR		GRACBFUSA
DIVASTI-, S	28	M	LABR		GRACBFUSA
LUNDE, P	20	M	LABR		GRACBFUSA
KABAS, L	32	M	LABR		GRACBFUSA
FORSBACKA, ABRAM	38	M	LABR		GRACBFUSA
KOSKI, J	31	M	LABR		GRACBFUSA
EISERMANN, CH	52	M	LABR		GRACBFUSA
HELPEROUSKY, MOSES	26	M	LABR		GRACBFUSA

PASSENGER	AGE	SEX	OCCUPATION	PRVL	DES
HABERMAN, A	42	M	LABR		GRACBFUSA
LUND, A	24	M	LABR		GRACBFUSA
KARKIT--, ELIAS	19	M	LABR		GRACBFUSA
JOHNSON, K	29	M	LABR		GRACBFUSA
ROOS, JOSEF	33	M	LABR		GRACBFUSA
S-ECKE, GEO	21	M	LABR		GRACBFUSA
SCHAELOT, ISAAC	20	M	LABR		GRACBFUSA
KOPEAK, PETER	38	M	LABR		GRACBFUSA
SARGOW, CASPAR	22	M	LABR		GRACBFUSA
ROVOSSER, JACOB	26	M	LABR		GRACBFUSA
KOL-ANER, AM-I	30	M	LABR		GRACBFUSA
HANSON, ABRAM	23	M	LABR		GRACBFUSA
HAVITA, S	28	M	LABR		GRACBFUSA
LOJA, JOHAN	28	M	LABR		GRACBFUSA
JACOB, DONALD	26	M	LABR		GRACBFUSA
GARA-IM, G	25	M	LABR		GRACBFUSA
KYN-JA, MIKKI	36	M	LABR		GRACBFUSA
SIMON, JOHN	28	M	LABR		GRACBFUSA
GEL-AND, S-UDE-	20	M	LABR		GRACBFUSA
HAMBA, SIMON	33	M	LABR		GRACBFUSA
NAWIKOSKI, ISK	32	M	LABR		GRACBFUSA
NY----, A	32	M	LABR		GRACBFUSA
LEIBMAN, MAILAK	38	M	LABR		GRACBFUSA
P	12	M	CH		GRACBFUSA
LAX, M	27	M	LABR		GRACBFUSA
WESTER-AL, S	34	M	LABR		GRACBFUSA
FRIEDMAN, MOSES	39	M	LABR		GRACBFUSA
GAVLOUSKY, JESSEL	24	M	LABR		GRACBFUSA
HANS, ANT-	26	M	LABR		GRACBFUSA

SHIP: STATE OF GEORGIA

FROM: GLASGOW AND LARNE
TO: NEW YORK
ARRIVED: 05 JULY 1888

PASSENGER	AGE	SEX	OCCUPATION	PRVL	DES
BENDELOW, JANKEL	25	M	GCR		GRAHRZUSA
COHN, MORITZ	16	M	LABR		GRAHRZUSA
FRIEDMANN, BEHR	24	M	BCHR		GRAHRZUSA
STRAUSS, FRANZ	24	M	BCHR		GRAHRZUSA
DERSSEL, CARL	27	M	BCHR		GRAHRZUSA
BAUER, GUTA	25	M	LABR		GRAHRZUSA
HEFTER, CARL	30	M	LABR		GRAHRZUSA
HILDEBRAND, CHRISTEN	39	M	LABR		GRAHRZUSA
WILHELMINE	41	F	W		GRAHRZUSA
EDWARD	8	M	CHILD		GRAHRZUSA
RUDOLPH	5	M	CHILD		GRAHRZUSA
MARIE	.09	F	INFANT		GRAHRZUSA
LAURIDSEN, LAURIDS	21	M	MSN		GRAHRZUSA
MALDER, CHRIST.	22	M	UNKNOWN		GRAHRZUSA
NEIMANN, A.B.	32	M	DLR		GRAHRZUSA
KEISCH, JOH.	48	M	LABR		GRAHRZUSA
ROSENBERG, MATTEL	45	M	PNTR		GRAHRZUSA
RUPP, JOHANN	60	M	FARMER		GRAHRZUSA
SOLM, ELIAS	18	M	BCHR		GRAHRZUSA
WURM, FRANZ	33	M	MCHT		GRAHRZUSA

SHIP: WERRA

FROM: BREMEN AND SOUTHAMPTON
TO: NEW YORK
ARRIVED: 05 JULY 1888

PASSENGER	AGE	SEX	OCCUPATION	PRVL	DES
KORDER, CHRIST	35	F	UNKNOWN		GRZZZZUSA
NEWBURG, J	25	M	TT		GRZZZZUSA

PASSENGER	AGE	SEX	OCCUPATION	PRVL-DES
POEPFER, A.	45	M	TT	GRAIDQUSA
ANNA	43	F	W	GRAIDQUSA
AGNES	11	F	CH	GRAIDQUSA
PANNEBACKER, WM.	58	F	W	GRAIDQUNK
HELENE	23	F	UNKNOWN	GRAIDQUSA
BOHLMANN, BERNH.	26	M	FARMER	GRZZZZUSA
LEIMKOHL, FRIEDA	26	F	UNKNOWN	GRZZZZUSA
RUPP, LIVA	32	F	UNKNOWN	GRADTHUSA
KREP, LINA	30	F	UNKNOWN	GRADTHUSA
BRAUN, ADAM	34	M	FARMER	BVZZZZUSA
RUDOLF, HERM.	35	M	MCHT	BVABQXUSA
HIMMLER, JOH	71	M	MCHT	BVZZZZUSA
BARB	74	F	W	BVZZZZUSA
FRANCKE, HULDA	40	F	W	GRZZZZUSA
HERBERDT	3	M	CHILD	GRZZZZUSA
HANS	.11	M	INFANT	GRZZZZUSA
FREY, BERTHA	25	F	UNKNOWN	GRADXCUSA
DALLDORF, EDITH	17	F	UNKNOWN	GRADXCUSA
MALKOMES, ELLA	20	F	UNKNOWN	GRADXCUSA
SCHWENKE, MARIE	21	F	UNKNOWN	GRZZZZUSA
GOEPEL, WILH	50	F	UNKNOWN	GRZZZZUSA
ZIEGLER, CARL	28	M	MCHT	GRAFQVUSA
CHRIST	26	F	W	GRAFQVUSA
HERTZ, MILTON	20	M	MCHT	GRAFQVUSA
FEINBERG, SIEGFRIED	30	M	MCHT	GRAFQVUSA
PEEROT, EUGEN	34	M	MCHT	GRAAZSUSA
ALEX	32	M	MCHT	GRAAZSUSA
RIEDEL, HEINR.	50	M	MCHT	GRAAZSUSA
SOPHIE	43	F	W	GRAAZSUSA
MALETZKI, MARIE	28	F	UNKNOWN	GRAAZQUSA
LACKMUND, J.A.	31	M	TT	GRAARRUSA
MARKER, FRED	58	M	TT	GRABDMUSA
WILH	62	F	W	GRABDMUSA
SCHWARICK, ROSALIE	16	F	UNKNOWN	GRAARRUSA
SCHWARZ, FRAN.CATH.	42	F	W	GRAARRUSA
LOUISE	16	F	UNKNOWN	GRAARRUSA
ELISE	.06	F	INFANT	GRAARRUSA
DATHE, FRIEDR.	69	M	WVR	GRZZZZUSA
MARIE	65	F	W	GRZZZZUSA
NECKER, HERM.	11	M	CH	GRADOKUSA
BERNH.	10	M	CH	GRADOKUSA
REDMANN, MINNE	54	F	W	GRAAUEUSA
LEVY, LAURA	18	F	UNKNOWN	GRABUTUSA
FADEL, JULIANNE	19	F	UNKNOWN	GRZZZZUSA
TAVENPORT, SOPHIE	57	F	UNKNOWN	GRAAFXUSA
KEONTKE, PAUL	35	F	W	GRZZZZUSA
ANNA	14	F	UNKNOWN	GRZZZZUSA
ROBERT	11	M	CH	GRZZZZUSA
CLARA	9	F	CHILD	GRZZZZUSA
FRIEDRICH, GEORG	45	M	LABR	GRAAFXUSA
CRESCENZIA	44	F	W	GRAAFXUSA
THERESE	17	F	UNKNOWN	GRAAFXUSA
MARG	11	F	CH	GRAAFXUSA
ANNA	11	F	CH	GRAAFXUSA
CRESCENZ	10	M	CH	GRAAFXUSA
JOSEPHA	8	F	CHILD	GRAAFXUSA
HAVER	7	M	CHILD	GRAAFXUSA
MARIA	6	F	CHILD	GRAAFXUSA
HABERREITER, HAVER	33	M	STCTR	GRAAFXUSA
MARCINKIWICH, ROSALIA	20	F	UNKNOWN	BVZZZZUSA
KANTOWSKI, JOH	24	M	SMH	BVZZZZUSA
ALBETZKI, JOSEF	30	M	LABR	BVZZZZUSA
LEICHAUER, MATH	25	F	UNKNOWN	BVACENUSA
ENGLHARD, BARB	31	F	W	BVACENUSA
BARB	.09	F	INFANT	BVACENUSA
SCHLETTERER, JOH	36	M	FARMER	BVZZZZUSA
ANNA	32	F	W	BVZZZZUSA
MARIA	3	F	CHILD	BVZZZZUSA
GEORG	.11	M	INFANT	BVZZZZUSA
MARIA	22	F	UNKNOWN	BVZZZZUSA
CATH.	19	F	UNKNOWN	BVZZZZUSA
HAIN, WILH	32	F	UNKNOWN	BVABQOUSA
PHILIPPE	32	F	W	BVABQOUSA
AUGUST	.09	M	INFANT	BVABQOUSA
WOLFF, WILH	43	M	JNR	BVAAKHUSA
HARMS, BERTHA	47	F	W	BVAAWVUSA
WILH	16	M	UNKNOWN	BVAAWVUSA
BRAUMANN, ALB.	22	M	FARMER	GRZZZZUSA
PFLUM, MARG	59	F	W	WMZZZZUSA
MARIE	19	F	UNKNOWN	WMZZZZUSA
GLOCKLER, REG.	24	F	UNKNOWN	WMZZZZUSA
DANZELMAIER, LORENZ	34	M	BRR	WMZZZZUSA
LUCAS	21	M	UNKNOWN	WMZZZZUSA
DREYERBERG, WILH	68	M	MLR	WMACBRUSA
HANS	10	M	CH	WMACBRUSA
KURT	7	M	CHILD	WMACBRUSA
BOHRMEISTER, WILH	65	M	FARMER	WMADKKUSA
HELENE	20	F	UNKNOWN	WMADKKUSA
WILLI	9	M	CHILD	WMADKKUSA
MICSAK, MAG.	35	M	UNKNOWN	HSZZZZUSA
SCHING, ANASTASIA	35	F	UNKNOWN	HSACUOUSA
HAELBER, LUDW.	00	M	LABR	HSABVIUSA
ALGAY, MINA	30	F	W	HSABVIUSA
MARIE	4	F	CHILD	HSABVIUSA
HAELBER, CHRIST	27	M	FARMER	HSAAGLUSA
LOUISE	4	F	CHILD	HSAAGLUSA
FRIDA	1	F	CHILD	HSAAGLUSA
BECK, NIKOLAUS	16	M	FARMER	HSZZZZUSA
SCHWINN, JOH	17	M	FARMER	HSZZZZUSA
SCHANERTE, HEIN.	17	M	FARMER	HSZZZZUSA
ALBAHN, CHRISTIANE	54	F	W	HSZZZZUSA
WILH	16	M	CGRMKR	HSZZZZUSA
JACOB	13	M	UNKNOWN	HSZZZZUSA
ENSINGER, MARIE	22	F	UNKNOWN	HSADHZUSA
WEBER, CATH	23	F	UNKNOWN	BVZZZZUSA
HOEPPEL, MARIA	18	F	UNKNOWN	GRZZZZUSA
SCHNEIDER, GUSTAV	20	M	LABR	GRADDQUSA
LANG, JOH	16	M	UNKNOWN	BVZZZZUSA
PAUL	21	M	LABR	GRZZZZUSA
OTTO, FR.WILH.	18	M	LABR	GRABJWUSA
EMRID, KATH.	17	F	UNKNOWN	BVZZZZUSA
SCHAEFER, GUSTAF	15	M	UNKNOWN	WMZZZZUSA
PFLUM, MART	23	M	FARMER	WMZZZZUSA
GUST.	3	M	CHILD	WMZZZZUSA
FULLEMANN, LOUISE	22	F	UNKNOWN	BVZZZZUSA
DITTER, GEORG	20	M	FARMER	GRZZZZUSA
FRIEDRICH, GEORG	14	M	FARMER	GRZZZZUSA
JALOVICAR, MARIA	28	F	W	GRZZZZUSA
MARIA	00	U	CH	GRZZZZUSA
LUDW.	00	U	UNKNOWN	GRZZZZUSA
JOSEF	.10	M	INFANT	GRZZZZUSA
SKUSA, EVA	23	F	UNKNOWN	GRAEXKUSA
STAUBWASSER, THOMAS	20	M	BCHR	BVZZZZUSA
GEISELBRECHT, BARB.	26	F	UNKNOWN	BVADUVUSA
HINZ, MICH.	62	M	FARMER	GRZZZZUSA
CAROL.	54	F	W	GRZZZZUSA
BEYER, AUGUSTE	28	F	W	GRZZZZUSA
MARTHA	.10	F	INFANT	GRZZZZUSA
BEHLE, CARL	16	M	LABR	GRAAZSUSA
KUMIN, JOH.	24	F	UNKNOWN	GRZZZZUSA
MATH.	14	F	UNKNOWN	GRZZZZUSA
GRZESSKOWIAK, JULIE	28	F	W	GRZZZZUSA
MARIE	3	F	CHILD	GRZZZZUSA
BANASCHINSKA, MARIA	20	F	UNKNOWN	GRZZZZUSA
DOERING, ANNA	35	F	UNKNOWN	GRAEACUSA
OEFELIN, MARIA	24	F	W	BVZZZZUSA
ANNA	2	F	CHILD	BVZZZZUSA
RAMKE, JOH	14	M	UNKNOWN	GRZZZZUSA
UHLIG, LOUIS	50	M	LABR	SYZZZZUSA
SCHNEIDER, WILH	30	M	LABR	BVZZZZUSA
ANNA	24	F	W	BVZZZZUSA
ANNA	3	F	CHILD	BVZZZZUSA
LINA	1	F	CHILD	BVZZZZUSA
ELISE	.06	F	INFANT	BVZZZZUSA
PFENFFEIER, HEDWIG	16	F	UNKNOWN	GRZZZZUSA
ARMBRUSTER, WILH	16	M	LABR	BVZZZZUSA
LINGER, HERM.	16	M	BKR	BVAFOIUSA
APPERT, CACILIA	30	F	UNKNOWN	BVZZZZUSA
MARKGRAF, JACOB	17	M	LABR	BVAFEIUSA
SINGER, WILH	21	M	MCHT	BVAFEIUSA

PASSENGER	AGE	SEX	OCCUPATION	PVRIVL	DES
SPANGEHL, BERTHA	24	F	UNKNOWN	GRZZZZ	USA
FRIEDA	21	F	UNKNOWN	GRZZZZ	USA
HUSTER, HERM.	27	M	LLD	GRZZZZ	USA
SCHAEFER, JACOB	30	M	SHMK	GRAAGJ	USA
HEIDEN, JOH	26	M	LABR	GRAGQG	USA
KUENZEL, LOUIS	22	M	LABR	GRAGQG	USA
KRENZWEISER, FRIEDERIKE	30	F	UNKNOWN	BDZZZZ	USA
GLANDER, HEINR	17	M	LABR	GRZZZZ	USA
SOTTUNG, CHRIST.	18	F	UNKNOWN	GRAJXW	USA
HELENA	17	F	UNKNOWN	GRAJXW	USA
BOGLE, MARIA	20	F	UNKNOWN	WMZZZZ	USA
LOHRMANN, MINNA	23	F	UNKNOWN	WMADYY	USA
KEMMLER, LOUIS	27	M	MCHT	WMAEXW	USA
WEISSLER, ERNST	19	M	BRR	WMAEXW	USA
SCHELLHORN, ANNA	19	F	UNKNOWN	GRZZZZ	USA
BERTHA, ANNA	18	F	UNKNOWN	GRZZZZ	USA
EYRICH, BARB.	22	F	UNKNOWN	GRACHY	USA
ANNA	14	F	UNKNOWN	GRACHY	USA
REPPLUM, KATH.	52	F	W	WMZZZZ	USA
ZIMMERMANN, REG.	16	F	UNKNOWN	WMZZZZ	USA
OELSCHLAEGER, ROSINA	15	F	UNKNOWN	WMZZZZ	USA
REPPLUM, JACOB	14	M	UNKNOWN	WMZZZZ	USA
BINDER, GEORG	24	M	BCHR	WMZZZZ	USA
STAHL, OTTO	16	M	FARMER	WMZZZZ	USA
LEHR, MARIA	49	F	W	GRZZZZ	USA
CAROL.	20	F	UNKNOWN	GRZZZZ	USA
PHILIPP	16	M	FARMER	GRZZZZ	USA
MARG	13	F	UNKNOWN	GRZZZZ	USA
CONRAD	11	M	CH	GRZZZZ	USA
SCHENERMANN, CONRAD	54	M	LABR	GRAAEA	USA
CHRIST.	56	F	W	GRAAEA	USA
MARIE	11	F	UNKNOWN	GRAAEA	USA
KOERNIG, THEOD.	24	M	MCHT	GRAAEA	USA
SCHMIDT, DANIEL	27	M	CGRMKR	GRZZZZ	USA
SYLVESTER, GUST.	20	M	BBR	GRAILB	USA
REIBSCHLAEGER, ROB.	22	M	FARMER	GRZZZZ	USA
CORDES, HEINR.	26	M	FARMER	GRACBR	USA
HOHENSTEIN, ADAM	64	M	LABR	GRACBR	USA
KOCH, HENNRIETTE	20	F	UNKNOWN	GRACBR	USA
POECK, GEORG	33	M	SHMK	GRAAMT	USA
ADE, LOUISE	22	F	UNKNOWN	GRAAWN	USA
VOLLE, MARIE	22	F	UNKNOWN	GRAAWN	USA
SILBERSACK, ADOLF	16	M	LABR	BVZZZZ	USA
HEIM, WILH	18	M	LABR	BVAFGO	USA
BOGUNN, FRANZ	27	M	LABR	GRZZZZ	USA
MARYANNA	26	F	W	GRZZZZ	USA
ANNA	.09	F	INFANT	GRZZZZ	USA
MARIANNA	5	F	CHILD	GRZZZZ	USA
MELCHERT, KAROL.	21	F	UNKNOWN	BDZZZZ	USA
MAINBERGER, ISIDOR	22	M	LABR	BDAAGL	USA
ROSINE	28	F	W	BDAAGL	USA
MUELLER, MARIE	45	F	W	HSZZZZ	USA
GEORG	16	M	UNKNOWN	HSZZZZ	USA
JACOB	11	M	CH	HSZZZZ	USA
ROSINE	9	F	CHILD	HSZZZZ	USA
MARIE	5	F	CHILD	HSZZZZ	USA
GUSTAV	3	M	CHILD	HSZZZZ	USA
NUTZHORN, JOH	41	M	LABR	HSACBR	USA
LUCKENBACH, EMIL	26	M	LABR	HSACBR	USA
SVOBECK, JOH.	00	M	LABR	GRZZZZ	USA
KUBIS, PAUL	15	M	LABR	GRZZZZ	USA
STELIK, ISTWAN	35	M	LABR	GRZZZZ	USA
ZACHER, ANDR	26	M	LABR	GRZZZZ	USA
KUBITA, GEORG	28	M	LABR	GRZZZZ	USA
DOLATA, LORENZ	28	M	LABR	GRZZZZ	USA
MONDRE, MICH.	37	M	LABR	GRZZZZ	USA
DETTKA, MICH	27	M	LABR	GRZZZZ	USA
KAMARCK, MICH.	43	M	LABR	GRZZZZ	USA
ROSTALISKI, MICH.	38	M	LABR	GRZZZZ	USA
CZISKA, FRIEDR.	35	M	LABR	GRZZZZ	USA
ORTWEIN, CLARA	17	F	UNKNOWN	GRZZZZ	USA
EMMA	19	F	UNKNOWN	GRZZZZ	USA
GIERSNEWSKI, FRANZ	26	M	FARMER	GRAARR	USA
BUENGER, AUGUST	35	M	FARMER	GRZZZZ	USA
VASIL, ZIELIP	26	M	FARMER	GRZZZZ	USA

SHIP: CITY OF ROME

FROM: LIVERPOOL AND QUEENSTOWN
TO: NEW YORK
ARRIVED: 06 JULY 1888

PASSENGER	AGE	SEX	OCCUPATION	PVRIVL	DES
KILEN, PHILIP	19	M	BCHR	GRADAX	USA
LUDWIG	18	M	BCHR	GRADAX	USA
DANIEL, ISAK	30	M	LABR	GRADAX	USA
EMMA	29	F	W	GRADAX	USA
SARAH	3	F	CHILD	GRADAX	USA
HANNY	2	M	CHILD	GRADAX	USA
IDA	1	F	CHILD	GRADAX	USA
LACHMAN, GEO	24	M	LABR	GRADAX	USA
U	22	F	W	GRADAX	USA
SLADKY, VAILAI	28	M	LABR	GRADAX	USA
ANNA	28	F	W	GRADAX	USA
OVEANELEK	11	M	CH	GRADAX	USA
MARIE	.11	F	INFANT	GRADAX	USA
DESONOIS, FRANCOIS	53	M	SHMK	GRADAX	USA
ALPHONSE	28	M	SHMK	GRADAX	USA
ALINE	18	F	SVNT	GRADAX	USA
PAULINE	8	F	CHILD	GRADAX	USA

SHIP: NOORDLAND

FROM: ANTWERP
TO: NEW YORK
ARRIVED: 06 JULY 1888

PASSENGER	AGE	SEX	OCCUPATION	PVRIVL	DES
ZWICK-, FR	65	M	ENGR	GRZZZZ	USA
TH-PSEN, E	35	M	MCHT	GRZZZZ	USA
BLUM, A	26	F	PVTW	GRZZZZ	USA
KOCH, B	30	F	PVTW	GRZZZZ	USA
ANDREAS, C	30	M	MCHT	GRADEI	USA
RUECKERT, F	24	F	PVTW	GRABOQ	USA
HELBERG, A	30	M	ENGR	GRZZZZ	USA
E	33	F	PVTW	GRZZZZ	USA
HEYMAN, E	17	F	PVTW	GRADNX	USA
E	14	F	PVTW	GRADNX	USA
R	00	F	PVTW	GRADNX	USA
GAPP, T	45	F	PVTW	GRACMG	USA
HOEFELD, R	18	F	PVTW	GRZZZZ	USA
STRUCK, W	28	F	PVTW	GRZZZZ	USA
TAE-ER, T	72	M	PVTW	GRZZZZ	USA
MRS	61	F	PVTW	GRZZZZ	USA
HARTING, C	30	M	MD	GRZZZZ	USA
TREUTRU-, U	21	M	MCHT	GRAAYA	USA
BERGMAN, A	30	M	ENGR	GRAAEC	USA
RIES, T	24	M	BKR	GRABOQ	USA
STEWINAGEL, C	64	M	BKMR	GRABOQ	USA
HAUBOLD, E	19	F	PVTW	GRAFJD	USA
BINGELL, C	23	M	FARMER	GRADEM	USA
MEYER, C	26	M	BKR	GRAEXW	USA
SCHAAFF, S	22	M	BKR	GRADEI	USA
POCKFUESS, MR	41	M	BCHR	GRADLD	USA
MRS	34	F	W	GRADLD	USA
SONNITZ, R	19	M	SMH	GRAANF	USA
WETTERGREN, J	21	M	TLR	GRZZZZ	USA
GRA-DM--TAYNE, A	26	M	LABR	GRAFJQ	USA
A	25	F	W	GRAFJQ	USA
WIG---ER, J	29	M	LABR	GRZZZZ	USA
NAURASKA, M	17	F	SVNT	GRZZZZ	USA
SIEBERT, T	25	M	ENGR	GRABHT	USA
E	27	F	W	GRABHT	USA
RIEGEL, G	19	M	LABR	GRABHT	USA
-ERASCAR, M	24	M	LABR	GRABHT	USA
WEINERT, A	25	M	LABR	GRABHT	USA
M	22	F	W	GRABHT	USA

PASSENGER	AGE	SEX	OCCUPATION	PRIVL	DES
GEN-ANATI, A	25	M	LABR		GRABHTUSA
-ARNISNEN, M	30	F	W		GRABHTUSA
T	00	F	INF		GRABHTUSA
MERTENS, T	5	M	CHILD		GRABHTUSA
HANSEN, A	22	M	LABR		GRZZZZUSA
CASPAR, F	20	M	LABR		GRZZZZSP
MERKEL, M	30	F	W		GRZZZZSP
A	00	F	INF		GRZZZZSP
MEWS, H	25	M	LABR		GRZZZZCLE
KUHL, A	27	M	LABR		GRZZZZUNK
GOTZ, TH	19	M	LABR		GRZZZZPA
HESSINGER, L	19	F	SVNT		GRAJZVNY
SCHWALL, J	55	F	W		GRZZZZNY
TH	10	F	CH		GRZZZZNY
BRENCKER, O	20	M	LABR		GRACACNY
LORENZ, O	17	M	LABR		GRACACBUF
BERNHOFEN, J	29	M	LABR		GRACACUNK
GUSE, J	54	M	LABR		GRZZZZUNK
W	23	F	SVNT		GRZZZZUNK
C	16	M	LABR		GRZZZZUNK
E	11	F	CH		GRZZZZUNK
WIEDER--EN, N	19	M	LABR		GRZZZZUNK
LERDERER, B	38	M	LABR		GRAFEECH
BERL-IER, J	21	F	SVNT		GRAFEENY
SARSCHOFF, J	50	F	W		GRAFEENY
M	00	F	INF		GRAFEENY
BERKMANN, W	25	M	LABR		GRZZZZNY
NARKUSKY, A	21	M	LABR		GRZZZZNY
HOFFMANN, E	18	F	W		GRZZZZUNK
PFEIFFER, L	25	M	LABR		GRZZZZNY
SCHR--D, S	34	M	LABR		GRZZZZKAS
P	34	F	W		GRZZZZKAS
PFISTER, G	22	M	LABR		GRAKXDKAS
FLECKS, C	29	F	SVNT		GRAKXDCH
MAISENHOLDER, C	16	F	SVNT		GRZZZZNY
KUHN, W	26	F	W		GRZZZZNY
A	4	M	CHILD		GRZZZZNY
E	00	M	INF		GRZZZZNY
JAEGER, H	65	M	LABR		GRABSONY
E	62	F	W		GRABSONY
ALBRECHT, C	32	F	W		GRABSONY
H	14	M	NN		GRABSONY
A	8	M	CHILD		GRABSONY
G	00	M	INF		GRABSONY
JAEGER, A	29	M	LABR		GRABSONY
C	4	F	CHILD		GRABSONY
L	00	F	INF		GRABSONY
SCHNELL, L	56	M	LABR		GRABSONY
M	46	F	W		GRABSONY
M	17	F	SVNT		GRABSONY
TH	14	M	LABR		GRABSONY
CLEMMER, E	25	F	W		GRABZVNY
J	2	M	CHILD		GRABZVNY
C	00	F	INF		GRABZVNY
ROTHENLEBER, J	50	M	LABR		GRADDWNY
A	48	F	W		GRADDWNY
C	21	F	SVNT		GRADDWNY
GROLLMANN, C	5	M	CHILD		GRADDWNY
C	6	F	CHILD		GRADDWNY
SCHMIDT, C	28	F	SVNT		GRZZZZNY
SCHIPP, J	26	M	LABR		GRADDWNY
SCHIELE, J	23	F	SVNT		GRAIPDNY
HANIERL, A	42	M	LABR		GRZZZZBUF
R	11	F	CH		GRZZZZBUF
KREUSS, J	36	M	LABR		GRABRCNY
REMMER, J	27	M	LABR		GRAECZNY
DIRSCHEL, J	18	M	LABR		GRAECZNY
DURSCHOWSKY, CH	35	M	LABR		GRACRANY
EDERER, J	22	F	SVNT		GRACDNNY
ANGEL, A	24	M	LABR		GRZZZZNY
HAFNER, C	34	M	LABR		GRZZZZNY
HAUSLADEN, G	37	M	LABR		GRZZZZBUF
URBAN, F	45	F	W		GRZZZZBUF
HOFFMANN, P	24	M	ENGR		GRABHTNY
STWIN, H	43	M	ENGR		GRABHTUNK
RIEUVE, A	23	M	LABR		GRABHTNY
E	15	F	SVNT		GRABHTNY
WENZAUER, O	30	M	BCHR		GRABHTNY
STEIGLEDER, S	44	M	SMH		GRABHTNY
WAHL, J	34	M	SMH		GRABHTNY
WEISS, B	26	F	W		GRABHTNY
BIEDERMAN, C	21	M	LABR		GRAAHUNY
A	22	M	LABR		GRAAHUNY
WINKLER, M	30	M	LABR		GRAAHUNY
STEINER, C	25	M	LABR		GRAAHUNY
CH	27	M	LABR		GRAAHUNY
BIEFER, E	37	M	SMH		GRAAHUNY
WEILLER, J	28	M	MCHT		GRAAHUNY
LUSCHER, C	25	M	LABR		GRAAHUNY
HAMMERLI, J	25	M	LABR		GRAAHUNY
BUSCH, C	25	M	LABR		GRAAHUNY
BAUER, J	37	F	SVNT		GRAAHUNY
KOLLIKER, J	32	F	SVNT		GRAAHUNY
E--OLF, J	27	F	SVNT		GRAAHUNY
M	26	F	SVNT		GRAAHUNY
DIETZIKER, O	43	F	W		GRAAHUNY
A	16	F	UNKNOWN		GRAAHUNY
A	12	M	CH		GRAAHUNY
WAGNER, L	27	M	UNKNOWN		GRAAHUNY
SUTHER, F	20	M	SMH		GRAAHUNY
SEEGER, FR	17	F	SVNT		GRAAHUNY
GRENTNER, E	23	F	SVNT		GRAAHUNY
WEIDMANN, M	24	F	SVNT		GRAAHUNY
THOMA, C	42	F	W		GRAAHUNY
FE-N, C	16	M	LABR		GRAAYANY
RAPP, G	51	M	LABR		GRAAYANY
M	50	F	W		GRAAYANY
E	11	F	CH		GRAAYANY
T	8	M	CHILD		GRAAYANY
M	7	F	CHILD		GRAAYANY
HUSS, T	27	M	LABR		GRZZZZNY
SENDER, E	20	F	SVNT		GRADLDNY
BAUER, M	22	M	LABR		GRADLDNY
BUCHHOLZ, H	19	M	LABR		GRADLDNY
E	11	F	CH		GRADLDNY
M	9	F	CHILD		GRADLDNY
P	7	M	CHILD		GRADLDNY
J	4	M	CHILD		GRADLDNY
W	2	M	CHILD		GRADLDNY
WEINIGER, O	17	M	LABR		GRZZZZNY
SCHL-NY, C	21	F	SVNT		GRZZZZNY
KISTNER, J	45	M	SHMK		GRZZZZNY
F	17	M	SHMK		GRZZZZNY
A	16	F	SVNT		GRZZZZNY
SCHERER, J	28	M	DRVR		GRZZZZNY
KEUMER, C	28	F	W		GRZZZZALB
S	3	F	CHILD		GRZZZZALB
M	2	F	CHILD		GRZZZZALB
A	00	M	INF		GRZZZZALB
BUBLA, J	37	M	LABR		GRAAYANY
FROHMANN, F	24	M	LABR		GRAAYANY
PULPIT, J	24	M	LABR		GRAAYANY
MATHIAS, N	17	M	LABR		GRZZZZNY
HAUPEL, G	20	M	GDSM		GRZZZZNY
PASTORET, D	19	M	LABR		GRAGTSNY
HILBERT, N	42	F	W		GRAGTSNY
M	11	F	CH		GRAGTSNY
HELSING, M	34	M	FARMER		GRZZZZNY
CLOOS, M	28	F	W		GRZZZZNY
J	4	M	CHILD		GRZZZZNY
C	00	M	INF		GRZZZZNY
GOST, W	55	M	LABR		GRAGFDNY
A	49	F	W		GRAGFDNY
T	15	M	NN		GRAGFDNY
E	11	M	CH		GRAGFDNY
SIMON, M	19	M	BCHR		GRAGFDNY
SEITZ, M	22	M	LABR		GRAGFDUNK
RAUCH, C	23	F	W		GRZZZZUNK
E	2	M	CHILD		GRZZZZUNK
MARX, A	38	M	LABR		GRAACTUNK

PASSENGER	AGE	SEX	OCCUPATION	PRVVL	DES
GERHARD, M	36	F	W		GRAACTUNK
MARX, M	13	F	NN		GRAACTUNK
C	11	F	CH		GRAACTUNK
A	10	M	CH		GRAACTUNK
C	8	F	CHILD		GRAACTUNK
CH	7	F	CHILD		GRAACTUNK
M	2	F	CHILD		GRAACTUNK
IRSCH, -	36	M	FARMER		GRZZZZNY
BLIASI, C	28	F	W		GRZZZZNY
C	3	M	CHILD		GRZZZZNY
J	2	M	CHILD		GRZZZZNY
M	00	M	INF		GRZZZZNY
WENTZ, W	18	F	SVNT		GRZZZZNY
STURZ, J	37	M	LABR		GRZZZZNY
TES-AR, W	24	M	LABR		GRAAYANY
HOLKER, C	22	M	LABR		GRAAYANY
RUCK, C	26	F	SVNT		GRABRCNY
REINIGHAUS, C	24	M	LABR		GRABRCNY
SCHUCK, C	42	M	LABR		GRABRCNY
MEYER, A	25	M	LABR		GRABRCNY
SCHAAFF, L	22	M	LABR		GRABRCNY
PFARRIUS, A	19	M	LABR		GRADDWNY
GULDIG, CH	40	M	LABR		GRADDWNY
KOTZLE, C	18	F	SVNT		GRADDWBUF
BLESSING, FR	15	M	LABR		GRADDWBUF
SCHECK, G	18	M	LABR		GRADDWBUF
SCHULER, C	35	M	LABR		GRAALNMIL
HIRTH, A	26	M	LABR		GRZZZZNY
E	19	F	LABR		GRZZZZNY
A	11	M	CH		GRZZZZNY
WAGNER, J	24	M	LABR		GRZZZZNY
DIRKELMAN, J	19	F	SVNT		GRZZZZNY
C	17	F	SVNT		GRZZZZNY
-OCHER, M	18	F	SVNT		GRZZZZNY
TRAUTH, CH	19	F	W		GRZZZZNY
ULLMANN, E	17	M	LABR		GRZZZZNY
BREITHMEYER, J	20	M	LABR		GRZZZZROC
WENDEL, M	21	F	SVNT		GRADTTCLE
B	19	F	SVNT		GRADTTCLE
DOLKER, M	26	F	SVNT		GRADTTNY
DEISSLER, M	66	F	W		GRADTTNY
HERMANN, P	42	M	LABR		GRADTTHEL
KOPF, J	27	M	LABR		GRAAZLNY
KLAUS, L	21	F	SVNT		GRZZZZNY
KOHLER, J	21	F	SVNT		GRZZZZNY
KROUT, E	21	F	SVNT		GRZZZZNY
NICHT, W	24	M	LABR		GRZZZZPHI
FROUK, J	45	M	LABR		GRAFDCPHI
BOSMANN, C	27	M	LABR		GRAFDCNY
LE-IER, TH	18	M	LABR		GRAFDCNY
-ERWE-RO, C	19	M	LABR		GRAFDCNY
MULLER, H	30	M	LABR		GRABTUNY
WEIL, A	27	F	W		GRABTUNY
LEY, P	29	M	LABR		GRZZZZUNK
EISEN-ECKEN, H	36	M	LABR		GRAFASNY
KRIESCH, TH	31	M	LABR		GRAFASNY
TOMMEL, P	32	M	LABR		GRAFASNY
VITTHORI, S	31	M	LABR		GRAFASSHN
DENBACHER, F	18	M	LABR		GRAFASNY
PEDERSEN, A	20	M	LABR		GRAFASBO
CARLSON, L	20	M	LABR		GRAFASBO
GUMAROSK-Y, U	33	M	LABR		GRAFASMIN
KESSELKAUL, P	35	M	LABR		GRAFASNY
BROUN, J	27	M	LABR		GRZZZZNY
KREMER, M	20	F	SVNT		GRZZZZCH
HARTMANN, V	54	M	LABR		GRAIBEPHI
C	50	F	W		GRAIBEPHI
STOCKER, A	00	F	SVNT		GRAIBESAN
HERMANN, J	17	M	LABR		GRAIBEROC
GASSER, C	25	M	LABR		GRZZZZBUF
PREUSSER, F	19	M	LABR		GRZZZZAKR
BADER, M	22	F	W		GRZZZZNY
C	00	F	INF		GRZZZZNY
CLEFF, C	20	M	LABR		GRZZZZNY
HOSCHLER, W	23	M	LABR		GRZZZZUNK

PASSENGER	AGE	SEX	OCCUPATION	PRVVL	DES
HORELMANN, J	22	M	LABR		GRZZZZUNK
MESCK, E	26	F	SVNT		GRAAKHCH
NEELMANN, H	20	M	LABR		GRAAKHNY
SOLUSKI, B	25	M	LABR		GRAAKHCH
SCHOTT, J	24	M	LABR		GRZZZZLAS
OLSEN, J	48	M	LABR		GRZZZZMIL
FR	53	F	W		GRZZZZMIL
GRUNDERSEN, G	28	M	LABR		GRZZZZNY
MILSON, M	41	M	LABR		GRZZZZNY
OLSEN, H	11	M	LABR		GRZZZZNY
WALTHER, J	25	M	LABR		GRZZZZNY
E	18	F	SVNT		GRZZZZNY
FATT, S	30	F	SVNT		GRZZZZNY
WERNER, B	24	F	SVNT		GRZZZZNY
ARM-ER, E	28	F	W		GRZZZZNY
A	5	F	CHILD		GRZZZZNY
M	3	F	CHILD		GRZZZZNY
G	00	F	INF		GRZZZZNY
SOTT, A	18	M	LABR		GRZZZZNY
KAMPER, C	30	M	LABR		GRAGBPMIL
RODERIA--, FR	18	M	LABR		GRAGBPCH
W	00	M	LABR		GRAGBPCH
GRUBERMA--R, M	30	M	LABR		GRZZZZNY
A	30	F	W		GRZZZZNY
A	4	F	CHILD		GRZZZZNY
DELLINGER, N	23	M	LABR		GRZZZZCIN
KARDONNSKY, A	30	F	SVNT		GRZZZZSTL
HARTMANN, J	38	M	LABR		GRACHOATK
SEEBALD, H	12	M	LABR		GRACHONY
ICHLE, A	22	F	W		GRZZZZNY
H	00	M	INF		GRZZZZNY
BALL, A	21	F	SVNT		GRZZZZNY
EBERSTEIN, M	24	F	SVNT		GRZZZZOTT
SCHENK, A	60	M	LABR		GRZZZZBET
DUG---, A	47	M	LABR		FRZZZZBET
S	4	F	CHILD		FRZZZZBET
ROCHER, L	31	M	LABR		GRZZZZBET
E	28	F	W		GRZZZZBET
D	3	M	CHILD		GRZZZZBET
M	00	F	INF		GRZZZZBET
DAGLA---D, A	37	M	LABR		GRZZZZBET
SEINER, F	17	F	SVNT		GRZZZZBET
ARBAGAST, A	24	M	LABR		GRZZZZOTT
KOTSCH, A	20	M	LABR		GRZZZZCH
UTZ, C	27	F	SVNT		GRZZZZROC
SCHMIDT, C	26	M	LABR		GRZZZZNY
E	37	F	W		GRZZZZNY
J	11	F	CH		GRZZZZNY
A	9	M	CHILD		GRZZZZNY
C	4	F	CHILD		GRZZZZNY
B	00	F	INF		GRZZZZNY
JUNGBLU--, L	23	F	SVNT		GRAEIHNY
PETER, G	25	M	LABR		GRACUONY
RO--SAIER, G	38	M	LABR		GRACUONY
BAUMANN, A	48	M	LABR		GRAEXKLOU
M	20	F	SVNT		GRAEXKLOU
GERES, J	28	M	LABR		GRZZZZLOU
IS-E--T, L	26	F	W		GRZZZZLOU
C	4	F	CHILD		GRZZZZLOU

SHIP: ALLER

FROM: BREMEN AND SOUTHAMPTON
TO: NEW YORK
ARRIVED: 07 JULY 1888

LATTMANN, A.	33	M	MCHT		GRZZZZUSA
VONTEMPSKY, GEORG	56	M	OFF		GRZZZZUSA
ANNA	46	F	W		GRZZZZUSA
EMMA	22	F	CH		GRZZZZUSA

201

PASSENGER	AGE	SEX	OCCUPATION	PRVL	DES
KRAEBE, FRITZ	48	M	MCHT	GRZZZZ	USA
LAPINI, JOSEF	22	M	MCHT	GRZZZZ	USA
KRONE, HERM.	40	M	RE	GRZZZZ	USA
RITTER, MARIE	30	F	NN	GRZZZZ	USA
RATHENBERGER, EMMA	30	F	NN	GRZZZZ	USA
ULRICH, SOPHIE	40	F	NN	GRZZZZ	USA
DAUB, MALCHEN	21	F	NN	GRZZZZ	USA
ROSENBAUM, BERTHA	17	F	NN	GRZZZZ	USA
NELDNER, CARL	26	M	MCHT	GRZZZZ	USA
SCHUETTE, HELENE	24	F	NN	GRZZZZ	USA
BEUTE, WALLY	36	F	NN	GRZZZZ	USA
LAZONI, ANNA	24	F	NN	GRZZZZ	USA
BAER, MAX	31	M	FARMER	GRZZZZ	USA
THUNN, GEORG	48	M	FARMER	GRZZZZ	USA
LAURIER, LOUISE	55	F	NN	GRZZZZ	USA
LOUISE	18	F	NN	GRZZZZ	USA
BANTJE, CARL	17	M	FARMER	GRZZZZ	USA
SCHMETTERER, HERMINE	26	F	NN	GRZZZZ	USA
KATSCHER, JOS.	23	M	MCHT	GRZZZZ	USA
HAASE, IDA	24	F	NN	GRZZZZ	USA
HULDA	3	F	CHILD	GRZZZZ	USA
KOCKLER, FRANZ	23	M	FARMER	GRZZZZ	USA
OTTO	21	M	FARMER	GRZZZZ	USA
RICHARD	22	M	FARMER	GRZZZZ	USA
JUENGLING, W.	56	M	FARMER	GRZZZZ	USA
GRUHLE, HEINR.	53	M	FARMER	GRZZZZ	USA
FISCHER, SANDER	6	M	CHILD	GRZZZZ	USA
RIEMER, JENNY	24	F	NN	GRZZZZ	USA
ELSA	.09	F	INFANT	GRZZZZ	USA
STERN, NATHAN	18	M	MCHT	GRZZZZ	USA
OVERBECK, BERNH.	30	M	MCHT	GRZZZZ	USA
WEISE, EDUARD	68	M	MCHT	GRZZZZ	USA
KOERNER, JOSEPHE	67	F	NN	GRZZZZ	USA
HERMAN	7	M	CHILD	GRZZZZ	USA
FILLY	5	F	CHILD	GRZZZZ	USA
FRIEDA	3	F	CHILD	GRZZZZ	USA
EMMA	.11	F	INFANT	GRZZZZ	USA
WITTIG, GUSTAV	26	M	FARMER	GRZZZZ	USA
TEUBNER, BRUNE	46	M	FARMER	GRZZZZ	USA
BUNTE, CECILIE	25	F	NN	GRZZZZ	USA
ENDERS, ALOIS	23	M	FARMER	GRZZZZ	USA
REICHEL, HUGO	23	M	FARMER	GRZZZZ	USA
SCHWERS, HEINR.	26	M	FARMER	GRZZZZ	USA
FUCHS, ANTON	60	M	FARMER	GRZZZZ	USA
STEUDER, HENRY	14	M	FARMER	GRZZZZ	USA
MUELLER, GERH.	23	M	FARMER	GRZZZZ	USA
SCHLUETER, WILH.	14	M	FARMER	GRZZZZ	USA
WAGNER, LEONH.	15	M	FARMER	GRZZZZ	USA
KREBS, GATTE	23	M	FARMER	GRZZZZ	USA
LIPPLE, LUDWIG	29	M	FARMER	GRZZZZ	USA
TROSCH, GEORG	25	M	FARMER	GRZZZZ	USA
HAAS, JOH.	30	M	FARMER	GRZZZZ	USA
KAUFMANN, FRIEDR.	16	M	FARMER	GRZZZZ	USA
HINZER, HEINR.	25	M	UNKNOWN	GRZZZZ	USA
HUMBURG	34	M	UNKNOWN	GRZZZZ	USA
MUTH, WILH.	28	M	FARMER	GRZZZZ	USA
KIRSCH, WILH.	19	M	UNKNOWN	GRZZZZ	USA
BENCK, AUG.	24	M	UNKNOWN	GRZZZZ	USA
STREHLA, LORENZ	31	M	UNKNOWN	GRZZZZ	USA
DECKER, JOH.	38	M	UNKNOWN	GRZZZZ	USA
ACKERMANN, WOLF	14	M	UNKNOWN	GRZZZZ	USA
ANNA, CARL	16	M	MLR	GRZZZZ	USA
SCHWAB, HEWER	27	M	LABR	GRZZZZ	USA
GRUENWALD, OTTE	17	M	LABR	GRZZZZ	USA
HAUSER, C.	22	M	LABR	GRZZZZ	USA
KRAETZ, ANTON	21	M	LABR	GRZZZZ	USA
STREB, FRIEDR.	26	M	LABR	GRZZZZ	USA
MUELLER, JOH.	26	M	LABR	GRZZZZ	USA
SIEVERS, FETER	40	M	FARMER	GRZZZZ	USA
SCHWITZGER, FETER	25	M	CPTR	GRZZZZ	USA
DAEN, CLAUS	17	M	CPTR	GRZZZZ	USA
DENNER, WILH.	18	M	CPTR	GRZZZZ	USA
SELIGER, AUG.	63	M	CPTR	GRZZZZ	USA
SUETZEN, U	24	M	CPTR	GRZZZZ	USA
U, U	23	M	CPTR	GRZZZZ	USA
DEUBER, DIEDR.	33	M	FARMER	GRZZZZ	USA
BOEHM, CARL	16	M	FARMER	GRZZZZ	USA
FLONSKIER, NATHAN	23	M	FARMER	PRZZZZ	USA
KATZ, ABRAH.	32	M	FARMER	PRZZZZ	USA
VITRIOL, ADOLF	32	M	FARMER	PRZZZZ	USA
TETERSEN, CHRIST.	32	M	FARMER	GRZZZZ	USA
HAUSEN, JOERGEN	67	M	FARMER	GRZZZZ	USA
MELJERS, HANS	14	M	FARMER	GRZZZZ	USA
SCHNEIDER, TETER	56	M	FARMER	GRZZZZ	USA
SAUER, JACOB	00	M	FARMER	GRZZZZ	USA
BEGENHEIMER, AUGEN	48	M	LABR	GRZZZZ	USA
DIPPEL, JACOB	19	M	LABR	GRZZZZ	USA
HOLLSTEIN, GEORG	56	M	LABR	GRZZZZ	USA
SCHLICHTING, GOTTF.	26	M	LABR	GRZZZZ	USA
HERM.	17	M	LABR	GRZZZZ	USA
STEHLE, MATHIAS	46	M	TLR	GRZZZZ	USA
SCHULZE, HUGO	28	M	BKR	GRZZZZ	USA
WALCH, ANNA	48	F	CL	GRZZZZ	USA
URBAN, CHR.	15	M	FARMER	GRZZZZ	USA
MEYER, HENRY	26	M	FARMER	GRZZZZ	USA
KORATKOWSKY, JAN	00	M	FARMER	GRZZZZ	USA
SLARTUNEWITZ, PIOTR	25	M	FARMER	GRZZZZ	USA
FUDAK, MATWEI	26	M	FARMER	GRZZZZ	USA
SUTKUS, IVAN	28	M	FARMER	GRZZZZ	USA
JUNEZUS, IVAN	27	M	FARMER	GRZZZZ	USA
MACZULEITIS, IVAN	25	M	FARMER	GRZZZZ	USA
SCHLEGELMILCH, FRANZ	25	M	FARMER	GRZZZZ	USA
HORLACHER, GEORG	23	M	FARMER	GRZZZZ	USA
BREUNER, JACOB	16	M	FARMER	GRZZZZ	USA
SCHMIS, GEORG	28	M	FARMER	GRZZZZ	USA
GAERTNER, SALON	16	M	FARMER	GRZZZZ	USA
FRAUTZ, ISIDOR	17	M	FARMER	GRZZZZ	USA
GAERTNER, WILH.	16	M	FARMER	GRZZZZ	USA
TFEIFLE, JOH.	21	M	TLR	GRZZZZ	USA
SCHINDLER, ED.	14	M	FARMER	GRZZZZ	USA
OTTOMAR	11	M	FARMER	GRZZZZ	USA
DOESCHER, JOHE.	25	M	FARMER	GRZZZZ	USA
MEYER, JOH.	21	M	FARMER	GRZZZZ	USA
KUNDSEN, ANDR.	20	M	FARMER	GRZZZZ	USA
THIME, FRIEDR.	20	M	FARMER	GRZZZZ	USA
GITFENT, HEINR.	20	M	FARMER	GRZZZZ	USA
REIFF, MATTH.	20	M	FARMER	GRZZZZ	USA
ULBEN, OTTO	26	M	FARMER	GRZZZZ	USA
HENIG, AD.	47	M	FARMER	GRZZZZ	USA
LEUCHTNER, AUG.	23	M	MCHT	GRZZZZ	USA
HRACH, FRANZ	18	M	MCHT	GRZZZZ	USA
RECH, JACOB	22	M	TLR	GRZZZZ	USA
BEHRMANN, HEINR.	19	M	FARMER	GRZZZZ	USA
BECKER, FRANZ	45	M	FARMER	GRZZZZ	USA
U--LA, ANTON	43	M	FARMER	GRZZZZ	USA
FIEBIG, GUSTAV	35	M	FARMER	GRZZZZ	USA
HOFFARTH, MARY	26	F	NN	GRZZZZ	USA
ANNA	18	F	NN	GRZZZZ	USA
SCHMIDT, LOUISE	25	F	NN	GRZZZZ	USA
FRIEDRICH, MINNA	17	F	NN	GRZZZZ	USA
LOEFFLER, ELISE	57	F	NN	GRZZZZ	USA
MEIER	20	F	NN	GRZZZZ	USA
KOMP, MARIE	17	F	NN	GRZZZZ	USA
WERLE, EMMA	23	F	NN	GRZZZZ	USA
THILL, MARIA	39	F	NN	GRZZZZ	USA
FLORA	26	F	NN	GRZZZZ	USA
MICHELS, SOPHIE	63	F	NN	GRZZZZ	USA
BAUER, THERESE	24	F	NN	GRZZZZ	USA
MAL-, MARIE	19	F	NN	GRZZZZ	USA
HAYMANN, MARIE	18	F	NN	GRZZZZ	USA
RITZ, MARIE	22	F	NN	GRZZZZ	USA
TFANDLER, MARIE	28	F	NN	GRZZZZ	USA
MATTKIESEN, KIERSTI	19	F	NN	GRZZZZ	USA
NOMENSEN, ANTONI	21	F	NN	GRZZZZ	USA
MEYER, ANNA	18	F	NN	GRZZZZ	USA
ANDERSON, ANNA	24	F	NN	GRZZZZ	USA
MOST, MARIE	24	F	NN	GRZZZZ	USA
KOENGER, AMALIE	36	F	NN	GRZZZZ	USA
LIPINSKI, WILHE.	25	F	NN	GRZZZZ	USA
ADE, BABETTE	43	F	NN	GRZZZZ	USA

SHIP: CELTIC

FROM: LIVERPOOL AND QUEENSTOWN
TO: NEW YORK
ARRIVED: 07 JULY 1888

PASSENGER	AGE	SEX	OCCUPATION	PRVL	DES
WESSNER, CHRE.	12	F	NN		GRZZZZUSA
WATSCHIE, AUGUSTE	36	F	NN		GRZZZZUSA
STRAUSS, EMILIE	23	F	NN		GRZZZZUSA
WEIL, CLARA	23	F	NN		GRZZZZUSA
FELDKAMP, GESINE	27	F	NN		GRZZZZUSA
STORZ, MARIE	19	F	NN		GRZZZZUSA
HEINZ, CATHI	22	F	NN		GRZZZZUSA
SCHAUB, DIENA	60	F	NN		GRZZZZUSA
SEPPEL, ANNA	19	F	NN		GRZZZZUSA
SIPP, FAUTINE	20	F	NN		GRZZZZUSA
EULE, BERTHA	35	F	NN		GRZZZZUSA
LEY, ROSINE	26	F	NN		GRZZZZUSA
FRANK, HENRIETTE	16	F	NN		GRZZZZUSA
GERBER, AUGUSTE	19	F	NN		GRZZZZUSA
GELPKE, ELISE	23	F	NN		GRZZZZUSA
NALTZ, JOHE.	22	F	NN		GRZZZZUSA
JOERGENSEN, METTE	63	F	NN		GRZZZZUSA
GAWICH, MARIE	19	F	NN		GRZZZZUSA
FELDMANN, ANNA	19	F	NN		GRZZZZUSA
GAUNAUER, ANNA	26	F	NN		GRZZZZUSA
RILS, HERMINE	20	F	NN		GRZZZZUSA
RECK, ANNA	20	F	NN		GRZZZZUSA
DONAT, JOH.	32	M	TLR		GRZZZZUSA
MARY	26	F	W		GRZZZZUSA
ERICH	4	M	CHILD		GRZZZZUSA
EDUARD	2	M	CHILD		GRZZZZUSA
ROESSWEY, AMALIE	43	F	NN		GRZZZZUSA
JULIUS	19	F	NN		GRZZZZUSA
AMALIE	18	F	NN		GRZZZZUSA
LINA	16	F	NN		GRZZZZUSA
JOSEFA	7	F	CHILD		GRZZZZUSA
ROBERT	4	M	CHILD		GRZZZZUSA
HIRSCH, ROSALIE	38	F	NN		GRZZZZUSA
JULIE	16	F	NN		GRZZZZUSA
JULIUS	7	M	CHILD		GRZZZZUSA
IDA	6	F	CHILD		GRZZZZUSA
CARL	4	M	CHILD		GRZZZZUSA
MARIE	2	F	CHILD		GRZZZZUSA
TEMPLIN, OTTO	31	M	FARMER		GRZZZZUSA
EMMA	27	F	W		GRZZZZUSA
MARTHA	5	F	CHILD		GRZZZZUSA
REINHARDT, ERNST	30	M	FARMER		GRZZZZUSA
ANNA	31	F	W		GRZZZZUSA
CATHI	7	F	CHILD		GRZZZZUSA
ELISE	5	F	CHILD		GRZZZZUSA
LISETTE	.06	F	INFANT		GRZZZZUSA
CARSTENSEN, DORIS	22	F	NN		GRZZZZUSA
BINE	2	F	CHILD		GRZZZZUSA
ANNA	.11	F	INFANT		GRZZZZUSA
TREIS, THERESE	23	F	NN		GRZZZZUSA
JOSEFA	.09	F	INFANT		GRZZZZUSA
BAUER, WOLFGANG	24	M	FARMER		GRZZZZUSA
ANNA	37	F	W		GRZZZZUSA
SCHMIDT, TRUELS	59	M	FARMER		GRZZZZUSA
MARIE	55	F	W		GRZZZZUSA
BERENDSEN	26	F	NN		GRZZZZUSA
ANNA	3	F	CHILD		GRZZZZUSA
NISSEN, NILS	27	M	BCK		GRZZZZUSA
AGATHE	33	F	W		GRZZZZUSA
LINDNER, CATHI	36	F	NN		GRZZZZUSA
CARL	3	M	CHILD		GRZZZZUSA
KUEHL, MARIE	36	F	NN		GRZZZZUSA
ANNA	6	F	CHILD		GRZZZZUSA
SCHUSTER, CATHI	36	F	NN		GRZZZZUSA
MARIE	7	F	CHILD		GRZZZZUSA
CATHI	4	F	CHILD		GRZZZZUSA
RADZIMANOWSKY, AUG.	35	M	LABR		GRZZZZUSA
CAROLE.	25	F	W		GRZZZZUSA
ANNA	2	F	CHILD		GRZZZZUSA
EMMA	.03	F	INFANT		GRZZZZUSA
SCHUELER, MARIE	28	F	NN		GRZZZZUSA
ANNA	6	F	CHILD		GRZZZZUSA
GERLINGER, JHOH.	31	M	FARMER		GRZZZZUSA
SUSA	27	F	W		GRZZZZUSA
MARY	2	F	CHILD		GRZZZZUSA
SUSA	2	F	CHILD		GRZZZZUSA
EULER, THEODOR	37	M	FARMER		GRZZZZUSA
JOHANNE	31	F	W		GRZZZZUSA
JOHAN	7	M	CHILD		GRZZZZUSA
JACOB	4	M	CHILD		GRZZZZUSA
FHILIPP	2	M	CHILD		GRZZZZUSA
OZECHOWSKY, ANT.	50	M	FARMER		GRZZZZUSA
LOUISE	40	F	W		GRZZZZUSA
JOSEF	35	M	NN		GRZZZZUSA
MUENZ, GOTTF.	45	M	FARMER		GRZZZZUSA
SOPHIE	28	F	W		GRZZZZUSA
FRIEDR.	7	M	CHILD		GRZZZZUSA
JOENG, WENDELIN	59	M	FARMER		GRZZZZUSA
FRANZ	25	F	W		GRZZZZUSA
CONRAD	21	M	NN		GRZZZZUSA
CARL	9	M	CHILD		GRZZZZUSA
REGINE	7	F	CHILD		GRZZZZUSA
GEORG	.04	M	INFANT		GRZZZZUSA
SCHOLZ, ANNA	43	F	NN		GRZZZZUSA
ELFRIEDA	7	F	CHILD		GRZZZZUSA
SPRINGER, HERM.	36	M	FARMER		GRZZZZUSA
BERTHA	27	F	W		GRZZZZUSA
JULIUS	7	M	CHILD		GRZZZZUSA
HERMAN	4	M	CHILD		GRZZZZUSA
HEINR.	2	M	CHILD		GRZZZZUSA
HERZBERG, JOH.	32	M	FARMER		GRZZZZUSA
MATE	32	F	W		GRZZZZUSA
ALBERT	7	M	CHILD		GRZZZZUSA
MARTHA	5	F	CHILD		GRZZZZUSA
HEDWIG	2	F	CHILD		GRZZZZUSA
MARIA	.03	F	INFANT		GRZZZZUSA
TOMPSON, ELISE	47	F	NN		GRZZZZUSA
CARL	6	M	CHILD		GRZZZZUSA
LAURIER, AUGENE	25	F	CH		GRZZZZUSA
FRANZ	68	F	CH		GRZZZZUSA
LUDWIG	7	F	CHILD		GRZZZZUSA
HOCHREITER, U	57	M	FARMER		GRZZZZUSA
CARL	7	M	CHILD		GRZZZZUSA
DENKER, CLARA	8	M	CHILD		GRZZZZUSA
CARL	10	M	CH		GRZZZZUSA
KAUFMAN, TAUBE	17	F	SVNT		GRACBFUSA
LEFELLHOLY, H	18	M	LABR		GRACBFUSA
LETOUSKA, AN-	23	M	LABR		GRACBFUSA
SCHAYBASK, SARAH	31	F	W		GRACBFUSA
CHAGE	35	M	MNR		GRACBFUSA
CHAUSE	18	F	SP		GRACBFUSA
BERL	11	F	SCH		GRACBFUSA
ISRAEL	5	M	CHILD		GRACBFUSA
SCHEFF, HERMAN	16	M	LABR		GRACBFUSA
CAMM, LEBYR-LY	20	M	LABR		GRACBFUSA
PUNCH, ABRAHAM	19	M	LABR		GRACBFUSA
ZISKA, CARL	16	M	LABR		GRACBFUSA
KENNIG, TRUDE	15	F	SP		GRACBFUSA
KAISER, SARA	20	F	SVNT		GRACBFUSA
SCHANGER, MOSES	20	M	LABR		GRACBFUSA
SILBER, BLUNE	40	F	W		GRACBFUSA
MALKE	11	M	SCH		GRACBFUSA
CHAGE	8	M	CHILD		GRACBFUSA
ONAS	5	M	CHILD		GRACBFUSA
SCHWAREZ, CHARGE	28	F	W		GRACBFUSA
L	9	F	CHILD		GRACBFUSA
C	7	F	CHILD		GRACBFUSA
SCHMISER, LE-SER	23	M	LABR		GRACBFUSA

PASSENGER	AGE	SEX	OCCUPATION	PVRIVL	DES
BRANS, F	67	M	LABR	GRACBFUSA	
HEINISCH, SUSANA	31	F	SVNT	GRACBFUSA	
ROG, NICOLAS	24	M	LABR	GRADXWUSA	
LOFFELHOLZ, MOSES	29	M	FARMER	GRACBFUSA	
ESTER	20	F	W	GRACBFUSA	
SAMUEL	.09	M	INFANT	GRACBFUSA	
SCHWARZBACH, LIEB	.10	M	INFANT	GRACBFUSA	
GUTMANN, SUSSMANN	11	F	SCH	GRACBFUSA	
SCHWARTZ, SAMUEL	16	M	LABR	GRACBFUSA	
ZISCHKA, ZIMAL	16	M	LABR	GRACBFUSA	
PILMUTH-, JONAS	53	M	FARMER	GRACBFUSA	
MARIE	50	F	W	GRACBFUSA	
SALIE	11	F	SCH	GRACBFUSA	
SCHLOMEL	9	F	CHILD	GRACBFUSA	
KRUS--BERG, JACOB	24	M	LABR	GRACBFUSA	
ENGELSBORG, ISAK	15	M	LABR	GRACBFUSA	
PACKER, BETTI	19	F	SVNT	GRACBFUSA	
NACHUM	26	M	LABR	GRACBFUSA	
LANKOPF, ISRAEL	26	M	LABR	GRACBFUSA	
BENTIERCH, SALOMON	24	M	LABR	GRACBFUSA	
KLEIN, ALBERT	38	M	LABR	GRACBFUSA	
HERMAN	8	M	CHILD	GRACBFUSA	
ARIN	3	M	CHILD	GRACBFUSA	
DEGIN	.10	M	INFANT	GRACBFUSA	
FRIDA	.10	M	INFANT	GRACBFUSA	
REISZ, SAML	27	M	LABR	GRACBFUSA	
KLEIN, JULIA	30	F	W	GRACBFUSA	
SCWARZ, ROSA	18	F	SVNT	GRACBFUSA	
NELD, HARTOG	32	M	RE	GRADBQUSA	
JULIA	30	F	W	GRADBQUSA	
GERT	6	F	CHILD	GRADBQUSA	
VOGRICH, MAX	36	M	CMP	GRADBQUSA	
MRS	29	F	W	GRADBQUSA	

SHIP: SORRENTO

FROM: HAMBURG
TO: NEW YORK
ARRIVED: 07 JULY 1888

PASSENGER	AGE	SEX	OCCUPATION	PVRIVL	DES
PRUSS, AUGUSTE	17	F	SGL	PRZZZZNY	
SCHIKAF, JOH.	25	F	SGL	PRZZZZNY	
STEIDING, ALBERTINE	30	F	SGL	PRZZZZNY	
WESSOLOWSKI, ANTONIA	13	F	SGL	PRZZZZNY	
FRANZISKA	9	F	CHILD	PRZZZZNY	
GAWORSKA, FRANZ	30	M	CPR	PRZZZZNY	
GELBART, JUSSMANN	15	M	MCHT	PRZZZZNY	
PUTGATSCHOW, MICHAEL	28	M	LABR	PRZZZZNY	
KNEIP, FRIEDRICH	28	M	LKSH	SYZZZZWI	
KUCHLER, FRIEDRICH	22	M	BKR	PRZZZZNY	
HABERLEIN, CAROLINE	17	F	SGL	BVZZZZNY	
HOFFMANN, KATHARINE	59	F	SGL	BVZZZZNY	
HIRSCH, LEOPOLD	27	M	MCHT	BDZZZZNY	
FANDRY, WILHELMINE	30	F	SGL	PRZZZZNY	
DUBBOCKE, OTTO	25	M	UNKNOWN	PRZZZZNY	
FARASIOWUZ, KASIMIR	23	M	LABR	PRZZZZNY	
BIZEWSKI, BOLESLAW	32	M	LABR	PRZZZZNY	
MARX, ROBERT	25	M	LABR	PRZZZZNY	
THOMAS, KARL	34	M	LABR	GRZZZZNY	
MINNA	30	F	W	GRZZZZNY	
FRANZ	9	M	CHILD	GRZZZZNY	
PAUL	7	M	CHILD	GRZZZZNY	
WILHELM	5	M	CHILD	GRZZZZNY	
MARTHA	.02	F	INFANT	GRZZZZNY	
SGEZECH, JOSEFA	20	F	SGL	PRZZZZNY	
FRANZ, CARL	24	M	FARMER	PRZZZZNY	
WOZINAK, FRANZIZEK	26	F	W	PRZZZZNY	
VICENTY	.11	M	INFANT	PRZZZZNY	
SHATH, ANDREAS	15	M	LABR	BDZZZZNY	
ORCHOLSKA, JOSEFA	16	F	SGL	PRZZZZNY	

PASSENGER	AGE	SEX	OCCUPATION	PVRIVL	DES
SCZEGLSKA, FRANZISKA	21	F	SGL	PRZZZZNY	
WELLMANN, ELISABETH	25	F	W	PRZZZZNY	
RICHARD	4	M	CHILD	PRZZZZNY	
MUEHEL, BERTHA	21	F	SGL	PRZZZZNY	
HEESE, THERESE	23	F	SGL	PRZZZZNY	
KRAFFT, ASMUS	54	M	FARMER	PRZZZZIA	
ANNA	53	F	W	PRZZZZIA	
EMMA	18	F	D	PRZZZZIA	
WILHELM	14	M	S	PRZZZZIA	
RHEDER, JACOB	16	M	BKR	PRZZZZSFC	
HAUSNER, ALIAS	28	M	CPR	BVZZZZNY	
HERZIG, LUDWIG	42	M	FUR	HBZZZZNY	
WERNER, MICHEL	27	M	LABR	PRZZZZNY	
MARIE	27	F	W	PRZZZZNY	
JOHANNA	.11	F	INFANT	PRZZZZNY	
B-DEWSKY, RICHARD	21	M	FUR	SYZZZZNY	
WEGNER, MAX	20	M	SLR	PRZZZZCH	
BLUHM, ALBERT	27	M	MCHT	PRZZZZNY	
JOHANNE	22	F	W	PRZZZZNY	
ELISE	.11	F	INFANT	PRZZZZNY	
KUPSTORUS, FRANZ	27	M	FARMER	PRZZZZNY	
NAGORSKA, ANIELA	31	F	UNKNOWN	PRZZZZNY	
APOLLINA	.11	F	INFANT	PRZZZZNY	
SAWALSKY, PAUL	35	M	FARMER	PRZZZZNY	
PATZSCHKY, RICHARD	30	M	DRVR	PRZZZZNY	
GRUNBERGER, HERM.	22	M	PNTR	PRZZZZBUF	
MERKEL, WILLY	28	M	WVR	PRZZZZNY	
THICDE, JOHANN	27	M	LABR	PRZZZZNY	
SMOLINSKY, ROSALIE	26	F	W	PRZZZZNY	
MARIANNA	3	F	CHILD	PRZZZZNY	
YOSEF, ISAAC	26	M	LABR	PRZZZZNY	
SGALSKI, FRANZ	24	M	LABR	PRZZZZNY	
BADT, HERMANN	16	M	LABR	PRZZZZNY	
BABLINSKI, VALENTIN	35	M	LABR	PRZZZZBUF	
MULKE, FRANZ	54	M	UNKNOWN	PRZZZZSTL	
SLAWSKI, VINCENT	18	M	MCHT	PRZZZZUNK	
WICHT, GUSTAV	21	M	LABR	PRZZZZUNK	
MOEHRING, CARL	38	M	LABR	PRZZZZUNK	
STREMPEL, AUGUST	16	M	MSN	PRZZZZOH	
WEBER, WILHELM	33	M	WVR	PRZZZZWI	
ANNA	33	F	W	PRZZZZWI	
JOS	7	F	CHILD	PRZZZZWI	
WILHELM	5	M	CHILD	PRZZZZWI	
GOTTFRIED	1	M	CHILD	PRZZZZWI	
ANNA	.05	F	INFANT	PRZZZZWI	
SCHUNKE, RICHARD	37	M	FARMER	PRZZZZNY	
JOSEFE	37	F	W	PRZZZZNY	
RICHARD	17	M	BY	PRZZZZNY	
ROMAN	8	M	CHILD	PRZZZZNY	
ANNA	4	F	CHILD	PRZZZZNY	
JOSEFA	3	F	CHILD	PRZZZZNY	
CAROLINA	62	F	WO	PRZZZZNY	
QUIRAM, JOHANN	42	M	FARMER	PRZZZZNY	
ANNA	33	F	W	PRZZZZNY	
HEDWIG	8	F	CHILD	PRZZZZNY	
META	7	F	CHILD	PRZZZZNY	
WILLY	.11	M	INFANT	PRZZZZNY	
KRAUSE, HUGO	32	M	CNF	PRZZZZNY	
ERNESTINE	33	F	W	PRZZZZNY	
WERTELOWSKY, FRIEDRICH	16	M	LABR	PRZZZZNY	
KUTZNER, HERMANN	42	M	BCHR	PRZZZZNY	
JESCHKE, AUGUST	74	M	UNKNOWN	PRZZZZNY	
KRAZEWSKI, ANTON	53	M	UNKNOWN	PRZZZZNY	
SYRACKI, ANTON	29	M	UNKNOWN	PRZZZZNY	
MARIANNE	30	F	W	PRZZZZNY	
SZWIZEYNSKI, ANTON	42	M	LABR	PRZZZZNY	
STROH, CHARLOTTE	23	F	SGL	PRZZZZNY	
PHILIPPINE	17	F	SGL	PRZZZZNY	
FRIEDERIKE	3	F	CHILD	PRZZZZNY	
DORRSCHUK, MARGARETHE	21	F	SGL	PRZZZZNY	
PAULIK, JOH.	28	M	FARMER	SYZZZZNY	
SCHEIDHAUER, CARL	36	M	SHMK	SYZZZZNY	
STEINBACH, EDUARD	27	M	JNR	BVZZZZIA	
HOBT, AGATHA	40	F	SVNT	BVZZZZUSA	
PUCHTA, KONRAD	30	M	SVNT	BVZZZZUSA	

PASSENGER	AGE	SEX	OCCUPATION	PRVVL	DES
HILLMANN, HEINRICH	57	M	LABR		SYZZZZMIL
HOFFMANN, JACOB	27	M	FARMER		WMZZZZNY
RUPPERT, CHR.ANDR.	27	M	SHMK		BVZZZZNY
KACKER, RICHARD	25	M	JNR		PRZZZZCH
AUGUSTE	63	F	SGL		PRZZZZNY
LOUIS	31	M	JNR		PRZZZZNY
B-RCHARDT, CHRISTIAN	48	M	GDNR		PRZZZZNY
JONES, JACOB	26	M	BKR		PRZZZZCH
MAISCH, ANDRAS	29	M	BKR		PRZZZZCH
SCHUSSLER, CARL	26	M	FARMER		PRZZZZNY
PAULSEN, CARL	26	M	SHMK		PRZZZZNY
WOLTER, JULIUS	41	M	FARMER		PRZZZZNY
JASARSKA, ELISABETH	21	F	SGL		PRZZZZNY
BERGER, DAVID	21	M	DLR		PRZZZZNY
MUELLER, MARGARETHA	17	F	SGL		PRZZZZNY
BUDZYNSKY, JOSEF	28	M	PNTR		PRZZZZNY
GOTTFELD, HIRSCH	30	M	LABR		PRZZZZNY

SHIP: WESER

FROM: BREMEN
TO: BALTIMORE
ARRIVED: 07 JULY 1888

PASSENGER	AGE	SEX	OCCUPATION	PRVVL	DES
BIRK, CAROLINA	22	F	NN		GRZZZZMD
KUHKE, MARIE	19	F	NN		GRZZZZMD
MIZGALSKI, HELENA	22	F	NN		GRZZZZWI
DELM, AUGUST	37	M	FARMER		GRZZZZMD
BAARS, HENRIETTE	50	F	NN		GRZZZZMD
LINA	18	F	NN		GRZZZZMD
HERMANN	10	M	CH		GRZZZZMD
GRIMM, HEINRICH	12	M	CH		GRZZZZMD
HELMUTH	10	M	CH		GRZZZZMD
KRAPPE, AUGUST	27	M	BKLYR		GRZZZZMD
PANZENHAGEN, CARL	24	M	LABR		GRZZZZIA
WILHELM	16	M	LABR		GRZZZZIA
KRUEGER, CARL	31	M	FARMER		GRZZZZIL
REGINE	29	F	NN		GRZZZZIL
AUGUSTE	9	F	CHILD		GRZZZZIL
HERMANN	4	M	CHILD		GRZZZZIL
MARIE	2	F	CHILD		GRZZZZIL
HAAK, WILHELM	34	M	FARMER		GRZZZZMN
WILHELMINA	36	F	NN		GRZZZZMN
OTTO	9	M	CHILD		GRZZZZMN
WILHELM	6	M	CHILD		GRZZZZMN
BERTHA	4	F	CHILD		GRZZZZMN
ANNA	2	F	CHILD		GRZZZZMN
FABBERT, FRIEDR.	67	M	TLR		GRZZZZMO
WILHE.	58	F	NN		GRZZZZMO
JULIE	25	M	FARMER		GRZZZZMO
GIESE, WILHELM	29	M	FARMER		GRZZZZKS
BERTHA	27	F	NN		GRZZZZKS
FRITZ	5	M	CHILD		GRZZZZKS
MARIE	4	F	CHILD		GRZZZZKS
WIENKE, ERNESTINE	22	F	CH		GRZZZZIL
KLEINCKE, FRANZ	21	M	FARMER		GRZZZZIL
SEIPE, GERTRUD	24	F	NN		GRZZZZIL
FLAMMERSFELD, JOHANN	53	M	LABR		GRZZZZKS
PETER	19	M	LABR		GRZZZZKS
LAMBRECHT, AUGUST	42	M	FARMER		GRZZZZOH
ALINA	43	F	NN		GRZZZZOH
AUGUSTE	21	F	NN		GRZZZZOH
WILHELM	17	M	FARMER		GRZZZZOH
BERTHA	16	F	FARMER		GRZZZZOH
ANNA	11	F	CH		GRZZZZOH
WILHELM	9	M	CHILD		GRZZZZOH
MARTHA	7	F	CHILD		GRZZZZOH
MANN, ALBERT	49	M	FARMER		GRZZZZIA
TRINE	42	F	NN		GRZZZZIA
EMILIA	18	F	NN		GRZZZZIA

PASSENGER	AGE	SEX	OCCUPATION	PRVVL	DES
AUGUSTE	21	F	NN		GRZZZZIA
GRUENEWALD, DORETTE	36	F	NN		GRAGFPIA
ANNA	11	F	CH		GRAGFPIA
ROSEN, DOROTHEA	60	F	NN		GRAGFPTN
BORTZ, AUGUST	53	M	LABR		GRAGFPIL
JOHANNE	52	F	NN		GRAGFPIL
RIEKE	22	F	NN		GRAGFPIL
HEINR.	19	M	LABR		GRAGFPIL
GUSTAV	15	M	LABR		GRAGFPIL
ANNA	12	F	NN		GRAGFPIL
FRIEDE, CAROLINE	36	F	NN		GRAGFPKY
RASZKOWSKA, BASSIA	12	F	NN		GRAGFPOH
NEUBAUER, OTTO	22	M	TLR		GRAGFPOH
PIEHLE, EMILIE	22	F	NN		GRAGFPMD
BASTIAN, WILH.	30	M	SMH		GRAGFPMD
SALK, EDUARD	23	M	TLR		GRAGFPMO
WILHELM	11	M	CH		GRAGFPMO
STOECKER, JOHANN	55	M	FARMER		GRAGFPMO
MARGA.	57	F	NN		GRAGFPMO
EMMA	19	F	NN		GRAGFPMO
SCHALK, JOHANNA	41	F	NN		GRAGFPWI
AUGUSTE	12	F	NN		GRAGFPWI
HEINRICH	9	M	CHILD		GRAGFPWI
ERNST	.01	M	INFANT		GRAGFPWI
SKOMSKA, STANISLAVA	22	F	NN		GRAGFPPA
PRUDLO, LUDWIG	26	M	LABR		GRAGFPOH
GOSZKA, VERONICA	19	F	NN		GRAGFPOH
JEZINSKA, CATHA.	22	F	NN		GRAGFPOH
MARIANNA	18	F	NN		GRAGFPOH
STANISLAUS	10	M	CH		GRAGFPOH
MARIANNA	10	F	CH		GRAGFPOH
FRANZISCA	2	F	CHILD		GRAGFPOH
ROSOLSKI, SIMON	27	M	MNR		GRAGFPOH
KONECZNY, STANISLAUS	31	M	MNR		GRAGFPOH
KALETHA, MARIANNA	50	F	NN		GRAGFPOH
AUGUST	16	M	LABR		GRAGFPOH
YAKOBEIT, MARIANNA	44	F	NN		GRAGFPNE
AUGUSTE	16	F	NN		GRAGFPNE
JAN	10	M	CH		GRAGFPNE
EMMA	6	F	CHILD		GRAGFPNE
GAWROWSKI, HERM.	23	M	FARMER		GRAGFPMD
SCHMEFEFSKI, MARTIN	56	M	FARMER		GRAGFPMD
TIGURSKI, MAX	31	M	SMH		GRAGFPIA
GABRICH, ELISABETH	22	F	NN		GRAGFPIL
SATZEK, CATHA.	50	F	NN		GRAGFPIL
OLSZEWSKI, LUDWIG	17	M	SHMK		GRAGFPIL
LYESEWSKI, STANISLAUS	25	M	SMH		GRAGFPKS
JUENGE, HANS	26	M	LABR		GRAGFPKS
DRILLER, FRIEDR.	24	M	LABR		GRAGFPOR
BETHGE, FERD.	25	M	LABR		GRAGFPMD
SINVECK, PAUL	15	M	SHMK		GRAGFPOH
NOLLER, ROSINE	19	F	NN		GRAGFPOH
KUCHINSKA, ANNA	66	F	NN		GRAGFPOH
MARTHA	6	F	CHILD		GRAGFPOH
BRZEZINSKI, LEON	33	M	CPTR		GRAGFPOH
CATHA.	36	F	NN		GRAGFPOH
BRUNO	5	M	CHILD		GRAGFPOH
DRSZANOWSKY, FRANZ	23	M	TLR		GRAGFPMI
STOECKER, CAROLINE	17	F	NN		GRAGFPOR
FRITZ	15	M	NN		GRAGFPOR
SALK, GOTTLIEBE	27	F	NN		GRAGFPMN
JOHNKE, AU	37	M	MLR		GRAGFPMN
WIEWAND, GUSTAV	37	M	SMH		GRAGFPOH
HULDA	37	F	NN		GRAGFPOH
FRANCISCA	3	F	CHILD		GRAGFPOH
PAUL	2	M	CHILD		GRAGFPOH
AUGUST	18	F	NN		GRAGFPOH
SCHULTZ, MARIE	17	F	NN		GRAGFPMI
EGGERT, JOHANN	55	M	SHMK		GRAGFPOH
MARIA	58	F	NN		GRAGFPOH
ANNA	25	F	NN		GRAGFPOH
HERM.	16	M	SHMK		GRAGFPOH
ELISABETH	13	F	NN		GRAGFPOH
BOGOLSKI, WILH.	23	M	SHMK		GRAGFPOH
CONRAD, GUSTAV	32	M	TNM		GRAGFPIL

PASSENGER	AGE	SEX	OCCUPATION	PRVL	DES
DRABER, WANDA	19	F	NN		GRAGFPIL
SINOCK, MARIE	27	F	NN		GRAGFPMO
HUTH, JACOB	39	M	MUSN		GRAGFPMD
NIEDERBIERMANN, HERMANN	13	M	CH		GRAGFPMD
KRIESCHER, ANNA	15	F	CH		GRAGFPMD
LEIMBACH, CATHA.	15	F	CH		GRAGFPMD
STEINWEG, MATHILDE	20	F	CH		GRAGFPMD
FRERICHS, JOHANN	20	M	FARMER		GRAGFPIA
HERMANN	19	M	FARMER		GRAGFPIA
ABCE, JOHANNE	18	F	NN		GRAGFPVA
FOLKERTS, WILHELMINE	19	F	NN		GRAGFPIA
STROECKER, HEINR.	14	M	NN		GRAGFPIA
WINTER, ADOLF	32	M	SMH		GRAGFPMO
HAUPT, ANNA	52	F	NN		GRAGFPMO
GOTTFRIED	8	M	CHILD		GRAGFPMO
CATHA.	11	F	CH		GRAGFPMO
KUHL, ANNA	30	F	NN		GRAGFPMO
TRETER, JOHN	55	M	BRR		GRAGFPMD
BRION, CHRISTIAN	27	M	FARMER		GRAGFPMD
DEMMER, MARIA	24	F	NN		GRAGFPOR
ANNA	2	F	CHILD		GRAGFPOR
JOSEPH	.02	M	INFANT		GRAGFPOR
BANGERT, WILHELM	14	M	INF		GRAGFPOH
RIES, MAGDALENE	39	F	INF		GRAGFPOH
JOHANNE	9	F	CHILD		GRAGFPOH
JOHANN	7	M	CHILD		GRAGFPOH
JOHANN	5	M	CHILD		GRAGFPOH
FRIEDR.	3	M	CHILD		GRAGFPOH
CHRISTINA	2	F	CHILD		GRAGFPOH
MAGDALENE	.03	F	INFANT		GRAGFPOH
WOHLERT, GOTTLIEBE	36	F	INF		GRAGFPKY
WILHELMINE	8	F	CHILD		GRAGFPKY
WILHELM	.11	M	INFANT		GRAGFPKY
SEIFERT, FRTIZ	16	M	WTR		GRAGFPKY
GRUNEWALD, CHRISTINA	34	F	NN		GRAGFPIL
CHRISTINA	11	F	CH		GRAGFPIL
HEINRICH	9	M	CHILD		GRAGFPIL
ORSCHL, MARIA	24	F	CH		GRAGFPIL
ARNOLD	.11	M	INFANT		GRAGFPIL
RICHTER, ANNA	18	F	INF		GRAGFPWI
ZDANCK, ANTON	28	M	FARMER		GRAGFPOH
ANTON	28	M	FARMER		GRAGFPOH
VERONICA	22	F	NN		GRAGFPOH
MARIANNA	3	F	CHILD		GRAGFPOH
STANISLAUS	.03	M	INFANT		GRAGFPOH
MEDLINSKY, JULIANA	24	F	NN		GRAGFPIA
JOSEPH	4	M	CHILD		GRAGFPIA
BERTHA	.11	F	INFANT		GRAGFPIA
VANFUREN, WILHE.	18	F	FARMER		GRAGFPPA
CORDES, FRANCISCA	30	F	NN		GRAGFPMN
JACOB	9	M	CHILD		GRAGFPMN
ALBERT	8	M	CHILD		GRAGFPMN
AGNISKA	4	F	CHILD		GRAGFPMN
MARIANNA	3	F	CHILD		GRAGFPMN
JOSEFA	.11	F	INFANT		GRAGFPMN
GRENZIN, HERMANN	48	M	BKLYR		GRAGFPMI
LOUISE	55	F	NN		GRAGFPMI
RICHARD	17	M	BKLYR		GRAGFPMI
PAUL	9	M	CHILD		GRAGFPMI
LUKASZA, SALONNJA	16	F	NN		GRAGFPMI
TIEDMANN, FRANZ	20	M	LABR		GRAGFPOH
WITT, AUGUST	30	M	LABR		GRAGFPOH
KERN, SAMUEL	56	M	FARMER		GRAGFPKY
TRRIEB, SOPHIE	17	F	NN		GRAGFPMO
DOEHLER, ALMA	47	F	NN		GRAGFPMO
MEYER, ANNA	20	F	NN		GRAGFPMO
SEIDEL, HEINR.	26	M	SMH		GRAGFPMO
HAIN, FRIEDR.	30	M	FARMER		GRAGFPMI
SEEFELD, LOMIN	28	F	NN		GRAGFPMI
TIEDMANN, CARL	48	M	FARMER		GRAGFPMN
JUSTINA	45	F	NN		GRAGFPMN
CARL	8	M	CHILD		GRAGFPMN
THERESE	6	F	CHILD		GRAGFPMN
HERMANN	2	M	CHILD		GRAGFPMN
SCHART, PETER	27	M	STCTR		GRAGFPMN
EMMA	23	F	NN		GRAGFPMN
HERMANN	.11	M	INFANT		GRAGFPMN
MORGENSTEIN, PHIIPPINE	40	F	NN		GRAGFPMN
CATHA.	19	F	NN		GRAGFPPA
HELENE	7	F	CHILD		GRAGFPPA
LACKE, TH.	23	M	LKSH		GRAGFPWI
BERGER, IDA	21	F	NN		GRAGFPTX
FENSAHRENS, CARL	14	M	NN		GRAGFPMD
KRAUSS, JOHANN	44	M	LABR		GRAGFPMI
DRUEHL, HEINR.	24	M	FARMER		GRAGFPIL
DIPPOLTMANN, ANNA	55	F	NN		GRAGFPMD
HEINR.	25	M	JNR		GRAGFPMD
GELERMANN, EDUARD	61	M	MCHT		GRAGFPMD
TIWE, CARL	40	M	LLD		GRAGFPMD
MEYER, THERESIA	32	F	NN		GRAGFPPA
JOSEPH	2	M	CHILD		GRAGFPPA
GEORG	.09	M	INFANT		GRAGFPPA
RUPNOW, EMIL	24	M	FARMER		GRAGFPMI
PEHL, MARIA	22	F	NN		GRAGFPIN
DEHN, AUGUST	33	M	GDNR		GRAGFPMN
DRUSCHKE, AUGUST	26	M	FARMER		GRAGFPMN
WILHE.	22	F	NN		GRAGFPMN
HERMANN	.11	M	INFANT		GRAGFPMN
HECKER, AMALIA	38	F	NN		GRAGFPMD
HILGE, LISETTE	17	F	NN		GRAGFPMD
OSTHOFF, HERM.	25	M	WTR		GRAGFPMI
ELLA	4	F	CHILD		GRAGFPMI
SCHMIDT, BRUNO	2	M	CHILD		GRAGFPMI
WILMER	.02	M	INFANT		GRAGFPMI
DRAPPER, H.	37	M	TCHR		GRAGFPWI
RIEGER, LOUIS	26	M	FARMER		GRAGFPMN
KONECZNY, MARIA	22	F	NN		GRAGFPIL
JOHANN	3	M	CHILD		GRAGFPIL
FRANZ	2	M	CHILD		GRAGFPIL
FUESE, DORETTE	20	F	CH		GRAGFPIL
ROENNECKER, HEIM.	30	M	FARMER		GRAGFPMD
HEINS, CLAUS	22	M	SHFM		GRAGFPIL
TRAPP, LUDWIG	34	M	PNTR		GRAGFPMN
MATHILDE	30	F	NN		GRAGFPMN
HERMANN	7	M	CHILD		GRAGFPMN
WILHELM	3	M	CHILD		GRAGFPMN
MARIE	3	F	CHILD		GRAGFPMN
MARTHA	2	F	CHILD		GRAGFPMN
MATHILDE	.10	F	INFANT		GRAGFPMN
WILHELM	3	M	CHILD		GRAGFPMN
MARIE	3	F	CHILD		GRAGFPMN
MARTHA	2	F	CHILD		GRAGFPMN
MATHILDE	.10	F	INFANT		GRAGFPMN
KLATTE, MARTHA	14	F	NN		GRAGFPMN
GRAF, GUSTAV	26	M	ENGR		GRAGFPPA
BVRANDES, BERTHA	18	F	NN		GRAGFPIL
WEINBERG, H.	28	M	FARMER		GRAGFPIL
GERHARDT, MARIE	32	F	NN		GRAGFPMD
WRUCK, CARL	32	M	LABR		GRAGFPMD
WESSLING, FRANZISCA	64	F	NN		GRAGFPMD
WENER, MICHAEL	27	M	LABR		GRAGFPIL
U., ALBERT	28	M	LABR		GRAGFPIL
SATTOWSKY, LOUISE	19	F	NN		GRAGFPMO
KREFT, JOHANN	36	M	TLR		GRAGFPMI
MARIE	35	F	NN		GRAGFPMI
FRIEDR.	3	M	CHILD		GRAGFPMI
FRIEDERIKE	.11	F	INFANT		GRAGFPMI
OZMINKOS, VALENTY	23	M	LABR		GRAGFPPA
KSZYZANOWSKI, JOSEPH	24	M	LABR		GRAGFPPA
UHL, ADAM	26	M	BRR		GRAGFPTN
ASCHKA, ELEONORA	34	F	NN		GRAGFPIL
MICHEL	10	M	CH		GRAGFPIL
ANNA	8	F	CHILD		GRAGFPIL
CATHA.	4	F	CHILD		GRAGFPIL
CRESCENZ	2	M	CHILD		GRAGFPIL
SCHIEBER, AMADEUS	15	M	CH		GRAGFPIL
JOHANN	14	M	CH		GRAGFPIL
ROTHLINGSHOEFER, LEONHA	27	M	UNKNOWN		GRAGFPMI
ROTHLINGSHOEFER, ANNA	18	F	NN		GRAGFPMI
PRESSER, MICHAEL	32	M	FARMER		GRAGFPOH

PASSENGER	AGE	SEX	OCCUPATION	PV RIVL	DES
KREISCHER, WILHELM	18	M	BRR	GRAGFPNY
HANDRACH, GOTTHELF	68	M	FARMER	GRAGFPPA
AUGUSTA	25	F	NN	GRAGFPPA
KIRSCHLING, FRANZISCA	54	F	NN	GRAGFPKS
MARIE	23	F	NN	GRAGFPKS
CLARA	11	F	CH	GRAGFPKS
JOHANNES	9	M	CHILD	GRAGFPKS
PAUL	8	M	CHILD	GRAGFPKS
GOYKE, JOSEPH	25	M	TLR	GRAGFPMD
TOMAZEWSKI, JOSEPH	29	M	SHMK	GRAGFPMD
REDWANZ, VALESCA	33	F	NN	GRAGFPIA
CURT	11	M	CH	GRAGFPIA
OLGA	9	F	CHILD	GRAGFPIA
SOPHIE	4	F	CHILD	GRAGFPIA
STUEMER, AUGUSTE	19	F	CH	GRAGFPNE
HEINRICH, JOHANNA	38	F	CH	GRAGFPOH
ALMA	15	F	CH	GRAGFPOH
EMILIE	11	F	CH	GRAGFPOH
NEUMANN, EMILIE	25	F	CH	GRAGFPMO
MAJEWSKA, VERONICA	23	F	CH	GRAGFPMO
MARIANNA	12	F	CH	GRAGFPMO
SCHULZ, WILHELMINE	16	F	CH	GRAGFPOH
JULIUS	8	M	CHILD	GRAGFPOH
BOIKI, FRANZ	47	M	FARMER	GRAGFPIA
SCHAFARKIEWICZ, LEON	29	M	JNR	GRAGFPMN
LEO	6	M	CHILD	GRAGFPMN
ANNA	4	F	CHILD	GRAGFPMN
STANISLAUS	2	M	CHILD	GRAGFPMN
MAX	.11	M	INFANT	GRAGFPMN
AMALIA	30	F	INF	GRAGFPMN
U, ROSALIA	16	F	INF	GRAGFPKY
BUDSISZ, JOHANN	25	M	FARMER	GRAGFPPA
ANNA	24	F	NN	GRAGFPPA
JOSEPH	.09	M	INFANT	GRAGFPPA
KOSS, MARIANNA	19	F	NN	GRAGFPMO
KRAUSE, DAVID	63	M	FARMER	GRAGFPMO
MARIA	62	F	NN	GRAGFPMO
SPIEWACK, JOSEPH	35	M	LABR	GRAGFPMI
MARIANNA	28	F	NN	GRAGFPMI
EVA	3	F	CHILD	GRAGFPMI
MICHAEL	.09	M	INFANT	GRAGFPMI
KRYESTECK, JOS.	24	M	LABR	GRAGFPPA
DIGUTES, SIMON	40	M	LABR	GRAGFPPA
LEMEITES, ANTONES	31	M	LABR	GRAGFPMD
LONDON, SOLOMON	4	M	CHILD	GRAGFPMD
RACHEL	3	F	CHILD	GRAGFPMD
WESTENDORF, BERHARDINA	56	F	NN	GRAGFPOH
PLASSMANN, MINNA	31	F	NN	GRAGFPMD
MINNA	7	F	CHILD	GRAGFPMD
JULIA	10	F	CH	GRAGFPMD
WATERKAMP, WILHELMINE	13	F	NN	GRAGFPPA
SOPHIA	18	F	NN	GRAGFPPA
LONDON, ANDREAS	36	M	LABR	GRAGFPMD
THEOPHILA	28	F	NN	GRAGFPMD
FRANZISCA	2	F	CHILD	GRAGFPMD
STANISLAUS	.09	M	INFANT	GRAGFPMD
ELFLEIN, GEORG	44	M	LABR	GRAGFPIL
KUNIGUNDE	29	F	NN	GRAGFPIL
JOHANN	6	M	CHILD	GRAGFPIL
MARGA.	4	F	CHILD	GRAGFPIL
JOHANN	2	M	CHILD	GRAGFPIL
DAVID	48	M	LABR	GRAGFPIL
CATHA.	44	F	NN	GRAGFPIL
ANNA	.03	F	INFANT	GRAGFPIL
SCHWARZ, LEOPOLD	23	M	LABR	GRAGFPWI
LAMA	18	F	NN	GRAGFPWI
TOMAZEWSKA, FELICIA	22	F	NN	GRAGFPMI
RUSS, ALOIS	25	M	BRR	GRAGFPKY
PFISTER, JOHANN	17	M	FARMER	GRAGFPKY
VOLK, JUSTUS	17	M	JNR	GRAGFPPA
WISMIERSKI, JOHANN	32	M	PVTM	GRAGFPPA
GLAUBITZ, CARL	32	M	CPR	GRAGFPKS
HELENE	30	F	NN	GRAGFPKS
EMIL	8	M	CHILD	GRAGFPKS
OTTO	7	M	CHILD	GRAGFPKS

PASSENGER	AGE	SEX	OCCUPATION	PV RIVL	DES
GRAUBETZ, FRIEDR.	3	M	CHILD	GRAGFPKS
MARTHA	.11	F	INFANT	GRAGFPKS
GOIKE, JOHANN	22	M	FARMER	GRAGFPMI
SELKE, JOSEPH	28	M	TNM	GRAGFPWI
SCHOENWALDE, ROSINE	45	F	NN	GRAGFPWI
EICHEL, ADOLF	24	M	FARMER	GRAGFPMD
HEMKER, FRIEDR.	18	M	JNR	GRAGFPMO
WENDT, ALBERT	26	M	CPTR	GRAGFPPA
BALZER, MARIA	60	F	NN	GRAGFPMD

SHIP: ANCHORIA

FROM: GLASGOW AND MOVILLE
TO: NEW YORK
ARRIVED: 09 JULY 1888

PASSENGER	AGE	SEX	OCCUPATION	PV RIVL	DES
ZENKOWITZ, MICHE.	48	F	CPTR	GRZZZZUSA
EMIL	16	F	CPTR	GRACSDUSA
HAREK, ARON	49	M	TLR	GRACSDUSA
ISRAEL	9	M	CHILD	GRACSDUSA
KAUSE, CARL	53	M	BKLYR	GRZZZZUSA
STUZMULLER, KARL-WILH.	28	M	TLR	GRAGALUSA
WINTE, ERNST	21	M	SMH	GRABEHUSA
SWIND, GEORG-A.	24	M	SMH	GRZZZZUSA
YARKE, FERDINANDE	44	M	LABR	GRZZZZUSA
ZOPF, JOHAN	47	M	LABR	GRACIOUSA
PFUNDHELLER, OTTO	36	M	MLR	GRADZVUSA
PEGLAN, LINA	19	F	NN	GRZZZZUSA
PRESTI, SILWO	19	M	STCTR	GRAFBGUSA

SHIP: ARIZONA

FROM: LIVERPOOL AND QUEENSTOWN
TO: NEW YORK
ARRIVED: 09 JULY 1888

PASSENGER	AGE	SEX	OCCUPATION	PV RIVL	DES
OCH, ANNA	32	F	W	GRACBFUSA
RAHN, HERMANN	28	M	PMBR	GRACBFUSA
GOEBEL, KALERINA	23	F	SP	GRACBFUSA
SCHWEIST, MARIE	21	F	SP	GRACBFUSA
ROSENBAUM, SALMEN	25	M	SHPMN	GRACBFUSA
RISKY, SAMUEL	21	M	LABR	GRZZZZUSA
KOPP, MARIE	48	F	W	GRZZZZUSA
JACOB	7	M	CHILD	GRZZZZUSA
KAUFMANN, JOSEPH	30	M	MECH	GRACBFUSA
BUFKOFGER, HUGO	19	M	FLABR	GRACBFUSA
EHRENSTEIN, ARON	31	M	SMH	GRACBFUSA
GIOVANIN, NANDI	32	M	FARMER	GRACBFUSA
BIRCHHOLZ, AUGUST	29	M	FTR	GRACBFUSA
MEYER, JOHAN	56	M	SMH	GRACBFUSA
SCHWARTZ, FREDRIK	38	M	GDNR	GRACBFUSA
STEINBOK, JAMES	30	M	ART	GRACBFUSA
ADA	31	F	W	GRACBFUSA
PETERS, S.	22	F	LDY	GRACBFUSA
BREM, F.MR	30	M	GENT	GRADAXUSA
GOLDBERG, J.MR	29	M	GENT	GRACBFUSA
MOREAN, A.	22	F	SVNT	GRADBQUSA
JACOB, KATE	23	F	LDY	GRADBQUSA
KATE	21	F	LDY	GRADBQUSA

SHIP: CATALONIA

FROM: LIVERPOOL AND QUEENSTOWN
TO: BOSTON
ARRIVED: 09 JULY 1888

PASSENGER	AGE	SEX	OCCUPATION	PRIVL / DES
SCHATZ, PAULINA	17	F	SVNT	GRZZZZUSA

SHIP: MARSEILLE

FROM: ANTWERP, BORDEAUX AND HAVRE
TO: NEW ORLEANS
ARRIVED: 09 JULY 1888

PASSENGER	AGE	SEX	OCCUPATION	PRIVL / DES
HEER, FRIT	16	M	UNKNOWN	GRZZZZUSA
OCREMAN, JEAN	62	M	FARMER	FRZZZZUSA
IRMA	38	F	UNKNOWN	FRZZZZUSA
COLIRA	9	F	CHILD	FRZZZZUSA
BLANCHE	7	F	CHILD	FRZZZZUSA
LEA	6	F	CHILD	FRZZZZUSA
GASTON	2	M	CHILD	FRZZZZUSA
FAK, JOSEPH	32	M	LKMKR	GRZZZZUSA
HEUBACH, EDOUARD	17	M	UNKNOWN	GRZZZZUSA
RUFF, OLBIN	18	M	WCHMKR	GRZZZZUSA
NEUGART, BERTHA	18	M	UNKNOWN	GRZZZZUSA
HERBSTRITT, ERNEST	4	M	CHILD	GRZZZZUSA
FELOMANN, FRIDOLIN	28	M	LABR	GRZZZZUSA
PRADELS, HIPPOLYTE	38	M	TCHR	FRZZZZUSA
BIROU, JEAN	44	M	FARMER	FRZZZZUSA
JEAN	40	M	FARMER	FRZZZZUSA
VINCENT, MARIE	19	F	SVNT	FRZZZZUSA
MOUCHOU, MARIE	17	F	SVNT	FRZZZZUSA
PARGADES, PIERRE	19	M	FARMER	FRZZZZUSA
VICTOR	16	M	FARMER	FRZZZZUSA
JOSEPH	14	M	FARMER	FRZZZZUSA
LARTIQUE, JEAN	35	M	FARMER	FRZZZZUSA
CELESTINE	37	F	W	FRZZZZUSA
MARIE	4	F	CHILD	FRZZZZUSA
HONTAAS, EULALI	18	F	CH	FRZZZZUSA
POUTS, LAPLACE	29	F	SVNT	FRZZZZUSA
HOUDEVILLE, MADELEINE	25	F	SVNT	FRZZZZUSA
BONNEU, VINCENT	22	M	FARMER	FRZZZZUSA
GAILLARDEU, HUGUES	24	M	FARMER	FRZZZZUSA
PRIGARDA, JEAN	22	M	FARMER	FRZZZZUSA
DEJEN, AUGUSTE	22	M	BKR	GRZZZZUSA
LESCURE, VICTOR	26	M	FARMER	FRZZZZUSA
LAPORTE, PIERRE	28	M	FARMER	FRZZZZUSA
PAYSSAN, JEAN	28	M	FARMER	FRZZZZUSA
BLAIZE, SYLVAIN	39	M	BCHR	FRZZZZUSA
MARIE	39	F	UNKNOWN	FRZZZZUSA
FRANCOIS	7	M	CHILD	FRZZZZUSA
HENRI	6	M	CHILD	FRZZZZUSA
MARIE	2	F	CHILD	FRZZZZUSA
BIE, HIPPOLYTE	23	M	CCHMN	FRZZZZUSA
CAARGOUN, PIERRE	20	M	CCHMN	FRZZZZUSA
LACASSIE, MARIE	16	M	CL	FRZZZZUSA
RIVIERRE, JEAN	53	M	MCHT	FRZZZZUSA
ALZIRE	40	F	UNKNOWN	FRZZZZUSA
MICHEL, PIERRE	41	M	FARMER	FRZZZZUSA
CHAIX, JOSEPH	40	M	FARMER	FRZZZZUSA
FIDELE	38	F	UNKNOWN	FRZZZZUSA
COURT, LEONE	33	F	UNKNOWN	FRZZZZUSA
MONTAGNER, MODESTE	70	F	UNKNOWN	FRZZZZUSA

SHIP: MORAVIA

FROM: HAMBURG AND HAVRE
TO: NEW YORK
ARRIVED: 09 JULY 1888

PASSENGER	AGE	SEX	OCCUPATION	PRIVL / DES
ATZEROTH, JOH	37	F	SGL	PRZZZZUSA
JUEDEN, EMMA	22	F	SGL	PRADWWUSA
ELLERBROCK, MARTHA	20	F	SGL	HBZZZZUSA
POKKES, THERESE	22	F	SGL	HBACBFUSA
SEYFRIED, CAROL.	37	F	WO	HBACBFUSA
SOPHIE	4	F	CHILD	HBACBFUSA
WILLIAMS, ALICE	22	F	SGL	HBACXVUSA
NAUMANN, LOUISE	50	F	WO	HBZZZZUSA
WUESTENBERG, HERM.	36	M	MLR	HBAAHRUSA
KRAKAUER, MICHAEL	15	M	S	HBAFZGUSA
SCHWECKHARDT, AUGUST	40	M	BKR	HBACBFUSA
HALBERSTADT, MAX	14	M	LABR	HBZZZZUSA
EMMA	9	F	CHILD	HBZZZZUSA
STERN, JENY	21	F	SGL	HBAADEUSA
WENGEMAIER, THERESE	17	F	SGL	HBAAFXUSA
ANDERSON, AGNES	16	M	SGL	BDZZZZUSA
JOHANNSEN, JOSEFINE	21	F	SGL	BDAGUZUSA
BRODY, SARA	25	F	WO	BDAGUZUSA
JENNE	.11	F	INFANT	BDAGUZUSA
BENDER, FRITZ	44	M	FARMER	BDALONUSA
CARL	16	M	FARMER	BDALONUSA
BUNBELIS, MARIANNE	27	F	WO	PRZZZZUSA
JOSEF	6	M	CHILD	PRZZZZUSA
VERONIKA	4	F	CHILD	PRZZZZUSA
HENNISGER, NICOLAUS	47	M	SMH	WMZZZZUSA
ALBERT.	46	F	W	WMZZZZUSA
WALBERGA	15	F	W	WMZZZZUSA
BARB.	13	F	CH	WMZZZZUSA
NICOL.	9	M	CHILD	WMZZZZUSA
LUDWIG	8	M	CHILD	WMZZZZUSA
ZSCHUNKE, OTTO	19	M	LABR	WMABVJUSA
KURZHALS, AUGUSTE	17	F	SGL	PRZZZZUSA
SCHLUNDT, AUGUST	57	M	LKSH	PRAADEUSA
ANNA	53	F	W	PRAADEUSA
CARL	9	M	CHILD	PRAADEUSA
SZATKOWSKY, MARIE	20	F	SGL	PRAAKHUSA
COHN, EVA	18	F	SGL	PRABMIUSA
SPRINGHORN, SOPHIE	20	F	SGL	HBZZZZUSA
MARQUARD, FRIEDRIKE	40	F	WO	PRZZZZUSA
HOLTZ, HERM.	20	M	FARMER	PRZZZZUSA
GUENTHER, EDUARD	52	M	STWD	PRZZZZUSA
RUHLAND, JOHANN	22	M	BKR	PRAHARUSA
COHN, DAVID	14	M	LABR	PRABMIUSA
HUNGER, EMIL	24	M	MCHT	PRABDMUSA
MARIE	24	F	W	PRABDMUSA
DAERGER, LOUISE	17	F	SGL	PRZZZZUSA
LOHSE, RUD.	14	M	MCHT	HBZZZZUSA
HAERTEL, FRIEDA	5	F	CHILD	PRZZZZUSA
HOLZBECHER, ANNA	21	F	SGL	PRZZZZUSA
PAUL	13	M	CH	PRZZZZUSA
EBERSBACH, FERD.	17	M	BTMKR	PRAIBVUSA
ADELHEID	15	F	SGL	PRAIBVUSA
ALEXANDER, MAX	29	M	TNM	PRZZZZUSA
KATZ, JOSEF	20	M	MCHT	PRADIJUSA
MUELLER, WILH.	27	M	MCHT	PRAAXKUSA
TRANC, JOHANN	16	M	LKSH	PRAAIFUSA
EILERS, ERNST	23	M	PNTR	HBZZZZUSA
DAMMAFT, FRITZ	28	M	MCHT	HBACARUSA
REICHARD, PETER	26	M	FARMER	PRZZZZUSA
KRANZ, ADRIAN	18	F	SGL	PRZZZZUSA
SIEVERS, MATHILDE	27	F	W	PRZZZZUSA
ALWINE	.09	F	INFANT	PRZZZZUSA
GREEN, GEORG	13	M	LABR	PRZZZZUSA
REESE, WILH	23	M	LABR	PRAEHOUSA
LAU, CARL	25	M	LABR	PRAJGMUSA
STEGMEIER, CHRISTINE	45	F	W	PRAHXIUSA
SCHMIDT, ELISAB.	25	F	SGL	PRZZZZUSA
BLEIDERER, ERNST	16	M	LABR	PRABVDUSA

PASSENGER	AGE	SEX	OCCUPATION	PRVL	DES
KOCH, CHRIST.	28	M	LABR	WMZZZ	USA
WIESENBACH, CAROLINE	24	F	SGL	PRZZZZ	USA
LEDERER, CAROLINE	22	F	SGL	PRAEYH	USA
MINNA	19	F	SGL	PRAEYH	USA
HARLACHER, BABETTE	18	F	SGL	PRAEYH	USA
BARTHOLOMAE, EMILIE	26	F	SGL	PRAFBV	USA
GAETH, FRIED	27	M	GDNR	PRAFOL	USA
EMMA	29	F	W	PRAFOL	USA
AHRENS, ALWINE	22	F	SGL	PRAFOL	USA
HENRY	32	M	LABR	PRAFOL	USA
WILH.	17	M	LABR	PRAFOL	USA
PIENNING, CARL	16	M	LABR	PRAFOL	USA
REHDERS, FRANZ	57	M	CPTR	PRAFOL	USA
ARNDT, ANNA	50	F	WO	PRAJOY	USA
ZIMMERMANN, ADOLF	34	M	BKBNDR	PRAEPZ	USA
KROENER, FRANZISKA	19	F	SGL	PRAGAS	USA
FRIEDRICHS, CLARA	23	F	SGL	PRAAYS	USA
MINNA	16	F	SGL	PRAAYS	USA
SNURSKA, MARIANNA	19	F	SGL	PRZZZZ	USA
LANGNESE, DOROTHEA	55	F	WO	PRZZZZ	USA
GREGOR, SUSANNE	30	F	W	PRZZZZ	USA
JULIANNE	9	F	CHILD	PRZZZZ	USA
CARL	8	M	CHILD	PRZZZZ	USA
CAROLINE	6	F	CHILD	PRZZZZ	USA
WILH.	4	M	CHILD	PRZZZZ	USA
EMILIE	2	F	CHILD	PRZZZZ	USA
ERNST	.03	M	INFANT	PRZZZZ	USA
GRAESER, MICHAEL	25	M	LABR	PRZZZZ	USA
KRAUTZ, ISAAC	23	M	CGRMKR	PRAFWJ	USA
WINKLER, VACLAV	15	M	LABR	PRZZZZ	USA
SPIZENETZKI, SCHLOMA	35	M	DLR	PRZZZZ	USA
ENDEL	28	F	W	PRZZZZ	USA
LEISER	38	M	FARMER	PRZZZZ	USA
JENTE	30	F	W	PRZZZZ	USA
MANIA	8	F	CHILD	PRZZZZ	USA
RISCHE	7	F	CHILD	PRZZZZ	USA
SARA	.11	F	INFANT	PRZZZZ	USA
ANNA	.01	F	INFANT	PRZZZZ	USA
KROKOWSKI, OTTO	30	M	LABR	PRZZZZ	USA
ANNA	21	F	W	PRZZZZ	USA
LAPINSKI, STANISLAUS	24	M	LABR	PRZZZZ	USA
HAERTEL, HENRIETTE	49	F	WO	PRZZZZ	USA
EMMA	15	F	CH	PRZZZZ	USA
HUGO	9	M	CHILD	PRZZZZ	USA
DEUTSCH, OTTILIE	20	F	SGL	BDZZZZ	USA
MARIE	18	F	SGL	BDZZZZ	USA
HAPPEL, MARIE	54	F	WO	BDZZZZ	USA
JAEKLE, CHRISTIAN	24	M	WCHMKR	BDAEPX	USA
STEGMANN, AGNES	23	F	SGL	BDAEPX	USA
FRIESELMANN, MARG.	28	F	WO	HBZZZZ	USA
ERNST	2	M	CHILD	HBZZZZ	USA
LAFRENTZ, AMALIE	19	F	SGL	PRZZZZ	USA
FRIEDRICH, WILH.	28	M	CNF	PRAADE	USA
SCHNOOR, PETER	60	M	FARMER	PRZZZZ	USA
DOROTHEA	63	F	W	PRZZZZ	USA
ULLWRIG, JUL.	58	M	LABR	PRZZZZ	USA
GICKEL, ERNEST	24	F	SGL	PRZZZZ	USA
RUEHMCKE, EDUARD	31	M	MCHT	HBZZZZ	USA
PRELL, GUSTAV	26	M	CK	HBZZZZ	USA
SZYMANSKY, NICODEMUS	26	M	MSN	PRZZZZ	USA
LUDWIG	28	M	MSN	PRZZZZ	USA
FRITSCH, EWALD	34	M	BCHR	PRAFGC	USA
SCHOLZ, FRANZ	37	M	GDNR	PRZZZZ	USA
ANNA	34	F	W	PRZZZZ	USA
CAECILIE	9	F	CHILD	PRZZZZ	USA
GREGOR	4	M	CHILD	PRZZZZ	USA
CATH.	.09	F	INFANT	PRZZZZ	USA
KUTTAS, JOHANN	33	M	LABR	SYZZZZ	USA
ZUCKOVSKI, CHAIE	18	F	SGL	SYZZZZ	USA
TIMM, AUGUST	28	M	LABR	PRZZZZ	USA
LORENZEN, MARY	26	F	SGL	PRAHZP	USA
ANDRESEN, ANNA	24	F	SGL	PRZZZZ	USA
HUSSEL, EMIL	22	M	CL	PRZZZZ	USA
GOTTLIEBE, LIEBUDA	24	F	SGL	PRAIEP	USA
BEER, EMMA	15	F	SGL	PRZZZZ	USA
MALECK, AUGUST	28	M	SHMK	PRAJAQ	USA
ERNST, BABETTI	49	F	WO	PRADRO	USA
KATI	23	F	D	PRADRO	USA
MUELLER, ELISE	16	F	D	PRADRO	USA
KALCZYNSKI, ANTON	25	M	LABR	PRZZZZ	USA
SCHUELER, MARIE	24	F	WO	PRAEXT	USA
ELISE	17	F	SI	PRAEXT	USA
MINNA	.09	F	INFANT	PRAEXT	USA
HORWITZ, FILLY	18	F	SGL	PRAEXT	USA
GORSKA, JOH	28	F	WO	PRZZZZ	USA
JOH.	.11	M	INFANT	PRZZZZ	USA
WENZEL, LUDWIG	26	M	TLR	PRAHSC	USA
POTZKOWSKY, MARIANNE	18	F	SGL	PRAHSC	USA
BERGHOLZ, BERTHA	18	F	SGL	PRAKYI	USA
TRAM, MARG.	22	F	WO	PRAAIF	USA
MATHILDE	4	F	CHILD	PRAAIF	USA
STEFFEN, FERD.	34	M	DR	PRAFUI	USA
STUHM, ANNA	19	F	SGL	PRADNX	USA
MEYER, WILH.	27	M	SMH	PRAEZF	USA
GREGOR, CARL	42	M	LABR	PRZZZZ	USA
GERDES, WILH.	26	M	JNR	PRZZZZ	USA
STEINBERG, GUST.	27	M	LABR	PRZZZZ	USA
PETERSEN, PETER	46	M	MLR	PRABIG	USA
IDA	45	F	W	PRABIG	USA
MOELLER, CARSTEN	54	M	FARMER	PRABIG	USA
MAREN	64	F	W	PRABIG	USA
BERTHA	23	F	D	PRZZZZ	USA
LORENZEN, CHRIST.	62	F	WO	PRAHZP	USA
SIEMSEN, CHRIST.	33	M	PNTR	PRACBR	USA
SONNICHSEN, CHRISTIAN	27	M	LABR	PRADVN	USA
STICK, JOH.	15	M	FARMER	PRZZZZ	USA
SCHRAMM, BERTHA	56	F	WO	PRAFSF	USA
SILBERSTEIN, ROSA	30	F	SGL	PRAFZG	USA
BOETTGER, HEINR.	36	M	CK	PRABNS	USA
POCKRANDT, ERNEST.	52	F	WO	PRZZZZ	USA
HIRSCH, SALI	31	M	TLR	PRAEAB	USA
EMILIE	30	F	W	PRAEAB	USA
GEORG	4	M	CHILD	PRAEAB	USA
ERNA	3	F	CHILD	PRAEAB	USA
KAUTER, WILH.	26	M	LABR	PRAAZQ	USA
DRESSEN, ANNA	19	F	SGL	PRZZZZ	USA
DIETRICHS, PETER	42	M	BCHR	PRAAOL	USA
HERM.	14	M	S	PRAAOL	USA
ELKE, MARIE	18	F	SGL	PRABVD	USA
BROSOWSKY, WILH.	24	M	LABR	PRZZZZ	USA
NIEHAUS, WILH.	16	M	LABR	PRZZZZ	USA
SCHEFFLER, JUL.	30	M	LABR	PRZZZZ	USA
FRANZISKA	25	F	W	PRZZZZ	USA
LANGNESE, WILHELMINA	26	F	WO	PRZZZZ	USA
MINNA	2	F	CHILD	PRZZZZ	USA
OTTO	.09	M	INFANT	PRZZZZ	USA
SCHNEIDER, FRANZ	60	M	LABR	PRALHC	USA
MARIE	9	F	CHILD	PRALHC	USA
DEUK, ADOLF	15	M	LABR	BDZZZZ	USA
BOETHER, JOH.	33	M	LABR	MKZZZZ	USA
ANNA	30	F	W	MKZZZZ	USA
CARL	9	M	CHILD	MKZZZZ	USA
ELISE	6	F	CHILD	MKZZZZ	USA
HERM.	4	M	CHILD	MKZZZZ	USA
WILH.	.11	M	INFANT	MKZZZZ	USA
ANNA	.01	F	INFANT	MKZZZZ	USA
WICH, WILH.	18	F	SGL	BVZZZZ	USA
BIBRO, ADOLF	16	M	SHMK	BVABUT	USA
CARSTENSEN, CARSTEN	16	M	FARMER	PRZZZZ	USA
ADAMSKIL, STANISL.	16	M	LABR	PRAHKM	USA
FRWEUND, WILH.	36	M	CPTR	PRAAKH	USA
WEISS, MARIANNE	29	F	WO	PRZZZZ	USA
STEFAN	.09	M	INFANT	PRZZZZ	USA
ARENDT, HERM.	34	M	LABR	PRZZZZ	USA
KLEIN, HERM.	28	M	LABR	PRAHVF	USA
ORANT, MARIE	23	F	WO	PRZZZZ	USA
ANNA	.11	F	INFANT	PRZZZZ	USA
LORENZEN, MARTIN	18	M	WTR	PRZZZZ	USA
JOSEF, HENRIETTE	22	F	SGL	PRZZZZ	USA
FECHNER, EMIL	26	M	FARMER	PRZZZZ	USA

PASSENGER	AGE	SEX	OCCUPATION	PRVL	DES
MEYER, HUGO	16	M	LABR	PRZZZZ	USA
OTTO, AUGUST	22	M	LABR	PRABDM	USA
KAISER, OSCAR	36	M	SMH	PRAAKH	USA
STEINBERG, SAMUEL	18	M	LABR	PRZZZZ	USA
GELTA, FRANCISKA	22	M	LABR	PRZZZZ	USA
JULIUS, DINES	00	F	INF	PR****	USA
MASOPUST, MARY	00	F	INF	PR****	USA
HIRSCH, S.	00	M	INF	PR****	USA
BLEILERN, VALENTIN	25	M	HTR	BDZZZZ	USA
FREY, VICTOR	17	M	JNR	BDZZZZ	USA
BLAESE, MAGDALENA	22	F	SGL	ACZZZZ	USA
LEPETITCORPS, MATHURIN	26	M	LABR	ACACDS	USA
SCHEU, HAVIER	25	M	SHMK	PRZZZZ	USA
HERZOG, WILHELM	22	M	LABR	PRAHRF	USA
GAMSCH, CATHARINE	26	F	SGL	PRAGVO	USA
RUOFF, CHRIST.	19	M	SHMK	WMZZZZ	USA
HEMMELER, EUGEN	19	M	FARMER	SRZZZZ	USA
SCHLEMINGER, WILHELM	50	M	FSHMN	SRADOI	USA
WIDMER, GUSTAV	26	M	BCHR	SRZZZZ	USA

SHIP: OHIO

FROM: LIVERPOOL AND QUEENSTOWN
TO: NEW YORK
ARRIVED: 09 JULY 1888

PASSENGER	AGE	SEX	OCCUPATION	PRVL	DES
ABRAMOWITZ, CHINE	58	F	W	GRZZZZ	NY
FEB.	18	F	SVNT	GRZZZZ	NY
BLUME	16	F	SVNT	GRZZZZ	NY
B.	24	M	LABR	GRZZZZ	NY
S.	9	M	CHILD	GRZZZZ	NY
BLANFELD, J.	19	M	LABR	GRZZZZ	PA
DEMBER, EYE	22	F	W	GRZZZZ	NY
C.	.06	F	INFANT	GRZZZZ	NY
ELOSSER, D.	22	M	LABR	GRZZZZ	NY
FUNEBERG, SANI	32	M	LABR	GRZZZZ	UNK
GEGEN, F.	20	M	LABR	GRZZZZ	NY
GUTKO, A.	24	M	LABR	GRZZZZ	NY
HOLLANDER, G.	17	M	LABR	GRZZZZ	NY
HERPHMANN, M.	31	M	LABR	GRZZZZ	NY
KOHN, JOE.	19	M	LABR	GRZZZZ	NY
KIMBELL, CHARLOTT.	21	F	SVNT	GRZZZZ	USA
MARIA	15	F	SVNT	GRZZZZ	USA
P.	12	F	SVNT	GRZZZZ	USA
KOHAN, SEIB	19	M	LABR	GRZZZZ	NY
LARUS, C.	23	M	LABR	GRZZZZ	NY
LEFKOWITZ, P.	32	M	LABR	GRZZZZ	NY
MARUTZ, A.	20	M	LABR	GRZZZZ	USA
MATUK, ALEX	25	M	LABR	GRZZZZ	NY
MEISEL, D.	25	M	LABR	GRZZZZ	NY
NOOK, F.	50	M	LABR	GRZZZZ	NY
HERMAN	14	M	LABR	GRZZZZ	NY
NAZOKS, A.	25	M	LABR	GRZZZZ	PA
OCKERF, J.	20	M	LABR	GRZZZZ	IA
RUSCHIN, S.	16	M	LABR	GRZZZZ	NY
REINEITZ, PAULINE	15	F	SP	GRZZZZ	NY
RATKEWICZ, J.	25	M	LABR	GRZZZZ	NY
ROSENTHAL, MINNE	24	F	SVNT	GRZZZZ	NY
SCHWARTZ, P.	36	M	LABR	GRZZZZ	NY
SEBORA	14	F	SP	GRZZZZ	NY
D.	11	F	CH	GRZZZZ	NY
SOLOMON, HY.	24	M	LABR	GRZZZZ	IL
SCHERSCHEWSKY, J.	45	M	LABR	GRZZZZ	PA
BELE	45	F	W	GRZZZZ	PA
TAUBE	18	F	SVNT	GRZZZZ	PA
EST.	10	F	CH	GRZZZZ	PA
J.	8	M	CHILD	GRZZZZ	PA
H.	3	M	CHILD	GRZZZZ	PA
TEZIERSKI, J.	26	M	LABR	GRZZZZ	NY
WEMBERGER, S.	22	M	LABR	GRZZZZ	NY

SHIP: SERVIA

FROM: LIVERPOOL AND QUEENSTOWN
TO: NEW YORK
ARRIVED: 09 JULY 1888

PASSENGER	AGE	SEX	OCCUPATION	PRVL	DES
LIEBACH, FRIEDRICH	31	M	LABR	GRADAX	NY
GRABINGE, JOHAN	29	M	BRR	GRADAX	NY
DAMER, ADAM	27	M	BLKSMH	GRADAX	NY
GLEICH, HARRY	30	M	LABR	GRADAX	NY
GREY, JULIA	18	F	SVNT	GRADAX	PA
DALIGARLT, JULIE	30	F	SVNT	GRADAX	PA
WAGENMAN, CARVIEL	35	M	MCHT	GRADAX	PA
SHIERHORST, BERNHARD	30	M	MRNR	GRADAX	PA
GAIWINE, ANNA	40	F	DRSMKR	GRADAX	PA
GOLDSMITH, SOLOMON	52	M	MCHT	GRADAX	PA

SHIP: EIDER

FROM: BREMEN AND SOUTHAMPTON
TO: NEW YORK
ARRIVED: 10 JULY 1888

PASSENGER	AGE	SEX	OCCUPATION	PRVL	DES
SCHROEDER, WILH.	40	M	TT	GRZZZZ	USA
V. ERNST	31	M	TT	GRZZZZ	USA
LEOOR, ROSA	17	F	UNKNOWN	GRZZZZ	USA
HESS, PHILIPPINE	16	F	UNKNOWN	GRZZZZ	USA
BRAUSER, CASPER	26	M	TT	GRZZZZ	USA
HANAUER, ESIDOR	24	M	TT	GRZZZZ	USA
BAUER, MEIER	18	M	TT	GRZZZZ	USA
ZUCHSCHWERS, BARBARA	20	F	UNKNOWN	GRZZZZ	USA
WUND, HEIN.	36	M	TT	GRZZZZ	USA
RALISKI, ADOLF	36	M	TT	GRZZZZ	USA
ULBRICH, RICH.	34	M	TT	GRZZZZ	USA
ROSENFELD, LEOP.	21	M	TT	GRZZZZ	USA
FENCKTMANGER, JOS.	16	M	TT	GRZZZZ	USA
ORDEMANN, W.	38	F	UNKNOWN	GRZZZZ	USA
GERTRUDE	23	F	UNKNOWN	GRZZZZ	USA
MEINBARDT, AUG.	22	M	BKBNDR	GRZZZZ	USA
KIESLING, ALWINE	21	F	SMSTS	GRZZZZ	USA
DRATH, BERTHA	17	F	SMSTS	GRZZZZ	USA
LAGOTZKI, ANDR.	76	M	FARMER	GRZZZZ	USA
KATHAR.	46	F	W	GRZZZZ	USA
ROST, FRIEDR.	19	M	FARMER	GRZZZZ	USA
ZBITMEWSKA, FRANZISKA	24	F	UNKNOWN	GRZZZZ	USA
IGNATZ	7	M	CHILD	GRZZZZ	USA
SALOMONEA	4	F	CHILD	GRZZZZ	USA
HELENA	1	F	CHILD	GRZZZZ	USA
WETTRICH, JOHAN	17	M	LABR	GRZZZZ	USA
MUELLER, JOHANN	17	M	LABR	GRZZZZ	USA
STEGMANN, EVA	22	F	SVNT	GRZZZZ	USA
MARCINIAK, IGNACI	22	M	MCHT	GRZZZZ	USA
LOEFFLER, STEFAN	43	M	MCHT	GRZZZZ	USA
APHALS, MARY	17	F	UNKNOWN	GRZZZZ	USA
HANNS, HEINR.	17	M	LABR	GRZZZZ	USA
KLANCKE, CHRIST.	16	M	LABR	GRZZZZ	USA
BEHMANN, FRIEDR.	18	M	LABR	GRZZZZ	USA
GANELS, FOCHE	32	M	LABR	GRZZZZ	USA
HENRI	19	M	LABR	GRZZZZ	USA
JOH.	8	F	CHILD	GRZZZZ	USA
FRIEDR.	7	M	CHILD	GRZZZZ	USA
MICH.	5	M	CHILD	GRZZZZ	USA
DORNSEIFF, SUSANNE	18	F	UNKNOWN	GRZZZZ	USA
VOIGT, FRITZ	58	M	FARMER	GRZZZZ	USA
JANECKE, WILH.	30	M	FARMER	GRZZZZ	USA
EMMA	28	F	W	GRZZZZ	USA
FRIEDR	4	M	CHILD	GRZZZZ	USA
WILHELM	00	M	CH	GRZZZZ	USA
DORELLE	.11	F	INFANT	GRZZZZ	USA

PASSENGER	AGE	SEX	OCCUPATION	PRVL	DES	PASSENGER	AGE	SEX	OCCUPATION	PRVL	DES
STENBER, DANIEL	26	M	MCHT		GRZZZZUSA	SPORNA, VALENTINE	30	F	UNKNOWN		GRZZZZUSA
DORNSEIFF, JOHS.	26	M	SHMK		GRZZZZUSA	MAX	4	M	CHILD		GRZZZZUSA
BECKER, JACOB	19	M	FARMER		GRZZZZUSA	BERTRAN, HEIN.	26	M	BKR		GRZZZZUSA
BOLZ, CARL	18	M	PNTR		GRZZZZUSA	SCHWAB, FRIEDR.	22	F	UNKNOWN		GRZZZZUSA
HALLER, CATH.	19	F	SMSTS		GRZZZZUSA	WILH.	20	F	UNKNOWN		GRZZZZUSA
BAUER, EMILIE	17	F	SMSTS		GRZZZZUSA	KRIEGER, GEORG	32	M	LABR		GRZZZZUSA
SEEGER, AGATHE	19	F	SMSTS		GRZZZZUSA	FLORIAN, MATH.	23	M	LABR		GRZZZZUSA
SCHMIDT, JOH.	59	M	LABR		GRZZZZUSA	LIERE, HERM.	32	F	LABR		GRZZZZUSA
SCHALLER, WILH.	11	M	UNKNOWN		GRZZZZUSA	KNUEZEL, BERTHA	34	F	SVNT		GRZZZZUSA
RICHTER, LONA	17	F	SMSTS		GRZZZZUSA	WALTER, ALBERT.	21	F	SVNT		GRZZZZUSA
MUELLER, KAETCHEN	24	F	SVNT		GRZZZZUSA	RINELING, ERNST	15	M	UNKNOWN		GRZZZZUSA
HUSCH, OSCAR	19	M	FARMER		GRZZZZUSA	WAGNER, MARIA	24	F	SVNT		GRZZZZUSA
GIESEL, WM.	21	M	MCHT		GRZZZZUSA	HOPPE, GUST.	26	M	PNTR		GRZZZZUSA
HAMMER, JOH.	24	M	MCHT		GRZZZZUSA	KNUEZEL, EMMA	23	F	UNKNOWN		GRZZZZUSA
JOS.	28	M	MCHT		GRZZZZUSA	SCHERM, MARGAR.	16	F	UNKNOWN		GRZZZZUSA
LOEW, AUGUSTA	30	F	UNKNOWN		GRZZZZUSA	DORNHEIM, GRETCHEN	26	F	UNKNOWN		GRZZZZUSA
ELSA	4	F	CHILD		GRZZZZUSA	JANCOHEN, FRIEDR.	29	M	MCHT		GRZZZZUSA
STEINERT, FRIEDR.	44	M	TLR		GRZZZZUSA	JAUDER, LUDW.	14	M	MCHT		GRZZZZUSA
WIORKOWSKA, MARYANNA	24	F	UNKNOWN		GRZZZZUSA	SCHROEDER, MATH.	40	M	FARMER		GRZZZZUSA
MONKA	3	F	CHILD		GRZZZZUSA	PHILIPP, BERNH.	18	M	PNTR		GRZZZZUSA
ANDRAS	.10	M	INFANT		GRZZZZUSA	BOETTCHER, LOUISE	17	F	PNTR		GRZZZZUSA
JABONISKI, JOSEPH	28	M	LABR		GRZZZZUSA	STAHL, GEORG	30	M	FARMER		GRZZZZUSA
MORUNDE, HERM.	24	M	LABR		GRZZZZUSA	EHRLICH, LEOP.	25	M	FARMER		GRZZZZUSA
ROISER, JULIUS	21	M	PNTR		GRZZZZUSA	SCHAAF, JOS.	28	M	FARMER		GRZZZZUSA
RASCHER, SIMON	18	M	PNTR		GRZZZZUSA	TENNEKEIT, SOPHIE	26	F	FARMER		GRZZZZUSA
HELNHOFER, JOSEF	17	M	BRR		GRZZZZUSA	HOENIG, M.	49	M	FARMER		GRZZZZUSA
HEINDEL, GEORG	28	M	MCHT		GRZZZZUSA	PFISTER, FRIEDERIKE	25	F	UNKNOWN		GRZZZZUSA
FLEISCHMAN, BARBARA	27	F	UNKNOWN		GRZZZZUSA	KNOFF, CATH	28	F	UNKNOWN		GRZZZZUSA
JABLEWSKI, FRANZ	20	M	TLR		GRZZZZUSA	FRANKE, ARMIN	24	M	MCHT		GRZZZZUSA
STUDAMSKI, JOSEF	28	M	CPTR		GRZZZZUSA	REINBARDT, GEORG	19	M	MCHT		GRZZZZUSA
BUSZER, JOH.	19	M	FARMER		GRZZZZUSA	BRATZ, GEORG	19	M	MCHT		GRZZZZUSA
CARL	16	M	FARMER		GRZZZZUSA	NEUWILLER, ERNST	66	M	PNTR		GRZZZZUSA
U, U	25	M	HTR		GRZZZZUSA	MUETZEL, JOH.	40	M	LABR		GRZZZZUSA
EICKERLING, WILH.	23	F	SMSTS		GRZZZZUSA	CHRISTINE	40	F	W		GRZZZZUSA
MATTES, WILH.	26	M	TLR		GRZZZZUSA	BARBARA	11	F	UNKNOWN		GRZZZZUSA
HORST, CONRAD	38	M	LABR		GRZZZZUSA	MARGARETHE	9	F	CHILD		GRZZZZUSA
MARGAR.	29	F	W		GRZZZZUSA	KARL	6	M	CHILD		GRZZZZUSA
HEINR.	11	M	UNKNOWN		GRZZZZUSA	MICHAEL	.09	M	INFANT		GRZZZZUSA
MARIA	8	F	CHILD		GRZZZZUSA	PIVANTKOWSKY, AUG.	36	M	FARMER		GRZZZZUSA
ELISA	3	F	CHILD		GRZZZZUSA	SCHIEMER, MATHIAS	24	M	BRR		GRZZZZUSA
ELISAB.	.11	F	INFANT		GRZZZZUSA	KUEHNE, DORA	23	F	UNKNOWN		GRZZZZUSA
SCHNEIDMUELLER, HERM.	17	M	SMH		GRZZZZUSA	KILBIS, JOSEF	19	M	LABR		GRZZZZUSA
WOLTERS, JACOB	19	M	LABR		GRZZZZUSA	ROSENBLUM, SORE	22	F	UNKNOWN		GRZZZZUSA
PETER	17	M	LABR		GRZZZZUSA	STINAR, THOMAS	15	M	LABR		GRZZZZUSA
STEGMAIER, HENRI	26	M	TLR		GRZZZZUSA	LUEBBING, WILH.	17	F	UNKNOWN		GRZZZZUSA
HERZBERG, FRIEDI	28	M	FARMER		GRZZZZUSA	FRITZSCHE, LOUIS	29	M	FARMER		GRZZZZUSA
ANTONIA	20	F	W		GRZZZZUSA	BAUMANN, JACOB	36	M	FARMER		GRZZZZUSA
MARIA	00	F	UNKNOWN		GRZZZZUSA	CHRISTINE	29	F	W		GRZZZZUSA
GROSS, -LB.	25	M	CPR		GRZZZZUSA	MEIER, CICHEL	33	M	FARMER		GRZZZZUSA
PANKRATZ, MART.	17	M	MLR		GRZZZZUSA	WILHELM, KATHAR.	25	F	UNKNOWN		GRZZZZUSA
HUNGER, EMIL	21	M	BKR		GRZZZZUSA	LITZ, PAUL	22	M	FARMER		GRZZZZUSA
ROWINSKA, VALERIE	24	F	UNKNOWN		GRZZZZUSA	SUSANNE	22	F	W		GRZZZZUSA
BRONISLAWA	2	F	CHILD		GRZZZZUSA	BERTHA	11	F	UNKNOWN		GRZZZZUSA
JOSEFA	.06	F	INFANT		GRZZZZUSA	ALBERT	11	M	UNKNOWN		GRZZZZUSA
MAERKEL, ELISAB.	17	F	UNKNOWN		GRZZZZUSA	FRANCISKA	9	F	CHILD		GRZZZZUSA
WALLERT, APOLLONIA	19	F	UNKNOWN		GRZZZZUSA	JOHANNAS	7	M	CHILD		GRZZZZUSA
HASSOLD, MARGAR.	19	F	UNKNOWN		GRZZZZUSA	ANNA	5	F	CHILD		GRZZZZUSA
TRAUTMANN, MART.	27	M	LABR		GRZZZZUSA	AGILKA	.09	F	INFANT		GRZZZZUSA
HEIN, IGNATZ	24	M	BCHR		GRZZZZUSA	CUSENAUER, JEAN	21	M	PNTR		GRZZZZUSA
MAUEJEWSKA, MICH.	21	F	UNKNOWN		GRZZZZUSA	WEBER, JOSEF	21	M	CPTR		GRZZZZUSA
IMBIROWSKI, MICH.	53	M	FARMER		GRZZZZUSA	MASONIG, FRITZ	26	M	CPTR		GRZZZZUSA
KATHAR.	40	F	W		GRZZZZUSA	KUFFNER, FRIEDR.	27	M	LABR		GRZZZZUSA
ATON	9	M	CHILD		GRZZZZUSA	HARTMANN, HEINR.	41	M	LABR		GRZZZZUSA
MARIANNE	6	F	CHILD		GRZZZZUSA	SEIFER, LOUISE	23	F	UNKNOWN		GRZZZZUSA
ANNA	3	F	CHILD		GRZZZZUSA						
FEHR, HEINR.	16	M	PNTR		GRZZZZUSA						
WOLSKI, ANNA	24	F	SVNT		GRZZZZUSA						
VOSS, EMMA	54	F	UNKNOWN		GRZZZZUSA						
KOEHLER, LOUISE	43	F	UNKNOWN		GRZZZZUSA						
ELLA	15	F	UNKNOWN		GRZZZZUSA						
MARTHA	9	F	CHILD		GRZZZZUSA						
LUCY	7	F	CHILD		GRZZZZUSA						
HINTZ, ANNA	26	F	SMSTS		GRZZZZUSA						
SKWIERTZ, PAUL	29	M	MCHT		GRZZZZUSA						
SEWING, WILH.	17	M	ENGR		GRZZZZUSA						

PASSENGER	AGE	SEX	OCCUPATION	PRIVL	DES
SHIP: LEERDAM					
FROM: ROTTERDAM					
TO: NEW YORK					
ARRIVED: 10 JULY 1888					
WALLNACH, JOHN	00	M	MCHT	GRZZZZUSA	
HORVATH, E	00	M	MCHT	GRZZZZUSA	
HEIFLER, L	00	M	MCHT	GRZZZZUSA	
B-RY, ADE-	00	M	MCHT	GRZZZZUSA	
BU-ER, R	00	M	MCHT	GRZZZZUSA	
GROBE, DORA	00	F	NN	GRZZZZUSA	
HAADE, G	00	M	MCHT	GRZZZZUSA	
SAMMEROCH, JAC	00	M	CPTR	GRZZZZUSA	
FRITSCHE, R	00	M	CPTR	GRZZZZUSA	
NETZ, HENRY	00	M	MCHT	GRZZZZUSA	
DAR-FUSS, BAB	00	F	NN	GRZZZZUSA	
B	00	F	NN	GRZZZZUSA	
FRITSCHE, M	00	F	NN	GRZZZZUSA	
RICHERS, L	00	M	LABR	GRZZZZUSA	
-ERE, GAB	00	F	NN	FRZZZZUSA	
BAHRENBACH, M	25	M	LABR	GRZZZZUSA	
EICHER, P	18	M	LABR	GRZZZZUSA	
HENGEL, CARL	18	M	LABR	GRZZZZUSA	
--OUCH, WILH	17	M	LABR	GRZZZZUSA	
KOPPERSCHMID, F	22	M	LABR	GRZZZZUSA	
RATTINER, D	34	M	LABR	GRZZZZUSA	
HABL--REL, JOH	31	M	LABR	FRZZZZUSA	
OLIVIER, JAN	27	M	LABR	FRZZZZUSA	
KREER, ANNA	24	F	SVNT	GRZZZZUSA	
RITSCHELE, CHRIST	22	F	SVNT	GRZZZZUSA	
HENKELMAN, ELIS	22	F	SVNT	GRZZZZUSA	
MACHE, SAM	47	M	FARMER	GRZZZZUSA	
ESTH	16	F	FARMER	GRZZZZUSA	
WIELAND, WILH	25	M	FARMER	GRZZZZUSA	
GOTTL	22	M	FARMER	GRZZZZUSA	
U	13	M	FARMER	GRZZZZUSA	
WOHLFAHR-, MARIE	21	F	SVNT	GRZZZZUSA	
EISERMANN, GOTTL	16	M	FARMER	GRZZZZUSA	
RACH	18	F	NN	GRZZZZUSA	
-ATZINA, ADOL	33	M	FARMER	GRZZZZUSA	
EILCHEN	28	M	FARMER	GRZZZZUSA	
ARNOLD	9	M	CHILD	GRZZZZUSA	
VICTOR	6	M	CHILD	GRZZZZUSA	
EDITH	4	F	CHILD	GRZZZZUSA	
ERICH	2	F	CHILD	GRZZZZUSA	
ORCHOLSKA, MAY	22	F	NN	GRZZZZUSA	
MARY	2	F	CHILD	GRZZZZUSA	
HIRSCHEL, ROSA	20	F	NN	GRZZZZUSA	
MITTENZWE-, EMIL	39	F	SMSTS	GRZZZZUSA	
HOEREGOTT, CARLO	39	M	FARMER	GRZZZZUSA	
LUIK, CHRIST	28	F	FARMER	GRZZZZUSA	
OTTO	3	M	CHILD	GRZZZZUSA	
GEORG	.06	M	INFANT	GRZZZZUSA	
LECHORO-TSKY, SALOM	30	M	FARMER	GRZZZZUSA	
SCHMITZ, TEOD	22	M	FARMER	GRZZZZUSA	
ROSENFELD, LUDW	26	M	FARMER	GRZZZZUSA	
VINZ, ANTON	18	M	FARMER	GRZZZZUSA	
HERSCHE, ANTON	43	M	FARMER	GRZZZZUSA	
VOTSKY, JOHANN	18	M	FARMER	GRZZZZUSA	
MEICHEL, -ER-O	18	M	FARMER	GRZZZZUSA	
URIC, DOLF	27	M	FARMER	GRZZZZUSA	
LANG, MART	58	M	FARMER	GRZZZZUSA	
A	58	F	FARMER	GRZZZZUSA	
SCHMIDT, CARL	19	M	FARMER	GRZZZZUSA	
BERENDS, W	29	M	FARMER	GRZZZZUSA	
SCHMIDT, EM	26	M	FARMER	GRZZZZUSA	
HOVIG, GEORG	17	M	LABR	GRZZZZUSA	
-ACH, U	19	M	SEMN	GRZZZZUSA	
HACHE, JOS	18	M	LABR	GRZZZZUSA	
BAUMEISTER, M	28	M	BKR	GRZZZZUSA	
WAGNER, ADAM	28	M	BKR	GRZZZZUSA	
HOLTLEISTER, JOH	26	M	BKR	GRZZZZUSA	
BAUMEISTER, E	24	F	BKR	GRZZZZUSA	
SCHMITZ, PETER	29	M	LABR	GRZZZZUSA	
ROEPF, MARIE	20	F	LABR	GRZZZZUSA	
HAUSLER, MARIE	19	F	LABR	GRZZZZUSA	
CATH	17	F	LABR	GRZZZZUSA	
ROERNER, H	20	F	LABR	GRZZZZUSA	
WIEDERMANN, M	20	F	LABR	GRZZZZUSA	
S-IGMANN, R	17	M	LABR	GRZZZZUSA	
GROSS, WILH	22	M	LABR	GRZZZZUSA	
SCHNEIDER, EMMA	17	F	LABR	GRZZZZUSA	
MUELLER, DORA	26	F	LABR	GRZZZZUSA	
SCHULTE, ANNA	20	F	LABR	GRZZZZUSA	
DANIEL, ABRAH	23	M	LABR	GRZZZZUSA	
SCHNEIDER, BAB	22	M	LABR	GRZZZZUSA	
KORUPSKY, LUDW	20	M	LABR	GRZZZZUSA	
STEGMUELLER, FRIED	25	M	LABR	GRZZZZUSA	
KONITZER, REINH	23	M	LABR	GRZZZZUSA	
STEGMUELLER, JOH	39	F	NN	GRZZZZUSA	
-IDDE, RICH	22	M	NN	GRZZZZUSA	
SPORING, WILH	23	M	NN	GRZZZZUSA	
HIRSCHFELD, -SIAS	30	M	NN	GRZZZZUSA	
MORSCH, ABRAH	24	M	NN	GRZZZZUSA	
MUELLER, HEINR	56	M	NN	GRZZZZUSA	
EMIL	18	F	NN	GRZZZZUSA	
EUGEN	8	M	CHILD	GRZZZZUSA	
BULLING, GOTT	16	M	LABR	GRZZZZUSA	
ELSINGER, FRIED	16	M	LABR	GRZZZZUSA	
KIEFER, GEORG	20	M	LABR	GRZZZZUSA	
BOEHRINGER, CARL	30	M	LABR	GRZZZZUSA	
SHEASER, CHRIST	21	M	LABR	GRZZZZUSA	
EISLER, ROSA	24	F	LABR	GRZZZZUSA	
LORENZEN, FR	29	M	LABR	GRZZZZUSA	
BADER, ROS	19	F	LABR	GRZZZZUSA	
MUELLER, KATH	20	F	LABR	GRZZZZUSA	
GROSSMANN, LAN	20	M	LABR	GRZZZZUSA	
KOSLOWSKY, MARIE	18	F	LABR	GRZZZZUSA	
GARTIN, PAUL	23	F	LABR	GRZZZZUSA	
-RYDIES, U	17	M	LABR	GRZZZZUSA	
KLEMER, EL	37	M	LABR	GRZZZZUSA	
WEISE, HERM	23	M	LABR	GRZZZZUSA	
SPAI, NACH	19	M	LABR	GRZZZZUSA	
DOEGGE, CARL	29	M	LABR	GRZZZZUSA	
HANNA	20	F	LABR	GRZZZZUSA	
GUSTAV	22	M	LABR	GRZZZZUSA	
SCHOENBRUEN, ROSA	40	F	LABR	GRZZZZUSA	
RANCORZINI, ANGELO	28	M	MCHT	FRZZZZUSA	
NICOLAS, RIZIA	32	F	MCHT	FRZZZZUSA	
THERESIA	32	F	MCHT	FRZZZZUSA	
ANLOINE, SOAVE	24	M	MCHT	FRZZZZUSA	
MARIE	27	F	MCHT	FRZZZZUSA	
BERNARDO, GENISIO	22	M	MCHT	FRZZZZUSA	
-ELORO, ANTONIO	28	M	MCHT	FRZZZZUSA	
HALUB, LINDA	29	F	NN	FRZZZZUSA	
-UKO	8	M	CHILD	FRZZZZUSA	
RICHARD	.01	M	INFANT	FRZZZZUSA	
FRANZ	1	M	CHILD	FRZZZZUSA	
WILLIE	.06	M	INFANT	FRZZZZUSA	
MASEIULLE, DOM	40	M	MCHT	FRZZZZUSA	
MONTANA, ANT	18	M	MCHT	FRZZZZUSA	
ZIESEL, EUG	22	M	LABR	GRZZZZUSA	
SCHERMER, ANNA	23	F	LABR	GRZZZZUSA	
SCHINDLER, FRANZ	28	M	SEMN	GRZZZZUSA	
PRIEMER, GEORG	21	M	WTR	GRZZZZUSA	

PASSENGER	AGE	SEX	OCCUPATION	PRVL	DES

SHIP: CASPIAN

FROM: LIVERPOOL
TO: BALTIMORE
ARRIVED: 11 JULY 1888

PASSENGER	AGE	SEX	OCCUPATION	PRVL	DES
WAGNER, JULIA	19	F	DMS		GRZZZZCLE
POTEK, DWUE	30	F	W		GRZZZZCLE
BONI	9	M	CHILD		GRZZZZCLE
CARRI	4	F	CHILD		GRZZZZCLE
RONI	4	M	CHILD		GRZZZZCLE
JACOB	3	M	CHILD		GRZZZZCLE
JESSIE	.08	F	INFANT		GRZZZZCLE
FREIMAN, ANNA	20	F	DMS		GRZZZZCLE
GUNTER, KALHARMA	19	F	UNKNOWN		GRZZZZCLE

SHIP: IOWA

FROM: LIVERPOOL
TO: BOSTON
ARRIVED: 11 JULY 1888

PASSENGER	AGE	SEX	OCCUPATION	PRVL	DES
BARENHOLZ, BV.	22	F	SP		GRZZZZUSA
CHARLOTTE, WALKER	27	F	SP		GRZZZZUSA
HORN, KARL	32	M	CPTR		GRZZZZUSA
HERDAN, RES.	24	M	MRNR		FRZZZZUSA
BERGER, RICHARD	27	M	CBTMKR		GRZZZZUSA

SHIP: MAIN

FROM: BREMEN
TO: BALTIMORE
ARRIVED: 12 JULY 1888

PASSENGER	AGE	SEX	OCCUPATION	PRVL	DES
CAMMANN, G.	18	F	TT		GRZZZZUNK
HEYDEMANN, FLORA	33	F	TT		GRZZZZUNK
EMMI	22	F	UNKNOWN		GRZZZZUNK
RIEDEBURG, MATHILDE	19	F	UNKNOWN		GRZZZZUNK
WERNSING, HERM.	45	M	UNKNOWN		GRZZZZUNK
BERGMANN, FRANZ	21	M	SVNT		GRZZZZBAL
KNABLER, WLH.	8	M	CHILD		GRZZZZBAL
BETHGE, DIEDR.	40	M	FARMER		GRZZZZBAL
SALADIN, JOSEF	26	M	WCHMKR		SRZZZZBAL
SINTEK, JOSEF	61	M	FARMER		GRZZZZBAL
LUDWIG	24	M	TLR		GRZZZZBAL
KUENTZ, HERM.	25	M	FUR		GRZZZZBAL
BAYER, JOHANN	17	M	FUR		GRZZZZBAL
BAIER, FRANZ	25	M	SHMK		GRZZZZBAL
PFEIFFER, KARL	42	M	BRR		GRZZZZBAL
PRIEM, ALBERT	30	M	LABR		GRZZZZBAL
KROLL, KASMIR	18	M	LABR		GRZZZZBAL
ARNSWALD, FRANZ	16	M	LABR		GRZZZZBAL
SCHINITZKI, CARL	29	M	FARMER		GRZZZZBAL
MUZIKOWSKI, FRANZ	23	M	FARMER		GRZZZZBAL
KAMPA, AUGUST	15	M	FARMER		GRZZZZBAL
MAERTL, JOSEF	18	M	FARMER		GRZZZZBAL
LEWENDOFSKI, JOSEF	21	M	FARMER		GRZZZZBAL
DALKE, ALBERT	17	M	FARMER		GRZZZZBAL
KEMMITZER, HEINR.	19	M	FARMER		GRZZZZBAL
WINTER, AUGUST	46	M	BRR		GRZZZZBAL
WAELKE, JULIUS	25	M	MLR		GRZZZZBAL
LUEDTKE, HERM.	29	M	MLR		GRZZZZBAL
VICK, JOHN	22	M	FARMER		GRZZZZMN
JORDAN, CARL	47	M	GZR		GRZZZZIL
VOIT, JOHANN	28	M	GZR		GRZZZZIL
MUELLER, JULIUS	36	M	GZR		GRZZZZMI
OBST, AUGUST	39	M	BKLYR		GRZZZZMN
BAYER, CARL	21	M	JNR		GRZZZZKY
KRAPF, LUDWIG	14	M	FARMER		GRZZZZBAL
VOELKER, JOSEPH	38	M	FARMER		GRZZZZBAL
OLENBACH, LEOPOLD	46	M	FARMER		GRZZZZBAL
STOCK, HERM.	26	M	FARMER		GRZZZZBAL
FLORCZAK, STANISLAUS	18	M	FARMER		GRZZZZBAL
MIKOLAICZAK, JAN	38	M	FARMER		GRZZZZBAL
JAST, JACOB	16	M	LABR		GRZZZZBAL
WENNISCHNER, LEIB	17	M	LABR		GRZZZZBAL
LITWINSKY, JAN	17	M	LABR		GRZZZZBAL
ARNDT, ANDREAS	24	M	LABR		GRZZZZMN
HORAK, WENZL	27	M	BRZ		GRZZZZBAL
KOEHNLEIN, JOHANN	17	M	TLR		GRZZZZBAL
FEIGE, AUGUST	25	M	PNTR		GRZZZZBAL
KAMPIEWSKY, SENIOR	27	M	LABR		GRZZZZBAL
KRUEGER, EDUARD	57	M	LABR		GRZZZZBAL
AICHELE, KONRAD	27	M	LABR		GRZZZZBAL
HARTMANN, PAUL	18	M	WVR		GRZZZZBAL
VAGES, ADOLPH	26	M	LABR		GRZZZZBAL
DAMRAU, CARL	25	M	LABR		GRZZZZBAL
FAHL, EMIL	22	M	LABR		GRZZZZBAL
DEUBER, SEBAST.	27	M	SDLR		GRZZZZBAL
HAHNENFELDER, GOTTFR.	10	M	CH		GRZZZZBAL
ZIMMERER, JOH.	27	M	FARMER		GRZZZZBAL
KRELLER, JOH.	25	M	FARMER		GRZZZZBAL
IGELINSKI, THEODOR	24	M	FARMER		GRZZZZBAL
RETZLAFFE, THEODOR	21	M	FARMER		GRZZZZBAL
HACHALSKI, KAZIMIR	26	M	FARMER		GRZZZZBAL
RINDERHAGEN, GUSTAV	15	M	FARMER		GRZZZZBAL
SCHMIDT, FRANZ	24	M	FARMER		GRZZZZBAL
BRANDT, CARL	25	M	TU		GRZZZZBAL
HORSCHIK, ANTON	15	M	TU		GRZZZZBAL
GRODMANN, IDEL	17	M	FARMER		GRZZZZBAL
GOEBEL, AUGUST	16	M	FARMER		GRZZZZBAL
ENGELBACH, AUGUST	18	M	FARMER		GRZZZZBAL
SCHMIDT, HEINR.	18	M	FARMER		GRZZZZBAL
MUTH, CARL	18	M	FARMER		GRZZZZBAL
UKOWSKI, JOSEF	21	M	LABR		GRZZZZBAL
SCHATTENKIRCHNER, MICH.	26	M	BKR		GRZZZZPA
HUEBEL, JOHANN	15	M	BKR		GRZZZZOH
BUCHNER, JULIUS	24	M	WVR		GRZZZZBAL
DEY, FRIEDR.	25	M	FARMER		GRZZZZMI
WEISS, JOHANN	22	M	FARMER		GRZZZZMI
RAPPAPORT, SALOMON	40	M	FARMER		GRZZZZMN
HUNEL, THEODOR	35	M	BKR		GRZZZZMN
GERTZEJANSSEN, HEINR.	22	M	FARMER		GRZZZZBAL
SCHWEIGEL, CARL	25	M	FARMER		GRZZZZBAL
STOEGBAUER, PETRON	24	M	FARMER		GRZZZZBAL
SOCK, THOMAS	20	M	FARMER		GRZZZZBAL
KOVARIK, FRANZ	21	M	FARMER		GRZZZZOH
CIEPLIK, JOSEF	25	M	SHMK		GRZZZZOH
KAZWACKI, S.	29	M	SHMK		GRZZZZOH
MAEDER, CHRISTIAN	15	M	BCHR		GRZZZZVA
EHRENBERG, WILH.	15	M	BCHR		GRZZZZVA
JENSEN, NICOLAUS	20	M	MCHT		GRZZZZNE
KOERNER, WILHELM	27	M	MCHT		GRZZZZIL
GLOWACKY, IGNATZ	37	M	FARMER		GRZZZZPA
SAMMER, CHRISTIAN	22	M	FARMER		GRZZZZUNK
TEWS, AUGUST	41	M	FARMER		GRZZZZOH
FREUND, ADOLF	30	M	FARMER		GRZZZZWI
SIEKMANN, LUDWIG	36	M	TNM		GRZZZZOH
BEHRENSWORTH, HEINR.	30	M	LABR		GRZZZZOH
HAGL, OTTO	30	M	BRR		GRZZZZIL
KELLER, AUG.	25	M	FARMER		GRZZZZIL
GENGNAGEL, CARL	15	M	FARMER		GRZZZZIL
GUTMANN, OSCAR	17	M	FARMER		GRZZZZIL
JASCHINSKI, JOH.	18	M	FUR		GRZZZZIL
GILSTER, HEINR.	17	M	FARMER		GRZZZZIL
SCHMIDT, WILH.	17	M	FARMER		GRZZZZIL
REUTER, JOHANN	16	M	FARMER		GRZZZZIL
BALDRUSCHAD, CARL	22	M	FARMER		GRZZZZIL
BOSCHARD, EDUARD	38	M	FARMER		GRZZZZIL

PASSENGER	AGE	SEX	OCCUPATION	PRVL / DES
SCHRADE, THADAEUS	32	M	FARMER	GRZZZZIL
HELLGOTH, NMARGARETHE	18	F	SVNT	GRZZZZBAL
BRANDT, BABETTE	33	F	W	GRZZZZBAL
FORSTER, MATHILDE	29	F	SVNT	GRZZZZBAL
NISSLBECK, MARIA	21	F	SVNT	GRZZZZBAL
GEISE, ALMA	20	F	SVNT	GRZZZZBAL
SCHLAF, BARBARA	20	F	SVNT	GRZZZZBAL
GABRICH, ZUZANNA	17	F	SVNT	GRZZZZBAL
JARZENBINSKI, MARIANNA	25	F	W	GRZZZZBAL
TURSKA, LUDWIGA	19	F	SVNT	GRZZZZBAL
POZORSKA, MARIANNA	30	F	W	GRZZZZBAL
SAVARIA	.01	F	INFANT	GRZZZZBAL
FORCKE, AGNES	49	F	W	GRZZZZBAL
HEDWIG	6	F	CHILD	GRZZZZBAL
GOSOROWSKI, MARIA	22	F	SVNT	GRZZZZBAL
JACOBUS, CAROLINE	25	F	SVNT	GRZZZZBAL
JOHN, EMMA	29	F	W	GRZZZZBAL
CHELEWSKA, MICHALINA	18	F	SVNT	GRZZZZBAL
SMOLINSKA, ANTONIA	18	F	SVNT	GRZZZZBAL
GROSS, WILH.	20	F	W	GRZZZZBAL
BEYL, JUSTINE	52	F	W	GRZZZZBAL
ALSCHESCHKY, CAROLINE	27	F	UNKNOWN	GRZZZZBAL
FALKOWSKY, BERTHA	15	F	SVNT	GRZZZZBAL
YOHN, BERTHA	26	F	W	GRZZZZBAL
RICHARD	.11	M	INFANT	GRZZZZBAL
EBERT, BERTHA	25	F	SVNT	GRZZZZBAL
LAWRENZ, EMILIE	22	F	SVNT	GRZZZZBAL
LEISTEKOW, CHARLOTTE	65	F	W	GRZZZZBAL
BAIER, KAROLINE	62	F	W	GRZZZZBAL
REHWINKEL, WILH.	31	F	W	GRZZZZBAL
U	3	F	CHILD	GRZZZZBAL
KUEBISIAK, KATERZYNA	30	F	W	GRZZZZBAL
VERONIKA	20	F	W	GRZZZZBAL
JOSEF	2	M	CHILD	GRZZZZBAL
MICHAEL	.01	M	INFANT	GRZZZZBAL
LEON	.01	M	INFANT	GRZZZZBAL
KLOSS, ANNA	50	F	W	GRZZZZBAL
WINTER, ELISE	16	F	SVNT	GRZZZZIL
OEHLSCHLAEGER, AMALIA	62	F	W	GRZZZZIL
AUGUSTE	32	F	W	GRZZZZIL
ANNA	22	F	D	GRZZZZIL
NOWAK, MARIANNE	34	F	W	GRZZZZIL
AGNES	16	F	SVNT	GRZZZZIL
STEPHAN	1	M	CHILD	GRZZZZIL
REHWINKEL, AUGUSTE	30	F	W	GRZZZZWI
BERTHA	.11	F	INFANT	GRZZZZWI
FRIEDRICH, AUGUUSTE	19	F	SVNT	GRZZZZIL
FENSKE, AUUGSTE	19	F	SVNT	GRZZZZIL
BORGES, HELENE	30	F	W	GRZZZZMO
HELENE	7	F	CHILD	GRZZZZMO
KURT	3	M	CHILD	GRZZZZMO
BAAKS, AGATHE	28	F	W	GRZZZZIA
HERM.	4	M	CHILD	GRZZZZIA
LABIG, MICHALINE	17	F	SVNT	GRZZZZBAL
STASTNY, ANNIE	21	F	SVNT	GRZZZZBAL
KRAMER, MINA	28	F	SVNT	GRZZZZBAL
LEY, ALMINA	25	F	W	GRZZZZBAL
HINRIKA	.11	F	INFANT	GRZZZZBAL
STUEMPF, MARGARETHA	21	F	W	GRZZZZBAL
KUNIGUNDE	.09	F	INFANT	GRZZZZBAL
ROHN, MARG.	18	F	SVNT	GRZZZZBAL
WISNIEWSKA, THEOPHILA	22	F	SVNT	GRZZZZBAL
WETZEL, PAULINE	18	F	SVNT	GRZZZZBAL
BILITZKA, VALENTINE	15	F	SVNT	GRZZZZBAL
ZARUL, CAROLINE	14	F	SVNT	GRZZZZBAL
BUSSE, EMILIE	18	F	SVNT	GRZZZZBAL
SCHERF, FRIEDERIKE	31	F	W	GRZZZZBAL
MARTHA	7	F	CHILD	GRZZZZBAL
LUTZ, ANNA	25	F	W	GRZZZZBAL
STENGLEIN, EVA	18	F	SVNT	GRZZZZBAL
FUNK, MARTHA	22	F	SVNT	GRZZZZBAL
KALM, BABETTE	22	F	SVNT	GRZZZZBAL
RADEMACHER, MINNA	21	F	SVNT	GRZZZZBAL
NUSSBAUM, BABETTE	51	F	W	GRZZZZBAL
ANNA	16	F	D	GRZZZZBAL
PAULINE	22	F	D	GRZZZZBAL
ISAAC	12	F	CH	GRZZZZBAL
KAUFMANN, AUGUSTE	16	F	SVNT	GRZZZZBAL
STANDTINGEN, JOH.	20	F	SVNT	GRZZZZBAL
HESSINGER, LINA	17	F	SVNT	GRZZZZBAL
KUSTER, GERTRUDE	21	F	SVNT	GRZZZZBAL
KIRMSE, BERTHA	23	F	SVNT	GRZZZZBAL
FOLKMANN, NETI	23	F	SVNT	GRZZZZBAL
ZERNAJAN, AUGUSTE	21	F	SVNT	GRZZZZBAL
VITSOCH, PELAGIA	19	F	SVNT	GRZZZZBAL
SEPKOWIAK, JULIANE	38	F	W	GRZZZZBAL
KOCH, KATHARIANA	17	F	SVNT	GRZZZZBAL
MENSEL, APOLLONIA	21	F	SVNT	GRZZZZBAL
DIECKMANN, ANNA	20	F	SVNT	GRZZZZBAL
MOHRIN, ANNA	21	F	UNKNOWN	GRZZZZIL
LEWANDOWSKA, MARIANNA	26	F	SVNT	GRZZZZMI
SCHLAF, ANNA	18	F	SVNT	GRZZZZIL
BASEL, CAROLINA	18	F	SVNT	GRZZZZBAL
BARTH, MARG.	18	F	SVNT	GRZZZZPA
LANG, MARG.	20	F	SVNT	GRZZZZMN
GRAHEL, AGNES	20	F	SVNT	GRZZZZWI
WAGNER, ANNA	21	F	SVNT	GRZZZZWI
JUNGWIRTH, ANNA	16	F	SVNT	GRZZZZBAL
BERANEK, MARG.	22	F	W	GRZZZZNE
KREMEL, CARL	8	M	CHILD	GRZZZZNE
MARIA	.10	F	INFANT	GRZZZZNE
MARTIN, HENRIETTE	20	F	SVNT	GRZZZZMI
AUGUSTE	30	F	W	GRZZZZMI
WOISKE, LOUISE	59	F	W	GRZZZZMI
PANEK, IDA	17	F	SVNT	GRZZZZMI
JOHANN	3	M	CHILD	GRZZZZMI
WIESNER, JULIE	20	F	SVNT	GRZZZZMI
HEIN, MARIE	29	F	SVNT	GRZZZZKS
KAPLAN, ANNA	21	F	SVNT	GRZZZZBAL
FRANZISKA	21	F	SVNT	GRZZZZBAL
KROLAK, STANISLAWA	20	F	W	GRZZZZUNK
ERWIGA	.06	F	INFANT	GRZZZZUNK
BUBERT, WILH.	36	F	W	GRZZZZMI
OTTO	6	M	CHILD	GRZZZZMI
DEYKE, OTTILIE	20	F	SVNT	GRZZZZMI
GOLOMBIEWSKI, ANNA	45	F	W	GRZZZZKS
WIESNIEWSKA, ANGELICA	21	F	SVNT	GRZZZZIL
TAMASCHINSKI, ADOLPHINE	20	F	SVNT	GRZZZZPA
GEBHARDT, MARIA	31	F	W	GRZZZZOH
JANKOWSKA, THEKLA	22	F	SVNT	GRZZZZWI
HAGEDORN, ANNA	19	F	SVNT	GRZZZZPA
LEIPOLD, BARB.	23	F	SVNT	GRZZZZIL
SALLER, ANNA	29	F	W	GRZZZZBAL
ANNA	2	F	CHILD	GRZZZZBAL
ROSINA	.10	F	INFANT	GRZZZZBAL
SCHMIDT, PAULA	23	F	W	GRZZZZMO
WALTER	.03	M	INFANT	GRZZZZMO
BRANDT, ANNA	35	F	W	GRZZZZMO
CLARA	6	F	CHILD	GRZZZZMO
TRUMPF, ANNA	31	F	W	GRZZZZMO
KUTZKA, LOUISE	18	F	SVNT	GRZZZZMO
MARGOLINER, AUGUSTE	19	F	SVNT	GRZZZZMO
ROBBERT, SOPHIE	20	F	SVNT	GRZZZZMO
VOIGT, LINA	18	F	SVNT	GRZZZZBAL
BARTELS, MARIA	21	F	SVNT	GRZZZZBAL
WITTE, LINA	15	F	SVNT	GRZZZZBAL
KRAUSE, LOUISE	48	F	W	GRZZZZBAL
CARL	11	M	CH	GRZZZZBAL
NAGEL, LOUISE	27	F	W	GRZZZZBAL
ROSENTHAL, ADELHEID	43	F	SVNT	GRZZZZBAL
ROLEWICZ, MARIANNA	17	F	SVNT	GRZZZZBAL
FROUCKOWIAK, FRANZISKA	27	F	W	GRZZZZBAL
THOZINSKY, MAXMIL	28	M	MCHT	GRZZZZBAL
EMILIE	20	F	W	GRZZZZBAL
BECK, ELISABETH	43	F	W	GRZZZZBAL
WENZEL	16	M	FARMER	GRZZZZBAL
FRANZ	10	M	CH	GRZZZZBAL
MARIA	7	F	CHILD	GRZZZZBAL
MODRZEWSKA, AUGUSTINE	44	F	W	GRZZZZBAL
MARG.	11	F	CH	GRZZZZBAL

PASSENGER	AGE	SEX	OCCUPATION	PRVL	DES
JOHANN	6	M	CHILD	GRZZZZBAL	
PAULINE	3	F	CHILD	GRZZZZBAL	
UKERT, WILHELM	23	M	FARMER	GRZZZZBAL	
EMMA	17	F	W	GRZZZZBAL	
SCHMIDT, AUGUST	57	M	SMH	GRZZZZBAL	
RIEKE	53	F	W	GRZZZZBAL	
RIEKE	19	F	D	GRZZZZBAL	
SCHOENFELD, PELAGIA	33	F	W	GRZZZZBAL	
STANISLAW	10	M	CH	GRZZZZBAL	
FLORINA	8	F	CHILD	GRZZZZBAL	
CLEMENTINA	6	F	CHILD	GRZZZZBAL	
LEONHART	3	M	CHILD	GRZZZZBAL	
CASIMIR	.09	M	INFANT	GRZZZZBAL	
HEINRIKOWSKI, FRANZ	17	M	FARMER	GRZZZZBAL	
LASER, JOHANN	38	M	FARMER	GRZZZZBAL	
CAROLINA	35	F	W	GRZZZZBAL	
REINHOLD	11	M	CH	GRZZZZBAL	
IDA	5	F	CHILD	GRZZZZBAL	
WITZKE, WILHELM	59	M	FARMER	GRZZZZBAL	
LINA	21	F	UNKNOWN	GRZZZZBAL	
BERTHA	18	F	UNKNOWN	GRZZZZBAL	
CAROLINA	58	F	W	GRZZZZBAL	
PAUL	3	M	CHILD	GRZZZZBAL	
KLEIST, GOTTL.	61	M	FARMER	GRZZZZBAL	
CAROLINA	57	F	W	GRZZZZBAL	
WILHELMINE	19	F	D	GRZZZZBAL	
BERTHA	4	F	CHILD	GRZZZZBAL	
PAWALSKA, WILHELMINE	30	F	W	GRZZZZBAL	
MARTIN	6	M	CHILD	GRZZZZBAL	
MARTHA	4	F	CHILD	GRZZZZBAL	
BRIGITTA	3	F	CHILD	GRZZZZBAL	
SEFELDT, WILH.	31	M	FARMER	GRZZZZBAL	
WILH.	26	F	W	GRZZZZBAL	
ELISABETH	4	F	CHILD	GRZZZZBAL	
ANNA	3	F	CHILD	GRZZZZBAL	
OTTO	.02	M	INFANT	GRZZZZBAL	
MAX	.02	M	INFANT	GRZZZZBAL	
KROLL, THOMAS	43	M	LABR	GRZZZZMI	
JUSTINE	43	F	W	GRZZZZMI	
AUGUSTE	16	F	D	GRZZZZMI	
CONRAD	14	M	LABR	GRZZZZMI	
RICHARD	11	M	CH	GRZZZZMI	
HEINRICH	9	M	CHILD	GRZZZZMI	
EMIL	7	M	CHILD	GRZZZZMI	
LOUISE	3	M	CHILD	GRZZZZMI	
MARIA	4	F	CHILD	GRZZZZMI	
SZUWARA, ANDR.	46	M	FARMER	GRZZZZIL	
FRANZISKA	66	F	W	GRZZZZIL	
MOLZAHN, FERDINAND	34	M	MCHT	GRZZZZWI	
MARIA	38	F	W	GRZZZZWI	
ANNA	7	F	CHILD	GRZZZZWI	
VOLESKA	22	F	CH	GRZZZZWI	
MARGARETHE	.11	F	INFANT	GRZZZZWI	
HELLER, CARL	32	M	LABR	GRZZZZWI	
HULDA	33	F	W	GRZZZZWI	
RAATZ, FRIEDR.	36	M	SHFM	GRZZZZIL	
HENRIETTE	33	F	W	GRZZZZIL	
IDA	8	F	CHILD	GRZZZZIL	
AUGUSTE	4	F	CHILD	GRZZZZIL	
ALWINE	2	F	CHILD	GRZZZZIL	
MARTHA	.06	F	INFANT	GRZZZZIL	
FEUSKE, MICHAEL	78	M	FARMER	GRZZZZIL	
JUSTINE	65	F	W	GRZZZZIL	
HAEGELE, HERM.	29	M	ART	GRZZZZKY	
CATHARINE	28	F	W	GRZZZZKY	
SCHOBER, AUGUST	27	M	PNTR	GRZZZZBAL	
KRATZ, BERENDT	50	M	BCHR	GRZZZZBAL	
ERNESTINE	16	F	SVNT	GRZZZZBAL	
ENGELE, CHRISTINE	27	F	W	GRZZZZBAL	
BECKER, TEOFIL	30	M	UNKNOWN	GRZZZZBAL	
CONSTANTIA	30	F	W	GRZZZZBAL	
STANISLAW	14	M	UNKNOWN	GRZZZZBAL	
BUDZUZ, ALEXANDER	27	M	FSHMN	GRZZZZBAL	
ANTON	.07	M	INFANT	GRZZZZBAL	
LECH, WILH.	33	M	LABR	GRZZZZBAL	
AUGUSTE	30	F	W	GRZZZZBAL	
MARY	.10	F	INFANT	GRZZZZBAL	
GUMPEL, HEINRICH	44	M	FARMER	GRZZZZBAL	
KATHARINA	31	F	W	GRZZZZBAL	
BICSIK, ZUZANNA	50	F	W	GRZZZZBAL	
IGNATZ	15	M	LABR	GRZZZZBAL	
FRANZ	11	M	CH	GRZZZZBAL	
KALEVA, FRIEDRICH	24	M	FARMER	GRZZZZBAL	
LOUISE	28	F	W	GRZZZZBAL	
ALBERT	2	M	CHILD	GRZZZZBAL	
FRIEDRICH	.06	M	INFANT	GRZZZZBAL	
SULEWSKI, FRANZ	35	M	TLR	GRZZZZBAL	
JULIANNE	36	F	W	GRZZZZBAL	
JOSEF	11	M	CH	GRZZZZBAL	
FRANZ	8	M	CHILD	GRZZZZBAL	
MARIA	7	F	CHILD	GRZZZZBAL	
JULIANNE	5	F	CHILD	GRZZZZBAL	
SCHULZ, JULIANNE	44	F	W	GRZZZZBAL	
ADOLF	48	M	JNR	GRZZZZBAL	
SARZOMKOWSKA, FRANZISKA	47	F	W	GRZZZZBAL	
GUSTAV	11	M	CH	GRZZZZBAL	
MARGR.	9	F	CHILD	GRZZZZBAL	
JANSSEN, MARIA	48	F	W	GRZZZZMN	
OTTO	15	M	LABR	GRZZZZMN	
WILHELM	11	M	CH	GRZZZZMN	
BETHGE, MARIE	32	F	W	GRZZZZBAL	
LINA	5	F	CHILD	GRZZZZBAL	
ANNA	3	F	CHILD	GRZZZZBAL	
EMMA	.11	F	INFANT	GRZZZZBAL	
DORA	.11	F	INFANT	GRZZZZBAL	
BERGMANN, CHARLOTTE	36	F	W	GRZZZZWI	
BERTHOLD	11	M	CH	GRZZZZWI	
FRITZ	9	M	CHILD	GRZZZZWI	
BERTHA	4	F	CHILD	GRZZZZWI	
HEINR.	.09	M	INFANT	GRZZZZWI	
HAENSLAIN, ELISAB.	46	F	W	GRZZZZMI	
SALOME	21	M	LABR	GRZZZZMI	
GEORG	8	M	CHILD	GRZZZZMI	
SCHMIDT, CARL	32	M	SHMK	GRZZZZBAL	
MARIA	27	F	W	GRZZZZBAL	
ELSA	7	F	CHILD	GRZZZZBAL	
AGNES	5	F	CHILD	GRZZZZBAL	
HELENE	.09	F	INFANT	GRZZZZBAL	
SCHNEIDER, HEINR.	48	M	LABR	GRZZZZIL	
MARIA	11	F	CH	GRZZZZIL	
LINA	4	F	CHILD	GRZZZZIL	
KUHLMANN, KATHARINE	50	F	W	GRZZZZNE	
SOPHIE	18	F	D	GRZZZZNE	
ANNA	16	F	D	GRZZZZNE	
MARIA	14	F	D	GRZZZZNE	
HELENE	10	F	CH	GRZZZZNE	
HERMANN	7	M	CHILD	GRZZZZNE	
WISNIEWSKA, JULIANNE	45	F	W	GRZZZZBAL	
EMMA	11	F	CH	GRZZZZBAL	
ALEXANDER	10	M	CH	GRZZZZBAL	
LEOKARJA	9	F	CHILD	GRZZZZBAL	
JOHANNES	8	M	CHILD	GRZZZZBAL	
GLOWIACKA, THEKLA	27	F	W	GRZZZZBAL	
FRANZISKA	7	F	CHILD	GRZZZZBAL	
WOZCIECT	5	M	CHILD	GRZZZZBAL	
JOSEF	3	M	CHILD	GRZZZZBAL	
MARIA	.03	F	INFANT	GRZZZZBAL	
WILEMSKI, JOHANN	38	M	FARMER	GRZZZZBAL	
AUGUSTE	37	F	W	GRZZZZBAL	
PAUL	10	M	CH	GRZZZZBAL	
AUGUSTE	5	F	CHILD	GRZZZZBAL	
WOJSNIAK, KATHARINE	45	F	W	GRZZZZBAL	
THOMAS	5	M	CHILD	GRZZZZBAL	
JOSEFA	4	F	CHILD	GRZZZZBAL	
MAGASAK	.11	M	INFANT	GRZZZZBAL	
WISCHNEWSKI, JACOB	39	M	FARMER	GRZZZZWI	
MATHILDE	38	F	W	GRZZZZWI	
DALMAR, ADOLF	32	M	JNR	GRZZZZMI	
WILHELMINE	32	F	W	GRZZZZMI	
RICHARD	11	M	CH	GRZZZZMI	

PASSENGER	AGE	SEX	OCCUPATION	PRVL	DES
WITTENBECHER, ERNST	34	M	LABR		GRZZZZWI
ANNA	34	F	W		GRZZZZWI
TRUMPF, WILHELM	00	M	INF		GR****WI

SHIP: STATE OF NEVADA

FROM: GLASGOW AND LARNE
TO: NEW YORK
ARRIVED: 12 JULY 1888

PASSENGER	AGE	SEX	OCCUPATION	PRVL	DES
GEDEON, AGNES	18	F	SVNT		GRAHRZUSA

SHIP: WIELAND

FROM: HAMBURG
TO: NEW YORK
ARRIVED: 12 JULY 1888

PASSENGER	AGE	SEX	OCCUPATION	PRVL	DES
HAMM, JOHANN	42	M	UNKNOWN		GRAHILUSA
ANNA	36	F	UNKNOWN		GRAHILUSA
DOROTHEA	15	F	UNKNOWN		GRAHILUSA
CARL	9	M	CHILD		GRAHILUSA
JOH.	8	M	CHILD		GRAHILUSA
CORNELSEN, JOHA.	21	F	SGL		GRAHILUSA
DONNER, FRIEDR.	60	M	LABR		PRZZZZUSA
BOHM, WM.	33	M	LABR		PRZZZZUSA
BERTHA	28	F	W		PRZZZZUSA
ANNA	9	F	CHILD		PRZZZZUSA
FRANZ	7	M	CHILD		PRZZZZUSA
AUG.	5	M	CHILD		PRZZZZUSA
MARIE	3	F	CHILD		PRZZZZUSA
EMILIE	.11	F	INFANT		PRZZZZUSA
FISCHEL, JACOB	25	M	FUR		PRACRXUSA
REGINA	33	F	W		PRACRXUSA
CARL	.11	M	INFANT		PRACRXUSA
WITZEL, JACOB	42	M	LABR		PRAAOOUSA
LOUISE	36	F	W		PRAAOOUSA
EMIL	9	M	CHILD		PRAAOOUSA
GEORG	8	M	CHILD		PRAAOOUSA
PAULINE	3	F	CHILD		PRAAOOUSA
RITTER, JACOB	61	M	LABR		PRABHUUSA
HENRIETTE	54	F	W		PRABHUUSA
KORDAN, ELISABETH	26	F	WO		PRABHUUSA
ANTONIE	4	F	CHILD		PRABHUUSA
OTTO	2	M	CHILD		PRABHUUSA
PAUL	.11	M	INFANT		PRABHUUSA
JACOBSOHN, ERNESTE.	29	F	SGL		PRZZZZUSA
SCHMIESECK, THERESE	23	F	SGL		BVZZZZUSA
VOHRER, ADOLF	17	M	MCHT		WMZZZZUSA
KLEIN, MARG.	27	F	SGL		PRZZZZUSA
KLUC, JOSEFINE	26	F	SGL		PRZZZZUSA
NORLACH, ADAM	57	M	LABR		PRAGDUUSA
JOSEFINE	42	F	W		PRAGDUUSA
ANDRZY	4	M	CHILD		PRAGDUUSA
FRANZISCA	1	F	CHILD		PRAGDUUSA
MARIANNE	.06	F	INFANT		PRAGDUUSA
ZABNISKA, ANNA	20	F	SGL		PRAGDUUSA
RABACZEWSKA, JOHANN	30	M	LABR		PRZZZZUSA
SKIBBE, ADELINE	22	F	SGL		PRZZZZUSA
POPPE, DIEDR.	25	M	LABR		PRAADEUSA
HAGENAH, MAX	16	M	SLR		PRZZZZUSA
KUNZE, OSWALD	27	M	MLR		SYZZZZUSA
RICHTER, EUGEN	16	M	BBR		SYAGAWUSA
KAHM, IWAN	17	M	MCHT		SYACBFUSA
KOESTER, HEINR.	25	M	SHMK		SYAECTUSA
KINNER, PAUL	23	M	BKR		SYAARZUSA
LIEBERMANN, JULS	21	M	CL		PRZZZZUSA
RICHTER, EUGEN	21	M	FARMER		PRAJWAUSA
LOUISE	20	F	W		PRAJWAUSA
GICKELLEITER, ANNA	35	F	SGL		PRAEXWUSA
WEIDE, LOUISE	23	F	WO		PRACBFUSA
TONY	.10	M	INFANT		PRACBFUSA
KOOR, MARTHA	21	F	SGL		PRACBFUSA
KALLING, CARL	18	M	LABR		PRACBFUSA
WORMECK, AUGE.	45	F	WO		PRAAKHUSA
HELENA	9	F	CHILD		PRAAKHUSA
SCHARFENBERG, LOUISE	19	F	SGL		MKZZZZUSA
MARTIN, MARGA.	46	F	WO		BVZZZZUSA
KARL	9	M	CHILD		BVZZZZUSA
JOHA	8	F	CHILD		BVZZZZUSA
CATHA.	6	F	CHILD		BVZZZZUSA
TARGAC, REWKO	19	M	LABR		BVZZZZUSA
MULLER, MARIE	68	F	WO		BVACBFUSA
NORDBERG, AGNES	28	F	SGL		BVACBFUSA
KRABBES, FRANZ	28	M	LKSH		BVAAKHUSA
KOEFER, MARIE	29	F	SGL		BVACBRUSA
GASSE, OSCAR	26	M	GDNR		PRZZZZUSA
FISCHER, MAD	22	M	ART		PRAGDHUSA
HAASE, MARIE	23	F	SGL		PRABVEUSA
GLENSKY, FRANZ	32	M	GDNR		PRZZZZUSA
KUSSINGER, MARIE	31	F	WO		PRZZZZUSA
CARL	.08	M	INFANT		BVZZZZUSA
KOPPEL, MENDEL	43	M	SHMK		BVAAKHUSA
JETTE	37	F	W		BVAAKHUSA
SIMON	9	M	CHILD		BVAAKHUSA
JOSEPH	8	M	CHILD		BVAAKHUSA
NATHAN	6	M	CHILD		BVAAKHUSA
ISAAC	6	M	CHILD		BVAAKHUSA
ROSA	5	F	CHILD		BVAAKHUSA
EDEL, JOHA.	22	F	SGL		BVAAKHUSA
RENNER, SALO	20	M	WCHMKR		BVACBFUSA
ROSENFELD, SIEBELUN	50	F	WO		BVAEABUSA
ARNOLD	22	M	S		BVAEABUSA
ANNA	15	F	D		BVAEABUSA
WOICK, VICTORIA	50	F	WO		PRZZZZUSA
THOMAS	9	M	CHILD		PRZZZZUSA
FRANZISKA	8	F	CHILD		PRZZZZUSA
MARIANNA	7	F	CHILD		PRZZZZUSA
GRZESKOWIAK, KATH.	26	F	WO		PRZZZZUSA
MICHALINA	9	F	CHILD		PRZZZZUSA
WENZEL, OTTO	42	M	MCHT		PRAAKHUSA
FAHNER, EMIL	25	M	SMH		PRADYYUSA
HERMANN, ROSALIE	22	F	SGL		PRACWTUSA
PAOLIK, LEOPOLD	25	M	FARMER		PRZZZZUSA
RUBIN, LEA	20	F	SGL		PRZZZZUSA
ROSENBLUM, ESTHER	34	F	WO		PRZZZZUSA
CHANE	9	F	CHILD		PRZZZZUSA
NORDER, MARIANNE	17	F	SGL		PRZZZZUSA
SACK, MOSES	35	M	LABR		PRZZZZUSA
MELACHOVSKIN, MORDCHE	20	M	LABR		PRZZZZUSA
ICHIMON	17	M	LABR		PRZZZZUSA
WARCHTER, JOH.	36	M	UNKNOWN		SRZZZZUSA
REUZUG, LORA	23	F	SGL		SRADWZUSA
NIELSEN, WIL.D.	45	M	BKR		BWZZZZUSA
JACOBSON, WILHE	33	F	SGL		BWADEPUSA
JANKOWSKI, CARL	48	M	LABR		BWADEPUSA
RENATE	54	F	W		BWADEPUSA
LOUISE	7	F	CHILD		BWADEPUSA
AUGUST	3	M	CHILD		BWADEPUSA
DOESCHER, PAULE.	21	F	SGL		MKZZZZUSA
KOSZMIDER, ADDAM	14	M	LABR		PRZZZZUSA
WREBLEVSKI, THEODOR	18	M	LABR		PRZZZZUSA
KRIMKE, JOH.	32	M	LABR		PRZZZZUSA
FRIED	.02	M	INFANT		PRZZZZUSA
DANBKOWSKA, MARIANNA	19	F	SGL		PRZZZZUSA
LIELAZNY, JOSEPH	37	M	LLD		PRZZZZUSA
CAROLINE	26	F	LLD		PRZZZZUSA
ALEXANDER	4	M	CHILD		PRZZZZUSA
MARIE	3	F	CHILD		PRZZZZUSA
PETRONELLA	.04	F	INFANT		PRZZZZUSA

PASSENGER	AGE	SEX	OCCUPATION	PRVL	DES
DUMALSKA, AGNISKA	19	F	SGL	PRZZZZUSA	
NOLL, ELISA	17	F	SGL	PRZZZZUSA	
PETER	15	M	LABR	PRZZZZUSA	
LANGE, HEINRICH	43	M	LABR	PRABHUUSA	
RANNS, PELAGIA	18	F	SGL	PRZZZZUSA	
HEIN, SOPHIE	16	F	SGL	PRZZZZUSA	
CAROLINE	14	F	SGL	PRZZZZUSA	
NIEDERMEYER, FRIEDOLIN	23	M	WVR	BDZZZZUSA	
DEMKER, ISIDOR	18	M	TLR	PRZZZZUSA	
PETERS, EMMA	20	F	SGL	PRZZZZUSA	
BERTENSCHVEN, HERM.	16	M	PNTR	PRADOIUSA	
PETERS, CARL	58	M	LABR	PRZZZZUSA	
ELISE	58	F	W	PRZZZZUSA	
KERBER, JOHANNE	60	F	WO	PRAARZUSA	
LANGE, MARIE	40	F	WO	PRABHUUSA	
MARIE	9	F	CHILD	PRABHUUSA	
JOHANNE	8	F	CHILD	PRABHUUSA	
PAUL	3	M	CHILD	PRABHUUSA	
ROBERT	.03	M	INFANT	PRABHUUSA	
EPSTEIN, JULIUS	27	M	MCHT	PRAAZQUSA	
SKWACZEWSKI, STANISLAUS	18	M	LABR	PRZZZZUSA	
THEIVOGH, PETER	16	M	FARMER	PRAAFGUSA	
WILH	14	M	FARMER	PRAAFGUSA	
KOPPE, AUGUST	35	M	FARMER	PRZZZZUSA	
VORBICK, AUG.	45	M	CPR	PRAEXJUSA	
CHRISTINE	41	F	W	PRAEXJUSA	
ERNST	16	M	CH	PRAEXJUSA	
OTTO	13	M	CH	PRAEXJUSA	
SCHIESSER, JOH.	27	M	LABR	BVZZZZUSA	
SCHNEIDER, CATHARINA	22	F	SGL	PRZZZZUSA	
KRAUSS, HEINRICH	18	M	LABR	PRZZZZUSA	
LENZ, RICHARD	24	M	PNTR	PRADZOUSA	
MULDUN, OSCAR	25	M	BRR	PRABZNUSA	
MEDEN, AUGUSTE	34	F	WO	PRAARZUSA	
FRITZ	4	M	CHILD	PRAARZUSA	
CARL	2	M	CHILD	PRAARZUSA	
ROBERT	.11	M	INFANT	PRAARZUSA	
JENSEN, CATHE.	30	F	WO	PRZZZZUSA	
SUWER	8	M	CHILD	PRZZZZUSA	
KRUSE, ASMINE	20	F	WO	PRZZZZUSA	
CATHE.	.11	F	INFANT	PRZZZZUSA	
SCHMIDT, ANNA	19	F	SGL	PRZZZZUSA	
JESSEN, ANNA	22	F	SGL	PRZZZZUSA	
JONNIKSEN, WILLADO	16	M	FARMER	PRZZZZUSA	
JEPSEN, BENJAMIN	20	M	FARMER	PRZZZZUSA	
MACHLER, MAGDALINA	27	F	SGL	PRZZZZUSA	
CARSTENS, LUDWIG	18	M	WTR	PRACKYUSA	
SELTENRIECH, CAROLINE	24	F	SGL	PRAARZUSA	
ZIMMERMANN, JOH.	32	M	LKSH	WMZZZZUSA	
GUETTRICH, OTTO	29	M	BCHR	PRZZZZUSA	
SERABECK, CLARA	13	F	SGL	SYZZZZUSA	
HULZBERG, GUSTAV	42	M	LABR	SYAEXJUSA	
WITTHAUS, MALTER	16	M	LABR	SYAEXJUSA	
SOMMER, BETTI	19	F	SGL	PRZZZZUSA	
BENDLER, FRIDKE	60	F	WO	PRAHRWUSA	
MARIE	25	F	D	PRAHRWUSA	
BLUM, ELISABETH	35	F	WO	PRAAKHUSA	
ELISABETH	8	F	CHILD	PRAAKHUSA	
GEORG	6	M	CHILD	PRAAKHUSA	
THOMSEN, NIELS	20	M	BKR	PRZZZZUSA	
HANS	18	M	BKR	PRZZZZUSA	
MILDE, CARL	26	M	PNTR	PRAAKHUSA	
STARASKE, ERNST	23	M	LABR	PRZZZZUSA	
BUSCHMANN, ADOLF	38	M	MCHT	PRZZZZUSA	
VOSS, GUSTAV	30	M	LABR	PRABXBUSA	
ALWINE	32	F	W	PRABXBUSA	
FRIEDKE	9	F	CHILD	PRABXBUSA	
CARL	6	M	CHILD	PRABXBUSA	
ANNA	5	F	CHILD	PRABXBUSA	
EMMA	2	F	CHILD	PRABXBUSA	
BERTHA	.04	F	INFANT	PRABXBUSA	
WILCKE, CHRISTIAN	15	M	MSN	PRZZZZUSA	
HANSEN, HELENE	23	F	SGL	PRZZZZUSA	
SOPHIE	19	F	SGL	PRZZZZUSA	
WOHLGEMUTH, EVA	29	F	SGL	PRZZZZUSA	

PASSENGER	AGE	SEX	OCCUPATION	PRVL	DES
SEUBERT, BARB.	18	F	SGL	BVZZZZUSA	
JAMMERMANN, EMIL	17	M	LABR	BVAAKHUSA	
MEMLER, MARIE	28	F	SGL	BVAAKHUSA	
WAGNER, JOHANN	18	M	LABR	BVZZZZUSA	
SCHULZE, GUSTAV	49	M	MCHT	BVACAWUSA	
ERNESTINE	49	F	W	BVACAWUSA	
MARY	15	F	CH	BVACAWUSA	
JOHE.	9	F	CHILD	BVACAWUSA	
ERNST	8	M	CHILD	BVACAWUSA	
WALTER	7	M	CHILD	BVACAWUSA	
HELENE	4	F	CHILD	BVACAWUSA	
RICHARD	3	M	CHILD	BVACAWUSA	
FREID	2	M	CHILD	BVACAWUSA	
ALMER, PAUL	50	M	LABR	WMZZZZUSA	
ELEONORE	47	F	W	WMZZZZUSA	
ANNA	26	F	CH	WMZZZZUSA	
PAULINE	20	F	CH	WMZZZZUSA	
EUGEN	16	M	CH	WMZZZZUSA	
SINDER, ZICHI	22	F	WO	WMZZZZUSA	
SARA	.01	F	INFANT	WMZZZZUSA	
MINKE, HEINRICH	28	M	WTR	PRZZZZUSA	
PETERS, MARY	21	F	SGL	PRZZZZUSA	
PEICH, WILH.	66	M	BCHR	PRACXVUSA	
ZAGORSKI, SALOMIA	30	F	WO	PRZZZZUSA	
ANNA	.11	F	INFANT	PRZZZZUSA	
DORRAIN, PHILOMENE	32	F	WO	FRZZZZUSA	
ADOLPH	8	M	CHILD	FRZZZZUSA	
JOSEPH	6	M	CHILD	FRZZZZUSA	
SIMON	4	M	CHILD	FRZZZZUSA	
MARTHA	2	F	CHILD	FRZZZZUSA	
MARIE	1	F	CHILD	FRZZZZUSA	
ROSALIE	.01	F	INFANT	FRZZZZUSA	
HUTH, LINA	21	F	SGL	FRZZZZUSA	
STAHLI, CARL	17	M	FARMER	FRAEZYUSA	
BURGER, ACHILLES	20	M	WCHMKR	FRACWPUSA	
MAY, EMMA	20	F	SGL	FRAAHUUSA	
STROHECKER, JOHANN	60	M	MNFTR	FRACBFUSA	
TROELTZSCH, ANNA	29	F	SGL	FRACBFUSA	
WAHLEN, BALTHASAR	50	M	MCHT	FRACBFUSA	
ITZIG, SAMUEL	70	M	MCHT	SRZZZZUSA	
STREMPEL, AUG.	36	M	MCHT	SRAEHQUSA	
BERTHA	29	F	W	SRAEHQUSA	
CLEMEND, WILLARD	24	M	CNF	SYZZZZUSA	
SCHROEDER, ROBERT	24	M	MCHT	SYACBFUSA	
FAUSTMANN, LOUISE	50	F	WO	SYAEKJUSA	
WUNDERLE, JOHN	45	M	ENGR	SYABPCUSA	
LANGENBAD, JOSEPH	25	M	MUSN	SYABPCUSA	

SHIP: EMS

FROM: BREMEN AND SOUTHAMPTON
TO: NEW YORK
ARRIVED: 13 JULY 1888

PASSENGER	AGE	SEX	OCCUPATION	PRVL	DES
STRAUSS, SALOMON	32	M	MCHT	SYABOQNY	
EMANUEL	16	M	MCHT	GRZZZZNY	
HECKEL, JOH	25	M	MCHT	GRZZZZNY	
WEISS, CHRIST	23	M	BKR	GRAEXWNY	
RUESTER, WILLY	20	M	BKR	GRADIJNY	
GOETJEN, HEINR	38	M	MCHT	GRZZZZNY	
GESCHE	42	F	W	GRZZZZNY	
EHLERT, LUDWIG	25	M	MCHT	GRACSDNY	
SIMON, MAX	26	M	MCHT	GRZZZZNY	
MERKT, CARL	43	M	MCHT	GRACPUNY	
HOLDERER, MAGD	20	F	NN	GRZZZZNY	
MAJER, CARL	28	M	BCHR	GRACSYNY	
HILLERT, GEORGINE	19	F	NN	GRAFNKNY	
KOTTLER, DINA	35	F	NN	GRAAZSNY	
HANSEN, ANNE	19	F	NN	GRZZZZNY	
DROST, LUDERICA	36	F	NN	GRAFNKNY	

PASSENGER	AGE	SEX	OCCUPATION	PRVVL	DES
GAUSELMAN, FRANZKA	21	F	NN		GRADKWNY
HUESSMANN, JOH	17	M	MCHT		GRAGKNNY
GUNDELSHEIMER, REGINA	22	F	NN		GRZZZZNY
SCHNEIDER, OTTO	29	M	MCHT		GRACXVNY
DIETZ, W	34	M	MD		GRAFCYNY
WILHNE	33	F	W		GRAFCYNY
EMILIE	4	F	CHILD		GRAFCYNY
OTTO	3	M	CHILD		GRAFCYNY
JENNY	2	F	CHILD		GRAFCYNY
KRUG, ROSAMUNDE	37	F	NN		GRAAKHNY
PREUSER, ELISE	20	F	NN		GRADDQNY
ERHARDT, CARL	45	M	GCR		GRADRONY
ENGEL, HUBERT	25	M	MCHT		GRAARZNY
ROBA, EMMA	24	F	NN		GRAARZNY
NEUMANN, ERNSTE	35	F	W		GRACZONY
IDA	10	F	CH		GRACZONY
MUELLER, CARL	76	M	GCR		GRAETSNY
-RERCKS, HEINR	24	M	MCHT		GRAADENY
V. JESK	22	M	MCHT		GRAAKHNY
SCHMIDT, HEDWIG	18	F	NN		GRAAKHNY
SCHROETER, WILHE	29	F	NN		GRACXVNY
WEINBERG, MICH	63	M	MCHT		GRAAXFNY
JOHA	20	F	NN		GRAAXFNY
FRIEDA	15	F	NN		GRAAXFNY
BRUENING, ANNA	17	F	NN		GRAARRNY
BOPP, GEO	15	M	NN		GRAARRNY
MARIE	19	F	NN		GRAARRNY
MARTOFEL, MORITZ	22	M	BKR		GRAARRNY
BRODERSEN, WILHM	23	M	MCHT		GRAARRNY
GUTERT, CARL	39	M	MCHT		GRAARRNY
HONS, CARLE	48	F	NN		GRAARRNY
UHLIG, LAURA	30	F	NN		GRAAUENY
BARSCHDORF, GUSTAV	18	M	LABR		GRAADHNY
SIEREDZKA, SALOME-A	24	F	W		GRAATNNY
MARIE	7	F	CHILD		GRAATNNY
CASMIRA	8	F	CHILD		GRAATNNY
ISABELLA	2	F	CHILD		GRAATNNY
PETER	.01	M	INFANT		GRAATNNY
STANISLAW	4	M	CHILD		GRAATNNY
SIERDZKI, WLADISLAW	16	M	FARMER		GRAEABNY
BUHL, ENGELINE	67	F	NN		GRZZZZNY
HOPP, RICHARD	16	M	LABR		GRADRONY
MILTENBERGER, VINCENT	37	M	LABR		GRZZZZNY
PETERS, JOH	32	M	LABR		GRAHXINY
SCHMIDT, MINA	28	F	NN		GRZZZZNY
ZEINBACH, IDA	18	F	NN		GRABSYNY
HEROLD, FRANZ	30	M	MCHT		GRADROPA
WEIDERER, BENED	33	M	FARMER		GRZZZZWI
LUDWIG	29	M	FARMER		GRZZZZWI
PENZENSTADLER, ALOIS	21	M	FARMER		GRACHOWI
LINKE, ROB	26	M	MCHT		GRABDMTX
HAGEN, SOPHIE	15	F	NN		GRACXHNY
BEHRENS, WILHE	20	F	NN		GRACXHNY
SCHINELZER, BERTHA	13	F	NN		GRZZZZNY
SAALFELD, ADOLF	23	M	MCHT		GRAAHBNY
KLOPFER, FRIEDKE	15	F	NN		GRABYCNY
WEIMANN, MARGA	22	F	NN		GRZZZZNY
VOLK, EMMA	22	F	NN		GRAEXWNY
ZINSER, MICH	16	M	LABR		GRZZZZNY
SIGEL, JOH	16	M	LABR		GRZZZZNY
WOLFF, WILHE	18	F	NN		GRAFHGNY
VETTER, MARIA	18	F	NN		GRAFHGNY
SCHWEIZER, CAROLE	19	F	NN		GRAFHGNY
SCHNEIDER, SOPHIE	20	F	NN		GRAIAKNY
MAIER, MARIA	21	F	NN		GRZZZZNY
HOFMANN, JOH	19	M	BSKM		GRZZZZNY
JOH	00	M	BSKM		GRZZZZNY
GRIESEMER, KATHA	17	F	NN		GRZZZZOH
WEMMER, CATHA	34	F	W		GRAKQPOH
ANNA	10	F	CH		GRAKQPOH
FRANZ	8	M	CHILD		GRAKQPOH
LIMBACH, MARGA	67	F	NN		GRADDWNY
HOEHRE, MARTHA	16	F	NN		GRADLUNY
GERBITZ, JOHS	31	M	MLR		GRAAESMN
EMILIE	31	F	W		GRAAESMN
LEOP	68	M	MLR		GRAAESMN
WILHE	63	F	W		GRAAESMN
MINNA	24	F	NN		GRAAESMN
ELISAB	7	F	CHILD		GRAAESMN
MARGA	6	F	CHILD		GRAAESMN
GERHARD	5	M	CHILD		GRAAESMN
MARTIN	3	M	CHILD		GRAAESMN
HERTHA	2	F	CHILD		GRAAESMN
PAUL	.02	M	INFANT		GRAAESMN
FRANZ	.02	M	INFANT		GRAAESMN
KAISER, CARL	27	M	FARMER		GRADLUNY
CAROLE	28	F	W		GRADLUNY
JUL	4	M	CHILD		GRADLUNY
JULCHEN	2	F	CHILD		GRADLUNY
FRIEDR	.02	M	INFANT		GRADLUNY
VAUPEL, THERSIA	16	F	NN		GRADLUNY
MEYER, JOS	32	M	LABR		GRADLUNY
KAELBER, CHRIST	33	M	LABR		GRADLUNY
KUNDSEN, KAREN	20	M	LABR		GRZZZZNY
CHRISTENSEN, WILH	33	F	W		GRZZZZNY
CHRIST	7	M	CHILD		GRZZZZNY
NIELS	7	M	CHILD		GRZZZZNY
HANSEN, JENS	15	M	LABR		GRZZZZNY
JOERGENSEN, HANS	16	M	FARMER		GRZZZZNY
NIELSEN, MARIE	21	F	NN		GRZZZZNY
MADSEN, PAUL	41	M	FARMER		GRZZZZNY
ANE	42	F	W		GRZZZZNY
PAUL	17	M	FARMER		GRZZZZNY
THOMAS	9	M	CHILD		GRZZZZNY
MADS	8	M	CHILD		GRZZZZNY
ANE	.09	F	INFANT		GRZZZZNY
THOMSEN, MARCUS	25	M	BKR		GRZZZZNY
HERGERT, MARIA	24	F	NN		GRZZZZNY
DIEL, FRANZ	39	M	LABR		GRZZZZNY
GEBELEIN, JOHS	15	M	LABR		GRAAKRNY
ADAM, HENRIETTE	30	F	W		GRAHQONY
ALFRED	.11	M	INFANT		GRAHQONY
FAUCH, GOTTL	65	M	LABR		GRAHQONY
LEISTRITZ, HEINR	40	M	LABR		GRAHQONY
MARIE	35	F	W		GRAHQONY
RAEDING, EMMA	19	F	NN		GRAEABIL
MAX	15	F	JNR		GRAEABIL
SCHAEFER, MINNA	20	F	NN		GRAATNIL
RICHARD	15	M	TLR		GRAATNIL
HEPPNER, JOSEF	21	M	SMH		GRZZZZIA
BLASER, CARL	17	M	LABR		GRZZZZIA
GROSS, JACOB	15	M	LABR		GRZZZZNY
GRAEFER, PAULE	56	F	NN		GRAAKHNY
FROSTDORFF, WILH	67	M	SMH		GRAAXKNY
AUGUSTE	60	F	W		GRAAXKNY
WEBER, GOTTFR	28	M	SMH		GRZZZZPA
OBERMEIER, MAX	28	M	LKSH		GRZZZZPA
HANSEN, JENS	24	M	LKSH		GRZZZZIL
PETERSEN, MARIE	22	F	NN		GRZZZZIL
DEYER, HANS	17	M	LABR		GRZZZZIL
SKOV, JOH	18	M	FARMER		GRZZZZIA
SCHULZ, PETER	23	M	SLR		GRAILBIA
PATRIAS, TEODOZIA	36	F	W		GRZZZZIA
JOSEFA	2	F	CHILD		GRZZZZIA
ANTON	5	M	CHILD		GRZZZZIA
KOSCHWITZKI, ADAL	24	M	SMH		GRZZZZIA
GALINSKY, WLADISLAW	26	M	SMH		GRADBDIA
BERENDS, ROELF	54	M	LABR		GRADBDIL
PLATZ, MATH	18	M	FARMER		GRADBDCAL
STOLLENWECK, WILH	19	M	LKSH		GRZZZZNY
HENTSCHEL, ALMA	39	F	NN		GRACZONY
HAGEN, MARGA	24	F	NN		GRADLNNY
HOELLERICH, JOH	25	M	FARMER		GRADKONY
REUTHER, JOHE	17	F	NN		GRADLNNY
HERMANN, CHRISTE	20	F	NN		GRADLNNY
PRECHT, HEINR	15	M	FARMER		GRAARRNY
GRAF, JOH	45	M	FARMER		GRZZZZNY
MUELLER, ERNST	25	M	PNTR		GRZZZZOR
LOEFFLER, LISETTE	24	F	NN		GRACEGOR
DOBARCZINKA, LOUISA	29	F	NN		GRAEABDAK

PASSENGER	AGE	SEX	OCCUPATION	PRVL	DES
HUETTEN, ANNA	18	F	NN		GRAEABNY
EBINGER, LOUISE	54	F	NN		GRACQENY
JACOB	15	M	LABR		GRACQENY
BUERKE, CARL	15	M	LABR		GRACQENY
LANDRISSEN, LENCHEN	22	F	NN		GRACQNNY
KLAUS, ERNST	25	M	JNR		GRAJZWNY
KAYERN, REGA	24	F	NN		GRAEVTNY
KAPPAS, CARL	38	M	BRR		GRZZZZNY
KUEBLER, FRANZ	22	M	CL		GRABOQNY
HECHT, LINA	39	F	W		GRZZZZNY
ROSA	11	F	CH		GRZZZZNY
SELMA	3	F	CHILD		GRZZZZNY
STOLTE, LISETTE	34	F	W		GRAFHJNE
LINA	14	F	NN		GRAFHJNE
EMMA	11	F	CH		GRAFHJNE
AUGUSTE	8	F	CHILD		GRAFHJNE
HEINR	6	M	CHILD		GRAFHJNE
PAULE	4	F	CHILD		GRAFHJNE
PAUL	3	M	CHILD		GRAFHJNE
CLARA	27	F	NN		GRAFHJNE
DOLLES, GEORG	37	M	FARMER		GRABERIA
BARBA	23	F	NN		GRABERIA
BIERTROCK, GOTTL	48	M	LABR		GRZZZZIL
HENRTE	43	F	W		GRZZZZIL
HECKE, WILH	26	M	LABR		GRZZZZIL
AMALIE	23	F	W		GRZZZZIL
HERM	4	M	CHILD		GRZZZZIL
HARTLIEB, CARL	22	M	SHMK		GRZZZZIL
GLASER, GEORG	31	M	LABR		GRZZZZNY
GRUBE, HEINR	60	M	LLD		GRZZZZTX
MARGA	39	F	W		GRZZZZTX
AUG	15	M	NN		GRZZZZTX
JOHE	13	F	NN		GRZZZZTX
DIEDR	10	M	CH		GRZZZZTX
ADOLF	8	M	CHILD		GRZZZZTX
CLAUS	3	M	CHILD		GRZZZZTX
WULFF, HERM	26	M	LABR		GRZZZZNY
GORRIES, HEINR	27	M	FARMER		GRAEQKTX
RUSSWURN, JOH	55	M	CGRMKR		GRZZZZNY
GOTSCHALK, CARL	29	M	LABR		GRZZZZOH
SCHMIDKORG, BABETTE	19	F	NN		GRADUVIA
HEINR	16	M	NN		GRADUVIA
MICH	15	M	NN		GRADUVIA
DAKERT, BERTHA	19	F	NN		GRZZZZWI
ROEGGE, ALWINE	16	F	NN		GRZZZZOH
PAUL	18	M	JNR		GRZZZZOH
GERNET, ANNA	20	F	NN		GRZZZZOH
ANDRAE, JACOB	32	M	LABR		GRAFSBUNK
WALETSCHKI, ANT	24	M	LABR		GRAFSBNY
ADAM, JOH	50	M	LABR		GRAEMANY
WILHE	21	M	NN		GRAEMANY
SCHROEDER, ELISE	35	F	NN		GRADJONY
MARGANSKA, STANISLAWA	22	F	W		GRALTJNY
JOH	.11	M	INFANT		GRALTJNY
FISCHER, EMIL	25	M	FARMER		GRABDMPA
SCHIMMEL, WILH	25	M	LABR		GRZZZZOR
THEIS, MAX	24	M	LABR		GRAESMNY
GLASER, LOUISE	16	F	NN		GRAFQVNY
DARMMEYER, BERNH	19	M	JNR		GRZZZZNY
MARTEN, EMIL	30	M	LABR		GRZZZZNY
BAUMGARTEN, WILH	27	M	LABR		GRZZZZCOU
RISSMANN, W	31	M	LABR		GRZZZZTX
OEGERSCHLAEGER, GERHARD	24	M	BCHR		GRAAGCNY
BANIKOW, AUGUSTE	22	F	NN		GRZZZZNY
ANDRES, JOSEF	35	M	LABR		GRZZZZNY
BUESING, JOH	22	M	BKR		GRAAQPNY
HINSTEDT, HEINR	26	M	JNR		GRAARRNY
BACHEL, JOHANN	30	M	LABR		GRAARRNY
MEYER, JOS	00	M	NN		GRAARRNY
LIESMANN, MARIE	13	F	NN		GRAARRNY
BENDER, MART	16	M	JNR		GRABLJNY
STOETZEL, MICH	16	M	JNR		GRZZZZNY
SCHAD, CATH	13	F	NN		GRZZZZNY
SCHERF, ROSA	19	F	NN		GRAAAGNY
ELISAB	17	F	NN		GRAAAGNY

PASSENGER	AGE	SEX	OCCUPATION	PRVL	DES
KEMPF, ADAM	18	M	SMH		GRZZZZNY
MEYER, LORENZ	18	M	MCHT		GRACJSNY
BRITSCH, CARL	24	M	BKR		GRZZZZNY
OESTERLE, JOH	17	M	BKLYR		GRZZZZOH
SCHWENGER, DAVID	18	M	TLR		GRAERMIL
LAUERWEIN, ADAM	16	M	TLR		GRZZZZOH
KREUSMANN, MARIE	16	F	NN		GRZZZZNY
HOFFMANN, EMMA	17	F	NN		GRZZZZNY
GRIESEMER, ADAM	18	M	BCHR		GRZZZZNY

SHIP: WAESLAND

FROM: ANTWERP
TO: NEW YORK
ARRIVED: 13 JULY 1888

PASSENGER	AGE	SEX	OCCUPATION	PRVL	DES
LANG-, W	48	M	MCHT		GRZZZZNY
PORGES, B	34	M	MCHT		GRZZZZNY
H	32	F	MCHT		GRZZZZNY
U	10	F	MCHT		GRZZZZNY
LAGES, W	28	M	MCHT		GRZZZZNY
BRINCK, L	34	M	MCHT		GRZZZZNY
KLEUTER, G	24	M	MCHT		GRZZZZNY
SCHWINDENHAMM, U	31	M	UNKNOWN		GRZZZZDET
MULLER, C	29	M	UNKNOWN		GRZZZZDET
BAUCHOR-, F	42	M	BKSL		FRZZZZDET
F	35	M	BKSL		FRZZZZDET
WALZ, F	30	F	NN		GRZZZZPHI
METZGER, F	73	M	DYR		GRZZZZNY
MRS	76	F	DYR		GRZZZZNY
FREY, U	48	F	DYR		GRZZZZNY
L	14	F	DYR		GRZZZZNY
E	12	F	DYR		GRZZZZNY
LOUISE	10	F	DYR		GRZZZZNY
KRAEMER, CATH	69	F	NN		GRZZZZNY
MARG	26	F	NN		GRZZZZNY
MARIA	23	F	NN		GRZZZZNY
LOUISE	00	F	NN		GRZZZZNY
BURKHARD, H	21	M	PNTR		GRZZZZNY
GROHMANN, G	19	M	JNR		GRZZZZNY
PFUISTER, E	27	M	BKBNDR		GRZZZZNY
KAMP, AUG	32	M	LABR		GRZZZZNY
BUHLER, SEAN	20	M	MCHT		GRZZZZNY
KAPPES, HCH	22	M	LABR		GRZZZZNY
FRANTZ, FCOIS	22	M	FARMER		GRZZZZNY
FLECKENSTEIN, NIC	19	M	ACHTT		GRZZZZNY
LUTZ, IDA	21	F	NN		GRZZZZMIL
KLEIN, ADAM	24	M	DLR		GRZZZZUSA
RESKA, ALOISE	20	M	BKR		GRZZZZCH
BONEZKOWSKA, JOHANNA	22	F	NN		GRZZZZCH
THALMANN, JOSEPH	26	M	CPTR		SRZZZZNY
KREISS, HERM	37	M	CBTMKR		GRZZZZNY
LEVIN, LEOP	23	M	GCR		GRZZZZNY
LEICH, MATHIAS	22	M	BLDR		GRZZZZSTO
JOSEPHE	25	F	BLDR		GRZZZZSTO
BECKMANN, LOUISE	21	F	NN		GRZZZZPHI
SCHUTTNER, JOHAN	21	M	MSN		GRZZZZCH
HIGLES, MARIA	30	F	NN		GRZZZZNY
FORIN, VICTOR	32	M	PLH		FRZZZZNY
KLEIN, PETER	26	M	MLR		GRZZZZPIT
COUTURIA, JEAN	20	M	MNR		FRZZZZMRL
GA-STER, CAROLINE	20	F	SVNT		GRZZZZALT
SEILER, CASPAR	25	M	FARMER		GRZZZZUNK
SO-CHULE, JOSEPHINE	35	F	NN		GRZZZZUNK
EMILY	9	F	CHILD		GRZZZZUNK
LOUISE	6	F	CHILD		GRZZZZUNK
CARL	4	M	CHILD		GRZZZZUNK
DUPREY, LORERET	24	M	MNR		FRZZZZUNK
ANAISE	21	F	MNR		FRZZZZUNK
JEANNE	2	F	CHILD		FRZZZZUNK

PASSENGER	AGE	SEX	OCCUPATION	PRVL	DES
LOUISE	00	F	INF		FRZZZZUNK
KACHELE, WILHE	15	F	SVNT		GRZZZZCLE
PIETER, FRANZ	15	M	NN		GRZZZZNY
KELLER, S	33	F	NN		GRZZZZNY
-OHR, ANTON	26	M	CBTMKR		GRZZZZNY
VERONIKE	21	F	CBTMKR		GRZZZZNY
WUERST, FRIED	36	M	FARMER		GRZZZZNY
FRIED	11	M	FARMER		GRZZZZNY
KOCHTE, MARIA	18	F	SVNT		GRZZZZNY
L-ABRAND, JACOB	26	M	BBR		GRZZZZNY
SCHAICH, BARBA	18	F	NN		GRZZZZNY
NOETZ, MARIE	18	F	NN		GRZZZZNY
STRAB, CHRISTINE	16	F	SVNT		GRZZZZNY
SANSEL, PHILIPP	47	F	NN		GRZZZZNY
NIK	9	M	CHILD		GRZZZZNY
PHILIP	5	M	CHILD		GRZZZZNY
SCHAEFFER, H	41	M	CH		GRZZZZNY
BERTHA	36	F	UNKNOWN		GRZZZZNY
HERMAN	16	M	UNKNOWN		GRZZZZNY
FRIEDH	15	M	UNKNOWN		GRZZZZNY
BACHMANN, FRZ	17	M	NN		GRZZZZNY
MAT-KEWIEZ, JOSEF	26	M	CPTR		GRZZZZNO
SALOME	50	M	CPTR		GRZZZZNO
MARIA	24	F	NN		GRZZZZNO
FUCHS, JOSEFINE	18	F	NN		GRZZZZNO
RUSCHEL, ALBERT	00	M	INF		GRZZZZNO
KESSLER, ANTON	24	M	ACHTT		GRZZZZEVA
DELL, BERN	30	M	MD		GRZZZZNY
ASCHERMANN, R	32	M	UNKNOWN		GRZZZZNY
BRUKELMAIER, GEO	21	M	BKR		GRZZZZNY
SCHU-TTS, HUGO	26	M	GLSR		GRZZZZNY
KLEIN, WILH	30	M	MSN		GRZZZZNY
HASSEL, CARL	66	M	BCHR		GRZZZZNY
ELISE	19	F	BCHR		GRZZZZNY
HANSSMANN, JULIUS	26	M	CBTMKR		GRZZZZNY
JORDAN, GIDEON	35	M	PDLR		GRZZZZNY
HESS, CARL	23	M	BCHR		GRZZZZNY
GRIMM, CARL	27	M	BCHR		GRZZZZNY
JULIUS	16	M	BCHR		GRZZZZNY
CHRISTINE	22	F	BCHR		GRZZZZNY
EMMA	19	F	BCHR		GRZZZZNY
EGELAND, FRANZ	30	M	PREST		GRZZZZNY
WEBER, CARL	16	M	NN		GRZZZZNY
HARTT, ANTON	24	M	MLR		GRZZZZNY
KAENDLER, ANNA	21	F	SVNT		GRZZZZNY
MARIA	22	F	SVNT		GRZZZZNY
UHL, HCH	29	M	LABR		GRZZZZNY
AHRENS, AUG	22	M	CL		GRZZZZNY
SCHICK, GEO	39	M	BLDR		GRZZZZNY
ROSSTENSCH, LEONH	42	M	MUSN		GRZZZZNY
ELISE	42	F	MUSN		GRZZZZNY
CARL	10	M	CH		GRZZZZNY
RUETGER, MAGDE	17	F	SVNT		GRZZZZNY
KOCH, ANNA	40	M	NN		GRZZZZNY
HCH	10	M	CH		GRZZZZNY
SCHWARTZ, ROSE	44	F	CK		GRZZZZNY
ROTH, ADAM	40	M	TRVLR		GRZZZZNY
HINZER, HENRY	26	M	CL		GRZZZZNY
RIVETT, ALF	19	M	FTR		GRZZZZNY
SPIEGEL, EMIL	17	M	NN		GRZZZZNY
FORSTNER, FRANC	23	F	NN		GRZZZZNY
NIEDERHOFER, PETER	6	M	CHILD		GRZZZZNY
FORSTNER, ANDREAS	.10	M	INFANT		GRZZZZNY
NIEDERHOFER, BARBA	50	F	SVNT		GRZZZZNY
BACKER, AUG	20	M	SMH		GRZZZZNY
FRANZ, FRANZ	23	M	CPR		GRZZZZNY
SAUERLEITER, GUST	16	M	UNKNOWN		GRZZZZNY
LIPP, JOHAN	17	M	BRR		GRZZZZNY
BRUCKELMAIER, JOSEF	27	M	LABR		GRZZZZJON
D-RVE-, HENRY	34	M	MNR		FRZZZZUNK
NIDETZKY, CARL	00	M	UNKNOWN		GRZZZZNY
ETTEL, JOHAN	00	M	MNR		GRZZZZNY
WEBER, CARL	22	M	MSN		SRZZZZNY
LE-, ANNA	25	F	SVNT		SRZZZZNY
FREY, THEOD	22	M	LABR		SRZZZZNY
SCHULTZ, CARL	19	M	SMH		SRZZZZNY
WANGLER, AUG	20	M	CBTMKR		SRZZZZNY
DIETRICH, GOTTL	43	M	LABR		SRZZZZNY
GLIESCH, PAUL	26	M	FARMER		SRZZZZNY
REISPACH, ELIS	49	F	SMSTS		GRZZZZNY
MARIA	15	F	SMSTS		GRZZZZNY
KAER, CHRISTIAN	23	M	FAB		GRZZZZNY
GLASER, WILHE	16	F	BKBNDR		GRZZZZNY
SCHREIER, MAX	24	M	LABR		GRZZZZNY
LOB, ISAAC	48	M	MCHT		GRZZZZNY
HITSCHER--, JOH	28	M	LABR		GRZZZZNY
KATH	23	F	LABR		GRZZZZNY
EVERLING, NIC	25	M	EGR		GRZZZZUSA
KEKA--ER, DOM	20	M	TLR		GRZZZZNY
THELL, NIC	26	M	GDNR		GRZZZZNY
LEICH, JULES	2	F	CHILD		GRZZZZNY
RISCHBACH, CATHA	58	F	LABR		GRZZZZNY
LEONARD	24	M	LABR		GRZZZZNY
HAACH, JAC	50	M	LABR		GRZZZZNY
BARBA	50	F	LABR		GRZZZZNY
MARIE	10	F	CH		GRZZZZNY
PIERRE	7	M	CHILD		GRZZZZNY
EPPERS, ERNST	20	M	BTMKR		GRZZZZNY
ENDRES, BARBA	22	F	SVNT		GRZZZZNY
SCHRUBEL, ANTON	29	M	MSN		GRZZZZNY
KREUER, JOHANN	28	M	FARMER		GRZZZZNY
TOUPAINS, PETER	22	M	LABR		GRZZZZNY
SCHENK, JOSEF	40	M	PNTR		GRZZZZNY
BRUECK, MARG	15	M	NN		GRZZZZNY
WAGNER, ANNA	26	F	NN		GRZZZZNY
ANNA	00	F	INF		GRZZZZNY
SEITZ, ELISAB	21	F	SVNT		GRZZZZPIT
BER--ER, RICH	26	M	FRD		GRZZZZPHI
LEHN, LUDWIG	21	M	UNKNOWN		GRZZZZNY
KLEMMER, GEO	43	M	UMKR		GRZZZZNY
BAUER, JOSEF	19	M	TLR		GRZZZZDYT
JACOB	16	M	TLR		GRZZZZDYT
FUCHES, PANKATZ	16	M	NN		GRZZZZNY
LON--ER, G	26	M	UNKNOWN		GRZZZZNY
DAERING, FRANZ	21	M	CBTMKR		GRZZZZNY
HENSEL, LUDWIG	26	M	UNKNOWN		GRZZZZNY
MULLER, JORDAN	29	M	FARMER		GRZZZZNY
CAROLINE	22	F	FARMER		GRZZZZNY
JOSEF	2	M	CHILD		GRZZZZNY
LIEGRIST, W	19	M	BRR		GRZZZZTOL
REMM--LE, ALOIS	19	M	SMH		GRZZZZWIO
SCHNEIDER, ELISAB	32	F	NN		GRZZZZNY
NE-OMER, LOUIS	14	M	NN		GRZZZZNY
FRYKE	10	F	CH		GRZZZZNY
CAROLINE	9	F	CHILD		GRZZZZNY
SALOMON	4	M	CHILD		GRZZZZNY
FREDERIC, ALFRED	27	M	BTMKR		GRZZZZPIT
JOSEFINE	27	F	BTMKR		GRZZZZPIT
WEIGAND, EUG	20	M	LABR		GRZZZZUNK
-UTZ, XAVER	30	M	WVR		GRZZZZUNK
ROSALIE	29	F	WVR		GRZZZZUNK
VERONIKA	7	F	CHILD		GRZZZZUNK
ROSALIE	2	F	CHILD		GRZZZZUNK
JEAN	00	M	INF		GRZZZZUNK
GOETZ, GOTTL	25	M	MACH		GRZZZZUNK
ERNST, MARIA	20	M	SVNT		GRZZZZUNK
SCHWARTZ, MATHIAS	00	M	WVR		GRZZZZUNK
MARIA	00	F	WVR		GRZZZZUNK
ANNA	15	F	WVR		GRZZZZUNK
ROBERT	4	M	CHILD		GRZZZZUNK
FREDERIKA	00	F	INF		GRZZZZUNK
RACHHOLD, FRITZ	23	M	BKR		GRZZZZUNK
STORZER, GUSTAV	38	M	BTMKR		GRZZZZUNK
BASTERN, ELISAB	25	F	SVNT		GRZZZZNY
DELBARRE, LOUIS	26	M	MNR		FRZZZZUNK
ROSALIE	25	F	MNR		FRZZZZUNK
JOSS, JACOB	38	M	WDCTR		SRZZZZSTJ
W	36	F	WDCTR		SRZZZZSTJ
JACOB	9	M	CHILD		SRZZZZSTJ
WITT, JACOB	19	M	LABR		GRZZZZMIL

PASSENGER	AGE	SEX	OCCUPATION	PRVL DES
STRUBENGER, MARIA	25	F	SVNT	GRZZZZUSA
HUBER, ROSA	46	F	NN	GRZZZZNY
GUTENBACHER, JOSEF	00	M	BKBNDR	GRZZZZNY
ENDRICH, OTTILIE	25	F	SVNT	GRZZZZNY
SCH---ZE, ELISE	28	F	SVNT	GRZZZZNY
SCHMIDT, AUG	22	M	LABR	GRZZZZNY
MUTZ, ROSALIE	29	F	NN	GRZZZZNY
WASLAND	00	M	INF	GR****NY

SHIP: DEVONIA

FROM: GLASGOW AND MOVILLE
TO: NEW YORK
ARRIVED: 16 JULY 1888

PASSENGER	AGE	SEX	OCCUPATION	PRVL DES
AIGRISE, JAQUES	51	M	LABR	FRZZZZUSA
SCONNING, ELIE	36	M	LABR	FRZZZZUSA
ERERS, RICH.	28	M	BLKSMH	GRZZZZUSA
LUI, WILHELM	24	M	LABR	GRZZZZUSA
MARX, HERMAN	46	M	LABR	GRZZZZUSA
URBAN, WILH.	52	M	BCHR	GRZZZZUSA
HARMS, JOHANNES	24	M	LABR	GRZZZZUSA

SHIP: EDAM

FROM: AMSTERDAM
TO: NEW YORK
ARRIVED: 16 JULY 1888

PASSENGER	AGE	SEX	OCCUPATION	PRVL DES
ERNER, ALB.	25	M	LABR	GRZZZZNY
ULRICH, H.	21	M	CPTR	GRZZZZNY
SCHUESSLER, FRZ.JOS.	00	M	LABR	GRZZZZNY
PETER	15	M	LABR	GRZZZZNY
GLASEM, JOSEF	40	M	LABR	GRZZZZNY
STEINER, TOBIAS	20	M	TLR	GRZZZZNY
MINTHEN, HUBERT	28	M	LABR	GRZZZZNY
OHE, ADOLF	20	M	WRT	GRZZZZNY
WELSLAW, JOS	22	M	MCHT	GRZZZZNY
MOEHLENHARD, FRIEDR.	20	M	LABR	GRZZZZMN
LANGE, KRIST	20	M	BTMKR	GRZZZZNY
RICKER, RUD.	18	M	MCHT	GRZZZZNY
PATSKE, MARIA	19	F	UNKNOWN	GRZZZZMIL
MICHEL	16	F	UNKNOWN	GRZZZZMIL
WILHA.	10	F	CH	GRZZZZMIL
PRUDNIT, G.	44	M	LABR	GRZZZZNY
HIEL, JOSEF	39	M	LABR	GRZZZZNY
DEJA, JOH.	10	M	CH	GRZZZZNY
KASPER, HELENA	20	F	SVNT	GRZZZZNY
BERBRAM, HEINR.	43	M	LABR	GRZZZZNY
BIEMIETH, AUG.	37	M	BTMKR	GRZZZZPA
KNUTZMAN, IGNATZ	23	M	LABR	GRZZZZNY
HENNIE, A.	41	M	MCHT	GRZZZZNY
DONELLI, LUIGI	20	M	LABR	FRZZZZNY
FORMAZO, DAMATO	27	M	LABR	FRZZZZNY
SALVATORE, DAMATO	17	M	LABR	FRZZZZNY
BABZANO, ANTONIO	17	M	LABR	FRZZZZNY
STORTI, GUISEPPE	19	M	LABR	FRZZZZNY
RASATI, ANTONO	20	M	LABR	FRZZZZNY
AYRAZAN, DAVID	29	M	LABR	FRZZZZCAL
TALCONA, PASGUELA	30	M	LABR	FRZZZZNY
VENERI, DOMENICO	28	M	LABR	FRZZZZNY
FUCCI, DOMENICO	31	M	LABR	FRZZZZNY
FELICIA	27	F	LABR	FRZZZZNY
EGENIO	.08	M	INFANT	FRZZZZNY
DITTEPHANO, T.	25	M	LABR	FRZZZZNY

PASSENGER	AGE	SEX	OCCUPATION	PRVL DES
STRUSCIOLO, ALESSANDRO	35	M	LABR	FRZZZZNY
DEMARTINO, MECHEL	27	M	LABR	FRZZZZNY
GRIFFONE, MARCO	30	M	LABR	FRZZZZNY
ANTONIA	10	F	CH	FRZZZZNY
FORTE, GIACINTO	31	M	LABR	FRZZZZNY
MAIER, MATH.	25	M	LABR	GRZZZZNY
JOH.	16	M	GDNR	GRZZZZNY
SKELL, MARGAR.	31	F	UNKNOWN	GRZZZZNY
HEDWIG	7	F	CHILD	GRZZZZNY
MICHELE, EMIL	29	M	LABR	FRZZZZCAL
RETIERI, FERDINAND	25	M	LABR	FRZZZZNY
STAIGER, JOH.	42	M	BKLYR	GRZZZZNY
HERMANN, LOUISE	40	F	SMSTS	GRZZZZNY
FIRIT, CHR.	17	M	TNM	GRZZZZNY
BENDER, MILH.	17	M	GDSM	GRZZZZNY
ROTHALER, VICTOR	21	M	BTMKR	GRZZZZNY
MANINCOR, ANNA	22	F	UNKNOWN	GRZZZZNY
ARBANJELA	.02	F	INFANT	GRZZZZNY
HEID, FRANCISCA	32	F	UNKNOWN	GRZZZZNY
HERMAN	5	M	CHILD	GRZZZZNY
CARL	3	M	CHILD	GRZZZZNY
FRANZ	2	M	CHILD	GRZZZZNY
FUENS, CARL	15	M	LABR	GRZZZZNY
DENKINGER, JACOB	32	M	LABR	GRZZZZNY
SCHAUPERT, WILHELM	18	M	LABR	GRZZZZNY
DRESELER, G.	16	M	LABR	GRZZZZSTL
SCHNEIDER, GUNDA	14	F	SVNT	GRZZZZNY
WALTER, JOHANNA	23	F	SVNT	GRZZZZNY
BLISEL, JOHAN	11	M	LABR	GRZZZZNY
NEIPERT, JOHAN	20	M	TLR	GRZZZZNY
ELISE	24	F	UNKNOWN	GRZZZZNY
KRAUS, MAX	20	M	WMCHT	GRZZZZNY
HORBOCH, JOSEPH	42	M	FARMER	GRZZZZNY
ELEONORA	25	F	UNKNOWN	GRZZZZNY

SHIP: UMBRIA

FROM: LIVERPOOL AND QUEENSTOWN
TO: NEW YORK
ARRIVED: 16 JULY 1888

PASSENGER	AGE	SEX	OCCUPATION	PRVL DES
BERING, RICHD.	27	M	FARMER	GRAAKHUSA
SCHROEDER, FREDK.	20	M	LABR	GRADAXUSA
SCH-M, WILH.	44	M	LABR	GRZZZZUSA
REGINE	36	F	W	GRZZZZUSA
HEDWIG	3	M	CHILD	GRZZZZUSA
ROSA	.08	F	INFANT	GRZZZZUSA
SPANGENBERG, IDA	31	F	UNKNOWN	GRACBFUSA
LEIERIN, LINA	24	F	SVNT	GRABDMUSA
DE, ADOLF	28	M	TRVLR	GRADBQUSA
PARROTT, CATHERINE	45	F	SVNT	GRADBQUSA
ASCH, LEAH	25	F	SVNT	GRADXWUSA
LEWIS, AUGUST	45	M	MCHT	GRADBQUSA
FRICK, ELISE	30	F	SP	GRADBQUSA
BUTNA, J.S.	48	M	MCHT	GRZZZZUSA
SCHERM, EDMUND	40	M	MCHT	GRADAXUSA
MARY	33	F	W	GRADAXUSA
SCHMIDT, JOHN	34	M	MCHT	GRAAKHUSA
MOSLE, FREDERICK	24	M	UNKNOWN	GRZZZZUSA
GEORGE-R.	23	M	UNKNOWN	GRZZZZUSA
HESSING, JULIUS-H.	27	M	VAL	GRADBQUSA
SCHRAMM, MENE.	33	M	MCHT	GRADAXUSA
BROWN, SAML.	50	M	MCHT	GRADBQUSA
SCHUBERTH, J.	33	M	UNKNOWN	GRZZZZUSA
LEVY, ROBERT	50	M	UNKNOWN	GRADAXUSA
HELMROTH, WILLM.	45	M	UNKNOWN	GRADBQUSA
ALBERT	22	M	UNKNOWN	GRADBQUSA
ROSENWALD, JULIA	89	M	UNKNOWN	GRADAXUSA
MANETTE, LOUIS	00	F	UNKNOWN	GRADAXUSA
ROSENTHAL, JULIUS	28	M	MCHT	GRADBQUSA

PASSENGER	AGE	SEX	OCCUPATION	PRVL	DES
JENNINGS, FRANCIS-C.	40	M	MCHT	GRADAXUSA	
FRANCIS-C.	41	F	W	GRADAXUSA	
ANNE-B.	5	F	CHILD	GRADAXUSA	
CRO-LEY, JACOB-M.	40	M	UNKNOWN	GRZZZZUSA	
SARAH	36	F	W	GRZZZZUSA	
FERGA, VICTOR	31	M	MCHT	GRADBQUSA	

SHIP: FULDA

FROM: BREMEN AND SOUTHAMPTON
TO: NEW YORK
ARRIVED: 17 JULY 1888

PASSENGER	AGE	SEX	OCCUPATION	PRVL	DES
PATAKY, WILHELM	26	M	TT	GRZZZZUSA	
CLAUSING, WILHELM	32	M	TT	GRZZZZUSA	
ZAHN, JOHANNA	28	F	UNKNOWN	GRZZZZUSA	
BAUER, KAETHE	30	F	UNKNOWN	GRZZZZUSA	
VALET, BARBARA	63	F	UNKNOWN	GRZZZZUSA	
SCHWARZKOPF, BERNHARD	34	M	SMH	GRZZZZUSA	
NICK, RICHARD	25	M	TT	GRZZZZUSA	
EGELING, AUGUST	27	M	TT	GRZZZZUSA	
HAGEMANN, VINZENS	83	M	TT	GRZZZZUSA	
HUPPER, ANNA	22	F	UNKNOWN	GRZZZZUSA	
SEIDEWITZ, PAUL	18	M	FARMER	GRZZZZUSA	
SCHAEFER, CARL	29	M	LABR	GRZZZZUSA	
NEUMANN, FANNY	19	F	UNKNOWN	GRZZZZUSA	
GEROMILLER, CRESENZIA	16	F	UNKNOWN	GRZZZZUSA	
THERESE	15	F	UNKNOWN	GRZZZZUSA	
RAPPELT, JOSEF	25	M	BCHR	GRZZZZUSA	
REUNER, ALB.	22	M	GDNR	GRZZZZUSA	
BERNHARDT, RUDOLF	52	M	LABR	GRZZZZUSA	
PUTZ, JOSEF	32	M	LABR	GRZZZZUSA	
JSOJARA, JOHANN	25	M	BKR	GRZZZZUSA	
WALA, ALEX	18	M	BKR	GRZZZZUSA	
TRASCH, MARIA	22	F	UNKNOWN	GRZZZZUSA	
REICHLE, JOH.	32	M	FARMER	GRZZZZUSA	
PAULINE	28	F	UNKNOWN	GRZZZZUSA	
HELENE	3	F	CHILD	GRZZZZUSA	
MARIE	.05	F	INFANT	GRZZZZUSA	
HAASE, FRANZ	14	M	LABR	GRZZZZUSA	
STOH, ELISABETH	19	F	UNKNOWN	GRZZZZUSA	
RICHTER, AUGUST	32	M	LABR	GRZZZZUSA	
CHRISTINE	28	F	UNKNOWN	GRZZZZUSA	
AUGUST	3	M	CHILD	GRZZZZUSA	
ERNESTINE	.04	F	INFANT	GRZZZZUSA	
KOHLER, ANDREAS	24	M	SMH	GRZZZZUSA	
FENTH, JEAN	25	M	BKBNDR	GRZZZZUSA	
MUELLER, BARB.	25	F	UNKNOWN	GRZZZZUSA	
LOOS, CATHARINA	51	F	UNKNOWN	GRZZZZUSA	
FRIEDRICH	6	M	CHILD	GRZZZZUSA	
LICHT, LYDIA	32	F	UNKNOWN	GRZZZZUSA	
CARL	7	M	CHILD	GRZZZZUSA	
ROBERT	5	M	CHILD	GRZZZZUSA	
WILHELMINE	2	F	CHILD	GRZZZZUSA	
HEINRICH	.09	M	INFANT	GRZZZZUSA	
WEBER, WILHELM	26	M	SHMK	GRZZZZUSA	
MARIE	24	F	UNKNOWN	GRZZZZUSA	
GRETCHEN	2	F	CHILD	GRZZZZUSA	
DESCHEIMER, LOUISE	17	F	CH	GRZZZZUSA	
REISINGER, LOUIS	39	M	MCHT	GRZZZZUSA	
NAEGELE, JOHANN	29	M	MCHT	GRZZZZUSA	
ZABEL, JOHANN	35	M	FARMER	GRZZZZUSA	
JOHANNE	31	F	UNKNOWN	GRZZZZUSA	
MARTHA	2	F	CHILD	GRZZZZUSA	
OTTO	.01	M	INFANT	GRZZZZUSA	
KUHULE, FRIEDE	22	F	UNKNOWN	GRZZZZUSA	
FLAUCHER, ANNA	28	F	UNKNOWN	GRZZZZUSA	
THEODOR	5	M	CHILD	GRZZZZUSA	
SCHLEICH, FRIEDA	16	F	UNKNOWN	GRZZZZUSA	
HARTMANN, ANNA	25	F	UNKNOWN	GRZZZZUSA	
ZEHNDER, FRANZ	31	M	TLR	GRZZZZUSA	
ATTINGER, CHRISTOPH	17	M	TNM	GRZZZZUSA	
SIEGEL, FRIEDRICH	24	M	TNM	GRZZZZUSA	
HAEFELE, NMATHIAS	25	M	BKR	GRZZZZUSA	
HEER, BARB.	21	F	UNKNOWN	GRZZZZUSA	
HIRSCH, ADAM	21	M	MCHT	GRZZZZUSA	
BECKMANN, OSCAR	40	M	FARMER	GRZZZZUSA	
ROSENBLATH, HEINRICH	15	M	FARMER	GRZZZZUSA	
SCHACK, FRIEDRICH	22	M	GDNR	GRZZZZUSA	
FROMBERG, WILHELM	21	M	LABR	GRZZZZUSA	
MOSSAKOWSKI, LUDWIG	27	M	LABR	GRZZZZUSA	
BRAUN, HERMAN	17	M	TLR	GRZZZZUSA	
JACOB, CARL	17	M	BKR	GRZZZZUSA	
WEBENGER, CASIMI	19	M	SMH	GRZZZZUSA	
FRITZ, IDA	18	F	UNKNOWN	GRZZZZUSA	
FRENTZEL, CAROLINE	61	F	UNKNOWN	GRZZZZUSA	
GRENZ, AUGUSTE	27	F	UNKNOWN	GRZZZZUSA	
JOHANNA	25	F	UNKNOWN	GRZZZZUSA	
RICHTER, CAROLINE	60	F	UNKNOWN	GRZZZZUSA	
FORBRECH, CARL	29	M	MLR	GRZZZZUSA	
EMME, HERMAN	30	M	MCHT	GRZZZZUSA	
WESELY, MARIE	7	F	CHILD	GRZZZZUSA	
MAHNKE, ANNA	21	F	UNKNOWN	GRZZZZUSA	
BURKEL, FRIEDRICH	16	M	FARMER	GRZZZZUSA	
CATHARINA	18	F	UNKNOWN	GRZZZZUSA	
BOO, ANTON	38	M	LABR	GRZZZZUSA	
SCHWEBACH, KATARINA	20	F	UNKNOWN	GRZZZZUSA	
RADER, JOHANN	35	M	TLR	GRZZZZUSA	
NADSTAWEK, VALENTIN	24	M	FARMER	GRZZZZUSA	
FUNKE, ANTON	33	M	BKR	GRZZZZUSA	
FLEISSNER, ANNA	34	F	UNKNOWN	GRZZZZUSA	
THOMAS	6	M	CHILD	GRZZZZUSA	
THERESIA	5	F	CHILD	GRZZZZUSA	
MARGARETHA	3	F	CHILD	GRZZZZUSA	
KARL	.09	M	INFANT	GRZZZZUSA	
HAIBACH, JOHANN	16	M	LABR	GRZZZZUSA	
WARNEBOLD, AUGUST	18	M	BKR	GRZZZZUSA	
BOCHLERT, CAROLINE	66	F	UNKNOWN	GRZZZZUSA	
LOUISE	31	F	BKR	GRZZZZUSA	
JUENKE, ARTHUR	4	M	CHILD	GRZZZZUSA	
MARIA	4	F	CHILD	GRZZZZUSA	
CHORHUMMEL, EMMA	18	F	UNKNOWN	GRZZZZUSA	
REMLER, BERNHARD	16	M	FARMER	GRZZZZUSA	
SCHWIEG, EUGEN	26	M	FARMER	GRZZZZUSA	
WEINMANN, VALENTIN	56	M	FARMER	GRZZZZUSA	
WALTER	19	M	FARMER	GRZZZZUSA	
BRENNER, CARL	22	M	MCHT	GRZZZZUSA	
FISCHER, ALMA	26	F	UNKNOWN	GRZZZZUSA	
BOHLE, GUSTAV	17	M	MCHT	GRZZZZUSA	
KUHBANDNER, JOHANN	16	M	MCHT	GRZZZZUSA	
GEISLER, CARL	25	M	BKR	GRZZZZUSA	
BOERGWER, META	20	F	UNKNOWN	GRZZZZUSA	
ZENKER, WILHELM	18	M	FARMER	GRZZZZUSA	
LAMMERS, NICOLAUS	15	M	FARMER	GRZZZZUSA	
LOSSE, DIEDRICH	15	M	FARMER	GRZZZZUSA	
WARNKE, EMILIE	20	F	UNKNOWN	GRZZZZUSA	
HOYNACKY, FRANZ	15	M	LABR	GRZZZZUSA	
JUNKER, SOPHIE	16	F	UNKNOWN	GRZZZZUSA	
FRIEDRICH	15	M	LABR	GRZZZZUSA	
GIES, MARGARETHA	23	F	UNKNOWN	GRZZZZUSA	
RUCK, SOPHIE	18	F	UNKNOWN	GRZZZZUSA	
HOEPPEL, JOHANN	28	M	BKR	GRZZZZUSA	
JANKEN, JOSEF	35	M	GDNR	GRZZZZUSA	
FRITSCHKA, LEOPOLD	22	M	GDNR	GRZZZZUSA	
ALTRUP, FRIEDRICH	25	M	WCHMKR	GRZZZZUSA	
JAEGER, GUSTAV	30	M	WCHMKR	GRZZZZUSA	
MOELLER, HEINRICH	16	M	MCHT	GRZZZZUSA	
HONANN, ANNA	28	F	UNKNOWN	GRZZZZUSA	
LISERT, CHARLOTTE	20	F	UNKNOWN	GRZZZZUSA	
MUELLER, JEAN	16	M	GDNR	GRZZZZUSA	
HENE, ROSA	22	F	UNKNOWN	GRZZZZUSA	
GRUENEBAUM, LLINA	19	F	UNKNOWN	GRZZZZUSA	
WERNER, JEAN	18	M	FARMER	GRZZZZUSA	
KAHRS, FRIEDR.	54	M	FARMER	GRZZZZUSA	
DORETHEA	51	F	UNKNOWN	GRZZZZUSA	

PASSENGER	AGE	SEX	OCCUPATION	PRVL	DES
FRIEDRICH	7	M	CHILD	GRZZZZUSA	
MARIE	5	F	CHILD	GRZZZZUSA	
CORDES, FRIEDRICH	29	M	FARMER	GRZZZZUSA	
HARMS, MARIE	25	F	UNKNOWN	GRZZZZUSA	
DECKER, IGNATZ	17	M	BKR	GRZZZZUSA	
RUHLAND, ANDREAS	18	M	LABR	GRZZZZUSA	
ARNOLD, ALEX	24	M	LLD	GRZZZZUSA	
DABIDSOHN, WOLF	39	M	LLD	GRZZZZUSA	
KOEHLER, HERMAN	26	M	LKSH	GRZZZZUSA	
MARX, HELENE	20	F	UNKNOWN	GRZZZZUSA	
FRISCH, ANNA	17	F	UNKNOWN	GRZZZZUSA	
DENZER, FRIEDRICH	14	M	LABR	GRZZZZUSA	
FLECK, ERNESTINE	18	F	UNKNOWN	GRZZZZUSA	
EMMA	20	F	UNKNOWN	GRZZZZUSA	
NATHAN	7	M	CHILD	GRZZZZUSA	
MALW.	6	F	CHILD	GRZZZZUSA	
LUDWIG	4	M	CHILD	GRZZZZUSA	
IDA	3	F	CHILD	GRZZZZUSA	
TRUDE	2	F	CHILD	GRZZZZUSA	
WUESTNER, HEINRICH	46	M	FARMER	GRZZZZUSA	
CAROLINE	47	F	UNKNOWN	GRZZZZUSA	
HEINRICH	17	M	FARMER	GRZZZZUSA	
MICHAEL	15	M	FARMER	GRZZZZUSA	
AUGUST	7	M	CHILD	GRZZZZUSA	
FIEDER, WILHELM	23	M	FARMER	GRZZZZUSA	
SEROHMAIER, JACOB	17	M	FARMER	GRZZZZUSA	
GRUBER, GOTTLIEB	19	M	LABR	GRZZZZUSA	
CIASZYNSKY, JOHANN	51	M	LABR	GRZZZZUSA	
HERDAM, AMALIE	14	F	UNKNOWN	GRZZZZUSA	
BOEHLIG, HEINRICH	15	M	LABR	GRZZZZUSA	
ALBRECHT, AUGUST	40	M	LABR	GRZZZZUSA	
KUNZLN, MARIE	30	F	UNKNOWN	GRZZZZUSA	
STOEHT, THERESE	25	F	UNKNOWN	GRZZZZUSA	
BULLERMANN, DORA	17	F	UNKNOWN	GRZZZZUSA	
STAGGE, HERMAN	30	M	FARMER	GRZZZZUSA	
HARZER, EDWALD	19	M	LABR	GRZZZZUSA	
KURNOTH, GUSTAV	38	M	LABR	GRZZZZUSA	
WILLE, JACOB	25	M	SHMK	GRZZZZUSA	
GERKEN, DIEDRICH	20	M	FARMER	GRZZZZUSA	
META	19	F	UNKNOWN	GRZZZZUSA	
EBERLEIN, CAROLINE	22	F	UNKNOWN	GRZZZZUSA	
LOUISE	20	F	UNKNOWN	GRZZZZUSA	
ANKER, LEOPOLD	15	M	HTR	GRZZZZUSA	
KODADO, KATHARINA	32	F	UNKNOWN	GRZZZZUSA	
JOSEF	4	M	CHILD	GRZZZZUSA	
MARIE	.10	F	INFANT	GRZZZZUSA	
DAUER, FRANCISCA	23	F	UNKNOWN	GRZZZZUSA	
MARIE	.10	F	INFANT	GRZZZZUSA	
SCHMENKEL, WILHELM	42	M	LABR	GRZZZZUSA	
LORLEY, BERNHARD	32	M	LABR	GRZZZZUSA	
NECKE, CARL	45	M	MCHT	GRZZZZUSA	
HAUCH, JACOB	26	M	MCHT	GRZZZZUSA	
RABEL, MICHAEL	50	M	MCHT	GRZZZZUSA	
STADLER, STEFAN	25	M	MCHT	GRZZZZUSA	
BRINKHOFF, HERMAN	31	M	CPTR	GRZZZZUSA	
JUNGE, ELISE	14	F	UNKNOWN	GRZZZZUSA	

SHIP: STATE OF NEBRASKA

FROM: GLASGOW AND LARNE
TO: NEW YORK
ARRIVED: 18 JULY 1888

PASSENGER	AGE	SEX	OCCUPATION	PRVL	DES
GEISBAUER, KATHARINA	19	F	SP	GRZZZZUSA	
BOLLE, MARIE	38	F	W	GRZZZZUSA	
MARGARETHA	8	F	CHILD	GRZZZZUSA	
REHDER, CHRISTIAN	35	M	FARMER	GRZZZZUSA	
MAXSEIN, JOHANN	16	M	NN	GRZZZZUSA	
SCHNEIER, ISAAK	14	M	NN	GRZZZZUSA	

SHIP: WISCONSIN

FROM: LIVERPOOL AND QUEENSTOWN
TO: NEW YORK
ARRIVED: 18 JULY 1888

PASSENGER	AGE	SEX	OCCUPATION	PRVL	DES
KNOPP, ROBERT	30	M	LABR	GRZZZZUSA	
FELDMAN, ZALEE	7	F	CHILD	GRZZZZUSA	
KNODT, MAX	22	M	MSN	GRZZZZUSA	
HIRBSCHAMAN, HERMAN	18	M	GZR	GRZZZZUSA	
HOMISCH, CONRAD	2	M	CHILD	GRZZZZUSA	
ROCHUS	.07	M	INFANT	GRZZZZUSA	
FENSTEIN, ISAAC	20	M	LABR	GRZZZZUSA	
NEOUZE, MARY	28	F	LDY	FRZZZZUSA	

SHIP: BELGENLAND

FROM: ANTWERP
TO: NEW YORK
ARRIVED: 19 JULY 1888

PASSENGER	AGE	SEX	OCCUPATION	PRVL	DES
SCHACHE, U	50	F	SVNT	FRACXVNY	
SCHINZEL, E.	18	M	CL	GRZZZZPHI	
LINDEN, H.	28	F	UNKNOWN	GRAFNKNY	
NEUMANN, W.G.	47	M	MCHT	GRACBFNY	
LUCA, LUDW.	21	M	LABR	GRZZZZNY	
WEISS, HULDA	19	F	UNKNOWN	GRZZZZNY	
AUGUSTE	17	F	UNKNOWN	GRZZZZNY	
OTTILIE	11	F	UNKNOWN	GRZZZZNY	
WAGNER, FRITZ	25	M	CL	GRALOFNY	
KNOBLAUCH, HERM.	45	M	PDLR	GRZZZZNY	
SCHULZE, MATH	43	F	UNKNOWN	GRABVWNY	
CARL	17	M	UNKNOWN	GRAAECNY	
EGER, CHRIST	53	M	LABR	GRAAECNY	
EUGEN	26	M	LABR	GRAAECNY	
SCHAERER, JOHANN	40	M	LWYR	GRAICHNY	
AGNES	11	F	CH	GRAICHNY	
SCHUENHOF, MARIA	30	F	UNKNOWN	GRAICHNY	
ANNA	7	F	CHILD	GRAICHNY	
STOLZ, ANNA	19	F	SVNT	GRZZZZNY	
GRABOWSKI, VAL.	57	M	MSN	GRAEBPCH	
DOROTHEA	52	F	UNKNOWN	GRAEBPCH	
FRZ.	8	M	CHILD	GRAEBPCH	
CLEYE	6	M	CHILD	GRAEBPCH	
HAAG, CATH.	28	F	HSKPR	GRADBQNY	
MANN, ERNST	48	M	BBR	GRZZZZIL	
HELENA	25	F	UNKNOWN	GRZZZZIL	
CAROLINE	2	F	CHILD	GRZZZZIL	
KOSAUKI, WILHELM	19	M	CPTR	GRZZZZMIL	
NEBENDAHL, AUGUST	20	M	CPTR	GRAIWINY	
RUTHARDT, PAUL	23	M	LABR	GRABECNY	
SATTEL, BENEDICT	22	M	FARMER	GRZZZZNY	
NILLERICH, JOHANNES	30	M	LABR	GRABKVNY	
REIS, ANNA	22	F	SVNT	LXZZZZUSA	
HAAG, LUDWIG	25	M	FARMER	LXALOFNY	
FLAUMER, MICH.	17	M	SHMK	GRZZZZNY	
PICKEL, PETER	18	M	SHMK	GRZZZZNY	
SCHERET, ELISABETH	18	F	SVNT	GRZZZZNY	
GRESER, MARKUS	27	M	UNKNOWN	GRZZZZUNK	
AUCHTER, JOSEPH	25	M	FARMER	GRZZZZLAN	
MESSER, FR.	28	F	UNKNOWN	GRZZZZLAN	
CHRIST.	4	M	CHILD	GRZZZZLAN	
LOUIS	3	F	CHILD	GRZZZZLAN	
WILH.	2	M	CHILD	GRZZZZLAN	
CARL	00	M	INF	GRZZZZLAN	
SCHUNTER, ERNST	14	M	UNKNOWN	GRZZZZNY	
HOFFMANN, GREGOR	18	M	STDNT	GRAAHPNY	
KIEWZER, CATH.	25	F	UNKNOWN	GRZZZZNY	
ANNA	00	F	INF	GRZZZZNY	

PASSENGER	AGE	SEX	OCCUPATION	PRVL	DES
TUTTER, JOHANN	28	M	TLR		GRZZZZNY
KUHN, LUDW.	17	M	LABR		GRZZZZNY
BAUSCH, JOH.	45	M	TLR		GRZZZZNY
LOUISE	44	F	UNKNOWN		GRZZZZNY
AULINE	9	F	CHILD		GRZZZZNY
FRIEDA	6	F	CHILD		GRZZZZNY
MEYER, JOHANN	21	M	FARMER		GRZZZZPIT
THIRY, MARIA	20	F	SMSTS		GRZZZZPIT
TIESSEL, SEBAST.	16	M	LABR		GRADQNPIT
ELISE	8	F	CHILD		GRADQNPIT
KLEMMER, JOH.	24	M	FARMER		GRZZZZPIT
WILKART, JACOB	25	M	FARMER		GRZZZZPIT
BOPP, PHIL	29	M	TNM		GRACDNNY
ELISE	32	F	UNKNOWN		GRACDNNY
MOEHR, CONRAD	17	M	TLR		GRACDNNY
METTER, CHRIST.	20	M	LABR		GRAGTKCH
SITTER, AMALIE	25	F	CK		GRAHGYCH
CRESCENZ	27	F	CK		GRAHGYCH
JOHANN	1	M	CHILD		GRAHGYCH
SCHNECK, JOHANN	23	M	LABR		GRZZZZCH
HUBER, JOHANN	32	M	LABR		GRZZZZCH
KERN, GOSEF	21	M	LABR		GRZZZZCH
CHRISTIANI, PHILY	34	M	BR		GRZZZZCH
CATH.	28	F	UNKNOWN		GRZZZZCH
ELISAB.	3	F	CHILD		GRZZZZCH
ANNA	00	F	INF		GRZZZZCH
METZGER, EDW.	18	M	SHMK		GRAAHBCH
WICKLES, ANTON	27	M	WTR		GRALQDCH
HIRSCHBERGER, BERNH.	17	M	CL		GRACRACH
HERBRICK, HCH.	16	M	LABR		GRZZZZCH
SCHAEFER, ANTON	18	M	LABR		GRZZZZCH
EICHSTEDTER, ELISAB.	21	F	SVNT		GRZZZZCH
BLATT, CHARLOTTE	35	F	SVNT		GRADODCH
LINA	10	F	CH		GRADODCH
LAURA	5	F	CHILD		GRADODCH
WILH.	3	M	CHILD		GRADODCH
LOUISE	00	F	INF		GRADODCH
DEBUS, LUDW.	37	M	GDSM		GRZZZZCH
JACOB	14	M	UNKNOWN		GRZZZZCH
JOSEF	11	M	UNKNOWN		GRZZZZCH
STOLTRMANN, ANTON	23	M	LABR		GRZZZZCH
CASPARI, HERIBERT	21	M	SEMN		GRZZZZCH
STEICHER, JEAN	25	M	LABR		LXZZZZNY
KECK, LOUIS	64	M	LABR		GRZZZZNY
KOHL, MARG.	24	F	MLNR		GRZZZZNY
NAGEL, FERD.	52	M	FARMER		SRZZZZNY
KRESZENZ	26	F	UNKNOWN		SRZZZZNY
WILH.	1	M	CHILD		SRZZZZNY
SEILER, CASPAR	25	M	UNKNOWN		SRZZZZNY
WACZAKOWSKI, MICH.	35	M	GDSM		GRZZZZNY
LEWY, NIC.	30	M	LABR		FRZZZZNY
KOHN, GUSTAV	21	M	CBTMKR		FRADBQNY
FRANTZ, WILL.	23	M	TLR		FRADBQNY
BZENTGEN, CARL	23	M	TLR		FRADBQNY
BECKMANN, PAUL	43	M	ENGR		FRADBQNY
FOX, LENA	26	F	CK		FRADBQNY
DONAVS, HIPPOLYTE	38	M	CK		FRADBQNY
U	38	F	UNKNOWN		FRADBQNY
THIES, ANNA	16	F	UNKNOWN		GRZZZZNY
REMFER, GEORGE	43	M	PNTR		GRACUXUNK
MARIA	44	F	UNKNOWN		GRACUXUNK
HOLUB, SIMON	23	M	CL		GRACXVNY
LEOPOLD	25	M	CL		GRACXVNY
HURKA, FRANZ	24	M	LABR		GRACXVNY
HAJEK, FRANZ	24	M	LABR		GRACXVNY
GAVUREK, WZL.	32	M	LABR		GRACXVNY
NEMASTA, C.F.	56	M	CL		GRACXVNY
FISCH, JOSEF	21	M	FARMER		GRACXVNY
DECAK, JOSEF	30	M	FARMER		GRZZZZNY
AHR, ENGELBERT	42	M	MSN		GRZZZZNY
NOLL, FRIED.	25	M	FARMER		GRZZZZNY
ANNA	24	F	UNKNOWN		GRZZZZNY
NICOLAUS	3	M	CHILD		GRZZZZNY
FRIED.	00	M	INF		GRZZZZNY
ERB, KATH.	19	F	SVNT		GRZZZZUSA
SATTLER, MARIE	19	F	SVNT		GRABQCUSA
LESMEISTER, GEORGE	18	M	LABR		GRZZZZUSA
KAPPLER, JACOB	36	M	BLKSMH		GRACBFNY
KATH.	34	F	UNKNOWN		GRACBFNY
MARIA	7	F	CHILD		GRACBFNY
JACOB	5	M	CHILD		GRACBFNY
KARL	2	M	CHILD		GRACBFNY
FRANZ.	00	F	INF		GRACBFNY
HEMMER, PETER	37	M	LABR		GRACBFNY
MARG.	37	F	UNKNOWN		GRACBFNY
ELISAB.	14	F	UNKNOWN		GRACBFNY
IDA	9	F	CHILD		GRACBFNY
JACOB	4	M	CHILD		GRACBFNY
HEIN.	2	M	CHILD		GRACBFNY
KOZELKA, VINZ.	19	M	UNKNOWN		GRACXVNY
GEISSLER, AUGUST	24	M	SHMK		GRZZZZNY
STENZEL, REINHOLD	38	M	UNKNOWN		GRAARZNY
WAGNER, JOSEPH	25	M	DRSMKR		GRZZZZNY
DOMINIGUE	21	M	FARMER		GRZZZZNY
LUTZ, CARL	23	M	BCHR		GRACVENY
SCHIERES, F.	32	M	FARMER		LXZZZZNY
ADAM, JACOB	21	M	SHMK		GRZZZZNY
PIESEN, HENRI	34	M	CPTR		LXZZZZNY
SCHOSSLER, PETER	19	M	TLR		LXZZZZNY
BICHLER, MICH.	22	M	FARMER		LXZZZZNY
MONTON, P.	22	M	SHMK		LXZZZZNY
RAPP, TERESA	36	F	UNKNOWN		GRZZZZNY
ROSA	13	F	UNKNOWN		GRZZZZNY
MARG.	00	F	INF		GRZZZZNY
LUDWIG, HEIN.	36	M	TLR		GRZZZZNY
ELIS.	37	F	UNKNOWN		GRZZZZNY
MARIA	14	F	UNKNOWN		GRZZZZNY
JOHANN	10	M	CH		GRZZZZNY
VOSSKUEHLER, CARL	24	M	BLKSMH		GRAKTDNY
CLASSEN, HEDWIG	14	M	UNKNOWN		GRAKTDKAS
VESTUNG, H.	56	M	SHMK		GRABHTKAS
ELLER, JOHANN	21	M	GDSM		GRAGKWCH
THIELE, CARL	26	M	LABR		GRABHTCH
WINHELLER, U	37	F	UNKNOWN		GRABHTCH
HENRIETTE	11	F	UNKNOWN		GRABHTCH
WULFRUEG, MAX	38	M	UNKNOWN		GRABHTCH
BREN, CHRIST	26	M	BKR		GRAAFXCH
GUEN, ANNA	23	F	UNKNOWN		GRAAFXCH
WALTER, KRESCENTIA	19	F	UNKNOWN		GRAAFXCH
WRISTEL, LOUISE	27	F	UNKNOWN		GRZZZZCH
EMIL	15	M	UNKNOWN		GRZZZZCH
ANNA	8	F	CHILD		GRZZZZCH
SAUBERLICH, CHRISTINE	18	F	UNKNOWN		GRZZZZCH
FREISEIS, CATH.	20	F	UNKNOWN		GRZZZZCH
DIENST, MARIE	17	F	UNKNOWN		GRABODCH
SCHMIEDBERG, CARL	14	M	LABR		GRZZZZCH
KOLB, VAL.	34	M	FARMER		GRZZZZCH
ALTVATER, HCH.	40	M	GDNR		GRZZZZCH
BAUER, JOSEF	39	M	FARMER		GRZZZZUNK
CRESCENZ	38	F	UNKNOWN		GRZZZZUNK
ALBERT	13	M	UNKNOWN		GRZZZZUNK
DYONIS	9	M	CHILD		GRZZZZUNK
MARIA	5	F	CHILD		GRZZZZUNK
CRESCENZ	4	F	CHILD		GRZZZZUNK
JOHANN	3	M	CHILD		GRZZZZUNK
JOHANNA	2	F	CHILD		GRZZZZUNK
LUDWIG	00	M	INF		GRZZZZUNK
FISCHER, HAVER	22	M	WTR		GRZZZZUNK
NOCHEL, JOHANN	22	M	LABR		GRACHWUNK
DECKER, EVA	15	F	SVNT		GRAETXUNK
KNAUSS, HCH.	17	M	UNKNOWN		GRZZZZNY
CHRISTIANE	21	F	SVNT		GRZZZZNY
KOLLUCK, FRANZ	24	M	LABR		GRADNUNY
FRANZ, ANNA	45	F	UNKNOWN		GRZZZZNY
ROSALIE	4	F	CHILD		GRZZZZNY
MARG.	11	F	UNKNOWN		GRZZZZNY
ROSINER, FRANZ	20	M	LABR		GRADEMNY
CNIABURG, F.	17	F	UNKNOWN		GRZZZZNY
HIRSCHSTELLER, CARL	15	M	UNKNOWN		GRZZZZNY
WAMECK, FRANZ	21	M	WTR		GRZZZZNY

PASSENGER	AGE	SEX	OCCUPATION	PRVL	DES
KOHLER, VICTOR	30	M	CL	GRZZZZNY	
MARIE	26	F	UNKNOWN	GRZZZZNY	
JULIETTE	1	F	CHILD	GRZZZZNY	
ALPHONS	00	M	INF	GRZZZZNY	
MULLER, ROBERT	18	M	LABR	GRZZZZNY	
ECKERICH, KATH.	18	F	UNKNOWN	GRZZZZNY	
CASSOLER, EDOUARD	17	M	STCTR	SRZZZZNY	
GACEK, ROBERT	16	M	CPTR	GRZZZZNY	
KUHLSHEINER, FRANZ	16	M	BKR	GRZZZZBUF	
SPAHN, BARBE	18	F	FARMER	GRZZZZBUF	
MENNINGER, CARL	16	M	WTR	GRZZZZBUF	
MALTRY, PETER	19	M	BLKSMH	GRABYNCLE	
KRZYZAMAK, WOWRSYN	23	M	LABR	GRZZZZUNK	
MERSCH, LUCIAN	19	M	LABR	LXZZZZUNK	
GOSSGART, MICHAEL	64	M	SHMK	GRZZZZNY	
RUPPERT, JOHANNES	22	M	FARMER	GRAAVDNY	
FONTENELL, CHRIST.	22	M	FARMER	GRZZZZNY	
HOFFMANN, GERARD	60	M	FARMER	GRZZZZNY	
MARY	50	F	UNKNOWN	GRZZZZNY	
ANNA	32	F	UNKNOWN	GRZZZZNY	
PETER	22	M	UNKNOWN	GRZZZZNY	
ZIMMER, CARL	25	M	CPTR	GRZZZZNY	
RIEWITZ, JOSEPHINE	24	F	UNKNOWN	GRZZZZNY	
WAHLSTER, GEORGE	24	M	UNKNOWN	GRZZZZNY	
BERTHA	28	F	UNKNOWN	GRZZZZNY	
IDA	7	F	CHILD	GRZZZZNY	
WILH.	00	M	INF	GRZZZZNY	
NILL, ANNA	16	F	UNKNOWN	GRZZZZNY	
FROEHLICH, FRANZ	22	M	LABR	GRZZZZNY	
FUTZ, ANDREAS	24	M	LABR	SRZZZZNY	
EGGER, JACOB	21	M	TLR	SRZZZZNY	
ASET, CECILIA	42	F	UNKNOWN	GRZZZZNY	
MARIA	13	F	UNKNOWN	GRZZZZNY	

SHIP: GOTHIA

FROM: STETTIN
TO: NEW YORK
ARRIVED: 19 JULY 1888

PASSENGER	AGE	SEX	OCCUPATION	PRVL	DES
REHFELD, HENRIETTE	24	F	SGL	PRZZZZUSA	
BATTSCH, JOHANN	62	M	SHMK	PRZZZZUSA	
MARIE	56	F	W	PRZZZZUSA	
BERTHA	18	F	CH	PRZZZZUSA	
U, U	24	M	UNKNOWN	PRZZZZUSA	
WENDT, LOUISE	29	F	CH	PRZZZZUSA	
OTTO	2	M	CHILD	PRZZZZUSA	
SCHIERMANN, CARL	60	M	UNKNOWN	PRZZZZUSA	
HENRIETTE	62	F	UNKNOWN	PRZZZZUSA	
MORAUZ, THOMAS	28	M	UNKNOWN	PRZZZZUSA	
JULIANA	25	F	W	PRZZZZUSA	
NEUMANN, GUSTAV	27	M	LABR	PRZZZZUSA	
BRIENIEWSKI, ANTON	35	M	TCHR	PRZZZZUSA	
SCHNEIDER, GOTTLIEB	58	M	LABR	PRZZZZUSA	
HAINZ, ADELE	15	F	SGL	PRZZZZUSA	
BERTHA	17	F	SGL	PRZZZZUSA	
KOLASKA, STANISLAWA	16	F	SGL	PRZZZZUSA	
WI------K, KATARZYNA	17	F	SGL	PRZZZZUSA	
NIMTZ, BERTHA	20	F	SGL	PRZZZZUSA	
KROGEL, MARTHA	20	F	SGL	PRZZZZUSA	
ROSE	21	F	SGL	PRZZZZUSA	
GOERS, FRIEDRICH	23	M	LABR	PRZZZZUSA	
ANNA	23	F	W	PRZZZZUSA	
CARL	68	M	LABR	PRZZZZUSA	
DOMNIK, JOSEF	45	M	LABR	PRZZZZUSA	
EVA	40	F	W	PRZZZZUSA	
JOHANN	11	F	CH	PRZZZZUSA	
ANASTASIA	4	F	CHILD	PRZZZZUSA	
KANNENBERG, FRIEDRICH	25	M	LABR	PRZZZZUSA	
KONNENBERG, WILHELMINE	24	F	W	PRZZZZUSA	

PASSENGER	AGE	SEX	OCCUPATION	PRVL	DES
PAUL	1	M	CHILD	PRZZZZUSA	
ALTENBURG, WILHELMINE	50	F	W	PRZZZZUSA	
AUGUSTE	19	F	CH	PRZZZZUSA	
REINHARDT, FRIEDRICH	31	M	FARMER	PRZZZZUSA	
WEGNER, HERMANN	29	M	LABR	PRZZZZUSA	
WILHELMINE	30	F	W	PRZZZZUSA	
AUGUSTE	5	F	CHILD	PRZZZZUSA	
ANNA	3	F	CHILD	PRZZZZUSA	
NEUMANN, ERNSTINE	29	F	SGL	PRZZZZUSA	
U., VACLAV	00	M	UNKNOWN	PRZZZZUSA	
LESKE, PAUL	30	M	LABR	PRZZZZUSA	
ANNA	21	F	W	PRZZZZUSA	
DIETRICH, LEOPOLD	26	M	SHMK	PRZZZZUSA	
JOHANNA	22	F	W	PRZZZZUSA	
ZORL, JOHANNA	56	F	W	PRZZZZUSA	
ROESNER, MARIE	28	F	SGL	PRZZZZUSA	
ROTH, FERDINAND	36	M	LABR	PRZZZZUSA	
MARIANNA	44	F	W	PRZZZZUSA	
THERESE	19	F	W	PRZZZZUSA	
ALEXANDER	16	M	W	PRZZZZUSA	
LUDWIG	9	M	CHILD	PRZZZZUSA	
ANTON	6	M	CHILD	PRZZZZUSA	
THEODOR	4	M	CHILD	PRZZZZUSA	
BERNHARD	.04	M	INFANT	PRZZZZUSA	
BECKER, HUGO	30	M	BCHR	PRZZZZUSA	
MARIOE	23	F	W	PRZZZZUSA	
BOHM, EMMA	25	F	SGL	PRZZZZUSA	
SCHUETT, AUGUSTE	19	F	SGL	PRZZZZUSA	
MARTSCHUNKE, FRIEDRICH	21	M	FARMER	PRZZZZUSA	
DIEVENSTEDT, OTTO	46	M	MCHT	PRZZZZUSA	
EMMA	38	F	W	PRZZZZUSA	
ELSE	16	F	CH	PRZZZZUSA	
LORENZ, M-SIE	30	F	SGL	PRZZZZUSA	
RAUBE, ELISABETH	14	F	SGL	PRZZZZUSA	
LEMKE, EMILIE	22	F	W	PRZZZZUSA	
WILHELM	.09	M	INFANT	PRZZZZUSA	
DARGA, ROSALIE	22	F	SGL	PRZZZZUSA	
SCHUBERTH, HERMANN	42	M	MECH	PRZZZZUSA	
OSCAR	15	M	SLSMH	PRZZZZUSA	
BARRA, JACOB	28	M	LABR	PRZZZZUSA	
KEILUS, MARIE	24	F	DRSMKR	PRZZZZUSA	
STOLZMANN, CAROLINE	41	F	W	PRZZZZUSA	
PAULINE	15	F	CH	PRZZZZUSA	
AUGUSTE	12	F	CH	PRZZZZUSA	
ERNSTINE	11	F	CH	PRZZZZUSA	
DOERING, EDUARD	27	M	TNSTH	PRZZZZUSA	
HIRSCH, JOHANNA	39	F	W	PRZZZZUSA	
JOSEPHA	19	F	CH	PRZZZZUSA	
KOPPEN, WILHELM	57	M	LABR	PRZZZZUSA	
WILHELMINE	30	F	W	PRZZZZUSA	
HERMANN	11	M	CH	PRZZZZUSA	
WILHELMINE	18	F	CH	PRZZZZUSA	
RAMMIN, HERMANN	44	M	LABR	PRZZZZUSA	
BERTHA	12	F	CH	PRZZZZUSA	
ANNA	9	F	CHILD	PRZZZZUSA	
RODD, FRANZ	59	M	TLR	PRZZZZUSA	
ROSA	58	F	W	PRZZZZUSA	
EDUARD	18	M	CH	PRZZZZUSA	
ANTON	15	M	CH	PRZZZZUSA	
ALBERT	12	M	CH	PRZZZZUSA	
MARIE	10	F	CH	PRZZZZUSA	
KRAUSE, CARL	25	M	SHMK	PRZZZZUSA	
SCHMIDT, ALBERT	48	M	LABR	PRZZZZUSA	
AUGUSTE	38	F	W	PRZZZZUSA	
EMIL	16	M	CH	PRZZZZUSA	
KLING, FRIEDRICH	27	M	SVNT	PRZZZZUSA	
PETER, WILHELM	36	M	CPRSMH	PRZZZZUSA	
ELISE	38	F	W	PRZZZZUSA	
ABRAHAM, EMMA	26	F	SGL	PRZZZZUSA	
BERTHA	21	F	SGL	PRZZZZUSA	
WASKOW, FRIEDRICH	54	M	CTW	PRZZZZUSA	
SOPHIE	45	F	W	PRZZZZUSA	
JULIUS	21	M	UNKNOWN	PRZZZZUSA	
AUGUST	15	M	UNKNOWN	PRZZZZUSA	
BERTHA	13	F	UNKNOWN	PRZZZZUSA	

PASSENGER	AGE	SEX	OCCUPATION	PRVL	DES
IDA	10	F	UNKNOWN	PRZZZZUSA
AUGUSTE	8	F	CHILD	PRZZZZUSA
BUETTNER, MAX	33	M	FARMER	PRZZZZUSA
WITTENBERG, FRIEDRICH	36	M	BLKSMH	PRZZZZUSA
MARIE	35	F	W	PRZZZZUSA
FRAESE, SUSANNE	65	F	W	PRZZZZUSA
WITTENBERG, ALBERT	11	M	CH	PRZZZZUSA
FRANZ	10	M	CH	PRZZZZUSA
OTTO	6	M	CHILD	PRZZZZUSA
ANNA	3	F	CHILD	PRZZZZUSA
HAAK, WILHELMINE	19	F	SGL	PRZZZZUSA
KAMINSKI, FRANZ	24	M	LABR	PRZZZZUSA
KACZMAREK, JOSEFA	20	F	W	PRZZZZUSA
CZAPIEWSKI, LEOPOLD	23	M	LABR	PRZZZZUSA
LADE, OTTO	16	M	JNR	PRZZZZUSA
MASCHUCKI, JOSEF	30	M	LABR	PRZZZZUSA
STEIN, CARL	39	M	LKSH	PRZZZZUSA
PALEKOWSKI, FERDINAND	39	M	LABR	PRZZZZUSA
WILHELMINE	36	F	W	PRZZZZUSA
JULIUS	11	M	CH	PRZZZZUSA
FERDINAND	9	M	CHILD	PRZZZZUSA
WILHELMINE	7	F	CHILD	PRZZZZUSA
ERNSTINE	4	F	CHILD	PRZZZZUSA
CAROLINE	3	F	CHILD	PRZZZZUSA
AUGUST	.10	M	INFANT	PRZZZZUSA
HARTMANN, AMANDA	24	F	SGL	PRZZZZUSA
UNRUH, MATHILDE	14	F	SGL	PRZZZZUSA
BUEGGE, FERDINAND	50	M	SHMK	PRZZZZUSA
THERESE	26	F	W	PRZZZZUSA
ANNA	3	F	CHILD	PRZZZZUSA
ELISABETH	1	F	CHILD	PRZZZZUSA
KRANIG, RUDOLF	28	M	LABR	PRZZZZUSA
BUCHDORN, CARL	38	M	LABR	PRZZZZUSA
ANNA	31	F	W	PRZZZZUSA
BRANDT, MICHAEL	60	M	SHFM	PRZZZZUSA
ANNA	50	F	W	PRZZZZUSA
HEINRICH	23	M	CH	PRZZZZUSA
MATHILDE	19	F	CH	PRZZZZUSA
PAULKE, WILHELM	33	M	BKR	PRZZZZUSA
WAGNER, ANNA	26	F	W	PRZZZZUSA
URBSCHEIT, TRAUGOTT	43	M	MCHT	PRZZZZUSA
GRUETZMACHER, JULIUS	28	M	FARMER	PRZZZZUSA
FROMMHOLZ, MATHILDE	24	F	SGL	PRZZZZUSA
BEHREND, FRIEDRICH	28	F	SGL	PRZZZZUSA
GREFFRATH, HANS	25	M	MCHT	PRZZZZUSA
LEIKIS, FRIEDERIKE	51	F	W	PRZZZZUSA
JENNYE	19	F	CH	PRZZZZUSA
HEROLD, EMIL	23	M	DT	PRZZZZUSA
LAFFLETH, ARTHUR	23	M	FARMER	PRZZZZUSA
KAMINSKY, VERONIKA	24	F	W	PRZZZZUSA
BELL, ALBERT	21	M	LABR	PRZZZZUSA
ZECHERT, MARIE	39	F	W	PRZZZZUSA
BERTHOLD	5	M	CHILD	PRZZZZUSA
BERTHA	4	F	CHILD	PRZZZZUSA
CARL	2	M	CHILD	PRZZZZUSA
STRECK, HERMANN	35	M	FARMER	PRZZZZUSA
WAGNER, HELLMUTH	.09	M	INFANT	PRZZZZUSA
GRUBNAU, FRIEDRICH	75	M	UNKNOWN	PRZZZZUSA
SIMMEL, MAX	26	M	FARMER	PRZZZZUSA

SHIP: ADRIATIC

FROM: LIVERPOOL AND QUEENSTOWN
TO: NEW YORK
ARRIVED: 20 JULY 1888

PASSENGER	AGE	SEX	OCCUPATION	PRVL	DES
LITTANER, B.	39	M	MCHT	PRADAXUSA
BRATNOBER, HY.	40	M	MNR	PRADAXUSA

SHIP: AMSTERDAM

FROM: ROTTERDAM
TO: NEW YORK
ARRIVED: 20 JULY 1888

PASSENGER	AGE	SEX	OCCUPATION	PRVL	DES
RITTER, GEO	24	M	MCHT	GRZZZZUSA
HACKL, ALBERT	32	M	MCHT	GRZZZZUSA
MAYRHOFER, JOHN	50	M	CLGYMN	GRZZZZUSA
WARUS--CH, CARL	39	M	NN	GRZZZZUSA
LEITHAUSER, FANY	37	F	NN	GRZZZZUSA
GERTRUDE	2	F	CHILD	GRZZZZUSA
ANNA	17	F	NN	GRZZZZUSA
KRETRZSCHMAR, EDUARD	50	F	NN	GRZZZZUSA
MERTSCHINSKY, PETER	25	M	MCHT	GRZZZZUSA
MATHILDE, MARIA	30	F	NN	GRZZZZUSA
CECILIA, MARIE	22	F	NN	GRZZZZUSA
HIERONYMA, MARIA	30	F	NN	GRZZZZUSA
SOPHIE, MARIE	36	F	NN	GRZZZZUSA
EUPH-ASI-, MARIA	27	F	NN	GRZZZZUSA
GONZAGA, MARIA	29	F	NN	GRZZZZUSA
FELICITAS, MARIA	31	F	NN	GRZZZZUSA
EPHREM, SOPHIE	26	F	NN	GRZZZZUSA
CORNELIA, SARA	25	F	NN	GRZZZZUSA
BERNARDINE, SOPHIE	29	F	NN	GRZZZZUSA
NORMANN, ANNA	29	F	NN	GRZZZZUSA
KAROLINA	4	F	CHILD	GRZZZZUSA
WILHELM	3	M	CHILD	GRZZZZUSA
LOUISE	.06	F	INFANT	GRZZZZUSA
ESCH, GERTRUDA	29	F	NN	GRZZZZUSA
GISELA	8	F	CHILD	GRZZZZUSA
EHRENBACH, ROBERTA	50	F	CH	GRZZZZUSA
MATHILDA	21	F	CH	GRZZZZUSA
AUGUSTA	24	F	CH	GRZZZZUSA
GOEDER, IDA	16	F	NN	GRZZZZUSA
EMMA	23	F	NN	GRZZZZUSA
SCHOERNER, GEO	26	M	LABR	GRZZZZUSA
NILES, JULEN	36	F	NN	GRZZZZUSA
MATHILDE	7	F	CHILD	GRZZZZUSA
MARIA	5	F	CHILD	GRZZZZUSA
JULES	3	F	CHILD	GRZZZZUSA
MARTHA	.08	F	INFANT	GRZZZZUSA
SCHMIDT, WALDA	25	F	NN	GRZZZZUSA
HOHENSLE, AUGUSTA	23	F	NN	GRZZZZUSA
ALFRED	17	M	MCHT	GRZZZZUSA
ZWECH, MARIA	18	F	NN	GRZZZZUSA
SNYERER, U	18	F	NN	GRZZZZUSA
MEURER, PRIST	45	M	MCHT	GRZZZZUSA
CAROLINA	43	F	NN	GRZZZZUSA
BLEECHNER, CHAS.	23	M	TLR	GRZZZZUSA
CABDEROT, M.	33	M	NN	GRZZZZUSA
HEIMANN, EDUARD	32	M	MCHT	GRZZZZUSA
EDMUND	31	F	NN	GRZZZZUSA
GRUENWALD, WALDER	26	M	STDNT	GRZZZZUSA
STEPHANS, ED.	27	M	NN	GRZZZZUSA
AHSEN, WILHELM	63	M	CPTR	GRZZZZUSA
CARBACH, PETER	59	M	NN	GRZZZZUSA
VONMAREIS, GEO	18	M	NN	GRZZZZUSA
SAUERHEIMER, LOUIS	32	M	NN	GRZZZZUSA
MULLER, LAURA	30	F	NN	GRZZZZUSA
KAROLINA	11	F	CH	GRZZZZUSA
GUNCSEN, CHAS.	38	M	MCHT	GRZZZZUSA
GALAMBOS, T.	36	M	MCHT	GRZZZZUSA
FRIEDRICH, ELLA	22	F	NN	GRZZZZUSA
MAYER, WANDA	23	F	NN	GRZZZZUSA
HENRY, JOSEF	22	M	LABR	FRZZZZUSA
NUSLIER, HENRI	32	M	LABR	FRZZZZUSA
DEBARD, FLORIAN	18	M	LABR	FRZZZZUSA
ERNESTO, VAGELIO	26	M	LABR	FRZZZZUSA
MONTEIN, GIUSEPPE	59	M	LABR	FRZZZZUSA
MARGARA.	14	F	NN	FRZZZZUSA
ANDREAS, CONATE	30	M	LABR	FRZZZZUSA
DUANE	27	M	LABR	FRZZZZUSA
BURATI, ANGELINA	24	F	NN	FRZZZZUSA

PASSENGER	AGE	SEX	OCCUPATION	PRVL	DES
GANDIOSO	19	M	NN	FRZZZZ	USA
GIUSEPPE	2	M	CHILD	FRZZZZ	USA
ALFONSO	1	M	CHILD	FRZZZZ	USA
RUOFF, ANNA	35	F	NN	GRZZZZ	USA
ANNA	10	F	CH	GRZZZZ	USA
CHRISTIAN	7	M	CHILD	GRZZZZ	USA
GOTLIEB	5	M	CHILD	GRZZZZ	USA
KASPRZIH, JOHAN	23	M	LABR	GRZZZZ	USA
KATHARINA	20	F	NN	GRZZZZ	USA
TRIPTAG, GERHARD	22	M	LABR	GRZZZZ	USA
KRAUS, MARIE	59	F	NN	GRZZZZ	USA
CATHARINA	38	F	NN	GRZZZZ	USA
MAYSER, GEORGE	8	M	CHILD	GRZZZZ	USA
KATHERINA	7	F	CHILD	GRZZZZ	USA
ANNA	34	F	NN	GRZZZZ	USA
KLUGE, OSWALD	39	M	LABR	GRZZZZ	USA
LANG, HEINRICH	63	M	LABR	GRZZZZ	USA
KLUGE, HELENE	44	F	NN	GRZZZZ	USA
AUGUSTA	11	F	CH	GRZZZZ	USA
ELISABETH	9	F	CHILD	GRZZZZ	USA
JOHANNA	6	F	CHILD	GRZZZZ	USA
JOSEF	5	M	CHILD	GRZZZZ	USA
KLEIN, CARL	16	M	CH	GRZZZZ	USA
SCHNEIDER, MARGA.	16	F	NN	GRZZZZ	USA
PFLANZENBAUER, PEPI	42	M	LABR	GRZZZZ	USA
DETZSO	19	M	NN	GRZZZZ	USA
BIRI	13	F	NN	GRZZZZ	USA
IDA	10	F	CH	GRZZZZ	USA
JETTA	7	F	CHILD	GRZZZZ	USA
KLARA	5	F	CHILD	GRZZZZ	USA
COHN, FRANZ	11	M	CH	GRZZZZ	USA
DUJARDIN, CHARLES	35	M	LABR	GRZZZZ	USA
MARIE	30	F	NN	GRZZZZ	USA
EUGENIE	7	F	CHILD	GRZZZZ	USA
CHARLES	4	M	CHILD	GRZZZZ	USA
MARIE	2	F	CHILD	GRZZZZ	USA
BELGE, CHARLES	43	M	LABR	GRZZZZ	USA
MARGARETHA	47	F	NN	GRZZZZ	USA
HEINRICH	13	M	NN	GRZZZZ	USA
LOUISE	9	F	CHILD	GRZZZZ	USA
CARL	7	M	CHILD	GRZZZZ	USA
OTTO	5	M	CHILD	GRZZZZ	USA
MARIE	3	F	CHILD	GRZZZZ	USA
PAULINE	.09	F	INFANT	GRZZZZ	USA
SAENGER, CATHARINA	70	F	NN	GRZZZZ	USA
PAPENGUT, EMMA	20	F	NN	GRZZZZ	USA
SZILAGGI, MADAR	27	M	TCHR	GRZZZZ	USA
REGINE	22	F	NN	GRZZZZ	USA
GEHRBIN, MARIA	20	F	NN	GRZZZZ	USA
PIOT, CATHARINA	21	F	NN	GRZZZZ	USA
MARIE	18	F	NN	GRZZZZ	USA
KRUSCHINSKI, CATHERINE	18	F	NN	GRZZZZ	USA
BERBERICH, JOHN	18	M	LABR	GRZZZZ	USA
DECKER, HERMAN	26	M	LABR	GRZZZZ	USA
BLAS, JOSEF	30	M	LABR	GRZZZZ	USA
VOGT, JOSEF	16	M	LABR	GRZZZZ	USA
URMAN, KATHERINE	38	F	NN	GRZZZZ	USA
METZGER, LOUISE	19	F	NN	GRZZZZ	USA
ERHARDT, FRIEDRICH	28	M	LABR	GRZZZZ	USA
MILA, MARIE	24	F	NN	GRZZZZ	USA
GAUSER, JOHAN	15	M	LABR	GRZZZZ	USA
SCHEFFNER, CHRISTIAN	59	M	TLR	GRZZZZ	USA
HERMANN	15	M	TLR	GRZZZZ	USA
KREJ, GERHARD	22	M	LABR	GRZZZZ	USA
MEIMER, ROSINA	19	F	NN	GRZZZZ	USA
BERNDT, HENRY	69	M	NN	GRZZZZ	USA
LEU, GODFRIED	21	M	LABR	GRZZZZ	USA
BRESSTEIN, JOHAN	19	M	MCHT	GRZZZZ	USA
SCHWEIZER, SOPHIE	24	F	NN	GRZZZZ	USA
WILHELM	19	M	BKR	GRZZZZ	USA
BAUER, JOHANNA	22	F	NN	GRZZZZ	USA
BARBARA	26	F	NN	GRZZZZ	USA
BRANT, CARL	19	M	LABR	GRZZZZ	USA
WYERS, HEINRICH	28	M	LABR	GRZZZZ	USA
MAEDER, FRIEDRICH	20	M	LABR	GRZZZZ	USA
STORTZ, KARE	26	M	LABR	GRZZZZ	USA
WEINGARTNER, JOH.	17	M	LABR	GRZZZZ	USA
TRAUBEL, KARN	15	M	LABR	GRZZZZ	USA
PARTHEL, JOHAN	19	M	LABR	GRZZZZ	USA
ZETTLER, JOSEF	11	M	LABR	GRZZZZ	USA
WERNER, GEORGE	19	M	LABR	GRZZZZ	USA
TRAMP, BARBARA	20	F	NN	GRZZZZ	USA
BAUMANN, EDUARD	53	M	LABR	GRZZZZ	USA
CHARLOTTE	48	F	NN	GRZZZZ	USA
AUGUST	20	M	LABR	GRZZZZ	USA
FERDINAND	18	M	LABR	GRZZZZ	USA
ROBERT	11	M	CH	GRZZZZ	USA
FRANS	9	M	CHILD	GRZZZZ	USA
ANTONIE	6	M	CHILD	GRZZZZ	USA
MARIA	3	F	CHILD	GRZZZZ	USA
LEHMAN, ANNA	19	F	CH	GRZZZZ	USA
MUELLER, ANDREAS	52	M	LABR	GRZZZZ	USA
EVA	43	F	NN	GRZZZZ	USA
MARGARETTA	20	F	NN	GRZZZZ	USA
MARIE	18	F	NN	GRZZZZ	USA
BERNARD	9	M	CHILD	GRZZZZ	USA
GEORG	4	M	CHILD	GRZZZZ	USA
TRUMP, ANDREAS	16	M	LABR	GRZZZZ	USA
SCHILLER, CARL	28	M	LABR	GRZZZZ	USA
ROCH, MARIE	23	F	NN	GRZZZZ	USA
BAUER, JOHAN	25	M	LABR	GRZZZZ	USA
ALTMAN, MORIS	22	M	LABR	GRZZZZ	USA
MAESCHESCHE, AUGUST	27	M	LABR	GRZZZZ	USA
ABRAHAMS, SELIG	19	M	LABR	GRZZZZ	USA
ZELINSKI, KAZMIR	18	M	LABR	GRZZZZ	USA
ROTH, CATHA.	21	F	NN	GRZZZZ	USA
JOHANN	19	M	LABR	GRZZZZ	USA
KUDER, CHRISTIAN	45	M	LABR	GRZZZZ	USA
HONDE, WILH.	35	M	LABR	GRZZZZ	USA
CAROLINE	30	F	NN	GRZZZZ	USA
CATHA.	10	F	CH	GRZZZZ	USA
SCHUELE, FRIEDRICKE	18	F	CH	GRZZZZ	USA
EMICH, NICOLAUS	64	F	CH	GRZZZZ	USA
ELISE	19	F	CH	GRZZZZ	USA
FISCHE, GEORGE	35	M	LABR	GRZZZZ	USA
KESSLER, MAX	24	M	CPTR	GRZZZZ	USA
GLASS, GEORG	33	M	FARMER	GRZZZZ	USA
MAISCH, RUDOLF	15	M	LABR	GRZZZZ	USA
MULLER, MARGA.	19	F	NN	GRZZZZ	USA
BOHLANDER, ELISE	21	F	NN	GRZZZZ	USA
BRAKER, FRANK	26	M	LABR	GRZZZZ	USA
RUPP, FRIEDRICH	33	M	LABR	GRZZZZ	USA
ROSENTHAL, ADOLF	28	M	TCHR	GRZZZZ	USA

SHIP: SAALE

FROM: BREMEN AND SOUTHAMPTON
TO: NEW YORK
ARRIVED: 20 JULY 1888

PASSENGER	AGE	SEX	OCCUPATION	PRVL	DES
RICHTER, ANNA	30	F	UNKNOWN	GRZZZZ	USA
HEINR.	7	M	CHILD	GRZZZZ	USA
HASSEL, ELISAB.	26	F	UNKNOWN	GRZZZZ	USA
PETERSEN, HERM.	26	M	BCHR	GRZZZZ	USA
KOCHS, AUG.	16	M	TLR	GRZZZZ	USA
ENGBRECHT, SOPHIE	52	F	UNKNOWN	GRZZZZ	USA
MANE	21	F	UNKNOWN	GRZZZZ	USA
FEDERLEIN, CATHINKA	17	F	UNKNOWN	GRZZZZ	USA
ROSA	19	F	UNKNOWN	GRZZZZ	USA
LUX, ERNSTINE	32	F	UNKNOWN	GRZZZZ	USA
RUBEL, FRIEDA	17	F	UNKNOWN	GRZZZZ	USA
WUNDERLICH, HENRIETTE	75	F	UNKNOWN	GRZZZZ	USA
RUBEL, FANNI	19	F	UNKNOWN	GRZZZZ	USA
REINLINGER, AUGUSTE	19	F	UNKNOWN	GRZZZZ	USA
DITTRICH, ELIZA	35	F	UNKNOWN	GRZZZZ	USA

PASSENGER	AGE	SEX	OCCUPATION	PRVL	DES
UNG-ATHEN, MARIE	22	F	UNKNOWN		GRZZZZUSA
U, CARL	32	M	MCHT		GRZZZZUSA
JACOBSOHN, MAX	16	M	MCHT		GRZZZZUSA
SCHLOSS, LOUIS	28	M	MCHT		GRZZZZUSA
WEBER, MARIE	18	F	UNKNOWN		GRZZZZUSA
MERKLE, SOPHIE	52	F	W		GRZZZZUSA
BARBARA	20	F	CH		GRZZZZUSA
FISCHER, WILLY	24	M	MCHT		GRZZZZUSA
SIEGLER, LOUISE	45	F	UNKNOWN		GRZZZZUSA
LOUISE	21	F	UNKNOWN		GRZZZZUSA
CARL	17	M	MCHT		GRZZZZUSA
ELISE	11	F	UNKNOWN		GRZZZZUSA
WEGNER, MAX	40	M	MCHT		GRZZZZUSA
SPIRA, THERESIA	15	F	UNKNOWN		GRZZZZUSA
STEPHAN	17	M	JNR		GRZZZZUSA
HERDENCK, ADAM	18	M	JNR		GRZZZZUSA
CASPER	21	M	JNR		GRZZZZUSA
HERBICH, JOH.	42	M	TLR		GRZZZZUSA
G--SS, WILH.	17	M	CNF		GRZZZZUSA
REIM---, FELIX	32	M	FARMER		GRZZZZUSA
STE----N, ANNA	32	F	UNKNOWN		GRZZZZUSA
JOLA	4	F	CHILD		GRZZZZUSA
WENZEL, DOROTHEA	58	F	UNKNOWN		GRZZZZUSA
NETTI	27	F	UNKNOWN		GRZZZZUSA
SCHEER, ANTON	27	M	TLR		GRZZZZUSA
KALITZKI, BERTHA	20	F	UNKNOWN		GRZZZZUSA
JORDAN, HERM.	24	M	SHMK		GRZZZZUSA
BLEIL, ANNA	37	F	UNKNOWN		GRZZZZUSA
BERTHA	16	F	UNKNOWN		GRZZZZUSA
HEINR.	11	M	UNKNOWN		GRZZZZUSA
GUST.	10	M	CH		GRZZZZUSA
HERM.	9	M	CHILD		GRZZZZUSA
MARGA.	2	F	CHILD		GRZZZZUSA
WENZEL, MARIA	29	F	UNKNOWN		GRZZZZUSA
LOEN--TEIN, MANNY	21	F	UNKNOWN		GRZZZZUSA
ROSOWSKA, ROSALIE	27	F	UNKNOWN		GRZZZZUSA
LO--ENSTEIN, LIEBMANN	56	M	LABR		GRZZZZUSA
HANNCHEN	16	F	CH		GRZZZZUSA
LEVY	14	M	CH		GRZZZZUSA
EMMA	10	F	CH		GRZZZZUSA
HERGENHAN, EUSTACH	23	M	FARMER		GRZZZZUSA
NIEBANK, ANTON	33	M	FARMER		GRZZZZUSA
KERLER, LOUISE	22	F	UNKNOWN		GRZZZZUSA
KNOEDLER, GUST.	14	M	UNKNOWN		GRZZZZUSA
MANCH, CARL	20	M	FARMER		GRZZZZUSA
KURZ, HEINR.	16	M	BKLYR		GRZZZZUSA
KRAPF, GOTTLOB	26	M	FARMER		GRZZZZUSA
GAIDE, GERTRUDE	58	F	UNKNOWN		GRZZZZUSA
MARIA	23	F	UNKNOWN		GRZZZZUSA
MORIN, ELISE	17	F	UNKNOWN		GRZZZZUSA
HEKM--N, OTTO	17	M	CL		GRZZZZUSA
HOFFMANN, JUL.	25	M	FARMER		GRZZZZUSA
STEGER, CONRAD	72	M	FARMER		GRZZZZUSA
STOBE, EMMA	11	F	UNKNOWN		GRZZZZUSA
SCHENRING, HEINR.	57	M	FARMER		GRZZZZUSA
KRAMER, ROMAN	16	M	FARMER		GRZZZZUSA
NOTHACKER, MICH.	23	M	FARMER		GRZZZZUSA
WESEMANN, GUST.	18	M	CL		GRZZZZUSA
NECKLER, JOH.	45	M	FARMER		GRZZZZUSA
ROSINE	44	F	W		GRZZZZUSA
WILH.	21	M	FARMER		GRZZZZUSA
JOHAN	19	M	FARMER		GRZZZZUSA
CATH.	16	F	CH		GRZZZZUSA
CARL	11	F	CH		GRZZZZUSA
FRIEDKE.	10	F	CH		GRZZZZUSA
GRANE, HERM.	20	M	JNR		GRZZZZUSA
BRUST, WILH.	39	M	JNR		GRZZZZUSA
HARTMANN, JOHN	17	M	TLR		GRZZZZUSA
LENZ, JACOB	25	M	BKR		GRZZZZUSA
WEBER, CATH.	21	F	UNKNOWN		GRZZZZUSA
SCHELLERT, HEINR.	20	M	CL		GRZZZZUSA
BLLASINS, CARL	35	M	FARMER		GRZZZZUSA
BANER, FRANZ	19	M	BKR		GRZZZZUSA
TANLERT, PAUL	24	M	FARMER		GRZZZZUSA
VOGEL, CARL	25	M	BKR		GRZZZZUSA
LEHMANN, JACOB	14	M	UNKNOWN		GRZZZZUSA
SCHWEMLE, JOHNE.	24	F	UNKNOWN		GRZZZZUSA
ROMMEL, CAREL	22	F	UNKNOWN		GRZZZZUSA
REISCHE, MARG.	33	F	UNKNOWN		GRZZZZUSA
CATH.	.07	F	INFANT		GRZZZZUSA
HANER, MATH.	28	M	FARMER		GRZZZZUSA
SIMET, ANTON	24	M	FARMER		GRZZZZUSA
ADELH.	24	F	W		GRZZZZUSA
JOSEPH	4	M	CHILD		GRZZZZUSA
KIEBIS, ANNA	21	F	UNKNOWN		GRZZZZUSA
KANTZ, PAULINE	22	F	UNKNOWN		GRZZZZUSA
DAENBLE, CARL	30	M	MCHT		GRZZZZUSA
RICK, HERM.	18	M	PNTR		GRZZZZUSA
STIERINGER, PAULINE	19	F	UNKNOWN		GRZZZZUSA
FISCHER, MAGD.	17	F	UNKNOWN		GRZZZZUSA
KAUTH, ELISAB.	26	F	UNKNOWN		GRZZZZUSA
ZEITZ, CARL	40	M	FARMER		GRZZZZUSA
REICHELT, MARG.	27	F	UNKNOWN		GRZZZZUSA
ELSA	5	F	CHILD		GRZZZZUSA
LUCIE	2	F	CHILD		GRZZZZUSA
MERTEN, MARIE	11	F	UNKNOWN		GRZZZZUSA
EMILIE	15	F	UNKNOWN		GRZZZZUSA
WITKOP, JOH.	27	M	FARMER		GRZZZZUSA
THERESIA	21	F	W		GRZZZZUSA
HILSDORF, MARTHA	52	F	UNKNOWN		GRZZZZUSA
GERBIG, CHRISTNE.	16	F	UNKNOWN		GRZZZZUSA
ER--T, CHRISTNE.	25	F	UNKNOWN		GRZZZZUSA
B----ERSPACHER, ANNA	24	F	UNKNOWN		GRZZZZUSA
BRENNEIS, ANNA	17	F	UNKNOWN		GRZZZZUSA
KOERNER, ANNA	18	F	UNKNOWN		GRZZZZUSA
STUECKRATH, WILH.	24	M	CL		GRZZZZUSA
HOLZBANER, BERTHA	20	F	UNKNOWN		GRZZZZUSA
FLEISCHMANN, MARG.	24	F	UNKNOWN		GRZZZZUSA
JOH.	4	M	CHILD		GRZZZZUSA
SCHANDEL, LORENZ	30	M	LABR		GRZZZZUSA
SCHWANDNER, ANNA	30	F	UNKNOWN		GRZZZZUSA
ANDR.	4	M	CHILD		GRZZZZUSA
FRANK, BARB.	40	F	UNKNOWN		GRZZZZUSA
GRAF, JOS.	32	M	LABR		GRZZZZUSA
GRUBER, KATHI	26	F	UNKNOWN		GRZZZZUSA
THERESE	.06	F	INFANT		GRZZZZUSA
BAUMMER, JOS.	23	M	FARMER		GRZZZZUSA
DOBMEIER, GEORG	30	M	FARMER		GRZZZZUSA
ZIMMERMANN, GEORG	59	M	SHMK		GRZZZZUSA
B--LK, THOMAS	24	M	BCHR		GRZZZZUSA
SCHAFER, GEORG	22	M	SMH		GRZZZZUSA
JOHE, ELISAB.	18	F	UNKNOWN		GRZZZZUSA
MARIE	16	F	UNKNOWN		GRZZZZUSA
WILH.	14	M	UNKNOWN		GRZZZZUSA
MICHLER, THERESIA	19	F	UNKNOWN		GRZZZZUSA
SCHIEDER, WILH.	25	M	BCHR		GRZZZZUSA
SCHWENTNER, JOH.	24	M	SMH		GRZZZZUSA
BARB.	26	F	W		GRZZZZUSA
ANNA	.09	F	INFANT		GRZZZZUSA
NEUBARGER, JANNY	16	F	UNKNOWN		GRZZZZUSA
BAUER, CARL	15	M	UNKNOWN		GRZZZZUSA
JOE-NS, FRIEDKE.	24	F	UNKNOWN		GRZZZZUSA
KULHN, MINNA	16	F	CH		GRZZZZUSA
LONK, AUG.	38	M	FARMER		GRZZZZUSA
GENF, FLORENCE	42	F	UNKNOWN		GRZZZZUSA
EMIL	14	M	UNKNOWN		GRZZZZUSA
SCHULZ, CARL	55	M	FARMER		GRZZZZUSA
AUG.	25	M	FARMER		GRZZZZUSA
HERSLER, KATCHEN	19	F	UNKNOWN		GRZZZZUSA
D----LE, CARL	17	M	TLR		GRZZZZUSA
LOUISE	19	F	UNKNOWN		GRZZZZUSA
MOCKEL, JOH.	17	M	JNR		GRZZZZUSA
SEILER, MINNA	24	F	UNKNOWN		GRZZZZUSA
SCHMIDT, GRETCHEN	28	F	UNKNOWN		GRZZZZUSA
NICKLAS, DIEDR.	16	M	WCHMKR		GRZZZZUSA
KOCH, JOHNE.	28	F	UNKNOWN		GRZZZZUSA
FRIEDA	7	F	CHILD		GRZZZZUSA
CARL	6	M	CHILD		GRZZZZUSA
ELSE	.11	F	INFANT		GRZZZZUSA
FOR-TER, MICH.	44	M	FARMER		GRZZZZUSA

PASSENGER	AGE	SEX	OCCUPATION	PVRIVL	DES
ANNA	35	F	W	GRZZZZUSA	
MARG.	11	F	CH	GRZZZZUSA	
GOTTFRIED	9	M	CHILD	GRZZZZUSA	
JOHNE.	7	F	CHILD	GRZZZZUSA	
MARIE	5	F	CHILD	GRZZZZUSA	
EICHHORN, ROSA	28	F	UNKNOWN	GRZZZZUSA	
CAPELANSKI, MATHAUS	27	M	SMH	GRZZZZUSA	
WEISOER, GEORG	42	M	MCHT	GRZZZZUSA	
ASSEL, JOHNE.	17	F	UNKNOWN	GRZZZZUSA	
BARK, FRIEDR.	23	M	BCHR	GRZZZZUSA	
LOUISE	30	F	W	GRZZZZUSA	
STIEFEL, JUDW.	16	M	BCHR	GRZZZZUSA	
NEIDHARDT, CHARLES	28	M	BRR	GRZZZZUSA	
EMILIE	22	F	W	GRZZZZUSA	
HALLER, MARG.	22	F	UNKNOWN	GRZZZZUSA	
REITZ, AUG.	14	M	UNKNOWN	GRZZZZUSA	
GRUN, HEINR.	15	M	UNKNOWN	GRZZZZUSA	
B--BACH, ELISAB.	58	F	UNKNOWN	GRZZZZUSA	
ED.	17	M	FARMER	GRZZZZUSA	
FERD.	14	M	UNKNOWN	GRZZZZUSA	
KONIG, ANNA	22	F	UNKNOWN	GRZZZZUSA	
VOLKART, HEINR.	57	M	LABR	GRZZZZUSA	
ELISE	45	F	W	GRZZZZUSA	
SCHLEC, LORENZ	23	M	BRR	GRZZZZUSA	
LABUS, OTTILIE	19	F	UNKNOWN	GRZZZZUSA	
ECKARD, ADAM	25	M	MLR	GRZZZZUSA	
ALTENDORFER, THERESE	27	F	UNKNOWN	GRZZZZUSA	
LANZ, JOH.	25	M	FARMER	GRZZZZUSA	
FONTER, ED.	33	M	FARMER	GRZZZZUSA	
SCHMOLDT, CARL	51	M	FARMER	GRZZZZUSA	
BORCHARDT, CARL	14	M	UNKNOWN	GRZZZZUSA	
GREGOROWICZ, JOS.	21	M	FARMER	GRZZZZUSA	
GRIESHAMER, JOH.	16	M	FARMER	GRZZZZUSA	
GUNTHER, MARIE	26	F	UNKNOWN	GRZZZZUSA	
SEIBEL, WILH.	16	M	SMH	GRZZZZUSA	
H-SSE, LOUISE	22	F	UNKNOWN	GRZZZZUSA	
KUHN, AUG.	19	M	PNTR	GRZZZZUSA	
STOLL, ANNA	56	F	UNKNOWN	GRZZZZUSA	
MUELLER, DIONIS	58	M	FARMER	GRZZZZUSA	
PIERZONKA, CARL	33	M	FARMER	GRZZZZUSA	
CAROL	32	F	W	GRZZZZUSA	
JOHNE.	8	F	CHILD	GRZZZZUSA	
MARIE	2	F	CHILD	GRZZZZUSA	
OTTO	.05	M	INFANT	GRZZZZUSA	
OLSOWSKI, FERD.	35	M	FARMER	GRZZZZUSA	
CAREL	30	F	W	GRZZZZUSA	
AD.	11	M	CH	GRZZZZUSA	
OTTO	7	M	CHILD	GRZZZZUSA	
CARL	3	M	CHILD	GRZZZZUSA	
MARIE	.05	F	INFANT	GRZZZZUSA	
BISCHOFF, GUSRT.	39	M	BKR	GRZZZZUSA	
LOY, JOSEPH	37	M	FARMER	GRZZZZUSA	
KOHLER, ANDR.	22	M	FARMER	GRZZZZUSA	
KATH, ELIAS	20	M	FARMER	GRZZZZUSA	
VENDT, U	24	F	UNKNOWN	GRZZZZUSA	
GOTZE, JOHNES.	27	M	TLR	GRZZZZUSA	
SELMA	17	F	UNKNOWN	GRZZZZUSA	
RESPOCHOWSKY, ANTON	22	M	LABR	GRZZZZUSA	
STERN, MAX	15	M	LABR	GRZZZZUSA	
LOWENSTEIN, LEVI	34	M	LABR	GRZZZZUSA	
SCHMIDT, JOS.	23	M	LABR	GRZZZZUSA	
CHR.	36	M	FARMER	GRZZZZUSA	
PETER	26	M	FARMER	GRZZZZUSA	
WEISMUELLER, MICH.	56	M	CPTR	GRZZZZUSA	
MARG.	47	F	W	GRZZZZUSA	
MARIE	14	F	CH	GRZZZZUSA	
MARG.	14	F	CH	GRZZZZUSA	
MICH.	11	M	CH	GRZZZZUSA	
ORZNOZKE, AUGUSTE	24	F	UNKNOWN	GRZZZZUSA	
HARTIG, EMIL	32	M	FARMER	GRZZZZUSA	
WILHNE.	29	F	W	GRZZZZUSA	
EMIL	.06	M	INFANT	GRZZZZUSA	
KIRINSE, MARG.	23	F	UNKNOWN	GRZZZZUSA	
BARBEL	4	F	CHILD	GRZZZZUSA	
MOETZ, CATH.	50	F	W	GRZZZZUSA	

PASSENGER	AGE	SEX	OCCUPATION	PVRIVL	DES
THE-L, MART.	23	M	FARMER	GRZZZZUSA	
WOLFF, AUBUST	28	M	JNR	GRZZZZUSA	

SHIP: AURANIA

FROM: LIVERPOOL AND QUEENSTOWN
TO: NEW YORK
ARRIVED: 23 JULY 1888

PASSENGER	AGE	SEX	OCCUPATION	PVRIVL	DES
RUBIN, FRANK	25	M	LABR	GRZZZZMI	
MARIE	14	F	SP	GRZZZZMI	
MULLER, CARL	31	M	LABR	GRZZZZNY	
SIRMAY, JENNY	17	F	SP	GRZZZZNY	
WEBER, HUGO	18	M	LABR	GRZZZZNY	
LISCHKL, SLATE	20	M	LABR	GRZZZZNY	
RUP, JOS.	24	M	LABR	GRZZZZNY	
FLITCHER, ROBERT	40	M	TRVLR	GRZZZZMA	
U	38	F	W	GRZZZZMA	
FRIEDSENDER, JACOB	00	M	LABR	GRZZZZBO	
MAUMANN, SENDEL	29	M	LABR	GRZZZZNY	
VANMURREB, ULOF	40	M	MCHT	GRZZZZNY	

SHIP: RHAETIA

FROM: HAMBURG AND HAVRE
TO: NEW YORK
ARRIVED: 23 JULY 1888

PASSENGER	AGE	SEX	OCCUPATION	PVRIVL	DES
RAAB, KARL	47	M	PT	GRZZZZUSA	
NEVE, HANS	65	M	FARMER	GRZZZZUSA	
UHL, NICOLAUS	30	M	BRR	GRZZZZUSA	
DELMONTE, JENNY	23	F	UNKNOWN	GRZZZZUSA	
SEUGER, MARIE	26	F	WO	GRZZZZUSA	
MARTHA	5	F	CHILD	GRZZZZUSA	
MARIE	3	F	CHILD	GRZZZZUSA	
FRANZ	.08	M	INFANT	GRZZZZUSA	
OFFERMANN, JOH.	20	F	SGL	GRZZZZUSA	
STENEBERG, FERD.	23	M	MCHT	GRZZZZUSA	
SCHOENROGGE, CARL	38	M	UNKNOWN	GRZZZZUSA	
ELISE	28	F	W	GRZZZZUSA	
HANS	5	M	CHILD	GRZZZZUSA	
BRUNO	2	M	CHILD	GRZZZZUSA	
ERNST	2	M	CHILD	GRZZZZUSA	
FRANZ	.11	M	INFANT	GRZZZZUSA	
PAGEL, ERNST	24	M	LABR	GRZZZZUSA	
GREUEL, BERTHA	25	F	SGL	GRZZZZUSA	
STOSS, CACILIA	29	F	SGL	GRZZZZUSA	
DORA	22	F	SGL	GRZZZZUSA	
SCHRAMM, OTTO	23	M	UNKNOWN	GRZZZZUSA	
LANE, OTTO	16	M	UNKNOWN	GRZZZZUSA	
ZIETLOW, HERRM.	26	M	FARMER	GRZZZZUSA	
EMILIE	20	F	SGL	GRZZZZUSA	
GOLDENITZ, CHRIST.	59	M	JNR	GRZZZZUSA	
MARIE	58	F	W	GRZZZZUSA	
JOH.	25	F	CH	GRZZZZUSA	
MARIE	22	F	CH	GRZZZZUSA	
SEEGELKEN, SOPHIE	35	F	WO	GRZZZZUSA	
WEISENBORN, LOUIS	21	M	FARMER	GRZZZZUSA	
HAUSEN, EMMA	30	F	UNKNOWN	GRZZZZUSA	
HEINRICH	2	M	CHILD	GRZZZZUSA	
DINGENS, PHILIPP	23	M	GLSR	GRZZZZUSA	
JACOBS, ANNA	21	F	UNKNOWN	GRZZZZUSA	
CLAUSEN, WILH.	24	M	UNKNOWN	GRZZZZUSA	
HARING, WILH.	18	M	UNKNOWN	GRZZZZUSA	
LARSEN, JOH.	38	F	WO	GRZZZZUSA	

PASSENGER	AGE	SEX	OCCUPATION	PRIVL	DES	PASSENGER	AGE	SEX	OCCUPATION	PRIVL	DES
EVA	9	F	CHILD		GRZZZZUSA	HELENE	5	F	CHILD		GRZZZZUSA
HELENE	8	F	CHILD		GRZZZZUSA	MAX	3	M	CHILD		GRZZZZUSA
WALDBURG	7	F	CHILD		GRZZZZUSA	KUEHNE, JOH.	25	M	FARMER		GRZZZZUSA
JOS.	4	M	CHILD		GRZZZZUSA	KRAUSE, GUSTAV	33	M	LABR		GRZZZZUSA
HOBYE	.09	M	INFANT		GRZZZZUSA	BIALKOWSKI, ANTON	35	M	FARMER		GRZZZZUSA
MOLITOR, WILH.	36	M	UPHST		GRZZZZUSA	MULLER, GUSTAV	24	M	MLR		GRZZZZUSA
MINNA	37	F	W		GRZZZZUSA	NAPARTY, JOSEF	58	M	LABR		GRZZZZUSA
ELISABETH	17	F	D		GRZZZZUSA	JUERGENSEN, FRITZ	34	M	SHMK		GRZZZZUSA
NEUBURGER, JOH.	28	M	FARMER		GRZZZZUSA	MARG.	36	F	W		GRZZZZUSA
LOEFFLER, CARL	16	M	SHMK		GRZZZZUSA	MAX	5	M	CHILD		GRZZZZUSA
FRITZ, PAULA	36	F	SGL		GRZZZZUSA	FRIDA	.09	F	INFANT		GRZZZZUSA
HAUSCHILD, META	25	F	SGL		GRZZZZUSA	TOBAKEN, MARIE	22	F	SGL		GRZZZZUSA
STRIFFLER, JOH.	27	M	LABR		GRZZZZUSA	GURSTEN, NISS	23	M	WVR		GRZZZZUSA
JANZEN, MARIE	37	F	WO		GRZZZZUSA	GONCZEROUSKY, JEANETTE	25	F	SGL		GRZZZZUSA
BERTHA	9	F	CHILD		GRZZZZUSA	ERDMANN, JOSEF	33	M	LABR		GRZZZZUSA
JOH.	5	M	CHILD		GRZZZZUSA	LOUISA	35	F	W		GRZZZZUSA
ROBERT	2	M	CHILD		GRZZZZUSA	PETER	3	M	CHILD		GRZZZZUSA
BERTRAM, WILH.	21	F	SGL		GRZZZZUSA	TEOFILA	2	F	CHILD		GRZZZZUSA
PIETSCH, ERDMANN	17	M	GDNR		GRZZZZUSA	JOSEF	.06	M	INFANT		GRZZZZUSA
ROEDER, PHILIPP	22	M	LABR		GRZZZZUSA	JOH.	.06	M	INFANT		GRZZZZUSA
ECKARDT, HERRM.	30	M	WVR		GRZZZZUSA	ZABLEFSKY, ROSA	60	F	WO		GRZZZZUSA
KEIL, ANNA	24	F	SGL		GRZZZZUSA	MORTIER, EMIL	45	M	MCHT		GRZZZZUSA
KARGER, JOSEFINE	30	F	WO		GRZZZZUSA	BARKHAUSEN, KARL	27	M	JNR		GRZZZZUSA
JENNY	7	F	CHILD		GRZZZZUSA	BAUMANN, TOMAS	67	M	LABR		GRZZZZUSA
FEIBUSCH, GUSTAV	26	M	LABR		GRZZZZUSA	CONSTANCIA	67	F	W		GRZZZZUSA
MASSMANN, FRITZ	25	M	FARMER		GRZZZZUSA	NIKLAS, IGNATZ	28	M	LABR		GRZZZZUSA
BALLHAUSEN, GUSTAV	30	M	CGRMKR		GRZZZZUSA	MARIE	19	F	SGL		GRZZZZUSA
CLARA	28	F	W		GRZZZZUSA	GRANDT, FRITZ	36	M	FARMER		GRZZZZUSA
META	4	F	CHILD		GRZZZZUSA	MARIE	33	F	W		GRZZZZUSA
HECKER, ERNST	23	M	MCHT		GRZZZZUSA	HEINR.	9	M	CHILD		GRZZZZUSA
LUNZ, GEORG	29	M	BKR		GRZZZZUSA	ELISE	8	F	CHILD		GRZZZZUSA
JOHANN	21	M	LABR		GRZZZZUSA	MARINE	7	F	CHILD		GRZZZZUSA
WOJCECHOWSKY, HEINR.	23	M	MCHT		GRZZZZUSA	EMMA	6	F	CHILD		GRZZZZUSA
PFEIFFER, LUDW.	58	M	LABR		GRZZZZUSA	GUSTAV	5	M	CHILD		GRZZZZUSA
BOSSOW, JOHANN	59	M	FARMER		GRZZZZUSA	BERTHA	3	F	CHILD		GRZZZZUSA
SHRISTIANSEN, BEILE	29	F	WO		GRZZZZUSA	KIMMICH, AMALIE	15	F	SGL		GRZZZZUSA
ENDRA	3	F	CHILD		GRZZZZUSA	FLAIG, CHR.	23	M	WVR		GRZZZZUSA
FRDK.	18	F	CH		GRZZZZUSA	ZERN, ALBERTINE	57	F	WO		GRZZZZUSA
SCHMIDT, NICOLAY	3	M	CHILD		GRZZZZUSA	HEDWIG	19	F	D		GRZZZZUSA
JOH.	9	F	CHILD		GRZZZZUSA	THIEDE, LOUISE	23	F	SGL		GRZZZZUSA
SCHMUL, JENNY	21	F	SGL		GRZZZZUSA	MARING, ROSINE	19	F	SGL		GRZZZZUSA
ROSA	19	F	SGL		GRZZZZUSA	LENOCH, HINRICH	33	M	LABR		GRZZZZUSA
MAHN, EMIL	24	M	LABR		GRZZZZUSA	DORIS	31	F	W		GRZZZZUSA
WILH.	35	F	W		GRZZZZUSA	WILH.	9	M	CHILD		GRZZZZUSA
HAUER, ANNA	36	F	SGL		GRZZZZUSA	CAROLINE	8	F	CHILD		GRZZZZUSA
SCHAUFUSS, HEINR.	30	M	TU		GRZZZZUSA	MARIE	7	F	CHILD		GRZZZZUSA
ZIEGLER, BRUNO	18	M	GDNR		GRZZZZUSA	TIETGEN, HANS	52	M	LABR		GRZZZZUSA
BERNDT, BERTHA	21	F	SGL		GRZZZZUSA	KOESTER, SOPHIE	9	F	CHILD		GRZZZZUSA
WALTER, WILH.	16	M	LABR		GRZZZZUSA	SCHWARZE, WILH.	26	M	LABR		GRZZZZUSA
PAUL	15	M	LABR		GRZZZZUSA	DORN, JULIUS	51	F	LABR		GRZZZZUSA
LITTMANN, WOLF	16	M	LABR		GRZZZZUSA	MERKENS, BERNH.	43	M	SMH		GRZZZZUSA
GARDHAUSEN, ALWINE	14	F	SGL		GRZZZZUSA	ZAUDER, EMMA	35	F	SGL		GRZZZZUSA
GROTZKE, REGINE	26	F	WO		GRZZZZUSA	SCHUETT, JOH.	34	F	WO		GRZZZZUSA
THEODOR	7	M	CHILD		GRZZZZUSA	MARTIN	8	M	CHILD		GRZZZZUSA
ALBERT	4	M	CHILD		GRZZZZUSA	JOSEPH.	4	F	CHILD		GRZZZZUSA
AUGUST	.11	M	INFANT		GRZZZZUSA	REINECKE, LOUIS	15	M	LABR		GRZZZZUSA
NEWAKOWSKA, FRANZISKA	20	F	WO		GRZZZZUSA	LIEBENDOERFER, KARL	16	M	FARMER		GRZZZZUSA
PELAGIA	.11	F	INFANT		GRZZZZUSA	KELLNER, CARL	22	F	MCHT		GRZZZZUSA
WOITZEL, AUGUST	15	M	LABR		GRZZZZUSA	GERSTANDT, HEINR.	41	M	FARMER		GRZZZZUSA
DREHER, IDA	18	F	SGL		GRZZZZUSA	MAGD.	32	F	W		GRZZZZUSA
JUERGENS, JOH.	21	F	SGL		GRZZZZUSA	MAX	13	M	CH		GRZZZZUSA
MEYER, ANNA	42	F	WO		GRZZZZUSA	HEINR.	12	M	CH		GRZZZZUSA
WUELFF, LOUISE	65	F	WO		GRZZZZUSA	DORA	9	F	CHILD		GRZZZZUSA
LUDWIG	33	M	FARMER		GRZZZZUSA	HELENE	8	F	CHILD		GRZZZZUSA
BOETIGER, RUDOLF	23	M	SLR		GRZZZZUSA	FRITZ	6	M	CHILD		GRZZZZUSA
KAUDLER, OTTO	24	M	SMH		GRZZZZUSA	MARTHA	5	F	CHILD		GRZZZZUSA
SCHONE, CARL	22	M	MCHT		GRZZZZUSA	GUSTAV	4	M	CHILD		GRZZZZUSA
HILLER, ALBERT	26	M	STDNT		GRZZZZUSA	JAUTKE, PAUL	26	M	UPHST		GRZZZZUSA
NIMTZ, BERNH.	22	M	MSN		GRZZZZUSA	BLICKE, CARL	26	F	BRR		GRZZZZUSA
REMMY, BRUNO	22	M	LABR		GRZZZZUSA	BREIDLINGER, ANNA	16	F	SGL		GRZZZZUSA
WENDT, WILH.	37	M	GDNR		GRZZZZUSA	LIEBEL, JOH.	30	M	LABR		GRZZZZUSA
MATH.	32	F	W		GRZZZZUSA	ERTELL, AUGUST	55	M	LABR		GRZZZZUSA
JOH.	2	M	CHILD		GRZZZZUSA	LUEHR, JOSEF	17	M	FARMER		GRZZZZUSA
FISCHER, ROBERT	22	M	LABR		GRZZZZUSA	LOTTES, THERESE	18	F	SGL		GRZZZZUSA
PIETSCHMANN, AUG.	30	F	WO		GRZZZZUSA	MOSSDORF, SELMA	48	F	SGL		GRZZZZUSA

PASSENGER	AGE	SEX	OCCUPATION	PRVL	DES
FISCHER, EUGEN	16	M	CNF	GRZZZZ	USA
WORBECK, MICHEL	28	M	LABR	GRZZZZ	USA
JUENGE, CATH.	51	F	WO	GRZZZZ	USA
LINA	16	F	WO	GRZZZZ	USA
ADOLF	9	M	CHILD	GRZZZZ	USA
ROEDER, FRANZ	26	M	SHMK	GRZZZZ	USA
LANGNER, BERTHA	33	F	WO	GRZZZZ	USA
ADELHEID	9	F	CHILD	GRZZZZ	USA
CARL	7	M	CHILD	GRZZZZ	USA
CLARA	.11	F	INFANT	GRZZZZ	USA
AGNES	.01	F	INFANT	GRZZZZ	USA
DURK, CONRAD	25	M	LKSH	GRZZZZ	USA
MUEHLHEISER, PETER	25	M	LABR	GRZZZZ	USA
RAZMANN, CHRIST.	30	M	FARMER	GRZZZZ	USA
BOEHN, FEDOR	30	M	MCHT	GRZZZZ	USA
MEISENBACH, ADAM	29	M	BCHR	GRZZZZ	USA
ANNA	20	F	W	GRZZZZ	USA
DIESTERBECK, HERRM.	34	M	LABR	GRZZZZ	USA
BAUMANN, MICHAEL	18	M	LABR	GRZZZZ	USA
PEPER, HANS	26	M	LABR	SRZZZZ	USA
HILPERT, EMIL	17	M	FARMER	SRZZZZ	USA
HERBST, AUGST.	36	M	LABR	GRZZZZ	USA
MARIA	21	F	W	GRZZZZ	USA
EICHE, FERDMAND	24	M	UPHST	GRZZZZ	USA
FREISS, CRESZENTIA	23	F	SGL	GRZZZZ	USA
MARKI, ANNA	27	F	SGL	SRZZZZ	USA
JEHLE, CORNEL	25	M	SHMK	GRZZZZ	USA
FISCHER, CATH.	22	F	SGL	GRZZZZ	USA
SCHWARZ, ROSINA	22	F	SGL	GRZZZZ	USA
GRAFF, WENDELIN	27	M	SHMK	GRZZZZ	USA
MARIE	22	F	W	GRZZZZ	USA
KUEBLER, JOSEF	26	M	LABR	GRZZZZ	USA
BERGER, BLASIUS	58	M	FARMER	SRZZZZ	USA
MARIE	40	F	W	SRZZZZ	USA
BLASIUS	11	M	UNKNOWN	SRZZZZ	USA
URSULA	10	F	CH	SRZZZZ	USA
FREY, MARIE	22	F	SGL	SRZZZZ	USA
HOLS, DANIEL	41	M	CK	GRZZZZ	USA
BRISS, ROSINE	54	F	WO	GRZZZZ	USA
RUPPRICHT, MARG.	29	F	SGL	GRZZZZ	USA
GERTZ, RICHARD	23	M	MCHT	GRZZZZ	USA
GINSBERG, JOSEF	28	F	SGL	GRZZZZ	USA
RIEMANN, SOPHIE	27	F	SGL	GRZZZZ	USA
HOFFMANN, OSCAR	9	M	CHILD	GRZZZZ	USA
LAUTERER, MARIE	21	F	SGL	GRZZZZ	USA
HAHN, OTTO	60	M	ADV	GRZZZZ	USA
ROESLE	46	F	W	GRZZZZ	USA
GUSTAV	22	M	CH	GRZZZZ	USA
OTTILIE	18	F	CH	GRZZZZ	USA
FRIEDA	16	F	CH	GRZZZZ	USA
FANNY	14	F	CH	GRZZZZ	USA
PAUL	13	M	CH	GRZZZZ	USA
WALTER	9	M	CHILD	GRZZZZ	USA
ANNA	8	F	CHILD	GRZZZZ	USA
EMANUEL	7	M	CHILD	GRZZZZ	USA
MARIE	5	F	CHILD	GRZZZZ	USA
MARTHA	4	F	CHILD	GRZZZZ	USA
SCHLOZ, PAULINE	43	F	WO	GRZZZZ	USA
GUSTAV	14	M	STDNT	GRZZZZ	USA
JACOBSEN, CHARLES	32	M	MCHT	GRZZZZ	USA
BERTHA	32	F	W	GRZZZZ	USA
WILKE, LOUISE	38	F	SGL	GRZZZZ	USA
HOLTHUSEN, CATH.	26	F	SGL	GRZZZZ	USA
HERTEL, AMANDA	56	F	WO	GRZZZZ	USA
NEUMANN, GUSTAV	16	M	STDNT	GRZZZZ	USA
BAEHRING, LOUISE	43	F	WO	GRZZZZ	USA
CORDS, H.	30	M	MCHT	GRZZZZ	USA
SCHMID, MAX	23	M	STDNT	GRZZZZ	USA
ALDRICH, EDWARD	18	M	MCHT	GRZZZZ	USA
DOELLIN, MAX	45	M	MCHT	GRZZZZ	USA
HENRIETTE	22	F	W	GRZZZZ	USA
JACOB, THEODOR	19	F	PRNTR	GRZZZZ	USA
BERGER, ANNA	35	F	SGL	GRZZZZ	USA
KOERNER, CHRISTINE	50	F	W	GRZZZZ	USA

SHIP: AMALFI

FROM: HAMBURG
TO: NEW YORK
ARRIVED: 24 JULY 1888

PASSENGER	AGE	SEX	OCCUPATION	PRVL	DES
THOM, HERMANN	34	M	LABR	PRZZZZ	USA
LAURA	30	F	W	PRZZZZ	USA
RICHARD	7	M	CHILD	PRZZZZ	USA
EMMA	5	F	CHILD	PRZZZZ	USA
AUGUSTE	3	F	CHILD	PRZZZZ	USA
ANNA	.11	F	INFANT	PRZZZZ	USA
LANGE, JOHANNA	33	F	WO	PRZZZZ	USA
ZARNIKAU, AUGUSTE	21	F	SGL	PRZZZZ	USA
BOECKER, ANNA	22	F	SGL	PRZZZZ	USA
DIEKOOS, WILHELM	36	M	LABR	PRZZZZ	USA
WILHEMINE	36	F	W	PRZZZZ	USA
ANNA	11	F	CH	PRZZZZ	USA
WILHELM	8	M	CHILD	PRZZZZ	USA
SPRENGER, CHRISTIAN	77	M	LABR	PRZZZZ	USA
HENTSCHEL, ERNST	34	M	FARMER	PRZZZZ	USA
LINA	32	F	W	PRZZZZ	USA
ANNA	11	F	CH	PRZZZZ	USA
ALBERT	3	M	CHILD	PRZZZZ	USA
HOCHMANN, EVA	24	F	W	PRZZZZ	USA
STANISLAV	2	M	CHILD	PRZZZZ	USA
STANISLAVA	.06	F	INFANT	PRZZZZ	USA
TOMKOWIAK, IGNATZ	60	M	LABR	PRZZZZ	USA
HEINE, KLARA	20	F	SGL	PRZZZZ	USA
NOTKE, MARIE	15	F	SGL	PRZZZZ	USA
MARTHA	4	F	CHILD	PRZZZZ	USA
SCHULTZ, ANNA	34	F	WO	PRZZZZ	USA
AUGNES	12	F	CH	PRZZZZ	USA
CHARLOTTE	10	F	CH	PRZZZZ	USA
CLARA	8	F	CHILD	PRZZZZ	USA
MARTIN	7	M	CHILD	PRZZZZ	USA
GEORG	5	M	CHILD	PRZZZZ	USA
GUSTAV	4	M	CHILD	PRZZZZ	USA
ALFRED	2	M	CHILD	PRZZZZ	USA
SULL, MARGARETHE	36	F	WO	PRZZZZ	USA
JOHN	14	M	CH	PRZZZZ	USA
BERTHA	11	F	CH	PRZZZZ	USA
JOSEF	4	M	CHILD	PRZZZZ	USA
FRYZYSKA, MARIANE	20	F	WO	PRZZZZ	USA
HELENA	1	F	CHILD	PRZZZZ	USA
FREUDE, VALERIA	40	F	WO	PRZZZZ	USA
IDA	5	F	CHILD	PRZZZZ	USA
HUGO	.10	M	INFANT	PRZZZZ	USA
EBLER, THEODOR	50	M	LABR	PRZZZZ	USA
LOUISE	53	F	W	PRZZZZ	USA
AMALIE	17	F	CH	PRZZZZ	USA
JULIUS	10	M	CH	PRZZZZ	USA
WUSTRAK, CARL	23	M	LABR	PRZZZZ	USA
ANNA	20	F	W	PRZZZZ	USA
PAUL	2	M	CHILD	PRZZZZ	USA
SABINOWICZ, MARIANE	18	F	WO	PRZZZZ	USA
KAZMIERZ, MIHALINA	26	F	WO	PRZZZZ	USA
STANISLAUS	3	M	CHILD	PRZZZZ	USA
MARTHA	2	F	CHILD	PRZZZZ	USA
WLADISLAV	1	M	CHILD	PRZZZZ	USA
FAERBER, OTTO	24	M	FARMER	PRZZZZ	USA
HANSEN, CAMILLA	20	F	WO	PRZZZZ	USA
KNUETT	.06	M	INFANT	PRZZZZ	USA
WEINBERG, ELSE	18	F	SGL	PRZZZZ	USA
ITZON, HANS	17	M	LABR	PRZZZZ	USA
BARTICH, CARL	56	M	LABR	PRZZZZ	USA
CAROLINE	54	F	W	PRZZZZ	USA
AUGUSTE	19	F	WO	PRZZZZ	USA
WOITRAIW	16	M	LABR	PRZZZZ	USA
KLAUS, MARIE	10	F	CH	PRZZZZ	USA
SASS, FRANZ	41	M	UNKNOWN	PRZZZZ	USA
WIACZEK, CARL	40	M	SMH	PRZZZZ	USA
CATHA.	39	F	W	PRZZZZ	USA
APOLINA	7	F	CHILD	PRZZZZ	USA

PASSENGER	AGE	SEX	OCCUPATION	PRVVL	DES
LEON	4	M	CHILD	PRZZZZUSA	
MIHAL	.09	M	INFANT	PRZZZZUSA	
HIRSCHKOWITZ, OSKAR	35	M	MCHT	PRZZZZUSA	
KOEHLER, ADOLF	34	M	LABR	PRZZZZUSA	
ZEISE, ANNA	15	F	SGL	PRZZZZUSA	
LETTNER, CARL	25	M	FARMER	PRZZZZUSA	
TOMHAWIAK, MARIANE	65	F	WO	PRZZZZUSA	
FUCHS, ALBERT	14	M	LABR	PRZZZZUSA	
KUNITZ, ALBERT	23	M	LABR	PRZZZZUSA	
EX, FRANZ	27	M	LABR	PRZZZZUSA	
AMALIE	65	F	WO	PRZZZZUSA	
POTRAFKA, GORRFIED	25	U	UNKNOWN	PRZZZZUSA	
KRUEGER, ERNST	27	M	UNKNOWN	PRZZZZUSA	
FRIEBEL, HANS	28	M	UNKNOWN	PRZZZZUSA	
KANITZ, BERNHARD	28	M	UNKNOWN	PRZZZZUSA	
BAUER, MARIE	21	F	SGL	BVZZZZUSA	
SCHEFFLER, HULDA	25	F	SGL	PRZZZZUSA	
ARND, HENRIETTE	32	F	SGL	PRZZZZUSA	
SCHEFFLER, ALBERT	23	M	LABR	PRZZZZUSA	
ULBER, ROBERT	28	M	SMH	SYZZZZUSA	
SELMA	23	F	W	SYZZZZUSA	
FRIEDA	.11	F	INFANT	SYZZZZUSA	
SCHELD, CARL	16	M	MCHT	HBZZZZUSA	

SHIP: DONAU

FROM: BREMEN
TO: BALTIMORE
ARRIVED: 25 JULY 1888

PASSENGER	AGE	SEX	OCCUPATION	PRVVL	DES
DOLLE, U	24	F	UNKNOWN	GRZZZZMD	
BERSCH, U	26	F	UNKNOWN	GRZZZZMD	
-ALKER, U	37	M	BLKSMH	GRZZZZIL	
U	00	M	CH	GRZZZZIL	
U	31	M	LABR	GRZZZZIL	
U	27	F	UNKNOWN	GRZZZZIL	
U	5	F	CHILD	GRZZZZIL	
U	4	F	CHILD	GRZZZZIL	
-CHSCHMIDT, U	16	M	LKSH	GRZZZZOH	
BANER, U	00	M	LKSH	GRZZZZMD	
WIEGAN, U	00	U	UNKNOWN	GRZZZZOH	
SETTELMAIER, JOHAN	24	M	FARMER	GRZZZZMD	
WIEGAND, MARIE	23	F	UNKNOWN	GRZZZZOH	
DUSSOLD, MARGO.	20	F	UNKNOWN	GRZZZZOH	
NICHOL, BARBARA	22	F	UNKNOWN	GRZZZZOH	
LODER, MARGA.	23	F	UNKNOWN	GRZZZZOH	
SCHMIDT, PETER	28	M	BRR	GRZZZZOH	
BLANKENBURG, JOHAN	54	M	FARMER	GRZZZZOH	
WILHELNE.	53	F	UNKNOWN	GRZZZZOH	
GOTTFRIED	10	M	CH	GRZZZZOH	
EMILIE	9	F	CHILD	GRZZZZOH	
JOHAN	1	M	CHILD	GRZZZZOH	
U	.11	M	INFANT	GRZZZZOH	
SCHMIDT, SELMA	14	F	UNKNOWN	GRZZZZPA	
BURANDT, THERESE	13	F	UNKNOWN	GRZZZZPA	
LEIPELT, PAUL	14	M	UNKNOWN	GRZZZZPA	
KANT, MARIA	32	F	UNKNOWN	GRZZZZPA	
KARL	6	M	CHILD	GRZZZZPA	
PAULINE	25	F	UNKNOWN	GRZZZZPA	
ALBERT	9	M	CHILD	GRZZZZPA	
OSKAR	8	M	CHILD	GRZZZZPA	
SCHIKANOWSKI, ANNA	10	F	CH	GRZZZZPA	
ALT, EDUARD	40	M	FARMER	GRZZZZMD	
LUTTERMANN, W.	19	F	UNKNOWN	GRZZZZIL	
TREBIATOWSKI, JOS.	28	M	LABR	GRZZZZMO	
U	24	F	UNKNOWN	GRZZZZMO	
---THA	1	F	CHILD	GRZZZZMO	
FRANZ	.06	M	INFANT	GRZZZZMO	
SCHEUDEL, FRIEDRICH	63	M	LABR	GRZZZZPA	
CHARLOTTE	53	F	UNKNOWN	GRZZZZPA	

PASSENGER	AGE	SEX	OCCUPATION	PRVVL	DES
FRIEDRICH	23	M	UNKNOWN	GRZZZZPA	
AMALIA	18	F	UNKNOWN	GRZZZZPA	
EHRICH, EMILIE	21	F	UNKNOWN	GRZZZZPA	
SCHIDLER, JULIANE	22	F	UNKNOWN	GRZZZZPA	
TSCHIMNA, MARZIANA	25	F	UNKNOWN	GRZZZZPA	
JOSEFA	5	F	CHILD	GRZZZZPA	
FRANZISKA	2	F	CHILD	GRZZZZPA	
STANISLAUS	.09	M	INFANT	GRZZZZPA	
MAJRZAK, MICHAEL	23	M	UNKNOWN	GRZZZZPA	
ROBINSKI, AGNES	22	F	UNKNOWN	GRZZZZPA	
JOSEF	.04	M	INFANT	GRZZZZPA	
KLEIN, HERMAN	28	M	UNKNOWN	GRZZZZPA	
BERTHA	34	F	UNKNOWN	GRZZZZPA	
MARIE	.03	F	INFANT	GRZZZZPA	
SCHAEFER, JOHAN	66	M	FARMER	GRZZZZIL	
WILHNE.	61	F	UNKNOWN	GRZZZZIL	
JABLONSKY, HAVER	26	M	UNKNOWN	GRZZZZIL	
LAMBRECHT, JULIUS	16	M	FARMER	GRZZZZIL	
KOTT, JULIANE	44	F	UNKNOWN	GRZZZZIL	
U	16	M	UNKNOWN	GRZZZZIL	
U	5	F	CHILD	GRZZZZIL	
-RYSZCZYNSKI, JAN	34	M	FARMER	GRZZZZMI	
SPLITTSTOSER, AUG.	49	F	UNKNOWN	GRZZZZMI	
HERMAN	11	M	UNKNOWN	GRZZZZMI	
BODENSTEDT, GUSTAV	10	M	CH	GRZZZZKS	
BOETTCHER, MARTIN	74	M	FARMER	GRZZZZKS	
JOHANNE	58	F	UNKNOWN	GRZZZZKS	
MARTHA	14	F	UNKNOWN	GRZZZZKS	
KNUTH, LOUISE	80	F	UNKNOWN	GRZZZZKS	
CAROLINE	42	F	UNKNOWN	GRZZZZKS	
PAUL	11	M	UNKNOWN	GRZZZZKS	
EMMA	7	F	CHILD	GRZZZZKS	
EMIL	5	M	CHILD	GRZZZZKS	
HEDWIG	2	F	CHILD	GRZZZZKS	
GRETE	.04	F	INFANT	GRZZZZKS	
BERNDT, JULIUS	50	M	UNKNOWN	GRZZZZIL	
MATHILDE	33	F	UNKNOWN	GRZZZZIL	
KIESOV, EMIL	9	M	CHILD	GRZZZZIL	
LOUISE	6	F	CHILD	GRZZZZIL	
PAUL	4	M	CHILD	GRZZZZIL	
KAPIBSCHKE, ALBERT	29	M	SHMK	GRZZZZIL	
MINNA	26	F	UNKNOWN	GRZZZZIL	
STRAWSKA, ANTONIA	39	F	UNKNOWN	GRZZZZIL	
MICHAEL	14	M	UNKNOWN	GRZZZZIL	
MARIA	9	F	CHILD	GRZZZZIL	
ANNA	8	F	CHILD	GRZZZZIL	
ANTON	7	M	CHILD	GRZZZZIL	
JOSEFA	4	F	CHILD	GRZZZZIL	
ANTONINA	3	F	CHILD	GRZZZZIL	
JOSEFINE	.08	F	INFANT	GRZZZZIL	
PFEIL, WILHNE.	33	F	UNKNOWN	GRZZZZMD	
MILLER, ALWINE	11	F	UNKNOWN	GRZZZZIL	
BERTHA	4	F	CHILD	GRZZZZIL	
THERESIA	2	F	CHILD	GRZZZZIL	
DREIER, WILHNE.	36	F	UNKNOWN	GRZZZZIL	
JOHANNE	63	F	UNKNOWN	GRZZZZIL	
HEIDEMANN, AUGUSTE	23	F	UNKNOWN	GRZZZZMD	
SELCHOW, THERESE	18	F	UNKNOWN	GRZZZZMD	
UTECHT, FRANZ	38	M	PT	GRZZZZPA	
IDA	30	F	UNKNOWN	GRZZZZPA	
IDA	4	F	CHILD	GRZZZZPA	
U	3	M	CHILD	GRZZZZPA	
KOWALSKI, U	30	F	UNKNOWN	GRZZZZPA	
SCHERLAV	.03	M	INFANT	GRZZZZPA	
SCHULZE, FRANZ	18	M	FARMER	GRZZZZPA	
SILL, AUGUSTA	21	F	UNKNOWN	GRZZZZPA	
TLAPO, FRANZ	17	M	LABR	GRZZZZPA	
GATZ, HERMAN	24	M	UNKNOWN	GRZZZZPA	
EMILIE	22	F	UNKNOWN	GRZZZZPA	
EMIL	.11	M	INFANT	GRZZZZPA	
NOWAKOWSKA, ANGELE	19	F	UNKNOWN	GRZZZZUNK	
SELESKI, MICHAEL	30	M	FARMER	GRZZZZUNK	
BOEHM, ANNA	22	F	UNKNOWN	GRZZZZUNK	
JAEGER, CATHA.	65	F	UNKNOWN	GRZZZZUNK	
GENSINSKA, ANTONIA	42	F	UNKNOWN	GRZZZZUNK	

PASSENGER	AGE	SEX	OCCUPATION	PR VL	DES
JOHANNA	9	F	CHILD	GRZZZZ	UNK
VALENTIA	5	F	CHILD	GRZZZZ	UNK
GRANETZKI, JOSEPH	17	M	FARMER	GRZZZZ	UNK
ZILZ, WILHNE.	17	F	UNKNOWN	GRZZZZ	UNK
AUGUSTA	15	F	UNKNOWN	GRZZZZ	UNK
GBUREK, JUSTINE	22	F	UNKNOWN	GRZZZZ	UNK
RINKOWSKI, ANNA	50	F	UNKNOWN	GRZZZZ	MN
FRANZISKA	24	F	UNKNOWN	GRZZZZ	MN
PAULINE	10	F	CH	GRZZZZ	MN
GOTTHARDT, JACOB	27	M	LABR	GRZZZZ	MN
KWIATKOWSKA, VICTORIA	22	F	UNKNOWN	GRZZZZ	MN
RINKUS, GEORTIE	46	F	UNKNOWN	GRZZZZ	OH
GERTRUD	40	F	UNKNOWN	GRZZZZ	OH
HENRIETTE	10	F	CH	GRZZZZ	OH
AUGUST	7	M	CHILD	GRZZZZ	OH
HERMAN	2	M	CHILD	GRZZZZ	OH
JOHANNA	.03	F	INFANT	GRZZZZ	OH
FELGNER, KAROLINE	52	F	UNKNOWN	GRZZZZ	OH
AUGUST	9	M	CHILD	GRZZZZ	OH
RATHKE, U	47	F	UNKNOWN	GRZZZZ	OH
MARIA	20	F	UNKNOWN	GRZZZZ	OH
EMMA	18	F	UNKNOWN	GRZZZZ	OH
ANNA	16	F	UNKNOWN	GRZZZZ	OH
GEORG	11	M	UNKNOWN	GRZZZZ	OH
JENNY	8	F	CHILD	GRZZZZ	OH
HELENE	6	F	CHILD	GRZZZZ	OH
OCHMANN, VALENTIN	40	M	FARMER	GRZZZZ	IL
TUENKE, JOSEPH	61	M	FARMER	GRZZZZ	IL
ANNA	24	F	UNKNOWN	GRZZZZ	IL
HAIDA, U	19	F	UNKNOWN	GRZZZZ	IL
ROEDLICH, U	30	F	UNKNOWN	GRZZZZ	IL
U	6	M	CHILD	GRZZZZ	IL
U	4	F	CHILD	GRZZZZ	IL
RUNOC, U	68	F	UNKNOWN	GRZZZZ	IL
HAASE, U	40	M	LABR	GRZZZZ	IL
WISCHER, U	41	F	UNKNOWN	GRZZZZ	IL
U	22	F	UNKNOWN	GRZZZZ	IL
U	18	F	UNKNOWN	GRZZZZ	IL
-SYENSKI, U	48	M	LABR	GRZZZZ	MO
MECH, U	35	M	LABR	GRZZZZ	MO
HESE, AMA.	22	F	UNKNOWN	GRZZZZ	MO
OSTROWSKA, MAGDALENE	31	F	UNKNOWN	GRZZZZ	NE
ROSALIA	8	F	CHILD	GRZZZZ	NE
MARIANNE	7	F	CHILD	GRZZZZ	NE
SCHELNIK, FRANZ	27	M	LABR	GRZZZZ	NE
BERNDT, AUGUST	23	M	LABR	GRZZZZ	NE
KARNAT, FRANZ	26	M	BLKSMH	GRZZZZ	NE
KUENSTER, BERTHA	53	F	UNKNOWN	GRZZZZ	MD
HERMAN	14	M	UNKNOWN	GRZZZZ	MD
U	9	M	CHILD	GRZZZZ	MD
KUHN, U	29	M	LABR	GRZZZZ	MD
HENRIETTE	28	F	UNKNOWN	GRZZZZ	MD
FRIEDRICH	2	M	CHILD	GRZZZZ	MD
CARL	.03	M	INFANT	GRZZZZ	MD
ROSENBERGER, FERD.	72	M	FARMER	GRZZZZ	MD
KOSIELSKI, MARTIN	26	M	LABR	GRZZZZ	MD
BORKOWSKI, ANDREAS	24	M	MLR	GRZZZZ	MD
SCHULTE, FRANZISKA	17	F	UNKNOWN	GRZZZZ	MD
IMHULSE, MARIA	16	F	UNKNOWN	GRZZZZ	MD
FRITZ	14	M	UNKNOWN	GRZZZZ	MD
SCHROEDER, SOPHIE	51	F	UNKNOWN	GRZZZZ	MD
SOPHIE	17	F	UNKNOWN	GRZZZZ	MD
WILHELM	15	M	UNKNOWN	GRZZZZ	MD
CARL	13	M	UNKNOWN	GRZZZZ	MD
HARTMANN, EMMA	23	F	UNKNOWN	GRZZZZ	MD
RAIBAND, HEINRICH	24	M	FARMER	GRZZZZ	MD
TEGELER, WILHELM	14	M	UNKNOWN	GRZZZZ	IL
KLEINHENZ, AUGUST	25	M	LABR	GRZZZZ	IL
BARBARA	21	F	UNKNOWN	GRZZZZ	IL
MEINWIESNER, MARIE	20	F	UNKNOWN	GRZZZZ	IL
EICHHAMMER, BARBARA	40	F	UNKNOWN	GRZZZZ	IL
PETER	14	M	UNKNOWN	GRZZZZ	IL
BARBARA	13	F	UNKNOWN	GRZZZZ	IL
GEORG	11	M	UNKNOWN	GRZZZZ	IL
JOSEPH	9	M	CHILD	GRZZZZ	IL
MAGDALENE	1	F	CHILD	GRZZZZ	IL
PFEIL, WILHELM	59	M	LABR	GRZZZZ	WI
SOPHIE	59	F	UNKNOWN	GRZZZZ	WI
THERESE	17	F	UNKNOWN	GRZZZZ	WI
MUELLER, ROBERT	7	M	CHILD	GRZZZZ	WI
DREIER, HERMAN	11	M	UNKNOWN	GRZZZZ	OH
EMMA	8	F	CHILD	GRZZZZ	OH
FRITZ	6	M	CHILD	GRZZZZ	OH
FRANZ	3	M	CHILD	GRZZZZ	OH
MARTHA	.09	F	INFANT	GRZZZZ	OH
GROTH, FERDINAND	62	M	UNKNOWN	GRZZZZ	MN
MAN, GOTTFRIED	59	M	UNKNOWN	GRZZZZ	MN
CHARLOTTE	56	F	UNKNOWN	GRZZZZ	IA
MARIE	17	F	UNKNOWN	GRZZZZ	IA
WILHNE.	15	F	UNKNOWN	GRZZZZ	IA
CARL	11	M	UNKNOWN	GRZZZZ	IA
SCHLAAK, FRIEDRICH	64	M	FARMER	GRZZZZ	IL
CAROLINE	64	F	UNKNOWN	GRZZZZ	IL
ROGGATZ, PAULINE	27	F	UNKNOWN	GRZZZZ	IL
EMIL	8	M	CHILD	GRZZZZ	IL
WERNER	.06	M	INFANT	GRZZZZ	IL
KUNDE, AUGUSTE	24	F	UNKNOWN	GRZZZZ	IL
SILL, BERTHA	21	F	UNKNOWN	GRZZZZ	IL
PUSCH, OTTO	31	M	BKR	GRZZZZ	WAS
ANNA	36	F	UNKNOWN	GRZZZZ	WAS
KUETER, CHRISTIAN	52	M	SHFM	GRZZZZ	MI
CHARLOTTE	52	F	UNKNOWN	GRZZZZ	MI
GUSTAV	24	M	UNKNOWN	GRZZZZ	MI
AUGUSTE	15	F	UNKNOWN	GRZZZZ	MI
MARIE	12	F	UNKNOWN	GRZZZZ	MI
KRETSCHMER, THOMAS	47	M	UNKNOWN	GRZZZZ	MO
LOUISE	46	F	UNKNOWN	GRZZZZ	MO
MARIE	17	F	UNKNOWN	GRZZZZ	MO
FERDINAND	14	M	UNKNOWN	GRZZZZ	MO
ANNA	12	F	UNKNOWN	GRZZZZ	MO
JOHAN	10	M	CH	GRZZZZ	MO
RICHARD	8	M	CHILD	GRZZZZ	MO
SONNENBERG, EMIL	23	M	LABR	GRZZZZ	OH
PRIDOEHL, CARL	24	M	FARMER	GRZZZZ	MI
WIKARSKI, LORENZ	33	M	LABR	GRZZZZ	MI
MARIANNE	26	F	UNKNOWN	GRZZZZ	MI
IGNATZ	5	M	CHILD	GRZZZZ	MI
STANISLAWA	3	F	CHILD	GRZZZZ	MI
MERTIN, OTTILIE	21	F	UNKNOWN	GRZZZZ	MI
WODTKE, MATHILDE	24	F	UNKNOWN	GRZZZZ	OH
SZYEMANKIEWITZ, FRANZ	28	M	FARMER	GRZZZZ	NE
MATZKOWSKI, JULIUS	18	M	LABR	GRZZZZ	IL
OPITZ, HERNIETTE	55	F	UNKNOWN	GRZZZZ	OH
GUSTAV	22	M	UNKNOWN	GRZZZZ	OH
OTTO	20	M	UNKNOWN	GRZZZZ	OH
MARIE	18	F	UNKNOWN	GRZZZZ	OH
EMMA	16	F	UNKNOWN	GRZZZZ	OH
LAUER, FRITZ	35	M	LKSH	GRZZZZ	IL
GAILUS, AUGUST	44	M	FARMER	GRZZZZ	NE
AUGUST	44	M	FARMER	GRZZZZ	NE
JUSTINE	35	F	UNKNOWN	GRZZZZ	NE
CARL	11	M	UNKNOWN	GRZZZZ	NE
WILHNE.	9	F	CHILD	GRZZZZ	NE
BERTHA	7	F	CHILD	GRZZZZ	NE
AUGUST	5	M	CHILD	GRZZZZ	NE
JUSTINE	3	F	CHILD	GRZZZZ	NE
AMALIA	.06	F	INFANT	GRZZZZ	NE
BOETTCHER, HERINRICH	20	M	MCHT	GRZZZZ	OH
GERZEWSKI, JACOB	39	M	GDNR	GRZZZZ	PA
AUGUSTE	34	F	UNKNOWN	GRZZZZ	PA
MARIE	8	F	CHILD	GRZZZZ	PA
FRANZ	7	M	CHILD	GRZZZZ	PA
ALBERT	.09	M	INFANT	GRZZZZ	PA
MATSCHKE, PAULINE	55	F	UNKNOWN	GRZZZZ	IN
BERNDT, BERTHA	30	F	UNKNOWN	GRZZZZ	IN
MARIE	10	F	CH	GRZZZZ	IN
GUSTAV	8	M	CHILD	GRZZZZ	IN
HAHN, GOTTLIEB	32	M	SHFM	GRZZZZ	IL
KALKE, FLORENTINE	62	F	UNKNOWN	GRZZZZ	IL
AUGUSTE	28	F	UNKNOWN	GRZZZZ	IL

PASSENGER	AGE	SEX	OCCUPATION	PRVVL	DES
DAALKE, OTTO	9	M	CHILD	GRZZZZIL	
ALBERT	7	M	CHILD	GRZZZZIL	
PETERS, ANTON	25	M	JNR	GRZZZZOH	
BILLATH, LUSWIG	35	M	FARMER	GRZZZZKY	
MEYER, JOHAN	29	M	FARMER	GRZZZZTX	
ROSENBAUER, WILHNE.	18	F	UNKNOWN	GRZZZZTX	
WOLFF, --ORG	62	M	FARMER	GRZZZZTX	
NAGEL, GOTTLIEB	16	M	UNKNOWN	GRZZZZUSA	
GEORG	14	M	UNKNOWN	GRZZZZUSA	
GLUNZ, ELISABETH	19	F	UNKNOWN	GRZZZZUSA	
STEINHILBER, MARIA	41	F	UNKNOWN	GRZZZZUSA	
MARIA	6	F	CHILD	GRZZZZUSA	
GAUSER, SOPHIE	18	F	UNKNOWN	GRZZZZUSA	
KRAUSS, FRANZISKA	48	F	UNKNOWN	GRZZZZUSA	
AMALIA	9	F	CHILD	GRZZZZUSA	
JOHAN	7	M	CHILD	GRZZZZUSA	
ALMA	7	F	CHILD	GRZZZZUSA	
MAURER, PHILIP	15	M	UNKNOWN	GRZZZZUSA	
PRESSLER, PETER	31	M	UNKNOWN	GRZZZZUSA	
KRAEMER, BERH.	31	M	UNKNOWN	GRZZZZUSA	
MARGA.	30	F	UNKNOWN	GRZZZZUSA	
BERNH.	7	M	CHILD	GRZZZZUSA	
MARIA	4	F	CHILD	GRZZZZUSA	
WALTER, PETER	22	M	BRR	GRZZZZWI	
GUESE, CARL	31	M	UNKNOWN	GRZZZZWI	
ANNA	29	F	UNKNOWN	GRZZZZWI	
DEMALADE, HEINRICH	47	M	FARMER	GRZZZZWI	
MOELLER, HANS	43	M	FARMER	GRZZZZWI	
CHRISTINE	40	F	UNKNOWN	GRZZZZWI	
EMMA	19	F	UNKNOWN	GRZZZZWI	
HEINRICH	17	M	UNKNOWN	GRZZZZWI	
WILHELM	11	M	UNKNOWN	GRZZZZWI	
ERNST	9	M	CHILD	GRZZZZWI	
ANNA	7	F	CHILD	GRZZZZWI	
GUSTAV	3	M	CHILD	GRZZZZWI	
TROHNAPFEL, JOHAN	32	M	CPTR	GRZZZZIL	
CAROLINE	32	F	UNKNOWN	GRZZZZIL	
LUDWIG	4	M	CHILD	GRZZZZIL	
SHOMAKER, KLAN	23	M	BLKSMH	GRZZZZMD	
WEBERS, HELENA	47	F	UNKNOWN	GRZZZZMD	
BERTUS	22	M	UNKNOWN	GRZZZZMD	
BERNHARD	14	M	UNKNOWN	GRZZZZMD	
GECHARD	10	M	CH	GRZZZZMD	
LENE	8	F	CHILD	GRZZZZMD	
ANGELE	2	F	CHILD	GRZZZZMD	
BANDEMER, MARIA	22	F	UNKNOWN	GRZZZZMD	
SCHADE, GEORG	22	M	SHMK	GRZZZZMD	
VOLKMAR, NICOL.	23	M	ENGR	GRZZZZMD	
MOELLER, CATHA.	46	F	UNKNOWN	GRZZZZMD	
HEINRTICH	15	F	UNKNOWN	GRZZZZMD	
CLARA	12	F	UNKNOWN	GRZZZZMD	
FRANZ	7	M	CHILD	GRZZZZMD	
HOERLE, FERDINAND	17	M	UNKNOWN	GRZZZZMD	
MUELLER, CHRISTINA	19	F	UNKNOWN	GRZZZZMD	
ANTES, LEONHARD	27	M	FARMER	GRZZZZMD	
GRAPP, THEODOR	11	M	UNKNOWN	GRZZZZMD	
BOETTER, WILHNE.	25	F	UNKNOWN	GRZZZZMD	
HOFFMANN, CHRISTIAN	47	M	FARMER	GRZZZZMD	
SIPPEL, ANNA	18	F	UNKNOWN	GRZZZZMD	
HOFFMANN, BARBARA	15	F	UNKNOWN	GRZZZZMD	
WALZ, MARGA.	20	F	UNKNOWN	GRZZZZMD	
SIMON, JOSEFA	15	F	UNKNOWN	GRZZZZMD	
SCHENERER, ROSINA	18	F	UNKNOWN	GRZZZZMD	
TISCHLER, FRANZISCA	22	F	UNKNOWN	GRZZZZMD	
FRUTH, FRANZISCA	19	F	UNKNOWN	GRZZZZMD	
GOCKE, CHRISTIAN	60	M	FARMER	GRZZZZMD	
MARIA	59	F	UNKNOWN	GRZZZZMD	
PAUL	8	M	CHILD	GRZZZZMD	
LANG, PAULUS	27	M	TLR	GRZZZZWI	
WOLFF, JOHAN	21	M	JNR	GRZZZZWI	
SCHORLE, BARBARA	16	F	UNKNOWN	GRZZZZIN	
LIEBONER, ANNA	18	F	UNKNOWN	GRZZZZIN	
FRITZ, BERNH.	18	M	STLR	GRZZZZIN	
LEHMANN, ARTHUR	14	M	UNKNOWN	GRZZZZIN	
SCHERER, PHILIPPINE	49	F	UNKNOWN	GRZZZZIN	
EMIL	14	M	UNKNOWN	GRZZZZIN	
AUGUSTINE	8	F	CHILD	GRZZZZIN	
HEISE, HEDWIG	58	F	UNKNOWN	GRZZZZIN	
MACKEBAN, WILHELM	25	M	UNKNOWN	GRZZZZIN	
LOUISE	28	F	UNKNOWN	GRZZZZIN	
WILHELM	3	M	CHILD	GRZZZZIN	
WILHELMINE	.03	F	INFANT	GRZZZZIN	
FORSTMANN, MINNA	22	F	UNKNOWN	GRZZZZIN	
TRISCHMANN, JOHAN	35	M	FARMER	GRZZZZCAL	
FELLNER, GEORG	61	M	FARMER	GRZZZZIL	
HAAS, CATHA.	59	F	UNKNOWN	GRZZZZIL	
HEIN, JOHANNES	45	M	FARMER	GRZZZZIL	
LISETTE	35	F	UNKNOWN	GRZZZZIL	
AUGUST	15	M	UNKNOWN	GRZZZZIL	
MINNA	13	F	UNKNOWN	GRZZZZIL	
ELISE	11	F	UNKNOWN	GRZZZZIL	
ANNA	3	F	CHILD	GRZZZZIL	
ULM, LUDWIG	58	M	UNKNOWN	GRZZZZIL	
THIEME, HEDWIG	24	F	UNKNOWN	GRZZZZIL	
NUELLE, LUCAS	24	M	FARMER	GRZZZZMN	
SCHUETTE, WILHELM	38	M	FARMER	GRZZZZMN	
ELEONORE	35	F	UNKNOWN	GRZZZZMN	
ELEONORE	10	F	CH	GRZZZZMN	
MARIE	8	F	CHILD	GRZZZZMN	
ANNA	6	F	CHILD	GRZZZZMN	
ENGEL	4	F	CHILD	GRZZZZMN	
ELISE	2	F	CHILD	GRZZZZMN	
CAROLINE	.06	F	INFANT	GRZZZZMN	
STOPPELHAEN, LUDWIG	38	M	JNR	GRZZZZMN	
BIELAWSKI, MARIANNE	22	F	UNKNOWN	GRZZZZPA	
MARIE	2	F	CHILD	GRZZZZPA	
FRANZ	.06	M	INFANT	GRZZZZPA	
WILLNER, MARIA	19	F	UNKNOWN	GRZZZZPA	
HENRIETTE	12	F	UNKNOWN	GRZZZZPA	
BOGUSCHEWSKI, AUGUSTA	24	F	UNKNOWN	GRZZZZPA	
ANASTASIA	3	F	CHILD	GRZZZZPA	
JOHAN	.10	M	INFANT	GRZZZZPA	
RUIAS, AUGUSTE	24	F	UNKNOWN	GRZZZZPA	
MARIE	.11	F	INFANT	GRZZZZPA	
JABLONSKI, IGNACI	27	M	SHMK	GRZZZZPA	
KRAUSE, AUGUST	27	M	FARMER	GRZZZZIL	
JOHAN	30	M	FARMER	GRZZZZIL	
ERNST	7	M	CHILD	GRZZZZIL	
MARIE	5	F	CHILD	GRZZZZIL	
BERTHA	2	F	CHILD	GRZZZZIL	
IDA	.09	F	INFANT	GRZZZZIL	
GRAJEWSKA, VALERIA	20	F	UNKNOWN	GRZZZZIL	
OLISCHEWSKA, ANNA	18	F	UNKNOWN	GRZZZZIL	
KATHKE, ADOLPH	26	M	LABR	GRZZZZIL	
SMOLINSKI, MARIAN	22	F	UNKNOWN	GRZZZZIL	
BENKE, AUGUST	36	M	FARMER	GRZZZZIL	
OTTILIE	45	F	UNKNOWN	GRZZZZIL	
EUGEN	10	M	CH	GRZZZZIL	
PALICKA, JOSEPHA	23	F	UNKNOWN	GRZZZZIL	
MADAG, MICHAEL	22	M	FARMER	GRZZZZIL	
LUTTE, HERMAN	16	M	UNKNOWN	GRZZZZIL	
MEIER, CARL	58	M	BCHR	GRZZZZIL	
SCHOPPE, FRIEDERIKE	45	F	UNKNOWN	GRZZZZIL	
FRANZISKA	19	F	UNKNOWN	GRZZZZIL	
ROSETTE	9	F	CHILD	GRZZZZIL	
CLARA	.03	F	INFANT	GRZZZZIL	
RIETH, JUSTUS	14	M	UNKNOWN	GRZZZZMI	
SCHLEGEL, EMILE	27	F	UNKNOWN	GRZZZZMI	
LISETTE	5	F	CHILD	GRZZZZMI	
IDA	4	F	CHILD	GRZZZZMI	
OTTO	2	M	CHILD	GRZZZZMI	
KUTSCHER, LEONORE	55	F	UNKNOWN	GRZZZZMI	
JABLONSKA, ANTONINA	25	F	UNKNOWN	GRZZZZMI	
STROHLEIN, ADAM	42	M	JNR	GRZZZZMI	
GRINDEL, VALENTIN	31	M	JNR	GRZZZZMI	
SCHUBERT, ADAM	23	M	FARMER	GRZZZZCAL	
LEHMANN, CARL	32	M	FARMER	GRZZZZCAL	
MARGA.	32	F	UNKNOWN	GRZZZZCAL	
HANNY	3	F	CHILD	GRZZZZCAL	
WILLY	.10	M	INFANT	GRZZZZCAL	

PASSENGER	AGE	SEX	OCCUPATION	PRVL DES
FICKE, HEINRICH	28	M	CPTR	GRZZZZWI
MEYER, ELISE	52	F	UNKNOWN	GRZZZZWI
ADELHEID	15	F	UNKNOWN	GRZZZZWI
CARL	15	M	UNKNOWN	GRZZZZWI
MARIE	11	F	UNKNOWN	GRZZZZWI
FEIGE, WILHELM	23	M	UNKNOWN	GRZZZZWI
RINGBERG, MARIE	35	F	UNKNOWN	GRZZZZMO
OTTO	3	M	CHILD	GRZZZZMO
PLAGENS, MARTIN	36	M	LABR	GRZZZZMI
CATHA.	35	F	UNKNOWN	GRZZZZMI
FRANZISKA	8	F	CHILD	GRZZZZMI
ANNA	4	F	CHILD	GRZZZZMI
FRANZ	3	M	CHILD	GRZZZZMI
ANDREAS	.06	M	INFANT	GRZZZZMI
WENTZEL, EMILIE	24	F	UNKNOWN	GRZZZZMI
SKOTSCHINSKY, ANDR.	24	M	FARMER	GRZZZZMD
BEMA, STANISL.	26	M	FARMER	GRZZZZMD
DRUENNER, LOUIS	14	M	UNKNOWN	GRZZZZMD
HILFER, MATHIAS	27	M	FARMER	GRZZZZMD
MIGINGER, PAULUS	32	M	FARMER	GRZZZZMD
HOFHENKE, JOHAN	18	M	FARMER	GRZZZZMD
HOLDT, NIKOLAUS	29	M	JNR	GRZZZZMD
MEYER, HUGO	17	M	LABR	GRZZZZIL
DEYERLING, EVA	21	F	UNKNOWN	GRZZZZIN
POLACZIK, JOSEPH	29	M	LABR	GRZZZZMN
MARIANNE	21	F	UNKNOWN	GRZZZZMN
BAUMBACH, AUGUST	17	M	CPTR	GRZZZZMN
KATZ, SAROH	15	F	UNKNOWN	GRZZZZMN
---MANN, JOSEPH	28	M	LABR	GRZZZZPA
ANNA	34	F	UNKNOWN	GRZZZZPA
KARL	.03	M	INFANT	GRZZZZPA
ANNA	65	F	UNKNOWN	GRZZZZPA
JOSEPH	13	M	UNKNOWN	GRZZZZPA
LANDECK, KARL	24	M	SHMK	GRZZZZMD
HUEBSCHER, KASPAR	24	M	UNKNOWN	GRZZZZMD
MEINERT, HEIRNICH	16	M	LABR	GRZZZZMD
REESE, WILHELM	27	M	MNR	GRZZZZOH
SAND, JOHAN	27	M	FARMER	GRZZZZOH
GERECHT, CHRIST.	23	M	FARMER	GRZZZZOH
BIESOMEIER, A.	37	M	FARMER	GRZZZZMO
SEIFERT, HERMAN	42	M	FARMER	GRZZZZPA
FRIEDERIKE	38	F	UNKNOWN	GRZZZZPA
CARL	9	M	CHILD	GRZZZZPA
ALWINE	8	F	CHILD	GRZZZZPA
KATHARINA	6	F	CHILD	GRZZZZPA
HERMAN	3	M	CHILD	GRZZZZPA
GIESE, MARGA.	24	F	UNKNOWN	GRZZZZIL
ANNA	5	F	CHILD	GRZZZZIL
MAGDA.	.11	F	INFANT	GRZZZZIL
LINK, JOHAN	43	M	TLR	GRZZZZMD
KLAUS, FRIEDRICH	65	M	SHMK	GRZZZZNE
ANNA	68	F	UNKNOWN	GRZZZZNE
FRIEDRICH	10	M	CH	GRZZZZNE
GOZKE, JOHAN	23	M	FARMER	GRZZZZMI
KUCHNOWSKY, JOHAN	29	M	LABR	GRZZZZMI
FRANZISKA	24	F	UNKNOWN	GRZZZZMI
FRANZ	3	M	CHILD	GRZZZZMI
FLOETER, BERNHARD	27	M	LABR	GRZZZZMD
EMILIE	23	F	UNKNOWN	GRZZZZMD
CARL	.04	M	INFANT	GRZZZZMD
HILL, JULIUS	18	M	UNKNOWN	GRZZZZPA
SZCZESNIAK, KATERZINA	22	F	UNKNOWN	GRZZZZPA
FEREDORE	.06	F	INFANT	GRZZZZPA
SZAFRAN, KATERZINA	20	F	UNKNOWN	GRZZZZPA
RUTKOWSKA, MARGA.	22	F	UNKNOWN	GRZZZZPA
DERBIN, AGNITZKA	.11	F	INFANT	GRZZZZPA
JUREZYK, KATHARINA	40	F	UNKNOWN	GRZZZZNE
CLARA	12	F	UNKNOWN	GRZZZZNE
JOSEPH	9	M	CHILD	GRZZZZNE
JULIUS	7	M	CHILD	GRZZZZNE
ANNA	4	F	CHILD	GRZZZZNE
FRANZ	2	M	CHILD	GRZZZZNE
DYSARZ, JOHN	31	M	LABR	GRZZZZNE
TOMEZAK, ELISABETH	23	F	UNKNOWN	GRZZZZNE
VOLKMANN, JOSEPH	18	M	LABR	GRZZZZNE
SKERT, LEOPOLD	50	M	LABR	GRZZZZNE
KALKE, CHRISTOPH	43	M	FARMER	GRZZZZIL
MATHILDE	14	F	UNKNOWN	GRZZZZIL
THEODOR	16	M	UNKNOWN	GRZZZZIL
HEINRICH	14	M	UNKNOWN	GRZZZZIL
HULDA	7	F	CHILD	GRZZZZIL
--HARD	5	M	CHILD	GRZZZZIL
U, U	18	F	UNKNOWN	GRZZZZIL
KIESPODZIANA, MARIANNE	20	F	UNKNOWN	GRZZZZIL
LACHLER, PAULINE	25	F	UNKNOWN	GRZZZZIL
MORAS, IGNATZ	24	M	JNR	GRZZZZIL
CZISZ, JOHAN	28	M	LABR	GRZZZZIA
HEDWIG	23	F	UNKNOWN	GRZZZZIA
FRANZ	.11	M	INFANT	GRZZZZIA
RECZEK, PRAXITTA	20	F	UNKNOWN	GRZZZZIA
NOWICKI, JOSEPH	16	M	UNKNOWN	GRZZZZIA
WOIJECH	9	M	CHILD	GRZZZZIA
PATKOWSKI, PAUL	41	M	LABR	GRZZZZMD
MELELKI, WLADILAW	28	M	LABR	GRZZZZMD
MASZAK, KONSTANZIA	34	F	UNKNOWN	GRZZZZMD
MARIANNE	11	F	UNKNOWN	GRZZZZMD
FRANZ	9	M	CHILD	GRZZZZMD
JOSEPH	7	M	CHILD	GRZZZZMD
ANNA	5	F	CHILD	GRZZZZMD
LIPKE, AUGUST	45	M	FARMER	GRZZZZIL
WILHELNE.	18	F	UNKNOWN	GRZZZZIL
ROSALIA	16	F	UNKNOWN	GRZZZZIL
U	10	F	CH	GRZZZZIL
SWIERSKI, U	62	M	FARMER	GRZZZZIL
--ERZINA	53	F	UNKNOWN	GRZZZZIL
KONSTANZIA	14	F	UNKNOWN	GRZZZZIL
WINCINTY	11	M	UNKNOWN	GRZZZZIL
MICHALINA	8	F	CHILD	GRZZZZIL
WLADISLAV	5	M	CHILD	GRZZZZIL
ZEILINGER, MARGA.	28	F	UNKNOWN	GRZZZZIL
V, JOHAN	56	M	LABR	GRZZZZPA
BECKER, AUGUST	34	M	LABR	GRZZZZPA
LAWRENTZ, LOUISE	17	F	UNKNOWN	GRZZZZPA
SCHULZ, ANNA	26	F	UNKNOWN	GRZZZZMD
HENZEL, ERNST	30	M	FARMER	GRZZZZMD
EMMA	30	F	UNKNOWN	GRZZZZMD
EMIL	11	M	UNKNOWN	GRZZZZMD
MASZAK, JOSEFA	5	F	CHILD	GRZZZZMD
HARTUNG, LOUISE	35	F	UNKNOWN	GRZZZZMI
WILHELM	8	M	CHILD	GRZZZZMI
PUGEHL, CLARA	21	F	UNKNOWN	GRZZZZMI
ROSCHER, EMILIE	63	F	UNKNOWN	GRZZZZMI
ALMA	39	F	UNKNOWN	GRZZZZMI
AGNES	37	F	UNKNOWN	GRZZZZMI
BERNHAGEN, EMILIE	20	F	UNKNOWN	GRZZZZMI
GERLACH, CARL	46	M	LLD	GRZZZZMI
IDA	36	F	UNKNOWN	GRZZZZMI
HELENE	11	F	UNKNOWN	GRZZZZMI
LULBINSKI, AUGUST	30	M	FARMER	GRZZZZMD
KOCZOR, VALENTIN	26	M	FARMER	GRZZZZMD
MARIANNE	25	F	UNKNOWN	GRZZZZMD
KUBARSZAK, ANTONIA	42	F	UNKNOWN	GRZZZZMD
IGNATZ	.06	M	INFANT	GRZZZZMD
WACHOWSKY, JOSEPH	26	M	UNKNOWN	GRZZZZMO
MARIANNA	28	F	UNKNOWN	GRZZZZMO
JAN	.05	M	INFANT	GRZZZZMO
SPIEWEG, ERNST	28	M	LABR	GRZZZZMO
JPESKA, MAGDALENE	22	F	UNKNOWN	GRZZZZMO
JACKOWITZ, VERONICA	24	F	UNKNOWN	GRZZZZMO
MARIANNE	26	F	UNKNOWN	GRZZZZMO
SZYSZ, U	25	M	SMH	GRZZZZUSA
ROSALIA	18	F	UNKNOWN	GRZZZZUSA
MUNDT, ALBERT	26	M	UNKNOWN	GRZZZZUSA
SCHMEIDER, WILHELM	38	M	FARMER	GRZZZZOH
FRANZISKA	34	F	UNKNOWN	GRZZZZOH
MARTHA	11	F	UNKNOWN	GRZZZZOH
PAUL	8	M	CHILD	GRZZZZOH
HELENE	5	F	CHILD	GRZZZZOH
ZINDAHL, HERMAN	25	M	LKSH	GRZZZZMD
GLUTH, IDA	22	F	UNKNOWN	GRZZZZMD

PASSENGER	AGE	SEX	OCCUPATION	PRVL	DES
NIEMERMANN, CARL	28	M	LABR		GRZZZZMD
GENZEL, EMIL	16	M	LABR		GRZZZZMD
HEINATT, VALERIA	36	F	UNKNOWN		GRZZZZMD
MOCEK, ROSALIA	23	F	UNKNOWN		GRZZZZUNK
JOSEPH	.11	M	INFANT		GRZZZZUNK
DOBLKOPF, REGINA	16	F	UNKNOWN		GRZZZZUNK
JOHAN	8	M	CHILD		GRZZZZUNK
AUMER, GERTRUDE	16	F	UNKNOWN		GRZZZZUNK
KRUEGER, EMILIE	33	F	UNKNOWN		GRZZZZMI
AUGUST	6	M	CHILD		GRZZZZMI
LEWIN, HANE	35	F	UNKNOWN		GRZZZZMI
ISRAEL	11	M	UNKNOWN		GRZZZZMI
REICHEL	9	F	CHILD		GRZZZZMI
LEISER	8	M	CHILD		GRZZZZMI
ISAAC	2	M	CHILD		GRZZZZMI
ESTER	.09	F	INFANT		GRZZZZMI
KLOESE, IDA	21	F	UNKNOWN		GRZZZZMI
BASILIUS, AGUST	60	M	FARMER		GRZZZZIL
WILHLENE.	50	F	UNKNOWN		GRZZZZIL
ALBERT	18	M	UNKNOWN		GRZZZZIL
BERTHA	15	F	UNKNOWN		GRZZZZIL
SITZLER, FRIEDERIKE	22	F	UNKNOWN		GRZZZZIL
FRIDA	2	F	CHILD		GRZZZZIL
ANNA	.06	F	INFANT		GRZZZZIL
PO--ASO, U	00	U	UNKNOWN		GRZZZZIL
JOHAN	00	M	UNKNOWN		GRZZZZIL
JOHANNE	16	F	UNKNOWN		GRZZZZIL
HEINRICH	8	M	CHILD		GRZZZZIL
FRIEDRICH	4	M	CHILD		GRZZZZIL
IRRGANG, MARIA	22	F	UNKNOWN		GRZZZZIL
MAX	.11	M	INFANT		GRZZZZIL
LAMPKE, URSULA	60	F	UNKNOWN		GRZZZZIL
HILDEBRAND, JACOB	34	M	FARMER		GRZZZZIL
JOSEFINE	31	F	UNKNOWN		GRZZZZIL
GERTRUD	4	F	CHILD		GRZZZZIL
MARIA	.11	F	INFANT		GRZZZZIL
ANNA	.11	F	INFANT		GRZZZZIL
REN---, U	00	U	UNKNOWN		GRZZZZMI
U, --WIG	13	F	UNKNOWN		GRZZZZMI
MARTHA	11	F	UNKNOWN		GRZZZZMI
PRZYBOVSKI, JAN	36	M	TLR		GRZZZZPA
JOSEFA	30	F	UNKNOWN		GRZZZZPA
FRANZISKA	3	F	CHILD		GRZZZZPA
VICTORIA	.11	F	INFANT		GRZZZZPA
HEINATH, MARIE	24	F	UNKNOWN		GRZZZZMI
RUDOLF, MARIE	20	F	UNKNOWN		GRZZZZIL
HUGE, FRITZ	28	M	GZR		GRZZZZIN
LOUISE	24	F	UNKNOWN		GRZZZZIN
LOUISE	.04	F	INFANT		GRZZZZIN
BUCKING, FRIEDRICH	22	M	UNKNOWN		GRZZZZOH
HAHNE, FRIEDRICH	52	M	UNKNOWN		GRZZZZOH
HOFELMANN, CARL	28	M	FARMER		GRZZZZOH
MARIA	22	F	UNKNOWN		GRZZZZOH
FRITZ	.03	M	INFANT		GRZZZZOH
DREYER, MARIE	46	F	UNKNOWN		GRZZZZOH
ELISE	17	F	UNKNOWN		GRZZZZOH
AUGUST	11	M	UNKNOWN		GRZZZZOH
HEINRICH	9	M	CHILD		GRZZZZOH
SCHMIER, MARIE	19	F	UNKNOWN		GRZZZZOH
WIELFF, REINHOLD	33	M	FARMER		GRZZZZOH
AUGUSTE	33	F	UNKNOWN		GRZZZZOH
FRED	8	M	CHILD		GRZZZZOH
MARIE	2	F	CHILD		GRZZZZOH
PAUL	.10	M	INFANT		GRZZZZOH
SCHWENKE, HERMAN	25	M	LABR		GRZZZZOH
HINZ, FRIEDRICH	67	M	LABR		GRZZZZMO
LOUISE	63	F	UNKNOWN		GRZZZZIL
U	37	M	UNKNOWN		GRZZZZIL
U	33	F	UNKNOWN		GRZZZZIL
U	9	M	CHILD		GRZZZZIL
BUSSE, U	37	M	LABR		GRZZZZIL
FRIEDERIKE	22	F	UNKNOWN		GRZZZZIL
CARL	9	M	CHILD		GRZZZZIL
FRITZ	4	M	CHILD		GRZZZZIL
WOLFER, GUSTAV	44	M	SMH		GRZZZZNE
JOHANNA	33	F	UNKNOWN		GRZZZZNE
HERMAN	13	F	UNKNOWN		GRZZZZNE
AGNES	11	F	UNKNOWN		GRZZZZNE
FRITZ	9	M	CHILD		GRZZZZNE
ROESSLER, AUGUST	32	M	LABR		GRZZZZWI
ERNSTINE	31	F	UNKNOWN		GRZZZZWI
GUSTAV	3	M	CHILD		GRZZZZWI
ANNA	1	F	CHILD		GRZZZZWI
ARNSDORFF, HENRIETTE	61	F	UNKNOWN		GRZZZZNE
LENZ, WILHELNE.	23	F	UNKNOWN		GRZZZZNE
CZAOHNKE, FRIEDERIKE	35	M	JNR		GRZZZZIL
IDA	27	F	UNKNOWN		GRZZZZIL
OLGA	5	F	CHILD		GRZZZZIL
ARTHUR	3	M	CHILD		GRZZZZIL
WILLY	.09	M	INFANT		GRZZZZIL
LULEG, SIMON	17	M	UNKNOWN		GRZZZZOH
MUTH, U	22	F	UNKNOWN		GRZZZZMD
KONKE, U	18	F	UNKNOWN		GRZZZZMD
KOWITZ, U	20	U	UNKNOWN		GRZZZZMD
U	20	M	UNKNOWN		GRZZZZMD
KEHLERT, U	24	F	UNKNOWN		GRZZZZMD
SCHREIBER, BARBARA	34	F	UNKNOWN		GRZZZZMD
WOLFGANG	8	M	CHILD		GRZZZZMD
JOSEPH	9	M	CHILD		GRZZZZMD
JOSEPHA	.09	F	INFANT		GRZZZZMD
KWIATKOFSKY, U	34	M	LABR		GRZZZZPA
NUERSCHE, U	20	F	UNKNOWN		GRZZZZOH
HEINZ, --ESTINE	00	F	UNKNOWN		GRZZZZUSA
WILHELNE.	18	F	UNKNOWN		GRZZZZUSA
AUGUST	16	M	UNKNOWN		GRZZZZUSA

SHIP: ELBE

FROM: BREMEN AND SOUTHAMPTON
TO: NEW YORK
ARRIVED: 25 JULY 1888

PASSENGER	AGE	SEX	OCCUPATION	PRVL	DES
WOLLENBERG, SIGMUND	38	M	TT		GRAARRNY
MATHIESEN, FRITZ	89	M	TT		GRZZZZNY
HILLMER, DORA	21	F	TT		GRABRYNY
WARNS, RUD.	21	M	TT		GRABMDNY
BARTHEL, CURT	19	M	TT		GRZZZZNY
SCHWEISHEIMER, JOS.	20	M	TT		GRZZZZNY
KOCH, JOS.	35	M	TT		GRADHENY
SPRINZ, LEON	23	M	TT		GRAAKHNY
BICHMANN, ROSA	20	F	TT		GRAARRNY
EVA	22	F	TT		GRAARRNY
SCHOENFELD, LOUISE	30	F	TT		GRAARRNY
HERM.	9	M	CHILD		GRAARRNY
GEORG	8	M	CHILD		GRAARRNY
LOUISE	.10	F	INFANT		GRAARRNY
SCHNEIDER, ANNA	25	F	TT		GRACXVNY
MENGELBIER, CARL	23	M	TT		GRACXVNY
LANG, SIGMUND	23	M	TT		GRACXVNY
MUESER, AUGUST	30	M	TT		GRACXVNY
STEIGER, FRANZISKA	45	F	UNKNOWN		GRADJWNY
FRANZISKA	4	F	CHILD		GRADJWNY
SCHMIDT, ANNA	12	F	CH		GRADJWNY
REGINA	12	F	CH		GRADJWNY
ANNA	22	F	UNKNOWN		GRADDQNY
MEYER, DORETHEA	54	F	UNKNOWN		GRZZZZNY
FICHTNER, PAUL	39	M	FUR		GRZZZZNY
CONRADENE	45	F	UNKNOWN		GRZZZZNY
MARGARETHE	11	F	UNKNOWN		GRZZZZNY
HEINR.	8	M	CHILD		GRZZZZNY
PAUL	5	M	CHILD		GRZZZZNY
WILHELM	3	M	CHILD		GRZZZZNY
FRIEDA	2	F	CHILD		GRZZZZNY
LOUISE	.06	F	INFANT		GRZZZZNY
DRUSKUS, MARIA	25	F	UNKNOWN		GRACBFNY

PASSENGER	AGE	SEX	OCCUPATION	PRVL	DES	PASSENGER	AGE	SEX	OCCUPATION	PRVL	DES
MICHELSON, AUGUSTE	30	F	UNKNOWN		GRACBFNY	AULBACH, ANNA	19	F	UNKNOWN		GRZZZZNY
KIEFFER, DENIS	39	M	LABR		GRAGLSNY	ZORN, ANNA	22	F	UNKNOWN		GRZZZZNY
SCHMIDT, ADELHEID	25	F	UNKNOWN		GRAARRNY	HASENSTAL, MARGARETHA	22	F	UNKNOWN		GRZZZZNY
HAHL, PHILOMENA	37	F	UNKNOWN		GRZZZZNY	FRIES, U	17	F	UNKNOWN		GRZZZZNY
ANTON	12	M	UNKNOWN		GRZZZZNY	VORDON, SUSANNE	46	F	UNKNOWN		GRAFWGNY
FRIEDR.	11	M	UNKNOWN		GRZZZZNY	HERBST, BARBARA	19	F	UNKNOWN		GRAFWGNY
JOSEPH	7	M	CHILD		GRZZZZNY	BEMREUTHER, ANNA	21	F	UNKNOWN		GRAFWGNY
BRUNO	6	M	CHILD		GRZZZZNY	BRUECKNER, ELEONORE	22	F	UNKNOWN		GRAEABNY
JOSEPHA	4	F	CHILD		GRZZZZNY	SPORING, ANNA	54	F	UNKNOWN		GRAEABNY
MAEIEJEWSKA, EMILIA	38	F	UNKNOWN		GRADNXNY	ZILSKE, BERTHA	21	F	UNKNOWN		GRAARRNY
FRANZISKA	11	F	UNKNOWN		GRADNXNY	PORAZEWSKA, AGNES	50	F	UNKNOWN		GRAARRNY
PAUL	9	M	CHILD		GRADNXNY	KROPF, NATHAN	17	M	LABR		GRAARRNY
MAX	7	M	CHILD		GRADNXNY	STANSWITZ, BERTHA	17	F	UNKNOWN		GRAARRNY
BERTHA	4	F	CHILD		GRADNXNY	PAULINE	12	F	UNKNOWN		GRAARRNY
FERSTNER, AUGUSTE	29	F	UNKNOWN		GRZZZZNY	RICHTBERG, EMILIE	19	F	UNKNOWN		GRAEABNY
KARL	4	M	CHILD		GRZZZZNY	EMILIE	16	F	UNKNOWN		GRAEABNY
MARIE	2	F	CHILD		GRZZZZNY	MERKEL, MARIE	18	F	UNKNOWN		GRAEABNY
KLEMS, ELISE	20	F	UNKNOWN		GRZZZZNY	FICKENWIRTH, HERM.	18	M	UNKNOWN		GRAEABNY
WINTER, AUG.	25	M	LABR		GRACSHNY	EHLEN, SOPHIE	28	F	UNKNOWN		GRAEABNY
RIEDMANN, ADAM	24	M	GDNR		GRZZZZNY	VIEHBROCK, META	14	F	UNKNOWN		GRAFTSNY
ZIMMERMANN, ANTON	25	M	BCHR		GRAFWZNY	DUBBELS, JOH.	14	M	LABR		GRZZZZNY
LUEDDEKE, HEINR.	22	M	MCHT		GRAARRNY	WALK, CARL	16	M	LABR		GRZZZZNY
SPERLICH, META	32	F	UNKNOWN		GRAARRNY	RIPMANN, EMIL	24	M	LABR		GRZZZZNY
PAUL	6	M	CHILD		GRAAURNY	REPNER, MARTHA	20	F	UNKNOWN		GRZZZZNY
MENKE, CHARLOTTE	57	F	UNKNOWN		GRAAURNY	REPP, JOSEF	25	M	CPR		GRAIZTNY
WERNER, HEDWIG	24	F	UNKNOWN		GRAAURNY	STOCK, SUSANNE	22	F	UNKNOWN		GRAIZTNY
MEYER, CARL	14	M	UNKNOWN		GRAENCNY	PFANNSTIEL, ERNESTINE	57	F	UNKNOWN		GRAEMTNY
MARGA.	9	F	CHILD		GRAENCNY	VOGEL, ERNST	27	M	BRR		GRADELNY
JUSTINE	39	F	UNKNOWN		GRAENCNY	SCHAICH, JACOB	28	M	BRR		GRZZZZNY
POPESCH, AGNES	27	F	UNKNOWN		GRZZZZNY	EGGERS, JOHANNE	22	F	UNKNOWN		GRZZZZNY
CARL	6	M	CHILD		GRZZZZNY	DREUTH, WILHELM	24	M	JNR		GRZZZZNY
JOH.	3	M	CHILD		GRZZZZNY	DRONBACH, WILHELMINE	15	F	UNKNOWN		GRZZZZNY
KELLERSOHN, AUGUST	26	M	BCHR		GRAKQPNY	BOCK, GEORG	18	M	FARMER		GRABBRMO
BUTZ, FRIEDR.	15	M	FARMER		GRAFGZNY	SCHAD, PAULINE	21	F	UNKNOWN		GRABBRNY
MARIA	22	F	UNKNOWN		GRAFGZNY	STASINSKI, SNTON	28	M	FARMER		GRAEABNY
SAHN, JACOB	14	M	FARMER		GRZZZZNY	FEUERBACH, BARBARA	13	F	UNKNOWN		GRAEABNY
KILLIEN, JOH.	21	M	FARMER		GRZZZZNY	GOLDEKE, GEORG	23	M	BKR		GRAEABGAL
LACHEMAYER, FRIEDKE	20	F	UNKNOWN		GRAILWNY	RUPPRECHT, GEORG	24	M	BCHR		GRAEABNY
KOCH, GEORG	17	M	FARMER		GRAFGZNY	U	25	F	UNKNOWN		GRAEABNY
FRIEDRKE.	16	F	UNKNOWN		GRAFGZNY	ANNA	.03	F	INFANT		GRAEABNY
HANNAUER, PAUL.	17	F	UNKNOWN		GRACAVNY	SCHIRMER, AMYNDA	17	F	UNKNOWN		GRAEABNY
SCHMIDT, AUGUSTE	22	F	UNKNOWN		GRABDMNY	TAPPEL, G.H.	17	M	FARMER		GRZZZZSTL
LEGLER, ANNA	22	F	UNKNOWN		GRABDMNY	ENGELBACH, LUDWIG	23	M	MCHT		GRAGFJERE
TREUTEN, ANNA	11	F	UNKNOWN		GRZZZZNY	NEUSTEL, CONRAD	25	M	BKR		GRAEYGERE
HERING, PAULINE	68	F	UNKNOWN		GRAEIQPA	EVA	21	F	UNKNOWN		GRAEYGERE
SCHEIDEL, JOH.	24	M	FARMER		GRZZZZPA	BRUMMER, BABETTA	15	F	UNKNOWN		GRAEYGERE
BRAUN, MARIANNA	23	F	UNKNOWN		GRZZZZIN	MUNCHIANDO, LUIZI	25	F	UNKNOWN		GRAEYJNY
HEMSHORN, STEPHAN	22	M	FARMER		GRABJXKS	MAZORINA, GUISEPE	28	M	LABR		GRAEYJNY
KORN, MARIA	16	F	UNKNOWN		GRZZZZOH	TRASCH, HAVER	38	M	LABR		GRZZZZNY
GECK, GEORG	15	M	FARMER		GRADEIMO	HEILBRUNN, JOS.	17	M	MCHT		GRZZZZNY
BARTH, MICH.	28	M	UNKNOWN		GRZZZZNY	HOEBER, JACOB	39	M	LABR		GRZZZZNY
LANGENBERG, JOHANNE	35	F	UNKNOWN		GRAAOKNY	FRIEDRIKE	30	F	UNKNOWN		GRZZZZNY
BRAND, ANNA	28	M	UNKNOWN		GRAGTTMO	EMILIE	4	F	CHILD		GRZZZZNY
ENGELHARDT, WILHELMINE	18	F	UNKNOWN		GRZZZZNY	MUTH, JOHS.	35	M	FARMER		GRABVHNE
SULDAN, MARTIN	15	M	MUSN		GRAAIHNY	FUNK, OTTO	27	M	FARMER		GRZZZZNY
MARTHA	18	F	UNKNOWN		GRAAIHNY	JUCHS, ALBERT	24	M	SDLR		GRACCINY
DITTMANN, LOUISE	31	F	UNKNOWN		GRZZZZNY	VOGEL, JOH.	23	M	FARMER		GRADLRNY
HINZ, EMILIE	22	F	UNKNOWN		GRZZZZNY	STROEBEL, MARIE	20	F	UNKNOWN		GRADLRNY
RISTAN, GOTTB.	21	M	UNKNOWN		GRZZZZNY	SILBERHORN, CARL	28	M	UNKNOWN		GRZZZZNY
KEIL, HANS	24	M	UNKNOWN		GRZZZZNY	MICHALS, SIBELLE	18	F	UNKNOWN		GRZZZZNY
CLAUSSNITZER, EMIL	24	M	UNKNOWN		GRZZZZNY	MARGA.	14	F	UNKNOWN		GRZZZZNY
BETZ, JACOB	33	M	UNKNOWN		GRZZZZNY	SCHULZE, AUGUSTE	21	F	UNKNOWN		GRADVHNY
ZALEWSKA, WERONIKA	24	F	UNKNOWN		GRZZZZNY	V., EBERH.	43	M	DLR		GRABHTNY
SPLETTSTOSSER, ANNA	20	F	UNKNOWN		GRAEASNY	CASSAGRANDA, JOH.	34	M	UNKNOWN		GRABHTCAL
SCHNEIDER, JOHS.	26	M	BKR		GRZZZZNY	BECK, GOTTLIEB	26	M	LABR		GRADYYNY
LOSER, CARL	46	M	SHMK		GRZZZZNY	SEEFELD, PAUL	22	M	LABR		GRZZZZNY
KRUEGER, AUGUSTE	18	F	UNKNOWN		GRZZZZNY	ZYWIEC, EVA	26	F	UNKNOWN		GRZZZZNY
WILH.	.03	M	INFANT		GRZZZZNY	BOHLMANN, HEINR.	16	M	UNKNOWN		GRACBRIL
ALBIG, CONRAD	33	M	SHMK		GRZZZZNY	BRODBECK, JOHS.	25	M	FARMER		GRZZZZNY
U	28	F	SHMK		GRAFWGNY	ESTELMANN, MARGA.	19	F	UNKNOWN		GRZZZZNY
AUGUSTE	.05	F	INFANT		GRAFWGNY	ERHARDT, LIZZI	19	F	UNKNOWN		GRZZZZNY
SCHNEIDER, PAUL	31	M	FARMER		GRAEWZNY	WITTMANN, ANDRAS	67	M	FARMER		GRAAGWNY
ZETTELMAIER, JOH.	32	M	UNKNOWN		GRAEWZNY	KIENZLER, MARIA	23	F	UNKNOWN		GRZZZZNY
DAISS, PAULINE	20	F	UNKNOWN		GRAFWGNY	KOLLERHOLZ, ELISAB.	22	F	UNKNOWN		GRZZZZNY
SCHULKOWSKI, JOSEPHINE	18	F	UNKNOWN		GRZZZZNY	FLICKINGER, JACOB	24	M	FARMER		GRZZZZNY

PASSENGER	AGE	SEX	OCCUPATION	PRV VL	DES
GRABINGER, JOSEF	26	M	CPR		GRZZZZNY
GLESZYUKA, MARIANNE	50	F	UNKNOWN		GRAEABNY
WEISNER, PAULINE	41	F	UNKNOWN		GRZZZZNY
AUGUSTE	17	F	UNKNOWN		GRZZZZNY
EMIL	11	M	UNKNOWN		GRZZZZNY
EMMA	6	F	CHILD		GRZZZZNY
RICHARD	4	M	CHILD		GRZZZZNY
IDA	.11	F	INFANT		GRZZZZNY
WOJTEYS, MARYJANNA	30	F	UNKNOWN		GRZZZZNY
AGNES	3	F	CHILD		GRZZZZNY
ANTONI	.11	F	INFANT		GRZZZZNY
PODANN, MARIANNE	19	F	UNKNOWN		GRZZZZNY
KOSIELMIKA, ANTONIA	20	F	UNKNOWN		GRAEABNY
SWOTTALA, ANTONIA	52	F	UNKNOWN		GRAEABNY
KRUEGER, GUST.	27	M	BKLYR		GRZZZZUNK
AUGUSTE	24	F	UNKNOWN		GRZZZZUNK
MARIE	3	F	CHILD		GRZZZZUNK
FEDOR	3	M	CHILD		GRZZZZUNK
KETZ, CAROLINE	62	F	UNKNOWN		GRZZZZUNK
ENGEL, JOH.	30	M	BKLYR		GRZZZZCLE
JULIANNE	22	F	UNKNOWN		GRZZZZCLE
JACOB	.03	M	INFANT		GRZZZZCLE
HINDERER, FRANZ	56	M	LABR		GRZZZZNY
MARIANNE	54	F	UNKNOWN		GRZZZZNY
MARTHE	14	F	UNKNOWN		GRZZZZNY
JOH.	10	M	CH		GRAIALNY
FRANCISKA	6	F	CHILD		GRAAXKNY
KOESTER, MORITZ	33	M	LABR		GRAAXKNY
PRZYBILSKI, MICHAEL	22	M	LABR		GRAARSNY
KUNDE, LOUIS	28	M	LABR		GRAEABNY
NOWIKA, APPOLONIE	30	F	UNKNOWN		GRAEABNY
STEMPINKA, MARIANNE	18	F	UNKNOWN		GRZZZZNY
CHIMEL, WICENTY	26	M	TLR		GRZZZZNY
NEKLEWSKI, JOHANN	24	M	TLR		GRZZZZNY
JOSEFA	24	F	UNKNOWN		GRZZZZNY
LEONA	.09	F	INFANT		GRADUXPA
KOWALSKI, ANTON	43	M	LABR		GRZZZZMN
ZWERZYCHA, LEONORE	22	F	UNKNOWN		GRZZZZIL
STAJKOWI, FRANZISKA	20	F	UNKNOWN		GRAAXHNY
WAGNER, PHILIPP	26	M	LABR		GRZZZZNY
FREISS, EDUARD	40	M	LABR		GRZZZZNY
PAKE, MICHAEL	25	M	PNTR		GRAEYGNY
--ENKE, U	40	M	JNR		GRAEYGNY
SUWATKA, FRANZ	27	M	LABR		GRACXVNY
PATZTAWA, FRANZ	23	M	LABR		GRAARRNY
MACORONSKI, ANTON	33	M	LABR		GRAABYNY
U	33	F	UNKNOWN		GRAABYNY
ROSALIE	6	F	CHILD		GRAABYNY
ANTON	.11	M	INFANT		GRAARRNY
BECK, GUST.	37	M	LABR		GRAARRNY
MARGARETHA	32	F	UNKNOWN		GRZZZZOH
BABETTA	2	F	CHILD		GRAARRNY
LORCHEN	.08	F	INFANT		GRAARRNY
STEENS, GOTTLIEB	56	M	LABR		GRAESBNY

SHIP: GELLERT

FROM: HAMBURG
TO: NEW YORK
ARRIVED: 25 JULY 1888

PASSENGER	AGE	SEX	OCCUPATION	PRV VL	DES
UNGER, ERNST	20	M	LABR		SYZZZZUSA
EHLIS, JOH.	19	F	SGL		HBZZZZUSA
WULF, HUGO	15	M	LABR		HBAADEUSA
KRETZER, GUSTAV	18	M	FARMER		HBZZZZUSA
KAYSER, ALBERT	17	M	LABR		HBZZZZUSA
BORDTHEISER, EMIL	25	M	CTW		HBZZZZUSA
WILKENS, JOH.	22	F	SGL		HBZZZZUSA
BEHRENDT, JOH.	44	M	SMH		HBZZZZUSA
JOSCHIN, CARL	25	M	SHMK		HBAAKHUSA

PASSENGER	AGE	SEX	OCCUPATION	PRV VL	DES
FEITSCHER, FRIEDRICH	23	M	UNKNOWN		HBAAKHUSA
KROH, HARRY	21	M	BKR		HBAAKHUSA
HINZ, WILH.	52	M	LABR		HBALPUUSA
WILH.	19	M	LABR		HBALPUUSA
MICHALEK, JOSEF	35	M	LABR		HBALPUUSA
GROSS, ALBERT	26	M	JNR		HBACGPUSA
PALMER, CATHA	21	F	UNKNOWN		WMZZZZUSA
BIERKAMP, AUGUSTE	46	F	WO		HBZZZZUSA
CARL	17	M	LABR		HBZZZZUSA
FAUL, JACOB	24	M	SHMK		BVZZZZUSA
BURGENS, WILH.	41	M	CGRMKR		BVAAKHUSA
ALLBERTINE	39		W		BVAAKHUSA
RAUSCH, LUISE	19	F	SGL		BVAEXWUSA
GOEZ, LUDW.	19	M	LABR		WMZZZZUSA
REISSER, ELISABETH	25	F	SGL		BVZZZZUSA
SCHWEITZER, ADAM	22	M	LABR		BVZZZZUSA
HUEGEL, JACOB	25	M	SHMK		BVZZZZUSA
RICHTER, MAX	17	M	LKSH		BVZZZZUSA
KLARY, HINRICH	45	M	LABR		HBZZZZUSA
GRISNAU, HANS	32	M	TCHR		PRZZZZUSA
BAUMANN, ANTON	25	M	FARMER		GRZZZZUSA
BRUECKMANN, DORIS	56	F	WO		MKZZZZUSA
AUGUSTE	20	F	D		MKZZZZUSA
BERG, CARL	49	M	SHMK		MKABWOUSA
AMALIA	52	F	W		MKABWOUSA
MARIE	21	F	W		MKABWOUSA
JOH.	16	F	W		MKABWOUSA
EMIL	9	M	CHILD		MKABWOUSA
ROSIE	8	F	CHILD		MKABWOUSA
HILLBURGER, ADAM	54	M	LABR		MKACWTUSA
MARGR.	48	F	W		MKACWTUSA
BOESCKE, THERESE	25	F	SGL		MKABPZUSA
HALL, CHRISTIAN	50	M	FARMER		PRZZZZUSA
CHRISTINE	50	F	W		PRZZZZUSA
JUERGEN	18	M	S		PRZZZZUSA
ANNA	14	F	D		PRZZZZUSA
ABRAHAM, JOSEF	55	M	LABR		PRZZZZUSA
JEANETTE	50	F	W		PRZZZZUSA
JULS	25	M	LABR		PRZZZZUSA
ROSALIE	16	F	D		PRZZZZUSA
SAMUEL	.11	M	INFANT		PRZZZZUSA
ATEINERT, AUGUST	16	M	FARMER		PRZZZZUSA
LIBISBAUSKI, MICHAEL	52	M	SHMK		PRZZZZUSA
HEDWIG	9	F	CHILD		PRZZZZUSA
FRIEDRICH, SUSANNE	38	F	SGL		PRZZZZUSA
PETERSEN, JOH.	25	M	CPR		PRZZZZUSA
POMMERENING, AUGUST	53	M	LABR		PRZZZZUSA
AMALIA	53	F	W		PRZZZZUSA
EMILIE	16	F	W		PRZZZZUSA
WILH.	15	M	CH		PRZZZZUSA
GUSTAV	9	M	CHILD		PRZZZZUSA
AUGUST	8	M	CHILD		PRZZZZUSA
GUERGENSEN, LUISE	18	F	SGL		PRACKYUSA
TEMPS, GUSTABV	17	M	FARMER		PRACKYUSA
BUCHHOLTZ, AUGUST	21	M	FARMER		PRACKYUSA
ROSE, FRIEDR.	42	M	JNR		PRACKYUSA
SOPHIE	36	F	W		PRACKYUSA
SOPHIE	5	F	CHILD		PRACKYUSA
HEINRICH	3	M	CHILD		PRACKYUSA
CHR.	.06	M	INFANT		PRACKYUSA
BEYER, RUDOLF	26	M	BKR		PRACBWUSA
ELISE	18	F	W		PRACBWUSA
ASMUSSEN, ANDR.	47	M	LABR		PRZZZZUSA
MARG.	43	F	W		PRZZZZUSA
JOHN	9	M	CHILD		PRZZZZUSA
MARIE	8	F	CHILD		PRZZZZUSA
MARIE	18	F	SGL		PRABNSUSA
MADAJEWSKA, MARIANNA	25	F	WO		PRAHWVUSA
EDWIG	.09	F	INFANT		PRAHWVUSA
RAUTENKRAUZ, EDUARD	19	M	MCHT		PRZZZZUSA
RATAJEWSKI, ADALBERT	24	M	UNKNOWN		PRZZZZUSA
SACH, GUSTAV	23	M	MCHT		PRZZZZUSA
RICHTER, PAUL	20	M	MCHT		PRADDQUSA
MASIEWSKI, ANDRAS	32	M	LABR		PRZZZZUSA
AGNES	30	F	W		PRZZZZUSA

PASSENGER	AGE	SEX	OCCUPATION	PRIVLS	DES
WOLSKA, MARIANNA	21	F	SGL	PRZZZZ	USA
BEDNARKIEWIEZ, AGNES	23	F	SGL	PRAGQX	USA
SEELAN, VICTOR	16	M	LABR	PRAAZQ	USA
GROSS, MARIE	32	F	SGL	PRAAZQ	USA
SCHMIDT, FRANCISKA	29	F	SGL	PRAAKH	USA
KUETTER, ELISABETH	38	F	WO	PRAAKH	USA
GEORG	7	M	CHILD	PRAAKH	USA
WOLFF, EMIL	36	M	JNR	PRAAKH	USA
MARIE	25	F	W	PRAAKH	USA
REINEKE, BERTHA	26	F	SGL	PRAAKH	USA
KIRCHNER, MINNA	54	F	WO	PRAAKH	USA
LOEBER, ELISABETH	21	F	SGL	PRAAKH	USA
ZENKEIT, CARL	25	M	LABR	PRZZZZ	USA
KRAUSE, JOHANN	30	M	LKSH	PRZZZZ	USA
CATH.	26	F	W	PRZZZZ	USA
MAX	3	M	CHILD	PRZZZZ	USA
RICHARD	.06	M	INFANT	PRZZZZ	USA
PAULINA	34	F	WO	PRACUA	USA
THERESE	9	F	CHILD	PRACUA	USA
BERNHARD	7	M	CHILD	PRACUA	USA
ANTON	4	M	CHILD	PRACUA	USA
HEDWIG	.09	F	INFANT	PRACUA	USA
ZACHER, FRIEDRICH	24	M	BKR	SYZZZZ	USA
HOPE, GEORG	23	M	BKR	SYZZZZ	USA
DORRNAN, FRANZ	26	M	GZR	SYADQZ	USA
NIKOLEIT, LOUISE	30	F	SGL	SYAAKH	USA
BADING, CARL	25	M	PRNTR	PRZZZZ	USA
TRONICKE, JULS	23	M	TNM	PRAAKH	USA
HEIDINGER, AGNES	24	F	SGL	PRADNY	USA
REINSCH, HUGO	26	M	BCHR	PRADNY	USA
ZIMMERMANN, JOSEFA	21	F	SGL	PRZZZZ	USA
CARL	27	M	WHR	PRZZZZ	USA
MARGR.	22	F	W	PRZZZZ	USA
RICHTER, PAUL	15	M	LABR	PRZZZZ	USA
BOLLHAMMMER, MARIE	23	F	SGL	BVZZZZ	USA
ACHRMANN, MAX	28	M	SMH	BVAAXK	USA
MUELLER, JOH.	58	M	PRNTR	BVACXV	USA
MEYER, HANS	20	M	LKSH	BVACAW	USA
ZWANGER, JULS.	16	M	GDNR	WMZZZZ	USA
HIRSCH, ABRAM	29	M	LABR	PRZZZZ	USA
ROSALIE	33	F	W	PRZZZZ	USA
DEMINSKA, MICHALINA	21	F	SGL	PRZZZZ	USA
MIERS, CARL	29	M	LABR	PRAFQO	USA
STRELITZ, MAX	34	M	MCHT	PRAAKH	USA
STAGEN, KARL	33	M	FARMER	PRAAKH	USA

SHIP: NEVADA

FROM: LIVERPOOL AND QUEENSTOWN
TO: NEW YORK
ARRIVED: 25 JULY 1888

PASSENGER	AGE	SEX	OCCUPATION	PRIVLS	DES
NATELSON, SCHIMEN	27	M	LKSH	GRZZZZ	USA
WACHTEL, LEON	18	M	LABR	GRZZZZ	USA
WEINSTEIN, ELEAZER	29	M	LABR	GRACBF	USA
SCHKLAR, ABRAM	27	M	LABR	GRACBF	USA
RISNER, ZEISSEN	17	M	LABR	GRACBF	USA
KLOTT, MINDEL	16	M	LABR	GRACBF	USA
WAIDER, CARL	14	M	LABR	GRACBF	USA
KNUR, HAFER	23	M	LABR	GRACBF	USA
DRIESSON, VICTOR	41	M	FARMER	GRACBF	USA
SOMMERER, WOLF	28	M	FARMER	GRACBF	USA
CHAIM	24	M	FARMER	GRACBF	USA
ROSENBLATT, CHAIM	34	M	LABR	GRACBF	USA
HOLLANDER, SALOMON	30	M	LABR	GRACBF	USA
HAUTER, JACOB	19	M	LABR	GRACBF	USA
KRAWZ, IGNAZ	65	M	FARMER	GRACBF	USA
HERMAN, MARTIN	28	M	FARMER	GRACBF	USA
GAUZEWISLER, HERM.	20	M	FARMER	GRACBF	USA
KLEINHAUER, P.	30	M	ENGR	GRACBF	USA

PASSENGER	AGE	SEX	OCCUPATION	PRIVLS	DES
TUER, LEOPOLD	23	M	LKSH	GRACBF	USA
FRANK, HENRY	25	M	LKSH	GRACBF	USA
PERKES, JUDEL	24	M	LKSH	GRACBF	USA
REITER, IGNATZ	7	M	CHILD	GRACBF	USA
FINKREISSER, Y.	22	M	LABR	GRACBF	USA
LUNA, MOTEL	19	M	LABR	GRACBF	USA
MULLER, HIRSCH	30	M	LABR	GRACBF	USA
FINKELSTEIN, RIFKY	19	F	SP	GRACBF	USA
WAGNER, REGINA	23	F	SP	GRACBF	USA
SEGLIN, HELKE	20	F	SP	GRACBF	USA
SPINGER, ROSA	23	F	W	GRACBF	USA
SAMUEL	.06	M	INFANT	GRACBF	USA
MELTZER, SCHIE	40	F	W	GRACBF	USA
GUDREICH, CHANNIE	24	F	SP	GRACBF	USA
CHERT, PHILIPPI	22	F	SP	GRACBF	USA
RIESER, MARTHA	31	F	W	GRACBF	USA
ANNA	7	F	CHILD	GRACBF	USA
RIBACK, LINKEL	33	F	W	GRACBF	USA
NANE	7	F	CHILD	GRACBF	USA
GITTEL	6	F	CHILD	GRACBF	USA
HERSCH	5	M	CHILD	GRACBF	USA
GODEL, CHANNE	30	F	SP	GRACBF	USA
SCHUMANN, MAGDALENA	24	F	SP	GRACBF	USA
SALTMANN, ABRAHAM	36	M	FARMER	GRACBF	USA
RALIEL	30	F	W	GRACBF	USA
BEILE	7	F	CHILD	GRACBF	USA
HELSCHE	6	M	CHILD	GRACBF	USA
EDELMANN, WOLF	48	M	FARMER	GRACBF	USA
DEBORA	30	F	W	GRACBF	USA
JOEL	6	M	CHILD	GRACBF	USA
SALOMON	3	M	CHILD	GRACBF	USA
SPOHRE, H.	28	M	LABR	GRACBF	USA
STEINHAUER, EM.	29	F	SP	GRACBF	USA
BROCKMANN, MARCUS	27	M	LABR	GRACBF	USA
JABELLA	24	F	W	GRACBF	USA
GALOMBEK, HIRSCH	21	M	LABR	GRACBF	USA
LENA	23	F	W	GRACBF	USA

SHIP: RHYNLAND

FROM: ANTWERP
TO: NEW YORK
ARRIVED: 26 JULY 1888

PASSENGER	AGE	SEX	OCCUPATION	PRIVLS	DES
WAGNER, PH.	78	M	PVTR	GRZZZZ	NY
SCHILD, CARL	49	M	PSTR	GRZZZZ	BUF
SCHULEMANN, F.	41	M	MCHT	GRZZZZ	NY
NEUBAUER, G.W.	39	M	SCP	GRZZZZ	UNK
U-MRS	34	F	UNKNOWN	GRZZZZ	UNK
MASTER-WILLIE	11	M	CH	GRZZZZ	UNK
ERKELING, JULIE-MISS	31	F	LDY	GRZZZZ	NY
ROSENBERG, GUSTAV-MR	19	M	CGR	GRZZZZ	NY
PERRI, FR.LEO	26	M	PREST	SRZZZZ	BUF
MULLER, OSWALD	26	M	PREST	SRZZZZ	BUF
SCHMAHL, J.G.MR	22	M	GCR	GRZZZZ	NY
DIRLAM, HUGO	15	M	GCR	GRZZZZ	NY
JONAS, JANNY-MISS	26	F	LDY	GRZZZZ	NY
SCHMELING, W.MRS	57	F	LDY	GRZZZZ	MIL
AUG.	26	M	LABR	GRZZZZ	MIL
LOEB, MOSES	17	M	BCHR	GRZZZZ	MIL
MULLER, FRED.	18	M	CGR	GRZZZZ	NY
SCHOETTLAENDER, H.	50	M	CGR	GRZZZZ	CH
RECKUM, F.	40	M	CGR	GRZZZZ	CH
MELCHIOR, W.	24	M	MCHT	SRZZZZ	UNK
HEES, H.	21	M	UPHST	GRZZZZ	PIT
GOLLER, HERM.	20	M	PREST	SRZZZZ	BUF
GARTNER, JULIUS	24	M	GCR	SRZZZZ	NY
SCHUSTER, ISAAC	24	M	SHMK	GRZZZZ	NY
HAEMFER, JOH.	23	M	SHMK	GRZZZZ	NY
ULLERICH, AUG.	48	M	MACH	GRZZZZ	NY

PASSENGER	AGE	SEX	OCCUPATION	PRVVLDES
AUG.	24	M	MACH	GRZZZZNY
TAUSCHER, JOHAN	18	M	MCHT	GRZZZZNY
PETER, KNAUS	26	M	CL	GRZZZZCH
SCHOO, ANNA	23	F	SVNT	GRZZZZNY
OHRABKA, FERENER	38	M	BCHR	GRZZZZNY
LICHTENFELD, IVAN	18	M	BCHR	GRZZZZNY
ESSER, EMILIE	33	F	UNKNOWN	GRZZZZNY
EMMA	32	F	W	GRZZZZNY
ANNA	8	F	CHILD	GRZZZZNY
CARL	6	M	CHILD	GRZZZZNY
ZIPPERMAAS, ALEX	30	M	MCHT	GRZZZZNY
STEIN, JOHANN	14	M	CH	GRZZZZNY
KRAUS, ANTON	50	M	FARMER	GRZZZZNY
CRESZENZ	48	F	W	GRZZZZNY
ANTON	22	M	CH	GRZZZZNY
BALTAZAR	17	M	CH	GRZZZZNY
CRESZENZ	8	F	CHILD	GRZZZZNY
BENEF	5	M	CHILD	GRZZZZNY
GOTTLIEB, HAAS	23	M	MLR	GRZZZZOH
URGEMACH, PAUL	24	M	DIACTR	GRZZZZPHI
THEIS, FERDINAND	36	M	NN	GRZZZZPHI
SCHROTH, ROSINE	15	F	SVNT	GRZZZZNY
BUCK, MARIE	24	F	SVNT	GRZZZZCH
GLUCK, FRIED.	3	M	CHILD	GRZZZZCH
GEORGE	4	M	CHILD	GRZZZZCH
MUELLER, PAULINE	19	F	CH	GRZZZZPHI
BARTHOLOME, WILLI	50	M	FARMER	GRZZZBUF
BEMSEL, AGNES	40	F	SVNT	GRZZZBUF
ZIMMERMANN, JOH.	40	M	LABR	GRZZZZNY
ENGELE, MARIE	16	F	SVNT	GRZZZZNY
BENZ, FRIEDR.	29	M	MLR	GRZZZZNY
RICK, GOTTLOB	25	M	LABR	GRZZZZNY
GLASSING, CHRISTINE	45	F	W	GRZZZZNY
FUCHS, CAROLINE	19	F	SVNT	GRZZZZNY
SCHWAIZER, PAULINA	14	F	SVNT	GRZZZZNY
RUHER, MARTIN	46	M	SMH	GRZZZZNY
ALBERT, LINA	18	F	SVNT	GRZZZZNY
HOLTSTEIM, SAMUEL	48	M	LABR	GRZZZZNY
ANNA	17	F	SVNT	GRZZZZNY
FRANK, EMIL	23	M	TU	GRZZZZNY
HEIPER, WM.	32	M	PNTR	GRZZZZNY
SCHNEIDER, JOSEF	21	M	NN	GRZZZZUNK
SASCHNER, EVA	28	F	SVNT	GRZZZZNY
BROM, PAULINE	20	F	SVNT	GRZZZZNY
DONERBERGER, MICH.	30	M	FARMER	GRZZZZNY
WEISS, M.JOH.	25	M	CPRSMH	GRZZZZNY
FLISSA, HCH.	44	M	SHMK	GRZZZZNY
BRENNER, EMILIE	22	F	SVNT	GRZZZZNY
DRASCH, JOH-B.	26	M	LABR	GRZZZZNY
ALBERT, JOH.	29	M	SHMK	GRZZZZNY
STEIN, PETER	72	M	UNKNOWN	GRZZZZNY
NANNENHORN, HCH.	22	M	BCHR	GRZZZZCH
WERKLE, WME.	26	F	W	GRZZZZNY
ARTHUR	5	M	CHILD	GRZZZZNY
OTTO	3	M	CHILD	GRZZZZNY
RUPPENSTEIN, CARL	27	M	CBTMKR	GRZZZZNY
SCHWEIZER, MATH.	36	M	BRR	GRZZZZNY
ZENDER, NICL.	25	M	FARMER	GRZZZZNY
BERG, HCH.	20	M	CL	GRZZZZNY
HIEMICKEL, GEO	23	M	CPRSMH	GRZZZZNY
SAMSTAG, FRIEDR.	35	M	SWMKR	GRZZZZNY
MARG.	32	F	W	GRZZZZNY
MAGD.	11	F	CH	GRZZZZNY
BARBARA	8	F	CHILD	GRZZZZNY
JACOB	1	M	CHILD	GRZZZZNY
RICKA, BEER	26	F	BCHR	GRZZZZNY
EMMA	3	F	CHILD	GRZZZZNY
HACKGEGEI, AUGUST	22	M	LABR	GRZZZZNY
GERBERICH, HEINR.	32	M	LABR	GRZZZZNY
LIWENSTEIN, RICH.	18	M	MCHT	GRZZZZNY
MAES, JEAN	40	M	LABR	FRZZZZUNK
JEAN	9	F	CHILD	FRZZZZUNK
KONIZERKA, ANDR.	22	M	LABR	GRZZZZCH
BUSCH, JOHANN	21	M	SHMK	GRZZZZUNK
BURKHARDT, JACOB	20	M	SHMK	GRZZZZUNK
FONTAINE, PH.	41	M	MNR	FRZZZZCLF
RAAS, JOH.CH.	00	M	LABR	SRZZZZNY
DEISENHOFER, JOH.	21	M	WCHMKR	SRZZZZNY
KUERZI, ALOIS	17	M	FARMER	SRZZZZNY
KARREN, MARTIN	25	M	FARMER	SRZZZZNY
HILGER, ROSALINDE	18	F	SVNT	GRZZZZNY
FRITZ, RIED	26	M	SHPWRT	GRZZZZNY
ZIERL, MAX	26	M	FARMER	GRZZZZNY
SCHWARZ, AUGUST	26	M	BCHR	GRZZZZMIL
MAIER, AGATHE	19	F	SVNT	GRZZZZNY
BACHMANN, ELIZA	24	F	SVNT	GRZZZZNY
SCHMITZ, ANNA	19	F	SVNT	GRZZZZNY
TONNAI, JEAN	38	M	MACH	GRZZZZNY
PASKATY, ANNA	22	F	SVNT	GRZZZZNY
SCHNEIDER, GEO	25	M	FARMER	GRZZZZNY
BILL, HCH.	23	M	FARMER	GRZZZZNY
SCHAEFER, JOH.	24	M	FARMER	GRZZZZNY
DAILLY, ED.	48	M	LABR	FRZZZZNY
LEONTINA	16	F	CH	FRZZZZNY
FELIOS	11	F	CH	FRZZZZNY
IRMA	18	F	CH	FRZZZZNY
DORG, ADOLF	35	M	LABR	FRZZZZNY
LANGE, WM.	39	M	LABR	GRZZZZNY
HELLBERG, DORA	40	F	W	GRZZZZNY
MARIA	10	F	CH	GRZZZZNY
ELISA	4	F	CHILD	GRZZZZNY
STOCKER, JOSEFA	22	F	W	GRZZZZCT
HEDWIG	3	M	CHILD	GRZZZZCT
ORTH, JOHANN	25	M	LABR	GRZZZZNY
ANNA	9	F	CHILD	GRZZZZNY
THEODOR, OLK	18	M	LABR	GRZZZZUNK
KETTENHOFEN, PETER	20	M	TLR	GRZZZZUNK
SCHWITTER, FRIDOLIN	00	M	FARMER	SRZZZZNY
SCHOENHALS, ELIZAB.	30	F	SVNT	GRZZZZNY
MARIA	9	F	CHILD	GRZZZZNY
LUKEY, JOHANN	19	M	UNKNOWN	GRZZZZNY
HENNWART, STEFANI	24	F	SVNT	GRZZZZNY
AMALIA	29	F	SVNT	GRZZZZNY
NOTHSTEIN, MARIA	18	F	SVNT	GRZZZZNY
SCHRAMM, JOH.	14	M	LABR	GRZZZZCH
GLUECK, OTTO	16	M	LABR	GRZZZZCH
CONCHY, ELEONORE	26	F	UNKNOWN	FRZZZZUNK
RIES, ELIZABETH	17	F	UNKNOWN	FRZZZZUNK
BURGER, JOH.	20	M	LABR	GRZZZZNY
SHIPPER, HCH.	20	M	TNSTH	GRZZZZNY
SCHWENK, CONRAD	23	M	FARMER	GRZZZZPA
KLIPPEL, HEDWIG	16	M	FARMER	GRZZZZNY
ELMI, JOH.W.	23	M	LABR	GRZZZZNY
JOLY, HENRY	32	M	MNR	FRZZZZCLF
HENRY	30	F	W	FRZZZZCLF
HENRY	9	M	CHILD	FRZZZZCLF
MARIE	7	F	CHILD	FRZZZZCLF
MATHILDE	6	F	CHILD	FRZZZZCLF
EMMANUEL	2	M	CHILD	FRZZZZCLF
JOSEF	00	M	INF	FRZZZZCLF
VISEUX, BENOIT	31	M	MNR	FRZZZZCLF
CELINE	25	F	W	FRZZZZCLF
DRIESEN, JOH.	33	M	SHMK	GRZZZZNY
POLASIK, ANNA	45	F	SVNT	GRZZZZUNK
STANISLAUS	10	M	CH	GRZZZZUNK
SCHMIDT, AUGUST	37	M	LABR	GRZZZZNY
HERRMANN, WILH.	47	M	WCHMKR	GRZZZZNY
ZAK, JOSEF	24	M	MCHT	GRZZZZNY
LUKAS	24	M	CL	GRZZZZNY
SCHUSTER, FILIP	24	M	SMH	GRZZZZNY
FAEBER, MARIA	26	F	SVNT	GRZZZZNY
RABAS, JOSEF	24	M	CBTMKR	GRZZZZNY
HUSSA, JOSEF	16	M	CL	GRZZZZNY
KRAL, CHRISTINE	40	F	W	GRZZZZNY
STANISLAUS	15	M	CH	GRZZZZNY
ANNA	11	F	CH	GRZZZZNY
OTAKAR	14	M	CH	GRZZZZNY
JANKE, ANTON	23	M	FARMER	GRZZZZCH
BUMICKI, VAL.	15	M	CH	GRZZZZUNK
FRIEDL, ADALB.	18	M	MCHT	GRZZZZCLE

PASSENGER	AGE	SEX	OCCUPATION	PRVL	DES
ANNA	15	F	SVNT	GRZZZZCLE
PIONTEK, WM.	26	M	LABR	GRZZZZBUF
SOBBE, ANTON	56	M	FARMER	GRZZZZCH
JEROME, ODILLE	27	F	W	FRZZZZUNK
ALBINE	8	F	CHILD	FRZZZZUNK
LOUIS	6	M	CHILD	FRZZZZUNK
ALPHONSE	4	M	CHILD	FRZZZZUNK
JULES	00	M	INF	FRZZZZUNK
HECHANEL, CATHE.	25	F	W	FRZZZZUNK
AUGUSTE	6	F	CHILD	FRZZZZUNK
MARIE	4	F	CHILD	FRZZZZUNK
HENRI	2	M	CHILD	FRZZZZUNK
EMMA	00	F	INF	FRZZZZUNK
DELABIES, MARIA	21	F	W	FRZZZZUNK
MARIA	7	F	CHILD	FRZZZZUNK
LEONIE	4	F	CHILD	FRZZZZUNK
HENRI	3	M	CHILD	FRZZZZUNK
MARIE	00	F	INF	FRZZZZUNK
HANDEGOND, DESSY	19	F	W	FRZZZZUNK
FRANCOIS	2	M	CHILD	FRZZZZUNK
FRANCOIS	00	M	INF	FRZZZZUNK
ZENE, CAMELLE	28	M	TRVLR	FRZZZZNY
CHONARAKI, NIC.	24	M	LABR	FRZZZZNY
MOUSSA, GAUTUS	28	M	TCHR	FRZZZZNY
HACHIM, NACHIL	22	M	CPTR	FRZZZZUNK
ZAMAR	20	M	CPTR	FRZZZZUNK
ZIRKEL, GERTRUD	25	F	SVNT	GRZZZZNY
HAHN, HUBERT	40	M	LABR	GRZZZZNY
FELINGMEIER, CASPAR	46	M	LABR	GRZZZZNY
ZIMMERMANN, E.	18	M	LABR	GRZZZZPTL

SHIP: ROMAN

FROM: LIVERPOOL
TO: BOSTON
ARRIVED: 26 JULY 1888

PASSENGER	AGE	SEX	OCCUPATION	PRVL	DES
BITTENBERG, ABRAM	19	M	LABR	GRZZZZNY
KIELMAN, FRANZ	17	M	LABR	GRZZZZBO
CHELMS, LOUIS	34	M	LABR	GRZZZZBO

SHIP: STATE OF INDIANA

FROM: GLASGOW AND LARNE
TO: NEW YORK
ARRIVED: 26 JULY 1888

PASSENGER	AGE	SEX	OCCUPATION	PRVL	DES
HITHEN, SIMON	22	M	LABR	GRZZZZUSA
SYRSUAKALO, PETER	18	M	LABR	GRZZZZUSA
TAUB, MOSES	42	M	LABR	GRZZZZUSA
LICHERT, THEODOR-A.	23	M	LABR	GRZZZZUSA
HASSER, ALBERT	38	M	PDLR	GRZZZZUSA
KIBESIN, RUEN	18	M	LABR	GRZZZZUSA
SHONGIN, SARA	33	F	W	GRZZZZUSA
RIWKE	2	F	CHILD	GRZZZZUSA
SAMUEL	1	M	CHILD	GRZZZZUSA
CAPLAN, HIRSCH	11	M	CH	GRZZZZUSA
FISCHMANN, LEAH	27	F	W	GRZZZZUSA
CHAISE	7	F	CHILD	GRZZZZUSA
ROSA	5	F	CHILD	GRZZZZUSA
MOSES	1	M	CHILD	GRZZZZUSA
GOLD, SARAH	46	F	W	GRZZZZUSA
ROCHE	10	M	CH	GRZZZZUSA
CHASSE	1	F	CHILD	GRZZZZUSA
ROSENBERG, FREIDE	27	F	W	GRZZZZUSA

PASSENGER	AGE	SEX	OCCUPATION	PRVL	DES
SAMUEL	11	M	CH	GRZZZZUSA
ABRAHAM	2	M	CHILD	GRZZZZUSA
ACKERMANN, LOUISE	36	F	W	GRZZZZUSA
FRANKE	8	M	CHILD	GRZZZZUSA
ABRAHAM	7	M	CHILD	GRZZZZUSA
BURCOH	1	M	CHILD	GRZZZZUSA
SHONZIN, FREIDE	18	F	DMS	GRZZZZUSA
GOLD, ZIWE	22	F	DMS	GRZZZZUSA
WELZER, SANE	17	F	DMS	GRZZZZUSA
BLUMBERG, BERTA	28	F	DMS	GRZZZZUSA
COHN, ROSE	24	F	DMS	GRZZZZUSA
MARIA	50	F	DMS	GRZZZZUSA

SHIP: GALLIA

FROM: LIVERPOOL AND QUEENSTOWN
TO: NEW YORK
ARRIVED: 27 JULY 1888

PASSENGER	AGE	SEX	OCCUPATION	PRVL	DES
KEMPNICK, JEAN	36	M	MLR	GRADXWUSA
TH.	32	M	MLR	GRADXWUSA
THOMA, PAUL	32	M	GCR	GRACBFUSA
RADY, H.	23	M	UNKNOWN	GRACBFUSA
BURKE, ED.	32	M	UNKNOWN	GRACBFUSA
RONTICH, CHRIST	37	M	UNKNOWN	GRACBFUSA
BENOCH, FRED.	34	M	UNKNOWN	GRACBFUSA
PAZKUEWITZ, WINCAS	27	M	PDLR	GRACBFUSA
PAZKNIVITZ, KASTA	25	F	W	GRACBFUSA

SHIP: BRITANNIC

FROM: LIVERPOOL AND QUEENSTOWN
TO: NEW YORK
ARRIVED: 28 JULY 1888

PASSENGER	AGE	SEX	OCCUPATION	PRVL	DES
SOFER, CHA--	25	F	W	GRADAXUSA
ELIE	7	M	CHILD	GRADAXUSA
SIMCHE	5	F	CHILD	GRADAXUSA
NICHOME	3	F	CHILD	GRADAXUSA
HERSCH	.09	M	INFANT	GRADAXUSA
MARKOWITZ, JOSEF	23	M	LABR	GRADAXUSA
JACOB, ISRAEL	24	M	LABR	GRADAXUSA
SITPESKI, SIMON	20	M	LABR	GRADAXUSA
GUINBURG, MOSES	34	M	LABR	GRADAXUSA
EFFENBACH, SAMUEL	36	M	LABR	GRADAXUSA
AFF-SIN, SCHULIN	24	M	LABR	GRADAXUSA
KOHN, SCHFIE	17	F	SP	GRADAXUSA
SE-RSINKY, DAVID	23	M	LABR	GRADAXUSA
DINN-ITZ, MEYER	23	M	LABR	GRADAXUSA
KRACKOW, --ATE	20	M	LABR	GRADAXUSA
HUT, HERMAN	36	M	LABR	GRADAXUSA
CLARA	25	F	W	GRADAXUSA
PURRA-UCK, INDEL	38	M	LABR	GRADAXUSA
KLIM, JOEL	21	M	LABR	GRADAXUSA
KROY, ONI--	45	M	LABR	GRADAXUSA
DEBRECINI, IST-A-	16	F	SP	GRADAXUSA
ROTTENBERG, BARRIE	35	F	W	GRADAXUSA
SCHAJE	6	F	CHILD	GRADAXUSA
ABRAHAM	1	M	CHILD	GRADAXUSA
SCHWARTZ, IDA	17	F	SP	GRADAXUSA
ZUCKER, FANNI	16	F	SP	GRADAXUSA
GOTTSGEN, MATI	35	F	W	GRADAXUSA
DEMANT, BENJM	35	M	LABR	GRADAXUSA
KLIM, PEPPI	29	F	SP	GRADAXUSA
GOTTSGEN, LEOPOLD	11	M	CH	GRADAXUSA

PASSENGER	AGE	SEX	OCCUPATION	PVRIVL	DES
LENI	9	F	CHILD		GRADAXUSA
THERESA	8	F	CHILD		GRADAXUSA
LIDI	7	F	CHILD		GRADAXUSA
CYLLI	4	F	CHILD		GRADAXUSA
D	3	M	CHILD		GRADAXUSA
NATIE	.09	M	INFANT		GRADAXUSA
KRAUSS, SALI	53	F	HSKPR		GRADAXUSA
KATZ, SIMON	39	M	LABR		GRADAXUSA
LASKI, DAVID	1	M	CHILD		GRADAXUSA
ME-ZER, CHI-N--E	17	F	SP		GRADAXUSA
KIRSCH	11	M	CH		GRADAXUSA
STRICK, FREDK	26	M	LABR		GRADAXUSA
WALL, G-NARDA	21	F	SVNT		GRADAXUSA
HABEL, -ISIM	23	M	LABR		GRADAXUSA
SCHLISSINGER, JACOB	48	M	LABR		GRADAXUSA
REISS, JACOB	47	M	LABR		GRADAXUSA
GLUCK, JACOB	37	M	LABR		GRADAXUSA
ATLAS, MA---NE	21	F	SVNT		GRADAXUSA
WENZEL, AUGUST	21	M	LABR		GRADAXUSA
SCHULTZ, CARL	27	M	LABR		GRADAXUSA
-CHALE, KERM	17	M	LABR		GRADAXUSA
CYRULI-, LOUIS	32	M	LABR		GRADAXUSA
BADERAM, INDEL	24	F	SVNT		GRADAXUSA
ASTRACHAN, MICHLE	23	M	LABR		GRADAXUSA
TELCHMANN, SCHERRI	16	F	SP		GRADAXUSA
ISAK	11	M	CH		GRADAXUSA
ABRAHAM	1	M	CHILD		GRADAXUSA
ELK, ABRAHAM	52	M	LABR		GRADAXUSA
SARAH	53	F	W		GRADAXUSA
BUCHMANN, SEN	25	M	LABR		GRADAXUSA
MACHTKE, BOUCHE	26	M	LABR		GRADAXUSA
PORZTEN, MOSES	20	M	LABR		GRADAXUSA
KRESCHIN, SELMA	20	M	LABR		GRADAXUSA
GROSS, AD-E	20	F	SP		GRADAXUSA
LANDAU, GERTIE	16	F	SP		GRADAXUSA
SOLOWEZIK, ABRAHAM	35	M	LABR		GRADAXUSA
BARON, CHAJE	24	F	W		GRADAXUSA
DAVID	18	M	LABR		GRADAXUSA
SINCHE	10	M	CH		GRADAXUSA
MAN--	9	F	CHILD		GRADAXUSA
CHAM	15	F	SP		GRADAXUSA
SCHUL	16	F	SP		GRADAXUSA
BER-I	.09	F	INFANT		GRADAXUSA
SZABO, EVZA	17	F	SP		GRADAXUSA
JAFFE, ANNE	18	F	SP		GRADAXUSA
RACHEL	11	F	CH		GRADAXUSA
LICHTMANN, JOSEF	18	M	LABR		GRADAXUSA
MARGOLIS, FANNY	22	F	SVNT		GRADAXUSA
MONS	18	M	LABR		GRADAXUSA
ISRALOWITZ, JIPE	16	F	SP		GRADAXUSA
RABINOWITZ, BENJ	31	M	LABR		GRADAXUSA
MASUR, PHILIP	32	M	LABR		GRADAXUSA
BLIEDIN, SARAH	35	F	W		GRADAXUSA
MARIE	12	F	CH		GRADAXUSA
EVIN	11	M	CH		GRADAXUSA
LINI	10	F	CH		GRADAXUSA
BERTHA	8	F	CHILD		GRADAXUSA
RA-E	6	M	CHILD		GRADAXUSA
MOSES	3	M	CHILD		GRADAXUSA
PLOTKIN, CHASE	22	F	SVNT		GRADAXUSA
JAFFE, AMALIS	20	F	SVNT		GRADAXUSA
STOCKECKER, INDEL	24	F	SVNT		GRADAXUSA
SCHLESINGER, LUKE	24	F	W		GRADAXUSA
BERNHARDT	.09	M	INFANT		GRADAXUSA
SVENSON, ES-JON	34	M	FARMER		GRADAXUSA
SJIESSON, PHER	34	M	FARMER		GRADAXUSA
GUNHILD	28	F	W		GRADAXUSA
MARTHA	.09	F	INFANT		GRADAXUSA
JACOBSON, ADOLF	33	M	LABR		GRADAXUSA
SCHROIN, EDWARD	21	M	LABR		GRADAXUSA
SLIP-ANSKY, JUDAH	1	F	CHILD		GRADAXUSA
ABRAH	1	M	CHILD		GRADAXUSA
GVIESE, CARL	26	M	LABR		GRADAXUSA
VERDIER, EMILIE	26	M	NN		GRADAXUSA

SHIP: CITY OF CHICAGO

FROM: LIVERPOOL AND QUEENSTOWN
TO: NEW YORK
ARRIVED: 28 JULY 1888

PASSENGER	AGE	SEX	OCCUPATION	PVRIVL	DES
JUDD, ARON	16	M	JWLR		GRACBFNY
KASEL, RISCHKE	19	M	LABR		GRACBFNY
KERPER, LEEF	30	M	LABR		GRACBFNY
BUPUSKY, MARCUS	28	M	TLR		GRACBFBUF
STOGGEN, ANOEN	20	M	LABR		GRACBFNY
GROLMAN, JOSEL	45	M	LABR		GRACBFPA
SORE	35	F	W		GRACBFPA
ESTHER	11	F	CH		GRACBFPA
ALGE	10	M	CH		GRACBFPA
GERSCHEN	5	M	CHILD		GRACBFPA
GROHMAN, IREINE	4	F	CHILD		GRACBFPA
BOSCHE	.07	M	INFANT		GRACBFPA
LEISEWITZ, RAPHAEL	19	M	LABR		GRACBFPA
ABRAMOWITZ, LEIB	30	M	LABR		GRACBFNY
FRIEDMANN, FERANZ	32	M	TLR		GRACBFNY
HAGENSEN, JOHANNA	24	M	SMH		GRACBFNY
SHHUELDON, ANTON	27	M	LABR		GRACBFNY
SCHUECHR, RICHA	28	M	LABR		GRACBFNY
WARNER, HENRI	21	M	SHMK		GRACBFNY
JUTTING, TH.	43	M	SEMN		GRZZZZNY
BERYLE, JULIUS	40	M	DSTLR		GRAGLENY
DE, AM.	24	M	GENT		GRADXWNY

SHIP: TRAVE

FROM: BREMEN AND SOUTHAMPTON
TO: NEW YORK
ARRIVED: 28 JULY 1888

PASSENGER	AGE	SEX	OCCUPATION	PVRIVL	DES
SCHWAB, N.	25	M	TT		GRAARRUSA
SURA	24	F	UNKNOWN		GRAARRUSA
BELLA	3	F	CHILD		GRAARRUSA
CARRY	2	F	CHILD		GRAARRUSA
ALFRED	.09	M	INFANT		GRAARRUSA
LEVI, PAULINE	22	F	UNKNOWN		GRAARRUSA
MATHEI, AUGUSTE	25	F	UNKNOWN		GRAARRUSA
BREITENBACH, ROSA	19	F	UNKNOWN		GRAARRUSA
LUCAS, HATTI	17	F	UNKNOWN		GRAFJDUSA
LANDGRAF, ALFRED	22	M	MCHT		GRAAXKUSA
GRAETZER, MARTHA	26	F	UNKNOWN		GRACBFUSA
ARTHUR	4	M	CHILD		GRACBFUSA
SCHUETTE, HERM.	17	M	CL		GRADQZUSA
FROEHLICH, HAENLEIN	15	M	UNKNOWN		GRAAIEUSA
LEHMANN, LOUIS	15	M	UNKNOWN		GRZZZZUSA
WIENECKE, CHRISTOF	57	M	MCHT		GRABAPUSA
GRUND, HELENE	33	F	UNKNOWN		GRAJXUSA
MARIA	7	F	CHILD		GRAJXUSA
ELISABETH	6	F	CHILD		GRAJXUSA
FRITZ	1	M	CHILD		GRAJXUSA
APPELIUS, EMMI	19	F	UNKNOWN		GRABHHUSA
FREUDENBERG, JACOB	42	M	MCHT		GRAEIHUSA
SPECHT, MAX	25	M	MCHT		GRAEIHUSA
SOERENSEN, NICOLAI	42	M	MCHT		GRZZZZUSA
RASMINE	28	F	W		GRZZZZUSA
META	14	F	UNKNOWN		GRZZZZUSA
JESS.	5	F	CHILD		GRZZZZUSA
ANNA	4	F	CHILD		GRZZZZUSA
MARIE	3	F	CHILD		GRZZZZUSA
JEF.	2	M	CHILD		GRZZZZUSA
KUENNE, WILHELMINE	47	F	UNKNOWN		GRZZZZUSA
SCHNEIDER, OSWALD	36	M	MCHT		GRABVWUSA
HEMMERDINGER, MAX	22	M	MCHT		GRADEIUSA
BAUR, CHAS.	34	M	TT		GRABPCUSA

PASSENGER	AGE	SEX	OCCUPATION	PRVVL	DES
HOCHFELDER, DAVID	32	M	MCHT	GRABPC	USA
ROTH, CARL	50	M	MCHT	GRACPE	USA
LAUTERJUNG, JOH.	50	F	UNKNOWN	GRAAKH	USA
ALMA	15	F	UNKNOWN	GRAAKH	USA
POLPER, IDA	28	F	UNKNOWN	GRAAKH	USA
WEILER, MATHILDE	16	F	UNKNOWN	GRAAKH	USA
SIMON, LAZARUS	57	M	MCHT	GRZZZZ	USA
REBECCA	58	F	W	GRZZZZ	USA
LINA	29	F	UNKNOWN	GRZZZZ	USA
MOLITOR, JULIA	20	F	UNKNOWN	GRACSY	USA
CARLICZEK, OTTOMAR	23	M	MCHT	GRAARZ	USA
FRIEDENSBURG, FRANZ	23	M	MCHT	GRAARZ	USA
STORZ, BERTHA	7	F	CHILD	GRAALY	USA
LOEBISCH, LAURA	30	F	UNKNOWN	GRZZZZ	USA
VEHMLE, HELENE	35	F	W	GRAAXB	USA
ALFRED	.09	M	INFANT	GRAAXB	USA
VANDER, U	60	F	UNKNOWN	GRAHSP	USA
HEINS, LOUISE	29	F	UNKNOWN	GRAHSP	USA
ENGELKE, ELISE	66	F	UNKNOWN	GRAHSP	USA
WALDEMAR	6	M	CHILD	GRAHSP	USA
MOHR, EMIL	25	M	TT	GRAAKH	USA
CLARA	23	F	W	GRAAKH	USA
KAISER, CHRISTINE	26	F	UNKNOWN	GRAAKH	USA
MARTE, U	40	M	RE	GRAARR	USA
PRAEGER, MAX	27	M	LABR	GRADDQ	USA
SCHRATZ, JOHN	26	M	LABR	GRZZZZ	USA
BORST, BABETTA	19	F	UNKNOWN	GRZZZZ	USA
SCHMIDT, BABETTA	19	F	UNKNOWN	GRZZZZ	USA
PFANNES, VALENTINE	16	F	UNKNOWN	GRZZZZ	USA
WIEDMANN, HEINR.	17	M	TLR	GRZZZZ	USA
CARL	14	M	UNKNOWN	GRZZZZ	USA
KLEINSCHRODT, CONRAD	13	M	JNR	GRADUC	USA
KUNZ, WILHELM	33	M	FARMER	GRAFWN	USA
RUSINELLI, OTTILIE	24	F	UNKNOWN	GRABDM	USA
LOESCHER, AGNES	16	F	UNKNOWN	GRZZZZ	USA
HORN, CONRAD	22	M	LABR	GRADOI	USA
PETER, LUDWIGE	47	M	LABR	GRADLO	USA
KASTECKY, JAN	26	M	LABR	GRZZZZ	USA
MALENOWSKA, FRANZISCA	22	F	UNKNOWN	GRAAZQ	USA
GEISLER, WILH.	14	M	UNKNOWN	GRZZZZ	USA
LINDEMANN, BERTHA	17	F	UNKNOWN	GRZZZZ	USA
HOPP, HEINR.	55	M	FARMER	GRZZZZ	USA
JUSTINE	51	F	W	GRZZZZ	USA
MARIA	25	F	UNKNOWN	GRZZZZ	USA
ELISAB.	22	F	UNKNOWN	GRZZZZ	USA
ERNST	7	M	CHILD	GRZZZZ	USA
AUGUST	6	M	CHILD	GRZZZZ	USA
ELISAB.	.09	F	INFANT	GRZZZZ	USA
SCHARKOWSKY, FRANZ	28	M	LABR	GRZZZZ	USA
HEINR.	.03	M	INFANT	GRZZZZ	USA
WALTER, CASPAR	32	M	BKLYR	GRZZZZ	USA
ELISAB.	27	F	W	GRZZZZ	USA
MARIA	5	F	CHILD	GRZZZZ	USA
JACOB	4	M	CHILD	GRZZZZ	USA
LIMBURG, GOTTFR.	15	M	UNKNOWN	GRZZZZ	USA
GRIMM, LORENZ	16	M	UNKNOWN	GRZZZZ	USA
KORSMEYER, JOHANN	18	M	SMH	GRZZZZ	USA
NIEPERT, ENGEL	17	M	LABR	GRACKN	USA
KRUSE, FRIEDR.	14	M	UNKNOWN	GRACKN	USA
FETTE, HERMANN	29	M	LABR	GRZZZZ	USA
LENGSTAKE, MARIE	26	F	UNKNOWN	GRZZZZ	USA
DULLINGER, MICHAEL	61	M	CPTR	GRZZZZ	USA
ANNA	45	F	UNKNOWN	GRZZZZ	USA
FRANZ	6	M	CHILD	GRZZZZ	USA
THERESE	7	F	CHILD	GRZZZZ	USA
GEORG	4	M	CHILD	GRZZZZ	USA
LINDECKE, WILH.	28	M	LABR	GRABPG	USA
FRIEDR.	27	M	CCHMN	GRABPG	USA
ANDUZIS, GEORG	25	M	TLR	GRZZZZ	USA
BREHM, FRIEDR.	26	M	LABR	GRZZZZ	USA
HUULGAARD, JENS	22	M	SHMK	GRZZZZ	USA
HAFNER, JOH.	18	M	MLR	GRZZZZ	USA
REICHERT, CARL	22	M	LLD	GRAELY	USA
HOESCH, PETER	24	M	FARMER	GRAELY	USA
DRESSLER, CHR.	60	F	UNKNOWN	GRZZZZ	USA
BARB.	21	F	UNKNOWN	GRZZZZ	USA
MAURER, ELISE	24	F	UNKNOWN	GRABOQ	USA
LEVY, MAX	30	M	FARMER	GRABOQ	USA
GLOSQUE, JOSEPHINE	70	F	UNKNOWN	GRABOQ	USA
ROTH, ANNA	28	F	UNKNOWN	GRABOQ	USA
REBHOLZ, JOSEPHINE	6	F	CHILD	GRABOQ	USA
KLINGEL, CAROLINE	16	F	UNKNOWN	GRABOQ	USA
HELBIG, ANNA	50	F	UNKNOWN	GRABOQ	USA
RUDOLF	7	M	CHILD	GRABOQ	USA
WEICK, JACOB	25	M	FARMER	GRAFGK	USA
ANNA	21	F	W	GRAFGK	USA
SCHWALB, MATTHAEUS	19	M	BCHR	GRZZZZ	USA
FREYTAG, MARIE	15	F	UNKNOWN	GRZZZZ	USA
DUERR, SEBAST.	22	M	BKLYR	GRZZZZ	USA
GORHAU, MARIA	20	F	UNKNOWN	GRZZZZ	USA
WIEMER, MARIE	22	F	UNKNOWN	GRAFNK	USA
WENDEL, CHRIST.	31	M	MCHT	GRAFNK	USA
EMMA	30	F	W	GRAFNK	USA
STEIN, CONRAD	24	M	FARMER	GRZZZZ	USA
CATH.	25	F	W	GRZZZZ	USA
DIERINGER, EMILIE	26	F	UNKNOWN	GRADTI	USA
HEER, GOTTLOB	22	M	LABR	GRAFBF	USA
BARWINSKI, AGNES	23	F	UNKNOWN	GRZZZZ	USA
AUG.	16	M	LABR	GRZZZZ	USA
PIETZ, EVA	16	F	UNKNOWN	GRZZZZ	USA
JUNGKUNZ, BARB.	27	F	UNKNOWN	GRAEIA	USA
ANNA	16	F	UNKNOWN	GRAEIA	USA
WIEGARTNER, JOH.	17	M	BBR	GRZZZZ	USA
LUTZ, FRIEDRICH	30	M	BCHR	GRZZZZ	USA
DAVID	24	M	FARMER	GRZZZZ	USA
LOUISE	18	F	UNKNOWN	GRZZZZ	USA
DERESER, LEO	24	M	TLR	GRAFRG	USA
KIESSLING, BARB.	22	F	UNKNOWN	GRACNZ	USA
GROSSMANN, JOH.	41	F	FARMER	GRZZZZ	USA
BARB.	43	F	W	GRZZZZ	USA
A.BARB.	16	M	CH	GRZZZZ	USA
JOH.G.	6	M	CHILD	GRZZZZ	USA
MARG.	7	F	CHILD	GRZZZZ	USA
JOH.CONR.	5	M	CHILD	GRZZZZ	USA
PFAFFENBERGER, JOH.	25	M	PNTR	GRZZZZ	USA
ZIMMERMANN, JOH.	25	M	LABR	GRZZZZ	USA
BAUMANN, AMALIE	28	F	UNKNOWN	GRAAZQ	USA
ANNA	59	F	UNKNOWN	GRAAZQ	USA
EMMA	20	F	UNKNOWN	GRAAZQ	USA
SCHMIDT, EDUARD	17	M	SMH	GRAFFY	USA
SEYFARTH, AUGUSTE	35	F	UNKNOWN	GRZZZZ	USA
BERTHOLD	7	M	CHILD	GRZZZZ	USA
ELLA	4	F	CHILD	GRZZZZ	USA
FRIDA	4	F	CHILD	GRZZZZ	USA
ANTONIE	2	F	CHILD	GRZZZZ	USA
ROSA	.06	F	INFANT	GRZZZZ	USA
KEPPES, ANNA	25	F	UNKNOWN	GRAMBF	USA
JAHRS, JOSEF	37	M	LABR	GRAGAR	USA
KRAKOWSKI, JACOB	32	M	LABR	GRAGAW	USA
MARIE	27	F	W	GRAGAW	USA
MARTHA	4	F	CHILD	GRAGAW	USA
BERNH.	2	M	CHILD	GRAGAW	USA
PAUL	.03	M	INFANT	GRAGAW	USA
MESLE, ELISAB.	21	F	UNKNOWN	GRZZZZ	USA
RAAB, KATH.	6	F	CHILD	GRZZZZ	USA
ENGELHARDT, JOSEF.	18	F	UNKNOWN	GRZZZZ	USA
SCHELL, MINA	30	F	W	GRABEW	USA
CARL	7	M	CHILD	GRABEW	USA
LOUISE	5	F	CHILD	GRABEW	USA
EMMA	3	F	CHILD	GRABEW	USA
FRITZ	.01	M	INFANT	GRABEW	USA
KRAFT, GEORG	14	M	UNKNOWN	GRAIUP	USA
LAKERMEYER, WILH.	16	M	LABR	GRAJIK	USA
JUNG, FRANZ	20	M	LABR	GRAABX	USA
LECHLEITNER, JOS.	28	M	FARMER	GRZZZZ	USA
SCHLEINKOFER, PETER	15	M	LABR	GRZZZZ	USA
STEPHAN, HEINR.	23	M	BCHR	GRAFNK	USA
KELLER, GEORG	27	M	LABR	GRZZZZ	USA
RUEPPEL, W.	47	M	LABR	GRAGVZ	USA
ULRICH, NICOL.	26	M	SMH	GRZZZZ	USA

PASSENGER	AGE	SEX	OCCUPATION	PRVL DES
HOEGL, FRANZ	24	M	CNF	GRADLDUSA
KUBISCH, SELMA	31	F	UNKNOWN	GRZZZZUSA
KLUBERTANZ, JOH.	36	M	LABR	GRZZZZUSA
ANNA	32	F	W	GRZZZZUSA
AUG.	7	M	CHILD	GRZZZZUSA
RUDOLF	4	M	CHILD	GRZZZZUSA
BARB.	2	F	CHILD	GRZZZZUSA
GEORG	.06	M	INFANT	GRZZZZUSA
HUEGE, HERM.	22	M	TLR	GRABXPUSA
KUEHNE, LOUIS	56	M	LABR	GRZZZZUSA
ERICH	6	M	CHILD	GRZZZZUSA
ROTTWEILER, ANDR.	21	M	SHMK	GRZZZZUSA
DUERINGER, JACOB	14	M	BCHR	GRZZZZUSA
PAUL	17	F	UNKNOWN	GRZZZZUSA
REINECK, JOH.	36	M	SHMK	GRZZZZUSA
BURDELSKI, ANDR.	23	M	LABR	GRZZZZUSA
KURZ, MARIA	20	F	UNKNOWN	GRACIOUSA
FUCHS, CATH.	18	F	UNKNOWN	GRACIOUSA
KLEINLEIN, JOH.	21	M	BRZ	GRZZZZUSA
ALBERT, DOROTHEA	18	F	UNKNOWN	GRZZZZUSA
HOFFMANN, AUG.	23	F	UNKNOWN	GRACHOUSA
FRITSCH, PHILIPPINE	25	F	W	GRAJIGUSA
CHR.	3	M	CHILD	GRAJIGUSA
ROSGA, JOH.	26	M	BKR	GRZZZZUSA
SZCZODROWSKI, MICH.	44	M	FSR	GRZZZZUSA
ROSALIE	41	F	W	GRZZZZUSA
IGNATZ	6	M	CHILD	GRZZZZUSA
JOH.	7	M	CHILD	GRZZZZUSA
MARIA	.11	M	INFANT	GRZZZZUSA
FANDREY, GOTTLIEB	38	M	FARMER	GRZZZZUSA
RUDOLF, ERNESTE.	35	F	UNKNOWN	GRABUTUSA
MIKULSKI, NDR.	22	M	CPTR	GRAEABUSA
DETLOFF, ROSALIA	27	F	UNKNOWN	GRZZZZUSA
WERNER, ANNA	18	F	UNKNOWN	GRZZZZUSA
SCHWARZER, PAUL	14	M	UNKNOWN	GRZZZZUSA
RUTKIEWICZ, JOH.	30	F	W	GRZZZZUSA
GREGOR	6	M	CHILD	GRZZZZUSA
THEOPHIL	7	M	CHILD	GRZZZZUSA
MARIE	4	F	CHILD	GRZZZZUSA
HEDWIG	.11	F	INFANT	GRZZZZUSA
KRAIN, FRITZ	18	M	WCHMKR	GRAARZUSA
SCHULZ, ALFRED	19	M	FARMER	GRZZZZUSA
SCHMIDT, EMIL	26	F	UNKNOWN	GRZZZZUSA
WERNER, MARIE	16	F	UNKNOWN	GRZZZZUSA
RICHTER, PAUL	21	M	BRR	GRAARZUSA
LEWANSKA, ROSALIE	23	F	UNKNOWN	GRZZZZUSA
PAUH, DAVID	27	M	LABR	GRAAZSUSA
ANDREAS, LUDW.	26	M	LABR	GRABKPUSA
FLAD, GEORG	26	M	WCHMKR	GRAJAPUSA
OTT, ADAM	26	M	LABR	GRAHRJUSA
PRINZING, JOH.FR.	30	M	SHMK	GRAFBFUSA
CARL	16	M	HRDRS	GRAFBFUSA
METZNER, LISETTE	25	F	UNKNOWN	GRACIJUSA
HERSTMANN, HERM.	22	M	BCHR	GRAEYKUSA
PRALLE, JUL.	23	M	CL	GRACBGUSA
HAHN, ANDR.	31	M	FARMER	GRZZZZUSA
SCHLICK, CHR.	56	M	FARMER	GRADHRUSA
DOROTHEA	50	F	W	GRADHRUSA
SALZER, MARTIN	20	M	LABR	GRADNPUSA
PREUSCH, DAVID	14	M	FARMER	GRABARUSA
LEKS, FRANZISKA	51	F	UNKNOWN	GRAHQGUSA
GLAENZER, GEORG	17	M	MCHT	GRABQKUSA
SCHUDT, HEINR.	15	M	MCHT	GRABGHUSA
AULBACH, BARB.	18	F	UNKNOWN	GRADTEUSA
MERZ, REG.	23	F	UNKNOWN	GRADTEUSA
GOTTFRIED, ANTON	26	M	LABR	GRADTEUSA
SCHMIDT, JUL.	25	M	LABR	GRADTEUSA
ANKENBRAND, CASPAR	44	M	LABR	GRABIVUSA
MARG.	49	F	UNKNOWN	GRABIVUSA
CONRAD	6	M	CHILD	GRABIVUSA
SCHILLER, JOH.	15	M	UNKNOWN	GRABIVUSA
HORNING, MARG.	26	F	UNKNOWN	GRABIVUSA
ZLAZYNSKI, JOH.	39	M	FARMER	GRAFTSUSA
VETTER, JOH.	41	M	GZR	GRAFTSUSA
MARIA	30	F	W	GRAFTSUSA
GOTTL.	14	M	CH	GRAFTSUSA
HERM.	6	M	CHILD	GRAFTSUSA
ELISE	4	F	CHILD	GRAFTSUSA
GOTTHILF	.11	M	INFANT	GRZZZZUSA
JOURRTERN, CARL	31	M	BCHR	GRADYYUSA
GROEGER, ED.	37	M	FARMER	GRZZZZUSA
AUGUSTE	24	F	W	GRZZZZUSA
NASSHOLZ, BERTHA	18	F	UNKNOWN	GRAGDHUSA
JAHN, HELENE	23	F	UNKNOWN	GRAARRUSA
REBECCA	19	F	UNKNOWN	GRAARRUSA
AMALIA	23	F	UNKNOWN	GRAARRUSA
RAAB, MARG.	18	F	UNKNOWN	GRZZZZUSA
WEIGLEIN, JOH.	21	M	LABR	GRZZZZUSA
BERENDT, ANNA	20	F	UNKNOWN	GRZZZZUSA
SCHREIBER, VALENT.	20	M	LABR	GRZZZZUSA
TREFFURT, MINNA	32	F	W	GRAFDWUSA
RICHARD	6	M	CHILD	GRAFDWUSA
GERETCHEN	3	F	CHILD	GRAFDWUSA
JOSEF, SALI	18	F	CH	GRAFDWUSA
VANPOELLNITZ, AUGUST	51	M	PVTR	GRADNDUSA
BERTHA	18	F	W	GRADNDUSA
KNITTEL, JULIUS	30	M	FARMER	GRAEXWUSA
MARIE	25	F	W	GRAEXWUSA
MEUSING, FRIEDR.	22	M	LABR	GRZZZZUSA
SCHRAGE, CARL	21	M	LABR	GRZZZZUSA
SCHULTE, CARL	5	M	CHILD	GRZZZZUSA
GROSSMANN, BARB.	21	F	UNKNOWN	GRZZZZUSA
RAUH, SIMON	34	M	LABR	GRZZZZUSA
GROSSMANN, PETER	16	M	LABR	GRZZZZUSA
KOCH, WILH.	21	F	UNKNOWN	GRZZZZUSA
SCHALK, JOH.	30	M	FARMER	GRACBRUSA
SIERICH, HEINR.	61	M	JNR	GRACBRUSA
PAULMANN, ALBERT	41	M	TNM	GRAARRUSA
MARIE	30	F	W	GRAARRUSA
WARNKE, META	15	F	UNKNOWN	GRZZZZUSA
BECKER, H.L.	26	M	FARMER	GRAFDFUSA
SOPHIE	26	F	W	GRAFDFUSA
ANNA	.04	F	INFANT	GRAFDFUSA
FR.H.	24	M	LABR	GRAFDFUSA
STRACK, JOHANN	15	M	UNKNOWN	GRZZZZUSA
SCHATZ, HEINR.	20	M	LABR	GRADNPUSA
SCHMID, JOHANN	63	M	LABR	GRZZZZUSA
BOLLONGINA, OTTO	26	M	MCHT	GRAAVGUSA
BOETTCHER, RUD.	26	M	MCHT	GRZZZZUSA
THOMS, HEINR.	51	M	FARMER	GRZZZZUSA
DORETTE	41	F	W	GRZZZZUSA
EMILIE	18	F	UNKNOWN	GRZZZZUSA
LOUIS	16	M	UNKNOWN	GRZZZZUSA
DORETTE	13	F	CH	GRZZZZUSA
HEINR.	6	M	CHILD	GRZZZZUSA
AUG.	5	M	CHILD	GRZZZZUSA
CHRISTEL	7	M	CHILD	GRZZZZUSA
GUSTAV	4	M	CHILD	GRZZZZUSA
ERNST	.06	M	INFANT	GRZZZZUSA
KOHNKE, FRANZ	30	M	LABR	GRZZZZUSA
QUAST, HERM.	16	M	BBR	GRAAKHUSA
RUNIENAPP, EMILIE	50	F	W	BWZZZZUSA
EDITH	6	F	CHILD	BWZZZZUSA
FUCHS, JOH.	32	M	LABR	GRZZZZUSA
RODENHAEUSEN, ERNST	25	M	LABR	GRZZZZUSA
FR.	20	M	LABR	GRZZZZUSA
STROEMER, GREGOR	18	M	LABR	GRACUXUSA
WOLF, HEINR.	26	M	BKR	GRACUXUSA
SANDBERG, O.F.	30	M	FARMER	GRAFNKUSA
SAUERHOEFER, DINA	19	F	UNKNOWN	GRAIKSUSA
MOSER, MARIA	16	F	UNKNOWN	GRAIKSUSA
WALTER, TILLI	19	F	W	GRAIKSUSA
ZIEGLER, PHILIPP.	23	F	UNKNOWN	GRAIKSUSA
DOROTHEA	25	F	UNKNOWN	GRAIKSUSA
BABETTA	18	F	UNKNOWN	GRAIKSUSA
NAGEL, AUG.	56	M	LLD	GRAFTBUSA
GIMMEL, WILH.	73	M	DLR	GRACKHUSA
WELCH, JOH.	25	M	FARMER	GRZZZZUSA
NITZE, CARL	22	M	WCHMKR	GRZZZZUSA
SCHNEIDER, MARIA	24	F	UNKNOWN	GRAIKSUSA

PASSENGER	AGE	SEX	OCCUPATION	PRVVL	DES
HAASE, CARL	22	M	SMH	GRAARRUSA	
MAHNKEN, HEINR.	26	M	BKR	GRAARRUSA	
FEICH, JACOB	18	M	FARMER	GRAARRUSA	
ENKHAUSEN, BERNHARD	17	M	PNTR	GRAARRUSA	
HELLWEG, JOSEF	24	M	FARMER	GRAARRUSA	
SCHICK, GUSTAV	19	M	BCHR	GRAETKUSA	
ADOLF	17	M	PNTR	GRAETKUSA	
SCHMALBACH, JOHANN	24	M	SMH	GRAETKUSA	
GROH, MARTIN	20	M	BRZ	GRAETKUSA	
BUCK, JULIUS	21	M	SHMK	GRAETKUSA	

SHIP: ALASKA

FROM: LIVERPOOL AND QUEENSTOWN
TO: NEW YORK
ARRIVED: 30 JULY 1888

BISSWANGER, ANDREAS	00	M	LABR	GRZZZZUSA	
WESSEL, ERNST	15	M	CL	GRZZZZUSA	
TRESSEL, WILHELM	25	M	LWYR	GRZZZZUSA	
DIDIER, JEAN	25	M	LABR	GRZZZZUSA	
SPA-LINGER, JOH	50	M	LABR	GRZZZZUSA	
GRASS, LUDWIG	50	M	LABR	GRZZZZUSA	

SHIP: ETRURIA

FROM: LIVERPOOL AND QUEENSTOWN
TO: NEW YORK
ARRIVED: 30 JULY 1888

RUCKERT, ADALBERT	27	M	ACHTT	GRACBFNY	
NESS, CHARLES	27	M	CTM	GRADAXNY	
RUDERMENSKY, ROSALIE	23	F	SP	GRACBFNY	
TENNANT, CHARLES	21	M	BCHR	GRADAXNY	
BARBARA	20	F	MA	GRADAXNY	
WEBER, OTILLIE	30	F	SVNT	SRZZZZNY	
GOLDSCHMIDT, PAUL	29	M	GENT	SRADXWNY	
BOBB, ROBERT	27	M	AR	SRADBQNY	
BIBB, LOUIS	26	M	GENT	SRADBQNY	
JANET	21	F	W	SRADBQNY	
GUNTHER, ELIZA	29	F	SVNT	GRZZZZNY	
MILLER, SOPHIA	38	F	SVNT	GRZZZZNY	
LANSOY, ELISE	36	F	SVNT	FRZZZZNY	
BALLY, ARNOLD	36	M	MNFTR	FRADBQNY	

SHIP: FURNESSIA

FROM: GLASGOW AND MOVILLE
TO: NEW YORK
ARRIVED: 30 JULY 1888

PA-KHAUS, FRED	53	M	LABR	FRAHRZUSA	
KALMANSBERGER, B	28	M	LABR	FRAHRZUSA	
MULLER, HUGO	16	M	CL	FRAHRZUSA	
SHAFFER, NICHOLAS	31	M	MLR	FRAHRZUSA	
SZYMANSKI, ANTON	35	M	TLR	FRAHRZUSA	
ISCHESCHOWKE, W	26	M	TLR	FRAHRZUSA	
WENTER, AUGUST	25	M	TLR	FRAHRZUSA	
VICTOR	18	M	TLR	FRAHRZUSA	
DECROIX, LAMER--T	25	M	SHMK	FRAHRZUSA	

PASSENGER	AGE	SEX	OCCUPATION	PRVVL	DES
ALPHONSE	50	M	SHMK	FRAHRZUSA	
TAMELART, LUCIEN	31	M	NTRL	FRAHRZUSA	
FINK, CHARLES	30	M	TT	FRAHRZUSA	
CEBELENZ, ELIZ	22	F	NN	FRAHRZUSA	
JOHAN	.09	M	INFANT	FRAHRZUSA	

SHIP: SUEVIA

FROM: HAMBURG AND HAVRE
TO: NEW YORK
ARRIVED: 31 JULY 1888

MEINS, FRIED	16	M	LABR	FRAGKAUSA	
LISKE, MICCILAUS	40	M	LABR	FRADLDUSA	
GISTE, LEONHARD	17	M	UNKNOWN	FRADLDUSA	
SAKOWSKI, FERD	32	M	LABR	FRAAKHUSA	
GLESMANN, CHRISTE	25	F	SGL	FRACBFUSA	
EGGERS, HEINR	44	M	JNR	FRACBFUSA	
SCHROEDER, ALBERT	26	M	TNM	FRACBFUSA	
TULINSKI, CACILINE	25	F	SGL	FRAAKHUSA	
MARTENS, SOPHIE	17	F	SGL	PRZZZZUSA	
BRUDKMAIER, MAGD	30	F	WO	MKZZZZUSA	
FRIDA	9	F	CHILD	MKZZZZUSA	
HENSLER, CAROLINE	21	F	SGL	MKABNUUSA	
MATHILDE	20	F	SGL	MKABNUUSA	
AMMON, LOUISE	30	F	SGL	PRZZZZUSA	
ROTHMANN, ALEXANDER	22	M	MCHT	PRAIHYUSA	
KU--RA, MARIE	20	F	SGL	PRZZZZUSA	
WAGNER, JOHN	71	M	LABR	PRZZZZUSA	
ROSALIE	62	F	W	PRZZZZUSA	
ZE--HLSDORF, CATH	35	F	WO	PRAGRRUSA	
MARIE	9	F	CHILD	PRAGRRUSA	
JULS	7	M	CHILD	PRAGRRUSA	
ELISABETH	5	F	CHILD	PRAGRRUSA	
JOSEF	3	M	CHILD	PRAGRRUSA	
ANNA	.11	F	INFANT	PRAGRRUSA	
KATZ, AUGUST	42	M	LABR	PRAASSUSA	
DINSKY, ANNA	24	F	SGL	PRAESLUSA	
DRU--BOERSKY, ANNA	19	F	SGL	PRZZZZUSA	
WITT, FRANZ	43	M	LABR	PRZZZZUSA	
PRANZKE, AUGUST	15	M	LABR	PRZZZZUSA	
DODINSKY, ADOLF	38	M	LABR	PRZZZZUSA	
SCHROEDER, HERMAN	16	M	FARMER	PRZZZZUSA	
HARTMANN, JOSEF	24	M	FARMER	PRZZZZUSA	
SCHIELE, CHRISTIAN	37	M	LABR	BVZZZZUSA	
WITTKOWSKA, FLORA	28	F	WO	BVAAKHUSA	
ADOLF	7	M	CHILD	BVAAKHUSA	
WIELAND, ROSA	18	F	SGL	BVZZZZUSA	
TREML, FRANZ	9	M	CHILD	BVZZZZUSA	
TALEVNA-KA, MARIENNA	54	F	WO	BVAFZGUSA	
STEDMANN, CATHA	15	F	SGL	PRZZZZUSA	
ANNA	25	F	SGL	PRZZZZUSA	
ZIELINSKI, JULIAN	15	M	CL	PRZZZZUSA	
TAIGLE, FRIEDERICH	30	M	BKR	WMZZZZUSA	
KRAEMER, FERDINANAD	31	M	MCHT	WMAFJHUSA	
DANKWERTH, HERM	22	M	LABR	WMAAKHUSA	
BENVIT, OTT	22	M	LABR	PRZZZZUSA	
AMMANN, AUGUST	30	M	FARMER	WMZZZZUSA	
WITT, SIMON	23	M	FARMER	WMAGPZUSA	
KOEHLER, LINA	21	F	SGL	BVZZZZUSA	
HAUSMANN, ANNA	14	F	SGL	BVABLVUSA	
HUB, ANNA	20	F	SGL	BVAAJNUSA	
BUSCH, WILHE	19	F	SGL	PRZZZZUSA	
SCHMIDT, AGNES	15	F	SGL	PRZZZZUSA	
LIND, CATHA	26	F	SGL	PRAJJJUSA	
STOSTH, NICOL	42	M	FARMER	PRABQRUSA	
ANNA	42	F	W	PRABQRUSA	
BARBA	16	F	CH	PRABQRUSA	
NICOLAUS	9	M	CHILD	PRABQRUSA	
LEOPOLD	8	M	CHILD	PRABQRUSA	

PASSENGER	AGE	SEX	OCCUPATION	PRIVL	DES
GERTRUD	7	F	CHILD	PRABQRUSA	
KUNIGUNDE	6	F	CHILD	PRABQRUSA	
MARIE	4	F	CHILD	PRABQRUSA	
AUG	1	F	CHILD	PRABQRUSA	
WEISSENBERGER, J	15	M	LABR	PRABQRUSA	
HEID, JOH	27	M	LABR	PRABQRUSA	
MUELLER, MAGD	47	F	WO	PRACMHUSA	
FRANZ	18	M	CH	PRACMHUSA	
LUDWIG	15	M	CH	PRACMHUSA	
OSCAR	9	M	CHILD	PRACMHUSA	
MARIE	8	F	CHILD	PRACMHUSA	
BERTHA	6	F	CHILD	PRACMHUSA	
HOFFMANN, AUGUSTE	53	F	WO	PRAAKHUSA	
ANNA	21	F	CH	PRAAKHUSA	
MAX	15	M	CH	PRAAKHUSA	
LEWIN, MATHILDE	17	F	SGL	PRZZZZUSA	
SIEKINGER, EMILIE	20	F	SGL	PRACBFUSA	
IKRZYSNIK, CLARA	20	F	SGL	PRZZZZUSA	
JOHANSEN, HENRIETTA	31	F	SGL	PRZZZZUSA	
BLEIDE, AMALIE	7	F	CHILD	PRZZZZUSA	
BARBA	34	F	W	PRZZZZUSA	
MARIE	6	F	CHILD	PRZZZZUSA	
JAR--LAWA	4	F	CHILD	PRZZZZUSA	
ANNA	2	F	CHILD	PRZZZZUSA	
VOTAVA, ALZLETA	17	F	SGL	PRZZZZUSA	
ANNA	15	F	SGL	PRZZZZUSA	
LOHMANN, CARL	31	M	BCHR	PRAAFTUSA	
BUCHHOLZ, ANNA	24	F	SGL	PRAAKHUSA	
REDE---EMMING, ALBERT	30	M	LABR	PRZZZZUSA	
SEITERT, LEOPOLD	47	M	DT	PRAFTDUSA	
SCHLESINGER, MAX	20	M	MCHT	PRAHPFUSA	
STEINER, ANNA	27	F	SGL	PRAFTDUSA	
IDA	26	F	SGL	PRAFTDUSA	
SCHMELKE, HEINR	23	M	FARMER	PRZZZZUSA	
JOSEFINE	33	F	WO	PRADETUSA	
WALDEMER	9	M	CHILD	PRADETUSA	
RHEINHOLD	5	M	CHILD	PRADETUSA	
ELISABETH	2	F	CHILD	PRADETUSA	
HABISCH, JULIUS	37	M	LABR	PRZZZZUSA	
HIRSCH, FRANZ	27	M	MCHT	PRAAKHUSA	
DIETZ, LOUISE	26	F	SGL	BDZZZZUSA	
TRAEGER, BERNHARD	49	M	BKR	BDABDMUSA	
SCHOEN, GOTT	27	M	BCHR	WMZZZZUSA	
JAKE-IEK, MARTHA	22	F	WO	WMAAKHUSA	
TONI	.05	F	INFANT	WMAAKHUSA	
JESSEN, JES	69	M	FARMER	WMAEFDUSA	
FRITZ	32	M	FARMER	WMAEFDUSA	
SKAK, ANNA	23	F	SGL	WMAEFDUSA	
KIRKETERP, ANNA	23	F	SGL	PRZZZZUSA	
JENSEN, ELSE	20	F	SGL	PRZZZZUSA	
CHRISTENSEN, PETER	20	M	CPTR	PRZZZZUSA	
OTTO, AUGUST	25	M	UNKNOWN	PRZZZZUSA	
JOSEPHE	28	F	W	PRZZZZUSA	
HEISIG, CARL	24	M	BCHR	PRABUTUSA	
STEINGRAEBER, FERD	24	M	LABR	PRZZZZUSA	
ANDREWS, ANNA	19	F	SGL	PRABIGUSA	
BLASBERG, WILH	25	M	FARMER	PRZZZZUSA	
TRUMMER, CARL	26	M	MD	PRZZZZUSA	
ECKERT, ANDR	46	M	FARMER	PRZZZZUSA	
MARCH, GUSTAV	25	M	JNR	PRAEIOUSA	
HENKE, JOH	64	M	LABR	PRABUTUSA	
HENRIETTE	23	F	SGL	PRABUTUSA	
BOE-, ANNA	46	F	WO	PRAAKHUSA	
HESSE, KATHA	47	F	WO	PRAAXFUSA	
JEAN	9	M	CHILD	PRAAXFUSA	
MINNA	7	F	CHILD	PRAAXFUSA	
FRITZ	3	M	CHILD	PRAAXFUSA	
PAPPERT, ADELHEIT	23	F	SGL	PRAAXFUSA	
SZYNATECKI, ANTON	35	M	LABR	PRZZZZUSA	
FIEBIG, MARIE	26	F	SGL	PRZZZZUSA	
ROSALIE	23	F	SGL	PRZZZZUSA	
SONNENBERG, EMMA	25	F	SGL	PRZZZZUSA	
KAISER, DANIL	25	M	LABR	PRABIJUSA	
KUEHN, MARIE	18	F	SGL	PRABIJUSA	
SIEGRECHT, GEORG	21	M	LABR	PRAAKHUSA	
ROSEN, GRUENBERG	27	F	W	PRAARZUSA	
SIMBRIDI, JOH	28	M	LABR	SRZZZZUSA	
BRUMEL, AUGUSTE	38	F	SGL	SRZZZZUSA	
SCHNEISSER, VALENTIN	26	M	LABR	SRZZZZUSA	
WITTERN, JOHN	27	M	LABR	SRZZZZUSA	
HUNZIKER, FRITZ	27	M	LABR	SRZZZZUSA	
FELBER, RICHARD	15	M	LABR	SRZZZZUSA	
MORATH, OTTO	27	M	LABR	SRZZZZUSA	
SCHNIDER, CARL	19	M	LABR	SRZZZZUSA	
SANTER, ARNOLD	27	M	LABR	SRZZZZUSA	
PREDMER, IGNATZ	42	M	LABR	SRZZZZUSA	
WOLF, WILHELM	19	M	LABR	SRZZZZUSA	
JAHNKE, MAGDEL	70	F	WO	PRZZZZUSA	
HIRSCHFELD, MARGR	40	F	WO	PRZZZZUSA	
NORDWALD, MAX	20	M	HTR	PRAADEUSA	
KRAUSE, FERDINAND	52	M	PVTM	PRADLUUSA	
OSTERBIND, MARIE	29	F	SGL	PRAAKHUSA	
BARNES, CH	20	M	MCHT	PRACXVUSA	
VATER, A	25	M	MCHT	PRACNTUSA	
GORSKA, JULIE	21	F	SGL	PRZZZZUSA	
HOCHKAMP, BETTI	28	F	WO	PRACBRUSA	
GEORG	8	M	CHILD	PRACBRUSA	
LOUISE	6	F	CHILD	PRACBRUSA	
FRIEDA	5	F	CHILD	PRACBRUSA	
VON, CARL	25	M	MCHT	PRAARRUSA	
MARTIN, HELENE	25	F	SGL	PRAAKHUSA	

SHIP: WERRA

FROM: BREMEN AND SOUTHAMPTON
TO: NEW YORK
ARRIVED: 31 JULY 1888

PASSENGER	AGE	SEX	OCCUPATION	PRIVL	DES
ARNETT, FRANK	20	M	MCHT	PRADLDUSA	
MEHLHOP, FRED.	21	M	MCHT	PRADLDUSA	
GOESSLING, ELISE	35	F	UNKNOWN	PRAAXFUSA	
BRANDT, LOUISE	24	F	UNKNOWN	PRAAXFUSA	
DUILLING, F.	38	M	MCHT	PRABOQUSA	
FABER, OTTO	24	M	MCHT	PRADROUSA	
BRANDT, RICHARD	26	M	MCHT	PRAAKHUSA	
VIEWEG, B.	35	F	MCHT	PRACXVUSA	
BRUENNING, HERM.	29	M	MCHT	PRAFECUSA	
HERMINE	24	F	W	PRAFECUSA	
KASTEN, CARL	24	M	MCHT	GRZZZZUSA	
GALITZ, MINNA	18	F	UNKNOWN	GRZZZZUSA	
SCHERF, CHARLES	52	M	FARMER	GRZZZZUSA	
ELISE	32	F	W	GRZZZZUSA	
ELSA	5	F	CHILD	GRZZZZUSA	
SCHRADER, ALWINE	39	F	W	GRZZZZUSA	
ERNST	11	M	CH	GRZZZZUSA	
WILLI	3	M	CHILD	GRZZZZUSA	
APPLER, AUG.	35	M	MCHT	BVZZZZUSA	
KNOTTERUS, AD.	24	M	CL	BVACBGUSA	
NEUBURGER, NTON	23	M	MCHT	BVABQZUSA	
RIECKE, BERTHA	50	F	W	BVAARRUSA	
CHARLOTTE	30	F	UNKNOWN	BVAARRUSA	
LIDLE, AUG.	25	M	TT	WMZZZZUSA	
WASSEMANN, JUL.	26	M	TT	WMADROUSA	
GRUBRICH, JENNY	19	F	UNKNOWN	WMADROUSA	
WIESE, OTTO	22	M	TT	WMAEAYUSA	
WERTHEIM, HERM.	24	M	TT	GRZZZZUSA	
WEBER, JOH.	33	M	TT	GRABDMUSA	
HARTER, CARL	33	M	TT	GRZZZZUSA	
HERM.	22	F	W	GRZZZZUSA	
ILBERG, MAX	21	M	MCHT	GRZZZZUSA	
KOENIGS, W.	54	M	MCHT	GRAGBPUSA	
MELSSHEIMER, CARL	27	M	MCHT	GRZZZZUSA	
MARIE	23	F	W	GRZZZZUSA	
KOHL, PETER	24	M	MCHT	GRZZZZUSA	
DOWAD, OTTO	40	M	MCHT	BDZZZZUSA	

PASSENGER	AGE	SEX	OCCUPATION	PRVL	DES
REINDL, FRIEDR.	22	M	MCHT	BDAIKJ	USA
DREISER, HUGO	20	M	MCHT	BDAIKJ	USA
ZINSSMANN, EMMA	17	F	UNKNOWN	GRZZZZ	USA
DAUBE, DAVID	11	F	MCHT	GRAHIT	USA
STRUWE, HELENE	19	F	UNKNOWN	GRAAQS	USA
WEBER, MARIA	48	F	UNKNOWN	GRAARZ	USA
WENZEL, LUCIE	30	F	UNKNOWN	GRABAH	USA
LARSEN, MAREN	32	M	FARMER	GRABZS	USA
STEINMETZ, ROSALIE	46	F	W	GRZZZZ	USA
ALFRED	10	M	CH	GRZZZZ	USA
JOH.	4	M	CHILD	GRZZZZ	USA
BERTHOLD	2	M	CHILD	GRZZZZ	USA
EILERS, AMALIE	17	F	UNKNOWN	GRZZZZ	USA
SIEH, ELSE	24	F	UNKNOWN	GRZZZZ	USA
WEIGELL, OTTO	23	M	MCHT	GRZZZZ	USA
WILKEN, WILLY	23	M	MCHT	GRADIJ	USA
SAMNELSON, MICHAELIS	40	M	MCHT	GRADIJ	USA
ZUMBULTE, MATH.	28	M	MCHT	GRADKW	USA
BLUMENFELD, JOH.	27	F	UNKNOWN	GRACBF	USA
RECHA	23	F	UNKNOWN	GRACBF	USA
RUFLE, MARG.	37	F	W	WMZZZZ	USA
EMMA	11	F	CH	WMZZZZ	USA
FRIEDR.	11	M	CH	WMZZZZ	USA
ORTSMANN, EMILIE	32	F	W	GRZZZZ	USA
CLARA	11	F	CH	GRZZZZ	USA
ANNA	10	F	CH	GRZZZZ	USA
WILLY	9	F	CHILD	GRZZZZ	USA
ALFRED	7	M	CHILD	GRZZZZ	USA
MAX	2	M	CHILD	GRZZZZ	USA
GRETCHEN	.06	F	INFANT	GRZZZZ	USA
SEMMER, RICHARD	30	F	UNKNOWN	GRAAKH	USA
SOMMER, OTTILIE	26	F	W	GRAAKH	USA
KATH.	3	F	CHILD	GRAAKH	USA
KASPAR, SAM.	42	F	MCHT	GRALSY	USA
HULDA	28	F	W	GRALSY	USA
ELKAN	3	F	CHILD	GRALSY	USA
HERTA	.10	F	INFANT	GRALSY	USA
MICHAELIS, HERM.	32	M	MCHT	GRAAKH	USA
MARIA	30	F	W	GRAAKH	USA
SCHILLING, LOUISE	25	F	UNKNOWN	GRAAKH	USA
MEYER, DORIS	18	F	UNKNOWN	GRAAKH	USA
GENREICH, MATH.	20	F	UNKNOWN	GRAAKH	USA
MELLIN, MARIE	54	F	W	GRAAKH	USA
KONICKA, ROSALIA	28	F	W	GRZZZZ	USA
IGNATZ	.09	F	INFANT	GRZZZZ	USA
BERTSCH, HENRIETTE	58	F	W	GRZZZZ	USA
WIEGARD, THERESSIA	26	F	UNKNOWN	GRZZZZ	USA
SCHIER, ELISAB.	30	F	W	GRAARR	USA
BERNH.	4	M	CHILD	GRAARR	USA
HENRIETTE	1	F	CHILD	GRAARR	USA
PAGEL, AUGUST	25	M	FARMER	GRZZZZ	USA
MARIA	24	F	W	GRZZZZ	USA
HERM.	1	M	CHILD	GRZZZZ	USA
KRANICH, AUGUSTE	63	F	W	GRZZZZ	USA
NOWAK, JACOB	27	M	BCHR	GRAEAB	USA
DIEGNER, WILH.	26	M	SHMK	GRAIWJ	USA
FROESE, HELENE	22	F	W	GRAIWJ	USA
MARIA	.11	F	INFANT	GRAIWJ	USA
HAASSBRUNNER, CATH.	22	F	UNKNOWN	GRADRO	USA
LAMMERS, JOH.	23	M	FARMER	GRADRO	USA
TEPERL, CATH.	49	F	W	GRADLD	USA
LUDW.	13	M	UNKNOWN	GRADLD	USA
GOEHL, HERM.	23	M	LABR	GRADBD	USA
REINHOLD	25	M	LABR	GRADBD	USA
SCHMIDT, CAROL.	52	F	W	GRZZZZ	USA
GERKEN, WILH.	14	M	UNKNOWN	GRZZZZ	USA
BRINKMANN, JOH.	17	M	FARMER	GRZZZZ	USA
WILLENBROCK, MARTIN	17	M	FARMER	GRAHTJ	USA
KREIBOHM, FRIEDR.	31	F	WTR	GRAHTJ	USA
LAMKE, HINR.	14	M	UNKNOWN	GRABXF	USA
ARMBRUSTER, ADOLPH	25	M	TLR	GRAEEA	USA
GOETZ, MARG.	17	F	UNKNOWN	GRAEEA	USA
ISCHINGER, CARL	25	M	BKR	WMZZZZ	USA
MACK, CATH.	25	F	W	WMZZZZ	USA
AUG.	2	M	CHILD	WMZZZZ	USA
CATH.	.06	F	INFANT	WMZZZZ	USA
FAUTH, CARL	24	M	LABR	WMZZZZ	USA
SPEIDEL, CARL	43	M	MCHT	WMZZZZ	USA
ROTHSCHILD, ALB.	16	M	MCHT	WMAAWT	USA
WEISSKOPF, CATH.	18	F	UNKNOWN	BDZZZZ	USA
OECHSLE, JULIANA	20	F	UNKNOWN	BDZZZZ	USA
CAROL.	18	F	UNKNOWN	BDZZZZ	USA
HESS, RUDOLF	14	M	UNKNOWN	BDZZZZ	USA
HOEHN, LUDW.	22	M	LABR	WMZZZZ	USA
HEGERMANN, ANTON	33	M	MCHT	WMADLD	USA
KEIL, JOH.A.	27	M	BKR	WMAECX	USA
BIHLMAYER, MARIE	23	F	UNKNOWN	WMZZZZ	USA
CHR.	16	M	UNKNOWN	WMZZZZ	USA
PETERSEN, JOH.	45	F	W	GRZZZZ	USA
NIELS	10	M	CH	GRZZZZ	USA
HARTWIG	8	M	CHILD	GRZZZZ	USA
ALFRED	3	M	CHILD	GRZZZZ	USA
BUCH, WILH.	26	M	LABR	GRZZZZ	USA
BAUER, JUST.	19	M	UNKNOWN	GRAAHB	USA
RETTNER, BARB.	20	F	UNKNOWN	GRAAHB	USA
HAETLEIN, EVA	30	F	UNKNOWN	BVZZZZ	USA
SCHLEGELMILCH, DORA	16	F	UNKNOWN	BVAFRX	USA
ZWIRNLEIN, MATH.	20	F	UNKNOWN	BVZZZZ	USA
HOFFMANN, JOH.	20	M	LABR	BVZZZZ	USA
JOSEF	21	M	LABR	BVZZZZ	USA
KOLB, KATH.	20	F	UNKNOWN	BVZZZZ	USA
WEBER, MARG.	24	F	UNKNOWN	BVZZZZ	USA
BEHR, MARIE	20	F	UNKNOWN	BVZZZZ	USA
SCHNEIDER, MARG.	26	F	UNKNOWN	BVZZZZ	USA
PUPEL, ANNA	30	F	W	BVZZZZ	USA
EMIL	7	M	CHILD	BVZZZZ	USA
JOHANN	.11	M	INFANT	BVZZZZ	USA
JENDRASZACK, IGNACZ	24	M	LABR	GRZZZZ	USA
LUBITZ, EMILIE	35	F	UNKNOWN	GRZZZZ	USA
KRASTSCHICK, MARIANNA	20	F	W	GRZZZZ	USA
SOFIA	.06	F	INFANT	GRZZZZ	USA
LUBITZ, JULIUS	34	M	LABR	GRZZZZ	USA
ANDRASZAK, ANTON	18	M	TLR	GRZZZZ	USA
KOLB, ANTON	73	M	LABR	GRAEZX	USA
BARB.	38	F	W	GRAEZX	USA
JACOB	28	M	LABR	GRAEZX	USA
ROSALIE	27	F	W	GRAEZX	USA
EDMUND	8	M	CHILD	GRAEZX	USA
ANTON	4	M	CHILD	GRAEZX	USA
BARB.	.10	F	INFANT	GRAEZX	USA
SCHMIDT, JOS.	60	M	FARMER	GRAIUP	USA
R--, JOH.	44	M	FARMER	GRADLD	USA
ZAHLGRIM, CARL	24	M	FARMER	GRABEH	USA
AUG.	22	F	W	GRABEH	USA
ESCHLER, NATHAN	37	M	LABR	GRAAKH	USA
BERTHA	27	F	W	GRAAKH	USA
BRUNO	4	M	CHILD	GRAAKH	USA
HAHN, JUL.	37	M	TLR	GRAAKH	USA
SCHMIDT, CARL	30	M	LABR	GRAAKH	USA
WILH.	26	F	W	GRAAKH	USA
MINNA	7	F	CHILD	GRAAKH	USA
OTTO	.04	M	INFANT	GRAAKH	USA
STRAUBER, CLARA	26	F	W	WMZZZZ	USA
GEORG	7	M	CHILD	WMZZZZ	USA
WESTPHAL, PAUL	7	M	CHILD	WMZZZZ	USA
STRAUBE, WILH.	26	M	BCHR	WMZZZZ	USA
WILH.	26	F	W	WMZZZZ	USA
CLARA	3	F	CHILD	WMZZZZ	USA
LOUISE	.07	F	INFANT	WMZZZZ	USA
SCHROEDER, CONRAD	45	M	SMH	WMAAXF	USA
REKINGER, JOH.	44	M	LABR	WMAHOU	USA
NOWAKOWSKI, JOH.	23	M	CPTR	GRZZZZ	USA
KINZURA, ANDR.	24	M	LABR	GRZZZZ	USA
RUDZINSKI, BRONISL.	23	M	MLR	GRZZZZ	USA
MERTENS, FERD.	55	M	FARMER	GRAIVQ	USA
SCHALLA, RICHARD	30	M	LABR	GRAILF	USA
FRIEDERIKE	26	F	W	GRAILF	USA
ANNA	.11	F	INFANT	GRAILF	USA
OTTO	.01	M	INFANT	GRAILF	USA
SCHMIDT, HERM.	26	M	LABR	GRAILF	USA

PASSENGER	AGE	SEX	OCCUPATION	PRVL	DES
MASGAY, MARIANNA	27	F	W	GRAIHYUSA	
JOSEFA	2	F	CHILD	GRAIHYUSA	
FISCHEL, CARL	18	M	LABR	GRAIHYUSA	
HAHN, SIM.	17	M	BKR	GRZZZZUSA	
SILGE, CARL	57	M	LABR	GRAFJKUSA	
EDMUND	14	M	LABR	GRAFJKUSA	
WALTHER, EMIL	43	M	MCHT	GRZZZZUSA	
SANCKE, KATH.	55	F	W	GRZZZZUSA	
ANNA	18	F	UNKNOWN	GRZZZZUSA	
ENDERWITZ, RICHARD	32	M	MLR	GRAARZUSA	
HULDA	24	F	W	GRAARZUSA	
ERWIN	3	M	CHILD	GRAARZUSA	
RICHARD	1	M	CHILD	GRAARZUSA	
LANDMANN, CHRIST.	33	M	LABR	BDZZZZUSA	
GRAEBER, MAGD.	19	F	UNKNOWN	BDZZZZUSA	
SCHUERHOFF, GEORG	26	M	CL	BDAAWCUSA	
FRIEDR.	25	M	CL	BDAAWCUSA	
JAKOBI, GEORG	65	M	LABR	GRZZZZUSA	
MAGD.	51	F	W	GRZZZZUSA	
HERM.	20	M	LABR	GRZZZZUSA	
BENNO	17	M	LABR	GRZZZZUSA	
HEINR.	14	M	UNKNOWN	GRZZZZUSA	
GUST.	9	M	CHILD	GRZZZZUSA	
KLEYMANN, LOUISE	61	F	W	GRZZZZUSA	
KAPPENSTEIN, ROB.	26	M	LABR	WMZZZZUSA	
KLINGER, GEORG	23	M	LABR	WMZZZZUSA	
CAROL.	19	F	UNKNOWN	WMZZZZUSA	
BANDORA, MART.	35	M	LABR	GRZZZZUSA	
MROTEK, JOH.	38	M	LABR	GRZZZZUSA	
LASKOWSKI, FRANZ	32	M	LABR	GRZZZZUSA	
NAGEL, MICH.	25	M	TCHR	GRAEOEUSA	
PRINZ, JACOB	44	M	SHMK	GRAAKHUSA	
GRIESCHEN, C.	16	M	UNKNOWN	GRZZZZUSA	
DOHRMANN, ANNA	20	F	UNKNOWN	GRACBRUSA	
RUSCH, MICH.	61	M	FARMER	BVZZZZUSA	
STERN, THOMAS	17	M	FARMER	BVZZZZUSA	
WIEMANN, K.	17	M	FARMER	BVAAQSUSA	
BERGER, MAX	16	M	UNKNOWN	BVACXVUSA	
CHRISTMANN, CATH.	21	F	UNKNOWN	BVZZZZUSA	
HUSSFELD, CONRAD	67	M	FARMER	BVAFNQUSA	
GUENTHER, FR.W.	23	M	MCHT	BVACXVUSA	
TAUFER, LEONH.	31	M	FARMER	BVZZZZUSA	
MAICHELE, WILH.	18	M	FARMER	WMZZZZUSA	
LOESER, CHRIST.FRANGOTH	51	M	FARMER	GRZZZZUSA	
EHBAUER, BARB.	18	F	UNKNOWN	BVZZZZUSA	
JOH.	16	M	UNKNOWN	BVZZZZUSA	
JOH.	15	M	UNKNOWN	BVZZZZUSA	
HEINR.	9	M	CHILD	BVZZZZUSA	
STURMER, DOROTHEA	64	F	UNKNOWN	GRZZZZUSA	
FUCHS, HEINR.	29	M	BRR	BVZZZZUSA	
SANDHERR, BARB.	20	F	UNKNOWN	WMZZZZUSA	
MEISTER, CAROL.	22	F	UNKNOWN	WMAEYJUSA	
JORDAN, JOH.	14	M	UNKNOWN	WMZZZZUSA	
VOLKER, ROSA	37	F	UNKNOWN	WMZZZZUSA	
SENN, EMMA	9	F	CHILD	WMZZZZUSA	
FUCHS, KATH.	22	F	UNKNOWN	WMZZZZUSA	
SUTTER, ALBERT	16	M	UNKNOWN	BVZZZZUSA	
MEYER, JOH.	31	M	LABR	BVZZZZUSA	
BRADL, MARG.	26	F	UNKNOWN	BVZZZZUSA	
KERSTENS, CATH.	14	F	UNKNOWN	BVAFDKUSA	
LERCH, JACOB	15	M	UNKNOWN	BVZZZZUSA	
MARG.	19	F	UNKNOWN	BVZZZZUSA	
WEBER, ANNA	17	F	UNKNOWN	BVADWUUSA	
LOEWE, JULIUS	21	M	LABR	GRZZZZUSA	
BEHRENS, FRAN.A.	28	F	W	GRABIOUSA	
HANS	3	M	CHILD	GRABIOUSA	

SHIP: ST. OF PENNSYLVANIA

FROM: GLASGOW AND LARNE
TO: NEW YORK
ARRIVED: 01 AUGUST 1888

PASSENGER	AGE	SEX	OCCUPATION	PRVL	DES
KIZEMINSKY, JOSEF	26	M	LABR	GRZZZZUSA	
FAUKUSKA, MARIANNE	44	F	W	GRZZZZUSA	
SOFIE	11	F	CH	GRZZZZUSA	

SHIP: WESTERNLAND

FROM: ANTWERP
TO: NEW YORK
ARRIVED: 01 AUGUST 1888

PASSENGER	AGE	SEX	OCCUPATION	PRVL	DES
BECKER, PETER	31	M	FARMER	GRZZZZBED	
THERESA	24	F	UNKNOWN	GRZZZZBED	
STEINTEL, VALENT.	31	M	FARMER	GRZZZZUSA	
TRANTWEIN, MARIE	65	F	UNKNOWN	GRZZZZUSA	
MADER, PAULINE	24	F	UNKNOWN	GRZZZZUSA	
MUHLHEISER, LUDWIG	19	M	FARMER	GRZZZZUSA	
MOLLE, CAROLINE	22	F	UNKNOWN	GRZZZZUSA	
BREMIDY, GRETCHEN	24	F	UNKNOWN	GRZZZZUSA	
STEIN, JULIE	16	F	UNKNOWN	GRZZZZUSA	
RUBING, AUGUSTE	23	M	FARMER	GRZZZZUSA	
KUNZLER, FRIEDR.	30	M	LABR	GRZZZZBO	
WEBER, CARL	41	M	FARMER	GRZZZZSTL	
SCHWER, CONRAD	31	M	SMH	GRZZZZNY	
EDER, CHRISTOPH	58	M	MCHT	GRZZZZNY	
WECKER, MARIA	17	F	UNKNOWN	GRZZZZNY	
GROSS, F.	32	M	CGRMKR	GRZZZZNY	
WISSERT, ADOLF	25	M	UNKNOWN	GRZZZZNY	
VANDERWEELE, ANNA	46	F	UNKNOWN	GRZZZZNY	
RIES, ANNA	41	F	UNKNOWN	GRZZZZPIT	
BRUGGE, AMALIE	24	F	UNKNOWN	GRZZZZRKV	
NEISS, CARL	18	M	FARMER	GRZZZZPHI	
PETER, JOHN	20	M	FARMER	GRZZZZMI	
DESSREE, JEAN	61	M	FARMER	GRZZZZUNK	
MARIE	50	F	F	GRZZZZUNK	
LATVAR, ALEX	11	M	UNKNOWN	GRZZZZUNK	
LOUIS	10	M	CH	GRZZZZUNK	
EDMUND	7	M	CHILD	GRZZZZUNK	
WOLPERT, GG.	23	M	LABR	GRZZZZUNK	
FINK, MARIA	17	F	UNKNOWN	GRZZZZCH	
BRAND, AGATHA	22	F	UNKNOWN	GRZZZZCH	
PETER	17	M	UNKNOWN	GRZZZZCH	
KUECHNER, MARGA	22	F	UNKNOWN	GRZZZZCH	
KRATZ, CATHA.	50	F	UNKNOWN	GRZZZZCH	
DOROTHEA	14	F	UNKNOWN	GRZZZZCH	
HENRIETTE	11	F	UNKNOWN	GRZZZZCH	
U, U	00	M	UNKNOWN	GRZZZZCH	
KURTZ, JOHN	24	M	LABR	GRZZZZCH	
KOCH, CATHA	48	F	UNKNOWN	GRZZZZCH	
WILBA	17	F	UNKNOWN	GRZZZZCH	
MARIE	15	F	UNKNOWN	GRZZZZCH	
ERNESTINE	11	F	UNKNOWN	GRZZZZCH	
WILHELM	10	M	CH	GRZZZZCH	
EMILIE	8	F	CHILD	GRZZZZCH	
BAUER, LOUISE	20	F	UNKNOWN	GRZZZZCH	
SCHMIDT, LEONARD	77	M	FARMER	GRZZZZSTL	
RECKOWSKY, FR.	26	M	FARMER	GRZZZZMIL	
ENNEPEL, FR.	23	M	FARMER	GRZZZZMIL	
KAISER, HCH.	44	M	FARMER	GRZZZZSCR	
MINA	15	F	UNKNOWN	GRZZZZSCR	
VALERIE	10	F	CH	GRZZZZSCR	
CARL	7	M	CHILD	GRZZZZSCR	
HENRIETTE	2	F	CHILD	GRZZZZSCR	
LAUER, AD.	18	M	LABR	GRZZZZKAS	

PASSENGER	AGE	SEX	OCCUPATION	PRVVL	DES	PASSENGER	AGE	SEX	OCCUPATION	PRVVL	DES
BOHREND, ED.	20	M	UNKNOWN	GRZZZZKAS		RORMER, ALOIS	27	M	BBR	GRZZZZNY	
SCHURFF, HELENE	14	F	UNKNOWN	GRZZZZKAS		GAUSBAUER, CHRIST.	17	M	FARMER	GRZZZZNY	
MORTEN, FR.	47	F	UNKNOWN	GRZZZZJON		CHRISTINE	30	F	UNKNOWN	GRZZZZNY	
CHS.	26	M	FARMER	GRZZZJON		STROHMAIER, LOUISE	25	F	UNKNOWN	GRZZZZNY	
LAIBER, DANIEL	33	M	WTR	GRZZZZPHI		SCHURR, MINA	38	F	UNKNOWN	GRZZZZNY	
KOCH, CONRAD	17	M	FARMER	GRZZZZPHI		AUG.	11	F	UNKNOWN	GRZZZZNY	
LEISCH, HUGO	18	M	FARMER	GRZZZZPIT		MINA	9	F	CHILD	GRZZZZNY	
GRASER, ADOLF	44	M	FARMER	GRZZZZNY		MARIE	7	F	CHILD	GRZZZZNY	
WAGNER, ERNEST	18	M	FARMER	GRZZZZNY		CHRISTINE	5	F	CHILD	GRZZZZNY	
KLOS, WENTEL	22	M	FARMER	GRZZZZNY		BURGER, FRIED	53	M	FARMER	GRZZZZNY	
KEISLER, FRIEDR.	21	M	FARMER	GRZZZZNY		EFIGE, CARL	15	M	UNKNOWN	GRZZZZNY	
MERTENS, GUILL.	56	M	CBTMKR	FRZZZZNY		GOMER, CARL	26	M	FARMER	GRZZZZPIT	
CHARLES	45	M	CBTMKR	FRZZZZNY		WILH.	21	F	UNKNOWN	GRZZZZPIT	
GUILLE.	34	M	CBTMKR	FRZZZZNY		CARL	7	M	CHILD	GRZZZZPIT	
ZOLLER, MARIE	22	F	UNKNOWN	GRZZZZNY		MILLER, CAROLINE	23	F	UNKNOWN	GRZZZZCH	
FRELINGSDORF, ADOLF	20	M	FARMER	GRZZZZNY		METZGER, LOUISE	26	F	UNKNOWN	GRZZZZCH	
DUPVIT, CH.	39	M	MECH	GRZZZZNY		HERMANN	4	M	CHILD	GRZZZZCH	
HEGNET, MARIE	25	F	UNKNOWN	GRZZZZNY		BOUMEISLER, GUST.	16	M	UNKNOWN	GRZZZZCH	
MERRMANN, JOHANN	64	M	FARMER	GRZZZZNY		HUAJORST, FR.	47	M	UNKNOWN	GRZZZZSTL	
HENRIETTE	56	F	UNKNOWN	GRZZZZNY		THEZAST, GUIS.	37	M	MCHT	GRZZZZSTL	
ALFRED	18	M	FARMER	GRZZZZNY		LING, JOH.	28	M	UNKNOWN	SRZZZZNY	
U, U	00	U	UNKNOWN	GRZZZZNY		DOLLENBACH, LUD.	26	M	FARMER	SRZZZZNY	
SCHMITZ, AMALIE	19	F	UNKNOWN	GRZZZZNY		HAEGLER, JOH.	26	M	FARMER	SRZZZZNY	
ELESAB.	22	F	UNKNOWN	GRZZZZNY		GRINSCHE, AUG.	19	M	CL	SRZZZZNY	
MARX, LEVI	25	M	CL	GRZZZZNY		UMLKA, VERENA	18	F	UNKNOWN	SRZZZZNY	
FIALOWSKI, ANTON	26	M	LABR	GRZZZZNY		LUGRIM, CONSTANT	47	M	FARMER	SRZZZZNY	
STAUTS, HENRY	22	M	LEDLR	GRZZZZNY		SCHUPBACH, VERONA	42	F	UNKNOWN	SRZZZZNY	
MUCH, H.	22	M	BKR	GRZZZZNY		WALTER	10	M	CH	SRZZZZNY	
MANDELOWITZ, D.	20	M	CL	GRZZZZNY		FRITZ	8	M	CHILD	SRZZZZNY	
SPEARER, HARIS	24	M	LABR	GRZZZZNY		FLEGNER, ANNA	53	F	UNKNOWN	SRZZZZNY	
LEARA	24	F	UNKNOWN	GRZZZZNY		LOUISE	26	F	UNKNOWN	SRZZZZNY	
SCHIEL, JOHN	23	M	LABR	GRZZZZPA		ELISA	27	F	UNKNOWN	SRZZZZNY	
WIRTH, THEOD.	18	M	FARMER	GRZZZZUNK		VILALMA	23	F	UNKNOWN	SRZZZZNY	
HIRSCH, SOPHIE	24	F	UNKNOWN	GRZZZZUNK		AUSTUTZ, ANNA	38	F	UNKNOWN	SRZZZZNY	
SEEL, HEINR.	53	M	CL	GRZZZZUNK		FELDMANN, ANTON	9	M	CHILD	SRZZZZPHI	
CATH.	37	F	UNKNOWN	GRZZZZUNK		SCHARLER, MINA	21	F	UNKNOWN	SRZZZZNY	
ANNA	11	F	UNKNOWN	GRZZZZUNK		U, U	00	U	UNKNOWN	SRZZZZNY	
CATH.	8	F	CHILD	GRZZZZUNK		HURNER, ANNA	25	F	UNKNOWN	SRZZZZNY	
MARIA	4	F	CHILD	GRZZZZUNK		LINA	27	F	UNKNOWN	SRZZZZNY	
ELISAB.	3	F	CHILD	GRZZZZUNK		LUSCHER, JOH.	21	M	FARMER	SRZZZZNY	
POSCHUNG, LEOP.	33	M	FARMER	GRZZZZUNK		VOGT, JAC.	27	M	LABR	SRZZZZNY	
MAGD.	25	F	UNKNOWN	GRZZZZUNK		LUNDEROGGEN, ARNOLD	17	M	LABR	SRZZZZNY	
HORAK, CATH.	30	F	UNKNOWN	GRZZZZUNK		AUG.	23	M	LABR	SRZZZZNY	
FRANZ.	4	M	CHILD	GRZZZZUNK		TROUDLE, MARIA	26	F	UNKNOWN	SRZZZZNY	
SIMON, JOHAN	34	M	TLR	GRZZZZUNK		LUTZ, THEO	37	M	BCHR	SRZZZZNY	
ANNA	33	F	UNKNOWN	GRZZZZUNK		MARIA	40	F	UNKNOWN	SRZZZZNY	
ANNA	3	F	CHILD	GRZZZZUNK		JULIUS	8	M	CHILD	SRZZZZNY	
FRANZ	1	M	CHILD	GRZZZZUNK		JOHANN	4	M	CHILD	SRZZZZNY	
BASTA, JOHANN	49	M	FARMER	GRZZZZNY		AUGUSTE	2	M	CHILD	SRZZZZNY	
MARIE	50	F	UNKNOWN	GRZZZZNY		HIERTZ, ELISE	21	F	UNKNOWN	GRZZZZNY	
MARIE	18	F	UNKNOWN	GRZZZZNY		KUEM--, ANNA	18	F	UNKNOWN	GRZZZZNY	
ELISAB.	16	F	UNKNOWN	GRZZZZNY		PAUMEUTIER, CHS.	25	M	LABR	FRZZZZNY	
ANTONIA	14	F	UNKNOWN	GRZZZZNY		SCHMIDT, CHS.	26	M	LABR	FRZZZZNY	
LERNY, F.J.	25	F	LABR	GRZZZZNY		GEROLD, FRANZ	31	M	LABR	FRZZZZNY	
MISKA, JOS.	31	M	FARMER	GRZZZZNY		LAUCE, MARIE	20	F	UNKNOWN	FRZZZZNY	
BASTER, JOHANN	16	M	UNKNOWN	GRZZZZNY		JUNG, HCH.	23	M	LABR	FRZZZZNY	
BLECHMANN, AB.	25	M	TLR	GRZZZZNY		LEVY, SOLOMON	39	M	LABR	FRZZZZNY	
MEYER, MICHAEL	27	M	TLR	GRZZZZNY		FERRING, MATH.	18	M	FARMER	GRZZZZNY	
SCHNEIDMANN, J.	18	M	SMH	GRZZZZNY		PETCHER, FRANZ	20	M	FARMER	GRZZZZNY	
DAMAR, JOSEF	46	M	LABR	GRZZZZNY		BILL, MICHEL	25	M	FARMER	GRZZZZNY	
WREIDOFF, ADOLF	24	M	LABR	GRZZZZTRA		PTCH, AMALIE	19	F	UNKNOWN	GRZZZZNY	
DRUMEL, GUST.	30	M	LABR	GRZZZZUNK		FENN, JOSEF	21	M	LABR	GRZZZZNY	
U, U	00	U	UNKNOWN	GRZZZZUNK		MELCHIOR, MICH.	67	M	FARMER	GRZZZZNY	
SCHOLEVCKER, G.	30	M	UNKNOWN	GRZZZZUNK		ELISE	65	F	UNKNOWN	GRZZZZNY	
BRADL, HENRITTE	24	F	UNKNOWN	GRZZZZUNK		GUST.	30	M	FARMER	GRZZZZNY	
BLOCH, MATHILDE	14	F	UNKNOWN	GRZZZZNY		JUNG, JOHANN	30	M	FARMER	GRZZZZNY	
STICHER, CAROLINA	20	F	UNKNOWN	GRZZZZNY		HOFFMANN, WM.	18	M	FARMER	GRZZZZNY	
KLING, WILH.	17	F	UNKNOWN	GRZZZZLOU		EISENKOFF, WM.	26	M	LABR	GRZZZZNY	
HOBIL, PHILI.	25	M	FARMER	GRZZZZNY		FLEISCHMANN, MARGA.	22	F	UNKNOWN	GRZZZZNY	
DICK, JACOB	21	M	FARMER	GRZZZZNY		BACKER, ANNA	22	F	UNKNOWN	GRZZZZNY	
MAY, CATH.	33	F	UNKNOWN	GRZZZZNY		SEIKIL, EMIL	34	M	CBTMKR	GRZZZZNY	
FRIED.	4	M	CHILD	GRZZZZNY		KNOFF, JOHANN	56	M	FARMER	GRZZZZNY	
LEICHE	3	F	CHILD	GRZZZZNY		CATHA	35	F	UNKNOWN	GRZZZZNY	
RICH.	1	M	CHILD	GRZZZZNY		GOTTL.	19	M	UNKNOWN	GRZZZZNY	
RUFFERTHAL, MINA	00	F	UNKNOWN	GRZZZZNY		CAROL.	17	F	UNKNOWN	GRZZZZNY	

PASSENGER	AGE	SEX	OCCUPATION	PRV	VIL	DES
MARIE	12	F	UNKNOWN	GRZZZZNY		
FRITZ, CH.	25	F	UNKNOWN	GRZZZZNY		
REISS, WM.	42	M	UNKNOWN	GRZZZZNY		
BARTENHEUER, WM.	24	M	UNKNOWN	GRZZZZNY		
JOH.	19	F	UNKNOWN	GRZZZZNY		
WEHRHEIMER, VERONIKA	19	F	UNKNOWN	GRZZZZNY		
KRAUS, MARIA	24	F	UNKNOWN	GRZZZZNY		
AMANN, CHARLOTTE	18	F	UNKNOWN	GRZZZZNY		
GAUCH, CHARLOTTE	43	F	UNKNOWN	GRZZZZNY		
JACOB	15	M	UNKNOWN	GRZZZZNY		
ELISE	11	F	UNKNOWN	GRZZZZNY		
MARGA.	10	F	CH	GRZZZZNY		
PFOFF, JOHANN	17	M	FARMER	GRZZZZNY		
WEIZNER, LISETTE	37	F	UNKNOWN	GRZZZZNY		
LOUISE	25	F	UNKNOWN	GRZZZZNY		
ROSSLER, LOUISE	31	F	UNKNOWN	GRZZZZNY		
STERPEL, FR.	16	F	UNKNOWN	GRZZZZNY		
BRUGGEMAN, ERNST	33	M	LABR	GRZZZZNY		
VOGEL, JOH.	22	M	LABR	GRZZZZNY		
BERGER, JULIUS	37	M	LABR	GRZZZZNY		
KROBS, DOMINICO	44	M	LABR	GRZZZZPIT		
WILHME.	24	F	UNKNOWN	GRZZZZPIT		
RILLBURGER, PET.	26	M	LABR	GRZZZZALT		
BOUDOUX, CARL	17	M	UNKNOWN	GRZZZZUNK		
MEISCHEID, MATH.	22	M	FARMER	GRZZZZNY		
ROEDER, JOHANN	16	M	UNKNOWN	GRZZZZNY		
EISENBEIN, PET.	62	M	UNKNOWN	GRZZZZNY		
BUR, EUGENE	34	F	UNKNOWN	GRZZZZBUF		
ALFRED	5	M	CHILD	GRZZZZBUF		
EWALD	3	M	CHILD	GRZZZZBUF		
LOUISE	1	F	CHILD	GRZZZZBUF		
BURGENHEIMER, MARIA	16	F	UNKNOWN	GRZZZZNY		
THOROT, FRANZ	52	M	FARMER	GRZZZZNY		
KUTZMACHER, HEINR.	44	M	FARMER	GRZZZZNY		
ELISAB.	44	F	UNKNOWN	GRZZZZNY		
CHRISTINA	20	F	UNKNOWN	GRZZZZNY		
ELISAB.	15	F	UNKNOWN	GRZZZZNY		
JACOB	12	M	UNKNOWN	GRZZZZNY		
HEINRICH	4	M	CHILD	GRZZZZNY		
MULLER, JACOB	24	M	FARMER	GRZZZZNY		
LANG, CATHA.	23	F	UNKNOWN	GRZZZZNY		
PHILIPP, CARL	17	M	FARMER	GRZZZZNY		
RIES, JACOB	24	M	FARMER	GRZZZZNY		
ZIMMERMANN, JOH.	28	M	UNKNOWN	GRZZZZNY		
FASSBENDER, HCH.	26	M	UNKNOWN	GRZZZZNY		
MEIKLE, JOH.	23	M	UNKNOWN	GRZZZZNY		
WEIDINGER, MICH.	22	M	UNKNOWN	GRZZZZSTL		
BURKHARD, LEON.	21	M	UNKNOWN	GRZZZZNY		
NAGEL, FR.	16	M	UNKNOWN	GRZZZZNY		
BEISLER, PETER	33	M	UNKNOWN	GRZZZZNY		
GILIN, EUGEN	17	M	FARMER	GRZZZZNY		
WEBER, ENGEL	21	M	FARMER	GRZZZZNY		
FUCHS, JOH.	25	M	UNKNOWN	GRZZZZNY		
JUNG, PHILIPP.	35	M	UNKNOWN	GRZZZZNY		
HERZL, JOHN	00	M	UNKNOWN	GRZZZZKAS		
GOEBEL, LINA	23	F	UNKNOWN	GRZZZZNY		
HERTEL, MAGD.	24	F	UNKNOWN	GRZZZZNY		
LUDWIG, CARL	24	M	LABR	GRZZZZNY		
REISS, PETER	26	M	LABR	GRZZZZNY		
HOFFMANN, OTTO	20	M	LABR	GRZZZZNY		
LANG, JOH.	19	M	LABR	GRZZZZNY		
LEINENDECKER, JOS.	17	M	LABR	GRZZZZNY		
BOSZEN, PETER	21	F	UNKNOWN	GRZZZZNAS		
SCHMITZ, F.	26	M	UNKNOWN	GRZZZZCLE		
PETER	21	M	UNKNOWN	GRZZZZCLE		
GERLACK, MARIE	60	F	UNKNOWN	GRZZZZCLE		
KLERBER, CARL	17	M	CL	GRZZZZCLE		
MORLANZ, PHILIPP.	31	M	SMH	GRZZZZCLE		
GOUKEL, HER.	25	M	MECH	GRZZZZCH		
SCHWARZKOFF, MARIA	17	M	UNKNOWN	GRZZZZNY		
REUM, ANTON	32	M	FARMER	GRZZZZNY		
JOSEFINE	32	F	UNKNOWN	GRZZZZNY		
ANNA	2	F	CHILD	GRZZZZNY		
ENDRES, MATH.	19	M	CBTMKR	GRZZZZCH		
NOTHDORFF, ROSLE	31	F	UNKNOWN	GRZZZZNY		
WEBER, GEORG	28	M	FARMER	GRZZZZNY		
CATHA.	24	F	UNKNOWN	GRZZZZNY		
PHILIMON	29	M	FARMER	GRZZZZNY		
VOGELMANN, CARL	26	M	LABR	GRZZZZLRT		
LIFFOTH, WM.	26	M	LABR	GRZZZZNY		
ROCHWEILER, JOH.	58	M	FARMER	GRZZZZCLF		
W.	25	M	FARMER	GRZZZZCLF		
SEUFT, M.	40	M	FARMER	GRZZZZCH		
THUNGER, FRZ.	25	M	FARMER	GRZZZZCH		
KELLER, GG.	27	M	FARMER	GRZZZZNY		
JOSEF	25	M	FARMER	GRZZZZNY		
MAIER, LUDWIG	22	M	SMH	GRZZZZBUF		
BOHRINGER, JOS.	23	M	FARMER	GRZZZZUNK		
SORENSEN, F.	32	M	LABR	GRZZZZCH		
ASLAG	30	M	UNKNOWN	GRZZZZCH		
ADAMS, MATHEU	23	M	FARMER	GRZZZZCH		
JOEKEN, HERMAN	22	M	LABR	GRZZZZCH		
MEIKES, ANTON	15	M	FARMER	GRZZZZCLE		
BUDDE, ANNA	22	F	UNKNOWN	GRZZZZCLE		
HCH.	4	M	CHILD	GRZZZZCLE		
WERNER	2	M	CHILD	GRZZZZCLE		
WILH.	1	M	CHILD	GRZZZZCLE		
FERRING, JOH.	48	M	FARMER	GRZZZZCLE		
MARG.	46	F	UNKNOWN	GRZZZZCLE		
U	00	F	UNKNOWN	GRZZZZCLE		
MARIE	3	F	CHILD	GRZZZZCLE		
CATH.	1	F	CHILD	GRZZZZCLE		
WURZ, PETER	45	M	SMH	GRZZZZCLE		
WIDERCORN, MARIE	14	F	UNKNOWN	GRZZZZCLE		
ISAAC	11	M	UNKNOWN	GRZZZZCLE		
HABERTY, JOHANN	32	M	FARMER	GRZZZZCLE		
UNGCHENER, FRITZ	18	M	BSKM	GRZZZZCLE		
GELHAUSEN, CATH.	24	F	UNKNOWN	GRZZZZCLE		
MEYER, ANNA	28	F	UNKNOWN	GRZZZZCLE		
BUCHLEIT, PETER	32	M	MNR	GRZZZZCLE		
GOBUL, LUD.	39	M	FARMER	GRZZZZALL		
SOPHIE	32	F	UNKNOWN	GRZZZZALL		
CAROLINE	7	F	CHILD	GRZZZZALL		
PHIL.	5	M	CHILD	GRZZZZALL		
LUDWIG	3	M	CHILD	GRZZZZALL		
ERNST	1	M	CHILD	GRZZZZALL		
BRAU, LEON	50	M	FARMER	GRZZZZUNK		
SCHULLE, GERARD	21	M	CL	GRZZZZUNK		
FORK, JEAN	27	M	CL	GRZZZZUNK		
BRUCK, MARIE	19	F	UNKNOWN	GRZZZZPIT		
SCHMELZER, PETER	19	M	LABR	GRZZZZPOT		
JOEGER, MICH.	27	M	CPTR	GRZZZZNY		
GRUTH, JACOB	25	M	LABR	GRZZZZNY		
LEINER, CATH.	22	F	UNKNOWN	GRZZZZNY		
WERLE, LOUISE	45	F	UNKNOWN	GRZZZZFTP		
BRAM, MARIE	36	F	UNKNOWN	GRZZZZNY		
WERLE, CROL.	19	F	UNKNOWN	GRZZZZFTP		
CATHA.	18	F	UNKNOWN	GRZZZZFTP		
JACOB	16	M	UNKNOWN	GRZZZZFTP		
LOUISE	22	F	UNKNOWN	GRZZZZFTP		
MULLER, JOHANNA	23	M	UNKNOWN	GRZZZZFTP		
BECKMANN, ELISAB.	17	F	UNKNOWN	GRZZZZFTP		
HEY, JACOB	28	M	FARMER	GRZZZZFTP		
DEPOSER, PETRUS	29	M	FARMER	GRZZZZPAT		
BECKMANN, H.	20	M	FARMER	GRZZZZCIN		
ENGELHARDT, BERTHA	28	F	UNKNOWN	GRZZZZNY		
ULRICH, ANNA	48	F	UNKNOWN	GRZZZZNY		
CLARA	18	F	UNKNOWN	GRZZZZNY		
HERMANN	11	M	UNKNOWN	GRZZZZNY		
LOUIS	8	M	CHILD	GRZZZZNY		
SEUSS, CATHA.	35	F	UNKNOWN	GRZZZZNY		
EMMA	11	F	UNKNOWN	GRZZZZNY		
WEILER, CATHA.	11	F	UNKNOWN	GRZZZZNY		
SEUFT, CATHA.	10	F	CH	GRZZZZNY		
ROSALIE	7	F	CHILD	GRZZZZNY		
FRANZ	4	M	CHILD	GRZZZZNY		
REBMANGER, JOH.	30	M	FARMER	GRZZZZNY		
TILLMANN, WILH.	35	M	UNKNOWN	GRZZZZNY		
CHRISTINE	34	F	UNKNOWN	GRZZZZNY		
WILH.	10	M	CH	GRZZZZNY		

PASSENGER	AGE	SEX	OCCUPATION	PRVL	DES
EMMA	7	F	CHILD	GRZZZZNY
LINA	6	F	CHILD	GRZZZZNY
CARL	2	M	CHILD	GRZZZZNY
EMIL	1	M	CHILD	GRZZZZNY
KAISER, ROSINE	32	F	UNKNOWN	GRZZZZNY
JACOB	16	M	UNKNOWN	GRZZZZNY
HENRI	4	M	CHILD	GRZZZZNY
STEIN, JOSEF	25	M	UNKNOWN	GRZZZZNY
BRAUDNER, HCH.	32	M	FARMER	GRZZZZNY
ELISAB.	26	F	UNKNOWN	GRZZZZNY
ANNA	3	F	CHILD	GRZZZZNY
KUMP, JOHA.	37	F	UNKNOWN	GRZZZZNY
JULIA	20	F	UNKNOWN	GRZZZZNY
DORMANN, W.	45	M	LABR	GRZZZZNY
SCHMIDT, CARL	35	M	CL	GRZZZZNY
TANGEMAN, B.	45	M	UNKNOWN	GRZZZZNY
HOLNIG, P.	40	M	MCHT	GRZZZZNY
OICH. H.	45	M	UNKNOWN	GRZZZZNY
RUCKSTUHL, F.	40	M	MCHT	GRZZZZNY
BURGDORF, H.	40	M	UNKNOWN	GRZZZZNY
BOEDEL, P.	28	M	UNKNOWN	GRZZZZNY
HISKUS, W.	48	M	UNKNOWN	GRZZZZNY
L.	45	F	UNKNOWN	GRZZZZNY
L.	20	F	UNKNOWN	GRZZZZNY
W.	17	M	UNKNOWN	GRZZZZNY
A.	14	F	UNKNOWN	GRZZZZNY
SCHULZ, H.	40	M	MCHT	GRZZZZNY
HYRONNUS, J.	42	F	UNKNOWN	GRZZZZNY
PAULUCCE, F.	41	F	UNKNOWN	GRZZZZNY
A.	50	M	UNKNOWN	GRZZZZNY
U	48	F	UNKNOWN	GRZZZZNY
U	28	F	UNKNOWN	GRZZZZNY
FU---, A.	25	M	UNKNOWN	GRZZZZNY
BUCHMANN, G.	28	M	UNKNOWN	GRZZZZNY
BIGLER, U	50	M	UNKNOWN	GRZZZZNY
J.	26	M	UNKNOWN	GRZZZZNY
C.	20	F	UNKNOWN	GRZZZZNY
E.	17	M	UNKNOWN	GRZZZZNY
F.	15	M	UNKNOWN	GRZZZZNY
G.	12	M	UNKNOWN	GRZZZZNY
SUSCHWUEDER, A.	28	F	UNKNOWN	GRZZZZNY
J.	20	M	UNKNOWN	GRZZZZNY
U, MARGARETHA	35	F	RE	GRZZZZNY
MAXMILLIAN	30	F	RE	GRZZZZNY
BRAUN, C.	26	F	UNKNOWN	GRZZZZNY
WILD, J.	25	F	UNKNOWN	GRZZZZNY
KOHLER, L.	30	M	MCHT	GRZZZZNY
KLEMER, W.	35	M	MCHT	GRZZZZNY
U	32	F	UNKNOWN	GRZZZZNY
LACCORN, P.	28	M	MECH	GRZZZZNY
EPP, A.	26	M	MECH	GRZZZZNY
GLIWZ, G.	30	M	UNKNOWN	GRZZZZNY
L.	25	F	UNKNOWN	GRZZZZNY
DECHERT, W.	28	M	MCHT	GRZZZZNY
KRINGS, W.	25	F	UNKNOWN	GRZZZZNY
BAYHOUSER, W.	45	M	UNKNOWN	GRZZZZNY
U	45	F	UNKNOWN	GRZZZZNY
ROYON, M.	25	F	UNKNOWN	GRZZZZNY
ROGAN, C.	25	F	UNKNOWN	GRZZZZNY
HENRY, F.	45	M	UNKNOWN	GRZZZZNY
BAER, H.	28	F	UNKNOWN	GRZZZZNY
METZGER, B.	23	F	UNKNOWN	GRZZZZNY
EWIG. C.	20	F	UNKNOWN	GRZZZZNY
F.	17	F	UNKNOWN	GRZZZZNY
VANSENTENDOLL, O.	40	M	MCHT	GRZZZZNY
U	41	F	UNKNOWN	GRZZZZNY
A.	17	M	UNKNOWN	GRZZZZNY
A.	15	M	UNKNOWN	GRZZZZNY
RUCKSTUHL, F.	18	M	UNKNOWN	GRZZZZNY
MERTOK, J.	42	M	UNKNOWN	GRZZZZNY
MICHEL, N.	45	M	UNKNOWN	GRZZZZNY
ZERNS, L.	25	F	UNKNOWN	GRZZZZNY
G.	17	M	UNKNOWN	GRZZZZNY
CAUDRIC, B.	30	F	UNKNOWN	GRZZZZNY
JAMBON, A.	26	F	UNKNOWN	FRZZZZNY

PASSENGER	AGE	SEX	OCCUPATION	PRVL	DES
M.	22	F	UNKNOWN	FRZZZZNY
CONROUNEAN, U	20	F	UNKNOWN	GRZZZZNY

SHIP: LAHN

FROM: BREMEN AND SOUTHAMPTON
TO: NEW YORK
ARRIVED: 03 AUGUST 1888

PASSENGER	AGE	SEX	OCCUPATION	PRVL	DES
ULLMANN, MOSES	42	M	TT	GRZZZZGR
ADLER, M.	28	M	TT	GRAAKHGR
KOHL, DAVID	16	M	TT	GRZZZZGR
BECKER, HERM.	23	M	TT	GRAEDPGR
REIFENSTUHL, OTTO	35	M	TT	GRAJHSGR
HAHN, WILHELM	58	M	TT	GRAJHSUNK
GRAEF, WILLIAM	40	M	TT	GRABZVUNK
KINDT, HERMANN	23	M	TT	GRABZVUNK
LEININGER, ABRAHAM	11	M	CH	GRADHWUNK
MANN, FRIEDR.	13	M	CH	GRABQVUNK
HORNSTEINER, HERM.	31	M	CH	GRAAKHUNK
GUGGENHEIM, JOSEPH	23	M	CH	GRZZZZUNK
WEIL, GUSTAV	16	M	CH	GRZZZZUNK
ULLMANN, SOPHIE	17	F	NN	GRZZZZUNK
MUELLER, JULIE	29	F	NN	GRZZZZUNK
MARIE	17	F	NN	GRZZZZUNK
DOERR, MAGDE.	17	F	NN	GRAARRUNK
SCHAEFFLER, MINNA	29	F	NN	GRAAHLUNK
LEVY, PAULINE	24	F	NN	GRAAHLUNK
POHL, AUGUST	30	M	TT	GRZZZZUNK
VOLKE, JOHANN	26	M	TT	GRZZZZUNK
KOENIG, OTTO	22	M	TT	GRADGOCH
FALK, DAVID	19	M	TT	GRADLDCH
SAMUEL, M.	31	M	TT	GRADLOCH
JOHANNA	55	F	W	GRADLOCH
ROSA	19	F	NN	GRADLOCH
JETTCHEN	11	F	CH	GRADLOCH
BOHLENS, WILHELM	45	M	TT	GRAARRCH
EBERHARDT, LEONHARDT	25	M	TT	GRZZZZCH
SMITH, EDWARD	40	M	TT	GRZZZZCH
HENRY	30	M	TT	GRZZZZCH
PHILLIPS, H.F.	32	M	TT	GRZZZZUNK
SICHERER, SIEGMUND	29	M	TT	GRAEXWUNK
WENDERLEIN, MARGA.	21	F	NN	GRZZZZUNK
MENK, LOUISE	28	F	NN	GRAAXFUNK
AHLERS, AUGUSTE	8	F	CHILD	GRAAXFUNK
SCHMIDT, AUGUSTE	25	F	NN	GRABOQUNK
GREUBLER, ELISE	20	F	NN	GRZZZZUNK
HAHN, LEOPOLD	24	M	TT	GRAARRUNK
HOEFT, MAX	36	M	MCHT	GRAAQYUNK
FICKEWIRTH, CARL	40	M	MCHT	GRAAQYUNK
HERBERTS, ALFRED	18	M	CL	GRAAHLUNK
BERRENBER, MARIA	21	F	NN	GRZZZZUNK
BOEHMKE, CLAUS	41	M	TT	GRZZZZUNK
BETTY	38	F	W	GRZZZZUNK
BRAUN, MARIE	30	F	W	GRAADEUSA
HANS	2	M	CHILD	GRAADEUSA
PARTHEYMUELLER, FRIEDR.	20	M	LABR	GRAAXYUSA
MOESTLE, BERNHD.	16	F	NN	GRABHUUSA
HEYER, HETTY	18	F	NN	GRZZZZUSA
LUSTIG, JACOB	20	M	FARMER	GRADITUSA
WELLHOEFER, MICHAEL	18	M	FARMER	GRZZZZUSA
NORDBROCK, LINE	44	F	NN	GRAAUPUSA
WOLTMANN, WILH.	28	M	LABR	GRZZZZUSA
JORDT, JACOB	23	M	LABR	GRAAYKUSA
MARSCHHAUSEN, AUGUSTE	26	F	NN	GRAAXFUSA
BERTHA	20	F	NN	GRAAXFUSA
SCHOELL, CATHA.	18	F	NN	GRABLVUSA
HAMMEL, MARIE	55	F	W	GRABLVUSA
EMIL	15	M	NN	GRABLVUSA
LOERSCH, EMILIE	16	F	NN	GRAEXWUSA

PASSENGER	AGE	SEX	OCCUPATION	PRVL	DES
HAAKER, AUGUSTE	26	F	NN		GRADMVUSA
THIEMANN, BERNHD.	63	M	FARMER		GRZZZZUSA
BERNHD.	26	M	FARMER		GRZZZZUSA
ANNA	21	F	NN		GRZZZZUSA
GERHARD	18	M	FARMER		GRZZZZUSA
FRANZ	16	M	NN		GRZZZZUSA
JOSEF	10	M	CH		GRAAXYUSA
JACOBI, LEOPOLD	57	M	MLR		GRABPNUSA
ERNESTE.	44	F	W		GRABPNUSA
BERTHA	20	F	NN		GRABPNUSA
JULIUS	14	M	NN		GRABPNUSA
RUDOLF	11	M	CH		GRABPNUSA
OLGA	9	F	CHILD		GRABPNUSA
AUGUSTE	6	F	CHILD		GRABPNUSA
WIDMANN, CARL	16	M	NN		GRZZZZUSA
SCHIEFER, SOPFIE	20	F	NN		GRZZZZUSA
HELLER, MARIE	28	F	NN		GRABEFUSA
ELISAB.	22	F	NN		GRABEFUSA
MALKUS, AUGUST	18	M	LABR		GRAJDMUSA
WELLER, LOUISE	22	F	NN		GRAJDMUSA
RUPP, CAROLE.	19	F	NN		GRAJDMUSA
KAEMPFER, WILHELM	14	M	NN		GRAEXCUSA
GUTBROD, ELISE	21	F	NN		GRAFRGUSA
ROMBACH, MARIA	21	F	NN		GRZZZZUSA
GUTMANN, BONIFAZ	30	M	SHMK		GRZZZZUSA
SCHMIDT, ANNA	18	F	NN		GRABOQUSA
KAMERER, CATHA.	16	F	NN		GRZZZZUSA
LEMP, CHRISTE.	21	F	NN		GRZZZZUSA
MEYER, MAGDE.	38	F	W		GRAAFXUSA
MAX	11	M	CH		GRAAFXUSA
BRENDLE, MARIA	31	F	W		GRACPSUSA
ELISABETH	11	F	CH		GRACPSUSA
SCHINDELBECK, JOSEF	26	M	FARMER		GRZZZZUSA
MATHE.	23	F	NN		GRZZZZUSA
JOST, MICHAEL	11	M	CH		GRABLGUSA
MEIER, SEBASTIAN	10	M	CH		GRAAFXUSA
GIERKING, HEINR.	26	M	CL		GRADIJUSA
BODENSOHN, AMALIE	17	F	NN		GRABOQUSA
AHLBRAND, MATHILDE	19	F	NN		GRADUXUSA
HEINZERLING, LOUISE	20	F	NN		GRAALWUSA
EDUARD, ROTH	25	M	BRR		GRZZZZUSA
RUPPE, HEINRICH	17	M	LABR		GRZZZZUSA
HUEBNER, MARGE.	22	F	NN		GRZZZZUSA
ESCHENBACH, MARIE	24	F	NN		GRZZZZUSA
MOEHRING, ANNA	11	F	CH		GRZZZZUSA
JUNG, JOHANN	29	M	FARMER		GRAAQZUSA
SCHMIDT, AUG.	45	M	FARMER		GRZZZZUSA
BETZ, ANNA	35	F	W		GRZZZZUSA
CARL	10	M	CH		GRZZZZUSA
WILHELM	9	M	CHILD		GRZZZZUSA
GOTTLIEB	7	M	CHILD		GRZZZZUSA
HEINR.	4	M	CHILD		GRZZZZUSA
FRIEDR.	2	M	CHILD		GRZZZZUSA
JOHANNES	.01	M	INFANT		GRZZZZUSA
NABEL, ADOLF	22	M	BKR		GRZZZZUSA
WANNINGER, PETER	27	M	LABR		GRADLDUSA
GENTI	4	F	CHILD		GRADLDUSA
MUELLER, HELENE	28	F	NN		GRZZZZUSA
SCHNERZINGER, LAURA	19	F	NN		GRZZZZUSA
SPRINGER, MINNA	19	F	NN		GRZZZZUSA
PFITZER, WILHELMINE	19	F	NN		GRZZZZUSA
SEITER, KATHA.	18	F	NN		GRAHKHUSA
CECH, PAULA.	30	F	NN		GRZZZZUSA
TOBI, THEODOR	29	M	LABR		GRABXPUSA
WEHNER, AMBROS	32	M	LABR		GRABSHUSA
KOENIG, CLARA	16	F	NN		GRACMHUSA
EMILIE	20	F	NN		GRACMHUSA
HAHN, FRANZ	22	M	LABR		GRZZZZUSA
KROSHA, CARL	28	M	LABR		GRZZZZUSA
MEYER, PAULINE	60	F	NN		GRAAKHUSA
GUTKIND, LOUIS	25	M	MCHT		GRAAKHUSA
MAAR, KUNIGUNDE	18	F	NN		GRZZZZUSA
KOCH, LOUISE	56	F	W		GRABDEUSA
BISCHOF, FRIEDR.	27	M	LABR		GRABDEUSA
MAUER, JACOB	27	M	LABR		GRABDEUSA
BRAUN, JACOB	26	M	FARMER		GRZZZZUSA
URSULA	25	F	W		GRABGIUSA
MICHAEL	17	M	FARMER		GRABGIUSA
SPRENG, LUDWIG	22	M	FARMER		GRZZZZUSA
LOHDE, AGNES	26	F	NN		GRZZZZUSA
SCHMIDT, JAKOB	18	M	PRNTR		GRAKVWUSA
KRAFT, JOHANN	28	M	SMH		GRAKVWUSA
MARGE.	36	F	W		GRAKVWUSA
KATHE.	3	F	CHILD		GRAKVWUSA
HEINRICH	.01	M	INFANT		GRAKVWUSA
REININGER, PETER	27	M	LABR		GRACRAUSA
WAGNER, JOH.	26	M	FARMER		GRACRAUSA
LOHMUELLER, ELISAB.	27	F	NN		GRACRAUSA
BERNETT, THEODOR	14	M	NN		GRAARRUSA
WASOWICZ, VERONIKA	29	F	W		GRZZZZUSA
STANISLAUS	.03	M	INFANT		GRZZZZUSA
WACOWICZ, DOMINIK	29	M	SDLR		GRZZZZUSA
RETTIG, RICHARD	19	M	LABR		GRAAKHUSA
BACHMANN, FRIEDR.	19	M	LABR		GRZZZZUSA
KUEHN, CARL	22	M	LABR		GRACARUSA
HOFMANN, EDUARD	23	M	LKSH		GRZZZZUSA
SCHILLING, JACOB	22	M	FARMER		GRACQOUSA
MERK, HERMANN	25	M	LABR		GRAFRPUSA
THEILMANN, CARL	14	M	NN		GRZZZZUSA
LOUISE	16	F	NN		GRZZZZUSA
SATTLER, NICOLAUS	23	M	LABR		GRZZZZUSA
CLEMEN, FRIEDR.	26	M	LABR		GRADEMUSA
HARTUNG, ELISABETH	19	F	NN		GRADEMUSA
GREBE, ANTON	48	M	GDNR		GRZZZZUSA
BIERE, WILHELMINE	20	F	NN		GRZZZZUSA
BUSCHING, WILHELM	25	M	FARMER		GRACXEUSA
HAESEMEIER, FRIEDR.	16	M	NN		GRACXEUSA
DEFFNER, SOPHIE	22	F	NN		GRAHAMUSA
DUX, HENRIETTE	37	F	NN		GRAHWIUSA
MINNA	11	F	CH		GRAHWIUSA
KREIKEL, AUGUSTE	25	F	CH		GRAAHLUSA
HENRIETTE	28	F	CH		GRAAHLUSA
SUPPUS, WILHELM	14	M	FARMER		GRADOIUSA
HIRSCH, DAVID	16	M	FARMER		GRZZZZUSA
PFARRER, RICHARD	14	M	NN		GRALWNUSA
STROHM, CHRIST.	24	M	SHMK		GRZZZZUSA
LEICHTENTRITT, PHILIPP	31	M	LABR		GRZZZZUSA
RUTISCHHAUSER, ROSINE	23	F	NN		GRADNPUSA
ZAPF, BARBARA	26	F	NN		GRAJZKUSA
HEINR.	24	M	MCHT		GRAJZKUSA
LEIPERT, LINA	19	F	NN		GRAITWUSA
BOETTCHER, CHRIST.	37	M	CPTR		GRZZZZUSA
THOMA, SUSANNA	48	F	W		GRAFLMUSA
JOHANN	9	M	CHILD		GRAFLMUSA
SAUER, MARIE	11	F	CH		GRAFLMUSA
OSWALD, ALBERT	24	M	LABR		GRAFLMUSA
OTT, MARGE.	23	F	NN		GRAFLMUSA
GROHE, FLORENTIN	27	M	LABR		GRZZZZUSA
HASENKAMP, DORETTE	29	F	W		GRZZZZUSA
MARIE	.09	F	INFANT		GRZZZZUSA
KLEMM, OTTO	32	M	FARMER		GRACGKUSA
SCHROEDER, HEINRICH	16	M	NN		GRZZZZUSA
WILHELM	14	M	NN		GRZZZZUSA
MEYER, WILHELM	15	M	NN		GRACJIUSA
CATTNER, SETTCHEN	15	F	NN		GRAFHAUSA
BLUMENFELD, JACOB	16	M	NN		GRZZZZUSA
GOLDSCHMIDT, A.	15	M	NN		GRACQKUSA
WEHNER, CLEMENTNE.	42	F	W		GRZZZZUSA
MARIE	11	F	CH		GRAFRIUSA
KLUEBER, KATHE.	6	F	CHILD		GRAFRIUSA
WEHNER, CARL	2	M	CHILD		GRAFRIUSA
JOHANN	.03	M	INFANT		GRAFRIUSA
WINTER, ADOLF	17	M	WCHMKR		GRADLRUSA
MONACI, MICHEL	30	M	LABR		GRZZZZUSA
SILVETTER, GRAZIOSA	26	F	W		GRZZZZUSA
GIO	21	M	LABR		GRZZZZUSA
MARCUS	23	M	LABR		GRZZZZUSA
WATSON, JOHANN	28	M	FARMER		GRAFDWUSA
HORSTMANN, ED.	25	M	FARMER		GRABWOUSA
BERTHA	27	F	W		GRABWOUSA

PASSENGER	AGE	SEX	OCCUPATION	PRVL	DES
MORENZ, MARIE	18	M	LABR		GRABWOUSA
WAETJEN, SOPHIE	18	F	NN		GRZZZZUSA
GRUENER, DOROTHEA	16	F	NN		GRAFRGUSA
MUELLER, KILIAN	25	M	LABR		GRAFRGUSA
HEROLD, EVA	17	F	NN		GRAAFCUSA
LOEFFLER, MARIA	22	F	NN		GRAAFCUSA
NEUHAUS, CATHA.	24	F	NN		GRAAAXUSA
KAUFHOLD, AUGUST	19	M	LABR		GRAARRUSA
KNIGGE, HEINRICH	18	M	TLR		GRAARRUSA
TABABEN, OTTO	36	M	FARMER		GRAADEUSA
MATHILDE	32	F	W		GRAADEUSA
PAULI, HERMANN	16	M	BCHR		GRACYYUSA
STEIDLE, FRIEDRICH	22	M	LABR		GRZZZZUSA
WEISS, GEORG	24	M	LABR		GRZZZZUSA
PAGENDARM, JOHANN	23	M	LABR		GRAARRUSA
KNIUEPPEL, JOHANN	37	M	LABR		GRAARRUSA
ABRAHAM, SARA	22	F	NN		GRAAEYUSA
DIERCKS, ANNA	14	F	NN		GRAECFUSA
WICHMANN, HEINR.	14	M	NN		GRAJXMUSA
SCHMIDT, ELISABETH	18	F	NN		GRAJXMUSA
BOEGER, MARIE	20	F	NN		GRAJXMUSA
BRINCKMANN, MARIE	23	F	NN		GRAJXMUSA
SANDER, MARIE	15	F	NN		GRAJXMUSA
GFEORG, CATHE.	18	F	NN		GRAJXMUSA
WINTER, LOUISE	24	F	NN		GRZZZZUSA
LOUISE	24	F	NN		GRACBRUSA
HANEKE, ELISE	18	F	NN		GRACBRUSA
SANDER, MINNA	20	F	NN		GRAJXMUSA
HENNINGER, ANNA	22	F	NN		GRZZZZUSA
KOZYROWSKI, RICHD.	23	M	LABR		GRZZZZUSA
SCHWARZ, JAKOB	17	M	LABR		GRZZZZUSA
ARTNET, JOHANN	29	M	LABR		GRAAIFUSA
BLUMENFELD, MARCUS	16	M	DLR		GRZZZZUSA
MYSEGADES, HEINR.	22	M	SLR		GRACXHUSA
ABRAHAM, JAKOB	26	M	MCHT		GRACUXUSA

SHIP: CELTIC

FROM: LIVERPOOL AND QUEENSTOWN
TO: NEW YORK
ARRIVED: 04 AUGUST 1888

PASSENGER	AGE	SEX	OCCUPATION	PRVL	DES
GABLONSKI, JOHADYR.	18	M	LABR		GRACBFUSA
STIPLEFSHAN, ROSALIER	19	M	LABR		GRACBFUSA
FORKMESON, KAREN	24	F	SVNT		GRACBFUSA
SCHUERTZ, NATIZA	18	F	SVNT		GRACBFUSA
GLOSOFREND, CHANE	16	F	SVNT		GRACBFUSA
BERKOWITZ, SCHENIDEL	45	M	LABR		GRACBFUSA
SARAH	20	F	SVNT		GRACBFUSA
NORVUSKY, LEON	25	M	LABR		GRACBFUSA
CHACKEL	15	M	LABR		GRACBFUSA
KUPFERSCHMID, LUDVIG	32	M	LABR		GRACBFUSA
CHUR, JACOB	23	M	LABR		GRACBFUSA
CALLMAN, SARAH	22	F	SVNT		GRACBFUSA
COHN, SIMON	57	M	LABR		GRACBFUSA
SUDLECI, BENJ	19	M	LABR		GRACBFUSA
GOLDENBERG, JANKEL	21	M	LABR		GRACBFUSA
WIEHSELS, SCHMIDEL	28	F	W		GRACBFUSA
DROORAH	3	F	CHILD		GRACBFUSA
HERMAN	.10	M	INFANT		GRACBFUSA
TEJERSTEIN, SCHAGI	48	F	HSKPR		GRACBFUSA
FEIGE	16	F	SP		GRACBFUSA
NORSI	8	M	CHILD		GRACBFUSA
SILBER, KINRIC	40	M	LABR		GRACBFUSA
GELLE	35	F	W		GRACBFUSA
DAVID	11	M	SCH		GRACBFUSA
LEREL	10	M	SCH		GRACBFUSA
ABR.	6	M	CHILD		GRACBFUSA
MOSES	4	M	CHILD		GRACBFUSA
ARON	2	M	CHILD		GRACBFUSA

PASSENGER	AGE	SEX	OCCUPATION	PRVL	DES
SCHLOME	.10	M	INFANT		GRACBFUSA
SAML.	.10	M	INFANT		GRACBFUSA
HOROWIETZ, WOLF	27	M	LABR		GRACBFUSA
FISCHER, BENHARD	29	M	LABR		GRACBFUSA
GRUN, JOSEF	59	M	LABR		GRACBFUSA
STERN, FANNY	40	F	SVNT		GRACBFUSA
FEDER, HANRY	14	F	SVNT		GRACBFUSA
KORMARCK, PETER	36	M	LABR		GRACBFUSA
ELZA	32	F	W		GRACBFUSA
KADZYK, WAZYN	28	M	LABR		GRACBFUSA
BIEKA, SCHOLA	46	M	LABR		GRACBFUSA
FELBERSTEIN, ETZIG	18	M	LABR		GRACBFUSA
WEMSTEIN, ISRAEL	34	M	LABR		GRACBFUSA
MILESKI, ANTON	18	M	LABR		GRACBFUSA
CHAUSTONSKI, BERY	43	M	LABR		GRACBFUSA
GOLDMAN, ABR.	32	M	LABR		GRACBFUSA
KAHN, LEIB	28	M	LABR		GRACBFUSA
LORE	23	F	W		GRACBFUSA
CHEVE	.10	M	INFANT		GRACBFUSA
MIHAL, SIKORA	18	M	SP		GRACBFUSA
GULZINSKI, IGNATZ	18	M	LABR		GRACBFUSA
MARSHALL, JETWAN	19	M	LABR		GRACBFUSA
DRESDNER, JINNE	48	M	LABR		GRACBFUSA
POKAMINSKI, SCHLOME	24	M	LABR		GRACBFUSA
LIPE	21	F	W		GRACBFUSA
ROSA	.09	F	INFANT		GRACBFUSA
GENS, CHAJI	43	F	HSKPR		GRACBFUSA
GELLE	15	F	SP		GRACBFUSA
AHE	9	F	CHILD		GRACBFUSA
ROSA	8	F	CHILD		GRACBFUSA
SIMI	3	M	CHILD		GRACBFUSA
TERL	.11	M	INFANT		GRACBFUSA
ROSENZARIG, JOSEL	11	M	SCH		GRACBFUSA
MIRELSON, BEER	35	M	LABR		GRACBFUSA
ESKE	30	F	W		GRACBFUSA
MERSLSON, JASSEL	9	M	CHILD		GRACBFUSA
GRUBMURE, ABR.MOSES	25	M	LABR		GRACBFUSA
IRE	21	F	W		GRACBFUSA
LABEKKI, ITZCHOK	34	M	LABR		GRACBFUSA
FIERSNIGER, SCHENIE	18	F	SP		GRACBFUSA
RUDOLF, JOHNN	38	M	LABR		GRACBFUSA
GRUNBERG, ISIDOR	33	M	LABR		GRACBFUSA
SPEISER, BRINSM	29	M	LABR		GRACBFUSA
TISCHLENSKI, TOBIAS	31	M	LABR		GRACBFUSA
PERZIKOW, WOLF	48	M	LABR		GRACBFUSA
USERKES, SCHLOME	30	M	LABR		GRACBFUSA
SCHILAM, NISCHUN	30	M	LABR		GRACBFUSA
KUSCHINAKY, JACOB	40	M	LABR		GRACBFUSA
FEWIELEM, MOSES	30	M	LABR		GRACBFUSA
GOLDBERG, JACOB	23	M	LABR		GRACBFUSA
GREVE, WM.	31	M	MCHT		GRABDMUSA
GROMANDZINSKY, CARL	39	M	GENT		GRACBFUSA

SHIP: ITALY

FROM: LIVERPOOL AND QUEENSTOWN
TO: NEW YORK
ARRIVED: 04 AUGUST 1888

PASSENGER	AGE	SEX	OCCUPATION	PRVL	DES
KOHL, JOSEPH	22	M	BKBNDR		GRZZZZNY
BACHEN, GEO	36	M	CL		GRADAXPHI
BELLINGER, CHAS	42	M	LABR		GRACBFNY
LEJEK, JOHN	25	M	CPTR		GRACBFNY

PASSENGER	AGE	SEX	OCCUPATION	PRVL	DES
SHIP: MARSALA					
FROM: HAMBURG					
TO: NEW YORK					
ARRIVED: 04 AUGUST 1888					
RISS, ANTON	26	M	SLR	HBZZZZNY	
KLEINE, LOUIS	27	M	SLR	HBZZZZNY	
IHSEN, CATHARINA	76	F	WO	HBZZZZNY	
KNUDSEN, GEORG	23	M	BKBNDR	HBAESDUNK	
KRUMHEUER, ERNST	51	M	JNR	HBABOQNY	
LOUISE	30	F	W	HBABOQNY	
PETERS, GEORG	27	M	JNR	HBAADESFC	
DAVID, HEINRICH	34	M	LABR	HBZZZZNY	
SAGER, JOHANN	21	M	LABR	PRZZZZIL	
FUENING, MAX	21	M	GDNR	PRAAKHCH	
NEUMANN, ROSA	36	F	WO	PRZZZZUNK	
EMILIE	9	F	CHILD	PRZZZZUNK	
CLARA	8	F	CHILD	PRZZZZUNK	
KNJAWSKI, JOH.	26	M	LABR	PRZZZZUNK	
SCHWALBACH, JOHANN	26	M	CGRMKR	BVZZZZNY	
NEITSCH, IDA	29	F	WO	SYZZZZNY	
HALLAS, OSW.	15	M	LABR	SYZZZZNY	
BRUDE, MARIE	18	F	SGL	SYADOIBAL	
SCHRAMM, JOH.	46	M	LABR	SYAEAJDET	
AUGUSTE	46	F	WO	SYAEAJDET	
HARMS, HERM.	64	M	LABR	SYAHILDAV	
CATHAR.	64	F	W	SYAHILDAV	
ZIMMER, CLARA	17	F	SGL	SYABRANY	
REBNER, ARTHUR	26	M	CNF	SYACXVNY	
VIESEL, ADOLF	24	M	FARMER	WMZZZZNY	
FUERST, MARIE	23	F	SGL	WMZZZZNY	
BALLE, ANTON	25	M	FARMER	WMZZZZNY	
RAPP, CHRISTINE	23	F	SGL	WMZZZZNY	
JACOB	18	M	CPR	WMZZZZNY	
HAPP, SAMUEL	16	M	BBR	PRZZZZNY	
KURTZAHN, WILH.	34	M	SMH	PRADHJNY	
BERTHA	28	F	W	PRADHJNY	
MANGELS, JOH.	30	M	FARMER	PRABIGNY	
ZARAMBA, AUGUSTE	25	F	WO	PRZZZZNY	
HERMANN	1	M	CHILD	PRZZZZNY	
PAUL	.06	M	INFANT	PRZZZZNY	
NOWACK, MARIANNE	20	F	SGL	PRZZZZNY	
ANDREAS	9	M	CHILD	PRZZZZNY	
PRZYSTACSZI, JOHANN	45	M	CPTR	PRAJJHNY	
DOROTHEA	36	F	W	PRAJJHNY	
ANNA	16	F	W	PRAJJHNY	
HEINRICH	14	M	W	PRAJJHNY	
BERTHA	9	F	CHILD	PRAJJHNY	
JAN	7	M	CHILD	PRAJJHNY	
BRUNO	.11	M	INFANT	PRAJJHNY	
APPEL, BERNHARD	18	M	LABR	SYZZZZNY	
EDUARD	16	M	LABR	SYZZZZNY	
HALLMANN, EMILIE	23	F	SGL	PRZZZZNY	
FRANK, AUGUSTE	16	F	SGL	PRAASSNY	
SALINGER, HENRIETTE	52	F	WO	PRAGRRNY	
SALOMON	46	M	LABR	PRAGRRNY	
GLINSKA, MARIANNE	19	F	SGL	PRAJSVNY	
SZYNKEWITZ, ROSALIE	36	F	WO	PRZZZZNY	
FRANZ	15	M	UNKNOWN	PRZZZZNY	
IGNATZ	9	M	CHILD	PRZZZZNY	
JAN	8	M	CHILD	PRZZZZNY	
MARIANNA	3	F	CHILD	PRZZZZNY	
JANITZKA, MARIANNA	20	F	WO	PRZZZZNY	
JAEGER, VALERIE	.11	F	INFANT	PRZZZZNY	
HOHNKE, FRIED.	51	M	LABR	PRABPNNY	
HENRIETTE	33	F	W	PRABPNNY	
CARL	9	M	CHILD	PRABPNNY	
AUGUSTE	8	F	CHILD	PRABPNNY	
PAULINE	2	F	CHILD	PRABPNNY	
PAUL	.04	M	INFANT	PRABPNNY	
AUERBACH, LUDWIG	26	M	MCHT	PRAETHNY	
JENSEN, JENS	15	M	FARMER	PRZZZZNY	
SCHULTZE, GEORG	20	M	MCHT	PRZZZZNY	
WITT, JOHANN	33	M	FARMER	PRZZZZNY	
NIELSEN, NIELS	32	M	FARMER	PRZZZZNY	
EMMA	27	F	W	PRZZZZNY	
ANNA	3	F	CHILD	PRZZZZNY	
ANDR.	.06	M	INFANT	PRZZZZNY	
VITZ, OTTILIA	22	F	SGL	PRZZZZNY	
LANGER, BERTHA	22	F	SGL	PRAEABNY	
KRINKE, PAUL	26	M	LKSH	PRACPSOH	
OSTROWSKI, HERM.	24	M	BCHR	PRACPSNY	
SZUBERT, FRANZISCA	38	F	SGL	PRAEIONY	
JANKOWSKA, JADWIGA	18	F	SGL	PRZZZZNY	
FRANK, CAROLINE	60	F	WO	PRAASSTRE	
ROTH, JOSEF	41	M	FARMER	PRAAKHNY	
LANGHOFF, BERTHOLD	29	M	MCHT	PRZZZZNY	
HEINRICH, ERNST	26	M	LABR	PRZZZZNY	
KREHER, OSCAR	31	M	LABR	PRZZZZNY	
MARIE	33	F	W	PRZZZZNY	
MARGR.	3	F	CHILD	PRZZZZNY	
HANS	.06	M	INFANT	PRZZZZNY	
HEISEN, NICOLINE	19	F	SGL	PRABNSNY	
MELTZER, OTTO	25	M	SCP	PRZZZZNY	
POLSTER, WILH.	33	M	WVR	PRADIXNY	
STORJOHUM, FRIED	30	M	LABR	PRZZZZNE	
ROSSOW, WILH.	21	M	LABR	PRADDZNY	
SCHEFFLER, ED.	23	M	GDNR	PRACZYNY	
SALINGER, OTTO	9	F	CHILD	PRAGRRNY	
JOSEF	8	M	CHILD	PRAGRRNY	
BENJAMIN	7	M	CHILD	PRAGRRNY	
CIRIS, JOH.	30	M	LABR	PRZZZZDET	
OSTROWSKY, IGNATZ	30	M	SHMK	PRACWTNY	
HUNGER, MARIE	39	F	SGL	PRAEOUNY	
SCHARN, FRANCISKA	27	F	SGL	PRABDMNY	
LINEK, JOH.	19	M	TCHR	PRAASZNY	
WEISSE, IDA	25	F	WO	PRABDMNY	
BERTHA	4	F	CHILD	PRABDMNY	
MEICKENSTRM, GREGOR	18	M	BRR	PRAKVVNY	
WETTERER, WILH.	66	M	BKR	PRAKVVNY	
STOSCH, HEDWIG	18	F	SGL	PRAEXQNY	
PUDA, MARIE	18	F	UNKNOWN	PRAEXQNY	
LEUCHTENBERG, BENJAMIN	28	M	CPTR	PRAHLINY	
REICHELT, WILHELM	17	M	CL	PRAHLINY	
HARTWIG, BOJE	23	M	BAR	PRABIGNY	
KROHN, AUGUST	36	M	LABR	HBZZZZNY	
ELISABETH	35	F	W	HBZZZZNY	
AUGUST	9	M	CHILD	HBZZZZNY	
HEINRICH	7	M	CHILD	HBZZZZNY	
EMIL	5	M	CHILD	HBZZZZNY	
BERTHA	5	F	CHILD	HBZZZZNY	
NOWAK, MARIANNE	32	F	WO	PRZZZZNY	
APOLONIA	4	F	CHILD	PRZZZZNY	
ANDRAS	3	M	CHILD	PRZZZZNY	
KASIMIR	.11	M	INFANT	PRZZZZNY	
MILDE, PAUL	36	M	LKSH	PRAARZNY	
GOLTZ, ALEXANDER	18	M	STDNT	PRAEVMNY	
SCHWARZ, ALBERT	29	M	MCHT	PRADESNY	
HERZOG, RICHARD	26	M	JNR	PRZZZZNY	
MENKE, LOUISE	37	F	SGL	PRZZZZUNK	
KOCH, HERM.	38	M	LABR	PRADDZUNK	
HOFFMANN, WILHELMINE	34	F	WO	PRZZZZNY	
GUSTAV	9	M	CHILD	PRZZZZNY	
RUCINSKA, ELSBETA	28	F	SGL	PRZZZZNY	
BRECKLINZHEMS, ANNA	26	F	WO	PRACIWNY	
ANNA	.11	F	INFANT	PRACIWNY	
SAMBOWSKA, MICHALINE	31	F	SGL	PRZZZZNY	
JAENCKE, OTTO	23	M	MCHT	PRAIRSNY	
SCHNEIDER, EMIL	15	M	LABR	PRAMBHPHI	
GRUBER, GODOHARD	23	M	MCHT	HBZZZZPHI	

PASSENGER	AGE	SEX	OCCUPATION	PRVL	DES

SHIP: RUGIA

FROM: HAMBURG AND HAVRE
TO: NEW YORK
ARRIVED: 04 AUGUST 1888

PASSENGER	AGE	SEX	OCCUPATION	PRVL·DES
NEUSTAAT, LINA	17	F	SGL	PRZZZZUSA
RUPPERT, ANNA	27	F	WO	BVZZZZUSA
ANNA	.09	F	INFANT	BVZZZZUSA
MEYER, HEINR.	28	M	LABR	BVAADEUSA
OTTO	3	M	CHILD	BVAADEUSA
SCHMIDT, ADOLF	33	M	PNTR	BVACBFUSA
PABST, LOUISE	63	F	WO	BVAEILUSA
KLINKER, ERNST	9	M	CHILD	BVAEILUSA
ORTLOPP, CARL	15	M	STDNT	BVAEILUSA
TROCK, MARTHA	23	F	SGL	BVAADEUSA
GARTZ, ROBERT	19	M	MCHT	BVACBFUSA
MARTIN, ADOLF	30	M	PNTR	BVAFBFUSA
DREYER, LOUISE	15	F	SGL	PRZZZZUSA
SCHWABE, BERTHA	35	F	WO	PRAAKHUSA
DEIHN, MARIE	18	F	SGL	PRZZZZUSA
CLARA	9	F	CHILD	PRZZZZUSA
FRANKE, LOUISE	30	F	SGL	PRACBFUSA
BONNESEN, KUND	20	M	LABR	PRZZZZUSA
KOHLSCHUTTER, EIML	24	M	UNKNOWN	PRAEABUSA
RISCH, BERTHA	66	F	WO	PRAEABUSA
GRAF, HEINR.	17	M	MCHT	PRADGCUSA
TRICK, HEINR.	33	M	UNKNOWN	PRAGMXUSA
GOEBEL, PAULA	25	F	SGL	PRABHUUSA
DABEL, ALEXANDRINE	24	F	SGL	PRAHXDUSA
BELLING, RUDOLF	44	M	TLR	MKZZZZUSA
WOGNER, CARL	39	M	TLR	MKZZZZUSA
ROTHER, CARL	16	M	LABR	PRZZZZUSA
GARSKI, ANTONIE	56	F	WO	PRZZZZUSA
KEMPINSKI, ROSA	16	F	SGL	PRZZZZUSA
LOUIS	13	M	B	PRZZZZUSA
SARA	9	F	CHILD	PRZZZZUSA
SLOMKA, ANNA	13	F	SGL	PRZZZZUSA
BASINSKA, STANISLAWA	23	F	WO	PRALTJUSA
PELAGIA	00	F	INF	PRALTJUSA
ROESELER, MARIE	29	F	WO	PRZZZZUSA
IDA	7	F	CHILD	PRZZZZUSA
KRUEGER, OTTO	24	M	LABR	PRZZZZUSA
WEBER, FLORIAN	22	M	MNFTR	SYZZZZUSA
BLOCH, JOHA.	19	F	SGL	PRZZZZUSA
MAGDALENA	19	F	WO	PRZZZZUSA
MICHAL	.06	M	INFANT	PRZZZZUSA
KUENZL, ADOLF	20	M	LABR	PRACBFUSA
BUNNING, WILLI	20	M	LABR	PRACBFUSA
KASPEROWITZ, MARIE	19	F	SGL	PRAEABUSA
GROTH, JOH.	30	M	ENGR	PRAADEUSA
BODE, GUSTAV	20	M	MCHT	PRACBRUSA
BAUMGARTH, MARTHA	24	F	SGL	PRAAZQUSA
ALBERT	23	M	SMH	PRAAZQUSA
SILZER, ELISE	22	F	SGL	HSZZZZUSA
BURMESTER, CARL	23	M	LABR	HSACBFUSA
SODEMANN, SOPHIE	31	F	WO	HSAJQAUSA
PAUL	6	M	CHILD	HSAJQAUSA
ERNA	4	F	CHILD	HSAJQAUSA
BAIER, MARGR.	19	F	SGL	HSZZZZUSA
SCHNEIDER, GUSTAV	23	M	TNM	HSADVHUSA
GOSCH, JUERGEN	22	M	CL	HSAKVLUSA
ERNST, MARGR.	68	F	WO	PRZZZZUSA
ANNA	35	F	SGL	PRZZZZUSA
CHRISTENSEN, MAREN	18	F	SGL	PRZZZZUSA
HELM, JOHS.	16	M	FARMER	PRZZZZUSA
STENER, CARL	31	M	UNKNOWN	PRAHNOUSA
LEVY, PAULA	23	F	SGL	PRACTQUSA
BUERINGER, FRANZ	30	M	BRR	PRABDMUSA
KRIEGMANN, LINE	18	F	SGL	HSZZZZUSA
HEINE, ALBERT	32	M	PNTR	HSACUXUSA
NEUMEYER, CARL	17	M	BCHR	WMZZZZUSA
BUHNOW, CARL	29	M	LABR	WMADNNUSA
GREGERSEN, ANNA	32	F	WO	PRZZZZUSA
MARIE	4	F	CHILD	PRZZZZUSA
VAGLER, ALBIN	16	M	CPR	PRZZZZUSA
APEL, FRDERIK	40	M	FARMER	PRZZZZUSA
BRANDIS, RUDOLF	42	M	UNKNOWN	PRZZZZUSA
DREIKUS, HEINR.	39	M	LABR	PRZZZZUSA
RAUT, JOH.	23	M	UNKNOWN	PRZZZZUSA
KAUFMANN, BERUHD.	44	M	MCHT	PRACBFUSA
LUCINDE	38	F	W	PRACBFUSA
EMANUEL	9	M	CHILD	PRACBFUSA
GEIER, BABETTE	23	F	SGL	BVZZZZUSA
OPPENHEIMER, ISAAC	18	M	TLR	BVAGKDUSA
DEGENER, ANNA	18	F	SGL	BVAJEUUSA
MITSCHKE, PAULINE	24	F	UNKNOWN	BVAAKHUSA
KLUTTIG, PAULINE	35	F	UNKNOWN	BVAAKHUSA
BERUHD.	7	M	CHILD	BVAAKHUSA
PAUL	9	M	CHILD	BVAAKHUSA
ARUCLD, ROBERT	32	M	UNKNOWN	PRZZZZUSA
KOSS, MAX	25	M	MSN	PRZZZZUSA
GRIMMER, KARL	31	M	LABR	SYZZZZUSA
BERTHA	28	F	W	SYZZZZUSA
OSWALD	4	M	CHILD	SYZZZZUSA
CURT	.11	M	INFANT	SYZZZZUSA
MARDAS, CATHA.	36	F	WO	PRZZZZUSA
KAMINSKI, IGNATZ	24	M	LABR	PRZZZZUSA
KIELDUZKA, SOFIE	26	F	SGL	PRAHZFUSA
PLEILIPP, ERNST	14	M	STDNT	PRABDMUSA
LESNICK, FRANZ	16	M	LABR	PRZZZZUSA
SPECHT, ALWINE	55	F	WO	PRZZZZUSA
RIEPER, JACOB	00	M	LABR	PRZZZZUSA
SCHNITZER, LOUIS	65	M	MCHT	PRAAKHUSA
STURZBAKER, CARL	60	M	MCHT	PRZZZZUSA
EMILIE	57	F	W	PRZZZZUSA
CARL	19	M	S	PRZZZZUSA
BETHKE, BERTHA	18	F	SGL	PRZZZZUSA
NAWROTH, THERESE	23	F	SGL	PRAARZUSA
BUJAK, PAULINE	25	F	SGL	PRAARZUSA
GERSCHNER, SOPHIE	28	F	SGL	PRZZZZUSA
STICK, JOHANN	72	M	LABR	PRABNOUSA
PAULINE	28	F	SGL	PRABNOUSA
BRONISLAWA	17	F	SGL	PRABNOUSA
FOETZKE, IDA	18	F	SGL	PRAFYDUSA
REISNER, JOSEPH	25	M	BKR	PRZZZZUSA
URBANSKI, STANISLAUS	27	M	BKR	PRZZZZUSA
BUROW, AMALIE	26	F	SGL	PRABTNUSA
REINHARDT, IDA	19	F	WO	PRAAKHUSA
AMALIE	.09	F	INFANT	PRAAKHUSA
BERNOW, MARIE	27	F	SGL	PRAETNUSA
THALMANN, PAUL	28	M	LABR	PRAAKHUSA
LICHTENSTEIN, HANNA	48	F	WO	PRZZZZUSA
ESTHER	22	F	CH	PRZZZZUSA
FRANZISKA	19	F	CH	PRZZZZUSA
DAVID	9	M	CHILD	PRZZZZUSA
ISAAC	9	M	CHILD	PRZZZZUSA
KRAFTMEYER, AUGUSTE	64	F	WO	PRAAKIUSA
MAX	22	M	S	PRAAKIUSA
FRANZ	9	M	CHILD	PRAAKIUSA
KOTHLO, OTTO	3	M	CHILD	PRAAKIUSA
STREN, HENRIETTE	38	F	WO	MKZZZZUSA
SOPHIE	15	F	D	MKZZZZUSA
KAEKEUMEISTER, GOTTLIEB	75	M	LABR	MKZZZZUSA
FRIEDRICH, FRDK.	32	F	WO	MKACBFUSA
NELLY	3	F	CHILD	MKACBFUSA
MATYSIAK, JADWIGA	28	F	WO	PRZZZZUSA
STANISLAV	.11	M	INFANT	PRZZZZUSA
SCHYMANSKY, HIPOLIT	39	M	CPR	PRZZZZUSA
KUNZ, MARTIN	42	M	CPR	PRZZZZUSA
ULRITZI, VICTOR	28	M	BRR	GRZZZZUSA
HARWEZYNSKY, FRANZ	23	M	BCHR	GRADOIUSA
BODENTHIN, FRIEDR.	63	M	JNR	GRABGHUSA
MUROWSKI, JOSEFA	27	F	WO	PRZZZZUSA
ROSALIE	4	F	CHILD	PRZZZZUSA
FRANZISKA	.06	F	INFANT	PRZZZZUSA
KAZOBOKI, CASIMIR	32	M	LKSH	PRAHWVUSA
GABRIEL, CHAS	39	M	CPR	PRAFVGUSA
LOUISE	36	F	W	PRAFVGUSA

PASSENGER	AGE	SEX	OCCUPATION	PRVIVL	DES
ENGSTER, CONRAD	33	M	FARMER	PRAHFI	USA
NETT, CHRISTINE	28	F	SGL	SRZZZZ	USA
WEIHERT, WALTER	17	M	MCHT	SRZZZZ	USA
KLOTER, ANNA	20	F	SGL	SRZZZZ	USA
EFFINGER, ANDREAS	22	M	WTR	GRZZZZ	USA
ADAM, OTTO	16	M	LABR	GRZZZZ	USA
MIMM, ALOIS	17	M	BRR	WMZZZZ	USA
BAST, MAGDALENE	44	F	WO	BDZZZZ	USA
DANIEL	14	M	S	BDZZZZ	USA
ANDIBERT, HORTENSE	33	F	WO	BDAGBU	USA
ELISE	9	F	CHILD	BDAGBU	USA
MOLDEHN, JOHA.	30	F	SGL	BDACSD	USA
CRAUZ, FRED.	37	M	MCHT	BDACBF	USA
V., FRIDH.	23	M	UNKNOWN	BDADMF	USA
ROHWEDDER, J.	47	M	FARMER	PRZZZZ	USA
MARGARETHA	39	F	W	PRZZZZ	USA
WILH.	9	M	CHILD	PRZZZZ	USA
DORA	8	F	CHILD	PRZZZZ	USA
CLAUS	3	M	CHILD	PRZZZZ	USA
AMANDA	.06	F	INFANT	PRZZZZ	USA
PFAFF, EMIL	33	M	MCHT	BDZZZZ	USA
SCHEWE, EDUARD	24	M	TCHR	BDAAKH	USA
LORENZEN, CARL	41	M	PVTM	BDADOI	USA
HEIDELBEREER, ANNA	15	F	SGL	BDAIUP	USA
EHLER, STEFANIE	17	F	SGL	BDAAVG	USA
NEHBER, ERNST	28	M	MD	BDAAKH	USA
SCHWEICKHARDT, ADOLF	22	M	MCHT	WMZZZZ	USA

SHIP: BOTHNIA

FROM: LIVERPOOL AND QUEENSTOWN
TO: BOSTON
ARRIVED: 06 AUGUST 1888

PASSENGER	AGE	SEX	OCCUPATION	PRVIVL	DES
DESGORDUILS, LOUIS	32	M	CL	FRZZZZ	MA
DETROIT, THEO	51	M	LABR	FRZZZZ	MA
BRUNO, EDWARD	26	M	CL	GRZZZZ	MA
ADOLF	25	M	CL	GRZZZZ	MA
LAROY, SUSSANE	28	F	MA	GRZZZZ	MA
LEARY, EMIL	10	M	CH	GRZZZZ	MA
KREMAR, CATHERINE	30	F	MA	GRZZZZ	MA
ANNA	6	F	CHILD	GRZZZZ	MA

SHIP: CITY OF RICHMOND

FROM: LIVERPOOL AND QUEENSTOWN
TO: NEW YORK
ARRIVED: 06 AUGUST 1888

PASSENGER	AGE	SEX	OCCUPATION	PRVIVL	DES
SALLY, ADOLPH	22	F	SP	GRZZZZ	NY
BAUNCK, S.	24	M	LABR	GRZZZZ	NY
THEKLA	19	F	SP	GRZZZZ	NY
EBHA, AUG.	26	M	LABR	GRZZZZ	NY
FYBAK, M.	25	M	LABR	GRZZZZ	NY
GRUBER, M.	19	M	LABR	GRZZZZ	NY
GRELLER, KAROLINA	20	F	SVNT	GRZZZZ	NY
F.	56	M	LABR	GRZZZZ	NY
GOLDBERG, H.	33	M	LABR	GRZZZZ	NY
KLEIN, OSCAR	25	M	LABR	GRZZZZ	NY
LECHLER, C.	18	M	LABR	GRZZZZ	NY
KOEMGSDORF, J.	11	M	CH	GRZZZZ	NY
PERIS, J.	26	M	LABR	GRZZZZ	NY
PELRUSCHKA, S.	23	M	LABR	GRZZZZ	NY
POLDZER, A.	23	M	LABR	GRZZZZ	NY
SHINE, S.	47	M	LABR	GRZZZZ	MA

PASSENGER	AGE	SEX	OCCUPATION	PRVIVL	DES
A.	17	M	LABR	GRZZZZ	MA
SHUMPFER, A.	25	M	LABR	GRAGFU	MA
SCHLICK, ABR.	18	M	LABR	GRAGFU	MA
SCHLANG, E.	28	M	LABR	GRAGFU	NY
ALLEN	30	F	W	GRAGFU	NY
J.	.06	F	INFANT	GRAGFU	NY
SCHOUBERG, J.	21	M	LABR	GRAGFU	NY
SCHENK, W.	21	M	LABR	GRAGFU	NY
SLOWEY, F.	22	M	LABR	GRAGFU	NY
SCHRODER, J.	48	M	LABR	GRAGFU	PA
WECHSMANN, GISELA	43	F	SVNT	GRAGFU	PA
L.	21	M	LABR	GRAGFU	PA
DIANA	16	F	SP	GRAGFU	PA
ROSA	14	F	SP	GRAGFU	PA
DAVID	8	M	CHILD	GRAGFU	PA
DAUL	.08	M	INFANT	GRAGFU	PA

SHIP: SERVIA

FROM: LIVERPOOL AND QUEENSTOWN
TO: NEW YORK
ARRIVED: 06 AUGUST 1888

PASSENGER	AGE	SEX	OCCUPATION	PRVIVL	DES
FERGAN, ARTHUR	25	M	CLGYMN	GRADAX	IL

SHIP: EIDER

FROM: BREMEN AND SOUTHAMPTON
TO: NEW YORK
ARRIVED: 07 AUGUST 1888

PASSENGER	AGE	SEX	OCCUPATION	PRVIVL	DES
LEHMANN, LEOPOLD	41	M	TT	GRZZZZ	USA
GEORGI, WILH.	24	F	TT	GRZZZZ	USA
GUDEMANN, A.	36	M	TT	GRZZZZ	USA
HUCH, WILH.	43	M	TT	GRZZZZ	USA
AUGUSTE	25	F	W	GRZZZZ	USA
WILH.	.02	M	INFANT	GRZZZZ	USA
SACHS, JOSEF	35	M	TT	GRZZZZ	USA
MUEGGE, AMALIE	29	F	UNKNOWN	GRZZZZ	USA
KAETCHEN	.10	F	INFANT	GRZZZZ	USA
MUEHLFELDER, DAVID	64	M	TT	GRZZZZ	USA
LOUIS	14	M	TT	GRZZZZ	USA
DRUEDING, MINNA	26	F	UNKNOWN	GRZZZZ	USA
RAN, HERM.	16	M	TT	GRZZZZ	USA
WISCHMEYER, WILH.	16	M	TT	GRZZZZ	USA
STEINKAMP, ELISE	22	F	UNKNOWN	GRZZZZ	USA
KOCH, MATH.	37	F	UNKNOWN	GRZZZZ	USA
BARBARA	17	F	UNKNOWN	GRZZZZ	USA
BILGER, MARIA	21	F	UNKNOWN	GRZZZZ	USA
COHEN, R.	38	F	UNKNOWN	GRZZZZ	USA
CHARTI	7	M	CHILD	GRZZZZ	USA
JESSI	2	M	CHILD	GRZZZZ	USA
OSWALD	.08	F	INFANT	GRZZZZ	USA
TOMSVCHAK, MARIA	36	F	UNKNOWN	GRZZZZ	USA
KUHNKE, CHR.	46	F	UNKNOWN	GRZZZZ	USA
MARX, JULIE	24	F	UNKNOWN	GRZZZZ	USA
VOLLHEIM, MARIE	20	F	UNKNOWN	GRZZZZ	USA
EISENBARTH, CAROLINE	26	F	UNKNOWN	GRZZZZ	USA
HANS	.08	M	INFANT	GRZZZZ	USA
HAAS, JACOB	70	M	TT	GRZZZZ	USA
JETTE	66	F	W	GRZZZZ	USA
ANERBACH, ABRAH.	19	M	TT	GRZZZZ	USA
SEIFELD, FRIEDR.	26	M	TT	GRZZZZ	USA
POMREHM, MATH.	16	F	UNKNOWN	GRZZZZ	USA
FERBER, MOLLY	32	F	UNKNOWN	GRZZZZ	USA

PASSENGER	AGE	SEX	OCCUPATION	PRVL	DES	PASSENGER	AGE	SEX	OCCUPATION	PRVL	DES
STEINBERG, BETTY	24	F	UNKNOWN	GRZZZZ	USA	KLUG, LUDW.	27	M	SHMK	GRZZZZ	USA
MAX	.09	M	INFANT	GRZZZZ	USA	GAUGER, JULIE	18	F	UNKNOWN	GRZZZZ	USA
STELLING, LOUISE	20	F	UNKNOWN	GRZZZZ	USA	RICH.	16	M	CNF	GRZZZZ	USA
SCHLEIT, ELISE	23	F	UNKNOWN	GRZZZZ	USA	BRAUN, MARIE	16	F	UNKNOWN	GRZZZZ	USA
WALLER, JOH.	23	F	UNKNOWN	GRZZZZ	USA	WEIDLICH, CATH.	30	F	UNKNOWN	GRZZZZ	USA
STRAUSS, DORIS	23	F	UNKNOWN	GRZZZZ	USA	FRIED.	8	M	CHILD	GRZZZZ	USA
DITTRICH, ROSA	19	F	UNKNOWN	GRZZZZ	USA	LOUISE	2	F	CHILD	GRZZZZ	USA
LEMME, FRIEDR.	18	M	TT	GRZZZZ	USA	CATH.	.06	F	INFANT	GRZZZZ	USA
BALZ, WILLY	16	M	TT	GRZZZZ	USA	SCHOELLER, JULIE	18	F	UNKNOWN	GRZZZZ	USA
MOEHL, CONR.	20	M	TT	GRZZZZ	USA	HERM.	4	M	CHILD	GRZZZZ	USA
HOHN, GEORG	24	M	TT	GRZZZZ	USA	FEILER, DANIEL	23	M	HTR	GRZZZZ	USA
WOLF, ELISE	52	F	UNKNOWN	GRZZZZ	USA	HALRER, JOSEPHA	18	F	UNKNOWN	GRZZZZ	USA
ANNA	26	F	UNKNOWN	GRZZZZ	USA	JACOB	24	M	UNKNOWN	GRZZZZ	USA
SCHUMACHER, ROSINE	44	F	UNKNOWN	GRZZZZ	USA	BARTH, ERNST	26	M	FARMER	GRZZZZ	USA
EISENBERG, MINNA	27	F	UNKNOWN	GRZZZZ	USA	SCHWEIZER, CARL	14	M	FARMER	GRZZZZ	USA
DRAENERT, EMELIE	25	F	UNKNOWN	GRZZZZ	USA	HOFMANN, FRIED.	15	M	FARMER	GRZZZZ	USA
MAX	4	M	CHILD	GRZZZZ	USA	SCHMID, ROSA	18	F	SMTS	GRZZZZ	USA
EMIL	.10	M	INFANT	GRZZZZ	USA	KAUFMANN, ROPERT	25	M	MCHT	GRZZZZ	USA
MARX, BERTHA	23	F	UNKNOWN	GRZZZZ	USA	CRESCENZ	25	F	W	GRZZZZ	USA
ROSINE	20	F	UNKNOWN	GRZZZZ	USA	JOSEFINE	.09	F	INFANT	GRZZZZ	USA
BENEKE, ANNA	19	F	UNKNOWN	GRZZZZ	USA	MORS, LISETTE	18	F	SMTS	GRZZZZ	USA
STEPHAN, AUG.	56	F	UNKNOWN	GRZZZZ	USA	SANGMEISTER, FRANZ	63	M	FARMER	GRZZZZ	USA
EHLERS, ELISE	18	F	UNKNOWN	GRZZZZ	USA	MARIE	60	F	W	GRZZZZ	USA
PRINME, MARIE	37	F	UNKNOWN	GRZZZZ	USA	WILHEL.	8	F	CHILD	GRZZZZ	USA
FANY	11	F	UNKNOWN	GRZZZZ	USA	MUENCH, MAGD.	22	F	UNKNOWN	GRZZZZ	USA
PAULA	7	F	CHILD	GRZZZZ	USA	WIELAND, PAULINE	8	F	CHILD	GRZZZZ	USA
DRENTLAN, VALENT.	75	M	TT	GRZZZZ	USA	HALLER, JOH.	54	M	FARMER	GRZZZZ	USA
JETTER, MARIE	52	F	UNKNOWN	GRZZZZ	USA	RECK, MATH.	15	F	UNKNOWN	GRZZZZ	USA
SOUPPOLD, MILH.	8	M	CHILD	GRZZZZ	USA	KOENIG, BARBARA	30	F	UNKNOWN	GRZZZZ	USA
CASBERG, MARIE	28	F	UNKNOWN	GRZZZZ	USA	JETTER, GOTTL	17	M	TLR	GRZZZZ	USA
BECKER, ANA	19	F	UNKNOWN	GRZZZZ	USA	HARRIS, ANNA	21	F	SMTS	GRZZZZ	USA
HELWIG, MINNA	24	F	UNKNOWN	GRZZZZ	USA	SPIESS, WILH.	15	M	UNKNOWN	GRZZZZ	USA
ANNA	22	F	UNKNOWN	GRZZZZ	USA	ROCK, KATH.	28	F	UNKNOWN	GRZZZZ	USA
HOHMANN, GEORG	20	M	TT	GRZZZZ	USA	GORN, LYDIA	27	F	UNKNOWN	GRZZZZ	USA
VOELKEL, CATH.	16	F	UNKNOWN	GRZZZZ	USA	GAERTNER, CARL	30	M	BKR	GRZZZZ	USA
FEVINK, JOS.	14	M	SMH	GRZZZZ	USA	GUENTNER, OTTO	19	M	BRR	GRZZZZ	USA
HEIMANN, REGINA	25	F	SMTS	GRZZZZ	USA	ROTH, CARL	15	M	UNKNOWN	GRZZZZ	USA
POPP, KUNIGUNDE	24	F	SVNT	GRZZZZ	USA	SCHAUB, FRIED.	25	M	SHMK	GRZZZZ	USA
KLEIN, FRANZ	48	M	FARMER	GRZZZZ	USA	NUTZEL, ELISE	16	F	SVNT	GRZZZZ	USA
GUST.	8	M	CHILD	GRZZZZ	USA	MORLOCH, GEORG	44	M	FARMER	GRZZZZ	USA
WILH.	7	M	CHILD	GRZZZZ	USA	HOLZER, CONR.	16	M	UNKNOWN	GRZZZZ	USA
EMILIE	6	F	CHILD	GRZZZZ	USA	PHIL.	31	M	FARMER	GRZZZZ	USA
REINKER, PAUL	15	F	SEMN	GRZZZZ	USA	WILH.	27	F	W	GRZZZZ	USA
FIEBER, EM.	6	F	CHILD	GRZZZZ	USA	PFETZING, CHR.	.05	M	INFANT	GRZZZZ	USA
GEORGI, CLARA	7	F	CHILD	GRZZZZ	USA	GRENZENBACH, ELIS.	42	F	SVNT	GRZZZZ	USA
HELENE	4	F	CHILD	GRZZZZ	USA	AUG.	53	F	UNKNOWN	GRZZZZ	USA
BOSER, ELEONORE	44	F	UNKNOWN	GRZZZZ	USA	HOLZER, EUG.	23	M	HTR	GRZZZZ	USA
ROB.	20	M	UNKNOWN	GRZZZZ	USA	BLUEMLER, MARG.	32	F	UNKNOWN	GRZZZZ	USA
FRIED.	6	M	CHILD	GRZZZZ	USA	JANSEN, CHR.	15	M	FARMER	GRZZZZ	USA
HENR.	7	F	CHILD	GRZZZZ	USA	SINGER, THERESE	35	F	UNKNOWN	GRZZZZ	USA
BUESCHEL, MARIE	19	F	UNKNOWN	GRZZZZ	USA	FERD.	8	M	CHILD	GRZZZZ	USA
SCHWERGER, OTTO	15	M	LABR	GRZZZZ	USA	MARIE	6	F	CHILD	GRZZZZ	USA
KOEHLER, FRIED.	21	F	SMTS	GRZZZZ	USA	THERESE	5	F	CHILD	GRZZZZ	USA
ROTH, ROB.	16	M	LABR	GRZZZZ	USA	GEORG	3	M	CHILD	GRZZZZ	USA
KAST, PAULINE	21	F	UNKNOWN	GRZZZZ	USA	FRANZ	.06	M	INFANT	GRZZZZ	USA
BERTHA	23	F	UNKNOWN	GRZZZZ	USA	FLEISCHMANN, KUNIG.	16	F	UNKNOWN	GRZZZZ	USA
MESSNER, CAROL.	30	F	UNKNOWN	GRZZZZ	USA	ROECKLEIN, GEORG	30	M	FARMER	GRZZZZ	USA
BERTHA	3	F	CHILD	GRZZZZ	USA	SCHLAPP, KUNIG.	25	F	UNKNOWN	GRZZZZ	USA
PAUL	.09	M	INFANT	GRZZZZ	USA	BARBARA	.10	F	INFANT	GRZZZZ	USA
SCHWARTING, BERTH.	19	F	SMTS	GRZZZZ	USA	LOEW, JOH.	27	M	UNKNOWN	GRZZZZ	USA
HOEPLE, CAROL.	28	F	SMTS	GRZZZZ	USA	LANKENAN, HELNE	5	F	CHILD	GRZZZZ	USA
LOUISE	23	F	SMTS	GRZZZZ	USA	WITTENBERG, PAUL	20	M	CPTR	GRZZZZ	USA
MOCK, JOSEF	23	M	BRR	GRZZZZ	USA	MISCH, WILH.	33	M	LABR	GRZZZZ	USA
RECK, AGNES	22	F	SVNT	GRZZZZ	USA	ANNA	36	F	W	GRZZZZ	USA
SOBRZYNKE, ANTON	62	F	UNKNOWN	GRZZZZ	USA	HELENE	1	F	CHILD	GRZZZZ	USA
RUECKERT, HEINR.	16	M	UNKNOWN	GRZZZZ	USA	ALFRED	.06	M	INFANT	GRZZZZ	USA
EDLER, WILH.	15	M	UNKNOWN	GRZZZZ	USA	FALKENSTEIN, DOROTH.	55	F	UNKNOWN	GRZZZZ	USA
ALBRECHT, GESINE	45	F	UNKNOWN	GRZZZZ	USA	BUEHL, JACOB	60	M	FARMER	GRZZZZ	USA
META	8	F	CHILD	GRZZZZ	USA	CHR.	7	M	CHILD	GRZZZZ	USA
LOUIS	5	M	CHILD	GRZZZZ	USA	WITSCHEN, OSCAR	3	M	CHILD	GRZZZZ	USA
BERTHA	3	M	CHILD	GRZZZZ	USA	MUELLER, EVA	41	F	UNKNOWN	GRZZZZ	USA
STRIELEN, AGNES	21	F	UNKNOWN	GRZZZZ	USA	LINA	23	F	UNKNOWN	GRZZZZ	USA
METZNER, PAULINE	23	F	UNKNOWN	GRZZZZ	USA	CHRIST.	16	F	UNKNOWN	GRZZZZ	USA
MELLER, WINCENT	25	M	LABR	GRZZZZ	USA	IDA	8	F	CHILD	GRZZZZ	USA
KRESS, PAUL	25	M	LABR	GRZZZZ	USA	OTTILIE	7	F	CHILD	GRZZZZ	USA

PASSENGER	AGE	SEX	OCCUPATION	PRVL	DES	PASSENGER	AGE	SEX	OCCUPATION	PRVL	DES
LISETTE	6	F	CHILD	GRZZZZ	USA	MARG.	24	F	W	GRZZZZ	USA
ANNA	.10	F	INFANT	GRZZZZ	USA	LOUISE	.11	F	INFANT	GRZZZZ	USA
GROSS, LISETTE	23	F	UNKNOWN	GRZZZZ	USA	HENNI	.01	M	INFANT	GRZZZZ	USA
WAGNER, AUGUSTE	22	F	UNKNOWN	GRZZZZ	USA	GRANBUER, THERESE	23	F	UNKNOWN	GRZZZZ	USA
SCHEIDIG, CAROLINE	23	F	UNKNOWN	GRZZZZ	USA	FLORA	.09	M	INFANT	GRZZZZ	USA
CHRISTINE	25	F	UNKNOWN	GRZZZZ	USA	WINKELMANN, DORA	23	F	SMSTS	GRZZZZ	USA
GAYKE, MICH.	27	M	LABR	GRZZZZ	USA	FAWORAT, MARIE	20	F	SMSTS	GRZZZZ	USA
LUDKE, AUG.	26	F	UNKNOWN	GRZZZZ	USA	KURTZ, CARL	10	M	CH	GRZZZZ	USA
RESSLING, CATH.	52	F	UNKNOWN	GRZZZZ	USA	FEULNER, KAROL.	25	F	UNKNOWN	GRZZZZ	USA
BUETTNER, HENR.	38	F	UNKNOWN	GRZZZZ	USA	KUNIGUNDE	.09	F	INFANT	GRZZZZ	USA
RITTER, ADAM	23	M	LABR	GRZZZZ	USA	ROPPE, PAUL	18	M	TLR	GRZZZZ	USA
LISNEWSKY, THERESE	28	F	UNKNOWN	GRZZZZ	USA	ZAPPE, GOTL.	36	M	SHMK	GRZZZZ	USA
BREHN, NICOL.	25	M	LABR	GRZZZZ	USA	HANG, EUGEN	27	M	ENGR	GRZZZZ	USA
KOERNER, FRANZ	42	M	UNKNOWN	GRZZZZ	USA	VETTER, PHILIPP	24	M	BBR	GRZZZZ	USA
IDA	42	F	W	GRZZZZ	USA	BEST, BALTASAR	27	M	BBR	GRZZZZ	USA
WERNER, HENRIETTE	20	F	UNKNOWN	GRZZZZ	USA	KIEGLER, ADAM	22	M	LABR	GRZZZZ	USA
ULRICH, OTTO	11	M	UNKNOWN	GRZZZZ	USA	DUESTERWALT, HENRIETTE	58	F	UNKNOWN	GRZZZZ	USA
SCHIFFER, MARG.	52	F	UNKNOWN	GRZZZZ	USA	WALTER	15	M	UNKNOWN	GRZZZZ	USA
PAPROCKI, ANNA	30	F	UNKNOWN	GRZZZZ	USA	WILLI	4	M	CHILD	GRZZZZ	USA
JOHN	11	M	UNKNOWN	GRZZZZ	USA	MEYER, MAX	38	M	FARMER	GRZZZZ	USA
JOSEF	8	F	CHILD	GRZZZZ	USA	HULDA	34	F	W	GRZZZZ	USA
ANTON	5	F	CHILD	GRZZZZ	USA	MAX	.06	M	INFANT	GRZZZZ	USA
CATH.	3	F	CHILD	GRZZZZ	USA	EIFERT, SIGM.	35	M	FARMER	GRZZZZ	USA
KWIATKOWSKI, MARIA	29	F	UNKNOWN	GRZZZZ	USA	BERTHA	22	F	W	GRZZZZ	USA
JOSEF	3	M	CHILD	GRZZZZ	USA	CARL	.11	M	INFANT	GRZZZZ	USA
ANTONI	.09	M	INFANT	GRZZZZ	USA	MEIER, GUST.	22	M	FARMER	GRZZZZ	USA
KURZAK, ANNA	22	F	UNKNOWN	GRZZZZ	USA	FRENDENTHAL, HULDA	17	F	UNKNOWN	GRZZZZ	USA
VICTORIA	2	F	CHILD	GRZZZZ	USA	MUEHLEFELDER, BLUEMCHEN	14	F	UNKNOWN	GRZZZZ	USA
LEW.	.10	M	INFANT	GRZZZZ	USA	FITZTHUM, ANTONL.	38	M	MCHT	GRZZZZ	USA
WICKERT, FRIED.	24	F	UNKNOWN	GRZZZZ	USA	CLARA	31	F	W	GRZZZZ	USA
MEIER, CAROL.	.06	M	INFANT	GRZZZZ	USA	MAX	8	M	CHILD	GRZZZZ	USA
AUKE, ADOLF	18	F	UNKNOWN	GRZZZZ	USA	ALMA	7	F	CHILD	GRZZZZ	USA
KOSEICHNA, MARIANNE	32	F	UNKNOWN	GRZZZZ	USA	PENBER, SOPHIE	19	F	SMSTS	GRZZZZ	USA
MAX	36	M	LABR	GRZZZZ	USA	LULLING, CHR.	58	F	SMSTS	GRZZZZ	USA
REISSMANN, LISIA	18	F	UNKNOWN	GRZZZZ	USA	BARB.	23	F	SMSTS	GRZZZZ	USA
GESSLER, ERNST	61	F	UNKNOWN	GRZZZZ	USA	ELSEBECK, BARB.	28	F	SMSTS	GRZZZZ	USA
VEISS, JULIA	28	F	UNKNOWN	GRZZZZ	USA	FALKENSTEIN, FRITZ	27	M	MCHT	GRZZZZ	USA
SOKOLOWSKI, MARIE	28	F	UNKNOWN	GRZZZZ	USA	VOLK, CATH.	14	F	UNKNOWN	GRZZZZ	USA
RUIGGL, WILH.	44	M	FARMER	GRZZZZ	USA	FREY, ANNA	24	F	UNKNOWN	GRZZZZ	USA
SOPHIE	43	F	UNKNOWN	GRZZZZ	USA	OSCAR	.11	M	INFANT	GRZZZZ	USA
WILH.	3	M	CHILD	GRZZZZ	USA	DINKEL, MARIA	15	F	UNKNOWN	GRZZZZ	USA
HERMINE	2	F	CHILD	GRZZZZ	USA	BARTH, NICOL.	22	M	LABR	GRZZZZ	USA
LINA	6	F	CHILD	GRZZZZ	USA	KOHLMANN, DIED.	16	M	LABR	GRZZZZ	USA
GERH.	.09	M	INFANT	GRZZZZ	USA	GEFFKEN, ADOLH.	19	F	UNKNOWN	GRZZZZ	USA
HERM.	39	M	FARMER	GRZZZZ	USA	WELLROCK, BERTH.	20	M	LABR	GRZZZZ	USA
WASCHKOWSKI, MARIE	25	F	UNKNOWN	GRZZZZ	USA	PAPER, META	16	F	UNKNOWN	GRZZZZ	USA
PROMMELB, RICH.	17	F	SHMK	GRZZZZ	USA	FISCZEN, HEINR.	17	M	MCHT	GRZZZZ	USA
MEIER, MARG.	20	F	UNKNOWN	GRZZZZ	USA	HAEGER, BARTH.	16	M	MCHT	GRZZZZ	USA
GROSS, PAUL	32	M	LABR	GRZZZZ	USA	HENSER, KATH.	19	F	UNKNOWN	GRZZZZ	USA
GERHOLD, LEOP.	49	M	LABR	GRZZZZ	USA	FOROTMEIER, JOH.	22	M	LABR	GRZZZZ	USA
DOROTH.	29	F	W	GRZZZZ	USA	ZAPF, GEORG	17	M	LABR	GRZZZZ	USA
FRIED.	8	M	CHILD	GRZZZZ	USA	KLOTZ, CARL	20	M	LABR	GRZZZZ	USA
SCHLOWIEDT, WILH.	16	M	UNKNOWN	GRZZZZ	USA	RENKEN, GEORG	38	M	LABR	GRZZZZ	USA
MENDEL, ISAAC	26	M	MCHT	GRZZZZ	USA	FELGES, HEINR.	16	M	LABR	GRZZZZ	USA
BODE, JOH.	39	M	MCHT	GRZZZZ	USA	SCHULZE, LUDW.	38	M	LABR	GRZZZZ	USA
LENK, LOUISE	25	F	UNKNOWN	GRZZZZ	USA	WILH.	13	F	UNKNOWN	GRZZZZ	USA
FRITZ	.10	M	INFANT	GRZZZZ	USA	AUG.	11	F	UNKNOWN	GRZZZZ	USA
PENERT, ERNST.	52	F	UNKNOWN	GRZZZZ	USA	LOUISE	11	F	UNKNOWN	GRZZZZ	USA
PARTOCH, EML.	29	F	UNKNOWN	GRZZZZ	USA	LUDW.	8	M	CHILD	GRZZZZ	USA
MARTHA	.11	F	INFANT	GRZZZZ	USA	ANNA	7	F	CHILD	GRZZZZ	USA
FLORA	6	F	CHILD	GRZZZZ	USA	SCHMIDT, DOEOTH.	49	F	SMSTS	GRZZZZ	USA
BECK, KAROL.	36	F	UNKNOWN	GRZZZZ	USA	GROMM, WILH.	22	F	UNKNOWN	GRZZZZ	USA
CAROL.	8	F	CHILD	GRZZZZ	USA	BERDA, GUST.	20	M	LABR	GRZZZZ	USA
REINH.	7	M	CHILD	GRZZZZ	USA	WILH.	22	F	W	GRZZZZ	USA
ANNA	6	F	CHILD	GRZZZZ	USA	BERTHA	.09	F	INFANT	GRZZZZ	USA
GUST.	.10	M	INFANT	GRZZZZ	USA	ZINNER, FRANZ	30	M	MCHT	GRZZZZ	USA
SCHUBERT, JOH.	21	M	LABR	GRZZZZ	USA	VOLLOMZ, VALENT.	22	M	CPTR	GRZZZZ	USA
JOHN, JOH.	16	M	LABR	GRZZZZ	USA	MICHEL, CARL	29	M	CPTR	GRZZZZ	USA
HEINR.	15	M	LABR	GRZZZZ	USA	SPIELKER, LOUISE	49	F	UNKNOWN	GRZZZZ	USA
JOH.	13	M	LABR	GRZZZZ	USA	EDW.	11	M	CH	GRZZZZ	USA
FRIEDER, JOH.	14	F	UNKNOWN	GRZZZZ	USA	HERMINE	8	F	CHILD	GRZZZZ	USA
BURHARD, MARG.	19	F	UNKNOWN	GRZZZZ	USA	SCHMIDT, CONR.	16	M	CNF	GRZZZZ	USA
JOH.	.03	M	INFANT	GRZZZZ	USA	BINDER, MART.	26	M	MCHT	GRZZZZ	USA
BROCKMANN, AUG.	15	M	LABR	GRZZZZ	USA	MUELLER, ELISE	65	F	UNKNOWN	GRZZZZ	USA
WALDHENSER, HENNI.	26	M	LABR	GRZZZZ	USA	BLOECHL, JOSEF	27	M	MCHT	GRZZZZ	USA

PASSENGER	AGE	SEX	OCCUPATION	PRVL	DES
BUTTERFASS, CARL	22	M	MCHT	GRZZZZUSA	
WYRKUS, ANT.	32	F	UNKNOWN	GRZZZZUSA	
RUBEL, MINNA	32	F	UNKNOWN	GRZZZZUSA	
ELEE	4	F	CHILD	GRZZZZUSA	
SOEHNGEN, CONR.	47	M	LABR	GRZZZZUSA	
AKERMANN, ISAAK	16	M	CNF	GRZZZZUSA	

SHIP: ETHIOPIA

FROM: GLASGOW AND MOVILLE
TO: NEW YORK
ARRIVED: 07 AUGUST 1888

PASSENGER	AGE	SEX	OCCUPATION	PRVL	DES
GLOTZBACH, LEONARD	21	M	LABR	GRZZZZUSA	
PARTYKA, KATAZYNA	50	F	HP	GRZZZZUSA	
MUNDT, HERMAN	22	M	LKSH	GRZZZZUSA	
SCHMIDT, ANTON	22	M	LABR	GRZZZZUSA	
HUMCKENS, HY.H.	30	M	HTLKPR	GRZZZZUSA	
F.CATH.ELISE	21	F	UNKNOWN	GRZZZZUSA	

SHIP: HERMANN

FROM: BREMEN
TO: BALTIMORE
ARRIVED: 08 AUGUST 1888

PASSENGER	AGE	SEX	OCCUPATION	PRVL	DES
ULLMANN, OTTO	19	M	TRVLR	GRZZZZMD	
ORF, U	20	F	UNKNOWN	GRZZZZMD	
CHRIST.	56	M	JNR	GRZZZZMD	
UHLMANN, THERESIA	63	F	UNKNOWN	SRZZZZMD	
BORST, KUNI.	34	F	UNKNOWN	GRZZZZMD	
HAHN, EMILIE	31	F	UNKNOWN	GRZZZZMD	
STROERER, HERM.	21	M	PVTR	GRZZZZMD	
HERMANN, M.	50	F	UNKNOWN	GRZZZZMD	
BADERNINSKY, JACOB	29	M	FARMER	GRZZZZMD	
SCHNEIDER, CONRAD	29	M	FARMER	GRZZZZMD	
NOCHELMANN, PETER	62	M	FARMER	GRZZZZMD	
REWALSKI, LUDWIG	56	M	BRR	GRZZZZMD	
KRAKOWSKI, BARBARA	30	F	UNKNOWN	GRZZZZMD	
SCHMIDT, GOTTFRIED	38	M	TLR	GRZZZZMD	
BERTHA	28	F	W	GRZZZZMD	
CARL	.11	M	INFANT	GRZZZZMD	
BOROWSKI, CHRIST.	60	M	SHMK	GRZZZZMD	
BARBARA	55	F	W	GRZZZZMD	
CIESIELSKI, PETER	31	M	FARMER	GRZZZZMD	
MACKENROTH, ADOLF	24	M	BLKSMH	GRZZZZMD	
ELISE	25	F	W	GRZZZZMD	
WILLY	1	M	CHILD	GRZZZZMD	
SZAFRANSKI, WAWR.	42	M	JNR	GRZZZZMD	
JULIA	59	F	W	GRZZZZMD	
MARIE	18	F	UNKNOWN	GRZZZZMD	
STANISLAUS	16	M	UNKNOWN	GRZZZZMD	
TUCHERA, HELENE	19	F	UNKNOWN	GRZZZZMD	
MIELKE, GUSTAV	26	M	FARMER	GRZZZZMD	
DEMERLING, FRANZ	27	M	PNTR	GRZZZZMD	
ELISABETH	23	F	W	GRZZZZMD	
ELISABETH	1	F	CHILD	GRZZZZMD	
LEMKE, EMMA	16	F	UNKNOWN	GRZZZZMD	
STUTZKE, FRIEDR.	17	M	UNKNOWN	GRZZZZMD	
KUJATH, CARL	18	M	TNM	GRZZZZMD	
SCHWARTZ, HERM.	25	M	TNM	GRZZZZMD	
SCHMIDT, CLARA	20	F	UNKNOWN	GRZZZZMD	
SIEG, AUGUSTE	20	F	UNKNOWN	GRZZZZMD	
DURSKA, ELISABETH	26	F	UNKNOWN	GRZZZZMD	
LISECKA, AGNISKA	22	F	UNKNOWN	GRZZZZMD	

PASSENGER	AGE	SEX	OCCUPATION	PRVL	DES
FRANZISKA	4	F	CHILD	GRZZZZMD	
MICHAEL	.09	M	INFANT	GRZZZZMD	
HEIN, EMILIE	21	F	UNKNOWN	GRZZZZMD	
GURSKI, SIMON	50	M	LABR	GRZZZZMD	
LAURA	63	F	W	GRZZZZMD	
LAURA	7	F	CHILD	GRZZZZMD	
MANN, CATHARINA	30	F	UNKNOWN	GRZZZZMD	
SCHWANKE, EMILIE	33	F	UNKNOWN	GRZZZZMD	
MATHILDE	19	F	CH	GRZZZZMD	
MARTHA	6	F	CHILD	GRZZZZMD	
MINNA	5	F	CHILD	GRZZZZMD	
OTTO	2	M	CHILD	GRZZZZMD	
AUGUST	.06	M	INFANT	GRZZZZMD	
KLINEK, JADWIGA	15	F	UNKNOWN	GRZZZZMD	
SCHULZ, JOHANN	16	M	UNKNOWN	GRZZZZMD	
GUSSMANN, LEOKADIA	22	F	UNKNOWN	GRZZZZMD	
MARIE	.09	F	INFANT	GRZZZZMD	
TILK, FRANZ	30	M	LKSH	GRZZZZMD	
ZELLER, HERM.	18	M	LKSH	GRZZZZMD	
KATTENBERG, EMILIE	25	F	UNKNOWN	GRZZZZMD	
KRUEGER, MINNA	21	F	UNKNOWN	GRZZZZMD	
NEIRITZKE, MARTIN	50	M	FARMER	GRZZZZMD	
MARIANNE	40	F	W	GRZZZZMD	
SALOME	10	F	CH	GRZZZZMD	
CLARA	6	F	CHILD	GRZZZZMD	
MICHEL	.01	M	INFANT	GRZZZZMD	
INSTERZENKA, THERESE	30	F	UNKNOWN	GRZZZZMD	
HALFPAPP, IDA	14	F	CH	GRZZZZMD	
KURZBEIN, AUGUST	18	F	UNKNOWN	GRZZZZMD	
ROGAZEWSKI, JOSEF	25	M	FARMER	GRZZZZMD	
PRANKE, PAULINE	23	F	UNKNOWN	GRZZZZMD	
KURZYNSKA, AMANDA	15	F	UNKNOWN	GRZZZZMD	
PRANKE, HERM.	2	M	CHILD	GRZZZZMD	
GRASSER, ANTON	36	M	FARMER	GRZZZZMD	
BEIROW, CARL	15	M	UNKNOWN	GRZZZZMD	
ANNA	12	F	CH	GRZZZZMD	
ECKENSTORFER, JOSEF	25	M	FARMER	GRZZZZMD	
ZIBELL, ROBERT	21	M	FARMER	GRZZZZMD	
LEBRECHT, LUISE	33	F	W	GRZZZZMD	
JOHANNA	4	F	CHILD	GRZZZZMD	
EDUARD	3	M	CHILD	GRZZZZMD	
RADESCHEWSKI, JULIANE	20	F	UNKNOWN	GRZZZZMD	
SELLESINSKY, ANNA	39	F	W	GRZZZZMD	
AGNES	9	F	CHILD	GRZZZZMD	
ALBERT	7	M	CHILD	GRZZZZMD	
FRIED.	2	M	CHILD	GRZZZZMD	
MARGARETHA	.09	F	INFANT	GRZZZZMD	
HETMANSKI, MARIE	13	F	CH	GRZZZZMD	
PLAMEISCH, EVA	22	F	UNKNOWN	GRZZZZMD	
NISIUS, FRIEDR.	53	M	FARMER	GRZZZZMD	
AMALIE	51	F	W	GRZZZZMD	
HULDA	21	F	UNKNOWN	GRZZZZMD	
LEHMANN, GUSTAF	18	M	UNKNOWN	GRZZZZMD	
HERMANN, ANNA	28	F	UNKNOWN	GRZZZZMD	
ALFRED	.01	M	INFANT	GRZZZZMD	
EITMER, SUSANNE	66	F	UNKNOWN	GRZZZZMD	
HAERSSNER, LUISE	28	F	UNKNOWN	GRZZZZMD	
KAZIEMIRSKA, PAULINE	25	F	UNKNOWN	GRZZZZMD	
CIECHOWICZ, JULIANE	20	F	UNKNOWN	GRZZZZMD	
WEINKAMP, HULDA	21	F	UNKNOWN	GRZZZZMD	
MAYER, OTTO	28	M	JNR	GRZZZZMD	
ALBERTINE	26	F	W	GRZZZZMD	
PAUL	2	M	CHILD	GRZZZZMD	
CARL	.09	M	INFANT	GRZZZZMD	
ERBACH, BERTHA	23	F	UNKNOWN	GRZZZZMD	
EHLERT, FERD.	13	M	CH	GRZZZZMD	
RADKE, CAROLINE	31	F	UNKNOWN	GRZZZZMD	
TOMASCHEFSKA, MARIA	56	F	UNKNOWN	GRZZZZMD	
MITSCHOFSKA, LEO	24	M	FARMER	GRZZZZMD	
ZERBEL, WILH.	52	M	UNKNOWN	GRZZZZMD	
CLARA	16	F	UNKNOWN	GRZZZZMD	
KRZLEWSKI, CATH.	36	F	UNKNOWN	GRZZZZMD	
MINNA	10	F	CH	GRZZZZMD	
OTTILIE	9	F	CHILD	GRZZZZMD	
JOHANN	6	M	CHILD	GRZZZZMD	

PASSENGER	AGE	SEX	OCCUPATION	PRVL	VLS
ANNA	.01	F	INFANT	GRZZZZMD	
BECKER, CARL	28	M	MNR	GRZZZZMD	
EMMA	25	F	W	GRZZZZMD	
LINNEMANN, LUISE	27	F	W	GRZZZZMD	
ERNST	28	M	MLR	GRZZZZMD	
PAUL	3	M	CHILD	GRZZZZMD	
ANNA	2	F	CHILD	GRZZZZMD	
IDA	.01	F	INFANT	GRZZZZMD	
KRUMMREI, HEINR.	29	M	LABR	GRZZZZMD	
DITTMANN, WILH.	60	M	LABR	GRZZZZMD	
BUTZIER, AUGUSTE	29	F	UNKNOWN	GRZZZZMD	
EMMA	2	F	CHILD	GRZZZZMD	
EICHHORN, CARL	41	M	LKSH	GRZZZZMD	
MEIHLENHAUPT, GUSTAF	17	M	CGRMKR	GRZZZZMD	
KRZYPOLSKA, FRZKA	26	F	W	GRZZZZMD	
ANNA	9	F	CHILD	GRZZZZMD	
JULIANA	.07	F	INFANT	GRZZZZMD	
BIERMANN, DORIS	54	F	W	GRZZZZMD	
MINNA	21	F	UNKNOWN	GRZZZZMD	
GEORGINE	18	F	UNKNOWN	GRZZZZMD	
WLHELMINE	15	F	UNKNOWN	GRZZZZMD	
BOETTCHER, ANDREAS	22	M	CL	GRZZZZMD	
REDEMSKY, FERD.	22	M	LABR	GRZZZZOH	
BERGUND, ANTONIE	19	F	UNKNOWN	GRZZZZMN	
SCHMURAN, HEDWIG	25	F	UNKNOWN	GRZZZZMN	
KLINGBEIL, MATHILDA	24	F	UNKNOWN	GRZZZZOH	
HAWRING, ANNA	52	F	W	GRZZZZWI	
JOHANNA	18	F	UNKNOWN	GRZZZZWI	
ELISE	12	F	CH	GRZZZZWI	
EUGEN.	9	M	CHILD	GRZZZZWI	
MASCHEE, HERM.	22	M	MLR	GRZZZZWI	
MUELLER, EMILIE	26	F	W	GRZZZZWI	
HERMANN	2	M	CHILD	GRZZZZWI	
ANNA	.06	F	INFANT	GRZZZZWI	
BUTZIN, BERTHA	24	F	UNKNOWN	GRZZZZWI	
LEHMANN, WILH.	26	M	BLKSMH	GRZZZZWI	
CHRISTIANS, PETER	50	M	FARMER	GRZZZZWI	
HEPKE	50	F	W	GRZZZZWI	
HEIKE	13	M	CH	GRZZZZWI	
WROTHMANN, ADAM	63	M	FARMER	GRZZZZWI	
MARIE	18	F	UNKNOWN	GRZZZZWI	
STEIN, LUISE	19	F	UNKNOWN	GRZZZZWI	
TOELKE, FERD.	21	M	MSN	GRZZZZWI	
JOHANNA	24	F	UNKNOWN	GRZZZZWI	
MINDERJAHN, HEINR.	25	M	FARMER	GRZZZZWI	
SPINDLER, JOHANN	26	M	FARMER	GRZZZZWI	
RHAEDE, WILH.	17	M	CL	GRZZZZWI	
GROHEUS, JOSEF	23	M	FARMER	GRZZZZWI	
MUELLER, JOHANN	24	M	FARMER	GRZZZZWI	
KNEUSTLE, JOHANN	20	M	GDNR	GRZZZZWI	
GRAF, FRANZISKA	19	F	UNKNOWN	GRZZZZWI	
HOEFLACHER, FRIEDR.	35	M	BKR	GRZZZZWI	
MEYER, JULIANE	35	F	W	GRZZZZMI	
EMMA	4	F	CHILD	GRZZZZMI	
EDUARD	.06	M	INFANT	GRZZZZMI	
BARELSKA, JOSEFA	24	F	UNKNOWN	GRZZZZMI	
MIKITTE, CHARLOTTE	20	F	UNKNOWN	GRZZZZMI	
GELFERT, ERNST	48	M	WVR	GRZZZZMI	
WINKLER, IDA	18	F	UNKNOWN	GRZZZZMI	
ZUELCH, PETER	18	M	CGRMKR	GRZZZZMI	
GOLDMEIER, ISAK	17	M	BCHR	GRZZZZMI	
KAHMANN, AUG.NOLTE	22	M	FARMER	GRZZZZMI	
LUKOWSKI, WILH.	52	M	SHMK	GRZZZZMI	
WALTER	11	M	CL	GRZZZZMI	
ANNA	.11	F	INFANT	GRZZZZMI	
HENRIETTE	35	F	W	GRZZZZMI	
WAESSMANN, LISETTE	20	F	W	GRZZZZMI	
FRIEDR.	.11	M	INFANT	GRZZZZMI	
WAPPLER, MARTHA	26	F	UNKNOWN	GRZZZZMI	
HAERTEL, CHRISTIAN	29	M	BCHR	GRZZZZMI	
LAURA	24	F	W	GRZZZZMI	
MARIE	2	F	CHILD	GRZZZZMI	
HEDWIG	.11	F	INFANT	GRZZZZMI	
CECILIE	65	F	UNKNOWN	GRZZZZMI	
MARTIN, CATHARINA	26	F	UNKNOWN	GRZZZZMI	
ADLOFF, MARGRETT	18	F	UNKNOWN	GRZZZZMI	
NISPEL, CHRISTINE	21	F	UNKNOWN	GRZZZZMI	
KOEHLER, ANTON	26	M	FARMER	GRZZZZMI	
BACH, HEINR.	36	M	FARMER	GRZZZZMI	
GRUENBAUM, SELEHE	18	F	UNKNOWN	GRZZZZMI	
SCHRAMM, MARIE	16	F	UNKNOWN	GRZZZZMI	
WALDMANN, ROSALIE	15	F	UNKNOWN	GRZZZZMI	
GRAF, ANASTASIA	34	F	UNKNOWN	GRZZZZMI	
SCHLENK, BABETTE	13	F	CH	GRZZZZMI	
ROSINA	14	F	CH	GRZZZZMI	
FISCHER, ERNST	17	M	UNKNOWN	GRZZZZMI	
KONKAWSKA, JULIUS	51	M	JNR	GRZZZZMI	
JULIE	55	F	UNKNOWN	GRZZZZMI	
DONAISKI, JACOB	24	M	SDLR	GRZZZZMI	
PETERS, MARGUARD	17	M	CL	GRZZZZMI	
SEITZ, JOHANN	40	M	FARMER	GRZZZZMI	
HEIN.	11	M	CH	GRZZZZMI	
GRUBNER, ANNA	4	F	CHILD	GRZZZZMI	
ALBRICH	2	M	CHILD	GRZZZZMI	
SMOLINSKI, PETER	34	M	TU	GRZZZZMI	
RUNJEWSKI, ANNA	30	F	UNKNOWN	GRZZZZMI	
MAIDOWSKY, JOH.	28	M	PNTR	GRZZZZMI	
KRUEGER, JOH.	23	M	DLR	GRZZZZMI	
JULIANE	29	F	W	GRZZZZMI	
SKERA, ANTONI	17	F	UNKNOWN	GRZZZZMI	
SCHMITTNER, ANTON	22	M	SHMK	GRZZZZWI	
FRANK, FRIEDR	33	M	TLR	GRZZZZWI	
SCHUSTER, JOHANN	15	M	UNKNOWN	GRZZZZWI	
KOKEMUELLER, LUDWIG	17	M	UNKNOWN	GRZZZZKY	
POHLMANN, ANGELA	52	F	UNKNOWN	GRZZZZOH	
MARIA	23	F	UNKNOWN	GRZZZZOH	
HENGAU, MARIA	26	F	UNKNOWN	GRZZZZOH	
SANDEL, ANNA	21	F	UNKNOWN	GRZZZZOH	
LUISE	7	F	CHILD	GRZZZZOH	
SUHR, ELISABETH	20	F	UNKNOWN	GRZZZZOH	
LOCH, CHARLES	42	M	MCHT	GRZZZZMD	
JANNING, AUGUST	26	M	FARMER	GRZZZZMD	
KIEHN, ALBERT	26	M	FARMER	GRZZZZMD	
DROESCHER, AUGUST	37	M	FARMER	GRZZZZNE	
BERTHA	27	F	W	GRZZZZNE	
GUSTAF	.03	M	INFANT	GRZZZZNE	
KELLER, ANNA	25	F	UNKNOWN	GRZZZZMD	
SCHRIEFER, ELISE	27	F	UNKNOWN	GRZZZZTX	
CATHARINA	4	F	CHILD	GRZZZZTX	
FRIEDA	2	F	CHILD	GRZZZZTX	
KORNINGBAUTEN, JAC.	55	M	FARMER	GRZZZZOH	
ELISABETH	48	F	W	GRZZZZOH	
CATHARINA	13	F	CH	GRZZZZOH	
LUISE	11	F	CH	GRZZZZOH	
MARIE	7	F	CHILD	GRZZZZOH	
STELLMACHER, AUG.	33	M	FARMER	GRZZZZOH	
ELISE	34	F	W	GRZZZZOH	
HEIN.	11	M	CH	GRZZZZOH	
EMILIE	8	F	CHILD	GRZZZZOH	
FRITZ	5	M	CHILD	GRZZZZOH	
MARTHA	3	F	CHILD	GRZZZZOH	
OSCAR	3	F	CHILD	GRZZZZOH	
BEYER, PAUL	22	M	GZR	GRZZZZMOB	
DIEWITZ, OTTILIE	28	F	UNKNOWN	GRZZZZMOB	
VOGT, JOHANN	18	F	UNKNOWN	GRZZZZMOB	
HANOLD, FRIEDR.	16	M	UNKNOWN	GRZZZZMOB	
MELCHING, DINA	19	F	UNKNOWN	GRZZZZMD	
SCHMIDT, MAX	28	M	WVR	GRZZZZNE	
LIPPRAND, WILH.	44	M	LABR	GRZZZZWI	
HERM.	18	M	LABR	GRZZZZWI	
OSCAR	7	M	CHILD	GRZZZZWI	
DICHTENHAHN, GEORG	28	M	FARMER	GRZZZZMOB	
FISCHER, JOHANN	16	M	UNKNOWN	GRZZZZMD	
SIELING, DIEDR.	36	M	FARMER	GRZZZZMD	
POHLMANN, LISETTE	18	F	UNKNOWN	GRZZZZMD	
BOEDEKER, HEINR.	16	M	UNKNOWN	GRZZZZMD	
GEISLER, AUGUST	36	M	BKLYR	GRZZZZIL	
BERTHA	31	F	W	GRZZZZIL	
ALBERT	8	M	CHILD	GRZZZZIL	
LUISE	1	F	CHILD	GRZZZZIL	

PASSENGER	AGE	SEX	OCCUPATION	PRVVL	DES
CATR.	00	F	INF	GRZZZZIL	
GROB, ANNA	17	F	UNKNOWN	GRZZZZMD	
TWELE, CARL	23	M	PNTR	GRZZZZMD	
HARMS, CARL	24	M	MCHT	GRZZZZUNK	
HEINR.	16	M	CL	GRZZZZUNK	
ORF, VALENTIN	49	M	FARMER	GRZZZZMD	
EMMA	46	F	W	GRZZZZMD	
LUISE	17	F	UNKNOWN	GRZZZZMD	
CARL	16	M	UNKNOWN	GRZZZZMD	
EDUARD	14	M	UNKNOWN	GRZZZZMD	
BERTHA	12	F	CH	GRZZZZMD	
AUGUSTE	3	F	CHILD	GRZZZZMD	
IDA	.09	F	INFANT	GRZZZZMD	
PALOSKA, EMILIE	52	F	UNKNOWN	GRZZZZMD	
SOSNOSKA, MARIA	25	F	W	GRZZZZMD	
JOHANN	4	M	CHILD	GRZZZZMD	
ANTON	3	M	CHILD	GRZZZZMD	
LIESLAK, MARIE	27	F	UNKNOWN	GRZZZZMD	
BUDAK, MARIE	27	F	UNKNOWN	GRZZZZMD	
ANNA	19	F	UNKNOWN	GRZZZZMD	
DOMBROWSKI, FRANZ	29	M	FARMER	GRZZZZMD	
ANNA	22	F	W	GRZZZZMD	
MARIAN	3	F	CHILD	GRZZZZMD	
BLOSS, HEDWIG	18	F	UNKNOWN	GRZZZZMD	
ERNST	16	M	UNKNOWN	GRZZZZMD	
WOLFRAM, MARIA	23	F	UNKNOWN	GRZZZZMD	
SKRZINSKA, ANASTA	26	F	UNKNOWN	GRZZZZMD	
AULBACH, MARG.	18	F	UNKNOWN	GRZZZZMD	
GOLSMEIER, MALCHEN	20	F	UNKNOWN	GRZZZZIL	
PFLUG, WILHELMINE	39	F	UNKNOWN	GRZZZZIL	
WILHELMINE	13	F	UNKNOWN	GRZZZZIL	
BENZING, CONRAD	53	M	FARMER	GRZZZZIL	
ANNA	46	F	W	GRZZZZIL	
ELISABETH	24	F	UNKNOWN	GRZZZZIL	
ADAM	10	M	CH	GRZZZZIL	
CATHARINA	10	F	CH	GRZZZZIL	
JOSEF	8	M	CHILD	GRZZZZIL	
OTTO	6	M	CHILD	GRZZZZIL	
BERGER, ANNA	28	F	UNKNOWN	GRZZZZOH	
BIESCHKE, ALBRECHT	33	M	FARMER	GRZZZZMI	
ALBERTINE	32	F	W	GRZZZZMI	
FRANZ	10	M	CH	GRZZZZMI	
GERTRUDE	9	F	CHILD	GRZZZZMI	
JOHANN	7	M	CHILD	GRZZZZMI	
FELIX	4	M	CHILD	GRZZZZMI	
ALBERT	2	M	CHILD	GRZZZZMI	
JULIANE	.06	F	INFANT	GRZZZZMI	
KUNKOWSKI, CAROLINE	34	F	UNKNOWN	GRZZZZMI	
CARL	3	M	CHILD	GRZZZZMI	
ALFRED	17	M	UNKNOWN	GRZZZZMI	
AUGUST	14	M	UNKNOWN	GRZZZZMI	
MEYER, FRANZ	23	M	PNTR	GRZZZZMD	
SCHREIBER, LOUIS	16	M	CL	GRZZZZIL	
SCHMIDT, WILH.	34	M	FARMER	GRZZZZMN	
EMMA	31	F	W	GRZZZZMN	
SCHULZ, BERTHA	21	F	UNKNOWN	GRZZZZMN	
BACH, CARL	16	M	CL	GRZZZZPA	
ERBECK, WILHELME	24	F	UNKNOWN	GRZZZZWI	
BARTSCH, MARGARETHE	20	F	UNKNOWN	GRZZZZMOB	
SCHAUER, AUGUST	27	M	FARMER	GRZZZZWI	
MUELLER, WILH.	17	M	BCHR	GRZZZZPA	
ANNA	15	F	UNKNOWN	GRZZZZPA	
OESER, RICHARD	25	M	MNR	GRZZZZIL	
MARIE	27	F	W	GRZZZZIL	
ERBISCH, JOHANNES	20	M	BLKSMH	GRZZZZIL	
LETTAU, MICHAEL	60	M	PVTR	GRZZZZIL	
AUGUST	56	F	W	GRZZZZIL	
JULIUS	16	M	UNKNOWN	GRZZZZIL	
SCHOLA, FRANZ	22	M	LABR	GRZZZZIL	
RIEDEMANN, LUISE	27	F	UNKNOWN	GRZZZZMD	
HEDWIG	2	F	CHILD	GRZZZZMD	
GLADE, JOHANNA	42	F	UNKNOWN	GRZZZZMD	
CARL	26	M	FARMER	GRZZZZMD	
SALIA	35	F	UNKNOWN	GRZZZZMD	
CLARA	5	F	CHILD	GRZZZZMD	
TSCHAMPEE, CHRIST.	31	M	FARMER	GRZZZZMD	
MURAWSKI, FRANZISKA	29	F	W	GRZZZZMD	
LEHONIA	6	F	CHILD	GRZZZZMD	
MARTHA	.10	F	INFANT	GRZZZZMD	
ZWANZIG, PETER	42	M	FARMER	GRZZZZMD	
MARIA	20	F	UNKNOWN	GRZZZZMD	
HEDWIG	.06	F	INFANT	GRZZZZMD	
KOHLWEZ, RICHARD	28	M	JWLR	GRZZZZMD	
SULJE, WILLI	22	M	CL	GRZZZZMD	
POHLMANN, HEINR.	50	M	FARMER	GRZZZZOH	
DINA	25	F	UNKNOWN	GRZZZZOH	
DE, OLLIG	36	M	LABR	GRZZZZIL	
HILKE	40	F	W	GRZZZZIL	
MATHIAS	7	F	CHILD	GRZZZZUNK	
JANNA	5	F	CHILD	GRZZZZUSA	
HARMKE	3	M	CHILD	GRZZZZUSA	
HEIKE	.09	F	INFANT	GRZZZZUSA	
STOEHR, JOHANN	11	M	CH	GRZZZZUSA	
HESS, CONRAD	17	M	CL	GRZZZZKY	
LOESCHER, LAURIN	28	M	CL	GRZZZZPA	
R---K. ELISE	33	F	UNKNOWN	GRZZZZMD	
HEINEMANN, HERM.	36	M	SDLR	GRZZZZMD	
GROB, GEORG	17	M	TU	GRZZZZMD	
KAISER, JOSEF	40	M	JNR	GRZZZZWI	
SOELTER, EMIL	29	M	CPTR	GRZZZZOH	
UCKMANN, CARL	29	M	MCHT	GRZZZZOH	
JOESSEN, FRIED.	3	M	CHILD	GRZZZZOH	
VANSELOW, AUGUSTE	11	F	CH	GRZZZZIA	
STECHMESSER, ERNESTINE	33	F	UNKNOWN	GRZZZZIA	
VANSELOW, CAROLINE	11	F	CH	GRZZZZIA	
WILHELM	8	M	CHILD	GRZZZZIA	
SCHOENFELD, LUISE	8	F	CHILD	GRZZZZIA	
LANNOCH, ERNST	18	M	CL	GRZZZZOH	
HEINZ, HEINR.	56	M	FARMER	GRZZZZMD	
MARGARETHE	56	F	W	GRZZZZMD	
CATHARINA	19	F	UNKNOWN	GRZZZZMD	
AMALIA	16	F	UNKNOWN	GRZZZZMD	
JACOB	8	M	CHILD	GRZZZZMD	
PETER	5	M	CHILD	GRZZZZMD	
RUSSMANN, WILHELMINE	36	F	W	GRZZZZMD	
BERTHA	9	F	CHILD	GRZZZZMD	
ROBERT	8	M	CHILD	GRZZZZMD	
ALBERT	5	M	CHILD	GRZZZZMD	
AUGUSTE	.11	F	INFANT	GRZZZZMD	
SCHUKAI, IDA	16	F	UNKNOWN	GRZZZZMD	
PAUL	3	M	CHILD	GRZZZZMD	
PLATT, CAROLINE	57	F	UNKNOWN	GRZZZZMD	
MARIE	21	F	UNKNOWN	GRZZZZMD	
AUGUSTE	15	F	UNKNOWN	GRZZZZMD	
KURRELMEYER, WILH.	56	M	LABR	GRZZZZMD	
FRIEDERIKE	51	F	W	GRZZZZMD	
HAESE, EDUARD	26	M	CL	GRZZZZMD	
HAMANN, EMILIE	16	F	UNKNOWN	GRZZZZMD	
STEGE, HERMANN	44	M	MUSN	GRZZZZMD	
ERNESTINE	42	F	W	GRZZZZMD	
OTTO	11	M	CH	GRZZZZMD	
AMALIE	9	F	CHILD	GRZZZZMD	
ABEL, JOHANN	31	M	MUSN	GRZZZZMD	
ANNA	26	F	W	GRZZZZMD	
EMMA	6	F	CHILD	GRZZZZMD	
EMIL	5	M	CHILD	GRZZZZMD	
OTTO	2	M	CHILD	GRZZZZMD	
HELENE	.02	F	INFANT	GRZZZZMD	
BEHLING, OTTO	22	M	LABR	GRZZZZMD	
PAULUS, JOHANN	36	M	LABR	GRZZZZMD	
GUENTHER, WILH.	58	M	WVR	GRZZZZMD	
AMALIE	55	F	W	GRZZZZMD	
ELISE	13	F	CH	GRZZZZMD	
TROMMEL, MARGARETHE	18	F	UNKNOWN	GRZZZZMD	
RENNER, ANNA	23	F	UNKNOWN	GRZZZZMD	
WENZEL, ELISE	26	F	UNKNOWN	GRZZZZMD	
KOTHE, ADAM	68	M	UNKNOWN	GRZZZZMD	
MARG.	24	F	UNKNOWN	GRZZZZMD	
HANKIEWICZ, MARIANNE	56	F	UNKNOWN	GRZZZZMD	
LINN, ANNA	13	F	CH	GRZZZZMD	

PASSENGER	AGE	SEX	OCCUPATION	PRIVL	DES
SCHUNTR, CATHARINA	29	F	UNKNOWN		GRZZZZMD
LAMBERT, LUISE	40	F	UNKNOWN		GRZZZZMD
NEINTZ, HANNA	19	F	UNKNOWN		GRZZZZMD
JANRYNSKY, JOH.	30	M	FARMER		GRZZZZMD
SERBENT, MARIA	24	F	UNKNOWN		GRZZZZMD
RAAB, ELISABETH	18	F	UNKNOWN		GRZZZZMD
ROTHLOW, ELISE	25	F	W		GRZZZZMD
MARGARETHE	5	F	CHILD		GRZZZZMD
ANNA	4	F	CHILD		GRZZZZMD
ELISABETH	3	F	CHILD		GRZZZZMD
JOHANNES	.01	F	INFANT		GRZZZZMD
BARLACH, WILHELMINE	59	F	UNKNOWN		GRZZZZMD
WEISSS, MICHAL	71	M	PVTR		GRZZZZMD
OSTREICHER, MINNA	26	F	UNKNOWN		GRZZZZMD
MINNA	4	F	CHILD		GRZZZZMD
WEISS, CATHARINA	69	F	UNKNOWN		GRZZZZMD
ZAPF, ANNA	12	F	CH		GRZZZZMD
TESTOVF, LUISE	34	F	UNKNOWN		GRZZZZMD
RANDEBROEK, ED.	28	M	MCHT		GRZZZZMOB
KREBS, WILH.	18	M	UNKNOWN		GRZZZZMOB
SEDE, ENGELBURGA	38	F	UNKNOWN		GRZZZZMD
GOLDMANN, JULIUS	32	M	BCHR		GRZZZZMD
RANFT, CHRISTINE	20	F	UNKNOWN		GRZZZZMD
TREBES, HEIN.	26	M	UNKNOWN		GRZZZZMD
HEINZE, GEORG	55	M	PVTR		GRZZZZMD
FANSLAU, MINNA	25	F	UNKNOWN		GRZZZZMD
TANZER, JOSEF	25	M	MCHT		GRZZZZMD
MARIE	23	F	W		GRZZZZMD
HILDESHEIM, MAX	26	M	MCHT		GRZZZZMD
WEBER, MAGDALENE	19	F	UNKNOWN		GRZZZZMD
SCHROLL, JOSEF	30	M	TLR		GRZZZZMD
MINNA	28	F	W		GRZZZZMD
LUIS	2	M	CHILD		GRZZZZMD
RETELBURGER, LEONH.	24	M	BKR		GRZZZZMD
RITTMANN, CARL	18	M	BKR		GRZZZZMD
MISLIK, PETER	36	F	LABR		GRZZZZMD
CATHARINE	33	F	W		GRZZZZMD
SCHRENEMANN, JACOB	20	M	LABR		GRZZZZMD

PASSENGER	AGE	SEX	OCCUPATION	PRIVL	DES
WIESENIEWSKI, PAUL	38	M	SHMK		GRAHRZUSA
LUTEAUX, FRANCIS	22	M	FARMER		GRAHRZUSA

SHIP: WYOMING

FROM: LIVERPOOL AND QUEENSTOWN
TO: NEW YORK
ARRIVED: 08 AUGUST 1888

PASSENGER	AGE	SEX	OCCUPATION	PRIVL	DES
GOSSMAN, OTTO	26	M	LABR		GRZZZZUSA
ANNA	24	F	W		GRZZZZUSA
AVRAMOWIEZ, SUSIE	21	F	SP		GRZZZZUSA
WEIL, MOSEL	38	U	SP		GRZZZZUSA
ROSE	30	F	SP		GRZZZZUSA
SIMON	7	M	CHILD		GRZZZZUSA
ADOLF	6	M	CHILD		GRZZZZUSA
REBICCA	5	F	CHILD		GRZZZZUSA
LEOPOLD	3	M	CHILD		GRZZZZUSA
DAVIDSON, LORE	46	F	UNKNOWN		GRZZZZUSA
DWUNED	7	U	CHILD		GRZZZZUSA
PERCHINSKA, OLESHA	17	F	UNKNOWN		GRZZZZUSA
PEZELEMSKI, ANTONI	19	U	UNKNOWN		GRZZZZUSA
GENULFELD, W.	39	U	UNKNOWN		GRZZZZUSA
ALDWINE	38	U	UNKNOWN		GRZZZZUSA
FUNK, J.	59	M	LABR		GRZZZZUSA
KAREN	50	F	W		GRZZZZUSA
GERTRUDE	57	F	SP		GRZZZZUSA
FRUME	17	F	SP		GRZZZZUSA
CAROLINE	15	F	SP		GRZZZZUSA
JOHAN	7	M	CHILD		GRZZZZUSA
JACOB	6	M	CHILD		GRZZZZUSA
MARCHAL, P.	22	M	LABR		GRZZZZUSA
SEHR, W.	39	M	LABR		GRZZZZUSA
SCHENLOHN, ESMIS	22	F	SP		GRZZZZUSA

SHIP: IOWA

FROM: LIVERPOOL
TO: BOSTON
ARRIVED: 08 AUGUST 1888

PASSENGER	AGE	SEX	OCCUPATION	PRIVL	DES
SISSILMANN, S.	45	M	TLR		GRZZZZUSA
FREIDMANN, MORITZ	32	M	TLR		GRZZZZUSA

SHIP: STATE OF GEORGIA

FROM: GLASGOW AND LARNE
TO: NEW YORK
ARRIVED: 08 AUGUST 1888

PASSENGER	AGE	SEX	OCCUPATION	PRIVL	DES
MOHR, JOHAN	27	M	MSN		GRAHRZUSA
MAJEWSKI, JUDWIG	17	M	SHMK		GRAHRZUSA
PANLKE, HERMAN	22	M	CK		GRAHRZUSA
RICHTER, MAX	19	M	CK		GRAHRZUSA
RAHLS, THEOD.	23	M	BCHR		GRAHRZUSA
SONNEWSCHEN, LEOPOLD	34	M	LABR		GRAHRZUSA
LINA	30	F	UNKNOWN		GRAHRZUSA
JOSEF	5	M	CHILD		GRAHRZUSA
EMMA	2	F	CHILD		GRAHRZUSA
OTTAKAR	1	M	CHILD		GRAHRZUSA
HEINRICH	.03	M	INFANT		GRAHRZUSA

SHIP: ENGLAND

FROM: LIVERPOOL AND QUEENSTOWN
TO: NEW YORK
ARRIVED: 09 AUGUST 1888

PASSENGER	AGE	SEX	OCCUPATION	PRIVL	DES
PURIS, WAKA	17	F	SVNT		GRAGFUNY
SAPHER, ELISAB.	46	M	LABR		GRAGFUNY
HEINE	44	F	W		GRAGFUNY
LASAR	7	M	CHILD		GRAGFUNY
MOSEFKE	4	F	CHILD		GRAGFUNY
HOCKE, HEINE	36	F	SVNT		GRAGFUNY

SHIP: HAMMONIA

FROM: HAMBURG AND HAVRE
TO: NEW YORK
ARRIVED: 09 AUGUST 1888

PASSENGER	AGE	SEX	OCCUPATION	PRIVL	DES
HOLTMANN, BERNH.	28	M	LABR		HBZZZZUSA
ROSA	42	F	W		HBZZZZUSA
OTTO	.06	M	INFANT		HBZZZZUSA
KOCH, GEORG	24	M	MCHT		HBAAKHUSA
BIOLUCHA, URBAN	34	M	BKR		HBADVVUSA
CZIAHOUSKA, ROSALIE	20	F	SGL		HBADVVUSA

PASSENGER	AGE	SEX	OCCUPATION	PRVL/DES
TEINBERG, MORITZ	44	M	MCHT	HBACSDUSA
MUELLER, WILH.	14	M	MCHT	HBZZZZUSA
VILWOCH, ARSEN	17	M	WCHMKR	PRZZZZUSA
WISSMANN, MARIE	30	F	W	PRAADEUSA
CAROL.	5	F	CHILD	PRAADEUSA
MARTENS, GUSTAV	27	M	LABR	PRAJSXUSA
MICHAELIS, FRANZ.	26	F	W	PRACBFUSA
EMMA	3	F	CHILD	PRACBFUSA
HETZEL, FRIEDRICH	25	M	WCHMKR	BVZZZZUSA
BUHR, DORA	28	F	W	HBZZZZUSA
CARL	.11	M	INFANT	HBZZZZUSA
MESSMER, URSULA	20	F	SGL	WMZZZZUSA
LAMPRECHT, JOH.	20	M	SHMK	BDZZZZUSA
MASHS, MARIE	20	F	SGL	PRZZZZUSA
KNEPF, CHR.	16	F	SGL	PRAFJAUSA
HOESER, MARIE	29	F	W	BVZZZZUSA
JOH.	4	F	CHILD	BVZZZZUSA
KRIEG, CARL	21	M	LABR	BVAHQWUSA
SCHNAUER, EMILIE	27	F	SGL	LUZZZZUSA
RALE, OTTO	28	M	MCHT	PRZZZZUSA
LEWENBERG, FRANKE	24	F	SGL	PRAAKHUSA
KLEIN, LINA	28	F	SGL	PRAAKHUSA
WEITZ, MARIE	24	F	SGL	BVZZZZUSA
MERZ, HEINR.	50	M	FARMER	BVZZZZUSA
ANNA	55	F	W	BVZZZZUSA
THERESE	17	F	CH	BVZZZZUSA
FRANZ	9	M	CHILD	BVZZZZUSA
GREF, JUL.	16	M	FARMER	BVZZZZUSA
WANKEL, ROBERT	16	M	PRNTR	BVZZZZUSA
MEIM, SOFIE	18	F	SGL	BVZZZZUSA
KLEBER, JOSEF	18	M	CL	BVZZZZUSA
WAGNER, GENNIA	16	F	SGL	BVACXVUSA
KLAPPENBACH, AUGUST	25	M	MCHT	BVACYJUSA
MANNLACH, MORITZ	16	M	MCHT	BVADGNUSA
VOLK, EMILIE	18	F	SGL	HSZZZZUSA
WIESE, HEINR.	46	M	CPTR	HSAHNOUSA
ANNA	43	F	W	HSAHNOUSA
ANDRAS	18	M	CH	HSAHNOUSA
CHRISTIAN	17	M	CH	HSAHNOUSA
HEINR.	7	M	CHILD	HSAHNOUSA
BANDMAN, ALLERS	18	M	UNKNOWN	HBZZZZUSA
DAVIDSOHN, HERM.	56	M	FARMER	HBABPVUSA
DINA	54	F	W	HBABPVUSA
JOH.	17	F	W	HBABPVUSA
SALLI	9	F	CHILD	HBABPVUSA
DAVID	7	M	CHILD	HBABPVUSA
SCHMIDT, HERMANN	22	M	LABR	SYZZZZUSA
PESCH, REBECCA	42	F	W	SYACPSUSA
PAULA	17	F	UNKNOWN	SYACPSUSA
MARIE	14	F	UNKNOWN	SYACPSUSA
EMIL	9	M	CHILD	SYACPSUSA
LOEDING, BERTHA	24	F	SGL	PRZZZZUSA
SOBOTKER, BERTHA	27	F	SGL	PRAEIOUSA
SZWENTIK, STANISL.	17	M	LABR	PRACPSUSA
PRAENKIL, MINCHA	50	F	W	PRZZZZUSA
PAULINE	20	F	W	PRZZZZUSA
SOMMER, LUDW.	30	M	MCHT	PRAAGGSUSA
BUNKER, HINRICH	72	M	WCHMKR	PRZZZZUSA
ERNST	15	M	CH	PRZZZZUSA
MARTIN	9	M	CHILD	PRZZZZUSA
CLAUSEN, MARIE	16	F	SGL	PRZZZZUSA
SKLAZ, ABRAM	21	M	CL	PRZZZZUSA
KAHN, ALBERT	39	M	LABR	PRABOQUSA
BAHNSEN, BAHNE	17	M	FARMER	PRZZZZUSA
HESSTRAMPF, HEM.	31	M	FARMER	PRAARZUSA
CEUL, EMIL	15	M	JNR	MKZZZZUSA
NICOND, JOH.	33	M	LABR	MKABKRUSA
CATH.	32	F	W	MKABKRUSA
JOH.	.07	M	INFANT	MKABKRUSA
LOPKEJES, LOUISE	20	F	SGL	MKADGOUSA
PALUCKI, ROSALIE	22	F	SGL	MKAHJJUSA
HANSEN, HANS	30	M	FARMER	PRZZZZUSA
MARIE	29	F	W	PRZZZZUSA
LINE	7	F	CHILD	PRZZZZUSA
KJERSTINE	3	F	CHILD	PRZZZZUSA
JUERGEN	2	M	CHILD	PRZZZZUSA
HANS	.06	M	INFANT	PRZZZZUSA
STRECKER, EMILIE	34	F	W	PRABPCUSA
MARTHA	9	F	CHILD	PRABPCUSA
ALBERT	6	M	CHILD	PRABPCUSA
HANSEN, AUGUSTE	24	F	SGL	PRAHZPUSA
DAVIDSOHN, MAX	15	M	LABR	PRAICOUSA
STEINKE, JOSNE.	65	F	W	PRZZZZUSA
JOH.	22	M	LABR	PRZZZZUSA
SCHMIDT, HENRIETTE	50	F	W	PRZZZZUSA
AUGUSTE	26	F	SGL	PRZZZZUSA
MAKHULCK, JULIAN	27	F	SGL	PRACPSUSA
BURKHARDT, MARIE	27	F	SGL	WMZZZZUSA
HEINRIKE	21	F	SGL	WMZZZZUSA
DAVISOHN, CLARA	18	F	SGL	WMAICOUSA
WANICEK, JOSEF	44	M	FARMER	WMAICOUSA
VAYTECH	15	M	UNKNOWN	WMAICOUSA
WIESEMANN, JPOH.	30	F	W	PRZZZZUSA
GRETE	4	F	CHILD	PRZZZZUSA
ELISABETH	3	F	CHILD	PRZZZZUSA
KNUDSEN, CATH.	21	F	SGL	PRZZZZUSA
PETERSEN, J.	22	M	FARMER	PRZZZZUSA
STAMERJOHANN, AMALIE	30	F	SGL	PRAHZPUSA
NEUMANN, JOS.	15	M	MCHT	PRAHZPUSA
WEISSENBORN, HELENE	54	F	W	PRAHZPUSA
HARRY	8	M	CHILD	PRAHZPUSA
UNDANP, ABRAM	47	M	LABR	PRAEXWUSA
NARR, EUGENE	16	M	SCP	PRAEXWUSA
WINHELBAUM, HEIN.	18	M	SHMK	PRABTTUSA
WILH.	15	M	SHMK	PRABTTUSA
HOLSMANN, ITTE	24	M	LABR	HBZZZZUSA
SHEUERMANN, MARIE	19	F	SGL	BVZZZZUSA
HESS, GOTTLIEB	21	M	BKR	WMZZZZUSA
HALLER, JOH.	24	M	LABR	WMAHNOUSA
AUG.	21	F	W	WMAHNOUSA
STUDENT, MAX	20	M	FARMER	PRZZZZUSA
LEWIN, JULIUS	23	M	FARMER	PRZZZZUSA
ANDERSEN, NIESS	52	M	FARMER	PRZZZZUSA
WME.	47	F	W	PRZZZZUSA
JOH.	14	F	UNKNOWN	PRZZZZUSA
LAURITZEN, CHRISTINE	21	F	SGL	PRZZZZUSA
SWISSMANN, FERD.	23	M	FARMER	PRAHZPUSA
POTONY, LEONORE	60	F	SGL	WMZZZZUSA
VOHRSE, EMILIE	25	F	SGL	WMZZZZUSA
BAESSLER, MARIE	15	F	SGL	WMZZZZUSA
STAFFA, MATILDE	26	F	SGL	WMZZZZUSA
WINKELBACH, GEORG	66	M	MCHT	WMAEXWUSA
GERZINE	22	F	SGL	WMAEXWUSA
RIEGE, IRMA	24	F	SGL	WMAEXWUSA
BOEDDINGHAUS, HUGO	27	M	MCHT	WMABHTUSA
ROTHAMEE, JOH.	17	F	SGL	WMAECMUSA
BALL, REG.	26	F	SGL	PRZZZZUSA
FRAENKEL, JACOB	29	M	MCHT	PRAAHBUSA
SCHMUCKERT, ELSE	17	F	SGL	PRAAKHUSA
BAER, BABETTE	56	F	W	WMZZZZUSA
MINNIE	18	F	D	WMZZZZUSA
ISAAC	24	M	BCHR	WMZZZZUSA
ARNDTS, JOS.	26	M	MCHT	WMAAYAUSA
WACHS, FANNY	22	F	SGL	WMAAKHUSA
SCHMOR, WILH.	29	F	SGL	WMAAKHUSA
HERRMANN, DORA	25	F	SGL	PRZZZZUSA
GAERTNER, CAECILIE	39	F	W	PRZZZZUSA
POLLSEN, NISS	23	M	FARMER	PRZZZZUSA
GOTTESLEBEN, JUL.	26	M	WTR	PRZZZZUSA
ALANAWITZ, JULIE	37	M	LABR	BVZZZZUSA
WEHNER, CHRIST.	30	M	TU	BVZZZZUSA
MARIE	30	F	W	BVZZZZUSA
BAUMGART, EMIL	30	M	WTR	BVAEGAUSA
ALMA	25	F	W	BVAEGAUSA
KANELD, PAUL	16	M	MCHT	BVAEGAUSA
DORGELCH, CARL	52	M	LKSH	BVAEGAUSA
WEBER, MARIE	34	F	SGL	PRZZZZUSA
BRAAGER, LAURIS	27	M	FARMER	PRZZZZUSA
BRORSEN, KYRSTINE	27	F	SGL	PRZZZZUSA
BERER, JOERGEN	30	M	FARMER	PRZZZZUSA

PASSENGER	AGE	SEX	OCCUPATION	PRVL	DES
DEGN, JOERGEN	53	M	FARMER		PRZZZZUSA
HENNING, FRIEDR.	25	M	BCHR		PRZZZZUSA
LENCE, ANNA	26	F	SGL		PRAEABUSA
STAMLER, HENRY	23	M	LABR		PRADXWUSA
---DREU, JOSEF	43	M	LABR		PRACDSUSA
HAUSER, CH.ALBERT	16	M	LABR		PRAAHUUSA
BUERKI, BERTA	25	F	SGL		PRAAHUUSA
GROSSENBACH, ROSINE	21	F	W		PRAAHUUSA
SURLER, ED.	18	M	LABR		PRAAHUUSA
RIBINSKY, MARIE	16	F	W		PRAAHUUSA
WANGER, GABRIEL	18	M	LABR		PRAAHUUSA
WOELFEL, ALFONS	17	M	LABR		PRAAHUUSA
TRENCK, MATH.	27	M	LABR		PRAAHUUSA
FRANK, JEAN	37	M	LABR		PRAAXBUSA
FRAKE	29	F	W		PRAAXBUSA
SAL.	10	M	CH		PRAAXBUSA
WERA	7	F	CHILD		PRAAXBUSA
ALEXANDER	.03	M	INFANT		PRAAXBUSA
SOFIE	6	F	CHILD		PRAAXBUSA
JACOB	6	M	CHILD		PRAAXBUSA
HOFSTETTER, WOLF	37	M	MCHT		PRAAHUUSA
EUHER, CARL	23	M	LABR		PRAAHUUSA
DENNINGER, JOSEF	30	M	LABR		PRAAHUUSA
MERKLE, MONIKA	20	F	SGL		PRAAHUUSA
WENGLER, ANNA	18	F	SGL		PRAAHUUSA
GABELMANN, JACQUES	26	M	LABR		PRACPEUSA
FRANZ, W.	44	M	MCHT		HBZZZZUSA
OLSEN, OTTO	16	M	STDNT		HBAADEUSA
KOCHENTALER, SARA	21	F	SGL		WMZZZZUSA
BOSCH, JACOB	34	M	APTC		SYZZZZUSA
VOLTER, AUG.	25	M	BKR		PRZZZZUSA
DIETSCH, THERESE	28	F	W		PRAEXWUSA
AUGUSTE	8	F	CHILD		PRAEXWUSA
BJENER, LOUISE	40	F	W		PRAEXWUSA
EUGENIE	18	F	CH		PRAEXWUSA
ANNA	5	F	CHILD		PRAEXWUSA
LUEBBERS, EMIL	38	F	SGL		PRAGOMUSA
BORTH, ANDREAS	70	M	JNR		PRAAKHUSA
SEIFERT, ELISE	32	F	W		PRAEWMUSA
HELENE	7	F	CHILD		PRAEWMUSA
SCHWARZ, RICKE	65	F	W		PRAEABUSA
STEIN, ROBERT	8	M	CHILD		PRAFRBUSA
SALI	7	F	CHILD		PRAFRBUSA
KORTHALS, CATH.	42	F	W		PRAAKHUSA
MESSLER, CAROLINE	23	F	SVNT		PRAEXWUSA
TAUCHER, MARY	29	F	SGL		PRADXWUSA

SHIP: ALLER

FROM: BREMEN AND SOUTHAMPTON
TO: NEW YORK
ARRIVED: 10 AUGUST 1888

PASSENGER	AGE	SEX	OCCUPATION	PRVL	DES
WEYERBUSCH, ARTHUR	40	F	NN		GRZZZZUSA
LOEWENHERZ, S.MR	45	M	MCHT		GRZZZZUSA
S.MR	40	F	W		GRZZZZUSA
GRANT, ALBERT	48	M	FARMER		GRZZZZUSA
BAUER, ARPAD	30	M	MCHT		GRZZZZUSA
LEMLE, RIKE	40	F	NN		GRZZZZUSA
LOEB, JOHANNE	22	F	NN		GRZZZZUSA
THECLA	25	F	NN		GRZZZZUSA
KRATZ, ANNA	57	F	NN		GRZZZZUSA
TAUCHLAUF, SALOMON	42	M	FARMER		GRZZZZUSA
GERKOWSKY, JOH.	52	M	FARMER		GRZZZZUSA
GEYER, AUG.	21	M	FARMER		GRZZZZUSA
NEBER, FRITZ	15	M	FARMER		GRZZZZUSA
HASELMANN, JOH.	23	M	FARMER		GRZZZZUSA
SCHUNIKI, CARL	18	M	FARMER		GRZZZZUSA
SCHUNETZ, JOH.	28	M	FARMER		GRZZZZUSA
SITTMANN, CARL	29	M	FARMER		GRZZZZUSA

PASSENGER	AGE	SEX	OCCUPATION	PRVL	DES
FREUTSCH, HENR.	20	M	FARMER		GRZZZZUSA
MACKOWITZ, JOH.	24	M	FARMER		GRZZZZUSA
BADENSTEIER, THOM.	40	M	LABR		GRZZZZUSA
MEYER, MARTIN	30	M	LABR		GRZZZZUSA
SEEDORF, CHARLES	25	M	LABR		GRZZZZUSA
SPINDLER, LUDWIG	21	M	LABR		GRZZZZUSA
HUNSICKER, CH.	29	M	LABR		GRZZZZUSA
SCHMIDT, JACOB	23	M	GDNR		GRZZZZUSA
BEUTTENMUELLER, RUD.	22	M	GDNR		GRZZZZUSA
SCHNEIDER, PAUL	17	M	GDNR		GRZZZZUSA
HERTLER, CARL	25	M	GDNR		GRZZZZUSA
RICK, OSCAR	17	M	GDNR		GRZZZZUSA
FIDELIS, RUDOLPH	26	M	GDNR		GRZZZZUSA
KAEPF	15	M	GDNR		GRZZZZUSA
RAPP, CHRISTOPH	47	M	FARMER		GRZZZZUSA
KINNRICH, JACOB	25	M	FARMER		GRZZZZUSA
HAUDEL, ADAM	22	M	FARMER		GRZZZZUSA
WAGNER, HEINR	17	M	FARMER		GRZZZZUSA
REICHALD, CONRAD	48	M	FARMER		GRZZZZUSA
KOPPMEIER, MICH.	26	M	GCR		GRZZZZUSA
WUNNER, GEORG	26	M	GCR		GRZZZZUSA
NEUHAUS, OTTO	21	M	BCHR		GRZZZZUSA
SCHWED, SIMON	32	M	FARMER		GRZZZZUSA
BALLING, NICOL.	62	M	FARMER		GRZZZZUSA
ALBERT, JOH.	18	M	FARMER		GRZZZZUSA
FELELBAUM, FLORIAN	16	M	FARMER		GRZZZZUSA
SCHULTHEISS, CONR.	14	M	FARMER		GRZZZZUSA
HOFFMANN, GUST.	18	M	FARMER		GRZZZZUSA
BERG, NILS	33	M	FARMER		GRZZZZUSA
EDWIN	24	M	FARMER		GRZZZZUSA
ERICSEN, AXEL	23	M	FARMER		GRZZZZUSA
STERN, SAMUEL	24	M	FARMER		GRZZZZUSA
EISERT, JOH.	15	M	FARMER		GRZZZZUSA
KLUGER, GITTEL	19	M	FARMER		GRZZZZUSA
GREINSKY, RUNZ	9	M	CHILD		GRZZZZUSA
MEYER, PAUL	30	M	CH		GRZZZZUSA
BABEL, ADAM	30	M	CH		GRZZZZUSA
FRIEDMANN, SIMON	17	M	MCHT		GRZZZZUSA
RUEB, FRANZ	30	M	FARMER		GRZZZZUSA
MEIER, FERD.	16	M	FARMER		GRZZZZUSA
SCHLOSS, SALOM	15	M	FARMER		GRZZZZUSA
BAHRENBERG, HEINR.	56	M	FARMER		GRZZZZUSA
NUSSBAUM, FETER-N.	56	M	FARMER		GRZZZZUSA
KLAWITTER, WILH.	34	M	FARMER		GRZZZZUSA
RANDECKER, JOH.	22	M	FARMER		GRZZZZUSA
WILH.	24	M	FARMER		GRZZZZUSA
HEIMANN, CARL	36	M	FARMER		GRZZZZUSA
HEILMANN, CARL	36	M	FARMER		GRZZZZUSA
FRIEDMANN, BENNO	18	M	FARMER		GRZZZZUSA
NEUBALD, CARL	31	M	FARMER		GRZZZZUSA
FOSE, CARL	22	M	FARMER		GRZZZZUSA
FABERLEIN, RICH.	15	M	LABR		GRZZZZUSA
ALBRECHT, ANDR.	29	M	LABR		GRZZZZUSA
WEGENER, FRANZ	21	M	LABR		GRZZZZUSA
FRERICHS, CHRIST.	22	M	LABR		GRZZZZUSA
FISCHER, BERTHOLD	21	M	LABR		GRZZZZUSA
OSTERLOH, JOH.	36	M	LABR		GRZZZZUSA
ELLFELD, CARL	15	M	FARMER		GRZZZZUSA
SEEMANN, MAX	16	M	FARMER		GRZZZZUSA
SCHULZ, OTTO	24	M	FARMER		GRZZZZUSA
BAUER, CHRIST	23	M	FARMER		GRZZZZUSA
KAISER, CHRIST	17	M	FARMER		GRZZZZUSA
DEININGER, WILH.	17	M	FARMER		GRZZZZUSA
WEBER, HEINR.	18	M	FARMER		GRZZZZUSA
FUCHS, CARL	15	M	FARMER		GRZZZZUSA
ARNOLD, W.	29	M	FARMER		GRZZZZUSA
BILFINGER, JUL.	16	M	FARMER		GRZZZZUSA
SCHMIDT, FHILIPP	21	M	FARMER		GRZZZZUSA
KRAUS, JACOB	39	M	FARMER		GRZZZZUSA
BLEIER, JOS.	31	M	FARMER		GRZZZZUSA
RUECKERT, WILH.	48	M	FARMER		GRZZZZUSA
FICK, LEOP.	36	M	FARMER		GRZZZZUSA
LIES, CHR.	20	M	FARMER		GRZZZZUSA
WINKLER, ERNST	17	M	FARMER		GRZZZZUSA
DRESSEL, FRANZ	24	M	FARMER		GRZZZZUSA

PASSENGER	AGE	SEX	OCCUPATION	PRVVL	DES
BAUKNECHT, CHR.	20	M	FARMER	GRZZZZ	USA
BOEHM, PETER	24	M	FARMER	GRZZZZ	USA
WEHRENBERG, ERNST	29	M	FARMER	GRZZZZ	USA
SIEMANN, HEINR.	30	M	FARMER	GRZZZZ	USA
SCHAEFER, HEINR.	16	M	FARMER	GRZZZZ	USA
HEMMER, CARL	32	M	FARMER	GRZZZZ	USA
BECKER, MICH.	30	M	FARMER	GRZZZZ	USA
DAHMANN, ERNST	7	M	CHILD	GRZZZZ	USA
NELS, JOSEF	23	M	FARMER	GRZZZZ	USA
WENTE, CARL	28	M	FARMER	GRZZZZ	USA
HARMS, BERNH.	38	M	FARMER	GRZZZZ	USA
KOEHLER, GOTTLIEB	36	M	FARMER	GRZZZZ	USA
ROTH, CATHI	21	F	NN	GRZZZZ	USA
ROGINA	20	F	NN	GRZZZZ	USA
ANNA	15	F	NN	GRZZZZ	USA
MUESKE, CHRISTINE	66	F	NN	GRZZZZ	USA
SCHROEDER, LOUISE	30	F	NN	GRZZZZ	USA
SCHMIDT, MARIA	22	F	NN	GRZZZZ	USA
STOLP, WILHE.	20	F	NN	GRZZZZ	USA
KRUEGER, LINA	14	F	NN	GRZZZZ	USA
GROENENWEG, HELENE	20	F	NN	GRZZZZ	USA
FUERNER, ROSINE	65	F	NN	GRZZZZ	USA
LIPPERT, MARY	46	F	NN	GRZZZZ	USA
HARMS, HELENE	20	F	NN	GRZZZZ	USA
BECKER, MARY	40	F	NN	GRZZZZ	USA
WEISSNER, CHRISTE.	64	F	NN	GRZZZZ	USA
SCHNEIDER, ANTONIE	19	F	NN	GRZZZZ	USA
STEPHAN, MARIE	17	F	NN	GRZZZZ	USA
BAJUS, MARIE	20	F	NN	GRZZZZ	USA
WOLFGANG, CATHI	15	F	NN	GRZZZZ	USA
DERT, MARIE	15	F	NN	GRZZZZ	USA
FISCHER, MARIE	20	F	NN	GRZZZZ	USA
STRAUSS, EMILIE	21	F	NN	GRZZZZ	USA
KIRSCH, GRETSCHEN	21	F	NN	GRZZZZ	USA
SOERG, FANNY	18	F	NN	GRZZZZ	USA
BAMBERGER, GETTY	20	F	NN	GRZZZZ	USA
GAST, EVA	28	F	NN	GRZZZZ	USA
VOGT, ANNA	20	F	NN	GRZZZZ	USA
GERZ, LOUISE	28	F	NN	GRZZZZ	USA
LORENZ, MARY	18	F	NN	GRZZZZ	USA
HAAS, MARY	19	F	NN	GRZZZZ	USA
FRELL, MARY	18	F	NN	GRZZZZ	USA
MUELLER, CHRISTE.	24	F	NN	GRZZZZ	USA
KALB, BABETTE	20	F	NN	GRZZZZ	USA
WICHTE, CAROLA.	64	F	NN	GRZZZZ	USA
SCHITTENHELM, RENATE	19	F	NN	GRZZZZ	USA
BUCHARSKY, ANNA	28	F	NN	GRZZZZ	USA
SMITH, ANNA	14	F	NN	GRZZZZ	USA
RADTKE, MARIA	16	F	NN	GRZZZZ	USA
MEILER, MARIA	28	F	NN	GRZZZZ	USA
GEIS, MARIA	26	F	NN	GRZZZZ	USA
HERTERDT, SIBILLE	29	F	NN	GRZZZZ	USA
ALTAR, MALGA	20	F	NN	GRZZZZ	USA
REBHOLZ, BABETTE	29	F	NN	GRZZZZ	USA
ALBRECHT, EMMA	23	F	NN	GRZZZZ	USA
RUNNEN, H.V.	50	F	NN	GRZZZZ	USA
SCHULBERG, HEDWIG	52	F	NN	GRZZZZ	USA
DIENER, FRANZA.	14	F	NN	GRZZZZ	USA
SCHULZ, ANNY	32	F	NN	GRZZZZ	USA
SCHWER, MARTHA	30	F	NN	GRZZZZ	USA
LANDAHN, ALWINE	18	F	NN	GRZZZZ	USA
SCHERNER, MARIE	25	F	NN	GRZZZZ	USA
UNGEMACH, MARIE	36	F	NN	GRZZZZ	USA
BREUNING, MARIE	29	F	NN	GRZZZZ	USA
RHEINICKE, MARIE	9	F	CHILD	GRZZZZ	USA
WEBER, BERTHA	24	F	CH	GRZZZZ	USA
LELLENBACH, VALERIE	40	F	CH	GRZZZZ	USA
KOEHLER, MAGDA.	25	F	CH	GRZZZZ	USA
KASTENS, JOHANNE	15	F	CH	GRZZZZ	USA
HARTHAM, MARY	19	F	CH	GRZZZZ	USA
REICHENBACH, IDA	15	F	CH	GRZZZZ	USA
HEINZ, NATALIE	18	F	CH	GRZZZZ	USA
BUECKING, MATHILDE	22	F	CH	GRZZZZ	USA
FRIED, JOHAN	67	M	FARMER	GRZZZZ	USA
CAROLA.	59	F	W	GRZZZZ	USA

PASSENGER	AGE	SEX	OCCUPATION	PRVVL	DES
AUGUSTE	14	F	CH	GRZZZZ	USA
WILHELM	6	M	CHILD	GRZZZZ	USA
HULDA	5	F	CHILD	GRZZZZ	USA
IKAPSCH, JOH.	29	M	FARMER	GRZZZZ	USA
AMALIE	25	F	W	GRZZZZ	USA
JOHANNE	.10	F	INFANT	GRZZZZ	USA
WITT, CARL	29	M	FARMER	GRZZZZ	USA
REGINE	25	F	W	GRZZZZ	USA
WEISSNER, AUGUST	22	M	FARMER	GRZZZZ	USA
WILHELM	6	F	CHILD	GRZZZZ	USA
SEUBERT, JOHAN	24	M	FARMER	GRZZZZ	USA
MARIA	22	F	W	GRZZZZ	USA
FRITZ	2	M	CHILD	GRZZZZ	USA
SCHEUERMANN, AUG.	51	M	FARMER	GRZZZZ	USA
ELISE	50	F	W	GRZZZZ	USA
HONDTMANN, ELISE	43	F	NN	GRZZZZ	USA
ELISE	9	F	CHILD	GRZZZZ	USA
JACOB	7	M	CHILD	GRZZZZ	USA
LOUISE	5	F	CHILD	GRZZZZ	USA
BLAZEK, ROSA	22	F	NN	GRZZZZ	USA
ANNA	.09	F	INFANT	GRZZZZ	USA
LANGE, MORITZ	42	M	GDNR	GRZZZZ	USA
EMILIE	38	F	W	GRZZZZ	USA
HELENE	7	F	CHILD	GRZZZZ	USA
HEDWIG	6	F	CHILD	GRZZZZ	USA
ROBERT	3	M	CHILD	GRZZZZ	USA
STEINHAUER, CONRAD	30	M	GDNR	GRZZZZ	USA
AMALIE	29	F	W	GRZZZZ	USA
CATTI	3	F	CHILD	GRZZZZ	USA
AMALIE	2	F	CHILD	GRZZZZ	USA
KRAFT, GEORG	55	M	GDNR	GRZZZZ	USA
CATHI	52	F	W	GRZZZZ	USA
BARBARA	5	F	CHILD	GRZZZZ	USA
IGNATZ	4	M	CHILD	GRZZZZ	USA
SCHAEFER, ALBERT	31	M	LABR	GRZZZZ	USA
MARIE	23	F	W	GRZZZZ	USA
WEISS, MORITZ	54	M	FARMER	GRZZZZ	USA
SOPHIE	46	F	W	GRZZZZ	USA
LINA	7	F	CHILD	GRZZZZ	USA
FANNY	5	F	CHILD	GRZZZZ	USA
STAMMERMANN, HEINR.	60	M	GDNR	GRZZZZ	USA
HEINR.	5	M	CHILD	GRZZZZ	USA
HOLMY, SELMA	21	F	NN	GRZZZZ	USA
MINNA	.11	F	INFANT	GRZZZZ	USA
FILZ, AGNES	30	F	INF	GRZZZZ	USA
ELSBETH	2	F	CHILD	GRZZZZ	USA
WICHEXRT, HERM.	35	M	FARMER	GRZZZZ	USA
HERM.	7	M	CHILD	GRZZZZ	USA
KATZ, DAVID	59	M	GDNR	GRZZZZ	USA
SARAH	58	F	W	GRZZZZ	USA
CLARA	7	F	CHILD	GRZZZZ	USA
ADOLF, PAUL	26	M	FARMER	GRZZZZ	USA
EMILIE	23	F	W	GRZZZZ	USA
GRIMM, ANNA	32	F	NN	GRZZZZ	USA
FRIEDA	.10	F	INFANT	GRZZZZ	USA
BRUMATE, FRIDRIKE	47	F	NN	GRZZZZ	USA
AUGUSTE	7	F	CHILD	GRZZZZ	USA
MUELLER, ANNA	22	F	CH	GRZZZZ	USA
WILLY	.11	M	INFANT	GRZZZZ	USA
CRAMER, FRITZ	46	M	FARMER	GRZZZZ	USA
FRIEDRE.	43	F	W	GRZZZZ	USA
HEINR.	16	M	CH	GRZZZZ	USA
ALBERT	15	M	CH	GRZZZZ	USA
FRIEDR.	12	M	CH	GRZZZZ	USA
AUGUSTE	10	F	CH	GRZZZZ	USA
WILHELM	8	M	CHILD	GRZZZZ	USA
JOHAN	7	M	CHILD	GRZZZZ	USA
HANNAH	5	F	CHILD	GRZZZZ	USA
FRIEDA	4	F	CHILD	GRZZZZ	USA
GUSTAV	3	M	CHILD	GRZZZZ	USA
MARIA	2	F	CHILD	GRZZZZ	USA
WEIGAND, MARIA	40	F	NN	GRZZZZ	USA
JOSEF	3	M	CHILD	GRZZZZ	USA
FRAENKEL, MALWINE	34	F	CH	GRZZZZ	USA
MAX	11	M	CH	GRZZZZ	USA

PASSENGER	AGE	SEX	OCCUPATION	PRVL	DES
ROSA	7	F	CHILD		GRZZZZUSA
ULLMANN, CAROLA.	36	F	CH		GRZZZZUSA
HEINR.	10	M	CH		GRZZZZUSA
KUNIGD.	7	F	CHILD		GRZZZZUSA
LINA	6	F	CHILD		GRZZZZUSA
MARY	4	F	CHILD		GRZZZZUSA
DINA	2	F	CHILD		GRZZZZUSA
BAAS, ALWINE	31	F	NN		GRZZZZUSA
CARL	6	M	CHILD		GRZZZZUSA

SHIP: CITY OF NEW YORK

FROM: LIVERPOOL AND QUEENSTOWN
TO: NEW YORK
ARRIVED: 10 AUGUST 1888

PASSENGER	AGE	SEX	OCCUPATION	PRVL	DES
SCHNETON, ISAK	17	M	UNKNOWN		GRACBFIL
WILENSSKI, ELLIV	18	M	UNKNOWN		GRACBFIL
STENBERG, ARON	38	M	UNKNOWN		GRACBFIL
SEBRENSE, SAM.	20	M	UNKNOWN		GRACBFIL
WASELOW, MOSES	23	M	UNKNOWN		GRACBFIL
FOUMEN, AUGUSTA	48	M	LABR		GRACBFNY
POLS, D.	22	M	LABR		GRACBFNY
SILK, FRANK	22	M	LABR		GRACBFNY
BLOM, JOSEPHE	26	F	UNKNOWN		GRACBFNY
URIEL	4	M	CHILD		GRACBFNY
JANKSE	00	M	INF		GRACBFNY
JACONTOB, EUG.	37	M	GENT		GRADAXNY
BECKER, EDWD.	25	M	GENT		GRADBQNY
EGGER, GEO.MAX	21	M	GENT		GRADBQNY

SHIP: NOORDLAND

FROM: ANTWERP
TO: NEW YORK
ARRIVED: 10 AUGUST 1888

PASSENGER	AGE	SEX	OCCUPATION	PRVL	DES
WITTHOF, CH.	52	M	MCHT		GRAAECUSA
HEILMANN, F.MR	27	M	MCHT		GRAGBPUSA
HEITMULLER, V.	24	F	PVTR		GRABVHUSA
KRUNNE, N.MISS	5	F	CHILD		GRABVHUSA
BABDANK, U-MR	36	M	PVTR		GRADXWUSA
LOUISE, U	43	F	SI		FRZZZZUSA
ETTINGER, E.	69	M	MCHT		FRZZZZUSA
U-MRS	63	M	MCHT		FRZZZZUSA
U-MR	29	M	MCHT		FRZZZZUSA
STRAUSS, B.MR	35	M	MCHT		FRAEXKUSA
U-MRS	34	F	W		FRAEXKUSA
A.	23	F	PVTR		FRAEXKUSA
A.	5	F	CHILD		FRAEXKUSA
D.	3	F	CHILD		FRAEXKUSA
B.	2	F	CHILD		FRAEXKUSA
KLAUG, CH.	47	M	SMH		GRZZZZUSA
CABEL, A.	30	M	MUSN		GRAGLYUSA
EUGARD, J.	42	F	PVTR		GRZZZZUSA
ROTH, M.	55	F	PVTR		GRZZZZUSA
TRIMPEL, W.MR	56	M	TLR		GRZZZZUSA
U-MRS	44	F	W		GRZZZZUSA
PENNER, P.MR	39	M	DLR		GRZZZZUSA
U-MRS	15	F	W		GRZZZZUSA
H.	11	M	CH		GRZZZZUSA
A.	10	F	CH		GRZZZZUSA
HERKNER, R.	25	M	MLR		GRADLDUSA
PROEHL, L.	28	F	PVTR		GRAAHLUSA
U	00	M	INF		GRAAHLUSA

PASSENGER	AGE	SEX	OCCUPATION	PRVL	DES
GROSS, J.	32	M	MCHT		GRAAYAUSA
FELLER, Z.	19	M	LABR		GRZZZZUNK
KATLER, M.	18	M	LABR		GRZZZZUNK
WAITT, B.	64	M	LABR		GRZZZZUNK
NICHOLS, M.	31	F	W		GRAAECUNK
FESSER, M.	28	M	LABR		GRZZZZUNK
BEERMANN, S.	60	M	LABR		GRZZZZUNK
WERTHEIMER, J.	39	M	LABR		GRZZZZUNK
BOLMANN, J.	17	M	LABR		GRZZZZUNK
AURBIAC, M.	72	F	W		GRZZZZUNK
HEININGER, M.	27	F	SVNT		GRZZZZPHI
BATL, C.	20	F	SVNT		GRZZZZPHI
REDLARSKI, M.	20	F	SVNT		GRZZZZCH
THORN, J.	18	M	LABR		GRZZZZCH
ROPP, M.	62	F	W		GRZZZZMIL
MAY, M.	31	F	W		GRZZZZRME
G.	4	M	CHILD		GRZZZZRME
VANHOFE, H.	26	M	LABR		GRAACDNY
EWEN, J.	20	M	LABR		GRAACDUNK
HOLLANDER, C.	22	F	W		GRAGVRDKK
M.	18	F	SVNT		GRAGVRDKK
WILHELM, J.	19	M	LABR		GRZZZZPHI
AHRENS, E.	32	F	W		GRADLDCH
C.	4	M	CHILD		GRADLDCH
KURZ, CH.G.	39	M	LABR		GRADLDPHI
SCHMIDT, A.	24	M	LABR		GRAGFBNY
SCHMITT, P.	20	M	LABR		GRZZZZPIT
KLEIN, M.	23	F	W		GRABLTPIT
FR.	4	M	CHILD		GRABLTPIT
B.	2	F	CHILD		GRABLTPIT
CH.	00	F	INF		GRABLTPIT
GOTTEN, E.	30	F	W		GRABLTPIT
W.	5	M	CHILD		GRABLTPIT
E.	4	F	CHILD		GRABLTPIT
ZOELLER, C.	52	F	W		GRABLTPIT
SCHWARZ, A.	56	F	W		GRZZZZDKK
L.	21	F	SVNT		GRZZZZDKK
J.	11	M	CH		GRZZZZDKK
KUSTER, A.	25	F	W		GRZZZZBUF
FR.	2	F	CHILD		GRZZZZBUF
W.	00	M	INF		GRZZZZBUF
MOLTER, M.	17	M	LABR		GRAEJQBAL
BLAISE, E.	16	F	SVNT		GRAAJZNY
FALKNER, L.	00	F	INF		GRAAJZNY
C.	2	F	CHILD		GRAAJZNY
DELLINGER, E.	00	F	W		GRAAJZNY
C.	1	F	CHILD		GRAAJZNY
HERMAN, O.	23	F	W		FRZZZZUNK
CL.	4	F	CHILD		FRZZZZUNK
A.	3	M	CHILD		FRZZZZUNK
NORMAND, A.	28	F	SVNT		FRZZZZNY
RIEGER, C.	60	F	W		FRABPCBUF
M.	26	F	SVNT		FRABPCBUF
LISBERGER, J.	35	M	LABR		GRZZZZBUF
M.	10	F	CH		GRZZZZBUF
HAGEN, P.	43	M	LABR		GRZZZZNY
L.	41	F	W		GRZZZZNY
L.	11	F	CH		GRZZZZNY
P.	9	M	CHILD		GRZZZZNY
ASADEN, P.	34	M	LABR		GRZZZZNY
C.	19	F	W		GRZZZZNY
HOFERMANN, C.	19	M	LABR		GRADLDNY
SCHULTHEIS, F.	27	M	LABR		GRABTUNY
SUIN, C.	35	F	W		GRZZZZUNK
FRAGH, N.	49	M	SEMN		GRZZZZNY
WUDY, G.	49	M	LABR		GRZZZZUNK
TH.	30	F	W		GRZZZZUNK
G.	9	M	CHILD		GRZZZZUNK
F.	8	M	CHILD		GRZZZZUNK
J.	4	M	CHILD		GRZZZZUNK
M.	3	F	CHILD		GRZZZZUNK
TH.	00	F	INF		GRZZZZUNK
FLOHR, G.	16	M	LABR		GRABRCNY
GEIL, J.	16	M	LABR		GRABRCNY
POPP, J.	17	M	LABR		GRABRCMIL

PASSENGER	AGE	SEX	OCCUPATION	PRVL DES
OSTHEIMER, G.	30	M	LABR	GRZZZZUNK
LOHMAN, M.	33	F	W	GRZZZZUNK
P.	4	M	CHILD	GRZZZZUNK
KLIER, J.	23	F	SVNT	GRZZZZNY
J.	29	M	LABR	GRADEINY
THURN, J.	29	M	LABR	GRZZZZNY
HEIFLING, J.	23	M	LABR	GRZZZZNY
MAIER, G.	24	M	LABR	GRZZZZNY
SEITZ, C.	30	F	W	GRZZZZNY
B.	7	M	CHILD	GRZZZZNY
L.	00	M	INF	GRZZZZNY
ALTMAIER, F.	18	M	LABR	GRZZZZCIN
GEHRINGER, B.	28	F	SVNT	GRZZZZPIT
RAPP, H.	36	M	LABR	GRZZZZNY
J.	50	M	LABR	GRZZZZNY
UDET, C.	25	M	MCHT	GRZZZZNY
VOGT, J.	34	M	WTR	GRAGFDCH
MULLER, V.	19	F	SVNT	GRAGFDCH
HEGGE, R.	35	M	BRR	GRAGFDNY
MISSWICER, A.	38	M	SLKP	GRADXWNY
E.	22	F	W	GRADXWNY
GIESEN, D.	75	M	LABR	GRACVINY
J.	60	F	W	GRACVINY
A.	34	F	SVNT	GRACVINY
C.	25	M	LABR	GRACVINY
H.	19	M	LABR	GRACVINY
R.	17	M	LABR	GRACVINY
O.	14	M	LABR	GRACVINY
PATT, J.	16	M	TLR	GRZZZZNY
VANTHIEL, W.	28	M	TLR	GRZZZZNY
W.	25	F	W	GRZZZZNY
H.	4	M	CHILD	GRZZZZNY
J.	1	F	CHILD	GRZZZZNY
H.	00	F	INF	GRZZZZNY
HILGEMAN, F.	21	M	LABR	GRZZZZNY
BRABAU, D.	58	F	W	GRABVWNY
FRITZ, F.	28	F	W	GRABVWNY
W.	4	M	CHILD	GRABVWNY
H.	00	M	INF	GRABVWNY
BAUER, C.	38	F	W	GRZZZZNY
STEFFAN, M.	23	F	SVNT	GRZZZZNY
ROSSI, G.	32	M	MNR	GRZZZZNY
GUNTHER, A.	30	F	W	GRZZZZNY
HOCHNER, H.	27	F	SVNT	GRZZZZBAL
E.	17	F	SVNT	GRZZZZBAL
J.	9	F	CHILD	GRZZZZBAL
E.	8	M	CHILD	GRZZZZBAL
BECKER, G.	27	M	LABR	GRZZZZUSA
BACKER, G.	35	M	LABR	GRZZZZUSA
A.	31	F	W	GRZZZZUSA
F.	10	M	CH	GRZZZZUSA
E.	4	F	CHILD	GRZZZZUSA
J.	00	M	INF	GRZZZZUSA
BECAK, J.	28	M	LABR	GRZZZZNY
WZEUZLIK, A.	44	M	LABR	GRZZZZNY
M.	32	F	W	GRZZZZNY
G.	12	M	CH	GRZZZZNY
W.	7	M	CHILD	GRZZZZNY
M.	4	F	CHILD	GRZZZZNY
FLECK, FR.	60	M	LABR	GRZZZZNY
A.	55	F	W	GRZZZZNY
A.	23	F	SVNT	GRZZZZNY
PESCK, J.	31	M	LABR	GRZZZZNY
ZAPCEK, C.	30	M	LABR	GRZZZZNY
A.	30	F	W	GRZZZZNY
C.	4	M	CHILD	GRZZZZNY
A.	2	F	CHILD	GRZZZZNY
SILHARZ, A.	24	M	LABR	GRACXVNY
ARDICKA, A.	34	M	LABR	GRACXVNY
POHANKA, A.	34	M	LABR	GRACXVNY
DOORAK, FR.	20	F	SVNT	GRACXVNY
HEMZA, C.	24	M	LABR	GRACXVNY
-AVADIL, J.	40	F	W	GRACXVNY
CACKA, J.	22	F	SVNT	GRACXVNY
BARTOS, J.	39	M	LABR	GRACXVNY
CERMAK, A.	26	M	LABR	GRACXVNY
KIEDERER, J.	26	M	LABR	GRACXVNY
MARCHIORI, B.	23	M	LABR	GRACXVNY
ANDREOLLI, A.	24	M	LABR	GRACXVNY
BAIER, FR.	29	M	LABR	GRACXVNY
THOMAS, G.	27	M	LABR	GRZZZZNY
FORSTER, C.	25	F	W	GRZZZZNY
TAKRSTORFER, M.	31	F	W	GRZZZZBUF
F.	3	M	CHILD	GRZZZZBUF
M.	2	F	CHILD	GRZZZZBUF
M.	1	F	CHILD	GRZZZZBUF
BERNAT, M.	23	M	MCHT	GRZZZZNY
ENER, J.	21	M	CL	GRZZZZUNK
FREITAG, A.	23	F	SVNT	GRZZZZUNK
AHRENS, G.	2	F	CHILD	GRZZZZUNK
LEONHARD, L.	24	M	MLR	GRZZZZUNK
SPEYERER, A.	20	F	SVNT	GRZZZZUNK
KNOLL, E.	23	M	SVNT	GRZZZZUNK
HAUBER, T.	41	M	LABR	GRZZZZUNK
E.	36	F	W	GRZZZZUNK
GRAF, R.	19	M	ENGR	GRAAGLUNK
FIRNEISEL, C.	39	M	SHMK	GRADEIUNK
LINDNER, G.	24	M	BCHR	GRADEICH
HECK, M.	36	F	W	GRZZZZNY
M.	8	F	CHILD	GRZZZZNY
G.	7	M	CHILD	GRZZZZNY
MOEKEL, S.	23	M	LABR	GRZZZZNY
HAAS, C.	24	F	SVNT	GRZZZZNY
HARZ, L.	18	F	SVNT	GRZZZZNY
JETTER, CH.	14	M	LABR	GRABLBNY
SCHMITT, J.	14	M	LABR	GRABLBNY
NEISE-, J.	36	M	LABR	GRZZZZCH
M.	34	F	W	GRZZZZCH
M.	11	F	CH	GRZZZZCH
J.	8	F	CHILD	GRZZZZCH
A.	4	F	CHILD	GRZZZZCH
C.	3	F	CHILD	GRZZZZCH
E.	2	F	CHILD	GRZZZZCH
M.	1	M	CHILD	GRZZZZCH
M.	00	M	INF	GRZZZZCH
HOLLANDER, NIC.	60	M	LABR	GRACXSDKK
M.	48	F	W	GRACXSDKK
TH.	19	M	LABR	GRACXSDKK
M.	6	F	CHILD	GRACXSDKK
C.	4	F	CHILD	GRACXSDKK
E.	3	F	CHILD	GRACXSDKK
RUPP, R.	49	M	LABR	GRAEGTPIT
WOLZ, G.	28	M	LABR	GRZZZZNY
LIEBLER, G.	25	M	LABR	GRAHYRNY
MOHNER, J.	16	M	LABR	GRAHYRNY
RISSEL, R.	30	M	LABR	GRABFKNY
A.	31	F	W	GRABFKNY
L.	4	F	CHILD	GRABFKNY
J.	2	M	CHILD	GRABFKNY
M.	00	F	INF	GRABFKNY
BRUCK, FR.	16	M	LABR	GRZZZZNY
JANSON, O.	30	M	LABR	GRZZZZNY
NEUMEISTER, E.	17	F	SVNT	GRAEXWNY
HAUER, J.	24	M	LABR	GRAEXWNY
SCHERER, C.	41	M	LABR	GRZZZZNY
M.	41	F	W	GRZZZZNY
M.	12	F	CH	GRZZZZNY
C.	11	M	CH	GRZZZZNY
E.	9	F	CHILD	GRZZZZNY
M.	5	F	CHILD	GRZZZZNY
M.	2	F	CHILD	GRZZZZNY
TH.	00	F	INF	GRZZZZNY
KRUG, A.E.	16	M	LABR	GRADDWNY
KAUDEWICK, M.	24	M	LABR	GRADDWNY
RULAND, S.	21	M	LABR	GRADDWBUF
TIMMNIGFER, J.	38	M	LABR	GRADDWPIT
AMFAHI, H.	39	M	LABR	GRAAYAPIT
SCHIRM, J.	31	M	WCHMKR	GRZZZZPIT
SABERGER, H.	21	M	LABR	GRZZZZPIT
HUIRICHS, J.	43	M	LABR	GRZZZZUNK

PASSENGER	AGE	SEX	OCCUPATION	PRIVL	DES
KAEMBOERSE, P.	47	M	LABR		FRZZZZNY
REUSS, V.	22	F	SVNT		FRZZZZNY
FUCHS, TH.	48	M	LABR		FRZZZZNY
BRILL, W.	27	M	LABR		FRZZZZNY
GASPAR, P.	38	M	FARMER		GRZZZZNY
PFETSCH, G.	42	M	MCHT		GRABUDNY
FR.	52	F	W		GRABUDNY
HUBER, S.	25	F	SVNT		GRZZZZNY
SCHAFER, C.	25	F	SVNT		GRZZZZNY
MARTIN, M.	31	F	W		GRAAYGNY
FR.	8	M	CHILD		GRAAYGNY
C.	3	M	CHILD		GRAAYGNY
HOPPE, E.	24	M	LABR		GRAAYGNY
WETSIEG, J.	18	F	SVNT		GRZZZZNY
STEFFENS, R.	22	M	LABR		GRZZZZNY
HERCHLER, H.	38	M	LABR		GRZZZZNY
KOFMANN, J.	38	M	LABR		GRZZZZNY
GUTBERLET, H.	36	F	W		GRAHSONY
E.	11	M	CH		GRAHSONY
A.	9	F	CHILD		GRAHSONY
M.	7	F	CHILD		GRAHSONY
WEBER, E.	22	M	LABR		GRAFJDNY
HUGER, C.	29	M	LABR		GRAFJDNY
C.	25	F	W		GRAFJDNY
BEUGOSCH, J.	21	M	LABR		GRZZZZNY
SCHULMAN, S.	28	M	LABR		GRZZZZNY
BUCHOW, L.	23	F	SVNT		GRZZZZNY
KATZ, D.	18	F	SVNT		GRZZZZNY
KLIBANOW, F.	19	F	SVNT		GRZZZZNY
KELLER, FR.	19	F	SVNT		GRZZZZUNK
L.	17	F	SVNT		GRZZZZUNK
LIENHARDT, A.	16	M	LABR		GRZZZZBUF
ROTH, E.	22	M	LABR		GRZZZZNY
VOTTELER, A.	26	M	LABR		GRZZZZNY
STADELMANN, H.	32	M	LABR		GRZZZZNY
THOMAS, R.	00	F	W		GRZZZZNY
MALONY, D.	19	M	LABR		GRZZZZNY
PELASNI, V.	00	M	LABR		GRZZZZNY
GALLINA, G.	00	M	LABR		GRZZZZNY
LEUZINGER, D.	25	F	SVNT		GRZZZZPIT
GALIA, M.	19	F	SVNT		GRADWTUSA
KLEIN, FR.	19	M	MCHT		GRZZZZNY
BACHIN, M.	20	M	MCHT		GRZZZZNY
SCHULTHEIS, A.	23	M	LABR		GRZZZZNY
PONSTER, H.	26	M	MSN		GRZZZZNY
SCHAUL, N.	54	M	MSN		GRZZZZNY
SCHILLEN, M.	30	M	MSN		GRZZZZNY
JACOBY, A.	17	M	LABR		GRZZZZNY
STOFFEL, H.	23	M	FARMER		GRZZZZNY
KLEIN, A.	16	F	SVNT		GRZZZZNY
THEIS, J.	23	M	LABR		GRZZZZNAS
NEMECEK, J.	28	M	LABR		GRZZZZNY
GOPFRICH, G.	24	M	TLR		GRZZZZUSA
A.	27	F	W		GRZZZZUSA
F.	00	M	INF		GRZZZZUSA
SCHIRG, U	21	M	LABR		GRZZZZNY
FUST, L.	25	M	LABR		GRZZZZNY
KESCH, J.	23	M	LABR		GRZZZZNY
WEISSENBACH, N.	46	M	LABR		GRZZZZNY
BRAUN, J.	46	F	W		GRZZZZNY
BUBEL, J.	34	M	LABR		GRZZZZNY
M.	28	F	W		GRZZZZNY
N.	7	M	CHILD		GRZZZZNY
M.	5	F	CHILD		GRZZZZNY
H.	3	M	CHILD		GRZZZZNY
MULLER, M.	55	F	W		GRZZZZNY
MAUSS, D.	23	M	LABR		GRACJONY
LEINER, G.	16	M	LABR		GRZZZZNY
DALPEZ, G.	34	M	LABR		GRZZZZNY
FERRARI, G.	18	M	LABR		GRZZZZNY
POLLI, A.	37	M	LABR		GRZZZZNY
FLEIN, G.	46	M	LABR		GRZZZZNY
THUNNER, A.	40	M	LABR		GRADLDNY
RHEINHEIMER, C.	44	M	MUSN		GRZZZZNY
C.	13	M	CH		GRZZZZNY
BOCK, J.	36	M	CH		GRZZZZNY
C.	33	M	CH		GRZZZZNY
KLARES, C.	14	M	CH		GRZZZZNY
RUTH, F.	17	M	CH		GRZZZZNY
HAAS, C.	24	M	CH		GRZZZZNY
BAYERN, J.	31	M	CH		GRZZZZNY

SHIP: POLYNESIA

FROM: HAMBURG
TO: NEW YORK
ARRIVED: 10 AUGUST 1888

PASSENGER	AGE	SEX	OCCUPATION	PRIVL	DES
BENSE, EMMA	17	F	SGL		PRZZZZNY
NOEBBE, PAULINE	40	F	WO		PRZZZZNY
PAUL	9	M	CHILD		PRZZZZNY
ERNST	3	M	CHILD		PRZZZZNY
PETRASCH, JOHANNES	18	M	UNKNOWN		PRZZZZNY
EVESS, RUDOLF	19	M	UNKNOWN		HBZZZZNY
GERSTEN, JOSEF	26	M	CL		BVZZZZNY
BLUM, JOHANNES	36	M	MSN		PRZZZZNY
VON, KARL	27	M	STDNT		PRZZZZNY
KRIEGEL, KARL	45	M	FARMER		PRZZZZNY
ERNEST.	38	F	W		PRZZZZNY
GUSTAV	14	M	CH		PRZZZZNY
HEMR.	9	M	CHILD		PRZZZZNY
MARIE	8	F	CHILD		PRZZZZNY
REINHOLD	7	F	CHILD		PRZZZZNY
RUEFFER, PAUL	18	F	CH		PRZZZZNY
HAENER, ALBERTINE	25	F	SGL		SRZZZZNY
GRUN, SOPHIE	18	F	UNKNOWN		WMZZZZNY
FRANTZEN, THEODOR	31	M	CGRMKR		PRZZZZNY
STASINS, HEINRICH	25	M	CGRMKR		PRZZZZNY
BERLINER, BERTHA	32	F	SGL		PRZZZZNY
BURENSDION, HANS	16	M	UNKNOWN		PRZZZZNY
KOEPKE, EMMA	20	F	SGL		WMZZZZNY
REBSTOCK, FABIAN	26	M	UNKNOWN		PRZZZZNY
NEHLS, AUGUST	25	M	LABR		PRZZZZNY
JOHA.	26	F	W		PRZZZZNY
AUGUSTE	4	F	CHILD		PRZZZZNY
ANNA	2	F	CHILD		PRZZZZNY
PAUL	.09	M	INFANT		PRZZZZNY
WILHWLM	29	M	LABR		PRZZZZNY
WILHE.	28	F	W		PRZZZZNY
WILHELM	5	M	CHILD		PRZZZZNY
ANNA	.09	F	INFANT		PRZZZZNY
REDE, SOPHIE	24	F	SGL		WMZZZZNY
OOEHLER, FRANK	17	M	MCHT		PRZZZZNY
PULCZYNSKA, JULIANE	17	F	SGL		PRZZZZNY
WINHEIMER, BABETTE	17	F	SGL		BVZZZZNY
LEWIN, WILHELM	67	M	LABR		PRZZZZNY
OLSEN, RICHARD	21	M	PNTR		PRZZZZNY
SOMMERFELD, ABRAM	18	M	LABR		PRZZZZNY
ISRAEL, ISIDOR	15	M	LABR		PRZZZZNY
BETTEN, EDUARD	30	M	SHMK		PRZZZZNY
JOSEFA	27	F	W		PRZZZZNY
HEDWIG	.02	F	INFANT		PRZZZZNY
KLEBING, WALDEMAR	20	M	LABR		PRZZZZNY
MELZER, EDUARD	32	M	UNKNOWN		PRZZZZNY
BUGS, EMMA	17	F	SGL		PRZZZZNY
SOMMERFELD, HERMANN	26	M	FARMER		PRZZZZNY
KARGER, AUGUST	35	M	LABR		PRZZZZNY
DAVIDSOHN, ARTHUR	17	M	MCHT		PRZZZZNY
SOELLNER, OSWSLD	31	M	UNKNOWN		BVZZZZNY
UTCKAL, LOUISE	39	F	SGL		PRZZZZNY
EMMA	9	F	CHILD		PRZZZZNY
REINSDORF, HERMANN	16	M	LABR		SYZZZZNY
GRAFF, ANTONINA	21	F	SGL		PRZZZZNY
HEILMANN, MAX	32	M	LABR		BVZZZZNY
SAPIR, JACOB	37	M	TCHR		PRZZZZNY

PASSENGER	AGE	SEX	OCCUPATION	PRVL	DES
GROTH, FRIEDR.	27	M	LABR	WMZZZZNY	
FINK, ADAM	37	M	LLD	PRZZZZNY	
CLAUS, HERM.	26	M	BRR	PRZZZZNY	
SCHMIDTKE, FRIEDR.	26	M	BKR	PRZZZZNY	
SCHAHL, HEINR.	26	M	LABR	WMZZZZNY	
RADE, HERMANN	30	M	LABR	SYZZZZNY	
KUEHNE, WILHELM	26	M	BCHR	PRZZZZNY	
MEYER, WALTER	29	M	BCHR	PRZZZZNY	
KALINOWSKA, MARIANNA	25	F	SGL	PRZZZZNY	
CISZEWSKA, KONSTANTE.	56	F	WO	PRZZZZNY	
WISZKOWSKA, BABINE	38	F	WO	PRZZZZNY	
VERONICA	4	F	CHILD	PRZZZZNY	
JOH.	.06	M	INFANT	PRZZZZNY	
KIST, BENEDICT	23	M	BRR	BDZZZZNY	
ROMPA, JOSEF	32	M	FARMER	PRZZZZNY	
GROSSER, WILHELM	33	M	FARMER	PRZZZZNY	
JOOS, ERNESTINE	48	F	SGL	PRZZZZNY	
SELL, FRANZ	20	M	CL	PRZZZZNY	
KAAD, MARGT.	20	F	SGL	PRZZZZNY	
MATHS.	14	M	FARMER	PRZZZZNY	
TRAUTMANN, JOHANN	30	M	LKSH	BVZZZZNY	
GOERTZ, LAURA	28	F	SGL	PRZZZZNY	
JASKOLSKA, MARIANNA	22	F	SGL	PRZZZZNY	
KIEMHOLZ, FRANZISCA	25	F	WO	PRZZZZNY	
TOMAS	4	M	CHILD	PRZZZZNY	
WIKLONIA	.06	F	INFANT	PRZZZZNY	
MASOHN, OTTO	25	M	MCHT	PRZZZZNY	

SHIP: ANCHORIA

FROM: GLASGOW AND MOVILLE
TO: NEW YORK
ARRIVED: 13 AUGUST 1888

PASSENGER	AGE	SEX	OCCUPATION	PRVL	DES
BAUMAN, JOHAN	33	M	SMH	GRZZZZUSA	
MARGARETTA	29	F	W	GRZZZZUSA	
LAT, JOSEF	16	M	LABR	GRZZZZUSA	
MARIE	22	F	HP	GRZZZZUSA	
SOSNOWSKI, THEOFIL	38	M	CPR	GRZZZZUSA	
KOSMANSKI, EDW.	51	M	MLR	GRZZZZUSA	
FABRI, JOHAN	30	M	JNR	GRZZZZUSA	
MATTHUS, JOHAN	23	M	JNR	GRZZZZUSA	
FRIEDRICH, MATT	26	M	LABR	GRZZZZUSA	
BALINSKY, JOSEF	23	M	UNKNOWN	GRZZZZUSA	
MAAS, JOSEF	31	M	UNKNOWN	GRZZZZUSA	
WAGNER, EMIL	25	M	UNKNOWN	GRZZZZUSA	
HAFER, HEINR.	19	M	UNKNOWN	GRZZZZUSA	
DEBOLDE, G.	34	F	UNKNOWN	GRACBRUSA	
ULKO, WILH.	28	M	UNKNOWN	GRZZZZUSA	

SHIP: ARIZONA

FROM: LIVERPOOL AND QUEENSTOWN
TO: NEW YORK
ARRIVED: 13 AUGUST 1888

PASSENGER	AGE	SEX	OCCUPATION	PRVL	DES
SCHOCK, ROSA	55	F	W	GRZZZZUSA	
TRESE	33	F	W	GRZZZZUSA	
EMMA	19	F	SP	GRZZZZUSA	
WITKOWSKY, MARTHA	16	F	SP	GRACBFUSA	
BECKER, CAESAR	30	M	MECH	FRZZZZUSA	
LOUISE	25	F	W	FRZZZZUSA	
BROUCHAR, MARIE	40	F	W	FRZZZZUSA	
ONASTHOFF, FRITZ	32	M	FARMER	FRACBFUSA	
ELISE	25	F	W	FRACBFUSA	

PASSENGER	AGE	SEX	OCCUPATION	PRVL	DES
JOHANNA	.05	F	INFANT	FRACBFUSA	
LEREN, MORITZ	35	M	ART	FRACBFUSA	

SHIP: EGYPT

FROM: LIVERPOOL AND QUEENSTOWN
TO: NEW YORK
ARRIVED: 13 AUGUST 1888

PASSENGER	AGE	SEX	OCCUPATION	PRVL	DES
LEITSLY, MOSES	26	M	LABR	FRADAXUSA	
LIPPINMAN, J.	20	M	LABR	FRADAXUSA	
KONDRATIGIN, S.	27	M	LABR	FRADAXUSA	
SERNER, LEISER	23	M	LABR	FRADAXUSA	
MECHALOREK, FELIX	45	M	LABR	FRADAXUSA	
JOK, E.	17	M	LABR	FRADAXUSA	
KORPAUSKY, JODEL	22	M	LABR	FRADAXUSA	
MANA, H.	35	M	LABR	FRADAXUSA	
SCHNEROX, G.	20	M	LABR	FRADAXUSA	
GEDENAUSKY, J.	18	M	LABR	FRADAXUSA	
GERZHALS, JACOB	22	M	LABR	FRADAXUSA	
SAMUEL	16	M	LABR	FRADAXUSA	
BASCHOUKY, S.	40	M	LABR	FRADAXUSA	
RANER, H.	30	M	LABR	FRADAXUSA	
BARDACK, JACOB	20	M	LABR	FRADAXUSA	
ELESTEIN, MOSES	18	M	LABR	FRADAXUSA	
ABERMAN, MOSES	16	M	LABR	FRADAXUSA	
ROMANKO, J.	24	M	LABR	FRADAXUSA	
KORLUNSKY, O.	19	M	LABR	FRADAXUSA	
KITOR, R.	31	M	LABR	FRADAXUSA	
WISCHINOVLY, M.	25	M	LABR	FRADAXUSA	
PLOGE, CARL	31	M	LABR	FRADAXUSA	
BARROD, ANTON	26	M	LABR	FRADAXUSA	
SCHUSELOME, S.	26	M	LABR	FRADAXUSA	
KAPLAN, ABRAHAM	18	M	LABR	FRADAXUSA	
PEVETZ, B.	22	M	LABR	FRADAXUSA	
RIBUCK, MOSES	25	M	LABR	FRADAXUSA	
MICHALHO, S.	26	M	LABR	FRADAXUSA	
PISELZNEK, GILLET	24	M	LABR	FRADAXUSA	
L.	4	M	CHILD	FRADAXUSA	
HENNE	00	M	INF	FRADAXUSA	
SWAN, MARY	28	F	W	FRADAXUSA	
J.	26	M	LABR	FRADAXUSA	
L.	3	M	CHILD	FRADAXUSA	
M.	00	M	INF	FRADAXUSA	
PYG-DTT, S.	22	M	LABR	FRADAXUSA	
RALMOWITZ, ALR.	30	M	LABR	FRADAXUSA	
S.	28	F	W	FRADAXUSA	
HISSEN	00	F	INF	FRADAXUSA	
KAPNER, C.	25	M	LABR	FRADAXUSA	
S.	5	M	CHILD	FRADAXUSA	
C.	3	M	CHILD	FRADAXUSA	
J.	00	M	INF	FRADAXUSA	
SELACLORCKY, M.	30	F	W	FRADAXUSA	
DAVID	00	M	INF	FRADAXUSA	
ZIPSKIN, R.	22	F	W	FRADAXUSA	
LIZZY	10	F	CH	FRADAXUSA	
DEBORA	11	M	CH	FRADAXUSA	
MALKE	9	M	CHILD	FRADAXUSA	
DOWORE	6	M	CHILD	FRADAXUSA	
F.	2	M	CHILD	FRADAXUSA	
B.	00	M	INF	FRADAXUSA	
GLESON, EFRAM	24	F	W	FRADAXUSA	
MOSES	00	M	INF	FRADAXUSA	
WEISS, B.	16	F	SP	FRADAXUSA	
PETERSON, MARTA	39	F	W	FRADAXUSA	
OSCAR	10	M	CH	FRADAXUSA	
A.	16	F	SP	FRADAXUSA	
CAROLIN	11	F	CH	FRADAXUSA	
SCHUMEL, SCHIE	45	F	LABR	FRADAXUSA	
LEA	48	F	W	FRADAXUSA	

PASSENGER	AGE	SEX	OCCUPATION	PRIVL	DES
C.	16	F	SP		FRADAXUSA
NEMLIRGE, MERE	23	M	LABR		FRADAXUSA
M.	20	F	W		FRADAXUSA
C.	3	F	CHILD		FRADAXUSA
RAHANORT, E.	37	F	W		FRADAXUSA
A.	10	F	CH		FRADAXUSA
SEHAMI	8	F	CHILD		FRADAXUSA
GUNAHER, CH.	44	M	LABR		FRADAXUSA
C.	40	F	W		FRADAXUSA
L.	16	F	SP		FRADAXUSA
BEILE	15	F	SP		FRADAXUSA
RACHEL	7	F	CHILD		FRADAXUSA
ELFMAN, S.	49	M	LABR		FRADAXUSA
SEHEME	45	F	W		FRADAXUSA
B.	18	F	SP		FRADAXUSA
J.	16	F	SP		FRADAXUSA
CHANI	10	M	CH		FRADAXUSA
IRDES	9	M	CHILD		FRADAXUSA
R.	7	M	CHILD		FRADAXUSA
GABRIEL	3	M	CHILD		FRADAXUSA
M.	5	F	CHILD		FRADAXUSA
LIZZY	00	F	INF		FRADAXUSA
SOCHMER, TOBIS	50	M	LABR		FRADAXUSA
C.	46	F	W		FRADAXUSA
N.	21	F	SP		FRADAXUSA
CARL	14	M	CH		FRADAXUSA
V.	16	F	SP		FRADAXUSA
KOLAEN, J.	40	M	LABR		FRADAXUSA
REBECCA	36	F	W		FRADAXUSA
S.	17	F	SP		FRADAXUSA

SHIP: EMS

FROM: BREMEN AND SOUTHAMPTON
TO: NEW YORK
ARRIVED: 13 AUGUST 1888

PASSENGER	AGE	SEX	OCCUPATION	PRIVL	DES
PESTALOZZI, A.	40	M	TT		FRAFTDNY
HOLTHAUS, HEINRICH	46	M	MCHT		FRAFTDNY
LEHMANN, GEORG	30	M	MCHT		FRAAKHNY
LIEBKER, EMILIE	20	F	UNKNOWN		FRAARRNY
ELISABETH	24	F	W		FRACAWNY
BRUETTING, BALTAHSAR	29	M	MCHT		FRAEXWNY
MARTHA	20	F	W		FRAEXWNY
BEROLZHEIMER, ERNST	20	M	MCHT		FRABOQNY
LUND, THEODOR	42	M	MCHT		GRZZZZNY
GEERS, HERMANN	22	M	MCHT		GRACHANY
JUNGE, MARGARETHE	30	F	W		GRAAKHNY
STELLMANN, GESINE	31	F	W		GRZZZZNY
BEYER, JOHANNA	30	F	W		GRAEVTNY
KATHARINA	16	F	UNKNOWN		GRAEVTNY
BARBARA	6	F	CHILD		GRAEVTNY
WAGNER, MINETTE	56	F	W		GRAEXWNY
BREDENBERG, LINA	26	F	UNKNOWN		GRZZZZNY
JOHANNA	24	F	UNKNOWN		GRZZZZNY
ANNA	17	F	UNKNOWN		GRZZZZNY
KOEPPE, ANNA	20	F	UNKNOWN		GRAAYCNY
KRAMER, WILHELM	23	M	MCHT		GRADUHNY
KRETSCHMAR, MARIA	23	F	UNKNOWN		GRAAYSNY
BUERCHARA, CARL	25	M	GCR		GRADLUWAS
FRIEDMANN, ROSA	37	F	W		GRAEAFNY
HENRIETTE	19	F	UNKNOWN		GRAEAFNY
ROSA	18	F	UNKNOWN		GRAEAFNY
RUETH, JOST	22	M	CL		GRZZZZNY
GOETTLER, CARL	28	M	SMH		GRAFBVNY
SCHMIDT, REGINE	20	F	UNKNOWN		GRAEDQNY
SCHWARZ, JENNY	17	F	UNKNOWN		GRAARRNY
WENDELKEN, HEINR.	29	M	LABR		GRAEFTNY
BERTHA	24	F	W		GRAEFTNY
ANNA	.11	F	INFANT		GRAEFTNY
KLESSOWSKY, FRIEDR.	22	M	WTR		GRAARRNY
RAUEB, EMMA	29	F	UNKNOWN		GRZZZZNY
FRANK, MARIE	26	F	UNKNOWN		GRAAVLNY
NACHARD, JACOB	15	M	MCHT		GRZZZZNY
HERRLER, JOHANN	35	M	FARMER		GRZZZZNY
JEZEWSKA, WIKTORIA	26	F	W		GRZZZZNY
PETER	4	M	CHILD		GRZZZZNY
STANISLAWA	2	F	CHILD		GRZZZZNY
VINCENT	.05	M	INFANT		GRZZZZNY
MIKOLAYWSKI, BAZYLI	20	F	UNKNOWN		GRZZZZNY
JAGOLDZINSKA, AGNISKA	25	F	W		GRZZZZNY
KONSTANZIA	2	F	CHILD		GRZZZZNY
SALOMYA	.01	F	INFANT		GRZZZZNY
GASZEZYNSKA, STANISLAWA	43	F	W		GRZZZZNY
MARIE	12	F	UNKNOWN		GRZZZZNY
THERESE	9	F	CHILD		GRZZZZNY
WLADISLAUS	8	M	CHILD		GRZZZZNY
LOTZ, ELISABETH	17	F	UNKNOWN		GRAARRNY
BERNETT, FRIEDR.	22	M	BBR		GRZZZZNY
WALKER, DORIS	24	F	UNKNOWN		GRAAOFNY
HUISMANN, HENDRICH	26	F	UNKNOWN		GRAAOFNY
VOEGE, ANNA	20	F	UNKNOWN		GRAAOFNY
BECKMANN, BERNARD	29	M	CPTR		GRZZZZNY
DOERING, AUGUSTE	56	F	W		GRABVWNY
MARIE	32	F	UNKNOWN		GRABVWNY
BRESSING, JOHANNES	21	M	SHMK		GRZZZZNY
WOLTER, ROSINE	23	F	UNKNOWN		GRZZZZNY
KRUSE, WILHELM	17	M	BKR		GRZZZZNY
HUBER, MARIE	22	F	UNKNOWN		GRADNANY
RUHN, JOHANNES	27	M	FARMER		GRADNANY
WOLLENSACH, FRANZ	15	M	FARMER		GRAEIFNY
HIPP, JORGEN	31	M	SDLR		GRZZZZNY
PAHL, EMIL	28	M	CPTR		GRAIISNY
MARIE	26	F	W		GRAIISNY
RICHARD	.08	M	INFANT		GRAIISNY
ATIPP, BARBARA	15	F	UNKNOWN		GRZZZZNY
SPECK, ANNIE	14	F	UNKNOWN		GRABLYNY
SCHUETER, WILHELMINE	18	F	UNKNOWN		GRACHBNY
GRAUNEMANN, CAROLINE	21	F	UNKNOWN		GRACHBNY
TOELLNER, SOPHIE	17	F	UNKNOWN		GRACHBNY
MEYER, MARIE	21	F	UNKNOWN		GRACHBNY
BRAND, SOPHIE	19	F	UNKNOWN		GRACHBNY
V., CHRISTIAN	16	M	FARMER		GRACHBNY
GERDING, FRIEDRICH	16	M	FARMER		GRACHBNY
BUSCHING, SOPHIE	18	F	UNKNOWN		GRZZZZNY
SAUER, ANDREAS	28	M	LABR		GRABOQNY
KROTH, FEBRONIA	26	F	UNKNOWN		GRABOQNY
MAIKRANTZ, WILHELM	38	F	LABR		GRACBOTX
MEYER, ANDREAS	25	M	FARMER		GRAFBVUNK
STIRNER, CARL	23	M	BCHR		GRZZZZUNK
MAIER, DOROTHEA	28	F	UNKNOWN		GRZZZZNY
HALLER, MARIE	17	F	UNKNOWN		GRZZZZNY
CATHARINA	15	F	UNKNOWN		GRZZZZNY
SCHAUBACHER, PAUL.	20	F	W		GRZZZZNY
HALLER, WILHELMINE	15	F	UNKNOWN		GRZZZZNY
HAHN, AMALIA	15	F	UNKNOWN		GRZZZZNY
SCHMILLE, WILHELM	27	M	SDLR		GRZZZZNY
CATHARINA	24	F	W		GRZZZZNY
ELISABETH	17	F	UNKNOWN		GRZZZZNY
DECKER, ANTON	29	M	FARMER		GRZZZZNY
EBERWEIN, LUDWIG	53	M	SHMK		GRAARPNY
GOTTLOB	10	M	CH		GRAARPNY
PFEIFFER, EMILIE	65	F	W		GRABDMNY
ROESE, ERNST	30	M	MCHT		GRAAKHNY
ANNA	27	F	W		GRAAKHNY
GEISSLER, SELMA	22	F	UNKNOWN		GRAAKHNY
SPEYER, ANNA	18	F	UNKNOWN		GRABOQNY
MAX, DOROTHEA	49	F	W		GRABOQNY
HERTZSCHUH, RICHARD	30	M	JNR		GRABOQNY
HEINRICH	28	M	CPTR		GRABOQNY
WEBERT, KAROLINA	60	F	W		GRACWTNY
JUZIKOWSKI, MAX	22	M	TNM		GRACWTNY
HOLZMANN, BABETTE	18	F	UNKNOWN		GRZZZZNY
SCHUELE, JACOB	21	M	LABR		GRZZZZNY
KNEISELRING, BERTHA	17	F	UNKNOWN		GRAABYNY

PASSENGER	AGE	SEX	OCCUPATION	PRV VL DIES
LIPPOT, JACOB	22	M	CL	GRZZZZNY
BUERKARD, JACOB	19	M	WTR	GRAARRNY
OPPENHEIMER, EMMA	19	F	UNKNOWN	GRAFSBNY
MUELLER, PETER	25	M	LABR	GRAAFCNY
SEIDEL, ERHARDT	25	M	PNTR	GRAAFCNY
BRAUN, JOHANN	24	M	SMH	GRAAFCNY
EBERT, AGNES	20	F	UNKNOWN	GRAEVVNY
STROELEIN, MARGARETHA	43	F	W	GRAEVVNY
BECKER, CATHARINA	14	F	UNKNOWN	GRAEVVNY
WEYMANN, CAROLINE	19	F	UNKNOWN	GRAEVVNY
ULBRICH, AMALIE	21	F	UNKNOWN	GRZZZZMN
KIRCHNER, JOHANN	25	M	FARMER	GRABTJROC
RIETH, WILHELMINE	18	F	UNKNOWN	GRAHCMOH
BOERRELI, SOPHIE	11	F	UNKNOWN	GRAHAOOH
HERZOG, ADAM	12	M	BKLYR	GRAHAOOH
WEBER, JOHANN	16	M	CL	GRAHAOOH
JAEGER, JOSEF	51	M	MLR	GRAEVYOH
KUNIGUNDE	45	F	W	GRAEVYOH
MARIE	12	F	UNKNOWN	GRAEVYOH
MARGARETHA	10	F	CH	GRAEVYOH
JOHANN	6	M	CHILD	GRAEVYOH
PETER	3	M	CHILD	GRAEVYOH
HAFER, WILHELMINE	14	F	UNKNOWN	GRAEONOH
SCHAFRANSKA, ROSALIA	29	F	W	GRAEONOH
ZBARAKA, LENORA	16	F	UNKNOWN	GRAEONOH
SCHAFRANSKA, CASIMIR	3	M	CHILD	GRAEONOH
MARIANNA	.09	F	INFANT	GRAEONOH
ANDRZYEWSKA, CATHARINA	23	F	W	GRAEONOH
STANISLAUS	.08	M	INFANT	GRAEONOH
GOHLE, SUSANNA	20	F	UNKNOWN	GRZZZZOH
SCHMIGELSKI, ERNSTINE	18	F	UNKNOWN	GRZZZZOH
KYNICKI, FRANCISKA	21	F	UNKNOWN	GRZZZZOH
JOSKOVIAK, MARYANNA	17	F	UNKNOWN	GRZZZZOH
ROSALIA	21	F	UNKNOWN	GRZZZZOH
PRZYWARSKA, JOSEFA	18	F	UNKNOWN	GRZZZZOH
ANDERS, HERMANN	26	M	TNM	GRZZZZOH
MATHES, REINHOLD	30	M	SHMK	GRZZZZOH
STEEB, ELIAS	20	M	BKLYR	GRAAOTOH
EBERHARDT, MICHAEL	30	M	FARMER	GRAAOTOH
BOETTCHER, LUDWIG	51	M	LABR	GRZZZZWI
ERNSTINE	45	F	UNKNOWN	GRZZZZWI
ROBERT	14	M	UNKNOWN	GRZZZZWI
HERMANN	10	M	CH	GRZZZZWI
BERTHA	4	F	CHILD	GRZZZZWI
DECKERT, AUGUSTE	19	F	UNKNOWN	GRZZZZNY
GRUNEWALD, GOTTLIEB	25	M	LABR	GRZZZZNY
AUGUSTE	19	F	UNKNOWN	GRZZZZNY
HOLLAD, LOUISE	48	F	W	GRZZZZNY
LASNISKI, ANTON	25	M	LABR	GRZZZZNY
SIEVERS, CHRISTIAN	36	M	LABR	GRAARRNY
KIESOW, AUGUST	29	M	LABR	GRAAKHIA
WENIGER, HULDA	33	F	W	GRAARZNY
ALFRED	7	M	CHILD	GRAARZNY
ULBRICHT, EMIL	17	M	LABR	GRZZZZNY
SUPLICKI, FRANZ	25	M	LABR	GRZZZZPA
STACHELBERG, MINNA	24	F	W	GRAAKHNY
PHILIPP	5	M	CHILD	GRAAKHNY
BERTHA	.10	F	INFANT	GRAAKHNY
CONITZER, ALEX.	29	M	MCHT	GRZZZZNY
JACOBSTHAL, BERTHA	22	F	UNKNOWN	GRZZZZNY
POST, AMALIE	26	F	UNKNOWN	GRAAKHNY
HEINKE, CARL	56	M	TLR	GRAAKHNY
BUERANDT, JULIUS	38	M	LABR	GRZZZZBUF
WILHELMINE	33	F	W	GRZZZZBUF
REINHARDT	9	M	CHILD	GRZZZZBUF
HELENE	6	F	CHILD	GRZZZZBUF
LAURA	5	F	CHILD	GRZZZZBUF
EMMA	3	F	CHILD	GRZZZZBUF
ERNST	.11	M	INFANT	GRZZZZBUF
HERZHEIM, ANNA	33	F	W	GRZZZZNY
JACOB	5	M	CHILD	GRZZZZNY
GUSE, AUGUSTE	18	F	UNKNOWN	GRZZZZNY
CARL	21	M	BKR	GRZZZZNY
KRUEGER, KARL	19	M	PNTR	GRZZZZNY
SCHWARZ, MARIE	20	F	UNKNOWN	GRAAACNY
PHIEL, WILHELM	27	M	SMH	GRZZZZNY
LOTZ, REINH.	14	M	LABR	GRAARRNY
SCHAEFER, BERTHA	21	F	UNKNOWN	GRZZZZNY
SEIBERT, WILHELM	25	M	BBR	GRZZZZNY
OBERNITZ, FRANZ	30	M	JNR	GRZZZZNY
SCHAUDER, ADAM	27	M	LABR	GRZZZZNY
HARR, JOHANN	28	M	PNTR	GRZZZZNY
RUDOLPH, ALVIN	26	M	LABR	GRZZZZNY
EISENMANN, JOSEF	21	M	FARMER	GRZZZZNY
JOHANN	21	M	FARMER	GRZZZZNY
SCHRAMM, ANNA	19	F	UNKNOWN	GRZZZZNY
EVERDING, WILHELMINE	21	F	UNKNOWN	GRZZZZNY
LIBRAK, LEON	25	M	TLR	GRAARZNY
HAPPEL, MARIA	18	F	UNKNOWN	GRZZZZNY
MINA	11	F	UNKNOWN	GRZZZZNY
HOFREUTER, JOHANN	42	M	FARMER	GRZZZZROC
KUHLMANN, MARIA	19	F	UNKNOWN	GRZZZZOH
HOEWELER, HEINR.	10	M	CH	GRZZZZOH
NIEHAUS, FRIEDR.	15	M	FARMER	GRZZZZOH
PIEPER, HENRIETTE	20	F	UNKNOWN	GRZZZZOH
WILHELMINE	10	F	CH	GRZZZZOH
BREMER, EMANUEL	34	M	FARMER	GRAARROH
EICHLER, HERMANN	38	M	FARMER	GRABHUMI
HENRIETTE	42	F	W	GRABHUMI
GUSTAV	13	M	UNKNOWN	GRABHUMI
HERMANN	11	M	UNKNOWN	GRABHUMI
JOHANNE	4	F	CHILD	GRABHUMI
KUEHN, ELISABETH	65	F	W	GRZZZZNY
GOETHEL, MARIE	28	F	W	GRZZZZNY
SCHEUERMANN, ADAM	26	M	LABR	GRAGFWNY
AMM, IDA	22	F	UNKNOWN	GRZZZZOH
AUSORGE, HUGO	24	M	FARMER	GRAFSYNY
LIEBLER, MARIE	56	F	W	GRABOQNY
BERGER, FRANZ	45	M	LABR	GRZZZZNY
RUEGE, PAUL	23	M	CPTR	GRABVWNY
AUGUSTE	23	F	W	GRABVWNY
SCHIEDER, JOHANN	31	M	LABR	GRZZZZNY
BUEHLER, MARIA	22	F	UNKNOWN	GRZZZZUNK
LOEHR, CHRISTOF	15	M	LABR	GRZZZZUNK
BUETTNER, MARIE	22	F	UNKNOWN	GRZZZZUNK
ADAM	17	M	LABR	GRZZZZUNK
GUTZKOW, CARL	23	M	LABR	GRZZZZIA
MONZ, PETER	24	M	LABR	GRZZZZNY
NICOLAUS	28	M	LABR	GRZZZZNY
GERHAEUSER, WILHELM	32	M	FARMER	GRZZZZNY
GOTTLIEB	27	M	FARMER	GRZZZZNY
LOUISE	4	F	CHILD	GRZZZZNY
CARL	.11	M	INFANT	GRZZZZNY
ALBERT	.11	M	INFANT	GRZZZZNY
BUEGER, MARIE	21	F	UNKNOWN	GRZZZZNY
STENGEL, FRIEDERIKE	18	F	UNKNOWN	GRZZZZNY
STUBER, CAROLINE	16	F	UNKNOWN	GRAGOINY
NAEGELE, CHRISTIAN	16	M	WTR	GRZZZZNY
CHRISTIAN	16	M	WTR	GRZZZZNY
KUHNER, JACOB	25	M	SHMK	GRZZZZNY
REBSTOCK, WILHELM	15	M	CL	GRZZZZNY
OEHLER, GOTTLIEB	22	M	LABR	GRZZZZNY
GRAEBER, HERMANN	16	M	LABR	GRAFMNOH
TIELKER, HERMANN	15	M	LABR	GRAFMNUNK
VOKURKA, ANNA	22	F	UNKNOWN	GRZZZZNY
EICHEL, ROSA	16	F	UNKNOWN	GRZZZZNY
DEUTSCH, ROSA	14	F	UNKNOWN	GRZZZZNY
CONRADI, JOHANN	48	M	WTR	GRACBONY
SCHAUBERGER, CHRIST.	18	M	LABR	GRAEVSPA
SPIELMANN, ADAM	24	M	LABR	GRAEVSPA
CHRISTINE	21	F	W	GRAEVSPA
LANG, LEONH.	40	M	LABR	GRAEVSNY
SIEVERT, MATHILDE	28	F	W	GRZZZZNY
FRIEDA	3	F	CHILD	GRZZZZNY
BECKER, GOTTFRIED	24	M	CPTR	GRZZZZNY
JAEGER, JACOB	55	M	FARMER	GRACBRNY
ANNA	36	F	W	GRACBRNY
FRANZ	8	M	CHILD	GRACBRNY
CLAUS	8	M	CHILD	GRACBRNY
NACHMANN, SIMON	40	M	SHMK	GRAESUNY

PASSENGER	AGE	SEX	OCCUPATION	PRVL	DES
JULIUS	.11	M	INFANT	GRAESUNY	
AUGUST, HENRY	31	M	JNR	GRACBRNY	
LOUISE	23	F	W	GRACBRNY	
ALFRED	3	M	CHILD	GRACBRNY	
GEHM, ELEONORE	16	F	UNKNOWN	GRACBRNY	
BOECKER, GUSTAV	30	M	PNTR	GRADLDNY	
PFEIFFER, JOSEF	30	M	BKLYR	GRADLDNY	
GROSSING, JOHANNA	41	F	W	GRAAKHNY	
FRANZ	13	M	UNKNOWN	GRAAKHNY	
MARTHA	10	F	CH	GRAAKHNY	
HOPF, NICOLAUS	18	M	DLR	GRZZZZNY	
SCHWIMMER, LORENZ	22	M	BKR	GRAFVPNY	
LOOS, CARL	51	M	LABR	GRZZZZNY	
KNIERIEMEN, PETER	16	M	BBR	GRADLDNY	
CHRISTMANN, ADAM	18	M	LABR	GRZZZZNY	
SCHUESSLER, PHILIPPA	23	F	UNKNOWN	GRZZZZNY	
BRAUN, ANNA	17	F	UNKNOWN	GRZZZZNY	
MARTINI, GEORGE	2	M	CHILD	GRZZZZNY	
GAMBERT, KATHARIANA	21	F	UNKNOWN	GRZZZZNY	
BRESLAUER, CARL	26	M	LABR	GRZZZZNY	
GUTH, ADOLF	28	M	BBR	GRAJXZNY	
JACOB, HERMANN	16	M	CPTR	GRACUXNY	
STAMMICH, RICHARD	18	M	SMH	GRABUKNY	
FUERMANOWICZ, PELAGIA	25	F	W	GRZZZZNY	
SIEGFRIED	.09	M	INFANT	GRZZZZNY	
MITTER, PETER	46	M	LABR	GRZZZZNY	
ILLING, ALMA	26	F	W	GRAAXKNY	
SCHNEIDER, PETER	18	M	CL	GRZZZZNY	
LINDENBLATT, WILHELMINE	24	F	UNKNOWN	GRAARRNY	
RINGEL, JOSEF	46	M	GDNR	GRACBRNY	
ANNA	45	F	W	GRACBRNY	
FRITZ	18	M	GDNR	GRACBRNY	
ANNA	16	F	UNKNOWN	GRACBRNY	
JOSEF	6	M	CHILD	GRACBRNY	
KOCH, EMILIE	16	F	UNKNOWN	GRZZZZNY	
KELLER, FRANCES	18	F	UNKNOWN	GRAARRNY	

SHIP: SLAVONIA

FROM: SWINEMUNDE
TO: NEW YORK
ARRIVED: 13 AUGUST 1888

PASSENGER	AGE	SEX	OCCUPATION	PRVL	DES
KOPPEN, CARL	36	M	LABR	PRZZZZUSA	
ALWINE	35	F	W	PRZZZZUSA	
ANNA	10	F	CH	PRZZZZUSA	
ALBERT	8	M	CHILD	PRZZZZUSA	
BERTHA	5	F	CHILD	PRZZZZUSA	
AUGUSTE	.11	F	INFANT	PRZZZZUSA	
KOWITZ, MICHAEL	53	M	LABR	PRZZZZUSA	
CARL	10	M	CH	PRZZZZUSA	
BINDER, AUGUSTE	19	F	UNKNOWN	PRZZZZUSA	
ERDMANN, CARL	26	M	LABR	PRAESTUSA	
AUGUSTE	24	F	W	PRAESTUSA	
WILHELM	.11	M	INFANT	PRAESTUSA	
MULLER, EMMA	23	F	SVNT	PRAESTUSA	
STEINKE, EMMA	19	F	UNKNOWN	PRADENUSA	
GAUGER, EMIL	22	M	JNR	PRZZZZUSA	
MODZELEWSKY, WLAD.	20	M	LABR	PRZZZZUSA	
LEWANDOWSKY, PAUL	57	M	LABR	PRZZZZUSA	
JOZWIAK, ANTONIA	30	F	WO	PRZZZZUSA	
FRANZISKA	10	F	CH	PRZZZZUSA	
ROSALIA	8	F	CHILD	PRZZZZUSA	
WOYTECH	6	M	CHILD	PRZZZZUSA	
MICHAEL	3	M	CHILD	PRZZZZUSA	
GUTZMER, ALBERT	26	M	FARMER	PRZZZZUSA	
PETROSCH, WILHELM	42	M	JNR	PRAAZQUSA	
KREBS, FRIEDERIKE	60	F	WI	PRZZZZUSA	
MARTHA	24	F	D	PRZZZZUSA	
ZIMMERMANN, MARTNIN	65	M	MUSN	PRZZZZUSA	

PASSENGER	AGE	SEX	OCCUPATION	PRVL	DES
HENRIETTE	54	F	W	PRZZZZUSA	
OTTO	25	M	CH	PRZZZZUSA	
EMME	15	F	CH	PRZZZZUSA	
ERNST, CARL	68	M	JNR	PRAGCHUSA	
WILHELMINE	66	F	W	PRAGCHUSA	
SCHONFELD, AUGUST	42	M	UNKNOWN	PRZZZZUSA	
SCHWESIG, CHARLOTTE	18	F	UNKNOWN	PRALNWUSA	
MAROINOWSKY, ACARL	31	M	TLR	PRAIHZUSA	
MARIANNE	27	F	W	PRAIHZUSA	
GEIRNATOWSKA, AGNISKA	36	F	WO	PRZZZZUSA	
LUDWIG	9	M	CHILD	PRZZZZUSA	
PELAGIA	.06	F	INFANT	PRZZZZUSA	
ZIEGLER, JANNETTE	66	F	WI	PRZZZZUSA	
BOHLMANN, EMILIE	39	F	WO	PRZZZZUSA	
TILLMANN, JOHANN	46	M	LABR	PRZZZZUSA	
STREHLOW, FRIEDRICH	24	M	SHMK	PRZZZZUSA	
GRUNOW, EMMA	17	F	UNKNOWN	PRZZZZUSA	
GEORG	9	M	CHILD	PRZZZZUSA	
RENTH, CARL	26	M	LABR	PRZZZZUSA	
EFFLER, BERTHA	36	F	WO	PRACTKUSA	
ANGELIKA	12	F	CH	PRACTKUSA	
BRUNO	10	M	CH	PRACTKUSA	
META	8	F	CHILD	PRACTKUSA	
GRETE	6	F	CHILD	PRACTKUSA	
HANS	6	M	CHILD	PRACTKUSA	
SCHULTZ, OTTO	35	M	BLKSMH	PRZZZZUSA	
LOUISE	25	F	W	PRZZZZUSA	
MARTHA	9	F	CHILD	PRZZZZUSA	
ANNA	4	F	CHILD	PRZZZZUSA	
MATHILDE	.11	F	INFANT	PRZZZZUSA	
ZASTROW, WILHWLM	25	M	LABR	PRAEWMUSA	
META	26	F	W	PRAEWMUSA	
META	.01	F	INFANT	PRAEWMUSA	
STEFANSKY, JOHANN	63	M	LABR	PRZZZZUNK	
DAMIN, JOSEPHA	28	F	WO	PRZZZZUNK	
LEWANDOWSKA, FRANZISKA	55	F	WO	PRZZZZUNK	
HERZBERG, JOHAN	72	M	LABR	PRAEQWUNK	
SOPHIE	68	F	W	PRAEQWUNK	
HULDA	28	F	D	PRAEQWUNK	
KRAUSE, EMMA	20	F	UNKNOWN	PRZZZZUNK	
SZUMANSKA, BARBARA	45	F	WO	PRZZZZUNK	
MARIANNA	17	F	CH	PRZZZZUNK	
JOHANN	14	M	CH	PRZZZZUNK	
PETER	11	M	CH	PRZZZZUNK	
WLADISLAWA	8	F	CHILD	PRZZZZUNK	
RATHER, OTTO	27	M	SHMK	PRAHPYUNK	
BROSE, JOAHANNES	44	M	TLR	PRAEWMUNK	
SCHONFELD, ERNESTINE	32	F	W	PRZZZZUNK	
ERNST	7	M	CHILD	PRZZZZUNK	
EMIL	1	M	CHILD	PRZZZZUNK	
MARCINKOWSKY, THEKLA	9	F	CHILD	PRZZZZUNK	
PELAGIA	6	F	CHILD	PRZZZZUNK	
THEOPHIL	3	M	CHILD	PRZZZZUNK	
STANIDLAUS	1	M	CHILD	PRZZZZUNK	
BODUAREK, FRANZISKA	23	F	SVNT	PRZZZZUNK	
KLATT, WILHELM	28	M	LABR	PRAAESUNK	
HARTKOPF, FERDINAND	58	M	JNR	PRAEWMUNK	
BUDOZINSKY, JOHANN	29	M	BLKSMH	PRAAZQUNK	
MARIE	24	F	W	PRAAZQUNK	
LUCIE	2	F	CHILD	PRAAZQUNK	
BETTY	.02	F	INFANT	PRAAZQUNK	
PREZIBIATOWSKY, ROSALIE	26	F	UNKNOWN	PRAAZQUNK	
HOFRICHTER, MAX	23	M	UNKNOWN	PRZZZZUNK	
SCHUMACHER, WILHELM	31	M	FARMER	PRZZZZUNK	
ELISABETH	24	F	W	PRZZZZUNK	
TIMM, GOTTLIEB	27	M	SLR	PRZZZZUNK	
LEIK, AUGUST	22	M	LABR	PRZZZZUNK	
NITZ, HEDWIG	17	F	UNKNOWN	PRZZZZUNK	
OLSCHEWSKA, ANNA	36	F	WO	PRZZZZUNK	
GUDERIAN, ADOLPH	17	M	MLR	PRZZZZUNK	
GRABOWSKY, FRANZ	26	M	WHLR	PRZZZZUNK	
SCHUPP, AUGUST	47	M	LABR	PRAAKHUNK	
CAROLINE	38	F	W	PRAAKHUNK	
GERTRUD	9	F	CHILD	PRAAKHUNK	
ANNA	9	F	CHILD	PRAAKHUNK	

PASSENGER	AGE	SEX	OCCUPATION	PRVVL/DES
PRILL, MINNA	40	F	UNKNOWN	PRAAKHUNK
MEHRWALD, LOUISE	28	F	UNKNOWN	PRAAKHUNK
WALTER, HERMANN	36	M	CK	PRAAKHUNK
FRANZISKA	30	F	W	PRAAKHUNK
OSCAR	7	M	CHILD	PRAAKHUNK
ANNA	5	F	CHILD	PRAAKHUNK
CARL	3	M	CHILD	PRAAKHUNK
FRITZ, AUGUSTE	30	F	WO	PRZZZZUNK
GUSTAV	9	M	CHILD	PRZZZZUNK
EMMA	1	F	CHILD	PRZZZZUNK
VOLKMANN, BERNHARDINE	35	F	WO	PRZZZZUNK
GEORG	8	M	CHILD	PRZZZZUNK
WENDT, JOHANNES	27	M	RPR	PRZZZZUNK
MAASS, ROBERT	34	M	TLR	PRZZZZUNK
SPLETTSTOEPER, OTTO	20	M	RPR	PRAEWMUNK
POCHOLKE, BERTHA	28	F	WO	PRZZZZUNK
BERTHA	5	F	CHILD	PRZZZZUNK
ANNA	3	F	CHILD	PRZZZZUNK
MINNA	.05	F	INFANT	PRZZZZUNK
NEMITZ, EMILIE	32	F	WO	PRZZZZUNK
PAUL	7	M	CHILD	PRZZZZUNK
MAX	4	M	CHILD	PRZZZZUNK
ADELINA	.03	F	INFANT	PRZZZZUNK
BERTHA	.03	F	INFANT	PRZZZZUNK
PLANOW, WILHELM	28	M	BCHR	PRZZZZUNK
DORLOFF, AGATHE	23	F	UNKNOWN	PRAAZQUNK
KANETHOVEN, GEORG	20	M	CL	PRAAZQUNK
JARKA, LEON	30	M	SHMK	PRZZZZUNK
CATHARINA	30	F	W	PRZZZZUNK
FRANZISKA	.06	F	INFANT	PRZZZZUNK
WIEDTKE, ERNST	24	M	MUSN	PRZZZZUNK
EGGORT, WILHELM	27	M	LABR	PRZZZZUNK
WILHELMINE	28	F	W	PRZZZZUNK
PAGEL, FRIEDERIKE	26	F	SVNT	PRZZZZUNK
EGGERT, ALBERT	3	M	CHILD	PRZZZZUNK
PAGEL, BERTHA	.11	F	INFANT	PRZZZZUNK
REIMER, WILHELM	20	M	FARMER	PRACSDUNK
LOESSER, OLGA	20	F	UNKNOWN	PRAAZQUNK
PYERITZ, AUGUSTE	23	F	WO	PRZZZZUNK
JOHANNA	3	F	CHILD	PRZZZZUNK
ANNA	2	F	CHILD	PRZZZZUNK
AUGUSTE	.03	F	INFANT	PRZZZZUNK
PASSEK, HERMANN	18	M	CL	PRACTKUNK
MALINOWSKY, FRANZ	24	M	TLR	PRZZZZUNK
TOMSA, CATHARINE	18	F	UNKNOWN	PRZZZZUNK
ELLIS	.09	F	INFANT	PRZZZZUNK
BEHNCKE, ERNST	40	M	FARMER	PRZZZZUNK
ADELE	17	F	UNKNOWN	PRZZZZUNK
KATHE	16	F	UNKNOWN	PRZZZZUNK
MAX	13	M	UNKNOWN	PRZZZZUNK
LIESBETH	12	F	CH	PRZZZZUNK
PAUL	11	M	CH	PRZZZZUNK
KURTH	10	M	CH	PRZZZZUNK
ALICE	7	F	CHILD	PRZZZZUNK
VONSCHEIDT, PAUL	19	M	UNKNOWN	PRAAZQUNK
KOEPKE, FRIEDRICH	27	M	LABR	PRAEWMUNK
WILHELMINE	29	F	W	PRAEWMUNK
MARIE	9	F	CHILD	PRAEWMUNK
ANNA	5	F	CHILD	PRAEWMUNK
NEUMANN, RICHARD	25	M	BLKSMH	PRAJKVUNK
KREUZBERGER, JOHANN	48	M	MSN	PRZZZZUNK
SCHUNEMANN, DAVID	33	M	UNKNOWN	PRZZZZUNK
AUGUSTE	23	F	W	PRZZZZUNK
MARGARETHE	6	F	CHILD	PRZZZZUNK
ROBERT	4	M	CHILD	PRZZZZUNK
IDA	1	F	CHILD	PRZZZZUNK

SHIP: UMBRIA

FROM: LIVERPOOL
TO: NEW YORK
ARRIVED: 13 AUGUST 1888

PASSENGER	AGE	SEX	OCCUPATION	PRVVL/DES
BOENTZES, JULIUS	22	M	BKR	PRADAXUSA
BRAUN, IGNAZ	16	M	SHMK	PRADAXUSA
BECKER, T.C.	35	M	LABR	PRADAXUSA
HEPPY, H.	36	M	LABR	PRADAXUSA
JAENBOWSKY, PAUL	30	M	LABR	PRADAXUSA
PIDBE, EMIL	22	M	LABR	PRADAXUSA
LINA	20	M	JWLR	PRADAXUSA
MENDLOWICZ, JOS	11	M	CH	PRADAXUSA
NAUCHEN, GIRLA	14	F	SVNT	GRZZZZUSA
JUSTINA	20	F	SVNT	GRZZZZUSA
KEINER, JOHAN	29	M	LABR	GRADAXUSA
SCHMEYER, CARL	37	M	LABR	GRZZZZUSA
SCHLUTZKI, PAULINE	19	F	SVNT	GRZZZZUSA
SURSTNY, JOSEFA	18	F	SVNT	GRZZZZUSA
THIELMANN, CATH.	54	F	MA	GRZZZZUSA
CARL	15	M	LABR	GRZZZZUSA
WILD, WILH.	36	M	GENT	GRADAXUSA
IDA	26	F	W	GRADAXUSA
ROSENTHAL, MARCUS	27	M	MCHT	GRADAXUSA
BUSH, THEO	48	M	MCHT	GRADAXUSA
HUFNAGEL, JOHN	52	M	MCHT	GRADAXUSA
SILIGMAN, LOUIS	56	M	MCHT	GRADAXUSA
GASENLEN, ALOF	48	M	CL	GRADBQUSA
FRANKFIELD, ALOF	59	M	JWLR	GRADBQUSA
LADENBURG, ADOLF	33	M	UNKNOWN	GRADBQUSA
EMILY	23	F	W	GRADBQUSA
HESS, LEO	26	M	MCHT	GRADBQUSA
WEITHEIMER, MATT.	45	M	MCHT	GRADBQUSA
CZIRMINSKI, MARY	25	F	SVNT	GRADBQUSA

SHIP: AMERICA

FROM: BREMEN
TO: BALTIMORE
ARRIVED: 14 AUGUST 1888

PASSENGER	AGE	SEX	OCCUPATION	PRVVL/DES
WEISS, WENDELIN	33	M	MCHT	GRZZZZMD
ELISE	39	F	UNKNOWN	GRZZZZMD
LINA	3	F	CHILD	GRZZZZMD
LUDWIG	.10	M	INFANT	GRZZZZMD
NAUMANN, FRIEDRICH	40	M	PVTR	GRZZZZBAL
LINDNER, BRUNO	45	M	PROF	GRZZZZMD
PAWLAK, WLADISLAW	19	M	SHMK	GRZZZZMD
KREFT, FRIEDRICH	37	M	LABR	GRZZZZMD
KOHN, FRITZ	59	M	LABR	GRZZZZMD
WIENBRANDT, MARIE	15	F	UNKNOWN	GRZZZZMD
WOLF, ANNA	65	F	UNKNOWN	GRZZZZMD
WEIN, ELISE	18	F	SVNT	GRZZZZMI
LENTZ, FRIEDERIK	00	M	FARMER	GRZZZZOH
EMILIE	33	F	UNKNOWN	GRZZZZOH
WILHELM	9	M	CHILD	GRZZZZOH
PAULINE	6	F	CHILD	GRZZZZOH
IDA	4	F	CHILD	GRZZZZOH
GRETE	.11	F	INFANT	GRZZZZOH
JOHANN	37	M	FARMER	GRZZZZOH
CAROLINE	35	F	UNKNOWN	GRZZZZOH
WILHELM	11	M	CH	GRZZZZOH
HULDA	9	F	CHILD	GRZZZZOH
JULIUS	7	M	CHILD	GRZZZZOH
FRIEDRICH	3	M	CHILD	GRZZZZOH
GUSTAV	2	M	CHILD	GRZZZZOH
RUDOLF	.11	M	INFANT	GRZZZZOH
HINZ, WILHELMINE	24	F	UNKNOWN	GRZZZZOH

PASSENGER	AGE	SEX	OCCUPATION	PRVL	DES
ROEDRER, MARGARETHE	56	M	UNKNOWN	GRZZZZIL	
HINRICHS, JOHANN	62	M	CPTR	GRZZZZOH	
GESKE	67	F	UNKNOWN	GRZZZZOH	
KABER, JOHANN	66	M	FARMER	GRZZZZCIN	
EMMA	5	F	CHILD	GRZZZZCIN	
DAHLKE, JUYLIUS	67	M	FARMER	GRZZZZCIN	
BELZ, EMIL	10	M	CH	GRZZZZCIN	
HIRSCHLEWICZ, FRANZ	30	M	MSN	GRZZZZWI	
ANNA	28	F	WO	GRZZZZWI	
JOHANN	4	M	CHILD	GRZZZZWI	
LEO	.06	M	INFANT	GRZZZZWI	
BLAYER, SIMON	28	M	LABR	GRZZZZNE	
SIBALSKY, SARA	23	F	UNKNOWN	GRZZZZMD	
SWIATKOWSKY, FRANZISZEK	32	M	SMH	GRZZZZMD	
CATHARINA	21	F	UNKNOWN	GRZZZZMD	
ILIANNA	2	F	CHILD	GRZZZZMD	
JOSEPH	.11	M	INFANT	GRZZZZMD	
SCHMIDT, HENRIETTE	43	F	UNKNOWN	GRZZZZMD	
PIECZENSKI, HEDWIG	33	F	UNKNOWN	GRZZZZDAK	
JOSEF	5	M	CHILD	GRZZZZDAK	
HELENE	.11	F	INFANT	GRZZZZDAK	
TZWANKOWSKI, PAULINE	23	F	UNKNOWN	GRZZZZOH	
LAMPERT, AUGUSTA	32	F	UNKNOWN	GRZZZZOH	
ZELINA	9	F	CHILD	GRZZZZOH	
NAWITZKI, MARIANNA	24	F	UNKNOWN	GRZZZZOH	
LEONORA	3	F	CHILD	GRZZZZOH	
STEFANIE	.11	F	INFANT	GRZZZZOH	
GRUND, HULDA	25	F	UNKNOWN	GRZZZZOH	
LOTZ, FRITZ	14	M	UNKNOWN	GRZZZZOH	
GRUND, IDA	.11	F	INFANT	GRZZZZOH	
UTECHT, JULIANNE	32	F	UNKNOWN	GRZZZZOH	
MARIE	6	F	CHILD	GRZZZZOH	
ANNA	.11	F	INFANT	GRZZZZOH	
KOPPER, ANNA	16	F	UNKNOWN	GRZZZZWI	
AUGUST	8	M	CHILD	GRZZZZWI	
SOBIER, THEODOR	29	M	LABR	GRZZZZWI	
POLTOCK, MATHILDE	18	F	UNKNOWN	GRZZZZNE	
MEYER, OTTO	34	M	JNR	GRZZZZCO	
WAHL, ARTHUR	21	M	MCHT	GRZZZZKS	
BORZYK, CONSTANTIN	26	M	LABR	GRZZZZKS	
FANDRY, CARL	64	M	SHFM	GRZZZZIN	
BERGFRIED, JOHANN	17	M	CL	GRZZZZMD	
JOHANN	17	M	CL	GRZZZZMD	
POLTRACK, FRIEDRICH	52	M	MLR	GRZZZZNE	
DAHLKE, AMALIE	31	F	UNKNOWN	GRZZZZCIN	
ROBERT	6	M	CHILD	GRZZZZCIN	
IDA	5	F	CHILD	GRZZZZCIN	
FRIEDRICH	4	M	CHILD	GRZZZZCIN	
RICHARD	.11	M	INFANT	GRZZZZCIN	
STUBRIS, MARIE	35	F	UNKNOWN	GRZZZZOH	
MARIE	11	F	CH	GRZZZZOH	
KROENKE, WILHELM	44	M	FARMER	GRZZZZWI	
ALBERTINE	39	F	UNKNOWN	GRZZZZWI	
IDA	15	F	UNKNOWN	GRZZZZWI	
MINNA	13	F	CH	GRZZZZWI	
HEINRICH	10	M	CH	GRZZZZWI	
LOUISE	5	F	CHILD	GRZZZZWI	
ALWINE	1	F	CHILD	GRZZZZWI	
WILKENING, OLGA	29	F	UNKNOWN	GRZZZZIL	
HANS	2	M	CHILD	GRZZZZIL	
DALLWIG, AUGUSTA	23	F	UNKNOWN	GRZZZZMD	
MATHILDE	2	F	CHILD	GRZZZZMD	
WILHELM	.03	M	INFANT	GRZZZZMD	
SCHULZ, LOUISE	12	F	CH	GRZZZZMD	
ERNST	9	M	CHILD	GRZZZZMD	
CARL	7	M	CHILD	GRZZZZMD	
BULLWINKEL, ANNA	17	F	UNKNOWN	GRZZZZMD	
KUECK, META	11	F	CH	GRZZZZMD	
GESELL, HERMANN	14	M	UNKNOWN	GRZZZZOH	
BOIEHME, MATTHAEUS	24	M	SMH	GRZZZZOH	
ALTVATER, AUGUST	21	M	TNM	GRZZZZOH	
KIRCHHAEFER, PETER	21	M	SDLR	GRZZZZOH	
STEUERNAGEL, CHRISTIAN	8	M	CHILD	GRZZZZCAL	
RUDOLF	17	M	UNKNOWN	GRZZZZCAL	
KROMBACH, GEORG	26	M	FARMER	GRZZZZCIN	
DICKMEYER, HEINRICH	16	M	UNKNOWN	GRZZZZCIN	
RICHTER, EMILIE	26	F	UNKNOWN	GRZZZZMD	
SCHUELEIN, JOHANN	49	M	FARMER	GRZZZZOH	
MARGARETHE	53	F	UNKNOWN	GRZZZZOH	
KRAUS, STANISLAWA	19	F	SVNT	GRZZZZOH	
KEBENSTOCK, GERTRUD	7	F	CHILD	GRZZZZOH	
CURT	5	M	CHILD	GRZZZZOH	
JENDRIAN, CATHRINA	44	F	UNKNOWN	GRZZZZWI	
AUGUST	9	M	CHILD	GRZZZZWI	
EMIL	7	M	CHILD	GRZZZZWI	
HERMANN	5	M	CHILD	GRZZZZWI	
EMMA	2	F	CHILD	GRZZZZWI	
HOEDL, LUDWIG	20	M	JNR	GRZZZZVA	
WELLERMANN, ELISABETH	14	F	UNKNOWN	GRZZZZVA	
WERKAMP, BERNARDINE	29	F	UNKNOWN	GRZZZZVA	
JOHANNE	5	F	CHILD	GRZZZZVA	
BLOMKE, CARL	16	M	UNKNOWN	GRZZZZPA	
GRONOWSKI, WLADISLAW	24	M	MSN	GRZZZZOH	
RASSINGER, MARIA	28	F	UNKNOWN	GRZZZZOH	
JOHANN	3	M	CHILD	GRZZZZOH	
RODISCH, THERESE	26	F	SVNT	GRZZZZOH	
SCHULZ, ELISABETH	50	F	UNKNOWN	GRZZZZOH	
DUBE, CATARINA	50	F	UNKNOWN	GRZZZZOH	
MANTHEI, OTTILIE	30	F	UNKNOWN	GRZZZZOH	
OTTO	3	M	CHILD	GRZZZZOH	
EMMA	.11	F	INFANT	GRZZZZOH	
DAVID, JOHANN	47	M	MCHT	GRZZZZIN	
ERNSTINE	36	F	UNKNOWN	GRZZZZIN	
EMMA	11	F	CH	GRZZZZIN	
AUGUSTE	10	F	CH	GRZZZZIN	
MARTHA	8	F	CHILD	GRZZZZIN	
BRUNO	6	M	CHILD	GRZZZZIN	
PAUL	4	M	CHILD	GRZZZZIN	
JESSNITZAN, ADELE	25	F	UNKNOWN	GRZZZZMD	
OFSCHINSKY, CAECILIA	30	F	UNKNOWN	GRZZZZKY	
HEDWIG	4	F	CHILD	GRZZZZKY	
YESKE, AUGUST	52	M	BKLYR	GRZZZZKY	
EMILIE	61	F	UNKNOWN	GRZZZZKY	
ALBERTINE	20	F	UNKNOWN	GRZZZZKY	
ALBERT	15	M	UNKNOWN	GRZZZZKY	
LABUDA, JOSEF	65	M	FARMER	GRZZZZKS	
ROSA	29	F	UNKNOWN	GRZZZZKS	
JULIANNA	4	F	CHILD	GRZZZZKS	
AUGUSTINA	3	F	CHILD	GRZZZZKS	
JOSEF	.10	M	INFANT	GRZZZZKS	
HAERSTENSTEINER, EMIL	10	M	CH	GRZZZZIN	
GREITENS, BERNHARD	23	M	LABR	GRZZZZIN	
MAIER, MARIA	45	F	UNKNOWN	GRZZZZIN	
MARIA	10	F	CH	GRZZZZIN	
GRUEBBEL, AUGUST	17	M	FARMER	GRZZZZOH	
RAISCH, JOHANN	22	M	TLR	GRZZZZOH	
FRITSCHE, FRANZ	16	M	UNKNOWN	GRZZZZOH	
JENNRICH, CARL	29	M	LABR	GRZZZZMD	
WIK, GEORG	26	M	JNR	GRZZZZMD	
JABLINSKI, CAROLINA	55	F	UNKNOWN	GRZZZZMD	
MARIE	10	F	CH	GRZZZZMD	
DREWNOWSKI, ELISABETH	42	F	UNKNOWN	GRZZZZMI	
BUCHHOLZ, AUGUST	24	M	TU	GRZZZZMI	
MOELLER, FERDINAND	50	M	HTR	GRZZZZMI	
HABERSTEIN, AUGUSTE	18	F	SVNT	GRZZZZMI	
HILSCHER, WILHELMINE	50	F	UNKNOWN	GRZZZZMI	
WILL, LUDWIG	15	M	UNKNOWN	GRZZZZMI	
MEYER, MARCYANNA	49	F	UNKNOWN	GRZZZZMN	
MARTHA	19	F	SVNT	GRZZZZMN	
LEON	10	M	CH	GRZZZZMN	
BUSCA, HENRIETTE	44	F	UNKNOWN	GRZZZZIL	
FRANZ	7	M	CHILD	GRZZZZIL	
MARIECHEN	6	F	CHILD	GRZZZZIL	
ALBERT	4	M	CHILD	GRZZZZIL	
KRUEGER, ERNST	49	M	UNKNOWN	GRZZZZWI	
KRAUSE, AUGUSTE	28	F	UNKNOWN	GRZZZZIL	
BERTHA	4	F	CHILD	GRZZZZIL	
ALBERT	3	M	CHILD	GRZZZZIL	
CARL	.11	M	INFANT	GRZZZZIL	
HARTMANN, HEINRICH	58	M	FARMER	GRZZZZOH	

PASSENGER	AGE	SEX	OCCUPATION	PVRVL	DES
MARIE	51	F	UNKNOWN	GRZZZZOH	
ANNA	18	F	UNKNOWN	GRZZZZOH	
HERMANN	16	M	FARMER	GRZZZZOH	
WILHELM	14	M	UNKNOWN	GRZZZZOH	
LUDWIG	11	M	CH	GRZZZZOH	
BOECKELMANN, HEINRICH	45	M	FARMER	GRZZZZOH	
CATHARINA	44	F	UNKNOWN	GRZZZZOH	
FRIEDRICH	17	M	FARMER	GRZZZZOH	
HEINRICH	15	M	CH	GRZZZZOH	
ELISE	13	F	CH	GRZZZZOH	
EMILIE	11	F	CH	GRZZZZOH	
JOHANNES	7	M	CHILD	GRZZZZOH	
CASPAR	5	M	CHILD	GRZZZZOH	
WILHELM	4	M	CHILD	GRZZZZOH	
ANNA	2	F	CHILD	GRZZZZOH	
MEIER, MARIA	18	F	SVNT	GRZZZZKS	
BOGATZ, LORE	26	F	UNKNOWN	GRZZZZKS	
KELI	6	F	CHILD	GRZZZZKS	
WALTHER, JOHANN	27	M	SMH	GRZZZZMD	
SCHMIDT, JOHANN	23	M	LABR	GRZZZZIL	
GAUL, MARIA	20	F	SVNT	GRZZZZIL	
SCHMIERLE, VALENTIN	16	M	UNKNOWN	GRZZZZIL	
FISCHER, LUDWIG	38	M	MSN	GRZZZZMI	
CATHARINA	36	F	UNKNOWN	GRZZZZMI	
WILHELM	7	M	CHILD	GRZZZZMI	
CARL	5	M	CHILD	GRZZZZMI	
JOHANNA	3	F	CHILD	GRZZZZMI	
OTTO	.10	M	INFANT	GRZZZZMI	
HORN, JOSEF	42	M	MCHT	GRZZZZPA	
MEYER, LINA	17	F	SVNT	GRZZZZMD	
SCHALZ, JOHANN	23	M	SMH	GRZZZZOH	
BEINKE, HEINRICH	18	M	FARMER	GRZZZZOH	
OTTO, RUDOLF	23	M	GDNR	GRZZZZIL	
HINGST, AUGUST	26	M	BKLYR	GRZZZZOH	
STEINLE, MARGARETHE	20	F	UNKNOWN	GRZZZZMI	
CORDES, CARL	22	M	LLD	GRZZZZMI	
WAGNER, CATHARINE	69	F	UNKNOWN	GRZZZZMI	
LERATZKI, CHRIST	25	M	LABR	GRZZZZMI	
PAWLIK, WILHELMINE	30	F	UNKNOWN	GRZZZZMI	
PANNECK, MARIE	25	F	UNKNOWN	GRZZZZMI	
SCHWEDER, GOTTFRIED	37	M	FARMER	GRZZZZMI	
LOUISE	39	F	UNKNOWN	GRZZZZMI	
FRIEDRICH	7	M	CHILD	GRZZZZMI	
RUDOLF	3	M	CHILD	GRZZZZMI	
WEIERSHAEUSER, CONRAD	31	M	MSN	GRZZZZIA	
CHRISTINE	3	F	CHILD	GRZZZZIA	
BRESMANN, FFRIEDRICH	17	M	JNR	GRZZZZWI	
BRUNS, BERTHA	34	F	UNKNOWN	GRZZZZIL	
FRIEDA	7	F	CHILD	GRZZZZIL	
LOUISE	.11	F	INFANT	GRZZZZIL	
WALLMEYER, ELISABETH	45	F	UNKNOWN	GRZZZZVA	
AGNES	13	F	CH	GRZZZZVA	
STEIN, GERTRUD	30	F	UNKNOWN	GRZZZZIL	
BERGES, JACOB	31	M	JNR	GRZZZZMI	
HUFNAGEL, EMIL	17	M	TLR	GRZZZZMI	
KIESER, MARIA	23	F	SVNT	GRZZZZIN	
KAISER, JACOB	21	M	SMH	GRZZZZIN	
HAMSTEDT, AUGUST	26	M	CPTR	GRZZZZIL	
SEIBT, RICHARD	24	M	MCHT	GRZZZZIL	
GETTEK, JOSEF	31	M	TLR	GRZZZZOH	
MOENNICH, FRITZ	26	M	LABR	GRZZZZVA	
DEIFECK, JOSEF	24	M	MSN	GRZZZZIL	

SHIP: BOHEMIA

FROM: HAMBURG
TO: NEW YORK
ARRIVED: 15 AUGUST 1888

PASSENGER	AGE	SEX	OCCUPATION	PVRVL	DES
JANSON, PAUL	27	M	PNTR	GRAAKHIL	
GRAMINSKI, FRANZ	24	M	LABR	PRZZZZIL	
SAKE, ANNA	35	F	WO	PRACWUIL	
SIMON, KARL	18	M	LABR	PRAEWZIL	
LASKOWSKA, EMILIE	23	F	SGL	PRZZZZIL	
SCHWEDER, FERD.	24	M	LABR	PRAESDNY	
LUDWIG, ALBERT	00	M	JNR	SZZZZZNY	
WEBER, MINNA	22	F	UNKNOWN	SZZZZZNY	
ULBRICH, GUSTAV	24	M	FARMER	PRZZZZNY	
PETERS, FRIEDR.	36	M	UNKNOWN	PRZZZZNY	
MIESKE, RICHARD	25	M	FARMER	PRZZZZCAN	
NEMITZ, ANNA	27	F	SGL	PRALZOUNK	
STRENGER, LOUISE	30	F	SGL	WMZZZZUNK	
BRUSGATIS, MARGARETHE	28	F	WO	WMAESDPA	
EMMA	9	F	CHILD	WMAESDPA	
CARL	7	M	CHILD	WMAESDPA	
EMIL	.11	M	INFANT	WMAESDPA	
MAIER, FREDRIKE	16	F	SGL	WMZZZZPA	
WLOSZYNSKI, MARIANNE	20	F	UNKNOWN	WMABNOOH	
PETRONELLA	18	F	UNKNOWN	WMABNOOH	
WIECZMARK, CARL	62	F	UNKNOWN	WMABNOOH	
SUSANNE	58	F	FARMER	PRZZZZDAK	
KAZMAREK, ANTON	44	M	MCHT	PRAIMFDAK	
ENGEL, ISAAC	30	M	LABR	PRZZZZDAK	
RIEGER, WILH.	26	M	JNR	PRAERUIL	
KUECKENMEISTER, FRIEDRI	16	M	FARMER	HSZZZZNY	
HOFFMANN, JOSEF	34	M	BLKSMH	HSAARZNY	
BALIEREK, VALENTIN	48	M	LABR	PRZZZZNE	
SCHAUER, WILH.	77	M	LABR	PRACTOIL	
BECK, THERESE	24	F	SGL	PRZZZZPA	
WALDENBURGER, GEORG	30	M	FARMER	BVZZZZPA	
MARG.	32	F	W	BVZZZZPA	
LUDWIG	3	M	CHILD	BVZZZZPA	
EVA	.09	F	INFANT	BVZZZZPA	
EGGERS, JOACHIM	70	M	LABR	MKZZZZPA	
SOFIE	64	F	W	MKZZZZPA	
WAWROCK, JOHANN	16	M	LABR	PRZZZZIL	
TOMCZAK, MICHALINE	22	F	SGL	PRZZZZNY	
SHACUFSKY, FIME	9	F	CHILD	PRZZZZNY	
PRZYBYSZ, ROSALIE	70	F	WO	PRZZZZNY	
ECKE, ANNA	32	F	WO	PRZZZZNY	
LISETTE	6	F	CHILD	PRZZZZNY	
FRIEDR.	4	M	CHILD	PRZZZZNY	
WILH.	2	M	CHILD	PRZZZZNY	
HUSTEDT, ROBERT	24	M	UNKNOWN	PRAGPTPA	
HOFFMANN, JOSEFA	35	F	WO	PRAARZPA	
BREUER, PAUL	25	M	FARMER	PRZZZZPA	
WERNER, ROBERT	22	M	BKLYR	PRZZZZPA	
MILLAHN, CLARA	26	F	SGL	HBZZZZPA	
MALINSKY, KASIMR	25	M	LABR	PRZZZZPA	
MALLEK, GOTTLIEB	26	M	LABR	PRZZZZPA	
CLAUSEN, NICKELS	30	M	FARMER	PRZZZZNE	
JUSCZYNSKA, ANNA	50	F	WO	PRALEBNE	
WOHLERS, HEINR.	22	M	LABR	PRZZZZNE	
GRUNDT, BODE	29	M	SHMK	PRACXHIA	
OTTE, HEINR.	34	M	FARMER	PRZZZZKS	
DOROTHEA	31	F	W	PRZZZZKS	
HEINR.	4	M	CHILD	PRZZZZKS	
CARL	.06	M	INFANT	PRZZZZKS	
BENECKE, CATH.	58	F	WO	PRZZZZKS	
SELLKE, CARL	24	M	LABR	PRAKSANY	
BERTHA	21	F	W	PRAKSANY	
SCHMIDT, GEORG	53	M	LABR	PRZZZZNY	
AMLIE	38	F	W	PRZZZZNY	
ELFRIEDE	9	F	CHILD	PRZZZZNY	
MINNA	6	F	CHILD	PRZZZZNY	
CHALOWSKI, NEPOMUK	27	M	SHMK	PRABUTOH	
BALCEREK, CAECILIE	17	F	SGL	PRAFPGOH	

PASSENGER	AGE	SEX	OCCUPATION	PRVL	DES
ULRICH, FERDINAND	27	M	LABR	PRAAKHOH	
BARUCH, SOPHIE	20	F	SGL	PRAAKHOH	
SABOR, MICHAEL	19	M	MCHT	PRABKPMO	
JACOBS, LEOPOLD	23	M	MCHT	PRAAKHNY	
SCHROETER, ANNA	19	F	SGL	PRAAKHNY	
PRUESSING, WILHELM	47	M	TNM	MKZZZZNY	
OGENSEN, META	17	F	SGL	MKZZZZNY	
GEHL, ANTON	24	M	LABR	ACZZZZNY	
BOEHMER, ANDREAS	41	M	LABR	ACAFRGWI	
CATH.	31	F	LABR	ACAFRGWI	
FRANZ	15	F	UNKNOWN	ACAFRGWI	
ALEXANDER	9	M	CHILD	ACAFRGWI	
BARBARA	4	F	CHILD	ACAFRGWI	
ISABELLA	.06	F	INFANT	ACAFRGWI	
BLOETHNER, GUSTAV	36	M	LKSH	ACAAXKIL	
WILHELMINE	26	F	W	ACAAXKIL	
CLARA	22	F	SGL	ACAAXKIL	
MERTEN, CARL	34	M	ENGR	ACAAZQNY	
EBERNHARDT, ERNST	26	M	BKR	WMZZZZNY	
MASOKE, SALLY	21	M	MCHT	WMACSXNY	
PETSCHKE, HERM.	27	M	LABR	WMAAXKIL	
WILH.	28	F	W	WMAAXKIL	
KUECHLER, JOS.	63	M	LABR	PRZZZZIL	
ADTLER, HEINR.	60	M	LABR	PRZZZZNY	
KOPFF, MAX	17	M	TNM	PRAIDONY	
FITTICHAUER, FELIX	18	M	MCHT	PRAAKHNY	

SHIP: KANSAS

FROM: LIVERPOOL
TO: BOSTON
ARRIVED: 15 AUGUST 1888

PASSENGER	AGE	SEX	OCCUPATION	PRVL	DES
ROSS, ANNA	41	F	NRS	GRZZZZBO	
SIBBERSON, PETER	32	M	LABR	GRZZZZUNK	
DILGEN, CARL	22	M	LABR	GRZZZZMO	
LARKIN, A.	32	M	CTM	FRZZZZBO	

SHIP: SCHIEDAM

FROM: AMSTERDAM
TO: NEW YORK
ARRIVED: 15 AUGUST 1888

PASSENGER	AGE	SEX	OCCUPATION	PRVL	DES
MULLER, ED	28	M	MCHT	GRZZZZUSA	
SNOCK, JOOST	41	M	PVTM	GRZZZZUSA	
ZUBER, ADOLF	16	M	LABR	SRZZZZUSA	
PREMFNER, LOUIS	34	M	UNKNOWN	GRZZZZUSA	
GUTEBIER, HEINR.L.	54	M	CLNT	GRZZZZUSA	
BLUME, JOH.FRIEDR.	49	M	FARMER	GRZZZZUSA	
KATHARINE	48	F	UNKNOWN	GRZZZZUSA	
ANNA	22	F	SVNT	GRZZZZUSA	
LOUISE	.08	F	INFANT	GRZZZZUSA	
SILBERHORN, CARL	22	M	GDSM	GRZZZZUSA	
ALBRECHT, JOHANN	22	M	JNR	GRZZZZUSA	
PERMANN, MATHIAS	42	M	UNKNOWN	GRZZZZUSA	
BAMBIC, JOSEF	33	M	UNKNOWN	GRZZZZUSA	
MUGAELS, MAX	36	M	UNKNOWN	FRZZZZUSA	
PIETRO, C---ERA	28	M	UNKNOWN	FRZZZZUSA	
HUTTER, MARGARETHA	22	F	SVNT	GRZZZZUSA	

SHIP: STATE OF NEVADA

FROM: GLASGOW AND LARNE
TO: NEW YORK
ARRIVED: 16 AUGUST 1888

PASSENGER	AGE	SEX	OCCUPATION	PRVL	DES
ALTINAN, JACOB	25	M	UNKNOWN	GRAHRZUSA	
HANSEN, ANDERS	18	M	FARMER	GRAHRZUSA	
OLSEN, HANS	18	M	FARMER	GRAHRZUSA	

SHIP: WAESLAND

FROM: ANTWERP
TO: NEW YORK
ARRIVED: 16 AUGUST 1888

PASSENGER	AGE	SEX	OCCUPATION	PRVL	DES
WIRTH, G.	40	M	ACHTT	GRZZZZSP	
DEAN, U	50	F	UNKNOWN	GRZZZZNY	
GERARDT, F.	35	M	MCHT	GRZZZZNY	
U	25	F	UNKNOWN	GRZZZZNY	
GRIFFIN, M.	45	F	UNKNOWN	GRZZZZNY	
ROEHL, J.	40	M	TPGPH	GRZZZZSP	
NOEVER, G.	39	M	PREST	GRZZZZWI	
DAHLEN, C.	31	M	LITGR	GRZZZZWI	
GERBERT, G.	26	M	LITGR	GRZZZZWI	
O.	18	M	UNKNOWN	GRZZZZWI	
DOLL, F.	24	F	UNKNOWN	GRZZZZWI	
LEISSNER, J.	24	F	UNKNOWN	GRZZZZNY	
ZIESING, B.	31	F	UNKNOWN	GRZZZZNY	
U	4	F	CHILD	GRZZZZNY	
U	3	F	CHILD	GRZZZZNY	
HETZEL, E.	34	F	PRNTR	GRZZZZWGT	
WAHNELT, W.	21	F	UNKNOWN	GRZZZZBO	
KRUSE, U	34	M	UNKNOWN	GRZZZZNY	
PELZER, G.	23	F	UNKNOWN	GRZZZZNY	
BROLHEN, L.	28	F	UNKNOWN	GRZZZZNY	
GUTGESELL, L.	21	F	UNKNOWN	GRZZZZNY	
KOMMELL, S.	28	M	CL	GRZZZZNY	
KABUS, U	34	F	UNKNOWN	GRZZZZNY	
ENGEL, CARL	52	M	CK	GRZZZZNY	
FERRIAUS, THEOD.	29	M	FARMER	GRZZZZCH	
BAELTSIN, ALB.	53	M	CPTR	GRZZZZCH	
WILHELM, WILH.	20	M	LABR	GRZZZZCH	
FISCHER, JEAN	19	M	LITGR	GRZZZZCH	
BAUSEN, RUD.	20	M	TCHR	GRZZZZNY	
CERWONKA, JOSEF	20	M	FARMER	GRZZZZUNK	
SZMIKOWSKI, AUG.	19	M	FARMER	GRZZZZBUF	
ROSINSKI, STAN.	22	M	FARMER	GRZZZZCH	
KREUSREITER, CARL	30	M	SMH	GRZZZZCH	
ZIMMER, MARIE	26	F	SVNT	GRZZZZCH	
MOSCHERROSCH, PAULINE	17	F	UNKNOWN	GRZZZZCH	
SOPHIE	15	F	UNKNOWN	GRZZZZCH	
LAWS, BERTHA	25	F	UNKNOWN	GRZZZZCH	
BERTHA	00	F	INF	GRZZZZCH	
SCHNEIDER, CAROLINE	21	F	SVNT	GRZZZZNY	
EUDERLE, EVA	30	F	UNKNOWN	GRZZZZNY	
HOLTZ, GEO	32	M	FARMER	GRZZZZNY	
SOEWER, JOH.	60	M	UNKNOWN	GRZZZZNY	
WEBER, VICTORIA	36	F	UNKNOWN	GRZZZZNY	
STEGERWALD, GEO	24	M	LABR	GRZZZZNY	
DINGER, PAULINE	21	F	UNKNOWN	GRZZZZNY	
PAUL	7	M	CHILD	GRZZZZNY	
FRITZ	3	M	CHILD	GRZZZZNY	
WINTER, ATHANASIA	51	F	UNKNOWN	GRZZZZNY	
HEDWIGA	15	F	UNKNOWN	GRZZZZNY	
GUSTAV	8	M	CHILD	GRZZZZNY	
KRAEMER, WILH.	57	M	CCHMN	GRZZZZUSA	
FRED.	54	F	UNKNOWN	GRZZZZUSA	
FRED.	20	M	UNKNOWN	GRZZZZUSA	

PASSENGER	AGE	SEX	OCCUPATION	PRVL	DES
HOFHAUER, PETER	29	M	PNTR		GRZZZZNY
ANNA	29	F	LABR		GRZZZZSTL
BRAUN, PHIL	25	M	LABR		GRZZZZNY
MOHR, HER.	24	M	SMH		GRZZZZNY
HESSLER, ELISE	16	F	SVNT		GRZZZZNY
REICKERT, PHIL.	21	M	BCHR		GRZZZZNY
SOPHIE	22	F	BCHR		GRZZZZNY
BRECHHEMMER, LUD.	16	M	BCHR		GRZZZZNY
ZIMMER, F.	16	M	LABR		GRZZZZNY
KRAUER, F.	27	M	MSN		GRZZZZCH
JUNG, THEOD.	28	M	MSN		GRZZZZNY
KEITLER, EUGEN	15	M	PH		GRZZZZNY
MULLER, LUD.	24	M	FARMER		GRZZZZNY
KUGELHARD, MICH.	37	M	FARMER		GRZZZZNY
JOS.	23	F	UNKNOWN		GRZZZZNY
SOLTONG, PHIL.	26	M	MSN		GRZZZZNY
FREIS, ELISE	21	F	FARMER		GRZZZZNY
MICHELS, JOH.	22	M	UNKNOWN		GRZZZZNY
HAAS, THEOD.	24	M	BKR		GRZZZZNY
MIST--LE, ALB.	36	M	CPR		GRZZZZNY
CAROLINE	36	F	CPR		GRZZZZNY
WEMMACHHER, GEO	32	M	WVR		GRZZZZNY
BERGER, PETER	28	M	UNKNOWN		GRZZZZNY
JOS.	22	M	UNKNOWN		GRZZZZNY
HAUER, MEIN.	24	M	FTR		GRZZZZNY
OBENDORFER, ANNA	28	F	UNKNOWN		GRZZZZNY
GRAMLICH, FRZ.	17	M	TLR		GRZZZZNY
SCHOLL, CARL	18	M	TLR		GRZZZZNY
WILH.	19	M	TLR		GRZZZZNY
ROLL, VERONIKA	22	F	UNKNOWN		GRZZZZNY
DEUSER, ROSA	28	F	UNKNOWN		GRZZZZNY
HOLLERBACH, GEWEOE	22	F	UNKNOWN		GRZZZZNY
GUSTAV	00	F	INF		GRZZZZNY
BUSHARD, MARIE	40	F	UNKNOWN		GRZZZZBUF
DEBOLD, ERNST	41	M	UNKNOWN		GRZZZZNY
FRK.	36	F	UNKNOWN		GRZZZZNY
EMMA	14	F	UNKNOWN		GRZZZZNY
MARIE	11	F	UNKNOWN		GRZZZZNY
CAROLINE	9	F	CHILD		GRZZZZNY
EUGENIE	7	F	CHILD		GRZZZZNY
LOUISE	4	F	CHILD		GRZZZZNY
CARL	00	M	INF		GRZZZZNY
DEBER, JACOB	18	M	FARMER		GRZZZZHAT
RICHTER, MARTIN	26	M	FARMER		GRZZZZCIN
MELLIS, WILH.	23	M	LABR		GRZZZZNY
MULLER, OTTO	25	M	LABR		GRZZZZNY
SCHELL, CARL	24	M	LABR		GRZZZZNY
NOTTE, CARL	21	M	TLR		GRZZZZNY
KIEFER, PETER	30	M	TCHR		GRZZZZNY
MARIA	25	F	TCHR		GRZZZZNY
HOFMANN, ALB.	25	M	LABR		GRZZZZUNK
BRUCK, JOS.	21	M	LABR		GRZZZZLOU
REISS, GOTFR.	30	M	LABR		GRZZZZNY
DENNIG, FRANZ	29	M	LABR		GRZZZZNY
STERZIK, ALB.	25	M	LABR		GRZZZZNY
WOLNEWITSCH, JOSEF	56	M	LABR		GRZZZZOMA
IGNAZ	17	F	LABR		GRZZZZOMA
BLASENBREIN, MAGD.	27	F	SVNT		GRZZZZUNK
WAGNER, JOSEF	29	M	WTR		GRZZZZUNK
HOFFMANN, CARL	24	M	FARMER		GRZZZZUNK
HCH.	23	M	FARMER		GRZZZZNY
DOBRINSKY, CARL	47	M	FARMER		GRZZZZNY
ANNA	60	F	UNKNOWN		GRZZZZNY
GUSTAV	17	M	UNKNOWN		GRZZZZNY
FEHRENBACH, ARTHUR	26	M	WCHMKR		GRZZZZNY
MARON, FRED.	31	M	CMST		GRZZZZNY
SPRINGEN, E.	25	M	SHMK		GRZZZZNY
CATH.	26	F	SHMK		GRZZZZNY
E.	00	M	INF		GRZZZZNY
KISTEL, A.	20	M	BKBNDR		GRZZZZNY
WOIDES, W.	27	M	CGRMKR		GRZZZZNY
BRUMMER, H.	38	M	HRDRS		GRZZZZNY
JOSEF.	41	F	HRDRS		GRZZZZNY
FRED.	3	F	CHILD		GRZZZZNY
GETTENS, ANNIL	38	F	UNKNOWN		GRZZZZNY
KATIE	14	F	UNKNOWN		GRZZZZNY
PIECK, LEOP.	24	M	MSN		GRZZZZNY
KASHENBUTH, MARG.	18	F	SVNT		GRZZZZNY
SCHAEFER, CHRIS.	24	M	CRDMKR		GRZZZZNY
KATZOSKEWITZ, ANTON	25	M	SMH		GRZZZZCH
BERCHEM, ALF.	18	M	MSN		GRZZZZNY
GEISS, MARG.	21	F	SVNT		GRZZZZNY
DUFNER, JOH.	32	M	MACH		GRZZZZNY
LOUISE	25	F	MACH		GRZZZZNY
HCH.	.07	M	INFANT		GRZZZZNY
GRAF, GUSTAF	37	M	LABR		SRZZZZNY
HONEGGER, ROB.	46	M	LABR		SRZZZZNY
BOOS, GENOVESA	22	M	LABR		SRZZZZNY
DIEK, CHR.	26	M	LABR		SRZZZZNY
ELISAB.	25	F	LABR		SRZZZZNY
JOST, HCH.	29	M	LABR		GRZZZZNY
LENIGANG, JACOB	17	M	LABR		GRZZZZNY
EHRLER, WILH.	24	M	LABR		GRZZZZPIT
WUENSCHEL, ANTON	23	M	SHMK		GRZZZZPIT
STIEBER, KAROLINA	21	F	SHMK		GRZZZZPIT
GREISMANN, BAP.	22	M	MLR		GRZZZZPHI
GLOSSTETTER, AMALIE	28	F	UNKNOWN		GRZZZZNY
ANNA	2	F	CHILD		GRZZZZNY
WEBER, STEFANIE	15	F	UNKNOWN		GRZZZZNY
LAUB, ANNA	15	F	UNKNOWN		GRZZZZNY
LAWS, ANTON	14	M	UNKNOWN		GRZZZZNY
FREI, JOH.	65	M	FARMER		GRZZZZNY
JOH.	30	F	FARMER		GRZZZZNY
EMMA	14	F	FARMER		GRZZZZNY
BURKART, KASPAR	21	M	UNKNOWN		GRZZZZNY
KELLER, JOHANN	34	M	UNKNOWN		GRZZZZNY
HCH.	9	M	CHILD		GRZZZZNY
METZLER, ERNST	28	M	LABR		GRZZZZPHI
MARIE	25	F	LABR		GRZZZZPHI
SCHMITT, ELISE	21	F	UNKNOWN		GRZZZZPHI
LUDWIG	16	M	WVR		GRZZZZPHI
THOEMER, WILH.	26	M	LABR		GRZZZZNY
MULLER, GEO	23	M	BCHR		GRZZZZNY
HAMMEL, GEO	21	M	LABR		GRZZZZNY
MEYER, RAES	20	M	MCHT		GRZZZZNY
WIRTH, PETER	26	M	FARMER		GRZZZZNY
MARSA, MARIA	20	F	SVNT		GRZZZZNY
PASCHKEWISKI, TOB.	28	F	LABR		GRZZZZNY
ANTONI	6	M	CHILD		GRZZZZNY
LAUDEN, SALOMON	30	M	CL		GRZZZZNY
PATTINOWICZ, BAR.	38	M	TLR		GRZZZZNY
PISZKOWSKI, NACT.	20	M	BCHR		GRZZZZNY
CHROBOBOWIEZ, SCHIFRE	20	F	SVNT		GRZZZZNY
ISAAESOHN, ARON	28	M	CBTMKR		GRZZZZNY
DEINI	27	F	UNKNOWN		GRZZZZNY
ROSEN	00	F	INF		GRZZZZNY
LUST, HCH.	36	M	TLR		GRZZZZNY
WALTER, GEO	19	M	MECH		GRZZZZNY
BAUER, GEO	21	M	BKR		GRZZZZNY
BRENNER, M.	20	F	SVNT		GRZZZZNY
CARMER, GEO	32	M	LABR		GRZZZZNY
AUGERER, ELISA	16	F	UNKNOWN		GRZZZZNY
CARL	14	M	UNKNOWN		GRZZZZNY
MADER, MARIA	36	F	UNKNOWN		GRZZZZNY
VOLEMER, ROSA	9	F	CHILD		GRZZZZNY
ASCHENBREMMER, HELENA	26	F	UNKNOWN		GRZZZZNY
MAGD.	3	F	CHILD		GRZZZZNY
LUDWIG	00	M	INF		GRZZZZNY
KRAUTZ, ADAM	14	M	UNKNOWN		GRZZZZNY
ROMER, THERESIA	22	F	UNKNOWN		GRZZZZNY
KAISER, CATH.	64	F	UNKNOWN		GRZZZZNY
MARG.	43	F	LABR		GRZZZZNY
GEO	00	M	LABR		GRZZZZNY
MARG.	7	F	CHILD		GRZZZZNY
BRAND, HCH.	30	M	SMH		GRZZZZNY
RAELTTER, CHRIST.	40	F	UNKNOWN		GRZZZZNY
AUGUST	13	F	UNKNOWN		GRZZZZNY
HCH.	12	M	UNKNOWN		GRZZZZNY
HERMANN	9	M	CHILD		GRZZZZNY
JOHANNA	4	F	CHILD		GRZZZZNY

PASSENGER	AGE	SEX	OCCUPATION	PRVL	DES
CHRISTINE	2	F	CHILD	GRZZZZNY	
DERUELLE, JOSEPHINE	18	F	UNKNOWN	FRZZZZUNK	
J.BTE.	00	M	INF	FRZZZZUNK	
SCHNEIDER, ARON	26	M	LABR	GRZZZZNY	
ROTH, PHIL.	28	M	MUSN	GRZZZZNY	
ERNST	25	M	MUSN	GRZZZZNY	
TAPPREICH, CATH.	10	F	CH	GRZZZZNY	
DAHM, THEOD.	20	M	FARMER	GRZZZZSP	
WOERNER, MARG.	20	F	PSSR	GRZZZZSP	
HAUSEN, MARIA	28	F	PSSR	GRZZZZSP	
ALEX	6	M	CHILD	GRZZZZSP	
ANNA	5	F	CHILD	GRZZZZSP	
BLACK, HENRI	47	M	CPR	GRZZZZNY	
BERCHEM, PETER	21	M	PNTR	GRZZZZNY	
HAUSEN, NIC	58	M	FARMER	GRZZZZNY	
ANNA	57	F	UNKNOWN	GRZZZZNY	
JEAN	17	M	UNKNOWN	GRZZZZNY	
KNERR, DANIEL	24	M	SHMK	GRZZZZNY	
LAROCHE, DOMINIQUE	27	M	MNR	FRZZZZNY	
U	27	F	UNKNOWN	FRZZZZNY	
JOSEPH	3	M	CHILD	FRZZZZNY	
SCHMIT, JOHANN	20	M	FARMER	GRZZZZNY	
THOMAS, JACOB	28	M	BCHR	GRZZZZNY	
KOESTNER, MARIA	32	F	SMSTS	GRZZZZNY	
FRISCHKORN, FRED.	19	M	FARMER	GRZZZZCH	
SCHELTENBECK, HEUGE	42	M	PNTR	GRZZZZCH	
WEISSWEILER, M.	35	M	CBTMKR	GRZZZZCH	
BAYER, E.	38	M	SLKP	GRZZZZCH	
PERSON, JOH.	30	M	MLR	GRZZZZCH	
STUSK, CHRETIEN	25	F	MLR	GRZZZZCH	
JAH---, LUDWIG	22	M	ENGR	GRZZZZCH	
U, ---H	00	M	FARMER	GRZZZZCH	
BECKE, ALB.	46	M	CTR	GRZZZZCH	
SCHULZ, HERM.	23	F	UNKNOWN	GRZZZZCH	
FRITZ	3	M	CHILD	GRZZZZCH	
THIEMANN, CARL	45	M	TRVLR	GRZZZZCH	
PREUSS, PAUL	19	M	SHMK	GRZZZZCH	
HOLTZMANN, H.	22	M	CL	GRZZZZCH	
RIDER, LOUISE	30	F	UNKNOWN	GRZZZZCH	
PAUL	5	M	CHILD	GRZZZZCH	
HOHL, CATH.	7	F	CHILD	GRZZZZCH	
EICHHORN, CHR.	15	M	UNKNOWN	GRZZZZCH	
WILTEMER, PHILIPPE	26	M	CBTMKR	GRZZZZCH	
SCHOENMANN, ELISAB.	50	F	UNKNOWN	GRZZZZCH	
CARL	17	M	JWLR	GRZZZZCH	
HERZ, HERM.	36	M	JWLR	GRZZZZCH	
EMMA	33	F	JWLR	GRZZZZCH	
ALMA	3	F	CHILD	GRZZZZCH	
SALY	00	F	INF	GRZZZZCH	
PASCHKEWITZ, ALBT.	00	M	INF	GR****CH	

SHIP: TAORMINA

FROM: HAMBURG
TO: NEW YORK
ARRIVED: 17 AUGUST 1888

PASSENGER	AGE	SEX	OCCUPATION	PRVL	DES
SCHRODER, SAMUEL	36	M	CGRMKR	BDZZZZNY	
KOOPMANN, LISETTE	23	F	SGL	HBZZZZNY	
KUEHN, FRITZ	23	M	CGRMKR	HBZZZZPHI	
POTER, ALBERTINE	27	F	WO	HBZZZZNY	
PAULA	6	M	CHILD	HBZZZZNY	
THEODOR	5	M	CHILD	HBZZZZNY	
GUSTAV	3	M	CHILD	HBZZZZNY	
OTTO	2	M	CHILD	HBZZZZNY	
WILLFOEFT, JACOB	56	M	LKSH	HBZZZZPHI	
JOHS.	14	M	CH	HBZZZZPHI	
TAENZGER, HERMAN	21	M	LABR	PRZZZZNY	
GOTTSCH, FRITZ	20	M	GLSR	HBZZZZCH	
PIEHL, WILH.	13	M	SCH	MKZZZZNY	

PASSENGER	AGE	SEX	OCCUPATION	PRVL	DES
WITTLER	26	M	GDNR	MKZZZZNY	
HICHMANN, FRIEDR.	52	M	TLR	SYZZZZCH	
PAULINE	44	F	W	SYZZZZNY	
GIMDELACH, THEODOR	32	M	UNKNOWN	BWZZZZNY	
WOLLERSCHLAEGER, HELENE	20	F	SGL	BVZZZZNY	
BESTHORN, FRIEDR.	21	M	FARMER	BVZZZZNY	
CLAUSEN, GUSTAV	16	M	TCHR	BVZZZZNY	
BUGE, FRIEDR.	19	M	FARMER	BVZZZZCH	
STAMPP, MARGR.	25	F	SGL	WMZZZZNY	
FICK, FRIEDR.	17	M	LABR	WMZZZZUNK	
MEYER, ROBERT	34	M	CPTR	PRZZZZBAL	
MISCH, JOSEPH	28	M	FARMER	PRZZZZBUF	
TOMAZEWSKI, FRANZ	22	M	FARMER	PRZZZZBUF	
MISCH, AUGUST	43	M	FARMER	PRZZZZBUF	
GROSSMANN, MARIE	12	F	SGL	PRZZZZNY	
CARL	16	M	LABR	PRZZZZNY	
BAUER, CAROLINE	33	F	WO	MKZZZZNY	
FREDA	9	F	CHILD	MKZZZZNY	
DORA	2	F	CHILD	MKZZZZNY	
META	6	F	CHILD	MKZZZZNY	
ERNA	2	F	CHILD	MKZZZZNY	
WICHMANN, ANNA	34	F	WO	PRZZZZNY	
WILLI	2	M	CHILD	PRZZZZNY	
OTTO	7	M	CHILD	PRZZZZNY	
BRUNO	5	M	CHILD	PRZZZZNY	
HANS	4	M	CHILD	PRZZZZNY	
MAX	3	M	CHILD	PRZZZZNY	
ELSA	.11	F	INFANT	PRZZZZNY	
VONDERSMISSEN, JOHS.	22	M	MCHT	GRZZZZNY	
CERA	16	F	SGL	GRZZZZNY	
VONSTOJENTIN, CAROLINA	60	F	WO	PRZZZZCH	
ERNSTINE	30	F	SGL	PRZZZZCH	
U, U	19	M	UNKNOWN	PRZZZZUSA	
HIRSCHBERGER, HUGO	21	M	ENGR	PRZZZZUSA	
DOBBERTHIN, WILHELMINE	36	F	WO	PRZZZZUNK	
AMANDA	9	F	CHILD	PRZZZZUNK	
LOUISE	8	F	CHILD	PRZZZZUNK	
MARIE	7	F	CHILD	PRZZZZUNK	
HELENE	4	F	CHILD	PRZZZZUNK	
COEMMERER, AUGUSTE	16	F	SGL	PRZZZZNY	
HEISSING, BERTHA	53	F	WO	PRZZZZNY	
BEERZ, AUGUSTE	18	F	SGL	PRZZZZMN	
KLINGER, ADOLPF	27	M	WVR	PRZZZZNY	
HOFFMANN, HEINR.	24	M	WVR	PRZZZZNY	
HECHT, BERTHOLD	35	M	LKSH	PRZZZZNY	
VOHS, ADOLPH	37	M	WVR	PRZZZZNY	
KARD	22	M	WVR	PRZZZZNY	
DOERINGER, ANTON	26	M	LABR	PRZZZZUNK	
WILCKE, ARCHER	17	M	LABR	PRZZZZDET	
VOSS, MARIE	23	F	SGL	PRZZZZCH	
PENKE, OSCAR	24	M	LABR	PRZZZZNY	
KRETSCHMANN, AUGUST	57	M	LABR	PRZZZZNY	
CAROLINE	52	F	W	PRZZZZNY	
ALBERT	17	M	CH	PRZZZZNY	
BUHSE, EVALINE	19	F	SGL	PRZZZZNY	
WEISS, HEINRICH	18	M	WHLR	PRZZZZNY	
KOBER, ADOLPH	25	M	LABR	PRZZZZNY	
BRAHOCKI, FRANZ	22	M	LABR	PRZZZZCH	
MUEHL, KATHA.	12	F	WO	BVZZZZCAL	
JOSEF	4	M	CHILD	BVZZZZCAL	
U, U	00	U	UNKNOWN	BVZZZZUSA	
WAGNER, JOSEF	32	M	MLR	BVZZZZKS	
CRESZENS	30	F	W	BVZZZZKS	
REISS, ISAAC	21	M	BCHR	HSZZZZNY	
REICHELT, MAX	35	M	LABR	SYZZZZNY	
FRANKE, FRIEDR.	38	M	LABR	SYZZZZNY	
LINE	35	F	W	SYZZZZNY	
ROBERT	24	M	CH	SYZZZZNY	
WILLI	2	M	CHILD	SYZZZZNY	
WALTER	.03	M	INFANT	SYZZZZNY	
HIRSCHBERGER, HUGO	21	M	ENGR	PRZZZZIA	
KLINGER, WILLM.	27	M	LABR	PRZZZZIA	
MAUERSBERG, RICHARD	28	M	MCHT	HBZZZZNY	
THOMSEN, PETER	27	M	MCHT	PRZZZZNY	
BODENBURG, HEINR.	27	M	FARMER	PRZZZZNY	

PASSENGER	AGE	SEX	OCCUPATION	PRV/VIL/DES
SCHNEIDER, HERM.	24	M	CL	SYZZZZUNK
ZUKERMANN, CHAIM	40	M	DLR	SYZZZZUNK
ROCHE	26	F	WO	SYZZZZUNK
STEIN, MICKEL	18	M	LABR	SYZZZZUNK
BERSING, JACOB	25	M	LABR	SYZZZZUNK
MLAWER, LIEBE	25	F	WO	SYZZZZUNK
ZWOIE	.11	F	INFANT	SYZZZZUNK
COHN, SARA	17	F	SGL	SYZZZZUNK
LYCK, CHRISTINE	00	M	LABR	SYZZZZUNK
HOROWITSCH, ABRAHAM	30	M	LABR	SYZZZZUNK
JACOB	20	M	LABR	SYZZZZUNK
SLAMM, SAMUEL	45	M	DLR	SYZZZZUNK
SAMUEL	45	M	DLR	SYZZZZUNK
JURA, MORITZ	45	M	LABR	SYZZZZUNK
MACHE	20	M	W	SYZZZZUNK
LASNACH, RUDOLPH	29	M	GDSM	PRZZZZNY
SCHMIDT, XAVER	34	M	MCHT	BVZZZZNY

SHIP: WIELAND

FROM: HAMBURG AND HAVRE
TO: NEW YORK
ARRIVED: 17 AUGUST 1888

PASSENGER	AGE	SEX	OCCUPATION	PRV/VIL/DES
RATHJE, MARIE	19	F	SGL	BVAIETUSA
LAMMBECK, FRANZISCA	60	F	WO	BVACBFUSA
BRAUCKMANN, AUGUSTE	19	F	SGL	BVAFCZUSA
ANDREAS, SOEN	35	M	UNKNOWN	HBZZZZUSA
VETTER, HERRMANN	25	M	MCHT	HBADOMUSA
REDER, META	50	F	WO	HBADOMUSA
PERSCH, HUGO	23	M	LABR	PRZZZZUSA
SUBBE, JOSCHIM	60	M	LLD	PRAIETUSA
OTTERSTEDT, AUGUST	28	M	BKR	PRAIETUSA
KAMMER, THERESE	41	F	WO	PRAADEUSA
OTTO	9	M	CHILD	PRAADEUSA
BOEHNKE, ROSETTE	24	F	SGL	PRZZZZUSA
MAHMENS, HELENE	17	F	SGL	PRAADEUSA
FECHNER, KARL	44	M	LABR	PRAHJVUSA
AUGUSTE	41	F	W	PRAHJVUSA
GOTTLIEB	15	M	CH	PRAHJVUSA
ANNA	9	F	CHILD	PRAHJVUSA
HERMANN	6	M	CHILD	PRAHJVUSA
FAHRENWALD, LUDWIG	22	M	TU	HBZZZZUSA
OTZEN, SOPHIE	19	F	SGL	HBAESDUSA
LAMBRECHT, WILH.	19	M	MCHT	HBACBFUSA
BENTHIEN, CAROLINE	28	F	SGL	HBACBFUSA
KRAUSE, ERNST	44	M	BKR	HBACBFUSA
CATHA.	34	F	W	HBACBFUSA
CATHA.	8	F	CHILD	HBACBFUSA
ADOLPH	6	M	CHILD	HBACBFUSA
JOHANNE	4	F	CHILD	HBACBFUSA
PAULA	2	F	CHILD	HBACBFUSA
ELISABETH	.03	F	INFANT	HBACBFUSA
PURUCKER, LORENZ	21	M	LABR	BVZZZZUSA
ECKSTEIN, MOSES	18	M	UPHST	BVACBFUSA
WERNER, ALOIS	52	M	MNR	BVABBTUSA
ANNA	52	F	W	BVABBTUSA
RAAB, JOSEPH	17	M	SVNT	BVABRCUSA
PCKULYK, THOMAS	29	M	LABR	PRZZZZUSA
LEHMANN, EMMA	29	F	WO	PRZZZZUSA
AUGUSTE	3	F	CHILD	PRZZZZUSA
GIMOWITZ, ANNA	20	F	LABR	PRZZZZUSA
HUENTSCH, PAUL	18	M	MCHT	PRZZZZUSA
CLEMENSEN, WILHELMINE	16	F	SGL	PRACKYUSA
NICOLAUSEN, WILHELMINE	16	F	SGL	PRZZZZUSA
GEISSLER, ERNST	19	M	DLR	PRACXVUSA
HEINEMANN, FELIX	22	M	BCHR	PRAEMTUSA
HUBEL, HELENE	43	F	WO	PRZZZZUSA
HENIR.	15	M	FARMER	PRZZZZUSA
KRUEGER, WHM.	15	M	FARMER	PRADJCUSA

PASSENGER	AGE	SEX	OCCUPATION	PRV/VIL/DES
JOOST, WILH.	41	M	BTMKR	PRZZZZUSA
DOROTHEA	36	F	W	PRZZZZUSA
WILH.	9	M	CHILD	PRZZZZUSA
DORA	7	F	CHILD	PRZZZZUSA
FULLIWEBER, LOUIS	26	M	WTR	PRADLDUSA
RUSCHENWEH, WILH.	23	M	CK	PRAAYGUSA
DOCKWEILER, PETER	25	M	FARMER	PRZZZZUSA
RIEWERT, MARTIN	25	M	LABR	PRAIPYUSA
HANSEN, IDA	19	F	SGL	PRZZZZUSA
TAUB, WOLF	41	M	LABR	PRZZZZUSA
SIME	36	F	W	PRZZZZUSA
TAPEL	9	M	CHILD	PRZZZZUSA
SUSCHE	7	F	CHILD	PRZZZZUSA
BRAUDEL	5	F	CHILD	PRZZZZUSA
PESSEL	.11	M	INFANT	PRZZZZUSA
JAMBOEITZ, LAMUEL	55	M	TLR	PRZZZZUSA
SCHLAGS, ESTHER	25	F	WO	PRZZZZUSA
RASMUSSEN, SIEGFRIEDE	22	M	GDNR	PRALJDUSA
BESTMANN, DIEDRICH	35	M	SMH	PRZZZZUSA
BUELL, FRANZISKA	18	F	SGL	PRAGNYUSA
SCHMIDT, JOHANN	20	M	FARMER	PRAGNYUSA
RYCHLEWSKI, STANISL.	23	M	LABR	PRZZZZUSA
SIMBILL, FRIEDR.	26	M	LABR	PRZZZZUSA
LEY, JOSEPH	34	M	FARMER	PRABVKUSA
COST, CARL	17	M	FARMER	HSZZZZUSA
ZIMMERMANN, KATCHEN	22	F	SGL	HSAAXBUSA
SCHMITZER, FRIDOLIN	26	M	BRR	HSAGMSUSA
DRESCENTIA	21	F	SGL	HSAGMSUSA
REBHOLZ, SIDONIA	24	F	SGL	HSABOQUSA
MOHR, HEINR.	43	M	CPTR	PRZZZZUSA
TEITZEL, FRIEDR.	18	M	BTMKR	PRZZZZUSA
BOCK, MINNA	20	F	SGL	PRZZZZUSA
TEITZEL, HERRM.	25	M	LABR	PRZZZZUSA
HOFFMANN, EMILIE	25	F	WO	PRZZZZUSA
MARIE	6	F	CHILD	PRZZZZUSA
EMILIE	4	F	CHILD	PRZZZZUSA
ANNA	2	F	CHILD	PRZZZZUSA
MINNA	.09	F	INFANT	PRZZZZUSA
STERNHEIM, WILLY	16	M	MCHT	PRZZZZUSA
MAHRT, JULIUS	15	M	FARMER	PRAGPBUSA
SPONAGEL, JACOB	27	M	BKBNDR	PRADEFUSA
MEYER, CARL	27	M	TLR	PRZZZZUSA
PENNER, AUGUSTE	20	F	SGL	PRAGNYUSA
EINHAUSEN, CATHA.	20	F	SGL	PRAGNYUSA
VENZMER, FRIEDRICH	25	M	BCHR	PRAFTWUSA
TEEYEN, HANS	55	M	FARMER	PRZZZZUSA
FANNY	50	F	W	PRZZZZUSA
AUGUST	15	M	CH	PRZZZZUSA
RUDOLF	13	M	CH	PRZZZZUSA
WILLI	8	M	CHILD	PRZZZZUSA
EMMA	7	F	CHILD	PRZZZZUSA
WIRTH, BABETTE	20	F	SGL	BVZZZZUSA
STRICKER, CHRISTIAN	20	M	WHLR	BVAEXWUSA
WEBER, ELISABETH	32	F	SGL	HSZZZZUSA
GLUECK, HUGO	36	M	MCHT	HSAFOCUSA
HETTLER, GOTTLIEB	18	M	FARMER	WMZZZZUSA
EISENHARDT, AUGUST	23	M	BRR	WMZZZZUSA
ZEISS, MARTIN	14	M	LABR	WMACJJUSA
SUNONSEN, MARIE	20	F	WO	WMABNSUSA
HANS	2	M	CHILD	WMABNSUSA
JOHS.	.03	M	INFANT	WMABNSUSA
KEMPERMANN, MATH.	47	M	WO	WMAARRUSA
LOTHAR	16	M	MCHT	WMAARRUSA
NINA	14	F	SGL	WMAARRUSA
CARSTENSEN, HANS	27	M	JNR	PRZZZZUSA
CZIELA, JOHANN	26	M	LABR	PRZZZZUSA
JAHNCKE, LUDOLPH	34	M	LABR	HBZZZZUSA
ELISABETH	21	F	W	HBZZZZUSA
HENRI	15	M	B	HBZZZZUSA
ALWINE	4	F	CHILD	HBZZZZUSA
LUDOLPH	2	M	CHILD	HBZZZZUSA
VIRUS, RUDOLPH	26	M	TLR	PRZZZZUSA
SCHMIDT, JOERGEN	49	M	FARMER	PRABNZUSA
NIELSEN, ANDREAS	32	M	FARMER	PRACFUUSA
NISSEN, META	30	F	SGL	PRACFUUSA

PASSENGER	AGE	SEX	OCCUPATION	PRVL	DES
RUSCH, SOFIE	26	F	SGL	PRADCRUSA	
DAEBBERT, AUGUSTE	26	F	SGL	PRAHYKUSA	
RUDOLPH, MATHEAS	56	M	FARMER	PRZZZZUSA	
GRUENEWALD, JOHANNE	16	F	SGL	PRACBRUSA	
WROBLEWSKI, MAX	25	M	SDLR	PRAEABUSA	
HELENE	18	F	W	PRAEABUSA	
MACHER, LEB	26	M	CPR	BVZZZZUSA	
MEYER, CARL	33	M	CL	BVAFSAUSA	
SUNDCHUS, CHRISTINE	74	F	WO	BVABNSUSA	
NISSEN, HARTWIG	25	M	MCHT	BVABNSUSA	
MARX, SIMON	16	M	BCHR	BVAERMUSA	
RUBRECHT, AUGUSTE	25	F	WO	BVAATSUSA	
WEIL, BERTHA	40	F	WO	BVABJAUSA	
SOPHIE	14	F	D	BVABJAUSA	
BACHALE, WILLS	24	M	BKR	BVABQVUSA	
HERRM.	18	M	FARMER	BVABQVUSA	
KROPP, HERRM.	29	M	MCHT	BVAALZUSA	
WULFF, FRIEDRICH	27	M	CL	BVAHOLUSA	
WEISSE, OSCAR	32	M	MCHT	SYZZZZUSA	
CZECHOWSKY, CARL	22	M	CL	PRZZZZUSA	
WEGNER, HANS	26	M	TLR	PRZZZZUSA	
LUFF, ANNA	24	F	SGL	PRACKYUSA	
FAWISCH, PAUL	24	M	LABR	PRZZZZUSA	
KLINKOV, WILH.	28	M	WTR	PRABSWUSA	
JAHNKE, HENNY	.11	F	INFANT	HBZZZZUSA	
DUTTWEILER, SALOME	13	F	UNKNOWN	HBACZAUSA	
TREMP, ALOIS	31	M	LKSH	SRZZZZUSA	
ANNA	33	F	W	SRZZZZUSA	
KARL	2	M	CHILD	SRZZZZUSA	
LIENHARD, GEORG	21	M	STCTR	BDZZZZUSA	
KLEIN, SEBASTIAN	20	M	SMH	BDAAJFUSA	
BOESCH, ARNOLD	21	M	GNMKR	SRZZZZUSA	
WECKERLE, AGNES	25	F	SGL	SRABJSUSA	
FREY, BERTHA	29	F	SGL	SRZZZZUSA	
EMBER, HAVER	18	M	LABR	ACZZZZUSA	
KASER, HERMANN	20	M	MCHT	SRZZZZUSA	
BERTHOLI, JAGUES	55	M	UNKNOWN	SRZZZZUSA	
GRUENER, RICHARD	21	M	TLR	SRAIEUUSA	
RADL, HIERWNIMUS	29	M	TLR	SRALWFUSA	
MARIA	24	F	W	SRALWFUSA	
HEDWIG	4	F	CHILD	SRALWFUSA	
MARIA	.09	F	INFANT	SRALWFUSA	
BLUM, JACOB	46	M	CTLDLR	SRADKIUSA	
JOHANN	37	M	FARMER	SRZZZZUSA	
HENSCH, J.E.	58	M	PVTM	SRACBFUSA	
DOROTHEA	45	F	W	SRACBFUSA	
FRANZISKA	15	F	D	SRACBFUSA	
KOHLER, WILHELM	36	M	MCHT	SRAAHLUSA	
LARSON, HELENE	32	F	WO	PRZZZZUSA	
KATIE	7	F	CHILD	PRZZZZUSA	
PLETT, ANNA	16	F	SGL	PRZZZZUSA	
OVERMANN, PAUL	34	M	HNTR	PRAAUSUSA	
EUGENIE	26	F	W	PRAAUSUSA	
WOLFF, ALBERT	18	M	MCHT	PRAEXWUSA	
SOLHEY, ROSALIE	34	F	WO	PRABDMUSA	
BERTHA	9	F	CHILD	PRABDMUSA	
RUESS, ADOLF	28	M	MCHT	PRAFBVUSA	
HEBERER, MAX	20	M	BKBNDR	PRAACOUSA	
MUERDEL, ROBERT	22	M	BCHR	PRAFBVUSA	
MAASS, THERESE	31	F	SGL	PRAAKHUSA	
KAHN, OLGA	18	F	SGL	PRZZZZUSA	
DREUFUSS, MAX	14	M	BY	PRACUDUSA	
LITZKENDORF, RICH.W.	27	M	MCHT	PRABDMUSA	
JUERGENS, JOHN	42	M	BKR	PRAFULUSA	
ROOS, SAMUEL	52	M	BCHR	BDZZZZUSA	
NANETTE	48	F	W	BDZZZZUSA	
CAROLINE	19	F	CH	BDZZZZUSA	
ROSA	16	F	CH	BDZZZZUSA	
LEA	11	F	CH	BDZZZZUSA	
EMMA	10	F	CH	BDZZZZUSA	
ANTON	8	M	CHILD	BDZZZZUSA	
KINZEL, AUGUSTE	26	M	TLR	BDAFTDUSA	

SHIP: CITY OF BERLIN

FROM: LIVERPOOL AND QUEENSTOWN
TO: NEW YORK
ARRIVED: 18 AUGUST 1888

PASSENGER	AGE	SEX	OCCUPATION	PRVL	DES
RUTER, SEMION	27	M	LABR	BDACBFPHI	
BERLMERBLUCH, SELIG	40	M	PNTR	BDACBFPHI	
FEIN, MORITZ	34	M	LABR	BDACBFNY	
SOKOLEWSKI, MOSES	47	M	BKR	BDACBFNY	
RAFAEL, LOUIS	34	M	TLR	BDACBFPA	
MICHAEL, BERY	24	M	SHMK	BDACBFNY	
OCHS, GUSTAV	18	M	LABR	BDACBFNY	
LEIBNER, C.	38	M	LABR	BDACBFNY	
WOHLBERG, BERND.	20	M	LABR	BDACBFNY	
SZEMANCZIK, ELIZ.	26	M	W	BDACBFNY	
GYULA	4	M	CHILD	BDACBFNY	
JOSEPH, S.	36	M	LABR	BDADXWNY	
FRANCISCO, ML.	21	M	LABR	BDADXWNY	
SOMERSET, U	30	F	LDY	BDACBFNY	
B.	4	F	CHILD	BDACBFNY	
L.	2	F	CHILD	BDACBFNY	

SHIP: SAALE

FROM: BREMEN AND SOUTHAMPTON
TO: NEW YORK
ARRIVED: 18 AUGUST 1888

PASSENGER	AGE	SEX	OCCUPATION	PRVL	DES
HEISTER, WILH.	26	M	MCHT	GRZZZZUSA	
LANGER, MARTHA	17	F	UNKNOWN	GRZZZZUSA	
WOLFF, GUIDO	42	M	MGR	GRZZZZUSA	
FEUCHTWANGER, ADOLPH	23	M	CL	GRZZZZUSA	
HEISSENBUETTEL, MARIE	17	F	UNKNOWN	GRZZZZUSA	
STUBENRAUCH, FANNY	32	F	UNKNOWN	GRZZZZUSA	
STE---, SELMA	23	F	UNKNOWN	GRZZZZUSA	
KRAUS, MARG.	21	F	UNKNOWN	GRZZZZUSA	
RUPPEL, JOS.	28	M	BCHR	GRZZZZUSA	
KLEE, RICH.	26	M	BKBNDR	GRZZZZUSA	
DILLENBERGER, ELISAB.	23	F	UNKNOWN	GRZZZZUSA	
ZIELINSKA, MARYANNA	20	F	UNKNOWN	GRZZZZUSA	
JOH.	56	M	LABR	GRZZZZUSA	
KLEAPHAS, AUG.	53	M	LABR	GRZZZZUSA	
FLORENTINE	54	F	W	GRZZZZUSA	
SCHWEDLER, OTTO	17	M	JNR	GRZZZZUSA	
BERGHORN, WILH.	26	M	FARMER	GRZZZZUSA	
NESTLER, CARL	36	M	FARMER	GRZZZZUSA	
GRIESSER, CONR.	24	M	FARMER	GRZZZZUSA	
ZIMMERER, JOS.	14	M	BCHR	GRZZZZUSA	
HAFNER, STEPHAN	23	M	BCHR	GRZZZZUSA	
JENSEN, CATH.	34	F	UNKNOWN	GRZZZZUSA	
ANDERS	7	M	CHILD	GRZZZZUSA	
ANDREAS	4	M	CHILD	GRZZZZUSA	
ELI.	.10	F	INFANT	GRZZZZUSA	
NISSEN, HANNA	49	F	UNKNOWN	GRZZZZUSA	
JOH.	14	F	UNKNOWN	GRZZZZUSA	
ANDERSEN, NIS.	11	M	UNKNOWN	GRZZZZUSA	
PABST, GEORG	17	M	CPTR	GRZZZZUSA	
BAYER, GEORGE	20	M	CPTR	GRZZZZUSA	
SCHMITT, AUG.	18	M	CPTR	GRZZZZUSA	
SCHNEIDER, FLOREAN	25	M	TLR	GRZZZZUSA	
PFAFF, FERD.	21	M	SMH	GRZZZZUSA	
GUENTHEN, RAYMOND	26	M	BRR	GRZZZZUSA	
MESSER, ELISE	16	F	UNKNOWN	GRZZZZUSA	
HAASE, HEINR.	25	M	GCR	GRZZZZUSA	
LOEW, JOH.	18	M	GDNR	GRZZZZUSA	
KAFFENGER, MARIE	17	F	UNKNOWN	GRZZZZUSA	
SCHMIDT, ELISAB.	20	F	UNKNOWN	GRZZZZUSA	
GLENZ, GEORG	17	M	BCHR	GRZZZZUSA	

PASSENGER	AGE	SEX	OCCUPATION	PRVVL	DES	PASSENGER	AGE	SEX	OCCUPATION	PRVVL	DES
HENDRICH, GEORG	21	M	JNR		GRZZZZUSA	JOSEPH	.08	M	INFANT		GRZZZZUSA
LINKO, HEINR.	19	M	BRR		GRZZZZUSA	ZIEME, PAUL	22	M	FARMER		GRZZZZUSA
MANN, ROSA	26	F	UNKNOWN		GRZZZZUSA	NICOLLEIT, HENRIETTE	42	F	UNKNOWN		GRZZZZUSA
WOERNER, WILH.	22	M	BKLYR		GRZZZZUSA	LUETZELBERGER, JOH.	17	M	BKBNDR		GRZZZZUSA
KNITTEL, PAUL	25	M	BKLYR		GRZZZZUSA	MARKOWSKA, EVA	30	F	UNKNOWN		GRZZZZUSA
SIEGLE, MARIE	22	F	UNKNOWN		GRZZZZUSA	FRANZ	.11	M	INFANT		GRZZZZUSA
BECK, AGATHE	22	F	UNKNOWN		GRZZZZUSA	ME----AEFER, HENRIETTE	26	F	UNKNOWN		GRZZZZUSA
BRAITSCH, FERD.	42	M	FARMER		GRZZZZUSA	WOLFRAM, MINNA	25	F	UNKNOWN		GRZZZZUSA
PRESSEL, MARIA	20	F	UNKNOWN		GRZZZZUSA	LOUISE	.06	F	INFANT		GRZZZZUSA
STRAUB, JOSEPHINE	18	F	UNKNOWN		GRZZZZUSA	SIEDENBURG, JOH.	16	M	TLR		GRZZZZUSA
HEDINGER, LOUISE	62	F	UNKNOWN		GRZZZZUSA	PAULY, MARIE	17	F	UNKNOWN		GRZZZZUSA
BREUSCH, CHRISTOPH	25	M	GZR		GRZZZZUSA	KNOPF, ALMA	36	F	UNKNOWN		GRZZZZUSA
VOLPP, MINNA	19	F	UNKNOWN		GRZZZZUSA	FRITZ	7	F	CHILD		GRZZZZUSA
BAESSLER, CARL	27	M	SHMK		GRZZZZUSA	EMMY	.04	F	INFANT		GRZZZZUSA
JOH.	22	M	SHMK		GRZZZZUSA	SCHACHTSCHABEL, JOH.	58	F	UNKNOWN		GRZZZZUSA
VE---, JOH.	43	M	SHMK		GRZZZZUSA	RUMMLER, CHRIST.	28	M	TLR		GRZZZZUSA
SCHMITT, MICHEL	29	M	FARMER		GRZZZZUSA	LUEHRS, BERTHA	29	F	UNKNOWN		GRZZZZUSA
WILH.	25	F	W		GRZZZZUSA	WEISS, BERTHA	19	F	UNKNOWN		GRZZZZUSA
JOSEPH	.05	M	INFANT		GRZZZZUSA	HOHNROT, SOPHIE	36	F	UNKNOWN		GRZZZZUSA
ILZHFER, WILH.	31	M	FARMER		GRZZZZUSA	GEFKE, OTTO	25	M	FARMER		GRZZZZUSA
HECKMANN, HEINR.	28	M	FARMER		GRZZZZUSA	S---, ADOLPH	23	M	MCHT		GRZZZZUSA
BERHOLD, CHRIST.	44	F	UNKNOWN		GRZZZZUSA	CATH.	22	F	UNKNOWN		GRZZZZUSA
FRIEDR.	4	M	CHILD		GRZZZZUSA	SCHOBET, JOH.	18	F	UNKNOWN		GRZZZZUSA
CONRAD, ERNST	27	M	JNR		GRZZZZUSA	KORMANN, MARIE	18	F	UNKNOWN		GRZZZZUSA
SCHNEIDER, PHILIPP	19	M	JNR		GRZZZZUSA	ANIER, GESINE	28	F	UNKNOWN		GRZZZZUSA
BLEML, CAROL.	25	F	UNKNOWN		GRZZZZUSA	ARNOLD	3	M	CHILD		GRZZZZUSA
FRANZ	29	M	BRR		GRZZZZUSA	GRETCHEN	2	F	CHILD		GRZZZZUSA
HILLENBRAND, JOSEPH	27	M	BRR		GRZZZZUSA	DREXLER, FRANCISCA	50	F	UNKNOWN		GRZZZZUSA
WERMRTH, MARIA	31	F	UNKNOWN		GRZZZZUSA	MARIE	48	F	UNKNOWN		GRZZZZUSA
L---S, THERESIA	52	F	UNKNOWN		GRZZZZUSA	SCHNITZLER, CARL	18	M	JNR		GRZZZZUSA
ALMA	19	F	UNKNOWN		GRZZZZUSA	SCHURCH, DOROTHEA	20	F	UNKNOWN		GRZZZZUSA
SCHMITT, ANNA	18	F	UNKNOWN		GRZZZZUSA	HOENOCH, JOH.	15	M	UNKNOWN		GRZZZZUSA
REFFERT, LOUISE	20	F	UNKNOWN		GRZZZZUSA	SALOMON, FRIEDR.	32	M	FARMER		GRZZZZUSA
DIETZ, JULIUS	22	M	FARMER		GRZZZZUSA	SCHAPER, LINA	24	F	UNKNOWN		GRZZZZUSA
MAUERER, WILH.	18	F	UNKNOWN		GRZZZZUSA	MARSCHALIC, MART	25	M	FARMER		GRZZZZUSA
EUNLE, GEO	14	M	UNKNOWN		GRZZZZUSA	GIEHL, JOH.	64	M	BRR		GRZZZZUSA
PIETRZAK, ANTONIE	38	F	UNKNOWN		GRZZZZUSA	EVA	62	F	W		GRZZZZUSA
KOWALCZIK, JOS.	24	M	FARMER		GRZZZZUSA	HUTNER, MARG.	22	F	UNKNOWN		GRZZZZUSA
MOHR, HENRIETTE	32	F	UNKNOWN		GRZZZZUSA	WITMANN, JOH.	23	M	SMH		GRZZZZUSA
KUREK, APPOLONIA	43	F	UNKNOWN		GRZZZZUSA	MARGUARD, LIBOR	48	M	SMH		GRZZZZUSA
WENZEL	11	M	UNKNOWN		GRZZZZUSA	BECKER, JOH.	31	M	FARMER		GRZZZZUSA
STANISLAWA	.11	F	INFANT		GRZZZZUSA	JACOBS, HEINR.	16	M	FARMER		GRZZZZUSA
JOH.	3	M	CHILD		GRZZZZUSA	KOENIG, CARL	15	M	FARMER		GRZZZZUSA
JENTTER, LOUISE	21	F	UNKNOWN		GRZZZZUSA	GAETJE, HERM.	15	M	FARMER		GRZZZZUSA
MAENNER, EMIL	20	M	SMH		GRZZZZUSA	FLACKE, RICH.	17	M	BKLYR		GRZZZZUSA
BRAENNING, GUST.	15	M	UNKNOWN		GRZZZZUSA	MISSENER, FRIEDR.	16	M	FARMER		GRZZZZUSA
KRAUTER, JACOB	40	M	FARMER		GRZZZZUSA	DELLER, MARG.	23	F	UNKNOWN		GRZZZZUSA
WILH.	33	F	W		GRZZZZUSA	JACOB.	24	M	FARMER		GRZZZZUSA
CHRIST.	14	M	CH		GRZZZZUSA	WITTE, AUG.	30	M	SHMK		GRZZZZUSA
JACOB	11	M	CH		GRZZZZUSA	FISCH, ALB.	16	M	SHMK		GRZZZZUSA
MARIE	9	F	CHILD		GRZZZZUSA	VOGT, LINA	24	F	UNKNOWN		GRZZZZUSA
ERNST	4	M	CHILD		GRZZZZUSA	SCHUHMANN, WILH.	57	F	UNKNOWN		GRZZZZUSA
ERNESTINE	3	F	CHILD		GRZZZZUSA	FRIEDA	8	F	CHILD		GRZZZZUSA
SCHWARZ, LOUISE	18	F	UNKNOWN		GRZZZZUSA	LIEBE, LOUIS	14	M	CH		GRZZZZUSA
HAICHER, ZIRIAKUS	32	M	FARMER		GRZZZZUSA	SCHAEFER, MARIA	32	F	UNKNOWN		GRZZZZUSA
CATH.	27	F	W		GRZZZZUSA	BARB.	8	F	CHILD		GRZZZZUSA
OLGA	4	F	CHILD		GRZZZZUSA	ROSS, AUG.	24	M	FARMER		GRZZZZUSA
GETTE	3	F	CHILD		GRZZZZUSA	----KA, FILOM	18	M	CPTR		GRZZZZUSA
MARIA	.06	F	INFANT		GRZZZZUSA	ALOISIE	13	F	UNKNOWN		GRZZZZUSA
MARIA	20	F	UNKNOWN		GRZZZZUSA	KUEHN, SELMA	21	F	UNKNOWN		GRZZZZUSA
FRYDENBORG, CHRIST.	21	F	UNKNOWN		GRZZZZUSA	MEINHARD, LINA	20	F	UNKNOWN		GRZZZZUSA
SCHOETTLE, CARL	21	M	FARMER		GRZZZZUSA	MRAZ, MART.	24	M	FARMER		GRZZZZUSA
WANENMACHER, ANTONIE	26	F	UNKNOWN		GRZZZZUSA	OETTEL, HERM.	23	M	FARMER		GRZZZZUSA
PFISTERER, EMMA	17	F	UNKNOWN		GRZZZZUSA	TERHELLEN, CHAINE	38	F	UNKNOWN		GRZZZZUSA
GAIRING, JOH.	45	M	BKLYR		GRZZZZUSA	WOLF, AMALIE	25	F	UNKNOWN		GRZZZZUSA
BA--, CHRIST.	21	M	BKLYR		GRZZZZUSA	BECKER, ALBERT	17	M	FARMER		GRZZZZUSA
WILH.	33	F	UNKNOWN		GRZZZZUSA	HABERMANN, STEPHAN	52	M	FARMER		GRZZZZUSA
B--	10	F	CH		GRZZZZUSA	GEORG	25	M	FARMER		GRZZZZUSA
FRANZ	6	M	CHILD		GRZZZZUSA	STRADLER, FRANZ	26	M	FARMER		GRZZZZUSA
GEORG	3	M	CHILD		GRZZZZUSA	BUNEMANN, HEINR.	34	M	FARMER		GRZZZZUSA
MINNA	2	F	CHILD		GRZZZZUSA	MARIE	34	F	W		GRZZZZUSA
ZIEGLER, ELISE	18	F	UNKNOWN		GRZZZZUSA	GUST.	.06	M	INFANT		GRZZZZUSA
DICHTENMUELLER, MARG.	20	F	UNKNOWN		GRZZZZUSA	DREYER, CARL	31	M	SHMK		GRZZZZUSA
GEORG	11	M	UNKNOWN		GRZZZZUSA	MARIE	28	F	W		GRZZZZUSA
RETZBACH, MARG.	23	F	UNKNOWN		GRZZZZUSA	ELISE	.09	F	INFANT		GRZZZZUSA

PASSENGER	AGE	SEX	OCCUPATION	PRVL	DES
KIRCHENBAUER, ANT.	21	M	PNTR	GRZZZZ	USA
SCHMEISSER, MARG.	19	F	UNKNOWN	GRZZZZ	USA
CRONHEIM, FRIED.	18	F	UNKNOWN	GRZZZZ	USA
JACOB, ARON	16	M	PNTR	GRZZZZ	USA
HENRIETTE	19	F	UNKNOWN	GRZZZZ	USA
SCHWARZ, THOMAS	38	M	JNR	GRZZZZ	USA
MARIE	10	F	CH	GRZZZZ	USA
ELISAB.	26	F	W	GRZZZZ	USA
BAENHOLZER, MARIA	24	F	UNKNOWN	GRZZZZ	USA
GERRIETS, GERH.	28	M	FARMER	GRZZZZ	USA
CATH.	28	F	W	GRZZZZ	USA
ANCHEN	3	F	CHILD	GRZZZZ	USA
HILLENBRAND, VAL.	17	M	JNR	GRZZZZ	USA
THEILEN, ANT.	28	M	JNR	GRZZZZ	USA
BECH, DOROTHEA	18	F	UNKNOWN	GRZZZZ	USA
PLECHER, JOSEPH	45	M	FARMER	GRZZZZ	USA
BURMESTER, HEINR.	16	M	FARMER	GRZZZZ	USA
BER---, DOROTL.	19	F	UNKNOWN	GRZZZZ	USA
----ES, DIEDR.	15	M	FARMER	GRZZZZ	USA
ESCHE----ORST, WILH.	17	M	FARMER	GRZZZZ	USA
U, WILH.	12	M	PNTR	GRZZZZ	USA
ESRNEST, --YOAGY	57	M	PNTR	GRZZZZ	USA
DURK, ILA	51	F	W	GRZZZZ	USA
HORMER, JANOS	18	F	UNKNOWN	GRZZZZ	USA
MEDWEDING, JANOS	23	F	UNKNOWN	GRZZZZ	USA
JANOS	21	M	BRR	GRZZZZ	USA
TEMASMANN, JANOS	20	F	UNKNOWN	GRZZZZ	USA
MATEJER, ANDR.	24	M	BRR	GRZZZZ	USA
RUETER, HERM.	17	M	CPTR	GRZZZZ	USA
HOELKEN, EMIL	31	M	FARMER	GRZZZZ	USA
BIEHLE, JOS.	24	M	FARMER	GRZZZZ	USA
WEIBERG, FRIED.	31	M	FARMER	GRZZZZ	USA
KEMMER, JACOB	27	M	FARMER	GRZZZZ	USA
JANSEN, ALFRED	27	M	MCHT	GRZZZZ	USA
----MANN, JOH.	33	F	UNKNOWN	GRZZZZ	USA
ENGERT, MIHAL	28	M	BRR	GRZZZZ	USA
COHEN, WOLF	17	M	FARMER	GRZZZZ	USA
R---, U	17	M	FARMER	GRZZZZ	USA
VOLKOVSKY, SALOMON	17	M	FARMER	GRZZZZ	USA
COHEN, LEIB	18	M	FARMER	GRZZZZ	USA
SESMON, LESSE	20	M	FARMER	GRZZZZ	USA
LUBECMSKI, STANISLAUS	33	M	FARMER	GRZZZZ	USA
BOTTCHER, AUG.	18	M	FARMER	GRZZZZ	USA
STOFFEL, CONRAD	34	M	FARMER	GRZZZZ	USA
WOLFMANN, EFRAIM	42	M	FARMER	GRZZZZ	USA
DEBORA	42	F	W	GRZZZZ	USA
RACHEL	55	F	UNKNOWN	GRZZZZ	USA
HIRSCH	10	M	CH	GRZZZZ	USA
AARON	11	M	CH	GRZZZZ	USA
FR---, ESTHER	11	F	UNKNOWN	GRZZZZ	USA
KONIGSBERG, RIFKA	25	F	UNKNOWN	GRZZZZ	USA
JOSEPH	6	M	CHILD	GRZZZZ	USA
JENNY	3	F	CHILD	GRZZZZ	USA
WINTER, ROSA	14	F	CH	GRZZZZ	USA
WOLFMANN, MARIA	16	F	UNKNOWN	GRZZZZ	USA
BOEH, JOH.	27	M	FARMER	GRZZZZ	USA
-----SON, MARG.	66	F	UNKNOWN	GRZZZZ	USA
SCHWECTMANN, CHRIST.	21	M	FARMER	GRZZZZ	USA
DALMAIDO, JOHN	28	M	FARMER	FRZZZZ	USA

SHIP: AURANIA

FROM: LIVERPOOL AND QUEENSTOWN
TO: NEW YORK
ARRIVED: 20 AUGUST 1888

PASSENGER	AGE	SEX	OCCUPATION	PRVL	DES
MANNO, FRANCISEA	17	F	SP	GRZZZZ	NY
WLOSCHNESKY, JOS.	72	M	LABR	GRZZZZ	OH
BERNOTRIN, SIMON	24	M	UNKNOWN	GRZZZZ	NY
BUCHANER, JOSEPH	27	M	LABR	GRZZZZ	NY

PASSENGER	AGE	SEX	OCCUPATION	PRVL	DES
EICHLAND, MINA	18	F	SP	GRZZZZ	NY
ZUMMER, MARIA	40	F	MA	GRZZZZ	NY
JACOB	17	M	LABR	GRZZZZ	NY
WILLIAM	10	M	CH	GRZZZZ	NY
SCHMIDT, LAMZ	38	M	LABR	GRZZZZ	NY
BURSCHUCK, WILH.	34	M	LABR	GRZZZZ	NY
PRONNER, AUG.	19	M	LABR	GRZZZZ	NY
WALBROL, CHAS.	19	M	LABR	GRZZZZ	NY
JUNGL, HERMAN	26	M	LABR	GRZZZZ	CH
VEHNER, ALAN	21	M	TLR	GRZZZZ	NY
UDLE, CON.	42	M	LABR	GRZZZZ	NY
BANPACH, WILH.	40	M	LABR	GRZZZZ	NY
LUSKI, ERNEST	50	M	LABR	GRZZZZ	NO
OSCAR	20	M	LABR	GRZZZZ	NO
ROSE	47	F	MA	GRZZZZ	NO
MARIA	11	F	CH	GRZZZZ	NO
PAULA	9	F	CHILD	GRZZZZ	NO
NACHAEL	7	F	CHILD	GRZZZZ	NO
FRITZ, ALB.	29	M	GENT	GRZZZZ	NY
MARCUS, HANNAH	53	F	MA	GRZZZZ	NY
GRIM, ABRAM	39	M	MCHT	GRZZZZ	CH
CROPP, JIANETTE	22	F	SP	GRZZZZ	NY
SIEBS, THOS.G.	35	M	MCHT	GRZZZZ	NY
BREHM, ELISE	38	F	SVNT	SRZZZZ	NY
DUBOIS, JULIS	26	M	GENT	FRZZZZ	NY

SHIP: DEVONIA

FROM: GLASGOW
TO: NEW YORK
ARRIVED: 20 AUGUST 1888

PASSENGER	AGE	SEX	OCCUPATION	PRVL	DES
FINKLEINER, MINNA	22	F	UNKNOWN	GRZZZZ	USA
FREIDBOTH, KARL	35	M	LABR	GRZZZZ	USA
ADELHEID	36	F	UNKNOWN	GRZZZZ	USA
HEINRICH	9	F	CHILD	GRZZZZ	USA
METHA	.06	F	INFANT	GRZZZZ	USA
HASKEL, GERSO	14	M	UNKNOWN	GRZZZZ	USA
HABIST, KARL	22	M	BCHR	GRZZZZ	USA
HAMAKER, JACOB	29	M	LABR	GRZZZZ	USA
HILDBRANDT, MARKUS	14	M	UNKNOWN	GRZZZZ	USA
KLEINHEIEZ, IGNATZ	22	M	CPTR	GRZZZZ	USA
MUNZINGER, RUDOLF	21	M	BKR	GRZZZZ	USA
WEBER, FRANZ	18	M	SHMK	GRZZZZ	USA

SHIP: LEERDAM

FROM: ROTTERDAM
TO: NEW YORK
ARRIVED: 20 AUGUST 1888

PASSENGER	AGE	SEX	OCCUPATION	PRVL	DES
LANGE, A.F.	26	M	TCHR	GRZZZZ	USA
RLEYN, AD.	34	M	JNLST	FRZZZZ	USA
ALTHOUS, W.	47	F	UNKNOWN	GRZZZZ	USA
L.	17	F	UNKNOWN	GRZZZZ	USA
STRUCK, L.	27	F	UNKNOWN	GRZZZZ	USA
LEVY, M.	27	F	UNKNOWN	GRZZZZ	USA
AD.	9	M	CHILD	GRZZZZ	USA
TH.	7	F	CHILD	GRZZZZ	USA
J.	2	M	CHILD	GRZZZZ	USA
LEADERMAN, C.	31	M	CL	GRZZZZ	USA
WALCHSHOFER, A.	22	F	UNKNOWN	GRZZZZ	USA
RODENTHAL, J.	24	M	STDNT	GRZZZZ	USA
DOPPEL, M.	30	F	UNKNOWN	GRZZZZ	USA
ALTSCHAUFFEL, M.	20	F	UNKNOWN	GRZZZZ	USA

PASSENGER	AGE	SEX	OCCUPATION	PRVL	DES
BREUNING, M.	26	F	UNKNOWN	GRZZZZUSA	
PREIT, F.	21	F	UNKNOWN	GRZZZZUSA	
ASCHINGER, AM.	22	F	UNKNOWN	GRZZZZUSA	
HUEBER, B.	20	F	UNKNOWN	GRZZZZUSA	
SPITZER, THER.	18	F	UNKNOWN	GRZZZZUSA	
SESSLER, F.	66	F	UNKNOWN	GRZZZZUSA	
VOLKMANN, AD.	31	M	MCHT	GRZZZZUSA	
CL.	3	F	CHILD	GRZZZZUSA	
ROTH, W.	32	M	UNKNOWN	GRZZZZUSA	
W.	36	F	UNKNOWN	GRZZZZUSA	
SCHMITH, JOS.	25	M	MCHT	GRZZZZUSA	
MEIER, F.	14	M	UNKNOWN	GRZZZZUSA	
R.	43	F	UNKNOWN	GRZZZZUSA	
JETER, M.	10	F	CH	GRZZZZUSA	
MERK, M.	26	M	ENGR	GRZZZZUSA	
KREUSSEN, V.	22	M	GDNR	GRZZZZUSA	
HAHN, TH.	46	M	WVR	GRZZZZUSA	
CH.	48	F	UNKNOWN	GRZZZZUSA	
E.	14	F	UNKNOWN	GRZZZZUSA	
M.	10	F	CH	GRZZZZUSA	
WH.	7	M	CHILD	GRZZZZUSA	
FURTH, JOS.	45	M	SHMK	GRZZZZUSA	
JOS.	17	M	SHMK	GRZZZZUSA	
ANNA	18	F	UNKNOWN	GRZZZZUSA	
WH.	15	M	UNKNOWN	GRZZZZUSA	
GERH.	11	F	UNKNOWN	GRZZZZUSA	
HOCHMUT, ALEN.	21	M	LABR	GRZZZZUSA	
BELZ, L.	22	F	UNKNOWN	GRZZZZUSA	
GLOECKNER, M.	46	F	UNKNOWN	GRZZZZUSA	
M.	18	F	UNKNOWN	GRZZZZUSA	
K.	16	F	UNKNOWN	GRZZZZUSA	
FINK, H.	44	F	UNKNOWN	GRZZZZUSA	
FR.	18	M	UNKNOWN	GRZZZZUSA	
RICH.	11	M	UNKNOWN	GRZZZZUSA	
AUG.	8	M	CHILD	GRZZZZUSA	
BENJ.	6	M	CHILD	GRZZZZUSA	
ADELL.	4	M	CHILD	GRZZZZUSA	
AZZEWSKY, ABE	20	M	TLR	GRZZZZUSA	
BENZ, JOH.	27	M	MSN	GRZZZZUSA	
CHRIST.	28	F	UNKNOWN	GRZZZZUSA	
GUTH, JOH.	45	M	LABR	GRZZZZUSA	
NOLLER, L.	55	M	UNKNOWN	GRZZZZUSA	
BISCHOFF, JOS.	24	F	UNKNOWN	GRZZZZUSA	
HOFFMANN, ANNA	14	F	UNKNOWN	GRZZZZUSA	
SHIPS, THER.	20	F	UNKNOWN	GRZZZZUSA	
JOS.	22	F	UNKNOWN	GRZZZZUSA	
TISCHKIN, K.	36	M	UNKNOWN	GRZZZZUSA	
WEGERN, C.	35	M	UNKNOWN	GRZZZZUSA	
HOEFLEIN, K.	20	M	BRR	GRZZZZUSA	
SENFFERT, N.	32	M	JNR	GRZZZZUSA	
SAEMONN, M.	22	M	BKR	GRZZZZUSA	
FURSTRER, H.	23	M	MCHT	GRZZZZUSA	
GRAF, WH.	53	M	LABR	GRZZZZUSA	
FELDBERG, JOH.	22	M	SHMK	GRZZZZUSA	
LAMBERT, P.	36	M	MCHT	GRZZZZUSA	
ZIEGLER, H.	19	M	LABR	GRZZZZUSA	
HAUESLER, ISOD.F.	21	M	TLR	GRZZZZUSA	
KLAUBER, ACH.	24	M	TLR	GRZZZZUSA	
WEBER, H.	17	M	SHMK	GRZZZZUSA	
SAPPELT, JOS.	27	M	LABR	GRZZZZUSA	
ZIELINSKIE, JOS.	22	M	LABR	GRZZZZUSA	
FREISSENHAUSEN, JOS.	19	M	PNTR	GRZZZZUSA	
BINDER, CHR.	24	M	WVR	GRZZZZUSA	
FLEISCHHONER, WH.	19	M	TLR	GRZZZZUSA	
CHR.	17	F	UNKNOWN	GRZZZZUSA	
ANNA	15	F	UNKNOWN	GRZZZZUSA	
SCHLAGENHEUSS, KASP.	16	M	SMH	GRZZZZUSA	
FRISCHHOLZ, JOHN	20	M	TLR	GRZZZZUSA	
HOFFMANN, KATH.	23	F	UNKNOWN	GRZZZZUSA	
FRISCHHOLZ, JOHANN	16	M	LABR	GRZZZZUSA	
BRUENHOLZE, ALB.	29	M	UNKNOWN	GRZZZZUSA	
MARIE	.11	F	INFANT	GRZZZZUSA	
STEEGER, ARN.	44	F	UNKNOWN	GRZZZZUSA	
JOH.	15	M	UNKNOWN	GRZZZZUSA	
JAC.	10	M	CH	GRZZZZUSA	
H.	8	M	CHILD	GRZZZZUSA	
CHR.	4	F	CHILD	GRZZZZUSA	
SCHOSEL, DEB.	18	F	UNKNOWN	GRZZZZUSA	
LORCHE, M.	51	F	UNKNOWN	GRZZZZUSA	
EBINGER, JAC.	28	M	BKR	GRZZZZUSA	
GROSSMANN, JOS.	33	M	TLR	GRZZZZUSA	
REIFSCHNEIDER, H.	27	M	SMH	GRZZZZUSA	
WEISHOUPT, GEORG	21	M	UNKNOWN	GRZZZZUSA	
DORSZYNSKI, M.	20	M	LABR	GRZZZZUSA	
DARNOCHER, A.M.	22	F	UNKNOWN	GRZZZZUSA	
SESSLER, JAC.	30	M	SHMK	GRZZZZUSA	
GLOECKNER, M.	69	F	UNKNOWN	GRZZZZUSA	
DROERFLER, A.	26	F	UNKNOWN	GRZZZZUSA	
K.	9	F	CHILD	GRZZZZUSA	
MOBUS, B.	32	F	UNKNOWN	GRZZZZUSA	
GEORG	2	M	CHILD	GRZZZZUSA	
KLEYN, L.	28	M	BCHR	GRZZZZUSA	
BALLERINI, A.	34	M	LABR	FRZZZZUSA	
ROSSI, BAS.	27	M	LABR	FRZZZZUSA	
ZORKI, EM.	25	M	LABR	FRZZZZUSA	
BENI	21	M	LABR	FRZZZZUSA	
VALENTIN, JOS.	27	M	LABR	FRZZZZUSA	
ADEL.	27	F	UNKNOWN	FRZZZZUSA	
ANGEL	.06	F	INFANT	FRZZZZUSA	
ROSENBERG, MAR.	23	M	TLR	FRZZZZUSA	
GARAFOLDA, F.	28	M	MCHT	FRZZZZUSA	
MARZEI, NIC.	28	M	MCHT	FRZZZZUSA	
TAZZI, LUIGI	47	M	MCHT	FRZZZZUSA	
TERRO, ANT.	24	M	MCHT	FRZZZZUSA	
LISTA, CAR.	20	M	MCHT	FRZZZZUSA	

SHIP: REPUBLIC

FROM: LIVERPOOL
TO: NEW YORK
ARRIVED: 20 AUGUST 1888

PASSENGER	AGE	SEX	OCCUPATION	PRVL	DES
KRUNT, ANNA	20	F	SVNT	FRADAXUSA	
BERGENDAHL, MARIA	30	F	W	FRADAXUSA	
EDW.	3	M	CHILD	FRADAXUSA	
WINIESH, M.	23	M	LABR	FRADAXUSA	
ZILBERGLERT, C.	20	F	W	FRADAXUSA	
ANN	.09	F	INFANT	FRADAXUSA	
RUBEN, CHAS	22	M	LABR	FRADAXUSA	
DOMSKI, RACHEL	11	F	CH	FRADAXUSA	
MINANN, M.	23	M	LABR	FRADAXUSA	
FANNY	23	F	W	FRADAXUSA	
NATEYE	5	F	CHILD	FRADAXUSA	
WELH, HERCH	11	M	CH	FRADAXUSA	
FREDMAN, FRED	22	M	LABR	FRADAXUSA	
GOTTLIEB, S.	26	M	LABR	FRADAXUSA	
KOOS, CARL	20	M	LABR	FRADAXUSA	
NOKLELY, SOFIE	23	F	SP	FRADAXUSA	
HAMMER, ELIZA	18	F	SP	FRADAXUSA	
JOLFINE	24	F	SP	FRADAXUSA	
OLE	28	M	LABR	FRADAXUSA	
CHANS, MARTH.	20	M	LABR	FRADAXUSA	
CHRISTIANSON, CARL	26	M	LABR	FRADAXUSA	
ANDERSON, EDGAR	.10	M	INFANT	FRADAXUSA	
BERGENDAHL, CARL	5	M	CHILD	FRADAXUSA	
TONLHENN, ERIK	21	M	LABR	FRADAXUSA	
HATALA, JOHN	24	M	LABR	FRADAXUSA	
WALKANKS, HECK	30	M	LABR	FRADAXUSA	
SODERBERG, J.A.	29	M	LABR	FRADAXUSA	
JOHANSON, EFRAIM	34	M	LABR	FRADAXUSA	
E.	28	F	W	FRADAXUSA	
GERDA	7	F	CHILD	FRADAXUSA	
BIDA	4	F	CHILD	FRADAXUSA	
PAUL	3	M	CHILD	FRADAXUSA	
LIFRIK	.11	M	INFANT	FRADAXUSA	

PASSENGER	AGE	SEX	OCCUPATION	PRVL	DES
RONING, PALER	30	M	LABR		FRADAXUSA
FOSISER, LIEB	26	M	LABR		FRADAXUSA
HERSCHE, FRAN	20	M	LABR		FRADAXUSA
FEINER, REGINA	20	F	SP		FRADAXUSA
PANCRUCHOWA, BRUCH	24	F	W		FRADAXUSA
ISAK	4	M	CHILD		FRADAXUSA
GAZER	.09	M	INFANT		FRADAXUSA
MIDNIK, BEILE	25	F	W		FRADAXUSA
HERSCH	7	M	CHILD		FRADAXUSA
WOLF	3	M	CHILD		FRADAXUSA
JANCHUN	.11	M	INFANT		FRADAXUSA
ABRAHAM, MANANA	19	F	SP		FRADAXUSA
LANGSFELD, BERTHA	27	F	SP		FRADAXUSA
GARHREN, HERMANN	49	M	FARMER		FRADAXUSA
STANKWIETZ, JOSEF	27	M	LABR		FRADAXUSA
WYERCH	22	M	LABR		FRADAXUSA
FORG, JOHAN	27	M	LABR		FRADAXUSA
SINFER, FRITZ	45	M	LABR		FRADAXUSA
MIAI	18	F	SP		FRADAXUSA
ADOLF	12	M	LABR		FRADAXUSA
HALPERN, RACHAIL	22	F	SP		FRADAXUSA
KISSNER, MORDCHI	32	F	SP		FRADAXUSA
SCHMIDT, CARL	47	M	LABR		FRADAXUSA
FREIDMAN, JOS.	19	M	LABR		FRADAXUSA
KATZENBERG, SARAH	20	F	SVNT		FRADAXUSA
HAGENDORF, JOHANN	25	M	LABR		FRACBDUSA

SHIP: FULDA

FROM: BREMEN AND SOUTHAMPTON
TO: NEW YORK
ARRIVED: 21 AUGUST 1888

PASSENGER	AGE	SEX	OCCUPATION	PRVL	DES
LIEBER, DOCTOR	45	M	MD		GRZZZZUSA
DOCTOR	45	M	MD		GRZZZZUSA
PFEIFER, FRANZ	31	M	TT		GRZZZZUSA
FRANZ	31	M	TT		GRZZZZUSA
MUENCHTHALER, WILHELMIN	26	F	NN		GRZZZZUSA
MUENCHTHALER, WILHELMIN	26	F	NN		GRZZZZUSA
UNNINGER, MARIA	43	F	NN		GRZZZZUSA
PETZOLT, MRS	45	F	NN		GRZZZZUSA
METGER, THERESIA	50	F	NN		GRZZZZUSA
BAUER, ABRAHAM	16	M	CL		GRZZZZUSA
KAISER, MARIA	50	F	NN		GRZZZZUSA
LUDWIG	17	M	TT		GRZZZZUSA
MANSCHETTE, ANNA	20	F	NN		GRZZZZUSA
SAUER, ELISE	17	F	NN		GRZZZZUSA
MECKES, OTTO	7	M	CHILD		GRZZZZUSA
BLATH, LINA	17	F	NN		GRZZZZUSA
BENNO	15	M	CL		GRZZZZUSA
HAAS, MORITZ	17	M	CL		GRZZZZUSA
WEILER, OSCAR	16	M	MCHT		GRZZZZUSA
LEVY, HELENE	22	F	NN		GRZZZZUSA
LENI	.03	F	INFANT		GRZZZZUSA
ROSS, MARIE	53	F	NN		GRZZZZUSA
ELISE	30	F	NN		GRZZZZUSA
HENRIETTE	20	F	NN		GRZZZZUSA
ERNESTINE	18	F	NN		GRZZZZUSA
EIGENRAUCH, ISRA	20	F	NN		GRZZZZUSA
LAPPENKOHRS, WILHELMINE	59	F	NN		GRZZZZUSA
WILHELMINE	59	F	NN		GRZZZZUSA
HOS, ROSINA	40	F	NN		GRZZZZUSA
SCHULZ, ANNA	15	F	NN		GRZZZZUSA
KNAUER, MARGARETHA	20	F	NN		GRZZZZUSA
ZAPF, EDWIN	25	M	FARMER		GRZZZZUSA
MAGDALENA	19	F	NN		GRZZZZUSA
OLGA	16	F	NN		GRZZZZUSA
KAUBER, ANDREAS	19	M	FARMER		GRZZZZUSA
PLISCH, AUGUSTE	55	F	NN		GRZZZZUSA
HERMINE	7	F	CHILD		GRZZZZUSA

PASSENGER	AGE	SEX	OCCUPATION	PRVL	DES
JANUSZAK, ANNA	48	F	CH		GRZZZZUSA
FRANZISKA	7	F	CHILD		GRZZZZUSA
ROJAHN, FRANZ	16	M	TLR		GRZZZZUSA
RENNINGER, GEORG	19	M	TLR		GRZZZZUSA
URBANSKA, MARIANNA	21	F	NN		GRZZZZUSA
HEMITSCHECK, MARIA	24	F	NN		GRZZZZUSA
LUKAS, MAGDALENA	21	F	NN		GRZZZZUSA
NERGE, WILHELM	26	M	LLD		GRZZZZUSA
KLUGKIST, JOHANN	14	M	FARMER		GRZZZZUSA
HERMINE	20	F	FARMER		GRZZZZUSA
HILBERS, JOHANN	45	M	BKR		GRZZZZUSA
WALKER, JOHANN	52	M	LABR		GRZZZZUSA
WILHELMINE	39	F	NN		GRZZZZUSA
GEBHARDT, AUGUST	7	M	CHILD		GRZZZZUSA
MARIE	6	F	CHILD		GRZZZZUSA
FRANK, CHR	24	M	SMH		GRZZZZUSA
BERGER, MARTHA	6	F	CHILD		GRZZZZUSA
BRUEM-EVE, CHRISTINE	22	F	NN		GRZZZZUSA
ROSA	17	F	NN		GRZZZZUSA
KULL, CHRISTIAN	18	M	LLD		GRZZZZUSA
RATHFUSS, WILHELM	17	M	LLD		GRZZZZUSA
HAGMANN, MARIA	29	F	NN		GRZZZZUSA
ROSA	3	F	CHILD		GRZZZZUSA
WITTMANN, JOHANN	30	M	BCHR		GRZZZZUSA
BAYER, ELISABETH	27	F	NN		GRZZZZUSA
EBERLE, FRIEDRICH	25	M	FARMER		GRZZZZUSA
HOESS, GOTTLIEB	25	M	FARMER		GRZZZZUSA
SCHWEIZER, CARL	25	M	SHMK		GRZZZZUSA
WITTMANN, LUDWIG	13	M	SHMK		GRZZZZUSA
ELISABETH	15	F	NN		GRZZZZUSA
ROTH, GEORG	16	M	LLD		GRZZZZUSA
HOFFMANN, FRIEDRICH	16	M	TLR		GRZZZZUSA
WITTMANN, LEONHARD	50	M	FARMER		GRZZZZUSA
HEGEMANN, VICTOR	36	M	GDNR		GRZZZZUSA
ALBERT	13	M	GDNR		GRZZZZUSA
BEHRENS, GOTTLIEB	79	M	FARMER		GRZZZZUSA
NIEBRICH, CHRISTINE	23	F	NN		GRZZZZUSA
KLAAS, CLEMENS	54	M	LABR		GRZZZZUSA
ANNA	54	F	NN		GRZZZZUSA
THERESE	16	F	NN		GRZZZZUSA
JOSEFA	7	F	CHILD		GRZZZZUSA
AUGUST	7	F	CHILD		GRZZZZUSA
CONNERMANN, AUGUST	29	M	BBR		GRZZZZUSA
KLASTER, HEINRICH	24	M	PNTR		GRZZZZUSA
BENDER, FRIEDRICH	28	M	LABR		GRZZZZUSA
GRIESMER, APOLLONIA	62	F	NN		GRZZZZUSA
ANNA	26	F	NN		GRZZZZUSA
AUGUSTE	4	F	CHILD		GRZZZZUSA
RICHARD	2	M	CHILD		GRZZZZUSA
ROETTKER, MARIA	23	F	NN		GRZZZZUSA
BRUMANN, LINA	20	F	NN		GRZZZZUSA
CATHARINE	.04	F	INFANT		GRZZZZUSA
WOHLRLE, JOHANNES	30	M	BCHR		GRZZZZUSA
MUELLER, MARIA	21	F	NN		GRZZZZUSA
BINDER, CATHARINA	24	F	NN		GRZZZZUSA
JOHANN	14	M	CL		GRZZZZUSA
LUTZ, CHRISTIAN	23	M	BCHR		GRZZZZUSA
BRAUN, CAROLINE	29	F	NN		GRZZZZUSA
GONDER, JOST	56	M	CPTR		GRZZZZUSA
HILBIG, HERMANN	31	M	FARMER		GRZZZZUSA
ORLUPP, CHR	26	M	LLD		GRZZZZUSA
ELISABETH	54	F	NN		GRZZZZUSA
ZWENGEL, HEINRICH	51	M	LABR		GRZZZZUSA
STUNTZNER, IDA	32	F	NN		GRZZZZUSA
GUIDO	6	M	CHILD		GRZZZZUSA
LOUIS	3	M	CHILD		GRZZZZUSA
PAUL	.09	M	INFANT		GRZZZZUSA
ENGLERT, KAROLINA	21	F	NN		GRZZZZUSA
EISOLD, EDMUND	21	M	BCHR		GRZZZZUSA
KRUECK, SUSANNA	18	F	NN		GRZZZZUSA
SCHICK, JOSEF	25	M	BBR		GRZZZZUSA
KOLB, MARTIN	25	M	BKR		GRZZZZUSA
SCHAPPMANN, AUGUST	28	M	JNR		GRZZZZUSA
SCHOETZ, SEBASTIAN	25	M	BKR		GRZZZZUSA
STARCH, ANNA	20	F	NN		GRZZZZUSA

PASSENGER	AGE	SEX	OCCUPATION	PRVL DES
LONGHAMER, CARL	16	M	LABR	GRZZZZUSA
FISCHER, FRIEDRICKE	28	F	NN	GRZZZZUSA
ROSA	7	F	CHILD	GRZZZZUSA
ANNA	5	F	CHILD	GRZZZZUSA
TO--Y	4	F	CHILD	GRZZZZUSA
IDA	.06	F	INFANT	GRZZZZUSA
OTTO, FRANZ	50	M	FARMER	GRZZZZUSA
ROSALIA	49	F	NN	GRZZZZUSA
PAUL, ELISABETH	16	F	NN	GRZZZZUSA
REUS, JOHANN	13	M	NN	GRZZZZUSA
KIELMANN, DORIS	19	F	NN	GRZZZZUSA
FROEHLKE, JOHANN	50	M	SMH	GRZZZZUSA
VOGELSANG, CHRISTINE	52	F	NN	GRZZZZUSA
MARIE	16	F	NN	GRZZZZUSA
ULLRICH, DOROTHEA	17	F	NN	GRZZZZUSA
HERR, JOHANN	23	M	LABR	GRZZZZUSA
DRESCHLER, JOHANN	30	M	GDNR	GRZZZZUSA
ZIEGLER, WILHELM	30	M	BBR	GRZZZZUSA
FORST, ANDREAS	17	M	FARMER	GRZZZZUSA
PAULINA	14	F	NN	GRZZZZUSA
P-PP, LORENZ	54	M	FARMER	GRZZZZUSA
KATHARINA	48	F	NN	GRZZZZUSA
ENGERT, JOSEFA	23	F	NN	GRZZZZUSA
BAUER, CARL	23	M	BRR	GRZZZZUSA
LANG, JACOB	23	M	BCHR	GRZZZZUSA
BACHMANN, ADAM	14	M	LABR	GRZZZZUSA
SANDER, JENNIE	16	F	NN	GRZZZZUSA
HAMM, MARIE	26	F	NN	GRZZZZUSA
WEBER, CONRAD	29	M	PNTR	GRZZZZUSA
DIETZ, ROSINE	59	F	NN	GRZZZZUSA
SELMA	16	F	NN	GRZZZZUSA
JOHANN	5	F	CHILD	GRZZZZUSA
SCHMIDT, JOSEF	28	M	LABR	GRZZZZUSA
TWARGOWSKA, KATARZYNA	21	F	NN	GRZZZZUSA
KIRSTE, JULIUS	17	M	LABR	GRZZZZUSA
WISCHLIE, JOHANN	27	M	SMH	GRZZZZUSA
SCHW--STKOWSKY, JOHAN	30	M	BKLYR	GRZZZZUSA
CACILIA	30	F	NN	GRZZZZUSA
BIEDENKOPP, JOHANNES	25	M	LLD	GRZZZZUSA
MILCH, SOPHIE	20	F	NN	GRZZZZUSA
THURN, -ANKRATZ	25	M	SHMK	GRZZZZUSA
GRUENAUER, THERESE	16	F	NN	GRZZZZUSA
BEIL, ANNA	23	F	NN	GRZZZZUSA
MARIE	3	F	CHILD	GRZZZZUSA
STRAUSS, BERTHA	19	F	NN	GRZZZZUSA
MUELLER, CONRAD	41	M	LABR	GRZZZZUSA
PAULI, OTTO	32	M	LABR	GRZZZZUSA
KA-UTH, CONRADA	26	F	NN	GRZZZZUSA
SOPHIE	4	F	CHILD	GRZZZZUSA
JOSEF	.10	M	INFANT	GRZZZZUSA
RASINSKY, MATHIAS	36	M	LABR	GRZZZZUSA
KASLOWSKY, RASIMIR	35	M	BCHR	GRZZZZUSA
VON, HEINRICH	15	M	MCHT	GRZZZZUSA
-LATZ, CASPAR	00	M	SMH	GRZZZZUSA
HIRNHEIMER, BERNHARD	15	M	MCHT	GRZZZZUSA
BRASFISCH, EMIL	17	M	GDNR	GRZZZZUSA
DETTMER, DIETRICH	65	M	TCHR	GRZZZZUSA
GAERTNER, ELISABETH	26	F	NN	GRZZZZUSA
GODDERKER, JOHANN	28	M	FARMER	GRZZZZUSA
GRUEN---, BERNHARD	17	M	FARMER	GRZZZZUSA
GRUESS, CATHARINA	21	F	NN	GRZZZZUSA
GRUENL--, JOSEF	16	M	LABR	GRZZZZUSA
MARIA	26	F	NN	GRZZZZUSA
KUEPER, MARIA	25	F	NN	GRZZZZUSA
CAROLINE	18	F	NN	GRZZZZUSA
THEDIECK, JOSEF	31	M	FARMER	GRZZZZUSA
CATHARINA	23	F	NN	GRZZZZUSA
BOECKENBRINK, ADOLF	63	M	FARMER	GRZZZZUSA
BAHNLEIN, U	24	M	FARMER	GRZZZZUSA
HEINRICH, ADAM	35	M	SHMK	GRZZZZUSA
HUFNAGEL, MARIE	29	F	NN	GRZZZZUSA
FRANKENBERGER, ANDREAS	24	M	FARMER	GRZZZZUSA
HIENE, CARL	16	M	SMH	GRZZZZUSA
WOELKENMEYER, ERNST	22	M	JNR	GRZZZZUSA
GOERLITZ, JACOB	24	M	FARMER	GRZZZZUSA
VOIGT, CLARA	24	F	NN	GRZZZZUSA
KINSMANN, GEORG	17	M	CPTR	GRZZZZUSA
KRESS, REGINE	21	F	NN	GRZZZZUSA
GASCH, THOMAS	48	M	BBR	GRZZZZUSA
KAEMMERER, HERMANN	33	M	LABR	GRZZZZUSA
ERNST	25	M	LABR	GRZZZZUSA
PERK, ANNA	23	F	NN	GRZZZZUSA
HELMSING, BERNHARD	39	M	LKSH	GRZZZZUSA
FRAN	27	F	NN	GRZZZZUSA
BERNHARD	2	M	CHILD	GRZZZZUSA
HEGGER, GESINE	30	F	NN	GRZZZZUSA
SCHROEDER, JOSEF	60	M	FARMER	GRZZZZUSA
FRAN	50	F	NN	GRZZZZUSA
-ASOLDT, PAUL	15	M	PNTR	GRZZZZUSA
STARCH, EDUARD	23	M	GDNR	GRZZZZUSA
LINDHORST, ANNA	15	F	NN	GRZZZZUSA
LANKENAU, HINRICH	16	M	BKR	GRZZZZUSA
BEHRENS, MINNA	24	F	NN	GRZZZZUSA
-OFF, FRIEDRICKE	50	F	NN	GRZZZZUSA
ACHARD, HERMANN	22	M	STDNT	GRZZZZUSA
ULLRICH, JOHANNA	17	F	NN	GRZZZZUSA
BAR, GEORG	16	M	BCHR	GRZZZZUSA
GE-ER, CHRISTIANA	00	F	NN	GRZZZZUSA
THOMAS, PAULINE	16	F	NN	GRZZZZUSA
BERTHOLD, MARGARETHA	17	F	NN	GRZZZZUSA
BAYER, CHRISTOPH	16	M	FARMER	GRZZZZUSA
KRAUSS, EVA	20	F	NN	GRZZZZUSA
-IELHAUER, JULIUS	16	M	TLR	GRZZZZUSA
LOUISE	18	F	NN	GRZZZZUSA
GOETZ, BURGHARD	29	M	FARMER	GRZZZZUSA
SCHLOTT, CONRAD	7	M	CHILD	GRZZZZUSA
BAUMGARTNER, ANNA	18	F	NN	GRZZZZUSA
HILPER, CARL	15	M	LABR	GRZZZZUSA
SCHMIDT, JOHANNE	13	F	NN	GRZZZZUSA
FOELL, FRIEDRICH	15	M	SMH	GRZZZZUSA
GUST, LORENZ	35	M	BKR	GRZZZZUSA
STUMPF, WILLIAM	51	M	MCHT	GRZZZZUSA
MEYER, JULIUS	17	M	MCHT	GRZZZZUSA
FUERST, JOSEF	38	M	FARMER	GRZZZZUSA
JANSSEN, MARGARETHA	19	F	NN	GRZZZZUSA
PICK, ELISABETH	21	F	NN	GRZZZZUSA
FEBINGER, LINA	18	F	NN	GRZZZZUSA
BAUER, AMALIE	19	F	NN	GRZZZZUSA
REICHERT, AUGUSTE	19	F	NN	GRZZZZUSA
PHILIPPINE	21	F	NN	GRZZZZUSA
ROEPER, ELISABETH	27	F	NN	GRZZZZUSA
CARL	.09	M	INFANT	GRZZZZUSA
VERECK, ANNA	16	F	NN	GRZZZZUSA
LIND, AUGUSTE	14	F	NN	GRZZZZUSA
GEORGI, ANNA	25	F	NN	GRZZZZUSA
BARTH, THERESIA	16	F	NN	GRZZZZUSA
SCHIMMER, MARIA	20	F	NN	GRZZZZUSA
MATH, THEODOR	21	M	LABR	GRZZZZUSA
SCHUMACHER, PETER	62	M	FARMER	GRZZZZUSA
HADELER, JOHANN	16	M	DLR	GRZZZZUSA
SOMMER, FRIEDRICH	26	M	GDNR	GRZZZZUSA
TRIESCHMANN, HEINRICH	32	M	BBR	GRZZZZUSA
SCH-K, MARGARETHA	19	F	NN	GRZZZZUSA
GARTELMANN, DIEDRICH	16	M	MCHT	GRZZZZUSA
MEINDE, PHILIPP	21	M	LABR	GRZZZZUSA
WILKENS, DIEDRICH	32	M	LABR	GRZZZZUSA
BLANK, M	21	M	LABR	GRZZZZUSA
GASTORFF, MAX	23	M	LABR	GRZZZZUSA
HARTMANN, HEINRICH	16	M	LABR	GRZZZZUSA
CARSTENN, CARS	23	M	FARMER	GRZZZZUSA
SIEMSEN, AUGUST	26	M	BKR	GRZZZZUSA
OLSCHA, GUSTAV	25	M	BBR	GRZZZZUSA
STANGE, HELENA	20	F	NN	GRZZZZUSA
SEIGER, BARBE	37	F	NN	GRZZZZUSA
SCHULZ, PAULINE	27	F	NN	GRZZZZUSA
WILHELM	4	M	CHILD	GRZZZZUSA
LINA	7	F	CHILD	GRZZZZUSA
EELESER, SOPHIE	20	F	NN	GRZZZZUSA
SZUMSKY, MARIANNA	54	F	NN	GRZZZZUSA
DITT--, MAGDALENA	18	F	NN	GRZZZZUSA

PASSENGER	AGE	SEX	OCCUPATION	PVRIVL	DES
REICHARD, KATHARINA	24	F	NN		GRZZZZUSA
BOERMANN, CARL	22	M	FARMER		GRZZZZUSA
LOOSE, ELISE	15	F	NN		GRZZZZUSA
O--WEIN, MARTH	14	M	NN		GRZZZZUSA
RUS, ANNA	64	F	NN		GRZZZZUSA
GIESE, AUGUST	45	M	JNR		GRZZZZUSA
SOM---SKA, JOSEFA	27	F	NN		GRZZZZUSA
SEIDLER, SAMUEL	36	M	MCHT		GRZZZZUSA
KA-OS, MARGARETHA	25	F	NN		GRZZZZUSA
CATHARINA	.11	F	INFANT		GRZZZZUSA
HASBERG, MARJANNA	35	F	NN		GRZZZZUSA
PEUSCH, STANIEL	7	M	CHILD		GRZZZZUSA
ANNA	6	F	CHILD		GRZZZZUSA
BALKEN, ANNA	15	F	NN		GRZZZZUSA
-MRE, VARGA	27	M	LABR		GRZZZZUSA
ECK, MICHAEL	37	M	GDNR		GRZZZZUSA
KUKINSKY, ISAAC	35	M	MCHT		GRZZZZUSA
FRAN	30	F	NN		GRZZZZUSA
SIMON	7	M	CHILD		GRZZZZUSA
LEWI	6	M	CHILD		GRZZZZUSA
PAUL	2	M	CHILD		GRZZZZUSA
MOSES	4	M	CHILD		GRZZZZUSA
JACOB	3	M	CHILD		GRZZZZUSA
SAMUEL	.11	M	INFANT		GRZZZZUSA
BARISKI, ELISABETH	21	F	NN		GRZZZZUSA

SHIP: MAIN

FROM: BREMEN
TO: BALTIMORE
ARRIVED: 22 AUGUST 1888

PASSENGER	AGE	SEX	OCCUPATION	PVRIVL	DES
STACHNIK, MARIA	60	F	TT		GRZZZZBAL
KRUEGER, ERNST	25	M	MCHT		GRZZZZBAL
GACHRING, FERD.	15	M	CL		GRZZZZBAL
DOEBLER, FERD.	22	M	LABR		GRZZZZBAL
REINHEIMER, FRITZ	43	M	FARMER		GRZZZZBAL
DEGELMANN, ERHARDT	19	M	FARMER		GRZZZZBAL
EICK, OTTO	17	M	FARMER		GRZZZZBAL
FROEHLKE, CARL	24	M	JWLR		GRZZZZBAL
SCHWANKE, HERM.	27	M	MNR		GRZZZZBAL
AHLMANN, LUDWIG	60	M	BKLYR		GRZZZZMN
LUND, CHRISTIAN	17	M	TU		GRZZZZBAL
WILLINN, THOMAS	18	M	LABR		GRZZZZBAL
VETTER, DANIEL	20	M	LABR		GRZZZZBAL
OHNMACHT, JOHN	13	M	LABR		GRZZZZBAL
MICHAEL, JACOB	17	M	JNR		GRZZZZMO
MONTAG, EWALD	16	M	CL		GRZZZZBAL
METZNER, CURT	17	M	FARMER		GRZZZZBAL
MAKONSKI, ANTON	32	M	FARMER		GRZZZZBAL
HADENSKI, JOSEF	36	M	FARMER		GRZZZZOH
JMOVALLE, HEINR.	17	M	FARMER		GRZZZZBAL
DRICHANS, ANTON	26	M	FARMER		GRZZZZBAL
KOEHLER, JOHANN	26	M	FARMER		GRZZZZBAL
TOYS, JOSEF	21	M	FARMER		GRZZZZBAL
JAMROZI, MICHAEL	50	M	FARMER		GRZZZZBAL
WALTER, ANDREAS	44	M	LABR		GRZZZZBAL
FRANZ	16	M	LABR		GRZZZZBAL
DOEPKE, ANTON	26	M	LABR		GRZZZZBAL
SCHALLA, EDUARD	25	M	LABR		GRZZZZBAL
HERZAG, JACOB	32	M	LABR		GRZZZZBAL
MAY, EDUARD	26	M	LABR		GRZZZZBAL
RIMERKEWITZ, PETER	27	M	SMH		GRZZZZBAL
ZEIDLER, LOUIS	54	M	SMH		GRZZZZBAL
NICKEL, EMIL	34	M	LABR		GRZZZZBAL
GREVE, JOHANN	31	M	LABR		GRZZZZBAL
KLATT, SAMUEL	63	M	LABR		GRZZZZBAL
SCHMIDTMANN, MICHAEL	11	M	CH		GRZZZZBAL
ADAM	9	M	CHILD		GRZZZZBAL
WOSCH, CARL	19	M	LABR		GRZZZZMD

PASSENGER	AGE	SEX	OCCUPATION	PVRIVL	DES
LUECKE, HERM.	45	M	LKSH		GRZZZZIA
MEYER, HEINR.	30	M	STCTR		GRZZZZMI
HAHN, JULIUS	25	M	FARMER		GRZZZZOH
CARL	39	M	FARMER		GRZZZZOH
BECKER, FRIEDR.	31	M	FARMER		GRZZZZOH
BALL, HEINR.	25	M	BKR		GRZZZZOH
LIPPERT, HEINR.	29	M	LABR		GRZZZZIL
LANGHEINRICHS, HEINR.	65	M	PVTM		GRZZZZIL
RAMSCHUESSEL, GUSTAV	16	M	FARMER		GRZZZZBAL
DRAGER, AUGUST	32	M	FARMER		GRZZZZCAL
FRIEDRICH	15	M	FARMER		GRZZZZCAL
SEITER, DANIEL	47	M	STNR		GRZZZZBAL
V., AUGUST	33	M	FARMER		GRZZZZMO
JOHANN	9	M	CHILD		GRZZZZMO
AUGUST	5	M	CHILD		GRZZZZMO
LANY, CHRISTIAN	35	M	BCHR		GRZZZZBAL
MAISSENHELDER, JOH.	22	M	BCHR		GRZZZZBAL
KNEICHEL, GEORG	27	M	LABR		GRZZZZBAL
HANSEN, WOLF	30	M	LABR		GRZZZZBAL
KAMMANN, HEINR.	37	M	MCHT		GRZZZZBAL
KATALINSKI, VACLAV	32	M	LABR		GRZZZZBAL
KOCKS, HEINR.	30	M	LABR		GRZZZZBAL
SCHOEBEL, JULIUS	30	M	LABR		GRZZZZBAL
MARIA	25	F	W		GRZZZZBAL
KOCH, AMALIE	19	F	SVNT		GRZZZZBAL
ROTH, MARIA	18	F	SVNT		GRZZZZBAL
LANGERER, SUSANNE	64	F	W		GRZZZZBAL
JOHANNE	22	F	D		GRZZZZBAL
STANCZIK, HELENE	15	F	SVNT		GRZZZZBAL
THOMA, ALOSIA	17	F	SVNT		GRZZZZBAL
ERNST, LOUISE	25	F	W		GRZZZZBAL
MARIA	3	F	CHILD		GRZZZZBAL
EICH, WILHNE.	17	F	SVNT		GRZZZZBAL
GIESA, JOSEFA	27	F	W		GRZZZZBAL
KORK, HENRIETTE	75	F	W		GRZZZZBAL
ZIMPEL, ANNA	16	F	SVNT		GRZZZZWI
BOHN, ADELHEIDE	43	F	W		GRZZZZWI
FRENZISCA	12	F	CH		GRZZZZWI
JOSEF	4	M	CHILD		GRZZZZWI
MARIA	3	F	CHILD		GRZZZZWI
TWICK, SAPPIE	17	F	SVNT		GRZZZZOH
SCHWANKE, AUGUSTE	21	F	SVNT		GRZZZZMO
LEWINSKI, MATHILDE	31	F	W		GRZZZZBAL
MARIA	4	F	CHILD		GRZZZZBAL
SHCLOSS, MARTHA	20	F	W		GRZZZZBAL
MARTHA	.01	F	INFANT		GRZZZZBAL
GROSSMANN, CHARLOTTE	22	F	SVNT		GRZZZZBAL
HAENZLER, CATHA.	34	F	W		GRZZZZBAL
BUCHOE-, MINE	25	F	W		GRZZZZBAL
LOTTY	.11	F	INFANT		GRZZZZBAL
OHR, MAIRA	16	F	SVNT		GRZZZZBAL
HANSSER, ELISAB.	16	F	SVNT		GRZZZZOH
HAHN, FRANZISKA	17	F	SVNT		GRZZZZOH
NICKEL, CATHA.	23	F	W		GRZZZZBAL
MICHEL	.09	M	INFANT		GRZZZZBAL
BORMLY, KATINKA	19	F	SVNT		GRZZZZBAL
STIELER, MARIA	18	F	SVNT		GRZZZZBAL
VONDRACEK, MARIA	10	F	CH		GRZZZZBAL
ENGELHARDT, MARIA	35	F	W		GRZZZZBAL
SCHUMANN, ANNA	16	F	SVNT		GRZZZZBAL
MATHEWS, LOUISE	17	F	SVNT		GRZZZZBAL
VESPER, MARIA	20	F	SVNT		GRZZZZBAL
NORDLAND, MARTHA	58	F	W		GRZZZZBAL
HASSE, PAULINE	24	F	W		GRZZZZBAL
MITTELSTEDT, ERNESTINE	21	F	SVNT		GRZZZZOH
HOHE, KUNIGUNDE	20	F	SVNT		GRZZZZKS
MEIER, KATHARINE	25	F	SVNT		GRZZZZOH
UPHOFF, AUGUSTE	29	F	W		GRZZZZBAL
BERNARDINE	30	F	W		GRZZZZBAL
FRITZ	11	M	CH		GRZZZZBAL
CARL	.06	M	INFANT		GRZZZZBAL
ELISABETH	54	F	W		GRZZZZBAL
MARIA	9	F	CHILD		GRZZZZBAL
KEMPER, THERESE	40	F	W		GRZZZZBAL
RUSSLER, CATH.	20	F	SVNT		GRZZZZBAL

286

PASSENGER	AGE	SEX	OCCUPATION	PRIVL	DES
DIESTER, KUNIGUND	28	F	W	GRZZZZBAL	
KEMPER, MARIA	14	F	SVNT	GRZZZZBAL	
WALTERS, GERTRUDE	26	F	W	GRZZZZBAL	
CAROLINE	5	F	CHILD	GRZZZZBAL	
MAX	2	M	CHILD	GRZZZZBAL	
RUEHALZ, MARIANNE	17	F	SVNT	GRZZZZBAL	
JARNIAK, AMALIE	40	F	W	GRZZZZBAL	
JOHANNA	6	F	CHILD	GRZZZZBAL	
JOSEF	4	M	CHILD	GRZZZZBAL	
DOEPKE, MATHILD.	24	F	W	GRZZZZBAL	
MARTHA	.10	F	INFANT	GRZZZZBAL	
KRONE, MARIA	15	F	SVNT	GRZZZZOH	
KOCK, MARIA	28	F	SVNT	GRZZZZOH	
WOLTER, MARIANNA	46	F	W	GRZZZZWI	
FRANZISKA	11	F	CH	GRZZZZWI	
VALERIA	10	F	CH	GRZZZZWI	
STANISLAWA	8	F	CHILD	GRZZZZWI	
JOSEFA	5	F	CHILD	GRZZZZWI	
MARIANNA	3	F	CHILD	GRZZZZWI	
HELENE	.06	F	INFANT	GRZZZZWI	
JAMROZI, MARIA	17	F	SVNT	GRZZZZWI	
PLATOSZINSKA, THERESIA	25	F	W	GRZZZZBAL	
AGNITZKA	5	F	CHILD	GRZZZZBAL	
ALBRECHT, AUGUSTE	37	F	W	GRZZZZBAL	
MARTHA	3	F	CHILD	GRZZZZBAL	
CLARA	.06	F	INFANT	GRZZZZBAL	
GRENUS, ANNA	21	F	SVNT	GRZZZZBAL	
ZINDARSCH, LOUISE	21	F	SVNT	GRZZZZBAL	
KRASEMANN, JOHNE.	63	F	W	GRZZZZBAL	
SCHNEIDERSCH, EMILIE	19	F	SVNT	GRZZZZBAL	
BECKER, EDA	19	F	SVNT	GRZZZZBAL	
NICKEL, LOUISE	28	F	W	GRZZZZWI	
AUGUSTE	5	F	CHILD	GRZZZZWI	
BERTHA	4	F	CHILD	GRZZZZWI	
EMIL	.11	M	INFANT	GRZZZZWI	
SCHALLER, CARLNE.	67	F	W	GRZZZZWI	
KLEIN, CAROLINE	25	F	W	GRZZZZBAL	
JULIUS	2	M	CHILD	GRZZZZBAL	
GEISSEL, ELISE	20	F	SVNT	GRZZZZBAL	
BORCKELMANN, ANNA	38	F	W	GRZZZZBAL	
DANIEL	6	M	CHILD	GRZZZZBAL	
MARIA	4	F	CHILD	GRZZZZBAL	
FITZBERGER, MARIA	55	F	W	GRZZZZBAL	
FOX, ANNA	27	F	W	GRZZZZBAL	
WASSERSTRASSE, AUGUSTE	36	F	W	GRZZZZBAL	
BIANKA	15	F	D	GRZZZZBAL	
GEORG	5	M	CHILD	GRZZZZBAL	
HERMANN	.06	M	INFANT	GRZZZZBAL	
OLSZEWSKI, KATHARINE	19	F	SVNT	GRZZZZBAL	
SCHULZ, HERMINE	27	F	W	GRZZZZBAL	
PAULINE	4	F	CHILD	GRZZZZBAL	
WACKAL, MARIANNE	61	F	W	GRZZZZBAL	
KATHARINE	17	F	D	GRZZZZBAL	
BRANDT, ELISE	16	F	SVNT	GRZZZZBAL	
MUELLER, MARGARETHE	21	F	SVNT	GRZZZZBAL	
GEBAUER, MAGAR.	22	F	W	GRZZZZBAL	
JADZIESKA, AUGUSTE	28	F	W	GRZZZZIL	
SCHWARTZ, ROSA	17	F	SVNT	GRZZZZBAL	
TOEPEL, ANNA	40	F	W	GRZZZZBAL	
BERNARD	10	M	CH	GRZZZZBAL	
HAMERL, MINNA	67	F	W	GRZZZZBAL	
KATHARINE	6	F	CHILD	GRZZZZBAL	
SCHAFELD, CAROLNE.	21	F	SVNT	GRZZZZBAL	
HAHN, JOSEPHINE	31	F	W	GRZZZZOH	
HOCK, ELISE	16	F	SVNT	GRZZZZOH	
BERCHBAUER, ANNA	38	F	W	GRZZZZWI	
FEREINAND	7	M	CHILD	GRZZZZWI	
LANZENLEHNER, THERESE	34	F	W	GRZZZZWI	
PIPPERT, ELISE	28	F	W	GRZZZZIL	
POKORNY, MARIA	40	F	W	GRZZZZBAL	
JOSEF	8	M	CHILD	GRZZZZBAL	
FRANZ	6	M	CHILD	GRZZZZBAL	
PHILIPP	.11	M	INFANT	GRZZZZBAL	
HEYM, ELISAB.	38	F	W	GRZZZZBAL	
BIEMUELLER, CAROLINE	16	F	SVNT	GRZZZZBAL	
DOROTHEA	15	F	SVNT	GRZZZZBAL	
AHLERT, ANNA	26	F	SVNT	GRZZZZBAL	
CHRISTINE	25	F	SVNT	GRZZZZBAL	
BACHOR, JOSEFA	26	F	W	GRZZZZMI	
BALOINA	4	F	CHILD	GRZZZZMI	
MARIANNA	.09	F	INFANT	GRZZZZMI	
THEEN, MAIRA	35	F	W	GRZZZTX	
PISCHERY, CLARA	35	F	W	GRZZZZWI	
JOHANN	11	M	CH	GRZZZZWI	
STERWINSKY, WANDA	23	F	SVNT	GRZZZZBAL	
NETZOLD, SELMA	22	F	SVNT	GRZZZZOH	
LEVI, MARIA	17	F	SVNT	GRZZZZBAL	
KORNHAAS, LESETTE	35	F	W	GRZZZZBAL	
RICHARD	5	M	CHILD	GRZZZZBAL	
HELENE	2	F	CHILD	GRZZZZBAL	
BADES, MARIA	34	F	W	GRZZZZBAL	
BABETTE	3	F	CHILD	GRZZZZBAL	
HEYDER, MARGR.	53	F	W	GRZZZZOH	
EMMA	11	F	CH	GRZZZZOH	
IDA	9	F	CHILD	GRZZZZOH	
NEUMER, URSULA	36	F	W	GRZZZZIL	
JOHANN	2	M	CHILD	GRZZZZIL	
SAPHIE	.02	F	INFANT	GRZZZZIL	
SEILER, KUNIGUNDE	18	F	SVNT	GRZZZZIL	
ZMUEDZINSKA, BRONISLAWA	28	F	W	GRZZZZBAL	
MIECZYSTOWA	.07	F	INFANT	GRZZZZBAL	
CUNAT, ANTONIA	21	F	W	GRZZZZBAL	
MARIA	.06	F	INFANT	GRZZZZBAL	
MUELLER, HEINR.	34	M	SHMK	GRZZZZBAL	
ANNA	34	F	W	GRZZZZBAL	
JOHANNE	6	F	CHILD	GRZZZZBAL	
REKS, PETER	69	M	FARMER	GRZZZZBAL	
OSTERBROCK, LUDWIG	27	M	JNR	GRZZZZBAL	
WILHELMINE	18	F	W	GRZZZZBAL	
BRANDT, WILHELM	24	M	LABR	GRZZZZBAL	
JUSTINE	17	F	W	GRZZZZBAL	
PETZ, WILHELM	42	M	FARMER	GRZZZZBAL	
ROSALIE	44	F	W	GRZZZZBAL	
MARIA	14	F	D	GRZZZZBAL	
AUGUSTE	9	F	CHILD	GRZZZZBAL	
KARZIN, PETER	36	M	ENGR	GRZZZZBAL	
LOUISE	30	F	W	GRZZZZBAL	
MARTHA	8	F	CHILD	GRZZZZBAL	
CARL	10	M	CH	GRZZZZBAL	
ZUDZEWITZ, LUDWIG	34	M	FARMER	GRZZZZBAL	
WILH.	34	F	W	GRZZZZBAL	
ANNA	9	F	CHILD	GRZZZZBAL	
HENRIETTE	7	F	CHILD	GRZZZZBAL	
JOHANN	5	M	CHILD	GRZZZZBAL	
ADOLF	3	M	CHILD	GRZZZZBAL	
LUDWIG	.09	M	INFANT	GRZZZZBAL	
ANKOWSKI, JOHANN	35	M	FARMER	GRZZZZIL	
FRANZISKA	31	F	W	GRZZZZIL	
WANDA	.11	F	INFANT	GRZZZZIL	
SEHER, JOHANN	41	M	FARMER	GRZZZZMI	
ANNA	38	F	W	GRZZZZMI	
BUEDNER, CONRAD	19	M	FARMER	GRZZZZMI	
GUROKI, JOHANN	55	M	FARMER	GRZZZZMI	
BARBARA	59	F	W	GRZZZZMI	
BACH, FRIEDR.	30	M	FARMER	GRZZZZBAL	
OLGA	28	F	W	GRZZZZBAL	
BERTHA	6	F	CHILD	GRZZZZBAL	
EUGEN	5	M	CHILD	GRZZZZBAL	
DORES, JOCOB	26	M	BRR	GRZZZZBAL	
ROSINA	21	F	W	GRZZZZBAL	
BARBARA	.01	F	INFANT	GRZZZZBAL	
SCHROER, ELISE	40	F	W	GRZZZZWI	
JOSEF	20	M	FARMER	GRZZZZWI	
HERMANN	7	M	CHILD	GRZZZZWI	
KRAUSE, JOHANN	48	M	LLD	GRZZZZWI	
EMILIE	28	F	W	GRZZZZWI	
AUGUSTE	17	F	D	GRZZZZWI	
ADOLPH	14	M	LABR	GRZZZZWI	
AMANDA	11	F	H	GRZZZZWI	
JULIUS	7	M	CHILD	GRZZZZWI	

PASSENGER	AGE	SEX	OCCUPATION	PROVL	DES
ALBERT	.11	M	INFANT	GRZZZZWI	
MARTHA	.11	M	INFANT	GRZZZZWI	
MIZERKA, VALENIN	28	M	FARMER	GRZZZZBAL	
ANTONIA	30	F	W	GRZZZZBAL	
STANISLAUS	4	M	CHILD	GRZZZZBAL	
MARIANNA	2	F	CHILD	GRZZZZBAL	
SUMER, MICHAEL	65	M	FARMER	GRZZZZMN	
ANNA	65	F	W	GRZZZZMN	
WEBER, HEINR.	45	M	FARMER	GRZZZZIA	
WILHELMINE	38	F	W	GRZZZZIA	
SOPHIE	10	F	CH	GRZZZZIA	
FRIEDR.	8	M	CHILD	GRZZZZIA	
WILHELM	6	M	CHILD	GRZZZZIA	
AUGUST	3	M	CHILD	GRZZZZIA	
CAROLINE	.09	F	INFANT	GRZZZZIA	
HOLTGNEFE, JOH.	60	M	FARMER	GRZZZZIA	
WILHNE.	55	F	W	GRZZZZIA	
LOUISE	25	F	D	GRZZZZIA	
HERMANN	15	M	FARMER	GRZZZZIA	
KIPP, FRITZ	50	M	LKSH	GRZZZZBAL	
AUGUSTE	33	F	W	GRZZZZBAL	
SCHALL, FRIEDR.	16	M	LKSH	GRZZZZBAL	
SIEMERS, ALBERT	52	M	LABR	GRZZZZMN	
MARGR.	55	F	W	GRZZZZMN	
SOPHIE	26	F	D	GRZZZZMN	
MARGR.	18	F	D	GRZZZZMN	
MARIA	16	F	D	GRZZZZMN	
FERDINAND	8	M	CHILD	GRZZZZMN	
ESCHSTRUTH, WILHELM	47	M	FARMER	GRZZZZPA	
OTTILIE	39	F	W	GRZZZZPA	
WILHELM	13	M	CH	GRZZZZPA	
LOUISE	11	F	CH	GRZZZZPA	
CARL	8	M	CHILD	GRZZZZPA	
MARIA	6	F	CHILD	GRZZZZPA	
SALIK, FRIEDRICH	25	M	FARMER	GRZZZZPA	

SHIP: MICHIGAN

FROM: LIVERPOOL
TO: BOSTON
ARRIVED: 22 AUGUST 1888

PASSENGER	AGE	SEX	OCCUPATION	PROVL	DES
PATAZKY, DAVID	19	M	TLR	GRZZZZUSA	
WALDSTEIN, SALOMON	16	M	TLR	GRZZZZUSA	
MARKS, JACK	20	M	TLR	GRZZZZUSA	
HARRIS, SAMUEL	35	M	TLR	GRZZZZUSA	
SLUTZKY, FREIDE	26	F	SP	GRZZZZUSA	
MULLIIN--, SCH--E	18	F	SP	GRZZZZUSA	
HARDMANN, MATILDE	28	F	SP	GRZZZZUSA	
TRUST--TZER, SCHOSI	50	M	LABR	GRZZZZUSA	
BREME	30	F	W	GRZZZZUSA	
WALDSTEIN, SARAH	40	F	W	GRZZZZUSA	

SHIP: STATE OF NEBRASKA

FROM: GLASGOW AND LARNE
TO: NEW YORK
ARRIVED: 22 AUGUST 1888

PASSENGER	AGE	SEX	OCCUPATION	PROVL	DES
TIZIENSKA, VALERIE	23	F	SP	GRZZZZUSA	
HEIDEWREICH, EMILIE	36	F	SP	GRZZZZUSA	
FESCHER, BARBARA	23	F	SP	GRZZZZUSA	
MARGARETHE	19	F	SP	GRZZZZUSA	
MENZEL, JOHANNA	54	F	WI	GRZZZZUSA	
FRANKE, ANGELIKE	32	F	W	GRZZZZUSA	

PASSENGER	AGE	SEX	OCCUPATION	PROVL	DES
MARGARETHE	11	F	CH	GRZZZZUSA	
CLARA	1	F	CHILD	GRZZZZUSA	
BERNSTEIN, DOROTHEA	29	F	W	GRZZZZUSA	
CAROLINE	6	F	CHILD	GRZZZZUSA	
LANGER, ERNESTINE	40	F	W	GRZZZZUSA	
MARTHA	11	F	CH	GRZZZZUSA	
ROBERT	9	M	CHILD	GRZZZZUSA	
HADLER, ERNESTINE	28	F	W	GRZZZZUSA	
EMMA	11	F	CH	GRZZZZUSA	
MARTHA	2	F	CHILD	GRZZZZUSA	
BARTELS, FRIEDRICH	34	M	CGRMKR	GRZZZZUSA	
ARTHUR	.03	M	INFANT	GRZZZZUSA	
BENKER, JOHANN	31	M	WVR	GRZZZZUSA	
SAINT, ELISE	61	F	SP	FRZZZZUSA	

SHIP: BELGENLAND

FROM: ANTWERP
TO: NEW YORK
ARRIVED: 23 AUGUST 1888

PASSENGER	AGE	SEX	OCCUPATION	PROVL	DES
PAULS, AUG.MR	37	M	MCHT	FRAAECNY	
U-MRS	20	F	UNKNOWN	FRAAECNY	
D-ANCHOLD, HENRI	21	M	STDNT	FRADXWNY	
BECKMANN, P.	30	M	MCHT	FRAIOYNY	
OPPENHEIM, MASE	45	M	CK	GRZZZZNY	
DUHAMEL, G.MR	36	M	CL	GRAGQWMRL	
ROHN, A.MISS	24	F	UNKNOWN	GRAGPLMRL	
MAY, G.MRS	34	F	UNKNOWN	GRAIKSUNK	
F.	9	F	CHILD	GRAIKSUNK	
THEO	5	M	CHILD	GRAIKSUNK	
HUGO	7	M	CHILD	GRAIKSUNK	
E.	3	F	CHILD	GRAIKSUNK	
OTTGIESER, P.	25	M	PREST	GRADXPKS	
KAMP, E.	23	M	PREST	GRADXPKS	
KRIEG, PHIL.	24	M	BBR	GRADBQNY	
HELBING, ANTONIETTE	26	F	UNKNOWN	GRAGPASCR	
FRITZ	7	M	CHILD	GRAGPASCR	
ANNA	4	F	CHILD	GRAGPASCR	
MARIA	1	F	CHILD	GRAGPASCR	
BOEFF, JEAN	22	M	LABR	GRZZZZNY	
LOHMANN, FRITZ	20	M	DRG	GRABOQNY	
ENDRESS, JOHANN	54	M	LABR	GRZZZZNY	
KAROLUS, MARTIN	22	M	LABR	GRZZZZNY	
LAWREUR, CARL	27	M	LABR	GRZZZZCH	
ECKEL, PHIL.	21	M	LABR	GRZZZZNY	
NIONEL, JACOB	26	M	CL	GRACFWNY	
CHARLOTTE	60	F	UNKNOWN	GRACFWNY	
SCHWAAB, ANTON	15	M	DRG	GRZZZZNY	
CHRISTOFFEL, EMIL	15	M	LABR	GRZZZZNY	
LORENTZ, CARL	21	M	BKR	GRZZZZNY	
WILH.	14	M	BKR	GRZZZZNY	
HERTEL, BERTHA	14	F	UNKNOWN	GRZZZZNY	
ZIEBWER, LOUISE	16	F	UNKNOWN	GRZZZZNY	
SCHAAL, EMMA	16	F	UNKNOWN	GRZZZZNY	
EBERLE, MARIE	20	F	SVNT	GRABNRNY	
SCHUSTER, FRIED	15	M	BCHR	GRZZZZPHI	
NEUMEISTER, ROSINE	54	F	UNKNOWN	GRZZZZCLE	
SCHUET, ROSINE	2	F	CHILD	GRZZZZCLE	
BAUER, SOFIE	22	F	SVNT	GRZZZZTOL	
THIEBER, CHRISTIAN	19	M	LABR	GRZZZZTOL	
CAESAR, OTTO	34	M	CK	GRZZZZNY	
WINDERLICH, CARL	37	M	CL	GRAFJDNY	
BECKER, CATHA.	19	F	SVNT	GRZZZZNY	
FOERSTER, LOUISE	18	F	SVNT	GRADYUNY	
BUTKAT, GEO	30	M	LABR	GRZZZZSTL	
SKRYPSAK, IGNAZ	20	M	LABR	GRZZZZUNK	
ELKER, JONATHAN	17	M	CPTR	GRZZZZNY	
SANDMANN, FRIED	23	M	LABR	GRZZZZNY	
PLUTINGHAUS, FRIED	26	M	LABR	GRZZZZNY	

PASSENGER	AGE	SEX	OCCUPATION	PRVL DES
RUTTMER, MICHAEL	65	M	LABR	GRZZZZNY
WEIS, CASPAR	26	M	CPTR	GRABESNY
BLUST, JULIA	21	F	UNKNOWN	GRAAGLNY
FELIX	00	M	INF	GRAAGLNY
SCHWANNBACH, SOPHIE	18	F	SVNT	GRZZZZNY
SCHLEHHUBER, FRANZ	14	M	TLR	GRZZZZNY
THIEN, CASPAR	64	M	LABR	GRZZZZNY
HADER, CATHNE.	21	F	CK	GRAKSMNY
FAEDORCH, GEO	22	M	LABR	GRAKSMNY
DIERAUF, CARL	27	M	LABR	GRZZZZNY
PAPENHEIM, HERM.	25	M	MNR	GRAGPASCR
STUEVE, HCH.	24	M	MNR	GRAGPASCR
HOEFFER, PETER	20	M	SHMK	GRAAPSSTL
GLASSMANN, GEO	00	M	LABR	GRAEUINY
ELINBERG, LEWIS	23	M	SHMK	GRADBQNY
VOSTER, LIZIE	24	F	SVNT	GRADBQNY
TREUKNAR, ROB.	21	M	TLR	GRADBQNY
OTTO, ADOLF	25	M	TLR	GRADBQNY
HORWITZ, JACOB	21	M	BKR	GRADBQCLE
KREMER, ELSE	8	F	CHILD	GRZZZZNY
HAAG, JACOB	22	M	BKR	GRZZZZNY
SCHWIND, PETER	49	M	LABR	GRAEWXNY
WILH.	11	M	CH	GRAEWXNY
KOHLEN, JOHANN	22	M	MNR	GRAEWXNY
ZIMMERMANN, WILH.	27	M	MNR	GRAEWXNY
COLIN, DESIRE	30	M	MNR	FRZZZZNY
AURELIE	25	F	UNKNOWN	FRZZZZNY
DUCON, TOURNANT	24	M	MNR	FRZZZZNY
LASSON, ERNSTE.	28	M	MNR	FRZZZZNY
BORGER, JOHS.	16	M	TLR	FRADAGNY
MEYERER, JOH.	42	M	LABR	FRADAGNY
JOH.	42	M	LABR	GRZZZZNY
APOLONIA	42	F	UNKNOWN	GRZZZZNY
ANNA	11	F	CH	GRZZZZNY
CATH.	9	F	CHILD	GRZZZZNY
GEOR.	7	M	CHILD	GRZZZZNY
CAROL.	6	F	CHILD	GRZZZZNY
ELISAB.	00	F	INF	GRZZZZNY
POMNIER, AUGUSTE	17	M	CH	GRADXWNY
BLICKLE, SEBAST.	18	M	SHMK	GRAFTDNY
EBERLI, THERESE	28	F	SVNT	GRADKJNY
BAUMER, THERESE	28	F	SVNT	GRADKJNY
FURNROHR, FRIEDR.	22	M	CPTR	GRAAHUNY
RUCH, MARIA	29	F	CK	GRAAHUNY
PIER, JACOB	25	M	PNTR	SRZZZZNY
STERN, SETTE	21	F	DRSMKR	GRZZZZNY
MRAZEK, CARL	42	M	BRR	GRZZZZNY
MARGA.	36	F	UNKNOWN	GRZZZZNY
ELISE	9	F	CHILD	GRZZZZNY
FRZKA.	7	F	CHILD	GRZZZZNY
MARIE	2	F	CHILD	GRZZZZNY
JOST, GEORGE	25	M	SHMK	GRADYUNY
SCHEUBLER, BERN.	30	M	CPTR	GRABSINY
PFEIFFER, MICHEL	57	M	FARMER	GRAJIZNY
MARIE	58	F	UNKNOWN	GRAJIZNY
MARIE	17	F	UNKNOWN	GRAJIZNY
ANNA	10	F	CH	GRZZZZNY
MARTEN, JOH.	66	M	FARMER	GRZZZZNY
MAUL, FRIED.	17	M	SHMK	GRAGLSNY
LETERLE, PETER	18	M	LABR	GRAEWXUNK
STERN, HEINR.	20	M	LABR	GRZZZZNY
NICOLAS, RCH.	20	M	LABR	GRZZZZNY
PISCES, FRIEDR.	21	M	CL	GRZZZZNY
STIEFEL, GEOGE	24	M	LABR	GRAGLSNY
LOEWEN, MARGA.	18	F	SVNT	GRZZZZNY
KLEIN, NICOLAS	24	M	LABR	GRZZZZNY
LOWEN, JOH.	14	M	LABR	GRZZZZNY
SCHWENDER, CHRIST.	27	M	MNR	GRZZZZNY
MARGA.	22	F	MNR	GRZZZZNY
WEISS, ALBERT	23	M	LABR	GRACUXNY
SEILER, CAROL.	17	F	UNKNOWN	GRAJTWPHI
ANTONI, WILH.	23	M	GLSMKR	GRZZZZPIT
NEUMANN, JASCHEL	27	M	LABR	GRZZZZNY
WIZENTY, MANKOCZ	21	M	LABR	GRAGRTNY
BETTICKE, HENRIETTE	26	F	UNKNOWN	GRZZZZCH

PASSENGER	AGE	SEX	OCCUPATION	PRVL DES
AUGUST	2	M	CHILD	GRZZZZCH
JULIUS	00	M	INF	GRZZZZCH
KLEIN, PAULINE	34	F	UNKNOWN	GRAEJDNY
CAHEN, NATHAN	00	M	BCHR	GRZZZZNY
RISSLING, LUDW.	28	M	BKR	GRZZZZNY
WENGERT, JOHS.	25	M	SHMK	GRAEXWCH
FOERGES, FRZ.	15	M	CPTR	GRACEDNY
KLEIN, ADERM	41	M	CPTR	GRACEDNY
KOBER, ROZINE	13	F	UNKNOWN	GRZZZZNY
DERTINGER, HERM.	23	M	BBR	GRZZZZNY
STIEGELE, LOUISE	23	F	UNKNOWN	GRZZZZCH
SCHWARZ, JOH.	23	M	LABR	GRABYQCH
DOVILLEZ, PAUL	35	M	LABR	GRAAECDET
ECKERT, SARAH	30	F	UNKNOWN	GRAAECNY
ERNST	9	M	CHILD	GRAAECNY
DOMBERGER, MATHILDE	23	F	UNKNOWN	GRAEXKLOS
JULIANA	17	F	UNKNOWN	GRAEXKLOS
LUDW.	19	M	CH	GRAEXKLOS
TABELLEON, LOUISE	29	F	CK	GRABZWOH
WITT, H.	16	M	LABR	GRADPHNY
METZGER, MARTIN	16	M	LABR	GRADPHNY
SCHWORER, SAMBERT	17	M	CGRMKR	GRADPHNY
OBERBILLIG, PETER	25	M	FARMER	GRAAECNY
SCHILLING, THERESE	25	F	SVNT	GRAFASNY
MULLER, CARL	29	M	BCHR	GRAFYWTWD
HAGENBRING, ANNA	26	F	CK	GRACXVCH
ZILLING, BRUNO	33	M	CL	GRACXVCH
MURAT, JEAN	33	M	TIREMN	GRAAECNY
GOOSENS, LOUISE	16	F	UNKNOWN	GRAAECNY
ENKEN, HERM.	21	M	LABR	FRZZZZNY
HAAS, JOSEF	18	M	BCHR	FRAFHRUNK
SCHEUERER, BARBA.	21	F	SVNT	FRZZZZUNK
U, U	28	F	SVNT	FRZZZZUNK
HEINR.	3	M	CHILD	FRZZZZUNK
CARL	2	M	CHILD	FRZZZZUNK
ZIESSEL, LOUIS	16	M	CPTR	LXZZZZUNK
GUNE, ANNE	19	M	LABR	LXZZZZUNK
KOEHL, XAVIER	28	M	LABR	LXZZZZUNK
LANER, CATH.	28	F	UNKNOWN	LXZZZZBUF
MARIA	3	F	CHILD	LXZZZZBUF
CATHA.	2	F	CHILD	LXZZZZBUF
PHILIPPE	1	M	CHILD	LXZZZZBUF
KLEIN, MARIA	35	F	UNKNOWN	LXZZZZBUF
BARBA.	.06	F	INFANT	LXZZZZBUF
HUBER, FRIED.	28	M	TLR	LXAEXKCH
STRASSEL, ELISAB.	45	F	UNKNOWN	LXAAECNY
BUND, LOUIS	42	M	LABR	LXAAECNY
STEIGER, BERTHA	21	F	SVNT	GRZZZZCIN
WIELAND, GEO	24	M	CNF	GRZZZZCIN
MARIE	25	F	UNKNOWN	GRZZZZCIN
MARIE	3	F	CHILD	GRZZZZCIN
CATH.	2	F	CHILD	GRZZZZCIN
MARG.	00	F	INF	GRZZZZCIN
AURICH, BRUNO	24	M	BKR	GRACXVCIN
KOCH, MARIE	00	F	SVNT	GRAAECCIN

SHIP: BRITANNIC

FROM: LIVERPOOL AND QUEENSTOWN
TO: NEW YORK
ARRIVED: 24 AUGUST 1888

PASSENGER	AGE	SEX	OCCUPATION	PRVL DES
HYKR--TZ, PATI	16	F	SP	GRADAXUSA
KOON, ROSA	17	F	SP	GRADAXUSA
TORSKI, M	28	F	SP	GRADAXUSA
ROTH, F-GE	11	M	CH	GRADAXUSA
GELBART, MENDEL	59	M	LABR	GRADAXUSA
SARA	59	F	W	GRADAXUSA
LIPPERT, HENSEL	23	F	SP	GRADAXUSA
F-NGOLD, E	29	F	W	GRADAXUSA

PASSENGER	AGE	SEX	OCCUPATION	PROVL	DIES
JOSEPH	6	M	CHILD		GRADAXUSA
BERNHARD	5	M	CHILD		GRADAXUSA
--ANDOV	2	F	CHILD		GRADAXUSA
AB	1	M	CHILD		GRADAXUSA
BEB-AKI, MARIA	20	F	W		GRADAXUSA
WAKINOR	1	M	CHILD		GRADAXUSA
DAVIDSON, MENDEL	25	M	LABR		GRADAXUSA
SOFI	19	F	W		GRADAXUSA
ISAK	1	M	CHILD		GRADAXUSA
CRASTIN, -ASHUM	30	M	LABR		GRADAXUSA
BICKER, MICHL	36	M	LABR		GRADAXUSA
STEGMAN, GITTEL	24	M	LABR		GRADAXUSA
SALOMON	24	M	LABR		GRADAXUSA
PAWN, JACOB	18	M	LABR		GRADAXUSA
L-RTGARTEN, HENRIETTE	14	F	SP		GRADAXUSA
HELGESON, U	32	M	LABR		GRADAXUSA
HANNA	9	F	CHILD		GRADAXUSA
HERMAN	5	M	CHILD		GRADAXUSA
LEWIS, INDE	42	F	W		GRADAXUSA
TRUME	28	F	SP		GRADAXUSA
BALNIA	16	F	SP		GRADAXUSA
ANNA	1	F	CHILD		GRADAXUSA
--UNK, LEA	20	F	SP		GRADAXUSA
KLEIN, JOSEF	14	M	LABR		GRADAXUSA
ALBERT	15	M	LABR		GRADAXUSA
GROSS, PEPI	17	M	LABR		GRADAXUSA
SETKN, ASUND	44	M	LABR		GRADAXUSA
EKVEM, GUSTA	22	F	SP		GRADAXUSA
HELLBERG, OLLINE	28	F	SP		GRADAXUSA
POLSEN, OLAF	20	M	LABR		GRADAXUSA
KAREN	18	F	W		GRADAXUSA
JONSON, W	25	M	LABR		GRADAXUSA
VOLESTHE, E	30	F	SVNT		GRADAXUSA
HELLE-ARTEN, LONAD	26	F	SVNT		GRADAXUSA
JULEN, ALBERT	28	M	LABR		GRADAXUSA
FRIEDENBERG, ESTEV	22	F	SP		GRADAXUSA
DAGVON, A	60	F	W		GRADAXUSA

SHIP: GALLIA

FROM: LIVERPOOL AND QUEENSTOWN
TO: NEW YORK
ARRIVED: 24 AUGUST 1888

PASSENGER	AGE	SEX	OCCUPATION	PROVL	DIES
SCHUBERT, JOHN	38	M	MLDR		GRADAXUSA
FELSENTHAL, JULIUS	26	M	FARMER		GRACBFUSA
HOJER, FRANS	32	M	TLR		GRACBFUSA
MOGRIDITSCH, THOMAS	32	M	TLR		GRACBFUSA
FABIAN, STEFAN	23	M	TLR		GRACBFUSA
GARATIAN, HAZAH	27	M	TLR		GRACBFUSA
GRUNDLER, CARL	22	M	LABR		GRACBFUSA
STEINMAN, LEWIS	38	M	TLR		GRACBFUSA
KRUMENAKER, PAUL	19	M	CL		GRAEXWUSA
ROBINSON, FOS.	17	M	LABR		GRACBFUSA
VARNAUSK, FANNY	21	F	SVNT		GRZZZZUSA
WIESNER, MARIE	28	F	TCHR		GRACBFUSA
HOCHE, EMIL	27	M	TLR		GRACBFUSA
FISCH, BERL	27	M	TLR		GRACBFUSA
LESORTZKEY, LEISER	24	M	TLR		GRACBFUSA
WAHERESCHAER, MIHER	24	M	LABR		GRACBFUSA
KOLZIN, HERSCH	38	M	LABR		GRACBFUSA
FRUCHL, LEIB	55	M	LABR		GRACBFUSA
ANISTEIN, JACOB	18	M	LABR		GRACBFUSA
HOLMANN, MOSES	25	M	TLR		GRACBFUSA
MOKOWITZ, KIWE	53	M	FARMER		GRACBFUSA
HASKORS, ADAM	35	M	TLR		GRACBFUSA
GOLDSTONG, DAVID	23	M	TLR		GRZZZZUSA
SKADOWSKY, JITE	18	F	SVNT		GRACBFUSA
SERESKY, RAHEL	19	F	SVNT		GRACBFUSA
GRUNDFELD, REBECCA	19	F	SVNT		GRACBFUSA

PASSENGER	AGE	SEX	OCCUPATION	PROVL	DIES
BINGEN, ELIAS	42	M	LABR		GRACBFUSA
HENRIETTE	26	F	W		GRACBFUSA
TACHAMOURTSCH, CHIRL	22	M	TLR		GRACBFUSA
SAVA	22	F	W		GRACBFUSA
GUSWOLD, ALICE	19	F	SP		FRZZZZUSA
WISTHOFF, CHARLES	43	M	UNKNOWN		GRZZZZUSA

SHIP: TRAVE

FROM: BREMEN AND SOUTHAMPTON
TO: NEW YORK
ARRIVED: 24 AUGUST 1888

PASSENGER	AGE	SEX	OCCUPATION	PROVL	DIES
FUNGER, FELIX	25	M	MCHT		SYZZZZUSA
VONESMARCH, ERVIN	30	M	TT		SYACQAUSA
GRAND, META	19	F	UNKNOWN		SYAERCUSA
LOEWEL, CURT	36	M	MCHT		SYABUKUSA
PETERS, EMIL	35	M	MCHT		SYZZZZUSA
VONESMARSCH, U	62	M	TT		GRZZZZUSA
HENR.	56	F	UNKNOWN		GRZZZZUSA
PAHL, EMILIE	23	F	SVNT		GRZZZZUSA
HERZFELD, JOSEF	25	M	TT		GRZZZZUSA
RALL, FRITZ	24	M	MCHT		GRZZZZUSA
KATHI	22	F	UNKNOWN		GRZZZZUSA
WALTER, OTTO	7	M	CHILD		GRZZZZUSA
KOLKMANN, FR.	30	M	MCHT		GRAFNKUSA
GERTRUDE	23	F	UNKNOWN		GRAFNKUSA
WEIGEL, IDA	30	F	UNKNOWN		GRAARRUSA
HAHN, MATHILDE	18	F	UNKNOWN		GRAABNUSA
HOEHN, CHR.	40	M	MCHT		GRAEMYUSA
OEHLERS, SOPHIE	16	F	UNKNOWN		GRACPEUSA
LUETTER, CARL	49	M	MCHT		GRAESMUSA
BISK, AUGUST	32	M	MCHT		GRAESMUSA
MOORE, JOHN	27	M	TT		GRZZZZUSA
KLEIN, META	20	F	UNKNOWN		GRADZZUSA
WEIL, EMMA	17	F	UNKNOWN		GRAEVZUSA
KELLER, HELENA	18	F	UNKNOWN		GRAEVZUSA
LOESMANN, GUST.	6	M	CHILD		GRADWUUSA
JERELSOHN, MORITZ	16	M	MCHT		GRADEIUSA
MURX--, CARL	16	M	MCHT		GRZZZZUSA
GLINGENSTEIN, ISAIS	16	M	MCHT		GRAFMIUSA
FLEISCHMANN, ISAIS	17	M	MCHT		GRAECHUSA
GIESSE, JOAHNNA	26	F	UNKNOWN		GRAFNKUSA
ISLINGER, ANNA	22	F	UNKNOWN		GRAAACUSA
KRAUSS, JOHANNE	16	F	UNKNOWN		GRZZZZUSA
GEYER, ROSINA	16	F	UNKNOWN		GRZZZZUSA
SCHUECKLING, MATHE.	17	F	UNKNOWN		GRZZZZUSA
SEUSS, NICOL	16	M	LABR		GRAJTSUSA
POEHLMANN, JOH.	16	M	LABR		GRAJTSUSA
KLIER, JOH.	63	M	LABR		GRZZZZUSA
CATHA.	67	F	UNKNOWN		GRZZZZUSA
PLATZNER, ELISE	16	F	UNKNOWN		GRAHNIUSA
LEDERMANN, MATHE.	20	F	UNKNOWN		GRAEPDUSA
STAHL, ANNA	15	F	UNKNOWN		GRZZZZUSA
MUELLER, MARIE	19	F	UNKNOWN		GRZZZZUSA
FRANZ, JPAULE.	22	F	UNKNOWN		GRZZZZUSA
KAMINSKI, CARL	27	M	TLR		GRADETUSA
MERTENS, CHRISTE.	53	F	UNKNOWN		GRAJAWUSA
ROSENTHAL, SOLOMON	30	M	MCHT		GRABQZUSA
ROSSLER, EVA	17	F	UNKNOWN		GRZZZZUSA
FERMER, AUGUSTE	19	F	UNKNOWN		GRAEHFUSA
ARCHINOL, ANNA	17	F	UNKNOWN		GRZZZZUSA
SCHUMANN, ELISE	14	F	UNKNOWN		GRZZZZUSA
BIVNBAUM, MORITZ	17	M	LABR		GRAEUBUSA
GRABHORN, ANNA	19	F	UNKNOWN		GRAFDKUSA
WACHSMANN, ERNESTINE	16	F	UNKNOWN		GRABNHUSA
HERM.	13	M	UNKNOWN		GRABNHUSA
SCHMIDT, ANNA	19	F	UNKNOWN		GRAJTSUSA
BROCK, EDUARD	22	M	JNR		GRZZZZUSA
HITZ, DOROTHEA	18	F	UNKNOWN		GRABKRUSA

PASSENGER	AGE	SEX	OCCUPATION	PRVVL	DES	PASSENGER	AGE	SEX	OCCUPATION	PRVVL	DES
PETZ, ANNA	22	F	UNKNOWN	GRABQZUSA		MEYER, LOUISE	59	F	UNKNOWN	GRACHBUSA	
EICHLER, OSWALD	29	M	FARMER	GRZZZZUSA		FREY, CATHA.	21	F	UNKNOWN	GRAECCUSA	
KERKHOFF, MINNA	5	F	CHILD	GRZZZZUSA		JOKEL, ELISAB.	17	F	UNKNOWN	GRAECCUSA	
BURKAMP, MINNA	18	F	UNKNOWN	GRZZZZUSA		HOCHSTAEDTER, AUGE.	17	F	UNKNOWN	GRAHVPUSA	
BEXTEN, AUGUST	28	M	BRR	GRZZZZUSA		ESSING, CATHA.	20	F	UNKNOWN	GRZZZZUSA	
ELLERBRUK, HEINR.	17	M	LABR	GRZZZZUSA		STEINMUELLER, MARIA	22	F	UNKNOWN	GRADZYUSA	
MEINKE, CHRIST.	26	M	LABR	GRZZZZUSA		HOCHREIN, DOROTHEA	22	F	UNKNOWN	GRADZYUSA	
MORCKEN, L.	26	M	LABR	GRAEFTUSA		MEYER, LOUIS	18	M	SMH	GRABLWUSA	
SPREEN, ALFRED	15	M	UNKNOWN	GRZZZZUSA		SHCEID, FRIEDR.	33	M	LABR	GRZZZZUSA	
MONSEES, FRIEDRICH	16	M	SMH	GRZZZZUSA		SCHNEIDER, FRANZ	15	M	LABR	GRZZZZUSA	
VONKAMPON, JOHANN	38	M	FARMER	GRZZZZUSA		BRENNER, JOH.	38	M	LLD	GRZZZZUSA	
U	30	F	UNKNOWN	GRZZZZUSA		WOHLGENANNT, MARIE	17	F	UNKNOWN	GRZZZZUSA	
FRIEDR.	5	M	CHILD	GRZZZZUSA		MUELLER, MARIE	20	F	UNKNOWN	GRAFORUSA	
JOH.	7	M	CHILD	GRZZZZUSA		HEINE, PAULE.	40	F	UNKNOWN	GRADFSUSA	
CARL	4	M	CHILD	GRZZZZUSA		ZEISS, WOLFGANG	22	M	BKR	GRABODUSA	
AUGUSTE	3	F	CHILD	GRZZZZUSA		KERN, MARGA.	22	F	UNKNOWN	GRABODUSA	
FRIEDERIKE	.06	F	INFANT	GRZZZZUSA		KOEHLER, EVA	17	F	UNKNOWN	GRAENDUSA	
BOETTGER, FRIEDRICH	28	M	LLD	GRZZZZUSA		ROELLER, MARGA.	20	F	UNKNOWN	GRZZZZUSA	
RUSS, PAULINE	21	F	UNKNOWN	GRAEXWUSA		REITZ, JOHANN	63	M	LABR	GRABEDUSA	
ESRAEL, JETTE	31	F	UNKNOWN	GRAHRAUSA		PHILIPPINE	61	F	UNKNOWN	GRABEDUSA	
REES, JACOB	28	M	LABR	GRALZEUSA		ANNA	5	F	CHILD	GRABEDUSA	
BLEYEL, CARL	14	M	UNKNOWN	GRABEDUSA		WEITKAMP, JOHANNA	14	F	UNKNOWN	GRZZZZUSA	
BASTIAN, WILHE.	18	F	UNKNOWN	GRZZZZUSA		NEUDECKER, MAGDA.	20	F	UNKNOWN	GRZZZZUSA	
GLUECK, JOH.	63	M	FARMER	GRADFCUSA		BLESS, MARIE	60	F	UNKNOWN	GRAFRGUSA	
MARG.	64	F	UNKNOWN	GRADFCUSA		EDELHAEUSER, GEORG	23	M	BCHR	GRZZZZUSA	
LEWINSOHN, MINNA	29	F	UNKNOWN	GRZZZZUSA		BARBA.	26	F	UNKNOWN	GRZZZZUSA	
SIEGFRIED	.08	M	INFANT	GRZZZZUSA		RODEMANN, L.	42	M	LABR	GRABHUUSA	
HEYEMANN, ROSA	22	F	UNKNOWN	GRZZZZUSA		SCHEFFER, GEORG	14	M	UNKNOWN	GRADQLUSA	
FUNK, FRIDA	24	F	UNKNOWN	GRAEOFUSA		KOERBER, SOPHIE	23	F	UNKNOWN	GRZZZZUSA	
EISSLER, CHRISTE.	18	F	UNKNOWN	GRAEOFUSA		BRUTTEL, ANNA	21	F	UNKNOWN	GRZZZZUSA	
LIELINGER, ELISAB.	71	F	UNKNOWN	GRAETSUSA		HERMANN, ELIS.	21	F	UNKNOWN	GRZZZZUSA	
HARTMANN, ANNA	15	F	UNKNOWN	GRAETSUSA		HENZEL, ANNA	16	F	UNKNOWN	GRZZZZUSA	
NADLER, AGATHE	22	F	UNKNOWN	GRZZZZUSA		VOGT, EMMA	20	F	UNKNOWN	GRAECXUSA	
FISCHER, REGINA	20	F	UNKNOWN	GRZZZZUSA		JAKOBS, ANNA	21	F	UNKNOWN	GRADWUUSA	
EHSTAND, ODA	21	F	UNKNOWN	GRZZZZUSA		FOETISCH, FRIEDKE.	52	F	UNKNOWN	GRAHFLUSA	
JUNG, ANNA	19	F	UNKNOWN	GRAFNKUSA		STURSZ, MINA	23	F	UNKNOWN	GRADWFUSA	
JOH.	.03	M	INFANT	GRAFNKUSA		RUEDER, ELISAB.	56	F	UNKNOWN	GRACHBUSA	
STIGGEN, MEHLE	21	F	UNKNOWN	GRACIUUSA		WURSTER, FRIEDKE.	17	F	UNKNOWN	GRABPMUSA	
LEISS, CATHA.	25	F	UNKNOWN	GRZZZZUSA		FROHNAPFEL, OTTILIE	18	F	UNKNOWN	GRZZZZUSA	
CATHA.	2	F	CHILD	GRZZZZUSA		DOSSOW, CARL	70	M	LLD	GRAAKHUSA	
ZINK, JOHANN	32	M	BBR	GRAJAPUSA		DRECHSLER, FRIEDR.	14	M	UNKNOWN	GRADNRUSA	
KESSLER, MICH.	23	M	FARMER	GRZZZZUSA		MOELLER, THERESE	20	F	UNKNOWN	GRZZZZUSA	
EHSER, MECHTILDA	19	F	UNKNOWN	GRZZZZUSA		OTTO, JUSTUS	16	M	BBR	GRZZZZUSA	
SCHWEIZER, ROBERT	6	M	CHILD	GRZZZZUSA		REICHHOLD, MARIA	17	F	UNKNOWN	GRZZZZUSA	
STUMPF, JOHANNA	19	F	UNKNOWN	GRAFRGUSA		SCHLAMM, GABRIEL	21	M	MLR	GRZZZZUSA	
MEIX, FREDERICH	26	M	BCHR	GRABODUSA		STOLL, BERTHA	21	F	UNKNOWN	GRAEABUSA	
KICK, GEORG	16	M	SHMK	GRABODUSA		HOHMANN, GEORGE	26	M	LABR	GRADDNUSA	
LEDERER, GOTTFRIED	23	M	LABR	GRABODUSA		HEINR.	25	M	LABR	GRADDNUSA	
METER, CARL	21	M	LABR	GRABODUSA		DECHAND, LOUISE	61	F	UNKNOWN	GRAAKHUSA	
JUNG, MARGA.	7	F	CHILD	GRAFNKUSA		MAGDA.	24	F	UNKNOWN	GRAAKHUSA	
SCHMIDT, APOLONIA	29	F	UNKNOWN	GRABOQUSA		SCHLEICHER, BERNH.	17	M	UNKNOWN	GRZZZZUSA	
WILH.	7	M	CHILD	GRABOQUSA		OPITZ, ERNST	25	M	UNKNOWN	GRACXVUSA	
CARL	.11	M	INFANT	GRABOQUSA		KEIDEL, CRESCHISIA	23	F	UNKNOWN	GRZZZZUSA	
HILLMANN, CARL	27	M	CPTR	GRAEGYUSA		HERBST, VERONICA	14	F	UNKNOWN	GRZZZZUSA	
SESSLER, CARL	16	M	BKR	GRZZZZUSA		SHNEIDER, RUDOLF	22	M	LKSH	GRZZZZUSA	
MAIER, FRIEDR.	15	M	BKR	GRZZZZUSA		NEHRING, ULRICH	16	M	LABR	GRZZZZUSA	
FREITAG, CARL	17	M	FARMER	GRZZZZUSA		WARWAS, ALBERT	24	M	MCHT	GRZZZZUSA	
SERGEL, ANNA	22	F	UNKNOWN	GRAETWUSA		HENTSCHEL, ALEX	33	M	MCHT	GRZZZZUSA	
AUGUSTA	.11	F	INFANT	GRAETWUSA		POETZ, JOH.	18	M	LABR	GRAKVWUSA	
KOEPPKE, ADOLF	17	M	LABR	GRAETWUSA		DAHM, WILH.	25	M	CGRMKR	GRAARRUSA	
KROENER, WILHELM	15	M	FARMER	GRZZZZUSA		MEYER, CATHA.	23	F	UNKNOWN	GRAARRUSA	
KOKENWADEL, CARL	16	M	LABR	GRZZZZUSA		ANNA	3	F	CHILD	GRAARRUSA	
WIMPFHEIMER, LINA	19	F	UNKNOWN	GRACNAUSA		HEINR.	.10	M	INFANT	GRAARRUSA	
THREN, CHRISTINE	19	F	UNKNOWN	GRAERBUSA		EBERHARDT, JOH.	21	M	WTR	GRAFBGUSA	
NEUGEBAUER, MARIE	17	F	UNKNOWN	GRAGEKUSA		FRANZKA.	23	F	UNKNOWN	GRAFBGUSA	
KRUSE, FRIEDRICH	34	M	FARMER	GRZZZZUSA		FRANZ	15	M	UNKNOWN	GRAFBGUSA	
MARIE	31	F	UNKNOWN	GRZZZZUSA		LUTZ, MARIA	6	F	CHILD	GRAFBGUSA	
SOPHIE	7	F	CHILD	GRZZZZUSA		WOBBE, DIEDR.	16	M	LABR	GRZZZZUSA	
FRIEDR.	3	M	CHILD	GRZZZZUSA		NEES, WILH.	25	M	FARMER	GRAIFGUSA	
LOUISE	.09	F	INFANT	GRZZZZUSA		WEINGARTNER, CARL	17	M	FARMER	GRAIGHUSA	
BECKEMEYER, LOUISE	59	F	UNKNOWN	GRZZZZUSA		DORSNER, ED	17	M	FARMER	GRAIGHUSA	
HADCKE, SOPHIE	15	F	UNKNOWN	GRZZZZUSA		GOETZ, CARL	25	M	FARMER	GRAIGHUSA	
BOEHNE, WILHE.	16	F	UNKNOWN	GRZZZZUSA		FISCHER, ED.	17	M	FARMER	GRAIGHUSA	
TIMANN, CAROLE.	17	F	UNKNOWN	GRZZZZUSA		HUCK, ANDR.	25	M	FARMER	GRZZZZUSA	
WEIHE, FR.	18	M	WCHMKR	GRZZZZUSA		BERCHTHOLD, CAROLE.	18	F	UNKNOWN	GRZZZZUSA	

PASSENGER	AGE	SEX	OCCUPATION	PRVL DES
FISCHER, CARL	26	M	FARMER	GRZZZZUSA
SCHNEIDER, PAULE.	22	F	UNKNOWN	GRAHJSUSA
SEWADE, CHRE.	28	F	UNKNOWN	GRADNEUSA
SCHUSTER, MINNA	21	F	UNKNOWN	GRAESKUSA
JOSEF, FLORA	23	F	UNKNOWN	GRZZZZUSA
STUTZMANN, CARL	15	M	LABR	GRZZZZUSA
JACHTLEBEN, CARL	16	M	LABR	GRAEAYUSA
OTTO	14	M	LABR	GRAEAYUSA
MEYER, RUD.	15	M	LABR	GRAEAYUSA
PUEHLHORN, MAGDA.	20	F	UNKNOWN	GRAEDYUSA
WICH, PAULUS	23	M	SMH	GRZZZZUSA
HARTUNG, SUSANNA	32	F	UNKNOWN	GRAEQBUSA
SKIBBE, JOH.	25	M	LABR	GRZZZZUSA
BIK, CATHA.	30	F	UNKNOWN	GRZZZZUSA
RODEMANN, MARIE	36	F	UNKNOWN	GRABHUUSA
OSGAR	6	M	CHILD	GRABHUUSA
ARTHUR	7	M	CHILD	GRABHUUSA
LIESCHEN	5	F	CHILD	GRABHUUSA
ANGELICA	2	F	CHILD	GRABHUUSA
MARTHA	.09	F	INFANT	GRABHUUSA
WEINBERGER, LEONGARD	22	M	LABR	GRAAIEUSA
LOER, MARGA.	21	F	UNKNOWN	GRAAHBUSA
EHLERT, ALBERT	18	M	LABR	GRAEWMUSA
JOCKISCH, ANNA	27	F	UNKNOWN	GRABVEUSA
OHRLEIN, ADAM	28	M	FARMER	GRZZZZUSA
CATHA.	25	F	UNKNOWN	GRZZZZUSA
BABETTA	18	F	UNKNOWN	GRZZZZUSA
HERGET, MARIA	26	F	UNKNOWN	GRZZZZUSA
KRAM, JOS.	34	M	TLR	GRZZZZUSA
MAGDA.	28	F	UNKNOWN	GRZZZZUSA
WILH.	5	M	CHILD	GRZZZZUSA
EMIL	3	M	CHILD	GRZZZZUSA
CAROLA.	2	F	CHILD	GRZZZZUSA
MARIA	.11	F	INFANT	GRZZZZUSA
WALBOHM, JOHS.	18	M	CL	GRAESDUSA
KLEIN, JUL.	24	M	MCHT	GRZZZZUSA
POTRZEBA, ANTON	30	M	BKLYR	GRAAKHUSA
BLUM, EMIL	22	M	JNR	GRAARRUSA
MEDER, AUGE.	20	F	UNKNOWN	GRAEMTUSA
AVANNARY, FANNY	23	F	UNKNOWN	GRACSDUSA
IMMLER, LISETTE	25	F	UNKNOWN	GRACSDUSA
BEIER, ANNA	16	F	UNKNOWN	GRABZFUSA
BANZL, CARL	21	M	FARMER	GRZZZZUSA
VOELDER, CARL	27	M	FARMER	GRZZZZUSA
WUNSCH, HEINR.	35	M	FARMER	GRABNEUSA
DIETRICH, MARTHA	24	F	FARMER	GRABNEUSA
KNAUST, GEORGE	14	M	FARMER	GRABNEUSA
BANZL, WILH.	14	M	FARMER	GRABNEUSA
LIEGLEIN, FRANZ	22	M	FARMER	GRZZZZUSA
WINKLER, CARL	16	M	LABR	GRZZZZUSA
SCHNEIDER, HEINR.	69	M	LABR	BVZZZZUSA
WENDLER, MARGA.	18	F	UNKNOWN	BVZZZZUSA
SEIDEL, MARGA.	21	F	UNKNOWN	BVAFJNUSA
SCHWARZ, CARL	28	M	LABR	BVAKUMUSA
MUELLER, EMILIE	33	F	UNKNOWN	BVAKUMUSA
FRANKE, EMILIE	33	F	UNKNOWN	BVAKUMUSA
HERM.	7	M	CHILD	BVAKUMUSA
HULDA	6	F	CHILD	BVAKUMUSA
BRUNO	5	M	CHILD	BVAKUMUSA
LOUIS	3	M	CHILD	BVAKUMUSA
ANTONIE	4	F	CHILD	BVAKUMUSA
WILHELM	.11	M	INFANT	BVAKUMUSA
WUNDERLICH, FR.	17	M	TLR	BVACIJUSA
BORGER, RICHARD	26	M	WTR	BVACIJUSA
HACKER, SIMON	42	M	FARMER	BVACIJUSA
SEMMELMANN, CATHA.	19	F	UNKNOWN	BVAFWGUSA
RATH, JOHE.	21	F	UNKNOWN	GRZZZZUSA
JUNG, CHRISTOFFER	15	M	LABR	GRZZZZUSA
SIEMER, GESINE	28	F	UNKNOWN	GRAARRUSA
APPMANN, DORA	36	F	UNKNOWN	GRAEULUSA
KUEKENHOENER, JOHE.	20	F	UNKNOWN	GRZZZZUSA
ILLIGE, CARL	16	M	TLR	GRZZZZUSA
PITZING, ANNA	20	F	UNKNOWN	GRZZZZUSA
KAPMEIER, AUGE.	18	F	UNKNOWN	GRAEATUSA
RALL, MARIA	26	F	UNKNOWN	GRZZZZUSA
MAIRE, ALB.	16	M	LABR	GRZZZZUSA
SCHEFFEL, JAK.	15	M	LABR	GRZZZZUSA
BAUER, MARIE	30	F	UNKNOWN	GRZZZZUSA
ALVIN	13	M	UNKNOWN	GRZZZZUSA
MARIE	3	F	CHILD	GRZZZZUSA
SCHIA, JAK	46	M	MLR	GRZZZZUSA
ELISA	34	F	UNKNOWN	GRZZZZUSA
MARGA.	7	F	CHILD	GRZZZZUSA
CATHA.	6	F	CHILD	GRZZZZUSA
HEINR.	5	M	CHILD	GRZZZZUSA
HAAS, EM.	36	M	MCHT	GRAHLDUSA
ROSA	30	F	UNKNOWN	GRAHLDUSA
SCHNEIDER, AUG.	26	M	FARMER	GRAFTMUSA
TEEPE, WILH.	25	M	FARMER	GRZZZZUSA
FRIEDKE.	27	F	UNKNOWN	GRZZZZUSA
LINA	3	F	CHILD	GRZZZZUSA
FRIEDR.	.02	M	INFANT	GRZZZZUSA
WINDSAUER, JOSEF	32	M	UNKNOWN	GRAFBGUSA
SWOBODA, LOUISE	45	F	UNKNOWN	GRACBRUSA
RUDOLF	19	M	LABR	GRACBRUSA
WILH.	17	M	LABR	GRACBRUSA
ALLWINE	7	F	CHILD	GRACBRUSA
ELISE	5	F	CHILD	GRACBRUSA
APEL, AUG.	17	M	LABR	GRACBRUSA
SCHMIDT, THEOD.	33	M	BBR	GRAARRUSA
FAJEM, HENRY	24	M	FARMER	GRAJBUUSA
HILGERMANN, FRIEDR.	18	M	WTR	GRZZZZUSA
LAIG, ERNST	22	M	FARMER	GRADWFUSA
LORPER, MARGA.	22	F	UNKNOWN	GRAECKUSA
KOENIG, MATHAEUS	17	M	JNR	GRZZZZUSA
SCHUERMANN, G.	20	M	FARMER	GRZZZZUSA
AMMERMANN, META	7	F	CHILD	GRZZZZUSA
SCHNEIDER, JOHANNA	24	F	UNKNOWN	GRABFGUSA
AUER, MARGA.	18	F	UNKNOWN	GRZZZZUSA
STEINKE, EMILIE	20	F	UNKNOWN	GRAAKHUSA
BERGER, LOUIS	22	M	LABR	GRZZZZUSA
SZOCINSKA, MARIANNA	17	F	UNKNOWN	GRZZZZUSA
JOSEF	7	M	CHILD	GRZZZZUSA
LEFKOEICZ, JACOB	35	M	LABR	GRAFZGUSA
DURSKY, VICENTY	43	M	LABR	GRAEIOUSA
VONKAMPEN, MARGA.	26	F	UNKNOWN	GRACZVUSA
KATT, MARGARETHE	5	F	CHILD	GRACZVUSA
TURINSZKI, SAROLTA	29	F	UNKNOWN	GRAFKEUSA
VONRUMMEL, VICTOR	30	M	UNKNOWN	GRAARRUSA
KNOCKE, LOUIS	28	M	UNKNOWN	GRAARRUSA
BEHRENS, WM.	17	M	UNKNOWN	GRAARRUSA
MASSILGE, WILHELM	25	M	UNKNOWN	GRAARRUSA

SHIP: WISCONSIN

FROM: LIVERPOOL AND QUEENSTOWN
TO: NEW YORK
ARRIVED: 24 AUGUST 1888

PASSENGER	AGE	SEX	OCCUPATION	PRVL DES
LAMB, CARL	24	M	TLR	GRZZZZUSA
ITIZBACH, GEO.	18	M	TLR	GRZZZZUSA
BERSTEIN, SORI	18	M	PMBR	GRZZZZUSA
PANKE, JULIUS	51	M	FARMER	GRZZZZUSA
AUGUST	50	M	FARMER	GRZZZZUSA
ANNE	18	F	SP	GRZZZZUSA
MENDERSCHEID, CLARA	22	F	SP	GRZZZZUSA
ANNA	21	F	SP	GRZZZZUSA
RARER, ADOLPH	23	M	JNR	GRZZZZUSA
ROSENTHAL, SIMON	23	M	MSN	GRZZZZUSA
RIKLER, ISRAEL	.11	M	INFANT	GRZZZZUSA
OTTEN, HENDRIK	45	M	FARMER	GRZZZZUSA
ABELIC, GERARD	18	M	FARMER	GRZZZZUSA
LUPCHY, SAMUEL	26	M	TLR	GRZZZZUSA

PASSENGER	AGE	SEX	OCCUPATION	PRVL	DES

SHIP: CITY OF CHESTER

FROM: LIVERPOOL AND QUEENSTOWN
TO: NEW YORK
ARRIVED: 25 AUGUST 1888

PASSENGER	AGE	SEX	OCCUPATION	PRVL	DES
JERZAK, JOSEPH	23	M	CL	GRACBFIL	
EWALD, FRED.	32	M	INWKR	GRZZZZNY	
GINNEL, OTTO	25	M	TCHR	GRZZZZNY	
JACKSEN, LORENZO	18	F	SVNT	GRACJPMN	
STAFF, CHRISTINA	21	M	BCHR	GRACBFNY	
LUDWIG	26	M	BLKSMH	GRACBFNY	
LANSBERG, N.	26	M	FARMER	GRACBFIL	

SHIP: CIRCASSIA

FROM: GLASGOW AND MOVILLE
TO: NEW YORK
ARRIVED: 27 AUGUST 1888

PASSENGER	AGE	SEX	OCCUPATION	PRVL	DES
KOCH, EMIL	20	M	MCHT	GRZZZZUSA	
HARTMAN, MAX	30	M	MCHT	GRZZZZUSA	
U	27	F	W	GRZZZZUSA	
WEISS, LEUB	25	F	W	GRZZZZUSA	
ISRAEL	7	M	CHILD	GRZZZZUSA	
MANDEL	3	M	CHILD	GRZZZZUSA	
GOLOUENSKA, JOHANNA	17	F	HP	GRZZZZUSA	
LAUNE, VERGINIA	22	F	HP	GRZZZZUSA	
VONBRUSSEL, SCHOLASKA	45	F	W	GRZZZZUSA	
GUSTAV	11	M	UNKNOWN	GRZZZZUSA	
ANNA	9	F	CHILD	GRZZZZUSA	
MANCHE, HENRIETTE	51	F	W	GRZZZZUSA	
NIDELMAN, JOSEF	18	M	LABR	GRZZZZUSA	
PEIL, JOHAN	47	M	UNKNOWN	GRZZZZUSA	
SCHOLLTORN, FRANZ	24	M	FARMER	GRZZZZUSA	
ADLER, KARL	32	M	FLSH	GRZZZZUSA	
KLOTT, KARL	21	M	FLSH	GRZZZZUSA	
HESSELSHON, ABR.	21	M	DLR	GRZZZZUSA	
KNOTT, JOHANN	32	M	FARMER	GRZZZZUSA	
FACK, FRED	29	M	FARMER	GRZZZZUSA	
LAMSPACK, BALLHASAR	30	M	FARMER	GRZZZZUSA	
KUSIN, F	36	M	MCHT	GRZZZZUSA	

SHIP: DUPUY DE LOME

FROM: ANTWERP
TO: NEW ORLEANS
ARRIVED: 27 AUGUST 1888

PASSENGER	AGE	SEX	OCCUPATION	PRVL	DES
EDMOND, KERSTEN	17	M	BRR	GRZZZZNO	
ALPHONSE, CORDIER	43	M	MCHT	FRZZZZUNK	
ANBDRIES, CAROLINE	44	F	NN	FRZZZZUNK	
CORDIER, HORTENSE	20	F	NN	FRZZZZUNK	
RICHARD	16	M	CL	FRZZZZUNK	
ADELE	14	F	NN	FRZZZZUNK	
CLEMENT	11	M	CL	FRZZZZUNK	
DEVENO, WIDOW	55	F	SMSTS	FRZZZZUNK	
EDWARD	30	M	MCHT	FRZZZZUNK	
MOREL, LOUIS	29	M	FLST	FRZZZZUNK	
VERHEYST, CHARLOTTE	20	F	NN	FRZZZZUNK	
DISCHL-R, CAROLINE	46	F	NRS	GRZZZZNO	
MARIE	20	F	HRDRS	GRZZZZNO	
SOPHIE	15	F	NRS	GRZZZZNO	
AUGUST	11	M	CL	GRZZZZNO	

PASSENGER	AGE	SEX	OCCUPATION	PRVL	DES
ANNA	9	F	CHILD	GRZZZZNO	
MAGDALENA	7	F	CHILD	GRZZZZNO	
LOUISE	6	F	CHILD	GRZZZZNO	
MENI-, PAULINE	20	F	NN	GRZZZZUNK	
BAUER, KARL-JOHANN	17	M	LABR	GRZZZZNO	
CARL, JACOB	25	M	LABR	GRZZZZNO	
SCHEMPF, BERNARD	18	M	LABR	GRZZZZTX	
CORDIER, LEON	18	M	CL	FRZZZZCAL	
DURAND, PIERRE	38	M	BCHR	FRZZZZUNK	
ARSINE, DUBRENIL	28	M	BCHR	FRZZZZUNK	
MONLOV, EUGENE	22	M	CPR	FRZZZZUNK	
BEAUD, FRANCOIS	15	M	CL	FRZZZZUNK	
COURBOUS, FRANCOIS	23	M	MNR	FRZZZZUNK	
RUDELLE, BAPTISTE	26	M	CTW	FRZZZZUNK	
EUGENIE	34	F	HSKPR	FRZZZZUNK	
ADOLPHE	11	M	CH	FRZZZZUNK	
RITON, ETIENNE	29	M	TNR	FRZZZZUNK	
ABADIE, ARNAUD	19	M	CL	FRZZZZUNK	
CAZEAUS, JEAN-MARIE	37	M	BKR	FRZZZZUNK	
MOUNICON, MARIE-LOUISE	13	F	NRS	FRZZZZUNK	
LALANNE, ANNA	15	F	NRS	FRZZZZUNK	
CIRET, CATHERINE	16	F	NRS	FRZZZZUNK	
EUGENE	17	M	CL	FRZZZZUNK	
BERNARD	4	M	CHILD	FRZZZZUNK	
COUDURES, MARIE	20	F	NRS	FRZZZZUNK	
BRU, JUSTIN	17	M	CL	FRZZZZUNK	
LAHUT, PAUL	37	M	CPR	FRZZZZUNK	
JEANNE-MARIE	31	F	SMSTS	FRZZZZUNK	
MARIE	6	F	CHILD	FRZZZZUNK	
BONNABEAU, FRANCISCO	20	M	CCHMN	FRZZZZUNK	
DARETTE, JEAN-PAUL	22	M	CCHMN	FRZZZZUNK	
GALAN, GRAT	27	M	CPR	FRZZZZUNK	
BUSTARRET, JEAN	29	M	MSN	FRZZZZUNK	
MARIE	29	F	HSKPR	FRZZZZUNK	
LAHORE, EDOUARD	18	M	CL	FRZZZZUNK	
FABRE, JEAN	34	M	GDNR	FRZZZZUNK	
DOASSAN, COURREGE-JEAN	20	M	CCHMN	FRZZZZUNK	
BONNECAZE, BERNARD	22	M	CPR	FRZZZZUNK	
TROUILLET, PIERRE	23	M	GDNR	FRZZZZUNK	
CASENAVE, FRANCOIS	18	M	CL	FRZZZZUNK	
LOUSTALOT, PIERRE	37	M	BKR	FRZZZZUNK	
LATERRADE, PIERRE	38	M	SHMK	FRZZZZUNK	
MARGUERITE	36	F	HSKPR	FRZZZZUNK	
FANNER, JACOB	25	M	CPR	SRZZZZUNK	
BUTTIKOFER, EDOUARD	20	M	WHLR	SRZZZZUNK	
MONLONG, JEAN	30	M	SHMK	FRZZZZUNK	
MARIE	20	F	HSKPR	FRZZZZUNK	
JEAN-BAPTISTE	2	F	CHILD	FRZZZZUNK	
BOURTHOUB, CAMILLE	18	M	CL	FRZZZZUNK	
BERNADON, BAPTISTE	33	M	MSN	FRZZZZUNK	
LAURAY, PIERRE	18	M	CPTR	FRZZZZUNK	
GOURSAU, PIERRE	22	M	CPTR	FRZZZZUNK	
DORE, ISIDORE	40	M	GDNR	FRZZZZUNK	
JOURDAN, JACQUES	42	M	GDNR	FRZZZZUNK	
VARIOL, ANGELINE	37	F	HRDRS	FRZZZZNO	
ANDRE	14	M	CL	FRZZZZNO	
MARIE	13	F	CH	FRZZZZNO	
MICHEL	10	M	NN	FRZZZZNO	
LEON	7	M	CHILD	FRZZZZNO	
ANNA	9	M	CHILD	FRZZZZNO	

SHIP: EDAM

FROM: AMSTERDAM
TO: NEW YORK
ARRIVED: 27 AUGUST 1888

PASSENGER	AGE	SEX	OCCUPATION	PRVL	DES
STEINBERG, ROB	26	M	LABR	GRZZZZNY	
REIBER, ERNST	26	M	GDNR	GRZZZZNY	
MITTENDORF, FRIEDR	30	M	CPTR	GRZZZZNY	

293   .

PASSENGER	AGE	SEX	OCCUPATION	PRVL	DES
MARIA	21	F	NN		GRZZZZNY
VOST, JOHAN	27	M	CMMSR		GRZZZZNY
KRIMMERMAN, J	25	M	LABR		GRZZZZNY
MIREL	24	F	NN		GRZZZZNY
-TTE	1	F	CHILD		GRZZZZNY
ROSA	.03	F	INFANT		GRZZZZNY
IDING, HEINRICH	20	M	LABR		GRZZZZNY
BABIE, JOSEF	27	M	LABR		GRZZZZNY
BURDIN, H	21	M	LABR		GRZZZZNY
VELTMAN, FRIEDR	20	M	LABR		GRZZZZNY
SCHMIDT, KATHI	22	F	MSVNT		GRZZZZPIT
GERBERS, HERMAN	57	M	LABR		GRZZZZNY
THERESA	55	F	NN		GRZZZZNY
HERM	25	M	LABR		GRZZZZNY
A-IDA	23	F	MSVNT		GRZZZZNY
AUGUST	13	M	NN		GRZZZZNY
SCHWARZ, MAGDA	20	F	MSVNT		GRZZZZNY
BAUR, ROSINA	40	F	MSVNT		GRZZZZROC
CARL	19	M	TLR		GRZZZZROC
OTTO	15	M	TLR		GRZZZZROC
RUDOLF	13	M	NN		GRZZZZROC
JACOB	11	M	CH		GRZZZZROC
FREDERIKE	9	F	CHILD		GRZZZZROC
MARIA	7	F	CHILD		GRZZZZROC
CATHARINE	5	F	CHILD		GRZZZZROC
JOHANNES	3	M	CHILD		GRZZZZROC
JOHANNES	36	M	TLR		GRZZZZROC
LEIMS, MARIA	20	F	MSVNT		GRZZZZNY
ROLLE, JOHANNA	21	F	MSVNT		GRZZZZNY
ROLLAR, JACOB	27	M	LABR		GRZZZZNY
SCHLEICHER, JOSEF	16	M	LABR		GRZZZZNY
SCHWARZ, FRANZ	16	M	LABR		GRZZZZNY
LA--, PETER	26	M	LABR		GRZZZZNY
FA-ITH, CARL	14	M	LABR		GRZZZZNY
HERMAN, FRIEDR	16	M	PNTR		GRZZZZCH
REICHERT, PAULINE	25	F	NN		GRZZZZNY
AUGUST	4	M	CHILD		GRZZZZNY
EMIL	.03	M	INFANT		GRZZZZNY
MERTZ, SOPHIE	20	F	MSVNT		GRZZZZNY
KAPANITZ, JACOB	30	M	LABR		GRZZZZNY
JOHANNA	30	F	NN		GRZZZZNY
LEOPOLDINE	10	F	CH		GRZZZZNY
AMALIA	8	F	CHILD		GRZZZZNY
JOHANN	6	M	CHILD		GRZZZZNY
JACOB	3	M	CHILD		GRZZZZNY
JOHANNA	1	F	CHILD		GRZZZZNY
RUDOLF	.06	M	INFANT		GRZZZZNY
NOTAR, LUKAS	25	M	LABR		GRZZZZNY
ANTONIE	20	F	NN		GRZZZZNY
FERDINAND	1	M	CHILD		GRZZZZNY
EPLER, FRIEDR	24	M	LABR		GRZZZZNY
KUNZ, EVA	24	F	MSVNT		GRZZZZNY
KATHARINA	17	F	MSVNT		GRZZZZNY
JUTZI, KONRAD	21	M	LABR		GRZZZZNY
MAUER, HEINR	15	M	LABR		GRZZZZNY
STRAATMA--, SOPHIE	19	F	MSVNT		GRZZZZNY
MASCHETZ, VICTORIA	30	F	MSVNT		GRZZZZNY
HUMMEL, ROSINA	15	F	MSVNT		GRZZZZNY
SCHWEN-B--, BARBARA	17	F	MSVNT		GRZZZZNY
KRAUTER, CARL	18	M	SMH		GRZZZZNY
HEFER, JOSEFA	16	F	MSVNT		GRZZZZNY
HOLSTEIN, ALBERT	30	M	BKBNDR		SRZZZZNY
PIEPER, GEORGE	21	M	LABR		SRZZZZNY
SPRENGER, U	43	M	CHMKRR		FRZZZZNY
MO--EAN, M	35	M	MNTR		FRZZZZNY
CONTER-E, MARIA	00	F	NN		FRZZZZNY
SPEN-LER, BARBARA	52	F	NN		FRZZZZNY
BI-LER, ALBERT	23	M	CHMKRR		FRZZZZNY
LOUISE	28	F	NN		FRZZZZNY
JOHANNA	.05	F	INFANT		FRZZZZNY
LUENT, JOZEF	22	M	CHMKRR		FRZZZZNY
NEIDHARD, FRANZ	30	M	CHMKRR		FRZZZZNY
FAUTH, CATHARINE	60	F	NN		FRZZZZNY
DICH, PETER	21	M	LABR		FRZZZZNY
STIET, GRETCHES	24	F	MSVNT		GRZZZZNY
VOLZ, JOSEF	40	M	MCHT		GRZZZZNY
JUL-ES, HAHN	19	M	WRT		GRZZZZNY
BEE-, VICTOR	24	M	LABR		FRZZZZNY
HERBAIN, JOSEF	28	M	LABR		FRZZZZNY
BROEALLE, ENG	24	F	NN		FRZZZZNY
HENRI	.11	M	INFANT		FRZZZZNY
DO-NER, OSCAR	29	M	LABR		FRZZZZNY
V, EMILLE	28	M	LABR		FRZZZZNY
CLAUS, AUGUST	49	M	LABR		FRZZZZNY
BUNDER, MAX	20	M	LABR		GRZZZZNY
MELK--, HERMAN	22	M	LABR		GRZZZZNY
LATOUR, EMIL	22	M	BCHR		FRZZZZNY
BUDDER, PAUL	22	M	BRR		GRZZZZNY
JELINECK, ANT	28	M	MCHT		GRZZZZNY
MUEN-EL, JOSEF	25	M	FARMER		GRZZZZNY
STANNA, FR	21	M	MCHT		GRZZZZNY
HELLMUTH, G	35	M	MCHT		GRZZZZNY
STEINBERG, PAUL	20	M	STDNT		GRZZZZNY
PRITZE, A	23	M	STDNT		GRZZZZNY
SCHEPPER, B	00	M	NN		GRZZZZNY
THIEL, MARIA	00	F	NN		GRZZZZNY
PETERSEN, KUNO	00	M	NN		GRZZZZNY
IDA	00	F	NN		GRZZZZNY
SCHWEFELIN-, ADOLF	00	M	NN		GRZZZZNY
MILLER, CHARL	00	M	FARMER		GRZZZZNY
GEORGINA	00	F	NN		GRZZZZNY
ROEDER, PAULINE	00	F	NN		GRZZZZNY
DIEMER, CARL	10	M	CH		GRZZZZNY
DEGRENNE, HENRI	00	M	RE		FRZZZZNY
KOMPFE, MRS	00	F	NN		GRZZZZNY
FERNINE, MARIA	00	F	NN		GRZZZZNY
CALISANTICA, MARIA	00	F	NN		GRZZZZNY
CAROLA, MARIA	00	F	NN		GRZZZZNY
BASILA, MARIA	00	F	NN		GRZZZZNY
IMILDA, MARIA	00	F	NN		GRZZZZNY
EYRIKA, MARIA	00	F	NN		GRZZZZNY
PRISCA, MARIA	00	F	NN		GRZZZZNY
MARIANA, MARIA	00	F	NN		GRZZZZNY

SHIP: ELBE

FROM: BREMEN AND SOUTHAMPTON
TO: NEW YORK
ARRIVED: 28 AUGUST 1888

PASSENGER	AGE	SEX	OCCUPATION	PRVL	DES
STREIBELEIN, ERNST	8	M	CHILD		GRAAXKNY
SCHROEDER, EMILIE	49	F	UNKNOWN		GRACBRNY
BETTY	58	F	UNKNOWN		GRACBRNY
STURTZKOPF, ROBERT	36	M	TT		GRZZZZNY
MARGA.	35	F	TT		GRZZZZNY
FRIEDEMANN, HERM.	37	M	TT		GRACZWNY
GOLDHAMMER, U	37	M	TT		GRAAKHNY
NEES, FRIEDR.	8	M	CHILD		GRAFJGNY
CAROLINE	5	F	CHILD		GRAFJGNY
EULER, LOUIS	26	M	TT		GRAFJGNY
SAPPER, ---IS	00	M	TT		GRAFJGNY
THEIS, SANCHEN	20	F	TT		GRAFJGNY
ITZIG, JOH.	18	F	TT		GRAFJGNY
JOSEPH, TRINE	55	F	UNKNOWN		GRAFJGNY
WEHRFRITZ, AUGUSTE	25	M	TT		GRADUXNY
STERN, SALZ	16	M	TT		GRADUXNY
VOVNHOLZ, BERNH.	23	M	TT		GRADUXNY
GRUENKLEE, MAX	22	M	TT		GRADUXNY
COHEN, PAUL	21	M	TT		GRADUXNY
BENDHEIM, LE.P	17	M	TT		GRADUXNY
GRUENEBAUM, AMALIE	20	F	UNKNOWN		GRADUXNY
JARACZEWER, SALOM.	30	M	UNKNOWN		GRADUXNY
ROEMKE, HUGO	40	M	UNKNOWN		GRADUXNY
BOERNER, HANS	28	M	TT		GRADBDNY
GOEGGEL, AUGUST	16	M	TT		GRZZZZNY

294

PASSENGER	AGE	SEX	OCCUPATION	PRVVL DES
MAHR, LINA	26	F	TT	GRAAHBNY
ANNA	7	F	CHILD	GRAAHBNY
BECK, ANNA	25	F	CH	GRAAHBNY
BLLUMMENSTENGEL, ROB.	27	M	TT	GRAARRNY
REH, EMIL	27	M	TT	GRAARRNY
FRIEBE, CARL	23	M	TT	GRAARRNY
SCHWARZENBERGER, S.	26	M	TT	GRAARRNY
LAU, EVELIN	28	F	TT	GRAARRNY
KUETT, MARG.	68	F	TT	GRAARRNY
WACKER, EMILIE	39	F	TT	GRAARRNY
PAUL	9	M	CHILD	GRAARRNY
WEBER, JOHANNE	17	F	UNKNOWN	GRAARRNY
LOEWNTHAL, LEOPOLD	16	M	TT	GRAARRNY
WETZFELD, WILHELLM	26	M	TT	GRAARRNY
FRIEDLAENDER, LAURA	21	F	TT	GRAARRNY
HENNE, RICH.	31	M	TT	GRAARRNY
MAAG, KATH.	14	F	UNKNOWN	GRZZZZNY
ALOIS	10	M	CH	GRZZZZNY
MANN, CARL	9	M	CHILD	GRZZZZNY
APMANN, HANNY	36	M	FARMER	GRAARRNY
BISCHOFF, HEINR.	16	M	FARMER	GRAAABNY
APMANN, CARL	16	M	FARMER	GRAAABNY
HUENEKE, ELISE	15	F	FARMER	GRAAABNY
HINZ, HENRIETTE	39	F	UNKNOWN	GRAAABNY
HERMANN	11	M	UNKNOWN	GRAAABNY
ANNA	3	F	CHILD	GRAAABNY
WILHEL.	.01	F	INFANT	GRAAABNY
WILEBINSKY, MARJANNY	18	F	INF	GRAAABNY
KESSLER, AUGUST	16	M	LABR	GRAAABNY
KACZMARK, JAN	22	M	SHMK	GRZZZZNY
DOGES, FRIEDR.	18	M	TLR	GRZZZZNY
NIKLIS, ANNA	28	F	UNKNOWN	GRAARZNY
ERICH	.07	M	INFANT	GRAARZNY
WEWINSKY, ZOFIA	18	F	UNKNOWN	GRZZZZNY
KOHNS, BERH.	32	M	LABR	GRZZZZNY
CLARA	28	F	UNKNOWN	GRZZZZNY
STIEBRITZ, EMILIE	46	F	UNKNOWN	GRADHENY
MARTHA	20	F	UNKNOWN	GRADHENY
RUDOLF	4	M	CHILD	GRADHENY
SUNDERER, ANA	15	F	UNKNOWN	GRZZZZNY
BARBARA	6	F	CHILD	GRZZZZNY
HOENS, JOHANN	19	M	UNKNOWN	GRADLCNY
ORDING, ADELH.	18	F	UNKNOWN	GRADLCNY
PILCHOWSKA, MARG.	23	F	UNKNOWN	GRZZZZNY
WALENZA	2	F	CHILD	GRZZZZNY
WEDEL, ANNA	28	F	UNKNOWN	GRZZZZNY
GEORG	.01	M	INFANT	GRZZZZNY
LEITNER, ULRICH	32	M	BRR	GRZZZZNY
SCHMIDT, HELENE	17	F	UNKNOWN	GRADZVNY
MALTER, MARGARETHE	22	F	UNKNOWN	GRADZVNY
GOLDSCHMIDT, JETTE	37	F	UNKNOWN	GRADZVNY
MEYER	.05	M	INFANT	GRADZVNY
BROEDEL, SELMA	17	F	UNKNOWN	GRZZZZNY
ZOBISCH, CARL	14	M	LABR	GRAJTDNY
AUGUSTE	18	F	UNKNOWN	GRAJTDNY
DUBE, HANNA	44	F	UNKNOWN	GRZZZZNY
LEHMANN, MARIA	21	F	UNKNOWN	GRZZZZNY
ERNST	11	M	CH	GRZZZZNY
LANGENDORF, FRIED.	24	M	BCHR	GRZZZZNY
WIEGAND, HELENE	23	F	UNKNOWN	GRZZZZNY
JOSEF	.11	M	INFANT	GRZZZZNY
BARTELS, CHR.	61	M	LABR	GRACXENY
CARL	11	M	UNKNOWN	GRACXENY
SAUER, MICH.	26	M	SHMK	GRZZZZNY
EICHHORN, MARIE	22	F	UNKNOWN	GRZZZZNY
RAAB, KATH.	20	F	UNKNOWN	GRZZZZNY
RICKER, PAULINE	21	F	UNKNOWN	GRZZZZNY
CARL	14	M	UNKNOWN	GRZZZZNY
MOEGELE, GEORG	38	M	LABR	GRZZZZNY
GOTTB.	15	M	LABR	GRZZZZNY
BEER, ALBERT	30	M	UNKNOWN	GRZZZZNY
WAGNER, ROSINE	20	F	UNKNOWN	GRZZZZNY
DIGEL, GOTTL.	18	M	TCHR	GRZZZZNY
BLANKENHORN, CATH.	21	F	UNKNOWN	GRAEZONY
KUEBLER, GOTTL.	25	M	LABR	GRAEZONY
SCHEUTFERLE, JOH.	22	M	LABR	GRZZZZNY
MAILER, U	26	F	UNKNOWN	GRZZZZNY
STEPHAN, JOH.	29	M	LABR	GRZZZZNY
RIEKERT, ANNA	18	F	UNKNOWN	GRAEZONY
BAUER, DOROTHEA	16	F	UNKNOWN	GRAEZONY
MAIER, AGNES	18	F	UNKNOWN	GRAEZONY
TALMON, CARL	16	M	SMH	GRAEXWNY
NONNE, HEINR.	18	M	CPR	GRAEXWNY
WOELFLE, LEO	25	M	CPR	GRAEXWNY
LUCKNER, MARIE	34	F	UNKNOWN	GRAEXWNY
FRIEDR.	10	F	CH	GRAEXWNY
EBER, ANNA	18	F	UNKNOWN	GRZZZZNY
RIETHEMMER, FRIEDRIKE	13	F	UNKNOWN	GRZZZZNY
SCHLOTZ, HERM.	14	M	UNKNOWN	GRADIRNY
BARTHOLD, OTTOMAR	23	M	LABR	GRZZZZNY
ALBERS, JOH.	27	M	LABR	GRZZZZNY
DUERR, CATH.	23	F	UNKNOWN	GRZZZZNY
VOELKER, BARB.	24	F	UNKNOWN	GRZZZZNY
KUECHENBRODT, SUSANNE	20	F	UNKNOWN	GRZZZZNY
DEMMERLEIN, CATH.	33	F	UNKNOWN	GRZZZZNY
MARIE	.09	F	INFANT	GRZZZZNY
HOFFMANN, JOH.	16	M	LABR	GRZZZZNY
STRICKER, KATH.	23	M	UNKNOWN	GRZZZZNY
HAEHNLEIN, CAROLINE	18	F	UNKNOWN	GRZZZZNY
KORNBECHER, MARG.	32	M	UNKNOWN	GRZZZZNY
FERD.	9	F	CHILD	GRZZZZNY
JOH.	8	M	CHILD	GRZZZZNY
MARIE	2	F	CHILD	GRZZZZNY
BARTHOLD, RICHARD	18	F	CPR	GRADIRNY
MARKERT, BARB.	24	F	UNKNOWN	GRADLDNY
BRANDT, THEOD.	23	M	BRR	GRADLDNY
REYNKEN, FRIEDR.	18	M	FARMER	GRAELGNY
HOHLWECK, WUIRIN	18	M	FARMER	GRZZZZNY
KUEHN, BERNH.	40	M	TLR	GRZZZZNY
HORSTMANN, HEINR.	15	M	LABR	GRZZZZNY
KRETNER, HEINR.	16	M	LABR	GRZZZZNY
RAISS, JOH.	19	M	CPR	GRAFITNY
ANGEMANN, PAUL	24	M	LABR	GRAAKHNY
KOHR, MARIE	21	F	UNKNOWN	GRAHVMNY
GERSTNER, REINHOLD	26	M	LABR	GRZZZZNY
HENKEL, ADAM	35	M	LABR	GRZZZZNY
REITZ, JOH.	28	M	LABR	GRZZZZNY
C.	19	M	LABR	GRZZZZNY
FRANK, CARL	17	M	LABR	GRZZZZNY
LAURI, ROSIE	15	F	UNKNOWN	GRZZZZNY
DALLMUS, FRIEDR.	16	M	UNKNOWN	GRZZZZNY
KULASEWICZ, VALENTIN	23	M	CPR	GRZZZZNY
KOZYCZKOWSKI, AUG.	20	M	UNKNOWN	GRZZZZNY
KREUZFELD, ANNA	19	F	UNKNOWN	GRAHWXNY
KOZYCZKOWSKI, MARIE	11	F	UNKNOWN	GRZZZZNY
LANGE, JACOB	53	M	SMH	GRACNZNY
WILHELMINE	49	F	UNKNOWN	GRACNZNY
BERTHA	17	F	UNKNOWN	GRACNZNY
EMIL	14	M	UNKNOWN	GRACNZNY
ANNA	9	F	CHILD	GRACNZNY
GUST.	6	M	CHILD	GRACNZNY
JAHN, ANNA	83	F	UNKNOWN	GRADWXNY
PFROMMER, CHRISTINE	19	F	UNKNOWN	GRADWXNY
FASS, EMILIE	21	F	UNKNOWN	GRADWXNY
ERHORN, FR.	20	M	UNKNOWN	GRABOQIA
FILBERT, NICOL.	21	M	TLR	GRADWFIA
REHLING, WILH.	25	M	BKLYR	GRADWFIA
NIEDERILAGE, FRANZ	30	M	FARMER	GRADWFOH
GERLING, ANNA	22	F	UNKNOWN	GRAFQVOH
WIEDEMANN, ANNA	23	F	UNKNOWN	GRZZZZOH
GUMPERT, PAULINE	46	F	UNKNOWN	GRADGKOH
LOUISE	14	F	UNKNOWN	GRADGKOH
GUTTMANN, EMILIE	15	F	UNKNOWN	GRADGKOH
SCHWARZLAENDER, MICHAEL	22	M	FARMER	GRADGKOH
HARTMANN, FRIEDR.	63	M	FARMER	GRACBROH
ANNA	63	F	UNKNOWN	GRACBROH
WILHELM	26	M	UNKNOWN	GRACBROH
MARIE	20	F	UNKNOWN	GRACBROH
POHLMANN, HENRIETTE	65	F	UNKNOWN	GRACBROH
AULBERT, HEINR.	15	M	FARMER	GRACBROH

PASSENGER	AGE	SEX	OCCUPATION	PRVL	DES
BEISKER, KAROLINE	25	F	UNKNOWN		GRZZZZNY
MENDLER, CHRIST.	27	M	UNKNOWN		GRAADWPA
HARST, JACOB	19	M	BKR		GRZZZZPA
FUNK, GEORG	15	M	BKR		GRZZZZPA
JOH.	9	M	CHILD		GRZZZZPA
WAGNER, ELISABETH	21	F	UNKNOWN		GRZZZZPA
FRIEDMANN, ANNA	18	F	UNKNOWN		GRZZZZNY
WEILER, FRANZ	23	M	LABR		GRZZZZNY
SPOERER, ANDR.	56	M	FARMER		GRZZZZNY
MARIE	49	F	UNKNOWN		GRZZZZNY
KLOTZER, HENRIETTE	17	F	FARMER		GRZZZZIL
WICH, CHRISTIANA	18	F	FARMER		GRZZZZIL
KLOETZER, JOH.	30	M	FARMER		GRZZZZIL
NAGEL, ERNST	24	M	JNR		GRZZZZIL
KREISS, LUDW.	21	M	JNR		GRABSONY
BREHM, BABETTA	29	F	UNKNOWN		GRZZZZNY
MAGD.	3	F	CHILD		GRZZZZNY
JOH.	.11	M	INFANT		GRZZZZNY
SCHREINER, KATH.	17	F	UNKNOWN		GRZZZZNY
KUNTZ, GEORG	30	M	LABR		GRALBLNY
HEINE, FRIEDR.	32	M	LABR		GRACHANY
BERTHA	28	F	LABR		GRACHANY
BERTHA	4	F	CHILD		GRACHANY
LENA	2	F	CHILD		GRACHANY
ERNST	.11	M	INFANT		GRACHANY
LINDER, IDA	20	F	UNKNOWN		GRALKAPA
WALTHER, JOHANN	8	M	CHILD		GRALKANY
RICH.	7	M	CHILD		GRALKANY
ANNA	5	F	CHILD		GRALKANY
ANNA	2	F	CHILD		GRALKANY
BARBARA	28	F	UNKNOWN		GRALKANY
U	34	M	LABR		GRALKANY
CAROLINE	32	F	UNKNOWN		GRALKANY
SCHWEIZER, CAROLINE	17	F	UNKNOWN		GRZZZZNY
HARTMANN, CATH.	16	F	UNKNOWN		GRABSONY
GEY, ERNST	21	M	BCHR		GRAARRNY
KAPPELMANN, SOPHIE	17	F	UNKNOWN		GRZZZZNY
DOHRMANN, MINNA	17	F	UNKNOWN		GRZZZZNY
GRAMS, AUGUSTE	16	F	UNKNOWN		GRZZZZNY
FRANK, THERESE	20	F	UNKNOWN		GRZZZZNY
TOEN, JOH.	20	M	FARMER		GRZZZZNY
NOLD, LEO	16	M	UNKNOWN		GRZZZZNY
UNZER, LUDWIG	17	M	UNKNOWN		GRZZZZNY
NOLD, OSWALD	30	M	LLD		GRZZZZNY
GOETZ, ROSE	26	F	UNKNOWN		GRZZZZNY
FETTIG, JOHANNE	60	F	UNKNOWN		GRZZZZNY
SOPHIE	21	F	UNKNOWN		GRZZZZNY
MAIER, ROSA	18	F	UNKNOWN		GRZZZZNY
JUNG, CAROLINE	20	F	UNKNOWN		GRZZZZNY
FISCHER, GOTTLIEB	16	M	UNKNOWN		GRZZZZNY
RICHARD, HEINR.	40	M	FARMER		GRZZZZOH
ELISE	40	F	FARMER		GRZZZZOH
HEIN.	15	M	FARMER		GRZZZZOH
MARIE	11	F	UNKNOWN		GRZZZZOH
GERTRUD	6	F	CHILD		GRZZZZOH
PETER	4	M	CHILD		GRZZZZOH
KUEMPEL, JACOB	15	M	CPR		GRZZZZOH
KIRSCHENBAUER, VICTORIA	22	F	UNKNOWN		GRZZZZIL
WICKENKAMP, DIEDR.	38	M	FARMER		GRZZZZNE
MARIE	32	F	UNKNOWN		GRZZZZNE
DIEDR.	10	M	CH		GRZZZZNE
MARIE	9	F	CHILD		GRZZZZNE
HEINR.	3	F	CHILD		GRZZZZNE
MICHAL, MARIE	17	F	UNKNOWN		GRZZZZNE
EDELBROCK, WILHELM	24	M	LABR		GRZZZZNE
ALTMANN, KATHIE	24	F	UNKNOWN		GRZZZZNE
BRANDINNEIER, MARIE	19	F	UNKNOWN		GRZZZZNY
SAUER, MARIA	9	F	CHILD		GRZZZZNY
WIEDER, MARG.	26	F	CH		GRZZZZNY
BARB.	.11	F	INFANT		GRZZZZNY
ROESE, JOSEF	26	M	LABR		GRZZZZNY
GEROSCH, JOHANNE	16	F	UNKNOWN		GRZZZZNY
FRIESEN, AUGUSTE	10	F	CH		GRZZZZNY
GERKEN, ANNA	18	F	UNKNOWN		GRACBRNY
SCHULD, ARNOLD	15	M	LABR		GRACBRNY
RICKHORN, MARIE	25	F	UNKNOWN		GRACBRNY
HEIN.	16	M	UNKNOWN		GRACBRNY
LEUMANN, ANNA	23	F	UNKNOWN		GRZZZZNY
GROSS, NATALI	23	F	UNKNOWN		GRZZZZNY
ED.	3	M	CHILD		GRZZZZNY
OBERMUELLER, BARBRA	23	F	UNKNOWN		GRZZZZNY
SCHUMACHER, FRANZ	30	M	LABR		GRAKVVNY
EBERHARD, JAC.	24	M	CPTR		GRZZZZNY
LAMKE, JOH.	17	M	CPTR		GRZZZZNY
WAETJEN, HERM.	16	M	CPTR		GRZZZZNY
HUMBRECHT, MARIE	26	F	UNKNOWN		GRZZZZROC
GOEDE, ROSINE	46	F	UNKNOWN		GRZZZZROC
MARTHA	9	F	CHILD		GRZZZZROC
ENICO	3	F	CHILD		GRZZZZROC
SCHULZ, ADOLF	24	M	UNKNOWN		GRZZZZIL
MINNA	21	F	UNKNOWN		GRZZZZIL
KUNKE, ANNA	14	F	UNKNOWN		GRZZZZIL
BOROWIAK, STANISLAUS	28	M	TLR		GRZZZZBUF
ANNA	22	F	UNKNOWN		GRZZZZBUF
HELENE	.04	F	INFANT		GRZZZZBUF
HAAS, JOH.	29	M	LABR		GRZZZZOH
GENOFERA, JUNG	20	F	UNKNOWN		GRZZZZIL
SEEFRIED, GREGOR	15	M	LABR		GRAAIEPA
BECK, FRIEDR.	19	M	LABR		GRAAIEPA
SCHMIDT, WILH.	18	M	LABR		GRAAIEPA
FRIEDR.	19	M	LABR		GRAAIEPA
FRIEDR.	16	M	LABR		GRAAIEPA
RICHELMANN, HEINR.	29	M	DLR		GRALEZPA
NEIDHARDT, GEORG	17	M	DLR		GRAAMYPA
PFITZNER, FERD.	34	M	DLR		GRAAMYPA
SCHOTT, JOS.	14	M	UNKNOWN		GRABKVNY
EBERT, ALOIS	14	M	UNKNOWN		GRABKVNY
WEIGERT, JOH.	26	M	UNKNOWN		GRABKVNY
SEITZ, MARIE	25	F	UNKNOWN		GRABKVNY
WEIGERT, JOHANNE	19	F	UNKNOWN		GRABKVNY
ROOS, BERTHA	20	F	UNKNOWN		GRADYYNY
FRANKE, FRIEDRIKE	00	F	UNKNOWN		GRADYYNY
SAPHIRSTEIN, ISIDOR	00	M	UNKNOWN		GRADYYNY
WOLF, PAUL	00	M	UNKNOWN		GRADYYNY
GRUENWALD, MARIE	00	F	UNKNOWN		GRADYYNY
ZARGE, CHRISTIAN	37	M	LABR		GRZZZZNY
OLSCHEWSKY, SIMON	28	M	LABR		GRZZZZNY
OETJEN, JOS.	16	M	LABR		GRZZZZNY
HORNUNG, PAUL	15	M	LABR		GRZZZZNY
PAUL	7	M	CHILD		GRZZZZNY
FOCKE, ARTHUR	10	M	CH		GRZZZZNY
PETERS, L.	23	M	CH		GRZZZZNY

SHIP: GELLERT

FROM: HAMBURG AND HAVRE
TO: NEW YORK
ARRIVED: 28 AUGUST 1888

PASSENGER	AGE	SEX	OCCUPATION	PRVL	DES
HARTUNG, CARL	18	M	MCHT		HBZZZZUSA
THUMB, FRANZ	22	M	MCHT		HBZZZZUSA
BEHR, ANNA	55	F	WO		HBAADEUSA
MEINKE, BERTHA	19	F	SGL		MKZZZZUSA
GERSTENKORN, EDUARD	22	M	FARMER		PRZZZZUSA
HILMERS, FERD.	22	M	JNR		PRAEDSUSA
MUELLER, WILH.	69	M	CMST		HBZZZZUSA
NIELSEN, CATH.	57	F	WO		HBABZSUSA
CARL	18	M	WTR		HBABZSUSA
PETERSEN, MARGA	24	F	SGL		HBACKYUSA
JANZEN, FRIEDRICH	34	M	LKSH		HBAFJIUSA
STAHLER, ERNESTINE	19	F	SGL		HBAAHUUSA
LOMBROWSKA, MARIE	20	F	SGL		PRZZZZUSA
MANNES, CARL	15	M	GZR		PRAFRBUSA
HUFELD, LOUISE	16	F	SGL		PRZZZZUSA
GENDEK, MARIANNE	24	F	WO		PRZZZZUSA

PASSENGER	AGE	SEX	OCCUPATION	PRVVL	DES
MICHAEL	.11	M	INFANT	PRZZZZ	USA
GROSSMANN, FRIEDR.	18	M	LABR	PRZZZZ	USA
PETERS, MARIE	20	F	SGL	HBZZZZ	USA
SCHELLHAAS, KATH	21	F	SGL	PRZZZZ	USA
BOUZIEL, RUDOLF	30	M	LKSH	PRZZZZ	USA
BERTHA	32	F	W	PRZZZZ	USA
ERICH	5	M	CHILD	PRZZZZ	USA
WALTHER	4	M	CHILD	PRZZZZ	USA
RUDOLF	.11	M	INFANT	PRZZZZ	USA
LEVY, CLARA	20	F	SGL	PRAEEP	USA
BRETTSCHNEIDER, LOUISE	22	F	SGL	SYZZZZ	USA
SCOPPE, ERNST	54	M	BKR	SYAAXK	USA
OCHMICHEN, ADOLF	40	M	BLKSMH	SYAENF	USA
SCHERWITZ, JOH.	32	M	FARMER	SYAFAB	USA
JANSEN, CLARA	16	F	SGL	SYACKY	USA
SAEHN, JOSS	21	M	LABR	PRZZZZ	USA
HENTSCHEL, MATHILDE	30	F	WO	PRZZZZ	USA
OSWALD	8	M	CHILD	PRZZZZ	USA
RICHARD	5	M	CHILD	PRZZZZ	USA
NIPOMINISCHTSCHI, NOECH	30	M	TLR	PRZZZZ	USA
GUTHNECHS, WILH.	40	M	FARMER	PRZZZZ	USA
AUGUSTE	39	F	W	PRZZZZ	USA
HERM.	19	M	W	PRZZZZ	USA
HELENE	16	F	CH	PRZZZZ	USA
ALBERT	14	M	CH	PRZZZZ	USA
IDA	12	F	CH	PRZZZZ	USA
WILH.	8	M	CHILD	PRZZZZ	USA
ANNA	7	F	CHILD	PRZZZZ	USA
ROB.	6	M	CHILD	PRZZZZ	USA
MARTHA	4	F	CHILD	PRZZZZ	USA
WEGNER, AUGUSTE	70	F	WO	PRZZZZ	USA
TEBERT, LOUISE	26	F	SGL	SYZZZZ	USA
FRICKE, LUDWIG	23	M	BKR	SYACQU	USA
HANG, JOH.	25	M	BLKSMH	WMZZZZ	USA
HECK, CHRISTINE	20	F	SGL	WMZZZZ	USA
NETH, AGNES	32	F	SGL	WMACDU	USA
FAHRION, AUGUST	25	M	BCHR	WMZZZZ	USA
BEYROW, FERD.	27	M	LABR	WMAGMJ	USA
ANNA	27	F	W	WMAGMJ	USA
HELENE	4	F	CHILD	WMAGMJ	USA
ERDMANN	3	M	CHILD	WMAGMJ	USA
MARIE	.11	F	INFANT	WMAGMJ	USA
FRIEDRICH	.01	M	INFANT	WMAGMJ	USA
GLEITSMANN, FRANZ	19	M	LABR	WMACAW	USA
WINKELMANN, JOSEPHA	16	F	SGL	PRZZZZ	USA
MUELLER, KARL	16	M	LABR	SYZZZZ	USA
BUSKER, ABEL	49	M	SLR	SYZZZZ	USA
JACOB	13	M	CH	SYZZZZ	USA
ALTMAN	8	M	CHILD	SYZZZZ	USA
GERHARD	7	M	CHILD	SYZZZZ	USA
LUKKEA	6	F	CHILD	SYZZZZ	USA
GESSINA	2	F	CHILD	SYZZZZ	USA
FRANZEN, HERMANDINE	21	F	WO	SYAADE	USA
KESSLER, CARL	28	M	LABR	HSZZZZ	USA
JENSEN, CARL	70	M	FARMER	PRZZZZ	USA
THEDENS, MAGDALENE	19	F	SGL	PRZZZZ	USA
BARGHUSEN, JOH.	25	M	CPTR	HBZZZZ	USA
STAHL, PETER	18	M	LABR	PRZZZZ	USA
HOLST, MARIE	27	F	WO	PRZZZZ	USA
MARCUS	6	M	CHILD	PRZZZZ	USA
FOERSTER, ANNA	34	F	SGL	PRZZZZ	USA
WIRTH, HERMANN	25	M	LABR	PRZZZZ	USA
MARIE	22	F	W	PRZZZZ	USA
FRANZISKA	1	F	CHILD	PRZZZZ	USA
FENGLER, ANNA	59	F	WO	PRZZZZ	USA
ERDMANN, RUDOLF	23	M	LABR	PRADEN	USA
ROSINE	56	F	W	PRADEN	USA
JUNGE, FRAN.	17	M	LABR	PRAHXE	USA
SCHROEDER, FRIEDR.	15	M	LABR	PRAHXE	USA
CORDS, EMMA	18	F	SGL	PRAAKH	USA
THIELKE, ERNST	24	M	JNR	PRAAKH	USA
BECKER, HEINR.	22	M	MCHT	PRAAKH	USA
QUAS, AUGUSTE	29	F	SGL	PRAAKH	USA
STOLL, HUGO	25	M	MUSN	PRAAKH	USA
SCHULTZE, HERRMAN	36	M	MUSN	PRAAKH	USA
KRAPP, MAX	28	M	LKSH	PRADZO	USA
ALBRECHT, BARBARA	21	F	SGL	PRAATV	USA
HONECK, KATHARINE	19	F	SGL	PRAATV	USA
HECKMANN, BARBARA	19	F	SGL	PRAATV	USA
HOFFMANN, JOH.	21	M	LABR	PRAATV	USA
MESSERSCHMIDT, GUSTAV	16	M	SMH	BDZZZZ	USA
HESS, ELISE	17	F	SGL	BDAHIT	USA
MESSERSCHMIDT, FREDRIKE	23	F	WO	BDAHIT	USA
HERTEL, MATHAEUS	30	M	FARMER	WMZZZZ	USA
CATH.	26	F	W	WMZZZZ	USA
CARL	3	M	CHILD	WMZZZZ	USA
EMILIE	.03	F	INFANT	WMZZZZ	USA
MESSERSCHMIDT, RUD.	37	M	FARMER	WMZZZZ	USA
KRUMM, CHRISTIAN	31	M	FARMER	WMZZZZ	USA
DESPANG, BRUNO	18	M	CGRMKR	WMABOK	USA
NISSEL, JULIUS	19	M	BBR	WMAEDF	USA
LESSMANN, WALDDEMAR	26	M	SLR	WMAAZQ	USA
WIEDEL, DOROTHEA	16	F	SGL	BVZZZZ	USA
MOHR, BERTHA	18	F	SGL	PRZZZZ	USA
FERBER, AUGUST	31	M	LKSH	PRABDM	USA
FLORA	32	F	W	PRABDM	USA
CURT	6	M	CHILD	PRABDM	USA
GERTRUD	4	F	CHILD	PRABDM	USA
WIEHN, CATHA.	40	F	WO	PRAJSM	USA
ANNA	17	F	CH	PRAJSM	USA
FRIEDR	8	M	CHILD	PRAJSM	USA
NICOLAUS	7	M	CHILD	PRAJSM	USA
CARL	5	M	CHILD	PRAJSM	USA
SEILER, AGNES	19	F	SGL	PRAAYS	USA
WINTER, CLARA	8	F	CHILD	PRAAYS	USA
FEIBEL, MATHILDE	19	F	SGL	PRACTQ	USA
STAUSS, KARL	21	M	BRR	WMZZZZ	USA
GROSSKOPF, JULIANE	16	F	SGL	WMACBF	USA
WEHLING, WILH.	68	M	LABR	PRZZZZ	USA
MARG.	62	F	W	PRZZZZ	USA
BRANDT, AMANDA	28	F	SGL	PRAADE	USA
BROSZEIT, KAROLINE	37	F	SGL	PRZZZZ	USA
FLESCHEL, JOHN	23	M	LABR	PRAFVV	USA
GERECKE, FRITZ	26	M	PRNTR	BWZZZZ	USA
WEINSCHMANN, REINHARDT	22	M	LABR	BWADNN	USA
HOMBURGER, CARL	23	M	MCHT	PRZZZZ	USA
SIMON, JOHANN	60	M	LABR	PRZZZZ	USA
JULIUS	43	M	LABR	PRZZZZ	USA
LOUISE	47	F	W	PRZZZZ	USA
HAAN, EDUARD	16	M	MCHT	PRAINK	USA
RAAWE, CHRISTIAN	25	M	LABR	SYZZZZ	USA
SCHWEISSINGER, AUG.	23	M	LABR	SYAFAB	USA
SALOMUN, AGNES	35	F	SGL	HBZZZZ	USA
HOPPMANN, SOPHIE	18	F	SGL	BWZZZZ	USA
GUHL, WILH.	34	M	TNM	PRZZZZ	USA
COHN, MARTIN	18	M	MCHT	PRZZZZ	USA
KUNERT, JENNY	31	F	SGL	PRZZZZ	USA
GUSTAFSON, WILH.	36	M	LABR	PRAADE	USA
WEISS, WOLFGANG	21	M	MCHT	BVZZZZ	USA
NEUHAUS, JOHANN	29	M	BTMKR	PRZZZZ	USA
WILHELMINE	26	F	W	PRZZZZ	USA
CARL	4	M	CHILD	PRZZZZ	USA
OTTO	.06	M	INFANT	PRZZZZ	USA
NARTEN, ANNA	14	F	SGL	HBZZZZ	USA
LANG, MARIE	15	F	SGL	WMZZZZ	USA
SEIDLER, ALFRED	24	M	MUSN	WMADGO	USA
RAIN, GEORG	36	M	LABR	WMABOQ	USA
KERN, BARB.	17	F	SGL	PRZZZZ	USA
SVHELLER, MARIE	42	F	WO	HBZZZZ	USA
PAUL, JERENNAS	45	M	LABR	SYZZZZ	USA
JAGELS, MICHAEL	24	M	SLR	PRZZZZ	USA
MAI, KARL	26	M	FARMER	BVZZZZ	USA
HOEFLING, CATH	26	F	SGL	BVZZZZ	USA
WOLFF, ROSINE	16	F	SGL	BVZZZZ	USA
KORNER, JOHANN	15	M	LABR	BVZZZZ	USA
SEIDEL, FERD.	32	M	BRR	SYZZZZ	USA
JAZAK, MARIANNE	20	F	WO	SYAHUZ	USA
JOSEF	3	M	CHILD	SYAHUZ	USA
MICHALINE	.08	F	INFANT	SYAHUZ	USA
KALINOWSKI, FRANZ	13	M	BY	SYAHSC	USA

PASSENGER	AGE	SEX	OCCUPATION	PRV/VIL/DES
DUDECK, WILH.	21	F	SGL	SYADABUSA
KLEIN, AMALIE	17	F	SGL	PRZZZZUSA
THUECHSEN, THOMAS	25	M	TLR	PRZZZZUSA
HENRICHSEN, CARSTEN	55	M	FARMER	PRZZZZUSA
LEICHNITZ, CARL	57	M	JNR	PRZZZZUSA
KNOBLAUCH, GUSTE	17	F	SGL	PRAEAQUSA
GRANEK, MARTHA	14	F	SGL	PRABAHUSA
GERSTEN, HENRIETTE	19	F	SGL	PRAFBBUSA
WOLOSCHEK, FRANZ	23	M	LABR	PRAAZQUSA
WEISS, JOHANNE	17	F	SGL	PRAEWMUSA
SELBIZER, BERTHA	17	F	SGL	PRAAKHUSA
LIETZ, AUGUSTE	25	F	WO	PRAFYBUSA
EMIL	3	M	CHILD	PRAFYBUSA
PAUL	.11	M	INFANT	PRAFYBUSA
RITOW, WM.	26	M	FARMER	PRAHUCUSA
HERIETTE	29	F	W	PRAHUCUSA
ANNA	5	F	CHILD	PRAHUCUSA
ALBERT	3	M	CHILD	PRAHUCUSA
MAARTHA	.11	F	INFANT	PRAHUCUSA
BARANIAK, ANDREAS	28	M	FARMER	PRAHUCUSA
AUGUSTE	28	F	W	PRAHUCUSA
ANNA	8	F	CHILD	PRAHUCUSA
MAX	3	M	CHILD	PRAHUCUSA
LOUISE	.09	F	INFANT	PRAHUCUSA
DAHLKE, GUSTAV	18	M	LABR	PRABNOUSA
CARES, KARL	21	M	SCH	PRAAKHUSA
RUTZKY, BRUNO	18	M	SCH	PRABHUUSA
BOSOLD, FRANZ	22	M	TCHR	PRAEVMUSA
LEMME, ANNA	26	F	SGL	PRAFPMUSA
HANSEN, FRDKE.	20	F	SGL	PRZZZZUSA
KOFFINKE, ROBERT	27	M	WCHMKR	PRZZZZUSA
SCHROEDER, JOHANN	22	M	MCHT	PRZZZZUSA
JULIUS	16	M	MCHT	PRZZZZUSA
DOMANN, MATHILDE	36	F	WO	PRAAKHUSA
LIENAU, ARNOLD	49	M	WTR	PRZZZZUSA
JOACHIMSTHAL, SIMON	26	M	WTR	PRAARZUSA
BRISKE, SIEGFRIED	26	M	MCHT	PRAEABUSA
COHN, HUGO	21	M	MCHT	PRAEWMUSA
JONAS, SALOMON	58	M	MCHT	PRAFZGUSA
HANNCHEN	60	F	W	PRAFZGUSA
HELENE	17	F	D	PRAFZGUSA
COHN, JACOB	19	M	LABR	PRAAKHUSA
KOPF, ARNOLD	18	M	LABR	PRZZZZUSA
SCHULZ, CARL	24	M	FSHMN	PRZZZZUSA
ECKSTEIN, EMIL	27	M	LKSH	PRZZZZUSA
GERWIEN, ABRAHAM	28	M	BCHR	PRZZZZUSA
KRIEM, HANS	19	M	PNTR	PRZZZZUSA
KNUEGLER, WILH.	16	M	MCHT	PRAAKXUSA
SCHMAL, JOSEF	27	M	BKBNDR	PRADLDUSA
BEEZ, ELISE	20	F	SGL	BVZZZZUSA
KAIN, ELISE	23	F	SGL	BVZZZZUSA
KUNZ, HUGO	27	M	BTMKR	BVAFKYUSA
KRAUSE, AUGUST	22	M	GZR	BVADZOUSA
GLAESER, AUGUSTE	20	F	SGL	BVZZZZUSA
BAUMGARN, HEINRICH	24	M	LABR	BVAJGSUSA
SOLTAN, HANS	52	M	LABR	BVAJGSUSA
MARG.	49	F	W	BVAJGSUSA
AUGUST	8	M	CHILD	BVAJGSUSA
JULIUS	7	M	CHILD	BVAJGSUSA
MINNA	6	F	CHILD	BVAJGSUSA
EMMA	16	F	SGL	BVAJGSUSA
WINKLER, WILH.	37	M	MLR	BVADGEUSA
PAULINE	40	F	W	BVADGEUSA
RICHTER, HERRM.	23	M	LABR	BVADGEUSA
BUCHMANN, GREJNON	8	M	CHILD	PRZZZZUSA
LEIZER	7	M	CHILD	PRZZZZUSA
ROST, WILH.	24	M	MCHT	SYZZZZUSA
HARKE, ERNESTINE	12	F	CH	SYAFYBUSA
ZALEWSKI, FRANZ	33	M	BTMKR	SYAEZVUSA
MARIANNE	3	F	CHILD	SYAEZVUSA
ECKSTEIN, CHRISTINE	25	F	WO	PRZZZZUSA
EMIL	5	M	CHILD	PRZZZZUSA
ELISE	3	F	CHILD	PRZZZZUSA
FORDMANN, CATH.	23	F	SGL	PRADKJUSA
REGNAULT, PIER	26	M	GDNR	FRZZZZUSA

PASSENGER	AGE	SEX	OCCUPATION	PRV/VIL/DES
VALENTIN, MARTIN	25	M	CPTR	PRZZZZUSA
EGLONT, EDUARD	29	M	FARMER	PRZZZZUSA
CLOSSE, FR.	31	M	FARMER	PRZZZZUSA
GFELLER, DANIEL	19	M	FARMER	PRAAKJUSA
GEISER, CHR.ALBERT	25	M	FARMER	PRACVVUSA
HOPPMANN, WILHELM	26	M	PNTR	PRACKPUSA
SCHEUBER, JOHANN	21	M	BCHR	SRZZZZUSA
EBERLE, GUSTAV	26	M	MCHT	BDZZZZUSA
HAENING, JOHN	35	M	LABR	PRZZZZUSA
HEST, OTTO	37	M	LABR	SRZZZZUSA
BEER, ALOIS	23	M	FARMER	SRZZZZUSA
BRUESTLE, MATHIAS	21	M	LABR	WMZZZZUSA
SERNI, JOSEF	36	M	FARMER	WMAHBWUSA
HUEGEL, FRIEDRICH	24	M	LABR	WMABPIUSA
HIRT, GELLERT	00	M	INF	WM****USA
FRIEDRICH, MARIE	00	F	INF	WM****USA
FLIEGE, LINE	53	F	SGL	WMAFABUSA
MARTENS, ALBERT	32	M	APTC	WMALAEUSA
SCHAEDING, WILLY	7	M	CHILD	WMAADEUSA
KOBYLYNSKA, MARIANNE	23	F	SGL	WMAFZGUSA
GRAUER, BERTHA	39	F	SGL	WMAAKHUSA
EISENBERG, MINNIE	15	F	SGL	WMAJICUSA
KUENZEL, ROSALIE	26	F	SGL	WMAAKHUSA
FROST, H.V.	27	M	CMST	WMABVHUSA
THEGE, JOHANNES	19	M	BKLYR	HBZZZZUSA
GUSTAV	22	M	BKLYR	HBZZZZUSA
GEBHARDT, DORA	17	F	SGL	HBAHSAUSA
ZIMMERMANN, MARIE	32	F	WO	WMZZZZUSA
ANNA	4	F	CHILD	WMZZZZUSA
HANS	3	M	CHILD	WMZZZZUSA
GEORG	.11	M	INFANT	WMZZZZUSA
HARLOFF, ERNA	19	F	SGL	WMABSYUSA
RUEDIZER, CHRIATIAN	16	M	MCHT	WMAGQLUSA
HERTZER, FRIEDR.	24	M	MCHT	PRZZZZUSA
HOLM, ERNST	28	M	DR	PRZZZZUSA
STEINBERG, RUDOLPH	29	M	MCHT	BRZZZZUSA
FRANKE, CARL	24	M	MCHT	BRAASGUSA
ROSENBERG, ISIDOR	14	M	MCHT	PRZZZZUSA

SHIP: NEVADA

FROM: LIVERPOOL AND QUEENSTOWN
TO: NEW YORK
ARRIVED: 29 AUGUST 1888

PASSENGER	AGE	SEX	OCCUPATION	PRV/VIL/DES
GELIKMAN, JACOB	21	M	LABR	PRACBFUSA
FARBER, ALDR.	35	M	FARMER	PRACBFUSA
GOLDBERG, HIRSCH	18	M	FARMER	PRACBFUSA
BERNSTEIN, MOSES	7	M	CHILD	PRACBFUSA
KAUFMAN, MANE	16	M	LABR	PRACBFUSA
MARREY, FREDERICK	17	M	LABR	PRACBFUSA
BREST, JOSSEL	18	M	LABR	PRACBFUSA
SPAMCHACK, FREIDR.	27	M	LABR	PRACBFUSA
ROSENSLIM, JOSSEL	18	M	LABR	PRACBFUSA
FISCHER, JOSEPH	18	M	LABR	PRACBFUSA
BECKER, EMIL	32	M	FARMER	PRACBFUSA
HASANGAGEN, WILLI	24	M	FARMER	PRACBFUSA
RUNTE, AUGUST	31	M	FARMER	PRACBFUSA
BLUM, MOSES	28	M	FARMER	PRACBFUSA
MARIE	26	F	W	PRACBFUSA
SIMON	.06	M	INFANT	PRACBFUSA
SCHAEIDER, AUGUST	7	M	CHILD	PRACBFUSA
LEWENSON, BEILE	.11	F	INFANT	PRACBFUSA
IVOLPH	.11	M	INFANT	PRACBFUSA
BASCHE	29	F	W	PRACBFUSA
MERE	7	F	CHILD	PRACBFUSA
MOSES	3	M	CHILD	PRACBFUSA
SCHERMAN, TONI	18	F	SP	PRACBFUSA
MELMIK, KEILE	18	F	SP	PRACBFUSA
JUSTER, RUSZE	23	F	W	PRACBFUSA

PASSENGER	A G E	S E X	OCCUPATION	P R V L	V I	D E S
WECHT, JETTE	35	F	W			PRACBFUSA
BORUSH	7	F	CHILD			PRACBFUSA
DWORE	5	F	CHILD			PRACBFUSA
LEIE	3	F	CHILD			PRACBFUSA
JUSTER, MICHL.	.11	M	INFANT			PRACBFUSA
KOHAUS, JOHANNA	19	F	SP			PRACBFUSA
NORAH	17	F	SP			PRACBFUSA
UDTERMAN, PEPPI	17	F	SP			PRACBFUSA
WEINSTEIN, FANNY	18	F	SP			PRACBFUSA
IMBER, MASCHE	22	F	SP			PRACBFUSA
WILKIE, HENRY	27	M	LABR			PRAAECUSA

SHIP: STATE OF INDIANA

FROM: GLASGOW AND LARNE
TO: NEW YORK
ARRIVED: 30 AUGUST 1888

PASSENGER	A G E	S E X	OCCUPATION	P R V L	V I	D E S
KLEIN, GUSTAF	26	M	LABR			PRAHRZUSA
SCHNEIKER, MOSES	23	M	UNKNOWN			PRAHRZUSA
BLOCH, ARON	41	M	PDLR			PRAHRZUSA
HANTZE, HENRY	35	M	LABR			PRAHRZUSA
FISETHEE, DAVED	26	M	PDLR			PRAHRZUSA
MARCUS	19	M	PDLR			PRAHRZUSA
ISAK	22	M	PDLR			PRAHRZUSA
LEIB, MOSES	16	M	PDLR			PRAHRZUSA
ROSENFILDT, MAX	18	M	LABR			PRAHRZUSA
NOCKER, U	28	M	PDLR			PRAHRZUSA
-ERNSTEIN, U	53	M	LABR			PRAHRZUSA
KLEIN, LOUISE	26	F	W			PRAHRZUSA
CARL	.09	M	INFANT			PRAHRZUSA
HERZBERG, GERSCHAN	11	M	CH			PRAHRZUSA
BERCHANROWITZ, ESELE	20	F	S			PRAHRZUSA
CHAUS	11	M	CH			PRAHRZUSA
DAVIDNITZ, MEYER	28	M	LABR			PRAHRZUSA
JEIHE	22	F	W			PRAHRZUSA
ISAAC	.03	M	INFANT			PRAHRZUSA
WILK, LASE	24	M	LABR			PRAHRZUSA
BASCHE	23	F	W			PRAHRZUSA
AOHEN, FENNY	36	F	W			PRAHRZUSA
BALIMEN	11	M	CH			PRAHRZUSA
PESASH	7	F	CHILD			PRAHRZUSA
BERSASEK, FREIDI	28	F	W			PRAHRZUSA
PERE	8	F	CHILD			PRAHRZUSA
RESE	6	F	CHILD			PRAHRZUSA
SCHMUL	2	M	CHILD			PRAHRZUSA
U	1	M	CHILD			PRAHRZUSA
LEWENSOHN, CHAIE	49	F	W			PRAHRZUSA
MOTHEL	11	M	CH			PRAHRZUSA
ESTHER	9	F	CHILD			PRAHRZUSA
CHAWESOHN, CHANE	25	F	W			PRAHRZUSA
HENE	.09	F	INFANT			PRAHRZUSA
PILDUS, SLATE	16	F	DMS			PRAHRZUSA
FINGERHUT, MINDEL	19	F	DMS			PRAHRZUSA
FEIGE	00	F	UNKNOWN			PRAHRZUSA
HELTEMAN, ISKE	28	F	UNKNOWN			PRAHRZUSA
GARFINKEL, U	18	F	UNKNOWN			PRAHRZUSA
BARASCH, JAKLIV	25	F	DMS			PRAHRZUSA
LEWENSOHN, CHAIE	17	F	DMS			PRAHRZUSA
KANESBERG, MINNIE	21	F	DMS			PRAHRZUSA
SRANKEL, LEAH	45	F	DMS			PRAHRZUSA

PASSENGER	A G E	S E X	OCCUPATION	P R V L	V I	D E S
SHIP: CITY OF ROME						
FROM: LIVERPOOL						
TO: NEW YORK						
ARRIVED: 31 AUGUST 1888						
CINGNERALLI, OTTO	28	M	GENT			GRZZZZUSA
CARL	25	M	GENT			GRZZZZUSA
MAX	21	M	GENT			GRZZZZUSA
U	29	M	GENT			GRZZZZUSA
U	27	F	LDY			GRZZZZUSA
CARMONELLI, CARL	32	M	GENT			GRZZZZUSA
U	28	F	LDY			GRZZZZUSA
U	34	M	GENT			GRZZZZUSA
U	32	M	GENT			GRZZZZUSA
U	30	M	GENT			GRZZZZUSA
WALLENTY, JOSEPH	22	M	LABR			GRZZZZUSA
CONDOR, ANTONIO	23	M	LABR			GRZZZZUSA

SHIP: LAHN

FROM: BREMEN
TO: NEW YORK
ARRIVED: 31 AUGUST 1888

PASSENGER	A G E	S E X	OCCUPATION	P R V L	V I	D E S
KNILLE, C.	36	M	TT			GRAAKHGR
VONVERSEN, U	38	F	W			GRAAKHGR
DODEL, H.	30	M	UNKNOWN			GRACXVGR
H.	26	F	W			GRACXVGR
MENSING, A.	42	M	CPT			GRABOQGR
WINDISCH, GUSTAV	39	M	TT			GRZZZZGR
VAUPEL, META	51	F	W			GRZZZZGR
SCHOMBURG, ELSE	24	F	UNKNOWN			GRZZZZGR
HOEATER, BETTY	30	F	W			GRZZZZGR
HEINRICH, SUCREZIA	28	F	UNKNOWN			GRACPEGR
NEUHAUS, EMIL	11	M	TT			GRAEMJGR
STRAUSS, ISAAC	48	M	TT			GRABTTGR
FANNY	45	F	W			GRABTTGR
ROSENHEIM, ROSALIE	46	F	W			GRABOQGR
BULTMANN, BERTHA	20	F	UNKNOWN			GRAFFNGR
SOELDNER, KARL	16	M	TT			GRADROGR
LANGHORST, LOUISE	19	F	UNKNOWN			GRABBCGR
VONDEYLEN, GEO	25	M	TT			GRZZZZGR
HEERE, MARIE	28	F	UNKNOWN			GRACBRGR
BACKHAUS, ELISAB.	27	F	UNKNOWN			GRAARRGR
TURIAN, WILHELM	16	M	UNKNOWN			GRZZZZUSA
SCHNEIDER, ALBERT	18	M	TLR			GRZZZZUSA
STAEBLEIN, CASPER	58	M	LABR			GRZZZZUSA
CATHE.	41	F	W			GRZZZZUSA
PAULE.	3	F	CHILD			GRZZZZUSA
KRAFT, KATHI	18	F	UNKNOWN			GRABQZUSA
HARTUNG, LOUISE	29	F	W			GRABVWUSA
CARL	3	M	CHILD			GRABVWUSA
FRITZ	.11	M	INFANT			GRABVWUSA
ROSENTHAL, SALAMON	58	M	TLR			GRZZZZUSA
KUEHLEWIND, HEINR.	17	M	LABR			GRADUOUSA
MATTHIES, FRITZ	27	M	FARMER			GRAFLIUSA
MORISSE, BETA	15	F	UNKNOWN			GRZZZZUSA
TIESTE, JULIE	22	F	UNKNOWN			GRADVHUSA
SCHULTE, JOHS.	14	M	UNKNOWN			GRAFSNUSA
SCHATZ, JOHANN	11	M	CH			GRZZZZUSA
HEROLD, JOHANN	16	M	UNKNOWN			GRAEHXUSA
VOGEL, ANDR.	25	M	LABR			GRZZZZUSA
BAECKER, NICL.	50	M	LABR			GRZZZZUSA
MARGA.	47	F	W			GRZZZZUSA
KATHA.	18	F	UNKNOWN			GRZZZZUSA
CONRAD	11	M	CH			GRZZZZUSA
SCHATZ, ANNA	22	F	UNKNOWN			GRACIJUSA
GRASS, JOHANN	20	M	FARMER			GRZZZZUSA

PASSENGER	AGE	SEX	OCCUPATION	PRVL	DES
KRAUSS, ANNA	22	F	UNKNOWN	GRZZZZ	USA
OTT, BABETTE	17	F	UNKNOWN	GRZZZZ	USA
REICHEL, ANNA	49	F	W	GRZZZZ	USA
GEORG	.09	M	INFANT	GRZZZZ	USA
NEESE, FRANZ	28	M	LABR	GRAFHU	USA
SREPUTHIS, MICH.	25	M	LABR	GRAFAB	USA
URTE	31	F	W	GRAFAB	USA
GUST	.11	M	INFANT	GRAEXR	USA
REHBURG, SOPHIE	20	F	UNKNOWN	GRAAUI	USA
HUSEMANN, WILH.	26	M	LABR	GRZZZZ	USA
MOENKEDICK, SOFIE	18	F	UNKNOWN	GRZZZZ	USA
KUHLMANN, HERM.	29	M	MCHT	GRAAUI	USA
V. WARNER	18	M	LABR	GRZZZZ	USA
SCHROEDER, HEINR.CARL	16	M	FARMER	GRAFDW	USA
LEDERER, REGINE	20	F	UNKNOWN	GRAEYH	USA
MICHAEL	15	M	UNKNOWN	GRAEYH	USA
PUCHTA, JOHANN	25	M	FARMER	GRZZZZ	USA
FISCHER, JOHANN	16	M	UNKNOWN	GRZZZZ	USA
SCHMALKUCHEN, LOUISE	26	F	UNKNOWN	GRACWL	USA
BUSER, BABETTE	23	F	UNKNOWN	GRZZZZ	USA
KROMMUELLER, CAROLA.	20	F	UNKNOWN	GRZZZZ	USA
SCHEIB, CATHA.	24	F	UNKNOWN	GRZZZZ	USA
WIELAND, MARIA	19	F	UNKNOWN	GRZZZZ	USA
KONZER, PAULINE	4	F	CHILD	GRZZZZ	USA
ROTH, LEONHARD	20	M	MLR	GRZZZZ	USA
KORB, ELISAB.	17	F	UNKNOWN	GRZZZZ	USA
MINZER, MARIA	35	F	W	GRZZZZ	USA
BELLA	14	F	UNKNOWN	GRZZZZ	USA
JOHA.	9	F	CHILD	GRZZZZ	USA
SUSE	6	F	CHILD	GRZZZZ	USA
HACHEM	4	M	CHILD	GRZZZZ	USA
HERING, JOHANN	53	M	FARMER	GRZZZZ	USA
MARG.	49	F	W	GRZZZZ	USA
JOSEF	16	M	FARMER	GRZZZZ	USA
ALFRED	11	M	FARMER	GRZZZZ	USA
BABETTE	7	F	CHILD	GRZZZZ	USA
FLORIAN	6	M	CHILD	GRZZZZ	USA
OTT, ANDR.	33	M	FARMER	GRZZZZ	USA
VOGLER, GEORG	22	M	LABR	GRZZZZ	USA
HAGER, GEORG	31	M	LABR	GRABTR	USA
KOESEL, UROULA	25	F	UNKNOWN	GRADMZ	USA
SCHMIDT, ADAM	25	M	SDLR	GRAECZ	USA
AGNES	28	F	W	GRAECZ	USA
MICHAEL	12	M	CH	GRAECZ	USA
REITER, HUGO	14	M	UNKNOWN	GRZZZZ	USA
METZ, JACOB	27	M	LABR	GRAAGW	USA
NIEDERMAYER, WENZL	42	M	SHMK	GRAEHP	USA
OTTO, LINA	17	F	UNKNOWN	GRAEHP	USA
SEIM, FRANZ	18	M	BKR	GRACIW	USA
SCHULTZE, PAUL	43	M	BKR	GRAASS	USA
OTT, JOHANN	24	M	FARMER	GRZZZZ	USA
WAGT, WILLY	15	M	LABR	GRZZZZ	USA
KRAKOWIAK, JUL.	48	M	TNM	GRAEWM	USA
MINNA	32	F	W	GRAEWM	USA
MARCUS	14	M	UNKNOWN	GRAEWM	USA
REGINA	10	F	CH	GRAEWM	USA
ADOLF	3	M	CHILD	GRAEWM	USA
ELLA	.04	F	INFANT	GRAEWM	USA
LORENZ, FRIEDR.	17	M	LABR	GRAEXW	USA
AKELSEN, CHRIST.	31	M	LABR	GRZZZZ	USA
BERTHA	26	F	W	GRZZZZ	USA
SIMON, SOPHIE	18	F	UNKNOWN	GRAFPJ	USA
CORDES, JOHANN	16	M	CGRMKR	GRZZZZ	USA
KUBIAK, JOHANN	40	M	LABR	GRZZZZ	USA
KRUPKE, LOUISE	28	F	W	GRAAKH	USA
WANDA	3	F	CHILD	GRAAKH	USA
MIETZKER, ANNA	31	F	UNKNOWN	GRZZZZ	USA
HILLER, THEOD.	18	M	LABR	GRAAKH	USA
GERHARDT, MARIE	25	F	UNKNOWN	GRZZZZ	USA
DRAUS, MARTIN	25	M	TLR	GRADLU	USA
MARIE	25	F	W	GRADLU	USA
HEINR.	7	M	CHILD	GRADLU	USA
ANNA	3	F	CHILD	GRADLU	USA
MARIE	.09	F	INFANT	GRADLU	USA
WELLY, EMIL	34	M	LABR	GRAHBB	USA
MARIE	30	F	W	GRAHBB	USA
CECILIE	7	F	CHILD	GRAHBB	USA
HANS	4	M	CHILD	GRAHBB	USA
REBISCHUNG, MARIE	24	F	UNKNOWN	GRZZZZ	USA
DRUEGES, BERNHD.	28	M	LABR	GRAJIG	USA
ANNA	42	F	W	GRAJIG	USA
ELISE	17	F	UNKNOWN	GRAJIG	USA
PETER	7	M	CHILD	GRAJIG	USA
SALDENBERGER, CONRAD	46	M	FARMER	GRAJIG	USA
MARGE.	38	F	W	GRAJIG	USA
CONRAD	15	M	UNKNOWN	GRAJIG	USA
HEINR.	7	M	CHILD	GRAJIG	USA
ADOLF	5	M	CHILD	GRAJIG	USA
LINA	3	F	CHILD	GRAJIG	USA
WILHELM	.09	M	INFANT	GRAJIG	USA
HILDEBRAND, MATHE.	6	F	CHILD	GRZZZZ	USA
NEUMILLER, JOHN	24	M	LABR	GRAEOY	USA
ECKMEIER, MARIA	24	F	UNKNOWN	GRZZZZ	USA
WICHERT, JULIANNA	23	F	UNKNOWN	GRAENL	USA
BALLING, JOHANN	17	M	LABR	GRZZZZ	USA
TETZNER, SILMA	19	F	UNKNOWN	GRAACO	USA
SCHUNAR, LOTHAR	21	M	LKSH	GRACBR	USA
BALZER, THERESE	29	F	UNKNOWN	GRACBR	USA
HASENEIER, MATHILDE	24	F	UNKNOWN	GRACBR	USA
GUTGESELL, FRANZ	26	M	LABR	GRACBR	USA
FEHR, CHRIST.	47	M	LABR	GRADLD	USA
PHILIPPE.	30	F	W	GRADLD	USA
PHILIPPE.	10	F	CH	GRADLD	USA
DORA	3	F	CHILD	GRADLD	USA
ELFA	.01	F	INFANT	GRADLD	USA
LUDWIG, ANTON	33	M	FARMER	GRZZZZ	USA
SOLF, BONIFAZ	15	M	UNKNOWN	GRACGM	USA
STINTZER, ROSA	19	F	UNKNOWN	GRACGM	USA
FOERSTER, KAROLE.	19	F	UNKNOWN	GRACGM	USA
HERBER, KATHA.	20	F	UNKNOWN	GRACGM	USA
THEN, ANTON	60	M	FARMER	GRACGM	USA
ANNA	57	F	W	GRACGM	USA
ENDERS, ANNA	15	F	UNKNOWN	GRACGM	USA
SANDHERR, MATHE.	16	F	UNKNOWN	GRAEXW	USA
KECK, LOUISE	30	F	UNKNOWN	GRAEXW	USA
SCHULTHEISS, CARL	15	M	TLR	GRAEXW	USA
BUTZ, DANIEL	22	M	LABR	GRZZZZ	USA
KELBERER, MARIA	19	F	UNKNOWN	GRZZZZ	USA
RUPF, JOHANN	24	M	SHMK	GRACWR	USA
BIBER, JOSEF	26	M	TLR	GRACWR	USA
NEUFFER, JOHANNES	51	M	FARMER	GRZZZZ	USA
ROSINE	32	F	W	GRZZZZ	USA
HEINR.	3	M	CHILD	GRZZZZ	USA
ALBERT	.08	M	INFANT	GRZZZZ	USA
SCHEFFOLD, FRANZISKA	13	F	UNKNOWN	GRZZZZ	USA
SOPHIE	15	F	UNKNOWN	GRZZZZ	USA
GEORG	15	M	UNKNOWN	GRZZZZ	USA
KOLBUS, ROSINE	20	F	UNKNOWN	GRAEML	USA
KANDERER, CHRISTE.	30	F	W	GRAEML	USA
GOTTLOB	8	M	CHILD	GRAEML	USA
LOUISE	4	F	CHILD	GRAEML	USA
CHRIST.	3	M	CHILD	GRAEML	USA
CHRISTE.	2	F	CHILD	GRAEML	USA
CARL	.06	M	INFANT	GRAEML	USA
KREMER, PHILPP	26	M	SHMK	GRAEML	USA
RAUCHMANN, MICHAEL	46	M	FARMER	GRZZZZ	USA
ELEONORE	35	F	W	GRZZZZ	USA
NEUBUAUER, PAULINE	40	F	W	GRZZZZ	USA
CARL	11	M	CH	GRZZZZ	USA
MARIA	7	F	CHILD	GRZZZZ	USA
JOSEF	6	M	CHILD	GRZZZZ	USA
ANNA	4	F	CHILD	GRZZZZ	USA
CAROLINE	2	F	CHILD	GRZZZZ	USA
BLOECHL, HEDWIG	32	F	UNKNOWN	GRZZZZ	USA
BAUMANN, AUGUSTE	38	F	W	GRAEPO	USA
PAULINE	21	F	UNKNOWN	GRAEPO	USA
SCHOLZ, GUSTAV	37	M	LABR	GRAEPO	USA
LOUISE	40	F	W	GRAEPO	USA
MARTHA	15	F	UNKNOWN	GRAEPO	USA
RICHARD	7	M	CHILD	GRAEPO	USA

PASSENGER	AGE	SEX	OCCUPATION	PRVVL	DES
GUSTAV	4	M	CHILD	GRAEPOUSA	
VONPARIS, AUG.	26	M	LABR	GRAEPOUSA	
KRESS, MAGMUS	20	M	LABR	GRZZZZUSA	
KOENIG, ELSBETH	15	F	UNKNOWN	GRACBRUNK	
VONBERGEN, GUST.	15	M	LABR	GRADXCUNK	
STILLT, HEINR.	22	M	LABR	GRZZZZUNK	
NOLTE, HEINR.	25	M	LABR	GRZZZZUNK	
EHRLING, HERMANN	17	M	LABR	GRZZZZUNK	
SCHUBERT, EMMA	23	F	UNKNOWN	GRADIJUNK	
KASTLER, KARL	16	M	UNKNOWN	GRAFBVUNK	
HERRMANN, KETHI	32	F	W	GRAFWNUNK	
CHRISTE.	.06	F	INFANT	GRAFWNUNK	
FELLHEIMER, SIEGFRD.	15	M	UNKNOWN	GRACHSUNK	
SOLGER, ANNA	17	F	UNKNOWN	GRADKOUNK	
APPEL, BERNHD.	19	M	LABR	GRALGCUNK	
ISAAC	18	M	LABR	GRALGCUNK	
NAEHLMANN, ANNA	15	F	UNKNOWN	GRZZZZUNK	
STOCKBAUER, JOSEF	22	M	LABR	GRACQFUNK	
HAFFKE, EMIL	28	M	LABR	GRAGFUUNK	
MARIA	22	F	W	GRAGFUUNK	
SCHELLER, AUGUST	21	M	LABR	GRADLDUNK	
ZICK, CATHA.	22	F	UNKNOWN	GRADEMUNK	
BRAUN, CATHA.	18	F	UNKNOWN	GRADEMUNK	
PURUCKER, JOHANN	21	M	LABR	GRZZZZUNK	
CHRISTOPH	16	M	LABR	GRZZZZUNK	
MUELLER, MAGE.	24	F	UNKNOWN	GRADFTUNK	
CATHE.	18	F	UNKNOWN	GRADFTUNK	
EBERT, WIEGAND	26	M	BCHR	GRZZZZUNK	
FROCHENBROD, EMIL	6	M	CHILD	GRZZZZUNK	
WESSEL, HEINR.	15	M	UNKNOWN	GRAARRUNK	
LOEWENSTEIN, DAVID	16	M	UNKNOWN	GRAESRUNK	
ZICK, FRIEDR.	11	M	CH	GRABQZUNK	
BRIGITTA	9	F	CHILD	GRABQZUNK	
GERDES, WILHELM	36	M	FARMER	GRAFSNUNK	
MAACK, JOHANN	23	M	FARMER	GRAFSNUNK	
MENGER, PHILIPP	31	M	LABR	GRADKKUNK	
MARIE	41	F	W	GRADKKUNK	
CARL	3	M	CHILD	GRADKKUNK	
MARIE	1	F	CHILD	GRADKKUNK	
ZULAIBZ, CATHA.	26	F	UNKNOWN	GRAEHTUNK	
WALTER, MINNA	20	F	UNKNOWN	GRZZZZUNK	
FAHLBUSCH, THERESE	10	F	CH	GRACBRUNK	
HUGEL, CHRIST.	24	M	UNKNOWN	GRZZZZUNK	
JOHA.	22	F	W	GRZZZZUNK	
FROATZ, WILHELM	24	M	LABR	GRADWRUNK	
RAUH, MATTHAUS	13	M	UNKNOWN	GRZZZZUNK	
EUCHNER, PAULINE	18	F	UNKNOWN	GRAHFTUNK	
VALTIN	4	M	CHILD	GRAHFTUNK	
SCHLOEDER, ANNA	18	F	UNKNOWN	GRZZZZUNK	
HERBIG, PETER	17	M	DYR	GRZZZZUNK	
BOHNSCH, KATHA.	19	F	UNKNOWN	GRAAYAUNK	
GILLITZER, FRIEDR.	22	M	LABR	GRZZZZUNK	
ENGELKEN, GESCHE	18	F	UNKNOWN	GRACBRUNK	
HOLSTEN, HERM.	14	M	UNKNOWN	GRACBRUNK	
LUETTGE, AUG.	14	M	UNKNOWN	GRACBRUNK	
DIERKS, DIEDRICH	16	M	UNKNOWN	GRACBRUNK	
CORDES, JOHANN	15	M	UNKNOWN	GRACBRUNK	
BENKE, DORA	18	F	UNKNOWN	GRAARRUNK	
HOFMANN, JOHANN	11	M	CH	GRAFVRUNK	
RENZ, HEINRICH	22	M	LABR	GRAFVRUNK	
DRUENER, MARIE	17	F	UNKNOWN	GRAFEEUNK	
PFEIFER, CACILIE	66	F	W	GRZZZZUNK	
SCHWARZE, HENRIETTE	70	F	W	GRACBRUNK	
SCHAEFERMEYER, HERM.	23	M	SDLR	GRAAURUNK	
MUELLER, DIEDR.	17	M	LABR	GRADUOUNK	
WEISS, FRIEDR.	22	M	LABR	GRZZZZUNK	
RIND, EILISAB.	36	F	UNKNOWN	GRZZZZUNK	
RING, ANTON	32	M	LKSH	GRABOQUNK	
BECK, CHRISTOPH	40	M	LKSH	GRABARUNK	
EISENRIECH, WILHELM	26	M	TLR	GRZZZZUNK	
KUECK, ADELINE	18	F	UNKNOWN	GRAARRUNK	
GEFFKEN, CATHA.	20	F	UNKNOWN	GRZZZZUNK	
BROCKMANN, HULDA	19	F	UNKNOWN	GRAAHLUNK	
WERFELMEYER, FRIEDKE.	25	F	UNKNOWN	GRAARRUNK	
REIFENBACH, FRIEDKE.	18	F	UNKNOWN	GRAARRUNK	
MINDERMANN, META	19	F	UNKNOWN	GRAARRUNK	
SIEG, JOHANN	23	M	LABR	GRZZZZUNK	
SIEBECK, HERMANN	15	M	UNKNOWN	GRZZZZUNK	
BAAR, ADOLPH	16	M	UNKNOWN	GRZZZZUNK	
LILIENTHAL, JULIE	17	F	UNKNOWN	GRZZZZUNK	
BEVERSEN, CLAUS	16	M	UNKNOWN	GRZZZZUNK	
OSTERMANN, CARL	27	M	LABR	GRAARRUNK	
HEUER, MINNA	22	F	UNKNOWN	GRADYMUNK	
BRUNGEN, HEINR.	14	M	UNKNOWN	GRAARRUNK	
KAUTZ, ADOLF	18	M	LABR	GRAENZUNK	
FREDL, EMILIE	16	F	UNKNOWN	GRZZZZUNK	
BOETH, WILHE.	46	F	W	GRZZZZUNK	
ELISE	19	F	UNKNOWN	GRZZZZUNK	
LOUISE	14	F	UNKNOWN	GRZZZZUNK	
BERTHA	9	F	CHILD	GRZZZZUNK	
ALBERT	6	M	CHILD	GRZZZZUNK	
MARIE	4	F	CHILD	GRZZZZUNK	
CREUZER, IDA	19	F	UNKNOWN	GRZZZZUNK	
SCHMIDT, HEINR.	55	M	LABR	GRZZZZUNK	
HORNING, JOSEF	61	M	LABR	GRZZZZUNK	
BARBA.	60	F	W	GRZZZZUNK	
ERB, MARGA.	19	F	UNKNOWN	GRACBRUNK	
FROEBEL, ERNST	19	M	LABR	GRAAFTUNK	
KOHRSEN, LOUISE	37	F	UNKNOWN	GRACBRUNK	
BUEDDENDORF, EILISAB.	24	F	UNKNOWN	GRAAAXUNK	
MUELLER, EMMA	32	F	UNKNOWN	GRAARRUNK	
BONNET, CHRIST.	18	M	LABR	GRABETUNK	
BVINDERNAGEL, ANNA	15	F	UNKNOWN	GRZZZZUNK	
HECKER, FRIEDKE.	46	F	W	GRZZZZUNK	
CARL	5	M	CHILD	GRZZZZUNK	
CHRICT.	59	M	FARMER	GRZZZZUNK	
KIESER, C.L.	35	M	LABR	GRACPUUNK	
KLEIN, MAX	32	M	LABR	GRADKWUNK	
PLESTER, FRITZ	47	M	LABR	GRADKWUNK	
HOEHLE, FRIEDKE.	19	F	UNKNOWN	GRADFMUNK	
HRONAU, WILHE.	30	F	W	GRAARSUNK	
WILHE.	7	F	CHILD	GRAARSUNK	
WILLY	4	M	CHILD	GRAARSUNK	
WAGENHAUSEN, MARIE	23	F	UNKNOWN	GRZZZZUNK	
HEDWOG	00	F	INF	GR****UNK	

SHIP: RHYNLAND

FROM: ANTWERP
TO: NEW YORK
ARRIVED: 31 AUGUST 1888

PASSENGER	AGE	SEX	OCCUPATION	PRVVL	DES
HOEGEN, MR	30	M	PNTR	GRZZZZUSA	
DELEPEE, MRS	25	F	NN	FRZZZZUSA	
GREINER, DAVID	54	M	ISP	GRZZZZUSA	
BETZ, PHIL	18	M	STDNT	GRZZZZUSA	
PIBERS, E	27	M	MCHT	FRZZZZUSA	
KLINGENSCHMIDT, KATH	26	F	PVTW	GRZZZZUSA	
BRANDT, G	30	M	PREST	GRZZZZUSA	
DITTEL, ANNA	16	F	SVNT	GRZZZZUSA	
MEIER, AUG	22	M	MCHT	SRZZZZUSA	
GRETERSOHN, O	12	M	CH	SRZZZZUSA	
WILH, BISCHOFF	23	M	LKSH	GRZZZZUSA	
FRAN, LECO--ITE	30	M	MNR	FRZZZZIN	
LEGRANDE, VICT	40	M	MNR	FRZZZZIN	
DUEZ, LOUIS	31	M	MNR	FRZZZZUNK	
HENRI	28	M	MNR	FRZZZZUNK	
EUGENIE	23	F	W	FRZZZZUNK	
HENRI	3	M	CHILD	FRZZZZUNK	
BIA, JULES	22	M	MNR	FRZZZZUNK	
ANGELA	9	F	CHILD	FRZZZZUNK	
HORACE	6	M	CHILD	FRZZZZUNK	
AUGUSTE	00	F	INF	FRZZZZUNK	
LEHRBACH, WILH	17	M	PPMKR	FRZZZZNY	
LESCHHORN, CHRIST	17	M	LABR	GRZZZZNY	

PASSENGER	AGE	SEX	OCCUPATION	PRVL	DES
WOLF, HEINR	55	M	LABR	GRZZZZNY	
ELISAB	20	F	SVNT	GRZZZZNY	
DREHER, JOHANN	25	M	FARMER	GRZZZZNY	
PE-TZ, JOHANN	24	M	FARMER	GRZZZZNY	
HECKHAUS, PHIL	43	M	CPTR	GRZZZZNY	
JAEGER, PETER	22	M	LNM	GRZZZZPHI	
GEIST, HEINR	17	M	BCHR	GRZZZZCH	
KURZ, CATHA	30	F	W	GRZZZZCH	
HEINR	3	M	CHILD	GRZZZZCH	
JOSEPH	00	M	INF	GRZZZZCH	
ZAGANSKI, BERTHA	18	F	SVNT	GRZZZZUSA	
HERMANS, ANTON-MRS	00	F	NN	GRZZZZNY	
HUBERTINE	00	F	NN	GRZZZZNY	
TRYSZEWSKI, MAROCLIE	19	M	CL	GRZZZZNY	
MEICHEL, CARL	23	M	MUSN	GRZZZZNY	
ANDES, JOHANN	23	M	LKSH	GRZZZZNY	
HOERNER, MINA	20	F	SVNT	GRZZZZNY	
LIEGOIS, LAURE	30	F	W	FRZZZZNY	
IDA	11	F	CH	FRZZZZNY	
BERTHE	7	F	CHILD	FRZZZZNY	
EVA	8	F	CHILD	FRZZZZNY	
RENE	2	M	CHILD	FRZZZZNY	
LUDWIG, FRED	18	M	MLR	GRZZZZNY	
DURAT, CELENE	30	F	W	FRZZZZUNK	
HOEN, JOHN	20	M	LKSH	GRZZZZDET	
SCHMIDT, H	20	M	CL	GRZZZZSTL	
WEBER, BERTHA	33	F	SVNT	GRZZZZSTL	
SCHLIESSER, WERNER	22	M	MCHT	GRZZZZPIT	
WOLF, GERH	18	M	MCHT	GRZZZZNY	
HOF, ANTON	56	M	LABR	GRZZZZNY	
DREYLING, THERESA	21	F	SVNT	GRZZZZNY	
BORG, CATHA	21	F	SVNT	GRZZZZNY	
DEMER, JACOB	16	M	NN	GRZZZZNY	
PROSCHASKA, FRANZ	45	M	LABR	GRZZZZPLY	
MARIE	40	F	W	GRZZZZPLY	
MARIE	19	F	D	GRZZZZPLY	
RINK, FRIED	49	M	LABR	GRZZZZNY	
ANOTNIA	39	F	W	GRZZZZNY	
MINNA	16	F	D	GRZZZZNY	
NORIS, ANNA	53	F	M	GRZZZZNY	
JOSEF	18	M	BCHR	GRZZZZNY	
JACOB	18	M	BCHR	GRZZZZNY	
BREGEL, PAUL	36	M	TRVLR	GRZZZZNY	
BACHMANN, G	18	M	MCHT	GRZZZZNY	
FISCHER, GOTTL	26	M	BCHR	GRZZZZOIL	
QUERBACH, G	36	M	SMH	GRZZZZTRE	
SOPHIE	29	F	W	GRZZZZTRE	
AUGUSTA	3	F	CHILD	GRZZZZTRE	
BOECK, ANNA	17	F	SVNT	GRZZZZNY	
MEN-ER, CARL	31	M	LABR	GRZZZZNY	
KATH	31	F	W	GRZZZZNY	
WALZ, J	30	M	LABR	GRZZZZNY	
WEBER, ADELBERT	30	M	LABR	GRZZZZNY	
THERESIA	30	F	W	GRZZZZNY	
GOSSLER, CARL	25	M	MACH	GRZZZZNY	
BUSIERE, DESIRE	20	M	MNR	FRZZZZUNK	
M-LIDOR, GERHARD	55	M	FARMER	GRZZZZNY	
MARIA	50	F	W	GRZZZZNY	
PHILIPP	23	M	LABR	GRZZZZNY	
FRANZ	21	M	LABR	GRZZZZNY	
CHRISTIAN	50	M	LABR	GRZZZZNY	
PROBST, CATH	23	F	SVNT	GRZZZZNY	
EDMUNDS, WILH	25	M	BKR	GRZZZZUNK	
HEIMANN, WILH	36	M	GZR	GRZZZZUNK	
MARGA	37	F	W	GRZZZZUNK	
MARGA	4	F	CHILD	GRZZZZUNK	
HELENA	1	F	CHILD	GRZZZZUNK	
FRANZ	00	M	INF	GRZZZZUNK	
THERESIA	68	F	M	GRZZZZUNK	
VAN, FERD	38	M	LABR	GRZZZZPHI	
BEYER, PETER	25	M	MCHT	GRZZZZNY	
NEUMUELLER, FRIDA	26	F	SVNT	GRZZZZNY	
LANGHARDT, LISETTE	22	F	W	GRZZZZJON	
AROLD	18	M	LABR	GRZZZZJON	
SELMA	1	F	CHILD	GRZZZZJON	
LEBON, JOSEPH	36	M	MNR	FRZZZZNY	
GRAULING, FRANZ	50	M	GDSM	GRZZZZNY	
MARIE	24	F	W	GRZZZZNY	
LEIGH, OTTO	21	M	CL	GRZZZZNY	
SCHUDEL, ELISE	21	F	SVNT	SRZZZZNY	
VOGELSANGER, ANNA	21	F	SVNT	SRZZZZNY	
KEEL, LEO	18	M	FARMER	SRZZZZNY	
ME-IKOMMER, EMI	29	F	SVNT	SRZZZZNY	
MOSER, ALBERT	26	M	CL	SRZZZZNY	
BIELSER, WALTER	17	M	FARMER	SRZZZZNY	
AMSLER, CARL	50	M	LABR	SRZZZZNY	
KEIDEL, H	15	M	WTR	GRZZZZNY	
SCHMIDT, ED	18	M	BBR	GRZZZZNY	
GRAULI, GERH	29	M	SDLR	GRZZZZNY	
BERGER, KARL	26	M	MCHT	GRZZZZNY	
ETZEL, MARGA	24	F	SVNT	GRZZZZNY	
WEBER, JOSEPH	24	M	LABR	GRZZZZNY	
BETZWEISER, ROSA	20	F	SVNT	GRZZZZIN	
WALDEIKER, SOPHIE	21	F	SVNT	GRZZZZCOU	
JOSEPH	18	F	SVNT	GRZZZZCOU	
SCHNEIDER, JOSEPHINA	26	F	SVNT	GRZZZZPHI	
SEIPO, GEORG	17	M	LABR	GRZZZZPIT	
LUTZ, ANNA	17	F	SVNT	GRZZZZPIT	
WOLPERTH, ELISE	18	F	SVNT	GRZZZZPIT	
EBERLE, MARGA	51	F	W	GRZZZZPIT	
RANDOLL, MARIE	26	F	SVNT	GRZZZZPIT	
MARIE	26	F	SVNT	GRZZZZPIT	
STOLL, CAROLINE	16	F	SVNT	GRZZZZNY	
WILL, GEORG	16	M	BKR	GRZZZZNY	
VOELPEL, ELISA	19	F	SVNT	GRZZZZNY	
LOVETIS, MARGA	22	F	SVNT	GRZZZZNY	
KEMP, MARIE	18	F	SVNT	GRZZZZNY	
-ERSE, KATHA	20	F	SVNT	GRZZZZNY	
HERBST, MARIE	24	F	SVNT	GRZZZZNY	
SCHEMPF, ANNA	26	F	W	GRZZZZNY	
DORA	3	F	CHILD	GRZZZZNY	
JOSEFA	.07	F	INFANT	GRZZZZNY	
LIPP, JOHANNES	56	M	LABR	GRZZZZBUF	
ANNA	55	F	W	GRZZZZBUF	
BARBE	21	F	SVNT	GRZZZZBUF	
WEIS, MARIA	26	F	SVNT	GRZZZZNY	
TESAR, ED	24	M	MCHT	GRZZZZNY	
VOJTA, JOSEF	52	M	LABR	GRZZZZNY	
ANNA	44	F	W	GRZZZZNY	
FRANZKE	16	F	CH	GRZZZZNY	
JOSEF	9	M	CHILD	GRZZZZNY	
VINCENZ	8	M	CHILD	GRZZZZNY	
ANNA	6	F	CHILD	GRZZZZNY	
BOZENA	1	F	CHILD	GRZZZZNY	
PICK, FRANZKA	22	F	SVNT	GRZZZZCH	
PISARIK, JOSEF	26	M	LABR	GRZZZZCH	
ADALBERT	24	M	BKR	GRZZZZCH	
HOVORKA, JOSEF	24	M	NN	GRZZZZCH	
ANDREAS, STIKA	26	M	TLR	GRZZZZCH	
KOPP, GEORG	35	M	LABR	GRZZZZROC	
MAMMOSKA, JULIE	24	F	SVNT	GRZZZZNY	
ADAM, RAPHAEL	30	M	LABR	GRZZZZNY	
KAUFMANN, ANNA	32	F	W	GRZZZZCH	
MAYER, S	00	M	SDLR	GRZZZZNY	
BLINDAUER, JOH	24	M	BCHR	GRZZZZNY	
BIRT, U	22	M	BCHR	GRZZZZNY	
MEYER, CARL	24	M	BCHR	GRZZZZNY	
HAMMER, ELIZ	48	F	W	GRZZZZNY	
FUNK, JOHANN	11	M	CH	GRZZZZNY	
BAUER, JACOB	28	M	LABR	GRZZZZNY	
LUPPER, FRANZ	37	M	LABR	GRZZZZNY	
ANNA	34	F	W	GRZZZZNY	
ANNA	11	F	CH	GRZZZZNY	
FREY, ELIZA	19	F	SVNT	GRZZZZNY	
BITZ, ANNA	20	F	SVNT	GRZZZZUNK	
CRESZ	18	F	SVNT	GRZZZZUNK	
DIETKE, CARL	19	M	NN	GRZZZZNY	
PAUL	17	M	NN	GRZZZZNY	
IMHOF, ADOLF	15	M	SHMK	GRZZZZNY	
BERDER, CLOT	19	F	SVNT	GRZZZZNY	

PASSENGER	AGE	SEX	OCCUPATION	PRVVL	DES
BRAIG, THEOD	20	M	LABR	GRZZZZNY	
ACHAIBLE, CATHA	19	F	SVNT	GRZZZZLOU	
WELKCH, JOHS	15	M	NN	GRZZZZUNK	
STOLL, CHRISTINE	17	F	SVNT	GRZZZZNY	
FROEHLICH, THERESA	29	F	SVNT	GRZZZZNY	
CLARA	19	F	SVNT	GRZZZZNY	
LANG, SOPHIE	22	F	SVNT	GRZZZZNY	
LEBER, AMALIE	32	F	W	GRZZZZNY	
EMILIE	9	F	CHILD	GRZZZZNY	
HUDELHOVEN, JOH	24	M	LABR	GRZZZZNY	
SCHMITZ, CATHA	26	F	SVNT	GRZZZZNY	
BASBACH, ELISE	20	F	SVNT	GRZZZZNY	
FIETTLER, LOUISE	17	F	SVNT	GRZZZZNY	
DERNESTHAL, FERD	31	M	BCHR	GRZZZZNY	
HAMPEL, -RA-GOTT	23	M	BKBNDR	GRZZZZNY	
SPICHLER, DANIEL	16	M	FARMER	SRZZZZNY	
MUSSER, WAL-URGER	44	F	SVNT	GRZZZZLOS	
THERES	19	F	SVNT	GRZZZZLOS	
HUBEL	18	M	BTMKR	GRZZZZNY	
LANDRISSER, LUDW	28	M	MUSN	GRZZZZNY	
HAAS, CATHA	22	F	W	GRZZZZNY	
URBAN	00	M	INF	GRZZZZNY	
BRAND, VINCENZ	51	M	LABR	GRZZZZNY	
SOPHIE	45	F	W	GRZZZZNY	
HEINR	16	M	CH	GRZZZZNY	
CARL	11	M	CH	GRZZZZNY	
PONGRATZ, CATH	19	F	SVNT	GRZZZZBUF	
MEYER, CARL	44	M	NN	GRZZZZCH	
WERNLEIN, JOHANNA	17	F	SVNT	GRZZZZBUF	
HA--E, LOUIS	18	M	LABR	SRZZZZUNK	
JONKE	00	M	NN	SRZZZZNY	
PROMERSBERGER, MARIA	27	F	W	GRZZZZNY	
CATHA	00	F	INF	GRZZZZNY	
GUTLING, ELISA	19	F	SVNT	GRZZZZNY	
ZIMMIER, ED	17	M	TLR	GRZZZZNY	
EVERLE, JOSEF	21	M	NN	GRZZZZUNK	
VANOIS, EUGENE	22	M	CPTR	FRZZZZCH	
GILLES, JOHANN	20	M	NN	GRZZZZCLE	
REIS, JOSEF	27	M	GENT	GRZZZZPIT	
GREIVER, CATHA	32	F	W	GRZZZZUNK	
ANNA	11	F	CH	GRZZZZUNK	
CLARA	10	F	CH	GRZZZZUNK	
JOSEFINE	8	F	CHILD	GRZZZZUNK	
MARIA	6	F	CHILD	GRZZZZUNK	
JOHANN	4	M	CHILD	GRZZZZUNK	
APPOLINA	2	F	CHILD	GRZZZZUNK	
HELENE	00	F	INF	GRZZZZUNK	
SCHWAAB, GEO	40	M	NN	GRZZZZNY	
REIHN, CARL	16	M	FARMER	GRZZZZCH	
STECH, PAULINA	23	F	SVNT	GRZZZZNY	
BEYER, MARIA	21	F	W	GRZZZZNY	
BELLER, MARIE	32	F	W	GRZZZZNY	
MARIE	8	F	CHILD	GRZZZZNY	
STEPHANIE	5	F	CHILD	GRZZZZNY	
CAROLINE	3	F	CHILD	GRZZZZNY	
MUELLER, MARIA	22	F	SVNT	GRZZZZPHI	
NOTHSTEIN, ROSA	20	F	SVNT	GRZZZZNY	
KLO-TER, LOUISA	15	F	CH	GRZZZZNY	
EMILIA	7	F	CHILD	GRZZZZNY	
U, M	00	M	BKR	GRZZZZNY	
FISCHER, THA	17	F	SVNT	GRZZZZCH	
BELLERT, ROSA	18	F	SVNT	GRZZZZCH	
ELL, WILL	15	M	GDNR	GRZZZZUNK	
KRUSE, FRANZIKA	20	F	SVNT	GRZZZZNY	
RAISCH, FRIED	20	M	BCHR	GRZZZZNY	
HEMMELN, WILH	12	M	NN	GRZZZZNY	
SCHLEGEL, ERNST	29	M	SMH	GRZZZZNY	
PETERMANN, CARL	21	M	LABR	GRZZZZNY	
DAEHNEN, MAX	22	M	LABR	GRZZZZNY	
BONGRAIN, AUG	38	M	LABR	FRZZZZUNK	

PASSENGER	AGE	SEX	OCCUPATION	PRVVL	DES
SHIP: ROMAN					
FROM: LIVERPOOL					
TO: BOSTON					
ARRIVED: 31 AUGUST 1888					
GREIG, JOHN	30	M	LABR	GRZZZZNY	
SHIP: WESER					
FROM: BREMEN					
TO: BALTIMORE					
ARRIVED: 31 AUGUST 1888					
STRAUSS, JACOB	40	M	MCHT	GRZZZZMD	
ERZ, MINNA	30	F	UNKNOWN	GRZZZZOH	
STREIT, AGNES	24	F	UNKNOWN	GRZZZZOH	
DAEHMS, HERMANN	27	M	MCHT	GRZZZZIL	
SCHNETZE, HERMANN	31	M	JNR	GRZZZZMD	
FISCHER, AUGUSTE	26	F	UNKNOWN	GRZZZZPA	
ERNST	4	M	CHILD	GRZZZZPA	
AUGUST	2	M	CHILD	GRZZZZPA	
WILHELMINE	62	F	UNKNOWN	GRZZZZPA	
BOLLMANN, LUDWIG	60	M	JNR	GRZZZZMD	
SOBOCHINSKI, FRANZ	38	M	BKR	GRZZZZIL	
OKSUSKA, MARIA	25	F	UNKNOWN	GRZZZZMN	
ELEONORA	3	F	CHILD	GRZZZZMN	
LUDWIG	.10	M	INFANT	GRZZZZMN	
RASENKIEWICZ, MICHALINA	19	F	UNKNOWN	GRZZZZIL	
MINDER, CECILIA	18	F	UNKNOWN	GRZZZZIL	
WEISSFUSS, MARTHA	21	F	UNKNOWN	GRZZZZPA	
MASCHNER, JULIUS	48	M	PNTR	GRZZZZMI	
MAX	14	M	PNTR	GRZZZZMI	
MUSCH, EDUARD	34	M	LABR	GRZZZZIL	
CAROLINE	29	F	UNKNOWN	GRZZZZIL	
EDUARD	9	M	CHILD	GRZZZZIL	
JOHANN	6	M	CHILD	GRZZZZIL	
PAULINE	5	F	CHILD	GRZZZZIL	
LENZ, ROSALIA	19	F	UNKNOWN	GRZZZZMD	
MEYER, HEINR.	37	M	LABR	GRZZZZIN	
KOTLEWSKY, KOSTEK	23	M	LABR	GRZZZZIL	
KLEIN, JOSEFINE	32	F	UNKNOWN	GRZZZZMO	
FRANZ	.11	M	INFANT	GRZZZZMO	
KOLSKA, JULIANA	50	F	UNKNOWN	GRZZZZIL	
TIEDEMANN, GUSTA	17	M	TNM	GRZZZZIL	
BEMER, ANNA	66	F	UNKNOWN	GRZZZZIN	
MELECKA, MARIANNA	35	F	UNKNOWN	GRZZZZIL	
MARIANNA	10	F	CH	GRZZZZIL	
JOSEPH	7	M	CHILD	GRZZZZIL	
PELAGIA	3	F	CHILD	GRZZZZIL	
WLADISLAUS	2	M	CHILD	GRZZZZIL	
LABUDDA, AUGUSTA	65	F	UNKNOWN	GRZZZZMI	
ANTONIE	10	M	CH	GRZZZZMI	
LICHTENBERG, ANNA	21	F	UNKNOWN	GRZZZZMI	
TANNENFREUND, AMALIA	24	F	UNKNOWN	GRZZZZMI	
KOTLEWSKI, JULIANA	21	F	UNKNOWN	GRZZZZMI	
KRONSCHLEGEL, ELEONORE	21	F	UNKNOWN	GRZZZZOH	
ZOELLER, PHILIPPINE	18	F	UNKNOWN	GRZZZZOH	
DREFKE, AUGUSTE	27	F	UNKNOWN	GRZZZZOH	
RICHTER, FRIEDERIKE	68	F	UNKNOWN	GRZZZZPA	
SPRENGLER, CARL	14	M	UNKNOWN	GRZZZZPA	
EBERHARDT, CRESENZ	19	M	BRR	GRZZZZMO	
NEUMEISTER, JOHANN	25	M	FARMER	GRZZZZPA	
DIERCKS, ANNA	19	F	UNKNOWN	GRZZZZPA	
WOIKE, EMILIE	16	F	UNKNOWN	GRZZZZOH	
SCHAEFER, WALTHER	21	M	FARMER	GRZZZZPA	
ZUELKE, EMMA	18	F	UNKNOWN	GRZZZZMD	
EBERHARDT, WILHELM	24	M	BRR	GRZZZZMO	
KRUSE, CATH.	51	F	UNKNOWN	GRZZZZMD	

303

PASSENGER	AGE SEX	OCCUPATION	PRVL DES
CATH.	13 F	UNKNOWN	GRZZZZMD
SOERGEL, OTTO	32 M	FARMER	GRZZZZMD
BLASEL, THERESE	23 F	UNKNOWN	GRZZZZMD
KREIB, CARL	16 M	BBR	GRZZZZMN
GEDULDIG, LUDWIG	27 M	FARMER	GRZZZZUNK
DOESS, EMILIE	22 F	UNKNOWN	GRZZZZKY
RICHTER, MARIE	6 F	CHILD	GRZZZZKY
WINTER, MARY	15 F	UNKNOWN	GRZZZZKY
LOOS, ROBERT	30 M	LKSH	GRZZZZMO
FRIES, MARIE	20 F	UNKNOWN	GRZZZZMO
NOLTE, CATH.	18 F	UNKNOWN	GRZZZZIL
ERNST, CONRAD	18 M	TNM	GRZZZZIL
SCHLOTTHAUER, HEIN.	17 M	TNM	GRZZZZIL
TOMCZAK, MARIANNA	36 F	UNKNOWN	GRZZZZPA
KOWALSKA, PAULINE	22 F	UNKNOWN	GRZZZZPA
ZYLA, AUGUST	15 M	UNKNOWN	GRZZZZPA
WINDER, MARG.	23 F	UNKNOWN	GRZZZZPA
KNOTT, ELISE	16 F	UNKNOWN	GRZZZZPA
KUEGEL, MARG.	21 F	UNKNOWN	GRZZZZOH
PHISTER, MARIE	18 F	UNKNOWN	GRZZZZOH
CONRAD	16 M	WTR	GRZZZZOH
MARG.	20 F	UNKNOWN	GRZZZZOH
LOSKAM, JOHANN	25 M	FARMER	GRZZZZMD
BOEH, PANKRATZ	67 M	FARMER	GRZZZZIL
BAYER, JACOBINA	24 F	UNKNOWN	GRZZZZIL
GEORG	52 M	LABR	GRZZZZIL
BARBARA	19 F	UNKNOWN	GRZZZZIL
NOWAKI, VALENTI	28 M	LABR	GRZZZZPA
JABLEWSKI, JOSEFA	24 F	UNKNOWN	GRZZZZPA
SCHWENCK, SOPHIE	26 F	UNKNOWN	GRZZZZOH
FREITAG, CATH.	24 F	UNKNOWN	GRZZZZIL
HUBERT, WILH.	45 M	FARMER	GRZZZZWI
DANIEL, AUGUSTE	64 F	UNKNOWN	GRZZZZWI
LANG, PPAULINE	33 F	UNKNOWN	GRZZZZMI
WILHELM	12 M	CH	GRZZZZMI
CARL	9 M	CHILD	GRZZZZMI
ANNA	7 F	CHILD	GRZZZZMI
DREIKE, FERDINAND	66 M	FARMER	GRZZZZMI
ERNESTINE	63 F	UNKNOWN	GRZZZZMI
IDA	25 F	UNKNOWN	GRZZZZMI
DUERFT, ANDREAS	16 M	WCHMKR	GRZZZZMO
SCHMIDT, JOHANN	50 M	FARMER	GRZZZZMO
JOHANNA	57 F	UNKNOWN	GRZZZZMO
JOHANN	28 M	FARMER	GRZZZZMO
MARG.	26 F	UNKNOWN	GRZZZZMO
KUNIGUNDE	11 F	UNKNOWN	GRZZZZMO
MARTHA	3 F	CHILD	GRZZZZMO
PANKRATZ	.03 M	INFANT	GRZZZZMO
MARGARETHA	16 F	INF	GRZZZZMO
PREISMEYER, CAROLINE	65 F	UNKNOWN	GRZZZZIN
MATHILDE	3 F	CHILD	GRZZZZIN
KREISS, ANDREAS	22 M	BRZ	GRZZZZOH
CRISTINE	22 F	UNKNOWN	GRZZZZOH
WIESE, FRIEDR.	45 M	LABR	GRZZZZWI
IDA	21 F	UNKNOWN	GRZZZZWI
SOEFKE, BARBARA	57 F	UNKNOWN	GRZZZZMO
THERESE	21 F	UNKNOWN	GRZZZZMO
HERMANN	18 M	BCHR	GRZZZZMO
SCHREIDER, ELISABETH	54 F	UNKNOWN	GRZZZZKY
MINNA	15 F	UNKNOWN	GRZZZZKY
JOSEPH	10 M	CH	GRZZZZKY
MARIA	8 F	CHILD	GRZZZZKY
VONBOKERN, WILH.	15 M	PNTR	GRZZZZMD
BUSSELMANN, WILH.	18 M	PNTR	GRZZZZIL
LUKASZIK, MARIANNA	23 F	UNKNOWN	GRZZZZOH
MALEK, MICHAEL	25 M	LABR	GRZZZZPA
MARKERT, BABETTE	18 F	UNKNOWN	GRZZZZKY
MEIERKIEWICZ, PELAGIA	24 F	UNKNOWN	GRZZZZOH
LEWENSON, PESCHA	18 F	UNKNOWN	GRZZZZWI
KIRSNER, SCHAIL	19 M	LABR	GRZZZZWI
WINDERLIN, EMILIE	20 F	UNKNOWN	SRZZZZWI
SIMON, MATHILDE	27 F	UNKNOWN	GRZZZZWI
HERBERT, ANNA	14 F	UNKNOWN	GRZZZZWI
LUDWIG, RUDOLF	52 M	FARMER	GRZZZZWI
ELISE	56 F	UNKNOWN	GRZZZZWI
HEINRICH	26 M	FARMER	GRZZZZWI
ANNA	25 F	UNKNOWN	GRZZZZWI
HANDKE, CHRISTINE	20 F	UNKNOWN	GRZZZZMD
REINKE, MARIE	53 F	UNKNOWN	GRZZZZUNK
ROSALIA	17 F	UNKNOWN	GRZZZZUNK
ANNA	9 F	CHILD	GRZZZZUNK
KWASNIEWSKI, CASMIR	13 M	UNKNOWN	GRZZZZUNK
NIEZGOSKA, ANTONIA	62 F	UNKNOWN	GRZZZZIL
NEIDBALSKA, CATH.	25 F	UNKNOWN	GRZZZZIL
WISCHMEIER, HEINRICH	16 M	WTR	GRZZZZKY
ZARELSKI, ANTON	28 M	LABR	GRZZZZIL
MARIANNE	24 F	UNKNOWN	GRZZZZIL
DERNBLUETH, HANS	26 M	GDNR	GRZZZZOH
GEUTSCH, BERNH.	22 M	BCHR	GRZZZZMO
ALTHABER, CARL	45 M	CPTR	GRZZZZKS
AUGUSTE	40 F	UNKNOWN	GRZZZZKS
FRANZ	10 M	CH	GRZZZZKS
MARIE	8 F	CHILD	GRZZZZKS
ROENNSPIESS, PAULINE	35 F	UNKNOWN	GRZZZZKS
HUSER, FRITZ	64 M	FARMER	GRZZZZOH
ELISABETH	59 F	UNKNOWN	GRZZZZOH
ANTON	16 M	LABR	GRZZZZOH
JOSEPH	10 M	CH	GRZZZZOH
MEYHAUS, HERM.	18 M	FARMER	GRZZZZOH
REMUCKER, HEINRICH	32 M	FARMER	GRZZZZOH
MOELLNMANN, HEINRICH	37 M	FARMER	GRZZZZOH
HERMANN	35 M	FARMER	GRZZZZOH
ELISABETH	31 F	UNKNOWN	GRZZZZOH
BERNHARD	28 M	TNM	GRZZZZOH
THEODOR	24 M	TNM	GRZZZZOH
WEBER, FRIEDR.	35 M	MCHT	GRZZZZTX
DOLLINGER, FRIEDR.	46 M	FARMER	GRZZZZMD
MARG.	47 F	UNKNOWN	GRZZZZMD
FRIEDR.	16 M	FARMER	GRZZZZMD
CAROLINE	9 F	CHILD	GRZZZZMD
CHRISTIAN	6 M	CHILD	GRZZZZMD
SCHMIDT, FR.	17 M	BRR	GRZZZZKY
BURCKHARDT, CATH.	20 F	UNKNOWN	GRZZZZIL
ZEN, EDUARD	28 M	FARMER	GRZZZZIA
KRUEGER, AUGUSTE	29 F	UNKNOWN	GRZZZZIA
FRANZ	2 M	CHILD	GRZZZZIA
MARTHA	.10 F	INFANT	GRZZZZIA
FENING, EUGEN	17 M	PNTR	GRZZZZIL
BRAUN, THERESIA	35 F	UNKNOWN	GRZZZZMO
EMILIE	8 F	CHILD	GRZZZZMO
HEINRICH	4 M	CHILD	GRZZZZMO
MARIA	2 F	CHILD	GRZZZZMO
BOEHLLKE, VALERIA	25 F	UNKNOWN	GRZZZZMD
PFEFFERLE, LEO	37 M	FARMER	GRZZZZMN
JOSEFINE	38 F	UNKNOWN	GRZZZZMN
MAX	10 M	CH	GRZZZZMN
BERTHOLD	6 M	CHILD	GRZZZZMN
ADOLF	3 M	CHILD	GRZZZZMN
KRUEGER, GOTTFRIED	69 M	GDNR	GRZZZZIL
JOHANNE	45 F	UNKNOWN	GRZZZZIL
EMIL	15 M	UNKNOWN	GRZZZZIL
BERTHA	12 F	UNKNOWN	GRZZZZIL
WETZEL, HULDA	20 F	UNKNOWN	GRZZZZIL
BECK, FRIEDR.	23 M	FARMER	GRZZZZIL
KUERKER, SOPHIE	15 F	UNKNOWN	GRZZZZMS
KEIDELBERGER, JACOB	16 M	SHMK	GRZZZZMD
KRIEG, ELISE	18 F	UNKNOWN	GRZZZZOH
DUNKER, FERDINAND	23 M	JNR	GRZZZZOH
MOORBRINK, AUGUST	25 M	BKR	GRZZZZOH
SCHWARTING, GEORG.	33 M	FARMER	GRZZZZOH
META	28 F	UNKNOWN	GRZZZZOH
WUESTNER, ANNA	15 F	UNKNOWN	GRZZZZOH
KOHALE, EMILIE	17 F	UNKNOWN	GRZZZZMN
STUTHMANN, FRIEDR.	17 M	LABR	GRZZZZMO
BLESNAWIG, DOROTHEA	79 F	UNKNOWN	GRZZZZMD
GERSTETTER, FANNY	28 F	UNKNOWN	GRZZZZMD
FRIEDR.	.05 M	INFANT	GRZZZZMD
WIEGE, FRITZ	25 M	JNR	GRZZZZIN
LINDNER, GEORG	32 M	SMH	GRZZZZMD
SEMDERMEYER, CARL	50 M	FARMER	GRZZZZNE

PASSENGER	AGE	SEX	OCCUPATION	PRVVL	DES
MARIA	47	F	UNKNOWN	GRZZZZNE	
MARIA	17	F	UNKNOWN	GRZZZZNE	
LOUISE	11	F	UNKNOWN	GRZZZZNE	
CARL	4	M	CHILD	GRZZZZNE	
HEINR.	2	M	CHILD	GRZZZZNE	
LISCHEN	14	F	UNKNOWN	GRZZZZNE	
STEFFEN, ANNA	18	F	UNKNOWN	GRZZZZIN	
STRAETER, HEINR.	52	M	LABR	GRZZZZNE	
CAROLINE	49	F	UNKNOWN	GRZZZZNE	
HEINRICH	18	M	LABR	GRZZZZNE	
CARL	15	M	UNKNOWN	GRZZZZNE	
CARL	15	M	UNKNOWN	GRZZZZNE	
LOUISA	11	F	UNKNOWN	GRZZZZNE	
CAROLINE	8	F	CHILD	GRZZZZNE	
HANE, E.H.	8	M	CHILD	GRZZZZNE	
KNIEPKAMP, HEINR.	17	M	FARMER	GRZZZZNE	
FRIESNER, SOPHIE	16	F	UNKNOWN	GRZZZZNE	
LIBERTI, WILHELM	42	M	LABR	GRZZZZIN	
WITTL, FRIEDREIKE	43	F	UNKNOWN	GRZZZZWI	
SCCHMIDT, FRIEDERIKE	43	F	UNKNOWN	GRZZZZWI	
LIPKE, JOHANNES	27	M	FARMER	GRZZZZMD	
SCHAFFER, CAROLINE	20	F	UNKNOWN	GRZZZZIA	
BRAUN, MINNA	35	F	UNKNOWN	GRZZZZIA	
FRITZ	10	M	CH	GRZZZZIA	
ALBERT	5	M	CHILD	GRZZZZIA	
HEDWIG	4	F	CHILD	GRZZZZIA	
EMIL	.11	M	INFANT	GRZZZZIA	
DOYAT, ALBERT	24	M	LABR	GRZZZZOH	
MUELLER, GEORG	16	M	LABR	GRZZZZOH	
CAROLINE	55	F	UNKNOWN	GRZZZZOH	
KEIL, LUCIA	23	F	UNKNOWN	GRZZZZOH	
ROMANKIEWICZ, ANASTASIA	70	F	UNKNOWN	GRZZZZKS	
GIESE, ANNA	13	F	UNKNOWN	GRZZZZOH	
CLARA	11	F	UNKNOWN	GRZZZZOH	
EMMA	8	F	CHILD	GRZZZZOH	
MUTH, JOHANN	43	M	LABR	GRZZZZTN	
ANNA	42	F	UNKNOWN	GRZZZZTN	
HERMANN	14	F	UNKNOWN	GRZZZZTN	
ANTON	11	M	UNKNOWN	GRZZZZTN	
CATH.	8	F	CHILD	GRZZZZTN	
OBERBECKMANN, GEORG	29	M	MCHT	GRZZZZPA	
VIEBISCH, ANNA	30	F	UNKNOWN	GRZZZZMD	
ROBERT	5	M	CHILD	GRZZZZMD	
EMIL	3	M	CHILD	GRZZZZMD	
MARIE	.08	F	INFANT	GRZZZZMD	
DIEHLER, ROBERT	23	M	BKR	GRZZZZIL	
BOHNENBERG, FERDINAND	31	M	FARMER	GRZZZZIL	
ORBANSEEK, IGNATZ	29	M	LABR	GRZZZZUNK	
GOLDENSKA, THERESIA	21	F	UNKNOWN	GRZZZZUNK	
TABEN, CARL	23	M	CPTR	GRZZZZMO	
GERDES, GERHARD	22	M	CPTR	GRZZZZMO	
ROSENTHAL, FRIEDERIKE	25	F	UNKNOWN	GRZZZZMO	
WOEHRMANN, WILH.	17	M	FARMER	GRZZZZMO	
WALDMANN, MARG.	16	F	UNKNOWN	GRZZZZOH	
SCHUMM, KUNIGUNDE	20	F	UNKNOWN	GRZZZZOH	
WIEST, CHRISTINA	37	F	UNKNOWN	GRZZZZOH	
VOLTE, AUGUSTE	18	F	UNKNOWN	GRZZZZOH	
CARL	15	M	UNKNOWN	GRZZZZOH	
MOELLER, THEODOR	50	M	LABR	GRZZZZIL	
CATH.	15	F	UNKNOWN	GRZZZZIL	
MATH, ADAM	30	M	LABR	GRZZZZIL	
WARNE, CATH.	20	F	UNKNOWN	GRZZZZKS	
BEIL, JOSEPH	29	M	JNR	GRZZZZOH	
FISCHER, CATH.	30	F	UNKNOWN	GRZZZZOH	
SMEDDINCH, GERHARD	43	M	FARMER	GRZZZZOH	
SUPPAU, MARIA	24	F	UNKNOWN	GRZZZZKY	
JOSEPH	4	M	CHILD	GRZZZZKY	
THERESE	1	F	CHILD	GRZZZZKY	
SIEMER, EPHEMIA	18	F	UNKNOWN	GRZZZZIA	
VOELKERS, HEIN.	75	M	UNKNOWN	GRZZZZMD	
KOCK, HERMANN	19	M	BBR	GRZZZZMD	
FISCHER, JOSEPH	31	M	LABR	GRZZZZUNK	
HOFFMANN, MARTHA	17	F	UNKNOWN	GRZZZZUNK	

SHIP: AMSTERDAM

FROM: ROTTERDAM
TO: NEW YORK
ARRIVED: 01 SEPTEMBER 1888

PASSENGER	AGE	SEX	OCCUPATION	PRVVL	DES
LEBINS, ANDERLY	29	M	AR	GRZZZZUSA	
ALEXANDER, ALFRED	26	M	AR	GRZZZZUSA	
WAYTHABER, ELLA	24	F	AR	GRZZZZUSA	
BAYLER, MATHILDE	20	F	NN	GRZZZZUSA	
U, U	54	M	AGT	GRZZZZUSA	
SPATZ, CHAS.	40	M	AGT	GRZZZZUSA	
SCHMIDT, HARRYE	42	M	AGT	LXZZZZUSA	
KUEFFNER, HARRY	20	M	STDNT	GRZZZZUSA	
SONNEMAIER, EMILIE	42	F	NN	GRZZZZUSA	
ROHLEDER, F.	34	M	TDR	GRZZZZUSA	
KNECHT, ARTHUR	26	M	MCHT	GRZZZZUSA	
RING, HELENE	46	F	NN	GRZZZZUSA	
LUCIE	13	F	NN	GRZZZZUSA	
ROBERT	15	M	NN	GRZZZZUSA	
SANFORD, LIZZIE	26	F	NN	GRZZZZUSA	
MEICHELBECK, RENOSSA	15	F	NN	GRZZZZUSA	
BRUCK, JOS.	50	M	AGT	GRZZZZUSA	
U	17	F	NN	GRZZZZUSA	
CHRISTEIN, MARY	27	F	NN	GRZZZZUSA	
HAARBRUECK, HERMINE	23	F	NN	GRZZZZUSA	
WEISS, CAROLINE	58	F	NN	GRZZZZUSA	
JAVILLIER, CAMILLE	27	M	SLD	FRZZZZUSA	
KUEHNEMANN, W.L.	29	M	FLST	GRZZZZUSA	
WEBER, LINA	22	F	NN	GRZZZZUSA	
RODA, ANNA	31	F	NN	GRZZZZUSA	
SISNONETTI, GIOVANNI	49	M	LABR	FRZZZZUSA	
POTERI, GIOVANNI	35	F	NN	FRZZZZUSA	
BASSO	38	M	LABR	FRZZZZUSA	
HUCCI	43	M	LABR	FRZZZZUSA	
-PEINER, MARTIN	32	M	LABR	FRZZZZUSA	
BABETTE	37	F	LABR	FRZZZZUSA	
THOUR, CHAS.	17	M	LABR	FRZZZZUSA	
STEPHAN, AURELIA	17	F	NN	FRZZZZUSA	
COLLETHI, TULGENSIE	29	M	LABR	FRZZZZUSA	
FABERI, JOSEF	26	M	LABR	GRZZZZUSA	
LEINEX, JOSEF	25	M	LABR	GRZZZZUSA	
KAHLE, CONRAD	25	M	LABR	GRZZZZUSA	
MICHEL, BARBARA	26	F	NN	GRZZZZUSA	
WATERKAMP, THEODOR	23	M	LABR	GRZZZZUSA	
LESHOR, AUGUST	20	M	BKR	GRZZZZUSA	
SCHUELLINGER, HERM.	26	M	BCHR	GRZZZZUSA	
LANGEN, JOSEF	27	M	LABR	GRZZZZUSA	
WALTER, FRIEDRICH	27	M	LABR	GRZZZZUSA	
MOHRER, ANTON	25	M	TLR	GRZZZZUSA	
SHRIVANICH, ANTON	23	M	TLR	GRZZZZUSA	
EISENHAUER, FRANZ	15	M	LABR	GRZZZZUSA	
DOWBOIA, WILHELMINE	39	F	NN	GRZZZZUSA	
ALEXANDER	14	M	NN	GRZZZZUSA	
RABINOWICZ, ABEL	34	M	LABR	GRZZZZUSA	
BOPP, FRIEDRIKE	26	F	NN	GRZZZZUSA	
BARBARA	22	F	NN	GRZZZZUSA	
HARTMANN, EMMA	20	F	NN	GRZZZZUSA	
MARLOH, JOSEF	40	M	LABR	GRZZZZUSA	
ALBERTINA	31	F	NN	GRZZZZUSA	
ANNA	11	F	CH	GRZZZZUSA	
FRANZ	9	M	CHILD	GRZZZZUSA	
AUGUST	7	M	CHILD	GRZZZZUSA	
MARTHA	4	F	CHILD	GRZZZZUSA	
ROSA	3	F	CHILD	GRZZZZUSA	
MARIA	.10	F	INFANT	GRZZZZUSA	
FULZ, ANNA	20	F	NN	GRZZZZUSA	
ELFNER, MARIA	19	F	NN	GRZZZZUSA	
HERZOG, MARGARETHA	25	F	NN	GRZZZZUSA	
RAUSER, CATH.	19	F	NN	GRZZZZUSA	
ZEBNER, ADOLF-FRIEDR.	19	M	CPTR	GRZZZZUSA	
DEEG, CHRISTINE	22	F	NN	GRZZZZUSA	
LEICHT, JOH.	25	M	BRR	GRZZZZUSA	
WITTING, KARL	29	M	LABR	GRZZZZUSA	

PASSENGER	AGE	SEX	OCCUPATION	PRVL	DES
U. PAULUS	24	M	BKR	GRZZZZZ	USA
REU---, JULIUS	21	M	BKR	GRZZZZZ	USA
SKARU-KA, CAROLA	24	F	NN	GRZZZZZ	USA
ROSA	21	F	NN	GRZZZZZ	USA
MARIA	1	F	CHILD	GRZZZZZ	USA
WEIS, ANTON	18	M	SHMK	GRZZZZZ	USA
ENI, GEORG	22	M	BKR	GRZZZZZ	USA
KOCHENDOERFER, LEONHARD	24	M	CPTR	GRZZZZZ	USA
EICHENLAUB, MATHIAS	30	M	FARMER	GRZZZZZ	USA
LUCKOW, MATHILDE	43	F	NN	GRZZZZZ	USA
HEDWIG	5	F	CHILD	GRZZZZZ	USA
FRIEDA	4	F	CHILD	GRZZZZZ	USA
EMMA	.11	F	INFANT	GRZZZZZ	USA
CARL	37	M	LABR	GRZZZZZ	USA
RAASCH, BERNHARD	19	M	LABR	GRZZZZZ	USA
LAURA	51	F	NN	GRZZZZZ	USA
ELISA	22	F	NN	GRZZZZZ	USA
IDA	17	F	NN	GRZZZZZ	USA
ANNA	11	F	CH	GRZZZZZ	USA
BERTHA	9	F	CHILD	GRZZZZZ	USA
CATHARINA	70	F	NN	GRZZZZZ	USA
NEUMANN, MARGARETHA	18	F	NN	GRZZZZZ	USA
RUCKABERLE, CATHARINA	51	F	NN	GRZZZZZ	USA
RAHNER, AUGUST	25	M	LABR	GRZZZZZ	USA
RIDER, ADAM	25	M	BBR	GRZZZZZ	USA
TRAUTH, GEORG	28	M	BBR	GRZZZZZ	USA
HAEUSERMANN, CAROLINE	19	F	NN	GRZZZZZ	USA
MOLL, JACOB	30	M	BKR	GRZZZZZ	USA
EDLER, JOSEF	15	M	NN	GRZZZZZ	USA
MAGDALENE	18	M	LABR	GRZZZZZ	USA
MEININGER, MARIA	22	F	NN	GRZZZZZ	USA
JOOST, JOHANN	26	M	LABR	GRZZZZZ	USA
FRIESE, FRANZ	21	M	LABR	GRZZZZZ	USA
SPROINGER, JOSEF	23	M	CPTR	GRZZZZZ	USA
FELDEN, JACOB	14	M	LABR	GRZZZZZ	USA
KLINGES, CATHERINA	25	F	NN	GRZZZZZ	USA
BREIER, LUDWIG	26	M	BL	GRZZZZZ	USA
HUCK, ERNST	16	M	LABR	GRZZZZZ	USA
ENGESZER, VALENT.	19	M	BBR	GRZZZZZ	USA
BAUMGARTEN, CHRISTOPH	21	M	SDLR	GRZZZZZ	USA
ICKLE, HEINRICK	40	M	SCH	GRZZZZZ	USA
IDA	32	F	NN	GRZZZZZ	USA
ETJEN, GEORG	19	M	LABR	GRZZZZZ	USA
HERREN, CARL	40	M	PNTR	GRZZZZZ	USA
ZWICKER, CARL	24	M	BCHR	GRZZZZZ	USA
FUNK, FRANZISKA	46	F	NN	GRZZZZZ	USA
SIMON, MORITZ	20	M	MCHT	GRZZZZZ	USA
SCHMITT, HEINRICH	23	M	LKSH	GRZZZZZ	USA
SCHANER, ALWIN	14	M	LABR	GRZZZZZ	USA
SCHLAPP, ANTON	13	M	LABR	GRZZZZZ	USA
SIEGLER, PETER	22	M	SHMK	GRZZZZZ	USA
SAUTER, ERNST	17	M	LABR	GRZZZZZ	USA
SOLLRIG, JOSEF	19	M	MECH	GRZZZZZ	USA
SAUTTER, AMALIA	22	F	NN	GRZZZZZ	USA
SCHWENCKER, WILHELMINE	66	F	NN	GRZZZZZ	USA
GESS, ELISABETH	26	F	NN	GRZZZZZ	USA
GEORG	5	M	CHILD	GRZZZZZ	USA
EMIL	2	M	CHILD	GRZZZZZ	USA
MINA	.09	F	INFANT	GRZZZZZ	USA
KOENIG, LOUISE	25	F	NN	GRZZZZZ	USA
URNBACH, HEINRICH	15	M	LABR	GRZZZZZ	USA
GLOECKNER, ANNA	24	F	NN	GRZZZZZ	USA
MARIA	.08	F	INFANT	GRZZZZZ	USA
MIGGEMEIER, ANTON	27	M	SHMK	GRZZZZZ	USA
LENCHEN	31	F	NN	GRZZZZZ	USA
METTENBUHLER, ALBERTINA	24	F	NN	GRZZZZZ	USA
HEIDER, CATGHERINA	22	F	NN	GRZZZZZ	USA
VOIGT, RUDOLF	27	M	MCHT	GRZZZZZ	USA
MARIA	26	F	NN	GRZZZZZ	USA
RUDOLF	4	M	CHILD	GRZZZZZ	USA
MARIA	.11	F	INFANT	GRZZZZZ	USA
OMMER, JOSEF	23	M	MCHT	GRZZZZZ	USA
HAUSSMANN, CHRISTINE	60	F	NN	GRZZZZZ	USA
LOUISE	28	F	NN	GRZZZZZ	USA
LOUISE	8	F	CHILD	GRZZZZZ	USA
CARL	5	M	CHILD	GRZZZZZ	USA
WILHELM	.09	M	INFANT	GRZZZZZ	USA
HOLZHERZ, MARIE	34	F	NN	GRZZZZZ	USA
POLNITZ, ANNA	18	F	NN	GRZZZZZ	USA
PISCHER, CARL	21	M	LABR	GRZZZZZ	USA
PABST, GEORG	28	M	UNKNOWN	GRZZZZZ	USA
PFITZEMAIER, CHRISTIAN	37	M	SMH	GRZZZZZ	USA
PAULINE	37	F	NN	GRZZZZZ	USA
PAULINE	11	F	CH	GRZZZZZ	USA
WILHELM	10	M	CH	GRZZZZZ	USA
CHRISTIAN	9	M	CHILD	GRZZZZZ	USA
HERMANN	8	M	CHILD	GRZZZZZ	USA
WILHELMINE	7	F	CHILD	GRZZZZZ	USA
GOTTLIEB	2	M	CHILD	GRZZZZ	***
KESSLER, GEORG	13	M	LKSH	GRZZZZZ	USA
KRAUSE, SARAH	39	F	NN	GRZZZZZ	USA
ROSE	8	F	CHILD	GRZZZZZ	USA
KOCH, ANNA	27	F	CH	GRZZZZZ	USA
VOGELGESANG, CATHARINA	27	F	CH	GRZZZZZ	USA
WITTE, CARL	57	M	LABR	GRZZZZZ	USA
EMMA	20	F	NN	GRZZZZZ	USA
WEY-ER, ELISABETH	18	F	NN	GRZZZZZ	USA
WEBER, CHARLES	22	M	PNTR	GRZZZZZ	USA
WARMUTH, JULIUS	18	M	LABR	GRZZZZZ	USA
WEIS, JACOB	21	M	LABR	GRZZZZZ	USA
ALBER, ROSA	23	F	NN	GRZZZZZ	USA
BRANDUS, BERHARD	31	M	LABR	GRZZZZZ	USA
JORDAN, LOUISE	43	F	NN	GRZZZZZ	USA
KASPAR, JACOB	61	M	TLR	GRZZZZZ	USA
JACOB, LINA	32	F	NN	GRZZZZZ	USA
SIMON	39	F	NN	GRZZZZZ	USA
ALFRED	6	M	CHILD	GRZZZZZ	USA
FRIEDA	4	F	CHILD	GRZZZZZ	USA
AMANDA	2	F	CHILD	GRZZZZZ	USA
BALTUS, JACOB	49	M	CRBLDR	GRZZZZZ	USA
U	43	F	NN	GRZZZZZ	USA
GERTRUD	20	F	NN	GRZZZZZ	USA
CHRISTIAN	18	M	NN	GRZZZZZ	USA
AGNES	8	F	CHILD	GRZZZZZ	USA
JACOB	6	M	CHILD	GRZZZZZ	USA
RAPHAEL	.01	M	INFANT	GRZZZZZ	USA
FASSBENDER, ANNA	21	F	INF	GRZZZZZ	USA
DIESER, JOSEFINE	22	F	SVNT	GRZZZZZ	USA
BOPP, JOSEF	22	M	UNKNOWN	GRZZZZZ	USA
BERNAU, FRANZ	37	M	PNTR	GRZZZZZ	USA
HEDWIG	21	F	NN	GRZZZZZ	USA
FERDINAND	10	M	CH	GRZZZZZ	USA
BEENEN, ULRICH	23	M	MCHT	GRZZZZZ	USA
BUCHS, FANNY	32	M	LABR	GRZZZZZ	USA
CATHAIRINA	3	F	CHILD	GRZZZZZ	USA
BENDEG, ROSA	22	F	CH	GRZZZZZ	USA
BRAUN, GUSTAV	18	M	BKR	GRZZZZZ	USA
MAURER, ANNA	23	F	NN	GRZZZZZ	USA
EDDIE	3	F	CHILD	GRZZZZZ	USA
ARTHUR	.11	M	INFANT	GRZZZZZ	USA
VALENTIN	61	M	LABR	GRZZZZZ	USA
ANNA-CATH.	60	F	NN	GRZZZZZ	USA
ROSINA	20	F	NN	GRZZZZZ	USA
MUEHLSTEIN, BERL	21	M	LABR	GRZZZZZ	USA
BEILE	19	F	NN	GRZZZZZ	USA
MATTES, GOTTLOB	18	M	LABR	GRZZZZZ	USA
GABELMANN, ELISE	33	F	LABR	GRZZZZZ	USA
JULIE	7	F	CHILD	GRZZZZZ	USA
CHARLES	4	M	CHILD	GRZZZZZ	USA
ADOLF	3	M	CHILD	GRZZZZZ	USA
HERMANN	2	M	CHILD	GRZZZZZ	USA
HORN, AUGUST-CARL	37	M	FARMER	GRZZZZZ	USA
WEBER, JOHANN	20	M	BBR	GRZZZZZ	USA
KESSLER, KARL	18	M	LABR	GRZZZZZ	USA
ALTMANN, JOSEF	19	M	MCHT	GRZZZZZ	USA
NIETHAMMER, CONRAD	27	M	SHMK	GRZZZZZ	USA
B-RMEIER, FRANZISKA	16	F	NN	GRZZZZZ	USA
HOCHSTETTER, PAUL	20	M	UNKNOWN	GRZZZZZ	USA
LAMPART, FRIEDR.ROB.	20	M	CVR	GRZZZZZ	USA
SCHUHMANN, ADOLF	26	M	LABR	GRZZZZZ	USA

PASSENGER	AGE	SEX	OCCUPATION	PRVL	DES
HAERTER, FRIEDR.	27	M	WVR	GRZZZZ	USA
ALLINGER, LOUISE	20	F	NN	GRZZZZ	USA
GABELMANN, ELIE	.09	M	INFANT	GRZZZZ	USA
ZINTNER, ANNA	20	F	INF	GRZZZZ	USA
VOGEL, JOHANN	20	M	BRR	GRZZZZ	USA
GLEIBER, JOHANN	36	M	LABR	GRZZZZ	USA
MATZERATT, A.	47	M	TLR	GRZZZZ	USA
KRUGER, JU	24	M	LABR	GRZZZZ	USA
LANDMEYER, CARL	11	M	NN	GRZZZZ	USA
BERTHA	10	F	CH	GRZZZZ	USA
EPHAUSEN, HANNAH	25	F	NN	GRZZZZ	USA
FROSH, SAM.	31	M	SEMN	GRZZZZ	USA
TOBIN, JAMES	52	M	ENGR	GRZZZZ	USA
MOFSKI, FANNIE	24	F	NN	GRZZZZ	USA
LISSLING, AUGUST	29	M	SHMK	GRZZZZ	USA
ANOTONIETTE	31	F	NN	GRZZZZ	USA
CLIFT, THOMAS	45	M	LABR	GRZZZZ	USA
CLARKE, JOHN	25	M	LABR	GRZZZZ	USA
FLORENCE	18	F	LABR	GRZZZZ	USA
SURPUTSKI, CHANE	21	F	NN	GRZZZZ	USA
ISAAC	1	M	CHILD	GRZZZZ	USA
SEGEL, ROSA	21	F	CH	GRZZZZ	USA
FURYE, ARTHUR	20	M	LABR	GRZZZZ	USA
GYESCHMAN, IBYE	20	M	LABR	GRZZZZ	USA
BERTR--S, ARTHUR	25	M	MCHT	GRZZZZ	USA
RISOT---, ANGELO	30	M	WTR	GRZZZZ	USA
U, MARKS	22	M	LABR	GRZZZZ	USA
GEO-A.	44	M	DCT	GRZZZZ	USA
BISKER	29	M	SHMK	GRZZZZ	USA
MORITZ	18	M	LABR	GRZZZZ	USA
GEORGE	33	M	ENGR	GRZZZZ	USA
HARRY	21	M	LABR	GRZZZZ	USA
DAVID	30	M	FRMN	GRZZZZ	USA
PAGGEL, HENRIETTE	40	F	NN	GRZZZZ	USA
EDWARD	16	M	LABR	GRZZZZ	USA

SHIP: CEPHALONIA

FROM: LIVERPOOL AND QUEENSTOWN
TO: BOSTON
ARRIVED: 03 SEPTEMBER 1888

PASSENGER	AGE	SEX	OCCUPATION	PRVL	DES
LEGROS, CLARA	40	F	SVNT	FRZZZZ	USA

SHIP: CITY OF CHICAGO

FROM: LIVERPOOL AND QUEENSTOWN
TO: NEW YORK
ARRIVED: 03 SEPTEMBER 1888

PASSENGER	AGE	SEX	OCCUPATION	PRVL	DES
BENZ, BARBRA	18	F	SVNT	FRACBF	NY
KAESELWITZ, FRITZ	27	M	LABR	FRACBF	NY
KUNZ, FRANZ	30	M	LABR	FRACBF	NY
GEANZ, AUG.N.	32	M	LABR	FRACBF	NY
KOHN, MATHILDA	15	F	UNKNOWN	FRACBF	NY
IKEN, FEIGE	20	F	SP	FRACBF	NY
SORENSON, CAROLINE	47	F	W	FRACBF	MN
ANDRE	14	M	SMH	FRACBF	MN
HELENE	11	F	CH	FRACBF	MN
PETER	6	M	CHILD	FRACBF	MN
MALVINE	00	F	INF	FRACBF	MN
HARLUNG, LAURITZ	20	M	BCHR	FRACBF	CH
JESSEN, MARTIN	17	M	LABR	FRACBF	IA
JENS	20	M	TNR	FRACBF	IA
BUCH, JENS	19	M	LABR	FRACBF	IA

PASSENGER	AGE	SEX	OCCUPATION	PRVL	DES
MICH.	15	M	LABR	FRACBF	IA
MARIE	16	F	SVNT	FRACBF	IA
LEIBRUSKIND, LEOPOLD	24	M	CL	FRADXW	NY
BRAND, ISSAK	28	M	CL	FRADXW	NY
BREWER, THOS.	23	M	TLR	FRACBF	NY
MANDEL, ESTER	10	F	CH	FRACBF	CAL
NEISEWSOHN, JON	25	M	HTR	FRACBF	USA
GEISCHUTZ, ANNA	18	F	SVNT	FRACBF	NY
GESTEA, DAN	31	M	TRVLR	FRADBQ	NY

SHIP: SUEVIA

FROM: HAMBURG AND HAVRE
TO: NEW YORK
ARRIVED: 03 SEPTEMBER 1888

PASSENGER	AGE	SEX	OCCUPATION	PRVL	DES
ANDERSEN, CARL	24	M	UNKNOWN	PRZZZZ	NY
SCHUTT, DETLEO	29	M	UNKNOWN	PRZZZZ	NY
REXHAUSEN, JOHS.	17	M	UNKNOWN	PRZZZZ	NY
JOSEPH, MALA	25	F	SGL	PRZZZZ	NY
ZURRNER, MARTHA	14	F	SGL	PRZZZZ	NY
SCHMIDT, LOUISE	17	F	SGL	PRZZZZ	NY
SEEMANN, OTTO	17	M	UNKNOWN	PRAADE	NY
JENSEN, PETER	31	M	UNKNOWN	PRZZZZ	NY
RUBBERT, EDO	18	M	LABR	PRACBW	NY
WIEDMANN, ROSINE	23	F	SGL	PRAACB	NY
STROHMEYER, CAROLINE	20	F	SGL	PRAEVV	NY
FABER, FREDKE	18	F	SGL	PRAJVT	NY
KRAUSBECK, PAUL	17	M	LKSH	WMZZZZ	NY
STAUCH, ANNA	38	F	WO	PRZZZZ	NY
MARGA.	8	F	CHILD	PRZZZZ	NY
KATTA.	7	F	CHILD	PRZZZZ	NY
ROSS, DORA	00	F	UNKNOWN	PRZZZZ	NY
HEINR.	13	M	BY	PRZZZZ	NY
HERTEL, CHRISTIANE	64	F	WO	PRAFTI	NY
PFLUGER, KARL	51	M	UNKNOWN	PRAFTI	NY
HOLZMANN, JOHANN	21	M	UNKNOWN	PRAITI	NY
OTTKE, LOUISE	21	F	SGL	PRAEZV	NY
GOPP, MARIE	20	F	SGL	PRAFNP	NY
KORSELT, WILH.	41	F	WO	SYZZZZ	NY
RAHEL	44	F	W	SYZZZZ	NY
AUGUSTE	17	F	CH	SYZZZZ	NY
PAULINAE	13	F	CH	SYZZZZ	NY
EMILIE	7	F	CHILD	SYZZZZ	NY
EMMA	5	F	CHILD	SYZZZZ	NY
EDEN, AMALIE	23	F	SGL	SYADVH	NY
AXT, ALBERT	14	M	LABR	SYAETN	NY
FLACHMILLER, HEINRICH	14	M	BY	HNZZZZ	NY
RICHTER, JOHANNE	42	F	WO	HNABPC	NY
CLARA	8	F	CHILD	HNABPC	NY
OSCAR	7	M	CHILD	HNABPC	NY
EMMA	6	F	CHILD	HNABPC	NY
NOWATZKA, STANISL.	28	F	WO	HNAAKH	NY
HANS	8	M	CHILD	HNAAKH	NY
KAMM, HEDWIG	18	F	SGL	HNACQO	NY
TASCH, ELISABETH	18	F	SGL	HSZZZZ	NY
EUCHNER, FRIDA	20	F	UNKNOWN	HSAFBD	NY
SCHUDGE, MARGA.	20	F	SGL	HSAIFG	NY
VIELHAUER, WILHELM	16	M	FARMER	WMZZZZ	NY
KATHA.	13	F	SGL	WMZZZZ	NY
SCHAUS, CHRISTIAN	37	M	FARMER	WMAFNK	NY
PAULINE	31	F	W	WMAFNK	NY
HERMANN	8	M	CHILD	WMAFNK	NY
AUGUST	7	M	CHILD	WMAFNK	NY
RUDOLF	4	M	CHILD	WMAFNK	NY
EMIL	2	M	CHILD	WMAFNK	NY
WILH.	.09	M	INFANT	WMAFNK	NY
SCHUHMANN, CURT	24	M	FARMER	WMACSD	NY
DOGGENHAUSEN, CATHA.	26	F	WO	WMACBF	NY
ELISABETH	.11	F	INFANT	WMACBF	NY

307

PASSENGER	AGE	SEX	OCCUPATION	PRVL	DES
STRASSER, GENOFEVA	32	F	WO		WMAECDNY
THERESE	8	F	CHILD		WMAECDNY
ULBRICHT, HEINR.	38	M	BCHR		PRZZZZNY
TIMMERMANN, FRANZ	22	M	LABR		PRACBFNY
BEIKE, HEINR.	26	M	CGRMKR		PRZZZZNY
TRIEBEL, FRDKE.	21	F	SGL		PRZZZZNY
BRAT, PAUL	43	M	TLR		PRADDQNY
AUGUSTE	38	F	W		PRADDQNY
JENNY	4	F	CHILD		PRADDQNY
FANNY	.02	F	INFANT		PRADDQNY
FITZAU, EDUARD	43	M	LABR		PRACBFNY
IDA	32	F	W		PRACBFNY
WENDT, WILHELM	20	M	LABR		PRADVINY
BRUEGMANN, CHRISTINE	19	F	SGL		PRAETHNY
GRIMM, AUGUST	25	M	LABR		PRALZCNY
FRIEDRICH	24	M	LABR		PRALZCNY
FRANKE, EDUARD	20	M	FARMER		SYZZZZNY
HOFMEISTER, ALBERT	25	M	UNKNOWN		BWZZZZNY
HARTIG, WILHELM	18	M	UNKNOWN		BWAFBFNY
SCHWALBE, CAECILIE	28	F	SGL		PRZZZZNY
JURGENS, FRIEDRICH	21	M	BBR		PRAECTNY
SCHMIDT, BERNH.	24	M	MCHT		PRABQWNY
KOCH, CARL	18	M	UNKNOWN		PRZZZZNY
NETZON, LOUIS	63	M	TLR		PRZZZZNY
LUDOMMER, JETTE	56	F	WO		PRZZZZNY
THIEMEL, HEINRICH	37	M	LABR		PRAKPSNY
ANNA	31	F	SGL		PRAKPSNY
GOERLICH, PAUL	37	M	JNR		PRAKPSNY
SEIBERLICH, ANNA	27	F	SGL		PRAKPSNY
WERTHMANN, MARIE	23	F	SGL		PRAFNPNY
HUPPERT, JOH.	23	M	UNKNOWN		BVZZZZNY
SCHARFF, SARA	56	F	WO		BVABQQNY
ISRAEL	23	M	WO		BVABQQNY
AKIBA	8	F	CHILD		BVABQQNY
LAZARUS	8	M	CHILD		BVABQQNY
KRUMMBACH, FRIEDR.	51	M	UNKNOWN		BVACJINY
WILHE.	59	F	UNKNOWN		BVACJINY
JOHANNETTE	18	F	UNKNOWN		BVACJINY
KARL	8	M	CHILD		BVACJINY
VIELHAUER, JOHS.	24	M	UNKNOWN		BVADFLNY
SEIFERT, HEINR.	24	M	UNKNOWN		BVAEAZNY
SCHURREK, ISCAR	16	M	UNKNOWN		BVAEXWNY
KLUMPP, GUSTAV	14	M	UNKNOWN		BVAEXWNY
GROS, CAROLINE	16	F	UNKNOWN		WMZZZZNY
SCHWAZZ, CATHA.	21	F	UNKNOWN		WMZZZZNY
MARIE	8	F	CHILD		WMZZZZNY
ROESNER, JOSEPH	53	M	UNKNOWN		PRZZZZNY
CAROLINE	54	F	UNKNOWN		PRZZZZNY
ANNA	25	F	WO		PRZZZZNY
OSCAR	.09	M	INFANT		PRZZZZNY
SCHADE, JOSEF	41	M	UNKNOWN		PRZZZZNY
BOSSLAU, LOUISE	16	F	SGL		PRZZZZNY
HOSER, SIMON	41	M	MCHT		PRAAKHNY
SCHATZEN, MICHAEL	24	M	JNR		PRZZZZNY
HENDEL, ANDR.	34	M	PNTR		PRAAUZNY
MARGA.	8	F	CHILD		PRAAUZNY
HIMMERICH, SUSANNE	15	F	SGL		PRAAUZNY
JPATZZYKAWSKI, GEORG	14	M	LABR		PRAAYFNY
LORENZ, ANNA	16	F	SGL		PRAEMANY
SCHJERLAND, KAREN	21	F	WO		PRZZZZNY
MARIE	.09	F	INFANT		PRZZZZNY
ROTHE, GOTTFRIED	24	M	LABR		SYZZZZNY
SCHOLLE, LOUISE	61	F	WO		SYAJYBNY
IWERSEN, LENE	24	F	SGL		SYADAANY
CAROLINE	17	F	SGL		SYADAANY
KUEPPER, HEINRICH	21	M	JNR		PRZZZZNY
STAATLICH, TONI	21	F	SGL		PRACSDNY
PAULA	21	F	SGL		PRACSDNY
LISBETH	19	F	SGL		PRACSDNY
LACHS, SALOMON	54	M	LABR		PRACPSNY
PAUL, FRIEDR.	24	M	UNKNOWN		PRZZZZNY
WITTE, CARL	23	M	CL		PRZZZZNY
PINKUS, EMMA	19	F	SGL		PRAJKUNY
DECKWART, AUGUST	68	M	LKSH		PRAJKUNY
WOELKEL, OTTO	29	M	JNR		PRAACQNY
LINA	21	F	SGL		PRAACONY
ITALIENER, MINA	22	F	SGL		PRACBFNY
SCHELLACK, MARIE	26	F	SGL		PRAEIXNY
REUPER, HEINR.	24	M	UNKNOWN		PRACXKNY
MARCUS, MAX	16	M	BBR		PRZZZZNY
HOEPNER, FRITZ	23	M	BBR		PRAEMANY
HUESKE, MARIE	19	F	SGL		PRZZZZNY
FIRCHAU, OTTILIE	26	F	SGL		PRZZZZNY
SEYFERT, CHRISTINE	30	F	WO		PRAADENY
PAUL	5	M	CHILD		PRAADENY
BOCK, WILHELM	26	M	MCHT		PRACBRNY
RIETSCH, ELISE	36	F	WO		SYZZZZNY
MORTNSEN, ABELINE	37	F	WO		PRZZZZNY
MARG.	6	F	CHILD		PRZZZZNY
ANNA	3	F	CHILD		PRZZZZNY
PETERSEN, CHRISTINE	39	F	LABR		PRAESDNY
WITT, MARIE	31	F	W		PRAESDNY
HEINR.	.09	M	INFANT		PRAESDNY
ALTENKIRCH, MARIE	36	F	WO		PRALJGNY
HELENE	8	F	CHILD		PRALJGNY
BAUER, AUGUSTE	28	F	WO		PRALJGNY
OTTO	28	M	S		PRALJGNY
KRUG, ROBERT	18	M	PNTR		PRAAKHNY
THIELE, FRIEDR.	16	F	SGL		PRZZZZNY
BATTIGE, AUG.	23	M	FARMER		PRZZZZNY
SIEG, ANTON	54	M	LABR		PRZZZZNY
KRONEMANN, WILH.	54	M	FARMER		PRAIWZNY
KRONBERGER, CATHA.	26	F	WO		PRACBFNY
MINNIE	.10	F	INFANT		PRACBFNY
USADEL, AUGUSTE	30	F	WO		PRAAKHNY
MAX	6	M	CHILD		PRAAKHNY
THIEROLF, CATHA.	22	F	SGL		HSZZZZNY
GERN, EVA	23	F	SGL		HSABKGNY
DIENES, ELISABETH	21	F	SGL		PRZZZZNY
GUTH, EVA	21	F	SGL		PRZZZZNY
MAYER, JETTCHEN	25	F	SGL		PRABTUNY
GUENEBAUM, NANNY	17	F	SGL		PRABOQNY
LINK, WILHELMINE	22	F	SGL		PRABVDNY
HUESKE, LUDWIG	65	M	UNKNOWN		PRZZZZNY
ALBERTINE	62	F	W		PRZZZZNY
BAHR, AUGUST	24	M	LABR		PRACSXNY
BOLTE, ERNST	24	M	LABR		SRZZZZNY
PFANGER, ADELBERT	24	M	LABR		SRZZZZNY
ADELHEIT	30	F	SGL		SRZZZZNY
MICHEL, MARIA	18	F	WO		SRZZZZNY
OESCHGER, JOSEF	25	M	LABR		SRZZZZNY
ROSINE	19	F	SGL		SRZZZZNY
WERNER, GUSTAV	21	M	LABR		SRZZZZNY
FROEHLICH, CARL	32	M	LABR		SRZZZZNY
WALIER, JACOB	25	M	LABR		SRZZZZNY
BASSI, JOSEFINE	31	F	SGL		FRZZZZNY
SITZLER, CATHARINE	41	F	SGL		SRZZZZNY
TEUBER, SIEGMUND	29	M	LABR		SRZZZZNY
VOLLMER, HERRMANN	29	M	LABR		SRAAKHNY
JULIE, CHRISTIANA	24	F	SGL		SRAAKHNY
DOMINIQUE, CHANGE	35	M	LABR		FRZZZZNY
FERDINAND	33	M	LABR		FRZZZZNY
JULIANE	30	F	SGL		FRZZZZNY
CONRAD, CHARLES	46	M	LABR		SRZZZZNY
SCHUUR, FRANZ	26	M	LABR		SRZZZZNY
HAIER, CARL	20	M	LABR		SRZZZZNY
HAILMUELLER, ANTON	21	M	LABR		SRZZZZNY
ROTHMANN, JOHANN	37	M	LABR		PRZZZZNY
SELMA	43	F	W		PRZZZZNY
ROSA	9	F	CHILD		PRZZZZNY
ANNA	8	F	CHILD		PRZZZZNY
FRIEDRICH	6	F	CHILD		PRZZZZNY
WILHELM	2	M	CHILD		PRZZZZNY
WAEHRLE, GEORG	26	M	LABR		PRZZZZNY
CATHARINE	26	F	W		PRZZZZNY
PANTHER, JOSEF	19	M	LABR		PRZZZZNY
SIEGFRIED	18	M	LABR		PRZZZZNY
HUELLER, CARL	17	M	LABR		PRZZZZNY
CONRAD	17	M	LABR		PRZZZZNY
EBVERS, RUDOLPH	53	M	MCHT		PRACBFNY

PASSENGER	AGE	SEX	OCCUPATION	PRVVL	DES
THIELSEN, WILHELMINE	27	F	SGL	PRACBFNY	
HOEFER, LOUISE	26	F	SGL	PRZZZZNY	
SHAW, JENNET	45	F	WO	PRACBRNY	
ANNIE	25	F	SGL	PRACBRNY	
KAUFMANN, HENRY	36	M	MCHT	PRZZZZNY	
MATHILDE	28	F	W	PRZZZZNY	
LEO	5	M	CHILD	PRZZZZNY	
SCHLICHTEN, HEINR.	16	M	FARMER	PRZZZZNY	
HARBECK, THEOD.	42	M	MCHT	PRABIGNY	
OTTILIE	25	F	W	PRABIGNY	
MARY	6	F	CHILD	PRABIGNY	
KLEINLAIN, ANNA	28	F	SGL	PRAAHBNY	
NEALE, ARTHUR	32	M	MCHT	BWZZZZNY	

SHIP: FURNESSIA

FROM: GLASGOW AND MOVILLE
TO: NEW YORK
ARRIVED: 04 SEPTEMBER 1888

PASSENGER	AGE	SEX	OCCUPATION	PRVVL	DES
MOELER, HENRY	60	M	CBLDR	GRZZZZUSA	
MALINSTRUS, FRANK	25	M	PDLR	GRZZZZUSA	
NILSON, JOHN	27	M	PDLR	GRZZZZUSA	
SANDBERG, GUTTFRID	21	M	LABR	GRZZZZUSA	
WALTHER, ALBERT	47	M	WVR	GRZZZZUSA	
WERKINASTER, GEORGE	27	M	LABR	GRZZZZUSA	
HAROWSTY, JENTE	18	F	HP	GRZZZZUSA	
MARKUS, CATEL	20	F	HP	GRZZZZUSA	
SALRUKA, MARYANA	27	F	HP	GRZZZZUSA	
DAVID, J.E.	28	M	FARMER	FRZZZZUSA	

SHIP: SORRENTO

FROM: HAMBURG
TO: NEW YORK
ARRIVED: 04 SEPTEMBER 1888

PASSENGER	AGE	SEX	OCCUPATION	PRVVL	DES
HELLMANN, HEINR.	21	M	SDLR	HBZZZZNY	
JAPKOWICH, SCHLOME	20	M	LABR	PRZZZZNY	
BESCHE	18	F	SGL	PRZZZZNY	
JEROM	8	M	CHILD	PRZZZZNY	
BENNIR	6	M	CHILD	PRZZZZNY	
ZIEWE, GITTE	38	F	WO	PRZZZZNY	
JOSEPH	15	M	CH	PRZZZZNY	
RACHMINE	8	F	CHILD	PRZZZZNY	
JOCHE	7	M	CHILD	PRZZZZNY	
JACOB	6	M	CHILD	PRZZZZNY	
HELM, WILHELMINE	58	F	WO	PRZZZZNY	
ALWINE	19	F	WO	PRZZZZNY	
HELLMANN, HEINR.	21	M	SDLR	HBZZZZNY	
LOPAN, HINRICH	22	M	WTR	PRZZZZNY	
DENSO, ANNA	25	F	WO	PRZZZZNY	
MARIE	4	F	CHILD	PRZZZZNY	
HENNIG, ARTHUR	19	M	BKR	PRZZZZPHI	
SILBERBERG, CLARA	17	F	SGL	PRZZZZBO	
WOHLENBERG, CHRRISTOPH	58	M	TCHR	PRAGKABO	
ALBRECHT, CARL	46	M	LABR	PRAGKACH	
HERING, THEODOR	56	M	MCHT	PRAGKANY	
SCHMURFEIL, AZUGUST	35	M	LABR	PRAGKAUNK	
KRAUSS, GUSTAV	18	M	WCHMKR	PRAGKANY	
NAREWSKI, JOHANN	23	M	TLR	PRAGKANY	
MALINOWSKY, MINA	28	F	SGL	PRAGKANY	

SHIP: WERRA

FROM: BREMEN AND SOUTHAMPTON
TO: NEW YORK
ARRIVED: 04 SEPTEMBER 1888

PASSENGER	AGE	SEX	OCCUPATION	PRVVL	DES
SALOMON, ARON	47	M	TT	GRZZZZUSA	
SCHMIDTHNSEN, MARIE	30	F	UNKNOWN	GRAFDDUSA	
SCHONE, GERH.	64	M	MCHT	GRAAKTUSA	
LOEB, ADELH.	24	F	UNKNOWN	GRZZZZUSA	
LEHMANN, LINA	19	F	UNKNOWN	GRZZZZUSA	
JOSEPH, ERNEST	17	F	UNKNOWN	GRZZZZUSA	
VOGT, MARIA	56	F	W	GRABUSUSA	
FRANZ	29	M	MCHT	GRABUSUSA	
ELMERS, META	14	F	UNKNOWN	GRACBRUSA	
EHNDZINSKA, MARIA	40	F	W	GRAHKMUSA	
STRAUSS, EMMA	18	F	UNKNOWN	GRZZZZUSA	
FRAENKEL, WELLA	22	F	UNKNOWN	GRZZZZUSA	
LAMPE, MARTHA	23	F	W	GRAAKHUSA	
HANS	1	M	CHILD	GRAAKHUSA	
STIEFEL, IGNAZ	24	M	MCHT	GRADLDUSA	
GUGGENHEIM, LINA	44	F	W	BVZZZZUSA	
CAROL.	16	F	UNKNOWN	BVZZZZUSA	
SALOMON	11	M	CH	BVZZZZUSA	
SARAH	9	F	CHILD	BVZZZZUSA	
FRIDA	7	F	CHILD	BVZZZZUSA	
GAGGENHEIM, SAMUEL	5	M	CHILD	BVZZZZUSA	
KURZ, SALOMON	11	M	CH	BVZZZZUSA	
LABES, OTTO	28	M	MCHT	GRZZZZUSA	
MUSSOTTER, FR.	17	M	MCHT	GRZZZZUSA	
VOGEL, LUI---	54	M	MCHT	GRZZZZUSA	
BLASS, CHARLES	40	M	MCHT	GRZZZZUSA	
MEYER, ADOLF	39	M	MCHT	GRZZZZUSA	
GESINE	28	F	W	GRZZZZUSA	
GERBER, AUG.	42	M	MCHT	GRZZZZUSA	
GERKEN, LOUIS	21	M	MCHT	GRZZZZUSA	
SCHWARZ, PHILIPP	60	M	MCHT	GRZZZZUSA	
HESSEN, JOHN	67	M	MCHT	GRZZZZUSA	
IDA	25	F	UNKNOWN	GRZZZZUSA	
KAUFMANN, RICH.	20	M	TT	GRZZZZUSA	
HOSBACH, EMMA	36	F	W	GRZZZZUSA	
MINNA	11	F	CH	GRZZZZUSA	
BROEHR, MARG.	24	F	UNKNOWN	GRAAKHUSA	
JACOBSOHN, MARG.	21	F	UNKNOWN	GRAAKHUSA	
KAHN, FANNY	63	F	W	GRAAKHUSA	
MARIE	22	F	W	GRAAKHUSA	
WEISS, ELISAB.	23	F	UNKNOWN	GRAIKSUSA	
EMMA	21	F	UNKNOWN	GRAIKSUSA	
RUSCHE, HENRIETTE	52	F	UNKNOWN	GRADWFUSA	
HEILIGENBRUEN, CAROL.	48	F	W	GRADOIUSA	
SARAH	15	F	UNKNOWN	GRADOIUSA	
BERTHA	12	F	UNKNOWN	GRADOIUSA	
JUSTIN	10	M	CH	GRADOIUSA	
PAUL.	6	F	CHILD	GRADOIUSA	
JOSEF, RACHEL	45	F	W	BVZZZZUSA	
THOGODE, JOH.	16	M	LABR	BVAALJUSA	
HUELSBERG, JOH.	16	M	LABR	BVALVLUSA	
STAMM, RICHARD	15	M	UNKNOWN	BVAESIUSA	
ULRICH, LOUIS	23	M	MCHT	GRZZZZUSA	
SOFKA, THERESE	18	F	UNKNOWN	GRZZZZUSA	
KERN, LUISE	15	F	UNKNOWN	BDZZZZUSA	
ALB.	11	M	UNKNOWN	BDZZZZUSA	
WEINERT, ROCHEL	48	M	LABR	BDABDMUSA	
HEYNE, RICHARD	34	M	LABR	BDABDMUSA	
LEHMANN, FABIAN	36	M	LABR	BDAAKHUSA	
JOHANNE	34	F	W	BDAAKHUSA	
ZERLINE	7	F	CHILD	BDAAKHUSA	
STRACK, MARIA	53	F	UNKNOWN	GRZZZZUSA	
SALOMON	16	M	UNKNOWN	GRZZZZUSA	
WATZ, JOH.	24	M	BRR	GRADLDUSA	
GARMS, MATH.	15	F	UNKNOWN	GRZZZZUSA	
HOFFMANN, CARL	56	M	FARMER	GRZZZZUSA	
AMALIE	53	F	W	GRZZZZUSA	
ALLERHOLT, HEINR.	32	M	SEMN	GRAARRUSA	

PASSENGER	AGE	SEX	OCCUPATION	PRVVL	DES	PASSENGER	AGE	SEX	OCCUPATION	PRVVL	DES
WERNER, AUGUST	26	M	SEMN		GRZZZZUSA	WOEHNERT, ELISAB.	21	F	UNKNOWN		BVZZZZUSA
MEYER, FRANZ	34	M	SEMN		GRAAKHUSA	DOERSCHEL, MARG.	21	F	UNKNOWN		BVABRAUSA
MEISSNER, EMMA	22	F	UNKNOWN		GRAEXWUSA	SCHMIDT, GENOFERA	25	F	UNKNOWN		BVZZZZUSA
FRANZ	17	M	LABR		GRAEXWUSA	LEIBINGER, JOSEF	13	M	UNKNOWN		BVZZZZUSA
KERNDEL, GEORG	45	M	LABR		BVZZZZUSA	MAERZ, JOSEF	23	M	BRR		BVZZZZUSA
MARG.	39	F	W		BVZZZZUSA	STAWOWA, FRANCISKA	21	F	UNKNOWN		GRZZZZUSA
THERES.	16	F	UNKNOWN		BVZZZZUSA	JOSEFA	11	F	UNKNOWN		GRZZZZUSA
VICTORIA	15	F	UNKNOWN		BVZZZZUSA	MINCH, ROSALIA	26	F	W		GRZZZZUSA
GEORG	12	M	CH		BVZZZZUSA	JAN	3	M	CHILD		GRZZZZUSA
U	9	F	CHILD		BVZZZZUSA	VALENTIN	.03	M	INFANT		GRZZZZUSA
MARIA	4	F	CHILD		BVZZZZUSA	MACHUKA, STANISL.	24	F	W		GRZZZZUSA
JOSEF	.09	M	INFANT		BVZZZZUSA	KASIMIR	2	M	CHILD		GRZZZZUSA
SCHUENKE, MARIE	17	F	UNKNOWN		GRZZZZUSA	STANISL	.06	M	INFANT		GRZZZZUSA
ECKHOFF, JOH.	26	M	LABR		GRZZZZUSA	GRUNKEMEYER, CHARL	16	M	UNKNOWN		GRABBRUSA
QUELL, HEINR.	16	M	LABR		GRAJMRUSA	PIRA, SWOLASHIKA	25	F	W		GRZZZZUSA
DANKERS, GEORG	16	M	LABR		GRZZZZUSA	SOPHIE	2	F	CHILD		GRZZZZUSA
VOGTS, CLAUS	16	M	LABR		GRAJMRUSA	REBER, GOTTL.	22	M	LABR		WMZZZZUSA
BRUENGES, MART.	30	M	LABR		GRAJMRUSA	PLAPPERT, FRIED.	17	F	UNKNOWN		WMZZZZUSA
ADELH.	34	F	W		GRAJMRUSA	LIPPS, WILH.	27	M	GDNR		WMZZZZUSA
HEIN.	9	M	CHILD		GRAJMRUSA	HERMLE, ANNA	14	F	UNKNOWN		WMZZZZUSA
DIEDR.	3	M	CHILD		GRAJMRUSA	SCHMIDT, MARIA	23	F	UNKNOWN		WMAFTFUSA
ALDAG, HERM.	15	M	UNKNOWN		GRAJMRUSA	GOLDNER, ALFRED	22	M	MCHT		WMADOIUSA
MEINEKE, ALICE	11	F	UNKNOWN		GRZZZZUSA	NITARDY, GOT.	21	M	LABR		GRZZZZUSA
OPPENHEIMER, ALB.	17	M	MCHT		GRZZZZUSA	HAECKER, PAUL.	26	F	UNKNOWN		GRADKJUSA
JUNG, BABETTA	17	F	UNKNOWN		BVZZZZUSA	CHRIST.	16	M	BKR		GRADKJUSA
MUENCH, JOS.	22	M	FARMER		BVAADFUSA	KLOTZ, MARTIN	52	M	TLR		BVZZZZUSA
MARIA	16	F	UNKNOWN		BVAADFUSA	LENGORS, JOSEPH.	25	F	UNKNOWN		GRZZZZUSA
HANDRICH, JACOB	65	M	FARMER		BVAADFUSA	PFEIFFER, ELISAB.	22	F	UNKNOWN		BVZZZZUSA
POLTE, THERESE	34	F	W		BVADYAUSA	PHILIPP	14	M	UNKNOWN		BVZZZZUSA
THERESE	10	F	CH		BVADYAUSA	LACHMANN, LENA	32	F	W		GRZZZZUSA
CATHA.	6	F	CHILD		BVADYAUSA	ADOLF	11	M	CH		GRZZZZUSA
JOSEPH	1	M	CHILD		BVADYAUSA	ALMA	8	F	CHILD		GRZZZZUSA
JOHANN	.03	M	INFANT		BVADYAUSA	LICHTENSTEIN, JOH.	16	F	UNKNOWN		GRZZZZUSA
TRAUTMANN, MARIE	44	F	UNKNOWN		BVZZZZUSA	ROSALIE	15	F	UNKNOWN		GRZZZZUSA
KLOTZ, MARG.	20	F	UNKNOWN		WMZZZZUSA	GREINDL, THERES	26	F	W		BVZZZZUSA
OTT, BARB.	21	F	UNKNOWN		WMZZZZUSA	JOH.	3	M	CHILD		BVZZZZUSA
SCHUMANN, ---RA	46	F	W		WMZZZZUSA	MARIA	.06	F	INFANT		BVZZZZUSA
-ERD.	10	M	CH		WMZZZZUSA	STRAUSS, AMALIE	17	F	UNKNOWN		GRZZZZUSA
SARA	9	F	CHILD		WMZZZZUSA	STUTZ, FRIED.	23	F	UNKNOWN		WMZZZZUSA
PAUL.	7	F	CHILD		WMZZZZUSA	SCHOENFELD, HUGO	17	M	BCHR		GRZZZZUSA
KELLER, OTTO	15	M	UNKNOWN		WMAFBVUSA	KNUSIUS, MICH.	21	M	FARMER		BVZZZZUSA
FUCHS, CATH.	17	F	UNKNOWN		WMAGMDUSA	BARNE, WILLY	15	M	UNKNOWN		BVAAAHUSA
GIHRING, HERM.	10	M	CH		WMACZLUSA	LINDEMANN, RICKA	20	M	UNKNOWN		GRZZZZUSA
FRIEDR.	6	M	CHILD		WMACZLUSA	SCHUBERT, ALBIN	18	M	FARMER		GRZZZZUSA
OHNGEMACH, ELISAB.	23	F	UNKNOWN		WMAENIUSA	KNUEPPEL, HERM.	15	M	UNKNOWN		GRAAMDUSA
HARTMANN, FRIED.	21	F	UNKNOWN		WMACZLUSA	WESTERHOLD, FRIED.	15	F	UNKNOWN		GRAAAHUSA
FEUCHT, BARB.	19	F	UNKNOWN		WMZZZZUSA	BLOCK, CATH.	15	F	UNKNOWN		GRAAAHUSA
MERG, CATH.	17	F	UNKNOWN		WMZZZZUSA	BRINKMANN, HERM.	25	M	LABR		GRAAQSUSA
HESS, SALOMON	19	M	BKR		WMAAXZUSA	JOH.	23	F	W		GRAAQSUSA
TANNENBAUM, JOH.	22	F	UNKNOWN		WMALGCUSA	JOH.	.04	F	INFANT		GRAAQSUSA
NOTHACKER, MAG.	22	F	UNKNOWN		WMZZZZUSA	CAMP, MARIA	18	F	UNKNOWN		GRAAAHUSA
MUELLER, CATH.	26	F	UNKNOWN		WMZZZZUSA	RELLING, HEINR.	42	M	LABR		GRAEXOUSA
BRUMMER, EMMA	17	F	UNKNOWN		WMZZZZUSA	GOETZ, FERD.	17	M	LABR		BDZZZZUSA
BETTING, BARB.	25	F	UNKNOWN		WMZZZZUSA	HAISCH, CATH.	17	F	UNKNOWN		BDABLVUSA
KRAUP, ROSINE	17	F	UNKNOWN		WMZZZZUSA	MEFFERT, ELISAB.	28	F	UNKNOWN		GRZZZZUSA
ROSEL, HELENE	25	F	UNKNOWN		WMABOQUSA	PETERS, GEORG	25	M	JNR		GRACBAUSA
KOHL, FRIED.	35	F	UNKNOWN		BVZZZZUSA	BADE, CARL	50	M	FARMER		GRZZZZUSA
LINKER, CATH.	22	F	UNKNOWN		GRZZZZUSA	AUGUSTE	25	F	W		GRZZZZUSA
WILHELME, JOH.	23	M	FARMER		GRZZZZUSA	FRIEDR.	1	M	CHILD		GRZZZZUSA
KOELL, CATH.	20	F	UNKNOWN		GRAAQZUSA	EMILIE	.06	F	INFANT		GRZZZZUSA
WEG---, FRITZ	16	M	UNKNOWN		GRZZZZUSA	LOEWE, ANNA	46	F	LABR		GRZZZZUSA
WILHELMI, MARIA	18	F	LABR		GRZZZZUSA	ELLA	17	F	UNKNOWN		GRZZZZUSA
PETER	16	M	UNKNOWN		GRZZZZUSA	FRAENKLE, ROSINE	21	F	UNKNOWN		WMZZZZUSA
JUNG, CARL	17	M	FARMER		BDZZZZUSA	WILH.	20	F	UNKNOWN		WMZZZZUSA
HOLLWEILER, LUDW.	16	M	UNKNOWN		BDZZZZUSA	WEYH, JOHO	24	M	FARMER		WMABHHUSA
HEIATZ, BARB.	20	F	UNKNOWN		BDZZZZUSA	SCHWEERS, WILH.	38	F	W		WMADIJUSA
FANLHABR, MARIE	18	F	UNKNOWN		BDZZZZUSA	MARIA	5	F	CHILD		WMADIJUSA
SCHMIDT, ISIDOR	63	M	DLR		GRZZZZUSA	SOMMERFELD, WILH.	23	M	UNKNOWN		WMAEHFUSA
AUGUSTE	51	F	W		GRZZZZUSA	MEYERSOHN, HERM.	16	M	UNKNOWN		WMALPKUSA
BERTHA	18	F	W		GRZZZZUSA	SCHROEDER, BERTHA	18	F	UNKNOWN		WMALPKUSA
VOWINKEL, FRANZ	22	M	MCHT		GRABOQUSA	THOMSON, WILH.	17	F	UNKNOWN		GRZZZZUSA
KOEHLER, CATH.	20	F	UNKNOWN		GRZZZZUSA	SCHWENNSEN, ANDR.	39	M	FARMER		GRZZZZUSA
JOLING, CAROL.	20	F	UNKNOWN		GRZZZZUSA	KAHN, JONAS	31	M	FARMER		GRAKYFUSA
KOEHLER, HEIN.	15	M	UNKNOWN		GRZZZZUSA	MINDROF, MONNE	50	F	W		GRZZZZUSA
HOFMANN, ANNA	21	F	UNKNOWN		BVZZZZUSA	KATH.	28	F	UNKNOWN		GRZZZZUSA

PASSENGER	AGE	SEX	OCCUPATION	PRVL	DES
HOFFMANN, KLARA	14	F	UNKNOWN	GRZZZZ	USA
MINDROP, VERONIKA	1	F	CHILD	GRZZZZ	USA
STUMPF, GEORG	26	M	BKLYR	GRAIIJ	USA
SENDNER, JOSEF	23	M	FARMER	GRAIIJ	USA
JU--, MARIE	20	F	UNKNOWN	GRAIIJ	USA
WOEHLING, PETER	16	M	TLR	GRAIIJ	USA
BROMDAN, FRIEDR.	15	M	UNKNOWN	GRAIIJ	USA
RUDOLF, PAUL	17	M	LABR	GRABOK	USA
THOMAS, ERNEST.	34	F	W	GRABOK	USA
EDM.	9	M	CHILD	GRABOK	USA
WAECHTER, GUST.	32	M	LABR	GRAJRZ	USA
LOUISE	32	F	W	GRAJRZ	USA
FANNY	6	F	CHILD	GRAJRZ	USA
ERNST	3	M	CHILD	GRAJRZ	USA
SIMON, BARB.	18	F	UNKNOWN	GRAFOI	USA
FORTLAGE, CHRIST.	53	F	W	GRADWF	USA
PLOHSE, ANNA	16	F	UNKNOWN	GRADWF	USA
ZIEGENBEIN, ERNST	15	M	UNKNOWN	GRAARR	USA
MEYER, ERNST	14	M	UNKNOWN	GRAARR	USA
TRAUBE, RICH.	19	M	GDNR	GRACBF	USA
GERLINGER, FRIEDR.	18	M	BKLYR	GRAFTF	USA
DINGER, JOS.	16	M	LKSH	GRAFTF	USA
SIMON, HEIN.	15	M	UNKNOWN	GRZZZZ	USA
HARMS, ANNA	46	F	UNKNOWN	GRZZZZ	USA
SCHOENE, FRANZ	19	M	FARMER	GRAAKT	USA
THEODOR	17	M	TLR	GRAAKT	USA
KOESTER, THEODOR	27	M	PNTR	GRAAKT	USA
KRUSE, JUL.	18	M	FARMER	GRZZZZ	USA
KRIEGSMANN, H.	16	M	FARMER	GRZZZZ	USA
KUEMPELMANN, MARIA	16	F	UNKNOWN	GRZZZZ	USA
HUSER, CATH.	59	F	W	GRZZZZ	USA
HEIM.	32	M	FARMER	GRZZZZ	USA
GERHARD	28	M	FARMER	GRZZZZ	USA
MARIA	18	F	UNKNOWN	GRZZZZ	USA
ELISAB.	22	F	UNKNOWN	GRZZZZ	USA
BEHRENS, HEIM.	18	M	TLR	GRZZZZ	USA
WAGENBAUER, ANT.	24	M	LABR	GRADLD	USA
THEIMER, GUST.	17	M	LABR	GRADLD	USA
WIRTH, JACOB	11	M	UNKNOWN	BVZZZZ	USA
KRAUSS, THERESE	23	F	UNKNOWN	BVABUS	USA
MERKLE, MARIE	18	F	UNKNOWN	BVACPE	USA
BAIER, CARL	17	M	FARMER	BVABUS	USA
WAGNER, EMIL	24	M	FARMER	BVABUS	USA
KLEMMER, GEORG	11	M	CH	BVABUS	USA
TE--KAMP, MINNA	26	F	UNKNOWN	GRZZZZ	USA
HUEHLFELD, FRANZ	67	M	LABR	GRZZZZ	USA
GERHARD	27	M	LABR	GRZZZZ	USA
FRANZ	11	M	CH	GRZZZZ	USA
KATH.	56	F	W	GRZZZZ	USA
KATH.	20	F	UNKNOWN	GRZZZZ	USA
KONEMANN, HEIN.	15	M	UNKNOWN	GRZZZZ	USA
RUDOLF, BERNH.	16	M	UNKNOWN	GRZZZZ	USA
STEINMETZ, LOUISE	16	F	UNKNOWN	GRABQK	USA
HENNES, GERHARD	39	M	FARMER	GRAAPL	USA
ELISAB.	33	F	W	GRAAPL	USA
MARIE	11	F	CH	GRAAPL	USA
DINA	9	F	CHILD	GRAAPL	USA
THEOD.	7	M	CHILD	GRAAPL	USA
ELISAB.	4	F	CHILD	GRAAPL	USA
AUGUST	2	M	CHILD	GRAAPL	USA
WEISEL, WOLF	34	M	FARMER	GRACQO	USA
ROSA	30	F	W	GRACQO	USA
DORA	7	F	CHILD	GRACQO	USA
LALLY	5	F	CHILD	GRACQO	USA
EMILIE	.10	F	INFANT	GRACQO	USA
BARTENBACH, LOUISE	30	F	W	WMZZZZ	USA
GEORG	4	M	CHILD	WMZZZZ	USA
SPAHR, CAROL.	23	F	UNKNOWN	WMZZZZ	USA
FASSNACHT, JOSEF	15	M	UNKNOWN	WMZZZZ	USA
WAHLS, MARIE	18	F	UNKNOWN	WMAAAH	USA
DANNEMANN, BERNH.	22	M	BCHR	WMAAAH	USA
MANOCHE	23	F	W	WMAAAH	USA
KELBER, ELISA	16	F	UNKNOWN	WMAAFT	USA
HARTMEIER, CHRIST.	15	F	UNKNOWN	WMAAFT	USA
STRAUSS, HERM.	25	M	LABR	WMADEM	USA
GROHBRUEGGE, ANNA	18	F	UNKNOWN	WMADDW	USA
MARIA	16	F	UNKNOWN	WMADDW	USA
SIMON, SOPHIE	16	F	UNKNOWN	WMADDW	USA
SEEDORF, JOH.	15	M	UNKNOWN	WMADDW	USA
WISCHHUSEN, GEVERT	17	M	UNKNOWN	WMADDW	USA
STEINBACH, MINNA	17	F	UNKNOWN	GRZZZZ	USA
BURKHARDT, CHRIST.	26	M	FARMER	WMZZZZ	USA
BANGE, HINR.	72	M	LABR	WMABZV	USA
WECHMANN, HERM.	19	M	LABR	GRZZZZ	USA
MEYER, JOH.	15	F	UNKNOWN	GRZZZZ	USA
HUCK, ANNA	15	F	UNKNOWN	GRZZZZ	USA
IDA	19	F	UNKNOWN	GRZZZZ	USA
HEUER, ALB.	14	M	UNKNOWN	GRABRY	USA
BAUER, SOPHIE	16	F	UNKNOWN	GRACAV	USA
HEINR.	15	M	UNKNOWN	GRACAV	USA
MALEK, MAX	24	M	LABR	GRAENA	USA
GRUNDMANN, LOUISE	62	F	W	GRAENA	USA
SZEFER, ALEX	14	M	UNKNOWN	GRAFRB	USA
HILGERS, MARIA	19	F	UNKNOWN	GRAFRB	USA
KOSMANSKI, WACLAW	29	M	LABR	GRZZZZ	USA
HAFTKA, FRANZ	34	M	LABR	GRZZZZ	USA
CHELMOWSKI, JOSEF	34	M	LABR	GRZZZZ	USA
JOH.	30	F	W	GRZZZZ	USA
ANTONIA	10	F	CH	GRZZZZ	USA
ANGELICA	7	F	CHILD	GRZZZZ	USA
AGNES	4	F	CHILD	GRZZZZ	USA
JOSEF	2	M	CHILD	GRZZZZ	USA
VALERIA	.03	F	INFANT	GRZZZZ	USA
CZERWINSKI, JAN	27	M	LABR	GRZZZZ	USA
FRANZISKA	25	F	W	GRZZZZ	USA
KYSA, JOSEF	40	M	LABR	GRZZZZ	USA
VEDDER, EMILIE	43	F	W	GRZZZZ	USA
GUST.	13	M	UNKNOWN	GRZZZZ	USA
ERNST	8	F	CHILD	GRZZZZ	USA
KELLER, JOH.	32	F	UNKNOWN	WMZZZZ	USA
WEGMANN, GERH.	47	M	LABR	GRZZZZ	USA
AHRENS, LENA	18	F	UNKNOWN	GRAELE	USA
WEBER, LUDW.	33	M	LABR	BVZZZZ	USA
BAUMANN, RICHARD	43	M	LABR	GRZZZZ	USA
PAUL	4	M	CHILD	GRZZZZ	USA
LAUTH, KARL	51	M	LABR	BDZZZZ	USA
GEORG	16	M	LABR	BDZZZZ	USA
KARL	11	M	CH	BDZZZZ	USA
SCHMIDT, CONRAD	37	M	LABR	BDAAIE	USA
FRIEDRICH, JOH.	28	M	LABR	BDAAIE	USA
CHRISTOPH	26	M	LABR	BDAAIE	USA
HUSSMANN, FR.	16	M	LABR	GRZZZZ	USA
WOLFER, GUST.	30	M	LABR	GRZZZZ	USA
KREMLER, HERM.	26	M	LABR	GRZZZZ	USA
SANNILOWITSCH, RACHEL	49	M	LABR	GRZZZZ	USA
JACOBSOHN, THERESE	25	F	UNKNOWN	GRZZZZ	USA
STURM, LOUISE	27	F	UNKNOWN	GRZZZZ	USA
HEITMUELLER, FR.	30	M	FARMER	GRACBR	USA
KERSTEN, FRAN.L.	55	F	W	GRADDQ	USA
BORN, CONRAD	17	M	FARMER	GRACGR	USA
HASSFELD, EDUARD	36	M	JNR	GRAARR	USA
JAEGER, MARIE	15	F	UNKNOWN	GRZZZZ	USA
CATH.	63	F	FARMER	GRZZZZ	USA

SHIP: DONAU

FROM: BREMEN
TO: BALTIMORE
ARRIVED: 05 SEPTEMBER 1888

ECKHARDT, GUSTAV	22	M	MCHT	GRZZZZ	MD
U. S---	40	M	UNKNOWN	GRZZZZ	MD
----SE	00	F	UNKNOWN	GRZZZZ	MD
FLORENCE	5	F	CHILD	GRZZZZ	MD
MABEL	8	F	CHILD	GRZZZZ	MD

PASSENGER	AGE	SEX	OCCUPATION	PRVL	DES
ISRAEL, MINNA	29	F	UNKNOWN	GRZZZZ	MD
TERN, GOTTLIEBE	45	F	UNKNOWN	GRZZZZ	MD
WILLRICH, HELENE	32	F	UNKNOWN	GRZZZZ	MD
AHA, GOTTHARD	29	M	FARMER	GRZZZZ	IL
MEYER, FELIX	20	M	FARMER	GRZZZZ	IL
MAKOWIAK, MARYANNA	21	F	UNKNOWN	GRZZZZ	IL
ANTONIA	.03	F	INFANT	GRZZZZ	IL
EHMANN, LINA	20	F	UNKNOWN	GRZZZZ	IL
YANKE, KARL	43	M	LABR	GRZZZZ	IL
THERESIA	50	F	UNKNOWN	GRZZZZ	IL
REDEMSKI, ADELINE	34	F	UNKNOWN	GRZZZZ	IL
PAUL	10	M	CH	GRZZZZ	IL
GUSTAV	3	M	CHILD	GRZZZZ	IL
EMIL	.08	M	INFANT	GRZZZZ	IL
INF, EMIL	.08	M	INFANT	GRZZZZ	IL
SCHOLZ, ALBERT	32	M	LABR	GRZZZZ	IL
MARIE	33	F	UNKNOWN	GRZZZZ	IL
JOHAN	10	M	CH	GRZZZZ	IL
ALBERT	2	M	CHILD	GRZZZZ	IL
FRANZ	21	M	LABR	GRZZZZ	IL
THESSING, HEINRICH	28	M	LABR	GRZZZZ	IL
WERNER, LISETTE	23	F	UNKNOWN	GRZZZZ	IL
KRZYZYNSKI, FRANZ	26	M	BKLYR	GRZZZZ	IL
POPPE, HERMAN	40	M	FARMER	GRZZZZ	IL
CHRISTINE	33	F	UNKNOWN	GRZZZZ	IL
---DRICH	10	M	CH	GRZZZZ	IL
MARIA	8	F	CHILD	GRZZZZ	IL
CARL	.03	M	INFANT	GRZZZZ	IL
KRIEGER, ANNA	50	F	UNKNOWN	GRZZZZ	IL
HULDA	19	F	UNKNOWN	GRZZZZ	IL
FRITZ	16	M	UNKNOWN	GRZZZZ	IL
SOMMER, ERNESTINE	23	F	UNKNOWN	GRZZZZ	IL
PUTZIGER, PAULINE	41	F	UNKNOWN	GRZZZZ	IL
JACOB	13	M	UNKNOWN	GRZZZZ	IL
HUGO	11	M	UNKNOWN	GRZZZZ	IL
MARTA	9	F	CHILD	GRZZZZ	IL
GORETZKA, MARIA	30	F	UNKNOWN	GRZZZZ	IL
JOHAN	8	M	CHILD	GRZZZZ	IL
STEFAN	5	M	CHILD	GRZZZZ	IL
JOSEF	.03	M	INFANT	GRZZZZ	IL
PRZESTWOR, APOLONIA	20	F	UNKNOWN	GRZZZZ	IL
ANDREAS	5	M	CHILD	GRZZZZ	IL
KATHARINA	10	F	CH	GRZZZZ	IL
GURSKE, MATHILDE	42	F	UNKNOWN	GRZZZZ	IL
AUUGSTE	15	F	UNKNOWN	GRZZZZ	IL
HERMINE	8	F	CHILD	GRZZZZ	IL
BORNEKA, ANNA	24	F	UNKNOWN	GRZZZZ	IL
WLADISLAW	3	M	CHILD	GRZZZZ	IL
STANISLAWS	.03	M	INFANT	GRZZZZ	IL
BANNOS, JOHANNA	16	F	UNKNOWN	GRZZZZ	IL
BUERGER, MORITZ	15	M	UNKNOWN	GRZZZZ	IL
ZWERNER, LEONHARD	25	M	FARMER	GRZZZZ	IL
MARG.	22	F	UNKNOWN	GRZZZZ	IL
MUELLER, ANNA	36	F	UNKNOWN	GRZZZZ	IL
KLAMETH, JOSEPH	55	M	LABR	GRZZZZ	IL
CAROLINE	52	F	UNKNOWN	GRZZZZ	IL
MARTHA	17	F	UNKNOWN	GRZZZZ	IL
PAUL	11	M	CH	GRZZZZ	IL
---T----KI, U	24	M	BKR	GRZZZZ	IL
KWADROWSKY, U	18	M	LABR	GRZZZZ	IL
BOLZ, U	32	M	LABR	GRZZZZ	IL
SCHMIDT, DORA	23	F	UNKNOWN	GRZZZZ	IL
IDA	14	F	UNKNOWN	GRZZZZ	IL
LUDWIG	11	M	CH	GRZZZZ	IL
DORA	10	F	CH	GRZZZZ	IL
HEINRICH	7	M	CHILD	GRZZZZ	IL
WILH.	4	F	CHILD	GRZZZZ	IL
AUGUST	.09	M	INFANT	GRZZZZ	IL
BECKER, DORA	17	F	UNKNOWN	GRZZZZ	IL
HAESSLEIN, ELISAB.	25	M	BCHR	GRZZZZ	IL
STAHL, ELISABETH	00	F	BCHR	GRZZZZ	IL
BAMACH, IGNATZ	28	M	FARMER	GRZZZZ	OH
HOASCH, AUGUST	55	M	FARMER	GRZZZZ	MN
WILHEL.	45	F	UNKNOWN	GRZZZZ	MN
BERTHA	24	F	UNKNOWN	GRZZZZ	MN
U	22	F	UNKNOWN	GRZZZZ	MN
BOLZ, -----INE	31	F	UNKNOWN	GRZZZZ	MI
WILDE, U	41	M	JNR	GRZZZZ	MI
KINSEROWSKI, ---B	62	M	LABR	GRZZZZ	OH
RINKUS, ----ST	28	M	UNKNOWN	GRZZZZ	OH
----LENE	29	F	UNKNOWN	GRZZZZ	OH
HELENE	4	F	CHILD	GRZZZZ	OH
AUGUST	3	M	CHILD	GRZZZZ	OH
MINNA	.03	F	INFANT	GRZZZZ	OH
JAHNKE, AUGUST	16	M	LABR	GRZZZZ	IN
AUGUSTE	14	F	UNKNOWN	GRZZZZ	IN
FIEDLER, ANNA	28	F	UNKNOWN	GRZZZZ	MO
MATHIS, HEINRICH	40	M	TU	GRZZZZ	MD
MINNA	40	F	UNKNOWN	GRZZZZ	MD
FRIEDRICH	15	M	UNKNOWN	GRZZZZ	MD
WILHELM	8	M	CHILD	GRZZZZ	MD
AUGUST	3	M	CHILD	GRZZZZ	MD
MINNA	2	F	CHILD	GRZZZZ	MD
HECKEL, LOUISE	20	F	UNKNOWN	GRZZZZ	MD
HEPPELER, WILH.	50	M	FARMER	GRZZZZ	MD
KATHARINA	45	F	UNKNOWN	GRZZZZ	MD
LOUISE	22	F	UNKNOWN	GRZZZZ	MD
ELISE	18	F	UNKNOWN	GRZZZZ	MD
WILHELM	11	M	UNKNOWN	GRZZZZ	MD
HECKEL, FRIEDERIKE	53	F	UNKNOWN	GRZZZZ	MD
EMMA	11	F	UNKNOWN	GRZZZZ	MD
CLASING, WILH.	22	F	UNKNOWN	GRZZZZ	MD
MERMHARDT, GEORG	17	M	GDNR	GRZZZZ	MD
MUELL, MARG.	28	F	UNKNOWN	GRZZZZ	MD
SCHULZ, FRANZISKA	28	F	UNKNOWN	GRZZZZ	MD
HUBER, CATHARINA	15	F	UNKNOWN	GRZZZZ	MD
BOHNENKAMP, SOFIE	25	F	UNKNOWN	GRZZZZ	MD
BULAUF, WILHELM	40	M	FARMER	GRZZZZ	PA
FLATTGEN, ANNA	25	F	UNKNOWN	GRZZZZ	OH
LUEBENJANS, MARIA	16	F	UNKNOWN	GRZZZZ	OH
GERHARD	16	M	UNKNOWN	GRZZZZ	OH
ANNA	14	F	UNKNOWN	GRZZZZ	OH
WILH.	11	F	UNKNOWN	GRZZZZ	OH
GEORG	9	M	CHILD	GRZZZZ	OH
EMMA	3	F	CHILD	GRZZZZ	OH
NEUMANN, MATHILDE	22	F	UNKNOWN	GRZZZZ	OH
RIPPERT, JOHAN	23	M	TNM	GRZZZZ	OH
THOMAS, AUGUST	17	M	TNM	GRZZZZ	OH
APPELGRUEN, WILH.	34	F	UNKNOWN	GRZZZZ	OH
MARIE	8	F	CHILD	GRZZZZ	OH
HAMM, WILHELM	61	M	FARMER	GRZZZZ	OH
THERESE	54	F	UNKNOWN	GRZZZZ	OH
HERMAN	22	M	UNKNOWN	GRZZZZ	OH
OTTO	17	M	UNKNOWN	GRZZZZ	OH
FRANZ	14	M	UNKNOWN	GRZZZZ	OH
EMMA	10	F	CH	GRZZZZ	OH
WUNDERLICH, JOHAN	27	M	FARMER	GRZZZZ	MD
WOLK, BABETTE	33	F	UNKNOWN	GRZZZZ	MD
LOSCHER, MARG.	34	F	UNKNOWN	GRZZZZ	MD
MOSER, BARBARA	29	F	UNKNOWN	GRZZZZ	MD
ALMA	26	F	UNKNOWN	GRZZZZ	MD
MOHN, MARG.	24	F	UNKNOWN	GRZZZZ	MD
METZGER, ELISE	11	F	CH	GRZZZZ	MD
--IMPEL, CHRISTINA	19	F	UNKNOWN	GRZZZZ	MD
KENRES, MARIA	35	F	UNKNOWN	GRZZZZ	MD
OTTILIE	11	F	CH	GRZZZZ	MD
PETER	10	M	CH	GRZZZZ	MD
CONRAD	6	M	CHILD	GRZZZZ	MD
VALENTIN	3	M	CHILD	GRZZZZ	MD
MARIA	.06	F	INFANT	GRZZZZ	MD
BEHM, WILHELM	23	M	FARMER	GRZZZZ	MD
FEICK, PHILIP	35	M	FARMER	GRZZZZ	MD
MARG.	24	F	UNKNOWN	GRZZZZ	MD
BIDRICH, HEDWIG	24	F	UNKNOWN	GRZZZZ	MD
ELISE	5	F	CHILD	GRZZZZ	MD
MARG.	3	F	CHILD	GRZZZZ	MD
GERTRUD	.07	F	INFANT	GRZZZZ	MD
WRAUZINIAK, ELISABETH	22	F	UNKNOWN	GRZZZZ	MD
FRANZISKA	.03	F	INFANT	GRZZZZ	MD
LIENTEK, JOSEPH	50	M	MCHT	GRZZZZ	MD

PASSENGER	AGE	SEX	OCCUPATION	PRV VIL DES
MUELLER, GOTTLIEB	32	M	FARMER	GRZZZZMD
DUEVEL, CHRISTIAN	33	M	UNKNOWN	GRZZZZMD
LOUISE	32	F	UNKNOWN	GRZZZZMD
HERMANN	2	M	CHILD	GRZZZZMD
AGNES	.03	F	INFANT	GRZZZZMD
ALWES, LOUISE	17	F	UNKNOWN	GRZZZZMD
VEDDER, HEINRICH	59	M	JNR	GRZZZZMD
CHARLOTTE	55	F	UNKNOWN	GRZZZZMD
LOUISE	25	F	UNKNOWN	GRZZZZMD
RUDOLF	11	M	CH	GRZZZZMD
ORDE, BERTHAMAN	23	F	UNKNOWN	GRZZZZMD
WILHELM	.03	M	INFANT	GRZZZZMD
HOENER, FRITZ	63	M	UNKNOWN	GRZZZZMD
EMILIE	33	F	UNKNOWN	GRZZZZMD
BUDZINSKI, THOMAS	21	M	FARMER	GRZZZZMD
BRIESCHKE, ALBERT	40	M	UNKNOWN	GRZZZZMD
AUGUSTE	38	F	UNKNOWN	GRZZZZMD
LOUISE	11	F	UNKNOWN	GRZZZZMD
MARIE	8	F	CHILD	GRZZZZMD
PAUL	6	M	CHILD	GRZZZZMD
ANNA	4	F	CHILD	GRZZZZMD
CARL	3	M	CHILD	GRZZZZMD
BREDA, ANNA	16	F	UNKNOWN	GRZZZZMD
ELISE	14	F	UNKNOWN	GRZZZZMD
STAEDLER, LYDIA	16	F	UNKNOWN	GRZZZZMD
SANDOW, MINNA	27	F	UNKNOWN	GRZZZZMD
HELENE	3	F	CHILD	GRZZZZMD
KESSLER, MARG.	18	F	UNKNOWN	GRZZZZMD
MOEHNE, WILH.	38	F	UNKNOWN	GRZZZZMD
WILHELM	12	M	UNKNOWN	GRZZZZMD
EHRLICH, FRIEDERIKE	53	F	UNKNOWN	GRZZZZMD
NOWITZKA, CECILIE	21	F	UNKNOWN	GRZZZZMD
BACHORIK, AUGUSTE	24	F	UNKNOWN	GRZZZZMD
GROTH, AUGUST	25	M	FARMER	GRZZZZMD
TEMPLIN, HULDA	21	F	UNKNOWN	GRZZZZMD
BUETTNER, MARG.	40	F	UNKNOWN	GRZZZZMD
LOEFFLER, JOHAN	14	M	UNKNOWN	GRZZZZMD
GEORG	9	M	CHILD	GRZZZZMD
BAUERNFEINDT, KUNIG.	25	F	UNKNOWN	GRZZZZMD
DOBERT, THERESE	19	F	UNKNOWN	GRZZZZMD
MARKWART, MINNA	24	F	UNKNOWN	GRZZZZMD
CLARA	2	F	CHILD	GRZZZZMD
MARTHA	.05	F	INFANT	GRZZZZMD
SCHULZ, AUGUSTE	32	F	UNKNOWN	GRZZZZMD
HARTMANN	5	M	CHILD	GRZZZZMD
MARTHA	11	F	CH	GRZZZZMD
SIGFRIED	3	M	CHILD	GRZZZZMD
HELLMUTH	.06	M	INFANT	GRZZZZMD
EWALD, AUGUST	35	M	FARMER	GRZZZZMD
HELENE	33	F	UNKNOWN	GRZZZZMD
ELISE	3	F	CHILD	GRZZZZMD
FRITZ	.05	M	INFANT	GRZZZZMD
BENKE, CARL	33	M	FARMER	GRZZZZMD
ANTONIA	30	F	UNKNOWN	GRZZZZMD
GERTRUDE	10	F	CH	GRZZZZMD
EMILIE	3	F	CHILD	GRZZZZMD
ELISE	2	F	CHILD	GRZZZZMD
MARTHA	.03	F	INFANT	GRZZZZMD
REICHENBERG, EMIL	23	M	BKR	GRZZZZMD
POKORA, FELIX	33	M	BCHR	GRZZZZMD
FEBB, JACOB	55	M	FARMER	GRZZZZMD
ELISE	31	F	UNKNOWN	GRZZZZMD
CATHARINA	11	F	CH	GRZZZZMD
PHILIPP	6	M	CHILD	GRZZZZMD
ANNA	.06	F	INFANT	GRZZZZMD
KALB, ADAM	18	M	LABR	GRZZZZMD
GREUG, ADELINE	21	F	UNKNOWN	GRZZZZMD
BUSCH, VALERIE	21	F	UNKNOWN	GRZZZZMD
HERINGHAUS, MARIA	54	F	UNKNOWN	GRZZZZMD
THERESA	30	F	UNKNOWN	GRZZZZMD
ANNA	17	F	UNKNOWN	GRZZZZMD
MATHILDE	14	F	UNKNOWN	GRZZZZMD
BERTHA	25	F	UNKNOWN	GRZZZZMD
JOHANNA	20	F	UNKNOWN	GRZZZZMD
TEGENKAMP, HEINRICH	41	M	LABR	GRZZZZMD
AGNES	34	F	UNKNOWN	GRZZZZMD
FRITZ	34	M	MCHT	GRZZZZMD
AUGUST	11	M	CH	GRZZZZMD
ANNA	9	F	CHILD	GRZZZZMD
AGNES	8	F	CHILD	GRZZZZMD
HEINRICH	5	M	CHILD	GRZZZZMD
MARIA	.03	F	INFANT	GRZZZZMD
SCHROEDER, HELENA	56	F	UNKNOWN	GRZZZZMD
LUDWIG, JULIUS	27	M	FARMER	GRZZZZMD
MARTENS, ANNA	26	F	UNKNOWN	GRZZZZMD
SCHNEIDER, KATHARINA	24	F	UNKNOWN	GRZZZZMD
LOUISE	.09	F	INFANT	GRZZZZMD
STANISLAWSKA, MARIANNE	21	F	UNKNOWN	GRZZZZMD
LUDWIG	.09	M	INFANT	GRZZZZMD
ANDRZEJEWSKA, JOSEFA	28	F	UNKNOWN	GRZZZZMD
MARIANNA	3	F	CHILD	GRZZZZMD
VERONICA	.03	F	INFANT	GRZZZZMD
CHOLEWSZYNSKA, KATARZIN	31	F	UNKNOWN	GRZZZZMD
CHOLEWSZYNSKA, JOHANNA	4	F	CHILD	GRZZZZMD
STANISLAUS	.03	M	INFANT	GRZZZZMD
URBANOWSKI, ROSALIA	27	F	UNKNOWN	GRZZZZMD
WATISLARA	3	F	CHILD	GRZZZZMD
STANISLAW	.06	M	INFANT	GRZZZZMD
ROZIK, VALENTIN	17	M	FARMER	GRZZZZMD
MARIANNA	10	F	CH	GRZZZZMD
WALISZESKA, FRANCISKA	25	F	UNKNOWN	GRZZZZMD
JOSEFA	4	F	CHILD	GRZZZZMD
KATHARINA	3	F	CHILD	GRZZZZMD
MICHAEL	.09	M	INFANT	GRZZZZMD
FRANKOWSKA, STANISLAWA	21	F	UNKNOWN	GRZZZZMD
WIKARZASZ, JOHAN	45	M	FARMER	GRZZZZMD
ROSALIA	40	F	UNKNOWN	GRZZZZMD
LORENZ	16	M	UNKNOWN	GRZZZZMD
KATH.	11	F	UNKNOWN	GRZZZZMD
THERESE	9	F	CHILD	GRZZZZMD
HEDWIG	6	F	CHILD	GRZZZZMD
CONSTANTIA	2	F	CHILD	GRZZZZMD
KATSCHMANN, KARL	22	M	TLR	GRZZZZMD
RATHERT, JOHAN	45	M	UNKNOWN	GRZZZZMD
GOETZE, JOHAN	53	M	LABR	GRZZZZNE
ANNA	51	F	UNKNOWN	GRZZZZNE
HELENE	11	F	UNKNOWN	GRZZZZNE
HEINRICH	9	M	CHILD	GRZZZZNE
KATHARINE	6	F	CHILD	GRZZZZNE
WINTER, GERHARD	25	M	FARMER	GRZZZZNE
BOESCHEN, FRIEDRICH	21	M	FARMER	GRZZZZNE
SCHUERLE, BARBRA	20	F	UNKNOWN	GRZZZZPA
KLENK, JOHAN	28	M	FARMER	GRZZZZWAS
SCHUERGER, KATH.	17	F	UNKNOWN	GRZZZZWAS
HANF, MARG.	19	F	UNKNOWN	GRZZZZWAS
JOHAN	22	M	FARMER	GRZZZZWAS
GRUND, MICHAEL	24	M	GDNR	GRZZZZWAS
SCHUESSLER, GEORG	14	M	UNKNOWN	GRZZZZWAS
VOGT, MARG.	14	F	UNKNOWN	GRZZZZWAS
ZOBEL, JOHAN	16	M	UNKNOWN	GRZZZZWAS
ZANZINGER, ROSINE	11	F	CH	GRZZZZWAS
SCHULZ, FRIEDRICH	27	M	UNKNOWN	GRZZZZWAS
BOTSCH, FRIED.	58	F	UNKNOWN	GRZZZZWAS
KORNHAAS, GOTTLIEB	33	M	PNTR	GRZZZZMD
WIECHMANN, W.T.	27	M	FARMER	GRZZZZMD
FRIEDERIKE	27	F	UNKNOWN	GRZZZZMD
ANNA	.11	F	INFANT	GRZZZZMD
LOUISE	.02	F	INFANT	GRZZZZMD
VOGELPOHL, WILHELM	63	M	FARMER	GRZZZZMD
CHRISTINE	24	F	UNKNOWN	GRZZZZMD
ELISE	18	F	UNKNOWN	GRZZZZMD
BRUNS, GESINA	25	F	UNKNOWN	GRZZZZMD
BERTRAM, JOHANNE	25	F	UNKNOWN	GRZZZZMD
META	23	F	UNKNOWN	GRZZZZMD
WILHELM	22	M	FARMER	GRZZZZMD
NEUBURGER, BARBARA	21	F	UNKNOWN	GRZZZZMD
KRAUS, GEORG	25	M	BRR	GRZZZZMD
MARG.	23	F	BRR	GRZZZZMD
SCHMIDT, HEINRICH	25	M	LABR	GRZZZZMD
JOHAN	22	M	UNKNOWN	GRZZZZMD

PASSENGER	AGE	SEX	OCCUPATION	PRVL	DES
THIERGARTNER, ELISAB.	20	F	UNKNOWN		GRZZZZMD
LEHMANN, CLEMENS	24	M	FARMER		GRZZZZOH
ELBRECHT, HEINRICH	29	M	DYR		GRZZZZOH
TRAPHOENER, AUGUST	24	M	UNKNOWN		GRZZZZOH
DREES, ANNA	19	F	UNKNOWN		GRZZZZOH
HAGEDORN, GERD.	24	M	FARMER		GRZZZZOH
LUETTEL, BERNHARD	23	M	FARMER		GRZZZZOH
HAVERLAUCH, AGNES	22	F	UNKNOWN		GRZZZZOH
KALB, KATHI	25	F	UNKNOWN		GRZZZZPA
HEGEMANN, THEODOR	35	M	FARMER		GRZZZZOH
ELISE	28	F	UNKNOWN		GRZZZZOH
ANNA	6	F	CHILD		GRZZZZOH
BERTHA	4	F	CHILD		GRZZZZOH
ELISABETH	.09	F	INFANT		GRZZZZOH
KINDERVATTER, DANIEL	38	M	ENGR		GRZZZZOH
EMMA	38	F	UNKNOWN		GRZZZZOH
WEISS, MATHILDE	30	F	UNKNOWN		GRZZZZMI
JOHANNES	.09	M	INFANT		GRZZZZMI
SOTMANN, WILHELM	36	M	FARMER		GRZZZZMO
WILH.	36	F	UNKNOWN		GRZZZZMO
WILHELM	10	M	CH		GRZZZZMO
CHARLOTTE	7	F	CHILD		GRZZZZMO
PAULINE	3	F	CHILD		GRZZZZMO
DIEHL, CLOTILDA	22	F	UNKNOWN		GRZZZZMO
HUSER, KATHARINA	20	F	UNKNOWN		GRZZZZMO
SPIEGEL, MATHILDE	18	F	UNKNOWN		GRZZZZMO
BECKER, ELISE	21	F	UNKNOWN		GRZZZZOH
STOCKHECKE, HEINRICH	24	M	TNM		GRZZZZIL
SCHNEIDER, ANNA	64	F	UNKNOWN		GRZZZZIL
LENCHEN	19	F	UNKNOWN		GRZZZZIL
WOLK, JOSEPH	7	M	CHILD		GRZZZZIL
SCHULZ, ROBERT	35	M	MNR		GRZZZZOH
ANNA	34	F	UNKNOWN		GRZZZZOH
LIDIE	11	F	CH		GRZZZZOH
ARNO	9	M	CHILD		GRZZZZOH
HEDWIG	.03	F	INFANT		GRZZZZOH
FRANKE, LINA	30	F	UNKNOWN		GRZZZZOH
KOEHLER, ANTON	28	M	FARMER		GRZZZZMO
ERNESTINE	26	F	UNKNOWN		GRZZZZMO
SOBRZAK, WOJCECK	31	M	TLR		GRZZZZPA
MICHALINE	20	F	UNKNOWN		GRZZZZPA
STANISLAW	.09	M	INFANT		GRZZZZPA
BRODNIAC, JAN	16	M	UNKNOWN		GRZZZZPA
DRESENER, CHRISTINA	20	M	SDLR		GRZZZZOH
ZWOSTE, CONRAD	29	M	LABR		GRZZZZIN
BARBARA	22	F	UNKNOWN		GRZZZZIN
KUNIGUNDE	3	F	CHILD		GRZZZZIN
ERHARD	.06	M	INFANT		GRZZZZIN
LANG, EDMUND	19	M	BKBNDR		GRZZZZIL
MINNA	16	F	UNKNOWN		GRZZZZIL
HUGO	12	M	UNKNOWN		GRZZZZIL
BOEHNKE, JUSTINE	64	F	UNKNOWN		GRZZZZPA
FRIEDRICH	25	M	LABR		GRZZZZMD
BUTH, WILHELM	27	M	BKLYR		GRZZZZIL
SCHMALZ, WILHELM	21	M	BCHR		GRZZZZIL
ONKEN, HERMAN	44	M	LABR		GRZZZZPA
MINNA	37	F	UNKNOWN		GRZZZZPA
JOHAN	15	M	UNKNOWN		GRZZZZPA
GESINE	11	F	UNKNOWN		GRZZZZPA
FRANZ	9	M	CHILD		GRZZZZPA
MARG.	5	F	CHILD		GRZZZZPA
PITTINGER, PHINE	16	M	FARMER		GRZZZZMD
REGMANN, PHICULA	27	F	UNKNOWN		GRZZZZMD
BENY	3	M	CHILD		GRZZZZMD
TINE	.11	F	INFANT		GRZZZZMD
PETERS, JOHANNA	18	F	UNKNOWN		GRZZZZIL
GERRJETS, HARM.	57	M	FARMER		GRZZZZIL
HINRICH	26	M	UNKNOWN		GRZZZZIL
EMMA	23	F	UNKNOWN		GRZZZZIL
JOHAN	20	M	UNKNOWN		GRZZZZIL
UBBO	18	M	UNKNOWN		GRZZZZIL
CHRISTINA	15	F	UNKNOWN		GRZZZZIL
AHL, PHILIPP	35	M	SHMK		GRZZZZMD
SCHMIDT, JOSEPH	33	M	BKLYR		GRZZZZMD
GEBHARD, GEORG	30	M	BRR		GRZZZZMD
HELBIG, GOTTFR.	38	M	SHMK		GRZZZZMD
SKLARZ, SIGMUND	17	M	LABR		GRZZZZMD
WANICHOWSKA, FRANZISKA	19	F	UNKNOWN		GRZZZZMD
WIENDL, JOHAN	18	M	FARMER		GRZZZZMD

SHIP: WESTERNLAND

FROM: ANTWERP
TO: NEW YORK
ARRIVED: 05 SEPTEMBER 1888

PASSENGER	AGE	SEX	OCCUPATION	PRVL	DES
FETTLING, CON	32	M	MLR		FRZZZZNY
EWALD, JOHA	17	M	FARMER		GRZZZZNY
KAMMERER, WILKE	23	F	UNKNOWN		GRZZZZNY
BISCHOFF, ANNA	23	F	UNKNOWN		GRZZZZNY
AIGNER, MARIE	21	F	UNKNOWN		GRZZZZNY
HOLZOPFEL, LOUISE	19	F	UNKNOWN		GRZZZZNY
SCHEIDT, WILH.	16	M	CL		GRZZZZNY
WINTER, ANNA	17	F	UNKNOWN		GRZZZZMIL
GRUNDL, JOSEF	28	M	LABR		GRZZZZMIL
WEBER, WILH.	18	M	CL		GRZZZZKS
DUERLING, ANDR.	25	M	LABR		GRZZZZCH
NOLL, ADAM	30	M	FARMER		GRZZZZNY
BENGEL, ANNA	18	F	UNKNOWN		GRZZZZNY
YUNGLING, THERESE	18	F	UNKNOWN		GRZZZZNY
SCHWICKEILATH, B.	22	M	SMH		GRZZZZNY
STIENER, FRIED.	19	M	CL		GRZZZZPHI
HOFFMANN, JOH.	25	M	LABR		GRZZZZPHI
HEBY, EMMA	24	F	UNKNOWN		GRZZZZNY
DENHAUR, ERNST	23	M	LABR		GRZZZZNY
NOWACK, ANNA	60	F	UNKNOWN		GRZZZZCH
PLEEZYNSKI, CH.	19	M	FARMER		GRZZZZYOU
WOLF, ANNA	23	F	UNKNOWN		GRZZZZNAT
DORMAIER, JOH.	27	F	UNKNOWN		GRZZZZSP
JOS.	7	F	CHILD		GRZZZZSP
FRANK, JOHS.	26	M	CL		GRZZZZPIT
LUDWIG, JOSEPHE	57	F	UNKNOWN		GRZZZZSPR
KICK, HEWER	25	M	LABR		GRZZZZNY
KREZA, RUD.	17	M	LABR		GRZZZZNY
KURZ, CAROL.	34	F	UNKNOWN		GRZZZZCH
WILHELM	10	M	CH		GRZZZZCH
MINA	8	F	CHILD		GRZZZZCH
EMILE	4	F	CHILD		GRZZZZCH
ROBT.	3	M	CHILD		GRZZZZCH
CARL	14	F	UNKNOWN		GRZZZZCH
BURSSENS, A.	42	M	FARMER		GRZZZZCH
ZURKELLER, JENNY	60	F	UNKNOWN		GRZZZZCH
CAMICHEL, JOHN	25	M	FARMER		GRZZZZNY
SANTONIS, LOUIS	17	M	FARMER		GRZZZZNY
MEIER, ANNA	27	F	UNKNOWN		GRZZZZNY
RITZMANN, HEL.	18	F	UNKNOWN		SRZZZZNY
BAUMGARTEN, JAC.	26	M	TRVLR		SRZZZZSTL
RENCKEN, JOHN	32	M	SMH		SRZZZZNY
PHIL.	32	F	UNKNOWN		SRZZZZNY
PAUL	1	M	CHILD		SRZZZZNY
LUTZ, ALOIS	29	M	FARMER		GRZZZZUNK
LOUISE	31	F	UNKNOWN		GRZZZZUNK
MARIE	2	F	CHILD		GRZZZZUNK
MEDGEFRAIR, CARL	45	M	FARMER		GRZZZZNY
EMIL	16	F	UNKNOWN		GRZZZZNY
SCHNEIDER, MAX	20	M	CL		GRZZZZCH
BUHLER, JOH.	29	M	LABR		GRZZZZPHI
MATHYSENS, MICH.	38	M	LABR		GRZZZZPHI
GERAADO, JOH.	48	M	LABR		GRZZZZPHI
KNOBLAUCH, CHRIST.	34	M	LABR		GRZZZZNY
NILISSEN, LEON	28	M	SMH		GRZZZZNY
JACOB	26	M	SMH		GRZZZZNY
DUNKEL, MICH.	25	M	FARMER		GRZZZZNY
MARIA	27	F	UNKNOWN		GRZZZZNY
KRANZ, JOSEF	19	M	LABR		GRZZZZNY

314

PASSENGER	AGE	SEX	OCCUPATION	PRVL	DES
POOS, MATH.	34	M	CBTMKR	GRZZZZNY	
GASZ, HCH.	23	M	LABR	GRZZZZNY	
REGNER, ELISA	20	M	LABR	GRZZZZNY	
LEINARZ, JOS.	25	M	LABR	GRZZZZNY	
ROMMERSBACH, PET.	30	M	BRR	GRZZZZNY	
RABBCETS, MICH.	44	M	LABR	GRZZZZCH	
MULMANS, CHS.	29	M	LABR	GRZZZZCH	
DECASTOR, MEOPH.	30	M	LABR	GRZZZZCH	
VADERS, AD.	39	M	FARMER	GRZZZZUNK	
CORNELIA	37	F	UNKNOWN	GRZZZZUNK	
HENDRICH	14	M	UNKNOWN	GRZZZZUNK	
GEKLING, JOH.	25	M	FARMER	GRZZZZQUI	
SCHLITING, MAR.	26	M	FARMER	GRZZZZNY	
WESLENMANN, BE.	26	F	UNKNOWN	GRZZZZNY	
BUFF, SEBA	30	F	UNKNOWN	GRZZZZNY	
MARIA	7	F	CHILD	GRZZZZNY	
BIRK, CHRIST.	38	M	FARMER	GRZZZZNY	
HAUPTE, CAROL.	18	F	UNKNOWN	GRZZZZNY	
HAJER, ABR.	31	M	FARMER	GRZZZZNY	
ENGELINA	38	F	UNKNOWN	GRZZZZNY	
ENGELINA	6	F	CHILD	GRZZZZNY	
AWAH	4	M	CHILD	GRZZZZNY	
SALOME	3	F	CHILD	GRZZZZNY	
PHIL.	1	M	CHILD	GRZZZZNY	
LYDIA	.02	F	INFANT	GRZZZZNY	
GROSSENBACHER, GOTH.	23	M	FARMER	SRZZZZNY	
CADONAN, M.	16	F	UNKNOWN	SRZZZZNY	
FELLER, ALW.	38	F	UNKNOWN	SRZZZZNY	
FEBER, JACOB	18	M	FARMER	SRZZZZNY	
WILLE, HELEN	10	F	CH	SRZZZZNY	
FURST, JEAN	23	M	FARMER	SRZZZZNY	
HAGER, SUS.	24	F	UNKNOWN	SRZZZZNY	
ELISA	22	F	UNKNOWN	SRZZZZNY	
MARIE	23	F	UNKNOWN	SRZZZZNY	
ROSINA	20	F	UNKNOWN	SRZZZZNY	
SOPHIE	17	F	UNKNOWN	SRZZZZNY	
FRIED	16	M	UNKNOWN	SRZZZZNY	
SUSE	51	F	UNKNOWN	SRZZZZNY	
GOST.	14	M	UNKNOWN	SRZZZZNY	
FESTIN, JOH.	28	M	FARMER	SRZZZZNY	
HUBSCHER, MARIE	18	F	UNKNOWN	SRZZZZNY	
GEORGES, DODANE	23	M	CL	SRZZZZNY	
BOHERGIN, JOSEF	25	M	FARMER	SRZZZZNY	
LIEBERMAN, JOH.	17	M	FARMER	SRZZZZNY	
SCHWEIDLER, FELIX	70	M	FARMER	SRZZZZNY	
KUFFER, ELISE	20	F	UNKNOWN	SRZZZZNY	
MEYER, VICTOR	22	M	LABR	SRZZZZNY	
COLOMBO, GUI	23	M	MNR	SRZZZZLEA	
REPP, MARIA	22	F	UNKNOWN	GRZZZZNY	
ROEFER, ANNA	13	F	UNKNOWN	GRZZZZNY	
BUCKLER, ELISA	36	F	UNKNOWN	GRZZZZNY	
ELISA	11	F	CH	GRZZZZNY	
HERMANN	2	M	CHILD	GRZZZZNY	
MORITZ, LINA	19	F	UNKNOWN	GRZZZZNY	
JOHN	15	M	UNKNOWN	GRZZZZNY	
HOLLINGER, WILH.	22	M	FARMER	GRZZZZNY	
ELISAB.	18	F	UNKNOWN	GRZZZZNY	
AMALIA	20	F	UNKNOWN	GRZZZZNY	
BENDEL, JOHANN	24	M	FARMER	GRZZZZCH	
WEBER, HCH.	55	M	FARMER	GRZZZZKS	
MARG.	16	F	UNKNOWN	GRZZZZKS	
ELISAB.	15	F	UNKNOWN	GRZZZZKS	
JULIUS	10	M	UNKNOWN	GRZZZZKS	
ANTONIE	11	F	UNKNOWN	GRZZZZKS	
GOLDSCHMIDT, GUSTAV	22	M	MACH	GRZZZZNY	
LAAS, MORITZ	37	M	FARMER	GRZZZZNY	
DUSEK, F.	20	F	UNKNOWN	GRZZZZNY	
MIKA, CARTHA.	25	F	UNKNOWN	GRZZZZNY	
MARIA	2	F	CHILD	GRZZZZNY	
ANNA	.07	F	INFANT	GRZZZZNY	
AMELY, MARIE	36	F	UNKNOWN	GRZZZZNY	
JOSEF	23	M	FARMER	GRZZZZNY	
SYNCK, JOSEF	24	M	FARMER	GRZZZZNY	
NOVAK, FANZ	32	M	FARMER	GRZZZZCH	
ZENALIK, FRANZ	24	M	MCHT	GRZZZZCH	
LEPIE, CARL	25	M	LABR	GRZZZZIA	
CERNEY, MARIE	34	F	UNKNOWN	GRZZZZIA	
WAUCK, FRANZ	25	M	CL	GRZZZZSP	
KOHN, MATH.	00	M	FARMER	GRZZZZSP	
ENGEL, MARIE	25	F	UNKNOWN	GRZZZZSP	
KEWEN, FRANZ	22	M	BRR	GRZZZZSP	
GELHAASEN, JOSEF	25	M	TLR	GRZZZZSP	
U, LOUIS	22	M	LABR	GRZZZZSP	
RABETH, ALBERT	21	M	FARMER	GRZZZZSP	
BECKER, LOUIS	20	M	MNR	GRZZZZSP	
KIHN, PIERRE	36	M	FARMER	GRZZZZSP	
MEYER, EUGEN	16	M	BBR	GRZZZZSP	
STRASS, NANETTE	15	F	UNKNOWN	GRZZZZSP	
HAEGER, CARL	33	M	FARMER	GRZZZZSP	
MARG.	34	F	UNKNOWN	GRZZZZSP	
CARL	3	M	CHILD	GRZZZZSP	
OTTO	1	M	CHILD	GRZZZZSP	
MAGD.	68	F	UNKNOWN	GRZZZZSP	
BEBUS, MICHAEL	25	M	LABR	GRZZZZCIN	
MOLK, JOSEF	28	M	LABR	GRZZZZBUF	
KATTUS, SYLESTER	26	M	LABR	GRZZZZBUF	
SCHMIDT, ADAM	31	M	CBTMKR	GRZZZZNY	
FURMKAS, JOHN	16	M	LABR	GRZZZZNY	
KODWERF, BARB.	51	F	UNKNOWN	GRZZZZNY	
BARB.	12	F	CH	GRZZZZNY	
WILH.	11	M	CH	GRZZZZNY	
LOT, FANNY	18	F	UNKNOWN	GRZZZZNY	
RANK, JOSEF	38	M	FARMER	GRZZZZNY	
--ECK, BERNH.	29	M	FARMER	GRZZZZNY	
BRAUN, HCH.	24	M	FARMER	GRZZZZNY	
ANTOWILL, ADOLF	24	M	FARMER	GRZZZZNY	
SCHMIDT, JOSEF	15	M	LABR	GRZZZZNY	
KASSNER, HELEN	18	F	UNKNOWN	GRZZZZNY	
ERBACHER, ANTON	17	M	LABR	GRZZZZNY	
SCHMITT, VERONIKA	18	M	LABR	GRZZZZNY	
KASCHER, MICHAEL	25	M	FARMER	GRZZZZNY	
MAGYER, F.	28	M	LABR	GRZZZZNY	
SABO, F.	25	M	LABR	GRZZZZNY	
WERNER, CATHA.	28	M	LABR	GRZZZZNY	
GOGER, FRANZ	33	M	BBR	GRZZZZNY	
RUF, CARL	28	M	LABR	GRZZZZNY	
HOLLMANN, WILH.	27	M	LABR	GRZZZZNY	
SCHMIEL, CARL	29	M	LABR	GRZZZZPIT	
WILHE.	28	F	UNKNOWN	GRZZZZPIT	
FENER, ROSALIE	18	F	UNKNOWN	GRZZZZNY	
JAMOS, C.	22	M	LABR	GRZZZZNY	
RETMANSKY, J	28	M	LABR	GRZZZZNY	
ROSENKRANZ, CARL	20	M	TLR	GRZZZZNY	
-EIKE, SOLOMON	24	M	MNR	GRZZZZNY	
U, U	17	M	LABR	GRZZZZNY	
U	00	U	UNKNOWN	GRZZZZNY	
MEND--S, LUDA	24	M	FARMER	GRZZZZNY	
SCHLATCHYN, KUSCH	29	M	FARMER	GRZZZZNY	
ZAKROI, HANISH	32	M	LABR	GRZZZZPHI	
SILBERSTEIN, HIRSCH	34	M	GDNR	GRZZZZPHI	
REITER, JEAN	55	M	FARMER	GRZZZZUNK	
CATHA.	20	F	UNKNOWN	GRZZZZUNK	
MARIA	16	F	UNKNOWN	GRZZZZUNK	
HAHLERT, MAX	16	M	FARMER	GRZZZZNY	
HERZOG, WM.	27	M	FARMER	GRZZZZNY	
AUSSER, CARL	72	M	LABR	GRZZZZRAC	
MICHEL, OTTO	18	M	LABR	GRZZZZNY	
MARTIN, CARL	17	M	FARMER	GRZZZZNY	
JULIE	16	F	UNKNOWN	GRZZZZNY	
KAHLUND, LOUISE	54	F	UNKNOWN	GRZZZZNY	
LOUISE	15	F	UNKNOWN	GRZZZZNY	
HAHLUND, MARIE	11	F	CH	GRZZZZNY	
CATH.	9	F	CHILD	GRZZZZNY	
FEGERT, SUSAN	43	F	UNKNOWN	GRZZZZNY	
WILHELM	17	M	FARMER	GRZZZZNY	
ELISE	14	F	UNKNOWN	GRZZZZNY	
AMALIA	11	F	CH	GRZZZZNY	
AUGUST	9	M	CHILD	GRZZZZNY	
REINHEIMEL, BABETTA	11	F	CH	GRZZZZNY	
SCHULZE, M.	19	M	LABR	GRZZZZNY	

PASSENGER	AGE	SEX	OCCUPATION	PRVL	DES
HENKE, WILH.	24	M	LABR		GRZZZZNY
THERESE	23	F	UNKNOWN		GRZZZZNY
SCHWARZE, F.	29	M	BBR		GRZZZZNY
LEGROIS, ADOLPH	31	M	FARMER		GRZZZZNY
WARZNISTA, M.	15	F	UNKNOWN		GRZZZZNY
BORREMAUS, JULIEN	30	M	CGRMKR		GRZZZZNY
JUNGERS, JEAN	24	M	LABR		GRZZZZNY
DIEDRICH, NIC.	16	M	LABR		GRZZZZNY
SCHEIDT, THERESE	22	F	UNKNOWN		GRZZZZNY
RUF, CHRISTINE	17	F	UNKNOWN		GRZZZZBO
STALDDER, ELISE	20	F	UNKNOWN		GRZZZZNY
JOSEF	13	M	CH		GRZZZZNY
CHRUGER, MARY	19	F	UNKNOWN		GRZZZZNY
BREIBRUGER, CAROL	18	F	UNKNOWN		GRZZZZNY
BOUNCOURC, GUI	20	M	MCHT		FRZZZZNY
NOSE, HENRI	17	M	LABR		GRZZZZCH
MECHESTER, RICH.	18	M	LABR		GRZZZZCH
STEINEGER, ANNA	18	F	UNKNOWN		GRZZZZNY
BUSCH, GRISECEA	20	F	UNKNOWN		GRZZZZNY
KRUKCH, CHRISTA	22	F	UNKNOWN		GRZZZZNY
OTTO	19	M	LABR		GRZZZZNY
STRANGE, JOHANNA	24	F	UNKNOWN		GRZZZZNY
JOHANNA	1	F	CHILD		GRZZZZNY
EMMA	.02	F	INFANT		GRZZZZNY
KOHL, AUG.	25	M	FARMER		GRZZZZPHI
BROGHE, CAROLINE	22	F	UNKNOWN		GRZZZZSAN
PRECHENA-AUDER, ANNA	21	F	UNKNOWN		GRZZZZCH
FRANZ	1	M	CHILD		GRZZZZCH
VONOGEN, AGATHA	33	F	UNKNOWN		GRZZZZCH
LAMBERTZ, LENA	21	F	UNKNOWN		GRZZZZCH
HANSEL, CATHER	22	F	UNKNOWN		GRZZZZCH
MARG.	4	F	CHILD		GRZZZZCH
CATHE.	1	F	CHILD		GRZZZZCH
MOLLER-TER, CATH.	17	F	UNKNOWN		GRZZZZCH
BREINER, ANNA	17	F	UNKNOWN		GRZZZZCH
VATTER, JACOB	17	M	FARMER		GRZZZZCH
MOSCHEL, CATH.	21	F	UNKNOWN		GRZZZZCH
MAHLER, ADAM	44	M	CPTR		GRZZZZUNK
KATE	16	F	UNKNOWN		GRZZZZUNK
SCHONEBECK, WILH.	33	M	LABR		GRZZZZNAT
PRUZINSKI, THEO	17	M	FARMER		GRZZZZCLE
PHIEL, AUG.	31	M	FARMER		GRZZZZNY
SAWITZKY, MAUSETTE	29	M	FARMER		GRZZZZNY
LETTLER, LUDWIG	49	M	FARMER		GRZZZZNY
WITTMANN, HCH.	39	M	LABR		GRZZZZNY
RIEDINGER, ME.	16	F	UNKNOWN		GRZZZZNY
BRIEHL, JAC.	29	M	LABR		GRZZZZCLE
HUBERACH, ROSALIE	26	F	UNKNOWN		GRZZZZCLE
AMALIE	19	F	UNKNOWN		GRZZZZCLE
HELLER, JOHANN	46	M	FARMER		GRZZZZNY
MARIE	35	F	UNKNOWN		GRZZZZNY
JOS.	11	M	CH		GRZZZZNY
WILH.	9	M	CHILD		GRZZZZNY
ALBERT	7	M	CHILD		GRZZZZNY
MARTIN	5	M	CHILD		GRZZZZNY
GOTT.	3	M	CHILD		GRZZZZNY
STRUD	2	M	CHILD		GRZZZZNY
LION, MEIER	49	M	UNKNOWN		GRZZZZNY
THEODOR	32	M	FARMER		GRZZZZNY
JULIUS	10	M	CH		GRZZZZNY
ALEX	7	M	CHILD		GRZZZZNY
ROSETTE	4	F	CHILD		GRZZZZNY
MORITZ	1	M	CHILD		GRZZZZNY
KAUFMANN, SALI	18	M	LABR		GRZZZZNY
BURKLE, ROSINE	20	F	UNKNOWN		GRZZZZNY
JOHULE, ROSINE	16	F	UNKNOWN		GRZZZZNY
SAUWALA, MAGDA.	19	F	UNKNOWN		GRZZZZNY
EISERMANN, JACOB	27	M	FARMER		GRZZZZNY
STOLL, ROSA	17	F	UNKNOWN		GRZZZZNY
BLUMENSTETTER, HER.	42	M	CL		GRZZZZNY
DIEBOSA, JOH.	17	M	CL		GRZZZZNY
LANGENSTEIN, HER.	44	M	JNR		GRZZZZNY
PHILPE.	41	M	CH		GRZZZZNY
ANTON	11	M	CH		GRZZZZNY
ASNNA	5	F	CHILD		GRZZZZNY
BOEPLER, HELENA	20	F	UNKNOWN		GRZZZZNY
HIBIG, ADOLF	19	M	CL		GRZZZZNY
AUG.	16	M	CL		GRZZZZNY
AST, JOH.	16	M	LABR		GRZZZZNY
A-T, REGINA	15	F	UNKNOWN		GRZZZZPIT
GEITE, THERESE	29	F	UNKNOWN		GRZZZZUNK
JOSEF	14	M	UNKNOWN		GRZZZZUNK
SCHENK, JOSEF	15	M	UNKNOWN		GRZZZZUNK
BERGER, JOSEF	27	M	FARMER		GRZZZZUNK
ANNA	21	M	FARMER		GRZZZZUNK
ANTON	1	M	CHILD		GRZZZZUNK
THERES	.02	F	INFANT		GRZZZZUNK
BISER, FRANCISKA	43	F	UNKNOWN		GRZZZZUNK
FRANCISKA	14	F	UNKNOWN		GRZZZZUNK
BAUER, ANTON	35	M	FARMER		GRZZZZSY
WALBURGA	37	F	UNKNOWN		GRZZZZSY
CRESCENZ	11	F	CH		GRZZZZSY
WALBURGA	7	F	CHILD		GRZZZZSY
MATHIAS	5	M	CHILD		GRZZZZSY
JOHANNAS	3	M	CHILD		GRZZZZSY
GAENSER, ELISE	16	F	UNKNOWN		GRZZZZSY
JUNG, ANTON	25	M	FARMER		GRZZZZLOU
LENTON, CLARA	34	F	UNKNOWN		GRZZZZNY
BECK, BABETTA	58	F	UNKNOWN		GRZZZZNY
CATHA.	16	F	UNKNOWN		GRZZZZNY
DEUCJH, ANNA	38	F	UNKNOWN		GRZZZZNY
LORENZOM, CHRISTOF	39	M	FARMER		GRZZZZNY
GENOFEVA	23	F	UNKNOWN		GRZZZZNY
HENLE, MARIA	26	F	UNKNOWN		GRZZZZNY
REGINA	2	F	CHILD		GRZZZZNY
VALENTIN	.05	M	INFANT		GRZZZZNY
BRESSART, JOHN	69	M	FARMER		GRZZZZNY
LOPPERT, CARTHAS	29	F	UNKNOWN		GRZZZZNY
BRESSART, FRANZ	9	M	CHILD		GRZZZZNY
PAULINE	1	F	CHILD		GRZZZZNY
STUPP, BARBA.	8	F	CHILD		GRZZZZNY
PFEIFFER, ANNA	17	F	UNKNOWN		GRZZZZNY
GEIGER, BERNH.	27	M	FARMER		GRZZZZNY
CATHA.	27	F	UNKNOWN		GRZZZZNY
STRUSS, JOH.	42	M	CL		GRZZZZNY
ANNA	42	F	UNKNOWN		GRZZZZNY
ELISA	18	F	UNKNOWN		GRZZZZNY
FRANZ	15	M	UNKNOWN		GRZZZZNY
FRANCISCA	12	F	UNKNOWN		GRZZZZNY
MARTHA	10	F	CH		GRZZZZNY
WALCH, ANNA	21	F	UNKNOWN		GRZZZZNY
EILITZ, ANNA	23	F	UNKNOWN		GRZZZZNY
HERMINE	3	F	CHILD		GRZZZZNY
HENRY	.07	M	INFANT		GRZZZZNY
SCHORZ, PHILIP	14	M	LABR		GRZZZZNY
LAUTENSCHAGER, LEVAH	19	M	FARMER		GRZZZZNY
FLUCK, ANNA	18	F	UNKNOWN		GRZZZZNY
HAAS, MAX	18	M	CL		GRZZZZNY
DIETZ, ROSINA	50	F	UNKNOWN		GRZZZZNY
GRUNDLER, FRIED.	27	M	FARMER		GRZZZZNY
ANNA	27	F	UNKNOWN		GRZZZZNY
FRIEDR.	.02	M	INFANT		GRZZZZNY
GOISCA, CHRISTINE	22	F	UNKNOWN		GRZZZZNY
BOUCH, MARIA	25	F	UNKNOWN		GRZZZZNY
ARNOLD, CATH.	19	F	UNKNOWN		GRZZZZNY
KENN, BARB.	16	F	UNKNOWN		GRZZZZNY
DU-SH, CAROL.	17	F	UNKNOWN		GRZZZZNY
RAISCH, GOB.	32	F	FARMER		GRZZZZNY
CLUSENROTH, NIC.	18	M	FARMER		GRZZZZNY
FLEUSS, MARIA	19	F	UNKNOWN		GRZZZZNY
BODENMUND, JOH.	28	M	FARMER		GRZZZZNY
FLERMEN, NIC.	28	M	FARMER		GRZZZZUNK
CATH.	10	F	CH		GRZZZZNY
GLASER, CAROLINE	34	F	UNKNOWN		GRZZZZNY
HELENA	10	F	CH		GRZZZZNY
ARTHUR	9	M	CHILD		GRZZZZNY
FELIX	4	M	CHILD		GRZZZZNY
ANTONIETTE	1	F	CHILD		GRZZZZNY
KRILL, FRIED.	19	M	PRNTR		GRZZZZUNK
WAGNER, FRIED	18	M	LABR		GRZZZZUNK

PASSENGER	AGE	SEX	OCCUPATION	PRV VIL DES
VOGT, WM.	18	M	LABR	GRZZZZUNK
SCHMIDT, PETER	23	M	FARMER	GRZZZZNY
BOSSERS, HCH.	41	M	LABR	GRZZZZNY
HCH.	10	M	CH	GRZZZZNY
GUISS, JOHANN	25	M	FARMER	GRZZZZNY
GERKE, WINE	46	F	UNKNOWN	GRZZZZNY
ROBERT	14	M	UNKNOWN	GRZZZZNY
MARIE	5	F	CHILD	GRZZZZNY
HOFFNER, MINA	37	F	UNKNOWN	GRZZZZNY
MARIA	8	F	CHILD	GRZZZZNY
FRIED.	6	M	CHILD	GRZZZZNY
LINA	3	F	CHILD	GRZZZZNY
WILHE.	1	F	CHILD	GRZZZZNY
GULDE, ANNA	18	F	UNKNOWN	GRZZZZNY
FUCHS, MARCUS	22	M	FARMER	GRZZZZNY
BUBLES, JOH.	15	M	LABR	GRZZZZNY
BOCKLE, GOTT.	16	M	LABR	GRZZZZNY
SCHRANKLER, PETER	58	M	FARMER	GRZZZZNY
MAGDO	56	F	UNKNOWN	GRZZZZNY
CATHA.	23	F	UNKNOWN	GRZZZZNY
SARAH	19	F	UNKNOWN	GRZZZZNY
SCHRANKER, LUDWIG	14	F	UNKNOWN	GRZZZZNY
FRANZ	10	F	UNKNOWN	GRZZZZNY
PETER	4	M	CHILD	GRZZZZNY
CHRIST, MAGDO	19	F	UNKNOWN	GRZZZZNY
RUFF, PETER	67	M	FARMER	GRZZZZNY
CATHA.	45	F	UNKNOWN	GRZZZZNY
ANGE	17	F	UNKNOWN	GRZZZZNY
GEORG	11	M	CH	GRZZZZNY
FULD	9	M	CHILD	GRZZZZNY
CATH.	4	F	CHILD	GRZZZZNY
ANDLBAUER, F.	22	M	FARMER	GRZZZZNY
BECK, WILH.	18	M	FARMER	GRZZZZNY
BIERMANN, CARL	26	M	FARMER	GRZZZZNY
SCHWARZ, JOHANN	50	M	TLR	GRZZZZNY
ELISAB.	50	F	UNKNOWN	GRZZZZNY
FRIED.	4	M	CHILD	GRZZZZNY
MAY, W.MRS	47	F	UNKNOWN	GRZZZZNY
MARIE	16	F	UNKNOWN	GRZZZZNY
MULLER, ELISE	29	F	UNKNOWN	GRZZZZNY
BAER, FRANZ	34	M	UNKNOWN	GRZZZZNY
CATHA.	32	F	UNKNOWN	GRZZZZNY
MESENHOLDEN, CAROLINE	17	F	UNKNOWN	GRZZZZNY
MAUBACH, PAUL	23	M	FARMER	GRZZZZNY
HOFFMANN, PETER	23	M	FARMER	GRZZZZNY
JOHANN	25	M	FARMER	GRZZZZNY
KORTING, HCH.	23	M	FARMER	GRZZZZNY
ARNOLD, JOHANN	43	M	FARMER	GRZZZZNY
MARGA.	48	F	UNKNOWN	GRZZZZNY
KUNZ	19	F	UNKNOWN	GRZZZZNY
JOHANN	16	M	UNKNOWN	GRZZZZNY
JOHANN	14	M	UNKNOWN	GRZZZZNY
BARBARA	11	F	UNKNOWN	GRZZZZNY
CATHA.	9	F	CHILD	GRZZZZNY
ANNA	7	F	CHILD	GRZZZZNY
OTRAUB, FLORIAN	20	M	LABR	GRZZZZNY
DOURLING, AMBROS	24	M	FARMER	GRZZZZNY
PREISS, JOHANN	35	M	FARMER	GRZZZZNY
BARB.	29	F	UNKNOWN	GRZZZZNY
ANNA	9	F	CHILD	GRZZZZNY
CATH.	3	F	CHILD	GRZZZZNY
STADER, JOHANN	16	M	MNR	GRZZZZNY
SEYKOMM, JOHANN	15	M	BCHR	GRZZZZNY
RUSS, HCH.	24	M	CL	GRZZZZNY
WOOLNEN, ERNST	37	M	CGR	GRZZZZNY
LOFF, MARTHA	19	F	UNKNOWN	GRZZZZNY
DREHER, CARL	35	M	CL	GRZZZZNY
MORDIAN, ADAM	58	M	LABR	GRZZZZNY
SEITZ, GEORG	15	M	CL	GRZZZZNY
FLOHFF, NIC.	38	M	FARMER	GRZZZZNY
SUSE	37	F	UNKNOWN	GRZZZZNY
ANTON	14	M	UNKNOWN	GRZZZZNY
JACOB	10	M	CH	GRZZZZNY
CATHA.	1	F	CHILD	GRZZZZNY
ABLOS, FRANZ	24	M	LABR	GRZZZZNY
FERTIG, MICHAEL	28	M	SMH	GRZZZZNY
SCHMIDT, ANTON	29	M	FARMER	GRZZZZNY
BAUER, MAX	18	M	FARMER	GRZZZZNY
SCHWEITER, PHILIP	38	M	FARMER	GRZZZZNY
CATH.	18	F	UNKNOWN	GRZZZZNY
VOGEL, CAMILLA	16	F	UNKNOWN	GRZZZZNY
WOHLFORTH, CATH.	32	M	BCHR	GRZZZZNY
MAILE, MARIE	27	F	UNKNOWN	GRZZZZNY
G-ATER, ROSA	34	F	UNKNOWN	GRZZZZNY
ARMENDINGE, ELISAB.	30	F	UNKNOWN	GRZZZZNY
CATH.	6	F	CHILD	GRZZZZNY
MICH.	4	M	CHILD	GRZZZZNY
ANNA	2	F	CHILD	GRZZZZNY
BACHMANN, ELISA	24	F	UNKNOWN	GRZZZZNY
CATH.	18	F	UNKNOWN	GRZZZZNY
HEUSEL, ANNA	18	F	UNKNOWN	GRZZZZNY
ACHOOF, JACOBINA	19	F	UNKNOWN	GRZZZZNY
GRAF, ELISA	47	F	UNKNOWN	GRZZZZNY
MARIE	18	F	UNKNOWN	GRZZZZNY
ELISE	15	F	UNKNOWN	GRZZZZNY
DANIEL	12	M	CH	GRZZZZNY
CHARLOTTE	10	F	CH	GRZZZZNY
DECK, DANIEL	25	M	FARMER	GRZZZZNY
ZIMMERMAN, LUDW.	17	M	FARMER	GRZZZZNY
REDERL, HCH.	16	M	CL	GRZZZZNY
SCHENKELBERKER, BARB.	20	F	UNKNOWN	GRZZZZNY
R--B, ELISAB.	19	F	UNKNOWN	GRZZZZNY
ZIMMER, PHILIPPE	25	F	UNKNOWN	GRZZZZNY
BANDEL, CATHE.	21	F	UNKNOWN	GRZZZZNY
WAHL, MARIE	21	F	UNKNOWN	GRZZZZNY
HENRICKS, LUDWICK	25	M	MLDR	GRZZZZNY
HEINRICHS, ANNA	24	F	UNKNOWN	GRZZZZNY
KARL	3	M	CHILD	GRZZZZNY
DRECKE, ANTON	25	M	LABR	GRZZZZNY
MULLER, MAGD.	66	F	UNKNOWN	GRZZZZNY
DEBR---, RICHARD	36	M	FARMER	GRZZZZNY
THOMAS, PHILOMENE	30	F	UNKNOWN	GRZZZZUNK
GUSTAV	7	M	CHILD	GRZZZZUNK
PAULA	4	F	CHILD	GRZZZZUNK
HUPEL, THERESIA	31	F	UNKNOWN	GRZZZZUNK
THERESIA	5	F	CHILD	GRZZZZUNK
ANNA	2	F	CHILD	GRZZZZUNK
SCHMALENBERGER, LENA	21	F	UNKNOWN	GRZZZZUSA
KL---, CATH.	23	F	UNKNOWN	GRZZZZNY
FRIES, ANNA	25	F	UNKNOWN	GRZZZZNY
UHLE, ANDREAS	23	M	FARMER	GRZZZZNY
JACOBINE	23	F	UNKNOWN	GRZZZZNY
MAGD.	58	F	UNKNOWN	GRZZZZNY
HORG	1	M	CHILD	GRZZZZNY
WESSMANN, MARIE	20	F	UNKNOWN	GRZZZZNY
RUY, E.	40	M	ART	GRZZZZNY
FISCHER, F.	40	M	WDCTR	GRZZZZNY
WIEGAND, C.MISS	26	F	UNKNOWN	GRZZZZNY
KOPPLER, GEO	45	M	FARMER	GRZZZZNY
CLAUSBERG, O.MR	42	M	MCHT	GRZZZZNY
FEHEGGEN, H.MR	22	M	CL	GRZZZZNY
BROSS, T.	26	M	CL	GRZZZZNY
HUMMEL, L.	23	F	UNKNOWN	GRZZZZNY
DERDELINGHE, J.	26	M	CL	GRZZZZNY
HOCK, L.MRS	30	F	UNKNOWN	GRZZZZUSA
COPMAN, A.	28	M	CL	GRZZZZUSA
LOBRY, E.	22	M	CL	GRZZZZUSA
BAUER, G.	28	M	PREST	GRZZZZUSA
ROTHEUL, H.	29	M	PREST	GRZZZZUSA
HAYGEN, J.	25	M	PREST	GRZZZZUSA
BALTZ, C.MR	45	M	SLKP	GRZZZZUSA
EMICH, K.	28	F	UNKNOWN	GRZZZZUSA
GERTICH, F.	26	F	UNKNOWN	GRZZZZUSA
PROEGGLER, F.MR	28	M	FARMER	GRZZZZUSA
SCHULHE, C.	38	F	UNKNOWN	GRZZZZUSA
HACKER, E.	23	F	UNKNOWN	GRZZZZUSA
MARY, U	25	F	RE	GRZZZZUSA
HERMAND, U	23	F	UNKNOWN	GRZZZZUSA
THEOPHAM, U	29	F	UNKNOWN	GRZZZZUSA
BERCHAN, U	27	F	UNKNOWN	GRZZZZUSA

PASSENGER	AGE	SEX	OCCUPATION	PRIVL	DES
STRATEN, H.MR	28	M	STDNT	GRZZZZUSA	
MAYFARTH, U-MRS	35	F	UNKNOWN	GRZZZZUSA	

SHIP: ALLER

FROM: BREMEN AND SOUTHAMPTON
TO: NEW YORK
ARRIVED: 07 SEPTEMBER 1888

PASSENGER	AGE	SEX	OCCUPATION	PRIVL	DES
BARNIGAN, MARIE	19	F	UNKNOWN	GRZZZZUSA	
SCHIMANECK, MARTHA	24	F	UNKNOWN	GRZZZZUSA	
BATTCHER, PAULA	22	F	UNKNOWN	GRZZZZUSA	
BLEGER, SINA	27	F	UNKNOWN	GRZZZZUSA	
SCHANER, EMMA	24	F	UNKNOWN	GRZZZZUSA	
VOETH, LOUISE	23	F	UNKNOWN	GRZZZZUSA	
NAUMANN, EMIL	28	M	MLR	GRZZZZUSA	
KORETZ, MARIE	17	F	UNKNOWN	GRZZZZUSA	
WEIL, BETTI	42	F	UNKNOWN	GRZZZZUSA	
BEIS, JOHN	24	M	MCHT	GRZZZZUSA	
SALZER, JOSEF	30	M	MCHT	GRZZZZUSA	
SALOMON, GUSTAV	22	M	MCHT	GRZZZZUSA	
SCHUSTER, CAROLA	50	F	UNKNOWN	GRZZZZUSA	
SCHELLING, PAUL	34	M	FARMER	GRZZZZUSA	
SCHULTHEIS, JACOB	28	M	FARMER	GRZZZZUSA	
BETTI	26	F	W	GRZZZZUSA	
HANSEN, MARIE	30	F	UNKNOWN	GRZZZZUSA	
BENTFELD, LOUIS	37	M	HTR	GRZZZZUSA	
ROEDEL, JOHAN	65	M	MCHT	GRZZZZUSA	
SCHAFFER, AUG.	38	M	MCHT	GRZZZZUSA	
LAEVENSTERN, JULIE	20	F	UNKNOWN	GRZZZZUSA	
HERZFELD, RIKE	28	F	UNKNOWN	GRZZZZUSA	
SENERIN, MARIE	38	F	UNKNOWN	GRZZZZUSA	
GALDWEIN, JULIE	11	F	UNKNOWN	GRZZZZUSA	
HELENE	9	F	CHILD	GRZZZZUSA	
HAGEDORN, BERTHA	30	F	UNKNOWN	GRZZZZUSA	
JULIE	8	F	CHILD	GRZZZZUSA	
MAX	4	M	CHILD	GRZZZZUSA	
BERNHARD	2	M	CHILD	GRZZZZUSA	
ABMANN, JOH.	17	M	FARMER	GRZZZZUSA	
BRUNING, JOH.	17	M	FARMER	GRZZZZUSA	
STARZ, GEORG	50	M	FARMER	GRZZZZUSA	
FRISE, LUDWIG	19	M	FARMER	GRZZZZUSA	
KAJAMA, ALE	6	M	CHILD	GRZZZZUSA	
KIRCHHUEBEL, FRIDR.	16	M	FARMER	GRZZZZUSA	
RODENBECK, AUG.	21	M	FARMER	GRZZZZUSA	
ALBERS, FRITZ	17	M	FARMER	GRZZZZUSA	
JATJE, FRITZ	40	M	FARMER	GRZZZZUSA	
BREDEN, HEINR.	40	M	LABR	GRZZZZUSA	
GROEPLER, MORITZ	40	M	LABR	GRZZZZUSA	
LIHMANN, GEORG	24	M	LABR	GRZZZZUSA	
GETTMANN, LUDW.	17	M	LABR	GRZZZZUSA	
ROEPPLE, FRITZ	17	M	LABR	GRZZZZUSA	
OSTERLAH, MICH.	23	M	LABR	GRZZZZUSA	
WILHELM, JOH.	30	M	LABR	GRZZZZUSA	
SCHWEINFURTH, FRANZ	40	M	LABR	GRZZZZUSA	
KROGGEL, FRANZ	22	M	GDNR	GRZZZZUSA	
PASCHE, HEINR.	30	M	GDNR	GRZZZZUSA	
LOEVENTRITT, BENJ.	18	M	GDNR	GRZZZZUSA	
VALKERT, FRANZ	72	M	GDNR	GRZZZZUSA	
WAHL, PETER	27	M	GDNR	GRZZZZUSA	
KRAEMER, JOHAN	21	M	GDNR	GRZZZZUSA	
KOEFF, MARTIN	25	M	GDNR	GRZZZZUSA	
RODENBECK, HEINR.	32	M	GDNR	GRZZZZUSA	
MUES, HEINR.	17	M	GDNR	GRZZZZUSA	
SCHUBERT, PIUS	23	M	GDNR	GRZZZZUSA	
MARX, ALBERT	15	M	GDNR	GRZZZZUSA	
KASKE, JUDWIG	59	M	GDNR	GRZZZZUSA	
SEEBUMACHER, FRANZ	25	M	GDNR	GRZZZZUSA	
SPIELMANN, OTTO	28	M	GDNR	GRZZZZUSA	
SENS, AUGUST	16	M	GDNR	GRZZZZUSA	
GREB, PHILIPP	17	M	GDNR	GRZZZZUSA	
LIPPERT, MARTIN	26	M	GDNR	GRZZZZUSA	
NOVATNY, THOMAS	51	M	GDNR	GRZZZZUSA	
BONDE, CARL	31	M	GDNR	GRZZZZUSA	
KLUTH, PAUL	28	M	MCHT	GRZZZZUSA	
LANDON, IGNATZ	17	M	MCHT	GRZZZZUSA	
STRAUSS, SAMUEL	16	M	FARMER	GRZZZZUSA	
BASSER, MICHEL	24	M	FARMER	GRZZZZUSA	
REGEN, JOHAN	24	M	FARMER	GRZZZZUSA	
SAKOW, ALFRED	24	M	FARMER	GRZZZZUSA	
WALLMEYER, AUGUST	27	M	FARMER	GRZZZZUSA	
LUEBBEN, DIEDR.	67	M	FARMER	GRZZZZUSA	
DOEHRMANN, CHRIST	21	M	FARMER	GRZZZZUSA	
RODEMALD, HERMAN	19	M	FARMER	GRZZZZUSA	
SCHNEIDER, CONR.	16	M	FARMER	GRZZZZUSA	
MARLANDER, WILLY	14	M	FARMER	GRZZZZUSA	
KAIN, JULIUS	15	M	FARMER	GRZZZZUSA	
WALTEMATE, EDUARD	25	M	FARMER	GRZZZZUSA	
MOSES, LEO	16	M	FARMER	GRZZZZUSA	
EBERT, ADOLF	7	M	CHILD	GRZZZZUSA	
STERN, HEINR.	21	M	CH	GRZZZZUSA	
EDINGER, JACOB	15	M	CH	GRZZZZUSA	
SPITZ, BAHEMIL	17	M	GDNR	GRZZZZUSA	
GEBHARDT, HEINR.	18	M	GDNR	GRZZZZUSA	
NEUKIRCHNER, ALWIN	16	M	GDNR	GRZZZZUSA	
MUENCHOW, FRIEDR.	49	M	GDNR	GRZZZZUSA	
JUNGES, CARL	28	M	GDNR	GRZZZZUSA	
MOELLER, JOHAN	49	M	GDNR	GRZZZZUSA	
HASELVENTER, GEORG	26	M	GDNR	GRZZZZUSA	
KIEPER, CARL	19	M	GDNR	GRZZZZUSA	
PREUSCHE, JOHAN	44	M	MCHT	GRZZZZUSA	
LEHNE, HENRY	42	M	MCHT	GRZZZZUSA	
VONTIN, FLORIAN	30	M	MCHT	GRZZZZUSA	
ULBRICHT, HERM.	31	M	FARMER	GRZZZZUSA	
KAUFMANN, JOHAN	33	M	FARMER	GRZZZZUSA	
WILMUNN, JOHAN	18	M	FARMER	GRZZZZUSA	
EMME, HERM.	33	M	FARMER	GRZZZZUSA	
WOLF, HERM.	28	M	FARMER	GRZZZZUSA	
VAGELSANG, AUGUST	20	M	GDNR	GRZZZZUSA	
BRANER, CHRIST	49	M	GDNR	GRZZZZUSA	
KAISER, JOHAN	33	M	GDNR	GRZZZZUSA	
SCHMITZ, FRANZ	26	M	GDNR	GRZZZZUSA	
SIMPER, FRANZ	55	M	GDNR	GRZZZZUSA	
VALTER, HEINR.	23	M	FARMER	GRZZZZUSA	
MAYER, WILH.	17	M	FARMER	GRZZZZUSA	
KOHN, IMAR	18	M	FARMER	GRZZZZUSA	
BASTING, BENNO	25	M	FARMER	GRZZZZUSA	
WAJE, HEINR.	22	M	FARMER	GRZZZZUSA	
FITZEN, CARSTEN	15	M	FARMER	GRZZZZUSA	
REDERS, CLAUS	16	M	FARMER	GRZZZZUSA	
SCHILL, CARL	20	M	FARMER	GRZZZZUSA	
SCHAEFER, AUGUST	24	M	FARMER	GRZZZZUSA	
FRITZ	27	M	FARMER	GRZZZZUSA	
BLAN, JULIUS	38	M	FARMER	GRZZZZUSA	
SCHMITTSCHNITT, JOS.	27	M	FARMER	GRZZZZUSA	
BOCK, GATTLE	27	M	FARMER	GRZZZZUSA	
KNORR, HERM.	40	M	FARMER	GRZZZZUSA	
BETZ, GEORG	38	M	FARMER	GRZZZZUSA	
RAHLFS, HENRY	36	M	FARMER	GRZZZZUSA	
MAXIMILIAN, VICT.	35	M	FARMER	GRZZZZUSA	
SEGALLY, JOHN	35	M	FARMER	GRZZZZUSA	
DERKEN, MARY	14	F	UNKNOWN	GRZZZZUSA	
JACKELMANN, LOUISE	7	F	CHILD	GRZZZZUSA	
STALIKOSKY, FRANZ.	20	F	UNKNOWN	GRZZZZUSA	
HAFFMANN, DORE	18	F	UNKNOWN	GRZZZZUSA	
ERENSTONF, WALBURGE	19	F	UNKNOWN	GRZZZZUSA	
PITTEL, THERESE	23	F	UNKNOWN	GRZZZZUSA	
HACK, MARIE	20	F	UNKNOWN	GRZZZZUSA	
OLESCH, CATI	55	F	UNKNOWN	GRZZZZUSA	
BRANDAN, LISE	22	F	UNKNOWN	GRZZZZUSA	
KREMLITZ, SELMA	15	F	UNKNOWN	GRZZZZUSA	
WIESLER, LOUISE	15	F	UNKNOWN	GRZZZZUSA	
SCHMEKT, VICTORE.	23	F	UNKNOWN	GRZZZZUSA	
DORSCH, MINNA	22	F	UNKNOWN	GRZZZZUSA	
BERTRAM, JOHANNE	22	F	UNKNOWN	GRZZZZUSA	

PASSENGER	AGE	SEX	OCCUPATION	PRVL	DES
EMMA	25	F	UNKNOWN	GRZ	ZZZUSA
KLIER, MARY	22	F	UNKNOWN	GRZ	ZZZUSA
MINNA	18	F	UNKNOWN	GRZ	ZZZUSA
GERRA, JULKA	13	F	UNKNOWN	GRZ	ZZZUSA
ZUPANI, AMALIE	32	F	UNKNOWN	GRZ	ZZZUSA
HUDAK, ANNA	20	F	UNKNOWN	GRZ	ZZZUSA
SCHINELZLE, MARIE	20	F	UNKNOWN	GRZ	ZZZUSA
KERN, BABARA.	17	F	UNKNOWN	GRZ	ZZZUSA
AMMAN, FRIEDA	18	F	UNKNOWN	GRZ	ZZZUSA
SPACEK, MARIE	34	F	UNKNOWN	GRZ	ZZZUSA
VOCEL, CATI	18	F	UNKNOWN	GRZ	ZZZUSA
FRANZEN, ANNI	30	F	UNKNOWN	GRZ	ZZZUSA
DAENBNER, MARIE	31	F	UNKNOWN	GRZ	ZZZUSA
DENATE	25	F	UNKNOWN	GRZ	ZZZUSA
KEHR, PHILPE.	47	F	UNKNOWN	GRZ	ZZZUSA
NEISSEL, EMILIE	7	F	CHILD	GRZ	ZZZUSA
BORNEMANN, FRIDA	38	F	CH	GRZ	ZZZUSA
ENDRESS, BARBARA	20	F	CH	GRZ	ZZZUSA
KRAFT, FRIEDA	18	F	CH	GRZ	ZZZUSA
BRADINGER, KATI	16	F	CH	GRZ	ZZZUSA
RAUSCHBACH, ANNA	17	F	CH	GRZ	ZZZUSA
BINZER, ELEONORE	24	F	CH	GRZ	ZZZUSA
RECHNER, EMMA	23	F	CH	GRZ	ZZZUSA
KOOPFER, MARIE	26	F	CH	GRZ	ZZZUSA
RIPPERT, MARIE	19	F	CH	GRZ	ZZZUSA
STOCK, MARIE	19	F	CH	GRZ	ZZZUSA
WACHTEL, BETTI	25	F	CH	GRZ	ZZZUSA
SCHROEDER, ANNI	16	F	CH	GRZ	ZZZUSA
BUBECK, FRIEDA	19	F	CH	GRZ	ZZZUSA
MERZ, CAROLA	18	F	CH	GRZ	ZZZUSA
MINNA	16	F	CH	GRZ	ZZZUSA
KAISER, BARBA.	22	F	CH	GRZ	ZZZUSA
KLAMMER, GUSTE	26	F	CH	GRZ	ZZZUSA
EGRING, SABINE	23	F	CH	GRZ	ZZZUSA
PFONTNER, BARB.	22	F	CH	GRZ	ZZZUSA
FABISIAK, CHRISTE.	22	F	CH	GRZ	ZZZUSA
ECKERT, MAGDA	21	F	CH	GRZ	ZZZUSA
GRASS, ANNA	31	F	CH	GRZ	ZZZUSA
SCHNEIDER, LISE	18	F	CH	GRZ	ZZZUSA
MAGER, MARIE	16	F	CH	GRZ	ZZZUSA
GROSCH, MARIE	19	F	CH	GRZ	ZZZUSA
SENGSTAK, META	13	F	UNKNOWN	GRZ	ZZZUSA
DAHLMANN, IDA	25	F	UNKNOWN	GRZ	ZZZUSA
RAGNET, ELISE	27	F	UNKNOWN	GRZ	ZZZUSA
LACROIX, MARG.	18	F	UNKNOWN	GRZ	ZZZUSA
ZEIS, MARG.	24	F	UNKNOWN	GRZ	ZZZUSA
WEBER, EVA	15	F	UNKNOWN	GRZ	ZZZUSA
MASZKA, GYULA	28	F	UNKNOWN	GRZ	ZZZUSA
BRATLEY, FRIDA	48	F	UNKNOWN	GRZ	ZZZUSA
KEIL, ELISE	16	F	UNKNOWN	GRZ	ZZZUSA
EBBRECHS, FRIEDE.	18	F	UNKNOWN	GRZ	ZZZUSA
STEBER, SARA	18	F	UNKNOWN	GRZ	ZZZUSA
ROECHLING, WILHE.	29	F	UNKNOWN	GRZ	ZZZUSA
DAEHRMANN, META	18	F	UNKNOWN	GRZ	ZZZUSA
EDINGER, CATI	24	F	UNKNOWN	GRZ	ZZZUSA
SCHNEIDER, CHRISTE.	21	F	UNKNOWN	GRZ	ZZZUSA
ZAISS, EMMA	14	F	UNKNOWN	GRZ	ZZZUSA
PASTOR, SINA	18	F	UNKNOWN	GRZ	ZZZUSA
MARK, ROSA	21	F	UNKNOWN	GRZ	ZZZUSA
GIGLEZ, MARIE	17	F	UNKNOWN	GRZ	ZZZUSA
CAROLA	15	F	UNKNOWN	GRZ	ZZZUSA
SCHROEDER, ANNA	25	F	UNKNOWN	GRZ	ZZZUSA
BENEDER, GRETCHEN	17	F	UNKNOWN	GRZ	ZZZUSA
REINECKE, MARIE	24	F	UNKNOWN	GRZ	ZZZUSA
SCHOENE, MARIE	51	F	UNKNOWN	GRZ	ZZZUSA
SEICHEL, ANNA	46	F	UNKNOWN	GRZ	ZZZUSA
-ULFES, ANNA	18	F	UNKNOWN	GRZ	ZZZUSA
RASCHE, FRIEDE.	18	F	UNKNOWN	GRZ	ZZZUSA
NATTMEIER, MINNA	20	F	UNKNOWN	GRZ	ZZZUSA
STUMPF, CATI	17	F	UNKNOWN	GRZ	ZZZUSA
GOSSLER, MARG.	18	F	UNKNOWN	GRZ	ZZZUSA
AUGE.	15	F	UNKNOWN	GRZ	ZZZUSA
WEIL, LINA	12	F	UNKNOWN	GRZ	ZZZUSA
SCHLEISTEHER, BETTY	60	F	UNKNOWN	GRZ	ZZZUSA
WEINDECKER, HANRIETTE	21	F	UNKNOWN	GRZ	ZZZUSA
PETERS, JOHE.	18	F	UNKNOWN	GRZ	ZZZUSA
OBRIEN, FLORA	29	F	UNKNOWN	GRZ	ZZZUSA
KLIPPERS, ELISE	14	F	UNKNOWN	GRZ	ZZZUSA
SCHAFER, MARTHA	19	F	UNKNOWN	GRZ	ZZZUSA
BRUECKNER, EMMA	26	F	UNKNOWN	GRZ	ZZZUSA
OKO, ROSA	19	F	UNKNOWN	GRZ	ZZZUSA
MANN, SOPHIE	21	F	UNKNOWN	GRZ	ZZZUSA
BEINLEIN, MARIE	17	F	UNKNOWN	GRZ	ZZZUSA
BETTY	5	F	CHILD	GRZ	ZZZUSA
OLANDER, HILDA	23	F	CH	GRZ	ZZZUSA
LUNDGREEN, JOHANNE	24	F	CH	GRZ	ZZZUSA
ZIMMER, CATI	22	F	CH	GRZ	ZZZUSA
SCHROTER, PAULA	22	F	CH	GRZ	ZZZUSA
U, PAULA	21	F	CH	GRZ	ZZZUSA
SAM, BELA	40	F	CH	GRZ	ZZZUSA
WILD, MARY	21	F	CH	GRZ	ZZZUSA
NEUBECK, JULIE	28	F	CH	GRZ	ZZZUSA
KATZ, REBECCA	25	F	CH	GRZ	ZZZUSA
JONSSON, NANA	26	F	CH	GRZ	ZZZUSA
KAJAWA, GOTTLB.	33	M	GDNR	GRZ	ZZZUSA
CAROLA	33	F	W	GRZ	ZZZUSA
AUGUST	3	M	CHILD	GRZ	ZZZUSA
WILHE.	2	F	CHILD	GRZ	ZZZUSA
HERM.	.07	M	INFANT	GRZ	ZZZUSA
ADOLF, MARIE	33	F	UNKNOWN	GRZ	ZZZUSA
PAUL	7	M	CHILD	GRZ	ZZZUSA
HEDWIG	5	F	CHILD	GRZ	ZZZUSA
RICHARD	4	M	CHILD	GRZ	ZZZUSA
GRANITZKY, AUGE.	27	F	UNKNOWN	GRZ	ZZZUSA
JOSEF	2	M	CHILD	GRZ	ZZZUSA
HERGENHAN, HELENE	32	F	UNKNOWN	GRZ	ZZZUSA
OLGA	6	F	CHILD	GRZ	ZZZUSA
ANNA	2	F	CHILD	GRZ	ZZZUSA
JOSEF	.06	M	INFANT	GRZ	ZZZUSA
ROEGER, CHARLES	36	M	TCHR	GRZ	ZZZUSA
EMILIE	00	F	W	GRZ	ZZZUSA
EMILIE	5	F	CHILD	GRZ	ZZZUSA
HAMJE, NICOL	47	M	HTR	GRZ	ZZZUSA
FRIEDRE.	9	F	CHILD	GRZ	ZZZUSA
WILHELM	7	M	CHILD	GRZ	ZZZUSA
NINNIC, ANNA	37	F	UNKNOWN	GRZ	ZZZUSA
WLADISL.	3	M	CHILD	GRZ	ZZZUSA
RAEPPLE, AMALIE	33	F	UNKNOWN	GRZ	ZZZUSA
HUGE	5	M	CHILD	GRZ	ZZZUSA
KAISER, SOPHIE	47	F	UNKNOWN	GRZ	ZZZUSA
HERMAN	7	M	CHILD	GRZ	ZZZUSA
BUEHLER, SARAH	24	F	UNKNOWN	GRZ	ZZZUSA
CHRIST	3	M	CHILD	GRZ	ZZZUSA
LUECKE, CHRISTE.	35	F	UNKNOWN	GRZ	ZZZUSA
GEORG	7	M	CHILD	GRZ	ZZZUSA
JACOB	4	M	CHILD	GRZ	ZZZUSA
OLESINSKI, AGNES	34	F	UNKNOWN	GRZ	ZZZUSA
FRANZ	3	M	CHILD	GRZ	ZZZUSA
MARIE	.09	F	INFANT	GRZ	ZZZUSA
MARX, WILHELM	59	M	FARMER	GRZ	ZZZUSA
ALWINE	35	F	W	GRZ	ZZZUSA
BERTHA	7	F	CHILD	GRZ	ZZZUSA
FRANZA.	6	F	CHILD	GRZ	ZZZUSA
MARG.	4	F	CHILD	GRZ	ZZZUSA
HERMAN	3	M	CHILD	GRZ	ZZZUSA
ULMSCHE--, MAGDE	40	F	UNKNOWN	GRZ	ZZZUSA
ANNA	7	F	CHILD	GRZ	ZZZUSA
ROSA	5	F	CHILD	GRZ	ZZZUSA
JOSEF	3	M	CHILD	GRZ	ZZZUSA
BOSCHE, ANDR.	35	M	TLR	GRZ	ZZZUSA
LISETTE	28	F	W	GRZ	ZZZUSA
ANNA	6	F	CHILD	GRZ	ZZZUSA
CHRISTIANSEN, CHRIST	24	M	FARMER	GRZ	ZZZUSA
AMALIE	23	F	W	GRZ	ZZZUSA
HERMAN	.06	M	INFANT	GRZ	ZZZUSA
BRAUN, MARY	60	F	UNKNOWN	GRZ	ZZZUSA
ELISE	30	F	UNKNOWN	GRZ	ZZZUSA
BEBETTE	26	F	UNKNOWN	GRZ	ZZZUSA
HANS	3	M	CHILD	GRZ	ZZZUSA
HUDAK, MAGDA	36	F	UNKNOWN	GRZ	ZZZUSA

PASSENGER	AGE	SEX	OCCUPATION	PRVL	DES
ELISE	7	F	CHILD	GRZZZZ	USA
JOHAN	5	M	CHILD	GRZZZZ	USA
HAUSMANN, MARIE	25	F	UNKNOWN	GRZZZZ	USA
AGNES	5	F	CHILD	GRZZZZ	USA
JAEGER, CARL	29	M	MCHT	GRZZZZ	USA
JAHE.	28	F	W	GRZZZZ	USA
WILHE.	2	F	CHILD	GRZZZZ	USA
COROLA	.03	F	INFANT	GRZZZZ	USA
SCHANZ, MARIE	24	F	UNKNOWN	GRZZZZ	USA
JOHN	3	M	CHILD	GRZZZZ	USA
MUELLER, HULDA	36	F	UNKNOWN	GRZZZZ	USA
GEORG	3	M	CHILD	GRZZZZ	USA
SCHAUBACHER, CHRISTE.	36	F	UNKNOWN	GRZZZZ	USA
CARL	7	M	CHILD	GRZZZZ	USA
BERNH.	5	M	CHILD	GRZZZZ	USA
SCHWINGER, CAROLA	38	F	UNKNOWN	GRZZZZ	USA
FRIEDR.	7	M	CHILD	GRZZZZ	USA
LINA	5	F	CHILD	GRZZZZ	USA
RUNGE, MINNA	34	F	UNKNOWN	GRZZZZ	USA
ANNA	7	F	CHILD	GRZZZZ	USA
CATI	5	F	CHILD	GRZZZZ	USA
FRIEDR.	3	M	CHILD	GRZZZZ	USA
LOUIS	.11	M	INFANT	GRZZZZ	USA
KAUL, GEORG	45	M	GDNR	GRZZZZ	USA
BETTI	33	F	W	GRZZZZ	USA
WILHE.	7	F	CHILD	GRZZZZ	USA
CAROLA	5	F	CHILD	GRZZZZ	USA
BETTI	4	F	CHILD	GRZZZZ	USA
FRIEDR.	2	M	CHILD	GRZZZZ	USA
HEINR.	.06	M	INFANT	GRZZZZ	USA
HORALD, AANA	62	F	UNKNOWN	GRZZZZ	USA
FRIEDE.	25	F	UNKNOWN	GRZZZZ	USA
VANGA, JOHAN	35	M	LABR	GRZZZZ	USA
PAULA	25	F	W	GRZZZZ	USA
JANOS	.06	M	INFANT	GRZZZZ	USA
GEORG	.06	M	INFANT	GRZZZZ	USA
GRASER, MARIE	33	F	UNKNOWN	GRZZZZ	USA
HEINR.	7	M	CHILD	GRZZZZ	USA
SCHNEIDER, ANDR.	31	M	TLR	GRZZZZ	USA
BARBA.	28	F	W	GRZZZZ	USA
FALKA, JOHAN	29	F	GCR	GRZZZZ	USA
AGNES	28	F	W	GRZZZZ	USA
STANIS.	2	M	CHILD	GRZZZZ	USA
CECILIE	.01	F	INFANT	GRZZZZ	USA
PICHL, JULIUS	40	M	BCHR	GRZZZZ	USA
MARIE	3	F	CHILD	GRZZZZ	USA
BUTTNER, JOHANNE	47	F	UNKNOWN	GRZZZZ	USA
WILHE.	16	F	UNKNOWN	GRZZZZ	USA
CARL	7	M	CHILD	GRZZZZ	USA
FERD	4	M	CHILD	GRZZZZ	USA
STAHL, MARIE	42	F	UNKNOWN	GRZZZZ	USA
EUGEN	12	M	UNKNOWN	GRZZZZ	USA
MARIE	9	F	CHILD	GRZZZZ	USA
EMMA	7	F	CHILD	GRZZZZ	USA
AMALIE	5	F	CHILD	GRZZZZ	USA
BERTHA	3	F	CHILD	GRZZZZ	USA
JOHANE.	2	F	CHILD	GRZZZZ	USA
SCHROEDER, CHRIST	56	M	MCHT	GRZZZZ	USA
AUGE.	40	F	W	GRZZZZ	USA
ELISE	7	F	CHILD	GRZZZZ	USA
WEITZEL, JOH.	24	M	TLR	GRZZZZ	USA
CHRISTE.	22	F	W	GRZZZZ	USA
HEINRICH	.04	F	INFANT	GRZZZZ	USA

PASSENGER	AGE	SEX	OCCUPATION	PRVL	DES
SHIP:	NOVA SCOTIAN				
FROM:	LIVERPOOL				
TO:	BALTIMORE				
ARRIVED: 07 SEPTEMBER 1888					
VERSEN, AUGUSTE	25	F	UNKNOWN	GRZZZZ	BAL
WERMEBURG, HENRY	21	M	LABR	GRZZZZ	OH
LOUISA	19	F	W	GRZZZZ	OH
DAMNE, MARIE	48	F	W	GRZZZZ	OH
LINA	2	F	CHILD	GRZZZZ	OH
TOMARZEWSKI, ANDREAS	25	M	LABR	GRZZZZ	CLE
SHIP:	BOTHNIA				
FROM:	LIVERPOOL AND QUEENSTOWN				
TO:	NEW YORK				
ARRIVED: 08 SEPTEMBER 1888					
THEIGEL, LEON	24	M	CTR	FRZZZZ	USA
FLEISHLER, HEYNE	21	M	LABR	GRZZZZ	USA
KALUDERMANN, JOHAN	57	M	TLR	GRZZZZ	USA
STALL, MOSES	36	M	TLR	GRZZZZ	USA
WOSINSKI, MICHAL	53	M	LABR	GRZZZZ	USA
KUPKA, CAROLINA	56	F	W	GRZZZZ	USA
WUITER, ALBERT	25	M	LABR	GRZZZZ	USA
BERTIE	20	F	LABR	GRZZZZ	USA
ERNEST	3	M	CHILD	GRZZZZ	USA
MATA	2	F	CHILD	GRZZZZ	USA
ANNA	.06	F	INFANT	GRZZZZ	USA
BERNSTEIN, FEIGE	40	F	W	GRZZZZ	USA
CHAJE	9	F	CHILD	GRZZZZ	USA
SURE	7	F	CHILD	GRZZZZ	USA
MALKE	9	M	CHILD	GRZZZZ	USA
SULZE, U	27	F	SP	GRZZZZ	USA
BROUN, JOSEFINE	32	F	W	FRZZZZ	USA
POPADOLPALOS, JOHN	34	M	BKPR	GRZZZZ	USA
LEVEGNE, A.	27	M	TCHR	FRZZZZ	USA
MANTON, CHARLS	32	M	UNKNOWN	FRZZZZ	USA
RAUX, GUSTAV	31	M	MCHT	FRZZZZ	USA
JOSEFINE	3	F	CHILD	FRZZZZ	USA
GRAF, JEAN	27	M	MCHT	FRZZZZ	USA
FONVUIS, U	48	F	SP	FRZZZZ	USA
JANNE	22	F	SP	FRZZZZ	USA
SHIP:	POLARIA				
FROM:	HAMBURG				
TO:	NEW YORK				
ARRIVED: 08 SEPTEMBER 1888					
WIERSZNISKY, JOH.	23	M	LABR	PRZZZZ	USA
ZNYCWICE, EVELINE	22	F	SGL	PRZZZZ	USA
ZUREWETS, ANTON	38	M	LABR	PRZZZZ	USA
METKETSONNER, BRONESLAW	18	F	SGL	PRZZZZ	USA
SAUERBERG, ERNESTINE	24	F	SGL	PRAGLS	USA
USDIWSKI, HENRIETTE	24	F	WO	PRACHOU	SA
AUGUSTE	.06	F	INFANT	PRACHOU	SA
JAWORSKA, ALBERTINE	22	F	SGL	PRZZZZ	USA
ZELINSKI, GOTTLIEBE	30	F	WO	PRZZZZ	USA
OTTO	6	M	CHILD	PRZZZZ	USA
AUGUSTE	5	F	CHILD	PRZZZZ	USA
EMMA	4	F	CHILD	PRZZZZ	USA
BERTHA	.11	F	INFANT	PRZZZZ	USA

PASSENGER	AGE	SEX	OCCUPATION	PVRIVL/DES
ARNDT, CHRIST.	39	M	LABR	PRAADEUSA
SCHWABE, GEORG	43	M	SHMK	PRAADEUSA
HELENE	23	F	W	PRAADEUSA
ALICE	2	F	CHILD	PRAADEUSA
GRAEF, AUGUST	26	M	BCHR	HBZZZZUSA
TROSCHIER, WILH.	31	M	TLR	PRZZZZUSA
TITZE, BERTHA	21	F	SGL	PRZZZZUSA
THULKE, JOH.	38	M	LABR	PRAGDHUSA
PAUL	14	M	LABR	PRAGDHUSA
KURZ, JOSEFA	36	F	WO	PRAEABUSA
MARTHA	15	F	UNKNOWN	PRAEABUSA
ROMAN	8	M	CHILD	PRAEABUSA
FRANZ	.08	M	INFANT	PRAEABUSA
RINNE, LOUISE	52	F	WO	PRAAUEUSA
CHRIST.	24	M	CH	PRAAUEUSA
ADOLF	9	M	CHILD	PRAAUEUSA
EICKMANN, ERNST	17	M	LABR	PRAAUEUSA
MUELLER, LOUISE	21	F	WO	PRZZZZUSA
FRANZ	27	M	BSKM	PRZZZZUSA
THIDE, WILHELMINE	34	F	SGL	PRAAKHUSA
KOCHANSKA, PAULINE	45	F	SGL	PRACWTUSA
MARX, KATIE	26	F	SGL	HSZZZZUSA
RAU, PAULINE	24	F	SGL	PRZZZZUSA
HOECK, AUGUST	37	M	FARMER	PRZZZZUSA
MARIE	39	F	W	PRZZZZUSA
MARG.	13	F	CH	PRZZZZUSA
DOROTHEA	8	F	CHILD	PRZZZZUSA
PETER	7	M	CHILD	PRZZZZUSA
STORTZ, CAROLINE	20	F	SGL	PRAEIEUSA
PFAFF, LOUISE	25	F	SGL	PRAEIEUSA
HELWIG, EUGEN	19	M	LABR	PRADEIUSA
HOENOW, EMMA	21	F	SGL	PRAAKHUSA
HOPPE, RICHARD	33	M	MCHT	PRZZZZUSA
STABY, HEINR.	25	M	BLKSMH	PRACQAUSA
BAUSTIAN, MARIE	28	F	SGL	PRAEPZUSA
HENRIK, JOSEF	28	M	JNR	PRAAKHUSA
LINDNER, MARIE	16	F	SGL	SYZZZZUSA
HETTLER, GERHARDT	26	M	FARMER	SYAHNUUSA
KISTOW, AUGUST	60	M	LABR	PRZZZZUSA
CAROLINE	38	F	W	PRZZZZUSA
PAULINE	18	F	SGL	PRZZZZUSA
FILIZOW, KATH.	24	F	WO	PRZZZZUSA
VALENTY	2	M	CHILD	PRZZZZUSA
VICTORIA	.06	F	INFANT	PRZZZZUSA
BEJKA, STANSL.	22	M	CPTR	PRABMIUSA
WOLTRAM, ANNE	33	F	WO	PRAAKHUSA
MARTHA	4	F	CHILD	PRAAKHUSA
WOLLAND, ERNST	38	M	FARMER	PRZZZZUSA
KLEINOWSKY, JOH.	50	M	LABR	PRZZZZUSA
JAHNKE, IDA	29	F	SGL	PRAHFWUSA
FLEYEL, ROBERT	32	M	MCHT	PRAARZUSA
BERTHA	32	F	W	PRAARZUSA
BRUYSCH, HEINR.	26	M	MCHT	PRAHQAUSA
FLEYEL, ALFR.	6	M	CHILD	PRAARZUSA
MARIE	3	F	CHILD	PRAARZUSA
ERNST	2	M	CHILD	PRAARZUSA
ELISAB.	.06	F	INFANT	PRAARZUSA
GROSS, GOTTFR.	69	M	FARMER	PRZZZZUSA
CAROLOINE	58	F	WO	PRZZZZUSA
EXNER, LUDW.	25	M	PNTR	PRAAXHUSA
KAUFMANN, LINA	59	F	WO	PRAAKHUSA
GROTTE, JOH.	14	M	BY	PRAAKHUSA
HOCHTRITT, EMILIE	24	F	SGL	PRAAKHUSA
ROTKOWSKI, LAURETTE	21	F	SGL	PRAAKHUSA
OWARZYSZECK, MARIE	28	F	WO	PRZZZZUSA
MARIANNE	7	F	CHILD	PRZZZZUSA
MALGORKATA	3	F	CHILD	PRZZZZUSA
HOINKE, WILH.	31	M	TCHR	PRAEACUSA
JANKE, MAX	24	M	TCHR	PRAAKHUSA
IMM, FRIEDR.	25	M	TCHR	PRZZZZUSA
WIEMANN, GUST.	28	M	TCHR	PRAAKHUSA
REITZ, FANNY	20	F	SGL	PRAAKHUSA
MOSESSOHN, MOSES	57	M	LABR	PRADLOUSA
MATHILDE	54	F	W	PRADLOUSA
SIEGFRIED	8	M	CHILD	PRADLOUSA

PASSENGER	AGE	SEX	OCCUPATION	PVRIVL/DES
ISIDOR	8	M	CHILD	PRADLOUSA
DOERGES, MINNA	37	F	WO	PRAAXHUSA
WILH.	14	M	CH	PRAAXHUSA
KARL	8	M	CHILD	PRAAXHUSA
AUG.	7	M	CHILD	PRAAXHUSA
HUNS	6	M	CHILD	PRAAXHUSA
ALTENHOFF, OTTO	38	M	LKSH	PRAJWOUSA
MINNA	41	F	W	PRAJWOUSA
LOUISE	14	F	CH	PRAJWOUSA
AUGUST	7	M	CHILD	PRAJWOUSA
BERTHA	4	F	CHILD	PRAJWOUSA
SCHEDEL, ADOLF	23	M	LABR	PRAAKHUSA
RAUSCH, PAUL	28	M	CPR	PRAFPMUSA
LEWIS, CAECILIE	21	F	SGL	PRAAKHUSA

SHIP: CITY OF RICHMOND

FROM: LIVERPOOL AND QUEENSTOWN
TO: NEW YORK
ARRIVED: 10 SEPTEMBER 1888

PASSENGER	AGE	SEX	OCCUPATION	PVRIVL/DES
KOBAL, CHRIS	26	M	LABR	PRACBFNY
SCHROEDER, CARL	40	M	LABR	PRACBFNY
BUNER, CARL	26	M	LABR	PRACBFNY
DENTSEL, LOGOSEL	19	M	LABR	PRACBFNY
WAFS, CHAM	22	M	LABR	PRACBFNY
EDELATEIN, CHIMS	28	M	LABR	PRACBFNY
SCHARAGMAN, SLATE	23	F	SP	GRZZZZNY
THOMPSON, EMMA	25	F	W	GRADAXUSA
MARY	3	F	CHILD	GRADAXUSA
JANSON, C.	25	M	GENT	GRZZZZNY

SHIP: GOTHIA

FROM: STETTIN
TO: NEW YORK
ARRIVED: 10 SEPTEMBER 1888

PASSENGER	AGE	SEX	OCCUPATION	PVRIVL/DES
KUPFERSCHMIDT, MARIE	26	F	SGL	PRZZZZUSA
MARTHA	19	F	SGL	PRZZZZUSA
SCHWAGINNIS, BERTHA	38	F	SGL	PRZZZZUSA
RICHARD	5	M	CHILD	PRZZZZUSA
BANG, PAULINA	24	F	SGL	PRZZZZUSA
MIELKE, MICHAEL	58	M	LABR	PRZZZZUSA
CAROLINE	57	F	W	PRZZZZUSA
ALWINE	9	F	CHILD	PRZZZZUSA
SCHEIL, HULDA	19	F	SGL	PRZZZZUSA
GUNDLACH, LUDWIG	68	M	UNKNOWN	PRZZZZUSA
WOYCHEKOWSKI, STANISL.	32	M	UNKNOWN	PRZZZZUSA
KLANK, CARL	33	M	LABR	PRZZZZUSA
KOTEMANN, KARL	42	M	LABR	PRZZZZUSA
FRIEDRIKE	36	F	W	PRZZZZUSA
ADELE	6	F	CHILD	PRZZZZUSA
ELISABETH	.04	F	INFANT	PRZZZZUSA
MARX, CLARA	16	F	SGL	PRZZZZUSA
GIELDON, MARIANA	34	F	SGL	PRZZZZUSA
RETKOWSKA, MARIE	19	F	SGL	PRZZZZUSA
WENDLAND, CARL	32	M	UNKNOWN	PRZZZZUSA
AUGUSTA	29	F	UNKNOWN	PRZZZZUSA
ANNA	5	F	CHILD	PRZZZZUSA
BRUNO	3	M	CHILD	PRZZZZUSA
PAUL	1	M	CHILD	PRZZZZUSA
OTTO	.03	M	INFANT	PRZZZZUSA
FISCHER, LUDWIG	70	M	LABR	PRZZZZUSA
LOUISE	64	F	W	PRZZZZUSA

PASSENGER	AGE	SEX	OCCUPATION	PRVL	DES
ERNSTINE	21	F	D		PRZZZZUSA
GRUEZINSKA, MAGDALENA	30	F	W		PRZZZZUSA
MARTHA	10	F	CH		PRZZZZUSA
VALERIA	8	F	CHILD		PRZZZZUSA
VICTOR	5	M	CHILD		PRZZZZUSA
FRANZ	4	M	CHILD		PRZZZZUSA
HELENE	.09	F	INFANT		PRZZZZUSA
FIJAL, AUGUSTINA	38	F	W		PRZZZZUSA
JOHANN	15	M	UNKNOWN		PRZZZZUSA
FRANZ	11	M	CH		PRZZZZUSA
JOSEPH	8	M	CHILD		PRZZZZUSA
LEON	4	M	CHILD		PRZZZZUSA
HUNDESTMARK, MARIA	40	F	W		PRZZZZUSA
META	10	F	CH		PRZZZZUSA
IDA	4	F	CHILD		PRZZZZUSA
KONOPATZKY, ADOLF	36	M	UNKNOWN		PRZZZZUSA
MARIE	40	F	W		PRZZZZUSA
WILHELM	7	M	CHILD		PRZZZZUSA
MARTHA	3	F	CHILD		PRZZZZUSA
U	1	F	CHILD		PRZZZZUSA
CARL	59	M	UNKNOWN		PRZZZZUSA
CHARLOTTE	64	F	W		PRZZZZUSA
AUGUSTE	29	F	D		PRZZZZUSA
ROTH, WILHELMINE	25	F	SGL		PRZZZZUSA
BAGEMEHL, MARIE	24	F	SGL		PRZZZZUSA
FUHLBRUGGE, JOHANNA	46	F	W		PRZZZZUSA
ANNA	16	F	D		PRZZZZUSA
AUGUSTE	10	F	H		PRZZZZUSA
ALBERT	8	M	CHILD		PRZZZZUSA
MARTHA	4	F	CHILD		PRZZZZUSA
JAHNKE, GUSTAV	36	M	TLR		PRZZZZUSA
BABIAK, ANDREAS	26	M	BCHR		PRZZZZUSA
SCHEFFLER, FRIEDRICH	20	M	FARMER		PRZZZZUSA
STOLP, ANNA	23	F	W		PRZZZZUSA
JANKOWSKI, STANISL.	24	M	LABR		PRZZZZUSA
GRONAU, BERTHA	21	F	W		PRZZZZUSA
HELENE	.11	F	INFANT		PRZZZZUSA
MERTINATIS, FRIEDRICH	60	M	BKR		PRZZZZUSA
CAROLINE	52	F	W		PRZZZZUSA
ERNST	18	M	CH		PRZZZZUSA
HADWIG	15	F	CH		PRZZZZUSA
LEWANDOWSKI, IGNATZ	23	M	SHMK		PRZZZZUSA
GORNY, WLADISLAUS	23	M	LABR		PRZZZZUSA
GARSZTACKA, MARIA	24	F	W		PRZZZZUSA
STANISLAUS	.11	M	INFANT		PRZZZZUSA
KOENIG, ALWINE	20	F	SGL		PRZZZZUSA
KORSUAK, RUCHARD	24	M	LKSH		PRZZZZUSA
HALFPAP, CARL	26	M	FARMER		PRZZZZUSA
LABANDT, MAGDALENA	23	F	W		PRZZZZUSA
ANTON	.09	M	INFANT		PRZZZZUSA
HARTWIG, GUSTAV	20	M	MCHT		PRZZZZUSA
BIEKUPSKY, WYEZACH	40	M	LABR		PRZZZZUSA
AFFMANN, CARL	34	M	UNKNOWN		PRZZZZUSA
MOEHRING, MARGARETHE	30	F	W		PRZZZZUSA
WILLY	7	M	CHILD		PRZZZZUSA
KATHIE	4	F	CHILD		PRZZZZUSA
ZITZELBERGER, KATHIE	24	F	SGL		PRZZZZUSA
BEHRENDT, MARTHA	23	F	W		PRZZZZUSA
SCHULER, CARL	42	M	LABR		PRZZZZUSA
RATENKE, FERD.	32	M	LABR		PRZZZZUSA
JANIAK, JOSEPH	30	M	BKPR		PRZZZZUSA
CORNEL, CLARA	34	F	W		PRZZZZUSA
MARGARETTE	9	F	CHILD		PRZZZZUSA
COURT	6	M	CHILD		PRZZZZUSA
MARIE	.06	F	INFANT		PRZZZZUSA
HEITMANN, JOHANN	64	M	LABR		PRZZZZUSA
WILHELM	21	M	LABR		PRZZZZUSA
HUNDERTMARK, JULIUS	.08	M	INFANT		PRZZZZUSA
BEHRENDT, MARIA	2	F	CHILD		PRZZZZUSA

SHIP: EIDER

FROM: BREMEN AND SOUTHAMPTON
TO: NEW YORK
ARRIVED: 11 SEPTEMBER 1888

PASSENGER	AGE	SEX	OCCUPATION	PRVL	DES
ESSER, ELISE	50	F	UNKNOWN		GRZZZZUSA
KUNIGUNDE	27	F	UNKNOWN		GRZZZZUSA
CETA	26	F	UNKNOWN		GRZZZZUSA
U	30	M	TT		GRZZZZUSA
HAARMANN, AUGUST	48	M	TT		GRZZZZUSA
UHLIG, G.U.	32	M	TT		GRZZZZUSA
C.H.	20	M	TT		GRZZZZUSA
LIEBMANN, OTTO	29	M	TT		GRZZZZUSA
WALDER, ANNA	24	F	UNKNOWN		GRZZZZUSA
LAMEYER, ED.	23	M	TT		GRZZZZUSA
DIEHL, ELISE	21	F	UNKNOWN		GRZZZZUSA
WIRTH, BABETTE	18	F	UNKNOWN		GRZZZZUSA
GEHLEN, HEUNR.	21	M	TT		GRZZZZUSA
POPP, SAPHIE	25	F	UNKNOWN		GRZZZZUSA
MEYE, HUGO	36	M	TT		GRZZZZUSA
MEIER, ELISAB.	68	F	UNKNOWN		SRZZZZUSA
ANNA	37	F	UNKNOWN		SRZZZZUSA
REIFF, AMALIE	20	F	UNKNOWN		SRZZZZUSA
CARLICZEK, MARTHA	24	F	UNKNOWN		SRZZZZUSA
ZIEGENBEIN, WILH.	28	M	TT		SRZZZZUSA
BRECHTEL, CATHAR.	30	F	UNKNOWN		SRZZZZUSA
ROBERT	7	M	CHILD		SRZZZZUSA
EDUARD	5	M	CHILD		SRZZZZUSA
ROSA	4	F	CHILD		SRZZZZUSA
ELISE	.01	F	INFANT		SRZZZZUSA
MOHR, JOHANNE	16	F	UNKNOWN		SRZZZZUSA
DIEKMANN, ELISAB.	63	F	UNKNOWN		SRZZZZUSA
AUGUSTE	28	F	UNKNOWN		SRZZZZUSA
RAHN, M.	51	F	TT		SRZZZZUSA
R.	45	F	TT		SRZZZZUSA
FANNY	9	F	CHILD		SRZZZZUSA
KLAPP, HEDWIG	20	F	UNKNOWN		SRZZZZUSA
HAMN, PAULINE	00	F	UNKNOWN		SRZZZZUSA
HERZ, JETTE	00	F	UNKNOWN		SRZZZZUSA
ROSALIE	00	F	UNKNOWN		SRZZZZUSA
ROSCHER, U	69	M	TT		SRZZZZUSA
KLOSTERMANN, HEINR.	18	M	LABR		SRZZZZUSA
HILBERT, MARIE	14	F	UNKNOWN		SRZZZZUSA
LIEDEG, JOSEPH	35	M	SHMK		SRZZZZUSA
KLANN, CARIA	18	F	SMSTS		SRZZZZUSA
TESSMANN, FRITZ	36	M	FARMER		SRZZZZUSA
AUGUSTE	35	F	W		SRZZZZUSA
MARTHA	9	F	CHILD		SRZZZZUSA
U	20	M	FARMER		SRZZZZUSA
QEITZ, FRIEDERIKE	36	F	UNKNOWN		SRZZZZUSA
PASCHE, SOPHIE	56	F	UNKNOWN		SRZZZZUSA
GALAS, VICTORIA	30	F	UNKNOWN		SRZZZZUSA
IGNATZ	6	M	CHILD		SRZZZZUSA
PALAZIA	1	F	CHILD		SRZZZZUSA
FRANZ	.09	M	INFANT		SRZZZZUSA
RWIATKOWSKA, MIHALINE	21	F	UNKNOWN		SRZZZZUSA
ANTONIA	.10	F	INFANT		SRZZZZUSA
MEINDL, MINNA	19	F	UNKNOWN		SRZZZZUSA
STAKES, JOH.	26	M	SHMK		SRZZZZUSA
CAROLINE	33	F	W		SRZZZZUSA
IDA	1	F	CHILD		SRZZZZUSA
ERNST	.11	M	INFANT		SRZZZZUSA
CYBART, FLORENZNA	23	F	UNKNOWN		SRZZZZUSA
BRANDT, JOH.	68	M	FARMER		SRZZZZUSA
WILHELMINE	55	F	W		SRZZZZUSA
MARTHA	21	F	UNKNOWN		SRZZZZUSA
U	17	M	FARMER		SRZZZZUSA
ROMIEJIVSKA, JOSEPH.	11	F	UNKNOWN		SRZZZZUSA
MAUESKE, JOS.	15	F	FARMER		SRZZZZUSA
RINGEL, MARIE	27	F	SMSTS		SRZZZZUSA
MAHR, HEINR.	21	M	BRR		SRZZZZUSA
AYPNIEWSKA, JOSEFA	26	F	UNKNOWN		SRZZZZUSA
MARIA	2	F	CHILD		SRZZZZUSA

PASSENGER	AGE	SEX	OCCUPATION	PRVL/VIL/DES
MOHR, LINA	21	F	SMSTS	SRZZZZUSA
BERTSCH, PETER	18	M	ENGR	SRZZZZUSA
MOELLER, ANNA	13	F	UNKNOWN	GRZZZZUSA
BREDE, MARIE	19	F	UNKNOWN	GRZZZZUSA
GARHAMER, FRANZ	47	M	FARMER	GRZZZZUSA
KOEGEL, SOPHIE	24	F	SWR	GRZZZZUSA
PARTENFELDER, MARG.	19	F	SWR	GRZZZZUSA
WAG---, JOH.	16	M	LABR	GRZZZZUSA
U, U	00	F	UNKNOWN	GRZZZZUSA
GRETZEN	20	F	UNKNOWN	GRZZZZUSA
BABETTE	18	F	UNKNOWN	GRZZZZUSA
ULMER, PILOUR	17	M	BKLYR	GRZZZZUSA
KRAIK, WILH.	24	M	BKLYR	GRZZZZUSA
KUNZ, ELISAB.	20	F	SMSTS	GRZZZZUSA
BLOCH, LEHURANN	14	M	CNF	GRZZZZUSA
ALEX	15	M	CNF	GRZZZZUSA
GRIMM, HEINR.	11	M	UNKNOWN	GRZZZZUSA
U, U	20	F	UNKNOWN	GRZZZZUSA
ADAM	17	M	CPTR	GRZZZZUSA
BAYER, EMMA	18	F	SWR	GRZZZZUSA
VOSSBRINCK, ELISE	16	F	SWR	GRZZZZUSA
WINKLER, LINA	29	F	UNKNOWN	GRZZZZUSA
EISENBERGER, JETTCHEN	20	F	SWR	GRZZZZUSA
GATZ, CARG.	24	F	SWR	GRZZZZUSA
HESS, KONRAD	16	M	UNKNOWN	GRZZZZUSA
SCHULZ, U	17	F	SMSTS	GRZZZZUSA
--FKEN, U	18	M	LABR	GRZZZZUSA
FRISCH, ANDR.	23	M	LABR	GRZZZZUSA
WILL, MARG.	22	F	UNKNOWN	GRZZZZUSA
GAHM, MARG.	25	F	UNKNOWN	GRZZZZUSA
SCHMALZBANER, JOH.	24	M	BRR	GRZZZZUSA
HUPFER, MARIE	25	F	SWR	GRZZZZUSA
PFAFF, KATHAR.	34	F	SWR	GRZZZZUSA
GRASS, JOH.	74	M	PNTR	GRZZZZUSA
JENSEN, SRTHUR	24	M	LABR	GRZZZZUSA
WEISBECKER, BARB.	66	F	UNKNOWN	GRZZZZUSA
SCHMIDT, ELISAB.	22	F	UNKNOWN	GRZZZZUSA
EHMER, APOLONIE	11	F	UNKNOWN	GRZZZZUSA
BREDEN, META	22	F	UNKNOWN	GRZZZZUSA
ANNA	16	F	UNKNOWN	GRZZZZUSA
HERRMANN, ANNA	20	F	UNKNOWN	GRZZZZUSA
RUSSEN, JOS.	29	M	BKR	GRZZZZUSA
LEHNERT, AUG.	23	M	BKR	GRZZZZUSA
LARKER, LODOVECZ	17	M	MCHT	SRZZZZUSA
SCHATZ, EVA	19	F	UNKNOWN	GRZZZZUSA
KOPPIL, ELISAB.	18	F	SMSTS	GRZZZZUSA
SCHATZ, ERHARD	26	M	SHMK	GRZZZZUSA
SCHNEIDER, JOH.	15	M	TLR	GRZZZZUSA
KOSTNER, U	17	F	SMSTS	GRZZZZUSA
SCHATZ, ELISE	19	F	SWR	GRZZZZUSA
SCHRAUNN, JOHANN	28	M	CPTR	GRZZZZUSA
DUMLING, CHRIST	14	M	UNKNOWN	GRZZZZUSA
PRENTSCH, LOUISE	16	F	SWR	GRZZZZUSA
NUSSBAUM, CONR.	17	M	CNF	GRZZZZUSA
WALDMANN, OTTO	11	M	UNKNOWN	GRZZZZUSA
REINHECKEL, WILH.	49	M	FARMER	GRZZZZUSA
ANNA	18	F	UNKNOWN	GRZZZZUSA
LAWRENZ, WANDA	25	F	UNKNOWN	GRZZZZUSA
HEIER, AUGUSTE	59	F	UNKNOWN	GRZZZZUSA
LAPPERT, IDA	25	F	UNKNOWN	GRZZZZUSA
ELSE	4	F	CHILD	GRZZZZUSA
WILLY	1	M	CHILD	GRZZZZUSA
DUENTCH, WILH.	39	M	FARMER	GRZZZZUSA
ANNA	27	F	W	GRZZZZUSA
EMIL	5	M	CHILD	GRZZZZUSA
MAX	.09	M	INFANT	GRZZZZUSA
JAEGER, MINNA	53	F	UNKNOWN	GRZZZZUSA
MIETENBERGER, MARIE	23	F	CNF	GRZZZZUSA
LECHENREYER, MARL	26	M	SHMK	GRZZZZUSA
RUECKEL, GEORG	16	M	UNKNOWN	GRZZZZUSA
JUNGKUNST, JOH.	25	M	BBR	GRZZZZUSA
FROBA, GEORG	15	M	UNKNOWN	GRZZZZUSA
BERGMANN, OTTILIE	32	F	UNKNOWN	GRZZZZUSA
ELISE	8	F	CHILD	GRZZZZUSA
GEORG	7	M	CHILD	GRZZZZUSA
WILHELMINE	5	F	CHILD	GRZZZZUSA
OTTILIE	3	F	CHILD	GRZZZZUSA
FISCHER, ERNST	22	M	BRR	GRZZZZUSA
GEISLER, MARIE	20	F	SMSTS	GRZZZZUSA
LANTER, ANNA	39	F	UNKNOWN	GRZZZZUSA
KOLB, CRESENTIA	28	F	UNKNOWN	GRZZZZUSA
STOEBER, ANNA	19	F	UNKNOWN	GRZZZZUSA
TIENEMANN, MARIE	20	F	SWR	GRZZZZUSA
LANGE, FRITZ	24	M	MCHT	GRZZZZUSA
KIRKEN, BERTHA	14	F	UNKNOWN	GRZZZZUSA
KELLNER, HEINR.	21	M	BCHR	GRZZZZUSA
SCHMALSTEIG, ALB.	24	M	BKR	GRZZZZUSA
WIESINGER, JOH.	57	M	FARMER	GRZZZZUSA
AUGUST	17	M	FARMER	GRZZZZUSA
BATEWA, EVA	54	F	UNKNOWN	GRZZZZUSA
WIEDMAIER, B.	25	M	FARMER	GRZZZZUSA
WALTER, U	15	M	LABR	GRZZZZUSA
BEIRE, LINA	31	F	UNKNOWN	GRZZZZUSA
SCHLOMERKAMPER, WILH.	16	M	UNKNOWN	GRZZZZUSA
BRUMMER, FRIED.	27	M	MCHT	GRZZZZUSA
KEITH, ROSE	16	F	UNKNOWN	GRZZZZUSA
KOOPMANN, JOH.	33	M	FARMER	GRZZZZUSA
ANNA	24	F	W	GRZZZZUSA
APPEL, KONRAD	27	M	ENGR	GRZZZZUSA
KOCH, RUDOLF	25	M	SLR	GRZZZZUSA
KRICK, FRANZ	23	M	TLR	GRZZZZUSA
FEHR, JANNI	18	F	SMSTS	GRZZZZUSA
STEINER, JACOB	27	M	FARMER	GRZZZZUSA
ELISE	24	F	W	GRZZZZUSA
MOLLE--, CHRIST	16	M	LABR	GRZZZZUSA
NEUMANN, HEINR.	46	M	BCHR	GRZZZZUSA
LORENZER, ALB.	31	M	BBR	GRZZZZUSA
MOOS, JULIUS	21	M	BRR	GRZZZZUSA
SCHMIDT, BARBARA	20	F	SWR	GRZZZZUSA
WINKLER, CHRIST	59	M	PNTR	GRZZZZUSA
MAIER, BARBARA	16	F	SWR	GRZZZZUSA
SCHOCKEL, KATHAR.	54	F	UNKNOWN	GRZZZZUSA
ANNA	26	F	UNKNOWN	GRZZZZUSA
MARG.	30	F	UNKNOWN	GRZZZZUSA
CONRAD	16	M	FARMER	GRZZZZUSA
GERKEN, ANNA	27	F	UNKNOWN	GRZZZZUSA
GEBERT, FR.	31	M	PNTR	GRZZZZUSA
BUSCHHAUSEN, AUG.	27	M	TU	GRZZZZUSA
BRINKMANN, HERM.	30	M	PNTR	GRZZZZUSA
FRANT, EDWIN	21	M	ENGR	GRZZZZUSA
RUVEKE, JOH.	35	M	FARMER	GRZZZZUSA
ANNA	30	F	W	GRZZZZUSA
ELLA	3	F	CHILD	GRZZZZUSA
ANNA	.07	F	INFANT	GRZZZZUSA
MUNKER, WILH.	30	M	TU	GRZZZZUSA
ROHN, AUG.	31	M	BRR	GRZZZZUSA
WAGNER, VALENT.	00	M	BKR	GRZZZZUSA
LIEBIEG, GOTTL.	45	M	FARMER	GRZZZZUSA
AUGUSTE	46	F	W	GRZZZZUSA
FREYNNITH, LINA	18	F	SWR	GRZZZZUSA
ROHRSCHEIDT, ELISAB.	20	F	SWR	GRZZZZUSA
HEILMANN, MARIA	22	F	UNKNOWN	GRZZZZUSA
FRANZISKA	18	F	UNKNOWN	GRZZZZUSA
KOSTER, SEBASTIAN	9	M	CHILD	GRZZZZUSA
DAHMS, U	16	M	CH	GRZZZZUSA
MEYER, JUL.	27	M	MCHT	GRZZZZUSA
BOHLEN, MARIA	18	F	SWR	GRZZZZUSA
FISCHER, H.L.	28	M	SLR	GRZZZZUSA
BELNER, FTIEDR.	67	M	FARMER	GRZZZZUSA
TOVER, SOPHIE	17	F	SWR	GRZZZZUSA
MOHRING, MARIA	17	F	SWR	GRZZZZUSA
HERTING, MARIA	31	F	UNKNOWN	GRZZZZUSA
PAULA	6	F	CHILD	GRZZZZUSA
ELSE	4	F	CHILD	GRZZZZUSA
LILIE	2	F	CHILD	GRZZZZUSA
GUNTHER, HELENE	25	F	SMSTS	GRZZZZUSA
GERSON, BERTHA	19	F	SMSTS	GRZZZZUSA
RUECKERT, FRAN.	45	F	SMSTS	GRZZZZUSA
DHONAN, WILH.	24	M	PNTR	GRZZZZUSA
KROECK, CATH.	21	F	SWR	GRZZZZUSA

PASSENGER	AGE	SEX	OCCUPATION	PRVL	DES
WIENER, ADOLF	15	M	UNKNOWN	GRZZZZUSA	
FORST, EMMA	24	F	SWR	GRZZZZUSA	
WERKMEISTER, FRITZ	40	M	ENGR	GRZZZZUSA	
MATHILDE	32	F	W	GRZZZZUSA	
MULLER, THEOD.	33	M	SMH	GRZZZZUSA	
GOOSMANN, JOSEF	12	M	UNKNOWN	GRZZZZUSA	
TEICHMUELLER, AD.	45	M	FARMER	GRZZZZUSA	
WEUEHOEFT, HEINR.	14	M	UNKNOWN	GRZZZZUSA	
HASEMANN, CHRISTINE	33	F	UNKNOWN	GRZZZZUSA	
WILH.	11	M	UNKNOWN	GRZZZZUSA	
FRANZ	10	M	UNKNOWN	GRZZZZUSA	
SOFIA	7	F	CHILD	GRZZZZUSA	
LENCHEN	5	F	CHILD	GRZZZZUSA	
SCHNEIDER, LUDW.	28	M	MCHT	GRZZZZUSA	
WOELFLEIN, GEORG	27	M	FARMER	GRZZZZUSA	
HARF, HERM.	22	M	LABR	GRZZZZUSA	
HOER, JOH.	35	M	LABR	GRZZZZUSA	
PELMAN, A.MARIA	23	F	SWR	GRZZZZUSA	
SCHMICKO, ALOIS	24	M	ENGR	GRZZZZUSA	
GERUM, LUDWIG	26	M	BRR	GRZZZZUSA	
HELLMANN, FRANZ	29	M	PNTR	GRZZZZUSA	
BORCKERS, U	26	F	SWR	GRZZZZUSA	
MEHNERT, EMIL	28	M	BKR	GRZZZZUSA	
SCHUGGEL, CONR.	.02	M	INFANT	GRZZZZUSA	
QUIATKOWSKI, ANTONIA	.09	F	INFANT	GRZZZZUSA	
HOLTBUHR, WILH.	23	M	LABR	GRZZZZUSA	
STUBE, ANDR.	34	M	GDNR	GRZZZZUSA	
RUPPRICH, AUG.	27	M	GDNR	GRZZZZUSA	
STACKER, CARL	.01	M	INFANT	GRZZZZUSA	
CARL	.01	M	INFANT	GRZZZZUSA	

SHIP: ETHIOPIA

FROM: GLASGOW AND MOVILLE
TO: NEW YORK
ARRIVED: 11 SEPTEMBER 1888

PASSENGER	AGE	SEX	OCCUPATION	PRVL	DES
LANGENBECK, PAUL	28	M	SDLR	GRZZZZUSA	
MARIA	25	F	UNKNOWN	GRZZZZUSA	
BERTHA	8	F	CHILD	GRZZZZUSA	
CHRISTINA	3	F	CHILD	GRZZZZUSA	
JOSEPH	2	M	CHILD	GRZZZZUSA	
MICHELE, HENRY	19	M	MCHT	GRZZZZUSA	
SCHNEIDER, MICHEL	24	M	BKR	GRZZZZUSA	
JOHANN	27	M	UNKNOWN	GRZZZZUSA	
RILZ, MATHILDA	30	F	HP	GRZZZZUSA	
STRAKOWITZ, LINA	20	F	HP	GRZZZZUSA	
ROSENWEICZ, G.	30	F	UNKNOWN	GRZZZZUSA	
BLUME	1	F	CHILD	GRZZZZUSA	

SHIP: WYOMING

FROM: LIVERPOOL AND QUEENSTOWN
TO: NEW YORK
ARRIVED: 11 SEPTEMBER 1888

PASSENGER	AGE	SEX	OCCUPATION	PRVL	DES
KESSLER, ALBR.	22	M	LABR	GRZZZZUSA	
DORECHANY, MATH.	20	M	LABR	GRZZZZUSA	
SCHOSSER, J.	17	M	LABR	GRZZZZUSA	
KLEIN, F.	25	M	LABR	GRZZZZUSA	
WEGAND, R.	22	F	W	GRZZZZUSA	
NOLL, J.	32	M	LABR	GRZZZZUSA	
PESCHKE, P.	26	M	LABR	GRZZZZUSA	
HAAB, CHRIST.	35	M	LABR	GRZZZZUSA	
STROUB, EMMA	29	F	W	GRZZZZUSA	

PASSENGER	AGE	SEX	OCCUPATION	PRVL	DES
MARIN	5	M	CHILD	GRZZZZUSA	
OTTO	3	M	CHILD	GRZZZZUSA	
CARR, E.	20	M	LABR	GRZZZZUSA	
LYIMGREN, ANNA	47	F	W	GRZZZZUSA	
AUGUST	14	M	LABR	GRZZZZUSA	
JULIA	24	F	SP	GRZZZZUSA	
JANSSON, JOHN	22	M	LABR	GRZZZZUSA	
HESTEIN, K.	22	M	UNKNOWN	GRZZZZUSA	
MUNARD, EVA	41	F	W	FRZZZZUSA	
FAVRE, JANNET	30	F	W	FRZZZZUSA	

SHIP: HERMANN

FROM: BREMEN
TO: BALTIMORE
ARRIVED: 12 SEPTEMBER 1888

PASSENGER	AGE	SEX	OCCUPATION	PRVL	DES
KUSLER, ALWINE	43	F	UNKNOWN	GRZZZZMD	
INGANG, RODERICH.	33	M	FARMER	GRZZZZMD	
CLARA	31	F	W	GRZZZZMD	
OTTO	10	M	CH	GRZZZZMD	
WILH.	6	M	CHILD	GRZZZZMD	
HERM.	4	M	CHILD	GRZZZZMD	
RICHARD	.03	M	INFANT	GRZZZZMD	
DITJENEIT, FRIEDR.	37	M	FARMER	GRZZZZMD	
FRIEDKE	33	F	W	GRZZZZMD	
OTTO	14	M	UNKNOWN	GRZZZZMD	
STEFFEN, AMANDA	17	F	UNKNOWN	GRZZZZMD	
PFAFF, ELISABETH	20	F	UNKNOWN	GRZZZZMD	
WETTER, FRIEDR.	35	M	FARMER	GRZZZZMD	
CHARLOTTE	43	F	W	GRZZZZMD	
WILHME.	10	M	CH	GRZZZZMD	
FRIEDR.	7	M	CHILD	GRZZZZMD	
CAROLINE	3	F	CHILD	GRZZZZMD	
LANGE, HERM.	28	M	SHMK	GRZZZZMD	
GAMJER, FRIEDRKE.	63	M	UNKNOWN	GRZZZZMD	
ALWINE	22	M	UNKNOWN	GRZZZZMD	
ALBERT	.05	M	INFANT	GRZZZZMD	
DAHEKE, JOHANN	49	M	LABR	GRZZZZMD	
JOHANNA	49	F	W	GRZZZZMD	
U. AUGUST.	22	F	UNKNOWN	GRZZZZMD	
VOGEL, CARL	25	M	LABR	GRZZZZMD	
SIEVERS, DORIS	25	F	UNKNOWN	GRZZZZMD	
LINA	4	F	CHILD	GRZZZZMD	
STILLER, OSCAR	28	M	CGRMKR	GRZZZZMD	
BRANDT, ANNA	49	F	UNKNOWN	GRZZZZMD	
CARL	14	M	UNKNOWN	GRZZZZMD	
WILHELM	12	M	CH	GRZZZZMD	
POHASKA, ROSA	18	F	UNKNOWN	GRZZZZMD	
MACHOLTZ, EVA	25	F	UNKNOWN	GRZZZZMD	
ZAKRZEASKI, MARIANE	18	F	UNKNOWN	GRZZZZMD	
RYMARKIEWICZ, FRZKA	32	F	UNKNOWN	GRZZZZMD	
MARIA	.06	F	INFANT	GRZZZZMD	
STEINKAMP, BEREND	21	M	LABR	GRZZZZMD	
HOEHNE, HERM.	22	M	FARMER	GRZZZZMD	
KOZLOWSKI, JOH.	12	M	FARMER	GRZZZZMD	
LIESKE, AUGUST	30	F	LABR	GRZZZZMD	
SZYDTOWSKA, JOSEFA	26	F	UNKNOWN	GRZZZZMD	
PELAGIA	3	F	CHILD	GRZZZZMD	
MARYANA	.09	F	INFANT	GRZZZZMD	
KONOPATZKY, PAULINE	25	F	UNKNOWN	GRZZZZMD	
KLEINNENT, AUG.	22	M	FARMER	GRZZZZMD	
LUISE	23	F	W	GRZZZZMD	
RUDOLF	.01	M	INFANT	GRZZZZMD	
BOROWSKA, MINNA	30	F	UNKNOWN	GRZZZZMD	
ANASTASIA	3	F	CHILD	GRZZZZMD	
WOHLGEMUTH, ANDR.	63	M	FARMER	GRZZZZMD	
HELENE	60	F	W	GRZZZZMD	
SEMRAM, CARL	49	M	PNTR	GRZZZZMD	
JOHANNA	64	F	UNKNOWN	GRZZZZMD	

PASSENGER	AGE	SEX	OCCUPATION	PRVL	DES
LASLOWSKA, FRANZKA	25	F	UNKNOWN	GRZZZZMD	
WLADISLAW	.06	M	INFANT	GRZZZZMD	
HOFFMANN, PAULINE	24	F	UNKNOWN	GRZZZZMD	
JOHANN	.09	M	INFANT	GRZZZZMD	
HABICHT, LAURA	27	F	UNKNOWN	GRZZZZMD	
OSCAR	2	M	CHILD	GRZZZZMD	
ADELE	.01	F	INFANT	GRZZZZMD	
SCHROEDER, ELISE	26	F	UNKNOWN	GRZZZZMD	
ANNA	6	F	CHILD	GRZZZZMD	
MARIA	4	F	CHILD	GRZZZZMD	
SCHALEN, JACOB	30	M	FARMER	GRZZZZMD	
BEDARF, ALEX	32	M	BLKSMH	GRZZZZMD	
ENGEMANN, CARL	17	M	UNKNOWN	GRZZZZMD	
STOLP, ELSA	18	F	UNKNOWN	GRZZZZIL	
OPPELT, GUSTAF	18	M	BRR	GRZZZZWI	
GERLACH, RICHARD	41	M	FARMER	GRZZZZWI	
MARTE	42	F	W	GRZZZZWI	
ROSA	13	F	CH	GRZZZZWI	
ARTHUR	12	M	CH	GRZZZZWI	
PRASCHECK, MARIA	25	F	UNKNOWN	GRZZZZWI	
GROSS, FRANZ	22	M	GZR	GRZZZZPA	
GEBBARDT, FRIEDR.	36	M	LKSH	GRZZZZPA	
MARTHA	32	F	W	GRZZZZPA	
FRIEDA	3	F	CHILD	GRZZZZPA	
WITTWER, ERNESTINE	26	F	UNKNOWN	GRZZZZWI	
KROGNE, MATIES	30	M	BCHR	GRZZZZTX	
BARBARA	26	F	W	GRZZZZTX	
OTTO	.05	M	INFANT	GRZZZZTX	
SCHAFFRINA, MARIA	30	F	UNKNOWN	GRZZZZTX	
CONRAD	3	M	CHILD	GRZZZZTX	
PAUL	.09	M	INFANT	GRZZZZTX	
NITSCHKE, PAUL	37	M	JNR	GRZZZZTX	
LUISE	29	F	W	GRZZZZTX	
ALFRED	3	M	CHILD	GRZZZZTX	
SCHUETZ, WILH.	14	M	UNKNOWN	GRZZZZMD	
WAGNER, ANNA	46	F	UNKNOWN	GRZZZZMD	
EZER, AUGUST	27	M	JNR	GRZZZZMD	
DAUM, AUGUST	26	M	BCHR	GRZZZZMD	
JAEGER, MARGR.	27	F	UNKNOWN	GRZZZZMD	
PRUSKI, EDMUND	22	M	FARMER	GRZZZZMD	
FAESSLER, CONSTANT.	17	M	FARMER	GRZZZZMD	
NEUER, ROSINE	14	F	UNKNOWN	GRZZZZMD	
SCHMIDT, CATHR.	22	F	UNKNOWN	GRZZZZMD	
DIEFFENBACH, ELISAB.	47	F	UNKNOWN	GRZZZZMD	
DIETZ, MARGR.	22	F	UNKNOWN	GRZZZZMD	
STAEBEL, THERESE	20	F	UNKNOWN	GRZZZZMD	
KRUMREG, ALBERT	19	M	CL	GRZZZZMD	
JARCHOW, FRIEDKE	42	F	UNKNOWN	GRZZZZMD	
ROSINE	12	F	CH	GRZZZZMD	
TRABER, ALBERT	21	M	UNKNOWN	GRZZZZMD	
LORSEN, DORIS	34	F	UNKNOWN	GRZZZZMD	
AUGUSTE	13	F	CH	GRZZZZMD	
SCHEFFLER, ADAM	23	M	FARMER	GRZZZZMD	
LASKOWSKA, JOSEFA	18	F	UNKNOWN	GRZZZZMD	
GRZEGORZEWSKI, FRZKA	16	F	UNKNOWN	GRZZZZMD	
CIZLAPINSKA, MARY	19	F	UNKNOWN	GRZZZZMD	
URSNACH, HEINR.	21	M	PDLR	GRZZZZMD	
ALBERTZKI, MARIE	50	F	UNKNOWN	GRZZZZMD	
FRITZ	15	M	UNKNOWN	GRZZZZMD	
SLOMOWIZ, MARY	23	F	UNKNOWN	GRZZZZMD	
VICTOR	.01	M	INFANT	GRZZZZMD	
STANISLAUS	.01	M	INFANT	GRZZZZMD	
NOWOWIEJSKO, MICHAELE.	21	F	UNKNOWN	GRZZZZMD	
MICHAEL	.01	M	INFANT	GRZZZZMD	
TREMMES, MAX	26	M	ENGR	GRZZZZMD	
GRAESSLE, CARL	28	M	TCHR	GRZZZZMD	
DOERING, CARL	21	M	FUR	GRZZZZMD	
THUENE, ANNA	17	F	UNKNOWN	GRZZZZMD	
SCHAFFER, EMMA	17	F	UNKNOWN	GRZZZZMD	
WEGE, ERNST	27	M	LABR	GRZZZZMD	
GAURONSKA, JOSEFA	26	F	UNKNOWN	GRZZZZMD	
MUSKATEWITZ, BERTHA	24	F	UNKNOWN	GRZZZZMD	
MUELLER, LENA	20	F	UNKNOWN	GRZZZZMD	
KELLEMANN, TRINA	17	F	UNKNOWN	GRZZZZMD	
WILBERDING, ANNA	21	F	UNKNOWN	GRZZZZMD	
WESSEL, AGNES	64	F	UNKNOWN	GRZZZZMD	
MICHALAK, MARGR.	28	F	UNKNOWN	GRZZZZMD	
JOSEF	9	M	CHILD	GRZZZZMD	
MARIANA	6	F	CHILD	GRZZZZMD	
ROSALIA	.06	F	INFANT	GRZZZZMD	
NOWAKOWSKI, JULIA	25	F	UNKNOWN	GRZZZZMD	
MARIANNA	2	F	CHILD	GRZZZZMD	
JOSEFA	.06	F	INFANT	GRZZZZMD	
JARACZEWSKA, ANTONIA	36	F	UNKNOWN	GRZZZZMD	
MICHALINA	6	F	CHILD	GRZZZZMD	
JOSEFA	3	F	CHILD	GRZZZZMD	
CATHRINA	.06	F	INFANT	GRZZZZMD	
LAULNER, ALEIS	20	M	BCHR	GRZZZZMD	
PEHEWSKY, FRANZ	26	M	SHFM	GRZZZZMD	
WIZECKA, FRZSKA	29	F	UNKNOWN	GRZZZZMD	
MICHAEL	3	M	CHILD	GRZZZZMD	
VINCENTI	.06	M	INFANT	GRZZZZMD	
RECHOWIAK, MARIANA	21	F	UNKNOWN	GRZZZZMD	
PELAGIA	5	F	CHILD	GRZZZZMD	
DOROTHEA	.09	F	INFANT	GRZZZZMD	
ICKLER, JOHANN	26	M	FARMER	GRZZZZMD	
LAWRENZ, MATHILDE	46	F	UNKNOWN	GRZZZZMD	
EMMA	19	F	UNKNOWN	GRZZZZMD	
EMIL	7	M	CHILD	GRZZZZMD	
HUGO	5	M	CHILD	GRZZZZMD	
SCHOLWIN, CARL	24	M	MCHT	GRZZZZMD	
KULBACH, WILHME	30	F	UNKNOWN	GRZZZZMD	
EMILIE	9	F	CHILD	GRZZZZMD	
OTTO	.06	M	INFANT	GRZZZZMD	
GRONAN, FRIEDR.	43	M	TU	GRZZZZMD	
AUGUSTE	39	F	W	GRZZZZMD	
BERTHA	3	F	CHILD	GRZZZZMD	
FRIEDRICH	.08	M	INFANT	GRZZZZMD	
KORNACKI, LUDWIG	62	M	BLKSMH	GRZZZZMD	
EMILIA	57	F	W	GRZZZZMD	
APOLLINIA	14	F	UNKNOWN	GRZZZZMD	
ANTONIA	12	F	CH	GRZZZZMD	
PRACEINS, FRIEDR.	20	M	JNR	GRZZZZMD	
LIPOWSKI, FRIEDR.	25	M	LABR	GRZZZZMD	
SALKOWSKI, JOH.	25	M	LABR	GRZZZZMD	
HOEPPA, PAUL	19	M	LABR	GRZZZZMD	
WILHM.	22	F	UNKNOWN	GRZZZZMD	
SEELIG, GEORG	26	M	PNTR	GRZZZZMD	
ROSALIA	24	F	W	GRZZZZMD	
TSCHENTSCHER, HERM.	35	M	SHMK	GRZZZZMD	
FRANZISKA	33	F	W	GRZZZZMD	
MAX	9	M	CHILD	GRZZZZMD	
ANNA	8	F	CHILD	GRZZZZMD	
IDA	.05	F	INFANT	GRZZZZMD	
SCHERMANN, ABRH.	16	M	UNKNOWN	GRZZZZPA	
MAYERLE, CRESCENZIA	18	F	UNKNOWN	GRZZZZIL	
KRUCZYNSKI, VAL.	21	M	FARMER	GRZZZZIL	
BLINZIG, LINA	21	F	UNKNOWN	GRZZZZOH	
VONWALDE, ANOTON	27	M	FARMER	GRZZZZIL	
PODKEMORSKI, EDW.	43	M	TLR	GRZZZZIL	
AUGUSTE	44	F	W	GRZZZZIL	
HEDWIG	6	F	CHILD	GRZZZZIL	
PETERS, CARL	22	M	BCHR	GRZZZZMI	
OSHOWSKI, PAUL	22	M	BCHR	GRZZZZIL	
KRIEHNKE, CARL	32	M	BCHR	GRZZZZWI	
FUMMHOLZ, FRUEDR.	54	M	LABR	GRZZZZWI	
EFFERT, WILH.	15	M	UNKNOWN	GRZZZZWI	
HINZ, OTTO	20	M	UNKNOWN	GRZZZZWI	
PFLUEGL, FRANZISKA	17	F	UNKNOWN	GRZZZZMD	
OTTILIE	1	F	CHILD	GRZZZZMD	
BELLIN, AUG.	32	M	SHMK	GRZZZZWI	
EMILIE	40	F	W	GRZZZZWI	
FRANZ	4	M	CHILD	GRZZZZWI	
MINNA	3	F	CHILD	GRZZZZWI	
BOETTCHER, FERD.	32	M	TLR	GRZZZZWI	
CARL	65	M	UNKNOWN	GRZZZZWI	
WILH.	20	F	UNKNOWN	GRZZZZWI	
HERMANIG, FR.	16	M	UNKNOWN	GRZZZZMD	
SATTHAU, MARIA	18	F	UNKNOWN	GRZZZZMD	
DEININGER, ALERS	36	M	LABR	GRZZZZMD	

PASSENGER	AGE	SEX	OCCUPATION	PRVL	DES
CATHRINA	6	F	CHILD	GRZZZZMD	
ANBACH, WILHME.	26	F	UNKNOWN	GRZZZZMD	
PRIETZ, BERNHDINE	35	F	UNKNOWN	GRZZZZMD	
ELISE	10	F	CH	GRZZZZMD	
BRUNO	6	M	CHILD	GRZZZZMD	
DAMERT, EDMUND	16	M	TLR	GRZZZZIL	
SEITZ, CHR.	53	M	FARMER	GRZZZZIL	
LUESE	63	F	W	GRZZZZIL	
SOPHIE	19	F	UNKNOWN	GRZZZZIL	
FRIEDR.	16	M	UNKNOWN	GRZZZZIL	
PIENING, BERNHD.	22	M	FARMER	GRZZZZOH	
THERESE	16	F	UNKNOWN	GRZZZZOH	
EKELMANN, AGNES	17	F	UNKNOWN	GRZZZZOH	
LRAMER, DINA	24	F	UNKNOWN	GRZZZZOH	
BUDT, FRANZ	35	M	SHMK	GRZZZZPA	
JUNG, EILH.	24	M	CPR	GRZZZZUSA	
REDIKER, MARIE	25	F	UNKNOWN	GRZZZZUSA	
MESCHEDE, MARIE	35	F	UNKNOWN	GRZZZZUSA	
PAULINE	4	F	CHILD	GRZZZZUSA	
BERGER, ANNA	20	F	UNKNOWN	GRZZZZOH	
KOEHLER, ANOTN	25	M	LABR	GRZZZZMN	
DIERKS, EILERT	46	M	FARMER	GRZZZZMD	
CAROLINE	42	F	W	GRZZZZMD	
CARL	19	M	UNKNOWN	GRZZZZMD	
ADOLF	15	M	UNKNOWN	GRZZZZMD	
MARTHA	9	F	CHILD	GRZZZZMD	
ALEXANDER	7	M	CHILD	GRZZZZMD	
HUGO	4	M	CHILD	GRZZZZMD	
BOEDEN, NANNE	27	F	CH	GRACOWMD	
GREETJE	26	F	W	GRACOWMD	
EILERT	.11	M	INFANT	GRACOWMD	
ENNEKING, BERNH.	18	M	UNKNOWN	GRACOWOH	
AUGUST	14	M	UNKNOWN	GRACOWOH	
WELSKI, CAROLINE	50	F	UNKNOWN	GRACOWMD	
MAIRE	14	F	UNKNOWN	GRACOWMD	
FRIEDR.	10	M	CH	GRACOWMD	
HENRIETTE	9	F	CHILD	GRACOWMD	
ALLENDORF, MARIE	60	F	UNKNOWN	GRACOWOH	
ACKEMANN, HEINR.	60	M	FARMER	GRACOWIL	
WILHME.	60	F	W	GRACOWIL	
HARTMANN, WILH.	15	M	UNKNOWN	GRACOWIL	
ENGELKING, AUG.	16	M	UNKNOWN	GRACOWIL	
HEIDORN, DIEDR.	21	M	LABR	GRACOWIL	
BERNHARD, ANTON	28	M	LABR	GRACOWMD	
FASCHER, EMMA	18	F	UNKNOWN	GRACOWMD	
MEITTNER, ANNA	38	F	UNKNOWN	GRACOWIL	
HOFFMANN, WILHE.	39	M	FARMER	GRACOWOH	
ELISE	32	F	W	GRACOWOH	
CATHRINA	7	F	CHILD	GRACOWOH	
ROSA	4	F	CHILD	GRACOWOH	
MARGRETE	2	F	CHILD	GRACOWOH	
BAYER, ANNA	77	F	UNKNOWN	GRACOWOH	
SCHULZ, MARTE	33	F	UNKNOWN	GRACOWMD	
ALBERT	2	M	CHILD	GRACOWMD	
BENKE, EMILIE	20	F	UNKNOWN	GRACOWMD	
JUSTINE	62	F	UNKNOWN	GRACOWMD	
HIRSCHBERG, SAM.	23	M	UNKNOWN	GRACOWMD	
SCHONLACK, MAYER	15	M	UNKNOWN	GRACOWMD	

SHIP: CALIFORNIA

FROM: HAMBURG
TO: NEW YORK
ARRIVED: 13 SEPTEMBER 1888

PASSENGER	AGE	SEX	OCCUPATION	PRVL	DES
KORUP, FRANZ	35	M	BCHR	GRABWAUSA	
HANS	8	M	CHILD	GRABWAUSA	
MOELLER, GUSTAF	16	M	LABR	PRZZZZUSA	
BAASCH, AUGUST	26	M	MCHT	HBZZZZUSA	
WULF, JOH.	25	M	DLR	HBAADEUSA	

PASSENGER	AGE	SEX	OCCUPATION	PRVL	DES
GOTTSCHAU, EMIL	19	M	MCHT	HBZZZZUSA	
MECKLENBURG, FRANZ	51	M	FARMER	MKZZZZUSA	
LOUISE	44	F	W	MKZZZZUSA	
JULIE	22	F	W	MKZZZZUSA	
MARIE	18	F	W	MKZZZZUSA	
INA	17	F	W	MKZZZZUSA	
CHARLOTTE	16	F	W	MKZZZZUSA	
WILHELM	.03	M	INFANT	MKZZZZUSA	
MANGELS, ANNA	24	F	SGL	MKABIGUSA	
DUCKSTEIN, ANNA	26	F	WO	MKAARZUSA	
ANNA	.11	F	INFANT	MKAARZUSA	
MATHES, HUGO	25	M	FARMER	PRZZZZUSA	
BUCKI, AMALIE	26	F	WO	PRZZZZUSA	
GERTRUD	3	F	CHILD	PRZZZZUSA	
REXIN, CARL	17	M	FARMER	PRALKBUSA	
PAULINE	19	F	SGL	PRALKBUSA	
GOERLITZ, LUCIA	26	F	SGL	PRAAKHUSA	
WEIMAR, CARL	37	M	JNR	PRACKYUSA	
BERNHARDT, EMIL	37	M	MCHT	HBZZZZUSA	
WEIMAR, MARIE	22	F	WO	HBACKYUSA	
BURGER, FR.JOSEF	23	M	GDSM	BDZZZZUSA	
CHRISTINE	20	F	W	BDZZZZUSA	
SCHWARZKOPF, JOHANNA	34	F	WO	BDAFBBUSA	
ANNA	4	F	CHILD	BDAFBBUSA	
MARIANNE	.11	F	INFANT	BDAFBBUSA	
FICHELOWICZ, KEILE	19	F	SGL	PRZZZZUSA	
KICKEL, CAROLINE	25	F	WO	PRZZZZUSA	
PAUL	.04	M	INFANT	PRZZZZUSA	
CIECMIEROWSKA, VICTORIA	25	F	WO	PRZZZZUSA	
MARG.	.11	F	INFANT	PRZZZZUSA	
KROCK, JOHANNA	16	F	SGL	PRALKBUSA	
KRATZ, FRANZ	20	M	LABR	PRAAKHUSA	
RYWELSKA, EMILIE	40	F	WO	PRZZZZUSA	
STANISLAWA	18	F	CH	PRZZZZUSA	
JOSEFA	15	F	CH	PRZZZZUSA	
MARIE	8	F	CHILD	PRZZZZUSA	
AGATHE	7	F	CHILD	PRZZZZUSA	
MARIANNE	5	F	CHILD	PRZZZZUSA	
KWIATKOWSKA, ROSALIE	57	F	WO	PRAGSOUSA	
SCHULZ, PAULINE	18	F	SGL	PRADLOUSA	
PAFFHAUSEN, BERTHA	38	F	WO	PRAAKHUSA	
SPYHALA, ANNA	21	F	WO	PRZZZZUSA	
JAN	.11	M	INFANT	PRZZZZUNK	
BLUHN, LEO	21	M	MCHT	PRAEABUSA	
KNAEKER, LUDWIG	39	M	SHMK	PRAAKHUSA	
RIETDORF, FRIEDRICH	44	M	LABR	PRZZZZUSA	
MARIE	30	F	W	PRZZZZUSA	
ANNA	5	F	CHILD	PRZZZZUSA	
THERESE	3	F	CHILD	PRZZZZUSA	
ERNST	.11	M	INFANT	PRZZZZUSA	
FRIEDR.	.01	M	INFANT	PRZZZZUSA	
ROSKIDA, CATH.	22	F	SGL	PRZZZZUSA	
SABROWSKA, GEORG	30	M	MCHT	PRAFABUSA	
BRANDT, WILHELM	29	M	MNR	PRAEVNUSA	
BOLLEI, WILHELM	22	M	SHMK	PRAAQUUSA	
TODTBERG, DORA	23	F	SGL	PRACKYUSA	
ANNA	21	F	SGL	PRACKYUSA	
MAERKER, ADOLF	25	M	MCHT	PRABYWUSA	
BREY, SOPHIE	33	F	WO	MKZZZZUSA	
FRIEDA	6	F	CHILD	MKZZZZUSA	
RAHLF, NICOLAUS	51	M	FARMER	MKAAVGUSA	
KNACKSTEDT, JOH.	26	M	LABR	MKAJSOUSA	
SCHOENFELDER, AUGUST	45	M	TLR	MKAARZUSA	
FEJA, THOMAS	34	M	TLR	MKAARZUSA	
HAESKE, HEDWIG	24	F	SGL	MKAJXBUSA	
NOWACK, JOSEF	24	M	BCHR	PRZZZZUSA	
OSPALEK, ALBIN	16	M	BBR	PRZZZZUSA	
BOETTCHER, MINNA	19	F	SGL	PRZZZZUSA	
WOLF, AUGUSTE	21	F	SGL	PRAIYMUSA	
ZERULL, OTTO	30	M	LABR	PRAFFYUSA	
MARKWARDT, WILHELM	48	M	FARMER	PRAEHQUSA	
MARIE	45	F	W	PRAEHQUSA	
AMALIE	22	F	CH	PRAEHQUSA	
HELENE	8	F	CHILD	PRAEHQUSA	
MAX	7	M	CHILD	PRAEHQUSA	

PASSENGER	AGE	SEX	OCCUPATION	PRVL	DES
MARTHA	6	F	CHILD	PRAEH	QUSA
HERMANN	5	M	CHILD	PRAEH	QUSA
LISBETH	4	F	CHILD	PRAEH	QUSA
MINNA	2	F	CHILD	PRAEH	QUSA
FRIDA	.09	F	INFANT	PRAEH	QUSA
MUELLER, HEINRICH	23	M	FARMER	PRAEB	JUSA
RIDZAWSKA, AUGUSTE	35	F	WO	PRAJSV	USA
HELENE	3	F	CHILD	PRAJSV	USA
MARIANNE	.06	F	INFANT	PRAJSV	USA
STOEBENAU, FRANZ	18	M	LABR	PRAJSV	USA
WILHELM	14	M	CH	PRAJSV	USA
OSKAR	12	M	CH	PRAJSV	USA
GUSTAV	8	M	CHILD	PRAJSV	USA
HAUS, SOPHIE	43	F	WO	PRAAKH	USA
LOUISE	14	F	CH	PRAAKH	USA
PAULA	8	F	CHILD	PRAAKH	USA
MARZINKEWITZ, JULIUS	25	M	LABR	PRAAZQ	USA
PEIN, GUSTAV	26	M	BCHR	PRZZZZ	USA
MARIE	29	F	W	PRZZZZ	USA
EHRICH	.09	M	INFANT	PRZZZZ	USA
WEINHOLD, FRIEDR.	17	M	TNM	SYZZZZ	USA
SCHRAFFL, JOSEPH	30	M	MCHT	SYADL	DUSA
DOSCH, MICHAEL	24	M	BRR	SYAFV	RUSA
TOEPFER, AUGUSTE	21	F	SGL	PRZZZZ	USA
MUEHLSTEDT, EMMA	39	F	WO	PRADIX	USA
EIGENIE	16	F	D	PRADIX	USA
REIBESTEIN, MINNA	21	F	SGL	PRADIX	USA
STOPP, EDUARD	43	M	LABR	SYZZZZ	USA
MENZ, FRITZ	32	M	TLR	SYALZN	USA
HEINRICH, REINHOLD	21	M	FARMER	SYAHGG	USA
LIETZ, HERMANN	29	M	LABR	SYAJFS	USA
STAUDER, HEINRICH	54	M	FARMER	SYADOI	USA
KAUSSEL, FRIEDR.	26	M	SHMK	PRZZZZ	USA
SCHMIDT, HEINRICH	30	M	MCHT	PRAHNP	USA
GOLLNIK, JOHANN	21	M	LABR	PRAEPY	USA
KORNBLUM, BRUNO	16	M	CL	PRAAKH	USA
LINDENAU, CARL	39	M	LABR	PRAEFL	USA
AUGUSTE	35	F	W	PRAEFL	USA
JOHANNA	8	F	CHILD	PRAEFL	USA
ERNST	7	M	CHILD	PRAEFL	USA
FERDINAND	6	M	CHILD	PRAEFL	USA
GUSTAV	3	M	CHILD	PRAEFL	USA
JOHANNA	.11	F	INFANT	PRAEFL	USA
HERMANN, CARL	17	M	LABR	PRAEFL	USA
LEDER, GUSTAV	17	M	LABR	PRAEFL	USA
WULFSOHN, SARAH	22	F	SGL	PRAEFL	USA
LIBBER, ABRAHAM	34	M	MCHT	PRAAOC	USA
OGAR, FRANZ	32	M	LABR	PRZZZZ	USA
DUDIKA, MARIE	28	F	SGL	PRAAKH	USA
JOSEF	24	M	BLKSMH	PRAAKH	USA
CARL	26	M	LKSH	PRAAKH	USA
GOEBLER, GUSTAV	34	M	CPTR	PRZZZZ	USA
ECKMEIER, ALOIS	38	M	FARMER	BVZZZZ	USA
MIXDORF, HEINRICH	31	M	FARMER	SYZZZZ	USA

SHIP: IOWA

FROM: LIVERPOOL
TO: BOSTON
ARRIVED: 13 SEPTEMBER 1888

PASSENGER	AGE	SEX	OCCUPATION	PRVL	DES
LOKETZ, SCHIE	19	M	TLR	FRZZZZ	USA
WIZAPSKY, ALBERT	23	M	LABR	GRZZZZ	USA

SHIP: ITALY

FROM: LIVERPOOL AND QUEENSTOWN
TO: NEW YORK
ARRIVED: 13 SEPTEMBER 1888

PASSENGER	AGE	SEX	OCCUPATION	PRVL	DES
RARTOW, HERMAN	50	M	LABR	GRACBF	NY
PEEHSTEIN, LAURA	33	F	SP	GRZZZZ	NY
RUCHUTOW, PAUL	20	M	LABR	GRZZZZ	NY
CASSIGNAUD, PAUL	26	M	GENT	GRADXW	NY
U	24	F	LDY	GRADXW	NY

SHIP: NOORDLAND

FROM: ANTWERP
TO: NEW YORK
ARRIVED: 13 SEPTEMBER 1888

PASSENGER	AGE	SEX	OCCUPATION	PRVL	DES
DOORAK, U	24	F	NRS	GRAAEC	USA
HUNGARTEN, B.	23	F	PVTR	GRAAEC	USA
WITHE, U	18	F	PVTR	GRAAEC	USA
STATTERS, A.	25	M	UNKNOWN	GRAAEC	USA
BECKER, J.	28	F	PVTR	GRAAEC	USA
H.	6	M	CHILD	GRAAEC	USA
M.	9	F	CHILD	GRAAEC	USA
SMITH, P.	32	M	MCHT	GRAAEC	USA
GLATT, E.	29	F	PVTR	GRAAEC	USA
SCHNEIDER, CATH.	30	F	PVTR	GRAAEC	USA
AUG.	29	F	PVTR	GRAAEC	USA
SCHAPPER, C.	38	M	DRG	GRAAEC	USA
U	33	F	UNKNOWN	GRAAEC	USA
ELLA	8	F	CHILD	GRAAEC	USA
CARL.	6	F	CHILD	GRAAEC	USA
MARIE	4	F	CHILD	GRAAEC	USA
WILLY	3	F	CHILD	GRAAEC	USA
U	00	F	INF	GRAAEC	USA
MARTIN, S.	23	M	PVTR	GRAAEC	USA
EDELBURG, U	22	F	SI	GRAAEC	USA
LIZNNIE	22	F	SI	GRAAEC	USA
ANNA	24	F	SI	GRAAEC	USA
LAZARA	19	F	SI	GRAAEC	USA
NOTHBURGA	54	F	SI	GRAAEC	USA
HUGEMEYER, L.	19	F	PVTR	GRAAEC	USA
MOTT, A.	65	F	PVTR	GRAAEC	USA
DAUM, A.	22	F	PVTR	GRAAEC	USA
KAISER, ROB.	14	M	PVTR	GRAAEC	USA
FUNCKE, M.	27	F	SI	GRAAEC	USA
MILLER, M.	00	F	SI	GRAAEC	USA
FEG, FR.	40	M	FARMER	GRAFRG	NY
FOCHS, GOTH.	20	M	FARMER	GRAFRG	NY
MUSER, CARL	21	M	FARMER	GRAFRG	NY
MATHISFEN, JACOB	47	M	BKR	GRAFRG	NY
LIPPMANN, MAX	23	M	LABR	GRAFRG	NY
SCHESFUECH, CARL	56	M	LABR	GRAFRG	NY
KITZING, OTTO	24	M	LABR	GRAFRG	NY
WOPPEL, B.	21	M	LABR	GRAFRG	NY
SCHOLTZ, GOTL.	23	M	LABR	GRAFRG	PHI
RIEXINGER, REGIUS	30	F	UNKNOWN	GRAFRG	NY
FLOWREZ, ELIS.	29	F	UNKNOWN	GRAFRG	UNK
DETREZ, OSCAR	29	M	LABR	GRAFRG	UNK
JACHMANN, HELENA	39	F	UNKNOWN	GRAFRG	UNK
HELENA	16	F	UNKNOWN	GRAFRG	UNK
EMIL	27	M	LABR	GRAFRG	UNK
WILLWERS, M.	42	M	MCHT	GRAFRG	CH
VANDERME, ERIK	39	M	MCHT	GRAFRG	DET
WELLE	34	F	UNKNOWN	GRAFRG	DET
JULIA	3	F	CHILD	GRAFRG	DET
LINK, LISETTE	21	F	UNKNOWN	GRAFRG	NY
VEREANTERSEN, AUG.	26	M	LABR	GRAFRG	NY

PASSENGER	AGE	SEX	OCCUPATION	PVR IVL DES
VANREUGHEN, F.	28	M	LABR	GRAFRGNY
GYWIGUS, HARRY	22	M	LABR	GRAFRGNY
JONSON, JOHN	25	M	LABR	GRAFRGPIT
VANBEESTEN, FRED.	31	M	LABR	GRAFRGNY
SCHNEIDER, B.	26	M	LABR	GRAFRGNY
FIESE, ELEONORE	20	F	UNKNOWN	GRAFRGNY
SCHODLER, BABETTE	22	F	UNKNOWN	GRAFRGNY
KAUFMANN, BAB.	19	F	UNKNOWN	GRAFRGBUF
PAIOLAK, VAL.	20	M	MCHT	GRAFRGBUF
FELDMANN, ANNA	21	F	UNKNOWN	GRAFRGBUF
BREISER, VERO.	55	F	UNKNOWN	GRAFRGBUF
SCHUNIS, JOH.	30	M	CPTR	GRAFRGUNK
ZIMMER, THEOD.	21	M	CPTR	GRAFRGUNK
MUELLER, SOPH.	30	F	UNKNOWN	GRAFRGUNK
BECKER, JEO.	19	M	LABR	GRAFRGNY
SCHOENFELTER, S.	32	M	LABR	GRAFRGNY
MEYER, MARTIN	17	M	LABR	GRAFRGROC
WEAVER, ROSE	48	F	UNKNOWN	GRZZZZNY
ELISAB.	16	F	UNKNOWN	GRZZZZNY
AUG.	14	M	UNKNOWN	GRZZZZNY
ROSE	19	F	UNKNOWN	GRZZZZNY
EMMA	12	F	UNKNOWN	GRZZZZNY
FRED.	10	M	CH	GRZZZZNY
FERD.	7	M	CHILD	GRZZZZNY
WILLMERTS, CH.	36	M	BCHR	GRZZZZNY
CATH.	36	F	UNKNOWN	GRZZZZNY
MASSARS, JOS.	29	M	LABR	GRZZZZUNK
SCHAKFSKY, SACHNE	22	M	LABR	GRZZZZNY
CLARE	22	F	UNKNOWN	GRZZZZNY
BEHR, ONRAD	50	M	LABR	GRZZZZNY
MARG.	58	F	UNKNOWN	GRZZZZNY
SCHORK, SOPHIE	16	F	UNKNOWN	GRZZZZNY
SCHRECK, M.	26	M	LABR	GRZZZZPHI
BIELER, ALB.	22	F	UNKNOWN	GRZZZZPHI
WELSCH, CATH.	38	F	UNKNOWN	GRZZZZUNK
W.	11	M	UNKNOWN	GRZZZZUNK
H.	9	M	CHILD	GRZZZZUNK
CATH.	7	F	CHILD	GRZZZZUNK
GERTRUDE	5	F	CHILD	GRZZZZUNK
HEINR.	00	M	INF	GRZZZZUNK
DECKER, J.	24	M	MCHT	GRZZZZSY
SCHWITZER, A.	58	M	MCHT	GRZZZZNY
KRAUSHAAR, FRIED.	59	M	MCHT	GRZZZZNY
ZOLLER, S.	39	M	MCHT	GRZZZZNY
MENTZER, TH.	26	M	MCHT	GRZZZZNY
SCHNELL, ANA	54	F	UNKNOWN	GRZZZZNY
FRANZ	21	M	SHMK	GRZZZZNY
ZOCHARIAS	15	F	UNKNOWN	GRZZZZNY
MARIA	19	F	UNKNOWN	GRZZZZNY
SOMMEL, ROSETTE	17	F	UNKNOWN	GRZZZZNY
DOENGLER, JOS.	30	M	LABR	GRZZZZNY
WINTER, ELISAB.	55	F	UNKNOWN	GRZZZZNY
STABER, A.	35	M	LABR	GRZZZZNY
KRUEGER, C.	37	M	LABR	GRZZZZNY
KLEIMANN, M.	19	F	UNKNOWN	GRZZZZNY
WAGNER, J.	43	M	LABR	GRZZZZNY
IDA	36	F	UNKNOWN	GRZZZZNY
BAYER, ELIS.	24	F	UNKNOWN	GRZZZZNY
BOLL, A.	22	M	LABR	GRZZZZNY
NAGEL, J.	24	M	LABR	GRZZZZNY
HOFMANN, ROSIUS	22	F	UNKNOWN	GRZZZZUSA
HELMER, S.	23	M	LABR	GRZZZZUSA
AGATHA	22	F	UNKNOWN	GRZZZZUSA
HEINTZELMANN, J.	22	M	LABR	GRZZZZNY
KIRSCHT, MATH.	39	M	LABR	GRZZZZALT
LINDNER, B.	62	M	LABR	GRZZZZBLO
MARIA	50	F	UNKNOWN	GRZZZZBLO
MARG.	21	F	UNKNOWN	GRZZZZBLO
MARIA	19	F	UNKNOWN	GRZZZZBLO
MARG.	17	F	UNKNOWN	GRZZZZBLO
MAGD.	1	F	CHILD	GRZZZZBLO
SUSANNA	16	F	UNKNOWN	GRZZZZBLO
OSCHSLE, JOSEF	58	M	BCHR	GRZZZZNY
MAGD.	20	F	UNKNOWN	GRZZZZNY
KOCH, MARIE	24	F	UNKNOWN	GRZZZZNY
SCHMIDT, SOPHIE	18	F	UNKNOWN	GRZZZZNY
BENZEL, ADOLF	22	M	MCHT	GRZZZZNY
REISS, MARKUS	22	M	MCHT	GRZZZZNY
SELLINGER, OSCAR	22	M	MCHT	GRZZZZNY
KAISER, GERH.	30	M	MCHT	GRZZZZNY
SCHILLER, ALFR.	17	M	LABR	GRZZZZNY
LEUFANE, VICT.	23	M	LABR	GRZZZZUNK
POFINEAN, JEAN	28	M	LABR	GRZZZZUNK
COULON, EMANUEL	22	M	LABR	GRZZZZUNK
DELEROIX, CH.	29	M	LABR	GRZZZZUNK
GYSEN, J.	32	M	LABR	GRZZZZNY
LAUVERGS, S.	45	M	LABR	GRZZZZNY
KREMER, P.	37	M	LABR	GRZZZZNY
GORTZ, J.	42	M	LABR	GRZZZZNY
LOKER, H.	32	M	LABR	GRZZZZNY
FELLER, P.	22	M	LABR	GRZZZZCH
MALLMANN, J.	21	M	LABR	GRZZZZCH
DEKORS, F.	29	M	LABR	GRZZZZNY
STOCHMANN, A.	25	M	LABR	GRZZZZNY
ROOG, L.J.	36	M	LABR	GRZZZZNY
SMITH, G.	26	M	LABR	GRZZZZNY
HEUSCH, P.	27	M	LABR	GRZZZZNY
SIERPIESZEWSKI, FR.	21	M	LABR	GRZZZZNY
KUBACKA, T.	21	M	LABR	GRZZZZBUF
PELAGIA	17	F	UNKNOWN	GRZZZZBUF
POLHENOVICH, MARIE	32	F	UNKNOWN	GRZZZZBUF
COATES, U	25	M	CPTR	GRZZZZNY
ANNIE	1	F	CHILD	GRZZZZNY
BERY	11	M	UNKNOWN	GRZZZZNY
FIBBY, T.	59	M	FARMER	GRZZZZNY
POHLMANN, L.	23	M	FARMER	GRZZZZNY
CHAPMANN, V.	26	M	FARMER	GRZZZZNY
MARG.	28	F	UNKNOWN	GRZZZZNY
RAEOLE, FRANK	23	M	LABR	GRZZZZNY
SOUND, G.	29	M	LABR	GRZZZZNY
BURSON, V.J.	35	M	LABR	GRZZZZNY
VOGT, G.	18	M	LABR	GRAAHUNY
E.	16	M	LABR	GRAAHUNY
LAUKER, J.	21	M	LABR	GRAAHUNY
HEYNER, MARIE	30	F	UNKNOWN	GRAAHUNY
CLARA	6	F	CHILD	GRAAHUNY
NACHHAUER, FR.	20	M	LABR	GRAAHUNY
HENNHAUSER, E.	19	M	LABR	GRAAHUNY
DABWYLER, AUG.	30	M	LABR	GRAAHUNY
SCHIEBLER, MARIA	30	F	UNKNOWN	GRAAHUNY
BLESI, H.	30	M	FARMER	GRAAHUNY
MEIER, ANNA	27	F	UNKNOWN	GRAAHUNY
ELVINA, B.	24	M	FARMER	GRAAHUNY
STBARIA, A.	32	M	FARMER	GRAAHUNY
ELISA	38	F	UNKNOWN	GRAAHUNY
BIELSER, AUG.	24	M	FARMER	GRAAHUNY
HUBMANN, FR.	23	M	LABR	GRAAHUNY
BLUMM, A.	37	M	LABR	GRAAHUPHI
GEMPERLI, MARIA	27	F	UNKNOWN	GRAAHUCH
NIERSMANN, S.	36	M	MCHT	GRAAHUUNK
LUSTENBACHER, L.	28	M	MCHT	GRAAHUUNK
HOFMANN, THERESE	20	F	UNKNOWN	GRAAHUUNK
L.	17	F	UNKNOWN	GRAAHUUNK
LEDERLE, AGNES	24	F	UNKNOWN	GRAAHUUNK
ERNESTINE	2	F	CHILD	GRAAHUUNK
HOLAST, P.	22	M	LABR	GRAAHUUNK
HIRSCH, CATH.	46	F	UNKNOWN	GRAAHUSY
MARTIN	12	M	UNKNOWN	GRAAHUSY
KLAMFIER, THERESE	38	F	UNKNOWN	GRAAHUNY
HERMINE	11	F	UNKNOWN	GRAAHUNY
EMMA	4	F	CHILD	GRAAHUNY
HERM, MOCKEL	24	M	LABR	GRAAHUNY
JANSKY, AD.	39	M	LABR	GRAAHUNY
KRILL, J.	49	M	LABR	GRAAHUNY
J.	24	M	LABR	GRAAHUNY
RUZIECKA, A.	24	M	LABR	GRAAHUNY
SESSAK, S.	24	M	LABR	GRAAHUCH
SCHMIDT, G.	31	M	LABR	GRAAHUCH
ANNA	26	F	UNKNOWN	GRAAHUCH
MARIE	7	F	CHILD	GRAAHUCH

PASSENGER	AGE	SEX	OCCUPATION	PRVL	DES
ALOIS	4	M	CHILD	GRAAHUCH	
ANT.	2	M	CHILD	GRAAHUCH	
KASSE, M.	37	M	MCHT	GRAAHUCH	
BARB.	31	F	UNKNOWN	GRAAHUCH	
MARIE	10	F	CH	GRAAHUCH	
SOFIE	8	F	CHILD	GRAAHUCH	
ANTONNIE	4	F	CHILD	GRAAHUCH	
RUZNIA	1	F	CHILD	GRAAHUCH	
BECKER, J.	28	F	UNKNOWN	GRAAYGNY	
SCHMIDT, J.	27	F	UNKNOWN	GRAAYGNY	
SCHUHMACHER, G.	24	F	UNKNOWN	GRAAYGNY	
REISS, ANNA	32	F	UNKNOWN	GRAAYGNY	
HURSA, J.	54	M	LABR	GRAAYGNY	
MEYER, AUG.	19	M	LABR	GRAAYGNY	
HOUCHARD, S.	50	M	LABR	GRAAYGNY	
SHUES, J.	58	M	LABR	GRAAYGNY	
EINMEISCH, LISA	18	F	UNKNOWN	GRAAYGNY	
CHABELEIN, MADELEINE	40	F	UNKNOWN	GRAAYGNY	
FUBER, J.B.	62	M	LABR	GRAAYGCH	
MARG.	62	F	UNKNOWN	GRAAYGCH	
HOFFMANN, S.	26	M	LABR	GRAAYGCH	
MERKT, ELISE	18	F	UNKNOWN	GRAAYGCH	
VOGELBACKER, MATH.	56	M	LABR	GRAAYGCH	
SCHNEIDER, ROSA	22	F	UNKNOWN	GRAAYGCH	
SCHRECH, R.	63	M	LABR	GRAAYGPHI	
MARG.	59	F	UNKNOWN	GRAAYGPHI	
STEIN, KATH.	18	F	UNKNOWN	GRAAYGPHI	
PISTER, V.	22	M	LABR	GRAAYGNY	
HARBWEIN, JOH.	16	M	UNKNOWN	GRAAYGCH	
KODERER, JOH.	28	M	UNKNOWN	GRAAYGNY	
KRUG, JOH.	25	M	UNKNOWN	GRAAYGNY	
LADRIEN, MARIE	28	F	UNKNOWN	GRAAYGUNK	
JANSEN, H.	55	M	LABR	GRAAYGCH	
CHRISTINA	48	F	UNKNOWN	GRAAYGCH	
W.	16	M	LABR	GRAAYGCH	
ANNA	14	M	UNKNOWN	GRAAYGCH	
ELISABETH	13	F	UNKNOWN	GRAAYGCH	
H.	10	M	CH	GRAAYGCH	
CATHERINE	8	F	CHILD	GRAAYGCH	
HESSERT, CARL	19	M	LABR	GRADDWKAS	
KOLAN, FR.	39	M	LABR	GRADDWKAS	
SKOSH, FRS.	24	M	LABR	GRADDWCLE	
AMMULLER, J.	30	M	LABR	GRADDWNY	
WM.	26	F	UNKNOWN	GRADDWNY	
WILLY	4	M	CHILD	GRADDWNY	
WILH.	2	F	CHILD	GRADDWNY	
ENGELHARDT, S.	47	M	MCHT	GRADDWNY	
HOINGMANN, AL.	17	M	UNKNOWN	GRADDWNY	
TUJENKA, EVA	19	F	UNKNOWN	GRADDWKIN	
SKAMERKINA, F.	28	M	TLR	GRADDWKIN	
BAUER, ELISE	41	F	UNKNOWN	GRADDWPIT	
BUTHERBACH, ELISE	44	F	UNKNOWN	GRADDWPIT	
EMMA	16	F	UNKNOWN	GRADDWPIT	
MARIE	14	F	UNKNOWN	GRADDWPIT	
FELIX	2	M	CHILD	GRADDWPIT	
JAST, CARL	24	M	LABR	GRADDWKAS	
GOEBEL, W.	27	M	LABR	GRADDWUNK	
BUTHER, FR.J.	38	M	LABR	GRADDWNY	
STUKI, P.	33	M	LABR	GRADDWNY	
BACHMANN, GOTTFR.	24	M	LABR	GRADDWNY	
REINERT, JOH.	30	M	LABR	GRADDWNY	
BOEHM, JOS.	42	M	LABR	GRADDWNY	
NEUMANN, JOS.	26	M	LABR	GRADDWNY	
CATH.	31	F	UNKNOWN	GRADDWCH	
GERTZEN, BERTHA	39	F	LABR	GRADDWNY	
DECKER, EMIL	28	M	UNKNOWN	GRADDWNY	
CAHN, MINA	30	F	UNKNOWN	GRADDWNY	
ANNA	10	F	CH	GRADDWNY	
P.	11	F	UNKNOWN	GRADDWNY	
BLODEL, C.	63	M	FARMER	GRADDWCH	
J.	28	F	UNKNOWN	GRADDWCH	
ELISABETH	33	F	UNKNOWN	GRADDWCH	
MARIA	5	F	CHILD	GRADDWCH	
WILH.	4	M	CHILD	GRADDWCH	
CARL	2	M	CHILD	GRADDWCH	
BARBARA	.11	F	INFANT	GRADDWCH	
SCHOTT, J.	38	M	FARMER	GRADDWNY	
H.	9	M	CHILD	GRADDWNY	
RUST, SOPHIE	26	F	UNKNOWN	GRADDWNY	
HAGER, E.	32	M	LABR	GRADDWNY	
WITTE, AUG.	55	M	LABR	GRADDWNY	
BECKER, HELENE	20	F	UNKNOWN	GRADDWNY	
HERSLENBERG, LOUISA	31	F	UNKNOWN	GRADDWNY	
ANTONIA	11	F	UNKNOWN	GRADDWNY	
ELISE	7	F	CHILD	GRADDWNY	
P.	5	F	CHILD	GRADDWNY	
TAPPERICH, J.	21	F	UNKNOWN	GRADDWCAI	
TAPPRICHHO, SYBILLA	20	F	UNKNOWN	GRADDWCAI	
LEOH.	52	M	UNKNOWN	GRADDWCAI	
ELISE	9	F	CHILD	GRADDWCAI	
MARIA	6	F	CHILD	GRADDWCAI	
R.	3	M	CHILD	GRADDWCAI	
VANLAERE, L.	45	M	LABR	GRADDWWI	
FLEMM, TH.	62	M	LABR	GRADDWNY	
TRIEBS, FR.	25	M	LABR	GRADDWSTL	
BAUMER, H.	27	M	LABR	GRADDWSTL	
SOSHER, WM.	17	M	LABR	GRADDWNY	
TENERSTEIN, C.	30	M	LABR	GRADDWNY	
BENDER, EMILIE	17	F	SVNT	GRADDWNY	
FRIDA	18	F	SVNT	GRADDWNY	
ROSSLER, FREDERIKE	18	F	SVNT	GRADDWNY	
BENDER, CAROLINE	24	F	SVNT	GRADDWNY	
MAIER, CATH.	24	F	SVNT	GRADDWNY	
ANNA	17	F	SVNT	GRADDWNY	
AHL, W.	17	M	LABR	GRADDWNY	
GEHRING, FR.	28	M	LABR	GRADDWNY	
ACKERMANN, FR.	26	M	LABR	GRADDWNY	
SCHAFER, CHRISTINE	17	F	SVNT	GRADDWNY	
U., W.	18	M	LABR	GRADDWNY	
A---	14	F	UNKNOWN	GRADDWNY	
H.	10	M	CH	GRADDWNY	
W.	8	M	CHILD	GRADDWNY	
BEIER, E.	45	M	LABR	GRADDWCH	
PETERSEN, MARIA	17	F	SVNT	GRADDWCH	
NIELSEN, MARIA	26	F	SVNT	GRADDWNPT	
HEGESCA, NARTHA	29	F	SVNT	GRADDWNPT	
ANNA	16	F	SVNT	GRADDWNPT	
GUSTAV	.11	M	INFANT	GRADDWNPT	
SCHLECKER, AUG.	44	M	FARMER	GRADDWCH	
SAUTHER, JOS.	22	M	FARMER	GRADDWNY	
KLENK, W.	25	M	FARMER	GRADDWNY	
BARB.	25	F	W	GRADDWNY	
MECHLER, CATH.	41	F	W	GRADDWNY	
RINK, HELENA	58	F	W	GRADDWNY	
SCHMIDT, V.	23	M	LABR	GRADDWNY	
SCHEVER, H.	35	M	LABR	GRADDWNY	
HEIN, ANNA	15	F	UNKNOWN	GRADDWNY	
DECK, CAROLINE	41	F	W	GRADDWNY	
TH.	17	M	W	GRADDWNY	
AUGUSTE	9	F	CHILD	GRADDWNY	
CATHARINA	7	F	CHILD	GRADDWNY	
FRIEDA	3	F	CHILD	GRADDWNY	
FUENEISEN, WM.	38	M	LABR	GRADDWNY	
BECKER, ERNESTINE	18	F	UNKNOWN	GRADDWNY	
PAUL, ELISAB.	22	F	UNKNOWN	GRADEICH	
NACHAR, J.	19	M	LABR	GRADEINY	
ABESHIAM, M.	21	M	LABR	GRADEINY	
HANDEL, MARIA	27	F	UNKNOWN	GRADEIUNK	
HAMMER, CATH.	32	F	UNKNOWN	GRADEIUNK	
MARG.	3	F	CHILD	GRADEIUNK	
SCHREIMER, P.	27	M	LABR	GRADEILAS	
MEUER, MARG.F.	16	F	UNKNOWN	GRADEINY	
KEHRLEIN, MARIA	25	F	UNKNOWN	GRADEINY	
SCHAUB, HAVER	17	M	LABR	GRADEINY	
ARNOLD, ROSINE	18	F	UNKNOWN	GRADEINY	
BECK, JOH.	28	M	LABR	GRADEINY	
ANDRES, FR.	19	M	LABR	GRADEINY	
FINGER, J.	15	M	LABR	GRADEINY	
WEHNER, THERESA	18	F	SVNT	GRADEINY	
KAUFMANN, ROSINE	15	F	SVNT	GRADEINY	

PASSENGER	AGE	SEX	OCCUPATION	PRVL	DES
GLUCKERT, EMILIE	18	F	SVNT	GRADEINY	
MUELLER, M.	21	M	MCHT	GRADEINY	
DEBUR, C.	15	M	LABR	GRADEICH	
GOETZ, CHR.	34	M	LABR	GRADEICH	

SHIP: STATE OF GEORGIA

FROM: GLASGOW AND LARNE
TO: NEW YORK
ARRIVED: 13 SEPTEMBER 1888

PASSENGER	AGE	SEX	OCCUPATION	PRVL	DES
LEDWAR, ANNA	22	F	SVNT	GRAHRZUSA	
JPHAN	1	M	CHILD	GRAHRZUSA	
KUBATH, BAERHA	18	F	SVNT	GRAHRZUSA	

SHIP: ADRIATIC

FROM: LIVERPOOL AND QUEENSTOWN
TO: NEW YORK
ARRIVED: 14 SEPTEMBER 1888

PASSENGER	AGE	SEX	OCCUPATION	PRVL	DES
ECK, B.	28	M	MCHT	GRZZZZUSA	
MARCUS, U	47	M	MCHT	GRADAXUSA	
PREYER, B.	33	M	MCHT	GRADAXUSA	

SHIP: EMS

FROM: BREMEN AND SOUTHAMPTON
TO: NEW YORK
ARRIVED: 14 SEPTEMBER 1888

PASSENGER	AGE	SEX	OCCUPATION	PRVL	DES
BAV-, FRED	45	M	TT	GRAARRNY	
FRED	18	M	TT	GRAARRNY	
KOPPEL, HUGO	30	M	TT	GRABDMNY	
MARTHA	28	F	W	GRABDMNY	
BODE, FREIDR	39	M	MCHT	GRABDMNY	
ANTONIE	28	F	W	GRABDMNY	
RICHARDS, H	39	M	PROF	GRACPENY	
WEIGEL, PAUL	28	M	MCHT	GRAAKHNY	
KORNING, CARL	11	M	CH	GRAEEANY	
FRIEDEL, PETER	62	M	TT	GRAAXYNY	
BERTHA	19	F	NN	GRAAXYNY	
K-MDE, DOROTHEA	64	F	W	GRAARRNY	
LANGE, HENRIETTA	56	F	W	GRZZZZNY	
PFEIFFER, FERDINAND	47	M	MCHT	GRZZZZNY	
STEFFENS, JOHN	70	M	PVTM	GRZZZZNY	
EMMA	18	F	NN	GRZZZZNY	
BEHRINGER, MARIA	53	F	W	GRZZZZNY	
HEINMANN, BERTA	18	F	NN	GRAFRGNY	
FANNENWALD, JETTE	66	F	W	GRAFRGNY	
MEITZEN, CLARA	30	F	W	GRAFRGNY	
ELLA	2	F	CHILD	GRAFRGNY	
EHLERS, ANNA	23	F	NN	GRAAHVNY	
KIRSCHBAUM, HENRY	20	F	NN	GRAARSNY	
MEYER, BERTHA	20	F	NN	GRAARSNY	
HIRSCHBUEHL, MATHILDE	21	F	NN	GRZZZZNY	
HARVERS, META	25	F	NN	GRAARRNY	
OPPENHEIMER, JULIUS	17	M	MCHT	GRACBONY	
NICGRIN, CHARLES	40	M	MCHT	GRACXVNY	
MARGARETHA	38	F	W	GRACXVNY	

PASSENGER	AGE	SEX	OCCUPATION	PRVL	DES
LIEBERMANN, FANNY	15	F	NN	GRZZZZNY	
MAX	15	M	NN	GRZZZZNY	
AC---TIUS, MARIE	25	F	NN	GRAIKSNY	
WALTER, ANNA	30	F	W	GRAIPZNY	
ELISE	5	F	CHILD	GRAIPZNY	
HAMMERLE, GERTRUDE	44	F	W	GRADEINY	
SCHRAG, MARTHA	35	F	W	GRZZZZNY	
SCHELLHORN, ELISE	20	F	NN	GRAAEQNY	
WAGNER, EMILY	15	F	NN	GRABPPNY	
KOCH, MINNA	22	F	NN	GRACPENY	
BERGER, PAULINE	45	F	W	GRZZZZNY	
RITTER, HERMANN	30	M	GCR	GRAAKHNY	
RAUSCH, MARIE	59	F	W	GRABQZNY	
B-SER, ANNA	26	F	NN	GRZZZZNY	
M-LTER, KATHARINE	66	F	W	GRACNWNY	
FIS-, FRIEDERIKE	53	F	W	GRAEXWNY	
EMILIE	19	F	CH	GRAEXWNY	
ALBERT	16	M	GCR	GRAEXWNY	
FROSSHAG, FRITZ	18	M	GCR	GRAAZSNY	
GIRTH, BERTHA	24	F	NN	GRABOQNY	
DAMASCH, LULU	16	F	NN	GRABRYNY	
BLAU, GUSSIE	25	F	NN	GRAARRNY	
KOLBE, ANNA	24	F	NN	GRAARRNY	
HAMPP, JOSEF	30	M	MCHT	GRAARRNY	
JOS	29	F	W	GRAARRNY	
MA-KE, GERHA	15	M	CGRMKR	GRACFNNY	
DEPKEN, MARIE	26	F	W	GRAARRNY	
SOPHIE	2	F	CHILD	GRAARRNY	
JULIUS	4	M	CHILD	GRAARRNY	
BOKCKSTOVER, LOUISE	20	F	NN	GRAARRNY	
BARTELS, WILHELM	20	F	NN	GRAAXFNY	
DREWES, JOHANNES	17	M	MCHT	GRAHSMNY	
REDDEHASE, JOHANNE	25	F	NN	GRACXHNY	
SUNI, JOHANN	26	M	FARMER	GRZZZZNY	
HUBER, PHILIPINE	15	F	NN	GRZZZZNY	
HEPPERLE, JOHANNES	26	M	FARMER	GRADMENY	
MUELLER, MARTIN	17	M	FARMER	GRZZZZNY	
BAUR, HERMANN	26	M	JNR	GRAHYWNY	
MARIE	24	F	W	GRAHYWNY	
BELL, LOUISE	25	F	W	GRZZZZNY	
THEOBALD	28	M	BCHR	GRZZZZNY	
AMPFER, CARL	17	M	BCK	GRZZZZNY	
WAHL, FRIEDR	24	M	SHMK	GRAGOSNY	
MERKLE, CARL	16	M	CPTR	GRAEXWNY	
BAIERLE, KAETCHEN	17	F	NN	GRAEXWUNK	
DREYER, HEINRICH	14	M	NN	GRZZZZUNK	
FISCHER, GOTTFRIED	44	M	LABR	GRALOOUNK	
ROEHRS, CATHARINA	10	F	CH	GRZZZZUNK	
BECHTHOLD, MARIE	18	F	NN	GRAAFXUNK	
HERBOLDSHEIM, CONR	17	M	CL	GRADROUNK	
STURM, MARIA	19	F	NN	GRZZZZUNK	
OTTMER, HEINRCIH	23	M	FARMER	GRZZZZUNK	
MINNA	23	F	W	GRZZZZUNK	
HEINRICH	.06	M	INFANT	GRZZZZUNK	
KRANT, HERMAN	32	M	TNM	GRACPEUNK	
HUSKE, HULDA	13	F	NN	GRAGLEUNK	
JAEGER, CARL	18	M	LABR	GRZZZZUNK	
KASER, SOPHIE	33	F	W	GRACVRUNK	
MACK, CHRISTIAN	20	M	FARMER	GRZZZZUNK	
FOERSTER, TRINCHEN	30	F	W	GRAARRUNK	
SOPHIE	11	F	CH	GRAARRUNK	
EDUARD	8	M	CHILD	GRAARRUNK	
TINA	4	F	CHILD	GRAARRUNK	
KOLL, PETER	49	M	FARMER	GRAARRMN	
ANNA	16	F	NN	GRAARRMN	
ALBRECHT, MARIA	4	F	CHILD	GRAARRNY	
DEGENHARDT, FRIEDR	16	M	FARMER	GRZZZZNY	
FISCHTLER, MARGARETHA	33	F	W	GRABSYNY	
MEYER, HEDWIG	25	F	NN	GRZZZZNY	
HINDERER, REGINE	21	F	NN	GRAACBNY	
MUELLER, ANNA	26	F	NN	GRADKJNY	
--NDANSKI, WILHELM	37	M	LABR	GRAAKHNY	
ERNESTINE	33	F	W	GRAAKHNY	
RICHARD	10	M	CH	GRAAKHNY	
HAHN, LISETTE	15	F	NN	GRAASSNY	

PASSENGER	AGE	SEX	OCCUPATION	PRVLS
KOTHE, FREDERICH	15	M	LABR	GRZZZZNY
NICODE, PAUL	23	M	MCHT	GRAAKHNY
MEYER, FRIEDRICH	16	M	FARMER	GRZZZZNY
STUMPF, CHRISTIANA	48	F	W	GRZZZZNY
WOBRANELK, FRANTISECK	22	M	LABR	GRZZZZNY
WOJTECH	20	M	LABR	GRZZZZNY
PICHA, FRANTISEK	18	M	LABR	GRZZZZNY
UHL, THEODOR	20	M	LABR	GRAAFTNY
MIELICH, FRANZ	24	M	LABR	GRAAFTNY
MEYER, JOSEF	23	M	BRR	GRAAFTNY
JOHANN	24	M	BRR	GRAAFTNY
ADLER, JOSEF	29	M	FARMER	GRADAAOH
FEIL, ANTON	26	M	FARMER	GRZZZZOH
PLIEMINGER, SOPHIE	18	F	NN	GRZZZZNY
SCHEUERLE, LOUISE	26	F	NN	GRZZZZNY
EGGER, JOSEF	19	M	JNR	GRAJTDNY
HANS, FRIEDR	23	M	PNTR	GRADCLNY
STUTE, RUDOLF	22	M	TLR	GRACXHNY
MARGUARDT, HERMANN	16	M	LABR	GRZZZZNY
HUDTWALKER, LUCINDE	24	F	NN	GRZZZZNY
MACKENTH--, GOTTFRIED	15	M	FARMER	GRAARTNY
ATLMANN, GEORGE	18	M	GDNR	GRAEGBNY
LANGE, HUGO	29	M	FARMER	GRABUDNY
KLUTE, HEINR	32	M	FARMER	GRAFKFNY
EMMA	25	F	W	GRAFKFNY
AUGUST	17	M	FARMER	GRAFKFNY
SCHNACKENBERG, ANNA	25	F	NN	GRZZZZNY
ELSASSER, ROBERT	22	M	TLR	GRADAQNY
FALKE, LISETTE	24	F	NN	GRZZZZNY
HAGER, HEINRICH	30	M	FARMER	GRAARRNY
SOPHIE	32	F	W	GRAARRNY
HEINRICH	4	M	CHILD	GRAARRNY
WILHELM	2	M	CHILD	GRAARRNY
ALBERT	.06	M	INFANT	GRAARRNY
FETTE, ERNST	31	M	FARMER	GRAARRNY
ELISABETH	36	F	W	GRAARRNY
ERNST	2	M	CHILD	GRAARRNY
HEINRICH	.02	M	INFANT	GRAARRNY
SCHNEIDER, AUGUSTE	21	F	NN	GRZZZZNY
MERTEN, GUSTAV	37	M	FARMER	GRACBRNY
HERRMANN, HEINRICH	23	M	WTR	GRZZZZNY
AUF, AUGUST	28	M	FARMER	GRZZZZNY
KOSLOWSKY, PETER	17	M	LABR	GRAHGRNY
ANDR	23	M	LABR	GRAHGRNY
DECKELT, ANNA	22	F	NN	GRAARRNY
SCHADE, ELISE	25	F	NN	GRAAXFNY
HOVELER, ANTON	21	M	LABR	GRACBRIA
KUHLMANN, UDO	30	M	MCHT	GRACZENY
GEREB, PETER	27	M	LABR	GRACZENY
ZEPLER, SAL-	27	M	BRR	GRAARZNY
HATTENDORF, RUDOLF	23	M	TLR	GRACBRNY
GROME, KATHARINA	20	F	NN	GRZZZZNY
GACH, BERTHA	20	F	NN	GRZZZZNY
KONIG, CARL	29	M	FARMER	GRADRONY

SHIP: HAMMONIA

FROM: HAMBURG AND HAVRE
TO: NEW YORK
ARRIVED: 14 SEPTEMBER 1888

PASSENGER	AGE	SEX	OCCUPATION	PRVLS
WOFF, AMALIE	26	F	UNKNOWN	HBZZZZNY
WACHTEL, EMMA	37	F	UNKNOWN	HBZZZZNY
SCHMEIL, ROBERT	35	M	UNKNOWN	HBZZZZNY
MARIE	30	F	UNKNOWN	HBZZZZNY
ELISABETH	8	F	CHILD	HBZZZZNY
GRETCHEN	7	F	CHILD	HBZZZZNY
BERNHARD	6	F	CHILD	HBZZZZNY
MARIE	2	F	CHILD	HBZZZZNY
LOUISE	.06	F	INFANT	HBZZZZNY

PASSENGER	AGE	SEX	OCCUPATION	PRVLS
WARNER, CARL	16	M	UNKNOWN	HBZZZZNY
WILHELM, ANNA	22	F	UNKNOWN	BVZZZZNY
SONNTAG, MATH	17	F	SGL	BVAFTDNY
MATH	17	F	SGL	BVAFTDNY
SCHNEIDER, ANNE	20	F	SGL	BVAFTDNY
ECKERT, PETER	24	M	LABR	BVAFTDNY
HUNTER, ALFRED	21	M	LABR	BVAAHUNY
SCHNEIDER, EUGENE	18	M	LABR	SRZZZZNY
MANIN, JEAN	20	M	LABR	SRAAHUNY
SCHMIDTHAUSER, J	26	M	LABR	SRADDKNY
RESTELLI, GASPARI	20	M	LABR	SRADDKNY
BEILMANN, ANNE	30	F	W	SRZZZZNY
ROSA	.06	F	INFANT	SRZZZZNY
VOEGTLE, ANSELM	23	M	LABR	SRZZZZNY
BOYER, B	41	M	LABR	SRZZZZNY
KAEPTER, MICHAEL	32	M	LABR	SRZZZZNY
BLATT, GEO	19	M	LABR	BDZZZZNY
FERNER, CAROLINE	23	F	SGL	BDZZZZNY
KENNEL, JOSEF	16	M	LABR	WMZZZZNY
LANGEL, MICHAEL	49	M	LABR	WMZZZZNY
KASPAR, LOUIS	20	M	LABR	WMZZZZNY
GAS-ARD, JOS	23	M	LABR	BVZZZZNY
KERN--, JOS	16	M	LABR	BVZZZZNY
LEHMANN, LEONH	16	M	LABR	WMZZZZNY
JAEGER, JOHANNES	28	M	LABR	WMZZZZNY
DELM, HERMINE	19	F	SGL	BDZZZZNY
VILLINGER, MARIE	19	F	SGL	BDZZZZNY
KAELIN, DIONIS	26	M	LABR	SRZZZZNY
SMITH, VIRGINIA	23	F	SGL	BVZZZZNY
VIRGINIA	23	F	SGL	BVZZZZNY
DIENDONNE, LOUISE	61	F	WO	BVAEXWNY
LILIENTHAL, CAROLINE	17	F	SGL	BVAEXWNY
JOHANNSEN, SOFIE	25	F	SGL	BVAEXWNY
BO-AR, IDA	17	F	SGL	BVAEXWNY
HARTMANN, JULIUS	20	M	IMKR	BVAEXWNY
B-BSIN, AUG	15	M	MCHT	BVAEXWNY
-ERS, LINA	22	F	SGL	BVAEXJNY
GUEH-, WILHELE	45	F	W	BVAFHBNY
EMMA	18	F	CH	BVAFHBNY
WM	8	M	CHILD	BVAFHBNY
ALBERT	7	M	CHILD	BVAFHBNY
LEHMANN, ANNA	15	F	SGL	BVABDMNY
CHRISTIANSEN, F	16	F	SGL	PRZZZZNY
DETTER, BERNHARD	23	M	JNR	PRADUHNY
KIMPA, FRIEDR	26	M	BKR	PRZZZZNY
-OCH, THOMAS	16	M	MACH	PRZZZZNY
LANDMANN, GOTTFR	27	M	WCHMKR	PRZZZZNY
MEYER, BERTA	16	F	SGL	PRZZZZNY
RABEN, BOY	52	M	FARMER	PRAESDNY
HELEN	46	F	W	PRAESDNY
ANNA	19	F	CH	PRAESDNY
CHRISTINE	18	F	CH	PRAESDNY
NICOLINE	16	F	CH	PRAESDNY
HELENE	7	F	CHILD	PRAESDNY
DETLEV	8	M	CHILD	PRAESDNY
PETER	6	M	CHILD	PRAESDNY
ARNOLD	.09	M	INFANT	PRAESDNY
FRANCK, CATHARINA	15	F	SGL	PRAIVVNY
LOOF, HEINRICH	27	M	BCHR	PRAESDUNK
NETZOW, JOHANNA	26	F	SGL	PRAESDNY
NIEMCZYCK, FRANZ	22	M	BCHR	PRAESDNY
DEPLAUGNE, ADOLF	28	M	JNR	PRAAKHNY
BOLI-, DORA	16	F	SGL	PRZZZZNY
WO-L, SIMON	20	M	GZR	PRAARZNY
D-OY, DOROTHEA	28	F	SGL	BDZZZZNY
DOROTHEA	28	F	SGL	BDZZZZNY
WARICH, FRANCOIS	36	M	LABR	BDAAHUNY
HELENE	53	F	W	BDAAHUNY
THOMAS	54	M	LABR	BDAAHUNY
BALL, THIF	16	M	LABR	SRZZZZNY
RUCH, GEORGES	19	M	LABR	SRZZZZNY
ACHERMANN, CATARINA	21	F	SGL	SRZZZZNY
MUELLER, JOHANNES	26	F	SGL	SRAAHUNY
BERNEGGER, ULRICH	21	F	SGL	SRAAHUNY
KAPPELER, JACOB	24	F	SGL	SRAAHUNY

PASSENGER	AGE	SEX	OCCUPATION	PRIVL	DES
OHRDORF, ANNA	25	F	SGL	SRAAHUNY
POPERT, ERNST	48	M	MCHT	SRAAHUNY
LUND, GEORG	45	M	MCHT	SRAAHUNY
WURR, EMIL	44	M	PVTM	SYZZZZNY
GREVE, PETRA	30	F	SGL	PRZZZZNY
KESSLER, WILH	28	M	HNTR	PRZZZZNY
SCHMINKE, ANNA	15	F	SGL	PRZZZZNY
ANDRESEN, N	17	M	CL	PRZZZZNY
OTT, DORA	23	F	SGL	HBZZZZNY
WITT, MATHILDE	18	F	SGL	PRZZZZNY
DETHMANN, LUDOLF	15	M	TKR	PRZZZZNY
ROSINE	18	F	SGL	PRZZZZNY
DABB-RT, JOHANNES	24	M	BLKSMH	PRZZZZNY
OHLSEN, PETER	42	M	FARMER	PRZZZZNY
JERSHI	42	F	W	PRZZZZNY
CARL	14	M	CH	PRZZZZNY
MARIE	13	F	CH	PRZZZZNY
HEINR	8	M	CHILD	PRZZZZNY
DOROTHEA	4	F	CHILD	PRZZZZNY
BERTA	.03	F	INFANT	PRZZZZNY
KRAUSE, HEDWIG	30	F	SGL	HBZZZZNY
KLAPP, BERTA	24	F	SGL	HNZZZZNY
SCHMI--DEL--, ALBERT	35	M	SCP	HNAIJWNY
KOHL, BRUNHILDE	31	F	SGL	HNAAKHNY
PAUL	22	M	MLR	HNAAKHNY
B--, ANNA	22	F	SGL	HNAEACNY
KLOPFER, AUG	56	M	LABR	HNAFKXNY
JOHANNE	54	F	W	HNAFKXNY
ROBERT	15	M	CH	HNAFKXNY
ANNE	19	F	CH	HNAFKXNY
GLASER, LYA--	19	F	SGL	PRZZZZNY
KLAPPER, HEINR	27	M	FARMER	PRZZZZNY
HAUBENSACH, OTTILIE	23	F	SGL	WMZZZZNY
LA--CHINGER, GOTTLIEB	21	M	BKR	WMAEXWNY
WAIDELISCH, GG	25	M	FARMER	WMAEXWNY
KLEPE--, ANNA	16	F	SGL	WMAEXWNY
ULMAN, MARIE	22	F	SGL	WMAEXWNY
WINKEL, HIENR	25	M	WHLR	HSZZZZNY
SCHWEIGER, VALENTIN	25	M	GDNR	HSZZZZNY
SCHILL, CARL	26	M	CPR	BDZZZZNY
DICK, ADOLF	14	M	FARMER	BDAADJNY
WOLTERSDORF, CARL	31	M	BKLYR	PRZZZZNY
WILHME	25	F	W	PRZZZZNY
HEDWIG	4	F	CHILD	PRZZZZNY
OTTO	3	M	CHILD	PRZZZZNY
EMMA	.11	F	INFANT	PRZZZZNY
HOLATZ, CARL	29	M	LABR	PRZZZZNY
FRAKE	25	F	W	PRZZZZNY
ELLY	3	F	CHILD	PRZZZZNY
BRICHE, AUGUST	31	M	JNR	HBZZZZNY
JACOBI, ALEXANDER	36	M	LABR	HBAAKHNY
B--NCHE, CHRISTIAN	26	M	LABR	MKZZZZNY
HANSEN, KLAUS	28	M	FARMER	MKAAJYNY
GREVE, PETER	14	M	FARMER	MKAAJYNY
USSATT, LEOPOLD	35	M	TLR	LUZZZZNY
MARIE	43	F	W	LUZZZZNY
DAVID, HEINR	23	M	BKR	LUZZZZNY
BOTE---R, PAUL	24	M	MCHT	HBZZZZNY
JEPSEN, ALWINE	20	F	SGL	HBADGLNY
MOELLER, ANNA	18	F	SGL	HBADGLNY
JOHANNSEN, MARIE	20	F	SGL	HBADGLNY
CHRISTEMEN, METTE	19	F	SGL	HBADGLNY
SCHILDKNECHT, CAROLINE	22	F	SGL	HBADGLNY
SCHULDT, CARL	26	M	FARMER	HBADGLNY
GRANZ-, CAROLINE	66	F	W	HBAAKHNY
MEYER, RICHARD	28	M	SVNT	HBAAKHNY
IDA	30	F	W	HBAAKHNY
IDA	3	F	CHILD	HBAAKHNY
BREMER, AUGUST	32	M	WMN	HBAAKHNY
WILHE	32	F	W	HBAAKHNY
SALZMANN, CARL	36	M	JNR	PRZZZZNY
WASILEWSKI, MARTIN	44	M	MCHT	PRZZZZNY
TREZYNSKI, RUD	32	M	LABR	PRZZZZNY
LOUISE	29	F	W	PRAENANY
BREITENGROSS, HELENE	18	F	SGL	PRAENANY

PASSENGER	AGE	SEX	OCCUPATION	PRIVL	DES
BLUEHMKE, HANS	25	M	LABR	PRAENANY
BUCHHOLZ, ROSA	19	F	SGL	PRAENANY
HART--, MARGR	18	F	SGL	SYZZZZNY
ARNUSKA	20	F	SGL	SYZZZZNY
SCHMIDT, EDUARD	23	M	LKSH	SYACDLNY
WEIST, MARG	22	F	SGL	SYACDLNY
ZUNDEL, CATHR	22	F	SGL	SYACDLNY
LUECKEL, CATHARINA	22	F	SGL	SYACDLNY
SCHMIDT, JACOB	16	M	JNR	SYACDLNY
MEISEL, KARL	16	M	BCHR	SYAAUMNY
RAUCH, JOH	54	M	FARMER	BDZZZZNY
CAROLINE	45	F	W	BDZZZZNY
CARL	21	M	CH	BDZZZZNY
CATARINE	19	F	CH	BDZZZZNY
MARIE	17	F	CH	BDZZZZNY
MINNA	8	F	CHILD	BDZZZZNY
FRIEDR	6	M	CHILD	BDZZZZNY
EMMA	3	M	CHILD	BDZZZZNY
ROTH, CAROLINE	23	F	SGL	BDZZZZNY
GERICKE, HEINR	32	M	CCHMN	PRZZZZNY
LALUDNE, ALBERTINE	42	F	WO	PRZZZZNY
SIBELITH, AGNES	8	F	CHILD	HBZZZZNY
RAUMM, JOH	29	M	BRR	PRZZZZNY
NIESSEN, NICOLAUS	17	M	FARMER	PRZZZZNY
MA-, BERTA	18	F	SGL	PRAFWJNY
HOLST, DORA	16	F	SGL	PRAFWJNY
PETERS, HELENE	49	F	W	PRZZZZNY
MEYER, AUGUST	36	M	CGRMKR	HBZZZZNY
ENGELHARDT, GUSTAV	39	M	CGRMKR	HBZZZZNY
ELISE	39	F	W	HBZZZZNY
HEDWIG	8	F	CHILD	HBZZZZNY
OLGA	7	F	CHILD	HBZZZZNY
GEORG	.09	M	INFANT	HBZZZZNY
SCHULZ, WILH	28	M	BRR	BDZZZZNY
RASMUSSEN, JOHANN	56	M	UNKNOWN	HBZZZZNY
BOLDT, HERM	16	M	BLKSMH	HBZZZZNY
HEINS---TER, EMMA	15	F	SGL	HBZZZZNY
WEISS, CLARA	48	F	W	PRZZZZNY
LEONORE	12	F	CH	PRZZZZNY
AGNES	8	F	CHILD	PRZZZZNY
BAUMANN, ANNA	19	F	SGL	HBZZZZNY
SELIGMANN, NATAN	19	M	MCHT	HBAAFLNY
BURGER, FRITZ	18	M	WTR	WMZZZZNY
KLA-E, AGNES	15	F	SGL	PRZZZZNY
LOWENSTEIN, MOSES	21	M	FARMER	PRZZZZNY
BISLER, CAROLINE	44	F	W	PRZZZZNY
RUDOLF	8	M	CHILD	PRZZZZNY
RUGG, JACOB	19	M	WVR	BVZZZZNY
TEMPEL, ADOLFINE	16	F	SGL	BVAEWBNY

SHIP: SAALE

FROM: BREMEN AND SOUTHAMPTON
TO: NEW YORK
ARRIVED: 14 SEPTEMBER 1888

	AGE	SEX	OCCUPATION	DES
DREYER, LOUISE	34	F	UNKNOWN	GRZZZZUSA
HERBORN, KATHIE	20	F	UNKNOWN	GRZZZZUSA
FRAENKEL, GUST.	28	M	MCHT	GRZZZZUSA
LINGENFELDT, PHILIPPINE	23	F	NN	GRZZZZUSA
POHLE, MAX	36	M	BKR	GRZZZZUSA
SIEBER, MARG.	36	F	NN	GRZZZZUSA
KAETCHEN	10	F	CH	GRZZZZUSA
WILH.	8	M	CHILD	GRZZZZUSA
WILH.	6	F	CHILD	GRZZZZUSA
HEINR.	4	M	CHILD	GRZZZZUSA
FRIEDR.	.01	M	INFANT	GRZZZZUSA
P-TSCH, JOHNES.	26	M	MCHT	GRZZZZUSA
SCHELLBER, MAX	25	M	MCHT	GRZZZZUSA
GROETCKE, LOUISE	18	F	MCHT	GRZZZZUSA

PASSENGER	AGE	SEX	OCCUPATION	PRVL	DES		PASSENGER	AGE	SEX	OCCUPATION	PRVL	DES
GRUENAGEL, PHILIPP	34	M	JNR	GRZZZZ	USA		MEYER, WILH.	23	M	FARMER	GRZZZZ	USA
LEWKOWITZ, SAM.	18	M	JNR	GRZZZZ	USA		MAUL, REGINE	22	F	NN	GRZZZZ	USA
LANTZ, ANNA	50	F	NN	GRZZZZ	USA		SCHINTZERLING, CONR.	25	M	FARMER	GRZZZZ	USA
ALI	30	F	NN	GRZZZZ	USA		WESS, AUGUSTA	17	F	NN	GRZZZZ	USA
CLARA	20	F	NN	GRZZZZ	USA		RITTER, LOUISE	21	F	NN	GRZZZZ	USA
WOCHNA, JOHANNA	23	F	NN	GRZZZZ	USA		ECKELDT, ANNA	22	F	NN	GRZZZZ	USA
FRANZ	2	M	CHILD	GRZZZZ	USA		BINDEWALD, FRIED.	22	F	NN	GRZZZZ	USA
WANDA	.11	F	INFANT	GRZZZZ	USA		HANS	28	M	FARMER	GRZZZZ	USA
WINKLER, MARG.	17	F	NN	GRZZZZ	USA		LAURA	25	F	W	GRZZZZ	USA
G-CK, SOPHIE	16	F	NN	GRZZZZ	USA		MARIE	3	F	CHILD	GRZZZZ	USA
B-LISKI, PAULINE	29	F	NN	GRZZZZ	USA		TRIP, EMIL	23	M	FARMER	GRZZZZ	USA
REINHARD	.06	M	INFANT	GRZZZZ	USA		SMITH, FRIEDR.	16	M	FARMER	GRZZZZ	USA
TIEFENBACHER, CARL	17	M	JNR	GRZZZZ	USA		TOFT, JOHNE.	20	F	NN	GRZZZZ	USA
RUDOLPH, JOSEPH	42	M	FARMER	GRZZZZ	USA		CHRISTIENSEN, ANDERS	62	M	FARMER	GRZZZZ	USA
STEFENS, MARIA	22	F	NN	GRZZZZ	USA		LOUISE	54	F	W	GRZZZZ	USA
WEYES, MARG.	15	F	NN	GRZZZZ	USA		JOHNE.	24	F	CH	GRZZZZ	USA
WILLIG, JOHNE.	18	F	NN	GRZZZZ	USA		NIELSEN, MATTHIAS	17	M	FARMER	GRZZZZ	USA
REHM, WILH.	7	M	CHILD	GRZZZZ	USA		WILHELM, HELENE	22	F	NN	GRZZZZ	USA
ARFMANN, ANNA	24	F	CH	GRZZZZ	USA		HEIDE, JOHNE.AUFDE	24	F	NN	GRZZZZ	USA
VOGT, JOH.	30	M	SMH	GRZZZZ	USA		VOLKLAND, AMALIE	69	F	NN	GRZZZZ	USA
JANSSEN, EILERT	56	M	FARMER	GRZZZZ	USA		FLEISCHER, FRANCISCA	17	F	NN	GRZZZZ	USA
MARIE	36	F	W	GRZZZZ	USA		KLINTWORT, ANNA	19	F	NN	GRZZZZ	USA
WILH.	11	M	CH	GRZZZZ	USA		SIEMS, HEINR.	16	M	PNTR	GRZZZZ	USA
AUG.	10	M	CH	GRZZZZ	USA		HERBIG, CARL	16	M	PNTR	GRZZZZ	USA
GUST.	8	M	CHILD	GRZZZZ	USA		HENRIETTE	18	F	NN	GRZZZZ	USA
AUGUSTE	6	F	CHILD	GRZZZZ	USA		--MIDT, ERNST	21	M	FARMER	GRZZZZ	USA
EMIL	4	M	CHILD	GRZZZZ	USA		LANGGUETH, JUL.	3	M	CHILD	GRZZZZ	USA
MARTHA	2	F	CHILD	GRZZZZ	USA		PFADENHAUER, JOH.	20	M	FARMER	GRZZZZ	USA
ILG, CARL	27	M	CH	GRZZZZ	USA		HOFFMANN, JOH.	37	M	FARMER	GRZZZZ	USA
FUCHS, AUGUSTE	22	F	NN	GRZZZZ	USA		VETTERS, CARL	15	M	BKR	GRZZZZ	USA
HOFFMANN, PHIL.	22	M	BRR	GRZZZZ	USA		BOSS, CARL	18	M	BKR	GRZZZZ	USA
FUESSLER, GEORG	16	M	BRR	GRZZZZ	USA		DEWALD, ELISE	17	F	NN	GRZZZZ	USA
RITTEL, FRIEDR.	20	M	PNTR	GRZZZZ	USA		GOMMLICH, AUG.	35	M	TLR	GRZZZZ	USA
BALSER, ELISAB.	21	F	NN	GRZZZZ	USA		DEDE, BECKA	15	F	NN	GRZZZZ	USA
LOTZ, H.	18	M	JNR	GRZZZZ	USA		SCHUMACHER, WOPKE	15	F	NN	GRZZZZ	USA
U, PETER	18	M	JNR	GRZZZZ	USA		MEYER, JOH.	16	M	JNR	GRZZZZ	USA
MICHEL, KAETCHEN	19	F	NN	GRZZZZ	USA		SCHREPFER, HEINR.	22	M	JNR	GRZZZZ	USA
HEYNER, DORIS	36	F	NN	GRZZZZ	USA		MARG.	18	F	W	GRZZZZ	USA
SCHUSTER, AUG.	29	M	FARMER	GRZZZZ	USA		VAETH, LUDW.	17	M	SMH	GRZZZZ	USA
REGINE	33	F	W	GRZZZZ	USA		KNEIKER, BARTEL	16	M	SMH	GRZZZZ	USA
GRETCHEN	10	F	CH	GRZZZZ	USA		HUBER, BABETTA	66	F	NN	GRZZZZ	USA
FRITZ	.09	M	INFANT	GRZZZZ	USA		WAGNER, FRIEDR.	16	M	FARMER	GRZZZZ	USA
ZANKE, MATHAEUS	17	M	PNTR	GRZZZZ	USA		BOHNE, ANNA	14	F	NN	GRZZZZ	USA
KLAUS, GUST.	15	M	PNTR	GRZZZZ	USA		LUIGIA	16	F	NN	GRZZZZ	USA
WOERNER, JOSEPH	22	M	FARMER	GRZZZZ	USA		GUST	21	M	JNR	GRZZZZ	USA
FROHULE, FRANCISCA	22	F	NN	GRZZZZ	USA		U, JOLA	14	F	NN	GRZZZZ	USA
STEINHAEUSER, AUG.	16	M	GDNR	GRZZZZ	USA		CHREINER, BABETTE	22	F	NN	GRZZZZ	USA
LEHMANN, MARIA	9	F	CHILD	GRZZZZ	USA		GEISSLER, FRIEDR.	50	M	CPTR	GRZZZZ	USA
LEI, FRIEDKE.	20	F	NN	GRZZZZ	USA		CRESCENZIA	47	F	W	GRZZZZ	USA
SUTOMIS, MARIE	20	F	NN	GRZZZZ	USA		ANNA	10	F	CH	GRZZZZ	USA
SCH-EIER, GEORG	30	M	BRR	GRZZZZ	USA		FRIEDR.	9	M	CHILD	GRZZZZ	USA
BARBARA	30	F	W	GRZZZZ	USA		HARTMANN, CRESCENZIA	19	F	NN	GRZZZZ	USA
FERD.	11	M	INF	GRZZZZ	USA		CASPAR	15	M	NN	GRZZZZ	USA
-ROSS, MARIA	14	F	NN	GRZZZZ	USA		STROBINGER, JOS.	27	M	FARMER	GRZZZZ	USA
KARBACHER, KUNIGUNDE	24	F	NN	GRZZZZ	USA		DEUENTHAL, HERM.	37	M	FARMER	GRZZZZ	USA
PETER	.06	M	INFANT	GRZZZZ	USA		HAEFNER, SOPHIE	14	F	FARMER	GRZZZZ	USA
BALLING, RUFINE	20	F	INF	GRZZZZ	USA		SEYBOLD, MARIE	15	F	FARMER	GRZZZZ	USA
SCHNECK, REGINE	19	F	INF	GRZZZZ	USA		BADEN, CATH.	15	F	FARMER	GRZZZZ	USA
GOTTHIB	17	M	FARMER	GRZZZZ	USA		LANDWEHR, ANTON	16	M	BRR	GRZZZZ	USA
KOEHLER, EVA	17	F	NN	GRZZZZ	USA		KLEINHEINTZ, GEORG	20	M	BRR	GRZZZZ	USA
GEDER, JACOB	35	M	FARMER	GRZZZZ	USA		SCHMOELZLE, CHRIST.	24	M	BRR	GRZZZZ	USA
PEPPLER, AUG.	22	M	FARMER	GRZZZZ	USA		FRIEDMANN, ISAAC	23	M	FARMER	GRZZZZ	USA
VONFRANTZINS, FRITZ	23	M	MCHT	GRZZZZ	USA		FISCHEL	22	M	FARMER	GRZZZZ	USA
FRESE, MINNA	23	F	NN	GRZZZZ	USA		DREYER, MARIE	20	F	NN	GRZZZZ	USA
KANN, MARIA	26	F	NN	GRZZZZ	USA		WAHLERS, JOH.	15	M	NN	GRZZZZ	USA
WEIDELING, GEORG	17	M	PNTR	GRZZZZ	USA		--HOP, MICH.	23	M	TLR	GRZZZZ	USA
AREND, AUG.	22	M	PNTR	GRZZZZ	USA		HESPOS, SOPHIE	18	F	NN	GRZZZZ	USA
CONRAD	24	M	PNTR	GRZZZZ	USA		FISCKEN, JOH.	31	M	FARMER	GRZZZZ	USA
KEPPER, FRITZ	28	M	LKSH	GRZZZZ	USA		--INKE, MARIA	26	F	NN	GRZZZZ	USA
BUETTNER, AUG.	28	M	FARMER	GRZZZZ	USA		MEYER, CONRAD	25	M	CPTR	GRZZZZ	USA
SEYBOLD, SOPHIE	16	F	NN	GRZZZZ	USA		MARIA	17	F	NN	GRZZZZ	USA
GUTER, OTTO	16	M	JNR	GRZZZZ	USA		SCHLUMBOHM, JOH.	16	M	CPTR	GRZZZZ	USA
WUEST, CAROL.	20	F	NN	GRZZZZ	USA		WIMMER, LOUIS	33	M	CPTR	GRZZZZ	USA
CATH.	18	F	NN	GRZZZZ	USA		ROOS, LINA	21	F	NN	GRZZZZ	USA
ZIMMERMANN, BERNH.	28	M	FARMER	GRZZZZ	USA		ZIECZEMAIER, HERM.	17	M	PNTR	GRZZZZ	USA

PASSENGER	AGE	SEX	OCCUPATION	PRVL	DES
ANNA	22	F	NN	GRZZZZUSA
ROSS, ADAM	17	M	BCHR	GRZZZZUSA
RUMP, WILH.	20	M	BCHR	GRZZZZUSA
ST--NKOPF, HULDREICH	15	M	NN	GRZZZZUSA
HESS, EDWIN	15	M	NN	GRZZZZUSA
STE-NKOPF, BERNH.	15	M	NN	GRZZZZUSA
U. HELENE	19	F	NN	GRZZZZUSA
FRIEDRICH, OSCAR	16	M	BCHR	GRZZZZUSA
MORGENROD, HUGO	17	M	BCHR	GRZZZZUSA
LIPPMANN, BERNH.	23	M	BCHR	GRZZZZUSA
KOENIG, WILH.	16	M	FARMER	GRZZZZUSA
LUDWIG, FRANZ	14	M	NN	GRZZZZUSA
WEISLEDER, PAUL	17	M	FARMER	GRZZZZUSA
BEUTEL, LOUISE	38	F	NN	GRZZZZUSA
SCHEIB, MARG.	51	F	NN	GRZZZZUSA
WILH.	9	M	CHILD	GRZZZZUSA
HOGE, SOPHIE	22	F	NN	GRZZZZUSA
WILHNE.	14	F	NN	GRZZZZUSA
DREHER, CARL	17	M	FARMER	GRZZZZUSA
PLAPPERT, ANNA	19	F	NN	GRZZZZUSA
CATHINKA	15	F	NN	GRZZZZUSA
KOST, EMILIE	2	F	CHILD	GRZZZZUSA
HEIL, PAULINE	24	F	NN	GRZZZZUSA
JAEGER, WILHNE.	21	F	NN	GRZZZZUSA
TONJES, JOH.	61	M	FARMER	GRZZZZUSA
WESTERBURG, LUDW.	26	M	FARMER	GRZZZZUSA
APPEL, LOUISE	20	F	NN	GRZZZZUSA
LEBMANN, ADOLPH	23	M	BRR	GRZZZZUSA
U. CARL	17	M	PNTR	GRZZZZUSA
FOCK, FABIAN	35	M	CPTR	GRZZZZUSA
MARK, ELISAB.	25	F	NN	GRZZZZUSA
PETER	2	M	CHILD	GRZZZZUSA
BIEBERSTEIN, CONSTANZE	30	F	NN	GRZZZZUSA
PEERS, AUGUSTE	16	F	NN	GRZZZZUSA
HOFFMANN, CATH.	46	F	NN	GRZZZZUSA
SCHROEDER, MARIE	7	F	CHILD	GRZZZZUSA
HALDENWANG, ANNA	26	F	CH	GRZZZZUSA
GEORG	5	M	CHILD	GRZZZZUSA
CATH.	17	F	CH	GRZZZZUSA
FAHRENFELD, VICTOR	24	M	LABR	GRZZZZUSA
KOEHLER, EVA	16	F	NN	GRZZZZUSA
HOFFMANN, CLEMENS	33	M	SMH	GRZZZZUSA
PFEIFFER, FRIEDR.	18	M	BKLYR	GRZZZZUSA
JAEGER, FRANZ	28	M	BRR	GRZZZZUSA
ANTON, CARL	16	M	PNTR	GRZZZZUSA
GROENE, CLARE	29	F	NN	GRZZZZUSA
WITTE, AUG.	19	M	FARMER	GRZZZZUSA
EBBERS, JOH.	15	M	NN	GRZZZZUSA
G--DEL, AUGUSTE	49	M	NN	GRZZZZUSA
U. MATHAEUS	28	M	LABR	GRZZZZUSA
SYLVEST, JOS.	24	M	BRR	GRZZZZUSA
HENING, ANTON	28	M	FARMER	GRZZZZUSA
KOHRT, EMMA	35	F	NN	GRZZZZUSA
CARL	11	M	CH	GRZZZZUSA
MELITA	9	F	CHILD	GRZZZZUSA
MARTIN, MINNA	29	F	CH	GRZZZZUSA
REUTER, GEORG	32	M	BRR	GRZZZZUSA
ROSA	28	F	W	GRZZZZUSA
KAETCHEN	2	F	CHILD	GRZZZZUSA
BARTOS, MARIA	22	F	CH	GRZZZZUSA
BASLER, PHILIPP	26	M	FARMER	GRZZZZUSA
IHLE, ALOISE	22	F	NN	GRZZZZUSA
BERTHA	20	F	NN	GRZZZZUSA
U. MARTH.	25	F	NN	GRZZZZUSA

PASSENGER	AGE	SEX	OCCUPATION	PRVL	DES
SHIP:			ANCHORIA		
FROM:			GLASGOW		
TO:			NEW YORK		
ARRIVED: 18 SEPTEMBER 1888					
RISSI, FREID	39	M	SHMK	GRZZZZUSA
SCHULZ, WILH.	27	M	LABR	GRABDMUSA
POHL, OTTO	22	M	LABR	GRABDMUSA
THIOBALD, ADAM	25	M	LABR	GRABDMUSA
KOLLINSKI, WAYSCH	35	M	LABR	GRZZZZUSA
BESSEL, FERDD.	20	M	LABR	GRZZZZUSA
WAGENKNECHT, KARL	17	M	LABR	GRZZZZUSA
KATZENBERGER, AND.	22	M	BKR	GRZZZZUSA
HEID, FRED.	22	M	TLR	GRZZZZUSA
SCHERER, FRED.	36	M	FARMER	GRACBFUSA
HERLING, CARL	51	M	LABR	GRAAKHUSA
MEREIER, EDUARD	54	M	MNR	FRZZZZUSA
ADELINE	48	F	W	FRZZZZUSA
MERCIER, HENRI	18	M	MNR	FRZZZZUSA
EDUARD	16	M	MNR	FRZZZZUSA
DESIRE	11	F	CH	FRZZZZUSA
SIDONIE	9	F	CHILD	FRZZZZUSA
LEONIE	1	F	CHILD	FRZZZZUSA
SENECHAL, HENRI	30	M	MNR	FRZZZZUSA
BADOMON, JULES	24	M	MNR	FRZZZZUSA
EUGENIE	19	F	W	FRZZZZUSA
GEORGES	2	M	CHILD	FRZZZZUSA
BERINQUE, LEOPOLD	30	M	MNR	FRZZZZUSA
ELISE	24	F	W	FRZZZZUSA
MARIE	1	F	CHILD	FRZZZZUSA

SHIP:			ARIZONA		
FROM:			LIVERPOOL AND QUEENSTOWN		
TO:			NEW YORK		
ARRIVED: 18 SEPTEMBER 1888					
KATSCHEROWSKY, STEPHAN	30	M	ART	FRACBFUSA
KEMMERER, R.	34	M	GENT	FRADAXGR
LANDAUER, J.A.	30	M	GENT	FRADBQGR
HORNER, R.	22	M	GENT	FRADBQSW

SHIP:			FULDA		
FROM:			BREMEN AND SOUTHAMPTON		
TO:			NEW YORK		
ARRIVED: 18 SEPTEMBER 1888					
LIEBMANN, G.	55	M	MD	GRZZZZUSA
FANNY	52	F	UNKNOWN	GRZZZZUSA
BLANKE	17	F	UNKNOWN	GRZZZZUSA
ALICE	15	F	UNKNOWN	GRZZZZUSA
WEBER, ERNST	29	M	TT	GRZZZZUSA
CHRIST, L.	33	M	TT	GRZZZZUSA
JABS, ASMUS	40	M	MCHT	GRZZZZUSA
KLINK, JULIE	20	M	UNKNOWN	GRZZZZUSA
NOHE, CARL	22	M	MCHT	GRZZZZUSA
ELISE	33	F	UNKNOWN	GRZZZZUSA
SCHELP, ARNOLD	18	M	CL	GRZZZZUSA
HEINBOCKEL, DORIS	26	F	UNKNOWN	GRZZZZUSA
PROPPER, MATHILDE	21	F	UNKNOWN	GRZZZZUSA
BUXMANN, GEORG	43	M	BBR	GRZZZZUSA
SCHOENEBECK, ELISAB.	30	F	UNKNOWN	GRZZZZUSA

PASSENGER	AGE	SEX	OCCUPATION	PRVL	DES
MAHLER, ADELE	22	F	UNKNOWN	GRZZZZUSA
STUBENRAUCH, CARL	31	M	ENGR	GRZZZZUSA
BROCHE, LYDIA	37	F	UNKNOWN	GRZZZZUSA
SCHKOEBZIGER, MAX	22	M	CLGYMN	GRZZZZUSA
KRAUSSE, CARL	43	M	ENGR	GRZZZZUSA
ROBERT	36	M	ENGR	GRZZZZUSA
ENGEL, WILHELM	18	M	CL	GRZZZZUSA
METTMANN, ANNA	26	F	UNKNOWN	GRZZZZUSA
KUCK, GRETCHEN	18	F	UNKNOWN	GRZZZZUSA
MAMMEN, JOHANN	20	M	LABR	GRZZZZUSA
LUCZAK, KATARZYNA	23	F	UNKNOWN	GRZZZZUSA
PELAGIA	.07	F	INFANT	GRZZZZUSA
STRIEGLER, KARL	38	M	FARMER	GRZZZZUSA
KELLNER, ELISE	20	F	UNKNOWN	GRZZZZUSA
UNSICKER, MARIA	14	F	UNKNOWN	GRZZZZUSA
MARTIN, LEO	34	M	BBR	GRZZZZUSA
MORSE, PAUL	17	M	CL	GRZZZZUSA
LOUISE	15	F	UNKNOWN	GRZZZZUSA
FRITZ, LOUISE	21	M	BKLYR	GRZZZZUSA
ARONOWSKY, EMMA	25	F	UNKNOWN	GRZZZZUSA
MAX	3	M	CHILD	GRZZZZUSA
JALEMSKA, FRANCISCA	24	F	UNKNOWN	GRZZZZUSA
KATARZYNA	2	F	CHILD	GRZZZZUSA
KUBIAK, VICTORIA	21	F	UNKNOWN	GRZZZZUSA
ELSBETHA	.01	F	INFANT	GRZZZZUSA
GARMOTH, CARL	27	M	JNR	GRZZZZUSA
PRADELLA, ADALBERT	23	M	BKR	GRZZZZUSA
SUESSBRICH, AUGUSTE	20	F	UNKNOWN	GRZZZZUSA
SCHWANZ, BERTHA	27	F	UNKNOWN	GRZZZZUSA
RUSCH, CARL	7	M	CHILD	GRZZZZUSA
FRIEDRICHS, GESINE	17	F	UNKNOWN	GRZZZZUSA
SCHRIEFER, LINA	16	F	UNKNOWN	GRZZZZUSA
ANNIE	15	F	UNKNOWN	GRZZZZUSA
DODT, FRIEDRICH	18	M	LABR	GRZZZZUSA
DRELL, AUGUST	60	M	FARMER	GRZZZZUSA
SILLS, FRIEDRICH	32	M	JNR	GRZZZZUSA
ANNA	31	F	UNKNOWN	GRZZZZUSA
ARMSTER, CHRISTIAN	16	M	UNKNOWN	GRZZZZUSA
DEUBLE, GEORGE	16	M	FARMER	GRZZZZUSA
CARL	7	M	CHILD	GRZZZZUSA
SPIELMANN, PAULINE	19	F	UNKNOWN	GRZZZZUSA
STECH, THEODOR	26	M	BCHR	GRZZZZUSA
DONATH, AUGUST	61	M	CPTR	GRZZZZUSA
BAHLS, HEINRICH	28	M	LABR	GRZZZZUSA
HUBER, AUGUST	34	M	LABR	GRZZZZUSA
SCHROEDER, BERTHA	27	F	UNKNOWN	GRZZZZUSA
WIRTH, MARGA.	30	F	UNKNOWN	GRZZZZUSA
GEORG	.11	M	INFANT	GRZZZZUSA
MICHAEL, WILHELM	27	M	BKR	GRZZZZUSA
FRENZ, FREDERICK	16	M	BKR	GRZZZZUSA
HESS, CARL	18	M	LABR	GRZZZZUSA
ZEHNDER, AGATHE	31	F	UNKNOWN	GRZZZZUSA
SIGMUND	14	M	UNKNOWN	GRZZZZUSA
STARK, MARGARETHA	21	F	UNKNOWN	GRZZZZUSA
ZIEGLER, EVA	59	F	UNKNOWN	GRZZZZUSA
HAFNER, MARIE	20	F	UNKNOWN	GRZZZZUSA
SCHMELZLE, CHRISTIAN	38	M	MCHT	GRZZZZUSA
MARIE	39	F	UNKNOWN	GRZZZZUSA
GEORG	7	M	CHILD	GRZZZZUSA
RENZ, FRIEDR.	24	M	SHMK	GRZZZZUSA
MUELLER, SOPHIE	18	F	UNKNOWN	GRZZZZUSA
BREMER, CATHA.	29	F	UNKNOWN	GRZZZZUSA
FRIEDR.	5	M	CHILD	GRZZZZUSA
BRAZ, LINA	24	F	UNKNOWN	GRZZZZUSA
HECK, ROSINE	17	F	UNKNOWN	GRZZZZUSA
NAEGELE, WILHELM	21	M	FARMER	GRZZZZUSA
BABETTE	19	F	UNKNOWN	GRZZZZUSA
BACH, JACOB	16	M	BBR	GRZZZZUSA
SEIFERT, RICHARD	32	M	JNR	GRZZZZUSA
HUGO	34	M	TLR	GRZZZZUSA
SEIDEL, FRANZ	39	M	LKSH	GRZZZZUSA
ZENKER, MAX	27	M	LABR	GRZZZZUSA
HELBIG, RICHARD	25	M	JNR	GRZZZZUSA
TAUSCHER, HEINRICH	48	M	LABR	GRZZZZUSA
DEPPKE, HEINRICH	24	M	MLR	GRZZZZUSA
HAUDICK, GOTTFIRED	37	M	SMH	GRZZZZUSA
ANNA	36	F	UNKNOWN	GRZZZZUSA
AGNES	18	F	UNKNOWN	GRZZZZUSA
BRINK, FRIEDR.	31	M	SMH	GRZZZZUSA
STEINWEG, WILHELM	21	M	LABR	GRZZZZUSA
LANGE, OTTO	33	M	SLKP	GRZZZZUSA
ERNESTINE	26	F	UNKNOWN	GRZZZZUSA
IDA	6	F	CHILD	GRZZZZUSA
HEDWIG	5	F	CHILD	GRZZZZUSA
MARGA.	3	F	CHILD	GRZZZZUSA
EMMA	2	F	CHILD	GRZZZZUSA
ERICH	.10	M	INFANT	GRZZZZUSA
GOEBEL, PAULINA	21	F	UNKNOWN	GRZZZZUSA
GALAESKA, MARIA	42	F	UNKNOWN	GRZZZZUSA
SPREEN, GEORG	15	M	UNKNOWN	GRZZZZUSA
TATGENHORST, SOPHIE	18	F	UNKNOWN	GRZZZZUSA
KAIBEL, GEORG	16	M	UNKNOWN	GRZZZZUSA
RAMSEIER, PAULINE	40	F	UNKNOWN	GRZZZZUSA
GOTTLIEB	15	M	UNKNOWN	GRZZZZUSA
WILHELM	7	M	CHILD	GRZZZZUSA
CARL	6	M	CHILD	GRZZZZUSA
MATHILDA	5	F	CHILD	GRZZZZUSA
WEISCHEDEL, PAULE.	18	F	UNKNOWN	GRZZZZUSA
AENGELE, FRIEDKE.	25	F	UNKNOWN	GRZZZZUSA
PAULINE	15	F	UNKNOWN	GRZZZZUSA
GUTEKUNST, GESINE	17	F	UNKNOWN	GRZZZZUSA
BAACH, CHRISTINE	24	F	UNKNOWN	GRZZZZUSA
BOMETSCH, FRIEDKE.	26	F	UNKNOWN	GRZZZZUSA
MUELLER, JOHANN	23	M	FARMER	GRZZZZUSA
EHMANN, JACOB	21	M	FARMER	GRZZZZUSA
WINTER, MARIA	18	F	UNKNOWN	GRZZZZUSA
GEISMANN, MINNA	17	F	UNKNOWN	GRZZZZUSA
HAUHEIDE, HEINRICH	56	M	LABR	GRZZZZUSA
JETTE	51	F	UNKNOWN	GRZZZZUSA
CARL	21	M	LABR	GRZZZZUSA
LUCA	17	F	UNKNOWN	GRZZZZUSA
MITTNACHT, CAROLINE	20	F	UNKNOWN	GRZZZZUSA
OHRMANN, ALWINA	20	F	UNKNOWN	GRZZZZUSA
MOOG, HERMANN	25	M	JNR	GRZZZZUSA
WACK, JOHANNES	18	M	FARMER	GRZZZZUSA
SCHWEIDER, LUDWIG	15	M	FARMER	GRZZZZUSA
FREY, GOTTLOB	16	M	BKR	GRZZZZUSA
RODELER, ELISABETH	17	F	UNKNOWN	GRZZZZUSA
KRAINZ, ANTON	40	M	PNTR	GRZZZZUSA
MARGA.	22	F	UNKNOWN	GRZZZZUSA
SIEMERS, ADELAIDE	16	F	UNKNOWN	GRZZZZUSA
SCHEUBLEIN, MARGA.	29	F	UNKNOWN	GRZZZZUSA
REINHARD, JOHANN	27	M	BCHR	GRZZZZUSA
HOFMANN, ELISE	18	F	UNKNOWN	GRZZZZUSA
BUCHNER, BETTY	15	F	UNKNOWN	GRZZZZUSA
WITSCH, SOPHIE	39	F	UNKNOWN	GRZZZZUSA
ERNESTINE	13	F	CH	GRZZZZUSA
MARGA.	7	F	CHILD	GRZZZZUSA
CHRISTOPH	6	M	CHILD	GRZZZZUSA
SOFIE	5	F	CHILD	GRZZZZUSA
ANNA	3	F	CHILD	GRZZZZUSA
BREITKREITZ, FRANCISCA	25	F	CH	GRZZZZUSA
STANISLAUS	.11	M	INFANT	GRZZZZUSA
ROBIEGA, FRANCISCA	21	F	UNKNOWN	GRZZZZUSA
VICTORIA	.10	F	INFANT	GRZZZZUSA
NOWAK, ANDR.	34	M	LABR	GRZZZZUSA
WUNK, JAN	27	M	LABR	GRZZZZUSA
SUFKA, ROSALIA	25	F	UNKNOWN	GRZZZZUSA
FRANCISZEK	2	M	CHILD	GRZZZZUSA
STANISLAW	.11	M	INFANT	GRZZZZUSA
NOWACKA, BARBA.	33	F	UNKNOWN	GRZZZZUSA
JADWIGA	7	F	CHILD	GRZZZZUSA
FRANZISZEK	4	M	CHILD	GRZZZZUSA
VERONICA	2	F	CHILD	GRZZZZUSA
JOSEFA	.11	F	INFANT	GRZZZZUSA
THROM, HEINR.	16	M	UNKNOWN	GRZZZZUSA
BECK, HEINR.	16	M	UNKNOWN	GRZZZZUSA
AUMUELLER, BABETTE	18	F	UNKNOWN	GRZZZZUSA
MAILA, JOHANNES	00	M	ENGR	GRZZZZUSA
FERSTEL, MICHAEL	16	M	LABR	GRZZZZUSA

PASSENGER	AGE	SEX	OCCUPATION	PRVL	DES
KURZ, JOS.	18	M	LABR		GRZZZZUSA
SPROESSLER, LEONH.	16	M	LABR		GRZZZZUSA
ALBRECHT, CARL	16	M	LABR		GRZZZZUSA
KRAMER, CARL	17	M	JNR		GRZZZZUSA
ELISAB.	16	F	UNKNOWN		GRZZZZUSA
EHLENBERGER, JULIUS	23	M	LABR		GRZZZZUSA
WILKE, AUGUST	30	M	BBR		GRZZZZUSA
BUMECK, ADAM	50	M	FARMER		GRZZZZUSA
CLARA	50	F	UNKNOWN		GRZZZZUSA
AUG.	7	M	CHILD		GRZZZZUSA
CLARA	6	F	CHILD		GRZZZZUSA
HEDWIG	4	F	CHILD		GRZZZZUSA
FRANZ	2	M	CHILD		GRZZZZUSA
SCHLICHTING, JOSEF	35	M	SDLR		GRZZZZUSA
SPLECK, AUGUST	23	M	MLR		GRZZZZUSA
POHLE, HELENE	23	F	UNKNOWN		GRZZZZUSA
PIRSIALCK, APOLONIA	30	F	UNKNOWN		GRZZZZUSA
AGNISKA	4	F	CHILD		GRZZZZUSA
ROZALIA	2	F	CHILD		GRZZZZUSA
BRINKMANN, ELISE	58	F	UNKNOWN		GRZZZZUSA
LOUIS	16	M	UNKNOWN		GRZZZZUSA
KONITZER, ROSA	24	F	UNKNOWN		GRZZZZUSA
SACK, FELIX	23	M	BKR		GRZZZZUSA
LENZ, PHILIPP	31	M	CPTR		GRZZZZUSA
MARG.	6	F	CHILD		GRZZZZUSA
JOERGENSEN, SUENKE	23	M	FARMER		GRZZZZUSA
SCHRAUB, MARIE	40	F	UNKNOWN		GRZZZZUSA
JOHANN	7	M	CHILD		GRZZZZUSA
HUTTELMAIER, CARL	25	M	BRR		GRZZZZUSA
GREINER, CATHA.	20	F	UNKNOWN		GRZZZZUSA
ROEHM, LINA	17	F	UNKNOWN		GRZZZZUSA
DATISMANN, SUSANNE	36	F	UNKNOWN		GRZZZZUSA
PITTROFF, GRETCHEN	28	F	UNKNOWN		GRZZZZUSA
MEISSEL, BARBA.	25	F	UNKNOWN		GRZZZZUSA
WESTJE, GERHARD	56	M	SLKP		GRZZZZUSA
CATHA.	55	F	UNKNOWN		GRZZZZUSA
KOPPBERGER, DANIEL	24	M	MCHT		GRZZZZUSA
NICKEL, MARIE	21	F	UNKNOWN		GRZZZZUSA
MILAK, TRHERESE	28	F	UNKNOWN		GRZZZZUSA
OTTO	.09	M	INFANT		GRZZZZUSA
FORDERER, MARIE	24	F	UNKNOWN		GRZZZZUSA
SCHMIDT, HEINRICH	22	M	TT		GRZZZZUSA
HINDERA, FELIX	20	M	MCHT		GRZZZZUSA
BUNDT, ED.	14	M	UNKNOWN		GRZZZZUSA
RENKEN, CHRIST.	16	M	CL		GRZZZZUSA
PROPPE, CARL	28	M	FARMER		GRZZZZUSA
GRIEBNER, CARL	30	M	CPTR		GRZZZZUSA
HOLLENBECK, LOUISE	25	F	UNKNOWN		GRZZZZUSA
KAMPMANN, WM.	14	M	UNKNOWN		GRZZZZUSA
WIENERS, JOSEF	63	M	LABR		GRZZZZUSA
HERM.	7	M	CHILD		GRZZZZUSA
SINGER, JACOB	18	M	LABR		GRZZZZUSA
MOELLER, FRIEDR.	17	M	BCHR		GRZZZZUSA
SCHWERING, AUGUSTE	19	F	UNKNOWN		GRZZZZUSA
PREKUHR, HEINRICH	16	M	JNR		GRZZZZUSA
MOHRMANN, FRITZ	15	M	JNR		GRZZZZUSA
GRAFERMANN, HEINR.	15	M	UNKNOWN		GRZZZZUSA
RITTERHOFF, AUGUST	15	M	UNKNOWN		GRZZZZUSA
SIEMERS, ANNA	15	F	UNKNOWN		GRZZZZUSA
GODE, FRITZ	15	M	UNKNOWN		GRZZZZUSA
UELZNER, ROSA	16	F	UNKNOWN		GRZZZZUSA
HARTIG, HANS	29	M	TLR		GRZZZZUSA
FRITZ	18	M	TLR		GRZZZZUSA
WILKENS, FRIEDR.	35	M	SMH		GRZZZZUSA
SPILLE, MARIE	25	F	UNKNOWN		GRZZZZUSA
HELENE	21	F	UNKNOWN		GRZZZZUSA
WILHELMINE	19	F	UNKNOWN		GRZZZZUSA
FRIEDRICH	15	M	UNKNOWN		GRZZZZUSA
SCHALTER, JACOB	21	M	JNR		GRZZZZUSA
U, U	48	M	BBR		GRZZZZUSA
MONSEES, META	16	F	UNKNOWN		GRZZZZUSA
BRUENJES, ANNA	19	F	UNKNOWN		GRZZZZUSA
HEITMANN, MINA	27	F	UNKNOWN		GRZZZZUSA
ANNA	6	F	CHILD		GRZZZZUSA
HEINR.	6	F	CHILD		GRZZZZUSA
OSCAR	2	M	CHILD		GRZZZZUSA
PAUGE, FRIEDR.	16	M	BKR		GRZZZZUSA
MEYER, CHARLOTTE	18	F	UNKNOWN		GRZZZZUSA
MINNA	21	F	UNKNOWN		GRZZZZUSA
SPRICK, HENRIETTE	20	F	UNKNOWN		GRZZZZUSA
CHARLOTTE	15	F	UNKNOWN		GRZZZZUSA
LIES, MINNA	18	F	UNKNOWN		GRZZZZUSA
ISBAUER, ROSALIA	18	F	UNKNOWN		GRZZZZUSA
STEINBORN, CATHARINA	18	F	UNKNOWN		GRZZZZUSA
KWASCHIGROCK, FRANZ	22	M	LABR		GRZZZZUSA
STUTZKE, ADALB.	15	M	BBR		GRZZZZUSA
REYEL, JOH.	25	M	UNKNOWN		GRZZZZUSA
KONITZER, ANASTASIA	21	F	UNKNOWN		GRZZZZUSA
FINK, ANNA	21	F	UNKNOWN		GRZZZZUSA
MEYER, AMIETTE	14	F	UNKNOWN		GRZZZZUSA
WOLFLE, URBAN	50	M	BRR		GRZZZZUSA
BANDEL, CHRISTINA	19	F	UNKNOWN		GRZZZZUSA
WOLFF, VALENTIN	60	M	WCHMKR		GRZZZZUSA
BILL, JACOB	19	M	CL		GRZZZZUSA
ELISAB.	43	F	UNKNOWN		GRZZZZUSA
HOPPE, MONIKA	19	F	UNKNOWN		GRZZZZUSA
REINERS, ELISABETH	28	F	UNKNOWN		GRZZZZUSA
STRUNK, WILHELM	19	M	BCHR		GRZZZZUSA
HASSMANN, JOH.	52	M	FARMER		GRZZZZUSA
GEORG	13	M	CH		GRZZZZUSA
HELENE	17	F	UNKNOWN		GRZZZZUSA
BEHLEN, HELENE	24	F	UNKNOWN		GRZZZZUSA
FRIEDR.	26	M	FARMER		GRZZZZUSA
HELENE	.08	F	INFANT		GRZZZZUSA
HARMS, HELENE	60	F	UNKNOWN		GRZZZZUSA
FRL.JOHANNE	19	F	UNKNOWN		GRZZZZUSA
KRUSE, GEORG	16	M	JNR		GRZZZZUSA
SANDER, GEORG	18	M	BKLYR		GRZZZZUSA
HARMS, HELENE	18	F	UNKNOWN		GRZZZZUSA
ANNA	7	F	CHILD		GRZZZZUSA
SCHNEIDER, MARIE	22	F	UNKNOWN		GRZZZZUSA
BUCHNER, LINA	25	F	UNKNOWN		GRZZZZUSA
WILH.	.11	M	INFANT		GRZZZZUSA
MARTHA	.11	F	INFANT		GRZZZZUSA
SCHMITTER, EMILIE	43	F	UNKNOWN		GRZZZZUSA
MARTHA	7	F	CHILD		GRZZZZUSA
LANG, KAROLINA	17	F	CH		GRZZZZUSA
TULKUC, ANTON	39	M	LABR		GRZZZZUSA
WENZLER, JOSEFINE	27	F	UNKNOWN		GRZZZZUSA
DIERKER, ARNOLD	26	M	BKLYR		GRZZZZUSA
MIDDENDORF, GERH.	30	M	CPTR		GRZZZZUSA
MERZ, MARGA.	27	F	UNKNOWN		GRZZZZUSA
MOHLENHOFF, HEINR.	15	M	FARMER		GRZZZZUSA
HEIDE, GERH.	16	M	FARMER		GRZZZZUSA
BRUEGGEMMANN, ANNA	15	F	UNKNOWN		GRZZZZUSA
KELLER, REINHARD	28	M	LABR		GRZZZZUSA
HALLER, ANNA	18	F	UNKNOWN		GRZZZZUSA
KLETT, REGINA	57	F	UNKNOWN		GRZZZZUSA
HAUDTE, DOROTHEA	18	F	UNKNOWN		GRZZZZUSA
WENTZEL, DAVID	22	M	TLR		GRZZZZUSA
SCHUETZ, WILHELM	23	M	JNR		GRZZZZUSA
MENZEL, ELISAB.	20	F	UNKNOWN		GRZZZZUSA
BERGMANN, ELOISAB.	24	F	UNKNOWN		GRZZZZUSA
SPERR, MARIA	23	F	UNKNOWN		GRZZZZUSA
TREME, KATHARINA	21	F	UNKNOWN		GRZZZZUSA
KRUEGEL, JOSEF	29	M	SHMK		GRZZZZUSA
HEINZE, HERMANN	43	M	FARMER		GRZZZZUSA
VOGES, CARL	26	M	BKLYR		GRZZZZUSA
KELLER, KATHA.	19	F	UNKNOWN		GRZZZZUSA
SCHWAN, JULIUS	17	M	JNR		GRZZZZUSA
WOLSKI, ANDR.	26	M	TLR		GRZZZZUSA
WEICHT, ALBERT	17	M	BCHR		GRZZZZUSA
ZABEL, EMMA	29	F	UNKNOWN		GRZZZZUSA
SCHROEDER, CARL	30	M	CPTR		GRZZZZUSA
HUCK, WILHELM	20	M	FARMER		GRZZZZUSA
KUEMMEL, BABETTE	26	F	UNKNOWN		GRZZZZUSA
STUMPP, THERESIA	22	F	UNKNOWN		GRZZZZUSA
FRIEDL, HEINRICH	18	M	FARMER		GRZZZZUSA
BRACKBUSCH, EWALD	39	M	MCHT		GRZZZZUSA
KLOEPER, CARL	28	M	SMH		GRZZZZUSA

PASSENGER	AGE	SEX	OCCUPATION	PRVL	DES
ANNA	22	F	UNKNOWN	GRZZZZUSA	
CARL	.05	M	INFANT	GRZZZZUSA	
BRANDT, ADOLF	18	M	SHMK	GRZZZZUSA	
GOENER, DORA	24	F	UNKNOWN	GRZZZZUSA	
BREIER, HEINR.	23	M	LKSH	GRZZZZUSA	
HASEMUELLER, ANT.	30	M	BKR	GRZZZZUSA	
ANTA.	50	F	UNKNOWN	GRZZZZUSA	
MARGA.	4	F	CHILD	GRZZZZUSA	
MART.	11	M	INF	GRZZZZUSA	
LUETTSCHWAGER, HERM.	31	M	BBR	GRZZZZUSA	
VOLKMANN, HERM.	22	M	WTR	GRZZZZUSA	
REIF, ELISAB.	37	F	UNKNOWN	GRZZZZUSA	
DORA	7	F	CHILD	GRZZZZUSA	
EMMA	5	F	CHILD	GRZZZZUSA	
ELISA	3	F	CHILD	GRZZZZUSA	
DISGUE, GEORG	17	M	BRR	GRZZZZUSA	
VOSS, THEODOR	24	M	FARMER	GRZZZZUSA	
BARBARA	23	F	UNKNOWN	GRZZZZUSA	
WINGERTER, PETER	29	M	LABR	GRZZZZUSA	
BELMANN, ANNA	17	F	UNKNOWN	GRZZZZUSA	
PRANGE, ANTON	18	M	JNR	GRZZZZUSA	
BRAME, LUDWIG	19	M	TLR	GRZZZZUSA	
STAHLHUT, FR.	28	M	FARMER	GRZZZZUSA	
MARIE	23	F	UNKNOWN	GRZZZZUSA	
BELMANN, HEINR.	15	M	UNKNOWN	GRZZZZUSA	
KEMENA, ALBERT	15	M	UNKNOWN	GRZZZZUSA	
GUESE, FRITZ	31	M	CPTR	GRZZZZUSA	
BEHRENDS, WILKE	60	M	FARMER	GRZZZZUSA	
H.M.	60	M	FARMER	GRZZZZUSA	
GESINE	18	F	UNKNOWN	GRZZZZUSA	
KRUSE, EILT	60	M	FARMER	GRZZZZUSA	
ETTA	58	F	UNKNOWN	GRZZZZUSA	
FREESE, DIEDR.	16	M	BRR	GRZZZZUSA	
OPPERMANN, CARL	45	M	FARMER	GRZZZZUSA	
CARL	16	M	FARMER	GRZZZZUSA	
-OTHDURFT, CARL	39	M	SMH	GRZZZZUSA	
AUGE.	32	F	UNKNOWN	GRZZZZUSA	
AUG.	6	F	CHILD	GRZZZZUSA	
EMILIE	4	F	CHILD	GRZZZZUSA	
EIDA	2	F	CHILD	GRZZZZUSA	
KLEE, ELISABETH	30	F	UNKNOWN	GRZZZZUSA	
RACKE, ELISABETH	36	F	UNKNOWN	GRZZZZUSA	
BANNER, MARGA.	44	F	UNKNOWN	GRZZZZUSA	
LENZ, GRETHE	16	F	UNKNOWN	GRZZZZUSA	
STELLWAGEN, EVA	32	F	UNKNOWN	GRZZZZUSA	
MAGDA.	26	F	UNKNOWN	GRZZZZUSA	
ADAM	.06	M	INFANT	GRZZZZUSA	
BUHL, PAUL	13	M	UNKNOWN	GRZZZZUSA	
WARKMEISTER, MARIE	17	F	UNKNOWN	GRZZZZUSA	
SCHERRER, JOSEF	16	M	BBR	GRZZZZUSA	
BENGEL, FRIEDR.	27	M	BRR	GRZZZZUSA	
HULLER, ADAM	42	M	LKSH	GRZZZZUSA	
KATHA.	39	F	UNKNOWN	GRZZZZUSA	
MICHAEL	7	M	CHILD	GRZZZZUSA	
FRIEDR.	4	M	CHILD	GRZZZZUSA	
MEYER, FRIEDRICH	18	M	WTR	GRZZZZUSA	
KAMPMANN, WILH.	28	M	MCHT	GRZZZZUSA	
FANNITZ, CARL	7	M	CHILD	GRZZZZUSA	
KUNZLI, W.J.	38	M	MCHT	GRZZZZUSA	
BRAUN, LORENZ	25	M	CPTR	GRZZZZUSA	

SHIP: KANSAS

FROM: LIVERPOOL
TO: BOSTON
ARRIVED: 19 SEPTEMBER 1888

PASSENGER	AGE	SEX	OCCUPATION	PRVL	DES
FOERSTER, CARL	32	M	LABR	GRZZZZBO	

SHIP: RHAETIA

FROM: HAMBURG AND HAVRE
TO: NEW YORK
ARRIVED: 19 SEPTEMBER 1888

PASSENGER	AGE	SEX	OCCUPATION	PRVL	DES
STAPELFELDT, MARG.	15	F	SGL	GRACBFUSA	
TOLKSDORF, WILKE	18	F	SGL	GRACBFUSA	
CHLEBOWSKA, ANTONIE	27	F	WO	GRACBFUSA	
WOYCICH	8	M	CHILD	GRACBFUSA	
FRANZ	.11	M	INFANT	GRACBFUSA	
ROSSELEV, ALBERTINE	17	F	SGL	GRACBFUSA	
SOTT, OTTO	25	M	MCHT	GRACBFUSA	
KRAUSE, FRIEDR.	70	M	DLR	GRACBFUSA	
SEGALL, ERNESTINE	32	F	WO	GRACBFUSA	
ADOLF	5	M	CHILD	GRACBFUSA	
THEODOR	3	M	CHILD	GRACBFUSA	
VOSS, LUDWIG	34	M	SVNT	GRACBFUSA	
TIMM, ELISAB.	25	F	SGL	GRACBFUSA	
KUEHN, MARIE	28	F	SGL	GRACBFUSA	
ROSENTHAL, SELMA	14	F	SGL	GRACBFUSA	
SCHULZ, FRIEDR.	28	M	FRMN	GRACBFUSA	
FRIEDRICH, CARL	22	M	ENGR	GRACBFUSA	
GEYER, FRIEDR.CHR.	22	M	CK	GRACBFUSA	
CONSIHR, JOH.	40	M	LABR	GRACBFUSA	
FR.	36	F	W	GRACBFUSA	
BERTHA	14	F	CH	GRACBFUSA	
FRANZ	8	M	CHILD	GRACBFUSA	
MICHAEL, HERRM.	22	M	LABR	GRACBFUSA	
KOLLOWA, HEINR.	23	M	SMH	GRACBFUSA	
HANFF, PAUL	16	M	GDSM	GRACBFUSA	
HEITNER, MAX	21	M	JNR	GRACBFUSA	
KNAPPE, ADOLF	21	M	PRNTR	GRACBFUSA	
ALBERT, HUGO	28	M	LABR	GRACBFUSA	
DONHAUSER, NEPOMUK	23	M	GDNR	GRACBFUSA	
HEMMANN, OSCAR	24	M	BCHR	GRACBFUSA	
VANBORSTEL, GEORG	24	M	FARMER	GRACBFUSA	
SIEGLE, FRIEDA	24	F	SGL	GRACBFUSA	
KUENICKE, FRANZ	20	M	LITGR	GRACBFUSA	
KLENKE, ELISAB.	21	F	SGL	GRACBFUSA	
BITTER, HANS	23	M	PRNTR	GRACBFUSA	
BAYER, HERRM.J.	36	M	FARMER	GRACBFUSA	
ELISAB.	30	F	W	GRACBFUSA	
ADAM	7	M	CHILD	GRACBFUSA	
HEINR.	6	M	CHILD	GRACBFUSA	
JOSEF	5	M	CHILD	GRACBFUSA	
JOH.	4	M	CHILD	GRACBFUSA	
GERTRUD	.09	F	INFANT	GRACBFUSA	
GOLLHARDT, PAUL	21	M	GZR	GRACBFUSA	
JUENGE, REBECA	23	F	SGL	GRACBFUSA	
ANNA	14	F	SGL	GRACBFUSA	
KREBS, KARL	45	M	WTR	GRACBFUSA	
SCHUELTZE, LOUIS	28	M	LABR	GRACBFUSA	
EMMA	25	F	W	GRACBFUSA	
ELISE	5	F	CHILD	GRACBFUSA	
AHLERS, CARL	17	M	LABR	GRACBFUSA	
SCHEUNEMANN, JOH.	13	M	BY	GRACBFUSA	
SCHIRMER, LAURA	21	F	SGL	GRACBFUSA	
HESS, ADOLF	30	M	DR	GRACBFUSA	
JARMUSCKIEWIEZ, JOSEF	48	M	SHMK	GRACBFUSA	
WALLIS, CHRIST.	49	M	SLR	GRACBFUSA	
WAGNER, MATH.	35	F	WO	GRACBFUSA	
MATHES, OSCAR	23	M	JNR	GRACBFUSA	
FRIED.	24	M	JNR	GRACBFUSA	
GOENS, HERRM.	33	M	FARMER	GRACBFUSA	
GOLLHARDT, HEINR.	26	M	SVNT	GRACBFUSA	
SCHRADEE, AUGU.	24	F	SGL	GRACBFUSA	
HORNEBERG, L.P.	57	M	GDSM	GRACBFUSA	
WEMER, CAROL.	17	F	SGL	GRACBFUSA	
ZIEGLER, AUG.	40	F	WO	GRACBFUSA	
HERRM.	7	M	CHILD	GRACBFUSA	
HAUSEN, MARTIN	68	M	BKLYR	GRACBFUSA	
GREINER, BARB.	19	F	SGL	GRACBFUSA	
HUELSEMANN, HERMINE	17	F	SGL	GRACBFUSA	

PASSENGER	AGE	SEX	OCCUPATION	PRVL	DES
MELFSEN, HERRM.	44	M	PRNTR	GRACBFUSA	
FIETZ, FERD.	31	M	LABR	GRACBFUSA	
VANLIESH, SOPHIE	18	F	SGL	GRACBFUSA	
RINNE, ANNA	17	F	SGL	GRACBFUSA	
ROLAND, BRUNO	32	M	BRR	GRACBFUSA	
ANNA	26	F	W	GRACBFUSA	
BAUMANN, HERMINE	25	F	SGL	GRACBFUSA	
HUEBNER, HERRM.	24	M	BKR	GRACBFUSA	
MARIE	21	F	W	GRACBFUSA	
OTTO	.11	M	INFANT	GRACBFUSA	
ANTON, HEDWIG	39	F	SGL	GRACBFUSA	
SCHLEGEL, FERD.	33	M	BLKSMH	GRACBFUSA	
MINNA	33	F	W	GRACBFUSA	
PAUL	3	M	CHILD	GRACBFUSA	
ARTHUR	2	M	CHILD	GRACBFUSA	
ELISABETH	.09	F	INFANT	GRACBFUSA	
LINDNER, VALESKA	23	F	SGL	GRACBFUSA	
FALLERT, MARIE	30	F	SGL	GRACBFUSA	
LENNINGER, PAUL	18	M	TLR	GRACBFUSA	
HECK, JEAN	22	M	JNR	GRACBFUSA	
ROSENDAHL, GEORG	48	M	BCHR	GRACBFUSA	
STUTSE, HEINR.	27	M	FARMER	GRACBFUSA	
ZAKSEWSKY, BALBINE	19	F	SGL	GRACBFUSA	
BOCKUSCHEFSKI, CARL	32	M	LABR	GRACBFUSA	
ROSALIA	25	F	W	GRACBFUSA	
BURGHARDT, BERTHA	32	F	WO	GRACBFUSA	
SCHMIDT, KONRAD	25	M	LABR	GRACBFUSA	
KIPFER, GOTTFRIED	25	M	LABR	GRACBFUSA	
AUBIN, MARTIN	40	M	WTR	GRACBFUSA	
MARIE	38	F	W	GRACBFUSA	
BRAENNING, MAX	17	M	GDNR	GRACBFUSA	
FASSLER, BERTHA	20	F	SGL	GRACBFUSA	
KREMER, PHILIPP	27	M	SMH	GRACBFUSA	
TIETJEN, HANRY	25	M	STDNT	GRACBFUSA	
BUCH, GRETCHEN	21	F	SGL	GRACBFUSA	
SCHLEGEL, RUD.	27	F	TCHR	GRACBFUSA	
TIEDE, HENRIETTE	60	F	WO	GRACBFUSA	
CLASEN, JOHANNA	35	F	SGL	GRACBFUSA	
JELINEK, MARCEL	36	M	ART	GRACBFUSA	
LINDT, JOHANNE	50	F	WO	GRACBFUSA	
JACOBSEN, ELSE	6	F	CHILD	GRACBFUSA	
LINDT, ROSA	22	F	SGL	GRACBFUSA	
FEDDERSEN, KATINKA	47	F	SGL	GRACBFUSA	
KELTING, AUG.	50	F	WO	GRACBFUSA	
EMMI	7	F	CHILD	GRACBFUSA	
ARNOLD, RICHARD	23	M	ENGR	GRACBFUSA	
KISTER, PAUL	20	M	MCHT	GRACBFUSA	
NEEF, SOFIE	34	F	SGL	GRACBFUSA	
LAPIERRE, ANNA	31	F	SGL	GRACBFUSA	
MUENDT, FRIEDR.	43	M	ENGR	GRACBFUSA	
BUROSE, ADOLF	30	M	ART	GRACBFUSA	

SHIP: RHEIN

FROM: BREMEN
TO: BALTIMORE
ARRIVED: 19 SEPTEMBER 1888

PASSENGER	AGE	SEX	OCCUPATION	PRVL	DES
KOCH, WALDEMAR	13	M	CH	GRZZZZMD	
HAEBERLE, HERM.	32	M	MCHT	GRZZZZMD	
BRAUNS, RICHARD	17	M	MCHT	GRZZZZMD	
RIEGEL, SUSANNA	32	F	NN	GRZZZZMD	
BRAUNS, RICHARD	17	M	MCHT	GRZZZZMD	
RIEGEL, SUSANNA	32	F	NN	GRZZZZMD	
JOHANN	2	M	CHILD	GRZZZZMD	
SCHMIDT, FOL.SOPHIE	40	F	NN	GRZZZZMD	
HAEBERLE, LOUIS	50	M	RE	GRZZZZMD	
FLORA	45	F	W	GRZZZZMD	
HULDA	18	F	NN	GRZZZZMD	
CHRIST.	25	M	MCHT	GRZZZZMD	

PASSENGER	AGE	SEX	OCCUPATION	PRVL	DES
SCHUERMANN, AUGUSTE	50	F	NN	GRZZZZMD	
ELLA	23	F	NN	GRZZZZMD	
WILLE, MINNA	20	F	NN	GRZZZZMD	
WEBER, JOSEPHINE	22	F	NN	GRZZZZMD	
NEUBERT, EMMA	5	F	CHILD	GRZZZZMD	
HEDWIG	3	F	CHILD	GRZZZZMD	
KALETA, ELISAB.	29	F	NN	GRZZZZMD	
FRANZ	.11	M	INFANT	GRZZZZMD	
STUBBE, HULDA	20	F	NN	GRZZZZMD	
LETTAN, ELISABETH	38	F	NN	GRZZZZMD	
KAPANKE, FRIEDR.	25	M	FARMER	GRZZZZMD	
MATHILDE	28	F	W	GRZZZZMD	
MARIA	.01	F	INFANT	GRZZZZMD	
STEFANIAK, VALERIA	16	F	NN	GRZZZZMD	
ZIELINSKA, ANNA	32	F	NN	GRZZZZMD	
CATHA.	7	F	CHILD	GRZZZZMD	
MARIANNA	.01	F	INFANT	GRZZZZMD	
BRUNNER, ALBERTINE	15	F	NN	GRZZZZMD	
EICHHORN, CHR.	22	M	TNM	GRZZZZMD	
SCHMIDT, ELISAB.	25	F	NN	GRZZZZMD	
BABETTE	1	F	CHILD	GRZZZZMD	
PEREGONTE, FRANZ	53	M	LABR	GRZZZZMD	
ULLRICH, FRIEDR.	17	M	FARMER	GRZZZZMD	
ROSENTHAL, BERTHA	62	F	NN	GRZZZZMD	
CARL	19	M	CH	GRZZZZMD	
KOLBE, FRITZ	27	M	CGRMKR	GRZZZZMD	
SIECKMANN, CATH.	37	F	NN	GRZZZZMD	
AUGUSTE	9	F	CHILD	GRZZZZMD	
OTTO	5	M	CHILD	GRZZZZMD	
THEODOR	3	M	CHILD	GRZZZZMD	
SCHULTZ, IDA	18	F	CK	GRZZZZMD	
LAMS, MATH.	68	M	FARMER	GRZZZZMD	
IDA	28	F	W	GRZZZZMD	
MARTHA	7	F	CHILD	GRZZZZMD	
GUST.	4	M	CHILD	GRZZZZMD	
PISCH, ANNA	27	F	LABR	GRZZZZMD	
KLAU, PHILIP	24	M	LABR	GRZZZZMD	
STREGE, MARIA	21	F	NN	GRZZZZMD	
MARGUARDT, ANNA	28	F	NN	GRZZZZMD	
LINEZUN, THEKLA	22	F	NN	GRZZZZMD	
STAWICKI, IGNATZ	31	M	SHMK	GRZZZZMD	
APPOLONIA	34	F	W	GRZZZZMD	
LAKONIA	7	F	CHILD	GRZZZZMD	
LEO	4	M	CHILD	GRZZZZMD	
HAAK, FRIEDERIKE	24	F	CK	GRZZZZMD	
GEORG	15	M	HTR	GRZZZZMD	
MILLNER, MINNA	23	F	NN	GRZZZZMD	
LEWANDOWSKI, MARIANNA	24	F	NN	GRZZZZMD	
WINKEL, ELISABETH	27	F	NN	GRZZZZMD	
MARIANNA	1	F	CHILD	GRZZZZMD	
WLADISLAW	.01	M	INFANT	GRZZZZMD	
BENTKOWSKI, SZECZEPAN	57	M	FARMER	GRZZZZMD	
CHELININIAK, MARIA	37	F	NN	GRZZZZMD	
JOSEPH	9	M	CHILD	GRZZZZMD	
CATHARINA	7	F	CHILD	GRZZZZMD	
STANISLAW	5	M	CHILD	GRZZZZMD	
ROSALIE	3	F	CHILD	GRZZZZMD	
MARIA	2	F	CHILD	GRZZZZMD	
OGORKOWSKI, ROZALIA	28	F	CH	GRZZZZMD	
ROSSOW, FRIEDR.	29	M	LABR	GRZZZZMD	
WILHE.	22	F	NN	GRZZZZMD	
HOHMANN, CHRISTINE	67	F	NN	GRZZZZMD	
ROBERT	3	M	CHILD	GRZZZZMD	
ANNA	.05	F	INFANT	GRZZZZMD	
SCHERBARTH, EMMA	20	F	NN	GRZZZZMD	
PAULINE	18	F	NN	GRZZZZMD	
HARTMANN, HEINR.	17	M	FARMER	GRZZZZMD	
KOERNER, MARIE	25	F	NN	GRZZZZMD	
NEUSSENDOERFER, MARIE	20	F	NN	GRZZZZMN	
STUBBE, MICHAEL	52	M	FARMER	GRZZZZIL	
PERGANTE, JULIUS	22	M	LABR	GRZZZZWI	
AUGUST	24	M	SMH	GRZZZZWI	
MAHLITZ, ANNA	20	F	NN	GRZZZZIL	
BEITZ, THERESE	57	F	NN	GRZZZZIL	
MAX	11	M	CH	GRZZZZIL	

PASSENGER	AGE	SEX	OCCUPATION	PRV VIL DES
ARNDT, WILH.	27	M	SMH	GRZZZZMN
OTTILIE	17	F	W	GRZZZZMN
OTTO	1	M	CHILD	GRZZZZMN
KRUKENBERG, GUST.	24	M	BKBNDR	GRZZZZKS
WEYH, JOHS.	55	M	BKLYR	GRZZZZMD
SCHERM, ELIZA	22	F	NN	GRZZZZMD
ZAHL, FERDINAND	59	M	FARMER	GRZZZZCAL
LOUISE	47	F	W	GRZZZZCAL
ALICE	20	F	NN	GRZZZZCAL
MARIE	18	F	NN	GRZZZZCAL
IDA	17	F	NN	GRZZZZCAL
CARL	16	M	FARMER	GRZZZZCAL
JULIUS	13	M	CH	GRZZZZCAL
ANNA	11	F	CH	GRZZZZCAL
FRANZ	10	M	CH	GRZZZZCAL
MARTHA	9	F	CHILD	GRZZZZCAL
HEDWIG	7	F	CHILD	GRZZZZCAL
ELSE	6	F	CHILD	GRZZZZCAL
OTTO	4	M	CHILD	GRZZZZCAL
ARNOLD, GEORG	33	M	BRR	GRZZZZOH
ANNA	27	F	W	GRZZZZOH
MATHIAS	5	M	CHILD	GRZZZZOH
BABETTE	2	F	CHILD	GRZZZZOH
ANNALIES	.06	F	INFANT	GRZZZZOH
BUDT, JOHANN	50	M	FARMER	GRZZZZMD
SOHPIE	38	F	W	GRZZZZMD
DIEDRICH	15	M	CH	GRZZZZMD
AUGUST	11	M	CH	GRZZZZMD
WILHELM	10	M	CH	GRZZZZMD
ANNA	5	F	CHILD	GRZZZZMD
FRITZ	.02	M	INFANT	GRZZZZMD
WILKENS, JOH.	34	M	FARMER	GRZZZZMD
HOLLDORF, HEINR.	31	M	FARMER	GRZZZZMD
ANNA	28	F	W	GRZZZZMD
EMMA	5	F	CHILD	GRZZZZMD
ALMA	1	F	CHILD	GRZZZZMD
U, JOSEPH	60	M	FARMER	GRZZZZMD
GRESSLER, BERTHOLD	16	M	FARMER	GRZZZZMD
BREIMER, ANNA	23	F	NN	GRZZZZMD
OTTO, MELCHIOR	21	M	DYR	GRZZZZIL
HOLLSCHEN, CATHA.	64	F	NN	GRZZZZMD
WILH.	26	M	FARMER	GRZZZZMD
SCHAEFER, KAETCHEN	23	F	CK	GRZZZZMD
KARL	25	M	FARMER	GRZZZZMD
RUPPERT, ANNA	16	F	NN	GRZZZZMD
FORKAS, ROSA	21	F	NN	GRZZZZMD
MRZENA, MARIA	21	F	NN	GRZZZZMD
GRAMBORT, DORA	19	F	NN	GRZZZZMD
FUERST, ANNA	65	F	NN	GRZZZZMD
WEDEL, KATHA.	19	F	NN	GRZZZZMD
BECKER, WEIGAND	63	M	FARMER	GRZZZZMD
BECK, EDUARD	18	M	FARMER	GRZZZZMD
THEURER, MARIE	28	F	NN	GRZZZZMD
MAIER, JOH.G.	21	M	THR	GRZZZZMD
KRAMER, MARIA	43	F	NN	GRZZZZMD
HELDT, ELISE	17	F	NN	GRZZZZMD
ROSENHILD, ADOLF	18	M	FARMER	GRZZZZMD
ELIAS	10	M	CH	GRZZZZMD
OTTO, CARL	45	M	FARMER	GRZZZZIA
ERNSTINE	36	F	W	GRZZZZIA
EMMA	17	F	NN	GRZZZZIA
ZUELOW, WILH.	37	M	TCHR	GRZZZZNE
EDWIN	10	M	CH	GRZZZZNE
ELFRIDA	7	F	CHILD	GRZZZZNE
AGNES	4	F	CHILD	GRZZZZNE
KATZNER, JOH.	33	M	CPTR	GRZZZZMI
CATH.	33	F	W	GRZZZZMI
JOHANN	3	M	CHILD	GRZZZZMI
PETER	.09	M	INFANT	GRZZZZMI
MOORWESSEL, J.B.	23	M	FARMER	GRZZZZMD
FRICK, CATH.	16	F	NN	GRZZZZMD
FERTING, AUG.	25	M	TLR	GRZZZZMD
HERM.	30	M	TLR	GRZZZZMD
MUELLER, KATHA.	17	F	NN	GRZZZZMD
ARISIUS, CARL	30	M	SLD	GRZZZZMD
BERGER, ROSINA	64	F	NN	GRZZZZMD
MARIA	19	F	SVNT	GRZZZZMD
NISSEL, PAULINE	30	F	NN	GRZZZZMD
SPIEWEG, WILHE.	33	F	NN	GRZZZZMD
OTTO	12	M	CH	GRZZZZMD
EMMA	6	F	CHILD	GRZZZZMD
ELISABETH	.01	F	INFANT	GRZZZZMD
LIPPKE, ROBERT	39	M	FARMER	GRZZZZMD
AUGUSTE	38	F	W	GRZZZZMD
JOHANNES	.02	M	INFANT	GRZZZZMD
HELENE	2	F	CHILD	GRZZZZMD
VANPEL, MARTHA	48	F	NN	GRZZZZMD
MINNA	13	F	CH	GRZZZZMD
SCHROEDERER, WILH.	57	F	NN	GRZZZZMD
ANNA	29	F	CK	GRZZZZMD
HEIKEL, JOSEF	30	M	PNTR	GRZZZZMD
MARIE	30	F	W	GRZZZZMD
CHOZELEWSKA, JULIA	20	F	NN	GRZZZZMD
LEWANDOWSKA, STANISLAWA	21	F	NN	GRZZZZMD
ANTONINA	30	F	NN	GRZZZZMD
JOSEFA	30	F	NN	GRZZZZMD
STEFANIE	.09	F	INFANT	GRZZZZMD
BRUEGGEMANN, CAROLINA	15	F	NN	GRZZZZMD
GRACZYK, FRANZISZEK	64	M	FARMER	GRZZZZMD
HELENA	64	F	W	GRZZZZMD
HUBER, THERESA	26	F	NN	GRZZZZMD
ANNA	4	F	CHILD	GRZZZZMD
FRANZ	1	M	CHILD	GRZZZZMD
SOPHIE	.06	F	INFANT	GRZZZZMD
PFEUFER, ROSINE	26	F	NN	GRZZZZMD
HOHNER, ANNA	16	F	NN	GRZZZZMD
REINHARDT, MICH.	16	M	BRR	GRZZZZMD
KAPLANOWSKI, VINCENT	38	M	FARMER	GRZZZZMD
JOSEPHINE	34	F	W	GRZZZZMD
JOHAN	7	M	CHILD	GRZZZZMD
MARCIA	5	F	CHILD	GRZZZZMD
ROBERT	.11	M	INFANT	GRZZZZMD
WAGNER, JOHS.	18	M	SMH	GRZZZZMD
KLEE, JOHS.	19	M	PRNTR	GRZZZZMD
ZANK, CLARA	18	F	NN	GRZZZZMD
SAUER, MARIA	22	F	NN	GRZZZZMD
STEGMANN, CONRAD	22	M	FARMER	GRZZZZMD
VIBUS	20	M	FARMER	GRZZZZMD
JACOB	18	M	FARMER	GRZZZZMD
JANKOWSKA, MARA.	40	F	NN	GRZZZZMD
STANISLAWA	12	F	CH	GRZZZZMD
BADER, CARL	44	M	JNR	GRZZZZMD
ELISABETH	44	F	W	GRZZZZMD
MARIA	9	F	CHILD	GRZZZZMD
KERHSENS, B.	39	M	MCHT	GRZZZZMD
MAJEWSKI, ANTON	27	M	FARMER	GRZZZZMD
BAKOVSKI, EDUARD	34	M	TLR	GRZZZZMD
CARL	5	M	CHILD	GRZZZZMD
LUSCHEN, SEBASTIAN	17	M	FARMER	GRZZZZMD
DIEDR.	19	M	FARMER	GRZZZZMD
SEIDEL, BERTHA	22	F	NN	GRZZZZMD
ALFRED	.05	M	INFANT	GRZZZZMD
ADAMCSAK, KATHA.	22	F	NN	GRZZZZMD
CATHA.	3	F	CHILD	GRZZZZMD
CWIKLINSKY, ANNA	24	F	NN	GRZZZZMD
FAHRENKAMP, AUGUST	16	M	SMH	GRZZZZMD
FENKER, HERM.	18	M	JNR	GRZZZZMD
PETZOLD, ROSA	21	F	NN	GRZZZZMD
BRAKEMEIER, WILHE.	21	F	NN	GRZZZZMD
KOTZIANER, PETER	27	M	LABR	GRZZZZMD
GOLTERMANN, HEINR.	25	M	FARMER	GRZZZZNE
HEINR.	3	M	CHILD	GRZZZZNE
BUTT, FRITZ	3	M	CHILD	GRZZZZNE
WEGHOEFT, FRIEDERIKE	18	F	NN	GRZZZZOH
WILHE.	16	F	NN	GRZZZZOH
ASCHEMOOR, ROSINE	16	F	NN	GRZZZZOH
BLUEMELIN, JOHANN	45	M	FARMER	GRZZZZWI
MARGA.	38	F	W	GRZZZZWI
GEORG	1	M	CHILD	GRZZZZWI
JOHANN	10	M	CH	GRZZZZWI

PASSENGER	AGE	SEX	OCCUPATION	PRVL	DES
FRIEDR.	7	M	CHILD		GRZZZZWI
KARL	5	M	CHILD		GRZZZZWI
BROEBKER, ROB.	14	M	CH		GRZZZZMO
BRANDT, HERMINE	33	F	NN		GRZZZZWI
OTTO	10	M	CH		GRZZZZWI
WRZEZINSKI, ANDR.	23	M	LABR		GRZZZZMD
KLATTE, FRIEDERIKE	19	F	NN		GRZZZZOH
PLITT, GEORG	24	M	MCHT		GRZZZZDAK
TOPP, MINNA	46	F	NN		GRZZZZNE
OLGA	22	F	NN		GRZZZZNE
ANTONIE	18	F	NN		GRZZZZNE
ARTHUR	11	M	CH		GRZZZZNE
KOPMANN, MARIE	18	F	NN		GRZZZZOH
BURMANN, MATHIAS	31	M	PNTR		GRZZZZOH
PUJE, MENOJE	70	M	PVTR		GRZZZZIL
MARGA.	64	F	W		GRZZZZIL
KLEIN, JOHANN	39	M	FARMER		GRZZZZIL
JOHANNE	31	F	W		GRZZZZIL
TRIENKE	10	F	CH		GRZZZZIL
MENSINE	9	F	CHILD		GRZZZZIL
JOHANN	4	M	CHILD		GRZZZZIL
ME---E	4	M	CHILD		GRZZZZIL
LINE	3	F	CHILD		GRZZZZIL
MARGA.	1	F	CHILD		GRZZZZIL
KREITEMEYER, CONRAD	18	M	FARMER		GRZZZZOH
KOSSENJANS, MATTH.	36	M	FARMER		GRZZZZMO
GESINE	21	F	W		GRZZZZMO
GRONDE, EMANUEL	50	M	FARMER		GRZZZZIL
CARL	46	M	FARMER		GRZZZZIL
AUGE.	48	F	W		GRZZZZIL
AUGE.	17	F	NN		GRZZZZIL
EMIL	11	M	CH		GRZZZZIL
ANNA	7	F	CHILD		GRZZZZIL
VOPEL, JAC.	18	M	FARMER		GRZZZZMO
ALBERTI, HEINR.	32	M	SHMK		GRZZZZOH
KAPPEL, CATH.	14	F	NN		GRZZZZOH
RUNGE, EMILIE	61	F	NN		GRZZZZOH
ANTON	14	M	CH		GRZZZZOH
JOSEF	17	M	BKR		GRZZZZOH
WAHLE, BERNH.	14	M	CH		GRZZZZOH
MOERSCHEN, HEINR.	34	M	FARMER		GRZZZZOH
ENGELBACH, BERTHA	16	F	SVNT		GRZZZZMD
CERMAK, ALOISIN	19	M	LABR		GRZZZZMD
CHOVALKOW, KAROLINA	24	F	NN		GRZZZZMD
KIESLER, ELISE	18	F	NN		GRZZZZMD
LIES, CLARA	11	F	CH		GRZZZZMD
KREUTZER, KUNIGE.	28	F	NN		GRZZZZMD
LANG, CHARLES	17	M	HTR		GRZZZZMD
HASEL, MARIE	32	F	CK		GRZZZZMD
MUELLER, FRIEDR.	27	M	FARMER		GRZZZZMD
GEMELIN, JULIUS	26	M	TNM		GRZZZZMD
PHILIPP, CONRAD	18	M	GDNR		GRZZZZMD
BISCHOF, LUDW.	18	M	FARMER		GRZZZZMD
LEFERS, JOH.	14	M	CH		GRZZZZNE
PARGMANN, FRIEDR.	62	M	FARMER		GRZZZZNE
MARGA.	52	F	W		GRZZZZNE
MARIE	21	F	NN		GRZZZZNE
ANNA	11	F	CH		GRZZZZNE
SOPHIE	9	F	CHILD		GRZZZZNE
HERM.	7	M	CHILD		GRZZZZNE
VOLKMANN, MARGA.	22	F	NN		GRZZZZNE
BOESCHE, HEINR.	59	M	BCHR		GRZZZZNE
ANNA	46	F	W		GRZZZZNE
SOPHIE	21	F	NN		GRZZZZNE
HEINR.	11	M	CH		GRZZZZNE
HERM.	7	M	CHILD		GRZZZZNE
DIEDR.	1	M	CHILD		GRZZZZNE
BECKMANN, HEINR.	16	M	JNR		GRZZZZIL
HEINE, BEKA	41	F	NN		GRZZZZNE
GESINE	15	F	NN		GRZZZZNE
MARIE	11	F	CH		GRZZZZNE
DORIA	9	F	CHILD		GRZZZZNE
ANNA	7	F	CHILD		GRZZZZNE
OTTO	4	M	CHILD		GRZZZZNE
META	.06	F	INFANT		GRZZZZNE
SCHONFELD, CARL	15	M	BKR		GRZZZZMD
WAGNER, JOH.	00	M	CL		GRZZZZMD
KOCH, GENOFEVA	50	F	NN		GRZZZZMD
NOWAK, MARIA	50	F	NN		GRZZZZMD
KONCELIK, ANNA	25	F	NN		GRZZZZMD
JARGONSKOWSKI, OTTO	34	M	LABR		GRZZZZMD
EMILIE	26	F	W		GRZZZZMD
CARL	5	M	CHILD		GRZZZZMD
MARTHA	.04	F	INFANT		GRZZZZMD
OTTO	11	M	CH		GRZZZZMD
FRIEDR.	77	M	LABR		GRZZZZMD
JEMUSCHEWSKI, BERTHA	35	F	NN		GRZZZZMD
LESCHMANN, CARL	59	M	FARMER		GRZZZZMD
BERTHA	59	F	W		GRZZZZMD
GUZIAK, FRANZISZEK	35	M	LABR		GRZZZZMD
STARZINSKI, STANISL.	16	M	LABR		GRZZZZMD
WERMEISTER, EMMA	40	F	NN		GRZZZZMD
ANNA	14	F	CH		GRZZZZMD
MAX	11	M	CH		GRZZZZMD
PAUL	00	M	CH		GRZZZZMD
HENRIETTE	3	F	CHILD		GRZZZZMD
FISCHER, KAROLINE	46	F	NN		GRZZZZMD
PLATE, LOUISE	16	F	NN		GRZZZZMD
DEGNER, AUGUSTA	45	F	NN		GRZZZZMD
OSCAR	11	M	CH		GRZZZZMD
HULDA	10	F	CH		GRZZZZMD
MORGENEIER, DOROTHA.	22	F	NN		GRZZZZIL
ANNA	.07	F	INFANT		GRZZZZIL
EILERMANN, AUG.	24	M	CPTR		GRZZZZOH
LEIPNITZ, GUSTAV	17	M	BKLYR		GRZZZZWI
HELD, ALWINE	16	F	NN		GRZZZZNE
MAYER, BERNH.	67	M	FARMER		GRZZZZOH
CHRISTINE	24	F	SVNT		GRZZZZOH
ALBRECHT, GEORG	67	M	FARMER		GRZZZZNE
BARBA.	24	F	NN		GRZZZZNE
SCHADEMANN, MARG.	40	F	NN		GRZZZZNE
MARIA	11	F	CH		GRZZZZNE
BARBA.	4	F	CHILD		GRZZZZNE
SCHEMM, FRIEDR.	35	M	FARMER		GRZZZZNE
ANNA	25	F	W		GRZZZZNE
ALBRECHT, JOH.	56	M	FARMER		GRZZZZNE
ANNA	57	F	W		GRZZZZNE
SCHEMM, GEORG	25	M	FARMER		GRZZZZNE
FUCHSHEBER, THERESE	40	F	NN		GRZZZZIL
GRENZINGER, ANNA	24	F	NN		GRZZZZMN
JANNSMUELLER, RICH.	20	M	MNR		GRZZZZKS
BOEHM, FRIEDR.	14	M	LKSH		GRZZZZPA
FALK, ANNA	19	F	CK		GRZZZZOH
REIFFENBERGER, WILH.	26	M	JNR		GRZZZZID
GIEBELER, ALBERT	27	M	TLR		GRZZZZID
ARNESEN, JOHANN	18	M	LABR		GRZZZZIL
CZINZOLL, CARL	24	M	LABR		GRZZZZIN
KRETSCHMANN, ROSA	21	F	NN		GRZZZZIN
ANNA	.11	F	INFANT		GRZZZZIN
KNAUS, KONRAD	25	M	FARMER		GRZZZZWI
ELISAB.	30	F	W		GRZZZZWI
KATHA.	3	F	CHILD		GRZZZZWI
KAEBELMANN, ANNA	23	F	NN		GRZZZZWI
TSCHUPPE, JACOB	27	M	CL		GRZZZZIL
AUGE.	24	F	W		GRZZZZIL
IDA	3	F	CHILD		GRZZZZIL
SCHMIDT, AMALIE	30	F	NN		GRZZZZWI
HUSTER, ADOLPH	28	M	FARMER		GRZZZZTN
HEDWIG	28	F	W		GRZZZZTN
MOULE, WENZL	22	M	LABR		GRZZZZMO
BLEINER, FRANS	22	M	LABR		GRZZZZMO
LUCKER, WM.	14	M	CH		GRZZZZMD
MENZE, FRITZ	21	M	FARMER		GRZZZZMD
HOPP, DIEDR.	25	M	TU		GRZZZZPA
HOLZ, MAX	20	M	UNKNOWN		GRZZZZMD
BARTH, CARL	26	M	GDNR		GRZZZZPA
HOEHN, WILH.	22	M	FARMER		GRZZZZMD
LUCKERT, RICHD.	15	M	FARMER		GRZZZZMD
EMMA	14	F	NN		GRZZZZMD
EICHBUCH, JOHANNA	11	F	CH		GRZZZZMD

PASSENGER	AGE	SEX	OCCUPATION	PRVVL	DES
KROENER, EMILIE	18	F	NN	GRZZZZMD
SCHERSCHING, BERTHA	26	F	NN	GRZZZZMD
MINNA	9	F	CHILD	GRZZZZMD
EMMA	.11	F	INFANT	GRZZZZMD
SCHREIBER, SUSANNA	18	F	NN	GRZZZZMD
BARK, OTTO	32	M	GDNR	GRZZZZMD
STEFFENS, WILHELM	15	M	CPTR	GRZZZZMD
SELZLE, CATHA.	32	F	NN	GRZZZZMD
EMMA	7	F	CHILD	GRZZZZMD
SCHWARZ, MARIE	30	F	NN	GRZZZZMD
CARL	10	M	CH	GRZZZZMD

SHIP: STATE OF NEVADA

FROM: GLASGOW AND LARNE
TO: NEW YORK
ARRIVED: 20 SEPTEMBER 1888

PASSENGER	AGE	SEX	OCCUPATION	PRVVL	DES
ANDRAS, ANTONI	20	M	LABR	PRZZZZUSA
BOSSET, ROCHE	42	F	MNR	PRZZZZUSA
SANIE	18	F	UNKNOWN	PRZZZZUSA
SENDER	11	M	FARMER	PRZZZZUSA
FANNY	10	F	CH	PRZZZZUSA
CHEITEL, ERNEST	20	M	WTR	GRZZZZUSA
CLAUSSEN, F.W.	21	M	FARMER	GRZZZZUSA
DAVIDOFF, JACOB	38	M	MCHT	GRZZZZUSA
WEINGART, AUG.	14	M	WTR	GRZZZZUSA
LINDMAN, GEO-L.	26	M	MCHT	GRZZZZUSA

SHIP: CITY OF BERLIN

FROM: LIVERPOOL
TO: NEW YORK
ARRIVED: 21 SEPTEMBER 1888

PASSENGER	AGE	SEX	OCCUPATION	PRVVL	DES
POLLERD, EUGENE	23	M	LABR	GRZZZZUNK
HANMESTROM, C.J.	24	M	LABR	GRZZZZNY
STOBEL, EDWARD	26	M	LABR	GRACBFNY
BEIVOITT, JOSEF	21	M	LABR	GRACBFNY
SCHULKENFSKI, FRANK	19	M	LABR	GRACBFNY
BOTHLEIN, BRUL	17	M	LABR	GRACBFNY
HEDDMEH, JACOB	26	M	LABR	GRACBFNY
HEBEDANK, CARL	27	M	LABR	GRACBFNY
ROINY, FRANZ	39	M	TLR	GRACBFHBK
KRNASH, GEORGE	16	M	LABR	GRACBFNY
SECHASE, CARL	21	M	BKR	GRACBFNY
KEYAWA, ANTENMA	22	F	W	GRZZZZPA
ALVA	00	F	INF	GRZZZZPA
LECHASE, JUDA	18	F	SVNT	GRZZZZUSA
EMMA	20	F	SVNT	GRZZZZUSA
MAYERS, A.	20	M	FARMER	GRZZZZNY
BLASE, U	21	F	LDY	GRZZZZNY

SHIP: PERUVIAN

FROM: LIVERPOOL
TO: BALTIMORE
ARRIVED: 21 SEPTEMBER 1888

PASSENGER	AGE	SEX	OCCUPATION	PRVVL	DES
BURPITT, JANUS	55	M	FARMER	GRZZZZUNK
U-MRS	50	F	W	GRZZZZUNK
ANDERSON, CAROLINE	29	F	W	GRZZZZOH
ELSA	2	F	CHILD	GRZZZZOH
AXEL	.09	M	INFANT	GRZZZZOH
ARNDT, AMALIA	28	F	DMS	GRZZZZCH
FRIEDLANDER, BERKO	18	M	BCHR	GRZZZZPIT
WEINER, DAVID	20	M	PNTR	GRZZZZBAL
EPSTEIN, DAVID	20	M	BKBNDR	GRZZZZOMA

SHIP: TRAVE

FROM: BREMEN AND SOUTHAMPTON
TO: NEW YORK
ARRIVED: 21 SEPTEMBER 1888

PASSENGER	AGE	SEX	OCCUPATION	PRVVL	DES
MEITTELHAUESER, ALB.	26	M	MCHT	GRZZZZUSA
JORDAN, OTTILIE	18	F	UNKNOWN	GRZZZZUSA
BECKER, ALB.	21	M	MCHT	GRZZZZUSA
LEIDEN, HANS	32	M	MCHT	GRZZZZUSA
STOCKHOFF, ADELHEID	63	F	UNKNOWN	GRZZZZUSA
OETJEN, J.	40	M	MCHT	GRZZZZUSA
DOEDERLEIN, KAROL.	45	F	UNKNOWN	GRZZZZUSA
BUERGER, LOUISE	46	F	UNKNOWN	GRZZZZUSA
LALSSING, LOUISE	26	F	UNKNOWN	GRZZZZUSA
BLAU, FANNY	40	F	UNKNOWN	GRZZZZUSA
HODT, JOH.	34	F	UNKNOWN	GRZZZZUSA
RIPPE, HEDWIG	32	F	UNKNOWN	GRZZZZUSA
STOCKHOFF, HERM.	36	M	MCHT	GRZZZZUSA
JOH.	31	F	UNKNOWN	GRZZZZUSA
HAUSGEN, LAURA	42	F	UNKNOWN	GRZZZZUSA
CHRIST.	6	M	CHILD	GRZZZZUSA
WEIL, CLARA	29	F	UNKNOWN	GRZZZZUSA
HERBERT	7	M	CHILD	GRZZZZUSA
ELSA	5	F	CHILD	GRZZZZUSA
BUERMEISTER, AUGUSTE	50	F	CH	GRZZZZUSA
ZINSE, AGNES	19	F	CH	GRZZZZUSA
GSIESLER, AGNES	30	F	UNKNOWN	GRZZZZUSA
WEIKMANN, THERESIA	22	F	UNKNOWN	GRZZZZUSA
CARD, JENNY	25	M	MCHT	GRZZZZUSA
LEMLE, JULIUS	26	M	MCHT	GRZZZZUSA
BEST, JACOB	5	M	CHILD	GRZZZZUSA
BRAUNCKHOFF, CLARA	25	F	UNKNOWN	GRZZZZUSA
KOEHLER, ELISAB.	16	F	UNKNOWN	GRZZZZUSA
WOHLTIMANN, MATH.	20	F	UNKNOWN	GRZZZZUSA
HEISSENBUETTEL, CHRIST.	15	F	UNKNOWN	GRZZZZUSA
KALINO, AUGUSTE	15	F	UNKNOWN	GRZZZZUSA
ECKHOFF, KATIE	20	F	UNKNOWN	GRZZZZUSA
EMMA	.10	F	INFANT	GRZZZZUSA
STAUGEL, CHRIST.	20	F	INF	GRZZZZUSA
HOESEL, AUGUSTE	16	F	INF	GRZZZZUSA
RISS, GEORG	25	M	MCHT	GRZZZZUSA
PFALLER, FRANZ	39	M	TLR	GRZZZZUSA
WESEMANN, CARL	63	M	FARMER	GRZZZZUSA
ALB.	28	M	FARMER	GRZZZZUSA
BLANKENBURG, WILH.	26	M	LKSH	GRZZZZUSA
ENGELKE, CARL	27	M	LABR	GRZZZZUSA
STURZEBECKER, HENRIETTE	26	F	UNKNOWN	GRZZZZUSA
AMORT, META	39	F	UNKNOWN	GRZZZZUSA
KATH.	25	F	UNKNOWN	GRZZZZUSA
SCHWAMBERGER, JOH.	22	M	LABR	GRZZZZUSA
HAHN, D.	52	F	UNKNOWN	GRZZZZUSA
ALEX	16	M	UNKNOWN	GRZZZZUSA

PASSENGER	AGE	SEX	OCCUPATION	PRVL	DES
LAURA	7	F	CHILD		GRZZZZUSA
CLARA	5	F	CHILD		GRZZZZUSA
SCHULZE, HEINR.	63	M	LABR		GRZZZZUSA
MARIE	54	F	UNKNOWN		GRZZZZUSA
VOLLTEN, FRIEDR.	28	M	SHMK		GRZZZZUSA
WILH.	25	M	TLR		GRZZZZUSA
WEISE, HEINR.	55	M	LABR		GRZZZZUSA
HERNITSCHEK, PHILIPP	28	M	FARMER		GRZZZZUSA
VANOEPEN, FRANZ	59	M	PVTR		GRZZZZUSA
U	52	F	UNKNOWN		GRZZZZUSA
PAUL	14	M	UNKNOWN		GRZZZZUSA
HELENE	7	F	CHILD		GRZZZZUSA
WILMS, MARG.	31	F	UNKNOWN		GRZZZZUSA
ERNST	7	M	CHILD		GRZZZZUSA
CARL	5	M	CHILD		GRZZZZUSA
PAULA	4	F	CHILD		GRZZZZUSA
GRETCHEN	2	F	CHILD		GRZZZZUSA
STOEVER, MINNA	23	F	CH		GRZZZZUSA
TIETJEN, LUEDER	31	M	LABR		GRZZZZUSA
KOSTERN, LOUISE	22	F	UNKNOWN		GRZZZZUSA
ROHRSSEN, JOH.	28	M	FARMER		GRZZZZUSA
MENCK, HERM.	31	M	PNTR		GRZZZZUSA
RHEIN, CHRIST.	18	M	UNKNOWN		GRZZZZUSA
NASSENBURG, HELENA	19	F	UNKNOWN		GRZZZZUSA
SCHULTZ, HELENE	18	F	UNKNOWN		GRZZZZUSA
DEUTSCH, THERESIA	13	F	UNKNOWN		GRZZZZUSA
BAUMANN, FERD.	19	M	MCHT		GRZZZZUSA
WILL, ELISE	24	F	UNKNOWN		GRZZZZUSA
REICHERT, MARIA	14	F	UNKNOWN		GRZZZZUSA
KUBBERNUSS, FROIEDR.	39	M	FARMER		GRZZZZUSA
WILH.	39	F	UNKNOWN		GRZZZZUSA
BERTHA	15	M	UNKNOWN		GRZZZZUSA
AUGUSTE	12	F	UNKNOWN		GRZZZZUSA
WILHELMINE	7	F	CHILD		GRZZZZUSA
FRIEDA	6	F	CHILD		GRZZZZUSA
CARL	4	M	CHILD		GRZZZZUSA
WILHELM	2	M	CHILD		GRZZZZUSA
FRIEDR.	.04	M	INFANT		GRZZZZUSA
BAUER, SOPHIE	24	F	UNKNOWN		GRZZZZUSA
WIEGERT, CHRIST	62	M	FARMER		GRZZZZUSA
GOELZ, LINA	19	F	UNKNOWN		GRZZZZUSA
PAUL	20	F	UNKNOWN		GRZZZZUSA
BEIETER, CONST.	14	M	LITGR		GRZZZZUSA
BITZER, WILH.	33	M	LABR		GRZZZZUSA
GOETZ, KARL	23	M	TLR		GRZZZZUSA
OTT, ANT.	26	M	FARMER		GRZZZZUSA
SCHMID, WILH.	16	F	UNKNOWN		GRZZZZUSA
BAUER, LOUISE	16	F	UNKNOWN		GRZZZZUSA
MARX, WILH.	21	M	MCHT		GRZZZZUSA
MATHILDE	18	F	UNKNOWN		GRZZZZUSA
MUELLER, MARIE	30	F	UNKNOWN		GRZZZZUSA
JEAN	2	M	CHILD		GRZZZZUSA
WUERTZ, HEINR.	26	M	FARMER		GRZZZZUSA
SCHEITT, JOH.	22	F	UNKNOWN		GRZZZZUSA
LEHI, ELISAB.	19	F	UNKNOWN		GRZZZZUSA
JER, JACOB	28	M	LKSH		GRZZZZUSA
MOELITOR, CHRIST.	20	F	UNKNOWN		GRZZZZUSA
KOEHLER, MARIA	21	F	UNKNOWN		GRZZZZUSA
KAYSER, MARIA	19	F	UNKNOWN		GRZZZZUSA
HADLER, LIZZIE	13	F	UNKNOWN		GRZZZZUSA
ROESENTHAL, SAM.	22	M	MCHT		GRZZZZUSA
BAUMANN, FRIEDR.	5	M	CHILD		GRZZZZUSA
PROBST, FRIED.	17	F	UNKNOWN		GRZZZZUSA
HOECKEL, WILH.	36	M	FARMER		GRZZZZUSA
CAROL.	39	F	UNKNOWN		GRZZZZUSA
MARIE	16	F	UNKNOWN		GRZZZZUSA
SOPHIE	12	F	UNKNOWN		GRZZZZUSA
CAROLINE	7	F	CHILD		GRZZZZUSA
LOUISE	5	F	CHILD		GRZZZZUSA
GOTTWALD, ANNA	25	F	UNKNOWN		GRZZZZUSA
PETERHAMEL, IDA	.03	F	INFANT		GRZZZZUSA
BRAEH, JOH.	30	M	MNR		GRZZZZUSA
RUEF, FANNY	34	F	UNKNOWN		GRZZZZUSA
HENN, AUGUSTE	20	F	UNKNOWN		GRZZZZUSA
BRECHT, JOH.	53	M	FARMER		GRZZZZUSA
HARTMANN, LINA	16	F	CH		GRZZZZUSA
ROEHLER, JOSEPH.	26	F	CH		GRZZZZUSA
SCHOTTLE, ANNA	12	F	CH		GRZZZZUSA
WOLK, ANTONIA	14	F	UNKNOWN		GRZZZZUSA
KESSLER, GEORG	18	M	SHMK		GRZZZZUSA
RAAB, HENRIETTE	22	F	UNKNOWN		GRZZZZUSA
WOLF, ELISAB.	19	F	UNKNOWN		GRZZZZUSA
GOLDNER, HENRIETTE	34	F	UNKNOWN		GRZZZZUSA
SIEGFRIED	2	M	CHILD		GRZZZZUSA
PAULA	3	F	CHILD		GRZZZZUSA
FREITAG, LUDW.	33	M	LABR		GRZZZZUSA
ENGEL, CONR.	30	M	FARMER		GRZZZZUSA
PETER	38	M	FARMER		GRZZZZUSA
ANNA	42	F	UNKNOWN		GRZZZZUSA
HEINR.	14	M	FARMER		GRZZZZUSA
GEORG	7	M	CHILD		GRZZZZUSA
CONRAD	6	M	CHILD		GRZZZZUSA
STEINBACH, DOROTHEA	28	F	UNKNOWN		GRZZZZUSA
WETJEN, META	23	F	UNKNOWN		GRZZZZUSA
LAM, MARG.	30	F	UNKNOWN		GRZZZZUSA
HARRER, KATH.	47	F	UNKNOWN		GRZZZZUSA
FERSCHING, FRANK.	21	F	FARMER		GRZZZZUSA
MAESENZCHE, MAG.	36	F	UNKNOWN		GRZZZZUSA
BAUMEITER, GEORG	19	M	WCHMKR		GRZZZZUSA
WERNER, MARG.	15	F	UNKNOWN		GRZZZZUSA
KREUZ, GERTRUD	24	F	UNKNOWN		GRZZZZUSA
NIECHERMEYER, ANNA	25	F	UNKNOWN		GRZZZZUSA
KLARA	.11	F	INFANT		GRZZZZUSA
ANNA	.01	F	INFANT		GRZZZZUSA
JOH.	16	M	LABR		GRZZZZUSA
HAECKER, KATH.	20	F	UNKNOWN		GRZZZZUSA
PEINEMANN, ANNA	24	F	UNKNOWN		GRZZZZUSA
EMMY	.11	F	INFANT		GRZZZZUSA
STADTMUELLER, AUG.	21	M	BRR		GRZZZZUSA
BAUMSTARK, --INSTEUS	47	M	BRR		GRZZZZUSA
FRIEDERIKE	48	F	BRR		GRZZZZUSA
KERN, EMMA	13	F	UNKNOWN		GRZZZZUSA
SCHOEBEL, ANNA	24	F	UNKNOWN		GRZZZZUSA
SCHWICH, KARL	22	M	JNR		GRZZZZUSA
SCH---, F.W.	57	M	BKLYR		GRZZZZUSA
AUGUSTE	47	F	UNKNOWN		GRZZZZUSA
RICHARD	13	M	UNKNOWN		GRZZZZUSA
ZDERENANY, HULDA	7	F	CHILD		GRZZZZUSA
MATHILDE	5	F	CHILD		GRZZZZUSA
SCHNEIDER, WILH.	6	M	CHILD		GRZZZZUSA
ALMA	5	F	CHILD		GRZZZZUSA
FRIEDA	2	F	CHILD		GRZZZZUSA
GERLACH, E.W.	26	M	FARMER		GRZZZZUSA
SPERL, LOUISE	20	F	UNKNOWN		GRZZZZUSA
BLOCK, DOROTHEA	16	F	UNKNOWN		GRZZZZUSA
HATTERMANN, LINA	22	F	UNKNOWN		GRZZZZUSA
HAASE, MATH.	23	F	UNKNOWN		GRZZZZUSA
EMMA	.11	F	INFANT		GRZZZZUSA
BAUMBACH, JULIE	18	F	INF		GRZZZZUSA
BECKER, ANNA	20	F	INF		GRZZZZUSA
SCHLEEDE, JOH.	15	F	INF		GRZZZZUSA
BELLMER, JOH.	24	M	FARMER		GRZZZZUSA
GOLLBACH, FERD.	25	M	MCHT		GRZZZZUSA
WILHELM, KATH.	16	F	UNKNOWN		GRZZZZUSA
GRELL, JACOB	39	M	FARMER		GRZZZZUSA
KUENDMUELLER, BARB.	20	F	UNKNOWN		GRZZZZUSA
LURZ, KUNIG.	17	F	UNKNOWN		GRZZZZUSA
JOERG, BARB.	30	F	UNKNOWN		GRZZZZUSA
MAHR, FRIEDR.	16	M	FARMER		GRZZZZUSA
-UETZ, BARB.	18	F	UNKNOWN		GRZZZZUSA
KRECKLER, FRED.	21	F	UNKNOWN		GRZZZZUSA
BEHLNER, ADELH.	14	F	UNKNOWN		GRZZZZUSA
KRUG, ANGELA	22	F	UNKNOWN		GRZZZZUSA
ROSINA	17	F	UNKNOWN		GRZZZZUSA
KARL	4	M	CHILD		GRZZZZUSA
FLACH, PETER	24	M	FARMER		GRZZZZUSA
MOEHRKE, OLGA	22	F	UNKNOWN		GRZZZZUSA
ELMA	.06	F	INFANT		GRZZZZUSA
BAAR, MINNA	24	F	INF		GRZZZZUSA
AUGUSTE	18	F	UNKNOWN		GRZZZZUSA

PASSENGER	AGE	SEX	OCCUPATION	PRV VL	DES
ZANG, ALOISIA	20	F	UNKNOWN	GRZZZZ	USA
WENDELKIN, DORA	20	F	UNKNOWN	GRZZZZ	USA
MATH.	18	F	UNKNOWN	GRZZZZ	USA
BETHWIESER, CONRAD	39	M	PNTR	GRZZZZ	USA
DINGWERTH, DIEDRICH	15	M	LABR	GRZZZZ	USA
HAFNER, JACOB	22	M	CPTR	GRZZZZ	USA
MARIA	24	F	UNKNOWN	GRZZZZ	USA
KRIETEMEYER, CHARLOTTE	18	F	UNKNOWN	GRZZZZ	USA
SCHMIDT, GUST.	21	M	FARMER	GRZZZZ	USA
STACH, JOS.	29	M	FARMER	GRZZZZ	USA
VOLLBRACHT, DORIS	16	F	UNKNOWN	GRZZZZ	USA
SCHNAKENBERG, FR.	16	M	LABR	GRZZZZ	USA
FUNKE, ANNA	17	F	UNKNOWN	GRZZZZ	USA
SCHWENTKER, FRITZ	15	M	LABR	GRZZZZ	USA
STALLHORN, AUG.	15	M	LABR	GRZZZZ	USA
SILKMAN, HEINR.	17	M	JNR	GRZZZZ	USA
STOCKHOFF, DIEDR.	32	F	CPTR	GRZZZZ	USA
ANNA	31	F	UNKNOWN	GRZZZZ	USA
MARIE	6	F	CHILD	GRZZZZ	USA
HEINR.	3	M	CHILD	GRZZZZ	USA
BROCKHORST, MARIE	18	F	UNKNOWN	GRZZZZ	USA
KEMUCH, ANNA	17	F	UNKNOWN	GRZZZZ	USA
SCHMIDT, LINA	21	F	UNKNOWN	GRZZZZ	USA
TILLMANN, BERTHA	18	F	UNKNOWN	GRZZZZ	USA
CAULDWELL, LOUISE	58	F	UNKNOWN	GRZZZZ	USA
VOGES, CAROLINE	56	F	UNKNOWN	GRZZZZ	USA
BUCK, JOH.	16	M	BKR	GRZZZZ	USA
LANE, AUGUSTE	21	F	UNKNOWN	GRZZZZ	USA
SEIFERT, EMIL	27	M	MCHT	GRZZZZ	USA
KLUESMEYER, WILH.	16	M	FARMER	GRZZZZ	USA
REICH, ADOLF	25	M	LABR	GRZZZZ	USA
SALINAR, JOH.	16	M	LABR	GRZZZZ	USA
KIES, JOSEPH	30	M	UNKNOWN	GRZZZZ	USA
LAUMANN, AUG.	29	M	TLR	GRZZZZ	USA
HEINTZEL, AGNES	18	F	UNKNOWN	GRZZZZ	USA
MEYER, PAUL	35	M	LABR	GRZZZZ	USA
LEND, ELISE	38	F	UNKNOWN	GRZZZZ	USA
MEYER, CHRIST.	15	M	LABR	GRZZZZ	USA
LAUER, WILH.	61	F	UNKNOWN	GRZZZZ	USA
BECK, LOUISE	22	F	UNKNOWN	GRZZZZ	USA
HOEXTER, FRANZISKA	18	F	UNKNOWN	GRZZZZ	USA
FUCH, ADOLPH	16	M	TLR	GRZZZZ	USA
APEL, HEINR.	23	M	LABR	GRZZZZ	USA
HUEFTLEIN, MICH.	16	M	FARMER	GRZZZZ	USA
GLOCK, FRIEDR.	14	M	LABR	GRZZZZ	USA
BRAEMER, FRIEDR.	17	M	FARMER	GRZZZZ	USA
SOEDER, MONIKA	17	M	FARMER	GRZZZZ	USA
HELDMANN, GEORG	27	M	PNTR	GRZZZZ	USA
RUEBENBAUER, JOSEF	23	M	BRR	GRZZZZ	USA
MAUERER, KATH.	30	F	UNKNOWN	GRZZZZ	USA
LUDW.	7	M	CHILD	GRZZZZ	USA
FANNY	4	F	CHILD	GRZZZZ	USA
OLGA	.11	F	INFANT	GRZZZZ	USA
DAUBENMERKE, FRANZ	34	M	LABR	GRZZZZ	USA
HEINECKE, CAROL.	48	F	UNKNOWN	GRZZZZ	USA
ERNSTBERGER, MICH.	29	M	LABR	GRZZZZ	USA
WENDELKEN, H.	24	M	FARMER	GRZZZZ	USA
KLINGEBERG, D.	39	M	MCHT	GRZZZZ	USA
WITT, FRANZ	37	M	FARMER	GRZZZZ	USA
JOSEPH	37	F	UNKNOWN	GRZZZZ	USA
MARTHA	7	F	CHILD	GRZZZZ	USA
ENDESCHT, CHRISTOPH	34	M	LABR	GRZZZZ	USA
KOCHANSKI, V.	52	M	LABR	GRZZZZ	USA
SCHILLER, PETER	40	M	FARMER	GRZZZZ	USA
PHILIPP.	36	F	UNKNOWN	GRZZZZ	USA
WILHELM	7	M	CHILD	GRZZZZ	USA
GEORG	6	M	CHILD	GRZZZZ	USA
GRETCHEN	4	F	CHILD	GRZZZZ	USA
ALBERT	3	M	CHILD	GRZZZZ	USA
KAISER, HEINR.	21	M	BKR	GRZZZZ	USA
STOEVER, SOPHIA	17	F	UNKNOWN	GRZZZZ	USA
SCHAEFER, CATH.	16	F	UNKNOWN	GRZZZZ	USA
GOTTLEB, PAUL.	20	F	UNKNOWN	GRZZZZ	USA
FELDNER, JETTE	17	F	UNKNOWN	GRZZZZ	USA
NIEDERLUECKE, AUG.	18	M	CPTR	GRZZZZ	USA
WILH.	15	M	CPTR	GRZZZZ	USA
DUSING, GEORG	24	M	FARMER	GRZZZZ	USA
BREITSCHWEILT, ROESLE	17	F	UNKNOWN	GRZZZZ	USA
WOLFF, WILH.	22	M	MCHT	GRZZZZ	USA
HOMANN, LOUISE	20	F	UNKNOWN	GRZZZZ	USA
NOEDING, CAARL	6	F	CHILD	GRZZZZ	USA
SCHLICHTING, OTTO	17	M	MCHT	GRZZZZ	USA
ROSENBOHM, HELENE	21	F	UNKNOWN	GRZZZZ	USA
MUELLER, MARTHA	18	F	UNKNOWN	GRZZZZ	USA
BERGER, ERNST	22	M	LABR	GRZZZZ	USA
MARIA	7	F	CHILD	GRZZZZ	USA
SCHROEDER, PAUL	28	F	UNKNOWN	GRZZZZ	USA
HERMANN, CATH.	21	F	UNKNOWN	GRZZZZ	USA
ABEL, JOH.	49	M	FARMER	GRZZZZ	USA
CATH.	51	F	UNKNOWN	GRZZZZ	USA
GRETCHEN	17	F	UNKNOWN	GRZZZZ	USA
ELISE	25	F	UNKNOWN	GRZZZZ	USA
HATTERMANN, BRUNE	16	M	LABR	GRZZZZ	USA
KLINKER, JOH.	29	M	LABR	GRZZZZ	USA
STADTLAUDER, GEORG	18	M	LABR	GRZZZZ	USA
KRACKE, HEINR.	16	M	LABR	GRZZZZ	USA
NIEBUHR, DIEDR.	31	M	LABR	GRZZZZ	USA
MEYER, JOH.	15	M	LABR	GRZZZZ	USA
WOHLERS, JOH.	24	M	LABR	GRZZZZ	USA
DUENKACK, DORA	16	F	UNKNOWN	GRZZZZ	USA
NIEMEYER, GEERD	16	M	BCHR	GRZZZZ	USA
LUEDECKE, HEINR.	15	M	LABR	GRZZZZ	USA
SCHWARTZ, WILLY	16	M	LABR	GRZZZZ	USA
STAHL, S.	52	M	LABR	GRZZZZ	USA
WILH.	21	F	UNKNOWN	GRZZZZ	USA
STELHJER, MARIE	24	F	W	GRZZZZ	USA
DIEDR.	.01	M	INFANT	GRZZZZ	USA
SCHMIDT, ELISE	21	F	UNKNOWN	GRZZZZ	USA
MADSEN, THOMINE	29	F	UNKNOWN	GRZZZZ	USA
MARTENSEN, THOMAS	18	M	LABR	GRZZZZ	USA
CLAUSSEN, PETER	17	M	LABR	GRZZZZ	USA
WOLF, CHRIST.	20	F	UNKNOWN	GRZZZZ	USA
JOERGENSEN, ANNA	32	F	UNKNOWN	GRZZZZ	USA
MOELLER, CHRIST.	7	F	CHILD	GRZZZZ	USA
LASSEN, METTE	18	F	UNKNOWN	GRZZZZ	USA
SORINE	17	F	UNKNOWN	GRZZZZ	USA
SEIDEL, MARG.	18	F	UNKNOWN	GRZZZZ	USA
HENRIETTE	17	F	UNKNOWN	GRZZZZ	USA
JOH.	27	F	FARMER	GRZZZZ	USA
HOLDT, SIMON	25	M	JNR	GRZZZZ	USA
REINEFELDT, MARIE	23	F	UNKNOWN	GRZZZZ	USA
SCHWIMM, JOH.	33	M	LABR	GRZZZZ	USA
BENNESSEN, C.P.	24	F	UNKNOWN	GRZZZZ	USA
GAUDERUP, HANNE	18	F	UNKNOWN	GRZZZZ	USA
BENNESSEN, ELLE	20	F	UNKNOWN	GRZZZZ	USA
GAUDERUP, CICILIE	18	F	UNKNOWN	GRZZZZ	USA
TIMMERMANN, KRIST.	22	F	UNKNOWN	GRZZZZ	USA
NIELSEN, NIELS	14	M	LABR	GRZZZZ	USA
BROEDERSEN, MARIE	22	F	UNKNOWN	GRZZZZ	USA
BOESSENS, CHR.	6	M	CHILD	GRZZZZ	USA
LAURITZEN, CATH.	18	F	UNKNOWN	GRZZZZ	USA
JEPSEN, LAURITZ	27	M	LABR	GRZZZZ	USA
ANDERSEN, ANDERS	25	M	FARMER	GRZZZZ	USA
KJER, ANNE	16	F	UNKNOWN	GRZZZZ	USA
NIELSEN, LUDW.	17	M	BCHR	GRZZZZ	USA
RUNGE, META	57	F	UNKNOWN	GRZZZZ	USA
SCHAEFER, VALENT.	19	M	LABR	GRZZZZ	USA
STREICH, CARL	25	M	LABR	GRZZZZ	USA
BRODERSEN, FREDER	25	M	LABR	GRZZZZ	USA
FREY, PETER	18	M	LABR	GRZZZZ	USA
STACHOWIAKS, AGNES	50	F	UNKNOWN	GRZZZZ	USA
STOCK, HERMANN	18	F	UNKNOWN	GRZZZZ	USA
TOFT, CARL	6	M	CHILD	GRZZZZ	USA
BECKER, CATH.	38	F	UNKNOWN	GRZZZZ	USA
BERNHARDT, MARIA	17	F	UNKNOWN	GRZZZZ	USA
MARG.	15	F	UNKNOWN	GRZZZZ	USA
DENTZER, JACOB	26	M	UNKNOWN	GRZZZZ	USA
KRIEG, ELISAB.	25	F	UNKNOWN	GRZZZZ	USA
KATH.	19	F	UNKNOWN	GRZZZZ	USA
STEINWEDEL, JOH.	30	M	WCHMKR	GRZZZZ	USA

PASSENGER	AGE	SEX	OCCUPATION	PRVL	DES
MARIE	45	F	UNKNOWN	GRZZZZUSA
FLEISCHMANN, MATH.	7	F	CHILD	GRZZZZUSA
GOTTWALD, JOS.	49	M	MCHT	GRZZZZUSA
ENGELMANN, HEINR.	28	M	MCHT	GRZZZZUSA
RHEIN, MARIA	22	F	UNKNOWN	GRZZZZUSA
ROEHRWEIN, ERNST	26	M	MCHT	GRZZZZUSA
DREYER, LOUIS	23	M	MCHT	GRZZZZUSA
GRAUL, LINA	18	F	UNKNOWN	GRZZZZUSA
CLARA	16	F	UNKNOWN	GRZZZZUSA
WILKEN, HERMANN	21	M	TLR	GRZZZZUSA
HASSBOCHER, JAC	35	M	MCHT	GRZZZZUSA
HARTING, EVA	24	F	UNKNOWN	GRZZZZUSA
KOENNECKE, NINA	22	F	UNKNOWN	GRZZZZUSA
SACHS, JUL.	29	M	MCHT	GRZZZZUSA
CARRERC, CATHARINA	33	F	UNKNOWN	FRZZZZUSA

SHIP: AMALFI

FROM: HAMBURG
TO: NEW YORK
ARRIVED: 22 SEPTEMBER 1888

PASSENGER	AGE	SEX	OCCUPATION	PRVL	DES
JENSEN, PAULA	29	F	WO	PRZZZZNY
ANTON	8	M	CHILD	PRZZZZNY
THEODOR	6	M	CHILD	PRZZZZNY
PAULA	00	F	CH	PRZZZZNY
SOEHL, CHRISTIAN	36	M	FARMER	PRZZZZNY
GLEY, ROBERT	38	M	CTHR	PRZZZZNY
HENRIETTE	39	F	W	PRZZZZNY
KUEHNLE, JACOB	22	M	JNR	WMZZZZCH
HAAGE, MAX	30	M	MCHT	SYZZZZNY
BLUM, MAGIAL	37	F	WO	PRZZZZNY
ALMA	4	F	CHILD	PRZZZZNY
HEICK, MARIE	23	F	SGL	PRZZZZIA
DIPPERN, AUGUSTE	65	F	SGL	PRZZZZIA
SCHMIDT, GEORG	31	M	TCHR	BDZZZZNY
SCHREIBER, CAROLINE	32	F	SGL	PRZZZZNY
MERKLE, PAULINE	22	F	SGL	WMZZZZNY
HUMMEL, PAULINE	22	F	SGL	WMZZZZNY
RUFF, ANNA	15	F	SGL	WMZZZZNY
HALLER, JOHE.	47	M	BRR	WMZZZZNY
JOHS.	14	M	CH	WMZZZZNY
WAGNER, ERNST	41	M	BRR	WMZZZZNY
NISSEN, JOHS.	23	M	FARMER	PRZZZZSTL
ANNA	24	F	W	PRZZZZSTL
KNUTZ, NICOLAI	43	M	FARMER	PRZZZZSTL
FRANKEN	37	F	W	PRZZZZSTL
ANDREAS	14	M	CH	PRZZZZSTL
GEORG	7	M	CHILD	PRZZZZSTL
U	6	M	CHILD	PRZZZZSTL
NICOLAI	4	M	CHILD	PRZZZZSTL
WILHELM	2	M	CHILD	PRZZZZSTL
ANNA	.06	F	INFANT	PRZZZZSTL
NISSEN, HANNDSEN	7	F	CHILD	PRZZZZSTL
LEESE, EMMA	19	F	SGL	PRZZZZNY
WILHELMINE	17	F	SGL	PRZZZZNY
LELAZNO, ELSBIETA	48	F	WO	PRZZZZNY
MARIANE	25	F	WO	PRZZZZNY
CASIMIR	7	F	CHILD	PRZZZZNY
CATHARINA	3	F	CHILD	PRZZZZNY
ZELAZNO, STANISLAUS	.11	M	INFANT	PRZZZZNY
MATOKAJASTE, KATHA.	17	F	SGL	PRZZZZNY
HOLST, ANNA	7	F	CHILD	PRZZZZNY
WILHELM	3	M	CHILD	PRZZZZNY
JOERGENSEN, HANSINE	39	F	WO	PRZZZZNY
JOERGINE	7	F	CHILD	PRZZZZNY
CHRISTINE	6	F	CHILD	PRZZZZNY
RASMUS	5	M	CHILD	PRZZZZNY
JOERGEN	4	M	CHILD	PRZZZZNY
MADSEN	3	M	CHILD	PRZZZZNY

PASSENGER	AGE	SEX	OCCUPATION	PRVL	DES
LINE	2	F	CHILD	PRZZZZNY
CARL	.02	M	INFANT	PRZZZZNY
JACOBSEN, MAREN	22	F	SGL	PRZZZZNY
EISFELD, FRANZISKA	43	F	WO	PRZZZZNY
MARIE	4	F	CHILD	PRZZZZNY
ZIMMERMANN, BESSI	40	F	WO	PRZZZZNY
RIWKE	20	F	CH	PRZZZZNY
NOCHEM	18	F	CH	PRZZZZNY
HENE	16	F	CH	PRZZZZNY
FRUME	7	F	CHILD	PRZZZZNY
DWORE	6	F	CHILD	PRZZZZNY
SCHUETT, HELENE	3	F	CHILD	PRZZZZNY
HOLST, AGATHE	59	F	WO	PRZZZZNY
HEINRICH	5	M	CHILD	PRZZZZNY
HANNEMAN, FRANZ	32	M	FARMER	PRZZZZCH
LEHMANN, EMIL	36	M	LABR	PRZZZZNY
ELS, MARIE	22	F	SGL	PRZZZZNY
EMMA	21	F	SGL	PRZZZZNY
MEIER, CARL	26	M	SLR	PRZZZZNY
ELISABETH	20	F	SGL	PRZZZZNY
POSTEL, EMIL	24	M	BCK	PRZZZZCH
KRAPF, EMILIE	22	F	SGL	SYZZZZNY
GROLLMA--, FERDINAND	22	M	FARMER	PRZZZZKS
SCHEPPE, JULIUS	26	M	MCHT	PRZZZZNY
PIESKER, HERMANN	37	M	JNR	PRZZZZNY
BAYER, EDWIN	18	M	MD	PRZZZZNY
ECK, U	34	M	JNR	PRZZZZNY
USTER, OTTO	32	M	JNR	PRZZZZNY

SHIP: DEVONIA

FROM: GLASGOW
TO: NEW YORK
ARRIVED: 24 SEPTEMBER 1888

PASSENGER	AGE	SEX	OCCUPATION	PRVL	DES
DAHL, ERNST-M.	55	M	GDNR	GRZZZZUSA
KASINSKA, REGINA	26	F	NN	GRZZZZUSA
AUGUSTA	4	F	CHILD	GRZZZZUSA
EMIL	.03	M	INFANT	GRZZZZUSA
LIPKA, JULIA	24	F	NN	GRZZZZUSA
WILHELM	.09	M	INFANT	GRZZZZUSA
MULLER, CARL	52	M	CPTR	GRZZZZUSA
WITT, FRITZ	27	M	CPTR	GRZZZZUSA
CHRISTOFFERSEN, CHRIS.	20	M	MCHT	GRZZZZUSA
JENSEN, ANNE-E.	26	F	SVNT	GRZZZZUSA

SHIP: ETRURIA

FROM: LIVERPOOL AND QUEENSTOWN
TO: NEW YORK
ARRIVED: 24 SEPTEMBER 1888

PASSENGER	AGE	SEX	OCCUPATION	PRVL	DES
BRISIAC, SALOMI	20	F	SVNT	GRADBQUSA
BLUMENTHAL, NATHANIEL	34	M	MCHT	GRADBQUSA
HERNAND, DUPORT	34	M	SEC	GRADBQUSA
RENAULT, EDOUARD	30	M	MCHT	GRADBQUSA
PICK, U	50	M	DR	GRADBQUSA
BOWNARDOT, ANNETTE	32	F	SVNT	GRADBQUSA
LIMBURGER, ANTHY	59	M	BNKR	GRADBQUSA
LORSH, ALBERT	42	M	MCHT	GRZZZZUSA
GITTERMANN, HENRY	53	M	MCHT	GRADBQUSA
ELLINGEN, LOUIS	38	M	MCHT	GRADBQUSA
CAYREL, MARIE	23	F	SP	GRADBQUSA
PETIT, ISABEL	35	F	SVNT	GRADBQUSA
STERNBACH, CHARLES	58	M	MCHT	GRADBQUSA

PASSENGER	AGE	SEX	OCCUPATION	PRVVL	DES
AURRAID, OCTORRE	24	F	SVNT		GRADBQUSA
MEYSENBURG, THEODORE	48	M	MNFTR		GRADBQUSA
LERRY, GREFFITH	20	M	STDNT		GRADBQUSA
REINHOLD, FRITZ	24	M	MCHT		GRZZZZUSA
JOHNSON, LOUISE	21	F	SVNT		GRADBQUSA
KUNTZ, CAROLINE	25	F	SVNT		GRADBQUSA
SCHALUS, WILLIAM	67	M	MCHT		GRADBQUSA
BOURJOLLY, ARTHYR	40	M	UNKNOWN		GRADBQUSA
WENSKOFF, EMILY	20	F	SVNT		GRADBQUSA
ZUBRANS, HORTENSE	19	F	SVNT		GRADBQUSA
DEMUTH, WILLIAM	53	M	MCHT		GRADBQUSA
HARRIET	48	F	W		GRADBQUSA
EDGER	16	M	CH		GRADBQUSA
AIMES	4	M	CHILD		GRADBQUSA
GOLDMAN, MARCUS	66	M	BKR		GRADBQUSA
BERTHA	59	F	W		GRADBQUSA
LEVY, MARK	49	M	MCHT		GRADBQUSA
ABRAM	47	M	MCHT		GRADBQUSA
GODE, HERMAN	36	M	MCHT		GRADBQUSA
GARIADOR, LEO.	28	M	MNSTR		GRADBQUSA
GARRITY, THOMAS	37	M	MCHT		FRZZZZUSA

SHIP: REPUBLIC

FROM: LIVERPOOL
TO: NEW YORK
ARRIVED: 24 SEPTEMBER 1888

PASSENGER	AGE	SEX	OCCUPATION	PRVVL	DES
KOLANSKI, ONKACS	30	M	LABR		GRZZZZUSA
BLOBHAVE, ANTON	37	M	LABR		GRZZZZUSA
LEWIN, CLARA	20	F	SVNT		GRZZZZUSA
MORITZ	22	M	LABR		GRZZZZUSA
HANN-, ABRAHAM	22	M	LABR		GRZZZZUSA
WOSMAH, ALBERT	22	M	LABR		GRZZZZUSA
BLOCH, ROSA	19	F	SVNT		GRZZZZUSA
TOBIAS, ALBR.	17	M	LABR		GRZZZZUSA
HANDMAN, HESSELE	29	M	LABR		GRZZZZUSA
TAILOR, ADAM	21	M	LABR		GRZZZZUSA
THESENGER, LEOPOLD	28	M	LABR		GRZZZZUSA
KASSER, MARTIN	30	M	LABR		GRZZZZUSA
KOGOSOWSKI, MORDEKE	29	M	LABR		GRZZZZUSA
PANKEWITZ, ALEX	18	M	LABR		GRZZZZUSA
RAFFORD, ARON	24	M	LABR		GRZZZZUSA

SHIP: AMERICA

FROM: BREMEN
TO: BALTIMORE
ARRIVED: 25 SEPTEMBER 1888

PASSENGER	AGE	SEX	OCCUPATION	PRVVL	DES
SEMMER, CHRISTINE	25	F	UNKNOWN		GRZZZZMD
BETZ, EMILIE	25	F	UNKNOWN		GRZZZZMD
HELBIG, AGNES	38	F	UNKNOWN		GRZZZZMD
VONBOECKMANN, ARTHUR	34	M	MCHT		GRZZZZMD
WILHELMINE	26	F	UNKNOWN		GRZZZZMD
ARTHUR	9	M	CHILD		GRZZZZMD
ANNA	4	F	CHILD		GRZZZZMD
KURT	4	M	CHILD		GRZZZZMD
BRANDT, ROSINE	24	F	UNKNOWN		GRZZZZOH
ALOIS	.09	M	INFANT		GRZZZZOH
ZALINKA, ANNA	31	F	UNKNOWN		GRZZZZVA
BEIGEL, ALOIS	15	M	CH		GRZZZZOH
ZANDER, FRIEDRICH	31	M	TNR		GRZZZZNE
STYBANIEWICZ, PETER	26	M	UNKNOWN		GRZZZZNE
KOSEIELMARK, MARGARETHE	16	F	UNKNOWN		GRZZZZOH

PASSENGER	AGE	SEX	OCCUPATION	PRVVL	DES
PAEZY, AUGUSTE	30	F	UNKNOWN		GRZZZZMO
ANNA	6	F	CHILD		GRZZZZMO
CARL	5	M	CHILD		GRZZZZMO
FRANZ	3	M	CHILD		GRZZZZMO
AUGUSTE	.01	F	INFANT		GRZZZZMO
KUEHN, JULIUS	13	M	UNKNOWN		GRZZZZOR
TROFAN, CAROLINE	61	F	UNKNOWN		GRZZZZWI
ILMA, ANNA	22	F	UNKNOWN		GRZZZZTN
KLANN, CARL	32	M	MNR		GRZZZZIN
ELISABETH	32	F	UNKNOWN		GRZZZZIN
KONRAD	4	M	CHILD		GRZZZZIN
EWALD, ULRIKE	47	F	UNKNOWN		GRZZZZDAK
BUTOW, HULDA	36	F	UNKNOWN		GRZZZZKS
MARTHA	4	F	CHILD		GRZZZZKS
BALKE, OLGA	24	F	UNKNOWN		GRZZZZKS
HEDWIG	4	F	CHILD		GRZZZZKS
HENKEN, JOSEPH	63	M	FARMER		GRZZZZMN
BOPP, MARGARETHE	19	F	SVNT		GRZZZZNE
SCHMIDT, FRANZ	25	M	FARMER		GRZZZZNE
KIZYJATHOWSKI, JULIUS	33	M	SHFM		GRZZZZDAK
ANNA	27	F	UNKNOWN		GRZZZZDAK
CLARA	4	F	CHILD		GRZZZZDAK
VICTOR	3	M	CHILD		GRZZZZDAK
ANNA	2	F	CHILD		GRZZZZDAK
AGNES	.06	F	INFANT		GRZZZZDAK
LESNAR, CAECILIE	19	F	SVNT		GRZZZZDAK
RUCINSHA, CATHARINA	55	F	UNKNOWN		GRZZZZMI
SCHWIATBOWSKA, ANNA	27	F	SVNT		GRZZZZMI
SCHMIDTKE, FRIEDRICH	52	M	FARMER		GRZZZZIL
FLORENTINE	56	F	UNKNOWN		GRZZZZIL
SCHULZ, CARL	25	M	SDLR		GRZZZZIL
NEUBERT, CAROLINE	56	F	UNKNOWN		GRZZZZIL
SCHRAMKE, FRIEDRICH	24	M	BKLYR		GRZZZZNE
FIDDA, MICHAEL	25	M	LABR		GRZZZZNE
HOERNSCHEMEYER, BERNHAR	14	M	UNKNOWN		GRZZZZOH
LEHMANN, BABETTA	24	F	SVNT		SRZZZZCAL
TUNBERT, LINA	20	F	UNKNOWN		GRZZZZPA
FUNK, BARBARA	22	F	UNKNOWN		GRZZZZOH
KUHNHEIM, JOHANN	14	M	UNKNOWN		GRZZZZOH
CASPARS, JOHANN	28	M	FARMER		GRZZZZOH
VONHOLDT, MARGARETHE-WI	26	F	UNKNOWN		GRZZZZIL
VONHOLDT, JULIUS	15	M	UNKNOWN		GRZZZZIL
HERMANN	11	M	CH		GRZZZZIL
KUNZE, ANNA	29	F	SVNT		GRZZZZIA
SCHMIDT, EUGEN	15	M	UNKNOWN		GRZZZZIA
ALTSCHT, GOTTFRIED	66	M	FARMER		GRZZZZIA
ZERBERICH, AUGUST	31	M	LABR		GRZZZZIL
ELISE	35	F	UNKNOWN		GRZZZZIL
KOCH, FRIEDRICH	24	M	MUSN		GRZZZZIL
STRIBICH, FRIDOLIN	42	M	TU		GRZZZZIL
HEIDELMANN, ELEONORE	28	F	UNKNOWN		GRZZZZDAK
PAWLOWSKA, PELAGIA	34	F	UNKNOWN		GRZZZZOH
ANTON	8	M	CHILD		GRZZZZOH
STANISLAUS	3	M	CHILD		GRZZZZOH
FRANZISZEK, CATHARINA	28	F	UNKNOWN		GRZZZZOH
JOSEFA	5	F	CHILD		GRZZZZOH
FRANZESCA	3	F	CHILD		GRZZZZOH
KAISER, MARIE	22	F	SVNT		SRZZZZCAL
CAROLINA	20	F	SVNT		SRZZZZCAL
WEIMANN, REGINA	26	F	UNKNOWN		GRZZZZKY
ROSA	.09	F	INFANT		GRZZZZKY
WIERSPECKA, WILHELM	22	M	FARMER		GRZZZZKY
HORSTMEIER, HENRIETTE	40	F	UNKNOWN		GRZZZZKY
RICHARD	10	M	CH		GRZZZZKY
PFEIFFER, BENEDICT	17	M	LABR		GRZZZZNE
SORECH, FRANCESCA	32	F	UNKNOWN		GRZZZZNE
ANDREAS	5	M	CHILD		GRZZZZNE
DOROTHEA	.09	F	INFANT		GRZZZZNE
STANIG, FRIEDRICH	46	M	BCHR		GRZZZZIL
MARIA	47	F	UNKNOWN		GRZZZZIL
ERNST	10	M	UNKNOWN		GRZZZZIL
HEDWIG	6	F	CHILD		GRZZZZIL
EDUARD	4	M	CHILD		GRZZZZIL
KORN, DOROTHEA	33	F	UNKNOWN		GRZZZZKS
CARL	10	M	CH		GRZZZZKS

PASSENGER	AGE	SEX	OCCUPATION	PVRIVL	DES	PASSENGER	AGE	SEX	OCCUPATION	PVRIVL	DES
THEODOR	5	M	CHILD	GRZZZZKS		MUELLER, FLORENTINE	49	F	UNKNOWN	GRZZZZCAL	
JULIUS	4	M	CHILD	GRZZZZKS		GESSNER, MARTHA	27	F	UNKNOWN	GRZZZZMD	
AUGUSTE	4	F	CHILD	GRZZZZKS		GEORG	5	M	CHILD	GRZZZZMD	
RUDOLF	3	M	CHILD	GRZZZZKS		PAPKE, MATHILDE	40	F	UNKNOWN	GRZZZZMD	
EMMA	2	F	CHILD	GRZZZZKS		OTTO	9	M	CHILD	GRZZZZMD	
FRIEDA	.03	F	INFANT	GRZZZZKS		PAUL	3	M	CHILD	GRZZZZMD	
ORZKOWSKI, JULIAN	24	M	FARMER	GRZZZZIL		MUELLER, META	20	F	UNKNOWN	GRZZZZOH	
SPLETTER, OTTILIE	19	F	SVNT	GRZZZZIL		MICHALSK, JOSEFA	34	M	UNKNOWN	GRZZZZOH	
KAHNKE, ROZALIE	29	F	SVNT	GRZZZZIL		BOGAZ, STANISLAWA	29	M	UNKNOWN	GRZZZZOH	
SKIRIEREZ, LOUISE	36	F	UNKNOWN	GRZZZZNE		MARIANNA	.09	F	INFANT	GRZZZZOH	
AUGUSTE	17	F	UNKNOWN	GRZZZZNE		STANICHEFSKI, VICTORIA	50	F	UNKNOWN	GRZZZZKS	
AUGUST	12	M	CH	GRZZZZNE		ANTON	11	M	CH	GRZZZZKS	
ALBERT	7	M	CHILD	GRZZZZNE		BYMAROWIECZ, ANNASTAZIA	27	F	UNKNOWN	GRZZZZPA	
ANDREAS	5	M	CHILD	GRZZZZNE		KARASIEWIECZ, FRANZ	19	M	TLR	GRZZZZPA	
ELISE	2	F	CHILD	GRZZZZNE		PICHOROWSKY, ANTON	44	M	LABR	GRZZZZPA	
JOHANNA	.11	F	INFANT	GRZZZZNE		JANKOWSKA, JOSEFA	26	F	SVNT	GRZZZZIL	
WITHOFFER, LINA	22	F	SVNT	GRZZZZWI		FISCHER, ANNA	43	F	UNKNOWN	GRZZZZIL	
FRIESELMANN, HEINRICH	9	M	CHILD	GRZZZZWI		ANNA	16	F	UNKNOWN	GRZZZZIL	
LOLBACH, HEINRICH	48	M	ENGR	GRZZZZDAK		MICHAEL	14	M	UNKNOWN	GRZZZZIL	
FRANZISCA	49	F	UNKNOWN	GRZZZZDAK		MASE	8	M	CHILD	GRZZZZIL	
ELEONORE	18	F	UNKNOWN	GRZZZZDAK		PINDACK, JOSEF	25	M	FARMER	GRZZZZOH	
FRIEDRICH	16	M	UNKNOWN	GRZZZZDAK		LAMMERT, FRANZ	56	M	LABR	GRZZZZIL	
SCHROEDER, LOUISE	25	F	UNKNOWN	GRZZZZDAK		JOHANN	17	M	LABR	GRZZZZIL	
KASTENS, ELISA	16	F	UNKNOWN	GRZZZZMN		MARIA	11	F	CH	GRZZZZIL	
RIPPE, FRIEDRICH	56	M	FARMER	GRZZZZTX		JOHANNE	6	F	CHILD	GRZZZZIL	
DOROTHEA	46	F	UNKNOWN	GRZZZZTX		HEIL, JOHANNE	18	F	SVNT	GRZZZZMD	
ANNA	17	F	UNKNOWN	GRZZZZTX		MEYER, CHRISTIAN	37	M	FARMER	GRZZZZCAL	
HERMANN	13	M	UNKNOWN	GRZZZZTX		ELSABEIN, CATHARINA	36	F	UNKNOWN	GRZZZZOH	
DOROTHEA	8	F	CHILD	GRZZZZTX		FLORENTINE	10	F	CH	GRZZZZOH	
HESPE, MARIE	13	F	CH	GRZZZZIL		HEINRICH	6	M	CHILD	GRZZZZOH	
WILHELM	11	M	CH	GRZZZZIL		CARL	3	M	CHILD	GRZZZZOH	
SCHMIDT, BABETTE	41	F	UNKNOWN	GRZZZZIL		AUGUSTE	.06	F	INFANT	GRZZZZOH	
KOESTER, LOUISE	21	F	SVNT	GRZZZZNE		MARIE	67	F	UNKNOWN	GRZZZZOH	
WILHELMINE	16	F	SVNT	GRZZZZNE		OSSENSCHMIDT, GOTTLIEB	35	M	FARMER	GRZZZZKY	
MEYER, WILHELM	50	M	FARMER	GRZZZZIN		CHARLOTTE	30	F	UNKNOWN	GRZZZZKY	
MARIE	47	F	UNKNOWN	GRZZZZIN		WILHELM	15	M	CH	GRZZZZKY	
MARIE	14	F	UNKNOWN	GRZZZZIN		BECKER, LUDWIG	18	M	FARMER	GRZZZZOH	
HEINRICH	10	M	CH	GRZZZZIN		UFFELMANN, WILHELM	24	M	BCHR	GRZZZZIL	
WILHELM	4	M	CHILD	GRZZZZIN		SCHMIDT, WALLY	30	F	UNKNOWN	GRZZZZOH	
ZOCKLEIN, CATHARINA	47	F	UNKNOWN	GRZZZZWI		KAETHIE	9	F	CHILD	GRZZZZOH	
PFAFF, SABINA	16	F	UNKNOWN	GRZZZZIL		MARIECHEN	7	F	CHILD	GRZZZZOH	
CILICHOWSKA, JOSEFA	26	F	UNKNOWN	GRZZZZIL		PAUL	4	M	CHILD	GRZZZZOH	
CONSTANTIN	2	M	CHILD	GRZZZZIL		EDMEIER, MICHAEL	32	M	BRR	GRZZZZMN	
PETER	3	M	CHILD	GRZZZZIL		BUSCHKE, ANNA	22	F	SVNT	GRZZZZMN	
JACOB	.06	M	INFANT	GRZZZZIL		LANGE, AGNES	18	F	SVNT	GRZZZZMN	
MJKA, MARIANNA	34	F	UNKNOWN	GRZZZZWI		LARMANN, STEPHAN	19	M	JNR	GRZZZZOH	
CATHARINA	9	F	CHILD	GRZZZZWI		FLURMA, GEORG	16	M	UNKNOWN	GRZZZZOH	
JOSEPH	6	M	CHILD	GRZZZZWI		HAEFER, MARGARETHE	19	F	SVNT	GRZZZZOH	
ANTONI	1	M	CHILD	GRZZZZWI		ZEITMEIER, JOSEF	22	M	FARMER	GRZZZZCOL	
ODENWALD, ROSA	28	F	UNKNOWN	GRZZZZOH		HINZE, WILHELM	33	M	CPTR	GRZZZZTX	
ANNA	4	F	CHILD	GRZZZZOH		AUGUSTE	36	F	UNKNOWN	GRZZZZTX	
WENIG, IDA	40	F	UNKNOWN	GRZZZZOH		FRIEDRICH	8	M	CHILD	GRZZZZTX	
SCHRAGE, FRIEDRICH	24	M	UNKNOWN	GRZZZZIL		HERMANN	4	M	CHILD	GRZZZZTX	
PAPENHAU--, FRIEDRICH	15	M	UNKNOWN	GRZZZZIL		GUENTHER, EMMA	16	F	SVNT	GRZZZZTX	
THEN, MICHAEL	22	M	BRR	GRZZZZPA		STAEFTING, HEINRICH	22	M	LABR	GRZZZZIL	
ZOECKLEIN, PHILIPP	11	M	CH	GRZZZZPA		WALTERS, JOHANN	26	M	LABR	GRZZZZIL	
OTTO	9	M	CHILD	GRZZZZPA		FABER, AUGUSTE	43	F	UNKNOWN	GRZZZZIL	
LEO	7	M	CHILD	GRZZZZPA		ALEXANDER	17	M	UNKNOWN	GRZZZZIL	
GRAUE, HEINRICH	57	M	FARMER	GRZZZZOH		EWERT, MARTHA	26	F	UNKNOWN	GRZZZZIL	
CATHARINA	54	F	UNKNOWN	GRZZZZOH		HANNES	4	M	CHILD	GRZZZZIL	
DINA	26	F	UNKNOWN	GRZZZZOH		CHARLOTTE	2	F	CHILD	GRZZZZIL	
FRANZ	24	M	FARMER	GRZZZZOH		CATHARINA	.06	F	INFANT	GRZZZZIL	
MINNA	22	F	UNKNOWN	GRZZZZOH		ABRANDT, CATHARINA	22	F	SVNT	GRZZZZIL	
LISETTE	20	F	UNKNOWN	GRZZZZOH		BRENNEKE, HEINRICH	10	M	CH	GRZZZZOH	
CATHARINA	17	F	UNKNOWN	GRZZZZOH		CARL	8	M	CHILD	GRZZZZOH	
HERMANN	16	M	UNKNOWN	GRZZZZOH		ERNST	6	M	CHILD	GRZZZZOH	
MAELMANN, HEINRICH	29	M	JNR	GRZZZZOH		MICHEL, CHRISTIANNE	40	F	UNKNOWN	GRZZZZOH	
OSTMANN, JOSEFINA	23	F	SVNT	GRZZZZOH		HERMANN	18	M	LABR	GRZZZZOH	
OSSENBECK, FRANZ	41	M	BCK	GRZZZZKS		ANNA	14	F	UNKNOWN	GRZZZZOH	
MUESER, BERNHARD	28	M	MCHT	GRZZZZKS		GUSTAV	11	M	CH	GRZZZZOH	
BASEMEYER, FRIEDRICH	23	M	FARMER	GRZZZZMN		CARL	10	M	CH	GRZZZZOH	
HAEPER, DOROTHEA	21	F	UNKNOWN	GRZZZZIL		SCHWECKENBACH, EMILIE	21	F	SVNT	GRZZZZIL	
GRUNDLING, ANNA	52	F	UNKNOWN	GRZZZZMN		LAUTAN, HANS	45	M	FARMER	GRZZZZKS	
FRIEDERIKE	21	F	UNKNOWN	GRZZZZMN		IDA	44	F	UNKNOWN	GRZZZZKS	
SCHUMANN, OTTO	10	M	CH	GRZZZZMN		THEODOR	18	M	FARMER	GRZZZZKS	

PASSENGER	AGE	SEX	OCCUPATION	PRVL	DES
CLARA	16	F	UNKNOWN		GRZZZZKS
ROBERT	4	M	CHILD		GRZZZZKS
FISBECK, FRIEDRICH	16	M	UNKNOWN		GRZZZZOH
SOPHIE	23	F	UNKNOWN		GRZZZZOH
RUDOLF	60	M	FARMER		GRZZZZOH
WILHELMINE	60	F	UNKNOWN		GRZZZZOH
ELISE	21	F	UNKNOWN		GRZZZZOH
SOPHIE	.11	F	INFANT		GRZZZZOH
KONE, DINA	20	F	SVNT		GRZZZZOH
LEHMANN, ERNST	32	M	ENGR		GRZZZZIN
FRIEDRICH, GUSTAV	31	M	WVR		GRZZZZIN
KAEMENA, HEINRICH	53	M	FARMER		GRZZZZOR
BECKE	57	F	UNKNOWN		GRZZZZOR
HEINRICH	23	M	FARMER		GRZZZZOR
DIEDRICH	16	M	UNKNOWN		GRZZZZOR
GRAEMLICH, LORENZ	54	M	FARMER		GRZZZZOH
URSULA	48	F	UNKNOWN		GRZZZZOH
CARL	15	M	UNKNOWN		GRZZZZOH
BERTHA	12	F	UNKNOWN		GRZZZZOH
GUSTAV	10	M	UNKNOWN		GRZZZZOH
EMMA	6	F	CHILD		GRZZZZOH
ANNA	2	F	CHILD		GRZZZZOH
WALTER, FRIEDRIKE	18	F	UNKNOWN		GRZZZZOH
GRIESEL, FRIEDRICH	43	M	FARMER		GRZZZZOH
CATHARINA	33	F	UNKNOWN		GRZZZZOH
ADAM	15	M	UNKNOWN		GRZZZZOH
CARL	11	M	CH		GRZZZZOH
KAETCHEN	9	F	CHILD		GRZZZZOH
FRIEDRICH	8	M	CHILD		GRZZZZOH
MILLER, MARGARETHE	65	F	UNKNOWN		GRZZZZMD
HEISIG, JOSEF	50	M	FARMER		GRZZZZMN
ERNESTINE	30	F	UNKNOWN		GRZZZZMN
ZOLINKA, JOHANN	4	M	CHILD		GRZZZZVA
WLADISLAW	3	M	CHILD		GRZZZZVA
BANGERL, JOSEF	22	M	UNKNOWN		GRZZZZIL
MILLER, CATHARINA	33	F	UNKNOWN		GRZZZZOH
CATHARINA	31	F	UNKNOWN		GRZZZZOH
GOTTLIEB	4	M	CHILD		GRZZZZOH
CRECRENCENZIA	1	F	CHILD		GRZZZZOH
WAGNER, JOSEF	35	M	UNKNOWN		GRZZZZOH
ZOLINKA, ALBANIA	.03	F	INFANT		GRZZZZVA

SHIP: EGYPT

FROM: LIVERPOOL
TO: NEW YORK
ARRIVED: 25 SEPTEMBER 1888

PASSENGER	AGE	SEX	OCCUPATION	PRVL	DES
LINDELL, JOHAN	30	M	LABR		GRZZZZUSA
DESETH, JOHAN	22	M	LABR		GRZZZZUSA
BUGOWOSKI, L.	19	M	LABR		GRZZZZUSA
GESELLA, JOS.	19	M	LABR		GRZZZZUSA
SCHUMACHER, K.	52	M	LABR		GRZZZZUSA
LAATREBER, S.	24	M	LABR		GRZZZZUSA
ROTH, JOSEPH	24	M	LABR		GRZZZZUSA
FRIEDMAN, MARCUS	28	M	LABR		GRZZZZUSA
CARLSON, S.	27	M	LABR		GRZZZZUSA
PETROURSKY, J.	35	M	LABR		GRZZZZUSA
M.	34	F	W		GRZZZZUSA
G.	00	M	INF		GRZZZZUSA
ANDERS	40	M	LABR		GRZZZZUSA
SOFIE	14	F	CH		GRZZZZUSA
FRANZ	11	M	CH		GRZZZZUSA
S.	5	M	CHILD		GRZZZZUSA
A.	00	M	INF		GRZZZZUSA
KARUTZ, ANNA	16	F	SP		GRZZZZUSA
PETROURSKY, VICTOR	32	M	LABR		GRZZZZUSA
ELENOR	23	F	W		GRZZZZUSA
VICTOR	00	M	INF		GRZZZZUSA
MONDSEHEIN, J.	35	M	LABR		GRZZZZUSA

PASSENGER	AGE	SEX	OCCUPATION	PRVL	DES
M.	7	M	CHILD		GRZZZZUSA
DANIEL	4	M	CHILD		GRZZZZUSA
ZANKEL	00	M	INF		GRZZZZUSA
EREKSON, H.	32	M	LABR		GRZZZZUSA
EMILE	9	F	CHILD		GRZZZZUSA
LINGMAN, ANNA	21	F	SP		GRZZZZUSA
ERICK	11	M	CH		GRZZZZUSA
CHRISTIAN	9	M	CHILD		GRZZZZUSA
ANN	5	F	CHILD		GRZZZZUSA
M.	00	F	INF		GRZZZZUSA
BEY, ANNA	16	F	SP		GRZZZZUSA
ASELAN, C.	39	M	LABR		GRZZZZUSA
D.	17	M	LABR		GRZZZZUSA
LARE	9	M	CHILD		GRZZZZUSA
MARIA	00	F	INF		GRZZZZUSA
LERNER, FANKEL	21	M	LABR		GRZZZZUSA
B.	19	F	W		GRZZZZUSA
SAMUEL	00	M	INF		GRZZZZUSA

SHIP: ELBE

FROM: BREMEN AND SOUTHAMPTON
TO: NEW YORK
ARRIVED: 25 SEPTEMBER 1888

PASSENGER	AGE	SEX	OCCUPATION	PRVL	DES
ROTHE, IDA	17	F	TT		GRACBRNY
BACHMANN, KONRAD	41	M	TT		GRAAHUNY
MEYER, LOUIS	16	M	TT		GRAARRNY
MUENCH, HUGO	16	M	TT		GRAARRNY
WANGNER, LUISE	46	F	TT		GRAEHGNY
WEISSENHORN, MATHILDE	18	F	TT		GRAFDKNY
SCHMALZ, SUSANNE	30	F	TT		GRAFDKNY
SEIBERT, MARTHA	35	F	TT		GRAABYNY
FINK, MINNIE	21	F	TT		GRAARRNY
SEIBERT, MARTHA	2	F	CHILD		GRAABYNY
ELEONORE	4	F	CHILD		GRAABYNY
SCHWAN, FRIEDR.	25	M	TT		GRZZZZNY
U, U	25	M	TT		GRZZZZNY
ZIESMER, CORNEL.	31	M	TT		GRZZZZNY
NUESCH, JOKOB	26	M	TT		GRAAKJNY
MANN, BERTHA	21	F	TT		GRAFABNY
SCHIFFER, HERMINE	29	F	TT		GRZZZZNY
FOERSTER, CHARLES	58	M	TT		GRADIJNY
BICKEL, FRANZ	21	M	TT		GRADIJNY
FLOER, ELISE	23	F	S		GRACPENY
WOLF, MARIE	27	F	S		GRADKWNY
KOCK, MARIE	22	F	S		GRADKWNY
WIEDAN, WILHELME.	20	F	S		GRADKWNY
NIEHAUS, JOSEPHE.	23	F	S		GRADKWNY
LOER, THERESIA	23	F	S		GRADKWNY
SCHLANTINAN, ANNA	22	F	S		GRADKWNY
JUNGESBLUT, AUGUSTE	23	F	S		GRADKWNY
BORGMANN, ELISABETH	22	F	S		GRADKWNY
KREMER, ELISABETH	19	F	S		GRADKWNY
GOEKS, MARTHA	23	F	UNKNOWN		GRAAKHNY
TONY	21	M	UNKNOWN		GRAAKHNY
BOEHM, HEDWIG	24	F	TT		GRAAKHNY
SEIBERT, FRITZ	24	M	TT		GRADLDNY
BABETTA	21	F	TT		GRADLDNY
MUENZING, FRITZ	11	M	UNKNOWN		GRZZZZNY
GEORG	10	M	CH		GRZZZZNY
BLOHM, HEINR.	47	M	TT		GRZZZZNY
KUESEL, U	23	F	TT		GRAARRNY
COHEN, U	36	M	TT		GRZZZZNY
GOETZ, BERTHA	40	F	UNKNOWN		GRZZZZNY
UCHLEIN, IDA	12	F	UNKNOWN		GRZZZZNY
HEIGEL, CARL	11	M	UNKNOWN		GRZZZZNY
FUCHS, AGATHE	23	F	UNKNOWN		GRADKJNY
ZANT, JOH.	27	M	FARMER		GRABTRNY
HORSCH, MICHAEL	16	M	UNKNOWN		GRABTRNY

PASSENGER	AGE	SEX	OCCUPATION	PRVL DES
BOCKELMANN, MINNIE	18	F	UNKNOWN	GRACZVNY
FROST, CARL	54	M	UNKNOWN	GRZZZZNY
FRIEDKE.	54	M	UNKNOWN	GRZZZZNY
GIERSCH, FRANZ	61	M	UNKNOWN	GRZZZZNY
CAROLINE	53	F	UNKNOWN	GRZZZZNY
DANKENBRINK, DOROTHEA	30	F	UNKNOWN	GRZZZZNY
WILH.	8	M	CHILD	GRZZZZNY
DOROTHEA	4	F	CHILD	GRZZZZNY
AUG.	.11	M	INFANT	GRZZZZNY
IMHOF, MICHAEL	16	M	UNKNOWN	GRZZZZNY
KONICZNA, MARIANNE	24	F	UNKNOWN	GRZZZZNY
BURLINSKA, VERONIKA	31	F	UNKNOWN	GRZZZZNY
KAPALENSKA, ROSALIE	19	F	UNKNOWN	GRZZZZNY
BURLINSKA, POLONIA	8	F	CHILD	GRZZZZNY
IGNATZ	6	M	CHILD	GRZZZZNY
SALOMAEA	2	F	CHILD	GRZZZZNY
JACOB	.09	M	INFANT	GRZZZZNY
SCHEITINGER, JOS.	27	M	FARMER	GRZZZZNY
MARGA.	32	F	UNKNOWN	GRZZZZNY
MARGA.	.09	F	INFANT	GRZZZZNY
OBERLE, FRANZ	50	M	MCHT	GRZZZZNY
V. MINNA	14	F	UNKNOWN	GRADXCNY
DESCH, JOST	22	M	CPR	GRZZZZNY
HEINR.	11	M	UNKNOWN	GRZZZZNY
CARL	9	M	CHILD	GRZZZZNY
PAULINE	7	F	CHILD	GRZZZZNY
MROSZKOWSKI, SIMON	42	M	UNKNOWN	GRAISTUSA
SCHMIDT, MARIE	24	F	UNKNOWN	GRZZZZUSA
RUEHR, JOH.	22	M	LABR	GRZZZZUSA
SCHMIDT, RUD.	2	M	CHILD	GRZZZZUSA
EMMA	.09	F	INFANT	GRZZZZUSA
ECKERT, CARL	34	M	LABR	GRAFBVUSA
HUENER, JOHA.	16	F	UNKNOWN	GRZZZZUSA
VOGT, LINA	62	F	UNKNOWN	GRACBRUSA
WOHLTMANN, ANNA	17	F	UNKNOWN	GRABZVUSA
PLATZ, REBECCA	24	F	UNKNOWN	GRABZVUSA
TREBE, CHR.	23	M	UNKNOWN	GRABZVUSA
BUECHLE, FRANZISKA	43	F	UNKNOWN	GRZZZZUSA
REGER, BALBE.	18	F	UNKNOWN	GRZZZZUSA
WAGNER, LEONHARD	17	M	LABR	GRZZZZUSA
KNAPP, CHRISTE.	16	F	UNKNOWN	GRAEXWUSA
SATTLER, JOHS.	21	M	UNKNOWN	GRZZZZUSA
THEURER, CARL	18	M	SDLR	GRAFRPUSA
HAUG, ANNA	18	F	UNKNOWN	GRAFRPUSA
WACHENDORFER, ANNA	18	F	UNKNOWN	GRAFRPUSA
GUBERAN, LOUISE	18	F	UNKNOWN	GRZZZZUSA
BLIND, JOHS.	16	M	LABR	GRAFKJUSA
HOHN, LOUISE	16	F	UNKNOWN	GRAFKJUSA
HAUSER, CATHA.	16	F	UNKNOWN	GRAFKJUSA
SCHNEIDER, MARIE	18	F	UNKNOWN	GRAFKJUSA
SCHNURBUSCH, FERD.	58	M	LABR	GRZZZZUSA
ELIZAB.	18	F	UNKNOWN	GRZZZZUSA
LUTZ, DOROTHEA	52	F	UNKNOWN	GRZZZZUSA
BOLZ, HEINR.	17	M	LABR	GRAARRUSA
ZAHN, CATHA.	16	F	UNKNOWN	GRZZZZUSA
SPOWZEL, BARBARA	19	F	UNKNOWN	GRZZZZUSA
DILG, HEINR.	23	M	LABR	GRZZZZUSA
HOFFMANN, JOH.	23	M	LABR	GRZZZZUSA
KELTSCH, CHR.	23	M	LABR	GRZZZZUSA
ALLES, HERM.	24	M	FARMER	GRABVAUSA
BOHRMANN, MART.	18	M	FARMER	GRABVAUSA
DENK, HEINRICH	26	M	UNKNOWN	GRZZZZUSA
STENGER, AGNES	22	F	UNKNOWN	GRZZZZUSA
BECKER, ADAM	18	M	JNR	GRZZZZUSA
RAAB, APOLLINA	34	F	UNKNOWN	GRAJBXUSA
BECKER, ELISAB.	23	F	UNKNOWN	GRAJBXUSA
STEINBRECHER, ANTON	17	M	LABR	GRAJBXUSA
GARTENHOF, ANNA	27	F	UNKNOWN	GRAJBXUSA
SAUER, PAULINA	24	F	UNKNOWN	GRABZBUSA
HERMINE	14	F	UNKNOWN	GRABZBUSA
HILLE, ELISE	15	F	UNKNOWN	GRAEQAUSA
GOEBBER, WILHELM	16	M	LABR	GRAEQAUSA
KOCH, GOTTLOB	23	M	UNKNOWN	GRZZZZUSA
WOLLBOLDT, KAROLE.	28	F	UNKNOWN	GRZZZZUSA
SELKE, KAROLINA	60	F	UNKNOWN	GRZZZZUSA
SUSANNE	26	F	UNKNOWN	GRAFTUUSA
MAJEWSKY, AUGUSTE	22	F	UNKNOWN	GRAFTUUSA
SKSYNECKA, CEVILIA	22	F	UNKNOWN	GRAFTUUSA
MEILER, GEORG	23	M	TLR	GRZZZZUSA
MARGA.	22	F	UNKNOWN	GRZZZZUSA
ZUERN, MICHAL	40	M	LABR	GRAFRGUSA
NAUMANN, MARTHA	18	F	UNKNOWN	GRAFRGUSA
DEMUTH, EMMA	26	F	UNKNOWN	GRZZZZUSA
REBECCA	3	F	CHILD	GRZZZZUSA
FRITZ	2	M	CHILD	GRZZZZUSA
SELMA	1	F	CHILD	GRZZZZUSA
BRACKMANN, HENRIETTE	34	F	UNKNOWN	GRAJKWUSA
EMMA	10	F	CH	GRAJKWUSA
WILHELM	7	M	CHILD	GRAJKWUSA
CARL	4	M	CHILD	GRAJKWUSA
ADELE	.11	F	INFANT	GRAJKWUSA
TISCHLAUTER, JOH.	26	M	FARMER	GRABBVUSA
MARIE	26	F	UNKNOWN	GRABBVUSA
OTTO	4	M	CHILD	GRABBVUSA
STEINERLING, ELISAB.	39	F	UNKNOWN	GRZZZZUSA
HENKEN, MARIE	21	F	UNKNOWN	GRZZZZUSA
SCHICKEL, MARGA.	29	F	UNKNOWN	GRZZZZNY
STEINIGER, CAROLINE	21	F	UNKNOWN	GRZZZZNY
KOEHNKE, MATHILDE	19	F	UNKNOWN	GRAAKHNY
GAETJENSS, HEINRICH	16	M	LABR	GRZZZZNY
HEUSER, ADOLF	14	M	LABR	GRZZZZNY
GAETJENS, HANS	16	M	LABR	GRZZZZNY
BENDER, MAX	17	M	LABR	GRZZZZNY
ZIMMERMANN, HIEMKE	56	M	UNKNOWN	GRZZZZNY
HELMERICHS, RICKLEF	45	M	UNKNOWN	GRZZZZNY
ANNA	42	F	UNKNOWN	GRZZZZNY
FRIEDR.	13	M	UNKNOWN	GRZZZZNY
ANNA	11	F	UNKNOWN	GRZZZZNY
JETTE	3	F	CHILD	GRZZZZNY
JOH.	.06	M	INFANT	GRZZZZNY
CURTH, LOUIS	22	M	LABR	GRACHANY
KOEMPEL, BARBA.	24	F	UNKNOWN	GRZZZZNY
DOUCKE, MINNIE	52	F	UNKNOWN	GRZZZZNY
HULDA	30	F	UNKNOWN	GRZZZZNY
GUST.	28	M	UNKNOWN	GRZZZZNY
MAERTZKE, CARL	26	M	LABR	GRZZZZMO
AUG.	47	M	LABR	GRZZZZMO
DOMKE, --ULIE	22	F	UNKNOWN	GRZZZZMO
FERD.	16	M	LABR	GRZZZZMO
BERTHA	11	F	UNKNOWN	GRZZZZMO
STAHLMANN, IDA	22	F	UNKNOWN	GRZZZZMO
HOFFMANN, IDA	18	F	UNKNOWN	GRZZZZIL
BRANDT, HEINRICH	26	M	LABR	GRAFBSIA
STROBEL, JOH.	22	M	LABR	GRAFBSPA
WIESNER, ANNA	24	F	UNKNOWN	GRZZZZPA
GOETZ, JOEF	18	M	LABR	GRZZZZPA
BEHRENS, BETTY	36	F	UNKNOWN	GRZZZZNY
PAULINA	11	F	UNKNOWN	GRZZZZNY
MAUSER, ERNST	19	M	FARMER	GRZZZZNY
ALBERTA.	19	F	UNKNOWN	GRZZZZNY
DICKJOST, JOH.	14	M	UNKNOWN	GRZZZZNY
OFFERJEST, FRITZ	23	M	BKLYR	GRZZZZNY
HEINR.	19	M	LABR	GRZZZZNY
KUHLMANN, CHRIST.	25	M	LABR	GRAAORNY
KAUFMANN, CHR.	27	M	LABR	GRAAORNY
BACHMANN, EUGENIE	27	M	LABR	GRAAORNY
OEHLER, KATHA.	17	F	UNKNOWN	GRZZZZNY
WILHELM	14	M	UNKNOWN	GRZZZZNY
SCHWEINLEIN, JOH.	25	M	CGRMKR	GRZZZZNY
GRAEBNBER, CHR.	25	M	BCHR	GRZZZZNY
LAMBRECHT, WILH.	30	M	UNKNOWN	GRZZZZNY
AHRENS, JOH.	28	M	BRR	GRZZZZNY
ELISAB.	24	F	UNKNOWN	GRZZZZNY
BETJA	2	F	CHILD	GRZZZZNY
MARGA.	.10	F	INFANT	GRZZZZNY
SAUTER, ANDREAS	55	M	UNKNOWN	GRAAACNY
BISSINGER, MATHILDE	36	F	UNKNOWN	GRAAACNY
ADELHEID	16	F	UNKNOWN	GRAAACNY
RODE, FRIEDRIKE	70	F	UNKNOWN	GRAAACNY
HAEGELE, PAULINE	20	F	UNKNOWN	GRAAACNY

PASSENGER	AGE	SEX	OCCUPATION	PRIVL	DES
HAEMMERLE, PAULINE	19	F	UNKNOWN	GRAAACNY	
BUNDSCHUH, WILHELMINE	16	F	UNKNOWN	GRAAACNY	
WICKE, JOS.	36	M	UNKNOWN	GRAAACNY	
JUNG, PHL.	48	M	MCHT	GRZZZZNY	
VOLLSTAEDT, FRANZ	24	M	UNKNOWN	GRZZZZNY	
LANGENBACH, FRANZ	53	M	UNKNOWN	GRZZZZNY	
KILLER, FRIEDR.	19	M	PNTR	GRZZZZNY	
GRAEFE, AUGUSTE	59	F	UNKNOWN	GRADFSNY	
BUSSINGER, ANNA	20	F	UNKNOWN	GRAAKHMI	
ZIEGENHAGEN, AUG.	22	M	MCHT	GRAAKHWI	
RICHTER, ERNST.	24	M	BKBNDR	GRAAKHNY	
HOFFMANN, BERNH.	24	M	CGRMKR	GRAAKHNY	
PAUL	30	M	SMH	GRAAKHNY	
ELISE	31	F	UNKNOWN	GRAAKHNY	
RITZ, MARIE	39	F	UNKNOWN	GRABUSNY	
SPECK, ELISAB.	31	F	UNKNOWN	GRABUSNY	
FRITZ, REINHD.	26	M	FARMER	GRAHBJNY	
MERKEL, HAVER	26	M	FARMER	GRAHBJNY	
HAAS, LOUISE	18	F	UNKNOWN	GRAHBJNY	
WUNSCH, CAECILIE	19	F	UNKNOWN	GRAHBJNY	
KRAEMER, MARIE	19	F	UNKNOWN	GRAHBJNY	
HAUSOTTE, ROB.	26	M	UNKNOWN	GRADFSNY	
WALTER, ANNA	22	F	UNKNOWN	GRZZZZNY	
LECHNER, MICH.	30	M	LABR	GRZZZZNY	
ELISABETH	26	F	UNKNOWN	GRZZZZNY	
MARIE	6	F	CHILD	GRZZZZNY	
JOH.	5	M	CHILD	GRZZZZNY	
LEONH.	4	M	CHILD	GRZZZZNY	
HANS	2	M	CHILD	GRZZZZNY	
MARGA.	.06	F	INFANT	GRZZZZNY	
ECKART, GEORG	31	M	LABR	GRZZZZNY	
MARGA.	30	F	UNKNOWN	GRZZZZNY	
GEORG	11	M	UNKNOWN	GRZZZZNY	
MARGOR, ELISABETH	5	F	CHILD	GRZZZZNY	
JOH.	3	M	CHILD	GRZZZZNY	
ELISAB.	.11	F	INFANT	GRZZZZNY	
HILLMANN, DIEDR.	24	M	LABR	GRACBRNY	
HERMANN, CATHA.	18	F	UNKNOWN	GRACBRNY	
PULSCH, REBEKA	15	F	UNKNOWN	GRACBRNY	
FEDDER, HELENE	29	F	UNKNOWN	GRZZZZNY	
KOLTZSCH, R.C.	11	M	UNKNOWN	GRADZONY	
KAUFHOLD, MARIE	30	F	UNKNOWN	GRABLTNY	
LINA	27	F	UNKNOWN	GRABLTNY	
HANS	9	M	CHILD	GRABLTNY	
EISMEYER, MARIE	21	F	UNKNOWN	GRABLTNY	
MILDENBERG, IDA	22	F	UNKNOWN	GRABLTNY	
SCHROEDER, PETER	16	M	LABR	GRZZZZNY	
PODRAZ, REGA.	14	F	UNKNOWN	GRZZZZNY	
SCHOLP, EUGEN	21	M	LABR	GRZZZZNY	
MAHNGOLD, MATHILDE	28	F	LABR	GRZZZZNY	
WILLINGHORST, WILH.	16	M	LABR	GRACBRNY	
KORMANN, HEINR.	16	M	LABR	GRACBRNY	
WAIZENEGGER, HELENE	20	F	UNKNOWN	GRAECDNY	
KRUG, GEORG	15	M	LABR	GRAECDNY	
STAPF, GEORG	20	M	LABR	GRAECDNY	
LAURENZ, DORA	24	F	UNKNOWN	GRACBRNY	
GRABAN, ADELHEID	29	F	UNKNOWN	GRACBRNY	
GESINE	5	F	CHILD	GRACBRNY	
STELLINS, ANNA	30	F	UNKNOWN	GRACBRNY	
FRIEDR.	6	M	CHILD	GRACBRNY	
HILPERT, LOUISE	36	F	UNKNOWN	GRACXHNY	
LOUISE	10	F	CH	GRACXHNY	
LUCIE	.07	F	INFANT	GRACXHNY	
HUEFTLE, PAULINE	16	F	UNKNOWN	GRAAWNNY	
TELL, WILHELM	36	M	UNKNOWN	GRAAKHNY	
MEINERS, WILHELM	27	M	UNKNOWN	GRAEZVNY	
WUNDER, MARTIN	39	M	UNKNOWN	GRAEZVNY	
WAHLERS, SOPHIE	26	F	UNKNOWN	GRABNMNY	
HAEGER, GEORG	31	M	LABR	GRABHHNY	
LANGAS, MARTIN	36	M	FARMER	GRZZZZNY	
PAULS, HELENE	25	F	UNKNOWN	GRZZZZNY	
WOLTMANN, H.C.	14	M	UNKNOWN	GRAARRNY	
PAVLIK, JOSEF	24	M	FARMER	GRAARRNY	
SCHMIDT, MARIE	18	F	UNKNOWN	GRZZZZNY	
KAMPS, THELA	26	F	UNKNOWN	GRZZZZNY	
WILKEN, BEREND	19	M	SEMN	GRABIYNY	
LAUTERER, MINNA	23	F	UNKNOWN	GRAARRNY	
SOBWATZKY, IGNATZ	26	M	LABR	GRAEWZNY	
KOLOZIEJEWSKA, PETRONEL	42	F	UNKNOWN	GRZZZZNY	
KOLOZIEJEWSKA, VLADISLA	9	F	CHILD	GRZZZZNY	
STASKIEWICZ, STANISL.	23	F	CH	GRZZZZNY	
THOMAS	3	M	CHILD	GRZZZZNY	
STANISLAUS	.09	F	INFANT	GRZZZZNY	

SHIP: WISCONSIN

FROM: LIVERPOOL AND QUEENSTOWN
TO: NEW YORK
ARRIVED: 25 SEPTEMBER 1888

PASSENGER	AGE	SEX	OCCUPATION	PRIVL	DES
FLEISCHMAN, JANKEL	36	M	TLR	GRZZZZUSA	
IDES	30	F	W	GRZZZZUSA	
ITZIG	6	M	CHILD	GRZZZZUSA	
U	3	F	CHILD	GRZZZZUSA	
ABRAM	.08	M	INFANT	GRZZZZUSA	
LANGMAN, ROBT.	31	M	PNTR	GRZZZZUSA	
SCHOLZ, WM.	41	M	PNTR	GRZZZZUSA	
GRIMBERG, ISAAC	30	M	PNTR	GRZZZZUSA	
SOCHLA, JOHAN	38	M	PNTR	GRZZZZUSA	
KUZMAR, FERDN.	32	M	PNTR	GRZZZZUSA	
OCHS, CONRAD	25	M	PNTR	GRZZZZUSA	
LANGENER, FLORENCE	30	F	SP	GRZZZZUSA	
MARGUARET, WM.	30	M	FARMER	GRZZZZUSA	
SCHEICHER, JOHAN	24	M	PMBR	GRZZZZUSA	
JOSEPH	20	M	PMBR	GRZZZZUSA	
BROCKE, ALFD.	23	M	PNTR	GRZZZZUSA	
CLARIA	20	F	W	GRZZZZUSA	
KAUFMAN, HENN	19	M	GZR	GRZZZZUSA	
MOHR, MARK	36	M	CPTR	GRZZZZUSA	
WITOSCH, ANTONIE	33	F	W	GRZZZZUSA	
LIETZ, FRANTZ	7	M	CHILD	GRZZZZUSA	
ALMENDINGER, FRIED	28	M	GZR	GRZZZZUSA	
KATH.	26	F	W	GRZZZZUSA	
FRIDA	2	F	CHILD	GRZZZZUSA	
REICHMAN, JOHAN	16	M	TLR	GRZZZZUSA	
MEIERHOFER, VERENA	58	F	MA	GRZZZZUSA	
ERNIE, KATH.	19	F	MA	GRZZZZUSA	
SIEGENTHALER, ROSE	28	F	MA	GRZZZZUSA	
SCHWIDLER, FRIED	27	M	TLR	GRZZZZUSA	
EGLI, NICHOLAUS	55	M	PMBR	GRZZZZUSA	
ANNA	55	F	W	GRZZZZUSA	
FRITZ	32	M	PMBR	GRZZZZUSA	
JOHAN	29	M	PMBR	GRZZZZUSA	
SINA	7	F	CHILD	GRZZZZUSA	
ROSA	7	F	CHILD	GRZZZZUSA	
BOSS, EMMA	18	F	SP	GRZZZZUSA	
RICHART, FRIED.	30	M	LABR	GRZZZZUSA	
SCHAINCK, JACOB	36	M	LABR	GRZZZZUSA	
VANLANWEN, HERMINE	28	F	W	GRZZZZUSA	
JOHANNA	4	F	CHILD	GRZZZZUSA	
ELSOBINA	2	F	CHILD	GRZZZZUSA	
MARIA	7	F	CHILD	GRZZZZUSA	
GERARDUS	.08	M	INFANT	GRZZZZUSA	
VIERTEL, WILHELA.	48	F	W	GRZZZZUSA	
HELENA	7	F	CHILD	GRZZZZUSA	
RICHD.	7	M	CHILD	GRZZZZUSA	
IBY, A.N.	28	M	GENT	GRZZZZGR	
MULLER, LEWIS	33	M	GENT	GRZZZZGR	

349

```
                    A S          P V  D
PASSENGER           G E OCCUPATION R I  E
                    E X          V L  S
```

SHIP: STATE OF NEBRASKA

FROM: GLASGOW AND LARNE
TO: NEW YORK
ARRIVED: 26 SEPTEMBER 1888

PASSENGER	AGE	SEX	OCCUPATION	PRVL	DES
HRUSCHKA, JOSEF	25	M	STDNT	GRAHRZUSA	
GAEGER, MARIA	24	F	SP	GRAHRZUSA	

SHIP: SCHIEDAM

FROM: AMSTERDAM
TO: NEW YORK
ARRIVED: 27 SEPTEMBER 1888

PASSENGER	AGE	SEX	OCCUPATION	PRVL	DES
SCHAUBELE, LUDWIG	27	M	MLW	GRZZZZUSA	
SEUBERT, CATH.	23	F	SVNT	GRZZZZUSA	
LANZ, CHR.GOTTL.	22	M	LABR	GRZZZZUSA	
ELLWANGER, LOUISE	8	F	CHILD	GRZZZZUSA	
RUHLE, PAULINE	18	F	SVNT	GRZZZZUSA	
ANNA	5	F	CHILD	GRZZZZUSA	
FREITAG, ALBERT	16	M	TLR	GRZZZZUSA	
HAUSMANN, ELISABETH	29	F	SVNT	GRZZZZUSA	
MOFFEL, PETER	26	M	SVNT	GRZZZZUSA	
MUCHA, J.	20	M	TLR	GRZZZZUSA	
NAWRODSKI, W.	22	M	SMH	GRZZZZUSA	
BESE, HANS	24	M	LABR	GRZZZZUSA	
OTT, GEORG	37	M	MCHT	GRZZZZUSA	
SEXANER, GOTTLIEB	16	M	BBR	GRZZZZUSA	
EHRHARDT, CARL	21	M	BRR	GRZZZZUSA	
SPOERRI, ANNA	20	F	SVNT	GRZZZZUSA	
HEITZMAN, MAGD.	25	F	SVNT	GRZZZZUSA	
SHERY, EUGEN	24	M	BKR	GRZZZZUSA	
OERHLE, MARIA	15	F	SVNT	GRZZZZUSA	
HOFFMANN, FRED	38	M	PVTM	GRZZZZUSA	
LOUISE	38	F	PVTW	GRZZZZUSA	
RAMSTEDT, W.	15	M	PVTM	GRZZZZUSA	
SCHUSSELE, OTTO	25	M	BBR	GRZZZZUSA	
F.	9	M	CHILD	GRZZZZUSA	
KLECK, C.L.	50	M	UNKNOWN	GRZZZZUSA	
RUBGE, SIEGBERT	16	M	MCHT	GRZZZZUSA	
ROHLFING, HEINRICH	34	M	CGRMKR	GRZZZZUSA	
BUCHERER, A.	25	M	STDNT	GRZZZZUSA	
GRASENACK, M.	28	M	PVTM	GRZZZZUSA	
HUGENTOBLER, A.	35	F	UNKNOWN	GRZZZZUSA	
AUG.	4	M	CHILD	GRZZZZUSA	
PAUL	2	M	CHILD	GRZZZZUSA	
SCHONFELD, CLARA	24	F	PVTW	GRZZZZUSA	
FLEISCHMAN, LAURA	38	F	UNKNOWN	GRZZZZUSA	
U	1	F	CHILD	GRZZZZUSA	
CHARLEZ	7	M	CHILD	GRZZZZUSA	
BAY, JOSEPH	49	M	PVTM	FRZZZZUSA	
BARNKLAN, W.	25	F	PVTW	FRZZZZUSA	
REUFMANN, PAUL	31	M	MCHT	FRZZZZUSA	

SHIP: LAHN

FROM: BREMEN AND SOUTHAMPTON
TO: NEW YORK
ARRIVED: 28 SEPTEMBER 1888

PASSENGER	AGE	SEX	OCCUPATION	PRVL	DES
HEUERMANN, CHARLOTTE	17	F	UNKNOWN	FRAAKHGR	
HERTZ, WILHE.	50	F	W	FRABEHGR	
MORGENSTERN, R.	40	M	TT	FRABOQGR	

PASSENGER	AGE	SEX	OCCUPATION	PRVL	DES
DREIFUSS, CAROLE.	21	F	UNKNOWN	GRZZZZGR	
HOLLAENDER, HEINR.	16	M	TT	GRZZZZGR	
ARENS, MARIE	28	F	UNKNOWN	GRADNUGR	
BUTTJER, HERM.	56	M	UNKNOWN	GRACXDGR	
MEYER, HERM.	53	M	UNKNOWN	GRACXDGR	
BORGMANN, THEODOR	59	M	TT	GRAIMSGR	
ANGELICA	54	F	W	GRAIMSGR	
DEDDO	17	M	UNKNOWN	GRAIMSGR	
HEINTZ, JOHANN	60	M	TT	GRADKKGR	
ROSENBAUM, CLARA	25	F	UNKNOWN	GRZZZZGR	
KOHN, JULIE	16	F	UNKNOWN	GRAECDGR	
JOSEPH, EMIL	15	M	TT	GRACMDGR	
LANDAU, SIEGFRD.	26	M	TT	GRAAKHGR	
SPIES, MARIA	29	F	UNKNOWN	GRAAKHGR	
SCHELTER, CHRISTA.	18	F	UNKNOWN	GRZZZZUSA	
TIEFENBACHER, CAROLE.	23	F	UNKNOWN	GRAEVIUSA	
SCHLEEHAUF, AUG.	15	M	UNKNOWN	GRAEVIUSA	
HECKERATH, JACOB	23	M	LABR	GRAFNKUSA	
MANNEL, LOUISE	18	F	UNKNOWN	GRZZZZUSA	
WILHELMI, FRIEDR.	17	M	FARMER	GRZZZZUSA	
KUECHENMEISTER, CHRIST.	19	M	LABR	GRZZZZUSA	
KLEPPICH, MARIE	18	F	W	GRZZZZUSA	
BEYER, CAROLA.	17	F	UNKNOWN	GRZZZZUSA	
MARX, EMIL	21	M	LABR	GRZZZZUSA	
HUSCH, ALFRED	14	M	UNKNOWN	GRABDMUSA	
ROECKER, FRANZ	25	M	LABR	GRZZZZUSA	
SEMPF, MARGA.	18	F	UNKNOWN	GRACIJUSA	
RETTKE, AUGE.	30	F	UNKNOWN	GRAAKHUSA	
DILLER, MARIA	18	F	UNKNOWN	GRAAHPUSA	
FESENFELD, ADELHE.	16	F	UNKNOWN	GRAARRUSA	
STEIN, JUDA	16	F	UNKNOWN	GRADKIUSA	
KUCK, GESINE	23	F	UNKNOWN	GRZZZZUSA	
SCHNAKENBERG, META	16	F	UNKNOWN	GRZZZZUSA	
FRIEMEL, MARIE	26	F	UNKNOWN	GRZZZZUSA	
WELLENSIECK, HERM.	16	M	UNKNOWN	GRADIJUSA	
HARTH, ANNA	37	F	UNKNOWN	GRZZZZUSA	
FISCHER, HEINR.	10	M	CH	GRZZZZUSA	
HARTH, JOHANN	30	M	FARMER	GRZZZZUSA	
HELDBERG, HEINR.	44	M	FARMER	GRACMQUSA	
DOROTHEA	39	F	W	GRACMQUSA	
FRIEDA	11	F	CH	GRACMQUSA	
ANNA	9	F	CHILD	GRACMQUSA	
HELENE	6	F	CHILD	GRACMQUSA	
DOROTHEA	3	F	CHILD	GRACMQUSA	
LOEWENSTEIN, SALOMON	68	M	LABR	GRAEXFUSA	
MATHILDE	52	F	W	GRAEXFUSA	
ELLA	16	F	UNKNOWN	GRAEXFUSA	
WAAKHUSEN, HERMINE	14	F	UNKNOWN	GRAJSUUSA	
BENCKEN, MARGE.	18	F	UNKNOWN	GRAHTJUSA	
HANKEN, CATHA.	16	F	UNKNOWN	GRZZZZUSA	
BUSCH, AUGE.	22	F	UNKNOWN	GRACBRUSA	
SCHAPER, BETTY	15	F	UNKNOWN	GRACXHUSA	
ETJEN, MARY	18	F	UNKNOWN	GRACXHUSA	
RUESKHARD, CHRIST.	18	M	LABR	GRZZZZUSA	
ECKHARDT, JAC.	17	M	TLR	GRABLMUSA	
FRANK, MORITZ	14	M	UNKNOWN	GRZZZZUSA	
HIEFNER, ELISE	16	F	UNKNOWN	GRZZZZUSA	
STROBEL, PAULINE	14	F	UNKNOWN	GRZZZZUSA	
BACHMANN, MARIE	21	F	UNKNOWN	GRZZZZUSA	
STICH, JOSEFE	18	F	UNKNOWN	GRZZZZUSA	
HEIDEMANN, FRIEDR.	16	M	UNKNOWN	GRZZZZUSA	
SIEGMANN, WILHELM	20	M	JNR	GRABOQUSA	
VOGT, MATHILDE	26	F	UNKNOWN	GRABOQUSA	
BINA	18	F	UNKNOWN	GRABOQUSA	
BERGDOLD, KAETCHEN	32	F	UNKNOWN	GRAGKIUSA	
HETTLING, CLAMOR	17	M	SHMK	GRABKHUSA	
HAMBURGER, ELISAB.	20	F	UNKNOWN	GRZZZZUSA	
MAERKLIN, MICH.	15	M	UNKNOWN	GRZZZZUSA	
STEGER, THERESE	27	F	UNKNOWN	GRAHIQUSA	
SCHOELLER, URSULA	25	F	W	GRAHIQUSA	
ANNA	2	F	CHILD	GRAHIQUSA	
BAUSCH, ADAM	21	M	FARMER	GRAEVTUSA	
ZIMMERMANN, ANNA	30	F	W	GRZZZZUSA	
CATHA.	10	F	CH	GRZZZZUSA	
MARIE	7	F	CHILD	GRZZZZUSA	

PASSENGER	AGE	SEX	OCCUPATION	PRVL	DES
BARBA.	4	F	CHILD	GRZZZZUSA
ANNA	3	F	CHILD	GRZZZZUSA
CHRISTN.	2	M	CHILD	GRZZZZUSA
ENGELMANN, GASCHE	60	M	LABR	GRZZZZUSA
SCHROEDER, FRITZ	15	M	UNKNOWN	GRZZZZUSA
KLINGMANN, SOPHIE	18	F	UNKNOWN	GRZZZZUSA
TRUNK, MICHAEL	17	M	FARMER	GRZZZZUSA
ADRIAN, JOCOB	46	M	LABR	GRZZZZUSA
BABETTE	27	F	W	GRZZZZUSA
SCHAEFER, CHRISTE.	11	F	CH	GRZZZZUSA
STENGEL, CHRIST.	22	M	MCHT	GRZZZZUSA
ZAPP, JULIUS	16	M	UNKNOWN	GRZZZZUSA
HEIDEL, WILHELM	14	M	UNKNOWN	GRABOKUSA
ROTH, MARIE	22	F	UNKNOWN	GRAEMLUSA
HEINZE, MARGE.	32	F	W	GRABOQUSA
ALBERT	8	M	CHILD	GRABOQUSA
DORA	4	F	CHILD	GRABOQUSA
HEINR.	2	M	CHILD	GRABOQUSA
ERNST	.02	M	INFANT	GRABOQUSA
REAROD, REGE.	24	F	UNKNOWN	GRACSAUSA
SCHAEFER, EVA	20	F	UNKNOWN	GRZZZZUSA
MUENCH, MARIE	21	F	UNKNOWN	GRZZZZUSA
RUEHL, MICHEL	26	M	LABR	GRACSAUSA
REGINE	27	F	W	GRACSAUSA
HEUSER, MARGE.	20	F	UNKNOWN	GRZZZZUSA
MUENCH, ANNA	15	F	UNKNOWN	GRZZZZUSA
LOEW, ALBERT	17	M	MCHT	GRZZZZUSA
PECH, TEOFILA	22	F	W	GRAEABUSA
THEODORE	.01	F	INFANT	GRAEABUSA
SCHLUEFER, ANNA	17	F	UNKNOWN	GRZZZZUSA
IDA	11	F	CH	GRZZZZUSA
STIER, EUGEN	15	M	UNKNOWN	GRAEXWUSA
LEUCKHARDT, ROSINA	64	F	W	GRZZZZUSA
LUTZ, GEORG	40	M	LABR	GRZZZZUSA
MARIA	30	F	W	GRZZZZUSA
MUENZ, JOHANN	16	M	UNKNOWN	GRZZZZUSA
KUCHN, GOTTLOB	21	M	FARMER	GRAKPGUSA
ROLL, MARGE.	14	F	UNKNOWN	GRZZZZUSA
OELSCHLAGER, CHRISTE.	19	F	UNKNOWN	GRADOLUSA
BLAICH, MATTHAEUS	31	M	FARMER	GRZZZZUSA
BARBARA	29	F	W	GRZZZZUSA
EVA	35	F	UNKNOWN	GRZZZZUSA
CATHA.	6	F	CHILD	GRZZZZUSA
MARIA	3	F	CHILD	GRZZZZUSA
CHRISTE.	2	F	CHILD	GRZZZZUSA
BARBA.	.07	F	INFANT	GRZZZZUSA
RIEDMAIER, JOH.	45	M	LABR	GRZZZZUSA
MAGDA.	44	F	W	GRZZZZUSA
FRIEDR.	15	M	UNKNOWN	GRZZZZUSA
JACOB	11	M	CH	GRZZZZUSA
WILHE.	10	F	CH	GRZZZZUSA
DAVID	8	M	CHILD	GRZZZZUSA
MARIE	7	F	CHILD	GRZZZZUSA
LOUISE	4	F	CHILD	GRZZZZUSA
GOTTLOB	3	M	CHILD	GRZZZZUSA
HERZER, GOTTLIEB	33	M	FARMER	GRZZZZUSA
KLOZ, FRIEDKE.	46	F	W	GRZZZZUSA
MARIE	16	F	UNKNOWN	GRZZZZUSA
GOTTLOB	10	M	CH	GRZZZZUSA
FRIEDKE.	9	F	CHILD	GRZZZZUSA
CAROLE.	7	F	CHILD	GRZZZZUSA
ALBERT	6	M	CHILD	GRZZZZUSA
FRIEDR.	4	M	CHILD	GRZZZZUSA
ANNA	2	F	CHILD	GRZZZZUSA
STAHL, MICHAEL	38	M	FARMER	GRZZZZUSA
FRIEDKE.	43	F	W	GRZZZZUSA
HERMANN	10	M	CH	GRZZZZUSA
WILHELE.	7	F	CHILD	GRZZZZUSA
ERNST	4	M	CHILD	GRZZZZUSA
PAULINE	3	F	CHILD	GRZZZZUSA
MARIE	2	F	CHILD	GRZZZZUSA
SIEBER, JOHANNES	16	M	UNKNOWN	GRAEEAUSA
SCHAEFER, MAGDA.	56	F	UNKNOWN	GRAFBDUSA
VETTER, ADOLF	21	M	LABR	GRAFBDUSA
WILDERMUTH, CARL	28	M	LABR	GRABEDUSA

PASSENGER	AGE	SEX	OCCUPATION	PRVL	DES
MESLE, STEPHAN	18	M	LABR	GRABEDUSA
STAEHLE, JOHANNES	15	M	UNKNOWN	GRABEDUSA
AICHELE, CARL	16	M	UNKNOWN	GRABEDUSA
KUERR, MARTIN	16	M	UNKNOWN	GRABENUSA
RUPP, JOSEF	17	M	MCHT	GRZZZZUSA
KOEPPNER, MARGE.	15	F	UNKNOWN	GRZZZZUSA
GOETHNER, ANNA	20	F	UNKNOWN	GRZZZZUSA
RIESS, EVA	18	F	UNKNOWN	GRZZZZUSA
LEIN, JOHANN	22	M	ENGR	GRZZZZUSA
HOHNER, MARIE	19	F	UNKNOWN	GRZZZZUSA
PITTROFF, DOROTHEA	18	F	UNKNOWN	GRZZZZUSA
HEMPFLING, CHRST.	28	M	FARMER	GRZZZZUSA
KOENIG, MARIE	16	F	UNKNOWN	GRZZZZUSA
MEINDL, MICHAEL	23	M	LABR	GRZZZZUSA
DREXLER, ALOIS	22	M	LABR	GRZZZZUSA
GAREIS, JOSEF	50	M	MCHT	GRZZZZUSA
ECKSTEIN, CAROLE.	22	F	UNKNOWN	GRZZZZUSA
KARGL, MARIA	19	F	UNKNOWN	GRAHQGUSA
BENDIX, LUDWIG	29	M	FARMER	GRACVNUSA
WENGENROTH, ANNA	28	F	UNKNOWN	GRZZZZUSA
BAYER, BEINH.	14	M	UNKNOWN	GRZZZZUSA
BREDE, CONRAD	26	M	LKSH	GRZZZZUSA
SIEBERT, HEINR.	28	M	SMH	GRZZZZUSA
DIETER, CATHA.	39	F	UNKNOWN	GRZZZZUSA
ESSENWEIN, GEORG	16	M	FARMER	GRZZZZUSA
HAEUSSLEY, CHRIST	25	M	JNR	GRADLMUSA
FUHRMERSTER, LOUISE	23	F	W	GRADLMUSA
HERM.	.05	M	INFANT	GRADLMUSA
APPEL, JOHS.	19	M	LABR	GRAIEJUSA
LANDWEHR, MARIE	19	F	UNKNOWN	GRZZZZUSA
MARZ, JOHANN	64	M	LABR	GRZZZZUSA
MARGA.	20	F	UNKNOWN	GRZZZZUSA
CATHA.	28	F	UNKNOWN	GRZZZZUSA
ELISABETH	3	F	CHILD	GRZZZZUSA
WUNSCHEL, KUNIGDE.	48	F	W	GRZZZZUSA
ELISAB.	17	F	UNKNOWN	GRZZZZUSA
KATHA.	14	F	UNKNOWN	GRZZZZUSA
MAGDA.	9	F	CHILD	GRZZZZUSA
KATHA.	7	F	CHILD	GRZZZZUSA
GEORG	6	M	CHILD	GRZZZZUSA
KIESSLING, JOHANN	39	M	LABR	GRZZZZUSA
BROETZ, MARIA	20	F	UNKNOWN	GRAAKHUSA
AUGUSTE	18	F	UNKNOWN	GRAAKHUSA
KENTE, ANNA	17	F	UNKNOWN	GRZZZZUSA
TELLMANN, DOMINIKA	18	F	UNKNOWN	GRZZZZUSA
BISPINGER, CATHA.	21	F	UNKNOWN	GRAFPGUSA
OBERSITZKY, JOHE.	16	F	UNKNOWN	GRAFPGUSA
RAPP, CARL	17	M	LABR	GRZZZZUSA
HACK, CATHA.	61	F	W	GRZZZZUSA
WALLER, CATHA.	27	F	UNKNOWN	GRZZZZUSA
THOBERS, REGINE	18	F	UNKNOWN	GRZZZZUSA
MEYER, CHRISTA.	19	F	UNKNOWN	GRZZZZUSA
KORB, JOHANNES	22	M	LABR	GRABAVUSA
WINTER, JOSEF	20	M	LABR	GRABAVUSA
WEIDNER, JOHANN	60	M	LABR	GRAENDUSA
WIESNOTH, GEORG	33	M	MLR	GRADPRUSA
RADATZ, WILHELME.	25	F	UNKNOWN	GRAHWIUSA
MEYER, EVA	54	F	UNKNOWN	GRAAYUUSA
FINGER, WILHELM	23	M	LABR	GRZZZZUSA
ZALEWSKA, AGNISZKA	20	F	W	GRZZZZUSA
MARTIN	.09	M	INFANT	GRZZZZUSA
WEBER, JOHANN	18	M	LABR	GRAFRGUSA
HARTENBACH, MAGDA.	18	F	UNKNOWN	GRAFQVUSA
FELDMANN, META	20	F	UNKNOWN	GRZZZZUSA
FREITAG, AUGUST	19	M	LABR	GRZZZZUSA
HAGEN, CARL	15	M	LABR	GRACENUSA
KUEHNE, EMMA	21	F	UNKNOWN	GRAIMSUSA
HELLER, LYDIA	17	F	UNKNOWN	GRAIMSUSA
FLOLL, IDA	17	F	UNKNOWN	GRAIMSUSA
DIECKHOFF, DIEDR.	15	M	UNKNOWN	GRZZZZUSA
EMMERT, ANNA	28	F	UNKNOWN	GRZZZZUSA
EMSHEIMER, AUGUST	17	M	MCHT	GRAFQVUSA
HONIG, ROBERT	14	M	UNKNOWN	GRAFQVUSA
HUGO	11	M	CH	GRAFQVUSA
KIEFER, SALOMON	17	M	MCHT	GRAFQVUSA

PASSENGER	AGE	SEX	OCCUPATION	PRVL	DES
AURICH, MARGE.	31	F	UNKNOWN	GRABOQUSA
PICHLER, ROSA	24	F	UNKNOWN	GRADLDUSA
KRUEGER, MINNA	21	F	W	GRADLDUSA
CARL	3	M	CHILD	GRADLDUSA
POLENZKA, AUGUSTE	18	F	UNKNOWN	GRAHWIUSA
PETRICK, WALDEMAR	9	M	CHILD	GRAAYXUSA
HEINRICH, GEORG	18	M	LABR	GRAJTDUSA
REINERT, CARL	21	M	LABR	GRZZZZUSA
SUTTER, MARIE	23	F	UNKNOWN	GRZZZZUSA
BERNHARD, JACOB	16	M	UNKNOWN	GRZZZZUSA
HOFMANN, THERESE	24	F	UNKNOWN	GRZZZZUSA
ILG, FRANZ	28	M	LABR	GRAEQTUSA
DINKELMANN, LUDWIG	17	M	LABR	GRAJIKUSA
FROMM, HERM.	17	M	LABR	GRAJIKUSA
HENER, FRITZ	24	M	LABR	GRAFDDUSA
SCHMIDT, PETER	23	M	LABR	GRADVHUSA
GERDAN, AUG.	24	M	LABR	GRACBRUSA
THEIL, FRITZ	24	M	LABR	GRACBRUSA
MUELLER, FRANZ	24	M	LABR	GRZZZZUSA
HANSEN, SOPHIE	17	F	UNKNOWN	GRACBRUSA
VIEBROCK, JOHA.	16	F	UNKNOWN	GRACBRUSA
OBST, CATHA.	18	F	UNKNOWN	GRAARRUSA
KUECK, CATHA.	15	F	UNKNOWN	GRABMPUSA
METTE, FRIEDKE.	20	F	UNKNOWN	GRZZZZUSA
DIERKS, JOHANNE	25	F	UNKNOWN	GRAARRUSA
HANAUER, FERD.	14	M	UNKNOWN	GRZZZZUSA
STELZNER, LINA	17	F	UNKNOWN	GRADQGUSA
OECHLER, DOROTHEA	18	F	UNKNOWN	GRAAXYUSA
SCHMIDT, CHRISTE.	17	F	UNKNOWN	GRAIEJUSA
WEITZEL, MARIE	19	F	UNKNOWN	GRAAULUSA
SICHEL, SARAH	18	F	UNKNOWN	GRAAULUSA
MARSTAELLER, JUSTUS	28	M	LABR	GRAIEHUSA
FARTZ, CARL	16	M	LABR	GRADHZUSA
KUEHN, ELISA	15	F	UNKNOWN	GRAEOHUSA
PEIN, LOUIS	15	M	UNKNOWN	GRACBRUSA
DIEFENBACH, MARTIN	22	M	LABR	GRZZZZUSA
MENGES, WILH.	19	M	LABR	GRZZZZUSA
KREBS, ELISE	16	F	UNKNOWN	GRAFNKUSA
GOEKEL, JOSEFA	21	F	UNKNOWN	GRAAQQUSA
GOETZ, HERTHA	24	F	W	GRZZZZUSA
STEUDLE, EMIL	29	M	LABR	GRAGXWUSA
LANG, MARGE.	17	F	UNKNOWN	GRADIRUSA
ROTHFUS-, LENE	40	F	W	GRAIACUSA
LINA	11	F	CH	GRAIACUSA
BAENDEL, PAULINE	16	F	UNKNOWN	GRZZZZUSA
EUGEN	14	M	UNKNOWN	GRZZZZUSA
HELLRIEGEL, ANNA	24	F	W	GRAAKHUSA
BURMEISTER, ALBERICH	17	M	UNKNOWN	GRACXHUSA
OHLAND, HEINR.	17	M	UNKNOWN	GRACVGUSA
HILDEBRANDT, JOHANN	16	M	UNKNOWN	GRZZZZUSA
MANGELS, MARIA	16	F	UNKNOWN	GRZZZZUSA
EHLEN, META	17	F	UNKNOWN	GRZZZZUSA
BERTHA	15	F	UNKNOWN	GRZZZZUSA
EICHTERSHEIMER, ISIDOR	16	M	UNKNOWN	GRZZZZUSA
HEGERFELD, GOTTLIEB	33	M	FARMER	GRZZZZUSA
LOUISE	25	F	W	GRZZZZUSA
WILHELM	4	M	CHILD	GRZZZZUSA
HEINRICH	.09	M	INFANT	GRZZZZUSA
KNETTER, CHARLOTTE	42	F	W	GRAFECUSA
MINNA	15	F	UNKNOWN	GRAFECUSA
MARIE	11	F	CH	GRAFECUSA
REISCH, ADOLF	15	M	UNKNOWN	GRZZZZUSA
RANDERMANN, HENRIETTE	19	F	UNKNOWN	GRZZZZUSA
AUGUST	15	M	UNKNOWN	GRZZZZUSA
DAUN, PAULINE	17	F	UNKNOWN	GRAAYRUSA
BERNETT, WILHELM	18	M	LABR	GRACBRUSA
HENZE, JOHANN	16	M	LABR	GRACBRUSA
GERCKEN, JOHANN	21	M	LABR	GRACBRUSA
DIECKMANN, JOHANN	16	M	LABR	GRACBRUSA
ROHDE, MATH.	23	M	LABR	GRACBRUSA
SEGELKEN, MARIE	10	F	CH	GRAAFXUSA
STRANGMEIER, WILHELM	15	M	LABR	GRADVXUSA
KIRSMANN, ALOIS	52	M	LABR	GRZZZZUSA
BARBA.	20	F	UNKNOWN	GRZZZZUSA
ALOIS	11	M	CH	GRZZZZUSA
CRESCENZ	6	M	CHILD	GRZZZZUSA
STEGMEYER, AUG.	23	M	LABR	GRAAJXUSA
SCHERMBACH, ROMIE	24	F	UNKNOWN	GRAAJXUSA
BEILNER, MARIE	22	F	UNKNOWN	GRZZZZUSA
KINDOVATER, KAROLE.	25	F	UNKNOWN	GRZZZZUSA
SCHROEDER, DOROTHEA	16	F	UNKNOWN	GRZZZZUSA
ULRICH, CHARLOTTE	20	F	UNKNOWN	GRZZZZUSA
SEIDL, JOHANN	40	M	LABR	GRAENZUSA
FRANZKA.	41	F	W	GRAENZUSA
JOHANN	14	M	UNKNOWN	GRAENZUSA
MARGA.	10	F	CH	GRAENZUSA
ELISABETH	6	F	CHILD	GRAENZUSA
NICOLAUS	3	M	CHILD	GRAENZUSA
BAR, CHRIST.	22	M	SHMK	GRABOQUSA
MELCHING, GEORG	26	M	LABR	GRACBRUSA
HELENE	25	F	W	GRACBRUSA
GRIES, BERNHD.	23	M	LABR	GRACBRUSA
BOLL, PETER	32	M	LABR	GRADJEUSA
HARTL, JOSEF	29	M	BKLYR	GRADJEUSA
GEORG	24	M	FARMER	GRADJEUSA
LIESERT, ALBERT	16	M	MCHT	GRADIJUSA
SONNTAG, KATHA.	16	F	UNKNOWN	GRABQKUSA
SCHREIER, CAROLE.	19	F	UNKNOWN	GRABQKUSA
LAMBERT, CAROLE.	19	F	UNKNOWN	GRABQKUSA
SEIBEL, FRANZKA	17	F	UNKNOWN	GRABQKUSA
KRAMER, ANNA	23	F	UNKNOWN	GRABQKUSA
KRONEMANN, KARL	17	M	TLR	GRABQKUSA
ZUELICH, ARNOLD	17	M	BCHR	GRABQKUSA
FERGER, CARL	24	M	BKR	GRZZZZUSA
ALTSTADT, ELISAB.	74	F	W	GRAHKJUSA
HELLER, MARIE	18	F	UNKNOWN	GRAHKJUSA
FUNK, CATHA.	18	F	UNKNOWN	GRAHKJUSA
KIRCHHOEFER, ELISE	45	F	UNKNOWN	GRAHKJUSA
HEENE, CATHA.	18	F	UNKNOWN	GRABTFUSA
WIRTH, MARGE.	23	F	UNKNOWN	GRZZZZUSA
HOERR, PETER	27	M	SHMK	GRZZZZUSA
GEORG	21	M	SHMK	GRZZZZUSA
WILHELM, FRANZISKUS	15	M	UNKNOWN	GRZZZZUSA
GREFE, MARIA	15	F	UNKNOWN	GRADXCUSA
STEFFENS, ERNST	16	M	UNKNOWN	GRACBFUSA
BECKMANN, MARIA	18	F	UNKNOWN	GRADNOUSA
SCHWAMANN, DORIS	24	F	UNKNOWN	GRADNOUSA
HARBES, GEORG	30	M	FARMER	GRADVHUSA
JOHA.	28	F	W	GRADVHUSA
HEINR.	4	M	CHILD	GRADVHUSA
OTTO	3	M	CHILD	GRADVHUSA
EMMA	1	F	CHILD	GRADVHUSA
HEINR.	34	M	FARMER	GRADVHUSA
ANNCHEN	24	F	W	GRADVHUSA
MARTHA	3	F	CHILD	GRADVHUSA
HEINR.	1	M	CHILD	GRADVHUSA
GEORG	.02	M	INFANT	GRADVHUSA
TAUBNER, RUDOLPH	21	M	LABR	GRAGFUUSA
MORISE, EILERT	49	M	LABR	GRADVHUSA
KATHA.	36	F	W	GRADVHUSA
BRUNO	10	M	CH	GRADVHUSA
LUEBBE	7	M	CHILD	GRADVHUSA
EILERT	.09	M	INFANT	GRADVHUSA
PETERING, WILHM.	59	M	LABR	GRADVHUSA
HELENE	53	F	W	GRADVHUSA
HERM.	15	M	CH	GRADVHUSA
AUG.	10	M	CH	GRADVHUSA
JOHANNE	17	F	UNKNOWN	GRADVHUSA
PFANNSTIEL, ANNA	16	F	UNKNOWN	GRZZZZUSA
CATHA.	15	F	UNKNOWN	GRZZZZUSA
STUETZ, ANNA	21	F	UNKNOWN	GRZZZZUSA
BERGHAUSEN, FRIEDR.	32	M	LABR	GRADAAUSA
SOPHIE	26	F	W	GRADAAUSA
MARIE	3	F	CHILD	GRADAAUSA
HELENE	.11	F	INFANT	GRADAAUSA
BINOTSCH, ROSA	57	F	UNKNOWN	GRAHTNUSA
RUSCHKE, PAUL	15	M	UNKNOWN	GRAHTNUSA
BLANK, GUST.	17	M	FARMER	GRADBZUSA
BRAUN, ANNA	48	F	UNKNOWN	GRABDMUSA
SCHULZ, JOHANNE	19	F	UNKNOWN	GRAJWOUSA

PASSENGER	AGE	SEX	OCCUPATION	PROVL DES
MEINECKE, DORA	25	F	UNKNOWN	GRAJWOUSA
BUETTNER, ELISE	44	F	UNKNOWN	GRAAKHUSA
BIERUCKA, VALERIA	23	F	UNKNOWN	GRZZZZUSA
ROSENOW, ERNST	36	M	LABR	GRAAKHUSA
EMMA	36	F	W	GRAAKHUSA
FRIEDR.	11	M	CH	GRAAKHUSA
ELSBETH.	10	F	CH	GRAAKHUSA
JOHANN	7	M	CHILD	GRAAKHUSA
ERNST	5	M	CHILD	GRAAKHUSA
WEIDMANN, AUGE.	45	F	UNKNOWN	GRAAKHUSA
KUERBIS, AUGUST	21	M	LABR	GRZZZZUSA
BISCHOF, ALBERT	65	M	LABR	GRAFWZUSA
KORTREY, GESINE	20	F	UNKNOWN	GRAJAWUSA
BARENBURG, ANNA	24	F	UNKNOWN	GRZZZZUSA
JAEGER, CHRIST.	18	M	LABR	GRAFFTUSA
BERGLE, MARIE	20	F	UNKNOWN	GRAEXWUSA
WILHELM	28	M	LABR	GRAEXWUSA
SIEBER, WILHELM	42	M	LABR	GRAEXWUSA
CAROLE	41	F	W	GRAEXWUSA
WILHELM	17	M	LABR	GRAEXWUSA
ERNST	12	M	CH	GRAEXWUSA
CARL	7	M	CHILD	GRAEXWUSA
ROBERT	3	M	CHILD	GRAEXWUSA
KIENZLE, LOUISE	15	F	UNKNOWN	GRZZZZUSA
SCHMIERER, CARL	22	M	LABR	GRZZZZUSA
KLAMT, ANNA	16	F	UNKNOWN	GRADOEUSA
ZEISBERG, MARIA	26	F	UNKNOWN	GRADOEUSA
DYCHTOWIC, WACLAW	27	M	LABR	GRZZZZUSA
DEGEN, CARL	18	M	LABR	GRAFQVUSA
PROBST, JOSEF	57	M	LABR	GRADLDUSA
SCHMIDT, HERM.	32	M	LABR	GRAEWMUSA
BORMUTH, CARL	16	M	LABR	GRAEWMUSA
KELLER, MARTINA	21	F	UNKNOWN	GRAAAGUSA
MATTHIS, JOHANN	25	M	LABR	GRZZZZUSA
KOLLER, ELISE	25	F	UNKNOWN	GRZZZZUSA
BUSCH, HANS	21	M	LABR	GRAAKHUSA
IBA, FRIEDR.	27	M	LABR	GRZZZZUSA
ROSENBERGER, JOSEF	24	M	LABR	GRACGJUSA
NIED, HEINR.	52	M	LABR	GRADKWUSA
SPALTHOFF, JOH.	22	M	LABR	GRADKWUSA
WIDMANN, ALFRED	22	M	LABR	GRZZZZUSA
WINHART, SIEGMUND	23	M	LABR	GRZZZZUSA
TRENSCH, BERNHD.	19	M	LABR	GRABKHUSA
ROLLER, KATHA.	20	F	UNKNOWN	GRADOIUSA
REISCHMANN, CATHA.	18	F	UNKNOWN	GRZZZZUSA
HARTMANN, SOPHIE	24	F	UNKNOWN	GRAFNKUSA
RUFA, JOHANN	37	M	FARMER	GRAFEJUSA
MARGA.	35	F	W	GRAFEJUSA
ADAM	11	M	CH	GRAFEJUSA
ELISAB.	7	F	CHILD	GRAFEJUSA
DIEFENBACH, KATHA.	15	M	UNKNOWN	GRAFEJUSA
RUFA, HEINR.	25	M	LABR	GRAFEJUSA
SCHICKEL, WILH.	18	M	LABR	GRAFEJUSA
BRUDER, ENGELBERT	29	M	LABR	GRZZZZUSA
HUMMEL, ANNA	18	F	UNKNOWN	GRZZZZUSA
HOFFMANN, BABETTE	21	F	UNKNOWN	GRZZZZUSA
DALZ, GOTTHILF	17	M	LKSH	GRAJYPUSA
DURIAN, CAROLE.	18	F	UNKNOWN	GRAJYPUSA
WALZ, ANNA	10	F	CH	GRAJYPUSA
GUENSER, CARL	16	M	BKR	GRAJYPUSA
BERG, LORENZ	18	M	LABR	GRZZZZUSA
EBERT, CONRAD	17	M	LABR	GRABLTUSA
LIZIE	19	F	CH	GRABLTUSA
JUENGERS, FRIEDKE.	19	F	UNKNOWN	GRZZZZUSA
WISELER, CHRISTOF	26	M	LABR	GRZZZZUSA
BINDER, MARIA	24	F	UNKNOWN	GRZZZZUSA
ETGETON, CARL	10	M	LABR	GRZZZZUSA
WEBER, ALBERT	15	M	UNKNOWN	GRAENLUSA
BROSIUS, ELISE	21	F	UNKNOWN	GRAENLUSA
LEUTHNER, EVA	25	F	UNKNOWN	GRACZUUSA
REUTHE, CATHA.	21	F	UNKNOWN	GRACZUUSA
STARICHA, JOHANN	25	M	LABR	GRABLTUSA
EBERT, CONRAD	47	M	FARMER	GRAJWOUSA
BEHRENS, JOHANNE	8	F	CHILD	GRADVHUSA
GROSS, MARIE	19	F	UNKNOWN	GRAAGLUSA

PASSENGER	AGE	SEX	OCCUPATION	PROVL DES
MUELLER, MARGE.	17	F	UNKNOWN	GRAAGLUSA
URBAN, MARIA	20	F	UNKNOWN	GRAAGLUSA
SCHMIDT, AMALIE	20	F	UNKNOWN	GRZZZZUSA
DORA	8	F	CHILD	GRZZZZUSA

SHIP: CITY OF CHESTER

FROM: LIVERPOOL AND QUEENSTOWN
TO: NEW YORK
ARRIVED: 29 SEPTEMBER 1888

PASSENGER	AGE	SEX	OCCUPATION	PROVL DES
WESTERLAIN, LOUIS	27	M	UNKNOWN	FRZZZZUSA
BURIERE, FIDELE	29	M	UNKNOWN	FRZZZZUSA
CAMPANY, FRANCAIS	33	M	UNKNOWN	FRZZZZUSA
GUENOF, PHIL.	40	F	UNKNOWN	FRZZZZUSA
SCHMIELT, KAPER	22	M	FARMER	FRACBFNY
FIAND, CHRISTIAN	24	M	FARMER	FRACBFNY
OELTEIN, HEMCH.	13	M	BY	FRACBFNY
BLANCKE, HERR.	22	M	BKLYR	FRADAXNY
BERKOWITZ, SOL.	19	M	TLR	FRACBFPHI
BURKTARDT, GUST.	54	M	BKLYR	FRACBFCH
BENDIT, RIEGEL	26	M	TLR	FRACBFNY
VOGEL, NATHAN	33	M	TLR	FRACBFNY
HERMANN, WILH.	16	M	TLR	FRACBFIL
LEMUNSCHNEDER, LIZZIE	23	F	UNKNOWN	FRACBFIL
JIEDRICH, KATIE	22	F	UNKNOWN	FRACBFIL
DEPRESLE, H.	32	M	GENT	FRADXWNY
BONNET, PAUL	30	M	GENT	FRADXWNY
APHRAATES, BRD.	66	M	B	FRADXWNY

SHIP: LEERDAM

FROM: ROTTERDAM
TO: NEW YORK
ARRIVED: 01 OCTOBER 1888

PASSENGER	AGE	SEX	OCCUPATION	PROVL DES
MAZEOND, A.M.J.	00	M	UNKNOWN	FRZZZZUSA
GLEASON, A.M.	00	F	UNKNOWN	GRZZZZUSA
WOHLOUER, O.	00	M	MCHT	GRZZZZUSA
RELLOGG, G.E.	00	F	UNKNOWN	GRZZZZUSA
JENNES, C.	35	F	UNKNOWN	FRZZZZUSA
U	16	F	UNKNOWN	FRZZZZUSA
B.	5	F	CHILD	FRZZZZUSA
F.	3	M	CHILD	FRZZZZUSA
MELNING, ELIS	46	F	UNKNOWN	GRZZZZUSA
WEYLAND, A.	00	F	UNKNOWN	GRZZZZUSA
MURPHY, C.	00	M	STDNT	FRZZZZUSA
C.	00	F	UNKNOWN	FRZZZZUSA
COLBERG, P.	00	M	UNKNOWN	GRZZZZUSA
ROCH, L.	00	M	UNKNOWN	GRZZZZUSA
BURBACH, A.	18	M	UNKNOWN	GRZZZZUSA
BOCHMEIER, J.	24	F	UNKNOWN	GRZZZZUSA
KEISER, NIC.	16	M	STDNT	GRZZZZUSA
WEBER, JOHN	60	M	MCHT	GRZZZZUSA
AICHINGER, G.	16	M	UNKNOWN	GRZZZZUSA
HELMBRECHT, A.	16	M	UNKNOWN	GRZZZZUSA
FRITZ, JOHN	25	M	MCHT	GRZZZZUSA
CASSERIR, TH.	27	M	UNKNOWN	GRZZZZUSA
TH.	20	F	UNKNOWN	GRZZZZUSA
RUEPPERS, P.	20	M	JNR	GRZZZZUSA
BUJAKOWSKI, ALB.	30	M	ENGR	GRZZZZUSA
A.	29	F	UNKNOWN	GRZZZZUSA
M.	4	M	CHILD	GRZZZZUSA
R.	2	M	CHILD	GRZZZZUSA
WEBER, C.L.	54	M	MCHT	GRZZZZUSA

PASSENGER	AGE	SEX	OCCUPATION	PRVL	DES
C.J.	53	F	UNKNOWN		GRZZZZUSA
COELL, SIB.	40	F	UNKNOWN		GRZZZZUSA
WEBER, MARIA	19	F	UNKNOWN		GRZZZZUSA
V, R.D.	65	M	UNKNOWN		GRZZZZUSA
JOESTEN, J.	20	M	STDNT		GRZZZZUSA
WENTZ, LOUIS	15	M	UNKNOWN		GRZZZZUSA
RANE, IDA	27	F	UNKNOWN		GRZZZZUSA
NIELSEN, A.	00	F	UNKNOWN		GRZZZZUSA
WOLF, J.	55	F	MCHT		GRZZZZUSA
M.	4	F	CHILD		GRZZZZUSA
SEUNLE, F.	24	M	TLR		GRZZZZUSA
SPEDT, FR.	38	M	MCHT		GRZZZZUSA
SPIEGEL, JOHAN	27	M	SHMK		GRZZZZUSA
CHRIST	21	F	UNKNOWN		GRZZZZUSA
ERNST	2	M	CHILD		GRZZZZUSA
WILH.	.05	F	INFANT		GRZZZZUSA
SCHMITZ, MICHAEL	45	M	FARMER		GRZZZZUSA
U	40	F	UNKNOWN		GRZZZZUSA
CESILIA	17	F	UNKNOWN		GRZZZZUSA
LENGEA	15	F	UNKNOWN		GRZZZZUSA
JOHANN	11	M	UNKNOWN		GRZZZZUSA
MICHAEL	8	M	CHILD		GRZZZZUSA
WILHEL.	26	M	FARMER		GRZZZZUSA
COHN, ISIDOR	30	M	FARMER		GRZZZZUSA
LANGEN, IDA	40	F	UNKNOWN		GRZZZZUSA
FRITZ	10	M	CH		GRZZZZUSA
MUELLER, WILH.	42	M	SHPKR		GRZZZZUSA
SYBIEL	32	F	UNKNOWN		GRZZZZUSA
SONNE, JANUS	18	M	LABR		GRZZZZUSA
HAUSEN, CHRIST.	19	M	LABR		GRZZZZUSA
VOGELSANG, E.	22	M	MCHT		GRZZZZUSA
BERGMANN, JAC.	25	M	LABR		GRZZZZUSA
FRIES, ANTON	60	M	LABR		GRZZZZUSA
MARIE	33	F	UNKNOWN		GRZZZZUSA
GROSSE, FRIED.	24	M	LABR		GRZZZZUSA
STADLER, LUDW.	18	M	SHMK		GRZZZZUSA
VOGLER, MART.	33	M	SHMK		GRZZZZUSA
BUSCH, PETER	18	M	SHMK		GRZZZZUSA
JEGER, BORTH.	25	M	BCHR		GRZZZZUSA
HEWED, RICHARD	16	M	CCHMN		GRZZZZUSA
HARNISCH, FRITZ	17	M	LABR		GRZZZZUSA
KUHN, W.	21	M	LABR		GRZZZZUSA
HAERLE, JOHANN	37	M	BKR		GRZZZZUSA
BORG, CARL	44	M	LABR		GRZZZZUSA
ROOS, ERHARD	21	M	LABR		GRZZZZUSA
HENNEMUTH, PETER	25	M	LABR		GRZZZZUSA
MISSERES, GEORG	19	M	LABR		GRZZZZUSA
DOERRLER, LEOPOLD	19	M	BKR		GRZZZZUSA
WEIKERT, ANTON	29	M	JNR		GRZZZZUSA
GROMLICH, JOH.	26	M	JNR		GRZZZZUSA
FRAUH, HERM.	23	M	LABR		GRZZZZUSA
SCHLEINER, WILH.	19	M	LABR		GRZZZZUSA
WOELFLE, JOH.	20	M	LABR		GRZZZZUSA
TRAUTMANN, JOH.	19	M	MUSN		GRZZZZUSA
EHINGER, EMIL	31	M	BKR		GRZZZZUSA
HERM.	18	M	BKR		GRZZZZUSA
EBERT, GUSTAV	24	M	SHMK		GRZZZZUSA
TROBOESE, HEINR.	43	M	STK		GRZZZZUSA
SCHNEIDER, WILH.	18	M	LABR		GRZZZZUSA
MONA	11	F	UNKNOWN		GRZZZZUSA
KOJCIECHOWSKI, MIKOLAY	22	M	LABR		GRZZZZUSA
JAKUBIAK, MAREIN	22	M	LABR		GRZZZZUSA
NAGEL, FANNY	25	F	UNKNOWN		GRZZZZUSA
HOEFNER, KAROL	30	F	UNKNOWN		GRZZZZUSA
FRITZ	3	M	CHILD		GRZZZZUSA
HOFFMANN, MARG.	73	F	UNKNOWN		GRZZZZUSA
VOGT, MARY	49	F	UNKNOWN		GRZZZZUSA
ADELE	9	F	CHILD		GRZZZZUSA
SHOPP, SUSETTE	20	F	UNKNOWN		GRZZZZUSA
GROSS, ANNA	16	F	UNKNOWN		GRZZZZUSA
MARG.	17	F	UNKNOWN		GRZZZZUSA
LINBRUNER, MARIE	26	F	UNKNOWN		GRZZZZUSA
THERESE	6	F	CHILD		GRZZZZUSA
PFEIFFER, VERONICA	28	F	CH		GRZZZZUSA
CALAR	6	F	CHILD		GRZZZZUSA
JENNE	.11	F	INFANT		GRZZZZUSA
GESCHEIDEE, CATH.	50	F	UNKNOWN		GRZZZZUSA
SOPHIE	18	F	UNKNOWN		GRZZZZUSA
BENZ, ELISE	15	F	UNKNOWN		GRZZZZUSA
KRAMER, EISAB.	63	F	UNKNOWN		GRZZZZUSA
PACH, ELIS.	35	F	UNKNOWN		GRZZZZUSA
LUCIA	17	F	UNKNOWN		GRZZZZUSA
MARIA	14	F	UNKNOWN		GRZZZZUSA
LINA	11	F	UNKNOWN		GRZZZZUSA
GEORG	9	M	CHILD		GRZZZZUSA
LAINDEMAIER, JOHANNA	30	F	UNKNOWN		GRZZZZUSA
PAULINE	4	F	CHILD		GRZZZZUSA
GEORGE	2	M	CHILD		GRZZZZUSA
ANZENBERGER, MARIA	17	F	UNKNOWN		GRZZZZUSA
SCHONIT, ELISE	18	F	UNKNOWN		GRZZZZUSA
REHLEIN, WILL.	25	M	LABR		GRZZZZUSA
ISSELSTEIN, WILH.	50	M	FARMER		GRZZZZUSA
AGNES	43	F	UNKNOWN		GRZZZZUSA
HEIMRICH	20	M	UNKNOWN		GRZZZZUSA
JULIUS	18	M	UNKNOWN		GRZZZZUSA
JOSEF	16	M	UNKNOWN		GRZZZZUSA
ROBERT	14	M	UNKNOWN		GRZZZZUSA
HUBERT	11	M	UNKNOWN		GRZZZZUSA
ANNA	8	M	CHILD		GRZZZZUSA
AUGUST	4	M	CHILD		GRZZZZUSA
E.	.03	F	INFANT		GRZZZZUSA
LIECK, JOHAN	17	M	LABR		GRZZZZUSA
WACHTER, CHRIST.	40	F	UNKNOWN		GRZZZZUSA
GEORG	8	M	CHILD		GRZZZZUSA
CAROL.	5	F	CHILD		GRZZZZUSA
BITSER, JOHS.	27	M	WVR		GRZZZZUSA
CATH.	29	F	UNKNOWN		GRZZZZUSA
SENDICK, PETER	19	M	LABR		GRZZZZUSA
SCHRODER, GUSTAV	36	M	SHMK		GRZZZZUSA
LUIDNER, EILH.	22	M	JNR		GRZZZZUSA
BOEHRNIGER, ALB.	18	M	GLSBR		GRZZZZUSA
WALTER, REINH.	32	M	LABR		GRZZZZUSA
GAHL, RUDOLF	24	M	LABR		GRZZZZUSA
SCHNUR, NICOLAS	11	M	LABR		GRZZZZUSA
EDUARD	9	M	CHILD		GRZZZZUSA
LIONTESEN, MORITZ	30	M	UNKNOWN		GRZZZZUSA
ZALOG, SIGM.	37	M	LABR		GRZZZZUSA
BORKOWIEZ, WALENTIN	22	M	FARMER		GRZZZZUSA
NILSON, NILS	29	M	LABR		GRZZZZUSA
LAKAJA, BIAGIO	58	M	LABR		FRZZZZUSA
FALOTIEO, ANTONIO	23	M	LABR		FRZZZZUSA
GIOVANNI, CINOTTO	22	M	LABR		FRZZZZUSA
GIOV.	26	M	LABR		FRZZZZUSA
LANGER, CESARE	26	M	LABR		FRZZZZUSA
MAZONE, EMILE	35	M	LABR		FRZZZZUSA
VIALENTINO, GUISEPPE	43	M	LABR		FRZZZZUSA
MARSAGLIA, LIGI	27	M	LABR		FRZZZZUSA
VILETTI, CUGGIO	43	M	LABR		FRZZZZUSA
GUILLARD, MARCO	35	M	LABR		FRZZZZUSA
COLLETI, MICHEL	25	M	LABR		FRZZZZUSA
PONS, ALPHONSE	26	M	LABR		FRZZZZUSA
RAMES, JEAN	55	M	LABR		FRZZZZUSA
CELESTIN, ABRAM	20	M	LABR		FRZZZZUSA
BARRIERE, PIERRE	31	M	LABR		FRZZZZUSA
SARCE, JULI	26	F	UNKNOWN		FRZZZZUSA
GUIBERT, ANTOINE	17	M	LABR		FRZZZZUSA
GOLDSTEIN, MANDEL	30	M	LABR		FRZZZZUSA
FURRATI, SIMON	31	M	LABR		FRZZZZUSA
DOOMS, FRANCOIS	35	M	LABR		FRZZZZUSA
TOURBOI, JEAN	37	M	LABR		FRZZZZUSA
ALBERTINA	26	F	UNKNOWN		FRZZZZUSA
ISOLO, MARGAR.	27	F	UNKNOWN		FRZZZZUSA
ROSA	8	F	CHILD		FRZZZZUSA
STRINGAT, CAROLINE	30	F	UNKNOWN		FRZZZZUSA
COZZA, ANTON	32	M	LABR		FRZZZZUSA
ROSMANI, ESTI	16	F	UNKNOWN		FRZZZZUSA
WAHL, MARY	18	F	UNKNOWN		GRZZZZUSA
LOEFFLER, GEO.	25	M	ENGR		GRZZZZUSA

PASSENGER	AGE	SEX	OCCUPATION	PRVL	DES
SHIP: MAIN					
FROM: BREMEN					
TO: BALTIMORE					
ARRIVED: 01 OCTOBER 1888					
RACKEMANN, JOSEF	19	M	CL	GRZZZZBAL	
RUTSCH, CURT	24	M	CL	GRZZZZBAL	
MUELLER, MAX	26	M	CL	GRZZZZBAL	
HAAG, JULIA	22	F	W	GRZZZZBAL	
THEKLA	60	F	W	GRZZZZBAL	
GOSE, MATHILDE	29	F	W	GRZZZZBAL	
BAUMGARTH, GOTTFR	40	M	FARMER	GRZZZZBAL	
HERMANN, EDUARD	27	M	TNR	GRZZZZBAL	
KALINOWSKI, ROMAN	28	M	JNR	GRZZZZBAL	
HOLZ, PAUL	31	M	FARMER	GRZZZZBAL	
KANIECKE, ANTON	16	M	FARMER	GRZZZZBAL	
MEYER, HENRY	30	M	FARMER	GRZZZZBAL	
KUZNICKA, VINCENT	26	M	FARMER	GRZZZZBAL	
KRUG, PAUL	16	M	LABR	GRZZZZBAL	
HONZIK, JOSEF	21	M	LABR	GRZZZZBAL	
BUENGER, GUSTAV	24	M	TU	GRZZZZBAL	
SCHUETTE, WILHELM	27	M	FARMER	GRZZZZBAL	
STUECKRADT, CHRIST	13	M	FARMER	GRZZZZIA	
MUEGGE, HARTWIG	50	M	TNR	GRZZZZIL	
DAUERHEIM, JOHANN	23	M	BRR	GRZZZZIL	
BECKER, CARL	16	M	LABR	GRZZZZIL	
KERSTING, FRIEDR	22	M	BKLYR	GRZZZZIL	
STENDER, RICHARD	28	M	FARMER	GRZZZZIL	
WENKEL, FRIEDR	17	M	FARMER	GRZZZZIL	
MADZEISESKY, JOH	30	M	FARMER	GRZZZZIL	
MOLDER, STEFAN	16	M	FARMER	GRZZZZIL	
ABBAN, JOHAN	16	M	FARMER	GRZZZZIL	
SIEMERS, JOSEF	19	M	FARMER	GRZZZZIL	
WIECHMANN, FRIEDR	18	M	WCHMKR	GRZZZZIL	
THIELE, GUSTAV	21	M	BKLYR	GRZZZZIL	
HAHN, HEINR	16	M	FARMER	GRZZZZIL	
EICHENHAUER, HEINR	17	M	FARMER	GRZZZZIL	
TATZEK, CARL	25	M	CPTR	GRZZZZIL	
HETZNER, LORENZ	27	M	BKR	GRZZZZIL	
WUEBBOLD, HEINR	24	M	FARMER	GRZZZZUNK	
KELLERMANN, WILH	20	M	TLR	GRZZZZUNK	
SCHUPP, LEONH	40	M	FARMER	GRZZZZIL	
EICKEL, FRANZ	17	M	FARMER	GRZZZZUNK	
STUTENKEMPER, HEINR	28	M	FARMER	GRZZZZUNK	
HOFFMANN, BERNH	18	M	FARMER	GRZZZZUNK	
ENTZNER, MICHAEL	28	M	FARMER	GRZZZZBAL	
BECKA, JOHANN	30	M	LABR	GRZZZZBAL	
STEENKEN, GEORG	24	M	LABR	GRZZZZUNK	
FRANKEL, FRIEDR	30	M	CPTR	GRZZZZNE	
STELLGES, HEINR	25	M	FARMER	GRZZZZBAL	
REITZ, WIEGAND	16	M	FARMER	GRZZZZBAL	
TRABANDT, AUGUST	16	M	GDNR	GRZZZZBAL	
SCHLARMANN, GERH	16	M	FARMER	GRZZZZUNK	
PUSCH, BRUNO	22	M	MNR	GRZZZZBAL	
GAMPERT, JOH	57	M	FARMER	GRZZZZBAL	
JOH	22	M	FARMER	GRZZZZBAL	
BARTEL, WILH	19	M	MCHT	GRZZZZBAL	
KRUEGER, CARL	22	M	FARMER	GRZZZZBAL	
HOFMANN, HERM	26	M	BCHR	GRZZZZBAL	
STEDRONSKY, JOSEF	24	M	LABR	GRZZZZBAL	
FRANK, JOH	26	M	LABR	GRZZZZBAL	
VEMEE, JOSEF	19	M	LABR	GRZZZZBAL	
SEEDL, JOSEF	23	M	MUSN	GRZZZZBAL	
GREGOR, EDWARD	16	M	FARMER	GRZZZZBAL	
JONAS, JULIUS	29	M	FARMER	GRZZZZBAL	
TUEMLER, AUG	36	M	BKR	GRZZZZUNK	
FUSS, AUG	30	M	LABR	GRZZZZIL	
STOEFER, BERNHARD	17	M	LABR	GRZZZZUNK	
-OERGENS, HEINR	18	M	FARMER	GRZZZZUNK	
WALTER, KONRAD	22	M	BRR	GRZZZZIL	
SUEDTKE, FRANZ	23	M	CL	GRZZZZIA	
PAUL	18	M	GZR	GRZZZZIA	
KREMELBERG, FRIEDR	50	M	MCHT	GRZZZZBAL	
REINE, JOSEF	23	M	FARMER	GRZZZZBAL	
KOERNER, GEORG	24	M	BCHR	GRZZZZUNK	
NOVAKI, MICHAEL	36	M	FARMER	GRZZZZUNK	
FRICKE, GEORG	26	M	FARMER	GRZZZZIL	
BAUERLE, HEINR	68	M	FARMER	GRZZZZBAL	
RASZEJA, FRANZ	24	M	FARMER	GRZZZZBAL	
WINTER, DAVID	45	M	FARMER	GRZZZZBAL	
HENNING, HEINR	44	M	FARMER	GRZZZZBAL	
BRINDZA, JOHANN	26	M	FARMER	GRZZZZBAL	
MEIER, ANDREAS	30	M	FARMER	GRZZZZBAL	
HAUCK, MARIA	18	F	SVNT	GRZZZZBAL	
WINTER, MARIA	31	F	W	GRZZZZBAL	
ESKOWSKA, ANNA	30	F	W	GRZZZZBAL	
HOHENDORF, ELISAB	35	F	W	GRZZZZBAL	
ROSA	7	F	CHILD	GRZZZZBAL	
JACOB, MARIA	32	F	W	GRZZZZBAL	
HEDWIG	6	F	CHILD	GRZZZZBAL	
PRIEGHAM, ALWINE	21	F	W	GRZZZZBAL	
ERNST	3	M	CHILD	GRZZZZBAL	
GUSTAV	.08	M	INFANT	GRZZZZBAL	
STACHOVIAK, FRANZISKA	27	F	W	GRZZZZBAL	
MARIA	3	F	CHILD	GRZZZZBAL	
BYGALL, ANNA	21	F	SVNT	GRZZZZBAL	
SCHMIDT, CLARA	28	F	W	GRZZZZBAL	
WALTER	.06	M	INFANT	GRZZZZBAL	
SKOCZINSKI, MARGR	24	F	SVNT	GRZZZZBAL	
RITSCHEWSKA, EMILIE	22	F	SVNT	GRZZZZBAL	
STERNA, AUGUSTE	13	F	SVNT	GRZZZZBAL	
CHACHULSKA, VERONIKA	28	F	W	GRZZZZBAL	
PETER	2	F	CHILD	GRZZZZBAL	
HORN, JOHANNA	15	F	SVNT	GRZZZZBAL	
WEIDNER, AUGUSTE	17	F	SVNT	GRZZZZBAL	
MARIA	15	F	SVNT	GRZZZZBAL	
HAMATH, JULIANA	20	F	SVNT	GRZZZZBAL	
KUNZE, ANNA	17	F	SVNT	GRZZZZBAL	
LENTZ, EMILIE	40	F	W	GRZZZZBAL	
HUEBSCH, LOUISE	24	F	W	GRZZZZNE	
REINHARD, ANNA	37	F	W	GRZZZZIA	
ALBRECHT, ELISE	13	F	SVNT	GRZZZZIA	
BARTELT, ANNA	35	F	W	GRZZZZUNK	
MARTHA	15	F	D	GRZZZZUNK	
OTTO	6	M	CHILD	GRZZZZUNK	
BERNTHALER, FRANZISKA	21	F	SVNT	GRZZZZBAL	
VOGEL, BERTHA	14	F	SVNT	GRZZZZBAL	
LEPPER, KATHR	16	F	SVNT	GRZZZZBAL	
ROLLWEGE, MINNA	17	F	SVNT	GRZZZZBAL	
ECHAUSEN, MARGR	25	F	W	GRZZZZBAL	
ANNA	.09	F	INFANT	GRZZZZBAL	
MAURER, KATHR	17	F	SVNT	GRZZZZBAL	
SE-BERT, LENCHEN	25	F	SVNT	GRZZZZBAL	
LEWANDOWSKA, JOSEF	27	F	W	GRZZZZBAL	
JOSEPH	3	M	CHILD	GRZZZZBAL	
MARIANNA	.06	F	INFANT	GRZZZZBAL	
NIERADZINSKA, FRANZISCA	50	F	W	GRZZZZBAL	
FORCH, KATHARINA	18	F	SVNT	GRZZZZBAL	
SCHORK, KATHARINA	21	F	SVNT	GRZZZZBAL	
MERK, EMMA	19	F	SVNT	GRZZZZBAL	
REUTTER, LINA	23	F	SVNT	GRZZZZBAL	
MEYER, AGNES	21	F	SVNT	GRZZZZBAL	
SCHMIDT, ANNA	44	F	W	GRZZZZBAL	
MARIA	11	F	CH	GRZZZZBAL	
JACOB	9	M	CHILD	GRZZZZBAL	
HABART, ANNA	9	M	CHILD	GRZZZZBAL	
HAHN, ANNA	21	F	SVNT	GRZZZZBAL	
FRIEDRICH, EMMA	18	F	SVNT	GRZZZZBAL	
LASKAWSKA, KATHARINE	55	F	W	GRZZZZBAL	
MARIANNE	10	F	CH	GRZZZZBAL	
BOLLESLAW	.10	F	INFANT	GRZZZZBAL	
VOBECKA, ANNA	65	F	W	GRZZZZBAL	
GUSKOWSKI, KATHR	54	F	W	GRZZZZBAL	
FRANZISKA	6	F	CHILD	GRZZZZBAL	
ANNA	4	F	CHILD	GRZZZZBAL	
KLOSSOWSKI, ELISABETH	58	F	W	GRZZZZBAL	
BRUNEK	.10	M	INFANT	GRZZZZBAL	
BREUSTEDT, EMMA	24	F	W	GRZZZZBAL	

PASSENGER	AGE	SEX	OCCUPATION	PRVL	DES
GRAFF, ROSALIA	24	F	W		GRZZZZBAL
HELENA	3	F	CHILD		GRZZZZBAL
ANNA	.01	F	INFANT		GRZZZZBAL
CONSTANCIA	50	F	W		GRZZZZBAL
GREMER, ELISABETH	20	F	SVNT		GRZZZZBAL
GENTHER, ANNA	18	F	SVNT		GRZZZZBAL
KAYSER, ANNA	25	F	W		GRZZZZBAL
MINNA	.01	F	INFANT		GRZZZZBAL
FREUDENBERG, HELENE	21	F	SVNT		GRZZZZBAL
KATHE, HELENE	19	F	SVNT		GRZZZZBAL
WAGNER, BARBARA	17	F	SVNT		GRZZZZBAL
MEYER, CATHR	18	F	SVNT		GRZZZZBAL
RICHERT, EMILIE	18	F	SVNT		GRZZZZBAL
KLAEHN, SOPHIE	28	F	W		GRZZZZBAL
WILLI	4	M	CHILD		GRZZZZBAL
BOEHM, THERESE	26	F	W		GRZZZZBAL
JOHNSON, MARIA	25	F	W		GRZZZZBAL
MINNA	.09	F	INFANT		GRZZZZBAL
SCHWANT, THEOP--LA	18	F	SVNT		GRZZZZBAL
SEEL, IDA	29	F	SVNT		GRZZZZBAL
ELISE	7	F	CHILD		GRZZZZBAL
THESING, MARIA	27	F	W		GRZZZZIL
LAMPEN, CHRISTINE	20	F	SVNT		GRZZZZBAL
MENKE, ANNA	20	F	SVNT		GRZZZZBAL
LOEWE, MINNA	25	F	SVNT		GRZZZZBAL
HOFMANN, MATHILDE	26	F	W		GRZZZZBAL
RENTHE, LOUISE	38	F	W		GRZZZZBAL
HIRSCHMUELLER, ANNA	32	F	W		GRZZZZBAL
SCHINNER, LIZZIE	25	F	W		GRZZZZBAL
EDMUND	.11	M	INFANT		GRZZZZBAL
VORNHORN, WILHELMINE	22	F	W		GRZZZZBAL
MARIA	2	F	CHILD		GRZZZZBAL
BOHLMANN, FRANZKA	16	F	SVNT		GRZZZZBAL
SCHAUER, MARIA	37	F	W		GRZZZZBAL
FRANZ	3	M	CHILD		GRZZZZBAL
BRUNO	.11	M	INFANT		GRZZZZBAL
LEWANDOWSKA, FRANZKA	26	F	W		GRZZZZBAL
THERESE	5	F	CHILD		GRZZZZBAL
MARY	3	F	CHILD		GRZZZZBAL
HELENE	.09	F	INFANT		GRZZZZBAL
MANKA, MARYANNA	21	F	W		GRZZZZBAL
VICTORIA	.09	F	INFANT		GRZZZZBAL
ZA--EWSKA, FRANZKA	16	F	SVNT		GRZZZZBAL
SABANSKA, MARGR	30	F	W		GRZZZZBAL
JACOB	2	M	CHILD		GRZZZZBAL
REKISS, HENRIETTE	54	F	W		GRZZZZBAL
OTTO, HEDWIG	8	F	CHILD		GRZZZZBAL
SZAMBELAU, MARIANNA	18	F	SVNT		GRZZZZBAL
JOSEPH	.06	M	INFANT		GRZZZZBAL
BRACK, MARIANNA	25	F	W		GRZZZZBAL
FRANZ	.11	M	INFANT		GRZZZZBAL
KIRK, MARTHA	19	F	SVNT		GRZZZZIL
ZINDARS, JOHANNE	26	F	W		GRZZZZIL
RENNEBAUM, MARIA	28	F	W		GRZZZZIL
NOWAKI, ANNA	24	F	W		GRZZZZIL
ELISABETH	4	F	CHILD		GRZZZZIL
KOCKS, MARIA	22	F	W		GRZZZZIL
MARIA	4	F	CHILD		GRZZZZIL
HEINRICH	2	F	CHILD		GRZZZZIL
ELISABETH	.07	F	INFANT		GRZZZZIL
FUCHS, MARGA	19	F	SVNT		GRZZZZIL
KNOTZER, ROSA	20	F	SVNT		GRZZZZIL
HOFFMANN, AUGUSTE	25	F	SVNT		GRZZZZIL
GRUENWALD, EMMA	21	F	SVNT		GRZZZZIL
KUCHCINSKA, I--SA	30	F	W		GRZZZZIL
LEO	2	M	CHILD		GRZZZZIL
WLADISLAUS	.02	M	INFANT		GRZZZZIL
SCHREINER, MARIA	36	F	W		GRZZZZIL
MICHAEL	6	M	CHILD		GRZZZZIL
GEORG	4	M	CHILD		GRZZZZIL
FRANZ	.09	M	INFANT		GRZZZZIL
SCHIMANOWSKI, PAULINE	35	F	W		GRZZZZIL
ANNA	10	F	CH		GRZZZZIL
FRANZ	8	M	CHILD		GRZZZZIL
BERTHA	7	F	CHILD		GRZZZZIL
JOSEPH	3	M	CHILD		GRZZZZIL
MARIA	.06	F	INFANT		GRZZZZIL
REICH, EMILIE	32	F	W		GRZZZZIL
MARGR	8	F	CHILD		GRZZZZIL
ANNA	6	F	CHILD		GRZZZZIL
FRITZ	4	M	CHILD		GRZZZZIL
CHARLOTTE	2	F	CHILD		GRZZZZIL
LOUISE	.06	F	INFANT		GRZZZZIL
FOLKERTO, FRIEDR	64	M	FARMER		GRZZZZIL
CATHA	18	F	D		GRZZZZIL
GRAF, THERESE	47	F	W		GRZZZZIL
ANNA	22	F	D		GRZZZZIL
LOUISE	15	F	D		GRZZZZIL
OSWALD	10	M	CH		GRZZZZIL
THERESE	8	F	CHILD		GRZZZZIL
JOHANNE	6	F	CHILD		GRZZZZIL
FRANZISKA	4	F	CHILD		GRZZZZIL
JOHANN	2	M	CHILD		GRZZZZIL
JOSEPH	.06	M	INFANT		GRZZZZIL
HARDER, JACOB	31	M	FARMER		GRZZZZIL
ANNA	26	F	W		GRZZZZIL
SCHULZ, MARTIN	30	M	JNR		GRZZZZIL
MARIA	30	F	W		GRZZZZIL
ANNA	4	F	CHILD		GRZZZZIL
MARTIN	3	M	CHILD		GRZZZZIL
GERTRUDE	.10	F	INFANT		GRZZZZIL
KOPP, JOSEF	25	M	BKLYR		SRZZZZIL
CRICENEIA	26	F	W		SRZZZZIL
WILHELM	.10	M	INFANT		SRZZZZIL
STIEGLITZ, MARIA	40	F	W		SRZZZZIL
HEINR	15	M	LABR		SRZZZZIL
MOELLER, CHRISTIAN	18	M	LABR		SRZZZZIA
ANNA	13	F	SVNT		SRZZZZIA
LOUISE	16	F	SVNT		SRZZZZIA
EURICH, JACOB	58	M	FARMER		SRZZZZBAL
MARIA	48	F	W		SRZZZZBAL
PHILIPP	8	M	CHILD		SRZZZZBAL
HOPPE, FRANZ	26	M	FARMER		SRZZZZBAL
MARTHA	26	F	W		SRZZZZBAL
HEIDMANN, GERTRUD	50	F	W		SRZZZZBAL
HEINRICH	20	M	CL		SRZZZZBAL
DINA	18	F	D		SRZZZZBAL
WILHELM	14	M	CL		SRZZZZBAL
ELISE	12	F	CH		SRZZZZBAL
JOSEF	6	M	CHILD		SRZZZZBAL
FREKING, CLEMM	35	M	TLR		SRZZZZBAL
LINA	24	F	W		SRZZZZBAL
BITTNER, FRIEDR	47	M	LABR		SRZZZZBAL
JOHANNE	49	F	W		SRZZZZBAL
HERRMANN, FRANZ	74	M	LABR		SRZZZZBAL
FRIEDERIKE	70	F	W		SRZZZZBAL
MILIAN, BARBARA	38	F	W		SRZZZZUNK
KUNIGUNDE	12	F	CH		SRZZZZUNK
VALENTIN	10	M	CH		SRZZZZUNK
MARGARETE	9	F	CHILD		SRZZZZUNK
JOHANN	8	M	CHILD		SRZZZZUNK
GEORG	7	M	CHILD		SRZZZZUNK
SOPHIE	5	F	CHILD		SRZZZZUNK
PANKRATZ	3	M	CHILD		SRZZZZUNK
JOHANN	1	M	CHILD		SRZZZZUNK
TEGELER, FERDINAND	25	M	SMH		SRZZZZUNK
WILHELMENE	24	F	W		SRZZZZUNK
HERMANN	4	M	CHILD		SRZZZZUNK
WILHNE	2	F	CHILD		SRZZZZUNK
BERNHOLD	26	M	SHMK		SRZZZZUNK
JANSSEN, ED	47	M	FARMER		SRZZZZIL
ANNA	49	F	W		SRZZZZIL
THEDA	23	F	D		SRZZZZIL
SCHAEFER, WILHELM	32	M	FARMER		SRZZZZUNK
MARIA	28	F	W		SRZZZZUNK
CARL	.01	M	INFANT		SRZZZZUNK
SCHREFFLER, VERONIKA	54	F	W		SRZZZZBAL
CONRAD	22	M	UNKNOWN		SRZZZZBAL
LE--ELER, JOHAN	32	M	FARMER		GRZZZZIL
META	28	F	W		GRZZZZIL

PASSENGER	AGE	SEX	OCCUPATION	PRVL	DES
JOHANN	4	M	CHILD	GRZZZZIL	
JOACHIM	2	M	CHILD	GRZZZZIL	
ANGELUS	2	M	CHILD	GRZZZZIL	
HENGGLER, JOSEPH	39	M	MD	SRZZZZBAL	
MARIA	28	F	W	SRZZZZBAL	
ANNA	11	F	CH	SRZZZZBAL	
ELISE	8	F	CHILD	SRZZZZBAL	
MUTH, JOHANNES	26	M	JNR	GRZZZZBAL	
ELISABETH	27	F	W	GRZZZZBAL	
HEINRICH	5	M	CHILD	GRZZZZBAL	
CONRAD	2	M	CHILD	GRZZZZBAL	
NANN--FSKY, JACOB	27	M	FARMER	GRZZZZBAL	
JACOB	6	M	CHILD	GRZZZZBAL	
ANNA	8	F	CHILD	GRZZZZBAL	
AUGSTIN, CLEMENS	36	M	FARMER	GRZZZZBAL	
MARIA	33	F	W	GRZZZZBAL	
AGNES	10	F	CH	GRZZZZBAL	
BERNHARD	8	M	CHILD	GRZZZZBAL	
JOSEF	5	M	CHILD	GRZZZZBAL	
MARIA	2	F	CHILD	GRZZZZBAL	
HAVEL, JOSEF	18	M	FARMER	GRZZZZBAL	
MEYER, FRANZ	56	M	FARMER	GRZZZZBAL	
ALWINE	54	F	W	GRZZZZBAL	
PAUL	11	M	CH	GRZZZZBAL	
BUELAU, EMILIE	32	F	W	GRZZZZBAL	
EDUARD	29	M	TU	GRZZZZBAL	
THEODOR	16	M	SMH	GRZZZZBAL	
FREY, LOUISE	55	F	W	GRZZZZBAL	
JOHANNES	17	M	LABR	GRZZZZBAL	
MARIA	12	F	CH	GRZZZZBAL	
K--SE, JOHANN	42	M	FARMER	GRZZZZNE	
MARGR	40	F	W	GRZZZZNE	
DIEDRICH	14	M	FARMER	GRZZZZNE	
WILHELM	9	M	CHILD	GRZZZZNE	
FRIEDRICH	4	M	CHILD	GRZZZZNE	
SZESZYCKI, THEODOZIA	30	F	W	GRZZZZBAL	
MARIANNA	11	F	CH	GRZZZZBAL	
PALAGIA	9	F	CHILD	GRZZZZBAL	
STANISLAWA	7	F	CHILD	GRZZZZBAL	
JOSEPH	5	M	CHILD	GRZZZZBAL	

SHIP: MARSALA

FROM: HAMBURG
TO: NEW YORK
ARRIVED: 01 OCTOBER 1888

PASSENGER	AGE	SEX	OCCUPATION	PRVL	DES
RATHKE, EMILIE	20	F	SGL	GRAEVVNY	
CORNELIUS, MARIE	22	F	SGL	BVZZZZNY	
SEIFERT, MAGARETHE	23	F	SGL	BVZZZZNY	
ROSMUS, MARIE	28	F	SGL	BVACBFNY	
LAURITZEN, CAROLINE	18	F	SGL	PRZZZZCH	
RINNERN, JOHANN	33	M	FARMER	PRZZZZCH	
U	31	F	W	PRZZZZCH	
FRIEDR.	7	M	CHILD	PRZZZZCH	
WILH.	6	M	CHILD	PRZZZZCH	
META	5	F	CHILD	PRZZZZCH	
JULIUS	4	M	CHILD	PRZZZZCH	
HERM.	3	M	CHILD	PRZZZZCH	
RUDOLF	.11	M	INFANT	PRZZZZCH	
POSSIN, PAUL	22	M	BKBNDR	PRZZZZNY	
GUELDIG, JOSEF	22	M	PRNTR	WMZZZZCH	
ANDREAS	26	M	PRNTR	WMZZZZCH	
KOWALSKA, MARIANE	22	F	WO	PRZZZZNY	
WOJTECH	.11	M	INFANT	PRZZZZNY	
SATOW, HERM.	32	M	MLR	MKZZZZCH	
RABENSTEIN, REINHOLD	32	M	LABR	PRZZZZDET	
ANNA	32	F	W	PRZZZZDET	
RIEMANN, F.W.	32	M	LABR	PRABLMNY	
DALLMANN, ERNESTINE	30	F	WO	PRAENLNY	

PASSENGER	AGE	SEX	OCCUPATION	PRVL	DES
GUSTAV	4	M	CHILD	PRAENLNY	
LOEFFELHARDT, DORATHEA	24	F	WO	PRACBFNY	
ANNA	4	F	CHILD	PRACBFNY	
DEJISKA, JOSEFA	21	F	SGL	PRAHSCNY	
STEFFEN, JULIUS	13	M	SCH	PRACBFUNK	
GAMBELLA, AUGUST	20	M	FARMER	PRZZZZIA	
AUGUSTE	27	F	SGL	PRZZZZIA	
ROLANDER, EMILIE	29	F	SGL	PRZZZZNY	
ZANG, ERNST	59	M	LABR	PRZZZZNY	
GRUENEBECK, U	27	F	SGL	PRZZZZUSA	
FROBOESE, JOHS.	25	M	LABR	PRZZZZCH	
KNISPEL, EMIL	16	M	LABR	PRZZZZNY	
KLOSE, EMANUEL	54	M	LABR	PRZZZZUSA	
SCHULTZ, SOPHIE	58	F	WO	PRAJWOUSA	
SCHLICKE, DORA	28	F	WO	PRAJWOUSA	
KARL	7	M	CHILD	PRAJWOUSA	
MARIE	6	F	CHILD	PRAJWOUSA	
EMMA	5	F	CHILD	PRAJWOUSA	
WILLI	4	M	CHILD	PRAJWOUSA	
ERNST	2	M	CHILD	PRAJWOUSA	
AUGUST	.09	M	INFANT	PRAJWOUSA	
SIMON, KATHA.	20	F	SGL	PRAJWOUSA	
JOH.	18	M	LABR	PRZZZZUSA	
FRANZISKA	15	F	SGL	PRZZZZUSA	
WOIGT, AUGST	58	M	TKR	PRAAKHNY	
CAROLINE	55	F	W	PRAAKHNY	
SCHILKE, MATHILDE	32	F	WO	PRAAKHNY	
FRIEDA	.09	F	INFANT	PRALKBNY	
META	6	F	CHILD	PRALKBNY	
DEMOLSKI, ALBERT	23	M	LABR	PRALKBNY	
PETZEL, LAURA	36	F	WO	PRALKBNY	
MAX	2	M	CHILD	PRALKBNY	
MIETHKE, --RIETTE	39	F	WO	PRAAKHNY	
SEIDEL, REBECKA	22	F	SGL	PRZZZZNY	
LAWA, JOHAN	27	M	BKR	PRAAVHNY	
SEIBOLD, FRIEDR.	25	M	GDNR	WMZZZZNY	
OESCHLE, CAROLINE	22	F	SGL	WMZZZZNY	
KOCH, THERESE	22	F	SGL	WMAEPPNY	
BURKART, CAROLINE	21	F	SGL	BDZZZZNY	
LOUISE	19	F	SGL	BDZZZZNY	
GARNER, MARIE	22	F	SGL	BDAEPPNY	
KRAUS, GEORG	39	M	SHMK	BDACEDNY	
CLARA	40	F	W	BDACEDNY	
EUGENIE	7	F	CHILD	BDACEDNY	
MARIE	2	F	CHILD	BDACEDNY	
BAER, PHILIPP	26	M	BCHR	BDABEUNY	
JAKOWSKY, JOHANNA	30	F	WO	BDAAKHNY	
JULEANE	7	F	CHILD	BDAAKHNY	
HEDWIG	5	F	CHILD	BDAAKHNY	
ELISE	.11	F	INFANT	BDAAKHNY	
SCHROEDER, HEINRICH	30	M	MCHT	BDADDDNY	
TELZEROW, LOUISE	52	F	WO	BDAAKHNY	
BEERMANN, WILH.	21	M	SDLR	BDACBFNY	
GOERNER, HERM.	46	M	HTR	SYZZZZNY	
RONSCHKE, LUDWIG	25	M	LABR	SYAJSXNY	
BIRKOMANN, JOHANN	25	M	LABR	SYABWCUSA	
VOGT, ADAM	52	M	LABR	PRZZZZNY	
LEU, CONRAD	32	M	FARMER	PRAEKYNY	
HAASS, JOHANN	25	M	FARMER	BVZZZZNY	
ARNOLD, MINNA	31	F	WO	SYZZZZNY	
MARTHA	7	F	CHILD	SYZZZZNY	
JULIUS	3	M	CHILD	SYZZZZNY	
MINNA	2	M	CHILD	SYZZZZNY	
ANNA	19	F	SGL	SYZZZZNY	
WULF, CAROLINE	31	F	WO	SYABYWNY	
RAUCHENBERG, FRIED.	20	M	MLR	SYADCRNY	
BOEHMER, GOTTE	38	M	TLR	SYZZZZUSA	
STEPPART, AMALIE	29	F	W	PRZZZZNY	
META	3	F	CHILD	PRZZZZNY	
MARTHA	.06	F	INFANT	PRZZZZNY	
EHLEBEN, AUGUSTE	25	F	WO	PRZZZZNY	
META	.06	F	INFANT	PRZZZZNY	
LOSZYNSKA, MARIANE	29	F	WO	PRAEIOBUF	
LEONHARD	.11	M	INFANT	PRAEIOBUF	
U	00	F	D	PRAEIOBUF	

PASSENGER	AGE	SEX	OCCUPATION	PRVL	DES
JOHANN	.01	M	INFANT	PRAEIOBUF	
SZEZCPANSKI, HUGO	25	M	BRR	PRAAKHNY	
WIETACH, CHTISTINE	30	F	WO	PRZZZZNY	
ANNA	3	F	CHILD	PRZZZZNY	
JOSEF	.11	M	INFANT	PRZZZZNY	

```
SHIP:     MORAVIA

FROM:     HAMBURG AND HAVRE
TO:       NEW YORK
ARRIVED:  01 OCTOBER 1888
```

PASSENGER	AGE	SEX	OCCUPATION	PRVL	DES
HELLMERICH, HERM.	21	M	MCHT	HBZZZZUSA	
KREUTER, HANS	14	M	SCH	HBZZZZUSA	
BLUME, HEINR.	43	M	MCHT	HBZZZZUSA	
HEYMANN, ARTHUR	25	M	MCHT	HBAAKHUSA	
KAROLEWSKY, CAROLINE	22	F	SGL	HBABOQUSA	
RAPPE, CARRY	14	F	SGL	HBABVHUSA	
BECKER, RICHARD	31	M	MCHT	HBZZZZUSA	
THEKLA	18	F	W	HBZZZZUSA	
CLAUSEN, CARL	15	M	LABR	HBACBFUSA	
STEINMETZ, CATH.	43	F	WO	HBACBWUSA	
SCHULTZ, ELZE	13	F	CH	BRZZZZUSA	
BUCKENDAHL, FRIEDRICH	27	M	GDNR	BRAFQBUSA	
KLUML, CARL	24	M	SVNT	PRZZZZUSA	
KOHN, KAROLINE	59	F	WO	PRZZZZUSA	
HOLSTEIN, AMALIE	18	F	SGL	PRAADEUSA	
PETERSEN, JUSTUS	16	M	BCHR	PRAADEUSA	
RUGE, MARIE	42	F	WO	HBZZZZUSA	
BERTHA	.11	F	INFANT	HBZZZZUSA	
SCHLUETOW, EMMA	50	F	WO	HBAINKUSA	
EMIL	15	M	CH	HBAINKUSA	
ELLA	7	F	CHILD	HBAINKUSA	
ALICE	6	F	CHILD	HBAINKUSA	
HERZ, ANNA	35	F	WO	HBAADEUSA	
MAX	3	M	CHILD	HBAADEUSA	
ANDRESEN, MARIE	28	F	SGL	PRZZZZUSA	
ELLING, MARIE	27	F	SGL	HBZZZZUSA	
LETKA, CHRISTIAN	69	M	LABR	HBAHUHUSA	
CAROLINE	59	F	W	HBAHUHUSA	
HERM.	15	M	S	HBAHUHUSA	
GROSS, JOH.	21	M	LABR	PRZZZZUSA	
GRAUMANN, CARL	25	M	LABR	PRADCVUSA	
LOUISE	24	F	W	PRADCVUSA	
WYSORKA, JOSEFA	45	F	WO	PRABSPUSA	
HELENE	7	F	CHILD	PRABSPUSA	
EWERT, BERTHA	19	F	SGL	PRAHWIUSA	
GRAMBOW, OTTO	14	M	BLKSMH	HBZZZZUSA	
LIENAU, THEODOR	15	M	LABR	HBABMIUSA	
POVTALA, VALENTIN	40	M	LABR	PRZZZZUSA	
ROSALIE	20	F	SGL	PRZZZZUSA	
STEUHOWSKA, JOSEFA	24	F	SGL	PRZZZZUSA	
FAUST, ALBERTINE	36	F	UNKNOWN	PRZZZZUSA	
JANSEN, GOENKE	46	F	WO	PRZZZZUSA	
BARTSCH, HERM.	16	M	LABR	PRZZZZUSA	
BAUER, MARIE	19	F	SGL	PRACIFUSA	
SCHWARTZ, MARG.	46	F	WO	PRABNSUSA	
META	15	F	D	PRABNSUSA	
SACH, FRITZ	26	M	SDLR	PRZZZZUSA	
BARGEND, ANNA	24	F	W	PRZZZZUSA	
TOKARSKI, MARIANNE	22	F	WO	PRACMHUSA	
FRANZ	6	M	CHILD	PRACMHUSA	
SOPHIE	3	F	CHILD	PRACMHUSA	
STANISLAUS	.09	M	INFANT	PRACMHUSA	
KOERNER, FRDKE	29	F	SGL	PRADUXUSA	
KLEVENHAGEN, LUDWIG	24	M	BCHR	PRZZZZUSA	
DIX, ERNESTINE	66	F	WO	PRZZZZUSA	
KOERNER, ANNA	23	F	SGL	PRAFSAUSA	
SEILLER, FRIDOLIN	23	M	SHMK	BVZZZZUSA	
JOHANNSEN, JOACHIM	34	M	LABR	HBZZZZUSA	
FELGEROW, ADOLF	22	M	LKSH	HBAAKHUSA	
MUELLER, HERRM.	61	M	LABR	HBAAKHUSA	
EUGEN	16	M	LABR	HBAAKHUSA	
STALTER, CAROLINE	43	F	WO	ACZZZZUSA	
MARIE	14	F	CH	ACZZZZUSA	
IGNAZ	12	M	CH	ACZZZZUSA	
PHILOMENE	11	F	CH	ACZZZZUSA	
EMIL	9	M	CHILD	ACZZZZUSA	
PETER	7	M	CHILD	ACZZZZUSA	
RIESCHER, OTTILIE	20	F	SGL	ACAIAGUSA	
RIEBER, FRIEDRICH	37	M	JNR	ACAIAGUSA	
JAUCH, ANTON	30	M	JNR	ACAIAGUSA	
MAUZ, THADAEUS	16	M	JNR	ACAIAGUSA	
STROHMAIER, CARL	18	M	MCHT	ACACOJUSA	
COUSSY, ROMAIN	44	M	WVR	ACAAYFUSA	
CAROLINE	47	F	W	ACAAYFUSA	
EMILIE	16	F	CH	ACAAYFUSA	
MARIE	11	F	CH	ACAAYFUSA	
EIGELDINGEN, JACQUES	7	M	CHILD	ACAAYFUSA	
FAVY, DENIS	19	M	LABR	FRZZZZUSA	
MUELLER, ERNST	17	M	LABR	SRZZZZUSA	
GAULOCHER, MATHIAS	19	M	FARMER	PRZZZZUSA	
ENDRESS, AGATHA	24	F	SGL	PRZZZZUSA	
LOHMUELLER, OTTO	40	M	HTR	PRAAKHUSA	
BRITSCHJI, ROSALIE	17	F	SGL	PRAGXBUSA	
SPINNENHORN, JOH.	34	M	FARMER	WMZZZZUSA	
REIHER, EMMA	.03	F	INFANT	WMAEXJUSA	
EHLERS, CESAR	23	M	LABR	HBZZZZUSA	
SCHNOOR, PETER	18	M	FARMER	PRZZZZUSA	
HINKELMANN, ANNA	50	F	WO	PRZZZZUSA	
LAURITZEN, LEONORE	21	F	SGL	PRZZZZUSA	
NATHAN, AUGUSTE	42	F	WO	PRZZZZUSA	
MANTEI, AMALIE	25	F	SGL	PRZZZZUSA	
NOWICKA, MARIANNA	21	F	SGL	PRZZZZUSA	
MACK, IDA	30	F	WO	PRZZZZUSA	
RASSMUSS, SOPHIE	23	F	SGL	PRZZZZUSA	
PETROWSKA, AGNESKA	27	F	SGL	PRZZZZUSA	
KRESS, ANNA	19	F	SGL	PRZZZZUSA	
STEPPAT, LEOPOLD	31	M	JNR	PRZZZZUSA	
KRZYZAWSKI, MICHEL	25	M	LABR	PRZZZZUSA	
BECKER, ERICH	24	M	LABR	PRZZZZUSA	
SORG, MARIE	14	F	SGL	BVZZZZUSA	
DEBROCK, META	32	F	WO	BVAHMCUSA	
CLARA	7	F	CHILD	BVAHMCUSA	
WULF, CARL	21	M	FARMER	BVAHMCUSA	
DUX, ALBERT	25	M	LABR	BVAAKHUSA	
HAAS, IDA	31	F	SGL	BVAAKHUSA	
LEVY, SIGISMUND	28	M	FUR	BVAAKHUSA	
KOLLIWER, AUGUSTE	25	F	SGL	BVAAKHUSA	
GRABOW, OTTO	46	M	CL	BVAAKHUSA	
BARGEND, JOHANN	24	M	LABR	PRZZZZUSA	
ROENSCH, THERESE	23	F	W	PRZZZZUSA	
SANDKUHL, ERNST	22	M	MCHT	PRAAXTUSA	
CALB, HENRIETTE	24	F	SGL	PRABOQUSA	
DICK, ERNST	27	M	LKSH	PRAFOYUSA	
RITTER, WILH.	16	M	SHMK	PRADLUUSA	
ZIEGELBAUER, PAULINE	7	F	CHILD	WMZZZZUSA	
GESELL, KARL	14	M	LABR	WMACBKUSA	
HARTUNG, CASPAR	27	M	LABR	WMACBKUSA	
QUARDT, ANNA	16	F	SGL	PRZZZZUSA	
HOERING, KARL	25	M	MCHT	SYZZZZUSA	
GUETLEIN, HEINR.	33	M	LABR	SYABESUSA	
BRAUER, JOSEPHA	51	F	WO	BVZZZZUSA	
GUSTAV	7	M	CHILD	BVZZZZUSA	
WECKER, FRNZ	15	M	MCHT	BVAIUPUSA	
WEISS, WILH.	15	M	LABR	WMZZZZUSA	
KUMPF, ANNA	30	F	WO	WMABOQUSA	
WILH.	7	M	CHILD	WMABOQUSA	
HUGO	4	M	CHILD	WMABOQUSA	
ALMA	.09	F	INFANT	WMABOQUSA	
ROWAZYNSKY, FRANZ	28	M	LABR	PRZZZZUSA	
SCHUMACHER, WILH.	22	M	LABR	PRZZZZUSA	
PEREWITZ, CAROLINE	20	F	SGL	PRZZZZUSA	
VORNDRAM, KASPAR	27	M	FARMER	BVZZZZUSA	
HOFMANN, KASPAR	23	M	FARMER	BVZZZZUSA	

PASSENGER	AGE	SEX	OCCUPATION	PRVVLS	DES
REIHER, CARL	28	M	LABR	BVZZZZUSA
HENRIETTE	27	F	W	BVZZZZUSA
JETA	7	F	CHILD	BVZZZZUSA
CARL	6	M	CHILD	BVZZZZUSA
JENSEN, CAROLINE	16	F	SGL	PRZZZZUSA
GAUL, ALWINE	28	F	WO	PRAADEUSA
THEODOR	.02	M	INFANT	PRAADEUSA
BLOECKER, DOROTGEA	28	F	SGL	HBZZZZUSA
BOETTGER, JOHANNA	25	F	SGL	HBZZZZUSA
KOFELDT, HEINR.	26	M	SVNT	HBZZZZUSA
SAUDERSSEN, CATH.	22	F	SGL	HBZZZZUSA
OLDENBURG, MINNA	16	F	SGL	PRZZZZUSA
GODENSCHWANG, JOHANNA	38	F	WO	HBZZZZUSA
VOLQUARDT, CHRISTIAN	52	M	MCHT	HBALMFUSA
ADERHOLD, FROKE	24	F	SGL	PRZZZZUSA
MUHS, JOHANN	44	M	LABR	HBZZZZUSA
PFLEGER, OTTO	24	M	FARMER	BVZZZZUSA
WERNER, GEORG	29	M	LKSH	BVAAKHUSA
FUERST, PETER	24	M	FARMER	PRZZZZUSA
SAMUELSEN, HARTWIG	22	M	BKR	PRZZZZUSA
HANKE, ANNA	28	F	SGL	PRAARZUSA
KEYSER, CARL	27	M	MCHT	PRAHZSUSA
WERNER, HERRMANN	33	M	LKSH	PRACNLUSA
BERTHA	29	F	W	PRACNLUSA
MARTIN	2	M	CHILD	PRACNLUSA
MAGDALENA	.08	F	INFANT	PRACNLUSA
GOMOLKA, JOSEF	30	M	JNR	PRZZZZUSA
BRAUN, ERNST	24	M	TNR	PRZZZZUSA
GOOTEL, JOH.	26	M	FARMER	PRZZZZUSA
JUERGENSEN, ANNA	22	F	SGL	PRAHZPUSA
SCHUETT, MARIE	15	F	SGL	PRAHZPUSA
OTTESGAARD, MAGD.	44	F	WO	PRZZZZUSA
MARIE	12	F	D	PRAHZPUSA
JUERGEN	7	M	CHILD	PRAHZPUSA
CHRISTINE	6	F	CHILD	PRAHZPUSA
MAGDALENE	3	F	CHILD	PRAHZPUSA
THOMSEN, ANNA	28	F	SGL	PRZZZZUSA
SCHOETT, MARIE	16	M	FARMER	PRAHILUSA
BLUNCK, CARL	15	M	FARMER	PRAGQLUSA
LAGE, AUGUST	48	M	PT	PRAGQLUSA
AUGUST	16	M	LABR	PRAGQLUSA
BECKER, MARIE	49	M	WO	PRZZZZUSA
GUSS, MAGDALENE	29	F	UNKNOWN	BVZZZZUSA
LUDWIG	7	M	CHILD	BVZZZZUSA
MARIE	6	F	CHILD	BVZZZZUSA
FERDINAND	5	M	CHILD	BVZZZZUSA
MILDENBERGER, LOUISE	30	F	SGL	BVAERUUSA
DINKELACKER, MARIE	14	F	SGL	BVAERUUSA
DENNER, JACOB	19	M	LABR	BVACFWUSA
HUBERT, JULIANE	48	F	WO	PRZZZZUSA
KLARA	7	F	CHILD	PRZZZZUSA
HULDA	.11	F	INFANT	PRZZZZUSA
MOELLER, MINNA	18	F	SGL	PRZZZZUSA
AMANDA	17	F	SGL	PRZZZZUSA
EUGEN, EMMA	20	F	SGL	MKZZZZUSA
BUERKEN, FRIED.	21	M	LABR	WMZZZZUSA
HAAS, GOTTLOB	20	M	LABR	WMZZZZUSA
KRETZER, ELISABETH	21	F	SGL	WMABOQUSA
KECK, CHRISTIAN	38	M	BCHR	WMABOQUSA
HENRIETTE	40	F	W	WMZZZZUSA
WILH.	13	M	CH	WMZZZZUSA
HENRIETTE	7	F	CHILD	WMZZZZUSA
FRITZ	.06	M	INFANT	WMZZZZUSA
ZIPP, MARIE	19	M	SGL	WMACFWUSA
MAIERHOFER, VICTORIA	50	F	WO	WMZZZZUSA
KRUEMPEL, JEAN	6	M	CHILD	WMZZZZUSA
WOLF, PAUL	16	M	BKR	WMAEXWUSA
KOERPER, JOH.	16	M	LABR	HSZZZZUSA
FEIL, PHILIPP	16	M	LABR	HSADQZUSA
FRANZ	6	M	CHILD	HSADQZUSA
RUHLE, ALBERT	35	M	CGRMKR	HSACBFUSA
AMALIE	33	F	W	HSACBFUSA
ANNA	7	F	CHILD	HSACBFUSA
HILDEGARD	6	F	CHILD	HSACBFUSA
RICHARD	5	M	CHILD	HSACBFUSA

PASSENGER	AGE	SEX	OCCUPATION	PRVVLS	DES
WILHELM	.09	M	INFANT	HSACBFUSA
SCHMIDT, AMALIE	30	F	SGL	HSACBFUSA
RAUCHFUSS, ADELHEID	20	F	SGL	PRZZZZUSA
ROENSCH, FRANZ	30	M	BCHR	PRZZZZUSA
BLUMER, DAVID	40	M	FARMER	SRZZZZUSA
HARTMANN, EDUARD	28	M	FARMER	SRADSUUSA
BACHMANN, ROSA	21	F	SGL	BDZZZZUSA
MATT, JACOB	21	M	FARMER	BDZZZZUSA
DUELLE, JOSEPH	37	M	DRVR	BDZZZZUSA
STREHLER, JACOB	38	M	FARMER	SRZZZZUSA
GOUILLON, EUGENE	29	F	GLDR	SRAAHUUSA
LOEHRER, FERDINAND	22	M	SDLR	SRAFGFUSA
RECHSTEINER, SALOMON	30	M	FARMER	SRZZZZUSA
SCHEU, JOSEPH	19	M	FARMER	SRAIAGUSA
SARTMANN, AUGUSTE	22	M	FARMER	WMZZZZUSA
MOELLER, HANS	21	M	BCHR	WMADBQUSA

SHIP: SLAVONIA

FROM: SWINEMUNDE
TO: NEW YORK
ARRIVED: 01 OCTOBER 1888

PASSENGER	AGE	SEX	OCCUPATION	PRVVLS	DES
MOLKENTHIN, WILHELM	44	M	JNR	PRZZZZUSA
THERESE	36	F	W	PRZZZZUSA
HELENE	11	F	CH	PRZZZZUSA
EMIL	9	M	CHILD	PRZZZZUSA
REINHOLD	7	M	CHILD	PRZZZZUSA
ALMA	5	F	CHILD	PRZZZZUSA
HUGO	.09	M	INFANT	PRZZZZUSA
WILHELM	9	M	CHILD	PRZZZZUSA
SCHMIDT, CHRISTIAN	41	M	UNKNOWN	PRZZZZUSA
FRIEDERIKE	47	F	W	PRZZZZUSA
RAGUSE, EDUARD	35	M	CPTR	PRZZZZUSA
KAMINSKA, FRANZISKA	20	F	UNKNOWN	PRZZZZUSA
ROZNIAK, MARIANNE	48	F	WO	PRABPNUSA
PAULINE	18	F	CH	PRABPNUSA
VALENTIN	12	M	CH	PRABPNUSA
KAULIN, ANNA	45	F	WO	PRZZZZUSA
REDDIN, AUGUST	26	M	LABR	PRAEVMUSA
EMILIE	24	F	W	PRAEVMUSA
LOUISE	.04	F	INFANT	PRAEVMUSA
WILHELMINE	58	F	M	PRAEVMUSA
RUDNICK, CAROLINE	21	F	UNKNOWN	PRAFQOUSA
CZENSKA, MARIANNA	29	F	WO	PRZZZZUSA
STANISLAUS	5	M	CHILD	PRZZZZUSA
JOHANN	3	M	CHILD	PRZZZZUSA
JOSEPHA	2	M	CHILD	PRZZZZUSA
MARIANNA	.03	F	INFANT	PRZZZZUSA
BLOCK, AUGUSTE	34	F	UNKNOWN	PRZZZZUSA
HERMANN, HEDWIG	17	F	UNKNOWN	PRAEABUSA
VANHOFEN, HENRIETTE	17	F	UNKNOWN	PRZZZZUSA
KOSS, JOHANNE	29	F	UNKNOWN	PRACWIUSA
BOAS, DAVID	19	M	UNKNOWN	PRAEWMUSA
MARTHA	4	F	CHILD	PRAEWMUSA
FRANZISKA	3	F	CHILD	PRAEWMUSA
LAUB, CAROLINE	28	F	WO	PRAJGMUSA
HERMANN	3	M	CHILD	PRAJGMUSA
ROSENTHAL, LUCIA	50	F	WO	PRALDDUSA
STACHOWIAK, FLORENINE	15	F	UNKNOWN	PRABUTUSA
MICHALAK, LUDWIKA	27	F	WO	PRZZZZUSA
AGNES	5	F	CHILD	PRZZZZUSA
VINSENT	3	M	CHILD	PRZZZZUSA
HERMANN	1	M	CHILD	PRZZZZUSA
FAHL, BERTHA	23	F	UNKNOWN	PRZZZZUSA
LINDONBERG, FERDINAND	50	M	LABR	PRACWIUSA
JOHANNA	45	F	W	PRACWIUSA
GUSTAV	11	M	CH	PRACWIUSA
CARL	9	M	CHILD	PRACWIUSA
JOHANN	7	M	CHILD	PRACWIUSA

PASSENGER	AGE	SEX	OCCUPATION	PRVVL	DES
ANNA	4	F	CHILD	PRACWIUSA
EMILIE	2	F	CHILD	PRACWIUSA
PAUL	.09	M	INFANT	PRACWIUSA
LADEMANN, OTTILIE	33	F	WO	PRAJMMUSA
THEODOR	15	M	S	PRAJMMUSA
BUZKOWSKY, MARTHA	19	F	UNKNOWN	PRZZZZUSA
BUTT, HERMANN	32	M	LABR	PRAEWMUSA
AUGUSTE	25	M	W	PRAEWMUSA
HEDWIG	6	F	CHILD	PRAEWMUSA
HELENE	3	F	CHILD	PRAEWMUSA
MIELKE, EDUARD	28	M	LABR	PRZZZZUSA
KOCH, HEINRICH	36	M	LABR	PRZZZZUSA
AUGUSTE	30	F	W	PRZZZZUSA
BERG, JOHANN	35	M	FARMER	PRALMVUSA
AUGUSTE	30	F	W	PRALMVUSA
LOEFFLER, FRIEDRICH	55	M	FARMER	PRACNZUSA
CAROLINE	40	F	W	PRACNZUSA
MAROHN, JULIUS	22	M	LABR	PRACNZUSA
BERTHA	11	F	CH	PRACNZUSA
LOEFFLER, MARTHA	8	F	CHILD	PRACNZUSA
PAUL	4	M	CHILD	PRACNZUSA
FENSKE, EMMA	21	F	UNKNOWN	PRADLOUSA
FRETTIN, EMMA	24	F	WO	PRZZZZUSA
CARL	.11	M	INFANT	PRZZZZUSA
SCHULZ, ERNESTINE	22	F	SVNT	PRZZZZUSA
REPP, CARL	34	M	UNKNOWN	PRAEWMUSA
ALWINE	24	F	W	PRAEWMUSA
GRUTZMACHER, DAVID	70	M	MLR	PRAEWMUSA
DOBERER, ERNESTINE	45	F	WO	PRZZZZUSA
ROBERT	10	M	CH	PRZZZZUSA
JOHANN	5	M	CHILD	PRZZZZUSA
GUTHNECHT, FERDINAND	40	M	LABR	PRZZZZUSA
KLUGE, GUSTAV	39	M	JNR	PRAEZVUSA
JOHANNA	26	F	W	PRAEZVUSA
ARTHUR	11	M	CH	PRAEZVUSA
FRANZ	10	M	CH	PRAEZVUSA
GUSTAV	9	M	CHILD	PRAEZVUSA
BLOSS, LOUISE	28	F	UNKNOWN	PRAEWMUSA
NEISE, WILHELM	49	M	LABR	PRALYZUSA
HENRIETTE	54	F	W	PRALYZUSA
CARL	24	M	FARMER	PRALYZUSA
EMILIE	15	F	CH	PRALYZUSA
ANNA	13	F	CH	PRALYZUSA
SZYMANSKA, FRANZISKA	25	F	WO	PRZZZZUSA
BAESTROW, MINNA	36	F	WO	PRAGDSUSA
WILLY	8	M	CHILD	PRAGDSUSA
EMMA	3	F	CHILD	PRAGDSUSA
PAUL	.11	M	INFANT	PRAGDSUSA
RZADKIEWA, STANISLAWA	28	F	WO	PRZZZZUSA
WLADISLAUS	1	M	CHILD	PRZZZZUSA
STANISLAUS	.06	M	INFANT	PRZZZZUSA
SCHUL--, CARL	21	M	UNKNOWN	PRZZZZUSA
ERDMANN, JOHANNA	35	F	WO	PRABWAUSA
MARIA	11	F	CH	PRABWAUSA
WALDEMAR	7	M	CHILD	PRABWAUSA
MARGARETHE	3	F	CHILD	PRABWAUSA
AMANDA	2	F	CHILD	PRABWAUSA
HERMANN, ANNA	20	F	UNKNOWN	PRZZZZUSA
WODISCHOCK, OTTO	26	M	CPR	PRAEWMUSA
KUEHL, ANNA	23	F	UNKNOWN	PRAGANUSA
KRUEGER, MATHILDE	46	F	WO	PRZZZZUSA
HEDWIG	8	F	CHILD	PRZZZZUSA
ELSBETH	5	F	CHILD	PRZZZZUSA
JOHANNA	4	F	CHILD	PRZZZZUSA
SASS, WILHELM	61	M	UNKNOWN	PRZZZZUSA
LADEMANN, MARTHA	11	F	CH	PRZZZZUSA
FRANZ	4	M	CHILD	PRZZZZUSA
PAUL	3	M	CHILD	PRZZZZUSA
DOMKE, WANDA	22	F	CK	PRABXGUSA
SCHMOLKE, AUGUSTE	28	F	WO	PRAEWZUSA
FROEBEL, OTTO	5	M	CHILD	PRAEWZUSA
SCHMOLKE, PAUL	.11	M	INFANT	PRAEWZUSA
STIEMKE, GERHARD	28	M	TLR	PRACBFUSA
SZYMANSKY, FRANZ	25	M	LABR	PRZZZZUSA
MATHILDE	21	F	W	PRZZZZUSA

PASSENGER	AGE	SEX	OCCUPATION	PRVVL	DES
ZAWATZKY, MARIA	42	F	WO	PRAJJYUSA
GOTTLIEB	15	M	CH	PRAJJYUSA
EMIL	9	M	CHILD	PRAJJYUSA
GUSTAV	6	M	CHILD	PRAJJYUSA
HORST, CAROLINE	28	F	WO	PRZZZZUSA
LOUISE	28	F	UNKNOWN	PRZZZZUSA
JOHANN	3	M	CHILD	PRZZZZUSA
HEDWIG	.11	F	INFANT	PRZZZZUSA
KOWALSKY, PELAGIA	16	F	UNKNOWN	PRAHZFUSA
NEHRING, BERTHA	30	F	SVNT	PRAGMLUSA
PAWLISCH, CARL	33	M	CPTR	PRAGMLUSA
OTTILIE	28	F	W	PRAGMLUSA
RICHARD	8	M	CHILD	PRAGMLUSA
ALBERT	2	M	CHILD	PRAGMLUSA
MAX	.03	M	INFANT	PRAGMLUSA
SIODA, THOMAS	16	M	FARMER	PRABNOUSA
HASSE, FRIEDRICH	22	M	LABR	PRZZZZUSA
AUGUSTE	26	F	W	PRZZZZUSA
LOUISE	.03	F	INFANT	PRZZZZUSA
MUELLER, FRIEDRICH	22	M	LABR	PRZZZZUSA
LAWRENZ, ADELINA	22	F	UNKNOWN	PRZZZZUSA
BOROWSKY, JOHANNA	47	F	WO	PRADGOUSA
MARIE	14	F	CH	PRADGOUSA
JOHN	9	M	CHILD	PRADGOUSA
ERDMANN, OLGA	00	F	INF	PR****USA

SHIP: CIRCASSIA

FROM: GLASGOW AND MOVILLE
TO: NEW YORK
ARRIVED: 02 OCTOBER 1888

PASSENGER	AGE	SEX	OCCUPATION	PRVVL	DES
BIRGMAN, LOUISA	23	F	HP	GRZZZZUSA
FRIEHLING, JACOB	21	M	FARMER	GRZZZZUSA
HORZ, HY.	46	M	FLSH	GRZZZZUSA
BECKER, E.	27	M	CNF	GRZZZZUSA
JACOBS, HRIN.	37	M	JNR	GRZZZZUSA
ROBERT, EMIL	30	M	MNR	FRZZZZUSA
ALPHE.	24	F	W	FRZZZZUSA

SHIP: CASPIAN

FROM: LIVERPOOL, QUEENSTOWN AND HALIFAX
TO: BALTIMORE
ARRIVED: 04 OCTOBER 1888

PASSENGER	AGE	SEX	OCCUPATION	PRVVL	DES
HAHN, JOHANN	20	M	DMS	GRZZZZIA
BORKOWSKA, EVA	27	F	HSWF	GRZZZZOH
FRANCESHEK	.07	F	INFANT	GRZZZZOH
SHULTZ, J.	22	M	TLR	GRZZZZNY
-ERVAIS, STRONGES	23	M	LABR	GRZZZZBAL
RORALIS, -OSIS	28	M	LABR	GRZZZZBAL
SHULTZ, KARL	58	M	LABR	GRZZZZBAL
CARICHOFF, W.	24	M	CL	GRZZZZBAL

PASSENGER	AGE	SEX	OCCUPATION	PRVVL	DES
SHIP: RHYNLAND					
FROM: ANTWERP					
TO: NEW YORK					
ARRIVED: 04 OCTOBER 1888					
YOUNG, JOHN	70	M	MD		SRZZZZBRO
GRANGER, A	40	F	LDY		SRZZZZNY
MEYLAN, MISS	25	F	GVNS		SRZZZZBRO
DECK, ALVI-A	24	F	PVTW		GRZZZZOH
BOEHLER, CLARA	34	M	PVTM		GRZZZZOH
HEIN, JULIUS	17	M	PVTM		GRZZZZNY
MUETTER, MAX	22	M	CMST		GRZZZZNY
OBERLE, EMILIE	22	F	LDY		GRZZZZNY
U	.01	M	INFANT		GRZZZZUNK
DIERR, BERTHA	16	F	LDY		GRZZZZCLE
SCHMITZ, ELISA	25	F	PVTW		GRZZZZOH
SCHUMANN, JOS	18	M	GDNR		GRZZZZNY
SERRES, ANTON	23	M	TCHR		GRZZZZNY
MAYER, MORITZ	15	M	BY		GRZZZZNY
WAGNER, ANNA	20	F	LDY		GRZZZZDET
OSBURG, GUSTAV	21	M	UPHST		GRZZZZNY
NEUSS, MRS	38	F	PVTW		GRZZZZUNK
KATH	3	F	CHILD		GRZZZZUNK
WILH	7	M	CHILD		GRZZZZUNK
PFLEGER, PH	48	F	PVTW		GRZZZZNY
EMMA	12	F	CH		GRZZZZNY
OLIVIER, MARIA	30	F	PVTW		FRZZZZNY
RENE	5	M	CHILD		FRZZZZNY
KOHLER, M	24	F	PVTW		GRZZZZMN
M	24	F	PVTW		GRZZZZMN
JOSEPH, EM	27	M	MCHT		GRZZZZLOU
RIEMECKE, PAUL	18	M	MCHT		GRZZZZNY
BRAJEWSKI, JOSEF	23	M	LABR		GRZZZZNY
SCHULER, HEINR	24	M	LABR		GRZZZZNY
BAUER, CARL	18	M	SHMK		GRZZZZNY
SIEBACH, JOHANN	19	M	NN		GRZZZZNY
SCHNEIDER, LOUISE	00	F	SVNT		GRZZZZNY
ROESSLER, JOHANN	38	M	LABR		GRZZZZUNK
LEFEBRE, EMIL	30	M	JNR		GRZZZZPIT
MANCHCCOURT, HENRI	29	M	MNR		FRZZZZUNK
HETTE, JOSEPH	29	M	MNR		FRZZZZUNK
PREIM, VICTOR	28	M	MCHT		GRZZZZNY
PA-MANO, AUG	25	M	BKBNDR		GRZZZZNY
GANSENEDER, JOHN	17	M	SMH		GRZZZZMIL
NUCHTEN, HERMANN	24	M	CL		GRZZZZASH
MAZIERA, JOHN	25	M	LABR		GRZZZZUNK
NOFKE, GUSTAV	18	M	LABR		GRZZZZFRE
DRECE-N, LOUISE	29	F	W		GRZZZZUNK
BOYER	7	M	CHILD		GRZZZZUNK
MARIA	4	F	CHILD		GRZZZZUNK
LOUISA	3	F	CHILD		GRZZZZUNK
CHARLES	2	M	CHILD		GRZZZZUNK
JACOB	00	M	INF		GRZZZZUNK
HAHN, AMELIA	28	F	W		GRZZZZUNK
GERTRUDE	16	F	SVNT		GRZZZZUNK
JOSEPH	14	M	S		GRZZZZUNK
VON, AGNES	3	F	CHILD		GRZZZZUNK
RUSKIEWIEZ, MA	36	F	W		GRZZZZBUF
FRANZ	11	M	CH		GRZZZZBUF
ANTON	9	M	CHILD		GRZZZZBUF
ALEX	00	M	INF		GRZZZZBUF
KOTTINSKI, ANTON	00	M	LABR		GRZZZZUNK
DRUART, FRANS	24	M	MNR		GRZZZZUNK
HURBY, ANNA	31	F	W		GRZZZZUNK
MARIA	11	F	CH		GRZZZZUNK
ELISABETH	9	F	CHILD		GRZZZZUNK
GUJA, MARIE	28	F	LDY		GRZZZZUNK
SCHOLSKI, MRS	52	F	LDY		GRZZZZCH
FRIDA	10	F	CH		GRZZZZCH
GRASSER, DOROTHEA	18	F	SVNT		GRZZZZUNK
ENGELTER, CATHA	22	F	SVNT		GRZZZZNY
BORK, GEORG	18	M	LABR		GRZZZZNY
HOEFLICH, EVA	18	F	LDY		GRZZZZNY
BECKER, HERM	18	M	LABR		GRZZZZNY
MINA	16	F	SVNT		GRZZZZNY
WEISSBECKER, LUDWIG	17	M	LABR		GRZZZZNY
ACKER, LOUISE	22	F	SVNT		GRZZZZNY
SCHENK, CARL	16	M	FARMER		GRZZZZNY
FREY, FRIEDR	18	M	TLR		GRZZZZNY
MAYER, PAULINE	18	F	SVNT		GRZZZZPHI
FALKNER, CATH	24	F	W		GRZZZZUNK
JOSEPH	00	M	INF		GRZZZZUNK
CARL	00	M	INF		GRZZZZUNK
DEITRICH, CAROLINE	21	F	SVNT		GRZZZZUNK
VELTEN, JACOB	24	M	LABR		GRZZZZNY
FAES, MARIA	22	F	SVNT		GRZZZZNY
BECKER, WM	21	M	LABR		GRZZZZUNK
BETZ, MATHILDE	22	F	SVNT		GRZZZZLEA
WIELAND, JOH	22	M	UNKNOWN		GRZZZZCH
SPONA-EL, WILH	43	M	BCHR		GRZZZZCH
SCHMIDT, G	27	M	SHMK		GRZZZZNY
EPRET, LUDWIG	20	M	NN		GRZZZZNY
STASSER, HCH	28	M	BCHR		GRZZZZNY
GERNER, SOPHIE	20	F	SVNT		GRZZZZNY
PETRI, JACOB	19	M	SHMK		GRZZZZUNK
DORR, JACOB	23	M	BKR		GRZZZZNY
ZIMMER, PH	18	M	LABR		GRZZZZNY
SOLLNER, EMIL	18	M	BCHR		GRZZZZNY
RITTER, CONRAD	24	M	BRR		GRZZZZNY
HARTOG, MARKUS	00	M	BCHR		GRZZZZNY
ROTH, MAX	24	M	BKR		GRZZZZNY
MEINZER, CARL	23	M	NN		GRZZZZUNK
KESEL, JACOB	26	M	LABR		GRZZZZSY
MUELLER, JACOB	17	M	BCHR		GRZZZZBUF
HERMANN, EVA	45	F	W		GRZZZZROC
FRANZ	15	M	CH		GRZZZZROC
VAL	8	M	CHILD		GRZZZZROC
KESEL, JOSEPH	25	M	LABR		GRZZZZROC
LOUISE	20	F	W		GRZZZZROC
ANNA	00	F	INF		GRZZZZROC
STADEL, GG	23	M	LABR		GRZZZZNY
PICKAVE, ERNST	17	M	LABR		GRZZZZNY
KAPEZIK, ADAM	26	M	LABR		GRZZZZNY
NUENLIST, ALBERT	21	M	LABR		SRZZZZNY
SCHOLTEN, FRANZKA	21	F	LDY		GRZZZZNY
AUGUSTE	19	F	LDY		GRZZZZNY
PHILIPPE, FAREY	43	M	MNR		FRZZZZNY
GI-JA, EMIL	36	M	PNTR		GRZZZZNY
SCHELSKI, NANNY	21	F	SVNT		GRZZZZCH
GSAND, MARIE	24	F	SVNT		GRZZZZNY
CONRAD, GEORGE	50	M	LABR		GRZZZZNY
HELENE	37	F	W		GRZZZZNY
MARIE	17	F	SVNT		GRZZZZNY
CONRAD	14	M	CH		GRZZZZNY
CLEMENTINE	6	M	CHILD		GRZZZZNY
MATHILDE	4	F	CHILD		GRZZZZNY
ALVINE	2	M	CHILD		GRZZZZNY
HEDWIG	00	M	INF		GRZZZZNY
HOELSCHER, CHRISTIAN	29	M	LKSH		GRZZZZUNK
MARIE	31	F	W		GRZZZZUNK
GODSTEIN, MISS	16	F	LDY		GRZZZZNY
MEINECKE, PAUL	26	M	LABR		GRZZZZPHI
SCHERER, JOHN	29	M	WCHMKR		GRZZZZSTL
BRAUN, RUPERT	21	M	SHMK		SRZZZZNY
SERAFINO, NABONI	14	M	LABR		SRZZZZNY
KNECHT, EMMA	19	F	LABR		SRZZZZNY
F	21	M	LABR		SRZZZZNY
SCHMID, PRULINE	17	F	SVNT		SRZZZZNY
BELLONI, ANTONIA	48	F	SVNT		SRZZZZNY
BRANDLE, MARIE	21	F	SVNT		SRZZZZLOU
WILD, WILH	28	M	LABR		SRZZZZLOU
BURGER, SUSANNA	53	F	CGRMKR		SRZZZZLOU
ELISA	20	F	CGRMKR		SRZZZZLOU
THEOBOLD	18	M	CGRMKR		SRZZZZLOU
LINA	11	F	CH		SRZZZZLOU
FRIEDA	10	F	CH		SRZZZZLOU
WILHELM	7	M	CHILD		SRZZZZLOU
OTTO	6	M	CHILD		SRZZZZLOU

PASSENGER	AGE	SEX	OCCUPATION	PRVL	DES
ZELLER, MAX	9	M	CHILD	SRZZZZPIT
BETSCH, MAGDA	17	F	SVNT	GRZZZZNY
WEINHARDT, ELIZA	20	F	TLR	GRZZZZSTL
ADLER, BERTHA	18	F	TRVLR	GRZZZZNY
STRAUB, MARIE	18	F	TRVLR	GRZZZZNY
METZGER, SARA	21	F	TRVLR	GRZZZZNY
GROMBACHER, LUDWIG	18	M	MCHT	GRZZZZCH
SCHRETZMANN, GUSTAV	16	M	BY	GRZZZZCH
KRAEMER, OTTO	15	M	NN	GRZZZZCH
WIELAND, CATHA	19	F	SVNT	GRZZZZCH
HOLZMANN, ANTON	17	M	BKR	GRZZZZCH
HOFMANN, ADAM	38	M	LABR	GRZZZZCH
JULIE	50	F	M	GRZZZZCH
CARL	12	M	CH	GRZZZZCH
ALBERT	11	M	CH	GRZZZZCH
ELISE	9	F	CHILD	GRZZZZCH
VEITH, DINA	20	F	SVNT	GRZZZZCH
SCHMITT, LOUISE	22	F	SVNT	GRZZZZCH
AUGUST	25	M	LKSH	GRZZZZCH
HAGEL, MARIE	19	F	SVNT	GRZZZZCH
HOLLERBACH, CAROLINE	22	F	SVNT	GRZZZZCH
KAUFMANN, KARL	24	M	BCHR	GRZZZZCH
MELBER, JOHANN	24	M	LABR	GRZZZZCH
JACOB	24	M	SHMK	GRZZZZPIT
STEFAN, MAGDA	29	F	SVNT	GRZZZZBUF
KUENZIG, MARGA	22	F	SVNT	GRZZZZUNK
GRAF, AMALIE	21	F	SVNT	GRZZZZNY
PLENDEL, AUG	16	M	SHMK	GRZZZZNY
BAUSENWEIN, LUDWIG	23	M	BKR	GRZZZZNY
SCHEUER, MINA	38	F	TLR	GRZZZZNY
SUSSMANN, BABETTE	32	F	SVNT	GRZZZZNY
FRANZ, FIALA	46	M	TLR	GRZZZZCH
ADALBERT	46	M	BKR	GRZZZZCH
EHRMANN, ROBERT	20	M	LABR	GRZZZZNY
KOHN, MARG	60	F	M	GRZZZZNY
MARIE	26	F	M	GRZZZZNY
MARG	4	F	CHILD	GRZZZZNY
JACOB	2	M	CHILD	GRZZZZNY
JOH	00	M	INF	GRZZZZNY
RIEDEL, JOSEPH	23	M	MCHT	GRZZZZNY
BUCHHOLZ, BARBARA	36	F	W	GRZZZZNY
MARIE	10	F	CH	GRZZZZNY
FERD	8	M	CHILD	GRZZZZNY
AUGUST	5	M	CHILD	GRZZZZNY
JOSEPHINE	4	F	CHILD	GRZZZZNY
MATHIAS	2	M	CHILD	GRZZZZNY
BLASENHAUER, F	20	M	LABR	GRZZZZNY
BONS, JOHANN	21	M	LABR	GRZZZZNY
GROS, MARIA	21	M	LABR	GRZZZZNY
WEILER, MARIA	21	M	LABR	GRZZZZNY
WILHELM, HELENE	22	F	SVNT	GRZZZZNY
SPENGLER, NICOL	22	M	MECH	GRZZZZNY
HEMMERON, JOSEF	28	M	MNR	FRZZZZNY
GILLIOT, GREG	30	M	MNR	FRZZZZNY
SCHMIDT, JOHAN	23	M	CPR	GRZZZZCH
KINNEN, ED	22	M	LKSH	GRZZZZPIT
SCHMIDT, WILH	24	M	SHMK	GRZZZZCIN
ECKEL, ADOLF	21	M	GDNR	GRZZZZCH
MAIER, JOHANN	24	M	NN	GRZZZZNY
KRUNNECK, GERTRUDE	18	F	SVNT	GRZZZZLOU
HEISSER, CARL	18	M	LABR	GRZZZZNY
SCHOENER, LUDWIG	34	M	BKBNDR	GRZZZZNY
SPECHT, HCH	27	M	BCHR	GRZZZZNY
NAUMANN, CATHA	20	F	SVNT	GRZZZZNY
KRONENBERGER, FRANZ	24	M	MCHT	GRZZZZNY
AMANN, JOSEF	00	M	BCHR	GRZZZZNY
SCHROEDER, ELISE	22	F	SVNT	GRZZZZNY
CALMAR, MATHILDE	21	F	SVNT	GRZZZZNY
PETERMANN, MARIE	24	F	SVNT	GRZZZZNY
DOERR, ELISE	27	F	SVNT	GRZZZZNY
KIEFER, FRIED	25	M	LABR	GRZZZZNY
JULIANE	28	F	W	GRZZZZNY
CASIMIA	00	F	INF	GRZZZZNY
HILLEN, MARG	49	F	W	GRZZZZNY
HCH	11	M	CH	GRZZZZNY

PASSENGER	AGE	SEX	OCCUPATION	PRVL	DES
PETER	9	M	CHILD	GRZZZZNY
HECK, WILHELMINE	34	F	W	GRZZZZNY
JACOB	11	M	CH	GRZZZZNY
ELISABETH	00	F	CH	GRZZZZNY
HCH	00	M	INF	GRZZZZNY
SCHUG, ANDREAS	18	M	BCHR	GRZZZZNY
LUTZ, HCH	24	M	BBR	GRZZZZNY
BUSBACH, PETER	25	M	LABR	GRZZZZCIN
LEPPERT, EMIL	16	M	NN	GRZZZZIND
KRAEMER, CARL	19	M	LABR	GRZZZZIND
KAUPFERLE, EMIL	24	M	LABR	GRZZZZNY
BORST, CATHE	56	F	SVNT	GRZZZZNY
ROSALIA	21	F	SVNT	GRZZZZNY
KOERBER, SOFIA	23	F	SVNT	GRZZZZNY
HOERNER, REGINA	18	F	SVNT	GRZZZZNY
BRAUN, CARL	16	M	NN	GRZZZZNY
NILSON, MATHILDA	22	F	SVNT	GRZZZZBO
MAURATH, CARL	18	M	SHMK	GRZZZZCLE
HESS, CARL	16	M	NN	GRZZZZCOU
HUERST, MARTIN	16	M	LABR	GRZZZZCOU
KALT, ED	24	M	NN	GRZZZZUNK
SEMMLER, JOSEPH	16	M	LABR	GRZZZZSTL
CREZCENT--	28	F	SVNT	GRZZZZSTL
DIETZ, PHILIPPE	15	M	TLR	GRZZZZNY
SCHMIDT, SALONE	20	F	SVNT	GRZZZZNY
DE-FUS, CARL	22	M	TRVLR	GRZZZZSFC

SHIP: ALLER

FROM: BREMEN AND SOUTHAMPTON
TO: NEW YORK
ARRIVED: 06 OCTOBER 1888

PASSENGER	AGE	SEX	OCCUPATION	PRVL	DES
FELDHOFF, AUG	20	M	MCHT	GRZZZZUSA
KA-RY, MARY	25	F	NN	GRZZZZUSA
JOHANNA	1	F	CHILD	GRZZZZUSA
FUCHS, FERD	52	M	MCHT	GRZZZZUSA
WOLFF, BERTHA	18	F	NN	GRZZZZUSA
GROTZ-CH, PAUL	25	M	MCHT	GRZZZZUSA
DOSHER, LOUIS	36	M	SHMK	GRZZZZUSA
ROEHRIG, BABETTE	23	F	NN	GRZZZZUSA
HERZNER, AUGUSTE	26	F	NN	GRZZZZUSA
WOLFF, GERTRUD	20	F	NN	GRZZZZUSA
HOMBERGER, CATHA	62	F	NN	GRZZZZUSA
KOTHE, WILH	22	M	SMH	GRZZZZUSA
STOECKEL, OTTO	24	M	SMH	GRZZZZUSA
MOHR, HERM	54	M	RTR	GRZZZZUSA
ANNA	46	F	W	GRZZZZUSA
ELSE	11	F	CH	GRZZZZUSA
DIECK, U	46	F	NN	GRZZZZUSA
U	16	F	NN	GRZZZZUSA
MARGA	15	F	NN	GRZZZZUSA
GERTRUD	11	F	CH	GRZZZZUSA
MARIE	10	F	CH	GRZZZZUSA
CLAUSSEN, JACOB	47	M	FARMER	GRZZZZUSA
ANNA	34	F	W	GRZZZZUSA
ANNA	16	F	CH	GRZZZZUSA
HEINR	15	M	CH	GRZZZZUSA
ABRAH	15	M	CH	GRZZZZUSA
MARIA	9	F	CHILD	GRZZZZUSA
HERM	4	M	CHILD	GRZZZZUSA
ELISE	.11	F	INFANT	GRZZZZUSA
JOHS	.02	M	INFANT	GRZZZZUSA
BENEVISTI, ENG	28	M	MCHT	GRZZZZUSA
BUHLER, LUDW	23	M	LABR	GRZZZZUSA
GRASS, HERM	26	M	LABR	GRZZZZUSA
MARTENS, HEINR	25	M	LABR	GRZZZZUSA
LATZBEWSKI, PAUL	23	M	LABR	GRZZZZUSA
HANSEN, PETER	24	M	LABR	GRZZZZUSA
FAHRIG, AUGUST	26	M	FARMER	GRZZZZUSA

PASSENGER	AGE	SEX	OCCUPATION	PRVL	DES
HILLBRECHT, FRANZ	34	M	FARMER	GRZZZZ	USA
MARK, WILH	25	M	FARMER	GRZZZZ	USA
KRAEFT, WILH	26	M	FARMER	GRZZZZ	USA
SCHIFFER, JOH	27	M	FARMER	GRZZZZ	USA
GALLE-, CONRAD	14	M	FARMER	GRZZZZ	USA
SCHAUB, JACOB	18	M	FARMER	GRZZZZ	USA
SCHMIDT, GOTTFR	34	M	TLR	GRZZZZ	USA
BREIMANN, AUGUST	32	M	FARMER	GRZZZZ	USA
REVER-S, JURGEN	25	M	FARMER	GRZZZZ	USA
SCHMID, HEINR	18	M	TLR	GRZZZZ	USA
MOSCHEROSCH, WILH	22	M	BKR	GRZZZZ	USA
STERN, RICH	24	M	FARMER	GRZZZZ	USA
LUEDSEL, HEINR	17	M	FARMER	GRZZZZ	USA
CONRAD	24	M	BCHR	GRZZZZ	USA
HERMANN, MICH	19	M	FARMER	GRZZZZ	USA
WEBER, PAUL	24	M	MCHT	GRZZZZ	USA
RUDOLPH, JOH	25	M	FARMER	GRZZZZ	USA
FRESH, CARL	17	M	SHMK	GRZZZZ	USA
FOGRASITZ, CARL	24	M	LABR	GRZZZZ	USA
NEBEL, BRUEMER	26	M	BRR	GRZZZZ	USA
HERMANN, JOH	21	M	BRR	GRZZZZ	USA
LAPPE, HEINR	20	M	LABR	GRZZZZ	USA
BELL, JOHS	17	M	TLR	GRZZZZ	USA
KLEIN, HEINR	17	M	BKLYR	GRZZZZ	USA
GE--NER, HUGO	26	M	BKLYR	GRZZZZ	USA
-ELLINGER, OTTO	16	M	MCHT	GRZZZZ	USA
SCHLAGBECK, BERNARD	22	M	MCHT	GRZZZZ	USA
BENTING, BERNARD	27	M	MCHT	GRZZZZ	USA
STE-ER, ANTON	54	M	SHMK	GRZZZZ	USA
KUETHER, HEINR	22	M	FARMER	GRZZZZ	USA
PETER, FRANZ	26	M	FARMER	GRZZZZ	USA
FOETSCH, OTTO	18	M	FARMER	GRZZZZ	USA
OHL, KARL	22	M	BCHR	GRZZZZ	USA
GEORG	16	M	BCHR	GRZZZZ	USA
MEIER, FRANZ	16	M	LABR	GRZZZZ	USA
MEISENZAHL, AUG	29	M	LABR	GRZZZZ	USA
KRAUSE, HEINR	21	M	MCHT	GRZZZZ	USA
SIEFERT, PETER	30	M	MCHT	GRZZZZ	USA
HERGEN---HER, PETER	17	M	LABR	GRZZZZ	USA
HOEPEKE, WILLY	15	M	MCHT	GRZZZZ	USA
-AMANN, U	18	M	LKSH	GRZZZZ	USA
ME-DLER, AD	29	M	BRR	GRZZZZ	USA
KLAMP, DIEDR	16	M	MCHT	GRZZZZ	USA
HA-BERG, CARL	26	M	SHMK	GRZZZZ	USA
DITTMER, PETER	15	M	SHMK	GRZZZZ	USA
CRAMER, PETER	46	M	LABR	GRZZZZ	USA
BECK, LUDW	51	M	FARMER	GRZZZZ	USA
GOTTFR	79	M	FARMER	GRZZZZ	USA
SCHERR--BL-, ANTON	25	M	FARMER	GRZZZZ	USA
LIEBLEIN, FRANZ	22	M	TLR	GRZZZZ	USA
WOL-LE, AUG	20	M	TLR	GRZZZZ	USA
ELBERT, HENRICH	17	M	TLR	GRZZZZ	USA
HARTMANN, CARL	11	M	CH	GRZZZZ	USA
JAHNKE, AUG	40	M	LABR	GRZZZZ	USA
GROSSHEIDER, HEINR	30	M	LABR	GRZZZZ	USA
OKER, ADOLF	28	M	BBR	GRZZZZ	USA
WOLTMANN, WILH	19	M	FARMER	GRZZZZ	USA
S--FFERTH, FRIEDR	59	M	BRR	GRZZZZ	USA
-IMMELLEBER, GEORG	18	M	MCHT	GRZZZZ	USA
KOEHL, CHRIST	20	M	MCHT	GRZZZZ	USA
MARKS, HEINR	30	M	FARMER	GRZZZZ	USA
NE-HOLD, ERNST	27	M	FARMER	GRZZZZ	USA
SCHMIDT, JOSEF	28	M	LABR	GRZZZZ	USA
NIERMEIER, JOSEF	25	M	LABR	GRZZZZ	USA
SCH--CK, JACOB	18	M	LABR	GRZZZZ	USA
MOHRMANN, CLAUS	30	M	SHMK	GRZZZZ	USA
SCHOERER, JOH	26	M	LABR	GRZZZZ	USA
BIEGER, ADOLF	18	M	LABR	GRZZZZ	USA
OVERHECK, BERNH	45	M	MCHT	GRZZZZ	USA
HACKMANN, LOUIS	27	M	MCHT	GRZZZZ	USA
HUMBKE, FRIEDR	25	M	MCHT	GRZZZZ	USA
MAZUREWSKY, MOJ	22	M	LABR	GRZZZZ	USA
GORSKI, ANTON	38	M	LABR	GRZZZZ	USA
SCHULZ, U	23	M	LABR	GRZZZZ	USA
RACH, LE-S	23	M	LABR	GRZZZZ	USA
THOMPSON, JOH	16	M	SHMK	GRZZZZ	USA
SCHAMER, MICH	50	M	FARMER	GRZZZZ	USA
HEINR	16	M	FARMER	GRZZZZ	USA
HEINBRUSH, FRIEDR	33	M	FARMER	GRZZZZ	USA
WIEDER, HEINR	36	M	FARMER	GRZZZZ	USA
HEIN, FERD	25	M	TLR	GRZZZZ	USA
CA-OW, HUGO	40	M	MCHT	GRZZZZ	USA
BEHRENS, FRIEDR	22	M	MCHT	GRZZZZ	USA
MEYER, HEINR	40	M	SMH	GRZZZZ	USA
STENTZ, WOLLMUTH	28	M	FARMER	GRZZZZ	USA
MOWOTNY, ANTON	31	M	FARMER	GRZZZZ	USA
KUETHER, HEINR	19	M	FARMER	GRZZZZ	USA
HEINRICH, ELEONORE	18	F	NN	GRZZZZ	USA
BLUMKE, MARIE	21	F	NN	GRZZZZ	USA
PETZHOLD, MARTHA	16	F	NN	GRZZZZ	USA
MA---MANN, HELENE	22	F	NN	GRZZZZ	USA
KN--AP, FRIED	52	F	NN	GRZZZZ	USA
MUELLER, ANNA	20	F	NN	GRZZZZ	USA
TUERKES, MARY	16	F	NN	GRZZZZ	USA
MARTENS, CLARA	25	F	NN	GRZZZZ	USA
BULLENKAMP, META	22	F	NN	GRZZZZ	USA
HERZBERG, BETTY	19	F	NN	GRZZZZ	USA
KUECK, MARY	27	F	NN	GRZZZZ	USA
ADAMS, MAGDA	21	F	NN	GRZZZZ	USA
BUEDMER, KATH	16	F	NN	GRZZZZ	USA
SIEBOLDS, ANNETTE	25	F	NN	GRZZZZ	USA
KIEL, ANNA	14	F	NN	GRZZZZ	USA
KRUPPENBACHER, SIBETTA	20	F	NN	GRZZZZ	USA
LE-CHEN	14	F	NN	GRZZZZ	USA
MEYER, MARGA	24	F	NN	GRZZZZ	USA
WERNER, CLARA	17	F	NN	GRZZZZ	USA
MUELLER, LOUISE	00	F	NN	GRZZZZ	USA
VESPER, LOUISE	17	F	NN	GRZZZZ	USA
KOCH, ELISE	20	F	NN	GRZZZZ	USA
WOELLINGER, APOLLA	17	F	NN	GRZZZZ	USA
BOHNE, DINA	22	F	NN	GRZZZZ	USA
S-AUB, DOROTHEA	17	F	NN	GRZZZZ	USA
RICHTER, BARBA	22	F	NN	GRZZZZ	USA
BENDER, MARGA	19	F	NN	GRZZZZ	USA
S---HR, ANNA	19	F	NN	GRZZZZ	USA
HAAS, MARIA	18	F	NN	GRZZZZ	USA
--EDE, WILH	18	F	NN	GRZZZZ	USA
WOELK, MARIA	21	F	NN	GRZZZZ	USA
KLAUS, LOUISE	16	F	NN	GRZZZZ	USA
FUEKEISEN, CAROLNE	16	F	NN	GRZZZZ	USA
WAGNER, AGNES	42	F	NN	GRZZZZ	USA
BELL, U	51	F	NN	GRZZZZ	USA
HOTH, VICTORIA	27	F	NN	GRZZZZ	USA
HASS, FANN-	18	F	NN	GRZZZZ	USA
KRAUSS, THERESE	26	F	NN	GRZZZZ	USA
ZENDELL, HENRIETTE	40	F	NN	GRZZZZ	USA
STEINER, AMALIA	51	F	NN	GRZZZZ	USA
MERKLE, SOPHIE	20	F	NN	GRZZZZ	USA
SCH---ELBACH, MARIA	18	F	NN	GRZZZZ	USA
--RABACHER, FRANZISKA	25	F	NN	GRZZZZ	USA
LOLLER, MARIA	21	F	NN	GRZZZZ	USA
SEIDEL, EMMA	26	F	NN	GRZZZZ	USA
AMALIE	24	F	NN	GRZZZZ	USA
KRETSCHMER, ANNA	19	F	NN	GRZZZZ	USA
H--RGEN--TTER, AGNES	15	F	NN	GRZZZZ	USA
DEL--, ELSA	27	F	NN	GRZZZZ	USA
MARTZEN, ADELHEIT	23	F	NN	GRZZZZ	USA
MARTENS, META	17	F	NN	GRZZZZ	USA
GRAMMLICH, CATHA	25	F	NN	GRZZZZ	USA
-UEHL, JOH	25	F	NN	GRZZZZ	USA
FROEHLICH, U	14	F	NN	GRZZZZ	USA
GRID--, FRANZISKA	20	F	NN	GRZZZZ	USA
KRAUS, MARIA	46	F	NN	GRZZZZ	USA
MESSL, MARGA	17	F	NN	GRZZZZ	USA
WOGER, CHRIST	30	F	NN	GRZZZZ	USA
ROHDE, DINA	20	F	NN	GRZZZZ	USA
ROLFS, MARIA	15	F	NN	GRZZZZ	USA
UHL, KRESZENZIA	26	F	NN	GRZZZZ	USA
STOFFEN, CHRIST	72	F	NN	GRZZZZ	USA
SCHNEIDER, ANNA	22	F	NN	GRZZZZ	USA

PASSENGER	AGE	SEX	OCCUPATION	PRVL	DES
WE-HSEL, BARB	63	F	NN		GRZZZZUSA
WEIS, LOUISE	19	F	NN		GRZZZZUSA
BAUMAN, ROSALIE	21	F	NN		GRZZZZUSA
MARG-ART, FRANZISKA	22	F	NN		GRZZZZUSA
SCHMIDT, MARGA	18	F	NN		GRZZZZUSA
NORDHEIM, AUGUSTE	20	F	NN		GRZZZZUSA
-USH, ALBERT	29	F	NN		GRZZZZUSA
SCHWELDT, JULIE	58	F	NN		GRZZZZUSA
HILLMANN, HENRIETTA	22	F	NN		GRZZZZUSA
GIEGULD, KATH	52	F	NN		GRZZZZUSA
METT, MARIE	18	F	NN		GRZZZZUSA
K--LINK--EISER, FRNZ	24	F	NN		GRZZZZUSA
STORTZ, KATH	22	F	NN		GRZZZZUSA
DREYER, EIBE	28	F	NN		GRZZZZUSA
BREDA, CATH	18	F	NN		GRZZZZUSA
BRANDT, MARIA	25	F	NN		GRZZZZUSA
T-KING, ADELE	18	F	NN		GRZZZZUSA
NEUMEYER, SOFIE	28	F	NN		GRZZZZUSA
STOL, AMALIE	22	F	NN		GRZZZZUSA
STOLL, WILH	15	F	NN		GRZZZZUSA
BRITZ, U	21	F	NN		GRZZZZUSA
BAUMEITER, CLAUDIA	11	F	NN		GRZZZZUSA
BRODKERB, JOH	23	F	NN		GRZZZZUSA
ELZER, BARB	16	F	NN		GRZZZZUSA
WEISHAU--, ELISABETH	24	F	NN		GRZZZZUSA
DUECK, FRANZ	14	F	NN		GRZZZZUSA
CZOLINSKA, JULIANNA	22	F	NN		GRZZZZUSA
MUELLER, WILH	68	F	NN		GRZZZZUSA
HELD, ANTONIA	32	F	NN		GRZZZZUSA
CE-CILEWSKA, JOSEFA	18	F	NN		GRZZZZUSA
KAZSER, JOHE	29	F	NN		GRZZZZUSA
LEDERER, KATH	26	F	NN		GRZZZZUSA
-ARTENFELS, PHILIPPINE	20	F	NN		GRZZZZUSA
BERLINECKE, LINA	20	F	NN		GRZZZZUSA
-RIGGE, JOH	60	M	FARMER		GRZZZZUSA
MARIA	59	F	W		GRZZZZUSA
MORITZ, IDA	33	F	NN		GRZZZZUSA
ALFRED	7	M	CHILD		GRZZZZUSA
WALDEMAR	6	M	CHILD		GRZZZZUSA
ADELE	.06	F	INFANT		GRZZZZUSA
DARGUSCH, EMMA	30	F	NN		GRZZZZUSA
AUGUSTE	7	F	CHILD		GRZZZZUSA
U	.09	M	INFANT		GRZZZZUSA
-HRIEMANN, GEORG	48	M	FARMER		GRZZZZUSA
LOUISE	45	F	W		GRZZZZUSA
GARTELMANN, HERM	17	M	FARMER		GRZZZZUSA
MARTIN	12	M	FARMER		GRZZZZUSA
STURM, WILH	40	M	FARMER		GRZZZZUSA
AUGTE	41	F	W		GRZZZZUSA
WI--BALD	7	M	CHILD		GRZZZZUSA
RUDOLPH	.09	M	INFANT		GRZZZZUSA
-UHL, WILH	37	M	FARMER		GRZZZZUSA
HENRIETTA	36	F	W		GRZZZZUSA
IDA	7	F	CHILD		GRZZZZUSA
ANNA	4	F	CHILD		GRZZZZUSA
MINNA	.10	F	INFANT		GRZZZZUSA
NIEMANN, HERM	36	M	FARMER		GRZZZZUSA
WILHE	30	F	W		GRZZZZUSA
BERTHA	7	F	CHILD		GRZZZZUSA
HELENA	6	F	CHILD		GRZZZZUSA
B	.09	M	INFANT		GRZZZZUSA
THIEMANN, LOUISE	45	F	NN		GRZZZZUSA
ANNA	.11	F	INFANT		GRZZZZUSA
ANTON, FRIEDR	35	M	FARMER		GRZZZZUSA
DOROTHEA	35	F	W		GRZZZZUSA
FRIEDR	64	M	LABR		GRZZZZUSA
FRIEDR	7	M	CHILD		GRZZZZUSA
ANNA	6	F	CHILD		GRZZZZUSA
HERME	.09	F	INFANT		GRZZZZUSA
DAKER, ELISAB	50	F	NN		GRZZZZUSA
CATH	16	F	NN		GRZZZZUSA
KOESLER, HEINR	27	M	LABR		GRZZZZUSA
GESINE	25	F	W		GRZZZZUSA
HEPP, PHILIPP	16	M	LABR		GRZZZZUSA
BEUSE, AUGUSTA	41	F	NN		GRZZZZUSA
ELISA	7	F	CHILD		GRZZZZUSA
JOH	.09	F	INFANT		GRZZZZUSA
FRIEDRICH, FRIEDERIKA	48	F	NN		GRZZZZUSA
MARIE	18	F	NN		GRZZZZUSA
GEORG	16	M	NN		GRZZZZUSA
SPINDLER, THERESIA	27	F	NN		GRZZZZUSA
DANIEL	5	M	CHILD		GRZZZZUSA
ALOIS	.09	M	INFANT		GRZZZZUSA
IGNATZ	.09	M	INFANT		GRZZZZUSA
LA---NE, JOH	29	F	NN		GRZZZZUSA
CH	.11	M	INFANT		GRZZZZUSA
NOLDE, ELISAB	29	F	INF		GRZZZZUSA
CATH	4	F	CHILD		GRZZZZUSA
U	.11	F	INFANT		GRZZZZUSA
HAUSLEIN, JOH	50	M	FARMER		GRZZZZUSA
IDA	48	F	W		GRZZZZUSA
M--NS, MINNA	56	F	NN		GRZZZZUSA
HERM	7	M	CHILD		GRZZZZUSA
GEISEL, MARIE	50	F	NN		GRZZZZUSA
CARL	7	M	CHILD		GRZZZZUSA
SCHUBER, CATH	27	F	NN		GRZZZZUSA
FRANZISKA	.10	F	INFANT		GRZZZZUSA
ANDLER, THEKLA	22	M	NN		GRZZZZUSA
MARYANNE	.06	F	INFANT		GRZZZZUSA
MEYER, JUL	31	M	FARMER		GRZZZZUSA
ADEL	27	F	W		GRZZZZUSA
ALURA	3	F	CHILD		GRZZZZUSA
HERM	.06	M	INFANT		GRZZZZUSA
LIPPERT, MARIA	50	F	NN		GRZZZZUSA
MARIA	21	F	NN		GRZZZZUSA
ADAM	7	M	CHILD		GRZZZZUSA
KOSLOWSKY, LADISLAUS	32	M	LABR		GRZZZZUSA
JULIE	26	F	W		GRZZZZUSA
STAU--, BERTHA	30	F	NN		GRZZZZUSA
-----F	2	M	CHILD		GRZZZZUSA
RUDOLF	.09	M	INFANT		GRZZZZUSA
BRINKMANN, FRIED	46	M	TLR		GRZZZZUSA
ELISAB	36	F	W		GRZZZZUSA
WILH	7	M	CHILD		GRZZZZUSA
JACOB	6	M	CHILD		GRZZZZUSA
AUG	.10	M	INFANT		GRZZZZUSA
FRIED	.10	M	INFANT		GRZZZZUSA
TRAMPAS--, FRANZ	33	F	NN		GRZZZZUSA
MARGA	.10	F	INFANT		GRZZZZUSA
LE-HMANN, MARIA	28	F	NN		GRZZZZUSA
ANNA	4	F	CHILD		GRZZZZUSA
JOSEPH	.09	M	INFANT		GRZZZZUSA
FRICKE, SOPHIE	24	F	NN		GRZZZZUSA
EUGEN	.10	M	INFANT		GRZZZZUSA
MEYER, PAUL	33	M	FARMER		GRZZZZUSA
ELISE	20	F	W		GRZZZZUSA
CATH	3	F	CHILD		GRZZZZUSA
ELISE	.11	F	INFANT		GRZZZZUSA
VOGEL, BABETTE	29	F	NN		GRZZZZUSA
MARIE	6	F	CHILD		GRZZZZUSA
BABETTE	.10	F	INFANT		GRZZZZUSA
-E-RSNER, POMA---	18	M	FARMER		GRZZZZUSA
KLINGENBERTH, ANTONIA	35	F	NN		GRZZZZUSA
MARIE	7	F	CHILD		GRZZZZUSA
IDA	.10	F	INFANT		GRZZZZUSA
FRITSCH, MARIE	30	F	NN		GRZZZZUSA
ELSA	.11	F	INFANT		GRZZZZUSA
GEIS, JACOB	39	M	BRR		GRZZZZUSA
CHARLOTTE	20	F	W		GRZZZZUSA
ORTMANN, PAUL	23	M	TLR		GRZZZZUSA
MARIE	20	F	W		GRZZZZUSA
BASSING, MARGA	47	F	NN		GRZZZZUSA
ANNA	7	F	CHILD		GRZZZZUSA
KNOBLAND, ANNA	60	F	CH		GRZZZZUSA
KRESZONIA	21	F	CH		GRZZZZUSA
KAPPLER, BERTHA	28	F	CH		GRZZZZUSA
BERTHA	4	F	CHILD		GRZZZZUSA
LOUISE	.10	F	INFANT		GRZZZZUSA
SCHWAGER, EVA	42	F	NN		GRZZZZUSA
CASIMIR	7	M	CHILD		GRZZZZUSA

PASSENGER	AGE	SEX	OCCUPATION	PRVL	DES
MAHLER, JOH	47	M	SHMK		GRZZZZUSA
MARGE	31	F	W		GRZZZZUSA
FRIEDR	6	M	CHILD		GRZZZZUSA
SOPHIE	5	F	CHILD		GRZZZZUSA
W	4	M	CHILD		GRZZZZUSA
DIEDR	.10	M	INFANT		GRZZZZUSA
ELISAB	.10	F	INFANT		GRZZZZUSA
DAUBL, MARGA	43	F	NN		GRZZZZUSA
ELISE	7	F	CHILD		GRZZZZUSA
GEORG	6	M	CHILD		GRZZZZUSA
BETZIE--A, FRIEDR	58	M	MCHT		GRZZZZUSA
SOPHIE	50	F	W		GRZZZZUSA
WILHE	6	F	CHILD		GRZZZZUSA
WAGNER, JOH	33	M	BCHR		GRZZZZUSA
ANNA	31	F	W		GRZZZZUSA
HEINR	7	M	CHILD		GRZZZZUSA
ERNST	4	M	CHILD		GRZZZZUSA
MARTHA	.09	F	INFANT		GRZZZZUSA
HUBER, GEORG	54	M	TLR		GRZZZZUSA
FRANZISKA	54	F	W		GRZZZZUSA
KAROLA	23	F	NN		GRZZZZUSA
MUEHLBAUER, FRANZ	47	M	FARMER		GRZZZZUSA
FRANZISKA	52	F	W		GRZZZZUSA
FRANZISKA	7	F	CHILD		GRZZZZUSA
HILBAUER, FRANZ	6	M	CHILD		GRZZZZUSA
ANNA	.10	F	INFANT		GRZZZZUSA
FRIEDRICH, PHIL	38	M	FARMER		GRZZZZUSA
MARIA	36	F	W		GRZZZZUSA
FRIEDR	7	M	CHILD		GRZZZZUSA
MARTHA	5	F	CHILD		GRZZZZUSA
ANNA	.08	F	INFANT		GRZZZZUSA
HEINR	.08	M	INFANT		GRZZZZUSA
WEIMAR, ELISABETH	17	F	NN		GRZZZZUSA
ANDR	11	M	CH		GRZZZZUSA
CARL	6	M	CHILD		GRZZZZUSA
GAR-, BERTHA	34	F	NN		GRZZZZUSA
FRIEDR	7	F	CHILD		GRZZZZUSA
PAUL	6	M	CHILD		GRZZZZUSA
HERMANN	3	M	CHILD		GRZZZZUSA
AUGUSTE	.09	F	INFANT		GRZZZZUSA
L-GNER, WALBURGA	39	F	NN		GRZZZZUSA
LOGNER, ELISABETH	2	F	CHILD		GRZZZZUSA
ALB	6	M	CHILD		GRZZZZUSA
ALOIS	4	M	CHILD		GRZZZZUSA
SIMON	.09	M	INFANT		GRZZZZUSA
WIEBE, JACOB	51	M	FARMER		GRZZZZUSA
MARIA	35	F	W		GRZZZZUSA
MARGA	7	F	CHILD		GRZZZZUSA
HELENE	6	F	CHILD		GRZZZZUSA
MAX	5	M	CHILD		GRZZZZUSA
FRANZ	4	M	CHILD		GRZZZZUSA
ANNA	3	F	CHILD		GRZZZZUSA
ELISE	2	F	CHILD		GRZZZZUSA
KURT	1	M	CHILD		GRZZZZUSA
GERTRUD	.09	F	INFANT		GRZZZZUSA
BRUCK, BETTY	28	F	NN		GRZZZZUSA
SELMA	5	F	CHILD		GRZZZZUSA
AUGUST	.03	M	INFANT		GRZZZZUSA

SHIP: CITY OF CHICAGO

FROM: LIVERPOOL AND QUEENSTOWN
TO: NEW YORK
ARRIVED: 06 OCTOBER 1888

PASSENGER	AGE	SEX	OCCUPATION	PRVL	DES
IEVEL, ANTON	26	M	TLR		GRZZZZNY
OLSEN, NILS	21	M	LABR		GRZZZZNY
JONASON, JONAS	40	M	LABR		GRZZZZNY
ISCHARKASKY, PINCUS	22	M	JWLR		GRACBFNY
WISMANN, HEINRICH	45	M	LABR		GRAEHFNY

PASSENGER	AGE	SEX	OCCUPATION	PRVL	DES
SUNKEWITZ, FRANZ	25	M	LABR		GRACBFPHI
WENZEL, GEORGE	22	M	SLR		GRACBFNY
HIRSHFIELD, WM.	22	M	SLR		GRZZZZNY
HINTZ, ELSE	23	F	LDY		GRADAXIA
BECKY, C.L.E.	45	M	MCHT		GRACBFWI
YOUNGMANN, BABEL	22	M	GENT		GRADAXNY

SHIP: GELLERT

FROM: HAMBURG AND HAVRE
TO: NEW YORK
ARRIVED: 06 OCTOBER 1888

PASSENGER	AGE	SEX	OCCUPATION	PRVL	DES
BENTHIEN, HELENE	28	F	WO		GRACBWUSA
JACOB, GEORGE	24	M	UNKNOWN		PRZZZZUSA
MARCUS	32	M	UNKNOWN		PRZZZZUSA
HERMANN, JULIUS	30	M	UNKNOWN		PRZZZZUSA
HARDER, EMMY	16	F	SGL		PRAHSAUSA
MARTHA	19	F	SGL		PRAHSAUSA
AGNES	41	F	WO		PRAHSAUSA
STERN, SIGMUND	16	M	BCHR		WMZZZZUSA
RIEDEMANN, LOUISE	32	F	WO		WMACBFUSA
LOUISE	7	F	CHILD		WMACBFUSA
HEINR.	5	M	CHILD		WMACBFUSA
SCHLUCHTER, CAROLINE	17	F	SGL		WMACBFUSA
LOHR, PETER	26	M	BTMKR		PRZZZZUSA
SCHALIPP, WILH.	43	M	SLR		PRAADEUSA
FISCHER, PAULINE	58	F	WO		PRALKWUSA
WALTER, CLARA	36	F	SGL		PRAIPJUSA
BRAUN, MARIA	27	F	WO		PRACSDUSA
BERTHA	6	F	CHILD		PRACSDUSA
KOPISCHKE, THERESE	14	F	SGL		PRACWIUSA
BOESE, EDUARD	14	M	WTR		PRADXCUSA
CAYKONSKA, JULIANA	31	F	WO		PRAEXKUSA
STANISLAV	.11	M	INFANT		PRAEXKUSA
WIESE, MARIE	50	F	WO		PRAADEUSA
BUEHRING, JOHANNE	45	F	WO		PRADIJUSA
OTTO	18	M	CH		PRADIJUSA
MARIE	13	F	CH		PRADIJUSA
HANS	7	M	CHILD		PRADIJUSA
ROHWEDDER, ANNA	24	F	SGL		PRZZZZUSA
PIEHLER, JOSEPH	29	M	LABR		PRAAKHUSA
FETZER, JOHANN	16	M	LABR		BVZZZZUSA
MARG.	19	F	SGL		BVZZZZUSA
DOESCHER, AUGUST	15	M	FARMER		HBZZZZUSA
LOEBENSTEIN, CLARA	17	F	SGL		HBADKJUSA
GINSBERG, LAURA	45	F	WO		PRZZZZUSA
IDA	6	F	CHILD		PRZZZZUSA
ERNST	5	M	CHILD		PRZZZZUSA
POSCHNER, ALBERT	26	M	GDNR		PRADHEUSA
STERN, PAUL	24	M	MCHT		PRAAKHUSA
WIECHMANN, AUGUST	25	M	FARMER		PRZZZZUSA
RARNEKOW, ANNA	26	F	SGL		PRAIAJUSA
KOGLIN, JOH.	36	M	LABR		PRZZZZUSA
FLEISCHER, PAUL	20	M	TKR		PRAEFLUSA
SCHROEDER, PAUL	35	M	TR		PRAAABUSA
ANNA	32	F	W		PRAAABUSA
BOOTH, FRIEDA	19	F	SGL		PRAHILUSA
JOENS, MARIE	18	F	SGL		PRAESDUSA
DORA	17	F	SGL		PRAESDUSA
MARGA	16	F	SGL		PRAESDUSA
ANNA	14	F	SGL		PRAESDUSA
GINSBERG, HERMINE	20	F	SGL		PRZZZZUSA
WAGNER, JACOB	38	M	BLKSMH		PRACUXUSA
WOLF, AUGUSTE	20	F	SGL		PRACBFUSA
ZIESKE, WILH.	33	M	LABR		PRAIQEUSA
META	30	F	W		PRAIQEUSA
PETER	3	M	CHILD		PRAIQEUSA
GUSTAV	.11	M	INFANT		PRAIQEUSA
HOEPFEL, HEINR.	14	M	SCH		PRACBRUSA

PASSENGER	AGE	SEX	OCCUPATION	PRVL	DES
KAHL, MARIE	42	F	WO	PRACBR	USA
ALMA	15	F	CH	PRAAKH	USA
CLARA	7	F	CHILD	PRAAKH	USA
CURT	4	M	CHILD	PRAAKH	USA
REDEPENNING, HERRM.	37	M	LABR	PRAAKH	USA
STREUSSLE, MARIE	21	F	SGL	PRAGFL	USA
AUSPACH, JACOB	14	M	LABR	PRAFJA	USA
KLENK, GOTTFRIED	25	M	SHFM	PRADCJ	USA
GROTKOPF, FRITZ	24	M	LABR	PRAEPZ	USA
GEORGES, CHRISTINE	58	F	WO	PRAFXV	USA
WAGENER, JOHANN	39	M	MLR	PRAEJM	USA
ELSE	33	F	W	PRAEJM	USA
SOPHIE	7	F	CHILD	PRAEJM	USA
CARL	6	M	CHILD	PRAEJM	USA
MARIE	3	F	CHILD	PRAEJM	USA
WILH.	1	M	CHILD	PRAEJM	USA
STANGE, CARL	17	M	BKLYR	PRAEPZ	USA
BITTER, EMILIE	17	F	SGL	PRAEJM	USA
FREIKARR, ZILLE	20	F	SGL	PRZZZZ	USA
MATHIESEN, ANNA	16	F	SGL	PRAHTP	USA
KONRAD, GABRIEL	27	M	BRR	PRAFBV	USA
FRDKE.	24	F	W	PRAFBV	USA
NEUNER, JULIUS	57	M	MCHT	PRAEEA	USA
BAUER, CHRISTIAN	7	M	CHILD	WMZZZZ	USA
BEHRINGER, MATH.	24	M	FARMER	WMAGMR	USA
FRANZ, MARIE	24	F	SGL	WMAGMR	USA
GEHRUNG, MARIE	31	F	WO	WMZZZZ	USA
ALBERT	3	M	CHILD	WMZZZZ	USA
DEININGER, MARIE	31	F	SGL	WMZZZZ	USA
HESS, LINE	20	F	SGL	WMAHIT	USA
FAUST, HEINR.	16	M	BLKSMH	PRZZZZ	USA
RENZ, JOHANNES	17	M	LABR	PRAHVX	USA
GOETZ, FRANZ	25	M	BBR	PRAFRG	USA
APOLLONIA	26	F	W	PRAFRG	USA
WEYRAUCH, CARL-E.J.	40	M	CPTR	PRABOQ	USA
MARIEK, LORENZ	45	M	LABR	PRZZZZ	USA
HERTEL, ANNA	18	F	SGL	PRAGPX	USA
METZNER, ALMA	21	F	SGL	PRAGPX	USA
RAU, EMMA	22	F	SGL	PRAAKH	USA
FINKLER, ADELHEID	22	F	SGL	BVZZZZ	USA
FERBER, WALBURGA	41	F	WO	BVZZZZ	USA
WALTHER, ELEONORE	62	F	WO	BVAAKH	USA
MINNA	23	F	SGL	BVAAKH	USA
ALWINE	19	F	SGL	BVAAKH	USA
PILZ, HEINR.	38	M	WVR	BVADFS	USA
PAULINE	31	F	W	BVADFS	USA
ANNO	7	M	CHILD	BVADFS	USA
CLARA	.11	F	INFANT	BVADFS	USA
FISCHER, JOHANNA	20	F	SGL	BVAHIL	USA
GORTH, LINE	18	F	SGL	HSZZZZ	USA
WIEDEMANN, ANNA	34	F	WO	HSAENI	USA
ELLA	7	F	CHILD	HSAENI	USA
FLORA	6	F	CHILD	HSAENI	USA
SCHAEFER, SOPHIE	15	F	SGL	HSAAGL	USA
ERXLEBEN, JOHANNA	29	F	WO	HBZZZZ	USA
HULDA	6	F	CHILD	HBZZZZ	USA
GUSTAV	3	M	CHILD	HBZZZZ	USA
WALTER	.10	M	INFANT	HBZZZZ	USA
JANOSCH, JOSEPH	23	M	MLR	HBAAKH	USA
BENECKE, HEINR.	16	M	LABR	PRZZZZ	USA
KLEINKAUT, ELISABETH	24	F	SGL	BVZZZZ	USA
PETERSEN, CATHA.	36	F	SGL	BVAGFU	USA
JUNG, THERESE	23	F	SGL	HSZZZZ	USA
RITSCHER, MARTHA	18	F	SGL	HSAIET	USA
REESE, HERRM.	32	M	LABR	PRZZZZ	USA
NEUMAUER, CHRISTINE	73	F	WO	PRZZZZ	USA
KLAVA, CATHA.	20	F	SGL	PRZZZZ	USA
ANDERSEN, ANE	38	F	WO	PRAHZP	USA
DORA	7	F	CHILD	PRAHZP	USA
ADLINE	3	F	CHILD	PRAHZP	USA
HAUS	3	M	CHILD	PRAHZP	USA
ERICHSEN, CARL	21	M	TU	PRAHZP	USA
HANSEN, LOUISE	71	F	WO	PRAHZP	USA
CHRISTIANSEN, HANS	16	M	FARMER	PRZZZZ	USA
BOH.	16	M	FARMER	PRZZZZ	USA
HANSEN, JUERGEN	16	M	FARMER	PRZZZZ	USA
HANS	14	M	FARMER	PRZZZZ	USA
LORENZEN, HAUS	21	M	FARMER	PRZZZZ	USA
KROGH, PETER	16	M	FARMER	PRZZZZ	USA
HINRICHSEN, JENS	21	M	FARMER	PRZZZZ	USA
TAFELMEYER, MARIE	72	F	WO	PRADXZ	USA
WILH.	48	M	BKBNDR	PRADXZ	USA
MARIE	32	F	W	PRADXZ	USA
ELISE	7	F	CHILD	PRADXZ	USA
ARNDT, GUSTAV	17	M	CL	PRAAKH	USA
OTTILIE	15	F	SGL	PRAAKH	USA
FERNBACH, JAMES	26	M	MCHT	PRAJVF	USA
KIEPER, ALBERT	27	M	FARMER	PRAAKH	USA
KUMBA, ELISABETH	21	F	SGL	PRAFQN	USA
MUETZEL, KATI	33	F	SGL	HSZZZZ	USA
KATI	33	F	SGL	HSZZZZ	USA
BALLING, BARBA.	18	F	SGL	HSZZZZ	USA
BURKHARDT, ANTON	26	M	GDSM	HSZZZZ	USA
KEMNITZER, HERRM.	29	M	MCHT	HSAFAR	USA
DEPRE, FRANZISCA	16	F	SGL	HSACSC	USA
STEMMLER, CARL	26	M	CPTR	HSAAYS	USA
METZGER, GEORG	26	M	GDNR	WMZZZZ	USA
HILL, CARL	38	M	BRR	WMZZZZ	USA
HIERNICKEL, JOSEF	27	M	BRR	BVZZZZ	USA
LEIS, BABETTE	18	F	SGL	BVADRO	USA
WENNINGER, MICHAEL	27	M	FARMER	BVZZZZ	USA
MAURER, ELISE	19	F	SGL	BVZZZZ	USA
GALLE, MORITZ	24	M	WHLR	BVABDM	USA
VICTOR, HELENE	23	M	WHLR	BVAAZD	USA
BEENK, MARIE	52	F	WO	HSZZZZ	USA
GEIGER, MARIE	24	F	SGL	HSZZZZ	USA
OTTILIE	24	F	SGL	HSADOI	USA
SCERZYNNA, FRANZ	21	M	MCHT	HSADOI	USA
MARIE	28	F	W	PRZZZZ	USA
RADNIK, HILLER	25	M	DLR	PRZZZZ	USA
VOLKES, DIEDRICH	20	M	BCKM	PRAARR	USA
GRIMPE, LOUIS	32	M	BCKM	PRZZZZ	USA
HOLTJE, FRIEDR.	27	M	LABR	PRACBF	USA
DOEFLER, ROBERT	55	M	SCP	PRADZO	USA
SWERSEN, ANTONIETTE	20	F	SGL	PRAHWX	USA
CHARLES, ANDRE-JULES	26	M	TLR	PRZZZZ	USA
BUECHLE, AUGUST	16	M	LABR	BDZZZZ	USA
BERTSCHIN, MARIE	27	F	SGL	BDAAHU	USA
BUCKENMAIER, AUGUST	24	M	MCHT	BDAEWM	USA
FRANCOIS, MARTHA	22	M	MCHT	BDAFWW	USA
BRUGGER, STEFANIE	20	M	MCHT	BDZZZZ	USA
CHARLES, CLEMENT	40	M	MNR	FRZZZZ	USA
CHRISTINE, GUHL	20	F	SGL	WMZZZZ	USA
MARIE	15	F	SGL	WMZZZZ	USA
ANTON, HOERING	22	M	MCHT	BDZZZZ	USA
EDUARD, HAENGGI	21	M	FARMER	SRZZZZ	USA
HELM, CARL	25	M	GDNR	PRZZZZ	USA
HUBER, JOHANN	42	M	GDNR	BDZZZZ	USA
HANS, AUGUST	30	M	CK	PRZZZZ	USA
KAUFMANN, JOSEPH	18	M	FARMER	PRZZZZ	USA
MATHIAS, KAISER	26	M	CTW	BDZZZZ	USA
PAULINE	25	F	W	BDZZZZ	USA
FRIEDRICH	3	M	CHILD	BDZZZZ	USA
HERMINE	2	F	CHILD	BDZZZZ	USA
LEON, LERNER	50	M	FARMER	BDAJPZ	USA
LEFENETRE, ANNA	18	F	SGL	BDAFWW	USA
MUETH, HELENE	21	F	SGL	FRZZZZ	USA
MUELLER, WILHELM	17	M	TLR	FRADEC	USA
STOLL, LINE	18	F	SGL	PRZZZZ	USA
SCHUERSCH, EMIL	19	M	LABR	PRAAKJ	USA
SCHNEIDER, EMMA	27	F	SGL	PRAEKY	USA
EMILIE	19	F	SGL	PRAEKY	USA
LINK, LUDWIG	22	M	BCK	PRAEIZ	USA
ZIMMERMANN, SIGMUND	22	M	FARMER	BDZZZZ	USA
HENRY	30	M	CPTR	BDAFTD	USA
MAACK, LOUISE	21	F	SGL	BDACBF	USA
SCHAEFLER, THEORDORE	38	F	SGL	BDACKY	USA
HOLZERLAND, LUCY	17	F	SGL	BDACBF	USA
DOERRIES, MARGARETHA	19	F	SGL	BDACBF	USA
MITTEL, PHILIPP	23	M	ART	BDADEI	USA

PASSENGER	AGE	SEX	OCCUPATION	PROV/VLS DES	

PASSENGER	AGE	SEX	OCCUPATION	PROV/VLS	DES
RODATZ, ANTON	22	M	MCHT	BDACBF	USA
KRETSCHMAR, ALMA	61	F	WO	SYZZZZ	USA
BAUM, HEINR.	22	M	MCHT	SYAAYG	USA
MEYER, ANNA	24	F	W	SYAARR	USA
LIPPSTREUER, HERMINE	29	F	SGL	PRZZZZ	USA
VONDERNBACH, WILH.	25	M	MCHT	PRACGM	USA
AGNESE.	39	F	W	PRACGM	USA
THERESE	2	F	CHILD	PRACGM	USA
LUDWIG	.11	M	INFANT	PRACGM	USA
GOEKSCH, HERMANN	30	M	MCHT	PRZZZZ	USA
OEHL, CONRAD	16	M	MCHT	PRAESD	USA
VONHUENERBEIN, GUSTV.	29	M	MILT	PRAIAI	USA
BECKER, ARTHUR	28	M	AR	PRAFWZ	USA
FRANCISCA	43	F	W	PRAFWZ	USA
VONBELLEVILLE, ELLI	24	F	WO	PRACBF	USA
HERMANN, TONI	25	F	SGL	PRAAKH	USA
EBERT, HERMINE	26	F	SGL	PRAAKH	USA
GERTRUD	3	F	CHILD	PRAAKH	USA
BAUER, PHILIPP	29	M	MCHT	PRACBF	USA
FUHRHOF, ALMA	30	F	SGL	PRACBF	USA
DOHRN, ANTJE	68	F	WO	PRAIDO***	
HELENE	25	F	SGL	PRAIDO	USA
CHRISTINE	35	F	W	PRAIDO	USA
ANNA	.02	F	INFANT	PRAIDO	USA
NACHMANN, REBECCA	28	F	SGL	PRAEWZ	USA
ASCHER, ROSALIE	60	F	WO	PRADYG	USA
OTTILIE	38	F	SGL	PRADYG	USA
HULDA	15	F	SGL	PRADYG	USA
EWERT, ERNESTINE	23	F	W	PRAJVR	USA
GOERTZ, HELENE	32	F	W	PRAJVR	USA
HEIN, MALWINE	20	F	W	PRACBF	USA
FELDHEIM, SELMA	19	F	SGL	PRAAKH	USA
BRAUER, CAROLINE	71	F	WO	PRAEZV	USA
PRINZ, JOHANNA	33	F	WO	PRAAKH	USA
ELSE	7	F	CHILD	PRAAKH	USA
GRETHE	6	F	CHILD	PRAAKH	USA
ERNST	5	M	CHILD	PRAAKH	USA
JAMES	4	M	CHILD	PRAAKH	USA
JULIUS	3	M	CHILD	PRAAKH	USA
WALLY	.11	F	INFANT	PRAAKH	USA
BEUCK, JOHANNA	70	F	WO	PRACQA	USA
HAAS, CARL	34	M	MCHT	PRABHT	USA
ZYDOWA, MAX	13	M	SCH	PRZZZZ	USA
ERNESTINE	14	F	SGL	PRZZZZ	USA
JARCH, MATTILDE	21	F	SGL	PRADTI	USA
VONBLOME, PAULA	38	F	WO	PRACEG	USA
RILLING, EMILIE	26	F	SGL	PRADHR	USA
STOCKFISCH, EMMA	20	F	SGL	PRACBF	USA
HELMI	2	M	CHILD	PRACBF	USA
CHRISTIAN	.11	M	INFANT	PRACBF	USA
KUEHLKE, MARY	38	F	SGL	PRAJEU	USA
SANDOW, LINA	26	F	SGL	PRAAKH	USA
HIMMEL, LINE	26	F	SGL	PRABOQ	USA
ROEPER, LUDWIG	23	M	BRR	PRADCR	USA
ROSSI, EMILIE	19	F	SGL	PRAAKH	USA
TROEPFER, RUDOLPH	30	M	MCHT	PRAAZQ	USA
BARTEKY, MARIE-KATHINKA	28	F	SGL	PRAAZS	USA
GRAENICHEN, S.	33	M	MD	SRZZZZ	USA
LOUISE	25	F	W	SRZZZZ	USA
WERNER	.06	M	INFANT	SRZZZZ***	
OSER, WILLIAM	25	M	MCHT	SRAAHU	USA
MARCHES, ERNST	25	M	MUSN	SRAAHU	USA
BAER, JETTCHEN	19	F	SGL	SRADEC	USA

SHIP: POLYNESIA

FROM: HAMBURG
TO: NEW YORK
ARRIVED: 06 OCTOBER 1888

PASSENGER	AGE	SEX	OCCUPATION	PROV/VLS	DES
LABES, CARL	40	M	LABR	SRABEH	NY
JULIE	39	F	W	SRABEH	NY
AMALIE	7	F	CHILD	SRABEH	NY
OTTILIE	6	F	CHILD	SRABEH	NY
AUGUSTE	5	F	CHILD	SRABEH	NY
MARTHA	.09	F	INFANT	SRABEH	NY
KRAEMER, JOH.	16	M	SHMK	HSZZZZ	NY
VOIGHT, LOUIS	23	M	BKLYR	HSACBF	NY
MASUSKIEWICZ, PELAGIO	34	F	SGL	PRZZZZ	NY
FRANK, AUGUSTE	24	F	SGL	PRZZZZ	NY
OTTERSTEDT, ANNA	28	F	WO	PRAADE	NY
MARY	.09	F	INFANT	PRAADE	NY
VILLRACK, EMIL	18	M	FARMER	PRZZZZ	NY
GREVE, HINR.	44	M	LABR	PRZZZZ	NY
ANNA	40	F	W	PRZZZZ	NY
HEINRICH	7	M	CHILD	PRZZZZ	NY
EMMA	6	F	CHILD	PRZZZZ	NY
HERM.	5	M	CHILD	PRZZZZ	NY
HANS	55	M	LABR	PRZZZZ	NY
ABEL	50	F	W	PRZZZZ	NY
ANNA	16	F	CH	PRZZZZ	NY
HINR.	7	M	CHILD	PRZZZZ	NY
BERTHA	6	F	CHILD	PRZZZZ	NY
ANNA	76	F	WO	PRZZZZ	NY
TRAMREN, CHRIST	27	M	FARMER	PRABNS	NY
KAY, HANS	71	M	FARMER	PRZZZZ	NY
EHLERS, HINR.	64	M	FARMER	PRAGEL	NY
MARGA.	62	F	W	PRAGEL	NY
MARGA.	21	F	CH	PRAGEL	NY
CAROLINE	16	F	CH	PRAGEL	NY
DUNKLAN, MARIE	59	F	WO	PRZZZZ	NY
JOHS.	20	M	BCHR	PRZZZZ	NY
AUGUSTE	25	F	W	PRZZZZ	NY
WILLY	.09	M	INFANT	PRZZZZ	NY
MUELLER, CAECILIE	58	F	WO	PRZZZZ	NY
LEHMANN, CHRISTINE	26	F	SGL	WMZZZZ	NY
BUROW, FRIDA	45	M	FARMER	PRZZZZ	NY
FRIEDERICKE	38	F	W	PRZZZZ	NY
WILHELMINE	14	F	CH	PRZZZZ	NY
ROBERT	7	M	CHILD	PRZZZZ	NY
ANNA	4	F	CHILD	PRZZZZ	NY
LOUISE	.11	F	INFANT	PRZZZZ	NY
DESSANER, ERNST	16	M	MUSN	PRAFSI	NY
SCHWARZ, WILHELM	23	M	LABR	WMZZZZ	NY
SCHETTLER, SIGMUND	20	M	FARMER	WMZZZZ	NY
HERBSTRICTTER, DOROTHEA	19	F	SGL	WMZZZZ	NY
ISRASCHECK, HERM	14	M	SCH	PRZZZZ	NY
EZARK, PETER	13	M	SCH	PRZZZZ	NY
REINHARD, AUGUSTE	19	F	SGL	PRZZZZ	NY
FRDKE.	24	F	WO	PRZZZZ	NY
ANNA	.06	F	INFANT	PRZZZZ	UNK
KANETKA, MARTIN	27	M	LABR	PRACBF	NY
SESCHEWITZ, HERM.	34	M	BLKSMH	PRAAZQ	NY
CAROLINE	38	F	W	PRAAZQ	NY
ZACHAL, AMALIE	19	F	SGL	PRAAZQ	NY
MARTHA	15	F	SGL	PRAAZQ	NY
GROSSTHAT, BERTHA	20	F	SGL	PRAAZQ	NY
SUTJAHR, HENRIETTE	20	F	SGL	PRAIGY	NY
BIESLER, MARTHA	27	F	SGL	PRAAKH	NY
TAMM, FRK.	24	F	SGL	MKZZZZ	NY
FRIISS, MATHILDE	20	F	SGL	PRZZZZ	NY
ANHAGE, WILHELMINE	51	F	WO	PRZZZZ	NY
DRESKE, BEATE	40	F	WO	PRZZZZ	NY
AUGUSTE	7	F	CHILD	PRZZZZ	NY
THIELMANN, MICHAEL	70	M	LABR	PRZZZZ	NY
FRIESE, GOTTLOB	58	M	LABR	PRZZZZ	NY
MUELLER, JACOB	34	M	SLT	PRACBI	USA
CAROLINE	32	F	W	PRACBI	USA

PASSENGER	AGE	SEX	OCCUPATION	PRIVL	DES
MARTHA	4	F	CHILD	PRACBIUSA	
JOHANNA	4	F	CHILD	PRACBIUSA	
BRANDT, DAVID	46	M	FARMER	PRZZZZUSA	
CATHA.	40	F	W	PRZZZZUSA	
ANNA	17	F	CH	PRZZZZUSA	
JACOB	15	M	CH	PRZZZZUSA	
MARGA.	14	F	CH	PRZZZZUSA	
EMMA	13	F	CH	PRZZZZUSA	
ALBERT	7	M	CHILD	PRZZZZUSA	
BERTHA	6	F	CHILD	PRZZZZUSA	
AUGUSTE	2	F	CHILD	PRZZZZUSA	
WOMLER, GUSTAV	33	M	FARMER	PRADGEUSA	
GORGANTESIEWICS, FRANZ	27	M	LABR	PRZZZZUSA	
AUGUSTE	28	F	W	PRZZZZUSA	
FRANZISKA	3	F	CHILD	PRZZZZUSA	
LORENZ	18	M	LABR	PRZZZZUSA	
NEUMANN, GUSTAV	34	M	MCHT	PRAAKHUSA	
HEILBRONN, JOHANN	14	M	FARMER	PRAFDWUSA	
MORTZFELD, ALBERT	22	M	FARMER	PRZZZZUSA	
KRUEGER, GUSTAV	23	M	BKR	PRADOKUSA	
GOLOWAKI, LORENZ	52	M	MUSN	PRZZZZUSA	
BATKOROSKI, APOLONARI	7	F	CHILD	PRZZZZUSA	
WEINERT, MATHILDE	26	F	SGL	PRAAKHUSA	
HEITMANN, JOH.	25	M	LABR	PRAFUIUSA	
SCHUETZ, OSCAR	24	M	BCHR	PRAAZQUSA	
BAERMROTH, MARIANNE	38	F	WO	PRZZZZUSA	
IDA	7	F	CHILD	PRZZZZUSA	
BERTHA	6	F	CHILD	PRZZZZUSA	
EWALD	5	M	CHILD	PRZZZZUSA	
EUGEN	3	M	CHILD	PRZZZZUSA	
WILLY	1	M	CHILD	PRZZZZUSA	
VOLKMER, WILHELM	24	M	FARMER	PRAITWUSA	
PORATH, CARL	29	M	MLR	PRAICHUSA	
ROHR, HERM.	14	M	CL	PRZZZZUSA	
FRANK, GUSTAV	60	M	FARMER	PRABAHUSA	
FREDR.	49	F	W	PRABAHUSA	
FRITZ	21	M	S	PRABAHUSA	
PARDUN, EMILIE	21	F	SGL	PRZZZZUSA	
ALWINE	17	F	SGL	PRZZZZUSA	
CYRNS, ROSALIE	26	F	WO	PRZZZZUSA	
MARIE	.08	F	INFANT	PRZZZZUSA	
FONFARA, ROSALIE	22	F	SGL	PRAHPRUSA	
GROCHOWINA, CONSTANTIN	23	M	LABR	PRAMBHUSA	
KAHL, EDUARD	37	M	JNR	PRAAKHUSA	
ERNESTINE	36	F	W	PRAAKHUSA	
ALMA	7	F	CHILD	PRAAKHUSA	
WENDEEIER, HERMANN	43	M	SHMK	PRAAKHUSA	
ROHWEDDER, HERRM.	28	M	CL	PRAAKHUSA	
DELITSCH, HERRM.	22	M	MCHT	PRAAKHUSA	
TREISSIG, WILH.	42	M	LABR	PRAAKHUSA	
MARIE	47	F	W	PRAAKHUSA	
MESZKATIS, WILH.	27	M	TLR	PRAAKHUSA	
V, JOSEF	30	M	FARMER	PRZZZZUSA	
SCHNETHEISS, JACOB	57	M	LABR	PRZZZZUSA	
HEINR.	19	M	LABR	PRZZZZUSA	
JOHS.	29	M	LABR	PRZZZZUSA	
ELISABETH	26	F	W	PRZZZZUSA	
ANNA	2	F	CHILD	PRZZZZUSA	
HEINR.	4	M	CHILD	PRZZZZUSA	
EMMA	.09	F	INFANT	PRZZZZUSA	
WOLLBRAND, HEINR.	30	M	CTHR	PRADOAUSA	
CATHA	32	F	W	PRADOAUSA	
MARIE	7	F	CHILD	PRADOAUSA	
CHRISTIANSEN, JOHANN	26	M	TCHR	PRAADEUSA	
BLATT, DANIEL	25	M	BBR	BVZZZZUSA	
PFLUG, AUGUSTA	24	F	SGL	BVAAKHUSA	
MUELLER, ADOLF	29	M	FARMER	BVAEABUSA	
ROSENBERGER, JOSEF	27	M	JNR	PRZZZZUSA	
HOFFMANN, CARL	33	M	CPTR	PRAHYEUSA	
GRUNER, PHILIPP	30	M	CPR	BVZZZZUSA	
SUCK, JULIUS	43	M	MCHT	PRZZZZUSA	
EMMA	33	F	W	PRZZZZUSA	
MAGDA	7	F	CHILD	PRZZZZUSA	
EMMA	4	F	CHILD	PRZZZZUSA	
HEINKE, AUGUSTE	42	F	WO	PRZZZZUSA	

PASSENGER	AGE	SEX	OCCUPATION	PRIVL	DES
OTTO	7	M	CHILD	PRZZZZUSA	
FRITZ	6	M	CHILD	PRZZZZUSA	
ALWINE	4	F	CHILD	PRZZZZUSA	
SCHOECKEL, ANTONIE	28	F	WO	PRZZZZUSA	
ANNA	4	F	CHILD	PRZZZZUSA	
GERKE, FRIEDR.	24	M	LABR	PRAAKHUSA	
BOTIER, JULIAN	28	M	LABR	PRZZZZUSA	
GUETMANN, LEIBE	33	F	WO	PRZZZZUSA	
SARA	7	F	CHILD	PRZZZZUSA	
KLARA	5	F	CHILD	PRZZZZUSA	
ANNA	4	F	CHILD	PRZZZZUSA	
SONI	.11	F	INFANT	PRZZZZUSA	
BERKER, ERICH	24	M	TKR	PRZZZZUSA	
KATHE, ALBERT	16	M	MCHT	SYZZZZUSA	
KOENIG, EDUARD	35	M	LKSH	SYAAZQUSA	
JABLOWSKY, PAUL	38	M	FARMER	PRAAKHUSA	
PFLUGE, ROBERT	22	M	LKSH	PRAAKHUSA	
RUH, JOSEPH	22	M	BLKSMH	BDZZZZUSA	
SACHER, JOHANN	23	M	LITGR	BVZZZZUSA	

SHIP: ALASKA

FROM: LIVERPOOL AND QUEENSTOWN
TO: NEW YORK
ARRIVED: 08 OCTOBER 1888

PASSENGER	AGE	SEX	OCCUPATION	PRIVL	DES
BEUS, M.	36	M	LABR	GRZZZZUSA	
SCHAWAST, MICHL.	24	M	LABR	GRZZZZUSA	
GOLDUER, MOSES	25	M	LABR	GRZZZZUSA	
WAGENKNECHTA, LUDWIG	50	M	LABR	GRZZZZUSA	
MARIA	48	F	W	GRZZZZUSA	
LOUISA	17	F	SP	GRZZZZUSA	
SOPHIA	11	F	CH	GRZZZZUSA	
MINNIE	14	F	SP	GRZZZZUSA	
FREDRICK	5	M	CHILD	GRZZZZUSA	
LODG, SOFIA	30	F	SP	GRZZZZUSA	
KLEIN, KATHA.	50	F	MA	GRZZZZUSA	
PETER	17	M	LABR	GRZZZZUSA	
HELENA	15	F	SP	GRZZZZUSA	
ANTONY	11	M	CH	GRZZZZUSA	
HASSELSTEIN, MICHL.	16	M	LABR	GRZZZZUSA	
DIEFENBRACHER, PHILIP	19	M	LABR	GRZZZZUSA	
OFFELT, ROB.	21	M	LABR	GRZZZZUSA	
BIRKHOLZ, HERMAN	24	M	LABR	GRZZZZUSA	
KIRST, IDA	42	F	MA	GRZZZZUSA	
THEIST, OTTO	25	M	TLR	GRZZZZUSA	
SCHIFFMAN, WOLF	17	M	LABR	GRZZZZUSA	
RAGEUZ, D.	28	F	SVNT	SRZZZZUSA	

SHIP: BOHEMIA

FROM: HAMBURG
TO: NEW YORK
ARRIVED: 09 OCTOBER 1888

PASSENGER	AGE	SEX	OCCUPATION	PRIVL	DES
BARTMANN, HENRY	24	M	JNR	SRACJONY	
DRAWERT, CAROLINE	19	F	SGL	PRZZZZNY	
SCHWANDT, JOSEFA	28	F	WO	PRZZZZNY	
CLARA	3	F	CHILD	PRZZZZNY	
SCHUSTERKA, ANTON	15	M	TLR	PRZZZZNY	
MARCE	20	F	SGL	PRZZZZNY	
MICHALOWSKI, PETER	27	M	LABR	PRZZZZNY	
ANTONI	20	F	W	PRZZZZNY	
STAAKE, MARIE	52	F	WO	PRAADENY	
KOHNE, GEORG	29	M	CL	PRAAVHNY	

PASSENGER	AGE	SEX	OCCUPATION	PRVL	DES
RISTAU, OTTO	14	M	LABR	PRZZZZ	NY
HELDMANN, JOH.	24	M	LABR	BVZZZZ	NY
MAGDALENA	23	F	W	BVZZZZ	NY
MUELLER, BERNH.	21	M	BKR	BVAACO	NY
PELTZNER, PAUL	36	M	DLR	BVAAKH	NY
MARIE	31	F	W	BVAAKH	NY
CARL	.06	M	INFANT	BVAAKH	NY
HARTMANN, MARGA.	7	F	CHILD	BVAAKH	NY
HEINR.	5	M	CHILD	BVAAKH	NY
MARIE	3	F	CHILD	BVAAKH	NY
PLACEK, JOSEF	39	M	LABR	PRZZZZ	NY
ROSINE	37	F	W	PRZZZZ	NY
BULAVA, MARIANE	23	F	SGL	PRZZZZ	NY
UGOREK, JOSEF	23	M	LABR	PRAFSF	NY
MUSAL, LUDWIG	55	M	BCHR	PRZZZZ	NY
FLORENTINE	55	F	W	PRZZZZ	NY
HERMAN	6	M	CHILD	PRZZZZ	NY
BINN, LOUISE	43	F	WO	PRZZZZ	NY
AUGUSTE	7	F	CHILD	PRZZZZ	NY
FRIEDR.	3	M	CHILD	PRZZZZ	NY
MEYER, HANS	7	M	CHILD	PRZZZZ	NY
WOELZ, ALBERT	40	M	LKSH	PRAAKH	NY
OSSWALD, MARIE	37	F	WO	WMZZZZ	NY
PAULINE	21	F	CH	WMZZZZ	NY
BARBA.	7	F	CHILD	WMZZZZ	NY
MARIE	6	F	CHILD	WMZZZZ	NY
EUGEN	5	M	CHILD	WMZZZZ	NY
EMILIE	4	F	CHILD	WMZZZZ	NY
ROSINE	68	F	WO	WMZZZZ	NY
ZOSCHKE, HERRMAN	30	M	BLKSMH	WMAIFY	NY
MOOR, LYDA	14	F	SGL	SYZZZZ	NY
GOLZ, ERNST	22	M	MCHT	SYAAKH	NY
OESTEREICH, HERM.	15	M	LABR	PRZZZZ	NY
TRAPPER, MARGA.	19	F	SGL	BVZZZZ	NY
SIKOCZYNSKA, JUSTINE	43	F	WO	PRZZZZ	NY
CATHA.	18	F	CH	PRZZZZ	NY
ANNA	7	F	CHILD	PRZZZZ	NY
HELENE	3	F	CHILD	PRZZZZ	NY
RAVN, ELISE	18	F	SGL	PRZZZZ	NY
ENGEL, EMILIE	16	F	SGL	PRZZZZ	NY
RITTER, FROKE	27	F	SGL	PRAAET	NY
SPAETH, WILH.	20	M	LABR	BDZZZZ	NY
JANUS, CARLINE	21	F	SGL	BDAAKH	NY
KAPLAN, MAX	24	M	TLR	BDAAKH	NY
GAUSKE, EMIL	22	M	LABR	BDAEWM	NY
SICHLER, RICHARD	23	M	LABR	BDADIJ	NY
NOTHDURFT, GUSTAV	13	M	SCH	BDAIDO	NY
GARSTEDT, HEINRICH	35	M	BSKM	BDACHA	NY
AUGUSTE	47	F	W	BDACHA	NY
W.	7	M	CHILD	BDACHA	NY
RIEBE, WILHE.	28	F	SGL	BDACBF	NY
KOLUPA, ANNA	28	F	WO	PRZZZZ	NY
HELENE	4	F	CHILD	PRZZZZ	NY
SOPHIE	2	F	CHILD	PRZZZZ	NY
ANTON	.04	M	INFANT	PRZZZZ	NY
MUELLER, HEINR.	64	M	FARMER	PRZZZZ	NY
RUSTWURM, PAULINE	17	F	SGL	PRZZZZ	NY
SCHMIDT, AUGUSTE	38	F	WO	PRAEAJ	NY
WM.	7	M	CHILD	PRAEAJ	NY
CLARA	6	F	CHILD	PRAEAJ	NY
MAX	3	M	CHILD	PRAEAJ	NY
ZENNE, AMALIE	18	F	SGL	SYZZZZ	NY
HEINS, DIEDR.	39	M	FARMER	SYAFSN	NY
ELISABETH	35	F	W	SYAFSN	NY
HEINRICH	3	M	CHILD	SYAFSN	NY
CATHA.	.05	F	INFANT	SYAFSN	NY
HUBICH, MALANE	28	F	SGL	SYAEEC	NY
AUGUSTE	18	F	SGL	SYAEEC	NY
V, JOH.	36	M	BCHR	PRZZZZ	NY
GRETE	26	F	W	PRZZZZ	NY
ELISE	3	F	CHILD	PRZZZZ	NY
HANS	.11	M	INFANT	PRZZZZ	NY
LENZ, AUGUST	30	M	LABR	PRZZZZ	NY
AUGUSTE	31	F	W	PRZZZZ	NY
REGINA	3	F	CHILD	PRZZZZ	NY

PASSENGER	AGE	SEX	OCCUPATION	PRVL	DES
FRNAZ	2	M	CHILD	PRZZZZ	NY
RADEMACHER, CARL	18	M	MD	PRZZZZ	NY
OTT, EDUARD	30	M	SDLR	PRAFUO	NY
PRANKE, JOH.	50	M	FARMER	PRZZZZ	NY
ELISABETH	50	F	W	PRZZZZ	NY
MARIE	7	F	CHILD	PRZZZZ	NY
BARTELS, AUGUSTE	47	F	WO	PRZZZZ	NY
JOHS	17	M	CH	PRZZZZ	NY
ADOLF	15	M	CH	PRZZZZ	NY
ALBERT	7	M	CHILD	PRZZZZ	NY
CARL	6	M	CHILD	PRZZZZ	NY
HAIN, FRITZ	31	M	LABR	PRACSD	NY
HACKER, FRIEDR.	25	M	FARMER	PRZZZZ	NY
OSOWSKY, VALENTIN	38	M	JNR	PRAAKH	NY
ROSALIE	42	F	W	PRAAKH	NY
EDMUND	7	M	CHILD	PRAAKH	NY
WOLFRAM, ANTON	15	M	FARMER	PRAAKH	NY
SCHNEIDERREICH, W.	46	M	FUR	PRAAKH	NY
ADELHEID	45	F	W	PRAAKH	NY
BETRAM, HULDA	23	F	SGL	PRZZZZ	NY
AFLER, OTTILIE	19	F	SGL	PRZZZZ	NY
ALEKSZEWICZ, L.	22	M	LKSH	PRZZZZ	NY
PFALZGRAF, ANNA	22	F	SGL	PRADGC	NY
THIEB, B.	34	M	WCHMKR	PRABUK	NY
WICH, ELISABETH	27	F	SGL	BVZZZZ	NY
JACOBSON, HILLMAR	26	M	MD	SYZZZZ	NY
SCHUMI, FRANZ	40	M	MCHT	SYACUQ	NY
LEWANDOWSKI, MICHAL	48	M	LABR	PRZZZZ	NY
LEHLE, JOH.	39	M	MLR	PRABSJ	NY
FRANZISKA	19	F	W	PRABSJ	NY
VOLDKNER, CLARA	19	F	SGL	PRACBF	NY
WITTKE, CARL	25	M	MLR	PRADZO	NY
HERBERG, BERTHA	36	F	SGL	PRZZZZ	NY
KOCH, WILH.	26	M	LABR	PRAAKH	NY
BURMANN, CARL	28	M	LABR	PRAAKH	NY
PTSCHZODY, HUGO	29	M	BBR	PRZZZZ	NY
ANNA	27	F	W	PRZZZZ	NY
KARL	.09	M	INFANT	PRZZZZ	NY
BONING, EMILIE	23	F	SGL	BRZZZZ	NY
LENSCH, LOUISE	20	F	SGL	BRAADE	NY
BERGMANN, ELISAGETH	37	F	SGL	BRACBF	NY
ULLRICH, ELISABETH	48	F	WO	BRAADE	NY
HEINRICH	7	M	CHILD	BRAADE	NY
POHL, HEINRICH	25	M	PNTR	PRZZZZ	NY
ENGELKE, ANNA	20	F	SGL	PRACGP	NY

SHIP: EIDER

FROM: BREMEN AND SOUTHAMPTON
TO: NEW YORK
ARRIVED: 09 OCTOBER 1888

PASSENGER	AGE	SEX	OCCUPATION	PRVL	DES
BANER, WILH.	36	M	TT	GRZZZZ	USA
ALTSCHUELER, JULIUS	21	M	TT	GRZZZZ	USA
GOELLNER, HEINR.	34	M	TT	GRZZZZ	USA
RUEPNITZ, FRIEDR.	21	M	TT	GRZZZZ	USA
WOENIGER, RUD.	39	M	TT	GRZZZZ	USA
ROSA	32	F	W	GRZZZZ	USA
FRANKE, CLARA	33	F	UNKNOWN	GRZZZZ	USA
BEIER, AUGUST	37	M	TT	GRZZZZ	USA
DAVIDSOHN, HERM.	26	M	TT	GRZZZZ	USA
STECHMANN, META	26	F	UNKNOWN	GRZZZZ	USA
SCHOEMANN, AMALIE	20	F	UNKNOWN	GRZZZZ	USA
COHN, HEDWIG	22	F	W	GRZZZZ	USA
PIEL, JEAN	31	M	TT	GRZZZZ	USA
HUETTENMOSER, JOH.	34	M	TT	SRZZZZ	USA
WILLMANN, ADOLF	21	M	MCHT	GRZZZZ	USA
LADWIG, AUG.	23	M	MCHT	GRZZZZ	USA
HOOS, KONRAD	18	M	MCHT	GRZZZZ	USA
FISCHER, F.C.	50	M	FARMER	GRZZZZ	USA

PASSENGER	AGE	SEX	OCCUPATION	PRVL DES
PITZOLD, OSCAR	26	M	FARMER	GRZZZZUSA
BUSCH, JOHANN	60	M	LABR	GRZZZZUSA
GERDES, JOH.	23	M	BKR	GRZZZZUSA
SCHLOBOHM, REBECCA	24	F	UNKNOWN	GRZZZZUSA
POLECKE, ADOLF	28	M	FARMER	GRZZZZUSA
SCHWEERS, JOHANNE	19	F	UNKNOWN	GRZZZZUSA
KOELSCH, MATH.	57	M	FARMER	GRZZZZUSA
MARIA	50	F	W	GRZZZZUSA
FRANZ	18	M	FARMER	GRZZZZUSA
HEMR.	15	M	FARMER	GRZZZZUSA
GISBERT	13	M	FARMER	GRZZZZUSA
KOELAH, MATHIAS	10	M	CH	GRZZZZUSA
HIRN, MATHILDE	49	F	UNKNOWN	GRZZZZUSA
STEINBANER, GEORG	24	M	MCHT	GRZZZZUSA
DORMEIER, JOHANN	24	M	MCHT	GRZZZZUSA
ALFLEN, MATH.	24	M	UNKNOWN	GRZZZZUSA
KERSCHER, FRIEDR.	27	M	MCHT	GRZZZZUSA
GERARD, FRIEDR.	62	M	FARMER	GRZZZZUSA
JOHANN	27	M	FARMER	GRZZZZUSA
KAHN, JACOB	25	M	MCHT	GRZZZZUSA
KACHELMANN, WILHE.	19	F	SVNT	GRZZZZUSA
MARSCHALL, GEORG	63	M	FARMER	GRZZZZUSA
SCHNEIDER, BARBARA	19	F	SVNT	GRZZZZUSA
RODEWALD, JOHS.	27	M	LABR	GRZZZZUSA
MARKMANN, CARL	28	M	LABR	GRZZZZUSA
FROMMHOLZ, ELISAB.	27	F	UNKNOWN	GRZZZZUSA
HIRSCH, CATH.	25	F	UNKNOWN	GRZZZZUSA
SCHULIER, MARIE	24	F	UNKNOWN	GRZZZZUSA
HENKE, JOHA.	35	F	UNKNOWN	GRZZZZUSA
ABERLE, JOHS.	31	M	BRR	GRZZZZUSA
SCWERKE, MARG.	43	F	UNKNOWN	GRZZZZUSA
FRITZ	12	M	UNKNOWN	GRZZZZUSA
DORIS	10	F	CH	GRZZZZUSA
REDEMANN, WILHE.	38	F	UNKNOWN	GRZZZZUSA
PUNZELT, MARG.	19	F	UNKNOWN	GRZZZZUSA
HOFFMANN, MARIE	21	F	UNKNOWN	GRZZZZUSA
POHL, ANNA	16	F	UNKNOWN	GRZZZZUSA
BRANDT, CHRISTINE	26	F	UNKNOWN	GRZZZZUSA
HOELTKE, WILLIAM	15	M	FARMER	GRZZZZUSA
JAHNKE, CAROLINE	33	F	UNKNOWN	GRZZZZUSA
KATTAN, ANNA	16	F	SVNT	GRZZZZUSA
BOCKELMANN, LINA	23	F	SVNT	GRZZZZUSA
FOLLMER, AMALIE	25	F	UNKNOWN	GRZZZZUSA
BERTHA	7	F	CHILD	GRZZZZUSA
WILLY	.11	M	INFANT	GRZZZZUSA
ROTH, U	37	M	LABR	GRZZZZUSA
BARBARA	18	F	UNKNOWN	GRZZZZUSA
DOPPEL, MARG.	11	F	UNKNOWN	GRZZZZUSA
GESSBIN, MARG.	21	F	UNKNOWN	GRZZZZUSA
GUNTZLER, HEMR.	31	M	FARMER	GRZZZZUSA
HEINKEN, ADELE	28	F	SVNT	GRZZZZUSA
ROEHRS, CARL	16	M	UNKNOWN	GRZZZZUSA
BANER, PHIL.	23	M	BRR	GRZZZZUSA
HOFFMANN, PETER	17	M	FARMER	GRZZZZUSA
BANER, LOUIS	25	M	FARMER	GRZZZZUSA
MULTER, MATH.	26	F	UNKNOWN	GRZZZZUSA
MAJEWSKI, JAN	42	M	LABR	GRZZZZUSA
LACHOWICZ, CARL	42	M	LABR	GRZZZZUSA
BACHMEIER, ALOIS	21	M	CPTR	GRZZZZUSA
WIESMANN, MAGDALENE	53	F	UNKNOWN	GRZZZZUSA
KRAUSE, AUGUST	46	M	FARMER	GRZZZZUSA
HANCK, FRIEDR.	23	M	ENGR	GRZZZZUSA
LEHMANN, EMIL	31	M	FARMER	GRZZZZUSA
MARIE	26	F	W	GRZZZZUSA
MAX	6	M	CHILD	GRZZZZUSA
CLARA	4	F	CHILD	GRZZZZUSA
PAUL	2	M	CHILD	GRZZZZUSA
EMIL	.06	M	INFANT	GRZZZZUSA
MEYER, CARL	25	M	WCHMKR	GRZZZZUSA
MERTZ, LOUISE	38	F	UNKNOWN	GRZZZZUSA
HAAS, JANNY	54	F	UNKNOWN	GRZZZZUSA
FRIEDERIKE	21	F	UNKNOWN	GRZZZZUSA
RUTKOWSKY, MAIRE	25	F	UNKNOWN	GRZZZZUSA
LIEB, ANNA	79	F	UNKNOWN	GRZZZZUSA
MARIA	18	F	UNKNOWN	GRZZZZUSA
VAGTS, MINNA	40	F	UNKNOWN	GRZZZZUSA
HAIDLE, JULIE	21	F	UNKNOWN	GRZZZZUSA
LIEB, AGNES	55	F	UNKNOWN	GRZZZZUSA
SCHMIDT, GUST.	36	M	TT	GRZZZZUSA
NICO, CAROL.	21	F	UNKNOWN	GRZZZZUSA
GROFFEL, DORIS	38	F	W	GRZZZZUSA
SEEGERS, IDA	50	F	UNKNOWN	GRZZZZUSA
KNOTTGE, CAROL.	60	F	UNKNOWN	GRZZZZUSA
WESTENDORP, W.L.	30	F	UNKNOWN	GRZZZZUSA
HEMMIGER, SOPHIE	17	F	UNKNOWN	GRZZZZUSA
ZIERENBERG, FRITZ	31	M	UNKNOWN	GRZZZZUSA
SCHWEMFURTH, JUDW.	17	M	SHMK	GRZZZZUSA
RANIH, JOH.	40	M	FARMER	GRZZZZUSA
SOLDNER, THERESE	17	F	UNKNOWN	GRZZZZUSA
HOLZ, ADELE	25	F	UNKNOWN	GRZZZZUSA
POHLEY, EDUARD	48	M	MCHT	GRZZZZUSA
HENRIETTE	45	F	W	GRZZZZUSA
CURT	19	M	MCHT	GRZZZZUSA
JENNY	16	F	UNKNOWN	GRZZZZUSA
FRITZ	10	M	CH	GRZZZZUSA
HANS	4	M	CHILD	GRZZZZUSA
TAUBNER, ARTHUR	18	M	CNF	GRZZZZUSA
MEISNEST, PAULINE	23	F	SMSTS	GRZZZZUSA
STOPPELHAAR, ROSALIE	41	F	UNKNOWN	GRZZZZUSA
MAN, GEORG	30	M	FARMER	GRZZZZUSA
GROSS, MARIA	18	F	SMSTS	PRZZZZUSA
STREUSKY, EMIL	10	M	CH	PRZZZZUSA
MACKEWICZ, TEKLA	25	F	SVNT	PRZZZZUSA
REGIELKI, TEOFILA	35	F	UNKNOWN	PRZZZZUSA
ANNA	12	F	UNKNOWN	PRZZZZUSA
FRANZISCA	10	F	CH	PRZZZZUSA
SIMON	4	M	CHILD	PRZZZZUSA
JOSEFA	3	F	CHILD	PRZZZZUSA
STEFAN	.09	M	INFANT	PRZZZZUSA
BESSMAN, IDA	79	F	SMSTS	PRZZZZUSA
GARFS, META	79	F	SMSTS	PRZZZZUSA
PLUCINSKI, MARYANNE	17	F	SVNT	GRZZZZUSA
JOSEFA	11	F	UNKNOWN	GRZZZZUSA
WILL, PAUL	15	M	UNKNOWN	GRZZZZUSA
ZANTOW, EMIL	16	M	UNKNOWN	GRZZZZUSA
NIEDZWITZKI, JOSEF	17	M	LABR	GRZZZZUSA
BRUCHINSKI, ROSALIE	26	F	SVNT	GRZZZZUSA
SCHOLTZ, EMILIE	48	F	UNKNOWN	GRZZZZUSA
WINKLER, AUGUSTE	20	F	SVNT	GRZZZZUSA
HAHLBOHM, JOH.	19	M	LABR	GRZZZZUSA
PAPPE, FRIEDR.	33	M	SMH	GRZZZZUSA
THODEN, WILHE.	23	F	SMSTS	GRZZZZUSA
RECK, WILH.	18	M	SHMK	GRZZZZUSA
ROEBER, C.	19	M	BDM	GRZZZZUSA
FELTEN, MINNA	21	F	SMSTS	GRZZZZUSA
SINAT, FRIEDR.	26	M	TLR	GRZZZZUSA
FUCHS, THERESA	17	F	SMSTS	GRZZZZUSA
BEHRENDS, HEINR.	30	M	CPTR	GRZZZZUSA
BAR, JOH.A.	18	M	BBR	GRZZZZUSA
FRESE, WILH.	30	M	FARMER	GRZZZZUSA
CAROLINE	24	F	W	GRZZZZUSA
WILHELM	3	M	CHILD	GRZZZZUSA
ANNA	1	F	CHILD	GRZZZZUSA
HACKER, JOHANN	70	M	PVTM	GRZZZZUSA
RUHOLT, LISETTE	60	F	UNKNOWN	GRZZZZUSA
BERNARDIN	22	M	FARMER	GRZZZZUSA
HEIDLE, OTTO	15	M	SMH	GRZZZZUSA
GAIDE, MARIA	12	F	UNKNOWN	GRZZZZUSA
KAPPENNANN, DIEDR.	16	M	FARMER	GRZZZZUSA
FUCKENSTEDT, AUG.	17	M	CNF	GRZZZZUSA
GUNDELACH, AMBROS	26	M	HTR	GRZZZZUSA
ROST, HERM.	16	M	FARMER	GRZZZZUSA
WETH, ANDREAS	44	M	FARMER	GRZZZZUSA
JOSEFA	38	F	W	GRZZZZUSA
KORB, MARIA	24	F	SVNT	GRZZZZUSA
RAMSANER, WILH.	24	M	TUT	GRZZZZUSA
WIECH, JOHS.	29	M	TLR	GRZZZZUSA
STOECKERT, EMMA	20	F	SVNT	GRZZZZUSA
MAURER, ROSE	29	F	UNKNOWN	GRZZZZUSA
SCHUHBANER, PHILIPP	30	M	FARMER	GRZZZZUSA

PASSENGER	AGE	SEX	OCCUPATION	PRVL	DES
ROTHENBURGER, CATHAR.	18	F	SVNT	GRZZZZUSA	
GENNER, EMILIE	22	F	SVNT	GRZZZZUSA	
ZIMMERMANN, PAULINE	58	F	SVNT	GRZZZZUSA	
KLINGE, MARTHA	33	F	UNKNOWN	GRZZZZUSA	
WILHELM	8	M	CHILD	GRZZZZUSA	
HEINR.	3	M	CHILD	GRZZZZUSA	
MARTHA	.09	F	INFANT	GRZZZZUSA	
ALTMANN, CHRISTINE	19	F	SVNT	GRZZZZUSA	
HERMANN, BABETTE	15	F	UNKNOWN	GRZZZZUSA	
CORDIER, JACOB	28	M	TLR	GRZZZZUSA	
WEISS, REGINA	15	F	UNKNOWN	GRZZZZUSA	
VERBARG, FREDR.	17	M	FARMER	GRZZZZUSA	
HOFACKER, CATH.	16	F	SVNT	GRZZZZUSA	
METZ, JOH.	14	M	UNKNOWN	GRZZZZUSA	
BAYER, F.	22	M	CPTR	GRZZZZUSA	
RUDLER, ANNA	17	F	SVNT	GRZZZZUSA	
RIEPLE, FRIEDA	17	F	SVNT	GRZZZZUSA	
NAUFERT, ANDR.	25	M	BBR	GRZZZZUSA	
HASSLER, HERM.	28	M	SHMK	GRZZZZUSA	
KAISER, BERTHA	26	F	SVNT	GRZZZZUSA	
SCHLEIHER, ANNA	22	F	SVNT	GRZZZZUSA	
BECK, KATH.	23	F	SVNT	GRZZZZUSA	
STEMMER, MARIA	25	F	SVNT	GRZZZZUSA	
BACHMANN, DINA	34	F	SVNT	GRZZZZUSA	
GOEBEL, PETER	22	M	FARMER	GRZZZZUSA	
LUCHS, IDA	31	F	UNKNOWN	GRZZZZUSA	
SCHUSTER, CATH.	46	F	UNKNOWN	GRZZZZUSA	
CHRISTINE	10	F	CH	GRZZZZUSA	
CAROLINE	8	F	CHILD	GRZZZZUSA	
MARGARETHE	4	F	CHILD	GRZZZZUSA	
BOEHEIM, JOHS.	23	M	PNTR	GRZZZZUSA	
WAGNER, FRIEDR.	40	M	FARMER	GRZZZZUSA	
CHARLOTTE	36	F	W	GRZZZZUSA	
FRIEDR.	15	M	FARMER	GRZZZZUSA	
FERDINAND	10	M	CH	GRZZZZUSA	
ANNA	9	F	CHILD	GRZZZZUSA	
CARL	8	M	CHILD	GRZZZZUSA	
BIEBER, MARTHA	22	F	UNKNOWN	GRZZZZUSA	
ANTON	2	M	CHILD	GRZZZZUSA	
ADAM	.05	M	INFANT	GRZZZZUSA	
GIES, MARIE	20	F	SVNT	GRZZZZUSA	
ALSTER, LINA	20	F	SVNT	GRZZZZUSA	
SZUMINSKA, ELEONORE	27	F	UNKNOWN	GRZZZZUSA	
JOHANN	.11	M	INFANT	GRZZZZUSA	
HERBST, LUDWIG	29	M	FARMER	GRZZZZUSA	
SCHULZ, MARG.	36	F	SVNT	GRZZZZUSA	
FEINBURG, CAROL.	25	F	SVNT	GRZZZZUSA	
FUHRY, NICKE	43	M	LABR	GRZZZZUSA	
SCHNEIDER, ANTON	33	M	LABR	GRZZZZUSA	
GUGGENNWOS, SYLVEST	30	M	LABR	GRZZZZUSA	
ULFER, K.W.	18	M	PNTR	GRZZZZUSA	
SCHULZ, LOUISE	26	F	SMSTS	GRZZZZUSA	
ROLLIN, ELSA	2	F	CHILD	GRZZZZUSA	
KRESS, ANNA	23	F	SVNT	GRZZZZUSA	
LINDEMEYER, AUG.	23	M	SHMK	GRZZZZUSA	
SHLASSLER, ADOLPH	15	M	UNKNOWN	GRZZZZUSA	
RIESER, JOH.	16	M	UNKNOWN	GRZZZZUSA	
OPITZ, LOUISE	36	F	UNKNOWN	GRZZZZUSA	
OTTO	11	M	UNKNOWN	GRZZZZUSA	
HEDWIG	10	F	CH	GRZZZZUSA	
ANNA	7	F	CHILD	GRZZZZUSA	
SCHNEIDER, JOSEPH	15	M	UNKNOWN	GRZZZZUSA	
ELSEN, MARIE	26	F	UNKNOWN	GRZZZZUSA	
WEISSKAUSS, NAFTALI	26	F	UNKNOWN	GRZZZZUSA	
KLOSINSKA, CAROLINE	55	F	UNKNOWN	GRZZZZUSA	
VERONIKA	21	F	UNKNOWN	GRZZZZUSA	
WOLFFS, ARON	16	M	MCHT	GRZZZZUSA	
PFINGST, CARL	23	M	MLR	GRZZZZUSA	
GERDES, ANNA	26	F	UNKNOWN	GRZZZZUSA	
DRAWIN, ANNI	17	F	UNKNOWN	GRZZZZUSA	
FRIEDA	19	F	UNKNOWN	GRZZZZUSA	
LECHNER, CARL	21	M	PRNTR	GRZZZZUSA	
SZUKAZ, MARIANNA	30	F	UNKNOWN	GRZZZZUSA	
CATHARINE	.06	F	INFANT	GRZZZZUSA	
KOWALSKA, MARIJANNE	21	F	UNKNOWN	GRZZZZUSA	

PASSENGER	AGE	SEX	OCCUPATION	PRVL	DES
OSTROWSKA, ANTONIA	70	F	UNKNOWN	GRZZZZUSA	
MAJEWSKI, ANNA	3	F	CHILD	GRZZZZUSA	
FINNBACH, AMALIE	16	F	CH	GRZZZZUSA	
CLARA	12	F	CH	GRZZZZUSA	
KUPFBERGER, BABETTE	25	F	CH	GRZZZZUSA	
WIESMANN, HELENE	19	F	CH	GRZZZZUSA	
TEUHMANN, EMIL	24	M	SHMK	GRZZZZUSA	
FOISTER, WALDEMAR	17	M	UNKNOWN	GRZZZZUSA	
SCHROTT, GEORG	36	M	BRR	GRZZZZUSA	
BLANKEMEYER, DIEDR.	19	M	FARMER	GRZZZZUSA	
SINN, CARL	30	M	FARMER	GRZZZZUSA	
BURMESTER, AUG.	16	M	UNKNOWN	GRZZZZUSA	
SEXANER, JAC.	26	M	PNTR	GRZZZZUSA	
BAR, ADAM	71	M	FARMER	GRZZZZUSA	
ERNA	52	F	W	GRZZZZUSA	
KOCH, CASPAR	15	M	UNKNOWN	GRZZZZUSA	
GOEPELE, LOUISE	18	F	UNKNOWN	GRZZZZUSA	
OEHLER, ELISE	26	F	UNKNOWN	GRZZZZUSA	
BEHRENS, CARL	20	M	MCHT	GRZZZZUSA	
HOFFMANN, LOUISE	16	F	UNKNOWN	GRZZZZUSA	
WESSELS, GESINE	16	F	UNKNOWN	GRZZZZUSA	
GROTELUESCHEN, LINA	27	F	SVNT	GRZZZZUSA	
HEINE, JOH.	49	M	FARMER	GRZZZZUSA	
ALBERS, ERWIN	52	M	FARMER	GRZZZZUSA	
MARG.	50	F	W	GRZZZZUSA	
ELISE	17	F	UNKNOWN	GRZZZZUSA	
GESINE	13	F	UNKNOWN	GRZZZZUSA	
ERNST	11	M	UNKNOWN	GRZZZZUSA	
HELENE	8	F	CHILD	GRZZZZUSA	
SCHWEERS, GERHARD	15	M	UNKNOWN	GRZZZZUSA	
HOTTER, THERESE	23	F	UNKNOWN	SRZZZZUSA	
JULIA	19	F	UNKNOWN	SRZZZZUSA	
EMMA	18	F	UNKNOWN	SRZZZZUSA	

SHIP: NORSEMAN

FROM: LIVERPOOL
TO: BOSTON
ARRIVED: 10 OCTOBER 1888

PASSENGER	AGE	SEX	OCCUPATION	PRVL	DES
KOBINSKA, ROSALIA	22	F	W	GRZZZZNY	
DENITCH, SAM.	41	M	TLR	GRZZZZBO	
MEUSKAFSKY, J.	20	M	LABR	GRZZZZBO	
SPR.	19	M	LABR	GRZZZZBO	
STANEISTCH, JAS.	24	M	LABR	GRZZZZBO	
ROSENFIELD, BEN	50	M	MCHT	GRZZZZBO	
BAS.	17	M	MCHT	GRZZZZBO	
SAFALL, ABRM.	37	M	MCHT	GRZZZZBO	

SHIP: ST. OF PENNSYLVANIA

FROM: GLASGOW AND LARNE
TO: NEW YORK
ARRIVED: 10 OCTOBER 1888

PASSENGER	AGE	SEX	OCCUPATION	PRVL	DES
THERMANSON, JOERGEN	19	M	FARMER	GRZZZZUSA	
THIMSEN, CARIUS	19	M	FARMER	GRZZZZUSA	
SOERENSEN, ANDERS	21	M	FARMER	GRZZZZUSA	
JACOBSEN, PEDER	20	M	FARMER	GRZZZZUSA	
HANSEN, HANS	20	M	FARMER	GRZZZZUSA	

PASSENGER	AGE	SEX	OCCUPATION	PRVVL	DES
SHIP: THE QUEEN					
FROM: LIVERPOOL AND QUEENSTOWN					
TO: NEW YORK					
ARRIVED: 10 OCTOBER 1888					
DRESSELHAUSEN, B.	24	M	LABR		GRACBFNY
MATTHES, FRANS	23	M	LABR		GRACBFNY
STOLZENBACH, U	27	F	CH		GRACBFNY
SHIP: EMS					
FROM: BREMEN AND SOUTHAMPTON					
TO: NEW YORK					
ARRIVED: 11 OCTOBER 1888					
H---, RUD.	27	M	MCHT		GRAFKYUSA
MEYER, CARL	24	M	FARMER		GRZZZZUSA
SEIDEWITZ, U	46	M	MCHT		GRZZZZUSA
LUEDECKE, LEOPOLD	21	M	MCHT		GRZZZZUSA
JOSEPHIE, CACILIA	19	F	UNKNOWN		GRAEABUSA
KUNST, MARGA.	23	F	UNKNOWN		GRAARRUSA
WINKLER, CARL	18	M	JNR		GRZZZZUSA
BOTHGE, MAX	22	M	MCHT		GRAAXFUSA
OSTHUS, LILLY	21	F	UNKNOWN		GRAAINUSA
FRANK, THERESIA	26	F	UNKNOWN		GRAFMIUSA
GOTTSCHALK, ROSA	17	F	UNKNOWN		GRADHZUSA
RUBEC, LINA	29	F	W		GRZZZZUSA
ROSI	3	F	CHILD		GRZZZZUSA
MOSINGER, DOROTHEA	44	F	W		GRABSOUSA
DOROTHEA	22	F	UNKNOWN		GRABSOUSA
ALTVATER, MARGA.	33	F	W		GRABSOUSA
MARIE	12	F	UNKNOWN		GRABSOUSA
CARL	8	M	CHILD		GRABSOUSA
ICKES, SOPHIE	68	F	W		GRABSOUSA
KERKMANN, KATHA.	54	F	W		GRABSDUSA
NEUMANN, JENNY	25	F	UNKNOWN		GRAAGLUSA
GLEISSNER, JOH.	22	M	MCHT		GRZZZZUSA
BLOHM, ERNST	19	M	BRR		GRZZZZUSA
OPPENHEIMER, JOSEF	16	M	BRR		GRAAIEUSA
JULIUS	16	M	TT		GRAAIEUSA
HOENIGSBERGER, HANS	17	M	TT		GRAAIEUSA
KIRSCHBAUM, GEORG	23	M	MCHT		GRAARRUSA
KAPPLER, ROSALIE	48	F	W		GRZZZZUSA
EICHMANN, MORITZ	33	M	FARMER		GRAAKHUSA
MARTHA	29	F	W		GRAAKHUSA
ROSA	9	F	CHILD		GRAAKHUSA
LUDWIG	6	M	CHILD		GRAAKHUSA
OSCAR	4	M	CHILD		GRAAKHUSA
ALFRED	2	M	CHILD		GRAAKHUSA
ARONSON, ADOLF	18	M	MCHT		GRAEABUSA
LOEW, AUGUSTE	30	F	UNKNOWN		GRABOQUSA
GREEL, META	22	F	UNKNOWN		GRZZZZNY
REBSTOCK, AUG.	16	M	MCHT		GRACXHNY
HEMMERICH, CATHA.	56	F	W		GRAARRNY
DIRCKS, ADOLF	6	M	CHILD		GRAARRNY
HATSCHMANN, JOSEF	27	M	TLR		GRAAXKNY
MARIA	26	F	W		GRAAXKNY
ELSA	3	F	CHILD		GRAAXKNY
MARTHA	.09	F	INFANT		GRAAXKNY
WOLB, AUGUSTE	17	F	UNKNOWN		GRAFNKNY
CARLE.	15	F	UNKNOWN		GRAFNKNY
SOMMER, ANNNA	22	F	UNKNOWN		GRZZZZNY
WAHL, MARIE	17	F	UNKNOWN		GRZZZZNY
CARL	15	M	UNKNOWN		GRZZZZNY
NORTRUP, WILH.	16	M	LABR		GRZZZZNY
V. ELSA	22	F	UNKNOWN		GRAEJCNY
BOSCH, MAGDA.	17	F	UNKNOWN		GRAAIENY
KIELE, MINNA	21	F	UNKNOWN		GRACBRNY
SEGERTH, JULIE	26	F	UNKNOWN		GRACBRNY
DITTMANN, EVA	18	F	UNKNOWN		GRZZZZNY
AMEND, FRANZ	23	M	FARMER		GRZZZZNY
MARIA	28	F	W		GRZZZZNY
ABENDROTH, CARL	15	M	LABR		GRAAGKNY
FRANK, SAMUEL	39	M	BKR		GRAFMINY
HABERLAU, CARL	54	M	BKR		GRAAKHNY
PAULE.	51	F	W		GRAAKHNY
PAUL	15	M	BKR		GRAAKHNY
EDUARD	11	M	UNKNOWN		GRAAKHNY
WANDA	8	F	CHILD		GRAAKHNY
VOGEL, MARIA	23	F	UNKNOWN		GRZZZZNY
WAGNER, LINA	25	F	W		GRACSYNY
SOPHIE	4	F	CHILD		GRACSYNY
CARL	.01	M	INFANT		GRACSYNY
KOENIG, CLARA	25	F	UNKNOWN		GRACSYNY
LEHR, ANNA	20	F	UNKNOWN		GRZZZZNY
HEIDEMEYER, WILH.	45	M	FARMER		GRZZZZNY
KEMNITZER, ERHARD	30	M	PNTR		GRAARRNY
BULLING, ANNA	50	F	W		GRAARRNY
HENNY	24	F	UNKNOWN		GRAAINNY
OSTHUS, STEPHAN	15	M	LABR		GRAAINNY
KIESEL, CAROLINE	18	F	UNKNOWN		GRZZZZNY
ROSINE	14	F	UNKNOWN		GRZZZZNY
ZELTWANGER, GOTTLOB	17	M	PNTR		GRZZZZNY
ENGELHARDT, CATHA.	18	F	UNKNOWN		GRZZZZNY
KUTTEROFF, MARIE	24	F	UNKNOWN		GRAFJANY
PODLICH, HENRIETTE	37	F	W		GRADWRNY
HEMR.	12	M	UNKNOWN		GRADWRNY
MARTHA	4	F	CHILD		GRADWRNY
KORFF, WILH.	17	M	JNR		GRZZZZNY
MEYER, HERM.	27	M	SHMK		GRZZZZNY
LOUISE	23	F	W		GRZZZZNY
WILH.	3	M	CHILD		GRZZZZNY
FRIEDR.	.03	M	INFANT		GRZZZZNY
FEIDNER, PHILIPP	18	M	LABR		GRZZZZNY
EIDAM, LOUIS	38	M	FARMER		GRADFSNY
MARTHA	10	F	CH		GRADFSNY
FRANZ	23	M	BCHR		GRADFSNY
EBERT, LUDWIG	30	M	JNR		GRABPVNY
ADELHD.	30	F	W		GRABPVNY
HERM.	8	M	CHILD		GRABPVNY
ELISE	4	F	CHILD		GRABPVNY
OTT, MARIA	25	F	UNKNOWN		GRABPVNY
EBERT, HERM.	24	M	LABR		GRABPVNY
AUGUSTE	26	F	W		GRABPVNY
HEMR.	4	M	CHILD		GRABPVNY
EMMA	.01	F	INFANT		GRABPVNY
OTT, ZIDONIA	19	F	UNKNOWN		GRAEKYNY
SCHROCK, EMILIE	70	F	W		GRAJNGNY
GUNDERIAN, WILHE.	53	F	W		GRAJNGNY
MATHE.	10	F	CH		GRAJNGNY
BOETTEHER, HANS	75	M	LABR		GRZZZZNY
FRIEDKE.	70	F	W		GRZZZZNY
JOH.	16	M	LABR		GRZZZZNY
LEWICKI, SALO	12	M	UNKNOWN		GRAEIONY
MUCK, MARGA.	24	F	UNKNOWN		GRZZZZWI
NICOLAY, JOSEF	24	M	LABR		GRZZZZNY
LUETT, EMMA	18	F	UNKNOWN		GRZZZZCAL
STEPHAN, JOH.	35	M	FARMER		GRAESHTX
RENADE	33	F	W		GRAESHTX
ELLA	9	F	CHILD		GRAESHTX
KLARA	2	F	CHILD		GRAESHTX
BRODZINSKY, GERTRUDE	36	F	W		GRZZZZNY
JULIANNA	11	F	UNKNOWN		GRZZZZNY
WLADISLAW	6	M	CHILD		GRZZZZNY
GRESCHKE, WILHE.	19	F	UNKNOWN		GRABTNNY
WIEDOVSKI, ANTON	62	M	LABR		GRZZZZNY
MATHDE.	54	F	W		GRZZZZNY
MARIE	11	F	UNKNOWN		GRZZZZNY
ZILLSTDORF, MARY	30	F	W		GRZZZZNY
MARIE	4	F	CHILD		GRZZZZNY
DOESCHER, LEON	28	M	BKR		GRZZZZNY
BOEHLE, JOSEPHE.	50	F	W		GRZZZZNY
AUGUSTE	11	F	UNKNOWN		GRZZZZNY

PASSENGER	AGE	SEX	OCCUPATION	PRVVL	DES
VERONIKA	9	F	CHILD	GRZZZZNY	
JOHANN	4	M	CHILD	GRZZZZNY	
BOETTCHER, AMANDA	24	F	W	GRAAKHNY	
ALEXANDER	2	M	CHILD	GRAAKHNY	
TROST, HEINR.	15	M	LABR	GRZZZZNY	
DIETRICH, JACOB	21	M	GDNR	GRACQOCAL	
WEIRICH, MARIE	20	F	UNKNOWN	GRZZZZNY	
FEULNER, RETA	17	F	UNKNOWN	GRACJSNY	
HENNIG, MARIA	17	F	UNKNOWN	GRACJSNY	
HUS, DORA	18	F	UNKNOWN	GRAFDWNY	
KESSER, DANIEL	56	M	FARMER	GRZZZZNY	
KATHIE	58	F	W	GRZZZZNY	
GEORGY	11	M	UNKNOWN	GRZZZZNY	
STIEHLER, ERNST	49	M	TLR	GRZZZZNY	
FEIL, FRITZ	15	M	FARMER	GRZZZZNY	
HOFFSTALL, WILHELM	17	M	LABR	GRAAGKNY	
GROTE, HEINR.	17	M	LABR	GRACBRNY	
LINDEMANN, HEINR.	17	M	LABR	GRACBRNY	
LAMPE, FRITZ	14	M	LABR	GRACBRNY	
VONFELDE, HEINR.	15	M	TLR	GRACBRNY	
RASCH, JOHA.	20	F	UNKNOWN	GRACBRNY	
WIELAND, HEINR.	24	M	SMH	GRZZZZNY	
POTH, JOHANNE	22	F	UNKNOWN	GRACBRNY	
POTTHAST, SOPHIE	60	F	W	GRACBRNY	
EMMA	20	F	UNKNOWN	GRACBRNY	
KORKMANN, WILHELM	11	M	UNKNOWN	GRABSDNY	
MUSTERMANN, HERM.	15	M	LABR	GRABSDNY	
BOERGER, HERM.	16	M	LABR	GRZZZZNY	
AHRENS, ELISABETH	25	F	UNKNOWN	GRABSDNY	
MARY, JULIUS	43	M	LABR	GRABDMNY	
BROCKMANN, ELISABETH	23	F	UNKNOWN	GRAARRNY	
SCHIERENBECK, HEINR.	18	M	CGRMKR	GRAARRNY	
SICK, LINE	19	F	UNKNOWN	GRAARRNY	
BUECHLER, CARL	21	M	BKR	GRZZZZNY	
SCHROEDER, JOHANN	26	M	BKR	GRZZZZNY	
MARIA	25	F	W	GRZZZZNY	
FATTHAUER, MARIE	22	F	UNKNOWN	GRACBRNY	
LAMMERS, ANNA	17	F	UNKNOWN	GRACBRNY	
ENGELKE, MARGA.	14	F	UNKNOWN	GRACBRNY	
SCHMEDES, ALBERT	22	M	FARMER	GRACBRNY	
THOELE, ADOLF	15	M	FARMER	GRACBRNY	
KUNST, WILHELMINE	17	F	UNKNOWN	GRACBRNY	
HAAL, MARKUS	16	M	TLR	GRACBRNY	
MANGELS, LOUISE	17	F	UNKNOWN	GRACBRNY	
MEYER, DOROTHEA	18	F	UNKNOWN	GRACBRNY	
DOESCHER, JOHN	45	M	LABR	GRACBRNY	
HEINSON, MINNA	56	F	W	GRACBRNY	
WENKE, WILHELMINE	17	F	UNKNOWN	GRACBRNY	
PAGELT, HEIM.	14	M	TLR	GRADVVNY	
HUELSMANN, SOPHIE	20	F	UNKNOWN	GRACBRNY	
OHLAND, KATHA.	16	F	UNKNOWN	GRACBRNY	
STAHNKE, PAULE.	18	F	UNKNOWN	GRZZZZNY	
SCHMIDT, HINR.	37	M	FARMER	GRZZZZNY	
LILIENTHAL, JOHE.	24	F	W	GRACBRNY	
JOH.	2	M	CHILD	GRACBRNY	
HINR.	.04	M	INFANT	GRACBRNY	
KAISER, JOHANN	22	M	LABR	GRZZZZNY	
FLEISCHAUER, FERD.	22	M	LABR	GRZZZZNY	
SCHOLZ, EVA	30	F	W	GRAHGXNY	
MARGA.	6	F	CHILD	GRAHGXNY	
HUTH, ADOLF	29	M	SHMK	GRALFLNY	
GRELL, HELENE	22	F	UNKNOWN	GRAJSVPA	
NOWACZYK, MAXIM	35	M	FARMER	GRABUTPA	
WESSLING, HERM.	17	M	FARMER	GRADBKPA	
LOHMANN, HEINR.	17	M	FARMER	GRADBKPA	
KAISER, JACOB	21	M	LABR	GRADCLPA	
THIELMANN, THERESE	22	F	W	GRADQZIL	
ANNA	3	F	CHILD	GRADQZIL	
MARGA.	2	F	CHILD	GRADQZIL	
THERESE	.02	F	INFANT	GRADQZIL	
SEGLER, OTTO	30	M	SDLR	GRADLDNY	
MARIE	21	F	W	GRADLDNY	
PHILIPP	.09	M	INFANT	GRADLDNY	
ELM, WILHELMINE	44	F	W	GRAARRNY	
SCHMETLER, BARTHOMEUS	23	M	SMH	GRZZZZNY	

PASSENGER	AGE	SEX	OCCUPATION	PRVVL	DES
ISSOUD, HUGO	11	M	UNKNOWN	GRZZZZNY	
BADER, ELISABETH	20	F	UNKNOWN	GRZZZZNY	
STADTLANDER, EMMA	35	F	W	GRAARRNY	
MARIA	5	F	CHILD	GRAARRNY	
PEPER, MARTIN	16	M	CH	GRAARRNY	
POIT, PETER	30	M	FARMER	GRAARRNY	

SHIP: AMSTERDAM

FROM: ROTTERDAM
TO: NEW YORK
ARRIVED: 13 OCTOBER 1888

PASSENGER	AGE	SEX	OCCUPATION	PRVVL	DES
KELFRIZE, OLGA	42	F	UNKNOWN	GRZZZZUSA	
JENNY	20	F	UNKNOWN	GRZZZZUSA	
MARTIN	15	M	UNKNOWN	GRZZZZUSA	
FRANZ	13	M	UNKNOWN	GRZZZZUSA	
STRAUB, EUGEN	28	M	AGNT	GRZZZZUSA	
DANKE, JOHN	36	M	AGNT	GRZZZZUSA	
MOREAN, HERNY	26	M	AGNT	FRZZZZUSA	
HENRIETTE	22	F	UNKNOWN	FRZZZZUSA	
TRAUH, LEOPOLD	22	M	UNKNOWN	GRZZZZUSA	
MEESER, PHILIP	36	M	TCHR	GRZZZZUSA	
PETZ, JOHN	66	M	UNKNOWN	GRZZZZUSA	
BRUNNER, BABET.	26	F	UNKNOWN	GRZZZZUSA	
ZICK, HENRY	29	M	TLR	GRZZZZUSA	
KRUEMEICH, PETER	31	M	AGNT	GRZZZZUSA	
GERTRUDE	23	F	UNKNOWN	GRZZZZUSA	
ZYEHR, HENRY	28	M	LABR	GRZZZZUSA	
EMBACH, GERTRUDE	24	F	UNKNOWN	GRZZZZUSA	
WEBER, HEINRICH	30	M	MCHT	GRZZZZUSA	
LIPP, LOUIS	24	M	MCHT	GRZZZZUSA	
MANE	52	F	UNKNOWN	GRZZZZUSA	
AGATHE	8	F	CHILD	GRZZZZUSA	
THERESE	11	F	CH	GRZZZZUSA	
TACSYTH, WILLEM	30	M	AGNT	GRZZZZUSA	
BECK, MANE	15	F	UNKNOWN	GRZZZZUSA	
DANGELMEYER, EMILIE	19	F	UNKNOWN	GRZZZZUSA	
SCHMULZER, FRIDA	17	F	UNKNOWN	GRZZZZUSA	
EHRLER, VICTORIA	18	F	UNKNOWN	GRZZZZUSA	
SCHLICK, MARIE	27	F	UNKNOWN	GRZZZZUSA	
SCHMIDT, BARBARA	23	F	UNKNOWN	GRZZZZUSA	
GROESE, MARIE	42	F	UNKNOWN	GRZZZZUSA	
LEDA	10	F	CH	GRZZZZUSA	
KESSLER, U	28	F	CH	GRZZZZUSA	
OCHSE, WILHELMINA	32	F	CH	GRZZZZUSA	
CARL	8	M	CHILD	GRZZZZUSA	
GEORG	6	M	CHILD	GRZZZZUSA	
CLOOS, GEORG	36	M	LABR	GRZZZZUSA	
METZGER, PHILIP	40	M	FARMER	GRZZZZUSA	
POOERMAN, FRANS	46	M	FARMER	GRZZZZUSA	
GUENTHER, ADOLF	59	M	FARMER	GRZZZZUSA	
STERN, BAREND	40	M	LABR	GRZZZZUSA	
GRAMLICH, WILHELM	35	M	LABR	GRZZZZUSA	
BRUEHN, JOHN	29	M	FARMER	GRZZZZUSA	
JOHANNA	26	F	UNKNOWN	GRZZZZUSA	
RINTEL, BELLA	29	F	UNKNOWN	GRZZZZUSA	
GROSS, BARBARA	58	F	UNKNOWN	GRZZZZUSA	
SCHMIDT, GEORGE	11	M	UNKNOWN	GRZZZZUSA	
HENCKE, ANNA	27	F	UNKNOWN	GRZZZZUSA	
SCHMIDT, CHRISTINA	34	F	UNKNOWN	GRZZZZUSA	
TOERTH, SERBINE	26	F	UNKNOWN	GRZZZZUSA	
HEGMEYER, HEDWIG	13	F	UNKNOWN	GRZZZZUSA	
TORSTER, BARBARA	22	F	UNKNOWN	GRZZZZUSA	
TRAUH, ANNA	20	F	UNKNOWN	GRZZZZUSA	
MANDEL, ANNA	19	F	UNKNOWN	GRZZZZUSA	
FRANCISCA	19	F	UNKNOWN	GRZZZZUSA	
RENHARD, CATHARINA	16	F	UNKNOWN	GRZZZZUSA	
SCHEN, BARBARA	17	F	UNKNOWN	GRZZZZUSA	
SAPPER, CARL	22	M	DR	GRZZZZUSA	

PASSENGER	AGE	SEX	OCCUPATION	PRV	VIL	DES
CHRIST, CAROLINE	26	F	UNKNOWN	GRZZZZ		USA
KLEIN, SOPHIE	23	F	UNKNOWN	GRZZZZ		USA
TECHTER, BARBARA	23	F	UNKNOWN	GRZZZZ		USA
CERVESON, GIOVANNI	24	M	LABR	FRZZZZ		USA
DOBRICH, TOMASO	25	M	LABR	FRZZZZ		USA
TRANCHETI, GIUSEPPE	22	M	LABR	FRZZZZ		USA
MAGGIO, MICHAELE	18	M	LABR	FRZZZZ		USA
BUONO, LUIGI	21	M	LABR	FRZZZZ		USA
BELTRAM, GIUSEPPE	28	M	LABR	FRZZZZ		USA
LOICONO, FRANCESA	33	M	LABR	FRZZZZ		USA
MANETTA, SALVATORE	26	M	LABR	FRZZZZ		USA
LACORTE, NICOLO	32	M	LABR	FRZZZZ		USA
TOMASETTI, GIANUTO	28	M	LABR	FRZZZZ		USA
GENTILE, GIUSEPPE	24	M	LABR	FRZZZZ		USA
PELLINI, GIOVANNO	18	M	LABR	FRZZZZ		USA
RACHIOLLI, GIACOMO	40	M	LABR	FRZZZZ		USA
GAUDENGIO, GUIDETTO	39	M	LABR	FRZZZZ		USA
GALETO, BATTISTA	34	M	LABR	FRZZZZ		USA
SAUDDRONO, FRANCESCO	20	M	LABR	FRZZZZ		USA
CARLO	23	M	LABR	FRZZZZ		USA
GANDIO, ANTONIO	42	M	LABR	FRZZZZ		USA
ROTHEY, MANE	23	F	UNKNOWN	FRZZZZ		USA
KNEBEL, CONRAD	54	M	LABR	GRZZZZ		USA
PAULINE	31	F	UNKNOWN	GRZZZZ		USA
SPARFELD, HERMAN	6	M	CHILD	GRZZZZ		USA
GUTTMAN, CHRIST	47	M	LABR	GRZZZZ		USA
HAUESER, MATHILDE	26	F	UNKNOWN	GRZZZZ		USA
TOMBO, WILHELM	45	M	LABR	GRZZZZ		USA
STEPHAN	10	M	CH	GRZZZZ		USA
STOCHOWICH, AUGUST	22	M	LABR	GRZZZZ		USA
EISERMANN, PAULINE	15	F	UNKNOWN	GRZZZZ		USA
BOY-, WILLIAM	19	M	LABR	GRZZZZ		USA
MILLER, CONRAD	19	M	LABR	GRZZZZ		USA
PFEIFER, KATHARINA	40	F	UNKNOWN	GRZZZZ		USA
U	16	M	LABR	GRZZZZ		USA
LUDWIG	14	M	UNKNOWN	GRZZZZ		USA
CAROLINE	11	F	UNKNOWN	GRZZZZ		USA
AUGUST	9	M	CHILD	GRZZZZ		USA
FREUND, THERESE	28	F	UNKNOWN	GRZZZZ		USA
HAEPP, ANNA	23	F	UNKNOWN	GRZZZZ		USA
RIEDT, CAROLINE	16	F	UNKNOWN	GRZZZZ		USA
ZILCH, PETER	26	M	LABR	GRZZZZ		USA
KATO	19	F	UNKNOWN	GRZZZZ		USA
STICHT, KONRAD	30	M	LABR	GRZZZZ		USA
KRUET, ANTON	25	M	LABR	GRZZZZ		USA
SCHWALBOCH, KATO	45	F	UNKNOWN	GRZZZZ		USA
MARIE	18	F	UNKNOWN	GRZZZZ		USA
GABRIEL, FRANS	46	M	LABR	GRZZZZ		USA
BELLAMAN, WILLEM	25	M	LABR	GRZZZZ		USA
EISENBACHER, CASPAR	27	M	LABR	GRZZZZ		USA
ANNA	25	F	UNKNOWN	GRZZZZ		USA
MARGARETHA	2	F	CHILD	GRZZZZ		USA
PETER	25	M	UNKNOWN	GRZZZZ		USA
MARGARDT, FRIEDRIKE	39	F	UNKNOWN	GRZZZZ		USA
PAULINE	9	F	CHILD	GRZZZZ		USA
FRIEDRICK	8	M	CHILD	GRZZZZ		USA
PETER, GABRIEL	54	M	UNKNOWN	GRZZZZ		USA
WILHELM, ELISA	18	F	UNKNOWN	GRZZZZ		USA
EGOLF, CARL	20	M	LABR	GRZZZZ		USA
GRAN, GEORG	32	M	LABR	GRZZZZ		USA
VASEL, ROSINE	22	F	UNKNOWN	GRZZZZ		USA
SANNDER, CARL	48	M	LABR	GRZZZZ		USA
CAROLINE	26	F	UNKNOWN	GRZZZZ		USA
MUEHLER, FRIEDRICA	14	M	UNKNOWN	GRZZZZ		USA
WOHLGEMUTH, JUL.	19	M	LABR	GRZZZZ		USA
KLEISEMAYER, CASPAR	51	M	LABR	GRZZZZ		USA
HEINRICH	23	M	LABR	GRZZZZ		USA
JOSEF	16	M	LABR	GRZZZZ		USA
FICHMEILER, ERNST	50	M	LABR	GRZZZZ		USA
KOPPEL, HEINRICH	17	M	LABR	GRZZZZ		USA
ASCHENBAUER, ANTON	18	M	LABR	GRZZZZ		USA
REINHARDT, FRANCISCA	17	F	UNKNOWN	GRZZZZ		USA
AMALIA	19	F	UNKNOWN	GRZZZZ		USA
BANDY, ELISABETH	23	F	UNKNOWN	GRZZZZ		USA
SCHNANBET, EDUARD	27	M	LABR	GRZZZZ		USA
FRERICHS, JURGEN	24	M	LABR	GRZZZZ		USA
HOCK, KATHARINA	21	F	UNKNOWN	GRZZZZ		USA
KUHN, CASPAR	23	M	LABR	GRZZZZ		USA
LOERNE, BERNARD	46	M	LABR	GRZZZZ		USA
WINKLER, ALOIS	41	M	LABR	GRZZZZ		USA
ERNESTINE	34	F	UNKNOWN	GRZZZZ		USA
KATZ, WILLEM	28	M	LABR	GRZZZZ		USA
SCHA--, JOSEF	34	M	LABR	GRZZZZ		USA
KUEREL, KATO	25	F	LABR	GRZZZZ		USA
SCHREINER, U	40	F	UNKNOWN	GRZZZZ		USA
ANTON	11	M	UNKNOWN	GRZZZZ		USA
ANNA	8	F	CHILD	GRZZZZ		USA
VINCENT	2	M	CHILD	GRZZZZ		USA
MARIA	.06	F	INFANT	GRZZZZ		USA
FRANZ	10	M	CH	GRZZZZ		USA
STEPHAN	24	M	LABR	GRZZZZ		USA
MUELLER, RICHARD	22	M	LABR	GRZZZZ		USA
FISCHE, WILHELM	19	M	LABR	GRZZZZ		USA
SCHWARZ, JOS.	19	M	LABR	GRZZZZ		USA
ADLER, PETER	22	M	LABR	GRZZZZ		USA
KIRCHMAYER, MARIE	24	F	UNKNOWN	GRZZZZ		USA
HELENE	.06	F	INFANT	GRZZZZ		USA
SCHMIDT, KARL	27	M	LABR	GRZZZZ		USA
WALDENBERGER, ANTON	14	M	LABR	GRZZZZ		USA
ZIMMERMAN, EMMA	34	F	UNKNOWN	GRZZZZ		USA
AHLPRECHT, AUGUST	29	M	LABR	GRZZZZ		USA
LOUIS	22	M	LABR	GRZZZZ		USA
KLEINFELD, LYDIA	26	F	UNKNOWN	GRZZZZ		USA
PETER	11	M	CH	GRZZZZ		USA
HERMAN	9	M	CHILD	GRZZZZ		USA
HEINRICH	7	M	CHILD	GRZZZZ		USA
HERR, ANTON	18	M	LABR	GRZZZZ		USA
MANGOLD, KATO	29	F	UNKNOWN	GRZZZZ		USA
OBERNAUER, JOHN	33	M	LABR	GRZZZZ		USA
KELLER, SUSSIE	52	F	UNKNOWN	GRZZZZ		USA
ANNA	10	F	CH	GRZZZZ		USA
REICHANDER, ANTON	10	M	CH	GRZZZZ		USA
PLETTE, ANDREAS	58	M	UNKNOWN	GRZZZZ		USA
MARIE	51	F	UNKNOWN	GRZZZZ		USA
KATIE	26	F	UNKNOWN	GRZZZZ		USA
BENNO	10	M	CH	GRZZZZ		USA
LEIDNER, ADAM	23	M	MCHT	GRZZZZ		USA
HERBER, JOHAN	23	M	MCHT	GRZZZZ		USA
GROSSMANN, ADOLF	60	M	UNKNOWN	GRZZZZ		USA
PETERSEN, CHRIST	55	M	LABR	GRZZZZ		USA
MUELLER, JOHN	23	M	LABR	GRZZZZ		USA
HEID, BERNARD	39	M	LABR	GRZZZZ		USA
HOFFMANN, LOUISE	18	F	UNKNOWN	GRZZZZ		USA
WEUMANN, OTTO	18	M	LABR	GRZZZZ		USA
OTT, JOHN	24	M	LABR	GRZZZZ		USA
BECKER, JACOB	44	M	LABR	GRZZZZ		USA
CHRISTINA	58	F	UNKNOWN	GRZZZZ		USA
MARIA	19	F	UNKNOWN	GRZZZZ		USA
JACOB	16	M	UNKNOWN	GRZZZZ		USA
PHILIPP	8	M	CHILD	GRZZZZ		USA
ZIMMERMAN, LIDIA	20	F	UNKNOWN	GRZZZZ		USA
BAUMER, MARIA	13	F	UNKNOWN	GRZZZZ		USA
MADOEN, ANTONIE	19	F	UNKNOWN	GRZZZZ		USA
LEIBBRAND, WILHELM	16	M	UNKNOWN	GRZZZZ		USA
----MANN, U	62	F	UNKNOWN	GRZZZZ		USA
KRACH, JOHAN	28	M	LABR	GRZZZZ		USA
WOLFURTH, LENE	19	M	LABR	GRZZZZ		USA
KRUMPHOLZ, JOSEF	30	M	LABR	GRZZZZ		USA
SCHAFER, HEINRICH	34	M	LABR	GRZZZZ		USA
SCHROEDER, HEINRICH	29	M	LABR	GRZZZZ		USA
PERLMANN, JUDEL	28	M	LABR	GRZZZZ		USA
SCHNEIDER, EMANUEL	21	F	UNKNOWN	GRZZZZ		USA
QUEISSER, MARIE	36	F	UNKNOWN	GRZZZZ		USA
WALTER	4	M	CHILD	GRZZZZ		USA
BUCHELE, CATO	44	F	UNKNOWN	GRZZZZ		USA
EMILIE	15	F	UNKNOWN	GRZZZZ		USA
JULIUS	9	M	CHILD	GRZZZZ		USA
ERNST	11	M	CH	GRZZZZ		USA
CARL	10	M	CH	GRZZZZ		USA
GOEBEL, MARGO	21	F	UNKNOWN	GRZZZZ		USA

PASSENGER	AGE	SEX	OCCUPATION	PRVVL	DES
MAYER, WILHELM	24	M	LABR	GRZZZZUSA	
BOLHOEFNER, HEINRICH	25	M	LABR	GRZZZZUSA	
OBREICH, FRIEDRICH	17	M	LABR	GRZZZZUSA	
WALDEIER, CARL	17	M	LABR	GRZZZZUSA	
SPREEN, WILHELM	25	M	LABR	GRZZZZUSA	
GROSFEAM, CONSTANT.	33	M	LABR	GRZZZZUSA	
SOPHIE	44	F	UNKNOWN	GRZZZZUSA	
FEUSSER, JULES	25	M	LABR	GRZZZZUSA	
GEBHARD, JACOB	30	M	LABR	GRZZZZUSA	
NUESS, JOHAN	61	M	LABR	GRZZZZUSA	
THIEMANN, HANRI	21	M	LABR	GRZZZZUSA	
KARL	17	M	LABR	GRZZZZUSA	
BLUMENFELD, MAX	20	M	LABR	GRZZZZUSA	
TJADEN, FRITZ	29	M	LABR	GRZZZZUSA	
MARTIN, SAM.	24	M	LABR	GRZZZZUSA	
HEINRICH, AUG.	19	M	LABR	GRZZZZUSA	
WEICHSEL, EMMA	22	F	UNKNOWN	GRZZZZUSA	
HERMANN, GERTRUD	52	F	UNKNOWN	GRZZZZUSA	
EMILIE	18	F	UNKNOWN	GRZZZZUSA	
LANG, FRIEDRIKE	25	F	UNKNOWN	GRZZZZUSA	
AUGUST	.11	M	INFANT	GRZZZZUSA	
WYDRA, VICTORIA	20	F	UNKNOWN	GRZZZZUSA	
HERM, FRANK	40	M	LABR	GRZZZZUSA	
MARGO	42	F	UNKNOWN	GRZZZZUSA	
SOPHIE	6	F	CHILD	GRZZZZUSA	
JOSEFINE	8	F	CHILD	GRZZZZUSA	
FRANS	10	M	CH	GRZZZZUSA	
STADLER, MARIE	20	F	UNKNOWN	GRZZZZUSA	
VIOOLTRAM, PETEL	50	M	LABR	FRZZZZUSA	
HORA	45	F	UNKNOWN	FRZZZZUSA	
LAZAR	21	M	LABR	FRZZZZUSA	
HERCON	18	M	LABR	FRZZZZUSA	
NEBIA	33	M	LABR	FRZZZZUSA	
HAKIN, CH.	32	M	LABR	FRZZZZUSA	
U, U	40	F	UNKNOWN	FRZZZZUSA	
LAID, FRANGOLA	18	F	UNKNOWN	FRZZZZUSA	
TOMMA, FRANGOLA	45	M	LABR	FRZZZZUSA	
ODKEREDJA, LARA	25	M	LABR	FRZZZZUSA	
FRANK, WILLEM	34	M	LABR	GRZZZZUSA	
ELISA	30	F	UNKNOWN	GRZZZZUSA	
JOHAN	11	M	UNKNOWN	GRZZZZUSA	
MARIA	6	F	CHILD	GRZZZZUSA	
WILHELM	4	M	CHILD	GRZZZZUSA	
HEINRICH	.04	M	INFANT	GRZZZZUSA	
BORYZESKA, VICTORIA	25	F	UNKNOWN	GRZZZZUSA	
ANTONIA	.10	F	INFANT	GRZZZZUSA	
BUSCH, MAGGIE	23	F	UNKNOWN	GRZZZZUSA	

SHIP: CITY OF RICHMOND

FROM: LIVERPOOL AND QUEENSTOWN
TO: NEW YORK
ARRIVED: 13 OCTOBER 1888

PASSENGER	AGE	SEX	OCCUPATION	PRVVL	DES
GOLDBERG, LEON	30	M	DR	GRADBQNY	
ENGEL, ISIDORE	17	M	SLR	GRACBFNY	
SCHWARZ, KEWE	19	M	SLR	GRACBFNY	
FUKURAN, AUG.	23	M	SLR	GRACBFNY	
FILTRUSER, FABEL	28	M	LABR	GRACBFPA	
BALZER, FRANZ	24	M	LABR	GRACBFNY	
GLASSEL, ROBT.	25	M	LABR	GRACBFNY	
JASCHKE, REINHOLD	22	M	LABR	GRACBFNY	
DROEGA, MARIA	24	F	SP	GRACBFNY	
JOHANA	19	F	SP	GRACBFNY	
PEERCHER, THERESIE	18	F	SP	GRACBFCAL	
GEBR, MALE	24	F	SP	GRADAXPHI	
BECHA, JULINA	51	F	W	GRACBFWI	
EVA	18	F	SP	GRACBFWI	
RUDOLPH	10	M	CH	GRACBFWI	
A.	00	F	INF	GRACBFWI	

SHIP: NANTES

FROM: BORDEAUX
TO: NEW ORLEANS
ARRIVED: 15 OCTOBER 1888

PASSENGER	AGE	SEX	OCCUPATION	PRVVL	DES
MICAELA, GLAIN	18	F	SVNT	FRZZZZUSA	
DUCAY, PAUL	38	M	CPTR	FRZZZZUSA	
LAGRAVE, ETIENNE	25	M	CL	FRZZZZUSA	
ASSEGUET, ADELE	36	F	SVNT	FRZZZZUSA	
ARSEGUCH, JEAN	16	M	CL	FRZZZZUSA	
CATHERINE, U	20	F	SMSTS	FRZZZZUSA	
CECILE, BELLECOURT	37	M	SVNT	FRZZZZUSA	
CHARLIE	11	M	NN	FRZZZZUSA	
STEWART, JOHN-ALEXANDRE	19	M	CL	FRZZZZUSA	
ABADIE, ALEXANDRE	35	M	GDNR	FRZZZZUSA	
MADELAINE	34	F	CK	FRZZZZUSA	
LOU--, BAPTISTE	50	M	FARMER	FRZZZZUSA	
MARIE	11	F	SVNT	FRZZZZUSA	
PAULINE	00	F	SVNT	FRZZZZUSA	
U, JEAN	35	M	FARMER	FRZZZZUSA	
EMILE	25	M	BKR	FRZZZZUSA	
BERGER, ANTONIETTE	20	F	SMSTS	FRZZZZUSA	
U, JEAN	49	M	FARMER	FRZZZZUSA	
LASSERRE, JEAN	37	M	CPTR	FRZZZZUSA	
JENS, JEAN	27	M	BKR	FRZZZZUSA	
-E-LIE, JUSTINE	19	M	CL	FRZZZZUSA	
DAMOUX, JEAN	24	M	CL	FRZZZZUSA	
VERGES, DOMINIQUE	38	M	WHLR	FRZZZZUSA	
JEANNE	30	F	SMSTS	FRZZZZUSA	
PAUL	10	M	CH	FRZZZZUSA	
DELOUT, PIERRE	34	M	FARMER	FRZZZZUSA	
LASSALLE, JEAN	40	M	FARMER	FRZZZZUSA	
LACOSTE, LEOPOLD-PIERRE	00	M	INF	FRZZZZUSA	
PHALIP, LEON	24	M	CL	FRZZZZUSA	
FAMES, JULIE	26	M	SVNT	FRZZZZUSA	
ABORA, EUGENIE	41	F	SMSTS	FRZZZZUSA	
GENTIE, ANTHONIE	39	M	FARMER	FRZZZZUSA	
GEULIE, MARIE	41	F	NN	FRZZZZUSA	
MARIE	4	F	CHILD	FRZZZZUSA	
BATH, JACK	18	M	FARMER	FRZZZZUSA	
AXOBIE, JEAN	20	M	FARMER	FRZZZZUSA	
SAUNBOURE, JEAN	20	M	FARMER	FRZZZZUSA	
LESLETTE, JEAN	15	M	FARMER	FRZZZZUSA	
LUISETTE, MANE	17	F	SVNT	FRZZZZUSA	
CICONLAR, CLEMENT	18	M	FARMER	FRZZZZUSA	
PILOT, PIERIE	19	M	FARMER	FRZZZZUSA	
GUICHANAND, PIERIE	31	M	FARMER	FRZZZZUSA	
MARIE	26	F	NN	FRZZZZUSA	
DESPOSSE, ALEXANDRE	55	M	JWLR	FRZZZZUSA	
FLORE	50	F	NN	FRZZZZUSA	
AUCE	18	F	NN	FRZZZZUSA	
ALBERT	11	M	CH	FRZZZZUSA	
PUSSEGNIE, ALEXANDRE	23	M	FARMER	FRZZZZUSA	
MA---NTO, MARIE	19	F	NN	FRZZZZUSA	
JEAN	16	M	NN	FRZZZZUSA	
BOZILE, MERANDE	29	M	MCHT	FRZZZZUSA	
LUCANTIS, JEAN-MARIE	28	M	FARMER	FRZZZZUSA	
COURTADE, ROSE	27	F	NN	FRZZZZUSA	
LABAT, J.	58	M	FARMER	FRZZZZUSA	
S.	56	F	NN	FRZZZZUSA	
THERESE	23	F	NN	FRZZZZUSA	
DARESA-, MARGUERITTE	28	F	NN	FRZZZZUSA	
HAURET, PIERRE	18	M	FLABR	FRZZZZUSA	
AUGLADE, BERNARD	19	M	FLABR	FRZZZZUSA	
LABOURDETTE, PIERRE	18	M	FLABR	FRZZZZUSA	
PIERIE, BOURDAT	17	M	FLABR	FRZZZZUSA	
LAILHACAN, MICHEL	17	M	FLABR	FRZZZZUSA	
BOURD---, MARIE	32	F	NN	FRZZZZUSA	
U, MARIANE	00	F	SVNT	FRZZZZUSA	
ROSSMANN, FRIED.	24	M	MCHT	GRZZZZNO	
PARMEBA, PAUL	32	M	CPTR	GRZZZZNO	
HULLMANN, OSKAR	30	M	MCHT	GRZZZZSAT	
MERBETH, GUSTAV	34	M	LABR	GRZZZZSAT	

PASSENGER	AGE	SEX	OCCUPATION	PRVL	DES
ELMA	25	F	NN		GRZZZZSAT
RICHARD	.06	M	INFANT		GRZZZZUNK
HERMANN, FRANKE	29	M	CPTR		GRZZZZUNK
MARIA	29	F	NN		GRZZZZUNK
RICHARD	6	M	CHILD		GRZZZZUNK
ALMA	7	F	CHILD		GRZZZZUNK
CARL	3	F	CHILD		GRZZZZUNK
GEORG	4	M	CHILD		GRZZZZUNK
HAEFNER, JOHANNES	25	M	BLKSMH		GRZZZZLOS
REIN, JOSEPH	42	M	FARMER		GRZZZZNO
MAGDALENA	39	F	NN		GRZZZZNO
JOSEPH	11	M	CH		GRZZZZNO
MARIA	10	F	CH		GRZZZZNO
STEPHAN	9	M	CHILD		GRZZZZNO
CONRAD	8	M	CHILD		GRZZZZNO
JOSEPH	5	M	CHILD		GRZZZZNO
BARBARA	3	F	CHILD		GRZZZZNO
MAGDALENA	1	F	CHILD		GRZZZZNO
LANGIER, CAROLINE	65	F	CH		FRZZZZNO
MENTZEL, RICHARD	31	M	FARMER		GRZZZZNO
FRANZISKA	27	F	NN		GRZZZZNO
WITTY	1	F	CHILD		GRZZZZNO
KLOV-K, WILHELM	59	M	FARMER		GRZZZZNO
U	58	F	NN		GRZZZZNO
ELISA	20	F	NN		GRZZZZNO
SEIBERT, MICHAEL	43	M	NN		GRZZZZNO
LOUISE	18	F	NN		GRZZZZNO
EMIL	2	M	CHILD		GRZZZZNO

SHIP: SCYTHIA

FROM: LIVERPOOL AND QUEENSTOWN
TO: BOSTON
ARRIVED: 15 OCTOBER 1888

PASSENGER	AGE	SEX	OCCUPATION	PRVL	DES
BELICKI, MICHEAL	23	M	WCHMKR		GRZZZZUNK
BARTASKE, JOSEPH	18	M	LABR		GRZZZZUNK
BO-, ISAK	19	M	LABR		GRZZZZNY
GARA-EIM, BEDROS	25	M	LABR		GRZZZZUNK
GHUM--, CARL	20	M	LABR		GRZZZZUNK
HEMMINGSEN, WALDIMAR	18	M	LABR		GRZZZZUNK
JOTEN, ANTON	20	M	LABR		GRZZZZUNK
LEONWICZ, MIKOS	20	M	TLR		GRZZZZUNK
RADRUJWORKY, LEO	19	M	LABR		GRZZZZUNK
RUSTIGRAN, SARKIS	22	M	CPTR		GRZZZZUNK
WILHELMSEN, AUGUST	28	M	SHMK		GRZZZZUNK
RICHTER, EMIL	20	M	NN		GRZZZZUNK

SHIP: SUEVIA

FROM: HAMBURG AND HAVRE
TO: NEW YORK
ARRIVED: 15 OCTOBER 1888

PASSENGER	AGE	SEX	OCCUPATION	PRVL	DES
FENDLE, LORENVE	24	M	LABR		BVZZZZMI
SIEVERS, MARGA.	60	F	WO		BVACBFMI
KRUSE, ERNESTINE	22	F	SGL		BVADOAMI
LORENZ, MARTHA	33	F	WO		BVABDMMI
ELISABETH	6	F	CHILD		BVABDMMI
HAUS	3	M	CHILD		BVABDMMI
MEINCKE, ALWINE	20	F	SGL		BVACBFNE
BOETTCHER, BERTHA	24	F	SGL		BVACBFNE
LIEBERMANN, HERRMANN	31	M	TCHR		BVACSDNE
HELENE	23	F	W		BVACSDNE
GINZBERG, HERM.	16	M	MCHT		BVACSDNE

PASSENGER	AGE	SEX	OCCUPATION	PRVL	DES
HAMPEL, ANNA	46	F	WO		PRZZZZMI
BERTHOLD	14	M	CH		PRZZZZMI
CARL	7	M	CHILD		PRZZZZMI
DREWES, CAROLINE	40	F	WO		PRACSLNY
EMILIE	7	F	CHILD		PRACSLNY
MARIE	6	F	CHILD		PRACSLNY
LEWIN, SARA	28	F	WO		PRADNYNY
ROSA	.11	F	INFANT		PRADNYNY
MOLL, AUGUST	22	M	CL		PRABZVNY
HAHN, CARL	28	M	SHMK		PRAADENY
MINNA	27	F	W		PRAADENY
EICHHORN, EMILIE	28	F	SGL		PRZZZZNY
MANTHEY, JULIUS	25	M	LABR		PRZZZZNY
AUGUSTE	25	F	W		PRZZZZNY
LEJO	.11	M	INFANT		PRZZZZNY
JACOBS, GEORG	43	M	LABR		PRAAKHNY
ALBERTINE	43	F	W		PRAAKHNY
ALFRED	17	M	CH		PRAAKHNY
FRIDA	14	F	CH		PRAAKHNY
SOHNBERT, LOUISE	48	F	WO		PRAARZNY
MARGA.	17	F	CH		PRAARZNY
OLGA	7	F	CHILD		PRAARZNY
WILBATH, EMMA	25	F	SGL		PRAEIZMD
PEICK, WILH.	21	M	CCHMN		PRAIONIL
RIEMER, RICHARD	32	M	TU		PRACPSOH
WILHE.	31	F	W		PRACPSOH
ARTHUR	.11	M	INFANT		PRACPSOH
CARL	4	M	CHILD		PRACPSOH
REIM, ERNST	15	M	TU		PRACPSOH
ZOLLMANN, WILH.	22	M	TU		PRAFNKOH
NAWROOKA, MALGORZATA	24	F	TU		PRZZZZOH
MARYANNE	3	F	CHILD		PRZZZZOH
ANNA	55	F	WO		PRZZZZOH
KENTOWSKI, JOHANNA	23	F	WO		PRAGAWOH
FITZNER, HEINR.	17	M	LABR		PRZZZZOH
DEHN, AUGUST	29	M	LABR		PRZZZZOH
EMILIE	24	F	W		PRZZZZOH
HERM.	2	M	CHILD		PRZZZZOH
RICHARD	.11	M	INFANT		PRZZZZOH
MUELLER, BERTHA	23	F	WO		PRZZZZPA
ULRICH, CARL	24	M	LABR		PRAEACIL
MUELLER, ELISABETH	64	F	SGL		BVZZZZPA
SCHLOTTMANN, FRIEDR.	16	M	LKSH		BVAEHQNY
HABECK, AUGUST	27	M	LABR		BVALZONY
JOHANNA	38	F	W		BVALZONY
CARL	2	M	CHILD		BVALZONY
GUSTAV	.11	M	INFANT		BVALZONY
CORNILS, HENRIETTE	21	F	SGL		BVAHMTNY
ASSMUSS, PETER	24	M	SHMK		BVAHMTNY
PAGEL, DIETRICH	36	M	BKLYR		PRZZZZIL
BABULKE, JOHANNE	23	F	SGL		PRZZZZIL
TUEMLER, FRITZ	30	M	MCHT		PRZZZZIL
BORDENHAGEN, JOHANN	19	M	MCHT		PRADWIIL
LASI, JOHS.	28	M	SLR		PRAHZPIL
WEINLE, CAROLINE	19	F	SGL		WMZZZZCH
LINDHOLM, MAREN	19	F	SGL		PRZZZZNY
MOJE, MARTHA	7	F	CHILD		PRACBFNY
HANSEL, ELISA	23	F	WO		SYZZZZNY
EMMA	.09	F	INFANT		SYZZZZNY
SCHIPPER, MARIE	45	F	WO		SYAHILNY
MARGA.	16	F	CH		SYAHILNY
LOUISE	13	F	CH		SYAHILNY
HEINR.	7	M	CHILD		SYAHILNY
TIETJENS, MATHILDE	18	F	SGL		SYAAVGPA
UKEN, META	19	F	SGL		SYAAVGPA
HAASE, GEORG	32	M	FARMER		PRZZZZPA
HERMINE	32	F	W		PRZZZZPA
WILH.	4	M	CHILD		PRZZZZPA
HERRM.	3	M	CHILD		PRZZZZPA
EMMA	.11	F	INFANT		PRZZZZPA
BOELLINGER, HERM.	16	M	FARMER		PRAAWKNY
MUELLER, ADAM	23	M	BKR		PRAAZSNY
HOFFMANN, ADOLF	17	M	SHMK		ANZZZZNY
SCHMIDT, GRETCHEN	24	F	SGL		ANABOQNY
HAENDLER, EMILIE	27	F	SGL		PRZZZZNY

PASSENGER	AGE	SEX	OCCUPATION	PRVL	DES
LADWIG, CARL	32	M	FARMER	PRZZZZNY	
JOHANNE	29	F	W	PRZZZZNY	
TRIBESS, ULRIKE	20	F	SGL	PRZZZZNY	
WAGENKNECHT, JOHANN	36	M	LABR	PRAKYJNY	
LOUISE	25	F	W	PRAKYJNY	
JOH.	3	M	CHILD	PRAKYJNY	
LOUISE	1	F	CHILD	PRAKYJNY	
KETTELMANN, MARGA.	21	F	SGL	PRACQONY	
BOLL, JACOB	46	M	BRR	WMZZZZMIL	
CATHA.	40	F	W	WMZZZZMIL	
GOTTFRIED	15	M	CH	WMZZZZMIL	
JACOB	7	M	CHILD	WMZZZZMIL	
MARTIN	6	M	CHILD	WMZZZZMIL	
CARL	5	M	CHILD	WMZZZZMIL	
MARIE	4	F	CHILD	WMZZZZMIL	
BEOHT, ANNA	18	F	SGL	WMAJKVMIL	
DENNER, CHRISTINE	28	F	WO	WMZZZZMIL	
MAIER, MATHAEUS	26	M	FARMER	WMAESYIL	
SOMMER, CATHA.	24	F	W	WMAEIFNY	
ANNA	16	F	SGL	WMAHSHNY	
CHRISTIANSEN, HAUS	55	M	FARMER	PRZZZZIL	
ELISABETH	61	F	W	PRZZZZIL	
ANNA	6	F	CHILD	PRZZZZIL	
JENSEN, BARBARA	15	F	SGL	PRZZZZIA	
BADURA, VALESKA	22	F	SGL	PRZZZZIA	
JACOBSEN, HAUS-P.	16	M	FARMER	PRZZZZIA	
BARTH, MINNA	26	F	SGL	SYZZZZNY	
STACHOWIAK, MARIANNE	25	F	WO	PRZZZZNY	
MARTHA	5	F	CHILD	PRZZZZNY	
ANTON	3	M	CHILD	PRZZZZNY	
PELOGIA	.06	F	INFANT	PRZZZZNY	
BOESE, FERD.	25	M	JNR	PRADNBIL	
JAHN, KARL	16	M	LABR	PRZZZZIL	
CHRISTIANSEN, MELE	18	F	SGL	PRZZZZIL	
WEEGE, FRANZ	35	M	BKR	PRAEIOIL	
HALLIER, OTTO	33	M	BCHR	MKZZZZIL	
FREITAG, ELISABETH	27	F	WO	MKZZZZIL	
WILH.	3	M	CHILD	MKZZZZIL	
LUDWIG	.11	M	INFANT	MKZZZZIL	
FROEHLICH, ERNST	28	M	LABR	MKAFWIIL	
AUGUSTE	32	F	W	MKAFWIIL	
WILH.	4	M	CHILD	MKAFWIIL	
EMMA	2	F	CHILD	MKAFWIIL	
FRIEDR.	44	M	LABR	MKAFWIIL	
LOUISE	25	F	WO	MKAEBUIL	
WILLI	3	M	CHILD	MKAEBUIL	
RUDOLF	.09	M	INFANT	MKAEBUIL	
DANZ, MINNA	16	F	SGL	MKAEBUNY	
SCHULZ, FRITZ	24	M	BKR	MKAAKHNY	
KAY, HEDWIG	32	F	WO	MKAAKHNY	
GEORG	4	M	CHILD	MKAAKHNY	
BOCOK, CARL	25	M	SVNT	MKAAKHIL	
KOSMANN, FRANK	38	M	JNR	MKACMHIL	
MUELLER, JOHANN	50	M	BRR	PRZZZZOH	
BERKOWITZ, JOSEF	19	M	MCHT	PRAMAIRSS	
ROST, MORITZ	35	M	MCHT	PRABDMRSS	
JENSEN, ANNA	49	F	WO	PRZZZZRSS	
MARTHA	7	F	CHILD	PRZZZZRSS	
COHRS, HEINR.	25	M	FARMER	PRAEUXIA	
KURTH, FRIEDR.	44	M	FARMER	PRZZZZIA	
WILHE.	39	F	W	PRZZZZIA	
IDA	15	F	CH	PRZZZZIA	
LOUISE	14	F	CH	PRZZZZIA	
ANNA	12	F	CH	PRZZZZIA	
GUSTAV	6	M	CHILD	PRZZZZIA	
EGGERT, WILH.	68	M	FARMER	PRZZZZIA	
MIEGEL, CARL	33	M	BLKSMH	PRZZZZMN	
ANNA	28	F	W	PRZZZZMN	
MINNA	7	F	CHILD	PRZZZZMN	
IDA	5	F	CHILD	PRZZZZMN	
HERM.	3	M	CHILD	PRZZZZMN	
SCHEIBE, EMMA	24	F	SGL	PRAIRSPA	
BIEDERMANN, MARIE	17	F	SGL	PRZZZZPA	
RUDACK, WILHELM	33	M	LABR	PRAFSANY	
PAULINE	39	F	W	PRAFSANY	
WYTZKA, LUDWIG	43	M	JNR	PRABZJIL	
JULIE	33	F	W	PRABZJIL	
GEORG	7	M	CHILD	PRABZJIL	
MARIE	6	F	CHILD	PRABZJIL	
GERTRUD	5	F	CHILD	PRABZJIL	
ERICH	4	M	CHILD	PRABZJIL	
HUBERT	1	M	CHILD	PRABZJIL	
HILDEBRANDT, GEORG	24	M	FARMER	PRADASWI	
NIX, CHRISTINE	16	F	SGL	PRABIFWI	
KUEBEL, EUGEN	18	M	MCHT	BVZZZZWI	
WILDE, GUSTAV	28	M	MCHT	SYZZZZWI	
BARTH, MINNA	26	M	LABR	SYZZZZWI	
RAHDER, PAULINE	16	F	SGL	SYZZZZWI	
DITTMER, JOHN	24	M	TKR	SYAFIGIL	
SCHNEPEL, HAUS	48	M	FARMER	SYZZZZIA	
ANNA	45	F	W	SYZZZZIA	
RUDOLPH	7	M	CHILD	SYZZZZIA	
CARL	6	M	CHILD	SYZZZZIA	
BERNHARD	4	M	CHILD	SYZZZZIA	
HEINR.	17	M	FARMER	SYZZZZIA	
VOLKERS, AMANDA	18	F	SGL	SYZZZZIA	
HELMKE, AUGUSTE	19	F	SGL	SYZZZZIA	
KURTH, ERNST	22	M	WTR	SYZZZZNY	
VONDERWUELBEKE, WM.	65	M	PVTR	PRZZZZNY	
KLINGBEIL, ALBERT	25	M	LABR	PRZZZZNY	
KASTNER, JACOB-F.	23	M	BKR	BDZZZZNY	
SCHLAUER, AUGUST	22	M	LABR	BDAACWIL	
BARGMANN, HEINRICH	25	M	JNR	BDAHSZIL	
HILSBERG, ERNST	47	M	BKR	BDABDMNY	
BOEHM, JOH.	40	M	LLD	BDADRONY	
LEVIN, MOSES	22	M	DLR	GRZZZZNY	
LIECHLE, MARIE	60	F	WO	GRADDKPA	
ELISE	.11	F	INFANT	GRADDKPA	
GEISSMANN, U	24	F	SGL	GRADDKPA	
JAUME, GUSTAVE	28	M	LABR	FRZZZZKS	
DESSORT, ALEXANDRE	17	M	LABR	FRZZZZKS	
HARDI, ARMAND	54	M	LABR	FRZZZZKS	
LEMARESCHALL, A.	32	M	LABR	FRZZZZKS	
BATTARD, ALBERT	32	M	LABR	FRZZZZCT	
GERROT, AUGUSTIN	22	F	SGL	FRZZZZCT	
BELLOT, ARISTID	38	M	LABR	FRZZZZCT	
ELISE	36	F	W	FRZZZZCT	
RUPP, OTTILIE	51	F	W	FRAFTDPA	
ELISABETH	18	F	CH	FRAFTDPA	
RENECON, ALBERT	22	M	CH	FRADXWKS	
DENIS, EMILIE	27	F	SGL	FRAGLYKS	
KRESCHMAR, HEINRICH	29	M	LABR	FRAAHUPA	
VOELKEL, CHRISITAN	20	M	LABR	FRABOQIL	
RICHERT, HEINRICH	55	M	LABR	FRAAHUPA	
KOHLER, GEORGE	48	M	LABR	FRAAHUUNK	
GORNICOURT, LYDIA	20	F	SGL	FRAFTDUNK	
KRAUSS, CONRAD	28	M	MCHT	FRAEOINY	
LIPPEL, JOHA.	53	F	WO	FRADCRNY	
RAND, JULIE	30	F	WO	FRAHSANY	
SCHOLERMANN, WILH.	26	M	AR	FRACBFNY	
AUGUSTIN, HEINR.	15	M	AR	FRAHSZNY	
SCHNABEL, CARL	29	M	MCHT	PRZZZZNY	
BECH, ELISE	35	F	SGL	PRZZZZNY	
LUHMANN, SOPHIE	72	F	WO	PRAARRNY	
PIENING, ADELE	19	F	SGL	PRACBFNY	
HASS, CAROLINE	24	F	SGL	MKZZZZNY	
MARCUSE, OSCAR	24	M	MCHT	PRZZZZNY	
CONRAD, REINHOLD	20	M	PNTR	PRAAKHNY	
STOECKER, FRIED.	34	M	MCHT	PRAGKTNY	
MENDELSOHN, RUDOLPH	28	M	MCHT	PRACSDNY	

PASSENGER	AGE	SEX	OCCUPATION	PRVL	DIES

SHIP: FULDA

FROM: BREMEN AND SOUTHAMPTON
TO: NEW YORK
ARRIVED: 16 OCTOBER 1888

PASSENGER	AGE	SEX	OCCUPATION	PRVL DIES
WERTHEIM, LOUIS	37	M	MCHT	GRZZZZUSA
PLODINS, MAX	34	M	MCHT	GRZZZZUSA
LUDWIG, MARIA	21	F	UNKNOWN	GRZZZZUSA
MANGELS, BARBA.	31	F	UNKNOWN	GRZZZZUSA
ELSA	7	F	CHILD	GRZZZZUSA
RUD.	6	M	CHILD	GRZZZZUSA
WALTER	4	M	CHILD	GRZZZZUSA
EDWIN	3	M	CHILD	GRZZZZUSA
ERISH	.05	M	INFANT	GRZZZZUSA
SCHLICK, JACOB	30	M	TT	GRZZZZUSA
ANNA	7	F	CHILD	GRZZZZUSA
BERG, KARL	16	M	MCHT	GRZZZZUSA
NEUMANN, U	38	F	UNKNOWN	GRZZZZUSA
BURT, LOUISE	26	F	UNKNOWN	GRZZZZUSA
THOMSSEN, MAGDA.	22	F	UNKNOWN	GRZZZZUSA
HOCH, ANNA	17	F	UNKNOWN	GRZZZZUSA
HAUNS, U	40	F	UNKNOWN	GRZZZZUSA
HARMS, ADELE	16	F	UNKNOWN	GRZZZZUSA
JOHE.	15	F	UNKNOWN	GRZZZZUSA
MENZEL, BENNO	24	M	LABR	GRZZZZUSA
WILKE, EMMO	15	M	LABR	GRZZZZUSA
ZIMMERMANN, NIKOL	63	M	LABR	GRZZZZUSA
NOWACK, FRANZ	26	M	LABR	GRZZZZUSA
NAWAJSKA, ROZALIA	44	F	UNKNOWN	GRZZZZUSA
KALDES, FR.	30	M	LABR	GRZZZZUSA
ZWANZIGER, CARL	23	M	LABR	GRZZZZUSA
SIMON, LINA	19	F	UNKNOWN	GRZZZZUSA
WEISSMANN, HANNI	18	F	UNKNOWN	GRZZZZUSA
DEDLOW, WILH.	17	M	CL	GRZZZZUSA
BANK, HERM.	22	M	SMH	GRZZZZUSA
GINAPP, WILH.	17	M	LABR	GRZZZZUSA
DURZEWSKY, FRAENK	15	M	LABR	GRZZZZUSA
TESCHE, WILH.	24	M	LABR	GRZZZZUSA
HAHN, ERNESTE.	24	F	UNKNOWN	GRZZZZUSA
EMIL	.10	M	INFANT	GRZZZZUSA
PHELKE, AUGUSTA	20	F	UNKNOWN	GRZZZZUSA
GRUEBNAU, HELENA	24	F	UNKNOWN	GRZZZZUSA
SCHULTZ, HERM.	24	M	LABR	GRZZZZUSA
KNUTHMANN, JOSEPH	44	M	LABR	GRZZZZUSA
ANNA	7	F	CHILD	GRZZZZUSA
KOHLBECHER, OTTILA	17	F	UNKNOWN	GRZZZZUSA
WILKE, LOUISE	30	F	UNKNOWN	GRZZZZUSA
LEO	3	M	CHILD	GRZZZZUSA
BEGRISCH, AUGUSTE	48	F	UNKNOWN	GRZZZZUSA
OPPERMANN, JOHN	34	M	FARMER	GRZZZZUSA
ELIS.	35	F	UNKNOWN	GRZZZZUSA
LOUISE	7	F	CHILD	GRZZZZUSA
MINNA	.11	F	INFANT	GRZZZZUSA
ROSENBAUM, TOBIAS	23	M	BBR	GRZZZZUSA
KLEBUCH, MARGANA	30	F	UNKNOWN	GRZZZZUSA
JULA	6	F	CHILD	GRZZZZUSA
JOSEF	5	M	CHILD	GRZZZZUSA
THIEL, HENRIETTE	54	F	UNKNOWN	GRZZZZUSA
HEINR.	15	M	CL	GRZZZZUSA
WILSCHEFFSKI, AGNES	22	F	UNKNOWN	GRZZZZUSA
BALKE, ADELE.	17	F	UNKNOWN	GRZZZZUSA
HESS, KUNIGDE.	18	F	UNKNOWN	GRZZZZUSA
REINERT, CAROLE.	49	F	UNKNOWN	GRZZZZUSA
NEIDHARDT, JOHA.	18	F	UNKNOWN	GRZZZZUSA
NEUMANN, EMMA	20	F	UNKNOWN	GRZZZZUSA
RYKOWSKA, ANNA	23	F	UNKNOWN	GRZZZZUSA
GLACZAK, THERESIA	33	F	UNKNOWN	GRZZZZUSA
STANISLAWA	7	F	CHILD	GRZZZZUSA
AGNES	4	F	CHILD	GRZZZZUSA
SIMON	.03	M	INFANT	GRZZZZUSA
RUESTAN, ANNA	28	F	UNKNOWN	GRZZZZUSA
EMMA	.10	F	INFANT	GRZZZZUSA
OSWALD, ELIS.	24	F	UNKNOWN	SRZZZZUSA
HOERAUF, FRIEDR.	24	M	SHMK	SRZZZZUSA
OSWALD, FRIEDR.	3	M	CHILD	SRZZZZUSA
SCHELL, JOH.	25	M	LABR	GRZZZZUSA
MADER, MICHAEL	19	M	LABR	GRZZZZUSA
GLOGSTEIN, MARIE	17	F	UNKNOWN	GRZZZZUSA
HEINS, SOPHIE	18	F	UNKNOWN	GRZZZZUSA
REPREGER, LOUISE	17	F	UNKNOWN	GRZZZZUSA
METSCHER, META	20	F	UNKNOWN	GRZZZZUSA
ULBRAND, OTTO	14	M	CL	GRZZZZUSA
SEGER, HENRY	15	M	LABR	GRZZZZUSA
WAGNER, SUSANA	26	F	UNKNOWN	GRZZZZUSA
U, U	19	F	UNKNOWN	GRZZZZUSA
NOWICKA, ANNA	22	F	UNKNOWN	GRZZZZUSA
PRAXEDA	2	F	CHILD	GRZZZZUSA
LACKARIA	.10	F	INFANT	GRZZZZUSA
LOEW, BERTHA	18	F	UNKNOWN	GRZZZZUSA
BORCHERDING, JOHE.	45	F	UNKNOWN	GRZZZZUSA
JOHANNES	18	M	GDNR	GRZZZZUSA
ADOLF	16	M	JNR	GRZZZZUSA
HENNI	15	F	UNKNOWN	GRZZZZUSA
JULIUS	13	M	CL	GRZZZZUSA
GRETCHEN	7	F	CHILD	GRZZZZUSA
FISCHER, ALONISE	24	F	UNKNOWN	GRZZZZUSA
BOENECKE, HEINR.	16	M	TLR	GRZZZZUSA
LUESER, HEINR.	18	M	LABR	GRZZZZUSA
FETH, MARIA	20	F	UNKNOWN	GRZZZZUSA
FRICK, ELIS.	22	F	UNKNOWN	GRZZZZUSA
ESSLINGER, CATHA.	25	F	UNKNOWN	GRZZZZUSA
STEIERWANDT, CATHA.	16	F	UNKNOWN	GRZZZZUSA
KECK, BARBA.	20	F	UNKNOWN	GRZZZZUSA
WINKLER, BERTHA.	22	F	UNKNOWN	GRZZZZUSA
GRUIS, LOUISE	26	F	UNKNOWN	GRZZZZUSA
UHL, EMMA	16	F	UNKNOWN	GRZZZZUSA
KOEBER, GUSTAV	32	M	FARMER	GRZZZZUSA
BISCHOFF, LOUISE	33	F	UNKNOWN	GRZZZZUSA
HORNICKEL, CONRAD	20	M	LABR	GRZZZZUSA
MEYER, WILH.	27	M	LABR	GRZZZZUSA
STERCH, ALEX	15	M	LABR	GRZZZZUSA
IDE	40	F	UNKNOWN	GRZZZZUSA
MOERING, ERNST	16	M	LABR	GRZZZZUSA
MANCH, WILH.	16	M	LABR	GRZZZZUSA
HAARMANN, HEINR.	46	M	LABR	GRZZZZUSA
WEISSBACH, PHILIP	26	M	CPTR	GRZZZZUSA
FUEHR, LOUIS	17	M	LABR	GRZZZZUSA
OTTO, ROBT.	32	M	LABR	GRZZZZUSA
CRASS, ELISE	16	F	UNKNOWN	GRZZZZUSA
LISETTE	20	F	UNKNOWN	GRZZZZUSA
ANDERS, BARBA.	13	F	UNKNOWN	GRZZZZUSA
MAYER, WILH.	32	M	MCHT	GRZZZZUSA
DOTTER, MARIE	26	F	UNKNOWN	GRZZZZUSA
BEUTZ, BARBARA.	17	F	UNKNOWN	GRZZZZUSA
FUCH, ANNA	22	F	UNKNOWN	GRZZZZUSA
JUSTE.	18	F	UNKNOWN	GRZZZZUSA
STRENGA, ROSINGA	22	F	UNKNOWN	GRZZZZUSA
KROEGER, ELISE	17	F	UNKNOWN	GRZZZZUSA
STOECKEL, MARIA	39	F	UNKNOWN	GRZZZZUSA
U, U	6	M	CHILD	GRZZZZUSA
ENDRESS, HEINR.	16	M	LABR	GRZZZZUSA
KOOP, HEINR.	50	M	LABR	GRZZZZUSA
MARIE	46	F	UNKNOWN	GRZZZZUSA
FRITZ	7	M	CHILD	GRZZZZUSA
AUG.	5	M	CHILD	GRZZZZUSA
MARIE	4	F	CHILD	GRZZZZUSA
JOH.	.08	M	INFANT	GRZZZZUSA
ZAHNER, JOH.	31	M	UNKNOWN	GRZZZZUSA
AUGUSTE	31	F	UNKNOWN	GRZZZZUSA
ROETSCH, CARL	42	M	LABR	GRZZZZUSA
BERGER, FEREL	53	M	LABR	GRZZZZUSA
METGER, EMMA	22	F	UNKNOWN	GRZZZZUSA
SCHUELER, E.	22	M	WTR	GRZZZZUSA
DUERSCH, CARL	23	M	FARMER	GRZZZZUSA
KESLINKA, JULIANA	24	F	UNKNOWN	GRZZZZUSA
MARIA	2	F	CHILD	GRZZZZUSA
GERTRUD	.10	F	INFANT	GRZZZZUSA
KREZENBINK, HEINR.	16	M	CL	GRZZZZUSA

PASSENGER	AGE	SEX	OCCUPATION	PVL	DES
MINNA	20	F	UNKNOWN		GRZZZZUSA
GAENZHIRT, EMIL	19	M	LKSH		GRZZZZUSA
HAFNER, ALB.	25	M	FARMER		GRZZZZUSA
SCHIELBAR, DIEDR.	45	M	FARMER		GRZZZZUSA
MARIE	36	F	UNKNOWN		GRZZZZUSA
SOPHIE	67	F	UNKNOWN		GRZZZZUSA
HEINR.	7	M	CHILD		GRZZZZUSA
BARGMANN, ELEONORE	21	F	UNKNOWN		GRZZZZUSA
REISS, ANNA	23	F	UNKNOWN		GRZZZZUSA
KALAMEIA, MARGA.	28	F	UNKNOWN		GRZZZZUSA
ANTONIA	.01	F	INFANT		GRZZZZUSA
KASPERCKA, STANISLAVA	24	F	UNKNOWN		GRZZZZUSA
BLASZCZYK, ELIS.	23	F	UNKNOWN		GRZZZZUSA
W---LEWSKA, ROSALIE	30	F	UNKNOWN		GRZZZZUSA
JOSEPH	6	M	CHILD		GRZZZZUSA
WOLSCHINSKA, ANNA	16	F	UNKNOWN		GRZZZZUSA
SCHLOH, CHRIST.	16	F	UNKNOWN		GRZZZZUSA
U., FRANZ	34	M	SHMK		GRZZZZUSA
BRUEMMER, E.	32	M	PNTR		GRZZZZUSA
KLEBER, JOS.	25	M	LABR		GRZZZZUSA
SCHOLLER, JUSTA.	22	F	UNKNOWN		GRZZZZUSA
PEDL, JOH.	16	M	LABR		GRZZZZUSA
SKELNICK, MARIE	18	F	UNKNOWN		GRZZZZUSA
LENZ, PEDER	24	M	LABR		GRZZZZUSA
BIERSACK, LUDWIG	23	M	LABR		GRZZZZUSA
KITZEL, P.	57	F	UNKNOWN		GRZZZZUSA
K----ZER, CAROLE.	21	F	UNKNOWN		GRZZZZUSA
DEWINSKA, W.	23	F	UNKNOWN		GRZZZZUSA
GOLDLIND---, PAULI	34	F	UNKNOWN		GRZZZZUSA
MEYER	7	M	CHILD		GRZZZZUSA
M.	3	F	CHILD		GRZZZZUSA
CHRISTINE	.01	F	INFANT		GRZZZZUSA
SCHAPIN, R.	28	M	LABR		GRZZZZUSA
MUND, U	18	F	UNKNOWN		GRZZZZUSA
HEITMANN, HEINR.	15	M	CL		GRZZZZUSA
HARTLAGE, HEINR.	35	M	FARMER		GRZZZZUSA
MARIE	34	F	UNKNOWN		GRZZZZUSA
WILH.	7	M	CHILD		GRZZZZUSA
AUG.	5	M	CHILD		GRZZZZUSA
CAROLE.	4	F	CHILD		GRZZZZUSA
HEINR.	2	M	CHILD		GRZZZZUSA
FRAIN, ARTHUR	22	M	LABR		GRZZZZUSA
MANDENUSCH, GEORG	30	M	LABR		GRZZZZUSA
HEITMANN, DOROTHEA	17	F	UNKNOWN		GRZZZZUSA
KLDER, CONRAD	40	M	SMH		GRZZZZUSA
BRUMLAND, TH.	24	M	LABR		GRZZZZUSA
QUAL, CATHA.	18	F	UNKNOWN		GRZZZZUSA
NEDDERMANN, MARGA.	15	F	UNKNOWN		GRZZZZUSA
HENZMANN, SOPHIE	23	F	UNKNOWN		GRZZZZUSA
MEINNKEN, JOH.	26	M	FARMER		GRZZZZUSA
TANZEA, MARGA.	31	F	UNKNOWN		GRZZZZUSA
GUST.	7	M	CHILD		GRZZZZUSA
ANNA	2	F	CHILD		GRZZZZUSA
HEIL, LISETTE	26	F	UNKNOWN		GRZZZZUSA
AUG.	3	M	CHILD		GRZZZZUSA
GERSTNER, LOUISE	21	F	UNKNOWN		GRZZZZUSA
DOERR, PETER	22	M	LABR		GRZZZZUSA
DOHT, F.	30	M	MCHT		GRZZZZUSA
CHRISTOFFERS, CATHA.	40	F	UNKNOWN		GRZZZZUSA
KUHLMANN, GESE.	47	F	UNKNOWN		GRZZZZUSA
MALINSKI, CASIMIR	25	M	LABR		GRZZZZUSA
PROZCHEWITZ, MICHAELE-M	21	F	UNKNOWN		GRZZZZUSA
GOMMER, EMMA	27	F	UNKNOWN		GRZZZZUSA
LINDNER, SEB.	22	M	SHMK		GRZZZZUSA
HEEREN, FR.	28	M	SMH		GRZZZZUSA
FORST, CAROLE.	23	F	UNKNOWN		GRZZZZUSA
WERTZEL, HEINR.	23	M	LABR		GRZZZZUSA
BRACKMANN, JOHE.	19	F	UNKNOWN		GRZZZZUSA
MAYER, SALOM.	17	M	MCHT		GRZZZZUSA
HOFER, ANNA	36	F	UNKNOWN		GRZZZZUSA
ELIS.	15	F	UNKNOWN		GRZZZZUSA
ENDERS, CARL	27	M	FARMER		GRZZZZUSA
KLOTH, FR.	25	M	FARMER		GRZZZZUSA
BERGER, WILH.	46	M	FARMER		GRZZZZUSA
GIESSER, ERNST	23	M	MCHT		GRZZZZUSA
FRAWNY, CARL	26	M	FARMER		GRZZZZUSA
SEIDLER, HERMINE	18	F	UNKNOWN		GRZZZZUSA
NICLAS, HERM.	54	M	FARMER		GRZZZZUSA
LOUISE	48	F	UNKNOWN		GRZZZZUSA
AUG.	7	M	CHILD		GRZZZZUSA
SCHAEFER, CATHA.	27	F	UNKNOWN		GRZZZZUSA
KAETHE	5	F	CHILD		GRZZZZUSA
JONK, WILH.	34	M	TLR		GRZZZZUSA
CZEMZAK, MAR.	23	M	LABR		GRZZZZUSA
REICHENBACH, BRUNO	31	M	BCHR		GRZZZZUSA
BERTHA	24	F	UNKNOWN		GRZZZZUSA
CARL	.09	M	INFANT		GRZZZZUSA
SCHOENBERGER, MARIE	28	F	UNKNOWN		GRZZZZUSA
GEROLD, E.	24	F	UNKNOWN		GRZZZZUSA
POETSCHNER, GOTTFR.	29	M	SMH		GRZZZZUSA
SCHOLL, BABETTE	23	F	UNKNOWN		GRZZZZUSA
SCHUTZLER, JOH.	25	M	LABR		GRZZZZUSA
BOESEL, ADAM	23	M	BKLYR		GRZZZZUSA
KLEPPER, MINNA	16	F	UNKNOWN		GRZZZZUSA
WETZEL, ADOLF	23	M	LABR		GRZZZZUSA
BECKER, ALOIS	36	M	LABR		GRZZZZUSA
CAROLE.	35	F	UNKNOWN		GRZZZZUSA
HENNINGER, WALBURGA	25	F	UNKNOWN		GRZZZZUSA
EISEMAN, CARL	16	M	BRR		GRZZZZUSA
FISCHER, ERNST	27	M	LABR		GRZZZZUSA
WIEGENER, MICH.	60	M	SHMK		GRZZZZUSA
IGEL, JOS.	27	F	FARMER		GRZZZZUSA
GRESSLE, FR.	20	M	LABR		GRZZZZUSA
HILKEN, META	18	F	UNKNOWN		GRZZZZUSA
ZACKER, EVA	22	F	UNKNOWN		GRZZZZUSA
LAUER, LOUISE	50	F	UNKNOWN		GRZZZZUSA
KNAPP, LUDW.	35	M	TLR		GRZZZZUSA
AUGUSTE	34	F	UNKNOWN		GRZZZZUSA
AUG.	7	M	CHILD		GRZZZZUSA
ERNA	4	F	CHILD		GRZZZZUSA
SOPHIE	.09	F	INFANT		GRZZZZUSA
GEHRIG, L.	40	M	LABR		GRZZZZUSA
GUENTHER, HERM.	40	M	LABR		GRZZZZUSA
WALZ, ELIS.	21	F	UNKNOWN		GRZZZZUSA
ROTH, ELIS.	26	F	UNKNOWN		GRZZZZUSA
SCHOTENER, MARGE.	20	F	UNKNOWN		GRZZZZUSA
WAGENHUT, JOH.	16	M	MCHT		GRZZZZUSA
WILD, CHARLOTTE	24	F	UNKNOWN		GRZZZZUSA
BECKER, HEINR.	32	M	FARMER		GRZZZZUSA
BERGST, ANNA	22	F	UNKNOWN		GRZZZZUSA
MEYER, LOUISE	32	F	UNKNOWN		GRZZZZUSA
LEONHARDT, LINA	31	F	UNKNOWN		GRZZZZUSA
MANGELS, DIEDR.	16	M	LABR		GRZZZZUSA
VOGT, HEINR.	16	M	LABR		GRZZZZUSA
TOENJES, ANNA	20	F	UNKNOWN		GRZZZZUSA
LOERSMANN, HEINR.	15	M	CL		GRZZZZUSA
FLEISSNER, JOSEF	45	M	LABR		GRZZZZUSA
WALTER, AUG.	50	M	LABR		GRZZZZUSA
ALB.	26	M	LABR		GRZZZZUSA
MARIE	14	F	UNKNOWN		GRZZZZUSA
HEINR.	7	M	CHILD		GRZZZZUSA
BERTHA	6	F	CHILD		GRZZZZUSA
FRANZ	4	M	CHILD		GRZZZZUSA
ROZNICKI, ADAM	49	M	LABR		GRZZZZUSA
FRANZ	17	M	LABR		GRZZZZUSA
GLAESER, JULIUS	25	M	LABR		GRZZZZUSA
ROSSWEILER, AUG.	23	M	LABR		GRZZZZUSA
WIEHLE, PAUL	24	M	LABR		GRZZZZUSA
WILDEMANN, LUDW.	24	M	FARMER		GRZZZZUSA
RASP, ALBERT	40	M	FARMER		GRZZZZUSA
BARBA.	40	F	UNKNOWN		GRZZZZUSA
OTILIE	17	F	UNKNOWN		GRZZZZUSA
KUNIGDE.	7	F	CHILD		GRZZZZUSA
JOHANN	3	M	CHILD		GRZZZZUSA
OBERMEYER, KATHA.	26	F	UNKNOWN		GRZZZZUSA
WEHRINGER, JOH.	29	M	TLR		GRZZZZUSA
WALBURGA	29	F	UNKNOWN		GRZZZZUSA
OTTO	.11	M	INFANT		GRZZZZUSA
BECKER, HERM.	28	M	LABR		GRZZZZUSA
KOCH, BERTHA	29	F	UNKNOWN		GRZZZZUSA

PASSENGER	AGE	SEX	OCCUPATION	PRVL	DES
MUELLER, MARIA	17	F	UNKNOWN		GRZZZZUSA
SEIFERT, LOUIS	30	M	LABR		GRZZZZUSA
ALWIN	7	M	CHILD		GRZZZZUSA
THILBAR, ANNA	26	F	UNKNOWN		GRZZZZUSA
LEHR, WM.	14	M	CL		GRZZZZUSA
HAMMER, GEORG	54	M	LABR		GRZZZZUSA
MARGA.	46	F	UNKNOWN		GRZZZZUSA
CATHA.	19	F	UNKNOWN		GRZZZZUSA
FRIEDR.	18	M	LABR		GRZZZZUSA
CARL	7	M	CHILD		GRZZZZUSA
HEINR.	15	M	LABR		GRZZZZUSA
WILH.	16	M	LABR		GRZZZZUSA
LEHR, ADAM	54	M	LABR		GRZZZZUSA
FICKEN, ELISE	19	F	UNKNOWN		GRZZZZUSA
HAGEN, WILHE.	48	F	UNKNOWN		GRZZZZUSA
FRIEDR.	16	M	MLR		GRZZZZUSA
CHRISTE.	7	F	CHILD		GRZZZZUSA
WILHE.	6	F	CHILD		GRZZZZUSA
HELENE	4	F	CHILD		GRZZZZUSA
NUERNBERG, MINNA	17	F	UNKNOWN		GRZZZZUSA
BECKER, SOPHIE	22	F	UNKNOWN		GRZZZZUSA
FRANKNER, W.	25	M	LABR		GRZZZZUSA
JUNKENBERG, LINNA	17	F	UNKNOWN		GRZZZZUSA
FREER, HELENE	14	F	UNKNOWN		GRZZZZUSA
HEINECKE, H.	18	M	LABR		GRZZZZUSA
ALBERS, LIEZZI	17	F	UNKNOWN		GRZZZZUSA
HERSH, ADELINE	18	F	UNKNOWN		GRZZZZUSA
REIF, SAM.	27	M	LABR		GRZZZZUSA
LOUISE	25	F	UNKNOWN		GRZZZZUSA
EPPLER, CATHA.	29	F	UNKNOWN		GRZZZZUSA
PAULE.	22	F	UNKNOWN		GRZZZZUSA
EVERTZ, CARL	32	M	MCHT		GRZZZZUSA
WIXFORT, FRIEDR.	22	M	MCHT		GRZZZZUSA
KRONENBARGERT, GEORG	17	M	MCHT		GRZZZZUSA
BALTZER, CARL	33	M	LABR		GRZZZZUSA
WENZEL, ISIDOR	24	M	LABR		GRZZZZUSA
WAGNER, JUL.	40	M	LABR		GRZZZZUSA
CAROLE.	33	F	UNKNOWN		GRZZZZUSA
MARIE	7	F	CHILD		GRZZZZUSA
BERTHA	3	F	CHILD		GRZZZZUSA
FLUNTSCHANIS, M.	28	M	LABR		GRZZZZUSA
RAGOIS, RAIZE	40	M	LABR		GRZZZZUSA
EPPLER, CHRISTINE	37	F	UNKNOWN		GRZZZZUSA
KAGERL, MICHAEL	32	M	LABR		GRZZZZUSA
KLEIN, JOHANN	32	M	LABR		GRZZZZUSA
MEYER, PHILIPP	45	M	CPTR		GRZZZZUSA
DRABENSKI, STEFAN	41	M	LABR		GRZZZZUSA
RICZYSKO, MARGANA	27	F	UNKNOWN		GRZZZZUSA
RALIE	4	F	CHILD		GRZZZZUSA
BICZYSKO, LAHASZ	37	M	LABR		GRZZZZUSA
JASTOWIZ, JOH.	20	M	LABR		GRZZZZUSA
KLEIN, JOH.	48	M	MCHT		GRZZZZUSA
WUKERMANN, FRIEDR.	31	M	LABR		GRZZZZUSA

SHIP: GALLIA

FROM: LIVERPOOL
TO: NEW YORK
ARRIVED: 16 OCTOBER 1888

PASSENGER	AGE	SEX	OCCUPATION	PRVL	DES
GROSSMAN, HATZE	18	M	SHMK		GRACBFUSA
LEID, MOSES	32	M	BKR		GRACBFUSA
LEIN, EMIL	24	M	SHMK		GRADBQUSA
SERABLE, ANTONIO	21	M	TLR		GRACBFUSA
WINDESCH, ELISABETH	18	F	TLR		GRACBFUSA
FRANKLE, EMINA	34	F	MA		GRACBFUSA
CHAR.	10	M	CH		GRACBFUSA
HG.	9	M	CHILD		GRACBFUSA
MARY	4	F	CHILD		GRACBFUSA
ADOLF	3	M	CHILD		GRACBFUSA

PASSENGER	AGE	SEX	OCCUPATION	PRVL	DES
RAJINA	.11	F	INFANT		GRACBFUSA
WETHENBERG, MERKE	45	F	MA		GRACBFUSA
NATHAN	11	M	CH		GRACBFUSA
RIFKE	11	F	CH		GRACBFUSA
FRIESL, ERNEST	27	M	TLR		GRADXWUSA
GIFFAN, EYGENE	30	M	ART		GRADXWUSA

SHIP: RUGIA

FROM: HAMBURG AND HAVRE
TO: NEW YORK
ARRIVED: 16 OCTOBER 1888

PASSENGER	AGE	SEX	OCCUPATION	PRVL	DES
KUCKLOW, JOHANN	29	M	LABR		GRAHVFUSA
EMILIE	23	F	W		GRAHVFUSA
LOUISE	6	F	CHILD		GRAHVFUSA
BONNIKSEN, ANNA	20	F	SGL		PRZZZZUSA
LINDNER, ANNA	20	F	SGL		SYZZZZUSA
ERNST	7	M	CHILD		SYZZZZUSA
MINNA	6	F	CHILD		SYZZZZUSA
GRUBE, ANNA	21	F	SGL		SYACXVUSA
BRANDT, BERTHA	23	F	SGL		SYACBFUSA
HOENER, BERTHA	22	F	SGL		SYADXCUSA
DAHLKE, EPHRAIM	28	M	FARMER		PRZZZZUSA
STRASSBURGER, HARTWIG	46	M	DLR		PRACBFUSA
THERESE	40	F	W		PRACBFUSA
VAROLINE	7	F	CHILD		PRACBFUSA
MAHNCHKE, CHRISTINE	26	F	SGL		PRAHPBUSA
SCHWARZ, ADOLF	27	M	FARMER		PRZZZZUSA
THENERKAUFT, CARL	61	M	MCHT		PRAFAQUSA
MATHILDE	48	F	W		PRAFAQUSA
EMMA	18	F	CH		PRAFAQUSA
CARL	13	M	CH		PRAFAQUSA
MARIE	16	F	CH		PRAFAQUSA
SCHMIDT, LUDWIG	24	M	WHLR		MKZZZZUSA
BAUSCH, LIZZIE	22	F	SGL		HSZZZZUSA
BRAUST, LINA	18	F	SGL		HSZZZZUSA
FRUEDRICH, MARIE	20	F	SGL		HSZZZZUSA
OLDENBURG, CHRISTINE	18	F	SGL		HSAADEUSA
JENSEN, ARTHUR	28	M	MD		HSACQAUSA
BAUSCH, LINA	17	F	SGL		HSABYHUSA
BAST, MARIE	17	F	SGL		HSZZZZUSA
MANK, MARGA.	24	F	WO		HSZZZZUSA
ANNA	00	F	INF		HSZZZZUSA
WEBER, ADELE	22	F	SGL		HSAAKHUSA
GIERMANN, JEACHIM	71	M	LABR		PRZZZZUSA
LOUISE	62	F	W		PRZZZZUSA
FRIEDR.	22	M	S		PRZZZZUSA
GUTOWSKY, JOHANN	28	M	TKR		PRADBDUSA
EMILIE	23	F	W		PRADBDUSA
HELENE	.06	F	INFANT		PRADBDUSA
HIPPNER, MARTHA	24	F	SGL		PRABDMUSA
HOGE, ADOLF	14	M	LABR		PRAFLAUSA
STOLL, GUSTAV	24	M	LABR		PRAFLAUSA
WENDT, AUGUST	41	M	FARMER		PRZZZZUSA
WILHELMINE	32	F	W		PRZZZZUSA
WM.	7	M	CHILD		PRZZZZUSA
ANNA	6	F	CHILD		PRZZZZUSA
MARIE	5	F	CHILD		PRZZZZUSA
PAUL	4	M	CHILD		PRZZZZUSA
GUSTAV	.11	M	INFANT		PRZZZZUSA
SPRUNG, EMILIE	23	F	WO		PRZZZZUSA
FRANZ	2	M	CHILD		PRZZZZUSA
KRUEGER, JOH.	27	M	LABR		PRZZZZUSA
FRDKE.	28	F	W		PRZZZZUSA
BEINHOLD	.11	M	INFANT		PRZZZZUSA
BONNICHSEN, HANS	25	M	FARMER		PRZZZZUSA
ANNA	28	F	CH		PRZZZZUSA
ANNA	.06	F	INFANT		PRZZZZUSA
KOPP, JULIUS	14	M	LABR		PRAACEUSA

PASSENGER	AGE	SEX	OCCUPATION	PRVL	DES
KOHN, CARL	21	M	MLR	PRZZZZ	USA
POHLMANN, META	48	F	WO	PRAGRZ	USA
WILH.	16	M	S		PRAGRZ	USA
SCHROETER, RUDOLF	43	M	LABR	PRAARZ	USA
AUGUSTE	43	F	W	PRAARZ	USA
DRASDEWSKA, THERESE	24	F	SGL	PRZZZZ	USA
WONSOWSKA, CHRISTINE	61	F	SGL	PRAEZV	USA
LUEDKE, MAX	24	M	FARMER	MKZZZZ	USA
JONAS, AUGUSTE	19	F	SGL	MKZZZZ	USA
HARDCKOPF, KLAUS	16	M	FARMER	PRZZZZ	USA
PATELSKA, STANISLAUS	25	M	LABR	PRZZZZ	USA
SULLIVAN, LOUISE	37	F	WO	MKZZZZ	USA
LEIPZIGER, HERSCH	18	M	CL	MKAAZD	USA
GESELL, ADELINE	25	F	WO	BDZZZZ	USA
KAROLINE	.10	F	INFANT	BDZZZZ	USA
DELHOLOFF, WILH.	43	M	FARMER	BDAFHQ	USA
WILHELMINE	36	F	W	BDAFHQ	USA
JOHANN	7	M	CHILD	BDAFHQ	USA
CARL	6	M	CHILD	BDAFHQ	USA
FRIEDR.	5	M	CHILD	BDAFHQ	USA
ALWINE	5	F	CHILD	BDAFHQ	USA
ELISE	2	F	CHILD	BDAFHQ	USA
RUMMELSBURG, ABR.	26	M	CL	PRZZZZ	USA
SIMON	18	M	CL	PRZZZZ	USA
SCHULZ, LOUISE	17	F	SGL	PRZZZZ	USA
FELSKE, HEINR.	29	M	LKSH	PRZZZZ	USA
OTTE, CARL	26	M	MCHT	PRAAKH	USA
HUEBNER, CHRISTIAN	76	M	PVTM	PRZZZZ	USA
WENDE, AUG.	34	M	FARMER	PRZZZZ	USA
WOLF, WILLI	16	M	TKR	PRAAYF	USA
ANEUSTING, FELIX	17	M	BBR	PRZZZZ	USA
SCHMIDT, JOH.	28	M	FARMER	PRZZZZ	USA
BERTHA	21	F	W	PRZZZZ	USA
JOH.	.06	M	INFANT	PRZZZZ	USA
WONSOWSKY, IGNATZ	66	M	JNR	PRZZZZ	USA
KIESSLING, MARIE	22	F	SGL	PRZZZZ	USA
PFEIFFER, IDA	39	F	WO	PRAARZ	USA
ERICH	.11	M	INFANT	PRAARZ	USA
CARL	.11	M	INFANT	PRAARZ	USA
WAWEREK, HELENE	7	F	CHILD	PRAARZ	USA
STARKER, MAGDALENE	7	F	CHILD	PRAARZ	USA
SCHNEIDER, BERTHA	16	F	SGL	PRAARZ	USA
LUNGNER, PAUL	15	M	LABR	PRZZZZ	USA
FLEGEL, MAX	15	M	LABR	PRAARZ	USA
UHLIG, CARL	44	M	CPTR	SYZZZZ	USA
THERESE	46	F	W	SYZZZZ	USA
OSWALD	25	M	CH	SYZZZZ	USA
MINNA	18	F	CH	SYZZZZ	USA
CLARA	7	F	CHILD	SYZZZZ	USA
MEINER, AGNES	52	F	WO	SYZZZZ	USA
FRIDA	7	F	CHILD	SYZZZZ	USA
KROEHNE, WIEGAND	43	M	LABR	SYABQZ	USA
GLASER, ALOIS	34	M	LABR	BDZZZZ	USA
ANNA	32	F	W	BDZZZZ	USA
FALKNER, RAIMUND	24	M	BKBNDR	BDADLD	USA
ARNOLD, OTTO	23	M	LABR	SYZZZZ	USA
KWASNITZA, NASTASIUS	48	M	FARMER	PRZZZZ	USA
JAWORSKY, JOHANN	39	M	LLD	PRZZZZ	USA
ANTONIE	29	F	W	PRZZZZ	USA
WLADISLAW	4	M	CHILD	PRZZZZ	USA
XAVERIUS	2	M	CHILD	PRZZZZ	USA
SCHMIDT, AUGUSTE	27	F	WO	PRAEPO	USA
PAUL	5	M	CHILD	PRAEPO	USA
JURISCH, WILLY	25	M	SGL	PRACBF	USA
KRUGER, MAX	22	M	PNTR	PRACBF	USA
HUEBNER, MARIE	28	F	SGL	PRZZZZ	USA
HELBIG, AUGUST	42	M	LABR	PRACXV	USA
GEISLER, THERESE	29	F	SGL	PRACXV	USA
WITTE, JOH.	27	M	FARMER	PRZZZZ	USA
NORING, ALFRED	30	M	LABR	PRAAKH	USA
BECKER, AUGUST	37	M	FARMER	PRZZZZ	USA
ANNA	33	F	W	PRZZZZ	USA
FRANZ	9	M	CHILD	PRZZZZ	USA
ANNA	3	F	CHILD	PRZZZZ	USA
JOH.	4	M	CHILD	PRZZZZ	USA

PASSENGER	AGE	SEX	OCCUPATION	PRVL	DES
MARIE	.11	F	INFANT	PRZZZZ	USA
HINZ, ALBERT	29	M	SMH	PRZZZZ	USA
ELISABETH	24	F	W	PRZZZZ	USA
ANNA	.09	F	INFANT	PRZZZZ	USA
ALBINES, KARL	27	M	LABR	PRABDM	USA
SCHLAUCH, ANNA	27	F	SGL	PRABEN	USA
WEGENER, ANNA	28	F	WO	PRZZZZ	USA
ANNA	5	F	CHILD	PRZZZZ	USA
LINA	3	F	CHILD	PRZZZZ	USA
LOEGLER, ANDREAS	25	M	BKR	BDZZZZ	USA
FOESSLER, HEINR.	34	M	BRR	BDAFZT	USA
ANATHINE	34	F	W	BDAFZT	USA
JOSEPHINE	6	F	CHILD	BDAFZT	USA
MARIE	4	F	CHILD	BDAFZT	USA
EHRBAR, JOH.	11	M	BY	SRZZZZ	USA
SCHEFER, ALBERT	23	M	LABR	SRZZZZ	USA
INAUER, HEINR.	21	M	LABR	SRZZZZ	USA
HAUSEN, ELISE	19	F	SGL	SRAGUH	USA
EBERLE, ANTON	24	M	FARMER	BDZZZZ	USA
DEMARIO, CASIMIR	38	M	LABR	FRZZZZ	USA
FLUHMANN, FRITZ	35	M	LABR	FRAAKJ	USA
ANNA	36	F	W	FRAAKJ	USA
FRITZ	15	M	CH	FRAAKJ	USA
ROBERT	8	M	CHILD	FRAAKJ	USA
ISCHI, ROSINE	25	F	SGL	FRAAKJ	USA
JAEUSCH, ALICE	28	F	SGL	FRAAKH	USA
ANOLLENBERGER, ELISE	52	F	SGL	FRACBF	USA
VONZELLER, ELISABETH	25	F	SGL	FRAESD	USA
DAVID, HANRIETTE	26	F	SGL	PRZZZZ	USA
HUWILER, J.	26	M	LABR	SRZZZZ	USA
KALIN, ADELRICH	22	M	STDNT	SRZZZZ	USA
PUTSCHER, CONRAD	22	M	STDNT	SRACSY	USA
WEHRLI, ALBERT	21	M	STDNT	SRZZZZ	USA
SCHAIBLE, CARL	24	M	STDNT	PRZZZZ	USA
STILLHART, ANTON	21	M	STDNT	SRZZZZ	USA
UNTERBERGER, CHRISTINE	23	F	SGL	SRZZZZ	USA

SHIP: WYOMING

FROM: LIVERPOOL AND QUEENSTOWN
TO: NEW YORK
ARRIVED: 16 OCTOBER 1888

PASSENGER	AGE	SEX	OCCUPATION	PRVL	DES
KORN, S.	39	M	LABR	GRZZZZ	USA
PETERSON, LARS	34	M	LABR	GRZZZZ	USA
CHRISTINE	32	F	W	GRZZZZ	USA
LEONORA	4	F	CHILD	GRZZZZ	USA
ERNELIA	3	F	CHILD	GRZZZZ	USA
ALINA	7	F	CHILD	GRZZZZ	USA
KARLSON, JOHN.	22	F	SP	GRZZZZ	USA
L---GRIST, ANDRIS	36	M	LABR	GRZZZZ	USA
MATH.	23	F	SP	GRZZZZ	USA
EMMA	26	F	SP	GRZZZZ	USA
JOHAN	8	M	CHILD	GRZZZZ	USA
E.	4	F	CHILD	GRZZZZ	USA
HANSON, A.	45	M	LABR	GRZZZZ	USA
ALMA	29	F	W	GRZZZZ	USA
JOHAN	7	M	CHILD	GRZZZZ	USA
GERTRUD.	4	F	CHILD	GRZZZZ	USA
HANS	3	M	CHILD	GRZZZZ	USA
ROSE	00	F	INF	GRZZZZ	USA
EKLUND, EMMA	25	F	SP	GRZZZZ	USA
LODERBERG, AMALIA	27	F	SP	GRZZZZ	USA
HIDING, JOHA.	25	F	SP	GRZZZZ	USA

SHIP: HAMMONIA

FROM: HAMBURG AND HAVRE
TO: NEW YORK
ARRIVED: 19 OCTOBER 1888

PASSENGER	AGE	SEX	OCCUPATION	PRVL/DES
GOSS, ELISE	24	F	SGL	PRZZZZUSA
ALMENRAEDER, HEINR.	23	M	BKR	HBZZZZUSA
SCHEWE, MARIE	7	F	CHILD	PRZZZZUSA
VOIGT, CAROLINE	23	F	UNKNOWN	PRZZZZUSA
GRUPE, EMMA	15	F	UNKNOWN	HBZZZZUSA
RHEDER, CLARA	24	F	UNKNOWN	PRZZZZUSA
BERTHA	23	F	UNKNOWN	PRZZZZUSA
PAHIEL, FRIEDR.	27	M	UNKNOWN	HBZZZZUSA
RIELOZ, EMILIE	16	F	SGL	HBZZZZUSA
CONRAD, ROSALIE	59	F	W	HBAARZUSA
NOLBICZKO, STANISL.	23	M	CH	HBAARZUSA
FANDRES, SAMUEL	15	M	CH	HBAAKHUSA
STRUWE, FRIEDR.	23	M	LABR	HBAAKHUSA
GRUENWALD, FRANZ	39	M	LABR	HBAENQUSA
CAROLINE	42	F	W	HBAENQUSA
LEIDNER, CARL	23	M	CLGYMN	HBAKPZUSA
BAUER, FRIEDR.	23	M	FARMER	HBAAKHUSA
HENSEL, ROSALIE	49	F	W	HBAAKHUSA
ERWIN	7	M	CHILD	HBAAKHUSA
DUHSING, HANS	5	M	CHILD	HBAAKHUSA
MEYER, JOH.VALT.	22	M	MCHT	HBACRAUSA
GEILICH, THERESE	20	F	SGL	HBABJEUSA
EVERS, FERDINAND	22	M	UPHST	PRZZZZUSA
OTTO, PAUL	27	M	MCHT	PRZZZZUSA
STRAUSS, LUDW.	18	M	MCHT	PRACQBUSA
HEISCH, HEINR.	16	M	FARMER	PRZZZZUSA
WRIEDT, DOROTHEA	38	F	W	PRADVHUSA
MANES, FRANZISKA	19	F	SGL	PRAANFUSA
JABINSKY, TEKLA	22	F	SGL	PRAHSCUSA
SCHLOBACH, FRANZ	24	M	ART	SYZZZZUSA
BARUCH, LINA	25	F	SGL	BVZZZZUSA
BERNBACH, HANNY	29	F	SGL	BVZZZZUSA
STRENGER, MARIE	17	F	SGL	PRZZZZUSA
PUFELEIN, ANTONIE	39	F	W	PRADLDUSA
RIES, EMMA	34	F	SGL	PRALTJUSA
CLAUSSEN, IDA	25	F	SGL	PRADVHUSA
HEIDESICH, JOHN	36	M	MCHT	PRACBFUSA
GROTH, JOHANNA	70	F	W	MKZZZZUSA
HENNINGSEN, MATILDE	19	F	SGL	PRZZZZUSA
SCHWASTEN, ERNST	28	M	TCHR	PRZZZZUSA
SEEKAMP, AUG.	23	M	MCHT	PRABPCUSA
SCHNEIDER, ROBERS	23	M	MCHT	PRABPCUSA
SIMONSEN, ERNST	18	M	STDNT	PRAAKHUSA
BERG, FRANZ	21	M	TCHR	PRACSDUSA
BLUMENAU, MAX	39	M	MCHT	PRABDMUSA
FEYER, WILH.	33	M	LABR	PRACBFUSA
THOMSEN, EDUARD	23	M	CL	PRACBFUSA
FREY, FRANGOTT	17	M	FARMER	PRZZZZUSA
SZIMKEITIS, MIHALIS	27	M	LABR	PRZZZZUSA
WIESE, NICOLAUS	50	M	FARMER	PRZZZZUSA
MARG.	60	F	W	PRZZZZUSA
SALOW, LOUIS	18	M	MCHT	PRACUMUSA
MAN, JOHANN	52	M	LABR	PRACUMUSA
SOFIE	49	F	W	PRACUMUSA
HERM.	20	M	CH	PRACUMUSA
ANNA	7	F	CHILD	MKZZZZUSA
AUNCK, WILH.	28	M	FARMER	MKADMVUSA
ARNDT, JOH.	29	M	FARMER	MKADMVUSA
WILH.	30	F	W	MKADMVUSA
HASSELMANN, SOFIE	50	F	W	MKADMVUSA
FESER, HERM.	17	M	ENGR	PRZZZZUSA
HAGEMEIER, ANNA	41	F	W	PRZZZZUSA
MONHAUPT, MARIE	40	F	W	PRZZZZUSA
VALISHA	4	F	CHILD	PRZZZZUSA
BERGER, HULDA	25	F	SGL	PRZZZZUSA
AULICH, EMMA	26	F	SGL	PRZZZZUSA
STREILICH, GUSTAV	27	M	PNTR	PRZZZZUSA
FILAREZYK, JOSEF	17	M	LABR	PRZZZZUSA
LESKOWITZ, HUGO	14	M	JNR	PRZZZZUSA
MUELLER, MAT.	45	M	LABR	PRAAHUUSA
KUMERANA	36	F	W	PRAAHUUSA
MARIE	12	F	CH	PRAAHUUSA
TSCHERDI, JOHANN	55	M	UNKNOWN	PRADDKUSA
ROSALIE	55	F	W	PRADDKUSA
EISELE, MARGR.	21	F	W	PRADDKUSA
FRIEDR.	20	M	LABR	PRADDKUSA
WYSER, ALBERTINE	24	F	SGL	PRADDKUSA
DPMA, FRAMZ	52	M	LABR	PRADDKUSA
DALMASO, ANNA	36	F	SGL	PRADDKUSA
FRICK, ALFRED	22	M	LABR	PRADDKUSA
HARTMANN, JACOB	28	M	LABR	SRZZZZUSA
MEYER, STEFAN	25	M	LABR	SRZZZZUSA
BLASER, FRIEDR.	25	M	LABR	SRAAHUUSA
GROL, ANNA	29	F	SGL	SRAAHUUSA
HOLZEN, GUISEPPE	24	M	LABR	SRZZZZUSA
DUDER, ANNA	39	F	LABR	SRZZZZUSA
PHILIP, ERNST	22	M	LABR	SRZZZZUSA
BAUMER, JACOB	26	M	LABR	SRZZZZUSA
MARTI, EDUARD	48	M	LABR	SRZZZZUSA
FEIL, JACQUES	25	M	LABR	SRAAHUUSA
FRIEDMANN, L.	45	M	LABR	SRAAHUUSA
PHILIPPINE	41	F	W	SRAAHUUSA
ANSELM	19	M	CH	SRAAHUUSA
ALBERT	9	M	CHILD	SRAAHUUSA
ADELHEID	7	F	CHILD	SRAAHUUSA
LEOPOLD	6	M	CHILD	SRAAHUUSA
MAGDALENA	4	F	CHILD	SRAAHUUSA
SCHULZ, AUGUST	32	M	LABR	SRABIJUSA
JENSEN, HANS	40	M	LABR	SRADEIUSA
MARIE	40	F	W	SRADEIUSA
HANS	10	M	CH	SRADEIUSA
MAX	7	M	CHILD	SRADEIUSA
SELMA	6	F	CHILD	SRADEIUSA
PAUL	4	M	CHILD	SRADEIUSA
U. MARIANNE	6	F	CHILD	PRZZZZUSA
ANTONIE	4	F	CHILD	PRZZZZUSA
ANASTASIA	.11	F	INFANT	PRZZZZUSA
BOCHNIG, ROBERT	24	M	FARMER	PRAAKHUSA
BAABE, GUSTAV	23	M	BKR	PRAAKHUSA
HELLING, MINE	25	F	SGL	PRZZZZUSA
ADAM, REINHOLD	24	M	SDLR	PRZZZZUSA
GOLLNIK, IDA	21	F	SGL	PRZZZZUSA
IDA	18	F	SGL	PRZZZZUSA
STOEHN, AUGUST	33	M	LABR	PRZZZZUSA
BAHR, EMMA	16	F	SGL	PRZZZZUSA
HECIAH, STANISLAUS	22	M	SHMK	PRZZZZUSA
SPITZER, CHRISTINE	65	F	W	PRZZZZUSA
BLOHM, JOHS.	5	M	CHILD	PRZZZZUSA
GEIDEL, BERTA	29	F	SGL	SYZZZZUSA
BATAGEY, JUDITH	42	F	SGL	SYAAHUUSA
LINEKE, FRITZ	34	M	LABR	SYAHGFUSA
MARIE	34	F	W	SYAHGFUSA
GEORG	4	M	CHILD	SYAHGFUSA
LOUISE	3	F	CHILD	SYAHGFUSA
ALBERT	2	M	CHILD	SYAHGFUSA
WESTENDORF, HANS	24	M	MCHT	SYACBFUSA
HUEBING, FRIEDR.	38	M	FARMER	PRZZZZUSA
WILHELMINE	31	F	W	PRZZZZUSA
LOUISE	7	F	CHILD	PRZZZZUSA
IDA	6	F	CHILD	PRZZZZUSA
MARTA	5	F	CHILD	PRZZZZUSA
MIX, MICHALINE	45	F	W	PRZZZZUSA
MARIANNE	7	F	CHILD	PRZZZZUSA
GABEL, JOSEF	44	M	LABR	PRZZZZUSA
JOSEF	7	M	CHILD	PRZZZZUSA
STEIF, MARIE	22	F	SGL	PRZZZZUSA
WIENER, MARIE	32	F	W	PRAAKHUSA
MAX	7	M	CHILD	PRAAKHUSA
BETTI	6	F	CHILD	PRAAKHUSA
GRETE	4	F	CHILD	PRAAKHUSA
HANS	3	M	CHILD	PRAAKHUSA
TRUTA	.11	F	INFANT	PRAAKHUSA
BERGMANN, AGNES	21	F	SGL	PRABOEUSA

PASSENGER	AGE	SEX	OCCUPATION	PRVL	DES
KROEGER, JOHA.	52	F	W		MKZZZZUSA
JOACHIM	19	M	S		MKZZZZUSA
CARL	17	M	LABR		MKZZZZUSA
COSELS, CARL	32	M	FARMER		MKZZZZUSA
MARIE	25	F	W		MKZZZZUSA
IDA	3	F	CHILD		MKZZZZUSA
BERTHA	.10	F	INFANT		MKZZZZUSA
KNITTLER, FRIEDR.	28	M	LABR		MKALKBUSA
KOWALSKA, ANNA	68	F	W		PRZZZZUSA
FUDE, MICHAEL	22	M	LABR		PRZZZZUSA
RATHJE, JUERGEN	16	M	FARMER		PRZZZZUSA
WULF, JOHS.	17	M	FARMER		PRZZZZUSA
MENCLA, IDA	14	F	SGL		MKZZZZUSA
ANNA	7	F	CHILD		MKZZZZUSA
LENDT, WILHELME	21	F	SGL		MKZZZZUSA
KASZUBA, JADWIGA	26	F	W		PRZZZZUSA
STANISLAUS	7	M	CHILD		PRZZZZUSA
MEHLHORN, MARTA	18	F	SGL		SYZZZZUSA
ESCHERICH, ALICE	20	F	SGL		SYACBFUSA
MILLER, HASTIE	7	F	CHILD		PRZZZZUSA
KARGL, FRANCIKA	26	F	SGL		PRACBFUSA
ROEPER, HANS	25	M	ENGR		PRZZZZUSA
NACKE, ROBERT	26	M	MCHT		PRAAXKUSA
RIZI, BERTA	19	F	SGL		PRACSYUSA
JOSAPHAT, EMMA	36	F	SGL		PRAAKHUSA
HAUSMANN, BERTA	18	F	SGL		HSZZZZUSA
MUELLER, OTTO	22	M	MCHT		HSACXVUSA
KURKA, MENL	23	M	MCHT		HSACBFUSA
OHLS, WILHELM.	21	F	SGL		PRZZZZUSA
CHLERT, AUG.	18	M	FARMER		PRAHXDUSA
BRUESER, CHRISTIAN	48	M	FARMER		PRZZZZUSA
MARIE	46	F	W		PRZZZZUSA
WILHELM.	21	F	CH		PRZZZZUSA
BERTA	19	F	CH		PRZZZZUSA
MARIE	17	F	CH		PRZZZZUSA
FRDKE.	15	F	CH		PRZZZZUSA
HERMINE	7	F	CHILD		PRZZZZUSA
LOUISE	6	F	CHILD		PRZZZZUSA
TIMM, JOHANN	39	M	FARMER		PRZZZZUSA
CAROLINE	35	F	W		PRZZZZUSA
CARL	5	M	CHILD		PRZZZZUSA
HERM.	.11	M	INFANT		PRZZZZUSA
FALCH, RIEKE	70	F	W		PRZZZZUSA
WOLF, PETER	20	M	PNTR		PRAFSBUSA
MEYER, CATHR.	18	F	SGL		WMZZZZUSA
MINUTH, ELISE	23	F	W		WMADDDUSA
BIERWISCH, ANNA	31	F	W		WMADDDUSA
WILLI	7	M	CHILD		WMADDDUSA
FRIEDA	6	F	CHILD		WMADDDUSA
MANNHEIM, EUGEN	22	M	MCHT		WMAEXWUSA
HULH, HEINR.	49	M	MCHT		WMABNSUSA
CATH.	59	F	W		WMABNSUSA
WILH.	15	M	S		WMABNSUSA
DIEDRICH, CARLA	51	M	GLSMKR		WMABNSUSA
JOHANNA	52	M	W		WMABNSUSA
HARST, ADOLF	16	M	LABR		MKZZZZUSA
JENNING, JOHANN	24	M	LABR		MKZZZZUSA
NISSEN, INGEB.	54	F	W		MKAAZFUSA
JULIANE	26	F	SGL		MKAAZFUSA
JENS	19	M	FARMER		MKAAZFUSA
HINSICHSEN, MARIE	20	F	SGL		PRZZZZUSA
SORENSEN, KATH.	24	F	W		PRZZZZUSA
HANS	4	M	CHILD		PRZZZZUSA
JOH.	2	M	CHILD		PRZZZZUSA
PETERSEN, CHRESTEN	54	M	FARMER		PRZZZZUSA
ANNA	47	F	W		PRZZZZUSA
PETER	18	M	CH		PRZZZZUSA
CHRIST.	14	M	CH		PRZZZZUSA
CAR.	7	M	CHILD		PRZZZZUSA
HANS	6	M	CHILD		PRZZZZUSA
BOTILDE	5	F	CHILD		PRZZZZUSA
WAMP, MARIE	52	F	W		PRZZZZUSA
JOH.	22	M	CH		PRZZZZUSA
THEODOR	17	M	CH		PRZZZZUSA
MINNA	13	F	CH		PRZZZZUSA
LABESQUE, JEAN	28	M	LABR		PRACDSUSA
BERTHE	29	F	W		PRACDSUSA
MARIE	29	F	S		PRACDSUSA
FRANCOIS	7	M	CHILD		PRACDSUSA
BERTHE	.06	F	INFANT		PRACDSUSA
EIGNER, HENRY	17	M	FARMER		PRZZZZUSA
PIEBRICH, BRUNO	18	M	BBR		PRZZZZUSA
SCHMIDT, MICHAEL	16	M	FARMER		WMZZZZUSA
WOERLER, JACOB	16	M	SHMK		WMZZZZUSA
GIEPERT, ANNA	18	F	SGL		WMAAXFUSA
PAWLOWSHI, JACOB	27	M	LABR		WMAAXFUSA
BOEHR, HERM.	32	M	DYR		WMALGGUSA
MORAWSHY, JOSEFA	35	F	WO		PRZZZZUSA
MICHALINA	16	F	CH		PRZZZZUSA
CATHARINA	3	F	CHILD		PRZZZZUSA
FRANZISKA	2	F	CHILD		PRZZZZUSA
MARSONIA	.05	F	INFANT		PRZZZZUSA
WEISER, THEODOR	26	M	BCHR		SYZZZZUSA
HOEFLOR, NIKOLAUS	26	M	GDNR		BVZZZZUSA
BURGERS, MARIE	30	F	SGL		BVACBFUSA
PESTE, GOTTFR.	24	M	SDLR		PRZZZZUSA
PLOHR, ADOLF	28	M	FARMER		PRACXVUSA
SOSERT, JULIUS	28	M	FARMER		PRZZZZUSA
BENNINGER, HELENE	40	F	W		PRACBFUSA
OLGA	17	F	CH		PRACBFUSA
HODKERS, JACOB	35	M	DLR		PRAIQKUSA
FELDT, MARG.	70	F	W		PRZZZZUSA
RESHOEFS, CATH.	48	F	W		PRZZZZUSA
EMMA	7	F	CHILD		PRZZZZUSA
MARG.	6	F	CHILD		PRZZZZUSA
SZIFLAT, BERTA	21	F	SGL		PRZZZZUSA
BIELENBERG, EMMA	18	F	SGL		PRZZZZUSA
KNAPHE, HELENE	21	F	SGL		PRAARZUSA
KNAPPHE, LOUISE	14	F	SGL		PRAARZUSA
ROBELEWSKA, EMILIE	19	F	SGL		PRZZZZUSA
ILSCHHEWIZ, ANNA	29	F	SGL		PRAHSCUSA
JOSEF	5	M	CHILD		PRAHSCUSA
HENRY	2	M	CHILD		PRAHSCUSA
URBAM, PAULINE	28	F	SGL		PRAHSCUSA
MEYER, JOHFR.	68	M	FARMER		PRAHFZUSA
ERNESTINE	60	F	W		PRAHFZUSA
FEHNIHLINZ, GUSTAV	32	M	FARMER		PRAHFZUSA
KROLL, JOHANN	24	M	LABR		PRZZZZUSA
U, WILH.	7	M	CHILD		PRZZZZUSA
MARIE	6	F	CHILD		PRZZZZUSA
WOLFF, CHR.	46	M	FARMER		PRAAKHUSA
FALCKE, AUGUST	21	M	ENGR		PRAAKHUSA
GRAUMANN, CARL	22	M	FARMER		PRAAKHUSA
BAY, ROSINE	21	F	SGL		PRAEXWUSA
KAISER, PAULINE	26	F	W		PRAEXWUSA
PFLOMM, PAULINE	28	F	SGL		WMZZZZUSA
SCHABER, CATHR.	21	F	SGL		WMAEDTUSA
HAGELE, ERNESTINE	24	F	SGL		BDZZZZUSA
WEBER, LOUISE	30	F	SGL		BDZZZZUSA
HANSEN, MARIE	24	F	SGL		PRZZZZUSA
SCHOOP, AUGUSTE	65	F	W		PRACBFUSA
MENCKE, FRIEDA	16	F	SGL		PRACBFUSA
SCHLUETER, ANNA	29	F	SGL		MKZZZZUSA
SALESKA, ANNA	23	F	SGL		MKACPSUSA
JORSCHHEWIZ, RICHE	23	F	SGL		MKACPSUSA
OESTREICH, HERM.	26	M	FARMER		MKAENHUSA
FRIDA	30	F	W		MKAENHUSA
AUGUSTE	3	F	CHILD		MKAENHUSA
ADOLF	.01	M	INFANT		MKAENHUSA
FRITZ	16	M	LABR		MKAENHUSA
ABFER, AUGUSTE	24	F	SGL		MKACBRUSA
FLIEGNER, JULIE	33	F	SGL		PRZZZZUSA
TIMRECH, HERMANN	24	M	FARMER		PRZZZZUSA
LAWRENTZ, BERTA	24	F	SGL		PRZZZZUSA
SCHUETZ, APOLLONIA	15	F	SGL		BVZZZZUSA
KEMSIRS, MATHILDE	45	F	W		PRZZZZUSA
ERNST	7	M	CHILD		PRZZZZUSA
HELENE	6	F	CHILD		PRZZZZUSA
FRIEDRICH, ANAR	26	M	LKSH		PRAHBQUSA
KAMINSKA, DOROTHEA	23	F	W		PRZZZZUSA

PASSENGER	AGE	SEX	OCCUPATION	PRVL/DES
LEOCADIA	.11	F	INFANT	PRZZZZUSA
PRAEFKE, CARL	27	M	FARMER	MKZZZZUSA
SOFIE	26	F	W	MKZZZZUSA
HEINR.	4	M	CHILD	MKZZZZUSA
ANNA	.11	F	INFANT	MKZZZZUSA
BECKER, MATHILDE	25	F	SGL	PRZZZZUSA
APITZSCH, LUDW.	20	M	CL	PRZZZZUSA
LENKE, HERMANN	27	M	BKLYR	PRZZZZUSA

SHIP: TRAVE

FROM: BREMEN AND SOUTHAMPTON
TO: NEW YORK
ARRIVED: 19 OCTOBER 1888

PASSENGER	AGE	SEX	OCCUPATION	PRVL/DES
BLOEM, HERMAN	40	M	MCHT	GRZZZZUSA
V, ADOLF	36	M	MCHT	GRZZZZUSA
VIEDOR, ADOLF	32	M	MCHT	GRZZZZUSA
MUELLER, EMILIE	23	F	UNKNOWN	GRZZZZUSA
SEICHT, EDWARD	29	M	MCHT	GRZZZZUSA
NANNDORFF, MIPETTE	35	F	UNKNOWN	GRZZZZUSA
SACK, AUGUSTE	55	F	UNKNOWN	GRZZZZUSA
GAELER, EMIL	24	M	MCHT	GRZZZZUSA
BUSER, LOUISE	33	F	UNKNOWN	GRZZZZUSA
PAULA	7	F	CHILD	GRZZZZUSA
HEDWIG	3	F	CHILD	GRZZZZUSA
CAPITAINE, CATHI	70	F	CH	GRZZZZUSA
HAUSER, ELISE	23	F	UNKNOWN	GRZZZZUSA
SHNEIDER, CONRAD	24	M	MCHT	GRZZZZUSA
LOEB, BABETTE	18	F	UNKNOWN	GRZZZZUSA
MAAS, BERTHA	26	F	UNKNOWN	GRZZZZUSA
SANDOZ, ELISE	18	F	UNKNOWN	GRZZZZUSA
DACHLER, MARIE	22	F	UNKNOWN	GRZZZZUSA
HERKSEN, CAPT.	39	M	CPTR	GRZZZZUSA
JUNGBLUTH, MARIE	40	F	UNKNOWN	GRZZZZUSA
ERHARDT, GUSTAV	21	M	MCHT	GRZZZZUSA
HUTSTEINER, WILHE.	21	F	UNKNOWN	GRZZZZUSA
SCHLUETER, ADELE	21	F	UNKNOWN	GRZZZZUSA
EGGERS, BECKA	16	F	UNKNOWN	GRZZZZUSA
SIEMER, MATHE.	18	F	UNKNOWN	GRZZZZUSA
KOCH, MARG.	17	F	UNKNOWN	GRZZZZUSA
KARL	.03	M	INFANT	GRZZZZUSA
KOMALKE, BABERT	24	M	GDNR	GRZZZZUSA
DECKER, ANNA	20	F	UNKNOWN	GRZZZZUSA
FOETZINGER, BABETTE	20	F	UNKNOWN	GRZZZZUSA
WUPPESAHL, META	23	F	UNKNOWN	GRZZZZUSA
DORIS	17	F	UNKNOWN	GRZZZZUSA
STANGE, MAIRE	21	F	UNKNOWN	GRZZZZUSA
CZEWINSKE, WILHE.	32	F	UNKNOWN	GRZZZZUSA
WUNDERLICH, MARIE	20	F	UNKNOWN	GRZZZZUSA
MEYER, MAGDA	20	F	UNKNOWN	GRZZZZUSA
ELFERS, ANNA	14	F	UNKNOWN	GRZZZZUSA
NITZ, CARL	57	M	LABR	GRZZZZUSA
PAULA	17	F	CH	GRZZZZUSA
JULIUS	14	M	CH	GRZZZZUSA
GUSTAV	28	M	LABR	GRZZZZUSA
EMILIE	.11	F	INFANT	GRZZZZUSA
HECKERT, THEO.	21	M	DLR	GRZZZZUSA
KOINECKE, EILH.	22	M	FARMER	GRZZZZUSA
HERMINE	19	F	W	GRZZZZUSA
HELLER, ALOIS	29	M	GDNR	GRZZZZUSA
BARRI, REBECCA	24	F	UNKNOWN	GRZZZZUSA
SIDER	2	M	CHILD	GRZZZZUSA
STRUSE, GESINE	28	F	UNKNOWN	GRZZZZUSA
HARMS, BECKA	23	F	UNKNOWN	GRZZZZUSA
HENRIETTE	2	F	CHILD	GRZZZZUSA
BEHRENDT, AUGUSTE	22	F	UNKNOWN	GRZZZZUSA
TEGELER, ANNA	25	F	UNKNOWN	GRZZZZUSA
BECKNAGE, WILH.	23	M	BRR	GRZZZZUSA
VALLMENDING, CATHI	18	F	UNKNOWN	GRZZZZUSA
HENKEN, CATHI	16	F	UNKNOWN	GRZZZZUSA
THONHALT, BERTHA	20	F	UNKNOWN	GRZZZZUSA
ELISE	17	F	UNKNOWN	GRZZZZUSA
MEYER, META	19	F	UNKNOWN	GRZZZZUSA
SPARNICHT, BETTY	22	F	UNKNOWN	GRZZZZUSA
BASSE, S.H.	35	M	BCHR	GRZZZZUSA
MOELLER, AUGUSTE	18	F	UNKNOWN	GRZZZZUSA
KIRCHHAFF, FRIEDR.	17	M	UNKNOWN	GRZZZZUSA
SIEGMANN, ELIZA	20	F	UNKNOWN	GRZZZZUSA
BORCHERT, HERMAN	24	M	BCHR	GRZZZZUSA
SANSSEN, HERM.	24	M	FARMER	GRZZZZUSA
HUSMANN, WILKE	27	M	BRR	GRZZZZUSA
RING, FRIEDR.	28	M	FARMER	GRZZZZUSA
FRIEDA	7	F	CHILD	GRZZZZUSA
MARIE	6	F	CHILD	GRZZZZUSA
SOPHIE	5	F	CHILD	GRZZZZUSA
MUELLER, WILHE.	54	F	UNKNOWN	GRZZZZUSA
BAGGENSTEIN, CECILIE	19	F	UNKNOWN	GRZZZZUSA
SCHWEIZER, ANNA	15	F	UNKNOWN	GRZZZZUSA
HEINERDINGEN, MARIE	7	F	CHILD	GRZZZZUSA
BATHENSCHLAG, ALFRED	22	M	BCHR	GRZZZZUSA
ENZINGER, FRANZ	28	M	FARMER	GRZZZZUSA
TRINZING, MARIE	56	F	UNKNOWN	GRZZZZUSA
MEYER, GOTTLIEB	17	M	FARMER	GRZZZZUSA
DUEGGNER, JOSEPHE	21	F	UNKNOWN	GRZZZZUSA
MEIER, KONDULA	20	F	UNKNOWN	GRZZZZUSA
PREISS, CAROLA	22	F	UNKNOWN	GRZZZZUSA
SCHNEIDER, CHEIST	22	M	FARMER	GRZZZZUSA
LEIBINGER, LINA	18	F	UNKNOWN	GRZZZZUSA
MUEHLHAUSER, JOH.	26	M	FARMER	GRZZZZUSA
SCHMIDT, ROSINE	21	F	UNKNOWN	GRZZZZUSA
ROSINE	19	F	UNKNOWN	GRZZZZUSA
WURSTER, CAROLINE	30	F	UNKNOWN	GRZZZZUSA
MUELLER, BENEDISE	33	M	GDNR	GRZZZZUSA
SIEGLER, WILH.	16	M	LABR	GRZZZZUSA
BUCK, MIRS	23	F	UNKNOWN	GRZZZZUSA
BALTHASAR, CATHI	47	F	UNKNOWN	GRZZZZUSA
FRAEHLICH, ANNA	22	F	UNKNOWN	GRZZZZUSA
BALTHASAR, GEORG	7	M	CHILD	GRZZZZUSA
KUEHN, HANIRETTE	26	F	UNKNOWN	GRZZZZUSA
CLARA	.06	F	INFANT	GRZZZZUSA
CLAUS, WILH.	41	M	MCHT	GRZZZZUSA
RUETTLER, FIREDR.	17	M	FARMER	GRZZZZUSA
RAAB, GUSTAV	17	M	FARMER	GRZZZZUSA
SCHUBERT, AMALIE	44	F	UNKNOWN	GRZZZZUSA
BEST, PHILIPP	17	M	LABR	GRZZZZUSA
ZSCHIRNER, GEORG	20	M	FARMER	GRZZZZUSA
LANGE, MARTHA	16	F	UNKNOWN	GRZZZZUSA
BREMER, ROSA	17	F	UNKNOWN	GRZZZZUSA
ECKLER, FRIEDR.	17	M	GDNR	GRZZZZUSA
HARTLIEB, ELISE	21	F	UNKNOWN	GRZZZZUSA
SENBERT, CARL	28	M	BCHR	GRZZZZUSA
BANER, PHILIPP	18	M	TLR	GRZZZZUSA
WINKLER, LUDWIG	15	M	FARMER	GRZZZZUSA
RITTER, BLUME	40	F	UNKNOWN	GRZZZZUSA
ROSA	28	F	UNKNOWN	GRZZZZUSA
MOOSBLECH, MARIE	21	F	UNKNOWN	GRZZZZUSA
BERWIND, MICHEL	25	M	BRR	GRZZZZUSA
STEINMUELLER, JULIE	22	F	UNKNOWN	GRZZZZUSA
SCHECKENBACH, JUSTINE	28	F	UNKNOWN	GRZZZZUSA
CORNEHL, WILH.	15	M	LABR	GRZZZZUSA
HERLING, JOHAN	22	M	FARMER	GRZZZZUSA
CLAMER	7	M	CHILD	GRZZZZUSA
BANER, ELEONORE	25	F	UNKNOWN	GRZZZZUSA
AGNES	4	F	CHILD	GRZZZZUSA
ANTON	2	M	CHILD	GRZZZZUSA
HARTMANN, MARG.	42	F	UNKNOWN	GRZZZZUSA
AULBACH, JOSEPHE	26	F	UNKNOWN	GRZZZZUSA
HEERLEIN, JOHAN	29	M	GDNR	GRZZZZUSA
WINDHAVER, IDA	23	F	UNKNOWN	GRZZZZUSA
ROSA	3	F	CHILD	GRZZZZUSA
MAY, CARL	30	M	SHMK	GRZZZZUSA
THERESE	28	F	W	GRZZZZUSA
CARL	3	M	CHILD	GRZZZZUSA
PAULA	.11	F	INFANT	GRZZZZUSA

PASSENGER	AGE	SEX	OCCUPATION	PRVL	DES
DITTER, PHILIPPE	17	F	UNKNOWN	GRZZZZ	USA
LAEHR, FRIDOLIN	16	M	LABR	GRZZZZ	USA
STOCK, JOHAN	46	M	LABR	GRZZZZ	USA
MARIE	40	F	W	GRZZZZ	USA
HANS	15	M	CH	GRZZZZ	USA
OSTENGAARD, BUNNE	22	M	FARMER	GRZZZZ	USA
STOCK, CHRISTE.	16	F	UNKNOWN	GRZZZZ	USA
BERG, MARIE	22	F	UNKNOWN	GRZZZZ	USA
ROEMER, JACOBE.	20	F	UNKNOWN	GRZZZZ	USA
FICKNITZ, LAURA	59	F	UNKNOWN	GRZZZZ	USA
BEHRENDT, MINNA	26	F	UNKNOWN	GRZZZZ	USA
WEBER, THEODOR	16	M	LABR	GRZZZZ	USA
KOWALSKI, MICHEL	25	M	FARMER	GRZZZZ	USA
FROESE, WILHELME.	17	F	UNKNOWN	GRZZZZ	USA
KUNTZ, LIOPOLD	29	M	FARMER	GRZZZZ	USA
MARIE	22	F	W	GRZZZZ	USA
HALBERG, HEINR.	25	M	GDNR	GRZZZZ	USA
SAELLNER, CATHI	21	F	UNKNOWN	GRZZZZ	USA
GROSCH, MARG.	14	F	UNKNOWN	GRZZZZ	USA
SCHUELER, ANNA	7	F	CHILD	GRZZZZ	USA
LE-RNER, CARL	40	M	MCHT	GRZZZZ	USA
LUECKE, MARTHA	19	F	UNKNOWN	GRZZZZ	USA
SCHEFFLER, ELISE	39	F	UNKNOWN	GRZZZZ	USA
HEIN, MECHEL	21	M	BCHR	GRZZZZ	USA
HEROLD, JULIUS	22	M	FARMER	GRZZZZ	USA
ULBRICH, VALENTIN	17	M	FARMER	GRZZZZ	USA
METZGER, ELISE	45	F	UNKNOWN	GRZZZZ	USA
AUGUST	7	M	CHILD	GRZZZZ	USA
BROLL, MARIE	50	F	UNKNOWN	GRZZZZ	USA
KUHL, ELISE	21	F	UNKNOWN	GRZZZZ	USA
KALBHEREN, ADAM	14	M	FARMER	GRZZZZ	USA
WEIGENT, JACOB	38	M	FARMER	GRZZZZ	USA
MARG.	37	F	W	GRZZZZ	USA
BECK, CALORA	28	F	UNKNOWN	GRZZZZ	USA
LOESER, MARIE	43	F	UNKNOWN	GRZZZZ	USA
FRANZ	16	M	UNKNOWN	GRZZZZ	USA
MINNA	12	F	UNKNOWN	GRZZZZ	USA
WILHELM	7	M	CHILD	GRZZZZ	USA
FRIEDRICH	5	M	CHILD	GRZZZZ	USA
GOTTFRIED	3	M	CHILD	GRZZZZ	USA
OTTO	.11	M	INFANT	GRZZZZ	USA
BEHRENS, FRIEDA	22	F	UNKNOWN	GRZZZZ	USA
SEMMELBRODT, CATHI	23	F	UNKNOWN	GRZZZZ	USA
SCHAPER, ANNA	20	F	UNKNOWN	GRZZZZ	USA
AUGUSTE	21	F	UNKNOWN	GRZZZZ	USA
KOESTER, CATHI	24	F	UNKNOWN	GRZZZZ	USA
ELLERMANN, ELISE	27	F	UNKNOWN	GRZZZZ	USA
STREG, PHILIPP	38	M	JNR	GRZZZZ	USA
SANDOASS, ALBERT	26	M	TLR	GRZZZZ	USA
RALFS, GUSTAV	26	M	FARMER	GRZZZZ	USA
LUEHR, CONRAD	23	M	BCHR	GRZZZZ	USA
HENSCH, MARIA	31	F	UNKNOWN	GRZZZZ	USA
KOCH, SOPHIE	35	F	UNKNOWN	GRZZZZ	USA
HARRIES, FRITZ	49	M	FARMER	GRZZZZ	USA
ADELHEIT	53	F	W	GRZZZZ	USA
SOPHIE	20	F	CH	GRZZZZ	USA
BULLWINKEL, LOUIS	16	M	BRR	GRZZZZ	USA
EDLER, FRIEDR.	18	M	GDNR	GRZZZZ	USA
WERFELMANN, HEINR.	16	M	GDNR	GRZZZZ	USA
HILSCHER, CARL	50	M	FARMER	GRZZZZ	USA
HENRIETTE	52	F	W	GRZZZZ	USA
MARTHA	28	F	CH	GRZZZZ	USA
MINNA	18	F	CH	GRZZZZ	USA
BERTHA	14	F	CH	GRZZZZ	USA
HIRSCHMANN, JOHAN	33	M	FARMER	GRZZZZ	USA
JANNER, MARGA	27	F	UNKNOWN	GRZZZZ	USA
HERLAND, AUGUSTE	26	F	UNKNOWN	GRZZZZ	USA
NOR, ALOIS	18	M	GDNR	GRZZZZ	USA
SCHNEIDER, ANTON	16	M	GCR	GRZZZZ	USA
SCHMIDT, THERESE	21	F	UNKNOWN	GRZZZZ	USA
WEBER, ANNA	15	F	UNKNOWN	GRZZZZ	USA
STEINBAUER, MARIE	19	F	UNKNOWN	GRZZZZ	USA
PETERS, GERHARD	17	M	FARMER	GRZZZZ	USA
FOCKERT, MARG.	16	F	UNKNOWN	GRZZZZ	USA
SKEN, MARG.	16	F	UNKNOWN	GRZZZZ	USA
HUSMANN, FRIEDR.	17	M	LABR	GRZZZZ	USA
LANDHERR, ALBERT	17	M	LABR	GRZZZZ	USA
WETZ, HEINR.	18	M	LABR	GRZZZZ	USA
BEHRE, FERDIN.	20	M	LABR	GRZZZZ	USA
SCHMIDT, ANNA	17	F	UNKNOWN	GRZZZZ	USA
THEILEN, JOHAN	32	M	GCR	GRZZZZ	USA
JANSEN, JOHAN	33	M	BCHR	GRZZZZ	USA
KOESTERS, LUDW.	65	M	JNR	GRZZZZ	USA
WALLIS, ELISE	30	F	UNKNOWN	GRZZZZ	USA
LOUIS	.11	M	INFANT	GRZZZZ	USA
KLEISCH, ALBERT	17	M	FARMER	GRZZZZ	USA
SCHMEERS, META	17	F	UNKNOWN	GRZZZZ	USA
MOHR, OTTILIE	16	F	UNKNOWN	GRZZZZ	USA
HEINTZ, WILHELM	25	M	GDNR	GRZZZZ	USA
ANNA	25	F	W	GRZZZZ	USA
FAUGNATZ, CATHI	19	F	UNKNOWN	GRZZZZ	USA
PAMMER, HELENE	21	F	UNKNOWN	GRZZZZ	USA
ROSINE	20	F	UNKNOWN	GRZZZZ	USA
BALKE, PAUL	25	M	FARMER	GRZZZZ	USA
WAETJEN, ANNA	20	F	UNKNOWN	GRZZZZ	USA
GAGERMEIER, JOHAN	25	M	SHMK	GRZZZZ	USA
FRANZISCA	22	F	W	GRZZZZ	USA
MARIE	1	F	CHILD	GRZZZZ	USA
GARBADEN, MARIE	16	F	UNKNOWN	GRZZZZ	USA
ALBEN	2	M	CHILD	GRZZZZ	USA
OTTO	.11	M	INFANT	GRZZZZ	USA
HERMSEN, WILHELM	16	M	FARMER	GRZZZZ	USA
HATTERMANN, HEINR.	27	M	FARMER	GRZZZZ	USA
SOPHIE	22	F	W	GRZZZZ	USA
HEINR.	.11	M	INFANT	GRZZZZ	USA
SCHMIDT, MARIE	40	F	UNKNOWN	GRZZZZ	USA
EDUARD	7	M	CHILD	GRZZZZ	USA
MENTZEN, ANNA	22	F	UNKNOWN	GRZZZZ	USA
LAGEMANN, ANNY	27	F	UNKNOWN	GRZZZZ	USA
SCHRAEDER, HEDWIG	20	F	UNKNOWN	GRZZZZ	USA
MATTFELD, SOPHIE	15	F	UNKNOWN	GRZZZZ	USA
LANDES, CATHI	20	F	UNKNOWN	GRZZZZ	USA
SOMMERMANN, ALWIN	22	M	FARMER	GRZZZZ	USA
HOPPE, AUGUST	16	M	GDNR	GRZZZZ	USA
HILLEBRECHT, FRIEDR.	15	M	MCHT	GRZZZZ	USA
DIEDRICHS, CARL	20	M	LABR	GRZZZZ	USA
WEGENER, PAULA	20	F	UNKNOWN	GRZZZZ	USA
HEINALD, JOHAN	18	M	FARMER	GRZZZZ	USA
MARG.	17	F	W	GRZZZZ	USA
MUNDL, MARG.	26	F	UNKNOWN	GRZZZZ	USA
SCHRAH, ELISE	18	F	UNKNOWN	GRZZZZ	USA
HOFFMANN, CATHI	25	F	UNKNOWN	GRZZZZ	USA
SISE	4	F	CHILD	GRZZZZ	USA
CATHI	2	F	CHILD	GRZZZZ	USA
HEINRICH	.06	M	INFANT	GRZZZZ	USA
SCHNEIDER, LATTCHEN	20	F	UNKNOWN	GRZZZZ	USA
HAHN, MARIE	18	F	UNKNOWN	GRZZZZ	USA
HEMANER, JACOB	48	M	FARMER	GRZZZZ	USA
ANNA	44	F	W	GRZZZZ	USA
JOHAN	24	M	CH	GRZZZZ	USA
JACOB	20	M	CH	GRZZZZ	USA
ALOIS	6	M	CHILD	GRZZZZ	USA
HAMBUECHER, PETER	26	M	FARMER	GRZZZZ	USA
HARTMANN, CONRAD	17	M	FARMER	GRZZZZ	USA
JOSEF	16	M	FARMER	GRZZZZ	USA
FRAEHLICH, ANNA	21	F	UNKNOWN	GRZZZZ	USA
MATLAGE, ANNA	54	F	UNKNOWN	GRZZZZ	USA
SOPHIE	16	F	UNKNOWN	GRZZZZ	USA
MINNA	5	F	CHILD	GRZZZZ	USA
FUCKS, DORA	31	F	UNKNOWN	GRZZZZ	USA
FRANZ	.11	M	INFANT	GRZZZZ	USA
MICHNIK, PAULA	22	F	UNKNOWN	GRZZZZ	USA
MATERNE, ERNSTINE	29	F	UNKNOWN	GRZZZZ	USA
EIBEN, AUGUST	26	M	TLR	GRZZZZ	USA
BRANDENBURG, IDA	20	F	UNKNOWN	GRZZZZ	USA
HAAREM, NICOL	16	M	GDNR	GRZZZZ	USA
WAHLTMANN, ANNA	18	F	UNKNOWN	GRZZZZ	USA
HILLMANN, JOHAN	15	M	FARMER	GRZZZZ	USA
SIEMERS, WILH.	14	M	FARMER	GRZZZZ	USA
HALLING, CATHI	23	F	UNKNOWN	GRZZZZ	USA

PASSENGER	AGE	SEX	OCCUPATION	PRVIVL DES
MIHRENS, ANNA	17	F	UNKNOWN	GRZZZZUSA
WAHLERS, ERNST	23	M	GCR	GRZZZZUSA
KAHRS, JOHAN	16	M	TLR	GRZZZZUSA
SENNIG, WILH.	16	M	BCHR	GRZZZZUSA
HEINS, HEINR.	16	M	LABR	GRZZZZUSA
MOHRMANN, ANNA	16	F	UNKNOWN	GRZZZZUSA
DROEGE, MARG.	20	F	UNKNOWN	GRZZZZUSA
HINR.	15	M	UNKNOWN	GRZZZZUSA
HULJUS, CLAUS	14	M	UNKNOWN	GRZZZZUSA
MEYER, DOROTHEA	15	F	UNKNOWN	GRZZZZUSA
SCHMIDT, ALWINE	18	F	UNKNOWN	GRZZZZUSA
HAHL, JOHAN	23	M	FARMER	GRZZZZUSA
MEINGERT, DOROTHEA	18	F	UNKNOWN	GRZZZZUSA
KIELMEYER, CARL	6	M	CHILD	GRZZZZUSA
SACHSE, FRITZ	22	M	BRR	GRZZZZUSA
SOPHIE	15	F	W	GRZZZZUSA
RUMP, CARL	22	M	FARMER	GRZZZZUSA
ZIPP, OTTO	16	M	FARMER	GRZZZZUSA
MUELLER, LINE	30	F	UNKNOWN	GRZZZZUSA
ARTHUR	3	M	CHILD	GRZZZZUSA
HUGO	.06	M	INFANT	GRZZZZUSA
RUDOLPH, LILLI	26	F	UNKNOWN	GRZZZZUSA
MOECKEL, ERNST	23	M	BRR	GRZZZZUSA
FRIEDA	22	F	W	GRZZZZUSA
LILIA	.09	F	INFANT	GRZZZZUSA
TAUSCHER, MAX	16	M	GDNR	GRZZZZUSA
BAHRER, GUST.	25	M	TLR	GRZZZZUSA
ROBERT, RUDOLPH	16	M	GCR	GRZZZZUSA
KRABBE, ELISE	23	F	UNKNOWN	GRZZZZUSA
WILHELM	3	M	CHILD	GRZZZZUSA
EGERT, ELIAS	23	M	LABR	GRZZZZUSA
KLEER, ANNA	28	F	W	GRZZZZUSA
LOEBICH, CHRISTE.	19	F	UNKNOWN	GRZZZZUSA
BECK, CAROLA	19	F	UNKNOWN	GRZZZZUSA
KUTTRUF, WILH.	25	M	GCR	GRZZZZUSA
SCHUHKNAFT, DANIEL	25	M	TLR	GRZZZZUSA
NOCK, PHILIPPE	20	F	UNKNOWN	GRZZZZUSA
ZIMMERMANN, PAUL	22	M	MCHT	GRZZZZUSA
RITTER, LOUIS	27	M	BRR	GRZZZZUSA
SEEGER, WILH.	40	M	JNR	GRZZZZUSA
WUNDERLICH, LUDWIG	32	M	MCHT	GRZZZZUSA
WIEGAND, LENA	36	F	UNKNOWN	GRZZZZUSA
WIEDT, HERMAN	20	M	FARMER	GRZZZZUSA
KLOMANN, MARY	17	F	UNKNOWN	GRZZZZUSA
LAEHR, FRITZ	28	M	BRR	GRZZZZUSA
ULTAMER, JOHAN	32	M	TLR	GRZZZZUSA
DAHLING, CARL	23	M	BLKSMH	GRZZZZUSA
GETTNER, REGINE	23	F	UNKNOWN	GRZZZZUSA
WAHLLEBEN, CARL	19	M	BCHR	GRZZZZUSA
ANGERMANN, CARL	44	M	MLR	GRZZZZUSA
OTLAMM, ERNST	22	M	GCR	GRZZZZUSA
THIESSMEIER, EMILIE	23	F	UNKNOWN	GRZZZZUSA
HIRSCHBERG, SAMUEL	24	M	MCHT	GRZZZZUSA
AMALIE	21	F	W	GRZZZZUSA
ROBERT	.03	M	INFANT	GRZZZZUSA
WALTER, GEORG	34	M	FARMER	GRZZZZUSA
MARIA	26	F	W	GRZZZZUSA
HOESEL, MAGDA	58	F	UNKNOWN	GRZZZZUSA
WALTER, GEORG	4	M	CHILD	GRZZZZUSA
JOHAN	.11	M	INFANT	GRZZZZUSA
GRAHLMANN, WILH.	16	M	BCHR	GRZZZZUSA
FICKE, JOHAN	21	M	GCR	GRZZZZUSA
RESS, URBAN	34	M	BRR	GRZZZZUSA
GROSS, HENRY	25	M	FARMER	GRZZZZUSA

SHIP: ANCHORIA

FROM: GLASGOW AND MOVILLE
TO: NEW YORK
ARRIVED: 22 OCTOBER 1888

PASSENGER	AGE	SEX	OCCUPATION	PRVIVL DES
MEER, LOUISE	25	F	NN	GRAHRZUSA
SAUL	3	M	CHILD	GRAHRZUSA
ABRAHAM	1	M	CHILD	GRZZZZUSA
LIPSCHITZ, SCHMUL	24	M	TLR	GRZZZZUSA
HERZE	12	M	CH	GRZZZZUSA
JALKOWSKI, MOREL	18	M	PDLR	GRZZZZUSA
GREIMAN, SCHIRA	16	M	PDLR	GRZZZZUSA
SAML.	10	M	PDLR	GRZZZZUSA
KOPEL, ABE	10	M	PDLR	GRZZZZUSA
BERKOWITZ, ABEL	17	M	TLR	GRZZZZUSA
KATE	17	F	W	GRZZZZUSA
SELMAN, ISAK	15	M	BBR	GRZZZZUSA
RATSIN, JOSEF	18	M	TLR	GRZZZZUSA
LIFSCHITZ, REUBEN	17	M	SHMK	GRZZZZUSA
GOLDSCHMIDT, JOSEF	58	M	UNKNOWN	GRZZZZUSA
KANTOR, ABRAHAM	40	M	LABR	GRZZZZUSA
GOLDSCHMIDT, CHANE	17	F	HP	GRZZZZUSA
SHUTZ, DOROTHEA	41	F	W	GRZZZZUSA
OTTO	14	M	LABR	GRZZZZUSA
ANNA	11	F	CH	GRZZZZUSA
RITCHARD	9	M	CHILD	GRZZZZUSA
LISA	2	F	CHILD	GRZZZZUSA
TREPOW, WILH.	22	M	SEMN	GRAAZQUSA
WULFF, PAUL	17	M	MNR	GRZZZZUSA
STARK, FERDD.	16	M	LABR	GRZZZZUSA
H-EMCZEWSKI, JOHAN	36	M	UNKNOWN	GRZZZZUSA
PEUDLEWICZ, LORENZ	38	M	LABR	GRAEABUSA

SHIP: ARIZONA

FROM: LIVERPOOL AND QUEENSTOWN
TO: NEW YORK
ARRIVED: 22 OCTOBER 1888

PASSENGER	AGE	SEX	OCCUPATION	PRVIVL DES
BECKER, U-MISS	34	F	LDY	GRADBQFR
SCHMIDT, JOHAN	25	M	CL	GRACBFUSA
VILAIN, ROSIN	37	F	W	GRADXWUSA
CONIMIANT, SELINA	20	F	SP	GRADXWUSA
AUGUSTINE	17	F	SP	GRADXWUSA
JOSEFINE	13	F	SP	GRADXWUSA
EDUARD	11	M	CH	GRADXWUSA
ROSINE	10	F	CH	GRADXWUSA
IVAN-B.	8	M	CHILD	GRADXWUSA
AUGUSTINE	6	M	CHILD	GRADXWUSA
JEAN-B.	4	M	CHILD	GRADXWUSA
ARONSOHN, SORE	30	F	W	GRACBFUSA
SAMUEL	15	M	LABR	GRACBFUSA
HERMAN	10	M	CH	GRACBFUSA
WOLF	7	M	CHILD	GRACBFUSA
BERNHARD	6	M	CHILD	GRACBFUSA
EMMA	5	F	CHILD	GRACBFUSA
SPADSY, ROCHEL	25	F	W	GRACBFUSA
ISAAC	11	M	CH	GRACBFUSA
BASCHE	7	M	CHILD	GRACBFUSA
MINE	6	F	CHILD	GRACBFUSA
DROGER, ANNA	20	F	SP	GRAAKHUSA
ARONSOHN, ANNA	.05	F	INFANT	GRACBFUSA
BICHHOLTZ, AUGUSTE	30	F	W	GRAAYKUSA
GATHE, SAMUEL	22	M	CL	GRAAECUSA
LANGENEGGER, U-MISS	24	F	SP	GRADAXUSA
BOWMANN, U-MISS	21	F	SP	GRADAXUSA
NAFFER, JULIUS	24	M	JNR	GRACBFUSA
MULLER, ERLA	18	F	SP	GRACBFUSA

PASSENGER	AGE	SEX	OCCUPATION	PRIVLS	DES
BOLDT, WILLIAM	51	M	ART	GRACBFUSA	
HENRIETTA	45	F	W	GRACBFUSA	
MARGARET	11	F	CH	GRACBFUSA	
ERNST	10	M	CH	GRACBFUSA	
FELD, PINCHES	11	M	CH	GRACBFUSA	
SCHMEER, PERL	17	F	SP	GRACBFUSA	
KELLER, HERMANN	18	M	FLABR	GRACBFUSA	
WOLFF, CHASKEL	20	F	SP	GRACBFUSA	
GROSS, SAMUEL	24	M	PNTR	GRACBFUSA	
JETTI	23	F	W	GRACBFUSA	
GRUNBAUM, LIPPMANN	20	M	FLABR	GRACBFUSA	
STEIN, HANS	19	M	FLABR	GRACBFUSA	

SHIP: STATE OF GEORGIA

FROM: GLASGOW
TO: NEW YORK
ARRIVED: 22 OCTOBER 1888

PASSENGER	AGE	SEX	OCCUPATION	PRIVLS	DES
DICHEN, JOHN	55	M	LABR	GRZZZZUSA	
FRANZEN, JOSEPH	22	M	FARMER	GRZZZZUSA	
HERMANN, OTTO	24	M	BLKSMH	GRZZZZUSA	
HARRISON, ABRAHAM	17	M	BKR	GRZZZZUSA	
HOID, WANDA-E.	15	F	SVNT	GRZZZZUSA	
MEITERS, MOSES	19	M	PHRS	GRZZZZUSA	
MARIE	21	F	SVNT	GRZZZZUSA	
SCHWEDER, HEINRICH	15	M	NN	GRZZZZUSA	
SCHULER, LOUISE	18	F	SVNT	GRZZZZUSA	
WEINHOLD, AUGUST	45	M	BKR	GRZZZZUSA	
HANNE	36	F	W	GRZZZZUSA	

SHIP: TAORMINA

FROM: HAMBURG
TO: NEW YORK
ARRIVED: 22 OCTOBER 1888

PASSENGER	AGE	SEX	OCCUPATION	PRIVLS	DES
STEGMESS, EDUARD	22	M	LABR	PRZZZZCIN	
RABE, MARIE	32	F	WO	PRZZZZNY	
PAUL	7	M	CHILD	PRZZZZNY	
ALBERT	6	M	CHILD	PRZZZZNY	
OTTO	5	M	CHILD	PRZZZZNY	
HARTUNG, EMIL	27	F	SGL	PRZZZZCH	
GUMALSKA, MARIANNE	28	F	WO	PRZZZZNY	
MARIE	7	F	CHILD	PRZZZZNY	
VERONIKA	6	F	CHILD	PRZZZZNY	
FRANZISKA	.09	F	INFANT	PRZZZZNY	
PAUL, JETTE	35	F	WO	PRZZZZNY	
AGNES	21	F	CH	PRZZZZNY	
CLARA	7	F	CHILD	PRZZZZNY	
SELMA	6	F	CHILD	PRZZZZNY	
ANNA	7	F	CHILD	PRZZZZNY	
GEORG	4	M	CHILD	PRZZZZNY	
HANNA	3	F	CHILD	PRZZZZNY	
MARTIN	2	M	CHILD	PRZZZZNY	
ELSE	.11	F	INFANT	PRZZZZNY	
WONDZINSKY, FRANZ	27	M	LABR	PRZZZZNY	
CATH	40	F	W	PRZZZZNY	
MARIE	14	M	CH	PRZZZZNY	
ANNA	7	M	CHILD	PRZZZZNY	
BURGHARDT, LINA	22	F	SGL	SCZZZZNY	
ZANDER, RICHARD	25	M	LABR	PRZZZZNY	
POSNANSKI, CARL	23	M	LABR	PRZZZZNY	
PIPRZINSKA, FRANZISKA	20	F	SGL	PRZZZZNY	
VOGELSANG, MARIE	26	F	SGL	PRZZZZNY	

PASSENGER	AGE	SEX	OCCUPATION	PRIVLS	DES
-ODING, HEINRICH	22	M	LABR	PRZZZZUNK	
KAYKA, FRIEDRICH	29	M	JNR	PRZZZZUNK	
POLNACK, WLADISLAV	.09	F	INFANT	PRZZZZUNK	
HEYNE, WILH	29	M	MCHT	PRZZZZUNK	
WEISS, MARTHA	37	F	WO	PRZZZZUNK	
PETERSEN, LINA	14	F	SGL	PRZZZZNY	
MEIER, D--SIS	68	F	WO	PRZZZZNY	
PETERSEN, MARTIN	23	M	BKR	PRZZZZCH	
PASCHKOWIAK, MARIANNE	42	F	WO	PRZZZZCH	
FRANZISCA	7	F	CHILD	PRZZZZCH	
INDIA	4	F	CHILD	PRZZZZCH	
MOELLER, EMILIA	12	F	SGL	PRZZZZCH	
FREICKE, ANNA	22	F	WO	PRZZZZNY	
HEINR	7	M	CHILD	PRZZZZNY	
GRETHE	6	F	CHILD	PRZZZZNY	
EMMA	.05	F	INFANT	PRZZZZNY	
EMMA	20	F	SGL	PRZZZZNY	
OL-NICSAK, MARIANNE	26	F	SGL	PRZZZZNY	
KREITLAV, MARIE	16	F	SGL	PRZZZZNY	
KR--SE, JOHANN	27	M	LABR	PRZZZZNY	
EMMA	7	F	CHILD	PRZZZZNY	
BISS, JOH	13	M	STDNT	PRZZZZMN	
MARIENKOWSKI, AUGUST	22	M	LLD	PRZZZZCH	
KEN-Y, MAX	23	M	MCHT	PRZZZZCIN	
HAASE, MA-THILDE	19	F	SGL	PRZZZZUNK	
GIERING, IDA	31	F	WO	PRZZZZPIT	
KARL	5	M	CHILD	PRZZZZPIT	
MARY	3	F	CHILD	PRZZZZPIT	
MATHIAS, EDUARD	39	M	CGRTW	PRZZZZNY	
ELISABETH	33	F	W	PRZZZZNY	
MARG	7	F	CHILD	PRZZZZNY	
CATH	6	F	CHILD	PRZZZZNY	
BRONIKOWSKI, PAUL	21	M	LABR	PRZZZZNAT	
GESSNER, MARGR	33	F	WO	BVZZZZNY	
RICHARD	7	M	CHILD	BVZZZZNY	
PHILOMENA	6	F	CHILD	BVZZZZNY	
HEDWIG	4	F	CHILD	BVZZZZNY	
ANNA	4	F	CHILD	BVZZZZNY	
ENGELBERT	00	M	CH	BVZZZZNY	
BARBA	2	F	CHILD	BVZZZZNY	
CIAZYNSKA, MARIE	40	F	WO	PRZZZZNY	
JOSEPH	.09	M	INFANT	PRZZZZNY	
BUDZINSKA, STANISLAUS	7	F	CHILD	PRZZZZNY	
ELISABETH	00	F	CH	PRZZZZNY	
KUNZMANN, HERMANN	41	M	LABR	PRZZZZNY	
CYRIA-, SOPHIE	27	F	WO	HBZZZZNY	
THERITE	.06	F	INFANT	HBZZZZNY	
KURZ, LORENZ	40	M	SHMK	PRZZZZNY	
MARTIN	7	M	CHILD	PRZZZZNY	
MOELLER, FELIX	24	M	CL	SYZZZZNY	
LANGOS, NICOLAUS	24	M	LABR	PRZZZZNY	
ANDRESEN, HEINRICH	35	M	SMH	PRZZZZCH	

SHIP: HERMANN

FROM: BREMEN
TO: BALTIMORE
ARRIVED: 24 OCTOBER 1888

PASSENGER	AGE	SEX	OCCUPATION	PRIVLS	DES
MERLI, RUDOLPH	25	M	FARMER	SRZZZZMD	
RUTA, MARIE	26	F	UNKNOWN	GRZZZZMD	
BOHMSTE, ELISABETH	56	F	UNKNOWN	GRZZZZMD	
JOSEFA	3	F	CHILD	GRZZZZMD	
JOSEF	.08	M	INFANT	GRZZZZMD	
ANASTASIA	24	F	UNKNOWN	GRZZZZMD	
JOTSCHKOWSKI, U	15	F	UNKNOWN	GRZZZZMD	
RETZLAFF, MARIE	19	F	UNKNOWN	GRZZZZMD	
TESCH, AUGUST	36	M	RPR	GRZZZZMD	
PRUSCH, THEODOR	37	M	FARMER	GRZZZZMD	
TESCH, WLHME.	20	F	W	GRZZZZMD	

PASSENGER	AGE	SEX	OCCUPATION	PRVL	DES
ZELINSKI, MARIANE	57	F	UNKNOWN	GRZZZZM	D
PUKAL, JULIUS	26	M	UNKNOWN	GRZZZZM	D
FORMELA, BARBARA	31	F	UNKNOWN	GRZZZZM	D
WLADISLAUS	7	M	CHILD	GRZZZZM	D
JOHANNA	5	F	CHILD	GRZZZZM	D
LEON	2	M	CHILD	GRZZZZM	D
VICTOR	.10	M	INFANT	GRZZZZM	D
SCHULTHEISS, MARIE	60	F	UNKNOWN	GRZZZZM	D
ZASTROW, AUGUST	44	M	LABR	GRZZZZM	D
CAROLINE	47	F	W	GRZZZZM	D
FRIEDRICH	19	M	UNKNOWN	GRZZZZM	D
WILHELM	12	M	CH	GRZZZZM	D
BERTHA	8	F	CHILD	GRZZZZM	D
AUGUST	3	M	CHILD	GRZZZZM	D
KLOTZ, ELEONORE	76	F	UNKNOWN	GRZZZZM	D
DIETRICH, MOSES	15	M	UNKNOWN	GRZZZZM	D
FROSCHAIETER, KATHR.	21	F	UNKNOWN	GRZZZZM	D
SCHMIDT, NICOL.	28	M	FARMER	GRZZZZM	D
BOCK, JOHANN	26	M	FARMER	GRZZZZM	D
MARGR.	23	F	W	GRZZZZM	D
TOMANN, ANTON	24	M	FARMER	GRZZZZI	A
HEIM, ANTON	15	M	UNKNOWN	GRZZZZM	D
KETZIERSKY, MICHEL	76	M	UNKNOWN	GRZZZZM	D
JOSEFA	57	F	W	GRZZZZM	D
SCHUECK, AUGUST	55	M	BCHR	GRZZZZM	D
WILHME.	45	F	W	GRZZZZM	D
AUGUSTE	14	F	UNKNOWN	GRZZZZM	D
EILHELM	7	M	CHILD	GRZZZZM	D
IDA	.01	F	INFANT	GRZZZZM	D
BECKER, BERTHA	27	F	UNKNOWN	GRZZZZM	D
FRAZKA.	.11	F	INFANT	GRZZZZM	D
WINTER, WILH.	25	M	BKR	GRZZZZM	D
EMILIE	20	F	W	GRZZZZM	D
EMIL	.09	M	INFANT	GRZZZZM	D
WITTWER, AUGUSTE	29	F	UNKNOWN	GRZZZZM	D
WITOSCH, REGINE	40	F	UNKNOWN	GRZZZZM	D
MICHEL	6	M	CHILD	GRZZZZM	D
JULIANE	5	F	CHILD	GRZZZZM	D
THERESE	3	F	CHILD	GRZZZZM	D
SCHNECK, FRIEDR.	77	M	BCHR	GRZZZZM	D
WEHL, HANS	17	M	UNKNOWN	GRZZZZM	D
KOEHLER, LUISE	29	F	UNKNOWN	GRZZZZM	D
HILDEBRAND, GOTTL.	70	M	FARMER	GRZZZZM	D
KORNKE, JULIUS	22	M	TLR	GRZZZZM	D
ZIEMKE, AUGUSTE	24	F	UNKNOWN	GRZZZZM	D
KOEHLER, AUGUSTE	21	F	UNKNOWN	GRZZZZM	D
WILHME.	18	F	UNKNOWN	GRZZZZM	D
EICKE, EMILIE	60	F	UNKNOWN	GRZZZZM	D
JOHANN	23	M	LKSH	GRZZZZM	D
MATHILDE	22	F	UNKNOWN	GRZZZZM	D
SCHULZ, ROSA	35	F	UNKNOWN	GRZZZZM	D
WILHME.	8	F	CHILD	GRZZZZM	D
BERTHA	6	F	CHILD	GRZZZZM	D
SCHWARTZ, JOHANN	45	M	FARMER	GRZZZZM	D
MARIANE	12	F	CH	GRZZZZM	D
CONSTANZE	9	F	CHILD	GRZZZZM	D
STANISLAUS	8	M	CHILD	GRZZZZM	D
WLADISLAW	5	M	CHILD	GRZZZZM	D
BAHR, HEINR.	33	M	JNR	GRZZZZM	D
STUEMPEL, AUGUSTE	31	F	UNKNOWN	GRZZZZM	D
CARL	6	M	CHILD	GRZZZZM	D
JANUSZEWSKI, JOH.	57	M	CPTR	GRZZZZM	D
MINNE	47	F	W	GRZZZZM	D
FRANZISKA	7	F	CHILD	GRZZZZM	D
THEODOR	4	M	CHILD	GRZZZZM	D
KLAUSCHEWSKI, WILHME.	57	F	UNKNOWN	GRZZZZM	D
AUGUSTE	18	F	UNKNOWN	GRZZZZM	D
ANNA	16	F	UNKNOWN	GRZZZZM	D
MIGAWA, VALERIA	25	F	UNKNOWN	GRZZZZM	D
GEORG	.01	M	INFANT	GRZZZZM	D
SZYMANSKA, ANNA	22	F	UNKNOWN	GRZZZZM	D
LEMKE, HEINR.	15	M	UNKNOWN	GRZZZZM	D
ELLEHERZ, HEINR.	14	M	UNKNOWN	GRZZZZM	D
LANGOWSKA, ANNA	36	F	UNKNOWN	GRZZZZM	D
IGNATZ	8	M	CHILD	GRZZZZM	D
ELISABETH	5	F	CHILD	GRZZZZM	D
MARIA	.11	F	INFANT	GRZZZZM	D
BRONISLAWA	.01	F	INFANT	GRZZZZM	D
ROGACZEWSKI, JOSEPH	25	M	FARMER	GRZZZZM	D
TYSIONZ, FRANZKA.	33	F	UNKNOWN	GRZZZZM	D
STANISLAUS	4	M	CHILD	GRZZZZM	D
ANILLA	.01	F	INFANT	GRZZZZM	D
OSINSKA, MARGR.	22	F	UNKNOWN	GRZZZZM	D
CATHA.	.01	F	INFANT	GRZZZZM	D
ICKERT, BERTHA	37	F	UNKNOWN	GRZZZZM	D
PAUL	15	M	UNKNOWN	GRZZZZM	D
GERTRUD	10	F	CH	GRZZZZM	D
ARTHUR	8	M	CHILD	GRZZZZM	D
IDA	.01	F	INFANT	GRZZZZM	D
TYSIONZ, JOSEPH	3	M	CHILD	GRZZZZM	D
HINZ, MINNA	24	F	UNKNOWN	GRZZZZM	D
SENKBEIL, FRIEDR.	50	M	JNR	GRZZZZM	D
LUISE	49	F	W	GRZZZZM	D
ANTONIE	20	F	UNKNOWN	GRZZZZM	D
HERM.	17	M	UNKNOWN	GRZZZZM	D
ROEPKE, BERTHA	26	F	UNKNOWN	GRZZZZM	D
PAHL, BERTHA	24	F	UNKNOWN	GRZZZZM	D
STELLMASCHIN, MARIA	33	F	UNKNOWN	GRZZZZM	D
DANIEL	2	M	CHILD	GRZZZZM	D
JOHANN	.01	M	INFANT	GRZZZZM	D
KLEIN, ANNA	53	F	UNKNOWN	GRZZZZM	D
EMILIE	18	F	UNKNOWN	GRZZZZM	D
FRIEDR.	11	M	CH	GRZZZZM	D
WIEDEMANN, HERM.	18	M	FARMER	GRZZZZM	D
SZEPANSKA, ROSA	18	F	UNKNOWN	GRZZZZM	D
HOLSTEIN, GOTTLIEB	58	M	BLKSMH	GRZZZZM	D
CAROLINE	49	F	W	GRZZZZM	D
CHARLOTTE	23	F	UNKNOWN	GRZZZZM	D
AUGUST	17	M	UNKNOWN	GRZZZZM	D
GUSTAF	7	M	CHILD	GRZZZZM	D
BRUNS, JOHANN	27	M	FARMER	GRZZZZM	D
KRANSKE, MICHEL	40	M	JNR	GRZZZZM	D
CONSTANTINE	30	F	W	GRZZZZM	D
CONSTANTIN	72	M	JNR	GRZZZZM	D
HELENE	9	F	CHILD	GRZZZZM	D
MARIANE	6	F	CHILD	GRZZZZM	D
FRANZ	2	M	CHILD	GRZZZZM	D
VERONIKA	.11	F	INFANT	GRZZZZM	D
GLAESER, ALBERTINE	44	F	UNKNOWN	GRZZZZM	D
AUGUSTE	10	F	CH	GRZZZZM	D
SCHOCH, AUGUST	11	M	CH	GRZZZZM	D
KRIPPENDORF, GOTTFR.	27	M	FARMER	GRZZZZM	D
NENNEMANN, CAROLINE	44	F	UNKNOWN	GRZZZZM	D
FRANZ	17	M	UNKNOWN	GRZZZZM	D
AUGUST	10	M	CH	GRZZZZM	D
CALLIER, HERM.	16	M	UNKNOWN	GRZZZZM	D
CARL	14	M	UNKNOWN	GRZZZZM	D
MAAS, WILHME.	63	F	UNKNOWN	GRZZZZM	D
WILHELM	17	M	FUR	GRZZZZM	D
BRUNKER, WILH.	22	M	TNM	GRZZZZM	D
FEITER, AUGUST	19	F	UNKNOWN	GRZZZZM	D
HEUSMANN, AUGUST	22	M	MNR	GRZZZZM	D
LISINSKI, ANTON	18	M	FARMER	GRZZZZM	D
MUZIK, WYNCENTZ	25	M	FARMER	GRZZZZM	D
TESCHOW, FRIEDKE	18	F	UNKNOWN	GRZZZZM	D
BRUST, LUISE	23	F	UNKNOWN	GRZZZZM	D
LAU, MARTIN	34	M	FARMER	GRZZZZM	D
MARIE	34	F	W	GRZZZZM	D
AUGUST	8	M	CHILD	GRZZZZM	D
WILHME.	6	F	CHILD	GRZZZZM	D
HELENE	3	F	CHILD	GRZZZZM	D
MARTE	.10	F	INFANT	GRZZZZM	D
KLEE, BERTHA	18	F	UNKNOWN	GRZZZZM	D
SCHLENK, JOHANN	23	M	BKR	GRZZZZM	D
TANNER, HEINR.	15	M	UNKNOWN	GRZZZZM	D
WEGNER, FRIEDR.	40	M	BLKSMH	GRZZZZM	D
EMMA	37	F	W	GRZZZZM	D
EMIL	11	M	CH	GRZZZZM	D
AGATHE	9	F	CHILD	GRZZZZM	D
ANNA	3	F	CHILD	GRZZZZM	D

PASSENGER	AGE	SEX	OCCUPATION	PRVVL DES
PLOTTKE, FRANZISKA	21	F	UNKNOWN	GRZZZZMD
STIEBER, AUGUSTE	20	F	UNKNOWN	GRZZZZMD
DOPKE, AUGUST	48	M	CPTR	GRZZZZMD
ELISE	51	F	W	GRZZZZMD
AUGUSTE	15	F	UNKNOWN	GRZZZZMD
KOBERSLEIN, AUG.	47	M	BLKSMH	GRZZZZMD
EMILIE	40	F	W	GRZZZZMD
ANNA	15	F	UNKNOWN	GRZZZZMD
AUGUST	11	M	CH	GRZZZZMD
ERNST	6	M	CHILD	GRZZZZMD
ADAMOWSKY, MARIA	27	F	UNKNOWN	GRZZZZMD
LARLIZ, EMILIE	22	F	UNKNOWN	GRZZZZMD
BERGMANN, HENRIETTE	15	F	UNKNOWN	GRZZZZMD
B, CARL	25	M	FARMER	GRZZZZMD
HELINZ, CARL	34	M	FARMER	GRZZZZMD
BERTHA	31	F	W	GRZZZZMD
BERNHARD	11	M	CH	GRZZZZMD
RICHARD	8	M	CHILD	GRZZZZMD
CARL	5	M	CHILD	GRZZZZMD
ROBERT	3	M	CHILD	GRZZZZMD
MARIE	.03	F	INFANT	GRZZZZMD
KOHL, CARL	43	M	FARMER	GRZZZZMD
FROEMING, CARL	24	M	FARMER	GRZZZZMD
VOIGT, CARL	28	M	TNM	GRZZZZMD
HERM.	26	M	WCHMKR	GRZZZZMD
OLDENBURG, THERESE	23	F	UNKNOWN	GRZZZZMD
EMIL	3	M	CHILD	GRZZZZMD
SCHLINKERT, MARIE	40	F	UNKNOWN	GRZZZZMD
ELISABETH	11	F	CH	GRZZZZMD
CATHARINA	9	F	CHILD	GRZZZZMD
EMILIE	7	F	CHILD	GRZZZZMD
JOSEPH	5	M	CHILD	GRZZZZMD
ANTONIA	4	F	CHILD	GRZZZZMD
ALEX	2	M	CHILD	GRZZZZMD
ZIMMERMANN, JOHA.	24	F	UNKNOWN	GRZZZZMD
BALFANZ, AUGUST	25	M	CGRMKR	GRZZZZMD
LIPKE, ALBERTINE	26	F	UNKNOWN	GRZZZZMD
DOERING, HERM.	58	M	LABR	GRZZZZMD
FRIEDKE	45	F	W	GRZZZZMD
JOHANN	15	M	UNKNOWN	GRZZZZMD
BERTHA	13	F	CH	GRZZZZMD
STORCH, FRIEDR.	30	M	LABR	GRZZZZMD
EMILIE	36	F	W	GRZZZZMD
ALWINE	6	F	CHILD	GRZZZZMD
WILHELM	4	M	CHILD	GRZZZZMD
ANNA	.09	F	INFANT	GRZZZZMD
BUEGE, KAROLINE	24	F	UNKNOWN	GRZZZZMD
FRITZ	5	M	CHILD	GRZZZZMD
CARL	23	M	BKR	GRZZZZMD
DROYER, FRIEDKE	24	F	UNKNOWN	GRZZZZMD
WENZLAFF, FRIEDR.	50	M	LABR	GRZZZZMD
SOLTNOW, WILH.	27	M	LABR	GRZZZZMD
MARIE	26	F	W	GRZZZZMD
HERM.	3	M	CHILD	GRZZZZMD
ANNA	.02	F	INFANT	GRZZZZMD
ROLCZYNSKA, MARIANA	22	F	UNKNOWN	GRZZZZIL
DOPKE, THEODOR	16	M	UNKNOWN	GRZZZZIL
ALBERT	11	M	CH	GRZZZZIL
HERMANN	9	M	CHILD	GRZZZZIL
SCHUETH, WILH.	48	M	JNR	GRZZZZWI
ALWINE	45	F	W	GRZZZZWI
EMILIE	21	F	UNKNOWN	GRZZZZWI
HELENE	18	F	UNKNOWN	GRZZZZWI
BERTHA	16	F	UNKNOWN	GRZZZZWI
CARL	14	M	UNKNOWN	GRZZZZWI
WILH.	10	M	CH	GRZZZZWI
AUGUSTE	7	F	CHILD	GRZZZZWI
IDA	2	F	CHILD	GRZZZZWI
ELISABETH	2	F	CHILD	GRZZZZWI
MARTHA	4	F	CHILD	GRZZZZWI
LENZ, AUGUST	49	M	FARMER	GRZZZZWI
ANTONIE	45	F	W	GRZZZZWI
ANNA	21	F	UNKNOWN	GRZZZZWI
BERTHA	17	F	UNKNOWN	GRZZZZWI
MARIE	15	F	UNKNOWN	GRZZZZWI
HAINKE, ERNST	41	M	FARMER	GRZZZZIL
SCHUMAN, U	24	M	LABR	GRZZZZMI
TESKE, GOTTFR.	70	M	LABR	GRZZZZMI
SAMSEL, MICHEL	67	M	FARMER	GRZZZZTX
WILHME.	68	F	W	GRZZZZTX
ALBERT	17	M	UNKNOWN	GRZZZZTX
WEICHAILL, AUGUST	34	M	FARMER	GRZZZZTX
MINNA	31	F	W	GRZZZZTX
DD-DZUWEIT, GEORG	29	M	TLR	GRZZZZTX
ALBERTINE	23	F	W	GRZZZZTX
MARTHA	.06	F	INFANT	GRZZZZTX
KOHLS, KARL	27	M	LABR	GRZZZZIL
LEITZKE, ALBERT	24	M	LABR	GRZZZZWI
HOLZ, FERDINAND	21	M	LABR	GRZZZZNE
KOTTKE, EMILIE	24	F	UNKNOWN	GRZZZZNE
PYANS, JULIUS	29	M	FARMER	GRZZZZNE
AUGUSTE	46	F	W	GRZZZZNE
EMMA	11	F	CH	GRZZZZNE
AGNES	4	F	CHILD	GRZZZZNE
IDA	5	F	CHILD	GRZZZZNE
SCHMIDT, BARBARA	22	F	UNKNOWN	GRZZZZIA
GUSTAV	4	M	CHILD	GRZZZZIA
KRIEN, EMILIE	21	F	UNKNOWN	GRZZZZMI
NITZ, WILHME.	17	F	UNKNOWN	GRZZZZMI
PIEPER, AMANDA	21	F	UNKNOWN	GRZZZZIL
LABUDA, JULIUS	23	M	LABR	GRZZZZIL
VONNAST, JOSEPH	34	M	JNR	GRZZZZIL
WEBER, MARTIN	20	M	WVR	GRZZZZUSA
TETENS, CLAUS	22	M	FARMER	GRZZZZTX
DEMANKOWSKI, CARL	24	M	PNTR	GRZZZZMD
DRESSTER, OTTO	35	M	FARMER	GRZZZZMD
TRYCK, MICHEL	33	M	FARMER	GRZZZZMD
BUSSAIKER, FLORENTINE	62	F	UNKNOWN	GRZZZZMD
HERM.	8	M	CHILD	GRZZZZMD
BEHRENS, MINNA	24	F	UNKNOWN	GRZZZZMD
MUENCHOW, RUDOLF	26	M	FARMER	GRZZZZMD
AUGUSTE	23	F	W	GRZZZZMD
DEMELADE, MARIE	44	F	UNKNOWN	GRZZZZMD
LUISE	22	F	UNKNOWN	GRZZZZMD
ANNA	20	F	UNKNOWN	GRZZZZMD
HEINR.	2	M	CHILD	GRZZZZMD
GOHRING, ELISABETH	58	F	UNKNOWN	GRZZZZMD
MARGRETHE	35	F	W	GRZZZZMD
JACOB	3	M	CHILD	GRZZZZMD
MUNSING, SOPHIA	20	F	UNKNOWN	GRZZZZMD
RIETHEL, APOLONIA	17	F	UNKNOWN	GRZZZZMD
WIETS, CATHRINA	22	F	UNKNOWN	GRZZZZMD
ERNST	3	M	CHILD	GRZZZZMD
PETER	.09	M	INFANT	GRZZZZMD
PETER, ADAM	35	M	MLR	GRZZZZMD
HAUSERMANN, JULIE	29	F	UNKNOWN	GRZZZZMD
JULIE	7	F	CHILD	GRZZZZMD
KNICKMAYER, CARL	19	M	FARMER	GRZZZZMD
VASACK, ANTONIA	15	F	UNKNOWN	GRZZZZMD
ARENDS, ARENS	21	M	FARMER	GRZZZZMD
BUETER, CATHR.	21	F	UNKNOWN	GRZZZZMD
SCHOTT, EMIL	29	M	GDNR	GRZZZZMD
GUETLIN, CHRISTINE	30	F	UNKNOWN	GRZZZZMD
CATHARINA	9	F	CHILD	GRZZZZMD
CARL	4	M	CHILD	GRZZZZMD
GEORG	2	M	CHILD	GRZZZZMD
LUISE	.01	F	INFANT	GRZZZZMD
KLAUSCH, AGATHE	19	F	UNKNOWN	GRZZZZMD
BORANIAK, U	27	F	UNKNOWN	GRZZZZMD
AGNES	7	F	CHILD	GRZZZZMD
CATHR.	4	F	CHILD	GRZZZZMD
VALENTIN	3	M	CHILD	GRZZZZMD
STANISLAWA	.06	F	INFANT	GRZZZZMD
TOBLEWSKA, AUGUSTE	30	F	UNKNOWN	GRZZZZMD
MAX	8	M	CHILD	GRZZZZMD
MARTHA	6	F	CHILD	GRZZZZMD
WIERZCHOLSKA, FRANSKA	24	F	UNKNOWN	GRZZZZMD
VINCENT	2	M	CHILD	GRZZZZMD
JOSEFA	4	F	CHILD	GRZZZZMD
IGNATZ	.06	M	INFANT	GRZZZZMD

PASSENGER	AGE	SEX	OCCUPATION	PRVL	DES
DENTER, WILHME.	27	F	UNKNOWN	GRZZZZMD	
DAHLEM, JOHANN	17	M	BBR	GRZZZZMD	
GEUINNER, ADAM	16	M	UNKNOWN	GRZZZZMD	
WEIGANOC, MARIA	58	F	UNKNOWN	GRZZZZMD	
AUGUT	17	M	CL	GRZZZZMD	
JULIE	12	F	CH	GRZZZZMD	
FRANZ	8	M	CHILD	GRZZZZMD	
ANTON	6	M	CHILD	GRZZZZMD	
BARBARA	.09	F	INFANT	GRZZZZMD	
WITZLAR, JOHANNA	.24	F	UNKNOWN	GRZZZZMD	
PAWLAK, ANDREAS	16	M	UNKNOWN	GRZZZZMD	
WATKOWIAK, MARIANA	23	F	UNKNOWN	GRZZZZMD	
JACOB	.09	M	INFANT	GRZZZZMD	
PIOTROWSKY, GUSTAF	32	M	MSN	GRZZZZMD	
BERTHA	33	F	W	GRZZZZMD	
ARTHUR	6	M	CHILD	GRZZZZMD	
RICHARD	5	M	CHILD	GRZZZZMD	
MARTHA	3	F	CHILD	GRZZZZMD	
RUDOLF	.11	M	INFANT	GRZZZZMD	
LENDER, RUDOLF	16	M	UNKNOWN	GRZZZZMD	
SCHULZ, HEINR.	34	M	BKR	GRZZZZMD	
-ETTENHAUSEN, U	20	M	UNKNOWN	GRZZZZMD	
U, U	19	M	FARMER	GRZZZZMD	
BUNGE, U	24	F	UNKNOWN	GRZZZZMD	
U	3	F	CHILD	GRZZZZMD	
WOLF, FRIEDR.	24	M	FARMER	GRZZZZMD	
HEINRIETTE	27	F	W	GRZZZZMD	
SHYJEWSKA, AUGUSTE	34	F	UNKNOWN	GRZZZZMD	
EDWIN	3	M	CHILD	GRZZZZMD	
HESSLAN, MARGR.	66	F	UNKNOWN	GRZZZZMD	
FRIEDSAM, NETTIE	25	F	UNKNOWN	GRZZZZMD	
SCHNEIDER, CATH.	58	F	UNKNOWN	GRZZZZMD	
NEUSS, CAROLINE	19	F	UNKNOWN	GRZZZZMD	
LEIPFELD, CARL	24	M	TU	GRZZZZMD	
SCHILLER, ANNA	22	F	UNKNOWN	GRZZZZMD	
BERNAK, CAROLINE	50	F	UNKNOWN	GRZZZZMD	
EVA	10	F	CH	GRZZZZMD	
GIELOW, CARL	31	M	LKSH	GRZZZZMD	
CAROLINE	33	F	W	GRZZZZMD	
RITZ	67	M	FARMER	GRZZZZMD	
LINA	9	F	CHILD	GRZZZZMD	
FRIEDR.	6	M	CHILD	GRZZZZMD	
WILLI	5	M	CHILD	GRZZZZMD	
HEINR.	3	M	CHILD	GRZZZZMD	
AUGUSTE	.04	F	INFANT	GRZZZZMD	
TOMKIEWICZ, EMILIE	21	F	UNKNOWN	GRZZZZMD	
U	16	M	UNKNOWN	GRZZZZMD	
--YZEWSKA, U	44	F	UNKNOWN	GRZZZZMD	
U	75	F	UNKNOWN	GRZZZZMD	
U	12	U	CH	GRZZZZMD	
ANTON	11	M	CH	GRZZZZMD	
JOHANN	4	M	CHILD	GRZZZZMD	
MARTHA	3	F	CHILD	GRZZZZMD	
KASPAREK, MARIA	16	F	UNKNOWN	GRZZZZMD	
ZZEDAONSKA, MARIANA	21	F	UNKNOWN	GRZZZZMD	
DUPONT, JOHANN	40	M	FARMER	GRZZZZKS	
JOHANN	18	M	FARMER	GRZZZZKS	
ORANSKI, STEFAN	58	M	CGRMKR	GRZZZZMI	
KIERZENKOWSKI, JOH.	23	M	CGRMKR	GRZZZZIL	
GALLMANN, FRANZ	21	M	CGRMKR	GRZZZZPA	
SCHYMANEK, JOSEF	28	M	LABR	GRZZZZPA	
FRANSISKA	20	F	W	GRZZZZPA	
HERMANN	00	M	INF	GR****PA	
KRUEGER, MINNA	37	F	UNKNOWN	GRZZZZIL	
HAHLE, FRIEDR.	50	M	FARMER	GRZZZZUSA	
FRIEDKE	42	F	W	GRZZZZUSA	
CAROLINE	19	F	UNKNOWN	GRZZZZUSA	
HERMANN	15	M	UNKNOWN	GRZZZZUSA	
HEINR.	11	M	CH	GRZZZZUSA	
FRIEDR.	9	M	CHILD	GRZZZZUSA	
AUGUST	8	M	CHILD	GRZZZZUSA	
LUISE	4	F	CHILD	GRZZZZUSA	
SIEMERS, GERHD.	23	M	FARMER	GRZZZZMD	
KERSE, JOHANN	33	M	SVNT	GRZZZZPA	
BRUMER, CAROLINE	20	F	UNKNOWN	GRZZZZUNK	
LUISE	24	F	UNKNOWN	GRZZZZUNK	
CATHARINA	13	F	CH	GRZZZZUNK	
CAROLINA	10	F	CH	GRZZZZUNK	
KLUGHARD, SOPHIE	35	F	UNKNOWN	GRZZZZPA	
WERNKE, HEINR.	27	M	FARMER	GRZZZZOH	
HERMES, CAROLINE	20	F	UNKNOWN	GRZZZZOH	
OHMSTEDE, FRIEDR.	15	M	UNKNOWN	GRZZZZNE	
BUSSDECKER, CAROLINE	21	F	UNKNOWN	GRZZZZOH	
SCHWARTZ, WILH.	54	M	JNR	GRZZZZWI	
ALBERTINE	47	F	W	GRZZZZWI	
ZUEHR, FRIEDR.	12	M	CH	GRZZZZWI	
VONGARREL, GESINE	22	F	UNKNOWN	GRZZZZOH	
JOHAS, JEANNETTE	18	F	UNKNOWN	GRZZZZMD	
VOSKOWIAK, MARYANA	39	F	UNKNOWN	GRZZZZWI	
SIMON	9	M	CHILD	GRZZZZWI	
FRANZISKA	8	F	CHILD	GRZZZZWI	
ANTONIA	4	F	CHILD	GRZZZZWI	
ANTON	.03	M	INFANT	GRZZZZWI	
CATHARINA	7	F	CHILD	GRZZZZWI	
AVERBECK, JOSEPH	13	M	FARMER	GRZZZZOH	
BAREWIAK, JOHANN	35	M	TU	GRZZZZWI	
WASCHIK, ADAM	40	M	UNKNOWN	GRZZZZWI	
CATHRINA	35	F	W	GRZZZZWI	
ADOLF	15	M	CH	GRZZZZWI	
JOHANN	11	M	CH	GRZZZZWI	
ANNA	7	F	CHILD	GRZZZZWI	
OTTILIE	4	F	CHILD	GRZZZZWI	
FRIEDKE	4	F	CHILD	GRZZZZWI	
AMOR	2	M	CHILD	GRZZZZWI	
AMALIE	.09	F	INFANT	GRZZZZWI	
BRUM, JOSEF	32	M	SVNT	GRZZZZOH	
BAUMGAERTNER, MARIE	23	F	UNKNOWN	GRZZZZOH	
LUISE	.10	F	INFANT	GRZZZZOH	
SCHWARZWALD, HENNI	20	F	UNKNOWN	GRZZZZMD	
HEIM, OTTILIE	22	F	UNKNOWN	GRZZZZMD	
EDLICH, THERESE	31	F	UNKNOWN	GRZZZZMN	
AUGUSTE	9	F	CHILD	GRZZZZMN	
KRAZEWSKI, JOHANN	52	M	LABR	GRZZZZOH	
LAURA	52	F	W	GRZZZZOH	
MARTHA	11	F	CH	GRZZZZOH	
JOHAMM	17	M	UNKNOWN	GRZZZZOH	
SMITA, STEFAN	41	M	MNR	GRZZZZIL	
MATSEK, CATHR.	30	F	UNKNOWN	GRZZZZKS	
FANNY	13	F	CH	GRZZZZKS	
RAIMOND	11	M	CH	GRZZZZKS	
KRAEMER, ADAM	30	M	FARMER	GRZZZZOH	
BARGMANN, EMILIE	20	F	UNKNOWN	GRZZZZIL	
AUGATHE	18	F	UNKNOWN	GRZZZZIL	
SHULZ, HERM.	18	M	LABR	GRZZZZIL	
WERNER, MATHILDE	20	F	UNKNOWN	GRZZZZOH	
KRAZEWSKI, AUGUST	28	M	LABR	GRZZZZOH	
CAROLINE	26	F	W	GRZZZZOH	
AUGUST	.10	M	INFANT	GRZZZZOH	
BECKER, WILH.	44	M	LABR	GRZZZZMD	
HUISINGA, LINA	50	F	UNKNOWN	GRZZZZIA	
KURK, JOSEFA	33	F	UNKNOWN	GRZZZZUNK	
FRANZISKA	10	F	CH	GRZZZZUNK	
JOSEF	6	M	CHILD	GRZZZZUNK	
FRANZ	5	M	CHILD	GRZZZZUNK	
MARIANNE	.01	F	INFANT	GRZZZZUNK	
FREG, JULIANE	21	F	UNKNOWN	GRZZZZUNK	
ELISABETH	16	F	UNKNOWN	GRZZZZUNK	
SMIAKOLIEWITZ, FRZKA.	58	F	UNKNOWN	GRZZZZUNK	
CONSTANZIA	16	F	UNKNOWN	GRZZZZUNK	
GERSTLER, HULDA	22	F	UNKNOWN	GRZZZZUNK	
EMIL	15	M	UNKNOWN	GRZZZZUNK	
KATHNER, JULIA	45	F	UNKNOWN	GRZZZZUNK	
STANISLAWA	15	F	UNKNOWN	GRZZZZUNK	
JOSEPH	13	M	CH	GRZZZZUNK	
MONSTANZIA	10	F	CH	GRZZZZUNK	
PETRONELA	9	F	CHILD	GRZZZZUNK	
MARIANA	7	F	CHILD	GRZZZZUNK	
PELAGIA	5	F	CHILD	GRZZZZUNK	
SMUDZINSKA, JOSEFA	27	F	UNKNOWN	GRZZZZUNK	
STANISLAUS	.06	M	INFANT	GRZZZZUNK	

PASSENGER	AGE	SEX	OCCUPATION	PRVL	DES
REINERD, MARGR.	30	F	UNKNOWN	GRZZZZ	UNK
NICHOLS, FRIEDR.	64	M	FARMER	GRZZZZ	UNK
MARGARETHE	58	F	W	GRZZZZ	UNK
FRIEDR.	15	M	UNKNOWN	GRZZZZ	UNK
GORG, ANNA	22	F	UNKNOWN	GRZZZZ	UNK
KLUETZ, BRUNO	18	M	UNKNOWN	GRZZZZ	UNK
KIRCHHOFF, WILHME.	25	F	UNKNOWN	GRZZZZ	UNK
HOFFMANN, FRANZ	25	M	FARMER	GRZZZZ	UNK
LANANZ, HEDWIG	25	M	UNKNOWN	GRZZZZ	UNK
ZBLEWSKA, ANTONIA	12	F	CH	GRZZZZ	UNK
LINDEMANN, FRIEDR.	17	M	LABR	GRZZZZ	UNK
STANCTZKY, ALBERT	23	M	TNM	GRZZZZ	MD
SCHULZ, BERTHA	15	F	UNKNOWN	GRZZZZ	MD
AUGUSTE	15	F	UNKNOWN	GRZZZZ	MD
LEPAK, SZYMON	17	M	SDLR	GRZZZZ	MD
KLEITZ, AUGUST	23	M	SDLR	GRZZZZ	MD
PRZYBILSKA, ELZBIETA	22	F	UNKNOWN	GRZZZZ	MD
STANISLAWA	3	F	CHILD	GRZZZZ	MD
IGNATZ	.09	M	INFANT	GRZZZZ	MD
LEJA, KATARINA	25	F	UNKNOWN	GRZZZZ	MD
JOSEPH	3	M	CHILD	GRZZZZ	MD
FRANZISKA	.10	F	INFANT	GRZZZZ	MD
MALEK, ROSALIE	24	F	UNKNOWN	GRZZZZ	MD
PETER	.06	M	INFANT	GRZZZZ	MD
RIGER, JOSEPHINE	17	F	UNKNOWN	GRZZZZ	MD
SCHINBECK, JUISE	27	F	UNKNOWN	GRZZZZ	MD
MATHILDE	15	F	UNKNOWN	GRZZZZ	MD
CLARA	7	F	CHILD	GRZZZZ	MD
EDUARD	2	M	CHILD	GRZZZZ	MD
IDA	.01	F	INFANT	GRZZZZ	MD
ROSKE, BERTHA	23	F	UNKNOWN	GRZZZZ	MD
LANGOWSKI, JACOB	33	M	BCHR	GRZZZZ	MD
LANGHOFER, JOSEF	23	M	GZR	GRZZZZ	MD
LANDMANN, ELISE	60	F	UNKNOWN	GRZZZZ	OH
MARGUARDT, ELISE	12	F	CH	GRZZZZ	OH
BIER, BERTHA	33	F	UNKNOWN	GRZZZZ	MD
HOFFMANN, EMMA	8	F	CHILD	GRZZZZ	MD
MAX	5	M	CHILD	GRZZZZ	MD
KETTLER, HEINR.	19	M	FARMER	GRZZZZ	KY
HOEPKE, MARTIN	18	M	FARMER	GRZZZZ	KY
HORSTMANN, HEIRN.	18	M	FARMER	GRZZZZ	KY
KAMPELMANN, MATH.	19	M	FARMER	GRZZZZ	KY
MEIER, PAUL	19	M	FARMER	GRZZZZ	KY
STORCK, CLARA	17	F	UNKNOWN	GRZZZZ	KY
AREND, FRIEDR.	57	M	FARMER	GRZZZZ	MOB
SCHNEIDES, EIBERT	26	M	FARMER	GRZZZZ	MOB
FAHL, MARHTA	3	F	CHILD	GRZZZZ	MOB
KOLBER, BERNAT	26	M	UNKNOWN	GRZZZZ	MOB
OLISZEWSKI, PETRONELLA	40	F	UNKNOWN	GRZZZZ	MOB
STANILSAUS	12	M	CH	GRZZZZ	MOB
MARTIN	10	M	CH	GRZZZZ	MOB
CATARZYNA	6	F	CHILD	GRZZZZ	MOB
WLADISLAWA	3	F	CHILD	GRZZZZ	MOB
MIHAL	.11	M	INFANT	GRZZZZ	MOB
SLAPIKOWSKA, ANASTASA	25	F	UNKNOWN	GRZZZZ	MOB
KIBSCHOLL, CAROLINE	26	F	UNKNOWN	GRZZZZ	MOB
KRUPMANN, LEOPOLD	21	M	LABR	GRZZZZ	MOB
FAHL, WILHME.	28	F	UNKNOWN	GRZZZZ	MOB
SCHUETT, MARTIN	23	F	UNKNOWN	GRZZZZ	WI
GEORGI, IDA	20	F	UNKNOWN	GRZZZZ	MD

SHIP: STATE OF NEVADA

FROM: GLASGOW AND LARNE
TO: NEW YORK
ARRIVED: 25 OCTOBER 1888

DORNBUSCH, HERM.	30	M	FARMER	GRAHRZ	USA
FICKS, OTTO	41	M	WCHMKR	GRAHRZ	USA
HEIM, ALB.	16	M	FARMER	GRAHRZ	USA

PASSENGER	AGE	SEX	OCCUPATION	PRVL	DES
KREWZ, PAULINA	21	F	UNKNOWN	GRAHRZ	USA
MARTHA	.09	F	INFANT	GRAHRZ	USA
OTTO, JAS	22	M	SHMK	GRAHRZ	USA
MARIA	22	F	W	GRAHRZ	USA
RETTIG, ADOLINA	21	F	SVNT	GRAHRZ	USA
RATKE, LOUISA	48	F	UNKNOWN	GRAHRZ	USA
MARIA	18	F	SVNT	GRAHRZ	USA
WILL, CARL	39	M	FARMER	GRAHRZ	USA
EMILIE	39	F	UNKNOWN	GRAHRZ	USA
EMILIE	18	F	UNKNOWN	GRAHRZ	USA
AUGUST	15	M	UNKNOWN	GRAHRZ	USA
AUGUSTA	14	F	UNKNOWN	GRAHRZ	USA
WM.	10	M	CH	GRAHRZ	USA
LUDWIG	9	M	CHILD	GRAHRZ	USA
MARIA	7	F	CHILD	GRAHRZ	USA
PAULINE	3	F	CHILD	GRAHRZ	USA
GERH.	1	M	CHILD	GRAHRZ	USA
----DKE, WM.	27	M	LABR	GRAHRZ	USA
---CHOFF, U	50	F	UNKNOWN	GRAHRZ	USA

SHIP: ITALY

FROM: LIVERPOOL AND QUEENSTOWN
TO: NEW YORK
ARRIVED: 26 OCTOBER 1888

RUGEL, JAN	21	M	LABR	GRACBF	NY
LICKMER, NICHOLAS	44	M	LABR	GRAAEC	NY
WEINBERGER, SAM.	18	M	LABR	GRACBF	NY
SZ-UND, JOSEFINA	28	F	W	GRACBF	NY
U	00	F	INF	GRACBF	NY
HEAGREW, HEDAY	24	F	W	GRACBF	NY
U	00	F	INF	GRACBF	NY
PRUMER, CHAGE	23	M	LABR	GRACBF	NY

SHIP: LAHN

FROM: BREMEN AND SOUTHAMPTON
TO: NEW YORK
ARRIVED: 26 OCTOBER 1888

VONMENGERSEN, CURT	44	M	TT	GRZZZZ	GR
U	28	F	W	GRZZZZ	GR
STUTZ, RICHARD	26	M	W	GRZZZZ	GR
FUCHS, JACOB	38	M	W	GRAGBP	GR
RITTER, CARL	35	M	W	GRAIEU	GR
WOERISHOFFER, W.L.	43	M	W	GRZZZZ	GR
GOERTZ, MAX	24	M	W	GRZZZZ	GR
BARTHMANN, ALBERT	37	M	W	GRAAKH	GR
MARIE	38	F	W	GRAAKH	GR
KIEL, ERNST	17	M	W	GRAARS	GR
VONOEPEN, EMIL	18	M	LABR	GRADLE	USA
KOEHLER, MICHAEL	53	M	LLD	GRZZZZ	USA
FRIEDKE.	43	F	W	GRZZZZ	USA
ROSA	16	F	UNKNOWN	GRZZZZ	USA
IDA	7	F	CHILD	GRZZZZ	USA
SCHMIDT, KAETCHEN	24	F	LABR	GRZZZZ	USA
KUIZEK, PROKOP	37	M	FARMER	GRZZZZ	USA
MARIA	34	F	W	GRZZZZ	USA
ANTON	10	M	CH	GRZZZZ	USA
PROKOP	9	M	CHILD	GRZZZZ	USA
FRANZ	5	M	CHILD	GRZZZZ	USA
MATTHIAS	2	M	CHILD	GRZZZZ	USA
HOFMANN, CHRISTE.	25	F	UNKNOWN	GRAAKH	USA
GEDAMOWSKI, JACOB	21	M	FARMER	GRAENL	USA

PASSENGER	AGE	SEX	OCCUPATION	PRVL	DES
KOLODZIEJSKI, MARTIN	25	M	LABR	GRZZZZ	USA
MARIANNA	22	F	W	GRZZZZ	USA
WISZ, JOSEFA	17	F	UNKNOWN	GRZZZZ	USA
NIEMANN, ALBERT	24	M	LABR	GRZZZZ	USA
TIMM, BERNHARDINE	28	F	UNKNOWN	GRZZZZ	USA
BERTHA	24	F	W	GRZZZZ	USA
ALWINE	4	F	CHILD	GRZZZZ	USA
WAGNER, MATHILDE	26	F	UNKNOWN	GRZZZZ	USA
ANNA	22	F	UNKNOWN	GRZZZZ	USA
BRANDES, ANNA	17	F	UNKNOWN	GRAACK	USA
WELBROCK, META	18	F	UNKNOWN	GRZZZZ	USA
HASECKER, MATHILDE	22	F	UNKNOWN	GRAEXF	USA
TIEFJEN, DIEDR.	18	M	LABR	GRAEXF	USA
SCHUMACHER, HERM.	25	M	LABR	GRAJCS	USA
EHLING, JOHN	16	M	UNKNOWN	GRAART	USA
SHLINGPLERRER, HEINR.	17	M	UNKNOWN	GRACXH	USA
SURHOFF, ANNA	17	F	UNKNOWN	GRAEXF	USA
BUENGER, CATHA.	22	F	UNKNOWN	GRAARR	USA
MARTIN	19	M	LABR	GRAARR	USA
ENGELKE, JOHANN	16	M	LABR	GRACBO	USA
HARTJEN, ANNA	18	F	UNKNOWN	GRAELE	USA
HELFRICK, ADAM	17	M	LABR	GRZZZZ	USA
LORECK, BERTHA	30	F	UNKNOWN	GRZZZZ	USA
ZIEGLER, HERMANN	23	M	MCHT	GRZZZZ	USA
MICHEL, GEORG	25	M	SHMK	GRZZZZ	USA
ANNA	23	F	W	GRZZZZ	USA
S, HELENA	17	F	UNKNOWN	GRACVS	USA
NOTL, KPJSMM	37	M	FARMER	GRAFAY	USA
ULMER, CHRISTE.	46	F	W	GRZZZZ	USA
CHRISTE.	16	F	UNKNOWN	GRZZZZ	USA
KLOEPFER, FRIEDR.	23	M	LABR	GRADCJ	USA
WAGNER, KATHA.	29	F	UNKNOWN	GRZZZZ	USA
SCHREIBER, EDUARD	18	M	BKLYR	GRAIWH	USA
MEZGER, MICHAEL	20	M	PNTR	GRZZZZ	USA
MOLL, MICHAEL	22	M	LABR	GRZZZZ	USA
MUELLER, EMIL	17	M	MCHT	GRAEXW	USA
ANDRAE, PAULINE	16	F	UNKNOWN	GRAEXW	USA
SCHMIDT, ELISAB.	16	F	UNKNOWN	GRABUI	USA
BAUMANN, MICHAEL	29	M	FARMER	GRZZZZ	USA
HIPP, MECHTILDE	27	F	W	GRZZZZ	USA
ROMALD	.11	M	INFANT	GRZZZZ	USA
RUOFF, MARIA	17	F	UNKNOWN	GRZZZZ	USA
DOROTHEA	15	F	UNKNOWN	GRZZZZ	USA
WILHELM	9	M	CHILD	GRZZZZ	USA
FRANK, JACOB	27	M	SHMK	GRZZZZ	USA
ROEHLING, SOPHIE	2	F	CHILD	GRZZZZ	USA
ANNA	.07	F	INFANT	GRZZZZ	USA
GANZENHUBER, JUSTE.	35	F	W	GRZZZZ	USA
HUGO	16	M	UNKNOWN	GRZZZZ	USA
WILHE.	10	F	CH	GRZZZZ	USA
JOHS.	9	M	CHILD	GRZZZZ	USA
CAROLE.	6	F	CHILD	GRZZZZ	USA
FRANZ	5	M	CHILD	GRZZZZ	USA
SCHMID, JOHANNES	53	M	FARMER	GRZZZZ	USA
MAGDA.	46	F	W	GRZZZZ	USA
CHRISTN.	18	M	FARMER	GRZZZZ	USA
LOUISE	14	F	UNKNOWN	GRZZZZ	USA
HAHN, GOTTFRIED	11	M	CH	GRZZZZ	USA
KUEHN, DOROTHEA	28	F	W	GRZZZZ	USA
CHRIST.	7	M	CHILD	GRZZZZ	USA
CATHA.	2	F	CHILD	GRZZZZ	USA
FRIEDA	.06	F	INFANT	GRZZZZ	USA
LOEB, ROSINE	19	F	UNKNOWN	GRZZZZ	USA
DEISS, GOTTLIEB	18	M	LABR	GRAEOF	USA
SCHMIDT, CHRIST.	40	M	LABR	GRABOQ	USA
HEUBERGER, GEORG	22	M	BKLYR	GRZZZZ	USA
ACKER, PHILIPP	22	M	LKSH	GRZZZZ	USA
SCHUTZ, JACOB	59	F	W	GRZZZZ	USA
JOHANN	27	M	FARMER	GRZZZZ	USA
MARGA.	20	F	UNKNOWN	GRZZZZ	USA
SALOME	17	F	UNKNOWN	GRZZZZ	USA
SONNTAG, MICHAEL	16	M	UNKNOWN	GRZZZZ	USA
MARZ, JACOB	20	M	LABR	GRZZZZ	USA
LANDMANN, LINA	29	F	W	GRZZZZ	USA
MINNA	10	F	CH	GRZZZZ	USA
HERRMANN, CARL	17	M	MCHT	GRAEXW	USA
DOMMERSHAUSEN, ANNA	42	F	UNKNOWN	GRAFNK	USA
SCHWELM, ANNA	22	F	W	GRACDX	USA
ISAAK	3	M	CHILD	GRACDX	USA
LANGENFELD, FRIEDA	17	F	UNKNOWN	GRAAXF	USA
HAERING, JACOB	22	M	LABR	GRADDR	USA
STRAUSS, JOSEF	17	M	MCHT	GRZZZZ	USA
WASHEIM, MAGDA.	19	F	UNKNOWN	GRABED	USA
KAISER, PHILIPPE.	4	F	CHILD	GRABED	USA
SCHMIDT, CENCI.	22	M	LABR	GRAAAB	USA
FRANK, MARIE	20	F	UNKNOWN	GRABED	USA
KOCH, ELISABETH	34	F	W	GRACUE	USA
ELISABETH	7	F	CHILD	GRACUE	USA
SCHNEIDER, JACOB	24	M	LABR	GRACUE	USA
RENZ, JOHANNA	29	F	UNKNOWN	GRADUX	USA
REITZ, KATINKA	23	F	UNKNOWN	GRADUX	USA
KAHL, JULIANNA	21	F	UNKNOWN	GRADUX	USA
EISELE, FRITZ	30	M	LABR	GRAAGW	USA
NEBEL, MARTIN	28	M	LABR	GRZZZZ	USA
GOETZ, REGINE	19	F	UNKNOWN	GRZZZZ	USA
HILDEBRAND, EMILIE	21	F	UNKNOWN	GRADUX	USA
MINNE	24	F	UNKNOWN	GRADUX	USA
STEDE, CATHA.	18	F	UNKNOWN	GRZZZZ	USA
SCHORK, LUDW.WILH.	36	M	LABR	GRZZZZ	USA
MARGA.	29	F	W	GRZZZZ	USA
MOELLER, MINNA	16	F	UNKNOWN	GRAJTH	USA
LOH, MARIA	14	F	UNKNOWN	GRZZZZ	USA
LUDWIG, CATHA.	19	F	UNKNOWN	GRZZZZ	USA
VONNEBELL, FRANZ	9	M	CHILD	GRABOQ	USA
CHARLOTTE	6	F	CHILD	GRABOQ	USA
GAERTNER, JOSEF	24	M	LABR	GRZZZZ	USA
SPATZ, MARIE	21	F	UNKNOWN	GRZZZZ	USA
SCHULTHEISS, GEORG	33	M	LABR	GRZZZZ	USA
HEDLER, MARGE.	44	F	UNKNOWN	GRZZZZ	USA
RASCH, JOHANNE	15	F	UNKNOWN	GRZZZZ	USA
LEHMANN, BABETTE	17	F	UNKNOWN	GRAJCF	USA
ROTH, PAULINE	17	F	UNKNOWN	GRAJCF	USA
MESSNER, MARKUS	24	M	LABR	GRZZZZ	USA
MUELLER, KUNIGDE.	18	F	UNKNOWN	GRAACB	USA
WIRTH, JOHANN	15	M	UNKNOWN	GRAACB	USA
RAEBEL, JOHANNA	20	F	UNKNOWN	GRAACB	USA
BOETTGER, ANNA	21	F	UNKNOWN	GRZZZZ	USA
HEGEMANN, LOUISE	43	F	W	GRAAUF	USA
ELISE	11	F	CH	GRAAUF	USA
FRIEDA	9	F	CHILD	GRAAUF	USA
JAROSZEWSKY, JOHANN	18	M	LABR	GRADBD	USA
SCHIEN, WILHELM	18	M	LABR	GRZZZZ	USA
KUEHNEMUND, CATHA.	28	F	UNKNOWN	GRZZZZ	USA
EINSCHUETZ, FERD.	17	M	LABR	GRZZZZ	USA
KLAHRINONT, SOFIE	25	F	UNKNOWN	GRAARR	USA
GLIESE, MARTHA	22	F	UNKNOWN	GRACRC	USA
BOCK, CARL	17	M	LABR	GRZZZZ	USA
LAEDER, CARL	23	M	LABR	GRAFKX	USA
BICHLER, GOTTL.	65	M	PVTM	GRAFKX	USA
MUELLER, ELIAS	62	M	LABR	GRAARR	USA
SCHNEIDERBANGER, MARGA.	17	F	UNKNOWN	GRZZZZ	USA
LIPPMANN, ANNA	20	F	UNKNOWN	GRZZZZ	USA
KAUFMANN, THERESE	17	F	UNKNOWN	GRACQF	USA
DREHER, GEORGE	15	M	LKSH	GRAALW	USA
HASENAUER, AUG.	26	M	JNR	GRZZZZ	USA
ANNA	26	F	W	GRZZZZ	USA
ZERAHN, OTTO	24	M	LABR	GRAJMM	USA
RHEINHOLZ, ANNA	22	F	UNKNOWN	GRADXR	USA
EVERS, ANNA	16	F	UNKNOWN	GRADXR	USA
KLAWER, ANTOINETTE	15	F	UNKNOWN	GRZZZZ	USA
FISCHER, NOTHBURGA	24	F	UNKNOWN	GRAEVQ	USA
BRAUN, SOPHIE	21	F	UNKNOWN	GRZZZZ	USA
REINER, MARGE.	50	F	W	GRADEO	USA
KUCAS	14	M	CH	GRADEO	USA
HIRSCH, ROSA	16	F	UNKNOWN	GRZZZZ	USA
SEIBOLD, JOHANN	24	M	LABR	GRZZZZ	USA
RIEGER, JOSEF	30	M	LABR	GRZZZZ	USA
LAURITZEN, ANNA	20	F	UNKNOWN	GRZZZZ	USA
SCHAU, ANNA	17	F	UNKNOWN	GRABOQ	USA
KRENZ, CATHA.	26	F	UNKNOWN	GRZZZZ	USA

PASSENGER	AGE	SEX	OCCUPATION	PRVL DES
BRUHN, ALBERT	22	M	FARMER	GRZZZZUSA
RITTER, JOHA.	72	F	W	GRZZZZUSA
HEINR.	26	M	FARMER	GRZZZZUSA
WIENK, JOACHIM	35	M	LABR	GRZZZZUSA
CAROLIE.	31	F	W	GRZZZZUSA
HERMANN	6	M	CHILD	GRZZZZUSA
IDA	4	F	CHILD	GRZZZZUSA
PAUL	1	M	CHILD	GRZZZZUSA
BREE, HERMANN	22	M	LABR	GRZZZZUSA
REBLIN, WILHELM	24	M	LABR	GRZZZZUSA
BECK, HERMANN	25	M	LABR	GRZZZZUSA
MARIE	25	F	W	GRZZZZUSA
GUSTAV	3	M	CHILD	GRZZZZUSA
HERMANN	.06	M	INFANT	GRZZZZUSA
LUECHT, CARL	59	M	LABR	GRZZZZUSA
FRIEDKE.	49	F	W	GRZZZZUSA
AUGUST	23	M	LABR	GRZZZZUSA
FAUSS, JACOB	23	M	LABR	GRZZZZUSA
GABEL, ELISABETH	19	F	UNKNOWN	GRZZZZUSA
HAACK, MICHAEL	52	M	LABR	GRAIXBUSA
MARIE	23	F	W	GRAIXBUSA
STEINKE, FERDINAND	25	M	LABR	GRADNOUSA
MARIE	23	F	W	GRADNOUSA
FRITZ	4	M	CHILD	GRADNOUSA
HELENE	3	F	CHILD	GRADNOUSA
WILHELM	1	M	CHILD	GRADNOUSA
KLUESPIES, LUDWIG	25	M	LABR	GRAFNPUSA
MEZGER, JOSEF	24	M	LABR	GRZZZZUSA
MERSCHKOTTER, CLEMENS	32	M	FARMER	GRAFLSUSA
WEISS, FRANZ	26	M	FARMER	GRADLDUSA
SAUM, MARIA	19	F	UNKNOWN	GRZZZZUSA
MAZIOSEK, LOUISE	33	F	UNKNOWN	GRZZZZUSA
FLOESCHEL, GERTRUD	10	F	CH	GRZZZZUSA
ELSE	2	F	CHILD	GRZZZZUSA
BUEHLER, THERESE	19	F	UNKNOWN	GRAEOIUSA
SCHMIEDER, MARIE	20	F	UNKNOWN	GRAEOIUSA
BEDNAREK, ANNA	20	F	W	GRABMIUSA
JOSEF	16	M	UNKNOWN	GRABMIUSA
STANISLAWA	.11	F	INFANT	GRABMIUSA
SCHLEMINSKI, MARTHA	24	F	UNKNOWN	GRZZZZUSA
JENEZYK, ANDR.	36	M	LABR	GRZZZZUSA
VICTOR, GUSTAV	21	M	LABR	GRAIALUSA
STEINACKER, CATHA.	24	F	UNKNOWN	GRAEMNUSA
WAHL, MARGE.	22	F	UNKNOWN	GRAEMNUSA
GOEBEL, JOHS.	82	M	PVTM	GRZZZZUSA
KRAFT, CARL	25	M	LABR	GRACKZUSA
RAUSCHER, LORENZ	23	M	LABR	GRZZZZUSA
HAEMMER, JOHANN	23	M	LABR	GRZZZZUSA
BAYER, FRITZ	33	M	LABR	GRAHARUSA
MOLLER, ANNA	22	F	UNKNOWN	GRACBRUSA
SCHARSCHMIDT, FRITZ	13	M	CH	GRZZZZUSA
FANNY	11	F	CH	GRZZZZUSA
SCHAUM, ELISAB.	30	F	UNKNOWN	GRZZZZUSA
MAIER, MARIE	26	F	UNKNOWN	GRZZZZUSA
JOESCH, ADAM	24	M	LABR	GRADJGUSA
SCHMITTINGER, ADAM	19	M	LABR	GRADJGUSA
PUESCHZEK, SERAFIM	17	M	LABR	GRZZZZUSA
CHMUELL, ROSA	26	F	UNKNOWN	GRZZZZUSA
SCHROEDER, HEINR.	24	M	LABR	GRADWRUSA
WELLBROCK, META	17	F	UNKNOWN	GRAJCCUSA
SCHROEDER, HEINR.	16	M	LABR	GRAJCCUSA
BRUENNING, ELISAB.	17	F	UNKNOWN	GRZZZZUSA
KUNZ, WILH.	27	M	LABR	GRACEDUSA
HOORHAMMER, JULIUS	22	M	LABR	GRZZZZUSA
OTERSEN, META	18	F	UNKNOWN	GRAARRUSA
BAUER, PHILIPP	29	M	LABR	GRZZZZUSA
HELMS, GEORG	17	M	LABR	GRAHUYUSA
STRICKER, JOSEPHE.	17	F	UNKNOWN	GRZZZZUSA
SEOBERT, BARBA.	18	F	UNKNOWN	GRZZZZUSA
ZINN, OTTO	17	M	UNKNOWN	GRZZZZUSA
NODING, WILHE.	38	F	W	GRAARSUSA
ELLA	18	F	UNKNOWN	GRAARSUSA
ELISE	16	F	UNKNOWN	GRAARSUSA
GEORG	10	M	CH	GRAARSUSA
THEODOR	8	M	CHILD	GRAARSUSA
MARIE	.08	F	INFANT	GRAARSUSA
RAMPE, JUSTUS	27	M	LABR	GRAARSUSA
DIEPOLDER, ALEXIUS	23	M	BKR	GRZZZZUSA
WIEDEMANN, GEORG	37	M	LABR	GRACSHUSA
MEYER, EVA	26	F	W	GRACSHUSA
JOHANN	.06	M	INFANT	GRACSHUSA
HAEGELE, MARIA	22	F	UNKNOWN	GRZZZZUSA
HACKER, IDA	14	F	UNKNOWN	GRZZZZUSA
SCHEIBE, LINA	17	F	UNKNOWN	GRZZZZUSA
HOFMANN, FRIEDR.	65	M	LABR	GRZZZZUSA
BARBA.	17	F	UNKNOWN	GRZZZZUSA
MEIER, MARIE	40	F	W	GRZZZZUSA
CARL	10	M	CH	GRZZZZUSA
MARIE	8	F	CHILD	GRZZZZUSA
BECKER, KATHA.	25	F	UNKNOWN	GRZZZZUSA
BRZUSCIK, FRANZ	25	M	SMH	GRZZZZUSA
PAULA.	19	F	W	GRZZZZUSA
FRIEDA	.01	F	INFANT	GRZZZZUSA
PAUL	.11	M	INFANT	GRZZZZUSA
FLOCK, EDUARD	59	M	FARMER	GRZZZZUSA
LISETTE	58	F	W	GRZZZZUSA
JACOBI, KATHA.	15	F	UNKNOWN	GRZZZZUSA
HELLER, MINNA	15	F	UNKNOWN	GRZZZZUSA
ABRAMS, CHRISTE.	24	F	UNKNOWN	GRADXRUSA
MENGER, HUBERT	18	M	LABR	GRZZZZUSA
RITTER, LINA	19	F	W	GRZZZZUSA
ANNA	.11	F	INFANT	GRZZZZUSA
SELZER, LOUSE	17	F	UNKNOWN	GRZZZZUSA
DRUSE, CATHA.	32	F	UNKNOWN	GRACXDUSA
THEILMANN, ADELE	18	F	UNKNOWN	GRAEXFUSA
BANER, GEORG	16	M	UNKNOWN	GRZZZZUSA
BLASSDOERFER, CASPAR	23	M	WTR	GRADBOUSA
ADORNA, ANNA	24	F	UNKNOWN	GRADBOUSA
WILKENS, GESCHE	21	F	UNKNOWN	GRZZZZUSA
OTTERSTEDT, BERTHA	15	F	UNKNOWN	GRZZZZUSA
BORWEGEN, HEINR.	39	M	JNR	GRADIBUSA
ZURMUEHLEN, FRITZ	28	M	LABR	GRZZZZUSA
SCHMIDT, SOPHIA	21	F	UNKNOWN	GRAECRUSA
PFENNIG, FRITZ	28	M	FARMER	GRZZZZUSA
JUSTA.	28	F	W	GRZZZZUSA
FRITZ	.09	M	INFANT	GRZZZZUSA
BRONNENMAYER, WILH.	18	M	LABR	GRABVDUSA
BRENNING, VALENTIN	24	M	LABR	GRAEMYUSA
BEGEMANN, BERNHD.	19	M	LABR	GRAARRUSA
POPP, ADAM	22	M	LABR	GRAAGLUSA
SCHMUCK, AMANDA	17	F	UNKNOWN	GRABKPUSA
MOELLEUNG, CAROLA.	20	F	UNKNOWN	GRABKPUSA
SULING, DIETRICH	31	M	LABR	GRAARRUSA
KUECK, META	25	F	UNKNOWN	GRACBRUSA
HELLWEGE, FRITZ	22	M	LABR	GRACBRUSA
THOELEN, HINRICH	16	M	LABR	GRACBRUSA
STEILEN, FRIEDR.	16	M	LABR	GRACBRUSA
LIEBERTZ, CARL	16	M	LABR	GRACBRUSA
MOELLE, WILH.	23	M	MCHT	GRACBRUSA
KOENIG, FRIEDR.	38	M	FARMER	GRZZZZUSA
LLOUISE	37	F	W	GRZZZZUSA
CAROLE.	10	F	CH	GRZZZZUSA
WILHELM	4	M	CHILD	GRZZZZUSA
MARIA	.09	F	INFANT	GRZZZZUSA
SCHABLONSKI, GUSTAF	24	M	FARMER	GRZZZZUSA
KRIEGER, AUGUSTE	23	F	UNKNOWN	GRZZZZUSA
FOLKS, AUGUSTE	16	F	UNKNOWN	GRZZZZUSA
WOLSCHEN, LENA	21	F	UNKNOWN	GRACBRUSA
KREME, EDUARD	18	M	LABR	GRACBRUSA
SCHMIDT, WOLKE	21	M	LABR	GRACBRUSA
EILERS, DINA	21	F	UNKNOWN	GRACBRUSA
GUTMANN, JOHN	31	M	FARMER	GRZZZZUSA
KLUG, CAROLA.	22	F	UNKNOWN	GRABNUUSA
BEST, WILHELMINE	19	F	UNKNOWN	GRABNUUSA
EICH, GEO	25	M	LABR	GRZZZZUSA
HARSTRICH, CARL	26	M	LABR	GRABXHUSA
WOLLMANN, ALBERT	31	M	LABR	GRAJERUSA
AHRFELD, REGINE	32	F	UNKNOWN	GRABNNUSA
HOFMANN, ALBERT	16	M	UNKNOWN	GRACGGUSA
MUELLER, ANNA	20	F	UNKNOWN	GRZZZZUSA

PASSENGER	AGE	SEX	OCCUPATION	PRVL	DES
NOAK, ROBERT	23	M	GCR	GRAARRUSA	
WIDMANN, EMIL	25	M	WTR	GRADBQUSA	

SHIP: WIELAND

FROM: HAMBURG
TO: NEW YORK
ARRIVED: 26 OCTOBER 1888

PASSENGER	AGE	SEX	OCCUPATION	PRVL	DES
BAIER, EMILIE	24	F	SGL	PRZZZZUSA	
SCHMIDT, OSCAR	7	M	CHILD	PRACBFUSA	
BEHR, HERHA	36	F	SGL	PRACBFUSA	
GERKEUS, JOHANNES	22	M	MCHT	PRACBFUSA	
WUGGALZER, PAUL	26	M	SDLR	PRAGLMUSA	
KAMOSS, ERNST	59	M	LABR	PRZZZZUSA	
HENRIETTE	52	F	W	PRZZZZUSA	
MINNA	22	F	CH	PRZZZZUSA	
OTTO	15	M	CH	PRZZZZUSA	
DENUHARDT, MAX	16	M	MCHT	PRACXVUSA	
PIMBER, KATHA.	35	F	SGL	PRAEXWUSA	
GRIMM, MARGA.	56	F	WO	PRZZZZUSA	
DOROTHEA	14	F	D	PRZZZZUSA	
ZIMMERMANN, OTTOLIE	27	F	SGL	PRZZZZUSA	
GRUENWALD, HELENE	24	F	SGL	PRZZZZUSA	
TACKMANN, HEINRICH	30	M	FARMER	PRAINJUSA	
SOPHIE	31	F	W	PRAINJUSA	
ALBERT	5	M	CHILD	PRAINJUSA	
AUGUSTE	3	F	CHILD	PRAINJUSA	
HEINR.	.09	M	INFANT	PRAINJUSA	
SCHRODER, ERNA	7	F	CHILD	PRAINJUSA	
HAAS, CARL	26	M	FARMER	PRZZZZUSA	
EMMA	22	F	W	PRZZZZUSA	
STASTNY, STEPHAN	19	M	JNR	PRZZZZUSA	
JESSEN, CAROLINE	44	F	WO	PRZZZZUSA	
MARTIN	14	M	CH	PRZZZZUSA	
CARL	7	M	CHILD	PRZZZZUSA	
MATHIAS	6	M	CHILD	PRZZZZUSA	
JUGEBORG	5	F	CHILD	PRZZZZUSA	
CARLINE	4	F	CHILD	PRZZZZUSA	
WEGENER, BERTHA	17	F	SGL	PRACBFUSA	
CARDEL, LAURA	23	F	WO	PRAGOIUSA	
MUELLER, ALBERT	22	M	MSN	PRAADEUSA	
HEITMANN, HEINRICH	14	M	STDNT	PRZZZZUSA	
MEUZLER, JOHS.	45	M	SLR	PRACBFUSA	
ROZNER, MINNIE	20	F	WO	PRAAKHUSA	
WAITZ, AUGUST	21	M	FARMER	PRAADEUSA	
DUWE, MINNA	45	F	WO	PRAEZVUSA	
KILB, GEORG	28	M	BRR	PRAAXGUSA	
ZIDEK, FRANZ	24	M	LABR	PRZZZZUSA	
PLANTZ, JULIUS	23	M	LABR	PRADHJUSA	
ROESING, WILHELM	16	M	LABR	PRZZZZUSA	
KOWALEWSKY, GEORG	47	M	LABR	PRZZZZUSA	
CAROLINE	63	F	W	PRZZZZUSA	
JANAN, CHRISTIAN	27	M	LABR	PRZZZZUSA	
THON, LOUISE	62	F	WO	BWZZZZUSA	
GELLERMANN, HERRMANN	25	M	LABR	BWZZZZUSA	
KORK, LOUISE	2	F	CHILD	BWZZZZUSA	
FRAAS, JOHANN	24	M	WVR	BVZZZZUSA	
KLUG, MARTHA	17	F	SGL	MKZZZZUSA	
KLEINDIENST, JOHE.	53	F	WO	PRZZZZUSA	
BERTHA	17	F	CH	PRZZZZUSA	
WILH.	7	M	CHILD	PRZZZZUSA	
BRESEMANN, JOHA.	20	F	SGL	PRZZZZUSA	
STRUCK, KARL	16	M	SLR	PRZZZZUSA	
HAGEDORN, CHRISTIAN	52	M	FARMER	PRZZZZUSA	
JOHE.	48	F	W	PRZZZZUSA	
MARIE	19	F	CH	PRZZZZUSA	
HERM.	16	M	CH	PRZZZZUSA	
CARL	14	M	CH	PRZZZZUSA	
MINE	7	F	CHILD	PRZZZZUSA	
EMMA	1	F	CHILD	PRZZZZUSA	
MINNA	.05	F	INFANT	PRZZZZUSA	
HASHAGE, HMR.	14	M	STDNT	PRZZZZUSA	
SCHLESINGER, ELISABETH	24	F	SGL	PRABHUUSA	
HINRICHSEN, FRITZ	16	M	FARMER	PRAGFUUSA	
CLAUSEN, PETER	15	M	LABR	PRZZZZUSA	
HELENE	17	F	SGL	PRZZZZUSA	
RABINOWICZ, SARA	26	F	WO	PRAFABUSA	
MOSES	7	M	CHILD	PRAFABUSA	
MIRE	6	F	CHILD	PRAFABUSA	
PETERSEN, CHR.	37	M	FARMER	PRAGNYUSA	
FRED	32	M	FARMER	PRAGNYUSA	
SIEWERT, WILH.	18	M	LABR	PRZZZZUSA	
CHRISTIANSEN, CARL	19	M	FARMER	PRZZZZUSA	
HANSEN, DORA	19	F	SGL	PRAGNYUSA	
NISSEN, PAULINE	21	F	SGL	PRZZZZUSA	
JULIANE	22	F	SGL	PRZZZZUSA	
PETERSEN, JUNS	51	M	FARMER	PRAGNYUSA	
GUSTARSON, ANNA	22	F	WO	PRAHROUSA	
MATHILDE	3	F	CHILD	PRAHROUSA	
ANNA	.09	F	INFANT	PRAHROUSA	
HOFFMANN, DORA	17	F	SGL	PRAGNYUSA	
MUELLER, CARL	16	M	FARMER	MKZZZZUSA	
ROBERT	25	M	FARMER	PRZZZZUSA	
HERMINE	20	F	W	PRZZZZUSA	
ANNA	.11	F	INFANT	PRZZZZUSA	
ELSE	.01	F	INFANT	PRZZZZUSA	
WILHE.	50	F	WO	PRZZZZUSA	
FRITZ	16	M	S	PRZZZZUSA	
GINRICHS, IDA	45	F	WO	PRZZZZUSA	
RUDOLPH	20	M	CH	PRZZZZUSA	
AUGUSTE	18	F	CH	PRZZZZUSA	
PLATIZITZKA, AMALIE	31	F	SGL	PRACBFUSA	
TIEBER, AUGUST	23	M	LABR	PRZZZZUSA	
FOLGNER, GOTTLIEB	22	M	LABR	PRABMPUSA	
KUBANICK, WILH.	23	M	BBR	PRZZZZUSA	
SCHWENIEBART, ANNA	30	F	WO	PRZZZZUSA	
KREBS, PHILIPP	22	M	BKR	BVZZZZUSA	
SENNE, EDUARD	21	M	BKBNDR	BVACBFUSA	
STEGEMANN, THEODOR	56	M	MSN	PRZZZZUSA	
AUGUSTE	54	F	W	PRZZZZUSA	
ANNA	17	F	CH	PRZZZZUSA	
FRIEDA	14	F	CH	PRZZZZUSA	
EMMA	7	F	CHILD	PRZZZZUSA	
REBENSDORF, JOHANN	22	M	LABR	MKZZZZUSA	
FRDKE.	28	F	W	MKZZZZUSA	
ANNA	7	F	CHILD	MKZZZZUSA	
FRDKE.	6	F	CHILD	MKZZZZUSA	
HERRM.	4	M	CHILD	MKZZZZUSA	
PAUL	3	M	CHILD	MKZZZZUSA	
EMMA	.06	F	INFANT	MKZZZZUSA	
PINNA, WILHE.	64	F	WO	MKZZZZUSA	
GROTH, FRITZ	18	M	LABR	PRZZZZUSA	
BENCHEL, MARGA.	15	F	SGL	PRACXVUSA	
WILDER, MINNA	27	F	SGL	PRZZZZUSA	
MENZ, FRITZ	32	M	LABR	MKZZZZUSA	
MARIE	26	F	W	MKZZZZUSA	
HERRM.	5	M	CHILD	MKZZZZUSA	
GUSTAV	3	M	CHILD	MKZZZZUSA	
FRIEDRICH	.11	M	INFANT	MKZZZZUSA	
SCHWIEGER, CHRISTOPH	52	M	FARMER	MKAEXJUSA	
MARIA	53	F	W	MKAEXJUSA	
HENRIETTA	21	F	CH	MKAEXJUSA	
GUSTAV	16	M	CH	MKAEXJUSA	
MINNA	7	F	CHILD	MKAEXJUSA	
CHRISTOPH	.11	M	INFANT	MKAEXJUSA	
OFFT, JOHANNA	25	F	SGL	MKADOAUSA	
WEILAND, ELISABETH	63	F	UNKNOWN	MKADUXUSA	
AMBELLAN, EMILIE	18	F	SGL	PRZZZZUSA	
HEITMANN, FIRIEDRICH	51	M	LABR	PRZZZZUSA	
JOHE.	53	F	W	PRZZZZUSA	
WILH.	24	M	CH	PRZZZZUSA	
CARL	16	M	CH	PRZZZZUSA	
HOHN, JASPER	26	M	TLR	PRZZZZUSA	
MARIE	30	F	W	PRZZZZUSA	

PASSENGER	AGE	SEX	OCCUPATION	PRVL	DES
AGNES	.06	F	INFANT	PRZZZZ	USA
VOSS, WILHE.	35	F	WO	PRZZZZ	USA
ANNA	13	F	D	PRZZZZ	USA
BERNER, CARL	56	M	FARMER	PRZZZZ	USA
EMMA	18	F	CH	PRZZZZ	USA
MINNA	15	F	CH	PRZZZZ	USA
ANNA	6	F	CHILD	PRZZZZ	USA
FRIEDA	.03	F	INFANT	PRZZZZ	USA
SIEMSEN, EDMUND	19	M	LABR	PRACBF	USA
JANISCHKER, JUDEL	18	M	LABR	PRZZZZ	USA
FRIED, EPHRAIM	42	M	LABR	PRAGRA	USA
MEIROWITZ, ITZIG	19	M	LABR	PRAGRA	USA
HARDLEBEN, WILHE.	51	F	WO	PRZZZZ	USA
MARTHA	7	F	CHILD	PRZZZZ	USA
BERG, JOHE.	80	F	WO	PRZZZZ	USA
NETZBAND, CHRISTOPH	39	M	LABR	MKZZZZ	USA
LOUISE	39	F	W	MKZZZZ	USA
ALBINE	15	F	CH	MKZZZZ	USA
FRIEDA	7	F	CHILD	MKZZZZ	USA
WILH.	4	M	CHILD	MKZZZZ	USA
ROBERT	.09	M	INFANT	MKZZZZ	USA
LAARTZ, JOHANN	68	M	LABR	MKZZZZ	USA
SCHUMACHER, CARL	38	M	MSN	MKADEA	USA
JOHE.	41	F	W	MKADEA	USA
ROBERT	14	M	CH	MKADEA	USA
BERNHARD	9	M	CHILD	MKADEA	USA
OTTO	7	M	CHILD	MKADEA	USA
ALMA	7	F	CHILD	MKADEA	USA
MICHEIL, HELMUCTH	24	M	FARMER	PRZZZZ	USA
SCHULZ, BERTHA	22	F	SGL	PRABAHU	USA
LORENZ, PAUL	24	M	FARMER	PRAGOTU	USA
HEITMANN, FRIEDR.	23	M	FARMER	PRZZZZ	USA
BERTHA	22	F	W	PRZZZZ	USA
ANNA	.11	F	INFANT	PRZZZZ	USA
KLUSCHKEWITZ, BERTHA	21	F	SGL	PRZZZZ	USA
HAGEN, ERNST	31	M	GDNR	PRZZZZ	USA
WILHE.	31	F	W	PRZZZZ	USA
LAURA	7	F	CHILD	PRZZZZ	USA
HIRSCH, LOACHIM	53	M	FARMER	PRZZZZ	USA
MARIE	58	F	W	PRZZZZ	USA
FRITZ	24	M	S	PRZZZZ	USA
HONERT, WILHE.	18	F	SGL	PRZZZZ	USA
FRANK, JOH.	34	M	FARMER	PRAFKJ	USA
ZAHRTE, WILHE.	73	F	WO	PRZZZZ	USA
ALMERSKI, BERTHA	41	F	WO	PRADWZ	USA
AMALIA	7	F	CHILD	PRADWZ	USA
JOHANN	6	M	CHILD	PRADWZ	USA
SCHULTZ, MARIE	63	F	WO	PRAECTU	USA
WANDOW, LOUISE	17	F	SGL	PRAAPJU	USA
BRUENING, FRIEDA	21	F	SGL	PRADCRU	USA
BREMER, HERMANN	15	M	LABR	MKZZZZ	USA
OHNER, HEINRICH	25	M	LABR	MKZZZZ	USA
LANGNER, STANISLAWA	24	F	SGL	PRZZZZ	USA
HARTISCH, CLARA	24	F	SGL	PRAAKHU	USA
FRUEBIS, ANNA	21	F	SGL	PRADOIU	USA
RUDOLPHSON, FERD.	16	M	LABR	PRZZZZ	USA
MARIE	18	F	SGL	PRZZZZ	USA
FELLER, KUNIGUNDE	16	F	SGL	BVZZZZ	USA
BARBA.	14	F	SGL	BVZZZZ	USA
BEHL, THEODOR	14	M	LABR	BVACSX	USA
KRUEGER, AMALIE	32	F	WO	PRZZZZ	USA
HERRM.	7	M	CHILD	PRZZZZ	USA
AUGUSTE	6	F	CHILD	PRZZZZ	USA
KLOSE, GUSTAV	23	M	LKSH	PRZZZZ	USA
WALKEWITZ, RACH	22	M	LABR	PRZZZZ	USA
ZASANICZEK, MICHALINE	28	F	WO	PRAHVN	USA
STANISLAW	5	M	CHILD	PRAHVN	USA
PIOTR	3	M	CHILD	PRAHVN	USA
MUELLER, GEORG	26	M	FARMER	PRADNO	USA
SCHAEFER, ANNA	29	F	WO	PRAGCB	USA
JOH.	7	M	CHILD	PRAGCB	USA
ANNA	3	F	CHILD	PRAGCB	USA
FRIEDR.	1	M	CHILD	PRAGCB	USA
POLONOVSKA, FRANZISCA	21	F	SGL	PRAGAO	USA
AHLF, CHARLOTTE	22	F	SGL	PRZZZZ	USA
GUENTSCHE, BERNHARD	25	M	MCHT	PRAEIL	USA
SPORL, JULS.	25	M	BKR	PRADLN	USA
PETERS, HENR.	16	M	FARMER	PRZZZZ	USA
BOEHRNSEN, FRIEDR.	15	M	FARMER	PRZZZZ	USA
LEPTIN, ADOLF	37	M	FARMER	PRAGHP	USA
KEY, MINE	17	F	SGL	PRAGHP	USA
BRUNCKHORST, CATHA.	27	F	SGL	PRALZN	USA
WINDMULLER, HEIRN.	42	M	CGRMKR	PRZZZZ	USA
PAULINE	48	F	W	PRZZZZ	USA
REGINE	5	F	CHILD	PRZZZZ	USA
PRUSS, MINNA	18	F	SGL	PRZZZZ	USA
KAHL, MARTHA	15	F	SGL	HBZZZZ	USA
STEFFENS, HEINR.	16	M	FARMER	HBZZZZ	USA
KNACK, DORA	33	F	SGL	PRZZZZ	USA
HANSEN, CATHA.	32	F	WO	PRZZZZ	USA
NIELS	7	M	CHILD	PRZZZZ	USA
ELLEN	6	F	CHILD	PRZZZZ	USA
MAREN	4	F	CHILD	PRZZZZ	USA
PETER	3	M	CHILD	PRZZZZ	USA
MAREN	63	F	WO	PRAHZP	USA
MARIE	55	F	WO	PRZZZZ	USA
HAGENSEN, AUGUSTE	22	F	SGL	PRZZZZ	USA
LECHLEITNER, JOH.	30	M	MSN	MKZZZZ	USA
MOELLER, FRIEDR.	26	M	FARMER	MKZZZZ	USA
SCHULZ, PAUL	16	M	BBR	MKACSX	USA
LOWINSKI, HUGO	20	M	MCHT	MKAAKH	USA
V, PAUL	32	M	MCHT	MKAAKH	USA
FRIESKA, IDA	22	F	WO	PRZZZZ	USA
HUGO	3	M	CHILD	PRZZZZ	USA
HEDWIG	1	F	CHILD	PRZZZZ	USA
DRUCKWITZ, WILH.	47	M	WVR	PRZZZZ	USA
MARIE	15	F	W	PRZZZZ	USA
ROHN, THEODOR	22	M	BCHR	PRAAKHU	USA
SCHWARZ, HENRIETTE	21	F	SGL	PRAAKHU	USA
KRUEGER, MARIE	22	F	SGL	PRAIBZ	USA
DANIEL, ERNST	32	M	LABR	PRZZZZ	USA
CHRISTIANE	33	F	W	PRZZZZ	USA
REINHOLD	3	M	CHILD	PRZZZZ	USA
FRITZ	.11	M	INFANT	PRZZZZ	USA
ONARG, DOROTHEA	57	F	WO	PRZZZZ	USA
DOROTHEA	21	F	CH	PRZZZZ	USA
GUSTAV	7	M	CHILD	PRZZZZ	USA
DANIEL, CHRISTIANE	20	F	SGL	PRZZZZ	USA
HAUBA, JOHS.	24	M	LABR	WMZZZZ	USA
ZIMMERMANN, LINE	28	F	SGL	SYZZZZ	USA
KOTHRADE, HERRM.	23	M	MCHT	SYAARRMX	
OTTO, MARGA.	15	F	SGL	BVZZZZ	USA
CRASSER, LORENZ	23	M	LABR	BVZZZZ	USA
ZEIFF, ANTON	32	M	BKR	BVAFHG	USA
SCHLAHN, FRIEDR.	22	M	FARMER	BVAHUP	USA
ABELE, CAROLINE	21	F	SGL	BDZZZZ	USA
MOSKOWINSKA, JULIANA	36	F	WO	PRZZZZ	USA
FRANZ	7	M	CHILD	PRZZZZ	USA
CATHA.	.09	F	INFANT	PRZZZZ	USA
BEHRENS, MINNA	18	F	SGL	PRACBF	USA
STOLL, MARIA	21	F	WO	PRZZZZ	USA
ANNA	.11	F	INFANT	PRZZZZ	USA
HELMUTH	17	M	FARMER	PRZZZZ	USA
KRAFF, FLORENTINE	67	F	WO	PRAAZQ	USA
PETERSEN, EMILIE	29	F	WO	PRAAZQ	USA
RIEDEL, GUSTAV	26	M	TNM	PRACPP	USA
LANGNER, ANDREAS	23	M	LABR	PRZZZZ	USA
LAWICKA, PELAGIA	21	F	SGL	PRZZZZ	USA
KEMSIS, RUDOLF	40	M	BKR	PRACSD	USA
FREYSCHMIDT, ALFRED	42	M	UNKNOWN	PRZZZZ	USA
MEIER, ERNESTE.	66	F	WO	PRAAKHU	USA
DESCHNER, CATHA.	18	F	SGL	BVZZZZ	USA
PECH, ELISABETH	48	F	WO	BVAEABU	USA
BELCKAMP, JOHANN	45	M	LABR	BVADZO	USA
WAGGEDORF, HANS	16	M	FARMER	BVAAJY	USA
ZILLHARDT, JACOB	20	M	MCHT	BVAANGU	USA
SUNIER, AUGUST	31	M	FARMER	SRZZZZ	USA
WEBER, OTTO	18	M	PNTR	BDZZZZ	USA
SCHMID, OTTO	19	M	LABR	SRZZZZ	USA
ERNI, J.CARL	40	M	WVR	SRZZZZ	USA

PASSENGER	AGE	SEX	OCCUPATION	PRVL	DES
KONIG, LOUIS	17	M	MCHT	SRAANGUSA	
FUCHS, CONRAD	28	M	SHMK	SRADHNUSA	
WILHELMINE	25	F	W	SRADHNUSA	
FRIEDA	1	F	CHILD	SRADHNUSA	
BROGLI, JOHANN	30	M	MSN	ACZZZZUSA	
JAEGER, JULIUS	21	M	SHMK	BDZZZZUSA	
URFER, LOUISA	23	F	SGL	SRZZZZUSA	
MARTI, EDUARD	48	M	WCHMKR	SRZZZZUSA	
GLADTRE, LOUIS	40	M	MCHT	ACZZZZUSA	
BLATTNER, JACOB	48	M	CPTR	ACAHEAUSA	
ANNA	48	F	W	ACAHEAUSA	
GUSTAV	8	M	CHILD	ACAHEAUSA	
JOHANN	6	M	CHILD	ACAHEAUSA	
MEYERHAUS, PAUL	42	M	JNR	SRZZZZUSA	
VARIOLI, ANNA	23	F	SGL	SRZZZZUSA	
SEMBER, BERTHA	26	F	SGL	SRACZDUSA	
KAHN, EMIL	26	M	MCHT	SRAADEUSA	
FANNY	28	F	W	SRAADEUSA	
LIZZIE	.11	F	INFANT	SRAADEUSA	
EGGERS, EDUARD	30	M	MCHT	SRACBFUSA	
V, ALFONS	27	M	PVTM	PRZZZZUSA	
WESSELHOEFF, EDWARD	30	M	SLR	PRACBFUSA	
ZAPSS, CAROL.	65	F	WO	PRAGFJUSA	
GRUNEBAUM, HENNY	30	F	WO	PRACBFUSA	
CARRY	6	F	CHILD	PRACBFUSA	
EDGAR	5	M	CHILD	PRACBFUSA	
ANNA	4	F	CHILD	PRACBFUSA	
SCHMAHL, CHARLOTTE	29	F	SGL	PRACBFUSA	
MALEHOW, DORIS	48	F	WO	PRADCRUSA	
STERN, ROSA	32	F	WO	PRAEIOUSA	
BECK, ARWIN	7	M	CHILD	WMZZZZUSA	
PIZA, ANITA	19	F	SGL	WMACBRUSA	
UNRAN, ARTHUR	34	M	MCHT	WMACBRUSA	
WERGEN, PETER	23	M	MCHT	WMABMRUSA	
SCHMIDT, CARL	22	M	MCHT	WMACBFUSA	
BECK, HILDA	7	F	CHILD	WMZZZZUSA	
BERLING, LOUISE	41	F	WO	WMAEPZUSA	
ANNA	17	F	SGL	WMAEPZUSA	
KLOOK, HENRICH	66	M	FARMER	WMAHWXUSA	
PRAEL, HERRM.	30	M	APTC	PRZZZZUSA	
DIEHL, KATHA.	57	F	WO	PRAJAPUSA	
PFEFFERMANN, JULIE	33	F	SGL	PRAAXFUSA	
FISCHER, CARL	27	M	BRR	PRACBRUSA	
MUELLER, SALLY	48	F	WO	PRABOQUSA	
JUSTINA	18	F	SGL	PRABOQUSA	
HENNY	16	F	SGL	PRABOQUSA	
HEDWIG	13	F	SGL	PRABOQUSA	
DIEBENOW, AGNES	25	F	WO	PRAAYAUSA	
IRMA	3	F	CHILD	PRAAYAUSA	
METZGER, NATHALIE	18	F	SGL	BVZZZZUSA	
RICHARDSEN, CARL	22	M	FARMER	PRZZZZUSA	
KRAUSE, HEDWIG	26	F	SGL	PRAAKHUSA	
SCOTT, NELLY	33	F	WO	PRADXWUSA	
GEORG	7	M	CHILD	PRADXWUSA	
STADELMANN, EMILE	27	M	MCHT	PRAFZTUSA	

SHIP: DEVONIA

FROM: GLASGOW
TO: NEW YORK
ARRIVED: 29 OCTOBER 1888

PASSENGER	AGE	SEX	OCCUPATION	PRVL	DES
ESSEN, BRAN	26	F	NN	GRZZZZUSA	
EBERT, BERNHARD	24	M	BCHR	GRZZZZUSA	
WIEDENMEYER, CARL	22	M	LABR	GRZZZZUSA	

SHIP: PAVONIA

FROM: LIVERPOOL AND QUEENSTOWN
TO: BOSTON
ARRIVED: 29 OCTOBER 1888

PASSENGER	AGE	SEX	OCCUPATION	PRVL	DES
NEUMANN, CARL	18	M	LABR	GRZZZZUNK	
KREJER, FRANTZ	26	M	LABR	GRZZZZUNK	
MULLER, ALVINE	20	F	SP	GRZZZZNE	
MARIA	16	F	SP	GRZZZZNE	
KLAWITTER, AN-TA	19	F	SP	GRZZZZNE	
KARFA, GOTTL	40	M	LABR	GRZZZZIA	
FREDERIEKA	38	F	W	GRZZZZIA	
LENA	13	F	CH	GRZZZZIA	
WILHELM	11	M	CH	GRZZZZIA	
MARTA	3	F	CHILD	GRZZZZIA	
WAGELE, JOHANNA	20	F	SP	GRZZZZUNK	

SHIP: POLARIA

FROM: HAMBURG
TO: NEW YORK
ARRIVED: 29 OCTOBER 1888

PASSENGER	AGE	SEX	OCCUPATION	PRVL	DES
NOWAK, KATHARINE	18	F	SGL	GRAIHYUSA	
JANSEN, DORA	19	F	SGL	GRACBFUSA	
LUKRIZ, ERNST	63	M	FARMER	PRZZZZUSA	
AUGUSTE	55	F	W	PRZZZZUSA	
EMMA	7	F	CHILD	PRZZZZUSA	
BRZESKI, FRANZ	16	M	LABR	PRAEVMUSA	
MUELLER, WILH.	46	M	BSKM	PRAAGCUSA	
KAECHELL, GEORG	24	M	SHMK	PRACBFUSA	
WINKLER, MAX	30	M	WTR	SYZZZZUSA	
SPIEGEL, ROBERT	26	M	WVR	PRZZZZUSA	
WOLFF, LUDWIG	35	M	LKSH	PRAJATUSA	
KUSS, JOHANN	37	M	BKR	PRABZSUSA	
SELB, JOHS.	25	M	LKSH	PRAJKTUSA	
NODDELMANN, HANS	72	M	FARMER	PRZZZZUSA	
MARGA.	60	F	W	PRZZZZUSA	
JOH.	36	M	SLR	PRZZZZUSA	
GROTRIAN, RUDOLF	32	M	TCHR	PRZZZZUSA	
EMILIE	20	F	W	PRZZZZUSA	
STEINKE, GUST.	22	M	LABR	PRZZZZUSA	
MUELLER, GOTTL.	25	M	FARMER	PRZZZZUSA	
ALBERTINE	24	F	W	PRZZZZUSA	
SPIKER, AUGUST	29	M	FARMER	PRZZZZUSA	
JOHANNA	35	F	W	PRZZZZUSA	
THEODOR	6	M	CHILD	PRZZZZUSA	
FRANZ	4	M	CHILD	PRZZZZUSA	
BOESEL, MARIA	23	F	SGL	PRZZZZUSA	
STEINHAUER, JOHANNA	23	F	SGL	PRZZZZUSA	
VIEK, HERM.	25	M	LABR	PRZZZZUSA	
BUZIER, HEINR.	36	M	FARMER	PRZZZZUSA	
WILHELMINE	32	F	W	PRZZZZUSA	
ALBERT	7	M	CHILD	PRZZZZUSA	
AUGUSTE	6	F	CHILD	PRZZZZUSA	
FRIEDRICH	5	M	CHILD	PRZZZZUSA	
LOUISE	4	F	CHILD	PRZZZZUSA	
HERMANN	3	M	CHILD	PRZZZZUSA	
ANNA	.11	F	INFANT	PRZZZZUSA	
STIETZEL, ANDREAS	36	M	LABR	PRZZZZUSA	
GERST, LOUISE	24	F	SGL	HSZZZZUSA	
TOGGOW, HEINR.	54	M	LABR	HSAJQLUSA	
MARIE	56	F	W	HSAJQLUSA	
HEINR.	17	M	CH	HSAJQLUSA	
ANNA	14	F	CH	HSAJQLUSA	
MARIE	7	F	CHILD	HSAJQLUSA	
JEDNIG, HERM.	24	M	BKBNDR	HSABIYUSA	
KIRCHHOFF, EMILIE	24	F	SGL	HSAHINUSA	

PASSENGER	AGE	SEX	OCCUPATION	PVRIVLES	PASSENGER	AGE	SEX	OCCUPATION	PVRIVLES
WILKE, AUGUST	28	M	SHFM	PRZZZZUSA	BOESEL, CAROLINE	20	F	SGL	PRZZZZUSA
BRANER, AUGUST	16	M	LABR	PRZZZZUSA	FRDKE	48	F	WO	PRZZZZUSA
LUETTJOHANN, EMMA	17	F	SGL	PRADOAUSA	PRESKERN, ELISB.	18	F	SGL	PRAIBQUSA
PETERSEN, ANDREAE	28	F	WO	PRZZZZUSA	FLESCHING, HUGO	34	M	SDLR	PRABDMUSA
CHRISTINE	7	F	CHILD	PRZZZZUSA	MUELLER, CARL	28	M	FARMER	PRAFAQUSA
OLENE	5	F	CHILD	PRZZZZUSA	WILHELMINE	31	F	W	PRAFAQUSA
HANS	.05	M	INFANT	PRZZZZUSA	HERM.	5	M	CHILD	PRAFAQUSA
GERIGK, ROSA	28	F	SGL	PRAAKHUSA	IDA	2	F	CHILD	PRAFAQUSA
JOENSEN, PETER	37	M	FARMER	PRZZZZUSA	MARTHA	.06	F	INFANT	PRAFAQUSA
MINA	27	F	W	PRZZZZUSA	REITZ, ANNA	7	F	CHILD	PRAFAQUSA
JOHS	22	M	FARMER	PRZZZZUSA	HOFFMANN, ADOLF	25	M	TLR	PRZZZZUSA
REIS, GEO.	65	M	LABR	PRZZZZUSA	HERBST, CARL	30	M	SHMK	PRZZZZUSA
GYDULE	45	F	W	PRZZZZUSA	EMILIE	28	F	W	PRZZZZUSA
ANDR.	7	M	CHILD	PRZZZZUSA	MARGOWSKY, JOHANNA	48	F	WO	PRZZZZUSA
ANNA	6	F	CHILD	PRZZZZUSA	MARIE	7	F	CHILD	PRZZZZUSA
GUTONIE	5	F	CHILD	PRZZZZUSA	GEORG	6	M	CHILD	PRZZZZUSA
SCHWAB, CARL	16	M	LABR	PRZZZZUSA	HUGO	5	M	CHILD	PRZZZZUSA
JOZWIAK, ILZBITA	27	F	WO	PRAHWVUSA	JACOBY, PHILIP	17	M	UNKNOWN	PRZZZZUSA
CATH.	6	F	CHILD	PRAHWVUSA	LANE, HUGO	18	M	MCHT	PRZZZZUSA
MARG.	1	F	CHILD	PRAHWVUSA	SCHLEMER, CONRAD	46	M	TLR	PRZZZZUSA
KOPELSKI, FRANZ	24	M	LABR	PRAJFMUSA	ANNA	22	F	W	PRZZZZUSA
FUSCHS, BERTHA	17	F	SGL	PRABAVUSA	CATHE.	15	F	CH	PRZZZZUSA
FRANZISCA	12	F	S	PRABAVUSA	MINNA	7	F	CHILD	PRZZZZUSA
KNUDER, GUST.	24	M	LABR	PRAJNFUSA	LEA	5	F	CHILD	PRZZZZUSA
WILHE.	24	F	W	PRAJNFUSA	MAIROOSKY, LEO	23	M	LABR	PRAAKHUSA
AMANDA	13	F	CH	PRAJNFUSA	NOUN, JULIE	49	F	WO	PRAAKHUSA
ROBERT	7	M	CHILD	PRAJNFUSA	CLARA	23	F	D	PRAAKHUSA
ANNA	6	F	CHILD	PRAJNFUSA	JOHANNA	16	F	D	PRAAKHUSA
BERTHA	5	F	CHILD	PRAJNFUSA	GUINAND, HEINR.	47	M	LABR	PRALZCUSA
ALBERT	3	M	CHILD	PRAJNFUSA	SCHMIDT, ALESANDRE	23	M	JNR	PRAARZUSA
MARTHA	.06	F	INFANT	PRAJNFUSA	NAWRODT, ANTON	23	M	PNTR	PRAARZUSA
RUNZEL, WILH.	66	M	LABR	PRZZZZUSA	MENDELSOHN, MORITZ	15	M	CL	PRAAKHUSA
WILHE.	58	F	W	PRZZZZUSA	BARTH, AUGUSTE	24	F	SGL	PRZZZZUSA
FRIEDR.	19	M	S	PRZZZZUSA	HOPP, FRITZ	17	M	LABR	PRAGFUUSA
BYHAHN, KARL	21	M	CHMKR	SYZZZZUSA	MILDNER, HERM.	25	M	TKR	PRABVEUSA
BEIER, PETER	18	M	FARMER	PRZZZZUSA	RAMTHAM, GUST.	24	M	FARMER	PRAHLPUSA
PAULSEN, ANNA	30	F	WO	PRZZZZUSA	HENTIETTE	16	F	SGL	PRAHLPUSA
ANDERS	3	M	CHILD	PRZZZZUSA	HOHL, JOHANN	34	M	BLKSMH	SRZZZZUSA
ANNE	.06	F	INFANT	PRZZZZUSA	FLECHL, RICHARD	22	M	MLR	SYZZZZUSA
STORGARD, KIRSTEN	60	F	WO	PRZZZZUSA	GUINAND, AMALIE	49	F	W	PRZZZZUSA
HANSEN, JORGEN	44	M	FARMER	PRZZZZUSA	ERNST	7	M	CHILD	PRZZZZUSA
FREDERIKSEN, JORGEN	22	M	FARMER	PRZZZZUSA	BERTHA	6	F	CHILD	PRZZZZUSA
DOMINICUSSEN, CHRISTINE	38	F	SGL	PRZZZZUSA	CARL	6	M	CHILD	PRZZZZUSA
LINDSTROEM, CARL	7	M	CHILD	PRABZSUSA	AGNES	3	F	CHILD	PRZZZZUSA
LAMTER, ANNA	27	F	SGL	PRZZZZUSA	GUENKOWSKY, CAROLINE	39	F	WO	PRAAIXUSA
REYGELIN, ANNA	21	F	SGL	PRZZZZUSA	MOHR, CARL	23	M	FARMER	PRZZZZUSA
HANSEN, HEINR.	18	M	CPTR	PRACKYUSA	MOSES, GEORG	18	M	MCHT	PRAARZUSA
REYGELIN, SABINE	25	F	WO	PRZZZZUSA	GOOATSKA, ANTONIE	40	F	W	PRACMHUSA
ANDREA	3	F	CHILD	PRZZZZUSA	JULIANE	7	F	CHILD	PRACMHUSA
JACOB	.11	M	INFANT	PRZZZZUSA	THERESE	6	F	CHILD	PRACMHUSA
KUEHL, ANGELUS	22	M	BKR	PRAESDUSA	EDMUND	5	M	CHILD	PRACMHUSA
REINBERGER, MARTHA	26	M	SGL	PRAARZUSA	STANISLAUS	3	M	CHILD	PRACMHUSA
JESCHEWSKA, MARIE	23	F	SGL	PRAEXKUSA	STANISLAWA	.11	F	INFANT	PRACMHUSA
TEICH, LUDW.	55	M	JNR	PRADCWUSA	WLADISLAW	.01	M	INFANT	PRACMHUSA
LUEDER, HEINR.	51	M	UNKNOWN	PRZZZZUSA	DEMMEL, KATHA.	60	F	W	PRZZZZUSA
MARIE	43	F	W	PRZZZZUSA	MIZISLAW	.11	M	INFANT	PRZZZZUSA
EMMA	21	F	CH	PRZZZZUSA	JABLONSKY, MARG.	43	F	W	PRZZZZUSA
HEINR.	18	M	CH	PRZZZZUSA	ANASTASIA	7	F	CHILD	PRZZZZUSA
BERTHA	15	F	CH	PRZZZZUSA	MIHAL	6	M	CHILD	PRZZZZUSA
AUGUST	7	M	CHILD	PRZZZZUSA	FRANZISKA	3	F	CHILD	PRZZZZUSA
FRIEDR.	6	M	CHILD	PRZZZZUSA	WITUKA, JOSEFA	27	F	W	PRZZZZUSA
CARL	5	M	CHILD	PRZZZZUSA	HELENE	18	F	CH	PRZZZZUSA
SCHALT, ANNA	25	F	SGL	PRZZZZUSA	MARIANNE	2	F	CHILD	PRZZZZUSA
RYDTA, LUCIE	19	F	SGL	PRAJFMUSA	STANISLAWA	.11	F	INFANT	PRZZZZUSA
SCHLIE, CHRISTIAN	26	M	FARMER	PRZZZZUSA	LORENZ, JOHANN	24	M	LABR	PRZZZZUSA
MUSSEHL, ANNA	26	F	WO	PRZZZZUSA	WISSMACH, HUGA	26	M	CGRMKR	PRAARZUSA
HEINR.	5	M	CHILD	PRZZZZUSA	POSEROWSKY, GUST.	28	M	MCHT	PRACSXUSA
EMMA	4	F	CHILD	PRZZZZUSA	HERKE, PAUL	17	M	MCHT	PRAAKHUSA
KUEGLER, ERNST	45	M	FARMER	PRZZZZUSA	DERKIEWIEZ, ROSALIE	38	F	W	PRZZZZUSA
SCHUBRENY, JULIUS	23	M	BKLYR	PRZZZZUSA	ANNA	17	F	SGL	PRZZZZUSA
STARKE, ALEXANDER	28	M	MCHT	PRZZZZUSA	MARIE	30	F	W	PRZZZZUSA
STELLING, HELENE	21	F	SGL	PRAAUIUSA	MUNDT, FRANZ	25	M	LABR	PRZZZZUSA
BERTHA	7	F	CHILD	PRAAUIUSA	KRAUSE, HERM.	24	M	LABR	PRZZZZUSA
KATTERMANN, HERM.	41	M	WVR	PRABOKUSA	KROLL, WILHLEMINE	57	F	WO	PRZZZZUSA
STEPKAN, EMIL	20	M	LABR	SYZZZZUSA	ANNA	10	F	CH	PRZZZZUSA

PASSENGER	AGE	SEX	OCCUPATION	PRIVL	DES	PASSENGER	AGE	SEX	OCCUPATION	PRIVL	DES
MARIE	7	F	CHILD	PRZZZZ	USA	KRENZ, EMILIE	28	M	LABR	GRZZZZ	UNK
SIEMSEN, CATHA.	26	F	W	PRADAA	USA	FALK, MARTHA	31	F	NN	GRZZZZ	UNK
CATHA.	7	F	CHILD	PRADAA	USA	AGNES	.10	F	INFANT	GRZZZZ	UNK
WILHELM	4	M	CHILD	PRADAA	USA	WADZINSKA, MARYANNA	37	F	NN	GRZZZZ	UNK
FRIDA	2	F	CHILD	PRADAA	USA	FRANZ	11	M	CH	GRZZZZ	UNK
BETHKE, AMALIE	24	F	SGL	PRADAA	USA	JOSEF	7	M	CHILD	GRZZZZ	UNK
						ROSALIE	5	F	CHILD	GRZZZZ	UNK
						KASIMIR	3	M	CHILD	GRZZZZ	UNK
						WLADISL	.11	M	INFANT	GRZZZZ	UNK
						KAMMINSKI, OSARI	33	F	NN	GRZZZZ	UNK
SHIP: MICHIGAN						JERSCHKE, JULIANE	32	F	NN	GRZZZZ	UNK
						BUSE, FRIEDR	33	M	LABR	GRZZZZ	UNK
FROM: LIVERPOOL						CAROLINE	32	F	W	GRZZZZ	UNK
TO: BOSTON						WILHELMINE	12	F	CH	GRZZZZ	UNK
ARRIVED: 30 OCTOBER 1888						CARL	10	M	CH	GRZZZZ	UNK
						JOHANNE	7	F	CHILD	GRZZZZ	UNK
						MARIE	6	F	CHILD	GRZZZZ	UNK
						ALWINE	3	F	CHILD	GRZZZZ	UNK
CZERFUS, CHAZI	28	M	TLR	GRZZZZ	USA	IDA	.11	F	INFANT	GRZZZZ	UNK
MITLER, SAMUEL	18	M	TLR	GRZZZZ	USA	A--E, CARL	63	M	LABR	GRZZZZ	UNK
MENDELES, JACOB	25	M	TLR	GRZZZZ	USA	LEWANDOWSKA, KATARINA	19	F	NN	GRZZZZ	UNK
DAVIDOVITCH, HERMAN	20	M	CL	GRZZZZ	USA	RANER, JOSEPH	38	M	TLR	GRZZZZ	UNK
HARRIS, ABRAHAM	27	M	TLR	GRZZZZ	USA	PAULINA	44	F	W	GRZZZZ	UNK
RUBIN, ABRAHAM	22	M	TLR	GRZZZZ	USA	ANNA	18	F	CK	GRZZZZ	UNK
FERRINS, ABRAHAM	24	M	TT	GRZZZZ	USA	KRUEGER, WILHE	60	F	NN	GRZZZZ	UNK
RUPERSTREK, SOLOMON	20	M	TLR	GRZZZZ	USA	AUGUST	38	M	FARMER	GRZZZZ	UNK
ZEPKAUSES, M.	25	M	TLR	GRZZZZ	USA	BERTHA	27	F	NN	GRZZZZ	UNK
JANKANISKA, U	24	M	TLR	GRZZZZ	USA	AUGE	24	F	NN	GRZZZZ	UNK
FRITZ, MOSES	17	M	TLR	GRZZZZ	USA	FRITZ	4	M	CHILD	GRZZZZ	UNK
SAUDLER, ABRAM	18	M	TLR	GRZZZZ	USA	MALKE	23	M	FARMER	GRZZZZ	UNK
SALMANOWITZ, MENDEL	17	M	TLR	GRZZZZ	USA	FRITZ, EMIL	16	M	FARMER	GRZZZZ	UNK
OLSHUNTZKUZ, BORIS	26	M	TLR	GRZZZZ	USA	SPIEWAK, ANTONIA	17	F	NN	GRZZZZ	UNK
PORTLASHROK, ISAAC	19	M	TLR	GRZZZZ	USA	KIND, WILHE	53	F	NN	GRZZZZ	UNK
WEZANSKY, BOB	24	M	SHMK	GRZZZZ	USA	JULIE	17	F	NN	GRZZZZ	UNK
ZIMMERMAN, ALTE	15	F	SP	GRZZZZ	USA	REICH, FRIEDR	16	M	HTR	GRZZZZ	UNK
KRAJEWSKY, ALTE	18	F	SP	GRZZZZ	USA	AUGE	9	F	CHILD	GRZZZZ	UNK
WEIN, KULE	20	F	SP	GRZZZZ	USA	BETHKE, BERNHARD	19	M	LABR	GRZZZZ	UNK
GWEMOSS, FEIGE	18	F	SP	GRZZZZ	USA	KORTHALS, EDUARD	23	M	BKR	GRZZZZ	UNK
ZIMMERMAN, CHAJE	40	F	W	GRZZZZ	USA	BERGER, HEDWIG	19	F	NN	GRZZZZ	UNK
BIALS, MICHAEL	47	M	SHMK	GRZZZZ	USA	KREBS, ANNA	24	F	NN	GRZZZZ	UNK
ANNA	46	F	W	GRZZZZ	USA	EDMUND	2	M	CHILD	GRZZZZ	UNK
KOTOWSKY, BUSCHE	40	F	W	GRZZZZ	USA	JANKOWSKA, JOSEFA	23	F	NN	GRZZZZ	UNK
KASCHDAN, ZUETE	23	F	W	GRZZZZ	USA	LOCHERBACH, JOSEPH	28	M	BCHR	GRZZZZ	UNK
BIALO, ALBERT	6	M	CHILD	GRZZZZ	USA	AUGUSTE	31	F	W	GRZZZZ	UNK
MARIA	4	F	CHILD	GRZZZZ	USA	OTTO	.11	M	INFANT	GRZZZZ	UNK
FRED	.09	M	INFANT	GRZZZZ	USA	BERK, ELISABETH	60	F	NN	GRZZZZ	UNK
WELENSKY, J.	.09	M	INFANT	GRZZZZ	USA	CARL	15	M	NN	GRZZZZ	UNK
KOTOWSKY, RUBIN	10	M	CH	GRZZZZ	USA	NEHLS, HERMANN	30	M	FARMER	GRZZZZ	UNK
SIMON	8	M	CHILD	GRZZZZ	USA	FRIEDERIKE	32	F	W	GRZZZZ	UNK
DWORA	6	F	CHILD	GRZZZZ	USA	GUSTAV	7	M	CHILD	GRZZZZ	UNK
SARAH	3	F	CHILD	GRZZZZ	USA	WILHELM	6	M	CHILD	GRZZZZ	UNK
KASCHDAN, ROSE	.08	F	INFANT	GRZZZZ	USA	OTTO	5	M	CHILD	GRZZZZ	UNK
						HERMANN	3	M	CHILD	GRZZZZ	UNK
						HERMINE	.06	F	INFANT	GRZZZZ	UNK
						KUNKEL, AUGUEST	24	F	CK	GRZZZZ	UNK
						KRIEG, EMILIE	25	F	CK	GRZZZZ	UNK
						RINDT, EMILIE	23	F	NN	GRZZZZ	UNK
SHIP: RHEIN						GUSTAV	2	M	CHILD	GRZZZZ	UNK
						TANDIEN, ERNST	12	M	TNM	GRZZZZ	UNK
FROM: BREMEN						MAESS, HERM	42	M	FARMER	GRZZZZ	UNK
TO: BALTIMORE						EMILIE	36	F	W	GRZZZZ	UNK
ARRIVED: 30 OCTOBER 1888						WILHELM	16	M	FARMER	GRZZZZ	UNK
						ANNA	4	F	CHILD	GRZZZZ	UNK
						MARIA	.11	F	INFANT	GRZZZZ	UNK
GROSCHEN, LISBETH	22	F	NN	GRZZZZ	UNK	B-RSS, MARTHA	22	F	NN	GRZZZZ	UNK
SCHULZ, RUDOLF	27	M	FARMER	GRZZZZ	UNK	LISMANN, ANNA	16	F	NN	GRZZZZ	UNK
MAN, JOHANN	31	M	FARMER	GRZZZZ	UNK	BAUMANN, MARIE	16	F	NN	GRZZZZ	UNK
MARIA	34	F	W	GRZZZZ	UNK	CAROLINE	33	F	NN	GRZZZZ	UNK
MINNA	14	F	CH	GRZZZZ	UNK	ROSMANN, ROSALIE	23	F	NN	GRZZZZ	UNK
JOHANNA	9	F	CHILD	GRZZZZ	UNK	MOSES	2	M	CHILD	GRZZZZ	UNK
AUGUSTE	6	F	CHILD	GRZZZZ	UNK	MORITZ	.11	M	INFANT	GRZZZZ	UNK
BONK, HEDWIG	20	F	CK	GRZZZZ	UNK	SCHMIDT, IDA	20	F	SVNT	GRZZZZ	UNK
SKONETZKI, ANNA	16	F	NN	GRZZZZ	UNK	W-TKI, EMILIE	18	F	SVNT	GRZZZZ	UNK
THIM, JULIANNA	31	F	NN	GRZZZZ	UNK	BASKE, BERTHA	31	F	NN	GRZZZZ	UNK
CHIKOWSKI, JOS	28	M	LABR	GRZZZZ	UNK	PAULINA	19	F	NN	GRZZZZ	UNK

PASSENGER	AGE	SEX	OCCUPATION	PRVVL DES	PASSENGER	AGE	SEX	OCCUPATION	PRVVL DES
LOSSMANN, THEODOR	31	M	FARMER	GRZZZZUNK	KLARA	13	F	CH	GRZZZZUNK
HERMINE	33	F	W	GRZZZZUNK	KASIMIR	10	M	CH	GRZZZZUNK
ANNA	7	F	CHILD	GRZZZZUNK	BROMISLAWA	9	F	CHILD	GRZZZZUNK
MARTHA	6	F	CHILD	GRZZZZUNK	ALEXANDRA	2	F	CHILD	GRZZZZUNK
MAX	3	M	CHILD	GRZZZZUNK	JOHANN	6	M	CHILD	GRZZZZUNK
EMMA	.04	F	INFANT	GRZZZZUNK	SHULTZ, THERSESIA	23	F	NN	GRZZZZUNK
FREESE, JOHANNES	66	M	FARMER	GRZZZZUNK	ABEL, DAVID	23	M	BCHR	GRZZZZUNK
BASKE, HERTHA	6	F	CHILD	GRZZZZMI	BELMAN, MART	16	M	FARMER	GRZZZZUNK
KURSZEWSKI, JOSEF	29	M	LABR	GRZZZZUNK	RELLERMANN, KATHA	25	F	NN	GRZZZZUNK
EVA	25	F	W	GRZZZZUNK	WIESSE, GERDJE	23	F	NN	GRZZZZUNK
JOSEF	.11	M	INFANT	GRZZZZUNK	GERHT	.09	M	INFANT	GRZZZZUNK
LORWEIN, GEORG	18	M	MCHT	GRZZZZUNK	KOHLER, JOSEPHINE	19	F	NN	GRZZZZUNK
BAATZ, HERMAN	17	M	LABR	GRZZZZUNK	JACOB, LOUISE	44	F	NN	GRZZZZUNK
GOLDMANN, H	35	M	FARMER	GRZZZZUNK	JAKOB	12	M	CH	GRZZZZUNK
VOIGT, CARL	23	M	FARMER	GRZZZZUNK	CAROLINE	7	F	CHILD	GRZZZZUNK
POTTER, AUGUST	23	M	TLR	GRZZZZUNK	GEIER, WILH	25	M	FARMER	GRZZZZUNK
KARUPKA, CATHA	40	F	NN	GRZZZZUNK	LOUISE	15	F	NN	GRZZZZUNK
JOSEPH	9	M	CHILD	GRZZZZUNK	LORENZ, PHILIPP	58	M	TNR	GRZZZZUNK
PAUL--	6	M	CHILD	GRZZZZUNK	LAFFERE, KARL	63	M	LABR	GRZZZZUNK
STANISL	2	M	CHILD	GRZZZZUNK	SHULMANN, JOHANNA	21	F	NN	GRZZZZUNK
WLADISLAWA	.09	F	INFANT	GRZZZZUNK	GARRELS, HINR	21	M	TU	GRZZZZUNK
KOEHLER, WILH	16	M	LABR	GRZZZZUNK	MODETZKA, MARIANNA	57	F	NN	GRZZZZUNK
EMILIE	19	F	NN	GRZZZZUNK	KOEFER, ELISE	38	F	NN	GRZZZZUNK
BERTHA	17	F	NN	GRZZZZUNK	SIEGFRIED	4	M	CHILD	GRZZZZUNK
MEINHARDT, WILH	24	M	CCHMN	GRZZZZUNK	STEMPENYAK, LUEZIA	43	F	NN	GRZZZZUNK
EMILIE	24	F	W	GRZZZZUNK	JOSEPH	11	M	CH	GRZZZZUNK
URBACH, WILHE	57	F	NN	GRZZZZUNK	VINCENY	9	F	CHILD	GRZZZZUNK
AMANDA	15	F	NN	GRZZZZUNK	LUDWIG	7	M	CHILD	GRZZZZUNK
GRETHA	16	F	NN	GRZZZZUNK	STANISLAW	5	M	CHILD	GRZZZZUNK
SEMER, EMIL	25	M	TNR	GRZZZZUNK	DEHMER, ANNA	23	F	NN	GRZZZZUNK
ROCKAHR, FERIN	40	M	TLR	GRZZZZMI	NIETZSCH, MINNA	19	F	NN	GRZZZZUNK
SOPHIE	53	F	NN	GRZZZZMI	STOLL, JOSEPH	37	M	FARMER	GRZZZZKY
BRANDT, HERM	23	M	LABR	GRZZZZMI	LOUISE	36	F	W	GRZZZZKY
RUDOLF	14	M	CH	GRZZZZMI	JULCHEN	11	F	CH	GRZZZZKY
ROCKAHR, HERMINE	15	F	CH	GRZZZZMI	LUISE	10	F	CH	GRZZZZKY
AUGUSTE	14	F	CH	GRZZZZMI	KARL	.11	M	INFANT	GRZZZZKY
LOUISE	11	F	CH	GRZZZZMI	HERBOERT, ANNA	14	F	CH	GRZZZZIL
KLEINSCHMIDT, FRIEDR	23	M	FARMER	GRZZZZWI	RIEGER, JOH	25	M	FARMER	GRZZZZIL
BERTHA	23	F	W	GRZZZZWI	EIFF, CHRISTOFF	49	M	FARMER	GRZZZZNE
BAUMANN, AUGUSTE	21	F	NN	GRZZZZWI	MUELLER, HEINRICH	46	M	FARMER	GRZZZZNE
LINDERMANN, EWALD	17	M	HTR	GRZZZZUNK	CATHARINA	36	F	W	GRZZZZNE
ROHL, CARL	58	M	FARMER	GRZZZZWI	ELISABETH	16	F	NN	GRZZZZNE
CHRISTINE	52	F	W	GRZZZZWI	GEORG	13	M	CH	GRZZZZNE
ROEHL, ANNA	23	F	NN	GRZZZZWI	CATHARINA	9	F	CHILD	GRZZZZNE
BERTHA	17	F	NN	GRZZZZWI	HEINRICH	7	M	CHILD	GRZZZZNE
ERNESTINE	14	F	NN	GRZZZZWI	SEITZ, CATHARINA	43	F	NN	GRZZZZUNK
CARL	11	M	CH	GRZZZZWI	JOHANN	9	M	CHILD	GRZZZZUNK
AUGUSTE	9	F	CHILD	GRZZZZWI	CHRISTIANA	5	F	CHILD	GRZZZZUNK
BARTELT, FRIEDR	24	M	LABR	GRZZZZWI	SGL	.09	F	INFANT	GRZZZZUNK
STOUCK, CARL	27	M	LABR	GRZZZZDAK	RUSS, KUNIGMUDE	56	M	NN	GRZZZZUNK
EMILIE	24	F	W	GRZZZZDAK	DUMLER, MARIA	48	M	NN	GRZZZZUNK
EMMA	4	F	CHILD	GRZZZZDAK	GEORG	16	M	BKR	GRZZZZUNK
WITTENHAGEN, ERNST	30	M	LABR	GRZZZZDAK	ROSENBUSCH, MARGA	19	F	NN	GRZZZZUNK
ALBERTINE	26	F	W	GRZZZZDAK	FRIEDMANN, MARGA	16	F	NN	GRZZZZUNK
WILHE	4	F	CHILD	GRZZZZDAK	ZWOSTA, KUNIGMUND	27	F	NN	GRZZZZUNK
HERMANN	2	M	CHILD	GRZZZZDAK	BAWRLEIN, MICH	29	M	TU	GRZZZZUNK
ANNA	.11	F	INFANT	GRZZZZDAK	MARIA	26	F	W	GRZZZZUNK
B--SS, FRIEDR	27	M	LABR	GRZZZZWI	JOHANN	3	M	CHILD	GRZZZZUNK
BETHKE, ANNA	27	F	NN	GRZZZZIL	CRESZENZ	2	M	CHILD	GRZZZZUNK
WILKE, ALBERT	16	M	SMH	GRZZZZIL	SCHUR-CH, JOSEPHA	24	F	NN	GRZZZZUNK
DALLMANN, FRANZ	22	M	BKR	GRZZZZIL	MARIA	.09	F	INFANT	GRZZZZUNK
TOLAGA, MARIANNA	30	F	NN	GRZZZZIL	BOLDA, ANNA	17	F	NN	GRZZZZUNK
VICTORIA	10	F	CH	GRZZZZIL	SPRUCK, ELISAB	29	F	NN	GRZZZZUNK
CASMIMIR	5	M	CHILD	GRZZZZIL	ROSALIE	2	F	CHILD	GRZZZZUNK
EDMUND	2	M	CHILD	GRZZZZIL	ELISAB	.09	F	INFANT	GRZZZZUNK
PELAGIA	.11	F	INFANT	GRZZZZIL	MARCHEM, MAGA	30	M	LABR	GRZZZZUNK
MARIANNA	.11	F	INFANT	GRZZZZIL	JULINS	4	M	CHILD	GRZZZZUNK
MUEHLENBECK, BERTHA	19	F	NN	GRZZZZWI	A	3	M	CHILD	GRZZZZUNK
KLUG, WILH	37	M	LABR	GRZZZZWI	TRZYBIATOWSKA, MARYANNA	22	F	NN	GRZZZZUNK
AUGUSTE	38	F	W	GRZZZZWI	MICHAEL	.02	M	INFANT	GRZZZZUNK
ZINGLER, WILHE	62	F	NN	GRZZZZWI	PETRONITZ, EVA	24	F	NN	GRZZZZUNK
WITTMER, KARL	20	M	GDNR	GRZZZZKY	BURCZYNSKA, MARTHA	18	F	NN	GRZZZZUNK
DABIS, HERM	22	M	MCHT	GRZZZZUNK	TIEMEYER, HERM	23	M	JNR	GRZZZZUNK
KREIMEIER, AUG	18	M	FARMER	GRZZZZUNK	LENSMANN, MARIE	41	F	NN	GRZZZZUNK
OLSZEWSKA, ANTONI	46	F	NN	GRZZZZUNK	HELENE	13	F	CH	GRZZZZUNK

PASSENGER	AGE	SEX	OCCUPATION	PRVL	DES
ALWINE	6	F	CHILD	GRZZZZUNK	
PICHORA, ANNA	20	F	NN	GRZZZZUNK	
MARIA	.10	F	INFANT	GRZZZZUNK	
HOFFER, MARIA	22	F	NN	GRZZZZUNK	
KLEIN, BERTHA	20	F	NN	GRZZZZUNK	
MAX	11	M	CH	GRZZZZUNK	
SIENS, ADELINE	24	F	NN	GRZZZZUNK	
SOPHIE	15	F	NN	GRZZZZUNK	
FETKENTAUER, MARIA	40	F	NN	GRZZZZUNK	
MINNA	18	F	NN	GRZZZZUNK	
CARL	10	M	CH	GRZZZZUNK	
GUSTAV	7	M	CHILD	GRZZZZUNK	
GUSTAV	6	M	CHILD	GRZZZZUNK	
RUDOLF	3	M	CHILD	GRZZZZUNK	
HERMANN	.10	M	INFANT	GRZZZZUNK	
BURREZYNSKA, MARIA	15	F	SVNT	GRZZZZUNK	
BLANK, THERESE	26	F	NN	GRZZZZWI	
JOS	4	M	CHILD	GRZZZZWI	
ZECH, GEORG	23	M	FARMER	GRZZZZUNK	
SCHMIDT, HEINR	23	M	FARMER	GRZZZZIL	
WESSELS, HERM	28	M	TLR	GRZZZZUNK	
ZUCHTOWSKA, ANNA	28	F	NN	GRZZZZUNK	
FRANZISKA	.09	F	INFANT	GRZZZZUNK	
JANDER, KAROLINE	31	F	NN	GRZZZZUNK	
DREWANS, THEODOR	24	M	SHMK	GRZZZZUNK	
ZAKRQEWSKA, ANNA	27	F	NN	GRZZZZUNK	
JOSEF	3	M	CHILD	GRZZZZUNK	
ASTANTIA	.11	F	INFANT	GRZZZZUNK	
LANENROTH, MARIA	27	F	NN	GRZZZZUNK	
EMILIE	2	F	CHILD	GRZZZZUNK	
HERMAN	.01	M	INFANT	GRZZZZUNK	
HERZBERG, AUG	23	M	CPTR	GRZZZZUNK	
KAININSKA, JOHANNA	31	F	NN	GRZZZZUNK	
HELENE	7	F	CHILD	GRZZZZUNK	
JOSEPH	6	M	CHILD	GRZZZZUNK	
LEOKADIA	4	F	CHILD	GRZZZZUNK	
MARIANNA	3	F	CHILD	GRZZZZUNK	
MARTHA	.10	F	INFANT	GRZZZZUNK	
HURTH, ANNA	21	F	W	GRZZZZUNK	
WILHELM	23	M	FARMER	GRZZZZUNK	
ZIGIELSKI, THOMAS	39	M	FARMER	GRZZZZUNK	
INARZLA, MARIANNA	30	F	NN	GRZZZZUNK	
JOSEFINA	4	F	CHILD	GRZZZZUNK	
JOSEPH	7	M	CHILD	GRZZZZUNK	
FRANZA	2	F	CHILD	GRZZZZUNK	
MARIANNA	.06	F	INFANT	GRZZZZUNK	
HURTH, ANNA	53	F	NN	GRZZZZUNK	
OTTILIE	10	F	CH	GRZZZZUNK	
SEMERAN, CHRISTINE	76	F	NN	GRZZZZUNK	
MOTZ, WILHE	28	F	NN	GRZZZZUNK	
FRANKOWSKI, JOHN	60	M	PVTM	GRZZZZUNK	
TEPPER, MARTINA	23	F	NN	GRZZZZUNK	
MARENTINA	4	F	CHILD	GRZZZZUNK	
WATISLAWA	.09	F	INFANT	GRZZZZUNK	
SCHAFRANZKI, MARIANNA	19	F	NN	GRZZZZUNK	
SIEGMUND, KARL	31	M	FARMER	GRZZZZUNK	
ERNSTINE	26	F	W	GRZZZZUNK	
SKORA, FRANZA	18	F	NN	GRZZZZUNK	
HARTWICH, MARYANNA	23	F	NN	GRZZZZUNK	
JOHANN	.06	M	INFANT	GRZZZZUNK	
LIPINSKI, ROSA	20	F	NN	GRZZZZUNK	
FRANZ	.11	M	INFANT	GRZZZZUNK	
PRZYBYLSKI, MICHEL	25	M	FUR	GRZZZZUNK	
MARYANNA	19	F	W	GRZZZZUNK	
WOJCIECHOWSKI, FRANZISZ	32	M	LABR	GRZZZZUNK	
JESILOWITZ, MARACHE	20	F	NN	GRZZZZUNK	
SALMEN	11	M	CH	GRZZZZUNK	
KEMPT, CHRISTIAN	40	M	FARMER	GRZZZZUNK	
WEBER, SOPHIE	22	F	NN	GRZZZZUNK	
HAWELKA, ANTON	42	M	MCHT	GRZZZZUNK	
WINTERMEYER, CARL	18	M	LABR	GRZZZZMPS	
VOGELSANG, LUER	17	M	FARMER	GRZZZZUNK	
CATHA	19	F	CK	GRZZZZUNK	
FRIEDR	16	M	FARMER	GRZZZZUNK	
NEUBAUER, CARL	16	M	FARMER	GRZZZZIL	
KREZESH--, JOHANN	22	M	FARMER	GRZZZZIL	
SIMON, SIMON	18	M	FARMER	GRZZZZUNK	
PFEIFFER, ROSA	19	F	NN	GRZZZZUNK	
-SMANN, CARL	26	M	JNR	GRZZZZUNK	
FRERICHS, M	27	M	MCHT	GRZZZZUNK	
CHARLOTTE	30	F	W	GRZZZZUNK	
TOPP, GOTTL	48	M	FARMER	GRZZZZOMA	
GLAMERT, WILHE	16	F	NN	GRZZZZPIT	
SOPHIE	22	F	NN	GRZZZZJDA	
KALKA, JOHANNA	28	M	HTR	GRZZZZPA	
DIETRICH, PAUL	15	M	FARMER	GRZZZZUNK	
BRAZTROL, JOHANN	57	M	FARMER	GRZZZZUNK	
MARIA	27	F	NN	GRZZZZUNK	
BALZER, BARBARA	27	F	NN	GRZZZZUNK	
GRUEN, CHRISTIAN	32	M	FARMER	GRZZZZUNK	
ROSA	31	F	W	GRZZZZUNK	
ROLAND, ANNA	21	F	NN	GRZZZZUNK	
BRETISLAV	6	M	CHILD	GRZZZZUNK	
JULIE	.08	F	INFANT	GRZZZZUNK	
SCHOTT, JOHANN	74	M	LABR	GRZZZZUNK	
BARBARA	65	F	W	GRZZZZUNK	
ANTONIE	35	F	NN	GRZZZZUNK	
KRATOCHVIL, MARIE	52	F	NN	GRZZZZUNK	
BARBA	22	F	NN	GRZZZZUNK	
KREME, JOSEF	20	M	LABR	GRZZZZUNK	
FRANZ	11	M	CH	GRZZZZUNK	
BERNARD, ROSALIE	35	F	NN	GRZZZZUNK	
CAROLINE	4	F	CHILD	GRZZZZUNK	
ORTHUBER, FRANZ	29	M	FARMER	GRZZZZKY	
ROSA	32	F	W	GRZZZZKY	
MARIE	10	F	CH	GRZZZZKY	
LUDVIK	6	M	CHILD	GRZZZZKY	
ROSA	6	F	CHILD	GRZZZZKY	
FRANZ	3	M	CHILD	GRZZZZKY	
HIRSCH, AGNES	25	F	CK	GRZZZZKY	
H-RBEK, JOSEF	18	M	LABR	GRZZZZKY	
TEIML, IGNACZ	33	M	LABR	GRZZZZKY	
MITT--HNER, ANTON	24	M	LABR	GRZZZZUNK	
SIKORA, KATHA	20	F	NN	GRZZZZNE	
N--OOTNY, JOSEF	62	M	LABR	GRZZZZNE	
KATHA	29	F	NN	GRZZZZNE	
FRANZ	3	F	CHILD	GRZZZZNE	
ANTON	.09	M	INFANT	GRZZZZNE	
MEDINA, WENZL	48	M	LABR	GRZZZZNE	
KONSCNY, FRANZ	24	M	LABR	GRZZZZUNK	
MARIE	23	F	W	GRZZZZUNK	
FRANZ	.11	M	INFANT	GRZZZZUNK	
JOSEF	23	M	LABR	GRZZZZUNK	
WACH, FRANZ	20	M	LABR	GRZZZZIL	
DENINGEN, ANONIA	38	F	NN	GRZZZZUNK	
LAURA	11	F	CH	GRZZZZUNK	
LINA	3	F	CHILD	GRZZZZUNK	
SICK, EMILIE	20	F	NN	GRZZZZUNK	
NERSSER, CHRIST	24	M	JNR	GRZZZZUNK	
OPIELENSKI, KATHA	39	M	NN	GRZZZZUNK	
MARIANNA	11	F	CH	GRZZZZUNK	
ANTONINA	9	F	CHILD	GRZZZZUNK	
PELAGIA	7	F	CHILD	GRZZZZUNK	
MICHEL	5	M	CHILD	GRZZZZUNK	
VERONIKA	2	F	CHILD	GRZZZZUNK	
STANISLAUS	.02	M	INFANT	GRZZZZUNK	
KRUEGER, WILHELM	55	M	FARMER	GRZZZZUNK	
ALBERTINE	54	F	W	GRZZZZUNK	
HERMANN	15	M	FARMER	GRZZZZUNK	
ADAN-CZYK, JOHANNA	36	F	NN	GRZZZZUNK	
WLADISL	9	M	CHILD	GRZZZZUNK	
MARIE	6	F	CHILD	GRZZZZUNK	
PEXITA	3	F	CHILD	GRZZZZUNK	
A-	.11	F	INFANT	GRZZZZUNK	
FRANZA	21	F	INF	GRZZZZUNK	
THESENWITZ, JOHANNE	43	F	NN	GRZZZZUNK	
WALTER	16	M	LABR	GRZZZZUNK	
FRITZ	9	M	CHILD	GRZZZZUNK	
FRIEDCHEN	4	F	CHILD	GRZZZZUNK	
STEFFEN, MINNA	73	F	NN	GRZZZZUNK	

PASSENGER	AGE	SEX	OCCUPATION	PRVVL	DES
FRIER	37	M	FARMER	GRZZZZ	UNK
AUGUSTE	36	F	W	GRZZZZ	UNK
CARL	11	M	CH	GRZZZZ	UNK
ANNA	10	F	CH	GRZZZZ	UNK
EMMA	9	F	CHILD	GRZZZZ	UNK
AUGUST	3	M	CHILD	GRZZZZ	UNK
MINNA	.03	F	INFANT	GRZZZZ	UNK
DOZEWIETZKA, JOSEFA	34	F	NN	GRZZZZ	UNK
FRANZ	7	M	CHILD	GRZZZZ	UNK
ROBERT	3	M	CHILD	GRZZZZ	UNK
HEDWIG	.01	F	INFANT	GRZZZZ	UNK
KAPELA, VERONIKA	28	F	NN	GRZZZZ	UNK
KASIMIR	.07	M	INFANT	GRZZZZ	UNK
BINDER, WILHE	15	F	CL	GRZZZZ	UNK
RESCHKE, ADOLF	32	M	SMH	GRZZZZ	MI
ERNESTINE	30	F	W	GRZZZZ	MI
FRIEDRICH	3	M	CHILD	GRZZZZ	MI
KRONE, JOHANN	50	M	FARMER	GRZZZZ	WI
REICHHARDT, WILH	28	M	FARMER	GRZZZZ	UNK
MARGA	28	F	W	GRZZZZ	UNK
MARTA	7	F	CHILD	GRZZZZ	UNK
ELISAB	6	F	CHILD	GRZZZZ	UNK
CONRAD	4	M	CHILD	GRZZZZ	UNK
PAUL	2	M	CHILD	GRZZZZ	UNK
MARIA	.08	F	INFANT	GRZZZZ	UNK
RATHE, CHR	50	M	FARMER	GRZZZZ	UNK
HEINR	21	M	FARMER	GRZZZZ	UNK
WOLKERMANN, MARIA	15	F	NN	GRZZZZ	UNK
KLEMME, WILH	44	M	LABR	GRZZZZ	UNK
RIEMANN, FRITZ	22	M	LABR	GRZZZZ	IL
FREISE, HEINR	22	M	LABR	GRZZZZ	IL
PANCK--, FLORIAN	38	M	LABR	GRZZZZ	UNK
KATARINA	17	F	W	GRZZZZ	UNK
ENGSTLER, BERTHA	30	F	NN	GRZZZZ	UNK
REBECCA	6	F	CHILD	GRZZZZ	UNK
SCHELLER, EMIL	40	M	FARMER	GRZZZZ	MN
MINEBURG, IDA	26	F	NN	GRZZZZ	UNK

SHIP: WERRA

FROM: BREMEN AND SOUTHAMPTON
TO: NEW YORK
ARRIVED: 30 OCTOBER 1888

PASSENGER	AGE	SEX	OCCUPATION	PRVVL	DES
VERGE, ETIENNE	20	F	NN	GRAAKH	USA
HEYE, HERMANN	24	M	TT	GRABEH	USA
KUESTERMANN, FRIEDR.	30	M	TT	GRACBF	USA
PREN. HEINR.	24	M	TT	GRABQZ	USA
FRIEDR.	22	M	TT	GRABQZ	USA
ROSENBAUM, LINA	19	F	NN	BVZZZZ	USA
SALOMON	17	M	TT	BVZZZZ	USA
KOHN, BETTY	30	F	W	BVADLD	USA
LOUIS	9	M	CHILD	BVADLD	USA
KARBER, IDA	49	F	W	BVABOQ	USA
BREIDENBACH, AMALIE	52	F	W	GRZZZZ	USA
EMILIE	22	F	NN	GRZZZZ	USA
MINNA	17	F	NN	GRZZZZ	USA
MORITZ	11	M	CH	GRZZZZ	USA
IDA	10	F	CH	GRZZZZ	USA
JUSTA	15	F	CH	GRZZZZ	USA
LOEFLAND, GUST.	40	M	MCHT	GRAEXW	USA
PRELLE, BERNHARD	28	M	MCHT	GRABDM	USA
DUNCKER, SIEGFRIED	16	M	NN	GRACBR	USA
FISCHER, LUD.	24	M	TT	GRAAGL	USA
HU-NER, JOSEFA.	34	F	W	GRADLD	USA
RAN, JOHANNA	38	F	NN	GRAARR	USA
JUNG, ELISE	22	F	NN	GRAARR	USA
GALL, ANTONIE	19	F	NN	WMZZZZ	USA
SCHONINGER, STEPHANIE	22	F	NN	WMZZZZ	USA
SICHEL, FANNY	22	F	NN	WMACRK	USA

PASSENGER	AGE	SEX	OCCUPATION	PRVVL	DES
MARK, LINA	20	F	NN	WMACQY	USA
KAHN, JOS.	18	M	MCHT	WMAAZS	USA
ZAHN, LOUISE	27	F	NN	WMAAKH	USA
EITNER, FELIX	23	M	MCHT	WMADIJ	USA
FISCHER, HEINR.	20	M	MCHT	WMABDM	USA
ANKER, REGE.	26	F	NN	GRZZZZ	USA
BORELL, FRIEDR.	32	M	MCHT	BDZZZZ	USA
WIEDEMANN, PAUL	18	M	MCHT	BDAAXK	USA
VONGEGHREN, CARL	42	M	TT	BDADEM	USA
HENNOCHSTEIN, DINA	21	F	NN	BDADLD	USA
MEYER, EMIL	14	M	NN	BVZZZZ	USA
HABERLUND, FRITZ	30	M	MCHT	BVAAKH	USA
EGGERS, MATHIAS	52	M	MCHT	GRZZZZ	USA
KATHA.	24	F	W	GRZZZZ	USA
MARTHA	3	F	CHILD	GRZZZZ	USA
PHILIPP	2	M	CHILD	GRZZZZ	USA
EDUARD	.08	M	INFANT	GRZZZZ	USA
SCHUMACHER, WILH.	21	M	MCHT	GRAARR	USA
WESEL, JOHA.	25	F	W	GRAARR	USA
CARL	3	M	CHILD	GRAARR	USA
EMILIE	.11	F	INFANT	GRAARR	USA
LIPPMANN, SOPHIA	37	F	W	GRZZZZ	USA
WILLIAM	3	M	CHILD	GRZZZZ	USA
WEIDL, ANNA	23	F	W	BVZZZZ	USA
ANNA	.09	F	INFANT	BVZZZZ	USA
BEISWENGER, CARL	18	M	FARMER	WMZZZZ	USA
JOZWIAK, MALGARZALA	20	F	W	GRZZZZ	USA
ANDR.	3	M	CHILD	GRZZZZ	USA
PETER	.11	M	INFANT	GRZZZZ	USA
BORKOWFSKA, ANTONIA	26	F	NN	GRZZZZ	USA
BORZICH, MARYANNA	20	F	W	GRZZZZ	USA
LEONORA	18	F	NN	GRZZZZ	USA
MARTINA	.09	F	INFANT	GRZZZZ	USA
ABRAHAM, LIPPMANN	15	M	NN	GRZZZZ	USA
HELENE	19	F	NN	GRZZZZ	USA
HAASE, SELMA	22	F	NN	GRZZZZ	USA
DUST, EMILIA	32	F	W	GRAENQ	USA
FRANZ	8	M	CHILD	GRAENQ	USA
WESTPHAL, ERNSTE.	30	F	W	GRADEN	USA
PAUL	6	M	CHILD	GRADEN	USA
ADLER, ANNA	27	F	NN	GRAATF	USA
MOENCH, ALFRED	36	M	FARMER	GRAAKH	USA
OTTO	11	M	CH	GRAAKH	USA
BLOCK, VINCENT	22	M	FARMER	GRZZZZ	USA
LASKOWSKI, PETER	16	M	FARMER	GRAEZV	USA
ANNA	14	F	NN	GRAEZV	USA
ZLANKE, HERM.	16	M	NN	GRAEXV	USA
LEICHMANN, FERD.	35	M	LABR	GRADNY	USA
DIEZ, MICH.	23	M	BKR	WMZZZZ	USA
WOHLHAUPTER, HEINR.	34	M	LABR	WMZZZZ	USA
UNMUSS, EMILIE	18	F	NN	GRZZZZ	USA
BUNANDT, AUGUSTE	40	F	W	GRACOS	USA
MARTHA	20	F	NN	GRACOS	USA
HELMUTH	14	M	NN	GRACOS	USA
GUSTAV	12	M	CH	GRACOS	USA
SELMA	9	F	CHILD	GRACOS	USA
LOUISE	.08	F	INFANT	GRACOS	USA
REINKE, GUSTAV	27	M	FARMER	GRZZZZ	USA
EMILIE	27	F	W	GRZZZZ	USA
HELLMUTH	2	M	CHILD	GRZZZZ	USA
FRIEDA	.06	F	INFANT	GRZZZZ	USA
EICHNER, MARIA	18	F	NN	BVZZZZ	USA
DISTLER, KATHA.	20	F	NN	BVZZZZ	USA
ADAMOWSKY, CHARLOTTE	38	F	W	BVAARR	USA
HEINR.	38	M	FARMER	BVAARR	USA
FRIEDKE.	10	F	CH	BVAARR	USA
HEINR.	11	M	CH	BVAARR	USA
BOEHLER, FRED.	20	M	LABR	GRZZZZ	USA
KUECK, META	19	F	NN	GRZZZZ	USA
DUETSCH, JOH.	17	M	FARMER	GRZZZZ	USA
BRANER, CHRISTE.	22	F	NN	GRABIY	USA
BUTSCHAROF, META	17	F	NN	GRAJYL	USA
LEOPOLD, META	18	F	NN	GRAALJ	USA
PUCKHABER, ANNA	18	F	NN	GRZZZZ	USA
KRIETE, ADELHD.	17	F	NN	GRZZZZ	USA

PASSENGER	AGE	SEX	OCCUPATION	PRVL	DES
SACHSENHAUSEN, MARIE	29	F	W		GRABKRUSA
CARL	4	M	CHILD		GRABKRUSA
MOLLE, BEBETTE	16	F	NN		BVZZZZUSA
WALDMANN, JOH.	16	M	LABR		BVADESUSA
DUSBILER, JACOB	15	M	NN		BVZZZZUSA
GRETCHEN	12	F	CH		BVZZZZUSA
OSTERLOH, HERM.	54	M	LABR		BVAHQTUSA
FRIEDR.	29	M	LABR		BVAHQTUSA
CHARLOTTE	25	F	W		BVAHQTUSA
HERM.	27	M	FARMER		BVAHQTUSA
HEINR.	24	M	FARMER		BVAHQTUSA
LUDWIG	15	M	FARMER		BVAHQTUSA
WILH.	11	M	CH		BVAHQTUSA
AUG.	9	M	CHILD		BVAHQTUSA
STEIN, CAROLE.	46	F	W		BVAHQTUSA
BERTHA	5	F	CHILD		BVAHQTUSA
WEISLER, MARIA	15	F	NN		BVZZZZUSA
KLOSS, MARIA	28	F	W		BVZZZZUSA
KARL	5	M	CHILD		BVZZZZUSA
BLOCK, MEYER	28	M	FARMER		BDZZZZUSA
KLAGMANN, ANNA	18	F	NN		BDZZZZUSA
MARTIN	18	M	NN		BDZZZZUSA
KUEMMEL, JOSEF	33	M	LKSH		BDADLDUSA
MEIER, ISAAK	16	M	NN		BDACSCUSA
WILLSTAEDTER, LEOP.	16	M	NN		BDABVZUSA
AUER, JACOB	15	M	NN		BDABVZUSA
HERTEL, JOHANN	22	M	LABR		BDAEBSUSA
EBERT, ALFRED	28	M	LABR		BDAEBSUSA
KLOPF, URSALA	59	F	W		BDAFSTUSA
LOUISE	7	F	CHILD		BDAFSTUSA
WEHNER, LISABETH	67	F	W		BDAFSTUSA
ZWIERLEIN, CATHA.	52	F	W		BDAFSTUSA
ENGLERT, MARGA.	40	F	W		BDAFSTUSA
MAGDA.	8	F	CHILD		BDAFSTUSA
RIEMENSCHNEIDER, JOH.	19	M	LABR		GRZZZZUSA
BERNHARDT, EVA	44	F	W		BVZZZZUSA
STRAUSS, SETTCHEN	19	F	NN		GRZZZZUSA
BOHNLEIN, ANNA	23	F	NN		BVZZZZUSA
VOLK, JOH.	75	M	LABR		BVAHVXUSA
SCHADT, CHRISTE.	18	F	NN		BVAAGLUSA
JUENGER, ADAM	14	M	NN		BVZZZZUSA
U, MAGDA.	18	F	NN		BVAARRUSA
NEUMEYER, JOH.	16	M	NN		BVAIECUSA
MARX, HERM.	17	M	LABR		BVAECXUSA
NAGENGAST, BARBA.	28	F	NN		BVZZZZUSA
GRONLE, MARTHA	29	F	NN		GRZZZZUSA
LIPSKI, ALEX	35	M	FARMER		GRAEABUSA
PREUSS, ANDR.	24	M	FARMER		GRAEABUSA
WITTENBERG, ANTONIA	30	F	NN		GRAAXYUSA
HOFFMANN, AUG.	24	M	LABR		GRAARZUSA
MAIER, THERESIA	19	F	NN		BDZZZZUSA
HERMANNSDOERFER, JOHN	30	M	LABR		BVZZZZUSA
ECKERT, LUDW.	16	M	LABR		BVAAXBUSA
VOITH, BARBA.	26	F	W		BVZZZZUSA
BAPTIST	.06	M	INFANT		BVZZZZUSA
KNEITH, KAETHA	22	F	NN		BVZZZZUSA
FISCHER, U	22	F	NN		BVADLDUSA
SKOETT, ERIK	37	M	LABR		BVABZSUSA
ANGINE	37	F	W		BVABZSUSA
THOMAS	9	M	CHILD		BVABZSUSA
STEFFEN	6	M	CHILD		BVABZSUSA
ELLEN	3	F	CHILD		BVABZSUSA
MADSEN, RASMUS	47	M	LABR		GRZZZZUSA
HENRIETTE	47	F	W		GRZZZZUSA
CARL	11	M	CH		GRZZZZUSA
PETER	10	M	CH		GRZZZZUSA
CAROLE.	9	F	CHILD		GRZZZZUSA
ZIPLINSKY, HEINR.	16	M	MCHT		GRAEXWUSA
GRONLE, EMILIE	29	F	NN		GRZZZZUSA
JUERGENS, MARGA.	30	F	NN		GRAEPZUSA
BRUECKEMANN, ADELGUNDE	10	F	CH		GRAEPZUSA
SCHROEDER, HENRIETTE	41	F	W		GRAEPZUSA
LOUISE	61	F	W		GRAEPZUSA
HERM.	8	M	CHILD		GRAEPZUSA
RUTZ, AUG.	28	M	LABR		GRAENAUSA
GLOECKNER, CARL	18	M	LABR		GRADLUUSA
RANSCH, ERNSTR	27	M	LABR		GRAGQUUSA
KOEHLER, GERHD.	18	M	NN		GRAJPOUSA
MARK, SEBAST.	39	M	LABR		GRAFRGUSA
MAGDA	4	F	CHILD		GRAFRGUSA
HEINR.	3	M	CHILD		GRAFRGUSA
OTTO	.09	M	INFANT		GRAFRGUSA
VOGELMANN, BABETTE	28	F	W		GRACEGUSA
BERTHA	3	F	CHILD		GRACEGUSA
EISELE, ANNA	17	F	NN		GRACEGUSA
OTT, FRANZISKA	50	F	W		GRAGVZUSA
BERTHA	13	F	NN		GRAGVZUSA
CATHA.	10	F	CH		GRAGVZUSA
WILDRUBE, F.	54	M	FARMER		GRZZZZUSA
ELISABETH	40	F	W		GRZZZZUSA
JOHA.	3	F	CHILD		GRZZZZUSA
LOUISE	.06	F	INFANT		GRZZZZUSA
VOIGT, MARTHA	15	M	NN		GRAEJBUSA
WERTHEIM, ELIAS	16	M	NN		GRAAUUUSA
JOSEPH, JETTCHEN	19	F	NN		GRAECXUSA
NUSSLOCH, ADAM	27	M	FARMER		GRAAMJUSA
OBENHAUS, JOHE.	17	F	NN		GRAEATUSA
SCHMIDT, CHRIST.	20	M	LABR		GRALSEUSA
FLEISCHER, FERD.	16	M	LABR		GRAAIFUSA
HAGEN, LUDW.	16	M	LABR		GRAAIFUSA
RAUFT, WILH.	18	M	LABR		GRAAKHUSA
ALTSCHUELHORST, ANNA	22	F	NN		GRZZZZUSA
CATHA.	17	F	NN		GRZZZZUSA
BUDDE, ARNOLD	15	F	NN		GRZZZZUSA
KAELBERER, GOTTL.	23	M	LABR		WMZZZZUSA
BADENHOEP, GEORG	15	M	NN		GRZZZZUSA
ALBERMANN, HERM.	15	M	NN		GRZZZZUSA
HARLE, JOHA.	42	F	NN		GRAAMHUSA
TOELL, LYDIA	16	F	NN		GRAAMHUSA
ROEHRIG, CARL	14	M	NN		GRZZZZUSA
BOEHM, SOPHIE	20	F	NN		GRZZZZUSA
BEYER, GEORG	28	M	FARMER		GRZZZZUSA
DIETZEL, JUL.	38	M	SHMK		GRAFKYUSA
EDMUND	9	M	CHILD		GRAFKYUSA
ROTHER, MORITZ	22	M	FARMER		GRAFKYUSA
BLUME, AUGUSTE	45	F	NN		GRACSDUSA
HUGO	18	M	LABR		GRACSDUSA
RANZINGER, GEORG	23	M	LABR		BVZZZZUSA
GRANGE, BETTI	29	F	NN		BVAARRUSA
SZIMANSKI, FILOMENA	18	F	NN		GRZZZZUSA
JOH.	16	M	NN		GRZZZZUSA
HAEWIG, CHRIST.	33	F	NN		GRZZZZUSA
NOWAK, ANNA	25	F	W		GRZZZZUSA
EDUARD	7	M	CHILD		GRZZZZUSA
SCHINDLER, JULIE	20	F	NN		GRZZZZUSA
FERD.	10	M	CH		GRZZZZUSA
GERKE, ELISE	21	F	NN		GRZZZZUSA
THERESE	18	F	NN		GRZZZZUSA
EMMA	9	F	CHILD		GRZZZZUSA
JOSEF	8	M	CHILD		GRZZZZUSA
MESSINGEN, ROB.	27	M	UNKNOWN		GRAFNKUSA
FUCHS, CARL	29	M	LABR		GRABMRUSA
MARIA	30	F	W		GRABMRUSA
CARL	3	M	CHILD		GRABMRUSA
LUDW.	.09	M	INFANT		GRABMRUSA
HAHN, MAX	22	M	LABR		BVZZZZUSA
ISIDOR	15	M	NN		BVZZZZUSA
MEYER, LOUISE	15	F	NN		BVAALJUSA
STERNBERG, GUSTAV	30	M	FARMER		BVADRUUSA
EMILIE	25	F	W		BVADRUUSA
WILHELM	.09	M	INFANT		BVADRUUSA
WEINMANN, JAC.	28	M	FARMER		BDZZZZUSA
SUSANNA	19	F	NN		BDZZZZUSA
HANK, HENRIETTE	21	F	NN		BDZZZZUSA
GRONBACH, WILHE.	16	F	NN		WMZZZZUSA
CATHA.	15	F	NN		WMZZZZUSA
FLATON, LEOPOLD	17	M	LABR		GRZZZZUSA
MASCHIK, MICHEL	35	M	LABR		GRZZZZUSA
BLOSCH, MARTIN	30	M	LABR		GRZZZZUSA
BARCZEKOWSKI, JOSEF	25	M	LABR		GRZZZZUSA

PASSENGER	AGE	SEX	OCCUPATION	PRVL	DES
BOSCHEK, ANDR.	25	M	LABR	GRZZZZ	USA
LICHTENSTEIN, EMIL	32	M	LABR	BVZZZZ	USA
DUFNER, JOH.	25	M	LABR	BDZZZZ	USA
RING, MOYS	55	M	LABR	WMZZZZ	USA
ANNA	56	F	W	WMZZZZ	USA
ANNA	24	F	W	WMZZZZ	USA
MARIA	23	F	NN	WMZZZZ	USA
KAROLE.	20	F	NN	WMZZZZ	USA
BABETTE	20	F	NN	WMZZZZ	USA
ALOYS	15	M	NN	WMZZZZ	USA
RESOEFT, FRITZ	36	M	LABR	GRZZZZ	USA
HENRIETTE	30	F	W	GRZZZZ	USA
BERTHA	7	F	CHILD	GRZZZZ	USA
MATHA.	3	F	CHILD	GRZZZZ	USA
WESSTERHOFF, LORENZ	53	F	CH	OLZZZZ	USA
FREIRICH, NATHAN	15	M	NN	OLAHJK	USA
SOPHIE	13	M	NN	OLAHJK	USA
U, U	00	U	UNKNOWN	GRZZZZ	USA
SCHMITT, ELISAB.	28	F	NN	GRAAIE	USA
VOELKER, EMMA	16	F	NN	GRAAIE	USA
PREISER, CECILIE	28	F	NN	GRACBR	USA
DOERFLER, FRIEDR.	41	M	LABR	GRACZE	USA
CATHA.	35	F	W	GRACZE	USA
ADAM	2	M	CHILD	GRACZE	USA
KUNIGDE.	.06	F	INFANT	GRACZE	USA
SCHNEIDER, MARG.	23	F	NN	GRZZZZ	USA
EISENBERG, ABRAM	25	M	FARMER	GRZZZZ	USA
WILD, MARIE	25	F	NN	GRAAGW	USA
GERDES, MARG.	23	F	NN	GRAEHY	USA
REBSCHER, WILH.	19	M	MCHT	GRABKH	USA
HOLDENBAUER, MARIE	19	F	NN	GRAHVP	USA
PITTINS, HERM.	41	M	LABR	GRZZZZ	USA
WAGNER, NATHAN	30	M	LABR	GRZZZZ	USA
THERESIA	19	F	W	GRZZZZ	USA
ALFONS	.08	M	INFANT	GRZZZZ	USA
KRAMER, WILH.	18	M	FARMER	GRZZZZ	USA
WOLTE, GERHD.	16	M	FARMER	GRZZZZ	USA
HORSTMANN, ELISE	21	F	NN	GRZZZZ	USA
WILH.	24	M	NN	GRZZZZ	USA
MARGA.	21	F	NN	GRZZZZ	USA
WEHRONIG, BLAS.	39	M	FARMER	GRZZZZ	USA
TIETJEN, MARGA.	24	F	NN	GRACBR	USA
HESS, WILH.	26	M	FARMER	GRZZZZ	USA
MUELLER, ROSA	23	F	NN	GRACBF	USA
ITZSCHLAN, KARSTEN	70	M	LABR	GRZZZZ	USA
U	64	F	W	GRZZZZ	USA
HORCHIS, MICKE	60	F	W	GRAFRA	USA
MUELLER, JOHANN	65	M	FARMER	GRAFRA	USA
U	60	F	W	GRAFRA	USA

SHIP: GOTHIA

FROM: STETTIN
TO: NEW YORK
ARRIVED: 31 OCTOBER 1888

PASSENGER	AGE	SEX	OCCUPATION	PRVL	DES
BORCHART, AUGUST	36	M	LABR	PRZZZZ	USA
JOHANNA	36	F	W	PRZZZZ	USA
DUVE, MICHAEL	70	M	NN	PRZZZZ	USA
BORCHART, AUGUSTE	11	F	CH	PRZZZZ	USA
CARL	9	M	CHILD	PRZZZZ	USA
MARIE	8	F	CHILD	PRZZZZ	USA
AUGUST	7	M	CHILD	PRZZZZ	USA
WILHELMINE	5	F	CHILD	PRZZZZ	USA
HERMANN	4	M	CHILD	PRZZZZ	USA
WILHELM	2	M	CHILD	PRZZZZ	USA
PAULINE	.09	F	INFANT	PRZZZZ	USA
ELSKE, AUGUSTE	18	F	SGL	PRZZZZ	USA
BURCZIK, FRANZ	34	M	LABR	PRZZZZ	USA
ANNA	32	F	W	PRZZZZ	USA

PASSENGER	AGE	SEX	OCCUPATION	PRVL	DES
LINA	2	F	CHILD	PRZZZZ	USA
GAFFKE, ROSALIE	18	F	SGL	PRZZZZ	USA
MANTHEI, WILHELM	66	M	LABR	PRZZZZ	USA
WEINKAUF, ERNSTINE	22	F	SGL	PRZZZZ	USA
BERTHA	20	F	SGL	PRZZZZ	USA
MATHILDE	16	F	SGL	PRZZZZ	USA
PESCH, AUGUSTE	22	F	W	PRZZZZ	USA
JAEGER, BERTHA	21	F	SGL	PRZZZZ	USA
LENG, HERMANN	29	M	LABR	PRZZZZ	USA
WILHELMINE	33	F	W	PRZZZZ	USA
LENZ, WILHELM	43	M	LABR	PRZZZZ	USA
WILHELMINE	47	F	W	PRZZZZ	USA
WILHELM	17	M	CH	PRZZZZ	USA
ALBERT	12	M	CH	PRZZZZ	USA
EMILIE	10	F	CH	PRZZZZ	USA
PETER	70	M	Y	PRZZZZ	USA
RANDIG, AUGUST	37	M	LABR	PRZZZZ	USA
LOUISE	35	F	W	PRZZZZ	USA
ANNA	8	F	CHILD	PRZZZZ	USA
STAHOWI-SZ, PAULINE	23	F	W	PRZZZZ	USA
MARTHA	.10	F	INFANT	PRZZZZ	USA
HUBERT, AUGUSTE	34	F	W	PRZZZZ	USA
WILHELM	14	M	CH	PRZZZZ	USA
ANNA	11	F	CH	PRZZZZ	USA
HERMANN	9	M	CHILD	PRZZZZ	USA
GUSTAV	7	M	CHILD	PRZZZZ	USA
MINNA	4	F	CHILD	PRZZZZ	USA
JULIUS	1	M	CHILD	PRZZZZ	USA
SPIEZAK, MARIANA	42	F	W	PRZZZZ	USA
MARIANA	18	F	CH	PRZZZZ	USA
KATHARINE	16	F	CH	PRZZZZ	USA
JOHANN	11	M	CH	PRZZZZ	USA
ANNA	10	F	CH	PRZZZZ	USA
MARTIN	4	M	CHILD	PRZZZZ	USA
LEON	3	M	CHILD	PRZZZZ	USA
AGNES	.10	F	INFANT	PRZZZZ	USA
VORPAHL, LOUISE	55	F	W	PRZZZZ	USA
ERNESTINE	22	F	CH	PRZZZZ	USA
CARL	20	M	CH	PRZZZZ	USA
BRZOZOWSKI, FRANZ	16	M	LABR	PRZZZZ	USA
MANIKOWSKI, VALENTIN	26	M	LABR	PRZZZZ	USA
BERTHA	22	F	W	PRZZZZ	USA
JOHANN	.04	M	INFANT	PRZZZZ	USA
WOLFF, ANNA	25	F	SGL	PRZZZZ	USA
WEISS, EMMA	20	F	SGL	PRZZZZ	USA
BALAU, RUDOLF	19	M	SMH	PRZZZZ	USA
EYLENFELDT, CARL	37	M	LABR	PRZZZZ	USA
ANNA	36	F	W	PRZZZZ	USA
OLGA	.11	F	INFANT	PRZZZZ	USA
MAXIMILIAN	8	M	CHILD	PRZZZZ	USA
GORZELANDA, MAGDALENA	21	F	SGL	PRZZZZ	USA
HOLTZ, FRIEDRICH	62	M	LABR	PRZZZZ	USA
FRIEDRICH	25	M	S	PRZZZZ	USA
SGLINSKA, ANTONIA	21	F	W	PRZZZZ	USA
JOHANN	1	M	CHILD	PRZZZZ	USA
KEPET, HEINRICH	25	M	LABR	PRZZZZ	USA
BARANOWSKA, MARIANA	31	F	W	PRZZZZ	USA
JOSEF	7	M	CHILD	PRZZZZ	USA
VALENTIN	5	M	CHILD	PRZZZZ	USA
STASZKIWITZ, THERSIA	31	F	W	PRZZZZ	USA
MARIANA	4	F	CHILD	PRZZZZ	USA
JADWIGA	2	F	CHILD	PRZZZZ	USA
PIMM, MARIE	16	F	SGL	PRZZZZ	USA
MUELLER, MINNA	21	F	SGL	PRZZZZ	USA
LUTZKE, CAROLINE	28	F	W	PRZZZZ	USA
EMILIE	7	F	CHILD	PRZZZZ	USA
WIRKUS, MATHILDE	28	F	W	PRZZZZ	USA
HERMAN	6	M	CHILD	PRZZZZ	USA
AUGUST	5	M	CHILD	PRZZZZ	USA
MARTIN	2	M	CHILD	PRZZZZ	USA
BERNHARD	.10	M	INFANT	PRZZZZ	USA
WETZLINSKY, JOSEPH	58	M	SEMN	PRZZZZ	USA
KRUGER, LOUISE	59	M	PVTM	PRZZZZ	USA
ADELHEID	14	F	CH	PRZZZZ	USA
IDA	15	F	CH	PRZZZZ	USA

403

PASSENGER	AGE	SEX	OCCUPATION	PRVL	DES
LEO	11	M	CH		PRZZZZZUSA
MARIE	9	F	CHILD		PRZZZZZUSA
HOCK, JOHANNA	52	F	W		PRZZZZZUSA
WILHELMINE	8	F	CHILD		PRZZZZZUSA
ANNA	5	F	CHILD		PRZZZZZUSA
RICHARD	3	M	CHILD		PRZZZZZUSA
OTTO	.09	M	INFANT		PRZZZZZUSA
PAUTZ, ANNA	24	F	SGL		PRZZZZZUSA
LAMPERT, DAVID	23	M	SDLR		PRZZZZZUSA
POSANSKI, AUGUSTE	31	F	W		PRZZZZZUSA
FRANZ	8	M	CHILD		PRZZZZZUSA
MARTHA	6	F	CHILD		PRZZZZZUSA
JOHANN	3	M	CHILD		PRZZZZZUSA
AUGUST	.06	M	INFANT		PRZZZZZUSA
BLOCK, EMILIE	48	F	W		PRZZZZZUSA
MATHILDE	19	F	SCH		PRZZZZZUSA
JULIUS	11	M	CH		PRZZZZZUSA
SCHAPPANSKI, AUGUST	30	M	LABR		PRZZZZZUSA
BERTHA	25	F	W		PRZZZZZUSA
THEODOR	1	M	CHILD		PRZZZZZUSA
ANDRES	1	M	CHILD		PRZZZZZUSA
MATKE, MARTHA	5	F	CHILD		PRZZZZZUSA
JUSTINA	56	F	W		PRZZZZZUSA
SCHMUDE, AUGUSTE	55	F	W		PRZZZZZUSA
HERMAN	10	M	S		PRZZZZZUSA
DETTLAFF, MARTIN	40	M	LABR		PRZZZZZUSA
MARIANA	40	F	W		PRZZZZZUSA
JULIANA	17	F	CH		PRZZZZZUSA
MARTHA	9	F	CHILD		PRZZZZZUSA
AUGUSTE	11	F	CH		PRZZZZZUSA
AUGUST	5	M	CHILD		PRZZZZZUSA
FELIX	3	M	CHILD		PRZZZZZUSA
JOHANN	.11	M	INFANT		PRZZZZZUSA
RISTAU, AUGUSTE	23	F	SGL		PRZZZZZUSA
PIMM, ERNST	58	M	LABR		PRZZZZZUSA
WILHELMINE	50	F	W		PRZZZZZUSA
STANK-ZWIECZ, PELAGIA	25	F	SGL		PRZZZZZUSA
LICH, WILHELMINE	53	F	W		PRZZZZZUSA
BERTHA	14	F	D		PRZZZZZUSA
LAEGKOWSKI, PETRONELLA	42	F	W		PRZZZZZUSA
JOSEF	11	M	CH		PRZZZZZUSA
MICHAEL	9	M	CHILD		PRZZZZZUSA
CACILIE	4	F	CHILD		PRZZZZZUSA
PAGEL, CHRISTIAN	38	M	LABR		PRZZZZZUSA
MARIA	33	F	W		PRZZZZZUSA
JOHAN	14	M	CH		PRZZZZZUSA
EMMA	13	F	CH		PRZZZZZUSA
MARTHA	10	F	CH		PRZZZZZUSA
ANNA	6	F	CHILD		PRZZZZZUSA
IDA	5	F	CHILD		PRZZZZZUSA
MINNA	3	F	CHILD		PRZZZZZUSA
BARTZ, WILHELM	15	M	BY		PRZZZZZUSA
JOHANES	10	M	BY		PRZZZZZUSA
BECKER, FRITZ	25	M	JNR		PRZZZZZUSA
PRONDEZIWSKI, KATHA	30	F	W		PRZZZZZUSA
LEON	7	M	CHILD		PRZZZZZUSA
PAUL	4	M	CHILD		PRZZZZZUSA
ANNA	3	M	CHILD		PRZZZZZUSA
ANTONIA	1	M	CHILD		PRZZZZZUSA
WITT, ANDREAS	28	M	PRNTR		PRZZZZZUSA
BROWN, CARL	28	M	MSN		PRZZZZZUSA
MUELLER, CARL	22	M	LABR		PRZZZZZUSA
AUGUSTA	22	F	W		PRZZZZZUSA
GOTTFRIED	.03	M	INFANT		PRZZZZZUSA
BURO-, BERTHA	20	F	SGL		PRZZZZZUSA
ROSSOW, MARIE	24	F	W		PRZZZZZUSA
HELENE	4	F	CHILD		PRZZZZZUSA
CARL	2	M	CHILD		PRZZZZZUSA
HASS, FRIEDRICH	26	M	CDR		PRZZZZZUSA
GUNTHER, DOROTHEA	38	F	SGL		PRZZZZZUSA
HARTMANN, AMANDA	17	F	SGL		PRZZZZZUSA
URBANCZYK, PAUL	30	M	SHMK		PRZZZZZUSA
A-SEZAK, FRANCISKA	24	F	SGL		PRZZZZZUSA
LIPINSKI, HENRIETTE	41	F	W		PRZZZZZUSA
GUSTAV	16	M	S		PRZZZZZUSA
MARIE	9	F	CHILD		PRZZZZZUSA
CHELMIENIEWICZ, VERONIK	.11	F	INFANT		PRZZZZZUSA
KUBICKI, VICTORIA	22	F	SGL		PRZZZZZUSA
LOCKSTADT, JULIUS	25	M	LABR		PRZZZZZUSA
GRUNO, EMIL	21	M	LABR		PRZZZZZUSA
MUELLER, OTTO	22	M	BCHR		PRZZZZZUSA
BARTELT, BERTHA	22	F	SGL		PRZZZZZUSA
J--CKEL, THEODOR	45	M	MCHT		PRZZZZZUSA
MELCHEN, HERMAN	17	M	FARMER		PRZZZZZUSA
SCHMIDT, FRIEDRIKE	52	F	W		PRZZZZZUSA
ELISABETH	14	F	D		PRZZZZZUSA
RAUSCHENBERGER, THEODOR	37	M	BKPR		PRZZZZZUSA
URBSCHEIT, JULIE	38	F	W		PRZZZZZUSA
MARGARETHE	11	F	CH		PRZZZZZUSA
META	8	F	CHILD		PRZZZZZUSA
OSKAR	4	M	CHILD		PRZZZZZUSA
MARIE	2	F	CHILD		PRZZZZZUSA
MUNDT, FRIEDRIKE	57	F	W		PRZZZZZUSA
KRUEGER, WILHELMINE	10	F	CH		PRZZZZZUSA
MAUS, PAULINE	55	F	CH		PRZZZZZUSA
WEHNER, ROBERT	54	M	GDNR		PRZZZZZUSA
PROCTER, JOHAN	43	M	LABR		PRZZZZZUSA
DOROTHEA	40	F	W		PRZZZZZUSA
JOHANNA	19	F	CH		PRZZZZZUSA
FRITZ	17	M	CH		PRZZZZZUSA
AUGUSTE	15	F	CH		PRZZZZZUSA
CARL	13	M	CH		PRZZZZZUSA
MARIE	9	F	CHILD		PRZZZZZUSA
JOHAN	3	F	CHILD		PRZZZZZUSA
MARTHA	1	F	CHILD		PRZZZZZUSA
GUENTHER, PAULINE	26	F	W		PRZZZZZUSA
FRIEDRICH	6	M	CHILD		PRZZZZZUSA
THRUN, CARL	24	M	LABR		PRZZZZZUSA
KAMINSKI, FRANZ	45	M	LABR		PRZZZZZUSA
FLORENTINE	43	F	W		PRZZZZZUSA
STEPHAN	15	M	CH		PRZZZZZUSA
MARIE	11	F	CH		PRZZZZZUSA
PETER	7	M	CHILD		PRZZZZZUSA
THERESE	5	F	CHILD		PRZZZZZUSA
PRILLWITZ, ANNA	11	F	CH		PRZZZZZUSA
HAHNEMAN, FRIEDRIKE	62	F	W		PRZZZZZUSA
LANGE, FRIEDRICH	25	M	TLR		PRZZZZZUSA
SEEGERT, EMMA	31	F	W		PRZZZZZUSA
PAUL	9	M	CHILD		PRZZZZZUSA
MARTHA	8	F	CHILD		PRZZZZZUSA
JOHANES	.10	M	INFANT		PRZZZZZUSA
KASTEN, EMILIE	28	F	W		PRZZZZZUSA
EMIL	7	M	CHILD		PRZZZZZUSA
ANNA	4	F	CHILD		PRZZZZZUSA
OTT	2	M	CHILD		PRZZZZZUSA
FRANZ	.08	M	INFANT		PRZZZZZUSA
KELM, AUGUST	23	M	LABR		PRZZZZZUSA
REDMAN, RUDOLF	25	M	CDR		PRZZZZZUSA
MELCH-OR, CARL	16	M	MCHT		PRZZZZZUSA
GERBER, AUGUST	23	M	BKR		PRZZZZZUSA
ZANDECKI, ANTON	23	M	FARMER		PRZZZZZUSA
-ORPAHL, AUGUST	.09	M	INFANT		PRZZZZZUSA
JAENICKE, HERMAN	24	M	MUSN		PRZZZZZUSA
ROTENHAGEN, HERMAN	34	M	SHMK		PRZZZZZUSA
KOEHLER, PAUL	26	M	UNKNOWN		PRZZZZZUSA
LINDSTADT, ALBERTINE	23	F	SGL		PRZZZZZUSA
ALBERT	16	M	B		PRZZZZZUSA
DETTLAFF, JOSEF	31	M	LABR		PRZZZZZUSA
HASSE, MARIE	22	F	SGL		PRZZZZZUSA
LOEWENTHAL, LOUIS	29	M	MCHT		PRZZZZZUSA
BERRBAUM, JULIUS	22	M	MCHT		PRZZZZZUSA
PESCH, CARL	1	M	CHILD		PRZZZZZUSA
STACHOWITZ, FRANZ	.01	M	INFANT		PRZZZZUNK
LUDTKE, ANNA	26	F	W		PRZZZZUNK

PASSENGER	AGE	SEX	OCCUPATION	PRVVL DIES

SHIP: PERUVIAN

FROM: HALIFAX AND LIVERPOOL
TO: BALTIMORE
ARRIVED: 31 OCTOBER 1888

PASSENGER	AGE	SEX	OCCUPATION	PRVVLDIES
LEMARGNE, THERESA	22	F	GVNS	FRZZZZBAL
WELL, CHRISTOPH	25	M	SMH	GRZZZZBAL
MOSCHKOWITZ, IGNAC	22	M	BBR	GRZZZZPIT
HAZUCOWE, MARIA	24	F	W	GRZZZZUNK
JOSEPH	.08	M	INFANT	GRZZZZUNK
WEIMMAN, HERMAN	25	M	GDNR	GRZZZZLOU
DIZKOWSKI, EMILIE	27	F	W	GRZZZZPIT
MARTHA	.02	F	INFANT	GRZZZZPIT
ELSE	.11	F	INFANT	GRZZZZPIT
KREICHEL, AUGUST	24	M	DSTLR	GRZZZZSTL

SHIP: WISCONSIN

FROM: LIVERPOOL AND QUEENSTOWN
TO: NEW YORK
ARRIVED: 31 OCTOBER 1888

PASSENGER	AGE	SEX	OCCUPATION	PRVVLDIES
SCHITKE, ZLATE	43	F	W	GRZZZZUSA
KLUGER, SIMON	23	M	GZR	GRZZZZUSA
SCHITKE, CIWIE	7	F	CHILD	GRZZZZUSA
ROLVE, MINNA	28	F	SP	GRZZZZUSA
FLIDEL, RIWKE	18	F	SP	GRZZZZUSA
SCHITKE, ETTEL	7	F	CHILD	GRZZZZUSA
GITLITZ, SOSSIE	20	F	SP	GRZZZZUSA
EHRENFURT, FRANZ	27	M	FARMER	GRZZZZUSA
KALWEK, JULIUS	25	M	PMBR	GRZZZZUSA
SCHILK, WM.	22	M	TLR	GRZZZZUSA
SCHAUB, CONRAD	45	M	GZR	GRZZZZUSA
ELIZA	39	F	W	GRZZZZUSA
CARL	19	M	PMBR	GRZZZZUSA
FRIDA	2	F	CHILD	GRZZZZUSA
PAULINE	.08	F	INFANT	GRZZZZUSA

SHIP: PENNLAND

FROM: ANTWERP
TO: NEW YORK
ARRIVED: 01 NOVEMBER 1888

PASSENGER	AGE	SEX	OCCUPATION	PRVVLDIES
LICHTER, F.	24	M	MCHT	GRAEDPUSA
WEIT, P.	21	M	MCHT	GRACEGUSA
LENAITE, P.	36	F	UNKNOWN	GRAAECUSA
ERB, E.	24	M	CAR	GRABHTUSA
STROTTHOTHE, H.	23	M	MCHT	GRAALZUSA
MEYER, J.	45	M	MCHT	GRAAECUSA
TIEMANN, H.	50	F	UNKNOWN	GRAAECUSA
COULUN, E.	60	M	ART	GRADXWUSA
BERGER, E.	38	M	ART	GRADXWUSA
U	29	F	ART	GRADXWUSA
LOUISE	3	F	CHILD	GRADXWUSA
LAFARGE, E.	26	M	ART	GRADXWNY
U	24	F	ART	GRADXWNY
LAMATTE, G.	31	M	ART	GRADXWNY
U	28	F	UNKNOWN	GRADXWNY
CLAVERIE, A.	28	M	ART	GRADXWNY
PLAIN, E.	42	M	ART	GRADXWNY
LENFANT, H.	43	M	ART	GRADXWNY
TETLINGER, F.	49	M	ART	GRADXWNY

PASSENGER	AGE	SEX	OCCUPATION	PRVVLDIES
PELISSON, J.	35	M	ART	GRADXWNY
PEQUILLAU, J.	30	M	ART	GRADXWNY
TAILLARD, J.	42	M	ART	GRADXWNY
DUEVS, L.	55	M	ART	GRADXWNY
MARECHAL, J.	25	M	ART	GRADXWNY
FLAEHAT, VANDIRIE	27	F	UNKNOWN	GRADXWNY
DEVOLTRY, LELIA	39	F	ART	GRADXWNY
DIDAU, E.	32	F	ART	GRADXWNY
PARIS, A.	23	F	ART	GRADXWNY
CHARPENTIER, B.	21	F	ART	GRADXWNY
E.	58	F	ART	GRADXWNY
DUCOS, M.	28	F	ART	GRADXWNY
BALMY, J.	26	F	ART	GRADXWNY
J.	3	F	CHILD	GRADXWNY
GUIBLOH, J.	22	F	ART	GRADXWNY
LERVY, J.	18	F	ART	GRADXWNY
FAUCONNIER, J.	36	M	ART	GRADXWNY
U	28	F	ART	GRADXWNY
U	.06	M	INFANT	GRADXWNY
A.	34	M	ART	GRADXWNY
U	25	F	UNKNOWN	GRADXWNY
FORIGAL, A.	43	M	ART	GRADXWNY
MANTE, E.	25	M	ART	GRADXWNY
GARNIER, E.	28	M	ART	GRADXWNY
BEUFORT, R.	20	M	ART	GRADXWNY
LOGRAYE, F.	31	M	ART	GRADXWNY
LECLERG, F.	19	M	ART	GRADXWNY
LENOM, A.	21	M	ART	GRADXWNY
WUERG, WILH.	42	F	UNKNOWN	GRAAABNY
MAIER, PHILIP.	22	F	SVNT	GRAFGJNY
SCHAPP, KATCHEN	17	F	SVNT	GRAFGJNY
ANNA	19	F	SVNT	GRAFGJNY
DIRKES, JOS.	17	M	LABR	GRZZZZCH
DZENSKI, OTTO	16	M	CPTR	GRAAKHMIL
MELLIES, ERNEST	18	M	LABR	GRZZZZCH
AHLGRIN, HCH.	28	M	LABR	GRADKKUSA
REINER, L.	17	F	UNKNOWN	GRZZZZNY
LINDNER, MARG.	21	F	UNKNOWN	GRAGFNSTL
ORLOWSKI, F.	28	M	MCHT	GRZZZZPHI
AUG.	23	F	UNKNOWN	GRZZZZPHI
BERTHA	.06	F	INFANT	GRZZZZPHI
LASKOWSKI, GUST.	24	M	TLR	GRZZZZCLE
KONIG, L.	42	M	LABR	GRZZZZUNK
U	8	F	CHILD	GRZZZZUNK
ELISE	7	F	CHILD	GRZZZZUNK
ANNA	4	F	CHILD	GRZZZZUNK
DUMPFERT, MARG.	20	F	UNKNOWN	GRZZZZRDG
WAGNER, O.	26	M	LABR	GRAGFDCH
KRUEGER, H.	59	F	UNKNOWN	GRAAKHCH
WOLLHOEFER, ELISA	22	F	SVNT	GRZZZZSTL
PIONTEK, AUG.	21	M	LABR	GRAHLIUNK
IRTLE, WILHELM	57	F	CK	GRAAKHNY
U	11	F	CH	GRAAKHNY
CLAUSS, WM.	19	F	CK	GRZZZZNY
MEYER, CAROLS	23	F	CK	GRAEIHNY
SCHEID, F.	35	M	SMH	GRAEIHNY
LOES, MARIA	21	F	SVNT	GRAGLSCH
SAMES, PETER	23	M	LABR	GRAATBCH
GRIMLING, MARIA	18	F	SVNT	GRZZZZNY
URBAN, ANNA	11	F	CH	GRZZZZNY
KUNIGUNDE	11	F	UNKNOWN	GRZZZZNY
RECLING, J.	24	M	CPTR	GRZZZZNY
MOENCH, WALBURGA	25	F	UNKNOWN	GRZZZZSP
EBERH.	4	M	CHILD	GRZZZZSP
JAEGER, MAR.	40	F	UNKNOWN	GRZZZZNY
LINA	10	F	CH	GRZZZZNY
KEPPICH, GOTTF.	22	M	LABR	GRADKONY
HAUSSLER, RUP.	29	M	LABR	GRZZZZNY
MADERHOF, SUS.	30	F	UNKNOWN	GRZZZZJON
JOH.	4	M	CHILD	GRZZZZJON
SCHULZ, MATH.	23	M	SMH	GRZZZZCIN
HERZIG, ERNST	30	M	CPTR	GRAAKHNY
SCHARMANN, JOH.	36	M	CPTR	GRAGOKNY
FAUSTMANN, FR.	19	M	LABR	GRZZZZNY
KESSEL, G.P.	41	M	FARMER	GRADEINY

405

PASSENGER	AGE	SEX	OCCUPATION	PRVL	DES
MAR.	44	F	UNKNOWN		GRADEINY
J.	19	M	UNKNOWN		GRADEINY
G.	17	M	UNKNOWN		GRADEINY
MAR.	15	F	UNKNOWN		GRADEINY
PH.	13	M	UNKNOWN		GRADEINY
J.	11	M	CH		GRADEINY
PH.	8	M	CHILD		GRADEINY
J.	5	M	CHILD		GRADEINY
KUCKES, OTTO	17	M	LABR		GRADEINY
GREFFEN, MARIE	23	F	UNKNOWN		GRZZZZPIT
F.	.06	M	INFANT		GRZZZZPIT
WOLFF, HCH.	26	M	SHMK		GRZZZZNY
BLUECHER, EMILIE	20	F	SVNT		GRZZZZNY
SEITZ, MAGD.	22	F	SVNT		GRAFNUNY
ARMBRUESTER, R.	21	M	LABR		GRZZZZNY
HACKER, GOTTL.	29	M	TLR		GRZZZZNY
STRENG, ADAM	45	M	BCHR		GRZZZZNY
SECGER, CHRISTINA	28	F	SVNT		GRABPMNY
HATZMANN, G.	14	M	LABR		GRZZZZNY
MULLER, WILH.	10	M	CH		GRZZZZNY
STROBEL, MICH.	23	M	FARMER		GRZZZZNY
LOCHMULLER, CATH.	18	F	SMSTS		GRZZZZNY
NIMSEL, ELISE	34	F	UNKNOWN		GRZZZZCIN
SCHWINDEL, JOS.	9	M	CHILD		GRZZZZCIN
NIMSEL, MAX	7	M	CHILD		GRZZZZCIN
OTTO	3	M	CHILD		GRZZZZCIN
WEIGAND, MARG.	59	F	UNKNOWN		GRZZZZBUF
JOSEFA	40	F	UNKNOWN		GRZZZZBUF
J.	2	M	CHILD		GRZZZZBUF
SCHOBERT, J.	23	M	BKR		GRZZZZBUF
KIRCHHOFER, FERD.	27	M	BKR		GRAGBPBUF
WEYERSTALL, EWALD	28	M	LABR		GRABHTBUF
NOTTENBAUM, H.	30	M	LABR		GRABHTBUF
ALTEN, A.	26	M	LABR		GRABHTSP
BEITGEL, F.	24	M	WVR		GRZZZZNY
PESTSCHEID, W.	19	M	WVR		GRAJRXNY
SCHWARZ, J.	20	M	CPTR		GRZZZZNY
BUECHEL, GUST.	44	M	LABR		GRAEWXNY
PFEIL, MATHIAS	43	M	LABR		GRAEWXNY
BUEMCKE, W.	45	M	LABR		GRAEWXNY
WEIZMANN, A.	23	M	LABR		GRZZZZNY
HILLEMANS, P.	28	M	LABR		GRAEWXNY
SEIFEL, J.	35	M	LABR		GRAJRXNY
BARBIAN, J.	21	M	LABR		GRZZZZNY
SAENGER, A.	45	M	WVR		GRABSYNY
AHLGRUEN, WILH.	18	F	UNKNOWN		GRZZZZCH
PHILIPP, AD.	24	M	LABR		GRZZZZCH
BERTHA	22	F	UNKNOWN		GRZZZZCH
LAURA	27	F	UNKNOWN		GRZZZZCH
WULLENJOHANN, C.	28	M	LABR		GRZZZZNY
MAR.	26	F	UNKNOWN		GRZZZZNY
ANNA	3	F	CHILD		GRZZZZNY
ELISA	.06	F	INFANT		GRZZZZNY
WEINBERG, LEAH	28	F	UNKNOWN		GRZZZZNY
RACHEL	3	F	CHILD		GRZZZZNY
SARAH	.06	F	INFANT		GRZZZZNY
MILCHICKEN, LEIBE	30	F	UNKNOWN		GRZZZZNY
CHAWE	10	F	CH		GRZZZZNY
SARAH	6	F	CHILD		GRZZZZNY
LENTHOFF, ERNEST	39	M	CPR		GRZZZZNY
ANT.	29	F	UNKNOWN		GRZZZZNY
ECKERT, M.	23	M	CMST		GRZZZZPHI
JOHANNA	25	F	UNKNOWN		GRZZZZPHI
SBORALSKI, F.	22	M	BKR		GRZZZZPHI
MULLER, MARG.	19	F	UNKNOWN		GRAHPAPHI
RINCK, MAGGIE	35	F	UNKNOWN		GRAAABNY
HOELLE, J.	21	M	LABR		GRZZZZNY
GOEBEL, MARG.	29	F	UNKNOWN		GRAAECNY
SATTER, MARIA	18	F	SVNT		GRZZZZNY
BACH, L.	20	M	LABR		GRABOQNY
FRANZ, DOROTHEA	22	F	CK		GRABOQNY
SCHMIDLI, ALBERTINE	20	F	CK		GRAAHUNY
LUTTEL, MARG.	22	F	SVNT		GRAAHUNY
FREY, MARIE	28	F	UNKNOWN		GRAAHUNY
STEPHANIE	1	F	CHILD		GRAAHUNY
FRIEDLI, ELISE	27	F	UNKNOWN		GRAAHUNY
SCHMALL, J.	53	M	FARMER		GRAAHUNY
TELL, ANNA	48	F	UNKNOWN		GRAAHUNY
SCHMALL, P.	25	M	FARMER		GRAAHUNY
A.	21	M	FARMER		GRAAHUNY
SUSANNE	18	F	UNKNOWN		GRAAHUNY
ANNA	16	F	UNKNOWN		GRAAHUNY
MARIE	13	F	UNKNOWN		GRAAHUNY
MARG.	11	F	UNKNOWN		GRAAHUNY
JACOB	8	M	CHILD		GRAAHUNY
FELL, CATH.	19	F	SVNT		GRAAHUNY
GALES, CATH.	26	F	SVNT		GRAAHUNY
ZAPP, J.	19	M	LABR		GRZZZZNY
MUELLER, C.	44	M	MCHT		GRZZZZNY
EMMA	42	F	UNKNOWN		GRZZZZNY
EMMA	19	F	UNKNOWN		GRZZZZNY
H.	11	M	CH		GRZZZZNY
WILLMUTH, J.B.	21	M	LKSH		GRZZZZNY
PFEIFFER, MICH.	22	M	LABR		GRZZZZHAT
GASPAR, J.	22	F	UNKNOWN		GRAGLSBUF
SCHWARZ, MARG.	17	F	UNKNOWN		GRAGLSBUF
G.	23	M	UNKNOWN		GRAGLSNY
WISSLER, H.	52	M	LABR		GRAGLSNY
MAGD.	48	F	UNKNOWN		GRAGLSNY
MARIE	19	F	UNKNOWN		GRAGLSNY
LOUIS	17	M	LABR		GRAGLSNY
JOSEPH	15	M	LABR		GRAGLSNY
P.	13	M	LABR		GRAGLSNY
C.	10	M	CH		GRAGLSNY
MARTIN	9	M	CHILD		GRAGLSNY
H.	7	M	CHILD		GRAGLSNY
MAGD.	6	F	CHILD		GRAGLSNY
NIC	3	M	CHILD		GRAGLSNY
ANNA	.10	F	INFANT		GRAGLSNY
ROOS, J.	28	M	CTR		GRAGLSNY
LAUF, J.P.	21	M	CPR		GRAGLSNY
MESSER, J.	21	M	STNR		GRABZWCIN
LEITER, J.	21	M	PNTR		GRZZZZCIN
HALBIG, CAROL.	17	F	UNKNOWN		GRAJYQUNK
WINDERLIN, MARG.	30	F	HSKPR		GRAAHUCH
MARG.	5	F	CHILD		GRAAHUCH
EGOLF, JACOB	59	M	LABR		SRZZZZNY
ERNEST	14	M	LABR		SRZZZZNY
LOUISE	4	F	CHILD		SRZZZZNY
CHELOMELA	49	F	UNKNOWN		SRZZZZNY
MUELLER, MARTHA	54	F	UNKNOWN		SRZZZZNY
MARIA	17	F	UNKNOWN		SRZZZZNY
JOSEPHINE	14	F	UNKNOWN		SRZZZZNY
SCHAFER, CAROL.	40	F	UNKNOWN		GRZZZZUNK
AUGUSTA	7	F	CHILD		GRZZZZUNK
H.	6	M	CHILD		GRZZZZUNK
C.	4	M	CHILD		GRZZZZUNK
LISA	2	F	CHILD		GRZZZZUNK
W.	.06	M	INFANT		GRZZZZUNK
BLUEMBACH, W.	30	M	LABR		GRAAOLDET
ANNA	24	F	UNKNOWN		GRAAOLDET
EMILIE	2	F	CHILD		GRAAOLDET
W.	.06	M	INFANT		GRAAOLDET
SACHERER, G.	20	M	LABR		GRAEIHUNK
FISCHBACH, H.	30	M	LABR		GRABHTNY
SALOMONS, ADA	21	F	UNKNOWN		GRZZZZNY
LEA	23	F	UNKNOWN		GRZZZZNY
MEYER, SER.	26	M	CPR		GRZZZZNY
WEBER, CATH.	29	F	CK		GRADBINY
JAHN, F.	38	M	CPTR		GRZZZZUNK
LERNIG, ANNA	28	F	UNKNOWN		GRZZZZUNK
STANER, MARION	20	F	SVNT		GRZZZZUNK
SCHWARTZ, J.	25	M	LABR		GRZZZZUNK
DAESGER, J.	36	M	LABR		LXZZZZUNK
VANBIRGELEN, J.	22	M	LABR		LXACBRMIN
BRAINEIER, A.	26	M	UNKNOWN		LXAEWXUNK
HELENE	.08	F	INFANT		LXAEWXUNK
LANOIS, ELISA	21	F	UNKNOWN		FRZZZZPIT
IRMA	2	F	CHILD		FRZZZZPIT
FRANC	.06	M	INFANT		FRZZZZPIT

PASSENGER	AGE	SEX	OCCUPATION	PRVVL	DES
KEMPF, LYDIA	25	F	SVNT	FRADLENY	
DUEFENBROUN, ANTON	30	M	FARMER	FRABZWNY	
MAPPS, CATH.	41	F	UNKNOWN	FRABZWNY	
HAULBERGER, MARIA	23	F	CK	FRABZWNY	
DEIS, G.	44	M	LABR	FRABZWNY	
CATH.	47	F	UNKNOWN	FRABZWNY	
JOS.	11	M	CH	FRABZWNY	
MARIE	10	F	CH	FRABZWNY	
HELENE	9	F	CHILD	FRABZWNY	
HERBER, E.	24	M	FARMER	FRAANGLOU	
BADINA, JOSEPHINA	78	F	UNKNOWN	FRABZWLOU	
FRISHLER, J.	31	M	FARMER	FRABZWCIN	
MAGD.	24	M	UNKNOWN	FRABZWCIN	
CH.	4	M	CHILD	FRABZWCIN	
JOS.	2	F	CHILD	FRABZWCIN	
MARIE	27	F	UNKNOWN	FRABZWCIN	
ANTON	.06	M	INFANT	FRABZWCIN	
GRUNDER, MAGD.	16	F	SMSTS	FRABZWCH	
MANGLER, ANNA	56	F	UNKNOWN	GRZZZZCIN	
URSULA	25	F	UNKNOWN	GRZZZZCIN	
JOHANN	.06	M	INFANT	GRZZZZCIN	
FUCHS, L.	27	M	LABR	GRZZZZCIN	
KEMMER, C.	24	M	CMST	GRADBQCIN	
DEIZGEN, ANNA	19	F	SVNT	LXZZZZCH	
FEDERHEIL, CHRIST.	18	M	CPTR	LXAGLSNY	
SCHILINGER, MARG.	51	F	UNKNOWN	LXAFGWCIN	
MAASS, MARIA	26	F	UNKNOWN	LXAFGWCIN	
FRANCISCA	17	F	UNKNOWN	LXAFGWCIN	
NICOLAUS	9	M	CHILD	LXAFGWCIN	
BILLEREY, J.	30	M	MNR	LXAGKHBUF	
MARIE	20	F	UNKNOWN	LXAGKHBUF	
DUEZ, E.	23	M	MNR	FRZZZZUNK	
J.	21	M	MNR	FRZZZZUNK	
LAURENT, JOSEPH	26	M	MNR	FRZZZZUNK	
DUPONT, FRANC	22	M	MNR	FRZZZZUNK	
DEBAUQUENNE, JULIE	26	M	HSKPR	FRZZZZUNK	
MANDERER, ELISA	17	F	UNKNOWN	FRZZZZNY	
HOEPP, GUST.	38	M	LABR	FRALKANY	
BERTHA	26	F	UNKNOWN	FRALKANY	
HELENA	5	F	CHILD	FRALKANY	
ELLA	.06	F	INFANT	FRALKANY	
DUBOIS, G.	23	M	MNR	FRZZZZUNK	
LEFORT, ARTH.	27	M	MNR	FRZZZZUSA	
SKAIEROSKY, WENZEL	29	M	MNR	FRACXVNY	
KOCH, NIC	25	M	LABR	FRACXVNY	
FRAEGER, HULDA	19	F	UNKNOWN	FRACXVNY	
FRANCK, WENZEL	17	M	LABR	FRACXVNY	
HONICK, F.	44	M	LABR	FRACXVNY	
ALOISIE	11	F	CH	FRACXVNY	
PENKAVA, MARIA	21	F	UNKNOWN	FRACXVNY	

SHIP: ROMAN

FROM: LIVERPOOL
TO: BOSTON
ARRIVED: 02 NOVEMBER 1888

PASSENGER	AGE	SEX	OCCUPATION	PRVVL	DES
KARRISKY, MORRIS	23	M	LABR	GRZZZZBO	

SHIP: SORRENTO

FROM: HAMBURG
TO: NEW YORK
ARRIVED: 02 NOVEMBER 1888

PASSENGER	AGE	SEX	OCCUPATION	PRVVL	DES
GROCHOWSKA, ANTONIA	22	F	SGL	PRZZZZNY	
AUGUSTIN, JOACHIM	70	M	LABR	MKZZZZCH	
SOPHIE	67	F	W	MKZZZZCH	
WICKMAN, CARL	30	M	LABR	MKZZZZCH	
AUGUSTE	29	F	W	MKZZZZCH	
AUGUSTE	4	F	CHILD	MKZZZZCH	
CARL	1	M	CHILD	MKZZZZCH	
HYMANN, JULIE	50	F	W	PRZZZZNY	
AUGUSTE	28	F	WO	PRZZZZNY	
EMMA	18	F	WO	PRZZZZNY	
KETTERER, PAULINE	21	F	SGL	BDZZZZNY	
CORMNELL, MARIA	22	F	SGL	MKZZZZCH	
LAUDAHN, JOHANN	46	M	FARMER	MKZZZZSP	
ELISABETH	47	F	WO	MKZZZZSP	
FRIEDRICH	17	M	UNKNOWN	MKZZZZSP	
MINNA	7	F	CHILD	MKZZZZSP	
WILH.	6	M	CHILD	MKZZZZSP	
ELISE	3	F	CHILD	MKZZZZSP	
WOSTENBERG, FRIEDRICH	23	M	FARMER	MKZZZZCIN	
MARIE	21	F	W	MKZZZZCIN	
SOPHIE	2	F	CHILD	MKZZZZCIN	
FRIEDA	.04	F	INFANT	MKZZZZCIN	
VOSS, JOH.	37	M	FARMER	MKZZZZNY	
ANNA	36	F	W	MKZZZZNY	
ERNST	6	M	CHILD	MKZZZZNY	
FRIEDERIKE	5	F	CHILD	MKZZZZNY	
OTTO	3	M	CHILD	MKZZZZNY	
FRIEDA	2	F	CHILD	MKZZZZNY	
JOH.	.11	M	INFANT	MKZZZZNY	
KAMPHENKEL, JOH.	16	M	MCHT	HBZZZZSP	
PUTZKE, LEOPOLD	34	M	LABR	PRZZZZNY	
OTTO	3	M	CHILD	PRZZZZNY	
CZOLLEK, EMILIE	47	F	W	PRZZZZNY	
PAUL	7	M	CHILD	PRZZZZNY	
KUMM, NALESKA	22	F	SGL	PRZZZZNY	
STENZEL, AMALIA	36	F	SGL	PRZZZZNY	
GROTH, WILH.	44	M	FARMER	MKZZZZCH	
SOPHIE	46	F	FARMER	MKZZZZCH	
HEINR.	14	M	BY	MKZZZZCH	
FRIEDR.	7	M	CHILD	MKZZZZCH	
KARRABAU, FRANZ	21	M	LABR	PRZZZZNY	
PIEPER, WILHELM	20	M	FARMER	PRZZZZNY	
LBERS, HERMAN	32	M	FARMER	PRZZZZNY	
MORATZ, PELAGIA	23	F	SGL	PRZZZZNY	
RUGUSZTKA, JOSEPH	7	M	CHILD	PRZZZZNY	
AGNISKA	6	F	CHILD	PRZZZZNY	
KIWAR, BALTIOMER	30	M	LABR	PRZZZZNY	
GOTTHARDT, FRANZISKA	26	M	SGL	PRZZZZNY	
LUDWIG, LOUISE	18	F	SGL	PRZZZZNY	
WENZKI, HINRICH	23	M	LABR	PRZZZZBUF	
KELLER, KATH.	16	F	SGL	BDZZZZNY	
BLASCH, AMALIE	26	F	SGL	PRZZZZNY	
BIBER, SALOMON	51	M	MCHT	GRZZZZNY	
BERGER, AUGUSTE	24	F	W	MKZZZZNY	
RAETKE, AUGUSTE	21	F	SGL	MKZZZZNY	
BERGER, HEINRICH	5	M	CHILD	MKZZZZNY	
BEHRENS, MARIE	24	F	SGL	PRZZZZNY	
KERNBACH, EMIL	39	M	LABR	PRZZZZNY	
MARIE	31	F	W	PRZZZZNY	
MALCHEN	7	F	CHILD	PRZZZZNY	
SELMA	3	F	CHILD	PRZZZZNY	
REHLAENDER, HEINR.	31	M	LABR	MKZZZZNY	
LOUISE	53	F	M	MKZZZZNY	
DAVIDS, OSKAR	18	M	FARMER	PRZZZZNY	
GOTTSCHALK, HEINR.	39	M	LABR	MKZZZZNY	
FRITZ	7	M	CHILD	MKZZZZNY	
AUGUSTE	4	F	CHILD	MKZZZZNY	
HARZ, JOH.	45	M	LABR	MKZZZZNY	

PASSENGER	AGE	SEX	OCCUPATION	PRV VIL DES
FREDERIKE	48	F	W	MKZZZZNY
JOH.	18	M	LABR	MKZZZZNY
LOUISE	16	F	D	MKZZZZNY
HERMANN	15	M	S	MKZZZZNY
WILH.	7	M	CHILD	MKZZZZNY
AUGUST	6	M	CHILD	MKZZZZNY
HEINR.	5	M	CHILD	MKZZZZNY
LOFF, KAROLINE	59	F	W	MKZZZZNY
LINSE, FRIEDR.	40	M	CNF	PRZZZZNY
BRESSEN, HANS	16	M	BKBNDR	PRZZZZCIN
GRAU, PETER	21	M	SLR	PRZZZZNY
GROENING, HEINRICH	45	M	LABR	PRZZZZNY
ANNA	40	F	W	PRZZZZNY
PRYTZKUWUZ, MICHAEL	23	M	LABR	PRZZZZNY
KRIEGER, ADOLF	23	M	MCHT	PRZZZZNY
BRUNS, HERMAN	36	M	LABR	MKZZZZNY
LOUISE	30	F	W	MKZZZZNY
WM.	7	M	CHILD	MKZZZZNY
ANNA	6	F	CHILD	MKZZZZNY
ERNST	2	M	CHILD	MKZZZZNY
HERM.	.06	M	INFANT	MKZZZZNY
MARIE	65	F	WO	MKZZZZNY
WIST, DORETHEA	63	F	WO	MKZZZZNY
STARK, WILH.	29	M	FARMER	MKZZZZNY
HOCHTRITH, HEDWIG	15	F	SGL	PRZZZZNY
BURGER, WILHELM	26	M	BKR	PRZZZZNY
KORNHAUSEL, JOHANN	22	M	LABR	PRZZZZNY
RABE, KARL	32	M	STDNT	PRZZZZMIL
PAWLETTA, LOUIS	32	M	LABR	PRZZZZNY
MARIE	22	F	W	PRZZZZNY
LENK, MARGR.	17	F	SGL	BVZZZZNY
HOLL, GEORG	36	F	WVR	BVZZZZNY
JUNGLING, FRANZ	20	M	BKR	BVZZZZNY
KINTZER, ALFRED	18	M	MLR	PRZZZZNY
KLEMCKE, FRIEDRICH	40	M	FARMER	PRZZZZNY
LOUISE	41	F	WO	PRZZZZNY
MAX	7	M	CHILD	PRZZZZNY
ALBERT	6	M	CHILD	PRZZZZNY
EMILIE	5	F	CHILD	PRZZZZNY
HEINR.	4	M	CHILD	PRZZZZNY
BRAUNE, ALBERT	37	M	MCHT	PRZZZZNY
SJOHOLM, ANNA	22	F	SGL	PRZZZZNY
SAMUELSDOTTER, FRDKE	26	F	SGL	PRZZZZNY
REHLAENDER, LOUISE	31	F	WO	MKZZZZNY
FRIEDR	6	M	CHILD	MKZZZZNY
JOH.	3	M	CHILD	MKZZZZNY
HERM.	.03	M	INFANT	MKZZZZNY
ANNA	.03	F	INFANT	MKZZZZNY
FRIEDA	20	F	WO	MKZZZZNY
PIEDT, FRIEDRICK	26	M	LABR	MKZZZZNY
FALKENBERG, WILHELM	25	M	LABR	MKZZZZNY
BACKALLA, ANNA	28	F	WO	PRZZZZNY
CLARA	6	F	CHILD	PRZZZZNY
OLGA	3	F	CHILD	PRZZZZNY
CARL	.03	M	INFANT	PRZZZZNY
WALLNER, JOHANN	61	M	LABR	PRZZZZNY
EMMA	15	F	D	PRZZZZNY
KNOLL, HUGO	26	M	SMH	PRZZZZNY
IDA	23	F	W	PRZZZZNY
HEYNE, ALFRED	24	M	APTC	PRZZZZNY
BUDASCHEWSKY, SALOMEA	37	F	WO	PRZZZZNY
JOSEFA	7	F	CHILD	PRZZZZNY
EDWARD	5	M	CHILD	PRZZZZNY
VERONA	3	F	CHILD	PRZZZZNY
GRIESBACH, JOH.	17	M	LABR	PRZZZZNY
CHARLOTTE	20	F	SGL	PRZZZZNY
ROGGOW, FRIEDERIKE	28	F	WO	PRZZZZNY
KARL	.11	M	INFANT	PRZZZZNY
HAUBOLDT, ADAM	24	M	SMH	BVZZZZNY
MAAG, RASMUS	47	M	SLR	PRZZZZNY
GOETZE, EDWIN	34	M	BCHR	SWZZZZNY
CLARA	28	F	WO	SWZZZZNY
PNKUS, HERM.	21	M	MCHT	PRZZZZNY
LEOPOLD, EMIL	35	M	GDNR	PRZZZZNY
JOSEPHINE	33	F	W	PRZZZZNY

PASSENGER	AGE	SEX	OCCUPATION	PRV VIL DES
TEICHMAN, ROBERT	24	M	BCHR	PRZZZZNY
KUNTZE, ERNST	30	M	FARMER	SYZZZZSTL
EPPINGER, CARL	17	M	LABR	PRZZZZNY

SHIP: WERRA

FROM: BREMEN AND SOUTHAMPTON
TO: NEW YORK
ARRIVED: 02 OCTOBER 1888 *

PASSENGER	AGE	SEX	OCCUPATION	PRV VIL DES
ROSENBAUM, U	40	M	MCHT	PRADLDUSA
U	32	F	W	PRADLDUSA
WALTER	12	M	CH	PRADLDUSA
MAND.	10	M	CH	PRADLDUSA
KATHE	8	M	CHILD	PRADLDUSA
HERBERT	6	M	CHILD	PRADLDUSA
M.	1	M	CHILD	PRADLDUSA
BECK, ERNST	56	M	MCHT	PRAEVQUSA
MARGE.	35	F	W	PRAEVQUSA
BARTELS, SOPHIE	30	F	NN	PRAEVQUSA
U, SOPHIE	30	F	NN	PRAEVQUSA
OLF, FRIEDKE.	48	F	NN	PRAEVQUSA
SCHAEFER, ELISE	23	F	NN	GRZZZZUSA
BLOCK, ANTON	22	M	TT	BVZZZZUSA
BOMEISLER, BERTHA	21	F	NN	BVZZZZUSA
STAEHLEIN, MARIANNA	59	F	W	BVZZZZUSA
BERGER, SOPHIE	27	F	NN	BVACBRUSA
LINK, ELISAB.	21	F	NN	BVAAGLUSA
ZIELECKE, GUST.	30	M	TT	BVAAKHUSA
SUSANNA	28	F	W	BVAAKHUSA
SCHMIDT, BERTHA	35	F	W	BVZZZZUSA
ZECHIEL, FRIDA	20	F	NN	BVAFJGUSA
DAMOSA, SCHWESTER	27	F	NN	BVAAABUSA
KOSKA, SCHWESTER	26	F	NN	BVAAABUSA
JOSEPHINE	28	F	NN	BVAAABUSA
SOPHIA	25	F	NN	BVAAABUSA
GERTRUD	21	F	NN	BVAAABUSA
JOSEPHA	23	F	NN	BVABOQUSA
GOETZ, BERTHA	33	F	NN	BVABOQUSA
STAMM, JUL.	16	M	TT	BVAAZSUSA
BAER, ELISA	20	F	NN	BVAEDGUSA
STEPHAN, PHILA.	30	F	NN	BVAAGLUSA
ZECHETNIAN, MARICE	60	F	W	BVADLDUSA
KATHA.	22	F	W	BVADLDUSA
MARY	.11	F	INFANT	BVADLDUSA
WALTHER, BERTHA	18	F	NN	BVAARRUSA
WILKENS, KAETHE	17	F	NN	BVAARRUSA
MITHOFER, MARIE	21	F	NN	BVADGJUSA
SEELIG, JUL.	69	M	TT	BVADCJUSA
GOEZ, CATHA.WM.	50	F	W	BVADCJUSA
ALEXANDER, EMMA	24	F	NN	BVAARRUSA
MUELLER, ANNA	16	F	NN	BVACBRUSA
DRESSEL, FRITZ	27	M	TT	BVAAZSUSA
ELISAB.	21	F	W	BVAAZSUSA
BUECHNER, ED.	37	M	TT	BVAEATUSA
MALER, ERNSTE.	30	F	NN	BVADKKUSA
MUELLER, MINNA	30	F	NN	BVABDMUSA
MENDYK, MATHIAS	33	M	LABR	BVAEUXUSA
BEDMANN, BERNHD.	49	M	LABR	GRZZZZUSA
PAULE.	40	F	W	GRZZZZUSA
LOUISE	18	F	NN	GRZZZZUSA
EDUARD	16	M	NN	GRZZZZUSA
BECHMANN, ALBRECHT	10	M	CH	GRZZZZUSA
MAX	8	M	CHILD	GRZZZZUSA
HULDA	6	F	CHILD	GRZZZZUSA
LINA	3	F	CHILD	GRZZZZUSA
BRAENTINGAM, DANIEL	16	M	NN	GRAIUJUSA
SEELIGMANN, JOHS.	16	M	NN	GRZZZZUSA
LORENZEN, LORENZ	21	M	TT	GRABNSUSA
AMALIA	27	F	W	GRABNSUSA

*Arrival date out of chronological order.

408

PASSENGER	AGE	SEX	OCCUPATION	PRVL	DES
LOESCHER, THEODOR	16	M	LABR	GRZZZZ	USA
ULLRICH, ANNA	19	F	NN	GRACPS	USA
NOVAK, AGNES	23	F	W	GRACPS	USA
STANISL.	.09	M	INFANT	GRACPS	USA
BROKOSKA, MICHA.	26	F	NN	GRZZZZ	USA
MIELKE, AUGUSTE	30	F	NN	GRADES	USA
PINZ, HERMNIE.	22	F	NN	GRADES	USA
NUNNER, KONRAD	21	M	LABR	GRAAIE	USA
BOLLAWSKI, BERTHA	19	F	NN	GRADBD	USA
CHACHILSKI, JOSEFA	33	F	W	GRADBD	USA
CLARA	8	F	CHILD	GRADBD	USA
SOFIA	6	F	CHILD	GRADBD	USA
BROMCK	3	M	CHILD	GRADBD	USA
HAUSMANN, KATHA.	19	F	NN	GRAESG	USA
OTEMANN, VICTORIA	20	F	NN	GRZZZZ	USA
LORFKOVITS, MARIA	19	F	NN	GRZZZZ	USA
LANGHENNIG, BERTHA	17	F	NN	GRADCD	USA
DEPNER, META	18	F	NN	GRADCD	USA
GRUENEWALD, ANNA	23	F	NN	GRAALJ	USA
BRODMANN, ANNA	19	F	NN	GRAFQW	USA
LOTH, JOSEF	27	M	LABR	GRABFJ	USA
HAGEDORN, AUGUST	11	M	CH	GRABFJ	USA
STERNER, FRANZ	11	M	CH	GRABFJ	USA
NEVE, CATHA.	21	F	CH	GRAESD	USA
FLEDDERMANN, ELISA	24	F	NN	GRAAKT	USA
SCHWAYER, RICH.	20	M	LABR	GRABDM	USA
ZITZER, AD.	19	M	LABR	GRAAIS	USA
STEINMEYER, DORA	20	F	NN	GRAEAT	USA
DAUME, ANNA	18	F	NN	GRZZZZ	USA
HEINR.	17	M	FARMER	GRZZZZ	USA
BLUME, HEINR.	22	M	PNTR	GRAEJW	USA
KRUG, SENZE	20	M	LABR	WMZZZZ	USA
LUMBIUS, CAROLE.	24	F	NN	WMAFNK	USA
BALZ, SOPHIE	19	F	NN	WMZZZZ	USA
MAIER, LOUISE	17	F	NN	WMZZZZ	USA
BURKHARDT, ADOLF	16	M	BKR	WMABET	USA
GRUBER, CARL	22	M	SHMK	WMZZZZ	USA
HIRLEMANN, THERESIA	25	F	NN	WMZZZZ	USA
WUTH, LOUIS	16	M	PNTR	WMAJNL	USA
HORR, KATHA.	18	F	NN	WMAAZS	USA
HUEGEL, PHILIPP	23	M	LABR	WMADGX	USA
EDINGER, GUST.	17	M	BCHR	WMADEI	USA
ACKER, GEORG	25	M	FARMER	WMABPC	USA
ROTHMANN, IDA	23	F	NN	WMABWI	USA
DEES, CASP.	25	M	LABR	BVZZZZ	USA
WETTIG, ANNA	19	F	NN	BVABVW	USA
BOCK, CARL	19	M	LKSH	BVABVW	USA
EICH, FRANCISCA	9	F	CHILD	BVABLT	USA
BUSCHDORF, AUGE.	17	F	NN	BVABLT	USA
SOMMER, MARIA	17	F	NN	BVZZZZ	USA
MUELLER, GEORG	21	M	FARMER	BVAATV	USA
KUHN, ADAM	25	M	BKR	BVZZZZ	USA
FREUND, JOSEF	34	M	LABR	BVZZZZ	USA
SCHMIDT, MARGA.	61	F	W	BVZZZZ	USA
ANNA	23	F	NN	BVZZZZ	USA
KARSTEKAMP, HEINR.	18	M	FARMER	GRZZZZ	USA
MEYERICKS, GEORG	17	M	FARMER	GRZZZZ	USA
WECKERLE, ROSALIA	40	F	W	GRABAR	USA
RECKWERTH, AUG.	15	M	NN	GRAEWD	USA
BECK, MAGDE.	59	F	W	GRAEWD	USA
MAGDE.	22	F	NN	GRAEWD	USA
ZINELL, WILH.	18	M	LABR	GRAEWD	USA
OTTO	16	M	LABR	GRABSO	USA
OTTO	16	M	LABR	GRABSO	USA
HEDDERICH, CATHA.	27	F	W	GRABSO	USA
FRIEDR.	6	M	CHILD	GRABSO	USA
SCHELBACH, HERM.	16	M	FARMER	GRAHJS	USA
BERTHA	18	F	NN	GRAHJS	USA
FLEISCHER, AUG.	27	M	LABR	GRZZZZ	USA
WOLF, EMILIE	21	F	NN	GRZZZZ	USA
SEILER, MARIE	27	F	NN	GRAAKH	USA
GOLTZ, MARIE	26	F	NN	GRAAKH	USA
WITOMSKI, JULIANNA	28	F	W	GRZZZZ	USA
MARIANNA	5	F	CHILD	GRZZZZ	USA
VICTORIA	.01	F	INFANT	GRZZZZ	USA
TOMROW, ELISE	25	F	NN	GRAAKH	USA
OLSSON, AMANDA	32	F	NN	GRAAKH	USA
SCHLUBATIS, LOUISE	17	F	NN	GRZZZZ	USA
RIHN, LOUISE	17	F	NN	GRZZZZ	USA
MORGENEIER, HELENE	18	F	NN	GRABSY	USA
SANDER, FRANZ	22	M	FARMER	GRAAKH	USA
WAGNER, CAROLE.	57	F	W	GRAJJK	USA
LOUISE	3	F	CHILD	GRAJJK	USA
CATHA.	25	F	W	GRAJJK	USA
CH.	19	M	LABR	GRAJJK	USA
MARIA	16	F	NN	GRAJJK	USA
HAUSMANN, FRIEDR.	39	M	LABR	GRAJJK	USA
GERLACH, ROBS.	26	M	FARMER	GRAAKH	USA
JULIANNA	25	F	W	GRAAKH	USA
BURESCH, RICHARD	18	M	FARMER	GRAAKH	USA
ZAKRZEWSKI, JOSEF	24	M	FARMER	GRAAKH	USA
MAJEROWICZ, KATARZYNA	26	F	W	GRZZZZ	USA
HELENE	.09	F	INFANT	GRZZZZ	USA
THEOD.	22	M	FARMER	GRZZZZ	USA
WENDT, IDA	23	F	W	GRZZZZ	USA
ARTHIUR	.09	M	INFANT	GRZZZZ	USA
MEYER, ANNA	45	F	W	GRZZZZ	USA
EMIL	9	M	CHILD	GRZZZZ	USA
BERTHA	8	F	CHILD	GRZZZZ	USA
BURGELEWITZ, ANBNA	50	F	W	GRAEND	USA
SCHAFFRENSKY, ANTONIA	4	F	CHILD	GRZZZZ	USA
AGNISKA	4	F	CHILD	GRZZZZ	USA
JOSEPHA	3	F	CHILD	GRZZZZ	USA
WIECZORECK, ANNA	53	F	W	GRAJSV	USA
JUL.	11	M	CH	GRAJSV	USA
WOLF, ARNO	26	M	LABR	GRAJSV	USA
LOHMANN, LOUISE	20	F	NN	GRAAKH	USA
BUCHHOLZ, AUGUSTE	18	F	NN	GRZZZZ	USA
PRIBE, PAULE.	21	F	NN	GRZZZZ	USA
METZER, CHRIST.	28	M	FARMER	GRACGA	USA
BEHRENS, JOH.	18	M	SMH	GRAJBU	USA
MUELLER, ANNA	17	F	NN	GRZZZZ	USA
DETERING, FR.	18	M	JNR	GRACHB	USA
BUEMNER, JOH.	22	M	FARMER	BDZZZZ	USA
SUSANNA	21	F	W	BDZZZZ	USA
BOEHM, AUG.	22	M	BCHR	BDACRA	USA
STURM, JOH.	17	M	LABR	BDZZZZ	USA
SCHAEDLER, FERD.	18	M	LABR	BDZZZZ	USA
WECKESSER, BABETTE	22	F	NN	BVZZZZ	USA
OECHSLE, ROB.	57	M	LABR	WMZZZZ	USA
SAMSON, HEINR.	24	M	LABR	WMAAUS	USA
STURCKMANN, EMIL	17	M	LABR	GRZZZZ	USA
FRIEDR.	68	M	LABR	GRZZZZ	USA
BOECKER, JOH.	46	M	LABR	GRZZZZ	USA
WALGO, CALETO	22	F	W	GRABDA	USA
UTTENWEILER, JOH.	27	M	FARMER	GRABDA	USA
RAPP, ANTON	47	M	FARMER	GRABDA	USA
AGATHA	49	F	W	GRABDA	USA
HYACINTA	22	F	NN	GRABDA	USA
MARIA	19	F	NN	GRABDA	USA
SALOMONIA	16	F	NN	GRABDA	USA
ROCHUS	14	M	NN	GRABDA	USA
THEOBALD	11	M	NN	GRABDA	USA
MONKA	20	M	NN	GRABDA	USA
KOHRS, METTA	19	M	NN	GRABXW	USA
MEINKE, CATHA.	22	M	NN	GRZZZZ	USA
SCHROEDER, ANNA	22	F	NN	GRABTQ	USA
HORSTMANN, ANNA	22	F	NN	GRABTQ	USA
NEUNABER, HEINR.	66	M	FARMER	GRZZZZ	USA
SCHULZ, WILH.	39	M	FARMER	GRAAKH	USA
PAULE.	36	F	W	GRAAKH	USA
SCHOEPER, JULIE	28	F	W	GRAAKH	USA
LOUISE	3	F	CHILD	GRAAKH	USA
SOPHIE	2	F	CHILD	GRAAKH	USA
NEHRBAS, JOHN	15	M	FARMER	GRADQN	USA
GUMBRECHT, APOLLONIA	27	F	NN	GRADQN	USA
DILLMANN, FRANZ	27	M	FARMER	BVZZZZ	USA
VISOSKY, JOHS.	18	M	FARMER	BVADEM	USA
BAUER, ADAM	21	M	FARMER	BVABKH	USA
LENZ, PETER	25	M	FARMER	BVABKH	USA

```
                      A  S           P V D                              A  S           P V D
PASSENGER             G  E OCCUPATION R I E        PASSENGER            G  E OCCUPATION R I E
                      E  X           V L S                              E  X           V L S
---------------------------------------------      ---------------------------------------------
SEIP, ANNA            20 F NN        BVABKHUSA      KUMMER, GHENRY       30 M FARMER    WMAEWZUSA
FEIGE, RICH.          31 M FARMER    BVACVAUSA        EMILIE             32 F W         WMAEWZUSA
GRUNNER, JOHANN       46 M FARMER    BVADCMUSA        HERTHA              2 F CHILD     WMAEWZUSA
  FRANZ               14 M NN        BVADCMUSA      KOENIG, GEORG        28 M FARMER    WMZZZZUSA
FRUEHWALD, CONRAD     28 M FARMER    BVAENQUSA      BUNKE, META          26 F NN        WMACBRUSA
HORN, BARBA.          24 F NN        BVAENQUSA      KRAKE, REBECCA       17 F NN        WMACBRUSA
SCHWOEDER, CARL       28 M LABR      GRZZZZUSA      STOCKMANN, ANNA      18 F NN        WMACBRUSA
  FRIEDKE.             26 F W         GRZZZZUSA        MARIA              15 F NN        WMACBRUSA
  ALBERT               9 M CHILD     GRZZZZUSA      PATRIZ, HUBER        24 M FARMER    WMZZZZUSA
  FRIEDA               6 F CHILD     GRZZZZUSA      REKER, LOUISE        45 F NN        GRZZZZUSA
  CHRISTA.             2 F CHILD     GRZZZZUSA        LINA               21 F NN        GRZZZZUSA
  AUGUSTE            .09 F INFANT    GRZZZZUSA      HAAG, ANNA           16 F NN        GRZZZZUSA
KUEMPEL, WILH.        30 M LABR      GRZZZZUSA      ENGELER, GOTTL.      35 M LABR      GRABZVUSA
  ELISE               34 F W         GRZZZZUSA      GIESELER, ANNA       28 F NN        GRACBRUSA
  KARL                 3 M CHILD     GRZZZZUSA      GERSCHAL, MARIANNA   27 F W         GRZZZZUSA
  ADAM               .06 M INFANT    GRZZZZUSA        CATHA.              3 F CHILD     GRZZZZUSA
HOMANN, CHRISTE.      28 F NN        GRABRYUSA        ANDREAS           .06 M INFANT    GRZZZZUSA
BENSDORF, IDA         16 F NN        GRAAZCUSA      KACZMARK, LORENZ     27 M LABR      GRZZZZUSA
GERKENS, BETHI        16 F NN        GRAAZCUSA      ROSENSTIEHL, CARL    18 M LABR      GRZZZZUSA
BORDEMANN, ELISE      41 F NN        GRAHMHUSA      FRIEDEL, BARBA.      51 F W         GRAEWFUSA
KRUSE, ELISE          28 F NN        GRAHMHUSA      HERMELING, MINNA     20 F NN        GRACBRUSA
  HEINR.              23 M FARMER    GRAHMHUSA      LIEBIG, MINE         32 F W         GRZZZZUSA
  HEINR.              22 F W         GRAHMHUSA        ARTHUR             11 M CH        GRZZZZUSA
DOEPKING, WILHE.      34 F W         GRABHGUSA        CONRAD              8 M CHILD     GRZZZZUSA
  FRIEDR.            .01 M INFANT    GRABHGUSA        ELSA                4 F CHILD     GRZZZZUSA
DESENER, NICOL.       16 M NN        GRABHGUSA        ANNA              .06 F INFANT    GRZZZZUSA
MANN, JOH.            55 M LABR      GRAEXWUSA      GIEGOLD, GEORG       52 M LABR      GRAAIEUSA
BRUNJES, JOH.         28 M LABR      GRAFQWUSA      MANDERLOH, SOPHIE    24 F NN        GRADVHUSA
TIETJEN, LINA         18 F NN        GRAFQWUSA      FREISS, ANDREAS      31 M FARMER    GRAAIEUSA
BRUNKHORST, AUG.      26 M FARMER    GRACBRUSA      BECKER, BRUNO        27 M LABR      GRACBRUSA
GURTNER, MARIE        21 F NN        GRACVEUSA      SUBR, JOSEF          25 M LABR      GRACBRUSA
MUELLER, ELISAB.      25 F NN        GRACVEUSA      BAUR, VALENTIN       25 M LABR      GRACBRUSA
ZINSMEISTER, ERMINE   20 F NN        GRACVAUSA      LEFKOWITZ, MORTON    26 M LABR      GRACBRUSA
  KAROLE.             45 F W         GRACVAUSA      ROEGNER, JOHANN      23 M FARMER    GRACBRUSA
PICHLER, ALOIS        43 M LABR      SRZZZZUSA      MEINKING, JOH.       15 M FARMER    GRZZZZUSA
  MARIE               43 F W         SRZZZZUSA      OTTEN, GESINE        24 F NN        GRAFRMUSA
  LUDWIG              11 M CH        SRZZZZUSA      SAUL, JOHN           20 M FARMER    GRAARRUSA
BOEHM, ANNA           18 F NN        BVZZZZUSA      ENTRES, FRANK        23 M WTR       GRABOQUSA
HAAG, AMBOS           27 M LABR      BVZZZZUSA
  MATHE.              23 F W         BVZZZZUSA
LUNDENSACK, HERM.     32 M LABR      BVZZZZUSA
HERZOG, BERNHARD      38 M FARMER    GRZZZZUSA
NESTHER, IDA          20 F NN        GRAAXKUSA      SHIP:    ALLER
KRUMBEIGEL, LINDA     16 F NN        GRAAXKUSA
FIRLEKE, GRETCHEN     14 F NN        GRACBRUSA      FROM:    BREMEN AND SOUTHAMPTON
NUESSLER, MINNA       19 F NN        GRAAXKUSA      TO:      NEW YORK
MICHAEL, AD.          21 M LABR      GRAERSUSA      ARRIVED: 03 NOVEMBER 1888
SAUL, HEINR.          17 M LABR      GRACBRUSA
THADEN, CATHA.        16 F NN        GRACBRUSA
ZAPP, HERM.           16 M LABR      GRACBRUSA
BUERKING, CARL        16 M LABR      GRACBRUSA      GUTTMANN, JOH.       25 M FARMER    GRZZZZUSA
HOBERG, WILHE.        23 F NN        GRACBRUSA      HENKEL, BERNH.       20 M FARMER    GRZZZZUSA
KRACH, EMMA           16 F NN        GRACBRUSA      MOHR, GEORG          16 M FARMER    GRZZZZUSA
HULSMANN, ANNA        17 F NN        GRACBRUSA      FRISCHMANN, FRANZ    36 M BCHR      GRZZZZUSA
MEYER, FRIEDR.        16 M FARMER    GRACBFUSA      WIPPENBEDS, DIONISS  44 M BRR       GRZZZZUSA
FRICK, WILH.          20 M FARMER    GRACBFUSA      FLEISCHMANN, LEONH.  18 M LABR      GRZZZZUSA
  FRIEDA              16 F NN        GRACBRUSA      HEIDENTHALER, ANTON  35 M MCHT      GRZZZZUSA
BOERGER, ELISE        21 F NN        GRACBRUSA      SEEGER, WM.          16 M TLR       GRZZZZUSA
RINGE, BETTY          17 F NN        GRZZZZUSA      PECK, HEINR.         18 M TLR       GRZZZZUSA
KRIUG, EMMA           22 F NN        WMZZZZUSA      OELLRICH, CLAUS      16 M TLR       GRZZZZUSA
GOEZ, CATHA.          21 F NN        WMZZZZUSA        CHRISTOFFER        22 M TLR       GRZZZZUSA
GRIMME, A.            28 M LABR      WMAAXFUSA      PFIFFNER, ANTON      30 M SHMK      GRZZZZUSA
ZELLER, GOTTL.        25 M LABR      WMZZZZUSA      ALEXANDER, MAX       15 M SHMK      GRZZZZUSA
  MARIA               21 F W         WMZZZZUSA      HAAS, EMIL           16 M FARMER    GRZZZZUSA
BARTOWSKA, OTTILIA    24 F NN        WMADBDUSA      WITHMANN, MECH.      23 M FARMER    GRZZZZUSA
KAROL, HERM.          33 M LABR      GRZZZZUSA      WAGNER, GOTTHILF     30 M FARMER    GRZZZZUSA
BLONNE, SOPHIE        33 F NN        GRACBRUSA      JACOB, LEONH.        23 M FARMER    GRZZZZUSA
KOESTER, ANNA         18 F NN        GRACBRUSA      DIETZ, PHIL.         69 M FARMER    GRZZZZUSA
KUECKS, META          19 F NN        GRAFSNUSA      WEIGAND, FRITZ       26 M FARMER    GRZZZZUSA
  JOHANN              16 M LABR      GRAFSNUSA      BECKER, AUG.         17 M FARMER    GRZZZZUSA
GLAENZEL, LOUISE      33 F W         BVZZZZUSA      DIETRICH, PETER      28 M FARMER    GRZZZZUSA
  ALB.                 3 M CHILD     BVZZZZUSA      FRISCHMANN, HEINR.   24 M FARMER    GRZZZZUSA
DREYER, FRIEDKE.      22 F NN        BVACBRUSA      ZACHMANN, ALB.       17 M FARMER    GRZZZZUSA
  AUGUSTE             27 F NN        BVACBRUSA      WOCHRLE, JACOB       54 M FARMER    GRZZZZUSA
MEINDEL, VERONIKA     17 F NN        WMZZZZUSA      SCHNEIDER, ED.       30 M SMH       GRZZZZUSA
```

PASSENGER	AGE	SEX	OCCUPATION	PROV VLS	DES	PASSENGER	AGE	SEX	OCCUPATION	PROV VLS	DES
JENSEN, MATTHIAS	19	M	SMH	GRZZZZ	USA	LINA	20	F	UNKNOWN	GRZZZZ	USA
ARZT, OSCAR	28	M	SMH	GRZZZZ	USA	ROHLEDER, KATHE.	22	F	UNKNOWN	GRZZZZ	USA
WEISS, CARL	30	M	FARMER	SRZZZZ	USA	FOERSTER, KAETHI	23	F	UNKNOWN	GRZZZZ	USA
FRIEDMANN, JULIUS	23	M	FARMER	GRZZZZ	USA	NOAK, SELMA	26	F	UNKNOWN	GRZZZZ	USA
EXEL, FRANS	28	M	FARMER	GRZZZZ	USA	BAECKER, MARIE	21	F	UNKNOWN	GRZZZZ	USA
HASL, ALOIS	24	M	FARMER	GRZZZZ	USA	DOELLINGER, ANNA	18	F	UNKNOWN	GRZZZZ	USA
HUSS, PHILIPP	17	M	FARMER	GRZZZZ	USA	NAKS, MINNA	29	F	UNKNOWN	GRZZZZ	USA
SCHLUETER, LOUIS	15	M	FARMER	GRZZZZ	USA	PEUBLER, PAULE.	17	F	UNKNOWN	GRZZZZ	USA
BUNDSCHUH, JEREMIAS	24	M	FARMER	GRZZZZ	USA	BABLIK, KAETHI	26	F	UNKNOWN	GRZZZZ	USA
KAMINSKY, ADOLF	34	M	FARMER	GRZZZZ	USA	DUHOLM, ANNA	29	F	UNKNOWN	GRZZZZ	USA
KACZON, TOMACZ	25	M	FARMER	GRZZZZ	USA	HAENASCH, MARIE	25	F	UNKNOWN	GRZZZZ	USA
LANT, FRIEDR.	20	M	FARMER	GRZZZZ	USA	KURL, EMMA	37	F	UNKNOWN	GRZZZZ	USA
IMSANDE, HEINR.	21	M	FARMER	GRZZZZ	USA	JENTER, AGNES	20	F	UNKNOWN	GRZZZZ	USA
JINGENS, FRANZ	39	M	CPTR	GRZZZZ	USA	MANTEL, MARG.	16	F	UNKNOWN	GRZZZZ	USA
TRABER, CARL	34	M	CPTR	GRZZZZ	USA	METZGER, CAROL.	19	F	UNKNOWN	GRZZZZ	USA
SCHREDS, JOHS.	34	M	CPTR	GRZZZZ	USA	FISCHER, ENGELB.	29	F	UNKNOWN	GRZZZZ	USA
SCHMIEG, MICH.	30	M	CPTR	GRZZZZ	USA	ENGELHART, KATHA.	20	F	UNKNOWN	GRZZZZ	USA
LOSSOW, MAX	29	M	FARMER	GRZZZZ	USA	FEIS, MARIA	20	F	UNKNOWN	GRZZZZ	USA
BONGARTZ, ADOLF	23	M	FARMER	GRZZZZ	USA	OETJEN, BESKA	17	F	UNKNOWN	GRZZZZ	USA
FEHRENKAMP, DIEDR.	16	M	FARMER	GRZZZZ	USA	FEIST, MARIANNE	22	F	UNKNOWN	GRZZZZ	USA
FLECKENSTEIN, FRANZ	16	M	WTR	GRZZZZ	USA	HUHN, ELISE	24	F	UNKNOWN	GRZZZZ	USA
SCHMIDT, JOS.	23	M	LKSH	GRZZZZ	USA	DOELL, LOUISE	16	F	UNKNOWN	GRZZZZ	USA
PRELLO-SS, LEON	25	M	FARMER	GRZZZZ	USA	SIX, AUGUSTE	17	F	UNKNOWN	GRZZZZ	USA
BADANN, HEINR.	26	M	FARMER	GRZZZZ	USA	SCHAEFER, KATH.	17	F	UNKNOWN	GRZZZZ	USA
JACOBS, FRIEDR.	14	M	FARMER	GRZZZZ	USA	GELHAAR, EMILIE	30	F	UNKNOWN	GRZZZZ	USA
PROHL, CARSTEN	20	M	FARMER	GRZZZZ	USA	FANNAS, ALWINE	22	F	UNKNOWN	GRZZZZ	USA
WENK, HUGO	32	M	FARMER	GRZZZZ	USA	HAAG, ANNA	19	F	UNKNOWN	GRZZZZ	USA
HECK, JOHS.	23	M	FARMER	GRZZZZ	USA	SCHROEDER, CARL	27	M	LABR	GRZZZZ	USA
KASELER, FRIEDR.	32	M	FARMER	GRZZZZ	USA	MINNA	25	F	W	GRZZZZ	USA
HOERR, AUG.	15	M	JNR	GRZZZZ	USA	HERM.	5	M	CHILD	GRZZZZ	USA
FROLSS, JOH.	38	M	JNR	GRZZZZ	USA	ALWINE	3	F	CHILD	GRZZZZ	USA
GEIDT, WILH.	43	M	JNR	GRZZZZ	USA	EMMA	2	F	CHILD	GRZZZZ	USA
KOESTER, JOH.	16	M	LABR	GRZZZZ	USA	ANNA	.01	F	INFANT	GRZZZZ	USA
FROHLICH, EMIL	16	M	LABR	GRZZZZ	USA	MOLLES, FR.	37	M	LABR	GRZZZZ	USA
ACKERMANN, JOH.	57	M	LABR	GRZZZZ	USA	ANNA	38	F	W	GRZZZZ	USA
FEIST, STEPHAN	22	F	FARMER	GRZZZZ	USA	WILH.	9	M	CHILD	GRZZZZ	USA
HOFFMANN, JOH.	16	M	FARMER	GRZZZZ	USA	EMMA	4	F	CHILD	GRZZZZ	USA
FROEHLIG, CARL	18	M	MCHT	GRZZZZ	USA	KARNATZ, SOPHIE	59	F	UNKNOWN	GRZZZZ	USA
GRUBE, HEINR.	31	M	MCHT	GRZZZZ	USA	MARIE	19	F	UNKNOWN	GRZZZZ	USA
SYBERTS, JOS.	23	M	TLR	GRZZZZ	USA	RABENALZ, HUGO	28	M	FARMER	GRZZZZ	USA
HIRSCH, WILH.	16	M	TLR	GRZZZZ	USA	MARGA.	25	F	W	GRZZZZ	USA
TERLE, PETER	55	M	FARMER	GRZZZZ	USA	HUGO	4	M	CHILD	GRZZZZ	USA
OTTO, KARL	28	M	FARMER	GRZZZZ	USA	EMMA	2	F	CHILD	GRZZZZ	USA
MALLBUCH, GERLG	36	M	FARMER	GRZZZZ	USA	OTTO	.01	M	INFANT	GRZZZZ	USA
HANDBINDER, JOSEPH	27	M	FARMER	GRZZZZ	USA	BERGH, ANNA	35	F	UNKNOWN	GRZZZZ	USA
KNAPSTEIN, ANT.	25	M	FARMER	GRZZZZ	USA	HUGO	9	M	CHILD	GRZZZZ	USA
OPITZ, JULIUS	27	M	SMH	GRZZZZ	USA	ANNA	7	F	CHILD	GRZZZZ	USA
MILLER, JOHS.	25	M	SHMK	GRZZZZ	USA	MAX	6	M	CHILD	GRZZZZ	USA
LUTTMANN, SOPHIE	12	F	UNKNOWN	GRZZZZ	USA	BRUNO	4	M	CHILD	GRZZZZ	USA
SCHMICK, BERTHA	21	F	UNKNOWN	GRZZZZ	USA	EMMA	2	F	CHILD	GRZZZZ	USA
GORBACH, ANNA	41	F	UNKNOWN	GRZZZZ	USA	PAUL	.09	M	INFANT	GRZZZZ	USA
FESSEMNAYER, CHARL.	20	F	UNKNOWN	GRZZZZ	USA	LUENEBURG, FERD.	60	M	FARMER	GRZZZZ	USA
BLUM, ANNA	18	F	UNKNOWN	GRZZZZ	USA	ANNA	43	F	W	GRZZZZ	USA
MICHEL, MARG.	20	F	UNKNOWN	GRZZZZ	USA	EMMA	18	F	CH	GRZZZZ	USA
RADLOFF, ANNA	28	F	UNKNOWN	GRZZZZ	USA	META	16	F	CH	GRZZZZ	USA
ABRAHAM, ADELE	26	F	UNKNOWN	GRZZZZ	USA	GUSTAV	7	M	CHILD	GRZZZZ	USA
RADSCHMEIER, MARIA	18	F	UNKNOWN	GRZZZZ	USA	JULIE	6	F	CHILD	GRZZZZ	USA
BELLMANN, ADELE	20	F	UNKNOWN	GRZZZZ	USA	HEDWIG	5	F	CHILD	GRZZZZ	USA
LOEWENSTEIN, FRIEDA	17	F	UNKNOWN	GRZZZZ	USA	HEYDT, WILH.	34	M	BCHR	GRZZZZ	USA
ABENDSCHEIN, MARG.	24	F	UNKNOWN	GRZZZZ	USA	MARIA	36	F	W	GRZZZZ	USA
ALLGAIER, LIZETTE	26	F	UNKNOWN	GRZZZZ	USA	ANNA	6	F	CHILD	GRZZZZ	USA
DIPPON, LOUISE	15	F	UNKNOWN	GRZZZZ	USA	KOLHAGEN, WILH.	23	M	SMH	GRZZZZ	USA
SCHWEITZER, HELENE	18	F	UNKNOWN	GRZZZZ	USA	LINA	20	F	W	GRZZZZ	USA
HAYN, ANNA	16	F	UNKNOWN	GRZZZZ	USA	SELPIN, MART.	47	M	FARMER	GRZZZZ	USA
SCHENK, WILHE.	18	F	UNKNOWN	GRZZZZ	USA	MARIE	59	F	W	GRZZZZ	USA
HESSEL, CAROL.	22	F	UNKNOWN	GRZZZZ	USA	WILHE.	18	F	D	GRZZZZ	USA
BACKER, WILHE.	17	F	UNKNOWN	GRZZZZ	USA	MUELLER, AUG.	30	M	FARMER	GRZZZZ	USA
ISKE, FRIEDERIKE	16	F	UNKNOWN	GRZZZZ	USA	KAETHER, WILHE.	25	F	W	GRZZZZ	USA
GELSEBACH, DOROTHEA	22	F	UNKNOWN	GRZZZZ	USA	ALB.	27	M	FARMER	GRZZZZ	USA
HOFFMANN, KAROL.	30	F	UNKNOWN	GRZZZZ	USA	WIEBADS, HENRY	18	M	FARMER	GRZZZZ	USA
GOLDMANN, MARIE	56	F	UNKNOWN	GRZZZZ	USA	HERM.	17	M	FARMER	GRZZZZ	USA
ARZT, MARTHA	15	F	UNKNOWN	GRZZZZ	USA	FRITZ, ANNA	53	F	UNKNOWN	GRZZZZ	USA
MUENNINGER, JOSEFA	70	F	UNKNOWN	GRZZZZ	USA	LOUISE	22	F	UNKNOWN	GRZZZZ	USA
URSULE	44	F	UNKNOWN	GRZZZZ	USA	ANNA	17	F	UNKNOWN	GRZZZZ	USA
ENSLIN, ANNA	16	F	UNKNOWN	GRZZZZ	USA	BERCKHEINER, CATHE.	40	F	UNKNOWN	GRZZZZ	USA

PASSENGER	AGE	SEX	OCCUPATION	PRVL	DES
EUGEN	13	M	UNKNOWN		GRZZZZUSA
MARTHA	10	F	CH		GRZZZZUSA
OSCAR	8	M	CHILD		GRZZZZUSA
JOHE.	7	F	CHILD		GRZZZZUSA
LOUISE	6	F	CHILD		GRZZZZUSA
MUELLER, ALOIS	30	M	FARMER		GRZZZZUSA
MARG.	29	F	W		GRZZZZUSA
CLASEN, FRITZ	30	M	FARMER		GRZZZZUSA
WILH.	26	F	W		GRZZZZUSA
ANNA	6	F	CHILD		GRZZZZUSA
HELMUTH	4	M	CHILD		GRZZZZUSA
HEINR.	2	M	CHILD		GRZZZZUSA
ALWINE	.06	F	INFANT		GRZZZZUSA
SCHROEDER, WILH.	38	M	FARMER		GRZZZZUSA
SOPHIA	41	F	W		GRZZZZUSA
WILHE.	7	F	CHILD		GRZZZZUSA
SOPHIE	4	F	CHILD		GRZZZZUSA
ALB.	2	M	CHILD		GRZZZZUSA
KRAUSS, KARL	68	M	BRR		GRZZZZUSA
URSULA	61	F	W		GRZZZZUSA
JOSEFA	22	F	D		GRZZZZUSA
JOHE.	19	F	D		GRZZZZUSA
HOEFER, ANNA	32	F	UNKNOWN		GRZZZZUSA
DOROTHEA	11	F	UNKNOWN		GRZZZZUSA
FRIEDR.	10	M	CH		GRZZZZUSA
ELISAB.	8	F	CHILD		GRZZZZUSA
MARIE	7	F	CHILD		GRZZZZUSA
CHRISTA.	7	F	CHILD		GRZZZZUSA
JOH.	3	M	CHILD		GRZZZZUSA
ELISABETH	2	F	CHILD		GRZZZZUSA
RUKOPF, MARIE	40	F	UNKNOWN		GRZZZZUSA
ERNST	15	M	UNKNOWN		GRZZZZUSA
MARTHA	11	F	UNKNOWN		GRZZZZUSA
ADOLF	7	M	CHILD		GRZZZZUSA
MARIE	5	F	CHILD		GRZZZZUSA
WOLFBERG, JOHA.	27	F	UNKNOWN		GRZZZZUSA
CARL	4	M	CHILD		GRZZZZUSA
SCHRAMM, DOROTHEA	25	F	UNKNOWN		GRZZZZUSA
HEINR.	4	M	CHILD		GRZZZZUSA
ANNA	2	F	CHILD		GRZZZZUSA
AUG.	.10	M	INFANT		GRZZZZUSA
RIBICH, MATH.	30	M	SHMK		GRZZZZUSA
MUELLER, CARL	38	M	SHMK		GRZZZZUSA
FRIEDA	19	F	D		GRZZZZUSA
WILHE.	14	F	D		GRZZZZUSA
MEYER, FR.	27	M	SHMK		GRZZZZUSA
JOHE.	19	F	W		GRZZZZUSA
GOEBEL, JOHE.	63	F	UNKNOWN		GRZZZZUSA
WILHE.	52	F	UNKNOWN		GRZZZZUSA
KATHE.	26	F	UNKNOWN		GRZZZZUSA
WILHE.	7	F	CHILD		GRZZZZUSA
JOHS.	6	M	CHILD		GRZZZZUSA
ZOERNER, KETHA.	22	F	UNKNOWN		GRZZZZUSA
HELENE	.10	F	INFANT		GRZZZZUSA
PFABE, CAROLE.	32	F	UNKNOWN		GRZZZZUSA
EMIL	7	M	CHILD		GRZZZZUSA
OTTO	6	M	CHILD		GRZZZZUSA
MARTHA	4	F	CHILD		GRZZZZUSA
WILLI	3	M	CHILD		GRZZZZUSA
FRIEDA	.10	F	INFANT		GRZZZZUSA
FROESS, CARL	44	M	JNR		GRZZZZUSA
SOPHIA	38	F	W		GRZZZZUSA
CARL	15	M	CH		GRZZZZUSA
PH.	11	M	CH		GRZZZZUSA
ANNA	7	F	CHILD		GRZZZZUSA
JACOB	6	M	CHILD		GRZZZZUSA
MARIE	5	F	CHILD		GRZZZZUSA
RAETHOHEN	4	F	CHILD		GRZZZZUSA
HEINR.	3	M	CHILD		GRZZZZUSA
LEON	.11	M	INFANT		GRZZZZUSA
GRETING, CATHE.	44	F	UNKNOWN		GRZZZZUSA
JOHE.	14	F	UNKNOWN		GRZZZZUSA
META	11	F	UNKNOWN		GRZZZZUSA
ERN, AUG.	39	M	FARMER		GRZZZZUSA
EMILIE	32	F	W		GRZZZZUSA
RICH.	8	M	CHILD		GRZZZZUSA
ELFRIEDE	6	F	CHILD		GRZZZZUSA
ERWIN	.06	M	INFANT		GRZZZZUSA
U, MINNA	20	F	UNKNOWN		GRZZZZUSA
LOUIS	18	M	FARMER		GRZZZZUSA
EMIL	16	M	FARMER		GRZZZZUSA
ENGELKING, CARL	40	M	LLD		GRZZZZUSA
CAROLE.	39	F	W		GRZZZZUSA
MINNA	15	F	CH		GRZZZZUSA
CARL	13	M	CH		GRZZZZUSA
HEINR.	11	M	CH		GRZZZZUSA
DIEDR.	7	M	CHILD		GRZZZZUSA
WILH.	4	M	CHILD		GRZZZZUSA
GEORG	.09	M	INFANT		GRZZZZUSA
BECK, CAROLE.	36	F	UNKNOWN		GRZZZZUSA
CATHE.	15	F	UNKNOWN		GRZZZZUSA
BABETTA	7	F	CHILD		GRZZZZUSA
KARL	4	M	CHILD		GRZZZZUSA
ERNST	3	M	CHILD		GRZZZZUSA
WILH.	2	M	CHILD		GRZZZZUSA
FRIEDKE.	.09	F	INFANT		GRZZZZUSA
HOEPPNER, ANNA	20	F	UNKNOWN		GRZZZZUSA
CARL	.04	M	INFANT		GRZZZZUSA
WEISOBARTH, HERM.	41	M	SHMK		GRZZZZUSA
FRIEDKE.	38	F	W		GRZZZZUSA
JETTI	11	F	CH		GRZZZZUSA
JEANETTE	9	F	CHILD		GRZZZZUSA
SALOMON	7	M	CHILD		GRZZZZUSA
ERNSTINE	6	F	CHILD		GRZZZZUSA
BERNHD.	5	M	CHILD		GRZZZZUSA
PAUL	.01	M	INFANT		GRZZZZUSA
SCHMELZER, FRIDA	26	F	UNKNOWN		GRZZZZUSA
FRIDA	.06	F	INFANT		GRZZZZUSA
KREITZNER, BARBARA	26	F	UNKNOWN		GRZZZZUSA
CATHE.	3	F	CHILD		GRZZZZUSA

SHIP: BOTHNIA

FROM: LIVERPOOL AND QUEENSTOWN
TO: NEW YORK
ARRIVED: 03 NOVEMBER 1888

BUCKLEY, PETER	27	M	BCHR		GRZZZZUSA

SHIP: CITY OF CHESTER

FROM: LIVERPOOL AND QUEENSTOWN
TO: NEW YORK
ARRIVED: 03 NOVEMBER 1888

SILSKI, EDWARD	45	M	TLR		GRACBFODE
ZIMERMANN, MICHAEL	27	M	TLR		GRACBFODE
RICHLETZKY, JACOB	29	M	TLR		GRACBFODE
PRELLWITZ, ROSALIA	17	F	SP		GRACBFOH

PASSENGER	AGE	SEX	OCCUPATION	PROV	DES
SHIP: RHAETIA					
FROM: HAMBURG AND HAVRE					
TO: NEW YORK					
ARRIVED: 05 NOVEMBER 1888					
RETHWISCH, ADOLF	26	M	LABR		GRZZZZUSA
SCHRAMM, BETTI	18	F	SGL		GRZZZZUSA
STRUBE, MELITA	19	F	SGL		GRZZZZUSA
GRUEN, JACOB	00	M	UNKNOWN		GRZZZZUSA
ROSA	00	F	UNKNOWN		GRZZZZUSA
PEPI	00	F	UNKNOWN		GRZZZZUSA
CAROLE.	00	F	UNKNOWN		GRZZZZUSA
MALI.	00	F	UNKNOWN		GRZZZZUSA
LUSTIG, IDES	00	F	UNKNOWN		GRZZZZUSA
BOEHME, MAX	15	M	STDNT		GRZZZZUSA
GUSKEWICZ, MARIE	50	F	WO		GRZZZZUSA
MARIE	16	F	CH		GRZZZZUSA
HELENE	13	F	CH		GRZZZZUSA
BARBA.	7	F	CHILD		GRZZZZUSA
ANNA	6	F	CHILD		GRZZZZUSA
FICK, BERTHA	24	F	SGL		GRZZZZUSA
ULIENOWSKA, MICHAEL	21	M	LABR		PRZZZZUSA
MAKERT, JOHA.	25	F	SGL		GRZZZZUSA
SCHMIDT, VALENTIN	18	M	CNF		GRZZZZUSA
LUETHKE, HENGO	21	M	FARMER		GRZZZZUSA
ERKEN, CHARLES	23	M	FARMER		GRZZZZUSA
WILDSTEIN, PEPI	00	M	UNKNOWN		GRZZZZUSA
SCHARFENBERG, OTTO	24	M	LABR		GRZZZZUSA
ANDERSEN, CHR.	22	M	LABR		GRZZZZUSA
REIMER, MARIE	14	F	SGL		GRZZZZUSA
BERMAN, ISAAC	30	M	LABR		PRZZZZUSA
KALMONOWICZ, ELKAN	14	M	LABR		GRZZZZUSA
MUSSER, JOHANN	29	M	LABR		GRZZZZUSA
RIWKEN, NACHMAN	16	M	LABR		GRZZZZUSA
STOCK, JOHS.	26	M	LABR		GRZZZZUSA
MARIE	30	F	W		GRZZZZUSA
NALT	6	M	CHILD		GRZZZZUSA
MARIE	.09	F	INFANT		GRZZZZUSA
HAUFF, LOUISE	17	F	SGL		GRZZZZUSA
KOHL, PAULINE	26	F	SGL		GRZZZZUSA
SAJEWSKA, MARIE	56	F	WO		GRZZZZUSA
STRAUB, PAUL	38	M	WTR		GRZZZZUSA
ROHDE, IDA	19	F	SGL		GRZZZZUSA
JAHNKE, FRIEDR.	38	M	MLR		GRZZZZUSA
BERTHA	36	F	W		GRZZZZUSA
AGNES	12	F	CH		GRZZZZUSA
ELLA	7	F	CHILD		GRZZZZUSA
EMIL	6	M	CHILD		GRZZZZUSA
HEDWIG	5	F	CHILD		GRZZZZUSA
HELLMUTH	3	M	CHILD		GRZZZZUSA
KERSCHNER, HEIMAN	66	M	LABR		GRZZZZUSA
FLORA	51	F	W		GRZZZZUSA
EVA	16	F	CH		GRZZZZUSA
HELLWOIG, CATHA.	16	F	SGL		GRZZZZUSA
HEINSOHN, MARIE	47	F	WO		GRZZZZUSA
ELISE	9	F	CHILD		GRZZZZUSA
GUNDER, PAULE.	57	F	WO		GRZZZZUSA
KATT, HEINR.	18	M	MCHT		GRZZZZUSA
GOETZE, CAROLINE	16	F	SGL		GRZZZZUSA
FRITZE, OTTO	24	M	BCHR		GRZZZZUSA
KOEHLER, JULS.	42	M	SMH		GRZZZZUSA
PAULE.	24	F	W		GRZZZZUSA
AGNES	9	F	CHILD		GRZZZZUSA
GUSTAV	4	M	CHILD		GRZZZZUSA
SEIDEL, HERMAN	34	M	BCHR		GRZZZZUSA
PESCH, ROBERT	19	M	CL		GRZZZZUSA
BURMEISTER, CARL	35	M	FARMER		GRZZZZUSA
CAROLE.	30	F	W		GRZZZZUSA
HERRM.	6	M	CHILD		GRZZZZUSA
OTTILIE	3	F	CHILD		GRZZZZUSA
ANNA	.11	F	INFANT		GRZZZZUSA
LUTZ, CAROLE.	21	F	SGL		GRZZZZUSA
ROLLE, ERNST	42	M	LABR		GRZZZZUSA
HENRIETTE	34	F	W		GRZZZZUSA
JOHA.	4	F	CHILD		GRZZZZUSA
KOSS, AUGSTE.	21	F	WO		GRZZZZUSA
EMMA	.11	F	INFANT		GRZZZZUSA
EHRARDT, MINNA	19	F	SGL		GRZZZZUSA
U, WILH.	00	M	BCHR		GRZZZZUSA
WOLFF, MAX	23	M	MCHT		GRZZZZUSA
WITH, HEINR.	9	M	CHILD		GRZZZZUSA
KRUETH, JOACHIM	60	M	FARMER		GRZZZZUSA
MARIE	52	F	W		GRZZZZUSA
FRITZ	19	M	CH		GRZZZZUSA
LINE	9	F	CHILD		GRZZZZUSA
VICK, JOHANN	22	M	LABR		GRZZZZUSA
KRUETH, HEINR.	25	M	LABR		GRZZZZUSA
ALMSTAEDT, JOH.	28	M	FARMER		GRZZZZUSA
ANNA	30	F	W		GRZZZZUSA
FRIEDR.	9	M	CHILD		GRZZZZUSA
LUDWIG	6	M	CHILD		GRZZZZUSA
ANNA	4	F	CHILD		GRZZZZUSA
META	2	F	CHILD		GRZZZZUSA
BECK, LOUISE	17	F	SGL		GRZZZZUSA
KARPP, BERNHD.	17	M	MCHT		GRZZZZUSA
LUEZ, HERRM.	26	M	FARMER		GRZZZZUSA
RAICH, AUGUST	17	M	BCHR		GRZZZZUSA
SAPHA, SIEGFRIED	27	M	MCHT		GRZZZZUSA
ELFRIEDE	22	F	W		GRZZZZUSA
GERGENSKI, GOTTFRIED	22	M	LABR		GRZZZZUSA
ADAMSKI, MARIANNE	27	F	WO		GRZZZZUSA
MARIANNE	4	F	CHILD		GRZZZZUSA
ANNA	3	F	CHILD		GRZZZZUSA
JOSEF	11	M	INF		GRZZZZUSA
ALBERS, HERRM.	28	M	LABR		GRZZZZUSA
SKRZPEZAK, MARIANE	25	F	WO		GRZZZZUSA
STANISL.	.11	M	INFANT		GRZZZZUSA
TASCHINSKA, ROSALIE	9	F	CHILD		GRZZZZUSA
LUEDWIG	8	M	CHILD		GRZZZZUSA
HAASE, MAX	21	M	LABR		GRZZZZUSA
DIEDRICHSEN, INKEN	28	F	WO		GRZZZZUSA
WM.	5	M	CHILD		GRZZZZUSA
CARL	3	M	CHILD		GRZZZZUSA
MOLL, ANNA	46	F	WO		GRZZZZUSA
BRAUN, ERNSTE.	47	F	WO		GRZZZZUSA
CARL	16	M	CH		GRZZZZUSA
ERNESTE.	14	F	CH		GRZZZZUSA
AUGST.	9	M	CHILD		GRZZZZUSA
MINNA	3	F	CHILD		GRZZZZUSA
KIELESZEWSKA, AGNISKA	21	F	SGL		GRZZZZUSA
WALNUT, MARIANE	35	F	SGL		GRZZZZUSA
REISIG, FRDKE.	52	F	WO		GRZZZZUSA
FRDKE.	9	F	CHILD		GRZZZZUSA
JULS.	8	M	CHILD		GRZZZZUSA
MINNA	7	F	CHILD		GRZZZZUSA
PETERSEN, C.	15	M	LABR		GRZZZZUSA
LIEDTKE, LEOPOLD	24	M	LABR		GRZZZZUSA
LAURA	24	F	W		GRZZZZUSA
SCHWARZ, LAURA	16	F	SGL		GRZZZZUSA
PIEPKE, EMMA	19	F	SGL		GRZZZZUSA
JUENGE, HERRM.	16	F	SGL		GRZZZZUSA
MAURITZ, BRUNO	17	M	LABR		GRZZZZUSA
WILLE, FRIEDA	24	F	WO		GRZZZZUSA
GERTRUD	.09	F	INFANT		GRZZZZUSA
POLEI, ANNA	23	F	SGL		GRZZZZUSA
MARIE	16	F	SGL		GRZZZZUSA
SCHOECKINCHOFF, BERNHD.	25	M	FARMER		GRZZZZUSA
PETERSEN, MARIE	21	F	SGL		GRZZZZUSA
MENZOW, ALBERT	27	M	LABR		GRZZZZUSA
CARL	23	M	LABR		GRZZZZUSA
JENSEN, JENS	17	M	MCHT		GRZZZZUSA
KRUEGER, AUGST	33	M	FARMER		GRZZZZUSA
MARIE	26	F	W		GRZZZZUSA
HEUMANN, CARL	57	M	LABR		GRZZZZUSA
MARIE	30	F	SGL		GRZZZZUSA
TEIGENBAUM, ESTER	32	F	WO		GRZZZZUSA
FISCHEL	9	M	CHILD		GRZZZZUSA
ABRAM	8	M	CHILD		GRZZZZUSA

413

PASSENGER	AGE	SEX	OCCUPATION	PRVL	DES
DAVID	5	M	CHILD	GRZZZZUSA	
ZISEL	.11	F	INFANT	GRZZZZUSA	
HIRSCH	.01	M	INFANT	GRZZZZUSA	
ZWANZIGER, JOHAN	17	M	BKR	GRZZZZUSA	
MUENCH, JOH.	16	M	BKR	GRZZZZUSA	
LOOS, GEORG	21	M	BKR	GRZZZZUSA	
HUEBER, CRECENTY	21	F	SGL	GRZZZZUSA	
LEDERER, ALOIS	22	M	FARMER	GRZZZZUSA	
HABERSTROH, ANNA	70	F	WO	GRZZZZUSA	
KUMMER, ELISE	13	F	CH	GRZZZZUSA	
ZIEGLER, LUDWEIG	25	M	GDNR	GRZZZZUSA	
BERTELSEN, PETER	25	M	SLR	GRZZZZUSA	
HERTEL, CATH.	22	F	WO	GRZZZZUSA	
JOHE.	.09	F	INFANT	GRZZZZUSA	
KRISCHKE, ANNA	30	F	WO	GRZZZZUSA	
RUDOLF	.09	M	INFANT	GRZZZZUSA	
MALINOWSKA, HELENE	36	F	WO	GRZZZZUSA	
PAUL	14	M	CH	GRZZZZUSA	
ALBERT	8	M	CHILD	GRZZZZUSA	
AUGUST	6	M	CHILD	GRZZZZUSA	
MARIE	4	F	CHILD	GRZZZZUSA	
ADOLF	.09	M	INFANT	GRZZZZUSA	
DAHM, AUGUST	23	M	LABR	GRZZZZUSA	
HARPE, CARL	21	M	LABR	GRZZZZUSA	
EICHHORN, SOPHIE	14	F	SGL	GRZZZZUSA	
ZRODELNY, THERESE	42	F	WO	GRZZZZUSA	
GAMMERDINGEN, CHRISTIAN	31	M	BKR	GRZZZZUSA	
SCHMIDT, WILH.	23	M	BCHR	GRZZZZUSA	
KIRCH, LEOPOLD	24	M	BCHR	GRZZZZUSA	
ALTENDORFER, JOSEF	25	M	CPTR	GRZZZZUSA	
RUEZER, ALBERT	28	M	JNR	GRZZZZUSA	
BECKER, LOUIS	23	M	CGRMKR	GRZZZZUSA	
REGLI, EMILIE	22	F	SGL	SRZZZZUSA	
OLGA	19	F	SGL	SRZZZZUSA	
HOSANG, MARIE	24	F	SGL	SRZZZZUSA	
STEBLER, BERTHA	15	F	SGL	SRZZZZUSA	
MARXZ, HENRI	23	M	BRR	ACZZZZUSA	
DIETIKER, J.F.	29	M	MCHT	SRZZZZUSA	
WELLNER, AUGSTE.	24	F	SGL	GRZZZZUSA	
HEEREN, HEINR.	23	M	FARMER	GRZZZZUSA	
KAYSER, HEINR.	45	M	PVTR	GRZZZZUSA	
MARIE	30	F	W	GRZZZZUSA	
ELISE	7	F	CHILD	GRZZZZUSA	
BERTHA	6	F	CHILD	GRZZZZUSA	
HARRY	5	M	CHILD	GRZZZZUSA	
CARSTENS, FANNY	40	F	WO	GRZZZZUSA	
JASTROW, HAUS	23	M	MCHT	GRZZZZUSA	
NACHMANN, JENNY	43	F	WO	GRZZZZUSA	
SELMA	20	F	CH	GRZZZZUSA	
IDA	18	F	CH	GRZZZZUSA	
HENRY	9	M	CHILD	GRZZZZUSA	
LUDWIG	9	M	CHILD	GRZZZZUSA	
BUSZYNSKY, NAPOLI	32	F	MD	GRZZZZUSA	
ORTLEPP, META	15	F	SGL	GRZZZZUSA	
HELLMANN, FRANZ	9	M	CHILD	GRZZZZUSA	

SHIP: CIRCASSIA

FROM: GLASGOW AND MOVILLE
TO: NEW YORK
ARRIVED: 07 NOVEMBER 1888

PASSENGER	AGE	SEX	OCCUPATION	PRVL	DES
KRAPP, AUGUST	30	M	MSN	GRAHRZUSA	
CHRISTIAN	23	M	MSN	GRAHRZUSA	
HERZOG, HUGO	18	M	MCHT	GRAHRZUSA	
BULSTER, THEODOR	21	M	CL	GRAHRZUSA	
PEDERSEN, ANTON	20	M	FARMER	GRAHRZUSA	
LACHER, BETTY	17	F	HP	GRAHRZUSA	
SOBEK, WINSENT	32	F	HP	GRAHRZUSA	

SHIP: EIDER

FROM: BREMEN AND SOUTHAMPTON
TO: NEW YORK
ARRIVED: 07 NOVEMBER 1888

PASSENGER	AGE	SEX	OCCUPATION	PRVL	DES
HILDEBRANDT, EUGEN	27	M	TT	GRZZZZUSA	
ROHRBACHER, HUGO	76	M	TT	GRZZZZUSA	
VOLKOUMMEN, JOS	24	M	TT	GRZZZZUSA	
JEBSEN, JOHANN	22	M	TT	GRZZZZUSA	
SCHLEGEL, FRANZ	24	M	TT	GRZZZZUSA	
SCHWARZ, CHARLOTTE	27	F	NN	GRZZZZUSA	
JACOB	5	M	CHILD	GRZZZZUSA	
BERTHA	.06	F	INFANT	GRZZZZUSA	
BURKHARDT, WILHELE	30	F	NN	GRZZZZUSA	
BREKENBERG, MARIA	25	F	NN	GRZZZZUSA	
BRAUN, FELIX	30	M	TT	GRZZZZUSA	
SONNTAG, MARIE	30	F	NN	GRZZZZUSA	
BUCK, ALI	45	F	NN	GRZZZZUSA	
HENRIETTE	24	F	NN	GRZZZZUSA	
ULLOTT, LUDWIG	25	M	TT	GRZZZZUSA	
BRUECKNER, MARIE	18	F	NN	GRZZZZUSA	
SCHAEFFER, FRIEDR	32	M	TT	GRZZZZUSA	
BAUER, LINA	18	F	NN	GRZZZZUSA	
MOESER, GEORG	17	M	TT	GRZZZZUSA	
KOONTZ, ANTHONY	16	M	TT	GRZZZZUSA	
BUCK, THERESE	15	F	NN	GRZZZZUSA	
NIEMES, BABETTE	20	F	NN	GRZZZZUSA	
PIECHOSKA, JOSEFA	28	F	NN	GRZZZZUSA	
OTTO, MATHE	18	F	NN	GRZZZZUSA	
JANKE, MARIANNE	24	F	NN	GRZZZZUSA	
ROSALIE	7	F	CHILD	GRZZZZUSA	
BA--K, CHARLOTTE	29	F	NN	GRZZZZUSA	
HAUSCHILD, FRANZ	55	M	FARMER	GRZZZZUSA	
WACHOWIAK, MAGDA	22	F	SVNT	GRZZZZUSA	
KORACK, AGNIESTKA	19	F	SVNT	GRZZZZUSA	
PUSCHA, JOH	24	M	LABR	GRZZZZUSA	
KAENTZ, AUGUST	23	M	LABR	GRZZZZUSA	
SIEG, ANNA	20	F	SVNT	GRZZZZUSA	
WESSOLLEK, FR	25	M	FARMER	GRZZZZUSA	
JANKOWSKI, CHARLOTTE	56	F	NN	GRZZZZUSA	
TORSCH, BARBARA	58	F	NN	GRZZZZUSA	
ANNA	19	F	NN	GRZZZZUSA	
ZECK, JULIE	45	F	NN	GRZZZZUSA	
CECILIA	15	F	NN	GRZZZZUSA	
JOSEPH	11	M	CH	GRZZZZUSA	
ELISABETH	10	F	CH	GRZZZZUSA	
LEO	3	M	CHILD	GRZZZZUSA	
SALEWSKI, AUGUSTE	30	F	SVNT	GRZZZZUSA	
HINZ, AMANDA	20	F	SVNT	GRZZZZUSA	
RAHN, EMILA	28	F	NN	GRZZZZUSA	
IDA	3	F	CHILD	GRZZZZUSA	
MARTHA	.09	F	INFANT	GRZZZZUSA	
MUELLER, MARIE	17	F	SVNT	GRZZZZUSA	
GOPP---R-T, JULIANE	59	F	NN	GRZZZZUSA	
HAMPEL, AUGUSTE	32	F	NN	GRZZZZUSA	
FRITZ	9	M	CHILD	GRZZZZUSA	
LUDWIG, AUGUSTE	19	F	SMSTS	GRZZZZUSA	
SCHMIDT, HERM	3	M	CHILD	GRZZZZUSA	
HARTFIELDT, AUGUSTE	38	F	SMSTS	GRZZZZUSA	
WIE-	8	M	CHILD	GRZZZZUSA	
FRANZ	7	M	CHILD	GRZZZZUSA	
ANNA	5	F	CHILD	GRZZZZUSA	
MARIA	3	F	CHILD	GRZZZZUSA	
JAHNKE, HENRIETTE	23	F	SVNT	GRZZZZUSA	
NEUMANN, ALBERT	25	M	FARMER	GRZZZZUSA	
JESSE, EMMA	15	F	SVNT	GRZZZZUSA	
PETERSEN, MAREN	25	F	SVNT	GRZZZZUSA	
RUEBSAM, OTTILIE	21	M	PNTR	GRZZZZUSA	
DOBECK, CARL	24	M	MCHT	GRZZZZUSA	
GERKEN, ADELE	17	F	SVNT	GRZZZZUSA	
HAHN, CATHAR	30	F	NN	GRZZZZUSA	
CATH	8	F	CHILD	GRZZZZUSA	
EHLERS, PETER	19	M	FARMER	GRZZZZUSA	

PASSENGER	AGE	SEX	OCCUPATION	PRVL	DES
RAUSCHER, MATTHAUS	23	M	FARMER	GRZZZZUSA	
SCHWANDNER, LOUISE	20	F	SVNT	GRZZZZUSA	
ERBELE, PAULINE	17	F	SVNT	GRZZZZUSA	
HARTMANN, CAROL	22	F	SVNT	GRZZZZUSA	
GEYER, CATHAR	21	F	NN	GRZZZZUSA	
FRIEDERIKE	.06	F	INFANT	GRZZZZUSA	
SCHA-BACHER, FRIEDERIKE	23	F	SVNT	GRZZZZUSA	
CATHARINE	17	F	SVNT	GRZZZZUSA	
SCHWEIZER, WILH	15	M	NN	GRZZZZUSA	
SCHWILLE, MART	68	M	FARMER	GRZZZZUSA	
ULRICH	43	M	FARMER	GRZZZZUSA	
GEORG	15	M	FARMER	GRZZZZUSA	
SCHMIDT, BETTIE	43	F	NN	GRZZZZUSA	
ITE	17	F	NN	GRZZZZUSA	
AUCHE	7	F	CHILD	GRZZZZUSA	
ZIMMERMANN, FRIEDR	34	M	FARMER	GRZZZZUSA	
ANNA	30	F	NN	GRZZZZUSA	
SCHULER, MARG	20	F	SVNT	GRZZZZUSA	
MEYER, AR-	19	M	FARMER	GRZZZZUSA	
HERM	63	M	FARMER	GRZZZZUSA	
BERNTJE	63	F	W	GRZZZZUSA	
ENGEL, DOROTHEA	18	F	SVNT	GRZZZZUSA	
FETT, CONRAD	29	M	PNTR	GRZZZZUSA	
BORUKESSLE, EVA	18	F	SVNT	GRZZZZUSA	
RUGHEIMMER, BABETTE	23	F	SVNT	GRZZZZUSA	
REIMANN, LOUISE	18	F	SVNT	GRZZZZUSA	
SCHULZ, AUG	53	M	FARMER	GRZZZZUSA	
AUGUSTE	51	F	W	GRZZZZUSA	
AUGUST	9	M	CHILD	GRZZZZUSA	
LOUISE	6	F	CHILD	GRZZZZUSA	
JOHANN	5	M	CHILD	GRZZZZUSA	
HERMANN	.11	M	INFANT	GRZZZZUSA	
MIELKE, LOUISE	50	F	NN	GRZZZZUSA	
HULDA	15	F	NN	GRZZZZUSA	
HERMANN	6	M	CHILD	GRZZZZUSA	
MARIA	10	F	CH	GRZZZZUSA	
ISLER, HULDA	23	F	SVNT	GRZZZZUSA	
FRAENKLER, MARIA	20	F	NN	GRZZZZUSA	
NEUBIG, PAULUS	26	M	FARMER	GRZZZZUSA	
FRAENKLER, ELISAB	.09	F	INFANT	GRZZZZUSA	
MAIER, ALOIS	25	M	MCHT	GRZZZZUSA	
TIET-EN, BERNHD	14	M	NN	GRZZZZUSA	
EHLERS, HINR	16	M	GDNR	GRZZZZUSA	
GOEDDE, HEINR	17	M	GDNR	GRZZZZUSA	
EBERLE, ROSA	19	F	SVNT	GRZZZZUSA	
GENOSEFA	18	F	SVNT	GRZZZZUSA	
LUDEMANN, JOHA	61	F	NN	GRZZZZUSA	
SCHOENLEIN, MARIE	20	F	SMSTS	GRZZZZUSA	
AMANT, KUNIGUNDE	18	F	SMSTS	GRZZZZUSA	
MUELLER, ANNA	21	F	SMSTS	GRZZZZUSA	
WIESER, MATH	44	M	CPTR	GRZZZZUSA	
HAUPT, AUGUST	17	M	GDNR	GRZZZZUSA	
CLANSSEN, GEORGE	38	M	MCHT	GRZZZZUSA	
LANGE, OSCAR	21	M	CNF	GRZZZZUSA	
GREIME, JOHANN	21	M	FARMER	GRZZZZUSA	
KRZYIMMSKI, LEOP	36	M	FARMER	GRZZZZUSA	
HARDT, ANNA	18	F	SMSTS	GRZZZZUSA	
ENGELHARDT, ANNA	22	F	SMSTS	GRZZZZUSA	
KNABE, IDA	25	F	NN	GRZZZZUSA	
ELISE	4	F	CHILD	GRZZZZUSA	
FRITZ	2	M	CHILD	GRZZZZUSA	
HELENE	.05	F	INFANT	GRZZZZUSA	
KAPIZYUSKA, ROZALIA	28	F	NN	GRZZZZUSA	
PELAZIA	2	F	CHILD	GRZZZZUSA	
STANISLAW	.06	M	INFANT	GRZZZZUSA	
MANRITZ, JOHN	34	M	FARMER	GRZZZZUSA	
MARIA	30	F	W	GRZZZZUSA	
WIE--	9	M	CHILD	GRZZZZUSA	
LOUISE	7	F	CHILD	GRZZZZUSA	
AUGUSTE	5	F	CHILD	GRZZZZUSA	
WILHELMINE	2	F	CHILD	GRZZZZUSA	
KNOBBE, MARIE	24	F	NN	GRZZZZUSA	
CARL	.10	M	INFANT	GRZZZZUSA	
GROCHOWALSKA, SUSANNE	60	F	NN	GRZZZZUSA	
CARL	8	M	CHILD	GRZZZZUSA	
OLSCHEWSKA, CATHAR	60	F	NN	GRZZZZUSA	
BUERGER, HEINR	26	M	TLR	GRZZZZUSA	
KAISER, ANNA	21	F	NN	GRZZZZUSA	
JOHANN	28	M	CL	GRZZZZUSA	
STE--ER, KATHAR	25	F	NN	GRZZZZUSA	
-ZEPCZENSKI, JOSEFA	25	F	NN	GRZZZZUSA	
KL--IS	3	M	CHILD	GRZZZZUSA	
STANISLAWA	1	F	CHILD	GRZZZZUSA	
STEFAN	.01	M	INFANT	GRZZZZUSA	
BREHMER, PAUL	20	M	TLR	GRZZZZUSA	
SCHWARZ, MICH	28	M	PNTR	GRZZZZUSA	
GEILINGER, THERESIA	25	F	NN	GRZZZZUSA	
WINDISCH, JOS	29	M	PRNTR	GRZZZZUSA	
HANNER, SEBAST	23	M	MCHT	GRZZZZUSA	
STEINHAUSER, JOSEF	25	M	SHMK	GRZZZZUSA	
ROHRMEIER, SEBAST	60	M	FARMER	GRZZZZUSA	
MARIA	5	F	CHILD	GRZZZZUSA	
MICHEL, ELISABE	30	F	NN	GRZZZZUSA	
ELISE	4	F	CHILD	GRZZZZUSA	
WILHELM	3	M	CHILD	GRZZZZUSA	
CONRAD	2	M	CHILD	GRZZZZUSA	
JUNG, ANNA	17	F	SMSTS	GRZZZZUSA	
JOHNSON, CATHAR	38	F	NN	GRZZZZUSA	
SCHWOGOSKA, AGNES	25	F	NN	GRZZZZUSA	
JACOBI, WILHELMINE	27	F	NN	GRZZZZUSA	
WILHE	3	F	CHILD	GRZZZZUSA	
ERNST	.07	M	INFANT	GRZZZZUSA	
WIEGAND, ELISAB	17	F	SVNT	GRZZZZUSA	
WIENECK, F	51	M	FARMER	GRZZZZUSA	
STRAUSS, JOHANN	16	M	SHMK	GRZZZZUSA	
HARTMANN, FRIEDR	67	M	FARMER	GRZZZZUSA	
DOEL, CHARE	68	M	FARMER	GRZZZZUSA	
RUIGEL, FRIEDR	27	M	FARMER	GRZZZZUSA	
SCHWEIER, CARL	38	M	BRR	GRZZZZUSA	
HUCK, BURKHARD	23	M	BCHR	GRZZZZUSA	
KIEFER, GUSTAF	18	M	BCHR	GRZZZZUSA	
FAUST, WALTER	50	M	FARMER	GRZZZZUSA	
NEUMANN, FRITZ	27	M	FARMER	GRZZZZUSA	
STENZEL, JOSEF	28	M	PNTR	GRZZZZUSA	
WERNER, JOSEF	29	M	BKR	GRZZZZUSA	
HEIM, SABINE	27	F	NN	GRZZZZUSA	
KLUG, ANTON	28	M	MCHT	GRZZZZUSA	
SEEKAMP, JOHANN	17	M	FARMER	GRZZZZUSA	
HE-SCHELL, ROSINE	23	F	NN	GRZZZZUSA	
PAULINE	.09	F	INFANT	GRZZZZUSA	
KLEPPER, PAULINE	19	F	SVNT	GRZZZZUSA	
ECK, ALOIS	18	M	SHMK	GRZZZZUSA	
WARZE--A, JOH	25	M	LABR	GRZZZZUSA	
ZE--ER, CHR	27	M	LABR	GRZZZZUSA	
STEDE, FRIEDR	24	M	LABR	GRZZZZUSA	
KUETHE, WILH	27	M	LABR	GRZZZZUSA	
FIEGE, LOUISE	18	F	NN	GRZZZZUSA	
VOSS, HEINR	26	M	FARMER	GRZZZZUSA	
ROBES, GEORGE	34	M	FARMER	GRZZZZUSA	
MARGA	23	F	W	GRZZZZUSA	
LENE	2	F	CHILD	GRZZZZUSA	
GEORGE	.10	M	INFANT	GRZZZZUSA	
VON, MARIE	20	F	NN	GRZZZZUSA	
ERNST	1	M	CHILD	GRZZZZUSA	
WALTHER	.07	M	INFANT	GRZZZZUSA	
SCHWARZER, BERTHA	16	F	NN	GRZZZZUSA	
KROENER, FRANZ	39	M	FARMER	GRZZZZUSA	
PAUL	14	M	FARMER	GRZZZZUSA	
HEDWIG	11	F	CH	GRZZZZUSA	
HAASE, GUSTAV	18	M	MCHT	GRZZZZUSA	
KARL	16	M	MCHT	GRZZZZUSA	
EBERT, KATIE	23	F	SMSTS	GRZZZZUSA	
REINKE-, MARG	27	F	SMSTS	GRZZZZUSA	
MARTE, JOSEPHINE	27	F	SMSTS	GRZZZZUSA	
LOCKEMEIER, MAGDAL	19	F	SMSTS	GRZZZZUSA	
KLINGER, BABETTE	20	F	SMSTS	GRZZZZUSA	
SCHNEIDER, ANNA	24	F	SMSTS	GRZZZZUSA	
GLAS, MOSES	24	M	MCHT	GRZZZZUSA	
PANCHOKE, WIE	23	M	BRR	GRZZZZUSA	
PFEIFFER, HEINR	23	M	BCHR	GRZZZZUSA	

PASSENGER	AGE	SEX	OCCUPATION	PRVL	DES
PAPENHANSEN, HEINR	26	M	FARMER		GRZZZZUSA
BERGMANN, MARG	18	F	SVNT		GRZZZZUSA
RABE, MARIA	11	F	CH		GRZZZZUSA
BAER, BARBARA	38	F	NN		GRZZZZUSA
MARG	12	F	CH		GRZZZZUSA
LERRACHER, KATH	20	F	NN		GRZZZZUSA
BUSCH, AUGUST	16	M	LABR		GRZZZZUSA
ROST, GEORG	30	M	SHMK		GRZZZZUSA
LESSER, THEO	31	M	CPTR		GRZZZZUSA
AC---TIUS, PETER	23	M	WTR		GRZZZZUSA
ALEXANDROWITSCH, BERTHA	32	F	NN		GRZZZZUSA
LYDIA	6	F	CHILD		GRZZZZUSA
EUGEN	5	M	CHILD		GRZZZZUSA
RICKA	4	F	CHILD		GRZZZZUSA
JETTA	.11	F	INFANT		GRZZZZUSA
BLASCOWITZ, VERONICA	22	F	NN		GRZZZZUSA
HORSTMANN, L	46	M	FARMER		GRZZZZUSA
KOSEL, HUGO	25	M	BBR		GRZZZZUSA
SCHULZ, FRIEDR	25	M	BKR		GRZZZZUSA
DUCH, FRANCISCA	35	F	NN		GRZZZZUSA
AGNES	10	F	CH		GRZZZZUSA
MARTIN	9	M	CHILD		GRZZZZUSA
STANSILAW	6	M	CHILD		GRZZZZUSA
VICTORIA	4	F	CHILD		GRZZZZUSA
BOROSKA, ROSALIE	25	F	NN		GRZZZZUSA
SOPHIA	1	F	CHILD		GRZZZZUSA
ROSALIA	.01	F	INFANT		GRZZZZUSA
HERRMANN, PHILIPP	19	M	MCHT		GRZZZZUSA
SCHALHORN, CAROLINE	61	F	NN		GRZZZZUSA
PETERS, HEINRICH	27	M	FARMER		GRZZZZUSA
HAURATH, AUGUST	26	M	WTR		GRZZZZUSA
SOPHIE	26	F	W		GRZZZZUSA
KLINGEBIEL, C	32	M	BDM		GRZZZZUSA
SCHAAF, WILLY	6	M	CHILD		GRZZZZUSA
RAUB, ALBERT	22	M	FARMER		GRZZZZUSA

SHIP: AMERICA

FROM: BREMEN
TO: BALTIMORE
ARRIVED: 08 NOVEMBER 1888

PASSENGER	AGE	SEX	OCCUPATION	PRVL	DES
SEIFERT, MATHILDE	51	F	NN		GRZZZZUNK
RAAB, CAROLINE	17	F	NN		GRZZZZUNK
PO--LEITNER, CREZENZ	39	F	NN		GRZZZZUNK
JOHANN	11	M	CH		GRZZZZUNK
LUDWIG	8	M	CHILD		GRZZZZUNK
JOSEPH	6	M	CHILD		GRZZZZUNK
ALOIS	3	M	CHILD		GRZZZZUNK
CARL	.09	M	INFANT		GRZZZZUNK
ARNDT, HEINRICH	58	M	TLR		GRZZZZNE
JOHANNA	50	F	NN		GRZZZZNE
AUGUST	24	M	SHMK		GRZZZZNE
BERTHA	17	F	SVNT		GRZZZZNE
EMILIE	10	F	CH		GRZZZZNE
GERHARDT, CATHARINA	15	F	NN		GRZZZZIA
BRUEHN, WILHELMINE	59	F	FARMER		GRZZZZIA
AUGUST	26	M	NN		GRZZZZIA
MARIA	20	F	NN		GRZZZZIA
AUGUSTE	16	F	NN		GRZZZZIA
CZWINSKI, ANDREAS	23	M	FARMER		GRZZZZMN
GUENTHER, CARL	22	M	BRR		GRZZZZUNK
S-KOTA, PAULINE	52	F	NN		GRZZZZIL
PETER	13	M	CH		GRZZZZIL
PAUL	9	M	CHILD		GRZZZZIL
WASIK, MARIA	23	F	NN		GRZZZZIL
FRANZ	10	M	CH		GRZZZZIL
VICTORIA	3	F	CHILD		GRZZZZIL
MARIANNA	.09	F	INFANT		GRZZZZIL
GEISLER, JOHANNE	63	F	NN		GRZZZZDAK

PASSENGER	AGE	SEX	OCCUPATION	PRVL	DES
GODZIZAKA, ANILA	16	F	NN		GRZZZZDAK
WOZINSKA, MARYANNA	26	F	NN		GRZZZZDAK
VALENTIN	.07	M	INFANT		GRZZZZDAK
S-YBIN, NA-AMMIA	28	F	NN		GRZZZZWI
MARIA	43	F	NN		GRZZZZWI
STANISLAWA	8	M	CHILD		GRZZZZWI
JOSEFA	.10	F	INFANT		GRZZZZWI
KOBUSS, KOSLESLA-	15	M	NN		GRZZZZWI
PAEGELAW, JOHANN	42	M	SMH		GRZZZZCIN
CAROLINE	40	F	NN		GRZZZZCIN
WILHELM	20	M	FARMER		GRZZZZCIN
FRITZ	15	M	NN		GRZZZZCIN
CARL	13	M	NN		GRZZZZCIN
IDA	11	F	NN		GRZZZZCIN
CAROLINE	9	F	CHILD		GRZZZZCIN
ANNA	5	F	CHILD		GRZZZZCIN
MARTHA	.11	F	INFANT		GRZZZZCIN
VON, OTTILIE	22	F	NN		GRZZZZMI
WENDORFF, WILHELMINE	30	F	NN		GRZZZZMI
JOHANNA	18	F	NN		GRZZZZMI
-IEGO, AUGUST	24	M	BCHR		GRZZZZIL
MOND, ALWINE	19	F	SVNT		GRZZZZIL
FICK, IDA	14	F	SVNT		GRZZZZIL
PORETH, ALBERTINE	18	F	SVNT		GRZZZZIL
BERTHA	16	F	SVNT		GRZZZZIL
BAUER, ROBERT	24	M	SDLR		GRZZZZIL
LIEBENAU, LOUISE	22	F	SVNT		GRZZZZIL
RAEPKE, WILHELMINE	23	F	SVNT		GRZZZZIL
P-OVINSKA, WILHELM	37	M	FARMER		GRZZZZIL
EMILIE	31	F	NN		GRZZZZIL
LUBKOWSKI, JOHANNES	32	M	JNR		GRZZZZIL
LANGE, JOHANN	36	M	SHMK		GRZZZZIL
REUMS, AUGUSTE	14	F	NN		GRZZZZUNK
PASCH, ALBERT	23	M	MSN		GRZZZZUNK
PIOTROWSKI, FRANZ	22	M	LABR		GRZZZZUNK
ROZENWIRZ, JOSEPHA	20	F	NN		GRZZZZUNK
STANISLAWA	.06	F	INFANT		GRZZZZUNK
MUELLER, OTTO	14	M	NN		GRZZZZUNK
BOHMKE, BERTHA	18	F	NN		GRZZZZUNK
LEPPIN, LUDWIG	38	M	FARMER		GRZZZZNE
PAULINA	32	F	NN		GRZZZZNE
FRIDA	10	F	CH		GRZZZZNE
HEINRICH	8	M	CHILD		GRZZZZNE
BERTHA	6	F	CHILD		GRZZZZNE
ANNA	3	F	CHILD		GRZZZZNE
HERMANN	.06	M	INFANT		GRZZZZNE
KLAUS, WILHELM	32	M	PRNTR		GRZZZZUNK
KOMORONSKI, WILHLEMINE	18	F	SVNT		GRZZZZUNK
SCHWARZ, CHRISTOPH	22	M	LABR		GRZZZZUNK
VOWRABLE, MARTIN	22	M	LABR		GRZZZZUNK
WEISSBERG, FRIEDRICH	22	M	FARMER		GRZZZZUNK
MARIE	16	F	SVNT		GRZZZZUNK
GUNTERBERG, OTTO	22	M	STCTR		GRZZZZUNK
BER-HOLZ, CARL	30	M	FARMER		GRZZZZDAK
MINNA	31	F	NN		GRZZZZDAK
BERTHA	9	F	CHILD		GRZZZZDAK
WILHELM	7	M	CHILD		GRZZZZDAK
HEINRICH	4	M	CHILD		GRZZZZDAK
CHAYNOWSKA, FRANZISCA	21	F	NN		GRZZZZPA
STEFFER, AUGUSTE	19	F	NN		GRZZZZPA
KUETBACH, FERDIN	30	M	SHFM		GRZZZZIL
WEISS, KATHERINA	40	F	NN		GRZZZZWI
ANNA	9	F	CHILD		GRZZZZWI
MARIE	4	F	CHILD		GRZZZZWI
MARTHA	3	F	CHILD		GRZZZZWI
KORKE, ELISABETH	18	F	SVNT		GRZZZZUNK
ME---DE, CLARA	34	F	NN		GRZZZZUNK
ALFRED	5	M	CHILD		GRZZZZUNK
ZINYDZINSKA, MARIANNA	19	F	NN		GRZZZZUNK
JULIANNA	18	F	NN		GRZZZZUNK
IDA	.07	F	INFANT		GRZZZZUNK
SCHWEDLER, JACOB	27	M	JNR		GRZZZZUNK
MECH, ROSALIE	39	F	NN		GRZZZZUNK
MARTHA	10	F	CH		GRZZZZUNK
STUEMER, ALMA	10	F	CH		GRZZZZUNK

PASSENGER	AGE	SEX	OCCUPATION	PRVL/DES
PUTSCHAK, GOTTLIEB	59	M	FARMER	GRZZZZUNK
WILHELMINE	42	F	NN	GRZZZZUNK
GUSTAV	16	M	NN	GRZZZZUNK
EDUARD	9	M	CHILD	GRZZZZUNK
AUGUSTE	6	F	CHILD	GRZZZZUNK
HULDA	10	F	CH	GRZZZZUNK
ADEL---	4	F	CHILD	GRZZZZUNK
MATHILDE	8	F	CHILD	GRZZZZUNK
WOLF, REINHOLD	22	M	MSN	GRZZZZUNK
MANUEL, LEON	38	M	MSN	GRZZZZMN
ANNA	36	F	NN	GRZZZZMN
MARIA	10	F	CH	GRZZZZMN
FRANZ	.11	M	INFANT	GRZZZZMN
SEM--, AUGUST	36	M	FARMER	GRZZZZWI
ELANORE	39	F	NN	GRZZZZWI
ADAM	11	M	CH	GRZZZZWI
ROSALIE	9	F	CHILD	GRZZZZWI
EMILIE	7	F	CHILD	GRZZZZWI
EMMA	3	F	CHILD	GRZZZZWI
OTTO	.11	M	INFANT	GRZZZZWI
RYPKE, ALBERTINE	25	F	SVNT	GRZZZZPA
KUTZ, JOHANN	37	M	LABR	GRZZZZPA
DOROTHEA	34	F	NN	GRZZZZPA
ANNA	8	F	CHILD	GRZZZZPA
JOHANNA	6	F	CHILD	GRZZZZPA
AUGUST	4	M	CHILD	GRZZZZPA
FRANZ	3	M	CHILD	GRZZZZPA
PAUL	.11	M	INFANT	GRZZZZPA
GROSSMANN, CARL	38	M	LABR	GRZZZZNE
ANNA	37	F	NN	GRZZZZNE
FRIEDRICH	10	M	CH	GRZZZZNE
AUGUSTE	6	F	CHILD	GRZZZZNE
HERMANN	4	M	CHILD	GRZZZZNE
HEINRICH	.08	M	INFANT	GRZZZZNE
MAGDOWSKA, JULIANNE	20	F	SVNT	GRZZZZUNK
STROSCHEIN, CARL	43	M	FARMER	GRZZZZUNK
WIESEN, CAROLINE	57	F	NN	GRZZZZUNK
KARKOWSKY, AUGUST	24	M	JNR	GRZZZZUNK
BEINHOLZ, GOTTFRIED	24	M	TLR	GRZZZZUNK
GOHLKE, HENRIETTE	18	F	SVNT	GRZZZZUNK
KITTER, FRIEDRICH	39	M	CPTR	GRZZZZMN
JACOBINE	35	F	NN	GRZZZZMN
JOHANN	14	M	CH	GRZZZZMN
MARIE	9	F	CHILD	GRZZZZMN
EMILIE	4	F	CHILD	GRZZZZMN
ANNA	2	F	CHILD	GRZZZZMN
PEPLINSKI, PETER	28	M	BLKSMH	GRZZZZMN
EMILIE	22	F	NN	GRZZZZMN
MARIE	.11	F	INFANT	GRZZZZMN
WASILEWSKA, APOLLONIA	30	F	NN	GRZZZZIL
MARIANNA	9	F	CHILD	GRZZZZIL
WLADISLAW	.03	M	INFANT	GRZZZZIL
GUTMEIDE, THERESE	46	F	NN	GRZZZZIL
CARL	13	M	CH	GRZZZZIL
JOHANN	11	M	CH	GRZZZZIL
MARIA	3	F	CHILD	GRZZZZIL
LANGER, PAUL	25	M	MCHT	GRZZZZIL
KRAMER, THEKLA	18	F	NN	GRZZZZIL
HERSSEN, CHRISTIAN	45	M	CK	GRZZZZIL
MARIE	35	F	NN	GRZZZZIL
KAWEL, CLARA	18	F	SVNT	GRZZZZIL
STRATHMANN, SOPHIE	30	F	NN	GRZZZZIL
LILLI	.09	F	INFANT	GRZZZZIL
ADES, SEIDEL	50	M	MCHT	GRZZZZIL
THNEN, JUERGEN	60	M	LABR	GRZZZZWI
HOFFNER, SOPHIE	62	F	NN	GRZZZZWI
EUCHNER, ADAM	17	M	SHFM	GRZZZZWI
KNASS, WALPURGA	66	F	NN	GRZZZZWI
VERONICA	24	F	NN	GRZZZZWI
WENIGER, JOSEF	19	M	LABR	GRZZZZIL
ZIMMERMANN, ERNESTINE	37	F	CK	GRZZZZIL
BRUNS, ETJE	35	F	CK	GRZZZZIL
LOEHR, CONRAD	16	M	NN	GRZZZZIL
TIEDMANN, MARIE	24	F	SVNT	GRZZZZIL
PLETOWSKI, ANDREAS	29	M	STCTR	GRZZZZIL
JASCHKA, MARTHA	22	F	NN	GRZZZZUNK
WILLY	1	M	CHILD	GRZZZZUNK
KRETSCHMANN, IGNATZ	21	M	MSN	GRZZZZUNK
LEWANDOWSKI, STANISLAUS	28	M	MSN	GRZZZZUNK
KLAUS, CAROLINE	30	F	NN	GRZZZZUNK
GOTTLIEBE	.09	F	INFANT	GRZZZZUNK
RASCHKE, JOHANN	27	M	BCKM	GRZZZZUNK
HELENE	24	F	NN	GRZZZZUNK
ALBERT	3	M	CHILD	GRZZZZUNK
JOHANN	2	M	CHILD	GRZZZZUNK
BUTSCHKOWSKI, FRANZ	59	M	FARMER	GRZZZZMN
SCHROETER, JOSEF	23	M	FARMER	GRZZZZMN
KOLBERG, JOHANNA	34	F	NN	GRZZZZCOL
CARL	9	M	CHILD	GRZZZZCOL
MAX	4	M	CHILD	GRZZZZCOL
OTTO	3	M	CHILD	GRZZZZCOL
MARX, AUGUST	55	M	UNKNOWN	GRZZZZIL
JOHANN	56	F	NN	GRZZZZIL
MARIA	11	F	CH	GRZZZZIL
BOTTCHER, CARL	34	M	FARMER	GRZZZZUNK
ADELINE	32	F	NN	GRZZZZUNK
ELISE	9	F	CHILD	GRZZZZUNK
ANNA	7	F	CHILD	GRZZZZUNK
GILT-	5	F	CHILD	GRZZZZUNK
FRANZ	6	M	CHILD	GRZZZZUNK
META	.11	F	INFANT	GRZZZZUNK
LEIBACH, JOSEPHINE	44	F	CK	GRZZZZUNK
FRANK, FERDINAND	18	M	TLR	GRZZZZUNK
HEINRICH, ANNA	12	F	NN	GRZZZZUNK
HARTMANN, ROSA	22	F	SVNT	GRZZZZPA
STAHL, LEOPOLD	24	M	LABR	GRZZZZPA
KALZ, JOSEPH	17	M	LABR	GRZZZZPA
SCHRADER, CARL	36	M	FARMER	GRZZZZMN
MINNA	33	F	NN	GRZZZZMN
FRIEDRICH	10	M	CH	GRZZZZMN
HEINRICH	9	M	CHILD	GRZZZZMN
JETTE	8	F	CHILD	GRZZZZMN
WILHELM	6	M	CHILD	GRZZZZMN
MINNA	4	F	CHILD	GRZZZZMN
ANNA	.09	F	INFANT	GRZZZZMN
ADAMEZEWSKI, FRANZISCA	27	F	NN	GRZZZZMI
ADALBERT	7	M	CHILD	GRZZZZMI
MARIANNA	4	F	CHILD	GRZZZZMI
ANTON	.10	M	INFANT	GRZZZZMI
BIERNAL, MARGARETHE	43	F	NN	GRZZZZMN
JOHANN	7	M	CHILD	GRZZZZMN
STANISLAUS	5	M	CHILD	GRZZZZMN
THOMAS	.09	M	INFANT	GRZZZZMN
PIOTNOWSKI, AGNES	26	F	NN	GRZZZZMN
MICHALINA	3	F	CHILD	GRZZZZMN
STANISLAW	2	M	CHILD	GRZZZZMN
SCHWEDER, ROBERT	17	M	LABR	GRZZZZMN
BRESMANN, ANNA	48	F	NN	GRZZZZMN
BERTHA	12	F	CH	GRZZZZMN
FRIEDRICH	12	M	CH	GRZZZZMN
LOBEZAK, ANNA	25	F	NN	GRZZZZMI
PAUL	4	M	CHILD	GRZZZZMI
ANTON	1	M	CHILD	GRZZZZMI
CONSTANZIA	.01	F	INFANT	GRZZZZMI
KAMPELL, FRANZ	47	M	LABR	GRZZZZUNK
HELENE	49	F	NN	GRZZZZUNK
JOHANN	6	M	CHILD	GRZZZZUNK
MORTZFELD, GOTTFRIED	47	M	FARMER	GRZZZZKY
LOUISE	46	F	NN	GRZZZZKY
WILHELM	14	M	CH	GRZZZZKY
WILHLMINE	10	F	CH	GRZZZZKY
AUGUST	8	M	CHILD	GRZZZZKY
AUGUSTE	3	F	CHILD	GRZZZZKY
MARE--ARDT, CARL	16	M	LABR	GRZZZZUNK
B-O-OFSKI, AUGUSTE	19	F	SVNT	GRZZZZUNK
DETLAF, DOROTHEA	17	F	SVNT	GRZZZZUNK
ROSALIE	19	F	SVNT	GRZZZZUNK
KOTLINSKA, AMANDA	19	F	SVNT	GRZZZZUNK
BEEKER, MINNA	27	F	SVNT	GRZZZZUNK
LEONARDT, HEINRICH	29	M	SHMK	GRZZZZIL

PASSENGER	AGE	SEX	OCCUPATION	PRV	VIL	DES
OLSOWSKI, RUDOLF	25	M	FARMER			GRZZZZIL
WILHELMINE	24	F	NN			GRZZZZIL
HOFFMANN, JULIUS	50	M	FARMER			GRZZZZUNK
LOUISE	50	F	NN			GRZZZZUNK
GUSTAV	10	M	CH			GRZZZZUNK
ELISE	8	F	CHILD			GRZZZZUNK
KARJENSKI, ANTONIA	47	F	NN			GRZZZZUNK
JOHANN	9	M	CHILD			GRZZZZUNK
HEDWIG	7	F	CHILD			GRZZZZUNK
STANISLAWA	3	F	CHILD			GRZZZZUNK
LEWANDOFSKI, ADAM	33	M	LABR			GRZZZZUNK
ASCHE-IN, CARL	33	M	LABR			GRZZZZUNK
AUGUSTE	30	F	NN			GRZZZZUNK
HUGO	6	M	CHILD			GRZZZZUNK
AMANDA	3	F	CHILD			GRZZZZUNK
MATHILDE	.11	F	INFANT			GRZZZZUNK
LIEDKE, MAX	23	M	MCHT			GRZZZZUNK
LEWANDOFSKI, MINNA	32	F	NN			GRZZZZUNK
AUGUSTE	5	F	CHILD			GRZZZZUNK
AUGUST	3	M	CHILD			GRZZZZUNK
JOHANN	.09	M	INFANT			GRZZZZUNK
WACKER, ROSA	25	F	SVNT			GRZZZZUNK
DETTLAF, WILHELM	29	M	FARMER			GRZZZZKY
FRIEDRIKE	29	F	NN			GRZZZZKY
LOUISE	10	F	CH			GRZZZZKY
ROBERT	4	M	CHILD			GRZZZZKY
IDA	3	F	CHILD			GRZZZZKY
CZERMIAKOWSKA, THERESE	29	F	SVNT			GRZZZZUNK
MERT, CAROLINE	38	F	NN			GRZZZZUNK
MARGARETHE	15	F	NN			GRZZZZUNK
MARIA	13	F	CH			GRZZZZUNK
CARL	12	M	CH			GRZZZZUNK
JOSEF	9	M	CHILD			GRZZZZUNK
WERNEKE, GEORG	17	M	MCHT			GRZZZZCOL
SCHERF, MARIA	21	F	SVNT			GRZZZZUNK
WAGNER, BERTHA	18	F	SVNT			GRZZZZUNK
KIRCHER, MARGARATHE	18	F	SVNT			GRZZZZUNK
JEPSEN, SOEREN	69	M	FARMER			GRZZZZIL
CATHARINA	65	F	NN			GRZZZZIL
DOHNE, WILHLEM	34	M	FARMER			GRZZZZIL
WILHELM	36	F	NN			GRZZZZIL
MARIE	9	F	CHILD			GRZZZZIL
CARL	6	M	CHILD			GRZZZZIL
PETROWSKY, CARL	42	M	GDNR			GRZZZZIL
GOTTLIEBE	38	F	NN			GRZZZZIL
ADOLF	10	M	CH			GRZZZZIL
AMO--	9	M	CHILD			GRZZZZIL
HERMANN	7	M	CHILD			GRZZZZIL
FRITZ	5	M	CHILD			GRZZZZIL
BERTHA	.03	F	INFANT			GRZZZZIL
GRUBBA, PAUL	16	M	NN			GRZZZZIL
MATSCHEFKOWSKI, FRIEDRI	27	M	FARMER			GRZZZZIL
MATSCHEFKOWSKI, GOTTLIE	26	F	NN			GRZZZZIL
MATSCHEFKOWSKI, ALEXA	15	F	NN			GRZZZZIL
MARIA	2	F	CHILD			GRZZZZIL
FRIEDRICH	.06	M	INFANT			GRZZZZIL
KUBIAK, MICHEL	24	M	FARMER			GRZZZZIL
SCHMIDT, WILHELM	17	M	FARMER			GRZZZZIL
KRISCHNICK, FERDINAND	26	M	FARMER			GRZZZZIL
BUSCHIKOWSKI, AUGUST	29	M	FARMER			GRZZZZIL
G-I-HE, CARL	28	M	FARMER			GRZZZZIL
CAROLINE	30	F	NN			GRZZZZIL
ADOLF	.03	M	INFANT			GRZZZZIL
HAES-, VALENTIN	27	M	FARMER			GRZZZZIL
ANNA	20	F	NN			GRZZZZIL
MARIA	.09	F	INFANT			GRZZZZIL
WITSCHINSKI, JOHANN	29	M	JNR			GRZZZZMI
WILLER, EMIL	20	M	MLR			GRZZZZMI
KOTECKA, VICTORIA	45	F	NN			GRZZZZUNK
STANISLAW	16	M	NN			GRZZZZUNK
BALESLAW	10	M	CH			GRZZZZUNK
MAX	4	M	CHILD			GRZZZZUNK
FRANZ	2	M	CHILD			GRZZZZUNK
RADIES, AUGUST	25	M	CPTR			GRZZZZUNK
SCHNEIDER, CARL	27	M	SMH			GRZZZZUNK
KROM--GA, JOHANNA	35	F	NN			GRZZZZIA
EBERHARD	17	M	SMH			GRZZZZIA
GERHARD	11	M	CH			GRZZZZIA
NAGEL, MARIA	19	F	SVNT			GRZZZZIA
VOLL, MARIA	20	F	SVNT			GRZZZZMN
BRANDT, REINHOLDT	27	M	MNR			GRZZZZMI
FRIEDRICKE	28	F	NN			GRZZZZMI
OTTO	4	M	CHILD			GRZZZZMI
WALTER	.03	M	INFANT			GRZZZZMI
MULLER, CHRISTIAN	30	M	LABR			GRZZZZUNK
BRAKE, JOSEF	22	M	MLR			GRZZZZUNK
SCHOENHEER, AUGUST	62	M	FARMER			GRZZZZUNK
NI--DEL	39	M	FARMER			GRZZZZUNK
CATHERINA	25	F	NN			GRZZZZUNK
AUGUST	11	M	CH			GRZZZZUNK
MARIE	10	F	CH			GRZZZZUNK
JOSEPH	4	M	CHILD			GRZZZZUNK
NICOLAUS	4	M	CHILD			GRZZZZUNK
DAHLE, CASPAR	25	M	JNR			GRZZZZUNK
SUBENEICHER, CARL	58	M	FARMER			GRZZZZUNK
IDA	28	F	NN			GRZZZZUNK
PAUL	3	M	CHILD			GRZZZZUNK
EMMA	.11	F	INFANT			GRZZZZUNK
SCHWEDER, JOHANN	24	M	GDNR			GRZZZZUNK
MARIANNA	2	F	CHILD			GRZZZZUNK
JOHANN	.01	M	INFANT			GRZZZZUNK
PRAUS--KE, LOUISE	44	F	NN			GRZZZZIL
CARL	11	M	CH			GRZZZZIL
LOUISE	7	F	CHILD			GRZZZZIL
PAUL	3	M	CHILD			GRZZZZIL
FUCHALSKI, CAROLINE	20	F	SVNT			GRZZZZIL
BANK, ANTONIA	27	F	NN			GRZZZZIL
MARIA	4	F	CHILD			GRZZZZIL
JOSEPH	2	M	CHILD			GRZZZZIL
JOHANN	.10	M	INFANT			GRZZZZIL
SCHRAE-ER, CARL	32	M	LABR			GRZZZZKY
CAROLINE	28	F	NN			GRZZZZKY
MARIA	21	F	NN			GRZZZZKY
KALISCH, AGNES	18	F	SVNT			GRZZZZUNK
REMSCH, FRANZ	22	M	LITGR			GRZZZZCOL
ELSNER, ERNST	11	M	CH			GRZZZZCOL
GREINER, JOHANN	24	M	TLR			GRZZZZUNK
GE-S, JOHANN	15	M	NN			GRZZZZUNK
HERBERGER, ELEANORE	68	F	NN			GRZZZZUNK
JOHANNA	25	F	NN			GRZZZZUNK
REINKE, AUGUSTE	41	F	NN			GRZZZZUNK
FERDINAND	10	M	CH			GRZZZZUNK
AUGUSTE	8	F	CHILD			GRZZZZUNK
PAULINE	6	F	CHILD			GRZZZZUNK
ANNA	3	F	CHILD			GRZZZZUNK
KUTSCHKE, ERNESTINE	17	F	SVNT			GRZZZZUNK
STRZELECKA, ROSALIA	15	F	SVNT			GRZZZZUNK
GROCHOWALCHA, STANISLAW	24	F	SVNT			GRZZZZUNK
MATHIS, MARIE	58	F	NN			GRZZZZPA
BLOHM, JOHANN	21	M	FARMER			GRZZZZUNK
SCHULMEISTER, FRIEDRICH	37	M	FARMER			GRZZZZUNK
KOTELMANN, SOPHIE	29	F	NN			GRZZZZUNK
HERMANN	5	M	CHILD			GRZZZZUNK
HARTMANN, FRIEDRICH	55	M	MSN			GRZZZZWI
CHRISTINE	56	F	NN			GRZZZZWI
MATHILDE	18	F	NN			GRZZZZWI
WILHELM	13	M	NN			GRZZZZWI
STEUR, CARL	27	M	HTR			GRZZZZWI
ALWINE	29	F	NN			GRZZZZWI
WILHELMINE	.11	M	INFANT			GRZZZZWI
MIERKE, AUGUST	32	M	FARMER			GRZZZZWI
EMILIE	25	F	NN			GRZZZZWI
CARL	.11	M	INFANT			GRZZZZWI
ZIMMERMANN, AUGUSTE	28	F	SVNT			GRZZZZWI
SCHUDLING, AUGUST	23	M	LABR			GRZZZZMI
KEMP, CARL	48	M	FARMER			GRZZZZMI
HENRIETTE	44	F	NN			GRZZZZMI
FRIEDRICH	16	M	NN			GRZZZZMI
CARL	11	M	CH			GRZZZZMI
ANNA	9	F	CHILD			GRZZZZMI

PASSENGER	AGE	SEX	OCCUPATION	PRVVL DES
GEILIS, HENRIETTE	17	F	SVNT	GRZZZZNE
KEISER, CHRISTIAN	28	M	MSN	GRZZZZNE
KRAFT, JULIUS	38	M	SHMK	GRZZZZNE
HENRIETTE	30	F	NN	GRZZZZNE
FRANZ	4	M	CHILD	GRZZZZNE
HERMANN	.11	M	INFANT	GRZZZZNE
ROESLER, GOTTFRIED	23	M	LABR	GRZZZZMI
GOTTLIEBE	21	F	NN	GRZZZZMI
JANICKA, ELISABETH	35	F	NN	GRZZZZUNK
BRONISLAUS	11	M	CH	GRZZZZUNK
KASIMIR	7	M	CHILD	GRZZZZUNK
STEFANIE	3	F	CHILD	GRZZZZUNK
LEO	2	M	CHILD	GRZZZZUNK
WLADISLAWA	.05	F	INFANT	GRZZZZUNK
STANISZEWOKA, FRANZISKA	11	F	CH	GRZZZZUNK
WISZOREK, JOSEF	40	M	PNTR	GRZZZZMI
CATHARINA	34	F	NN	GRZZZZMI
HERMAN, DOROTHEA	34	F	NN	GRZZZZUNK
JOHANN	8	M	CHILD	GRZZZZUNK
DANKEN, ANNIE	18	F	NN	GRZZZZUNK
DATZLER, WILHELM	25	M	FARMER	GRZZZZUNK
MARIA	27	F	NN	GRZZZZUNK
AUGUST	.09	M	INFANT	GRZZZZUNK
ROLFS, DIETRICH	34	M	FARMER	GRZZZZUNK
MARGARETHE	28	F	NN	GRZZZZUNK
HENRIETTE	9	F	CHILD	GRZZZZUNK
DIETRICH	7	M	CHILD	GRZZZZUNK
HEINRICH	.11	M	INFANT	GRZZZZUNK
LEWANDOWSKI, ADAM	31	M	FARMER	GRZZZZIL
TEOFILE	26	F	NN	GRZZZZIL
MAX	2	M	CHILD	GRZZZZIL
WLADISLAUS	.09	M	INFANT	GRZZZZIL
SCHWAETER, ANNA	15	F	NN	GRZZZZUNK
AUGUSTE	4	F	CHILD	GRZZZZUNK
JOHANN	3	M	CHILD	GRZZZZUNK
FRITZ	2	M	CHILD	GRZZZZUNK
MARIE	.09	F	INFANT	GRZZZZUNK
HINZ, FRANZ	33	M	SMH	GRZZZZMI
LORA	26	F	NN	GRZZZZMI
MARIE	4	F	CHILD	GRZZZZMI
AUGUST	2	M	CHILD	GRZZZZMI
AUGUSTE	.09	F	INFANT	GRZZZZMI
LANGE, FRIEDRIKE	64	F	NN	GRZZZZMI
SCHOENBERGER, ANNA	23	F	NN	GRZZZZMI
JOSEPH	3	M	CHILD	GRZZZZMI
ZINN, EMILIE	14	F	NN	GRZZZZMI
MATZA-, FRIEDRICH	24	M	SMH	GRZZZZIL
ZLIKOWSKA, JULIA	26	F	SVNT	GRZZZZIL
ZIMMERMANN, JACOB	26	M	LABR	GRZZZZIL
ZLICKOWSKA, EMIL	11	M	CH	GRZZZZIL
GUSTAV	.10	M	INFANT	GRZZZZIL
WAGNER, OTTO	28	M	JNR	GRZZZZUNK
SIVATZKY, FRANZ	26	M	BCHR	GRZZZZPA

SHIP: SAALE

FROM: BREMEN AND SOUTHAMPTON
TO: NEW YORK
ARRIVED: 10 NOVEMBER 1888

PASSENGER	AGE	SEX	OCCUPATION	PRVVL DES
IMMERMANN, ELISAB.	19	F	UNKNOWN	GRZZZZUSA
SECHLMAYER, WILH.	40	M	MCHT	GRZZZZUSA
THERESE	35	F	W	GRZZZZUSA
V, U	28	M	MCHT	GRZZZZUSA
HOERMANN, CLARA	11	F	UNKNOWN	GRZZZZUSA
GROEPPEL, ANTONIE	20	F	UNKNOWN	GRZZZZUSA
PETZKE, GEORG	23	M	MCHT	GRZZZZUSA
MAI, MARG.	22	F	UNKNOWN	GRZZZZUSA
FLECKENSTEIN, CATH.	23	F	UNKNOWN	GRZZZZUSA
ROSINA	18	F	UNKNOWN	GRZZZZUSA

PASSENGER	AGE	SEX	OCCUPATION	PRVVL DES
LUDWIG, ELISA	22	F	UNKNOWN	GRZZZZUSA
KLEINMANN, CARL	16	M	TLR	GRZZZZUSA
PHILIPP, WILH.	20	F	UNKNOWN	GRZZZZUSA
OPIELINSKI, CZESLAUS	26	M	SMH	GRZZZZUSA
KRASMANN, ED.	15	M	UNKNOWN	GRZZZZUSA
BLUM, CATH.	25	F	UNKNOWN	GRZZZZUSA
KRAFF, NANETTE	52	F	UNKNOWN	GRZZZZUSA
BABETTE	21	F	UNKNOWN	GRZZZZUSA
ANNA	15	F	UNKNOWN	GRZZZZUSA
GRIESNER, CHRISTINE	6	F	CHILD	GRZZZZUSA
KRAUZUSCH, OTTILIE	19	F	UNKNOWN	GRZZZZUSA
HAHN, LOUISE	20	F	UNKNOWN	GRZZZZUSA
STRZYZEWSKI, FRANZ	35	M	FARMER	GRZZZZUSA
MARIE	40	F	W	GRZZZZUSA
MARIE	14	F	CH	GRZZZZUSA
BERNHARD	12	F	CH	GRZZZZUSA
SOPHIE	7	F	CHILD	GRZZZZUSA
JULIUS	5	M	CHILD	GRZZZZUSA
FRANZ	3	M	CHILD	GRZZZZUSA
STANISLAUS	.11	M	INFANT	GRZZZZUSA
BROSCHKIEWWICZ, MARIE	20	F	UNKNOWN	GRZZZZUSA
KNOHL, ANNA	27	F	UNKNOWN	GRZZZZUSA
JEUSCH, EMMA	24	F	UNKNOWN	GRZZZZUSA
SELMA	2	F	CHILD	GRZZZZUSA
RIESCHWELER, FRIEDR.	74	M	LABR	GRZZZZUSA
KAMIENSKI, IGNATZ	40	M	LABR	GRZZZZUSA
CLARA	28	F	W	GRZZZZUSA
RISS, ARTHUR	19	M	LABR	GRZZZZUSA
WALTER, GEORG	42	M	TLR	GRZZZZUSA
VETEWALER, CAROL.	18	F	UNKNOWN	GRZZZZUSA
GERT, RICH.	15	M	UNKNOWN	GRZZZZUSA
HEINSOHN, MARIE	21	F	UNKNOWN	GRZZZZUSA
MEIER, DOROTHEA	20	F	UNKNOWN	GRZZZZUSA
EHRHARDT, ANNA	24	F	UNKNOWN	GRZZZZUSA
THEILENGERDES, GEORG	39	M	FARMER	GRZZZZUSA
ANNA	37	F	W	GRZZZZUSA
JOH.	9	F	CHILD	GRZZZZUSA
FRITZ	7	M	CHILD	GRZZZZUSA
AUG.	5	M	CHILD	GRZZZZUSA
SCHAEFER, HERM.	15	M	UNKNOWN	GRZZZZUSA
SCHUFELD, THERESA	16	F	UNKNOWN	GRZZZZUSA
STEIN, RICH.	11	M	UNKNOWN	GRZZZZUSA
ASMUS, WILH.	22	M	JNR	GRZZZZUSA
FISCHER, BARB.	24	F	UNKNOWN	GRZZZZUSA
HAAG, WILH.	25	M	TLR	GRZZZZUSA
TRAUTMANN, SEBAST.	24	M	TLR	GRZZZZUSA
LOSCH, JOH.	25	M	FARMER	GRZZZZUSA
VOTTELER, LOUISE	21	F	UNKNOWN	GRZZZZUSA
GUDERDING, LOUISE	14	F	UNKNOWN	GRZZZZUSA
GLANDE, CAROL.	22	F	UNKNOWN	GRZZZZUSA
MADER, ADAM	57	M	BKR	GRZZZZUSA
WUCHERER, WILH.	23	M	BKR	GRZZZZUSA
KRUEGER, HERM.	16	M	TLR	GRZZZZUSA
WAGNER, MINE	20	F	UNKNOWN	GRZZZZUSA
FRANKENBERGER, PIUS	18	M	SHMK	GRZZZZUSA
KOHL, CARL	16	M	SMH	GRZZZZUSA
GILSTER, MARIE	53	F	UNKNOWN	GRZZZZUSA
AHRENS, ELISAB.	26	F	UNKNOWN	GRZZZZUSA
MACHALETT, ERNST	58	M	FARMER	GRZZZZUSA
REB.	16	M	FARMER	GRZZZZUSA
SCHAEFFNER, FRANZ	31	M	TLR	GRZZZZUSA
STAMM, GEORG	22	M	PNTR	SRZZZZUSA
DONNERSTAG, EMIL	18	M	CPTR	GRZZZZUSA
SCHNEIDER, ANNA	23	F	UNKNOWN	GRZZZZUSA
SOEDER, ROSINA	17	F	UNKNOWN	GRZZZZUSA
KATZENBERGER, LORENZ	36	M	FARMER	GRZZZZUSA
WEISS, LEONH.	32	M	FARMER	GRZZZZUSA
ZIMMERMANN, MARG.	54	F	UNKNOWN	GRZZZZUSA
MARIE	7	F	CHILD	GRZZZZUSA
BANOLSKA, OTTILIE	45	F	UNKNOWN	GRZZZZUSA
AGNES	11	F	CH	GRZZZZUSA
JOH.	7	F	CHILD	GRZZZZUSA
CESLAP	14	M	UNKNOWN	GRZZZZUSA
PUNDT, JOH.	14	M	UNKNOWN	GRZZZZUSA
ERBRICH, ELISAB.	20	F	UNKNOWN	GRZZZZUSA

PASSENGER	AGE	SEX	OCCUPATION	PRVL	DES
ZUEMPEL, HUGO	35	M	BRR		GRZZZZUSA
MATHILDE	39	F	W		GRZZZZUSA
GOTTSCHALK, BERTHA	31	F	UNKNOWN		GRZZZZUSA
FELIX	10	M	CH		GRZZZZUSA
ROBERT	8	M	CHILD		GRZZZZUSA
OTTILIE	7	F	CHILD		GRZZZZUSA
ALFRED	4	M	CHILD		GRZZZZUSA
ELSBETH	.11	F	INFANT		GRZZZZUSA
BUTKEREIT, HERM.	34	M	JNR		GRZZZZUSA
STROEHLEIN, MARIE	39	F	UNKNOWN		GRZZZZUSA
LOUISE	10	F	CH		GRZZZZUSA
LOUISE	8	F	CHILD		GRZZZZUSA
CARL	.01	M	INFANT		GRZZZZUSA
GROESER, BERNH.	34	M	FARMER		GRZZZZUSA
LISETTE	25	F	W		GRZZZZUSA
BERNH.	3	M	CHILD		GRZZZZUSA
SCHUESSLER, GERTRUD	18	F	UNKNOWN		GRZZZZUSA
KIEFER, EMMA	22	F	UNKNOWN		GRZZZZUSA
SAUNER, DORA	28	F	UNKNOWN		GRZZZZUSA
CARL	6	M	CHILD		GRZZZZUSA
MEYER, PETER	16	M	FARMER		GRZZZZUSA
GRIM, JOS.	21	M	FARMER		GRZZZZUSA
SCHMIDT, WILH.	22	F	UNKNOWN		GRZZZZUSA
FREYER, GUSTAV	36	M	CPTR		GRZZZZUSA
EMMA	32	F	W		GRZZZZUSA
IDA	9	F	CHILD		GRZZZZUSA
RUDOLPH	6	M	CHILD		GRZZZZUSA
KIRSCHNER, GOTTL.	27	M	TLR		GRZZZZUSA
ANNA	27	F	W		GRZZZZUSA
BAUER, MICHEL	19	M	SHMK		GRZZZZUSA
SCHMITALLA, ALB.	32	M	FARMER		GRZZZZUSA
KRASSMANN, ELFRIEDE	11	F	UNKNOWN		GRZZZZUSA
SCHMIDT, GEORG	28	M	FARMER		GRZZZZUSA
SPILGER, CATH.	22	F	UNKNOWN		GRZZZZUSA
WEDER, MARIA	19	F	UNKNOWN		GRZZZZUSA
BANZERT, CARL	16	M	FARMER		GRZZZZUSA
KNITTEL, ALBERTINE	21	F	UNKNOWN		GRZZZZUSA
BARON, ED.	43	M	BRR		GRZZZZUSA
MUELLER, GERTRUD	11	M	UNKNOWN		GRZZZZUSA
SZCZICINSKA, MARTHA	21	F	UNKNOWN		GRZZZZUSA
KRAUSE, FRIEDR.	28	M	FARMER		GRZZZZUSA
ENGLISCH, JOSEPH	24	M	FARMER		GRZZZZUSA
PARTSCH, ALOIS	50	M	FARMER		GRZZZZUSA
AMALIE	44	F	W		GRZZZZUSA
RUD.	19	M	FARMER		GRZZZZUSA
RICH.	17	M	JNR		GRZZZZUSA
MARIE	11	F	CH		GRZZZZUSA
CARL	7	M	CHILD		GRZZZZUSA
ANNA	.10	F	INFANT		GRZZZZUSA
HERFERT, FRITZ	18	M	FARMER		GRZZZZUSA
WIEBMER, PAULINE	47	F	UNKNOWN		GRZZZZUSA
DITTMER, HEINR.	16	M	JNR		GRZZZZUSA
OBENAUF, BERNH.	24	M	JNR		GRZZZZUSA
MARIE	24	F	W		GRZZZZUSA
HAEGELE, MARIE	22	F	UNKNOWN		GRZZZZUSA
WOLLMANN, ADOLPH	23	M	FARMER		GRZZZZUSA
SCHEURER, JOSEPH	14	M	UNKNOWN		GRZZZZUSA
LOHMANN, ANNA	56	F	UNKNOWN		GRZZZZUSA
RAUSCH, PAUL	28	M	FARMER		GRZZZZUSA
JANOWSKA, CILA	28	F	UNKNOWN		GRZZZZUSA
FANNY	6	F	CHILD		GRZZZZUSA
IHLEFEHDT, PAUL	26	M	FARMER		GRZZZZUSA
MUEGGE, PETER	16	M	FARMER		GRZZZZUSA
OPPEL, CASPAR	27	M	FARMER		GRZZZZUSA
MEYER, HEINR.	31	M	FARMER		GRZZZZUSA
WILH.	26	M	SMH		GRZZZZUSA
MARIE	23	F	W		GRZZZZUSA
HEINZ, LEONH.	17	M	BKR		GRZZZZUSA
MUELLER, JOH.	17	M	TLR		GRZZZZUSA
MEYER, BARB.	24	F	UNKNOWN		GRZZZZUSA
WILH.	20	F	UNKNOWN		GRZZZZUSA
SCHLUIFER, LOUISE	23	F	UNKNOWN		GRZZZZUSA
KUHN, EVA	24	M	UNKNOWN		GRZZZZUSA
ANNA	4	F	CHILD		GRZZZZUSA
GREGOR	.11	M	INFANT		GRZZZZUSA

PASSENGER	AGE	SEX	OCCUPATION	PRVL	DES
KREBS, MICH.	68	M	BRR		GRZZZZUSA
SCHELLMANN, ANNA	15	F	UNKNOWN		GRZZZZUSA
WOLFMANN, ERNST	15	M	UNKNOWN		GRZZZZUSA
OSTMORS, CHR.	15	M	UNKNOWN		GRZZZZUSA
TEWES, JOH.	16	M	TLR		GRZZZZUSA
HERM.	24	M	TLR		GRZZZZUSA
LINDENFELDER, JOS.	24	M	BRR		GRZZZZUSA
EUBELL, DORA	33	F	UNKNOWN		GRZZZZUSA
ADOLPH	9	M	CHILD		GRZZZZUSA
ALTSCHULSHORST, JAC.	21	M	FARMER		GRZZZZUSA
MILLER, NIKOLAUS	24	M	FARMER		GRZZZZUSA
REISS, PAULINE	40	F	UNKNOWN		GRZZZZUSA
ANNA	9	F	CHILD		GRZZZZUSA
ANTON	6	M	CHILD		GRZZZZUSA
AUG.	3	M	CHILD		GRZZZZUSA
HANCK, MARIA	24	F	UNKNOWN		GRZZZZUSA
KRUSE, CHR.	30	M	SHMK		GRZZZZUSA
LEWIN, WILH.	25	M	FARMER		GRZZZZUSA
WILKENS, JOH.	17	F	UNKNOWN		GRZZZZUSA
HENRY, HEINR.	15	M	UNKNOWN		GRZZZZUSA

SHIP: ALASKA

FROM: LIVERPOOL AND QUEENSTOWN
TO: NEW YORK
ARRIVED: 12 NOVEMBER 1888

PASSENGER	AGE	SEX	OCCUPATION	PRVL	DES
NOLL, HEINRICH	22	M	LABR		GRZZZZUSA
STAIGER, MATILDA	55	F	MA		GRZZZZUSA
AUGUSTE	26	F	MA		GRZZZZUSA
EDWARD	4	M	CHILD		GRZZZZUSA
ANNA	3	F	CHILD		GRZZZZUSA
LOUISA	19	F	SP		GRZZZZUSA
MUNNER, HEINRICH	62	M	LABR		GRZZZZUSA
SEGALL, JOSSEL	24	M	BCHR		GRZZZZUSA
MUSFELD, LOUISA	48	F	MA		GRZZZZUSA
HOFFMANN, WILH.	21	M	LABR		GRZZZZUSA
LECOTNET, JULES	21	M	LABR		FRZZZZUSA
PINGE, LEIDEN	45	M	LABR		FRZZZZUSA
ALLAERT, EDWD.	32	M	LABR		FRZZZZUSA
DANGIGER, JACOB	50	M	JWLR		GRZZZZUSA

SHIP: BELGENLAND

FROM: ANTWERP
TO: NEW YORK
ARRIVED: 12 NOVEMBER 1888

PASSENGER	AGE	SEX	OCCUPATION	PRVL	DES
GREEF, CL.	43	F	UNKNOWN		GRAAECNY
SEUFBERT, GERT.	22	F	SVNT		GRAAECNY
VANALBERTIN, A.	22	F	DR		GRAAECNY
HUTH, ERNST	25	M	ENGR		GRZZZZNY
OSCHATZ, HEIN.	23	M	ENGR		GRZZZZNY
BENEDICT, NAIMA	22	F	UNKNOWN		GRZZZZNY
DESCAMPS, VICTOR	45	M	MNR		FRZZZZUNK
ASSUM, JOSEF	20	M	BKR		FRABOQNY
BURCK, MARIA	24	F	UNKNOWN		GRZZZZPHI
EISELEN, CAROL.	19	F	UNKNOWN		GRZZZZPHI
ELLWAUGER, CONRAD	18	M	BCHR		GRZZZZPHI
MAYER, PHIL.	35	M	CPTR		GRACUENY
DINA	33	F	UNKNOWN		GRACUENY
ALVINA	1	F	CHILD		GRACUENY
HAUSMANN, CARL	27	M	WTR		GRZZZZNY
ZINKE, GUSTAV	23	M	LABR		GRZZZZMIL
KOWALSKI, ANNA	17	F	SVNT		GRZZZZMIL

420

PASSENGER	AGE SEX	OCCUPATION	PV RIVL DES
HAIMERL, ALVIG	17 M	BCHR	GRZZZZPIT
SCHULZ, GUSTAV	25 M	LABR	GRZZZZUNK
LIGMANN, JOHANN	20 M	SHMK	GRZZZZCH
WEICHLEIN, REGINA	45 F	UNKNOWN	GRABRAUNK
MARIA	18 F	UNKNOWN	GRABRAUNK
EMIL	16 M	UNKNOWN	GRABRAUNK
JOSEFINE	14 F	UNKNOWN	GRABRAUNK
ELISAB.	10 F	CH	GRABRAUNK
AMBERG, HEINR.	18 M	FARMER	GRZZZZUNK
HARTMANN, OTTILIE	19 F	SVNT	GRZZZZNY
MARCUS, LOUIS	20 M	BCHR	GRAGQZNY
LINSNER, MARG.	27 F	CK	GRZZZZPHI
LIPERT, SUPPLIA	27 F	UNKNOWN	FRZZZZUNK
POLONIE	00 F	INF	FRZZZZUNK
RICHARD, FRANZ	48 M	MNR	FRZZZZUNK
HONORE	18 F	MNR	FRZZZZUNK
JVACHIN, ANNA	18 F	SVNT	GRZZZZCIN
BAUER, PHILIPINE	28 F	UNKNOWN	GRZZZZCIN
ANNA	5 F	CHILD	GRZZZZCIN
THEODORE	1 M	CHILD	GRZZZZCIN
THEISEN, ANNA	24 F	UNKNOWN	GRZZZZCH
SIEGEMUELLER, DANIEL	17 M	BRR	GRZZZZALT
LUTZ, THERESIA	16 F	SVNT	GRAFRGCH
STRECKER, MARTIN	26 M	LABR	GRZZZZNY
FRIEDR.	23 M	LABR	GRZZZZNY
PFANNER, BARB.	31 F	UNKNOWN	GRZZZZCH
ELISAB.	2 F	CHILD	GRZZZZCH
ROECKELEIN, PHIL.	16 M	BKR	GRZZZZNY
EHRENHUBER, HAVER	26 M	MLR	GRZZZZCH
WIDMANN, EMIL	20 M	LABR	GRZZZZNY
ROCKENBERGER, CHRIST	26 M	LABR	GRZZZZNY
TRAUTMANN, MINA	26 F	SVNT	GRZZZZNY
HESSINGER, MINA	18 F	SVNT	GRZZZZNY
BLUM, ELISAB.	35 F	UNKNOWN	GRZZZZNY
MEININGER, JOH.	27 M	BKR	GRZZZZNY
GABEL, HEIN.	65 M	ENGR	GRZZZZNY
BERG, RUD.	31 M	ENGR	GRZZZZNY
BORT, CHRIST	23 M	BKR	GRADHWNY
HECK, MICH.	25 M	LABR	GRAAICNY
MARIAN	36 F	UNKNOWN	GRAAICNY
PETER	38 M	UNKNOWN	GRAAICNY
MUELLER, CONR.	28 F	UNKNOWN	GRABHTNY
ELISAB.	3 F	CHILD	GRABHTNY
EMILIE	00 F	INF	GRABHTNY
HARTMANN, WILH.	22 M	SHMK	GRZZZZROC
LABRIC, MARG.	29 F	CK	GRAGTKNY
HAGERMEIER, HEIN.	45 M	SHMK	GRAAYAUNK
DEMMER, PETER	43 M	CPTR	GRZZZZUNK
ROBER, CHRIST	14 M	FARMER	GRAFOOUNK
SCHMIDT, ANNA	24 F	SVNT	GRALXQOH
MUELLER, JOH.VAL.	28 M	LABR	GRZZZZCIN
GRUBER, EMERAU	38 M	BCHR	GRZZZZNY
SCHWARZMANN, FRIEDR.	24 M	LABR	GRADNONY
MARY	28 F	UNKNOWN	GRADNONY
HEINR.	2 M	CHILD	GRADNONY
ZETTNER, GEO	16 M	LABR	GRADNONY
REH, MELCHIOR	30 M	CPTR	GRADNONY
HUMMER, JOSEPH	29 F	UNKNOWN	GRZZZZNY
REIDEMANN, K.	25 M	IMKR	GRAEXWNY
HELLMUTH, ANNA	35 F	UNKNOWN	GRZZZZNY
AUGUST	9 M	CHILD	GRZZZZNY
CARL	6 M	CHILD	GRZZZZNY
LOUISE	3 F	CHILD	GRZZZZNY
HUCKENBROICH, JEAN	38 M	ENGR	GRAHELNY
WEBER, JOSEF	28 M	LABR	GRZZZZCH
FUCHS, WOLF	18 M	BKR	GRZZZZNY
SCHIFFGENS, MATH.	27 M	LABR	GRAAABUNK
WICHMANN, EMIL	20 M	LABR	GRAAABNY
MEYER, BERH	21 M	CL	GRZZZZNY
JOCHIM, THERESE	27 F	UNKNOWN	GRZZZZNY
MILLER, JOHANN	00 M	INF	GR****NY
NEUPERT, CHRISTIAN	50 M	WVR	GRZZZZNY
CAROLINE	42 F	WVR	GRZZZZNY
MATHILDE	20 F	UNKNOWN	GRZZZZNY
MINA	18 F	UNKNOWN	GRZZZZNY
ALMA	16 F	UNKNOWN	GRZZZZNY
OTTO	9 M	CHILD	GRZZZZNY
WIESEMER, FRIEDR	38 M	BBR	GRAABXNY
KATH.	28 F	UNKNOWN	GRAABXNY
PREUSS, PHIL.	15 M	UNKNOWN	GRAABXNY
KEBBE, FRIED	31 M	MNR	GRAKQPJON
FRAN.	26 F	UNKNOWN	GRAKQPJON
BERTHA	21 F	UNKNOWN	GRAKQPJON
FRITZ	5 M	CHILD	GRAKQPJON
WILH.	3 M	CHILD	GRAKQPJON
SELMA	.07 F	INFANT	GRAKQPJON
DRUART, EMILE	29 M	MNR	FRZZZZJON
LOUIS	27 M	MNR	FRZZZZJON
GAERTNER, JOH.	57 F	UNKNOWN	FRADGTNY
LOUISE	23 F	UNKNOWN	FRADGTNY
JOH.	25 F	UNKNOWN	FRADGTNY
ELIS	11 F	UNKNOWN	FRADGTNY
HCH.	10 M	CH	FRADGTNY
FRIED	8 M	CHILD	FRADGTNY
KEBBE, FRIED	8 M	CHILD	FRAKQPJON
LAMOTTE, HELENE	00 F	SVNT	FRADBQNY
HEINRICH, HENRI	28 M	FARMER	FRADBQNY
PASQUELIN, LOUISE	26 F	HSKPR	LXZZZZNY
BACK, MONTEMACH	30 M	LABR	LXZZZZNY
JOHANN	10 M	CH	LXZZZZNY
HEINRICH	8 M	CHILD	LXZZZZNY
JAKOB	6 M	CHILD	LXZZZZNY
MICHEL	4 M	CHILD	LXZZZZNY
LOUIS	2 M	CHILD	LXZZZZNY
FISCH, MICH.	34 M	FARMER	LXZZZZNY
CATH.	28 F	UNKNOWN	LXZZZZNY
LEONHARD	.10 M	INFANT	LXZZZZNY
KALM, LEOPOLD	40 M	CL	LXACUXNY
STREIT, CATH.	24 F	SVNT	LXAHCHCH
WILTZ, JOH.	17 M	LABR	GRZZZZTRE
WEILER, NICOL	18 M	WCHMKR	LXZZZZUNK
COURTOIS, FRANCOIS	26 M	CL	FRZZZZNY
HAAGERE, JACOB	24 M	LABR	GRZZZZNY
THAN, FRANZ	17 M	CGRMKR	GRZZZZNY
GEIS, SOFIE	27 F	CK	GRZZZZNY
GRASS, MICHEL	18 M	LABR	GRZZZZSP
KATH.	9 F	CHILD	GRZZZZSP
THERESIA	9 F	CHILD	GRZZZZSP
HOLLOSCH, MICHEL	51 M	LABR	GRZZZZSP
JUL.	61 F	LABR	GRZZZZSP
THERESA	18 F	UNKNOWN	GRZZZZSP
SCHWEIGER, FRANZ	30 M	LABR	GRZZZZCH
KLETT, CAROL.	19 F	SVNT	GRAJYPCH
CHRIST.	16 M	ENGR	GRAJYPCH
MAIER, LOUISE	18 F	SVNT	GRZZZZPTL
RICHNER, PHIL.	38 M	LABR	GRAEUINY
SCHROEBEL, MAGD.	24 F	UNKNOWN	GRAEUINY
PFLUGER, ANNA	26 F	UNKNOWN	GRZZZZCH
SCHULE, BARB.LISETTE	17 F	UNKNOWN	GRZZZZCH
MEIER, ADOLF	16 M	BKR	GRAAWTCH
SCHMIDT, JOH.	26 M	SHMK	GRAIUNCH
WELLER, ERNST	15 M	ENGR	GRAAWTCH
HABERLE, BERTHA	23 F	UNKNOWN	GRABVDCH
BERTHA	00 F	INF	GRABVDCH
WEWZ, EUGEN	23 M	CON	GRAESMCH
PRIEGER, JOHANN	32 M	BKR	GRABHTNY
WILH.	32 F	UNKNOWN	GRABHTNY
STEUDLE, LOUISE	18 F	UNKNOWN	GRZZZZBUF
HASSMANN, HEODOR	38 M	BKR	GRZZZZNY
ROSA	28 F	UNKNOWN	GRZZZZNY
THEODOR	9 M	CHILD	GRZZZZNY
EUGEN	6 M	CHILD	GRZZZZNY
FRIEDR.	5 M	CHILD	GRZZZZNY
KLUMP, GENOFEVA	29 F	CK	GRZZZZNY
THROM, CARL	27 M	LABR	GRZZZZNY
BAUMANN, CAROLINE	24 F	SVNT	GRZZZZNY
AMALIA	23 F	SVNT	GRZZZZNY
BEAUX, MARIE	23 F	HSKPR	GRAGKHNY
WINKEL, AMALIE	27 F	UNKNOWN	GRAGKHNY
EDM.	7 M	CHILD	GRAGKHNY

PASSENGER	AGE	SEX	OCCUPATION	PRVL	DES
LUCIE	2	F	CHILD	GRAGKHNY	
LEONIE	00	F	INF	GRAGKHNY	
ZEIDLER, GEO	18	M	SHMK	FRZZZZNY	
HILDENBREMD, MARIE	21	F	SVNT	FRAGVZNY	
RUEB, SEBAST	19	M	LABR	FRAFNPSTL	
SCHENK, MINA	22	F	SVNT	FRZZZZCIN	
EBERHARD, JACOB	25	M	BCHR	FRAEOINY	
JEROME, U	43	F	UNKNOWN	FRAGKHPHI	
EMILIE	1	M	CHILD	FRAGKHPHI	
EMILIE	13	M	CH	FRAGKHPHI	
JOSEPHINE	11	F	UNKNOWN	FRAGKHPHI	
DELVALEE, VICTOR	27	M	MNR	FRZZZZPHI	
GESCHITZKI, JOSEF	26	M	LABR	GRZZZZNY	
KOWALEWSKA, MARIANNA	24	F	SVNT	GRZZZZRDG	
SOOBODA, JOHN	54	M	MLR	GRADZCRDG	
JOSEFA	43	F	UNKNOWN	GRADZCRDG	
CARPENTIER, CECILE	00	F	UNKNOWN	FRZZZZPIT	
CECILE	4	F	CHILD	FRZZZZPIT	
AEPPEL, AUG.	24	M	BCHR	FRABHTNY	
HOHNWALD, BTE.	39	M	LABR	GRZZZZNY	
MORGAITHALER, ANTON	23	M	BKR	GRAEDQNY	
EIBS, JOSEPHINE	21	F	SVNT	GRZZZZNY	
BRENNER, JOHANN	14	M	CPTR	GRAGTKNY	
GARTNER, CAROL	27	F	CK	GRADGTNY	
BRUGBACHER, MARIA	00	F	SVNT	GRADGTNY	
FREERMANN, AUG.	22	M	LABR	GRAFHPDYE	
WEBER, ELIS.	22	F	UNKNOWN	GRAFHPDYE	
SCHMIDT, JOS.	19	M	PPMKR	GRAAFXNY	
KRIEG, GOTTL.	17	M	FARMER	SRZZZZNY	
GOTTL.	21	M	FARMER	SRZZZZNY	
WEBER, ROSALIE	20	F	UNKNOWN	SRZZZZCIN	
FLUCKEGER, CATH.	00	F	SVNT	SRZZZZCH	
BAER, CARL	21	M	CL	SRAAHUNY	
BARTOLOME, ARNOLD	23	M	LABR	SRZZZZNY	
TOBLER, JOH.	31	M	LABR	SRZZZZNY	
EGGENBERGER, JOH.	21	M	UNKNOWN	SRAHMHNY	
KOLLER, HULDREICH	21	M	UNKNOWN	SRAHMHNY	
SOLA, UBALDO	24	M	LABR	SRZZZZCO	
SALLER, JOH.	24	M	BKR	SRADLDBUF	
ABELE, MARIE	26	F	UNKNOWN	SRADLDBUF	
WEHNER, VAL.	23	M	FARMER	GRZZZZBUF	
ZFELLER, DAVID	26	M	FARMER	GRAAHUBUF	

SHIP: CITY OF CHICAGO

FROM: LIVERPOOL AND QUEENSTOWN
TO: NEW YORK
ARRIVED: 12 NOVEMBER 1888

PASSENGER	AGE	SEX	OCCUPATION	PRVL	DES
HOLLAENRER, MALKE	18	F	TCHR	GRACBFNY	
BRAND, ABRAM	19	M	LABR	GRACBFNY	
SIHER, ROCHEL	20	F	SVNT	GRACBFNY	
SRINE, SCHAGE	22	M	LABR	GRACBFNY	
WELRY, MARIA	21	F	SP	GRAAECNY	
BUSCH, JOHN	29	M	CPTR	GRAAECCH	

SHIP: GELLERT

FROM: HAMBURG
TO: NEW YORK
ARRIVED: 12 NOVEMBER 1888

PASSENGER	AGE	SEX	OCCUPATION	PRVL	DES
SANDLER, JAN	66	M	LABR	GRACBFUSA	
PETERSEN, CHRISTE	23	F	WO	PRZZZZUSA	
HEINR.	.11	M	INFANT	PRZZZZUSA	

PASSENGER	AGE	SEX	OCCUPATION	PRVL	DES
SOPHIE	22	F	SGL	PRZZZZUSA	
STREHLKE, AUGUSTE	18	F	SGL	PRZZZZUSA	
KRUMBEIN, FRIEDR.	22	M	LABR	PRZZZZUSA	
SONTOWSKI, ALBRECHT	34	M	LABR	PRZZZZUSA	
FRANZISKA	22	F	W	PRZZZZUSA	
JOHANN	5	M	CHILD	PRZZZZUSA	
ALALBERT	.09	E	INFANT	PRZZZZ***	
USZAKOWSKY, MICHAEL	60	M	LABR	PRZZZZUSA	
CONRAD, FRIDRICKE	23	F	SGL	PRACQAUSA	
HANSEN, INGEBORG	45	F	WO	PRZZZZUSA	
LENE	7	F	CHILD	PRZZZZUSA	
KOTSCH, PAUL	16	M	LABR	SYZZZZUSA	
BARTEL, ADOLF	17	M	LKSH	SYAFPTUSA	
WARSCHAUER, HANNCHEN	21	F	SGL	SYAHWSUSA	
HA--IUS, ERNST	25	M	MCHT	SYABOQUSA	
GOPPERT, JOHN	24	M	BCHR	SYAAEBUSA	
SCHIRMER, EMIL	22	M	FARMER	SYZZZZUSA	
ANTON, EMIL	26	M	BCHR	SYAAKHUSA	
ALBERT, CATHA.	30	F	WO	SYAAKHUNK	
ALFRED	5	M	CHILD	SYAAKHUNK	
ERNA	4	F	CHILD	SYAAKHUNK	
MOHR, MINNA	25	F	WO	SYAAKHUNK	
BEITZEL, RUDOLF	44	M	FARMER	MKZZZZUNK	
CHRISTINE	38	F	W	MKZZZZUNK	
RUDOLPH	16	M	CH	MKZZZZUNK	
HEINR.	14	M	CH	MKZZZZUNK	
FRIEDA	7	F	CHILD	MKZZZZUNK	
ERNA	6	F	CHILD	MKZZZZUNK	
MARTHA	5	F	CHILD	MKZZZZUNK	
ALBERT	4	M	CHILD	MKZZZZUNK	
ANA	.09	F	INFANT	MKZZZZUNK	
EVERT, HEINR.	29	M	LABR	MKZZZZUNK	
DOROTHEA	31	F	W	MKZZZZUNK	
DORA	4	F	CHILD	MKZZZZUNK	
HANS	2	M	CHILD	MKZZZZUNK	
ROGGENBAUM, FRITZ	16	M	FARMER	MKZZZZUNK	
CATHA.	21	F	SGL	MKZZZZUNK	
HEINR.	23	M	LABR	MKZZZZUNK	
CAROLE.	23	F	W	MKZZZZUNK	
ANNA	2	F	CHILD	MKZZZZUNK	
SUDROW, FRIEDRICH	31	M	FARMER	MKZZZZUNK	
WILHE.	28	F	W	MKZZZZUNK	
ANNA	5	F	CHILD	MKZZZZUNK	
ALBERT	3	M	CHILD	MKZZZZUNK	
WILH.	27	M	FARMER	MKZZZZUNK	
SCHURSTEIN, HANNA	60	F	WO	MKZZZZUNK	
RADLOFF, FRIEDRICH	49	M	LABR	MKZZZZUNK	
WILHE.	49	F	W	MKZZZZUNK	
KARL	17	M	CH	MKZZZZUNK	
WILHE.	15	F	CH	MKZZZZUNK	
AUGUST	7	M	CHILD	MKZZZZUNK	
WM.	14	M	CH	MKZZZZUNK	
BERNDT, JOHANN	44	M	LABR	MKABXBUNK	
CHRISTINE	42	F	W	MKABXBUNK	
LOUISE	22	F	CH	MKABXBUNK	
FRANZ	18	M	CH	MKABXBUNK	
EMIL	17	M	CH	MKABXBUNK	
ANNA	7	F	CHILD	MKABXBUNK	
BERTHA	.11	F	INFANT	MKABXBUNK	
LANTZE, KARL	17	M	LKSH	MKAAXFUNK	
KRAFT, MARIE	20	F	SGL	MKAIAIUNK	
ZWICK, KATHA	16	F	SGL	BVZZZZUNK	
CONRAD, ANNA	19	F	SGL	BVAEYJUNK	
HAHN, BRUNO	25	M	SHMK	BVADQZUNK	
OST, SOPHIE	33	F	WO	BVAINKUNK	
TIMMERMANN, JOH.	47	M	FARMER	PRZZZZUNK	
DOROTHEA	40	F	W	PRZZZZUNK	
OTTO	9	M	CHILD	PRZZZZUNK	
FERNANDO	8	M	CHILD	PRZZZZUNK	
OLGA	7	F	CHILD	PRZZZZUNK	
HUGO	6	M	CHILD	PRZZZZUNK	
CONRAD	5	M	CHILD	PRZZZZUNK	
BERNHARDT	3	M	CHILD	PRZZZZUNK	
WILLY	2	M	CHILD	PRZZZZUNK	
META	1	F	CHILD	PRZZZZUNK	

PASSENGER	AGE	SEX	OCCUPATION	PRVL DIES
JOHES.	.11	M	INFANT	PRZZZZUNK
HOLM, JEPPE	52	M	LABR	PRZZZZUNK
KRUGER, CARL	32	M	LABR	PRAAUEUNK
JOHA.	30	F	W	PRAAUEUNK
WILH.	6	M	CHILD	PRAAUEUNK
ANNA	4	F	CHILD	PRAAUEUNK
HAHN, FRIEDA	7	F	CHILD	PRAAUEUNK
ASMUSSEN, HANS	59	M	LABR	PRZZZZUNK
PHILIPP, WILH.	26	M	LABR	MKZZZZUNK
RADLOFF, FERD.	22	M	LABR	MKAFWAUNK
STUDIER, JOH.	52	M	LABR	MKZZZZUNK
FRIEDR.	23	M	LABR	MKZZZZUNK
HEKEL, ROSINE	18	F	SGL	WMZZZZUNK
SCHMALENBERGER, MAGDALE	21	F	SGL	BVZZZZUNK
BOTH, PETER	45	M	BCHR	BVAHILUNK
HERZAN, CARL	42	M	SHMK	BVACAWUNK
JANICKI, EMILIE	53	F	WO	PRZZZZUNK
JANICKE, WLEDISLAUS	24	M	SHMK	PRZZZZUNK
KRETSCHMER, BARBA.	21	F	WO	PRZZZZUNK
WLADISLAUS	.01	M	INFANT	PRZZZZUNK
MOELLER, CHRISTOPH	25	M	LABR	PRZZZZUNK
KUEHLING, JOHANN	40	M	LABR	PRZZZZUNK
MARIE	35	F	W	PRZZZZUNK
RICHARD	7	M	CHILD	PRZZZZUNK
ERNST	6	M	CHILD	PRZZZZUNK
ANNA	5	F	CHILD	PRZZZZUNK
WITT, JOHANN	22	M	LABR	MKZZZZUNK
FRIDRICKE	25	F	W	MKZZZZUNK
WM.	4	M	CHILD	MKZZZZUNK
OTTO	.03	M	INFANT	MKZZZZUNK
MAHN, MARIE	18	F	SGL	MKZZZZUNK
KRENZ, EMMA	18	F	SGL	PRZZZZUNK
JACOBSEN, HEINR.	20	M	LABR	PRAESDUNK
BOLZ, FRIEDR.	32	M	LABR	PRZZZZUNK
WILHE.	28	F	W	PRZZZZUNK
MARIE	7	F	CHILD	PRZZZZUNK
AUGUSTE	4	F	CHILD	PRZZZZUNK
HERM.	.06	M	INFANT	PRZZZZUNK
BREDLAN, MARIE	17	F	SGL	PRZZZZUNK
FROST, HENRY	30	M	LABR	PRAGOEUNK
MARLOW, CARL	60	M	FARMER	MKZZZZUNK
FRIDRIKE	62	F	W	MKZZZZUNK
MEYER, WILL	53	M	TLR	PRZZZZUNK
DUTSCHEK, FRANCISCA	62	F	WO	SYZZZZUNK
ZWOMIRAK, DOROTHEA	25	F	WO	PRZZZZUNK
ROSALIE	.11	M	INFANT	PRZZZZUNK
PIETSCHKE, KARL	16	M	LABR	PRZZZZUNK
SCHULTZ, LUDWIG	48	M	LABR	PRZZZZUNK
MARIE	46	F	W	PRZZZZUNK
PAUL	7	M	CHILD	PRZZZZUNK
TAK, WILHE.	32	F	WO	MKZZZZUNK
EMMA	2	F	CHILD	MKZZZZUNK
MORDSFELD, MATHILDE	18	F	SGL	PRZZZZUNK
JOHANNSEN, PETER	64	M	LABR	PRABQBUNK
MARIE	61	F	W	PRABQBUNK
MATZ, BAJE	13	M	CH	PRABQBUNK
KARSTENS, MARIE	7	F	CHILD	PRABQBUNK
MUELLER, AMALIE	21	F	SGL	PRZZZZUNK
SADOFSKI, PAULE	28	F	SGL	PRAAZQUNK
SCHULTZ, AUGUST	26	M	LABR	PRZZZZUNK
OTTO	4	M	CHILD	PRZZZZUNK
WILH.	.09	M	INFANT	PRZZZZUNK
THIELKE, SOPHIE	24	F	SGL	MKZZZZUNK
JUERSS, JOHANN	39	M	FARMER	MKZZZZUNK
ELISE	37	F	W	MKZZZZUNK
WILH.	15	M	CH	MKZZZZUNK
MARTIN	7	M	CHILD	MKZZZZUNK
CAROLE.	6	F	CHILD	MKZZZZUNK
CHRISTE	5	F	CHILD	MKZZZZUNK
ADOLF	4	M	CHILD	MKZZZZUNK
JOH.	.11	M	INFANT	MKZZZZUNK
RISSE, MARIE	22	F	SGL	MKAAKHUNK
AUGUSTE	16	F	SGL	MKAAKHUNK
JACOBS, LOUIS	30	M	LABR	MKAFWIUNK
HENRIETTE	30	F	W	MKAFWIUNK

PASSENGER	AGE	SEX	OCCUPATION	PRVL DIES
BRUNO	6	M	CHILD	MKAFWIUNK
ALBERT	4	M	CHILD	MKAFWIUNK
HUGO	2	M	CHILD	MKAFWIUNK
GERHARDT	.08	M	INFANT	MKAFWIUNK
OCHS, ANTON	22	M	LABR	BDZZZZUNK
PETER	22	M	LABR	BDZZZZUNK
PETER	20	M	LABR	BDZZZZUNK
PUKALLUS, GOTTFRIED	31	M	LABR	PRZZZZUNK
EMIL	3	M	CHILD	PRZZZZUNK
MARIE	.08	F	INFANT	PRZZZZUNK
SELK, JOHE.	66	F	WO	MKZZZZUNK
KRUTZFELDT, DORA	24	F	SGL	PRZZZZUNK
PENTZIN, SOPHIE	24	F	SGL	MKZZZZUNK
DIETRICH, ALB.	25	M	LABR	MKAAKHUNK
DLUZEWSKY, MICHAEL	22	M	LABR	PRZZZZUNK
KREUZ, OTTO	16	M	LABR	PRZZZZUNK
MARLOW, LINA	18	F	SGL	PRZZZZUNK
HERM.	15	M	LABR	PRZZZZUNK
EWERT, WILH.	28	M	LABR	PRZZZZUNK
CHRISTINE	22	F	W	PRZZZZUNK
KOCH, FRITZ	25	M	FARMER	PRZZZZUNK
FRDRIKE.	29	F	W	PRZZZZUNK
LOUISE	2	F	CHILD	PRZZZZUNK
PAUL	.11	M	INFANT	PRZZZZUNK
EPPINGER, CLARA	22	F	SGL	PRAAKHUNK
FISCHER, BERTHA	22	F	SGL	PRACPSUNK
LINK, MARG.	35	F	SGL	PRACTPUNK
WILZ, PHILIPP	25	M	LABR	BVZZZZUNK
LIPPERT, EVA	60	F	W	BVZZZZUNK
ELISABETH	24	F	CH	BVZZZZUNK
LANG, FRITZ	24	M	LABR	BVADYYUNK
MUELLER, ADOLF	17	M	LABR	BVADYYUNK
JENSEN, BOTHILDE	48	F	WO	BVADYYUNK
JOST, PETER	7	M	CHILD	BVADYYUNK
HEINTZE, HEINR.	29	M	SHMK	BVABXBUNK
FRANCIK, JOH.	26	M	TLR	PRZZZZUNK
PRENTZLIN, CARL	37	M	LABR	PRACBFUNK
JOHS.	7	M	CHILD	PRACBFUNK
KUEHNE, EMILIE	29	F	SGL	PRACBFUNK
WOLF, JOSEF	28	M	SDLR	BDZZZZUNK
TAAP, ALBERT	24	M	LABR	PRZZZZUNK
NEUMANN, EDUARD	26	M	LABR	PRZZZZUNK
MARCINIAK, LORENZ	28	M	SMH	PRAETNUNK
VEHRS, DETLEV	49	M	FARMER	PRAHIOUNK
FRAENKEL, FRANZISKA	16	F	SGL	PRACXVUNK
GRUNDT, KARL	21	M	MCHT	PRAFWZUNK
BOCK, HERM.	25	M	MCHT	PRAFWZUNK
PASTOR, JOSEF	47	M	MCHT	PRACBFUNK
GRAVENHORST, FRIEDRICH	19	M	STDNT	PRAEUXUNK
LEHMANN, DORIS	22	F	SGL	PRAAKHUNK

SHIP: SAALE

FROM: BREMEN AND SOUTHAMPTON
TO: NEW YORK
ARRIVED: 13 OCTOBER 1888 *

BLUMBERGER, JOH.	33	M	MCHT	GRZZZZGR
SCHNEIDER, EMIL	43	M	MCHT	GRZZZZGR
BJOERNSEN, EMMA	19	F	NN	GRZZZZGR
KNICKE, ELLA	23	F	NN	GRZZZZGR
HAAS, CATH.	52	F	W	GRZZZZGR
FUESSLER, CAROL.	21	F	NN	GRZZZZGR
MUELLER, ELISE	23	F	NN	GRZZZZUSA
WUNNER, PAULINE	29	F	NN	GRZZZZUSA
ZEPF, MAX	14	M	NN	GRZZZZUSA
VOLTMANN, BERTHA	23	F	NN	GRZZZZUSA
SCHEURENBRAND, ANDR.	34	M	BRR	GRZZZZUSA
TOMBOEDDE, ENGELB.	50	M	FARMER	GRZZZZUSA
ANNA	46	F	W	GRZZZZUSA

*Arrival date out of chronological order.

423

PASSENGER	AGE	SEX	OCCUPATION	PRVL	DES
FRANZ	4	M	CHILD		GRZZZZUSA
HEINROCK, AUG.	34	M	SMH		GRZZZZUSA
SCHUSTER, KAETCHEN	24	F	NN		GRZZZZUSA
STRUTH, FRIEDR.	22	M	PNTR		GRZZZZUSA
LAMPERT, MARG.	21	F	NN		GRZZZZUSA
MEINANN, MINNA	17	F	NN		GRZZZZUSA
STARKE, SOPHIA	16	F	NN		GRZZZZUSA
MUELLER, ELISE	22	F	NN		GRZZZZUSA
WUNNER, PAULINE	29	F	NN		GRZZZZUSA
ZEPF, MAX	14	M	NN		GRZZZZUSA
VOLTMANN, BERTHA	23	F	NN		GRZZZZUSA
SCHEURENBRAND, ANDR.	34	M	BRR		GRZZZZUSA
TOMBOEDDE, ENGELB.	50	M	FARMER		GRZZZZUSA
ANNA	46	F	W		GRZZZZUSA
FRANZ	4	M	CHILD		GRZZZZUSA
HEIROCK, AUG.	34	M	SMH		GRZZZZUSA
SCHUSTER, KAETCHEN	24	F	NN		GRZZZZUSA
STRUTH, FRIEDR.	22	M	PNTR		GRZZZZUSA
LAMPERT, MARG.	21	F	NN		GRZZZZUSA
NIEMANN, MINNA	17	F	NN		GRZZZZUSA
STARKE, SOPHIA	16	F	NN		GRZZZZUSA
ULLRICH, ADAM	17	M	LABR		GRZZZZUSA
CAHN, CARL	21	M	CL		GRZZZZUSA
ANDERSEN, HANS	34	M	MLR		GRZZZZUSA
SUSANNE	33	F	W		GRZZZZUSA
MATHIESEN, HANS	16	M	FARMER		GRZZZZUSA
MARTENSEN, INGEBORG	25	F	NN		GRZZZZUSA
SINE	6	F	CHILD		GRZZZZUSA
JOHNSEN, HENRY	29	M	FARMER		GRZZZZUSA
JENSEN, MARIE	28	F	NN		GRZZZZUSA
JESSEN, CAECILIE	24	F	NN		GRZZZZUSA
SCHAEFER, HEINR.	26	M	BKLYR		GRZZZZUSA
JUERGENSEN, WILH.	25	M	BKLYR		GRZZZZUSA
REHBEIN, WILH.	32	M	GDNR		GRZZZZUSA
HARTMANN, HEINR.	48	M	GDNR		GRZZZZUSA
DICKMANN, MINNA	21	F	NN		GRZZZZUSA
TUERK, PETER	19	M	SHMK		GRZZZZUSA
EISENBRAND, FRANZ	24	M	SHMK		GRZZZZUSA
BALD, JOSEPH	23	M	FARMER		GRZZZZUSA
WILL, KILIAN	31	M	JNR		GRZZZZUSA
OHN, DOROTHEA	23	F	NN		GRZZZZUSA
SCHERER, DANIEL	24	M	BRR		GRZZZZUSA
TODT, BABETTE	28	F	NN		GRZZZZUSA
GEORG	3	M	CHILD		GRZZZZUSA
KAHN, JOHNE.	17	F	CH		GRZZZZUSA
MINDERMANN, HENNY	19	F	CH		GRZZZZUSA
FRINKWALTER, EVA	29	F	CH		GRZZZZUSA
STAUBER, MICH.	15	M	CH		GRZZZZUSA
WENK, FRIEDA	18	F	CH		GRZZZZUSA
LIPPMANN, BERTHA	20	F	CH		GRZZZZUSA
MOZZEBACH, MARIE	18	F	NN		GRZZZZUSA
KNUTZ, MART.	17	M	FARMER		GRZZZZUSA
FRANZ, CASPAR	26	M	FARMER		GRZZZZUSA
ROTTINGER, GEORG	26	M	FARMER		GRZZZZUSA
STEINMETZ, ANNA	19	F	NN		GRZZZZUSA
HUTH, MARIE	20	F	NN		GRZZZZUSA
PUEHLER, ANNA	20	F	NN		GRZZZZUSA
GRUNAUER, ROSA	22	F	NN		GRZZZZUSA
PUEHLER, BARB.	23	F	NN		GRZZZZUSA
FRANZ	2	M	CHILD		GRZZZZUSA
BODENSTEINER, JOSEPH	26	M	BRR		GRZZZZUSA
THIEROFF, HEINR.	34	M	BRR		GRZZZZUSA
JOHNE.	34	F	W		GRZZZZUSA
ADOLPH	10	M	CH		GRZZZZUSA
HERMANN	.08	M	INFANT		GRZZZZUSA
DOERNHOFER, JOH.	40	M	CPTR		GRZZZZUSA
CATH.	36	F	W		GRZZZZUSA
HAEUSSLER, LUDW.	30	M	CPTR		GRZZZZUSA
MARIE	25	F	W		GRZZZZUSA
FRITZ, KAETCHEN	21	F	NN		GRZZZZUSA
JOHNE.	.11	F	INFANT		GRZZZZUSA
BAUER, CATH.	21	F	INF		GRZZZZUSA
TRUNK, SEBAST.	24	M	FARMER		GRZZZZUSA
MANN, ROSA	14	F	NN		GRZZZZUSA
SCHIMMEL, CATH.	15	F	NN		GRZZZZUSA
MAGNUS, ELINA	19	F	NN		GRZZZZUSA
STARK, BARB.	18	F	NN		GRZZZZUSA
KLUSSMEYER, DORA	22	F	NN		GRZZZZUSA
SOPHIE	20	F	NN		GRZZZZUSA
DAHL, LOUISE	22	F	NN		GRZZZZUSA
WEISS, CATH.	21	F	NN		GRZZZZUSA
HAGENBACHER, PAULINE	17	F	NN		GRZZZZUSA
SCHWAMM, WILH.	17	M	GDNR		GRZZZZUSA
SEEMANN, LAZARUS	33	M	MCHT		GRZZZZUSA
HENRIETTE	29	F	W		GRZZZZUSA
ROSA	7	F	CHILD		GRZZZZUSA
HANNCHEN	3	F	CHILD		GRZZZZUSA
BECKER, MARG.	20	F	NN		GRZZZZUSA
ZIEGLER, LUCIE	26	F	NN		GRZZZZUSA
JOH.	4	M	CHILD		GRZZZZUSA
THERESIA	1	F	CHILD		GRZZZZUSA
ROSINE	.06	F	INFANT		GRZZZZUSA
GRIEB, MINNA	18	F	NN		GRZZZZUSA
KOBELINSKA, STANISL.	21	M	SMH		GRZZZZUSA
SCHOEN, LUDW.	23	M	FARMER		GRZZZZUSA
SCHEN, OTTO	54	M	FARMER		GRZZZZUSA
OTTILIE	44	F	W		GRZZZZUSA
HEDWIG	15	F	CH		GRZZZZUSA
WILH.	11	M	CH		GRZZZZUSA
JULIUS	10	M	CH		GRZZZZUSA
MARG.	8	F	CHILD		GRZZZZUSA
ERNESTINE	3	F	CHILD		GRZZZZUSA
KALTE, MAGD.	31	F	NN		GRZZZZUSA
JOHNES.	.09	M	INFANT		GRZZZZUSA
ALBERT, WILHNE.	27	F	INF		GRZZZZUSA
CORDES, JOH.	15	M	INF		GRZZZZUSA
VONELM, MAGD.	31	F	INF		GRZZZZUSA
THEOD.	3	M	CHILD		GRZZZZUSA
MAGD.	1	F	CHILD		GRZZZZUSA
KUHLMANN, ALWIN	16	M	LKSH		GRZZZZUSA
LANAMERS, JOH.	23	M	LKSH		GRZZZZUSA
SCHICK, CLARA	18	F	NN		GRZZZZUSA
AMEND, GEORG	23	M	JNR		GRZZZZUSA
CHRISTINE	18	F	NN		GRZZZZUSA
DIONIADA	8	F	CHILD		GRZZZZUSA
NELSON, JOHNE.	39	F	NN		GRZZZZUSA
DREWES, FRIEDR.	30	M	BCHR		GRZZZZUSA
BOESCHEN, ANNA	22	F	NN		GRZZZZUSA
FRAENKEL, HANNCHEN	42	F	NN		GRZZZZUSA
ROSA	14	F	NN		GRZZZZUSA
JONAS	10	M	NN		GRZZZZUSA
PAULINE	8	F	CHILD		GRZZZZUSA
FERD.	5	M	CHILD		GRZZZZUSA
OBERLAENDER, GEORG	30	M	FARMER		GRZZZZUSA
PACZINSKI, JOS.	40	M	FARMER		GRZZZZUSA
CATH.	40	F	W		GRZZZZUSA
CASIMIR	15	M	CH		GRZZZZUSA
HEILER, MARIE	21	F	NN		GRZZZZUSA
DIEHM, FRIEDKE.	21	F	NN		GRZZZZUSA
WEISSENSEEL, CATH.	28	F	NN		GRZZZZUSA
AGATHE	5	F	CHILD		GRZZZZUSA
SOEDER, BARB.	8	F	CHILD		GRZZZZUSA
THOMAS, HEINR.	54	M	FARMER		GRZZZZUSA
CATH.	55	F	W		GRZZZZUSA
MARIA	14	F	CH		GRZZZZUSA
STEINMETZ, OTTO	17	M	MCHT		GRZZZZUSA
SCHLEYER, ANNA	18	F	NN		GRZZZZUSA
ROHDE, FRANZ	29	M	FARMER		GRZZZZUSA
BRAUN, HERM.	25	M	FARMER		GRZZZZUSA
ARNOLD, FRANZ	25	M	JNR		GRZZZZUSA
REINHARD, MICH.	18	M	JNR		GRZZZZUSA
HOFMANN, BARB.	23	F	NN		GRZZZZUSA
GORUFLO, ERNESTINE	21	F	NN		GRZZZZUSA
BARRIE, LINA	9	F	CHILD		GRZZZZUSA
WIECHMANN, BERTHA	19	F	NN		GRZZZZUSA
FROBOESE, MARIE	19	F	NN		GRZZZZUSA
GREWEN, HEINR.	23	M	PNTR		GRZZZZUSA
ELSE	23	F	W		GRZZZZUSA
KOEHLER, JOHNE.	16	F	W		GRZZZZUSA
WIEBOLD, MARG.	17	F	W		GRZZZZUSA

PASSENGER	AGE	SEX	OCCUPATION	PRIVL	DES
HAAS, HEINR.	16	M	BCHR		GRZZZZUSA
MUELLER, JOH.	27	M	BCHR		GRZZZZUSA
HEISSENBECK, WILHNE.	22	F	NN		GRZZZZUSA
LILIENTHAL, ALB.	19	M	JNR		GRZZZZUSA
FLEISCHBAUER, ROB.	16	M	JNR		GRZZZZUSA
NAU, ELISAB.	17	F	NN		GRZZZZUSA
GLASER, JACOB	65	M	FARMER		GRZZZZUSA
SCHMELZ, GOTTFR.	36	M	FARMER		GRZZZZUSA
PONSOLD, CAROL.	26	F	NN		GRZZZZUSA
MOELLER, HUGO	14	M	NN		GRZZZZUSA
STAENGLEN, HERM.	21	M	JNR		GRZZZZUSA
FUNK, ALB.	43	M	BKR		GRZZZZUSA
SOPHIE	36	F	W		GRZZZZUSA
ALB.	13	M	CH		GRZZZZUSA
CARL	11	M	CH		GRZZZZUSA
LOUISE	5	F	CHILD		GRZZZZUSA
BADEN, CHRISTOPH	20	M	TLR		GRZZZZUSA
JOCKENS, JAC.	23	M	TLR		GRZZZZUSA
ALP, GEORG	16	M	GZR		GRZZZZUSA
SCHUCKMANN, GEORG	36	M	FARMER		GRZZZZUSA
DUERER, HENRIETTE	19	F	NN		GRZZZZUSA
WOLSNOWSKA, ANASTASIE	26	F	NN		GRZZZZUSA
BORCHARD, MARTHA	18	F	NN		GRZZZZUSA
STANDT, SABINA	23	F	NN		GRZZZZUSA
KAST, ANTONIE	30	F	NN		GRZZZZUSA
TREBER, WILH.	24	M	FARMER		GRZZZZUSA
JONSSON, ANNA	27	F	FARMER		GRZZZZUSA
ERIKSON, MARIA	38	F	FARMER		GRZZZZUSA
OLSSON, JOHNE.	26	F	FARMER		GRZZZZUSA
OJAHALA, ERITZ	26	M	FARMER		GRZZZZUSA
PACHELANDEN, ESAIAS	22	M	FARMER		GRZZZZUSA
AROLA, SOPHIA	28	F	NN		GRZZZZUSA
JACOB	.02	M	INFANT		GRZZZZUSA
ALAPORET, MARIA	20	F	NN		GRZZZZUSA
PEKARI, CARL	30	M	CPTR		GRZZZZUSA
TUNNO, AUG.	18	M	CPTR		GRZZZZUSA
STENBERG, CARL	19	M	CPTR		GRZZZZUSA
SANDBERG, EMIL	25	M	CPTR		GRZZZZUSA
KIVIJARVI, ANDERS	35	M	CPTR		GRZZZZUSA
PFIRRMANN, LOUIS	41	M	BRR		GRZZZZUSA
MARTERN, CONRAD	27	M	TCHR		GRZZZZUSA
HILD, ANNA	32	F	NN		GRZZZZUSA
MARIA	29	F	NN		GRZZZZUSA
BREDCHORST, DIEDR.	28	M	FARMER		GRZZZZUSA
SEIFART, JOLA	22	F	NN		GRZZZZUSA
WELLBROCK, HEINR.	15	M	FARMER		GRZZZZUSA
GROTHER, JOH.	16	M	FARMER		GRZZZZUSA
KREUGEL, GESINE	20	F	NN		GRZZZZUSA
SCHLOETTELBURG, HEINR.	20	M	FARMER		GRZZZZUSA
GISCHEN, HEINR.	16	M	FARMER		GRZZZZUSA
FINCKEN, META	16	F	NN		GRZZZZUSA
WELFORT, JAC.	30	M	SMH		GRZZZZUSA
HORONCZYK, CHAIN	28	M	SMH		GRZZZZUSA
WAHL, EMILIE	18	F	NN		GRZZZZUSA
SOLTAN, JUL.	20	M	TLR		GRZZZZUSA
LODERHOSE, MARIA	19	F	NN		GRZZZZUSA
WAHL, ANNA	16	F	NN		GRZZZZUSA
HIMMELMANN, JOH.	18	M	SHMK		GRZZZZUSA
BEYER, JOHANNE	54	F	NN		GRZZZZUSA
FACKINER, JOH.	14	M	NN		GRZZZZUSA
FINGER, HEINR.	18	M	CL		GRZZZZUSA
HINZE, AUG.	38	M	JNR		GRZZZZUSA
STEIN, FRANZ	29	M	JNR		GRZZZZUSA
WEISENSSEL, CRYSOST.	35	M	FARMER		GRZZZZUSA
NIEMANN, FERD.	17	M	JNR		GRZZZZUSA
GILDNER, MARIE	54	F	NN		GRZZZZUSA
ADAM	68	M	FARMER		GRZZZZUSA
RUDNER, HANNE	36	F	NN		GRZZZZUSA
FANNY	16	F	NN		GRZZZZUSA
BERTHA	14	F	NN		GRZZZZUSA
ANNA	.11	F	INFANT		GRZZZZUSA
WAHLBERG, MINNA	26	F	NN		GRZZZZUSA
WOBBE, ANTONIE	24	F	NN		GRZZZZUSA
BECKER, AMALIE	33	F	NN		GRZZZZUSA
NAGEL, META	23	F	NN		GRZZZZUSA
AHRENS, CATH.	30	F	NN		GRZZZZUSA
ENGELBERT, JOHN	8	M	CHILD		GRZZZZUSA
GUNDMANN, FRANZ	50	M	MCHT		GRZZZZUSA
SANDERS, HEINR.	30	M	MCHT		GRZZZZGR

SHIP: FULDA

FROM: BREMEN AND SOUTHAMPTON
TO: NEW YORK
ARRIVED: 14 NOVEMBER 1888

PASSENGER	AGE	SEX	OCCUPATION	PRIVL	DES
RAGENCOWICH, PETER	24	M	MCHT		GRAARRNY
BETHMANN, HOLLWEG	34	M	TT		GRAARRUNK
SANDMANN, MARGARETHA	23	F	UNKNOWN		GRAARRUNK
KESSLER, HUGO	32	M	MCHT		GRAARRUNK
HESTHAL, FR.E.	26	M	DR		GRAARRUNK
HACKEL, MANON	18	F	UNKNOWN		GRAEABUNK
GESELSCHAP, MARIE	17	F	UNKNOWN		GRAFNKUNK
KOHLMANN, ERNST	40	M	AGNT		GRACXVUNK
MARSCHALL, E.L.	50	M	TT		GRADBQUNK
SAUTTER, FRIDR.	20	M	FARMER		GRZZZZNY
KRAUL, CARL	34	M	MCHT		GRAEJCNY
DOERKEN, JOHANN	28	M	MCHT		GRZZZZNY
DOERNHOEFER, ALBERT	35	M	MCHT		GRAAYANY
ANNA	28	F	W		GRAAYANY
GEORG	5	M	CHILD		GRAAYANY
EMMA	2	F	CHILD		GRAAYANY
ALBERT	.06	M	INFANT		GRAAYANY
STEGE, HEINRICH	41	M	GCR		GRAEFTNY
HOHENBROECKEN, ARTHUR	18	M	FARMER		GRZZZZNY
THOMSEN, CHRISTINE	20	F	UNKNOWN		GRAFDDNY
SUHREN, HELENE	37	F	UNKNOWN		GRACBRNY
SCHROEDER, LINA	36	F	UNKNOWN		GRZZZZNY
MEHRMANN, HEINR.	23	M	MCHT		GRACBGNY
KOEHNEMANN, WILHELM	30	M	MCHT		GRAAKHNY
VONRADZIBOR, U	23	F	W		GRAAKHNY
FEILCHENFELD, HEINR.	24	M	MCHT		GRAEPZNY
SEIBEL, HENRIETTE	30	F	W		GRAEABNY
SCHWABACHER, PAULINE	48	F	W		GRAEXWNY
SOPHIE	20	F	CH		GRAEXWNY
NATALIE	16	F	CH		GRAEXWNY
IDA	14	F	CH		GRAEXWNY
HELD, GEORG	30	M	MCHT		GRABFQNY
JOHANNE	26	F	W		GRABFQNY
KOCH, EDUARD	22	M	CL		GRAAKHNY
TSCHIPKE, ALBERT	24	M	FARMER		GRZZZZNY
RAKOWSKY, CARL	20	M	MCHT		GRAARRNY
ROSENSTERN, LOUIS	18	M	CL		GRAEQNNY
SCHUMAN, FRED.	33	M	MD		GRAEQNNY
GRUENWALD, ALFRED	26	M	MCHT		GRAAKHNY
JEPSEN, LOUIS	22	M	MCHT		GRAGFUNY
WINDECKER, JACOB	35	M	MCHT		GRAAOONY
SAALFELD, ELSA	18	F	UNKNOWN		GRABOQNY
SCHUMANN, GUSTAV	32	M	MCHT		GRAAHBNY
MEYER, MINNI	8	F	CHILD		GRAEFTNY
LOUIS	7	M	CHILD		GRAEFTNY
GRAF, LEOPOLD	24	M	MCHT		GRAARRNY
ARNDT, JOHANN	31	M	MCHT		GRADRONY
HASCHKE, ERNST	50	M	FARMER		GRZZZZNY
WUSZYERSKA, JULYANNA	25	F	W		GRAICJNY
BARBARA	6	F	CHILD		GRAICJNY
MAGDLA.	.03	F	INFANT		GRAICJNY
FABER, BETA	20	F	UNKNOWN		GRZZZZNY
BRUNS, HEINRICH	58	M	CGRMKR		GRZZZZNY
ERNSTINE	20	F	UNKNOWN		GRZZZZNY
MICHALIS, WILHELM	25	M	BKLYR		GRAFVPNY
MANN, FERDINAND	42	M	GYP		GRZZZZNY
AUGUSTE	48	F	W		GRZZZZNY
ALBERT	16	M	SLT		GRZZZZNY
BERTHA	16	F	CH		GRZZZZNY

PASSENGER	AGE	SEX	OCCUPATION	PRVL	DES
EMILIE	10	F	CH		GRZZZZNY
IDA	7	F	CHILD		GRZZZZNY
OTTO	4	M	CHILD		GRZZZZNY
WILHELMINE	4	F	CHILD		GRZZZZNY
GOETZKI, WILHELMINE	25	F	UNKNOWN		GRZZZZNY
BRUEHN, HENRIETTE	43	F	W		GRZZZZNY
FERDINAND	26	M	EGR		GRZZZZNY
JOHANN	16	M	EGR		GRZZZZNY
CARL	11	M	CH		GRZZZZNY
WILHELMINE	9	F	CHILD		GRZZZZNY
HENNANN	8	M	CHILD		GRZZZZNY
HENRIETTE	6	F	CHILD		GRZZZZNY
DOLMA, MAGDALENA	17	F	UNKNOWN		GRAEABNY
PENSKI, GUSTI	33	M	BKLYR		GRZZZZNY
ERBER, GUSTAV	21	M	CPTR		GRAEABNY
BACH, GOTTLIEB	58	M	FARMER		GRZZZZNY
CHRISTINE	58	F	W		GRZZZZNY
JOHANNE	24	F	CH		GRZZZZNY
ELISABETH	20	F	CH		GRZZZZNY
HEINRICH	17	M	FARMER		GRZZZZNY
AUGUST	15	M	FARMER		GRZZZZNY
ANNA	11	F	CH		GRZZZZNY
MUEHLMEISTER, FEIGE	36	F	UNKNOWN		GRZZZZNY
KLINGE, PAULINE	18	F	UNKNOWN		GRZZZZNY
BOERCHRDT, FRANZISKA	19	F	UNKNOWN		GRAAKHNY
BUELLECKE, AUGUSTE	19	F	UNKNOWN		GRZZZZNY
STREHL, SUDWIG	24	M	CL		GRZZZZNY
GRONAU, JOHANN	27	M	CNF		GRZZZZNY
JULIA	24	F	W		GRZZZZNY
GUSTAV	.06	M	INFANT		GRZZZZNY
VONELM, WILHELM	26	M	MCHT		GRZZZZNY
WILKENS, AUGUST	18	M	FARMER		GRZZZZNY
JOHANN	16	M	FARMER		GRZZZZNY
WOEHLKENS, GUSTAV	20	M	LABR		GRADNINY
WEISSGRAF, ANNA	28	F	UNKNOWN		GRAARRNY
FECKE, META	40	F	W		GRZZZZNY
HERMINE	10	F	CH		GRZZZZNY
DIETRICH	8	M	CHILD		GRZZZZNY
SCHWAB, LUDWIG	18	M	FARMER		GRZZZZNY
SERRAND, JACOB	24	M	FARMER		GRZZZZNY
ZEEB, PAULA	21	F	UNKNOWN		GRZZZZNY
SCHIRMER, BERTHA	28	F	W		GRZZZZMI
EMMA	.07	F	INFANT		GRZZZZMI
BORCHARDT, IDA	50	F	W		GRZZZZIL
BRAUN, FRIEDR.	23	M	JNR		GRZZZZOH
HEILMANN, CHR.	14	M	CL		GRACOJIN
DREHER, CATHARINA	26	F	UNKNOWN		GRAEEANY
HANEMANN, GOTTLIEB	26	M	JNR		GRZZZZNY
GEORG	24	M	FARMER		GRZZZZNY
STIESS, CARL	36	M	BKR		GRZZZZNY
CHRISTINE	29	F	W		GRZZZZNY
LINA	6	F	CHILD		GRZZZZNY
WILHELM	5	M	CHILD		GRZZZZNY
SOPHIE	3	F	CHILD		GRZZZZNY
V. CELESTINE	33	F	UNKNOWN		GRAEABMI
DEYHLE, WILHELM	22	M	BKR		GRAIWNNY
MUELLER, ELISABETH	45	F	W		GRAIWNNY
FUELLKRUG, AUGUSTE	15	F	UNKNOWN		GRZZZZNY
TOMASZEVSKI, CAESAR	19	M	FARMER		GRAMAZMI
SHIEBE, MARIA	29	F	UNKNOWN		GRZZZZIL
KIEHN, ROSINA	20	F	UNKNOWN		GRADHWNY
STOLL, MARGARETHA	61	F	W		GRAARRNY
GEISS, BARBARA	61	F	W		GRADOINY
ANTONIA	21	F	CH		GRADOINY
RIEDLING, MARIA	23	F	UNKNOWN		GRAFLZNY
KLUCZ, MARYANNA	18	F	UNKNOWN		GRZZZZNY
SCHELLER, ELISABETH	22	F	UNKNOWN		GRAFRGNY
JAHNKE, JACOB	28	M	LABR		GRZZZZNY
ALBERTINE	21	F	W		GRZZZZNY
IDA	.11	F	INFANT		GRZZZZNY
NUESSEN, AUGUSTE	21	F	UNKNOWN		GRZZZZNY
ZANG, ELISABETH	31	F	W		GRADXPNY
EMMA	6	F	CHILD		GRADXPNY
HELENA	4	F	CHILD		GRADXPNY
MEYER, CARL	19	M	CL		GRAFBVNY
SEYFRIED, EMILIE	18	F	UNKNOWN		GRADEUNY
OBERMEIER, NICOLAUS	22	M	LABR		GRZZZZNY
SCHROEDER, GEORG	32	M	LABR		GRZZZZNY
BAZMARYNOSKA, STANISL.	34	F	W		GRAGPJNY
MEYER, MARIE	22	F	UNKNOWN		GRZZZZNY
LUBASKI, JAN	44	M	LABR		GRAGMLNY
BARBARA	45	F	W		GRAGMLNY
ZELZ, JACOB	55	M	LABR		GRZZZZNY
WILHNE.	54	F	W		GRZZZZNY
ROSENBROCK, HENRICH	16	M	CL		GRZZZZNY
KAMMERER, ROSA	22	F	UNKNOWN		GRZZZZNY
BORNGESSER, BALTHASAR	16	M	WTR		GRZZZZNY
GRESER, ERNSTINE	38	F	W		GRZZZZNY
EMMA	10	F	CH		GRZZZZNY
OTTILIE	5	F	CHILD		GRZZZZNY
EBELING, PETER	24	M	CPR		GRZZZZNY
MINNA	20	F	W		GRZZZZNY
NUELLE, HEINRICH	10	M	CH		GRZZZZNY
FRITZ	8	M	CHILD		GRZZZZNY
ELISABETH	5	F	CHILD		GRZZZZNY
CHRISTIAN	4	M	CHILD		GRZZZZNY
DIETRICH	2	M	CHILD		GRZZZZNY
DETTLING, CONRAD	24	M	CPTR		GRAEXKOH
SCHETTEL, THEODOR	22	M	DYR		GRADXPNM
KOLASKA, STANISLAWA	21	F	UNKNOWN		GRAJFMIL
NEGRASZUS, FRITZ	30	M	BKR		GRAFABOH
KOENIG, CARL	33	M	BKLYR		GRAFABOH
SCHONHALS, HEINR.	43	M	FARMER		GRZZZZMI
GEORG	15	M	FARMER		GRZZZZMI
HEINRICH	11	M	CH		GRZZZZMI
KALBFLEISCH, KATHARINA	26	F	W		GRZZZZMI
MARIA	9	F	CHILD		GRZZZZMI
CHRISTIAN	2	M	CHILD		GRZZZZMI
CHRISTINE	20	F	UNKNOWN		GRZZZZMI
GEORG	10	M	CH		GRZZZZMI
ZELZ, BERTHA	23	F	UNKNOWN		GRZZZZNY
AUGUSTE	7	F	CHILD		GRZZZZNY
WEIDNER, CARL	21	M	FARMER		GRZZZZTX
HAFER, FRIEDR.	25	M	FARMER		GRZZZZNY
KRUDENER, HENR.	25	M	FARMER		GRADNONY
BEER, JOHANN	33	M	CPR		GRZZZZBUF
SCHUCK, ANTON	34	M	MLR		GRAAFCNY
KETTLER, LOUISE	55	F	W		GRACASNY
HOFFMANN, FRIEDR.	18	M	JNR		GRZZZZNY
SCHUBERTH, CHRISTINE	21	F	UNKNOWN		GRADLNNY
WAGENER, JEKA	24	F	UNKNOWN		GRAARRNY
KOS, JOSEF	63	M	LABR		GRAARRNY
MATHAES, EMIL	23	M	FARMER		GRAKUOIL
SCHUMACHER, WILHELM	18	M	FARMER		GRABAZOH
FRIEDRICHS, DOROTHEA	31	F	UNKNOWN		GRACBFMN
KUHN, ANNA	20	F	UNKNOWN		GRZZZZNY
PELLENS, WILHELM	46	M	SHMK		GRACBRNY
FRIEDRICHS, FERDINAND	18	M	BCHR		GRAGHPNY
JOHANN	22	M	BRR		GRAGHPNY
BRUENING, FRIEDRICH	16	M	FARMER		GRAAQINY
SCHEELE, HINRICH	14	M	CL		GRAAQINY
PRECHT, FRIEDRICH	16	M	PNTR		GRAAQINY
MEINEKE, JOHANN	46	M	LABR		GRZZZZNY
MEYER, MARIE	21	F	UNKNOWN		GRZZZZNY
JANSON, WILKE	41	F	W		GRZZZZNY
GELLERT, HELENE	24	F	UNKNOWN		GRABXFNY
RAUCH, AUGUST	33	M	LABR		GRZZZZNY
BENSER, KATHARINA	18	F	UNKNOWN		GRZZZZNY
STRAUSS, LEOPOLD	23	M	LABR		GRADKWOH
SCHMIEL, HERMANN	25	M	DLR		GRAAYAPA
JUSTE	64	F	W		GRAAYAPA
AUGUSTE	25	F	UNKNOWN		GRAAYAPA
ROSS, JOHANN	27	M	LABR		GRAEUXNY
MAASS, LOUISE	18	F	UNKNOWN		GRAFDDNY
KRIOGLSTEINER, MARIA	20	F	UNKNOWN		GRADDPNY
MUELLER, JULIUS	29	M	PNTR		GRABDMNY
DIETZMANN, CARL	26	M	LITGR		GRAFFNTX
NIESSEN, MARIE	32	F	W		GRAESDCH
SIEGFRIED	11	M	CH		GRAESDCH
LUDWIG	10	M	CH		GRAESDCH

PASSENGER	AGE	SEX	OCCUPATION	PRVL	DES
LUBOTZKI, AUGUST	24	M	LABR		GRABHTBUF
ROSALIE	19	F	W		GRABHTBUF
WENZEL, ERNSTINE	22	F	UNKNOWN		GRZZZZNLB
BECK, AUGUST	22	M	FARMER		GRAAKHSTL
WENZEL, AUGUST	34	M	CNF		GRZZZZNY
NIEDENNEYER, AMALIE	42	F	W		GRZZZZNY
SCHEELE, HEINR.	15	M	FARMER		GRAAQINY
PANEK, WOJCIECH	24	M	LABR		GRZZZZNY
MEYERDIRCKS, DANIEL	15	M	MCHT		GRZZZZNY
SAGEOWA, LUCIE	22	F	UNKNOWN		GRZZZZNY
RIEHM, ANNA	16	F	UNKNOWN		GRADOINY
MUELLER, HEINR.	16	M	JNR		GRZZZZNY
RIEHM, KATHARINA	38	F	W		GRADOINY
JOSEF	4	M	CHILD		GRADOINY
MAHLE, SOPHIE	23	F	UNKNOWN		GRABLVNY
HENVIG, REINHARD	24	M	FARMER		GRZZZZIL
KLOERS, JOHANNE	21	F	UNKNOWN		GRZZZZIL
GEBAUER, HOHN	36	M	CPR		GRZZZZNY
EMILIE	26	F	W		GRZZZZNY
BAIERLE, PETER	31	M	TLR		GRZZZZNY
AMALIE	24	F	W		GRZZZZNY
HUGO	.10	M	INFANT		GRZZZZNY
LETNER, RATZEL	35	F	W		GRAARRNY
JOHANN	2	M	CHILD		GRAARRNY
JORDEN, HERMANN	26	M	WTR		GRAARRNY
KOEHNKE, MARIA	20	F	UNKNOWN		GRACXHNY
SZTARINESAK, MARIA	21	F	UNKNOWN		GRACXHNY
RIES, GERHARD	51	M	CPTR		GRAARRNY
KOMMER, JOHANN	19	M	TLR		GRAARRNY

SHIP: FURNESSIA

FROM: GLASGOW AND MOVILLE
TO: NEW YORK
ARRIVED: 15 NOVEMBER 1888

PASSENGER	AGE	SEX	OCCUPATION	PRVL	DES
ABRAHAM, EMIL	21	M	CL		GRZZZZUSA
HOLZ, CARL	24	M	SLR		GRZZZZUSA
KLIER, FRANZ	28	M	CLR		GRZZZZUSA
MICHSELS, LUDWIG	33	M	LABR		GRZZZZUSA
SCHNEIDER, WECH.	43	M	JNR		GRZZZZUSA
JENSEN, MICHAEL-JESP.	21	M	FLABR		GRZZZZUSA
TRAPP, ANTON	20	M	CLR		GRZZZZUSA
HARTINGSEN, CAROLINE	28	F	NN		GRZZZZUSA
HARLWEGEN, PETER	32	M	NN		GRZZZZUSA
GEBAUER, T.	24	M	LABR		GRZZZZUSA
DRAUTMANN, M.	24	M	LABR		GRZZZZUSA

SHIP: MAIN

FROM: BREMEN
TO: BALTIMORE
ARRIVED: 15 NOVEMBER 1888

PASSENGER	AGE	SEX	OCCUPATION	PRVL	DES
PRETZFELDER, MICHAEL	15	M	TT		GRZZZZBAL
ROSCHEN, ANNA	28	F	TT		GRZZZZBAL
SIEGERT, CARL	32	M	TT		GRZZZZBAL
EMMA	28	M	TT		GRZZZZBAL
LANGE, FRIEDR.	23	M	FARMER		GRZZZZBAL
SCHIDZIK, ANDR.	23	M	BCHR		GRZZZZBAL
NAHA, MARCUS	25	M	CPTR		GRZZZZBAL
MOSCHCENSKI, CHRIST.	63	M	FARMER		GRZZZZBAL
DRECONICK, AUGUST	56	M	FARMER		GRZZZZBAL
BOLDT, WILH.	25	M	TLR		GRZZZZBAL
NOFFKE, WILH.	16	M	TLR		GRZZZZBAL

PASSENGER	AGE	SEX	OCCUPATION	PRVL	DES
UTECH, HEINR.	32	M	LKSH		GRZZZZBAL
GIESE, ALBERT	27	M	BKR		GRZZZZBAL
BEERMANN, CARL	25	M	BCHR		GRZZZZMI
SCHUMACHER, CARL	42	M	BKR		GRZZZZMI
ECKERT, LEONH.	25	M	BRR		GRZZZZPA
ROTHLINGSHOEFER, CHR.	18	M	BRR		GRZZZZIN
NOWAK, JOHANN	22	M	JNR		GRZZZZPA
NEUMANN, JOHANN	37	M	FARMER		GRZZZZBAL
MENNING, THEODOR	24	M	FARMER		GRZZZZBAL
BUSCH, CARL	55	M	FARMER		GRZZZZBAL
FRITZ	16	M	FARMER		GRZZZZBAL
GEINR.	13	M	FARMER		GRZZZZBAL
SMERZ, JOSEPH	28	M	FARMER		GRZZZZBAL
VOLLBRECHT, FRIEDR.	24	M	MUSN		GRZZZZBAL
SWIDERSKI, JAN	26	M	FARMER		GRZZZZBAL
FROEBA, THOMAS	24	M	FUR		GRZZZZWI
LOEFFLER, CHRISTOPHER	35	M	LABR		GRZZZZWI
IGLEWSKI, STANISL	24	M	LABR		GRZZZZWI
BAUM, DAVID	20	M	FARMER		GRZZZZBAL
SCHARONN, ANTON	24	M	PVTR		GRZZZZBAL
BREINER, MAURITIUS	23	M	FARMER		GRZZZZBAL
MORLOCK, OTTO	14	M	LABR		GRZZZZBAL
MAX	15	M	LABR		GRZZZZBAL
MENDELOWSKA, JOSEF	16	M	LABR		GRZZZZBAL
KRYGIER, JOSEF	17	M	JNR		GRZZZZBAL
KRAPFS, HEINR.	17	M	LABR		GRZZZZBAL
LASKOWSKI, JOH.	22	M	LABR		GRZZZZBAL
BAER, JOHANN	15	M	LABR		GRZZZZBAL
GRAMS, JOSEF	25	M	LABR		GRZZZZBAL
BRAUN, SAMUEL	23	M	MCHT		GRZZZZBAL
FREY, FRANZ	21	M	FARMER		GRZZZZBAL
JENDRASZEK, MELCHIOR	13	M	FARMER		GRZZZZBAL
HANEKAMP, HERM.	23	M	SMH		GRZZZZBAL
RADMINE, MAREL	29	M	LABR		GRZZZZBAL
JONAS, AUGUST	24	M	SDLR		GRZZZZBAL
WENDT, JOHN	24	M	SDLR		GRZZZZBAL
ERNST, FRIEDR.	25	M	LABR		GRZZZZBAL
BORNZKI, LORENZ	27	M	FARMER		GRZZZZBAL
MILLNER, JANKEL	18	M	LABR		GRZZZZBAL
SCHERMISKI, LEON	27	M	LABR		GRZZZZBAL
DISCHLER, JACOB	23	M	LABR		GRZZZZBAL
WOJTKOWSKI, VINCENT	27	M	LABR		GRZZZZBAL
GEROLD, ERNST	16	M	LABR		GRZZZZBAL
KINZLIN, GREGOR	24	M	LABR		GRZZZZBAL
SWIKOWSKI, HEINR.	24	M	LABR		GRZZZZBAL
KAHN, ARON	16	M	LABR		GRZZZZBAL
GRUBRECHTS, FRIEDR.	18	M	FARMER		GRZZZZDAK
HAUG, JOHANN	23	M	FARMER		GRZZZZDAK
SCHMERBECK, PAUL	30	M	FARMER		GRZZZZOH
SCHMERTSKE, AUG.	29	M	LABR		GRZZZZBAL
PROKOP, MATHIAS	28	M	LABR		GRZZZZBAL
ZANDLER, EMIL	18	M	FARMER		GRZZZZBAL
ALBRECHT, EMIL	19	M	LABR		GRZZZZBAL
ENGELHARDT, OTTO	37	M	TLR		GRZZZZBAL
ZULAWUSKI, JOH.	23	M	CPTR		GRZZZZBAL
SUHR, HERM.	29	M	SMH		GRZZZZBAL
REHMKE, BERNH.	17	M	FARMER		GRZZZZBAL
AMMANDSEN, FREDRIK	29	M	JNR		GRZZZZBAL
URBACH, GEORG	64	M	PVTR		GRZZZZBAL
PISTROWSKI, IGNATZ	23	M	FARMER		GRZZZZBAL
JANKOWSKY, JOHN	24	M	BKR		GRZZZZBAL
WESTPHAL, JOH.	4	M	CHILD		GRZZZZMI
KUESSNER, RUDOLF	40	M	LABR		GRZZZZMI
WINTER, GOTFRIED	24	M	LABR		GRZZZZMI
SCHAEFER, ADAM	39	M	LABR		GRZZZZOH
STUBENRAUCH, MARTIN	24	M	GZR		GRZZZZOH
FALK, JULIUS	24	M	SDLR		GRZZZZOH
BADE, CHRIST.	26	M	FARMER		GRZZZZBAL
KAUFMANN, EMIL	17	M	FARMER		GRZZZZBAL
BOLEN, JOCKE	45	M	FARMER		GRZZZZBAL
KOEHLER, WILH.	31	M	FARMER		GRZZZZBAL
GOLTNERMANN, JAN	44	M	FARMER		GRZZZZBAL
KAUFMANN, VICTOR	30	M	FARMER		GRZZZZBAL
GRAUZEN, BERNH.	24	M	FARMER		GRZZZZBAL
FISCHER, JOHANN	17	M	FARMER		GRZZZZBAL

PASSENGER	AGE	SEX	OCCUPATION	PRIVL	DES
WEIGLI, HENRIETTE	26	F	SVNT	GRZZZZBAL	
GUSS, PAULINE	36	F	W	GRZZZZBAL	
FRANZ	5	M	CHILD	GRZZZZBAL	
FRANZA	3	F	CHILD	GRZZZZBAL	
ANASTASIA	.07	F	INFANT	GRZZZZBAL	
LUECK, EMILIE	36	F	W	GRZZZZBAL	
MARIA	9	F	CHILD	GRZZZZBAL	
MATHILDE	8	F	CHILD	GRZZZZBAL	
BAAL, ELISE	59	F	W	GRZZZZBAL	
MOROCZKOWSKA, CHRISTINE	37	F	W	GRZZZZBAL	
OTTILIE	15	F	SVNT	GRZZZZBAL	
WILHELMINE	11	F	CH	GRZZZZBAL	
ALBERT	8	M	CHILD	GRZZZZBAL	
BECKMANN, HULDA	16	M	SVNT	GRZZZZBAL	
SIRUCEK, ANNA	23	F	SVNT	GRZZZZBAL	
WOHL, MARTHA	18	F	SVNT	GRZZZZBAL	
EMMA	16	F	SVNT	GRZZZZBAL	
FRIESEN, JUSTINE	39	F	W	GRZZZZBAL	
MARIA	2	F	CHILD	GRZZZZBAL	
NOWAK, MARIANNA	38	F	W	GRZZZZBAL	
JOSEPHA	12	F	CH	GRZZZZBAL	
ANASTASIA	4	F	CHILD	GRZZZZBAL	
CATH.	3	F	CHILD	GRZZZZBAL	
GROHOWSKA, JOSEPHA	29	F	W	GRZZZZBAL	
YANZ, WILH.	32	F	W	GRZZZZBAL	
RUDOLF	4	M	CHILD	GRZZZZBAL	
THERESE	.09	F	INFANT	GRZZZZBAL	
MAICHOZAK, HELENE	66	F	W	GRZZZZBAL	
UCRBANECK, MARIANNE	20	F	W	GRZZZZBAL	
FRANZISCA	.11	F	INFANT	GRZZZZBAL	
SCHIMANSKI, CAROLINE	20	F	SVNT	GRZZZZBAL	
BETIN, AUGUSTE	18	F	SVNT	GRZZZZBAL	
JULIUS	9	M	CHILD	GRZZZZBAL	
ROGASCHEFSKA, JULIANE	22	F	W	GRZZZZBAL	
JOSEPHINE	19	F	SVNT	GRZZZZBAL	
LESZEZYNSKA, MARYANNE	40	F	W	GRZZZZBAL	
FRANZISCA	16	F	SVNT	GRZZZZBAL	
MANSKE, BERTHA	29	F	W	GRZZZZBAL	
REINHOLD	9	M	CHILD	GRZZZZBAL	
CARL	.06	M	INFANT	GRZZZZBAL	
GIESE, WILHELM	49	F	W	GRZZZZBAL	
SCHWARZ, AUGUSTE	22	F	SVNT	GRZZZZBAL	
KILIAN, MARIA	26	F	SVNT	GRZZZZBAL	
LIPSKA, JULIANE	25	F	SVNT	GRZZZZBAL	
MARSCHALK, ROSALIE	48	F	W	GRZZZZMN	
CLARA	17	F	SVNT	GRZZZZMN	
HEDWIG	16	F	SVNT	GRZZZZMN	
PATZER, BERTHA	21	F	SVNT	GRZZZZMN	
RISTAER, EMILIE	23	F	SVNT	GRZZZZMN	
GROSSMANN, CATHA.	29	F	W	GRZZZZOH	
EVA	11	F	CH	GRZZZZOH	
SCHAEFF, KATH.	19	F	SVNT	GRZZZZOH	
JOHANNSON, HELENE	23	F	W	GRZZZZBAL	
CARL	.11	M	INFANT	GRZZZZBAL	
SCHOENBECK, WILH.	21	F	SVNT	GRZZZZBAL	
KORZUMBECK, JULIA	23	F	W	GRZZZZBAL	
MARIA	.11	F	INFANT	GRZZZZBAL	
GRZESCHITZ, JOSEPHA	26	F	W	GRZZZZBAL	
SIELEFSKI, FRANZISCA	25	F	W	GRZZZZBAL	
CLARA	3	F	CHILD	GRZZZZBAL	
JOHANNE	.09	F	INFANT	GRZZZZBAL	
FRIEDRICH, EMILIE	37	F	W	GRZZZZBAL	
AUGUSTE	10	F	CH	GRZZZZBAL	
BERTHA	4	F	CHILD	GRZZZZBAL	
OTTILIE	3	F	CHILD	GRZZZZBAL	
MAX	.09	M	INFANT	GRZZZZBAL	
JURKEWICZ, MARIANNE	22	F	SVNT	GRZZZZBAL	
WIECZORKIEWICZ, KATERZY	31	F	W	GRZZZZBAL	
WIECZORKIEWICZ, ANASTAS	2	F	CHILD	GRZZZZBAL	
WIECZORKIEWICZ, MARIANN	4	F	CHILD	GRZZZZBAL	
BOHINSKI, ROSALIE	28	F	W	GRZZZZBAL	
CONSTANCIA	3	F	CHILD	GRZZZZBAL	
STANISLAW	.09	M	INFANT	GRZZZZBAL	
SKOROWSKA, AGNES	24	F	W	GRZZZZBAL	
MICHAL	.11	M	INFANT	GRZZZZBAL	
THOMASCHEFSKA, KATH.	34	F	W	GRZZZZBAL	
IGNATZ	8	M	CHILD	GRZZZZBAL	
TEKLA	6	F	CHILD	GRZZZZBAL	
BRONISLAW	.11	F	INFANT	GRZZZZBAL	
SACKSCHENSKA, ANNA	11	F	UNKNOWN	GRZZZZBAL	
KOELCZYNSKA, ANTONIE	17	F	SVNT	GRZZZZBAL	
GLASENAPP, PAULINE	18	F	SVNT	GRZZZZBAL	
BORGIEWICZ, ANTONI	29	F	W	GRZZZZBAL	
MALETZKA, MARIANNA	28	F	W	GRZZZZBAL	
HEDWIG	4	F	CHILD	GRZZZZBAL	
STANISLAW	.11	M	INFANT	GRZZZZBAL	
FUCHS, GOTTLIEBE	23	F	W	GRZZZZBAL	
WILHELM	4	M	CHILD	GRZZZZBAL	
AUGUST	.11	M	INFANT	GRZZZZBAL	
KOLACZEK, FRANEISEA	30	F	W	GRZZZZBAL	
MARTENS, LOUISE	22	F	SVNT	GRZZZZBAL	
BUSCH, HULDA	52	F	W	GRZZZZMI	
AUGUSTE	11	F	CH	GRZZZZMI	
SCHIRMER, MARGR.	35	F	W	GRZZZZWI	
JOSEF	9	M	CHILD	GRZZZZWI	
JOHANN	7	M	CHILD	GRZZZZWI	
GEORG	3	M	CHILD	GRZZZZWI	
INGELMANN, THERESE	16	F	SVNT	GRZZZZBAL	
PLOEGER, HENRIETTE	24	F	SVNT	GRZZZZBAL	
NIENABER, REGINE	29	F	W	GRZZZZBAL	
ENGEL, ANNA	22	F	SVNT	GRZZZZBAL	
RHEINHEIMER, LINA	21	F	SVNT	GRZZZZBAL	
MUELLER, ANNA	20	F	SVNT	GRZZZZBAL	
SCHENDLER, ELISAB.	21	F	SVNT	GRZZZZBAL	
NEEF, CATH.	45	F	W	GRZZZZBAL	
CAROLINE	16	F	SVNT	GRZZZZBAL	
MATHILDE	10	F	CH	GRZZZZBAL	
LOUISE	9	F	CHILD	GRZZZZBAL	
JULIUS	3	M	CHILD	GRZZZZBAL	
RUPP, BARBARA	17	F	SVNT	GRZZZZBAL	
SEEGER, BERTHA	21	F	SVNT	GRZZZZBAL	
STEINBACH, MINNA	17	F	SVNT	GRZZZZBAL	
LEWANDOWSKA, ANTONIA	23	F	W	GRZZZZBAL	
STANISLAW	5	M	CHILD	GRZZZZBAL	
CASIMIR	.11	M	INFANT	GRZZZZBAL	
KRAUSE, MARIA	17	F	SVNT	GRZZZZBAL	
RENACHEWSKA, JOSEPHINE	24	F	SVNT	GRZZZZBAL	
SZCZECHOWSKI, AGNES	18	F	SVNT	GRZZZZBAL	
KONCZAL, ROSALYA	37	F	W	GRZZZZBAL	
THEODORIA	8	F	CHILD	GRZZZZBAL	
FRANZISCA	.11	F	INFANT	GRZZZZBAL	
JUST, MATHILDE	17	F	SVNT	GRZZZZBAL	
GRABOWSKA, ELISE	20	F	SVNT	GRZZZZBAL	
FENBURG, MARIA	20	F	SVNT	GRZZZZBAL	
LAUBE, AGNES	21	F	SVNT	GRZZZZBAL	
GORALSKI, ROSALIE	30	F	W	GRZZZZBAL	
JOSEF	10	M	CH	GRZZZZBAL	
KATHARINE	6	F	CHILD	GRZZZZBAL	
JAN	3	M	CHILD	GRZZZZBAL	
WLADISLAUS	.01	M	INFANT	GRZZZZBAL	
BARUCH, CONSTANTIA	40	F	W	GRZZZZBAL	
MICHAEL	.06	F	INFANT	GRZZZZBAL	
MARCHEB, MARIA	23	F	SVNT	GRZZZZBAL	
FUCHS, ANNA	16	F	SVNT	GRZZZZBAL	
STUBENRAUCH, GRETA	59	F	W	GRZZZZBAL	
ZANDEISEK, EMILIE	42	F	W	GRZZZZBAL	
THERESIA	13	F	CH	GRZZZZBAL	
PROSCHASKA, MARIA	19	F	SVNT	GRZZZZBAL	
POLKOVA, JOHANNE	32	F	W	GRZZZZBAL	
FRANZ	8	M	CHILD	GRZZZZBAL	
WENZL.	9	M	CHILD	GRZZZZBAL	
MASEK, MARIA	57	F	W	GRZZZZBAL	
RAFFEL, ELISAB.	28	F	W	GRZZZZBAL	
RUZENA	4	F	CHILD	GRZZZZBAL	
VALCHAZ, EMIL	9	M	CHILD	GRZZZZBAL	
ZIBELL, ELISAB.	48	F	W	GRZZZZBAL	
BAUMGARTEN, ERNESTINE	20	F	W	GRZZZZBAL	
ALBERT	.09	F	INFANT	GRZZZZBAL	
GORALZYK, APOLLONIA	60	F	W	GRZZZZBAL	
CZARNECKA, KATERCYNA	20	F	SVNT	GRZZZZBAL	

PASSENGER	AGE	SEX	OCCUPATION	PRV VIL DES
KIERCZYNSKA, FRANZISKA	34	F	W	GRZZZZBAL
ROMAN	8	M	CHILD	GRZZZZBAL
FRANZ	5	M	CHILD	GRZZZZBAL
JAHNS, BERTHA	25	F	W	GRZZZZBAL
HANSEN, ANNA	58	F	W	GRZZZZBAL
WIECINSKA, MARIA	29	F	UNKNOWN	GRZZZZMI
JOHANN	4	M	CHILD	GRZZZZMI
AUGUST	.10	M	INFANT	GRZZZZMI
DOMBROWSKA, EVA	63	F	W	GRZZZZMI
STOECHER, EVA	18	F	SVNT	GRZZZZBAL
STOECHER, MARG.	56	F	W	GRZZZZBAL
MUELLER, ELISE	21	F	SVNT	GRZZZZBAL
WROBLUSKA, MARIA	37	F	W	GRZZZZBAL
MARIA	11	F	CH	GRZZZZBAL
SMOLINSKA, ROSALIA	26	F	W	GRZZZZBAL
WLADISE	3	F	CHILD	GRZZZZBAL
REHBEIN, CAROLINE	33	F	W	GRZZZZBAL
TECHAU, MARGR.	17	F	SVNT	GRZZZZBAL
SKALICKI, MARIANNE	26	F	W	GRZZZZBAL
JOHANN	5	M	CHILD	GRZZZZBAL
LORENZ	3	M	CHILD	GRZZZZBAL
MARIA	.07	F	INFANT	GRZZZZBAL
SUWALSKA, APELLONIA	19	F	SVNT	GRZZZZBAL
ZALEWSKA, VICTORIA	30	F	W	GRZZZZBAL
TEKLA	3	F	CHILD	GRZZZZBAL
LEON.	.10	F	INFANT	GRZZZZBAL
REHMKE, ALWINE	17	F	SVNT	GRZZZZBAL
FAUSTMANN, CARMILLA	18	F	SVNT	GRZZZZBAL
MEYER, BERTHA	25	F	W	GRZZZZBAL
WILLIGARD	.08	M	INFANT	GRZZZZBAL
HAAS, BERTHA	19	F	SVNT	GRZZZZBAL
SEEROCKA, GOTTLIEBE	46	F	W	GRZZZZBAL
ANGE	.05	F	INFANT	GRZZZZBAL
BUTZBACH, CAROLINE	28	F	W	GRZZZZBAL
MATELSKA, ROSALIE	26	F	W	GRZZZZBAL
SCHULZ, AUGUSTE	29	F	W	GRZZZZWI
JACKOUBECK, BARBARA	15	F	SVNT	GRZZZZBAL
ZELENSKA, CAROLINE	33	F	W	GRZZZZBAL
FRANZISCA	.05	F	INFANT	GRZZZZBAL
HOCHDOERFER, MARIA	44	F	W	GRZZZZBAL
KOTERSK, MARIANNA	30	F	W	GRZZZZBAL
MARIANNA	7	F	CHILD	GRZZZZBAL
KOENEZA, MARIANNA	21	F	W	GRZZZZBAL
JOSEFA	.11	F	INFANT	GRZZZZBAL
TRZASKOWSKA, MARIANNA	25	F	W	GRZZZZBAL
AGNES	1	F	CHILD	GRZZZZBAL
MARIANNA	.01	F	INFANT	GRZZZZBAL
KNITTEL, JOSEFA	56	F	W	GRZZZZBAL
ALBERTINE	32	F	W	GRZZZZBAL
LOUISE	6	F	CHILD	GRZZZZBAL
GALASCHEWSKI, FRANZ	42	M	FARMER	GRZZZZBAL
ROSALIE	36	F	W	GRZZZZBAL
JOSEF	11	M	CH	GRZZZZBAL
FRANZ	10	M	CH	GRZZZZBAL
AGNES	8	F	CHILD	GRZZZZBAL
ROSALIE	7	F	CHILD	GRZZZZBAL
AUGUST	.11	M	INFANT	GRZZZZBAL
FORST, MARIANNA	34	F	W	GRZZZZBAL
JULIUS	9	M	CHILD	GRZZZZBAL
JOHANN	7	M	CHILD	GRZZZZBAL
JULIA	4	F	CHILD	GRZZZZBAL
ELISE	3	F	CHILD	GRZZZZBAL
ANTON	.10	M	INFANT	GRZZZZBAL
BLAHOLZKI, JULIUS	17	M	FARMER	GRZZZZBAL
WISNIEFSKI, ANNA	69	F	W	GRZZZZBAL
JOHANN	16	M	FARMER	GRZZZZBAL
MARIA	11	F	CH	GRZZZZBAL
JUST, JOHANN	27	M	FARMER	GRZZZZBAL
MARTHA	26	F	W	GRZZZZBAL
FRANZ	.10	M	INFANT	GRZZZZBAL
ACKERMANN, AUGUST	41	M	FARMER	GRZZZZBAL
DOROTHEA	42	F	W	GRZZZZBAL
WILH.	14	F	CH	GRZZZZBAL
RAJEWICZ, WOJTEK	36	M	FARMER	GRZZZZBAL
ANNA	31	F	W	GRZZZZBAL
STEFAN	7	M	CHILD	GRZZZZBAL
MARIA	.09	F	INFANT	GRZZZZBAL
SAGUSCH, DANIEL	32	M	SMH	GRZZZZBAL
CAROLINE	30	F	W	GRZZZZBAL
EMILIE	6	F	CHILD	GRZZZZBAL
AUGUSTE	3	F	CHILD	GRZZZZBAL
MARTHA	.10	F	INFANT	GRZZZZBAL
HOFSCHILD, FRIED.	67	M	FARMER	GRZZZZBAL
JOHANNE	60	F	W	GRZZZZBAL
EMILIE	28	F	W	GRZZZZBAL
FERDINAND	28	M	FARMER	GRZZZZBAL
FRANZ	2	M	CHILD	GRZZZZBAL
LESZCZYNSKA, JOHANN	24	M	FARMER	GRZZZZBAL
HUEBNER, PETER	54	M	FARMER	GRZZZZBAL
MINNA	16	F	D	GRZZZZBAL
SOPHIA	14	F	D	GRZZZZBAL
FRIEDRICH	12	M	CH	GRZZZZBAL
BRUHN, FRIEDRICH	55	M	FARMER	GRZZZZBAL
HEINRICH	25	M	FARMER	GRZZZZBAL
DORIS	28	F	W	GRZZZZBAL
NINNEMANN, ERNEST	44	F	W	GRZZZZBAL
ANNA	18	F	D	GRZZZZBAL
CARL	15	M	FARMER	GRZZZZBAL
IDA	9	F	CHILD	GRZZZZBAL
BOERNER, OTTO	24	M	TU	GRZZZZTX
MARIA	23	F	W	GRZZZZTX
ELSA	3	F	CHILD	GRZZZZTX
ALBERT	2	M	CHILD	GRZZZZTX
LONG, CARL	36	M	FARMER	GRZZZZBAL
MARIA	24	F	W	GRZZZZBAL
HERMANN	5	M	CHILD	GRZZZZBAL
WILHELM	3	M	CHILD	GRZZZZBAL
ANNA	2	F	CHILD	GRZZZZBAL
EMMA	.11	F	INFANT	GRZZZZBAL
GLODAUSKY, JOSEF	40	M	FARMER	GRZZZZBAL
JULIANE	42	F	W	GRZZZZBAL
HOLLER, ERDMUND	32	M	FARMER	GRZZZZBAL
FRIEDERIKA	35	F	W	GRZZZZBAL
LEOPOLD	11	M	CH	GRZZZZBAL
EMMA	9	F	CHILD	GRZZZZBAL
ANNA	7	F	CHILD	GRZZZZBAL
BERTHA	4	F	CHILD	GRZZZZBAL
YOST, AUGUST	25	M	SDLR	GRZZZZBAL
CAROLINE	23	F	W	GRZZZZBAL
AUGUSTE	.07	F	INFANT	GRZZZZBAL
STACHOWSKY, JAN	28	M	FARMER	GRZZZZBAL
JULIANNE	28	F	W	GRZZZZBAL
ANTONIE	5	F	CHILD	GRZZZZBAL
ANNA	3	F	CHILD	GRZZZZBAL
VALERIA	.09	F	INFANT	GRZZZZBAL
RADZMIEZOWSKI, JOHANN	42	M	FARMER	GRZZZZBAL
SALINE	33	F	W	GRZZZZBAL
FRANZ	9	M	CHILD	GRZZZZBAL
JOHANN	6	M	CHILD	GRZZZZBAL
ROBERT	3	M	CHILD	GRZZZZBAL
PAUL	.11	M	INFANT	GRZZZZBAL
KOEPPER, AUGUST	47	M	FARMER	GRZZZZBAL
WILHELMINE	42	F	W	GRZZZZBAL
LOUISE	16	F	D	GRZZZZBAL
WILHELMINE	12	F	CH	GRZZZZBAL
MARIA	10	F	CH	GRZZZZBAL
HERMANN	6	M	CHILD	GRZZZZBAL
AUGUSTE	3	F	CHILD	GRZZZZBAL
WILHELM	.09	M	INFANT	GRZZZZBAL
SCHMUCK, JOSEF	26	M	SMH	GRZZZZBAL
AGNES	23	F	W	GRZZZZBAL
SCHLICKER, JOHANN	25	M	FARMER	GRZZZZOH
JOHANNE	25	F	W	GRZZZZOH
HERMANN	.09	M	INFANT	GRZZZZOH
RETAT, EDUARD	28	M	FARMER	GRZZZZIL
EMILIE	24	F	W	GRZZZZIL
FRIEDRICH	3	M	CHILD	GRZZZZIL
HUGO	2	M	CHILD	GRZZZZIL
LUTTKA, RICHARD	38	M	TLR	GRZZZZKY
MARIA	38	F	W	GRZZZZKY

PASSENGER	AGE	SEX	OCCUPATION	PRVL	DES
MARIA	11	F	CH		GRZZZZKY
JOHANN	9	M	CHILD		GRZZZZKY
WILHELM	4	M	CHILD		GRZZZZKY
WIEGAND, CATH.	61	F	W		GRZZZZBAL
THEODOR	25	M	MCHT		GRZZZZBAL
MARGR.	27	F	W		GRZZZZBAL
STEINHEBEL, AUGUST	26	M	FARMER		GRZZZZBAL
MARIA	28	F	W		GRZZZZBAL
JOHANN	4	M	CHILD		GRZZZZBAL
WILHELM	.11	M	INFANT		GRZZZZBAL
KLAROWSKI, KASIMIR	26	M	FARMER		GRZZZZBAL
AUGUSTE	27	F	W		GRZZZZBAL
KAROLINE	5	F	CHILD		GRZZZZBAL
HENRIETTE	.11	F	INFANT		GRZZZZBAL
KELLERBAUM, JOSEPH	31	M	FARMER		GRZZZZBAL
ALFRINA	33	F	W		GRZZZZBAL
JOSEF	5	M	CHILD		GRZZZZBAL
JOSEFINE	.11	F	INFANT		GRZZZZBAL
SCHOLL, SIMON	42	M	TU		GRZZZZBAL
LOUISE	13	F	CH		GRZZZZBAL
BAMBICH, JOSEF	46	M	FARMER		GRZZZZBAL
ANNA	40	F	W		GRZZZZBAL
JOSEF	16	M	FARMER		GRZZZZBAL
ANNA	14	F	CH		GRZZZZBAL
TEFA	6	F	CHILD		GRZZZZBAL
ANTON	4	M	CHILD		GRZZZZBAL
ANTIM	.06	M	INFANT		GRZZZZBAL
PAVLONSKI, FRIEDR.	22	M	FARMER		GRZZZZBAL
GOTTLIEBE	29	F	W		GRZZZZBAL
HERMANN	4	M	CHILD		GRZZZZBAL
FRITZ	3	M	CHILD		GRZZZZBAL
ANNA	.09	F	INFANT		GRZZZZBAL
WESTPHAL, JOACHIM	35	M	FARMER		GRZZZZBAL
FRIEDERIKE	26	F	W		GRZZZZBAL
BERTHA	16	F	D		GRZZZZBAL
FRANZ	11	M	CH		GRZZZZBAL
MINNA	7	F	CHILD		GRZZZZBAL
AUGUSTE	5	F	CHILD		GRZZZZBAL
RUDOLPH	48	M	FARMER		GRZZZZBAL
RUDJE, MARTIN	69	M	FARMER		GRZZZZBAL
REGINE	59	F	W		GRZZZZBAL
BEUDICK, HERM.	26	M	FARMER		GRZZZZBAL
GOTTLIEBE	25	F	W		GRZZZZBAL
WILH.	.03	F	INFANT		GRZZZZBAL
BUECHNER, AUGUST	54	M	FARMER		GRZZZZMO
MARIA	52	F	W		GRZZZZMO
KLINGE, CARL	37	M	MSN		GRZZZZMO
FRIEDERIKE	32	F	W		GRZZZZMO
SCHMIDT, FRIEDR.	27	M	BKR		GRZZZZMO
SELMA	24	F	W		GRZZZZMO
RODADT, CARL	44	M	FARMER		GRZZZZOH
AMALIE	23	F	D		GRZZZZOH
KLEINE, WILHELM	24	M	FARMER		GRZZZZOH
BITZER, GOTTLIEB	29	M	FARMER		GRZZZZDAK
CATHARINA	23	F	W		GRZZZZDAK
MATHILDE	3	F	CHILD		GRZZZZDAK
CATRHARINE	.11	F	INFANT		GRZZZZDAK
BUCHHOLZ, JACOB	31	M	FARMER		GRZZZZDAK
ELISE	25	F	W		GRZZZZDAK
LYDIA	3	F	CHILD		GRZZZZDAK
PHILIPP	.11	M	INFANT		GRZZZZDAK
KRAUSS, PHILIPP	28	M	FARMER		GRZZZZDAK
PAULINE	22	F	W		GRZZZZDAK
WIESE, AUGUST	34	M	GDNR		GRZZZZDAK
MARIE	22	F	W		GRZZZZDAK
CARL	4	M	CHILD		GRZZZZDAK
EMIL	18	M	GDNR		GRZZZZDAK
KAISER, CARL	31	M	FARMER		GRZZZZMI
MARIA	30	F	W		GRZZZZMI
MARIA	2	F	CHILD		GRZZZZMI
ANNA	.03	F	INFANT		GRZZZZMI
GRIBOWSKY, ADAM	29	M	LABR		GRZZZZMI
AUGUSTE	30	F	W		GRZZZZMI
KAENEHL, ROBERT	26	M	LABR		GRZZZZMI
MARIA	28	F	W		GRZZZZMI
GUSTAV	.11	M	INFANT		GRZZZZMI
KEIL, ADOLPH	40	M	LABR		GRZZZZPA
GOTTLIEBE	34	F	W		GRZZZZPA
EMILIE	11	F	CH		GRZZZZPA
WILHELMINE	4	F	CHILD		GRZZZZPA
KARSTENS, ELISE	43	F	W		GRZZZZBAL
CATH.	21	F	D		GRZZZZBAL
HEINR.	16	M	FARMER		GRZZZZBAL
WILHELM	12	M	CH		GRZZZZBAL
ANNA	10	F	CH		GRZZZZBAL
JULIUS	8	M	CHILD		GRZZZZBAL
MICHAEL	6	M	CHILD		GRZZZZBAL
WILHELM	4	M	CHILD		GRZZZZBAL
MATHIAS	.11	M	INFANT		GRZZZZBAL
STOLNICKA, SCHIFRAM	42	M	MCHT		GRZZZZBAL
BERTHA	18	F	D		GRZZZZBAL
SCHIPSE	21	F	D		GRZZZZBAL
ISAAC	23	M	MCHT		GRZZZZIL
DEZYKAWSKI, MICHAEL	42	M	GZR		GRZZZZIL
APOLLONIA	33	F	W		GRZZZZIL
FRANZ	2	M	CHILD		GRZZZZIL
GERJETS, HINDERIKUS	46	M	LKSH		GRZZZZMI
BEREND	2	M	CHILD		GRZZZZMI
BATT, ANTON	28	M	FARMER		GRZZZZBAL
FRANZISKA	30	F	W		GRZZZZBAL
MARIA	7	F	CHILD		GRZZZZBAL
MARGARETHA	2	F	CHILD		GRZZZZBAL
CARL	1	M	CHILD		GRZZZZBAL
KLOCKGETER, GERHARD	25	M	FARMER		GRZZZZMO
ANNA	28	F	W		GRZZZZMO
SCHROEDER, FRANZ	38	M	FARMER		GRZZZZTX
GERTRUD	33	F	W		GRZZZZTX
WILHELM	4	M	CHILD		GRZZZZTX
ANTON	3	M	CHILD		GRZZZZTX
ALBERT	2	M	CHILD		GRZZZZTX
CATHARINE	.03	F	INFANT		GRZZZZTX
SEIFERT, WM.	29	M	SHMK		GRZZZZBAL
CHRISTINE	24	F	W		GRZZZZBAL
THOMAS	24	M	SHMK		GRZZZZBAL
HANITZKA, AGNES	50	F	W		GRZZZZBAL
ROMAN	15	M	LABR		GRZZZZBAL
ANTONIA	11	F	CH		GRZZZZBAL
LEONHARD	6	M	CHILD		GRZZZZBAL
ADALBERT	4	M	CHILD		GRZZZZBAL
ROUHUT, FRIEDRICH	29	M	TLR		GRZZZZBAL
ANNA	2	F	CHILD		GRZZZZBAL

SHIP: CASPIAN

FROM: LIVERPOOL
TO: BALTIMORE
ARRIVED: 16 NOVEMBER 1888

PASSENGER	AGE	SEX	OCCUPATION	PRVL	DES
SUMMSKI, SAME.	19	M	CPTR		GRZZZZUNK
JOSSEL	16	M	CPTR		GRZZZZUNK
RIGELEWITZ, SIMON	20	M	CPTR		GRZZZZUNK
KNOSKOWSKI, ROSALIE	20	F	DMS		GRZZZZBAL
CHAIE	16	F	DMS		GRZZZZBAL
KAMOWITSCJH, BREINE	22	M	LABR		GRZZZZBAL
JERNANIK, FERDINAND	26	M	LABR		GRZZZZOH
FANNY	30	F	W		GRZZZZOH
STANISLAUS	4	M	CHILD		GRZZZZOH
JULIA	3	F	CHILD		GRZZZZOH
FERDINAND	2	M	CHILD		GRZZZZOH
HANNAH	.08	F	INFANT		GRZZZZOH

```
                        A  S        P  V  D                                   A  S        P  V  D
PASSENGER               G  E OCCUPATION R  I  E        PASSENGER              G  E OCCUPATION R  I  E
                        E  X        V  L  S                                   E  X        V  L  S
--------------------------------------------------    --------------------------------------------------
SHIP:     LEERDAM                                        JULIANE               8 F CHILD     GRZZZZUSA
                                                        FRIEDR.               6 M CHILD     GRZZZZUSA
FROM:     ROTTERDAM                                     ADOLPH               3 M CHILD     GRZZZZUSA
TO:       NEW YORK                                    ROSEMANN, KATH.        27 F UNKNOWN   GRZZZZUSA
ARRIVED: 16 NOVEMBER 1888                               ERNST                3 M CHILD     GRZZZZUSA
                                                        HELENE               2 F CHILD     GRZZZZUSA
                                                      KOLLER, REGINA         32 F UNKNOWN   GRZZZZUSA
KOHN, IGN.SAM           00 M MCHT       GRZZZZUSA     RENNENBERG, GOTTFRIED  22 M GDNR      GRZZZZUSA
   IGN.SAM              00 F MCHT       GRZZZZUSA        MARIA               18 F UNKNOWN   GRZZZZUSA
   ROSA                 00 F UNKNOWN    GRZZZZUSA     ZAFFARA, LUIGI         23 M DLR       FRZZZZUSA
   ANNA                 11 F CH         GRZZZZUSA     SPINELE, DOMENICO      19 M DLR       FRZZZZUSA
CAMPBELL, H.            00 F UNKNOWN    GRZZZZUSA     PINTO, RAFFEL          17 M UNKNOWN   FRZZZZUSA
DI, JARD.               00 M UNKNOWN    FRZZZZUSA     OLIVIER, VICTOR        25 M LABR      FRZZZZUSA
WEISMANN, N.            28 M MCHT       GRZZZZUSA     PADJEN, JOSA           32 M LABR      FRZZZZUSA
STOCK, JOH.            17 M MCHT       GRZZZZUSA     DESANTI, VINCENZO      26 M LABR      FRZZZZUSA
KISTNER, JOH.H.         25 M MCHT       GRZZZZUSA     U, JACOB               38 M DLR       FRZZZZUSA
GRETSCH, CARL          26 M MCHT       GRZZZZUSA     BONDAVOLLI, FILOM.     29 F UNKNOWN   FRZZZZUSA
FROHNENBURG, JOH.       21 M UNKNOWN    GRZZZZUSA     BARBIERI, LUIGI        40 M LABR      FRZZZZUSA
STERN, EMIL            29 M MCHT       GRZZZZUSA     LUCHETTI, MICH.        27 M LABR      FRZZZZUSA
WILLIG, CHR.           46 F UNKNOWN    GRZZZZUSA     BONAPEA, PASQUALE      26 M LABR      FRZZZZUSA
   MARG.               11 F UNKNOWN    GRZZZZUSA     GELBERG, NOSEN         17 M LABR      FRZZZZUSA
SCHNEDL, ANTON         30 M LABR       GRZZZZUSA     CORPORATE, EMIDIA      25 M LABR      FRZZZZUSA
HELBRICGH, JOH.        20 M LABR       GRZZZZUSA        TERES.              24 F LABR      FRZZZZUSA
VORNDRAN, RAPH.        40 M LABR       GRZZZZUSA        MICH.               .11 F INFANT    FRZZZZUSA
JOERG, BARBARO         12 F CH         GRZZZZUSA
MIDLINSKY, MOSES       38 M DLR        GRZZZZUSA
VOGT, ADOL.G.          23 M LABR       GRZZZZUSA
REINKE, H.             22 M FARMER     GRZZZZUSA
MEYER, H.              22 M FARMER     GRZZZZUSA
MANTL, JOS.            19 M DLR        GRZZZZUSA     SHIP:     DONAU
SCHOTT, ADAM           29 M DLR        GRZZZZUSA
GILBERT, MICH.         20 M DLR        GRZZZZUSA     FROM:     BREMEN
HORATH, PAUL           17 M DLR        GRZZZZUSA     TO:       BALTIMORE
GROTHAUS, WILH.        23 M SMH        GRZZZZUSA     ARRIVED: 17 NOVEMBER 1888
VERGAI, REINH.         15 M UNKNOWN    GRZZZZUSA
HOLZMAN, JOH.          22 M LABR       GRZZZZUSA
KOCH, EMMA             25 F UNKNOWN    GRZZZZUSA     REIF, JOHAN            50 M MCHT       GRZZZZMD
SCHWIND, GEORG         27 M FARMER     GRZZZZUSA     JUELICH, HERMAN        20 M MCHT       GRZZZZMD
LINDNER, EMIL          23 F UNKNOWN    GRZZZZUSA     GRIESE, WILHELM        25 M MCHT       GRZZZZMD
HOFMEIER, ANNA         16 F UNKNOWN    GRZZZZUSA     SCHILLER, CHRISTINE    61 F UNKNOWN    GRZZZZMD
KOEPFLER, ANNA         17 F UNKNOWN    GRZZZZUSA     SCHOTTKY, BERTHA       22 F UNKNOWN    GRZZZZMD
KLEIN, SALI            28 F UNKNOWN    GRZZZZUSA     BRANDES, MATHILDE      40 F UNKNOWN    GRZZZZMD
TESSLER, LUDW.         42 M LABR       GRZZZZUSA     RO--, FRIEDRICH        25 M MCHT       GRZZZZMD
   PEPI                36 F UNKNOWN    GRZZZZUSA     HERBST, ELISE          52 F UNKNOWN    GRZZZZMD
   MALOI                4 F CHILD      GRZZZZUSA     WEYNA, BERTHA          15 F UNKNOWN    GRZZZZMD
PELAK, MAXIM           23 M LABR       GRZZZZUSA     GELINSKY, BERTHA       22 F UNKNOWN    GRZZZZMD
FRITZ, JOSEF           52 M LABR       GRZZZZUSA     MEBES, MINNA           24 F UNKNOWN    GRZZZZMD
   KATH.               54 F LABR       GRZZZZUSA     MEDEN, MARIA           20 F UNKNOWN    GRZZZZMD
LUCK, GUSTAV           20 M FARMER     GRZZZZUSA     KRUMBHOLZ, KARL        14 M UNKNOWN    GRZZZZMD
TOEPFER, GEORG         17 M UNKNOWN    GRZZZZUSA     THOMAS, ANNA           20 F UNKNOWN    GRZZZZMD
ECKFELDER, KARL        17 M UNKNOWN    GRZZZZUSA     STUPIK, HEDWIG         19 F UNKNOWN    GRZZZZMD
GLASER, PH.            27 M WTR        GRZZZZUSA     WRYECOL, JOHAN         42 M FARMER     GRZZZZMD
RINOFER, BLAS.         30 M WTR        GRZZZZUSA        BARBARA             40 F UNKNOWN    GRZZZZMD
TSCHENDER, ROMAN       19 M WTR        GRZZZZUSA        EMANUEL             11 M CH         GRZZZZMD
HAUSER, ANNA           20 F UNKNOWN    GRZZZZUSA        ROBERT               9 M CHILD      GRZZZZMD
SCHMITH, CONST.        19 M SMH        GRZZZZUSA        ELISABETH            7 F CHILD      GRZZZZMD
IBSEN, C.F.            58 M UNKNOWN    GRZZZZUSA        WALERKA              4 F CHILD      GRZZZZMD
LOEFF, ARTH.           17 M MCHT       GRZZZZUSA        AGNES                2 F CHILD      GRZZZZMD
CHRISTMAN, HEINR.      24 M MCHT       GRZZZZUSA        NATALIA            .03 F INFANT     GRZZZZMD
WEISSMANN, ISAC        19 M MCHT       GRZZZZUSA     SCHMATLOK, ALOIS       26 M FARMER     GRZZZZMD
MINDELOWER, DAVID      19 M MCHT       GRZZZZUSA     BAUMGARTEN, MARIA      39 F UNKNOWN    GRZZZZMD
STRUNH, ALONIS         20 M LABR       GRZZZZUSA        HEDWIG               9 F CHILD      GRZZZZMD
SCHEIBER, CARL         23 M MECH       GRZZZZUSA        ANNA                 8 F CHILD      GRZZZZMD
HEUN, HEINR.           21 M MECH       GRZZZZUSA     FISCHER, CATHA.        24 F UNKNOWN    GRZZZZMD
BROCKMANN, KARL        25 M CGRMKR     GRZZZZUSA     NEUBAUER, GEORG        14 M UNKNOWN    GRZZZZMD
STOLZE, GERTR.         25 F UNKNOWN    GRZZZZUSA     HUCKENBROECKEN, JOHNA. 19 F UNKNOWN    GRZZZZMD
SCHLAUTMANN, F.H.      26 F UNKNOWN    GRZZZZUSA     SCHULZE, BERTHA        30 F UNKNOWN    GRZZZZMD
SCHOTT, THERESIA       29 F UNKNOWN    GRZZZZUSA        CLARA               20 F UNKNOWN    GRZZZZMD
LINK, HERM.            16 M UNKNOWN    GRZZZZUSA     STEINCKE, AUGUSTE      23 F UNKNOWN    GRZZZZMD
WALCHER, JULIA         39 F UNKNOWN    GRZZZZUSA     SPRENGER, AUGUSTE      20 F UNKNOWN    GRZZZZMD
   JULIA               11 F CH         GRZZZZUSA     KATNY, MICHAEL         55 M FARMER     GRZZZZMD
BECKMANN, FR.          43 M LKSH       GRZZZZUSA        STANISLAUS          17 M UNKNOWN    GRZZZZMD
LUTSCHI, KATH.         30 F UNKNOWN    GRZZZZUSA        CATHA.               9 F CHILD      GRZZZZMD
   KATH.               11 F CH         GRZZZZUSA        MARIA                7 F CHILD      GRZZZZMD
   ANNA                 9 F CHILD      GRZZZZUSA     KASACK, AUGUST         24 M FARMER     GRZZZZMD
```

431

PASSENGER	AGE	SEX	OCCUPATION	PRVL	DES
WILHNE.	27	F	UNKNOWN		GRZZZZMD
SOPHIE	18	F	UNKNOWN		GRZZZZMD
IDA	.06	F	INFANT		GRZZZZMD
HASELOW, JOHN	59	M	UNKNOWN		GRZZZZMD
FRIEDERIKE	58	F	UNKNOWN		GRZZZZMD
IDA	20	F	UNKNOWN		GRZZZZMD
ADOLF	.09	M	INFANT		GRZZZZMD
BROECHERT, FRIEDRICH	36	M	UNKNOWN		GRZZZZMD
FRIEDERIKE	29	F	UNKNOWN		GRZZZZMD
RUDOLF	4	M	CHILD		GRZZZZMD
HERMAN	3	M	CHILD		GRZZZZMD
IDA	.03	F	INFANT		GRZZZZMD
BOETTCHER, MARIA	75	F	UNKNOWN		GRZZZZMD
KOOS, CARL	24	M	FARMER		GRZZZZMD
WILKORZ, VERONICA	23	F	UNKNOWN		GRZZZZMD
IGNATZ	.11	M	INFANT		GRZZZZMD
LIPKO, JOHAN	54	M	UNKNOWN		GRZZZZMD
BERTHA	44	F	UNKNOWN		GRZZZZMD
SCHUENKE, CHRISTOPH	54	M	FARMER		GRZZZZMD
BUCHHOLZ, ALBERT	28	M	TU		GRZZZZMD
WALIGURSKA, MICHALINA	20	F	UNKNOWN		GRZZZZMD
DRIEZINSKI, AUGUSTE	22	F	UNKNOWN		GRZZZZMD
PAPE, ELISABETH	18	F	UNKNOWN		GRZZZZMD
DOBEZKA, VALERIA	25	F	UNKNOWN		GRZZZZMD
TOEPPEL, LOUISE	22	F	UNKNOWN		GRZZZZMD
SUESS, U	22	F	UNKNOWN		GRZZZZMD
ANNA	14	F	UNKNOWN		GRZZZZMD
JOSEPH	3	M	CHILD		GRZZZZMD
BLAB, ANNA	31	F	UNKNOWN		GRZZZZMD
MARIA	6	F	CHILD		GRZZZZMD
ELISE	3	F	CHILD		GRZZZZMD
BUCHINGER, ANNA	30	F	UNKNOWN		GRZZZZMD
ANNA	3	F	CHILD		GRZZZZMD
CATHA.	1	F	CHILD		GRZZZZMD
LEMKE, FRIEDRICH	21	M	FARMER		GRZZZZMD
HARNISCH, PAULINE	26	F	UNKNOWN		GRZZZZMD
KAJETIGNON, CARL	22	M	FARMER		GRZZZZMD
WILHELM	48	M	FARMER		GRZZZZMD
JUSTINE	50	F	UNKNOWN		GRZZZZMD
MARIE	16	F	UNKNOWN		GRZZZZMD
MINNA	7	F	CHILD		GRZZZZUNK
MAAS, ERNESTINE	22	F	UNKNOWN		GRZZZZUNK
WAIDL, ELISABETH	17	F	UNKNOWN		GRZZZZUNK
STOLZER, MARIE	18	F	UNKNOWN		GRZZZZUNK
WOLK, CAROLINE	20	F	UNKNOWN		GRZZZZUNK
KONILI, JOSEPH	33	M	LABR		GRZZZZUNK
WAGNER, FRIEDRICH	26	M	FARMER		GRZZZZUNK
SPECHT, AUGUST	30	M	LABR		GRZZZZUNK
AUGUSTE	19	F	UNKNOWN		GRZZZZUNK
THEOPHIL	.03	M	INFANT		GRZZZZUNK
KRIESSIEN, KATE	26	F	UNKNOWN		GRZZZZUNK
HASS, U	26	F	UNKNOWN		GRZZZZUNK
MARIA	3	F	CHILD		GRZZZZUNK
ALEXANDER	.02	M	INFANT		GRZZZZUNK
BRUCK, ERNESTINE	18	F	UNKNOWN		GRZZZZUNK
WRABLEWSKA, MARIE	22	F	UNKNOWN		GRZZZZUNK
REIMAS, WILHNE.	70	F	UNKNOWN		GRZZZZUNK
KALINOWSKI, TADEUSZ	27	M	JNR		GRZZZZUNK
LAMBRECHT, AUGUST	25	M	SMH		GRZZZZUNK
BRZOSKA, TECLA	36	F	UNKNOWN		GRZZZZUNK
ANGELA	6	F	CHILD		GRZZZZUNK
BRONISLAWA	5	F	CHILD		GRZZZZUNK
HELENA	.04	F	INFANT		GRZZZZUNK
LEHMANN, BERTHA	26	F	UNKNOWN		GRZZZZUNK
SCHEEL, WILHELM	54	M	SHMK		GRZZZZUNK
ELISABETH	49	F	UNKNOWN		GRZZZZUNK
ELISABETH	15	F	UNKNOWN		GRZZZZUNK
WILLICH, MARTHA	22	F	UNKNOWN		GRZZZZUNK
CAROLINE	31	F	UNKNOWN		GRZZZZUNK
SIMON	4	M	CHILD		GRZZZZUNK
GRUNDMEIER, AUGUST	30	M	FARMER		GRZZZZUNK
AMALIE	34	F	UNKNOWN		GRZZZZUNK
AUGUST	5	M	CHILD		GRZZZZUNK
FRIEDRICH	2	M	CHILD		GRZZZZUNK
AMALIA	.11	F	INFANT		GRZZZZUNK
SCHWANDT, MINNA	15	F	UNKNOWN		GRZZZZUNK
KULKA, JOSEPHA	57	F	UNKNOWN		GRZZZZUNK
LENTZ, CARL	25	M	FARMER		GRZZZZUNK
NOACK, WILHELM	63	M	FARMER		GRZZZZUNK
U	46	F	FARMER		GRZZZZUNK
KRUEGER, FRIEDRICH	61	M	LKSH		GRZZZZUNK
EMILIE	51	F	UNKNOWN		GRZZZZUNK
OLGA	19	F	UNKNOWN		GRZZZZUNK
KARL	16	M	UNKNOWN		GRZZZZUNK
WENDLER, JULIUS	50	M	FARMER		GRZZZZUNK
MATHILDE	45	F	UNKNOWN		GRZZZZUNK
ADOLF	16	M	UNKNOWN		GRZZZZUNK
WILHELM	16	M	UNKNOWN		GRZZZZUNK
RUIDOLF	14	M	UNKNOWN		GRZZZZUNK
CARL	7	M	CHILD		GRZZZZUNK
MINNA	5	F	CHILD		GRZZZZUNK
WIECKE, WILHE.	19	F	CH		GRZZZZUNK
KRUEGER, LOUISE	62	F	UNKNOWN		GRZZZZUNK
ZIELKE, AUGUSTE	52	F	UNKNOWN		GRZZZZUNK
GRUENN, LOUISE	24	F	UNKNOWN		GRZZZZUNK
LOBEGOTT, FRIEDRICH	64	M	CPTR		GRZZZZUNK
FRANZ, WILH.	37	M	FARMER		GRZZZZUNK
WILHNE.	37	F	UNKNOWN		GRZZZZUNK
FRIEDERIKE	10	F	CH		GRZZZZUNK
ANNA	8	F	CHILD		GRZZZZUNK
WILHELM	5	M	CHILD		GRZZZZUNK
HERMAN	2	M	CHILD		GRZZZZUNK
FRITZ	.11	M	INFANT		GRZZZZUNK
BYECZYENSKA, MARIANNE	41	F	UNKNOWN		GRZZZZUNK
ANTON	6	M	CHILD		GRZZZZUNK
KLEWE, AUGUST	22	M	LABR		GRZZZZUNK
KLENFELDT, U	32	M	FARMER		GRZZZZUNK
FRIEDERIKE	33	F	UNKNOWN		GRZZZZUNK
WILHNE.	10	F	CH		GRZZZZUNK
ANNA	3	F	CHILD		GRZZZZUNK
BEUTEL, WILH.	38	M	FARMER		GRZZZZUNK
AUGUSTE	34	F	UNKNOWN		GRZZZZUNK
BERTHA	10	F	CH		GRZZZZUNK
KARL	9	M	CHILD		GRZZZZUNK
ANNA	7	F	CHILD		GRZZZZUNK
WILHELM	5	M	CHILD		GRZZZZUNK
AUGUSTE	3	F	CHILD		GRZZZZUNK
JOHANNA	.04	F	INFANT		GRZZZZUNK
MARTENS, ANNA	16	F	UNKNOWN		GRZZZZUNK
KARBE, CARL	28	M	FARMER		GRZZZZUNK
AUGUSTE	32	F	UNKNOWN		GRZZZZUNK
---LIE	4	F	CHILD		GRZZZZUNK
KERBE, KARL	.09	M	INFANT		GRZZZZUNK
FRIESE, WILHELM	36	M	TU		GRZZZZUNK
AUGUSTE	27	F	UNKNOWN		GRZZZZUNK
BERTHA	7	F	CHILD		GRZZZZUNK
HERMAN	3	M	CHILD		GRZZZZUNK
STAFFELDT, WILHELM	39	M	LABR		GRZZZZUNK
CAROLINE	43	F	UNKNOWN		GRZZZZUNK
MARIE	16	F	UNKNOWN		GRZZZZUNK
WILHELM	12	M	CH		GRZZZZUNK
CARL	12	M	CH		GRZZZZUNK
ELFRIEDE	7	F	CHILD		GRZZZZUNK
AUGUST	5	M	CHILD		GRZZZZUNK
KALLENBERG, U	50	F	UNKNOWN		GRZZZZUNK
ANNA	15	F	UNKNOWN		GRZZZZUNK
GRITZKA, WILHELM	37	M	BLKSMH		GRZZZZUNK
JULIA	36	F	UNKNOWN		GRZZZZUNK
CHRISTIAN	11	M	CH		GRZZZZUNK
GERSKI, JOHAN	37	M	UNKNOWN		GRZZZZUNK
EMILIE	42	F	UNKNOWN		GRZZZZUNK
JOHAN	9	M	CHILD		GRZZZZUNK
BERTHA	8	F	CHILD		GRZZZZUNK
MARGA.	3	F	CHILD		GRZZZZUNK
LAURA	2	F	CHILD		GRZZZZUNK
EHLKE, AUGUST	41	M	CCHMN		GRZZZZUNK
BERTHA	39	F	UNKNOWN		GRZZZZUNK
ROBERT	10	M	CH		GRZZZZUNK
ANNA	12	F	CH		GRZZZZUNK
EMMA	5	F	CHILD		GRZZZZUNK

PASSENGER	AGE	SEX	OCCUPATION	PRV VL DES
ELSA	3	F	CHILD	GRZZZZUNK
NEUMANN, FRIEDRICH	66	M	LABR	GRZZZZUNK
JULIANE	58	F	UNKNOWN	GRZZZZUNK
EMILIE	19	F	UNKNOWN	GRZZZZUNK
ANNA	16	F	UNKNOWN	GRZZZZUNK
WERTH, GUSTAV	33	M	LABR	GRZZZZUNK
KLAPPER, ALOIS	19	M	LABR	GRZZZZUNK
JEHMKE, WILHNE.	38	F	UNKNOWN	GRZZZZUNK
THERESE	7	F	CHILD	GRZZZZUNK
EMMA	11	M	CH	GRZZZZUNK
WILHELM	2	M	CHILD	GRZZZZUNK
ROHLOFF, THERESE	30	F	UNKNOWN	GRZZZZUNK
WILHELM	2	M	CHILD	GRZZZZUNK
HEDWIG	.03	F	INFANT	GRZZZZUNK
HAASCH, ALBERTINE	55	F	UNKNOWN	GRZZZZUNK
AUGUSTE	18	F	UNKNOWN	GRZZZZUNK
POLAND, FRANZISCA	23	F	UNKNOWN	GRZZZZUNK
LEISTV, AUGUST	49	M	FARMER	GRZZZZUNK
EMILIE	19	F	UNKNOWN	GRZZZZUNK
BERTHA	18	F	UNKNOWN	GRZZZZUNK
GUSTAV	15	M	UNKNOWN	GRZZZZUNK
HELENE	14	F	UNKNOWN	GRZZZZUNK
WILHELM	8	M	CHILD	GRZZZZUNK
ANNA	3	F	CHILD	GRZZZZUNK
RATZMANN, JOHAN	68	M	UNKNOWN	GRZZZZUNK
FRIEDERICKE	40	F	UNKNOWN	GRZZZZUNK
KREUZKE, FRIEDRICH	60	M	UNKNOWN	GRZZZZUNK
POSKE, WILHNE.	24	F	UNKNOWN	GRZZZZUNK
ROBERT	3	M	CHILD	GRZZZZUNK
ENGEL, AUGUST	25	M	PVTR	GRZZZZMI
AUGUSTINE	34	F	UNKNOWN	GRZZZZMI
THERESE	11	F	CH	GRZZZZMI
ADOLF	9	M	CHILD	GRZZZZMI
FRIEDRICH	7	M	CHILD	GRZZZZMI
OTTO	6	M	CHILD	GRZZZZMI
CARL	4	M	CHILD	GRZZZZMI
HUGO	.11	M	INFANT	GRZZZZMI
MZYEK, CARL	46	M	MNR	GRZZZZIL
ZEILLER, ANDREAS	23	M	LABR	GRZZZZOH
STEINER, THERESE	21	F	UNKNOWN	GRZZZZOH
WIEDERHIH, ALBERTINE	30	F	UNKNOWN	GRZZZZDAK
GUSTAV	6	M	CHILD	GRZZZZDAK
GOTTLIEB	1	M	CHILD	GRZZZZDAK
BUSSE, WILHNE.	20	F	UNKNOWN	GRZZZZIL
BEJENKE, FRANZISKA	15	F	UNKNOWN	GRZZZZIL
BENDIG, FRANZISKA	28	F	UNKNOWN	GRZZZZIL
WITTLIEF, TEOPHILE	20	M	MCHT	GRZZZZMI
FLAUM, CARL	47	M	SMH	GRZZZZOH
HENRIETTE	37	F	UNKNOWN	GRZZZZOH
WILHNE.	18	F	UNKNOWN	GRZZZZOH
WILHELM	4	M	CHILD	GRZZZZOH
HERMAN	4	M	CHILD	GRZZZZOH
FRIEDRICH	39	M	UNKNOWN	GRZZZZPA
WILHNE.	35	F	UNKNOWN	GRZZZZPA
ASUGUSTE	18	F	UNKNOWN	GRZZZZPA
HERMAN	16	M	UNKNOWN	GRZZZZPA
CARL	6	M	CHILD	GRZZZZPA
ELISABETH	.11	F	INFANT	GRZZZZPA
ZILLGIT, CARL	64	M	FARMER	GRZZZZPA
JUSTINE	69	F	UNKNOWN	GRZZZZPA
FEDDER, WILHNE.	54	F	UNKNOWN	GRZZZZMD
ERNESTINE	11	F	CH	GRZZZZMD
NEUBAUER, CHRISTINA	67	F	UNKNOWN	GRZZZZMD
ANNA	67	F	UNKNOWN	GRZZZZMD
BARTEL, DANIEL	65	M	LABR	GRZZZZOH
WILHNE.	53	F	UNKNOWN	GRZZZZOH
EMILIE	21	F	UNKNOWN	GRZZZZOH
WILHELM	18	M	UNKNOWN	GRZZZZOH
U	13	M	UNKNOWN	GRZZZZOH
ZANDER, CARL	35	M	LABR	GRZZZZOH
WILHNE.	34	F	UNKNOWN	GRZZZZOH
BARTEL, AUGUSTE	16	F	UNKNOWN	GRZZZZOH
BERTHA	13	F	UNKNOWN	GRZZZZOH
WILHNE.	11	F	UNKNOWN	GRZZZZOH
ZANDER, EMILIE	5	F	CHILD	GRZZZZOH
CHRISTINE	63	F	UNKNOWN	GRZZZZOH
WILHNE.	26	F	UNKNOWN	GRZZZZOH
PAUL	.11	M	INFANT	GRZZZZOH
IHLENFELDT, CARL	35	M	ISP	GRZZZZMI
WILHNE.	32	F	UNKNOWN	GRZZZZMI
HERMINE	9	F	CHILD	GRZZZZMI
CARL	4	M	CHILD	GRZZZZMI
WILH.	.06	M	INFANT	GRZZZZMI
SCHULZ, CARL	29	M	SHFM	GRZZZZMI
ERNESTINE	25	F	UNKNOWN	GRZZZZMI
BERTHA	.03	F	INFANT	GRZZZZMI
IHLENFELDT, JOHE.	62	F	UNKNOWN	GRZZZZMI
DRUECKHAEMER, MARIE	21	F	UNKNOWN	GRZZZZCAL
LEIN, LIDIE	11	F	CH	GRZZZZIL
DEHN, ERNST	23	M	LABR	GRZZZZWI
MEINHARDT, FERD.	18	M	LABR	GRZZZZOH
MEINKE, FERD.	23	M	FARMER	GRZZZZWI
PFEUDER, CARL	68	M	FARMER	GRZZZZWI
DEHN, ALBERT	22	M	LABR	GRZZZZWI
WILHNE.	30	F	UNKNOWN	GRZZZZWI
MINNA	1	F	CHILD	GRZZZZWI
EMMA	.07	F	INFANT	GRZZZZWI
NEUMANN, EMMA	10	F	CH	GRZZZZWI
SCHMIDT, CARL	36	M	FARMER	GRZZZZWI
IDA	37	F	UNKNOWN	GRZZZZWI
LOUISE	9	F	CHILD	GRZZZZWI
MARTHA	9	F	CHILD	GRZZZZWI
EMIL	4	M	CHILD	GRZZZZWI
DLUGOSCH, THEOPHILE	36	M	FARMER	GRZZZZIL
ANASTASIA	30	F	UNKNOWN	GRZZZZIL
HELENE	8	F	CHILD	GRZZZZIL
MATHILDE	6	F	CHILD	GRZZZZIL
JOACHIM	4	M	CHILD	GRZZZZIL
FALLKOWSKI, FRANZ	63	M	FARMER	GRZZZZNE
CATHA.	61	F	UNKNOWN	GRZZZZNE
WENDLANDT, CARL	26	M	FARMER	GRZZZZMI
MARIE	20	F	UNKNOWN	GRZZZZMI
ANNA	.06	F	INFANT	GRZZZZMI
HULDA	19	F	UNKNOWN	GRZZZZMN
HAASCH, EMILIE	24	F	UNKNOWN	GRZZZZWI
CARL	15	M	UNKNOWN	GRZZZZWI
HENSEL, FRANZ	23	M	UNKNOWN	GRZZZZMO
BORKERT, JOSEPH	22	M	FARMER	GRZZZZMO
STREI, WILHE.	23	F	UNKNOWN	GRZZZZMD
ANNA	.06	F	INFANT	GRZZZZMD
EMILIE	20	F	UNKNOWN	GRZZZZMD
BERTHA	2	F	CHILD	GRZZZZMD
VOTH, AUGUSTE	24	F	UNKNOWN	GRZZZZMD
RUDALL, WILHELM	25	M	LABR	GRZZZZMD
SAEMERT, AUGUSTE	18	F	UNKNOWN	GRZZZZMD
MUETZEL, CHRISTIAN	55	M	UNKNOWN	GRZZZZMD
MARIA	54	F	UNKNOWN	GRZZZZMD
REGINE	26	F	UNKNOWN	GRZZZZMD
MARIA	24	F	UNKNOWN	GRZZZZMD
GEORG	13	M	UNKNOWN	GRZZZZMD
U	00	F	UNKNOWN	GRZZZZMD
POHLMANN, U	25	M	FUR	GRZZZZMD
BERZ, AUGUSTE	20	F	UNKNOWN	GRZZZZMD
LEMCKE, AUGUST	57	M	TNM	GRZZZZMD
BEILFUSS, BERTHA	16	F	UNKNOWN	GRZZZZMD
EGGERT, EMIL	30	M	FARMER	GRZZZZMD
IDA	23	F	UNKNOWN	GRZZZZMD
BRUNS, JOSEPH	64	M	MCHT	GRZZZZMD
KUHLMANN, JOHAN	30	M	FARMER	GRZZZZMD
SCHACHTSCHNEIDER, ADELB	18	M	UNKNOWN	GRZZZZMD
JACOB, MARTHA	16	F	UNKNOWN	GRZZZZMD
KICKBUSCH, FERD.	38	M	BKR	GRZZZZMD
WILHNE.	29	F	UNKNOWN	GRZZZZMD
LOUISE	6	F	CHILD	GRZZZZMD
FRANY	4	M	CHILD	GRZZZZMD
MARIE	.11	F	INFANT	GRZZZZMD
DLUGOSCH, SERAPHIN	.10	M	INFANT	GRZZZZIL
RUBE, ROSA	18	F	UNKNOWN	GRZZZZMD
KLINK, CAROLINE	20	F	UNKNOWN	GRZZZZMD
HORST, ANNA	18	F	UNKNOWN	GRZZZZMD

PASSENGER	AGE	SEX	OCCUPATION	PRVL	DES
KRUSE, GRETCHEN	21	F	UNKNOWN		GRZZZZMD
VANDETTEN, HERM.	16	M	UNKNOWN		GRZZZZMD
BAUMGARTEN, LOUISE	23	F	UNKNOWN		GRZZZZMD
MARTHA	3	F	CHILD		GRZZZZMD
FRANZ	.09	M	INFANT		GRZZZZMD
SEILER, CAECILIA	43	F	UNKNOWN		GRZZZZMD
HARTUNG, ANNA	20	F	UNKNOWN		GRZZZZMD
PREM, MARIA	21	F	UNKNOWN		GRZZZZMD
JANZER, JOHN	19	M	BRR		GRZZZZMD
-OGES, U	26	F	UNKNOWN		GRZZZZMD
MINNA	4	F	CHILD		GRZZZZMD
FRIEDA	.11	F	INFANT		GRZZZZMD
HERKEN, MEUNE	53	M	FARMER		GRZZZZMD
OCKJE	48	F	UNKNOWN		GRZZZZMD
WAHNE	17	F	UNKNOWN		GRZZZZMD
ANNA	12	F	CH		GRZZZZMD
JUSTINE	10	F	CH		GRZZZZMD
REHME	8	F	CHILD		GRZZZZMD
MINNA	6	F	CHILD		GRZZZZMD
HOFFMANN, WILHELM	17	M	CL		GRZZZZMD
WENZ, PHILIPPINA	30	F	UNKNOWN		GRZZZZMD
WILHNE.	11	F	CH		GRZZZZMD
KRAFT, MARIA	15	F	UNKNOWN		GRZZZZMD
THORHAUER, DOROTHEA	40	F	UNKNOWN		GRZZZZMD
ANNA	10	F	CH		GRZZZZMD
JULIUS	8	M	CHILD		GRZZZZMD
SCHLIENITZ, LOUISE	47	F	UNKNOWN		GRZZZZMD
ERNST	16	M	UNKNOWN		GRZZZZMD
JOHAN	7	M	CHILD		GRZZZZMD
ALBERT	5	M	CHILD		GRZZZZMD
ZUCKEN, THERESE	33	F	UNKNOWN		GRZZZZMD
HETTI	3	F	CHILD		GRZZZZMD
FRANKI	1	M	CHILD		GRZZZZMD
GISCHEL, CARL	30	M	UNKNOWN		GRZZZZMD
SEGFRIED, KAROLINE	14	F	UNKNOWN		GRZZZZMD
BEUCHERT, HEINRICH	16	M	FARMER		GRZZZZMD
STENGLE, FRANZISKA	21	F	UNKNOWN		GRZZZZMD
SEITZ, CARL	27	M	FARMER		GRZZZZMD
WOERNER, ALOIS	16	M	UNKNOWN		GRZZZZMD
DORN, ELISAB.	18	F	UNKNOWN		GRZZZZMD
HILDEBRANDT, ELISAB.	21	F	UNKNOWN		GRZZZZMD
KATHA.	9	F	CHILD		GRZZZZMD
OFFHENSEN, EMILIE	46	F	UNKNOWN		GRZZZZMD
PAULA	10	F	CH		GRZZZZMD
MARTHA	6	F	CHILD		GRZZZZMD
DORN, JOHAN	16	M	UNKNOWN		GRZZZZMD
POST, AUGUSTE	20	F	UNKNOWN		GRZZZZMD
ROTTENBERGER, AMBROSE	15	F	UNKNOWN		GRZZZZMD
HAUSLER, JACOBINE	21	F	UNKNOWN		GRZZZZMD
PRIEBE, HENRIETTE	22	F	UNKNOWN		GRZZZZMD
BELZ, SOPHIE	27	F	UNKNOWN		GRZZZZMD
SCHNAPP, VERONICA	19	F	UNKNOWN		GRZZZZMD
GOETZ, AUGUST	20	M	BRR		GRZZZZMD
DIEDRICH, LOUISE	38	F	UNKNOWN		GRZZZZMD
U	00	M	UNKNOWN		GRZZZZMD
TECLA	9	F	CHILD		GRZZZZMD
MAX	7	M	CHILD		GRZZZZMD
REIMANN, AUGUST	23	M	SMH		GRZZZZMD
EISENHUT, AUGUST	11	M	CH		GRZZZZMD
KUGELBERG, WILHELM	22	M	SMH		GRZZZZMD
HANNEMANN, LOUISE	52	F	UNKNOWN		GRZZZZMD
DIGLER, HERMAN	28	M	TLR		GRZZZZMD
BELZ, HEINRICH	31	M	JNR		GRZZZZMD
PFEIFFER, SIMON	24	M	FARMER		GRZZZZMD
OESTERWINTER, JOHAN	35	M	FARMER		GRZZZZTX
PAUL, CHRIST.	23	M	FARMER		GRZZZZMD
WIENERS, BERN.	18	M	FARMER		GRZZZZPA
GAERTNER, LOUISE	37	F	UNKNOWN		GRZZZZMD
HERMAN	11	M	CH		GRZZZZMD
KELLER, CAROLIE	34	M	CH		GRZZZZMD
TRINKAUS, GUST.	23	M	LABR		GRZZZZMO
HOLK, HERM.	24	M	SHMK		GRZZZZPA
RUST, DIEDR.	15	M	UNKNOWN		GRZZZZMN
BRANDT, WILHELM	17	M	UNKNOWN		GRZZZZNE
RUEBENHAGEN, ROB.	28	M	BKR		GRZZZZWI
WALKER, ANDREAS	21	M	FARMER		GRZZZZPA
BARBARA	27	F	UNKNOWN		GRZZZZPA
MANJER, JOSEPH	21	M	TLR		GRZZZZPA
WEBER, MICHAEL	27	M	TLR		GRZZZZPA
RUST, HEINRICH	27	M	LABR		GRZZZZMN
MEYER, FRITZ	51	M	UNKNOWN		GRZZZZOH
MINNA	39	F	UNKNOWN		GRZZZZOH
JOSEPHINE	18	F	UNKNOWN		GRZZZZOH
HEINRICH	16	M	UNKNOWN		GRZZZZOH
GERHARD	11	M	CH		GRZZZZOH
BERNHARD	29	M	UNKNOWN		GRZZZZOH
U	27	F	UNKNOWN		GRZZZZOH
VONDERLINDEN, MARIA	18	F	UNKNOWN		GRZZZZMD
NEUMANN, HEINRICH	11	M	CH		GRZZZZMD
FRITZ, EMMA	23	F	UNKNOWN		GRZZZZMD
OFFKENSEN, ERNST	27	M	BKR		GRZZZZMD
DAMM, LOUISE	34	F	UNKNOWN		GRZZZZMD
CARL	11	M	CH		GRZZZZMD
KATINKA	9	F	CHILD		GRZZZZMD
TRUTH, MARIA	22	F	UNKNOWN		GRZZZZMD
PETER	15	M	UNKNOWN		GRZZZZMD
FUCHS, JOHANNA	19	F	UNKNOWN		GRZZZZMD
LOTER	15	M	UNKNOWN		GRZZZZMD
ANTON	10	M	UNKNOWN		GRZZZZMD
DOLLINGER, LINA	26	F	UNKNOWN		GRZZZZMD
HERRMANN, KASPAR	25	M	FARMER		GRZZZZMD
THIERAUFF, JOHAN	23	M	FARMER		GRZZZZMD
HERRMANN, WOLFGANG	29	M	FARMER		GRZZZZMD
ANNA	27	F	FARMER		GRZZZZMD
JOSEPH	3	M	CHILD		GRZZZZMD
BARBARA	.03	F	INFANT		GRZZZZMD
FINGER, MARIE	27	F	UNKNOWN		GRZZZZMD
APPEL, ERNESTINE	47	F	UNKNOWN		GRZZZZMD
M.	15	M	UNKNOWN		GRZZZZMD
HELENE	11	F	CH		GRZZZZMD
HERMANN	9	M	CHILD		GRZZZZMD
U, U	22	F	UNKNOWN		GRZZZZMD
URBANIAK, AGNITZKA	23	F	UNKNOWN		GRZZZZMD
LUDWIG	2	M	CHILD		GRZZZZMD
STANISLAUS	.09	M	INFANT		GRZZZZMD
BLUM, GRETCHEN	20	F	UNKNOWN		GRZZZZMD
POPPEN, GEORG	16	M	UNKNOWN		GRZZZZMD
BLUME, SOPHIE	16	F	UNKNOWN		GRZZZZMD
HOHMANN, JOHAN	16	M	UNKNOWN		GRZZZZMD
SCHWABE, FRANZ	29	F	UNKNOWN		GRZZZZMD
WVA.	27	F	UNKNOWN		GRZZZZMD
MARTHA	1	F	CHILD		GRZZZZMD
MARTHA	1	M	CHILD		GRZZZZMD
U	.09	F	INFANT		GRZZZZMD
LETTAN, PETER	48	M	TLR		GRZZZZMD
LOUISE	41	F	UNKNOWN		GRZZZZMD
HERMAN	10	M	CH		GRZZZZMD
MARTHA	8	F	CHILD		GRZZZZMD
LOBREITSCHAK, JOSEFA	23	F	UNKNOWN		GRZZZZMD
NADOLSKI, JOHN	33	M	FARMER		GRZZZZMD
MARIA	28	F	UNKNOWN		GRZZZZMD
ROSA	9	F	CHILD		GRZZZZMD
MARIANNA	7	F	CHILD		GRZZZZMD
ANNA	5	F	CHILD		GRZZZZMD
JOSEPH	.11	M	INFANT		GRZZZZMD
BERNH.	.01	M	INFANT		GRZZZZMD
MICHALAK, MAREIN	23	M	INF		GRZZZZMD
KATHA.	24	F	UNKNOWN		GRZZZZMD
FRANZ	2	M	CHILD		GRZZZZMD
WEHRENBURG, AUGUST	18	M	FARMER		GRZZZZMD
OTTERPOHL, BERNH.	18	M	FARMER		GRZZZZMD
BENDER, SOPHIE	22	F	UNKNOWN		GRZZZZMD
LUCHTING, EMILIE	14	F	UNKNOWN		GRZZZZMD
BERTELS, MINNA	14	F	UNKNOWN		GRZZZZMD
KRACK, KUNIGUNDE	21	F	UNKNOWN		GRZZZZMD
JAEGER, ELISAB.	23	F	UNKNOWN		GRZZZZMD
RENSCH, PHILIP	17	M	JNR		GRZZZZMD
HOHLMANN, CHRISTINA	21	F	UNKNOWN		GRZZZZMD
KISSERING, FOKKE	37	M	SMH		GRZZZZIL
RENIA	36	F	UNKNOWN		GRZZZZIL

PASSENGER	AGE	SEX	OCCUPATION	PRVL DES
PETER	13	M	CH	GRZZZZIL
HERMSIENE	11	F	CH	GRZZZZIL
FREICH	10	M	CH	GRZZZZIL
ANNA	8	F	CHILD	GRZZZZIL
RENDSKE	5	F	CHILD	GRZZZZIL
RENIA	3	F	CHILD	GRZZZZIL
FADA	1	F	CHILD	GRZZZZIL
PETER, MARGA.	36	F	UNKNOWN	GRZZZZPA
U	13	F	UNKNOWN	GRZZZZPA
JOSWEPH	11	M	CH	GRZZZZPA
WILHELM	9	M	CHILD	GRZZZZPA
STEPHAN	7	M	CHILD	GRZZZZPA
MARGA.	3	F	CHILD	GRZZZZPA
JESPERSEN, HANS	60	M	FARMER	GRZZZZWI
MARGA.	59	F	UNKNOWN	GRZZZZWI
BIESNICK, FRANZ	52	M	FARMER	GRZZZZMN
MARDA	47	F	UNKNOWN	GRZZZZMN
JOHAN	19	M	UNKNOWN	GRZZZZMN
VICTOR	16	M	UNKNOWN	GRZZZZMN
CENEILI	11	F	CH	GRZZZZMN
JULIA	9	F	CHILD	GRZZZZMN
CHRIST	5	M	CHILD	GRZZZZMN
BIALUCHA, JOHAN	28	M	FARMER	GRZZZZMN
MUELLER, WILHELM	59	M	FARMER	GRZZZZMD
U	54	F	UNKNOWN	GRZZZZMD
--DERS, U	63	F	UNKNOWN	GRZZZZMD
U, U	35	F	UNKNOWN	GRZZZZMD
ROEDER, HERMAN	30	M	LABR	GRZZZZMD
SCHNEIDER, PETER	56	M	FARMER	GRZZZZIA
JACOB	19	M	UNKNOWN	GRZZZZIA
GERTRUD	14	F	UNKNOWN	GRZZZZIA
JOSEPH	12	M	UNKNOWN	GRZZZZIA
JOHAN	9	M	CHILD	GRZZZZIA
MAR.	7	F	CHILD	GRZZZZIA
U, U	5	M	CHILD	GRZZZZIA
U	00	M	FARMER	GRZZZZUSA
CATHA.	45	F	UNKNOWN	GRZZZZUSA
LOUISE	16	F	UNKNOWN	GRZZZZUSA
ANNA	13	F	UNKNOWN	GRZZZZUSA
ILSEBEIN	6	F	CHILD	GRZZZZUSA
HEINRICH	5	M	CHILD	GRZZZZUSA
CHRISTINE	4	F	CHILD	GRZZZZUSA
HERMAN	.09	M	INFANT	GRZZZZUSA
SCHUMACHER, ENGEL	29	M	FARMER	GRZZZZUSA
GARSETZKI, ANNA	28	F	UNKNOWN	GRZZZZMD
AICHELE, WILHELM	24	M	FARMER	GRZZZZMD
GEISSLER, MARIA	23	F	UNKNOWN	GRZZZZMD
THEISSEN, MARIA	23	F	UNKNOWN	GRZZZZMD
EZEL, EVA	22	F	UNKNOWN	GRZZZZPA
TOENIES, U	30	F	UNKNOWN	GRZZZZPA
STUCKENBRECK, U	15	F	UNKNOWN	GRZZZZPA
SEEGA, HERMAN	26	M	LABR	GRZZZZPA
DRUSCHKI, RUDOLPH	41	M	BCHR	GRZZZZWI
ALEXANDRINE	39	F	UNKNOWN	GRZZZZWI
HELENE	14	F	UNKNOWN	GRZZZZWI
GEORG	13	M	UNKNOWN	GRZZZZWI
RUDOLPH	8	M	CHILD	GRZZZZWI
ERNST	3	M	CHILD	GRZZZZWI
BOEHNKE, JOHAN	29	M	TLR	GRZZZZIA
JOSINE	25	F	UNKNOWN	GRZZZZIA
CATHARINE	3	F	CHILD	GRZZZZIA
U	.11	M	INFANT	GRZZZZIA
BOETTCHER, PAULINE	30	F	UNKNOWN	GRZZZZIA
WIEBER, ANNA	39	F	UNKNOWN	GRZZZZIA
EMMA	9	F	CHILD	GRZZZZIA
HERMAN	7	M	CHILD	GRZZZZIA
LIPKE, SUSANNA	44	F	UNKNOWN	GRZZZZIA
JOHANNA	8	F	CHILD	GRZZZZIA
HELENE	5	F	CHILD	GRZZZZIA
STOLP, CHRISTIAN	49	M	FARMER	GRZZZZIA
KRZWEINSKA, ANTONIA	15	F	UNKNOWN	GRZZZZMD
LIS, MARTHA	13	F	UNKNOWN	GRZZZZMD
EWERDOWSKI, IGNATZ	23	M	FARMER	GRZZZZMD
LYESS, PAULINE	18	F	UNKNOWN	GRZZZZMD
GROESCH, CARL	29	M	GDNR	GRZZZZMD
ZARASKI, MARIANNE	18	F	UNKNOWN	GRZZZZMD
PIATKOWSKA, DOROTA	21	F	UNKNOWN	GRZZZZMD
RETZLAFF, CARL	25	M	JNR	GRZZZZMD
LOUISE	24	F	UNKNOWN	GRZZZZMD
HEDWIG	.04	F	INFANT	GRZZZZMD
SCHROEDER, MATHILDA	19	F	UNKNOWN	GRZZZZMD
DORNGUART, U	25	F	UNKNOWN	GRZZZZMD
U, U	00	U	UNKNOWN	GRZZZZMD
KILINSKY, U	00	F	UNKNOWN	GRZZZZMD
FRANZISKA	25	F	UNKNOWN	GRZZZZMD
ENGELSKIND, U	14	M	TLR	GRZZZZMD
TURKOWSKI, U	25	F	UNKNOWN	GRZZZZMD
MARIE	.09	F	INFANT	GRZZZZMD
NIESPODZIANY, PETER	65	M	GDNR	GRZZZZMD
FRANZISKA	65	F	UNKNOWN	GRZZZZMD
BEUTLER, HAENRICH	41	M	UNKNOWN	GRZZZZMD
NACHTIGALL, MARIA	43	F	UNKNOWN	GRZZZZMD
RAPLOCHOWSKA, MARYANNA	21	F	UNKNOWN	GRZZZZMD
STEPHAN, ELISABETH	16	F	UNKNOWN	GRZZZZMD
CARL	25	M	LABR	GRZZZZMD
FERDERICH, WOZACH	23	M	LABR	GRZZZZMD
ROZMARINOWSKA, U	66	F	UNKNOWN	GRZZZZMD
WIELITZKA, U	22	M	FARMER	GRZZZZMD
JOGODZINSKA, U	32	F	UNKNOWN	GRZZZZMD
MARTHA	9	F	CHILD	GRZZZZMD
JULIUS	6	M	CHILD	GRZZZZMD
BRONISLAVA	4	F	CHILD	GRZZZZMD
LEONHARDT	2	M	CHILD	GRZZZZMD
MARIANNA	.09	F	INFANT	GRZZZZMD
FILSZINSKI, JOHN	24	M	UNKNOWN	GRZZZZMD
LOBCZAK, MARYE	23	F	UNKNOWN	GRZZZZMD
BESMER, EMILIE	34	F	UNKNOWN	GRZZZZMD
CARL	9	M	CHILD	GRZZZZMD
MARGA.	7	F	CHILD	GRZZZZMD
HEINRICH	5	M	CHILD	GRZZZZMD
OLGA	3	F	CHILD	GRZZZZMD
EDUARD	.11	M	INFANT	GRZZZZMD
AHRENDT, U	15	F	UNKNOWN	GRZZZZMD
HERZBERG, A.	40	M	FARMER	GRZZZZMD
U	39	F	UNKNOWN	GRZZZZMD
U	00	F	UNKNOWN	GRZZZZMD
U	3	F	UNKNOWN	GRZZZZMD
KUCHENBACKER, U	25	F	UNKNOWN	GRZZZZMD
MINGE, PAUL	16	M	UNKNOWN	GRZZZZMD
WACHOWSKI, FRANZ	31	M	UNKNOWN	GRZZZZMD
THERESE	25	F	UNKNOWN	GRZZZZMD
MARTHA	6	F	CHILD	GRZZZZMD
MARGA.	3	F	CHILD	GRZZZZMD
U	.06	M	INFANT	GRZZZZMD
WILL, FRANZISKA	20	M	INF	GRZZZZMD
SIMON, HERMAN	29	M	FARMER	GRZZZZMD
HELMKE, LOUISE	20	F	UNKNOWN	GRZZZZMD
BLASEJZYEK, LUDWIG	25	M	FARMER	GRZZZZMD
MIENE, WILHNE.	18	F	UNKNOWN	GRZZZZMD
KOSTRZEWSKA, STANISLAWA	25	F	UNKNOWN	GRZZZZMD
MARIE	2	F	CHILD	GRZZZZMD
SCHLEUERSTAHL, GEORG	22	M	TCHR	GRZZZZMD
HAFNER, JACOB	28	M	LABR	GRZZZZMD
THEOBALD, CATHA.	26	F	UNKNOWN	GRZZZZMD
U	5	M	CHILD	GRZZZZMD
U	2	F	CHILD	GRZZZZMD
WILHELM	.06	M	INFANT	GRZZZZMD
KREBS, MARGA.	16	F	UNKNOWN	GRZZZZMD
BATZ, MARGA.	3	F	CHILD	GRZZZZMD
BETTENBROK, FRITZ	18	M	CH	GRZZZZMD
LINDENBLAM, MARIA	17	F	CH	GRZZZZMD
SCHOBER, U	25	F	UNKNOWN	GRZZZZWI
U	.09	M	INFANT	GRZZZZWI
HENNING, MARIE	22	F	UNKNOWN	GRZZZZWI
BRENDEMUEHL, ROSA	22	F	UNKNOWN	GRZZZZWI
BOETGER, EDUARD	24	M	FARMER	GRZZZZOH
BRUEHL, MARGA.	26	F	UNKNOWN	GRZZZZIL
EISENMANN, KATHA.	38	F	UNKNOWN	GRZZZZWI
MUELLER, MARIE	21	F	UNKNOWN	GRZZZZWI
FICK, LEONH.	51	M	FARMER	GRZZZZWI

PASSENGER	AGE	SEX	OCCUPATION	PRVL	DES
ANNA	56	F	UNKNOWN	GRZZZZWI	
MICHAEL	17	M	FARMER	GRZZZZWI	
BERGMANN, CHRISTOPH	52	M	UNKNOWN	GRZZZZMO	
JOHN	11	M	CH	GRZZZZMO	
POECKER, GUIDO	18	M	CL	GRZZZZIL	
JARMUSCH, GOTTLIEB	39	M	UNKNOWN	GRZZZZOH	
HERMANN	14	M	CH	GRZZZZOH	
U	8	F	CHILD	GRZZZZOH	
-ENA	4	F	CHILD	GRZZZZOH	
EMMA	2	F	CHILD	GRZZZZOH	
BERTHA	.09	F	INFANT	GRZZZZOH	
RAPELIUS, CARL	27	M	PVTR	GRZZZZWI	
BATZER, LINA	18	F	UNKNOWN	GRZZZZWI	
HEIN, AUGUSTE	62	F	UNKNOWN	GRZZZZWI	
SCHAEFER, FRANZ	19	M	CL	GRZZZZIL	
KOPF, FRIEDRICH	29	M	SMH	GRZZZZMI	
RIESS, MARGA.	24	F	UNKNOWN	GRZZZZOH	
REIMANN, ERNSTINE	27	F	UNKNOWN	GRZZZZDAK	
ALPERS, U	30	M	LABR	GRZZZZMD	
STEFFENS, JACOB	18	M	LABR	GRZZZZMD	
STOLP, MATHILDE	40	F	UNKNOWN	GRZZZZMD	
LOEHN, HEINRICH	60	M	FARMER	GRZZZZMO	
HENRIETTE	60	F	UNKNOWN	GRZZZZMO	
WALLBAUM, AMALIA	30	F	UNKNOWN	GRZZZZMO	
ANNA	7	F	CHILD	GRZZZZMO	
MEYER, JULIE	19	F	UNKNOWN	GRZZZZMO	
ADAM, RUDOLPH	21	M	FARMER	GRZZZZMD	
STANISLAWSKA, FRANZKA.	22	F	UNKNOWN	GRZZZZMD	
FRANZKA.	.11	F	INFANT	GRZZZZMD	
BAUMER, THERESIA	22	F	UNKNOWN	GRZZZZMD	
CABYE	.09	F	INFANT	GRZZZZMD	
DIEDRICH, U	00	M	INF	GRZZZZUNK	

SHIP: IOWA

FROM: LIVERPOOL
TO: BOSTON
ARRIVED: 17 NOVEMBER 1888

PASSENGER	AGE	SEX	OCCUPATION	PRVL	DES
KOLOSNER, AUGUSTA	20	M	LABR	GRZZZZUSA	
MASHERLIEN, JOHANNA	18	F	SP	GRZZZZUSA	
BL-CHER, PEPPE	29	F	W	GRZZZZUSA	
BLECHER, FANNIE	7	F	CHILD	GRZZZZUSA	
ROSA	5	F	CHILD	GRZZZZUSA	

SHIP: RHYNLAND

FROM: ANTWERP
TO: NEW YORK
ARRIVED: 19 NOVEMBER 1888

PASSENGER	AGE	SEX	OCCUPATION	PRVL	DES
V, ALMA	32	F	LDY	GRZZZZUSA	
BUTTNER, U	23	M	DR	GRZZZZNY	
MAGUS, C.	38	M	MCHT	GRZZZZNY	
LUCY	10	F	CH	GRZZZZNY	
OSCAR	9	M	CHILD	GRZZZZNY	
EUGEN	7	M	CHILD	GRZZZZNY	
CLAUSS, U	39	M	DR	GRZZZZCO	
FALK, U	27	F	UNKNOWN	GRZZZZPHI	
BONILLIE, U	52	F	UNKNOWN	FRZZZZPTL	
U	22	F	UNKNOWN	FRZZZZPTL	
MILTENBERG, U	32	M	MCHT	GRZZZZCH	
U	30	F	UNKNOWN	GRZZZZCH	
ALFRED	5	M	CHILD	GRZZZZCH	
SELIGMANN, U	72	F	UNKNOWN	GRZZZZCH	

PASSENGER	AGE	SEX	OCCUPATION	PRVL	DES
KOENIG, U	29	M	ART	GRZZZZNY	
U	24	F	UNKNOWN	GRZZZZNY	
ELZER, U	23	F	UNKNOWN	GRZZZZSTL	
KUHN, U	24	F	UNKNOWN	GRZZZZNY	
U	1	F	CHILD	GRZZZZNY	
FRIEDMANN, U	20	F	UNKNOWN	GRZZZZSTL	
PFLICHINGER, U	34	F	UNKNOWN	GRZZZZSTL	
STEIN, KURT	25	M	MCHT	GRZZZZMX	
WOLZ, U	26	F	UNKNOWN	GRZZZZNY	
THIEMANN, U	35	F	UNKNOWN	GRZZZZMIL	
PRENDENBORWECH, FRANZ	25	M	BKR	GRZZZZNY	
SCHWEITZER, SIMON	19	M	SHMK	GRZZZZNY	
REICH, HEINR.	24	M	LABR	GRZZZZNY	
MOSSON, MAX	18	M	LABR	GRZZZZNY	
KNUTH, CARL	23	M	TLR	GRZZZZMIL	
WECHSLER, FRED.W.	26	M	LABR	GRZZZZDET	
FRIEDRICH, SOFIA	20	F	SVNT	GRZZZZFRA	
KURTZWEG, JULIUS	59	M	LABR	GRZZZZBUF	
PAULINE	54	F	W	GRZZZZBUF	
CAROLINE	12	F	CH	GRZZZZBUF	
HEINRICH	18	M	LABR	GRZZZZBUF	
BOSKOWSKI, FRANZ	24	M	TLR	GRZZZZCH	
MATZE, BERTHA	19	F	LDY	GRZZZZNY	
ANNA	16	F	UNKNOWN	GRZZZZNY	
CHARLES	9	M	CHILD	GRZZZZNY	
SCHMIDT. CATH.	27	F	SVNT	GRZZZZNY	
BARTHELEMY, JULES	31	M	LABR	GRZZZZUNK	
HAMBACHER, JACOB	18	M	LABR	GRZZZZNY	
V, PHILOMENE	13	F	UNKNOWN	GRZZZZNY	
LEONIE	11	F	UNKNOWN	GRZZZZNY	
BROEDEL, ADA	19	F	SVNT	GRZZZZSAN	
BURGER, CATH.	60	M	LABR	GRZZZZPIT	
WAL.	24	M	LABR	GRZZZZPIT	
FRANK, WILH.	18	M	UNKNOWN	GRZZZZNLB	
BRAND, ALOIS	40	M	LABR	GRZZZZUNK	
SHARMANN, ELISAB.	46	F	W	GRZZZZUNK	
EWALD, CATH.	41	F	W	GRZZZZNY	
FANNY	19	F	D	GRZZZZNY	
CLARA	15	F	D	GRZZZZNY	
JULIE	10	F	CH	GRZZZZNY	
NICOLA	9	F	CHILD	GRZZZZNY	
CARL	7	M	CHILD	GRZZZZNY	
MARIE	4	F	CHILD	GRZZZZNY	
JOHANN	00	M	INF	GRZZZZNY	
ROBERT, HUBERT	46	M	LABR	GRZZZZUNK	
SCHELLENBURGER, U	28	F	W	GRZZZZNY	
OTTO	5	M	CHILD	GRZZZZNY	
PAULA	4	F	CHILD	GRZZZZNY	
KERN, ANDR.	20	M	GDSM	GRZZZZNY	
BRUECK, LORENZ	62	M	LABR	GRZZZZNY	
MARG.	61	F	W	GRZZZZNY	
CAROLINE	22	F	SVNT	GRZZZZNY	
CARL	18	M	LABR	GRZZZZNY	
GRETCHEN	2	F	CHILD	GRZZZZNY	
SANDER, WILH.	23	M	SP	GRZZZZNY	
TRAPP, CARL	26	M	LKSH	GRZZZZUNK	
BAER, FRANSISCA	32	F	W	GRZZZZHTD	
FRAN.	4	F	CHILD	GRZZZZUNK	
ANNA	1	F	CHILD	GRZZZZUSA	
STELZER, JOSEF	36	M	LABR	GRZZZZCH	
BECKERT, CAROLINE	20	F	SVNT	GRZZZZNY	
RONNOSER, S.	31	F	SVNT	GRZZZZNY	
MARIA	24	F	SVNT	GRZZZZNY	
WACHTER, CARL	31	M	LABR	GRZZZZNY	
ANTON	25	M	LABR	GRZZZZNY	
OEYNER, CHRISTINA	21	F	WO	GRZZZZNY	
UOLD, CORNEL	57	M	LABR	GRZZZZNY	
BRIGETTA	60	F	W	GRZZZZNY	
JOSEF	31	M	LABR	GRZZZZNY	
ALBERT	19	M	LABR	GRZZZZNY	
VAL.	17	M	LABR	GRZZZZNY	
HARTMANN, ENGELBERT	21	M	LABR	GRZZZZNY	
REICKERT, REGINA	26	F	WI	GRZZZZNY	
JOSEF	00	M	INF	GRZZZZNY	
WIRSNIG, -EUZENTIA	31	F	W	GRZZZZNY	

PASSENGER	AGE	SEX	OCCUPATION	PRVVL	DES
WILH.	11	M	CH		GRZZZZNY
HERMANN	9	M	CHILD		GRZZZZNY
ANNA	5	F	CHILD		GRZZZZNY
LUTZ, JULIE	16	F	SVNT		GRZZZZNY
SCHMAUSCH, BABETTE	19	F	UNKNOWN		GRZZZZNY
HIRT, FRIEDR.	27	M	LABR		GRZZZZUNK
WEIDEMANN, LISETTE	27	F	W		GRZZZZUNK
WINZIG, GEORG	20	M	SHMK		GRZZZZCIN
JULIANNE	12	F	SVNT		GRZZZZCIN
WEIGLEIN, WM.	17	M	LABR		GRZZZZNY
MARTIN, JOHANN	18	M	LABR		GRZZZZNY
STREIT, EMILIE	34	F	SVNT		GRZZZZNY
BACHMANN, CARL	25	M	MCHT		GRZZZZNY
SEITZER, OTTO	25	M	MECH		GRZZZZUNK
LINSSEN, HCH.	22	M	CMST		GRZZZZCIN
KOSFWIG, GOTTFRIED	49	M	BKR		GRZZZZCIN
DEETERICKS, MICH.	24	M	LABR		GRZZZZNY
LEUCHS, ANDREAS	28	M	SMH		GRZZZZNY
SANDER, LOUIS	27	M	MCHT		GRZZZZNY
EMMA	29	F	W		GRZZZZNY
BLANCKERT, CHARLES	36	M	LABR		FRZZZZDET
BERLIN, ALBERT	30	M	UNKNOWN		GRZZZZNY
ORTSMANN, JOHANN	30	M	LABR		GRZZZZNY
WEBER, JOHANN	25	M	LABR		GRZZZZNY
SCHWEIZER, MARIA	20	F	SVNT		GRZZZZNY
PETERS, EDMUND	28	M	BKBNDR		GRZZZZNY
SIMON, HCH.	25	M	BKBNDR		GRZZZZNY
SOMMER, MARIE	60	F	LDY		GRZZZZNY
FUND, ELISE	33	F	W		GRZZZZUNK
ELISE	14	F	CH		GRZZZZUNK
DALLAFIOR, DOMINICO	24	M	LABR		GRZZZZUNK
FRANZ	28	M	LABR		GRZZZZUNK
FRIEDRICH, MAX	21	M	GDNR		GRZZZZNY
KLUCKNER, ALEX	25	M	GDNR		GRZZZZNY
WOLFSON, WOLF	21	M	MCHT		GRZZZZNY
HAMBUCHER, ADAM	6	M	CHILD		GRZZZZNY
MICH.	15	M	CH		GRZZZZNY
CATH.	13	F	CH		GRZZZZNY
GEORG	10	M	CH		GRZZZZNY
MARIE	3	F	CHILD		GRZZZZNY
GENSHEIMER, MARIE	19	F	SVNT		GRZZZZNY
SCHWERTFEGER, HCH.	19	M	MECH		GRZZZZNY
LEONHARD, FERD.	19	M	STCTR		GRZZZZNY
STARK, CARL	17	M	MCHT		GRZZZZNY
SCHWEIZER, ALOIS	22	M	BKR		GRZZZZNY
ZUGENBUHLER, MARTIN	43	M	CPTR		SRZZZZNY
JOHANNA	36	F	W		SRZZZZNY
ANNA	7	F	CHILD		SRZZZZNY
MARIA	4	F	CHILD		SRZZZZNY
STOCK, DOROTHEA	70	F	UNKNOWN		SRZZZZNY
ANNA	31	F	UNKNOWN		SRZZZZNY
GALLIARD, MARIA	24	F	SVNT		SRZZZZNY
LENDELOTTI, CESARINA	24	F	SVNT		SRZZZZNY
CHRIST, ELISE	20	F	SVNT		SRZZZZNY
KRONENBERG, ANTON	40	M	TLR		GRZZZZNY
ELISE	42	F	W		GRZZZZNY
ERNST	7	M	CHILD		GRZZZZNY
BLIND, ALEX	30	M	SHMK		GRZZZZNY
LEYZI, VALENTIN	27	M	LABR		SRZZZZNY
CELESTINA	27	F	W		SRZZZZNY
PORINO, GUISEPPE	19	M	LABR		SRZZZZNY
MERLO, ENRICO	23	M	LABR		SRZZZZNY
CERFOGLIA, ENRICO	23	M	LABR		SRZZZZNY
SCHWARZ, MATHIAS	24	M	BKR		SRZZZZNY
DREIXLER, THEODOR	21	M	SMH		SRZZZZNY
TREVISEAU, ANNA	30	F	W		FRZZZZNY
GERTRUDE	11	F	CH		FRZZZZNY
ANGELS	2	M	CHILD		FRZZZZNY
MARIE	00	F	INF		FRZZZZNY
KOEHLER, F.LUD.	21	M	ART		GRZZZZNY
---LING, JOH.	24	M	SHMK		GRZZZZNY
BAUDEL, FRANZ	49	M	LABR		GRZZZZNY
SEYFRIED, JACOB	27	M	LABR		GRZZZZNY
KLEIBER, JOH.	22	M	LABR		GRZZZZPIT
HOLZWARTH, GG.	28	M	BKBNDR		GRZZZZNY
SOPHIE	25	F	W		GRZZZZNY
SCHELLER, LOUISE	00	F	LDY		GRZZZZNY
KOBER, CATH.	21	F	SVNT		GRZZZZNY
DOBLER, ANTONIE	21	F	W		GRZZZZNY
MINA	00	F	INF		GRZZZZNY
WILLI, THERESIA	26	F	SVNT		GRZZZZCH
MUELLER, LEOPOLD	16	M	BY		GRZZZZBO
MILZ, CATH.	34	F	W		GRZZZZUNK
CATH.	9	F	CHILD		GRZZZZUNK
WILH.	6	M	CHILD		GRZZZZUNK
LEOPOLD	3	M	CHILD		GRZZZZUNK
LEONORA	00	F	INF		GRZZZZUNK
JAINICKI, BRUNO	18	M	SHMK		GRZZZZCH
SANASKI, MICHAEL	59	M	LABR		GRZZZZWI
MARIE	16	F	UNKNOWN		GRZZZZWI
SOUTOWSKI, FRANZ	26	M	LABR		GRZZZZWI
ANNA	22	F	W		GRZZZZWI
GRABOWSKA, GOTTLIEBE	30	F	W		GRZZZZWI
BERHARD	00	M	INF		GRZZZZWI
TREMLER, JOH.	21	M	LABR		GRZZZZNY
BUSCH, LUD.	30	M	TLR		GRZZZZNY
HARTL, JOSEF	55	M	MECH		GRZZZZNY
FISCHER, MICHAEL	53	M	MECH		GRZZZZPEO
MONICKA	45	F	W		GRZZZZPEO
EUGENIE	20	F	SVNT		GRZZZZPEO
ANTON	15	M	BY		GRZZZZPEO
EMIL	11	M	CH		GRZZZZPEO
KNERR, LUDWIG	21	M	BKR		GRZZZZNY
PFEIFFER, JACOB	29	M	LABR		GRZZZZNY
BROM, JOHANN	37	M	LABR		GRZZZZNY
RUTER, WENZL	39	M	LABR		GRZZZZNY
CEUKOWITZ, JOHANN	28	M	LABR		GRZZZZNY
MARIE	28	F	W		GRZZZZNY
STANISLAUS	00	M	INF		GRZZZZNY
NOVOTING, MAGD.	18	F	SVNT		GRZZZZNY
MUSIL, FRANCISKA	21	F	W		GRZZZZNY
MARIA	2	F	CHILD		GRZZZZNY
ZIB, WENZL	24	M	LABR		GRZZZZNY
DOZEZAL, THERESA	23	F	SVNT		GRZZZZNY
GRILL, JOSEFA	20	F	SVNT		GRZZZZNY
PISANKOW, MARIE	31	F	SVNT		GRZZZZUNK
KRISTA, BARBARA	20	F	SVNT		GRZZZZPIT
KUSTER, LINDA	18	F	SVNT		GRZZZZPIT
SCHNEIDER, MARIA	20	F	SVNT		GRZZZZNY
KEYENBURG, THEO.	26	M	LKSH		GRZZZZUNK
TIPPERMAAS, JETTCHEN	30	F	W		GRZZZZNY
LEO	00	M	INF		GRZZZZNY
HEULENSER, GG.	58	M	MECH		GRZZZZNY
STEPHANIE, ED.	35	M	LABR		GRZZZZNY
JEHL, FLORENZ	38	M	LABR		GRZZZZNY
JECKERT, ANTON	39	M	LABR		GRZZZZNY
KOPFER, GEORG	21	M	BKR		GRZZZZNY
FANURICH, MAGD.	24	F	W		GRZZZZPIT
CARL	00	M	INF		GRZZZZPIT
U	51	M	W		GRZZZZPIT
ANTON	11	M	CH		GRZZZZPIT
LOUISE	10	F	CH		GRZZZZPIT
JOSEPHINE	8	F	CHILD		GRZZZZPIT
MOHRMANN, ALFRED	26	M	BBR		GRZZZZNY
POEHNE, PAUL	21	M	BBR		GRZZZZNY
HEAFFSTADT, ELIS	17	F	SVNT		GRZZZZCH
FAEHNRICH, H.	00	M	LABR		GRZZZZPIT

PASSENGER	AGE	SEX	OCCUPATION	PRVL	DES

SHIP: ST. OF PENNSYLVANIA

FROM: GLASGOW AND LARNE
TO: NEW YORK
ARRIVED: 19 NOVEMBER 1888

PASSENGER	AGE	SEX	OCCUPATION	PRVL DES
ASMUSSEN, CHRISTIAN	22	M	LABR	GRZZZZUSA
PEDERSEN, LAURITZ	15	M	LABR	GRZZZZUSA
FARBOL, BODIL	47	F	W	GRZZZZUSA
ANNA	20	F	SP	GRZZZZUSA
HEINRICH	15	M	LABR	GRZZZZUSA
KJERSTINE	2	F	CHILD	GRZZZZUSA

SHIP: TRAVE

FROM: BREMEN
TO: NEW YORK
ARRIVED: 20 NOVEMBER 1888

PASSENGER	AGE	SEX	OCCUPATION	PRVL DES
V, AD.	21	M	TT	GRZZZZGR
HEINR.	24	M	TT	GRZZZZGR
HEIL, JACOB	34	M	MCHT	GRZZZZGR
MUELLER, FLORENTE	21	F	UNKNOWN	GRZZZZGR
HERBERG, GUST.	27	M	MCHT	GRZZZZGR
SCHULZ, ADAM	40	M	MCHT	GRZZZZGR
WOLLHEIM, HEINR.	35	M	MCHT	GRZZZZGR
THOMAS, K.	22	F	UNKNOWN	GRZZZZGR
COHEN, ALMA	13	F	UNKNOWN	GRZZZZGR
STRAUSS, ADAM	38	M	MCHT	GRZZZZGR
BAND, CL.H.	45	M	MCHT	GRZZZZGR
U	40	F	UNKNOWN	GRZZZZGR
A.	17	F	UNKNOWN	GRZZZZGR
B.	16	F	UNKNOWN	GRZZZZGR
BREVANNES, U	47	F	UNKNOWN	FRZZZZFR
MARTIN, ARTHUR	35	M	MCHT	GRZZZZGR
SCHUPP, ANNA	30	F	UNKNOWN	GRZZZZGR
ENDRES, AUG.	24	M	MCHT	SRZZZZSW
STEIN, FRIEDKE.	63	F	UNKNOWN	GRZZZZGR
MUELLER, SOPHIE	26	F	UNKNOWN	GRZZZZGR
MUSELINS, CARL	21	M	MCHT	GRZZZZGR
BETTMANN, JUSTUS	16	M	MCHT	GRZZZZGR
KOHLMEYER, LEO	15	M	UNKNOWN	GRZZZZGR
RAUCH, EUGEN	16	M	UNKNOWN	GRZZZZGR
ZIEBOLD, EMILIE	26	F	UNKNOWN	GRZZZZGR
GELLNER, HELENE	25	F	UNKNOWN	GRZZZZGR
ULLMANN, HEINR.	43	M	MCHT	GRZZZZGR
ROSA	28	F	UNKNOWN	GRZZZZGR
MAGDA.	7	F	CHILD	GRZZZZGR
HARRY	3	M	CHILD	GRZZZZGR
SCHMIDTMANN, BERNHD.	16	M	MCHT	GRZZZZGR
DORA	18	F	UNKNOWN	GRZZZZGR
FRIEST, KARL	17	M	MCHT	GRZZZZGR
FREUND, BABETTE	33	F	UNKNOWN	GRZZZZGR
SCHMIEDER, MARTHA	28	F	UNKNOWN	GRZZZZGR
BACHRACH, SIGM.	16	M	MCHT	GRZZZZGR
SCHANZ, JOHA.	20	F	UNKNOWN	GRZZZZGR
MEYERLOFF, LINA	20	F	UNKNOWN	GRZZZZGR
WALTER, DORA	60	F	UNKNOWN	GRZZZZGR
DUBE, LOUIS	20	M	MCHT	GRZZZZGR
KLEIN, ANTONIE	27	F	UNKNOWN	GRZZZZGR
WINKLER, MARIE	23	F	UNKNOWN	SRZZZZSW
SCHMAHL, KATHA.	22	F	UNKNOWN	GRZZZZGR
KIRSCHNER, LOUIS	32	M	MCHT	GRZZZZGR
HOCH, MARY	58	F	UNKNOWN	GRZZZZGR
PFRETZSCHNER, ADOLF	21	M	MCHT	GRZZZZGR
V, HUGO	21	M	MCHT	GRZZZZGR
STEINMETZ, HANS	20	M	MCHT	GRZZZZGR
KRIEGL, LUDW.	60	M	MCHT	GRZZZZGR
LENFF, ERNST	27	M	MCHT	GRZZZZGR

PASSENGER	AGE	SEX	OCCUPATION	PRVL DES
AHRENS, HENRY	46	M	MCHT	GRZZZZGR
ANNA	18	F	UNKNOWN	GRZZZZGR
THORMANN, A.	54	M	MCHT	GRZZZZGR
C.	26	M	MCHT	GRZZZZGR
BACHMANN, BERNHD.	48	M	MCHT	GRZZZZGR
EMMA	20	F	UNKNOWN	GRZZZZGR
KUCTZEIN, FRANZ	35	M	DR	GRZZZZGR
BOECKER, ADOLPHINE	19	F	UNKNOWN	GRZZZZGR
GRAEFENSTEIN, BERNHD.	31	M	MCHT	GRZZZZUSA
KELLER, BARBA.	68	F	UNKNOWN	GRZZZZUSA
HECHT, MARIA	32	F	UNKNOWN	GRZZZZUSA
ROSALIA	7	F	CHILD	GRZZZZUSA
LIND, CAROLE.	24	F	UNKNOWN	GRZZZZUSA
KINDERMANN, MISNIE	24	F	UNKNOWN	GRZZZZUSA
BELAU, BERTHA	23	F	UNKNOWN	GRZZZZUSA
RAPP, AUG.	42	M	FARMER	GRZZZZUSA
ROSALIE	44	F	UNKNOWN	GRZZZZUSA
ALB.	15	M	MCHT	GRZZZZUSA
FRANZ	7	M	CHILD	GRZZZZUSA
PAUL	5	M	CHILD	GRZZZZUSA
WALTHER, CHRIST	15	M	BKR	GRZZZZUSA
KOENIG, ROSA	15	F	UNKNOWN	GRZZZZUSA
GRESS, FRANZISKA	27	F	UNKNOWN	GRZZZZUSA
STERZE, MATH.	5	M	CHILD	GRZZZZUSA
LAKORTIN, JOH.	41	M	FARMER	GRZZZZUSA
MARIA	36	F	UNKNOWN	GRZZZZUSA
GRESKOWICZ, ANNA	62	F	UNKNOWN	GRZZZZUSA
SENF, AUGUSTE	18	F	UNKNOWN	GRZZZZUSA
HOHMAYER, MARIE	24	F	UNKNOWN	GRZZZZUSA
BAIER, MATH.	16	M	JNR	GRZZZZUSA
FUCHS, ARNHOLD	17	M	MCHT	GRZZZZUSA
BLESSING, MARGE.	19	F	UNKNOWN	GRZZZZUSA
GERKEN, ANNA	20	F	UNKNOWN	GRZZZZUSA
SCHMIDT, OTTILIE	17	F	UNKNOWN	GRZZZZUSA
ZIGELMANN, CHR.	31	M	BKR	GRZZZZUSA
MOCHEL, MARIE	16	F	UNKNOWN	GRZZZZUSA
STANGENMUELLER, LOUISE	22	F	UNKNOWN	GRZZZZUSA
KOHBRUSS, WILH.	16	M	FARMER	GRZZZZUSA
RAN, FRIEDERIKE	20	F	UNKNOWN	GRZZZZUSA
BRENNER, JOH.	30	M	FARMER	GRZZZZUSA
TEISS, MINA	23	F	UNKNOWN	GRZZZZUSA
WALTMANN, CHR.	58	F	UNKNOWN	GRZZZZUSA
NOLTEMAYER, SOPHIE	16	F	UNKNOWN	GRZZZZUSA
DOBRINER, ADOLF	35	M	TLR	GRZZZZUSA
ZIRKLIN, ADOLF	25	M	BBR	GRZZZZUSA
ERKES, HERM.	22	M	SMH	GRZZZZUSA
RAUH, CONRAD	25	M	UNKNOWN	GRZZZZUSA
BRAND, GERHR.	27	F	UNKNOWN	GRZZZZUSA
PFAFFENZELLER, TH.	24	M	FARMER	GRZZZZUSA
KUPPRINGER, HEINR.	35	M	BCHR	GRZZZZUSA
SCHEUNING, STEPH.	21	M	LABR	GRZZZZUSA
REININGER, NICOL.	21	M	LABR	GRZZZZUSA
HIRSCHMANN, GEORG	47	M	FARMER	GRZZZZUSA
SCHUESSLER, MARIE	17	F	UNKNOWN	GRZZZZUSA
VOGT, KATHA.	28	F	UNKNOWN	GRZZZZUSA
RICH.	7	M	CHILD	GRZZZZUSA
JOH.	3	M	CHILD	GRZZZZUSA
CARL	.01	M	INFANT	GRZZZZUSA
MARKL, ADAM	32	M	LABR	GRZZZZUSA
DESKLE, MARIA	22	F	UNKNOWN	GRZZZZUSA
SCHWARZ, RITTER	40	M	LABR	GRZZZZUSA
MARIA	32	F	UNKNOWN	GRZZZZUSA
JOHS.	7	M	CHILD	GRZZZZUSA
HEINRICH	.10	M	INFANT	GRZZZZUSA
RUENGELKE, HERM.	26	M	FARMER	GRZZZZUSA
MEISLER, JOH.	21	M	FARMER	GRZZZZUSA
PETERSEN, ANNA	25	F	UNKNOWN	GRZZZZUSA
SEELIG, WILH.	18	M	FARMER	GRZZZZUSA
MARKERT, HERM.	24	M	LABR	GRZZZZUSA
HELLMERS, DIEDR.	16	M	CL	GRZZZZUSA
SCHWICHTENBERG, BERTHA	18	F	UNKNOWN	GRZZZZUSA
MOSSMANN, MARIE	21	F	UNKNOWN	GRZZZZUSA
BRANDT, RUD.	25	M	MCHT	GRZZZZUSA
BOEHME, FRIEDR.	17	M	FARMER	GRZZZZUSA
RESCH, BAPTISH	20	M	FARMER	GRZZZZUSA

PASSENGER	AGE	SEX	OCCUPATION	PRV/VIL/DES
FRIEDRICH, MAGDE.	18	F	UNKNOWN	GRZZZZUSA
FRANTZ, CARL	24	M	BBR	GRZZZZUSA
ZIMMERMANN, ERNESTE.	20	F	UNKNOWN	GRZZZZUSA
SUESS, FRIEDR.	45	M	SHMK	GRZZZZUSA
CHRISTE.	43	F	UNKNOWN	GRZZZZUSA
PHILIPPE	21	F	UNKNOWN	GRZZZZUSA
JOH.	19	F	UNKNOWN	GRZZZZUSA
MAGDA.	14	F	UNKNOWN	GRZZZZUSA
FRIEDR.	7	M	CHILD	GRZZZZUSA
ZIMMERMANN, FR.	15	M	CL	GRZZZZUSA
HEILMANN, CATHE.	22	F	UNKNOWN	GRZZZZUSA
PFISTER, VALTIN	15	M	FARMER	GRZZZZUSA
RAEHNER, JOH.	29	M	BCHR	SRZZZZUSA
STAUBACH, WILH.	25	M	MCHT	GRZZZZUSA
BEIN, WILH.	32	M	MCHT	GRZZZZUSA
GRUENEWALD, JAKOB	17	M	UNKNOWN	GRZZZZUSA
WEIGLEIN, JOH.	52	M	LABR	GRZZZZUSA
BABO, JOSEF	27	M	LABR	GRZZZZUSA
SCHULTZ, HR.	40	M	BBR	GRZZZZUSA
LUENEBERG, HERM.	30	M	FARMER	GRZZZZUSA
ALPERSMEIER, HEINR.	69	M	FARMER	GRZZZZUSA
ANTONIE	58	F	UNKNOWN	GRZZZZUSA
ROSENBAUM, HEINR.	25	M	SMH	GRZZZZUSA
GEIER, KARL	16	M	JNR	GRZZZZUSA
DETTMANN, GEORG	36	M	FARMER	GRZZZZUSA
POHLMEYER, WILHE.	44	F	UNKNOWN	GRZZZZUSA
LINA	22	F	UNKNOWN	GRZZZZUSA
WILH.	14	M	CL	GRZZZZUSA
HEINR.	7	M	CHILD	GRZZZZUSA
MATTFELDT, ADELHD.	16	F	UNKNOWN	GRZZZZUSA
MEINKEN, JOHA.	16	F	UNKNOWN	GRZZZZUSA
BOESE, CATHA.	18	F	UNKNOWN	GRZZZZUSA
GEBAUER, JUL.	30	M	FARMER	GRZZZZUSA
MATHE.	29	F	UNKNOWN	GRZZZZUSA
MERZ, WILH.	15	M	SHMK	GRZZZZUSA
KAUPER, JOH.	22	M	FARMER	GRZZZZUSA
SAYER, THERESINA	56	F	UNKNOWN	GRZZZZUSA
DONNER, ELIAS	16	M	FARMER	GRZZZZUSA
SAYER, EGBERT	15	M	FARMER	GRZZZZUSA
RIDHART, CARL	50	M	MCHT	GRZZZZUSA
MARIE	29	F	UNKNOWN	GRZZZZUSA
SACHSENHAEUSER, JOH.	28	M	LABR	GRZZZZUSA
SCHEIBEL, AUG.	28	M	LABR	GRZZZZUSA
BRUNJES, JOHANN	15	M	FARMER	GRZZZZUSA
TIEFJEN, ADELINE	21	F	UNKNOWN	GRZZZZUSA
ROEFER, HINRICH	25	M	SMH	GRZZZZUSA
KOSCHER, FRANZ	18	M	JNR	GRZZZZUSA
KOENIG, JOSEF	19	M	BKR	GRZZZZUSA
NAGY, STEFAN	28	M	LABR	GRZZZZUSA
U	22	F	UNKNOWN	GRZZZZUSA
MERKEL, MARGE.	40	F	UNKNOWN	GRZZZZUSA
GRASHORN, DIEDR.	40	M	FARMER	GRZZZZUSA
PAPST, VALENTY	21	M	FARMER	GRZZZZUSA
FELLER, JULIUS	32	M	FARMER	GRZZZZUSA
BAUMANN, SEBASTIAN	20	M	FARMER	GRZZZZUSA
MANGOLD, WENDELIN	26	M	FARMER	GRZZZZUSA
BARBARA	25	F	UNKNOWN	GRZZZZUSA
WENDELIN	3	M	CHILD	GRZZZZUSA
MARGA.	.11	F	INFANT	GRZZZZUSA
HESS, GEORG	16	M	FARMER	GRZZZZUSA
REDER, JOS.B.	40	M	FARMER	GRZZZZUSA
WILHE.	61	F	UNKNOWN	GRZZZZUSA
WILH.	7	M	CHILD	GRZZZZUSA
FRANK	35	M	FARMER	GRZZZZUSA
JOSEFA	25	F	UNKNOWN	GRZZZZUSA
HELDKAMP, BERNHD.	65	F	UNKNOWN	GRZZZZUSA
HINNERS, HERM.	23	M	FARMER	GRZZZZUSA
RUPPERT, MINA	19	F	UNKNOWN	GRZZZZUSA
BEHLAJEWSKA, FRANZISKA	17	F	UNKNOWN	GRZZZZUSA
WINNIENSKA, JOHA.	6	F	CHILD	GRZZZZUSA
THOMAS, CARL	27	M	FARMER	GRZZZZUSA
COORSEN, JESINE	30	F	UNKNOWN	GRZZZZUSA
LOEWENTHAL, CAROLE.	26	F	UNKNOWN	GRZZZZUSA
STEPIC, MART.	28	M	LABR	GRZZZZUNK
PLLAUM, JOH.	49	M	LABR	GRZZZZUSA
FRIEDKE.	50	F	UNKNOWN	GRZZZZUSA
MAGE.	27	F	UNKNOWN	GRZZZZUSA
SCHOENINGER, PIA	20	F	UNKNOWN	GRZZZZUSA
BUECKEL, HEINR.	29	M	FARMER	GRZZZZUSA
MARIA	26	F	UNKNOWN	GRZZZZUSA
MARIA	2	F	CHILD	GRZZZZUSA
HEIM.	.01	M	INFANT	GRZZZZUSA
SCHUETZ, JOHA.	38	F	UNKNOWN	GRZZZZUSA
HEIM.	7	M	CHILD	GRZZZZUSA
THEOD.	6	M	CHILD	GRZZZZUSA
JOHA.	5	F	CHILD	GRZZZZUSA
MAYER, CAROLA.	22	F	UNKNOWN	GRZZZZUSA
FRIEDR.	17	M	FARMER	GRZZZZUSA
ZIMMERMANN, HEINR.	25	M	JNR	GRZZZZUSA
KUHSIECK, SIMONDE	6	F	CHILD	GRZZZZUSA
STEINBACH, JACOB	32	M	MCHT	GRZZZZUSA
REISENAUER, ALFRED	29	M	MCHT	GRZZZZUSA
NIGGEL, MAX	14	M	CL	GRZZZZUSA
SCHUSTER, BABETTE	12	F	UNKNOWN	GRZZZZUSA
GAWRONSKA, KATARGYNA	16	F	UNKNOWN	GRZZZZUSA
GUENTHER, PAULE.	29	F	UNKNOWN	GRZZZZUSA
ALBRTS, CATHA.	38	F	UNKNOWN	GRZZZZUSA
LANGFERMANN, JOSEFE.	20	F	UNKNOWN	GRZZZZUSA
MARIE	15	F	UNKNOWN	GRZZZZUSA
WENDT, CARL	24	M	FARMER	GRZZZZUSA
STEIN, AUG.CARL	26	M	MCHT	GRZZZZUSA
BENNIGAERTHER, CATHARIN	26	F	UNKNOWN	GRZZZZUSA

SHIP: ELBE

FROM: BREMEN AND SOUTHAMPTON
TO: NEW YORK
ARRIVED: 21 NOVEMBER 1888

PASSENGER	AGE	SEX	OCCUPATION	PRV/VIL/DES
BUSCH, ANTON	29	M	TT	GRAAXFNY
SCHULDER, HUGO	31	M	TT	GRZZZZNY
FORTMANN, FRITZ	60	M	TT	GRAARTNY
GIESE, CARLES	31	M	TT	GRAARTNY
LIEBHARDT, JUL.	26	M	TT	GRAAHLNY
BUHMANN, GEORG	25	M	TT	GRADLDNY
MARX, LUD.	30	M	TT	GRZZZZNY
WOLLUHN, EUG.	29	M	TT	GRAAKHNY
MARK, MARIE	26	F	TT	GRAAIENY
JANSEN, BERUH	34	M	TT	GRZZZZNY
SCHLUTOW, HEINR.	62	M	TT	GRAARRNY
KNOOP, ALMER	30	M	TT	GRZZZZNY
SCHWIERSKI, FRITZ	40	M	LABR	GRAAPJNY
SCHRIFFER, PETER	23	M	LABR	GRZZZZNY
MARIE	20	F	UNKNOWN	GRZZZZNY
HERMANUTZ, FRIEDR.	18	M	LABR	GRADELNY
LOEWENSTEIN, HENRIETTE	19	F	SVNT	GRABTUNY
MARKEDT, MARIA	22	F	SVNT	GRZZZZNY
ADAM	16	M	LABR	GRZZZZNY
MORITZ, CHRIST.	16	M	LABR	GRZZZZNY
STENSEL, ALWINA	21	F	UNKNOWN	GRZZZZNY
AUGUSTE	19	F	SVNT	GRZZZZNY
IDA	2	F	CHILD	GRZZZZNY
SCHMERCKER, GEORGE	26	M	FARMER	GRAARRNY
HINZE, BERNH.	25	M	SEMN	GRZZZZNY
GAUKOWSKY, SUSANNA	29	F	UNKNOWN	GRZZZZNY
STEFAN	.06	F	INFANT	GRZZZZNY
ANNA	3	F	CHILD	GRZZZZNY
ANDERSKOWSKY, AUG.	55	F	UNKNOWN	GRAASSNY
DRZEWRECKI, SOPHIE	23	F	UNKNOWN	GRAASSNY
MART.	.01	M	INFANT	GRAASSNY
KEDROWSKY, ANNA	28	F	SVNT	GRZZZZNY
ROSALIE	24	F	SVNT	GRZZZZNY
STEINKE, FRIED.	60	F	W	GRAEABNY
HEIDER, HEINR.	26	M	LABR	GRAAZWNY
KREIE, ETTIE	19	F	SVNT	GRACBRNY

PASSENGER	AGE	SEX	OCCUPATION	PRVVL	DES
HAUSNER, MARG.	25	F	SVNT	GRZZZZNY	
ROTH, ALBERT	14	M	LABR	GRZZZZNY	
BOSSONG, CATH.	21	F	SVNT	GRZZZZNY	
AUSPACH, FRIED.	25	F	SVNT	GRABOQNY	
BERNH.	17	M	LABR	GRABOQNY	
KREISELMEYER, B.	18	M	FARMER	GRZZZZNY	
MERZ, CARL	26	M	FARMER	GRAJYQNY	
SCHUHNERICK, PETER	16	M	FARMER	GRZZZZNY	
FRENZEL, THERESE	18	F	SVNT	GRZZZZNY	
HECKELER, WILH.	22	M	DLR	GRACGKNY	
DIETRICK, LUD.	57	M	FARMER	GRZZZZNY	
MARG.	43	F	UNKNOWN	GRZZZZNY	
LUD.	12	M	CH	GRZZZZNY	
VOGELFAENGER, MAGD.	26	F	WO	GRZZZZNY	
SCHEIB, ANNIE	15	F	WO	GRABHTNY	
WALKOWIAK, WERONIKA	30	F	W	GRZZZZNY	
MAGD.	5	F	CHILD	GRZZZZNY	
LEHRMANN, HANS	9	M	CHILD	GRACZWNY	
BACHMANN, MAX	28	M	JNR	GRACZWNY	
ROCKSTROH, LINE	21	F	SVNT	GRABDMNY	
HUMERT, MARG.	56	F	W	GRABQZNY	
MARG.	2	F	CHILD	GRABQZNY	
HAVCK, GEORG	60	M	FARMER	GRADLDNY	
KOIL, FRIED.	20	M	JNR	GRADLDUNK	
HILGARD, KATH.	48	F	W	GRADLDWI	
ANNA	25	F	SVNT	GRADLDWI	
SCHAEFER, CHR.	39	M	GDNR	GRZZZZOH	
KUHL, WILH.	23	M	SHMK	GRZZZZOH	
LENZ, HEIN.	20	M	FARMER	GRZZZZOH	
LEHRMANN, GUST.	41	M	TCHR	GRACZWOH	
SCHUELZE, GEORG	15	M	LABR	GRZZZZMO	
WEGWERTH, BERTHA	20	F	SVNT	GRZZZZMN	
FREITAG, EMMA	15	F	SVNT	GRZZZZMN	
DOLL, KATH.	18	F	SVNT	GRAINHCAL	
TILLACK, JOH.	38	F	W	GRZZZZCAL	
BOTTJER, HERM.	55	M	FARMER	GRAJMRCAL	
ENGLERTH, JOS.	34	M	FARMER	GRADOINY	
MARG.	30	F	FARMER	GRADOINY	
OTTE, JOSEPH	10	M	CH	GRADOINY	
EVA	5	F	CHILD	GRADOINY	
MICH.	4	M	CHILD	GRADOINY	
FRANZ	.09	M	INFANT	GRADOINY	
SCHWARZ, ERNST	15	M	LABR	GRAAKHNY	
STEIN, WILH.	16	M	LABR	GRAARRNY	
SCHNEIDER, BETTY	21	F	SVNT	GRAARRNY	
SCHULZ, WILH.	48	M	BKR	GRAARRNY	
GRZEBYTA, FAUSTINA	51	F	W	GRAAZQOH	
FRANZ	25	M	LABR	GRAAZQOH	
LORENZ	18	M	SVNT	GRAAZQOH	
MARTHA	11	F	UNKNOWN	GRAAZQOH	
MARIA	9	F	CHILD	GRAAZQOH	
STEPHAN	7	M	CHILD	GRAAZQOH	
BUSKA, LORENZ	30	M	LABR	GRZZZZOH	
KERN, JACOB	16	M	LABR	GRZZZZOH	
MEYER, EDUARD	25	M	LABR	GRACBROH	
ANNA	23	F	W	GRACBROH	
ERNST	3	M	CHILD	GRACBROH	
SOPHIE	.09	F	INFANT	GRACBROH	
RINGELHARDT, ROB.	30	M	MLR	GRABDMOH	
ZERREMER, BERTHA	27	F	SVNT	GRZZZZWI	
RUPPERT, AUGUST	24	M	LABR	GRZZZZNY	
WEINBERG, MICH.	23	M	LABR	GRZZZZNY	
LANG, ALB.	36	M	LABR	GRADLDUT	
RODICK, AREND	25	M	MCHT	GRZZZZTX	
ZEHUBER, BARB.	40	F	W	GRZZZZTX	
MICH.	12	M	UNKNOWN	GRZZZZTX	
MARIE	8	F	CHILD	GRZZZZTX	
ADAM	3	M	CHILD	GRZZZZTX	
CHRIST.	2	M	CHILD	GRZZZZTX	
GEORG	.09	M	INFANT	GRZZZZTX	
VOGEL, GEORG	33	M	BKR	GRAJXSTX	
MARG.	28	F	UNKNOWN	GRAJXSTX	
SCHALLER, GRETHA	11	F	UNKNOWN	GRAJXSTX	
BOETJER, TRINA	19	F	SVNT	GRZZZZTX	
WIECKHORST, CAECILIE	18	M	SVNT	GRZZZZUNK	

PASSENGER	AGE	SEX	OCCUPATION	PRVVL	DES
SEIDEL, MARIA	25	F	W		GRAFFQNY
SCHULTE, ULRICH	32	M	LABR		GRZZZZNY
ROTH, GEORG	58	M	LABR		GRZZZZNY
WALTHER, GOTTL.	28	M	LABR		GRADCLNY
HERTKERN, AUG.	39	M	FARMER		GRABUSPHI
JOSEPHINE	34	F	W		GRABUSPHI
JULIUS	10	M	CH		GRABUSPHI
FRIEDA	8	F	CHILD		GRABUSPHI
WEBER, ADAM	27	M	FARMER		GRZZZZNY
LEVI, EMANUEL	22	M	FARMER		GRABOQNY
SCHMIDT, FRAN.	9	M	CHILD		GRZZZZNY
JOH.	43	M	LKSH		GRZZZZNY
HUEBNER, CHRIST.	44	M	FARMER		GRZZZZNY
ANTONOWICZ, WIN.	27	M	LABR		GRAARRNY
ELISAB.	25	F	UNKNOWN		GRAARRNY
NAUJOKS, ANTON	28	M	LABR		GRAARRNY
ROEBER, BERNNH.	20	M	LABR		GRAARRNY
KECH, WILH.	32	M	LABR		GRAARRNY
FREIBERGER, BERTHALAN	40	M	LABR		GRAARRNY
DORA	16	F	SVNT		GRAARRNY
EVERS, HENRY	36	M	LABR		GRAARRNY

SHIP: SLAVONIA

FROM: STETTIN
TO: NEW YORK
ARRIVED: 21 NOVEMBER 1888

PASSENGER	AGE	SEX	OCCUPATION	PRVVL	DES
SZUSTER, JOSEPH	31	M	LABR		PRZZZZUSA
ANNA	23	F	W		PRZZZZUSA
MARIE	2	F	CHILD		PRZZZZUSA
ANTONIE	1	F	CHILD		PRZZZZUSA
JOHANN	.03	M	INFANT		PRZZZZUSA
BARWITZKY, JOHANN	36	M	LABR		PRZZZZUSA
MARIANNA	30	F	W		PRZZZZUSA
WLADISLAUS	3	M	CHILD		PRZZZZUSA
MARTHA	2	F	CHILD		PRZZZZUSA
DOSS, HENRIETTE	17	F	SVNT		MKZZZZUSA
CARL	15	M	B		MKZZZZUSA
SCHMIDT, CARL	35	M	LABR		PRZZZZUSA
MATHILDE	34	F	W		PRZZZZUSA
LOUISE	11	F	CH		PRZZZZUSA
AUGUSTE	8	F	CHILD		PRZZZZUSA
ANNA	2	F	CHILD		PRZZZZUSA
GEHL, JOACHIM	42	M	LABR		PRZZZZUSA
MARIA	36	F	W		PRZZZZUSA
ROBERT	11	M	CH		PRZZZZUSA
FRIEDRICH	10	M	CH		PRZZZZUSA
FRIEDERIKE	10	F	CH		PRZZZZUSA
EMMA	9	F	CHILD		PRZZZZUSA
AUGUSTE	8	F	CHILD		PRZZZZUSA
ANNA	5	F	CHILD		PRZZZZUSA
LINA	2	F	CHILD		PRZZZZUSA
MUELLER, AUGUST	66	M	LABR		PRZZZZUSA
LEOPOLD	6	M	CHILD		PRZZZZUSA
LEOPOLD	6	M	CHILD		PRZZZZUSA
BLOEDAN, CAROLINE	46	F	WO		PRZZZZUSA
EMMA	15	F	CH		PRZZZZUSA
DANIEL	13	M	CH		PRZZZZUSA
ADOLPH	11	M	CH		PRZZZZUSA
EDUARD	.06	M	INFANT		PRZZZZUSA
WACHOWIAK, MARIANNA	18	F	UNKNOWN		PRAFTUUSA
FENGLER, FRIEDRICH	71	M	CTW		PRABWAUSA
BOEHL, JOHANN	12	M	CH		PRABWAUSA
ANNA	11	F	CH		PRABWAUSA
EHRENFRIED	9	M	CHILD		PRABWAUSA
NORMANN, AUGUSTE	18	F	SVNT		PRZZZZUSA
PLEHWE, OTTO	25	M	MLR		PRZZZZUSA
BOEHL, JOHANN	45	M	LABR		PRABWAUSA
CARL	18	M	CH		PRABWAUSA

440

PASSENGER	AGE	SEX	OCCUPATION	PRVL	DES
CAROLINE	15	F	CH	PRABWAUSA	
SCHULDT, AUGUSTE	17	F	UNKNOWN	PRABWAUSA	
ZUSKE, CAROLINE	51	F	WO	PRABYHUSA	
ALBRT	13	M	CH	PRABYHUSA	
EMILIE	9	F	CHILD	PRABYHUSA	
SOKOLSKA, MARIANNA	38	F	WO	PRZZZZUSA	
VERONIKA	17	F	CH	PRZZZZUSA	
NASTKA	15	F	CH	PRZZZZUSA	
JOSEFA	11	F	CH	PRZZZZUSA	
LEON	7	M	CHILD	PRZZZZUSA	
MAXIMA	3	F	CHILD	PRZZZZUSA	
SCHULZ, OTTO	32	M	WDCTR	PRZZZZUSA	
CHARLOTTE	30	F	W	PRZZZZUSA	
ROMAN	7	M	CHILD	PRZZZZUSA	
CARL	5	M	CHILD	PRZZZZUSA	
ADOLPH	3	M	CHILD	PRZZZZUSA	
META	.06	F	INFANT	PRZZZZUSA	
HERMANN, BERTHA	18	F	UNKNOWN	PRZZZZUSA	
ZCIENICWICZ, ANNA	14	F	SVNT	PRZZZZUSA	
HAGEMEISTER, FRIEDERIKE	22	F	UNKNOWN	PRAFUIUSA	
HERTOG, PAULINE	40	F	WO	PRZZZZUSA	
EMMA	10	F	CH	PRZZZZUSA	
HERMANN	3	M	CHILD	PRZZZZUSA	
WOICZESCHOWSKY, JOHANN	28	M	BLKSMH	PRZZZZUSA	
CAECILIE	23	F	W	PRZZZZUSA	
SOPHIE	.10	F	INFANT	PRZZZZUSA	
DRECHSLER, WILHELMINE	40	F	WO	PRAFZIUSA	
ELISABETH	9	F	CHILD	PRAFZIUSA	
LEMKE, MARIE	2	F	CHILD	PRAFZIUSA	
POMMERENIG, LUDWIG	24	M	LABR	PRZZZZUSA	
PROCH, FRANZ	21	M	LABR	PRZZZZUSA	
DZUBINSKA, AGNISKA	23	F	UNKNOWN	PRZZZZUSA	
AGNISKA	23	F	UNKNOWN	PRZZZZUSA	
SEIDLITZ, LOUISE	20	F	UNKNOWN	PRZZZZUSA	
KAMIN, CARTIN	24	M	BLKSMH	PRAFBUUSA	
GOERTZ, MARIE	16	F	UNKNOWN	PRAFTUUSA	
HERZ, BERTHA	19	F	UNKNOWN	PRACWIUSA	
BLOEDAU, CARL	55	M	LABR	PRZZZZUSA	
GOTTSCHALK, JOHANN	37	M	LABR	PRADNEUSA	
AUGUSTE	33	F	W	PRADNEUSA	
ZICHM, GUSTAV	15	M	CH	PRADNEUSA	
GOTTSCHALK, ANNA	6	F	CHILD	PRADNEUSA	
ALBERT	4	M	CHILD	PRADNEUSA	
NOEFFKE, BERNHARD	25	M	BCHR	PRZZZZUSA	
MUELLER, JULIUS	23	M	LABR	PRABRQUSA	
MEYER, EMILIE	16	F	UNKNOWN	PRZZZZUSA	
JAGUSCH, MICHAEL	41	M	LABR	PRAGEWUSA	
CAROLINE	38	F	W	PRAGEWUSA	
WILHELMINE	15	F	CH	PRAGEWUSA	
FRIEDRICH	8	M	CHILD	PRAGEWUSA	
HERMANN	.11	M	INFANT	PRAGEWUSA	
WINCKLER, EMILIE	48	F	WO	PRAEABUSA	
MARTHA	23	F	D	PRAEABUSA	
JAGUSCH, SAMUEL	28	M	LABR	PRZZZZUSA	
WILHELMINE	26	F	W	PRZZZZUSA	
BERTHA	1	F	CHILD	PRZZZZUSA	
ANNA	.05	F	INFANT	PRZZZZUSA	
FISCHER, JOHANN	66	M	LABR	PRZZZZUSA	
CAROLINE	69	F	W	PRZZZZUSA	
MARIE	28	F	CH	PRZZZZUSA	
JOHANN	8	M	CHILD	PRZZZZUSA	
BIENNECK, MICHAEL	31	M	LABR	PRZZZZUSA	
WILHELMINE	28	F	W	PRZZZZUSA	
AUGUST	3	M	CHILD	PRZZZZUSA	
HERMANN	2	M	CHILD	PRZZZZUSA	
EMMA	.08	F	INFANT	PRZZZZUSA	
STRANKOWSKA, ANNA	36	F	WO	PRZZZZUSA	
ANNA	9	F	CHILD	PRZZZZUSA	
PHILIPPSKY, JOHANNA	32	F	WO	PRZZZZUSA	
KLATT, OTTO	11	M	CH	PRZZZZUSA	
PHILIPPSKY, MARTHA	9	F	CHILD	PRZZZZUSA	
ELISABETH	9	F	CHILD	PRZZZZUSA	
ROSALIE	7	F	CHILD	PRZZZZUSA	
AMANDA	.11	F	INFANT	PRZZZZUSA	
REIMANN, CLEMENTINE	20	F	UNKNOWN	PRZZZZUSA	
ZAHN, FRIEDRICH	25	M	TLR	PRZZZZUSA	
SCHWARZ, MARIA	20	F	SMSTS	PRZZZZUSA	
DAEHN, THEODOR	28	M	PT	PRAAKHUSA	
OTTILIE	32	F	W	PRAAKHUSA	
KAETHE	2	F	CHILD	PRAAKHUSA	
DREWS, OTTO	7	M	CHILD	PRAAKHUSA	
HANDSCHU, MARIE	38	F	UNKNOWN	PRZZZZUSA	
DREWS, AMALIE	17	F	UNKNOWN	PRZZZZUSA	
OTTILIE	20	F	UNKNOWN	PRZZZZUSA	
MUSOLL, EMILIE	18	F	CK	PRZZZZUSA	
WULFF, OTTO	26	M	SHMK	PRZZZZUSA	
MARIA	25	F	W	PRZZZZUSA	
HASS, JULIUS	54	M	LABR	PRZZZZUSA	
ELEONORE	54	F	W	PRZZZZUSA	
LAURA	11	F	CH	PRZZZZUSA	
OTTO	9	M	CHILD	PRZZZZUSA	
SIEBAU, JOHANN	18	M	LKSH	PRAAZQUSA	
FUSCHS, RICHARD	17	M	GSMH	PRAEWZUSA	
MARGUART, BERTHA	15	F	SVNT	PRZZZZUSA	
DREWS, WILHELMINE	49	F	WO	PRZZZZUSA	
ZIMMERMANN, RICHARD	29	M	CL	PRAEVMUSA	
LABRENZ, CAROLINE	50	F	WO	PRZZZZUSA	
WADARSZAK, VALENTIN	36	M	LABR	PRACSDUSA	
WENER, ALFRED	26	M	CL	PRZZZZUSA	
KUNZ, MICHALINA	50	F	WO	PRAEABUSA	
KUHRT, WILHELM	16	M	TLR	PRAEWMUSA	
DREWS, WILHELM	27	M	FARMER	PRABWAUSA	
SEIDLITZ, AUGUSTE	19	F	SVNT	PRZZZZUSA	
BARWITZKY, SOPHIE	.06	F	INFANT	PRZZZZUSA	
NEUMANN, FRANZ	25	M	FARMER	PRZZZZUSA	
EHLERT, HEINRICH	19	M	CL	PRACSDUSA	
SEIDEL, JOSEPH	23	M	BKR	PRAAKHUSA	
WALTERSDORF, MINNA	39	F	WO	PRAEZVUSA	
WERNICKE, CARL	35	M	CTL	PRAAKHUSA	
GARBRECHT, GUSTAV	23	M	FARMER	PRZZZZUSA	
JANUSCHEWSKY, JAN	32	M	JNR	PRZZZZUSA	
KUHRT, RUDOLPH	30	M	CL	PRAEWMUSA	
DENZ, LOUISE	38	F	WO	PRZZZZUSA	
JOHANN	14	M	CH	PRZZZZUSA	
MARIE	11	F	CH	PRZZZZUSA	
MARTHA	10	F	CH	PRZZZZUSA	
ROSALIE	7	F	CHILD	PRZZZZUSA	
JOSEPH	4	M	CHILD	PRZZZZUSA	
AGATHE	2	F	CHILD	PRZZZZUSA	
ANNA	.04	F	INFANT	PRZZZZUSA	
SELKE, HERMANN	54	M	LABR	PRACWIUSA	
CAROLINE	54	F	W	PRACWIUSA	
JOHANNA	23	F	CH	PRACWIUSA	
EMILIE	18	F	CH	PRACWIUSA	
ANNA	.09	F	INFANT	PRACWIUSA	
RABESKE, ANNA	24	F	SVNT	PRZZZZUSA	
MATHILDE	23	F	SVNT	PRZZZZUSA	
ROSA	21	F	SVNT	PRZZZZUSA	
KAMISCHKE, REINHOLD	19	M	LABR	PRAJSQUSA	
MINNA	16	F	S	PRAJSQUSA	
SETTEKOMM, MAX	26	M	TCHR	PRAEWMUSA	
BARTELT, JOHANN	43	M	LABR	PRZZZZUSA	

SHIP: WESTERNLAND

FROM: ANTWERP
TO: NEW YORK
ARRIVED: 22 NOVEMBER 1888

PASSENGER	AGE	SEX	OCCUPATION	PRVL	DES
SCHONLAUB, MARIA	53	F	UNKNOWN	GRZZZZNY	
KONDRA, WILH.	19	M	TLR	GRZZZZNY	
NELLER, LUDWIG	18	M	FARMER	GRZZZZNY	
ENGEL, HENRICH	17	M	LABR	GRZZZZNY	
SCHMIDT, SUSANNA	26	F	UNKNOWN	GRZZZZNY	
HANDEGARD, GERARD	27	M	FARMER	GRZZZZUNK	

PASSENGER	AGE	SEX	OCCUPATION	PRVL	DES
LETZER, PHILLIPE	58	F	UNKNOWN	GRZZZZUNK	
BABETTE	30	F	UNKNOWN	GRZZZZUNK	
RIES, JOB	16	M	CL	GRZZZZPA	
HELMBRACHT, JOB	29	M	FARMER	GRZZZZAPP	
SCHMIDT, CATHE.	20	F	UNKNOWN	GRZZZZUSA	
HEINES, FRED	63	M	FARMER	GRZZZZUNK	
PELSTER, HERMAN	31	M	CL	GRZZZZUNK	
MARKEN, GEORG	18	M	BBR	GRZZZZPHI	
BECKER, CATHE.	65	F	UNKNOWN	GRZZZZUNK	
HCH.	34	M	FARMER	GRZZZZUNK	
DIENDONE, MARIE	19	F	UNKNOWN	GRZZZZROC	
WELTER, BERNARD	20	M	FARMER	GRZZZZDET	
FRANTZEN, ELOIE	25	F	UNKNOWN	GRZZZZCH	
MOSS, MAGGIE	20	F	UNKNOWN	GRZZZZSP	
LESHLER, CAROLINE	22	F	UNKNOWN	GRZZZZNY	
FEY, JOSEF	66	M	FARMER	GRZZZZNY	
CAROLINE	17	F	UNKNOWN	GRZZZZNY	
FLACK, CHRISTINE	22	F	UNKNOWN	GRZZZZLAN	
SCHELLHAMMER, ANNA	15	F	UNKNOWN	GRZZZZUNK	
LACHMANN, MECHILDA	17	F	UNKNOWN	GRZZZZBO	
BERGER, GOTTFR.	18	M	FARMER	GRZZZZNY	
SPESK, BARBA.	49	F	UNKNOWN	GRZZZZPHI	
B--CH, LOUISE	32	F	UNKNOWN	GRZZZZPHI	
WILLIE	8	M	CHILD	GRZZZZPHI	
MUHLBANER, SYLVESTER	17	M	FARMER	GRZZZZBUF	
SCHARF, MARGA.	26	F	UNKNOWN	GRZZZZNY	
GROTZ, CHRISTIAN	17	M	LABR	GRZZZZNY	
GWISSLER, VALENT	38	M	MACH	GRZZZZNY	
WAGER, CASPAR	26	M	FARMER	GRZZZZNY	
KOCH, THER.	20	F	UNKNOWN	GRZZZZNY	
BOECKER, CATH.	16	F	UNKNOWN	GRZZZZNY	
GUTTLER, CARL	39	M	FARMER	GRZZZZNY	
MAGTT.	36	F	UNKNOWN	GRZZZZNY	
MARIA	6	F	CHILD	GRZZZZNY	
HEFF, ELIZTH.	39	F	UNKNOWN	GRZZZZNY	
ANT.	13	M	CH	GRZZZZNY	
HCH.	6	M	CHILD	GRZZZZNY	
GROSS, MARIE	21	F	UNKNOWN	GRZZZZNY	
WASST, OTTO	20	M	FARMER	GRZZZZNY	
GERLACH, CAROLINE	41	F	UNKNOWN	GRZZZZNY	
CATH.	12	F	CH	GRZZZZNY	
WILH.	10	M	CH	GRZZZZNY	
PLASSER, EMMA	24	F	UNKNOWN	GRZZZZNY	
GEIER, ALOIS	23	M	CL	GRZZZZNY	
KRACKEL, FRIED.	23	M	FARMER	GRZZZZNY	
DIESEL, FRIED.	44	M	FARMER	GRZZZZNY	
KRASKEL, CARLE.	65	M	UNKNOWN	GRZZZZNY	
CAROLINE	18	F	UNKNOWN	GRZZZZNY	
BLUMENSTELLER, PAULINE	37	F	UNKNOWN	GRZZZZNY	
STEFANIE	15	F	UNKNOWN	GRZZZZNY	
HERMIN	11	M	CH	GRZZZZNY	
MARIE	8	F	CHILD	GRZZZZNY	
HAID, ANNA	16	F	UNKNOWN	GRZZZZNY	
CHOUNER, ERNEST	31	M	FARMER	GRZZZZNY	
SHANT, MARG.	28	F	UNKNOWN	GRZZZZNY	
REISS, JOB.	18	M	FARMER	GRZZZZNY	
LICHTER, NICL.	86	M	FARMER	GRZZZZNY	
A.	16	M	FARMER	GRZZZZNY	
ESIG, JOSEFINE	28	F	UNKNOWN	GRZZZZNY	
CHRISTE.	23	F	UNKNOWN	GRZZZZNY	
DEG, FRIED	14	M	LABR	GRZZZZNY	
WEING, ROSINE	23	F	UNKNOWN	GRZZZZNY	
LACKLER, MARIE	16	F	UNKNOWN	GRZZZZNY	
REBENACK, JACOB	17	M	FARMER	GRZZZZNY	
REIFFEL, WILL	24	M	FARMER	GRZZZZNY	
MEYER, COUR	17	M	SMH	GRZZZZNY	
HASSENT, CHRIST.	52	M	MACH	GRZZZZNY	
PWANDS, WALTER	32	M	SMH	GRZZZZNY	
MESZ, M.	35	F	UNKNOWN	GRZZZZNY	
HELMBRECHT, ANNA	24	F	UNKNOWN	GRZZZZNY	
LAITH, WOLFGANG	23	M	FARMER	GRZZZZNY	
SCHWAB, FRIEDRH.	15	M	UNKNOWN	GRZZZZNY	
GOUILLART, HENRY	26	M	FARMER	GRZZZZNY	
GUSTAV	20	M	LABR	GRZZZZNY	
MULLER, FRITZ	23	M	LABR	GRZZZZNY	
MAX	18	M	LABR	GRZZZZNY	
MEYER, HUGO	19	M	FARMER	GRZZZZLIT	
TOLLER, FRANCIS	30	M	FARMER	GRZZZZNY	
OS, VALENTIN	38	M	FARMER	GRZZZZNY	
GRUMWALD, JULIUS	25	M	FARMER	GRZZZZNY	
AUGUISTE	23	F	FARMER	GRZZZZNY	
GEHRING, JOHANN	22	M	SDLR	GRZZZZCH	
SUSHOMSKE, STANISL.	25	M	FARMER	GRZZZZBUF	
ANNA	24	F	UNKNOWN	GRZZZZBUF	
KARMINESZ	1	M	CHILD	GRZZZZBUF	
SNIZERA, JOHANN	57	M	FARMER	GRZZZZBUF	
BARBARA	20	F	UNKNOWN	GRZZZZBUF	
BECKER, CHARLOTTE	23	F	UNKNOWN	GRZZZZNY	
WELKER, GEORG	31	M	CL	GRZZZZNY	
SEWRYNK, C.	20	M	FARMER	GRZZZZDET	
WEINBERG, ISAAC	38	M	TLR	GRZZZZNY	
FEDERGRUN, ABRAH.	20	M	FARMER	GRZZZZNY	
VEITH, ALBERT	11	M	CH	GRZZZZNY	
KELLER, PHILIP	22	M	LABR	GRZZZZCO	
THEODOR, M.	15	M	LABR	GRZZZZCH	
OCHS, LEOPOLD	17	M	LABR	GRZZZZNY	
GASSMANN, WM.	25	M	LABR	GRZZZZNY	
DURR, JOHANN	21	M	LABR	GRZZZZNY	
SUMMER, CATH.	20	F	UNKNOWN	GRZZZZNY	
OFFENBAUER, BERNHARD	17	M	FARMER	GRZZZZNY	
BAMMBUSCH, MARIE	26	F	UNKNOWN	GRZZZZNY	
GUNTLIER, MARG.	36	F	UNKNOWN	GRZZZZNY	
SCHMIDT, MATHIAS	36	M	FARMER	GRZZZZNY	
JEAN	10	M	CH	GRZZZZNY	
JEANE	8	F	CHILD	GRZZZZNY	
NICHOLAS	7	M	CHILD	GRZZZZNY	
MATH.	5	M	CHILD	GRZZZZNY	
ANNA	4	F	CHILD	GRZZZZNY	
ADOLF	3	M	CHILD	GRZZZZNY	
WESTER, PETER	18	M	SMH	GRZZZZNY	
CASEL, BERNARD	21	M	LABR	GRZZZZNY	
GOMERING, JEAN	20	M	FARMER	GRZZZZNY	
BISERIUS, WILH.	29	M	FARMER	GRZZZZNY	
LANTZERT, F.	22	M	FARMER	GRZZZZNY	
SCHMITZ, ANTON	25	M	FARMER	GRZZZZNY	
WIES, MICHEL	21	M	CPTR	GRZZZZNY	
KRUMER, JOHN	27	M	JNR	GRZZZZNY	
WERLAND, MARIE	41	F	UNKNOWN	GRZZZZCH	
MATH.	41	M	FARMER	GRZZZZCH	
CATH.	18	F	UNKNOWN	GRZZZZCH	
MATH.	11	M	CH	GRZZZZCH	
NIC.	7	M	CHILD	GRZZZZCH	
BERCHAM, MARIE	38	F	UNKNOWN	GRZZZZSP	
MATHIAS	9	M	CHILD	GRZZZZSP	
ADELE	5	F	CHILD	GRZZZZSP	
ANNA	4	F	CHILD	GRZZZZSP	
JEAN	2	M	CHILD	GRZZZZSP	
WILHELM, LOUISE	21	F	UNKNOWN	GRZZZZNY	
SEIDEL, WILH.	22	M	FARMER	GRZZZZNY	
PAULI, CARL	23	M	FARMER	GRZZZZNY	
SICHNER, MARG.	19	F	UNKNOWN	GRZZZZNY	
HEFFRICH, MARIE	18	F	UNKNOWN	GRZZZZNY	
KNUTH, LOUISE	24	F	UNKNOWN	GRZZZZNY	
WELH, PETER	22	M	FARMER	GRZZZZNY	
FRITTEN, CATH.	33	F	UNKNOWN	SRZZZZNY	
CATH.	8	M	CHILD	SRZZZZNY	
HERNING, JULIUS	22	M	CPTR	SRZZZZNY	
REITER, CAROLINA	76	F	UNKNOWN	SRZZZZNY	
SCHAEFER, RUDOLF	19	M	LABR	SRZZZZNY	
BAER, EUGENIA	34	F	UNKNOWN	SRZZZZNY	
GILLYUSS, JOH.	22	M	FARMER	SRZZZZNY	
RUPP, ANTON	28	M	FARMER	SRZZZZNY	
ZIMMERLI, HERM.	35	M	FARMER	SRZZZZNY	
BRUMER, UBRICH	26	M	FARMER	SRZZZZNY	
WACKER, MARIA	22	F	UNKNOWN	SRZZZZNY	
HEUMAGIN, JOSEF	22	M	FARMER	GRZZZZGBY	
JOHOWTZKI, FRIED	20	M	FARMER	GRZZZZNY	
SPALENTA, JOHANNA	22	F	UNKNOWN	GRZZZZNY	
MARIA	1	F	CHILD	GRZZZZNY	
SELESTA, MATH.	26	M	LABR	GRZZZZNY	

PASSENGER	AGE	SEX	OCCUPATION	PRVVL DES	PASSENGER	AGE	SEX	OCCUPATION	PRVVL DES
RUBA, ANNA	16	F	UNKNOWN	GRZZZZNY	LARSIZ, JOSEF	27	M	LABR	GRZZZZNY
ANNA	16	F	UNKNOWN	GRZZZZNY	THURANSS, ANNA	60	F	UNKNOWN	GRZZZZDET
WUGTSCH, WILHELM	20	F	UNKNOWN	GRZZZZNY	CLARA	22	F	UNKNOWN	GRZZZZDET
RAMPKAR, WILHELME	27	F	UNKNOWN	GRZZZZNY	GUTHORSLIN, JACOB	18	M	MSN	GRZZZZPIT
MARIE	53	F	UNKNOWN	GRZZZZNY	HORNBERGER, AUG.	16	M	LABR	GRZZZZSPR
VALENTIN	16	M	LABR	GRZZZZNY	HELFER, JACOB	22	M	FARMER	GRZZZZNY
CARL	13	M	CH	GRZZZZNY	SCHILLS, MAGDE.	31	F	UNKNOWN	GRZZZZNY
BERNAR	2	M	CHILD	GRZZZZNY	EWALD	9	M	CHILD	GRZZZZNY
THUMPF, LINA	15	F	UNKNOWN	GRZZZZNY	MARTIN	6	M	CHILD	GRZZZZNY
GROSS, VALENTINE	20	M	FARMER	GRZZZZNY	GEORG	3	M	CHILD	GRZZZZNY
BICHOLZ, BERNHARD	30	M	UNKNOWN	GRZZZZNY	MULLER, LOUIS	15	M	LABR	GRZZZZNY
GERMAN, FANNY	20	F	UNKNOWN	GRZZZZNY	KUHNE, OTTO	23	M	CL	GRZZZZUNK
VOIGHT, KEUGEL	23	M	LABR	GRZZZZNY	WETUSHING, BEROS	30	M	FARMER	GRZZZZUNK
KRAUSS, CHRISTIAN	36	M	LABR	GRZZZZNY	BOL, U	23	F	UNKNOWN	GRZZZZCIN
ERNST, LOUISE	29	F	UNKNOWN	GRZZZZNY	ESCHBACHER, LINA	22	F	UNKNOWN	GRZZZZUNK
DIETZ, JACOB	14	M	UNKNOWN	GRZZZZNY	MARZURKOWSKY, MARGA	35	F	UNKNOWN	GRZZZZNY
FRAND, FRIED	15	M	UNKNOWN	GRZZZZNY	ELISA	16	F	UNKNOWN	GRZZZZNY
TURNER, CHRISTINE	18	F	UNKNOWN	GRZZZZNY	MARG.	10	F	CH	GRZZZZNY
REB, WILHELM	19	F	UNKNOWN	GRZZZZNY	GEORG	5	M	CHILD	GRZZZZNY
RAMKER, MARIA	1	F	CHILD	GRZZZZNY	HASEL, ADELE	31	F	UNKNOWN	GRZZZZASH
RAUPP, CAROLINE	19	F	UNKNOWN	GRZZZZNY	JOSEF	7	M	CHILD	GRZZZZASH
LINDNER, JOSEF	24	M	FARMER	GRZZZZCIN	GAROT, CATH.	60	F	UNKNOWN	GRZZZZASH
LEIBSERSBERGER, CARL	18	M	CL	GRZZZZNY	VERSHASEN, OCTAVIE	20	M	UNKNOWN	GRZZZZCH
ZIMMERMANN, HCH.	37	M	JNR	GRZZZZNY	STRANG, BARBA	20	F	UNKNOWN	GRZZZZCH
HAMSTER, ANNA	18	F	UNKNOWN	GRZZZZNY	OLSCHOWSKY, JOHN	30	M	LABR	GRZZZZUNK
RINZIGER, THERESEA	18	M	UNKNOWN	GRZZZZNY	MEYERS, HCH.	24	M	UNKNOWN	GRZZZZUNK
GARDON, CAROLINE	20	F	UNKNOWN	GRZZZZNY	STERBENZ, JOSEFA	24	F	UNKNOWN	GRZZZZNY
PISER, VALENTINE	15	M	LABR	GRZZZZNY	HEIDS, CARL	17	M	CL	GRZZZZROC
RITTM---, ADAM	22	M	MACH	GRZZZZNY	RANSKER, JOH	39	M	LABR	GRZZZZNY
FURNOK, ADAM	30	M	UNKNOWN	GRZZZZNY	MULLER, EVA	39	F	UNKNOWN	GRZZZZPIT
MARGE	22	F	UNKNOWN	GRZZZZNY	CATH.	14	F	UNKNOWN	GRZZZZPIT
JACOB, JOH.	2	M	CHILD	GRZZZZNY	CHRISTIANA	10	F	CH	GRZZZZPIT
MUHLUM, JOSEF	28	M	LABR	GRZZZZNY	ELISE	9	F	CHILD	GRZZZZPIT
SPENGNETHE, HERMAN	29	M	LABR	GRZZZZCH	ANNA	7	F	CHILD	GRZZZZPIT
STOCK, JOS.	25	M	SMH	GRZZZZOMA	MARIA	5	F	CHILD	GRZZZZPIT
PELDBECK, GUSTAV	35	M	CL	GRZZZZNY	PETER	1	M	CHILD	GRZZZZPIT
HILTENBACH, LISETTE	56	F	UNKNOWN	GRZZZZNY	MOCK, JOSEFINE	31	F	UNKNOWN	GRZZZZUNK
PETER	14	M	UNKNOWN	GRZZZZNY	ALBERT	7	M	CHILD	GRZZZZNY
EBERHARD, ADOLF	24	M	MSN	GRZZZZNY	STANISLAW	5	M	CHILD	GRZZZZNY
WILKESMANN, ELISE	29	F	UNKNOWN	GRZZZZNY	MARIANNE	1	F	CHILD	GRZZZZNY
IDA	5	F	CHILD	GRZZZZNY	JOHN	.02	M	INFANT	GRZZZZNY
FELDMANN, EMILIE	21	F	UNKNOWN	GRZZZZNY	URBAMICK, HEDWIG	22	M	FARMER	GRZZZZNY
DRESDEN, HUGO	52	M	FARMER	GRZZZZNY	SCHETIN, MARTIN	19	M	FARMER	GRZZZZNY
GRIESBACH, CASHE	24	F	UNKNOWN	GRZZZZNY	MEYER, IDA	24	F	UNKNOWN	GRZZZZNY
BORIG, VALENTINE	36	M	CPTR	GRZZZZNY	GUNTHER, HUGO	31	M	LABR	GRZZZZNY
SCHMITZ, FRANZ	32	M	LABR	GRZZZZUNK	MYER, ALB.	21	M	LABR	GRZZZZNY
HOCK, JACOB	18	M	LABR	GRZZZZNY	DETHISE, L.	40	M	MCHT	FRZZZZNY
LORAND, ERMELINE	20	F	UNKNOWN	GRZZZZPHI	U-MRS	38	F	UNKNOWN	FRZZZZNY
TELESPHORN	18	F	UNKNOWN	GRZZZZPHI	YENSETTE, L.	40	M	GENT	FRZZZZNY
PIERRE	14	M	UNKNOWN	GRZZZZPHI	MARBESOME, L.	40	M	GENT	FRZZZZNY
ECK, CATH.	26	F	UNKNOWN	GRZZZZPHI	SAMBERLINI, U	37	M	CL	FRZZZZNY
REILING, JOSEF	52	M	FARMER	GRZZZZNY	MAISSY, M	26	F	UNKNOWN	GRZZZZNY
XAIRE	54	F	UNKNOWN	GRZZZZNY	RAPSARD, A.	35	M	ART	GRZZZZNY
CECILIA	24	F	UNKNOWN	GRZZZZNY	MASSART, N.	25	F	UNKNOWN	GRZZZZNY
ANTON	11	M	CH	GRZZZZNY	REISELL, R.	35	F	UNKNOWN	GRZZZZNY
BRAUER, BERNHARD	33	M	FARMER	GRZZZZNY	SCHLUBDEBRER, E.	45	F	UNKNOWN	GRZZZZNY
AUGUSTE	26	F	UNKNOWN	GRZZZZNY	W.	12	M	CH	GRZZZZNY
HERBERT	4	M	CHILD	GRZZZZNY	LINE	6	F	CHILD	GRZZZZNY
WALTER	13	M	CH	GRZZZZNY	MARGARETA, U	18	F	SI	GRZZZZNY
FRIEDRICH	1	M	CHILD	GRZZZZNY	ELIZABETH	27	F	SI	GRZZZZNY
MEYER, ALBERT	21	M	TLR	GRZZZZNY	SUSANNA	23	F	SI	GRZZZZNY
KUMMER, MARTIN	22	M	TLR	GRZZZZNY	HUND, ANNA	19	F	SI	GRZZZZNY
MATHIS, CATHA.	28	F	UNKNOWN	GRZZZZSY	OLIWIER	24	F	SI	GRZZZZNY
SALOMI	4	F	CHILD	GRZZZZSY	EUPHROSIA	21	F	SI	GRZZZZNY
PAUL	1	M	CHILD	GRZZZZSY	MARIA-KAPTIG	27	F	SI	GRZZZZNY
MAGD.	22	F	UNKNOWN	GRZZZZSY	ADELINA	20	F	SI	GRZZZZNY
MICHEL	1	M	CHILD	GRZZZZSY	FISCHER, HELENA	25	F	SI	GRZZZZNY
MATHIAS, FRIED	56	M	FARMER	GRZZZZSY	STETCH, ROSALIA	23	F	SI	GRZZZZNY
CATH.	52	F	UNKNOWN	GRZZZZSY	PILKE, SOFIE	27	F	SI	GRZZZZNY
JACOB	11	M	CH	GRZZZZSY	BARBARA, GARIER	20	F	SI	GRZZZZNY
JULIUS	10	M	CH	GRZZZZSY	SPAT, FRANCISCAN	23	F	SI	GRZZZZNY
LOUISE	9	F	CHILD	GRZZZZSY	ROMER, PAULINE	19	F	SI	GRZZZZNY
ERNST	4	M	CHILD	GRZZZZSY	HEPTIG, CATHA.	26	F	SI	GRZZZZNY
CAROLINE	24	F	UNKNOWN	GRZZZZNY	SCHMIDT, L.	25	M	WCHMKR	GRZZZZNY
BERKOWITZ, ABUL	22	M	LABR	GRZZZZNY	WUNDERLIN, A.	40	F	UNKNOWN	GRZZZZNY

PASSENGER	AGE	SEX	OCCUPATION	PRVL	DES
RIESE, E.	63	F	UNKNOWN	SRZZZZNY
BEYERLE, L.	27	F	UNKNOWN	GRZZZZNY
VANGULPER, A.	28	M	MCHT	GRZZZZNY
ERNST	30	M	MCHT	GRZZZZNY
FIRMAIN, H.	26	F	UNKNOWN	GRZZZZNY
LOW, U	26	F	UNKNOWN	GRZZZZNY
ROBERT, U	20	F	UNKNOWN	GRZZZZNY
ROTHGANG, C.	26	F	UNKNOWN	GRZZZZNY
WANG, CHAS.	25	M	MNSTR	GRZZZZNY

SHIP: WYOMING

FROM: LIVERPOOL AND QUEENSTOWN
TO: NEW YORK
ARRIVED: 22 NOVEMBER 1888

PASSENGER	AGE	SEX	OCCUPATION	PRVL	DES
EDELMANN, B.	26	F	W	GRZZZZUSA
MOSES	7	M	CHILD	GRZZZZUSA
LEA	6	F	CHILD	GRZZZZUSA
RACHEL	3	F	CHILD	GRZZZZUSA

SHIP: AMALFI

FROM: HAMBURG
TO: NEW YORK
ARRIVED: 23 NOVEMBER 1888

PASSENGER	AGE	SEX	OCCUPATION	PRVL	DES
BAIER, CAROLINE	17	F	SGL	MKZZZZUSA
PIERNITZKI, FRED	17	M	LABR	PRZZZZUSA
ROSALIE	19	F	SGL	PRZZZZUSA
SPRINGER, ERNST	57	M	LABR	MKZZZZUSA
ANNA	53	F	W	MKZZZZUSA
BACH, ANNA	28	F	SGL	MKZZZZUSA
ZIELINSKI, MARIE	30	F	SGL	PRZZZZUSA
GALOFSKA, ROSALIE	30	F	SGL	PRZZZZUSA
GOLINOWSKA, VERONIKA	35	F	WO	PRZZZZUSA
MARIE	55	F	WO	PRZZZZUSA
JOSEFA	9	F	CHILD	PRZZZZUSA
MARIA	3	F	CHILD	PRZZZZUSA
VERONIKA	1	F	CHILD	PRZZZZUSA
MARLOW, CHRISTIAN	46	M	LABR	PRZZZZUSA
MARIE	41	F	W	PRZZZZUSA
FRIEDR	19	M	W	PRZZZZUSA
BICH.	17	F	CH	PRZZZZUSA
GUSTE	14	F	CH	PRZZZZUSA
WILHELM	9	M	CHILD	PRZZZZUSA
CARL	8	M	CHILD	PRZZZZUSA
EMMA	6	F	CHILD	PRZZZZUSA
ALBERT	4	M	CHILD	PRZZZZUSA
MINNA	.09	F	INFANT	PRZZZZUSA
RADLOFF, CHRISTIAN	49	M	LABR	PRZZZZUSA
CAROLINE	27	F	W	PRZZZZUSA
WILHELMINE	18	F	CH	PRZZZZUSA
ERNESTINE	11	F	CH	PRZZZZUSA
CARL	9	M	CHILD	PRZZZZUSA
AUGUST	1	M	CHILD	PRZZZZUSA
CIESLAK, KATH	22	F	SGL	PRZZZZUSA
HAUSWURZ, CLARA	13	F	CH	PRZZZZUSA
RICHARD	16	M	CH	PRZZZZUSA
ENNO	7	M	CHILD	PRZZZZUSA
ELSA	6	F	CHILD	PRZZZZUSA
MALINOWSKA, ANIELA	22	F	WO	PRZZZZUSA
MARTHA	.06	F	INFANT	PRZZZZUSA
BORS, FRIEDRICH	56	M	LABR	PRZZZZUSA
DOROTHEA	51	F	W	PRZZZZUSA

PASSENGER	AGE	SEX	OCCUPATION	PRVL	DES
LOUISE	11	F	CH	PRZZZZUSA
GUSTAV	16	M	CH	PRZZZZUSA
TAUBE, JOH.	54	M	LABR	PRZZZZUSA
CAROLINE	43	F	W	PRZZZZUSA
JULIUS	23	M	S	PRZZZZUSA
EMMA	11	F	CH	PRZZZZUSA
HULDA	4	F	CHILD	PRZZZZUSA
ALLA	.06	F	INFANT	PRZZZZUSA
WILS, KAROLINE	23	F	WO	MKZZZZUSA
OTTO	5	M	CHILD	MKZZZZUSA
CLARA	.09	F	INFANT	MKZZZZUSA
BEHLEIN, MARTHA	15	F	SGL	PRZZZZUSA
SCHUHMACHER, ROBERT	19	M	LABR	PRZZZZUSA
WITZEL, VALENTINE	25	M	FARMER	PRZZZZUSA
JANISZEWSKA, STEFAN	14	M	LABR	PRZZZZUSA
HINZ, ANNA	20	F	SGL	PRZZZZUSA
OEHMANN, FRITZ	35	M	TLR	HBZZZZUSA
CHRISTINE	29	F	W	HBZZZZUSA
PINGEL, CARL	25	M	LABR	MKZZZZUSA
FRIEDERIKE	35	F	W	MKZZZZUSA
STIENE	11	F	CH	MKZZZZUSA
HEINRICH	2	M	CHILD	MKZZZZUSA
HINZMANN, CAROLINE	68	F	WO	PRZZZZUSA
LEIPOLD, ANNA	32	F	WO	BVZZZZUSA
HANS	8	M	CHILD	BVZZZZUSA
URSULA	4	F	CHILD	BVZZZZUSA
ANNA	.11	F	INFANT	BVZZZZUSA
KOESELING, WILHELMINE	42	F	WO	PRZZZZUSA
FRANZISKA	3	F	CHILD	PRZZZZUSA
FLEISCHER, BEILE	20	F	SGL	PRZZZZUSA
FRIMET	18	F	SGL	PRZZZZUSA
KOMALSKI, LEIE	28	F	WO	PRZZZZUSA
LIEBE	10	F	CH	PRZZZZUSA
FEIGE	7	M	CHILD	PRZZZZUSA
RUCHEL	6	F	CHILD	PRZZZZUSA
CHANE	4	F	CHILD	PRZZZZUSA
KOWALSKI, ABRAM	3	M	CHILD	PRZZZZNY
ANNA	1	F	CHILD	PRZZZZNY
HELMST, HEINRICH	41	M	LABR	HBZZZZIA
MOELLER, KARL	26	M	JNR	PRZZZZNE
ASSMUSS, JOHANN	24	M	LABR	PRZZZZNE
TUEBEL, WILHELM	17	M	MLR	BVZZZZNY
MILLING, FLORENTINE	28	F	SGL	PRZZZZNY
BAM, HERMANN	27	M	LABR	PRZZZZNY
MELKER, MARTIN	51	M	LABR	PRZZZZNY
CHRISTINE	35	F	W	PRZZZZNY
ALBERT	9	M	CHILD	PRZZZZNY
AGMANN, FRIEDERIKE	15	F	SGL	PRZZZZNY
WINKEL, ADOLF	39	M	LABR	PRZZZZNY
NEUMANN, GUSTAV	27	M	LABR	PRZZZZNY
ENDERLEIN, PAUL	29	M	MCHT	SYZZZZNY
FEHRS, MINNA	24	F	UNKNOWN	PRZZZZNY
STENDER, JOH.	28	M	FARMER	PRZZZZNY
DORIS	24	F	W	PRZZZZNY
FRIEDR.	4	M	CHILD	PRZZZZNY
OTTO	2	M	CHILD	PRZZZZNY
ECKHORST, WILHELM	41	M	LABR	PRZZZZNY
LOUISE	44	F	W	PRZZZZNY
BERTHA	5	F	CHILD	PRZZZZNY
MARTHA	1	F	CHILD	PRZZZZNY
SCHOENING, LINE	7	F	CHILD	PRZZZZNY
SCHUHMACHER, HEINR.	20	M	LABR	PRZZZZNY
ENGEL, GUSTAV	33	M	LABR	PRZZZZNY
REHBERG, AUGUSTE	23	F	SGL	PRZZZZNY
MATEJEWSKI, LEO	24	M	MCHT	PRZZZZNY
ANNA	42	F	WO	PRZZZZNY
WEIDEMANN, AUGUTE	18	F	SGL	PRZZZZIA
CHOINACKI, MICHAL	34	M	LABR	PRZZZZNY
SCHULZ, JOH.	23	M	LABR	MKZZZZNY
HILBERT, GUSTAV	17	M	LABR	MKZZZZMI
SEIDEL, AUGUSTE	25	F	WO	PRZZZZNY
ALBERT	.09	M	INFANT	PRZZZZNY
DUERING, AUGUST	26	M	LABR	PRZZZZIA
ELLERMANN, CHRISTIAN	38	M	LABR	MKZZZZIA
MARIE	31	F	W	MKZZZZIA

PASSENGER	AGE	SEX	OCCUPATION	PRVL	DES
WILHELM	10	M	CH		MKZZZZIA
FRIEDR.	7	M	CHILD		MKZZZZIA
TIMM, HERMANN	29	M	LABR		PRZZZZTX
MINNA	30	F	W		PRZZZZTX
ELISABETH	6	F	CHILD		PRZZZZTX
ELFRIEDE	4	F	CHILD		PRZZZZTX
MARY	3	F	CHILD		PRZZZZTX
WALTER	.06	M	INFANT		PRZZZZTX
PACKLEP, AUGUSTE	20	F	SGL		PRZZZZMI
BLOHM, CARL	24	M	LABR		MKZZZZMI
JOH.	25	F	W		MKZZZZMI
MOELLER, JOH.	43	M	LABR		MKZZZZROC
LOUISE	41	F	W		MKZZZZROC
WILHELMINE	17	F	CH		MKZZZZROC
AUGUSTE	15	F	CH		MKZZZZROC
JOH.	11	F	CH		MKZZZZROC
JOH.	5	M	CHILD		MKZZZZROC
ELISE	4	F	CHILD		MKZZZZROC
FROEHLICH, LEOPOLD	31	M	FARMER		MKZZZZROC
WILH.	26	F	W		MKZZZZROC
HELENE	4	F	CHILD		MKZZZZROC
GUSTAV	3	M	CHILD		MKZZZZROC
ANNA	2	F	CHILD		MKZZZZROC
FICK, CARL	24	M	LABR		MKZZZZROC
LOUISE	27	F	W		MKZZZZROC
CARL	3	M	CHILD		MKZZZZROC
EMMA	1	F	CHILD		MKZZZZROC
FRITZ	57	M	FARMER		MKZZZZROC
FRITZ	15	M	FARMER		MKZZZZROC
NIEMANN, JOHANN	34	M	LABR		MKZZZZROC
CAROLINE	35	F	W		MKZZZZROC
SIHLICKER, FRIEDERICKE	65	F	WO		MKZZZZROC
MARZAHN, FRIEDA	11	F	UNKNOWN		MKZZZZROC
CARL	9	M	CHILD		MKZZZZROC
LUDWIG	7	M	CHILD		MKZZZZROC
NIEMANN, AUGUSTE	3	F	CHILD		MKZZZZROC
AUGUST	.09	M	INFANT		MKZZZZROC
KLICKAN, JOHANN	53	M	FARMER		MKZZZZIL
SOPHIE	50	F	W		MKZZZZIL
WILHELMINE	22	F	CH		MKZZZZIL
FRIEDERIKE	19	F	CH		MKZZZZIL
ERNST	15	M	CH		MKZZZZIL
WILHELM	4	M	CHILD		MKZZZZIL
KRAMENER, HEINRICH	31	M	FARMER		MKZZZZIL
ROSENBAUM, WILHELM	47	M	LABR		MKZZZZNY
BERTHA	18	F	CH		MKZZZZNY
AUGUST	15	M	CH		MKZZZZNY
EMMA	8	F	CHILD		PRZZZZNY
ANNA	4	F	CHILD		PRZZZZNY
SOPHIE	71	F	WO		PRZZZZNY
GOLDSTEIN, LIEBE	25	F	WO		PRZZZZNY
JANKEL	8	M	CHILD		PRZZZZNY
GERSON	5	M	CHILD		PRZZZZNY
TROST, HEINRICJH	56	M	LABR		PRZZZZIL
JOH.	55	F	W		PRZZZZIL
MAGDALENE	21	F	CH		PRZZZZIL
ANNA	19	F	CH		PRZZZZIL
LOUISE	18	F	CH		PRZZZZIL
MINNA	16	F	CH		PRZZZZIL
FISCHER, ALBERT	22	M	LABR		PRZZZZNY
BREESE, FRITZ	26	M	LABR		PRZZZZNY
SOPHIE	27	F	W		PRZZZZNY
GUSTAV	2	M	CHILD		PRZZZZNY
FISCHER, EMMA	11	F	CH		PRZZZZNY
BUCK, THEODOR	24	M	LABR		PRZZZZNY
WENDLAND, CHRISTIAN	30	M	LABR		PRZZZZIL
MARIE	29	F	W		PRZZZZIL
WILHELM	7	M	CHILD		PRZZZZIL
EMMA	6	F	CHILD		PRZZZZIL
ANNA	.09	F	INFANT		PRZZZZIL
SCHROEDER, FRIEDERICH	27	M	LABR		PRZZZZIN
KAISER, EMIL	39	M	LABR		PRZZZZMI
WALISZEWSKI, ANDREAS	28	M	LABR		PRZZZZPA
SOSNOWSKI, AUGUST	30	M	LABR		PRZZZZPA
ANNA	24	F	SGL		PRZZZZPA
VICTORIA	24	F	LABR		PRZZZZPA
EVA	56	F	WO		PRZZZZPA
JAGUSZEWSKI, STANISLAVA	23	F	SGL		PRZZZZBUF
ANTON	15	M	PNTR		PRZZZZBUF
WALLISZEWSKI, MARYANNA	27	F	WO		PRZZZZBUF
JOH.	4	F	CHILD		PRZZZZBUF
STANISLAW	3	M	CHILD		PRZZZZBUF
KONSTANTIN	1	M	CHILD		PRZZZZBUF
SCHARFIG, KARL	21	M	LABR		PRZZZZPA
ROBLINSKA, MARIANNA	37	F	WO		PRZZZZBUF
STANISLAW	16	M	CH		PRZZZZBUF
MARIANNA	6	F	CHILD		PRZZZZBUF
MAGDALENA	1	F	CHILD		PRZZZZBUF
DORNEA, HEINRICH	31	M	MCHT		BVZZZZBUF
SCHICKORA, ROBERT	20	M	MCHT		PRZZZZNE
OSTROWSKI, JAKOB	29	M	MCHT		MKZZZZNY
MUELLER, ADOLF	33	M	MCHT		PRZZZZNY
WILHELMINE	40	F	W		PRZZZZNY
JUEDEL, ALBIN	20	M	PRNTR		PRZZZZNY
STEMPLE, BARBARA	26	F	SGL		WMZZZZNY
HAENNERMUELLER, HERMANN	17	M	TNM		SYZZZZNY
MITTERER, BARBA	23	F	SGL		BVZZZZOH
SCHWAENZEL, MIHAEL	26	M	LABR		BVZZZZNY
THERESE	4	F	CHILD		BVZZZZNY
PFEIFFER, EDUARD	60	M	LABR		PRZZZZNY
FISCHER, MATHIAS	38	M	TNR		PRZZZZNY
CAROL.	36	F	W		PRZZZZNY
NICOLAUS	11	M	CH		PRZZZZNY
JOSEF	9	M	CHILD		PRZZZZNY
GEORG	8	M	CHILD		PRZZZZNY
ANNA	2	F	CHILD		PRZZZZNY
CARL.	1	F	CHILD		PRZZZZNY
KR---, MARTHA	31	F	WO		PRZZZZNY
ROSE, SOPHIE	22	F	SGL		PRZZZZIL
GEBHARDT, JULIUS	23	M	LABR		MKZZZZNY
HEIDORN, CATHARINE	17	F	SGL		PRZZZZNY
NIKISCH, FRANZ	22	M	TCHR		PRZZZZNY
MEMFRASS, THEODOR	26	M	LABR		PRZZZZOH
JOH.	22	F	W		PRZZZZOH
EMMA	3	F	CHILD		PRZZZZOH
ANNA	1	F	CHILD		PRZZZZOH
ALBERT	6	M	CHILD		PRZZZZOH
MATEJEWSKI, LEO	24	M	MCHT		PRZZZZIL
ANNE	42	F	WO		PRZZZZIL
WENDLAND, FRIEDA	.01	F	INFANT		PRZZZZIL

SHIP: ELBE

FROM: BREMEN AND SOUTHAMPTON
TO: NEW YORK
ARRIVED: 23 OCTOBER 1888*

PASSENGER	AGE	SEX	OCCUPATION	PRVL	DES
WEICHMANN, JULIUS	36	M	UNKNOWN		PRAARRNY
MATHILDE	34	F	UNKNOWN		PRAARRNY
LUDWIG	2	M	CHILD		PRAARRNY
SIMSON, ERNESTINE	62	F	UNKNOWN		PRAARRNY
HOLLAENDER, MAX	28	M	UNKNOWN		PRAARRNY
FORRER, RUPPECHT	20	M	UNKNOWN		GRZZZZNY
WIEST, FRANZISKA	45	F	UNKNOWN		GRAARRNY
HERMANN, MARIE	20	F	UNKNOWN		GRAARRNY
WOLF, BERTHA	20	F	UNKNOWN		GRZZZZNY
MORITZ, AUGUST	23	M	UNKNOWN		GRZZZZNY
HEERKLOTZ, RICHARD	26	M	UNKNOWN		GRAFNXNY
WICHEL, SOPHIE	29	M	UNKNOWN		GRAFNXNY
VEHBER, CARL	22	M	UNKNOWN		GRAARRNY
ANNA	19	F	UNKNOWN		GRAARRNY
LEVY, EVA	39	F	UNKNOWN		GRAEABNY
MARTHA	11	F	UNKNOWN		GRAEABNY
AUGUSTE	10	F	UNKNOWN		GRAEABNY
MELAMET, DAVID	27	M	UNKNOWN		GRAEABNY

*Arrival date out of chronological order.

PASSENGER	AGE	SEX	OCCUPATION	PRVVL	DES
WALKHOFF, JULIE	57	M	UNKNOWN		GRAEABNY
SICK, MATHILDE	57	F	UNKNOWN		GRAEABNY
LUEBBE, FRANZ	62	M	UNKNOWN		GRAARRNY
STECKHAHN, OTTO	38	M	UNKNOWN		GRAAKHNY
ROSA	35	F	UNKNOWN		GRAAKHNY
HENRIETTE	60	F	UNKNOWN		GRAAKHNY
HANS	9	M	CHILD		GRAAKHNY
U, CANDIDA	25	F	RE		GRAFMKNY
ARMILLA	27	F	RE		GRAFMKNY
JACOBINE	21	F	RE		GRAFMKNY
MONICA	23	F	RE		GRAFMKNY
LARENTE	25	F	RE		GRAFMKNY
IDA	29	F	RE		GRAFMKNY
PAULA	28	F	RE		GRAFMKNY
SCHOLASTICA	27	F	RE		GRAFMKNY
ANNA	22	F	RE		GRAFMKNY
EUPHROSINA	21	F	RE		GRAFMKNY
THERESIA	24	F	RE		GRAFMKNY
ENSTACHINE	20	F	RE		GRAFMKNY
GERKE, MARIE	20	F	RE		GRACBRNY
ARMENDINGEN, KAETCHEN	18	F	RE		GRACBRNY
MICHAELIS, JOHA.	29	F	UNKNOWN		GRZZZZNY
SCHWOHL, JOH.	52	M	MCHT		GRAAZQNY
SUSANNE	62	F	UNKNOWN		GRAAZQNY
KOSTRZEWA, JOHN	26	M	LABR		GRAAZQNY
DREWICK, PRACKSEDA	26	F	UNKNOWN		GRAAZQNY
KOHL, AUGUSTE	30	F	UNKNOWN		GRZZZZNY
FESS, BERTHA	20	F	UNKNOWN		GRZZZZNY
FISCHER, IDA	19	F	UNKNOWN		GRZZZZNY
ZITZMANN, ERNST	16	M	LABR		GRZZZZNY
DEUTZER, ANNA	24	F	UNKNOWN		GRZZZZNY
PLAMBECK, ALWINE	30	F	UNKNOWN		GRADVHNY
HEFTER, ANNA	22	F	UNKNOWN		GRZZZZNY
VENGELS, BERTHA	43	F	UNKNOWN		GRZZZZNY
REHM, MARIE	17	F	UNKNOWN		GRAARRNY
LEMKE, WILHELMINE	16	F	UNKNOWN		GRZZZZNY
LUEHRS, AHLRICH	17	M	LABR		GRACBRNY
MEYER, HEINR.	26	M	MCHT		GRAAXFNY
WINDHORST, CARL	25	M	MCHT		GRAARRNY
BRUMMERLOH, JOHA.	19	F	UNKNOWN		GRZZZZUNK
JOH.	.08	M	INFANT		GRZZZZBUF
MOESSNER, CARL	26	M	CPR		GRAEXWNY
KOCH, NELLY	17	F	UNKNOWN		GRADWQMI
CARL	30	M	SMH		GRADWQMI
STOEFFLER, WILHELM	18	M	JNR		GRZZZZMI
HEINZ, DOROTHEA	30	F	UNKNOWN		GRACQEMI
AMALIE	7	F	CHILD		GRACQEMI
MARIE	3	F	CHILD		GRACQEMI
HELENE	2	F	CHILD		GRACQEMI
KOCH, EMILIE	16	F	UNKNOWN		GRAEXWMI
GUTJAHR, CHRISTE.	65	F	UNKNOWN		GRZZZZMI
DEIFEL, ALBERT	15	M	LABR		GRZZZZMI
AIRLE, AGNES	19	F	UNKNOWN		GRZZZZMI
STUETZ, MARIE	29	F	UNKNOWN		GRZZZZMI
FISCHER, JOHA.	16	M	LABR		GRAFMAMI
SCHLEEHAUPT, ADOLF	20	M	LABR		GRAFMAMI
SCHMIDT, AUGUST	19	M	LABR		GRAFMAMI
STENDER, MATHILDE	28	F	UNKNOWN		GRAENRMI
OTTO	7	M	CHILD		GRAENRMI
WILHELMINE	6	F	CHILD		GRAENRMI
AUGST, LOUISE	24	F	UNKNOWN		GRZZZZMI
FENSTERMACHER, CHRISTIA	45	M	UNKNOWN		GRZZZZMI
FENSTERMACHER, --NE	24	F	UNKNOWN		GRZZZZMI
MINNA	3	F	CHILD		GRZZZZMI
ERBE, AUGUSTE	58	F	UNKNOWN		GRACZKMI
DANZ, AUGUSTE	16	F	UNKNOWN		GRAARRMI
AMANN, HELENE	21	F	UNKNOWN		GRAARRMI
SCHILLING, CATHA.	20	F	UNKNOWN		GRZZZZMI
FUSS, JOH.	25	M	LABR		GRAAHBMI
ROOS, JOH.	23	M	LABR		GRAAHBMI
BRAUN, ANBNA	22	F	UNKNOWN		GRAAHBMI
WENZEL, FRANZ	26	M	LABR		GRZZZZMI
PAAR, JOH.	17	M	LABR		GRZZZZMI
OKESSON, WILH.	15	M	LABR		GRAKVLMI
KOCH, HEINR.	18	M	LABR		GRAARRMI
BEAUPEIN, HELENE	19	F	UNKNOWN		GRABZVMI
RUCHHOLZ, KAETHI	56	F	UNKNOWN		GRAARRMI
LACKMANN, ANNA	22	F	UNKNOWN		GRAAFFNY
KEUNECKE, F.F.	25	M	FARMER		GRAAFFNY
WYESITZKI, AUG.	24	M	FARMER		GRAARRNY
HUMMER, MICHAEL	30	M	UNKNOWN		GRAARRNY
FRANCISCA	22	F	UNKNOWN		GRAARRNY
JOH.	2	M	CHILD		GRZZZZKS
FRANZ	.03	M	INFANT		GRZZZZKS
PLATZ, MARIANNE	23	F	UNKNOWN		GRZZZZPA
WIETRZYKOWSKI, JOSEF	23	M	LABR		GRZZZZNY
DEGA, AGNES	19	F	UNKNOWN		GRZZZZNY
HAMMERL, BARBARA	34	F	UNKNOWN		GRZZZZNY
PETER	2	M	CHILD		GRZZZZNY
EMMERLING, FRITZ	13	M	LABR		GRZZZZNY
BAUER, PHILIPP	25	M	LABR		GRAAQWNY
KATHA.	24	F	UNKNOWN		GRAAQWNY
CHRISTE.	2	F	CHILD		GRAAQWNY
KORNPROBST, JOSEF	20	M	LABR		GRZZZZNY
KEHR, JOH.	44	M	LABR		GRZZZZNY
HABERLAND, WILHE.	33	F	UNKNOWN		GRZZZZNY
HERM.	10	M	CH		GRZZZZNY
EMMA	7	F	CHILD		GRZZZZNY
KARL	3	M	CHILD		GRZZZZNY
MARTEM, WILHE.	25	F	UNKNOWN		GRZZZZNY
WILHE.	62	F	UNKNOWN		GRZZZZNY
WM.	.10	M	INFANT		GRZZZZNY
FESENFELDT, HEINR.	38	M	FARMER		GRAJMZNY
MARIE	28	F	UNKNOWN		GRAJMZNY
BOEHME, MAX	7	M	CHILD		GRAASGNY
BARTSCH, LOUISE	46	F	UNKNOWN		GRAAKHNY
FALTER, FRANZ	53	M	FARMER		GRADNPNY
BLUEMEL, CAROLINE	17	F	UNKNOWN		GRADNPNY
GEUSSLER, BABETTE	33	F	UNKNOWN		GRADNPNY
KOEHLER, PAULINE	38	F	UNKNOWN		GRADNPNY
ANNA	19	F	UNKNOWN		GRADNPNY
OSCAR	15	M	UNKNOWN		GRADNPNY
GUST.	7	M	CHILD		GRADNPNY
PAUL	5	M	CHILD		GRADNPNY
IDA	3	F	CHILD		GRADNPNY
BERTHA	.10	F	INFANT		GRADNPNY
RICHTER, ROSALIE	66	F	UNKNOWN		GRADNPNY
RESSNER, BERL	23	M	LABR		GRADNPNY
MEYER, FRITZ	16	M	UNKNOWN		GRZZZZNY
ROWOHLT, CHRIST.	14	M	UNKNOWN		GRZZZZNY
MINNERMANN, HINR.	15	M	UNKNOWN		GRZZZZNY
WITTROCK, HEINR.	14	M	UNKNOWN		GRADXENY
BECKER, CATHA.	16	F	UNKNOWN		GRACBRIL
KIRCHNER, THERESIA	23	F	UNKNOWN		GRZZZZMO
STIEF, CATHARINE	67	F	UNKNOWN		GRZZZZMO
ANNA	30	F	UNKNOWN		GRZZZZMO
AUGUSTE	21	F	UNKNOWN		GRZZZZMO
MIELKE, CARL	48	M	FARMER		GRZZZZMO
BUESCHEL, AMALIE	25	F	UNKNOWN		GRZZZZMO
MIELKE, BERTHA	10	F	CH		GRZZZZMO
ANNA	7	F	CHILD		GRZZZZMO
REISS, NATHAN	25	M	LABR		GRADGOMO
LOEPER, CARL	50	M	LABR		GRZZZZMO
AUGUSTE	45	F	UNKNOWN		GRZZZZMO
ERNST	15	M	UNKNOWN		GRZZZZMO
PAUL	11	M	CH		GRZZZZMO
LEPCYK, JOSEFA	21	F	UNKNOWN		GRZZZZNY
WAWRZYN	30	M	LABR		GRZZZZNY
JOH.	.09	M	INFANT		GRZZZZNY
BUZDZIAK, ANNA	31	F	UNKNOWN		GRZZZZNY
JACOB	7	M	CHILD		GRZZZZNY
VALENTIN	5	M	CHILD		GRZZZZNY
PETER	3	M	CHILD		GRZZZZNY
JOH.	.10	M	INFANT		GRZZZZNY
SKUZA, AMALIE	22	F	UNKNOWN		GRADNRNY
AHLERS, JOHA.	16	F	UNKNOWN		GRAARRNY
CLAUSING, BERTHA	21	F	UNKNOWN		GRAARRNY
BULTMANN, MARIE	67	F	UNKNOWN		GRAARRNY
WALLMANN, ANNA	23	F	UNKNOWN		GRAJEROH
HULDA	.09	F	INFANT		GRAJEROH

PASSENGER	AGE	SEX	OCCUPATION	PRVL	DES
CATHA.	22	F	UNKNOWN	GRAJEROH	
HEINRICH, ERNST	45	M	CPR	GRZZZZNY	
HARMS, DOROTHEA	25	F	UNKNOWN	GRADQLNY	
GERHARD, LUDW.	32	M	FARMER	GRAARTNY	
MEYER, FRIEDR.	17	M	LABR	GRZZZZNY	
PAPE, JOH.	59	M	SMH	GRZZZZNY	
JOH.	18	M	UNKNOWN	GRZZZZNY	
CATHA.	16	F	UNKNOWN	GRZZZZNY	
LAUTER, ANNA	18	F	UNKNOWN	GRZZZZNY	
BRELL, MARIE	23	F	UNKNOWN	GRZZZZNY	
KRESZENZ	22	M	BKLYR	GRZZZZNY	
OPPEL, BABATTE	22	F	UNKNOWN	GRZZZZNY	
ADLER, MAX	14	M	UNKNOWN	GRZZZZNY	
MEYER, FANNY	18	F	UNKNOWN	GRZZZZNY	
REHME, SOPHIE	19	F	UNKNOWN	GRABOQOH	
CZRIACK, CATHA.	28	F	UNKNOWN	GRAARRNY	
SPARENBERG, HERM.	26	M	JNR	GRAARRNY	
U, U	24	M	BRR	GRAARRNY	
U	23	M	BRR	GRAARRNY	
MEYER, JOHANN	30	M	FARMER	GRZZZZBUF	
MARGA.	20	F	UNKNOWN	GRZZZZBUF	
LEIPOLD, THERESIA	17	F	UNKNOWN	GRZZZZBUF	
KOTAKI, WAIZICK	30	M	LABR	GRZZZZBUF	
PIANOWSKA, JAN	30	M	LABR	GRZZZZBUF	
REICH, MICH.	23	M	LABR	GRZZZZBUF	
NOE, LOUISE	16	F	UNKNOWN	GRAFRGNY	
JENA, BABETTA	35	F	UNKNOWN	GRAAEXNY	
ADOLF	15	M	LABR	GRAAEXNY	
THERESA	10	F	CH	GRAAEXNY	
ADELE	8	F	CHILD	GRAAEXNY	
MAX	6	M	CHILD	GRAAEXNY	
GUST.	4	M	CHILD	GRAAEXNY	
HANS	2	M	CHILD	GRAAEXNY	
FRIEDR.	.06	M	INFANT	GRAAEXNY	
U, U	18	F	UNKNOWN	GRACHTNY	
STALLMANN, HINRICH	16	M	UNKNOWN	GRAEXFIL	
DOESCHER, WILHELM	17	M	UNKNOWN	GRZZZZIL	
BERTHA	15	F	UNKNOWN	GRZZZZIL	
SIEFKEN, ANNA	23	F	UNKNOWN	GRACBRIL	
BOETJER, HINRICH	16	M	UNKNOWN	GRACBRIL	
THOENEMANN, KAROLINE	25	F	UNKNOWN	GRACBRIL	
MEYER, ANNA	15	F	UNKNOWN	GRACBRIL	
OHLAND, ANNA	14	F	UNKNOWN	GRACBRIL	
HEINR.	11	M	CH	GRACBRIL	
WIESEMANN, LINA	19	F	UNKNOWN	GRACBRIL	
KAARS, HINR.	19	M	SMH	GRAARRNY	
KUMPFER, GEORG	30	M	BCHR	GRZZZZNY	
MARGA.	28	F	UNKNOWN	GRZZZZNY	
WALTER, MARGA.	16	F	UNKNOWN	GRZZZZNY	
BLUM, MATHILDE	40	F	UNKNOWN	GRZZZZNY	
GUST.	7	M	CHILD	GRZZZZNY	
HARSTRICH, JULIUS	32	M	FARMER	GRACBRNY	
EMMA	24	F	UNKNOWN	GRACBRNY	
HERMINE	16	F	UNKNOWN	GRACBRNY	
BACHMANN, ANNA	32	F	UNKNOWN	GRACBRNY	
VOSS, GEORG	18	M	LABR	GRADKWNY	
HAVERKAMP, GERTRUD	51	F	UNKNOWN	GRADKWNY	
SCHILDE, AMANDE	24	F	UNKNOWN	GRADXCNY	
JUDETZKI, GUST.	29	M	LABR	GRACBRNY	
ZUMDOWITZ, FRANZ	30	M	LABR	GRACBRNY	
EBMEIER, RIEKE	14	F	UNKNOWN	GRACBRNY	
KARBER, MARIE	34	F	UNKNOWN	GRACBRNY	
MIMI	6	F	CHILD	GRACBRNY	
HEMPEL, BERTHA	20	F	UNKNOWN	GRACBRNY	
HASE, IDA	20	F	UNKNOWN	GRZZZZNY	
SCHIEBEL, FRIEDR.	18	M	LABR	GRZZZZNY	
SCHWENDER, REINH.	17	M	LABR	GRZZZZNY	
NOORMANN, ERDMANN	18	M	LABR	GRZZZZNY	
OEHLER, ANNA	49	F	UNKNOWN	GRACPENY	
STASKIEWIECZ, M.	24	M	LABR	GRACBRNY	
GROSS, ELISAB.	49	F	UNKNOWN	GRACBRNY	
JACOB	23	M	LABR	GRACBRNY	
STAHL, THERESE	34	F	UNKNOWN	GRZZZZNY	
CHRIST.	11	M	CH	GRZZZZNY	
HEINR.	7	M	CHILD	GRZZZZNY	
MATHILDE	4	F	CHILD	GRZZZZNY	
NUESSLEIN, JOHANN	30	M	BLKSMH	GRADKVNY	
KLETTNER, ANTON	35	M	BRR	GRADKVNY	
WENZEL, CESAK	38	M	LABR	GRZZZZNY	
SACHS, FRANZ	43	M	FARMER	GRADLDNY	
BORCHERS, JUERGEN	16	M	LABR	GRACBRNY	
HARMS, HEINR.	27	M	JNR	GRACBRNY	
HORN, JOHANNE	23	F	UNKNOWN	GRACBRNY	
RAHM, JOHANNES	22	M	BCHR	GRACBRNY	
STROEBEL, LEONHD.	26	M	MCHT	GRACBRNY	
CARLSON, JOHANNE	18	F	UNKNOWN	GRACBRNY	

SHIP: HAMMONIA

FROM: HAMBURG
TO: NEW YORK
ARRIVED: 24 NOVEMBER 1888

PASSENGER	AGE	SEX	OCCUPATION	PRVL	DES
HOEFSMANN, ANNA	31	F	SGL	GRACTCUSA	
ROSENTHAL, JOHANNA	30	F	W	GRAFOZUSA	
KONOPINSKI, LEONH.	31	M	CL	GRAFOZUSA	
---ENA	22	F	WO	GRAEOLUSA	
ANTON	.01	M	INFANT	GRAEOLUSA	
GEORG	.11	M	INFANT	GRAEOLUSA	
LORENSIUS, NANNIENZ	15	M	FARMER	PRZZZZUSA	
DABESHAHL, FERD.	41	M	LABR	PRZZZZUSA	
DUEMLING, GEORG	15	M	LABR	BVZZZZUSA	
HANNEMANN, WILH.	21	M	LABR	BVAJUGUSA	
ROMICKE, JULIUS	38	M	TLR	BVAJUGUSA	
ZIMMER, HERM.	22	M	MCHT	BVAAKHUSA	
FREITAG, JOHAN	29	M	SHMK	BVAAKHUSA	
BRETTSCHNEIDER, SELMA	35	F	W	BVABDMUSA	
ANNA	15	F	D	BVABDMUSA	
WEIDINGER, ELISE	39	F	W	BVABDMUSA	
GRABAWSKA, ANTONIA	16	F	SGL	SYZZZZUSA	
NADOLNA, MICHALINE	25	F	SGL	SYZZZZUSA	
SCHNEIDER, FRANZ	25	M	MLR	SYZZZZUSA	
REDDIG, ELISABETH	20	F	SGL	PRZZZZUSA	
THRUN, VICTORIA	60	F	W	PRZZZZUSA	
JOSEF	22	M	CH	PRZZZZUSA	
VINCENT	16	M	CH	PRZZZZUSA	
WODTHE, EMILIE	23	F	SGL	PRZZZZUSA	
PROTZOWSKY, GUSTAV	25	M	LABR	PRZZZZUSA	
WILHELMINE	16	F	W	PRZZZZUSA	
RITZ, FRANZ	25	M	LABR	PRZZZZUSA	
STECKMANN, HERM.	24	M	LABR	PRZZZZUSA	
KAMINSKI, JOH.	57	M	LABR	PRZZZZUSA	
WANDEL, WM.	23	M	FARMER	PRZZZZUSA	
KRICKE, GOTTL.	23	M	FARMER	PRZZZZUSA	
LANGE, FRANZ	37	M	LABR	PRZZZZUSA	
JUSTINE	38	F	W	PRZZZZUSA	
AUGUSTE	8	F	CHILD	PRZZZZUSA	
CARL	7	M	CHILD	PRZZZZUSA	
HERM.	6	M	CHILD	PRZZZZUSA	
GUSTAV	5	M	CHILD	PRZZZZUSA	
EMIL	2	M	CHILD	PRZZZZUSA	
RUDOLF	.09	M	INFANT	PRZZZZUSA	
PELGEN, HEINR.	24	M	LABR	PRZZZZUSA	
MUELLER, LOUISE	22	F	SGL	PRZZZZUSA	
KLEINSDER, CONRAD	33	M	CPTR	BVZZZZUSA	
ELISABETH	28	F	W	BVZZZZUSA	
MARGARETHE	4	F	CHILD	BVZZZZUSA	
KAFFKA, ALBERT	49	M	PNTR	PRZZZZUSA	
BUSCH, JOHANNA	34	F	WO	OLZZZZUSA	
WILH.	7	F	CHILD	OLZZZZUSA	
MICHAEL, JOHANN	29	M	LABR	MKZZZZUSA	
THERESE	22	F	W	MKZZZZUSA	
FRIEDA	3	F	CHILD	MKZZZZUSA	
BERTHA	.01	F	INFANT	MKZZZZUSA	
NEHLS, CARL	24	M	LABR	MKZZZZUSA	

PASSENGER	AGE	SEX	OCCUPATION	PRIVL	DES
REGNER, LUDW.	28	M	LKSH	MKADROUSA	
GERLINGER, LEONHARD	20	M	SMH	BVZZZZUSA	
DAHL, CAROLINE	25	F	SGL	PRZZZZUSA	
ANDERSEN, ANDERS	16	M	FARMER	PRZZZZUSA	
BRACKE, THEODRO	40	M	MCHT	PRAIALUSA	
SCHLUETER, CHRIST.	22	F	SGL	PRZZZZUSA	
MESER, MARG.	23	F	SGL	PRZZZZUSA	
JOHNSON, ANDREAS	24	M	FARMER	PRADGHUSA	
PETER	21	M	FARMER	PRADGHUSA	
MORTENSEN, TOMAS	22	M	FARMER	PRADGHUSA	
PETERSEN, MARG.	25	F	SGL	PRADGHUSA	
NIELSEN, PETER	28	M	FARMER	PRADGHUSA	
SCHULZ, MARIE	22	F	SGL	PRADGHUSA	
CHRISTENSEN, JENS	27	M	FARMER	PRADGHUSA	
ANNA	24	F	W	PRADGHUSA	
SCHUHMACHER, CATH.	23	F	W	PRADGHUSA	
HERM.	.06	M	INFANT	PRADGHUSA	
MUNDSTOCH, FR.	25	M	LABR	PRADGHUSA	
CHRIS.	23	M	LABR	PRADGHUSA	
BURAND, AUGUSTE	27	F	SGL	PRADGHUSA	
BRUSS, HINR.	34	M	LABR	PRADGHUSA	
BEHBERG, HERM.	27	M	LABR	PRADGHUNK	
REINHARDT, OSWALD	15	M	BKBNDR	SYZZZZUNK	
LOEFFLER, LORENZ	24	M	FARMER	SYABVKUNK	
LOCHETAMPFER, ROSA	15	F	SGL	SYACAVUNK	
BATTUGE, BERTA	23	F	SGL	PRZZZZUNK	
STOLSMANN, JOHN	22	M	MCHT	PRACBFUNK	
WESTPHAL, FRIEDR.	24	M	LABR	LUZZZZUNK	
MUELLER, MARG.	26	F	W	BVZZZZUNK	
HAHN, LOUIS	15	M	BBR	MKZZZZUNK	
ROSENTHAL, FERD.	49	M	LABR	MKACSDUNK	
MARTIN, AURELIUS	24	M	TNM	BVZZZZUNK	
CZARNIAH, TOMAS	28	M	FARMER	PRZZZZUNK	
KAEMMESER, HERM.	23	M	MCHT	PRAEPZUNK	
JACOB, ELIAS	22	M	MCHT	PRAAKHUNK	
ROSENBAUM, FRANZISKA	28	F	SGL	PRAAKHUNK	
SCHOENEMANN, BETTI	25	F	SGL	PRAAKHUNK	
HOLTZ, LOUIS	38	M	UNKNOWN	PRZZZZUNK	
AMELIA	21	F	W	PRZZZZUNK	
FUCHS, LOUIS	32	M	ENGR	PRZZZZUSA	
NATHAN, LUDW.	39	M	MCHT	HBZZZZUSA	
PIETZNER, HENNRIETTE	37	F	W	HBAAKHUSA	
GERTRUDE	7	F	CHILD	HBAAKHUSA	
NIRSHEIM, PAUL	22	M	MCHT	HBAAKHUSA	
RICHENBACH, FRITZ	23	M	MCHT	HBAAKHUSA	
SPIELDOCH, GEDALIE	80	M	PVTR	HBAAKHUSA	
RELING, JOHN	24	M	MCHT	HBAAKHUSA	
UHLMANN, GEORG	24	M	UNKNOWN	HBAAXKUSA	

SHIP: LAHN

FROM: BREMEN AND SOUTHAMPTON
TO: NEW YORK
ARRIVED: 24 NOVEMBER 1888

PASSENGER	AGE	SEX	OCCUPATION	PRIVL	DES
GLASER, JOS.	38	M	TT	GRZZZZGR	
STEINBERGER, H.	18	M	TT	GRAARRGR	
VONHAUPTMANN, MONTBE	39	M	TT	GRAARRGR	
U	28	F	TT	GRAARRGR	
BOELKEN, CARL	21	M	TT	GRAARRGR	
BETTAGUE, KATHE.	28	F	ART	GRAARRGR	
BERTHOLD, ADEH.	38	F	W	GRABVHGR	
VICTORIA	14	F	UNKNOWN	GRABVHGR	
ADDA	11	F	CH	GRABVHGR	
HUGO	6	M	CHILD	GRABVHGR	
CARLA	.01	F	INFANT	GRABVHGR	
FREY, CHARLES	30	M	TT	GRABOQGR	
CARRY	24	F	W	GRABOQGR	
MORAN, FANNY	34	F	ART	GRABOQGR	
CARL	38	M	TT	GRABOQGR	

PASSENGER	AGE	SEX	OCCUPATION	PRIVL	DES
LIPS, AUGUSTE	37	F	W	GRABOQGR	
EDWARD	10	M	CH	GRABOQGR	
PAULA	8	F	CHILD	GRABOQGR	
ROJAHN, GEORG	41	M	TT	GRACXVGR	
KUNREDE, ANNA	18	F	UNKNOWN	GRZZZZGR	
OETTING, JULIUS	22	M	TT	GRACBFGR	
WULF, EMMA	30	F	UNKNOWN	GRAARRGR	
VORWERK, FRIEDKE.	25	F	UNKNOWN	GRAETSGR	
LERSCH, FERDINAND	19	M	TT	GRACPEGR	
REINHARDRT, CACILIE	22	F	UNKNOWN	GRACPEGR	
ALBERS, THEOD.	33	M	TT	GRZZZZGR	
MUELLER, BERHD.	18	M	TT	GRADVHGR	
REIS, HERM.	18	M	TT	GRABOQGR	
STRAUSS, CARL	17	M	TT	GRAFNKGR	
REDER, HEINRICH	26	M	TT	GRADLDGR	
BORMANN, AURORA	26	F	UNKNOWN	GRADEPGR	
ALTHEIMER, BERTHA	22	F	UNKNOWN	GRADEIGR	
PITTHAU, FRIEDKE.	22	F	UNKNOWN	GRABTUGR	
HAEGELE, WILH.	23	M	TT	GRAFBVGR	
TISCHLER, CLARA	23	F	SVNT	GRAAYAGR	
HAMMERSTEIN, OTTILIE	22	F	SVNT	GRZZZZGR	
TIPPNER, FRANZ	23	M	TT	GRZZZZGR	
SCHAAF, AUGUST	28	M	TT	GRZZZZGR	
BERTHA	32	F	W	GRZZZZGR	
WILLY	4	M	CHILD	GRZZZZGR	
CLARA	.06	F	INFANT	GRZZZZGR	
LAUFKOETTER, GEORG	20	M	TT	GRACBRGR	
BOSENKRANZ, PAUL	21	M	TT	GRACBRGR	
BEHRENS, AHA	27	F	UNKNOWN	GRZZZZGR	
HILGERMANN, AUGUA.	49	F	W	GRZZZZGR	
HEDWIG	12	M	CH	GRZZZZGR	
OTTO	11	M	CH	GRZZZZGR	
GEORG	8	M	CHILD	GRZZZZGR	
ANNA	6	F	CHILD	GRZZZZGR	
MAYER, SIMON	35	M	TT	GRADEIGR	
ANNA	27	F	W	GRADEIGR	
BERTHA	51	F	W	GRADEIGR	
RICHARD	2	M	CHILD	GRADEIGR	
RUTH, HEDWIG	36	F	UNKNOWN	GRAEABGR	
PETERSEN, ANNE	56	F	UNKNOWN	GRAEABGR	
BOROWSKI, ELISAB.	30	F	UNKNOWN	GRACSDGR	
WEHDE, OTTO	15	M	UNKNOWN	GRACSDGR	
BLESSING, CLARA	21	F	UNKNOWN	GRAARRGR	
WEBER, ROSA	4	F	CHILD	GRAARRGR	
HOLLWEGS, EIKE	17	M	UNKNOWN	GRZZZZUSA	
JENTZ, HEINR.	15	M	UNKNOWN	GRADRBUSA	
WITZ, AUGUST	27	M	LABR	GRADRBUSA	
FALKENSTEIN, ROSA	17	F	UNKNOWN	GRAEEQUSA	
AELLERT, GUSTAV	23	M	LABR	GRAKXYUSA	
SZYPERSKA, EMILIA	28	F	W	GRAEABUSA	
MARIA	3	F	CHILD	GRAEABUSA	
IGNATZ	.09	M	INFANT	GRAEABUSA	
BADASZEWSKA, JOSEFA	19	F	UNKNOWN	GRAEABUSA	
KUSCHINSKI, MICHAEL	57	M	LABR	GRZZZZUSA	
ANNA	57	F	W	GRZZZZUSA	
ANDREAS	23	M	LABR	GRZZZZUSA	
JULIANNA	23	F	W	GRZZZZUSA	
ANDREAS	.03	M	INFANT	GRZZZZUSA	
DORSCH, CARL	26	M	LABR	GRZZZZUSA	
CZARNETZKI, CARL	27	M	LABR	GRZZZZUSA	
EVA	25	F	W	GRZZZZUSA	
KRACKE, AUGUST	15	M	UNKNOWN	GRAELEUSA	
KOESTER, JUERGEN	29	M	LABR	GRZZZZUSA	
JUERGEN	29	M	LABR	GRZZZZUSA	
DORIS	27	F	W	GRZZZZUSA	
GRETE	7	F	CHILD	GRZZZZUSA	
JOHANN	5	M	CHILD	GRZZZZUSA	
KATHA.	1	F	CHILD	GRZZZZUSA	
HEIN, JOHANN	22	M	LABR	GRZZZZUSA	
HENRICHS, ELISE	30	F	UNKNOWN	GRZZZZUSA	
TRILOCH, IDA	28	F	UNKNOWN	GRZZZZUSA	
RAMEL, JULIUS	29	M	LABR	GRZZZZUSA	
BERTHA	29	F	W	GRZZZZUSA	
IDA	.11	F	INFANT	GRZZZZUSA	
HOEPKE, FRIEDKE.	18	F	UNKNOWN	GRACBRUSA	

PASSENGER	AGE	SEX	OCCUPATION	PRVL	DES
TIETJEN, CHRISTOPH	16	M	UNKNOWN	GRACBRUSA	
IHLEN, EMMA	16	F	UNKNOWN	GRACBRUSA	
GROENWALD, HERM.	15	M	UNKNOWN	GRACBRUSA	
ROTTMERSHUSEN, HENRY	15	M	UNKNOWN	GRACBRUSA	
VONBORSTEL, WILHELM	15	M	UNKNOWN	GRAARRUSA	
BECKMANN, JOH.N.	66	M	LABR	GRZZZZUSA	
POSTEL, HENRY	15	M	UNKNOWN	GRZZZZUSA	
SCHOELERMANN, JOH.W.	16	M	UNKNOWN	GRZZZZUSA	
MEYER, HEINR.	16	M	UNKNOWN	GRAFMGUSA	
BOHLIN, LENA	22	F	UNKNOWN	GRAAWVUSA	
HUBER, CATHA.	24	F	UNKNOWN	GRZZZZUSA	
GOERMER, MARIA	22	F	UNKNOWN	GRZZZZUSA	
HEYD, BARBA.	17	F	UNKNOWN	GRACJIUSA	
BAESSLER, FRIEDKE.	21	F	UNKNOWN	GRALALUSA	
MUELLER, FRIEDKE.	15	F	UNKNOWN	GRALALUSA	
DEMUTH, LINA	30	F	UNKNOWN	GRAIACUSA	
KLEYENSTUEBER, ANNA	36	F	UNKNOWN	GRAEVTUSA	
BERNER, MARIE	25	F	UNKNOWN	GRZZZZUSA	
BELZNER, CARL	36	M	LABR	GRAIACUSA	
DEMUTH, MARGE.	25	F	UNKNOWN	GRZZZZUSA	
BUTSCH, EMIL	15	M	UNKNOWN	GRAEXWUSA	
MAST, CHRIST.	28	M	BCHR	GRAEXWUSA	
KAUFMANN, FELICITS	18	F	UNKNOWN	GRZZZZUSA	
SCHILL, EUGEN	14	M	UNKNOWN	GRZZZZUNK	
BEYER, CHEIST.	25	M	SMH	GRZZZZUNK	
BAIERSCHMIDT, AUG.	21	M	LABR	GRAGKIUNK	
HEIL, ANNA	15	F	UNKNOWN	GRABETUNK	
MAHLER, CAROLE.	38	F	W	GRZZZZUNK	
JOSEFE	14	F	UNKNOWN	GRZZZZUNK	
JOSEF	13	M	CH	GRZZZZUNK	
CAROLE.	10	F	CH	GRZZZZUNK	
MAGDE.	9	F	CHILD	GRZZZZUNK	
LUDWIG	7	M	CHILD	GRZZZZUNK	
ELISAB.	5	F	CHILD	GRZZZZUNK	
ADAM	3	M	CHILD	GRZZZZUNK	
SAFER	2	M	CHILD	GRZZZZUNK	
MAULHARDT, CHRIST.	30	M	LABR	GRZZZZUNK	
STRUBE, GOTTLIEB	23	M	LABR	GRZZZZUNK	
MESSERSCHMIDT, ANT.	26	M	SMH	GRZZZZUNK	
LANGSDORF, JOHANN	25	M	LABR	GRZZZZUNK	
ECKHARDT, ANTON	16	M	CK	GRZZZZUNK	
HOERSCHER, ANNA	18	F	UNKNOWN	GRZZZZUNK	
SITTELMEIER, MARGA.	19	F	UNKNOWN	GRAHPAUNK	
LEHR, ANNA	25	F	UNKNOWN	GRAEOWUNK	
HELLER, CATHA.	16	F	UNKNOWN	GRZZZZUNK	
STRAUSS, LEOPOLD	15	M	UNKNOWN	GRZZZZUNK	
HUBER, PETER	30	M	LABR	GRAAFCUNK	
HARTMANN, PAUL	17	M	MCHT	GRZZZZUNK	
GEORG	54	M	MCHT	GRZZZZUNK	
KUENZIG, BABETTE	27	F	UNKNOWN	GRZZZZUNK	
WIEHLE, REINHD.	28	M	UPHST	GRAAKHUNK	
BALDES, MARIE	37	F	W	GRAEUTUNK	
HOFFMANN, MICH.	56	M	LABR	GRZZZZUNK	
CAROLE.	56	F	W	GRZZZZUNK	
EMMA	17	F	UNKNOWN	GRZZZZUNK	
MARTHA	10	F	CH	GRZZZZUNK	
CHRISTENSEN, LARS	26	M	JNR	GRZZZZUNK	
DIEDRICHSEN, NIELS	17	M	SMH	GRZZZZUNK	
VOGEL, JULIANNA	28	F	UNKNOWN	GRACUEUNK	
ZIEFLE, EVA	15	F	UNKNOWN	GRALALUNK	
SCHIEFER, SOPHIE	22	F	UNKNOWN	GRABARUNK	
HEISE, JUSTUS	17	M	LKSH	GRAFFDUNK	
MEYER, THOMAS	22	M	MLR	GRZZZZUNK	
HAAS, ALBERTE.	44	F	W	GRADHZUNK	
ANNA	16	F	UNKNOWN	GRADHZUNK	
PHILIPP	14	M	UNKNOWN	GRADHZUNK	
BEBETTE	13	F	CH	GRADHZUNK	
WILHELM	10	M	CH	GRADHZUNK	
MARIA	9	F	CHILD	GRADHZUNK	
GRETCHEN	7	F	CHILD	GRADHZUNK	
JAKOB	3	M	CHILD	GRADHZUNK	
HOECKER, KARL	40	M	LABR	GRZZZZUNK	
FRANZKA	35	F	W	GRZZZZUNK	
FRANZKA	11	F	CH	GRZZZZUNK	
THERESE	9	F	CHILD	GRZZZZUNK	
JOHANN	7	M	CHILD	GRZZZZUNK	
KARL	5	M	CHILD	GRZZZZUNK	
IGNAZ	4	M	CHILD	GRZZZZUNK	
LUDWIG	3	M	CHILD	GRZZZZUNK	
JOSEF	.01	M	INFANT	GRZZZZUNK	
MEIER, THERESE	40	F	W	GRZZZZUNK	
THERESE	20	F	UNKNOWN	GRZZZZUNK	
ANNA	11	F	CH	GRZZZZUNK	
JOSEF	8	M	CHILD	GRZZZZUNK	
MARIA	7	F	CHILD	GRZZZZUNK	
CRESZENS	4	M	CHILD	GRZZZZUNK	
LUDWINA	3	F	CHILD	GRZZZZUNK	
OTTILIA	.02	F	INFANT	GRZZZZUNK	
AX, FRIEDR.	26	M	LABR	GRABLTUNK	
SCHULTE, WILHELM	26	M	CPTR	GRABLTUNK	
RAPP, JOHANN	16	M	BKR	GRZZZZUNK	
WEIGMANN, RICHARD	22	M	CNF	GRZZZZUNK	
SALBECK, FRANZ	18	M	LABR	GRZZZZUNK	
BEHLING, FRANZ	24	M	LABR	GRZZZZUNK	
MARGUARDT, MATHILDE	21	F	UNKNOWN	GRZZZZUNK	
GEISSEL, WILHE.	17	F	UNKNOWN	GRZZZZUNK	
HAERER, GOTTLOB	10	M	CH	GRZZZZUNK	
LINK, ERNESTE.	22	F	UNKNOWN	GRABOQUNK	
OPPERMANN, CARL	22	M	BKBNDR	GRZZZZUNK	
PFEFFER, ERNESTE.	38	F	W	GRZZZZUNK	
ADAM	11	M	CH	GRZZZZUNK	
SOPHIE	10	F	CH	GRZZZZUNK	
HEINRICH	9	M	CHILD	GRZZZZUNK	
JOHANETTE	6	F	CHILD	GRZZZZUNK	
CHRISTINE	2	F	CHILD	GRZZZZUNK	
HARDTMANN, ADAM	22	M	SHMK	GRZZZZUNK	
AMEND, MARIE	22	F	UNKNOWN	GRABTUUNK	
MENZEL, HEINR.	25	M	PNTR	GRAEVVUNK	
SCHROEDER, META	21	F	UNKNOWN	GRAADEUNK	
SCHEMALLEK, MAX	23	M	SLR	GRAAKHUNK	
EHLEN, JOHANN	45	M	FARMER	GRADXMUNK	
SWOBODA, HEINR.	10	M	CH	GRABVEUNK	
FEUBNER, JOHANN	25	M	BKR	GRAAIFUNK	
SCHREIBER, SOPHIE	20	F	UNKNOWN	GRZZZZUNK	
BUELKEN, HEINRICH	15	M	UNKNOWN	GRADXCUNK	
STRUSS, HERMANN	16	M	UNKNOWN	GRADXCUNK	
STEGEMANN, HERMANN	17	M	UNKNOWN	GRADXCUNK	
PFISTERER, FRIEDA	22	F	UNKNOWN	GRAHYCUNK	
GADE, ELISABETA	23	F	UNKNOWN	GRZZZZUNK	
KROEGER, ANNA	17	F	UNKNOWN	GRZZZZUNK	
KAUPER, JOHN	35	M	MCHT	GRZZZZUNK	
STROEBER, THOMAS	53	M	CPTR	GRZZZZUNK	
CATHA.	47	F	W	GRZZZZUNK	
BARBARA	11	F	CH	GRZZZZUNK	
JOHANN	9	M	CHILD	GRZZZZUNK	
HEINRICH	3	M	CHILD	GRZZZZUNK	
LANDAU, ROBERT	22	M	MCHT	GRAIKJUNK	
JUNG, CARL	26	M	LABR	GRAIHNUNK	
RETZLAFF, LOUISE	46	F	W	GRZZZZUNK	
MARTHA	.10	F	INFANT	GRZZZZUNK	
HERMANN, CHRIST.	29	M	LABR	GRZZZZUNK	
AUGUSTE	29	F	W	GRZZZZUNK	
OTTO	4	M	CHILD	GRZZZZUNK	
WILHELM	.04	M	INFANT	GRZZZZUNK	
SCHIKOWSKI, ANTON	24	M	LABR	GRZZZZUNK	
KOEHN, THERESE	62	F	W	GRAAKHUNK	
STAHL, HELENE	22	F	UNKNOWN	GRAAKHUNK	
KEMPER, THEODOR	23	M	GDNR	GRAAAXUNK	
MENSE, THEODOR	37	M	CPTR	GRZZZZUNK	
STEINMANN, FRIEDR.	29	M	LABR	GRZZZZUNK	
WEHNER, OTTO	29	M	LABR	GRAFRGUNK	
WILLOX, DANIEL	29	M	LABR	GRACBRUNK	
IDEN, JOHANN	38	M	BKSL	GRAARRUNK	
FRISCHE, JOH.H.	50	M	LABR	GRZZZZUNK	
MAHRMANN, TRINA	17	F	UNKNOWN	GRZZZZUNK	
MUEGGE, WILH.	21	M	FARMER	GRABRYUNK	
HAUCK, MARGA.	19	F	UNKNOWN	GRADOIUNK	
DIESSEL, BABETTE	19	F	UNKNOWN	GRADOIUNK	
WENDLER, ANNA	17	F	UNKNOWN	GRABZSUNK	
PAULSEN, ANNA	21	F	UNKNOWN	GRABZSUNK	

449

PASSENGER	AGE	SEX	OCCUPATION	PRIVL	DES
PETERSON, PAULE.	20	F	UNKNOWN	GRZZZZUNK	
LYDIKSEN, MARIE	19	F	W	GRZZZZUNK	
IVER	2	M	CHILD	GRZZZZUNK	
PETERSEN, MARIE	22	F	UNKNOWN	GRZZZZUNK	
CHRISTIANSEN, CHRISTN.	24	M	FARMER	GRABZSUNK	
SUEHRIG, AUGUST	30	M	FARMER	GRACBRUNK	
HAMMELEF, CHRIST.	26	M	FARMER	GRZZZZUNK	
THOMSEN, KJESTEN	30	M	FARMER	GRZZZZUNK	
HOEI, MATTHIAS	10	M	CH	GRAHXAUNK	
MAGNUSSEN, SARA	23	F	UNKNOWN	GRABZSUNK	
STUBBE, JOHANN	16	M	UNKNOWN	GRAFPSUNK	
STENDER, HEINR.	60	M	LABR	GRACBRUNK	
HENRIETTE	50	F	W	GRACBRUNK	
GOTTLIEB	24	M	LABR	GRACBRUNK	
BENTRUP, MARIE	19	F	UNKNOWN	GRZZZZUNK	
SOENDERGAARD, METTE	21	F	UNKNOWN	GRAHUOUNK	
MATTHIESEN, ANNA	26	F	UNKNOWN	GRZZZZUNK	
MARIE	20	F	UNKNOWN	GRZZZZUNK	
ANDREASEN, JOERGEN	36	M	LABR	GRZZZZUNK	
LAGONI, CHRIST.	26	M	LABR	GRZZZZUNK	
WENZEL, ANNE	26	F	UNKNOWN	GRZZZZUNK	
HAHN, EDMUND	24	M	FARMER	GRZZZZUNK	
GARBRISCH, JOSEF	25	M	MLR	GRAARZUNK	
MATIBA, FRIEDR.	53	M	BRR	GRZZZZUNK	
BOEK, JOKOB	31	M	LABR	GRADPJUNK	
ANNA	28	F	W	GRADPJUNK	
ANNA	3	F	CHILD	GRADPJUNK	
MARIE	.02	F	INFANT	GRADPJUNK	
SCHEROCHING, MINNA	26	F	UNKNOWN	GRAEHFUNK	
ROTH, GEORG	41	M	BCHR	GRADLDUNK	
MARIE	36	F	W	GRADLDUNK	
GEORG	16	M	WTR	GRADLDUNK	
WALLY	14	M	UNKNOWN	GRADLDUNK	
MAX	3	M	CHILD	GRADLDUNK	
DANIELZIK, LUDWIG	30	M	TLR	GRZZZZUNK	
ROGOTTA, GOTTLOB	33	M	SMH	GRZZZZUNK	
PRZEZINSKA, BERTHA	35	F	W	GRZZZZUNK	
FRIEDRICH	10	M	CH	GRZZZZUNK	
JOHANN	4	M	CHILD	GRZZZZUNK	
VAGO, WILHELNE	60	F	W	GRZZZZUNK	
BOYE, MARIA	30	F	UNKNOWN	GRZZZZUNK	
REINSDORF, HEINR.	14	M	UNKNOWN	GRADRDUNK	
CAMPBELL, RICHARD	37	M	TT	GRADBQUNK	
R.	25	F	W	GRADBQUNK	

SHIP: THE QUEEN

FROM: LIVERPOOL AND QUEENSTOWN
TO: NEW YORK
ARRIVED: 24 NOVEMBER 1888

PASSENGER	AGE	SEX	OCCUPATION	PRIVL	DES
WEISENBERG, JETA	9	F	CHILD	GRACBFNY	
SAM.	7	M	CHILD	GRACBFNY	
SARAH	5	F	CHILD	GRACBFNY	
HYMAN	3	M	CHILD	GRACBFNY	
ANNIE	1	F	CHILD	GRACBFNY	
WEINSTEIN, ISRAEL	44	M	LABR	GRADBQNY	
ROSE	42	F	W	GRADBQNY	
MORIS	21	M	LABR	GRADBQNY	
BETSY	12	F	CH	GRADBQNY	
SOLOMON	10	M	CH	GRADBQNY	
RACHEL	8	F	CHILD	GRADBQNY	
EPHRAIM	3	M	CHILD	GRADBQNY	
WISENBERG, M	31	M	LABR	GRACBFNY	
U	29	F	W	GRACBFNY	
WILLICKS, ANTON	39	M	LABR	GRACBFNY	
PHILIPP	10	M	CH	GRACBFNY	
ISTAMY, ANTON	23	M	LABR	GRZZZZNY	
GREENSPAN, ROSA	20	F	SP	GRACBFNY	
WILLKE, ALBERT	25	M	LABR	GRADBQBO	

PASSENGER	AGE	SEX	OCCUPATION	PRIVL	DES
DORN, AUGUST	64	M	LABR	GRACBFNY	
CAROLINA	52	F	W	GRACBFNY	
ROSALIE	30	F	SP	GRACBFNY	
ALBERT	11	M	CH	GRACBFNY	
RUDOLF	8	M	CHILD	GRACBFNY	
LANGE, JULIUS	34	M	LABR	GRZZZZNY	
ERENOVI, CHELE	39	M	LABR	GRZZZZBO	
PHWENHUR, LEO	41	M	LABR	GRZZZZBO	
LACKRRUR, JOSEPH	42	M	LABR	GRZZZZBO	
DE, JUS.	20	M	LABR	GRZZZZNY	
BRISURS, ED.	30	M	LABR	GRZZZZNY	
SPERMAN, H.	40	M	LABR	GRADBQNY	
KR-PP, CAROLINE	24	F	SP	GRADBQNY	
INAYE, ISIDOR	31	M	LABR	GRADAXNY	

SHIP: CITY OF RICHMOND

FROM: LIVERPOOL AND QUEENSTOWN
TO: NEW YORK
ARRIVED: 26 NOVEMBER 1888

PASSENGER	AGE	SEX	OCCUPATION	PRIVL	DES
SEIG, CARL	62	M	LABR	GRACBFNY	
RASOTKOWSKY, JOS	42	M	LABR	GRACBFNY	
SALOMON, M.	16	M	LABR	GRACBFNY	
BOSSER, FLYNZ	23	M	LABR	GRACBFNY	
ATTMORLT, SOFLIN	24	M	LABR	GRACBFNY	
KELLER, LOUIS	52	M	LABR	GRADXWNY	
MILLER, G.	16	F	SP	GRACBFNY	
PERET, ISRAEL	60	M	LABR	GRACBFNY	
ESTHER	53	F	W	GRACBFNY	
LINA	22	F	UNKNOWN	GRACBFNY	
L.	19	F	UNKNOWN	GRACBFNY	
MENDEL	12	F	CH	GRACBFNY	
G.	10	M	CH	GRACBFNY	
KATZEN, JOHAN	25	M	LABR	GRACBFWI	
J.	36	F	W	GRACBFWI	
AN.	12	F	CH	GRACBFWI	
AN.	60	F	W	GRACBFWI	
KLEIN, HERMAN	24	F	W	GRACBFNY	
REISE	26	M	LABR	GRACBFNY	
KURATKOWSKI, WOL.	61	M	LABR	GRACBFNY	
CATH.	60	F	W	GRACBFNY	
JOHAN	20	M	LABR	GRACBFNY	
PETER	17	M	LABR	GRACBFNY	

SHIP: ARIZONA

FROM: LIVERPOOL AND QUEENSTOWN
TO: NEW YORK
ARRIVED: 27 NOVEMBER 1888

PASSENGER	AGE	SEX	OCCUPATION	PRIVL	DES
HAAS, MINNIE	24	F	SP	GRACBFUSA	
MILLER, ANNA	21	F	SP	GRACBFUSA	
FALKNER, CARL	24	M	SHPMN	GRACBFUSA	
VAKE, HERMANN	17	M	LABR	GRAAECUSA	
BERG, GEORGE	21	M	LABR	GRACBFUSA	
SCHOPFLOCHER, S.	22	M	GENT	GRAAIEUSA	
STEINER, CARL	31	M	GENT	GRADBQUSA	
ROUX, P.	30	M	GENT	GRADXWUSA	
LESPERANCE, W.	54	M	GENT	GRADBQUSA	

SHIP: GALLIA

FROM: LIVERPOOL AND QUEENSTOWN
TO: NEW YORK
ARRIVED: 27 NOVEMBER 1888

PASSENGER	AGE	SEX	OCCUPATION	PRVL	DES
TROHLICH, EMIL	30	M	TLR		GRACBFUSA
SCHLAKMAN, SENDER	21	M	LABR		GRACBFUSA
BRANDENBURGEN, DANIEL	16	M	SHMK		GRACBFUSA
JOSEF	20	M	SHMK		GRACBFUSA
BOHN, LOUISA	19	F	SP		GRACBFUSA
GAY, EMIL	31	M	UNKNOWN		GRACDSUSA
HENNRIETTA	22	F	W		GRACDSUSA

SHIP: POLYNESIA

FROM: HAMBURG
TO: NEW YORK
ARRIVED: 27 NOVEMBER 1888

PASSENGER	AGE	SEX	OCCUPATION	PRVL	DES
DRZEWICKI, FRANZ	35	M	PNTR		GRACBFNY
ZACHARIAS, FRIEDRICH	25	M	LABR		GRAASPNY
U, U	16	M	LABR		PRZZZZNY
MEYER, WILHELMINE	27	F	SGL		PRZZZZNY
HARLOSSA, MACIEJ	48	M	LABR		PRZZZZNY
CLARA	48	F	W		PRZZZZNY
MARIANNE	16	F	CH		PRZZZZNY
AGNISZKA	7	F	CHILD		PRZZZZNY
FRANZISKA	6	F	CHILD		PRZZZZNY
PETERS, CARL	32	M	LABR		PRAFYKNY
FRDCKE.	35	F	W		PRAFYKNY
WM.	7	F	CHILD		PRAFYKNY
BERTHA	6	F	CHILD		PRAFYKNY
MARTHA	20	F	CH		PRAFYKNY
CARL	14	F	CH		PRAFYKNY
BODZINSKI, JOSEF	32	M	LABR		PRZZZZNY
WIETZSCHOWSKI, MINE	57	M	WO		PRAECBNY
LASKOWSKI, EDUARD	25	M	LABR		PRAECBNY
PETERSEN, ELISABETH	21	F	SGL		PRAHILNY
HORN, CATHA.	16	F	SGL		PRAHKVNY
CZESLIKOWSKI, JOHANN	23	M	TLR		PRAAZQNY
ROSALIE	29	F	W		PRAAZQNY
WAGENER, HEINR.	27	M	MCHT		PRAARZNY
BAEHNKE, JOH.	35	M	FARMER		PRZZZZNY
HINRISCHSEN, LOUISE	24	F	SGL		PRACQANY
ERICH, FERD.	29	M	LABR		PRAEPZNY
MARIE	29	F	W		PRAEPZNY
SKRONIECKY, VALENTIN	16	M	LABR		PRZZZZNY
POGLETTKI, PAUL	16	M	LABR		PRZZZZNY
NAWROTZKA, NIEPOMACZINA	22	M	LABR		PRZZZZNY
BONZKOWIAK, ANNA	19	F	SGL		PRZZZZNY
PRZYBYTOWICZ, PELAGIA	21	F	SGL		PRAAYFNY
FRANZISCA	7	F	CHILD		PRAAYFNY
REINHARDT, ADOLF	26	M	SHMK		PRAAKHNY
GRABISNA, MARIA	23	F	SGL		PRADVVNY
ANNE, ERNST	16	M	BKR		PRACZENY
SCHNEIDER, ALOIS	20	M	LABR		PRAAFCNY
MAI, KARL	32	M	FARMER		PRZZZZNY
MARIANNE	30	F	W		PRZZZZNY
MINNA	5	F	CHILD		PRZZZZNY
MARIANNE	2	F	CHILD		PRZZZZNY
GROSSKOPH, CARL	29	M	SLR		PRZZZZNY
KLAT, CARL	31	M	LABR		PRAEVMNY
JUETZOW, CARLE.	38	F	WO		PRAAKHNY
ERICH	16	M	WO		PRAAKHNY
ANNA	14	F	WO		PRAAKHNY
MARGR.	7	F	CHILD		PRAAKHNY
GERTRUDE	5	F	CHILD		PRAAKHNY
CARL	3	M	CHILD		PRAAKHNY
META	.09	F	INFANT		PRAAKHNY
NIELSEN, HANS	50	M	TLR		PRZZZZNY
BERTHOLD, JOSEF	27	M	JNR		PRABDMNY
EMTMANN, JOHANN	25	M	BRR		BVZZZZNY
RUSSINE	24	F	W		BVZZZZNY
MERZ, ADOLF	25	M	BKR		WMZZZZNY
WILMERSDORFER, ARON	47	M	LABR		WMABNYNY
FREIBERGER, JOHAN	22	M	SMH		WMADLDNY
HOEHN, JOHANNE	21	F	SGL		WMZZZZNY
REGINE	19	F	SGL		WMZZZZNY

SHIP: WERRA

FROM: BREMEN AND SOUTHAMPTON
TO: NEW YORK
ARRIVED: 28 NOVEMBER 1888

PASSENGER	AGE	SEX	OCCUPATION	PRVL	DES
PAGENS, JUAN	26	M	TT		WMACBFUSA
SANVALLE, ELIZA	65	F	W		WMACBFUSA
JULIA	38	F	UNKNOWN		WMACBFUSA
SOHIFF, HENRY	38	M	MCHT		WMACBFUSA
U	36	F	W		WMACBFUSA
GUSTAV	10	M	CH		WMACBFUSA
DOEHR, JOHANNA	22	F	UNKNOWN		GRZZZZUSA
MARBURG, ALFRED	23	M	TT		GRACBFUSA
V, W.	22	M	TT		GRACBRUSA
VILMAR, RUD.	30	M	TT		GRAAKHUSA
HONIGHAUSEN, ANNA	56	F	W		GRAIPJUSA
LILLY	20	F	UNKNOWN		GRAIPJUSA
LAURA	8	F	CHILD		GRAIPJUSA
LUECKMANN, JOHE.	16	F	UNKNOWN		GRZZZZUSA
POPPE, ANNA	63	F	W		GRAFOAUSA
HOFFMANN, PAUL	23	M	MCHT		GRABUJUSA
THERESE	20	F	W		GRABUJUSA
SADROSINSKY, AUGUSTE	32	F	W		GRZZZZUSA
ARTHUR	.11	M	INFANT		GRZZZZUSA
GEYER, MICH.	26	M	TT		BDZZZZUSA
JACOB	25	M	TT		BDZZZZUSA
BRAUN, CATHA.	21	F	UNKNOWN		GRZZZZUSA
REICHENPFADER, ENGELB.	29	M	TT		GRAAOOUSA
GUTENSTEIN, FRIEDA	16	F	UNKNOWN		GRAAOOUSA
LOUIS	14	M	UNKNOWN		GRAAOOUSA
MUELLER, EURENTIA	53	F	W		GRAAGLUSA
BECK, THERES.	24	F	UNKNOWN		GRAARRUSA
ROTH, HELENE	36	F	W		BDZZZZUSA
GAERTNER, MARIA	20	F	UNKNOWN		GRZZZZUSA
PICHOCH, MICH.	51	M	LABR		GRZZZZUSA
RINADE	47	F	W		GRZZZZUSA
FRIEDRICH	9	M	CHILD		GRZZZZUSA
MITLENER, MARIA	59	F	W		BVZZZZUSA
BENECKE, WILHE.	17	F	UNKNOWN		BVAAAHUSA
HILBICH, BERTHA	21	F	UNKNOWN		BVACSLUSA
KRENZER, RIENHOLD	22	M	LABR		GRZZZZUSA
IDEM, ROSALIE	17	F	UNKNOWN		GRZZZZUSA
DAMRATH, FRIEDR.	22	M	LABR		GRZZZZUSA
LILIENTHAL, PETER	25	M	LABR		GRZZZZUSA
WILHE.	26	F	W		GRZZZZUSA
OTTO	4	M	CHILD		GRZZZZUSA
MARIE	.02	F	INFANT		GRZZZZUSA
KORTAS, HELENE	18	F	UNKNOWN		GRAHRSUSA
KREIER, MICH.	35	M	LABR		GRZZZZUSA
ROSALIE	34	F	W		GRZZZZUSA
MARIE	9	M	CHILD		GRZZZZUSA
JOH.	4	M	CHILD		GRZZZZUSA
ANNA	.11	F	INFANT		GRZZZZUSA
FELITAN, CONSTANZ	58	M	LABR		GRZZZZUSA
MARIE	50	F	W		GRZZZZUSA
AUGUST	15	M	LABR		GRZZZZUSA
BLOCK, MICHEL	35	M	LABR		GRZZZZUSA
LOUISE	27	F	W		GRZZZZUSA

PASSENGER	AGE	SEX	OCCUPATION	PRVL	DES
JOH.	8	M	CHILD	GRZZZZ	USA
ANNA	5	F	CHILD	GRZZZZ	USA
ROSE	5	F	CHILD	GRZZZZ	USA
HANNE	.09	F	INFANT	GRZZZZ	USA
KAMBROWSKI, ELISAB.	15	F	UNKNOWN	GRZZZZ	USA
WICHERT, HELENE	22	F	UNKNOWN	GRZZZZ	USA
GAJEWSKI, JOH.	72	M	LABR	GRAHRS	USA
BAUGNOWSKI, ANNA	16	F	UNKNOWN	GRZZZZ	USA
GRABOWSKI, BARBARA	35	F	UNKNOWN	GRAHRS	USA
ROSCHINSKI, FLORENT.	59	F	W	GRAHRS	USA
ROSALIE	26	F	UNKNOWN	GRAHRS	USA
GRABOWSKI, CAROLE.	60	F	W	GRZZZZ	USA
ADAM	23	M	LABR	GRZZZZ	USA
SCHMICK, JOH.	26	M	LABR	GRZZZZ	USA
EMILIE	27	F	W	GRZZZZ	USA
AUGUSTE	4	F	CHILD	GRZZZZ	USA
JOHANN	3	M	CHILD	GRZZZZ	USA
WILHE.	.06	F	INFANT	GRZZZZ	USA
PINZLAK, JOHN	29	M	LABR	GRZZZZ	USA
ANNA	31	F	W	GRZZZZ	USA
MARIA	4	F	CHILD	GRZZZZ	USA
FRANZISKA	.01	F	INFANT	GRZZZZ	USA
MEDING, FRANZ	25	M	LABR	GRZZZZ	USA
KOWALEWSKY, AUG.	24	M	LABR	GRZZZZ	USA
BERTHA	17	F	UNKNOWN	GRZZZZ	USA
RESCHKE, JOH.	35	M	FARMER	GRZZZZ	USA
JUSTINE	34	F	W	GRZZZZ	USA
ANNA	13	F	UNKNOWN	GRZZZZ	USA
CARL	7	M	CHILD	GRZZZZ	USA
ADELGUNDE	2	F	CHILD	GRZZZZ	USA
JOH.	.09	M	INFANT	GRZZZZ	USA
BEHNKE, JOH.	16	M	FARMER	GRZZZZ	USA
BRANDT, WILH.	25	M	FARMER	GRZZZZ	USA
PAUL, CARL	26	M	FARMER	GRAAXF	USA
SELINSKI, JOH.	60	M	FARMER	GRZZZZ	USA
DOROTHEA	60	F	W	GRZZZZ	USA
MATHIAS, AUG.	25	M	FARMER	GRZZZZ	USA
CHARLOTTE	19	F	UNKNOWN	GRZZZZ	USA
GOLUMBKI, JAKOB	32	M	LABR	GRZZZZ	USA
JUSTINE	26	F	W	GRZZZZ	USA
JOH.	7	M	CHILD	GRZZZZ	USA
LISBETH	6	F	CHILD	GRZZZZ	USA
MARIE	4	F	CHILD	GRZZZZ	USA
CAROL	.09	M	INFANT	GRZZZZ	USA
SMIKORSKI, WERONIKA	15	F	UNKNOWN	GRZZZZ	USA
BENDIG, AUG.	67	M	LABR	GRZZZZ	USA
HELENE	62	F	W	GRZZZZ	USA
AUG.	38	M	LABR	GRZZZZ	USA
ANNA	35	F	W	GRZZZZ	USA
RASCHKE, MICHEL	40	M	LABR	GRZZZZ	USA
HELENE	38	F	W	GRZZZZ	USA
FRIEDR.	35	M	LABR	GRZZZZ	USA
CAROLINE	34	F	W	GRZZZZ	USA
BENDIG, MARIA	22	F	UNKNOWN	GRZZZZ	USA
MAROHN, OLGA	21	F	UNKNOWN	GRZZZZ	USA
FLOCINSKY, FRANZ	17	M	LABR	GRZZZZ	USA
GRASSE, FRIEDR.	32	M	LABR	GRZZZZ	USA
AUGUSTE	32	F	W	GRZZZZ	USA
ANNA	4	F	CHILD	GRZZZZ	USA
THUMSER, CHRISTOPH	17	M	LABR	BVZZZZ	USA
BRANDES, LUDWIG	44	M	LABR	GRZZZZ	USA
GRABOWSKI, GOTTL.	51	M	LABR	GRZZZZ	USA
CAROL.	50	F	W	GRZZZZ	USA
JOH.	17	M	LABR	GRZZZZ	USA
MARIE	11	F	UNKNOWN	GRZZZZ	USA
ELIS	6	F	CHILD	GRZZZZ	USA
EGGERT, JULIUS	38	M	LABR	GRZZZZ	USA
ROCK, FRITZ	52	M	FARMER	GRACBR	USA
WILKENS, HEINR.	34	M	FARMER	GRADIB	USA
BROMDENBURG, FRITZ	24	M	FARMER	GRAGOI	USA
LOUISE	23	F	FARMER	GRAGOI	USA
GANLER, GOTTL.	29	M	BCHR	GRZZZZ	USA
SCHIMPF, REINHD.	23	M	LABR	GRZZZZ	USA
HEINZ, GOTTL.	25	M	LABR	WMZZZZ	USA
SCHMID, JOH.	23	M	LABR	WMZZZZ	USA
SORG, WILHE.	69	F	W	BVZZZZ	USA
WILH.	28	M	FARMER	BVZZZZ	USA
PETERS, ANNA	21	F	UNKNOWN	GRZZZZ	USA
FRIESS, MARIE	18	F	UNKNOWN	WMZZZZ	USA
BRADER, MICH.	18	M	FARMER	BVZZZZ	USA
FAUSTLIN, MARGA.	18	F	UNKNOWN	BVZZZZ	USA
KREUZMANN, ELISAB.	28	F	W	BVZZZZ	USA
THEDA	9	F	CHILD	BVZZZZ	USA
WILH.	7	M	CHILD	BVZZZZ	USA
ADAM	6	M	CHILD	BVZZZZ	USA
BREDL, OTTOMAR	23	M	LABR	BVZZZZ	USA
LUTHER, BARBA.	20	F	UNKNOWN	BVZZZZ	USA
SAPPER, ROSINE	20	F	UNKNOWN	BVZZZZ	USA
WOERLER, ELISE	20	F	UNKNOWN	BVZZZZ	USA
KOENIG, MARGA.	27	F	UNKNOWN	BVZZZZ	USA
SCHUESSLER, CONRAD	25	M	FARMER	BVZZZZ	USA
HERRHAMER, AD.H.	17	M	FARMER	BVZZZZ	USA
MUELLER, CARL	17	M	FARMER	BVZZZZ	USA
KRICK, CATHA.	21	F	UNKNOWN	BVAAFT	USA
HERHOLD, FERDINAND	59	M	LABR	GRZZZZ	USA
AUGUSTE	54	F	W	GRZZZZ	USA
KALDOWSKI, JOS.	32	M	LABR	GRAEVM	USA
MARIE	26	F	W	GRAEVM	USA
LEOKADEA	3	F	CHILD	GRAEVM	USA
NORBERT	.11	M	INFANT	GRAEVM	USA
LUBENSKI, AGNES	29	F	W	GRZZZZ	USA
HELENE	2	F	CHILD	GRZZZZ	USA
SOPHIE	.11	F	INFANT	GRZZZZ	USA
WANZLAW	.01	M	INFANT	GRZZZZ	USA
PILZWEGER, MARIA	69	F	W	GRADRO	USA
GOESS, CONRAD	13	M	UNKNOWN	GRADRO	USA
KELLNER, HEINR.	18	M	LABR	GRZZZZ	USA
KUGLMAYER, MICHL.	37	M	LABR	BVZZZZ	USA
POPPE, AUG.	20	M	LABR	BVAFOA	USA
NIEMANN, JOSEPH	23	M	LABR	BVAFDF	USA
RODE, HEINR.	20	M	LABR	BVADAA	USA
REBHORN, GEORG	28	M	LABR	BVZZZZ	USA
WACHTER, BABETTE	22	F	UNKNOWN	BVAEVV	USA
JIENAN, MARIE	20	F	UNKNOWN	GRZZZZ	USA
ROGACKI, AGNISZKA	30	F	W	GRZZZZ	USA
WLADISLAW	5	M	CHILD	GRZZZZ	USA
IGNATZ	4	M	CHILD	GRZZZZ	USA
STANISLAW	3	M	CHILD	GRZZZZ	USA
JOSEPH	.03	M	INFANT	GRZZZZ	USA
QUARTIER, EMILIE	15	F	UNKNOWN	GRZZZZ	USA
BENDIG, HELENE	7	F	CHILD	GRZZZZ	USA
MARIE	3	F	CHILD	GRZZZZ	USA
ANNA	.02	F	INFANT	GRZZZZ	USA
RESCHKE, FRIEDR.	11	M	CH	GRZZZZ	USA
JOH.	8	M	CHILD	GRZZZZ	USA
ANDREAS	5	M	CHILD	GRZZZZ	USA
HELENE	3	F	CHILD	GRZZZZ	USA
MARIE	.09	F	INFANT	GRZZZZ	USA
MARIE	10	F	CH	GRZZZZ	USA
FRIEDR.	8	M	CHILD	GRZZZZ	USA
JOSEF	6	M	CHILD	GRZZZZ	USA
HERM.	3	M	CHILD	GRZZZZ	USA
PAUL	.03	M	INFANT	GRZZZZ	USA
ELISAB.	.03	F	INFANT	GRZZZZ	USA
MARKOWSKA, MARIE	19	F	UNKNOWN	GRZZZZ	USA
HERHOLD, MARIE	21	F	UNKNOWN	GRZZZZ	USA
PAULE.	17	F	UNKNOWN	GRZZZZ	USA
ROHMANN, AUG.	24	M	LABR	GRZZZZ	USA
WOHLFAHRT, LUDW.	15	M	LABR	BVZZZZ	USA
ZEITZLER, CHESZENZ	19	M	LABR	BVACVF	USA
DREMSEL, AND.	23	M	LABR	BVZZZZ	USA
STINDT, HANSEINE	20	F	UNKNOWN	GRZZZZ	USA
HELENE	29	F	UNKNOWN	GRZZZZ	USA
SZUKAY, ANTONIA	25	F	W	GRZZZZ	USA
FRANZ	.09	M	INFANT	GRZZZZ	USA
LAKOMSKY, WALENTY	35	M	LABR	GRZZZZ	USA
RYDZENSKA, AGNISZKA	22	F	W	GRZZZZ	USA
FRANZISKA	.05	F	INFANT	GRZZZZ	USA
SIEBERT, JOH.	58	M	LABR	GRZZZZ	USA
MARIE	56	F	W	GRZZZZ	USA

PASSENGER	AGE	SEX	OCCUPATION	PROVL	DES
WILH.	16	M	LABR	GRZZZZUSA
AUGUSTE	10	F	CH	GRZZZZUSA
FICKERS, AUG.	16	M	UNKNOWN	GRADAFUSA
CATTAN, FRIEDR.	20	M	LABR	GRAHLUUSA
CORDES, H.	23	M	LABR	GRZZZZUSA
MARKIEWITZ, BRONISLAWA	17	F	UNKNOWN	GRABUTUSA
LOGEMANN, JASPER	32	M	BCHR	GRAFGPUSA
FREITAG, CARL	24	M	BCHR	GRZZZZUSA
SCHECH, JOH.	23	M	BCHR	GRZZZZUSA
CAROLE.	22	F	W	GRZZZZUSA
WILHE.	.02	F	INFANT	GRZZZZUSA
KUPJISCH, FRIEDR.	16	M	UNKNOWN	GRAFFYUSA
LAKOMSKI, JOSEFE.	35	F	W	GRZZZZUSA
PETRONELLA	7	F	CHILD	GRZZZZUSA
RADWILSKI, IGNATZ	40	M	FARMER	GRAENIUSA
CAROLE.	47	F	W	GRAENIUSA
WEGNER, AUGUSTE	23	F	UNKNOWN	GRAENIUSA
FREITZG, AUGUSTE	18	F	UNKNOWN	GRZZZZUSA
MEYER, THEOBALD	23	M	LABR	BDZZZZUSA
FREITAG, GOTTL.	26	M	LABR	GRZZZZUSA
FRIEDR.	2	M	CHILD	GRZZZZUSA
AUGUSTE	.03	F	INFANT	GRZZZZUSA
MEHREN, AUGUSTE	17	F	UNKNOWN	GRAETVUSA
STERZER, WILHE.	27	F	W	GRACAWUSA
FRIEDR.	7	M	CHILD	GRACAWUSA
OTTO	3	M	CHILD	GRACAWUSA
POSER, ANNA	24	F	UNKNOWN	GRZZZZUSA
BANOMER, BERTHA	18	F	UNKNOWN	GRZZZZUSA
GEBHARDT, AUG.	23	M	LABR	GRAAKHUSA
CLARA	21	F	W	GRAAKHUSA
HAECKER, ANTON	32	M	FARMER	GRADZYUSA
MARIE	30	F	W	GRADZYUSA
BABETTE	6	F	CHILD	GRADZYUSA
JOSEPH	5	M	CHILD	GRADZYUSA
GERHARD	2	M	CHILD	GRADZYUSA
JOSEPH	.06	M	INFANT	GRADZYUSA
WITTHOLM, CHR.	17	M	LABR	GRZZZZUSA
HUONDER, URSALA	56	F	W	WMZZZZUSA
CATHA.	20	F	UNKNOWN	WMZZZZUSA
BIPPUS, JOHS.	55	M	LABR	WMZZZZUSA
ANNA	27	F	W	WMZZZZUSA
JOHS.	2	M	CHILD	WMZZZZUSA
SCHNEIDER, JACOB	23	M	JNR	WMAFDKUSA
GOEHRING, MARTIN	24	M	FARMER	WMAIARUSA
MAMMEN, CAROLE.	18	F	UNKNOWN	WMAIARUSA
KRAFT, EMIL	46	M	FARMER	WMAIARUSA
ECKSTEIN, DORA	29	F	UNKNOWN	WMAARRUSA
KUEMMEL, CHR.	24	M	LABR	WMADNUUSA
MUELLER, JACOB	27	M	LABR	GRZZZZUSA
WINTER, MATHIAS	37	M	LABR	GRAAYAUSA
KOCH, JACOB	43	M	LABR	GRAAYAUSA
MARIA	18	F	UNKNOWN	GRAAYAUSA
EDELBLUTH, PETER	37	M	LABR	GRAFASUSA
LUDW.	16	M	LABR	GRAFASUSA
SCHEEL, KARL	51	M	LABR	GRZZZZUSA
EVA	46	F	W	GRZZZZUSA
GOTTFR.	17	M	LABR	GRZZZZUSA
MARGA.	11	F	CH	GRZZZZUSA
CATHA.	11	F	CH	GRZZZZUSA
HEINR.	4	M	CHILD	GRZZZZUSA
ELISAB.	8	F	CHILD	GRZZZZUSA
MEYERHOLD, G.	28	M	FARMER	GRACYBUSA
JULIANNE	24	F	W	GRACYBUSA
SEMMLER, AMALIE	20	F	UNKNOWN	GRZZZZUSA
HAAS, ANNA	30	F	UNKNOWN	BVZZZZUSA
KANZ, JOS.	24	M	CPTR	GRZZZZUSA
HIMGERBUHLER, REGERL	41	F	W	GRAFTDUSA
FRIDR.	13	M	UNKNOWN	GRAFTDUSA
EMMA	11	F	UNKNOWN	GRAFTDUSA
GEIB, FRIEDR.	17	M	LABR	BVZZZZUSA
SCHWEDOWSKI, ANNA	28	F	W	GRZZZZUSA
MARIA	.08	F	INFANT	GRZZZZUSA
JANS, ANTON	23	M	LABR	GRZZZZUSA
PEHRSSON, P.J.	23	M	FARMER	GRADCRUSA
KOCH, ADOLF	23	M	FARMER	GRZZZZUSA

PASSENGER	AGE	SEX	OCCUPATION	PROVL	DES
JORDAN, JUNO	17	M	FARMER	GRZZZZUSA
KARPINSKI, IGNATZ	44	M	FARMER	GRZZZZUSA
LANGENECKER, JOHN	33	M	LABR	GRADLDUSA
HOFFMANN, FRIEDA	3	F	CHILD	GRABRYUSA
MARIE	.11	F	INFANT	GRABRYUSA
CLOTH, M.	40	M	TT	FRZZZZUSA

SHIP: ANCHORIA

FROM: GLASGOW AND MOVILLE
TO: NEW YORK
ARRIVED: 30 NOVEMBER 1888

PASSENGER	AGE	SEX	OCCUPATION	PROVL	DES
NAGEL, FREID	36	M	LABR	GRZZZZUSA
CAROLINE	35	F	W	GRZZZZUSA
WILHELMINE	3	F	CHILD	GRZZZZUSA
WILHELM	1	M	CHILD	GRZZZZUSA
FRIEDRICH	7	M	CHILD	GRZZZZUSA
SOPPE, AUGUST	21	F	HP	GRZZZZUSA
BENKE, AUGUSTE	11	F	CH	GRZZZZUSA
STRUTZ, JOHANN	48	M	LABR	GRZZZZUSA
EMILIE	40	F	W	GRZZZZUSA
HANS	13	M	UNKNOWN	GRZZZZUSA
CARL	11	M	UNKNOWN	GRZZZZUSA
MARTHA	6	F	CHILD	GRZZZZUSA
ELITZ, WILLIAM	28	M	LABR	GRZZZZUSA
FREDERIKE	26	F	W	GRZZZZUSA
U	3	F	CHILD	GRZZZZUSA
U	1	F	CHILD	GRZZZZUSA

SHIP: SPAIN

FROM: LIVERPOOL
TO: NEW YORK
ARRIVED: 30 NOVEMBER 1888

PASSENGER	AGE	SEX	OCCUPATION	PROVL	DES
GOLD, HENRY	24	M	LABR	GRADAXUSA
JOUNAGAN, AMELIA	24	F	SP	GRAEXKUSA
KAPLAN, MARCUS	20	M	LABR	GRAEXKUSA
SARAH	18	F	SP	GRAEXKUSA
LEA	48	F	W	GRAEXKUSA
RIEVE	6	F	CHILD	GRAEXKUSA
SCHLAUK, G.	27	F	SP	GRAEXKUSA
A.	26	F	SP	GRAEXKUSA
KINETA, SCHOLEM	23	M	LABR	GRAEXKUSA
CHEYRELLAY, VINCENT	23	M	LABR	GRAEXKUSA
HERMURTY, MARCUS	45	M	LABR	GRAEXKUSA
ROSENBLATT, B.	49	M	LABR	GRAEXKUSA
JOHANSON, HANNA	20	F	SP	GRAEXKUSA
BLANBERG, HANNA	22	F	SP	GRAEXKUSA
BECKER, L.	24	M	GENT	GRADBQUSA
HEREN, BERTHA	20	M	GENT	GRADBQUSA

Index

457

INDEX

471

INDEX

RAIT, IGNATZ 127
RAJAHN, ANNA 186
RAJEWICZ, ANNA 429
  MARIA 429
  STEFAN 429
  WOJTEK 429
RAJTAJCZAK, ANDRO 29
RAK, PAUL 56
RAKOFSKY, MARGARETHE
  81
  MATTHIAS 81
RAKOWSKI, GUSTAV 81
RAKOWSKY, CARL 425
RAKUSEN, SARAH 114
RAL--, BERTHA 43
  LUDWIG 43
  SOPHIE 43
RALE, OTTO 263
RALFS, GUSTAV 385
  SOPHIE 144
RALISKI, ADOLF 210
RALL, FRITZ 290
  KATHI 290
  MARIA 292
RALMOWITZ, ALR. 269
  HISSEN 269
  S. 269
RAM, MARIA 29
RAMBACH, A 196
  CHRIS 196
  JOSEPH 196
  MARGR 196
  PAULINE 197
RAMEL, BERTHA 448
  IDA 448
  JULIUS 448
RAMES, JEAN 354
RAMISCHERZKA, PAULINE
  168
RAMKE, JOH 198
RAMKER, MARIA 443
RAMM, EDUARD 189
  JOHE. 85
  O.H. 89
  WILHELM 85
RAMMEL, MARIA 36
RAMMER, HEINRICH 27
RAMMGER, ED 14
RAMMIN, ANNA 225
  BERTHA 225
  HERMANN 225
RAMPE, JUSTUS 393
RAMPKAR, BERNAR 443
  CARL 443
  MARIE 443
  VALENTIN 443
  WILHELME 443
RAMROTH, ELISABETH
  188
  FRITZ 188
  MAGNUS 188
RAMSANER, WILH. 370
RAMSAUER, JOS. 30
  THERESIA 30
RAMSCHUESSEL, GUSTAV
  286
RAMSEIER, CARL 335
  GOTTLIEB 335
  MATHILDA 335
  PAULINE 335
  WILHELM 335
RAMSTEDT, W. 350
RAMTHAM, GUST. 397
  HENTIETTE 397
RAN, AUGUST 89
  FRIEDERIKE 438
  HERM. 256
  JOHANNA , 401

RAN, MARTHA 144
RANCHE, JOH 103
RANCORZINI, ANGELO
  212
RAND, JULIE 377
RANDAL, ERNST 158
RANDEBROEK, ED. 262
RANDECKER, JOH. 264
  WILH. 264
RANDERMANN, AUGUST
  352
  HENRIETTE 352
RANDIG, ANNA 403
  AUGUST 403
  LOUISE 403
RANDOLL, MARIE 302
RANE, IDA 354
RANER, ANNA 398
  H. 269
  JOSEPH 398
  PAULINA 398
RANFT, CHRISTINE 262
RANGE, JOHS. 113
RANH, ELISAB 131
RANIH, JOH. 370
RANK, HERM 174
  JOH. 177
  JOSEF 315
  MARIE 176
RANNS, PELAGIA 217
RANSCH, ERNSTR 402
RANSKER, JOH 443
RANTENBERG, DOROTHEA
  141
  ROB. 141
RANTZ, AUGUST 113
RANUBACHER, BABETTE
  191
  DORA 191
RANZINGER, GEORG 402
RAON, ANNE 87
  JOERGLINE 87
  KIESTE. 87
  NIELS 87
RAPELIUS, CARL 436
RAPLOCHOWSKA, MARYANNA
  435
RAPP, AGATHA 409
  ALB. 438
  ANTON 409
  AUG. 438
  CARL 351
  CHR 130
  CHRISTINE 254
  CHRISTOPH 264
  E 200
  FRANZ 438
  G 200
  GEORG 87
  H. 267
  HYACINTA 409
  J. 267
  JACOB 254
  JOHANN 449
  K.H. 119
  LOUISE 60
  M 200
  MARG. 224
  MARIA 31 , 409
  MONKA 409
  PAUL 438
  ROCHUS 409
  ROSA 224
  ROSALIE 438
  SALOMONIA 409
  SOPHIE 129
  T 200
  TERESA , 224

RAPP, THEOBALD 409
RAPPAPORT, SALOMON
  213
RAPPE, CARRY 358
RAPPEL, SAINVALET 11
RAPPELT, JOSEF 222
RAPPEPORT, ESTHER 173
  PERCEL 173
  POTE 173
  SALMEN 173
RAPPORT, HIRSCH 137
  JOSEF 137
RAPSARD, A. 443
RARER, ADOLPH 292
RARNEKOW, ANNA 365
RARTOW, HERMAN 327
RASATI, ANTONO 221
RASCH, EMILIE 64
  FRIEDRICH 64
  JOHA. 373
  JOHANNE 392
RASCHE, FRIEDE. 319
RASCHER, SIMON 211
RASCHKA, MINNA 169
RASCHKE, ALBERT 417
  CAROLINE 452
  FRIEDR. 452
  HELENE 452 , 417
  JOHANN 417
  MICHEL 452
  THEOVILL 171
RASCHKOWSKY, C. 83
RASE, MARIE 74
RASENKIEWICZ, MICHALINA
  303
RASINSKY, MATHIAS 285
RASMUSSEN, HANNE 139
  JOHANN 332
  MARIE 139
  SIEGFRIEDE 279
RASOTKOWSKY, JOS 450
RASP, ALBERT 379
  BARBA. 379
  JOHANN 379
  KUNIGDE. 379
  OTILIE 379
RASPEDA, CONST. 84
RASPERKA, JOSEFA 7
RASS, FRIEDR. 31
RASSINGER, JOHANN 274
  MARIA 274
RASSLER, MARIE 45
RASSMUSS, SOPHIE 358
RAST, HCH 94
RASZAREK, FRANZISKA
  45
  JULIANE 45
  LUDWIG 45
  MARIANNE 45
RASZEJA, FRANZ 355
RASZINSKI, MICHAL 19
RASZKOWSKA, BASSIA
  205
RASZMARK, VALENZ 105
RASZUBKIEWITZ,
  KONSTANZIA 154
RATAEZAK, FRANZICECK
  1
RATAJCZAK, JOH 39
RATAJEWSKI, ADALBERT
  238
RATAJEZAK, LUDWIG 35
RATAPSAK, STANISLAW
  52
RATENKE, FERD. 322
RATER, EDMUND 31
RATH, CATHI 143
  JOHE. , 292

RATH, MARIE 143
RATHAUS, AUGUSTE 143
RATHBUCHNER, ANNA 144
  AUGUST 144
  ELISE 144
RATHE, CHR 401
  HEINR 401
RATHENAU, JOSEPH 26
RATHENBERGER, EMMA
  202
RATHER, ELISAB. 58
  OTTO 272
RATHERT, JOHAN 313
RATHFUSS, WILHELM 284
RATHGEBER, AUGUSTE
  105
  FRIEDR. 105
  JULIE 105
RATHIEN, EMMA 148
RATHJE, BERTHA 89
  INGA 121
  JUERGEN E. 383
  MARIE 279
RATHJEN, FRIEDR 13
  OTTO 13
RATHKE, ANNA 233
  EMILIE 357
  EMMA 233
  GEORG 233
  HELENE 233
  JENNY 233
  MARIA 233
  U 233
RATKA, LUDWIG 113
RATKE, EVA 169
  LOUISA 391
  MARIA 391
RATKEWICZ, J. 210
RATLUK, AND. 7
RATSIN, JOSEF 386
RATTINER, D 212
RATTONY, ADELINE 91
RATZKOWSKI, JOSEPH 79
RATZMANN, FRIEDERICKE
  433
  JOHAN 433
RAU, EMMA 366
  JACOB 58
  MAGD 94
  MARG 45
  PAULINE 321
  ROESLE 44
  WILH 45
RAUB, ALBERT 416
RAUBE, ELISABETH 225
RAUCH, AUGUST 426
  BARBARA 111
  C 200
  CARL 332
  CAROLINE 332 , 94
  CATARINE 332
  E 200
  EMMA 332
  EUGEN 438
  FRIEDR 332
  GEORG 111
  JOH 332
  JOSEF 111
  KARL 57
  LUDWIG 94
  MARG 94
  MARIA 94
  MARIE 332
  MINNA 332
RAUCHENBERG, FRIED.
  357
RAUCHFUSS, ADELHEID
  359

VIKAMP, HERM 103
VILAIN, ROSIN 386
VILEIN, GALIE 61
  PEPPI 61
VILETTI, CUGGIO 354
VILLHARD, MARIA 158
VILLINGER, MARIE 331
VILLRACK, EMIL 367
VILMAR, RUD. 451
VILOE, JULE 128
VILWOCH, ARSEN 263
VINCENT, MARIE 208
VINTER, PETER-N. 85
VINZ, ANTON 212
VIOOLTRAM, HERCON 375
  HORA 375
  LAZAR 375
  NEBIA 375
  PETEL 375
VIRUS, RUDOLPH 279
VISEUX, BENOIT 240
  CELINE 240
VISOSKY, JOHS. 409
VITRIOL, ADOLF 202
VITSOCH, PELAGIA 214
VITTHORI, S 201
VITZ, OTTILIA 254
VLACH, J. 119
VOBECKA, ANNA 355
VOCEL, CATI 319
VOCK, PAULA. 9
VOEGE, ANNA 270
VOEGEL, HENRY 151
VOEGELI, JACOB 171
VOEGTLE, ANSELM 331
VOELDER, CARL 292
VOELK, CARL 146
VOELKE, LUDW 131
VOELKEL, CATH. 257
  CHRISITAN 377
VOELKER, BARB. 295
  EMIL 195
  EMMA 403
  GEORG 160
  JOSEPH 213
VOELKERS, HEIN. 305
VOELKL, JOH 131
  WOLFGANG 29
VOELLINGER, JOS 175
VOELLM, GUSTAV 113
VOELPEL, ELISA 302
VOETH, LOUISE 318
VOGE, EMMA 191
VOGEL, ANDR. 299
  BABETTE 364
  BERTHA 355
  CAMILLA 317
  CARL 228 , 324
  CATHA. 141
  ERNST 237
  FR. 155
  FRANCISCA 81
  GEORG 440
  HEINRICH 137
  JOH. 71 , 237 , 250
  JOHANN 307
  JOHN 139
  JULIANNA 449
  LUI--- 309
  MARG. 440
  MARIA 60 , 372
  MARIE 364
  META 148
  NATHAN C. 353
  PAUL 81
VOGELBACKER, MATH. 329
VOGELFAENGER, MAGD.

VOGELFAENGER, MAGD. 440
VOGELGESANG, CATHARINA 306
VOGELMANN, BABETTE 402
  BERTHA 402
  CARL 250
VOGELPOHL, CHRISTINE 313
  ELISE 313
  WILHELM 313
VOGELSANG, CATHA 400
  CHRISTINE 285
  E. 354
  FRIEDR 400
  LUER 400
  MARIE 285 , 387 , 120
VOGELSANGER, ANNA 302
VOGES, CARL 336
  CAROLINE 343
  ELISABETH 71
  MINNA 28
  WILH. 60
VOGLER, ADAM 174
  ANTON 174
  GEORG 300 , 193
  MART. 354
  OTTILIE 174
VOGRICH, MAX 204
  MRS 204
VOGT, ADAM 357
  ADELE 354
  ADOL.G. 431
  ANNA 265
  BINA 350
  CARL 438
  E. 328
  EMMA 291
  FRANZ 309
  FRIEDRICH 89
  G. 328
  HEINR. 379
  HEINRICH 40
  J. 267
  JAC. 249
  JOH. 438 , 333
  JOHANN 260
  JOSEF 227
  KATHA. 438
  L. 119
  LINA 281 , 348
  MARG. 313
  MARIA 99 , 309
  MARY EL. 354
  MATHILDE 350
  RICH. 438
  U 194
  WM. 317
VOGTLI, URSULA 50
VOGTMANN, PETER 156
VOGTS, CLAUS 310
  DOROTHEA 89
VOHANCK, ARNOSTA 149
VOHRER, ADOLF 216
VOHRSE, EMILIE 263
VOHS, ADOLPH 278
  KARD 278
VOIGHT, KEUGEL 443
  LOUIS 367
VOIGL, JOSEF 134
VOIGT, ADAM 41
  AGNES 160
  ANNA 59 , 17
  AUGUST 48
  CARL 399 , 39 , 389
  CAROLINE , 382 , 8

VOIGT, CLARA 285
  EMIL 160
  FRIDA 9
  FRITZ 210
  GEORG 160
  GUSTAV 17
  HENRIETTE 17
  HERM 39
  HERM. 389
  JEANETTE 160
  JOHANN 59
  LINA 214
  LOUISE 39
  MARIA 306
  MARIE 59
  MARTHA 402
  MINNA 39
  PAUL 17
  RICHARD 17
  RUDOLF 306
  WILH 17
VOIGTMANN, PAUL 137
VOIGTR, EDUARD 160
  PAUL 160
VOIT, CHAS. 83
  JOHANN 213
VOITH, BAPTIST 402
  BARBA. 402
VOJER, LEONHARD 8
VOJTA, ANNA 302
  BOZENA 302
  FRANZKE 302
  JOSEF 302
  VINCENZ 302
VOKURKA, ANNA 271
VOLCK, ADALBUS 6
  MARIE 6
VOLDKNER, CLARA 369
VOLEMER, ROSA 277
VOLESTHE, E 290
VOLK, C. 119
  CATH. 258
  EMILIE 263
  EMMA 218
  JOH. 402
  JOSEF 173
  JUSTUS 207
VOLKART, ELISE 229
  HEINR. 229
VOLKE, JOHANN 251
VOLKER, H 67
  ROSA 248
VOLKERDINY, JAS. 27
VOLKERS, AMANDA 377
VOLKES, DIEDRICH 366
VOLKLAND, AMALIE 333
VOLKMANN, AD. 283
  BENNO 186
  BERNHARDINE 273
  CL. 283
  EILHELM 186
  EMIL 186 , 138
  FRANCISCA 186
  FRANZ 138
  GEORG 273
  HERM. 337
  HULDA 138
  JOHANNA 186
  JOSEPH 235
  JULIUS 65
  LEA 186
  MARGA. 340
  MINNA 138
  PAUL 186
  ROBERT 186
  WANDA 186
  WILLIBALD 138
  WILLY , 65

VOLKMAR, NICOL. 234
VOLKMER, WILHELM 368
VOLKOUMMEN, JOS 414
VOLKOVSKY, SALOMON 282
VOLL, MARIA 418
VOLLACZINSKOVO, CATH. 16
VOLLBRACHT, DORIS 343
VOLLBRECHT, FRIEDR. 427
VOLLE, MARIE 199
VOLLHEIM, MARIE 256
VOLLMAN, JOH. 158
VOLLMANN, AMALIE 162
  ESTHER 92
  JACOB 92
VOLLMAR, ELISABETH 146
  EMIL 43
  LUDWIG 140
  PAULINE 146
  PETER 140
VOLLMER, HERRMANN 308
VOLLOMZ, VALENT. 258
VOLLSTAEDT, FRANZ 349
VOLLTEN, FRIEDR. 342
  WILH. 342
VOLMER, GEORG 122
VOLPP, MINNA 281
VOLQUARDT, CHRISTIAN 359
VOLTER, AUG. 264
VOLTMANN, BERTHA 424 , 423
VOLZ, CATH. 191
  GENOVEVA 178
  JACOB 150
  JAN 136
  JOSEF 294
  MARIA 177
VON BREMEN, META 191
VON E-EN, ERNST 415
  MARIE 415
  WALTHER 415
VON HALM, HEINRICH 285
VON PICHOWSKA, OTTILIE 416
VON REI, AGNES 361
VON WILLE, CARL 246
VON ZALUSKOWSKY, KARL 268
VONBARGEN, CHRIST. 105
VONBELLEVILLE, ELLI 367
VONBERGEN, GUST. 301
VONBLOME, PAULA 367
VONBOECKMANN, ANNA 345
  ARTHUR 345
  KURT 345
  WILHELMINE 345
VONBOHR, PHA. 30
VONBOKERN, WILH. 304
VONBORSTEL, WILHELM 449
VONBRUSSEL, ANNA 293
  GUSTAV 293
  SCHOLASKA 293
VONDERHEIDE, CLEMENS 58
VONDERLIETH, CAROLINE 60
VONDERLINDEN, MARIA 434
VONDERNBACH, AGNESE.

INDEX

643